MORNINGSTAR®

Funds 500™

Annual Sourcebook
2007 Edition

Introduction by
Scott Berry
and Russel Kinnel,
Co-Editors

For general information on our other products and services or for technical support, please contact our Customer Care Department within the United States at (800) 762-2974, outside the United States at (317) 572-3993 or fax (317) 572-4002.

For general information about Morningstar's other products and services, please contact Morningstar's product sales line at 866-608-9570 or visit www.morningstar.com.

Wiley also publishes its books in a variety of electronic formats. Some content that appears in print may not be available in electronic books. For more information about Wiley products, visit our web site at www.wiley.com.

Library of Congress Cataloging-in-Publication Data:

ISBN-13 978-0-471-78664-1
ISBN-10 0-471-78664-0

Printed in the United States of America

10 9 8 7 6 5 4 3 2 1

Table of Contents

It was a good year to be a fund investor. From world-stock funds to real estate funds to high-yield bond funds, returns were strong. As you sift through all the results of 2006, we encourage you to remember that, while useful, looking at last year's returns amounts to looking in the rearview mirror. Our analyses are focused on looking through the windshield at what's coming up that can lead a fund to superior return. When recommending funds, we look for a combination of low costs, skilled managers, proven strategies, solid long-term performance, and shareholder-friendly advisors. We've found that those traits are the best indicators of future success.

We've taken the roughly 7,000 member mutual fund universe and selected 500 of the best and most notable funds. For each of these funds, we provide a one-page report that provides all the data and analysis needed to put a mutual fund through its paces. The reports include performance history, portfolio analysis, the fund's Morningstar rating, and Morningstar's take on the fund and its prospects. Our analysts dig through the financial statements and SEC filings of each fund to see if it offers sustainable advantages over competitors, while also speaking regularly with fund managers and paying visits to fund companies to see how their research and resources stack up. Taking all of that into consideration, the analyst forms an opinion of whether a given fund is worth owning.

That research has helped our analysts identify young funds that have the potential to be big winners, as well as older funds that have hit a rough patch but that are poised for a rebound. For example, we like the two-year-old Champlain Small Company, and we think Oakmark Select and Fidelity Dividend Growth are due to recapture their past glory.

If these 500 reports seem daunting, we'd suggest you start off with our Fund Analyst Picks. This list highlights our very favorite funds. If you're in the market for a new fund or two, consider this the place to start. In most fund categories, our analysts select a small number of funds that they consider to be the very best options for investors. Some of these funds end up being options in Morningstar's own 401(k) plan and are among the first our analysts recommend when cornered by friends and relatives at social gatherings. One size never fits all, but if you're looking for a short list of favorites, this is the list for you.

There's much more to this book than picks and fund reports, though. Many fund investors surely own funds that aren't included in this book and are interested to know if they could be doing better. For that purpose we've included performance summaries of all the major fund categories and index benchmarks going back 15 years, so you can see how your fund stacks up against the competition. We've also included expense ratios for each category, so you can see if you're overpaying for your fund or if you're manager is worth every penny.

We hope you get as much out of this book as we've put into it. The mutual fund universe stretches farther and wider than investors need to go, but we've studied the universe and narrowed it down considerably. And we're confident that the recommendations, data, and analysis we've provided in this book will help you make the choices that best fit your own investment needs.

Scott Berry
Co-Editor
Morningstar Funds 500

Russel Kinnel
Co-Editor
Morningstar Funds 500

How To Use This Book

by Christine Benz,
Director of
Fund Analysis

Just as most professional stock-pickers agree that it's impossible to pick securities based solely on their past performance patterns, we at Morningstar have long argued that successful fund investing begins with fundamental analysis—and not by checking last year's leaders' lists. True, looking at the best-performing funds for any given time period can provide important clues about certain funds and market trends, and that's why this book includes plenty of fund rankings. (See Pages 542-544.) But to truly understand a fund and the role it might play in a portfolio, investors have to drill down into its holdings, understand the manager's strategy, assess the shareholder-friendliness of the fund company, and evaluate the fund's risk level.

Toward that end, this year's *Morningstar Funds 500* is chock-full of all the data and analysis you need to make informed decisions. Read on as we walk through some of the best tools for doing just that. (The Glossary that begins on Page 562 provides you with specific definitions of all of the data points in this book.)

Analyst Picks

Analyst Picks, a complete listing of which appears on Page 22, are Morningstar fund analysts' "best ideas." The analysts responsible for the picks within each fund category are charged with finding those offerings with strong track records, reasonable volatility, compelling strategies, great managers, and low expenses. We also look for our Analyst Picks to hail from firms that have a strong record of putting shareholders' interests first.

Many of our choices are fairly obvious. From low-cost intermediate bond funds such as Dodge & Cox Income to high-octane mid-growth offerings such as Turner Midcap Growth, our list of picks is full of well-known, well-run "category killers." Of course, some categories may be inappropriate for some investors. But once

you've determined that you're looking for a certain type of fund, the Analyst Picks list is a natural next step.

Morningstar's Take

The text box in the lower left-hand quadrant of each individual fund page is the analysis, or "Morningstar's Take." Reading the analysis is an essential first step as you attempt to determine whether a fund is appropriate for your goals and risk tolerance. In it, the analyst sums up all of a fund's salient points by assessing its historical risk/reward profile relative to its peer group, discussing the manager's strategy, and/or noting any recent changes to the portfolio or its management. And because Morningstar analysts generally speak with each fund manager and have Morningstar's extensive database at their fingertips, the analysis can provide glimpses into a fund that you won't find anywhere else.

Stewardship Grade

In an effort to summarize all of the factors that determine whether a fund company is shareholder-friendly, we developed our Stewardship Grades. The lettergrades, which appear on each individual fund page, right below the fund's name, range from A to F. The grades take into account whether the fund company has had prior run-ins with securities regulators, the quality of the fund's board, the structure of the fund's manager incentives, the fund's expenses relative to its peers', and its corporate culture.

The Stewardship Grade serves as a handy way to assess key intangibles—such as the quality of a fund's board of directors or a fund firm's corporate culture—that can make the difference between a great investment and one to avoid. The grades are not meant to be used in isolation or as simplistic buy or sell signals. Rather, they represent yet another valuable addition to our suite of investing research and tools, alongside our analysis and Morningstar Rating for funds.

Star Ratings

For years, the Morningstar Rating for funds—the "star rating"—has been our best-known tool. This risk-adjusted rating is designed to give you a quick look at a fund's historical risk/reward profile, with 5 stars being the best rating and 1 star being the worst. The star rating is derived from a fund's standing within its category, rather than within a broad asset class. That helps show you how well a fund has executed its particular style.

The star rating has shown itself to be a decent predictor of performance and searching for 5- and 1-star funds can be an effective way to quickly determine which funds merit further investigation and which do not. However, there may well be situations in which a fund's star rating doesn't reflect its worthiness. For example, a fund that just gained a topnotch manager may sport a relatively low star rating, even though its prospects have recently improved. And the reverse could also be true, as a 5-star fund could lose a great manager and be less appealing than its star rating might imply.

Style Boxes/Morningstar Categories

The Morningstar style box, the nine-square grid that appears toward the bottom right-hand corner of each individual fund page, is designed to give you a visual snapshot of the type of securities a fund is holding. For stock funds, the style box shows you the size of companies in which a fund invests, as well as whether the fund manager buys growth- or value-oriented securities. For bond funds, the style box depicts a fund's sensitivity to interest rates as well as the average credit quality of the bonds in the portfolio. Armed with three years' worth of style boxes, we determine a fund's Morningstar Category placement, which reflects how the fund has invested its assets over the past three years.

As a general rule of thumb, large-cap blend or large-cap value funds make the best core stock holdings, because they invest in the well-established companies that tend to dominate the market. For those seeking a core bond-fund holding, the intermediate-term bond category is generally the best hunting ground. Such funds are typically well-diversified across government and corporate bonds and have some (although not extreme) sensitivity to interest-rate changes.

Just as Morningstar's style boxes and categories can help you make smart fund selections, they can also help you determine how to put the funds together into a well-diversified package. While you need not buy a fund in every single Morningstar Category, building a portfolio of funds with varying investment styles is a sensible diversification strategy.

Sector Weightings

Sector weightings, which appear in the bottom right-hand corner of each stock and bond-fund page, pick up where a fund's investment style box leaves off. Eyeballing a fund's sector weightings is an essential step on the road to understanding how a fund will behave and how you might use it (or not use it) to build a diversified portfolio. After all, funds may land in different Morningstar Categories, but if their sector compositions are similar, it's possible that their performances will be, too.

Tax Analysis

Since the bear-market losses in the early part of this decade, many funds have posted solid returns, meaning that sizable capital gains could be in the offing. In an effort to help you know whether a fund is best suited to a taxable or tax-deferred account, we've developed our tax-analysis section, which is located on the left-hand side of every fund page. The section gives you an estimate of how much of a fund's return an investor in the highest tax bracket would be able to pocket after taxes. Pay particularly close attention to a fund's tax-adjusted return ranking within its category. If a fund's tax-adjusted return ranking is higher than its raw-return ranking, that could indicate that management is using a tax-efficient strategy. If the opposite is true, you might want to consider holding that fund in a tax-sheltered account such as an IRA. Tax-adjusted returns are load adjusted, so the rankings may not be as meaningful for front-load funds.

Tables and Charts

For those of you who love lists, Pages 536-550 include an impressive array of fund data and rankings. In general, selecting funds from a list of short-term leaders is a poor investment strategy. But checking the lists of top-performing funds over longer time frames—over the past five and 10 years, for example—can provide you with great ideas for further research. The lists of leaders and laggards over various time frames can also be a good way to get up to speed on recent market trends. Specialty real estate funds dominate the three- and five-year domestic-equity funds' leader list on Page 542, for example, whereas large-cap-dominated funds bring up the rear over these time frames. ▥

The Morningstar Stock-Fund Page

In this eight-page walk-through, we briefly describe how each section of the page is relevant to your fund research and offer some tips on using these features to better analyze funds. More-detailed discussions of the elements presented in this section appear in the Glossary.

A Historical Investment Style Boxes

B Morningstar Rating

C Portfolio Manager(s) Profile and Stewardship Grade

D Manager Strategy

E Performance

F Tax Analysis

G Morningstar's Take

H Operations

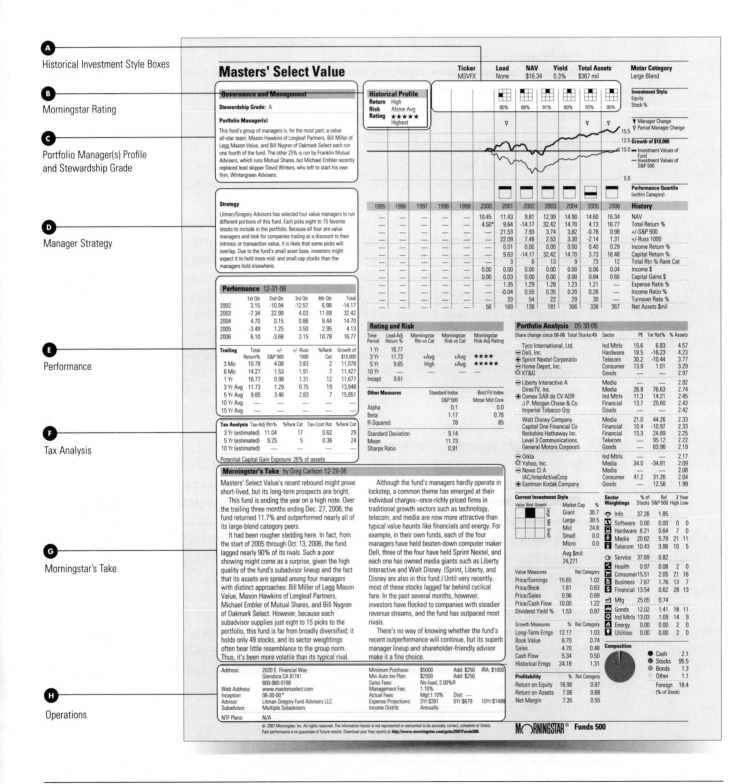

Commentary

Ⓐ Historical Investment Style Boxes

Does the manager stick with a consistent investment style year to year, or does he or she invest in different areas of the market as they become attractive? These are important questions to ask when building a portfolio. If you buy a fund to occupy a particular investment area, you will want it to maintain that position.

Ⓑ Morningstar Rating

The star rating is a good way to identify funds that have provided the best balance of risk and return within their Morningstar Category. It sets out to separate the long-term winners from the losers. It's best used as a first screen, as a tool to narrow the field to a manageable group of funds to look at in-depth. Using it in other ways, such as a timing device or the sole reason to buy a fund, is not a good strategy.

Ⓒ Governance and Management

The portfolio manager is the individual or individuals responsible for the overall fund strategy, as well as the buying and selling decisions for the securities in a fund's portfolio. To help investors know who is running a fund, we detail the fund's management with a brief biography. We note the manager's background, experience, analytical support, other funds managed, and/or whether the manager invests in his or her own fund. If a fund has a great record but new management, beware: The fund's best days may be behind it. This section also includes our analysts' Stewardship Grades.

Ⓓ Manager Strategy

While the Morningstar Category gives investors an idea of the kind of investments a manager makes, it does not fully capture the nuances of a manager's approach to picking stocks or bonds. In this section, Morningstar's analysts explain what criteria a manager uses in selecting securities, and how risky a given approach may be. On the equity side, the strategy description often focuses on what size and type of company a manager prefers, along with a discussion regarding how he or she balances growth and value factors. With bond funds, the strategy section explains whether the manager makes interest-rate and credit-quality bets,

or whether management attempts to add value with individual security selection.

Ⓔ Performance

The quarterly returns show the performance investors have seen over each calendar quarter in the past five years. This section is a good spot to quickly test your risk tolerance. Find the largest quarterly loss; if it makes you uneasy, you should probably look for less-volatile funds. The trailing returns section illustrates performance over short and long periods. We compare returns against appropriate benchmarks and peers: 1 is the best percentile; 100 is the worst.

Ⓕ Tax Analysis

This section lists a fund's tax-adjusted returns and the percentage-point reduction in annualized returns that results from taxes, called the tax-cost ratio. For context, each figure is then given a percentile rank in the fund's category (1 is the best percentile; 100 is the worst). Examine the two returns figures together because high tax-adjusted returns do not necessarily mean the fund is tax-efficient. Also, a fund could be very tax-efficient, but if returns are poor to begin with, an investor will still pocket a low sum. This section is perhaps best used to determine whether a fund should be held in a tax-deferred or taxable account. Note that tax-adjusted returns are also adjusted for loads.

Ⓖ Morningstar's Take

Our analysts interpret the data on the page and interview the fund's manager to uncover the strategies guiding investment decisions. They then succinctly detail how and why a fund has succeeded or failed, and what role—if any—it should play in your portfolio.

Ⓗ Operations

Here we list where to obtain investment information from the fund. We also list the fund's minimum initial purchase and break down a fund's expenses into their components.

The Morningstar Stock-Fund Page (continued)

Morningstar Category

Investment Value Graph

Performance Quartile Graph

History

Rating and Risk

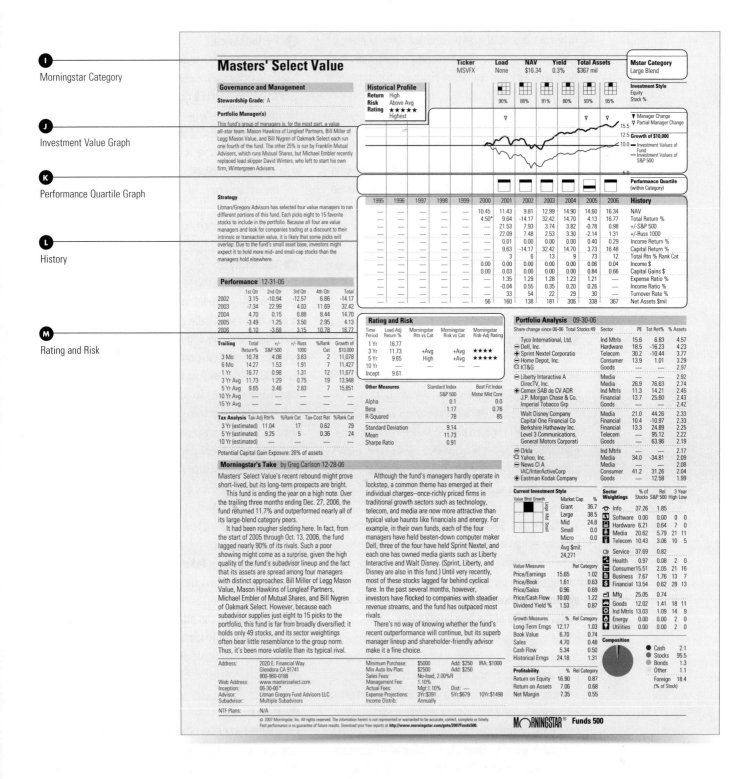

❶ Morningstar Category

The Morningstar Category is the first stage of digging into the fund's portfolio. We sort funds into peer groups based on the types of securities the funds hold. Each category is assigned using a fundamental analysis of a fund's portfolio over a three-year period. It is important to analyze the types of securities a fund holds. Portfolio analysis, and a fund's category, can tell you a lot about a fund's performance and future volatility. For example, investors can expect bumpier rides with funds in the small-cap growth category—those that focus on small, rapidly growing companies—than with large-cap value funds, which focus on well-established companies that are trading cheaply. In addition to portfolio analysis, the Morningstar categories also can help you diversify and evaluate the role a fund might play in your portfolio. For example, you might head to the more-volatile categories (the small-cap groups or emerging markets) if you decided to spice up your large-cap-laden portfolio. Or you might want to tone down a growth-oriented portfolio with a value fund or two.

❶ Investment Value Graph

The Investment Value graph line shows a fund's performance trend, derived from the fund's historical growth of $10,000. It provides a visual depiction of how a fund has amassed its returns, including the performance swings its shareholders have endured along the way. The growth of $10,000 begins at the date of the fund's inception, or if the fund has been in existence for more than 12 years, then growth of $10,000 begins at the first year listed on the graph. Also, featured in the graph is the performance of an index, which allows investors to compare the performance of the fund with the performance of the benchmark index.

❶ Performance Quartile Graph

Here we show in which quartile a fund's calendar-year returns landed relative to its category. You can quickly gauge how consistent the fund's returns have been year to year.

❶ History

Use this table to spot trends over the past 12 years. Pay particular attention to the following statistics.

Expense Ratio

This percentage tells you how much it costs to own the fund each year. Generally, stick to funds with expense ratios lower than 1.25%. Many great domestic-stock funds keep expenses below 1%, and topnotch bond funds often charge less than 0.75%. Raise the bar a little for international funds, because it costs more to do business overseas.

Turnover Rate

A low turnover figure (less than 30%) indicates a buy-and-hold strategy. A high rate (more than 100%) means the manager is doing a lot of buying and selling. (The average annual turnover for domestic-stock funds is about 85%.) If a fund has a high turnover rate, make sure the manager has a proven record as a good stock-picker; investors will end up the losers if a high-trading manager consistently buys and sells at the wrong time. Also, high turnover drives up a fund's costs because more brokerage commissions are being paid. High-turnover funds also tend to be less tax-efficient, although that is not always the case if the manager is offsetting gains with losses. Still, if a fund has a high turnover rate, check the fund's tax efficiency. And watch for significant year-to-year changes in the turnover rate: It could indicate a new management style or a change in the fund's investment strategy. Turnover is not as meaningful for bond funds, as it can be driven higher by certain cash-management strategies.

Net Assets

A fund's asset size can also be an important consideration, especially for funds that focus on small-cap stocks or specialized areas of the market. In these cases, generally, the smaller the fund the better, because smaller funds can maneuver more nimbly in and out of market areas. Many small-cap funds close to new investors to keep a handle on asset size.

❶ Rating and Risk

This section breaks down the fund's risk, returns, and overall star rating over the three-, five-, and 10-year time

Portfolio Analysis

Other Measures

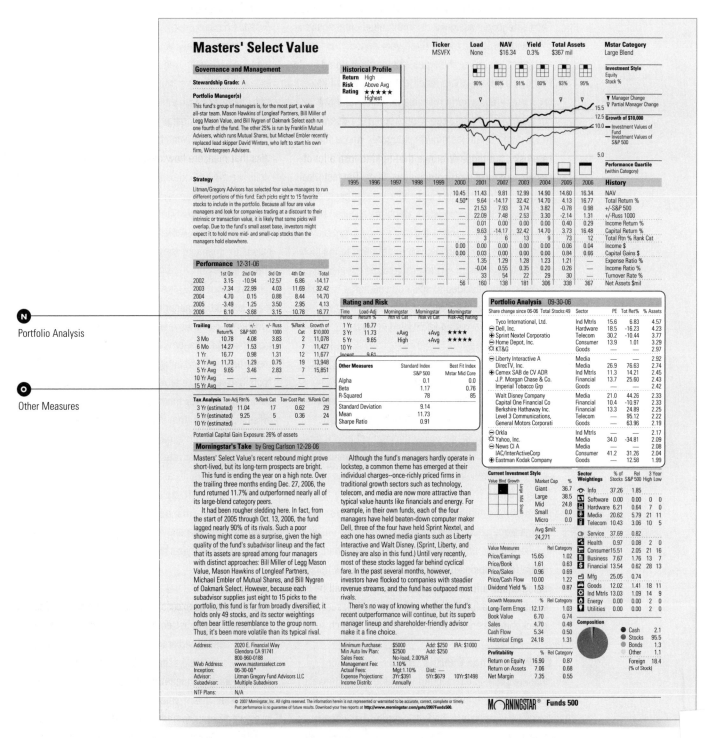

periods. The Return vs. Category section shows how the fund's returns compare with those of its peer group. The top 10% receive a high rating, the next 22.5% garner an "above-average" designation, and the middle 35% are rated "average." The next 22.5% of funds land in the "below-average" group, while the bottom 10% receive "low" ratings. Similarly, the Risk versus Category section ranks a fund's historical volatility versus that of its peer group, with those funds that have exhibited a lot of downside volatility faring worse than those that have not. The rationale here is that highly volatile funds are risky, but those offerings that tend to lose a lot of money are most worrisome to investors. The historical star ratings offer some clues regarding the consistency of a fund's historical risk-adjusted performance. Those with 5-star three-, five-, and 10-year results have often put up consistently strong risk-adjusted results, while those with universally poor marks have often languished year after year. Funds with markedly different short- and long-term results may have extreme strategies that produce feast-or-famine returns, or they may have experienced a manager change that has materially affected performance. The section also lists the fund's load-adjusted returns over the one-, three-, five-, and 10-year periods, as well as the annualized return since inception.

Ⓝ Portfolio Analysis

Analyzing a fund's portfolio will give you an understanding of the fund's performance and potential volatility. First, note the fund's total holdings: The fund with fewer stocks will get more kick from its best performers, but if just a few holdings falter, the fund will lag. All things being equal, a fund with 50 or fewer stocks will be more volatile than a fund holding twice as many issues. Next, check the percentage of assets devoted to each security. A manager who follows a concentrated strategy will have large hunks of the fund's assets (more than 5% per stock) invested in its top holdings. Now identify each stock's sector to gain insight into where a fund's top holdings are concentrated and where its vulnerabilities lie. Then check the stocks' price/earnings ratios; high P/E's are another indication of possible future volatility. Each stock's year-to-date returns tell you which securities in which sectors are driving the performance of the fund up or down. Keep tabs on which positions

the manager has increased or trimmed. A plus sign (⊕) means the fund has added shares to that holding; a minus sign (⊖) indicates a reduction. New additions are noted with a star burst (✳). If a position in a losing stock is new or expanded, the manager could be bargain-hunting.

Ⓞ Other Measures

These numbers provide more views of risk. Alpha, beta, and R-squared are three Modern Portfolio Theory statistics that measure how much you can expect a fund to follow a market index and whether the fund has added or subtracted value versus that benchmark. We compare all domestic- and international-equity funds with the S&P 500 and a Best Fit Index (the index with which the fund has the highest correlation).

R-squared

For beta and alpha to be reliable measures of risk and reward, a fund must have a high correlation with its index, as measured by R-squared. R-squared indicates how market-like a fund is. A high R-squared (between 85 and 100) indicates the fund's performance patterns have been in line with the index's. A fund with a low R-squared (70 or less) doesn't act much like the index.

Beta

Beta measures a fund's volatility relative to its benchmark. A beta of more than 1.0 means the fund is more volatile than the index and should outperform it when the index is rising and underperform it when the index is falling. A beta of less than 1.0 works the opposite way.

Alpha

Alpha measures excess returns per unit of risk. The higher the alpha, the better. A positive alpha indicates the fund performed better in the past than its beta would predict. A negative alpha indicates the fund performed worse. Below these statistics, standard deviation measures risk as volatility by showing the range within which a fund's monthly returns have landed. The larger the number, the wider the range and more volatile the fund's returns have been. To set a fund's standard deviation in context, compare it with others in the fund's category. The mean represents the annualized total return for a fund over the trailing three years.

The Morningstar Stock-Fund Page (continued)

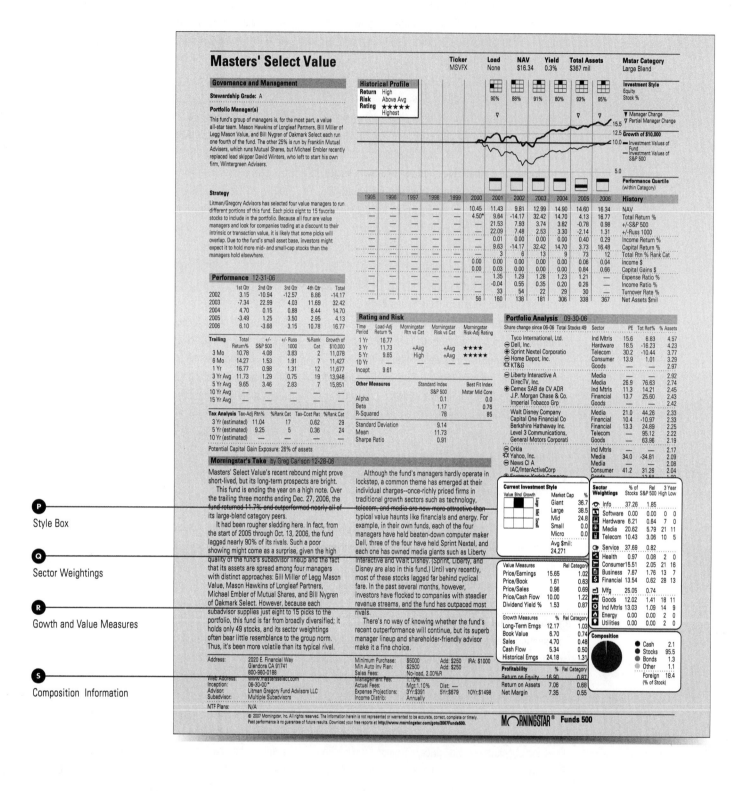

Style Box

Sector Weightings

Gowth and Value Measures

Composition Information

Sharpe Ratio

The Sharpe ratio is a risk-adjusted measure similar to the star rating. The higher the Sharpe ratio (1.0 is pretty good), the better the fund's risk-adjusted performance has been.

ⓟ Style Box

For stock funds, Morningstar assigns style-box classifications based on portfolios' scores for Growth Measures, Value Measures, and average weighted market cap. For example, funds that invest predominantly in large-cap, fast-growing firms with high valuations typically land in large growth. By contrast, funds that specialize in smaller, slower-growing firms with modest valuations are assigned to the small-value style box.

ⓠ Sector Weightings

Learn which sectors of the economy the fund invests in to gauge how diversified the fund is. A fund that has more than 25% of assets concentrated in one sector is almost certain to carry more risk than a more-diversified offering. Knowing the fund's weightings can help you maintain a well-diversified portfolio. Weightings are displayed relative to the S&P 500 for domestic-stock funds and relative to the MSCI EAFE for international stock funds. (We show relative subsector breakdowns for funds in our specialty categories.) The last two columns of the section give a fund's historical range of the percentage of assets held in each sector; here, you can see if a fund is bullish or bearish on particular sectors, based on its past weightings.

ⓡ Growth and Value Measures

This section lists a fund portfolio's current averages for various portfolio statistics, including price/earnings, price/cash flow, and historical earnings growth. To provide perspective, we compare these measures with the funds' category average.

ⓢ Composition Information

This section shows the percentage of assets devoted to cash, stocks, bonds, and other, along with what percentage of stock assets are invested in foreign securities. A large percentage of cash in Composition might indicate the fund is taking a defensive position.

The Morningstar Bond-Fund Page

In this two-page walk-through, we spotlight sections that are unique to the bond-fund page and offer some advice on using the page to select a bond fund. More-detailed discussions of the elements presented in this section appear in the Glossary.

A — Yield

B — Expense Ratio %

C — Current Investment Style/ Duration Management

D — Credit Analysis

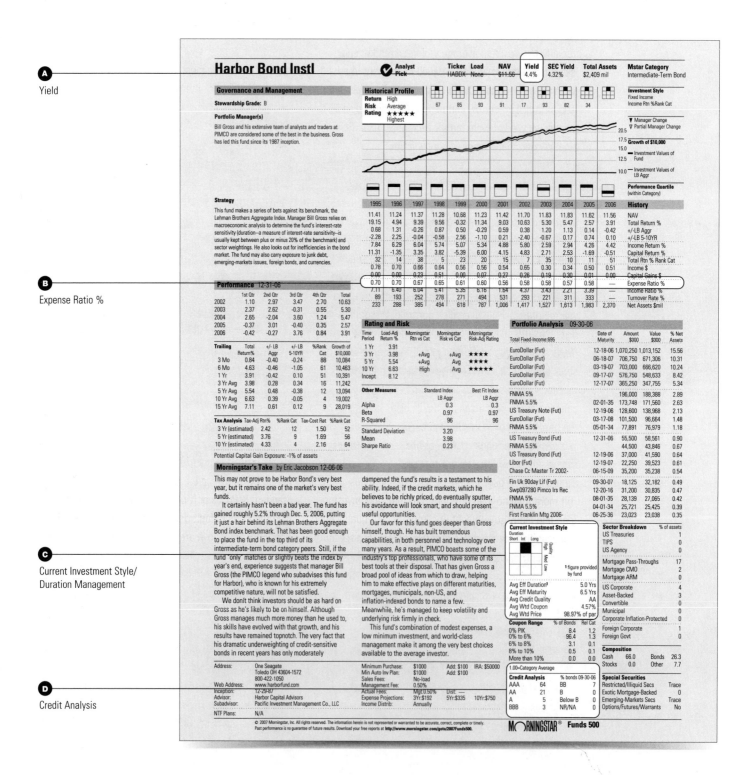

A Yield

Yield provides instant gratification in the form of regular income payments, but basing your buy decision on a fund's high yield instead of total returns could cost you in the end. To pump up yields some funds use accounting tricks that can erode a fund's NAV over time. In other words, part of the "income" they are distributing to you is a return of your principal. Others invest in lower-quality debt and/or complex derivatives in an effort to enhance yield. Shrinking principal leads to smaller income checks, though, even if the yield percentage stays the same. Imagine a $10,000 investment in a fund carrying an NAV of $10 and yielding 7%. One year later, the fund still yields 7%, but its NAV has slipped to $9. Income would have dropped to $630 from $700. Be wary if a fund has a high payout relative to its category and an NAV that is eroding, particularly in years when interest rates have declined. That fund may have to fight hard to keep writing big income checks.

B Expense Ratio %

It's critical to look for bond funds with low expenses. Expenses can eat into total returns, and typically, only a narrow difference separates the returns of the leaders and laggards of a bond category. Also, high-cost bond funds tend to be riskier than low-cost funds. Expenses are deducted from a fund's income payments. To keep yields at high-cost funds competitive, managers often make riskier investments, such as buying longer-duration issues, lower-quality debt, or complex derivatives. Managers with lower expense hurdles can offer the same returns without taking on the extra risk. How much is too much to pay? In general, broker-sold funds cost a bit more than no-load offerings, but that said, investors can find many government or corporate high-quality bond funds with expense ratios of 0.75% or less. For specialty bond funds, such as high yield or international bond, don't pay much more than 1%.

C Current Investment Style / Duration

The bond style box is based on a fund's credit quality and its duration. Check the fund's average credit quality and average effective duration in the column next to the style box. Credit quality is an important aspect of any bond fund, as it measures the creditworthiness of the fund's holdings. A fund with an average credit quality of AAA, for example, is less likely to get stung by defaults than a fund with an average credit quality of BBB. Duration is equally important, as it measures a fund's overall interest-rate risk. The longer a fund's duration, the more sensitive the fund is to shifts in interest rates. When interest rates fall, funds with longer durations benefit; when rates climb, shorter-duration funds benefit.

Most managers keep duration either pegged to a benchmark or within a prescribed range around a benchmark. For most investors, a fund with a disciplined duration strategy makes the most sense. First, such an approach confines managers' interest-rate bets. Few managers have proved they can consistently time the short-term direction of interest rates. Second, a fund with a consistent duration strategy may be easier to place in a portfolio. For example, a bond fund whose duration fluctuates dramatically poses asset-allocation problems for investors, as it's difficult to tell how it will react to interst rate changes.

First-time bond-fund buyers, especially those looking to cushion their stock-heavy portfolios, probably should stick with funds in the intermediate-term range (3.5 to six years). Intermediate-term bond funds have offered yields and returns similar to long-term bond funds but with less volatility.

D Credit Analysis

Average credit quality provides a snapshot of a portfolio's overall credit quality, while the Credit Analysis section shows the percentage of fixed-income securities that fall within each credit-quality rating, as assigned by Standard & Poor's or Moody's. The lower a bond's rating, the greater its default risk and the higher its yield. Bonds rated BBB and above are considered investment-grade issues; those rated BB and below are high yield, commonly called junk bonds. Pay particularly close attention to a fund's weightings in below B and nonrated bonds. Often these issues are riskier bonds that are in danger of defaulting or that have already defaulted. They are also typically less liquid than higher-quality bonds.

Diversify with a good mix of high- and low-quality bonds (lean more toward the high-quality side), if not in one of the multisector bond funds (which tend to cost more), then in a portfolio of two or three bond funds.

The Best Funds for 2007

**by Scott Berry and
Russel Kinnel,
Co-Editors, Morningstar
Funds 500**

Savvy investors get excited when great opportunities for long-term winners come up. Less successful investors get excited by a chance to hop on a trend for a few weeks. The former way is the way to wealth. The latter is the way to disappointment.

So when we gather up some of our favorite ideas for 2007, we're talking about something that we expect to be rewarding if you buy in 2007 and hold until 2017 or 2027. It's that long-term perspective that can have a powerful effect on your wealth down the line.

Assessing the investment landscape for 2007, we see a lot of attractive investments but we don't really have an opinion on whether 2007 will be a good year for the market.

One of the strongest themes we're hearing from smart fund managers is that large-cap stocks look cheap. Historically they have traded at a premium to small caps because there's safety in companies that dominate their market and because most of the valuable brand names are large caps. Yet today small caps trade at a premium because they've had such a long runup.

Another theme worth exploring is the advantages that small funds will have over bloated funds. Many of the best managers are running so much money that it will be very hard for them to add value in a meaningful way. That's a big opportunity for more flexible managers with small sums to run. You have to look harder to find them, often at fund companies that aren't household names, but they're there.

Finally, we end with the most dependable theme: Low-cost funds make great investments. Today bond yields are kind of small, and some experts say stock returns won't be much better. Bond managers point out that today's market doesn't pay you much for taking on more credit risk or interest-rate risk. So the best way is to instead work on the other end of the return equation: costs. If you lower your fund costs, then you will get more out of the low-return environment. We've done study after study to show low-cost funds consistently beat high-cost funds.

Growth Is Good

Primecap Odyssey Aggressive Growth

It's funny: When investors move into funds with higher-risk strategies, they often throw caution to the wind and pick whatever fund has the best one-year returns. But experience and discipline are actually most important with higher-risk strategies. So for an aggressive mid-growth fund, we want good fundamental investors who won't throw caution to the wind. The Primecap team fits the bill, and the fund doesn't yet have a lot in assets.

Harbor International Growth

Don't let the fund's bland record fool you; this is a keeper. The fund had some rough years in the past, but in 2004 it was handed to Jim Gendelman of Marsico Capital Management, and he's done a great job here and at a similar fund he runs under the Marsico banner. As you'd expect from someone running money at Marsico, Gendelman is a focused aggressive-growth manager who mixes in fundamental research with macroeconomic analysis. Gendelman takes on plenty of risk with emerging-markets stocks among other things, but his long-term record shows he makes the most of the risks.

Big Is Beautiful

Bridgeway Ultra 35

This fund has underperformed simply because the market has had a strong bias against blue chips over the past few years. That makes this fund all the more attractive because markets rotate, and blue chips are likely set to outperform for a while. If you've let your small-cap funds grow to become larger parts of your portfolio, this fund is a quick way to realign your market-cap allocation. Its average market cap is a huge $107 billion. It's also cheap at just 0.15%.

Dreyfus Appreciation

This fund is one of many plays on blue-chip names, but management's preference for companies with proven and well-known brands separates it from the pack. It holds more consumer-goods companies and fewer technology names than the typical large-blend fund. Management likes firms with high-quality earnings, clean balance sheets, and lots of free cash flow. The portfolio is more concentrated in individual stocks than many rivals. Management takes a buy-and-hold approach, which translates into strong tax efficiency. The fund is subadvised by Fayez Sarofim, a firm with a great record and a deep staff of analysts and managers.

Small
Schneider Value

With just over $150 million in assets, this fund is hardly a household name. But we think the fund's small asset base adds to its appeal, as it allows manager Arnie Schneider plenty of flexibility to go where the values take him. Recently, for example, the fund has loaded up on financials, a number of which have delivered strong returns. The fund's record isn't as long as others, but its early results have been most impressive. We also like this fund for its reasonable costs. Often new funds are priced high until assets build and costs can be lowered.

Masters Select Smaller Companies

This fund provides one-stop access to a number of skilled small-cap managers. The managers, including Bob Rodriguez of FPA Capital and John Rogers of Ariel Fund, run the gamut from deep value to aggressive growth, so shareholders are getting diversified small-cap exposure here. Though the managers run money elsewhere, this fund's small asset base means their best ideas can go here. We like the fund's management lineup, and we like that advisor Litman/Gregory plans on keeping the fund small by closing it at $450 million. The fund is near $300 million now.

T. Rowe Price Global Stock

This fund was a pick for 2006, and it remains a pick for 2007. The key attraction here is the fund's management. Rob Gensler took over the portfolio in August 2005, after delivering strong results at T. Rowe Price Media & Telecom. Gensler employs a go-anywhere approach, ranging freely across regions (including emerging markets) while maintaining a concentrated, growth-oriented style. That bold style and a nimble asset base ($330 million) make for a potent combination. Gensler's bets on

lesser-known stocks may create some added short-term volatility here, but we're confident in his research capabilities and expect this fund will be a long-term winner.

Cheap
Vanguard Total Bond Market Index

It might seem like we're throwing our hands in the air by picking an index fund, but costs play such a huge role in separating bond fund winners and losers that this fund's expense advantage can't be ignored. The fund charges just 0.20% per year, while its median no-load intermediate bond peer charges 0.72%. To put that difference in perspective, it basically equates to a little more than one extra monthly dividend payment per year at current yield levels. Not surprisingly, the fund's income returns typically rank in category best quartile. Finally, with many fund managers complaining about a lack of opportunities in the bond market, we think just owning the market makes good sense.

Fidelity Intermediate Municipal

At 0.42%, the fund's expense ratio ranks among the cheapest no-load intermediate muni funds. And Fidelity is careful not to put the fund's expense advantage at too much risk. Manager Mark Sommer avoids low-rated bonds and interest-rate bets, focusing instead on issues, sectors, and bond structures that he considers to be undervalued. That approach isn't flashy, but backed by Fidelity's considerable research capabilities, it has delivered consistently solid results here. And with longer-term bonds and low-rated issues offering little added yield, we don't think investors are sacrificing much return for this fund's relative stability.

Dodge & Cox Income

This fund is another perennial favorite. The fund's proven and experienced management team relies on the bottom-up research of its large analyst staff to build this portfolio bond by bond. The team's rigorous credit research helped the fund shine in 2002 when others faltered, while low costs have provided a meaningful and sustainable advantage year in and year out. The overall results have been quite remarkable, as the fund's volatility checks in well below the intermediate bond category norm, while its long-term returns rank among the group's elite. We expect continued success in 2007. ▮

How We Choose Funds for the 500

**by Russel Kinnel,
Co-Editor, Morningstar
Funds 500**

An important part of investing is simply narrowing the list of ideas down to a manageable group that you can investigate more thoroughly. After all, there are thousands of funds and stocks to choose from. Here's how I go about narrowing the field for the *Morningstar Funds 500*.

Our Complete Coverage List

We track more than 7,000 mutual funds in our database, which includes virtually every mutual fund in the U.S. Out of that universe, we select 2,000 funds to analyze in depth. Analyzing a fund means we interview the manager, review SEC filings, conduct research on the fund using our in-house tools, and dig into the individual holdings of the fund's portfolio.

All 2,000 Analyst Reports are in the Premium section of Morningstar.com. We choose the 2,000 funds based on a few key factors: asset size, performance, quality of management, expense ratio, and strategy. We give extra points to unique strategies or formats. For instance, only a handful of funds track commodity prices directly, and we quickly covered the first two after their inceptions. While we generally add funds with strong track records, we'll sometimes add funds quickly if we like their managers. For example, we added Marsico Focus and Primcecap Odyssey Aggressive Growth soon after they were launched.

The Morningstar Funds 500

Morningstar Funds 500 readers use this publication for two distinct purposes: to monitor their existing investments and to find great new ideas to buy. So when I'm winnowing the group of 2,000 funds down to 500, I look for big funds that are popular with our readers. On the other hand, I also look for great funds—or at least intriguing new ones—that are worth a look. The two groups aren't mutually exclusive, of course, but I think about both roles when adding new names.

To illustrate, let's look at a couple of new additions to the *Morningstar Funds 500*. I added Primecap Odyssey Aggressive Growth because I know that the Primecap management team is one of the best in the business. We've followed them for a long time at Vanguard Primecap and Vanguard Capital Opportunity. I even visited them in Pasadena, and we named them Managers of the Year a couple years ago. The fund is so new that its track record isn't very meaningful but that didn't matter because Primecap has a very long track record at other funds.

On the other hand, there are funds that have to build long successful track records before they get in. Osterweis Fund was around for 12 years before it made it in. It's a nifty little mid-blend fund with a small asset base that gives it room to grow. Not exactly a household name, but we like Osterweis' eclectic stock selection, which is driven by a focus on cash flow. The fund's 10-year returns top 90% of mid-blend funds'.

To make room for attractive funds like Osterweis, I cull funds that have slipped a notch or two. For example, I cut a fund if it loses a good manager or raises its expense ratio, or if its fundamentals have deteriorated to the point where it isn't all that attractive any more.

Is the Morningstar Funds 500 a Buy List?

Not quite. The *Morningstar Funds 500* contains a lot of attractive funds, but it isn't exactly a buy list. For one thing, I don't kick funds off the list once they close to new investors. For another, I'll keep a giant fund on the list even if it's not quite topnotch. However, most big funds are decent investments, as they usually offer skilled management and modest costs. This leads us to what is a buy list.

Our Fund Analyst Picks List

The Fund Analyst Picks list represents our best ideas for new investments. We limit it to just those funds we consider to be outstanding. There's no set number of picks for each category.

A pick just has to be a fund we like so much we'd consider buying it ourselves. Thus, we have no current picks in the Japan stock category due to a lack of well-managed funds with reasonable expenses.

On the other hand, we have eight Analyst Picks in the large-value category—a stock-picker's haven. The Fund Analyst Picks list is a subset of the *Morningstar Funds 500*. All picks except for single-state municipal-bond funds are included in the 500. If you're looking for a fund to add in a particular category, the Analyst Picks are a quick way to narrow the field to the very best.

What We Look For
Only funds with strong competitive advantages make our Analyst Picks list. We look for low costs, outstanding management with strong support from analysts and traders, a sound strategy, and a healthy corporate culture that puts fundholders' interests first. We also want a fund with bright prospects, so we keep an eye out for signals that the outlook could change. We monitor for such warning signs as asset growth, turnover in the analyst or manager ranks, or portfolio changes that don't jibe with our expectations given the stated strategy.

Let's take a look at how some picks stack up on those criteria.

Dodge & Cox International Stock scores well on all fronts. The fund charges just 0.70%, and it boasts a great management team with tremendous experience. Moreover, the fund uses a conservative, value-driven strategy that makes all of Dodge & Cox's funds easy for investors to buy and hold without being tempted by fear or greed the way they can be at more volatile funds. The fund has a number of competitive advantages: strong, stable management that competitors couldn't quickly match and low costs that only a handful of foreign funds can touch. It certainly passes the test of being a fund we'd invest in—I own it.

Stewardship Grades
Only funds with a Stewardship Grade of A or B earn a place on our picks list. Those that rate lower can be bad risks because of poor corporate culture, high manager turnover, a bad track record with regulators, or other problems that could hurt a fund in the future.

Inside the Process
Each category is assigned to a specialist who gets to know the funds inside and out. We have regular reviews in which the analysts submit their recommendations for category picks to a committee of four that vets the selections and submits suggestions of its own. We review the recommendations and make a final call. We engage in a vigorous debate that will often bring up new avenues to investigate before we make a final decision. Thus, every pick goes through a rigorous process.

Why Funds Get Removed
Culling funds from our picks list is a process based on the same criteria used to build the list. The most frequent reasons for removing Analyst Picks are manager changes and rising expense ratios. Sometimes a combination of a few factors leads us to conclude a fund is no longer a standout.

For example, we dropped Gabelli Small Cap Growth because its expense ratio remained high even as assets grew. At the same time, performance had tailed off and there were serious stewardship issues at Gabelli.

Conclusion
The *Morningstar Funds 500* and Fund Analyst Picks list is the culmination of a lot of hard work by our 30-strong analyst staff. Like the managers we admire most, we're constantly on the look out for ways to improve our picks list. However, because the process is fundamentally driven, our actual turnover is fairly low. ∎

Getting the Most Out of Star Ratings and Analyst Picks

**by Christine Benz,
Director of
Fund Analysis**

Morningstar analysts tend to receive e-mail that relates to whatever investment type they specialize in. No matter what the analyst's specialty, however, one type of question seems to crop up more than any other. "If Fund X is so great, why does it have only a 3-star rating from Morningstar?" I also tend to see a lot of variations on a related question. "Fund Y has a 5-star rating from Morningstar, so why isn't it an Analyst Pick?"

Fund star ratings and Analyst Picks can be great additions to your research process, but it's essential to understand how we come up with them and how best to use them (and perhaps just as important, how not to use them). In this article, I'll discuss the basics of getting the most out of both sets of tools.

The Morningstar Rating for Funds

Morningstar's fund star rating is designed to give investors a snapshot of how a mutual fund has balanced risk and return in the past. We calculate a fund's star rating relative to other offerings that operate within the same category. We arrive at a large-cap value fund's star rating by evaluating how it has performed relative to other large-cap value funds, for example, and we compare short-term bond funds with other short-term bond funds.

The fund star rating is strictly quantitative; analysts can't add stars to funds they like or yank them from those they don't. Because the star rating captures only a fund's past risk/reward profile, there will definitely be occasions when a fund with a low star rating has terrific future prospects, and vice versa. For example, American Funds Washington Mutual, a 2-star fund, is one of our Analyst Picks within the large-value category. Yes, it has struggled recently, but we like its management's consistent approach, which has delivered good results over the life of the fund.

How to Use It

The fund universe, at more than 17,000 offerings, is a little bit overwhelming. That's where the star rating comes in. If you know you want a given type of fund, you can use the star rating to winnow that group down to a more manageable list of options that deserves further research. In so doing, you can reduce the large-growth universe from more than 500 funds to those that fit your criteria and merit further investigation. True, you might miss out on that 1-star fund with bright prospects, but that's a small price to pay for greatly streamlining the number of funds you have to research further.

You can also use the star rating to help monitor your funds' performance. If your onetime 5-star fund is now sporting a single star, you should research what has driven the downturn. It's possible that the manager's style is simply out of favor and will eventually rebound. But a dramatic shift in a fund's star rating could indicate that there's something more substantive going on—maybe the fund is taking bigger risks than it once did, or perhaps its management team has changed.

How Not to Use It

Although the star rating can be a handy tool for monitoring your funds' performance, you shouldn't view it as a buy or sell signal. Because we recalculate funds' star ratings every month, funds frequently gain or lose a star, and that action can best be described as "noise" that you should tune out.

Moreover, a fund isn't automatically worth buying just because it earns a 5-star rating. There are 5-star funds in every category, so job one is determining which categories make sense for you in the first place. (A 5-star large-value fund might make sense for a broad swath of investors, but a 5-star precious-metals fund might not.)

In addition, a fund's rating may not reflect underlying changes—a manager or strategy change, for example—that make it more or less attractive. Finally, remember that the star rating is just a starting point for your research—not the be-all end-all for determining its future prospects. Although we'd stand by the assertion that 5-star funds are a generally better lot than 1-star offerings, you'll need to assess a number of other factors—notably, its strategy, costs, and management—to determine whether a given fund makes sense for you.

Fund Analyst Picks

That brings us to our Analyst Picks, which pick up where the star rating leaves off. True, we pay attention to a fund's past risk/reward profile when culling each category's elite. But in searching for funds that will be winners in the future, we spend even more time scouting out those offerings with the best "fundamentals"—those with sensible strategies, enough experienced management and analyst support to distinguish themselves from others using that same approach, and strong risk controls, among other factors. We also pay a lot of attention to expenses, because expenses are the single-best predictor of a fund's long-term performance.

In contrast to our star ratings, which are strictly quantitative, our Analyst Picks are qualitative all the way. For each category, we assign an analyst to serve as the Analyst Picks guru, meaning that he or she is responsible for knowing the funds in that group inside and out and for staying abreast of the best and brightest (and also the worst) within that category.

How to Use Them

Whereas the star rating can lend a helping hand to investors who like to do their own research, our Analyst Picks list does the work for you. If you're looking at our Analyst Picks list for ideas, you can rest assured we've put all of the funds through their paces and believe that they have a strong shot at outperforming their rivals. (Our Analyst Pick criteria are so stringent that if we can't find any worthy funds within a given category, we'll go without; that's currently the case with the Japan-stock category, for example.)

Our Analyst Picks list is also an ideal way to surface off-the-beaten-path funds whose strong future prospects aren't reflected in their past records. For example, we made Wasatch Heritage Growth an Analyst Pick shortly after it launched in 2004. Although the fund was brand new and its managers unproven, we're impressed by the research effort that infuses all Wasatch funds. We also appreciate the firm's shareholder-friendliness, as evidenced by its timely closing of other Wasatch funds.

How Not to Use Them

As with the star rating, it's a mistake to view the Analyst Picks as a "must-own" list. While all of the funds on the list are tops within their categories, you may simply not need a fund within a given group.

Also, think twice before supplanting a fund you own with one on our Analyst Picks list. It may well make sense to make the switch, but you should take tax and transaction costs into account before swapping out of a perfectly serviceable fund.

By the same token, you shouldn't overreact if and when we take one of your holdings off our Analyst Picks list. For example, we recently removed Fidelity Asset Manager 50% from our moderate-allocation Analyst Picks list because we were concerned about a recent management change. The change dampens the fund's appeal, but its other attractions remain. Although we no longer believe the fund to be in the top tier of the moderate-allocation category, we'd definitely recommend that current shareholders hang on to it. ▥

Analyst Picks
Morningstar Funds 500 Universe

Domestic Equity

Page	Fund Name	Category Name	Morningstar Rating
36	Allianz RCM Technology Instl	Specialty-Technology	★★★★
65	American Funds Inc Fund of Amer A	Moderate Allocation	★★★★
72	American Funds Washington Mutual A	Large Value	★★
77	Ariel Appreciation	Mid-Cap Blend	★★★
85	Aston/Montag & Caldwell Growth N	Large Growth	★★★★
95	Bogle Small Cap Growth Inv	Small Blend	★★★★
96	Brandywine	Mid-Cap Growth	★★★★
105	Buffalo Mid Cap	Mid-Cap Growth	★★★★
108	Calamos Growth & Income A	Convertibles	★★★★
112	Century Small Cap Select Inv	Small Growth	★★★★
114	Champlain Small Company Adv	Small Growth	—
117	Clipper	Large Blend	★★★★
122	Davis Appreciation & Income A	Convertibles	★★★★
123	Davis Financial A	Specialty-Financial	★★★
127	Diamond Hill Small Cap A	Small Value	★★★★
128	Dodge & Cox Balanced	Moderate Allocation	★★★★★
131	Dodge & Cox Stock	Large Value	★★★★★
139	Eaton Vance Utilities A	Specialty-Utilities	★★★★★
219	FPA Capital	Small Value	★★
222	FPA Paramount	Mid-Cap Blend	★★
142	Fairholme	Mid-Cap Blend	★★★★★
159	Fidelity Dividend Growth	Large Blend	★★★
203	Fidelity Spartan 500 Index Investor	Large Blend	★★★
205	Fidelity Spartan Total Market Index Inv	Large Blend	★★★★
234	Harbor Capital Appreciation Instl	Large Growth	★★★
259	JPMorgan U.S. Real Estate A	Specialty-Real Estate	★★★
250	Janus Mid Cap Value Investor	Mid-Cap Value	★★★
268	Longleaf Partners	Large Blend	★★★★
270	Longleaf Partners Small-Cap	Small Value	★★★★★
276	MainStay ICAP Select Equity I	Large Value	★★★★
287	Masters' Select Equity	Large Blend	★★★
288	Masters' Select Smaller Companies	Small Growth	★★★★
299	Morgan Stanley Inst US Real Estate A	Specialty-Real Estate	★★★★★
318	Oakmark I	Large Blend	★★★★
321	Oakmark Select I	Large Blend	★★★★
343	PRIMECAP Odyssey Aggressive Growth	Mid-Cap Growth	—
328	Pax World Balanced	Moderate Allocation	★★★★
351	Royce Special Equity Inv	Small Value	★★
358	Schneider Small Cap Value	Small Value	★★★★★
359	Schneider Value	Large Value	★★★★★
361	Selected American Shares S	Large Blend	★★★★★
362	Selected Special Shares S	Mid-Cap Blend	★★★
365	Sound Shore	Large Value	★★★★
373	T. Rowe Price Equity Income	Large Value	★★★★
374	T. Rowe Price Financial Services	Specialty-Financial	★★★★
380	T. Rowe Price Health Sciences	Specialty-Health	★★★★
386	T. Rowe Price Media & Telecom	Specialty-Communications	★★★★★
388	T. Rowe Price Mid-Cap Value	Mid-Cap Value	★★★★★
389	T. Rowe Price New America Growth	Large Growth	★★★
394	T. Rowe Price Personal Strat Income	Conservative Allocation	★★★★

Domestic Equity

Page	Fund Name	Category Name	Morningstar Rating
395	T. Rowe Price Real Estate	Specialty-Real Estate	★★★★
412	TCW Value Opportunities I	Mid-Cap Blend	★
418	Third Avenue Real Estate Value	Specialty-Real Estate	★★★
419	Third Avenue Small-Cap Value	Small Blend	★★★★
427	Turner Midcap Growth	Mid-Cap Growth	★★★
433	USAA Aggressive Growth	Large Growth	★★★
441	Vanguard 500 Index	Large Blend	★★★
445	Vanguard Capital Opportunity	Mid-Cap Growth	★★★★★
447	Vanguard Convertible Securities	Convertibles	★★★★
454	Vanguard Explorer	Small Growth	★★★
460	Vanguard Growth Equity	Large Growth	★★★
461	Vanguard Health Care	Specialty-Health	★★★★★
482	Vanguard Mid Capitalization Index	Mid-Cap Blend	★★★★
485	Vanguard PRIMECAP	Large Blend	★★★★★
486	Vanguard PRIMECAP Core	Large Growth	—
488	Vanguard Selected Value	Mid-Cap Value	★★★
501	Vanguard Tax-Managed Balanced	Conservative Allocation	★★★★
503	Vanguard Tax-Managed Small Cap Ret	Small Blend	★★★
504	Vanguard Total Stock Mkt Idx	Large Blend	★★★★
509	Vanguard U.S. Value	Large Value	★★★
511	Vanguard Wellesley Income	Conservative Allocation	★★★★★
512	Vanguard Wellington	Moderate Allocation	★★★★★
517	Wasatch Heritage Growth	Mid-Cap Growth	—
522	Weitz Hickory	Mid-Cap Blend	★★★
524	Weitz Value	Large Value	★★★★

Analyst Picks

Morningstar Funds 500 Universe

International Equity

Page	Fund Name	Category Name	Morningstar Rating
41	American Century Global Gold Inv	Specialty-Precious Metals	★★
59	American Funds Capital Inc Bldr A	World Allocation	★★★★
62	American Funds EuroPacific Gr A	Foreign Large Blend	★★★★
68	American Funds New Perspective A	World Stock	★★★
69	American Funds New World A	Diversified Emerging Mkts	★★
78	Artisan International Inv	Foreign Large Growth	★★★★
80	Artisan International Small Cap	Foreign Small/Mid Growth	★★★★
94	BlackRock Global Allocation A	World Allocation	★★★★
111	Causeway International Value Inv	Foreign Large Value	★★★
130	Dodge & Cox International Stock	Foreign Large Value	★★★★
204	Fidelity Spartan International Index Inv	Foreign Large Blend	★★★★
235	Harbor International Growth Inv	Foreign Large Growth	★★★
236	Harbor International Instl	Foreign Large Value	★★★★
275	MainStay ICAP International I	Foreign Large Value	★★★★
290	Masters' Select International	Foreign Large Blend	★★★★
292	Matthews Pacific Tiger	Pacific/Asia ex-Japan Stk	★★★★
317	Oakmark Global I	World Stock	★★★★★
322	Oppenheimer Developing Markets A	Diversified Emerging Mkts	★★★★
323	Oppenheimer Global A	World Stock	★★★★
325	Oppenheimer International Growth A	Foreign Large Growth	★★★
372	T. Rowe Price Emerging Markets Stock	Diversified Emerging Mkts	★★★★
375	T. Rowe Price Global Stock	World Stock	★★★★
385	T. Rowe Price Latin America	Latin America Stock	★★★★
390	T. Rowe Price New Asia	Pacific/Asia ex-Japan Stk	★★★★
453	Vanguard European Stock Index	Europe Stock	★★★
468	Vanguard International Explorer	Foreign Small/Mid Growth	★★★★
484	Vanguard Precious Metals and Mining	Specialty-Precious Metals	★★★★★
506	Vanguard Total Intl Stock Index	Foreign Large Blend	★★★★

Fixed Income

Page	Fund Name	Category Name	Morningstar Rating
129	Dodge & Cox Income	Intermediate-Term Bond	★★★★★
137	Eaton Vance Floating Rate A	Bank Loan	★
138	Eaton Vance Income Fund of Boston A	High Yield Bond	★★★★
221	FPA New Income	Intermediate-Term Bond	★★★
164	Fidelity Floating Rate High Income	Bank Loan	★★
168	Fidelity Government Income	Intermediate Government	★★★★
175	Fidelity Intermediate Municipal Income	Muni National Interm	★★★★
186	Fidelity Municipal Income	Muni National Long	★★★★
187	Fidelity New Markets Income	Emerging Markets Bond	★★★
197	Fidelity Short-Intermediate Muni Income	Muni National Short	★★★
198	Fidelity Short-Term Bond	Short-Term Bond	★★★★
206	Fidelity Strategic Income	Multisector Bond	★★★★
208	Fidelity Tax-Free Bond	Muni National Long	★★★★
211	Fidelity Ultra-Short Bond	Ultrashort Bond	★★★★
224	Franklin Federal Tax-Free Income A	Muni National Long	★★★★
233	Harbor Bond Instl	Intermediate-Term Bond	★★★★★
271	Loomis Sayles Bond Ret	Multisector Bond	★★★★★
272	Loomis Sayles Global Bond Ret	World Bond	★★★★
297	Metropolitan West Total Return Bond M	Intermediate-Term Bond	★★★★
313	Northeast Investors	High Yield Bond	★★★
332	PIMCO Emerging Markets Bond D	Emerging Markets Bond	★★★
333	PIMCO Foreign Bond (USD-Hedged) D	World Bond	★★★
334	PIMCO Foreign Bond (Unhedged) D	World Bond	—
335	PIMCO High Yield D	High Yield Bond	★★★
330	Payden Limited Maturity	Ultrashort Bond	★★★
381	T. Rowe Price High-Yield	High Yield Bond	★★★★
382	T. Rowe Price International Bond	World Bond	★★★
401	T. Rowe Price Spectrum Income	Multisector Bond	★★★
404	T. Rowe Price Tax-Free High-Yield	High Yield Muni	★★★
403	T. Rowe Price Tax-Free Short-Interm	Muni National Short	★★★★
410	TCW Total Return Bond I	Intermediate-Term Bond	★★★★★
435	USAA Tax Exempt Intermediate-Term	Muni National Interm	★★★★★
437	USAA Tax Exempt Short-Term	Muni National Short	★★★★
457	Vanguard GNMA	Intermediate Government	★★★★★
462	Vanguard High-Yield Corporate	High Yield Bond	★★★
463	Vanguard High-Yield Tax-Exempt	Muni National Interm	★★★★★
472	Vanguard Interm-Term Tax-Ex	Muni National Interm	★★★★
478	Vanguard Long-Term Investment-Grade	Long-Term Bond	★★★★
477	Vanguard Long-Term Tax-Exempt	Muni National Long	★★★★
479	Vanguard Long-Term U.S. Treasury	Long Government	★★★
480	Vanguard Ltd-Term Tax-Ex	Muni National Short	★★★★
489	Vanguard Short-Term Bond Index	Short-Term Bond	★★★★
490	Vanguard Short-Term Federal	Short Government	★★★★
493	Vanguard Short-Term Tax-Ex	Muni National Short	★★
505	Vanguard Total Bond Market Index	Intermediate-Term Bond	★★★★
526	Western Asset Core Bond Institutional	Intermediate-Term Bond	★★★★★

Analyst Pans
Morningstar's Open-End Fund Universe

Fund Name	Category Name	Morningstar Rating	Fund Name	Category Name	Morningstar Rating
AIM Opportunities I A	Small Blend	★	Midas Special	Large Blend	★★
AIM Opportunities II A	Mid-Cap Blend	★	Monetta Select Technology	Specialty-Technology	★
AIM Opportunities III A	Large Blend	★	Morgan Stanley Natural Resource Dev B	Specialty-Natural Res	★★
AXA Enterprise Mergers & Acquisitions A	Mid-Cap Blend	★★	Munder Internet A	Specialty-Technology	★★★
AllianceBernstein Bond Corp Bd A	Intermediate-Term Bond	★★★	PL Inflation Managed 529 AZ A	Inflation-Protected Bond	★
AllianceBernstein Bond U.S. Govt A	Intermediate Government	★★	Pacific Advisors Growth A	Large Growth	★★★★
American Eagle Twenty	Mid-Cap Growth	★★	Payden Value Leaders	Large Value	★★
American Growth D	Large Growth	★	Phoenix Market Neutral A	Long-Short	★★
American Heritage	World Stock	★	Phoenix Nifty Fifty A	Large Growth	★
Berkshire Focus	Specialty-Technology	★	ProFunds Biotechnology UltraSector Inv	Specialty-Health	★★
Chicken Little Growth	Large Growth	—	ProFunds UltraBull Inv	Large Blend	★★★
Columbia Asset Allocation A	Moderate Allocation	★★	Putnam Europe Equity A	Europe Stock	★★
Columbia Federal Securities A	Intermediate Government	★★	Saratoga Financial Service B	Specialty-Financial	★★
Columbia Small Cap Growth I Z	Small Growth	★★★★	Saratoga Health & Biotechnology A	Specialty-Health	★
Dreyfus Founders Passport F	Foreign Small/Mid Value	★★★	Saratoga Technology & Comm A	Specialty-Technology	★★
Dreyfus Premier Short Term Income D	Short-Term Bond	★★★	Seligman Global Growth A	World Stock	★
Eastern European Equity	Europe Stock	★★★	State Farm LifePath 2010 A Legacy	Target-Date 2000-2014	★★★
Federated Equity-Income A	Large Value	★★	State Farm LifePath 2020 A Legacy	Target-Date 2015-2029	★★
Federated International Equity A	Foreign Large Growth	★★	State Farm LifePath 2030 A Legacy	Target-Date 2030+	★★
Federated International Small Co A	Foreign Small/Mid Growth	★★	State Farm LifePath 2040 A Legacy	Target-Date 2030+	★★
Federated Limited Term Municipal A	Muni National Short	★★	SunAmerica Balanced Assets A	Moderate Allocation	★
Fifth Third Interm Muni Bond A	Muni National Interm	★	SunAmerica Focused Gr A	Mid-Cap Growth	★★★
First American Large Cap Value A	Large Value	★★	SunAmerica New Century A	Mid-Cap Growth	★★★
First Investors Insured Tax-Exempt A	Muni National Long	★★	U.S. Global Investors Eastern Europe	Europe Stock	★★★★★
Frontier MicroCap	Small Blend	★	U.S. Global Investors Gold Shares	Specialty-Precious Metals	★★
FundX Conservative Upgrader	Large Blend	★★★★	UBS PACE Municipal Fixed-Income A	Muni National Interm	★
FundX Upgrader	World Stock	★★★★	Van Kampen Technology A	Specialty-Technology	★★
GAMCO Mathers	Conservative Allocation	★	Van Wagoner Emerging Growth	Small Growth	★
Genomics Y	Specialty-Health	★★	Waddell & Reed Adv Muni High-Inc A	High Yield Muni	★★★
Granum Value	Mid-Cap Value	★★	Waddell & Reed Adv Municipal Bond A	Muni National Long	★
ING MagnaCap A	Large Value	★			
Integrity Technology A	Specialty-Technology	★★★			
Ivy International Growth A	Foreign Large Blend	★			
Jacob Internet	Specialty-Technology	★★★★★			
Jundt Growth A	Large Growth	★			
Jundt Opportunity A	Large Growth	★			
Jundt Twenty-Five A	Large Growth	★			
Kinetics Internet	Mid-Cap Growth	★★★			
MainStay Tax-Free Bond A	Muni National Long	★			
MegaTrends	Large Growth	★★★★			

Rating the Performance of the Star Rating

**by Russel Kinnel,
Co-Editor, Morningstar
Funds 500**

In 2002 we launched the revised Morningstar Rating for funds, and each year since we've updated a study on how the rating has performed. For background, the rating is a quantitative measure of risk-adjusted performance relative to a category over the past three-, five-, and 10-year periods.

For this year we look at how the ratings as of June 2002, June 2003, and June 2004 have fared at predicting relative performance and future star ratings.

Now that the ratings are four years old and we're on our third study, we can be more certain about how it's working. Fund investing is about long-term success, so the best measure of the star rating will be long-term performance. We are starting to get there with four-year returns, but we're still a ways away. We looked at shorter periods, too, for purposes of tracking how the rating is faring, but we do not want to read too much into two-year returns.

I also looked at ways to improve upon the performance of 5-star funds and what funds in the *Morningstar Funds 500* pass the test. I found that adding in low costs to a screen for 5-star funds produced better results than using either screen on its own. Here, I'll provide more names of funds that pass both screens.

How Do 5-Star Funds Perform?

Consistent with past studies, the new study shows that 5-star funds tend to outperform 4-star funds and so on. Thus, the biggest performance gap is from 5-star funds to 1-star funds. This was the case when measured by relative performance and the three-year star rating.

Looking out over the three time periods tested, it's apparent that this trend is holding up and may be getting stronger. Consider that 5-star domestic-stock funds from

2002 produced top-47% returns while 2003 improved to top-43% and 2004 to top-39%.

I'm not yet certain if this means that the rating is best at predicting near-term performance or if the rating simply performed better in the ensuing years. As you recall, 2002 was an inflection point—the last brutal year of the bear market. Thus, returns were less useful as a predictor of future performance that year than they would be in a more normal year.

The 2004 ratings are notable for the fact that they were the first to reflect our style-specific foreign-stock categories such as foreign large-growth. For the ensuing two-year period, 5-star international-stock funds averaged top-40% returns while 1-star funds were in the bottom 45%.

Bond Ratings Work Best

The rating for bond funds and balanced funds is even more powerful than it is for stock funds. Consider that the gap between 5-star and 1-star funds over the three time periods was an average of 26 percentage points for balanced funds, 27 percentage points for taxable-bond funds, and 40 percentage points for municipal-bond funds.

The most likely explanation is that within a bond-fund category the returns are closely bunched because bonds tend to perform pretty closely to each other with only modest differences in returns. That means that expense ratios have a big impact on relative performance rankings and expense ratios hardly change at all. Thus, the star ratings capture a source of persistent outperformance. Moreover, the top bond shops are head and shoulders above the rest of the crowd, and they are more consistent in their outperformance than stock-fund managers again. These two factors combined make the star rating a strong measure for bond funds and balanced funds.

An Anomaly Disappears

I was interested to see that one anomaly that stood out in last year's study is no longer there. Last year, I reported that 1-star international funds from 2002 had produced a surprisingly strong top-43% return ranking over the ensuing three years. One year later, that top-43% has melted to bottom-63%. What happened? In two words: emerging markets.

The star rating is a risk-adjusted measure, but from 2003 to 2005 emerging markets were a risk that paid off wonderfully. Thus, international funds penalized by the star rating for risk were in the clover. In the second quarter of 2006, that risk came home to roost as emerging markets were clobbered and funds with excessive bets on them took a beating. That's an encouraging sign that our risk measure is working at capturing funds with big underlying risk.

What About Batting Averages?

In my report on performance of our Fund Analyst Picks, I introduced batting averages as a way to track success. That is the percentage of Fund Analyst Picks that outperformed their category peers. As you may recall, our overall batting averages for the trailing three- and five-year periods ended June 30, 2006, were 67% for both periods.

I took a look at the batting averages for star ratings, too, and here's what I found. For 2002 through summer 2006 the average was 62%, for the class of 2003 it was 66%, and for 2004 it was 72%. So, on the whole, it looks like the Fund Analyst Picks have held up a little better.

Low-Cost 5-Star Funds

As I reported in February, low-cost 5-star funds have a good track record. Yet even with the field narrowed down you have to analyze the fundamentals to make sure it has a shot at producing performance to match its strong past returns. I've narrowed the list of 55 *Morningstar Funds 500* funds that have bottom-quartile costs and 5 stars to 11 still-open funds that look quite rewarding.

Dodge & Cox Income DODIX is exactly what most of us want in a bond fund: a conservative, dependable fund that outperforms year in and year out. Dodge does it by focusing on issue selection with a team of skilled analysts. The result is a fund that just keeps chugging along.

Fairholme Fund FAIRX is a great old-fashioned investor's fund at a time when funds have become more bland and corporate. Managers Bruce Berkowitz and Larry Pitkowsky invest in the styles of Buffett and Graham. They look for good companies on the cheap (Buffett) and supercheap turnaround plays (Graham).

Fidelity Municipal Income FHIGX has the best muni managers in the business, and the fund charges less than 96% of its peers. Tell me again about how you have to pay up for great management. (I own **Fidelity Tax-Free Bond** FTABX, but the idea's the same.)

Harbor Bond HABDX boasts the venerable Bill Gross and PIMCO as managers. It's not quite as good as Bill Miller's streak, but this fund has beaten the Lehman Brothers Aggregate in nine out of the past 11 years.

Homestead Value HOVLX is a relative newcomer to the Morningstar *Funds 500* but it certainly looks like a winner. Stuart Teach and Peter Morris look for companies that have hit hard times but that they think are fundamentally strong. They keep turnover and costs low and let stock selection do the rest.

Mairs & Power Growth MPGFX has been in a bit of a slump since George Mairs III retired, but we don't think the two are related. After all, the fund has 3% turnover. Manager Bill Frels likes steady-growing Midwest companies such as **3M** MMM and **Target** TGT, and I'm sure the market will like those stocks again.

Oakmark Global OAKGX managers Robert Taylor and Clyde McGregor are value stalwarts who take a creative approach to value investing. They keep a focused portfolio of their favorite names without much concern for country or sector weightings. For example, Switzerland is their second-largest country weighting.

Schneider Value SCMLX has a small asset base, low costs, and a great manager in Arnie Schneider. The only catch is you have to invest directly or pony up the transaction fee and buy through Vanguard. But that's a small price to pay for a great deep-value manager who is as interested in clients' returns as he is in his own.

Vanguard Global Equity VHGEX is a slightly odd mix of two traditional value managers from Marathon and AllianceBernstein with a faster-trading benchmark-focused team from Acadian Asset Management.

How the Star Rating Has Performed

Broad Asset Class	Rating as of June 2002	Total Return % Rank	3yr Rating as of June 30, 2005	Rating as of June 2003	Total Return % Rank	3yr Rating as of June 30, 2006	Rating as of June 2004	Total Return % Rank
2002				**2003**			**2004**	
Domestic Equity	★★★★★	47	3.18	★★★★★	43	3.24	★★★★★	39
	★★★★	50	3.12	★★★★	48	2.98	★★★★	45
	★★★	53	2.88	★★★	52	2.82	★★★	51
	★★	55	2.65	★★	54	2.67	★★	55
	★	52	2.37	★	49	2.70	★	57
International Equity	★★★★★	40	3.29	★★★★★	42	3.28	★★★★★	40
	★★★★	47	3.08	★★★★	47	2.91	★★★★	44
	★★★	51	2.81	★★★	50	2.83	★★★	48
	★★	57	2.52	★★	55	2.56	★★	56
	★	63	2.16	★	52	2.55	★	55
Balanced	★★★★★	34	3.73	★★★★★	35	3.41	★★★★★	26
	★★★★	42	3.45	★★★★	44	3.11	★★★★	40
	★★★	54	2.90	★★★	51	2.77	★★★	52
	★★	57	2.59	★★	54	2.69	★★	61
	★	55	2.00	★	63	2.22	★	63
Taxable Bond	★★★★★	39	3.60	★★★★★	35	3.47	★★★★★	22
	★★★★	44	3.38	★★★★	41	3.29	★★★★	37
	★★★	49	2.95	★★★	50	2.72	★★★	50
	★★	56	2.43	★★	57	2.20	★★	62
	★	53	2.53	★	56	2.36	★	67
Municipal Bond	★★★★★	27	4.15	★★★★★	28	4.02	★★★★★	27
	★★★★	39	3.50	★★★★	40	3.30	★★★★	36
	★★★	45	2.99	★★★	46	2.79	★★★	45
	★★	56	2.60	★★	53	2.41	★★	58
	★	65	2.32	★	63	2.21	★	74

Percentile Rank: 1=best   100=worst

Even so, you get good management and low costs, if not style purity.

Vanguard High-Yield Tax-Exempt VWAHX is a great way to earn a lot of tax-free income without sweating that your principal is at stake. This fund doesn't qualify for our muni high-yield category because it actually has a lot of holdings that are rated A or better. So, this is the chicken's way to high-yield munis, but with an expense ratio of just 0.15%, you still get a nice yield (currently 4.07% by Vanguard's estimate).

Vanguard Wellesley Income VWINX has it all. You get two managers with more than 20 years at the helm—Earl McEvoy and John Ryan of Wellington Asset Management—and ridiculously low expenses: 0.24%. If you are looking for a conservative fund, this is a fine one.

Stepping Back

Now that you have the details of our study, it's a good idea to step back and think about the ideas behind the numbers and why they might work together. Long-term returns are largely the result of costs and management skill, with a little randomness, or luck, thrown in. Because expense ratios are pretty stable, historical expense ratios make very good predictors of future expense ratios and therefore of returns.

The star rating has three components: loads, risk, and returns. Loads are another element of cost and are even more stable than expenses, so it's easy to see why they would have predictive value. Risk isn't quite as stable, but a number of studies have found that fund risk is fairly consistent, so it's clearly helpful in finding funds with attractive risk/reward profiles. Now for the trickiest bit. In order for past returns to be valuable predictors, they must be an indicator of future management skill. The results above are encouraging but hardly conclusive. In fact, most studies have found little persistence in above-average performance. Long-term returns probably tell you about manager skill, but you're bound to get luck wrapped up in the numbers, too.

That's where we believe fundamental analysis can help. Morningstar's fund analysts are able to talk with portfolio managers and analysts at fund companies in order to better assess whether past success was purely luck or also due to skill. Good indicators that the success stems from the latter include stability among analysts and managers, a sound strategy, and success at other funds run by the same management team, among other things. We can also examine asset growth at the mutual fund and firmwide to make sure that a manager's skill is not being swamped by cash.

Viewed from that perspective, you can see why expenses and star ratings can be a big help in getting you there, but you still need to do fundamental research. You can let the *Morningstar Funds 500* do a lot of that work for you with our Analyst Picks list, or you can do more of that legwork yourself using our data and reading shareholder reports and brushing up on management. ▌▌

New Morningstar Categories Highlight New Options

by Morningstar Analysts

In March 2006, Morningstar rolled out five new fund categories to help investors better assess three fast-growing strategies. Our new long-short category is the home to funds that employ hedge-fund-like strategies. Our new Treasury Inflation-Protected Securities category is for bond funds focused on inflation-protected bonds. And finally, we created three new target-date categories for investors looking for an all-in-one solution that automatically adjusts their asset allocation over time.

The Long and Short of It

First we'll give you a little background on what long-short funds are. These funds buy stocks (or take "long" positions) just like other equity funds. In addition, they also short stocks or indexes with the expectation that these securities' prices will go down. Funds that use shorting strategies usually borrow shares from a broker and sell those shares to another investor hoping that they can later buy back the shares at a lower price. To be included in the category, mutual funds must have a significant shorting component to their strategy (with shorts of roughly 20% of total net assets as a general guideline).

What Investors Can Expect

Despite the inherent risks of shorting, funds that combine long and short positions have the potential to reduce overall volatility, because their net exposure to stock market swings is lower than that of funds with all-long portfolios. If a sharp correction lowers stock prices across the market, for example, a fund's long positions will lose value while the short positions can gain ground.

Risk reduction is a central element to most market-neutral funds, which we have also included in our long-short category. The major difference between long-short and market-neutral funds is that market-neutral funds balance their short positions with their long positions in a way that brings the net exposure to the broad market close to zero. Long-short funds, meanwhile, either have a consistent long bias or a strategy that opportunistically looks to alter the percentage of long and short positions over time.

Avoiding the Pitfalls

To be sure, the long-short category is filled with unique strategies. Having an understanding of the risks and rewards of a strategy is sound advice in any case, but it is especially true for funds in this category. Also beware of funds with short track records that haven't been fully tested by the market. Our decision to create a long-short category should not be considered a blanket endorsement of this type of fund. Too many funds in the category suffered from tepid returns and high fees.

TIPS Come of Age and Get a New Category

What's so unusual about TIPS? Conventional bonds pay a fixed rate of interest on a face (also known as par, or principal) value of $1,000 per bond, an immutable number that never changes. Like conventional bonds, TIPS also pay a fixed rate of interest, expressed as a percentage of their face values. What makes them special, though, is that TIPS' face values are adjusted in line with the government's consumer price index. So while a TIPS issue may always carry a fixed rate of say, 3%, the amount of income it pays each year will be 3% of whatever its face value is at the time. The end result is that investors get an assurance that their principal will be indexed directly to the consumer price index. And by extension, their interest payments, while expressed as a fixed percentage, will be a fixed percentage of a principal amount that should increase along with inflation.

Does Everyone Need TIPS?

So, does that mean everyone should run out and buy a TIPS fund? Well, not necessarily. The unique profile and appeal of TIPS do argue that almost any long-term investor should find a portfolio slot for a TIPS allocation. Although there are other investments available that offer the promise of an inflation hedge—natural resources and precious metals, for example—there aren't really any that provide as direct and certain a link to what the U.S. government considers to be the cost of living.

There's a common misconception, however, that the indexing of principal inherent with TIPS makes them safe in all circumstances. The fact is, however, that over short periods of time, TIPS funds can lose money when interest rates rise, just as is the case with conventional bonds. How TIPS behave depends a lot on where we are in the interest-rate cycle and the overall level of income that investors are demanding from the bond market. In fact, over short time periods, TIPS can be as volatile as other bond funds, rising or falling as many as a few percentage points in a single month, for example.

Who's Got the Goods?

At the moment, most TIPS funds pursue a pretty plain-vanilla strategy, holding mostly U.S. Treasury-issued bonds and little else. If that's what you're looking for, we'd recommend keeping a sharp eye on costs. There are a handful of particularly cheap options including one of our favorites, Vanguard Inflation-Protected Securities, which charges just 0.17% per annum. Until recently, small investors who were willing to take on some risk with more complex and profitable strategies had little choice but to go with one of the pricey share classes of the otherwise excellent PIMCO Real Return. Harbor funds, though, recently rolled out a fund subadvised by PIMCO, run by the same manager, with the same strategy. And that fund, Harbor Real Return, will be charging a modest 0.57% for the foreseeable future. It's certainly a more aggressive pick than the Vanguard option, but one that we think makes sense for investors willing to put their trust in PIMCO and manager John Brynjolfsson. The bottom line is that this category represents a true innovation for bond investors. And while we would counsel some caution we think it makes sense for just about any long-term investor to carve out some portfolio space for a TIPS-focused fund.

Taking Aim at Target-Date Funds

Target-date funds, which Fidelity first launched in 1996, tended to reside in the moderate-allocation, conservative-allocation, and large-blend categories. But they have very different mandates than their former peers. They're designed to serve as one-stop-shopping options for investors with a specific time horizon in mind. If an investor expects to retire in 28 years, for example, he or she might choose a fund with a target date of 2035. The funds, which typically hold other offerings from within their fund family, become more conservative over time. In order to provide more stability as retirement approaches, the advisor reduces a fund's equity weighting in favor of bonds as the target date draws near. Although most of these funds are designed for investors' retirement assets, we think they can also be a good place to stash college savings, too. In order to provide better comparisons, we've split the funds into three categories: target-date 2000-2014, target-date 2015-2029, and target-date 2030+.

What to Look For

When sorting through these new categories, investors should keep in mind that competing funds with similar time horizons can have markedly different asset allocations. First, check out how the funds shift from stocks to bonds over time. T. Rowe Price, for example, strongly believes that investors should own significant equity stakes well into retirement due to the corrosive effects of inflation. Second, investigate how much foreign-stock exposure you're getting and whether you'll need to get small-cap exposure from other funds. The underlying funds should also boast accomplished managers, prudent strategies, and relatively low expense ratios.

Finally, because target-date funds are meant to be held for very long periods, costs play a crucial role. Expense ratios for funds of funds often have two components: the price tags of the underlying holdings and fees that the fund company charges for overseeing the aggregate portfolio. Some charge additional management fees for the minimal effort required to occasionally adjust their asset allocations, but the better ones don't. Also, given the often hefty fixed-income weightings of target-date funds, investors should expect to pay less than they would for most pure-equity funds.

The lowest-cost offerings are (no surprise) from Vanguard, which uses only its ultracheap index funds in its Target Retirement series; thus, the funds' total costs are less than 0.25% per year, which make them very attractive choices. However, we're also impressed with T. Rowe Price's target-date funds, given the quality of their underlying holdings and their modest costs. ▥

Fund Manager Changes

American Century International Growth TWIEX | Impact: Negative | 07-05-06

Manager Michael Perelstein has left the firm and was replaced by Alexander Tedder, who amassed a strong record at DWS International Select Equity (MGINX). **I** Our Take: Perelstein's record at this fund was middling at best, but we're a little worried by frequent manager and analyst departures in American Century's foreign group.

American Century Small Cap Value ASVIX | Impact: Negative | 11-17-06

Comanager Kevin Laub left to join a small investment firm in Ohio. Comanager Ben Giele who has been with the fund since inception remains on board. **I** Our Take: While we don't expect a big change in strategy or performance, it's still disappointing to lose a manager. American Century has had a few departures recently raising questions about their ability to retain top talent.

American Funds | Impact: Neutral | 03-01-06

As a part of a broad plan to split its investment staff into two identical research organizations, the fund boards of American Balanced (ABALX), Investment Company of America (AIVSX), and Fundamental Investors (ANCFX) approved a slew of manager changes. The idea behind the division is to spread out decision-making responsibilities among more people so that the growing firm can mitigate the costs of buying and selling larger blocks of shares. Each fund will now have one subadvisor. Changes include Gordon Crawford leaving Fundamental Investors, though he will remain at Growth Fund of America (AGTHX), Smallcap World (SMCWX), and New Economy (ANEFX). At American Balanced, Alan Berro and Dina Perry have replaced J. Dale Harvey. **I** Our Take: While some funds lost prominent managers, they picked up other good managers from American. Historically, manager changes at American have not led to big shifts in portfolios or performance. It's encouraging to see American tackle the asset bloat issue, but we'd rather see the firm do it directly by closing funds.

Baron Fifth Avenue Growth BFTHX | Impact: Negative | 03-05-06

Manager Mitch Rubin departed to run a hedge fund. Randy Haase, who put up middling results at Alliance Quasar in the 1990s, was hired to replace him. **I** Our Take: Rubin produced nice results at the fund, so he'll be missed. Haase produced good returns in the mid-1990s but lagged in 1998 and 1999 because he was a valuation-sensitive growth manager. That's not such a bad thing, and he's certainly consistent with Baron's strategy.

Clipper Fund CFIMX | Impact: Positive | 01-01-06

This fund's board has switched gears. Rather than hand management duties over to Barrow, Hanley—which just happens to be owned by the same firm that owns Clipper—the board has hired Chris Davis and Ken Feinberg of Selected American (SLASX). In addition, the fund's expense ratio is coming down by 50 basis points because Davis and Feinberg's management fee is half that of the old Clipper team's. The new managers will own about 15 to 20 stocks, but they won't move into cash and bonds the way the former team did. **I** Our Take: This is great news. You get low costs, outstanding managers, and a board that has done the right thing for shareholders.

Fidelity Asset Manager 50% FASMX | Impact: Negative | 07-19-06

Charles Mangum was replaced by a committee of sector-fund managers. The fund's sector weightings are now kept in line with those of the Wilshire 5000, and the sector-fund analysts pick their favorite names in their sector. The fixed-income side remains unchanged. **I** Our Take: This fund went from great management to bland management just as the market was swinging Mangum's way. We removed the fund from our picks list.

Fidelity Blue Chip Growth FBGRX | Impact: Negative | 11-13-06

John McDowell retired and Jennifer Uhrig took the reins at this fund. Uhrig is an experienced manager who has put up middling returns at Fidelity Advisor Equity Growth (EPGAX). **I** Our Take: This is a little disappointing. Both Uhrig and McDowell put up middling returns during their tenures at the funds, but McDowell was focused on much larger stocks and therefore had a better excuse for producing mediocre returns in a small-cap-dominated market.

Fidelity Disciplined Equity FDEQX | Impact: Negative | 10-09-06

Steven Snider stepped down to focus on running money for Fidelity's institutional wing, Pyramis. He was replaced by Keith Quinton, who also manages Fidelity Tax-Managed Stock (FTXMX) and Fidelity Advisor Tax Managed Stock (FTAMX). **I** Our Take: Quinton's record in two years at those funds has been respectable though the funds are tiny. Thus, Quinton's record isn't nearly as impressive as Snider's. Snider has posted top-quintile returns in his six years at the helm of Fidelity Disciplined Equity (FDEQX). We'd wait until Quinton has shown what he can do at this fund before buying.

Fidelity Equity-Income II FEQTX | Impact: Neutral | 11-13-06

C. Robert Chow took over Fidelity Equity-Income II for Stephen M. DuFour who is slated for a new assignment. Chow will continue to manage Fidelity Advisor Equity Income (EQPIX), which he has managed since 1996. **I** Our Take: Hard to get real excited here. Chow has a slightly better record than DuFour, though he runs a rather bland, plain-vanilla style. The fund has built up capital gains of about 20%, so look for the fund to make a sizable distribution in 2007.

Fidelity Europe FIEUX | Impact: Negative | 01-16-05

After five months at this fund, Frederic Gautier left Fidelity and was replaced by Trygve Toraasen, who has run Fidelity Nordic (FNORX) since 1998. Toraasen has a decent record at Nordic and a middling one at a Europe fund run for overseas investors. **I** Our Take: Fidelity needs to do a better job of retaining good managers. Toraasen's middling record means he'll have to prove his abilities here before we can recommend the fund.

Fidelity Independence FDFFX | Impact: Negative | 11-13-06

Jason Weiner left this fund to replace Uhrig at Fidelity Advisor Equity Growth (EPGAX). Bob Bertelson will take his place. Bertelson has run a slew of Fidelity funds over the course of his career. At Fidelity Aggressive Growth (FDEGX), Bertelson's fund lost 75% versus a 35% loss for the average mid-growth fund during his tenure from 2000 to 2002. **I** Our Take: Ouch! Weiner had a great record and Bertelson's is dismal. This fund's appeal has fallen significantly. There is a precedent for a Fidelity manager to follow a poor showing with a strong one. Bob Haber put up awful returns at Fidelity Balanced but more recently has put up good returns at Fidelity Focused Stock (FTQGX).

Fidelity Interm Govt FSTGX | **Fidelity Mtg Sec** FMSFX | Impact: Negative | 10-02-06

Brett Kozlowski took the helm at these two funds—replacing George Fischer. This is Kozlowski's first management assignment, but he has been with Fidelity's bond group since 1997. **I** Our Take: Since Fischer is a known quantity and Kozlowski isn't, we consider this a slight negative. However, manager changes at Fidelity's bond group are rarely worrisome. They use a team approach and manager changes don't result in a change in strategy. In this case, Kozlowski has plenty of experience with government and mortgage securities at Fidelity.

Fidelity New Millennium FMILX | Impact: Negative | 07-01-06

Neal Miller retired and was replaced by John Roth, who has served as an analyst at Fidelity. | Our Take: Neal Miller is one of the best managers around whereas Roth is unproven. Fidelity must think highly of him to put him at this fund, but Roth has big shoes to fill and won't likely even attempt to run Miller's eclectic strategy.

Fidelity Overseas FOSFX | Impact: Positive | 01-01-06

Rick Mace is being replaced by Ian Hart, former manager of Fidelity Europe Capital Appreciation (FECAX). | Our Take: Mace's record was mediocre, while Hart's five-year performance at Europe Capital Appreciation has been quite strong. Thus, we're more optimistic about this fund's prospects than we've been in a long time.

Fidelity Small Cap Retirement FSCRX | Impact: Neutral | 03-14-06

Charles Myers replaced Lionel Harris. This marks the second manager change for the fund in less than a year. | Our Take: In moving from Harris to Myers, Fidelity is going from one unknown to another, so it's hard to get too worked up. However, two changes in a year is disappointing, and this fund was once rather promising.

Fidelity Small Cap Value FCPVX | Impact: Negative | 03-05-06

Kathy Lieberman left the firm and was replaced by Thomas Hense. Hense joined Fidelity as a high-income analyst in 1993 and became director of high-income research in 1999. In 2000, he joined Fidelity's equity division and soon after became codirector of equity research. Hense has also managed small-cap-oriented institutional accounts for the firm since 2004. | Our Take: Lieberman had produced good results here and was regarded within Fidelity as a rising star, so this is a real blow. On the plus side, Hense is a more seasoned investor than you typically get taking over a smallish Fidelity fund.

Fidelity Worldwide FWWFX | Impact: Positive | 01-01-06

Bill Kennedy and Jeffrey Feingold replaced Brian Hogan and Rick Mace as comanagers. | Our Take: It's a positive for the same reasons we cited for Fidelity Overseas. However, this new team's U.S. manager is new to running a diversified portfolio, so we wouldn't rush in. Kennedy is a veteran who built a strong record at Fidelity Pacific Basin (FPBFX), but we don't have much to go on with Feingold, who has run some sector funds only for brief stints.

Janus Fund JANSX | Impact: Positive | 02-01-06

Janus Mercury (JAMRX) manager David Corkins took over the struggling flagship fund. | Our Take: Corkins is Janus' top manager, so this is a big upgrade. His success at Janus Growth & Income (JAGIX) and Mercury give us confidence.

Janus Mercury JAMRX | Impact: Negative | 02-01-06

David Corkins was moved off this fund, and it was handed over to the analyst staff. | Our Take: It's a big letdown to go from the shop's best manager to a collection of analysts. While Janus has some good analysts, we think Corkins was adding value. Thus, the fund has lost a fair amount of appeal.

Masters' Select Smaller Companies MSSFX | Impact: Positive | 07-15-06

Masters' hired Tucker Walsh and Michael Malouf of Copper Capital Partners to join its existing lineup of managers. The move enabled Masters' to reopen the fund to new investors. | Our Take: We like the fund and are happy to see it reopen, even though the latest additions aren't the biggest draw. Walsh produced decent returns at the now merged-away State Street Research Emerging Growth, while Malouf oversaw a steep rise and fall at Neuberger Berman Millennium (NBMIX) .

Oak Value OAKVX | Impact: Negative | 05-09-06

Comanager Matthew Sauer left the firm to take a job at Ariel, leaving comanagers David Carr and Larry Coats at the helm. | Our Take: The fund has lost two of its four managers in the past three years. In addition, the advisor has lost two analysts. We removed the fund from our Analyst Picks list because we find the loss of talent worrisome. In addition, the fund's performance has been poor. That could turn around with an energy sell-off, but we still feel the fund is one notch below our standard for Analyst Picks.

Putnam Fund for Growth & Income PGRWX | Impact: Positive | 04-12-06

After years of poor performance, managers Hugh Mullin and Chris Miller were let go. Team members Josh Brooks and David King remained and they were joined by Eric Harthun, comanager of Putnam Small Cap Value (PSLAX). | Our Take: Brooks and King are able investors, and we think this fund's prospects have improved. That said, we're still lukewarm on most Putnam funds because, three years into Ed Haldeman's overhaul of the firm, we've seen only slight improvements in performance.

T. Rowe Price Global Technology PRGTX | Impact: Negative | 04-01-06

Manager Rob Gensler stepped down to focus on T. Rowe Price Global Stock (PRGSX). Jeffrey Rottinghaus, who has a little less than one year of experience running a fund (T. Rowe Price Developing Technology PRDTX) has taken over. | Our Take: Rottinghaus may prove to be a good manager, but we knew for certain that Gensler was. We removed this fund from our Fund Analyst Picks list as a result.

Vanguard Global Equity VHGEX | Impact: Negative | 04-16-06

Vanguard added a third subadvisor, AllianceBernstein, to this fund. Vanguard will gradually ramp up AllianceBernstein's share of the fund by directing most new inflows to them. | Our Take: AllianceBernstein is a decent manager, but adding a third subadvisor dilutes the fund's portfolio a bit. In addition, this fund's great record was built by a single manager, Jeremy Hosking of Marathon Asset Management, but Marathon's relative contribution continues to diminish because Vanguard doesn't want to close the fund. Even before this move, Marathon's share of the fund's total assets had fallen to less than one half.

Vanguard Morgan Growth VMRGX | Impact: Neutral | 12-31-06

Robert D. Rands, of Wellington, retired at the end of the year. Wellington runs one third of this fund. Paul E. Marrkand, who has served as comanager of Wellington's portion of the fund since 2005, will assume Rands' responsibilities. | Our Take: Wellington has a deep team, so we don't expect a drop-off.

Vanguard Windsor II VWNFX | Impact: Neutral | 01-04-06

Vanguard added advisor Armstrong Shaw Associates to the lineup of Barrow, Hanley, Mewhinney & Strauss, Equinox Capital Management, Hotchkis and Wiley Capital Management, Tukman Capital Management, and Vanguard. Armstrong Shaw has a good record running large-value separate accounts, and also has done a nice job at Harbor Large Cap Value (HAVLX). | Our Take: Armstrong Shaw is a good shop, and its disciplined, low-turnover value approach should fit in well at Windsor II.

Report Pages

This section offers a full-page report on each of the 500 funds.

Aegis Value

	Ticker	Load	NAV	Yield	Total Assets	Mstar Category
	AVALX	None	$14.41	0.7%	$384 mil	Small Value

Governance and Management

Stewardship Grade: C

Portfolio Manager(s)

Scott Barbee joined the fund's advisor, Aegis Financial Corporation, in 1997. He previously worked at deep-value advisor Donald Smith & Co. He's supported here by two analysts, Tom Saberhagen and David Shapiro, who both joined Aegis in 2002.

Strategy

Manager Scott Barbee looks for stocks sporting very low price/earnings, price/cash-flow, and price/book ratios. (That approach has typically led him to buy very small companies, but he's willing to look at larger names if they meet his strict criteria.) He then narrows the field to firms going through problems that he deems temporary, such as a weak division masking the power of a more productive one. He buys when a firm sells at a discount to his estimates of its intrinsic value. He'll sell when a stock hits that value. Barbee is willing to hoard cash when he can't find buying opportunities.

Performance 12-31-06

	1st Qtr	2nd Qtr	3rd Qtr	4th Qtr	Total
2002	3.92	1.70	-9.24	5.65	1.35
2003	-6.95	20.97	10.18	9.47	35.75
2004	5.25	0.68	0.06	7.03	13.48
2005	-1.32	2.68	-2.39	5.01	3.85
2006	5.66	1.45	-2.37	12.55	17.79

Trailing	Total Return%	+/- S&P 500	+/- Russ 2000 VL	%Rank Cat	Growth of $10,000
3 Mo	12.55	5.85	3.52	2	11,255
6 Mo	9.88	-2.86	-1.93	30	10,988
1 Yr	17.79	2.00	-5.69	44	11,779
3 Yr Avg	11.55	1.11	-4.93	84	13,881
5 Yr Avg	13.82	7.63	-1.55	48	19,103
10 Yr Avg	—	—	—	—	—
15 Yr Avg	—	—	—	—	—

Tax Analysis	Tax-Adj Rtn%	%Rank Cat	Tax-Cost Rat	%Rank Cat
3 Yr (estimated)	8.75	86	2.51	79
5 Yr (estimated)	11.66	58	1.90	78
10 Yr (estimated)	—	—	—	—

Potential Capital Gain Exposure: -6% of assets

Historical Profile

Return	Average
Risk	Low
Rating	★★★ Neutral

Investment Style: Equity, Stock %

Percentages across top: 99% | 58% | 57% | 65% | 45% | 75% | 70%

▼ Manager Change
▽ Partial Manager Change

Growth of $10,000
— Investment Values of Fund
— Investment Values of S&P 500

Performance Quartile (within Category)

	1995	1996	1997	1998	1999	2000	2001	2002	2003	2004	2005	2006	History
NAV	—	—	—	9.79	8.81	9.14	13.00	12.66	16.77	18.15	16.95	14.41	
Total Return %	—	—	—	-0.85*	9.55	14.67	42.66	1.35	35.75	13.48	3.85	17.79	
+/-S&P 500	—	—	—	-11.49	23.77	54.55	23.45	7.07	2.60	-1.06	2.00		
+/-Russ 2000 VL	—	—	—	-11.04	-8.16	28.64	12.78	-10.28	-8.77	-0.86	-5.69		
Income Return %	—	—	—		1.53	2.04	0.03	0.15	0.00	0.00	1.05	0.81	
Capital Return %	—	—	—		8.02	12.63	42.63	1.20	35.75	13.48	2.80	16.98	
Total Rtn % Rank Cat	—	—	—		29	68	2	5	79	96	74	44	
Income $	—	—	—	0.08	0.15	0.18	0.00	0.02	0.00	0.00	0.19	0.14	
Capital Gains $	—	—	—	0.04	1.70	0.76	0.04	0.49	0.41	0.87	1.67	5.30	
Expense Ratio %	—	—	—		1.50	1.50	1.50	1.50	1.50	1.50	1.42		
Income Ratio %	—	—	—		1.46	0.04	0.89	1.41	0.31	-0.34	0.83		
Turnover Rate %	—	—	—		33	50	10	29	15	27	18		
Net Assets $mil	—	—	—	1	1	2	72	174	470	823	384		

Rating and Risk

Time Period	Load-Adj Return %	Morningstar Rtn vs Cat	Morningstar Risk vs Cat	Morningstar Risk-Adj Rating
1 Yr	17.79			
3 Yr	11.55	-Avg	Low	★★
5 Yr	13.82	Avg	Low	★★★★
10 Yr	—			
Incept	15.21			

Other Measures	Standard Index S&P 500	Best Fit Index Mstar Small Value
Alpha	1.4	-0.1
Beta	0.98	0.67
R-Squared	44	63
Standard Deviation	10.09	
Mean	11.55	
Sharpe Ratio	0.82	

Portfolio Analysis 08-31-06

Share change since 05-06 Total Stocks:62	Sector	PE	Tot Ret%	% Assets
⊖ Alliance One International	Goods	—	81.03	6.53
☼ Pma Cap	Financial	—	—	6.21
Audiovox Corporation A	Ind Mtrls	—	1.66	3.64
⊕ Cf Industries Holdings,	Ind Mtrls	—	—	3.60
⊕ Royal Group Technologies	Consumer	—	—	3.39
⊖ Dillard's, Inc.	Consumer	14.2	41.62	3.20
⊖ Imperial Sugar Company	Goods	23.0	101.35	3.07
⊖ Scpie Holdings, Inc.	Financial	22.5	25.67	2.99
Air France-Klm Adr	Business	11.2	96.86	2.87
⊕ Superior Industries Inte	Ind Mtrls	—	-10.49	2.64
⊖ Reliant Energy, Inc.	Utilities	—	37.69	1.98
⊖ California First Nationa	Financial	14.5	10.25	1.91
⊕ Bassett Furniture Indust	Goods	24.3	-7.56	1.76
Head Nv	Goods	17.6	29.02	1.57
Delta Apparel, Inc.	Goods	10.8	11.01	1.56
⊖ Books-A-Million, Inc.	Consumer	23.4	139.13	1.48
Mair Holdings, Inc.	Business	—	52.23	1.47
Duckwall-Alco Stores, In	Consumer	23.7	70.75	1.22
Usec Inc.	Ind Mtrls	11.4	6.44	1.20
⊖ Sea Containers, Ltd. A	Ind Mtrls	—	-94.42	1.17

Current Investment Style

Value Blnd Growth — Large Mid Small

Market Cap	%
Giant	0.0
Large	0.0
Mid	19.4
Small	9.1
Micro	71.5

Avg $mil: 353

Value Measures		Rel Category
Price/Earnings	20.88	1.36
Price/Book	0.89	0.50
Price/Sales	0.24	0.30
Price/Cash Flow	2.13	0.35
Dividend Yield %	1.50	0.95

Growth Measures	%	Rel Category
Long-Term Erngs	10.24	0.82
Book Value	-2.95	NMF
Sales	-1.11	NMF
Cash Flow	-16.18	NMF
Historical Erngs	5.67	0.50

Profitability	%	Rel Category
Return on Equity	-4.23	NMF
Return on Assets	-4.13	NMF
Net Margin	-1.50	NMF

Sector Weightings

	% of Stocks	Rel S&P 500	3 Year High Low
Info	1.51	0.08	
Software	0.02	0.01	1 0
Hardware	1.35	0.15	3 0
Media	0.09	0.02	0 0
Telecom	0.05	0.01	1 0
Service	44.64	0.97	
Health	0.01	0.00	0 0
Consumer	17.23	2.25	22 17
Business	6.96	1.65	7 4
Financial	20.44	0.92	23 18
Mfg	53.85	1.59	
Goods	23.42	2.74	23 16
Ind Mtrls	27.58	2.31	32 20
Energy	0.00	0.00	6 0
Utilities	2.85	0.81	8 3

Composition

● Cash	26.6	
● Stocks	69.8	
● Bonds	0.0	
● Other	3.7	
	Foreign	12.9
	(% of Stock)	

Morningstar's Take by Katherine Yang 12-11-06

Our endorsement of Aegis Value is drawing to a close.

We've been patient with this fund during its rough patches because we like its sensible deep-value strategy. Manager Scott Barbee's strategy is simple. He invests in mostly micro-caps that are having temporary problems with a potential for turnaround and holds cash when he can't find a suitable alternative. He buys stocks with low price-to-book ratios and holds on for the long haul. Despite the approach, we're losing confidence. Granted, the fund has outperformed its benchmark, the Russell 2000 Value Index, and category peers since its May 1998 inception. However, since 2003, the fund has underperformed the index and category by nearly eight and five percentage points in annualized returns, respectively.

What's most troubling is a series of recent stock blowups. For example, the fund's top holding, Sea Containers, has plummeted more 95% since its February 2005 high. Many of Barbee's stock picks have similarly disappointed. Both Dominion Homes and Quanta Capital Holdings have fallen more than 75% since their 2004 highs. Finally, Quaker Fabric has lost more than 90% since a January 2004 spike. They are also year-to-date underperformers. These frequent blowups make us question whether Barbee and his two analysts have overlooked their picks' fundamental issues due to low valuations.

We usually praise managers for having contrarian and long-term strategies. However, an investor would need a lot of tolerance to be comfortable with Barbee's implementation and stock selection. This patience can be rewarding in one sense; Barbee rarely sells positions, which results in a low turnover ratio--this can reduce trading costs and increase tax efficiency. However, the fund's stock-picking, along with its above-average expense ratio, makes us wary.

Address:	1100 North Glebe Rd Arlington VA 22201 800-528-3780	Minimum Purchase:	$10000 Add: $1000 IRA: $4000
		Min Auto Inv Plan:	$100 Add: $100
		Sales Fees:	No-load
Web Address:	www.aegishighyieldfund.com	Management Fee:	1.20%, 0.10%A
Inception:	05-15-98*	Actual Fees:	Mgt:1.20% Dist: —
Advisor:	Aegis Financial Corporation	Expense Projections:	3Yr:$446 5Yr:$771 10Yr:$1691
Subadvisor:	None	Income Distrib:	Annually
NTF Plans:	N/A		

Allianz RCM Tech Ins

Analyst Pick ✓

	Ticker	Load	NAV	Yield	Total Assets	Mstar Category
	DRGTX	None	$41.51	0.0%	$1,250 mil	Specialty-Technology

Governance and Management

Stewardship Grade:

Portfolio Manager(s)

Seasoned. Huachen Chen and Walter Price have been running institutional tech money together for more than 10 years and have managed this fund since its late-1995 inception. Chen left Allianz, apparently frustrated by internal politics, early in 2003 but continued to work on the fund as an independent contractor. He returned as a comanager in early 2004, however, having reconciled whatever differences he had with Allianz.

Strategy

This fund cuts a broad swath across the technology sector. It is typically well diversified across subsectors and market-cap ranges. Management splits the fund into three categories: emerging stocks (which includes more-speculative issues), core blue chips, and opportunistic value plays. The fund is required to own securities in at least three countries, but, despite its global name, it has typically invested the bulk of its assets in U.S. companies. Management will hold cash and use options and shorts to give the fund a defensive cast at times and will also use ETFs to manage near-term sector exposure.

Performance 12-31-06

	1st Qtr	2nd Qtr	3rd Qtr	4th Qtr	Total
2002	-9.95	-24.80	-21.95	12.83	-40.37
2003	-1.43	37.05	15.33	8.53	69.08
2004	3.09	3.37	-8.93	21.52	17.93
2005	-9.61	3.69	11.14	4.55	8.90
2006	7.08	-13.13	3.05	9.53	4.98

Trailing	Total Return%	+/- S&P 500	+/- ArcaEx Tech 100	%Rank Cat	Growth of $10,000
3 Mo	9.53	2.83	3.90	10	10,953
6 Mo	12.86	0.12	1.21	25	11,286
1 Yr	4.98	-10.81	0.30	65	10,498
3 Yr Avg	10.47	0.03	2.59	13	13,481
5 Yr Avg	6.33	0.14	1.37	9	13,592
10 Yr Avg	15.13	6.71	1.42	1	40,915
15 Yr Avg	—	—	—		

Tax Analysis	Tax-Adj Rtn%	%Rank Cat	Tax-Cost Rat	%Rank Cat
3 Yr (estimated)	10.47	11	0.00	1
5 Yr (estimated)	6.33	7	0.00	1
10 Yr (estimated)	14.28	1	0.74	23

Potential Capital Gain Exposure: 9% of assets

Morningstar's Take by Christopher Davis 11-13-06

A distinctive approach and skilled management make Allianz RCM Technology a top-flight choice.

Managers Huachen Chen and Walter Price look for stocks poised to rise at least 50% in the coming year or two. Chen and Price see potential for such gains in both blue chips and up-and-comers. In the former, the managers eye companies whose earnings they think will accelerate. For instance, they expect Microsoft, which they scooped up in 2006's second quarter, to post improved earnings following the impending launch of a new operating system and a new Xbox video game console.

Although the managers have been ratcheting up their exposure to large-cap names like Microsoft and Oracle lately, mid caps such as Nintendo and Red Hat remain their sweet spot and nearly account for half of the fund's assets. They say such firms have grown beyond the immaturity of tech small fry, yet they still have the potential to be the next big thing. In contrast to the proprietary Unix and Microsoft platforms, Red Hat's Linux is open-source software, which the managers say is more innovative and can take market share from its rivals.

The managers' bold streak extends beyond their reliance on mid caps. Their portfolio is relatively compact, and they've been willing to bet big on their favorites. Google stood at 2.6% of assets in September 2006, but they've stashed as much as 9.2% of assets in Google in the past. The managers will delve into health-care and energy stocks, and they're not shy about raising cash when good tech ideas are scarce.

All of that is a tough act to pull off successfully, but we're confident that the managers can. They've worked together for more than 20 years and have delivered fine results here for more than 10. It's true that no one needs this fund and those who want it must have a very strong stomach (witness its 40% losses in both 2001 and 2002). But for those intrepid enough, this offering remains one of the best means to get tech exposure.

Address:	2187 Atlantic Street
	Stamford, CT 06902
	800-498-5413
Web Address:	www.allianzinvestors.com
Inception:	12-27-95*
Advisor:	Allianz Global Investors Fund Mgmt LLC
Subadvisor:	NFJ Investment Group LP
NTF Plans:	N/A

Minimum Purchase:	$5000000	Add: $0	IRA: $5000000
Min Auto Inv Plan:	$0	Add: —	
Sales Fees:	No-load, 2.00%R		
Management Fee:	0.90%, 0.30%A		
Actual Fees:	Mgt:0.90%	Dist: —	
Expense Projections:	3Yr:$393	5Yr:$681	10Yr:$1500
Income Distrib:	Annually		

Historical Profile

Return	High
Risk	Average
Rating	★★★★ Above Avg

Investment Style: Equity, Stock %

| | 96% | 96% | 79% | 93% | 88% | 95% | 95% | 97% | 91% |

▼ Manager Change
▽ Partial Manager Change

Growth of $10,000
— Investment Values of Fund
— Investment Values of S&P 500

Performance Quartile (within Category)

1995	1996	1997	1998	1999	2000	2001	2002	2003	2004	2005	2006	History
10.04	12.60	13.69	21.47	59.21	50.32	30.54	18.21	30.79	36.31	39.54	41.51	NAV
0.40*	26.41	27.08	61.06	182.95	-14.33	-39.31	-40.37	69.08	17.93	8.90	4.98	Total Return %
—	3.45	-6.28	32.48	161.91	-5.23	-27.42	-18.27	40.40	7.05	3.99	-10.81	+/-S&P 500
—	6.38	7.11	6.46	66.55	1.89	-23.72	-7.04	16.94	6.20	1.54	0.30	+/-ArcaEx Tech 100
—	0.90	0.00	0.00	0.00	0.00	0.00	0.00	0.00	0.00	0.00	0.00	Income Return %
—	25.51	27.08	61.06	182.95	-14.33	-39.31	-40.37	69.08	17.93	8.90	4.98	Capital Return %
1	21	4	32	6	8	64	37	16	6	29	65	Total Rtn % Rank Cat
0.00	0.09	0.00	0.00	0.00	0.00	0.00	0.00	0.00	0.00	0.00	0.00	Income $
0.00	0.00	2.21	0.57	1.38	0.43	0.00	0.00	0.00	0.00	0.00	0.00	Capital Gains $
—	1.73	1.75	1.75	1.50	1.21	1.56	1.29	1.36	1.36	1.32	1.24	Expense Ratio %
—	-1.34	-1.15	-0.99	-1.02	-0.26	-0.15	-0.85	-0.92	-1.16	-0.87	-0.75	Income Ratio %
—		156	189	266	119	451	386	343	237	206	238	272	Turnover Rate %
1	5	7	18	197	366	200	81	194	245	337	334	Net Assets $mil

Rating and Risk

Time Period	Load-Adj Return %	Morningstar Rtn vs Cat	Morningstar Risk vs Cat	Morningstar Risk-Adj Rating
1 Yr	4.98			
3 Yr	10.47	+Avg	Avg	★★★★
5 Yr	6.33	+Avg	Avg	★★★★
10 Yr	15.13	High	Avg	★★★★
Incept	16.14			

Other Measures	Standard Index S&P 500	Best Fit Index ArcaEx Tech 100
Alpha	-5.3	2.3
Beta	1.96	1.14
R-Squared	56	78
Standard Deviation	18.02	
Mean	10.47	
Sharpe Ratio	0.46	

Portfolio Analysis 11-30-06

Share change since 10-06 Total Stocks:41

	Sector	PE	Tot Ret%	% Assets
Nintendo	Goods			5.65
⊖ Google, Inc.	Business	61.5	11.00	5.19
Cisco Systems, Inc.	Hardware	30.1	59.64	4.60
Microsoft Corporation	Software	23.8	15.83	4.32
⊕ Apple Computer, Inc.	Hardware	37.6	18.01	3.64
⊖ Research in Motion, Ltd.	Hardware	72.5	93.58	3.39
⊖ NVIDIA Corporation	Hardware	33.4	102.46	3.14
⊖ Comverse Technology, Inc	Hardware	—	-20.61	3.10
⊖ NII Holdings, Inc.	Telecom	45.9	47.53	3.07
Hewlett-Packard Company	Hardware	19.3	45.21	3.03
⊕ Marvell Technology Group	Hardware	35.9	-31.57	2.85
⊕ Ericsson Telephone Compa	Hardware	19.7	18.23	2.78
⊕ QLogic Corporation	Hardware	31.5	34.85	2.71
⊕ Seagate Technology	Hardware	23.7	34.47	2.70
Tencent Hldgs	Telecom			2.35
⊕ Red Hat, Inc.	Software	58.8	-15.63	2.34
⊕ Merrill Lynch Intl	—			2.32
⊖ Intel Corporation	Hardware	21.0	-17.18	2.32
Chartered Semiconductor	Hardware	—	—	2.14
Cognizant Technology Sol	Business	52.9	53.49	2.10

Current Investment Style

Value Blnd Growth — Large Mid Small

Market Cap	%
Giant	43.9
Large	25.0
Mid	25.7
Small	5.4
Micro	0.0

Avg $mil: 20,903

Value Measures		Rel Category
Price/Earnings	28.96	1.19
Price/Book	3.99	1.24
Price/Sales	3.57	1.28
Price/Cash Flow	16.00	1.23
Dividend Yield %	0.45	1.02

Growth Measures	%	Rel Category
Long-Term Erngs	19.59	1.14
Book Value	7.82	0.81
Sales	14.23	1.14
Cash Flow	17.50	0.88
Historical Erngs	26.16	0.95

Profitability	%	Rel Category
Return on Equity	17.32	1.11
Return on Assets	11.23	1.21
Net Margin	16.21	1.17

Industry Weightings	% of Stocks	Rel Cat
Software	28.0	1.3
Hardware	13.5	1.2
Networking Eq	6.2	0.8
Semis	13.5	0.8
Semi Equip	2.6	0.5
Comp/Data Sv	10.9	1.2
Telecom	6.5	2.2
Health Care	2.5	0.5
Other	16.4	0.9

Composition

	%
● Cash	3.7
● Stocks	90.9
● Bonds	2.3
● Other	3.1
Foreign	24.6

(% of Stock)

MORNINGSTAR® Funds 500

AmCent Capital Val Inv

	Ticker	Load	NAV	Yield	Total Assets	Mstar Category
	ACTIX	None	$8.35	1.5%	$531 mil	Large Value

Governance and Management

Stewardship Grade: C

Portfolio Manager(s)

Charles Ritter and Mark Mallon have been managers at this fund since its 1999 inception. During that time they've amassed an impressive record relative to the large-value category. Ritter and Mallon also manage American Century Large Company Value in a nearly identical manner. They're assisted by portfolio manager Brendan Healy and analyst Lon West, who came from USAA. Analyst Matt Titus joined the team from Bank One in 2005.

Strategy

Management begins with quantitative screens, looking for stocks that rank in the cheapest 30% of its large-cap universe. Its valuation model incorporates measures such as price-to-cash flow and dividends. It then does fundamental research to choose those with decent growth prospects and solid balance sheets. Cheaper stocks get more play in the portfolio, as do companies with larger market caps and those that the managers know best. Management tries to avoid big sector bets relative to its Russell 1000 Value benchmark. It runs the fund with an eye for tax efficiency.

Performance 12-31-06

	1st Qtr	2nd Qtr	3rd Qtr	4th Qtr	Total
2002	3.62	-7.32	-17.95	9.52	-13.70
2003	-6.07	17.67	2.01	13.71	28.21
2004	2.07	1.88	0.15	9.71	14.25
2005	-1.27	0.86	2.55	1.55	3.70
2006	3.77	0.40	7.09	7.29	19.71

Trailing	Total Return%	+/- S&P 500	+/- Russ 1000 Vl	%Rank Cat	Growth of $10,000
3 Mo	7.29	0.59	-0.71	48	10,729
6 Mo	14.90	2.16	0.18	14	11,490
1 Yr	19.71	3.92	-2.54	29	11,971
3 Yr Avg	12.35	1.91	-2.74	49	14,181
5 Yr Avg	9.43	3.24	-1.43	28	15,692
10 Yr Avg	—	—	—	—	—
15 Yr Avg	—	—	—	—	—

Tax Analysis	Tax-Adj Rtn%	%Rank Cat	Tax-Cost Rat	%Rank Cat
3 Yr (estimated)	11.72	31	0.56	22
5 Yr (estimated)	8.87	18	0.51	28
10 Yr (estimated)	—	—	—	—

Potential Capital Gain Exposure: 24% of assets

Morningstar's Take by Christopher Davis 11-20-06

American Century Capital Value is looking better these days, though there are better reasons than that to jump in.

This offering has been perking up lately. Avoiding racier energy names hurt in 2005, but it's helped more recently as oil and gas prices have fallen from their lofty highs. Meanwhile, management's decision to emphasize giant integrated energy firms such as ExxonMobil and Chevron has paid off nicely. Its preference for giant caps also is finally starting to work in the fund's favor. Bigger banks such as Bank of America and Wells Fargo have posted handsome gains this year. In all, the fund is up 16% for the year to date through Nov. 17, 2006, placing in the large-value group's top third.

That standing is more like what long-term investors have grown accustomed to here. Last year marked the first in which the fund lagged its typical peer--it beat the category average in each of the prior five years. In addition, the fund has also been

less volatile (as measured by standard deviation) than its typical rival.

What's more important, of course, is whether the fund will enjoy lasting success. We think it's likely that it will. Management is very experienced and is plying a disciplined strategy. Chuck Ritter and his team screen for stocks ranking in the cheapest 30% of their large-cap universe using a valuation model that incorporates metrics such as price-to-cash flow and price-to-earnings. They tend to sell when valuations rise well above historical norms, enabling the fund to benefit from rallying picks while still protecting it from excessive price risk. It also helps the managers keep turnover low, resulting in lower transaction costs and reducing the likelihood of taxable gains (an important trait given the fund's tax-managed mandate).

This fund should be cheaper--its costs are higher than the investor shares of similarly managed American Century Large Company Value--but it's still a respectable choice.

Historical Profile

Return	Above Avg
Risk	Average
Rating	★★★★ Above Avg

Investment Style: Equity, Stock %

94% | 89% | 89% | 90% | 95% | 94% | 97% | 96%

▼ Manager Change
▽ Partial Manager Change

Growth of $10,000
— Investment Values of Fund
— Investment Values of S&P 500

17.5 / 15.0 / 12.5 / 10.0 / 6.0

Performance Quartile (within Category)

	1995	1996	1997	1998	1999	2000	2001	2002	2003	2004	2005	2006	History
NAV	—	—	—	—	5.08	5.49	5.80	4.94	6.27	7.09	7.17	8.35	
Total Return %	—	—	—	—	2.60*	9.75	6.78	-13.70	28.21	14.25	3.70	19.71	
+/-S&P 500	—	—	—	—	—	18.85	18.67	8.40	-0.47	3.37	-1.21	3.92	
+/-Russ 1000 Vl	—	—	—	—	—	2.74	12.37	1.82	-1.82	-2.24	-3.35	-2.54	
Income Return %	—	—	—	—	—	1.60	1.10	1.12	1.25	1.16	1.44	1.74	
Capital Return %	—	—	—	—	—	8.15	5.68	-14.82	26.96	13.09	2.26	17.97	
Total Rtn % Rank Cat	—	—	—	—	—	50	11	20	47	34	75	29	
Income $	—	—	—	—	0.05	0.08	0.06	0.07	0.06	0.07	0.10	0.12	
Capital Gains $	—	—	—	—	0.00	0.00	0.00	0.00	0.00	0.00	0.08	0.11	
Expense Ratio %	—	—	—	—	1.10	1.10	1.10	1.10	1.10	1.10	1.10	—	
Income Ratio %	—	—	—	—	1.14	1.56	1.18	1.32	1.54	1.44	1.42	—	
Turnover Rate %	—	—	—	—	—	—	73	56	42	22	15	28	
Net Assets $mil	—	—	—	—	45	40	53	62	116	331	457	481	

Rating and Risk

Time Period	Load-Adj Return %	Morningstar Rtn vs Cat	Morningstar Risk vs Cat	Morningstar Risk-Adj Rating
1 Yr	19.71			
3 Yr	12.35	Avg	-Avg	★★★
5 Yr	9.43	+Avg	Avg	★★★★
10 Yr	—			
Incept	8.53			

Other Measures	Standard Index S&P 500	Best Fit Index Russ 1000 Vl
Alpha	2.9	-1.0
Beta	0.83	0.87
R-Squared	87	92
Standard Deviation	6.17	
Mean	12.35	
Sharpe Ratio	1.42	

Portfolio Analysis 09-30-06

Share change since 06-06 Total Stocks:78

	Sector	PE	Tot Ret%	% Assets
⊕ Citigroup, Inc.	Financial	13.1	19.55	4.66
⊖ ExxonMobil Corporation	Energy	11.1	39.07	4.58
⊖ Bank of America Corporat	Financial	12.4	20.68	3.55
⊕ Freddie Mac	Financial	23.3	7.06	3.03
Chevron Corporation	Energy	9.0	33.76	2.95
Royal Dutch Shell PLC AD	Energy	8.7	19.33	2.73
⊖ J.P. Morgan Chase & Co.	Financial	13.6	25.60	2.55
⊕ Wells Fargo Company	Financial	14.7	16.82	2.24
⊖ Pfizer Inc.	Health	15.2	15.22	2.07
AT&T, Inc.	Telecom	18.2	51.59	1.96
ConocoPhillips	Energy	6.5	26.53	1.81
⊕ Time Warner, Inc.	Media	19.6	26.37	1.75
Wachovia Corporation	Financial	12.9	12.02	1.66
American International G	Financial	17.0	6.05	1.62
⊖ Morgan Stanley	Financial	12.3	45.93	1.57
⊖ Microsoft Corporation	Software	23.8	15.83	1.54
Merrill Lynch & Company,	Financial	14.2	39.28	1.54
Wyeth	Health	17.2	12.88	1.47
⊖ Exelon Corporation	Utilities	—	19.79	1.46
⊖ Allstate Corporation	Financial	8.7	23.38	1.45

Current Investment Style

Value Blnd Growth — Large Mid Small

Market Cap	%
Giant	62.8
Large	28.5
Mid	8.6
Small	0.2
Micro	0.0

Avg $mil: 66,559

Value Measures		Rel Category
Price/Earnings	13.03	0.95
Price/Book	2.19	0.99
Price/Sales	1.34	1.03
Price/Cash Flow	2.19	0.33
Dividend Yield %	2.58	1.11

Growth Measures	%	Rel Category
Long-Term Erngs	9.87	0.95
Book Value	8.06	1.02
Sales	9.33	1.04
Cash Flow	6.83	1.13
Historical Erngs	11.62	0.72

Profitability	%	Rel Category
Return on Equity	18.71	1.04
Return on Assets	11.01	1.12
Net Margin	14.20	1.10

Sector Weightings	% of Stocks	Rel S&P 500	3 Year High	Low
⊙ Info	15.56	0.78		
Software	2.55	0.74	3	2
Hardware	3.56	0.39	5	3
Media	3.75	0.99	4	2
Telecom	5.70	1.62	6	4
⊆ Service	49.63	1.07		
Health	7.89	0.65	8	6
Consumer	5.79	0.76	6	4
Business	1.86	0.44	4	2
Financial	34.09	1.53	34	32
Mfg	34.81	1.03		
Goods	7.20	0.84	11	7
Ind Mtrls	11.03	0.92	12	10
Energy	13.30	1.36	14	10
Utilities	3.28	0.94	4	3

Composition

	%
● Cash	3.8
● Stocks	96.2
● Bonds	0.0
○ Other	0.0
Foreign	4.0
(% of Stock)	

Address:	4500 Main Street Kansas City MO 64111 800-345-2021	Minimum Purchase:	$2500	Add: $50	IRA: $2500
		Min Auto Inv Plan:	$2500	Add: $50	
		Sales Fees:	No-load	
Web Address:	www.americancentury.com	Management Fee:	1.10% mx./0.90% mn.	
Inception:	03-31-99*	Actual Fees:	Mgt:1.10%	Dist: —
Advisor:	American Century Investment MGMT Inc.	Expense Projections:	3Yr:$349	5Yr:$604	10Yr:$1334
Subadvisor:	None	Income Distrib:	Annually	
NTF Plans:	Fidelity Retail-NTF, Schwab OneSource			

AmCent Equity Growth Inv

Ticker	Load	NAV	Yield	Total Assets	Mstar Category
BEQGX	None	$25.64	0.9%	$3,388 mil	Large Blend

Governance and Management

Stewardship Grade: B

Portfolio Manager(s)

William Martin and Thomas Vaiana lead the fund's portfolio-management team. Martin has worked on the fund since June 1997 and has been employed as a portfolio manager and analyst at American Century since 1989. Vaiana has been part of the management team since 2001 and has worked for American Century since 1997. Several quantitative analysts help them.

Strategy

This fund keeps its sector weightings near the S&P 500 Index's, and managers use computers to try to pick better stocks in each sector. The fund's quantitative models look for low-valuation stocks that have growth potential as indicated by growth rates and other earnings and price-momentum factors.

Historical Profile
Return Above Avg
Risk Above Avg
Rating ★★★★ Above Avg

| | 94% | 95% | 93% | 91% | 98% | 98% | 99% | 99% | 100% |

Investment Style
Equity
Stock %

▼ Manager Change
▽ Partial Manager Change

37.0
32.0
25.0 Growth of $10,000
20.0 — Investment Values of Fund
15.0 — Investment Values of S&P 500
10.0

Performance Quartile (within Category)

1995	1996	1997	1998	1999	2000	2001	2002	2003	2004	2005	2006	History
14.24	15.96	19.04	22.71	26.23	21.77	19.24	15.19	19.60	22.08	23.37	25.64	NAV
34.56	27.34	36.06	25.45	18.47	-10.95	-11.01	-20.32	30.27	13.98	7.30	14.14	Total Return %
-3.02	4.38	2.70	-3.13	-2.57	-1.85	0.88	1.78	1.59	3.10	2.39	-1.65	+/-S&P 500
-3.21	4.89	3.21	-1.57	-2.44	-3.16	1.44	1.33	0.38	2.58	1.03	-1.32	+/-Russ 1000
1.96	1.85	1.54	1.08	0.83	0.53	0.60	0.78	1.11	1.24	0.98	0.99	Income Return %
32.60	25.49	34.52	24.37	17.64	-11.48	-11.61	-21.10	29.16	12.74	6.32	13.15	Capital Return %
49	8	6	39	59	87	41	34	22	12	30	53	Total Rtn % Rank Cat
0.22	0.26	0.24	0.20	0.19	0.14	0.13	0.15	0.17	0.24	0.22	0.23	Income $
1.01	1.85	2.31	0.88	0.43	1.47	0.00	0.00	0.00	0.00	0.10	0.79	Capital Gains $
0.71	0.63	0.69	0.69	0.68	0.67	0.68	0.69	0.69	0.68	0.67	—	Expense Ratio %
1.96	1.74	1.39	1.07	0.77	0.53	0.64	0.86	1.00	1.24	0.98	—	Income Ratio %
126	131	161	89	86	79	79	100	95	97	106	—	Turnover Rate %
159	274	771	2,019	2,317	1,912	1,477	988	1,194	1,548	1,959	2,488	Net Assets $mil

Performance 12-31-06

	1st Qtr	2nd Qtr	3rd Qtr	4th Qtr	Total
2002	-0.42	-10.94	-16.80	7.99	-20.32
2003	-2.03	15.14	3.30	11.80	30.27
2004	3.08	1.81	-1.41	10.16	13.98
2005	-0.72	2.27	4.35	1.27	7.30
2006	3.60	-0.63	3.67	6.95	14.14

Trailing	Total Return%	+/- S&P 500	+/- Russ 1000	%Rank Cat	Growth of $10,000
3 Mo	6.95	0.25	0.00	35	10,695
6 Mo	10.87	-1.87	-1.49	63	11,087
1 Yr	14.14	-1.65	-1.32	53	11,414
3 Yr Avg	11.76	1.32	0.78	19	13,959
5 Yr Avg	7.70	1.51	0.88	18	14,490
10 Yr Avg	8.79	0.37	0.15	21	23,221
15 Yr Avg	10.72	0.08	-0.08	29	46,067

Tax Analysis	Tax-Adj Rtn%	%Rank Cat	Tax-Cost Rat	%Rank Cat
3 Yr (estimated)	11.17	16	0.53	25
5 Yr (estimated)	7.21	17	0.45	29
10 Yr (estimated)	7.63	24	1.07	48

Potential Capital Gain Exposure: 17% of assets

Rating and Risk

Time Period	Load-Adj Return %	Morningstar Rtn vs Cat	Morningstar Risk vs Cat	Morningstar Risk-Adj Rating
1 Yr	14.14			
3 Yr	11.76	+Avg	+Avg	★★★★
5 Yr	7.70	+Avg	Avg	★★★★
10 Yr	8.79	+Avg	+Avg	★★★★
Incept	11.39			

Other Measures	Standard Index S&P 500	Best Fit Index Russ 1000
Alpha	0.4	0.1
Beta	1.12	1.09
R-Squared	91	91
Standard Deviation	8.10	
Mean	11.76	
Sharpe Ratio	1.02	

Morningstar's Take by Arijit Dutta 12-12-06

American Century Equity Growth's measured approach can still produce powerful results.

This fund's quantitative strategy imposes a nice balance. Management uses a set of valuation, momentum, and earnings-stability characteristics to quantitatively predict which stocks have higher future expected returns than the overall market. At the same time, however, management restricts the model to make sure the portfolio's sector weights and risk characteristics mimic those of the S&P 500 Index. The twin goals here are to let stock selection do the talking, and limit volatility. American Century devotes an experienced group of quant specialists to the upkeep of the firm's numerical models, which adds to the strategy's inherent strength.

Results have indeed been pleasing. Recent examples include ExxonMobil, the portfolio's largest holding. While the stock didn't keep pace with smaller, less diversified rivals in 2005, Exxon is easily among this year's best energy stocks. (A steep decline in oil prices has made Exxon relatively

attractive due to the company's low costs and multiple sources of revenue.) Overall, the quantitative models here have consistently identified the better bargains in any sector, leading to the fund's strong long-term record.

Also, the models' attention to risk makes the fund especially appealing as a core choice. The portfolio takes on minimal sector bets relative to the benchmark, which limits how far performance can stray due to market swings in any industry. True, this didn't prevent a sharp loss in 2000, when the portfolio paid the price for matching the index's large stake in overheated technology and telecom stocks. Still, the fund made up ground as the bear market of 2000-02 deepened. The models' valuation component should continue to steer the portfolio away from pricey fare in a timely fashion.

We think the fund will sustain its enviable risk/return profile.

Portfolio Analysis 09-30-06

Share change since 06-06 Total Stocks:142	Sector	PE	Tot Ret%	% Assets
⊖ ExxonMobil Corporation	Energy	11.1	39.07	4.78
⊕ Citigroup, Inc.	Financial	13.1	19.55	3.53
⊕ J.P. Morgan Chase & Co.	Financial	13.6	25.60	2.84
⊕ IBM	Hardware	17.1	19.77	2.61
⊕ Hewlett-Packard Company	Hardware	19.3	45.21	2.52
⊕ Bank of America Corporat	Financial	12.4	20.68	2.50
⊖ Chevron Corporation	Energy	9.0	33.76	2.15
⊖ Goldman Sachs Group, Inc	Financial	12.4	57.41	2.06
⊕ Merck & Co., Inc.	Health	19.1	42.66	2.04
⊕ Amgen, Inc.	Health	29.1	-13.38	1.96
⊖ TXU Corporation	Utilities	12.8	11.19	1.94
⊕ Morgan Stanley	Financial	12.3	45.93	1.94
⊕ McKesson, Inc.	Health	18.1	-1.26	1.74
⊖ Coca-Cola Company	Goods	21.7	23.10	1.65
Colgate-Palmolive Compan	Goods	27.6	21.51	1.64
⊕ Accenture, Ltd.	Business	22.0	29.32	1.62
⊕ Cummins, Inc.	Ind Mtrls	8.4	33.23	1.61
⊕ Humana	Health	21.8	1.80	1.60
⊕ Nucor Corp.	Ind Mtrls	10.3	70.67	1.52
⊕ Lockheed Martin Corporat	Ind Mtrls	17.3	46.98	1.47

Current Investment Style

Value Blnd Growth — Large Mid Small

Market Cap	%
Giant	40.1
Large	33.9
Mid	22.5
Small	3.5
Micro	0.0
Avg $mil:	28,638

Value Measures		Rel Category
Price/Earnings	13.26	0.86
Price/Book	2.62	1.02
Price/Sales	0.95	0.68
Price/Cash Flow	4.19	0.50
Dividend Yield %	1.62	0.93

Growth Measures	%	Rel Category
Long-Term Erngs	11.07	0.94
Book Value	10.29	1.14
Sales	11.67	1.20
Cash Flow	26.46	2.56
Historical Erngs	23.72	1.28

Profitability	%	Rel Category
Return on Equity	23.95	1.23
Return on Assets	11.64	1.12
Net Margin	12.54	0.93

Sector Weightings	% of Stocks	Rel S&P 500	3 Year High	Low
↻ Info	16.19	0.81		
Software	0.59	0.17	3	1
Hardware	8.86	0.96	10	8
Media	4.13	1.09	6	3
Telecom	2.61	0.74	5	2
⊂ Service	52.78	1.14		
Health	14.47	1.20	16	10
Consumer	8.54	1.12	12	6
Business	5.82	1.38	6	3
Financial	23.95	1.08	24	18
Mfg	31.02	0.92		
Goods	6.37	0.75	16	5
Ind Mtrls	9.50	0.80	13	7
Energy	11.85	1.21	12	7
Utilities	3.30	0.94	5	3

Composition

● Cash	0.4
● Stocks	99.6
● Bonds	0.0
● Other	0.0
Foreign	0.2
(% of Stock)	

Address:	4500 Main Street	Minimum Purchase:	$2500	Add: $50	IRA: $2500
	Kansas City MO 64111	Min Auto Inv Plan:	$2500	Add: $50	
	800-345-2021	Sales Fees:	No-load		
Web Address:	www.americancentury.com	Management Fee:	0.67%		
Inception:	05-09-91	Actual Fees:	Mgt:0.67%	Dist: —	
Advisor:	American Century Investment MGMT Inc.	Expense Projections:	3Yr:$214	5Yr:$373	10Yr:$833
Subadvisor:	None	Income Distrib:	Quarterly		
NTF Plans:	Fidelity Retail-NTF, Schwab OneSource				

MORNINGSTAR® Funds 500

AmCent Equity Income Inv

	Ticker	Load	NAV	Yield	Total Assets	Mstar Category
	TWEIX	None	$8.58	2.1%	$6,408 mil	Large Value

Governance and Management

Stewardship Grade: C

Portfolio Manager(s)

Phil Davidson has been at the helm since the fund's inception. Before that, Davidson spent 11 years as a manager for Boatmen's Trust Co. Scott Moore has roughly a decade of experience as an analyst and portfolio manager. Kevin Toney joined the group in 2003 after serving as one of the fund's analysts.

Strategy

Phil Davidson and Scott Moore employ an all-cap approach, focusing on stocks that are cheap based on at least two valuation measures, such as P/E or dividend yield. They also aim to create a portfolio with a yield that is 2 percentage points greater than the S&P 500 Index's by emphasizing higher-yielding stocks and holding a slew of convertibles. This income mandate means the fund has big stakes in dividend-rich utilities, energy, financials, and industrials. The managers are quick to sell stocks they think have gotten too pricey; turnover is well above the mid-value norm.

Performance 12-31-06

	1st Qtr	2nd Qtr	3rd Qtr	4th Qtr	Total
2002	3.59	-4.71	-10.74	7.83	-5.00
2003	-4.14	13.63	2.31	11.49	24.25
2004	1.30	2.80	0.97	7.03	12.53
2005	-0.36	0.78	1.21	0.80	2.46
2006	4.27	1.00	6.89	6.11	19.45

Trailing	Total Return%	+/- S&P 500	+/- Russ 1000 Vl	%Rank Cat	Growth of $10,000
3 Mo	6.11	-0.59	-1.89	85	10,611
6 Mo	13.43	0.69	-1.29	38	11,343
1 Yr	19.45	3.66	-2.80	33	11,945
3 Yr Avg	11.26	0.82	-3.83	69	13,773
5 Yr Avg	10.21	4.02	-0.65	15	16,259
10 Yr Avg	12.30	3.88	1.30	3	31,901
15 Yr Avg	—	—	—	—	—

Tax Analysis	Tax-Adj Rtn%	%Rank Cat	Tax-Cost Rat	%Rank Cat
3 Yr (estimated)	9.01	77	2.02	79
5 Yr (estimated)	8.24	29	1.79	85
10 Yr (estimated)	9.08	11	2.87	99

Potential Capital Gain Exposure: 12% of assets

Historical Profile

Return	Above Avg
Risk	Low
Rating	★★★★ Above Avg

Investment Style: Equity, Stock %

Percentages: 77% 82% 64% 63% 65% 74% 68% 69% 69%

▼ Manager Change
▽ Partial Manager Change

Growth of $10,000
■ Investment Values of Fund
— Investment Values of S&P 500

42.2 / 32.4 / 24.0 / 17.0 / 10.0

Performance Quartile (within Category)

	1995	1996	1997	1998	1999	2000	2001	2002	2003	2004	2005	2006	History
NAV	5.76	6.34	6.66	6.31	5.60	6.62	7.14	6.53	7.78	8.11	7.82	8.58	
Total Return %	29.62	23.31	28.26	12.97	-0.18	21.91	11.33	-5.00	24.25	12.53	2.46	19.45	
+/-S&P 500	-7.96	0.35	-5.10	-15.61	-21.22	31.01	23.22	17.10	-4.43	1.65	2.46	3.66	
+/-Russ 1000 Vl	-8.74	1.67	-6.92	-2.66	-7.53	14.90	16.92	10.52	-5.78	-3.96	-4.59	-2.80	
Income Return %	3.96	3.29	4.14	3.28	3.48	3.24	2.67	2.27	3.01	2.56	2.10	2.58	
Capital Return %	25.66	20.02	24.12	9.69	-3.66	18.67	8.66	-7.27	21.24	9.97	0.36	16.87	
Total Rtn % Rank Cat	72	17	39	42	76	9	4	1	85	58	89	33	
Income $	0.19	0.19	0.26	0.22	0.22	0.18	0.18	0.16	0.19	0.20	0.17	0.20	
Capital Gains $	0.45	0.55	1.16	0.96	0.48	0.00	0.04	0.14	0.12	0.42	0.32	0.55	
Expense Ratio %	1.00	0.98	1.00	1.00	1.00	1.00	1.00	1.00	1.00	1.00	0.99	0.98	
Income Ratio %	4.04	3.51	3.46	3.52	3.31	3.41	3.02	2.49	2.60	2.95	2.56	2.53	
Turnover Rate %	—	170	159	158	180	141	169	139	120	91	174	150	
Net Assets $mil	97	187	297	326	328	385	832	1,241	2,105	2,919	3,820	4,621	

Rating and Risk

Time Period	Load-Adj Return %	Morningstar Rtn vs Cat	Morningstar Risk vs Cat	Morningstar Risk-Adj Rating
1 Yr	19.45			
3 Yr	11.26	Avg	Low	★★★
5 Yr	10.21	+Avg	Low	★★★★
10 Yr	12.30	High	Low	★★★★★
Incept	14.07			

Other Measures	Standard Index S&P 500	Best Fit Index Russ 1000 Vl
Alpha	3.0	-0.2
Beta	0.66	0.70
R-Squared	76	82
Standard Deviation	5.29	
Mean	11.26	
Sharpe Ratio	1.46	

Portfolio Analysis 09-30-06

Share change since 06-06 Total Stocks:69	Sector	PE	Tot Ret%	% Assets
⊕ General Electric Company	Ind Mtrls	20.0	9.35	4.68
⊕ ExxonMobil Corporation	Energy	11.1	39.07	4.68
⊕ Amer Intl Grp Cv				4.58
⊕ Bank of America Corporat	Financial	12.4	20.68	3.20
☼ AT&T, Inc.	Telecom	18.2	51.59	2.99
⊖ Ameren Corporation	Utilities	21.1	10.14	2.24
⊕ H.J. Heinz Company	Goods	29.0	37.89	2.21
⊕ Commerce Bancshares, Inc	Financial	15.6	-0.55	2.14
⊕ FNMA Pfd 144A				2.14
⊖ SunTrust Banks, Inc.	Financial	14.1	19.81	2.06
⊕ Commonwealth Tel Enterpr				2.04
⊕ Consolidated Edison Comp	Utilities	17.3	9.14	1.97
☼ SPDRs				1.96
⊖ Southern Company	Utilities	17.6	11.69	1.91
⊖ Hasbro Cv 2.75%				1.84
⊕ Westar Energy, Inc.	Utilities	14.3	26.11	1.73
⊕ Watson Pharmaceuticals C				1.72
⊕ LINCARE HLDGS				1.65
⊕ BP PLC ADR	Energy	10.4	7.94	1.62
⊖ Freddie Mac	Financial	23.3	7.06	1.57

Current Investment Style

Value Blnd Growth — Large Mid Small

Market Cap	%
Giant	38.5
Large	32.2
Mid	24.5
Small	4.5
Micro	0.3

Avg $mil: 29,275

Value Measures		Rel Category
Price/Earnings	15.07	1.10
Price/Book	2.43	1.09
Price/Sales	1.43	1.10
Price/Cash Flow	3.21	0.48
Dividend Yield %	3.43	1.47

Growth Measures	%	Rel Category
Long-Term Erngs	8.33	0.80
Book Value	6.61	0.83
Sales	8.54	0.95
Cash Flow	1.20	0.20
Historical Erngs	7.66	0.47

Profitability	%	Rel Category
Return on Equity	18.19	1.01
Return on Assets	8.99	0.92
Net Margin	12.25	0.95

Sector Weightings	% of Stocks	Rel S&P 500	3 Year High	Low
Info	7.29	0.36		
Software	0.10	0.03	1	0
Hardware	0.72	0.08	2	0
Media	0.43	0.11	2	0
Telecom	6.04	1.72	6	1
Service	32.91	0.71		
Health	3.06	0.25	8	3
Consumer	4.63	0.61	5	0
Business	4.51	1.07	8	2
Financial	20.71	0.93	28	19
Mfg	59.80	1.77		
Goods	13.07	1.53	16	10
Ind Mtrls	18.84	1.58	22	15
Energy	10.75	1.10	15	11
Utilities	17.14	4.90	18	10

Composition

● Cash		3.0
● Stocks		69.5
● Bonds		3.6
● Other		24.0
Foreign (% of Stock)		3.4

Morningstar's Take by Christopher Davis 11-20-06

American Century Equity Income isn't perfect, but it's still plenty appealing.

The typical large-value fund's turnover runs about 60% annually. That means this fund's typical rival holds its picks for just less than two years. Turnover here is much higher, clocking in at 150% in 2005, implying a typical holding period of just six months. The heavy trading stems in large part from management's valuation discipline, which involves adding to holdings on declines and cutting them loose when they rise to perceived fair value.

Undoubtedly, that strategy makes some intuitive sense. After all, it makes sense to own more of a stock when it's cheaper and less of it when it's more expensive. But management's high sensitivity to short-term stock price movements has downsides. For one, trading stocks isn't free, and high turnover racks up transaction costs. It also can lead to heavy taxable gains, which historically have taken a big bite out of the fund's pretax returns. Finally, management's trading strategy puts the fund in closer competition with hedge funds and other short-term investors, which have proliferated in recent years. Looking ahead, we worry that this trend could diminish the fund's edge.

On balance, though, we like what we see here. Management is highly experienced and has delivered strong long-term returns under its watch. And in contrast with many equity income funds, which merely pay lip service to income generation, this one takes its mandate seriously. Management favors higher-yielding stocks and keeps a large slug of the portfolio in income-rich convertibles, an approach that helps limit losses. Indeed, its worst calendar-year loss was just 5% in 2002 (the average large-value fund lost 18%).

To be sure, the fund's income orientation means it's likely to lag when racier fare leads the way. But historically, it's earned its keep in rough markets. Conservative investors will feel at home here; though given this fund's lackluster tax efficiency, they should hold it in a tax-protected account.

Address:	4500 Main Street Kansas City MO 64111 800-345-2021
Web Address:	www.americancentury.com
Inception:	08-01-94
Advisor:	American Century Investment MGMT Inc.
Subadvisor:	None
NTF Plans:	Fidelity Retail-NTF, Schwab OneSource

Minimum Purchase:	$2500	Add: $50 IRA: $0
Min Auto Inv Plan:	$2500	Add: $50
Sales Fees:	No-load	
Management Fee:	1.00% mx./0.80% mn.	
Actual Fees:	Mgt:0.98%	Dist: —
Expense Projections:	3Yr:$311	5Yr:$540 10Yr:$1196
Income Distrib:	Quarterly	

 Morningstar® Funds 500

AmCent Ginnie Mae Inv

	Ticker	Load	NAV	Yield	SEC Yield	Total Assets	Mstar Category
	BGNMX	None	$10.16	4.9%	4.80%	$1,330 mil	Intermediate Government

Governance and Management

Stewardship Grade: B

Portfolio Manager(s)

Alejandro H. Aguilar and Dan Shiffman took over here in September 2004 (from prior manager Casey Colton). Both previously worked at the California pension system known as CalPERS and have several years of experience in the industry. Prior to joining CalPERS, Aguilar also managed portfolios for New York-based manager TIAA-CREF.

Strategy

Until recently, the fund held GNMAs and other issues with the full backing of Uncle Sam and used a blended mortgage/Treasury index. But while supporting team members remain the same, two new arrivals took on day-to-day responsibility in early September 2004. The team may now hold up to 20% in mortgages and bonds from government-linked agencies such as FNMA and FHLMC. They may also use asset-backed and commercial mortgage securities. The fund's duration (a measure of interest-rate sensitivity) will typically stay within six months of the Salomon Brothers GNMA Index.

Performance 12-31-06

	1st Qtr	2nd Qtr	3rd Qtr	4th Qtr	Total
2002	0.99	3.37	2.45	1.27	8.30
2003	0.69	0.41	0.29	0.62	2.02
2004	1.06	-0.91	2.05	0.91	3.12
2005	0.05	1.74	0.05	0.97	2.83
2006	-0.27	-0.66	3.58	1.34	3.99

Trailing	Total Return%	+/- LB Aggr	+/- LB Govt	%Rank Cat	Growth of $10,000
3 Mo	1.34	0.10	0.50	16	10,134
6 Mo	4.97	-0.12	0.56	11	10,497
1 Yr	3.99	-0.34	0.51	23	10,399
3 Yr Avg	3.31	-0.39	0.11	22	11,026
5 Yr Avg	4.03	-1.03	-0.61	42	12,184
10 Yr Avg	5.37	-0.87	-0.64	36	16,872
15 Yr Avg	5.77	-0.73	-0.53	25	23,197

Tax Analysis	Tax-Adj Rtn%	%Rank Cat	Tax-Cost Rat	%Rank Cat
3 Yr (estimated)	1.63	27	1.63	80
5 Yr (estimated)	2.24	48	1.72	80
10 Yr (estimated)	3.18	45	2.08	85

Potential Capital Gain Exposure: -6% of assets

Historical Profile

Return Average
Risk Below Avg
Rating ★★★ Neutral

	30	14	19	12	11	13	12	11	

Growth of $10,000
— Investment Values of Fund
— Investment Values of LB Aggr

▼ Manager Change
▽ Partial Manager Change

Performance Quartile (within Category)

1995	1996	1997	1998	1999	2000	2001	2002	2003	2004	2005	2006	History
10.68	10.49	10.68	10.69	10.14	10.49	10.62	10.90	10.61	10.45	10.26	10.16	NAV
15.86	5.21	8.79	6.32	0.99	10.35	7.43	8.30	2.02	3.12	2.83	3.99	Total Return %
-2.61	1.58	-0.86	-2.37	1.81	-1.28	-1.01	-1.95	-2.08	-1.22	0.40	-0.34	+/-LB Aggr
-2.48	2.44	-0.80	-3.53	3.22	-2.89	0.20	-3.20	-0.34	-0.36	0.18	0.51	+/-LB Govt
7.78	6.94	6.88	6.23	6.28	6.72	6.21	5.60	4.72	4.64	4.68	4.94	Income Return %
8.08	-1.73	1.91	0.09	-5.29	3.63	1.22	2.70	-2.70	-1.52	-1.85	-0.95	Capital Return %
63	6	50	84	8	74	27	70	37	49	5	23	Total Rtn % Rank Cat
0.74	0.72	0.70	0.65	0.65	0.66	0.63	0.58	0.50	0.48	0.48	0.50	Income $
0.00	0.00	0.00	0.00	0.00	0.00	0.00	0.00	0.00	0.00	0.00	0.00	Capital Gains $
0.58	0.58	0.55	0.58	0.59	0.59	0.59	0.59	0.59	0.59	0.58	0.57	Expense Ratio %
7.08	6.98	6.84	6.49	5.98	6.57	6.57	5.75	5.19	2.77	3.58	4.15	Income Ratio %
120	64	105	133	119	133	143	218	356	356	315	315	Turnover Rate %
1,111	1,131	1,234	1,377	1,298	1,288	1,646	2,069	1,732	1,517	1,400	1,238	Net Assets $mil

Rating and Risk

Time Period	Load-Adj Return %	Morningstar Rtn vs Cat	Morningstar Risk vs Cat	Morningstar Risk-Adj Rating
1 Yr	3.99			
3 Yr	3.31	+Avg	-Avg	★★★★
5 Yr	4.03	Avg	-Avg	★★★
10 Yr	5.37	Avg	Low	★★★
Incept	7.23			

Other Measures	Standard Index LB Aggr	Best Fit Index LB Mort
Alpha	-0.2	-0.7
Beta	0.64	0.86
R-Squared	88	95
Standard Deviation	2.23	
Mean	3.31	
Sharpe Ratio	0.03	

Portfolio Analysis 09-30-06

Total Fixed-Income:2163	Date of Maturity	Amount $000	Value $000	% Net Assets
GNMA 5.5%	11-20-34	180,000	134,412	6.86
GNMA 6%	10-15-34	130,000	131,584	6.71
G2sf 6%	10-20-36	109,000	110,057	5.61
GNMA 5.5%	07-15-33	268,548	109,529	5.59
GNMA 5%	10-15-35	102,000	99,099	5.06
GNMA 5.5%	10-15-35	70,000	69,541	3.55
GNMA 6.5%	10-15-34	58,000	59,486	3.03
GNMA CMO	02-16-33	110,000	47,854	2.44
GNMA 6%	09-20-34	72,100	46,389	2.37
GNMA 5%	08-15-33	65,182	35,034	1.79
GNMA 6%	07-20-34	55,882	33,402	1.70
GNMA 5%	09-15-33	61,622	32,344	1.65
GNMA 5.5%	03-20-36	33,120	32,055	1.64
GNMA	05-20-31	59,000	31,830	1.62
GNMA 5.5%	12-20-34	41,000	31,048	1.58
GNMA 5%	08-15-33	53,160	30,234	1.54
GNMA 5.5%	03-15-34	50,175	27,032	1.38
GNMA 5.5%	06-15-33	55,302	26,681	1.36
GNMA CMO 5%	10-20-27	35,565	24,236	1.24
GNMA 5%	09-15-33	52,218	23,750	1.21

Current Investment Style

Duration: Short Int Long
Quality: High Med Low

¹ figure provided by fund

Avg Eff Duration¹	4.0 Yrs
Avg Eff Maturity	6.4 Yrs
Avg Credit Quality	AAA
Avg Wtd Coupon	5.28%
Avg Wtd Price	67.75% of par

Coupon Range	% of Bonds	Rel Cat
0% PIK	2.5	0.3
0% to 6%	88.7	1.1
6% to 8%	10.5	0.7
8% to 10%	0.7	0.3
More than 10%	0.1	0.1

1.00=Category Average

Credit Analysis	% bonds 09-30-06		
AAA	100	BB	0
AA	0	B	0
A	0	Below B	0
BBB	0	NR/NA	0

Sector Breakdown	% of assets
US Treasuries	1
TIPS	0
US Agency	1
Mortgage Pass-Throughs	62
Mortgage CMO	11
Mortgage ARM	0
US Corporate	6
Asset-Backed	0
Convertible	0
Municipal	0
Corporate Inflation-Protected	0
Foreign Corporate	0
Foreign Govt	0

Composition			
Cash	19.7	Bonds	80.3
Stocks	0.0	Other	0.0

Special Securities	
Restricted/Illiquid Secs	0
Exotic Mortgage-Backed	—
Emerging-Markets Secs	0
Options/Futures/Warrants	No

Morningstar's Take by Andrew Gunter 12-11-06

American Century Ginnie Mae does right by investors.

This mutual fund treats investors well on a number of measures. Its trailing one-, three-, five-, and 10-year returns stand within the intermediate government-bond category's top half, and it's provided a smooth ride for shareholders who reinvest dividends. Of the 27 quarters from January 1, 2000, through September 30, 2006, this fund had negative total returns in only four of them.

At the heart of comanagers Hando Aguilar and Dan Shiffman's strategy is an effort to find Ginnie Mae bonds whose prepayment risk is mispriced by the market. For each mortgage bond they research, they investigate whether the market is over- or underestimating how quickly its pool of homeowners will pay down the principal of their mortgages. When the market overestimates prepayment risk on a Ginnie Mae, the bond is discounted too much and carries a higher yield than it logically should. Aguilar and Shiffman, like other

Ginnie Mae managers, try to find these bonds before others do, and then wait for the market to revalue them correctly--at a higher price.

American Century's managers are good bond-pickers, so they can afford to be conservative in other areas such as interest-rate positioning. Aguilar and Shiffman incorporate theses on such topics, developed by American Century's economic strategy team, into the portfolio's construction. Yet even when they strongly believe in their thesis--in this case, that interest rates should start to fall soon--their tinkering is restrained. For example, as the fall of 2006 drew near, they extended the fund's duration (a measure of interest rate sensitivity) to one tenth of a year beyond its benchmark.

The comanagers' close attention to valuation, and moderation in areas where wrong moves can be disastrous, all get a boost from the fund's below-average expenses. For investors seeking a Ginnie Mae fund, this is a worthwhile candidate.

Address:	4500 Main Street Kansas City MO 64111 800-345-2021	Minimum Purchase:	$2500	Add: $50	IRA: $2500
		Min Auto Inv Plan:	$2500	Add: $50	
		Sales Fees:	No-load		
Web Address:	www.americancentury.com	Management Fee:	0.65% mx./0.53% mn.		
Inception:	09-23-85	Actual Fees:	Mgt:0.57%	Dist:—	
Advisor:	American Century Investment MGMT Inc.	Expense Projections:	3Yr:$182	5Yr:$318	10Yr:$712
Subadvisor:	None	Income Distrib:	Monthly		
NTF Plans:	Fidelity Retail-NTF, Schwab OneSource				

MORNINGSTAR® Funds 500

AmCent Global Gold Inv

		Ticker	Load	NAV	Yield	Total Assets	Mstar Category
		BGEIX	None	$19.63	0.2%	$1,077 mil	Specialty-Precious Metals

Governance and Management

Stewardship Grade: B

Portfolio Manager(s)

Bill Martin has run this fund since 1992, giving him one of the longest tenures in the precious-metals category. Two comanagers, John Schniedwind, American Century's CIO, and Joe Sterling, assist with stock selection.

Strategy

Manager Bill Martin runs this offering as a pure gold fund and stays away from other metals, such as palladium and platinum. He selects stocks to buy and sell using a combination of fundamental analysis and a computer-driven risk-management model. Martin doesn't stick to any one geographic region, and the fund typically holds a mix of North American, Australian, and South African companies.

Performance 12-31-06

	1st Qtr	2nd Qtr	3rd Qtr	4th Qtr	Total
2002	40.19	11.83	-1.33	11.84	73.00
2003	-13.47	16.50	19.65	21.63	46.70
2004	-2.05	-17.89	15.22	-0.91	-8.17
2005	-5.67	-0.80	19.41	15.59	29.17
2006	18.65	1.56	-7.52	14.00	27.03

Trailing	Total Return%	+/- MSCI EAFE	+/- MSCI W Me&M	%Rank Cat	Growth of $10,000
3 Mo	14.00	3.65	-2.95	78	11,400
6 Mo	5.42	-9.27	-6.27	84	10,542
1 Yr	27.03	0.69	-7.53	76	12,703
3 Yr Avg	14.64	-5.29	-12.35	60	15,066
5 Yr Avg	30.77	15.79	4.41	59	38,242
10 Yr Avg	6.85	-0.86	—	69	19,397
15 Yr Avg	7.21	-0.65	—	73	28,414

Tax Analysis	Tax-Adj Rtn%	%Rank Cat	Tax-Cost Rat	%Rank Cat
3 Yr (estimated)	14.50	57	0.12	7
5 Yr (estimated)	30.47	47	0.23	14
10 Yr (estimated)	6.43	65	0.39	32

Potential Capital Gain Exposure: 44% of assets

Historical Profile

Return	Average
Risk	Above Avg
Rating	★★ Below Avg

96%	98%	93%	93%	91%	98%	99%	99%	98%

Investment Style
Equity
Stock %

▼ Manager Change
▽ Partial Manager Change

19.6 / 14.0 / 10.0 / 3.0

Growth of $10,000
— Investment Values of Fund
— Investment Values of MSCI EAFE

Performance Quartile (within Category)

1995	1996	1997	1998	1999	2000	2001	2002	2003	2004	2005	2006	History
12.37	11.33	6.34	5.52	5.29	4.00	5.30	9.13	13.17	12.00	15.50	19.63	NAV
9.25	-2.76	-41.47	-12.18	-23.95	34.09	73.00	46.70	-8.17	29.17	27.03		Total Return %
-1.96	-8.81	-43.25	-32.11	-30.21	-9.76	55.51	88.94	8.11	-28.42	15.63	0.69	+/-MSCI EAFE
—	—	—	—	-53.22	-0.39	32.99	77.28	-17.63	-22.05	-4.49	-7.53	+/-MSCI W Me&M
0.08	0.47	0.83	0.76	0.94	0.49	1.44	0.69	2.26	0.59	0.00	0.30	Income Return %
9.17	-3.23	-42.30	-12.94	-4.12	-24.44	32.65	72.31	44.44	-8.76	29.17	26.73	Capital Return %
39	91	65	71	81	85	4	19	82	52	64	76	Total Rtn % Rank Cat
0.01	0.06	0.09	0.05	0.05	0.03	0.06	0.04	0.21	0.08	0.00	0.05	Income $
0.00	0.64	0.20	0.00	0.00	0.00	0.00	0.00	0.00	0.00	0.00	0.00	Capital Gains $
0.61	0.62	0.67	0.69	0.68	0.67	0.68	0.69	0.69	0.68	0.67	—	Expense Ratio %
0.17	0.46	0.93	0.75	1.04	1.19	0.99	0.57	0.22	-0.03	0.11	—	Income Ratio %
28	45	28	68	53	17	17	34	22	14	5	—	Turnover Rate %
540	433	249	228	202	142	193	421	737	695	777	1,071	Net Assets $mil

Rating and Risk

Time Period	Load-Adj Return %	Morningstar Rtn vs Cat	Morningstar Risk vs Cat	Morningstar Risk-Adj Rating
1 Yr	27.03			
3 Yr	14.64	Avg	+Avg	★★
5 Yr	30.77	Avg	+Avg	★★
10 Yr	6.85	-Avg	+Avg	★★
Incept	4.88			

Other Measures	Standard Index MSCI EAFE	Best Fit Index JSE Gold ND
Alpha	-19.6	10.2
Beta	2.29	0.72
R-Squared	43	82
Standard Deviation	32.93	
Mean	14.64	
Sharpe Ratio	0.48	

Morningstar's Take by Karen Wallace 12-20-06

Despite seemingly average risk-adjusted returns, American Century Global Gold is one of the better options for pure gold exposure.

Longtime manager Bill Martin runs this fund using a straightforward strategy. He over- or underweights certain stocks relative to an internally devised custom index if he thinks they're attractively valued and have favorable risk characteristics. The portfolio permanently focuses on the world's largest gold producers: More than 17% of assets are devoted to the two largest gold producers, Newmont Mining and Barrick Gold. The fund also has limited positions in the smaller and more-speculative exploration and production companies that are common elsewhere in the category, as he also tends to favor stocks that are less sensitive to gold prices.

Investors here should be aware of some positives and negatives of Martin's consistent approach. Because of the fund's pure focus on gold producers, it tracks the gold price fairly reliably and

has a low correlation with domestic-equity markets. Additionally, its focus on larger, more-diversified gold producers gives it a little more stability than peers focusing on smaller-cap companies, if the price of gold takes a turn for the worse. This is because smaller companies are generally more sensitive to gold prices.

But the converse is also true: Peers that focus on smaller, less-diversified producers have more upside potential than this fund during gold rallies. Another factor is that the fund's nearly pure focus on gold producers means its volatility, as measured by standard deviation, is above the category median. It also means the fund will likely lag peers that delve into other areas such as aluminum or coal when gold prices stink.

So we think it's a sensible choice for investors seeking pure exposure to gold producers. Investors in this fund have two major bonuses: The fund is run in a dependable style, and its fees are among the cheapest in the group.

Portfolio Analysis 09-30-06

Share change since 06-06 Total Stocks:77	Sector	Country	% Assets
Barrick Gold Corporation	Ind Mtrls	Canada	9.49
⊕ Newmont Mining	Ind Mtrls	United States	7.58
Glamis Gold, Ltd.	Ind Mtrls	Canada	5.38
⊕ Goldcorp, Inc.	Ind Mtrls	Canada	5.38
Kinross Gold Corporation	Ind Mtrls	Canada	4.98
Oxiana Ltd	Ind Mtrls	Australia	4.93
Agnico-Eagle Mines	Ind Mtrls	Canada	4.30
Gold Fields Ltd	Ind Mtrls	South Africa	3.87
Newcrest Mining Ltd	Ind Mtrls	Australia	3.72
Lihir Gold Ltd	Ind Mtrls	Australia	3.34
Yamana Gold, Inc.	Ind Mtrls	Canada	3.32
Meridian Gold, Inc.	Ind Mtrls	Canada	3.03
Bema Gold Corporation	Ind Mtrls	Canada	2.73
Centerra Gold	Ind Mtrls	Canada	2.32
Harmony Gold Mining	Ind Mtrls	South Africa	2.31
⊕ Anglogold Ashanti, Ltd.	Ind Mtrls	South Africa	2.25
Anglogold Ashanti Ltd	Ind Mtrls	South Africa	2.24
Randgold Resources, Ltd.	Ind Mtrls	U.K.	2.07
⊕ Iamgold Corporation	Ind Mtrls	Canada	1.88
Miramar Mining Corporati	Ind Mtrls	Canada	1.73

Current Investment Style

Value Blnd Growth — Large Mid Small

Market Cap	%
Giant	9.7
Large	32.0
Mid	42.7
Small	13.6
Micro	2.1
Avg $mil:	3,762

Value Measures		Rel Category
Price/Earnings	20.41	0.99
Price/Book	3.37	0.96
Price/Sales	5.40	1.01
Price/Cash Flow	13.87	1.13
Dividend Yield %	0.73	0.59

Growth Measures	%	Rel Category
Long-Term Erngs	20.45	1.08
Book Value	6.08	0.56
Sales	19.51	0.90
Cash Flow	20.88	0.51
Historical Erngs	5.87	0.22

Composition			
Cash	1.5	Bonds	0.0
Stocks	98.3	Other	0.2
Foreign (% of Stock)	90.2		

Sector Weightings	% of Stocks	Rel MSCI EAFE	3 Year High	Low
⊙ Info	0.00	0.00		
▩ Software	0.00	0.00	0	0
▤ Hardware	0.00	0.00	0	0
▤ Media	0.00	0.00	0	0
▤ Telecom	0.00	0.00	0	0
⊕ Service	0.00	0.00		
▤ Health	0.00	0.00	0	0
▤ Consumer	0.00	0.00	0	0
▤ Business	0.00	0.00	0	0
▤ Financial	0.00	0.00	0	0
⊡ Mfg	100.00	2.44		
▤ Goods	0.00	0.00	0	0
▦ Ind Mtrls	100.00	6.48	100	100
▤ Energy	0.00	0.00	0	0
▤ Utilities	0.00	0.00	0	0

Regional Exposure			% Stock
UK/W. Europe	2	N. America	69
Japan	0	Latn America	0
Asia X Japan	15	Other	14

Country Exposure			% Stock
Canada	59	United States	10
Australia	15	U.K.	2
South Africa	14		

Address:	4500 Main Street Kansas City MO 64111 800-345-2021
Web Address:	www.americancentury.com
Inception:	08-17-88
Advisor:	American Century Investment MGMT Inc.
Subadvisor:	None
NTF Plans:	Fidelity Retail-NTF, Schwab OneSource

Minimum Purchase:	$2500	Add: $50	IRA: $2500
Min Auto Inv Plan:	$2500	Add: $50	
Sales Fees:	No-load, 1.00%R		
Management Fee:	0.67%		
Actual Fees:	Mgt:0.67%	Dist: —	
Expense Projections:	3Yr:$214	5Yr:$373	10Yr:$833
Income Distrib:	Semi-Annually		

MORNINGSTAR® Funds 500

41

AmCent Global Gr Inv

	Ticker	Load	NAV	Yield	Total Assets	Mstar Category
	TWGGX	None	$10.74	0.5%	$448 mil	World Stock

Governance and Management

Stewardship Grade: B

Portfolio Manager(s)

Keith Creveling, who also manages American Century International Stock and is a comanager of American Century International Growth, took over from Matthew Hudson in November 2005. Helen O'Donnell was promoted from analyst to comanager at the same time.

Strategy

Companies with growing sales or profits are attractive to this fund's management, and the portfolio is full of fast-growers, regardless of their countries, sectors, sizes, or price multiples. Management also favors firms with competent management and niche products, and earnings disappointments send a stock packing from the portfolio.

Performance 12-31-06

	1st Qtr	2nd Qtr	3rd Qtr	4th Qtr	Total
2002	0.95	-4.08	-17.97	0.40	-20.25
2003	-4.76	16.46	7.33	13.00	34.52
2004	4.57	-0.99	-2.99	14.60	15.11
2005	-0.64	3.31	8.01	6.53	18.11
2006	9.20	-4.21	3.04	9.64	18.16

Trailing	Total Return%	+/- MSCI EAFE	+/- MSCI World	%Rank Cat	Growth of $10,000
3 Mo	9.64	-0.71	1.27	31	10,964
6 Mo	12.97	-1.72	-0.24	49	11,297
1 Yr	18.16	-8.18	-1.91	61	11,816
3 Yr Avg	17.12	-2.81	2.44	34	16,065
5 Yr Avg	11.50	-3.48	1.53	44	17,234
10 Yr Avg	—	—	—		
15 Yr Avg	—	—	—		

Tax Analysis	Tax-Adj Rtn%	%Rank Cat	Tax-Cost Rat	%Rank Cat
3 Yr (estimated)	16.93	22	0.16	11
5 Yr (estimated)	11.39	36	0.10	9
10 Yr (estimated)	—	—	—	—

Potential Capital Gain Exposure: 28% of assets

Morningstar's Take by Kai Wiecking 12-20-06

American Century Global Growth remains an uninspiring choice.

This fund has undergone numerous manager changers in recent years, and its supporting analyst staff has also experienced turnover. We were encouraged when the talented Matt Hudson took charge in August 2005, but he was hired away by Wellington Management just three months later. And Keith Creveling, the former comanager who took the reins here when Hudson left, has mixed results at American Century International Growth and American Century International Stock.

The fund's trailing three-year average return of 18.2% is ahead of its typical world-stock category rival. But that's largely due to its top-decile performance in 2005, when growth funds such as this one dominated the group, and another momentum-driven rally in recent months. During the severe correction in May and June of 2006, the tables temporarily turned in favor of more-valuation-conscious offerings.

American Century's earnings-momentum-oriented strategy tends to work well when markets reward accelerating growth more than sustainability and stability of earnings. The fund's emerging-markets exposure, after hurting it in May and June, provided a major boost. But disappointing results from several technology stocks held back returns, such as U.S. storage firm EMC, which has since been sold. But there were other contributors: British hedge-fund group Man Investments performed well, as did the fund's oil service provider holdings, led by Schlumberger.

While we still think American Century's growth investment approach is viable in the long run, we're not ready to recommend this fund. This category offers several more proven, and cheaper alternatives, such as analyst pick T Rowe Price Global Stock. In the short run, investors should brace themselves for considerable volatility.

Historical Profile
Return Average
Risk Average
Rating ★★★ Neutral

	90%	91%	85%	95%	94%	98%	98%	98%	100%

Investment Style
Equity
Stock %

▼ Manager Change
▽ Partial Manager Change

Growth of $10,000
━ Investment Values of Fund
— Investment Values of MSCI EAFE

20.8
16.6
13.0
10.0
6.0

Performance Quartile (within Category)

1995	1996	1997	1998	1999	2000	2001	2002	2003	2004	2005	2006	History
—	—	—	5.43	9.81	8.50	6.32	5.04	6.78	7.79	9.13	10.74	NAV
—	—	—	8.60*	86.09	-5.77	-25.65	-20.25	34.52	15.11	18.11	18.16	Total Return %
—	—	—		59.06	8.42	-4.23	-4.31	-4.07	-5.14	4.57	-8.18	+/-MSCI EAFE
—	—	—		61.14	7.42	-8.85	-0.36	1.41	0.39	8.62	-1.91	+/-MSCI World
—	—	—		0.00	0.00	0.00	0.00	0.00	0.20	0.90	0.53	Income Return %
—	—	—		86.09	-5.77	-25.65	-20.25	34.52	14.91	17.21	17.63	Capital Return %
—	—	—		6	37	86	55	51	51	9	61	Total Rtn % Rank Cat
—	—	0.00	0.00	0.00	0.00	0.00	0.00	0.00	0.01	0.07	0.05	Income $
—	—	0.00	0.00	0.26	0.75	0.00	0.00	0.00	0.00	0.00	0.00	Capital Gains $
—	—	—				1.30	1.30	1.30	1.32	1.31	1.30	—	Expense Ratio %
—	—	—				-0.60	-0.48	-0.06	0.13	0.00	-0.12	—	Income Ratio %
—	—	—				133	123	232	278	152	79	—	Turnover Rate %
—	—	—		73	318	412	275	201	262	312	427	Net Assets $mil

Rating and Risk

Time Period	Load-Adj Return %	Morningstar Rtn vs Cat	Morningstar Risk vs Cat	Morningstar Risk-Adj Rating
1 Yr	18.16			
3 Yr	17.12	+Avg	+Avg	★★★★
5 Yr	11.50	Avg	Avg	★★★
10 Yr	—	—	—	—
Incept	11.67			

Other Measures	Standard Index MSCI EAFE	Best Fit Index MSCI World
Alpha	-2.2	-0.8
Beta	0.99	1.29
R-Squared	79	89
Standard Deviation	10.55	
Mean	17.12	
Sharpe Ratio	1.26	

Portfolio Analysis 09-30-06

Share change since 06-06 Total Stocks:93	Sector	Country	% Assets
⊕ American Tower Corporati	Telecom	United States	2.29
⊕ Schlumberger, Ltd.	Energy	United States	2.10
⊖ ORIX	Financial	Japan	1.78
⊕ American Express Company	Financial	United States	1.71
⊕ Carphone Warehouse Grp	Consumer	U.K.	1.62
⊕ America Movil SA ADR	Telecom	Mexico	1.61
⊕ Reckitt Benckiser	Goods	U.K.	1.57
⊕ Automatic Data Processin	Business	United States	1.56
⊕ National Bank of Greece	Financial	Greece	1.54
⊕ Allergan, Inc.	Health	United States	1.51
⊕ Man Grp	Financial	U.K.	1.49
⊖ BHP Billiton Ltd	Ind Mtrls	Australia	1.45
⊕ Amdocs Ltd.	Software	United States	1.42
⊕ Air Products and Chemica	Ind Mtrls	United States	1.41
Societe Generale Grp	Financial	France	1.38
⊖ Comcast Corporation A	Media	United States	1.37
Danaher Corporation	Ind Mtrls	United States	1.34
Roche Holding	Health	Switzerland	1.32
☼ Cisco Systems, Inc.	Hardware	United States	1.32
⊖ Suncor Energy, Inc.	Energy	Canada	1.32

Current Investment Style

Value Blnd Growth — Large / Mid / Small

	Market Cap	%
	Giant	42.2
	Large	40.7
	Mid	17.2
	Small	0.0
	Micro	0.0
	Avg $mil:	24,535

Value Measures		Rel Category
Price/Earnings	18.86	1.23
Price/Book	3.24	1.36
Price/Sales	1.44	1.10
Price/Cash Flow	11.89	1.37
Dividend Yield %	1.58	0.73

Growth Measures	%	Rel Category
Long-Term Erngs	14.69	1.16
Book Value	11.04	1.23
Sales	9.95	1.19
Cash Flow	15.50	1.58
Historical Erngs	25.60	1.37

Composition

Cash	0.0	Bonds	0.0
Stocks	100.0	Other	0.0
Foreign (% of Stock)			56.6

Sector Weightings

Sector Weightings	% Stocks	Rel MSCI EAFE	3 Year High	Low
⟳ Info	19.12	1.62		
🖥 Software	4.85	8.66	5	1
💻 Hardware	6.54	1.69	8	3
🎙 Media	2.48	1.36	5	2
📶 Telecom	5.25	0.94	7	4
⚙ Service	51.58	1.09		
🏥 Health	11.35	1.59	16	9
🛒 Consumer	8.55	1.73	9	6
📋 Business	10.44	2.06	12	5
💲 Financial	21.24	0.71	26	19
🏭 Mfg	29.31	0.72		
🏬 Goods	9.82	0.75	14	8
⚙ Ind Mtrls	13.39	0.87	16	12
🛢 Energy	6.08	0.85	10	5
💡 Utilities	0.02	0.00	0	0

Regional Exposure % Stock

UK/W. Europe	35	N. America	45
Japan	10	Latn America	2
Asia X Japan	9	Other	0

Country Exposure % Stock

United States	43	Switzerland	7
Japan	10	France	6
U.K.	8		

Address:	4500 Main Street, Kansas City MO 64111, 800-345-3533
Web Address:	www.americancentury.com
Inception:	12-01-98*
Advisor:	American Century Global Invsmt Mgt, Inc.
Subadvisor:	American Century Investment MGMT Inc.
NTF Plans:	Fidelity Retail-NTF, Schwab OneSource

Minimum Purchase:	$2500	Add: $50	IRA: $0
Min Auto Inv Plan:	$2500	Add: $50	
Sales Fees:	No-load, 2.00%R		
Management Fee:	1.30% mx./1.05% mn.		
Actual Fees:	Mgt:1.30%	Dist: —	
Expense Projections:	3Yr:$410	5Yr:$710	10Yr:$1558
Income Distrib:	Annually		

 **Funds 500**

AmCent Growth Inv

	Ticker	Load	NAV	Yield	Total Assets	Mstar Category
	TWCGX	None	$22.20	0.1%	$4,779 mil	Large Growth

Governance and Management

Stewardship Grade: C

Portfolio Manager(s)

Greg Woodhams and Prescott LeGard were named comanagers here in mid-1998 and mid-2000, respectively. The managers served as analysts at other firms before joining American Century.

Strategy

Management screens for companies with accelerating earnings-growth rates and favors those that can continue to deliver improving rates of growth. Although the fund has plenty of exposure to typical growth sectors, such as health care and technology, it will also pick up less-traditional industrial or consumer-staples names if their earnings are accelerating. Management's emphasis on sustainable growth means the fund is dominated by more-stable blue chips. With a median market cap that's among the highest in the group, management's giant-cap bias is evident.

Performance 12-31-06

	1st Qtr	2nd Qtr	3rd Qtr	4th Qtr	Total
2002	-1.33	-15.42	-16.39	5.87	-26.13
2003	-2.15	12.47	2.14	10.67	24.41
2004	1.62	0.93	-1.90	9.24	9.91
2005	-4.01	2.11	3.47	3.37	4.84
2006	2.53	-3.65	5.02	4.05	7.94

Trailing	Total Return%	+/- S&P 500	+/- Russ 1000Gr	%Rank Cat	Growth of $10,000
3 Mo	4.05	-2.65	-1.88	83	10,405
6 Mo	9.27	-3.47	-0.83	35	10,927
1 Yr	7.94	-7.85	-1.13	40	10,794
3 Yr Avg	7.54	-2.90	0.67	42	12,437
5 Yr Avg	2.71	-3.48	0.02	49	11,430
10 Yr Avg	6.56	-1.86	1.12	41	18,877
15 Yr Avg	6.46	-4.18	-1.56	87	25,574

Tax Analysis	Tax-Adj Rtn%	%Rank Cat	Tax-Cost Rat	%Rank Cat
3 Yr (estimated)	7.48	33	0.06	4
5 Yr (estimated)	2.67	44	0.04	5
10 Yr (estimated)	5.11	43	1.36	68

Potential Capital Gain Exposure: -1% of assets

Morningstar's Take by Christopher Davis 11-12-06

American Century Growth has looked good lately, but we're not sure it has staying power.

While most large-growth funds have eked out modest gains in 2006, this one has done better. It's gained 7% for the year to date through Nov. 10, 2006, good enough to rank in the large-growth category's top third. An outsized technology stake could have sunk returns, but managers Prescott LeGard and Greg Woodhams bet on the right horses, including Cisco Systems and Freescale Semiconductor. Strong-performing financials and industrials stocks, such as Bank of America and Emerson Electric, have also lent a boost.

Earlier in the year, LeGard and Woodhams had ramped up its exposure to Cisco on the belief that earnings growth would improve over the next few quarters. That move proved prescient, but management's strategy of identifying companies whose near-term earnings are accelerating has enjoyed mixed success overall. In 2005, for instance, soaring oil and gas prices juiced energy

firms' earnings, but the fund's relatively light weighting in the sector led to a subpar showing for the year. Management was also slow to recognize tech companies' improving fortunes in 2003, helping explain the fund's bottom-third showing for the year.

To be sure, this fund boasts some appealing traits. Whereas other American Century growth funds have been beset by manager turnover in recent years, Woodhams and LeGard have been at the helm for eight and six years, respectively. Their process is also disciplined and consistent. Although the fund's long-term returns are middling, volatility has been modest relative to the typical growth fund.

In the end, however, we don't see where the fund gets its edge. Betting on short-term earnings, as this fund does, is a tough game to win because it's one most other growth investors also play. Without confidence it can outrun the competition, we can't get behind this fund.

Address:	4500 Main Street Kansas City MO 64111 800-345-3533
Web Address:	www.americancentury.com
Inception:	06-30-71
Advisor:	American Century Investment MGMT Inc.
Subadvisor:	None
NTF Plans:	Fidelity Retail-NTF, Schwab OneSource

Minimum Purchase:	$2500	Add: $50	IRA: $2500
Min Auto Inv Plan:	$2500	Add: $50	
Sales Fees:	No-load		
Management Fee:	1.00% mx./0.80% mn.		
Actual Fees:	Mgt:1.00%	Dist: —	
Expense Projections:	3Yr:$318	5Yr:$551	10Yr:$1219
Income Distrib:	Annually		

Historical Profile

Return	Average
Risk	Average
Rating	★★★ Neutral

	91%	93%	92%	87%	91%	98%	99%	99%	99%

▼ Manager Change
▽ Partial Manager Change

Growth of $10,000
— Investment Values of Fund
— Investment Values of S&P 500

Performance Quartile (within Category)

1995	1996	1997	1998	1999	2000	2001	2002	2003	2004	2005	2006	History
19.39	21.88	24.01	27.16	32.28	24.00	19.52	14.42	17.94	19.71	20.58	22.20	NAV
20.35	15.01	29.28	36.77	34.68	-14.71	-18.67	-26.13	24.41	9.91	4.84	7.94	Total Return %
-17.23	-7.95	-4.08	8.19	13.64	-5.61	-6.78	-4.03	-4.27	-0.97	-0.07	-7.85	+/-S&P 500
-16.83	-8.11	-1.21	-1.94	1.52	7.71	1.75	1.75	-5.34	3.61	-0.42	-1.13	+/-Russ 1000Gr
0.37	0.94	0.00	0.00	0.00	0.00	0.00	0.00	0.00	0.04	0.43	0.07	Income Return %
19.98	14.07	29.28	36.77	34.68	-14.71	-18.67	-26.13	24.41	9.87	4.41	7.87	Capital Return %
96	78	35	27	51	60	44	45	74	34	62	40	Total Rtn % Rank Cat
0.07	0.18	0.00	0.00	0.00	0.00	0.00	0.00	0.00	0.01	0.09	0.01	Income $
3.06	0.25	4.17	5.39	4.14	3.58	0.00	0.00	0.00	0.00	0.00	0.00	Capital Gains $
1.00	1.00	1.00	1.00	1.00	1.00	1.00	1.00	1.00	1.00	1.00	—	Expense Ratio %
0.40	-0.10	0.02	-0.02	-0.24	-0.30	-0.01	-0.04	0.05	-0.07	0.38	—	Income Ratio %
141	122	75	126	92	102	114	135	159	131	77	—	Turnover Rate %
4,849	4,667	5,166	7,093	9,631	8,376	6,273	3,832	4,482	4,350	4,100	3,919	Net Assets $mil

Rating and Risk

Time Period	Load-Adj Return %	Morningstar Rtn vs Cat	Morningstar Risk vs Cat	Morningstar Risk-Adj Rating
1 Yr	7.94			
3 Yr	7.54	Avg	-Avg	★★★
5 Yr	2.71	Avg	-Avg	★★★
10 Yr	6.56	Avg	Avg	★★★
Incept	13.54			

Other Measures	Standard Index S&P 500	Best Fit Index Russ 1000Gr
Alpha	-3.0	1.0
Beta	1.06	0.89
R-Squared	83	89
Standard Deviation	7.98	
Mean	7.54	
Sharpe Ratio	0.55	

Portfolio Analysis 09-30-06

Share change since 06-06 Total Stocks:89	Sector	PE	Tot Ret%	% Assets
⊖ Cisco Systems, Inc.	Hardware	30.1	59.64	3.41
Bank of America Corporat	Financial	12.4	20.68	3.32
⊖ PepsiCo, Inc.	Goods	21.5	7.86	2.89
⊖ General Electric Company	Ind Mtrls	20.0	9.35	2.63
⊕ Schering-Plough Corporat	Health	36.6	14.63	2.57
⊕ Oracle Corporation	Software	26.7	40.38	2.53
Emerson Electric Company	Ind Mtrls	19.6	20.68	2.49
⊖ Motorola, Inc.	Hardware	11.8	-8.17	2.37
⊖ Textron Incorporated	Ind Mtrls	18.3	23.94	2.11
✵ Intel Corporation	Hardware	21.0	-17.18	2.10
⊖ J.P. Morgan Chase & Co.	Financial	13.6	25.60	2.04
⊖ Becton, Dickinson and Co	Health	23.9	18.34	2.02
⊖ Amgen, Inc.	Health	29.1	-13.38	2.01
⊕ Hewlett-Packard Company	Hardware	19.3	45.21	1.96
⊕ Google, Inc.	Business	61.5	11.00	1.90
⊖ United Technologies	Ind Mtrls	17.8	13.65	1.86
⊖ IBM	Hardware	17.1	19.77	1.75
Gilead Sciences, Inc.	Health	40.6	23.51	1.59
Cooper Industries, Ltd.	Ind Mtrls	18.4	26.02	1.54
⊕ Goldman Sachs Group, Inc	Financial	12.4	57.41	1.53

Current Investment Style

Value Blnd Growth — Large Mid Small

Market Cap	%
Giant	44.2
Large	39.5
Mid	15.7
Small	0.6
Micro	0.0

Avg $mil: 36,547

Value Measures		Rel Category
Price/Earnings	18.10	0.94
Price/Book	3.35	1.01
Price/Sales	1.78	0.92
Price/Cash Flow	11.40	1.00
Dividend Yield %	1.19	1.16

Growth Measures	%	Rel Category
Long-Term Erngs	12.84	0.89
Book Value	8.02	0.69
Sales	9.24	0.80
Cash Flow	19.08	1.14
Historical Erngs	19.53	0.85

Profitability	%	Rel Category
Return on Equity	18.87	0.93
Return on Assets	9.83	0.89
Net Margin	12.75	0.89

Sector Weightings	% of Stocks	Rel S&P 500	3 Year High	Low
☎ Info	25.76	1.29		
Software	6.28	1.82	8	4
Hardware	17.48	1.89	19	15
Media	0.00	0.00	7	0
Telecom	2.00	0.57	2	0
☞ Service	45.68	0.99		
Health	17.87	1.48	24	18
Consumer	10.68	1.40	12	3
Business	5.50	1.30	9	1
Financial	11.63	0.52	15	6
Mfg	28.56	0.85		
Goods	7.73	0.90	15	7
Ind Mtrls	16.64	1.39	23	10
Energy	3.50	0.36	6	2
Utilities	0.69	0.20	1	0

Composition

● Cash	1.1
● Stocks	99.0
● Bonds	0.0
○ Other	0.0
Foreign	4.5 (% of Stock)

AmCent Inc & Growth Inv

	Ticker	Load	NAV	Yield	Total Assets	Mstar Category
	BIGRX	None	$33.30	1.7%	$4,807 mil	Large Value

Governance and Management

Stewardship Grade: B

Portfolio Manager(s)

John Schniedwind, Kurt Borgwardt, and Zili Zhang are the day-to-day portfolio managers. Several quantitative analysts help with the fund's models.

Strategy

Like its sibling American Century Equity Growth, this fund keeps its sector and market-cap weightings close to the S&P 500 Index's and uses quantitative models to pick stocks based on valuations and a host of growth, momentum, and earnings-quality factors. The fund's models have more of a bias for cheap stocks than Equity Growth's, however, and they emphasize yield and risk control. To that end, the fund holds more than 250 names and keeps an eye on individual-position bets against the S&P 500 Index. Outperforming the benchmark with lower volatility is the goal.

Historical Profile

Return Average
Risk Above Avg
Rating ★★★ Neutral

Investment Style Equity Stock %

93% 96% 94% 95% 98% 99% 99% 98% 100%

▼ Manager Change
▽ Partial Manager Change

Growth of $10,000
— Investment Values of Fund
— Investment Values of S&P 500

31.0
24.0
17.0
10.0

Performance Quartile (within Category)

	1995	1996	1997	1998	1999	2000	2001	2002	2003	2004	2005	2006	History
	17.81	20.16	24.30	29.25	34.05	30.19	27.35	21.74	27.70	30.67	30.33	33.30	NAV
	36.88	24.15	34.45	27.67	17.96	-10.54	-8.37	-19.37	29.62	12.98	4.79	17.17	Total Return %
	-0.70	1.19	1.09	-0.91	-3.08	-1.44	3.52	2.73	0.94	2.10	-0.12	1.38	+/-S&P 500
	-1.48	2.51	-0.73	12.04	10.61	-17.55	-2.78	-3.85	-0.41	-3.51	-2.26	-5.08	+/-Russ 1000 Vl
	3.07	2.52	1.94	1.46	1.15	0.85	1.01	1.20	1.98	2.13	1.97	1.99	Income Return %
	33.81	21.63	32.51	26.21	16.81	-11.39	-9.38	-20.57	27.64	10.85	2.82	15.18	Capital Return %
	15	15	4	1	4	97	78	60	36	52	61	64	Total Rtn % Rank Cat
	0.42	0.44	0.38	0.35	0.33	0.29	0.30	0.33	0.43	0.59	0.59	0.59	Income $
	0.75	1.44	2.29	1.30	0.07	0.00	0.00	0.00	0.00	0.00	1.22	1.56	Capital Gains $
	0.67	0.62	0.66	0.69	0.68	0.67	0.68	0.69	0.69	0.68	0.67	—	Expense Ratio %
	2.61	2.32	1.81	1.31	1.08	0.89	1.07	1.34	1.80	2.10	1.86	—	Income Ratio %
	70	92	102	86	58	64	61	67	67	74	70	—	Turnover Rate %
	374	715	1,786	4,285	6,347	5,417	4,475	3,147	3,820	3,972	3,665	3,615	Net Assets $mil

Performance 12-31-06

	1st Qtr	2nd Qtr	3rd Qtr	4th Qtr	Total
2002	1.14	-11.29	-17.05	8.34	-19.37
2003	-3.65	16.41	2.05	13.25	29.62
2004	2.73	2.05	-1.76	9.70	12.98
2005	-1.32	1.82	4.09	0.20	4.79
2006	2.97	-0.14	4.89	8.65	17.17

Trailing	Total Return%	+/- S&P 500	+/- Russ 1000 Vl	%Rank Cat	Growth of $10,000
3 Mo	8.65	1.95	0.65	6	10,865
6 Mo	13.96	1.22	-0.76	30	11,396
1 Yr	17.17	1.38	-5.08	64	11,717
3 Yr Avg	11.53	1.09	-3.56	63	13,873
5 Yr Avg	7.71	1.52	-3.15	61	14,497
10 Yr Avg	9.18	0.76	-1.82	43	24,067
15 Yr Avg	11.15	0.51	-1.88	49	48,825

Tax Analysis	Tax-Adj Rtn%	%Rank Cat	Tax-Cost Rat	%Rank Cat
3 Yr (estimated)	10.16	58	1.23	49
5 Yr (estimated)	6.67	59	0.97	52
10 Yr (estimated)	7.93	31	1.14	26

Potential Capital Gain Exposure: 23% of assets

Rating and Risk

Time Period	Load-Adj Return %	Morningstar Rtn vs Cat	Morningstar Risk vs Cat	Morningstar Risk-Adj Rating
1 Yr	17.17			
3 Yr	11.53	Avg	+Avg	★★★
5 Yr	7.71	Avg	Avg	★★★
10 Yr	9.18	Avg	+Avg	★★★
Incept	12.82			

Other Measures	Standard Index S&P 500	Best Fit Index S&P 500
Alpha	0.3	0.3
Beta	1.10	1.10
R-Squared	92	92
Standard Deviation	7.94	
Mean	11.53	
Sharpe Ratio	1.02	

Morningstar's Take by Arijit Dutta 12-11-06

American Century Income & Growth makes a tidy case for itself.

This fund's quantitative approach strikes a nice balance. Management uses a set of valuation, momentum, and earnings-stability characteristics to quantitatively predict which stocks have higher future expected returns than the overall market. The valuation characteristics dominate the model, including one that favors income-generating stocks, as indicated by the portfolio's cheap price multiples and rich dividend yield relative to the large-value category. Still, the model's momentum and quality components point it toward a fair number of growth stocks. Moreover, management restricts the model to make sure the portfolio's sector weights mimic those of the S&P 500, which means growth sectors such as technology get adequate representation. Thus, traditional value plays such as Cummins rub shoulders here with fallen growth stocks like IBM .

This balanced approach hasn't been helpful in recent years as value stocks have dominated. Still, the model has chosen stocks well enough to allow the fund to hang close to the category's middle. Also, the fund's approach really helped it shine in the late 1990s, when pure value managers struggled amidst a growth rally.

Thus, while the style won't please value purists, we think its inherent stability is appealing. Also, management has access to a large team of quantitative analysts whose research on value and momentum characteristics keeps the model in shape. This bodes well for continued strength in stock selection here. Moreover, management has shown it will adhere to the model with discipline, even when the chips are down. For example, it has held on to Cummins and IBM through difficult times (both have shown strength in recent months, which has helped the fund). The fund's expenses are also very competitive.

Portfolio Analysis 09-30-06

Share change since 06-06 Total Stocks:150

	Sector	PE	Tot Ret%	% Assets
⊖ ExxonMobil Corporation	Energy	11.1	39.07	5.13
⊕ IBM	Hardware	17.1	19.77	4.74
⊖ Citigroup, Inc.	Financial	13.1	19.55	4.53
Bank of America Corporat	Financial	12.4	20.68	3.77
⊕ Morgan Stanley	Financial	12.3	45.93	3.56
⊕ Pfizer Inc.	Health	15.2	15.22	2.81
⊖ Washington Mutual, Inc.	Financial	13.4	9.62	2.73
Merck & Co., Inc.	Health	19.1	42.66	2.72
⊖ Chevron Corporation	Energy	9.0	33.76	2.59
Hewlett-Packard Company	Hardware	19.3	45.21	2.43
⊖ Cummins, Inc.	Ind Mtrls	8.4	33.23	2.37
⊖ Goldman Sachs Group, Inc	Financial	12.4	57.41	2.16
Kimberly-Clark Corporati	Goods	22.7	17.55	2.02
Northrop Grumman Corpora	Ind Mtrls	16.7	14.63	1.99
⊕ Verizon Communications	Telecom	15.9	34.88	1.97
⊖ ConocoPhillips	Energy	6.5	26.53	1.82
⊕ ACE, Ltd.	Financial	10.6	15.41	1.78
⊖ Lyondell Chemical Compan	Energy	10.1	11.52	1.61
⊖ Microsoft Corporation	Software	23.8	15.83	1.58
⊖ Johnson & Johnson	Health	17.5	12.45	1.47

Current Investment Style

Value Blnd Growth — Large Mid Small

Market Cap	%
Giant	47.3
Large	22.9
Mid	23.0
Small	6.8
Micro	0.0

Avg $mil: 31,561

Value Measures		Rel Category
Price/Earnings	11.44	0.83
Price/Book	2.05	0.92
Price/Sales	0.82	0.63
Price/Cash Flow	4.89	0.73
Dividend Yield %	2.36	1.01

Growth Measures	%	Rel Category
Long-Term Erngs	9.99	0.96
Book Value	9.69	1.22
Sales	13.43	1.49
Cash Flow	22.53	3.72
Historical Erngs	19.89	1.23

Profitability	%	Rel Category
Return on Equity	19.93	1.11
Return on Assets	11.22	1.14
Net Margin	13.21	1.02

Sector Weightings

	% of Stocks	Rel S&P 500	3 Year High	Low
⌖ Info	17.01	0.85		
Software	1.70	0.49	4	2
Hardware	9.42	1.02	10	8
Media	0.74	0.20	4	1
Telecom	5.15	1.47	6	5
⌖ Service	50.41	1.09		
Health	12.58	1.04	15	10
Consumer	4.89	0.64	8	4
Business	4.95	1.17	5	3
Financial	27.99	1.26	28	21
⌖ Mfg	32.58	0.96		
Goods	4.87	0.57	14	5
Ind Mtrls	10.71	0.90	11	6
Energy	14.29	1.46	14	7
Utilities	2.71	0.77	6	3

Composition

● Cash		0.3
● Stocks		99.7
● Bonds		0.0
● Other		0.0
Foreign		1.0
(% of Stock)		

Address:	4500 Main Street Kansas City MO 64111 800-345-2021	Minimum Purchase:	$2500	Add: $50	IRA: $2500
		Min Auto Inv Plan:	$2500	Add: $50	
		Sales Fees:	No-load		
Web Address:	www.americancentury.com	Management Fee:	0.67%		
Inception:	12-17-90	Actual Fees:	Mgt:0.67%	Dist: —	
Advisor:	American Century Investment MGMT Inc.	Expense Projections:	3Yr:$214	5Yr:$373	10Yr:$833
Subadvisor:	None	Income Distrib:	Quarterly		
NTF Plans:	Fidelity Retail-NTF, Schwab OneSource				

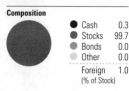

MORNINGSTAR® Funds 500

AmCent Intl Disc Inv

	Ticker	Load	NAV	Yield	Total Assets	Mstar Category
	TWEGX	Closed	$15.20	0.0%	$1,605 mil	Foreign Small/Mid Growth

Governance and Management

Stewardship Grade: B

Portfolio Manager(s)

Mark Kopinski has run this fund since January 1998, although he was also its manager for 10 months when American Century launched it in April 1994. Brian Brady joined the portfolio-management team in November 1998. Two emerging-markets analysts support the team (after two in Singapore resigned earlier in 2005). American Century is currently looking for two more analysts after recently hiring one to cover European stocks.

Strategy

Like most American Century funds, this offering bulks up on stocks with improving trends in profitability. More so than its domestic counterparts, however, the managers also focus on other factors, emphasizing companies with good management, niche products, or rapidly growing revenues (even when profits are absent). The team buys small- and mid-cap stocks in the $1.5 billion to $5 billion range. American Century uses fair value pricing when necessary. It does not engage in currency hedging.

Performance 12-31-06

	1st Qtr	2nd Qtr	3rd Qtr	4th Qtr	Total
2002	7.13	-3.37	-15.94	0.18	-12.83
2003	-2.81	18.36	14.63	14.79	51.38
2004	9.51	-4.14	-1.63	12.58	16.26
2005	-0.46	1.44	18.49	9.91	30.50
2006	15.11	-2.10	1.17	15.37	31.52

Trailing	Total Return%	+/- MSCI EAFE	+/- MSCI Wd xUS	%Rank Cat	Growth of $10,000
3 Mo	15.37	5.02	5.25	17	11,537
6 Mo	16.71	2.02	2.49	47	11,671
1 Yr	31.52	5.18	5.81	25	13,152
3 Yr Avg	26.21	6.28	6.11	42	20,104
5 Yr Avg	21.55	6.57	6.30	38	26,532
10 Yr Avg	16.61	8.90	8.65	10	46,490
15 Yr Avg	—				

Tax Analysis	Tax-Adj Rtn%	%Rank Cat	Tax-Cost Rat	%Rank Cat
3 Yr (estimated)	21.52	71	3.72	96
5 Yr (estimated)	18.78	59	2.28	95
10 Yr (estimated)	14.64	17	1.69	70

Potential Capital Gain Exposure: 23% of assets

Morningstar's Take by Kai Wiecking 12-18-06

American Century International Discovery is a good option for the long term, but its risks may soon become more apparent.

Lead manager Mark Kopinski, who has been in charge here for more than eight years, is aware of the portfolio's vulnerability to the changing economic environment and is taking steps to adjust to it without abandoning the firm's long-standing investment philosophy. He's added to positions that show slower but more sustainable growth characteristics than typically found in this fund. Chewing-tobacco maker Swedish Match and several utility holdings serve as examples. On the flip side, Kopinski lightened up on some of the cyclically sensitive materials stocks that served the fund so well in 2004 and 2005.

This fund is one of the few options within the foreign small/mid-growth category that focus on mid-caps. This specific focus goes a long way toward explaining why the fund lagged its peers so badly in 2004, when the smallest stocks led the market, and why it is holding up better than most of its rivals now that a renewed focus on sustainability of earnings growth is favoring the larger stocks within this asset class.

But in order to understand the fund's behavior in various markets, it's also important to analyze American Century's style of growth investing. Its focus on stocks with accelerating earnings tends to work well when overall growth is accelerating and momentum is strong. However, when the economic expansion begins to decelerate and investors become more risk-averse, this process doesn't work nearly as well. In the latter part of 2006, investors seem to ignore risk altogether, but 2007 may turn out to be a very different story.

While we are reasonably confident that Kopinski's stock-picking skills will continue to make this offering an attractive option for the long term, we also think it's a good time for investors to check whether its role in their portfolios has become too large.

Address:	4500 Main Street Kansas City MO 64111 800-345-2021
Web Address:	www.americancentury.com
Inception:	04-04-94
Advisor:	American Century Global Invsmt Mgt, Inc.
Subadvisor:	American Century Investment MGMT Inc.
NTF Plans:	Schwab OneSource

Minimum Purchase:	Closed	Add: —	IRA: —
Min Auto Inv Plan:	Closed	Add: —	
Sales Fees:	No-load, 2.00%R		
Management Fee:	1.75% mx./1.20% mn.		
Actual Fees:	Mgt:1.46%	Dist: —	
Expense Projections:	3Yr:$463	5Yr:$798	10Yr:$1745
Income Distrib:	Annually		

Historical Profile

Return	Above Avg
Risk	Above Avg
Rating	★★★ Neutral

	92%	95%	82%	94%	95%	96%	98%	99%	96%

Growth of $10,000
- Investment Values of Fund
- Investment Values of MSCI EAFE

64.6 / 46.4 / 33.8 / 24.0 / 17.0 / 10.0

Investment Style: Equity, Stock %

Performance Quartile (within Category)

1995	1996	1997	1998	1999	2000	2001	2002	2003	2004	2005	2006	History
5.88	7.36	8.15	9.57	17.16	13.09	10.24	8.91	13.46	13.47	14.61	15.20	NAV
9.89	31.18	17.48	17.86	88.54	-14.21	-21.77	-12.83	51.38	16.26	30.50	31.52	Total Return %
-1.32	25.13	15.70	-2.07	61.51	-0.02	-0.35	3.11	12.79	-3.99	16.96	5.18	+/-MSCI EAFE
-1.52	24.31	15.21	-0.83	60.56	-0.85	-0.38	2.97	11.96	-4.12	16.03	5.81	+/-MSCI Wd xUS
0.60	0.29	0.28	0.00	0.00	0.00	0.00	0.15	0.30	0.00	0.96	0.00	Income Return %
9.29	30.89	17.20	17.86	88.54	-14.21	-21.77	-12.98	51.08	16.26	29.54	31.52	Capital Return %
1	1	10	34	32	55	45	37	45	91	20	25	Total Rtn % Rank Cat
0.03	0.02	0.02	0.00	0.00	0.00	0.00	0.02	0.03	0.00	0.13	0.00	Income $
0.00	0.32	0.47	0.03	0.81	1.64	0.00	0.00	0.00	2.09	2.82	3.92	Capital Gains $
2.00	1.88	1.70	1.64	1.55	1.36	1.45	1.53	1.57	1.49	1.47	—	Expense Ratio %
0.27	-0.31	-0.37	-0.36	-0.65	-0.64	0.10	0.35	0.27	-0.06	1.02	—	Income Ratio %
168	130	146	178	110	113	180	224	215	201	145	—	Turnover Rate %
121	390	622	799	1,723	1,576	1,016	794	1,077	1,105	1,236	1,495	Net Assets $mil

Rating and Risk

Time Period	Load-Adj Return %	Morningstar Rtn vs Cat	Morningstar Risk vs Cat	Morningstar Risk-Adj Rating
1 Yr	31.52			
3 Yr	26.21	Avg	+Avg	★★★
5 Yr	21.55	Avg	+Avg	★★★
10 Yr	16.61	+Avg	Avg	★★★
Incept	16.77			

Other Measures	Standard Index MSCI EAFE	Best Fit Index MSCI Wd xUS
Alpha	-1.8	-1.8
Beta	1.48	1.46
R-Squared	81	81
Standard Deviation	15.58	
Mean	26.21	
Sharpe Ratio	1.37	

Portfolio Analysis 09-30-06

Share change since 06-06 Total Stocks:100	Sector	Country	% Assets
⊖ CSL Ltd	Health	Australia	2.64
⊕ Carphone Warehouse Grp	Consumer	U.K.	2.59
⊕ Neopost	Ind Mtrls	France	2.32
Enagas	Energy	Spain	2.13
⊖ Kon Bam Groep Nv	—	Netherlands	2.00
⊖ Topdanmark	Financial	Denmark	1.98
⊖ The Japan Steel Works, L	Ind Mtrls	Japan	1.95
⊕ Kingspan Grp	Business	Ireland	1.82
⊕ Punch Taverns	Consumer	U.K.	1.78
⊖ Schwarz Pharma	Health	Germany	1.73
⊕ Gildan Activewear, Inc.	Goods	Canada	1.71
⊕ Red Electrica de Espana	Utilities	Spain	1.51
⊖ HOCHTIEF	Business	Germany	1.49
⊕ Geberit	Consumer	Switzerland	1.43
⊕ Hagemeyer	Business	Netherlands	1.41
⊖ United Internet	Business	Germany	1.39
⊖ Tullow Oil	Energy	U.K.	1.39
⊕ High-Tech Computer	Hardware	Taiwan	1.36
⊖ Banca Italease	Financial	Italy	1.35
⊕ Tokyo Tatemono	Financial	Japan	1.29

Current Investment Style

Value Blnd Growth		Market Cap	%
		Giant	1.5
Large		Large	16.3
Mid		Mid	79.5
Small		Small	2.8
		Micro	0.0
		Avg $mil: 3,552	

Value Measures		Rel Category
Price/Earnings	19.12	1.22
Price/Book	2.82	1.17
Price/Sales	1.14	1.04
Price/Cash Flow	6.64	0.85
Dividend Yield %	1.46	0.71

Growth Measures	%	Rel Category
Long-Term Erngs	16.99	0.83
Book Value	7.88	0.83
Sales	9.51	0.76
Cash Flow	17.75	1.18
Historical Erngs	29.44	1.30

Composition			
Cash	4.3	Bonds	0.0
Stocks	95.7	Other	0.0
Foreign (% of Stock)			99.2

Sector Weightings	% of Stocks	Rel MSCI EAFE	3 Year High	3 Year Low
⊙ Info	8.45	0.71		
Software	0.60	1.07	3	0
Hardware	5.23	1.35	11	4
Media	0.86	0.47	5	0
Telecom	1.76	0.32	10	0
⊙ Service	48.00	1.02		
Health	8.35	1.17	12	4
Consumer	9.08	1.83	17	5
Business	15.27	3.01	15	4
Financial	15.30	0.51	18	8
⊙ Mfg	43.56	1.06		
Goods	10.79	0.82	21	5
Ind Mtrls	20.90	1.35	30	16
Energy	6.35	0.89	12	2
Utilities	5.52	1.05	6	1

Regional Exposure	% Stock
UK/W. Europe 65	N. America 3
Japan 14	Latn America 1
Asia X Japan 17	Other 0

Country Exposure	% Stock
Japan 14	Australia 6
U.K. 13	Netherlands 6
Germany 9	

AmCent Intl Growth Inv

	Ticker	Load	NAV	Yield	Total Assets	Mstar Category
	TWIEX	None	$12.52	0.7%	$2,833 mil	Foreign Large Growth

Governance and Management

Stewardship Grade: B

Portfolio Manager(s)

Alex Tedder took over in July 2006 from Michael Perelstein, who had a short but ultimately unsuccessful stint here. Tedder comes with the recommendation of a strong record at DWS International Select Equity, his prior charge. Keith Creveling remains on board; he was promoted from a large-cap Europe analyst to portfolio manager in 2002.

Strategy

There have been adjustments over the past couple of years. Working with fund consultants, American Century has made changes, including the addition of quantitative analysis and screening. New manager Alex Tedder is set to further increase the emphasis on sustainability begun by his predecessor. The fund continues to look for companies with improving trends in revenues and earnings.

Historical Profile

Return: Average
Risk: Average
Rating: ★★★ Neutral

Investment Style: Equity Stock %

97% 96% 81% 92% 95% 99% 98% 99% 99%

▼ Manager Change
▽ Partial Manager Change

Growth of $10,000
— Investment Values of Fund
— Investment Values of MSCI EAFE

Performance Quartile (within Category)

	1995	1996	1997	1998	1999	2000	2001	2002	2003	2004	2005	2006	History
	7.78	7.96	8.19	9.58	14.97	10.93	7.97	6.38	7.94	9.06	10.09	12.52	NAV
	11.89	14.43	19.72	19.01	64.44	-15.01	-26.79	-19.25	25.38	15.31	13.34	25.00	Total Return %
	0.68	8.38	17.94	-0.92	37.41	-0.82	-5.37	-3.31	-13.21	-4.94	-0.20	-1.34	+/-MSCI EAFE
	0.48	7.56	17.45	0.32	36.46	-1.65	-5.40	-3.45	-14.04	-5.07	-1.13	-0.71	+/-MSCI Wd xUS
	0.10	0.00	0.35	0.20	0.06	0.00	0.28	0.70	0.90	1.16	1.95	0.90	Income Return %
	11.79	14.43	19.37	18.81	64.38	-15.01	-27.07	-19.95	24.48	14.15	11.39	24.10	Capital Return %
	26	41	7	17	30	33	71	55	96	54	64	27	Total Rtn % Rank Cat
	0.01	0.00	0.03	0.02	0.01	0.00	0.03	0.06	0.06	0.09	0.18	0.09	Income $
	0.00	0.92	1.28	0.14	0.46	1.75	0.00	0.00	0.00	0.00	0.00	0.00	Capital Gains $
	1.77	1.65	1.38	1.33	1.27	1.20	1.21	1.25	1.28	1.26	1.23	—	Expense Ratio %
	0.25	-0.07	0.04	0.33	-0.06	-0.16	0.48	0.76	0.84	0.57	1.22	—	Income Ratio %
	169	158	163	190	117	116	178	215	169	118	89	—	Turnover Rate %
	1,258	1,361	1,784	2,640	4,521	4,755	3,311	2,318	2,617	2,471	2,340	2,350	Net Assets $mil

Performance 12-31-06

	1st Qtr	2nd Qtr	3rd Qtr	4th Qtr	Total
2002	-0.88	-2.28	-19.69	3.81	-19.25
2003	-9.09	16.03	4.31	13.95	25.38
2004	4.79	-2.16	-1.47	14.16	15.31
2005	-1.10	-0.11	8.60	5.64	13.34
2006	10.11	-2.16	3.77	11.81	25.00

Trailing	Total Return%	+/- MSCI EAFE	+/- MSCI Wd xUS	%Rank Cat	Growth of $10,000
3 Mo	11.81	1.46	1.69	24	11,181
6 Mo	16.03	1.34	1.81	25	11,603
1 Yr	25.00	-1.34	-0.71	27	12,500
3 Yr Avg	17.77	-2.16	-2.33	48	16,334
5 Yr Avg	10.59	-4.39	-4.66	72	16,542
10 Yr Avg	9.20	1.49	1.24	21	24,112
15 Yr Avg	10.38	2.52	2.34	12	43,990

Tax Analysis	Tax-Adj Rtn%	%Rank Cat	Tax-Cost Rat	%Rank Cat
3 Yr (estimated)	17.29	36	0.41	33
5 Yr (estimated)	10.18	66	0.37	35
10 Yr (estimated)	7.92	17	1.17	75

Potential Capital Gain Exposure: 14% of assets

Rating and Risk

Time Period	Load-Adj Return %	Morningstar Rtn vs Cat	Morningstar Risk vs Cat	Morningstar Risk-Adj Rating
1 Yr	25.00			
3 Yr	17.77	Avg	-Avg	★★★
5 Yr	10.59	-Avg	-Avg	★★
10 Yr	9.20	+Avg	Avg	★★★★
Incept	10.61			

Other Measures	Standard Index MSCI EAFE	Best Fit Index MSCI EAFE
Alpha	-2.7	-2.7
Beta	1.06	1.06
R-Squared	95	95
Standard Deviation	10.31	
Mean	17.77	
Sharpe Ratio	1.34	

Portfolio Analysis 09-30-06

Share change since 06-06 Total Stocks:114	Sector	Country	% Assets
⊖ Roche Holding	Health	Switzerland	2.06
⊕ DANONE Grp	Goods	France	1.81
⊖ ORIX	Financial	Japan	1.69
⊖ Reckitt Benckiser	Goods	U.K.	1.69
⊕ ING Groep	Financial	Netherlands	1.68
⊖ Novartis	Health	Switzerland	1.68
⊖ UBS AG	Financial	Switzerland	1.66
☼ TOTAL	Energy	France	1.58
Societe Generale Grp	Financial	France	1.44
⊕ Samsung Electronics	Goods	Korea	1.43
⊖ GlaxoSmithKline	Health	U.K.	1.37
⊖ Toyota Motor	Goods	Japan	1.37
⊕ Fresenius Medical Care	Health	Germany	1.36
☼ Tesco	Consumer	U.K.	1.35
⊖ America Movil SA ADR	Telecom	Mexico	1.33
AXA	Financial	France	1.31
⊕ National Bank of Greece	Financial	Greece	1.27
⊖ Hon Hai Precision Indust	Hardware	Taiwan	1.24
⊖ BHP Billiton Ltd	Ind Mtrls	Australia	1.23
⊕ Banco Popolare di Verona	Financial	Italy	1.22

Current Investment Style

Value Blnd Growth — Large Mid Small

	Market Cap	%
	Giant	47.5
	Large	42.6
	Mid	9.9
	Small	0.0
	Micro	0.0
	Avg $mil:	27,286

Value Measures		Rel Category
Price/Earnings	16.02	1.04
Price/Book	2.67	1.02
Price/Sales	1.22	0.87
Price/Cash Flow	7.07	0.73
Dividend Yield %	2.54	1.05

Growth Measures	%	Rel Category
Long-Term Erngs	13.19	0.97
Book Value	11.07	1.01
Sales	6.51	0.75
Cash Flow	11.87	0.97
Historical Erngs	26.23	1.15

Composition

Cash	0.5	Bonds	0.0
Stocks	99.4	Other	0.1
Foreign (% of Stock)			100.0

Sector Weightings	% of Stocks	Rel MSCI EAFE	3 Year High	Low
☎ Info	11.16	0.94		
🖥 Software	1.57	2.80	3	0
💻 Hardware	3.76	0.97	5	1
🎬 Media	1.01	0.55	4	0
📞 Telecom	4.82	0.87	9	4
⚒ Service	52.40	1.11		
⚕ Health	7.57	1.06	15	8
🛒 Consumer	9.25	1.87	9	5
💼 Business	8.41	1.66	10	3
💲 Financial	27.17	0.90	27	21
⚙ Mfg	36.44	0.89		
🏭 Goods	16.61	1.27	21	13
⚙ Ind Mtrls	11.86	0.77	18	10
🔋 Energy	7.17	1.00	11	5
💡 Utilities	0.80	0.15	5	0

Regional Exposure	% Stock		
UK/W. Europe	67	N. America	0
Japan	18	Latn America	2
Asia X Japan	11	Other	2

Country Exposure	% Stock		
Japan	18	France	11
U.K.	18	Germany	7
Switzerland	12		

Morningstar's Take by Kai Wiecking 12-21-06

We think new management stands a good chance of fixing American Century International Growth.

This fund has had numerous manager changes in recent years as American Century's international-equity team went through a period of high employee turnover. That's disconcerting, even if the basic investment philosophy has remained intact: All of its managers look for stocks exhibiting accelerating earnings growth.

That approach has worked rather well at this blue-chip fund's mid-cap and small-cap siblings, American Century International Discovery and American Century International Opportunities. This offering, however, has assembled a disappointing track record over the trailing five years through Dec. 20, 2006: Its average return of 10.9% trails that of 73% of its peers in the foreign large-growth category. The fund had been much more successful in the latter half of the 1990s, when its large-cap focus and its fairly aggressive growth style were much more in vogue. But the fact that managers

and analysts kept coming and going certainly hasn't helped.

Alex Tedder is the latest at trying his hand at this fund. He brings along a good deal of experience gained at his former employer, DWS, where he amassed a strong track record at DWS International Select Equity. In his first month in charge since joining in July 2006, he has already implemented some subtle but important tweaks to the investment process that increase its viability in our opinion: He has complemented the quantitative filters that emphasize accelerating earnings with metrics measuring the sustainability of earnings trends. This should prove a better fit for the large-cap space, where rapid growth is hard to come by and long-term winners are most often those firms with slow, but resilient, growth.

All told, we are cautiously optimistic that this fund can regain its footing, provided that the staff turnover finally settles down. Early results are encouraging.

Address:	4500 Main Street Kansas City MO 64111 800-345-2021	Minimum Purchase:	$2500	Add: $50	IRA: $0
		Min Auto Inv Plan:	$2500	Add: $50	
		Sales Fees:	No-load, 2.00%R		
Web Address:	www.americancentury.com	Management Fee:	1.23%		
Inception:	05-09-91	Actual Fees:	Mgt:1.23%	Dist: —	
Advisor:	American Century Global Invsmt Mgt. Inc.	Expense Projections:	3Yr:$389	5Yr:$673	10Yr:$1480
Subadvisor:	American Century Investment MGMT Inc.	Income Distrib:	Annually		
NTF Plans:	Fidelity Retail-NTF, Schwab OneSource				

MORNINGSTAR® Funds 500

AmCent Large Co Val Inv

	Ticker	Load	NAV	Yield	Total Assets	Mstar Category
	ALVIX	None	$7.58	1.7%	$2,666 mil	Large Value

Governance and Management

Stewardship Grade: B

Portfolio Manager(s)

Charles Ritter and Mark Mallon have managed this fund since its 1999 inception. During that time they have amassed an impressive record relative to the large-value category. Ritter and Mallon also manage American Century Capital Value in a nearly identical manner. They are assisted by portfolio manager Brendan Healy and analyst Lon West, who came from USAA. Analyst Matt Titus joined the team from Bank One in 2004.

Strategy

Management begins with quantitative screens, looking for stocks that rank in the cheapest 30% of its large-cap universe. Its valuation model incorporates measures such as price-to-cash flow and dividends. It then does fundamental research to choose those with decent growth prospects and solid balance sheets. Cheaper stocks get more play in the portfolio, as do companies with larger market caps and those that the managers know best. Management tries to avoid big sector bets relative to its Russell 1000 Value benchmark.

Performance 12-31-06

	1st Qtr	2nd Qtr	3rd Qtr	4th Qtr	Total
2002	3.66	-7.44	-17.67	9.53	-13.47
2003	-5.58	17.47	2.01	13.99	28.97
2004	2.01	1.91	0.29	9.62	14.28
2005	-1.16	1.01	2.69	1.60	4.17
2006	3.84	0.47	7.00	7.33	19.81

Trailing	Total Return%	+/- S&P 500	+/- Russ 1000 Vl	%Rank Cat	Growth of $10,000
3 Mo	7.33	0.63	-0.67	47	10,733
6 Mo	14.84	2.10	0.12	15	11,484
1 Yr	19.81	4.02	-2.44	28	11,981
3 Yr Avg	12.56	2.12	-2.53	44	14,261
5 Yr Avg	9.74	3.55	-1.12	21	15,916
10 Yr Avg	—	—	—	—	—
15 Yr Avg	—	—	—	—	—

Tax Analysis	Tax-Adj Rtn%	%Rank Cat	Tax-Cost Rat	%Rank Cat
3 Yr (estimated)	11.59	33	0.86	34
5 Yr (estimated)	8.92	18	0.75	40
10 Yr (estimated)	—	—	—	—

Potential Capital Gain Exposure: 19% of assets

Morningstar's Take by Christopher Davis 11-20-06

American Century Large Company Value has regained its footing lately, but that's not the main reason why we like it.

This offering is looking better these days. Avoiding racier energy names hurt in 2005, but it's helped more recently as oil and gas prices have fallen. Meanwhile, management's decision to emphasize giant integrated energy firms such as ExxonMobil and Chevron instead also pays off nicely. Its preference for giant caps also is finally starting to work in the fund's favor. Bigger banks such as Bank of America and Wells Fargo have posted handsome gains this year. In all, the fund is up 17% for the year to date through Nov. 17, 2006, placing in the large-value group's top third.

That standing is more like what long-term investors have grown accustomed to here. Last year marked the first in which the fund lagged its typical peer--it beat the category average in each of the prior five years. In addition to delivering good long-term returns, the fund has also been less volatile (as measured by standard deviation) than most peers.

What's more important, of course, is whether the fund can continue to stay ahead of the competition. We think it can. Management is very experienced. And we like its disciplined strategy. Chuck Ritter and his team screen for stocks ranking in the cheapest 30% of their large-cap universe using a valuation model that incorporates metrics such as price-to-cash flow and price-to-earnings. They tend to sell when valuations rise well above historical norms, enabling the fund to benefit from rallying picks while still protecting it from excessive price risk. It also helps keep turnover low, resulting in lower transaction costs.

We wish this fund were cheap for new shareholders, who must buy through the higher-cost A shares. Do-it-yourselfers, though, can buy similarly managed American Century Capital Value without paying a load.

Address:	4500 Main Street Kansas City MO 64111 800-345-2021
Web Address:	www.americancentury.com
Inception:	07-30-99*
Advisor:	American Century Investment MGMT Inc.
Subadvisor:	None
NTF Plans:	Fidelity Retail-NTF, Schwab OneSource

Minimum Purchase:	$2500	Add: $50	IRA: $0
Min Auto Inv Plan:	$2500	Add: $50	
Sales Fees:	No-load		
Management Fee:	0.90% mx./0.70% mn.		
Actual Fees:	Mgt:0.84%	Dist: —	
Expense Projections:	3Yr:$268	5Yr:$465	10Yr:$1034
Income Distrib:	Quarterly		

Historical Profile

Return	Above Avg
Risk	Average
Rating	★★★★ Above Avg

95%	89%	87%	90%	95%	95%	95%	96%

Investment Style
Equity
Stock %

▼ Manager Change
▽ Partial Manager Change

16.4
14.4
12.0
Growth of $10,000
— Investment Values of Fund
— Investment Values of S&P 500
10.0

6.0

Performance Quartile (within Category)

	1995	1996	1997	1998	1999	2000	2001	2002	2003	2004	2005	2006	History
NAV	—	—	—	—	4.67	5.04	5.35	4.56	5.79	6.49	6.50	7.58	
Total Return %	—	—	—	—	-5.97*	9.68	7.47	-13.47	28.97	14.28	4.17	19.81	
+/-S&P 500	—	—	—	—	—	18.78	19.36	8.63	0.29	3.40	-0.74	4.02	
+/-Russ 1000 Vl	—	—	—	—	—	2.67	13.06	2.05	-1.06	-2.21	-2.88	-2.44	
Income Return %	—	—	—	—	—	1.62	1.28	1.35	1.78	1.72	1.66	2.05	
Capital Return %	—	—	—	—	—	8.06	6.19	-14.82	27.19	12.56	2.51	17.76	
Total Rtn % Rank Cat	—	—	—	—	—	51	9	18	41	34	69	28	
Income $	—	—	—	—	0.03	0.08	0.06	0.07	0.08	0.10	0.11	0.13	
Capital Gains $	—	—	—	—	0.00	0.00	0.00	0.00	0.00	0.02	0.15	0.06	
Expense Ratio %	—	—	—	—	—	—	0.90	0.90	0.90	0.90	0.90	0.84	
Income Ratio %	—	—	—	—	—	—	1.72	1.62	1.34	1.75	1.58	1.75	
Turnover Rate %	—	—	—	—	—	—	51	55	34	30	14	16	
Net Assets $mil	—	—	—	—	—	12	14	57	121	305	541	1,471	

Rating and Risk

Time Period	Load-Adj Return %	Morningstar Rtn vs Cat	Morningstar Risk vs Cat	Morningstar Risk-Adj Rating
1 Yr	19.81			
3 Yr	12.56	Avg	-Avg	★★★
5 Yr	9.74	+Avg	Avg	★★★★
10 Yr	—	—	—	—
Incept	7.95			

Other Measures	Standard Index S&P 500	Best Fit Index Russ 1000 Vl
Alpha	3.1	-0.8
Beta	0.83	0.87
R-Squared	88	92
Standard Deviation	6.15	
Mean	12.56	
Sharpe Ratio	1.45	

Portfolio Analysis 09-30-06

Share change since 06-06 Total Stocks:78

	Sector	PE	Tot Ret%	% Assets
⊕ Citigroup, Inc.	Financial	13.1	19.55	4.67
⊕ ExxonMobil Corporation	Energy	11.1	39.07	4.55
⊕ Bank of America Corporat	Financial	12.4	20.68	3.47
⊕ Freddie Mac	Financial	23.3	7.06	3.00
⊕ Chevron Corporation	Energy	9.0	33.76	2.87
⊕ Royal Dutch Shell PLC AD	Energy	8.7	19.33	2.63
⊕ J.P. Morgan Chase & Co.	Financial	13.6	25.60	2.46
⊕ Wells Fargo Company	Financial	14.7	16.82	2.16
⊕ Pfizer Inc.	Health	15.2	15.22	2.04
⊕ AT&T, Inc.	Telecom	18.2	51.59	1.93
⊕ ConocoPhillips	Energy	6.5	26.53	1.81
⊕ Time Warner, Inc.	Media	19.6	26.37	1.76
⊖ Microsoft Corporation	Software	23.8	15.83	1.69
⊕ American International G	Financial	17.0	6.05	1.68
⊕ Wachovia Corporation	Financial	12.9	12.02	1.66
⊖ Morgan Stanley	Financial	12.3	45.93	1.58
⊕ Merrill Lynch & Company,	Financial	14.2	39.28	1.49
⊕ Johnson & Johnson	Health	17.5	12.45	1.45
⊖ Exelon Corporation	Utilities	—	19.79	1.44
⊕ Allstate Corporation	Financial	8.7	23.38	1.43

Current Investment Style

Value Blnd Growth — Large Mid Small

Market Cap	%
Giant	62.6
Large	28.7
Mid	8.5
Small	0.2
Micro	0.0

Avg $mil: 66,497

Value Measures		Rel Category
Price/Earnings	13.04	0.95
Price/Book	2.17	0.98
Price/Sales	1.34	1.03
Price/Cash Flow	2.20	0.33
Dividend Yield %	2.58	1.11

Growth Measures	%	Rel Category
Long-Term Ergns	9.88	0.95
Book Value	8.10	1.02
Sales	9.33	1.04
Cash Flow	6.85	1.13
Historical Ergns	11.67	0.72

Profitability	%	Rel Category
Return on Equity	18.70	1.04
Return on Assets	11.00	1.12
Net Margin	14.18	1.09

Sector Weightings	% of Stocks	Rel S&P 500	3 Year High Low	
⊙ Info	15.67	0.78		
Software	2.51	0.73	3	2
Hardware	3.68	0.40	5	3
Media	3.76	0.99	4	2
Telecom	5.72	1.63	6	4
⊏ Service	49.43	1.07		
Health	7.79	0.65	8	6
Consumer	5.82	0.76	6	4
Business	1.82	0.43	4	2
Financial	34.00	1.53	34	33
⊔ Mfg	34.90	1.03		
Goods	7.22	0.84	11	7
Ind Mtrls	11.25	0.74	12	10
Energy	13.16	1.34	14	10
Utilities	3.27	0.93	4	3

Composition

		%
●	Cash	4.4
●	Stocks	95.6
●	Bonds	0.0
●	Other	0.0
	Foreign (% of Stock)	3.9

© 2007 Morningstar, Inc. All rights reserved. The information herein is not represented or warranted to be accurate, correct, complete or timely. Past performance is no guarantee of future results. Download your free reports at http://www.morningstar.com/goto/2007Funds500.

Morningstar® Funds 500   47

AmCent Select Inv

	Ticker	Load	NAV	Yield	Total Assets	Mstar Category
	TWCIX	None	$36.73	0.4%	$2,714 mil	Large Growth

Governance and Management

Stewardship Grade: C

Portfolio Manager(s)

Harold Bradley was named manager in March 2006, replacing John Sykora, who left for personal reasons. Bradley is chief investment officer of American Century's small- and mid-cap growth strategies. Keith Lee and Michael Li, who worked alongside Sykora, remain as comanagers.

Strategy

New lead manager Harold Bradley uses a quantitative model that ranks stocks based on earnings and price momentum, valuation, and balance-sheet quality. Bradley and his team favor stocks that score in the top decile of their investment universe and generally sell those landing in the bottom 40%. They keep a fairly compact portfolio of between 50 and 65 holdings, equally weighting each of their positions. A more aggressive version of the fund's model has been used by American Century's mid- and small-growth funds for some time, which has led to high turnover and heavy concentration in fast-growing areas.

Performance 12-31-06

	1st Qtr	2nd Qtr	3rd Qtr	4th Qtr	Total
2002	-0.70	-12.90	-15.44	5.59	-22.77
2003	-2.39	15.92	1.43	8.68	24.74
2004	1.83	1.16	-4.48	9.10	7.35
2005	-4.62	1.40	0.95	3.30	0.86
2006	-0.24	-6.94	-1.04	6.90	-1.79

Trailing	Total Return%	+/- S&P 500	+/- Russ 1000Gr	%Rank Cat	Growth of $10,000
3 Mo	6.90	0.20	0.97	17	10,690
6 Mo	5.78	-6.96	-4.32	83	10,578
1 Yr	-1.79	-17.58	-10.86	96	9,821
3 Yr Avg	2.07	-8.37	-4.80	97	10,634
5 Yr Avg	0.48	-5.71	-2.21	82	10,242
10 Yr Avg	5.31	-3.11	-0.13	60	16,776
15 Yr Avg	6.22	-4.42	-1.80	91	24,723

Tax Analysis	Tax-Adj Rtn%	%Rank Cat	Tax-Cost Rat	%Rank Cat
3 Yr (estimated)	1.83	95	0.24	16
5 Yr (estimated)	0.32	79	0.16	17
10 Yr (estimated)	3.84	62	1.40	70

Potential Capital Gain Exposure: 10% of assets

Morningstar's Take by Christopher Davis 11-10-06

American Century Select's look is new, but we're not sure it's improved.

This offering has charted a markedly different course under current lead manager Harold Bradley, who took charge after the March 2006 departure of John Sykora. The head of American Century's research and development efforts, Bradley was a key player in the development of the quantitative models that drive small- and mid-growth siblings like American Century New Opportunities, which he also runs. Not surprisingly, his models identify firms with improving earnings and revenues--that's always been American Century's modus operandi. But Bradley doesn't stop there; his models also screen for earnings quality, valuation, and price momentum.

Sykora, too, looked for high-quality companies trading at modest valuations. But Bradley argues his models do so more systematically and rigorously. And by requiring strong price momentum, he says he'll avoid areas of the market that aren't running. Whereas Sykora stuck with big-cap consumer and health-care names even as their share prices stagnated, Bradley has shifted the fund's focus to better-performing areas like energy, basic materials, and especially, financials. Reflecting the relative strength of small cap and foreign stocks in recent years, he's also brought down the fund's market cap and given it a bit more international flavor.

We're a little wary of Bradley's strategy. At siblings like New Opportunities, it's led to heavy concentration in fast-growing areas of the market, rapid-fire trading, and high volatility. He's toned down his approach here in appreciation of this fund's mild-mannered roots, but it still requires him to consistently make accurate short-term calls, a tough act to pull off over the long haul. While he's had some success in the small- and mid-cap arena, he has never been put to the test in the large-cap realm. Until Bradley proves he can deliver in diverse markets, we'd look elsewhere.

Address:	4500 Main Street Kansas City MO 64111 800-345-2021
Web Address:	www.americancentury.com
Inception:	06-30-71
Advisor:	American Century Investment MGMT Inc.
Subadvisor:	None
NTF Plans:	Fidelity Retail-NTF, Schwab OneSource

Minimum Purchase:	$2500	Add: $50	IRA: $2500
Min Auto Inv Plan:	$2500	Add: $50	
Sales Fees:	No-load		
Management Fee:	1.00% mx./0.80% mn.		
Actual Fees:	Mgt:1.00%	Dist: —	
Expense Projections:	3Yr:$318	5Yr:$551	10Yr:$1219
Income Distrib:	Annually		

Historical Profile

Return	Below Avg
Risk	Below Avg
Rating	★★ Below Avg

Investment Style: Equity, Stock %

92% 93% 91% 90% 91% 98% 99% 98% 100%

▼ Manager Change
▽ Partial Manager Change

Growth of $10,000
— Investment Values of Fund
— Investment Values of S&P 500

Performance Quartile (within Category)

1995	1996	1997	1998	1999	2000	2001	2002	2003	2004	2005	2006	History
35.62	38.53	42.59	47.39	52.68	45.29	37.00	28.50	35.55	38.08	38.15	36.73	NAV
22.67	19.22	32.19	35.72	22.23	-8.71	-18.16	-22.77	24.74	7.35	0.86	-1.79	Total Return %
-14.91	-3.74	-1.17	7.14	1.19	0.39	-6.27	-0.67	-3.94	-3.53	-4.05	-17.58	+/-S&P 500
-14.51	-3.90	1.70	-2.99	-10.93	13.71	2.26	5.11	-5.01	1.05	-4.40	-10.86	+/-Russ 1000Gr
0.81	0.91	0.51	0.40	0.00	0.00	0.14	0.20	0.00	0.23	0.69	0.42	Income Return %
21.86	18.31	31.68	35.32	22.23	-8.71	-18.30	-22.97	24.74	7.12	0.17	-2.21	Capital Return %
93	52	16	31	79	39	41	21	72	55	93	96	Total Rtn % Rank Cat
0.27	0.32	0.20	0.17	0.00	0.00	0.06	0.07	0.00	0.08	0.26	0.16	Income $
4.66	3.68	7.93	9.79	5.10	2.79	0.00	0.00	0.00	0.00	0.00	0.58	Capital Gains $
1.00	1.00	1.00	1.00	1.00	1.00	1.00	1.00	1.00	1.00	1.00	—	Expense Ratio %
0.90	0.50	0.33	0.25	0.03	-0.11	0.15	0.21	0.03	-0.01	0.42	—	Income Ratio %
106	105	94	165	130	67	98	168	84	48	55	—	Turnover Rate %
3,983	4,060	5,006	6,498	7,674	6,475	4,973	3,444	3,984	3,818	3,361	2,531	Net Assets $mil

Rating and Risk

Time Period	Load-Adj Return %	Morningstar Rtn vs Cat	Morningstar Risk vs Cat	Morningstar Risk-Adj Rating
1 Yr	-1.79			
3 Yr	2.07	Low	-Avg	★
5 Yr	0.48	-Avg	-Avg	★★
10 Yr	5.31	Avg	-Avg	★★★
Incept	12.89			

Other Measures	Standard Index S&P 500	Best Fit Index Russ 1000Gr
Alpha	-8.5	-4.4
Beta	1.11	0.96
R-Squared	76	85
Standard Deviation	8.72	
Mean	2.07	
Sharpe Ratio	-0.09	

Portfolio Analysis 09-30-06

Share change since 06-06 Total Stocks:62	Sector	PE	Tot Ret%	% Assets
J.P. Morgan Chase & Co.	Financial	13.6	25.60	2.88
⊕ Loews Corporation	Financial	14.9	32.04	2.67
Johnson & Johnson	Health	17.5	12.45	2.66
Baxter International Inc	Health	24.3	24.81	2.62
Diageo	Goods	—	—	2.61
⊕ US Bancorp	Financial	13.9	26.29	2.61
⊖ Bank of America Corporat	Financial	12.4	20.68	2.58
⊕ MEMC Electronic Material	Hardware	32.6	76.55	2.54
⊕ St. Paul Travelers Compa	Financial	11.6	22.90	2.52
⊕ Verizon Communications	Telecom	15.9	34.88	2.46
⊖ American Tower Corporati	Telecom		37.57	2.39
Colgate-Palmolive Compan	Goods	27.6	21.51	2.32
⊖ International Game Tech.	Consumer	34.3	52.07	2.28
Omnicom Group, Inc.	Business	21.4	24.14	2.20
✵ PNC Financial Services G	Financial	8.7	23.60	2.17
Phelps Dodge Corp.	Ind Mtrls	12.7	76.29	2.14
✵ Medco Health Solutions,	Health	28.4	-4.23	2.11
✵ Genzyme Corporation	Health	50.8	-13.00	2.09
✵ Microsoft Corporation	Software	23.8	15.83	2.08
✵ WellPoint, Inc.	Health	17.2	-1.38	2.08

Current Investment Style

Value Blnd Growth — Large Mid Small

	Market Cap	%
	Giant	35.9
	Large	44.7
	Mid	19.4
	Small	0.0
	Micro	0.0
	Avg $mil:	29,056

Value Measures		Rel Category
Price/Earnings	16.20	0.84
Price/Book	3.02	0.91
Price/Sales	2.08	1.07
Price/Cash Flow	11.86	1.04
Dividend Yield %	1.42	1.38

Growth Measures	%	Rel Category
Long-Term Erngs	13.33	0.93
Book Value	4.45	0.38
Sales	6.56	0.57
Cash Flow	13.87	0.83
Historical Erngs	20.84	0.91

Profitability	%	Rel Category
Return on Equity	23.07	1.13
Return on Assets	11.78	1.07
Net Margin	15.59	1.09

Sector Weightings	% of Stocks	Rel S&P 500	3 Year High Low	
↻ Info	25.67	1.28		
Software	6.71	1.94	7	0
Hardware	12.19	1.32	12	4
Media	1.91	0.50	3	0
Telecom	4.86	1.38	5	0
Œ Service	53.55	1.16		
Health	19.55	1.62	25	11
Consumer	6.79	0.89	22	7
Business	4.29	1.01	9	4
Financial	22.92	1.03	23	12
Mfg	20.77	0.61		
Goods	6.18	0.72	18	6
Ind Mtrls	8.80	0.74	20	2
Energy	4.04	0.41	9	0
Utilities	1.75	0.50	2	0

Composition

● Cash	0.2	
● Stocks	99.8	
● Bonds	0.0	
● Other	0.0	
Foreign	13.7	(% of Stock)

MORNINGSTAR® Funds 500

AmCent Small Cap Val Inv

	Ticker	Load	NAV	Yield	Total Assets	Mstar Category
	ASVIX	Closed	$9.74	0.5%	$2,179 mil	Small Value

Governance and Management

Stewardship Grade: B

Portfolio Manager(s)

Manager Ben Giele has been here right from the start. Prior to February 1999, he was an analyst on the fund. He is assisted by Steve Roth, who had been an analyst for the fund since November 2002 and was named co-manager in November 2006 following the departure of Kevin Laub.

Strategy

Managers Ben Giele and Steve Roth look for stocks that are cheap based on measures such as dividends, cash flow, earnings, and book value. They are quick to sell stocks that they think have appreciated beyond their fair value estimates, giving the fund a turnover rate considerably above the small-value norm. Sector weightings are kept within 10 percentage points of the Russell 2000 Value Index's.

Historical Profile
Return	Average
Risk	Below Avg
Rating	★★★ Neutral

Investment Style: Equity Stock %

96% 90% 85% 90% 91% 93% 98% 95% 95%

▼ Manager Change
▽ Partial Manager Change

Growth of $10,000
- ■ Investment Values of Fund
- — Investment Values of S&P 500

Performance Quartile (within Category)

	1995	1996	1997	1998	1999	2000	2001	2002	2003	2004	2005	2006	History
	—	—	—	5.12	4.73	6.32	8.02	6.79	9.18	10.17	9.64	9.74	NAV
	—	—	—	3.31*	-0.86	39.41	30.52	-11.38	36.11	21.81	8.40	15.52	Total Return %
	—	—	—	—	-21.90	48.51	42.41	10.72	7.43	10.93	3.49	-0.27	+/-S&P 500
	—	—	—	—	0.63	16.58	16.50	0.05	-9.92	-0.44	3.69	-7.96	+/-Russ 2000 VL
	—	—	—	—	1.06	1.08	0.59	0.00	0.75	0.31	0.65	0.63	Income Return %
	—	—	—	—	-1.92	38.33	29.93	-11.38	35.36	21.50	7.75	14.89	Capital Return %
	—	—	—	—	66	3	7	64	77	43	26	58	Total Rtn % Rank Cat
	—	—	—	0.00	0.05	0.05	0.04	0.00	0.05	0.03	0.06	0.06	Income $
	—	—	—	0.04	0.28	0.20	0.18	0.32	0.00	0.95	1.34	1.33	Capital Gains $
	—	—	—	—	1.25	1.25	1.25	1.25	1.25	1.25	1.26	1.25	Expense Ratio %
	—	—	—	—	1.02	1.04	1.10	0.27	0.37	0.59	0.58	Income Ratio %
	—	—	—	—	153	178	144	73	104	110	111	Turnover Rate %
	—	—	—	—	12	19	66	1,090	784	972	1,248	1,281	Net Assets $mil

Performance 12-31-06

	1st Qtr	2nd Qtr	3rd Qtr	4th Qtr	Total
2002	7.48	-3.71	-19.04	5.76	-11.38
2003	-4.85	18.62	5.24	14.57	36.11
2004	5.94	3.67	-1.29	12.36	21.81
2005	-0.85	3.38	4.36	1.34	8.40
2006	8.54	-4.78	4.02	7.46	15.52

Trailing	Total Return%	+/- S&P 500	+/- Russ 2000 VL	%Rank Cat	Growth of $10,000
3 Mo	7.46	0.76	-1.57	75	10,746
6 Mo	11.78	-0.96	-0.03	14	11,178
1 Yr	15.52	-0.27	-7.96	58	11,552
3 Yr Avg	15.11	4.67	-1.37	38	15,252
5 Yr Avg	12.97	6.78	-2.40	62	18,400
10 Yr Avg	—	—	—	—	—
15 Yr Avg	—	—	—	—	—

Tax Analysis	Tax-Adj Rtn%	%Rank Cat	Tax-Cost Rat	%Rank Cat
3 Yr (estimated)	11.81	54	2.87	89
5 Yr (estimated)	10.58	76	2.12	86
10 Yr (estimated)	—	—	—	—

Potential Capital Gain Exposure: 14% of assets

Morningstar's Take by Christopher Davis 12-28-06

American Century Small Cap Value's appeal has shrunk, but it hasn't vanished.

American Century has dealt with a spate of manager departures across its lineup in recent years. This closed offering is no exception. In October, comanager Kevin Laub left to join another fund manager. In his place, the firm elevated Steve Roth, who had been an analyst for the fund since November 2002. He joins Ben Giele, who was one of the original analysts at the fund's 1998 launch and was named manager in 1999.

There's reason to believe Laub's exit won't have a detrimental impact on the fund. After all, Giele remains on board. And because Roth has worked closely with him for four years, he's well acquainted with the fund's strict valuation discipline. All along, its strategy has required management to seek stocks in the cheapest third of the small-cap universe and sell them quickly when they get pricey. It's an approach that's led to solid, if unspectacular, long-term returns here, and in a similar incarnation at American Century Value.

Still, not all is rosy. The departed Laub was here from the start, so he played a big role in the fund's success. Losing such a key player means there's no guarantee execution will remain as strong. Other American Century funds, such as Ultra and Growth, have retained their strategies amid manager turnover and yet had returns weaken. Also, we're increasingly worried about the fund's size. Assets have continued to grow despite its 2001 closure and now stand at $2.2 billion. That's a sizable sum given the fund's high-turnover strategy. Some telltale signs of asset bloat have also emerged. For instance, the number of holdings, now at 240, is nearly a hundred more than a couple of years ago.

While not as appealing as in the past, this fund is still led by experienced, successful management. That might be reason to hang on, especially if you'd take a tax hit for selling, but this isn't a top-rate small-value investment.

Address:	4500 Main Street Kansas City MO 64111 800-345-2021
Web Address:	www.americancentury.com
Inception:	07-31-98*
Advisor:	American Century Investment MGMT Inc.
Subadvisor:	None
NTF Plans:	Schwab OneSource

Minimum Purchase:	Closed	Add: —	IRA: —
Min Auto Inv Plan:	Closed	Add: —	
Sales Fees:	No-load		
Management Fee:	1.25% mx./1.00% mn.		
Actual Fees:	Mgt:1.25%	Dist: —	
Expense Projections:	3Yr:$395	5Yr:$683	10Yr:$1503
Income Distrib:	Quarterly		

Rating and Risk

Time Period	Load-Adj Return %	Morningstar Rtn vs Cat	Morningstar Risk vs Cat	Morningstar Risk-Adj Rating
1 Yr	15.52			
3 Yr	15.11	Avg	-Avg	★★★★
5 Yr	12.97	Avg	-Avg	★★★
10 Yr	—			
Incept	15.76			

Other Measures	Standard Index S&P 500	Best Fit Index Mstar Small Core
Alpha	1.8	1.3
Beta	1.39	0.77
R-Squared	81	92
Standard Deviation	10.55	
Mean	15.11	
Sharpe Ratio	1.09	

Portfolio Analysis 09-30-06

Share change since 06-06 Total Stocks:240	Sector	PE	Tot Ret%	% Assets
⊕ iShares Russell 2000 Ind	—	—	—	3.49
⊖ Sybase Inc.	Software	22.7	12.99	1.89
⊖ Washington Federal Inc.	Financial	14.1	5.98	1.20
⊖ Platinum Underwriters Ho	Financial	21.1	0.68	1.19
⊕ Beckman Coulter, Inc.	Health	33.7	6.21	1.11
⊕ Minerals Technologies, I	Ind Mtrls	22.1	5.58	1.05
⊕ International Speedway C	Goods	16.8	6.73	1.02
⊖ Perot Systems Corporatio	Business	26.6	15.91	1.01
⊖ Lifepoint Hospitals, Inc	Health	14.3	-10.13	1.01
⊖ South Financial Group, I	Financial	33.0	-0.90	1.01
⊖ Parametric Technology Co	Software	38.1	18.16	1.00
⊖ WGL Holdings, Inc.	Utilities	17.3	13.29	0.97
⊖ First Midwest Bancorp	Financial	17.0	13.70	0.97
⊖ Aspen Insurance Holdings	Financial	8.3	14.24	0.96
⊖ Getty Realty Corporation	Financial	17.1	25.09	0.94
⊖ Schnitzer Steel Industri	Ind Mtrls	8.5	30.03	0.90
⊕ Kaydon Corporation	Ind Mtrls	19.1	25.23	0.81
⊕ CEC Entertainment, Inc.	Consumer	19.6	18.24	0.77
⊕ Kennametal Inc.	Ind Mtrls	8.3	16.85	0.76
⊖ Puget Energy, Inc.	Utilities	16.8	29.99	0.76

Current Investment Style

Value Blnd Growth — Large / Mid / Small

Market Cap	%
Giant	0.0
Large	0.0
Mid	36.1
Small	54.2
Micro	9.7
Avg $mil: 1,315	

Value Measures		Rel Category
Price/Earnings	14.81	0.96
Price/Book	1.72	0.97
Price/Sales	0.94	1.17
Price/Cash Flow	6.88	1.12
Dividend Yield %	1.80	1.14

Growth Measures	%	Rel Category
Long-Term Erngs	11.91	0.95
Book Value	7.96	1.47
Sales	9.15	1.24
Cash Flow	7.05	0.86
Historical Erngs	8.72	0.77

Profitability	%	Rel Category
Return on Equity	12.09	1.12
Return on Assets	6.80	1.11
Net Margin	11.31	1.25

Sector Weightings	% of Stocks	Rel S&P 500	3 Year High	Low
☊ Info	12.43	0.62		
🖭 Software	4.83	1.40	7	4
🖥 Hardware	5.39	0.58	7	4
🗐 Media	1.53	0.40	3	2
📶 Telecom	0.68	0.19	1	0
☞ Service	51.38	1.11		
🕂 Health	8.55	0.71	10	6
🛒 Consumer	6.24	0.82	10	6
🗏 Business	10.77	2.55	12	10
💲 Financial	25.82	1.16	26	18
🏭 Mfg	36.19	1.07		
🛢 Goods	9.21	1.08	11	8
⚙ Ind Mtrls	18.65	1.56	19	16
🔥 Energy	4.18	0.43	9	4
🗲 Utilities	4.15	1.19	5	4

Composition

	%
● Cash	4.4
● Stocks	94.9
● Bonds	0.0
● Other	0.7
Foreign (% of Stock)	0.3

AmCent Tax-Free Bond Inv

	Ticker	Load	NAV	Yield	SEC Yield	Total Assets	Mstar Category
	TWTIX	None	$10.79	3.8%	3.45%	$640 mil	Muni National Interm

Governance and Management

Stewardship Grade: B

Portfolio Manager(s)

Robert Miller became lead manager in April 2006. He joined American Century in 1998 and started working on this fund in April 2000. He is supported by two comanagers and three experienced muniicipal-bond analysts.

Strategy

This fund employs a pretty conservative strategy. Its credit quality is generally high (with more than 70% of assets in AA or AAA rated bonds), and manager Robert Miller keeps duration within a tight range of a self-selected peer group. He also looks for undervalued bonds and makes bets on the yield curve, adding or subtracting lower-rated securities as market yields dictate.

Historical Profile

Return	Above Avg
Risk	Average
Rating	★★★★ Above Avg

Performance Quartile (within Category)

History	1995	1996	1997	1998	1999	2000	2001	2002	2003	2004	2005	2006
NAV	10.48	10.37	10.54	10.58	9.99	10.46	10.45	10.96	10.99	10.91	10.77	10.79
Total Return %	11.92	3.86	7.44	6.74	-0.93	9.77	5.25	9.12	4.04	2.65	2.43	4.10
+/-LB Muni	-5.54	-0.57	-1.75	0.26	1.13	-1.91	0.12	-0.48	-1.27	-1.83	-1.08	-0.74
+/-LB Muni 10YR	-5.25	-0.68	-1.79	-0.02	0.32	-0.99	0.63	-1.05	-1.66	-1.50	-0.31	-0.61
Income Return %	5.00	4.65	4.80	4.67	4.56	4.92	4.51	3.99	3.50	3.37	3.66	3.89
Capital Return %	6.92	-0.79	2.64	2.07	-5.49	4.85	0.74	5.13	0.54	-0.72	-1.23	0.21
Total Rtn % Rank Cat	83	42	55	3	22	42	12	33	55	55	25	26
Income $	0.48	0.48	0.49	0.48	0.47	0.48	0.46	0.41	0.38	0.36	0.39	0.41
Capital Gains $	0.07	0.02	0.09	0.17	0.02	0.00	0.09	0.02	0.03	0.00	0.01	0.00
Expense Ratio %	0.60	0.60	0.58	0.51	0.51	0.51	0.51	0.51	0.51	0.51	0.50	0.49
Income Ratio %	4.77	4.66	4.71	4.62	4.52	4.75	4.65	4.14	3.62	3.34	3.46	3.73
Turnover Rate %	32	39	35	17	32	107	106	86	57	60	77	79
Net Assets $mil	82	79	133	147	161	163	316	556	605	590	639	632

Investment Style
Fixed Income
Income Rtn %Rank Cat

▼ Manager Change
▽ Partial Manager Change

Growth of $10,000
— Investment Values of Fund
— Investment Values of LB Muni

Performance 12-31-06

	1st Qtr	2nd Qtr	3rd Qtr	4th Qtr	Total
2002	0.87	3.48	4.51	0.03	9.12
2003	0.78	2.25	-0.13	1.10	4.04
2004	1.07	-2.09	2.83	0.88	2.65
2005	-0.63	2.31	0.02	0.74	2.43
2006	0.18	-0.08	3.17	0.79	4.10

Trailing	Total Return%	+/- LB Muni	+/- LB Muni 10YR	%Rank Cat	Growth of $10,000
3 Mo	0.79	-0.32	-0.13	35	10,079
6 Mo	3.99	-0.56	-0.78	32	10,399
1 Yr	4.10	-0.74	-0.61	26	10,410
3 Yr Avg	3.06	-1.22	-0.80	36	10,946
5 Yr Avg	4.44	-1.09	-1.02	37	12,426
10 Yr Avg	5.01	-0.75	-0.69	21	16,304
15 Yr Avg	5.77	-0.49	-0.51	21	23,197

Tax Analysis	Tax-Adj Rtn%	%Rank Cat	Tax-Cost Rat	%Rank Cat
3 Yr (estimated)	3.05	26	0.01	5
5 Yr (estimated)	4.42	29	0.02	8
10 Yr (estimated)	4.90	18	0.10	44

Potential Capital Gain Exposure: 1% of assets

Rating and Risk

Time Period	Load-Adj Return %	Morningstar Rtn vs Cat	Morningstar Risk vs Cat	Morningstar Risk-Adj Rating
1 Yr	4.10			
3 Yr	3.06	Avg	-Avg	★★★
5 Yr	4.44	Avg	Avg	★★★
10 Yr	5.01	+Avg	Avg	★★★★
Incept	5.83			

Other Measures	Standard Index LB Muni	Best Fit Index LB Muni
Alpha	-1.0	-1.0
Beta	0.85	0.85
R-Squared	97	97
Standard Deviation	2.68	
Mean	3.06	
Sharpe Ratio	-0.06	

Portfolio Analysis 09-30-06

Total Fixed-Income:326

	Date of Maturity	Amount $000	Value $000	% Net Assets
PITTSBURGH PA GO REF BD	09-01-16	15,805	17,618	2.31
New Jersey St Transn Tr	12-15-20	15,000	16,921	2.22
Engy Northwest Wash Elec	07-01-18	10,000	11,152	1.46
Mississippi St 5.25%	11-01-13	7,925	8,587	1.13
New Jersey St Transn Tr	12-15-12	7,400	8,055	1.06
California St 5%	06-01-26	7,500	7,907	1.04
Snohomish Cnty Wash Sch	12-01-17	6,715	7,298	0.96
Los Alamos Cnty N Mex 5%	07-01-11	6,675	7,087	0.93
New Jersey St Tran 5%	10-01-13	5,595	6,017	0.79
CHARLESTON EDL EXCELLENC	12-01-19	5,455	5,844	0.77
New York N Y 5.75%	03-01-20	5,000	5,629	0.74
New York N Y 5%	11-01-17	5,195	5,610	0.74
Tulsa Cnty Okla Indl Aut	05-15-10	5,225	5,485	0.72
Tacoma Wash Elec Sys 5.6	01-01-21	5,000	5,450	0.71
Univ Colo Regts Partn In	10-01-22	5,000	5,446	0.71

Current Investment Style

¹Avg Eff Duration	5.5 Yrs
Avg Eff Maturity	7.7 Yrs
Avg Credit Quality	AA
Avg Wtd Coupon	5.02%
Avg Wtd Price	107.28% of par

¹figure provided by fund

Credit Analysis	% bonds 09-30-06		
AAA	62	BB	0
AA	11	B	0
A	7	Below B	0
BBB	20	NR/NA	0

Special Securities	
Restricted/Illiqud Secs	0
Options/Futures/Warrants	No

Top 5 States	% bonds		
WA	8.4	AZ	6.0
TX	8.3	NJ	5.6
IL	7.6		

Composition			
Cash	16.1	Bonds	84.0
Stocks	0.0	Other	0.0

Sector Weightings	% of Bonds	Rel Cat
General Obligation	38.1	1.03
Utilities	11.0	1.16
Health	8.4	0.93
Water/Waste	6.4	0.71
Housing	1.1	0.22
Education	20.5	1.59
Transportation	2.6	0.49
COP/Lease	5.1	2.07
Industrial	5.2	0.56
Misc Revenue	0.0	—
Demand	1.6	4.21

Morningstar's Take by Andrew Gunter 12-11-06

Investors shouldn't worry about the manager change at American Century Tax-Free Bond.

American Century Investments named Robert Miller lead manager of this fund after Ken Salinger left the firm in April. Salinger had final say on investment decisions, but execution of this fund's strategy has long been a team effort: Miller worked with Salinger for six years to deliver average annual returns of 5.19%--besting 70% of category peers during that time.

We're comfortable with this change for several reasons. Miller is a successful municipal-bond manager in his own right: His five-year record as manager of the firm's California Tax-Free fund tops more than 68% of its rivals. Plus this fund retains three dedicated municipal-bond analysts and two comanagers. Finally, and most importantly, Miller won't change the strategy that drove this fund's past success.

That strategy includes avoiding big bets on the direction of interest rates--a quick way to ruin a fund's returns if the bet is wrong--and tightly monitoring credit risk. So while Miller now has a tactical bet on bonds that mature in 10 years, he offsets it with bonds near maturity to make sure the portfolio's duration, a measure of interest-rate sensitivity, stays within a close two tenths of a year of its benchmark.

Miller's team is equally careful with credit risk, devoting nearly two thirds of assets to AAA rated issues. The team spreads the remaining dollars across bonds with risk it thoroughly evaluates. For example, it'll seek BBB rated issuers it deems as financially healthy as many A rated issuers in order to gain more income at little added risk.

This strategy isn't designed to produce home runs. But it provides steady returns with curtailed downside risk. With below-average expenses of only 0.51% and an experienced management team, this fund remains a good choice for conservative bond investors.

Address:	4500 Main Street
	Kansas City MO 64111
	800-345-2021
Web Address:	www.americancentury.com
Inception:	03-02-87
Advisor:	American Century Investment MGMT Inc.
Subadvisor:	None
NTF Plans:	Fidelity Retail-NTF, Schwab OneSource

Minimum Purchase:	$5000	Add: $50	IRA: $0
Min Auto Inv Plan:	$5000	Add: $50
Sales Fees:	No-load
Management Fee:	0.57% mx./0.45% mn., 0.11%A
Actual Fees:	Mgt:0.48%	Dist:—
Expense Projections:	3Yr:$157	5Yr:$274	10Yr:$615
Income Distrib:	Monthly

Morningstar® Funds 500

AmCent Ultra Inv

	Ticker	Load	NAV	Yield	Total Assets	Mstar Category
	TWCUX	None	$27.11	0.0%	$14,298 mil	Large Growth

Performance 12-31-06

	1st Qtr	2nd Qtr	3rd Qtr	4th Qtr	Total
2002	-1.05	-11.26	-15.41	3.47	-23.15
2003	-1.23	13.86	2.39	9.27	25.83
2004	3.41	1.74	-4.35	9.99	10.69
2005	-4.92	0.89	2.12	4.24	2.12
2006	0.27	-6.26	-1.10	4.05	-3.28

Trailing	Total Return%	+/- S&P 500	+/- Russ 1000Gr	%Rank Cat	Growth of $10,000
3 Mo	4.05	-2.65	-1.88	83	10,405
6 Mo	2.91	-9.83	-7.19	96	10,291
1 Yr	-3.28	-19.07	-12.35	97	9,672
3 Yr Avg	3.02	-7.42	-3.85	94	10,934
5 Yr Avg	1.12	-5.07	-1.57	73	10,573
10 Yr Avg	5.42	-3.00	-0.02	58	16,952
15 Yr Avg	7.97	-2.67	-0.05	58	31,590

Tax Analysis	Tax-Adj Rtn%	%Rank Cat	Tax-Cost Rat	%Rank Cat
3 Yr (estimated)	2.65	92	0.36	24
5 Yr (estimated)	0.88	72	0.24	25
10 Yr (estimated)	4.16	57	1.20	58

Potential Capital Gain Exposure: -5% of assets

Morningstar's Take by Christopher Davis 11-17-06

Our view toward American Century Ultra continues to sour.

This offering recently lost two of its most seasoned managers. In June 2006, comanager Bruce Wimberly stepped down from the helm of this offering after nearly a decade. And this month, Jerry Sullivan, who had been a comanager since 2001, left with analyst Rob Brookby to focus on their other charge, American Century Fundamental Equity. Given both managers' experience, we consider their departures losses. Still, Wade Slome, named comanager in 2002, remains. He's joined by Tom Telford, who still runs American Century Technology and comanaged small-growth American Century New Opportunities II before assuming management duties here.

It hasn't been business as usual since Telford arrived. He's drawn on his quantitative background to beef up the fund's strategy, bringing in the earnings- and price-momentum-focused quantitative model used by American Century's

mid- and small-growth offerings. He's added quant screens for earnings growth, quality, and valuation--metrics he argues have also been good predictors of future returns in large caps.

The model helps shape portfolio construction, with management overweighting sectors that score the highest under the screen. In 2006's third quarter, for instance, the managers pared their outsized weighting in Internet stocks, which the model singled out for weak price momentum.

That bet on Internet stocks partly explains the fund's misfortunes this year and last. But while it has cut back exposure to names such as Yahoo, the fund remains aggressively positioned, with larger stakes in pricier, faster-growing names such as Cisco Systems. Thus, the fund could look better in an improved environment for large-growth stocks.

That said, we've long regarded the fund as a solid, but not topnotch, choice. Now with management turnover and a restyled strategy, it's tough to pound the table for this offering.

Address:	4500 Main Street Kansas City MO 64111 800-345-2021
Web Address:	www.americancentury.com
Inception:	11-02-81
Advisor:	American Century Investment MGMT Inc.
Subadvisor:	None
NTF Plans:	Fidelity Retail-NTF, Schwab OneSource

Minimum Purchase:	$2500	Add: $50	IRA: $2500
Min Auto Inv Plan:	$2500	Add: $50	
Sales Fees:	No-load		
Management Fee:	1.00% mx./0.80% mn.		
Actual Fees:	Mgt:0.99%	Dist: —	
Expense Projections:	3Yr:$314	5Yr:$545	10Yr:$1208
Income Distrib:	Annually		

Historical Profile

Return	Below Avg
Risk	Average
Rating	★★★ Neutral

	97%	99%	95%	87%	99%	98%	99%	99%	98%

▼ Manager Change
▽ Partial Manager Change

Growth of $10,000
— Investment Values of Fund
— Investment Values of S&P 500

31.0
24.0
17.0
10.0

Investment Style
Equity
Stock %

Performance Quartile (within Category)

1995	1996	1997	1998	1999	2000	2001	2002	2003	2004	2005	2006	History
26.11	28.09	27.30	33.41	45.78	32.37	27.64	21.18	26.65	29.50	30.09	27.11	NAV
37.68	13.85	23.13	34.56	41.46	-19.91	-14.61	-23.15	25.83	10.69	2.12	-3.28	Total Return %
0.10	-9.11	-10.23	5.98	20.42	-10.81	-2.72	-1.05	-2.85	-0.19	-2.79	-19.07	+/-S&P 500
0.50	-9.27	-7.36	-4.15	8.30	2.51	5.81	4.73	-3.92	4.39	-3.14	-12.35	+/-Russ 1000Gr
0.00	0.00	0.05	0.00	0.00	0.00	0.00	0.23	0.00	0.00	0.12	0.00	Income Return %
37.68	13.85	23.08	34.56	41.46	-19.91	-14.61	-23.38	25.83	10.69	2.00	-3.28	Capital Return %
21	83	65	36	35	79	25	24	64	26	86	97	Total Rtn % Rank Cat
0.00	0.00	0.01	0.00	0.00	0.00	0.00	0.06	0.00	0.00	0.04	0.00	Income $
1.30	1.69	7.07	3.12	1.38	4.41	0.00	0.00	0.00	0.00	0.00	2.01	Capital Gains $
1.00	1.00	1.00	1.00	1.00	0.99	0.98	0.99	1.00	0.99	0.99	—	Expense Ratio %
-0.30	-0.20	0.03	-0.08	-0.39	-0.64	-0.18	0.24	-0.09	-0.20	0.09	—	Income Ratio %
87	87	107	128	42	62	86	92	82	34	33	—	Turnover Rate %
14,551	18,419	22,420	30,076	43,193	33,784	26,911	17,972	21,744	21,998	19,103	12,939	Net Assets $mil

Rating and Risk

Time Period	Load-Adj Return %	Morningstar Rtn vs Cat	Morningstar Risk vs Cat	Morningstar Risk-Adj Rating
1 Yr	-3.28			
3 Yr	3.02	Low	Avg	★
5 Yr	1.12	-Avg	-Avg	★★★
10 Yr	5.42	Avg	Avg	★★★
Incept	12.53			

Other Measures	Standard Index S&P 500	Best Fit Index Russ 1000Gr
Alpha	-8.0	-3.7
Beta	1.17	1.03
R-Squared	76	88
Standard Deviation	9.16	
Mean	3.02	
Sharpe Ratio	0.02	

Portfolio Analysis 09-30-06

Share change since 06-06 Total Stocks:75

	Sector	PE	Tot Ret%	% Assets
⊖ UnitedHealth Group, Inc.	Health	20.8	-13.49	3.22
⊖ Electronic Arts, Inc.	Software	91.2	-3.73	3.09
⊕ Cisco Systems, Inc.	Hardware	30.1	59.64	2.98
⊖ International Game Tech.	Consumer	34.3	52.07	2.77
⊕ Monsanto Company	Ind Mtrls	39.8	36.78	2.61
⊕ Google, Inc.	Business	61.5	11.00	2.55
⊕ Fisher Scientific Intern	Health	—	—	2.28
⊖ SLM Corporation	Financial	14.1	-9.76	2.26
⊕ Wells Fargo Company	Financial	14.7	16.82	2.19
⊕ Walgreen Company	Consumer	26.6	4.36	2.08
⊖ First Data Corporation	Business	12.3	9.88	1.98
⊕ Apple Computer, Inc.	Hardware	37.6	18.01	1.88
⊕ T Rowe Price Group	Financial	26.1	23.27	1.86
☼ Danaher Corporation	Ind Mtrls	22.0	30.02	1.85
☼ Motorola, Inc.	Hardware	11.8	-8.17	1.83
☼ PepsiCo, Inc.	Goods	21.5	7.86	1.79
⊕ CarMax, Inc.	Consumer	32.2	93.75	1.78
⊕ Stryker Corporation	Health	30.3	24.53	1.72
☼ America Movil SA ADR	Telecom	27.7	55.53	1.65
⊖ Paychex, Inc.	Business	30.4	5.62	1.63

Current Investment Style

Value Blnd Growth — Large Mid Small

Market Cap	%
Giant	39.5
Large	46.0
Mid	14.3
Small	0.1
Micro	0.0

Avg $mil: 31,382

Value Measures		Rel Category
Price/Earnings	20.48	1.06
Price/Book	3.70	1.11
Price/Sales	1.90	0.98
Price/Cash Flow	13.09	1.15
Dividend Yield %	0.86	0.83

Growth Measures	%	Rel Category
Long-Term Erngs	14.81	1.03
Book Value	14.48	1.25
Sales	11.31	0.98
Cash Flow	18.46	1.10
Historical Erngs	21.66	0.94

Profitability	%	Rel Category
Return on Equity	20.65	1.02
Return on Assets	12.85	1.17
Net Margin	15.45	1.08

Sector Weightings	% of Stocks	Rel S&P 500	3 Year High	Low
↻ Info	18.88	0.94		
Software	4.66	1.35	8	5
Hardware	11.25	1.22	11	7
Media	0.59	0.16	4	1
Telecom	2.38	0.68	2	0
Service	63.70	1.38		
Health	19.22	1.59	20	14
Consumer	17.48	2.28	29	17
Business	10.18	2.41	14	7
Financial	16.82	0.76	17	13
Mfg	17.41	0.52		
Goods	4.15	0.49	10	3
Ind Mtrls	8.80	0.74	9	0
Energy	4.44	0.45	5	2
Utilities	0.02	0.01	0	0

Composition

● Cash	1.8
● Stocks	98.2
● Bonds	0.0
● Other	0.0
Foreign (% of Stock)	9.2

AmCent Value Inv

	Ticker	Load	NAV	Yield	Total Assets	Mstar Category
	TWVLX	None	$7.59	1.5%	$3,198 mil	Large Value

Governance and Management

Stewardship Grade: B

Portfolio Manager(s)

Prior to taking the helm upon this fund's inception in 1993, Phil Davidson spent 11 years as a manager for Boatmen's Trust Company. Comanager Scott Moore has about a decade of experience as an analyst and portfolio manager. Davidson and Moore also lead American Century Equity Income, which has one of the mid-value category's better risk/reward profiles. After serving as one of the fund's analysts since 1998, Michael Liss was appointed comanager in early 2004. Five analysts support this offering and Equity Income.

Strategy

Managers Phil Davidson, Scott Moore, and Michael Liss employ an all-cap approach, looking for stocks that are cheap on measures such as dividends, cash flow, earnings, and book value. They apply these criteria rather strictly, so the fund has traditionally had scant exposure to growth sectors, including technology. The pair is quick to sell stocks that have gotten too pricey, which has given the fund high turnover in past years.

Performance 12-31-06

	1st Qtr	2nd Qtr	3rd Qtr	4th Qtr	Total
2002	3.03	-6.60	-16.28	8.37	-12.69
2003	-5.41	15.72	3.72	13.68	29.06
2004	3.09	3.05	-1.00	8.74	14.36
2005	-0.89	1.32	0.71	3.86	5.03
2006	3.70	-0.79	7.33	7.32	18.51

Trailing	Total Return%	+/- S&P 500	+/- Russ 1000 VI	%Rank Cat	Growth of $10,000
3 Mo	7.32	0.62	-0.68	47	10,732
6 Mo	15.19	2.45	0.47	9	11,519
1 Yr	18.51	2.72	-3.74	47	11,851
3 Yr Avg	12.49	2.05	-2.60	46	14,234
5 Yr Avg	9.91	3.72	-0.95	19	16,039
10 Yr Avg	10.88	2.46	-0.12	14	28,089
15 Yr Avg	—	—	—	—	—

Tax Analysis	Tax-Adj Rtn%	%Rank Cat	Tax-Cost Rat	%Rank Cat
3 Yr (estimated)	9.27	73	2.86	93
5 Yr (estimated)	7.63	40	2.07	91
10 Yr (estimated)	7.82	34	2.76	97

Potential Capital Gain Exposure: 12% of assets

Historical Profile

Return	Above Avg
Risk	Below Avg
Rating	★★★★ Above Avg

| | 100% | 98% | 79% | 81% | 87% | 97% | 95% | 96% | 95% | Investment Style: Equity / Stock % |

Growth of $10,000
— Investment Values of Fund
— Investment Values of S&P 500

▼ Manager Change
▽ Partial Manager Change

1995	1996	1997	1998	1999	2000	2001	2002	2003	2004	2005	2006	History
5.90	6.59	6.95	6.05	5.49	6.38	7.00	5.95	7.50	7.39	6.95	7.59	NAV
32.80	24.25	26.01	4.99	-0.80	18.27	12.86	-12.69	29.06	14.36	5.03	18.51	Total Return %
-4.78	1.29	-7.35	-23.59	-21.84	27.37	24.75	9.41	0.38	3.48	0.12	2.72	+/-S&P 500
-5.56	2.61	-9.17	-10.64	-8.15	11.26	18.45	2.83	-0.97	-2.13	-2.02	-3.74	+/-Russ 1000 VI
2.72	1.89	1.80	1.23	1.49	1.81	1.30	0.93	1.43	1.16	1.27	1.76	Income Return %
30.08	22.36	24.21	3.76	-2.29	16.46	11.56	-13.62	27.63	13.20	3.76	16.75	Capital Return %
52	14	65	83	81	16	3	12	40	33	57	47	Total Rtn % Rank Cat
0.13	0.11	0.12	0.08	0.09	0.10	0.08	0.06	0.08	0.09	0.09	0.12	Income $
0.48	0.61	1.20	1.15	0.41	0.00	0.11	0.10	0.08	1.05	0.72	0.51	Capital Gains $
1.00	0.97	1.00	1.00	1.00	1.00	1.00	1.00	1.00	1.00	0.99	0.99	Expense Ratio %
2.65	2.17	1.86	1.38	1.19	1.48	1.71	1.19	1.19	1.26	1.16	1.71	Income Ratio %
145	145	111	130	130	115	150	151	102	122	130	134	Turnover Rate %
652	1,548	2,419	2,083	1,605	1,516	1,929	1,700	2,051	2,346	2,282	2,585	Net Assets $mil

Rating and Risk

Time Period	Load-Adj Return %	Morningstar Rtn vs Cat	Morningstar Risk vs Cat	Morningstar Risk-Adj Rating
1 Yr	18.51			
3 Yr	12.49	Avg	-Avg	★★★
5 Yr	9.91	+Avg	-Avg	★★★★
10 Yr	10.88	+Avg	Avg	★★★★
Incept	12.78			

Other Measures	Standard Index S&P 500	Best Fit Index S&P 500
Alpha	3.0	3.0
Beta	0.84	0.84
R-Squared	84	84
Standard Deviation	6.31	
Mean	12.49	
Sharpe Ratio	1.40	

Portfolio Analysis 09-30-06

Share change since 06-06 Total Stocks:88

	Sector	PE	Tot Ret%	% Assets
⊖ Bank of America Corporat	Financial	12.4	20.68	3.67
⊕ Kimberly-Clark Corporati	Goods	22.7	17.55	3.58
⊕ Beckman Coulter, Inc.	Health	33.7	6.21	2.74
⊖ Freddie Mac	Financial	23.3	7.06	2.56
⊖ American International G	Financial	17.0	6.05	2.56
⊖ Equitable Resources, Inc	Energy	21.8	16.51	2.47
⊕ SunTrust Banks, Inc.	Financial	14.1	19.81	2.43
⊖ International Flavors &	Ind Mtrls	23.0	49.66	2.38
⊕ H.J. Heinz Company	Goods	29.0	37.89	2.17
⊕ HCA, Inc.	Health			2.07
⊖ Intel Corporation	Hardware	21.0	-17.18	2.04
⊕ ExxonMobil Corporation	Energy	11.1	39.07	1.98
☼ AT&T, Inc.	Telecom	18.2	51.59	1.97
⊕ SPDRs	—			1.96
⊖ Fannie Mae	Financial		24.34	1.88
⊕ General Electric Company	Ind Mtrls	20.0	9.35	1.85
⊕ Fifth Third Bancorp	Financial	15.4	12.99	1.83
⊕ Dollar General Corporati	Consumer	17.3	-14.94	1.75
⊖ Kraft Foods, Inc.	Goods	18.0	30.52	1.64
⊖ Anheuser-Busch Companies	Goods	18.8	17.41	1.58

Current Investment Style

Value Blnd Growth — Large Mid Small

Market Cap	%
Giant	35.9
Large	31.4
Mid	28.1
Small	3.9
Micro	0.8

Avg $mil: 23,933

Value Measures		Rel Category
Price/Earnings	15.09	1.10
Price/Book	2.45	1.10
Price/Sales	1.39	1.07
Price/Cash Flow	2.69	0.40
Dividend Yield %	2.46	1.06

Growth Measures	%	Rel Category
Long-Term Erngs	10.05	0.97
Book Value	6.88	0.87
Sales	9.39	1.04
Cash Flow	3.24	0.53
Historical Erngs	7.41	0.46

Profitability	%	Rel Category
Return on Equity	18.55	1.03
Return on Assets	8.78	0.90
Net Margin	12.10	0.93

Sector Weightings	% of Stocks	Rel S&P 500	3 Year High	Low
☎ Info	9.14	0.46		
🖥 Software	0.47	0.14	3	0
💻 Hardware	4.80	0.52	5	2
🎙 Media	0.38	0.10	6	0
📱 Telecom	3.49	0.99	4	2
☞ Service	45.47	0.98		
🏥 Health	10.49	0.87	12	5
🛒 Consumer	5.92	0.77	10	2
💼 Business	3.80	0.90	11	1
💲 Financial	25.26	1.13	27	21
🏭 Mfg	45.38	1.34		
🏠 Goods	18.29	2.14	21	14
🏭 Ind Mtrls	12.88	1.08	15	9
🔋 Energy	7.89	0.81	10	6
💡 Utilities	6.32	1.81	8	3

Composition

		%
● Cash		5.0
● Stocks		95.0
● Bonds		0.0
○ Other		0.0
Foreign		1.9
(% of Stock)		

Morningstar's Take by Christopher Davis 11-20-06

American Century Value could take a cue from another member of its family, but it's still a worthwhile choice.

Like sibling American Century Large Company Value, this offering employs a strict valuation discipline, screening for the cheapest stocks in their investment universes. This fund, though, owns more mid-caps, and its turnover is much higher. Large Company Value lead manager Chuck Ritter trades modestly and generally sticks with his picks until valuations rise well above historical norms, which keeps turnover low. By contrast, this fund's managers trade more rapidly, adding to their holdings on declines while quickly trimming appreciating picks. That tack results in relatively high turnover: The fund's 134% annual turnover rate is more than twice the large-value average.

To be sure, the underlying rationale for all that trading makes intuitive sense. After all, you'd want to own more of a stock when it's cheaper and less of it once it gets expensive. But management's high sensitivity to short-term stock price movements has downsides. For one, trading stocks isn't free, and high turnover racks up transaction costs. It also can lead to heavy taxable gains, which historically have taken a big bite out of the fund's pretax returns. Finally, management's trading strategy puts the fund in closer competition with hedge funds and other short-term investors, which have proliferated in recent years. Looking ahead, we worry that this trend could diminish the fund's edge.

That said, we think the fund is still appealing. Management is very experienced and has executed its strategy consistently all along. It's also delivered solid long-term results, and despite a slug of mid- and small caps, has kept volatility below average. Lackluster tax efficiency means this offering is best held in nontaxable accounts, but overall, it's a respectable option. The fund isn't as appealing, though, for new investors, who must buy it through higher-cost A shares.

Address:	4500 Main Street Kansas City MO 64111 800-345-2021
Web Address:	www.americancentury.com
Inception:	09-01-93
Advisor:	American Century Investment MGMT Inc.
Subadvisor:	None
NTF Plans:	Fidelity Retail-NTF, Schwab OneSource

Minimum Purchase:	$2500 Add: $50 IRA: $0
Min Auto Inv Plan:	$2500 Add: $50
Sales Fees:	No-load
Management Fee:	1.00% mx./0.85% mn.
Actual Fees:	Mgt:0.99% Dist:—
Expense Projections:	3Yr:$314 5Yr:$545 10Yr:$1208
Income Distrib:	Quarterly

MORNINGSTAR® Funds 500

AmCent Veedot Inv

	Ticker	Load	NAV	Yield	Total Assets	Mstar Category
	AMVIX	None	$6.43	0.0%	$162 mil	Mid-Cap Growth

Governance and Management

Stewardship Grade: C

Portfolio Manager(s)

In February 2004, Jim Stowers III relinquished management duties to comanager John Small, whom he worked with since this fund's 1999 inception. Small worked closely with Stowers, managing the fund on a day-to-day basis from the start.

Strategy

Like all growth-oriented American Century offerings, this fund uses quantitative models to identify a universe of companies whose earnings-growth or revenue-growth rates are increasing. But management then employs technical analysis to home in on stocks with upward price momentum. Top holdings are typically kept to less than 2% of assets to minimize the risk of individual blowups, but the fund has no limits on sector concentration. It can invest in stocks in any market-cap and valuation range, so its holdings span the Morningstar Style Box.

Historical Profile

Return	Average
Risk	Average
Rating	★★★ Neutral

	91%	95%	98%	99%	99%	100%	100%	98%

Investment Style
Equity
Stock %

▼ Manager Change
▽ Partial Manager Change

14.0
12.0
Growth of $10,000
■ Investment Values of Fund
— Investment Values of S&P 500
10.0

6.0

Performance Quartile (within Category)

	1995	1996	1997	1998	1999	2000	2001	2002	2003	2004	2005	2006	History
	—	—	—	—	5.92	5.84	4.66	3.63	5.17	5.54	5.84	6.43	NAV
	—	—	—	—	18.40*	-1.35	-20.21	-22.10	42.42	7.16	5.42	10.10	Total Return %
	—	—	—	—	—	7.75	-8.32	0.00	13.74	-3.72	0.51	-5.69	+/-S&P 500
	—	—	—	—	—	10.40	-0.06	5.31	-0.29	-8.32	-6.68	-0.56	+/-Russ MG
	—	—	—	—	—	0.00	0.00	0.00	0.00	0.00	0.00	0.00	Income Return %
	—	—	—	—	—	-1.35	-20.21	-22.10	42.42	7.16	5.42	10.10	Capital Return %
	—	—	—	—	—	48	57	33	22	92	82	40	Total Rtn % Rank Cat
	—	—	—	—	0.00	0.00	0.00	0.00	0.00	0.00	0.00	0.00	Income $
	—	—	—	—	0.00	0.00	0.00	0.00	0.00	0.00	0.00	0.00	Capital Gains $
	—	—	—	—	—	1.50	1.50	1.50	1.50	1.30	1.50	—	Expense Ratio %
	—	—	—	—	—	-0.92	-0.09	-0.31	-0.68	-0.37	-0.51	—	Income Ratio %
	—	—	—	—	—	250	410	330	415	344	399	—	Turnover Rate %
	—	—	—	—	73	343	245	175	236	232	179	152	Net Assets $mil

Performance 12-31-06

	1st Qtr	2nd Qtr	3rd Qtr	4th Qtr	Total
2002	2.58	-8.58	-14.42	-2.94	-22.10
2003	-3.03	20.74	7.53	13.13	42.42
2004	2.51	-0.38	-5.11	10.58	7.16
2005	-4.33	2.64	6.99	0.34	5.42
2006	11.82	-7.81	-1.66	8.61	10.10

Trailing	Total Return%	+/- S&P 500	+/- Russ MG	%Rank Cat	Growth of $10,000
3 Mo	8.61	1.91	1.66	18	10,861
6 Mo	6.81	-5.93	-1.09	37	10,681
1 Yr	10.10	-5.69	-0.56	40	11,010
3 Yr Avg	7.54	-2.90	-5.19	85	12,437
5 Yr Avg	6.65	0.46	-1.57	46	13,798
10 Yr Avg	—	—	—		—
15 Yr Avg	—	—	—		—

Tax Analysis	Tax-Adj Rtn%	%Rank Cat	Tax-Cost Rat	%Rank Cat
3 Yr (estimated)	6.82	81	0.00	1
5 Yr (estimated)	6.65	37	0.00	1
10 Yr (estimated)	—	—	—	—

Potential Capital Gain Exposure: -31% of assets

Morningstar's Take by Christopher Davis 12-13-06

American Century Veedot may need the human touch.

This offering employs a two-pronged strategy that blends American Century's longstanding reliance on fundamental analysis with models that focus on stock-price momentum. Manager John Small uses quantitative screens that first look for companies with accelerating earnings and revenues. He then whittles down the universe further using technical analysis, a study of stock-market action. The models look to relative strength and other technical measures to identify stocks whose price trends are on the upswing.

This isn't the only American Century fund that marries fundamental and technical analysis. But it's the only one with a purely quantitative approach. Siblings American Century Vista and Heritage also screen for instances of improving earnings and strong price momentum, but in both instances, management also looks ahead to assess whether or not a good story has legs. While that's led the

funds to big winners, more importantly, it has helped keep them out of trouble. Vista, for instance, outperformed in the early 2000s' bear market in part because it began ratcheting down its tech stake by mid-2000.

This fund's quant-driven strategy has done a good job spotting companies and stocks on the upswing, but it's not as adept in spotting problem areas before they happen. And while incorporating price momentum in the process is supposed to improve the timing of buy and sell decisions, the fund's success in that regard has been mixed. In 2005, for example, the fund's models rightly homed in on rallying energy stocks, but it also emphasized faltering technology stocks to its detriment.

All told, this fund's long-term record is middling. And its fast-trading, momentum-driven strategy is one that investors have had a tough time getting right historically. This offering has yet to prove its worth, so we'd stay away.

Rating and Risk

Time Period	Load-Adj Return %	Morningstar Rtn vs Cat	Morningstar Risk vs Cat	Morningstar Risk-Adj Rating
1 Yr	7.90			
3 Yr	6.82	-Avg	+Avg	★★
5 Yr	6.65	Avg	Avg	★★★
10 Yr	—	—	—	
Incept	3.61			

Other Measures	Standard Index S&P 500	Best Fit Index Russ 2000 Gr
Alpha	-7.2	-1.8
Beta	1.75	0.86
R-Squared	71	91
Standard Deviation	14.23	
Mean	7.54	
Sharpe Ratio	0.36	

Portfolio Analysis 09-30-06

Share change since 06-06 Total Stocks:107	Sector	PE	Tot Ret%	% Assets
Technitrol, Inc.	Ind Mtrls	19.2	41.82	1.97
The Geo Group, Inc.	Business	58.2	145.44	1.92
Tempur-Pedic Internation	Consumer	16.8	77.91	1.41
AT&T, Inc.	Telecom	18.2	51.59	1.40
WellCare Health Plans, I	Health	30.9	68.67	1.36
FactSet Research Systems	Business	33.8	37.91	1.32
Gilead Sciences, Inc.	Health	40.6	23.51	1.29
Cisco Systems, Inc.	Hardware	30.1	59.64	1.26
Capital Trust, Inc. A	Financial	13.6	85.85	1.25
Volvo AB ADR	Ind Mtrls	15.3	51.75	1.23
Triad Guaranty Inc.	Financial	12.5	24.73	1.22
⊖ Heico Corporation	Ind Mtrls	33.5	50.48	1.11
Healthways, Inc.	Health	50.4	5.44	1.07
Luminent Mortgage Capita	Financial	—	42.14	1.07
☼ First Marblehead Corpora	Financial	14.2	152.13	1.05
Movado Group, Inc.	Goods	19.5	60.15	1.05
Ralcorp Holdings, Inc.	Goods	22.6	27.51	1.04
Entertainment Properties	Financial	23.1	51.98	1.02
Belden CDT, Inc.	Hardware	26.9	60.98	1.01
Bank of America Corporat	Financial	12.4	20.68	0.97

Current Investment Style

Value Blnd Growth — Large Mid Small

	Market Cap	%
	Giant	7.2
	Large	19.1
	Mid	26.1
	Small	37.2
	Micro	10.4
	Avg $mil:	2,932

Value Measures		Rel Category
Price/Earnings	15.75	0.77
Price/Book	2.49	0.78
Price/Sales	1.37	0.78
Price/Cash Flow	9.93	0.87
Dividend Yield %	1.15	1.83

Growth Measures	%	Rel Category
Long-Term Erngs	13.82	0.85
Book Value	3.66	0.29
Sales	11.06	1.11
Cash Flow	14.43	0.78
Historical Erngs	14.48	0.58

Profitability	%	Rel Category
Return on Equity	15.49	0.86
Return on Assets	7.83	0.84
Net Margin	12.64	1.09

Sector Weightings	% of Stocks	Rel S&P 500	3 Year High	Low
⟳ Info	23.48	1.17		
▣ Software	3.70	1.07	10	3
▣ Hardware	12.90	1.40	21	7
▣ Media	1.73	0.46	2	0
▣ Telecom	5.15	1.47	5	1
☞ Service	47.05	1.02		
▣ Health	16.65	1.38	17	8
▣ Consumer	5.00	0.65	12	5
▣ Business	9.03	2.13	13	7
▣ Financial	16.37	0.74	22	9
▣ Mfg	29.48	0.87		
▣ Goods	5.81	0.68	9	3
▣ Ind Mtrls	18.75	1.57	22	10
▣ Energy	4.06	0.41	19	4
▣ Utilities	0.86	0.25	5	0

Composition

- ● Cash 1.9
- ● Stocks 98.1
- ● Bonds 0.0
- ● Other 0.0
- Foreign 13.1 (% of Stock)

Address:	4500 Main Street Kansas City MO 64111 800-345-2021
Web Address:	www.americancentury.com
Inception:	11-30-99 *
Advisor:	American Century Investment MGMT Inc.
Subadvisor:	None
NTF Plans:	Schwab OneSource

Minimum Purchase:	$2500	Add: $50	IRA: $2500
Min Auto Inv Plan:	$2500	Add: $50	
Sales Fees:	No-load, 2.00%R		
Management Fee:	1.25% mx./1.00% mn.		
Actual Fees:	Mgt:1.25%	Dist: —	
Expense Projections:	3Yr:$618	5Yr:$683	10Yr:$1503
Income Distrib:	Annually		

AmCent Vista Inv

	Ticker	Load	NAV	Yield	Total Assets	Mstar Category
	TWCVX	None	$17.11	0.0%	$2,362 mil	Mid-Cap Growth

Governance and Management

Stewardship Grade: C

Portfolio Manager(s)

Experienced. Comanager Glenn Fogle has been a member of this fund's team since 1993. David Hollond joined the team as an analyst in 1998 and became comanager in March 2004 when David Rose, who had worked on the fund since February 2001, left. Analysts Brad Eixman and Matthew Dennis round out the team.

Strategy

This fund applies American Century's earnings-acceleration strategy to the mid-cap universe. Management uses models to screen for companies with improving prospects, looking primarily at earnings-growth rates, but it also considers relative price strength. It researches companies to determine which can keep up earnings growth. The fund holds between 60 and 90 names, often stashing a good amount of assets in top holdings. If management finds several companies with accelerating earnings in a particular area, it will often make rather large sector bets.

Performance 12-31-06

	1st Qtr	2nd Qtr	3rd Qtr	4th Qtr	Total
2002	0.36	-6.37	-10.93	-5.49	-20.90
2003	0.11	18.32	6.54	13.18	42.82
2004	8.61	1.17	-6.10	12.21	15.79
2005	0.48	-1.30	9.31	0.44	8.88
2006	9.99	-3.05	-6.11	8.92	9.05

Trailing	Total Return%	+/- S&P 500	+/- Russ MG	%Rank Cat	Growth of $10,000
3 Mo	8.92	2.22	1.97	15	10,892
6 Mo	2.26	-10.48	-5.64	84	10,226
1 Yr	9.05	-6.74	-1.61	47	10,905
3 Yr Avg	11.20	0.76	-1.53	46	13,750
5 Yr Avg	9.21	3.02	0.99	20	15,535
10 Yr Avg	6.69	-1.73	-1.93	71	19,109
15 Yr Avg	8.16	-2.48	-1.97	65	32,434

Tax Analysis	Tax-Adj Rtn%	%Rank Cat	Tax-Cost Rat	%Rank Cat
3 Yr (estimated)	11.15	32	0.04	3
5 Yr (estimated)	9.18	13	0.03	3
10 Yr (estimated)	5.55	65	1.07	36

Potential Capital Gain Exposure: 21% of assets

Morningstar's Take by Christopher Davis 12-11-06

American Century Vista pulls off its high-wire act well.

The path to long-term success in investing has been paved with many different strategies, but there's one lesson worth gleaning from them all: You can't beat the market by imitating it. Managers Glenn Fogle and David Hollond wouldn't disagree. They are no slaves to benchmarks or peer group comparisons. For example, the fund's telecom weighting accounts for 17% of assets, versus just 3% for the typical mid-growth offering.

The fund's portfolio stems from a strategy that's just as bold. The managers seek instances where earnings are not only accelerating but stock prices are rising, too. Their reliance on the latter means they gravitate toward pricier fare--the portfolio's aggregate valuations are well above the category norm. And because they trade furiously in response to fluctuating prices, turnover is sky-high, clocking in at 284% last year.

Fogle says his strategy is well grounded in academic studies demonstrating that stocks with rising stock prices keep going up. But the same studies point out that profiting from these trends is difficult because it requires a lot of trading, leading to high transaction costs that eat into returns and additional tax headaches. Here, however, trading costs have been restrained and are on the decline, accounting for 0.4% of assets at last count. And the managers' tax-loss selling and avoidance of short-term gains has led to good tax efficiency.

Of course, mindlessly following the crowd can lead one off a cliff. But management's focus on the fundamentals has helped it stay away from trouble while leading it to big winners when stocks are rallying. The fund's strategy doesn't work well when the market's winds shift abruptly--it badly lagged in 2006's third quarter, for example--but no approach works all the time. For those looking to add some punch to a diversified portfolio, we think this offering is a worthwhile choice.

Address:	4500 Main Street
	Kansas City MO 64111
	800-345-2021
Web Address:	www.americancentury.com
Inception:	11-25-83
Advisor:	American Century Investment MGMT Inc.
Subadvisor:	None
NTF Plans:	Fidelity Retail-NTF, Schwab OneSource

Minimum Purchase:	$2500	Add: $50	IRA: $2500
Min Auto Inv Plan:	$2500	Add: $50	
Sales Fees:	No-load		
Management Fee:	1.00%		
Actual Fees:	Mgt:1.00%	Dist: —	
Expense Projections:	3Yr:$318	5Yr:$551	10Yr:$1219
Income Distrib:	Annually		

Historical Profile

Return	Average
Risk	Average
Rating	★★★ Neutral

												Investment Style
95%	97%	96%	93%	91%		99%	98%	99%	97%			Equity Stock %

▼ Manager Change
▽ Partial Manager Change

Growth of $10,000
■ Investment Values of Fund
— Investment Values of S&P 500

Performance Quartile (within Category)

1995	1996	1997	1998	1999	2000	2001	2002	2003	2004	2005	2006	History
14.60	14.51	12.42	10.65	22.21	15.33	11.10	8.78	12.54	14.52	15.81	17.11	NAV
46.13	7.56	-8.68	-14.25	119.11	-0.98	-27.59	-20.90	42.82	15.79	8.88	9.05	Total Return %
8.55	-15.40	-42.04	-42.83	98.07	8.12	-15.70	1.20	14.14	4.91	3.97	-6.74	+/-S&P 500
12.15	-9.92	-31.22	-32.11	67.82	10.77	-7.44	6.51	0.11	0.31	-3.22	-1.61	+/-Russ MG
0.00	0.00	0.00	0.00	0.00	0.00	0.00	0.00	0.00	0.00	0.00	0.00	Income Return %
46.13	7.56	-8.68	-14.25	119.11	-0.98	-27.59	-20.90	42.82	15.79	8.88	9.05	Capital Return %
13	92	99	98	11	46	77	27	21	33	63	47	Total Rtn % Rank Cat
0.00	0.00	0.00	0.00	0.00	0.00	0.00	0.00	0.00	0.00	0.00	0.00	Income $
1.03	1.18	0.80	0.00	0.95	6.33	0.00	0.00	0.00	0.00	0.00	0.13	Capital Gains $
0.98	0.99	1.00	1.00	1.00	1.00	1.00	1.00	1.00	1.00	1.00	—	Expense Ratio %
-0.60	-0.70	-0.73	-0.42	-0.40	-0.65	0.31	-0.34	-0.57	-0.48	-0.26	—	Income Ratio %
89	91	96	229	187	135	290	293	280	255	284	—	Turnover Rate %
1,775	2,236	1,651	955	1,800	2,081	1,251	907	1,295	1,568	1,992	2,031	Net Assets $mil

Rating and Risk

Time Period	Load-Adj Return %	Morningstar Rtn vs Cat	Morningstar Risk vs Cat	Morningstar Risk-Adj Rating
1 Yr	9.05			
3 Yr	11.20	Avg	+Avg	★★★
5 Yr	9.21	+Avg	-Avg	★★★★
10 Yr	6.69	-Avg	+Avg	★★
Incept	10.58			

Other Measures	Standard Index S&P 500	Best Fit Index S&P Mid 400
Alpha	-2.7	-3.8
Beta	1.59	1.26
R-Squared	60	85
Standard Deviation	14.08	
Mean	11.20	
Sharpe Ratio	0.60	

Portfolio Analysis 09-30-06

Share change since 06-06 Total Stocks:80	Sector	PE	Tot Ret%	% Assets
⊕ NII Holdings, Inc.	Telecom	45.9	47.53	5.36
⊕ Thermo Electron Corp.	Health	37.4	50.32	3.41
⊕ America Movil SA ADR	Telecom	27.7	55.53	3.16
⊕ Alliance Data Systems Co	Business	29.1	75.48	3.12
⊖ McDermott International	Energy	23.4	71.02	3.04
⊕ Monsanto Company	Ind Mtrls	39.8	36.78	2.70
⊕ American Tower Corporati	Telecom	—	37.57	2.67
⊕ SBA Communications Corpo	Telecom	—	53.63	2.61
⊕ Pharmaceutical Product D	Health	24.3	4.26	2.28
⊖ Precision Castparts Corp	Ind Mtrls	25.4	51.40	2.28
✹ Leap Wireless Internatio	Telecom	81.7	57.00	2.23
⊖ Covance, Inc.	Health	28.4	21.34	2.13
✹ Nintendo	Goods	—	—	2.10
✹ Humana	Health	21.8	1.80	2.07
✹ American Eagle Outfitter	Consumer	21.6	105.48	2.04
⊖ Las Vegas Sands, Inc.	Consumer	75.7	126.70	1.93
⊕ BE Aerospace	Ind Mtrls	15.3	16.73	1.91
✹ Kohl's Corporation	Consumer	22.6	40.80	1.91
⊖ Tetra Technologies, Inc.	Energy	18.9	67.63	1.58
⊕ Akamai Technologies, Inc	Software	26.0	166.53	1.57

Current Investment Style

Value Blnd Growth		Market Cap	%
	Large Mid Small	Giant	5.4
		Large	26.6
		Mid	58.5
		Small	9.5
		Micro	0.0
		Avg $mil: 7,073	

Value Measures		Rel Category
Price/Earnings	22.03	1.07
Price/Book	3.34	1.04
Price/Sales	2.07	1.18
Price/Cash Flow	12.36	1.08
Dividend Yield %	0.50	0.79

Growth Measures	%	Rel Category
Long-Term Erngs	16.18	1.00
Book Value	8.86	0.70
Sales	-9.38	NMF
Cash Flow	14.47	0.78
Historical Erngs	19.28	0.77

Profitability	%	Rel Category
Return on Equity	17.20	0.96
Return on Assets	8.16	0.87
Net Margin	9.64	0.83

Sector Weightings

	% of Stocks	Rel S&P 500	3 Year High	Low
⊙ Info	28.43	1.42		
Software	4.37	1.27	14	1
Hardware	6.31	0.68	14	3
Media	0.00	0.00	2	0
Telecom	17.75	5.06	18	2
⊂ Service	47.53	1.03		
Health	17.37	1.44	26	9
Consumer	11.74	1.53	32	7
Business	8.23	1.95	16	2
Financial	10.19	0.46	14	2
⊔ Mfg	24.04	0.71		
Goods	4.44	0.52	12	1
Ind Mtrls	12.18	1.02	27	2
Energy	5.84	0.60	15	5
Utilities	1.58	0.45	4	0

Composition

● Cash	3.3	
● Stocks	96.7	
● Bonds	0.0	
● Other	0.0	
Foreign (% of Stock)	9.6	

Morningstar® Funds 500

Amer Funds Amcap A

	Ticker	Load	NAV	Yield	Total Assets	Mstar Category
	AMCPX	5.75%	$20.02	0.8%	$25,237 mil	Large Growth

Governance and Management

Stewardship Grade: B

Portfolio Manager(s)

The fund is managed by a very seasoned group of portfolio counselors. The average member boasts more than two decades of experience with advisor Capital Reserach and Management. A talented group of 22 analysts also runs a slice of the fund. The firm has reorganized its investment staff into two groups, which has reduced the fund's portfolio manager lineup from five members to four.

Strategy

The fund favors established companies with proven records of steady, above-average growth. It owns its share of highfliers, but it's also willing to scoop up names that aren't very common in other growth portfolios. The resulting portfolio is well diversified across industries and individual names, and a usually large cash stake further keeps a lid on risk.

Historical Profile
Return: Above Avg
Risk: Low
Rating: ★★★★ Above Avg

Investment Style: Equity / Stock %

Stock % by year: 78% 82% 73% 71% 69% 78% 81% 83% 84%

▼ Manager Change
▽ Partial Manager Change

Growth of $10,000
— Investment Values of Fund
— Investment Values of S&P 500

Scale: 38.0 / 31.0 / 24.0 / 17.0 / 10.0

Performance Quartile (within Category)

	1995	1996	1997	1998	1999	2000	2001	2002	2003	2004	2005	2006	History
	13.67	14.16	15.65	17.71	18.78	17.78	16.12	13.00	16.85	18.33	19.12	20.02	NAV
	28.71	14.16	30.55	30.02	21.78	7.50	-5.01	-18.66	29.64	9.80	6.98	8.63	Total Return %
	-8.87	-8.80	-2.81	1.44	0.74	16.60	6.88	3.44	0.96	-1.08	2.07	-7.16	+/-S&P 500
	-8.47	-8.96	0.06	-8.69	-11.38	29.92	15.41	9.22	-0.11	3.50	1.72	-0.44	+/-Russ 1000Gr
	1.47	0.90	0.73	0.85	0.58	0.59	0.49	0.15	0.02	0.26	0.50	0.82	Income Return %
	27.24	13.26	29.82	29.17	21.20	6.91	-5.50	-18.81	29.62	9.54	6.48	7.81	Capital Return %
	71	81	27	51	81	6	4	10	40	32	43	34	Total Rtn % Rank Cat
	0.17	0.12	0.10	0.13	0.10	0.11	0.09	0.02	0.00	0.04	0.09	0.16	Income $
	1.19	1.31	2.47	2.29	2.48	2.26	0.71	0.10	0.00	0.13	0.39	0.58	Capital Gains $
	0.71	0.71	0.69	0.68	0.67	0.68	0.67	0.71	0.77	0.73	0.68	0.65	Expense Ratio %
	1.16	1.16	0.81	0.62	0.70	0.72	1.18	0.58	0.25	0.11	0.36	0.66	Income Ratio %
	18	35	24	31	36	34	39	25	18	17	16	20	Turnover Rate %
	3,533	3,784	4,537	5,830	7,188	7,655	7,596	6,683	10,322	13,319	15,568	17,194	Net Assets $mil

Performance 12-31-06

	1st Qtr	2nd Qtr	3rd Qtr	4th Qtr	Total
2002	-0.31	-11.29	-14.34	7.37	-18.66
2003	-0.85	15.62	2.75	10.06	29.64
2004	2.61	1.85	-3.07	8.39	9.80
2005	-2.78	3.14	2.37	4.22	6.98
2006	3.24	-2.58	2.52	5.36	8.63

Trailing	Total Return%	+/- S&P 500	+/- Russ 1000Gr	%Rank Cat	Growth of $10,000
3 Mo	5.36	-1.34	-0.57	52	10,536
6 Mo	8.01	-4.73	-2.09	56	10,801
1 Yr	8.63	-7.16	-0.44	34	10,863
3 Yr Avg	8.47	-1.97	1.60	30	12,762
5 Yr Avg	6.12	-0.07	3.43	12	13,458
10 Yr Avg	11.00	2.58	5.56	4	28,394
15 Yr Avg	11.26	0.62	3.24	10	49,555

Tax Analysis	Tax-Adj Rtn%	%Rank Cat	Tax-Cost Rat	%Rank Cat
3 Yr (estimated)	5.86	58	0.46	30
5 Yr (estimated)	4.54	20	0.31	32
10 Yr (estimated)	8.80	6	1.40	70

Potential Capital Gain Exposure: 23% of assets

Rating and Risk

Time Period	Load-Adj Return %	Morningstar Rtn vs Cat	Morningstar Risk vs Cat	Morningstar Risk-Adj Rating
1 Yr	2.39			
3 Yr	6.35	Avg	Low	★★★
5 Yr	4.87	+Avg	-Avg	★★★★
10 Yr	10.35	High	Low	★★★★★
Incept	12.19			

Other Measures	Standard Index S&P 500	Best Fit Index Russ MG
Alpha	-1.6	-0.7
Beta	0.98	0.62
R-Squared	83	91
Standard Deviation	7.38	
Mean	8.47	
Sharpe Ratio	0.71	

Morningstar's Take by Paul Herbert 11-15-06

Amcap Fund remains a solid large-growth offering, despite some uncertainty.

This fund is rather selective. The managers and analysts who choose stocks here look for firms that have consistently delivered strong growth in the past and can keep that up for a half-decade or more into the future. And, they want to buy these companies when their growth prospects aren't fully appreciated by other investors. They tend to hang on to stocks for a while, too, which sets them apart in the large-growth group.

The fund hasn't been wanting for new ideas lately. Some growth favorites that became quite cheap earlier in the year now occupy large positions in the fund's portfolio. The managers picked up shares of giant chipmaker Intel earlier this year. Intel's rival, Advanced Micro Devices, has turned out some winning designs in recent years. As a result, some investors have shunned Intel's shares, creating a buying opportunity for those confident in Intel's strong brand and commitment to research.

The fund also added to its stake in managed-care firm UnitedHealth Group. Its stock price swooned upon news of questionable options-granting policies for the firm's executives. New bosses are in place, and the firm's scale and operational performance give it appeal.

Shareholders have clearly benefited from this emphasis on cheap, proven growers. In recent years and over time, it has been able to consistently beat the large-growth pack. And it has also done so with less volatility, which owes to both its stock-selection approach and management's willingness to hold some cash, currently around 14% of assets.

Though we like what this fund has to offer, American Funds' rapid asset growth in recent years is a concern. Though this fund isn't particularly bulky, it shares holdings (and managers) with some of the larger offerings, causing us to wonder if it will be able to trade positions without sacrificing performance as easily in the future.

Portfolio Analysis 09-30-06

Share change since 06-06 Total Stocks:136

	Sector	PE	Tot Ret%	% Assets
☼ Intel Corporation	Hardware	21.0	-17.18	2.63
Oracle Corporation	Software	26.7	40.38	2.47
⊕ Lowe's Companies Inc.	Consumer	15.6	-6.05	2.41
Cisco Systems, Inc.	Hardware	30.1	59.64	2.39
WellPoint, Inc.	Health	17.2	-1.38	2.18
Target	Consumer	19.3	4.65	2.16
⊕ UnitedHealth Group, Inc.	Health	20.8	-13.49	2.09
Fannie Mae	Financial	—	24.34	2.04
Google, Inc.	Business	61.5	11.00	1.75
⊕ eBay, Inc.	Consumer	40.1	-30.43	1.71
⊕ Carnival Corporation	Goods	18.7	-6.15	1.69
Capital One Financial Co	Financial	10.4	-10.97	1.63
⊖ Best Buy Co., Inc.	Consumer	19.8	13.89	1.43
⊖ Microsoft Corporation	Software	23.8	15.83	1.40
⊖ Schlumberger, Ltd.	Energy	22.3	31.07	1.39
⊖ American International G	Financial	17.0	6.05	1.33
First Data Corporation	Business	12.3	9.88	1.29
⊖ Medco Health Solutions,	Health	28.4	-4.23	1.15
⊕ Forest Laboratories, Inc	Health	22.5	24.39	1.10
⊕ Sprint Nextel Corporatio	Telecom	30.2	-10.44	1.10

Current Investment Style

Value Blnd Growth — Large Mid Small (Large Growth box marked)

Market Cap	%
Giant	33.1
Large	42.3
Mid	22.8
Small	1.8
Micro	0.0
Avg $mil:	27,695

Value Measures		Rel Category
Price/Earnings	17.45	0.91
Price/Book	2.59	0.78
Price/Sales	1.49	0.77
Price/Cash Flow	5.74	0.50
Dividend Yield %	1.02	0.99

Growth Measures	%	Rel Category
Long-Term Erngs	13.94	0.97
Book Value	13.39	1.15
Sales	12.94	1.12
Cash Flow	13.66	0.81
Historical Erngs	19.72	0.86

Profitability	%	Rel Category
Return on Equity	19.07	0.94
Return on Assets	10.35	0.94
Net Margin	13.29	0.93

Sector Weightings	% of Stocks	Rel S&P 500	3 Year High	Low
↻ Info	22.12	1.11		
Software	5.26	1.52	7	2
Hardware	10.52	1.14	13	7
Media	3.61	0.95	6	3
Telecom	2.73	0.78	3	1
⊂ Service	56.03	1.21		
Health	19.34	1.60	21	17
Consumer	17.42	2.28	21	17
Business	8.90	2.10	11	8
Financial	10.37	0.47	13	10
⊐ Mfg	21.86	0.65		
Goods	9.75	1.14	10	7
Ind Mtrls	5.06	0.42	7	4
Energy	6.85	0.70	8	4
Utilities	0.20	0.06	1	0

Composition

● Cash	15.8
● Stocks	84.3
● Bonds	0.0
● Other	0.0
Foreign (% of Stock)	1.6

Address:	333 S Hope St - 55th FL Los Angeles CA 90071 800-421-0180
Web Address:	www.americanfunds.com
Inception:	05-01-67
Advisor:	Capital Research and Management Company
Subadvisor:	None
NTF Plans:	Federated Tr NTF

Minimum Purchase:	$250	Add: $50	IRA: $250
Min Auto Inv Plan:	$250	Add: $50	
Sales Fees:	5.75%L, 0.22%S		
Management Fee:	0.49% mx./0.29% mn.		
Actual Fees:	Mgt:0.32%	Dist:0.22%	
Expense Projections:	3Yr:$780	5Yr:$932	10Yr:$1373
Income Distrib:	Semi-Annually		

Amer Funds Amer Bal A

Ticker	Load	NAV	Yield	Total Assets	Mstar Category
ABALX	5.75%	$19.02	2.4%	$55,880 mil	Moderate Allocation

Governance and Management

Stewardship Grade: B

Portfolio Manager(s)

Like most American funds, this one is steered by a very experienced team. This fund's seven portfolio counselors have been with American Funds or affiliates for between 11 and 31 years, as of the March 2006 prospectus. The managers are backed by a seasoned and deep team of research analysts, who are also responsible for managing a portion of the fund's assets.

Strategy

This fund keeps it simple. Its management tends to invest about 60% of the fund's assets in equities, while devoting the remainder to high-quality bonds and cash. The fund's stock portfolio is broadly diversified across sectors and individual names, with a bias toward value-priced securities. The managers typically own large-cap stocks.

Performance 12-31-06

	1st Qtr	2nd Qtr	3rd Qtr	4th Qtr	Total
2002	3.47	-5.57	-11.53	8.44	-6.27
2003	-2.43	12.76	2.37	9.05	22.82
2004	2.48	0.58	-0.33	6.01	8.92
2005	-1.37	1.67	0.92	1.89	3.12
2006	2.81	-0.55	4.49	4.66	11.81

Trailing	Total Return%	+/- DJ Mod	+/- DJ US Mod	%Rank Cat	Growth of $10,000
3 Mo	4.66	-0.93	-0.01	68	10,466
6 Mo	9.35	0.56	1.45	35	10,935
1 Yr	11.81	-0.49	1.54	35	11,181
3 Yr Avg	7.89	-2.83	-1.23	59	12,559
5 Yr Avg	7.65	-2.37	0.05	17	14,457
10 Yr Avg	9.69	1.14	1.10	9	25,216
15 Yr Avg	10.44	1.23	1.05	16	44,350

Tax Analysis	Tax-Adj Rtn%	%Rank Cat	Tax-Cost Rat	%Rank Cat
3 Yr (estimated)	4.59	88	1.12	56
5 Yr (estimated)	5.25	42	1.06	64
10 Yr (estimated)	7.07	14	1.81	70

Potential Capital Gain Exposure: 14% of assets

Morningstar's Take by Gregg Wolper 12-27-06

Keep American Funds American Balanced in mind for a slim-portfolio plan.

In recent years many funds of funds have come onto the market intended for investors who'd like to get diversification without buying a lot of different funds. In some areas, this offering won't give you the very broad diversification of many of those choices; it doesn't own small-cap stocks or junk bonds, for example, and it's light on foreign issues. But its mixture of big-company stocks and higher-quality bonds can provide such a solid anchor that you wouldn't need to add many other funds in order to provide a suitably well-diversified and rewarding portfolio.

Of course, the fund's structure alone wouldn't qualify it for this role. After all, there are other moderate-allocation funds with similar makeups. It's the skill with which its managers have invested that gives it that status. Over the trailing 10-year period ending Nov. 30, 2006, the fund's return beats nearly 90% of the 149 offerings in the category that

have been around that long. And impressively, its volatility (as measured by standard deviation) over that period has been milder than the vast majority of its peers. True, its performance over the trailing three-year stretch through Dec. 26, 2006, has not been eye-catching; its return is in the middle of the pack. But in fact, that's a more-than-respectable showing, given that the type of huge blue-chip stocks that fill its equity portfolio generally have not been in investors' favor during that period.

As with other funds in American's lineup, asset growth does raise concerns here about whether it will be able to continue its fine performance. But as yet, it isn't a reason to steer away from this fund. In fact, this is still one of the category's better choices--especially if used as a high-quality core with a few topnotch supplemental funds. Its low expense ratio--which has fallen sharply in recent years--is another plus.

Address:	One Market - Steuart Tower San Francisco CA 94105 800-325-3590
Web Address:	www.americanfunds.com
Inception:	01-03-33
Advisor:	Capital Research and Management Company
Subadvisor:	None
NTF Plans:	Federated Tr NTF

Minimum Purchase:	$250	Add: $50	IRA: $250
Min Auto Inv Plan:	$50	Add: $50	
Sales Fees:	5.75%L, 0.25%S		
Management Fee:	0.42% mx./0.21% mn.		
Actual Fees:	Mgt:0.24%	Dist:0.25%	
Expense Projections:	3Yr:$759	5Yr:$896	10Yr:$1293
Income Distrib:	Quarterly		

Historical Profile

Return Average
Risk Below Avg
Rating ★★★ Neutral

	56%	55%	57%	58%	59%	64%	67%	66%	65%

▼ Manager Change
▽ Partial Manager Change

Growth of $10,000
■ Investment Values of Fund
— Investment Values of DJ Mod

Investment Style
Equity
Stock %

Performance Quartile (within Category)

	1995	1996	1997	1998	1999	2000	2001	2002	2003	2004	2005	2006	History
NAV	14.15	14.55	15.68	15.76	14.42	15.47	15.85	14.42	17.29	18.00	17.82	19.02	
Total Return %	27.13	13.17	21.04	11.13	3.47	15.86	8.19	-6.27	22.82	8.92	3.12	11.81	
+/-DJ Mod	7.33	2.51	9.14	-1.19	-13.86	17.53	10.99	0.50	-4.56	-4.05	-3.87	-0.49	
+/-DJ US Mod	2.36	1.83	1.84	-1.26	-9.38	11.42	8.03	4.27	-1.24	-2.25	-2.88	1.54	
Income Return %	4.74	4.03	3.93	3.63	3.63	3.94	3.68	2.74	2.59	2.10	2.24	2.66	
Capital Return %	22.39	9.14	17.11	7.50	-0.16	11.92	4.51	-9.01	20.23	6.82	0.88	9.15	
Total Rtn % Rank Cat	41	64	37	66	85	5	3	7	27	50	80	35	
Income $	0.56	0.56	0.56	0.56	0.56	0.56	0.56	0.43	0.37	0.36	0.40	0.47	
Capital Gains $	0.47	0.85	1.30	1.05	1.30	0.58	0.30	0.02	0.00	0.44	0.34	0.41	
Expense Ratio %	0.67	0.67	0.65	0.63	0.66	0.69	0.68	0.70	0.67	0.62	0.59	—	
Income Ratio %	4.38	4.01	3.74	3.57	3.59	3.93	3.26	2.79	2.38	2.23	2.31	—	
Turnover Rate %	39	44	44	54	48	16	50	41	32	25	35	—	
Net Assets $mil	3,048	3,941	5,036	5,881	5,981	6,042	8,915	12,405	19,951	29,162	33,009	35,294	

Rating and Risk

Time Period	Load-Adj Return %	Morningstar Rtn vs Cat	Morningstar Risk vs Cat	Morningstar Risk-Adj Rating
1 Yr	5.38			
3 Yr	5.78	-Avg	Low	★★
5 Yr	6.38	Avg	+Avg	★★★
10 Yr	9.04	+Avg	-Avg	★★★★
Incept	6.55			

Other Measures	Standard Index DJ Mod	Best Fit Index S&P 500
Alpha	-0.1	0.3
Beta	0.64	0.60
R-Squared	77	91
Standard Deviation	4.33	
Mean	7.89	
Sharpe Ratio	1.05	

Portfolio Analysis 09-30-06

Total Stocks:118
Share change since 06-30-06

		Sectors	P/E Ratio	YTD Return %	% Net Assets
⊕	Microsoft Corporation	Software	23.8	0.23	2.73
	Wal-Mart Stores, Inc.	Consumer	16.9	1.78	2.08
⊖	Oracle Corporation	Software	26.7	4.20	1.86
⊕	Altria Group, Inc.	Goods	16.3	2.52	1.67
⊕	IBM	Hardware	17.1	1.80	1.59
⊖	Citigroup, Inc.	Financial	13.1	-1.17	1.52
	General Electric Company	Ind Mtrls	20.0	0.91	1.48
⊕	Chevron Corporation	Energy	9.0	-2.83	1.44
	Berkshire Hathaway Inc. A	Financial	—	—	1.35

Total Fixed-Income:717

	Date of Maturity	Amount $000	Value $000	% Net Assets
US Treasury Note 4.25%	01-15-10	300,000	383,370	0.71
US Treasury Note 4.25%	08-15-13	385,625	377,550	0.70
FHLMC	10-01-36	324,197	325,870	0.60
US Treasury Bond 6.875%	08-15-25	233,250	291,453	0.54
US Treasury Note 5.625%	05-15-08	250,000	253,418	0.47
US Treasury Bond 8.875%	08-15-17	180,000	243,196	0.45
GNMA	08-20-36	204,029	205,894	0.38
US Treasury Bond 5.25%	02-15-29	153,000	161,822	0.30
US Treasury Bond 7.875%	02-15-21	113,000	148,560	0.28

Equity Style
Style: Blend
Size: Large-Cap

Value Measures		Rel Category
Price/Earnings	14.74	0.96
Price/Book	2.55	1.03
Price/Sales	1.41	1.03
Price/Cash Flow	6.35	0.78
Dividend Yield %	2.15	1.11

Growth Measures	%	Rel Category
Long-Term Erngs	10.97	0.94
Book Value	8.14	0.94
Sales	11.28	1.27
Cash Flow	8.57	0.87
Historical Erngs	15.84	0.89

Market Cap %			
Giant	66.5	Small	0.0
Large	32.0	Micro	0.0
Mid	1.5	Avg $mil:	72,718

Fixed-Income Style
Duration: Interm-Term
Quality: High

Avg Eff Duration [1]	4.3 Yrs
Avg Eff Maturity	—
Avg Credit Quality	AA
Avg Wtd Coupon	5.51%

[1]figure provided by fund as of 09-30-06

Sector Weightings	% of Stocks	Rel DJ Mod	3 Year High Low
⚙ Info	26.67	—	
🖳 Software	7.11	—	7 2
🖥 Hardware	12.66	—	13 9
🎬 Media	2.74	—	4 2
📞 Telecom	4.16	—	7 4
☎ Service	39.80	—	
🏥 Health	11.87	—	13 11
🛒 Consumer	9.00	—	12 8
🏢 Business	3.09	—	4 3
💲 Financial	15.84	—	19 16
🏭 Mfg	33.53	—	
🚗 Goods	8.44	—	11 8
🔩 Ind Mtrls	15.79	—	17 14
🔋 Energy	8.58	—	10 7
🔌 Utilities	0.72	—	2 1

Composition

		%
●	Cash	7.0
●	Stocks	64.5
●	Bonds	28.0
○	Other	0.5
	Foreign (% of Stock)	10.5

MORNINGSTAR® Funds 500

Amer Funds Amer Mut A

	Ticker	Load	NAV	Yield	Total Assets	Mstar Category
	AMRMX	5.75%	$29.21	1.9%	$19,359 mil	Large Value

Governance and Management

Stewardship Grade: B

Portfolio Manager(s)

As with other American Funds, this fund's managers oversee several portfolios. The five portfolio counselors on this offering boast an average of more than 25 years of investment experience with the firm. Manager James Dunton has more than 40 years of experience. The firm's research staff, which plays a vital role, is equally seasoned. Many analysts at the firm follow a career analyst track and have covered their respective industries for decades. We find it laudable that short-term performance isn't rewarded here, as investment professionals are evaluated over four-year periods.

Strategy

The fund aims to meet three goals: current income, capital growth, and conservation of principal. In pursuit of these objectives, management favors established, dividend-paying companies. And like most funds in the firm's roster, management likes to buy shares on the cheap. To smooth volatility, the fund typically has a sizable cash stake. Finally, the fund won't invest in companies that derive the majority of their revenues from tobacco or alcohol.

Performance 12-31-06

	1st Qtr	2nd Qtr	3rd Qtr	4th Qtr	Total
2002	3.62	-6.29	-15.73	7.33	-12.18
2003	-3.70	13.05	2.14	10.90	23.32
2004	1.52	1.79	0.28	6.87	10.74
2005	-0.87	1.33	2.51	1.91	4.94
2006	3.84	0.38	4.36	6.86	16.24

Trailing	Total Return%	+/- S&P 500	+/- Russ 1000 Vl	%Rank Cat	Growth of $10,000
3 Mo	6.86	0.16	-1.14	64	10,686
6 Mo	11.52	-1.22	-3.20	77	11,152
1 Yr	16.24	0.45	-6.01	74	11,624
3 Yr Avg	10.54	0.10	-4.55	80	13,507
5 Yr Avg	7.91	1.72	-2.95	56	14,632
10 Yr Avg	9.45	1.03	-1.55	36	24,669
15 Yr Avg	10.80	0.16	-2.23	54	46,569

Tax Analysis	Tax-Adj Rtn%	%Rank Cat	Tax-Cost Rat	%Rank Cat
3 Yr (estimated)	7.34	92	0.96	38
5 Yr (estimated)	5.57	79	1.00	54
10 Yr (estimated)	6.75	55	1.89	71

Potential Capital Gain Exposure: 23% of assets

Morningstar's Take by Arijit Dutta 12-27-06

For those seeking stability, American Funds American Mutual is one of the best options.

This fund has stuck with its conservative ways for decades. Since the fund debuted in 1950, its mandate has been to provide investors a smooth ride, and avoid loss of capital. Management loads the portfolio with overlooked, dividend-paying stocks (its current dividend yield of 2% is twice the large-value average). For example, top-holdings General Electric, Citigroup, and IBM have steadily increased their dividends over the years, though their stocks have languished. Also, management will prefer cash if the market doesn't field enough stocks with rich-enough dividends or cheap valuations (the portfolio's current cash stake is at 13%, while the category average is 4%). The dividend and cash cushions, along with management's preference for stocks with limited downside, fulfill the fund's twin objectives.

Indeed, the fund has delivered on its stability goal. As measured by standard deviation, both the fund's long- and short-term volatility are rock-bottom in the large-value category. Also, the fund has avoided big losses. It held up very well during the bear market, and more recently, the fund was among the least affected in the sharp market correction in May and June 2006.

While relative returns haven't been nearly as attractive here, we're not discouraged. Dividend-paying stalwarts have hardly been star performers in recent years, but management has good reason to believe that could change. Management points out that for more than two decades now, stocks overall have returned sharply more than their long-term historical average. Understandably, investors have not valued dividends in this high-return environment. If, as management thinks, and the logic of valuations is on its side, stock returns are modest in the years ahead, dividends could regain center stage. Meanwhile, the fund offers great protection from market volatility, at a very attractive expense ratio.

Address:	333 S Hope St - 55th FL
	Los Angeles CA 90071
	800-421-0180
Web Address:	www.americanfunds.com
Inception:	02-21-50
Advisor:	Capital Research and Management Company
Subadvisor:	None
NTF Plans:	Federated Tr NTF

Minimum Purchase:	$250	Add: $50	IRA: $250
Min Auto Inv Plan:	$50	Add: $50	
Sales Fees:	5.75%L, 0.22%S		
Management Fee:	0.38% mx./0.23% mn.		
Actual Fees:	Mgt:0.26%	Dist:0.22%	
Expense Projections:	3Yr:$750	5Yr:$880	10Yr:$1259
Income Distrib:	Quarterly		

Historical Profile

Return Below Avg
Risk Low
Rating ★★★ Neutral

| | 72% | 69% | 73% | 77% | 76% | 79% | 85% | 82% | 87% | Investment Style Equity Stock % |

▼ Manager Change
▽ Partial Manager Change

Growth of $10,000
■ Investment Values of Fund
— Investment Values of S&P 500

Performance Quartile (within Category)

1995	1996	1997	1998	1999	2000	2001	2002	2003	2004	2005	2006	History
24.33	25.76	29.21	29.65	23.83	23.87	24.05	20.32	24.38	26.48	26.27	29.21	NAV
31.38	16.22	26.39	14.76	-0.12	9.12	6.67	-12.18	23.32	10.74	4.94	16.24	Total Return %
-6.20	-6.74	-6.97	-13.82	-21.16	18.22	18.56	9.92	-5.36	-0.14	0.03	0.45	+/-S&P 500
-6.98	-5.42	-8.79	-0.87	-7.47	2.11	12.26	3.34	-6.71	-5.75	-2.11	-6.01	+/-Russ 1000 Vl
4.24	3.50	3.14	2.77	2.52	3.14	3.05	2.18	2.58	1.82	1.90	2.19	Income Return %
27.14	12.72	23.25	11.99	-2.64	5.98	3.62	-14.36	20.74	8.92	3.04	14.05	Capital Return %
65	80	60	32	76	54	12	9	75	59	74	Total Rtn % Rank Cat
0.84	0.84	0.80	0.80	0.74	0.74	0.72	0.52	0.52	0.44	0.50	0.57	Income $
1.15	1.61	2.48	2.93	5.04	1.25	0.65	0.31	0.09	0.05	1.01	0.71	Capital Gains $
0.59	0.59	0.58	0.56	0.57	0.59	0.59	0.60	0.62	0.60	0.56	—	Expense Ratio %
3.92	3.36	2.95	2.75	2.67	3.29	2.67	2.15	2.32	1.97	2.06	—	Income Ratio %
23	24	19	29	42	29	45	31	24	17	22	—	Turnover Rate %
6,946	7,982	9,739	10,629	9,652	8,515	9,002	8,028	10,449	12,986	14,331	16,308	Net Assets $mil

Rating and Risk

Time Period	Load-Adj Return %	Morningstar Rtn vs Cat	Morningstar Risk vs Cat	Morningstar Risk-Adj Rating
1 Yr	9.56			
3 Yr	8.38	Low	Low	★★
5 Yr	6.64	-Avg	Low	★★★
10 Yr	8.81	Avg	Low	★★★
Incept	12.36			

Other Measures	Standard Index S&P 500	Best Fit Index S&P 500
Alpha	1.9	1.9
Beta	0.73	0.73
R-Squared	92	92
Standard Deviation	5.29	
Mean	10.54	
Sharpe Ratio	1.34	

Portfolio Analysis 09-30-06

Share change since 06-06 Total Stocks:123	Sector	PE	Tot Ret%	% Assets
⊕ General Electric Company	Ind Mtrls	20.0	9.35	2.82
⊕ Citigroup, Inc.	Financial	13.1	19.55	2.35
⊖ BellSouth Corporation	Telecom	—	—	2.20
⊕ IBM	Hardware	17.1	19.77	2.12
⊕ Fannie Mae	Financial		24.34	1.76
Marathon Oil Corporation	Energy	6.1	54.68	1.75
Abbott Laboratories	Health	24.3	26.88	1.74
⊕ Microsoft Corporation	Software	23.8	15.83	1.61
Bank of America Corporat	Financial	12.4	20.68	1.48
⊕ Hewlett-Packard Company	Hardware	19.3	45.21	1.47
Eli Lilly & Company	Health	17.3	-5.16	1.41
⊖ Bristol-Myers Squibb Com	Health	23.1	19.93	1.35
ExxonMobil Corporation	Energy	11.1	39.07	1.35
Norfolk Southern Corpora	Business	14.0	13.73	1.28
United Technologies	Ind Mtrls	17.8	13.65	1.23
R.R. Donnelley & Sons Co	Business	48.2	7.19	1.22
⊖ J.P. Morgan Chase & Co.	Financial	13.6	25.60	1.22
⊕ Lowe's Companies Inc.	Consumer	15.6	-6.05	1.20
Freddie Mac	Financial	23.3	7.06	1.19
⊕ United Parcel Service, I	Business	19.7	1.76	1.17

Current Investment Style

Value Blnd Growth — Large Mid Small

Market Cap	%
Giant	45.2
Large	40.0
Mid	14.8
Small	0.0
Micro	0.0
Avg $mil:	42,079

Value Measures		Rel Category
Price/Earnings	14.29	1.04
Price/Book	2.39	1.08
Price/Sales	1.30	1.00
Price/Cash Flow	4.32	0.64
Dividend Yield %	2.53	1.09

Growth Measures	%	Rel Category
Long-Term Erngs	10.40	1.00
Book Value	7.85	0.99
Sales	9.26	1.03
Cash Flow	4.50	0.74
Historical Erngs	11.69	0.72

Profitability	%	Rel Category
Return on Equity	18.43	1.03
Return on Assets	9.25	0.94
Net Margin	12.47	0.96

Sector Weightings	% of Stocks	Rel S&P 500	3 Year High	Low
↻ Info	17.73	0.89		
Software	2.79	0.81	3	0
Hardware	7.61	0.82	8	6
Media	1.57	0.41	2	0
Telecom	5.76	1.64	8	6
☞ Service	42.78	0.93		
Health	10.55	0.87	12	9
Consumer	6.98	0.91	7	5
Business	6.51	1.54	7	4
Financial	18.74	0.84	22	18
Mfg	39.49	1.17		
Goods	7.05	0.82	10	7
Ind Mtrls	17.37	1.45	19	16
Energy	8.50	0.87	11	9
Utilities	6.57	1.88	8	6

Composition

	%
● Cash	12.7
● Stocks	87.1
● Bonds	0.0
● Other	0.3
Foreign	0.4
(% of Stock)	

Amer Funds Amer H/I A

	Ticker	Load	NAV	Yield	SEC Yield	Total Assets	Mstar Category
	AHITX	3.75%	$12.61	7.3%	6.78%	$11,996 mil	High Yield Bond

Governance and Management

Stewardship Grade: B

Portfolio Manager(s)

This fund is run by a team of managers (including David Barclay, Susan Tolson, and Abner Goldstine), each of whom is responsible for a segment of the portfolio. The managers communicate regularly and have access to vast research resources.

Strategy

The fund's management team targets issues with improving revenues and cash flows, much like stock-pickers do. The strategy has been capably executed over the long stretch, and it relies on a division of labor, with each of the fund's portfolio counselors getting a slice of the fund to manage individually. The group works together and shares resources, but each member has the final say on his or her portion of the portfolio. In general, the team has managed the fund more conservatively than its average high-yield fund peer.

Performance 12-31-06

	1st Qtr	2nd Qtr	3rd Qtr	4th Qtr	Total
2002	-0.58	-9.06	-3.09	10.16	-3.59
2003	7.52	9.46	3.64	5.67	28.88
2004	1.70	-0.92	3.83	4.86	9.78
2005	-1.63	2.64	1.58	1.04	3.63
2006	3.19	0.45	3.37	4.71	12.19

Trailing	Total Return%	+/- LB Aggr	+/- CSFB Glb HY	%Rank Cat	Growth of $10,000
3 Mo	4.71	3.47	0.26	12	10,471
6 Mo	8.24	3.15	0.09	13	10,824
1 Yr	12.19	7.86	0.26	10	11,219
3 Yr Avg	8.47	4.77	-0.15	20	12,762
5 Yr Avg	9.66	4.60	-1.41	28	15,858
10 Yr Avg	7.28	1.04	0.19	13	20,192
15 Yr Avg	8.78	2.28	-0.12	14	35,337

Tax Analysis	Tax-Adj Rtn%	%Rank Cat	Tax-Cost Rat	%Rank Cat
3 Yr (estimated)	4.37	51	2.55	59
5 Yr (estimated)	5.77	46	2.81	66
10 Yr (estimated)	3.42	18	3.23	43

Potential Capital Gain Exposure: 3% of assets

Morningstar's Take by Lawrence Jones 12-19-06

American Funds American High Income Trust's success suggests that the whole can indeed be more than the sum of its parts.

This fund's team follows Capital Research's trademark multiple-manager system--to good effect. Five different portfolio managers divide roughly three fourths of the fund's $12 billion asset base between them, with the final fourth run by a team of more than a dozen credit analysts. Each segment is run in an autonomous fashion, with differing styles and disciplines, but the aggregate portfolio is strengthened by the diversity of approaches within it. This is partly because not all portfolio segments react to market changes in the same way, offering a degree of low correlation.

We're also encouraged by the team's impressive level of experience. On average, members of the team have been investment professionals with Capital Research for 19 years and have been working on the portfolio for nine years. Analysts here are also quite seasoned. All of this gives us

confidence that the research-intensive approach used here can be effective.

While the team occasionally takes its risks, caution has been the watchword lately. This is partly because management doesn't believe investors are being adequately compensated for taking added credit risk, given the narrow range of yields between credit-quality tiers. Other tools against problem bonds are strict holdings limits on industry, issuer, and issue-position size. This approach results in a diversified portfolio of several hundred issues and limits the damage that might be caused by issue-specific credit problems.

While the approach has led to excellent results in both the short term and long term, success has also produced a potentially cumbersome asset base. Still, investors also see benefits from the asset size, too, as with the fund's low cost. In fact, it is the least costly front-load fund on offer in the category. In sum, the issue is worth keeping an eye on, and the fund still impresses.

Address:	333 S Hope St - 55th FL
	Los Angeles CA 90071
	800-421-0180
Web Address:	www.americanfunds.com
Inception:	02-19-88
Advisor:	Capital Research and Management Company
Subadvisor:	None
NTF Plans:	Federated Tr NTF

Minimum Purchase:	$250	Add: $50	IRA: $250
Min Auto Inv Plan:	$50	Add: $50	
Sales Fees:	3.75%L, 0.24%S		
Management Fee:	0.30% mx./0.14% mn.		
Actual Fees:	Mgt:0.33%	Dist:0.24%	
Expense Projections:	3Yr:$587	5Yr:$745	10Yr:$1201
Income Distrib:	Monthly		

Historical Profile

Return	Above Avg	
Risk	Above Avg	
Rating	★★★★ Above Avg	

	52	42	59	50	36	45	44	13			

▽

23.8
19.6
16.0
13.0
10.0

Investment Style
Fixed Income
Income Rtn %Rank Cat

▼ Manager Change
▽ Partial Manager Change

Growth of $10,000
— Investment Values of Fund
— Investment Values of LB Aggr

Performance Quartile (within Category)

1995	1996	1997	1998	1999	2000	2001	2002	2003	2004	2005	2006	History
14.42	15.03	15.20	14.13	13.84	12.14	11.83	10.33	12.33	12.61	12.11	12.61	NAV
20.71	13.88	12.62	1.54	7.54	-3.31	7.44	-3.59	28.88	9.78	3.63	12.19	Total Return %
2.24	10.25	2.97	-7.15	8.36	-14.94	-1.00	-13.84	24.78	5.44	1.20	7.86	+/-LB Aggr
3.32	1.46	-0.01	0.96	4.26	1.90	1.66	-6.70	0.95	-2.18	1.37	0.26	+/-CSFB Glb HY
9.91	9.22	8.71	8.68	9.68	9.47	10.20	9.23	8.84	7.31	7.69	7.87	Income Return %
10.80	4.66	3.91	-7.14	-2.14	-12.78	-2.76	-12.82	20.04	2.47	-4.06	4.32	Capital Return %
6	30	59	37	23	22	13	73	19	51	18	10	Total Rtn % Rank Cat
1.25	1.28	1.26	1.27	1.31	1.25	1.19	1.04	0.88	0.87	0.94	0.92	Income $
0.08	0.02	0.34	0.05	0.00	0.00	0.00	0.00	0.00	0.00	0.00	0.00	Capital Gains $
0.89	0.87	0.82	0.81	0.82	0.82	0.83	0.88	0.75	0.67	0.65	0.65	Expense Ratio %
9.72	8.90	8.35	8.76	9.21	8.87	9.75	9.99	8.49	7.19	7.17	7.52	Income Ratio %
30	40	54	55	30	46	44	34	41	39	39	41	Turnover Rate %
1,211	1,671	2,194	2,573	2,871	2,620	3,290	3,892	6,831	7,408	7,484	8,749	Net Assets $mil

Rating and Risk

Time Period	Load-Adj Return %	Morningstar Rtn vs Cat	Morningstar Risk vs Cat	Morningstar Risk-Adj Rating
1 Yr	7.98			
3 Yr	7.10	Avg	Avg	★★★
5 Yr	8.83	Avg	+Avg	★★★
10 Yr	6.87	+Avg	+Avg	★★★★
Incept	9.09			

Other Measures	Standard Index LB Aggr	Best Fit Index CSFB Glb HY
Alpha	4.8	-0.2
Beta	0.41	1.02
R-Squared	12	93
Standard Deviation	3.86	
Mean	8.47	
Sharpe Ratio	1.31	

Portfolio Analysis 09-30-06

Total Fixed-Income:680	Date of Maturity	Amount $000	Value $000	% Net Assets
Triton Pcs 8.5%	06-01-13	113,840	106,156	0.93
Windstream 144A 8.625%	08-01-16	90,575	97,368	0.85
General Mtrs 7.2%	01-15-11	96,220	89,124	0.78
Nextel Comms 7.375%	08-01-15	85,378	88,177	0.77
Sanmina Sci 8.125%	03-01-16	77,725	76,559	0.67
Warner Chilcott 8.75%	02-01-15	71,014	73,855	0.65
United Airlines Term Loa	02-01-12	67,045	67,548	0.59
Amer Tower 7.125%	10-15-12	64,360	66,291	0.58
LINENS N THINGS	01-15-14	66,350	64,360	0.56
3815688 Cda Inc/Canwest	09-15-12	62,808	62,337	0.55
DRAX GROUP		3,970	61,924	0.54
Cinemark Usa 9%	02-01-13	58,743	61,240	0.54
Hughes Net Sys 144A 9.5%	04-15-14	58,375	60,418	0.53
Fuji Jgb Invt 144A FRN	12-31-49	52,248	55,982	0.49
Amer Cellular 10%	08-01-11	52,725	55,493	0.49
Jsg Hldgs 11.5%	10-01-15	41,591	53,912	0.47
Charter Com Term Loan Fa	04-28-13	51,500	51,822	0.45
Georgia-Pacific Term Loa	12-23-13	49,475	50,032	0.44
Young Broadcstg 10%	03-01-11	52,810	49,575	0.43
Grupo Posadas S A De C V	10-04-11	46,225	48,536	0.43

Current Investment Style

Duration: Short Int Long
Quality: High Med Low

¹ figure provided by fund

Avg Eff Duration¹	3.5 Yrs
Avg Eff Maturity	—
Avg Credit Quality	BB
Avg Wtd Coupon	8.01%
Avg Wtd Price	178.70% of par

Coupon Range	% of Bonds	Rel Cat
0% PIK	4.2	0.8
0% to 8%	46.3	0.9
8% to 11%	50.3	1.1
11% to 14%	3.1	0.7
More than 14%	0.3	1.9

1.00=Category Average

Credit Analysis	% bonds 09-30-06		
AAA	7	BB	27
AA	0	B	46
A	1	Below B	11
BBB	9	NR/NA	0

Sector Breakdown

	% of assets
US Treasuries	0
TIPS	0
US Agency	0
Mortgage Pass-Throughs	0
Mortgage CMO	0
Mortgage ARM	0
US Corporate	77
Asset-Backed	2
Convertible	0
Municipal	0
Corporate Inflation-Protected	0
Foreign Corporate	9
Foreign Govt	2

Composition

Cash	9.3	Bonds	86.3
Stocks	1.8	Other	2.6

Special Securities

Restricted/Illiquid Secs	16
Exotic Mortgage-Backed	0
Emerging-Markets Secs	4
Options/Futures/Warrants	No

MORNINGSTAR® Funds 500

Amer Funds CpIncBldr A

Analyst Pick ✓

	Ticker	Load	NAV	Yield	Total Assets	Mstar Category
	CAIBX	5.75%	$61.11	3.6%	$80,853 mil	World Allocation

Governance and Management

Stewardship Grade: A

Portfolio Manager(s)

American Funds uses a multimanager system in which each of the fund's managers runs a portion of assets independently of the other managers. Many of the managers (also known as counselors) on this fund have been managing money for years, and many run other American Funds' portfolios as well.

Strategy

This fund has a razor-sharp focus on income. Its stock portfolio, for example, is filled with high-yielding names. Its bond portfolio consists mostly of U.S. Treasuries, investment-grade corporates, and mortgages. Although the fund's stock stake has hovered between 50% and 65%, its bond stake has varied widely: It has been as high as 40% and as low as 10% (with the remainder in cash).

Historical Profile

Return	Average
Risk	Below Avg
Rating	★★★★ Above Avg

Equity %: 58% 63% 59% 59% 47% 62% 67% 65% 64%

▼ Manager Change
▽ Partial Manager Change

Investment Style — Equity Stock %

Growth of $10,000
— Investment Values of Fund
— Investment Values of DJ Mod

Scale: 38.0 / 31.0 / 24.0 / 17.0 / 10.0

Performance Quartile (within Category)

	1995	1996	1997	1998	1999	2000	2001	2002	2003	2004	2005	2006	History
	37.23	41.03	46.90	47.47	42.67	44.82	43.59	41.33	47.87	53.26	53.03	61.11	NAV
	25.05	17.64	23.33	11.75	-2.77	12.52	4.75	0.65	21.57	17.40	4.94	22.04	Total Return %
	5.25	6.98	11.43	-0.57	-20.10	14.19	7.55	7.42	-5.81	4.43	-2.05	9.74	+/-DJ Mod
	4.33	4.16	7.57	-12.57	-27.72	25.71	21.55	20.54	-11.54	2.68	-4.55	1.97	+/-MSCI World
	5.63	5.01	4.68	4.22	4.17	4.80	4.73	4.76	4.84	3.85	4.04	4.27	Income Return %
	19.42	12.63	18.65	7.53	-6.94	7.72	0.02	-4.11	16.73	13.55	0.90	17.77	Capital Return %
	1	1	1	34	100	22	10	33	64	13	60	9	Total Rtn % Rank Cat
	1.75	1.83	1.89	1.95	1.95	2.01	2.08	2.04	1.97	1.82	2.12	2.23	Income $
	0.50	0.73	1.61	2.81	1.54	0.94	1.17	0.52	0.17	0.90	0.69	1.17	Capital Gains $
	0.72	0.71	0.65	0.64	0.64	0.67	0.66	0.67	0.65	0.59	0.57	—	Expense Ratio %
	4.96	5.19	4.04	4.35	4.15	4.67	4.36	4.19	4.04	3.65	3.79	—	Income Ratio %
	18	28	28	24	21	41	37	36	27	24	20	—	Turnover Rate %
	4,809	5,809	7,803	9,239	8,392	7,708	8,428	11,078	20,605	32,505	44,688	60,669	Net Assets $mil

Performance 12-31-06

	1st Qtr	2nd Qtr	3rd Qtr	4th Qtr	Total
2002	4.08	0.66	-8.60	5.10	0.65
2003	-2.12	10.49	2.36	9.82	21.57
2004	2.51	-0.08	4.03	10.18	17.40
2005	-1.66	2.30	3.00	1.28	4.94
2006	4.89	1.69	5.84	8.11	22.04

Trailing	Total Return%	+/- DJ Mod	+/- MSCI World	%Rank Cat	Growth of $10,000
3 Mo	8.11	2.52	-0.26	16	10,811
6 Mo	14.42	5.63	1.21	2	11,442
1 Yr	22.04	9.74	1.97	9	12,204
3 Yr Avg	14.56	3.84	-0.12	28	15,035
5 Yr Avg	12.97	2.95	3.00	35	18,400
10 Yr Avg	11.26	2.71	3.62	23	29,066
15 Yr Avg	11.76	2.55	3.07	40	53,002

Tax Analysis	Tax-Adj Rtn%	%Rank Cat	Tax-Cost Rat	%Rank Cat
3 Yr (estimated)	10.57	56	1.56	78
5 Yr (estimated)	9.78	69	1.67	97
10 Yr (estimated)	8.36	38	2.03	75

Potential Capital Gain Exposure: 21% of assets

Rating and Risk

Time Period	Load-Adj Return %	Morningstar Rtn vs Cat	Morningstar Risk vs Cat	Morningstar Risk-Adj Rating
1 Yr	15.03			
3 Yr	12.32	Avg	-Avg	★★★
5 Yr	11.64	Avg	-Avg	★★★
10 Yr	10.60	Avg	-Avg	★★★★
Incept	11.59			

Other Measures	Standard Index DJ Mod	Best Fit Index Russ 1000 VI
Alpha	4.9	2.6
Beta	0.80	0.72
R-Squared	72	76

Standard Deviation	5.61
Mean	14.56
Sharpe Ratio	1.91

Portfolio Analysis 09-30-06

Total Stocks:252

Share change since 06-30-06	Sectors	P/E Ratio	YTD Return %	% Net Assets
⊕ E.ON	Utilities	—	—	1.75
BellSouth Corporation	Telecom	—	—	1.57
⊖ AT&T, Inc.	Telecom	18.2	-5.43	1.54
Altria Group, Inc.	Goods	16.3	2.52	1.44
Exelon Corporation	Utilities	—	-2.67	1.15
⊕ National Grid Transco	Utilities	—	—	1.08
⊕ Veolia Environnement	Business	—	—	1.07
Koninklijke KPN	Telecom	—	—	1.05
⊕ General Electric Company	Ind Mtrls	20.0	0.91	1.01

Total Fixed-Income:785

	Date of Maturity	Amount $000	Value $000	% Net Assets
FHLMC	10-01-36	389,643	390,909	0.55
GNMA	10-01-36	250,000	252,208	0.36
US Treasury Note 6%	08-15-09	200,000	207,344	0.29
US Treasury Bond 11.75%	11-15-14	95,000	114,341	0.16
US Treasury Bond 5.375%	02-15-31	104,000	112,352	0.16
Cardinal Health 6.75%	02-15-11	100,250	104,946	0.15
FHLMC 5.875%	03-21-11	100,000	103,195	0.15
US Treasury Note 3.625%	07-15-09	105,000	102,293	0.14

Current Investment Style

Value Blnd Growth — Large / Mid / Small

Market Cap	%
Giant	45.6
Large	40.6
Mid	12.9
Small	0.9
Micro	0.0

Avg $mil: 29,514

Value Measures	Rel Category
Price/Earnings	13.74	0.91
Price/Book	2.11	0.93
Price/Sales	1.36	1.05
Price/Cash Flow	3.57	0.47
Dividend Yield %	4.45	1.52

Growth Measures	%	Rel Category
Long-Term Erngs	10.53	0.92
Book Value	8.05	0.97
Sales	6.70	1.04
Cash Flow	3.31	0.50
Historical Erngs	11.65	0.68

Composition

Cash	15.0	Bonds	19.7
Stocks	64.3	Other	0.9
Foreign (% of Stock)			56.1

Sector Weightings	% of Stocks	Rel DJ Mod	3 Year High Low
⟳ Info	14.92	—	
📄 Software	0.91	—	1 0
💻 Hardware	1.03	—	1 0
🎙 Media	1.27	—	1 0
📞 Telecom	11.71	—	15 12
⚙ Service	44.84		
🏥 Health	4.92	—	5 2
🛒 Consumer	3.45	—	3 2
🏢 Business	6.15	—	6 3
💲 Financial	30.32	—	32 30
🏭 Mfg	40.23	—	
🏠 Goods	11.44	—	14 11
⚙ Ind Mtrls	7.66	—	10 7
🔥 Energy	6.82	—	8 7
💡 Utilities	14.31	—	17 14

Regional Exposure

	% Stock		
UK/W. Europe	37	N. America	46
Japan	0	Latn America	0
Asia X Japan	16	Other	1

Country Exposure

	% Stock		
United States	44	Netherlands	5
U.K.	9	Australia	5
France	7		

Morningstar's Take by Kai Wiecking 12-26-06

American Funds Capital Income Builder remains the one to beat among world-allocation funds.

This fund's long-term record is solid on an absolute basis as well as compared with its world-category competitors. It held up well in the recent bear market thanks to its emphasis on large-value stocks. And with its significant bond and cash stake, the odds are good that it will continue to outperform its more aggressive peers when the going gets tough. We think the fund's steadiness in difficult periods, one of which may be sooner rather than later given the signs of slowing economic growth around the world, more than makes up for its lagging returns in frothy markets.

Remarkably, this offering's performance remains strong even in the face of continuing massive inflows. With assets now exceeding $80 billion, this offering is the largest in the group by a huge margin. If this were any other category, we'd be concerned about the fund losing its maneuverability. But since it truly is a go-anywhere option, this is less of a worry. In fact, the fund's size has the positive effect of creating economies of scale, which American Funds is passing on to shareholders: At 0.57%, the fund's expense ratio is by far the lowest of all retail funds in the world-allocation category.

While those low costs are a crucial underpinning for long-term success, the fund's strong showing so far in 2006 has more to do with the stabilizing effect its bond and cash stakes provided during the market turmoil in May and June, as well as with its exposure to high-yielding utility and telecom stocks as those sectors came back in vogue.

We're reasonably confident that this fund will continue to thrive, supported by American Fund's vast pool of skilled managers executing a prudent and proven strategy at a low price. It's rare that a world-stock allocation fund is among the best a large fund company has to offer, but that's certainly the case here.

Address:	333 S Hope St - 55th FL Los Angeles CA 90071 800-325-3590	
Web Address:	www.americanfunds.com	
Inception:	07-30-87	
Advisor:	Capital Research and Management Company	
Subadvisor:	None	
NTF Plans:	Federated Tr NTF	

Minimum Purchase:	$250	Add: $50	IRA: $250
Min Auto Inv Plan:	$50	Add: $50	
Sales Fees:	5.75%L, 0.23%S		
Management Fee:	0.26%		
Actual Fees:	Mgt:0.26%	Dist:0.23%	
Expense Projections:	3Yr:$753	5Yr:$885	10Yr:$1270
Income Distrib:	Quarterly		

Amer Funds CapWrldBd A

	Ticker	Load	NAV	Yield	SEC Yield	Total Assets	Mstar Category
	CWBFX	3.75%	$19.22	3.3%	4.20%	$3,728 mil	World Bond

Governance and Management

Stewardship Grade: B

Portfolio Manager(s)

Five individual managers and a group of analysts each manage a slice of the fund. The managers have between seven and 19 years' experience on the fund. They also work on other bond offerings from American Funds, such as Intermediate Bond Fund of America and U.S. Government Securities. Their setup is slightly different than at other American funds, with a couple of the managers acting more as specialists in their sectors.

Strategy

This fund primarily invests in investment-grade debt, but shareholders have voted to allow it to put up to 25% of assets in high-yield and emerging-markets bonds, although the managers generally stick to investment-grade debt in emerging markets. Management does make currency bets and country bets. However, the fund recently moved from a mostly foreign-currency benchmark to one that's normally about 50% exposed to the U.S. dollar.

Performance 12-31-06

	1st Qtr	2nd Qtr	3rd Qtr	4th Qtr	Total
2002	-0.21	6.80	1.83	7.31	16.45
2003	4.09	6.21	2.28	5.11	18.86
2004	2.03	-3.57	4.39	8.45	11.38
2005	-1.96	0.26	-0.05	-1.12	-2.86
2006	0.32	0.93	2.94	3.24	7.60

Trailing	Total Return%	+/- LB Aggr	+/- SB Wld Govt	%Rank Cat	Growth of $10,000
3 Mo	3.24	2.00	1.15	15	10,324
6 Mo	6.28	1.19	3.29	10	10,628
1 Yr	7.60	3.27	0.66	19	10,760
3 Yr Avg	5.20	1.50	2.32	14	11,643
5 Yr Avg	10.01	4.95	0.51	15	16,112
10 Yr Avg	5.84	-0.40	1.14	30	17,640
15 Yr Avg	6.69	0.19	0.34	28	26,415

Tax Analysis	Tax-Adj Rtn%	%Rank Cat	Tax-Cost Rat	%Rank Cat
3 Yr (estimated)	2.40	32	1.42	35
5 Yr (estimated)	7.72	18	1.33	17
10 Yr (estimated)	3.77	26	1.58	25

Potential Capital Gain Exposure: 3% of assets

Morningstar's Take by Lawrence Jones 12-21-06

American Funds Capital World Bond provides broadly diversified global bond exposure in an attractive package.

This fund's wide-ranging approach helps dampen volatility. By spreading the fund's assets across more than 600 different holdings and by keeping the portfolio's top holdings at modest weightings (the top 10 holdings account for 17% of assets, the category's lowest percentage), management effectively limits the damage that issue-specific credit problems might cause. Further, the team will hold bonds issued by many different countries and companies, denominated in various currencies. These will include issues from developed nations, as well as emerging markets (currently around 20% of assets), in both the investment-grade and high-yield (10.5% of assets) ranges of the credit-quality scale.

The fund, for instance, holds a 1.64% position in Israeli sovereign debt, denominated in shekels. The team has liked Israel for a while, particularly for the country's positive current-accounts position, improving inflation picture, and strong currency. Even during the country's war with Hezbollah in Lebanon, the bonds held up surprisingly well. The fund's regional exposure to the Middle East is quite small in an absolute sense, but with other modest positions in Egypt, Turkey, Qatar, and a very small one in Iraq, management illustrates its willingness to cast a wide net. While this approach can court country-specific risk, we feel that the fund's broad diversification and management's experience should keep large troubles at bay.

The fund's experienced management and below-average expense ratio add to its appeal. Five managers each run a segment of the portfolio, and the five have been working on the fund for between seven and 19 years. Over the years, the team has shown it can navigate the fund's risks quite well. Add in the fund's built-in cost advantage, and we think it is a fine choice for investors.

Address:	333 S Hope St - 55th FL
	Los Angeles CA 90071
	800-421-0180
Web Address:	www.americanfunds.com
Inception:	08-04-87
Advisor:	Capital Research and Management Company
Subadvisor:	None
NTF Plans:	Federated Tr NTF

Minimum Purchase:	$250	Add: $50	IRA: $250
Min Auto Inv Plan:	$50	Add: $50	
Sales Fees:	3.75%L, 0.24%S		
Management Fee:	0.57% mx./0.45% mn.		
Actual Fees:	Mgt:0.52%	Dist:0.24%	
Expense Projections:	3Yr:$669	5Yr:$886	10Yr:$1509
Income Distrib:	Quarterly		

Historical Profile

Return	Average
Risk	Average
Rating	★★★ Neutral

| 53 | 75 | 77 | 82 | 81 | 59 | 62 | 52 |

Growth of $10,000
- Investment Values of Fund
- Investment Values of LB Aggr

Performance Quartile (within Category)

	1995	1996	1997	1998	1999	2000	2001	2002	2003	2004	2005	2006	History
NAV	17.09	16.95	15.75	16.18	14.96	14.63	14.53	16.49	18.80	20.01	18.48	19.22	NAV
	21.41	6.34	-0.36	10.09	-3.12	1.46	1.53	16.45	18.86	11.38	-2.86	7.60	Total Return %
	2.94	2.71	-10.01	1.40	-2.30	-10.17	-6.91	6.20	14.76	7.04	-5.29	3.27	+/-LB Aggr
	1.86	2.26	3.90	-7.70	1.95	4.09	5.07	-5.54	0.34	-0.76	6.34	0.66	+/-SB Wld Govt
	8.14	5.67	5.17	5.18	4.08	3.59	2.21	2.78	4.68	4.23	3.76	3.51	Income Return %
	13.27	0.67	-5.53	4.91	-7.20	-2.13	-0.68	13.67	14.18	7.15	-6.62	4.09	Capital Return %
	26	75	72	43	49	59	48	38	22	21	38	19	Total Rtn % Rank Cat
	1.20	0.95	0.86	0.80	0.65	0.53	0.32	0.40	0.76	0.78	0.74	0.64	Income $
	0.00	0.23	0.28	0.32	0.07	0.00	0.00	0.00	0.00	0.10	0.22	0.00	Capital Gains $
	1.12	1.09	1.07	1.06	1.08	1.12	1.12	1.08	1.04	1.02	0.93	0.91	Expense Ratio %
	6.83	6.07	5.21	5.15	4.66	4.66	5.46	5.38	4.22	3.74	3.76	4.19	Income Ratio %
	105	91	79	101	129	52	61	48	83	79	72	91	Turnover Rate %
	698	815	710	626	515	417	383	544	935	1,427	1,921	2,438	Net Assets $mil

Rating and Risk

Time Period	Load-Adj Return %	Morningstar Rtn vs Cat	Morningstar Risk vs Cat	Morningstar Risk-Adj Rating
1 Yr	3.56			
3 Yr	3.87	+Avg	Avg	★★★
5 Yr	9.17	Avg	Avg	★★★★
10 Yr	5.44	Avg	Avg	★★★
Incept	7.41			

Other Measures	Standard Index LB Aggr	Best Fit Index SB Wld Govt
Alpha	1.5	2.1
Beta	1.04	0.71
R-Squared	39	86
Standard Deviation	5.43	
Mean	5.20	
Sharpe Ratio	0.37	

Portfolio Analysis 09-30-06

Total Fixed-Income:638	Date of Maturity	Amount $000	Value $000	% Net Assets
Germany (Federal Republi	01-04-13	69,000	91,663	2.37
US Treasury Bond 4.5%	02-15-36	86,330	82,742	2.14
Jpy Fwd Pur From Usd10/1		7,946,859	67,422	1.75
Jpy Fwd Pur From Usd11/1		7,756,141	66,144	1.71
Germany (Federal Republi	01-04-24	39,300	64,590	1.67
State Of Israel	03-31-14	254,545	63,413	1.64
Japan (Government Of) 1.	09-20-14	7,270,000	61,581	1.59
Sweden (Kingdom Of) 5.25	03-15-11	393,250	57,409	1.49
US Treasury Note 3.875%	02-15-13	58,250	55,956	1.45
Sweden (Kingdom Of) 6.75	05-05-14	326,925	53,839	1.39
Japan (Government Of) 0.	12-22-08	5,623,501	47,866	1.24
Japan (Government Of) 1.	03-22-10	5,355,001	46,750	1.21
South Korea (Republic Of	09-28-15	40,067,685	43,894	1.14
Singapore Govt Sgd3.125%	02-01-11	67,685	42,791	1.11
Germany (Federal Republi	01-04-11	29,525	39,827	1.03
Eur Fwd Pur From Usd11/9		30,771	39,134	1.01
US Treasury Bond 8.5%	02-15-20	27,625	37,656	0.97
Federal Republic Of Germ	07-04-14	28,000	36,886	0.95
Jpy Fwd Pur From Usd11/3		4,300,001	36,732	0.95
Aries Vermoegensverwaltu	10-25-14	28,000	36,260	0.94

Current Investment Style

Duration: Short Int Long
Quality: High Med Low

1 figure provided by fund

Avg Eff Duration[1]	5.5 Yrs
Avg Eff Maturity	7.7 Yrs
Avg Credit Quality	AA
Avg Wtd Coupon	5.61%
Avg Wtd Price	401.37% of par

Coupon Range	% of Bonds	Rel Cat
0% PIK	2.3	0.6
0% to 6%	67.2	0.8
6% to 8%	19.6	1.5
8% to 10%	9.4	2.1
More than 10%	3.8	1.7

1.00=Category Average

Credit Analysis		% bonds 09-30-06	
AAA	48	BB	6
AA	9	B	7
A	18	Below B	1
BBB	12	NR/NA	0

Sector Breakdown	% of assets
US Treasuries	—
TIPS	—
US Agency	—
Mortgage Pass-Throughs	—
Mortgage CMO	—
Mortgage ARM	—
US Corporate	—
Asset-Backed	—
Convertible	—
Municipal	—
Corporate Inflation-Protected	—
Foreign Corporate	—
Foreign Govt	—

Composition			
Cash	20.1	Bonds	77.2
Stocks	0.0	Other	2.7

Special Securities	
Restricted/Illiquid Secs	5
Exotic Mortgage-Backed	0
Emerging-Markets Secs	—
Options/Futures/Warrants	No

Investment Style
Fixed Income
Income Rtn %Rank Cat

▼ Manager Change
▽ Partial Manager Change

MORNINGSTAR® Funds 500

Amer Funds CapWrldGl A

Ticker	Load	NAV	Yield	Total Assets	Mstar Category
CWGIX	5.75%	$41.93	2.1%	$79,964 mil	World Stock

Governance and Management

Stewardship Grade: B

Portfolio Manager(s)

Like other American Funds, this offering uses a multimanager approach. Each manager--or counselor, as they are called here--runs his or her portion of assets independently. The newest manager on the team joined Capital Research in 1990. The managers also help run other American Funds offerings. As with all American Funds offerings, a portion of this fund's assets are managed by Capital Research & Management's analyst staff.

Strategy

This fund's managers are focused on yield. They buy a lot of blue-chip stocks with healthy dividends and hold them for the long term. They usually try to pick up stocks on the cheap, so the portfolio's price multiples are below the group norm. The managers use cash to moderate volatility, typically keeping the fund's stake in the double digits. The fund usually has a stake in emerging-markets companies and will sometimes hold preferred stock and convertibles debt.

Performance 12-31-06

	1st Qtr	2nd Qtr	3rd Qtr	4th Qtr	Total
2002	5.43	-5.78	-15.18	10.21	-7.15
2003	-5.77	18.20	8.38	15.21	39.07
2004	4.09	-0.70	2.10	13.16	19.42
2005	0.08	0.54	8.96	4.64	14.72
2006	6.10	0.45	5.20	9.14	22.36

Trailing	Total Return%	+/- MSCI EAFE	+/- MSCI World	%Rank Cat	Growth of $10,000
3 Mo	9.14	-1.21	0.77	39	10,914
6 Mo	14.82	0.13	1.61	18	11,482
1 Yr	22.36	-3.98	2.29	22	12,236
3 Yr Avg	18.79	-1.14	4.11	17	16,763
5 Yr Avg	16.70	1.72	6.73	7	21,645
10 Yr Avg	13.79	6.08	6.15	6	36,395
15 Yr Avg	—	—	—	—	—

Tax Analysis	Tax-Adj Rtn%	%Rank Cat	Tax-Cost Rat	%Rank Cat
3 Yr (estimated)	14.90	41	1.35	73
5 Yr (estimated)	13.95	13	1.20	86
10 Yr (estimated)	11.19	10	1.71	86

Potential Capital Gain Exposure: 24% of assets

Morningstar's Take by Kai Wiecking 12-26-06

As long as shareholders of American Funds Capital World Growth & Income manage their expectations, they should remain happy campers indeed.

There's no arguing with the excellent job the many managers of this fund have done over the years. Its trailing average 10-year return of 13.5% through Nov. 30 , 2006, bests that of 95% of its rivals in the competitive world-stock category. More importantly, it has done well throughout various market environments. The fact that it only lost 5.0% and 7.2% of its value, respectively, in the tough bear market years of 2001 and 2002 goes a long way toward explaining its muted volatility.

The prudent investment approach employed here is a major factor in those achievements. Management places a big emphasis on dividends, and it restricts itself to investing in large, stable companies. The managers pay close attention to valuations, too. This approach doesn't preclude them from investing in emerging markets, however. And as that area of the market has enjoyed an extended boom until recently, this fund has participated.

The fund's vast diversification across all sectors and regions protects it from being overly exposed to any particular risk. But it's also a reflection of its increasing bloat, as assets here have reached $80 billion. This could restrict the managers' ability to maneuver. We would thus caution investors not to expect this fund to indefinitely perform as well as it has in the past. So far in 2006, however, the fund is still beating up on most of its rivals in the group. Its positions in pharma stocks, such as Roche Holding, have been a boon, as has its stake in the energy names, such as Total.

The fund's rock-bottom expense ratio of 0.73% is another factor favoring its long-term viability. We wish American Funds would consider closing the fund to protect existing shareholders, but even without that step, they would do well to stay put.

Address:	333 S Hope St - 55th FL
	Los Angeles CA 90071
	800-421-0180
Web Address:	www.americanfunds.com
Inception:	03-26-93
Advisor:	Capital Research and Management Company
Subadvisor:	None
NTF Plans:	Federated Tr NTF

Minimum Purchase:	$250	Add: $50	IRA: $250
Min Auto Inv Plan:	$250	Add: $50	
Sales Fees:	5.75%L, 0.23%S		
Management Fee:	0.60% mx./0.36% mn.		
Actual Fees:	Mgt:0.39%	Dist:0.23%	
Expense Projections:	3Yr:$804	5Yr:$973	10Yr:$1463
Income Distrib:	Quarterly		

Historical Profile

Return	High
Risk	Below Avg
Rating	★★★★★ Highest

75% 87% 70% 75% 75% 80% 83% 87% 87%

▼ Manager Change
▽ Partial Manager Change

Growth of $10,000
— Investment Values of Fund
— Investment Values of MSCI EAFE

43.6
32.4
24.0
17.0
10.0

Performance Quartile (within Category)

1995	1996	1997	1998	1999	2000	2001	2002	2003	2004	2005	2006	History
20.26	22.97	24.51	25.42	29.83	26.47	24.50	22.25	29.88	33.89	36.57	41.93	NAV
21.39	21.54	17.99	16.20	27.30	1.38	-4.96	-7.15	39.07	19.42	14.72	22.36	Total Return %
10.18	15.49	16.21	-3.73	0.27	15.57	16.46	8.79	0.48	-0.83	1.18	-3.98	+/-MSCI EAFE
0.67	8.06	2.23	-8.12	2.35	14.57	11.84	12.74	5.96	4.70	5.23	2.29	+/-MSCI World
3.59	3.50	2.83	2.31	2.00	1.78	1.91	2.14	2.86	2.91	2.38	2.48	Income Return %
17.80	18.04	15.16	13.89	25.30	-0.40	-6.87	-9.29	36.21	16.51	12.34	19.88	Capital Return %
30	15	34	50	58	17	11	6	26	14	27	22	Total Rtn % Rank Cat
0.62	0.70	0.64	0.56	0.51	0.52	0.50	0.52	0.63	0.86	0.80	0.90	Income $
0.27	0.85	1.87	2.37	1.81	3.20	0.16	0.00	0.29	0.80	1.44	1.80	Capital Gains $
0.88	0.85	0.82	0.78	0.79	0.79	0.78	0.82	0.81	0.77	0.73	—	Expense Ratio %
3.24	3.28	2.53	2.25	1.93	2.08	2.05	2.22	2.70	2.28	2.41	—	Income Ratio %
26	30	32	39	34	41	45	32	27	21	26	—	Turnover Rate %
3,723	5,213	7,359	8,697	10,964	11,122	10,480	9,419	16,216	26,906	42,102	60,265	Net Assets $mil

Rating and Risk

Time Period	Load-Adj Return %	Morningstar Rtn vs Cat	Morningstar Risk vs Cat	Morningstar Risk-Adj Rating
1 Yr	15.33			
3 Yr	16.47	+Avg	-Avg	★★★★
5 Yr	15.33	+Avg	-Avg	★★★★
10 Yr	13.12	High	-Avg	★★★★★
Incept	14.26			

Other Measures	Standard Index MSCI EAFE	Best Fit Index MSCI World
Alpha	1.3	4.8
Beta	0.85	0.98
R-Squared	93	95
Standard Deviation	8.33	
Mean	18.79	
Sharpe Ratio	1.75	

Portfolio Analysis 09-30-06

Share change since 06-06 Total Stocks:377	Sector	Country	% Assets
⊕ Roche Holding	Health	Switzerland	1.52
Altria Group, Inc.	Goods	United States	1.36
⊕ Diageo	Goods	U.K.	1.33
⊕ Bayer	Ind Mtrls	Germany	1.32
⊕ E.ON	Utilities	Germany	1.25
⊕ Novo-Nordisk A S	Health	Denmark	1.11
⊕ UniCredito Italiano Grp	Financial	Italy	1.07
⊕ AT&T, Inc.	Telecom	United States	1.02
⊕ Vivendi Universal	Media	France	1.02
Royal Dutch Shell	Energy	U.K.	1.01
Koninklijke KPN	Telecom	Netherlands	0.99
⊕ AstraZeneca	Health	U.K.	0.96
⊕ HSBC Hldgs	Financial	U.K.	0.95
⊕ Microsoft Corporation	Software	United States	0.92
Veolia Environnement	Business	France	0.90
⊕ TOTAL	Energy	France	0.87
⊕ Chevron Corporation	Energy	United States	0.86
⊕ BNP Paribas	Financial	France	0.85
⊕ Citigroup, Inc.	Financial	United States	0.82
⊕ General Electric Company	Ind Mtrls	United States	0.79

Current Investment Style

Value Blnd Growth / Large Mid Small

Market Cap	%
Giant	58.9
Large	34.7
Mid	6.4
Small	0.1
Micro	0.0

Avg $mil: 36,777

Value Measures		Rel Category
Price/Earnings	12.16	0.79
Price/Book	2.12	0.89
Price/Sales	1.08	0.82
Price/Cash Flow	6.68	0.77
Dividend Yield %	3.61	1.66

Growth Measures	%	Rel Category
Long-Term Erngs	12.13	0.96
Book Value	9.64	1.07
Sales	6.47	0.78
Cash Flow	5.03	0.51
Historical Erngs	11.35	0.61

Sector Weightings	% of Stocks	Rel MSCI EAFE	3 Year High	Low
⌖ Info	16.70	1.41		
Software	1.65	2.95	2	0
Hardware	4.46	1.16	5	3
Media	2.03	1.11	3	1
Telecom	8.56	1.54	12	8
Service	42.34	0.90		
Health	8.92	1.25	9	6
Consumer	5.61	1.13	7	6
Business	4.66	0.92	5	2
Financial	23.15	0.77	25	21
Mfg	40.97	1.00		
Goods	13.16	1.00	18	13
Ind Mtrls	14.14	0.92	16	14
Energy	9.06	1.27	10	6
Utilities	4.61	0.88	6	3

Regional Exposure	% Stock		
UK/W. Europe 46		N. America	26
Japan 6		Latn America	3
Asia X Japan 17		Other	2

Composition

| Cash | 11.0 | Bonds | 0.5 |
| Stocks | 86.6 | Other | 1.9 |

Foreign (% of Stock) 75.8

Country Exposure	% Stock		
United States	24	Germany	7
U.K.	10	Japan	6
France	9		

Amer Funds EuroPac A

✔ Analyst Pick	**Ticker** AEPGX	**Load** 5.75%	**NAV** $46.56	**Yield** 1.6%	**Total Assets** $95,301 mil	**Mstar Category** Foreign Large Blend

Governance and Management

Stewardship Grade: A

Portfolio Manager(s)

Like all American Funds, this offering boasts many experienced managers, most of whom have been with the company for more than a decade. Each manager runs his or her portion of assets independently of the others. A portion of the portfolio (less than 25% of assets) is run by the firm's analyst staff.

Strategy

The fund divides assets among several portfolio counselors (managers) whose investment philosophies vary from growth-focused to value-oriented. In the aggregate, the fund's portfolio is well diversified across countries and sectors, and its price multiples usually stay close to the category norms. Several of the managers like to pick up stocks on the cheap and then hold them for the long haul. The fund's turnover is quite low.

Historical Profile
Return: Above Avg
Risk: Below Avg
Rating: ★★★★ Above Avg

Investment Style: Equity Stock %

82% 86% 79% 82% 85% 86% 90% 86% 90%

▼ Manager Change
▽ Partial Manager Change

Growth of $10,000
— Investment Values of Fund
— Investment Values of MSCI EAFE

33.0 / 26.0 / 20.0 / 15.0 / 10.0

Performance Quartile (within Category)

	1995	1996	1997	1998	1999	2000	2001	2002	2003	2004	2005	2006	History
	23.13	26.04	26.02	28.40	42.66	31.35	26.87	22.97	30.21	35.63	41.10	46.56	NAV
	12.87	18.64	9.19	15.54	56.97	-17.84	-12.17	-13.61	32.91	19.69	21.12	21.87	Total Return %
	1.66	12.59	7.41	-4.39	29.94	-3.65	9.25	2.33	-5.68	-0.56	7.58	-4.47	+/-MSCI EAFE
	1.46	11.77	6.92	-3.15	28.99	-4.48	9.22	2.19	-6.51	-0.69	6.65	-3.84	+/-MSCI Wd xUS
	2.33	1.90	1.78	1.40	1.03	0.50	2.09	0.90	1.35	1.68	2.02	1.88	Income Return %
	10.54	16.74	7.41	14.14	55.94	-18.34	-14.26	-14.51	31.56	18.01	19.10	19.99	Capital Return %
	31	14	36	40	12	62	5	20	49	20	7	82	Total Rtn % Rank Cat
	0.49	0.43	0.45	0.36	0.29	0.19	0.66	0.24	0.31	0.51	0.72	0.77	Income $
	0.21	0.89	1.93	1.26	1.39	3.74	0.00	0.00	0.00	0.00	1.32	2.71	Capital Gains $
	0.97	0.95	0.90	0.86	0.84	0.84	0.84	0.88	0.90	0.87	0.82	0.76	Expense Ratio %
	1.80	2.09	1.77	1.64	1.45	0.93	1.89	1.21	1.06	1.08	1.31	1.58	Income Ratio %
	16	22	26	31	32	29	37	27	29	25	30	35	Turnover Rate %
	10,922	15,727	18,854	20,798	34,783	31,496	27,153	22,601	29,908	36,920	45,485	54,836	Net Assets $mil

Performance 12-31-06

	1st Qtr	2nd Qtr	3rd Qtr	4th Qtr	Total
2002	1.56	-4.32	-17.58	7.87	-13.61
2003	-9.66	17.98	9.27	14.13	32.91
2004	6.79	-1.83	0.47	13.63	19.69
2005	0.00	0.79	12.25	7.06	21.12
2006	7.54	-0.68	4.99	8.67	21.87

Trailing	Total Return%	+/- MSCI EAFE	+/- MSCI Wd xUS	%Rank Cat	Growth of $10,000
3 Mo	8.67	-1.68	-1.45	87	10,867
6 Mo	14.10	-0.59	-0.12	59	11,410
1 Yr	21.87	-4.47	-3.84	82	12,187
3 Yr Avg	20.89	0.96	0.79	14	17,667
5 Yr Avg	15.20	0.22	-0.05	16	20,289
10 Yr Avg	11.23	3.52	3.27	6	28,988
15 Yr Avg	11.96	4.10	3.92	1	54,443

Tax Analysis	Tax-Adj Rtn%	%Rank Cat	Tax-Cost Rat	%Rank Cat
3 Yr (estimated)	17.27	53	1.06	56
5 Yr (estimated)	12.94	37	0.79	62
10 Yr (estimated)	9.27	9	1.18	60

Potential Capital Gain Exposure: 34% of assets

Rating and Risk

Time Period	Load-Adj Return %	Morningstar Rtn vs Cat	Morningstar Risk vs Cat	Morningstar Risk-Adj Rating
1 Yr	14.86			
3 Yr	18.53	Avg	Avg	★★★
5 Yr	13.84	Avg	-Avg	★★★
10 Yr	10.57	+Avg	-Avg	★★★★★
Incept	13.81			

Other Measures	Standard Index MSCI EAFE	Best Fit Index MSCI Wd xUS
Alpha	0.9	0.9
Beta	1.00	0.98
R-Squared	91	91
Standard Deviation	9.91	
Mean	20.89	
Sharpe Ratio	1.66	

Morningstar's Take by Kai Wiecking 12-27-06

Recent results are an indication that this fund's glorious past will be hard to repeat.

There's no denying the fact that American Funds EuroPacific has been a terrific pick for its many shareholders and made them a lot of money in recent years. The fund's track record is outstanding, both on an absolute and a relative basis. But the worry persists that this fund's increasing girth will eventually limit its maneuverability, as the fund has delivered uncharacteristically weak performance so far in 2006. Its 20.4% return through Dec. 19 may look impressive at first glance, yet it trails what 85% of its rivals in the foreign large-blend category have achieved.

We're not saying by any means that this fund is doomed to deliver mediocre results going forward. Its vastly experienced team of portfolio managers consists of excellent stockpickers--although American Funds won't disclose who did what--and the shop's ability to train and retain talent is unmatched in the industry. But each talent pool is finite, and at close to $100 billion in assets, managers' ability to invest meaningfully in new, high-conviction ideas is significantly reduced.

This year, however, the problem was more that their portfolios' biases were out of sync with the market. The shortfall was concentrated in the latter half of the year, when many erstwhile strong performers, including top holdings Roche Holdings and Samsung, retreated amid profit-taking and lowered earnings outlooks. Managers were also surprised by the resiliency of the British stock market, which they had significantly underweighted. Many of the fund's tech positions also trailed the market. But instead of hopping on the momentum bandwagon, management sensibly increased exposure to defensive areas, such as insurance and pharmaceuticals.

All told, this well-run, cheap fund remains a solid choice, but investors should manage their expectations.

Portfolio Analysis 09-30-06

Share change since 06-06 Total Stocks:278

	Sector	Country	% Assets
⊕ Roche Holding	Health	Switzerland	3.03
Nestle	Goods	Switzerland	1.88
⊕ Bayer	Ind Mtrls	Germany	1.68
Samsung Electronics	Goods	Korea	1.57
America Movil SA ADR	Telecom	Mexico	1.53
⊖ Kookmin Bank	Financial	Korea	1.45
AstraZeneca	Health	U.K.	1.34
Novo-Nordisk A S	Health	Denmark	1.27
⊕ Hon Hai Precision Indust	Hardware	Taiwan	1.19
⊕ ING Groep	Financial	Netherlands	1.17
⊕ AXA	Financial	France	1.17
Inditex Grp	Goods	Spain	1.00
⊕ Continental	Ind Mtrls	Germany	0.98
Taiwan Semiconductor Mfg	Hardware	Taiwan	0.95
⊖ Koninklijke Ahold	Consumer	Netherlands	0.92
⊕ BNP Paribas	Financial	France	0.90
⊕ Sun Hung Kai Properties	Financial	Hong Kong	0.85
Hynix Semiconductor	Hardware	Korea	0.85
Royal Dutch Shell	Energy	U.K.	0.81
⊕ Mitsubishi UFJ Financial	Financial	Japan	0.80

Current Investment Style

Value Blnd Growth — Large/Mid/Small

Market Cap	%
Giant	56.1
Large	38.0
Mid	5.7
Small	0.0
Micro	0.1

Avg $mil: 28,170

Value Measures		Rel Category
Price/Earnings	9.82	0.75
Price/Book	2.10	0.97
Price/Sales	1.16	1.00
Price/Cash Flow	7.65	0.92
Dividend Yield %	2.59	0.89

Growth Measures	%	Rel Category
Long-Term Erngs	11.72	0.99
Book Value	11.29	1.24
Sales	6.53	1.00
Cash Flow	7.09	0.86
Historical Erngs	8.51	0.42

Composition

Cash	7.8	Bonds	0.0
Stocks	90.4	Other	1.8
Foreign (% of Stock)			99.5

Sector Weightings	% of Stocks	Rel MSCI EAFE	3 Year High	Low
⟳ Info	19.22	1.63		
Software	0.51	0.91	1	0
Hardware	8.96	2.32	9	4
Media	2.38	1.30	4	2
Telecom	7.37	1.32	17	7
⟳ Service	43.09	0.91		
Health	9.86	1.38	12	9
Consumer	4.72	0.95	6	4
Business	3.61	0.71	4	1
Financial	24.90	0.83	26	19
⟳ Mfg	37.69	0.92		
Goods	18.59	1.42	20	15
Ind Mtrls	10.65	0.69	11	8
Energy	6.45	0.90	9	5
Utilities	2.00	0.38	3	1

Regional Exposure		% Stock
UK/W. Europe	50	N. America	3
Japan	16	Latn America	5
Asia X Japan	23	Other	3

Country Exposure		% Stock
Japan	16	Switzerland	8
U.K.	9	Germany	8
South Korea	9		

Address:	333 S Hope St - 55th FL Los Angeles CA 90071 800-421-0180
Web Address:	www.americanfunds.com
Inception:	04-16-84
Advisor:	Capital Research and Management Company
Subadvisor:	None
NTF Plans:	Federated Tr NTF

Minimum Purchase:	$250	Add: $50	IRA: $250
Min Auto Inv Plan:	$250	Add: $50	
Sales Fees:	5.75%L, 0.25%S		
Management Fee:	0.69% mx./0.40% mn.		
Actual Fees:	Mgt:0.43%	Dist:0.25%	
Expense Projections:	3Yr:$819	5Yr:$999	10Yr:$1519
Income Distrib:	Annually		

MORNINGSTAR® Funds 500

Amer Funds Fundamen A

	Ticker	Load	NAV	Yield	Total Assets	Mstar Category
	ANCFX	5.75%	$40.05	1.4%	$38,375 mil	Large Blend

Governance and Management

Stewardship Grade: A

Portfolio Manager(s)

The fund's five portfolio counselors boast an average of more than 16 years of investment experience. Investors would be hard-pressed to find managers and analysts who know their industries better. The managers oversee other portfolios as well and are backed by a legion of analysts. We find it laudable that short-term performance isn't rewarded here, as investment professionals are evaluated over four-year periods.

Strategy

This fund's investment team employs rigorous fundamental analysis to search for undervalued or overlooked companies that have solid long-term growth potential. Often, the managers let winners ride or pick up depressed growth stocks, occasionally pushing the fund into large-blend territory. The team doesn't limit its search to U.S. stocks, either, and generally devotes a sizable portion of assets to foreign stocks.

Historical Profile

Return Above Avg
Risk Average
Rating ★★★★★ Highest

Investment Style: Equity, Stock %

89% 90% 85% 90% 89% 92% 93% 96% 91%

▼ Manager Change
▽ Partial Manager Change

Growth of $10,000
— Investment Values of Fund
— Investment Values of S&P 500

40.8
31.0
24.0
17.0
10.0

Performance Quartile (within Category)

	1995	1996	1997	1998	1999	2000	2001	2002	2003	2004	2005	2006	History
NAV	22.29	24.54	27.40	28.92	32.59	31.16	27.45	22.23	28.85	32.25	35.40	40.05	NAV
	34.21	19.99	26.67	16.72	24.58	4.27	-9.55	-17.34	31.96	13.91	11.68	19.24	Total Return %
	-3.37	-2.97	-6.69	-11.86	3.54	13.37	2.34	4.76	3.28	3.03	6.77	3.45	+/-S&P 500
	-3.56	-2.46	-6.18	-10.30	3.67	12.06	2.90	4.31	2.07	2.51	5.41	3.78	+/-Russ 1000
	2.32	1.82	1.74	1.47	1.41	1.25	1.30	1.82	1.81	1.95	1.84	1.59	Income Return %
	31.89	18.17	24.93	15.25	23.17	3.02	-10.85	-19.16	30.15	11.96	9.84	17.65	Capital Return %
	54	66	63	67	22	17	30	16	15	13	6	5	Total Rtn % Rank Cat
	0.40	0.40	0.42	0.40	0.40	0.40	0.40	0.50	0.40	0.56	0.59	0.56	Income $
	0.68	1.76	3.13	2.59	2.79	2.36	0.38	0.00	0.56	0.56	0.00	1.57	Capital Gains $
	0.70	0.66	0.63	0.63	0.63	0.64	0.65	0.67	0.66	0.63	0.60	—	Expense Ratio %
	2.08	1.78	1.54	1.47	1.33	1.28	1.41	1.68	2.08	2.05	1.75	—	Income Ratio %
	25	39	45	53	46	43	29	38	31	30	24	—	Turnover Rate %
	4,754	7,165	10,465	12,713	16,603	19,872	19,331	15,201	19,212	21,543	24,391	31,687	Net Assets $mil

Performance 12-31-06

	1st Qtr	2nd Qtr	3rd Qtr	4th Qtr	Total
2002	2.43	-8.56	-17.59	7.10	-17.34
2003	-5.85	16.24	3.70	16.28	31.96
2004	1.69	1.08	0.94	9.79	13.91
2005	-0.62	1.44	7.96	2.61	11.68
2006	7.35	1.37	2.17	7.24	19.24

Trailing	Total Return%	+/- S&P 500	+/- Russ 1000	%Rank Cat	Growth of $10,000
3 Mo	7.24	0.54	0.29	27	10,724
6 Mo	9.57	-3.17	-2.79	84	10,957
1 Yr	19.24	3.45	3.78	5	11,924
3 Yr Avg	14.90	4.46	3.92	3	15,169
5 Yr Avg	10.60	4.41	3.78	4	16,549
10 Yr Avg	11.14	2.72	2.50	7	28,754
15 Yr Avg	12.78	2.14	1.98	9	60,741

Tax Analysis	Tax-Adj Rtn%	%Rank Cat	Tax-Cost Rat	%Rank Cat
3 Yr (estimated)	11.79	11	0.76	35
5 Yr (estimated)	8.49	9	0.73	47
10 Yr (estimated)	8.97	10	1.37	63

Potential Capital Gain Exposure: 22% of assets

Rating and Risk

Time Period	Load-Adj Return %	Morningstar Rtn vs Cat	Morningstar Risk vs Cat	Morningstar Risk-Adj Rating
1 Yr	12.38			
3 Yr	12.65	+Avg	+Avg	★★★★
5 Yr	9.29	High	+Avg	★★★★★
10 Yr	10.48	+Avg	-Avg	★★★★★
Incept	7.48			

Other Measures	Standard Index S&P 500	Best Fit Index MSCI World
Alpha	3.7	-0.2
Beta	1.05	1.04
R-Squared	72	88
Standard Deviation	8.56	
Mean	14.90	
Sharpe Ratio	1.30	

Portfolio Analysis 09-30-06

Share change since 06-06 Total Stocks:210	Sector	PE	Tot Ret%	% Assets
⊕ Suncor Energy, Inc.	Energy	33.1	25.42	3.66
⊕ Microsoft Corporation	Software	23.8	15.83	2.49
⊕ Altria Group, Inc.	Goods	16.3	19.87	2.28
Oracle Corporation	Software	26.7	40.38	1.77
Roche Holding	Health	—	—	1.74
Deere & Company	Ind Mtrls	14.8	42.27	1.35
⊕ Lowe's Companies Inc.	Consumer	15.6	-6.05	1.26
⊕ Eli Lilly & Company	Health	17.3	-5.16	1.23
AT&T, Inc.	Telecom	18.2	51.59	1.22
⊕ Citigroup, Inc.	Financial	13.1	19.55	1.20
Royal Dutch Shell PLC AD	Energy	8.7	19.33	1.20
⊕ Target	Consumer	19.3	4.65	1.15
⊕ Allied Irish Banks	Financial	—	—	1.10
KDDI	Telecom	—	—	1.08
Texas Instruments, Inc.	Hardware	16.9	-9.82	1.08
Washington Mutual, Inc.	Financial	13.4	9.62	1.06
Union Pacific Corporatio	Business	17.4	15.87	1.05
Merck & Co., Inc.	Health	19.1	42.66	1.05
Caterpillar Inc.	Ind Mtrls	11.8	7.86	1.01
⊕ Chevron Corporation	Energy	9.0	33.76	0.94

Current Investment Style

Value Blnd Growth — Large Mid Small

Market Cap	%
Giant	43.7
Large	42.1
Mid	14.0
Small	0.1
Micro	0.0

Avg $mil: 37,401

Value Measures		Rel Category
Price/Earnings	15.37	1.00
Price/Book	2.64	1.03
Price/Sales	1.41	1.01
Price/Cash Flow	5.82	0.69
Dividend Yield %	2.04	1.17

Growth Measures	%	Rel Category
Long-Term Erngs	11.56	0.98
Book Value	8.77	0.97
Sales	9.54	0.98
Cash Flow	7.87	0.76
Historical Erngs	17.57	0.95

Profitability	%	Rel Category
Return on Equity	20.78	1.07
Return on Assets	9.49	0.91
Net Margin	13.07	0.97

Sector Weightings	% of Stocks	Rel S&P 500	3 Year High Low
Info	18.26	0.91	
Software	4.69	1.36	5 2
Hardware	7.08	0.77	8 6
Media	0.98	0.26	5 1
Telecom	5.51	1.57	9 4
Service	35.20	0.76	
Health	11.68	0.97	12 4
Consumer	6.68	0.87	7 6
Business	4.43	1.05	5 3
Financial	12.41	0.56	13 11
Mfg	46.54	1.38	
Goods	8.80	1.03	9 5
Ind Mtrls	18.73	1.57	30 19
Energy	16.08	1.64	21 12
Utilities	2.93	0.84	6 2

Composition

- Cash 8.8
- Stocks 90.8
- Bonds 0.0
- Other 0.4

Foreign 27.7 (% of Stock)

Morningstar's Take by Arijit Dutta 12-27-06

American Funds Fundamental Investors should continue to thrive on its forward-looking approach.

This fund has had a great run. The portfolio's large energy overweighting--its current 15% stake is nearly 50% higher than the S&P 500 Index's--has proved a huge winner over the past few years (though that sector has tumbled sharply in recent months). The portfolio has also freely ventured into foreign stocks (28% of its assets are currently in non-U.S. stocks), which continues to benefit the fund.

This fund has an aggressive mandate relative to American Funds' large-value offerings--so much so that we recently moved it to the large-blend group. It deserves credit for making excellent use of that leeway, though. Management upped the portfolio's energy stake back in 2004, early enough to make the most of the sector's massive rally. Moreover, stock selection has also been great. For example, Canadian oil-explorer Suncor Energy, which has been in the portfolio for almost a decade, has

trounced even the energy sector's heady gains. Management correctly identified Suncor's immense production capacity, which it still believes will generate hefty profits even at much lower oil prices. Management was also looking ahead when it started buying heavily in foreign markets back in 2001. It noticed much stronger dividend growth in foreign stocks (though the fund emphasizes capital appreciation, it has a dividend mandate as well), and much cheaper valuations than domestic equities.

Management's thoughtful, opportunistic style strikes a nice balance. It will make bold bets, but only when it spots good value, and while maintaining the fund's dividend goal. While we don't expect this fund to protect capital as well as the more-conservative American Fund choices, it has shown great upside potential to compensate. Its rock-bottom expenses further cement the fund's claim as a great core holding.

Address:	One Market - Steuart Tower San Francisco CA 94105 800-421-0180	Minimum Purchase:	$250	Add: $50	IRA: $250
		Min Auto Inv Plan:	$250	Add: $50	
		Sales Fees:	5.75%L, 0.24%S		
Web Address:	www.americanfunds.com	Management Fee:	0.39% mx./0.24% mn.		
Inception:	12-30-32	Actual Fees:	Mgt:0.27% Dist:0.24%		
Advisor:	Capital Research and Management Company	Expense Projections:	3Yr:$762 5Yr:$901 10Yr:$1305		
Subadvisor:	None	Income Distrib:	Quarterly		
NTF Plans:	Federated Tr NTF				

Amer Funds Grth Fund A

	Ticker	Load	NAV	Yield	Total Assets	Mstar Category
	AGTHX	5.75%	$32.87	0.8%	$161,166 mil	Large Growth

Governance and Management

Stewardship Grade: B

Portfolio Manager(s)

First-rate. Ten seasoned managers call most of the shots here, and a huge staff of career analysts also runs a part of the fund. Each counselor manages money without the input of his counterparts. American Funds has named new managers to the fund as assets have poured in during the past few years, but it still appears that everyone's running more money than they did a few years ago. An ongoing reorganization of the firm's investment staff introduces some uncertainty.

Strategy

The fund's portfolio managers invest independently of one another but with a common flexible-growth strategy. The team will invest in a mix of traditional growth stocks, turnaround situations, and cyclical names. The resulting portfolio is well diversified across industries and individual issues. Management also tends to park a good chunk of assets in cash at times, and the team is very sensitive to how much it pays for a stock. As a result, it may not be a chart-topper when speculative fare rules the roost, but the fund tends to be less volatile than most growth offerings.

Performance 12-31-06

	1st Qtr	2nd Qtr	3rd Qtr	4th Qtr	Total
2002	-1.27	-14.48	-13.64	6.93	-22.02
2003	-2.49	17.21	3.65	12.19	32.90
2004	3.46	1.06	-2.34	9.63	11.95
2005	-1.83	3.57	6.93	5.06	14.23
2006	4.37	-1.58	1.45	6.46	10.94

Trailing	Total Return%	+/- S&P 500	+/- Russ 1000Gr	%Rank Cat	Growth of $10,000
3 Mo	6.46	-0.24	0.53	24	10,646
6 Mo	8.00	-4.74	-2.10	57	10,800
1 Yr	10.94	-4.85	1.87	17	11,094
3 Yr Avg	12.37	1.93	5.50	5	14,189
5 Yr Avg	8.01	1.82	5.32	5	14,700
10 Yr Avg	12.94	4.52	7.50	2	33,766
15 Yr Avg	12.92	2.28	4.90	5	61,882

Tax Analysis	Tax-Adj Rtn%	%Rank Cat	Tax-Cost Rat	%Rank Cat
3 Yr (estimated)	9.73	12	0.40	27
5 Yr (estimated)	6.48	9	0.24	25
10 Yr (estimated)	11.03	2	1.10	52

Potential Capital Gain Exposure: 24% of assets

Historical Profile

Return	High
Risk	Average
Rating	★★★★ Highest

Investment Style: Equity, Stock %

85% 85% 80% 79% 82% 88% 89% 88% 87%

▼ Manager Change
▽ Partial Manager Change

Growth of $10,000
— Investment Values of Fund
— Investment Values of S&P 500

40.8
31.0
24.0
17.0
10.0

Performance Quartile (within Category)

1995	1996	1997	1998	1999	2000	2001	2002	2003	2004	2005	2006	History
15.27	16.57	18.78	22.40	29.14	27.08	23.71	18.47	24.54	27.38	30.86	32.87	NAV
29.75	14.84	26.86	31.78	45.70	7.49	-12.28	-22.02	32.90	11.95	14.23	10.94	Total Return %
-7.83	-8.12	-6.50	3.20	24.66	16.59	-0.39	0.08	4.22	1.07	9.32	-4.85	+/-S&P 500
-7.43	-8.28	-3.63	-6.93	12.54	29.91	8.14	5.86	3.15	5.65	8.97	1.87	+/-Russ 1000Gr
1.14	0.72	0.78	0.48	0.20	0.50	0.17	0.08	0.03	0.37	0.69	0.89	Income Return %
28.61	14.12	26.08	31.30	45.50	6.99	-12.45	-22.10	32.87	11.58	13.54	10.05	Capital Return %
64	78	46	46	28	6	13	18	21	17	7	17	Total Rtn % Rank Cat
0.14	0.11	0.13	0.09	0.05	0.14	0.05	0.02	0.01	0.09	0.19	0.27	Income $
1.14	0.86	2.06	2.21	3.19	4.09	0.00	0.00	0.00	0.00	0.23	1.10	Capital Gains $
0.75	0.75	0.72	0.70	0.70	0.70	0.71	0.75	0.76	0.70	0.66	0.63	Expense Ratio %
0.90	0.90	0.73	0.48	0.28	0.58	0.76	0.18	0.28	0.20	0.76	0.89	Income Ratio %
27	27	34	39	46	47	36	30	25	19	20	22	Turnover Rate %
7,891	9,675	12,248	16,247	27,407	37,006	36,347	31,104	48,074	60,323	73,623	84,112	Net Assets $mil

Rating and Risk

Time Period	Load-Adj Return %	Morningstar Rtn vs Cat	Morningstar Risk vs Cat	Morningstar Risk-Adj Rating
1 Yr	4.56			
3 Yr	10.17	+Avg	-Avg	★★★★
5 Yr	6.74	High	Avg	★★★★★
10 Yr	12.27	High	Avg	★★★★★
Incept	—			

Other Measures	Standard Index S&P 500	Best Fit Index Russ MG
Alpha	1.1	2.0
Beta	1.11	0.72
R-Squared	79	92
Standard Deviation	8.56	
Mean	12.37	
Sharpe Ratio	1.04	

Portfolio Analysis 09-30-06

Share change since 06-06 Total Stocks:266	Sector	PE	Tot Ret%	% Assets
Google, Inc.	Business	61.5	11.00	2.32
⊕ Roche Holding	Health	—		2.18
⊖ Oracle Corporation	Software	26.7	40.38	1.93
⊖ Schlumberger, Ltd.	Energy	22.3	31.07	1.81
⊕ Microsoft Corporation	Software	23.8	15.83	1.74
⊕ Lowe's Companies Inc.	Consumer	15.6	-6.05	1.69
⊕ Target	Consumer	19.3	4.65	1.58
⊕ Altria Group, Inc.	Goods	16.3	19.87	1.56
⊕ Fannie Mae	Financial	—	24.34	1.44
⊖ Cisco Systems, Inc.	Hardware	30.1	59.64	1.41
⊕ General Electric Company	Ind Mtrls	20.0	9.35	1.33
⊕ American International G	Financial	17.0	6.05	1.31
⊕ Medtronic, Inc.	Health	23.8	-6.29	1.20
⊕ Carnival Corporation	Goods	18.7	-6.15	1.19
⊖ Applied Materials	Hardware	19.5	3.89	1.10
⊕ Sprint Nextel Corporatio	Telecom	30.2	-10.44	1.04
WellPoint, Inc.	Health	17.2	-1.38	0.93
⊕ Suncor Energy, Inc.	Energy	33.1	25.42	0.92
Tyco International, Ltd.	Ind Mtrls	15.7	6.83	0.88
Best Buy Co., Inc.	Consumer	19.8	13.89	0.85

Current Investment Style

Value Blnd Growth — Large Mid Small

Market Cap	%
Giant	45.0
Large	42.8
Mid	11.9
Small	0.3
Micro	0.0

Avg $mil: 37,267

Value Measures		Rel Category
Price/Earnings	16.92	0.88
Price/Book	2.66	0.80
Price/Sales	1.70	0.88
Price/Cash Flow	5.28	0.46
Dividend Yield %	1.21	1.17

Growth Measures	%	Rel Category
Long-Term Erngs	14.07	0.98
Book Value	11.79	1.02
Sales	11.31	0.98
Cash Flow	14.38	0.86
Historical Erngs	21.17	0.92

Profitability	%	Rel Category
Return on Equity	19.72	0.97
Return on Assets	10.43	0.95
Net Margin	14.56	1.02

Sector Weightings

	% of Stocks	Rel S&P 500	3 Year High Low
⟳ Info	23.22	1.16	
🖥 Software	5.11	1.48	5 3
💻 Hardware	13.22	1.43	14 12
🎬 Media	2.43	0.64	12 6
📞 Telecom	2.46	0.70	4 2
⟲ Service	43.73	0.95	
⚕ Health	16.10	1.33	16 12
🛒 Consumer	11.18	1.46	14 11
📋 Business	7.27	1.72	8 5
💲 Financial	9.18	0.41	10 8
⚒ Mfg	33.05	0.98	
🏭 Goods	7.57	0.89	8 6
⚙ Ind Mtrls	11.19	0.94	11 9
🔋 Energy	14.29	1.46	18 8
💡 Utilities	0.00	0.00	1 0

Composition

- ● Cash 11.6
- ● Stocks 87.0
- ● Bonds 0.1
- ● Other 1.3

Foreign 20.3 (% of Stock)

Morningstar's Take by Paul Herbert 11-16-06

We're holding to our previously stated views on American Funds Growth Fund of America.

For those who haven't read our stance before, during the past few years we have been somewhat skeptical of this fund's ability to continue to put up topnotch returns because of its considerable and growing asset base. Already a large fund with nearly $40 billion in assets in early 2002, the fund has grown to $156 billion in late 2006. Running more money can increase trading costs or force a fund to tweak its approach in ways that can lead to moderate performance.

American Funds' advisor has an answer to the problem that others have faced managing size. It employs a multiple-manager system designed to prevent individuals from having responsibility for too much of a fund's assets. This fund has 10 chiefs and its lead portfolio manager says that no one is running more than 10% of the fund's assets.

Up until now, at least, it appears that the setup has worked, as the fund has continued to perform very strongly as it has grown. As before, the managers have continued to uncover winning ideas. Spot-on broad moves such as turning to non-U.S. stocks and overweighting energy names have helped, as have strong stock picks such as Google. In all, the fund has trounced relevant peer groups and benchmarks in recent years.

We're impressed by this feat, but some uncertainty makes us concerned about the fund's future. Despite the firm's reassurances, we still don't know how much managers here are running. Several of Growth Fund's decision makers run parts of other charges and the firm doesn't disclose individual manager burdens. It would be easier for us to appreciate the benefits of the system if we had this information. Plus, we still think that the firm's move to divide its investment staff into two groups, while it may have benefits, could disrupt interactions.

In the end, we continue to worry that the fund will be a less-stellar performer over the long run.

Address:	One Market - Steuart Tower San Francisco CA 94105 800-421-0180	Minimum Purchase:	$250	Add: $50	IRA: $250
		Min Auto Inv Plan:	$250	Add: $50	
		Sales Fees:	5.75%L, 0.25%S		
Web Address:	www.americanfunds.com	Management Fee:	0.50% mx./0.24% mn.		
Inception:	01-01-59	Actual Fees:	Mgt:0.28%	Dist:0.25%	
Advisor:	Capital Research and Management Company	Expense Projections:	3Yr:$771	5Yr:$916	10Yr:$1339
Subadvisor:	None	Income Distrib:	Annually		
NTF Plans:	Federated Tr NTF				

MORNINGSTAR® Funds 500

Amer Funds Inc Fund A

	Ticker	Load	NAV	Yield	Total Assets	Mstar Category
	AMECX	5.75%	$20.36	4.3%	$76,353 mil	Moderate Allocation

Governance and Management

Stewardship Grade: B

Portfolio Manager(s)

The fund's nine named portfolio "counselors" (managers) are a very seasoned bunch, with an average of more than 18 years with the fund's advisor, Capital Research and Management. Moreover, the firm boasts one of the deepest and most skilled research benches in the fund business.

Strategy

The fund's managers favor stocks that pay high dividends, which typically leads them to large stakes in financials and utilities stocks and scant exposure to technology shares. On the bond side, the team keeps the fund's interest-rate risk fairly moderate and won't invest more than 20% of assets in issues rated below investment-grade--that sliver has been a tad below 10% of late.

Historical Profile

Return	Above Avg
Risk	Below Avg
Rating	★★★★ Above Avg

Investment Style: Equity / Stock %

47% 51% 51% 48% 44% 56% 63% 63% 64%

▼ Manager Change
▽ Partial Manager Change

Growth of $10,000
■ Investment Values of Fund
— Investment Values of DJ Mod

37.0 32.0 25.0 20.0 15.0 10.0

Performance Quartile (within Category)

	1995	1996	1997	1998	1999	2000	2001	2002	2003	2004	2005	2006	History
	15.87	16.52	17.77	17.34	15.74	15.94	15.82	14.35	17.18	18.56	18.11	20.36	NAV
	29.08	15.23	22.16	9.47	0.52	9.98	5.41	-4.37	25.27	12.92	3.41	20.29	Total Return %
	9.28	4.57	10.26	-2.85	-16.81	11.65	8.21	2.40	-2.11	-0.05	-3.58	7.99	+/-DJ Mod
	4.31	3.89	2.96	-2.92	-12.33	5.54	5.25	6.17	1.21	1.75	-2.59	10.02	+/-DJ US Mod
	6.45	5.79	5.17	5.04	5.11	5.18	5.11	4.99	4.97	3.87	3.88	5.00	Income Return %
	22.63	9.44	16.99	4.43	-4.59	4.80	0.30	-9.36	20.30	9.05	-0.47	15.29	Capital Return %
	23	47	28	74	91	12	4	4	12	7	75	1	Total Rtn % Rank Cat
	0.83	0.90	0.82	0.88	0.87	0.80	0.80	0.78	0.70	0.66	0.71	0.89	Income $
	0.18	0.81	1.48	1.19	0.81	0.48	0.16	0.02	0.00	0.13	0.36	0.46	Capital Gains $
	0.65	0.62	0.61	0.59	0.59	0.63	0.62	0.61	0.61	0.57	0.54	0.53	Expense Ratio %
	6.12	5.56	5.09	4.75	4.99	5.52	5.18	4.66	4.98	4.15	4.26	4.35	Income Ratio %
	26	38	41	35	44	35	44	36	28	27	24	35	Turnover Rate %
	13,778	16,192	20,221	22,909	21,450	18,568	19,853	20,836	31,955	42,536	48,701	58,910	Net Assets $mil

Performance 12-31-06

	1st Qtr	2nd Qtr	3rd Qtr	4th Qtr	Total
2002	3.22	-3.61	-10.29	7.13	-4.37
2003	-1.13	11.37	2.43	11.07	25.27
2004	1.96	0.15	2.71	7.67	12.92
2005	-1.37	2.12	2.21	0.45	3.41
2006	4.94	1.75	5.62	6.67	20.29

Trailing	Total Return%	+/- DJ Mod	+/- DJ US Mod	%Rank Cat	Growth of $10,000
3 Mo	6.67	1.08	2.00	6	10,667
6 Mo	12.67	3.88	4.77	2	11,267
1 Yr	20.29	7.99	10.02	1	12,029
3 Yr Avg	11.99	1.27	2.87	5	14,046
5 Yr Avg	10.97	0.95	3.37	2	16,828
10 Yr Avg	10.12	1.57	1.53	7	26,222
15 Yr Avg	11.11	1.90	1.72	7	48,562

Tax Analysis	Tax-Adj Rtn%	%Rank Cat	Tax-Cost Rat	%Rank Cat
3 Yr (estimated)	8.01	26	1.63	82
5 Yr (estimated)	7.81	6	1.69	93
10 Yr (estimated)	6.99	15	2.27	94

Potential Capital Gain Exposure: 19% of assets

Rating and Risk

Time Period	Load-Adj Return %	Morningstar Rtn vs Cat	Morningstar Risk vs Cat	Morningstar Risk-Adj Rating
1 Yr	13.38			
3 Yr	9.80	+Avg	Avg	★★★★
5 Yr	9.66	High	Avg	★★★★★
10 Yr	9.47	+Avg	Low	★★★★
Incept	11.01			

Other Measures	Standard Index DJ Mod	Best Fit Index Russ 1000 Vl
Alpha	3.0	0.6
Beta	0.74	0.69
R-Squared	71	83
Standard Deviation	5.20	
Mean	11.99	
Sharpe Ratio	1.62	

Morningstar's Take by Christine Benz 12-27-06

We're fans of American Funds Income Fund of America's prudent approach to income generation.

Any time you see a fund with a relatively high yield--and this fund's payout is among the highest in the moderate-allocation category--it's worth investigating what it's investing in to achieve it. Many funds are marketed on the basis of their yields, and some will venture into high-risk securities in order to deliver a tempting payout. Companies with shaky credit qualities have to pay high bond yields to compensate for risk that they'll welch on their debts, of course, and very high stock-dividend yields often result when a company's share price has plummeted on bad fundamental news.

Yet we're satisfied that this fund's management team isn't taking undue risks to help it achieve its compelling payout. For starters, the fund has one of the lowest expense ratios in the category, meaning that more of its income automatically flows through to shareholders. And the fund's stock and bond portfolios rest on a solid foundation. Its experienced equity management team employs a time-tested value-leaning approach, limits individual positions to mitigate company-specific risk, and leans on the firm's fine international team as a source of additional stock ideas. On the fixed-income side, management limits risk by capping its stake in below-investment-grade credits at 20%.

Recent performance has been exceptional, but it's worth noting that the fund won't thrive in every market environment. When pricey growth stocks lead the way, this fund will almost certainly look slow. Perhaps a bigger worry is the fund's girth, particularly when you consider that many of its top holdings appear in other portfolios within the American Funds complex. That's an issue we're watching closely, but it's reassuring that most of its holdings are highly liquid and its turnover has typically been quite low.

Income-seekers should find a happy home here.

Portfolio Analysis 09-30-06

Total Stocks:178

Share change since 06-30-06	Sectors	P/E Ratio	YTD Return %	% Net Assets
⊖ AT&T, Inc.	Telecom	18.2	-5.43	2.36
⊖ Chevron Corporation	Energy	9.0	-2.83	2.11
⊖ BellSouth Corporation	Telecom	—		1.94
⊕ Citigroup, Inc.	Financial	13.1	-1.17	1.84
⊕ General Electric Company	Ind Mtrls	20.0	0.91	1.82
⊖ Bristol-Myers Squibb Comp	Health	23.1	0.22	1.34
⊕ Verizon Communications	Telecom	15.9	-0.07	1.32
Merck & Co., Inc.	Health	19.1	1.58	1.14
⊕ Washington Mutual, Inc.	Financial	13.4	-0.79	1.13

Total Fixed-Income:1125

	Date of Maturity	Amount $000	Value $000	% Net Assets
US Treasury Note 4.25%	08-15-13	273,875	268,140	0.39
Nextel Comms 7.375%	08-01-15	165,240	170,656	0.25
QWEST COMMUNICATIONS INTL	11-15-25	100,000	163,250	0.24
Electnc Data Sys New 6.5%	08-01-13	137,150	139,319	0.20
Cwalt CMO 5.5%	11-25-35	137,303	136,062	0.20
Sb Treas 144A FRN	12-29-49	124,434	132,286	0.19
General Mtrs 7.2%	01-15-11	138,470	128,258	0.18
Nextel Comms 6.875%	10-31-13	125,730	128,122	0.18
Gmac 7.25%	03-02-11	104,895	105,593	0.15

Equity Style
Style: Value
Size: Large-Cap

Value Measures		Rel Category
Price/Earnings	14.38	0.94
Price/Book	2.33	0.94
Price/Sales	1.39	1.01
Price/Cash Flow	9.57	1.18
Dividend Yield %	3.99	2.07

Growth Measures	%	Rel Category
Long-Term Erngs	8.87	0.76
Book Value	5.69	0.66
Sales	5.45	0.61
Cash Flow	-0.76	NMF
Historical Erngs	10.65	0.60

Market Cap %			
Giant	46.7	Small	0.7
Large	39.7	Micro	0.0
Mid	12.9	Avg $mil:	37,365

Fixed-Income Style
Duration: Interm-Term
Quality: Medium

Avg Eff Duration [1]	4.2 Yrs
Avg Eff Maturity	6.2 Yrs
Avg Credit Quality	BBB
Avg Wtd Coupon	6.63%

[1]figure provided by fund as of 09-30-06

Sector Weightings	% of Stocks	Rel DJ Mod	3 Year High Low
⊙ Info	13.40	—	
Software	0.56	—	1 0
Hardware	0.33	—	1 0
Media	0.13	—	1 0
Telecom	12.38	—	14 11
⊏ Service	40.88		
Health	8.54	—	9 3
Consumer	2.36	—	4 2
Business	1.92	—	3 0
Financial	28.06	—	29 27
Mfg	45.71		
Goods	13.18	—	14 10
Ind Mtrls	11.93	—	18 12
Energy	8.20	—	12 8
Utilities	12.40	—	15 10

Composition

● Cash	9.3
● Stocks	64.4
● Bonds	22.7
● Other	3.7
Foreign (% of Stock)	23.2

Address:	One Market - Steuart Tower San Francisco CA 94105 800-421-0180
Web Address:	www.americanfunds.com
Inception:	12-31-70
Advisor:	Capital Research and Management Company
Subadvisor:	None
NTF Plans:	Federated Tr NTF

Minimum Purchase:	$250	Add: $50	IRA: $250
Min Auto Inv Plan:	$50	Add: $50	
Sales Fees:	5.75%L, 0.23%S		
Management Fee:	0.25%		
Actual Fees:	Mgt:0.25%	Dist:0.23%	
Expense Projections:	3Yr:$744	5Yr:$870	10Yr:$1236
Income Distrib:	Quarterly		

Amer Funds Inv Co Am A

	Ticker	Load	NAV	Yield	Total Assets	Mstar Category
	AIVSX	5.75%	$33.51	2.1%	$88,703 mil	Large Value

Governance and Management

Stewardship Grade: B

Portfolio Manager(s)

The fund is managed by a veteran nine-person team. The firm's research capabilities are hard to match as it employs more than 140 investment pros globally. Investors will also be hard-pressed to find analysts with greater industry expertise. Joyce Gordon, for example, has followed banks since 1987. Both managers and analysts are compensated in part based on how their picks perform versus a benchmark over a four-year moving average.

Strategy

The fund favors established blue-chip companies, many of which pay dividends. As a result, the fund devotes a decent portion of assets to stocks in industries such as oil services, financials, and tobacco. But management is also willing to scoop up shares in depressed growth names. Thus, it isn't surprising to see stocks that are typically considered growth stocks in its portfolio. Management will also keep a decent chunk of assets parked in bonds and cash at times.

Historical Profile

Return	Average
Risk	Low
Rating	★★★ Neutral

81% 85% 78% 79% 72% 82% 84% 84% 83%

Investment Style
Equity
Stock %

▼ Manager Change
▽ Partial Manager Change

Growth of $10,000
— Investment Values of Fund
— Investment Values of S&P 500

38.0
31.0
24.0
17.0
10.0

Performance Quartile (within Category)

1995	1996	1997	1998	1999	2000	2001	2002	2003	2004	2005	2006	History
21.61	24.23	28.25	31.07	32.46	31.06	28.53	23.48	28.84	30.75	31.36	33.51	NAV
30.63	19.35	29.81	22.94	16.56	3.84	-4.59	-14.47	26.31	9.78	6.87	15.94	Total Return %
-6.95	-3.61	-3.55	-5.64	-4.48	12.94	7.30	7.63	-2.37	-1.10	1.96	0.15	+/-S&P 500
-7.73	-2.29	-5.37	7.31	9.21	-3.17	1.00	1.05	-3.72	-6.71	-0.18	-6.31	+/-Russ 1000 VI
2.86	2.33	2.08	1.83	1.66	1.63	1.70	1.84	2.23	1.82	2.23	2.38	Income Return %
27.77	17.02	27.73	21.11	14.90	2.21	-6.29	-16.31	24.08	7.96	4.64	13.56	Capital Return %
68	54	25	4	9	74	55	24	65	85	33	78	Total Rtn % Rank Cat
0.50	0.50	0.50	0.51	0.51	0.52	0.52	0.52	0.52	0.52	0.68	0.74	Income $
0.91	1.03	2.60	2.94	3.04	2.08	0.59	0.46	0.21	0.36	0.81	2.06	Capital Gains $
0.60	0.59	0.56	0.55	0.55	0.56	0.57	0.59	0.59	0.57	0.55	—	Expense Ratio %
2.70	2.17	1.90	1.65	1.54	1.74	1.49	1.89	2.14	2.06	2.06	—	Income Ratio %
21	17	26	25	28	25	22	27	24	19	19	—	Turnover Rate %
25,678	30,875	39,718	48,498	56,095	56,212	54,315	46,129	58,353	64,880	66,959	73,978	Net Assets $mil

Performance 12-31-06

	1st Qtr	2nd Qtr	3rd Qtr	4th Qtr	Total
2002	2.02	-9.06	-14.51	7.84	-14.47
2003	-4.43	14.47	2.39	12.75	26.31
2004	1.48	0.59	-0.10	7.65	9.78
2005	-0.89	1.06	4.23	2.37	6.87
2006	4.15	1.51	4.08	5.37	15.94

Trailing	Total Return%	+/- S&P 500	+/- Russ 1000 VI	%Rank Cat	Growth of $10,000
3 Mo	5.37	-1.33	-2.63	93	10,537
6 Mo	9.67	-3.07	-5.05	92	10,967
1 Yr	15.94	0.15	-6.31	78	11,594
3 Yr Avg	10.80	0.36	-4.29	76	13,603
5 Yr Avg	8.00	1.81	-2.86	54	14,693
10 Yr Avg	10.47	2.05	-0.53	19	27,067
15 Yr Avg	11.40	0.76	-1.63	40	50,498

Tax Analysis	Tax-Adj Rtn%	%Rank Cat	Tax-Cost Rat	%Rank Cat
3 Yr (estimated)	7.36	92	1.17	46
5 Yr (estimated)	5.56	79	1.10	59
10 Yr (estimated)	8.09	30	1.58	53

Potential Capital Gain Exposure: 0% of assets

Rating and Risk

Time Period	Load-Adj Return %	Morningstar Rtn vs Cat	Morningstar Risk vs Cat	Morningstar Risk-Adj Rating
1 Yr	9.27			
3 Yr	8.63	Low	Low	★★
5 Yr	6.73	-Avg	Low	★★★
10 Yr	9.82	+Avg	-Avg	★★★★
Incept	12.81			

Other Measures	Standard Index S&P 500	Best Fit Index Russ 1000 VI
Alpha	1.7	-2.0
Beta	0.80	0.83
R-Squared	88	91
Standard Deviation	5.90	
Mean	10.80	
Sharpe Ratio	1.24	

Morningstar's Take by Karen Dolan 12-27-06

American Funds Investment Company of America is well positioned, but we think its siblings are a better bet.

This fund has not been able to outshine its competition in recent years. It has lagged the typical large-cap value fund on a trailing three-year basis for several months now. The fund's giant-cap bias has held it back as smaller companies have led the way. And while the fund has benefited from a healthy stake in rallying energy stocks, bets on media and telecom have largely worked against it.

Even so, the fund's portfolio looks strong on a fundamental basis and could be due for a comeback. Its aggregate valuation measures such as price/earnings and price/cash flow are below those of the S&P 500 Index. Meanwhile, the fund enjoys higher dividend yields from its stocks. The fund also has a meaningful cost advantage: It is the cheapest front-load large-cap value fund available.

The fund's large size could stand in the way of its future competitiveness, though. With more than $85 billion in assets, it is the biggest large-value fund. As is the case with all American Funds, the fund's multimanager setup better equips it to deal with its size. The portfolio is cut 10 ways among nine different managers and a group of research analysts. Each sleeve is managed independently of the others. Yet, we're still concerned that the fund's girth makes trading more difficult and could trap the portfolio in mega-caps indefinitely. What's more, the fund also faces the risk that the managers' high-conviction bets will cancel each other out as its manager roster grows.

For these reasons, we think investors should consider other funds. Within the American Fund lineup, Fundamental Investors is smaller and more nimble. And although Washington Mutual Investors also has a huge asset base, its stricter commitment to dividend-paying stocks is appealing. What's more, those funds have managed their downside well without diluting the portfolio with cash and bonds, as this fund does.

Address:	333 S Hope St - 55th FL Los Angeles CA 90071 800-421-0180
Web Address:	www.americanfunds.com
Inception:	01-02-34
Advisor:	Capital Research and Management Company
Subadvisor:	None
NTF Plans:	Federated Tr NTF

Minimum Purchase:	$250	Add: $50	IRA: $0
Min Auto Inv Plan:	$0	Add: $0	
Sales Fees:	5.75%L, 0.23%S		
Management Fee:	0.39% mx./0.22% mn.		
Actual Fees:	Mgt:0.24%	Dist:0.23%	
Expense Projections:	3Yr:$747	5Yr:$875	10Yr:$1248
Income Distrib:	Quarterly		

Portfolio Analysis 09-30-06

Share change since 06-06 Total Stocks:172

Sector	PE	Tot Ret%	% Assets
⊖ Altria Group, Inc. — Goods	16.3	19.87	4.31
⊖ AT&T, Inc. — Telecom	18.2	51.59	2.64
⊕ General Electric Company — Ind Mtrls	20.0	9.35	2.04
⊕ Citigroup, Inc. — Financial	13.1	19.55	1.84
⊕ Lowe's Companies Inc. — Consumer	15.6	-6.05	1.77
⊖ Microsoft Corporation — Software	23.8	15.83	1.76
Oracle Corporation — Software	26.7	40.38	1.74
Fannie Mae — Financial	—	24.34	1.71
Schlumberger, Ltd. — Energy	22.3	31.07	1.69
⊖ BellSouth Corporation — Telecom	—	—	1.63
Tyco International, Ltd. — Ind Mtrls	15.7	6.83	1.56
Chevron Corporation — Energy	9.0	33.76	1.55
⊕ Target — Consumer	19.3	4.65	1.47
Royal Dutch Shell PLC AD — Energy	8.7	19.33	1.41
Washington Mutual, Inc. — Financial	13.4	9.62	1.31
⊕ IBM — Hardware	17.1	19.77	1.15
PepsiCo, Inc. — Goods	21.5	7.86	1.10
⊕ Roche Holding — Health	—	—	1.03
Best Buy Co., Inc. — Consumer	19.8	13.89	0.99
⊖ Merck & Co., Inc. — Health	19.1	42.66	0.98

Current Investment Style

Value Blnd Growth — Large Mid Small

Market Cap	%
Giant	60.5
Large	35.8
Mid	3.6
Small	0.0
Micro	0.0

Avg $mil: 63,949

Value Measures		Rel Category
Price/Earnings	14.66	1.07
Price/Book	2.48	1.12
Price/Sales	1.31	1.01
Price/Cash Flow	6.27	0.94
Dividend Yield %	2.44	1.05

Growth Measures	%	Rel Category
Long-Term Erngs	11.31	1.09
Book Value	8.69	1.10
Sales	7.97	0.89
Cash Flow	9.38	1.55
Historical Erngs	15.04	0.93

Profitability	%	Rel Category
Return on Equity	20.06	1.12
Return on Assets	9.92	1.01
Net Margin	12.85	0.99

Sector Weightings	% of Stocks	Rel S&P 500	3 Year High	Low
↻ Info	23.10	1.16		
🖥 Software	4.21	1.22	4	1
💻 Hardware	10.32	1.12	10	8
🎤 Media	1.46	0.39	4	1
📱 Telecom	7.11	2.03	9	6
☁ Service	35.78	0.77		
🏥 Health	11.12	0.92	11	6
🛒 Consumer	7.96	1.04	8	6
💼 Business	2.48	0.59	3	2
💲 Financial	14.22	0.64	15	12
🏭 Mfg	41.11	1.22		
🛍 Goods	13.53	1.58	15	12
⚙ Ind Mtrls	14.51	1.22	20	15
🔥 Energy	10.30	1.05	14	10
💡 Utilities	2.77	0.79	3	2

Composition

	%
● Cash	16.5
● Stocks	83.2
● Bonds	0.0
● Other	0.3
Foreign	11.8
(% of Stock)	

MORNINGSTAR® Funds 500

Amer Funds New Econ A

	Ticker	Load	NAV	Yield	Total Assets	Mstar Category
	ANEFX	5.75%	$26.70	0.7%	$8,682 mil	Large Growth

Governance and Management

Stewardship Grade: B

Portfolio Manager(s)

The team here is seasoned and influential. Its most senior member, Gordon Crawford, has been in the business for 34 years and wields significant influence with many of the media industry's top executives. The portfolio counselors are backed by an experienced and extensive team of research analysts who are based around the globe. We think there is a risk that a recent reorganization may strain communications channels among these investors.

Strategy

This fund invests in companies whose prospects are tied to the information and services areas of the economy. The upshot of this approach is that the fund tends to have large stakes in technology and telecom, and it also boasts significant exposure to financial services and media. Management sometimes maintains a double-digit cash stake and will invest a good chunk of assets overseas. It generally prefers a growth-at-a-reasonable-price approach, but the fund owns everything from value names to hypergrowth stocks.

Performance 12-31-06

	1st Qtr	2nd Qtr	3rd Qtr	4th Qtr	Total
2002	-1.20	-15.21	-19.24	9.37	-26.01
2003	-4.51	22.82	5.29	12.33	38.71
2004	3.84	-0.26	-3.50	12.51	12.45
2005	-4.61	3.69	5.29	7.71	12.17
2006	4.31	-3.60	4.75	8.92	14.73

Trailing	Total Return%	+/- S&P 500	+/- Russ 1000Gr	%Rank Cat	Growth of $10,000
3 Mo	8.92	2.22	2.99	5	10,892
6 Mo	14.10	1.36	4.00	3	11,410
1 Yr	14.73	-1.06	5.66	5	11,473
3 Yr Avg	13.11	2.67	6.24	3	14,471
5 Yr Avg	8.23	2.04	5.54	4	14,850
10 Yr Avg	9.56	1.14	4.12	7	24,918
15 Yr Avg	11.20	0.56	3.18	11	49,155

Tax Analysis	Tax-Adj Rtn%	%Rank Cat	Tax-Cost Rat	%Rank Cat
3 Yr (estimated)	10.68	8	0.20	14
5 Yr (estimated)	6.82	7	0.13	14
10 Yr (estimated)	7.89	9	0.94	45

Potential Capital Gain Exposure: 23% of assets

Morningstar's Take by Paul Herbert 11-15-06

American Funds New Economy Fund's designers deserve credit for their foresight.

Simply reading this fund's name might cause some cringing, particularly among investors who suffered the worst when the tech bubble burst in 2000. This fund owns a healthy dose of technology, telecom, and media stocks, and it did post sharp losses during the 2000 to 2002 period. But it would be unwise to throw it in with the many narrow, aggressive offerings that crashed and burned earlier this decade. (Although the fund slid during the bear market, it didn't fare worse than other large-growth funds.) First, its managers' vision of the future--which took shape before this fund was launched in 1983--includes financial-services, energy-services, retail, and drug firms. Second, as part of the American Funds family, the fund is backed by a stout research effort and features a long-term outlook.

Those two factors have worked for the fund in recent years, but one could argue that a third has

been more important. To be sure, exposure to non-technology stocks such as Schlumberger and Wells Fargo has helped the fund to deliver lights-out performance during the past four years as tech has generally struggled. But the fund's top-flight results may owe more to its nearly-40% stake in non-U.S. stocks, considering that the typical fund in the category sticks less than 7% of assets abroad. Foreign equities have benefited from higher growth abroad, as well as the decline of the U.S. dollar. For the fund, holding stocks such as Roche, Societe Generale, and many others, has been quite a coup.

While the fund's success is nice, the remaining challenge for investors is determining how to use the fund in a portfolio. Its emphasis on the software, hardware, media, telecom, consumer-services, and business-services areas mean it will work best for investors whose portfolios are more geared toward "old economy" stocks. That may be a limited audience indeed.

Address:	333 S Hope St - 55th FL Los Angeles CA 90071 800-421-0180
Web Address:	www.americanfunds.com
Inception:	12-01-83
Advisor:	Capital Research and Management Company
Subadvisor:	None
NTF Plans:	Federated Tr NTF

Minimum Purchase:	$250	Add: $50	IRA: $250
Min Auto Inv Plan:	$50	Add: $50	
Sales Fees:	5.75%L, 0.24%S		
Management Fee:	0.58% mx./0.35% mn.		
Actual Fees:	Mgt:0.41%	Dist:0.24%	
Expense Projections:	3Yr:$825	5Yr:$1009	10Yr:$1541
Income Distrib:	Annually		

Historical Profile

Return	High
Risk	Above Avg
Rating	★★★★ Above Avg

Investment Style: Equity Stock %

86% | 85% | 86% | 90% | 86% | 91% | 90% | 89% | 91%

▼ Manager Change
▽ Partial Manager Change

Growth of $10,000
— Investment Values of Fund
— Investment Values of S&P 500

33.0
26.0
20.0
15.0
10.0

Performance Quartile (within Category)

1995	1996	1997	1998	1999	2000	2001	2002	2003	2004	2005	2006	History
16.18	16.98	19.97	22.95	29.82	22.14	18.30	13.54	18.77	21.03	23.44	26.70	NAV
24.37	12.89	28.85	28.84	45.87	-16.20	-17.34	-26.01	38.71	12.45	12.17	14.73	Total Return %
-13.21	-10.07	-4.51	0.26	24.81	-7.10	-5.45	-3.91	10.03	1.57	7.26	-1.06	+/-S&P 500
-12.81	-10.23	-1.64	-9.87	12.71	6.22	3.08	1.87	8.96	6.15	6.91	5.66	+/-Russ 1000Gr
1.39	0.87	0.77	0.70	0.79	0.00	0.00	0.00	0.08	0.40	0.71	0.82	Income Return %
22.98	12.02	28.08	28.14	45.08	-16.20	-17.34	-26.01	38.63	12.05	11.46	13.91	Capital Return %
88	87	38	57	28	66	36	44	9	13	12	5	Total Rtn % Rank Cat
0.19	0.14	0.13	0.14	0.18	0.00	0.00	0.00	0.01	0.07	0.15	0.19	Income $
0.69	1.13	1.72	2.54	3.18	2.92	0.00	0.00	0.00	0.00	0.00	0.00	Capital Gains $
0.88	0.84	0.81	0.79	0.78	0.81	0.82	0.89	0.89	0.84	0.79	—	Expense Ratio %
1.33	0.85	0.66	0.60	0.42	0.42	0.02	-0.01	0.09	0.32	0.73	—	Income Ratio %
27	30	32	39	48	54	41	37	38	35	32	—	Turnover Rate %
3,546	4,132	4,985	6,531	10,865	10,438	8,159	5,262	6,885	7,151	7,218	7,654	Net Assets $mil

Rating and Risk

Time Period	Load-Adj Return %	Morningstar Rtn vs Cat	Morningstar Risk vs Cat	Morningstar Risk-Adj Rating
1 Yr	8.13			
3 Yr	10.90	High	Avg	★★★★★
5 Yr	6.96	High	High	★★★★
10 Yr	8.91	+Avg	Avg	★★★★
Incept	12.24			

Other Measures	Standard Index S&P 500	Best Fit Index Russ MG
Alpha	0.4	1.9
Beta	1.32	0.82
R-Squared	85	89
Standard Deviation	9.87	
Mean	13.11	
Sharpe Ratio	0.98	

Portfolio Analysis 09-30-06

Share change since 06-06 Total Stocks:177	Sector	PE	Tot Ret%	% Assets
Google, Inc.	Business	61.5	11.00	3.12
Target	Consumer	19.3	4.65	2.28
Cisco Systems, Inc.	Hardware	30.1	59.64	1.78
⊖ Schlumberger, Ltd.	Energy	22.3	31.07	1.66
Freddie Mac	Financial	23.3	7.06	1.59
⊕ UniCredito Italiano Grp	Financial	—	—	1.50
⊕ Intel Corporation	Hardware	21.0	-17.18	1.45
⊖ Microsoft Corporation	Software	23.8	15.83	1.42
⊕ Bayer	Ind Mtrls	—	—	1.42
Societe Generale Grp	Financial	—	—	1.40
Hynix Semiconductor	Hardware	—	—	1.39
Symantec Corporation	Software	50.9	19.14	1.39
⊕ Lowe's Companies Inc.	Consumer	15.6	-6.05	1.30
⊕ eBay, Inc.	Consumer	40.1	-30.43	1.30
⊕ Erste Bank	Financial	—	—	1.29
⊕ Roche Holding	Health	—	—	1.19
Affiliated Computer Serv	Business	16.0	-17.47	1.14
Oracle Corporation	Software	26.7	40.38	1.13
⊕ Sprint Nextel Corporatio	Telecom	30.2	-10.44	1.06
⊕ Wells Fargo Company	Financial	14.7	16.82	1.04

Current Investment Style

Value Blnd Growth — Large Mid Small

Market Cap	%
Giant	35.0
Large	42.1
Mid	19.9
Small	3.0
Micro	0.0

Avg $mil: 21,132

Value Measures		Rel Category
Price/Earnings	17.89	0.93
Price/Book	2.35	0.71
Price/Sales	1.69	0.87
Price/Cash Flow	3.46	0.30
Dividend Yield %	1.58	1.53

Growth Measures	%	Rel Category
Long-Term Erngs	14.24	0.99
Book Value	9.96	0.86
Sales	9.04	0.78
Cash Flow	11.19	0.67
Historical Erngs	15.59	0.68

Profitability	%	Rel Category
Return on Equity	18.40	0.91
Return on Assets	8.86	0.80
Net Margin	14.67	1.03

Sector Weightings	% of Stocks	Rel S&P 500	3 Year High	Low
⟳ Info	33.07	1.65		
Software	5.46	1.58	6	2
Hardware	13.39	1.45	17	12
Media	7.07	1.87	15	7
Telecom	7.15	2.04	11	7
⟱ Service	58.06	1.26		
Health	12.48	1.03	12	12
Consumer	13.37	1.75	21	13
Business	11.99	2.83	14	10
Financial	20.22	0.91	22	17
⟰ Mfg	8.86	0.26		
Goods	2.90	0.34	5	3
Ind Mtrls	3.17	0.27	4	0
Energy	1.98	0.20	6	2
Utilities	0.81	0.23	2	0

Composition

● Cash		8.5
● Stocks		90.7
● Bonds		0.0
○ Other		0.8
Foreign (% of Stock)		40.4

Amer Funds New Persp A

	Ticker	Load	NAV	Yield	Total Assets	Mstar Category
	ANWPX	5.75%	$31.74	1.5%	$52,548 mil	World Stock

Governance and Management

Stewardship Grade: B

Portfolio Manager(s)

American Funds uses a multimanager system at its offerings. Each portfolio manager runs a portion of assets, investing independently of the others. The managers' styles range from moderately aggressive to conservative. The average manager tenure here spans approximately two decades. All the managers also comanage other successful offerings, such as American Funds EuroPacific Growth and American Funds New Economy.

Strategy

This fund's managers typically buy out-of-favor companies and hold them for the long run. Although they tend to shop for bargains, they allow their winners to run, which pushes the fund into large-cap growth territory. The managers never chase speculative stocks, though. The fund always has a sizable cash position. American Funds uses a fair-value pricing policy, although it only implemented such an approach within the past few years.

Historical Profile

Return	Average
Risk	Average
Rating	★★★ Neutral

Investment style: 83% 85% 81% 82% 85% 87% 91% 90% 90%

▼ Manager Change
▽ Partial Manager Change

Growth of $10,000
— Investment Values of Fund
— Investment Values of MSCI EAFE

38.0 / 31.0 / 24.0 / 17.0 / 10.0

Performance Quartile (within Category)

1995	1996	1997	1998	1999	2000	2001	2002	2003	2004	2005	2006	History
16.38	18.17	19.36	22.95	29.44	24.05	21.69	18.04	24.49	27.72	28.63	31.74	NAV
20.43	17.28	14.98	28.53	40.07	-7.24	-8.30	-16.05	36.76	14.27	11.28	19.87	Total Return %
9.22	11.23	13.20	8.60	13.04	6.95	13.12	-0.11	-1.83	-5.98	-2.26	-6.47	+/-MSCI EAFE
-0.29	3.80	-0.78	4.21	15.12	5.95	8.50	3.84	3.65	-0.45	1.79	-0.20	+/-MSCI World
2.17	1.98	1.60	1.35	0.74	0.66	1.54	0.77	0.98	1.05	1.43	1.74	Income Return %
18.26	15.30	13.38	27.18	39.33	-7.90	-9.84	-16.82	35.78	13.22	9.85	18.13	Capital Return %
35	38	50	13	44	43	18	26	40	59	55	48	Total Rtn % Rank Cat
0.31	0.32	0.29	0.26	0.17	0.20	0.37	0.17	0.18	0.26	0.40	0.50	Income $
0.60	0.69	1.21	1.57	2.34	3.10	0.00	0.00	0.00	0.00	1.82	2.06	Capital Gains $
0.83	0.82	0.79	0.77	0.77	0.79	0.78	0.82	0.82	0.78	0.74	0.71	Expense Ratio %
2.12	2.00	1.56	1.27	1.06	1.00	1.40	0.84	0.84	0.93	1.36	1.63	Income Ratio %
22	18	26	30	29	34	32	26	28	19	30	32	Turnover Rate %
9,292	12,895	16,203	21,257	32,173	31,304	27,787	22,166	29,053	33,735	36,756	42,805	Net Assets $mil

Performance 12-31-06

	1st Qtr	2nd Qtr	3rd Qtr	4th Qtr	Total
2002	2.12	-8.85	-18.28	10.35	-16.05
2003	-8.20	19.99	7.35	15.67	36.76
2004	3.23	-0.28	-1.19	12.34	14.27
2005	-2.20	0.18	8.73	4.46	11.28
2006	5.76	0.36	4.44	8.12	19.87

Trailing	Total Return%	+/- MSCI EAFE	+/- MSCI World	%Rank Cat	Growth of $10,000
3 Mo	8.12	-2.23	-0.25	63	10,812
6 Mo	12.93	-1.76	-0.28	51	11,293
1 Yr	19.87	-6.47	-0.20	48	11,987
3 Yr Avg	15.08	-4.85	0.40	53	15,241
5 Yr Avg	11.84	-3.14	1.87	41	17,498
10 Yr Avg	11.91	4.20	4.27	16	30,810
15 Yr Avg	12.58	4.72	3.89	10	59,145

Tax Analysis	Tax-Adj Rtn%	%Rank Cat	Tax-Cost Rat	%Rank Cat
3 Yr (estimated)	11.67	79	1.03	55
5 Yr (estimated)	9.70	52	0.74	57
10 Yr (estimated)	9.87	20	1.24	62

Potential Capital Gain Exposure: 32% of assets

Rating and Risk

Time Period	Load-Adj Return %	Morningstar Rtn vs Cat	Morningstar Risk vs Cat	Morningstar Risk-Adj Rating
1 Yr	12.97			
3 Yr	12.83	-Avg	Avg	★★
5 Yr	10.52	Avg	Avg	★★★
10 Yr	11.25	+Avg	Avg	★★★★
Incept	13.67			

Other Measures	Standard Index MSCI EAFE	Best Fit Index MSCI World
Alpha	-2.8	-1.1
Beta	0.91	1.14
R-Squared	88	94
Standard Deviation	9.16	
Mean	15.08	
Sharpe Ratio	1.24	

Morningstar's Take by Kai Wiecking 12-26-06

American Funds New Perspective is still a good choice, but investors shouldn't expect miracles from it.

This fund sports an enviable long-term record. Its trailing 10-year average return of 11.6% is remarkable not only on an absolute basis; it also bests that of 85% of its rivals in the world-stock category. Yet that success hasn't been consistent. The fund tends to fare better than most in difficult markets, while it more or less tracks the competition in bullish environments.

This profile was evident in 2004 and 2005, when the fund's performance fell slightly short of its peers, many of which invested more heavily in mid-caps and small caps than this fund. During the correction of May-June 2006, though, that large-cap bias came in handy, as the fund held up better than most. Its large stake in pharmaceuticals such as Roche Holdings, as well as its exposure to mining stocks such as Newmont Mining, helped it weather that downturn. Since then, however, the markets have resumed their exuberant path, and the fund is struggling to keep pace.

The portfolio's continuously growing bulk is a mounting concern, however, as it can reduce management's ability to meaningfully add value through initiating new positions and make it harder to unload its sizable top holdings if warranted. With now more than $52 billion in assets, American Funds still shows no willingness to close this or any other of its bloated funds to new investors. It's true that its ability to invest anywhere in the world and its focus on very liquid stocks helps mitigate those concerns, as does the fact that management responsibilities are spread among six experienced managers, each running separate portions of the fund. Still, we're increasingly concerned that more assets could hamper future returns.

For the time being, though, we recommend holding on to this well-managed and moderately priced offering.

Address:	333 S Hope St - 55th FL Los Angeles CA 90071 800-421-0180	Minimum Purchase:	$250 Add: $50 IRA: $250
		Min Auto Inv Plan:	$50 Add: $50
		Sales Fees:	5.75%L, 0.24%S
Web Address:	www.americanfunds.com	Management Fee:	0.60% mx./0.37% mn.
Inception:	03-13-73	Actual Fees:	Mgt:0.39% Dist:0.24%
Advisor:	Capital Research and Management Company	Expense Projections:	3Yr:$801 5Yr:$968 10Yr:$1452
Subadvisor:	None	Income Distrib:	Annually
NTF Plans:	Federated Tr NTF		

Portfolio Analysis 09-30-06

Share change since 06-06 Total Stocks:231	Sector	Country	% Assets
Roche Holding	Health	Switzerland	3.04
Altria Group, Inc.	Goods	United States	1.83
⊕ Microsoft Corporation	Software	United States	1.55
Samsung Electronics	Goods	Korea	1.42
AstraZeneca	Health	U.K.	1.38
Nestle	Goods	Switzerland	1.35
⊕ Barrick Gold Corporation	Ind Mtrls	Canada	1.33
⊕ General Electric Company	Ind Mtrls	United States	1.30
ING Groep	Financial	Netherlands	1.23
⊕ Oracle Corporation	Software	United States	1.21
Erste Bank	Financial	Austria	1.19
Allianz	Financial	Germany	1.18
⊖ Taiwan Semiconductor Mfg	Hardware	Taiwan	1.18
⊕ Novo-Nordisk A S	Health	Denmark	1.17
⊕ Bayer	Ind Mtrls	Germany	1.15
Royal Dutch Shell	Energy	U.K.	1.14
⊖ Societe Generale Grp	Financial	France	1.11
Koninklijke KPN	Telecom	Netherlands	1.10
⊕ Newmont Mining	Ind Mtrls	United States	1.02
⊕ Applied Materials	Hardware	United States	0.99

Current Investment Style

Value Blnd Growth — Large / Mid / Small

	Market Cap	%
	Giant	60.9
	Large	34.4
	Mid	4.7
	Small	0.0
	Micro	0.1
	Avg $mil:	44,704

Value Measures		Rel Category
Price/Earnings	15.40	1.00
Price/Book	2.35	0.98
Price/Sales	1.35	1.03
Price/Cash Flow	9.12	1.05
Dividend Yield %	2.53	1.17

Growth Measures	%	Rel Category
Long-Term Erngs	11.34	0.89
Book Value	8.79	0.98
Sales	5.67	0.68
Cash Flow	6.37	0.65
Historical Erngs	20.22	1.08

Composition

Cash	9.3	Bonds	0.0
Stocks	90.1	Other	0.6
Foreign (% of Stock)			70.1

Sector Weightings	% of Stocks	Rel MSCI EAFE	3 Year High	Low
↻ Info	22.17	1.88		
🖥 Software	3.44	6.14	3	1
💻 Hardware	12.03	3.12	15	12
🎬 Media	2.82	1.54	6	3
📞 Telecom	3.88	0.70	10	4
⚙ Service	35.89	0.76		
🏥 Health	10.48	1.47	11	9
🛒 Consumer	4.59	0.93	5	3
🏢 Business	4.24	0.84	4	1
💲 Financial	16.58	0.55	17	11
🏭 Mfg	41.93	1.02		
🏷 Goods	16.77	1.28	18	16
🔧 Ind Mtrls	14.11	0.91	17	14
🔋 Energy	9.31	1.30	11	5
💡 Utilities	1.74	0.33	2	2

Regional Exposure	% Stock		
UK/W. Europe 44	N. America	33	
Japan 9	Latn America	3	
Asia X Japan 10	Other	1	

Country Exposure	% Stock		
United States 30	France	8	
Japan 9	Switzerland	7	
U.K. 9			

MORNINGSTAR® Funds 500

Amer Funds New World A

✓ Analyst Pick

	Ticker	Load	NAV	Yield	Total Assets	Mstar Category
	NEWFX	5.75%	$48.44	1.8%	$10,908 mil	Diversified Emerging Mkts

Governance and Management

Stewardship Grade: B

Portfolio Manager(s)

The fund's managers, all of whom have been on the fund since its 1999 inception, have long tenures at Capital Research & Management, the fund's parent, and several comanage other foreign offerings at the firm. In general, American Funds boasts an impressive lineup of international managers and research analysts. As with every American Fund, each manager here oversees his or her portion of assets independently.

Strategy

This fund splits its equity portfolio between emerging-market stocks and developed-market names. However, stocks that come from developed economies must conduct business in emerging markets. Typically, the fund's developed-market stake has hovered between one fourth and one third of assets. The portfolio holds a slug of multinationals such as Samsung and Coca-Cola and lacks many of the smaller-cap, speculative picks that are typical of emerging-markets funds. The fund can also put up to 25% of its assets in bonds.

Performance 12-31-06

	1st Qtr	2nd Qtr	3rd Qtr	4th Qtr	Total
2002	10.54	-6.86	-12.98	6.45	-4.62
2003	-3.66	17.30	9.68	15.67	43.36
2004	6.37	-5.02	6.48	12.28	20.79
2005	1.05	3.47	12.27	4.10	22.20
2006	11.71	-3.01	8.11	13.91	33.42

Trailing	Total Return%	+/- MSCI EAFE	+/- MSCI EmrMkt	%Rank Cat	Growth of $10,000
3 Mo	13.91	3.56	-3.37	94	11,391
6 Mo	23.15	8.46	1.06	59	12,315
1 Yr	33.42	7.08	4.24	37	13,342
3 Yr Avg	25.35	5.42	-1.91	86	19,696
5 Yr Avg	21.91	6.93	-1.61	89	26,928
10 Yr Avg	—	—	—	—	—
15 Yr Avg	—	—	—	—	—

Tax Analysis	Tax-Adj Rtn%	%Rank Cat	Tax-Cost Rat	%Rank Cat
3 Yr (estimated)	21.82	91	0.88	36
5 Yr (estimated)	19.54	96	0.78	46
10 Yr (estimated)	—	—	—	—

Potential Capital Gain Exposure: 30% of assets

Historical Profile

Return Low
Risk Low
Rating ★★ Below Avg

| | 66% | 70% | 74% | 69% | 74% | 74% | 69% | 75% | Investment Style Equity Stock % |

▼ Manager Change
▽ Partial Manager Change

Growth of $10,000
— Investment Values of Fund
— Investment Values of MSCI EAFE

Performance Quartile (within Category)

1995	1996	1997	1998	1999	2000	2001	2002	2003	2004	2005	2006	History
—	—	—	—	28.29	22.01	20.58	19.38	27.18	32.27	38.70	48.44	NAV
—	—	—	—	20.97*	-20.90	-3.96	-4.62	43.36	20.79	22.20	33.42	Total Return %
—	—	—	—	-6.71	17.46	11.32	4.77	0.54	8.66	7.08	+/-MSCI EAFE
—	—	—	—	11.00	0.72	3.35	-8.23	-1.66	-8.11	4.24	+/-MSCI EmrMkt
—	—	—	—	1.31	2.48	1.22	3.02	2.01	2.26	2.36	Income Return %
—	—	—	—	-22.21	-6.44	-5.84	40.34	18.78	19.94	31.06	Capital Return %
—	—	—	—	6	58	39	89	68	89	37	Total Rtn % Rank Cat
—	—	—	—	0.20	0.37	0.55	0.25	0.59	0.55	0.73	0.91	Income $
—	—	—	—	0.00	0.00	0.00	0.00	0.00	0.00	0.00	2.23	Capital Gains $
—	—	—	—		1.44	1.35	1.29	1.34	1.31	1.22	—	Expense Ratio %
—	—	—	—		1.83	1.61	2.15	1.65	1.86	1.68	—	Income Ratio %
—	—	—	—			30	40	32	30	20	—	Turnover Rate %
—	—	—	—	1,050	1,222	1,137	1,114	1,728	2,606	8,319	Net Assets $mil

Rating and Risk

Time Period	Load-Adj Return %	Morningstar Rtn vs Cat	Morningstar Risk vs Cat	Morningstar Risk-Adj Rating
1 Yr	25.75			
3 Yr	22.90	Low	Low	★
5 Yr	20.48	Low	Low	★★
10 Yr	—	—	—	—
Incept	11.89			

Other Measures	Standard Index MSCI EAFE	Best Fit Index MSCI EmrMkt
Alpha	3.3	5.4
Beta	1.10	0.66
R-Squared	77	96
Standard Deviation	11.85	
Mean	25.35	
Sharpe Ratio	1.72	

Portfolio Analysis 09-30-06

Share change since 06-06 Total Stocks:201

	Sector	Country	% Assets
America Movil SA ADR	Telecom	Mexico	1.72
⊕ Doosan Heavy Industry &	—	Korea	1.72
Telekomunikasi Indonesia	Telecom	Indonesia	1.68
Fomento Economico Mexica	Goods	Mexico	1.57
⊕ Erste Bank	Financial	Austria	1.44
Nestle	Goods	Switzerland	1.44
Grupo Financiero Banorte	Financial	Mexico	1.37
⊕ Oil & Natural Gas	Energy	India	1.35
Philippine Long Distance	Telecom	Philippines	1.23
Bank Rakyat Indonesia (P	Financial	Indonesia	1.13
Tesco	Consumer	U.K.	1.11
Mol Magyar Olaj- Es Gazi	Energy	Hungary	1.07
Murray & Roberts Hldgs L	Ind Mtrls	South Africa	0.98
⊕ Bbva(Bilb-Viz-Arg)	Financial	Spain	0.97
ICICI Bank	Financial	India	0.97
Samsung Electronics	Goods	Korea	0.97
⊖ Rao Ues Of Russia	Utilities	Russia	0.94
⊕ Taiwan Cement	Ind Mtrls	Taiwan	0.94
Petroleo Brasileiro S.A.	Energy	Brazil	0.93
Thai Airways Intl	Business	Thailand	0.91

Current Investment Style

Value Blnd Growth — Large Mid Small

Market Cap	%
Giant	32.5
Large	48.3
Mid	15.1
Small	4.1
Micro	0.1

Avg $mil: 11,188

Value Measures		Rel Category
Price/Earnings	14.32	1.11
Price/Book	2.45	1.12
Price/Sales	1.15	1.05
Price/Cash Flow	8.26	1.25
Dividend Yield %	3.11	0.95

Growth Measures	%	Rel Category
Long-Term Erngs	15.48	1.00
Book Value	11.12	1.11
Sales	16.55	1.05
Cash Flow	9.35	0.85
Historical Erngs	23.81	1.33

Composition

Cash	14.1	Bonds	8.3
Stocks	74.7	Other	3.0
Foreign (% of Stock)			95.0

Sector Weightings

	% of Stocks	Rel MSCI EAFE	3 Year High	Low
↻ Info	18.13	1.53		
🖥 Software	0.00	0.00	0	0
🖥 Hardware	3.02	0.78	4	2
🎤 Media	1.02	0.56	3	1
📶 Telecom	14.09	2.53	19	13
☁ Service	34.61	0.73		
🏥 Health	2.72	0.38	4	2
🛒 Consumer	5.28	1.07	6	3
💼 Business	6.41	1.26	10	6
💲 Financial	20.20	0.67	20	15
🏭 Mfg	47.25	1.15		
🛢 Goods	16.28	1.24	21	15
⚙ Ind Mtrls	16.17	1.05	22	15
🔋 Energy	9.50	1.33	11	4
💡 Utilities	5.30	1.01	8	0

Regional Exposure % Stock

UK/W. Europe	22	N. America	6
Japan	3	Latn America	15
Asia X Japan	40	Other	14

Country Exposure % Stock

India	8	Thailand	6
Brazil	8	South Korea	6
Mexico	7		

Morningstar's Take by Kai Wiecking 12-26-06

Investors who can fit the quirky American Funds New World in their portfolios should be happy with it in the long run.

It follows a somewhat unusual investment strategy. It provides exposure to economic growth in the developing world through a combination of direct investment in emerging stock markets and stakes in companies residing in industrialized nations, but with significant earnings exposure to those fast-growing regions in Asia, Eastern Europe, and Latin America. Almost a third of its current portfolio is invested in North American, Western European, and Japanese stocks.

Swiss food giant Nestle, which sells an increasingly important share of its product in emerging markets, is among the top holdings, as is Austria's Erste Bank. The company has made excellent use of Vienna's position as the main gateway to Eastern Europe to build a dominant position in many countries of that region.

This significant stake in established markets has helped keep volatility in check, especially when compared with its pure-play peers in the diversified emerging-markets category. But it has also meant that the fund's returns have lagged in times when emerging markets have rallied sharply, as has been the case since late 2002. But during the sharp correction in May and June 2006, the fund held up much better than most of its peers. Still, the fund's trailing five-year average annual return of 22.0% lags 88% of its rivals in the group.

We think this fund is one of the most sensible ways to participate in the long-term growth of emerging economies without incurring the full brunt of the risks commonly associated with that asset class. Investors shouldn't forget that while the balance sheets of many of those countries are much more solid these days, geopolitical and regulatory risks remain. The seasoned, skilled managers of this low-cost offering are well aware of those caveats, and we think they can be trusted to deliver in the long run.

Address:	333 S Hope St - 55th FL Los Angeles CA 90071 800-421-0180	Minimum Purchase:	$250	Add: $50	IRA: $250
		Min Auto Inv Plan:	$250	Add: $50	
Web Address:	www.americanfunds.com	Sales Fees:	5.75%L, 0.23%S		
Inception:	06-17-99*	Management Fee:	0.85% mx./0.54% mn.		
Advisor:	Capital Research and Management Company	Actual Fees:	Mgt:0.63% Dist:0.23%		
Subadvisor:	None	Expense Projections:	3Yr:$893 5Yr:$1126 10Yr:$1795		
		Income Distrib:	Annually		
NTF Plans:	Federated Tr NTF				

Amer Funds Sm World A

	Ticker	Load	NAV	Yield	Total Assets	Mstar Category
	SMCWX	5.75%	$39.07	1.6%	$20,368 mil	World Stock

Governance and Management

Stewardship Grade: B

Portfolio Manager(s)

Experienced, deep, and perhaps in flux. Every one of this fund's seven managers has plenty of tenure and experience. The managers also contribute to other American Funds. The fund's advisor has a group of analysts dedicated to researching small-cap companies. The managerial lineup could change in 2006, since a reorganization at the advisor has led to personnel shuffling at some of its funds.

Strategy

This fund's managers scour the globe for small-cap stocks with sound fundamentals. Normally, at least 80% of assets is invested in stocks that court market capitalizations between $50 million and $2 billion. In picking stocks, the team focuses on companies with experienced management, strong product lines, and solid balance sheets. The team also pays attention to how much it pays for a stock, which can cause the portfolio to swing between the growth and blend sections of the Morningstar style box.

Performance 12-31-06

	1st Qtr	2nd Qtr	3rd Qtr	4th Qtr	Total
2002	2.27	-8.83	-17.97	1.65	-22.25
2003	-5.05	23.64	10.99	15.42	50.40
2004	7.28	-2.40	-0.75	13.32	17.76
2005	-0.13	2.34	9.03	4.57	16.53
2006	12.16	-3.87	2.24	11.54	22.96

Trailing	Total Return%	+/- MSCI EAFE	+/- MSCI World	%Rank Cat	Growth of $10,000
3 Mo	11.54	1.19	3.17	12	11,154
6 Mo	14.03	-0.66	0.82	28	11,403
1 Yr	22.96	-3.38	2.89	18	12,296
3 Yr Avg	19.05	-0.88	4.37	14	16,873
5 Yr Avg	14.56	-0.42	4.59	16	19,732
10 Yr Avg	9.59	1.88	1.95	35	24,987
15 Yr Avg	11.25	3.39	2.56	37	49,488

Tax Analysis	Tax-Adj Rtn%	%Rank Cat	Tax-Cost Rat	%Rank Cat
3 Yr (estimated)	15.55	34	1.01	53
5 Yr (estimated)	12.52	23	0.61	48
10 Yr (estimated)	7.83	40	1.02	49

Potential Capital Gain Exposure: 25% of assets

Historical Profile

Return	Above Avg
Risk	Above Avg
Rating	★★★ Neutral

Investment Style: Equity / Stock %

89% 89% 86% 88% 90% 90% 92% 91% 89%

▼ Manager Change
▽ Partial Manager Change

Growth of $10,000
— Investment Values of Fund
— Investment Values of MSCI EAFE

32.0 / 25.0 / 20.0 / 15.0 / 10.0

Performance Quartile (within Category)

1995	1996	1997	1998	1999	2000	2001	2002	2003	2004	2005	2006	History
23.50	25.61	25.98	24.63	39.14	27.78	22.92	17.82	26.77	31.20	35.27	39.07	NAV
22.70	19.75	11.83	0.38	61.64	-15.56	-17.35	-22.25	50.40	17.76	16.53	22.96	Total Return %
11.49	13.70	10.05	-19.55	34.61	-1.37	4.07	-6.31	11.81	-2.49	2.99	-3.38	+/-MSCI EAFE
1.98	6.27	-3.93	-23.94	36.69	-2.37	-0.55	-2.36	17.29	3.04	7.04	2.89	+/-MSCI World
1.08	0.51	0.39	0.35	0.06	0.00	0.14	0.00	0.17	1.16	1.31	1.97	Income Return %
21.62	19.24	11.44	0.03	61.58	-15.56	-17.49	-22.25	50.23	16.60	15.22	20.99	Capital Return %
21	25	67	87	25	75	55	73	6	29	16	18	Total Rtn % Rank Cat
0.23	0.12	0.10	0.09	0.02	0.00	0.04	0.00	0.03	0.31	0.41	0.70	Income $
2.45	2.35	2.50	1.29	0.61	5.29	0.00	0.00	0.00	0.00	0.68	3.61	Capital Gains $
1.13	1.09	1.07	1.06	1.09	1.10	1.09	1.17	1.19	1.12	1.04	1.01	Expense Ratio %
0.97	0.68	0.40	0.27	0.12	—	-0.01	-0.32	-0.07	0.06	0.76	0.68	Income Ratio %
46	43	42	44	50	63	60	51	49	48	45	45	Turnover Rate %
4,766	7,073	8,667	8,109	12,374	11,329	8,723	6,180	9,200	11,117	13,237	16,636	Net Assets $mil

Rating and Risk

Time Period	Load-Adj Return %	Morningstar Rtn vs Cat	Morningstar Risk vs Cat	Morningstar Risk-Adj Rating
1 Yr	15.89			
3 Yr	16.73	+Avg	+Avg	★★★★
5 Yr	13.21	+Avg	+Avg	★★★★
10 Yr	8.94	Avg	+Avg	★★
Incept	11.31			

Other Measures	Standard Index MSCI EAFE	Best Fit Index MSCI World
Alpha	-2.1	1.9
Beta	1.10	1.32
R-Squared	79	87
Standard Deviation	11.75	
Mean	19.05	
Sharpe Ratio	1.28	

Portfolio Analysis 09-30-06

Share change since 06-06 Total Stocks:582	Sector	Country	% Assets
The Daegu Bank Ltd	Financial	Korea	0.99
⊕ OPTI Canada Inc	Energy	Canada	0.99
Kingboard Chemical Hldgs	Ind Mtrls	Hong Kong	0.94
Quicksilver Resources, I	Energy	United States	0.91
Pusan Bank	Financial	Korea	0.81
✻ Beckman Coulter, Inc.	Health	United States	0.75
⊖ Michaels Store	Consumer	United States	0.74
Samsung Engineering	Business	Korea	0.71
⊕ Corrections Corporation	Business	United States	0.70
⊕ Medicis Pharmaceuticals	Health	United States	0.68
⊖ Kyphon, Inc.	Health	United States	0.67
Advanced Medical Optics,	Health	United States	0.62
Container Corp. of India	Business	India	0.60
CNET Networks, Inc.	Media	United States	0.58
⊕ Schibsted	Media	Norway	0.54
⊖ CarMax, Inc.	Consumer	United States	0.53
✻ Time Warner Telecom, Inc	Telecom	United States	0.49
⊕ Central European Media E	Media	United States	0.48
Big Lots, Inc.	Consumer	United States	0.48
Lindt & Sprungli	Goods	Switzerland	0.48

Current Investment Style

Value Blnd Growth / Large Mid Small

Market Cap	%
Giant	0.0
Large	11.3
Mid	45.1
Small	38.2
Micro	5.5
Avg $mil:	1,412

Value Measures		Rel Category
Price/Earnings	17.29	1.12
Price/Book	2.13	0.89
Price/Sales	1.10	0.84
Price/Cash Flow	8.45	0.98
Dividend Yield %	1.62	0.75

Growth Measures	%	Rel Category
Long-Term Erngs	17.70	1.40
Book Value	10.58	1.18
Sales	11.19	1.34
Cash Flow	3.54	0.36
Historical Erngs	16.25	0.87

Composition

Cash	9.8	Bonds	0.1
Stocks	89.1	Other	0.9
Foreign (% of Stock)			57.6

Sector Weightings	% of Stocks	Rel MSCI EAFE	3 Year High	Low
↻ Info	16.97	1.44		
☒ Software	2.12	3.79	4	2
☐ Hardware	8.02	2.08	11	7
♒ Media	4.17	2.28	6	4
☎ Telecom	2.66	0.48	3	1
☞ Service	50.32	1.07		
♥ Health	14.80	2.08	15	8
☒ Consumer	11.44	2.31	16	11
⚑ Business	13.10	2.58	16	12
⚖ Financial	10.98	0.36	11	9
⚒ Mfg	32.70	0.80		
☒ Goods	7.73	0.59	9	7
☒ Ind Mtrls	16.51	1.07	17	14
⚡ Energy	6.73	0.94	10	6
⚐ Utilities	1.73	0.33	2	0

Regional Exposure			% Stock
UK/W. Europe	14	N. America	47
Japan	3	Latn America	4
Asia X Japan	30	Other	2

Country Exposure			% Stock
United States	42	India	4
South Korea	9	Australia	4
Canada	5		

Morningstar's Take by Paul Herbert 12-21-06

We think it's wise for investors to maintain measured expectations about this fund.

Smallcap World Fund has delivered some strong returns in recent years, posting an annualized five-year surge of 15% as of Dec. 20, 2006. Its focus on rallying smaller-cap stocks deserves much of the credit for its fine showing, which ranks in the world-stock category's best 20%. The fund sticks the bulk of its assets in small and smaller mid-cap companies, while the typical fund in the category focuses more on large-cap names.

But given how well the fund's favorite spots have fared in recent years, we think it makes sense to keep a sober outlook. After rallying for many years, small caps are looking more expensive relative to large caps than they have in some time. Emerging markets, another area of emphasis of the fund, have also dominated in recent years. The fund would be in for some extra volatility if these areas were to cool off. Investors got a sense of that when these areas swooned in the May-to-June time

frame, since the fund declined by 16% from peak to trough. To be fair, that wasn't a large loss compared with other global small-cap funds, but it's still significant on an absolute basis.

Another area of concern for us continues to be the fund's relatively large $20-billion asset base. That has led to some portfolio changes such as a migration toward bigger cap stocks (its advisor increased its upper market-cap limit from $2 billion to $3.5 billion in May) and diversification among more names. As we've indicated before, American has more resources than other small-cap managers and can hire enough analysts to expertly research this fund's nearly 600 stock holdings. Plus, a handful of other advisors have managed this much in the space well. However, the changes that the fund has undergone and the tougher sledding for its stomping grounds make it harder for us to envision that it will sustain its winning ways.

Address:	333 S Hope St - 55th FL Los Angeles CA 90071 800-421-0180	Minimum Purchase:	$250	Add: $50 IRA: $250
		Min Auto Inv Plan:	$50	Add: $50
		Sales Fees:	5.75%L, 0.24%S	
Web Address:	www.americanfunds.com	Management Fee:	0.80% mx./0.60% mn.	
Inception:	04-30-90	Actual Fees:	Mgt:0.64%	Dist:0.24%
Advisor:	Capital Research and Management Company	Expense Projections:	3Yr:$899	5Yr:$1136 10Yr:$1816
Subadvisor:	None	Income Distrib:	Annually	
NTF Plans:	Federated Tr NTF			

MORNINGSTAR® Funds 500

Amer Funds T/E Bd A

	Ticker	Load	NAV	Yield	SEC Yield	Total Assets	Mstar Category
	AFTEX	3.75%	$12.53	4.0%	3.39%	$5,600 mil	Muni National Interm

Governance and Management

Stewardship Grade: B

Portfolio Manager(s)

The management team splits this fund's portfolio, with each manager responsible for a specific portion. The group has seen managers come and go over the years but currently includes Neil Langberg (who joined the fund in 1979), Brenda Ellerin (1998), and Karl Zeile (2004).

Strategy

This fund's multiple managers have historically favored municipal issues with good structure, particularly noncallable bonds carrying predictable duration characteristics. The portfolio holds a larger stake in midgrade bonds rated A or BBB than most rivals in the muni national intermediate category, as well. Because the fund holds more than 1,000 names, though, the effect of a possible default in one issue is diminished.

Performance 12-31-06

	1st Qtr	2nd Qtr	3rd Qtr	4th Qtr	Total
2002	0.88	3.45	4.09	-0.18	8.44
2003	0.99	2.45	0.20	1.46	5.18
2004	1.67	-1.83	3.43	1.11	4.37
2005	-0.19	2.88	-0.03	0.67	3.35
2006	0.26	0.21	3.32	0.93	4.76

Trailing	Total Return%	+/- LB Muni	+/- LB Muni 10YR	%Rank Cat	Growth of $10,000
3 Mo	0.93	-0.18	0.01	15	10,093
6 Mo	4.28	-0.27	-0.49	17	10,428
1 Yr	4.76	-0.08	0.05	7	10,476
3 Yr Avg	4.16	-0.12	0.30	6	11,301
5 Yr Avg	5.21	-0.32	-0.25	10	12,891
10 Yr Avg	5.36	-0.40	-0.34	7	16,856
15 Yr Avg	6.00	-0.26	-0.28	7	23,966

Tax Analysis	Tax-Adj Rtn%	%Rank Cat	Tax-Cost Rat	%Rank Cat
3 Yr (estimated)	2.84	32	0.00	1
5 Yr (estimated)	4.40	31	0.01	4
10 Yr (estimated)	4.90	17	0.06	26

Potential Capital Gain Exposure: 3% of assets

Historical Profile

Return	Above Avg
Risk	Average
Rating	★★★★ Above Avg

	10	11	7	8	10	11	13	16

Investment Style Fixed Income
Income Rtn %Rank Cat

▼ Manager Change
▽ Partial Manager Change

Growth of $10,000
— Investment Values of Fund
— Investment Values of LB Muni

20.8
18.8
16.4
14.0
12.0
10.0

Performance Quartile (within Category)

1995	1996	1997	1998	1999	2000	2001	2002	2003	2004	2005	2006	History
12.23	12.09	12.47	12.41	11.50	11.97	12.01	12.42	12.52	12.54	12.45	12.53	NAV
17.28	4.57	8.98	6.07	-2.32	9.67	5.57	8.44	5.18	4.37	3.35	4.76	Total Return %
-0.18	0.14	-0.21	-0.41	-0.26	-2.01	0.44	-1.16	-0.13	-0.11	-0.16	-0.08	+/-LB Muni
0.11	0.03	-0.25	-0.69	-1.07	-1.09	0.95	-1.73	-0.52	0.22	0.61	0.05	+/-LB Muni 10YR
6.20	5.38	5.39	5.04	4.87	5.43	5.01	4.79	4.34	4.19	4.08	4.09	Income Return %
11.08	-0.81	3.59	1.03	-7.19	4.24	0.56	3.65	0.84	0.18	-0.73	0.67	Capital Return %
15	13	12	24	55	45	6	53	12	7	6	7	Total Rtn % Rank Cat
0.67	0.64	0.64	0.61	0.59	0.61	0.59	0.56	0.53	0.51	0.50	0.50	Income $
0.09	0.04	0.04	0.19	0.04	0.00	0.03	0.02	0.00	0.00	0.00	0.00	Capital Gains $
0.66	0.68	0.68	0.66	0.65	0.67	0.66	0.63	0.61	0.61	0.57	0.56	Expense Ratio %
5.87	5.35	5.27	4.98	4.78	5.22	4.98	4.73	4.33	4.23	4.08	4.04	Income Ratio %
49	27	14	23	15	29	21	8	8	8	9	9	Turnover Rate %
1,502	1,513	1,666	1,863	1,816	1,898	2,254	2,799	3,028	3,208	3,768	4,640	Net Assets $mil

Rating and Risk

Time Period	Load-Adj Return %	Morningstar Rtn vs Cat	Morningstar Risk vs Cat	Morningstar Risk-Adj Rating
1 Yr	0.84			
3 Yr	2.84	+Avg	Avg	★★★★
5 Yr	4.41	+Avg	Avg	★★★★
10 Yr	4.96	+Avg	Avg	★★★★
Incept	7.29			

Other Measures	Standard Index LB Muni	Best Fit Index LB Muni
Alpha	0.0	0.0
Beta	0.90	0.90
R-Squared	99	99
Standard Deviation	2.78	
Mean	4.16	
Sharpe Ratio	0.32	

Portfolio Analysis 09-30-06

Total Fixed-Income:1365	Date of Maturity	Amount $000	Value $000	% Net Assets
NEW YORK ST DORM AUTH RE	11-15-23	44,845	48,145	0.92
New York N Y City Indl D	03-01-15	35,000	37,244	0.71
TENNESSEE ENERGY ACQUISI	09-01-20	30,000	33,513	0.64
Tobacco Settlement Fing	05-15-30	30,920	32,067	0.61
Atlanta Ga Arpt Passenge	01-01-34	26,955	28,167	0.54
BADGER TOB ASSET SECURIT	06-01-27	25,655	27,514	0.53
San Antonio Tex Elec & G	02-01-15	24,000	26,639	0.51
New Jersey St Transn Tr	12-15-22	20,000	22,614	0.43
Central Puget Sound Wash	02-01-28	21,940	22,185	0.42
NEW YORK N Y CITY TRANSI	11-01-26	20,300	21,996	0.42
CALIFORNIA ST	09-01-30	20,000	21,079	0.40
Chicago Ill O Hare Intl	01-01-33	20,000	20,988	0.40
Houston Tex Indpt Sch Di	02-15-32	20,000	20,908	0.40
Detroit Mich City Sch Di	05-01-16	19,000	20,538	0.39
Indiana Health & Edl Fac	02-15-39	19,000	19,523	0.37

Current Investment Style

¹Avg Eff Duration	5.3 Yrs
Avg Eff Maturity	—
Avg Credit Quality	AA
Avg Wtd Coupon	5.38%
Avg Wtd Price	106.58% of par

¹figure provided by fund

Credit Analysis	% bonds 09-30-06		
AAA	51	BB	8
AA	20	B	2
A	10	Below B	0
BBB	9	NR/NA	0

Special Securities	
Restricted/Illiquid Secs	0
Options/Futures/Warrants	No

Sector Weightings	% of Bonds	Rel Cat
General Obligation	28.2	0.76
Utilities	10.9	1.15
Health	17.3	1.93
Water/Waste	5.8	0.64
Housing	3.2	0.60
Education	11.9	0.92
Transportation	4.5	0.86
COP/Lease	2.8	1.15
Industrial	14.1	1.53
Misc Revenue	0.0	—
Demand	1.2	3.13

Top 5 States	% bonds		
TX	14.2	CA	7.6
IL	10.7	FL	5.9
NY	8.3		

Composition			
Cash	4.5	Bonds	95.5
Stocks	0.0	Other	0.0

Morningstar's Take by Marta Norton 12-21-06

There's not much missing at American Funds Tax-Exempt Bond Fund of America.

This fund has consistently produced superior returns relative to other muni national intermediate funds. Over the 10-year period ending Nov. 30, 2006, it gained 5.37% per annum on average, which places it in the top 10% of funds in the category. Much of its outperformance can be attributed to strong security selection. An experienced credit research team explores the ins and outs of each holding before the fund invests. That's no easy feat, considering the size of its portfolio. As of Sept. 30 it held more than 1,300 bonds. This also acts in the fund's interest, as it limits the impact of any one poorly performing bond.

American Funds views its skills with security selection as a competitive advantage, so the fund focuses much of its risk-taking on credit selection. It generally holds more midquality bonds than its average competitor, although its managers have trimmed some lately, as they think midquality bonds haven't offered enough reward for their added risk. The fund has stepped lightly in some riskier sectors, such as tobacco, and held on to insured and prefunded bonds. But as of Sept. 30, it still held 20% of its assets in bonds rated BBB and below, which is noticeably higher than its category average. As has long been the case, if lower-quality bonds hit the skids, this fund could feel it more than its rivals.

That's no reason to lose faith, though. The fund's traditionally heavy slug of midquality bonds hasn't produced above-average volatility over the long term. In fact, for periods of three years and longer, this fund's standard deviation (a measure of return volatility) is lower than that of its typical peer.

What's more, the fund's 0.56% expense ratio, which is partly the result of a fee waiver, is a better deal than what most front-load rivals offer. Investors looking for a tax-free intermediate-bond exposure should consider this worthy option.

Address:	333 S Hope St - 55th FL Los Angeles CA 90071 800-421-0180	Minimum Purchase:	$250 Add: $50 IRA: $0
		Min Auto Inv Plan:	$250 Add: $50
		Sales Fees:	3.75%L, 0.25%S
Web Address:	www.americanfunds.com	Management Fee:	0.30% mx./0.13% mn.
Inception:	10-03-79	Actual Fees:	Mgt:0.29% Dist:0.25%
Advisor:	Capital Research and Management Company	Expense Projections:	3Yr:$557 5Yr:$692 10Yr:$1085
Subadvisor:	None	Income Distrib:	Monthly
NTF Plans:	Federated Tr NTF, Schwab Instl NTF		

Amer Funds WashingtonA

Analyst Pick ✓

	Ticker	Load	NAV	Yield	Total Assets	Mstar Category
	AWSHX	5.75%	$34.86	1.8%	$83,998 mil	Large Value

Performance 12-31-06

	1st Qtr	2nd Qtr	3rd Qtr	4th Qtr	Total
2002	3.63	-7.36	-17.90	8.04	-14.85
2003	-4.92	15.94	1.25	12.73	25.83
2004	1.62	1.36	0.30	6.40	9.92
2005	-1.43	1.38	2.00	1.59	3.55
2006	4.44	0.69	5.55	6.35	18.04

Trailing	Total Return%	+/- S&P 500	+/- Russ 1000 VI	%Rank Cat	Growth of $10,000
3 Mo	6.35	-0.35	-1.65	81	10,635
6 Mo	12.25	-0.49	-2.47	63	11,225
1 Yr	18.04	2.25	-4.21	53	11,804
3 Yr Avg	10.34	-0.10	-4.75	82	13,434
5 Yr Avg	7.56	1.37	-3.30	64	14,396
10 Yr Avg	9.88	1.46	-1.12	28	25,656
15 Yr Avg	11.89	1.25	-1.14	28	53,935

Tax Analysis	Tax-Adj Rtn%	%Rank Cat	Tax-Cost Rat	%Rank Cat
3 Yr (estimated)	7.21	93	0.91	36
5 Yr (estimated)	5.36	83	0.87	47
10 Yr (estimated)	7.63	39	1.46	45

Potential Capital Gain Exposure: 30% of assets

Historical Profile

Return	Below Avg
Risk	Below Avg
Rating	★★ Below Avg

	95%	96%	95%	94%	96%	96%	97%	98%	97%

Investment Style Equity / Stock %

▼ Manager Change
▽ Partial Manager Change

Growth of $10,000
- Investment Values of Fund
- Investment Values of S&P 500

38.0 / 31.0 / 24.0 / 17.0 / 10.0

Performance Quartile (within Category)

1995	1996	1997	1998	1999	2000	2001	2002	2003	2004	2005	2006	History
21.97	24.54	30.35	32.91	29.56	29.03	28.25	23.51	28.78	30.78	30.84	34.86	NAV
41.22	20.18	33.29	19.37	1.16	9.06	1.51	-14.85	25.83	9.92	3.55	18.04	Total Return %
3.64	-2.78	-0.07	-9.21	-19.88	18.16	13.40	7.25	-2.85	-0.96	-1.36	2.25	+/-S&P 500
2.86	-1.46	-1.89	3.74	-6.19	2.05	7.10	0.67	-4.20	-6.57	-3.50	-4.21	+/-Russ 1000 VI
3.73	2.85	2.55	2.02	1.77	1.98	1.91	1.93	2.32	2.07	1.96	2.12	Income Return %
37.49	17.33	30.74	17.35	-0.61	7.08	-0.40	-16.78	23.51	7.85	1.59	15.92	Capital Return %
2	47	6	9	66	55	25	26	71	84	77	53	Total Rtn % Rank Cat
0.62	0.62	0.62	0.61	0.58	0.58	0.55	0.54	0.54	0.59	0.60	0.65	Income $
1.09	1.20	1.66	2.60	3.10	2.50	0.64	0.04	0.19	0.23	0.43	0.84	Capital Gains $
0.69	0.66	0.64	0.62	0.61	0.63	0.65	0.65	0.67	0.64	0.60	0.57	Expense Ratio %
3.57	2.98	2.56	2.08	1.84	1.91	1.95	1.72	2.28	2.14	2.24	2.13	Income Ratio %
26	23	20	18	28	26	25	22	21	12	16	13	Turnover Rate %
18,786	25,374	38,246	51,774	53,136	47,414	48,751	42,436	55,575	63,079	62,375	67,795	Net Assets $mil

Rating and Risk

Time Period	Load-Adj Return %	Morningstar Rtn vs Cat	Morningstar Risk vs Cat	Morningstar Risk-Adj Rating
1 Yr	11.26			
3 Yr	8.19	Low	Low	★
5 Yr	6.29	-Avg	-Avg	★★
10 Yr	9.23	Avg	-Avg	★★★
Incept	12.74			

Other Measures	Standard Index S&P 500	Best Fit Index Russ 1000 VI
Alpha	1.3	-2.2
Beta	0.79	0.81
R-Squared	90	90
Standard Deviation	5.80	
Mean	10.34	
Sharpe Ratio	1.19	

Portfolio Analysis 09-30-06

Share change since 06-06 Total Stocks:135	Sector	PE	Tot Ret%	% Assets
⊕ General Electric Company	Ind Mtrls	20.0	9.35	3.43
⊖ Chevron Corporation	Energy	9.0	33.76	3.12
⊖ J.P. Morgan Chase & Co.	Financial	13.6	25.60	2.84
ExxonMobil Corporation	Energy	11.1	39.07	2.78
⊖ Citigroup, Inc.	Financial	13.1	19.55	2.67
⊖ AT&T, Inc.	Telecom	18.2	51.59	2.60
⊖ Bank of America Corporat	Financial	12.4	20.68	2.30
⊖ BellSouth Corporation	Telecom	—	—	1.94
⊕ Fannie Mae	Financial	—	24.34	1.88
⊕ Wells Fargo Company	Financial	14.7	16.82	1.87
⊕ United Parcel Service, I	Business	19.7	1.76	1.86
⊕ IBM	Hardware	17.1	19.77	1.83
⊖ Bristol-Myers Squibb Com	Health	23.1	19.93	1.81
⊕ Lowe's Companies Inc.	Consumer	15.6	-6.05	1.80
⊕ Washington Mutual, Inc.	Financial	13.4	9.62	1.75
⊕ Microsoft Corporation	Software	23.8	15.83	1.67
⊕ Eli Lilly & Company	Health	17.3	-5.16	1.65
⊕ Wal-Mart Stores, Inc.	Consumer	16.9	0.13	1.64
⊕ Abbott Laboratories	Health	24.3	26.88	1.60
⊕ Pfizer Inc.	Health	15.2	15.22	1.57

Current Investment Style

Value Blnd Growth — Large Mid Small

Market Cap	%
Giant	58.9
Large	38.0
Mid	3.0
Small	0.1
Micro	0.0

Avg $mil: 66,574

Value Measures		Rel Category
Price/Earnings	14.02	1.02
Price/Book	2.41	1.09
Price/Sales	1.39	1.07
Price/Cash Flow	4.90	0.73
Dividend Yield %	2.54	1.09

Growth Measures	%	Rel Category
Long-Term Erngs	10.41	1.00
Book Value	10.11	1.28
Sales	10.87	1.21
Cash Flow	6.64	1.10
Historical Erngs	13.90	0.86

Profitability	%	Rel Category
Return on Equity	19.54	1.09
Return on Assets	10.23	1.04
Net Margin	13.69	1.06

Sector Weightings	% of Stocks	Rel S&P 500	3 Year High Low	
⟳ Info	15.09	0.75		
🖳 Software	2.70	0.78	3	1
💻 Hardware	5.04	0.55	5	3
🖥 Media	0.38	0.10	1	0
📶 Telecom	6.97	1.99	8	7
⟳ Service	47.16	1.02		
🩺 Health	12.64	1.05	13	10
🛒 Consumer	8.19	1.07	8	7
📊 Business	3.23	0.76	3	2
💲 Financial	23.10	1.04	25	22
⟳ Mfg	37.75	1.12		
🏭 Goods	6.88	0.80	12	7
⚙ Ind Mtrls	14.36	1.20	16	14
🔋 Energy	10.89	1.11	11	9
💡 Utilities	5.62	1.61	8	6

Composition

- Cash 3.4
- Stocks 96.6
- Bonds 0.0
- Other 0.0
- Foreign 1.3 (% of Stock)

Morningstar's Take by Karen Dolan 12-27-06

There's a strong case for owning American Funds Washington Mutual right now.

This fund's focus on dividend-paying stalwarts has served investors well over the long haul, but it hasn't led to competitive results during the past three years. Its recent underperformance is a function of the current market environment rather than flaws in its approach, in our view. Markets have rallied around real estate, energy, and smaller companies during the past several years, while established players such as IBM and Wal-Mart--key holdings at this offering--have puttered along and consequently held this fund back.

One could argue that the fund took on its mega-cap posture too soon. Granted, mega-cap stocks make sense here given the fund's dividend criteria, but the portfolio hasn't always looked as big. In the late 1990s, for example, the fund's average market cap was a fraction of what it is today and smaller than the typical large-cap value fund. The fund evolved into its current stance as management became drawn to what it views as inescapable values among many of the market's largest companies. (With total assets now topping $80 billion, though, the fund's girth could hamper its flexibility to move away from huge companies in the future.)

Although recent relative returns have been lackluster, the fund looks fundamentally strong. The portfolio's aggregate valuation statistics such as price/earnings and price/cash flow are well below the S&P 500 Index. And on average, the companies in its portfolio pay 40% more in dividends than the S&P 500. What's more, the managers stick with a longer time horizon than most; the fund's low turnover ratio suggests an average holding period between five and 10 years and helps rein in volatility here.

Regardless of what's working on Wall Street, the fund's cheap expense ratio will always give it a leg up against competitors. We think this fund is ripe for a turnaround and well worth sticking with.

MORNINGSTAR® Funds 500

American Beacon IntEq Ins

Ticker	Load	NAV	Yield	Total Assets	Mstar Category
AAIEX	None	$23.91	2.2%	$3,069 mil	Foreign Large Value

Governance and Management

Stewardship Grade: B

Portfolio Manager(s)

Gary Motyl is a longtime subadvisor who has succeeded with his value style at other charges. The Lazard team, which came aboard in March 1999, has also succeeded elsewhere. The Causeway team, which returned in September 2001 after a short hiatus, has produced strong results elsewhere. Kirk Henry, who leads The Boston Company team, has also succeeded on other funds. William Quinn, Douglas Herring and Kirk Brown of American Beacon oversee the subadvisors.

Strategy

Assets are divided among four value-oriented subadvisors. Templeton's Gary Motyl seeks stocks that are cheap relative to their assets or earnings. The Causeway Capital team focuses on dividend and earnings yields. A team from Lazard looks for attractive returns on equity and fetching prices. And The Boston Company team pursues stocks that are in the cheapest 40% of their market and less expensive than most of their global peers. American Beacon tightly limits which emerging markets the fund's subadvisors can invest in, and South Korea is the only developing nation where the teams can now buy.

Historical Profile

Return Average
Risk Average
Rating ★★★ Neutral

Investment Style: Equity Stock %: 95% 93% 93% 93% 88% 93% 94% 94% 93%

▼ Manager Change
▽ Partial Manager Change

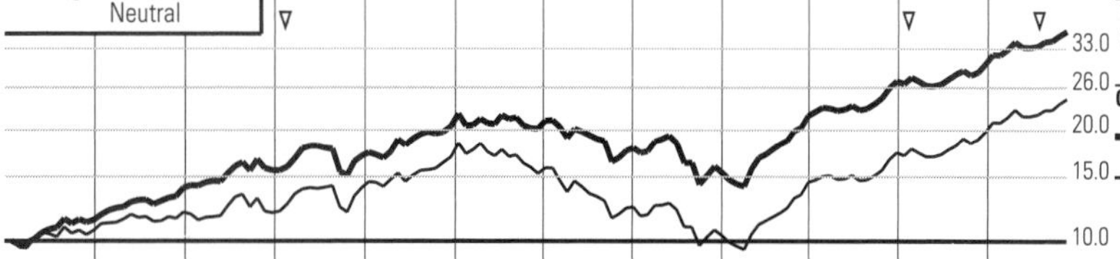

Performance Quartile (within Category)

1995	1996	1997	1998	1999	2000	2001	2002	2003	2004	2005	2006	History
13.42	15.36	16.01	17.05	19.60	17.27	14.34	11.96	16.55	20.26	20.76	23.91	NAV
17.69	19.78	9.56	11.73	26.91	-4.14	-15.43	-14.09	41.88	23.92	11.10	26.45	Total Return %
6.48	13.73	7.78	-8.20	-0.12	10.05	5.99	1.85	3.29	3.67	-2.44	0.11	+/-MSCI EAFE
6.28	12.91	7.29	-6.96	-1.07	9.22	5.96	1.71	2.46	3.54	-3.37	0.74	+/-MSCI Wd xUS
2.29	2.63	2.19	2.16	1.84	1.13	1.49	2.48	3.39	1.48	2.10	2.75	Income Return %
15.40	17.15	7.37	9.57	25.07	-5.27	-16.92	-16.57	38.49	22.44	9.00	23.70	Capital Return %
23	24	43	51	37	59	67	61	30	31	66	50	Total Rtn % Rank Cat
0.27	0.35	0.34	0.35	0.31	0.22	0.26	0.36	0.41	0.24	0.42	0.57	Income $
0.24	0.35	0.48	0.49	1.64	1.24	0.00	0.00	0.00	0.00	1.33	1.74	Capital Gains $
0.85	0.85	0.83	0.80	0.64	0.72	0.78	0.75	0.79	0.76	0.70	—	Expense Ratio %
2.37	2.19	2.35	2.05	2.00	1.64	1.54	1.56	1.97	1.69	2.17	—	Income Ratio %
21	19	15	24	63	45	36	43	44	36	37	—	Turnover Rate %
31	74	247	462	652	607	559	551	797	1,134	1,348	1,619	Net Assets $mil

Performance 12-31-06

	1st Qtr	2nd Qtr	3rd Qtr	4th Qtr	Total
2002	3.91	-0.87	-22.41	7.50	-14.09
2003	-8.03	21.82	8.71	16.48	41.88
2004	4.83	1.61	1.08	15.09	23.92
2005	-0.05	-1.83	8.75	4.11	11.10
2006	9.15	1.32	4.18	9.75	26.45

Trailing	Total Return%	+/- MSCI EAFE	+/- MSCI Wd xUS	%Rank Cat	Growth of $10,000
3 Mo	9.75	-0.60	-0.37	58	10,975
6 Mo	14.34	-0.35	0.12	51	11,434
1 Yr	26.45	0.11	0.74	50	12,645
3 Yr Avg	20.30	0.37	0.20	52	17,410
5 Yr Avg	16.24	1.26	0.99	46	21,222
10 Yr Avg	10.33	2.62	2.37	53	26,726
15 Yr Avg	11.11	3.25	3.07	55	48,562

Tax Analysis	Tax-Adj Rtn%	%Rank Cat	Tax-Cost Rat	%Rank Cat
3 Yr (estimated)	18.58	46	1.43	55
5 Yr (estimated)	14.78	49	1.26	71
10 Yr (estimated)	8.74	52	1.44	52

Potential Capital Gain Exposure: 28% of assets

Rating and Risk

Time Period	Load-Adj Return %	Morningstar Rtn vs Cat	Morningstar Risk vs Cat	Morningstar Risk-Adj Rating
1 Yr	26.45			
3 Yr	20.30	Avg	-Avg	★★★
5 Yr	16.24	Avg	Avg	★★★
10 Yr	10.33	Avg	Avg	★★★
Incept	10.97			

Other Measures	Standard Index MSCI EAFE	Best Fit Index MSCI EAFE
Alpha	1.4	1.4
Beta	0.93	0.93
R-Squared	95	95
Standard Deviation	8.99	
Mean	20.30	
Sharpe Ratio	1.76	

Morningstar's Take by William Samuel Rocco 12-11-06

Reserved investors will find a lot to like at American Beacon International Equity.

This fund has an edge on the important issue of costs. This share class has an expense ratio that's 37 basis points below the median for institutional foreign large-cap funds. And the retail share class of the fund ranks in the cheapest quartile of no-load foreign large-cap funds.

For these low costs, the fund provides exposure to four outside management teams who have all been successful using distinctive value styles. The Causeway team has thrived at its primary fund by pursuing stocks that are cheap on a variety of metrics. Gary Motyl of Templeton has had significant success by focusing on stocks that are undervalued relative to their assets or earnings, while the Lazard team has earned solid results at its main charge by favoring stocks with fetching prices and returns on equity. And The Boston Company team has succeeded elsewhere by focusing on stocks that are cheap relative to their market and peers.

Meanwhile, the fund sports a relatively conservative portfolio. The fund has far less emerging-markets exposure than its typical peer because American Beacon has tight limits on which developing markets the subadvisors can consider and three of the teams have pronounced developed-markets biases. Its average market cap is much bigger than the group norm because two of the teams have giant-cap biases and the other two pay no more attention to smaller caps than do most foreign large-value managers. And it has more issue and sector diversification than most of its peers, because its four teams rely on a mix of styles.

All this and a solid risk/reward profile make the fund a worthy option for reserved investors. But such investors should note that this fund is unlikely to be a long-term returns leader and that it's at a disadvantage when emerging-markets or smaller-cap names lead the way.

Address:	4151 Amon Carter Boulevard Fort Worth TX 76155 800-658-5811	Minimum Purchase:	$2000000 Add: $0 IRA: $0
		Min Auto Inv Plan:	$0 Add: —
		Sales Fees:	No-load, 2.00%R
Web Address:	www.americanbeaconfunds.com	Management Fee:	0.35%
Inception:	08-07-91	Actual Fees:	Mgt:0.35% Dist: —
Advisor:	American Beacon Advisors, Inc.	Expense Projections:	3Yr:$224 5Yr:$390 10Yr:$871
Subadvisor:	Multiple Subadvisors	Income Distrib:	Annually
NTF Plans:	N/A		

Portfolio Analysis 11-30-06

Share change since 10-06 Total Stocks:195	Sector	Country	% Assets
Sanofi-Synthelabo	Health	France	2.35
France Telecom	Telecom	France	2.01
Vodafone Grp	Telecom	U.K.	1.89
⊕ GlaxoSmithKline	Health	U.K.	1.87
⊖ Total SA	Energy	France	1.71
⊕ BAE Systems	Ind Mtrls	U.K.	1.65
Deutsche Post	Business	Germany	1.62
Royal Bank Of Scotland G	Financial	U.K.	1.55
⊕ BP	Energy	U.K.	1.47
BNP Paribas	Financial	France	1.46
Philips Elec	Goods	Netherlands	1.43
Siemens	Hardware	Germany	1.26
UniCredito Italiano Grp	Financial	Italy	1.25
Credit Suisse Grp	Financial	Switzerland	1.20
⊖ Axa	Financial	France	1.18
Telefonica	Telecom	Spain	1.18
ING Groep	Financial	Netherlands	1.18
Novartis	Health	Switzerland	1.15
HSBC Hldgs	Financial	U.K.	1.09
TNT NV	Business	Netherlands	1.02

Current Investment Style

Value Blnd Growth; Large Mid Small

Market Cap	%
Giant	56.1
Large	37.1
Mid	6.5
Small	0.3
Micro	0.0
Avg $mil: 37,407	

Value Measures		Rel Category
Price/Earnings	13.62	1.08
Price/Book	2.02	1.13
Price/Sales	1.11	1.17
Price/Cash Flow	7.17	1.00
Dividend Yield %	3.71	1.13

Growth Measures	%	Rel Category
Long-Term Erngs	10.38	1.01
Book Value	8.03	1.03
Sales	4.96	0.90
Cash Flow	5.27	1.47
Historical Erngs	17.94	1.10

Composition

Cash	5.1	Bonds	0.0
Stocks	93.0	Other	2.0
Foreign (% of Stock)			99.9

Sector Weightings	% of Stocks	Rel MSCI EAFE	3 Year High	3 Year Low
Info	15.30	1.29		
Software	0.00	0.00	0	0
Hardware	3.38	0.88	4	2
Media	2.95	1.61	4	2
Telecom	8.97	1.61	11	7
Service	46.23	0.98		
Health	7.70	1.08	10	7
Consumer	5.57	1.13	6	2
Business	6.44	1.27	7	6
Financial	26.52	0.88	29	23
Mfg	38.47	0.94		
Goods	16.45	1.25	17	14
Ind Mtrls	9.21	0.60	15	9
Energy	8.71	1.22	10	6
Utilities	4.10	0.78	5	2

Regional Exposure	% Stock		
UK/W. Europe	76	N. America	2
Japan	13	Latn America	0
Asia X Japan	9	Other	0

Country Exposure	% Stock		
U.K.	26	Germany	8
France	14	Switzerland	8
Japan	13		

American Beacon SmCVI Pln

	Ticker	Load	NAV	Yield	Total Assets	Mstar Category
	AVPAX	Closed	$21.38	0.6%	$3,252 mil	Small Value

Governance and Management

Stewardship Grade: B

Portfolio Manager(s)

As of September 2005, the fund has eight subadvisors. They are Brandywine; Hotchkis & Wiley; Barrow, Hanley, Mewhinney & Strauss; Boston Company; Opus Capital; Dreman Value Management; Metropolitan West Capital Management; and SSgA Funds Management. The last three managers were added Aug. 31, 2005, and are expected to receive the bulk of new inflows.

Strategy

The fund used to divide the assets among five different subadvisors, but it added another three late in 2005 and intends to send future inflows to the new members. Each subadvisor has a separate sleeve that it manages in a particular style, but they all look for companies that have below-average price/earnings ratios and above-average growth measures relative to the Russell 2000 Index.

Historical Profile

Return	Above Avg
Risk	Above Avg
Rating	★★★★ Above Avg

88% 97% 95% 93% 96% 95%

▼ Manager Change
▽ Partial Manager Change

Growth of $10,000
■ Investment Values of Fund
— Investment Values of S&P 500

Performance Quartile (within Category)

Investment Style
Equity
Stock %

	1995	1996	1997	1998	1999	2000	2001	2002	2003	2004	2005	2006	History
	—	—	—	—	9.30	10.69	12.73	11.45	16.84	19.91	20.03	21.38	NAV
	—	—	—	—	4.04*	19.03	27.24	-6.92	51.28	23.19	5.51	15.36	Total Return %
	—	—	—	—	—	28.13	39.13	15.18	22.60	12.31	0.60	-0.43	+/-S&P 500
	—	—	—	—	—	-3.80	13.22	4.51	5.25	0.94	0.80	-8.12	+/-Russ 2000 VL
	—	—	—	—	—	1.98	0.75	0.95	0.28	0.33	0.47	0.67	Income Return %
	—	—	—	—	—	17.05	26.49	-7.87	51.00	22.86	5.04	14.69	Capital Return %
	—	—	—	—	—	—	54	13	31	16	26	63	59	Total Rtn % Rank Cat
	—	—	—	—	0.02	0.18	0.08	0.12	0.03	0.06	0.09	0.13	Income $
	—	—	—	—	0.17	0.17	0.77	0.28	0.44	0.77	0.89	1.56	Capital Gains $
	—	—	—	—	—	—	—	—	1.11	1.16	1.15	—	Expense Ratio %
	—	—	—	—	—	—	—	—	0.52	0.39	0.33	—	Income Ratio %
	—	—	—	—	—	—	—	—	81	75	35	—	Turnover Rate %
	—	—	—	—	—	—	—	1	35	86	756	1,377	Net Assets $mil

Performance 12-31-06

	1st Qtr	2nd Qtr	3rd Qtr	4th Qtr	Total
2002	11.55	-2.96	-20.90	8.71	-6.92
2003	-5.41	24.75	8.88	17.75	51.28
2004	8.08	-0.06	1.04	12.87	23.19
2005	-2.41	4.01	3.22	0.71	5.51
2006	8.89	-3.16	-0.05	9.46	15.36

Trailing	Total Return%	+/- S&P 500	+/- Russ 2000 VL	%Rank Cat	Growth of $10,000
3 Mo	9.46	2.76	0.43	23	10,946
6 Mo	9.41	-3.33	-2.40	37	10,941
1 Yr	15.36	-0.43	-8.12	59	11,536
3 Yr Avg	14.46	4.02	-2.02	49	14,996
5 Yr Avg	16.12	9.93	0.75	17	21,112
10 Yr Avg	—	—	—	—	—
15 Yr Avg	—	—	—	—	—

Tax Analysis	Tax-Adj Rtn%	%Rank Cat	Tax-Cost Rat	%Rank Cat
3 Yr (estimated)	13.04	33	1.24	31
5 Yr (estimated)	14.77	15	1.16	40
10 Yr (estimated)	—	—	—	—

Potential Capital Gain Exposure: 16% of assets

Rating and Risk

Time Period	Load-Adj Return %	Morningstar Rtn vs Cat	Morningstar Risk vs Cat	Morningstar Risk-Adj Rating
1 Yr	15.36			
3 Yr	14.46	Avg	Avg	★★★
5 Yr	16.12	+Avg	+Avg	★★★★
10 Yr	—			
Incept	16.58			

Other Measures	Standard Index S&P 500	Best Fit Index Mstar Small Value
Alpha	1.0	-0.7
Beta	1.43	0.94
R-Squared	73	95
Standard Deviation	11.49	
Mean	14.46	
Sharpe Ratio	0.96	

Portfolio Analysis 11-30-06

Share change since 10-06 Total Stocks:513

Sector		PE	Tot Ret%	% Assets
Ingram Micro, Inc.	Business	13.3	2.41	0.94
American Financial Group	Financial	10.9	42.43	0.88
⊖ AGCO Corporation	Ind Mtrls	—	86.72	0.87
Men's Wearhouse	Consumer	16.6	30.69	0.78
Avnet, Inc.	Business	16.5	6.64	0.77
Flowserve Corporation	Ind Mtrls	39.2	27.58	0.73
Great Plains Energy, Inc	Utilities	—	20.32	0.70
Hanover Insurance Group,	Financial	26.9	17.57	0.67
Lubrizol Corporation	Ind Mtrls	16.6	18.17	0.64
⊖ Delphi Financial Group	Financial	14.8	33.00	0.64
Mentor Graphics Corporat	Software	NMF	74.37	0.62
⊕ Brunswick Corporation	Goods	9.1	-20.12	0.61
NSTAR	Utilities	17.4	24.73	0.61
⊖ Atmos Energy Corporation	Utilities	17.3	27.57	0.61
BJ's Wholesale Club, Inc	Consumer	18.1	5.24	0.59
Lear Corporation	Ind Mtrls	—	4.93	0.59
AGL Resources, Inc	Utilities	13.1	16.49	0.57
Century Aluminum Company	Ind Mtrls	—	70.36	0.56
⊕ Con-way, Inc.	Business	10.2	-20.59	0.55
⊖ Swift Transportation Co.	Business	13.0	29.41	0.55

Current Investment Style

Value Blnd Growth — Large Mid Small

Market Cap	%
Giant	0.0
Large	0.3
Mid	40.4
Small	51.3
Micro	8.1
Avg $mil:	1,487

Value Measures		Rel Category
Price/Earnings	14.94	0.97
Price/Book	1.73	0.97
Price/Sales	0.67	0.84
Price/Cash Flow	6.59	1.08
Dividend Yield %	1.65	1.04

Growth Measures	%	Rel Category
Long-Term Erngs	11.41	0.91
Book Value	7.35	1.36
Sales	-5.96	NMF
Cash Flow	-0.17	NMF
Historical Erngs	11.01	0.97

Profitability	%	Rel Category
Return on Equity	12.65	1.18
Return on Assets	7.05	1.16
Net Margin	8.78	0.97

Sector Weightings

	% of Stocks	Rel S&P 500	3 Year High	Low
↻ Info	11.23	0.56		
Software	2.28	0.66	3	0
Hardware	5.97	0.65	7	1
Media	2.01	0.53	3	2
Telecom	0.97	0.28	1	0
☞ Service	51.82	1.12		
Health	3.60	0.30	7	3
Consumer	12.31	1.61	16	11
Business	11.61	2.74	13	8
Financial	24.30	1.09	30	21
Mfg	36.94	1.09		
Goods	6.75	0.79	10	7
Ind Mtrls	18.28	1.53	19	9
Energy	5.41	0.55	7	4
Utilities	6.50	1.86	15	7

Composition

	%
● Cash	4.7
● Stocks	95.3
● Bonds	0.0
○ Other	0.0
Foreign (% of Stock)	1.4

Morningstar's Take by Marta Norton 12-19-06

American Beacon Small Cap Value is not the nimble gem it once was.

Most of the things that made this fund one of our favorites in the small-value category are still intact. The fund still splits its assets between stellar management teams at Brandywine; the Boston Company; Hotchkis & Wiley; Barrow, Hanley, Mewhinney, & Strauss; and Opus Capital. And the fund continues to keep expenses low, which gives it a built-in advantage over other small-cap funds. These strengths have added up to excellent long-term returns. The fund's 17.2% gain for the five-year stretch through Dec. 15, 2006, outstripped more than 80% of its rivals.

Unfortunately, we're not sure the fund will continue to produce such impressive results. In its early years, it had the advantage of a nimble asset base. But after several years of big gains, particularly in 2003 when it soared 52%, money has flooded in. A 2005 close to new investors did little to stem the tide. Since then, additional money from current investors and market appreciation has added more than $1 billion in assets. The fund is now one of the biggest in the small-value category. And even so, management has not moved for a hard close. Instead, the fund has lined up three more subadvisors, Dreman Value Management, Metropolitan West Capital Management, and SSgA Funds Management, to handle any extra money investors throw its way.

This fund also now has spread its money over more individual stocks, which could be a recipe for mediocrity. The fund's number of holdings has climbed from less than 300 in 2003 to more than 500 in 2006. And should its asset base grow more, it could add even more stocks. With so many holdings, it will be increasingly difficult for the fund to distinguish itself from index funds.

We're disappointed to see a fund with so many strengths lose its edge. But because of its burgeoning size, we've lost our enthusiasm for this fund.

Address:	4151 Amon Carter Boulevard Fort Worth TX 76155 800-388-3344	Minimum Purchase:	Closed	Add: —	IRA: —
		Min Auto Inv Plan:	Closed	Add: —	
		Sales Fees:	No-load		
Web Address:	www.americanbeaconfunds.com	Management Fee:	0.65%		
Inception:	03-01-99*	Actual Fees:	Mgt:0.50%	Dist: —	
Advisor:	American Beacon Advisors, Inc.	Expense Projections:	3Yr:$350	5Yr:$606	10Yr:$1340
Subadvisor:	Multiple Subadvisors	Income Distrib:	Annually		
NTF Plans:	Fidelity Retail-NTF, Schwab OneSource				

© 2007 Morningstar, Inc. All rights reserved. The information herein is not represented or warranted to be accurate, correct, complete or timely. Past performance is no guarantee of future results. Download your free reports at http://www.morningstar.com/goto/2007Funds500.

MORNINGSTAR® Funds 500

Ameristock

	Ticker	Load	NAV	Yield	Total Assets	Mstar Category
	AMSTX	None	$43.79	3.7%	$601 mil	Large Value

Portfolio Manager(s)

Nicholas Gerber has been the lead manager on this offering since its August 1995 inception and continues to make the final call on all buy and sell decisions. Andrew Ngim was added as a comanager in January 2000 and currently runs the day-to-day operations of the fund. Although Gerber has come a long way from the time when he ran the fund out of his basement, his research staff is still limited to Ngim and two other analysts.

Strategy

Nicholas Gerber sticks with stocks that have market caps of $15 billion or higher, looking for cheaply priced companies with high-dividend yields or fallen-growth stocks with bright long-term outlooks and reasonable valuations. He tends to hold on to stocks for the long haul, resulting in low turnover.

Performance 12-31-06

	1st Qtr	2nd Qtr	3rd Qtr	4th Qtr	Total
2002	3.17	-9.86	-18.45	10.76	-16.00
2003	-5.24	14.76	0.72	10.72	21.27
2004	-0.74	1.07	-1.80	7.09	5.52
2005	-2.69	0.53	-1.24	0.51	-2.88
2006	4.13	0.87	6.30	5.63	17.95

Trailing	Total Return%	+/- S&P 500	+/- Russ 1000 VI	%Rank Cat	Growth of $10,000
3 Mo	5.63	-1.07	-2.37	90	10,563
6 Mo	12.29	-0.45	-2.43	62	11,229
1 Yr	17.95	2.16	-4.30	54	11,795
3 Yr Avg	6.52	-3.92	-8.57	99	12,086
5 Yr Avg	4.25	-1.94	-6.61	99	12,313
10 Yr Avg	10.48	2.06	-0.52	18	27,092
15 Yr Avg	—	—	—	—	—

Tax Analysis	Tax-Adj Rtn%	%Rank Cat	Tax-Cost Rat	%Rank Cat
3 Yr (estimated)	5.49	99	0.97	38
5 Yr (estimated)	3.36	99	0.85	46
10 Yr (estimated)	9.54	8	0.85	13

Potential Capital Gain Exposure: 7% of assets

Morningstar's Take by Kerry O'Boyle 12-27-06

Investors that have stuck by Ameristock are beginning to see the light at the end of the tunnel.

As expected, it took a rally in mega-cap stocks to get this fund back on its feet. After three consecutive calendar years of bottom-decile returns versus its large-value rivals, the fund surged during the third quarter of 2006 along with some of the market's biggest stocks. Powered by resurgent large-cap pharmaceutical and telecom stocks, including Bristol-Myers Squibb, Pfizer, SBC (now AT&T) and Verizon Communications, the fund has gained nearly 18% in 2006.

This sequence of events isn't entirely surprising. The fund's deep-value leanings and focus on the bluest of the blue chips in terms of size have left it lagging most of its peers as smaller, seemingly more-speculative stocks have carried the stage since 2003. The portfolio's bias is evident in its $78 billion average market capitalization--greater than 97% of its rivals. So any rebound in mega-cap stocks was likely to work in favor of this fund and

shareholders willing to stick with it.

Unfortunately, not everyone was able to show such patience. Fickle investors fleeing the fund sent assets down to $610 million from more than $1.7 billion at the beginning of 2005. That has forced manager Nick Gerber to trim back stakes across the board, possibly at inopportune times, in order to meet redemptions. In addition, Gerber himself loosened the criteria for buying and selling stocks at the end of 2005 in the hopes of improving performance, though thus far, he has yet to wield that added flexibility.

Still, we reiterate our view that the rationale for owning this fund--low costs, tax efficiency, modest volatility, and a disciplined approach to picking stocks--remains the same. Although the market winds have been against it for some time, we think the fund has shown that it's able to deliver the goods in an environment more favorable to its style.

Address:	1480 Moraga Rd 200 Moraga CA 94556 800-394-5064	Minimum Purchase: Min Auto Inv Plan: Sales Fees:	$1000 $0 No-load	Add: $100 Add: —	IRA: $1000
Web Address: Inception: Advisor: Subadvisor:	www.ameristock.com 08-31-95* Ameristock Corporation None	Sales Fees: Management Fee: Actual Fees: Expense Projections: Income Distrib:	1.00% mx./0.70% mn. Mgt:0.78% Dist: — 3Yr:$252 5Yr:$439 Annually	10Yr:$977	
NTF Plans:	Fidelity Retail-NTF, Schwab OneSource				

Historical Profile

Return: Below Avg
Risk: Below Avg
Rating: ★★ Below Avg

	1995	1996	1997	1998	1999	2000	2001	2002	2003	2004	2005	2006	History
	16.96	21.18	26.81	34.91	35.11	40.22	40.40	33.04	39.41	40.54	38.51	43.79	NAV
	14.29*	27.68	32.86	31.98	2.73	20.70	1.25	-16.00	21.27	5.52	-2.88	17.95	Total Return %
	—	4.72	-0.50	3.40	-18.31	29.80	13.14	6.10	-7.41	-5.36	-7.79	2.16	+/-S&P 500
	—	6.04	-2.32	16.35	-4.62	13.69	6.84	-0.48	-8.76	-10.97	-9.93	-4.30	+/-Russ 1000 VI
	—	2.31	2.02	0.90	1.19	1.28	0.71	1.02	1.92	2.63	2.14	4.25	Income Return %
	—	25.37	30.84	31.08	1.54	19.42	0.54	-17.02	19.35	2.89	-5.02	13.70	Capital Return %
	—	7	8	1	59	12	26	36	96	98	99	54	Total Rtn % Rank Cat
	0.18	0.39	0.42	0.24	0.42	0.45	0.29	0.41	0.63	1.04	0.87	1.64	Income $
	0.00	0.04	0.83	0.22	0.34	1.63	0.04	0.49	0.04	0.00	0.00	0.00	Capital Gains $
	—	0.00	0.56	0.90	0.94	0.99	0.83	0.77	0.78	0.77	0.77	0.79	Expense Ratio %
	—	2.40	2.40	1.48	1.22	1.51	1.50	1.31	1.97	1.96	2.10	2.21	Income Ratio %
	—	—	22	12	9	31	6	14	3	6	—	10	Turnover Rate %
	—	5	7	36	110	164	1,313	1,400	1,925	1,711	817	601	Net Assets $mil

Rating and Risk

Time Period	Load-Adj Return %	Morningstar Rtn vs Cat	Morningstar Risk vs Cat	Morningstar Risk-Adj Rating
1 Yr	17.95			
3 Yr	6.52	Low	Low	★
5 Yr	4.25	Low	-Avg	★
10 Yr	10.48	+Avg	Avg	★★★★
Incept	12.90			

Other Measures	Standard Index S&P 500	Best Fit Index Mstar Large Core TR
Alpha	-1.8	-2.5
Beta	0.72	0.77
R-Squared	72	73
Standard Deviation	5.97	
Mean	6.52	
Sharpe Ratio	0.56	

Portfolio Analysis 09-30-06

Share change since 06-06 Total Stocks:43	Sector	PE	Tot Ret%	% Assets
Colgate-Palmolive Compan	Goods	27.6	21.51	4.50
⊖ Bank of America Corporat	Financial	12.4	20.68	4.50
IBM	Hardware	17.1	19.77	4.39
Sara Lee Corporation	Goods	22.6	10.03	4.09
⊖ Citigroup, Inc.	Financial	13.1	19.55	4.08
Dell, Inc.	Hardware	18.4	-16.23	3.93
⊖ Washington Mutual, Inc.	Financial	13.4	9.62	3.83
☼ Progressive Corporation	Financial	12.4	-16.93	3.62
Fannie Mae	Financial	—	24.34	2.81
PNC Financial Services G	Financial	8.7	23.60	2.53
Comcast Corporation A	Media	45.2	63.31	2.53
Microsoft Corporation	Software	23.8	15.83	2.51
Procter & Gamble Company	Goods	23.9	13.36	2.50
Merck & Co., Inc.	Health	19.1	42.66	2.47
⊕ Texas Instruments, Inc.	Hardware	16.9	-9.82	2.46
⊖ Pfizer Inc.	Health	15.2	15.22	2.46
Dow Chemical Company	Ind Mtrls	10.0	-5.44	2.43
Chevron Corporation	Energy	9.0	33.76	2.42
ExxonMobil Corporation	Energy	11.1	39.07	2.39
General Electric Company	Ind Mtrls	20.0	9.35	2.37

Current Investment Style

Value Blnd Growth — Large Mid Small

Market Cap	%
Giant	66.9
Large	32.4
Mid	0.7
Small	0.0
Micro	0.0

Avg $mil: 78,611

Value Measures		Rel Category
Price/Earnings	14.84	1.08
Price/Book	2.94	1.32
Price/Sales	1.60	1.23
Price/Cash Flow	9.60	1.43
Dividend Yield %	2.64	1.13

Growth Measures	%	Rel Category
Long-Term Erngs	9.77	0.94
Book Value	9.27	1.17
Sales	9.40	1.05
Cash Flow	3.78	0.62
Historical Erngs	12.83	0.79

Profitability	%	Rel Category
Return on Equity	25.20	1.40
Return on Assets	11.65	1.19
Net Margin	14.45	1.11

Sector Weightings	% of Stocks	Rel S&P 500	3 Year High Low	
☎ Info	21.68	1.08		
Software	2.51	0.73	3	0
Hardware	11.63	1.26	12	6
Media	3.33	0.88	3	2
Telecom	4.21	1.20	10	4
Service	41.99	0.91		
Health	12.00	1.00	20	12
Consumer	4.77	0.62	6	3
Business	0.91	0.22	3	1
Financial	24.31	1.09	25	22
Mfg	36.33	1.08		
Goods	15.52	1.82	16	11
Ind Mtrls	11.88	0.99	14	11
Energy	6.83	0.70	8	5
Utilities	2.10	0.60	5	2

Composition

● Cash	0.0
● Stocks	100.0
● Bonds	0.0
● Other	0.0
Foreign	2.0
(% of Stock)	

Ariel

	Ticker	Load	NAV	Yield	Total Assets	Mstar Category
	ARGFX	None	$51.81	0.0%	$4,214 mil	Mid-Cap Blend

Governance and Management

Stewardship Grade: A

Portfolio Manager(s)

John Rogers, founder of Ariel Capital Management and architect of the firm's investment strategy, has managed this fund since its inception. He has more than 20 years of investment experience, specializing in small- and mid-cap stocks. John Miller formally became comanager on Nov. 20, 2006; he's been with Ariel since 1989 and has worked on the fund for years. Rogers works with about eight analysts. The analysts follow companies on their assignment lists closely, providing regular updates and recommendations.

Strategy

Manager John Rogers seeks out smaller-cap stocks that are selling at a discount of 40% or more to his estimate of their intrinsic values. He favors firms with strong brands or franchises that operate in consistent and stable industries, have sound balance sheets, generate lots of cash, and have strongly motivated management teams. The upshot of this approach is that the fund tends to have scant exposure to volatile sectors, such as technology and biotech, and big stakes in consumer goods, services, and industrial materials. The portfolio is typically concentrated in about 40 or fewer stocks.

Performance 12-31-06

	1st Qtr	2nd Qtr	3rd Qtr	4th Qtr	Total
2002	7.64	-3.55	-10.16	1.66	-5.18
2003	-5.51	17.63	4.26	10.48	28.04
2004	6.74	4.78	0.32	8.72	21.97
2005	-0.32	1.68	1.22	-1.63	0.92
2006	8.11	-6.21	2.42	6.25	10.35

Trailing	Total Return%	+/- S&P 500	+/- S&P Mid 400	%Rank Cat	Growth of $10,000
3 Mo	6.25	-0.45	-0.74	79	10,625
6 Mo	8.83	-3.91	3.00	51	10,883
1 Yr	10.35	-5.44	0.03	70	11,035
3 Yr Avg	10.75	0.31	-2.34	79	13,584
5 Yr Avg	10.52	4.33	-0.37	42	16,489
10 Yr Avg	13.11	4.69	-0.36	22	34,278
15 Yr Avg	12.48	1.84	-1.15	62	58,362

Tax Analysis	Tax-Adj Rtn%	%Rank Cat	Tax-Cost Rat	%Rank Cat
3 Yr (estimated)	9.72	67	0.93	40
5 Yr (estimated)	9.83	38	0.62	37
10 Yr (estimated)	11.40	20	1.51	38

Potential Capital Gain Exposure: 19% of assets

Morningstar's Take by Todd Trubey 11-29-06

Ariel Fund has happily plodded along to a big milestone.

Some key changes occurred around this fund's 20th birthday. John Miller, the longtime deputy at the fund, became a named comanager on Nov. 20, 2006. That doesn't portend real change--since-inception manager John Rogers isn't going anywhere--but reflects Miller's true role here. Less happy news comes from the board, where Bert Mitchell, the independent chairman, had to step down after a 20-year stint; his accounting firm merged with another that disallows him from being on Ariel's board. Taking his place will be Mellody Hobson, President of Ariel Capital Management. The firm says that her passion for the funds, historical understanding of the board, and business sense made her the clear choice. We don't dispute any of that, but firmly prefer independent chairs.

Still, stability abounds at this fund, as John Rogers has led it with the same strategy from inception to a great record that's tough to measure.

Only 94 domestic-stock funds have a manager tenure of more than 19 years, and Ariel's 13.4% annualized 20-year return ranks 21st among them. Still that group includes sector funds and team-managed funds as well as funds of all styles. Moreover, it's nearly impossible to say how many funds have lost their original managers or come and gone over the two-decade span. Ultimately, we'd simply say that on an absolute basis the fund's rewards have been ample, especially when one considers the fund's relatively low volatility.

Our overall stance here remains the same: The fund remains sound. Our one misgiving is that the fund spreads $4.3 billion dollars among 36 smaller mid-cap firms. That's fewer holdings than 80% of its mid-blend category peers, yet the asset base is seventh highest out of 191 funds. That makes it tougher to reach down the market-cap ladder into its favored small-caps. Still, the fund's focus, deep research, and endurance are the keys, and they're intact.

Address:	200 East Randolph Drive
	Chicago IL 60601
	800-292-7435
Web Address:	www.arielmutualfunds.com
Inception:	11-06-86
Advisor:	Ariel Capital Management, LLC
Subadvisor:	None
NTF Plans:	Fidelity Retail-NTF, Schwab OneSource

Minimum Purchase:	$1000	Add: $50	IRA: $250
Min Auto Inv Plan:	$0	Add: $50	
Sales Fees:	No-load, 0.25%S		
Management Fee:	0.65% mx./0.55% mn.		
Actual Fees:	Mgt:0.57%	Dist:0.25%	
Expense Projections:	3Yr:$328	5Yr:$569	10Yr:$1260
Income Distrib:	Annually		

Historical Profile

Return	Average
Risk	Below Avg
Rating	★★★★ Above Avg

| 93% | 99% | 90% | 97% | 95% | 88% | 82% | 99% | 99% |

Investment Style
Equity
Stock %

▼ Manager Change
▽ Partial Manager Change

Growth of $10,000
— Investment Values of Fund
— Investment Values of S&P 500

43.6
32.4
24.0
17.0
10.0

Performance Quartile (within Category)

1995	1996	1997	1998	1999	2000	2001	2002	2003	2004	2005	2006	History
27.32	31.96	39.88	39.96	31.11	33.61	37.72	35.24	45.12	53.17	50.07	51.81	NAV
18.52	23.51	36.44	9.89	-5.76	28.77	14.21	-5.18	28.04	21.97	0.92	10.35	Total Return %
-19.06	0.55	3.08	-18.69	-26.80	37.87	26.10	16.92	-0.64	11.09	-3.99	-5.44	+/-S&P 500
-12.41	4.26	4.19	-9.23	-20.48	11.26	14.82	9.35	-7.58	5.49	-11.64	0.03	+/-S&P Mid 400
1.62	0.00	0.45	0.20	0.19	0.79	0.33	0.00	0.00	0.05	0.30	0.00	Income Return %
16.90	23.51	35.99	9.69	-5.95	27.98	13.88	-5.18	28.04	21.92	0.62	10.35	Capital Return %
88	29	11	44	95	6	16	8	88	10	94	70	Total Rtn % Rank Cat
0.44	0.00	0.14	0.08	0.08	0.25	0.11	0.00	0.00	0.02	0.15	0.00	Income $
4.18	1.78	3.57	3.72	6.04	5.75	0.53	0.52	0.00	1.79	3.48	3.40	Capital Gains $
1.37	1.31	1.25	1.21	1.25	1.24	1.19	1.19	1.10	1.07	1.03	1.07	Expense Ratio %
1.18	0.57	0.23	0.30	0.27	0.65	0.59	-0.12	-0.05	0.06	0.08	0.19	Income Ratio %
16	17	20	22	38	48	24	6	4	16	19	28	Turnover Rate %
121	120	174	202	205	286	619	1,190	2,380	4,197	4,703	4,214	Net Assets $mil

Rating and Risk

Time Period	Load-Adj Return %	Morningstar Rtn vs Cat	Morningstar Risk vs Cat	Morningstar Risk-Adj Rating
1 Yr	10.35			
3 Yr	10.75	-Avg	-Avg	★★
5 Yr	10.52	Avg	-Avg	★★★
10 Yr	13.11	+Avg	-Avg	★★★★★
Incept	13.55			

Other Measures	Standard Index S&P 500	Best Fit Index Mstar Small Value
Alpha	-0.4	-0.9
Beta	1.12	0.67
R-Squared	70	75
Standard Deviation	9.16	
Mean	10.75	
Sharpe Ratio	0.81	

Portfolio Analysis 11-30-06

Share change since 10-06 Total Stocks:36	Sector	PE	Tot Ret%	% Assets
⊖ Markel Corporation	Financial	12.2	51.43	4.85
Hewitt Associates, Inc.	Business	—	-8.07	4.52
Janus Capital Group, Inc	Financial	42.2	16.13	4.49
⊖ Jones Lang LaSalle, Inc.	Financial	18.6	84.32	4.25
Energizer Holdings, Inc.	Goods	17.6	42.58	3.62
Idex Corporation	Ind Mtrls	19.6	16.76	3.59
Tribune Company	Media	16.0	4.15	3.56
⊕ Mohawk Industries, Inc.	Goods	13.0	-13.93	3.50
Investors Financial Serv	Financial	17.9	16.09	3.50
⊖ HCC Insurance Holdings I	Financial	16.5	9.39	3.44
BearingPoint, Inc.	Business	—	0.13	3.35
IMS Health, Inc.	Health	17.4	10.77	3.21
H & R Block, Inc.	Consumer	25.3	-3.95	3.13
⊖ Career Education Corpora	Consumer	19.6	-26.51	3.04
Black & Decker Corporati	Ind Mtrls	12.2	-6.37	2.99
Anixter International	Ind Mtrls	12.6	38.80	2.76
McClatchy Company A	Media	12.6	-25.53	2.76
J.M. Smucker Co.	Goods	19.5	12.99	2.76
Interpublic Group of Com	Business	—	26.84	2.75
A.G. Edwards, Inc.	Financial	17.9	37.15	2.72

Current Investment Style

Value Blnd Growth — Large Mid Small

Market Cap	%
Giant	0.0
Large	0.0
Mid	82.8
Small	17.3
Micro	0.0
Avg $mil:	3,127

Value Measures		Rel Category
Price/Earnings	16.69	1.04
Price/Book	2.28	1.01
Price/Sales	1.25	1.12
Price/Cash Flow	11.44	1.35
Dividend Yield %	0.97	0.75

Growth Measures	%	Rel Category
Long-Term Erngs	11.35	0.90
Book Value	7.64	0.92
Sales	9.44	1.06
Cash Flow	-4.16	NMF
Historical Erngs	8.34	0.47

Profitability	%	Rel Category
Return on Equity	18.13	1.14
Return on Assets	8.20	1.02
Net Margin	10.48	0.96

Sector Weightings	% of Stocks	Rel S&P 500	3 Year High Low	
Info	12.59	0.63		
Software	0.00	0.00	0	0
Hardware	0.00	0.00	4	0
Media	12.59	3.32	16	11
Telecom	0.00	0.00	0	0
Service	59.12	1.28		
Health	6.93	0.57	10	3
Consumer	8.92	1.17	20	8
Business	10.69	2.53	14	2
Financial	32.58	1.46	35	20
Mfg	28.29	0.84		
Goods	14.38	1.68	17	13
Ind Mtrls	13.91	1.16	15	7
Energy	0.00	0.00	0	0
Utilities	0.00	0.00	0	0

Composition

		%
●	Cash	0.7
●	Stocks	99.3
●	Bonds	0.0
●	Other	0.0
	Foreign	0.0
	(% of Stock)	

MORNINGSTAR® Funds 500

Ariel Appreciation

Analyst Pick ✓ | Ticker CAAPX | Load None | NAV $48.33 | Yield 0.0% | Total Assets $2,770 mil | Mstar Category Mid-Cap Blend

Governance and Management

Stewardship Grade: A

Portfolio Manager(s)

Firm founder John Rogers, who also manages Ariel Fund, runs the show here. Rogers boasts more than 20 years of investment experience, specializing in small- and mid-cap stocks. His tenure here began Sept. 30, 2002. Matt Sauer became comanager on Nov. 20, 2006. He arrived at Ariel Capital after 13 years at Oak Value, another stellar Buffett-inspired fund.

Strategy

Management hunts for stocks that are selling at discounts of 40% or more to its estimates of their intrinsic value. Following Warren Buffett's lead, it favors firms with strong brands or franchises that operate in consistent and stable industries, have sound balance sheets, generate lots of cash, and have strongly motivated management teams. The portfolio is typically concentrated in 40 or fewer stocks, heavy in financials and consumer stocks, and light in technology fare.

Performance 12-31-06

	1st Qtr	2nd Qtr	3rd Qtr	4th Qtr	Total
2002	8.56	-6.77	-15.96	5.38	-10.36
2003	-7.05	21.84	4.14	11.05	30.97
2004	3.72	-0.04	-0.60	9.76	13.10
2005	-2.69	2.63	1.49	1.54	2.92
2006	1.86	-3.03	5.01	6.96	10.94

Trailing	Total Return%	+/- S&P 500	+/- S&P Mid 400	%Rank Cat	Growth of $10,000
3 Mo	6.96	0.26	-0.03	61	10,696
6 Mo	12.31	-0.43	6.48	16	11,231
1 Yr	10.94	-4.85	0.62	65	11,094
3 Yr Avg	8.90	-1.54	-4.19	94	12,915
5 Yr Avg	8.68	2.49	-2.21	75	15,162
10 Yr Avg	12.76	4.34	-0.71	31	33,232
15 Yr Avg	12.32	1.68	-1.31	67	57,129

Tax Analysis	Tax-Adj Rtn%	%Rank Cat	Tax-Cost Rat	%Rank Cat
3 Yr (estimated)	7.99	84	0.84	36
5 Yr (estimated)	8.12	64	0.52	31
10 Yr (estimated)	11.43	18	1.18	23

Potential Capital Gain Exposure: 28% of assets

Morningstar's Take by Todd Trubey 11-28-06

Ariel Appreciation remains fundamentally strong.

Two notable changes occurred in November 2006. Matt Sauer, who came to Ariel Capital Management in May 2006 from Oak Value Capital Management became comanager on Nov. 20, 2006. Sauer proved his skill at the similarly Buffett-inspired Oak Value, and lead manager John Rogers says he made an immediate, heavy impact here. Less happy news comes from the fund's board of directors, where Bert Mitchell, the independent chairman, stepped down after a 20-year stint; his accounting firm merged with another that disallows him from being on Ariel's board. Mellody Hobson, president of Ariel Capital Management, takes his place. The firm says her passion for the funds, historical understanding of the board, and business sense made her the clear choice. We don't dispute any of that but hold firmly to our preference for independent chairs.

This Analyst Pick, like many Buffett-style funds, has lagged lately, but we encourage investors to be patient. As commodity firms and risky fare of many stripes surged, the steady-Eddie businesses favored here lagged. That's the key reason why the fund's 10% annualized three-year return through Nov. 27, 2006, trails nearly 90% of mid-blend peers. When high quality returns to favor, as it has very recently, the fund should thrive: Over the past three months, the fund's 11% gain tops nearly 90% of peers.

Our faith here rests on Ariel's constant research of business fundamentals. Over time, Ariel develops deep knowledge of favored niche industries, as in the office product, outsourcing, and newpaper arenas. The latter has been a drag here, but the Ariel crew notes that the four holdings here are attractively priced given recent mergers. They argue that while the market focuses on dropping daily circulations, the newspapers' Internet audience and cash flows are improving.

Long term, we believe the fund remains a winner.

Address:	200 East Randolph Drive
	Chicago IL 60601
	800-292-7435
Web Address:	www.arielmutualfunds.com
Inception:	12-01-89
Advisor:	Ariel Capital Management, LLC
Subadvisor:	None
NTF Plans:	Fidelity Retail-NTF, Schwab OneSource

Minimum Purchase:	$1000	Add: $50	IRA: $250
Min Auto Inv Plan:	$0	Add: $50	
Sales Fees:	No-load, 0.25%S		
Management Fee:	0.75% mx./0.65% mn.		
Actual Fees:	Mgt:0.67%	Dist:0.25%	
Expense Projections:	3Yr:$362	5Yr:$627	10Yr:$1384
Income Distrib:	Annually		

Historical Profile

Return Below Avg
Risk Below Avg
Rating ★★★ Neutral

	94%	98%	94%	97%	97%	96%	96%	99%	99%	

Growth of $10,000
— Investment Values of Fund
— Investment Values of S&P 500

Performance Quartile (within Category)

1995	1996	1997	1998	1999	2000	2001	2002	2003	2004	2005	2006	History
22.24	26.07	32.82	35.69	30.97	32.53	37.02	33.06	43.30	47.67	46.72	48.33	NAV
24.16	23.72	37.95	19.55	-3.79	18.82	16.23	-10.36	30.97	13.10	2.92	10.94	Total Return %
-13.42	0.76	4.59	-9.03	-24.83	27.92	28.12	11.74	2.29	2.22	-1.99	-4.85	+/-S&P 500
-6.77	4.47	5.70	0.43	-18.51	1.31	16.84	4.17	-4.65	-3.38	-9.64	0.62	+/-S&P Mid 400
1.02	0.33	0.26	0.11	0.12	0.38	0.20	0.00	0.00	0.11	0.29	0.05	Income Return %
23.14	23.39	37.69	19.44	-3.91	18.44	16.03	-10.36	30.97	12.99	2.63	10.89	Capital Return %
70	28	9	20	93	21	14	18	74	82	90	65	Total Rtn % Rank Cat
0.20	0.07	0.07	0.04	0.04	0.12	0.06	0.00	0.00	0.05	0.13	0.02	Income $
1.77	1.37	3.07	3.46	3.15	3.95	0.71	0.12	0.00	1.20	2.20	3.46	Capital Gains $
1.36	1.36	1.33	1.26	1.26	1.31	1.26	1.26	1.20	1.15	1.14	1.16	Expense Ratio %
0.61	0.50	0.07	0.05	0.13	0.25	0.35	-0.06	-0.06	0.01	0.17	0.27	Income Ratio %
18	26	19	20	24	31	28	13	32	19	25	25	Turnover Rate %
139	146	204	284	335	340	771	1,420	2,508	3,265	3,323	2,770	Net Assets $mil

Rating and Risk

Time Period	Load-Adj Return %	Morningstar Rtn vs Cat	Morningstar Risk vs Cat	Morningstar Risk-Adj Rating
1 Yr	10.94			
3 Yr	8.90	-Avg	Low	★★
5 Yr	8.68	-Avg	-Avg	★★
10 Yr	12.76	Avg	-Avg	★★★★
Incept	12.55			

Other Measures	Standard Index S&P 500	Best Fit Index Mstar Large Core TR
Alpha	-1.5	-2.5
Beta	1.02	1.10
R-Squared	79	82
Standard Deviation	7.93	
Mean	8.90	
Sharpe Ratio	0.71	

Portfolio Analysis 11-30-06

Share change since 10-06 Total Stocks:31	Sector	PE	Tot Ret%	% Assets
⊖ Accenture, Ltd.	Business	22.0	29.32	5.79
⊖ Tribune Company	Media	16.0	4.15	4.93
⊖ Pitney Bowes Inc.	Ind Mtrls	19.7	12.57	4.89
Carnival Corporation	Goods	18.7	-6.15	4.51
⊖ Northern Trust Corporati	Financial	20.9	19.11	4.49
Yum Brands, Inc.	Consumer	20.4	26.76	4.25
Black & Decker Corporati	Ind Mtrls	12.2	-6.37	3.98
Gannett Co., Inc.	Media	12.3	1.92	3.85
⊖ Franklin Resources	Financial	23.6	17.79	3.82
⊖ Omnicom Group, Inc.	Business	21.4	24.14	3.80
Mohawk Industries, Inc.	Goods	13.0	-13.93	3.77
CBS, Inc. B	Media	—	33.16	3.71
Janus Capital Group, Inc	Financial	42.2	16.13	3.52
T Rowe Price Group	Financial	26.1	23.27	3.34
H & R Block, Inc.	Consumer	25.3	-3.95	3.18
Baxter International Inc	Health	24.3	24.81	3.18
IMS Health, Inc.	Health	17.4	10.77	3.11
⊖ Interpublic Group of Com	Business	—	26.84	2.95
☀ Thermo Fisher Scientific	Health	37.4	50.32	2.85
⊖ Career Education Corpora	Consumer	19.6	-26.51	2.81

Current Investment Style

Value Blnd Growth — Large Mid Small

Market Cap	%
Giant	0.0
Large	43.0
Mid	57.0
Small	0.0
Micro	0.0

Avg $mil: 9,860

Value Measures		Rel Category
Price/Earnings	17.49	1.09
Price/Book	2.86	1.27
Price/Sales	1.72	1.54
Price/Cash Flow	11.86	1.40
Dividend Yield %	1.29	0.99

Growth Measures	%	Rel Category
Long-Term Ergns	11.19	0.88
Book Value	-1.13	NMF
Sales	8.71	0.98
Cash Flow	2.76	0.33
Historical Ergns	9.05	0.51

Profitability	%	Rel Category
Return on Equity	19.43	1.22
Return on Assets	8.13	1.01
Net Margin	9.17	0.84

Sector Weightings	% of Stocks	Rel S&P 500	3 Year High	Low
↻ Info	16.85	0.84		
Software	0.00	0.00	0	0
Hardware	0.00	0.00	0	0
Media	16.85	4.45	18	6
Telecom	0.00	0.00	3	0
☞ Service	62.19	1.35		
Health	9.19	0.76	14	6
Consumer	12.38	1.62	16	4
Business	17.44	4.12	29	17
Financial	23.18	1.04	33	23
Mfg	20.96	0.62		
Goods	12.05	1.41	12	6
Ind Mtrls	8.91	0.75	12	6
Energy	0.00	0.00	0	0
Utilities	0.00	0.00	0	0

Composition

		%
● Cash		0.6
● Stocks		99.4
● Bonds		0.0
● Other		0.0
Foreign		0.0
(% of Stock)		

Artisan International Inv

	Ticker	Load	NAV	Yield	Total Assets	Mstar Category
	ARTIX	None	$28.99	1.4%	$10,532 mil	Foreign Large Growth

Governance and Management

Stewardship Grade: B

Portfolio Manager(s)

Mark Yockey came to start this fund for Artisan Partners in 1996. He won Morningstar's 1998 International Fund Manager of the Year for his record here and for delivering strong long-term returns on previous charge, United International Growth (now Waddell & Reed Advisors International Growth), where he got his start in 1990. He's supported here by ten analysts divided mostly by sector, but also by region. Because of Artisan Partners unique structure, Yockey's San Francisco-based team is distinct from those of others at the shop.

Strategy

The fund favors companies that are poised to enjoy superior earnings growth, but it is flexible in its pursuit of such issues. Thus, nontraditional growth stocks such as banks and insurers are often well represented in the portfolio. Yockey is more willing than most peers to look at smaller developed markets and emerging markets. The fund normally does not hedge its foreign currency risk, levies a 2% redemption fee on shares held fewer than 90 days, and uses fair value pricing whenever necessary.

Historical Profile

Return	Above Avg
Risk	Above Avg
Rating	★★★★ Above Avg

Investment Style
Equity
Stock %

83% | 92% | 91% | 93% | 87% | 96% | 98% | 97% | 99%

▼ Manager Change
▽ Partial Manager Change

Growth of $10,000
— Investment Values of Fund
— Investment Values of MSCI EAFE

39.4
32.4
24.0
17.0
10.0

Performance Quartile (within Category)

1995	1996	1997	1998	1999	2000	2001	2002	2003	2004	2005	2006	History
10.00	13.32	12.46	16.12	28.50	21.90	18.36	14.79	18.91	22.14	25.31	28.99	NAV
0.00*	34.37	3.46	32.18	81.29	-10.59	-15.86	-18.90	29.14	17.76	16.27	25.56	Total Return %
—	28.32	1.68	12.25	54.26	3.60	5.56	-2.96	-9.45	-2.49	2.73	-0.78	+/-MSCI EAFE
—	27.50	1.19	13.49	53.31	2.77	5.53	-3.10	-10.28	-2.62	1.80	-0.15	+/-MSCI Wd xUS
—	0.00	1.48	0.28	0.15	0.00	0.30	0.55	1.19	0.65	1.85	1.72	Income Return %
—	34.37	1.98	31.90	81.14	-10.59	-16.16	-19.45	27.95	17.11	14.42	23.84	Capital Return %
—	3	70	1	13	20	17	51	79	29	42	23	Total Rtn % Rank Cat
0.00	0.00	0.20	0.04	0.02	0.00	0.07	0.10	0.18	0.12	0.41	0.43	Income $
0.00	0.11	1.13	0.24	0.54	3.55	0.00	0.00	0.00	0.00	0.00	2.33	Capital Gains $
—	2.50	1.61	1.45	1.38	1.27	1.22	1.21	1.20	1.22	1.19	1.20	Expense Ratio %
—	1.60	1.07	0.37	0.59	-0.10	0.45	0.82	1.35	0.64	0.94	0.66	Income Ratio %
—	57	104	109	79	99	72	51	15	55	56	58	Turnover Rate %
—	192	301	505	2,240	3,665	4,059	4,814	5,962	7,130	7,414	10,821	Net Assets $mil

Performance 12-31-06

	1st Qtr	2nd Qtr	3rd Qtr	4th Qtr	Total
2002	0.87	-2.00	-21.38	4.35	-18.90
2003	-14.13	23.07	5.82	15.47	29.14
2004	6.08	-1.30	-2.37	15.21	17.76
2005	-0.54	-1.41	12.39	5.50	16.27
2006	10.63	-1.04	3.75	10.54	25.56

Trailing	Total Return%	+/- MSCI EAFE	+/- MSCI Wd xUS	%Rank Cat	Growth of $10,000
3 Mo	10.54	0.19	0.42	63	11,054
6 Mo	14.69	0.00	0.47	47	11,469
1 Yr	25.56	-0.78	-0.15	23	12,556
3 Yr Avg	19.80	-0.13	-0.30	22	17,194
5 Yr Avg	12.48	-2.50	-2.77	47	18,004
10 Yr Avg	12.88	5.17	4.92	7	33,587
15 Yr Avg	—	—	—		—

Tax Analysis	Tax-Adj Rtn%	%Rank Cat	Tax-Cost Rat	%Rank Cat
3 Yr (estimated)	18.84	21	0.80	49
5 Yr (estimated)	11.81	45	0.60	54
10 Yr (estimated)	11.43	6	1.28	83

Potential Capital Gain Exposure: 29% of assets

Rating and Risk

Time Period	Load-Adj Return %	Morningstar Rtn vs Cat	Morningstar Risk vs Cat	Morningstar Risk-Adj Rating
1 Yr	25.56			
3 Yr	19.80	+Avg	Avg	★★★★
5 Yr	12.48	Avg	+Avg	★★★
10 Yr	12.88	+Avg	+Avg	★★★★
Incept	14.67			

Other Measures	Standard Index MSCI EAFE	Best Fit Index MSCI EAFE
Alpha	-1.4	-1.4
Beta	1.09	1.09
R-Squared	94	94
Standard Deviation	10.66	
Mean	19.80	
Sharpe Ratio	1.47	

Portfolio Analysis 09-30-06

Share change since 06-06 Total Stocks:96	Sector	Country	% Assets
⊕ UBS AG	Financial	Switzerland	3.77
⊕ RWE	Utilities	Germany	3.05
⊕ Credit Saison	Financial	Japan	2.82
⊕ Allianz	Financial	Germany	2.41
Nestle	Goods	Switzerland	2.26
⊖ Mizuho Financial Grp	Financial	Japan	2.25
ORIX	Financial	Japan	2.16
⊕ Kookmin Bank	Financial	Korea	2.09
⊕ Fortum Oyj	Energy	Finland	2.01
⊖ China Mobile	Telecom	Hong Kong	1.83
⊖ ASML Holding	Hardware	Netherlands	1.83
⊕ Swiss Re	Financial	Switzerland	1.80
Roche Holding	Health	Switzerland	1.75
⊖ UniCredito Italiano Grp	Financial	Italy	1.74
⊖ Fortis	Financial	Belgium	1.73
⊖ Grupo Televisa SA ADR	Media	Mexico	1.73
Carrefour	Consumer	France	1.72
⊕ Publishing & Broadcastin	Media	Australia	1.61
⊕ William Morrison Supermk	Consumer	U.K.	1.53
⊖ Kingfisher	Consumer	U.K.	1.52

Current Investment Style

Value Blnd Growth — Large/Mid/Small

	Market Cap	%
Giant		55.3
Large		38.3
Mid		6.4
Small		0.0
Micro		0.0
Avg $mil:		27,337

Value Measures		Rel Category
Price/Earnings	4.77	0.31
Price/Book	2.14	0.82
Price/Sales	1.23	0.87
Price/Cash Flow	9.66	1.00
Dividend Yield %	2.17	0.89

Growth Measures	%	Rel Category
Long-Term Erngs	12.32	0.91
Book Value	11.34	1.03
Sales	5.87	0.67
Cash Flow	6.41	0.53
Historical Erngs	23.24	1.02

Composition

Cash	0.5	Bonds	0.0
Stocks	98.5	Other	1.0
Foreign (% of Stock)			100.0

Sector Weightings

	% of Stocks	Rel MSCI EAFE	3 Year High	Low
⟳ Info	13.23	1.12		
🗗 Software	1.01	1.80	1	0
💻 Hardware	2.80	0.73	7	3
📺 Media	4.11	2.25	11	3
📞 Telecom	5.31	0.95	11	4
⊆ Service	59.86	1.27		
🏥 Health	6.01	0.84	6	3
🛒 Consumer	6.24	1.26	13	6
🏢 Business	8.79	1.73	9	5
💲 Financial	38.82	1.29	39	25
🏭 Mfg	26.92	0.66		
🚗 Goods	10.87	0.83	14	11
⚙ Ind Mtrls	5.11	0.33	8	5
🔋 Energy	6.00	0.84	9	5
💡 Utilities	4.94	0.94	5	0

Regional Exposure

	% Stock		% Stock
UK/W. Europe	53	N. America	1
Japan	23	Latn America	3
Asia X Japan	18	Other	2

Country Exposure

	% Stock		% Stock
Japan	23	France	8
Switzerland	13	Hong Kong	7
Germany	9		

Morningstar's Take by Dan Lefkovitz 12-17-06

Artisan International still has what it takes to be a Fund Analyst Pick.

We've long been fans of this fund. Mark Yockey has managed the portfolio since 1996 and has built an impressive team, recently bolstered by Laurie Fitch, a former research director at TIAA-CREF. Yockey practices a growth-at-a-reasonable-price discipline and is willing to source growth ideas across a wide range of sectors. He pays little attention to the country weightings of the popular EAFE Index; for example, he's currently investing far less in the popular U.K. market and far more in smaller developed markets like Italy and emerging markets like Korea.

This independent thinking has resulted in great long-term returns. Since 1996, the fund has averaged a 12.75% annual gain, roughly 5 percentage points better than both EAFE and the typical fund in the foreign large-growth category. Yockey owned hot growth stocks in the late 1990s, but his valuation discipline led him to trim,

especially in telecom, and the fund survived the 2000-02 bear market better than most.

Yockey's flexible, value-conscious style has helped the fund in recent years. This year's big winners include Swiss bank UBS and German utility RWE, considered by many to be "value" stocks. Yet Yockey sees European financials growing due to economic activity on the continent and utilities benefiting from government investment. Such flexibility, as well as a significant emerging markets stake, has helped the fund beat its foreign-large-growth peers over the past three-years. And though the fund, like most of its growth-oriented peers, has not beaten EAFE for the trailing three- or five-year period, it will be well positioned if growth comes back into favor.

Two words of caution. First, don't expect the fund to continue posting such gaudy absolute returns. Second, asset growth--Yockey now runs $25 billion across the strategy--has made the fund less nimble than it once was.

Address:	875 East Wisconsin Ave Ste 800 Milwaukee WI 53202 800-344-1770	Minimum Purchase:	$1000	Add: $50	IRA: $1000
		Min Auto Inv Plan:	$50	Add: $50	
		Sales Fees:	No-load, 2.00%R		
Web Address:	www.artisanfunds.com	Management Fee:	1.00% mx./0.90% min.		
Inception:	12-28-95*	Actual Fees:	Mgt:0.93%	Dist: —	
Advisor:	Artisan Partners Limited Partnership	Expense Projections:	3Yr:$381	5Yr:$660	10Yr:$1455
Subadvisor:	None	Income Distrib:	Annually		
NTF Plans:	Fidelity Retail-NTF, Schwab OneSource				

MORNINGSTAR® Funds 500

Artisan Intl Val

	Ticker	Load	NAV	Yield	Total Assets	Mstar Category
	ARTKX	None	$27.93	1.5%	$1,532 mil	Foreign Small/Mid Value

Governance and Management

Stewardship Grade: A

Portfolio Manager(s)

Manager David Samra came to Artisan Partners to start this fund in 2002. He previously worked at Harris Associates, where he was a senior analyst on the team managing Oakmark International and Oakmark International Small Cap. Dan O'Keefe, an analyst who was named a comanager in October 2006, came with Samra from Harris Associates. A small analyst team supports the fund. Although the team shares a trader with Artisan's international-growth team (see Artisan International), the two groups are located in different locations in San Francisco and don't regularly interact.

Strategy

Management looks for stocks cheap enough to offer a 30% return. Ideas are generated using right screens that search for stocks with features such as low P/E ratios and high returns on capital. These ideas are researched further, with about 60 stocks making the final list. (Unlike some value funds, expect this offering to avoid firms that are highly leveraged or in financial distress.) The most undervalued stocks occupy the largest stakes in the portfolio. Additionally, emerging markets are limited to 20% of the portfolio, no one country can exceed 35% of assets, and currency hedging is rare.

Performance 12-31-06

	1st Qtr	2nd Qtr	3rd Qtr	4th Qtr	Total
2002	—	—	—	6.85	6.00 *
2003	-3.68	27.42	10.07	15.91	56.59
2004	8.90	4.71	0.49	15.43	32.26
2005	1.23	-4.08	9.49	3.55	10.09
2006	13.74	0.92	5.49	11.05	34.46

Trailing	Total Return%	+/- MSCI EAFE	+/- MSCI Wd xUS	%Rank Cat	Growth of $10,000
3 Mo	11.05	0.70	0.93	79	11,105
6 Mo	17.15	2.46	2.93	13	11,715
1 Yr	34.46	8.12	8.75	5	13,446
3 Yr Avg	25.10	5.17	5.00	32	19,578
5 Yr Avg	—	—	—	—	—
10 Yr Avg	—	—	—	—	—
15 Yr Avg	—	—	—	—	—

Tax Analysis	Tax-Adj Rtn%	%Rank Cat	Tax-Cost Rat	%Rank Cat
3 Yr (estimated)	23.68	32	1.14	29
5 Yr (estimated)	—	—	—	—
10 Yr (estimated)	—	—	—	—

Potential Capital Gain Exposure: 18% of assets

Historical Profile

Return Average
Risk Below Avg
Rating ★★★★ Above Avg

Investment Style
Equity
Stock %

90% 87% 90% 91%

▼ Manager Change
▽ Partial Manager Change

28.4
22.8
18.0
14.0 — Investment Values of Fund
— Investment Values of MSCI EAFE
10.0

Growth of $10,000

Performance Quartile (within Category)

1995	1996	1997	1998	1999	2000	2001	2002	2003	2004	2005	2006	History
—	—	—	—	—	—	—	10.60	16.18	21.06	22.06	27.93	NAV
—	—	—	—	—	—	—	6.00*	56.59	32.26	10.09	34.46	Total Return %
—	—	—	—	—	—	—	—	18.00	12.01	-3.45	8.12	+/-MSCI EAFE
—	—	—	—	—	—	—	—	17.17	11.88	-4.38	8.75	+/-MSCI Wd xUS
—	—	—	—	—	—	—	—	0.85	0.67	2.25	2.01	Income Return %
—	—	—	—	—	—	—	—	55.74	31.59	7.84	32.45	Capital Return %
—	—	—	—	—	—	—	—	21	12	98	5	Total Rtn % Rank Cat
—	—	—	—	—	—	—	0.00	0.09	0.11	0.47	0.44	Income $
—	—	—	—	—	—	—	0.00	0.30	0.21	0.60	1.28	Capital Gains $
—	—	—	—	—	—	—	—	—	2.45	1.56	1.25	Expense Ratio %
—	—	—	—	—	—	—	—	—	1.14	1.61	2.18	Income Ratio %
—	—	—	—	—	—	—	—	—	9	15	43	Turnover Rate %
—	—	—	—	—	—	—	3	20	458	1,532		Net Assets $mil

Rating and Risk

Time Period	Load-Adj Return %	Morningstar Rtn vs Cat	Morningstar Risk vs Cat	Morningstar Risk-Adj Rating
1 Yr	34.46			
3 Yr	25.10	Avg	-Avg	★★★★
5 Yr	—	—	—	
10 Yr	—	—	—	
Incept	31.78			

Other Measures	Standard Index MSCI EAFE	Best Fit Index MSCI EAFE
Alpha	5.1	5.1
Beta	0.95	0.95
R-Squared	80	80
Standard Deviation	10.05	
Mean	25.10	
Sharpe Ratio	1.98	

Portfolio Analysis 09-30-06

Share change since 06-06 Total Stocks:42	Sector	Country	% Assets
⊕ Diageo	Goods	U.K.	4.98
⊕ Tyco International, Ltd.	Ind Mtrls	United States	4.83
⊕ Countrywide	Financial	U.K.	4.77
⊕ Wolters Kluwer	Media	Netherlands	4.28
⊕ Vodafone Group PLC ADR	Telecom	U.K.	3.85
⊕ Pfeiffer Vacuum Technolo	Ind Mtrls	Germany	3.57
⊕ Central Japan Railway	Business	Japan	3.17
⊕ Meitec	Business	Japan	3.02
⊕ Benfield Grp Ltd	Business	U.K.	2.95
⊕ Givaudan	Ind Mtrls	Switzerland	2.94
⊕ Unicharm	Goods	Japan	2.93
⊕ Signet Grp	Goods	U.K.	2.82
⊕ Sekisui House, Ltd	Consumer	Japan	2.60
⊕ Vivendi Universal	Media	France	2.59
⊕ Willis Group Holdings, L	Financial	Bermuda	2.56
⊕ CanWest Global Communica	Media	Canada	2.43
⊕ GUS	Consumer	U.K.	2.36
⊕ Unilever PLC ADR	Goods	U.K.	2.36
⊕ Kimberly-Clark de Mexico	Ind Mtrls	Mexico	2.33
⊕ Guoco Grp Ltd	Financial	Hong Kong	2.31

Current Investment Style

Value Blnd Growth — Large/Mid/Small

Market Cap	%
Giant	23.0
Large	23.0
Mid	39.5
Small	13.3
Micro	1.2
Avg $mil: 6,952	

Value Measures		Rel Category
Price/Earnings	15.34	1.04
Price/Book	2.64	1.32
Price/Sales	1.27	1.43
Price/Cash Flow	7.51	1.19
Dividend Yield %	2.56	0.97

Growth Measures		Rel Category
Long-Term Erngs	10.35	0.69
Book Value	3.50	0.45
Sales	4.02	0.54
Cash Flow	7.83	0.87
Historical Erngs	46.68	2.40

Composition

Cash	7.9	Bonds	0.0
Stocks	91.1	Other	1.1
Foreign (% of Stock)			91.6

Sector Weightings	% of Stocks	Rel MSCI EAFE	3 Year High	Low
♈ Info	20.75	1.76		
🖳 Software	3.13	5.59	3	0
🖰 Hardware	0.00	0.00	1	0
🖵 Media	12.02	6.57	12	6
🕿 Telecom	5.60	1.01	6	3
☞ Service	34.40	0.73		
⚕ Health	0.00	0.00	3	0
🛒 Consumer	7.32	1.48	7	1
🏢 Business	10.04	1.98	12	5
💲 Financial	17.04	0.57	23	17
🏭 Mfg	44.86	1.10		
🏠 Goods	24.75	1.89	30	25
⚙ Ind Mtrls	18.89	1.22	26	19
🛢 Energy	0.00	0.00	1	0
🔋 Utilities	1.22	0.23	2	0

Regional Exposure % Stock

UK/W. Europe	58	N. America	11
Japan	13	Latn America	11
Asia X Japan	7	Other	0

Country Exposure % Stock

U.K.	33	Mexico	7
Japan	13	Germany	6
United States	8		

Morningstar's Take by Dan Lefkovitz 12-11-06

For a bold investor, Artisan International Value could be a core foreign holding.

The fund possesses many traits that point to long-term success. Manager David Samra and recently named comanager Dan O'Keefe apply a consistent, value-oriented process. They build portfolios of 40-odd stocks and trade infrequently. Expenses are reasonable. Although the fund has only existed since 2002, Samra and O'Keefe are experienced. They spent years working on Oakmark International.

Investors may note that, while the fund is having a boffo 2006, annual return rankings have been uneven. That's partly because the high-conviction strategies can cause bumpy results and partly because of the fund's category designation. Although judged against the foreign small-/mid category, the fund is all-cap in nature, and in 2005, exposure to large caps held it back versus peers that were fully exposed to red-hot small caps. Not surprisingly, Samra has found an increasing number of undervalued opportunities among large caps with each passing year.

Small has not trounced large in 2006, and this fund, with its gaudy 32% gain for the year to date through Dec. 8, 2006, sits near the top of the category heap. Returns have been boosted by several takeover offers for key portfolio holdings, such as Countrywide, a British real estate broker that Samra bought in 2004 when concerns over the U.K. real estate market depressed its price. The offer is a sign of the boom in private equity firms, which tend to share this fund's attraction to cash-rich businesses.

It's important to moderate expectations. Chances are slim that absolute returns over the coming few years will match those of the past few. But this fund can play a useful long-term role in a portfolio. Its emphasis on high-quality stocks trading cheaply limits volatility and counteracts the effects of smaller stocks and significant emerging-markets exposure.

Address:	875 East Wisconsin Ave Ste 800 Milwaukee WI 53202 800-399-1770	Minimum Purchase:	$1000	Add: $50	IRA: $1000
		Min Auto Inv Plan:	$50	Add: $50	
Web Address:	www.artisanfunds.com	Sales Fees:	No-load, 2.00%R		
Inception:	09-23-02*	Management Fee:	1.00% mx./0.93% mn.		
Advisor:	Artisan Partners Limited Partnership	Actual Fees:	Mgt:0.98% Dist: —		
Subadvisor:	None	Expense Projections:	3Yr:$397 5Yr:$686 10Yr:$1511		
NTF Plans:	Fidelity Retail-NTF, Schwab OneSource	Income Distrib:	Annually		

Artisan Intl Sm Cap

	Ticker	Load	NAV	Yield	Total Assets	Mstar Category
	ARTJX	Closed	$21.83	2.7%	$1,039 mil	Foreign Small/Mid Growth

Governance and Management

Stewardship Grade: A

Portfolio Manager(s)

Mark Yockey, who also runs Artisan International and was named Morningstar's International-Stock Manager of the Year in 1998, is the lead manager here. He's supported here by ten analysts divided mostly by sector, but also by region. Because of Artisan Partners unique structure, Yockey's San Francisco-based team is distinct from those of others at the shop.

Strategy

Lead manager Mark Yockey focuses on firms with market caps of less than $3 billion that have good earnings prospects and reasonable valuations. Yockey, who considers opportunities from all over the globe and makes full use of the industry spectrum, readily builds country and sector weightings that are quite different from his bogy or peer group. The fund normally does not hedge its foreign-currency risk. Meanwhile, it charges a 2% redemption fee on shares held fewer than 90 days, and it uses fair-value pricing whenever necessary.

Performance 12-31-06

	1st Qtr	2nd Qtr	3rd Qtr	4th Qtr	Total
2002	4.07	0.10	-13.43	9.41	-1.34
2003	-3.83	26.83	14.46	16.75	63.00
2004	7.05	-1.50	-0.36	19.64	25.70
2005	3.08	-0.44	15.76	5.82	25.71
2006	15.55	-4.63	4.31	15.87	33.18

Trailing	Total Return%	+/- MSCI EAFE	+/- MSCI Wd xUS	%Rank Cat	Growth of $10,000
3 Mo	15.87	5.52	5.75	15	11,587
6 Mo	20.86	6.17	6.64	6	12,086
1 Yr	33.18	6.84	7.47	19	13,318
3 Yr Avg	28.15	8.22	8.05	21	21,045
5 Yr Avg	27.61	12.63	12.36	15	33,839
10 Yr Avg	—	—	—	—	—
15 Yr Avg	—	—	—	—	—

Tax Analysis	Tax-Adj Rtn%	%Rank Cat	Tax-Cost Rat	%Rank Cat
3 Yr (estimated)	24.34	45	2.97	91
5 Yr (estimated)	25.04	16	2.01	90
10 Yr (estimated)	—	—	—	—

Potential Capital Gain Exposure: 30% of assets

Morningstar's Take by Dan Lefkovitz 12-17-06

Artisan International Small Cap, while superb, won't always look this good.

This closed Fund Analyst Pick is set to record another sensational year. Midway through December 2006, it has gained 30%. That's after posting 25% gains in both 2005 and 2004 and climbing a gravity-defying 63% in 2003. Even by the standards of the red-hot foreign small/mid growth category, its record is enviable.

But shareholders must understand that numbers of that magnitude aren't sustainable. The yawning valuation gap that once existed between foreign large caps and foreign small caps has closed, which is why manager Mark Yockey says that the team is finding fewer undervalued small caps. Also, the fund has thrived partly by stashing more than 25% of assets in emerging markets like China and Mexico, and that asset class has been on a long run.

Still, for investors who understand that volatility is inevitable here, this fund makes a great

long-term holding. Yockey, who also runs the outstanding large-cap fund Artisan International, is patient as well as valuation sensitive, a trait that served him well during the 2000-2002 bear market. He's also flexible. That means he sources ideas from a wide range of sectors and countries. For instance, he is committing nearly 30% of assets to financial services sector, a traditional favorite of value investors, due to his belief in the growth of banking, insurance, investing, and real estate in many markets. One of the fund's top holdings, Indiabulls Financials, is involved in all of those activities in one of the world's fast growing economies. It has been a big winner this year.

Another plus is that the fund is a good diversifier. Yockey focuses on smaller stocks than most of his peers, and the portfolio's geographic breakdown--including not only emerging markets but smaller developed markets like Singapore and Norway--gives investors exposure they might lack in their core foreign fund.

Address:	875 East Wisconsin Ave Ste 800 Milwaukee WI 53202 800-344-1770
Web Address:	www.artisanfunds.com
Inception:	12-21-01*
Advisor:	Artisan Partners Limited Partnership
Subadvisor:	None
NTF Plans:	Fidelity Retail-NTF, Schwab OneSource

Minimum Purchase:	Closed	Add: —	IRA: —
Min Auto Inv Plan:	Closed	Add: —	
Sales Fees:	No-load, 2.00%R		
Management Fee:	1.25%		
Actual Fees:	Mgt:1.25%	Dist: —	
Expense Projections:	3Yr:$483	5Yr:$834	10Yr:$1824
Income Distrib:	Annually		

Historical Profile

Return	Above Avg
Risk	Average
Rating	★★★★ Above Avg

	80%	93%	95%	94%	93%

Investment Style
Equity
Stock %

▼ Manager Change
▽ Partial Manager Change

Growth of $10,000
— Investment Values of Fund
— Investment Values of MSCI EAFE

Performance Quartile (within Category)

1995	1996	1997	1998	1999	2000	2001	2002	2003	2004	2005	2006	History
—	—	—	—	—	—	10.08	9.92	15.61	17.56	19.81	21.83	NAV
—	—	—	—	—	—	0.80*	-1.34	63.00	25.70	25.71	33.18	Total Return %
—	—	—	—	—	—	—	14.60	24.41	5.45	12.17	6.84	+/-MSCI EAFE
—	—	—	—	—	—	—	14.46	23.58	5.32	11.24	7.47	+/-MSCI Wd xUS
—	—	—	—	—	—	—	0.00	0.36	0.75	1.13	3.54	Income Return %
—	—	—	—	—	—	—	-1.34	62.64	24.95	24.58	29.64	Capital Return %
—	—	—	—	—	—	—	1	17	41	51	19	Total Rtn % Rank Cat
—	—	—	—	—	—	0.00	0.00	0.04	0.12	0.20	0.70	Income $
—	—	—	—	—	—	0.00	0.02	0.49	1.77	1.88	3.76	Capital Gains $
—	—	—	—	—	—	—	1.91	1.77	1.57	1.53		Expense Ratio %
—	—	—	—	—	—	—	-0.02	0.28	0.95	0.41		Income Ratio %
—	—	—	—	—	—	—		38	13	81	62	Turnover Rate %
—	—	—	—	—	—	—	108	164	621	1,039		Net Assets $mil

Rating and Risk

Time Period	Load-Adj Return %	Morningstar Rtn vs Cat	Morningstar Risk vs Cat	Morningstar Risk-Adj Rating
1 Yr	33.18			
3 Yr	28.15	+Avg	Avg	★★★★
5 Yr	27.61	+Avg	Avg	★★★★
10 Yr	—	—	—	—
Incept	27.65			

Other Measures	Standard Index MSCI EAFE	Best Fit Index MSCI EAFE
Alpha	1.8	1.8
Beta	1.35	1.35
R-Squared	87	87
Standard Deviation	13.63	
Mean	28.15	
Sharpe Ratio	1.67	

Portfolio Analysis 09-30-06

Share change since 06-06 Total Stocks:78	Sector	Country	% Assets
Empresas ICA Sociedad Co	Business	Mexico	3.26
Buhrmann	Ind Mtrls	Netherlands	3.07
Fraser & Neave Ltd	Ind Mtrls	Singapore	2.57
⊕ Sibir Energy	Energy	U.K.	2.56
⊕ Creed	Financial	Japan	2.24
⊕ Korea Invest Hldgs	—	Korea	2.19
⊖ Elekta	Health	Sweden	2.15
⊕ Geodis	Business	France	2.00
⊖ Banco Latinoamericano de	Financial	Panama	1.91
⊕ Commrcl Intl Bk	Financial	Egypt	1.89
⊕ Bank Sarasin & Cie	Financial	Switzerland	1.84
Schindler Hldg	Ind Mtrls	Switzerland	1.78
⊖ Indiabulls Financial Ser	Financial	India	1.74
NTT Urban Development	Financial	Japan	1.74
Hong Kong Exchanges & Cl	Financial	Hong Kong	1.70
Kaufman & Broad	Consumer	France	1.66
⊖ Kangwon Land	Consumer	Korea	1.60
Socotherm	Business	Italy	1.58
⊖ Sulzer	Ind Mtrls	Switzerland	1.57
Beijing Capital Int'l Ai	Business	Hong Kong	1.56

Current Investment Style

Value Blnd Growth / Large Mid Small

	Market Cap	%
	Giant	0.0
	Large	19.5
	Mid	49.4
	Small	29.4
	Micro	1.8
	Avg $mil: 1,630	

Value Measures		Rel Category
Price/Earnings	16.11	1.03
Price/Book	2.09	0.86
Price/Sales	1.02	0.93
Price/Cash Flow	4.20	0.54
Dividend Yield %	2.37	1.16

Growth Measures	%	Rel Category
Long-Term Erngs	16.38	0.80
Book Value	5.90	0.63
Sales	6.23	0.50
Cash Flow	11.70	0.78
Historical Erngs	23.01	1.02

Composition

Cash	4.5	Bonds	0.0
Stocks	92.9	Other	2.6
Foreign (% of Stock)			100.0

Sector Weightings

	% of Stocks	Rel MSCI EAFE	3 Year High	Low
⊙ Info	1.76	0.15		
🗔 Software	0.00	0.00	1	0
🖥 Hardware	0.13	0.03	3	0
🎙 Media	0.00	0.00	15	0
📞 Telecom	1.63	0.29	7	2
☞ Service	66.03	1.40		
🩺 Health	3.55	0.50	10	4
🛒 Consumer	13.60	2.75	14	10
🏢 Business	20.41	4.03	20	6
💲 Financial	28.47	0.95	28	14
🏭 Mfg	32.22	0.79		
🏪 Goods	5.69	0.43	11	2
⚙ Ind Mtrls	17.65	1.14	21	15
🔋 Energy	7.07	0.99	15	4
💡 Utilities	1.81	0.35	2	0

Regional Exposure	% Stock		
UK/W. Europe 43	N. America	3
Japan 13	Latn America	8
Asia X Japan 28	Other	5

Country Exposure	% Stock		
Japan	13	Singapore	7
Hong Kong	11	Switzerland	7
U.K.	7		

MORNINGSTAR® Funds 500

Artisan Mid Cap Inv

Ticker	**Load**	**NAV**	**Yield**	**Total Assets**	**Mstar Category**
ARTMX	Closed	$30.46	0.0%	$4,762 mil	Mid-Cap Growth

Governance and Management

Stewardship Grade: A

Portfolio Manager(s)

Andy Stephens has managed the fund since its inception in 1997. Before coming aboard here, he was a comanager at Strong Balanced. Jim Hamel, originally an analyst here and then an associate portfolio manager, was promoted to portfolio manager in July 2006. At the same time, Tom Wooden, who has been on board as an analyst since 1999, was bumped up to associate portfolio manager. Six additional analysts support the fund and related non-fund accounts.

Strategy

Manager Andy Stephens and his team look for dominant companies with accelerating profit cycles that are selling at attractive valuations. They seek a balance of stable and aggressive-growth stocks, and they pay more attention to valuations than many in the mid-growth set.

Historical Profile

Return	Average
Risk	Average
Rating	★★★ Neutral

Investment Style: Equity Stock %

93% 96% 91% 95% 95% 96% 98% 97% 97%

▼ Manager Change
▽ Partial Manager Change

Growth of $10,000
— Investment Values of Fund
— Investment Values of S&P 500

40.8 / 31.0 / 24.0 / 17.0 / 10.0

Performance Quartile (within Category)

	1995	1996	1997	1998	1999	2000	2001	2002	2003	2004	2005	2006	History
NAV	—	—	12.01	14.36	21.69	26.60	25.79	19.56	25.78	29.56	30.92	30.46	NAV
	—	—	28.14*	33.37	57.89	27.16	-3.05	-24.16	31.80	14.66	9.11	9.65	Total Return %
	—	—	4.79	36.85	36.26	8.84	-2.06	3.12	3.12	3.78	4.20	-6.14	+/-S&P 500
	—	—	15.51	6.60	38.91	17.10	3.25	-10.91	-0.82	-2.99	-1.01	+/-Russ MG
	—	—	0.00	0.00	0.00	0.00	0.00	0.00	0.00	0.00	0.00	Income Return %
	—	—	28.14	33.37	57.89	27.16	-3.05	-24.16	31.80	14.66	9.11	9.65	Capital Return %
	—	—	13	44	6	14	40	71	45	62	43	Total Rtn % Rank Cat
	—	0.00	0.00	0.00	0.00	0.00	0.00	0.00	0.00	0.00	0.00	0.00	Income $
	—	0.79	1.27	0.83	1.03	0.00	0.00	0.00	0.00	1.33	3.47	Capital Gains $
	—	0.00	2.00	2.00	1.40	1.31	1.22	1.20	1.19	1.18	Expense Ratio %
	—	0.00	-0.77	-1.13	-0.79	0.52	-0.77	-0.56	-0.77	-0.55	Income Ratio %
	—	—	236	203	246	154	121	27	101	74	Turnover Rate %
	—	—	9	25	98	773	1,997	2,333	2,706	4,763	4,762	Net Assets $mil

Performance 12-31-06

	1st Qtr	2nd Qtr	3rd Qtr	4th Qtr	Total
2002	-2.06	-12.39	-18.07	7.89	-24.16
2003	-3.22	15.21	6.01	11.51	31.80
2004	5.04	1.77	-5.19	13.13	14.66
2005	-3.08	2.79	4.75	4.54	9.11
2006	7.41	-4.85	0.54	6.71	9.65

Trailing	Total Return%	+/- S&P 500	+/- Russ MG	%Rank Cat	Growth of $10,000
3 Mo	6.71	0.01	-0.24	52	10,671
6 Mo	7.29	-5.45	-0.61	32	10,729
1 Yr	9.65	-6.14	-1.01	43	10,965
3 Yr Avg	11.11	0.67	-1.62	47	13,717
5 Yr Avg	6.52	0.33	-1.70	48	13,714
10 Yr Avg	—	—	—	—	—
15 Yr Avg	—	—	—	—	—

Tax Analysis	Tax-Adj Rtn%	%Rank Cat	Tax-Cost Rat	%Rank Cat
3 Yr (estimated)	10.24	43	0.78	39
5 Yr (estimated)	6.02	47	0.47	33
10 Yr (estimated)	—	—	—	—

Potential Capital Gain Exposure: 23% of assets

Rating and Risk

Time Period	Load-Adj Return %	Morningstar Rtn vs Cat	Morningstar Risk vs Cat	Morningstar Risk-Adj Rating
1 Yr	9.65			
3 Yr	11.11	Avg	Avg	★★★
5 Yr	6.52	Avg	Avg	★★★
10 Yr	—			
Incept	17.30			

Other Measures	Standard Index S&P 500	Best Fit Index Russ MG
Alpha	-2.7	-1.7
Beta	1.55	1.04
R-Squared	77	94
Standard Deviation	12.10	
Mean	11.11	
Sharpe Ratio	0.67	

Morningstar's Take by Greg Carlson 12-11-06

Artisan Mid Cap gets enough things right to make it a worthy holding.

There's plenty to like about this closed mid-growth fund. It's been run by the same lead manager, Andy Stephens, since its mid-1997 inception. What's more, Stephens has built a deep, experienced eight-person team. The team's size allows for in-depth research into companies' financial statements and pay schemes; as a result, this fund has suffered through fewer major misfires than many of its rivals in this racy category.

We're also comforted by the fact that the fund's advisor, Artisan Partners, has generally closed its offerings in a timely manner, and Stephens and comanager Jim Hamel have better aligned their interests with shareholders' by stashing more than $1 million apiece in this fund. Thus, the fund earns a Stewardship Grade of A.

Yet despite the fund's attributes, it's not a slam-dunk choice. It closed in 2002 at a relatively modest size, but the fund continued to grow through its presence in retirement plans, and the team ran more than $10 billion as of September 2005 (a figure that includes identically run separate accounts, and has since shrunk a bit due to redemptions). We think that hefty asset load is at least partially responsible for the fund's middling performance over the past five years--Stephens and company tend to trade at a substantial clip. Although the team hasn't swamped the shares of more than a couple of its favorites, it's had some difficulty building full positions in stocks before they rally, and thus had to forgo some gains. It's also worth noting that despite the fund's hefty asset base, it's a bit pricier than the typical no-load mid-cap fund; we'd like to see more breakpoints added to its management fee schedule.

All told, we're not sure the fund can repeat the superb showings of its early years, but management's abilities and commitment to the fund give shareholders reason to stay the course.

Address:	875 East Wisconsin Ave Ste 800 Milwaukee WI 53202 800-344-1770
Web Address:	www.artisanfunds.com
Inception:	06-27-97 *
Advisor:	Artisan Partners Limited Partnership
Subadvisor:	None
NTF Plans:	Fidelity Retail-NTF, Schwab OneSource

Minimum Purchase:	Closed	Add: —	IRA: —
Min Auto Inv Plan:	Closed	Add: —	
Sales Fees:	No-load		
Management Fee:	1.00% mx./0.93% mn.		
Actual Fees:	Mgt:0.93%	Dist: —	
Expense Projections:	3Yr:$375	5Yr:$649	10Yr:$1432
Income Distrib:	Annually		

Portfolio Analysis 09-30-06

Share change since 06-06 Total Stocks:94

	Sector	PE	Tot Ret%	% Assets
⊖ Fisher Scientific Intern	Health	—		3.82
Electronic Arts, Inc.	Software	91.2	-3.73	2.57
Allergan, Inc.	Health	—	11.33	2.54
⊖ Freescale Semiconductor,	Hardware	—		2.45
⊖ McDermott International	Energy	23.4	71.02	2.19
⊕ Juniper Networks, Inc.	Hardware	34.3	-15.07	2.16
⊕ MGIC Investment Corporat	Financial	9.5	-3.39	1.98
⊖ Precision Castparts Corp	Ind Mtrls	25.4	51.40	1.89
⊖ NII Holdings, Inc.	Telecom	45.9	47.53	1.80
⊕ Equifax, Inc.	Business	19.1	7.27	1.78
⊖ Cerner Corporation	Software	37.1	0.10	1.72
⊕ Cooper Industries, Ltd.	Ind Mtrls	18.4	26.02	1.68
⊕ TJX Companies	Consumer	16.9	24.05	1.68
⊖ Coventry Health Care, In	Health	15.4	-12.13	1.66
⊖ Intermec, Inc.	Business	30.1	-28.20	1.65
⊖ Alliance Data Systems Co	Business	29.1	75.48	1.61
⊕ Advanced Micro Devices	Hardware	18.5	-33.50	1.56
⊕ Adobe Systems Inc.	Software	48.1	11.26	1.51
⊕ Investors Financial Serv	Financial	17.9	16.09	1.50
⊖ Smith International, Inc	Energy	17.0	11.59	1.41

Current Investment Style

Value Blnd Growth — Large / Mid / Small (Mid/Growth box marked)

Market Cap	%
Giant	0.0
Large	30.5
Mid	65.4
Small	4.2
Micro	0.0

Avg $mil: 7,428

Value Measures		Rel Category
Price/Earnings	21.29	1.04
Price/Book	2.87	0.89
Price/Sales	1.89	1.07
Price/Cash Flow	13.04	1.14
Dividend Yield %	0.45	0.71

Growth Measures	%	Rel Category
Long-Term Erngs	15.45	0.95
Book Value	16.81	1.32
Sales	8.05	0.81
Cash Flow	15.23	0.82
Historical Erngs	20.48	0.82

Profitability	%	Rel Category
Return on Equity	19.01	1.06
Return on Assets	9.54	1.02
Net Margin	10.83	0.93

Sector Weightings	% of Stocks	Rel S&P 500	3 Year High	Low
↻ Info	28.44	1.42		
Software	10.72	3.11	11	6
Hardware	13.05	1.41	19	12
Media	1.94	0.51	5	2
Telecom	2.73	0.78	3	0
⊆ Service	47.81	1.03		
Health	17.33	1.44	20	14
Consumer	7.68	1.00	14	6
Business	10.60	2.51	15	10
Financial	12.20	0.55	12	7
↥ Mfg	23.75	0.70		
Goods	4.48	0.52	5	3
Ind Mtrls	13.49	1.13	14	8
Energy	5.78	0.59	9	4
Utilities	0.00	0.00	1	0

Composition

● Cash	2.7
● Stocks	97.3
● Bonds	0.0
● Other	0.0
Foreign	0.3
(% of Stock)	

Artisan Mid Cap Value

	Ticker	Load	NAV	Yield	Total Assets	Mstar Category
	ARTQX	Closed	$20.18	0.3%	$2,848 mil	Mid-Cap Value

Governance and Management

Stewardship Grade: B

Portfolio Manager(s)

James Kieffer and Scott Satterwhite worked together at Wachovia before joining Artisan in 1997. George Sertl joined them as an analyst a few years later, and was promoted to portfolio manager for this fund, as well as Artisan Small Cap Value, in May 2006. The trio also manages Artisan Opportunistic Value. They invest their own money in their funds and have equity stakes in Artisan Partners, the fund's advisor.

Strategy

Managers James Kieffer, Scott Satterwhite, and George Sertl look for 40 to 60 cash-producing companies with strong financial positions that sell at low valuations. They focus on companies with market caps between $1.5 billion and $10 billion. Because of the managers' value discipline, investors can expect them to buy stocks in distressed industries and hold them until their prices appreciate close to their intrinsic values. The managers trade infrequently and don't spend much time meeting with company management.

Performance 12-31-06

	1st Qtr	2nd Qtr	3rd Qtr	4th Qtr	Total
2002	5.94	-3.65	-14.51	10.16	-3.87
2003	-1.86	16.40	4.98	14.10	36.83
2004	7.45	2.11	3.53	11.11	26.20
2005	5.20	5.38	4.26	-0.10	15.46
2006	5.55	-2.37	2.85	7.76	14.20

Trailing	Total Return%	+/- S&P 500	+/- Russ MV	%Rank Cat	Growth of $10,000
3 Mo	7.76	1.06	-0.74	57	10,776
6 Mo	10.83	-1.91	-1.50	41	11,083
1 Yr	14.20	-1.59	-6.02	68	11,420
3 Yr Avg	18.50	8.06	-0.27	4	16,640
5 Yr Avg	16.96	10.77	1.08	2	21,887
10 Yr Avg	—	—	—	—	—
15 Yr Avg	—	—	—	—	—

Tax Analysis	Tax-Adj Rtn%	%Rank Cat	Tax-Cost Rat	%Rank Cat
3 Yr (estimated)	17.24	2	1.06	35
5 Yr (estimated)	16.10	2	0.74	27
10 Yr (estimated)	—	—	—	—

Potential Capital Gain Exposure: 13% of assets

Morningstar's Take by Greg Carlson 11-29-06

Despite a wart or two, Artisan Mid Cap Value is a solid holding.

There's a lot to like about this closed fund. Veteran skippers Scott Satterwhite and Jim Kieffer--as well as recently promoted comanager George Sertl--ply a fairly conservative approach. The team seeks out companies that generate plenty of cash and have sturdy balance sheets, yet trade cheaply relative to their average earnings per share over a full business cycle ("normalized" earnings). That strategy has generated fine returns during Satterwhite and Kieffer's five-year tenure here, and the team owns a similarly strong record in its nine years running Artisan Small Cap Value (where the team uses a nearly identical strategy). We also like the fact that management invests with conviction--the fund's portfolio is typically compact, with 40-60 stocks, and the team trades at a restrained pace (which keeps brokerage commissions down). Finally, thanks to a 2005 decision to close the fund at a modest size, the managers have plenty of flexibility to invest in smaller, less-liquid mid-cap names.

Despite the fund's positive attributes, it does come with a couple of caveats. First, management will buy some businesses that are subject to commodity price swings; witness the fund's recent hefty stake in energy names such as oil driller Pioneer Natural Resources, as well as chicken distributors like Tyson Foods. So, the fund may look sluggish relative to its rivals in an economic slowdown. However, we're encouraged by the team's refusal to chase hot corners of the market such as REITs, where the fund has very little exposure.

Another concern is the fund's costs--it recently charged a relatively lofty 0.96% management fee, resulting in an expense ratio that's a bit higher than that of the fund's typical no-load rival. However, given its modest trading costs, superb pedigree, and appealing strategy, shareholders have plenty of reason to stay the course here.

Address:	875 East Wisconsin Ave Ste 800 Milwaukee WI 53202 800-344-1770
Web Address:	www.artisanfunds.com
Inception:	03-28-01 *
Advisor:	Artisan Partners Limited Partnership
Subadvisor:	None
NTF Plans:	Fidelity Retail-NTF, Schwab OneSource

Minimum Purchase:	Closed	Add: —	IRA: —
Min Auto Inv Plan:	Closed	Add: —	
Sales Fees:	No-load		
Management Fee:	1.00% mx./0.93% mn.		
Actual Fees:	Mgt:0.95%	Dist: —	
Expense Projections:	3Yr:$381	5Yr:$660	10Yr:$1455
Income Distrib:	Annually		

Historical Profile

Return	High
Risk	Average
Rating	★★★★★ Highest

▼ Manager Change
▽ Partial Manager Change

Growth of $10,000
— Investment Values of Fund
— Investment Values of S&P 500

19.6
16.0
13.0
10.0
7.0

87% 95% 94% 97% 96%

Investment Style
Equity
Stock %

Performance Quartile (within Category)

1995	1996	1997	1998	1999	2000	2001	2002	2003	2004	2005	2006	History
—	—	—	—	—	—	10.60	10.19	13.69	16.96	18.75	20.18	NAV
—	—	—	—	—	—	6.93*	-3.87	36.83	26.20	15.46	14.20	Total Return %
—	—	—	—	—	—	—	18.23	8.15	15.32	10.55	-1.59	+/-S&P 500
—	—	—	—	—	—	—	5.77	-1.24	2.49	2.81	-6.02	+/-Russ MV
—	—	—	—	—	—	—	0.00	0.00	0.01	0.08	0.30	Income Return %
—	—	—	—	—	—	—	-3.87	36.83	26.19	15.38	13.90	Capital Return %
—	—	—	—	—	—	—	6	37	1	2	68	Total Rtn % Rank Cat
—	—	—	—	—	—	0.00	0.00	0.00	0.00	0.01	0.06	Income $
—	—	—	—	—	—	0.08	0.00	0.24	0.30	0.82	1.18	Capital Gains $
—	—	—	—	—	—	—	1.95	1.78	1.39	1.20		Expense Ratio %
—	—	—	—	—	—	—	-0.82	-0.34	0.73	0.33		Income Ratio %
—	—	—	—	—	—	—	168	12	54	48		Turnover Rate %
—	—	—	—	—	—	15	36	52	720	2,848		Net Assets $mil

Rating and Risk

Time Period	Load-Adj Return %	Morningstar Rtn vs Cat	Morningstar Risk vs Cat	Morningstar Risk-Adj Rating
1 Yr	14.20			
3 Yr	18.50	High	+Avg	★★★★★
5 Yr	16.96	High	Avg	★★★★★
10 Yr	—			
Incept	15.91			

Other Measures	Standard Index S&P 500	Best Fit Index S&P Mid 400
Alpha	6.7	6.1
Beta	1.10	0.85
R-Squared	56	77
Standard Deviation	9.97	
Mean	18.50	
Sharpe Ratio	1.43	

Portfolio Analysis 09-30-06

Share change since 06-06 Total Stocks:52	Sector	PE	Tot Ret%	% Assets
⊖ Student Loan Corporation	Financial	13.7	1.62	4.19
⊖ Alleghany Corporation	Financial	12.4	30.59	3.48
⊕ Avnet, Inc.	Business	16.5	6.64	3.36
⊖ Pioneer Natural Resource	Energy	11.4	-22.11	2.77
⊕ Claire's Stores, Inc.	Consumer	19.2	14.94	2.74
⊖ Zale Corporation	Goods	26.4	12.17	2.65
⊖ Ingram Micro, Inc.	Business	13.3	2.41	2.56
⊖ Lubrizol Corporation	Ind Mtrls	16.6	18.17	2.55
⊖ Leggett & Platt, Inc.	Ind Mtrls	16.0	7.01	2.43
⊖ Liz Claiborne, Inc.	Goods	17.9	22.05	2.36
⊖ Pilgrim's Pride Corporat	Goods	—	-10.93	2.35
⊖ White Mountains Insuranc	Financial	15.2	5.27	2.32
⊖ Annaly Capital Managemen	Financial	—	32.85	2.28
⊖ Foot Locker, Inc.	Consumer	14.8	-5.67	2.26
⊕ Hewitt Associates, Inc.	Business	—	-8.07	2.25
⊕ Con-way, Inc.		10.2	-20.59	2.25
⊖ Marvel Enterprises, Inc.	Media	34.5	64.29	2.21
⊖ Noble Energy, Inc.	Energy	11.7	22.48	2.19
⊖ AutoZone, Inc.	Consumer	15.3	25.95	2.10
⊖ Apache Corporation	Energy	7.8	-2.30	2.02

Current Investment Style

Value Blnd Growth — Large Mid Small

Market Cap	%
Giant	0.0
Large	3.0
Mid	89.0
Small	8.0
Micro	0.0

Avg $mil: 3,645

Value Measures		Rel Category
Price/Earnings	13.16	0.89
Price/Book	1.66	0.83
Price/Sales	0.65	0.67
Price/Cash Flow	6.53	0.86
Dividend Yield %	1.34	0.74

Growth Measures	%	Rel Category
Long-Term Erngs	11.24	1.02
Book Value	9.91	1.42
Sales	9.17	1.20
Cash Flow	13.69	3.45
Historical Erngs	18.40	1.25

Profitability	%	Rel Category
Return on Equity	16.48	1.14
Return on Assets	7.79	1.06
Net Margin	12.81	1.22

Sector Weightings

	% of Stocks	Rel S&P 500	3 Year High	Low
↻ Info	5.17	0.26		
Software	1.10	0.32	7	0
Hardware	1.69	0.18	4	0
Media	2.38	0.63	2	0
Telecom	0.00	0.00	1	0
⚙ Service	54.41	1.18		
Health	0.00	0.00	6	0
Consumer	12.91	1.69	13	3
Business	17.17	4.06	17	7
Financial	24.33	1.09	39	24
Mfg	40.42	1.20		
Goods	16.03	1.87	19	15
Ind Mtrls	8.44	0.71	8	0
Energy	15.95	1.63	23	16
Utilities	0.00	0.00	4	0

Composition

	%
● Cash	3.6
● Stocks	96.3
● Bonds	0.0
● Other	0.0
Foreign (% of Stock)	4.1

Artisan Small Cap

	Ticker	Load	NAV	Yield	Total Assets	Mstar Category
	ARTSX	Closed	$18.20	0.0%	$1,294 mil	Small Growth

Governance and Management

Stewardship Grade: A

Portfolio Manager(s)

Carlene Murphy Ziegler has been on the job here since the fund's 1995 inception. She was joined by Marina Carlson in April 1999. Craigh Cepukenas recently became the third comanager after serving as an analyst on the fund for nine years. Two analysts round out the team. Both Ziegler and Carlson previously worked at Stein Roe and Strong Capital Management.

Strategy

The team here is more price-conscious than the average small-growth manager. It searches for stocks selling at discounts to its estimates of the private market values. Firms with improving returns on invested capital and positive free cash flow rank highly. Management tends to spread assets widely across sectors and stocks.

Historical Profile

Return	Average
Risk	Average
Rating	★★★ Neutral

Investment Style: Equity / Stock %

Percentages across chart: 92% 98% 96% 95% 99% 96% 97% 95% 96%

▼ Manager Change
▽ Partial Manager Change

Growth of $10,000
— Investment Values of Fund
— Investment Values of S&P 500

31.0 / 25.0 / 20.0 / 15.0 / 10.0

Performance Quartile (within Category)

1995	1996	1997	1998	1999	2000	2001	2002	2003	2004	2005	2006	History
13.18	13.64	14.15	11.16	13.30	12.48	13.94	9.88	14.18	16.76	17.36	18.20	NAV
32.84*	11.86	22.67	-13.47	19.18	-1.40	12.21	-28.67	43.52	22.10	6.97	6.92	Total Return %
—	-11.10	-10.69	-42.05	-1.86	7.70	24.10	-6.57	14.84	11.22	2.06	-8.87	+/-S&P 500
—	0.60	9.72	-14.70	-23.91	21.03	21.44	1.59	-5.02	7.79	2.82	-6.43	+/-Russ 2000 Gr
—	0.00	0.00	0.00	0.00	0.00	0.00	0.00	0.00	0.00	0.00	0.00	Income Return %
—	11.86	22.67	-13.47	19.18	-1.40	12.21	-28.67	43.52	22.10	6.97	6.92	Capital Return %
—	76	30	99	82	40	11	60	55	10	41	75	Total Rtn % Rank Cat
0.00	0.00	0.00	0.00	0.00	0.00	0.00	0.00	0.00	0.00	0.00	0.00	Income $
0.10	1.07	2.58	0.96	0.00	0.66	0.06	0.06	0.00	0.53	0.57	0.36	Capital Gains $
2.00	1.52	1.41	1.33	1.37	1.35	1.34	1.31	1.39	1.27	1.18	1.15	Expense Ratio %
-0.59	-0.75	-0.73	-0.74	-0.67	-0.79	-0.68	-1.00	-0.98	-0.95	-0.80	-0.70	Income Ratio %
—	—	105	87	135	155	194	147	140	30	119	79	102	Turnover Rate %
270	296	39	67	59	139	154	102	100	425	1,014	1,294	Net Assets $mil

Performance 12-31-06

	1st Qtr	2nd Qtr	3rd Qtr	4th Qtr	Total
2002	-1.51	-12.67	-24.10	9.27	-28.67
2003	-2.73	23.83	5.29	13.17	43.52
2004	6.98	5.08	-5.14	14.51	22.10
2005	-4.59	5.63	6.28	-0.12	6.97
2006	12.73	-9.25	-1.41	6.00	6.92

Trailing	Total Return%	+/- S&P 500	+/- Russ 2000 Gr	%Rank Cat	Growth of $10,000
3 Mo	6.00	-0.70	-2.77	81	10,600
6 Mo	4.51	-8.23	-2.35	59	10,451
1 Yr	6.92	-8.87	-6.43	75	10,692
3 Yr Avg	11.77	1.33	1.26	27	13,963
5 Yr Avg	7.41	1.22	0.48	41	14,296
10 Yr Avg	7.18	-1.24	2.30	59	20,005
15 Yr Avg	—	—	—	—	—

Tax Analysis	Tax-Adj Rtn%	%Rank Cat	Tax-Cost Rat	%Rank Cat
3 Yr (estimated)	11.07	20	0.63	23
5 Yr (estimated)	6.98	36	0.40	22
10 Yr (estimated)	6.12	57	0.99	36

Potential Capital Gain Exposure: 11% of assets

Rating and Risk

Time Period	Load-Adj Return %	Morningstar Rtn vs Cat	Morningstar Risk vs Cat	Morningstar Risk-Adj Rating
1 Yr	6.92			
3 Yr	11.77	+Avg	Avg	★★★★
5 Yr	7.41	Avg	Avg	★★★
10 Yr	7.18	Avg	-Avg	★★★
Incept	9.71			

Other Measures	Standard Index S&P 500	Best Fit Index Russ 2000 Gr
Alpha	-3.0	1.8
Beta	1.72	0.89
R-Squared	67	94
Standard Deviation	14.37	
Mean	11.77	
Sharpe Ratio	0.62	

Morningstar's Take by Greg Carlson 12-18-06

Despite its recent struggles, Artisan Small Cap is a fine choice.

This small-growth fund appears headed for a poor 2006 showing: As of Dec. 15, it sat on the cusp of the category's bottom quartile. That subpar performance is due primarily to the fund's light exposure to the economically sensitive fare that has led the post-bear-market rally. Its management team prefers modestly priced companies with a history of solid earnings, cash flow, and returns on invested capital--many cyclical businesses fail to clear the latter hurdle. Thus, the portfolio is chock full of service-oriented companies less likely to go through boom-and-bust cycles. For example, the fund's health-care weighting includes fewer racy biotech firms than it does contract research organizations such as ICON, which provides testing services to drug developers of all sizes and has a diversified customer base. And although the fund has a hefty stake in the tech sector, where product cycles are notoriously short, its biggest overweight

is in software makers, which tend to generate steadier revenues than, say, semiconductor makers.

The fund's moderate approach has paid off over the longer term. Since the 1999 arrival of Marina Carlson, who instituted significant strategy tweaks (and previously worked with longest-tenured skipper Carlene Ziegler for eight years), the fund has outpaced roughly 60% of its rivals and held up well in tough times.

Besides its prudent strategy, the fund has several charms that should stand it in good stead in the future. It closed at a modest size--the team runs about $3 billion in all, which affords some flexibility--its expense ratio is reasonable, and both Ziegler and Carlson have over $1 million invested in the fund's shares, which aligns their interests with shareholders'. (These traits contribute to the fund's Stewardship Grade of A.) All told, we think shareholders have plenty of reason to hang on here.

Address:	875 East Wisconsin Ave Ste 800 Milwaukee WI 53202 800-344-1770
Web Address:	www.artisanfunds.com
Inception:	03-28-95*
Advisor:	Artisan Partners Limited Partnership
Subadvisor:	None
NTF Plans:	Fidelity Retail-NTF, Schwab OneSource

Minimum Purchase:	Closed	Add: —	IRA: —
Min Auto Inv Plan:	Closed	Add: —	
Sales Fees:	No-load		
Management Fee:	1.00% mx./0.93% mn.		
Actual Fees:	Mgt:0.97%	Dist: —	
Expense Projections:	3Yr:$365	5Yr:$633	10Yr:$1398
Income Distrib:	Annually		

Portfolio Analysis 09-30-06

Share change since 06-06 Total Stocks:73	Sector	PE	Tot Ret%	% Assets
⊖ Avocent Corporation	Hardware	34.7	24.49	2.16
⊖ Interline Brands, Inc.	Consumer	25.2	-1.23	2.01
⊕ ESCO Technologies, Inc.	Hardware	38.4	2.14	1.88
⊕ Carter's, Inc.	Goods	29.3	-13.34	1.81
⊕ HealthExtras, Inc.	Consumer	40.7	-3.98	1.76
⊕ Guitar Center, Inc.	Consumer	16.6	-9.10	1.73
⊖ Bright Horizons Family S	Consumer	26.3	4.35	1.71
⊕ Open Solutions, Inc.	Business	40.7	64.22	1.70
⊖ Strayer Education, Inc.	Consumer	30.1	14.34	1.70
⊖ CRA International, Inc.	Business	22.1	9.88	1.69
⊕ Keystone Automotive Indu	Ind Mtrls	22.8	7.81	1.67
⊖ Progress Software	Software	25.4	-1.59	1.67
⊕ Pacer International, Inc	Business	16.3	16.54	1.67
⊕ F5 Networks, Inc.	Hardware	49.5	29.76	1.65
⊕ Euronet Worldwide, Inc.	Business	25.7	6.80	1.63
⊕ United Natural Foods, In	Consumer	31.1	36.00	1.63
⊖ Tessera Technologies, In	Hardware	35.4	56.05	1.61
⊕ DSP Group	Software	24.6	-13.41	1.61
⊕ Global Cash Access Holdi	Business	—	—	1.58
⊕ Advisory Board Company	Business	41.0	12.31	1.57

Current Investment Style

Value Blnd Growth — Large Mid Small

Market Cap	%
Giant	0.0
Large	0.0
Mid	4.2
Small	89.1
Micro	6.7
Avg $mil:	1,020

Value Measures		Rel Category
Price/Earnings	18.88	0.90
Price/Book	2.02	0.74
Price/Sales	1.31	0.83
Price/Cash Flow	9.67	1.00
Dividend Yield %	0.52	1.13

Growth Measures	%	Rel Category
Long-Term Erngs	17.02	0.96
Book Value	19.16	1.83
Sales	15.63	1.31
Cash Flow	28.00	1.32
Historical Erngs	24.35	1.00

Profitability	%	Rel Category
Return on Equity	12.84	1.04
Return on Assets	7.91	1.19
Net Margin	10.21	1.18

Sector Weightings	% of Stocks	Rel S&P 500	3 Year High Low	
↻ Info	25.45	1.27		
▣ Software	10.80	3.13	14	10
▣ Hardware	13.48	1.46	17	10
▣ Media	0.00	0.00	3	0
▣ Telecom	1.17	0.33	3	1
☞ Service	56.47	1.22		
▣ Health	10.42	0.86	17	10
▣ Consumer	15.61	2.04	22	9
▣ Business	18.08	4.27	18	11
▣ Financial	12.36	0.56	13	8
⊞ Mfg	18.07	0.53		
▣ Goods	3.73	0.46	4	1
▣ Ind Mtrls	8.96	0.75	11	7
▣ Energy	5.38	0.55	7	4
▣ Utilities	0.00	0.00	0	0

Composition

- Cash 3.7
- Stocks 96.3
- Bonds 0.0
- Other 0.0
- Foreign 1.5 (% of Stock)

Artisan Small Cap Value

	Ticker	Load	NAV	Yield	Total Assets	Mstar Category
	ARTVX	Closed	$18.08	0.0%	$2,199 mil	Small Value

Governance and Management

Stewardship Grade: B

Portfolio Manager(s)

Scott Satterwhite has been on board since the fund's inception in late 1997. Before that, he amassed a strong record as manager of Wachovia Special Values. James Kieffer has been with the fund since its inception, starting as an analyst and moving up to comanager in mid-2000. George Sertl, an analyst with the team since 2000, was recently promoted to comanager.

Strategy

Managers Scott Satterwhite, James Kieffer, and George Sertl like small-cap stocks that are really cheap. They look for names that are selling at 30% to 50% discounts to their estimates of the companies' private-market values. They won't simply own a stock because it's on sale, however. They also want the safety that comes with owning cash-rich companies with limited debt loads. The managers also limit position sizes to 5% of assets.

Historical Profile

Return Above Avg
Risk Below Avg
Rating ★★★★ Above Avg

90% 88% 89% 90% 93% 93% 92% 95% 93%

▼ Manager Change
▽ Partial Manager Change

Growth of $10,000
— Investment Values of Fund
— Investment Values of S&P 500

30.0 25.0 20.0 15.0 10.0

Performance Quartile (within Category)

	1995	1996	1997	1998	1999	2000	2001	2002	2003	2004	2005	2006	History
	—	—	10.31	9.14	10.16	11.70	12.68	11.60	16.08	17.61	17.25	18.08	NAV
	—	—	3.10*	-5.76	15.42	20.83	15.04	-4.44	40.54	21.15	11.06	19.11	Total Return %
	—	—	—	-34.34	-5.62	29.93	26.93	17.66	11.86	10.27	6.15	3.32	+/-S&P 500
	—	—	—	0.69	16.91	-2.00	1.02	6.99	-5.49	-1.10	6.35	-4.37	+/-Russ 2000 VL
	—	—	—	0.00	0.30	0.52	0.14	0.00	0.00	0.00	0.00	0.00	Income Return %
	—	—	—	-5.76	15.12	20.31	14.90	-4.44	40.54	21.15	11.06	19.11	Capital Return %
	—	—	—	49	19	47	54	20	52	48	6	28	Total Rtn % Rank Cat
	—	—	0.00	0.00	0.03	0.05	0.02	0.00	0.00	0.00	0.00	0.00	Income $
	—	—	0.00	0.54	0.35	0.49	0.71	0.50	0.20	1.78	2.32	2.47	Capital Gains $
	—	—	—	1.93	1.66	1.35	1.20	1.20	1.21	1.18	1.18	1.17	Expense Ratio %
	—	—	—	-0.50	-0.45	0.60	0.45	-0.10	-0.21	-0.17	-0.16	-0.09	Income Ratio %
	—	—	—	53	49	38	41	34	12	41	56	59	Turnover Rate %
	—	—	24	54	143	335	523	566	616	1,400	1,662	2,199	Net Assets $mil

Performance 12-31-06

	1st Qtr	2nd Qtr	3rd Qtr	4th Qtr	Total
2002	9.38	-2.81	-16.39	7.51	-4.44
2003	-3.97	18.04	3.95	19.26	40.54
2004	3.73	3.90	1.73	10.50	21.15
2005	2.21	1.89	6.38	0.24	11.06
2006	9.62	-3.81	5.39	7.18	19.11

Trailing	Total Return%	+/- S&P 500	+/- Russ 2000 VL	%Rank Cat	Growth of $10,000
3 Mo	7.18	0.48	-1.85	80	10,718
6 Mo	12.96	0.22	1.15	9	11,296
1 Yr	19.11	3.32	-4.37	28	11,911
3 Yr Avg	17.02	6.58	0.54	8	16,024
5 Yr Avg	16.57	10.38	1.20	12	21,525
10 Yr Avg	—	—	—	—	—
15 Yr Avg	—	—	—	—	—

Tax Analysis	Tax-Adj Rtn%	%Rank Cat	Tax-Cost Rat	%Rank Cat
3 Yr (estimated)	14.32	15	2.31	73
5 Yr (estimated)	14.64	17	1.66	71
10 Yr (estimated)	—	—	—	—

Potential Capital Gain Exposure: 17% of assets

Rating and Risk

Time Period	Load-Adj Return %	Morningstar Rtn vs Cat	Morningstar Risk vs Cat	Morningstar Risk-Adj Rating
1 Yr	19.11			
3 Yr	17.02	+Avg	Avg	★★★★
5 Yr	16.57	+Avg	-Avg	★★★★
10 Yr	—			
Incept	13.98			

Other Measures	Standard Index S&P 500	Best Fit Index Mstar Small Core
Alpha	4.3	2.7
Beta	1.28	0.80
R-Squared	54	78
Standard Deviation	11.97	
Mean	17.02	
Sharpe Ratio	1.11	

Morningstar's Take by Greg Carlson 12-18-06

Artisan Small Cap Value's shareholders remain a fortunate group.

This closed fund continues to chug along. It's beaten 80% of its rivals for the year to date through Dec. 15, 2006. More importantly, the fund has been remarkably steady: Since its mid-1997 inception, the fund has avoided the small-value category's bottom third in every calendar year, and its average annual returns over that time span surpass all but one if its peers.

Its consistently solid results owe to the management team's mix of caution and well-timed opportunism. Lead manager Scott Satterwhite and company tend to avoid the most troubled businesses; they attempt to find those that have relatively clean balance sheets and at least average-quality business models, yet trade at low valuations. Thus, the fund hasn't owned a lot of debt-heavy industrial fare, a stance that helped buoy returns in the latter stages of the bear market. It has, however, owned a hefty stake in energy

firms for several years, as the team recognized the severity of the supply/demand imbalance in the sector. (That bet has been trimmed considerably this year as the stocks have continued to rally.)

The fund's strong showing in 2006 is especially noteworthy, since it's had virtually no stake in REITs, the market's hottest area; the team has been skeptical of REIT valuations after a lengthy rally. Instead, the fund benefited from solid picks such as human-resources consultant Watson Wyatt, which the team bought for its low fixed costs and fee-based business model.

On an absolute basis, this fund's recent returns are likely unsustainable, but its prospects are bright. Although the team, which consists of Satterwhite, two other managers, and an analyst, may be stretched a bit thin since it now manages both a mid-value and a recently introduced large-value fund, Artisan has done a solid job of limiting its asset load. What's more, its veteran managers and modest costs engender confidence.

Address:	875 East Wisconsin Ave Ste 800 Milwaukee WI 53202 800-344-1770
Web Address:	www.artisanfunds.com
Inception:	09-29-97 *
Advisor:	Artisan Partners Limited Partnership
Subadvisor:	None
NTF Plans:	Fidelity Retail-NTF, Schwab OneSource

Minimum Purchase:	Closed	Add: —	IRA: —
Min Auto Inv Plan:	Closed	Add: —	
Sales Fees:	No-load		
Management Fee:	1.00% mx./0.93% mn.		
Actual Fees:	Mgt:0.96%		
Expense Projections:	3Yr:$372	5Yr:$644	10Yr:$1420
Income Distrib:	Annually		

Portfolio Analysis 09-30-06

Share change since 06-06 Total Stocks:100

	Sector	PE	Tot Ret%	% Assets
⊖ Watson Wyatt Worldwide,	Business	19.9	63.12	3.25
⊖ Hilb Rogal & Hobbs Compa	Financial	17.5	10.67	3.15
Zale Corporation	Goods	26.4	12.17	2.73
Stewart Information Serv	Financial	19.0	-9.18	2.56
St. Mary Land & Explorat	Energy	11.5	0.33	2.32
⊕ Lawson Software	Software	—	—	2.23
⊖ Sanderson Farms, Inc.	Goods	—	0.92	1.90
Furniture Brands Interna	Goods	10.6	-25.10	1.88
⊕ Manhattan Associates, In	Software	39.7	46.88	1.82
Cimarex Energy Company	Energy	6.4	-14.79	1.81
⊕ Ethan Allen Interiors, I	Goods	15.4	0.80	1.78
⊕ Cross Country Healthcare	Business	37.0	22.38	1.75
⊖ AMN Healthcare Services,	Business	28.6	39.23	1.54
Kellwood Company	Goods	36.4	39.16	1.52
⊕ Orbotech, Ltd.	Hardware	19.2	6.17	1.49
● Lone Star Technologies	Ind Mtrls	8.7	-6.29	1.48
● Applebee's International	Consumer	21.9	10.16	1.48
Stone Energy Corporation	Energy	13.0	-22.36	1.48
Conmed Corporation	Health	35.8	-2.28	1.42
⊕ Quanex Corporation	Ind Mtrls	8.0	5.38	1.38

Current Investment Style

Value Blnd Growth — Large Mid Small

Market Cap	%
Giant	0.0
Large	0.0
Mid	16.2
Small	70.5
Micro	13.3

Avg $mil: 962

Value Measures		Rel Category
Price/Earnings	15.17	0.99
Price/Book	1.61	0.90
Price/Sales	0.78	0.97
Price/Cash Flow	5.98	0.98
Dividend Yield %	0.90	0.57

Growth Measures	%	Rel Category
Long-Term Erngs	11.86	0.95
Book Value	10.09	1.86
Sales	9.41	1.27
Cash Flow	14.47	1.77
Historical Erngs	7.86	0.69

Profitability	%	Rel Category
Return on Equity	10.80	1.00
Return on Assets	5.97	0.98
Net Margin	8.21	0.91

Sector Weightings	% of Stocks	Rel S&P 500	3 Year High Low
↻ Info	17.93	0.90	
Software	6.66	1.93	7 0
Hardware	5.53	0.60	6 0
Media	1.70	0.45	2 1
Telecom	4.04	1.15	4 1
☎ Service	42.26	0.91	
Health	4.61	0.38	5 1
Consumer	6.52	0.85	11 5
Business	16.57	3.92	19 15
Financial	14.56	0.65	17 12
⬐ Mfg	39.80	1.18	
Goods	12.61	1.47	13 8
Ind Mtrls	12.96	1.09	18 12
Energy	12.99	1.33	22 13
Utilities	1.24	0.35	5 1

Composition

	%
● Cash	7.2
● Stocks	92.8
● Bonds	0.0
● Other	0.0
Foreign	2.9
(% of Stock)	

Investment Style
Equity
Stock %

MORNINGSTAR® Funds 500

Aston/Montag Growth N

Analyst Pick ✓	**Ticker** MCGFX	**Load** None	**NAV** $25.49	**Yield** 0.2%
	Total Assets $2,051 mil		**Mstar Category** Large Growth	

Governance and Management

Stewardship Grade: B

Portfolio Manager(s)

Ron Canakaris has been in charge of this fund since its 1994 inception and has a strong record in his 26 years with near-clone AXA Enterprise Growth. Although Canakaris is the architect of the fund's strategy and leader of the research team, specific investment decisions are made by a committee of 12 portfolio managers with the help of four analysts.

Strategy

Manager Ron Canakaris and his 16-person investment team mix macroeconomic analysis with fundamental research. They stick to large-cap names, favoring those with earnings-growth rates of at least 10%. They're not willing to pay through the nose, however, and will consider selling a stock when it reaches a 20% premium to their calculation of its intrinsic value.

Historical Profile

Return	Average
Risk	Low
Rating	★★★★ Above Avg

	99%	99%	99%	96%	95%	98%	97%	100%	100%

Investment Style: Equity Stock %

▼ Manager Change
▽ Partial Manager Change

Growth of $10,000
■ Investment Values of Fund
— Investment Values of S&P 500

Performance Quartile (within Category)

1995	1996	1997	1998	1999	2000	2001	2002	2003	2004	2005	2006	History
13.52	17.80	23.25	29.65	34.64	27.83	24.12	18.60	21.79	22.65	23.80	25.49	NAV
38.68	32.72	31.85	31.85	22.51	-7.36	-13.33	-22.89	17.24	4.10	5.36	8.07	Total Return %
1.10	9.76	-1.51	3.27	1.47	1.74	-1.44	-0.79	-11.44	-6.78	0.45	-7.72	+/-S&P 500
1.50	9.60	1.36	-6.86	-10.65	15.06	7.09	4.99	-12.51	-2.20	0.10	-1.00	+/-Russ 1000Gr
0.27	0.04	0.00	0.00	0.00	0.00	0.00	0.09	0.15	0.29	0.24	Income Return %
38.41	32.68	31.85	31.85	22.51	-7.36	-13.33	-22.89	17.15	3.95	5.07	7.83	Capital Return %
17	2	18	46	77	33	18	22	97	86	58	39	Total Rtn % Rank Cat
0.03	0.00	0.00	0.00	0.00	0.00	0.00	0.02	0.03	0.06	0.06	Income $
0.00	0.14	0.21	0.94	1.65	4.08	0.00	0.00	0.00	0.00	0.18	Capital Gains $
1.30	1.28	1.23	1.12	1.05	1.03	1.06	1.06	1.06	1.02	1.03	—	Expense Ratio %
0.20	-0.06	-0.37	-0.22	-0.16	-0.14	0.10	0.23	0.29	0.20	0.20	—	Income Ratio %
—	26	19	30	32	67	60	38	39	53	52	—	Turnover Rate %
49	196	549	1,157	1,736	1,299	947	698	1,001	1,062	959	821	Net Assets $mil

Performance 12-31-06

	1st Qtr	2nd Qtr	3rd Qtr	4th Qtr	Total
2002	-0.12	-13.62	-14.08	4.03	-22.89
2003	-0.59	8.92	-0.50	8.82	17.24
2004	1.70	2.26	-4.55	4.87	4.10
2005	-1.77	1.08	6.38	-0.25	5.36
2006	2.42	-2.22	2.02	5.77	8.07

Trailing	Total Return%	+/- S&P 500	+/- Russ 1000Gr	%Rank Cat	Growth of $10,000
3 Mo	5.77	-0.93	-0.16	43	10,577
6 Mo	7.90	-4.84	-2.20	58	10,790
1 Yr	8.07	-7.72	-1.00	39	10,807
3 Yr Avg	5.83	-4.61	-1.04	68	11,853
5 Yr Avg	1.39	-4.80	-1.30	69	10,715
10 Yr Avg	6.24	-2.18	0.80	45	18,318
15 Yr Avg	—				

Tax Analysis	Tax-Adj Rtn%	%Rank Cat	Tax-Cost Rat	%Rank Cat
3 Yr (estimated)	5.72	60	0.10	7
5 Yr (estimated)	1.32	65	0.07	8
10 Yr (estimated)	5.73	33	0.48	18

Potential Capital Gain Exposure: 16% of assets

Rating and Risk

Time Period	Load-Adj Return %	Morningstar Rtn vs Cat	Morningstar Risk vs Cat	Morningstar Risk-Adj Rating
1 Yr	8.07			
3 Yr	5.83	Avg	Low	★★★
5 Yr	1.39	-Avg	Low	★★★
10 Yr	6.24	Avg	Low	★★★★
Incept	10.31			

Other Measures	Standard Index S&P 500	Best Fit Index Russ 1000Gr
Alpha	-3.8	-0.3
Beta	0.94	0.79
R-Squared	77	81
Standard Deviation	7.40	
Mean	5.83	
Sharpe Ratio	0.37	

Morningstar's Take by David Kathman 11-13-06

We still like ABN AMRO/Montag & Caldwell Growth for the long term.

There's no doubt that this fund, soon to be known as Aston/Montag & Caldwell Growth when ABN AMRO completes the sale of its mutual funds, has put up some disappointing numbers lately. It badly trailed the large-growth category in 2003 and 2004, and despite some promising results in the first half of 2006, its three- and five-year returns are nothing to write home about. But we remain fans of the fundamental research and valuation discipline behind the fund, and think that patient investors will be rewarded here.

One of the biggest reasons for the fund's recent underperformance is its emphasis on mega-caps, resulting from the management team's preference for big, relatively stable growth names. Essentially all of the portfolio is in large-cap stocks, and more than half of those are mega-caps such as top-10 holdings PepsiCo, Procter & Gamble, and General Electric. That has hurt the fund during a period when mega-caps, and especially mega-cap growth stocks, have lagged the rest of the market.

We consider the fund's valuation discipline to be one of its long-term strengths, but that, too, has hurt in the past few years, when risk has been excessively rewarded in the market. The team comes up with a present value for each stock, using relatively conservative long-term growth assumptions, and sells a stock if it gets more than 20% over that present value. That hasn't prevented it from buying some highfliers such as Google, but for the most part it's stayed away from overly speculative growth stocks.

This has been a very solid large-growth fund overall, beating the category in seven of its first eight years of existence, but its recent travails have masked that fact. It has also been one of the least volatile funds in the category, making it an especially good option for investors who want some growth exposure but not the ups and downs that typically come with it.

Address:	161 North Clark St Chicago IL 60601 800-992-8151
Web Address:	www.abnamrofunds.com
Inception:	11-02-94
Advisor:	Montag & Caldwell Inc /GA /Adv
Subadvisor:	None
NTF Plans:	Fidelity Retail-NTF, Schwab OneSource

Minimum Purchase:	$2500	Add: $50	IRA: $500
Min Auto Inv Plan:	$50	Add: $50	
Sales Fees:	No-load, 0.25%S		
Management Fee:	0.80% mx./0.60% mn., 0.05%A		
Actual Fees:	Mgt:0.65%	Dist:0.25%	
Expense Projections:	3Yr:$328	5Yr:$569	10Yr:$1259
Income Distrib:	Quarterly		

Portfolio Analysis 11-30-06

Share change since 10-06 Total Stocks:33

	Sector	PE	Tot Ret%	% Assets
⊖ Schlumberger, Ltd.	Energy	22.3	31.07	5.28
⊖ Procter & Gamble Company	Goods	23.9	13.36	4.83
⊖ General Electric Company	Ind Mtrls	20.0	9.35	4.64
⊖ Research in Motion, Ltd.	Hardware	72.5	93.58	4.61
⊖ Halliburton Company	Energy	11.2	1.11	4.35
⊖ Hewlett-Packard Company	Hardware	19.3	45.21	4.09
⊖ Google, Inc.	Business	61.5	11.00	4.08
⊕ American International G	Financial	17.0	6.05	3.99
⊖ PepsiCo, Inc.	Goods	21.5	7.86	3.98
⊖ Genentech, Inc.	Health	48.7	-12.29	3.73
⊖ Paychex, Inc.	Business	30.4	5.62	3.57
⊖ Stryker Corporation	Health	30.3	24.53	3.57
⊖ Baker Hughes Inc.	Energy	9.9	23.68	3.56
⊖ Apple Computer, Inc.	Hardware	37.6	18.01	3.54
⊖ Starbucks Corporation	Consumer	49.3	18.03	3.47
⊖ Colgate-Palmolive Compan	Goods	27.6	21.51	3.37
⊖ American Express Company	Financial	20.9	19.09	3.35
⊖ Qualcomm, Inc.	Hardware	26.6	-11.32	3.16
⊖ Merrill Lynch & Company,	Financial	14.2	39.28	2.99
⊖ Walgreen Company	Consumer	26.6	4.36	2.97

Current Investment Style

Value Blnd Growth — Large/Mid/Small — Large Giant

Market Cap	%
Giant	61.1
Large	38.9
Mid	0.0
Small	0.0
Micro	0.0

Avg $mil: 60,246

Value Measures		Rel Category
Price/Earnings	20.36	1.06
Price/Book	4.15	1.25
Price/Sales	2.26	1.16
Price/Cash Flow	15.25	1.34
Dividend Yield %	1.14	1.11

Growth Measures	%	Rel Category
Long-Term Erngs	14.52	1.01
Book Value	13.27	1.14
Sales	11.98	1.03
Cash Flow	11.48	0.68
Historical Erngs	23.53	1.02

Profitability	%	Rel Category
Return on Equity	24.62	1.21
Return on Assets	13.28	1.21
Net Margin	15.26	1.07

Sector Weightings

	% of Stocks	Rel S&P 500	3 Year High	Low
↻ Info	17.17	0.86		
⬚ Software	0.00	0.00	7	0
⬚ Hardware	15.39	1.67	15	5
⬚ Media	1.78	0.47	6	0
⬚ Telecom	0.00	0.00	0	0
⬚ Service	44.93	0.97		
⬚ Health	14.28	1.18	27	14
⬚ Consumer	12.67	1.66	15	8
⬚ Business	7.65	1.81	13	6
⬚ Financial	10.33	0.46	10	2
⬚ Mfg	37.90	1.12		
⬚ Goods	13.75	1.61	20	14
⬚ Ind Mtrls	8.92	0.75	12	5
⬚ Energy	15.23	1.55	19	4
⬚ Utilities	0.00	0.00	0	0

Composition

● Cash	0.0
● Stocks	100.0
● Bonds	0.0
● Other	0.0
Foreign	4.6
(% of Stock)	

Morningstar® Funds 500

Aston/TAMRO Small Cap N

	Ticker	Load	NAV	Yield	Total Assets	Mstar Category
	ATASX	None	$19.55	0.0%	$294 mil	Small Blend

Governance and Management

Stewardship Grade: B

Portfolio Manager(s)

Philip Tasho founded TAMRO Capital in 2000 with two partners and has managed this fund since its November 2000 inception. He previously spent a decade at Riggs Investment Management, where he was chief executive for four years and managed Riggs Small Company Stock from November 1995 to June 2000. He has three analysts assisting him with this fund, as well as a trader and a quantitative analyst.

Strategy

Manager Philip Tasho's five-step process starts with quantitative screens that rank small-cap stocks on the basis of PEG ratio, relative valuations, and changes in earnings estimates. From the top third of this group, he looks for companies fitting at least one of three themes: consolidation, restructuring, and new products. He holds about 40 to 60 names at any one time, keeping position sizes roughly equal and sector weightings within reasonable limits. He'll let winners run unless they reach 10% of total assets, although the fund's largest position has been about 5%.

Performance 12-31-06

	1st Qtr	2nd Qtr	3rd Qtr	4th Qtr	Total
2002	8.80	-1.87	-21.53	6.13	-11.08
2003	-2.11	25.28	8.82	17.53	56.86
2004	5.59	-1.95	-6.04	15.09	11.95
2005	-5.19	3.00	4.99	-0.19	2.34
2006	19.41	-5.43	1.48	11.57	27.84

Trailing	Total Return%	+/- S&P 500	+/- Russ 2000	%Rank Cat	Growth of $10,000
3 Mo	11.57	4.87	2.67	9	11,157
6 Mo	13.22	0.48	3.84	5	11,322
1 Yr	27.84	12.05	9.47	3	12,784
3 Yr Avg	13.57	3.13	0.01	47	14,648
5 Yr Avg	15.36	9.17	3.97	15	20,430
10 Yr Avg	—	—	—	—	—
15 Yr Avg	—	—	—	—	—

Tax Analysis	Tax-Adj Rtn%	%Rank Cat	Tax-Cost Rat	%Rank Cat
3 Yr (estimated)	12.77	35	0.70	15
5 Yr (estimated)	14.15	15	1.05	47
10 Yr (estimated)	—	—	—	—

Potential Capital Gain Exposure: 28% of assets

Morningstar's Take by David Kathman 12-07-06

Aston/TAMRO Small Cap has justified our confidence in a big way in 2006.

This fund, known until recently as ABN AMRO/TAMRO Small Cap, has achieved considerable success with a theme-based approach to stock-picking. Manager Philip Tasho looks for small-cap stocks that have reasonable valuations and rising earnings estimates, and that fit into one of three themes: consolidation, restructuring, or new products. It's a somewhat concentrated portfolio of about 50 stocks, and that concentration has contributed to higher volatility than the average small-blend fund.

That volatility has resulted in quite a few ups and downs since the fund's inception in late 2000. It put together very strong results in its first three years, then hit the skids in 2004 and 2005, ranking in or near the small-blend category's bottom decile both years. During that time we expressed our optimism that the fund would bounce back, and it has done so with a vengeance. As of December 7,

2006, it had gained 29% for the year to date, putting it in the top 3% of small-blend funds.

Increased merger activity over the past year has been one factor boosting the fund. Much of the good performance has come from consolidation-themed stocks such as NBTY, which has been buying up other makers of nutritional supplements, and First Marblehead, which has become dominant in its niche as a one-stop service provider for issuers of student loans. In addition, a half dozen holdings have themselves been acquired in 2006, mostly for good premiums. Restructuring plays such as Knight Capital Group and Bob Evans Farms have also helped.

This fund has a fair amount of appeal as a slightly quirky small-cap option, though with some necessary caveats. Investors who can't handle big year-to-year performance swings may be happier with a tamer fund, but those who can tough out the occasional low points are likely to be satisfied in the long term.

Address:	161 North Clark St Chicago IL 60601 800-992-8151
Web Address:	www.abnamrofunds.com
Inception:	11-30-00*
Advisor:	TAMRO Capital Partners LLC
Subadvisor:	None
NTF Plans:	Fidelity Retail-NTF, Schwab OneSource

Minimum Purchase:	$2500	Add: $50	IRA: $500
Min Auto Inv Plan:	$50	Add: $50	
Sales Fees:	No-load, 0.25%S		
Management Fee:	0.90%, 0.05%A		
Actual Fees:	Mgt:0.90%	Dist:0.25%	
Expense Projections:	3Yr:$435	5Yr:$761	10Yr:$1681
Income Distrib:	Quarterly		

Historical Profile

Return	Above Avg
Risk	Above Avg
Rating	★★★★ Above Avg

| 79% | 88% | 94% | 99% | 97% | 100% | 100% |

Investment Style
Equity
Stock %

▼ Manager Change
▽ Partial Manager Change

Growth of $10,000
— Investment Values of Fund
— Investment Values of S&P 500

Performance Quartile (within Category)

1995	1996	1997	1998	1999	2000	2001	2002	2003	2004	2005	2006	History
—	—	—	—	—	10.92	12.27	10.91	15.04	15.81	16.18	19.55	NAV
—	—	—	—	—	9.20*	13.57	-11.08	56.86	11.95	2.34	27.84	Total Return %
—	—	—	—	—	—	25.46	11.02	28.18	1.07	-2.57	12.05	+/-S&P 500
—	—	—	—	—	—	11.08	9.40	9.61	-6.38	-2.21	9.47	+/-Russ 2000
—	—	—	—	—	—	0.40	0.00	0.00	0.00	0.00	0.00	Income Return %
—	—	—	—	—	—	13.17	-11.08	56.86	11.95	2.34	27.84	Capital Return %
—	—	—	—	—	—	26	21	7	91	88	3	Total Rtn % Rank Cat
—	—	—	—	—	0.00	0.04	0.00	0.00	0.00	0.00	0.00	Income $
—	—	—	—	—	0.00	0.08	0.00	2.03	0.00	0.00	1.14	Capital Gains $
—	—	—	—	—	—	—	1.30	1.30	1.30	1.30	—	Expense Ratio %
—	—	—	—	—	—	—	0.67	-0.12	-0.07	-0.77	—	Income Ratio %
—	—	—	—	—	—	—	175	267	115	103	—	Turnover Rate %
—	—	—	—	—	—	6	41	66	143	211	Net Assets $mil

Rating and Risk

Time Period	Load-Adj Return %	Morningstar Rtn vs Cat	Morningstar Risk vs Cat	Morningstar Risk-Adj Rating
1 Yr	27.84			
3 Yr	13.57	Avg	+Avg	★★★
5 Yr	15.36	+Avg	+Avg	★★★★
10 Yr	—	—	—	—
Incept	16.51			

Other Measures	Standard Index S&P 500	Best Fit Index Russ 2000 Gr
Alpha	-1.5	3.6
Beta	1.72	0.87
R-Squared	70	94
Standard Deviation	14.18	
Mean	13.57	
Sharpe Ratio	0.75	

Portfolio Analysis 11-30-06

Share change since 10-06 Total Stocks:51	Sector	PE	Tot Ret%	% Assets
⊕ Hain Celestial Group, In	Goods	31.3	47.50	3.37
⊕ NBTY, Inc.	Health	27.0	155.82	2.98
⊕ General Cable Corporatio	Ind Mtrls	23.9	121.88	2.83
⊕ JetBlue Airways Corporat	Business		-7.67	2.75
⊕ Netflix, Inc.	Consumer	22.1	-4.44	2.62
⊕ Packeteer, Inc.	Software	34.2	75.03	2.45
⊕ Steelcase, Inc.	Goods	37.8	17.77	2.44
⊕ Baldor Electric Company	Ind Mtrls	22.5	33.18	2.34
⊕ Whiting Petroleum Corpor	Energy	9.7	16.50	2.33
⊕ Willbros Group, Inc.	Business		30.89	2.32
⊕ L-1 Identity Solutions,	Business		-14.08	2.32
⊕ ValueClick, Inc.	Business	46.8	30.48	2.31
⊕ TIBCO Software, Inc.	Software	33.0	26.37	2.31
⊖ First Marblehead Corpora	Financial	14.2	152.13	2.30
⊕ Manitowoc Company, Inc.	Business	27.2	137.42	2.25
⊕ Acco Brands Corporation	Ind Mtrls	62.1	8.04	2.24
⊕ Emulex Corporation	Hardware	44.7	-1.42	2.21
⊕ Helmerich & Payne, Inc.	Energy	10.7	-20.48	2.20
⊕ SunOpta, Inc.	Goods	50.4	67.30	2.20
⊕ Polycom, Inc.	Hardware	50.6	102.03	2.17

Current Investment Style

Value Blnd Growth — Large Mid Small

Market Cap	%
Giant	0.0
Large	0.0
Mid	31.5
Small	53.1
Micro	15.5
Avg $mil:	1,275

Value Measures		Rel Category
Price/Earnings	20.14	1.21
Price/Book	2.09	0.99
Price/Sales	1.00	1.02
Price/Cash Flow	9.03	1.29
Dividend Yield %	0.53	0.50

Growth Measures	%	Rel Category
Long-Term Erngs	17.24	1.24
Book Value	4.76	0.63
Sales	12.20	1.38
Cash Flow	11.16	0.88
Historical Erngs	8.33	0.50

Profitability	%	Rel Category
Return on Equity	6.55	0.51
Return on Assets	5.30	0.74
Net Margin	6.89	0.71

Sector Weightings	% of Stocks	Rel S&P 500	3 Year High Low
↻ Info	20.37	1.02	
🖥 Software	9.89	2.87	11 5
💻 Hardware	10.48	1.13	13 2
🔊 Media	0.00	0.00	7 0
📶 Telecom	0.00	0.00	0 0
⬤ Service	48.44	1.05	
🏥 Health	7.57	0.63	20 7
🛒 Consumer	12.69	1.66	24 12
💲 Business	16.02	3.79	16 10
💲 Financial	12.16	0.55	15 8
🏭 Mfg	31.20	0.92	
🏗 Goods	8.81	1.03	14 9
⚙ Ind Mtrls	14.65	1.23	15 6
🔋 Energy	7.74	0.79	12 3
💡 Utilities	0.00	0.00	0 0

Composition

● Cash	0.0
● Stocks	100.0
● Bonds	0.0
● Other	0.0
Foreign (% of Stock)	2.2

Morningstar® Funds 500

Atlas Global Growth A

	Ticker	Load	NAV	Yield	Total Assets	Mstar Category
	AGRAX	None	$26.61	0.6%	$456 mil	World Stock

Governance and Management

Stewardship Grade: C

Portfolio Manager(s)

Management is in flux. Since its inception in 1996, OppenheimerFunds managers--first Bill Wilby, then Rajeev Bhaman--ran this fund as a near-clone of Oppenheimer Global. If shareholders approve a proposed merger (already approved by the board), fund management will transfer to Metropolitan West Capital Management LLC, a large-value manager owned by new advisor Evergreen Investments. MetWest is led by Howard Gleicher, Gary Lisenbee, and David Graham, who all have decades of experience. We don't yet know who specifically will be responsible for this fund.

Strategy

MetWest Capital will likely take over this fund in May 2007. MetWest specializes in large-cap value investing, especially on the domestic side, where it uses the Russell 1000 Value as a benchmark. On the international side, it uses the MSCI EAFE Index. MetWest tends to build compact portfolios (roughly 40 stocks) and trade infrequently (annual turnover rates around 30%). We don't yet know how it will run this global portfolio and how it will address issues such as currency hedging. Former manager Oppenheimer used a flexible growth approach that included mid-caps and emerging markets.

Performance 12-31-06

	1st Qtr	2nd Qtr	3rd Qtr	4th Qtr	Total
2002	1.45	-8.95	-18.55	2.57	-22.82
2003	-7.76	20.66	8.88	15.79	40.31
2004	4.58	-0.86	-1.51	15.34	17.79
2005	-3.09	2.26	9.36	4.29	13.02
2006	6.89	-3.40	3.85	8.19	16.02

Trailing	Total Return%	+/- MSCI EAFE	+/- MSCI World	%Rank Cat	Growth of $10,000
3 Mo	8.19	-2.16	-0.18	61	10,819
6 Mo	12.36	-2.33	-0.85	65	11,236
1 Yr	16.02	-10.32	-4.05	82	11,602
3 Yr Avg	15.59	-4.34	0.91	48	15,444
5 Yr Avg	10.83	-4.15	0.86	50	16,722
10 Yr Avg	13.14	5.43	5.50	8	34,369
15 Yr Avg	—	—	—	—	—

Tax Analysis	Tax-Adj Rtn%	%Rank Cat	Tax-Cost Rat	%Rank Cat
3 Yr (estimated)	15.28	37	0.27	18
5 Yr (estimated)	10.65	42	0.16	13
10 Yr (estimated)	12.18	6	0.85	34

Potential Capital Gain Exposure: 27% of assets

Morningstar's Take by Dan Lefkovitz 12-19-06

Atlas Global Growth's future is murky.

The stability that this fund enjoyed for its first 10 years of life was recently shattered. Earlier in 2006, Wachovia acquired Golden West Financial, the parent company of Atlas Advisors. Pending shareholder approval, Wachovia's asset management division, Evergreen Investments, will take over the Atlas funds. In May 2007, Atlas shareholders are likely to become owners of various Evergreen funds.

That means that OppenheimerFunds, which has racked up a great track record running this fund as a clone of broker-sold Oppenheimer Global, will no longer manage the portfolio. A team from MetWest that specializes in large-cap-value investing will take over the fund, which is to be renamed Evergreen Intrinsic World Equity Fund. Evergreen recently acquired MetWest, which is distinct from the bond shop of the same name.

The change raises several concerns. First, shareholders will lose a superb flexible growth manager in Rajeev Bhaman of OppenheimerFunds. Oppenheimer Global is a Morningstar Fund Analyst Pick. Second, this seems like an inopportune time to be changing the fund's mandate from growth to value, as the value style of investing has been on top for several years now, and markets are cyclical. Third, while MetWest has strong records running U.S. large-cap value and international strategies on the institutional side, it doesn't have a record running a global portfolio. Nor does it have a publicly available record on a mutual fund.

These changes beg the question: How did the Atlas fund board sign off on the changes to this fund? After all, a fund's board is supposed to look out for shareholders. As we point out in this fund's Stewardship Grade, the Atlas board is marked by key conflicts of interest. They have signed off on changes that leave investors with a very different fund than the one they bought.

In short, we'd seek other options.

Address:	794 Davis Street, First Floor
	San Leandro CA 94577
	800-933-2852
Web Address:	www.atlasfunds.com
Inception:	04-30-96*
Advisor:	Atlas Advisers Inc
Subadvisor:	OppenheimerFunds, Inc.
NTF Plans:	Fidelity Retail-NTF, Schwab OneSource

Minimum Purchase:	$2500	Add: $250	IRA: $250
Min Auto Inv Plan:	$2500	Add: $250	
Sales Fees:	No-load, 0.25%S, 2.00%R		
Management Fee:	0.80% mx./0.70% mn.		
Actual Fees:	Mgt:0.77%	Dist:0.25%	
Expense Projections:	3Yr:$415	5Yr:$718	10Yr:$1579
Income Distrib:	Annually		

Historical Profile

Return Above Avg
Risk Above Avg
Rating ★★★★ Above Avg

Investment Style: Equity Stock %

▼ Manager Change
▽ Partial Manager Change

Growth of $10,000
— Investment Values of Fund
— Investment Values of MSCI EAFE

Performance Quartile (within Category)

	1995	1996	1997	1998	1999	2000	2001	2002	2003	2004	2005	2006	History
	—	10.96	12.69	14.56	19.28	18.69	16.52	12.75	17.89	21.02	23.65	26.61	NAV
	—	10.89*	24.35	16.19	55.85	3.24	-11.61	-22.82	40.31	17.79	13.02	16.02	Total Return %
	—	—	22.57	-3.74	28.82	17.43	9.81	-6.88	1.72	-2.46	-0.52	-10.32	+/-MSCI EAFE
	—	—	8.59	-8.13	30.90	16.43	5.19	-2.93	7.20	3.07	3.53	-4.05	+/-MSCI World
	—	—	0.00	0.00	0.00	0.01	0.00	0.00	0.00	0.30	0.51	0.69	Income Return %
	—	—	24.35	16.19	55.85	3.23	-11.61	-22.82	40.31	17.49	12.51	15.33	Capital Return %
	—	6	51	30	14	28	76	24	28	41	82		Total Rtn % Rank Cat
	0.01	0.00	0.00	0.00	0.00	0.00	0.00	0.00	0.05	0.11	0.16		Income $
	0.28	0.94	0.18	3.41	1.21	0.00	0.00	0.00	0.00	0.00	0.67		Capital Gains $
	—	—	1.62	1.53	1.48	1.34	1.38	1.48	1.54	1.35	—		Expense Ratio %
	—	—	0.14	0.04	0.49	0.15	-0.08	-0.03	0.06	0.22	—		Income Ratio %
	—	—	64	75	103	54	44	39	38	20	—		Turnover Rate %
	—	13	27	36	70	127	115	89	159	241	456		Net Assets $mil

Rating and Risk

Time Period	Load-Adj Return %	Morningstar Rtn vs Cat	Morningstar Risk vs Cat	Morningstar Risk-Adj Rating
1 Yr	16.02			
3 Yr	15.59	Avg	Avg	★★★
5 Yr	10.83	Avg	Avg	★★★
10 Yr	13.14	High	+Avg	★★★★
Incept	13.36			

Other Measures	Standard Index MSCI EAFE	Best Fit Index MSCI World
Alpha	-2.8	-1.6
Beta	0.94	1.24
R-Squared	79	90
Standard Deviation	10.04	
Mean	15.59	
Sharpe Ratio	1.18	

Portfolio Analysis 09-30-06

Share change since 06-06 Total Stocks:138

	Sector	Country	% Assets
⊕ Ericsson AB (publ)	Hardware	Sweden	3.38
⊖ Vodafone Grp	Telecom	U.K.	2.00
⊕ H&M Hennes & Mauritz	Consumer	Sweden	1.87
⊕ Microsoft Corporation	Software	United States	1.81
⊕ Sanofi-Synthelabo	Health	France	1.62
⊕ Royal Bank Of Scotland G	Financial	U.K.	1.62
⊖ Reckitt Benckiser	Goods	U.K.	1.54
⊕ eBay, Inc.	Consumer	United States	1.49
⊕ Advanced Micro Devices	Hardware	United States	1.46
⊕ Roche Holding	Health	Switzerland	1.38
⊕ Carnival Corporation	Goods	United States	1.34
⊕ Morgan Stanley	Financial	United States	1.33
⊕ LVMH Moet Hennessy L.V.	Goods	France	1.28
⊕ Adobe Systems Inc.	Software	United States	1.26
⊕ Credit Suisse Grp	Financial	Switzerland	1.26
⊕ Koninklijke Philips Elec	Goods	Netherlands	1.25
⊕ Corning Inc.	Hardware	United States	1.22
⊕ Automatic Data Processin	Business	United States	1.22
⊕ Allianz	Financial	Germany	1.22
⊕ Siemens	Hardware	Germany	1.21

Current Investment Style

Value Blnd Growth Large Mid Small

Market Cap	%
Giant	47.0
Large	40.9
Mid	10.4
Small	1.6
Micro	0.2
Avg $mil:	30,075

Value Measures		Rel Category
Price/Earnings	14.91	0.97
Price/Book	2.43	1.02
Price/Sales	1.68	1.28
Price/Cash Flow	10.05	1.16
Dividend Yield %	2.09	0.96

Growth Measures	%	Rel Category
Long-Term Erngs	11.94	0.94
Book Value	7.91	0.88
Sales	9.18	1.10
Cash Flow	9.25	0.94
Historical Erngs	25.95	1.39

Composition

Cash	1.5	Bonds	0.0
Stocks	98.5	Other	0.0
Foreign	(% of Stock)		59.3

Sector Weightings	% of Stocks	Rel MSCI EAFE	3 Year High	Low
⊙ Info	27.92	2.36		
🖳 Software	5.93	10.59	7	4
🖥 Hardware	14.01	3.63	14	11
🎙 Media	3.47	1.90	9	3
📞 Telecom	4.51	0.81	10	5
⊂ Service	38.47	0.81		
🏥 Health	12.61	1.77	17	13
🛒 Consumer	7.23	1.46	8	6
💼 Business	2.65	0.52	3	2
$ Financial	15.98	0.53	20	15
⚒ Mfg	33.61	0.82		
⚙ Goods	19.79	1.51	20	11
⚙ Ind Mtrls	6.88	0.45	7	3
🔥 Energy	6.94	0.97	10	6
💡 Utilities	0.00	0.00	1	0

Regional Exposure	% Stock		
UK/W. Europe 39	N. America		43
Japan 11	Latn America		4
Asia X Japan 4	Other		0

Country Exposure	% Stock		
United States 41	France		7
U.K. 13	Sweden		6
Japan 11			

Baron Asset

	Ticker	Load	NAV	Yield	Total Assets	Mstar Category
	BARAX	None	$59.80	0.0%	$3,649 mil	Mid-Cap Growth

Governance and Management

Stewardship Grade: C

Portfolio Manager(s)

Ron Baron has been at the helm since 1987. His firm employs roughly 18 analysts and portfolio managers, but he's the driving force behind this fund's portfolio. Andrew Peck was named comanager in July 2003. Peck, who worked as an analyst on the fund for five years before being named comanager, focuses on mid-cap stocks.

Strategy

Manager Ron Baron buys companies he thinks can double in price over the next four years, focusing on steady growers trading at prices that don't yet reflect their potential. He keeps turnover low and gets to know a company's management thoroughly before buying a full position. His emphasis on steady growers tends to keep the fund out of the technology sector, but it has frequently owned tech- and communications-related service companies.

Performance 12-31-06

	1st Qtr	2nd Qtr	3rd Qtr	4th Qtr	Total
2002	6.03	-8.02	-17.78	-0.21	-19.99
2003	-7.09	17.73	6.37	9.44	27.34
2004	7.69	2.52	-1.03	16.35	27.13
2005	-0.61	2.66	5.47	4.51	12.46
2006	9.33	-2.62	0.25	7.40	14.64

Trailing	Total Return%	+/- S&P 500	+/- Russ MG	%Rank Cat	Growth of $10,000
3 Mo	7.40	0.70	0.45	37	10,740
6 Mo	7.67	-5.07	-0.23	28	10,767
1 Yr	14.64	-1.15	3.98	12	11,464
3 Yr Avg	17.90	7.46	5.17	2	16,389
5 Yr Avg	10.80	4.61	2.58	10	16,699
10 Yr Avg	9.35	0.93	0.73	36	24,445
15 Yr Avg	12.81	2.17	2.68	7	60,984

Tax Analysis	Tax-Adj Rtn%	%Rank Cat	Tax-Cost Rat	%Rank Cat
3 Yr (estimated)	16.85	2	0.89	44
5 Yr (estimated)	10.06	9	0.67	47
10 Yr (estimated)	8.62	24	0.67	17

Potential Capital Gain Exposure: 44% of assets

Historical Profile

Return	Above Avg
Risk	Below Avg
Rating	★★★★ Above Avg

Investment Style: Equity Stock %

98% 99% 100% 99% 99% 96% 92% 98% 84%

▽ Partial Manager Change

▼ Manager Change
▽ Partial Manager Change

Growth of $10,000
— Investment Values of Fund
— Investment Values of S&P 500

31.0
24.0
17.0
10.0

Performance Quartile (within Category)

1995	1996	1997	1998	1999	2000	2001	2002	2003	2004	2005	2006	History
29.74	36.23	48.51	50.54	58.77	54.39	44.46	34.42	43.83	52.52	56.29	59.80	NAV
35.28	21.96	33.89	4.27	16.28	0.36	-10.12	-19.99	27.34	27.13	12.46	14.64	Total Return %
-2.30	-1.00	0.53	-24.31	-4.76	9.46	1.77	2.11	-1.34	16.25	7.55	-1.15	+/-S&P 500
1.30	4.48	11.35	-13.59	-35.01	12.11	10.03	7.42	-15.37	11.65	0.36	3.98	+/-Russ MG
0.00	0.00	0.00	0.08	0.00	0.00	0.00	0.00	0.00	0.00	0.00	0.00	Income Return %
35.28	21.96	33.89	4.19	16.28	0.36	-10.12	-19.99	27.34	27.13	12.46	14.64	Capital Return %
39	25	7	83	87	42	29	22	88	1	32	12	Total Rtn % Rank Cat
0.00	0.00	0.00	0.04	0.00	0.00	0.00	0.00	0.00	0.00	0.00	0.00	Income $
0.03	0.04	0.00	0.00	0.00	4.61	4.07	1.18	0.00	2.99	2.81	4.68	Capital Gains $
1.40	1.40	1.30	1.32	1.31	1.33	1.37	1.33	1.34	1.34	1.34	1.33	Expense Ratio %
-0.50	-0.30	-0.50	0.11	-0.57	-1.09	-1.14	-1.16	-1.14	-0.90	-0.91	-0.49	Income Ratio %
35	19	13	23	16	3	4	6	28	20	11	22	Turnover Rate %
353	1,326	3,793	5,672	6,147	4,257	3,063	1,945	1,949	2,376	2,901	3,649	Net Assets $mil

Rating and Risk

Time Period	Load-Adj Return %	Morningstar Rtn vs Cat	Morningstar Risk vs Cat	Morningstar Risk-Adj Rating
1 Yr	14.64			
3 Yr	17.90	High	-Avg	★★★★★
5 Yr	10.80	High	-Avg	★★★★★
10 Yr	9.35	Avg	-Avg	★★★
Incept	13.31			

Other Measures	Standard Index S&P 500	Best Fit Index DJ Wilshire 4500
Alpha	5.2	4.2
Beta	1.25	0.86
R-Squared	62	78
Standard Deviation	10.84	
Mean	17.90	
Sharpe Ratio	1.28	

Portfolio Analysis 09-30-06

Share change since 03-06 Total Stocks:62	Sector	PE	Tot Ret%	% Assets
⊖ Charles Schwab Corporati	Financial	26.3	32.87	4.67
Wynn Resorts, Ltd.	Consumer	—	82.52	4.51
⊖ Choicepoint, Inc.	Business	26.2	-11.53	4.45
Chicago Mercantile Excha	Financial	49.3	39.48	3.62
Vail Resorts, Inc.	Consumer	37.2	35.70	3.56
⊖ Xto Energy, Inc.	Energy	9.0	12.16	2.94
Alexander's Inc.	Financial	NMF	70.94	2.89
Manor Care, Inc.	Health	24.6	19.65	2.33
Polo Ralph Lauren Corpor	Goods	25.5	38.77	2.02
CH Robinson Worldwide, I	Business	30.1	11.88	1.98
Arch Capital Group, Ltd.	Financial	18.2	23.49	1.88
Southern Union Company	Energy	—	20.09	1.76
⊕ Whole Foods Market, Inc.	Consumer	32.8	-37.19	1.72
⊕ Iron Mountain, Inc.	Business	44.8	-2.09	1.66
Wellpoint, Inc.	Health	17.2	-1.38	1.60
⊕ Kerzner International, L	Consumer	—	—	1.54
⊕ CB Richard Ellis Group,	Financial	30.3	69.24	1.46
Assurant, Inc.	Financial	12.2	28.01	1.35
Nuveen Investments, Inc.	Financial	23.9	24.13	1.29
Brown & Brown, Inc.	Financial	22.9	-6.98	1.27

Current Investment Style

Value Blnd Growth — Mid, Small

Market Cap	%
Giant	0.0
Large	16.8
Mid	74.2
Small	8.9
Micro	0.0

Avg $mil: 5,371

Value Measures		Rel Category
Price/Earnings	20.12	0.98
Price/Book	3.17	0.99
Price/Sales	1.92	1.09
Price/Cash Flow	10.40	0.91
Dividend Yield %	0.64	1.02

Growth Measures	%	Rel Category
Long-Term Erngs	15.45	0.95
Book Value	10.57	0.83
Sales	14.86	1.49
Cash Flow	20.87	1.13
Historical Erngs	25.85	1.04

Profitability	%	Rel Category
Return on Equity	18.51	1.03
Return on Assets	12.07	1.29
Net Margin	12.69	1.09

Sector Weightings

	% of Stocks	Rel S&P 500	3 Year High Low
↻ Info	0.00	0.00	
Software	0.00	0.00	0 0
Hardware	0.00	0.00	1 0
Media	0.00	0.00	6 0
Telecom	0.00	0.00	0 0
☞ Service	87.71	1.90	
Health	14.98	1.24	15 10
Consumer	22.32	2.92	42 22
Business	19.09	4.51	19 16
Financial	31.32	1.41	31 15
⊔ Mfg	12.30	0.36	
Goods	3.64	0.43	4 3
Ind Mtrls	0.00	0.00	0 0
Energy	8.66	0.88	9 4
Utilities	0.00	0.00	3 0

Composition

	%
● Cash	7.9
● Stocks	83.9
● Bonds	0.0
● Other	8.2
Foreign (% of Stock)	0.0

Morningstar's Take by Kerry O'Boyle 12-07-06

Investing, not trading, has kept Baron Asset sitting pretty versus its rivals.

When most people think of growth investing, they likely picture high-flying technology stocks, momentum, and a rapid-trading high-turnover style. You'll find little of that here. Veteran manager Ron Baron and comanager Andrew Peck look for companies with significant competitive advantages that can sustain steady growth for many years. They buy for the long haul--as reflected in the fund's minimal turnover relative to other mid-growth offerings--and mostly shun the mainstream tech sector, where Baron dislikes the short product cycles. Instead, they tend to invest in niche areas of the market--such as gaming and asset managers--with companies with proven pricing power that allows for continued revenue growth.

That doesn't mean that this is a staid option, however. The fund's main advantage has been Baron's keen eye in discovering small companies with the ability to grow rapidly into large firms. For example, financial outsourcing firm First Marblehead has more than doubled this year. One of the fund's more recent additions is Lamar Advertising. As the largest billboard operator in second-tier markets, the firm has no meaningful competitor, says Peck, and there's yet to be a technological substitute for billboard advertising. Plus, the firm is experimenting with digital billboards with the potential to boost existing revenues tenfold.

The fund has had its fair share of mistakes. An investment in consulting firm Hewitt Associates didn't pan out and was sold in the third quarter. And Baron called the recent purchase of Getty Images a mistake, saying it faces increased competition and isn't as unique as he first thought.

Still, powered by a patient approach, the fund's winners have far outweighed the losers in most years. Despite its relatively rich price tag, we think this is a solid option.

Address:	767 Fifth Ave New York NY 10153 800-442-3814	
Web Address:	www.baronfunds.com	
Inception:	06-12-87	
Advisor:	Bamco Inc.	
Subadvisor:	None	
NTF Plans:	Fidelity Retail-NTF, Schwab OneSource	

Minimum Purchase:	$2000	Add: $0	IRA: $2000
Min Auto Inv Plan:	$500	Add: $50	
Sales Fees:	No-load, 0.25%S		
Management Fee:	1.00%		
Actual Fees:	Mgt:1.00%	Dist:0.25%	
Expense Projections:	3Yr:$425	5Yr:$734	10Yr:$1613
Income Distrib:	Annually		

Morningstar® Funds 500

Baron FifthAveGr

	Ticker	Load	NAV	Yield	Total Assets	Mstar Category
	BFTHX	None	$13.11	0.0%	$123 mil	Large Growth

Governance and Management

Stewardship Grade: B

Portfolio Manager(s)

Randy Haase took charge in May 2006 from a group of interim managers that looked after the fund following the departure of Mitch Rubin, who left to start his own hedge fund in March 2006. Haase spent the previous five and a half years at hedge fund Duquesne Capital under the tutelage of Stanley Druckenmiller. Prior to that, Haase was an analyst and fund manager at Alliance, where he ultimately ran Alliance Quasar (now AllianceBernstein Small Cap Growth) from June 1994 to January 2000.

Strategy

Randy Haase breaks the portfolio down into three "buckets" that represent different types of growth stocks. Classic growth consists of proven industry leaders that are reasonably priced and represents roughly 65% of the portfolio. Misunderstood growth stocks are former highfliers going through a transition, and make up 25% of assets. The remaining 10% of assets are devoted to what are traditionally known as cyclical growth stocks. Underlying all of that is a high-quality, valuation-conscious bias, and an emphasis on strong company management teams.

Performance 12-31-06

	1st Qtr	2nd Qtr	3rd Qtr	4th Qtr	Total
2002	—	—	—	—	—
2003	—	—	—	—	—
2004	—	—	-1.20	10.92	—*
2005	-4.74	7.08	3.31	2.94	8.48
2006	4.12	-4.20	2.95	7.28	10.17

Trailing	Total Return%	+/- S&P 500	+/- Russ 1000Gr	%Rank Cat	Growth of $10,000
3 Mo	7.28	0.58	1.35	13	10,728
6 Mo	10.45	-2.29	0.35	19	11,045
1 Yr	10.17	-5.62	1.10	21	11,017
3 Yr Avg	—	—	—	—	—
5 Yr Avg	—	—	—	—	—
10 Yr Avg	—	—	—	—	—
15 Yr Avg	—	—	—	—	—

Tax Analysis	Tax-Adj Rtn%	%Rank Cat	Tax-Cost Rat	%Rank Cat
3 Yr (estimated)	—	—	—	—
5 Yr (estimated)	—	—	—	—
10 Yr (estimated)	—	—	—	—

Potential Capital Gain Exposure: 20% of assets

Morningstar's Take by Kerry O'Boyle 11-10-06

As Baron Fifth Avenue Growth tries to find its way, investors may want to find something else.

When manager Randy Haase took charge of this fund in May 2006, he said he was generally content with the condition of the portfolio and laid out a philosophy for segmenting the fund's holdings into six different types of growth buckets. Well, scrap that plan. After the stock market's early summer swoon, Haase has now completely overhauled the fund--selling 31 stocks and adding 19 new ones to build a more compact portfolio of 50 holdings.

Citing a changed environment and a renewed consciousness regarding risk, Haase is also talking about the portfolio in a different way. Gone are the six buckets, now replaced by three that he calls classic, misunderstood, and cyclical growth stocks. Steady, more-traditional growers such as Procter & Gamble, PepsiCo, and Johnson & Johnson have migrated to the top of the portfolio. Indeed, recently sluggish-grower Microsoft--which Haase was not all keen on back in May--has now found a place in the fund's top 10 holdings.

While the sudden change of heart disturbs us, it does strike us as more in line with what we know about Haase. When he was running Alliance Quasar (now AllianceBernstein Small Cap Growth) during the 1990s, Haase was known for keeping an eye on valuation and picking up stocks when they were out of favor with the market. High-quality mega-caps have certainly been out of favor in recent years, and were on sale during the summer.

Then again, Haase's most recent prior stint was at a hedge fund, so we hope he hasn't picked up that industry's penchant for short-term thinking and rapid trading. Of greater import to shareholders, though, is that this fund no longer looks like the fast-growing, large-cap fund it was originally billed as. Baron doesn't have much of a track record in picking large-cap stocks, and the fees here are well in excess of the median for a no-load large-cap offering. We don't recommend this fund.

Address:	767 Fifth Ave New York NY 10153 800-442-3814
Web Address:	www.baronfunds.com
Inception:	04-30-04
Advisor:	Bamco Inc.
Subadvisor:	None
NTF Plans:	Fidelity Retail-NTF, Schwab OneSource

Minimum Purchase:	$2000	Add: $0	IRA: $2000
Min Auto Inv Plan:	$500	Add: $50	
Sales Fees:	No-load, 0.25%S		
Management Fee:	1.00% mx./0.80% mn.		
Actual Fees:	Mgt:1.00%	Dist:0.25%	
Expense Projections:	3Yr:$462	5Yr:$805	10Yr:$1772
Income Distrib:	Annually		

Historical Profile

Return —
Risk —
Rating Not Rated

Investment Style: Equity, Stock %

92% 93% 100%

▼ Manager Change
▽ Partial Manager Change

Growth of $10,000
— Investment Values of Fund
— Investment Values of S&P 500

Performance Quartile (within Category)

1995	1996	1997	1998	1999	2000	2001	2002	2003	2004	2005	2006	History
—	—	—	—	—	—	—	—	—	10.97	11.90	13.11	NAV
—	—	—	—	—	—	—	—	—	—	8.48	10.17	Total Return %
—	—	—	—	—	—	—	—	—	—	3.57	-5.62	+/-S&P 500
—	—	—	—	—	—	—	—	—	—	3.22	1.10	+/-Russ 1000Gr
—	—	—	—	—	—	—	—	—	—	0.00	0.00	Income Return %
—	—	—	—	—	—	—	—	—	—	8.48	10.17	Capital Return %
—	—	—	—	—	—	—	—	—	—	30	21	Total Rtn % Rank Cat
—	—	—	—	—	—	—	—	0.00	0.00	0.00	0.00	Income $
—	—	—	—	—	—	—	—	0.00	0.00	0.00	0.00	Capital Gains $
—	—	—	—	—	—	—	—	—	1.40	1.39		Expense Ratio %
—	—	—	—	—	—	—	—	—	-0.79	-0.16		Income Ratio %
—	—	—	—	—	—	—	—	—	8	106		Turnover Rate %
—	—	—	—	—	—	—	—	—	60	123		Net Assets $mil

Rating and Risk

Time Period	Load-Adj Return %	Morningstar Rtn vs Cat	Morningstar Risk vs Cat	Morningstar Risk-Adj Rating
1 Yr	10.17			
3 Yr	—	—	—	—
5 Yr	—	—	—	—
10 Yr	—	—	—	—
Incept	10.68			

Other Measures	Standard Index S&P 500	Best Fit Index
Alpha	—	—
Beta	—	—
R-Squared	—	—
Standard Deviation	—	
Mean	—	
Sharpe Ratio	—	

Portfolio Analysis 09-30-06

Share change since 03-06 Total Stocks:50	Sector	PE	Tot Ret%	% Assets
✲ Procter & Gamble Company	Goods	23.9	13.36	4.21
⊕ American Express Company	Financial	20.9	19.09	4.17
✲ Microsoft Corporation	Software	23.8	15.83	3.61
✲ PepsiCo, Inc.	Goods	21.5	7.86	3.39
⊖ Las Vegas Sands, Inc.	Consumer	75.7	126.70	3.28
⊖ Charles Schwab Corporati	Financial	26.3	32.87	3.22
✲ Diageo PLC ADR	Goods	16.1	40.66	3.12
✲ Johnson & Johnson	Health	17.5	12.45	3.12
⊕ Walt Disney Company	Media	21.0	44.26	3.09
⊖ Apple Computer, Inc.	Hardware	37.6	18.01	2.77
⊕ Alliancebernstein Holdin		20.8	50.15	2.76
⊕ WellPoint, Inc.	Health	17.2	-1.38	2.71
⊕ Target Corporation	Consumer	19.3	4.65	2.65
✲ Wells Fargo Company	Financial	14.7	16.82	2.60
✲ Comcast	Media			2.50
⊕ American Tower Corporati	Telecom		37.57	2.48
⊕ Marriott International,	Consumer	27.7	43.41	2.38
⊕ UnitedHealth Group, Inc.	Health	20.8	-13.49	2.36
Chicago Mercantile Excha	Financial	49.3	39.48	2.29
✲ Federated Department Sto	Consumer	20.8	16.54	2.25

Current Investment Style

Value Blnd Growth — Large Mid Small

Market Cap	%
Giant	38.1
Large	45.9
Mid	16.0
Small	0.0
Micro	0.0

Avg $mil: 32,193

Value Measures		Rel Category
Price/Earnings	20.91	1.09
Price/Book	2.95	0.89
Price/Sales	2.20	1.13
Price/Cash Flow	13.70	1.20
Dividend Yield %	1.03	1.00

Growth Measures	%	Rel Category
Long-Term Erngs	14.80	1.03
Book Value	12.92	1.11
Sales	13.09	1.13
Cash Flow	14.69	0.87
Historical Erngs	21.74	0.95

Profitability	%	Rel Category
Return on Equity	19.81	0.97
Return on Assets	12.18	1.11
Net Margin	14.90	1.05

Sector Weightings

Sector Weightings	% of Stocks	Rel S&P 500	3 Year High Low
↻ Info	17.92	0.90	
▣ Software	3.71	1.08	4 1
▣ Hardware	2.85	0.31	9 3
▣ Media	8.81	2.32	13 5
▣ Telecom	2.55	0.73	5 0
☞ Service	61.49	1.33	
▣ Health	12.32	1.02	12 6
▣ Consumer	19.34	2.53	34 19
▣ Business	7.12	1.68	12 6
▣ Financial	22.71	1.02	27 15
▫ Mfg	20.59	0.61	
▣ Goods	15.59	1.82	16 4
▣ Ind Mtrls	0.00	0.00	0 0
▣ Energy	5.00	0.51	6 4
▣ Utilities	0.00	0.00	0 0

Composition

● Cash		0.0
● Stocks		100.0
● Bonds		0.0
○ Other		0.0
Foreign (% of Stock)		4.5

Baron Growth

	Ticker	Load	NAV	Yield	Total Assets	Mstar Category
	BGRFX	None	$49.88	0.0%	$5,858 mil	Small Growth

Governance and Management

Stewardship Grade: C

Portfolio Manager(s)

Ron Baron handles the stock-picking responsibilities here. He has run Baron Asset since 1987 and this fund since its inception. The advisory firm employs more than 15 analysts and portfolio managers.

Strategy

Manager and firm founder Ron Baron looks for businesses he thinks can double in price during the next four to five years, based on fundamentals such as rapidly growing earnings or cash flow, or improving margins. He also emphasizes quality of management and stays in close contact with the executives at the fund's holdings. Technology stocks rarely meet the fund's criteria, but the business-services, media, and communications sectors have been favorites.

Historical Profile
Return High
Risk Low
Rating ★★★★★ Highest

Investment Style: Equity Stock %

96% 89% 98% 83% 99% 90% 86% 89% 95%

▼ Manager Change
▽ Partial Manager Change

Growth of $10,000
— Investment Values of Fund
— Investment Values of S&P 500

63.2 46.4 33.8 24.0 17.0 10.0

Performance Quartile (within Category)

	1995	1996	1997	1998	1999	2000	2001	2002	2003	2004	2005	2006	History
NAV	15.11	19.04	24.88	24.87	33.68	28.82	30.67	26.90	35.44	44.87	45.40	49.88	NAV
	52.54	27.72	31.07	0.10	44.71	-4.59	12.67	-12.29	31.75	26.61	5.71	15.50	Total Return %
	14.96	4.76	-2.29	-28.48	23.67	4.51	24.56	9.81	3.07	15.73	0.80	-0.29	+/-S&P 500
	21.50	16.46	18.12	-1.13	1.62	17.84	21.90	17.97	-16.79	12.30	1.56	2.15	+/-Russ 2000 Gr
	0.37	0.60	0.09	0.14	0.00	0.00	0.00	0.00	0.00	0.00	0.00	0.00	Income Return %
	52.17	27.12	30.98	-0.04	44.71	-4.59	12.67	-12.29	31.75	26.61	5.71	15.50	Capital Return %
	9	12	10	65	58	48	10	2	93	3	51	17	Total Rtn % Rank Cat
	0.04	0.09	0.02	0.04	0.00	0.00	0.00	0.00	0.00	0.00	0.00	0.00	Income $
	0.11	0.16	0.06	0.00	1.88	3.19	1.64	0.00	0.00	0.00	2.05	2.54	Capital Gains $
	2.00	1.50	1.40	1.37	1.37	1.36	1.36	1.35	1.36	1.33	1.31	1.31	Expense Ratio %
	1.10	1.20	0.40	0.20	-0.20	-0.78	-0.79	-1.16	-1.11	-0.89	-0.73	-0.61	Income Ratio %
	—	40	25	40	53	39	35	18	33	27	15	21	Turnover Rate %
	41	244	415	344	620	500	721	1,214	2,521	4,049	5,122	5,858	Net Assets $mil

Performance 12-31-06

	1st Qtr	2nd Qtr	3rd Qtr	4th Qtr	Total
2002	4.53	-5.12	-11.37	-0.22	-12.29
2003	-2.49	17.96	5.53	8.55	31.75
2004	7.28	1.68	0.67	15.29	26.61
2005	1.43	1.56	-0.56	3.20	5.71
2006	11.23	-3.88	-2.70	11.02	15.50

Trailing	Total Return%	+/- S&P 500	+/- Russ 2000 Gr	%Rank Cat	Growth of $10,000
3 Mo	11.02	4.32	2.25	7	11,102
6 Mo	8.02	-4.72	1.16	24	10,802
1 Yr	15.50	-0.29	2.15	17	11,550
3 Yr Avg	15.62	5.18	5.11	5	15,456
5 Yr Avg	12.30	6.11	5.37	6	17,861
10 Yr Avg	13.81	5.39	8.93	9	36,459
15 Yr Avg	—	—	—		—

Tax Analysis	Tax-Adj Rtn%	%Rank Cat	Tax-Cost Rat	%Rank Cat
3 Yr (estimated)	15.09	3	0.46	17
5 Yr (estimated)	11.99	4	0.28	15
10 Yr (estimated)	13.11	4	0.62	14

Potential Capital Gain Exposure: 34% of assets

Rating and Risk

Time Period	Load-Adj Return %	Morningstar Rtn vs Cat	Morningstar Risk vs Cat	Morningstar Risk-Adj Rating
1 Yr	15.50			
3 Yr	15.62	High	Low	★★★★★
5 Yr	12.30	High	Low	★★★★★
10 Yr	13.81	High	Low	★★★★★
Incept	17.74			

Other Measures	Standard Index S&P 500	Best Fit Index DJ Wilshire 4500
Alpha	2.7	1.1
Beta	1.34	0.97
R-Squared	59	81
Standard Deviation	11.96	
Mean	15.62	
Sharpe Ratio	1.01	

Portfolio Analysis 09-30-06

Share change since 03-06 Total Stocks:128

	Sector	PE	Tot Ret%	% Assets
⊕ Jefferies Group, Inc.	Financial	19.7	21.21	2.57
⊕ CB Richard Ellis Group,	Financial	30.3	69.24	2.29
Four Seasons Hotel, Inc.	Consumer	—	65.03	2.16
Dick's Sporting Goods, I	Consumer	27.2	47.38	2.14
⊖ Amerigroup Corporation	Financial	21.6	84.43	2.06
Arch Capital Group, Ltd.	Financial	18.2	23.49	1.97
⊖ First Marblehead Corpora	Financial	14.2	152.13	1.86
Station Casinos Inc.	Consumer	38.6	22.46	1.85
Manor Care, Inc.	Health	24.6	19.65	1.77
Edwards Lifesciences Cor	Health	25.7	13.05	1.75
⊕ WellCare Health Plans, I	Health	30.9	68.67	1.60
⊖ Encore Acquisition Compa	Energy	9.8	-23.44	1.56
⊕ Wynn Resorts, Ltd.	Consumer	—	82.52	1.55
⊕ Cheesecake Factory, Inc.	Consumer	23.9	-34.21	1.55
International Securities	Financial	—	70.81	1.54
DeVry, Inc.	Consumer	34.4	40.26	1.48
Wynn Resorts 144A Cv 6%	—	—		1.46
⊕ Copart, Inc.	Business	25.4	30.10	1.45
⊕ Carter's, Inc.	Goods	29.3	-13.34	1.44
Strayer Education, Inc.	Consumer	30.1	14.34	1.42

Current Investment Style

Value Blnd Growth — Large Mid Small

Market Cap	%
Giant	0.0
Large	0.0
Mid	46.4
Small	51.0
Micro	2.6

Avg $mil: 1,851

Value Measures		Rel Category
Price/Earnings	20.28	0.96
Price/Book	2.79	1.02
Price/Sales	1.18	0.75
Price/Cash Flow	9.65	1.00
Dividend Yield %	0.39	0.85

Growth Measures	%	Rel Category
Long-Term Erngs	15.43	0.87
Book Value	9.32	0.89
Sales	12.64	1.06
Cash Flow	9.76	0.46
Historical Erngs	22.70	0.93

Profitability	%	Rel Category
Return on Equity	14.96	1.21
Return on Assets	8.29	1.24
Net Margin	8.41	0.97

Sector Weightings	% of Stocks	Rel S&P 500	3 Year High	Low
↻ Info	3.95	0.20		
🖩 Software	0.82	0.24	2	1
🖥 Hardware	0.41	0.04	1	0
📺 Media	1.90	0.50	6	2
☎ Telecom	0.82	0.23	3	1
⊂ Service	76.21	1.65		
🩺 Health	13.24	1.10	14	11
🛒 Consumer	31.15	4.07	35	30
📇 Business	8.98	2.12	12	9
💲 Financial	22.84	1.03	23	19
⊔ Mfg	19.85	0.59		
🏭 Goods	10.13	1.18	10	4
⚙ Ind Mtrls	2.61	0.22	3	1
🔋 Energy	6.12	0.62	7	6
💡 Utilities	0.99	0.28	2	1

Composition

● Cash	2.7	
● Stocks	95.5	
● Bonds	0.0	
○ Other	1.8	
	Foreign	2.9
	(% of Stock)	

Morningstar's Take by Kerry O'Boyle 12-27-06

We find Baron Growth's reopening inexplicable.

In August 2006, the fund announced that it was once again open to all investors effective immediately. What's shocking is that it was only recently getting a handle on its girth despite originally closing to retail investors in September 2003. Inflows from institutional clients caused assets to more than double in size in the subsequent 18 months, before the fund then instituted a hard close in May 2005.

Only two other small-growth funds are bigger than this offering--one of them has multiple subadvisors, and the other has been big for a long time. And there's evidence to suggest that the surge in flows has altered the fund's investment approach. Since the end of 2000, for instance, the number of holdings in the portfolio has grown to 128 from 61, and the percentage of assets devoted to mid-cap stocks increased to 56% of assets in early 2006 from less than 30%.

Granted, part of that style drift is likely reflective of manager Ron Baron's willingness to let his winners ride. Baron is a gifted stock-picker who's had tremendous success investing in niche growth industries like gaming and asset managers, while largely avoiding volatile technology stocks. We like his long-term approach to investing, as evident by the fund's consistently low turnover relative to its peers, and willingness to hold on to stocks he has conviction in even during rough stretches. That light trading style is also of some benefit in helping the fund manage its increasing size.

It is harder for a small-cap manager to run ever-larger amounts of assets, with the result often being mediocrity. Although Baron has been increasing the size of his analyst staff to assist with the growing number of holdings, nearly half have only been with the firm since 2005. We're also disappointed that economies of scale have not been passed along to investors, as Baron's management fee remains fixed at 1%. We don't think investors should be sending new assets here.

Address:	767 Fifth Ave New York NY 10153 800-442-3814	Minimum Purchase:	$2000 Add: $0 IRA: $2000
		Min Auto Inv Plan:	$500 Add: $50
		Sales Fees:	No-load, 0.25%S
Web Address:	www.baronfunds.com	Management Fee:	1.00%
Inception:	12-30-94	Actual Fees:	Mgt:1.00% Dist:0.25%
Advisor:	Bamco Inc.	Expense Projections:	3Yr:$415 5Yr:$718 10Yr:$1579
Subadvisor:	None	Income Distrib:	Annually
NTF Plans:	Fidelity Retail-NTF, Schwab OneSource		

M🌑RNINGSTAR® Funds 500

Baron Partners

	Ticker	Load	NAV	Yield	Total Assets	Mstar Category
	BPTRX	None	$22.34	0.0%	$2,302 mil	Mid-Cap Growth

Governance and Management

Stewardship Grade: C

Portfolio Manager(s)

Ron Baron has been at the helm since the fund's 1992 inception, and given that he owns the advisor, he should be here for a long time. His firm employs roughly 18 analysts and portfolio managers, but he's the driving force behind this fund's portfolio.

Strategy

Manager Ron Baron buys companies he thinks can double in price over the next four years, focusing on rapidly growing firms trading at prices that don't yet reflect their potential. His dislike of short product cycles keeps the fund out of the technology sector. This fund, a partnership until it was converted to a mutual fund in 2003, can also short stocks and use leverage. Typically, individual short positions are quite small. The fund uses leverage (borrows money) to amplify its equity exposure when the manager is bullish on stocks, up to a maximum of one third of its assets including leverage.

Historical Profile

Return	High
Risk	High
Rating	★★★★ Above Avg

Investment Style: Equity Stock %

96% 83% 99% 99%

▼ Manager Change
▽ Partial Manager Change

Growth of $10,000
— Investment Values of Fund
— Investment Values of S&P 500

64.6 / 46.4 / 33.8 / 24.0 / 17.0 / 10.0

Performance Quartile (within Category)

1995	1996	1997	1998	1999	2000	2001	2002	2003	2004	2005	2006	History
5.39	6.45	10.44	11.62	14.07	14.70	12.34	10.07	12.17	16.85	18.43	22.34	NAV
45.68	19.67	61.86	11.30	21.08	4.48	-16.05	-18.40	34.76	42.35	14.37	21.55	Total Return %
8.10	-3.29	28.50	-17.28	0.04	13.58	-4.16	3.70	6.08	31.47	9.46	5.76	+/-S&P 500
11.70	2.19	39.32	-6.56	-30.21	16.23	4.10	9.01	-7.95	26.87	2.27	10.89	+/-Russ MG
0.00	0.00	0.00	0.00	0.00	0.00	0.00	0.00	0.00	0.00	0.00	0.00	Income Return %
45.68	19.67	61.86	11.30	21.08	4.48	-16.05	-18.40	34.76	42.35	14.37	21.55	Capital Return %
14	30	1	66	83	37	46	17	55	1	18	2	Total Rtn % Rank Cat
0.00	0.00	0.00	0.00	0.00	0.00	0.00	0.00	0.00	0.00	0.00	0.00	Income $
0.00	0.00	0.00	0.00	0.00	0.00	0.00	1.36	0.43	0.78	0.06		Capital Gains $
—	—	—	—	—	—	—	—	1.45	1.46	—		Expense Ratio %
—	—	—	—	—	—	—	—	-1.79	-0.83	—		Income Ratio %
—	—	—	—	—	—	—	—	37	58	—		Turnover Rate %
—	—	—	—	—	—	—	164	633	2,302			Net Assets $mil

Performance 12-31-06

	1st Qtr	2nd Qtr	3rd Qtr	4th Qtr	Total
2002	4.05	-7.40	-22.04	8.63	-18.40
2003	-8.34	19.93	6.14	15.49	34.76
2004	12.69	4.11	2.32	18.58	42.35
2005	-0.74	5.39	2.97	6.17	14.37
2006	12.81	-2.65	1.14	9.43	21.55

Trailing	Total Return%	+/- S&P 500	+/- Russ MG	%Rank Cat	Growth of $10,000
3 Mo	9.43	2.73	2.48	11	10,943
6 Mo	10.68	-2.06	2.78	11	11,068
1 Yr	21.55	5.76	10.89	2	12,155
3 Yr Avg	25.54	15.10	12.81	1	19,785
5 Yr Avg	16.82	10.63	8.60	1	21,756
10 Yr Avg	15.33	6.91	6.71	4	41,632
15 Yr Avg	—				

Tax Analysis	Tax-Adj Rtn%	%Rank Cat	Tax-Cost Rat	%Rank Cat
3 Yr (estimated)	24.92	1	0.49	25
5 Yr (estimated)	16.11	1	0.61	43
10 Yr (estimated)	14.98	3	0.30	6

Potential Capital Gain Exposure: 27% of assets

Rating and Risk

Time Period	Load-Adj Return %	Morningstar Rtn vs Cat	Morningstar Risk vs Cat	Morningstar Risk-Adj Rating
1 Yr	21.55			
3 Yr	25.54	High	+Avg	★★★★★
5 Yr	16.82	High	High	★★★★★
10 Yr	15.33	High	High	★★★
Incept	18.30			

Other Measures	Standard Index S&P 500	Best Fit Index DJ Wilshire 4500
Alpha	10.4	9.0
Beta	1.47	1.02
R-Squared	57	73
Standard Deviation	13.28	
Mean	25.54	
Sharpe Ratio	1.54	

Portfolio Analysis 09-30-06

Share change since 03-06 Total Stocks:47	Sector	PE	Tot Ret%	% Assets
⊕ Wynn Resorts, Ltd.	Consumer	—	82.52	5.72
⊕ Las Vegas Sands, Inc.	Consumer	75.7	126.70	5.51
⊕ Boyd Gaming Corporation	Consumer	32.8	-3.73	4.74
⊕ Iron Mountain, Inc.	Business	44.8	-2.09	4.68
⊕ Jefferies Group, Inc.	Financial	19.7	21.21	4.39
⊖ Charles Schwab Corporati	Financial	26.3	32.87	4.24
Manor Care, Inc.	Health	24.6	19.65	4.21
⊕ Alliancebernstein Holdin	Financial	—	20.8	50.15	3.97
ChoicePoint, Inc.	Business	26.2	-11.53	3.39
✻ Fastenal Company	Business	27.8	-7.37	2.74
Chicago Mercantile Excha	Financial	49.3	39.48	2.72
⊕ International Securities	Financial	—	70.81	2.50
Nuveen Investments, Inc.	Financial	23.9	24.13	2.49
⊕ Toll Brothers, Inc.	Consumer	6.2	-6.96	2.36
Four Seasons Hotel, Inc.	Consumer	—	65.03	2.33
Dick's Sporting Goods, I	Consumer	27.2	47.38	2.27
✻ Brookdale Senior Living,	Health	—		2.20
⊕ Penn National Gaming	Goods	21.8	26.31	2.16
Arch Capital Group, Ltd.	Financial	18.2	23.49	2.11
⊕ Whole Foods Market, Inc.	Consumer	32.8	-37.19	2.04

Current Investment Style

Value Blnd Growth — Large Mid Small

Market Cap	%
Giant	0.0
Large	21.1
Mid	64.7
Small	14.2
Micro	0.0

Avg $mil: 4,980

Value Measures		Rel Category
Price/Earnings	22.95	1.12
Price/Book	3.58	1.12
Price/Sales	2.23	1.27
Price/Cash Flow	13.72	1.20
Dividend Yield %	0.91	1.44

Growth Measures	%	Rel Category
Long-Term Erngs	16.14	0.99
Book Value	11.02	0.87
Sales	15.30	1.53
Cash Flow	19.25	1.04
Historical Erngs	27.15	1.09

Profitability	%	Rel Category
Return on Equity	18.08	1.01
Return on Assets	9.88	1.05
Net Margin	13.72	1.18

Sector Weightings	% of Stocks	Rel S&P 500	3 Year High Low
⟳ Info	0.00	0.00		
Software	0.00	0.00	0	0
Hardware	0.00	0.00	0	0
Media	0.00	0.00	4	0
Telecom	0.00	0.00	0	0
☞ Service	90.38	1.96		
Health	8.58	0.71	9	5
Consumer	35.05	4.58	55	24
Business	17.82	4.21	24	17
Financial	28.93	1.30	36	17
Mfg	9.62	0.28		
Goods	5.73	0.67	6	1
Ind Mtrls	0.00	0.00	1	0
Energy	2.61	0.27	8	0
Utilities	1.28	0.37	2	0

Composition

● Cash	0.0
● Stocks	99.3
● Bonds	0.0
● Other	0.7
Foreign (% of Stock)	3.5

Morningstar's Take by Kerry O'Boyle 12-07-06

Gambling anyone?

Baron Partners is the fund where veteran small- and mid-cap growth manager Ron Baron lets it all hang out. This fund, a former partnership that was converted into a mutual fund in 2003, can short stocks and use leverage (borrow money) to boost its equity exposure. It's the most compact offering that Baron runs at 47 holdings, and nearly 50% of the fund's assets are in its top 10 stocks. He's also willing to load up more here on the industries he thinks offer the greatest opportunity than he is at other, more-diversified offerings that he runs.

As evidence, more than 20% of assets, including the portfolio's top three holdings--Wynn Resorts, Las Vegas Sands, and Boyd Gaming--are devoted to casino operators. Baron, a longtime fan of these so-called "gaming" stocks, thinks that the price/earnings multiples for these fast-growing firms remain low because of the "sin" stigma attached to gambling. But Baron cites the continuing expansion of the industry across the U.S.

and overseas, with the building boom in Macau being the latest example of gaming's popularity. Thanks in large part to that bet, the fund's results thus far in 2006 have been spectacular. Its 23.5% gain for the year to date through December 4 bests its typical mid-growth rival by nearly 13 percentage points.

Investors should be aware, however, that this fund's style involves considerable risk. Although the fund currently has no short positions and is only minimally levered (104% invested), its concentrated positions can just as quickly turn south. The greater risk also causes Baron to trade a bit more here--a departure from his normally low-turnover style--in an attempt to keep volatility in check.

While Baron has proven himself to be a savvy stock-picker in his nearly 20 years as a mutual fund manager, this fund's aggressive profile is not for the faint of heart. Only the most risk-tolerant investors need apply.

Address:	767 Fifth Ave New York NY 10153 800-442-3814	Minimum Purchase: Min Auto Inv Plan: Sales Fees:	$2000 Add: $0 IRA: $0 $500 Add: $50 No-load, 0.25%S
Web Address:	www.baronfunds.com	Management Fee:	1.00%
Inception:	01-31-92	Actual Fees:	Mgt:1.00% Dist:0.25%
Advisor:	Bamco Inc.	Expense Projections:	3Yr:$511 5Yr:$881 10Yr:$1922
Subadvisor:	None	Income Distrib:	Annually
NTF Plans:	Fidelity Retail-NTF, Schwab OneSource		

Baron Small Cap

	Ticker	Load	NAV	Yield	Total Assets	Mstar Category
	BSCFX	None	$22.83	0.0%	$3,093 mil	Small Growth

Governance and Management

Stewardship Grade: B

Portfolio Manager(s)

Cliff Greenberg has managed the fund since its inception, and he has only two dedicated analysts working with him. But Greenberg also shares information with founder Ron Baron, and he can draw upon the firm's 15 other analysts and portfolio managers for ideas.

Strategy

Manager Cliff Greenberg invests in firms that he thinks can double in price over the next four years, but he doesn't trade nearly as often as his rivals. He favors firms with strong competitive advantages and, above all, astute executive teams, but he will buy fallen angels, too. Greenberg's long-term bent keeps him clear of the volatile technology sector.

Historical Profile

Return	High
Risk	Low
Rating	★★★★ Highest

95%	83%	97%	88%	96%	91%	87%	95%	94%

Investment Style
Equity
Stock %

▼ Manager Change
▽ Partial Manager Change

Growth of $10,000
— Investment Values of Fund
— Investment Values of S&P 500

26.8
22.8
18.0
14.0
10.0

Performance Quartile (within Category)

	1995	1996	1997	1998	1999	2000	2001	2002	2003	2004	2005	2006	History
	—	—	10.31	10.54	18.00	14.46	15.21	13.37	18.56	22.08	23.17	22.83	NAV
	—	—	3.10*	2.23	70.78	-17.53	5.19	-9.66	38.82	22.16	8.34	11.83	Total Return %
	—	—	—	-26.35	49.74	-8.43	17.08	12.44	10.14	11.28	3.43	-3.96	+/-S&P 500
	—	—	—	1.00	27.69	4.90	14.42	20.60	-9.72	7.85	4.19	-1.52	+/-Russ 2000 Gr
	—	—	—	0.00	0.00	0.00	0.00	0.00	0.00	0.00	0.00	0.00	Income Return %
	—	—	—	2.23	70.78	-17.53	5.19	-9.66	38.82	22.16	8.34	11.83	Capital Return %
	—	—	—	54	32	84	18	1	72	9	30	40	Total Rtn % Rank Cat
	—	—	0.00	0.00	0.00	0.00	0.00	0.00	0.00	0.00	0.00	0.00	Income $
	—	—	0.00	0.00	0.00	0.38	0.00	0.38	0.00	0.55	0.74	3.06	Capital Gains $
	—	—	1.39	1.34	1.33	1.35	1.36	1.36	1.33	1.33	1.33		Expense Ratio %
	—	—	-0.20	-0.99	-0.90	-0.68	-0.97	-0.87	-0.88	-0.48	-0.73		Income Ratio %
	—	—	—	43	53	56	55	30	33	25	40		Turnover Rate %
	—	—	285	470	1,089	746	704	748	1,426	2,252	2,930	3,093	Net Assets $mil

Performance 12-31-06

	1st Qtr	2nd Qtr	3rd Qtr	4th Qtr	Total
2002	9.01	-1.45	-15.97	0.08	-9.66
2003	0.22	19.55	7.74	7.53	38.82
2004	7.22	1.61	-5.14	18.21	22.16
2005	0.45	3.38	0.65	3.64	8.34
2006	11.31	-7.41	-1.21	9.83	11.83

Trailing	Total Return%	+/- S&P 500	+/- Russ 2000 Gr	%Rank Cat	Growth of $10,000
3 Mo	9.83	3.13	1.06	16	10,983
6 Mo	8.50	-4.24	1.64	20	10,850
1 Yr	11.83	-3.96	-1.52	40	11,183
3 Yr Avg	13.96	3.52	3.45	12	14,800
5 Yr Avg	13.17	6.98	6.24	4	18,563
10 Yr Avg	—	—	—		—
15 Yr Avg	—	—	—		—

Tax Analysis	Tax-Adj Rtn%	%Rank Cat	Tax-Cost Rat	%Rank Cat
3 Yr (estimated)	12.95	9	0.89	34
5 Yr (estimated)	12.44	3	0.65	37
10 Yr (estimated)	—	—	—	—

Potential Capital Gain Exposure: 28% of assets

Rating and Risk

Time Period	Load-Adj Return %	Morningstar Rtn vs Cat	Morningstar Risk vs Cat	Morningstar Risk-Adj Rating
1 Yr	11.83			
3 Yr	13.96	+Avg	-Avg	★★★★
5 Yr	13.17	High	Low	★★★★★
10 Yr	—	—	—	—
Incept	12.19			

Other Measures	Standard Index S&P 500	Best Fit Index Russ MG
Alpha	1.1	1.4
Beta	1.38	0.99
R-Squared	53	74
Standard Deviation	12.99	
Mean	13.96	
Sharpe Ratio	0.82	

Portfolio Analysis 09-30-06

Share change since 03-06 Total Stocks:91	Sector	PE	Tot Ret%	% Assets
⊕ CB Richard Ellis Group,	Financial	30.3	69.24	2.53
⊖ American Tower Corporati	Telecom	—	37.57	2.50
⊖ SBA Communications Corpo	Telecom	—	53.63	2.29
Brookdale Senior Living,	Health	—		2.22
Gaylord Entertainment	Consumer	—	16.84	2.10
⊖ FLIR Systems, Inc.	Ind Mtrls	28.6	42.54	2.00
Wynn Resorts, Ltd.	Consumer	—	82.52	1.98
☼ Eagle Materials, Inc.	Consumer	10.6	7.77	1.84
⊕ Covanta Holding Corporat	Business	33.8	46.35	1.84
Penn National Gaming	Goods	21.8	26.31	1.75
Flowserve Corporation	Ind Mtrls	39.2	27.58	1.73
⊖ Actuant Corporation A	Ind Mtrls	15.6	-14.47	1.71
⊕ United Surgical Partners	Health	35.6	-11.82	1.66
Strayer Education, Inc.	Consumer	30.1	14.34	1.64
DSW, Inc.	Goods	—		1.62
⊖ Immucor, Inc.	Health	48.7	87.70	1.61
Intuitive Surgical, Inc.	Health	35.2	-18.22	1.53
Acco Brands Corporation	Ind Mtrls	62.1	8.04	1.52
⊕ Navigant Consulting	Business	22.4	-10.10	1.51
⊕ United Auto Group, Inc.	Consumer	17.2	24.98	1.44

Current Investment Style

Value Blnd Growth — Large Mid Small

Market Cap	%
Giant	0.0
Large	2.7
Mid	38.5
Small	45.3
Micro	13.4
Avg $mil:	1,569

Value Measures		Rel Category
Price/Earnings	21.29	1.01
Price/Book	2.41	0.88
Price/Sales	1.11	0.71
Price/Cash Flow	10.59	1.10
Dividend Yield %	0.18	0.39

Growth Measures	%	Rel Category
Long-Term Erngs	16.50	0.93
Book Value	8.66	0.83
Sales	12.92	1.09
Cash Flow	10.19	0.48
Historical Erngs	23.74	0.98

Profitability	%	Rel Category
Return on Equity	11.09	0.89
Return on Assets	6.65	1.00
Net Margin	5.75	0.66

Sector Weightings

	% of Stocks	Rel S&P 500	3 Year High	Low
↻ Info	9.71	0.49		
⬛ Software	0.73	0.21	2	0
⬛ Hardware	1.02	0.11	2	0
⬛ Media	1.79	0.47	8	1
⬛ Telecom	6.17	1.76	11	6
⬛ Service	64.68	1.40		
⬛ Health	11.43	0.95	16	11
⬛ Consumer	29.56	3.86	39	30
⬛ Business	16.97	4.01	20	14
⬛ Financial	6.72	0.30	8	2
⬛ Mfg	25.61	0.76		
⬛ Goods	11.61	1.36	12	6
⬛ Ind Mtrls	14.00	1.17	14	3
⬛ Energy	0.00	0.00	1	0
⬛ Utilities	0.00	0.00	0	0

Composition

● Cash	3.2
● Stocks	94.1
● Bonds	0.0
● Other	2.7
Foreign	5.2
(% of Stock)	

Morningstar's Take by Kerry O'Boyle 12-27-06

Baron Small Cap's reopening is puzzling.

In August 2006, this offering announced that it was once again open to new investors effective immediately. While not as bloated as sibling Baron Growth in absolute terms, assets here have tripled since 2003. That makes it the sixth-largest small-growth fund in our database. We've found that managers, especially small-cap skippers, generally have a harder time delivering stand-out returns as assets rise.

The fund's size, though, can't be blamed for its middling showing in 2006. Big stakes in consumer stocks, including restaurant chains P.F. Chang's China Bistro and Texas Roadhouse, real-estate-related firms, and industrials were hit hard during an early summer sell-off in the stock market. A slim weighting in the battered technology sector has helped to cushion the blow, and the fund has since bounced back strongly on the strength of top holdings like commercial realtor CB Richard Ellis. All told, the fund is up more than 11% for the year to date through Dec. 22.

That shows the benefits of sticking to one's guns. Manager Cliff Greenberg used the correction as an opportunity to add to some of his favorite holdings at cheaper prices. One example was luxury boat-maker MarineMax--down roughly 40% from its earlier highs--which Greenberg thinks has a dominant brand. That kind of conviction is evident in the fund's low turnover rate, which has historically been well under the 91% median for the small-growth category. Low turnover also helps in managing the fund's larger asset base.

Still, we're wary of the fund's reopening. While the number of holdings in the portfolio had increased somewhat with the growth in assets, the fund's style hadn't much changed. But things could turn very quickly should more assets pour in. Although shareholders have benefited nicely over the long haul from Greenberg's patient approach, we'd be hesitant to send new money here.

Address:	767 Fifth Ave New York NY 10153 800-442-3814	Minimum Purchase:	$2000 Add: $0 IRA: $2000
		Min Auto Inv Plan:	$500 Add: $50
		Sales Fees:	No-load, 0.25%S
Web Address:	www.baronfunds.com	Management Fee:	1.00%
Inception:	09-30-97 *	Actual Fees:	Mgt:1.00% Dist:0.25%
Advisor:	Bamco Inc.	Expense Projections:	3Yr:$421 5Yr:$729 10Yr:$1601
Subadvisor:	None	Income Distrib:	Annually
NTF Plans:	Fidelity Retail-NTF, Schwab OneSource		

MORNINGSTAR® Funds 500

Bjurman, Barry MicroCp Gr

	Ticker	Load	NAV	Yield	Total Assets	Mstar Category
	BMCFX	Closed	$20.87	0.0%	$379 mil	Small Growth

Governance and Management

Portfolio Manager(s)

Tom Barry has been managing this offering since its March 1997 inception. He relies on sell-side analysts, primarily from regional brokerages, for earnings projections, but he also works with a couple of in-house analysts. Barry also runs Bjurman, Barry's other funds, Bjurman, Barry Mid Cap Growth and Bjurman, Barry Small Cap Growth. Barry has worked for Bjurman, Barry as a portfolio manager since 1978.

Strategy

Manager Tom Barry screens the stock universe with market caps between $30 million and $300 million. Barry uses five models. Four look for fairly common growth criteria, including 12-month trailing earnings growth, 12-month forecasted earnings growth, P/E ratios relative to earnings-growth rates, and earnings revision. One, however, is less common and examines price/cash-flow ratios. Barry limits positions to 5% of assets and typically owns roughly 150 stocks.

Performance 12-31-06

	1st Qtr	2nd Qtr	3rd Qtr	4th Qtr	Total
2002	1.26	-2.93	-19.04	3.62	-17.54
2003	-3.10	28.35	14.81	16.86	66.86
2004	0.78	-3.84	-7.97	15.96	3.42
2005	-4.42	2.93	6.48	5.76	10.79
2006	9.84	-7.42	-4.90	8.08	4.52

Trailing	Total Return%	+/- S&P 500	+/- Russ 2000 Gr	%Rank Cat	Growth of $10,000
3 Mo	8.08	1.38	-0.69	48	10,808
6 Mo	2.78	-9.96	-4.08	79	10,278
1 Yr	4.52	-11.27	-8.83	91	10,452
3 Yr Avg	6.19	-4.25	-4.32	84	11,974
5 Yr Avg	10.51	4.32	3.58	14	16,482
10 Yr Avg	—	—	—	—	—
15 Yr Avg	—	—	—	—	—

Tax Analysis	Tax-Adj Rtn%	%Rank Cat	Tax-Cost Rat	%Rank Cat
3 Yr (estimated)	3.15	89	2.86	90
5 Yr (estimated)	8.59	21	1.74	82
10 Yr (estimated)	—	—	—	—

Potential Capital Gain Exposure: 23% of assets

Morningstar's Take by Kerry O'Boyle 12-27-06

As the market shuns risk, Bjurman, Barry Micro-Cap Growth has been left holding the bag, but we don't think that's reason enough to dismiss it.

Manager Tom Barry employs a quantitative-based model that screens for the fastest-growing micro-cap stocks. They have the potential to generate huge returns quickly, as evidenced by the fund's 67% gain in 2003, but they can also be quite volatile. Despite its focus on stocks with reasonable price/cash-flow ratios, the fund was rocked during the summer by a flight to more-stable stocks. It lost more than 20% in just a three-month period during that time, although the fund has since recovered somewhat to be up nearly 8% for the year to date through Dec. 22, 2006.

Still, Barry says that the fastest-growing companies in his universe have underperformed for much of the past 18 months except for a strong rally in the fourth quarter of 2005. He adds that this is not unusual for micro-cap stocks during a rising interest-rate cycle and favorable economic environment. He acknowledges the extreme volatility of micro-caps, but he emphasizes long-term potential for outperformance in this area of the market, citing the strong returns of the group over rolling five- and 10-year periods.

Such sharp losses may be more than most investors can stomach though. This isn't the first time the fund has posted double-digit losses in such a brief period; it's happened more than a few times before during its nine-year existence. Such volatility may make it difficult for shareholders to stick with the fund.

But stick with it they should. Although we recommend that investors limit this offering to the fringes of their overall portfolio because of the excessive volatility, micro-caps offer worthwhile diversification. This closed fund has come to grips with its previous struggles with asset bloat and is once again more dedicated to its micro-cap strategy. Hold on long and tight, though, for the ride is likely to be a rocky one.

Address:	10100 Santa Monica Blvd	Minimum Purchase:	Closed	Add: —	IRA: —
	Los Angeles CA 90067-4103	Min Auto Inv Plan:	Closed	Add: —	
	800-227-7264	Sales Fees:	No-load, 0.25%S, 2.00%R		
Web Address:	www.bjurmanbarry.com	Management Fee:	1.00%		
Inception:	03-31-97 *	Actual Fees:	Mgt:1.00%	Dist:0.25%	
Advisor:	Bjurman, Barry & Associates	Expense Projections:	3Yr:$480	5Yr:$829	10Yr:$1813
Subadvisor:	None	Income Distrib:	Annually		
NTF Plans:	Fidelity Retail-NTF, Schwab OneSource				

Historical Profile
Return	Average
Risk	Above Avg
Rating	★★★ Neutral

	100%	100%	96%	99%	95%	99%	100%	100%	100%

Investment Style
Equity
Stock %

▼ Manager Change
▽ Partial Manager Change

Growth of $10,000
— Investment Values of Fund
— Investment Values of S&P 500

Performance Quartile (within Category)

1995	1996	1997	1998	1999	2000	2001	2002	2003	2004	2005	2006	History
—	—	8.96	10.02	15.17	20.60	24.63	20.31	33.89	30.75	30.69	20.87	NAV
—	—	49.33*	11.83	53.31	45.57	19.56	-17.54	66.86	3.42	10.79	4.52	Total Return %
—	—	—	-16.75	32.27	54.67	31.45	4.56	38.18	-7.46	5.88	-11.27	+/-S&P 500
—	—	—	10.60	10.22	68.00	28.79	12.72	18.32	-10.89	6.64	-8.83	+/-Russ 2000 Gr
—	—	—	0.00	0.00	0.00	0.00	0.00	0.00	0.00	0.00	0.00	Income Return %
—	—	—	11.83	53.31	45.57	19.56	-17.54	66.86	3.42	10.79	4.52	Capital Return %
—	—	—	26	49	1	4	10	7	88	17	91	Total Rtn % Rank Cat
—	—	0.00	0.00	0.00	0.00	0.00	0.00	0.00	0.00	0.00	0.00	Income $
—	—	0.00	0.00	0.18	1.35	0.00	0.00	0.00	4.13	3.47	10.85	Capital Gains $
—	—	—	1.80	1.80	1.80	1.80	1.80	1.59	1.46	1.54	1.52	Expense Ratio %
—	—	—	-1.41	-1.58	-1.65	-1.05	-1.40	-1.16	-1.19	-1.14	-0.88	Income Ratio %
—	—	—	110	234	337	159	105	54	65	28	62	Turnover Rate %
—	—	4	10	16	91	275	400	898	650	587	379	Net Assets $mil

Rating and Risk

Time Period	Load-Adj Return %	Morningstar Rtn vs Cat	Morningstar Risk vs Cat	Morningstar Risk-Adj Rating
1 Yr	4.52			
3 Yr	6.19	-Avg	High	★★
5 Yr	10.51	+Avg	+Avg	★★★★
10 Yr	—			
Incept	22.68			

Other Measures	Standard Index S&P 500	Best Fit Index Russ 2000 Gr
Alpha	-11.8	-4.6
Beta	2.34	1.14
R-Squared	71	89
Standard Deviation	19.09	
Mean	6.19	
Sharpe Ratio	0.24	

Portfolio Analysis 10-31-06

Share change since 09-06 Total Stocks:120	Sector	PE	Tot Ret%	% Assets
Palomar Medical Technolo	Health	27.3	44.61	3.43
Middleby Corporation	Ind Mtrls	24.1	21.01	3.39
Diodes Inc.	Hardware	24.9	14.27	3.38
World Fuel Services Corp	Energy	22.4	32.34	3.05
Ceradyne, Inc.	Ind Mtrls	15.0	29.00	2.94
MGP Ingredients, Inc.	Goods	26.5	93.27	2.80
Smith Micro Software	Software	46.0	142.56	2.46
Steven Madden	Goods	17.6	84.89	2.27
Healthcare Services Grou	Business	32.2	42.74	2.26
Andersons, Inc.	Ind Mtrls	21.0	97.73	2.17
Dynamic Materials Corpor	Ind Mtrls	19.9	-5.94	2.14
Pioneer Drilling Company	Energy	8.0	-25.93	2.10
McCormick & Schmicks Sea	Consumer	26.7	6.61	1.85
Fuel Tech, Inc.	Business	80.6	171.67	1.68
Smith & Wesson Holding C	Ind Mtrls	46.3	163.10	1.61
⊕ American Physicians Capi	Financial	13.4	31.16	1.59
RC2 Corporation	Goods	17.3	23.87	1.45
U.S. Global Investors, I	Financial	42.5	383.24	1.38
Verint Systems, Inc.	Software	—	-0.55	1.36
Air Methods Corp.	Health	18.1	61.39	1.34

Current Investment Style

Value Blnd Growth		Market Cap	%
	Large	Giant	0.0
	Mid	Large	0.0
	Small	Mid	1.4
		Small	30.0
		Micro	68.6
		Avg $mil: 413	

Value Measures		Rel Category
Price/Earnings	17.52	0.83
Price/Book	2.89	1.06
Price/Sales	0.84	0.54
Price/Cash Flow	6.69	0.69
Dividend Yield %	0.21	0.46

Growth Measures	%	Rel Category
Long-Term Erngs	18.39	1.04
Book Value	11.73	1.12
Sales	14.12	1.19
Cash Flow	28.96	1.37
Historical Erngs	37.00	1.52

Profitability	%	Rel Category
Return on Equity	19.01	1.53
Return on Assets	12.32	1.85
Net Margin	10.41	1.20

Sector Weightings	% of Stocks	Rel S&P 500	3 Year High	Low
Info	19.00	0.95		
Software	8.71	2.52	15	8
Hardware	9.53	1.03	19	10
Media	0.38	0.10	1	0
Telecom	0.38	0.11	1	0
Service	38.62	0.84		
Health	7.76	0.64	20	8
Consumer	9.53	1.25	10	4
Business	13.82	3.27	15	11
Financial	7.51	0.34	8	3
Mfg	42.38	1.25		
Goods	9.66	1.13	13	7
Ind Mtrls	27.17	2.28	27	15
Energy	5.55	0.57	7	1
Utilities	0.00	0.00	0	0

Composition

		%
●	Cash	0.0
●	Stocks	100.0
●	Bonds	0.0
○	Other	0.0
	Foreign	1.6
	(% of Stock)	

BlackRock Global Alloc A

Analyst Pick ✓

	Ticker	Load	NAV	Yield	Total Assets	Mstar Category
	MDLOX	5.25%	$18.16	1.9%	$16,649 mil	World Allocation

Governance and Management

Stewardship Grade: C

Portfolio Manager(s)

Dennis Stattman has been at the helm since the fund's 1989 inception, making him one of the category's longest-serving managers. Veteran analyst Dan Chamby became associate manager in 2004. They are supported by longtime analysts Karene Morley Wescott, James Wei, Catherine Brady Rauscher, and Lisa O'Donnell. The team also added a quantitative analyst in 2004.

Strategy

The fund invests in out-of-favor stocks and bonds that its managers think will rebound. For example, it loaded up on emerging-markets bonds in 1998 when few others would touch them. And in 2002 it moved into equities (particularly technology stocks) and corporate bonds when the near-term outlook for them was bleak. The portfolio's broad diversification takes the edge off its contrarian bent. It owns hundreds of securities, which limits the effects of individual blowups.

Performance 12-31-06

	1st Qtr	2nd Qtr	3rd Qtr	4th Qtr	Total
2002	3.43	-5.65	-14.26	10.00	-7.96
2003	-1.93	18.05	5.57	11.25	35.98
2004	3.34	0.13	0.98	9.37	14.27
2005	0.67	0.60	6.32	2.47	10.33
2006	6.16	0.45	2.66	5.92	15.94

Trailing	Total Return%	+/- DJ Mod	+/- MSCI World	%Rank Cat	Growth of $10,000
3 Mo	5.92	0.33	-2.45	52	10,592
6 Mo	8.73	-0.06	-4.48	67	10,873
1 Yr	15.94	3.64	-4.13	54	11,594
3 Yr Avg	13.49	2.77	-1.19	50	14,617
5 Yr Avg	12.84	2.82	2.87	41	18,294
10 Yr Avg	11.17	2.62	3.53	28	28,832
15 Yr Avg	—	—	—	—	—

Tax Analysis	Tax-Adj Rtn%	%Rank Cat	Tax-Cost Rat	%Rank Cat
3 Yr (estimated)	9.79	69	1.51	72
5 Yr (estimated)	10.05	61	1.42	82
10 Yr (estimated)	7.92	48	2.40	95

Potential Capital Gain Exposure: 19% of assets

Historical Profile

Return	Average
Risk	Average
Rating	★★★★ Above Avg

| 44% | 53% | 48% | 47% | 18% | 60% | 62% | 56% | 52% |

Growth of $10,000
- ■ Investment Values of Fund
- — Investment Values of DJ Mod

▼ Manager Change
▽ Partial Manager Change

Performance Quartile (within Category)

	1995	1996	1997	1998	1999	2000	2001	2002	2003	2004	2005	2006	History
NAV	13.87	14.54	14.13	12.60	14.01	13.10	12.83	11.41	14.97	16.47	16.89	18.16	NAV
	23.29	15.96	11.12	0.37	27.75	8.57	1.88	-7.96	35.98	14.27	10.33	15.94	Total Return %
	3.49	5.30	-0.78	-11.95	10.42	10.24	4.68	-1.19	8.60	1.30	3.34	3.64	+/-DJ Mod
	2.57	2.48	-4.64	-23.95	2.80	21.76	18.68	11.93	2.87	-0.45	0.84	-4.13	+/-MSCI World
	6.25	6.20	7.54	3.74	7.02	2.52	3.88	3.15	4.45	2.90	2.18	2.26	Income Return %
	17.04	9.76	3.58	-3.37	20.73	6.05	-2.00	-11.11	31.53	11.37	8.15	13.68	Capital Return %
	25	18	55	87	4	36	28	78	10	50	20	54	Total Rtn % Rank Cat
	0.76	0.85	1.08	0.52	0.87	0.35	0.50	0.40	0.50	0.43	0.36	0.37	Income $
	0.43	0.65	0.94	1.05	1.13	1.69	0.01	0.00	0.00	0.18	0.92	0.98	Capital Gains $
	1.16	1.10	1.08	1.10	1.16	1.13	1.19	1.19	1.18	1.13	1.09	—	Expense Ratio %
	5.63	5.04	4.38	4.40	4.61	3.11	2.92	2.85	2.28	1.54	1.79	—	Income Ratio %
	37	51	55	50	27	54	45	58	45	43	49	—	Turnover Rate %
	304	1,091	1,454	1,269	1,275	1,441	2,053	2,034	2,586	3,818	4,741	6,137	Net Assets $mil

Investment Style
Equity
Stock %

Rating and Risk

Time Period	Load-Adj Return %	Morningstar Rtn vs Cat	Morningstar Risk vs Cat	Morningstar Risk-Adj Rating
1 Yr	9.86			
3 Yr	11.47	Avg	Avg	★★★
5 Yr	11.63	Avg	+Avg	★★★
10 Yr	10.57	Avg	Avg	★★★★
Incept	11.60			

Other Measures	Standard Index DJ Mod	Best Fit Index MSCI Wd xUS
Alpha	2.8	-0.1
Beta	0.97	0.62
R-Squared	85	93
Standard Deviation	6.19	
Mean	13.49	
Sharpe Ratio	1.57	

Portfolio Analysis 10-31-06

Total Stocks:474 Share change since 07-31-06	Sectors	P/E Ratio	YTD Return %	% Net Assets
⊖ General Electric Company	Ind Mtrls	20.0	0.91	0.80
Reliance Industries Ltd	Ind Mtrls	—	—	0.78
⊖ American International Gr	Financial	17.0	-0.18	0.72
⊖ ExxonMobil Corporation	Energy	11.1	-5.19	0.72
⊖ Microsoft Corporation	Software	23.8	0.23	0.68
Foster Wheeler, Ltd.	Business	—	-8.43	0.59
⊕ Millea Hldgs	Financial	—	—	0.57
⊕ Vodafone Grp	Telecom	—	—	0.51
⊕ HSBC Hldgs	Financial	—	—	0.51

Total Fixed-Income:83	Date of Maturity	Amount $000	Value $000	% Net Assets
US Treasury Note	01-15-16	558,800	557,664	3.33
US Treasury Note 2.375%	04-15-11	521,500	532,823	3.18
US Treasury Note 4.875%	05-31-11	269,425	272,709	1.63
US Treasury Note 0.875%	04-15-10	259,875	263,560	1.57
US Treasury Note 2.5%	07-15-16	230,250	235,797	1.41
US TREASURY NOTE	07-15-15	233,574	235,739	1.41
Germany(Fed Rep) 4%	07-04-16	176,500	229,994	1.37
US Treasury Note 4.25%	11-15-14	178,500	174,365	1.04

Current Investment Style

Value Blnd Growth — Large / Mid / Small

Market Cap	%
Giant	45.9
Large	35.5
Mid	14.4
Small	3.8
Micro	0.3

Avg $mil: 23,894

Value Measures		Rel Category
Price/Earnings	13.85	0.91
Price/Book	1.84	0.81
Price/Sales	1.25	0.96
Price/Cash Flow	7.06	0.92
Dividend Yield %	2.57	0.88

Growth Measures	%	Rel Category
Long-Term Erngs	10.75	0.94
Book Value	9.05	1.09
Sales	-12.47	NMF
Cash Flow	5.10	0.77
Historical Erngs	18.94	1.10

Composition

Cash	6.4	Bonds	27.3
Stocks	52.5	Other	13.8
Foreign (% of Stock)			58.8

Sector Weightings	% of Stocks	Rel DJ Mod	3 Year High	Low
☎ Info	18.20	—		
🖥 Software	2.75	—	5	3
Hardware	4.43	—	5	4
Media	1.93	—	2	1
Telecom	9.09	—	9	6
☞ Service	42.64			
Health	7.43	—	9	6
Consumer	3.40	—	5	3
Business	7.00	—	9	4
Financial	24.81	—	26	22
✋ Mfg	39.17			
Goods	9.12	—	11	8
Ind Mtrls	13.62	—	17	13
Energy	11.96	—	16	12
Utilities	4.47	—	4	2

Regional Exposure % Stock

UK/W. Europe	21	N. America	44
Japan	14	Latn America	3
Asia X Japan	18	Other	0

Country Exposure % Stock

United States	41	India	4
Japan	14	South Korea	4
U.K.	7		

Morningstar's Take by Arijit Dutta 12-26-06

Even in an unremarkable year for BlackRock Global Allocation, we continue to see signs of sound management.

After a strong start to 2006, this fund has slowed down in recent months. The stock portfolio's 14% stake in Japan (almost twice the world-allocation category average) was one of its star performers in 2005 and helped out this year as well until May, but it has struggled bad since. Also, the portfolio's significant energy overweight has caused problems over the past month or so, as oil prices have turned sharply lower. Moreover, the dollar's weakness has hurt the U.S.-heavy bond portfolio. As a result of these setbacks, the fund has fallen back to the category's middle for the year to date.

Veteran lead manager Dennis Stattman is taking things in stride, however. Stattman isn't one to make sudden moves (the portfolio's turnover is almost half the category average); he took his time building the portfolio's positions in energy and Japan as he became convinced of their long-term

merit. He still thinks Japanese stocks have robust earnings prospects, so he has bought more on weakness. Stattman is more circumspect in energy due to the sector's massive gains in recent years, so he has been taking profits and has avoided especially volatile commodities like natural gas (which has benefited the fund this year). Yet, he sees enough long-term demand for energy (while supplies remain tight) to not make big changes in the portfolio's energy weight. Stattman also continues to find relatively more value in the U.S. bond market.

We appreciate Stattman's approach. He will make decisive bets, and the portfolio may court short-term volatility as a result. However, Stattman is valuation-conscious and doesn't get swayed by market sentiment. That style tempers losses and allows time for the portfolio's bolder positions to deliver their potential gains. The fund retains its appeal as a one-stop portfolio anchor.

Address:	P O Box 9011 Princeton NJ 08543 800-441-7762	Minimum Purchase:	$1000 Add: $50 IRA: $100
		Min Auto Inv Plan:	$1000 Add: $50
		Sales Fees:	5.25%L, 0.25%S, 2.00%R
Web Address:	www.mlim.ml.com	Management Fee:	0.75%
Inception:	10-21-94	Actual Fees:	Mgt:0.75% Dist:0.25%
Advisor:	Blackrock Investment Management LLC	Expense Projections:	3Yr:$877 5Yr:$1135 10Yr:$1871
Subadvisor:	Blackrock Asset Management Uk Limited	Income Distrib:	Annually
NTF Plans:	DATALynx NTF, Federated Tr NTF		

MORNINGSTAR® Funds 500

Bogle Small Cap Gr Inv

Analyst Pick ✓

	Ticker	Load	NAV	Yield	Total Assets	Mstar Category
	BOGLX	Closed	$24.48	0.0%	$359 mil	Small Blend

Governance and Management

Stewardship Grade: B

Portfolio Manager(s)

John Bogle Jr. has run this fund since its 1999 inception, when he set up his own firm. Previously, he worked at Numeric Investors for nearly a decade and built a strong record running N/I Numeric Investors Emerging Growth from June 1996 until February 1999. He's assisted here by director of research Keith Hartt (a six-year Fidelity veteran) and a staff of three analysts.

Strategy

Manager John Bogle Jr. typically looks for stocks within the market-cap range of its benchmark, the Russell 2000 Index. He normally keeps the fund's sector weightings close to those of the index, attempting to beat it through stock selection. (But he has lately made modest sector bets.) He employs a series of quantitative screens that focus on factors such as upward earnings-estimate revisions, straightforward accounting, and relatively low price/sales ratios. Portfolio turnover is a bit higher than the small-blend norm.

Historical Profile

Return	Above Avg
Risk	Above Avg
Rating	★★★★ Above Avg

Investment Style: Equity, Stock %

87% 97% 99% 99% 99% 100% 100% 100%

▼ Manager Change
▽ Partial Manager Change

Growth of $10,000
■ Investment Values of Fund
— Investment Values of S&P 500

32.0 / 27.0 / 20.0 / 15.0 / 10.0 / 6.0

Performance Quartile (within Category)

	1995	1996	1997	1998	1999	2000	2001	2002	2003	2004	2005	2006	History
	—	—	—	—	15.61	19.13	20.10	16.57	26.29	26.33	26.44	24.48	NAV
	—	—	—	—	30.08*	26.83	5.07	-17.56	58.66	10.78	17.26	15.29	Total Return %
	—	—	—	—	—	35.93	16.96	4.54	29.98	-0.10	12.35	-0.50	+/-S&P 500
	—	—	—	—	—	29.85	2.58	2.92	11.41	-7.55	12.71	-3.08	+/-Russ 2000
	—	—	—	—	—	0.00	0.00	0.00	0.00	0.00	0.00	0.00	Income Return %
	—	—	—	—	—	26.83	5.07	-17.56	58.66	10.78	17.26	15.29	Capital Return %
	—	—	—	—	—	10	60	61	6	94	3	46	Total Rtn % Rank Cat
	—	—	—	—	0.00	0.00	0.00	0.00	0.00	0.00	0.00	0.00	Income $
	—	—	—	—	0.00	0.66	0.00	0.00	0.00	2.48	3.96	5.79	Capital Gains $
	—	—	—	—	—	1.35	1.35	1.27	1.35	1.35	1.35	1.35	Expense Ratio %
	—	—	—	—	—	-0.68	-0.46	-0.20	-0.69	-0.70	-0.83	-0.65	Income Ratio %
	—	—	—	—	—	94	126	140	122	129	129	127	Turnover Rate %
	—	—	—	—	6	27	69	81	133	139	144	157	Net Assets $mil

Performance 12-31-06

	1st Qtr	2nd Qtr	3rd Qtr	4th Qtr	Total
2002	6.72	-5.41	-18.93	0.73	-17.56
2003	-3.20	24.31	12.49	17.21	58.66
2004	5.52	-1.23	-3.36	9.98	10.78
2005	-2.70	4.45	9.49	5.37	17.26
2006	15.62	-6.31	-2.34	8.98	15.29

Trailing	Total Return%	+/- S&P 500	+/- Russ 2000	%Rank Cat	Growth of $10,000
3 Mo	8.98	2.28	0.08	23	10,898
6 Mo	6.43	-6.31	-2.95	66	10,643
1 Yr	15.29	-0.50	-3.08	46	11,529
3 Yr Avg	14.41	3.97	0.85	32	14,976
5 Yr Avg	14.39	8.20	3.00	20	19,586
10 Yr Avg	—	—	—	—	—
15 Yr Avg	—	—	—	—	—

Tax Analysis	Tax-Adj Rtn%	%Rank Cat	Tax-Cost Rat	%Rank Cat
3 Yr (estimated)	11.07	56	2.92	86
5 Yr (estimated)	12.38	25	1.76	77
10 Yr (estimated)	—	—	—	—

Potential Capital Gain Exposure: 14% of assets

Rating and Risk

Time Period	Load-Adj Return %	Morningstar Rtn vs Cat	Morningstar Risk vs Cat	Morningstar Risk-Adj Rating
1 Yr	15.29			
3 Yr	14.41	+Avg	High	★★★
5 Yr	14.39	+Avg	+Avg	★★★★
10 Yr	—			
Incept	18.36			

Other Measures	Standard Index S&P 500	Best Fit Index Russ 2000 Gr
Alpha	-1.3	4.1
Beta	1.82	0.91
R-Squared	68	90

Standard Deviation	15.20
Mean	14.41
Sharpe Ratio	0.75

Morningstar's Take by Greg Carlson 12-19-06

Does Bogle Small Cap Growth's subpar 2006 indicate the small-value rally is finally nearing an end?

This closed small-blend fund's strategy is straightforward. It aims to beat the Russell 2000 Index through stock selection, and its sector bets against the benchmark are rather limited. To achieve this goal, manager John Bogle Jr. and his team use a series of quantitative models to identify companies with upward earnings-estimate revisions, improving earnings quality, and modest valuations. But while the fund has handily beaten the index since its 1999 inception, it's 3.5 percentage points behind in 2006.

This isn't the first year the fund has lagged its bogy, but the way it has underperformed is perhaps telling. Typically, when the trend-following models aren't clicking--as has been the case for the past six months--the fund's valuation measures keep it on an even keel. However, in 2006, even as companies with the biggest earnings-estimate revisions have

lagged--reflective of value stocks' leadership this year--those with lower price multiples haven't especially stood out. That's likely due to the fact that the same value-oriented sectors that have rallied for years--REITs, energy, and utilities--have continued to lead the market, and due to their relatively lofty valuations, this fund has been underweighted in those areas compared with the index. Given their seeming lack of a valuation edge, as well as their slower profit growth, it's fair to wonder whether small-value stocks will soon cool after a seven-year run.

When the shift in leadership to growth stocks occurs, this fund may perform even better than it has in the past. Bogle and company believe their models work best with growth stocks; thus the fund has often held bigger stakes in tech and health care than its typical rival or the index. And, timing aside, this fund's other traits--a veteran team, modest asset base, and shareholder-friendly policies--make it a fine holding.

Portfolio Analysis 12-31-06

Share change since 11-06 Total Stocks:174

	Sector	PE	Tot Ret%	% Assets
⊖ Jack In The Box, Inc.	Consumer	19.8	74.75	1.16
NBTY, Inc.	Health	27.0	155.82	1.07
⊖ Interactive Intelligence	Software	37.0	340.24	0.96
⊖ Zoll Medical Corporation	Health	74.1	131.20	0.95
Arch Capital Group, Lto.	Financial	18.2	23.49	0.93
⊕ The Phoenix Companies, I	Financial	15.3	17.87	0.90
⊕ Wimm Bill Dann Foods ADR	Goods	93.0	180.79	0.90
Steven Madden	Goods	17.6	84.89	0.89
Dade Behring Holdings, I	Health	26.3	-2.13	0.88
⊕ Argonaut Group, Inc.	Financial	14.7	6.38	0.88
⊕ Zenith National Insuranc	Financial	7.4	4.36	0.85
⊕ SWS Group, Inc.	Financial	20.1	81.12	0.85
⊕ CorVel Corporation	Financial	53.6	275.75	0.85
Platinum Underwriters Ho	Financial	21.1	0.68	0.85
Reinsurance Group of Ame	Financial	12.5	17.46	0.84
ICT Group, Inc.	Business	26.7	86.37	0.84
Robbins & Myers, Inc.	Ind Mtrls	—	127.64	0.84
⊕ Odyssey Re Holdings Corp	Financial	7.9	49.39	0.84
⊕ IntercontinentalExchange	Financial	—	—	0.83
⊖ Core Laboratories N.V.	Energy	33.5	116.81	0.82

Current Investment Style

Value Blnd Growth — Large Mid Small

Market Cap	%
Giant	0.0
Large	0.0
Mid	23.1
Small	50.1
Micro	26.8

Avg $mil: 967

Value Measures		Rel Category
Price/Earnings	17.10	1.03
Price/Book	2.40	1.14
Price/Sales	1.12	1.14
Price/Cash Flow	5.05	0.72
Dividend Yield %	0.34	0.32

Growth Measures	%	Rel Category
Long-Term Erngs	15.87	1.14
Book Value	3.55	0.47
Sales	8.20	0.93
Cash Flow	15.88	1.25
Historical Erngs	15.52	0.93

Profitability	%	Rel Category
Return on Equity	12.93	1.00
Return on Assets	8.27	1.16
Net Margin	8.19	0.85

Sector Weightings

	% of Stocks	Rel S&P 500	3 Year High	Low
↻ Info	25.92	1.30		
🖥 Software	9.44	2.74	12	4
💻 Hardware	13.44	1.45	18	8
📶 Media	1.66	0.44	2	0
☎ Telecom	1.38	0.39	5	1
⊂ Service	54.60	1.18		
🏥 Health	13.24	1.10	17	9
🛒 Consumer	8.66	1.13	14	9
🏢 Business	13.82	3.27	15	8
💲 Financial	18.88	0.85	19	16
↥ Mfg	19.48	0.58		
🏠 Goods	8.35	0.98	8	3
🔧 Ind Mtrls	8.68	0.73	21	8
⬢ Energy	2.45	0.25	6	2
⚡ Utilities	0.00	0.00	1	0

Composition

● Cash	0.0
● Stocks	100.0
● Bonds	0.0
○ Other	0.0
Foreign	8.8
(% of Stock)	

Address:	57 River Street, Suite 206 Wellesley MA 02481 877-264-5346	
Web Address:	www.boglefunds.com	
Inception:	09-30-99*	
Advisor:	Bogle Investment Management, LP	
Subadvisor:	None	
NTF Plans:	N/A	

Minimum Purchase:	Closed	Add: —	IRA: —
Min Auto Inv Plan:	Closed	Add: —	
Sales Fees:	No-load		
Management Fee:	1.00%		
Actual Fees:	Mgt:1.00%	Dist: —	
Expense Projections:	3Yr:$472	5Yr:$830	10Yr:$1839
Income Distrib:	Annually		

Brandywine

	Analyst Pick	Ticker BRWIX	Load None	NAV $34.29	Yield 0.0%	Total Assets $4,230 mil	Mstar Category Mid-Cap Growth

Governance and Management

Stewardship Grade: A

Portfolio Manager(s)

Bill D'Alonzo, fund family CEO and manager since inception, has the lead portfolio manager role. D'Alonzo also steers the larger-cap Brandywine Blue, as well as Brandywine Advisors, another mid-cap offering. In addition, roughly 30 analysts conduct stock-specific research for this portfolio. Fund family founder Foster Friess is the fund's largest shareholder, while D'Alonzo has all of his investments in Brandywine Funds.

Strategy

Brandywine is always on the hunt for companies it expects will beat Wall Street's expectations in the near term. The management team considers only profitable companies that are trading at reasonable P/Es. It doesn't stick with them for long, though, quickly selling when a firm's valuation heats up or better opportunities come up. As a result of its rapid-fire approach, the fund generally has a high turnover ratio. Investing purely based on company-by-company considerations, the portfolio can become heavily skewed toward just a couple of sectors.

Performance 12-31-06

	1st Qtr	2nd Qtr	3rd Qtr	4th Qtr	Total
2002	-1.93	-3.93	-13.27	-4.19	-21.71
2003	-1.48	15.82	2.11	12.82	31.46
2004	4.41	-2.15	-1.47	12.36	13.11
2005	1.07	2.73	11.62	-1.30	14.39
2006	9.30	-5.24	0.22	7.02	11.09

Trailing	Total Return%	+/- S&P 500	+/- Russ MG	%Rank Cat	Growth of $10,000
3 Mo	7.02	0.32	0.07	47	10,702
6 Mo	7.26	-5.48	-0.64	32	10,726
1 Yr	11.09	-4.70	0.43	33	11,109
3 Yr Avg	12.85	2.41	0.12	26	14,372
5 Yr Avg	8.14	1.95	-0.08	29	14,789
10 Yr Avg	7.96	-0.46	-0.66	57	21,509
15 Yr Avg	11.58	0.94	1.45	21	51,736

Tax Analysis	Tax-Adj Rtn%	%Rank Cat	Tax-Cost Rat	%Rank Cat
3 Yr (estimated)	12.81	16	0.04	3
5 Yr (estimated)	8.12	22	0.02	2
10 Yr (estimated)	6.03	59	1.79	70

Potential Capital Gain Exposure: 16% of assets

Morningstar's Take by Karen Dolan 12-10-06

Brandywine's process is unmatched.

Competition is fierce in the mutual fund universe, so funds need a sustainable edge that is repeatable. We think this fund has one. Its main advantage comes from how the work of its researchers, traders, writers, quantitative analysts, and senior leaders is intertwined.

For example, 30 researchers spend all of their time talking to firms' suppliers, customers, competitors, and industry pundits. Each researcher looks for stocks that are on a better earnings trajectory than Wall Street suspects. Because they are looking for earnings surprises that are going to happen soon, speed is critical. That's where Brandywine's trading desk steps in. In management's eyes, the traders are in the best position to assess liquidity and position sizes. That allows researchers to quickly refocus their attention to existing holdings or new ideas.

A team of writers keeps it all connected. The writing team relays messages from researchers who are on the road to those in the office. This team also helps coordinate the fund's outstanding quarterly shareholder reports and newsletters. We applaud management's devotion to making sure that fund shareholders are informed

Not only has this system led to peer-beating long-term returns, but investors have bought and sold the fund well. Morningstar recently started calculating investor returns, which measure how the typical investor fared considering the impact of cash flows. If investors bought a fund after big gains and sold at weak points, investor returns would be lower than the fund's total returns. Brandywine's investor returns are actually higher than its total returns for the five- and 10-year periods. Its 10-year showing likely has to do with the fund's poor relative results in 1997 and 1998, which kept some hot money out, but we think it also owes to the fund's candid and clear communication. This fund's edge is deeply embedded in its standout process.

Address:	3908 Kennett Pike Greenville DE 19807 800-656-3017
Web Address:	www.brandywinefunds.com
Inception:	12-12-85
Advisor:	Friess Associates
Subadvisor:	Friess Associates of Delaware, LLC
NTF Plans:	N/A

Minimum Purchase:	$10000	Add: $1000	IRA: $10000
Min Auto Inv Plan:	$0	Add: —	
Sales Fees:	No-load		
Management Fee:	1.00%		
Actual Fees:	Mgt:1.00%	Dist: —	
Expense Projections:	3Yr:$343	5Yr:$595	10Yr:$1317
Income Distrib:	Annually		

Historical Profile

Return	Above Avg
Risk	Below Avg
Rating	★★★★ Above Avg

Investment Style: Equity Stock %

95% 95% 91% 96% 97% 98% 97% 97% 98%

▼ Manager Change
▽ Partial Manager Change

Growth of $10,000
— Investment Values of Fund
— Investment Values of S&P 500

Performance Quartile (within Category)

1995	1996	1997	1998	1999	2000	2001	2002	2003	2004	2005	2006	History
28.08	33.69	30.89	30.28	42.88	29.39	23.35	18.28	24.03	27.18	31.09	34.29	NAV
35.75	24.92	12.02	-0.65	53.50	7.10	-20.55	-21.71	31.46	13.11	14.39	11.09	Total Return %
-1.83	1.96	-21.34	-29.23	32.46	16.20	-8.66	0.39	2.78	2.23	9.48	-4.70	+/-S&P 500
1.77	7.44	-10.52	-18.51	2.21	18.85	-0.40	5.70	-11.25	-2.37	2.29	0.43	+/-Russ MG
0.00	0.00	0.00	0.86	0.00	0.00	0.00	0.00	0.00	0.00	0.00	0.00	Income Return %
35.75	24.92	12.02	-1.51	53.50	7.10	-20.55	-21.71	31.46	13.11	14.39	11.09	Capital Return %
38	10	85	92	48	32	60	31	74	56	18	33	Total Rtn % Rank Cat
0.00	0.00	0.00	0.26	0.00	0.00	0.00	0.00	0.00	0.00	0.00	0.00	Income $
3.84	1.35	7.02	0.07	3.12	16.11	0.00	0.00	0.00	0.00	0.00	0.25	Capital Gains $
1.07	1.06	1.04	1.04	1.05	1.04	1.06	1.08	1.09	1.08	1.08	1.08	Expense Ratio %
-0.40	-0.40	-0.30	0.60	-0.70	-0.60	-0.30	-0.50	-0.53	-0.55	-0.25	-0.31	Income Ratio %
194	203	192	264	209	244	284	273	279	247	183	200	Turnover Rate %
4,210	6,547	8,414	4,890	5,515	5,771	4,265	2,997	3,796	3,731	3,954	4,230	Net Assets $mil

Rating and Risk

Time Period	Load-Adj Return %	Morningstar Rtn vs Cat	Morningstar Risk vs Cat	Morningstar Risk-Adj Rating
1 Yr	11.09			
3 Yr	12.85	+Avg	Avg	★★★★
5 Yr	8.14	+Avg	-Avg	★★★★
10 Yr	7.96	Avg	-Avg	★★★
Incept	13.54			

Other Measures	Standard Index S&P 500	Best Fit Index Mstar Small Core
Alpha	-1.4	-2.2
Beta	1.60	0.91
R-Squared	73	86
Standard Deviation	12.86	
Mean	12.85	
Sharpe Ratio	0.76	

Portfolio Analysis 09-30-06

Share change since 06-06 Total Stocks:106	Sector	PE	Tot Ret%	% Assets
Hewlett-Packard Company	Hardware	19.3	45.21	4.52
⊕ Fisher Scientific Intern	Health	—	—	4.25
⊖ Kohl's Corporation	Consumer	22.6	40.80	4.20
Precision Castparts Corp	Ind Mtrls	25.4	51.40	4.19
Weatherford Internationa	Energy	15.2	16.56	4.16
✿ TJX Companies	Consumer	16.9	24.05	4.03
⊕ Comcast Corporation A	Media	45.2	63.31	3.99
⊕ Baker Hughes Inc.	Energy	9.9	23.68	3.42
✿ Best Buy Co., Inc.	Consumer	19.8	13.89	2.89
Harris Corporation	Hardware	24.8	7.57	2.85
⊕ Rockwell Collins, Inc.	Ind Mtrls	23.7	37.70	2.75
✿ Phelps Dodge Corp.	Ind Mtrls	12.7	76.29	2.70
✿ Allegheny Technologies C	Ind Mtrls	17.1	152.95	2.42
✿ Baxter International Inc	Health	24.3	24.81	2.32
Davita, Inc.	Health	21.1	12.32	2.13
✿ Frontline, Ltd.	Business	3.9	7.02	2.00
⊕ Flextronics Internationa	Hardware	45.1	9.96	1.97
✿ St. Jude Medical, Inc.	Health	34.9	-27.17	1.83
✿ NVIDIA Corporation	Hardware	33.4	102.46	1.83
⊕ McDermott International	Energy	23.4	71.02	1.78

Current Investment Style

Value Blnd Growth — Large Mid Small

Market Cap	%
Giant	8.7
Large	28.2
Mid	53.1
Small	10.0
Micro	0.0

Avg $mil: 8,180

Value Measures		Rel Category
Price/Earnings	16.82	0.82
Price/Book	2.92	0.91
Price/Sales	1.24	0.70
Price/Cash Flow	11.04	0.97
Dividend Yield %	1.24	1.97

Growth Measures	%	Rel Category
Long-Term Erngs	17.82	1.10
Book Value	9.45	0.74
Sales	8.46	0.85
Cash Flow	15.70	0.85
Historical Erngs	22.71	0.91

Profitability	%	Rel Category
Return on Equity	21.29	1.19
Return on Assets	8.74	0.93
Net Margin	9.78	0.84

Sector Weightings	% of Stocks	Rel S&P 500	3 Year High Low	
⊙ Info	23.87	1.19		
▨ Software	2.31	0.67	9	0
▦ Hardware	17.48	1.89	27	8
▥ Media	4.08	1.08	4	0
▤ Telecom	0.00	0.00	3	0
⊈ Service	43.48	0.94		
▨ Health	18.53	1.54	19	5
▤ Consumer	13.68	1.79	17	9
▣ Business	10.75	2.54	17	5
$ Financial	0.52	0.02	20	1
▱ Mfg	32.65	0.97		
▨ Goods	3.34	0.39	8	1
▨ Ind Mtrls	18.12	1.52	28	7
▨ Energy	11.19	1.14	21	2
▨ Utilities	0.00	0.00	0	0

Composition

●	Cash	2.1
●	Stocks	97.8
●	Bonds	0.0
●	Other	0.0
	Foreign	6.2
	(% of Stock)	

MORNINGSTAR® Funds 500

Brandywine Blue

	Ticker	Load	NAV	Yield	Total Assets	Mstar Category
	BLUEX	None	$31.70	0.0%	$2,131 mil	Large Growth

Governance and Management

Stewardship Grade: A

Portfolio Manager(s)

Fund family founder and chairman Foster Friess is no longer involved with the day-to-day portfolio-management process. Bill D'Alonzo, who is also the fund shop's CEO, has been leading the team of analysts here since the fund's 1991 inception. D'Alonzo and team also steer the fund's more famous sibling, Brandywine Fund, as well as Brandywine Advisors. Both D'Alonzo and Friess have substantial investments in all three Brandywine funds.

Strategy

The same team that runs Brandywine Fund uses an identical approach here, but this fund focuses on larger names and tends to own fewer holdings (typically around 35 stocks). The team looks for companies whose earnings are increasing rapidly (preferably in the 20% to 30% range annually), but it also requires that a company have three years of earnings history, $3 million in aftertax income, and a reasonable P/E ratio. Because its investments are based on company-specific considerations, the portfolio can become skewed toward just a couple of sectors. Management also trades frequently.

Performance 12-31-06

	1st Qtr	2nd Qtr	3rd Qtr	4th Qtr	Total
2002	-2.54	-0.24	-11.55	0.60	-13.49
2003	-1.36	15.64	1.90	11.31	29.39
2004	6.97	-1.18	0.12	12.69	19.27
2005	-2.50	3.83	8.97	-1.74	8.39
2006	7.57	-4.31	2.30	5.30	10.89

Trailing	Total Return%	+/- S&P 500	+/- Russ 1000Gr	%Rank Cat	Growth of $10,000
3 Mo	5.30	-1.40	-0.63	53	10,530
6 Mo	7.72	-5.02	-2.38	62	10,772
1 Yr	10.89	-4.90	1.82	17	11,089
3 Yr Avg	12.76	2.32	5.89	4	14,337
5 Yr Avg	9.92	3.73	7.23	1	16,047
10 Yr Avg	8.84	0.42	3.40	9	23,328
15 Yr Avg	12.17	1.53	4.15	7	55,995

Tax Analysis	Tax-Adj Rtn%	%Rank Cat	Tax-Cost Rat	%Rank Cat
3 Yr (estimated)	12.05	4	0.63	42
5 Yr (estimated)	9.51	1	0.37	38
10 Yr (estimated)	7.09	15	1.61	80

Potential Capital Gain Exposure: 13% of assets

Historical Profile
Return High
Risk Average
Rating ★★★★ Highest

Investment Style: Equity Stock %

94% 93% 95% 93% 96% 94% 94% 98% 96%

▼ Manager Change
▽ Partial Manager Change

Growth of $10,000
— Investment Values of Fund
— Investment Values of S&P 500

33.0
26.0
20.0
15.0
10.0

Performance Quartile (within Category)

1995	1996	1997	1998	1999	2000	2001	2002	2003	2004	2005	2006	History
21.48	26.47	26.58	25.91	36.24	27.57	21.28	18.41	23.82	28.41	29.58	31.70	NAV
32.33	23.23	19.25	-0.98	49.36	6.81	-22.81	-13.49	29.39	19.27	8.39	10.89	Total Return %
-5.25	0.27	-14.11	-29.56	28.32	15.91	-10.92	8.61	0.71	8.39	3.48	-4.90	+/-S&P 500
-4.85	0.11	-11.24	-39.69	16.20	29.23	-2.39	14.39	-0.36	12.97	3.13	1.82	+/-Russ 1000Gr
0.00	0.00	0.00	0.77	0.00	0.00	0.00	0.00	0.00	0.00	0.00	0.00	Income Return %
32.33	23.23	19.25	-1.75	49.36	6.81	-22.81	-13.49	29.39	19.27	8.39	10.89	Capital Return %
49	22	80	99	23	6	63	3	42	1	31	17	Total Rtn % Rank Cat
0.00	0.00	0.00	0.20	0.00	0.00	0.00	0.00	0.00	0.00	0.00	0.00	Income $
1.11	0.00	5.09	0.13	2.18	10.71	0.00	0.00	0.00	0.00	1.14	1.10	Capital Gains $
1.31	1.13	1.08	1.06	1.08	1.04	1.09	1.13	1.14	1.13	1.12	—	Expense Ratio %
-0.44	-0.40	-0.50	0.60	-0.70	-0.60	-0.20	-0.30	-0.41	-0.32	-0.13	—	Income Ratio %
174	197	202	300	228	246	275	311	300	247	181	—	Turnover Rate %
190	383	590	357	399	388	257	240	379	663	1,352	2,131	Net Assets $mil

Rating and Risk

Time Period	Load-Adj Return %	Morningstar Rtn vs Cat	Morningstar Risk vs Cat	Morningstar Risk-Adj Rating
1 Yr	10.89			
3 Yr	12.76	High	+Avg	★★★★★
5 Yr	9.92	High	-Avg	★★★★★
10 Yr	8.84	+Avg	Avg	★★★★
Incept	13.76			

Other Measures	Standard Index S&P 500	Best Fit Index Mstar Small Value
Alpha	-0.6	-2.1
Beta	1.45	0.93
R-Squared	71	88
Standard Deviation	11.78	
Mean	12.76	
Sharpe Ratio	0.81	

Portfolio Analysis 09-30-06

Share change since 06-06 Total Stocks:38	Sector	PE	Tot Ret%	% Assets
⊕ Comcast Corporation A	Media	45.2	63.31	4.85
⊕ Hewlett-Packard Company	Hardware	19.3	45.21	4.69
✷ TJX Companies	Consumer	16.9	24.05	4.41
⊕ Fisher Scientific Intern	Health	—	—	4.39
✷ Best Buy Co., Inc.	Consumer	19.8	13.89	3.89
⊕ General Dynamics	Ind Mtrls	19.1	32.17	3.86
⊕ Rockwell Collins, Inc.	Ind Mtrls	23.7	37.70	3.53
⊕ Bank of New York Company	Financial	18.9	26.85	3.27
⊕ Baker Hughes Inc.	Energy	9.9	23.68	3.21
⊕ Coach, Inc.	Goods	32.1	28.85	3.15
⊖ Weatherford Internationa	Energy	15.2	16.56	3.12
⊕ Exelon Corporation	Utilities		19.79	3.01
✷ NII Holdings, Inc.	Telecom	45.9	47.53	2.74
✷ Phelps Dodge Corp.	Ind Mtrls	12.7	76.29	2.65
✷ Emerson Electric Company	Ind Mtrls	19.6	20.68	2.62
⊕ Flextronics Internationa	Hardware	45.1	9.96	2.59
✷ Forest Laboratories, Inc	Health	22.5	24.39	2.52
⊖ Kohl's Corporation	Consumer	22.6	40.80	2.45
✷ Entergy Corporation	Utilities	19.7	38.40	2.37
⊕ Precision Castparts Corp	Ind Mtrls	25.4	51.40	2.30

Current Investment Style

Value Blnd Growth — Large Mid Small

Market Cap	%
Giant	13.7
Large	54.5
Mid	31.8
Small	0.0
Micro	0.0

Avg $mil: 19,077

Value Measures		Rel Category
Price/Earnings	18.50	0.96
Price/Book	3.35	1.01
Price/Sales	1.63	0.84
Price/Cash Flow	13.69	1.20
Dividend Yield %	0.77	0.75

Growth Measures	%	Rel Category
Long-Term Erngs	17.27	1.20
Book Value	9.27	0.80
Sales	9.78	0.84
Cash Flow	10.66	0.63
Historical Erngs	19.43	0.84

Profitability	%	Rel Category
Return on Equity	21.19	1.04
Return on Assets	10.06	0.91
Net Margin	10.27	0.72

Sector Weightings

	% of Stocks	Rel S&P 500	3 Year High Low
↻ Info	23.92	1.20	
Software	0.17	0.05	9 0
Hardware	13.51	1.46	20 8
Media	7.40	1.95	7 0
Telecom	2.84	0.81	4 0
⊂ Service	40.56	0.88	
Health	18.92	1.57	19 0
Consumer	15.12	1.98	26 11
Business	3.13	0.74	14 2
Financial	3.39	0.15	28 3
⊔ Mfg	35.51	1.05	
Goods	3.27	0.38	7 0
Ind Mtrls	20.10	1.68	31 6
Energy	6.57	0.67	19 0
Utilities	5.57	1.59	6 0

Composition

	%
● Cash	3.6
● Stocks	96.4
● Bonds	0.0
○ Other	0.0
Foreign (% of Stock)	2.7

Morningstar's Take by Karen Dolan 11-10-06

Brandywine Blue remains best of breed.

A lot of moving parts keep this fund going. A group of 30 researchers spend their time talking to firms' suppliers, customers, and competitors, as well as industry pundits. Each researcher looks for companies that are on a better earnings trajectory than Wall Street suspects. Because they are looking for earnings surprises that are going to take place in the near term, speed is critical.

That's where Brandywine's trading desk steps in. Researchers don't spend time worrying about liquidity or position sizes. In management's eyes, the traders are in the best position to assess a stock's liquidity and figure out how to build a full position. That allows researchers to quickly refocus their attention to existing holdings or new ideas.

Keeping it all connected is a team of writers. The writing team relays messages from researchers who are on the road to those in the office. This team also helps coordinate the fund's outstanding quarterly shareholder reports and newsletters. We

applaud management's devotion to making sure that fund shareholders are tuned in to what is happening.

This system has helped deliver strong returns for shareholders by several measures. Not only has the fund generated peer-beating long-term returns, but investors have bought and sold the fund well. Morningstar recently started calculating investor returns, which measure how the typical investor fared considering the impact of cash flows. If investors bought a fund after big gains and sold at weak points, investor returns would be lower than the fund's total returns. For the five- and 10-year periods, however, Brandywine Blue's investor returns are higher than its total returns. That shows that shareholders haven't been chasing past returns or fleeing during tough periods. This fund's candid and clear communication is a definite reason why and increases the chance that investors will continue to be successful.

This is a great choice.

Address:	P.O. Box 4166 Greenville DE 19807 800-656-3017	Minimum Purchase:	$10000	Add: $1000	IRA: $10000
		Min Auto Inv Plan:	$0	Add: —	
		Sales Fees:	No-load		
Web Address:	www.brandywinefunds.com	Management Fee:	1.00%		
Inception:	01-10-91	Actual Fees:	Mgt:1.00%	Dist: —	
Advisor:	Friess Associates	Expense Projections:	3Yr:$356	5Yr:$617	10Yr:$1363
Subadvisor:	Friess Associates of Delaware, LLC	Income Distrib:	Annually		
NTF Plans:	N/A				

Bridgeway Balanced

	Ticker	Load	NAV	Yield	Total Assets	Mstar Category
	BRBPX	None	$12.54	2.2%	$87 mil	Conservative Allocation

Governance and Management

Stewardship Grade: A

Portfolio Manager(s)

Richard Cancelmo, who is also Bridgeway's head of equity trading, has been at the helm since the fund's mid-2001 inception. His two decades in the investment industry include extensive options-trading experience and a stint from 1995 to 2000 managing the West University Fund (which trailed peers during the bull market because of its low-beta strategy).

Strategy

Manager Richard Cancelmo's chief goal is low volatility. He aims for a beta of no more than 0.40 relative to the S&P 500. At least 25% of assets is parked in high-quality bonds, mainly government issues; 30% is split between focused portfolios of growth and value stocks chosen by quantitative models; and the rest is in a basket of stocks meant to mimic the S&P 500. Cancelmo writes call or put options against most of the stocks in the growth and value portions and against a smaller percentage of stocks in the index portion.

Historical Profile

Return	Above Avg
Risk	Above Avg
Rating	★★★★ Above Avg

Investment Style: Equity Stock %

58% 57% 52% 54% 57%

▼ Manager Change
▽ Partial Manager Change

Growth of $10,000
— Investment Values of Fund
— Investment Values of DJ Mod

14.0 12.0 10.0 8.0

Performance Quartile (within Category)

1995	1996	1997	1998	1999	2000	2001	2002	2003	2004	2005	2006	History
—	—	—	—	—	—	9.72	9.31	10.92	11.57	12.16	12.54	NAV
—	—	—	—	—	—	-2.29*	-3.51	17.82	7.61	6.96	6.65	Total Return %
—	—	—	—	—	—	3.26	-9.56	-5.36	-0.03	-5.65	+/-DJ Mod
—	—	—	—	—	—	0.51	0.16	-1.40	2.27	-0.81	+/-DJ 40%
—	—	—	—	—	—	0.64	0.52	0.71	0.94	2.26	Income Return %
—	—	—	—	—	—	-4.15	17.30	6.90	6.02	4.39	Capital Return %
—	—	—	—	—	—	56	14	21	2	71	Total Rtn % Rank Cat
—	—	—	—	—	0.05	0.06	0.05	0.08	0.11	0.27	Income $
—	—	—	—	—	0.00	0.01	0.00	0.10	0.11	0.15	Capital Gains $
—	—	—	—	—	—	0.94	0.94	0.94	0.94	Expense Ratio %
—	—	—	—	—	—	0.49	1.06	0.60	1.81	Income Ratio %
—	—	—	—	—	—	18	98	124	50	Turnover Rate %
—	—	—	—	—	—	2	6	14	28	87	Net Assets $mil

Performance 12-31-06

	1st Qtr	2nd Qtr	3rd Qtr	4th Qtr	Total
2002	3.19	-1.60	-5.88	0.95	-3.51
2003	-0.32	8.30	2.59	6.39	17.82
2004	3.11	0.36	-0.80	4.83	7.61
2005	0.78	2.40	2.76	0.86	6.96
2006	2.88	1.12	0.40	2.12	6.65

Trailing	Total Return%	+/- DJ Mod	+/- DJ 40%	%Rank Cat	Growth of $10,000
3 Mo	2.12	-3.47	-0.92	91	10,212
6 Mo	2.52	-6.27	-4.04	98	10,252
1 Yr	6.65	-5.65	-0.81	71	10,665
3 Yr Avg	7.08	-3.64	0.04	23	12,278
5 Yr Avg	6.89	-3.13	0.16	14	13,954
10 Yr Avg	—	—	—	—	—
15 Yr Avg	—	—	—	—	—

Tax Analysis	Tax-Adj Rtn%	%Rank Cat	Tax-Cost Rat	%Rank Cat
3 Yr (estimated)	6.36	13	0.67	26
5 Yr (estimated)	6.37	8	0.49	7
10 Yr (estimated)	—		—	

Potential Capital Gain Exposure: 6% of assets

Rating and Risk

Time Period	Load-Adj Return %	Morningstar Rtn vs Cat	Morningstar Risk vs Cat	Morningstar Risk-Adj Rating
1 Yr	6.65			
3 Yr	7.08	+Avg	+Avg	★★★★
5 Yr	6.89	+Avg	+Avg	★★★★
10 Yr	—	—	—	—
Incept	5.79			

Other Measures	Standard Index DJ Mod	Best Fit Index Mstar Mid Growth TR
Alpha	-0.3	0.8
Beta	0.56	0.28
R-Squared	67	76
Standard Deviation	3.97	
Mean	7.08	
Sharpe Ratio	0.93	

Portfolio Analysis 09-30-06

Total Stocks:243 Share change since 06-30-06	Sectors	P/E Ratio	YTD Return %	% Net Assets
⊕ Bristol-Myers Squibb Comp	Health	23.1	0.22	2.06
⊕ Verizon Communications	Telecom	15.9	-0.07	1.50
⊕ Dress Barn, Inc.	Consumer	18.0	-4.93	1.36
⊕ McDermott International	Energy	23.4	-8.69	1.19
⊕ Washington Mutual, Inc.	Financial	13.4	-0.79	0.94
⊕ Bank of America Corporati	Financial	12.4	0.11	0.92
US Bancorp	Financial	13.9	-1.49	0.89
AT&T, Inc.	Telecom	18.2	-5.43	0.82
Archer Daniels Midland	Ind Mtrls	13.8	0.09	0.80

Total Fixed-Income:28	Date of Maturity	Amount $000	Value $000	% Net Assets
US Treasury Note 4.375%	01-31-08	3,000	2,982	3.40
US Treasury Note 5.125%	05-15-16	2,000	2,075	2.37
US Treasury Note 4.875%	04-30-11	2,000	2,022	2.31
US Treasury Note 4.25%	01-15-11	2,000	1,973	2.25
Leucadia Natl 7.75%	08-15-13	1,550	1,604	1.83
US Treasury Note 4.875%	07-31-11	1,000	1,012	1.15
US Treasury Note 4.75%	03-31-11	1,000	1,006	1.15
US Treasury Note 4.625%	03-31-08	1,000	998	1.14
US Treasury Note 4.5%	02-28-11	1,000	996	1.14

Equity Style

Style: Blend
Size: Large-Cap

Value Measures		Rel Category
Price/Earnings	14.95	0.99
Price/Book	2.59	1.07
Price/Sales	1.24	0.89
Price/Cash Flow	7.24	0.91
Dividend Yield %	1.53	0.71

Growth Measures	%	Rel Category
Long-Term Erngs	11.47	1.02
Book Value	8.89	1.12
Sales	9.67	1.09
Cash Flow	11.26	1.25
Historical Erngs	22.43	1.30

Market Cap %			
Giant	23.8	Small	4.7
Large	47.9	Micro	0.0
Mid	23.6	Avg $mil:	21,453

Fixed-Income Style

Duration: —
Quality: —

Avg Eff Duration [1]	—
Avg Eff Maturity	—
Avg Credit Quality	—
Avg Wtd Coupon	4.34%

[1]figure provided by fund

Sector Weightings	% of Stocks	Rel DJ Mod	3 Year High	Low
↻ Info	18.77	—		
🖥 Software	1.97	—	5	2
💻 Hardware	8.81	—	15	8
🎙 Media	2.95	—	4	2
📶 Telecom	5.04	—	8	4
⊆ Service	50.41			
🩺 Health	13.56	—	17	11
🛒 Consumer	11.07	—	11	7
📋 Business	4.37	—	5	3
💲 Financial	21.41	—	22	17
🏭 Mfg	30.82			
🔩 Goods	6.11	—	11	6
🏗 Ind Mtrls	13.13	—	15	10
🔥 Energy	8.87	—	9	5
💡 Utilities	2.71	—	3	2

Composition

- Cash 19.5
- Stocks 57.2
- Bonds 23.0
- Other 0.3
- Foreign 0.0 (% of Stock)

Morningstar's Take by Reginald Laing 12-13-06

Bridgeway Balanced's unique approach has merit.

Manager Dick Cancelmo aims for solid returns without taking on much risk. As with most Bridgeway offerings, this fund relies on the firm's quantitative models to seek out stocks displaying the factors management thinks are predictive of high returns.

Cancelmo won't necessarily buy these stocks outright, though. Often he'll sell a put option on the stock--giving the put's owner the right to sell that stock at a specified price within a given amount of time. Essentially, this is a way to bet the share price will go up or stay the same without taking a position in the stock itself. Or, if the fund owns a particular stock, Cancelmo might sell a call--the right to buy the stock at a given "strike price" within a certain amount of time. If the stock rises above the strike price, the shares will get called away by the holder of the option. So, by selling the call, Cancelmo gives up some of the stock's potential upside in exchange for a boost to returns from the proceeds of the option sale.

Though the strategy here sounds complex, it tempers risk rather than magnifies it. First, options only affect a small fraction of the overall portfolio--and if anything, they allow Cancelmo to protect capital losses within the portfolio. He also keeps roughly one fourth of assets in bonds at all times--which gives this fund ballast during stock market sell-offs. Moreover, most of the bond holdings are Treasuries, which carry no credit risk. Plus Cancelmo owns each maturity in roughly equal amounts, which keeps interest-rate risk low.

We like the strategy here, and Cancelmo has proved his ability to execute it. For the trailing five years through Dec. 12, 2006, the fund's 7.1% annualized gain tops 87% of its conservative-allocation peers'. The fund's cheap 0.94% expense ratio gives it a bit of a tailwind, historically and going forward.

We think there's a lot to like about this fund; it could use more attention from investors.

Address:	5615 Kirby Drive Suite 518 Houston TX 77005-2448 800-661-3550	Minimum Purchase:	$2000	Add: $500	IRA: $2000
		Min Auto Inv Plan:	$2000	Add: $200	
		Sales Fees:	No-load		
Web Address:	www.bridgeway.com	Management Fee:	0.60%		
Inception:	06-29-01 *	Actual Fees:	Mgt:0.60%	Dist: —	
Advisor:	Bridgeway Capital Management Inc	Expense Projections:	3Yr:$300	5Yr:$520	10Yr:$1155
Subadvisor:	None	Income Distrib:	Annually		
NTF Plans:	ETrade No Load ETF				

MORNINGSTAR® Funds 500

Bridgeway Blue-Chip 35

	Ticker	Load	NAV	Yield	Total Assets	Mstar Category
	BRLIX	None	$8.06	1.4%	$75 mil	Large Blend

Governance and Management

Stewardship Grade: A

Portfolio Manager(s)

Bridgeway Funds' founder, John Montgomery, is the lead manager here. Montgomery's background is unique: Prior to starting Bridgeway in 1993, he worked in mass-transit management. With experience in statistics, he used quantitative models on his personal investment portfolio. In May 2006, Elena Khoziaeva and Michael Whipple were named comanagers of this fund. Prior to joining the management team, Khoziaeva and Whipple served as quantitative analysts, helping to create and maintain the firm's quant models.

Strategy

Manager John Montgomery is attempting to track an index of his own creation. It is an equally weighted index that is composed of 35 of the market's largest names, meaning that Montgomery must rebalance the portfolio every quarter to ensure that the fund's assets are divided equally among the index's constituents. No industry is represented by more than four names. Montgomery also attempts to avoid paying capital gains distributions.

Performance 12-31-06

	1st Qtr	2nd Qtr	3rd Qtr	4th Qtr	Total
2002	0.15	-12.28	-15.35	10.23	-18.02
2003	-2.94	16.07	1.30	12.91	28.87
2004	-0.57	1.30	-3.85	8.21	4.79
2005	-3.62	-0.87	1.60	3.07	0.05
2006	2.26	-0.41	7.07	5.85	15.42

Trailing	Total Return%	+/- S&P 500	+/- Russ 1000	%Rank Cat	Growth of $10,000
3 Mo	5.85	-0.85	-1.10	79	10,585
6 Mo	13.34	0.60	0.98	12	11,334
1 Yr	15.42	-0.37	-0.04	30	11,542
3 Yr Avg	6.56	-3.88	-4.42	95	12,100
5 Yr Avg	5.04	-1.15	-1.78	67	12,787
10 Yr Avg	—	—	—	—	—
15 Yr Avg	—	—	—	—	—

Tax Analysis	Tax-Adj Rtn%	%Rank Cat	Tax-Cost Rat	%Rank Cat
3 Yr (estimated)	6.00	89	0.53	25
5 Yr (estimated)	4.53	63	0.49	32
10 Yr (estimated)	—	—	—	—

Potential Capital Gain Exposure: 11% of assets

Historical Profile

Return	Below Avg
Risk	Above Avg
Rating	★★ Below Avg

	100%	100%		100%	100%	99%	100%	100%	95%

Investment Style Equity Stock %

▼ Manager Change
▽ Partial Manager Change

Growth of $10,000
— Investment Values of Fund
— Investment Values of S&P 500

18.0 / 16.0 / 14.0 / 12.0 / 10.0

Performance Quartile (within Category)

	1995	1996	1997	1998	1999	2000	2001	2002	2003	2004	2005	2006	History
	—	—	5.00	6.92	8.95	7.51	6.75	5.45	6.97	7.18	7.08	8.06	NAV
	—	—	0.00*	39.11	30.34	-15.12	-9.07	-18.02	28.87	4.79	0.05	15.42	Total Return %
	—	—		10.53	9.30	-6.02	2.82	4.08	0.19	-6.09	-4.86	-0.37	+/-S&P 500
	—	—		12.09	9.43	-7.33	3.38	3.63	-1.02	-6.61	-6.22	-0.04	+/-Russ 1000
	—	—		0.61	0.96	0.98	1.08	1.29	0.97	1.78	1.47	1.59	Income Return %
	—	—		38.50	29.38	-16.10	-10.15	-19.31	27.90	3.01	-1.42	13.83	Capital Return %
	—	—	2	13	95	27	19	31	95	95	30	Total Rtn % Rank Cat
	—	—	0.00	0.03	0.07	0.09	0.08	0.09	0.05	0.12	0.11	0.11	Income $
	—	—	0.00	0.00	0.00	0.00	0.00	0.00	0.00	0.00	0.00	0.00	Capital Gains $
	—	—		0.15	0.15	0.15	0.15	0.15	0.15	0.15	0.15	0.15	Expense Ratio %
	—	—		1.47	1.06	0.98	1.15	1.35	1.65	1.64	1.90	Income Ratio %
	—	—		72	17	26	24	41	25	5	41	Turnover Rate %
	—	—		2	6	7	6	6	23	39	75	Net Assets $mil

Rating and Risk

Time Period	Load-Adj Return %	Morningstar Rtn vs Cat	Morningstar Risk vs Cat	Morningstar Risk-Adj Rating
1 Yr	15.42			
3 Yr	6.56	Low	Avg	★
5 Yr	5.04	-Avg	+Avg	★★
10 Yr	—			
Incept	6.37			

Other Measures	Standard Index S&P 500	Best Fit Index S&P 500
Alpha	-3.2	-3.2
Beta	0.95	0.95
R-Squared	84	84
Standard Deviation	7.21	
Mean	6.56	
Sharpe Ratio	0.48	

Portfolio Analysis 09-30-06

Share change since 06-06 Total Stocks:36	Sector	PE	Tot Ret%	% Assets
⊕ Oracle Corporation	Software	26.7	40.38	3.89
⊕ J.P. Morgan Chase & Co.	Financial	13.6	25.60	3.82
⊕ Bank of America Corporat	Financial	12.4	20.68	3.51
⊕ Google, Inc.	Business	61.5	11.00	3.42
⊕ United Technologies	Ind Mtrls	17.8	13.65	3.37
⊕ Wachovia Corporation	Financial	12.9	12.02	3.24
⊕ Chevron Corporation	Energy	9.0	33.76	2.90
⊕ AT&T, Inc.	Telecom	18.2	51.59	2.89
⊕ United Parcel Service, I	Business	19.7	1.76	2.73
⊕ Merck & Co., Inc.	Health	19.1	42.66	2.72
⊕ Pfizer Inc.	Health	15.2	15.22	2.71
⊕ Microsoft Corporation	Software	23.8	15.83	2.63
⊕ PepsiCo, Inc.	Goods	21.5	7.86	2.58
⊕ American International G	Financial	17.0	6.05	2.52
⊕ Procter & Gamble Company	Goods	23.9	13.36	2.51
⊖ Cisco Systems, Inc.	Hardware	30.1	59.64	2.50
⊕ Texas Instruments, Inc.	Hardware	16.9	-9.82	2.46
⊕ ExxonMobil Corporation	Energy	11.1	39.07	2.46
⊕ Johnson & Johnson	Health	17.5	12.45	2.44
⊕ Intel Corporation	Hardware	21.0	-17.18	2.43

Current Investment Style

Value Blend Growth — Large/Mid/Small

	Market Cap	%
	Giant	95.1
	Large	4.9
	Mid	0.0
	Small	0.0
	Micro	0.0

Avg $mil: 119,999

Value Measures		Rel Category
Price/Earnings	15.17	0.99
Price/Book	2.77	1.08
Price/Sales	1.81	1.29
Price/Cash Flow	10.93	1.30
Dividend Yield %	2.04	1.17

Growth Measures	%	Rel Category
Long-Term Erngs	10.74	0.91
Book Value	8.69	0.96
Sales	13.11	1.35
Cash Flow	10.03	0.97
Historical Erngs	15.07	0.81

Profitability	%	Rel Category
Return on Equity	21.47	1.10
Return on Assets	12.37	1.19
Net Margin	16.66	1.24

Sector Weightings	% of Stocks	Rel S&P 500	3 Year High Low	
↻ Info	29.84	1.49		
🖥 Software	6.88	1.99	7	5
🖴 Hardware	14.90	1.61	18	15
🎙 Media	2.50	0.66	6	3
📞 Telecom	5.56	1.58	6	5
⊆ Service	45.81	0.99		
🏥 Health	13.14	1.09	14	13
🛒 Consumer	4.91	0.64	9	5
📊 Business	6.49	1.53	7	2
💲 Financial	21.27	0.96	21	16
🏭 Mfg	24.34	0.72		
⚙ Goods	7.82	0.91	12	8
⚙ Ind Mtrls	8.58	0.72	9	8
⚡ Energy	7.94	0.81	9	5
💡 Utilities	0.00	0.00	0	0

Composition

Composition	%
● Cash	5.2
● Stocks	94.8
● Bonds	0.0
○ Other	0.0
Foreign (% of Stock)	0.0

Morningstar's Take by Reginald Laing 12-13-06

Bridgeway Blue-Chip 35 Index is showing signs of life.

Investors here have had to be patient in recent years, as the mega-cap companies that this index offering tracks have lagged the broader market by a wide margin. The fund's sector allocation also has hurt. Because sectors are pretty evenly weighted in Bridgeway's proprietary blue-chip index, the portfolio has been comparatively light (versus the large-blend peer group) in energy stocks--the hottest-performing sector in recent years. Since the middle of 2006, however, performance has picked up, as the market has rewarded mega-caps due to their favorable valuations and relative stability.

Our reasons for liking this fund extend beyond recent performance. First, indexing makes sense in the mega-cap arena, where it's difficult for actively managed funds to differentiate themselves. This fund is something of an admission by John Montgomery that his quantitative models (which have had notable success selecting smaller-cap stocks) have limited effectiveness in picking closely followed, highly efficient mega-caps. A fund that passively owns a cross-section of the mega-cap market and charges a pittance (as this one does) stands a good chance of outperforming more-expensive mega-cap funds over time.

Moreover, Montgomery rebalances the fund each quarter in order to keep its components weighted equally. By regularly lowering exposure to stocks that have appreciated in value, and raising stakes in companies that have gone down, he eliminates the price risk taken on by market-cap-weighted indexes--which are forced to own more of a company as it becomes a bigger part of the index (and hence gets more expensive).

This fund is subject to dry spells, of course. And by its nature, the stocks it owns have limited room to grow. Still, it provides an attractive dividend, is highly tax-efficient, and is easily supplemented with funds that invest down the market-cap ladder. This is a solid choice for a core fund.

Address:	5615 Kirby Drive Suite 518 Houston TX 77005-2448 800-661-3550	Minimum Purchase:	$2000	Add: $500 IRA: $2000
		Min Auto Inv Plan:	$2000	Add: $100
		Sales Fees:	No-load	
Web Address:	www.bridgeway.com	Management Fee:	0.08%	
Inception:	07-31-97 *	Actual Fees:	Mgt:0.08%	Dist: —
Advisor:	Bridgeway Capital Management Inc	Expense Projections:	3Yr:$48	5Yr:$85 10Yr:$192
Subadvisor:	None	Income Distrib:	Annually	
NTF Plans:	ETrade No Load ETF			

Bridgeway Small-Cap Gr

	Ticker	Load	NAV	Yield	Total Assets	Mstar Category
	BRSGX	None	$14.27	0.0%	$176 mil	Small Growth

Governance and Management

Stewardship Grade: A

Portfolio Manager(s)

Bridgeway Funds' founder, John Montgomery, is the lead manager on all but one of the firm's 11 funds. Montgomery's background is unique: Prior to starting Bridgeway, he worked in mass-transit management. With experience in statistics, he used quantitative models on his personal investment portfolio. In May 2006, Elena Khoziaeva and Michael Whipple were named comanagers of this fund. Prior to joining the management team, Khoziaeva and Whipple served as quantitative analysts, helping to create and maintain the firm's quant models.

Strategy

Manager John Montgomery slices the investment universe into four distinct sections: large value, large growth, small value, and small growth. For this fund, he then applies several of his quantitative computer models, including some looking for value, to the small-growth list. He also aims to keep taxable distributions to a minimum by working to offset gains with losses.

Historical Profile

Return	Above Avg
Risk	Above Avg
Rating	★★★ Neutral

▼ Manager Change
▽ Partial Manager Change

Growth of $10,000
— Investment Values of Fund
— Investment Values of S&P 500

Performance Quartile (within Category)

History	1995	1996	1997	1998	1999	2000	2001	2002	2003	2004	2005	2006
NAV	—	—	—	—	—	—	—	—	10.27	11.46	13.55	14.27
Total Return %	—	—	—	—	—	—	—	—	—	11.59	18.24	5.31
+/-S&P 500	—	—	—	—	—	—	—	—	—	0.71	13.33	-10.48
+/-Russ 2000 Gr	—	—	—	—	—	—	—	—	—	-2.72	14.09	-8.04
Income Return %	—	—	—	—	—	—	—	—	—	0.00	0.00	0.00
Capital Return %	—	—	—	—	—	—	—	—	—	11.59	18.24	5.31
Total Rtn % Rank Cat	—	—	—	—	—	—	—	—	—	52	2	84
Income $	—	—	—	—	—	—	—	—	0.00	0.00	0.00	0.00
Capital Gains $	—	—	—	—	—	—	—	—	0.00	0.00	0.00	0.00
Expense Ratio %	—	—	—	—	—	—	—	—	—	—	0.94	0.81
Income Ratio %	—	—	—	—	—	—	—	—	—	—	-0.74	-0.19
Turnover Rate %	—	—	—	—	—	—	—	—	—	—	17	41
Net Assets $mil	—	—	—	—	—	—	—	—	—	10	38	176

Performance 12-31-06

	1st Qtr	2nd Qtr	3rd Qtr	4th Qtr	Total
2002	—	—	—	—	—
2003	—	—	—	—	—*
2004	2.43	3.04	-9.23	16.46	11.59
2005	-2.18	7.67	8.70	3.28	18.24
2006	13.58	-4.16	-8.34	5.55	5.31

Trailing	Total Return%	+/- S&P 500	+/- Russ 2000 Gr	%Rank Cat	Growth of $10,000
3 Mo	5.55	-1.15	-3.22	87	10,555
6 Mo	-3.25	-15.99	-10.11	98	9,675
1 Yr	5.31	-10.48	-8.04	84	10,531
3 Yr Avg	11.59	1.15	1.08	27	13,896
5 Yr Avg	—	—	—	—	—
10 Yr Avg	—	—	—	—	—
15 Yr Avg	—	—	—	—	—

Tax Analysis	Tax-Adj Rtn%	%Rank Cat	Tax-Cost Rat	%Rank Cat
3 Yr (estimated)	11.59	18	0.00	1
5 Yr (estimated)	—	—	—	—
10 Yr (estimated)	—	—	—	—

Potential Capital Gain Exposure: 10% of assets

Rating and Risk

Time Period	Load-Adj Return %	Morningstar Rtn vs Cat	Morningstar Risk vs Cat	Morningstar Risk-Adj Rating
1 Yr	5.31			
3 Yr	11.59	+Avg	+Avg	★★★
5 Yr	—	—	—	—
10 Yr	—	—	—	—
Incept	11.88			

Other Measures	Standard Index S&P 500	Best Fit Index Mstar Mid Growth TR
Alpha	-4.6	-4.0
Beta	1.97	1.26
R-Squared	64	89
Standard Deviation	16.89	
Mean	11.59	
Sharpe Ratio	0.54	

Morningstar's Take by Reginald Laing 12-20-06

Bridgeway Small-Cap Growth is a fine long-term holding for those who can take its volatility.

Even by the standards of the volatile small-growth category, this is a volatile offering. For instance, from May 1, 2006, through Aug. 31, 2006, the fund lost 15.3% (versus a 10.5% loss, over the same period, for its average peer). Significant dips in performance will occur from time to time here, when the stock characteristics that management thinks are predictive of high future returns fall out of favor with the market. Such was the case during the performance downturn, when Bridgeway's growth-focused models led management to buy semiconductor-related holdings like Amkor Technology, Zoran, and BTU International--just as their share prices deteriorated.

The fund has come back in recent months. We think long-term investors will be compensated for being patient with this fund's volatility. The quantitative models that drive stock-picking here

have had extraordinary success at Bridgeway's older funds--particularly in the growth and small-cap areas of the Morningstar Style Box, where this fund looks for opportunities.

That this is one of a number of Bridgeway funds that seek opportunities in the small-growth corner of the style box might raise worries that the firm is depleting those opportunities. But lead manager John Montgomery has an exemplary record of closing funds well before they reach capacity. So we don't think that's a big concern here.

Montgomery closely guards the specific factors that the model takes into account. We do know, however, that this fund has one of the cheapest expense ratios (0.81%) among no-load small-cap funds. The fund's low expenses are more remarkable when you consider that it has $268 million in assets. (The typical small-cap fund has $320 million and charges a lot more.) This cheap, well-pedigreed offering has much to recommend it.

Portfolio Analysis 09-30-06

Share change since 06-06 Total Stocks:126

	Sector	PE	Tot Ret%	% Assets
American Commercial Line	Business	—	—	3.43
⊕ Hansen Natural Corporati	Goods	37.9	70.94	2.88
Dril-Quip, Inc.	Energy	22.9	65.93	1.97
CommScope, Inc.	Hardware	17.5	51.42	1.71
Ansoft Corporation	Software	38.6	63.29	1.63
Ocwen Financial Corporat	Financial	6.0	82.30	1.62
Guess ?, Inc.	Goods	29.8	78.17	1.62
Kendle International, In	Health	27.4	22.18	1.54
Holly Corporation	Energy	12.8	75.88	1.48
Encore Wire Corporation	Ind Mtrls	3.5	-3.30	1.47
✿ LifeCell Corporation	Health	45.6	26.79	1.45
BTU International, Inc.	Hardware	8.6	-22.28	1.36
Cognizant Technology Sol	Business	52.9	53.49	1.36
Ladish Company, Inc.	Ind Mtrls	19.9	65.91	1.35
NutriSystem, Inc.	Goods	33.2	75.99	1.31
Vital Images, Inc.	Health	67.4	33.08	1.30
BMC Software, Inc.	Software	39.5	57.15	1.27
Baldor Electric Company	Ind Mtrls	22.5	33.18	1.22
Abaxis, Inc.	Health	47.4	16.81	1.14
✿ Broadwing Corporation	Telecom	—	158.18	1.14

Current Investment Style

Value Blnd Growth — Large Mid Small

Market Cap	%
Giant	0.3
Large	0.4
Mid	30.5
Small	41.5
Micro	27.4

Avg $mil: 1,022

Value Measures		Rel Category
Price/Earnings	16.49	0.78
Price/Book	3.21	1.18
Price/Sales	1.61	1.03
Price/Cash Flow	9.82	1.02
Dividend Yield %	0.30	0.65

Growth Measures	%	Rel Category
Long-Term Erngs	19.27	1.09
Book Value	10.06	0.96
Sales	17.65	1.48
Cash Flow	36.10	1.71
Historical Erngs	45.78	1.89

Profitability	%	Rel Category
Return on Equity	20.17	1.63
Return on Assets	12.30	1.84
Net Margin	11.85	1.37

Sector Weightings

	% of Stocks	Rel S&P 500	3 Year High Low	
☊ Info	20.65	1.03		
Software	6.33	1.83	8	2
Hardware	11.13	1.20	18	4
Media	0.00	0.00	2	0
Telecom	3.19	0.91	4	2
☞ Service	38.51	0.83		
Health	12.49	1.04	24	10
Consumer	5.33	0.70	30	5
Business	13.80	3.26	17	9
Financial	6.89	0.31	7	2
◷ Mfg	40.85	1.21		
Goods	6.97	0.82	13	3
Ind Mtrls	19.35	1.62	19	6
Energy	14.53	1.48	17	2
Utilities	0.00	0.00	2	0

Composition

● Cash	0.0	
● Stocks	100.0	
● Bonds	0.0	
○ Other	0.0	
Foreign (% of Stock)	0.0	

Address:	5615 Kirby Drive Suite 518 Houston TX 77005-2448 800-661-3550
Web Address:	www.bridgeway.com
Inception:	10-31-03
Advisor:	Bridgeway Capital Management Inc
Subadvisor:	None
NTF Plans:	Schwab Instl NTF

Minimum Purchase:	$2000	Add: $500	IRA: $2000
Min Auto Inv Plan:	$2000	Add: $100	
Sales Fees:	No-load		
Management Fee:	0.60%		
Actual Fees:	Mgt:0.61%	Dist: —	
Expense Projections:	3Yr:$259	5Yr:$450	10Yr:$1002
Income Distrib:	Annually		

 **Morningstar® Funds 500**

Bridgeway Sm-Cap Val N

	Ticker	Load	NAV	Yield	Total Assets	Mstar Category
	BRSVX	None	$16.16	0.0%	$258 mil	Small Value

Governance and Management

Stewardship Grade: A

Portfolio Manager(s)

Bridgeway Funds' founder, John Montgomery, is the lead manager on all but one of the firm's 11 funds. Montgomery's background is unique: Prior to starting Bridgeway, he worked in mass-transit management. With experience in statistics, he used quantitative models on his personal investment portfolio. In May 2006, Elena Khoziaeva and Michael Whipple were named comanagers of this fund. Prior to joining the management team, Khoziaeva and Whipple served as quantitative analysts, helping to create and maintain the firm's quant models.

Strategy

Manager John Montgomery slices the investment universe into four sections: large-value, large-growth, small-value, and small-growth. For this fund, he then applies several of his quantitative computer models, including some looking for growth, to the small-value list. He also aims to keep taxable distributions to a minimum by working to offset gains with losses.

Historical Profile
Return Above Avg
Risk High
Rating ★★★ Neutral

Investment Style: Equity
Stock %: 100% 98% 97% 100%

▼ Manager Change
▽ Partial Manager Change

Growth of $10,000
— Investment Values of Fund
— Investment Values of S&P 500

Performance Quartile (within Category)

	1995	1996	1997	1998	1999	2000	2001	2002	2003	2004	2005	2006	History
NAV	—	—	—	—	—	—	—	—	10.27	12.05	14.33	16.16	NAV
Total Return %	—	—	—	—	—	—	—	—	—	17.33	18.92	12.77	Total Return %
+/-S&P 500	—	—	—	—	—	—	—	—	—	6.45	14.01	-3.02	+/-S&P 500
+/-Russ 2000 VL	—	—	—	—	—	—	—	—	—	-4.92	14.21	-10.71	+/-Russ 2000 VL
Income Return %	—	—	—	—	—	—	—	—	—	0.00	0.00	0.00	Income Return %
Capital Return %	—	—	—	—	—	—	—	—	—	17.33	18.92	12.77	Capital Return %
Total Rtn % Rank Cat	—	—	—	—	—	—	—	—	—	84	1	77	Total Rtn % Rank Cat
Income $	—	—	—	—	—	—	—	—	0.00	0.00	0.00	0.00	Income $
Capital Gains $	—	—	—	—	—	—	—	—	0.00	0.00	0.00	0.00	Capital Gains $
Expense Ratio %	—	—	—	—	—	—	—	—	—	—	0.94	0.77	Expense Ratio %
Income Ratio %	—	—	—	—	—	—	—	—	—	—	-0.42	-0.03	Income Ratio %
Turnover Rate %	—	—	—	—	—	—	—	—	—	—	20	49	Turnover Rate %
Net Assets $mil	—	—	—	—	—	—	—	—	8	30	258		Net Assets $mil

Performance 12-31-06

	1st Qtr	2nd Qtr	3rd Qtr	4th Qtr	Total
2002	—	—	—	—	—
2003	—	—	—	—	—*
2004	3.41	-1.51	-0.86	16.20	17.33
2005	1.99	4.07	10.01	1.85	18.92
2006	13.82	-1.78	-5.18	6.39	12.77

Trailing	Total Return%	+/- S&P 500	+/- Russ 2000 VL	%Rank Cat	Growth of $10,000
3 Mo	6.39	-0.31	-2.64	89	10,639
6 Mo	0.87	-11.87	-10.94	100	10,087
1 Yr	12.77	-3.02	-10.71	77	11,277
3 Yr Avg	16.31	5.87	-0.17	17	15,734
5 Yr Avg	—	—	—	—	—
10 Yr Avg	—	—	—	—	—
15 Yr Avg	—	—	—	—	—

Tax Analysis	Tax-Adj Rtn%	%Rank Cat	Tax-Cost Rat	%Rank Cat
3 Yr (estimated)	16.31	2	0.00	1
5 Yr (estimated)	—	—	—	—
10 Yr (estimated)	—	—	—	—

Potential Capital Gain Exposure: 20% of assets

Rating and Risk

Time Period	Load-Adj Return %	Morningstar Rtn vs Cat	Morningstar Risk vs Cat	Morningstar Risk-Adj Rating
1 Yr	12.77			
3 Yr	16.31	+Avg	High	★★★
5 Yr	—	—	—	—
10 Yr	—	—	—	—
Incept	16.36			

Other Measures	Standard Index S&P 500	Best Fit Index Mstar Small Core
Alpha	0.3	-2.0
Beta	1.86	1.15
R-Squared	62	88

Standard Deviation	16.19
Mean	16.31
Sharpe Ratio	0.82

Morningstar's Take by Reginald Laing 12-20-06

Bridgeway Small-Cap Value will be volatile, but we like its long-term prospects.

This fund's merits begin, but don't end, with its low fees. Its 0.77% expense ratio is one of the cheapest for an actively managed small-value fund and will give this fund an enduring advantage. It's also remarkable given the fund's modest $268 million under management--an asset size that's far more nimble than those of many other successful small-value funds, which have been swamped with money during the recent multiyear small-value rally. And we're encouraged that lead manager John Montgomery has demonstrated that he'll close funds (such as the successful Bridgeway Aggressive Investors 1) before assets become unwieldy, so we don't think he'll let this young fund grow to a size that will hamper performance.

The fund's approach is disciplined and sound, too. Montgomery and his team draw on proprietary quantitative models that have delivered stellar long-term returns at older Bridgeway offerings. We

don't know as much about the firm's models as we'd like, but they display a contrarian streak we admire at nonquant offerings. Lately, for instance, management has given the fund a slight tilt toward growth stocks, which have significantly lagged their value counterparts in recent years. (Hence the presence in the fund of fast-growers like medical-device maker ICU Medical.) That tilt should help relative returns if more-growth-oriented small caps pull ahead of their hotter-performing value peers.

Contrarianism will, as it has recently, lead to volatility and stretches of underperformance: For the year to date through Dec. 18, 2006, the fund's 13.1% gain lagged the returns of more than two thirds of small-value peers.

Those still are strong absolute returns, and investors should be careful not to overallocate to this fund now, as small-value stocks have been on a remarkable multiyear run. However, we expect this to be a long-term winner.

Portfolio Analysis 09-30-06

Share change since 06-06 Total Stocks:93	Sector	PE	Tot Ret%	% Assets
Quanta Services, Inc.	Ind Mtrls	39.6	49.36	3.44
⊕ Ocwen Financial Corporat	Financial	6.0	82.30	2.38
McDermott International	Energy	23.4	71.02	2.34
General Cable Corporatio	Ind Mtrls	23.9	121.88	2.30
Celadon Group	Business	17.2	30.86	2.12
EZCorp, Inc.	Financial	28.8	219.07	1.94
Knight Capital Group, In	Business	14.3	93.83	1.93
Dress Barn, Inc.	Consumer	18.0	20.85	1.85
Steven Madden, Inc.	Goods	17.6	84.89	1.76
Technitrol, Inc.	Ind Mtrls	19.2	41.82	1.73
Clean Harbors, Inc.	Business	33.7	68.03	1.71
AAR Corporation	Ind Mtrls	26.2	21.88	1.69
Emcor Group, Inc.	Business	26.9	68.37	1.67
⊖ OGE Energy Corp	Utilities	15.8	55.73	1.64
⊖ Armor Holdings, Inc.	Ind Mtrls	15.3	28.61	1.63
Carpenter Technology Cor	Ind Mtrls	11.7	46.55	1.60
Alaska Air Group, Inc.	Business	—	10.58	1.60
LMI Aerospace, Inc.	Ind Mtrls	17.1	9.32	1.59
ICU Medical, Incorporate	Health	26.1	3.75	1.55
Dillard's, Inc.	Consumer	14.2	41.62	1.54

Current Investment Style

Value Blnd Growth — Large Mid Small

Market Cap	%
Giant	0.0
Large	0.3
Mid	25.0
Small	49.4
Micro	25.3
Avg $mil:	1,011

Value Measures		Rel Category
Price/Earnings	14.33	0.93
Price/Book	2.29	1.29
Price/Sales	0.70	0.87
Price/Cash Flow	4.74	0.77
Dividend Yield %	0.37	0.23

Growth Measures	%	Rel Category
Long-Term Erngs	13.84	1.11
Book Value	6.53	1.20
Sales	4.92	0.66
Cash Flow	11.64	1.42
Historical Erngs	34.82	3.06

Profitability	%	Rel Category
Return on Equity	16.56	1.54
Return on Assets	8.91	1.46
Net Margin	8.19	0.90

Sector Weightings	% of Stocks	Rel S&P 500	3 Year High Low	
Info	8.11	0.41		
Software	0.08	0.02	5	0
Hardware	6.87	0.74	13	3
Media	0.00	0.00	4	0
Telecom	1.16	0.33	2	0
Service	50.02	1.08		
Health	6.20	0.51	9	3
Consumer	14.27	1.87	21	13
Business	18.65	4.41	19	12
Financial	10.90	0.49	12	8
Mfg	41.88	1.24		
Goods	2.19	0.26	8	2
Ind Mtrls	28.23	2.36	29	15
Energy	8.28	0.84	12	4
Utilities	3.18	0.91	3	1

Composition

● Cash	0.3	
● Stocks	99.7	
● Bonds	0.0	
○ Other	0.0	
Foreign	0.0	
(% of Stock)		

Address:	5615 Kirby Drive Suite 518 Houston TX 77005-2448 800-661-3550	Minimum Purchase:	$2000	Add: $500	IRA: $2000
		Min Auto Inv Plan:	$2000	Add: $100	
		Sales Fees:	No-load		
Web Address:	www.bridgeway.com	Management Fee:	0.60%		
Inception:	10-31-03	Actual Fees:	Mgt:0.60%	Dist: —	
Advisor:	Bridgeway Capital Management Inc	Expense Projections:	3Yr:$246	5Yr:$428	10Yr:$954
Subadvisor:	None	Income Distrib:	Annually		
NTF Plans:	Schwab Instl NTF				

Bridgeway Ul-Sm Co Mkt

	Ticker	Load	NAV	Yield	Total Assets	Mstar Category
	BRSIX	None	$19.54	0.4%	$1,176 mil	Small Blend

Governance and Management

Stewardship Grade: A

Portfolio Manager(s)

Bridgeway Funds' founder John Montgomery runs all but one of Bridgeway's 11 funds. Two quantitative analysts assist him in testing new variables to potentially add to his models and in creating new models. Montgomery's background is unique: Prior to starting Bridgeway, he worked in mass-transit management, and with experience in statistics, he used quantitative models on his personal investment portfolio.

Strategy

This passively managed fund follows the CRSP Cap-Based Portfolio 10 Index--a benchmark consisting of the smallest 10% of NYSE-listed equities (based on market cap). Manager John Montgomery tries to replicate the index's returns by holding a representative sampling of stocks. The fund's diversification, Montgomery argues, offsets the company-specific risk that comes with investing in these tiny firms, some of which ultimately will go out of business. He pays close attention to tax implications, rebalancing less often than the bogy--which can lead to higher tracking error than that of an ordinary index fund.

Performance 12-31-06

	1st Qtr	2nd Qtr	3rd Qtr	4th Qtr	Total
2002	10.93	-1.47	-14.37	12.08	4.90
2003	0.48	30.87	15.94	17.69	79.43
2004	9.04	-0.92	-4.09	15.93	20.12
2005	-8.84	4.69	5.96	2.92	4.08
2006	12.88	-6.52	-2.01	7.81	11.48

Trailing	Total Return%	+/- S&P 500	+/- Russ 2000	%Rank Cat	Growth of $10,000
3 Mo	7.81	1.11	-1.09	57	10,781
6 Mo	5.65	-7.09	-3.73	75	10,565
1 Yr	11.48	-4.31	-6.89	80	11,148
3 Yr Avg	11.70	1.26	-1.86	74	13,937
5 Yr Avg	21.27	15.08	9.88	1	26,228
10 Yr Avg	—	—	—	—	—
15 Yr Avg	—	—	—	—	—

Tax Analysis	Tax-Adj Rtn%	%Rank Cat	Tax-Cost Rat	%Rank Cat
3 Yr (estimated)	11.30	51	0.36	8
5 Yr (estimated)	21.00	1	0.22	6
10 Yr (estimated)	—	—	—	—

Potential Capital Gain Exposure: 34% of assets

Morningstar's Take by Reginald Laing 12-28-06

Performance might have slowed at Bridgeway Ultra-Small Company Market, but it remains a fine long-term holding.

For the trailing five years through Dec. 23, 2006, this fund's 21.8% annualized gain topped those of 99% of its small-blend peers. However, that relative five-year ranking masks the fact that this fund underperformed in calendar year 2005 (it finished behind 74% of its peers) and will likely do so again in 2006 (it's lagging 85% of its peers through Dec. 23).

So is this fund's remarkable multiyear run over? It appears that way, but that doesn't mean you should sell the fund, as the qualities that have made it a long-term winner are intact. First, it offers passive exposure to roughly 700 of the smallest publicly traded companies. A broadly diversified portfolio should somewhat dampen the risks associated with this volatile segment of the market (some ultrasmall companies lack the diversification and financial strength to withstand difficult economic times). And this offering serves as a good diversifier in a portfolio tilted toward larger-cap names. Also, studies suggest that micro-caps, on the whole, have delivered higher returns (albeit with higher volatility) than larger-cap stocks over many decades.

This offering looks even better from a tax and expense perspective. Lead manager John Montgomery, using proprietary methods that he won't entirely reveal, has avoided paying out sizable taxable dividends during this fund's lifespan. And even though the fund now has more than $1 billion is assets (which may make it harder to track the returns of its benchmark), Bridgeway has passed on the attendant cost savings by lowering the fund's expense ratio to a very cheap 0.65%. Tax efficiency and low fees mean investors here can expect to keep a higher percentage of gross returns than at the typical small-blend fund.

This remains a fine choice--though investors should be careful not overallocate to it.

Address:	5615 Kirby Drive Suite 518
	Houston TX 77005-2448
	800-661-3550
Web Address:	www.bridgeway.com
Inception:	07-31-97 *
Advisor:	Bridgeway Capital Management Inc
Subadvisor:	None
NTF Plans:	ETrade No Load ETF

Minimum Purchase:	$2000	Add: $500	IRA: $2000
Min Auto Inv Plan:	$2000	Add: $200	
Sales Fees:	No-load, 2.00%R		
Management Fee:	0.50%		
Actual Fees:	Mgt:0.50%	Dist: —	
Expense Projections:	3Yr:$208	5Yr:$362	10Yr:$810
Income Distrib:	Annually		

Historical Profile
Return Above Avg
Risk Above Avg
Rating ★★★★ Above Avg

	100%	99%		99%	90%	90%	98%	96%	99%

Investment Style
Equity
Stock %

▼ Manager Change
▽ Partial Manager Change

Growth of $10,000
■ Investment Values of Fund
— Investment Values of S&P 500

39.4
32.4
24.0
17.0
10.0

Performance Quartile (within Category)

1995	1996	1997	1998	1999	2000	2001	2002	2003	2004	2005	2006	History
—	—	4.98	4.89	6.43	6.43	7.96	8.35	14.94	17.77	17.94	19.54	NAV
—	—	-0.40*	-1.81	31.49	0.67	23.98	4.90	79.43	20.12	4.08	11.48	Total Return %
—	—	—	-30.39	10.45	9.77	35.87	27.00	50.75	9.24	-0.83	-4.31	+/-S&P 500
—	—	—	0.74	10.23	3.69	21.49	25.38	32.18	1.79	-0.47	-6.89	+/-Russ 2000
—	—	—	0.00	0.00	0.66	0.18	0.00	0.00	0.18	0.16	0.46	Income Return %
—	—	—	-1.81	31.49	0.01	23.80	4.90	79.43	19.94	3.92	11.02	Capital Return %
—	—	—	29	16	88	9	1	2	40	74	80	Total Rtn % Rank Cat
—	—	0.00	0.00	0.00	0.04	0.01	0.00	0.00	0.03	0.03	0.08	Income $
—	—	0.00	0.00	0.00	0.00	0.00	0.00	0.04	0.15	0.53	0.37	Capital Gains $
—	—	—	0.75	0.75	0.75	0.75	0.75	0.75	0.67	0.73	0.65	Expense Ratio %
—	—	—	-0.38	-0.51	0.53	0.77	-0.05	-0.14	0.11	0.15	0.27	Income Ratio %
—	—	—	68	48	40	215	56	18	19	13	26	Turnover Rate %
—	—	40	58	69	64	59	100	752	806	758	1,176	Net Assets $mil

Rating and Risk

Time Period	Load-Adj Return %	Morningstar Rtn vs Cat	Morningstar Risk vs Cat	Morningstar Risk-Adj Rating
1 Yr	11.48			
3 Yr	11.70	-Avg	+Avg	★★
5 Yr	21.27	High	+Avg	★★★★★
10 Yr	—	—	—	
Incept	16.49			

Other Measures	Standard Index S&P 500	Best Fit Index Russ 2000 Gr
Alpha	-3.6	1.7
Beta	1.79	0.90
R-Squared	71	95
Standard Deviation	14.54	
Mean	11.70	
Sharpe Ratio	0.61	

Portfolio Analysis 09-30-06

Share change since 06-06 Total Stocks:693	Sector	PE	Tot Ret%	% Assets
iShares Russell 2000 Val	—	—	—	1.34
iShares Russell 2000 Ind	—	—	—	1.30
Giant Industries, Inc.	Energy	10.2	44.25	0.99
LCA-Vision, Inc.	Health	20.3	-26.75	0.91
LifeCell Corporation	Health	45.6	26.79	0.88
Oregon Steel Mills, Inc.	Ind Mtrls	14.0	112.14	0.75
ATP Oil & Gas Corporatio	Energy	—	6.92	0.63
Andersons, Inc.	Ind Mtrls	21.0	97.73	0.63
Clean Harbors, Inc.	Business	33.7	68.03	0.62
Amedisys, Inc.	Health	20.7	3.76	0.62
Hub Group, Inc. A	Business	25.2	55.87	0.60
inVentiv Health, Inc.	Business	21.0	49.66	0.58
Spartan Stores, Inc.	Consumer	19.9	103.47	0.53
Umpqua Holdings Corporat	Financial	18.3	5.37	0.49
Hurco Companies, Inc.	Ind Mtrls	10.9	3.12	0.48
Sciele Pharma, Inc.	Health	21.5	39.13	0.48
Lufkin Industries, Inc.	Energy	13.4	17.68	0.46
Ceradyne, Inc.	Ind Mtrls	15.0	29.00	0.46
Lamson & Sessions	Ind Mtrls	7.4	-3.04	0.44
First Cash Financial Ser	Financial	28.1	77.44	0.43

Current Investment Style

Value Blnd Growth — Large Mid Small

Market Cap	%
Giant	0.5
Large	0.0
Mid	1.9
Small	17.3
Micro	80.3

Avg $mil: 304

Value Measures		Rel Category
Price/Earnings	16.76	1.01
Price/Book	1.94	0.92
Price/Sales	1.01	1.03
Price/Cash Flow	6.07	0.87
Dividend Yield %	0.63	0.59

Growth Measures	%	Rel Category
Long-Term Erngs	15.91	1.14
Book Value	3.72	0.49
Sales	6.46	0.73
Cash Flow	7.87	0.62
Historical Erngs	17.94	1.07

Profitability	%	Rel Category
Return on Equity	7.47	0.58
Return on Assets	3.99	0.56
Net Margin	8.77	0.91

Sector Weightings	% of Stocks	Rel S&P 500	3 Year High Low
↻ Info	19.05	0.95	
🔲 Software	6.60	1.91	7 5
🔲 Hardware	9.77	1.06	11 9
🔲 Media	1.18	0.31	1 1
🔲 Telecom	1.50	0.43	2 1
☎ Service	59.42	1.29	
🔲 Health	17.66	1.46	19 17
🔲 Consumer	8.18	1.07	9 7
🔲 Business	11.13	2.63	11 10
🔲 Financial	22.45	1.01	24 20
🔲 Mfg	21.50	0.64	
🔲 Goods	4.48	0.52	7 4
🔲 Ind Mtrls	11.98	1.00	14 12
🔲 Energy	3.97	0.41	5 4
🔲 Utilities	1.07	0.31	1 1

Composition

● Cash	1.0	
● Stocks	99.0	
● Bonds	0.0	
● Other	0.0	
Foreign	0.2	(% of Stock)

MORNINGSTAR® Funds 500

Brown Cap Small Co Instl

	Ticker	Load	NAV	Yield	Total Assets	Mstar Category
	BCSIX	Closed	$32.60	0.0%	$347 mil	Small Growth

Governance and Management

Stewardship Grade: C

Portfolio Manager(s)

Keith Lee leads the management team of Robert Hall, Kempton Ingersol, and Amy Zhang. Lee has been with Brown Capital Management since 1991.

Strategy

This fund's managers search for promising growth businesses that they can invest in for the long haul. Because the managers look for companies with $250 million or less in operating revenue, the fund holds everything from micro- to mid-cap names. The fund sports huge weightings in volatile sectors such as technology and biotech.

Historical Profile

Return	Below Avg
Risk	Average
Rating	★★ Below Avg

Manager Change ▼
Partial Manager Change ▽

Growth of $10,000

— Investment Values of Fund
— Investment Values of S&P 500

Investment Style
Equity
Stock %

93% 91% 100% 92% 92% 92% 97% 95% 99%

Performance Quartile (within Category)

1995	1996	1997	1998	1999	2000	2001	2002	2003	2004	2005	2006	History
13.99	16.00	18.29	21.42	28.70	31.23	35.17	20.98	29.73	29.80	31.24	32.60	NAV
33.91	17.08	15.78	18.39	44.02	15.30	13.33	-40.34	41.71	0.24	4.83	15.67	Total Return %
-3.67	-5.88	-17.58	-10.19	22.98	24.40	25.22	-18.24	13.03	-10.64	-0.08	-0.12	+/-S&P 500
2.87	5.82	2.83	17.16	0.93	37.73	22.56	-10.08	-6.83	-14.07	0.68	2.32	+/-Russ 2000 Gr
0.00	0.00	0.00	0.00	0.00	0.00	0.00	0.00	0.00	0.00	0.00	0.00	Income Return %
33.91	17.08	15.78	18.39	44.02	15.30	13.33	-40.34	41.71	0.24	4.83	15.67	Capital Return %
53	54	57	16	58	11	9	89	61	95	61	16	Total Rtn % Rank Cat
0.00	0.00	0.00	0.00	0.00	0.00	0.00	0.00	0.00	0.00	0.00	0.00	Income $
1.04	0.36	0.24	0.23	2.12	1.81	0.22	0.00	0.00	0.00	0.00	3.58	Capital Gains $
2.00	1.69	1.50	1.50	1.50	1.43	1.35	1.24	1.23	1.18	1.18	1.19	Expense Ratio %
-0.90	-0.50	-0.30	-0.68	-0.98	-0.94	-0.23	-0.83	-1.05	-1.03	-0.95	-0.97	Income Ratio %
33	23	13	12	28	28	8	7	1	1	11	10	Turnover Rate %
3	6	10	16	45	126	365	373	719	647	373	347	Net Assets $mil

Performance 12-31-06

	1st Qtr	2nd Qtr	3rd Qtr	4th Qtr	Total
2002	-3.55	-22.88	-26.95	9.79	-40.34
2003	-4.58	21.93	8.77	11.98	41.71
2004	1.61	-3.97	-6.55	9.92	0.24
2005	-9.26	8.47	5.80	0.68	4.83
2006	11.72	-4.27	-2.96	11.46	15.67

Trailing	Total Return%	+/- S&P 500	+/- Russ 2000 Gr	%Rank Cat	Growth of $10,000
3 Mo	11.46	4.76	2.69	6	11,146
6 Mo	8.15	-4.59	1.29	23	10,815
1 Yr	15.67	-0.12	2.32	16	11,567
3 Yr Avg	6.72	-3.72	-3.79	79	12,155
5 Yr Avg	0.54	-5.65	-6.39	93	10,273
10 Yr Avg	10.24	1.82	5.36	32	26,509
15 Yr Avg	—	—	—		

Tax Analysis	Tax-Adj Rtn%	%Rank Cat	Tax-Cost Rat	%Rank Cat
3 Yr (estimated)	6.19	73	0.50	18
5 Yr (estimated)	0.25	92	0.29	15
10 Yr (estimated)	9.69	21	0.50	11

Potential Capital Gain Exposure: 25% of assets

Rating and Risk

Time Period	Load-Adj Return %	Morningstar Rtn vs Cat	Morningstar Risk vs Cat	Morningstar Risk-Adj Rating
1 Yr	15.67			
3 Yr	6.72	-Avg	Avg	★★
5 Yr	0.54	Low	+Avg	★
10 Yr	10.24	Avg	Avg	★★★
Incept	11.76			

Other Measures	Standard Index S&P 500	Best Fit Index Russ 2000 Gr
Alpha	-7.9	-2.8
Beta	1.77	0.91
R-Squared	60	84
Standard Deviation	15.80	
Mean	6.72	
Sharpe Ratio	0.29	

Portfolio Analysis 09-30-06

Share change since 06-06 Total Stocks:42	Sector	PE	Tot Ret%	% Assets
DTS, Inc	Goods	43.8	63.45	5.08
FEI Company	Hardware	—	37.56	4.55
⊖ Macrovision Corporation	Software	66.5	68.92	4.44
Concur Technologies, Inc	Software	17.6	24.44	4.44
FLIR Systems, Inc.	Ind Mtrls	28.6	42.54	3.85
Dolby Laboratories, Inc.	Goods	—	81.94	3.61
Symyx Technologies, Inc.	Ind Mtrls	92.8	-20.89	3.46
⊖ Ansys, Inc.	Software	NMF	1.87	3.42
SPSS, Inc.	Software	32.5	-2.78	3.33
Cognex Corporation	Hardware	27.3	-19.80	3.24
⊕ Techne Corporation	Health	29.5	-1.12	3.23
⊕ Talx Corporation	Business	28.7	-9.28	3.22
⊕ Blackbaud, Inc.	Business	41.7	54.25	3.13
Manhattan Associates, In	Software	39.7	46.88	3.01
Green Mountain Coffee Ro	Goods	43.0	21.26	2.96
Radisys Corporation	Hardware	—	-3.86	2.80
⊕ Kensey Nash Corporation	Health	72.1	44.35	2.54
Fair Isaac, Inc.	Business	25.4	-7.78	2.51
⊕ Affymetrix, Inc.	Health	72.6	-51.71	2.51
⊖ Transaction Systems Arch	Software	20.8	13.13	2.40

Current Investment Style

Value Blnd Growth — Large Mid Small

Market Cap	%
Giant	0.0
Large	0.0
Mid	12.5
Small	51.3
Micro	36.2
Avg $mil:	792

Value Measures		Rel Category
Price/Earnings	29.87	1.42
Price/Book	2.95	1.08
Price/Sales	2.93	1.87
Price/Cash Flow	14.65	1.52
Dividend Yield %	0.13	0.28

Growth Measures	%	Rel Category
Long-Term Erngs	18.64	1.05
Book Value	3.79	0.36
Sales	8.24	0.69
Cash Flow	13.30	0.63
Historical Erngs	18.06	0.74

Profitability	%	Rel Category
Return on Equity	9.19	0.74
Return on Assets	6.19	0.93
Net Margin	11.89	1.37

Sector Weightings

	% of Stocks	Rel S&P 500	3 Year High Low
↻ Info	38.09	1.91	
Software	26.28	7.62	26 19
Hardware	10.72	1.16	13 9
Media	0.00	0.00	2 0
Telecom	1.09	0.31	2 1
⊏ Service	42.71	0.92	
Health	27.77	2.30	41 28
Consumer	1.71	0.22	5 2
Business	13.23	3.13	13 8
Financial	0.00	0.00	0 0
⊔ Mfg	19.19	0.57	
Goods	11.79	1.38	12 3
Ind Mtrls	7.40	0.62	11 6
Energy	0.00	0.00	0 0
Utilities	0.00	0.00	0 0

Composition

● Cash	1.2	
● Stocks	98.8	
● Bonds	0.0	
○ Other	0.0	
	Foreign	0.0
	(% of Stock)	

Morningstar's Take by Arijit Dutta 12-27-06

Brown Capital Management Small Company should see better days.

After a number of dismal years, this fund is making some headway in 2006, despite the odds. The portfolio is heavily into software and health-care stocks (its combined stake of 58% in those two sectors dwarfs the small-growth average of 23%), which have both been anemic. The fund's complete lack of energy stocks (the category average is 7%) has also continued to hurt. Still, stock-specific successes such as Macrovision, a leader in antipiracy software, have powered the fund to a respectable showing thus far this year.

It'll take more such hits to repair the damage done to the fund's record in recent years, but it's a relevant example nonetheless. Management looks for companies that can exploit their strong industry position for years. For example, Macrovision's antipiracy products have remained key in protecting intellectual property like films and music, even as modes of delivering entertainment continue to evolve. The approach requires plenty of patience because markets will often overlook a company's long-term strengths. Management has indeed shown great patience: The portfolio's close-to-single-digit turnover rates in recent years are practically unheard of in the small-growth arena. Concur Technologies, which makes specialty software in the business-expense reimbursement area, is another example of this long-term focus. Management has reaped rich rewards by sticking with that stock through its slumps over the years.

We think this is a fine approach to growth investing, although it isn't practiced by many. Most investors obsess over short-term earnings prospects of small companies, but this fund's focus on identifying eventual winners should prove effective. Indeed, the fund's 10-year record is still solid, despite the setbacks in recent years. Thus, shareholders who bought here to nvest in companies with innovative technologies and sound business plans have good reason to stay.

Address:	116 South Franklin Street Rocky Mount NC 27802 877-892-4226	Minimum Purchase:	Closed	Add: — IRA: —
		Min Auto Inv Plan:	Closed	Add: —
		Sales Fees:	No-load	
Web Address:	www.ncfunds.com	Management Fee:	1.00%	
Inception:	07-23-92	Actual Fees:	Mgt:1.00%	Dist: —
Advisor:	Brown Capital Management Inc.	Expense Projections:	3Yr:$378	5Yr:$654 10Yr:$1443
Subadvisor:	None	Income Distrib:	Monthly	
NTF Plans:	Schwab OneSource			

Buffalo MicroCp

	Ticker	Load	NAV	Yield	Total Assets	Mstar Category
	BUFOX	None	$13.03	0.0%	$57 mil	Small Growth

Governance and Management

Stewardship Grade: A

Portfolio Manager(s)

A three-person team from advisor Kornitzer Capital Management runs this fund. Kent Gasaway and Robert Male have comanaged Buffalo Small Cap since its April 1998 inception. Grant Sarris, a former small-cap manager with Waddell & Reed, joined in late 2003. Eight analysts support the team in its effort.

Strategy

The managers employ numerous themes to direct stock selection, such as those related to demographic patterns and technological innovation. Within those themes, they use a growth-at-a-reasonable-price philosophy. Firms with strong earnings and cash flows, competitive products, and rock-solid balance sheets are fund favorites. Such stocks often sell for a premium, but management gets edgy when prices climb too high. The fund focuses on stocks with market caps of less than $600 million. Initial positions in any one issue are small, but it holds on to winners. Expect turnover to be low.

Performance 12-31-06

	1st Qtr	2nd Qtr	3rd Qtr	4th Qtr	Total
2002	—	—	—	—	—
2003	—	—	—	—	—
2004	—	—	-6.32	16.08	—*
2005	-5.09	5.18	5.37	4.10	9.50
2006	10.49	-8.23	0.81	10.11	12.54

Trailing	Total Return%	+/- S&P 500	+/- Russ 2000 Gr	%Rank Cat	Growth of $10,000
3 Mo	10.11	3.41	1.34	13	11,011
6 Mo	11.00	-1.74	4.14	5	11,100
1 Yr	12.54	-3.25	-0.81	33	11,254
3 Yr Avg	—	—	—	—	—
5 Yr Avg	—	—	—	—	—
10 Yr Avg	—	—	—	—	—
15 Yr Avg	—	—	—	—	—

Tax Analysis	Tax-Adj Rtn%	%Rank Cat	Tax-Cost Rat	%Rank Cat
3 Yr (estimated)	—	—	—	—
5 Yr (estimated)	—	—	—	—
10 Yr (estimated)	—	—	—	—

Potential Capital Gain Exposure: 20% of assets

Historical Profile

Return
Risk
Rating   Not Rated

Investment Style: Equity, Stock %

83% | 95% | 96%

▼ Manager Change
▽ Partial Manager Change

Growth of $10,000
— Investment Values of Fund
— Investment Values of S&P 500

Performance Quartile (within Category)

	1995	1996	1997	1998	1999	2000	2001	2002	2003	2004	2005	2006	History
	—	—	—	—	—	—	—	—	—	11.19	12.20	13.03	NAV
	—	—	—	—	—	—	—	—	—	—	9.50	12.54	Total Return %
	—	—	—	—	—	—	—	—	—	—	4.59	-3.25	+/-S&P 500
	—	—	—	—	—	—	—	—	—	—	5.35	-0.81	+/-Russ 2000 Gr
	—	—	—	—	—	—	—	—	—	—	0.00	0.00	Income Return %
	—	—	—	—	—	—	—	—	—	—	9.50	12.54	Capital Return %
	—	—	—	—	—	—	—	—	—	—	22	33	Total Rtn % Rank Cat
	—	—	—	—	—	—	—	—	—	0.00	0.00	0.00	Income $
	—	—	—	—	—	—	—	—	—	0.00	0.05	0.69	Capital Gains $
	—	—	—	—	—	—	—	—	—	—	1.51	—	Expense Ratio %
	—	—	—	—	—	—	—	—	—	—	-1.09	—	Income Ratio %
	—	—	—	—	—	—	—	—	—	—	50	—	Turnover Rate %
	—	—	—	—	—	—	—	—	—	—	32	57	Net Assets $mil

Rating and Risk

Time Period	Load-Adj Return %	Morningstar Rtn vs Cat	Morningstar Risk vs Cat	Morningstar Risk-Adj Rating
1 Yr	12.54			
3 Yr	—	—	—	—
5 Yr	—	—	—	—
10 Yr	—	—	—	—
Incept	13.09			

Other Measures	Standard Index S&P 500	Best Fit Index
Alpha	—	—
Beta	—	—
R-Squared	—	—
Standard Deviation	—	
Mean	—	
Sharpe Ratio	—	

Portfolio Analysis 09-30-06

Share change since 06-06 Total Stocks:54	Sector	PE	Tot Ret%	% Assets
⊖ ICON PLC ADR	Health	—	83.28	3.18
Align Technology, Inc.	Health	—	115.92	3.13
DTS, Inc	Goods	43.8	63.45	3.11
LifeCell Corporation	Health	45.6	26.79	3.04
Cohen & Steers, Inc.	Financial	—	119.24	3.00
⊕ Heidrick & Struggles Int	Business	23.2	32.17	2.66
⊕ A.C. Moore Arts & Crafts	Consumer	56.1	48.94	2.65
MarketAxess Holdings, In	Financial	93.1	18.72	2.38
LifeCore Biomedical	Health	33.7	9.93	2.36
⊕ AngioDynamics, Inc.	Health	45.5	-15.83	2.36
Golf Galaxy, Inc.	Consumer	—	—	2.30
Trump Entertainment Reso	Consumer	—	-9.39	2.30
⊕ Educate, Inc.	Consumer	—	-39.66	2.24
⊕ Dixie Group, Inc.	Goods	16.9	-8.27	2.24
⊕ NeuroMetrix, Inc.	Health	45.4	-45.35	2.16
CRA International, Inc.	Business	22.1	9.88	2.09
⊕ Morton's Restaurant Grou	—	—	—	2.08
⊕ Clayton Holdings, Inc.	Business	—	—	2.04
⊕ eCollege.com	Business	58.3	-13.20	1.96
Stellent, Inc.	Software	—	—	1.85

Current Investment Style

Value Blnd Growth — Large Mid Small

Market Cap	%
Giant	0.0
Large	0.0
Mid	1.4
Small	38.1
Micro	60.5
Avg $mil: 448	

Value Measures		Rel Category
Price/Earnings	23.22	1.10
Price/Book	1.74	0.64
Price/Sales	1.06	0.68
Price/Cash Flow	9.27	0.96
Dividend Yield %	0.21	0.46

Growth Measures	%	Rel Category
Long-Term Erngs	17.43	0.98
Book Value	20.86	1.99
Sales	9.92	0.83
Cash Flow	12.80	0.61
Historical Erngs	8.30	0.34

Profitability	%	Rel Category
Return on Equity	8.08	0.65
Return on Assets	4.64	0.70
Net Margin	5.90	0.68

Sector Weightings	% of Stocks	Rel S&P 500	3 Year High Low	
↻ Info	10.42	0.52		
Software	5.07	1.47	7	3
Hardware	5.35	0.58	14	5
Media	0.00	0.00	0	0
Telecom	0.00	0.00	0	0
☞ Service	75.70	1.64		
Health	30.39	2.52	34	24
Consumer	18.65	2.44	29	19
Business	14.14	3.34	14	5
Financial	12.52	0.56	13	5
Mfg	13.88	0.41		
Goods	10.59	1.24	13	9
Ind Mtrls	3.29	0.28	6	1
Energy	0.00	0.00	0	0
Utilities	0.00	0.00	0	0

Composition

- ● Cash 4.4
- ● Stocks 95.6
- ● Bonds 0.0
- ○ Other 0.0
- Foreign 6.0 (% of Stock)

Morningstar's Take by Reginald Laing 12-29-06

Despite its risks, Buffalo Micro Cap is intriguing.

This fund isn't for short-term or risk-averse investors. The management team (from the well-regarded Kornitzer Capital Management) mostly buys companies with between $100 million and $600 million in market cap. These are among the smallest publicly traded firms. As such, they tend to be less diversified and have fewer financial resources with which to weather lean economic times, so their share prices can be highly volatile.

What's more, this fund's managers are willing to own these companies in a concentrated manner: Presently, the portfolio consists of 54 holdings. That means individual picks can have a sizable impact--both positive and negative--on performance. Last, management focuses on long-term trends and aims to buy and hold the companies that will benefit from them. That approach will lead to sizable overweights (relative to the small-growth peer group) in the sectors--such as health-care and consumer-related stocks--where

their trends play out. And the sector risk that management is willing to court can lead to high volatility of returns.

A recent pick in financials is asset manager Cohen & Steers. The firm specializes in real estate portfolios, whose relatively high income payouts will be increasingly attractive to aging baby boomers, according to this fund's managers. So far Cohen & Steers has been a good stock pick, contributing to this fund's solid start. Moreover, this fund's managers have demonstrated their ability to make such winning picks consistently at Buffalo's small- and mid-cap offerings.

While this fund's 1.51% expense ratio is well above the 1.26% median for similar no-load funds, assets are still quite modest. What's more, the prospectus states that management intends to close the fund to new investors when assets reach $250 million. That commitment to controlling asset growth, coupled with talented management, gives this fund a bright future.

Address:	PO Box 219757 Kansas City, MO 64121 800-492-8332	Minimum Purchase:	$2500	Add: $100	IRA: $250
		Min Auto Inv Plan:	$100	Add: $100	
		Sales Fees:	No-load, 2.00%R		
Web Address:	www.buffalofunds.com	Management Fee:	1.45%		
Inception:	05-21-04	Actual Fees:	Mgt:1.45%	Dist: —	
Advisor:	Kornitzer Capital Management, Inc.	Expense Projections:	3Yr:$477	5Yr:$824	10Yr:$1802
Subadvisor:	None	Income Distrib:	Annually		
NTF Plans:	Federated Tr NTF, TD Waterhouse Ins NT				

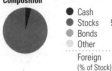
Morningstar® Funds 500

Buffalo Mid Cap

Analyst Pick ✓

Ticker BUFMX	**Load** None	**NAV** $15.01	**Yield** 0.0%	**Total Assets** $375 mil	**Mstar Category** Mid-Cap Growth

Governance and Management

Stewardship Grade: A

Portfolio Manager(s)

Kent Gasaway and Robert Male have run this fund since its December 2001 inception. They are part of Kansas City-based Kornitzer Capital Management, which manages several Buffalo funds, including Buffalo Small Cap and Buffalo Large Cap.

Strategy

The managers employ numerous themes to help direct stock selection. Demographic trends are always important in building the portfolio. Thus, consumer and financial stocks that benefit from growing population segments are prevalent. In terms of stock-specific criteria, management uses a growth-at-a-reasonable-price philosophy. It likes companies with solid earnings potential and little or no debt that are trading at reasonable valuations. The fund defines mid-cap stocks as those having market caps between $1.5 billion and $10 billion at the time of purchase.

Performance 12-31-06

	1st Qtr	2nd Qtr	3rd Qtr	4th Qtr	Total
2002	0.90	-13.24	-18.56	9.23	-22.13
2003	-3.46	22.02	7.50	13.45	43.66
2004	10.78	-1.53	-6.29	14.05	16.60
2005	-2.94	4.55	3.48	5.80	13.83
2006	6.77	-8.21	2.47	5.24	5.68

Trailing	Total Return%	+/- S&P 500	+/- Russ MG	%Rank Cat	Growth of $10,000
3 Mo	5.24	-1.46	-1.71	75	10,524
6 Mo	7.84	-4.90	-0.06	26	10,784
1 Yr	5.68	-10.11	-4.98	75	10,568
3 Yr Avg	11.94	1.50	-0.79	34	14,027
5 Yr Avg	9.43	3.24	1.21	17	15,692
10 Yr Avg	—	—	—	—	—
15 Yr Avg	—	—	—	—	—

Tax Analysis	Tax-Adj Rtn%	%Rank Cat	Tax-Cost Rat	%Rank Cat
3 Yr (estimated)	11.61	27	0.29	14
5 Yr (estimated)	9.23	13	0.18	13
10 Yr (estimated)	—	—	—	—

Potential Capital Gain Exposure: 16% of assets

Morningstar's Take by Karen Wallace 12-15-06

We think Buffalo Mid Cap deserves the benefit of investors' doubt.

This fund's 6.2% return for the year to date through Dec. 15, 2006, is not bad in absolute terms, but it lands in only the bottom quintile of the mid-growth category. A combination of having zero exposure to this year's hottest-performing sectors (utilities, telecommunications, and energy) and the managers' conviction in some lagging stock picks have held the fund back this year.

But the managers are still investing according to the fund's sound strategy. They look for stocks that stand to benefit from major demographic or technological trends and that have attractive earnings potential, reasonable valuations, and low debt. For instance, some of the trends they've identified include the aging of the baby boomers, productivity in the workplace, and outsourcing. Their favored trends tend to lead to heavy exposure to the technology, consumer services, and health-care sectors. Also, the managers tend to be

patient with their stock picks. For instance, the fund's second-largest holding, Linux distributor Red Hat, has fallen more than 35% this year on perceived competitive threats. The managers are holding on because they think the market for Linux will continue to grow, and Red Hat has strong competitive advantages that will allow it to retain its market share.

In general, it can be difficult to gain an information edge that would allow one to benefit from macroeconomic themes. But we think the managers here distinguish their strategy in some meaningful ways. For starters, we like their attention to valuation, which has meaningfully reduced volatility here--the fund's standard deviation is in line with the category median, despite big sector bets, which tend to court volatility. In addition, we like the low-turnover approach, which has kept the fund tax-efficient and has limited trading costs.

Address:	PO Box 219757 Kansas City, MO 64121 800-492-8332	Minimum Purchase:	$2500 Add: $100 IRA: $250
		Min Auto Inv Plan:	$100 Add: $100
		Sales Fees:	No-load, 2.00%R
Web Address:	www.buffalofunds.com	Management Fee:	1.00%
Inception:	12-14-01*	Actual Fees:	Mgt:1.00% Dist: —
Advisor:	Kornitzer Capital Management, Inc.	Expense Projections:	3Yr:$325 5Yr:$563 10Yr:$1248
Subadvisor:	None	Income Distrib:	Semi-Annually
NTF Plans:	Fidelity Retail-NTF, Schwab OneSource		

Historical Profile

Return	Above Avg
Risk	Above Avg
Rating	★★★★ Above Avg

Investment Style: Equity, Stock %

93% 97% 97% 90% 91% 97%

▼ Manager Change
▽ Partial Manager Change

Growth of $10,000
— Investment Values of Fund
— Investment Values of S&P 500

14.0
12.0
10.0
7.0

Performance Quartile (within Category)

	1995	1996	1997	1998	1999	2000	2001	2002	2003	2004	2005	2006	History
NAV	—	—	—	—	—	—	10.03	7.81	11.22	12.92	14.48	15.01	
Total Return %	—	—	—	—	—	—	0.30*	-22.13	43.66	16.60	13.83	5.68	
+/-S&P 500	—	—	—	—	—	—	—	-0.03	14.98	5.72	8.92	-10.11	
+/-Russ MG	—	—	—	—	—	—	—	5.28	0.95	1.12	1.73	-4.98	
Income Return %	—	—	—	—	—	—	—	0.00	0.00	0.00	0.00	0.00	
Capital Return %	—	—	—	—	—	—	—	-22.13	43.66	16.60	13.83	5.68	
Total Rtn % Rank Cat	—	—	—	—	—	—	—	33	17	27	21	75	
Income $	—	—	—	—	—	—	0.00	0.00	0.00	0.00	0.00	0.00	
Capital Gains $	—	—	—	—	—	—	0.00	0.00	0.00	0.16	0.22	0.29	
Expense Ratio %	—	—	—	—	—	—	—	1.16	1.10	1.03	1.02		
Income Ratio %	—	—	—	—	—	—	—	-0.71	-0.59	-0.48	-0.21		
Turnover Rate %	—	—	—	—	—	—	—	3	8	24	19		
Net Assets $mil	—	—	—	—	—	—	—	47	75	167	375		

Rating and Risk

Time Period	Load-Adj Return %	Morningstar Rtn vs Cat	Morningstar Risk vs Cat	Morningstar Risk-Adj Rating
1 Yr	5.68			
3 Yr	11.94	+Avg	Avg	★★★
5 Yr	9.43	+Avg	+Avg	★★★★
10 Yr	—	—	—	
Incept	9.40			

Other Measures	Standard Index S&P 500	Best Fit Index Russ MG
Alpha	-1.6	-0.6
Beta	1.50	1.00
R-Squared	70	86
Standard Deviation	12.30	
Mean	11.94	
Sharpe Ratio	0.72	

Portfolio Analysis 09-30-06

Share change since 06-06 Total Stocks:57	Sector	PE	Tot Ret%	% Assets
Amylin Pharmaceuticals	Health	—	-9.64	3.00
⊕ Red Hat, Inc.	Software	58.8	-15.63	2.89
Endo Pharmaceutical Hold	Health	17.7	-8.86	2.66
⊕ Charles River Laboratori	Health	—	2.08	2.64
IMS Health, Inc.	Health	17.4	10.77	2.50
Iron Mountain, Inc.	Business	44.8	-2.09	2.45
⊕ Barr Pharmaceuticals, In	Health	18.7	-19.54	2.37
BEA Systems, Inc.	Software	34.6	33.83	2.29
⊕ F5 Networks, Inc.	Hardware	49.5	29.76	2.26
⊕ Morningstar, Inc.	Media	43.1	30.05	2.25
Medicis Pharmaceuticals	Health	—	10.05	2.19
Novellus Systems, Inc.	Hardware	35.3	42.70	2.17
⊕ MedImmune, Inc.	Health	—	-7.57	2.14
Shire PLC ADR	Health	40.2	59.84	2.11
Qiagen NV	Health	38.1	28.77	2.07
⊕ Checkfree Corporation	Software	30.2	-12.51	2.04
Hewitt Associates, Inc.	Business	—	-8.07	1.97
Altera Corp.	Hardware	24.8	6.21	1.94
Janus Capital Group, Inc	Financial	42.2	16.13	1.84
PetSmart Inc.	Consumer	23.0	12.99	1.83

Current Investment Style

Value Blnd Growth — Large Mid Small

Market Cap	%
Giant	0.0
Large	4.1
Mid	84.9
Small	11.0
Micro	0.0
Avg $mil:	4,122

Value Measures		Rel Category
Price/Earnings	21.89	1.07
Price/Book	2.83	0.88
Price/Sales	2.12	1.20
Price/Cash Flow	12.19	1.07
Dividend Yield %	0.45	0.71

Growth Measures	%	Rel Category
Long-Term Erngs	15.71	0.97
Book Value	13.50	1.06
Sales	12.69	1.27
Cash Flow	14.07	0.76
Historical Erngs	17.11	0.69

Profitability	%	Rel Category
Return on Equity	13.33	0.74
Return on Assets	7.55	0.81
Net Margin	8.88	0.76

Sector Weightings	% of Stocks	Rel S&P 500	3 Year High	Low
↻ Info	27.10	1.36		
🖥 Software	10.11	2.93	10	5
💻 Hardware	14.67	1.59	24	12
🎙 Media	2.32	0.61	2	0
📞 Telecom	0.00	0.00	0	0
⊆ Service	57.51	1.24		
🏥 Health	26.83	2.22	27	16
🛒 Consumer	17.27	2.26	29	17
📋 Business	6.96	1.65	10	4
💲 Financial	6.45	0.29	11	6
🏭 Mfg	15.41	0.46		
🏠 Goods	10.11	1.18	11	6
⚙ Ind Mtrls	5.30	0.44	6	3
🔋 Energy	0.00	0.00	0	0
💡 Utilities	0.00	0.00	0	0

Composition

● Cash	2.9
● Stocks	97.1
● Bonds	0.0
○ Other	0.0
Foreign (% of Stock)	6.2

Buffalo Small Cap

	Ticker	Load	NAV	Yield	Total Assets	Mstar Category
	BUFSX	None	$26.94	0.0%	$2,019 mil	Small Growth

Governance and Management

Stewardship Grade: A

Portfolio Manager(s)

Kent Gasaway and Robert Male have both comanaged the fund since its April 1998 inception. Grant Sarris, a former small-cap manager with Waddell & Reed, has been with the fund since November 2003. Four analysts support Male, Gasaway, and Sarris.

Strategy

Using a growth-at-a-reasonable-price philosophy, the managers employ numerous themes to direct stock selection, such as those related to demographic patterns and technological innovation. Firms with strong earnings and cash flow, competitive products, and rock-solid balance sheets are fund favorites. Such stocks often trade at a premium, but management gets edgy when prices climb too high. Although its initial position in any one issue is small, it holds on to winners. Turnover is very low.

Historical Profile

Return	Above Avg
Risk	Above Avg
Rating	★★★★ Above Avg

Investment Style: Equity, Stock %

68% 98% 96% 91% 96% 93% 91% 99% 99%

▼ Manager Change
▽ Partial Manager Change

Growth of $10,000
— Investment Values of Fund
— Investment Values of S&P 500

Performance Quartile (within Category)

	1995	1996	1997	1998	1999	2000	2001	2002	2003	2004	2005	2006	History
	—	—	—	9.63	12.76	15.24	19.96	14.80	22.18	27.65	25.44	26.94	NAV
	—	—	—	-3.29*	34.79	33.69	31.18	-25.75	51.23	28.82	3.22	13.95	Total Return %
	—	—	—	—	13.75	42.79	43.07	-3.65	22.55	17.94	-1.69	-1.84	+/-S&P 500
	—	—	—	—	-8.30	56.12	40.41	4.51	2.69	14.51	-0.93	0.60	+/-Russ 2000 Gr
	—	—	—	—	0.00	0.00	0.00	0.00	0.00	0.08	0.00	0.00	Income Return %
	—	—	—	—	34.79	33.69	31.18	-25.75	51.23	28.74	3.22	13.95	Capital Return %
	—	—	—	—	68	2	1	42	24	1	78	25	Total Rtn % Rank Cat
	—	—	—	0.04	0.00	0.00	0.00	0.00	0.00	0.02	0.00	0.00	Income $
	—	—	—	0.00	0.21	1.67	0.03	0.03	0.20	0.88	3.11	2.04	Capital Gains $
	—	—	—	—	—	—	1.12	1.04	1.01	1.02	1.01	1.01	Expense Ratio %
	—	—	—	—	—	—	-0.27	-0.12	-0.44	-0.55	-0.53	-0.42	Income Ratio %
	—	—	—	—	—	—	42	31	6	23	22	27	Turnover Rate %
	—	—	—	—	—	24	49	1,027	857	1,418	1,971	2,019	Net Assets $mil

Performance 12-31-06

	1st Qtr	2nd Qtr	3rd Qtr	4th Qtr	Total
2002	5.61	-13.25	-23.00	5.26	-25.75
2003	-6.82	30.38	11.12	12.03	51.23
2004	15.87	-0.32	-3.01	15.00	28.82
2005	-4.88	4.33	1.64	2.33	3.22
2006	12.85	-9.40	3.54	7.65	13.95

Trailing	Total Return%	+/- S&P 500	+/- Russ 2000 Gr	%Rank Cat	Growth of $10,000
3 Mo	7.65	0.95	-1.12	56	10,765
6 Mo	11.46	-1.28	4.60	3	11,146
1 Yr	13.95	-1.84	0.60	25	11,395
3 Yr Avg	14.86	4.42	4.35	7	15,153
5 Yr Avg	11.22	5.03	4.29	10	17,018
10 Yr Avg	—	—	—	—	—
15 Yr Avg	—	—	—	—	—

Tax Analysis	Tax-Adj Rtn%	%Rank Cat	Tax-Cost Rat	%Rank Cat
3 Yr (estimated)	13.46	6	1.22	47
5 Yr (estimated)	10.37	8	0.76	44
10 Yr (estimated)	—	—	—	—

Potential Capital Gain Exposure: 25% of assets

Morningstar's Take by Reginald Laing 12-27-06

We recommend Buffalo Small Cap--but with reservations about its size.

This fund--which new investors can only buy directly from Buffalo Funds--has appeal. The management team's strategy of looking for companies that will benefit from long-term trends works well in the small-cap arena: Smaller companies tend to focus on particular businesses, and this fund's managers can find firms that are pure beneficiaries of trends and are the likeliest to succeed if their trend analysis is on-target.

Of course, the portfolio is subject to performance swings. The managers tend to cluster holdings in a handful of industries where they predict their trends will play out, particularly in health care and consumer-related stocks. So, the fund can prosper or sink on the strength or weakness of individual sectors. But management is patient with its picks. For instance, slot machine maker WMS Industries has been in the portfolio since mid-2003. The managers think this company will benefit from two

long-term trends: An aging population spending more disposable income playing slots and the growing popularity of slots abroad. They also think WMS will gain from a cyclical upturn, as many casinos will upgrade their slots soon.

Over time, management has executed this strategy well, giving the fund one of the best long-term records in Morningstar's small-growth category. But has success come at a cost? With inflows and capital appreciation, this is now one of the biggest small-cap funds around--a particular concern in the relatively illiquid small-cap arena. For instance, management owns roughly 10 times the average daily trading volume of executive-search consultant Heidrick & Struggles, which could be a difficult position to unwind without lowering its share price.

But investors have reason to stay put. For now, cheap expenses, talented management, and a low-turnover strategy should keep asset size from being a major impediment.

Address:	5420 West 61st Street	Minimum Purchase:	$2500	Add: $100	IRA: $250
	Shawnee Mission, KS 66205	Min Auto Inv Plan:	$100	Add: $100	
	800-492-8332	Sales Fees:	No-load, 2.00%R		
Web Address:	www.buffalofunds.com	Management Fee:	1.00%		
Inception:	04-14-98*	Actual Fees:	Mgt:1.00%	Dist: —	
Advisor:	Kornitzer Capital Management, Inc.	Expense Projections:	3Yr:$322	5Yr:$558	10Yr:$1236
Subadvisor:	None	Income Distrib:	Semi-Annually		
NTF Plans:	Fidelity Retail-NTF, Schwab OneSource				

Rating and Risk

Time Period	Load-Adj Return %	Morningstar Rtn vs Cat	Morningstar Risk vs Cat	Morningstar Risk-Adj Rating
1 Yr	13.95			
3 Yr	14.86	High	Avg	★★★★★
5 Yr	11.22	+Avg	+Avg	★★★★
10 Yr	—			
Incept	16.87			

Other Measures	Standard Index S&P 500	Best Fit Index Mstar Small Growth
Alpha	-0.1	5.8
Beta	1.68	0.79
R-Squared	69	85
Standard Deviation	13.89	
Mean	14.86	
Sharpe Ratio	0.84	

Portfolio Analysis 09-30-06

Share change since 06-06 Total Stocks:61	Sector	PE	Tot Ret%	% Assets
⊖ Amylin Pharmaceuticals	Health	—	-9.64	3.48
WMS Industries, Inc.	Consumer	38.0	38.94	3.27
Gamestop Corporation B	Goods	—	—	2.84
Covance, Inc.	Health	28.4	21.34	2.68
⊖ Pharmaceutical Product D	Health	24.3	4.26	2.65
Mentor Corporation	Health	52.4	7.70	2.51
Heidrick & Struggles Int	Business	23.2	32.17	2.36
⊕ P.F. Chang's China Bistr	Consumer	29.6	-22.67	2.31
Penn National Gaming	Goods	21.8	26.31	2.27
Immucor, Inc.	Health	48.7	87.70	2.18
Adtran	Hardware	19.4	-22.46	2.17
Medicis Pharmaceuticals	Health	—	10.05	2.08
Borders Group, Inc.	Consumer	50.2	5.14	2.00
Orient-Express Hotels, L	Consumer	50.0	50.53	1.96
DeVry, Inc.	Consumer	34.4	40.26	1.95
⊕ Dolby Laboratories, Inc.	Goods	—	81.94	1.93
Manhattan Associates, In	Software	39.7	46.88	1.90
Fairchild Semiconductor	Hardware	92.0	-0.59	1.90
MKS Instruments, Inc.	Hardware	16.1	26.22	1.87
Central Garden & Pet Com	Ind Mtrls	16.0	5.40	1.87

Current Investment Style

Value Blnd Growth — Large Mid Small

Market Cap	%
Giant	0.0
Large	0.0
Mid	31.2
Small	68.0
Micro	0.8
Avg $mil:	1,428

Value Measures		Rel Category
Price/Earnings	21.50	1.02
Price/Book	2.67	0.98
Price/Sales	1.62	1.03
Price/Cash Flow	12.84	1.33
Dividend Yield %	0.45	0.98

Growth Measures	%	Rel Category
Long-Term Erngs	15.87	0.89
Book Value	9.65	0.92
Sales	12.53	1.05
Cash Flow	3.73	0.18
Historical Erngs	12.30	0.51

Profitability	%	Rel Category
Return on Equity	11.41	0.92
Return on Assets	6.81	1.02
Net Margin	6.43	0.74

Sector Weightings	% of Stocks	Rel S&P 500	3 Year High	Low
℧ Info	23.57	1.18		
Software	6.39	1.85	9	3
Hardware	15.57	1.69	17	10
Media	1.61	0.42	2	0
Telecom	0.00	0.00	0	0
Service	61.39	1.33		
Health	27.50	2.28	30	22
Consumer	20.64	2.70	33	20
Business	7.23	1.71	7	0
Financial	6.02	0.27	10	6
Mfg	15.04	0.45		
Goods	10.40	1.22	12	6
Ind Mtrls	4.64	0.39	7	4
Energy	0.00	0.00	0	0
Utilities	0.00	0.00	0	0

Composition

● Cash	1.4	
● Stocks	98.6	
● Bonds	0.0	
● Other	0.0	
Foreign	5.2	(% of Stock)

Morningstar® Funds 500

Calamos Convertible A

	Ticker	Load	NAV	Yield	Total Assets	Mstar Category
	CCVIX	Closed	$19.03	4.0%	$801 mil	Convertibles

Governance and Management

Stewardship Grade: B

Portfolio Manager(s)

John Calamos wrote the book on convertibles and has more than 20 years of experience investing in convertible securities. Nick Calamos, who has comanaged the fund since 1988, developed the firm's quantitative models. New investors seeking access to their skills might consider Calamos Growth & Income, a slightly bolder convertibles-focused fund, given that this fund is closed.

Strategy

Comanagers John and Nick Calamos have traditionally focused on high-credit-quality issues that are trading at moderate conversion premiums, meaning the convertible security is somewhat correlated with the underlying equity. Management uses a quantitative approach to identify attractively valued issues and backs that up with fundamental analysis and company visits. In February 2003, the fund dropped its investment-grade average credit-quality requirement and will likely carry more lower-rated credits.

Performance 12-31-06

	1st Qtr	2nd Qtr	3rd Qtr	4th Qtr	Total
2002	2.21	-2.50	-9.13	5.39	-4.56
2003	-1.08	11.83	2.40	10.36	25.01
2004	5.37	-1.52	-2.48	6.27	7.54
2005	-3.68	0.98	4.52	1.14	2.82
2006	3.96	-0.99	2.02	3.93	9.13

Trailing	Total Return%	+/- DJ Mod	+/- Merrill Lynch Convert	%Rank Cat	Growth of $10,000
3 Mo	3.93	-1.66	-0.89	76	10,393
6 Mo	6.03	-2.76	-1.62	71	10,603
1 Yr	9.13	-3.17	-2.90	70	10,913
3 Yr Avg	6.46	-4.26	-0.13	75	12,066
5 Yr Avg	7.56	-2.46	-0.05	56	14,396
10 Yr Avg	10.42	1.87	1.81	13	26,945
15 Yr Avg	10.99	1.78	1.09	29	47,781

Tax Analysis	Tax-Adj Rtn%	%Rank Cat	Tax-Cost Rat	%Rank Cat
3 Yr (estimated)	2.35	98	2.29	93
5 Yr (estimated)	4.73	74	1.68	76
10 Yr (estimated)	7.69	16	1.99	37

Potential Capital Gain Exposure: 13% of assets

Historical Profile

Return	Average	
Risk	Average	
Rating	★★★ Neutral	

12%	6%	17%	21%	23%	20%	21%	14%	18%

Growth of $10,000

— Investment Values of Fund
— Investment Values of DJ Mod

▼ Manager Change
▽ Partial Manager Change

Performance Quartile (within Category)

1995	1996	1997	1998	1999	2000	2001	2002	2003	2004	2005	2006	History
13.85	14.41	15.87	16.87	21.80	20.38	18.56	17.41	21.24	21.20	19.21	19.03	NAV
29.25	16.70	20.81	11.64	35.11	7.25	-4.28	-4.56	25.01	7.54	2.82	9.13	Total Return %
9.45	6.04	8.91	-0.68	17.78	8.92	-1.48	2.21	-2.37	-5.43	-4.17	-3.17	+/-DJ Mod
5.29	4.58	5.30	-0.57	-0.88	14.77	-1.37	-1.44	2.04	-0.77	3.01	-2.90	+/-Merrill Lynch Convert
3.16	3.53	3.21	2.71	2.96	2.62	3.09	1.67	2.80	2.69	4.67	4.36	Income Return %
26.09	13.17	17.60	8.93	32.15	4.63	-7.37	-6.23	22.21	4.85	-1.85	4.77	Capital Return %
1	45	28	11	20	26	47	12	46	65	54	70	Total Rtn % Rank Cat
0.37	0.47	0.45	0.43	0.50	0.54	0.62	0.31	0.48	0.56	0.93	0.81	Income $
1.00	1.18	1.05	0.38	0.37	2.44	0.31	0.00	0.00	1.04	1.62	1.09	Capital Gains $
1.60	1.50	1.50	1.40	1.40	1.40	1.20	1.20	1.20	1.15	1.11	1.12	Expense Ratio %
3.30	3.00	2.80	3.30	2.60	2.30	2.50	2.70	3.80	2.36	1.80	1.78	Income Ratio %
42	65	52	76	78	91	93	37	36	67	51	34	Turnover Rate %
21	32	52	68	86	129	250	461	632	554	420	348	Net Assets $mil

Rating and Risk

Time Period	Load-Adj Return %	Morningstar Rtn vs Cat	Morningstar Risk vs Cat	Morningstar Risk-Adj Rating
1 Yr	3.95			
3 Yr	4.75	Low	Avg	★
5 Yr	6.52	-Avg	Avg	★★
10 Yr	9.88	+Avg	Avg	★★★★
Incept	10.61			

Other Measures	Standard Index DJ Mod	Best Fit Index Merrill Lynch Convert
Alpha	-4.5	-0.3
Beta	1.09	1.08
R-Squared	81	90
Standard Deviation	7.11	
Mean	6.46	
Sharpe Ratio	0.47	

Portfolio Analysis 10-31-06

Total Fixed-Income:22	Date of Maturity	Amount $000	Value $000	% Net Assets
Merrill Lynch	03-13-32	20,500	25,746	3.03
LOCKHEED MARTIN	08-15-33	20,000	25,492	3.00
US Treasury Note 3.375%	02-15-08	24,600	24,169	2.84
Laboratory	09-11-21	25,600	23,744	2.79
Genzyme 1.25%	12-01-23	18,500	20,188	2.38
DST SYS	08-15-23	14,350	19,839	2.33
Csx Cv	10-30-21	14,600	18,816	2.21
Gilead Sciences 144A Cv	05-01-11	17,400	18,401	2.16
Cadence Design Sys Cv	08-15-23	14,900	17,768	2.09
Genworth Finl		485	17,484	2.06
Carnival Cv 2%	04-15-21	13,350	17,088	2.01
Travelers Ppty Cas Pfd	04-15-32	635	16,510	1.94
Symantec 144A Cv 0.75%	06-15-11	13,900	16,141	1.90
Fluor 1.5%	02-15-24	10,600	15,450	1.82
Csg Sys Intl 144A 2.5%	06-15-24	13,300	15,278	1.80
Wachovia 25%	12-15-10	14,300	14,306	1.68
Disney Walt Cv 2.125%	04-15-23	12,500	14,266	1.68
Washington Mut		261	14,103	1.66
Intl Game Tech Cv	01-29-33	15,500	14,086	1.66
Metlife Pfd		457	13,531	1.59

Investment Style

Equity
Stock %

Avg Eff Maturity	3.3 Yrs
Avg Credit Quality	BBB
Avg Wtd Coupon	1.48%
Avg Wtd Price	119.74% of par

Coupon Range	% of Bonds	Rel Cat
0% PIK	25.8	1.8
0% to 8%	100.0	1.0
8% to 11%	0.0	0.0
11% to 14%	0.0	0.0
More than 14%	0.0	0.0
1.00=Category Average		

Special Securities

Restricted/Illiquid Secs	15
Emerging-Markets Secs	0
Options/Futures/Warrants	No

Credit Analysis   % bonds 10-31-06

AAA	9	BB	5
AA	10	B	6
A	16	Below B	0
BBB	31	NR/NA	23

Composition

Cash	3.8
Stocks	18.2
Bonds	31.2
Convertibles	35.4
Other	11.4

Morningstar's Take by Kerry O'Boyle 12-11-06

Is mediocrity setting in at Calamos Convertible?

Once a standout in the convertibles category, this fund has treated shareholders to middling returns over the past five years. In 2006 in particular, the fund's bias toward higher-quality companies and investment-grade convertibles hasn't helped in a market largely favoring lower-quality issues. It has no exposure to CCC converts and only a minimal 7% stake in B rated holdings (versus 24% for the overall market), the two best-performing credit segments of the market.

Still, there are many variables in convertible investing, and a high-quality bias doesn't fully explain all its past woes. The fund is somewhat caught in the middle relative to its peers. While more moderate than sibling Calamos Growth & Income and other aggressive offerings in the category, it has carried sizable stakes in straight equities in the past (nearly 11% as of the end of September) that make it more sensitive to the stock market than more-pure-play convertible funds. Thus, it hasn't excelled in recent years against its rivals during extreme markets favoring either stocks or converts.

That doesn't mean the fund has lost its touch, however. It has remained true to its mild approach to investing in convertibles and continues to provide an attractive risk/reward profile for investors. And should investment-grade converts regain favor, something that Calamos thinks will happen and it has further increased its stake, the fund could be poised to shine once again.

While the fund's current rough patch has lasted longer than previous dry spells, we think that shareholders have reason to stick with it. Calamos is one of the more highly regarded convertible specialists in the mutual fund arena, as its long-term record here and at Growth & Income will attest. While its record doesn't look as good as it has in years past, we think it still holds appeal for shareholders.

Address:	2020 Calamos Court Naperville IL 60563 800-823-7386	Minimum Purchase:	Closed	Add: —	IRA: —
		Min Auto Inv Plan:	Closed	Add: —	
		Sales Fees:	4.75%L, 0.25%S, 2.00%R		
Web Address:	www.calamos.com	Management Fee:	0.75% mx./0.65% mn.		
Inception:	06-21-85	Actual Fees:	Mgt:0.72% Dist:0.25%		
Advisor:	Calamos Advisors LLC	Expense Projections:	3Yr:$814 5Yr:$1063 10Yr:$1773		
Subadvisor:	None	Income Distrib:	Quarterly		
NTF Plans:	DATALynx NTF, Federated Tr NTF				

Calamos Gr & Inc A

	Analyst Pick	Ticker	Load	NAV	Yield	Total Assets	Mstar Category
	✓	CVTRX	4.75%	$31.46	1.9%	$6,500 mil	Convertibles

Governance and Management

Stewardship Grade: B

Portfolio Manager(s)

John Calamos wrote the book on convertibles. And he has more than 20 years of experience investing in convertible securities. Nick Calamos has comanaged the fund since 1988 and developed the firm's quantitative models. The pair also guides the highly successful Calamos Growth, which invests exclusively in stocks. The managers eat their own cooking: Most of their wealth is invested in the funds.

Strategy

Comanagers John and Nick Calamos couple convertible bonds and stocks in this fund. The convertibles are often low- and midquality issues from typically small- and mid-cap firms. Management uses a quantitative approach to identify attractively valued issues and backs that up with fundamental analysis and company visits.

Historical Profile

Return	Above Avg
Risk	Above Avg
Rating	★★★★ Above Avg

Investment Style: Equity / Stock %

13% 14% 5% 24% 22% 37% 49% 43% 40%

▼ Manager Change
▽ Partial Manager Change

Growth of $10,000
— Investment Values of Fund
— Investment Values of DJ Mod

50.6
43.6
32.4
24.0
17.0
10.0

Performance Quartile (within Category)

	1995	1996	1997	1998	1999	2000	2001	2002	2003	2004	2005	2006	History
	14.74	15.46	16.59	17.95	26.51	25.05	23.60	22.21	27.78	29.82	30.83	31.46	NAV
	29.14	19.22	23.34	17.62	52.94	6.86	-2.38	-4.10	27.57	9.67	8.06	9.84	Total Return %
	9.34	8.56	11.44	5.30	35.61	8.53	0.42	2.67	0.19	-3.30	1.07	-2.46	+/-DJ Mod
	5.18	7.10	7.83	5.41	16.95	14.38	0.53	-0.98	4.60	1.36	8.25	-2.19	+/-Merrill Lynch Convert
	3.52	2.09	2.53	1.96	2.64	2.30	2.49	1.80	2.28	1.65	2.04	2.09	Income Return %
	25.62	17.13	20.81	15.66	50.30	4.56	-4.87	-5.90	25.29	8.02	6.02	7.75	Capital Return %
	5	23	10	3	1	37	22	8	30	45	2	61	Total Rtn % Rank Cat
	0.43	0.29	0.38	0.32	0.47	0.59	0.61	0.42	0.50	0.46	0.60	0.63	Income $
	0.71	1.68	2.00	1.17	0.28	2.73	0.21	0.00	0.00	0.16	0.76	1.74	Capital Gains $
	2.00	2.00	2.00	2.00	2.00	1.70	1.40	1.30	1.30	1.14	1.08	1.05	Expense Ratio %
	3.00	2.60	2.40	2.00	2.30	1.80	2.60	2.20	3.30	1.63	1.42	1.35	Income Ratio %
	85	86	92	116	88	117	82	40	27	50	65	42	Turnover Rate %
	4	8	10	16	24	65	173	474	1,634	2,507	3,007	3,568	Net Assets $mil

Performance 12-31-06

	1st Qtr	2nd Qtr	3rd Qtr	4th Qtr	Total
2002	1.85	-2.65	-8.06	5.19	-4.10
2003	1.05	11.74	2.82	9.87	27.57
2004	3.56	-1.71	-1.21	9.06	9.67
2005	-1.41	1.63	6.32	1.43	8.06
2006	5.84	-3.35	2.44	4.82	9.84

Trailing	Total Return%	+/- DJ Mod	+/- Merrill Lynch Convert	%Rank Cat	Growth of $10,000
3 Mo	4.82	-0.77	0.00	44	10,482
6 Mo	7.38	-1.41	-0.27	31	10,738
1 Yr	9.84	-2.46	-2.19	61	10,984
3 Yr Avg	9.19	-1.53	2.60	23	13,018
5 Yr Avg	9.75	-0.27	2.14	12	15,923
10 Yr Avg	13.93	5.38	5.32	1	36,845
15 Yr Avg	13.63	4.42	3.73	1	67,982

Tax Analysis	Tax-Adj Rtn%	%Rank Cat	Tax-Cost Rat	%Rank Cat
3 Yr (estimated)	6.28	33	1.07	41
5 Yr (estimated)	7.68	20	0.93	28
10 Yr (estimated)	11.40	5	1.75	22

Potential Capital Gain Exposure: 16% of assets

Rating and Risk

Time Period	Load-Adj Return %	Morningstar Rtn vs Cat	Morningstar Risk vs Cat	Morningstar Risk-Adj Rating
1 Yr	4.63			
3 Yr	7.43	Avg	High	★★★
5 Yr	8.69	+Avg	+Avg	★★★★
10 Yr	13.38	High	+Avg	★★★★★
Incept	13.63			

Other Measures	Standard Index DJ Mod	Best Fit Index Russ 2000
Alpha	-3.7	0.0
Beta	1.34	0.57
R-Squared	85	86
Standard Deviation	8.55	
Mean	9.19	
Sharpe Ratio	0.70	

Portfolio Analysis 06-30-06

Total Fixed-Income:43	Date of Maturity	Amount $000	Value $000	% Net Assets
US Treasury Note 3.375%	02-15-08	307,000	298,486	4.76
Merrill Lynch	03-13-32	134,000	146,730	2.34
Infosys Technologies, Lt		1,800	137,538	2.19
Microsoft Corporation		4,876	113,611	1.81
LIBERTY MEDIA	03-30-23	105,720	112,724	1.80
Thermo Electron Corp.		3,000	108,720	1.73
Valero Engy Cv		800	105,700	1.69
Home Depot, Inc.		2,900	103,791	1.66
Halliburton Cv 3.125%	07-15-23	47,500	95,475	1.52
Nokia		4,500	91,227	1.46
Washington Mutual, Inc.		2,000	91,168	1.45
Amgen 144A Cv 0.125%	02-01-11	90,000	84,600	1.35
Nii Hldgs 144A Cv 2.75%	08-15-25	63,500	84,455	1.35
PepsiCo, Inc.		1,375	82,555	1.32
Host Marriott L P 144A 3	04-15-24	60,000	79,800	1.27
Medtronic 1.25%	09-15-21	78,800	78,505	1.25
Pfizer Inc.		3,250	76,278	1.22
Goldman Sachs Group, Inc		485	72,959	1.16
NVIDIA Corporation		3,400	72,386	1.15
ANGLO AMERICAN PLC	04-17-07	40,250	72,048	1.15

Investment Style

Avg Eff Maturity	3.3 Yrs
Avg Credit Quality	BBB
Avg Wtd Coupon	2.29%
Avg Wtd Price	114.89% of par

Coupon Range	% of Bonds	Rel Cat
0% PIK	12.5	0.9
0% to 8%	98.7	1.0
8% to 11%	1.3	1.5
11% to 14%	0.0	0.0
More than 14%	0.0	0.0

1.00=Category Average

Special Securities

Restricted/Illiquid Secs	13
Emerging-Markets Secs	3
Options/Futures/Warrants	No

Credit Analysis

	% bonds 06-30-06		
AAA	13	BB	18
AA	10	B	10
A	13	Below B	1
BBB	12	NR/NA	23

Composition

Cash	3.7
Stocks	39.6
Bonds	29.6
Convertibles	24.0
Other	3.0

Morningstar's Take by Kerry O'Boyle 12-11-06

A big stake in equities has taken its toll on Calamos Growth & Income in 2006.

It's been a rough year thus far for this fund versus its convertible fund peers. Unlike in 2005, when a hedge-fund fueled selling frenzy rocked the convert market in the spring, the attractive risk/reward characteristics of converts have shone in 2006. These hybrid securities sailed through the stormy early summer stock market correction largely unscathed thanks to a relatively stable credit market. Such has not been the case at this fund, however, which has invested well more than 30% of its assets in stocks for several years now.

Not that this is cause for concern at Calamos. It has positioned this fund to be more aggressive than sibling Calamos Convertible and its typical peer. In addition to the large equity stakes, management also tends to buy converts that are more sensitive to the movements of their underlying stocks than most rivals. What's more, during the year it has again increased the fund's stock holdings to more than 45% of assets. Management thinks the early-summer correction has made stocks more attractive, while converts are no longer trading at the discounts they did last year.

This sort of big picture analysis isn't unusual for Calamos, which has made a number of prudent macro calls in the past to go along with its topnotch bottom-up convertible research. The firm continues to be bullish on the stock market and the overall state of the economy despite the recent turmoil. Shareholders can take heart in that the recent swoon is likely a blip given the fund's outstanding long-term record.

To be sure, investors shouldn't confuse this offering with a pure-play convertible fund. With more than $6 billion in assets--3 times the size of its next largest rival--the fund will likely always need to turn to equities given the relatively small convertible market. But it still offers moderate volatility compared with an equity fund, and we're standing by this Analyst Pick.

Address:	2020 Calamos Court Naperville IL 60563 800-823-7386
Web Address:	www.calamos.com
Inception:	09-22-88
Advisor:	Calamos Advisors LLC
Subadvisor:	None
NTF Plans:	DATALynx NTF, Federated Tr NTF

Minimum Purchase:	$2500	Add: $50	IRA: $500
Min Auto Inv Plan:	$2500	Add: $50	
Sales Fees:	4.75%L, 0.25%S, 2.00%R		
Management Fee:	1.00% mx./0.80% mn.		
Actual Fees:	Mgt:0.66%	Dist:0.25%	
Expense Projections:	3Yr:$796	5Yr:$1032	10Yr:$1708
Income Distrib:	Quarterly		

M⊖RNINGSTAR® Funds 500

Calamos Growth A

	Ticker	Load	NAV	Yield	Total Assets	Mstar Category
	CVGRX	4.75%	$53.90	0.0%	$16,919 mil	Mid-Cap Growth

Governance and Management

Stewardship Grade: B

Portfolio Manager(s)

Calamos Asset Management, known for its convertible-bond expertise, employs techniques at this fund that are similar to those it uses in assessing underlying firms in the convertibles market. John and Nick Calamos have managed the fund since its September 1990 inception, and John's son, John Jr., came on board in 1994.

Strategy

Management uses quantitative models to search for companies growing faster than their industries and sector peers as measured by earnings growth and returns on invested capital. It then digs deeply into company balance sheets to understand the business and looks for strong free cash flows and sustainable growth. Finally, in constructing the portfolio, management uses top-down macroeconomic analysis to identify promising sectors and themes to exploit with higher/lower weightings.

Historical Profile

Return: Above Avg
Risk: Average
Rating: ★★★★ Above Avg

97%	98%	100%	98%	85%	98%	99%	99%	99%

Growth of $10,000
— Investment Values of Fund
— Investment Values of S&P 500

Performance Quartile (within Category)

1995	1996	1997	1998	1999	2000	2001	2002	2003	2004	2005	2006	History
14.46	18.13	17.21	21.91	35.71	40.51	37.40	31.46	44.78	52.98	55.06	53.90	NAV
27.50	37.91	24.22	27.31	77.70	26.59	-7.68	-15.88	42.34	18.65	8.47	1.45	Total Return %
-10.08	14.95	-9.14	-1.27	56.66	35.69	4.21	6.22	13.66	7.77	3.56	-14.34	+/-S&P 500
-6.48	20.43	1.68	9.45	26.41	38.34	12.47	11.53	-0.37	3.17	-3.63	-9.21	+/-Russ MG
0.51	0.00	0.00	0.00	0.00	0.00	0.00	0.00	0.00	0.00	0.00	0.00	Income Return %
26.99	37.91	24.22	27.31	77.70	26.59	-7.68	-15.88	42.34	18.65	8.47	1.45	Capital Return %
75	2	32	21	28	7	22	11	22	14	66	94	Total Rtn % Rank Cat
0.07	0.00	0.00	0.00	0.00	0.00	0.00	0.00	0.00	0.00	0.00	0.00	Income $
2.97	1.75	5.50	0.00	3.13	4.99	0.00	0.00	0.00	0.14	2.34	1.97	Capital Gains $
2.00	2.00	2.00	2.00	2.00	2.00	1.50	1.55	1.40	1.31	1.23	1.19	Expense Ratio %
0.20	-0.80	-1.30	-1.50	-1.60	-1.70	-0.70	-1.10	-1.10	-0.96	-0.74	-0.71	Income Ratio %
104	252	174	206	184	175	91	79	60	54	63	41	Turnover Rate %
3	6	8	12	26	102	642	1,521	4,458	9,680	12,879	12,081	Net Assets $mil

Investment Style: Equity, Stock %

▼ Manager Change
▽ Partial Manager Change

Performance 12-31-06

	1st Qtr	2nd Qtr	3rd Qtr	4th Qtr	Total
2002	0.64	-4.44	-10.98	-1.75	-15.88
2003	0.70	16.16	10.60	10.02	42.34
2004	6.34	3.04	-3.85	12.61	18.65
2005	-5.81	1.84	7.46	5.23	8.47
2006	5.90	-6.96	-1.59	4.62	1.45

Trailing	Total Return%	+/- S&P 500	+/- Russ MG	%Rank Cat	Growth of $10,000
3 Mo	4.62	-2.08	-2.33	84	10,462
6 Mo	2.96	-9.78	-4.94	78	10,296
1 Yr	1.45	-14.34	-9.21	94	10,145
3 Yr Avg	9.29	-1.15	-3.44	68	13,054
5 Yr Avg	9.35	3.16	1.13	18	15,635
10 Yr Avg	17.77	9.35	9.15	2	51,327
15 Yr Avg	15.80	5.16	5.67	2	90,288

Tax Analysis	Tax-Adj Rtn%	%Rank Cat	Tax-Cost Rat	%Rank Cat
3 Yr (estimated)	7.11	79	0.40	20
5 Yr (estimated)	8.03	23	0.24	18
10 Yr (estimated)	15.57	2	1.39	50

Potential Capital Gain Exposure: 20% of assets

Rating and Risk

Time Period	Load-Adj Return %	Morningstar Rtn vs Cat	Morningstar Risk vs Cat	Morningstar Risk-Adj Rating
1 Yr	-3.37			
3 Yr	7.54	-Avg	+Avg	★★
5 Yr	8.29	+Avg	Avg	★★★★
10 Yr	17.20	High	Avg	★★★★★
Incept	16.95			

Other Measures	Standard Index S&P 500	Best Fit Index Mstar Mid Growth TR
Alpha	-6.1	-5.0
Beta	1.85	1.13
R-Squared	71	90

Standard Deviation	14.96
Mean	9.29
Sharpe Ratio	0.45

Portfolio Analysis 10-31-06

Share change since 09-06   Total Stocks:180

Sector		PE	Tot Ret%	% Assets
Apple Computer, Inc.	Hardware	37.6	18.01	4.89
Google, Inc.	Business	61.5	11.00	4.03
Gilead Sciences, Inc.	Health	40.6	23.51	2.72
⊕ Oracle Corporation	Software	26.7	40.38	2.23
Hewlett-Packard Company	Hardware	19.3	45.21	2.18
Express Scripts	Health	22.7	-14.56	2.05
NII Holdings, Inc.	Telecom	45.9	47.53	1.83
Weatherford Internationa	Energy	15.2	16.56	1.71
☼ Danaher Corporation	Ind Mtrls	22.0	30.02	1.54
⊕ Garmin, Ltd.	Hardware	28.2	69.45	1.44
Lehman Brothers Holdings	Financial	12.2	22.75	1.32
⊕ Caremark RX, Inc.	Health	23.6	10.90	1.28
Celgene Corporation	Health	—	77.56	1.26
⊕ Coach, Inc.	Goods	32.1	28.85	1.26
Charles Schwab Corporati	Financial	26.3	32.87	1.20
Caterpillar Inc.	Ind Mtrls	11.8	7.86	1.20
Best Buy Co., Inc.	Consumer	19.8	13.89	1.15
Baker Hughes Inc.	Energy	9.9	23.68	1.13
SanDisk Corporation	Hardware	24.2	-31.50	1.11
⊕ Las Vegas Sands, Inc.	Consumer	75.7	126.70	1.07

Current Investment Style

Value Blnd Growth — Large/Mid/Small

Market Cap	%
Giant	15.4
Large	36.0
Mid	44.1
Small	4.5
Micro	0.0

Avg $mil: 12,283

Value Measures		Rel Category
Price/Earnings	21.83	1.06
Price/Book	3.82	1.19
Price/Sales	1.88	1.07
Price/Cash Flow	12.97	1.14
Dividend Yield %	0.42	0.67

Growth Measures	%	Rel Category
Long-Term Erngs	16.44	1.01
Book Value	9.25	0.73
Sales	10.95	1.10
Cash Flow	23.39	1.27
Historical Erngs	23.82	0.95

Profitability	%	Rel Category
Return on Equity	20.40	1.14
Return on Assets	11.48	1.23
Net Margin	13.77	1.18

Sector Weightings	% of Stocks	Rel S&P 500	3 Year High	Low
⚲ Info	32.24	1.61		
▣ Software	6.41	1.86	10	2
▣ Hardware	20.15	2.18	26	17
▣ Media	1.26	0.33	6	0
▣ Telecom	4.42	1.26	4	3
☞ Service	49.82	1.08		
▣ Health	15.09	1.25	22	9
▣ Consumer	10.33	1.35	23	9
▣ Business	11.88	2.81	15	5
▣ Financial	12.52	0.56	13	4
⊔ Mfg	17.95	0.53		
▣ Goods	4.84	0.57	6	1
▣ Ind Mtrls	8.63	0.72	12	5
▣ Energy	4.48	0.46	12	4
▣ Utilities	0.00	0.00	0	0

Composition

● Cash	0.6	
● Stocks	98.9	
● Bonds	0.0	
● Other	0.5	
Foreign	1.9	(% of Stock)

Morningstar's Take by Kerry O'Boyle 12-15-06

Calamos Growth may be a victim of its own success.

While we consider this fund's awful year in 2006 to be a bit of an aberration, we also think the fund's asset size will prevent it from being the standout offering it once was. After delivering five straight top-quartile finishes in the mid-growth category--through bull and bear markets--from 1998 to 2002, the fund saw assets explode from $1.5 billion to nearly $20 billion in the subsequent three years. That's a huge amount of money for a manager to run in a mid-cap style. Already there's been evidence of a change in the fund's approach, in the form of greater number of holdings in the portfolio and lower turnover as assets have grown.

While there have been instances of mid-cap funds of this size maintaining their excellence, they are few and far between. A number of factors work against this fund. The asset growth likely came too far too fast to allow for a smooth adjustment to running such a big fund. Also, top-down,

sector-shifting moves that have served the fund well in the past are now more difficult to pull off given its less nimble size. Finally, given the shop's expanding fund lineup (all run by the same team) and the greater responsibilities associated with being a public company, we wonder if management has the necessary time to devote to the fund's nearly 200 holdings.

That said, we don't necessarily blame the fund's poor showing this year on asset bloat. A longstanding bet on technology, especially hardware stocks, continues to hold the fund back. Plus, the fund cut its heretofore neutral energy weighting in half amid the summer correction in commodity prices, only to see that sector bounce back strongly in recent months.

Still, those may be prudent moves over the long haul, and shareholders that jumped in the past few years would be wise to give them time to pan out. Prospective investors, however, should look at cheaper and nimbler options.

Address:	2020 Calamos Court	Minimum Purchase:	$2500 Add: $50 IRA: $500
	Naperville IL 60563	Min Auto Inv Plan:	$2500 Add: $50
	800-823-7386	Sales Fees:	4.75%L, 0.25%S, 2.00%R
Web Address:	www.calamos.com	Management Fee:	1.00% mx./0.70% mn.
Inception:	09-04-90	Actual Fees:	Mgt:0.79% Dist:0.25%
Advisor:	Calamos Advisors LLC	Expense Projections:	3Yr:$838 5Yr:$1103 10Yr:$1860
Subadvisor:	None	Income Distrib:	Annually
NTF Plans:	DATALynx NTF, Federated Tr NTF		

Calamos Mrkt Ntrl Inc A

	Ticker	Load	NAV	Yield	Total Assets	Mstar Category
	CVSIX	4.75%	$12.73	4.1%	$934 mil	Long-Short

Governance and Management

Stewardship Grade:

Portfolio Manager(s)

Convertibles are this shop's bread and butter, as founder John Calamos Sr. has more than 20 years of experience investing in convertible securities. Also included on the team is Nick Calamos, who has more than 15 years of investing experience and who developed the firm's quantitative models.

Strategy

This fund employs a complex convertibles-arbitrage strategy in an attempt to reduce the risk inherent in equities. Management holds convertible securities, and it shorts its underlying stock (a strategy that benefits from a decline in the stock's price). The team may also use options on occasion to further hedge its positions. Income received from the convertibles and short sales fuel much of the fund's performance.

Performance 12-31-06

	1st Qtr	2nd Qtr	3rd Qtr	4th Qtr	Total
2002	1.01	1.45	0.57	3.44	6.60
2003	1.48	3.05	0.46	4.09	9.36
2004	2.18	-2.46	1.70	3.53	4.94
2005	-3.63	0.10	1.89	-0.36	-2.05
2006	3.51	-0.14	2.53	2.29	8.42

Trailing	Total Return%	+/- S&P 500	+/- Russell3000	%Rank Cat	Growth of $10,000
3 Mo	2.29	-4.41	-4.83	47	10,229
6 Mo	4.88	-7.86	-7.21	28	10,488
1 Yr	8.42	-7.37	-7.30	28	10,842
3 Yr Avg	3.67	-6.77	-7.52	57	11,142
5 Yr Avg	5.37	-0.82	-1.80	45	12,989
10 Yr Avg	8.29	-0.13	-0.35	1	22,176
15 Yr Avg	8.06	-2.58	-2.73	67	31,987

Tax Analysis	Tax-Adj Rtn%	%Rank Cat	Tax-Cost Rat	%Rank Cat
3 Yr (estimated)	-0.53	84	2.49	92
5 Yr (estimated)	1.94	63	2.31	89
10 Yr (estimated)	5.46	50	2.13	100

Potential Capital Gain Exposure: -3% of assets

Morningstar's Take by Kerry O'Boyle 12-11-06

Low correlation with most standard indexes gives the hedge-fund-like Calamos Market Neutral Income appeal as a portfolio diversifier.

This fund is one of the few mutual funds employing an alternative investment strategy that has actually earned its keep over the years. Targeting absolute annual returns of 8% to 10%, the fund has delivered on that goal over the long haul while keeping volatility to roughly a third of that of the S&P 500 Index. It has done this by employing a convertible-arbitrage strategy that seeks to exploit pricing inefficiencies by buying convertibles and short-selling the underlying stock for steady returns regardless of the direction the overall market moves.

Granted, the fund posted lackluster gains in 2004, as convertibles became severely overpriced, and it actually lost money in 2005 during a sharp sell-off in the convert market. Still, such blips have been few and far between. Plus, beginning in 2006 Calamos has initiated a covered call strategy, in which it sells options on a portion of the fund's stock portfolio; that component currently comprises 30% of the portfolio and will generate additional income and balance out some of the risk associated with the quirky convertible market. Management will also buy short-term, out-of-the-money puts to protect against steep stock market declines. Thus far this year returns are looking better.

Investors still need to be cautious of the potential drawbacks of alternative strategies, though. Like most other offerings in the long-short category, this fund isn't cheap. In addition, the emphasis on income and the high turnover involved typically results in lousy tax efficiency, making it best suited for tax-deferred accounts.

That said, the fund's risk/reward profile is impressive. Investors looking for a hedging strategy to provide consistent returns regardless of the direction the stock market moves have a strong candidate here.

Address:	2020 Calamos Court
	Naperville IL 60563
	800-823-7386
Web Address:	www.calamos.com
Inception:	09-04-90
Advisor:	Calamos Advisors LLC
Subadvisor:	None
NTF Plans:	DATALynx NTF, Federated Tr NTF

Minimum Purchase:	$2500	Add: $50	IRA: $500
Min Auto Inv Plan:	$10000	Add: $50	
Sales Fees:	4.75%L, 0.25%S, 2.00%R		
Management Fee:	0.75% mx./0.65% mn.		
Actual Fees:	Mgt:0.75%	Dist:0.25%	
Expense Projections:	3Yr:$947	5Yr:$1290	10Yr:$2254
Income Distrib:	Quarterly		

Historical Profile

Return	Average
Risk	Low
Rating	★★★ Neutral

Investment Style
Equity
Stock %

▼ Manager Change
▽ Partial Manager Change

Growth of $10,000
— Investment Values of Fund
— Investment Values of S&P 500

Performance Quartile (within Category)

1995	1996	1997	1998	1999	2000	2001	2002	2003	2004	2005	2006	History
10.88	10.75	11.85	11.64	12.43	13.00	13.67	14.18	14.20	13.51	12.24	12.73	NAV
14.46	8.17	14.00	10.04	13.69	10.32	8.49	6.60	9.36	4.94	-2.05	8.42	Total Return %
-23.12	-14.79	-19.36	-18.54	-7.35	19.42	20.38	28.70	-19.32	-5.94	-6.96	-7.37	+/-S&P 500
-22.34	-13.65	-17.78	-14.10	-7.21	17.78	19.95	28.14	-21.70	-7.01	-8.17	-7.30	+/-Russell3000
4.61	5.14	3.19	4.19	4.42	3.80	3.14	2.80	6.95	6.42	7.49	4.37	Income Return %
9.85	3.03	10.81	5.85	9.27	6.52	5.35	3.80	2.41	-1.48	-9.54	4.05	Capital Return %
34	100	34	50	14	35	32	26	45	29	93	28	Total Rtn % Rank Cat
0.45	0.55	0.34	0.49	0.51	0.46	0.40	0.38	0.95	0.88	0.99	0.53	Income $
0.00	0.45	0.04	0.86	0.26	0.25	0.02	0.00	0.31	0.48	0.00	0.00	Capital Gains $
2.40	2.20	2.00	2.10	2.10	1.50	1.50	1.30	1.50	1.51	1.32	1.57	Expense Ratio %
4.00	4.60	4.30	3.90	3.10	3.90	5.00	3.10	3.70	3.64	3.45	4.34	Income Ratio %
60	81	152	398	193	265	265	161	117	123	74	137	Turnover Rate %
2	1	1	2	4	46	296	367	416	326	140	556	Net Assets $mil

Rating and Risk

Time Period	Load-Adj Return %	Morningstar Rtn vs Cat	Morningstar Risk vs Cat	Morningstar Risk-Adj Rating
1 Yr	3.27			
3 Yr	2.01	-Avg	-Avg	★★
5 Yr	4.35	Avg	Low	★★★
10 Yr	7.76	—	—	—
Incept	8.11			

Other Measures	Standard Index S&P 500	Best Fit Index Merrill Lynch Convert
Alpha	-2.3	-1.3
Beta	0.39	0.53
R-Squared	50	74
Standard Deviation	3.84	
Mean	3.67	
Sharpe Ratio	0.12	

Portfolio Analysis 10-31-06

Share change since 09-06 Total Stocks:97	Sector	PE	Tot Ret%	% Assets
Slm FRN	—	—	—	1.62
Bankunited Finl 3.125%	—	—	—	1.60
Prudential Finl FRN	—	—	—	1.60
Biomarin Pharma Cv 2.5%	—	—	—	1.48
⊕ Edwards Lifesciences Cv	—	—	—	1.48
Ford Mtr Pfd	—	—	—	1.45
FNMA 4.625%	—	—	—	1.43
Webmd 3.125%	—	—	—	1.42
FHLMC 3.625%	—	—	—	1.41
ITRON	—	—	—	1.23
Triumph Grp 144A	—	—	—	1.20
☼ FINISAR	—	—	—	1.15
Drs Tech 144A	—	—	—	1.14
Coherent 144A 2.75%	—	—	—	1.12
Omnicare 3.25%	—	—	—	1.11
⊕ ExxonMobil Corporation	Energy	11.1	39.07	1.10
☼ Wesco Intl 144A Cv 1.75%	—	—	—	1.10
⊕ General Electric Company	Ind Mtrls	20.0	9.35	1.10
Chesapeake Engy Pfd	—	—	—	1.09
On Semicon 1.875%	—	—	—	1.08

Current Investment Style

Value Blnd Growth — Large Mid Small

Market Cap	%
Giant	66.8
Large	29.7
Mid	3.5
Small	0.0
Micro	0.0
Avg $mil:	76,341

Value Measures		Rel Category
Price/Earnings	14.72	0.95
Price/Book	2.69	1.12
Price/Sales	1.67	1.38
Price/Cash Flow	10.01	1.27
Dividend Yield %	2.05	1.34

Growth Measures	%	Rel Category
Long-Term Erngs	10.72	0.88
Book Value	9.15	1.23
Sales	12.09	1.26
Cash Flow	11.68	1.06
Historical Erngs	18.09	0.94

Profitability	%	Rel Category
Return on Equity	20.88	1.25
Return on Assets	11.91	1.37
Net Margin	15.53	1.33

Sector Weightings	% of Stocks	Rel S&P 500	3 Year High	Low
⊙ Info	17.80	0.89		
Software	2.83	0.82	3	3
Hardware	9.28	1.00	10	8
Media	3.77	0.99	4	3
Telecom	1.92	0.55	2	1
Œ Service	48.10	1.04		
Health	10.69	0.89	11	9
Consumer	8.93	1.17	10	9
Business	4.55	1.08	6	4
Financial	23.93	1.07	27	24
Mfg	34.10	1.01		
Goods	9.56	1.12	10	8
Ind Mtrls	10.91	0.91	12	9
Energy	10.62	1.08	12	10
Utilities	3.01	0.86	3	2

Composition

● Cash	15.0
● Stocks	33.3
● Bonds	28.7
● Other	22.9
Foreign (% of Stock)	0.0

Morningstar® Funds 500

Causeway Intl Value Inv

Analyst Pick ✓

	Ticker	Load	NAV	Yield	Total Assets	Mstar Category
	CIVVX	Closed	$19.70	0.9%	$5,179 mil	Foreign Large Value

Governance and Management

Stewardship Grade: A

Portfolio Manager(s)

Sarah Ketterer and Harry Hartford managed Mercury HW International Value with success until June 2001. Ketterer directed the day-to-day operations at that fund from its inception in 1990; Hartford joined in 1994. Together with their long-time colleague James Doyle, they started this fund in October 2001. The trio's long-time associates Jonathan Eng and Kevin Durkin became comanagers on this fund in January 2006. The five managers have an impressive support team composed of eight fundamental analysts and three quantitative analysts.

Strategy

The managers rely on the same value style here as they did at their former charge. They pursue stocks that are cheap on many metrics, have superior return prospects, and pay dividends or repurchase their shares. They focus on larger caps from developed markets, and they don't mind if their sector and country weights stand out. Meanwhile, they normally keep the fund's currency exposure unhedged. The fund has a 2% redemption fee on shares sold within 90 days, and Causeway uses a third-party fair-valuation vendor.

Performance 12-31-06

	1st Qtr	2nd Qtr	3rd Qtr	4th Qtr	Total
2002	5.72	0.62	-22.40	7.60	-11.18
2003	-8.12	25.47	9.45	15.34	45.53
2004	7.86	2.01	0.20	14.56	26.31
2005	0.06	-0.80	5.30	3.22	7.87
2006	8.29	1.84	3.90	9.73	25.74

Trailing	Total Return%	+/- MSCI EAFE	+/- MSCI Wd xUS	%Rank Cat	Growth of $10,000
3 Mo	9.73	-0.62	-0.39	60	10,973
6 Mo	14.01	-0.68	-0.21	56	11,401
1 Yr	25.74	-0.60	0.03	57	12,574
3 Yr Avg	19.66	-0.27	-0.44	62	17,134
5 Yr Avg	17.24	2.26	1.99	33	22,150
10 Yr Avg	—	—	—	—	—
15 Yr Avg	—	—	—	—	—

Tax Analysis	Tax-Adj Rtn%	%Rank Cat	Tax-Cost Rat	%Rank Cat
3 Yr (estimated)	18.27	52	1.16	39
5 Yr (estimated)	16.20	31	0.89	40
10 Yr (estimated)	—	—	—	—

Potential Capital Gain Exposure: 24% of assets

Historical Profile

Return	Average
Risk	Average
Rating	★★★ Neutral

93% 92% 94% 95% 97% 93% Investment Style: Equity / Stock %

▼ Manager Change
▽ Partial Manager Change

Growth of $10,000
— Investment Values of Fund
— Investment Values of MSCI EAFE

22.6 / 19.6 / 16.0 / 13.0 / 10.0

Performance Quartile (within Category)

	1995	1996	1997	1998	1999	2000	2001	2002	2003	2004	2005	2006	History
NAV	—	—	—	—	—	—	10.66	9.36	13.36	16.17	16.52	19.70	NAV
Total Return %	—	—	—	—	—	—	6.66*	-11.18	45.53	26.31	7.87	25.74	Total Return %
+/-MSCI EAFE	—	—	—	—	—	—	—	4.76	6.94	6.06	-5.67	-0.60	+/-MSCI EAFE
+/-MSCI Wd xUS	—	—	—	—	—	—	—	4.62	6.11	5.93	-6.60	0.03	+/-MSCI Wd xUS
Income Return %	—	—	—	—	—	—	—	0.61	1.73	1.78	2.08	1.12	Income Return %
Capital Return %	—	—	—	—	—	—	—	-11.79	43.80	24.53	5.79	24.62	Capital Return %
Total Rtn % Rank Cat	—	—	—	—	—	—	—	40	18	13	95	57	Total Rtn % Rank Cat
Income $	—	—	—	—	—	—	0.01	0.07	0.16	0.24	0.34	0.19	Income $
Capital Gains $	—	—	—	—	—	—	0.00	0.04	0.09	0.45	0.58	0.89	Capital Gains $
Expense Ratio %	—	—	—	—	—	—	—	—	1.27	1.27	1.23	—	Expense Ratio %
Income Ratio %	—	—	—	—	—	—	—	—	1.69	1.55	1.31	—	Income Ratio %
Turnover Rate %	—	—	—	—	—	—	—	—	47	32	21	—	Turnover Rate %
Net Assets $mil	—	—	—	—	—	—	18	164	435	947	1,573		Net Assets $mil

Rating and Risk

Time Period	Load-Adj Return %	Morningstar Rtn vs Cat	Morningstar Risk vs Cat	Morningstar Risk-Adj Rating
1 Yr	25.74			
3 Yr	19.66	Avg	-Avg	★★★
5 Yr	17.24	Avg	+Avg	★★★
10 Yr	—	—	—	—
Incept	18.05			

Other Measures	Standard Index MSCI EAFE	Best Fit Index MSCI EAFE
Alpha	1.8	1.8
Beta	0.87	0.87
R-Squared	84	84
Standard Deviation	8.96	
Mean	19.66	
Sharpe Ratio	1.70	

Morningstar's Take by William Samuel Rocco 12-08-06

The closed Causeway International Value has a lot more potential than its recent returns would suggest.

This fund has been an uninspiring performer the past two years. It has earned only average gains in 2006, as several of its telecom and other picks have helped but its market-cap and developed-country biases have not. And it finished in its category's bottom decile in 2005, stung by its emphasis on the upper end of the market-cap spectrum, its dearth of emerging-markets names, and its paltry exposure to Japan.

The traits that have slowed the fund the past two years are central to its conservative value strategy, though. Its managers are strict bargain-hunters who focus on large-cap and giant-cap stocks from developed markets. The fund's average market cap is normally much bigger than the category norm, and the sole developing market where they consider opportunities is South Korea, which many observers consider to be developed. The managers have always had trouble finding good values in Japan--the fund has never had much more than 13% of its assets there--because Japanese stocks tend to be pricey relative to their prospects in their view.

Meanwhile, there's ample reason to think the managers will be able to deliver strong returns with their style over the long run. They posted good results in their early years here, when small-cap and emerging-markets names also outperformed, by making way more than their share of good stock picks. So, the fund has outpaced its typical peer since opening in late 2001--despite its recent slump and the fact that its style has been out of favor most of its life. And the managers earned good risk-adjusted returns at their prior charge using the same approach as they do here.

Due to that success, the quality of the managers and their support team, and their firm's commitment to fundholders, we remain confident about the fund's long-term prospects.

Address:	11111 Santa Monica Blvd Los Angeles CA 90025 866-947-7000	Minimum Purchase:	Closed	Add: —	IRA: —
		Min Auto Inv Plan:	Closed	Add: —	
Web Address:	www.causewayfunds.com	Sales Fees:	No-load, 0.23%S, 2.00%R	
Inception:	10-26-01*	Management Fee:	0.80%	
Advisor:	Causeway Capital Markets, Inc.	Actual Fees:	Mgt:0.80% Dist:0.23%	
Subadvisor:	None	Expense Projections:	3Yr:$384 5Yr:$665 10Yr:$1466	
NTF Plans:	Fidelity Retail-NTF, Schwab OneSource	Income Distrib:	Annually	

Portfolio Analysis 09-30-06

Share change since 06-06 Total Stocks:64

	Sector	Country	% Assets
⊕ Samsung Electronics	Goods	Korea	3.13
⊕ British American Tobacco	Goods	U.K.	2.95
⊕ Sanofi-Synthelabo	Health	France	2.78
⊕ Vinci	Business	France	2.66
⊕ AXA	Financial	France	2.31
⊕ ING Groep	Financial	Netherlands	2.20
⊕ BAE Systems	Ind Mtrls	U.K.	2.17
⊕ PetroChina	Energy	Hong Kong	2.11
⊕ France Telecom	Telecom	France	2.09
⊕ Royal Bank Of Scotland G	Financial	U.K.	2.08
⊕ Deutsche Post	Business	Germany	1.98
⊕ Zurich Financial Service	Financial	Switzerland	1.96
⊕ Koninklijke Philips Elec	Goods	Netherlands	1.94
⊕ BNP Paribas	Financial	France	1.91
⊕ Telefonica	Telecom	Spain	1.85
⊕ Honda Motor	Goods	Japan	1.85
⊕ Credit Suisse Grp	Financial	Switzerland	1.78
⊕ Manulife Finl	Financial	Canada	1.69
⊕ Takeda Chemical Industri	Health	Japan	1.61
⊕ Aviva	Financial	U.K.	1.58

Current Investment Style

Value Blnd Growth — Large/Mid/Small

Market Cap	%
Giant	62.7
Large	28.7
Mid	8.4
Small	0.2
Micro	0.0

Avg $mil: 40,376

Value Measures		Rel Category
Price/Earnings	12.71	1.01
Price/Book	1.92	1.08
Price/Sales	1.01	1.06
Price/Cash Flow	7.13	1.00
Dividend Yield %	3.71	1.13

Growth Measures	%	Rel Category
Long-Term Erngs	10.80	1.05
Book Value	9.86	1.26
Sales	5.53	1.01
Cash Flow	4.70	1.31
Historical Erngs	22.97	1.40

Composition

Cash	4.8	Bonds	0.0
Stocks	92.8	Other	2.5
Foreign (% of Stock)			100.0

Sector Weightings

Sector Weightings	% of Stocks	Rel MSCI EAFE	3 Year High	Low
⊙ Info	13.34	1.13		
Software	0.00	0.00	0	0
Hardware	2.33	0.60	2	1
Media	2.32	1.27	3	2
Telecom	8.69	1.56	14	8
⊖ Service	50.50	1.07		
Health	7.68	1.08	10	6
Consumer	4.86	0.98	5	3
Business	10.36	2.04	13	10
Financial	27.60	0.92	29	26
⊔ Mfg	36.17	0.88		
Goods	17.01	1.30	21	15
Ind Mtrls	5.50	0.36	8	5
Energy	9.96	1.39	10	4
Utilities	3.70	0.71	4	0

Regional Exposure

	% Stock		% Stock
UK/W. Europe	77	N. America	3
Japan	6	Latn America	0
Asia X Japan	13	Other	1

Country Exposure

	% Stock		% Stock
U.K.	27	Germany	8
France	20	South Korea	7
Netherlands	8		

Century Sm-Cp Sel Inv

Analyst Pick ✓

	Ticker	Load	NAV	Yield	Total Assets	Mstar Category
	CSMVX	Closed	$23.94	1.2%	$887 mil	Small Growth

Governance and Management

Stewardship Grade: B

Portfolio Manager(s)

Lanny Thorndike has been the fund's lead manager since its December 1999 inception. Before working for the advisor he was an analyst at William Blair. Kevin Callahan, who joined the firm in 2001, is the director of research and comanager of the fund. They are currently supported by four equity analysts. The pair also head sibling Century Shares Trust.

Strategy

This fund is tilted toward service-oriented companies that boast strong brands, competitive advantages, and high returns on equity. Prospective companies must also generate large amounts of cash sufficient to fund internal growth. A typical stock in the portfolio will have a minimum return on equity of 15% over five-year rolling periods and will also have the potential to double its book value over that same time frame.

Historical Profile

Return	Above Avg
Risk	Low
Rating	★★★★ Above Avg

Investment Style: Equity, Stock %

Investment Style %: 100% | 100% | 99% | 93% | 94% | 91% | 92%

▼ Manager Change
▽ Partial Manager Change

Growth of $10,000
— Investment Values of Fund
— Investment Values of S&P 500

Performance Quartile (within Category)

	1995	1996	1997	1998	1999	2000	2001	2002	2003	2004	2005	2006	History
NAV	—	—	—	—	—	14.98	15.83	15.44	21.54	23.52	24.09	23.94	NAV
Total Return %	—	—	—	—	—	51.70*	5.87	0.18	46.73	11.93	3.75	9.27	Total Return %
+/-S&P 500	—	—	—	—	—	17.76	22.28	18.05	1.05	-1.16	-6.52	+/-S&P 500	+/-S&P 500
+/-Russ 2000 Gr	—	—	—	—	—	15.10	30.44	-1.81	-2.38	-0.40	-4.08	+/-Russ 2000 Gr	+/-Russ 2000 Gr
Income Return %	—	—	—	—	—	0.00	0.41	5.89	0.00	0.13	1.39		Income Return %
Capital Return %	—	—	—	—	—	5.87	-0.23	40.84	11.93	3.62	7.88		Capital Return %
Total Rtn % Rank Cat	—	—	—	—	—	17	1	40	51	74	59		Total Rtn % Rank Cat
Income $	—	—	—	—	0.00	0.00	0.07	0.91	0.00	0.03	0.32		Income $
Capital Gains $	—	—	—	—	0.19	0.03	0.35	0.19	0.56	0.28	2.01		Capital Gains $
Expense Ratio %	—	—	—	—	—	—	1.80	1.80	1.61	1.50	—		Expense Ratio %
Income Ratio %	—	—	—	—	—	—	-0.48	-1.05	-0.86	-0.69	—		Income Ratio %
Turnover Rate %	—	—	—	—	—	—	24	48	123	88	103		Turnover Rate %
Net Assets $mil	—	—	—	—	—	2	11	13	78	180	344		Net Assets $mil

Performance 12-31-06

	1st Qtr	2nd Qtr	3rd Qtr	4th Qtr	Total
2002	6.19	-4.05	-9.24	8.32	0.18
2003	-0.58	17.98	9.83	13.90	46.73
2004	3.85	0.18	-2.14	9.94	11.93
2005	0.17	1.74	2.25	-0.44	3.75
2006	8.39	-5.17	0.65	5.63	9.27

Trailing	Total Return%	+/- S&P 500	+/- Russ 2000 Gr	%Rank Cat	Growth of $10,000
3 Mo	5.63	-1.07	-3.14	86	10,563
6 Mo	6.31	-6.43	-0.55	37	10,631
1 Yr	9.27	-6.52	-4.08	59	10,927
3 Yr Avg	8.26	-2.18	-2.25	66	12,688
5 Yr Avg	13.28	7.09	6.35	4	18,654
10 Yr Avg	—	—	—	—	—
15 Yr Avg	—	—	—	—	—

Tax Analysis	Tax-Adj Rtn%	%Rank Cat	Tax-Cost Rat	%Rank Cat
3 Yr (estimated)	7.20	62	0.98	38
5 Yr (estimated)	12.12	4	1.02	58
10 Yr (estimated)	—	—	—	—

Potential Capital Gain Exposure: 7% of assets

Rating and Risk

Time Period	Load-Adj Return %	Morningstar Rtn vs Cat	Morningstar Risk vs Cat	Morningstar Risk-Adj Rating
1 Yr	9.27			
3 Yr	8.26	Avg	Low	★★★
5 Yr	13.28	High	Low	★★★★★
10 Yr	—			
Incept	17.37			

Other Measures	Standard Index S&P 500	Best Fit Index DJ Wilshire 4500
Alpha	-3.3	-4.3
Beta	1.22	0.84
R-Squared	68	85
Standard Deviation	10.15	
Mean	8.26	
Sharpe Ratio	0.52	

Morningstar's Take by Andrew Gogerty 12-20-06

Century Small Cap Select's main appeal is its consistent approach.

This closed Analyst Pick is one of the more level-headed members of the hairy small-growth category. Manager Lanny Thorndike focuses on companies that generate plump cash flows relative to their peers to fund internal growth. Hence, more than 60% of the fund's assets are stashed in service-oriented firms, and he generally shies away from companies in the energy, utility, and industrial sectors that require constant capital investment.

What Thorndike's picks tend to have in common are plush margins from entrenched competitive advantages, solid balance sheets, and consistently high returns on equity and sane valuations. Ideal holdings will have a history of 15% return on equity and the potential to double book value over a five-year time frame. As such, the fund typically sports higher profitability metrics but lower valuations, compared with its peers. Railroad car leasing company GATX, for example, occupies a top spot in the portfolio because Thorndike believes the firm's dominant position in industry, combined with a shortage of rail cars amid increased industry demand, gives the firm strong pricing power in the coming years. This dynamic could lead to steady earnings growth. He is also fond of the firm's decision to sell off a non-core division and use the proceeds to pay down debt.

Thorndike's style leads to predictable but not always chart-topping returns; however, that is not a reason to cut loose here. The fund will likely preserve capital during down or choppy markets but, as we previously noted, lag during strong cyclical or momentum rallies such as those seen in the past three years. The trade-off has been one of the lowest standard deviations of returns measures in the category, which calms investors' urge to buy and sell at the exact wrong time.

In the end, this fund is a keeper. Its clearly defined style of focusing on internal growth to create shareholder value holds appeal.

Portfolio Analysis 09-30-06

Share change since 06-06 Total Stocks:71

	Sector	PE	Tot Ret%	% Assets
⊕ GATX Corporation	Consumer	—	22.62	3.27
⊖ Usana Health Sciences, I	Goods	23.3	34.67	2.75
⊖ Waddell & Reed Financial	Financial	62.4	34.04	2.63
⊕ Wright Express Corporati	Business	—	41.68	2.54
RPM International, Inc.	Goods	—	24.55	2.36
⊕ Global Imaging Systems,	Ind Mtrls	16.4	26.77	2.23
⊖ Micros Systems, Inc.	Software	33.4	9.07	2.21
⊕ SurModics, Inc.	Ind Mtrls	31.4	-15.87	2.15
⊕ Tractor Supply	Consumer	20.7	-15.55	2.12
⊕ Scientific Games Corpora	Consumer	40.4	10.81	2.07
⊖ Guitar Center, Inc.	Consumer	16.6	-9.10	2.07
⊖ Mercury Interactive Corp	Software	—	—	2.01
⊕ LCA-Vision, Inc.	Health	20.3	-26.75	1.97
⊕ Qiagen NV	Health	38.1	7.73	1.94
⊖ Blackbaud, Inc.	Business	41.7	54.25	1.93
⊖ Jarden Corporation	Goods	32.0	15.39	1.93
⊕ Quality Systems, Inc.	Software	36.1	-0.48	1.87
⊕ SMART Modular Technologi	Hardware	—	—	1.79
⊕ Healthways, Inc.	Health	50.4	5.44	1.78
⊖ Cognos Inc.	Software	33.2	22.33	1.74

Current Investment Style

Value Blnd Growth — Large Mid Small

Market Cap	%
Giant	0.0
Large	0.0
Mid	39.1
Small	51.6
Micro	9.3
Avg $mil:	1,388

Value Measures		Rel Category
Price/Earnings	17.62	0.84
Price/Book	2.59	0.95
Price/Sales	1.08	0.69
Price/Cash Flow	8.26	0.86
Dividend Yield %	0.70	1.52

Growth Measures	%	Rel Category
Long-Term Erngs	15.39	0.87
Book Value	13.73	1.31
Sales	19.65	1.65
Cash Flow	23.31	1.10
Historical Erngs	16.71	0.69

Profitability	%	Rel Category
Return on Equity	17.80	1.44
Return on Assets	10.71	1.61
Net Margin	10.69	1.23

Sector Weightings

	% of Stocks	Rel S&P 500	3 Year High	Low
⌖ Info	16.89	0.84		
Software	8.78	2.54	12	5
Hardware	7.54	0.82	14	5
Media	0.00	0.00	0	0
Telecom	0.57	0.16	3	0
Service	60.53	1.31		
Health	18.13	1.50	25	16
Consumer	13.45	1.76	21	7
Business	13.39	3.17	15	9
Financial	15.56	0.70	21	11
Mfg	22.58	0.67		
Goods	9.83	1.15	10	5
Ind Mtrls	7.29	0.61	10	2
Energy	5.46	0.56	7	1
Utilities	0.00	0.00	0	0

Composition

● Cash	8.5
● Stocks	91.5
● Bonds	0.0
● Other	0.0
Foreign	4.0
(% of Stock)	

Address:	100 Federal Street, 29th Floor
	Boston, MA 02110
	800-303-1928
Web Address:	www.centuryfunds.com
Inception:	02-24-00*
Advisor:	Century Capital Management, LLC
Subadvisor:	None
NTF Plans:	Fidelity Retail-NTF, Schwab OneSource

Minimum Purchase:	Closed	Add: —	IRA: —
Min Auto Inv Plan:	Closed	Add: —	
Sales Fees:	No-load, 0.15%S, 1.00%R		
Management Fee:	0.95%		
Actual Fees:	Mgt:0.95%	Dist:0.15%	
Expense Projections:	3Yr:$428	5Yr:$739	10Yr:$1624
Income Distrib:	Annually		

MORNINGSTAR® Funds 500

CGM Focus

	Ticker	Load	NAV	Yield	Total Assets	Mstar Category
	CGMFX	None	$34.69	2.1%	$2,276 mil	Large Blend

Governance and Management

Stewardship Grade:

Portfolio Manager(s)

Ken Heebner has been at the helm of this offering since its 1997 inception. But he has run CGM Capital Development for 30 years. He also runs CGM Mutual, and CGM Realty. Before helping to start CGM in 1990, Heebner began his career as an economist in 1965 and put in time as a portfolio manager at Scudder, Stevens & Clark, and Loomis Sayles & Co.

Strategy

This fund is even more gutsy than its sibling CGM Capital Development. Manager Ken Heebner often invests in fewer than 25 stocks, and he trades furiously among stocks and sectors. He makes big sector bets relative to the typical mid-blend fund, and he has changed the fund's market-cap emphasis based on where he sees opportunity. Heebner also has free rein to short--and he sometimes shorts a large portion of the portfolio.

Historical Profile
Return High
Risk High
Rating ★★★★
Highest

Investment Style
Equity
Stock %

98% | 89% | 99% | 100% | 99% | 98% | 99% | 99%

▼ Manager Change
▽ Partial Manager Change

Growth of $10,000
— Investment Values of Fund
— Investment Values of S&P 500

46.4
33.8
24.0
17.0
10.0

Performance Quartile (within Category)

1995	1996	1997	1998	1999	2000	2001	2002	2003	2004	2005	2006	History
—	—	9.38	9.71	10.50	15.80	21.87	17.98	29.93	29.49	33.41	34.69	NAV
—	—	-6.20*	3.52	8.45	53.93	47.65	-17.79	66.46	12.33	25.37	14.95	Total Return %
—	—	—	-25.06	-12.59	63.03	59.54	4.31	37.78	1.45	20.46	-0.84	+/-S&P 500
—	—	—	-23.50	-12.46	61.72	60.10	3.86	36.57	0.93	19.10	-0.51	+/-Russ 1000
—	—	—	0.00	0.31	3.43	0.06	0.00	0.00	0.13	1.49	2.42	Income Return %
—	—	—	3.52	8.14	50.50	47.59	-17.79	66.46	12.20	23.88	12.53	Capital Return %
—	—	—	97	86	1	1	18	1	24	1	39	Total Rtn % Rank Cat
—	—	0.00	0.00	0.03	0.36	0.01	0.00	0.00	0.04	0.44	0.81	Income $
—	—	0.00	0.00	0.00	1.44	0.00	0.00	4.07	3.12	2.92		Capital Gains $
—	—	1.20	1.20	1.20	1.20	1.20	1.20	1.18	1.12	1.07	—	Expense Ratio %
—	—	-0.83	-0.65	0.23	3.02	0.11	-0.98	-0.92	0.14	1.55	—	Income Ratio %
—	—	—	340	288	551	254	155	204	327	282	—	Turnover Rate %
—	—	110	69	69	246	385	774	925	1,636	2,276		Net Assets $mil

Performance 12-31-06

	1st Qtr	2nd Qtr	3rd Qtr	4th Qtr	Total
2002	10.15	-0.79	-21.34	-4.36	-17.79
2003	-7.40	34.65	10.70	20.59	66.46
2004	5.55	-4.91	7.12	4.48	12.33
2005	10.95	3.06	17.44	-6.64	25.37
2006	10.33	4.53	-6.85	7.01	14.95

Trailing	Total Return%	+/- S&P 500	+/- Russ 1000	%Rank Cat	Growth of $10,000
3 Mo	7.01	0.31	0.06	33	10,701
6 Mo	-0.32	-13.06	-12.68	99	9,968
1 Yr	14.95	-0.84	-0.51	39	11,495
3 Yr Avg	17.42	6.98	6.44	1	16,189
5 Yr Avg	17.25	11.06	10.43	1	22,160
10 Yr Avg	—	—	—	—	—
15 Yr Avg	—	—	—	—	—

Tax Analysis	Tax-Adj Rtn%	%Rank Cat	Tax-Cost Rat	%Rank Cat
3 Yr (estimated)	14.92	1	2.13	84
5 Yr (estimated)	15.74	1	1.29	80
10 Yr (estimated)	—	—	—	—

Potential Capital Gain Exposure: 12% of assets

Morningstar's Take by Federico Cepeda 11-17-06

CGM Focus is too risky for most, but perhaps not for all.

This fund is atypical. It invests in both growth and value stocks, regardless of their size. It also holds foreign stocks. It may invest in bonds of all types. It can even sell stocks short. Unlike most peers, manager Ken Heebner combines fundamental analysis with top-down macro calls. He's not afraid of concentrating his bets in a few sectors or radically changing the portfolio composition.

Such concentrated bets court risk. For instance, Heebner held only 23 stocks as of June 30, 2006, and these holdings were confined to only two sectors: energy and industrial materials. If a few stocks or, worse, one of these sectors, perform poorly, the portfolio will suffer greatly. Because of this concentration, the fund is extremely volatile, exposed not just to big gains but also to sharp losses. The fund lost 21% in the third quarter of 2002. And, more recently, the fund shed almost 7%

during the third quarter of 2006, as energy pulled back. Volatility makes the fund hard to use, because investors tend to get in and out in the wrong periods. They will plunge in during euphoria when the underlying shares are dearest, only to sell after large losses, when such stocks are cheap. And the fund's high turnover makes it one of the most tax-inefficient equity funds around.

But, the fund has some niche appeal. Heebner has run CGM Capital Development for almost 30 years and has built an impressive record. He is a high conviction investor who gives investors something different. And the fund moves moves independently of any index, which makes it a good diversifier.

For most investors, this fund is too hard to use. Daring types may want to devote a small portion of their portfolio to it and tiptoe in through dollar-cost averaging. But they certainly must not get scared away after a big dip--that is the nature of this animal.

Rating and Risk

Time Period	Load-Adj Return %	Morningstar Rtn vs Cat	Morningstar Risk vs Cat	Morningstar Risk-Adj Rating
1 Yr	14.95			
3 Yr	17.42	High	High	★★★★★
5 Yr	17.25	High	High	★★★★★
10 Yr	—	—	—	—
Incept	19.59			

Other Measures	Standard Index S&P 500	Best Fit Index GS NATR RES
Alpha	6.6	-6.4
Beta	1.21	0.99
R-Squared	16	82
Standard Deviation	20.87	
Mean	17.42	
Sharpe Ratio	0.72	

Portfolio Analysis 09-30-06

Share change since 06-06 Total Stocks:22

	Sector	PE	Tot Ret%	% Assets
Southern Copper Corporat	Ind Mtrls	8.5	79.47	5.99
⊕ Allegheny Technologies C	Ind Mtrls	17.1	152.95	5.83
⊖ Tenaris SA ADR	Ind Mtrls	22.1	120.18	5.78
⊕ Schlumberger, Ltd.	Energy	22.3	31.07	5.76
✲ Advanced Micro Devices	Hardware	18.5	-33.50	5.72
✲ Goldman Sachs Group, Inc	Financial	12.4	57.41	5.67
✲ Vimpel-Communications AD	Telecom	25.6	78.50	5.60
✲ America Movil SA ADR	Telecom	27.7	55.53	5.59
✲ Morgan Stanley	Financial	12.3	45.93	5.41
✲ Merrill Lynch & Company,	Financial	14.2	39.28	5.35
⊖ Phelps Dodge Corp.	Ind Mtrls	12.7	76.29	5.30
✲ AT&T, Inc.	Telecom	18.2	51.59	5.19
⊖ Petroleo Brasileiro S.A.	Energy	10.4	51.12	4.61
✲ Legg Mason	Financial	25.1	-19.99	4.24
⊕ CNOOC, Ltd. ADR	Energy	11.9	44.14	4.08
⊖ Suncor Energy, Inc.	Energy	33.1	25.42	4.03
⊖ Canadian Natural Resourc	Energy	29.1	7.84	3.77
⊖ Empresa Brasileira de Ae	Ind Mtrls	—	8.23	3.74
✲ Lehman Brothers Holdings	Financial	12.2	22.75	3.37
⊖ Freeport-McMoRan Copper	Ind Mtrls	7.7	13.08	2.19

Current Investment Style

Value Blnd Growth — Large Mid Small

	Market Cap	%
	Giant	59.3
	Large	32.1
	Mid	8.6
	Small	0.0
	Micro	0.0
	Avg $mil: 30,418	

Value Measures		Rel Category
Price/Earnings	12.26	0.80
Price/Book	2.72	1.06
Price/Sales	2.30	1.64
Price/Cash Flow	6.72	0.80
Dividend Yield %	1.10	0.63

Growth Measures	%	Rel Category
Long-Term Erngs	18.62	1.58
Book Value	15.19	1.68
Sales	17.10	1.76
Cash Flow	33.09	3.21
Historical Erngs	34.82	1.88

Profitability	%	Rel Category
Return on Equity	26.25	1.35
Return on Assets	14.01	1.35
Net Margin	18.22	1.36

Sector Weightings	% of Stocks	Rel S&P 500	3 Year High	Low
☎ Info	22.95	1.15		
Software	0.00	0.00	5	0
Hardware	6.41	0.69	14	0
Media	0.00	0.00	3	0
Telecom	16.54	4.71	17	0
☞ Service	25.52	0.55		
Health	0.00	0.00	3	0
Consumer	0.00	0.00	31	0
Business	0.00	0.00	12	0
Financial	25.52	1.15	26	0
Mfg	51.53	1.53		
Goods	0.00	0.00	14	0
Ind Mtrls	29.09	2.44	56	10
Energy	22.44	2.29	54	13
Utilities	0.00	0.00	0	0

Composition

● Cash	0.9	
● Stocks	99.1	
● Bonds	0.0	
○ Other	0.0	
Foreign	43.6	(% of Stock)

Address:	One International Place Boston MA 02110 800-343-5678	Minimum Purchase:	$2500	Add: $50	IRA: $1000
		Min Auto Inv Plan:	$2500	Add: $50	
Web Address:	www.cgmfunds.com	Sales Fees:	No-load		
Inception:	09-03-97 *	Management Fee:	0.90% mx./0.75% mn.		
Advisor:	Capital Growth Mgt Ltd Partnership	Actual Fees:	Mgt:0.96%	Dist: —	
Subadvisor:	None	Expense Projections:	3Yr:$387	5Yr:$670	10Yr:$1477
NTF Plans:	N/A	Income Distrib:	Annually		

Champlain Small Co Adv

Ticker CIPSX	**Load** None	**NAV** $12.33	**Yield** 0.0%	**Total Assets** $103 mil	**Mstar Category** Small Growth

Governance and Management

Stewardship Grade: C

Portfolio Manager(s)

Scott Brayman is the lead manager and decision-maker, with the other four listed managers in supporting roles. Brayman put together a great record at Sentinel Small Company before founding Champlain Investment Partners in late 2004. The other listed managers include David O'Neal and Deborah Healey, who worked on Brayman's Sentinel fund as analyst and trader, respectively; Van Harissis, former manager of Sentinel Common Stock; and Dan Butler, formerly an analyst at Principal. By early 2007, all the comanagers will have ownership stakes in Champlain.

Strategy

Lead manager Scott Brayman and his team concentrate on five sectors (industrials, consumer, health care, technology, and financials), and within those sectors, they use a bottom-up approach to find attractive stocks with market caps under $3 billion. They prefer companies with consistent cash flows, credible management, and superior growth relative to their industries. The team uses four different methods for valuing companies, buying stocks at a discount to their fair values and selling them as soon as they get too expensive.

Performance 12-31-06

	1st Qtr	2nd Qtr	3rd Qtr	4th Qtr	Total
2002	—	—	—	—	—
2003	—	—	—	—	—
2004	—	—	—	—	—*
2005	-2.45	6.44	6.33	-0.32	10.05
2006	9.18	-4.08	1.39	7.39	14.03

Trailing	Total Return%	+/- S&P 500	+/- Russ 2000 Gr	%Rank Cat	Growth of $10,000
3 Mo	7.39	0.69	-1.38	60	10,739
6 Mo	8.88	-3.86	2.02	18	10,888
1 Yr	14.03	-1.76	0.68	25	11,403
3 Yr Avg	—	—	—	—	—
5 Yr Avg	—	—	—	—	—
10 Yr Avg	—	—	—	—	—
15 Yr Avg	—	—	—	—	—

Tax Analysis	Tax-Adj Rtn%	%Rank Cat	Tax-Cost Rat	%Rank Cat
3 Yr (estimated)	—	—	—	—
5 Yr (estimated)	—	—	—	—
10 Yr (estimated)	—	—	—	—

Potential Capital Gain Exposure: 7% of assets

Morningstar's Take by David Kathman 12-19-06

There's a lot to like about Champlain Small Company Fund.

This Fund Analyst Pick has been around only for a little more than two years, but its pedigree goes back more than a decade. Lead manager Scott Brayman compiled an outstanding record at Sentinel Small Company from 1996 to 2004, and he brought over several colleagues from Sentinel when he co-founded Champlain Investment Partners in late 2004. So far the results here have been good, with returns ranking in the top quartile of the small-growth category in 2005, and in 2006 through Dec. 18.

Those results are certainly encouraging, but what really makes us confident is the fund's strategy, which Brayman also brought over with him wholesale. He and his team focus on five sectors where they're likely to find promising small caps, and they spend a lot of time researching stocks before buying them. They like to see rapid growth, skilled management, and abundant cash flows, but

they also pay lots of attention to valuation, using several different methods. As a result, the fund tends to land near the blend side of the small-growth area of the style box.

The fund's solid performance in 2006 has been all the more impressive given that the small-cap market's leaders have tended to be the speculative stocks that Brayman shuns. This portfolio's top holdings include such unsexy names as medical instrument maker Mettler-Toledo, which Brayman likes for its world-class franchise, and industrial conglomerate Idex. Both stocks have posted good gains in 2006, but Brayman tends to trim stocks that do well, preferring to give more space to those with greater upside potential.

Champlain has said it won't let its total small-cap assets exceed $1.5 billion; it expects to be halfway to that limit by February 2007, though only about $100 million of that is in the mutual fund. Potential investors should get into this gem while they still have the chance.

Address:	PO Box 219009 Kansas City, MO 64121 866-773-3238	
Web Address:	www.cipvt.com	
Inception:	11-30-04	
Advisor:	Champlain Investment Partners, LLC	
Subadvisor:	None	
NTF Plans:	Fidelity Retail-NTF, Schwab OneSource	

Minimum Purchase:	$10000	Add: $0	IRA: $3000
Min Auto Inv Plan:	$0	Add: —	
Sales Fees:	No-load, 0.25%S		
Management Fee:	0.90%, 0.10%A		
Actual Fees:	Mgt:0.90%	Dist:0.25%	
Expense Projections:	3Yr:$706	5Yr:$1210	10Yr:$2595
Income Distrib:	Annually		

Historical Profile
Return —
Risk —
Rating Not Rated

Investment Style: Equity Stock %
94% 92% 90%

▼ Manager Change
▽ Partial Manager Change

Growth of $10,000
— Investment Values of Fund
— Investment Values of S&P 500

12.1
11.4
10.7
10.0
9.0

Performance Quartile (within Category)

	1995	1996	1997	1998	1999	2000	2001	2002	2003	2004	2005	2006	History
	—	—	—	—	—	—	—	—	—	10.19	11.00	12.33	NAV
	—	—	—	—	—	—	—	—	—	—	10.05	14.03	Total Return %
	—	—	—	—	—	—	—	—	—	—	5.14	-1.76	+/-S&P 500
	—	—	—	—	—	—	—	—	—	—	5.90	0.68	+/-Russ 2000 Gr
	—	—	—	—	—	—	—	—	—	—	0.06	0.00	Income Return %
	—	—	—	—	—	—	—	—	—	—	9.99	14.03	Capital Return %
	—	—	—	—	—	—	—	—	—	—	20	25	Total Rtn % Rank Cat
	—	—	—	—	—	—	—	—	—	0.02	0.01	0.00	Income $
	—	—	—	—	—	—	—	—	—	0.00	0.21	0.21	Capital Gains $
	—	—	—	—	—	—	—	—	—	—	—	1.41	Expense Ratio %
	—	—	—	—	—	—	—	—	—	—	—	-0.22	Income Ratio %
	—	—	—	—	—	—	—	—	—	—	—	94	Turnover Rate %
	—	—	—	—	—	—	—	—	—	—	2	103	Net Assets $mil

Rating and Risk

Time Period	Load-Adj Return %	Morningstar Rtn vs Cat	Morningstar Risk vs Cat	Morningstar Risk-Adj Rating
1 Yr	14.03			
3 Yr	—	—	—	—
5 Yr	—	—	—	—
10 Yr	—	—	—	—
Incept	12.61			

Other Measures	Standard Index S&P 500	Best Fit Index
Alpha	—	—
Beta	—	—
R-Squared	—	—
Standard Deviation	—	
Mean	—	
Sharpe Ratio	—	

Portfolio Analysis 12-31-06

Share change since 09-06 Total Stocks:77

	Sector	PE	Tot Ret%	% Assets
⊕ AptarGroup, Inc.	Goods	21.1	14.89	2.61
⊕ ABM Industries, Inc.	Business	28.6	18.98	2.20
⊕ WD-40 Company	Energy	20.1	36.55	1.98
⊕ Idex Corporation	Ind Mtrls	19.6	16.76	1.97
⊕ Regis Corporation	Consumer	16.4	2.96	1.87
⊕ Universal Technical Inst	Consumer	19.8	-28.22	1.79
⊕ Harte-Hanks, Inc.	Media	20.6	5.94	1.77
⊕ eFunds Corporation	Business	24.9	17.32	1.74
⊕ Schawk, Inc.	Business	17.3	-5.22	1.56
⊕ Laureate Education, Inc.	Consumer	27.1	-7.39	1.56
⊕ First Advantage Corporat	Business	20.8	-14.04	1.45
⊕ CACI International, Inc.	Business	20.9	-1.53	1.45
⊕ American Medical Systems	Health	69.9	3.87	1.43
⊕ Cooper Companies	Health	35.7	-13.14	1.42
⊕ Lancaster Colony Corpora	Goods	17.7	22.65	1.41
⊕ Euronet Worldwide, Inc.	Business	25.7	6.80	1.41
⊕ Church & Dwight Company,	Goods	22.2	30.00	1.36
⊕ WebEx Communications, In	Software	36.5	61.30	1.32
⊕ Stewart Enterprises	Consumer	27.5	17.54	1.30
⊕ Corinthian Colleges, Inc	Consumer	35.6	15.80	1.29

Current Investment Style

Value Blnd Growth — Large/Mid/Small

Market Cap	%
Giant	0.0
Large	0.0
Mid	26.4
Small	66.4
Micro	7.1
Avg $mil:	1,358

Value Measures		Rel Category
Price/Earnings	21.06	1.00
Price/Book	2.36	0.86
Price/Sales	1.56	0.99
Price/Cash Flow	11.20	1.16
Dividend Yield %	0.60	1.30

Growth Measures	%	Rel Category
Long-Term Erngs	14.84	0.84
Book Value	13.94	1.33
Sales	-5.91	NMF
Cash Flow	8.86	0.42
Historical Erngs	17.76	0.73

Profitability	%	Rel Category
Return on Equity	12.86	1.04
Return on Assets	7.91	1.19
Net Margin	10.81	1.25

Sector Weightings

	% of Stocks	Rel S&P 500	3 Year High	Low
☏ Info	10.87	0.54		
Software	6.37	1.85	7	2
Hardware	1.43	0.15	3	0
Media	3.07	0.81	3	2
Telecom	0.00	0.00	0	0
☞ Service	61.79	1.34		
Health	17.05	1.41	22	15
Consumer	10.01	1.31	17	8
Business	21.11	4.99	22	15
Financial	13.62	0.61	18	12
Mfg	27.35	0.81		
Goods	8.59	1.00	10	6
Ind Mtrls	12.91	1.08	18	13
Energy	5.85	0.60	7	2
Utilities	0.00	0.00	0	0

Composition

	%
● Cash	9.4
● Stocks	90.3
● Bonds	0.0
● Other	0.4
Foreign (% of Stock)	1.1

Morningstar® Funds 500

Chase Growth

Ticker	Load	NAV	Yield	Total Assets	Mstar Category
CHASX	None	$18.99	0.3%	$590 mil	Large Growth

Governance and Management

Stewardship Grade:

Portfolio Manager(s)

The founder of Chase Growth, Derwood Chase, Jr., has been in institutional asset management since the 1950s. He and comanager David Scott launched this fund in December 1997. Brian Lazorishak, who also assists with the fund's quantitative screening, was named a portfolio manager in January 2006. The management team is backed by analysts Peter Tuz and Peter Wood.

Strategy

Lead manager David Scott buys large- and mega-cap companies that have shown consistently strong earnings growth and are attractively priced. The investment process begins with a quantitative screen that seeks out companies with earnings growth of more than 10% in seven of the previous 10 years. Next, the team conducts fundamental analysis (looking at factors like return on equity, debt/equity ratio, and reinvestment of profits) and technical analysis (looking for stock purchases by insiders, price momentum, and unusually high trading volumes). The portfolio will hold between 35 and 45 names.

Historical Profile

Return Above Avg
Risk Below Avg
Rating ★★★★★ Highest

Investment Style: Equity Stock %

1998	1999	2000	2001	2002	2003	2004	2005	2006
92%	90%	81%	85%	87%	97%	92%	96%	100%

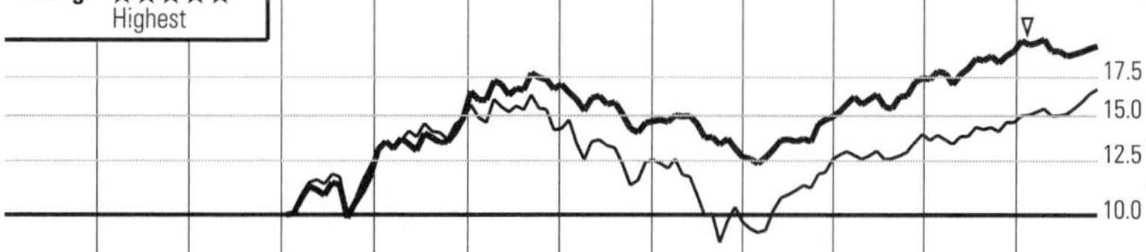

17.5
15.0
12.5
10.0

▼ Manager Change
▽ Partial Manager Change

Growth of $10,000
— Investment Values of Fund
— Investment Values of S&P 500

Performance Quartile (within Category)

History

1995	1996	1997	1998	1999	2000	2001	2002	2003	2004	2005	2006	History
—	—	10.19	13.21	16.73	16.99	14.62	12.64	14.90	17.42	19.40	18.99	NAV
—	—	2.01*	29.64	26.65	2.93	-13.73	-13.54	17.88	16.91	11.37	1.41	Total Return %
—	—	—	1.06	5.61	12.03	-1.84	8.56	-10.80	6.03	6.46	-14.38	+/-S&P 500
—	—	—	-9.07	-6.51	25.35	6.69	14.34	-11.87	10.61	6.11	-7.66	+/-Russ 1000Gr
—	—	—	0.00	0.00	1.38	0.22	0.00	0.00	0.00	0.00	0.32	Income Return %
—	—	—	29.64	26.65	1.55	-13.95	-13.54	17.88	16.91	11.37	1.09	Capital Return %
—	—	—	53	65	9	20	3	96	3	16	89	Total Rtn % Rank Cat
—	—	0.01	0.00	0.00	0.23	0.04	0.00	0.00	0.00	0.00	0.06	Income $
—	—	0.00	0.00	0.00	0.00	0.00	0.00	0.00	0.00	0.00	0.62	Capital Gains $
—	—	—	1.47	1.48	1.48	1.48	1.48	1.42	1.37	1.18	—	Expense Ratio %
—	—	—	-0.17	-0.59	-0.06	0.34	-0.32	-0.55	-0.77	-0.27	—	Income Ratio %
—	—	—	—	62	74	95	96	174	84	87	—	Turnover Rate %
—	—	1	6	11	27	37	61	121	221	545	590	Net Assets $mil

Performance 12-31-06

	1st Qtr	2nd Qtr	3rd Qtr	4th Qtr	Total
2002	2.39	-3.41	-8.09	-4.89	-13.54
2003	-0.08	7.76	-1.03	10.62	17.88
2004	8.32	1.05	-0.98	7.86	16.91
2005	1.89	1.97	5.08	2.00	11.37
2006	3.30	-3.19	-0.21	1.62	1.41

Trailing	Total Return%	+/- S&P 500	+/- Russ 1000Gr	%Rank Cat	Growth of $10,000
3 Mo	1.62	-5.08	-4.31	99	10,162
6 Mo	1.41	-11.33	-8.69	99	10,141
1 Yr	1.41	-14.38	-7.66	89	10,141
3 Yr Avg	9.71	-0.73	2.84	17	13,205
5 Yr Avg	6.12	-0.07	3.43	12	13,458
10 Yr Avg	—	—	—	—	—
15 Yr Avg	—	—	—	—	—

Tax Analysis	Tax-Adj Rtn%	%Rank Cat	Tax-Cost Rat	%Rank Cat
3 Yr (estimated)	9.49	14	0.20	14
5 Yr (estimated)	5.99	11	0.12	13
10 Yr (estimated)	—	—	—	—

Potential Capital Gain Exposure: 10% of assets

Rating and Risk

Time Period	Load-Adj Return %	Morningstar Rtn vs Cat	Morningstar Risk vs Cat	Morningstar Risk-Adj Rating
1 Yr	1.41			
3 Yr	9.71	+Avg	Avg	★★★★
5 Yr	6.12	+Avg	Low	★★★★★
10 Yr	—	—	—	—
Incept	7.94			

Other Measures	Standard Index S&P 500	Best Fit Index S&P Mid 400
Alpha	-0.7	-1.4
Beta	1.03	0.82
R-Squared	58	83
Standard Deviation	9.18	
Mean	9.71	
Sharpe Ratio	0.70	

Portfolio Analysis 09-30-06

Share change since 06-06 Total Stocks:38	Sector	PE	Tot Ret%	% Assets
⊕ Bank of America Corporat	Financial	12.4	20.68	4.53
⊕ Lockheed Martin Corporat	Ind Mtrls	17.3	46.98	4.52
PepsiCo, Inc.	Goods	21.5	7.86	4.51
⊕ Wells Fargo Company	Financial	14.7	16.82	4.38
⊖ Oracle Corporation	Software	26.7	40.38	4.23
United Technologies	Ind Mtrls	17.8	13.65	4.13
☆ Pfizer Inc.	Health	15.2	15.22	4.10
☆ Johnson & Johnson	Health	17.5	12.45	4.03
⊕ General Dynamics	Ind Mtrls	19.1	32.17	3.86
☆ Procter & Gamble Company	Goods	23.9	13.36	3.55
J.C. Penney Company, Inc	Consumer	17.3	40.59	3.27
☆ ExxonMobil Corporation	Energy	11.1	39.07	3.08
☆ Microsoft Corporation	Software	23.8	15.83	3.06
☆ CVS Corporation	Consumer	19.7	17.60	2.99
Kohl's Corporation	Consumer	22.6	40.80	2.93
Metropolitan Life Insura	Financial	16.0	21.67	2.85
Marriott International,	Consumer	27.7	43.41	2.65
⊕ Danaher Corporation	Ind Mtrls	22.0	30.02	2.62
☆ McDonald's Corporation	Consumer	18.9	34.63	2.61
☆ Walt Disney Company	Media	21.0	44.26	2.55

Current Investment Style

Market Cap	%
Giant	50.5
Large	47.9
Mid	1.5
Small	0.0
Micro	0.0
Avg $mil: 57,669	

Value Measures		Rel Category
Price/Earnings	17.10	0.89
Price/Book	3.32	1.00
Price/Sales	1.76	0.91
Price/Cash Flow	13.24	1.16
Dividend Yield %	1.62	1.57

Growth Measures	%	Rel Category
Long-Term Erngs	11.42	0.80
Book Value	11.27	0.97
Sales	10.84	0.93
Cash Flow	11.02	0.66
Historical Erngs	16.72	0.73

Profitability	%	Rel Category
Return on Equity	22.83	1.12
Return on Assets	11.00	1.00
Net Margin	14.05	0.99

Sector Weightings	% of Stocks	Rel S&P 500	3 Year High	3 Year Low
Info	9.84	0.49		
Software	7.29	2.11	7	0
Hardware	0.00	0.00	9	0
Media	2.55	0.67	3	0
Telecom	0.00	0.00	5	0
Service	51.52	1.11		
Health	20.60	1.71	32	4
Consumer	14.45	1.89	18	6
Business	1.03	0.24	8	1
Financial	15.44	0.69	19	6
Mfg	38.65	1.14		
Goods	13.27	1.55	13	6
Ind Mtrls	19.71	1.65	29	7
Energy	4.14	0.42	19	4
Utilities	1.53	0.44	2	0

Composition

Cash	0.0
Stocks	100.0
Bonds	0.0
Other	0.0
Foreign (% of Stock)	6.3

Morningstar's Take by Reginald Laing 11-06-06

We're not concerned with Chase Growth's recent dip in relative performance.

This offering follows a benchmark-spurning approach; given lead manager David Scott's talent, we think it's a good thing he goes his own way. Still, that will lead to occasional dry spells, such as the one the fund has experienced lately: For the trailing 12 months through Nov. 3, 2006, its 3.1% gain lagged those of roughly three fourths of its peers in Morningstar's large-growth category.

That underperformance doesn't stem from errant stock-picking. Rather, it was the fund's highly successful three-year bet on energy stocks that finally went against it, as that sector cooled due to valuation concerns and a drop (from August through October 2006) in crude-oil prices. Scott was already reducing the portfolio's energy exposure at the time of the energy sell-off, though, as he'd grown worried about the stocks' valuations and loss of price momentum--key factors in his buy and sell decisions. The energy stake now stands at 4.1% of assets, down from 18.3% in September 2005 and below the 6.5% stake for the average large-growth offering. Meanwhile, Scott has raised the fund's exposure to large pharmaceutical companies, taking positions in Pfizer, Wyeth, and Johnson & Johnson. Scott thinks these companies have moderate to depressed valuations and points to their revived earnings and price momentum as reasons to buy them now.

Such moves in and out of industries, which amount to de facto bets for and against those industries, can be difficult to time well with consistency (hence the occasional dry spells here). But in this fund's lifetime, Scott and his team have demonstrated a knack for doing so, avoiding carnage from downturns and buying into attractive areas of the market at opportune times. That accounts for this fund's excellent long-term record. And though it hasn't looked its best recently, we expect it to rebound--maybe sooner rather than later.

Address:	615 E Michigan Street Milwaukee, WI 53202 888-861-7556
Web Address:	www.chaseinv.com
Inception:	12-02-97*
Advisor:	Chase Investment Counsel Corporation
Subadvisor:	None
NTF Plans:	Fidelity Retail-NTF, Schwab OneSource

Minimum Purchase:	$2000	Add: $250	IRA: $0
Min Auto Inv Plan:	$250	Add: $250	
Sales Fees:	No-load, 2.00%R		
Management Fee:	1.00%		
Actual Fees:	Mgt:1.00%	Dist: —	
Expense Projections:	3Yr:$375	5Yr:$649	10Yr:$1432
Income Distrib:	Annually		

Chesapeake Core Growth

	Ticker	Load	NAV	Yield	Total Assets	Mstar Category
	CHCGX	None	$18.07	0.0%	$827 mil	Large Growth

Governance and Management

Stewardship Grade: B

Portfolio Manager(s)

Whit Gardner and John Lewis founded the Chesapeake fund family in 1990 after spending a few years as analysts at Friess Associates, which runs Brandywine Fund. Gardner and Lewis serve as managers of this fund and all of Chesapeake's offerings. William Zantzinger leads the risk-management and trading efforts and also oversees the nine-member analyst staff. Analysts are generalists who are encouraged to roam the market-cap and sector spectra. Gardner-Lewis maintains an extensive database cataloging all company contacts.

Strategy

Whit Gardner and John Lewis have adapted an approach they learned as analysts at Friess Associates. The research-intensive process involves identifying companies poised to beat earnings estimates and relies on constant contact with a variety of sources: a company, its competitors, suppliers, and customers. They also pay attention to valuation relative to growth rates and look for strong balance sheets. They tend to avoid cyclical industries. The team limits the portfolio to 50 stocks and often owns fewer, and it makes an effort to control risk by limiting its sector bets.

Performance 12-31-06

	1st Qtr	2nd Qtr	3rd Qtr	4th Qtr	Total
2002	-2.41	-14.50	-14.25	6.33	-23.92
2003	-0.37	18.86	8.09	11.26	42.42
2004	4.57	0.37	-6.22	12.48	10.71
2005	-4.37	2.53	3.01	0.30	1.30
2006	4.14	-4.26	2.96	4.44	7.22

Trailing	Total Return%	+/- S&P 500	+/- Russ 1000Gr	%Rank Cat	Growth of $10,000
3 Mo	4.44	-2.26	-1.49	75	10,444
6 Mo	7.53	-5.21	-2.57	65	10,753
1 Yr	7.22	-8.57	-1.85	48	10,722
3 Yr Avg	6.34	-4.10	-0.53	59	12,025
5 Yr Avg	5.43	-0.76	2.74	16	13,026
10 Yr Avg	—	—	—	—	—
15 Yr Avg	—	—	—	—	—

Tax Analysis	Tax-Adj Rtn%	%Rank Cat	Tax-Cost Rat	%Rank Cat
3 Yr (estimated)	6.23	52	0.10	7
5 Yr (estimated)	5.37	14	0.06	7
10 Yr (estimated)	—	—	—	—

Potential Capital Gain Exposure: 11% of assets

Historical Profile

Return	Above Avg
Risk	Above Avg
Rating	★★★ Above Avg

Investment Style: Equity, Stock %

100% 100% 91% 100% 100% 99% 99% 100% 99%

▼ Manager Change
▽ Partial Manager Change

Growth of $10,000
■ Investment Values of Fund
— Investment Values of S&P 500

Performance Quartile (within Category)

	1995	1996	1997	1998	1999	2000	2001	2002	2003	2004	2005	2006	History
	—	—	9.92	12.63	17.12	16.20	14.13	10.75	15.31	16.95	16.92	18.07	NAV
	—	—	-0.63*	27.32	47.60	6.36	-12.72	-23.92	42.42	10.71	1.30	7.22	Total Return %
	—	—	—	-1.26	26.56	15.46	-0.83	-1.82	13.74	-0.17	-3.61	-8.57	+/-S&P 500
	—	—	—	-11.39	14.44	28.78	7.70	3.96	12.67	4.41	-3.96	-1.85	+/-Russ 1000Gr
	—	—	—	0.00	0.00	0.00	0.00	0.00	0.00	0.00	0.00	0.00	Income Return %
	—	—	—	27.32	47.60	6.36	-12.72	-23.92	42.42	10.71	1.30	7.22	Capital Return %
	—	—	—	63	24	6	15	30	6	26	90	48	Total Rtn % Rank Cat
	—	—	0.02	0.00	0.00	0.00	0.00	0.00	0.00	0.00	0.00	0.00	Income $
	—	—	0.00	0.00	1.37	2.10	0.01	0.00	0.00	0.00	0.26	0.07	Capital Gains $
	—	—	—	1.24	1.39	1.15	1.25	1.23	1.31	1.33	1.35	—	Expense Ratio %
	—	—	—	-0.24	-0.55	-0.49	-0.50	-0.59	-0.61	-0.56	-0.51	—	Income Ratio %
	—	—	—	30	174	130	106	111	71	60	90	—	Turnover Rate %
	—	—	6	6	10	16	28	21	110	357	642	827	Net Assets $mil

Rating and Risk

Time Period	Load-Adj Return %	Morningstar Rtn vs Cat	Morningstar Risk vs Cat	Morningstar Risk-Adj Rating
1 Yr	7.22			
3 Yr	6.34	Avg	+Avg	★★★
5 Yr	5.43	+Avg	+Avg	★★★★
10 Yr	—			
Incept	9.21			

Other Measures	Standard Index S&P 500	Best Fit Index Mstar Small Growth
Alpha	-6.0	-0.9
Beta	1.36	0.60
R-Squared	76	84
Standard Deviation	10.71	
Mean	6.34	
Sharpe Ratio	0.33	

Portfolio Analysis 09-30-06

Share change since 06-06 Total Stocks:45	Sector	PE	Tot Ret%	% Assets
⊕ Goldman Sachs Group, Inc	Financial	12.4	57.41	3.96
⊕ Humana	Health	21.8	1.80	3.77
⊕ Comcast	Media	—	—	3.56
⊕ Monsanto Company	Ind Mtrls	39.8	36.78	3.44
⊕ Google, Inc.	Business	61.5	11.00	3.01
⊕ MEMC Electronic Material	Hardware	32.6	76.55	2.99
⊕ Capital One Financial Co	Financial	10.4	-10.97	2.96
⊕ Cigna Corporation	Health	13.3	17.89	2.95
⊕ American Express Company	Financial	20.9	19.09	2.95
⊕ Procter & Gamble Company	Goods	23.9	13.36	2.72
⊕ Best Buy Co., Inc.	Consumer	19.8	13.89	2.71
⊕ CVS Corporation	Consumer	19.7	17.60	2.70
⊕ Corning Inc.	Hardware	25.5	-4.83	2.66
⊕ TXU Corporation	Utilities	12.8	11.19	2.46
⊕ Applied Materials	Hardware	19.5	3.89	2.38
✿ American Capital Strateg	Financial	8.8	39.34	2.26
⊕ Xerox Corporation	Ind Mtrls	13.4	15.70	2.21
⊕ Chicago Mercantile Excha	Financial	49.3	39.48	2.19
⊕ GlaxoSmithKline PLC ADR	Health	17.6	7.95	2.18
⊕ Qualcomm, Inc.	Hardware	26.6	-11.32	2.18

Current Investment Style

Value Blnd Growth — Large Mid Small

Market Cap	%
Giant	21.9
Large	66.7
Mid	11.4
Small	0.0
Micro	0.0

Avg $mil: 25,250

Value Measures		Rel Category
Price/Earnings	17.76	0.92
Price/Book	2.98	0.90
Price/Sales	1.46	0.75
Price/Cash Flow	12.01	1.06
Dividend Yield %	0.97	0.94

Growth Measures	%	Rel Category
Long-Term Erngs	13.62	0.95
Book Value	14.26	1.23
Sales	9.76	0.84
Cash Flow	6.61	0.39
Historical Erngs	26.13	1.14

Profitability	%	Rel Category
Return on Equity	19.77	0.97
Return on Assets	10.99	1.00
Net Margin	13.03	0.91

Sector Weightings	% of Stocks	Rel S&P 500	3 Year High	Low
↻ Info	22.14	1.11		
▣ Software	2.01	0.58	9	2
▣ Hardware	14.53	1.57	21	15
▣ Media	5.60	1.48	9	5
▣ Telecom	0.00	0.00	0	0
☞ Service	55.94	1.21		
▣ Health	20.43	1.69	22	16
▣ Consumer	15.98	2.09	16	8
▣ Business	3.05	0.72	5	3
▣ Financial	16.48	0.74	17	13
▣ Mfg	21.93	0.65		
▣ Goods	6.60	0.77	9	3
▣ Ind Mtrls	9.64	0.81	12	5
▣ Energy	3.20	0.33	8	3
▣ Utilities	2.49	0.71	3	0

Composition

● Cash	0.0
● Stocks	98.9
● Bonds	0.0
● Other	1.1
Foreign (% of Stock)	6.3

Morningstar's Take by Dan Lefkovitz 11-10-06

We still see Chesapeake Core Growth as an elite member of the large-growth category.

Some readers may be wondering why we continue to stand by this fund. After all, it is lagging the large-growth category average for the second year in a row. Its returns for the trailing three-year period through November 9, 2006, put it near the peer group's bottom quartile.

The reason for our faith is that Chesapeake Core Growth has much of what we look for in a fund: experienced, proven management and a sound, consistently applied strategy. Comanagers Whit Gardner and John Lewis have been working together for more than 20 years--17 as partners in Gardner-Lewis Asset Management. They apply a research-intensive process they learned as analysts on the topnotch Brandywine Fund; they look for companies with catalysts for serious earnings growth that are not recognized by the market. They build portfolios of roughly 50 names and spread assets around, so that every stock will have an impact but no one stock will sink the fund.

Subpar recent returns can partly be blamed on a bias inherent in the fund's process. Gardner and Lewis tend to favor health-care, technology, and consumer-services stocks, because they see those sectors as driven by internal as opposed to macro-level forces. Those sectors happen to be three of the four worst performers in recent years. Stocks such as Humana and Qualcomm are recent detractors, and in 2005 the fund's lack of exposure to energy was a drag.

Investors need to keep their eyes on the long term. Even the best investors misfire. And this fund's 9% average annual gain since inception in 1997 is twice as good as its typical category peer. The fund preserved investor capital far better than most during the rough years of 2000-03. And it was enjoying a strong 2006 until a market pullback in May.

If fees were lower, we would bang the table harder for the fund.

Address:	116 South Franklin Street Rocky Mount NC 27802 800-430-3863	Minimum Purchase:	$2500 Add: $500 IRA: $2500
		Min Auto Inv Plan:	$2500 Add: $100
		Sales Fees:	No-load, 0.25%S
Web Address:	www.ncfunds.com	Management Fee:	1.00%, 0.08%A
Inception:	09-29-97*	Actual Fees:	Mgt:1.00% Dist:0.25%
Advisor:	Gardner Lewis Asset Management LP	Expense Projections:	3Yr:$454 5Yr:$787 10Yr:$1731
Subadvisor:	None	Income Distrib:	Quarterly
NTF Plans:	Fidelity Retail-NTF, Schwab OneSource		

MORNINGSTAR Funds 500

Clipper

		Ticker	Load	NAV	Yield	Total Assets	Mstar Category
✓	Analyst Pick	CFIMX	None	$91.98	1.1%	$3,432 mil	Large Blend

Governance and Management

Stewardship Grade: B

Portfolio Manager(s)

The board of directors hired Chris Davis and Ken Feinberg of Davis Selected Advisors to run the fund starting in 2006. Davis has been at the firm since 1991. Feinberg began as a financial-stock analyst with the firm in 1994. Davis' family owns the firm and invests heavily in its funds, which include Selected American and Davis New York Venture. Davis is investing $50 million in Clipper.

Strategy

Chris Davis and Ken Feinberg of Davis Selected Advisors took over here at the start of 2006. Davis and Feinberg try to buy great companies whose shares are temporarily depressed, estimating a firm's intrinsic value based on their own earnings analysis, in which they try to assess a firm's true cash earnings. They then look at those cash earnings relative to a return on adjusted invested capital. The idea is to figure out how well the company has historically allocated its capital.

Performance 12-31-06

	1st Qtr	2nd Qtr	3rd Qtr	4th Qtr	Total
2002	5.71	-6.22	-12.34	8.74	-5.50
2003	-10.17	17.32	3.63	9.27	19.35
2004	-2.76	2.71	-2.31	8.51	5.87
2005	-3.06	1.20	0.48	1.20	-0.24
2006	1.44	-0.11	4.11	9.27	15.28

Trailing	Total Return%	+/- S&P 500	+/- Russ 1000	%Rank Cat	Growth of $10,000
3 Mo	9.27	2.57	2.32	5	10,927
6 Mo	13.76	1.02	1.40	9	11,376
1 Yr	15.28	-0.51	-0.18	33	11,528
3 Yr Avg	6.78	-3.66	-4.20	94	12,175
5 Yr Avg	6.55	0.36	-0.27	31	13,733
10 Yr Avg	12.22	3.80	3.58	3	31,674
15 Yr Avg	13.75	3.11	2.95	5	69,067

Tax Analysis	Tax-Adj Rtn%	%Rank Cat	Tax-Cost Rat	%Rank Cat
3 Yr (estimated)	5.87	90	0.85	39
5 Yr (estimated)	5.57	36	0.92	60
10 Yr (estimated)	9.99	7	1.99	86

Potential Capital Gain Exposure: 24% of assets

Morningstar's Take by Kerry O'Boyle 12-27-06

The new management team has placed its stamp on the Clipper portfolio, and we think investors will like the results.

Chris Davis and Ken Feinberg, Morningstar's Fund Managers of the Year in 2005 for their work on Selected American and Davis NY Venture, took the reins here on Jan. 1, 2006, and have recently put the finishing touches on their overhaul of the portfolio. Gone are Marsh & McLennan and Time Warner, among others. They view the former as too tainted from investigations into questionable fee practices and point to increased transparency in pricing that will likely affect margins in the firm's insurance business. With Time Warner, Davis and Feinberg didn't have enough conviction in management (a key criterion for them to own a company) to merit holding what they considered to be a relatively pricey stock.

Coming into the portfolio are Procter & Gamble and News Corporation. Both represent dominant brands in their respective fields with management teams that Davis and Feinberg think are innovative and capable of delivering better growth than is currently priced into their stocks. All told, only nine stocks remain in the portfolio from December 2005, and the number of holdings has decreased from 24 to 19.

Although the fund has retained its concentrated, value-oriented approach, it's no longer the deep-value stalwart it once was. Davis and Feinberg are certainly bargain hunters, but they're more focused on a firm's future cash flows and enterprise value than finding stocks trading at the biggest discounts. Thus, we've shifted the fund to our large-blend category, where the overhauled portfolio lands and is likely to stay.

Performance has perked up for the first time in years in the fourth quarter of 2006. Plus, investors are getting a topnotch management team at a better price--currently 0.70%. We have enough faith in Davis and Feinberg that we've once again made this fund an Analyst Pick.

Address:	2949 E. Elvira Road Tucson AZ 85706 800-432-2504	Minimum Purchase:	$25000 Add: $1000 IRA: $4000
		Min Auto Inv Plan:	$25000 Add: $200
Web Address:	www.clipperfund.com	Sales Fees:	No-load
Inception:	02-29-84	Management Fee:	0.65% mx./0.49% mn.
Advisor:	Davis Selected Advisers LP	Actual Fees:	Mgt:0.50% Dist:—
Subadvisor:	Davis Selected Advisers - NY, Inc.	Expense Projections:	3Yr:$224 5Yr:$390 10Yr:$871
		Income Distrib:	Annually
NTF Plans:	Fidelity Retail-NTF, CommonWealth NTF		

Historical Profile
Return	Above Avg
Risk	Below Avg
Rating	★★★★ Above Avg

	61%	67%	60%	65%	92%	74%	79%	81%	98%

Investment Style
Equity
Stock %

▼ Manager Change
▽ Partial Manager Change

50.6
43.6
32.4
24.0 ■ Investment Values of Fund
17.0 — Investment Values of S&P 500
10.0

Growth of $10,000

Performance Quartile (within Category)

1995	1996	1997	1998	1999	2000	2001	2002	2003	2004	2005	2006	History
60.74	67.57	76.86	75.37	65.28	79.25	83.53	75.73	87.97	89.68	88.18	91.98	NAV
45.22	19.43	30.44	19.20	-2.02	37.40	10.26	-5.50	19.35	5.87	-0.24	15.28	Total Return %
7.64	-3.53	-2.92	-9.38	-23.06	46.50	22.15	16.60	-9.33	-5.01	-5.15	-0.51	+/-S&P 500
7.45	-3.02	-2.41	-7.82	-22.93	45.19	22.71	16.15	-10.54	-5.53	-6.51	-0.18	+/-Russ 1000
1.64	1.37	2.01	2.26	2.98	2.87	1.36	1.30	0.96	0.65	1.44	1.31	Income Return %
43.58	18.06	28.43	16.94	-5.00	34.53	8.90	-6.80	18.39	5.22	-1.68	13.97	Capital Return %
3	69	44	60	97	1	3	2	96	91	96	33	Total Rtn % Rank Cat
0.76	0.83	1.36	1.63	2.25	1.87	1.08	1.09	0.73	0.57	1.29	1.10	Income $
5.42	4.27	9.83	12.86	6.16	8.38	2.75	2.11	1.62	2.81	0.00	8.01	Capital Gains $
1.11	1.08	1.08	1.06	1.10	1.09	1.08	1.07	1.13	1.12	1.11	—	Expense Ratio %
1.39	1.32	1.84	2.13	2.54	2.88	1.72	1.65	0.98	0.65	0.97	—	Income Ratio %
31	24	31	65	63	46	23	48	25	16	13	—	Turnover Rate %
404	543	824	1,234	961	1,366	2,685	5,002	6,556	7,057	6,658	3,432	Net Assets $mil

Rating and Risk

Time Period	Load-Adj Return %	Morningstar Rtn vs Cat	Morningstar Risk vs Cat	Morningstar Risk-Adj Rating
1 Yr	15.28			
3 Yr	6.78	Low	Low	★★
5 Yr	6.55	+Avg	Avg	★★★★
10 Yr	12.22	High	Low	★★★★★
Incept	14.74			

Other Measures	Standard Index S&P 500	Best Fit Index Mstar Large Core TR
Alpha	-1.2	-2.0
Beta	0.68	0.74
R-Squared	57	62
Standard Deviation	6.30	
Mean	6.78	
Sharpe Ratio	0.57	

Portfolio Analysis 09-30-06

Share change since 06-06   Total Stocks:19

	Sector	PE	Tot Ret%	% Assets
Tyco International, Ltd.	Ind Mtrls	15.7	6.83	9.44
American International G	Financial	17.0	6.05	9.17
American Express Company	Financial	20.9	19.09	8.52
ConocoPhillips	Energy	6.5	26.53	7.70
Costco Wholesale Corpora	Consumer	23.3	7.90	6.94
⊖ Wal-Mart Stores, Inc.	Consumer	16.9	0.13	6.89
Altria Group, Inc.	Goods	16.3	19.87	6.19
Procter & Gamble Company	Goods	23.9	13.36	5.60
Harley-Davidson, Inc.	Goods	18.5	38.81	5.52
Ameriprise Financial, In	Financial	—	—	4.70
Microsoft Corporation	Software	23.8	15.83	4.60
Berkshire Hathaway Inc.	Financial	—	—	4.04
Merrill Lynch & Company,	Financial	14.2	39.28	3.87
J.P. Morgan Chase & Co.	Financial	13.6	25.60	3.66
⊕ News Corporation, Ltd. A	Media	—	—	3.27
⊖ Golden West Fin	Financial	—	—	3.25
⊖ Coca-Cola Company	Goods	21.7	23.10	2.14
Johnson & Johnson	Health	17.5	12.45	1.80
⊖ Sprint Nextel Corporatio	Telecom	30.2	-10.44	0.77

Current Investment Style

Value Blnd Growth — Large Mid Small

Market Cap	%
Giant	79.5
Large	20.5
Mid	0.0
Small	0.0
Micro	0.0

Avg $mil: 82,587

Value Measures		Rel Category
Price/Earnings	13.82	0.90
Price/Book	2.28	0.89
Price/Sales	1.05	0.75
Price/Cash Flow	8.55	1.01
Dividend Yield %	2.20	1.26

Growth Measures	%	Rel Category
Long-Term Ergns	10.88	0.92
Book Value	10.91	1.21
Sales	13.51	1.39
Cash Flow	14.55	1.41
Historical Ergns	20.58	1.11

Profitability	%	Rel Category
Return on Equity	19.10	0.98
Return on Assets	12.45	1.20
Net Margin	11.42	0.85

Sector Weightings	% of Stocks	Rel S&P 500	3 Year High	Low
↻ Info	8.80	0.44		
🗔 Software	4.69	1.36	5	0
🖥 Hardware	0.00	0.00	0	0
🎙 Media	3.33	0.88	3	1
📶 Telecom	0.78	0.22	2	0
⊜ Service	53.88	1.17		
🩺 Health	1.83	0.15	22	2
🛒 Consumer	14.10	1.84	15	7
🏛 Business	0.00	0.00	10	0
💲 Financial	37.95	1.70	42	34
⊟ Mfg	37.31	1.10		
🏭 Goods	19.84	2.32	20	11
🔧 Ind Mtrls	9.62	0.81	11	7
🔋 Energy	7.85	0.80	9	4
💡 Utilities	0.00	0.00	0	0

Composition

●	Cash	1.9
●	Stocks	98.1
●	Bonds	0.0
○	Other	0.0
	Foreign (% of Stock)	0.0

Columbia Acorn A

	Ticker	Load	NAV	Yield	Total Assets	Mstar Category
	LACAX	5.75%	$29.02	0.1%	$18,970 mil	Mid-Cap Growth

Governance and Management

Stewardship Grade: B

Portfolio Manager(s)

In September 2003, legendary manager Ralph Wanger relinquished his position as head of the fund. His longtime comanager Chuck McQuaid is now at the helm, with Rob Mohn joining as his comanager. Mohn has served as a manager on Columbia Acorn USA for several years and has delivered fine results.

Strategy

Comanagers Chuck McQuaid, Rob Mohn, and their colleagues use a combination of top-down themes and fundamental research to put together this fund's sprawling portfolio of about 400 holdings. The managers are far more price-sensitive than their typical small-growth rival, and the portfolio usually has lower valuations and a much smaller technology weighting than the category norm. They have often favored business-services companies and financials.

Performance 12-31-06

	1st Qtr	2nd Qtr	3rd Qtr	4th Qtr	Total
2002	4.83	-8.25	-16.53	7.35	-13.82
2003	-2.80	19.85	8.79	14.30	44.85
2004	7.12	1.51	-0.91	12.35	21.05
2005	-1.35	4.00	6.71	2.99	12.76
2006	9.83	-3.81	0.42	7.59	14.13

Trailing	Total Return%	+/- S&P 500	+/- Russ MG	%Rank Cat	Growth of $10,000
3 Mo	7.59	0.89	0.64	33	10,759
6 Mo	8.03	-4.71	0.13	25	10,803
1 Yr	14.13	-1.66	3.47	14	11,413
3 Yr Avg	15.93	5.49	3.20	7	15,581
5 Yr Avg	14.23	8.04	6.01	2	19,449
10 Yr Avg	—	—	—	—	—
15 Yr Avg	—	—	—	—	—

Tax Analysis	Tax-Adj Rtn%	%Rank Cat	Tax-Cost Rat	%Rank Cat
3 Yr (estimated)	12.62	18	0.92	46
5 Yr (estimated)	12.26	4	0.55	39
10 Yr (estimated)	—	—	—	—

Potential Capital Gain Exposure: 37% of assets

Historical Profile

Return High
Risk Below Avg
Rating ★★★★ Highest

	92%	92%	83%	91%	91%	93%	92%

Investment Style
Equity
Stock %

▼ Manager Change
▽ Partial Manager Change

Growth of $10,000
— Investment Values of Fund
— Investment Values of S&P 500

19.6
16.6
13.0
10.0
5.0

Performance Quartile (within Category)

1995	1996	1997	1998	1999	2000	2001	2002	2003	2004	2005	2006	History
—	—	—	—	—	17.19	17.80	15.34	22.20	25.93	27.57	29.02	NAV
—	—	—	—	—	6.92*	-13.82	44.85	21.05	12.76	14.13		Total Return %
—	—	—	—	—	17.45	8.28	16.17	10.17	7.85	-1.66		+/-S&P 500
—	—	—	—	—	25.71	13.59	2.14	5.57	0.66	3.47		+/-Russ MG
—	—	—	—	—	0.00	0.00	0.00	0.00	0.28	0.15		Income Return %
—	—	—	—	—	5.56	-13.82	44.85	21.05	12.48	13.98		Capital Return %
—	—	—	—	—	6	5	13	29	14			Total Rtn % Rank Cat
—	—	—	—	—	0.06	0.00	0.00	0.00	0.00	0.07	0.04	Income $
—	—	—	—	—	1.86	0.35	0.00	0.02	0.91	1.56	2.38	Capital Gains $
—	—	—	—	—	1.03	1.42	1.42	1.33	1.20	1.03	—	Expense Ratio %
—	—	—	—	—	0.39	-0.33	-0.45	-0.36	-0.21	0.28	—	Income Ratio %
—	—	—	—	—	29	20	13	10	20	16	—	Turnover Rate %
—	—	—	—	—	17	304	713	2,000	2,668	3,353	4,079	Net Assets $mil

Rating and Risk

Time Period	Load-Adj Return %	Morningstar Rtn vs Cat	Morningstar Risk vs Cat	Morningstar Risk-Adj Rating
1 Yr	7.57			
3 Yr	13.66	+Avg	-Avg	★★★★
5 Yr	12.88	High	-Avg	★★★★★
10 Yr	—	—	—	
Incept	12.43			

Other Measures	Standard Index S&P 500	Best Fit Index Russ 2000 Gr
Alpha	2.5	6.8
Beta	1.40	0.68
R-Squared	77	96
Standard Deviation	10.93	
Mean	15.93	
Sharpe Ratio	1.12	

Morningstar's Take by Todd Trubey 12-12-06

Columbia Acorn continues to defy the odds.

A torrent of mergers and acquisitions has had a big impact here. Twenty-six stocks in this fund became takeout targets in 2006 through early December. Lead manager Chuck McQuaid says that meant about $1 billion worth of transactions here--more than 5% of this giant fund's assets. He usually thinks such deals are worthy and says investors here thrived when Western Gas went out at a 50% premium and top-25 holding Michaels Stores gained a 30% windfall. Still, he dislikes takeouts with measly 15% premiums on firms that his analysts think will double in size in a few years.

Wanger Asset Management (WAM) would say that it's largely a bottom-up stock-picker, but it does lean a bit on macroeconomic views. McQuaid thinks risk is high in today's markets: Some tiny, unprofitable firms have big valuations, and junk-bond yields are low. So the fund is tamping down risk, whittling its foreign stake largely by selling a few emerging-markets stocks. It has a

modest energy overweighting versus its Russell 2500 Growth benchmark, but it's leaning toward drillers that have locked-in contracts. WAM isn't afraid to be contrarian, either: It's overweighted consumer fare all year.

As noted before, this analyst-driven behemoth's future success rests on two key things. As always, the staff must find smaller-growth stocks that can thrive for years--and hold on through temporary troubles. Consumer specialist Susie Hultquist did the latter when Coach and Abercrombie & Fitch suffered early this year, which looks very smart today. Also, as the fund grows, WAM must keep adding to its big roster of analysts. The firm is clearly committed: It has hired two more analysts in the last six months and now seems on a permanent prowl for talent.

We continue to prefer the two smaller Acorn siblings but believe that this fund's large investor base can do quite well here. Despite its size, its record of outperformance remains impressive.

Address:	227 W Monroe Ste 3000 Chicago IL 60606 800-345-6611	Minimum Purchase:	$75000 Add: $0 IRA: $75000
		Min Auto Inv Plan:	$50 Add: $50
		Sales Fees:	5.75%L, 0.25%S
Web Address:	www.columbiafunds.com	Management Fee:	0.74% mx./0.63% mn., 0.05%A
Inception:	10-16-00*	Actual Fees:	Mgt:0.64% Dist:0.25%
Advisor:	Columbia Wanger Asset Management, LP	Expense Projections:	3Yr:$887 5Yr:$1116 10Yr:$1773
Subadvisor:	None	Income Distrib:	Semi-Annually
NTF Plans:	DATALynx NTF, Federated Tr NTF		

Portfolio Analysis 11-30-06

Share change since 10-06 Total Stocks:379	Sector	PE	Tot Ret%	% Assets
Coach, Inc.	Goods	32.1	28.85	1.66
Expeditors International	Business	34.4	20.54	1.31
People's Bank	Financial	45.5	47.71	1.01
⊕ Abercrombie & Fitch Comp	Consumer	17.5	8.01	1.01
FMC Technologies, Inc.	Energy	19.7	43.59	0.89
Genlyte Group Inc.	Ind Mtrls	15.1	45.81	0.87
⊕ Chico's FAS, Inc.	Consumer	19.2	-52.90	0.86
⊕ Eaton Vance Corporation	Financial	25.8	22.47	0.83
Crown Castle Internation	Telecom	—	20.94	0.81
ITT Educational Services	Consumer	26.8	12.59	0.81
AmeriCredit Corporation	Financial	11.2	-1.80	0.80
Ultra Petroleum Corporat	Energy	30.4	-14.44	0.76
SEI Investments Company	Business	26.8	61.73	0.75
⊕ Ametek, Inc.	Ind Mtrls	18.9	12.94	0.75
⊕ BOK Financial Corp.	Financial	17.3	22.36	0.74
Tellabs, Inc.	Hardware	18.0	-5.87	0.72
Scotts Miracle-Gro Compa	Ind Mtrls	21.6	15.43	0.71
Fugro	Business	—	—	0.71
American Tower Corporati	Telecom	—	37.57	0.70
Harley-Davidson, Inc.	Goods	18.5	38.81	0.68

Current Investment Style

Value Blnd Growth — Large Mid Small

Market Cap	%
Giant	0.1
Large	9.2
Mid	55.8
Small	29.4
Micro	5.6

Avg $mil: 2,574

Value Measures		Rel Category
Price/Earnings	18.78	0.92
Price/Book	2.84	0.88
Price/Sales	1.60	0.91
Price/Cash Flow	9.97	0.87
Dividend Yield %	1.00	1.59

Growth Measures	%	Rel Category
Long-Term Erngs	15.29	0.94
Book Value	8.71	0.68
Sales	-4.50	NMF
Cash Flow	13.28	0.72
Historical Erngs	14.97	0.60

Profitability	%	Rel Category
Return on Equity	16.58	0.92
Return on Assets	9.04	0.96
Net Margin	11.27	0.97

Sector Weightings	% of Stocks	Rel S&P 500	3 Year High Low
Info	16.83	0.84	
Software	4.59	1.33	8 4
Hardware	6.32	0.68	7 5
Media	1.98	0.52	2 2
Telecom	3.94	1.12	4 2
Service	52.92	1.15	
Health	9.63	0.80	12 9
Consumer	12.69	1.66	15 12
Business	12.75	3.01	14 12
Financial	17.85	0.80	18 14
Mfg	30.24	0.89	
Goods	8.44	0.99	10 7
Ind Mtrls	14.41	1.21	16 11
Energy	6.69	0.68	9 6
Utilities	0.70	0.20	1 1

Composition

● Cash	6.8
● Stocks	92.3
● Bonds	0.0
● Other	0.9
Foreign (% of Stock)	12.9

MORNINGSTAR® Funds 500

Columbia Acorn Intl A

	Ticker	Load	NAV	Yield	Total Assets	Mstar Category
	LAIAX	5.75%	$40.07	0.7%	$4,341 mil	Foreign Small/Mid Growth

Governance and Management

Stewardship Grade: B

Portfolio Manager(s)

Zach Egan and Louis Mendes joined the fund as analysts in 1999 and 2001, respectively, and were promoted to comanagers in May 2003. They're supported by seven analysts. Each member of the team is responsible for stock selection in his area of expertise.

Strategy

Management searches for smaller companies that are growing at above-average rates. The team also looks for strong balance sheets, cash flows, and dividend yields, and it pays a lot of attention to valuations and diversification. Zach Egan and Louis Mendes monitor the aggregate portfolio to make sure its sector and other bets aren't too aggressive. The fund levies a 2% redemption fee on shares held less than 60 days.

Historical Profile

Return	Below Avg
Risk	Below Avg
Rating	★★ Below Avg

86%　91%　83%　93%　88%　93%　92%

Investment Style
Equity
Stock %

▽ Partial Manager Change
▼ Manager Change

Growth of $10,000
— Investment Values of Fund
— Investment Values of MSCI EAFE

15.5
12.5
10.0
5.0

Performance Quartile (within Category)

	1995	1996	1997	1998	1999	2000	2001	2002	2003	2004	2005	2006	History
	—	—	—	—	—	23.85	18.35	15.32	22.45	28.75	33.20	40.07	NAV
	—	—	—	—	—	-5.28*	-21.62	-16.46	46.94	28.91	21.42	34.16	Total Return %
	—	—	—	—	—	—	-0.20	-0.52	8.35	8.66	7.88	7.82	+/-MSCI EAFE
	—	—	—	—	—	—	-0.23	-0.66	7.52	8.53	6.95	8.45	+/-MSCI Wd xUS
	—	—	—	—	—	—	0.00	0.05	0.30	0.69	1.86	0.98	Income Return %
	—	—	—	—	—	—	-21.62	-16.51	46.64	28.22	19.56	33.18	Capital Return %
	—	—	—	—	—	—	43	67	75	25	63	17	Total Rtn % Rank Cat
	—	—	—	—	—	0.00	0.00	0.01	0.05	0.15	0.53	0.32	Income $
	—	—	—	—	—	3.59	0.39	0.02	0.05	1.08	3.91	Capital Gains $
	—	—	—	—	—	0.59	1.65	1.56	1.59	1.48	1.30	—	Expense Ratio %
	—	—	—	—	—	0.40	0.03	0.30	0.57	0.61	0.72	—	Income Ratio %
	—	—	—	—	—	63	45	52	40	40	27	—	Turnover Rate %
	—	—	—	—	—	12	27	34	53	71	142	313	Net Assets $mil

Performance 12-31-06

	1st Qtr	2nd Qtr	3rd Qtr	4th Qtr	Total
2002	2.23	-1.44	-19.96	3.58	-16.46
2003	-6.59	21.37	10.68	17.11	46.94
2004	6.77	1.63	1.86	16.63	28.91
2005	3.17	-0.33	13.10	4.40	21.42
2006	15.45	-1.16	2.81	14.36	34.16

Trailing	Total Return%	+/- MSCI EAFE	+/- MSCI Wd xUS	%Rank Cat	Growth of $10,000
3 Mo	14.36	4.01	4.24	38	11,436
6 Mo	17.57	2.88	3.35	29	11,757
1 Yr	34.16	7.82	8.45	17	13,416
3 Yr Avg	28.06	8.13	7.96	22	21,001
5 Yr Avg	20.85	5.87	5.60	45	25,777
10 Yr Avg	—	—	—	—	—
15 Yr Avg	—	—	—	—	—

Tax Analysis	Tax-Adj Rtn%	%Rank Cat	Tax-Cost Rat	%Rank Cat
3 Yr (estimated)	24.30	46	1.00	35
5 Yr (estimated)	18.68	60	0.63	45
10 Yr (estimated)	—	—	—	—

Potential Capital Gain Exposure: 28% of assets

Rating and Risk

Time Period	Load-Adj Return %	Morningstar Rtn vs Cat	Morningstar Risk vs Cat	Morningstar Risk-Adj Rating
1 Yr	26.44			
3 Yr	25.55	Avg	-Avg	★★★
5 Yr	19.43	-Avg	-Avg	★★
10 Yr	—	—	—	—
Incept	9.97			

Other Measures	Standard Index MSCI EAFE	Best Fit Index MSCI EAFE
Alpha	3.3	3.3
Beta	1.24	1.24
R-Squared	91	91
Standard Deviation	12.25	
Mean	28.06	
Sharpe Ratio	1.84	

Portfolio Analysis 11-30-06

Share change since 10-06 Total Stocks:174	Sector	Country	% Assets
Hexagon	Ind Mtrls	Sweden	1.44
Fugro	Business	Netherlands	1.40
C&C Grp	Goods	Ireland	1.21
SES GLOBAL	Telecom	Luxembourg	1.19
Housing Development Fina	Financial	India	1.13
Aalberts Industries	Ind Mtrls	Netherlands	1.08
⊖ IAWS Grp	Goods	Ireland	1.05
Hong Kong Exchanges & Cl	Financial	Hong Kong	1.05
Geberit	Consumer	Switzerland	1.03
Bank of Ireland	Financial	Ireland	1.02
Atwood Oceanics, Inc.	Energy	United States	1.02
Northern Rock	Financial	U.K.	0.98
Suzano Bahia Sul Papel E	—	Brazil	0.98
DEPFA Bank	Financial	Germany	0.97
Rhoen Klinikum	Health	Germany	0.96
Expro International Grp	Energy	U.K.	0.95
⊖ Anglo Irish Bank	Financial	Ireland	0.95
Wincor Nixdorf	Hardware	Germany	0.94
Synthes	Health	Switzerland	0.92
⊖ Usg People Nv	Business	Netherlands	0.92

Current Investment Style

Value Blnd Growth — Large Mid Small

	Market Cap	%
	Giant	0.0
	Large	19.2
	Mid	53.2
	Small	25.9
	Micro	1.8
	Avg $mil: 2,570	

Value Measures		Rel Category
Price/Earnings	17.41	1.11
Price/Book	2.89	1.19
Price/Sales	1.28	1.16
Price/Cash Flow	9.58	1.22
Dividend Yield %	1.89	0.92

Growth Measures	%	Rel Category
Long-Term Erngs	16.35	0.80
Book Value	6.15	0.65
Sales	14.53	1.16
Cash Flow	14.41	0.96
Historical Erngs	4.88	0.22

Composition

Cash	5.1	Bonds	0.0
Stocks	92.3	Other	2.6
Foreign (% of Stock)			98.1

Sector Weightings	% of Stocks	Rel MSCI EAFE	3 Year High	3 Year Low
↻ Info	8.16	0.69		
▣ Software	1.29	2.30	2	1
▣ Hardware	3.03	0.78	4	2
▣ Media	1.71	0.93	2	1
▣ Telecom	2.13	0.38	3	1
☗ Service	52.21	1.11		
▣ Health	6.31	0.89	9	6
▣ Consumer	10.03	2.03	14	9
▣ Business	18.36	3.62	21	15
▣ Financial	17.51	0.58	20	12
▣ Mfg	39.63	0.97		
▣ Goods	12.37	0.94	15	8
▣ Ind Mtrls	20.43	1.32	22	18
▣ Energy	5.32	0.74	6	4
▣ Utilities	1.51	0.29	2	1

Regional Exposure % Stock

UK/W. Europe	59	N. America	5
Japan	15	Latn America	4
Asia X Japan	13	Other	4

Country Exposure % Stock

Japan	15	Netherlands	8
France	10	Germany	8
U.K.	8		

Morningstar's Take by William Samuel Rocco 12-23-06

Columbia Acorn International has real allure as a supplemental international holding.

This fund is more attractively priced than most other supplemental international holdings (foreign smaller-cap funds and emerging-markets offerings). Indeed, it has an expense ratio of 1.30%, whereas the median expense ratio for front-load foreign smaller-cap funds is 1.72% and the median expense ratio for front-load emerging markets offerings is 1.94%.

What's more, this fund has quite a bit of diversification value. Many foreign smaller-cap funds pay lots of attention to larger caps, but this one does not, and its average market cap tends to be slightly below the norm for such funds as a result. It also provides more emerging-markets exposure than most other foreign smaller-cap funds do, and its universe extends beyond the biggest developing markets. As of Sept. 30, in fact, it had investments in Poland, the Czech Republic, Indonesia, and Chile.

This fund has more than price and portfolio appeal. It has been much less volatile than most of its foreign small/mid-growth peers, because Zach Egan and Louis Mendes are quality- and valuation-conscious growth investors who shun big country, sector, and stock bets. And this fund has outgained its average category peer by a small margin since Egan and Mendes took the helm in early 2003, as their stock selection have been pretty good overall.

All this is encouraging, and this fund is well worth a look from foreign small/mid-growth fans and others who are seeking supplemental international exposure. But such investors need to be sure they understand that this fund is quite volatile in absolute terms and that the big gains it and other supplemental foreign holdings have posted in recent years aren't sustainable.

Address:	227 W Monroe Ste 3000 Chicago IL 60606 800-345-6611	
Web Address:	www.columbiafunds.com	
Inception:	10-16-00*	
Advisor:	Columbia Wanger Asset Management, LP	
Subadvisor:	None	
NTF Plans:	DATALynx NTF, Federated Tr NTF	

Minimum Purchase:	$2500	Add: $50　IRA: $1000
Min Auto Inv Plan:	$50	Add: $50
Sales Fees:	5.75%L, 0.25%S, 2.00%R	
Management Fee:	1.19% mx./0.74% mn., 0.05%A	
Actual Fees:	Mgt:0.79%	Dist:0.25%
Expense Projections:	3Yr:$969	5Yr:$1257　10Yr:$2074
Income Distrib:	Semi-Annually	

Columbia Acorn Select A

Ticker	Load	NAV	Yield	Total Assets	Mstar Category
LTFAX	5.75%	$26.18	0.1%	$2,238 mil	Mid-Cap Growth

Governance and Management

Stewardship Grade: B

Portfolio Manager(s)

Ben Andrews took charge here in April 2004, replacing longtime manager John Park. Andrews cut his teeth as a software analyst at Wanger Asset Management and also has experience with debt analysis. Andrews receives considerable support from Acorn's large analyst staff.

Strategy

Historically, this fund's manager and the Acorn analyst team use a combination of investment themes and fundamental research to look for promising growth companies trading at discounts to the team's estimates of their worth. This fund is limited to fewer than 50 holdings and will take large individual positions. It favors mid-caps to provide the needed liquidity to buy and sell such stakes.

Historical Profile

Return	High
Risk	Low
Rating	★★★★ Highest

Investment Style: Equity Stock %

95% | 93% | 95% | 94% | 87% | 95% | 94%

▼ Manager Change
▽ Partial Manager Change

Growth of $10,000
— Investment Values of Fund
— Investment Values of S&P 500

Performance Quartile (within Category)

	1995	1996	1997	1998	1999	2000	2001	2002	2003	2004	2005	2006	History
	—	—	—	—	—	14.12	15.17	13.93	18.01	20.83	22.47	26.18	NAV
	—	—	—	—	—	6.32*	7.65	-8.17	29.95	18.16	10.78	19.32	Total Return %
	—	—	—	—	—	—	19.54	13.93	1.27	7.28	5.87	3.53	+/-S&P 500
	—	—	—	—	—	—	27.80	19.24	-12.76	2.68	-1.32	8.66	+/-Russ MG
	—	—	—	—	—	—	0.00	0.00	0.00	0.00	0.00	0.10	Income Return %
	—	—	—	—	—	—	7.65	-8.17	29.95	18.16	10.78	19.22	Capital Return %
	—	—	—	—	—	4	1	81	16	46	3		Total Rtn % Rank Cat
	—	—	—	—	—	0.00	0.00	0.00	0.00	0.00	0.00	0.02	Income $
	—	—	—	—	—	0.20	0.03	0.00	0.09	0.44	0.59	0.59	Capital Gains $
	—	—	—	—	—	1.70	1.70	1.70	1.63	1.47	1.26	—	Expense Ratio %
	—	—	—	—	—	-0.61	-0.79	-0.79	-1.15	-0.86	-0.42	—	Income Ratio %
	—	—	—	—	—	116	82	40	16	34	19	—	Turnover Rate %
	—	—	—	—	—	3	12	32	260	515	745	941	Net Assets $mil

Performance 12-31-06

	1st Qtr	2nd Qtr	3rd Qtr	4th Qtr	Total
2002	-0.79	-4.45	-8.55	5.93	-8.17
2003	1.72	14.26	6.67	4.81	29.95
2004	5.27	1.79	-3.11	13.80	18.16
2005	-5.38	5.40	4.21	6.59	10.78
2006	7.74	-2.27	2.68	10.37	19.32

Trailing	Total Return%	+/- S&P 500	+/- Russ MG	%Rank Cat	Growth of $10,000
3 Mo	10.37	3.67	3.42	8	11,037
6 Mo	13.32	0.58	5.42	3	11,332
1 Yr	19.32	3.53	8.66	3	11,932
3 Yr Avg	16.03	5.59	3.30	6	15,621
5 Yr Avg	13.26	7.07	5.04	3	18,637
10 Yr Avg	—	—	—	—	—
15 Yr Avg	—	—	—	—	—

Tax Analysis	Tax-Adj Rtn%	%Rank Cat	Tax-Cost Rat	%Rank Cat
3 Yr (estimated)	13.30	14	0.40	20
5 Yr (estimated)	11.64	4	0.26	19
10 Yr (estimated)	—	—	—	—

Potential Capital Gain Exposure: 31% of assets

Morningstar's Take by Todd Trubey 12-12-06

Columbia Acorn Select's success doesn't stem from luck.

This fund has a great record, but that's not why we like it. The oldest share class has gained 15% annually from Nov. 11, 1998, to Dec. 11, 2006, and on Ben Andrew's watch the A shares have also gained 15% annually since April 1, 2004. Over both time frames the fund tops 90% of mid-growth category rivals. That's the outgrowth of a strong game plan. Wanger Asset Management plies a valuation-sensitive growth style and holds stocks for years. Here, the small-cap outfit owns mid-caps it knew before they got big and puts them in a compact three-dozen-stock portfolio. Such focused investing can produce great results.

Still, we wouldn't endorse such a strategy unless there was talent in place. WAM rests largely on the work of its two-dozen seasoned, committed analysts. This year many investors were spooked over consumers' future woes, so holdings here such as Coach and Abercrombie & Fitch plummeted. But consumer analyst Susie Hultquist saw strong fundamentals and held tight; the stocks have rallied 48% and 26%, respectively, since July 31. It's been hard to make money in telecom firms lately, but firm CEO and analyst Chuck McQuaid's American Tower pick here has more than doubled in less than two years.

Even at an analyst-driven shop, though, you want a solid manager like Ben Andrews here. He wanted to raise exposure to commodity firms to capitalize on supply/demand imbalances--but only wants the right firms. In December 2005 he bought Potash Corporation of Saskatchewan after it fell more than 30% without a real change in fundamentals. He likes it because it's the dominant industry player, has the lowest costs and best reserves, and especially because management adjusts production as commodity prices impact profit margins to maximize value.

The $50,000 minimum investment is a high bar to entry, but it's a worthy fund.

Address:	227 W Monroe Ste 3000
	Chicago IL 60606
	800-345-6611
Web Address:	www.columbiafunds.com
Inception:	10-13-00*
Advisor:	Columbia Wanger Asset Management, LP
Subadvisor:	None
NTF Plans:	Schwab OneSource

Minimum Purchase:	$50000	Add: $0	IRA: $50000
Min Auto Inv Plan:	$50	Add: $50	
Sales Fees:	5.75%L, 0.25%S		
Management Fee:	0.85% mx./0.80% mn., 0.05%A		
Actual Fees:	Mgt:0.82%	Dist:0.25%	
Expense Projections:	3Yr:$958	5Yr:$1237	10Yr:$2031
Income Distrib:	Semi-Annually		

Rating and Risk

Time Period	Load-Adj Return %	Morningstar Rtn vs Cat	Morningstar Risk vs Cat	Morningstar Risk-Adj Rating
1 Yr	12.46			
3 Yr	13.76	+Avg	Low	★★★★
5 Yr	11.93	High	Low	★★★★★
10 Yr	—	—	—	—
Incept	11.89			

Other Measures	Standard Index S&P 500	Best Fit Index DJ Wilshire 4500
Alpha	3.6	3.0
Beta	1.24	0.81
R-Squared	71	81
Standard Deviation	10.07	
Mean	16.03	
Sharpe Ratio	1.22	

Portfolio Analysis 11-30-06

Share change since 10-06 Total Stocks:34	Sector	PE	Tot Ret%	% Assets
⊕ Urasia Engy	Energy	—	—	5.15
⊕ Tellabs, Inc.	Hardware	18.0	-5.87	5.09
Safeway Inc.	Consumer	20.4	47.22	5.09
⊕ ITT Educational Services	Consumer	26.8	12.59	4.70
⊕ Abercrombie & Fitch Comp	Consumer	17.5	8.01	4.39
American Tower Corporati	Telecom	—	37.57	4.05
⊕ Avid Technology, Inc.	Software	56.0	-31.96	3.85
Liberty Global, Inc.	Media	—	—	3.59
⊕ Expedia, Inc.	Consumer	—	-12.44	3.30
⊕ Janus Capital Group, Inc	Financial	42.2	16.13	3.25
Potash Corporation of Sa	Ind Mtrls	26.0	80.04	3.14
⊖ Coach, Inc.	Goods	32.1	28.85	3.12
Pride International, Inc	Energy	17.6	-2.41	3.00
SkillSoft ADR	Business	33.2	12.91	2.79
Expeditors International	Business	34.4	20.54	2.78
⊖ Harley-Davidson, Inc.	Goods	18.5	38.81	2.65
Quanta Services, Inc.	Ind Mtrls	39.6	49.36	2.58
Markel Corporation	Financial	12.2	51.43	2.33
Nuveen Investments, Inc.	Financial	23.9	24.13	2.25
Waste Management, Inc.	Business	16.6	24.21	2.21

Current Investment Style

Value Blnd Growth — Large Mid Small

Market Cap	%
Giant	0.0
Large	26.1
Mid	58.9
Small	14.8
Micro	0.2
Avg $mil:	5,017

Value Measures		Rel Category
Price/Earnings	21.75	1.06
Price/Book	2.37	0.74
Price/Sales	1.22	0.69
Price/Cash Flow	8.69	0.76
Dividend Yield %	0.59	0.94

Growth Measures	%	Rel Category
Long-Term Erngs	13.48	0.83
Book Value	8.90	0.70
Sales	7.78	0.78
Cash Flow	8.90	0.48
Historical Erngs	10.10	0.40

Profitability	%	Rel Category
Return on Equity	20.03	1.12
Return on Assets	10.67	1.14
Net Margin	9.42	0.81

Sector Weightings	% of Stocks	Rel S&P 500	3 Year High	Low
↻ Info	25.25	1.26		
Software	5.86	1.70	18	2
Hardware	7.24	0.78	11	3
Media	6.74	1.78	9	0
Telecom	5.41	1.54	5	0
Service	48.14	1.04		
Health	1.69	0.14	15	2
Consumer	23.89	3.12	28	15
Business	11.95	2.83	21	9
Financial	10.61	0.48	18	9
Mfg	26.61	0.79		
Goods	8.02	0.94	17	7
Ind Mtrls	8.14	0.68	10	0
Energy	10.45	1.07	10	0
Utilities	0.00	0.00	0	0

Composition

	%
● Cash	5.9
● Stocks	94.1
● Bonds	0.0
● Other	0.0
Foreign	12.3
(% of Stock)	

MORNINGSTAR® Funds 500

Columbia Acorn USA A

	Ticker	Load	NAV	Yield	Total Assets	Mstar Category
	LAUAX	5.75%	$28.02	0.0%	$1,577 mil	Small Growth

Governance and Management

Stewardship Grade: B

Portfolio Manager(s)

Robert Mohn has been with Columbia Acorn USA's advisor, Columbia Wanger Asset Management, since 1992 and has managed this fund since its late-1996 inception. He became comanager on Columbia Acorn in mid-2003. Mohn draws heavily on the advisor's staff of domestic-equity analysts and portfolio managers. Like all Wanger portfolio managers, Mohn also has analyst duties. He covers financial-services stocks.

Strategy

Like its bigger sibling Columbia Acorn, Columbia Acorn USA hunts for fast-growing companies trading at discounts to its manager's estimates of their values. A proprietary valuation model, in-house research, and investment themes drive management's picks. This fund takes large positions in individual names.

Performance 12-31-06

	1st Qtr	2nd Qtr	3rd Qtr	4th Qtr	Total
2002	5.94	-10.03	-21.40	8.16	-18.97
2003	-2.75	23.06	7.78	13.40	46.26
2004	4.87	4.55	-4.05	14.17	20.12
2005	-0.04	5.42	4.24	2.59	12.68
2006	6.79	-4.44	1.04	4.70	7.95

Trailing	Total Return%	+/- S&P 500	+/- Russ 2000 Gr	%Rank Cat	Growth of $10,000
3 Mo	4.70	-2.00	-4.07	94	10,470
6 Mo	5.79	-6.95	-1.07	42	10,579
1 Yr	7.95	-7.84	-5.40	68	10,795
3 Yr Avg	13.47	3.03	2.96	16	14,610
5 Yr Avg	11.61	5.42	4.68	8	17,319
10 Yr Avg	—	—	—	—	—
15 Yr Avg	—	—	—	—	—

Tax Analysis	Tax-Adj Rtn%	%Rank Cat	Tax-Cost Rat	%Rank Cat
3 Yr (estimated)	10.82	22	0.39	13
5 Yr (estimated)	10.03	10	0.24	12
10 Yr (estimated)	—	—	—	—

Potential Capital Gain Exposure: 25% of assets

Historical Profile

Return Above Avg
Risk Below Avg
Rating ★★★★ Above Avg

	97%	89%	90%	93%	91%	91%	93%

Investment Style
Equity
Stock %

▼ Manager Change
▽ Partial Manager Change

Growth of $10,000
— Investment Values of Fund
— Investment Values of S&P 500

19.6
16.6
13.0
10.0
5.0

Performance Quartile (within Category)

1995	1996	1997	1998	1999	2000	2001	2002	2003	2004	2005	2006	History
—	—	—	—	—	14.88	17.50	14.18	20.74	24.77	26.52	28.02	NAV
—	—	—	—	—	6.90*	18.65	-18.97	46.26	20.12	12.68	7.95	Total Return %
—	—	—	—	—	—	30.54	3.13	17.58	9.24	7.77	-7.84	+/-S&P 500
—	—	—	—	—	—	27.88	11.29	-2.28	5.81	8.53	-5.40	+/-Russ 2000 Gr
—	—	—	—	—	—	0.00	0.00	0.00	0.00	0.00	0.00	Income Return %
—	—	—	—	—	—	18.65	-18.97	46.26	20.12	12.68	7.95	Capital Return %
—	—	—	—	—	—	5	15	41	14	9	68	Total Rtn % Rank Cat
—	—	—	—	—	0.00	0.00	0.00	0.00	0.00	0.00	0.00	Income $
—	—	—	—	—	0.00	0.15	0.00	0.00	0.14	1.37	0.61	Capital Gains $
—	—	—	—	—	—	—	1.84	1.74	1.65	1.51	—	Expense Ratio %
—	—	—	—	—	—	—	-1.13	-1.21	-1.26	-1.08	—	Income Ratio %
—	—	—	—	—	49	39	24	31	7	18	—	Turnover Rate %
—	—	—	—	—	—	1	20	33	91	112	245	Net Assets $mil

Rating and Risk

Time Period	Load-Adj Return %	Morningstar Rtn vs Cat	Morningstar Risk vs Cat	Morningstar Risk-Adj Rating
1 Yr	1.74			
3 Yr	11.25	+Avg	Low	★★★★
5 Yr	10.29	+Avg	-Avg	★★★★
10 Yr	—	—	—	—
Incept	12.44			

Other Measures	Standard Index S&P 500	Best Fit Index Mstar Small Growth
Alpha	0.5	5.3
Beta	1.38	0.65
R-Squared	73	92
Standard Deviation	11.00	
Mean	13.47	
Sharpe Ratio	0.91	

Portfolio Analysis 11-30-06

Share change since 10-06 Total Stocks:176	Sector	PE	Tot Ret%	% Assets
Crown Castle Internation	Telecom	—	20.94	2.18
Oxford Industries, Inc.	Goods	17.0	-8.01	2.03
Genlyte Group Inc.	Ind Mtrls	15.1	45.81	2.01
Avid Technology, Inc.	Software	56.0	-31.96	1.92
ITT Educational Services	Consumer	26.8	12.59	1.80
Abercrombie & Fitch Comp	Consumer	17.5	8.01	1.69
Edwards Lifesciences Cor	Health	25.7	13.05	1.67
AmeriCredit Corporation	Financial	11.2	-1.80	1.66
Scotts Miracle-Gro Compa	Ind Mtrls	21.6	15.43	1.66
ESCO Technologies, Inc.	Hardware	38.4	2.14	1.62
Time Warner Telecom, Inc	Telecom	—	102.34	1.59
FMC Technologies, Inc.	Energy	19.7	43.59	1.52
World Acceptance Corpora	Financial	21.8	64.74	1.48
Kronos, Inc.	Software	25.5	-12.23	1.47
⊕ Ametek, Inc.	Ind Mtrls	18.9	12.94	1.43
Quicksilver Resources, I	Energy	26.3	-12.90	1.40
⊕ HCC Insurance Holdings I	Financial	16.5	9.39	1.36
Pentair, Inc.	Business	16.7	-7.49	1.35
PDL BioPharma, Inc.	Health	—	-29.13	1.27
⊕ Integrated Device Techno	Hardware	—	17.45	1.25

Current Investment Style

Value Blnd Growth — Large Mid Small

Market Cap	%
Giant	0.0
Large	3.0
Mid	50.2
Small	40.0
Micro	6.8

Avg $mil: 1,901

Value Measures		Rel Category
Price/Earnings	19.61	0.93
Price/Book	2.52	0.92
Price/Sales	1.69	1.08
Price/Cash Flow	10.05	1.04
Dividend Yield %	0.63	1.37

Growth Measures	%	Rel Category
Long-Term Erngs	15.33	0.86
Book Value	11.36	1.09
Sales	-3.15	NMF
Cash Flow	12.70	0.60
Historical Erngs	20.34	0.84

Profitability	%	Rel Category
Return on Equity	11.79	0.95
Return on Assets	7.26	1.09
Net Margin	7.52	0.87

Sector Weightings	% of Stocks	Rel S&P 500	3 Year High	Low
⚓ Info	27.44	1.37		
🖥 Software	8.02	2.32	14	6
💻 Hardware	9.00	0.97	10	8
🎬 Media	2.46	0.65	4	2
📶 Telecom	7.96	2.27	9	7
⚙ Service	44.59	0.96		
🏥 Health	13.65	1.13	16	12
🛒 Consumer	11.15	1.46	13	9
📋 Business	8.98	2.12	15	9
💲 Financial	10.81	0.49	12	9
🏭 Mfg	27.97	0.83		
🔧 Goods	8.64	1.01	9	3
⚙ Ind Mtrls	11.62	0.97	12	5
🔥 Energy	7.03	0.72	10	6
💡 Utilities	0.68	0.19	2	1

Composition

	%
● Cash	7.1
● Stocks	92.8
● Bonds	0.0
○ Other	0.0
Foreign	2.2
(% of Stock)	

Morningstar's Take by Todd Trubey 12-14-06

Columbia Acorn USA is already a standout but works hard to improve.

This fund trails nearly 70% of small-growth category rivals in 2006 with an 8.6% gain through Dec. 12, and there are some easy explanations for that. First and foremost, the fund's portfolio is now evenly split between small and mid-caps, and the former continue to outperform. Cash, recently a 7% stake here, has been a bit of a drag. And although Wanger Asset Management (WAM) has been a groundbreaker in foreign small-growth investing, this fund is light by mandate on international fare, which has done well this year.

To his credit, Manager Rob Mohn isn't concentrating on the above factors but rather a couple of other things. He wants to be sure that the stock-picking at WAM is strong across all industries so that the fund won't miss out anywhere. He says this is a crucial issue in biotechnology, which has a 6% weighting in the Russell 2000 Growth Index. For years, WAM would buy a basket of such fare when

it looked cheap. Mohn says that more work is as crucial now as a biotech analyst with a science background. Enter 2006 hire Rich Watson, with a degree in biosciences and experience as a finance director at a pharmaceutical firm. Also, this year, WAM missed out on the nifty gains of steel mills. Such firms have short cycles, but Mohn doesn't believe in saying "it's not our type of thing." The firm's new industrial analyst Greg Pinsky is researching the area now.

We still think of WAM as a small-growth firm, but now that Acorn has moved up to the mid-growth category, this is the only domestic small-growth offering the firm has left. That's fine, because we think the fund is a keeper and has a nice risk/reward profile. Like perennial standout Acorn, its success and advantage over rivals rests on the growth-at-a-reasonable-price strategy that the large crew all practice. But unlike that gentle giant, it leans more on technology, health, and telecom firms.

Address:	227 W Monroe Ste 3000 Chicago IL 60606 800-345-6611	Minimum Purchase:	$75000 Add: $0 IRA: $75000
		Min Auto Inv Plan:	$50 Add: $50
		Sales Fees:	5.75%L, 0.25%S
Web Address:	www.columbiafunds.com	Management Fee:	0.94% mx./0.84% mn., 0.05%A
Inception:	10-16-00*	Actual Fees:	Mgt:0.87% Dist:0.25%
Advisor:	Columbia Wanger Asset Management, LP	Expense Projections:	3Yr:$960 5Yr:$1242 10Yr:$2042
Subadvisor:	None	Income Distrib:	Semi-Annually
NTF Plans:	DATALynx NTF, Federated Tr NTF		

Davis Appr & Income A

© Analyst Pick

	Ticker	Load	NAV	Yield	Total Assets	Mstar Category
	RPFCX	4.75%	$29.71	2.0%	$584 mil	Convertibles

Governance and Management

Stewardship Grade: A

Portfolio Manager(s)

Andrew Davis has managed this fund since joining the firm in 1993 from PaineWebber, where he managed convertible securities research. Davis also manages Davis Real Estate, and at both funds he has shown a willingness to follow mandates loosely. In September 2005 Keith Sabol replaced comanager Jason Voss. Sabol had a six-year stint at Federated, then three-plus years at a hedge fund before coming to Davis.

Strategy

Managers Andrew Davis and Keith Sabol prefer to own securities from about 30 to 40 firms with strong management and reasonable valuations. They believe that a portfolio largely invested in convertibles can offer 80% of the S&P 500 Index's upside return while avoiding 50% of its downside risk. When they can't find an ideal convertible, they'll mix a convert with the firm's common stock or bundle stock and straight debt.

Performance 12-31-06

	1st Qtr	2nd Qtr	3rd Qtr	4th Qtr	Total
2002	5.43	-3.14	-11.43	9.21	-1.21
2003	2.86	10.39	2.43	9.15	26.94
2004	4.69	-1.66	2.45	7.20	13.08
2005	-1.85	4.14	2.38	1.57	6.29
2006	4.90	0.89	3.35	5.31	15.19

Trailing	Total Return%	+/- DJ Mod	+/- Merrill Lynch Convert	%Rank Cat	Growth of $10,000
3 Mo	5.31	-0.28	0.49	19	10,531
6 Mo	8.83	0.04	1.18	10	10,883
1 Yr	15.19	2.89	3.16	4	11,519
3 Yr Avg	11.45	0.73	4.86	4	13,843
5 Yr Avg	11.67	1.65	4.06	2	17,365
10 Yr Avg	8.54	-0.01	-0.07	40	22,693
15 Yr Avg	—	—	—	—	—

Tax Analysis	Tax-Adj Rtn%	%Rank Cat	Tax-Cost Rat	%Rank Cat
3 Yr (estimated)	8.39	12	1.16	51
5 Yr (estimated)	9.30	7	1.16	36
10 Yr (estimated)	6.41	37	1.48	7

Potential Capital Gain Exposure: 13% of assets

Morningstar's Take by Lawrence Jones 12-21-06

We like that management runs this fund with a flexible but disciplined approach.

Davis Appreciation & Income veteran manager Andrew Davis and new comanager Keith Sabol run a fund that looks little like the typical convertible bond offering, but that's just fine with us. Management's goal here is not style purity, but rather is to provide 80% of the total return potential of the fund's S&P 500 Index benchmark, while limiting downside risk to 50% of index declines.

Formerly called Davis Convertible Securities, the board decided to remain true to these goals, rather than to the asset class. Since 2003, when the fund changed its name and mandate, its convertible stake has gradually declined, recently falling to 49% of assets. When the team is dissatisfied with the converts on offer, they turn to other options, such as creating bundled converts by buying a firm's debt and matching it to its equity. This flexibility allows them to focus on the risk/reward goal, without the constraints rivals operate under.

While the mandate is flexible the investment approach taken by Davis and Sabol is rigorously disciplined. The team adheres to a long-term, low-turnover philosophy that focuses on purchasing the securities of strong companies with proven management teams. In fact, turnover in 2005 was the lowest in the category. That shields investors from trading costs and makes the fund more tax efficient than most rivals. Valuation is also key here; the team will attempt to secure a margin of safety in the price they pay for securities, which can protect the fund during market downturns. For example, in the first quarter of 2005 the typical converts fund declined by 3.5%, due to hedge fund selling; this fund only suffered by 1.85%.

For the trailing 10-year period ending Nov. 30, 2006, the fund's returns have topped the benchmark's, with less than three fourths of the index's volatility. This differs somewhat from the 80:50 goal sought here, but we'll take it.

Address:	2949 E. Elvira Road
	Tucson AZ 85706
	800-279-0279
Web Address:	www.davisfunds.com
Inception:	05-01-92
Advisor:	Davis Selected Advisers LP
Subadvisor:	Davis Selected Advisers - NY, Inc.
NTF Plans:	DATALynx NTF, Federated Tr NTF

Historical Profile

Return	Above Avg
Risk	Average
Rating	★★★★ Above Avg

31%	31%	29%	39%	16%	26%	31%	22%	32%

Investment Style
Equity
Stock %

▼ Manager Change
▽ Partial Manager Change

Growth of $10,000
■ Investment Values of Fund
— Investment Values of DJ Mod

Performance Quartile (within Category)

	1995	1996	1997	1998	1999	2000	2001	2002	2003	2004	2005	2006	History
NAV	18.22	21.22	25.26	23.76	25.21	23.96	21.36	20.30	24.95	27.50	27.94	29.71	NAV
Total Return %	26.68	29.46	28.68	-1.79	12.97	-0.97	-7.56	-1.21	26.94	13.08	6.29	15.19	Total Return %
+/-DJ Mod	6.88	18.80	16.78	-14.11	-4.36	0.70	-4.76	5.56	-0.44	0.11	-0.70	2.89	+/-DJ Mod
+/-Merrill Lynch Convert	2.72	17.34	13.17	-14.00	-23.02	6.55	-4.65	1.91	3.97	4.77	6.48	3.16	+/-Merrill Lynch Convert
Income Return %	4.30	4.06	3.49	3.05	3.30	3.35	3.17	3.80	3.67	2.69	2.28	2.35	Income Return %
Capital Return %	22.38	25.40	25.19	-4.84	9.67	-4.32	-10.73	-5.01	23.27	10.39	4.01	12.84	Capital Return %
Total Rtn % Rank Cat	10	1	4	75	80	60	59	2	34	7	19	4	Total Rtn % Rank Cat
Income $	0.66	0.73	0.73	0.76	0.77	0.83	0.75	0.80	0.74	0.67	0.62	0.64	Income $
Capital Gains $	0.78	1.54	1.23	0.28	0.77	0.21	0.04	0.00	0.00	0.00	0.64	1.79	Capital Gains $
Expense Ratio %	1.14	1.05	1.07	1.16	1.12	1.07	1.09	1.09	1.10	1.08	1.07	—	Expense Ratio %
Income Ratio %	3.87	3.34	3.00	3.27	2.99	3.02	3.31	3.69	3.38	2.52	2.12	—	Income Ratio %
Turnover Rate %	54	43	24	14	33	25	20	34	33	21	17	—	Turnover Rate %
Net Assets $mil	60	43	90	134	117	103	89	81	114	150	223	392	Net Assets $mil

Rating and Risk

Time Period	Load-Adj Return %	Morningstar Rtn vs Cat	Morningstar Risk vs Cat	Morningstar Risk-Adj Rating
1 Yr	9.72			
3 Yr	9.66	+Avg	Low	★★★★
5 Yr	10.58	High	Avg	★★★★★
10 Yr	8.01	Avg	Avg	★★★
Incept	10.60			

Other Measures	Standard Index DJ Mod	Best Fit Index Mstar Mid Value
Alpha	2.1	-0.1
Beta	0.80	0.57
R-Squared	72	74
Standard Deviation	5.55	
Mean	11.45	
Sharpe Ratio	1.42	

Portfolio Analysis 09-30-06

Total Fixed-Income:7	Date of Maturity	Amount $000	Value $000	% Net Assets
Lehman Bros Hldgs 0.25%	08-23-11	12,400	20,105	4.07
Intel Cv 2.95%	12-15-35	20,000	17,975	3.64
School Specialty Cv 3.75	08-01-23	15,710	16,201	3.28
Universal Health Service		257	15,378	3.11
SL Green Realty Corporat		135	15,097	3.06
Quanta Svcs Cv 4.5%	10-01-23	8,500	13,898	2.81
Sealed Air 144A Cv 3%	06-30-33	13,500	13,230	2.68
Coca-Cola Company		275	12,287	2.49
General Growth Propertie		246	11,706	2.37
AMERICAN EXPRESS	12-01-33	11,100	11,280	2.28
Aes Tr Iii Cv		221	10,822	2.19
Vornado Rlty L P 3.875%	04-15-25	8,500	10,731	2.17
Avon Products		339	10,400	2.10
Intl Rectifier Cv 4.25%	07-15-07	10,220	10,143	2.05
Waste Connections 144A C	04-01-26	10,000	10,050	2.03
Tyson Foods, Inc. A		617	9,803	1.98
J.C. Penney Company, Inc		140	9,599	1.94
News Amer Cv	02-28-21	16,050	9,288	1.88
Kohl's Corporation		136	8,829	1.79
Masco	07-20-31	17,600	8,272	1.67

Investment Style	
Avg Eff Maturity	—
Avg Credit Quality	BBB
Avg Wtd Coupon	2.99%
Avg Wtd Price	107.44% of par

Coupon Range	% of Bonds	Rel Cat
0% PIK	0.0	0.0
0% to 8%	100.0	1.0
8% to 11%	0.0	0.0
11% to 14%	0.0	0.0
More than 14%	0.0	0.0
1.00=Category Average		

Special Securities	
Restricted/Illiquid Secs	5
Emerging-Markets Secs	0
Options/Futures/Warrants	No

Credit Analysis	% bonds 09-30-06		
AAA	0	BB	5
AA	8	B	31
A	30	Below B	0
BBB	26	NR/NA	0

Composition	
Cash	25.9
Stocks	32.0
Bonds	11.1
Convertibles	28.9
Other	2.1

Minimum Purchase:	$1000	Add: $25	IRA: $1000
Min Auto Inv Plan:	$25	Add: $25	
Sales Fees:	4.75%L, 0.18%S		
Management Fee:	0.75% mx./0.55% mn.		
Actual Fees:	Mgt:0.72%	Dist:0.18%	
Expense Projections:	3Yr:$799	5Yr:$1037	10Yr:$1719
Income Distrib:	Quarterly		

MORNINGSTAR® Funds 500

Davis Financial A

	Analyst Pick	Ticker	Load	NAV	Yield	Total Assets	Mstar Category
	✓	RPFGX	4.75%	$47.48	0.0%	$1,021 mil	Specialty-Financial

Governance and Management

Stewardship Grade: A

Portfolio Manager(s)

Ken Feinberg joined the firm in 1994 and became comanager of the fund in 1997. (Chris Davis is also listed as a comanager of this offering--a position he's held since 1991--but he doesn't make day-to-day stock-picking decisions.) Feinberg has a considerable portion of his net worth invested in this and other Davis offerings. He also owns some of the portfolios' individual securities.

Strategy

Ken Feinberg, the primary decision-maker at this offering, focuses on companies with sound financials and high-quality management that are trading at attractive valuations. He is an opportunistic buyer and will often invest in companies that are under a cloud. The fund tends to hold each stock for several years, making for good tax efficiency. Its portfolio is quite compact, with only 30 names or so. Although management builds the portfolio stock by stock, the fund doesn't steer away from major industry bets when favorite names are found in the same line of business.

Performance 12-31-06

	1st Qtr	2nd Qtr	3rd Qtr	4th Qtr	Total
2002	-0.15	-9.96	-16.66	8.13	-18.98
2003	-6.29	21.77	4.56	14.71	36.86
2004	6.51	-2.36	-2.18	10.22	12.11
2005	-2.22	-0.95	2.57	8.75	8.03
2006	2.15	-0.83	7.89	8.65	18.74

Trailing	Total Return%	+/- S&P 500	+/- DJ Finance	%Rank Cat	Growth of $10,000
3 Mo	8.65	1.95	1.68	13	10,865
6 Mo	17.22	4.48	2.30	9	11,722
1 Yr	18.74	2.95	-0.68	32	11,874
3 Yr Avg	12.88	2.44	-0.09	36	14,383
5 Yr Avg	9.78	3.59	-1.03	53	15,945
10 Yr Avg	12.10	3.68	-0.33	23	31,337
15 Yr Avg	15.79	5.15	0.46	34	90,171

Tax Analysis	Tax-Adj Rtn%	%Rank Cat	Tax-Cost Rat	%Rank Cat
3 Yr (estimated)	10.51	43	0.50	12
5 Yr (estimated)	8.39	53	0.30	8
10 Yr (estimated)	11.21	21	0.30	1

Potential Capital Gain Exposure: 48% of assets

Historical Profile

Return Average
Risk Average
Rating ★★★ Neutral

	90%	99%	96%	87%	93%	100%	100%	100%	99%	Investment Style Equity Stock %

▼ Manager Change
▽ Partial Manager Change

Growth of $10,000

■ Investment Values of Fund
— Investment Values of S&P 500

Performance Quartile (within Category)

1995	1996	1997	1998	1999	2000	2001	2002	2003	2004	2005	2006	History
14.50	18.06	25.68	29.32	29.07	36.30	32.98	26.72	36.57	41.00	42.40	47.48	NAV
50.51	31.50	44.53	14.17	-0.85	32.16	-9.15	-18.98	36.86	12.11	8.03	18.74	Total Return %
12.93	8.54	11.17	-14.41	-21.89	41.26	2.74	3.12	8.18	1.23	3.12	2.95	+/-S&P 500
-0.35	-2.49	-4.41	6.66	-2.37	5.22	-2.77	-6.63	4.63	-1.28	1.57	-0.68	+/-DJ Finance
0.66	1.03	0.69	0.00	0.00	0.00	0.00	0.00	0.00	0.00	0.00	0.00	Income Return %
49.85	30.47	43.84	14.17	-0.85	32.16	-9.15	-18.98	36.86	12.11	8.03	18.74	Capital Return %
10	46	56	17	39	23	85	92	28	63	40	32	Total Rtn % Rank Cat
0.07	0.15	0.13	0.00	0.00	0.00	0.00	0.00	0.00	0.00	0.00	0.00	Income $
1.50	0.87	0.30	0.00	0.00	1.93	0.00	0.00	0.00	0.00	1.91	2.77	Capital Gains $
1.18	1.15	1.07	1.06	1.04	1.05	1.08	1.11	1.10	1.01	0.98	—	Expense Ratio %
0.53	0.92	0.77	0.34	0.36	-0.21	-0.20	0.18	0.27	0.05	0.10	—	Income Ratio %
42	26	6	11	18	35	18	15	9		5	—	Turnover Rate %
80	108	288	461	425	633	600	417	535	583	610	817	Net Assets $mil

Rating and Risk

Time Period	Load-Adj Return %	Morningstar Rtn vs Cat	Morningstar Risk vs Cat	Morningstar Risk-Adj Rating
1 Yr	13.10			
3 Yr	11.06	Avg	Avg	★★★
5 Yr	8.72	-Avg	+Avg	★★
10 Yr	11.55	Avg	Avg	★★★
Incept	16.25			

Other Measures	Standard Index S&P 500	Best Fit Index Mstar Large Core TR
Alpha	2.0	0.9
Beta	1.04	1.12
R-Squared	65	69
Standard Deviation	8.94	
Mean	12.88	
Sharpe Ratio	1.05	

Portfolio Analysis 09-30-06

Share change since 06-06 Total Stocks:21	Sector	PE	Tot Ret%	% Assets
American Express Company	Financial	20.9	19.09	11.87
Transatlantic Holdings,	Financial	12.6	-6.80	9.37
Tyco International, Ltd.	Ind Mtrls	15.7	6.83	7.45
Dun & Bradstreet Corpora	Business	23.1	23.64	7.20
Moody's Corporation	Financial	32.6	12.95	6.20
First Marblehead Corpora	Financial	14.2	152.13	6.13
Loews Corporation	Financial	14.9	32.04	6.05
American International G	Financial	17.0	6.05	5.95
⊖ Golden West Fin	Financial	—	—	5.24
J.P. Morgan Chase & Co.	Financial	13.6	25.60	5.20
Commerce Bancorp, Inc.	Financial	23.6	3.89	4.82
Markel Corporation	Financial	12.2	51.43	3.93
Ameriprise Financial, In	Financial	—	—	3.36
Progressive Corporation	Financial	12.4	-16.93	3.32
Altria Group, Inc.	Goods	16.3	19.87	2.87
Sealed Air Corporation	Goods	22.8	16.85	2.70
Everest Re Group, Ltd.	Financial	—	-1.62	2.38
H & R Block, Inc.	Consumer	25.3	-3.95	1.87
China Life Insurance Com	Financial	84.2	283.24	1.77
FPIC Insurance Group, In	Financial	11.6	12.31	1.45

Current Investment Style

Value Blnd Growth — Large Mid Small

Market Cap	%
Giant	37.6
Large	20.1
Mid	40.8
Small	0.0
Micro	1.5

Avg $mil: 18,066

Value Measures		Rel Category
Price/Earnings	14.31	1.08
Price/Book	2.40	1.25
Price/Sales	1.81	0.79
Price/Cash Flow	9.26	1.46
Dividend Yield %	1.22	0.49

Growth Measures	%	Rel Category
Long-Term Erngs	13.48	1.20
Book Value	3.66	0.40
Sales	3.80	0.45
Cash Flow	6.46	0.28
Historical Erngs	6.54	0.47

Profitability	%	Rel Category
Return on Equity	16.30	1.06
Return on Assets	17.24	1.42
Net Margin	13.54	0.66

Industry Weightings	% of Stocks	Rel Cat
Intl Banks	6.0	0.3
Banks	5.3	0.3
Real Estate	0.0	0.0
Sec Mgmt	0.0	0.0
S & Ls	0.0	0.0
Prop & Reins	29.1	1.8
Life Ins	2.0	0.4
Misc. Ins	6.7	2.1
Other	51.0	3.9

Composition

● Cash		0.6
● Stocks		99.4
● Bonds		0.0
○ Other		0.0
Foreign (% of Stock)		2.0

Morningstar's Take by Laura Pavlenko Lutton 12-21-06

This fund's pluses outweigh its risks.

Davis Financial is an unusual sector offering. To be sure, it focuses primarily on financials stocks, as its name suggests. But within that sector, manager Ken Feinberg has a few favorite industries, with insurance being the most prominent and representing about one third of the fund's assets. (The typical financials fund has about a quarter of its assets in insurance.)

In addition to this industry-specific risk, the fund also courts stock-specific risk. The offering currently invests in just 21 companies, and it lets top positions grow quite large. American Express represents more than 11% of the fund's assets, for example.

As one might expect, given this fund's strategy, short-term returns here can be lumpy depending on whether Feinberg's favorite areas are in style. The fund got some help earlier in 2006 from its large position in Golden West Financial, which agreed to a buyout from Wachovia. And although lagging

insurance stocks hurt relative returns in recent years, a few of them have contributed to the fund's strong rebound this year. It was leading 68% of its peers in 2006 as December approached.

Over the longer term, however, Feinberg has demonstrated that he is a skilled and thoughtful money manager, and this offering has beaten the general market amid considerably lower volatility. (The fund's 20% stake in nonfinancials and its very low turnover have contributed to smoother returns.)

In the end, we think this fund is too focused to serve as a core holding, and we wouldn't own it alongside siblings Davis NY Venture or Selected American; however, it could be an interesting addition for long-term investors with otherwise growth-heavy portfolios. Among financials funds, it remains a top choice.

Address:	2949 E. Elvira Road Tucson AZ 85706 800-279-0279	Minimum Purchase: Min Auto Inv Plan: Sales Fees:	$1000 $25 4.75%L, 0.19%S	Add: $25 Add: $25	IRA: $1000
Web Address:	www.davisfunds.com	Management Fee:	0.75% mx./0.55% mn.		
Inception:	05-01-91	Actual Fees:	Mgt:0.63%	Dist:0.19%	
Advisor:	Davis Selected Advisers LP	Expense Projections:	3Yr:$775	5Yr:$996	10Yr:$1630
Subadvisor:	Davis Selected Advisers - NY, Inc.	Income Distrib:	Annually		
NTF Plans:	DATALynx NTF, Federated Tr NTF				

Davis NY Venture A

	Ticker	Load	NAV	Yield	Total Assets	Mstar Category
	NYVTX	4.75%	$38.52	0.7%	$43,669 mil	Large Blend

Governance and Management

Stewardship Grade: A

Portfolio Manager(s)

Chris Davis started at the firm in 1991 and has been a comanager on this fund since 1995. He plans to stick around--the Davis family owns the firm and invests heavily in the funds. Comanager Ken Feinberg began as a financial-stock analyst with the firm in 1994 and became comanager in 1998. Other employees are also significant owners, and the bonus plan here is set up with an eye toward long-term outperformance.

Strategy

The managers try to buy great companies whose shares are temporarily depressed. They estimate a firm's intrinsic value based on their own earnings analysis in which they try to assess a firm's true cash earnings. They then look at those earnings relative to a return on adjusted invested capital. The idea is to figure out how well the company has historically allocated its capital.

Historical Profile

Return	Above Avg
Risk	Below Avg
Rating	★★★★ Above Avg

| 88% | 91% | 87% | 90% | 88% | 98% | 98% | 99% | 95% |

Investment Style
Equity
Stock %

▼ Manager Change
▽ Partial Manager Change

40.8
31.0
24.0 **Growth of $10,000**
17.0 — Investment Values of Fund
— Investment Values of S&P 500
10.0

Performance Quartile (within Category)

1995	1996	1997	1998	1999	2000	2001	2002	2003	2004	2005	2006	History
14.52	17.50	22.33	25.01	28.76	28.74	25.43	20.94	27.52	30.69	33.70	38.52	NAV
40.56	26.54	33.68	14.73	17.59	9.92	-11.41	-17.16	32.34	12.37	10.68	15.12	Total Return %
2.98	3.58	0.32	-13.85	-3.45	19.02	0.48	4.94	3.66	1.49	5.77	-0.67	+/-S&P 500
2.79	4.09	0.83	-12.29	-3.32	17.71	1.04	4.49	2.45	0.97	4.41	-0.34	+/-Russ 1000
1.34	1.24	1.31	0.47	0.01	0.19	0.10	0.51	0.88	0.88	0.88	0.80	Income Return %
39.22	25.30	32.37	14.26	17.58	9.73	-11.51	-17.67	31.46	11.53	9.80	14.32	Capital Return %
5	11	13	75	62	11	45	15	13	24	8	37	Total Rtn % Rank Cat
0.15	0.18	0.23	0.11	0.00	0.05	0.03	0.13	0.19	0.23	0.27	0.27	Income $
1.01	0.70	0.83	0.48	0.62	2.64	0.00	0.00	0.00	0.00	0.00	0.00	Capital Gains $
0.90	0.87	0.89	0.91	0.90	0.88	0.89	0.92	0.95	0.92	0.89	0.87	Expense Ratio %
1.11	1.30	0.98	0.80	0.56	0.31	0.50	0.49	0.85	0.77	0.98	0.79	Income Ratio %
15	19	24	11	25	29	15	22	10	6	3	6	Turnover Rate %
1,798	2,659	4,655	6,820	8,139	10,600	10,463	8,258	11,563	15,108	19,395	27,035	Net Assets $mil

Performance 12-31-06

	1st Qtr	2nd Qtr	3rd Qtr	4th Qtr	Total
2002	-0.67	-9.94	-13.49	7.04	-17.16
2003	-5.59	18.66	2.43	15.33	32.34
2004	4.03	0.42	-1.18	8.85	12.37
2005	0.07	1.79	4.54	3.94	10.68
2006	3.20	0.00	3.62	7.65	15.12

Trailing	Total Return%	+/- S&P 500	+/- Russ 1000	%Rank Cat	Growth of $10,000
3 Mo	7.65	0.95	0.70	19	10,765
6 Mo	11.55	-1.19	-0.81	50	11,155
1 Yr	15.12	-0.67	-0.34	37	11,512
3 Yr Avg	12.71	2.27	1.73	11	14,318
5 Yr Avg	9.44	3.25	2.62	7	15,699
10 Yr Avg	10.67	2.25	2.03	9	27,561
15 Yr Avg	13.01	2.37	2.21	7	62,626

Tax Analysis	Tax-Adj Rtn%	%Rank Cat	Tax-Cost Rat	%Rank Cat
3 Yr (estimated)	10.72	20	0.16	8
5 Yr (estimated)	8.20	10	0.17	11
10 Yr (estimated)	9.56	8	0.53	20

Potential Capital Gain Exposure: 31% of assets

Rating and Risk

Time Period	Load-Adj Return %	Morningstar Rtn vs Cat	Morningstar Risk vs Cat	Morningstar Risk-Adj Rating
1 Yr	9.65			
3 Yr	10.90	+Avg	Low	★★★★
5 Yr	8.38	+Avg	-Avg	★★★★
10 Yr	10.14	+Avg	Avg	★★★★
Incept	13.30			

Other Measures	Standard Index S&P 500	Best Fit Index S&P 500
Alpha	3.2	3.2
Beta	0.83	0.83
R-Squared	83	83
Standard Deviation	6.32	
Mean	12.71	
Sharpe Ratio	1.43	

Portfolio Analysis 10-31-06

Share change since 07-06 Total Stocks:77	Sector	PE	Tot Ret%	% Assets
Altria Group, Inc.	Goods	16.3	19.87	4.88
American Express Company	Financial	20.9	19.09	4.87
American International G	Financial	17.0	6.05	4.23
⊕ ConocoPhillips	Energy	6.5	26.53	3.80
⊕ Tyco International, Ltd.	Ind Mtrls	15.7	6.83	3.59
J.P. Morgan Chase & Co.	Financial	13.6	25.60	3.57
Costco Wholesale Corpora	Consumer	23.3	7.90	3.15
⊕ HSBC Hldgs	Financial	—	—	2.90
Berkshire Hathaway Inc.	Financial	—	—	2.88
⊕ Wells Fargo Company	Financial	14.7	16.82	2.80
Comcast Corporation	Media	—	—	2.67
☼ Wachovia Corporation	Financial	12.9	12.02	2.35
Devon Energy Corporation	Energy	9.2	8.06	2.35
Citigroup, Inc.	Financial	13.1	19.55	2.32
Progressive Corporation	Financial	12.4	-16.93	2.32
Microsoft Corporation	Software	23.8	15.83	2.19
Loews Corporation	Financial	14.9	32.04	2.12
Sealed Air Corporation	Goods	22.8	16.85	1.89
EOG Resources	Energy	10.1	-14.62	1.86
⊕ News Corporation, Ltd. A	Media	—	—	1.66

Current Investment Style

Value Blnd Growth — Large Mid Small

	Market Cap	%
	Giant	52.9
	Large	34.5
	Mid	12.6
	Small	0.0
	Micro	0.0
	Avg $mil: 43,511	

Value Measures		Rel Category
Price/Earnings	14.21	0.92
Price/Book	2.31	0.90
Price/Sales	1.34	0.96
Price/Cash Flow	8.56	1.01
Dividend Yield %	2.00	1.14

Growth Measures	%	Rel Category
Long-Term Erngs	11.15	0.94
Book Value	8.88	0.98
Sales	10.92	1.13
Cash Flow	14.02	1.36
Historical Erngs	17.78	0.96

Profitability	%	Rel Category
Return on Equity	19.79	1.02
Return on Assets	12.52	1.21
Net Margin	14.15	1.05

Sector Weightings	% of Stocks	Rel S&P 500	3 Year High Low
⊙ Info	12.21	0.61	
Software	2.29	0.66	2 1
Hardware	1.52	0.16	3 1
Media	6.28	1.66	6 3
Telecom	2.12	0.60	2 0
⊆ Service	57.14	1.24	
Health	2.97	0.25	4 3
Consumer	8.51	1.11	9 6
Business	3.80	0.90	6 4
Financial	41.86	1.88	55 41
Mfg	30.64	0.91	
Goods	13.29	1.55	13 11
Ind Mtrls	6.54	0.55	7 6
Energy	10.81	1.10	12 6
Utilities	0.00	0.00	0 0

Composition

● Cash	4.2
● Stocks	95.5
● Bonds	0.3
● Other	0.0
Foreign	10.4 (% of Stock)

Morningstar's Take by Kerry O'Boyle 11-01-06

Davis NY Venture is a topnotch large-blend option.

Consistency and excellence have been hallmarks of this fund for more than a decade. Managers Chris Davis and Ken Feinberg don't wed themselves to any particular valuation metric; instead, they seek well-managed firms trading at a discount to their estimate of its intrinsic value. This holistic approach is heavily reliant on digging through balance sheets to root out the sustainability of future cash flows as well as company management's ability to deploy future capital effectively.

That can be a challenge. One of the portfolio's laggards this year has been Sprint Nextel. Despite the firm's proven track record of absorbing acquisitions in the past, management has taken a number of missteps since the two entities merged at the end of 2004. Davis and Feinberg have pared their estimates of the firm but continue to hold on as they don't view the stock as overpriced. Overall, the fund has slipped a bit thus far in 2006 relative

to past years and now trails a majority of its category peers.

Nonetheless, we continue to like management's long-term outlook and thoughtful approach. Annual turnover at the fund remains well below the category median of 58%, reflecting their conviction in their research and the fund's holdings. Davis and Feinberg are constantly looking at the market from different angles. For instance, they trimmed back on struggling Avon Products, putting those assets to work in rival Procter & Gamble--the theme being that revitalized industry leaders such as McDonald's and Hewlett-Packard have regained their dominance after sorting through short-term problems. They saw P&G as the next in line to stage such a comeback when the fund bought it at depressed prices during 2006.

Despite a slightly off year, the fund's long-term focus, reasonable fees, and shareholder-friendly practices make it an offering worth owning.

Address:	2949 E. Elvira Road Tucson AZ 85706 800-279-0279
Web Address:	www.davisfunds.com
Inception:	02-17-69
Advisor:	Davis Selected Advisers LP
Subadvisor:	Davis Selected Advisers - NY, Inc.
NTF Plans:	DATALynx NTF, Federated Tr NTF

Minimum Purchase:	$1000	Add: $25	IRA: $1000
Min Auto Inv Plan:	$25	Add: $25	
Sales Fees:	4.75%L, 0.25%S		
Management Fee:	0.75% mx./0.44% mn.		
Actual Fees:	Mgt:0.49% Dist:0.25%		
Expense Projections:	3Yr:$742	5Yr:$939	10Yr:$1508
Income Distrib:	Annually		

MORNINGSTAR® Funds 500

Delafield

	Ticker	Load	NAV	Yield	Total Assets	Mstar Category
	DEFIX	None	$25.64	0.7%	$531 mil	Mid-Cap Value

Governance and Management

Stewardship Grade:

Portfolio Manager(s)

Dennis Delafield and Vincent Sellecchia have managed this fund since its 1993 inception. One analyst, who has been with the fund since 2003, rounds out the team. All three share research responsibilities.

Strategy

The fund combs the list of stocks hitting new lows in search of special situations--firms in the midst of a reorganization or management change--with lots of free cash flow. The pure bottom-up portfolio-construction process often leads to significant sector bets and a fairly concentrated portfolio. Management is willing to hold large cash stakes when compelling ideas are scarce, so the fund is rarely fully invested.

Performance 12-31-06

	1st Qtr	2nd Qtr	3rd Qtr	4th Qtr	Total
2002	10.86	-6.14	-18.34	8.90	-7.46
2003	-5.76	22.88	6.63	13.49	40.14
2004	3.63	5.04	-0.04	11.07	20.85
2005	-0.32	-1.07	4.34	3.01	6.00
2006	10.28	-2.84	3.40	8.65	20.38

Trailing	Total Return%	+/- S&P 500	+/- Russ MV	%Rank Cat	Growth of $10,000
3 Mo	8.65	1.95	0.15	31	10,865
6 Mo	12.34	-0.40	0.01	20	11,234
1 Yr	20.38	4.59	0.16	12	12,038
3 Yr Avg	15.53	5.09	-3.24	34	15,420
5 Yr Avg	14.86	8.67	-1.02	8	19,991
10 Yr Avg	13.21	4.79	-0.44	19	34,582
15 Yr Avg	—	—	—	—	—

Tax Analysis	Tax-Adj Rtn%	%Rank Cat	Tax-Cost Rat	%Rank Cat
3 Yr (estimated)	13.44	33	1.81	64
5 Yr (estimated)	13.24	13	1.41	73
10 Yr (estimated)	11.86	10	1.19	29

Potential Capital Gain Exposure: 16% of assets

Morningstar's Take by Karen Wallace 11-29-06

Delafield Fund is a smart way to get exposure to small and mid-caps.

Dennis Delafield and Vincent Sellecchia look for hidden gems among stocks whose prices have gotten bruised in the market. Specifically, they examine lists of 52-week laggards, looking for what they consider to be "special situations," which they define as financially sound companies where there is a catalyst for positive change in place that is not yet priced into the stock. For example, if a company has undergone a management change, Delafield and Sellecchia get to know the management team and the company's board and try to assess whether the new managers are particularly shareholder-friendly and skilled at allocating investors' capital.

Such was the case with top holding Thermo Fisher Scientific. Delafield and Sellecchia purchased Thermo Electron when its share price was drooping in 2001, long before its merger with Fisher Scientific. The catalyst that attracted

Delafield and Sellecchia was the fact that firm had begun to restructure and refocus on core businesses under a new CEO. Since their purchase, the company has risen more than 14% per year.

Just as they're sensitive to valuation when they buy a stock, Delafield and Sellecchia are not slow to sell a stock when they think it is reasonably valued. They concede that they will occasionally leave money on the table with this strategy but would rather sell the stock when they perceive that the market risk outweighs the potential benefit to shareholders and redeploy that capital into another undervalued stock.

This valuation-sensitive approach has led to very competitive returns relative to the category over time. But importantly, it has also preserved investors' capital well in difficult markets for stocks, such as 2001 and 2002, and has done so with reasonable volatility. We think the managers' consistently applied, sensible strategy will continue to be successful.

Address:	600 Fifth Avenue 8th Floor New York NY 10020-2302 800-221-3079	Minimum Purchase:	$5000	Add: $0	IRA: $250
		Min Auto Inv Plan:	$5000	Add: —	
		Sales Fees:	No-load, 0.25%S, 2.00%R		
Web Address:	www.delafieldfund.com	Management Fee:	0.80% mx./0.70% mn., 0.21%A		
Inception:	11-19-93	Actual Fees:	Mgt:0.78%	Dist:0.25%	
Advisor:	Reich & Tang Asset Management, LLC	Expense Projections:	3Yr:$456	5Yr:$787	10Yr:$1724
Subadvisor:	None	Income Distrib:	Monthly		
NTF Plans:	Fidelity Retail-NTF, Schwab OneSource				

Historical Profile

Return	Above Avg
Risk	Above Avg
Rating	★★★★ Above Avg

	99%	99%	94%	75%	92%	75%	82%	86%	92%		

Investment Style
Equity
Stock %

▼ Manager Change
▽ Partial Manager Change

50.6
43.6

Growth of $10,000
32.4
24.0 ▬ Investment Values of Fund
17.0 ▬ Investment Values of S&P 500
10.0

Performance Quartile (within Category)

1995	1996	1997	1998	1999	2000	2001	2002	2003	2004	2005	2006	History
12.26	13.49	14.88	13.06	14.07	15.80	19.70	18.23	23.17	25.21	23.63	25.64	NAV
27.41	26.35	19.66	-11.47	8.40	13.98	32.19	-7.46	40.14	20.85	6.00	20.38	Total Return %
-10.17	3.39	-13.70	-40.05	-12.64	23.08	44.08	14.64	11.46	9.97	1.09	4.59	+/-S&P 500
-7.52	6.09	-14.71	-16.55	8.51	-5.20	29.86	2.18	2.07	-2.86	-6.65	0.16	+/-Russ MV
1.41	1.29	1.54	0.81	0.65	0.52	0.36	0.00	0.00	0.00	0.11	0.81	Income Return %
26.00	25.06	18.12	-12.28	7.75	13.46	31.83	-7.46	40.14	20.85	5.89	19.57	Capital Return %
43	9	76	91	49	75	1	15	25	34	77	12	Total Rtn % Rank Cat
0.14	0.16	0.21	0.12	0.09	0.07	0.06	0.00	0.00	0.00	0.03	0.19	Income $
0.89	1.84	1.03	0.00	0.00	0.16	1.13	0.00	2.38	2.78	3.07	2.63	Capital Gains $
1.65	1.29	1.29	1.24	1.25	1.25	1.25	1.20	1.32	1.32	1.33	—	Expense Ratio %
1.35	1.18	1.64	0.83	0.56	0.52	0.33	-0.09	-0.32	-0.10	0.11	—	Income Ratio %
70	76	55	82	105	100	98	79	78	55	71	—	Turnover Rate %
45	61	146	104	86	99	199	144	247	345	372	531	Net Assets $mil

Rating and Risk

Time Period	Load-Adj Return %	Morningstar Rtn vs Cat	Morningstar Risk vs Cat	Morningstar Risk-Adj Rating
1 Yr	20.38			
3 Yr	15.53	Avg	+Avg	★★★
5 Yr	14.86	+Avg	+Avg	★★★★
10 Yr	13.21	+Avg	+Avg	★★★★
Incept	14.61			

Other Measures	Standard Index S&P 500	Best Fit Index Mstar Mid Core
Alpha	2.4	1.8
Beta	1.35	0.91
R-Squared	74	87
Standard Deviation	10.81	
Mean	15.53	
Sharpe Ratio	1.10	

Portfolio Analysis 06-30-06

Share change since 12-05 Total Stocks:59

	Sector	PE	Tot Ret%	% Assets
⊖ Thermo Electron Corp.	Health	37.4	50.32	4.49
Kennametal Inc.	Ind Mtrls	8.3	16.85	3.68
Foot Locker, Inc.	Consumer	14.8	-5.67	3.61
⊕ Hercules, Inc.	Ind Mtrls	—	70.89	3.39
☼ RadioShack Corporation	Consumer	58.6	-19.05	2.81
⊖ Aleris International, In	Ind Mtrls	—	—	2.80
⊕ International Rectifier	Hardware	24.0	20.78	2.77
⊕ Navistar International	Ind Mtrls	—	16.81	2.76
⊕ Ashland	Energy	2.5	42.83	2.76
☼ Southern Union Company	Energy	—	20.09	2.72
⊖ Cytec Industries	Ind Mtrls	20.0	19.52	2.70
⊕ Furniture Brands Interna	Goods	10.6	-25.10	2.46
☼ Tyco International, Ltd.	Ind Mtrls	15.7	6.83	2.44
⊕ Commercial Metals Compan	Ind Mtrls	8.8	38.66	2.43
⊕ Symbol Technologies	Hardware	35.6	16.64	2.36
⊖ Acuity Brands, Inc.	Ind Mtrls	22.2	66.05	2.30
⊕ YRC Worldwide, Inc.	Business	7.7	-15.42	2.21
⊕ Paxar	Goods	20.2	17.47	2.19
⊕ Chemtura Corporation	Ind Mtrls	—	-22.61	2.10
⊕ Stanley Works	Ind Mtrls	15.9	7.22	1.95

Current Investment Style

Value Blnd Growth — Large Mid Small

Market Cap	%
Giant	2.7
Large	2.3
Mid	60.5
Small	26.7
Micro	7.9
Avg $mil:	2,245

Value Measures		Rel Category
Price/Earnings	14.46	0.98
Price/Book	1.73	0.86
Price/Sales	0.67	0.69
Price/Cash Flow	5.84	0.77
Dividend Yield %	1.00	0.56

Growth Measures	%	Rel Category
Long-Term Erngs	12.59	1.14
Book Value	6.70	0.96
Sales	7.00	0.91
Cash Flow	5.24	1.32
Historical Erngs	24.31	1.65

Profitability	%	Rel Category
Return on Equity	11.26	0.78
Return on Assets	5.01	0.68
Net Margin	5.66	0.54

Sector Weightings	% of Stocks	Rel S&P 500	3 Year High	Low
⊙ Info	13.73	0.69		
Software	0.98	0.28	4	0
Hardware	12.75	1.38	14	4
Media	0.00	0.00	4	0
Telecom	0.00	0.00	2	0
⊆ Service	26.98	0.58		
Health	6.83	0.57	11	6
Consumer	8.60	1.12	9	3
Business	9.07	2.14	20	8
Financial	2.48	0.11	4	2
Mfg	59.28	1.75		
Goods	8.03	0.94	12	8
Ind Mtrls	41.91	3.51	50	34
Energy	9.34	0.95	9	2
Utilities	0.00	0.00	1	0

Composition

● Cash	7.8	
● Stocks	92.2	
● Bonds	0.0	
● Other	0.0	
Foreign	0.8	
(% of Stock)		

DFA U.S. Micro Cap

	Ticker	Load	NAV	Yield	Total Assets	Mstar Category
	DFSCX	None	$15.70	1.8%	$4,881 mil	Small Blend

Governance and Management

Stewardship Grade: B

Portfolio Manager(s)

A team of portfolio managers, led by Robert Deere, runs this offering. These folks are focused on implementing the fund's strategy. DFA's investment committee, which includes many famous academics, designed this strategy.

Strategy

The fund invests in the smallest 5% of U.S. exchange-listed stocks to take advantage of the small-cap effect. The portfolio contains anywhere between 2,500 and 3,000 holdings, but it does not contain REITs, newly minted IPOs, or firms that management identifies as merger candidates or too highly leveraged.

Historical Profile

Return	Above Avg
Risk	Above Avg
Rating	★★★ Neutral

Investment Style: Equity, Stock %

99% 97% 98% 98% 99% 98% 98% 98%

▼ Manager Change
▽ Partial Manager Change

Growth of $10,000
— Investment Values of Fund
— Investment Values of S&P 500

50.6 / 43.6 / 32.4 / 24.0 / 17.0 / 10.0

Performance Quartile (within Category)

	1995	1996	1997	1998	1999	2000	2001	2002	2003	2004	2005	2006	History
NAV	10.53	11.20	11.78	10.76	12.61	9.64	10.01	8.53	13.32	15.12	14.77	15.70	NAV
Total Return %	34.48	17.65	22.78	-7.32	29.79	-3.60	22.77	-13.27	60.72	18.39	5.69	16.16	Total Return %
+/-S&P 500	-3.10	-5.31	-10.58	-35.90	8.75	5.50	34.66	8.83	32.04	7.51	0.78	0.37	+/-S&P 500
+/-Russ 2000	6.03	1.16	0.42	-4.77	8.53	-0.58	20.28	7.21	13.47	0.06	1.14	-2.21	+/-Russ 2000
Income Return %	0.51	0.26	0.23	1.28	3.49	3.89	0.51	0.16	2.42	2.04	2.38	2.02	Income Return %
Capital Return %	33.97	17.39	22.55	-8.60	26.30	-7.49	22.26	-13.43	58.30	16.35	3.31	14.14	Capital Return %
Total Rtn % Rank Cat	15	80	72	69	18	92	10	29	5	55	61	36	Total Rtn % Rank Cat
Income $	0.04	0.03	0.03	0.15	0.38	0.49	0.05	0.02	0.21	0.27	0.36	0.30	Income $
Capital Gains $	0.84	1.16	1.89	0.00	0.89	1.99	1.71	0.14	0.18	0.36	0.84	1.13	Capital Gains $
Expense Ratio %	0.62	0.61	0.60	0.59	0.61	0.56	0.56	0.56	0.56	0.16	0.55	—	Expense Ratio %
Income Ratio %	0.45	0.22	0.21	0.18	0.30	0.34	0.41	0.24	0.25	0.64	0.48	—	Income Ratio %
Turnover Rate %	25	24	28	26	23	37	—	—	—	—	—	—	Turnover Rate %
Net Assets $mil	946	1,187	1,437	1,360	1,452	1,378	1,663	1,533	2,685	3,380	3,912	4,881	Net Assets $mil

Performance 12-31-06

	1st Qtr	2nd Qtr	3rd Qtr	4th Qtr	Total
2002	6.99	-3.92	-20.70	6.39	-13.27
2003	-3.99	27.35	12.56	16.77	60.72
2004	6.46	0.14	-4.32	16.06	18.39
2005	-6.43	3.93	6.78	1.78	5.69
2006	14.39	-7.11	-0.21	9.55	16.16

Trailing	Total Return%	+/- S&P 500	+/- Russ 2000	%Rank Cat	Growth of $10,000
3 Mo	9.55	2.85	0.65	16	10,955
6 Mo	9.32	-3.42	-0.06	22	10,932
1 Yr	16.16	0.37	-2.21	36	11,616
3 Yr Avg	13.27	2.83	-0.29	52	14,533
5 Yr Avg	15.16	8.97	3.77	16	20,254
10 Yr Avg	13.48	5.06	4.04	27	35,415
15 Yr Avg	15.45	4.81	3.98	8	86,280

Tax Analysis	Tax-Adj Rtn%	%Rank Cat	Tax-Cost Rat	%Rank Cat
3 Yr (estimated)	11.68	46	1.40	41
5 Yr (estimated)	13.94	16	1.06	48
10 Yr (estimated)	11.26	27	1.96	72

Potential Capital Gain Exposure: 28% of assets

Rating and Risk

Time Period	Load-Adj Return %	Morningstar Rtn vs Cat	Morningstar Risk vs Cat	Morningstar Risk-Adj Rating
1 Yr	16.16			
3 Yr	13.27	Avg	+Avg	★★★
5 Yr	15.16	+Avg	+Avg	★★★★
10 Yr	13.48	+Avg	+Avg	★★★
Incept	14.01			

Other Measures	Standard Index S&P 500	Best Fit Index Russ 2000
Alpha	-2.5	-0.5
Beta	1.83	1.03
R-Squared	74	97
Standard Deviation	14.60	
Mean	13.27	
Sharpe Ratio	0.71	

Portfolio Analysis 08-31-06

Share change since 05-06 Total Stocks:0

	Sector	PE	Tot Ret%	% Assets
⊕ Dimensional U.S. Micro C	—	—	—	100.00

Morningstar's Take by Sonya Morris 12-22-06

This fund is a respectable choice, but only for those who can accept its risks.

DFA U.S. Micro Cap focuses on the tiniest stocks in the market. Its passively managed portfolio consists of those stocks that make up the smallest 5% of the U.S. stock market, as measured by market capitalization. As a result, the fund's aggregate market cap is a fraction of the small-value category norm. That positioning makes this a fairly racy offering because small companies can be risky investments. Their fortunes may be tied to a small menu of products or services, and many of these firms may also be dependent on a limited number of customers. And some may have taken on substantial debt to finance growth. As a result, micro-cap stocks can be extremely volatile, and this fund has experienced its share of turbulence. As measured by standard deviations of returns (a statistical measure of volatility), it has been more volatile than 80% of its category peers.

But this fund's advisor, Dimensional Fund

Advisors, doesn't necessarily try to avoid risk. Instead, the firm uses years of academic research to identify those risks that stand the best chance of being adequately compensated over time, and it positions its portfolios accordingly. The fund's results lend credence to this approach: Its five-year returns rank in the category's top 15%.

This offering has other attractive traits. Its passive approach means it can handle asset growth more than competing small-cap funds. And even though it traffics in the market's smallest, least liquid stocks, the firm has developed a trading expertise that focuses on minimizing the market impact of trades, which should also help it manage its girth. Finally, its modest 0.55% expense ratio adds to its appeal.

Despite these strengths, this fund isn't for everyone. Risk-averse investors should steer clear. And those who do decide to hop aboard here should limit this fund to no more than 5% of their portfolios.

Address:	1299 Ocean Ave Santa Monica CA 90401 310-395-8005
Web Address:	www.dfafunds.com
Inception:	12-22-81
Advisor:	Dimensional Fund Advisors Ltd
Subadvisor:	None
NTF Plans:	N/A

Minimum Purchase:	$2000000	Add: $0	IRA: $0
Min Auto Inv Plan:	$0	Add: —	
Sales Fees:	No-load		
Management Fee:	0.50%		
Actual Fees:	Mgt:0.50%	Dist:—	
Expense Projections:	3Yr:$176	5Yr:$307	10Yr:$689
Income Distrib:	Annually		

Current Investment Style

Value Blnd Growth — Large Mid Small

Market Cap	%
Giant	0.0
Large	0.0
Mid	0.2
Small	38.6
Micro	61.2
Avg $mil:	289

Value Measures		Rel Category
Price/Earnings	17.08	1.03
Price/Book	1.72	0.82
Price/Sales	0.71	0.72
Price/Cash Flow	4.27	0.61
Dividend Yield %	0.57	0.53

Growth Measures	%	Rel Category
Long-Term Erngs	14.78	1.06
Book Value	0.22	0.03
Sales	0.75	0.08
Cash Flow	-24.01	NMF
Historical Erngs	1.16	0.07

Profitability	%	Rel Category
Return on Equity	3.29	0.26
Return on Assets	0.21	0.03
Net Margin	2.89	0.30

Sector Weightings	% of Stocks	Rel S&P 500	3 Year High	Low
⟳ Info	18.66	0.93		
Software	5.61	1.63	6	6
Hardware	10.17	1.10	10	10
Media	1.40	0.37	1	1
Telecom	1.48	0.42	1	1
⟶ Service	50.45	1.09		
Health	15.15	1.26	15	15
Consumer	10.36	1.35	10	10
Business	11.77	2.78	12	12
Financial	13.17	0.59	13	13
Mfg	30.89	0.91		
Goods	7.29	0.85	7	7
Ind Mtrls	17.06	1.43	17	17
Energy	5.12	0.52	5	5
Utilities	1.42	0.41	1	1

Composition

	%
● Cash	0.5
● Stocks	98.4
● Bonds	0.0
● Other	1.1
Foreign (% of Stock)	0.1

MORNINGSTAR® Funds 500

Diamond Hill Small Cap A

 Analyst Pick

Ticker DHSCX	**Load** Closed	**NAV** $25.03	**Yield** 0.3%	**Total Assets** $516 mil	**Mstar Category** Small Value

Governance and Management

Stewardship Grade: B

Portfolio Manager(s)

Ric Dillon, Diamond Hill's chief investment officer, and his comanager, Tom Schindler, have run this fund since its inception. Although he has a limited public record, Dillon has managed assets in this style for more than 20 years at both Loomis, Sayles & Co. and his own firm, Dillon Capital Management. Previously, Schindler was an analyst at Dillon Capital and Gartmore Group. The team is supported by three other managers at the firm, Chuck Bath, Chris Bingaman, and Chris Welch.

Strategy

Management seeks small-cap companies with competitive advantages that are trading below its estimates of intrinsic value. The team is not benchmark-sensitive and thus will go wherever values can be found; however, sector weightings can't exceed 25% of assets. Management is also willing to let the fund's cash balance grow if equity valuations become too steep to meet its strict criterion. The team tends to run a fairly compact portfolio of 40-50 stocks. Its universe approximates the Russell 2000 Index.

Performance 12-31-06

	1st Qtr	2nd Qtr	3rd Qtr	4th Qtr	Total
2002	11.39	-5.55	-19.03	7.72	-8.23
2003	-8.97	28.68	11.22	15.27	50.18
2004	6.66	3.57	3.98	12.54	29.26
2005	-2.01	4.39	7.95	2.25	12.90
2006	6.47	-2.94	-4.69	8.66	7.03

Trailing	Total Return%	+/- S&P 500	+/- Russ 2000 VL	%Rank Cat	Growth of $10,000
3 Mo	8.66	1.96	-0.37	43	10,866
6 Mo	3.57	-9.17	-8.24	96	10,357
1 Yr	7.03	-8.76	-16.45	97	10,703
3 Yr Avg	16.03	5.59	-0.45	21	15,621
5 Yr Avg	16.57	10.38	1.20	12	21,525
10 Yr Avg	—				
15 Yr Avg	—				

Tax Analysis	Tax-Adj Rtn%	%Rank Cat	Tax-Cost Rat	%Rank Cat
3 Yr (estimated)	13.65	22	0.36	4
5 Yr (estimated)	15.08	10	0.26	4
10 Yr (estimated)	—			

Potential Capital Gain Exposure: 10% of assets

Rating and Risk

Time Period	Load-Adj Return %	Morningstar Rtn vs Cat	Morningstar Risk vs Cat	Morningstar Risk-Adj Rating
1 Yr	1.68			
3 Yr	14.06	Avg	Avg	★★★
5 Yr	15.38	+Avg	Avg	★★★★
10 Yr	—			
Incept	16.99			

Other Measures	Standard Index S&P 500	Best Fit Index Mstar Small Core
Alpha	4.2	2.2
Beta	1.17	0.77
R-Squared	50	80
Standard Deviation	11.24	
Mean	16.03	
Sharpe Ratio	1.09	

Historical Profile
Return Above Avg
Risk Average
Rating ★★★★ Above Avg

Investment Style: Equity, Stock %

88% 83% 76% 69% 85%

23.6
18.0
14.0
10.0
6.0

▼ Manager Change
▽ Partial Manager Change

Growth of $10,000
— Investment Values of Fund
— Investment Values of S&P 500

Performance Quartile (within Category)

	1995	1996	1997	1998	1999	2000	2001	2002	2003	2004	2005	2006	History
NAV	—	—	—	—	—	10.00	12.29	11.26	16.82	21.41	23.95	25.03	
Total Return %	—	—	—	—	—	0.00*	25.46	-8.23	50.18	29.26	12.90	7.03	
+/-S&P 500	—	—	—	—	—		37.35	13.87	21.50	18.38	7.99	-8.76	
+/-Russ 2000 VL	—	—	—	—	—		11.44	3.20	4.15	7.01	8.19	-16.45	
Income Return %	—	—	—	—	—		0.06	0.00	0.00	0.00	0.03	0.36	
Capital Return %	—	—	—	—	—		25.40	-8.23	50.18	29.26	12.87	6.67	
Total Rtn % Rank Cat	—	—	—	—	—		15	42	18	1	2	97	
Income $	—	—	—	—	—	0.00	0.01	0.00	0.00	0.00	0.01	0.09	
Capital Gains $	—	—	—	—	—	0.00	0.25	0.02	0.09	0.32	0.21	0.52	
Expense Ratio %	—	—	—	—	—			1.75	1.50	1.50	1.50	—	
Income Ratio %	—	—	—	—	—			2.71	-0.70	-0.57	-0.35	—	
Turnover Rate %	—	—	—	—	—			43	49	53	24	—	
Net Assets $mil	—	—	—	—	—		2	6	12	55	430		

Portfolio Analysis 11-30-06

Share change since 10-06 Total Stocks:59	Sector	PE	Tot Ret%	% Assets
⊖ Encore Acquisition Compa	Energy	9.8	-23.44	3.72
⊖ Cimarex Energy Company	Energy	6.4	-14.79	3.72
⊖ Whiting Petroleum Corpor	Energy	9.7	16.50	3.18
⊖ Helmerich & Payne, Inc.	Energy	10.7	-20.48	3.16
AirTran Holdings, Inc.	Business	86.6	-26.76	2.73
⊖ Berry Petroleum Company	Energy	10.8	9.51	2.63
American Greetings Corpo	Media	27.9	10.23	2.60
Acco Brands Corporation	Ind Mtrls	62.1	8.04	2.39
Werner Enterprises, Inc.	Business	14.2	-10.49	2.00
WPS Resources	Utilities	15.0	2.11	1.97
Finish Line	Goods	15.6	-17.40	1.96
Trinity Industries, Inc.	Ind Mtrls	16.0	20.56	1.87
⊕ United Fire & Casualty	Financial	—	-11.48	1.85
Greenbrier Companies	Ind Mtrls	11.5	6.63	1.81
Callaway Golf Company	Goods	63.5	6.18	1.81
Apria Healthcare Group	Health	17.0	10.54	1.74
Hornbeck Offshore Servic	Business	12.5	9.17	1.66
Century Aluminum Company	Ind Mtrls	—	70.36	1.63
Belo Corporation	Media	16.3	-12.02	1.63
⊖ Buckeye Technologies, In	Ind Mtrls	76.1	48.82	1.62

Current Investment Style

Value Blnd Growth — Large Mid Small

Market Cap	%
Giant	0.0
Large	0.0
Mid	26.3
Small	60.5
Micro	13.2

Avg $mil: 1,285

Value Measures		Rel Category
Price/Earnings	15.31	1.00
Price/Book	1.87	1.05
Price/Sales	0.96	1.20
Price/Cash Flow	6.65	1.09
Dividend Yield %	0.82	0.52

Growth Measures	%	Rel Category
Long-Term Erngs	12.22	0.98
Book Value	9.46	1.75
Sales	-6.91	NMF
Cash Flow	11.78	1.44
Historical Erngs	24.70	2.17

Profitability	%	Rel Category
Return on Equity	14.07	1.31
Return on Assets	6.81	1.12
Net Margin	11.43	1.26

Sector Weightings	% of Stocks	Rel S&P 500	3 Year High Low
Info	7.26	0.36	
Software	2.29	0.66	4 2
Hardware	0.00	0.00	3 0
Media	4.97	1.31	13 5
Telecom	0.00	0.00	0 0
Service	38.13	0.83	
Health	3.81	0.32	13 4
Consumer	3.84	0.50	11 1
Business	13.36	3.16	16 5
Financial	17.12	0.77	17 10
Mfg	54.61	1.62	
Goods	0.00	1.17	1 3
Ind Mtrls	16.86	1.41	26 14
Energy	23.92	2.44	31 11
Utilities	3.83	1.09	6 0

Composition

- Cash 14.9
- Stocks 85.1
- Bonds 0.0
- Other 0.0
- Foreign 0.0 (% of Stock)

Morningstar's Take by Sonya Morris 12-22-06

Diamond Hill Small Cap's risks are fully apparent right now, but shareholders should stand pat.

Many shareholders here are relatively new to the fund, which saw its total assets balloon from just $70 million at the end of 2004 to $530 million today. This small-value fund experienced such growth in 2005 that Diamond Hill elected to close the fund to new investors at the end of that year.

It's understandable if newest shareholders here are a little concerned. They joined the fund just as it hit a rough patch. After three years of stellar results, it has struggled in 2006. Its year-to-date returns rank in the category's bottom 10%. That poor result can partly be attributed to the fund's large energy bet. Energy firms have long played a key role here. (They currently consume about 25% of assets.) In the middle of the year, many of these stocks--particularly those heavily involved in the natural-gas industry--stumbled when commodity prices tanked.

These sorts of short-term price fluctuations aren't likely to rattle this fund's management team, though. Managers Ric Dillon and Tom Schindler are patient, long-term investors, and they base their valuation estimates on forecasts that look out at least five years. Furthermore, the two are disciplined value hounds who won't admit a stock into the portfolio unless it trades well below their estimate of intrinsic value. They're so insistent about that standard that they'll let the fund's cash stake build if they can't find stocks that meet their criterion. The fund's cash balance has recently been as high as 20%, but it has shrunk recently, as management used the mid-year pullback in energy stocks to add to some of their favorite names.

That move is consistent with management's discipline and commitment to a strategy that has yielded impressive results over the long haul. We're further heartened by this firm's record of shareholder-friendly practices. All told, we think this fine fund has earned shareholders' patience.

Address:	325 John H. Mcconnell Boulevard Columbus OH 43215 888-226-5595	Minimum Purchase:	Closed	Add: — IRA: —
		Min Auto Inv Plan:	Closed	Add: —
		Sales Fees:	5.00%L, 0.25%S	
Web Address:	www.diamond-hill.com	Management Fee:	0.75%	
Inception:	12-29-00*	Actual Fees:	Mgt:0.80%	Dist:0.25%
Advisor:	Diamond Hill Capital Management Inc	Expense Projections:	3Yr:$924	5Yr:$1233 10Yr:$2106
Subadvisor:	None	Income Distrib:	Annually	
NTF Plans:	Schwab OneSource, DATAlynx NTF			

Dodge & Cox Balanced

	Ticker	Load	NAV	Yield	Total Assets	Mstar Category
	DODBX	Closed	$87.08	2.4%	$27,064 mil	Moderate Allocation

Governance and Management

Stewardship Grade: A

Portfolio Manager(s)

The fund's management team is deep, experienced, and talented. Stock selection and asset allocation are handled by the team from Dodge & Cox Stock. The bond portfolio is run by the squad from Dodge & Cox Income. The average tenure of the team members is more than 15 years. They are supported by a bevy of industry and credit analysts.

Strategy

Management only moderately adjusts its typical mix of 60% to 65% stocks and 30% to 35% bonds. The equity position mirrors the mid- to large-cap value Dodge & Cox Stock, and management sticks to government and midquality corporate bonds on the fixed-income side of the portfolio.

Historical Profile

Return High
Risk Average
Rating ★★★★ Highest

| | 59% | 59% | 61% | 61% | 63% | 63% | 59% | 62% | 63% |

Investment Style
Equity
Stock %

▼ Manager Change
▽ Partial Manager Change

Growth of $10,000
— Investment Values of Fund
— Investment Values of DJ Mod

38.0
31.0
24.0
17.0
10.0

Performance Quartile (within Category)

	1995	1996	1997	1998	1999	2000	2001	2002	2003	2004	2005	2006	History
NAV	54.60	59.82	66.78	65.22	65.71	63.42	65.42	60.75	73.04	79.35	81.34	87.08	NAV
	28.02	14.76	21.19	6.69	12.06	15.14	10.05	-2.94	24.44	13.30	6.59	13.86	Total Return %
	8.22	4.10	9.29	-5.63	-5.27	16.81	12.85	3.83	-2.94	0.33	-0.40	1.56	+/-DJ Mod
	3.25	3.42	1.99	-5.70	-0.79	10.70	9.89	7.60	0.38	2.13	0.59	3.59	+/-DJ US Mod
	4.90	3.70	3.77	3.41	3.47	3.91	3.44	2.91	2.76	2.21	2.34	2.73	Income Return %
	23.12	11.06	17.42	3.28	8.59	11.23	6.61	-5.85	21.68	11.09	4.25	11.13	Capital Return %
	32	49	34	87	40	2	2	2	17	5	22	14	Total Rtn % Rank Cat
	2.18	1.99	2.22	2.23	2.22	2.47	2.14	1.88	1.66	1.60	1.84	2.20	Income $
	0.91	0.69	3.27	3.74	4.98	9.22	2.05	0.88	0.67	1.68	1.32	3.20	Capital Gains $
	0.57	0.56	0.55	0.54	0.53	0.53	0.53	0.53	0.54	0.54	0.53	—	Expense Ratio %
	3.85	3.60	3.39	3.29	3.18	3.70	3.28	3.12	2.57	1.97	2.15	—	Income Ratio %
	20	17	32	26	17	23	21	25	19	18	18	—	Turnover Rate %
	1,800	3,630	5,077	5,693	5,138	4,909	6,040	7,885	13,196	20,741	23,611	27,064	Net Assets $mil

Performance 12-31-06

	1st Qtr	2nd Qtr	3rd Qtr	4th Qtr	Total
2002	3.28	-2.93	-8.94	6.32	-2.94
2003	-2.86	12.32	3.78	9.88	24.44
2004	4.03	0.27	0.47	8.12	13.30
2005	-0.09	1.07	3.41	2.09	6.59
2006	3.54	0.53	4.26	4.91	13.86

Trailing	Total Return%	+/- DJ Mod	+/- DJ US Mod	%Rank Cat	Growth of $10,000
3 Mo	4.91	-0.68	0.24	56	10,491
6 Mo	9.38	0.59	1.48	35	10,938
1 Yr	13.86	1.56	3.59	14	11,386
3 Yr Avg	11.20	0.48	2.08	8	13,750
5 Yr Avg	10.68	0.66	3.08	2	16,609
10 Yr Avg	11.79	3.24	3.20	2	30,481
15 Yr Avg	12.51	3.30	3.12	3	58,596

Tax Analysis	Tax-Adj Rtn%	%Rank Cat	Tax-Cost Rat	%Rank Cat
3 Yr (estimated)	10.33	5	0.78	37
5 Yr (estimated)	9.59	2	0.98	59
10 Yr (estimated)	9.71	2	1.86	73

Potential Capital Gain Exposure: 22% of assets

Rating and Risk

Time Period	Load-Adj Return %	Morningstar Rtn vs Cat	Morningstar Risk vs Cat	Morningstar Risk-Adj Rating
1 Yr	13.86			
3 Yr	11.20	High	Avg	★★★★★
5 Yr	10.68	High	Avg	★★★★★
10 Yr	11.79	High	-Avg	★★★★★
Incept	—			

Other Measures	Standard Index DJ Mod	Best Fit Index DJ Mod
Alpha	2.0	2.0
Beta	0.78	0.78
R-Squared	86	86
Standard Deviation	4.95	
Mean	11.20	
Sharpe Ratio	1.53	

Morningstar's Take by Dan Culloton 11-20-06

Dodge & Cox Balanced is closed but not forgotten.

This fund is the cream of its crop. A large, veteran team manages it with a patient, detail-oriented, contrarian style. The fund's advisor is an exemplary steward of fund owners' wealth; it never rolls out trendy funds, keeps fees low, and values capital preservation as much as capital appreciation. Its record speaks for itself.

Performance may speak too well. The fund has garnered a torrent of assets in the last several years, even after it closed to new investors in 2004, and is now the fourth-biggest moderate-allocation fund, with nearly $27 billion in assets.

Indeed, we are frequently asked if this fund will open again. The answer, based on conversations with the fund's managers, is, when you least expect it, expect it. It would take a harrowing drop in the stock market or this fund's relative performance for the fund to take in new money again. In short, don't look for the fund to reopen unless it gets smaller and/or less popular. This isn't surprising from a firm

that was founded in the Great Depression.

As for the equity sleeve, it's hard for a portfolio this large to invest successfully without getting in its own way (especially when the managers also run a nearly $60 billion equity fund in the same style). That the fund has been able to preserve performance so far is testimony to the decision to close, as well as to the fund's approach. It doesn't trade much and often buys when most others are selling. For example, the fund added Dell in the second quarter because the managers thought the market had gotten too pessimistic about the computer maker. On the bond side, managers focus on individual security selection, recently adding to mortgage-backed securities.

Taxes may be a chink in this fund's armor. The fund's aftertax returns look good because its pretax returns are so good, but it distributes capital gains like clockwork. In 2006 the fund said it would pay out more than $3, or more than 3% of its NAV. This fund is still a keeper, though.

Address:	555 California St San Francisco CA 94104 800-621-3979
Web Address:	www.dodgeandcox.com
Inception:	06-26-31
Advisor:	Dodge & Cox
Subadvisor:	None
NTF Plans:	N/A

Minimum Purchase:	Closed	Add: —	IRA: —
Min Auto Inv Plan:	Closed	Add: —	
Sales Fees:	No-load		
Management Fee:	0.50%		
Actual Fees:	Mgt:0.50%	Dist: —	
Expense Projections:	3Yr:$170	5Yr:$296	10Yr:$665
Income Distrib:	Quarterly		

Portfolio Analysis 09-30-06

Total Stocks:86 Share change since 06-30-06	Sectors	P/E Ratio	YTD Return %	% Net Assets
⊖ Hewlett-Packard Company	Hardware	19.3	1.89	2.61
Comcast Corporation A	Media	45.2	0.33	2.37
Pfizer Inc.	Health	15.2	1.00	2.13
News Cl A	Media	—	—	1.90
⊕ Chevron Corporation	Energy	9.0	-2.83	1.70
McDonald's Corporation	Consumer	18.9	-1.40	1.64
Sony Corporation ADR	Goods	43.2	4.62	1.60
⊕ Time Warner, Inc.	Media	19.6	2.71	1.60
⊕ Cardinal Health, Inc.	Health	20.8	-0.43	1.56

Total Fixed-Income:302	Date of Maturity	Amount $000	Value $000	% Net Assets
US Treasury Note 3.75%	05-15-08	350,000	344,545	1.33
US Treasury Note 3.625%	07-15-09	307,000	299,073	1.15
FNMA 6%	04-01-35	280,436	282,345	1.09
FNMA 6.5%	12-01-32	225,694	230,762	0.89
US Treasury Note 3.375%	02-15-08	200,000	196,227	0.76
Gmac 6.875%	09-15-11	173,670	172,750	0.67
FNMA 5%	03-01-34	176,131	169,841	0.66
FNMA FRN	07-01-35	152,212	151,448	0.58
FNMA 6%	06-01-35	143,001	144,194	0.56

Equity Style
Style: Value
Size: Large-Cap

Value Measures		Rel Category
Price/Earnings	14.83	0.97
Price/Book	2.18	0.88
Price/Sales	1.12	0.82
Price/Cash Flow	9.38	1.16
Dividend Yield %	1.65	0.85

Growth Measures	%	Rel Category
Long-Term Erngs	10.84	0.92
Book Value	5.31	0.62
Sales	8.05	0.91
Cash Flow	6.98	0.71
Historical Erngs	19.15	1.07

Market Cap %			
Giant	47.8	Small	0.0
Large	42.4	Micro	0.0
Mid	9.8	Avg $mil:	42,741

Fixed-Income Style
Duration: Interm-Term
Quality: High

Avg Eff Duration[1]	3.9 Yrs
Avg Eff Maturity	6.3 Yrs
Avg Credit Quality	AA
Avg Wtd Coupon	5.62%

[1]figure provided by fund as of 09-30-06

Sector Weightings	% of Stocks	Rel DJ Mod	3 Year High	Low
⟳ Info	21.64	—		
🖳 Software	0.85	—	1	1
🖥 Hardware	9.22	—	9	5
🎬 Media	10.61	—	11	7
☎ Telecom	0.96	—	6	1
⟐ Service	48.69	—		
🩺 Health	17.81	—	18	11
🛒 Consumer	7.42	—	8	6
🏢 Business	7.68	—	9	8
💲 Financial	15.78	—	20	16
⚒ Mfg	29.69			
⚙ Goods	5.94	—	7	6
🏭 Ind Mtrls	13.95	—	16	13
🔥 Energy	9.37	—	10	8
💡 Utilities	0.43	—	4	0

Composition

		%
●	Cash	6.6
●	Stocks	63.0
●	Bonds	30.2
●	Other	0.2
	Foreign (% of Stock)	16.2

M⟋RNINGSTAR® Funds 500

Dodge & Cox Income

Analyst Pick ✔

Ticker	Load	NAV	Yield	SEC Yield	Total Assets	Mstar Category
DODIX	None	$12.57	4.9%	—	$11,709 mil	Intermediate-Term Bond

Governance and Management

Stewardship Grade: A

Portfolio Manager(s)

A deep, nine-member management team is responsible for the fund and all of the firm's institutional fixed-income accounts. Sector specialists on the team have both research and trading responsibilities. Dodge & Cox's 20-member analyst staff provides individual credit analysis and also supports the firm's equity products.

Strategy

Management strives to better its bogy, the Lehman Brothers Aggregate Bond Index, mainly through security selection. Thus, the fund is typically overweighted in corporate bonds, especially mid-grade issues. Management targets corporate bonds and mortgage-backed securities with call-protection features so that it can hold on to its bonds for the long haul.

Performance 12-31-06

	1st Qtr	2nd Qtr	3rd Qtr	4th Qtr	Total
2002	0.98	3.12	3.81	2.45	10.75
2003	1.42	2.82	0.54	1.08	5.97
2004	1.86	-2.07	2.69	1.17	3.64
2005	-0.47	2.14	-0.24	0.55	1.98
2006	0.08	0.00	3.43	1.73	5.30

Trailing	Total Return%	+/- LB Aggr	+/- LB 5-10YR	%Rank Cat	Growth of $10,000
3 Mo	1.73	0.49	0.65	13	10,173
6 Mo	5.22	0.13	-0.46	24	10,522
1 Yr	5.30	0.97	1.49	11	10,530
3 Yr Avg	3.63	-0.07	-0.01	33	11,129
5 Yr Avg	5.49	0.43	-0.43	14	13,063
10 Yr Avg	6.52	0.28	-0.16	5	18,807
15 Yr Avg	6.93	0.43	-0.06	12	27,321

Tax Analysis	Tax-Adj Rtn%	%Rank Cat	Tax-Cost Rat	%Rank Cat
3 Yr (estimated)	2.86	6	0.74	6
5 Yr (estimated)	4.23	4	1.19	18
10 Yr (estimated)	4.58	2	1.82	28

Potential Capital Gain Exposure: -1% of assets

Morningstar's Take by Dan Culloton 11-17-06

Dodge & Cox Income deftly balances caution and opportunism.

The managers had kept the portfolio's duration (a measure of interest-rate sensitivity) more than a year short of the Lehman Brothers Aggregate Bond Index for about two years to guard against the risk of higher interest rates and inflation. Since the middle of 2005, however, this fund's managers have been gradually extending duration.

It would be a mistake though to say the fund has turned offensive. The portfolio's duration is still about 80% of that of the benchmark, and the managers have gotten the fund there via a thoughtful and measured route. For example, the fund increased its stake in mortgage-backed securities to 44% of the portfolio, including bonds backed by hybrid adjustable-rate mortgages (loans that offer a fixed rate for five years before switching to a variable one) that were trading below their par values. The managers say such securities offered a good combination of yield,

quality, and return potential because many of the borrowers probably will seek to refinance before their loan rates start floating.

That same focus on balancing opportunity and risk has been on display in the fund's still-substantial corporate-bond stake. Large positions in the debt of the lending arms of the major automakers have helped the fund in the past year. Managers also bought the securities of some foreign companies who recently sold U.S. dollar-denominated debt for the first time, such as French basic materials company Lafarge. Dodge & Cox's analysts were familiar with the company because Dodge & Cox International Stock owns it. So when the yield on Lafarge's U.S. dollar bonds rose due to the market's unfamiliarity with them, this fund bought.

Such cross-pollination between the firm's equity and fixed-income operations (all Dodge & Cox analysts cover both the stock and bonds of their companies) gives this fund a big advantage.

Address:	555 California St	Minimum Purchase:	$2500	Add: $100	IRA: $1000
	San Francisco CA 94104	Min Auto Inv Plan:	$2500	Add: $100	
	800-621-3979	Sales Fees:	No-load		
Web Address:	www.dodgeandcox.com	Management Fee:	0.50% mx./0.40% mn.		
Inception:	01-03-89	Actual Fees:	Mgt:0.40%	Dist: —	
Advisor:	Dodge & Cox	Expense Projections:	3Yr:$141	5Yr:$246	10Yr:$555
Subadvisor:	None	Income Distrib:	Quarterly		
NTF Plans:	N/A				

Historical Profile

Return	High
Risk	Below Avg
Rating	★★★★ Highest

Investment Style: Fixed Income — Income Rtn %Rank Cat

▼ Manager Change
▽ Partial Manager Change

Growth of $10,000
— Investment Values of Fund
— Investment Values of LB Aggr

Performance Quartile (within Category)

1995	1996	1997	1998	1999	2000	2001	2002	2003	2004	2005	2006	History
12.02	11.68	12.08	12.25	11.40	11.80	12.20	12.77	12.92	12.84	12.54	12.57	NAV
20.21	3.61	10.00	8.08	-0.81	10.70	10.32	10.75	5.97	3.64	1.98	5.30	Total Return %
1.74	-0.02	0.35	-0.61	0.01	-0.93	1.88	0.50	1.87	-0.70	-0.45	0.97	+/-LB Aggr
-1.22	0.92	0.57	-2.06	2.07	-1.74	1.50	-2.28	0.00	-1.66	0.15	1.49	+/-LB 5-10YR
7.74	6.31	6.40	6.11	5.94	7.02	6.42	5.52	4.78	4.25	4.35	5.00	Income Return %
12.47	-2.70	3.60	1.97	-6.75	3.68	3.90	5.23	1.19	-0.61	-2.37	0.30	Capital Return %
20	37	18	34	36	36	5	6	28	65	40	11	Total Rtn % Rank Cat
0.81	0.74	0.73	0.72	0.71	0.78	0.74	0.66	0.60	0.54	0.55	0.62	Income $
0.03	0.00	0.00	0.06	0.04	0.00	0.06	0.05	0.00	0.00	0.00	0.00	Capital Gains $
0.54	0.50	0.49	0.47	0.46	0.46	0.45	0.45	0.45	0.44	0.44	—	Expense Ratio %
6.85	6.65	6.32	6.00	6.10	6.67	6.18	5.67	4.81	3.61	3.99	—	Income Ratio %
53	37	28	35	24	34	40	31	41	30	24	—	Turnover Rate %
303	533	705	952	974	1,021	1,512	3,405	5,697	7,870	9,610	11,709	Net Assets $mil

Rating and Risk

Time Period	Load-Adj Return %	Morningstar Rtn vs Cat	Morningstar Risk vs Cat	Morningstar Risk-Adj Rating
1 Yr	5.30			
3 Yr	3.63	+Avg	Low	★★★★
5 Yr	5.49	+Avg	Low	★★★★
10 Yr	6.52	High	-Avg	★★★★★
Incept	7.93			

Other Measures	Standard Index LB Aggr	Best Fit Index LB. U.S. Univ. Bd
Alpha	0.1	-0.3
Beta	0.69	0.72
R-Squared	92	95
Standard Deviation	2.38	
Mean	3.63	
Sharpe Ratio	0.16	

Portfolio Analysis 09-30-06

Total Fixed-Income:373

	Date of Maturity	Amount $000	Value $000	% Net Assets
US Treasury Note 3%	11-15-07	475,000	465,352	4.19
US Treasury Note 3.25%	01-15-09	400,000	387,938	3.50
US Treasury Note 3.625%	07-15-09	335,000	326,350	2.94
Gmac 6.875%	09-15-11	227,980	226,772	2.04
FNMA 6%	04-01-35	222,266	223,779	2.02
Ford Motor Cr 7.25%	10-25-11	229,015	215,979	1.95
FNMA 5.5%	05-01-34	214,613	212,033	1.91
FNMA 6.5%	12-01-32	205,524	210,139	1.89
FNMA 6%	07-01-35	186,099	187,472	1.69
FNMA 6%	04-01-35	169,946	171,200	1.54
FNMA	07-01-35	147,739	147,007	1.33
US Treasury Note 3.375%	09-15-09	150,000	144,926	1.31
FNMA 5%	03-01-34	149,451	144,114	1.30
At&T 8%	11-15-31	113,850	139,154	1.25
Aol Time Warner 7.625%	04-15-31	119,983	132,542	1.19
US Treasury Note 3.125%	10-15-08	125,000	121,250	1.09
Aol Time Warner 7.7%	05-01-32	101,284	113,108	1.02
FNMA 5.5%	12-01-18	112,758	113,080	1.02
Wyeth 5.5%	02-01-14	110,465	110,674	1.00
FNMA 6%	03-01-33	109,377	110,184	0.99

Current Investment Style

Duration: Short / Int / Long
Quality: High / Med / Low

¹ figure provided by fund

Avg Eff Duration¹	3.9 Yrs
Avg Eff Maturity	6.2 Yrs
Avg Credit Quality	AA
Avg Wtd Coupon	5.52%
Avg Wtd Price	100.99% of par

Coupon Range	% of Bonds	Rel Cat
0% PIK	6.0	0.9
0% to 6%	61.6	0.8
6% to 8%	35.4	1.6
8% to 10%	3.0	0.8
More than 10%	0.0	0.0

1.00=Category Average

Credit Analysis	% bonds 09-30-06		
AAA	65	BB	8
AA	3	B	0
A	7	Below B	0
BBB	15	NR/NA	2

Sector Breakdown % of assets

US Treasuries	13
TIPS	0
US Agency	3
Mortgage Pass-Throughs	40
Mortgage CMO	4
Mortgage ARM	0
US Corporate	30
Asset-Backed	1
Convertible	0
Municipal	0
Corporate Inflation-Protected	0
Foreign Corporate	1
Foreign Govt	0

Composition

Cash	8.0	Bonds	91.8
Stocks	0.0	Other	0.2

Special Securities

Restricted/Illiquid Secs	1
Exotic Mortgage-Backed	0
Emerging-Markets Secs	0
Options/Futures/Warrants	No

Dodge & Cox Intl Stock

✓ Analyst Pick

Ticker	Load	NAV	Yield	Total Assets	Mstar Category
DODFX	None	$43.66	1.3%	$28,486 mil	Foreign Large Value

Governance and Management

Stewardship Grade: A

Portfolio Manager(s)

This fund is run by the Dodge & Cox International Policy Committee. The eight-person team is deep, talented, and experienced. Committee members have been at Dodge & Cox for an average of 16 years. Several members also serve on the committee that runs large-value Analyst Pick Dodge & Cox Stock. Finally, all the firm's analysts are tasked with finding ideas for this fund, because they cover sectors on a global basis.

Strategy

This fund's management team invests in stocks that it considers undervalued on a range of variables. It favors companies with good management, dominant competitive positions, and good growth potential. Because management takes such a long-term view, turnover is generally low. Finally, management normally runs an unhedged portfolio and uses fair-value pricing whenever it thinks such an approach is warranted.

Historical Profile

Return	Above Avg
Risk	High
Rating	★★★★ Above Avg

Investment Style: Equity, Stock %

71% 93% 83% 90% 93% 96%

▼ Manager Change
▽ Partial Manager Change

Growth of $10,000
— Investment Values of Fund
— Investment Values of MSCI EAFE

20.8
16.6
13.0
10.0
6.0

Performance Quartile (within Category)

	1995	1996	1997	1998	1999	2000	2001	2002	2003	2004	2005	2006	History
	—	—	—	—	—	—	18.42	15.81	23.48	30.64	35.03	43.66	NAV
	—	—	—	—	—	—	-8.51*	-13.11	49.42	32.46	16.75	28.01	Total Return %
	—	—	—	—	—	—	—	2.83	10.83	12.21	3.21	1.67	+/-MSCI EAFE
	—	—	—	—	—	—	—	2.69	10.00	12.08	2.28	2.30	+/-MSCI Wd xUS
	—	—	—	—	—	—	—	0.72	0.90	1.02	1.14	1.61	Income Return %
	—	—	—	—	—	—	—	-13.83	48.52	31.44	15.61	26.40	Capital Return %
	—	—	—	—	—	—	—	56	8	1	16	33	Total Rtn % Rank Cat
	—	—	—	—	—	—	0.14	0.13	0.14	0.24	0.35	0.57	Income $
	—	—	—	—	—	—	0.02	0.06	0.00	0.22	0.39	0.62	Capital Gains $
	—	—	—	—	—	—	—	0.90	0.90	0.82	0.77	—	Expense Ratio %
	—	—	—	—	—	—	—	1.74	1.30	1.54	1.90	—	Income Ratio %
	—	—	—	—	—	—	—	23	12	11	6	—	Turnover Rate %
	—	—	—	—	—	—	25	117	655	4,203	28,486		Net Assets $mil

Performance 12-31-06

	1st Qtr	2nd Qtr	3rd Qtr	4th Qtr	Total
2002	7.71	-5.04	-22.77	10.00	-13.11
2003	-11.70	22.64	18.46	16.49	49.42
2004	7.71	2.17	3.64	16.14	32.46
2005	1.79	-0.06	9.72	4.59	16.75
2006	9.91	1.19	3.31	11.41	28.01

Trailing	Total Return%	+/- MSCI EAFE	+/- MSCI Wd xUS	%Rank Cat	Growth of $10,000
3 Mo	11.41	1.06	1.29	27	11,141
6 Mo	15.10	0.41	0.88	43	11,510
1 Yr	28.01	1.67	2.30	33	12,801
3 Yr Avg	25.56	5.63	5.46	6	19,795
5 Yr Avg	20.78	5.80	5.53	11	25,702
10 Yr Avg	—	—	—		—
15 Yr Avg	—	—	—		—

Tax Analysis	Tax-Adj Rtn%	%Rank Cat	Tax-Cost Rat	%Rank Cat
3 Yr (estimated)	25.10	1	0.37	4
5 Yr (estimated)	20.35	9	0.36	7
10 Yr (estimated)	—		—	

Potential Capital Gain Exposure: 22% of assets

Rating and Risk

Time Period	Load-Adj Return %	Morningstar Rtn vs Cat	Morningstar Risk vs Cat	Morningstar Risk-Adj Rating
1 Yr	28.01			
3 Yr	25.56	High	High	★★★★★
5 Yr	20.78	+Avg	High	★★★★
10 Yr	—	—	—	
Incept	16.28			

Other Measures	Standard Index MSCI EAFE	Best Fit Index MSCI Wd xUS
Alpha	3.6	3.7
Beta	1.07	1.06
R-Squared	91	91
Standard Deviation	10.58	
Mean	25.56	
Sharpe Ratio	1.92	

Portfolio Analysis 09-30-06

Share change since 06-06 Total Stocks:83	Sector	Country	% Assets
⊕ Sanofi-Synthelabo	Health	France	3.37
News Cl A	Media	United States	2.78
⊕ HSBC Hldgs	Financial	Hong Kong	2.41
⊕ Nokia	Hardware	Finland	2.35
⊕ Matsushita Electric Indu	Ind Mtrls	Japan	2.33
⊕ Royal Bank Of Scotland G	Financial	U.K.	2.29
⊕ Infineon Technologies	Hardware	Germany	2.27
⊕ GlaxoSmithKline PLC ADR	Health	U.K.	2.16
⊕ Hitachi, Ltd	Hardware	Japan	2.16
⊕ Mitsubishi UFJ Financial	Financial	Japan	2.16
⊕ Swiss Re	Financial	Switzerland	2.09
⊕ Royal Dutch Shell PLC AD	Energy	Netherlands	2.08
⊕ Tesco	Consumer	U.K.	2.08
Volvo	Ind Mtrls	Sweden	2.04
⊕ Honda Motor ADR	Goods	Japan	1.99
⊕ Credit Suisse Grp	Financial	Switzerland	1.98
Central Japan Railway	Business	Japan	1.98
Nestle	Goods	Switzerland	1.88
⊖ Vodafone Group PLC ADR	Telecom	U.K.	1.85
⊕ Sony	Goods	Japan	1.85

Current Investment Style

Value Blnd Growth — Large Mid Small

Market Cap	%
Giant	51.8
Large	28.6
Mid	18.7
Small	0.9
Micro	0.0

Avg $mil: 24,006

Value Measures		Rel Category
Price/Earnings	14.43	1.15
Price/Book	1.73	0.97
Price/Sales	0.83	0.87
Price/Cash Flow	9.47	1.32
Dividend Yield %	2.37	0.72

Growth Measures	%	Rel Category
Long-Term Erngs	10.37	1.01
Book Value	7.33	0.94
Sales	5.44	0.99
Cash Flow	-5.46	NMF
Historical Erngs	20.53	1.25

Composition

Cash	4.1	Bonds	0.0
Stocks	95.9	Other	0.0
Foreign	(% of Stock)		94.9

Sector Weightings	% of Stocks	Rel MSCI EAFE	3 Year High	Low
⌾ Info	17.06	1.44		
▣ Software	0.00	0.00	0	0
▣ Hardware	8.71	2.26	9	1
▣ Media	4.55	2.49	5	0
▣ Telecom	3.80	0.68	6	4
⌾ Service	37.49	0.79		
▣ Health	6.65	0.93	9	1
▣ Consumer	3.41	0.69	6	3
▣ Business	5.07	1.00	5	0
▣ Financial	22.36	0.74	23	19
⌾ Mfg	45.46	1.11		
▣ Goods	14.50	1.11	23	15
▣ Ind Mtrls	21.50	1.39	30	21
▣ Energy	8.88	1.24	13	9
▣ Utilities	0.58	0.11	3	0

Regional Exposure		% Stock
UK/W. Europe 51	N. America	6
Japan 23	Latn America	8
Asia X Japan 10	Other	2

Country Exposure		% Stock
Japan 23	Switzerland	9
U.K. 11	Netherlands	8
France 9		

Morningstar's Take by Gregg Wolper 12-16-06

It's still easy to feel comfortable owning Dodge & Cox International Stock.

This fund's performance has been excellent. Over the trailing five-year period through Dec. 15, 2006, it has posted a 21.1% annualized return that beats roughly 85% of its foreign large-value rivals. The fund has had another strong year in 2006; it is well into the category's top half and ahead of the MSCI EAFE Index, with a 26.2% gain so far.

Past performance itself isn't enough, but this one has much more going for it. It's only five years old, but it relies on the same strategy and many of the same members of a skilled and experienced group of investment professionals as other Dodge & Cox funds with much longer records of success. This fund's patience is also an attraction: With a turnover rate of only 6% in 2004 and 7% in 2005, it really does invest for the long term, and its affordability is another reason to favor this offering.

When the fund does make moves, they are often contrarian. For example, comanager Diana Strandberg says the fund's industrial-materials weighting has fallen substantially since its inception, even as that sector's weighting in the MSCI EAFE Index has nearly doubled. Conversely, she says the fund had been low but is now overweighted in what she calls "intellectual property" stocks, such as drug firms.

The only concern here is the growth of the fund's asset base from less than $1 billion at 2003's end to more than $26 billion now. Strandberg says the managers have determined that all things considered, the fund could grow much larger without being hampered by its size. From other families, that might sound simply like an excuse to keep gathering assets, but given this firm's shareholder-friendly history, its resources, and the fund's methods, we think this fund does still deserve to be considered a top choice in its field.

Address:	555 California St San Francisco CA 94104 800-621-3979	Minimum Purchase:	$2500 Add: $100 IRA: $1000
		Min Auto Inv Plan:	$2500 Add: $100
		Sales Fees:	No-load
Web Address:	www.dodgeandcox.com	Management Fee:	0.60%
Inception:	05-01-01*	Actual Fees:	Mgt:0.60% Dist: —
Advisor:	Dodge & Cox	Expense Projections:	3Yr:$224 5Yr:$390 10Yr:$871
Subadvisor:	None	Income Distrib:	Annually
NTF Plans:	N/A		

MORNINGSTAR® Funds 500

Dodge & Cox Stock

Ticker	**Load**	**NAV**	**Yield**	**Total Assets**	**Mstar Category**
DODGX	Closed	$153.46	1.3%	$64,843 mil	Large Value

Governance and Management

Stewardship Grade: A

Portfolio Manager(s)

This fund has an experienced and deep management team. The Dodge & Cox equity investment policy committee, which runs this fund, has nine members. The team is supported by nearly 20 analysts and five research assistants.

Strategy

This fund's management team invests in mid- and large-cap stocks that look cheap on a range of valuation measures. It favors companies with good management, dominant competitive positions, and good growth potential, but usually doesn't get interested until these stocks are under some sort of cloud. Because management takes such a long-term view, the fund's turnover is just a fraction of the large-value category average.

Performance 12-31-06

	1st Qtr	2nd Qtr	3rd Qtr	4th Qtr	Total
2002	4.89	-6.22	-15.84	8.06	-10.54
2003	-5.29	16.59	5.24	13.88	32.34
2004	4.96	1.06	-0.26	12.64	19.17
2005	0.12	0.56	5.45	3.01	9.37
2006	5.30	0.81	4.82	6.54	18.53

Trailing	Total Return%	+/- S&P 500	+/- Russ 1000 VI	%Rank Cat	Growth of $10,000
3 Mo	6.54	-0.16	-1.46	75	10,654
6 Mo	11.67	-1.07	-3.05	74	11,167
1 Yr	18.53	2.74	-3.72	47	11,853
3 Yr Avg	15.60	5.16	0.51	6	15,448
5 Yr Avg	12.84	6.65	1.98	3	18,294
10 Yr Avg	14.23	5.81	3.23	1	37,827
15 Yr Avg	15.34	4.70	2.31	1	85,055

Tax Analysis	Tax-Adj Rtn%	%Rank Cat	Tax-Cost Rat	%Rank Cat
3 Yr (estimated)	14.71	4	0.77	30
5 Yr (estimated)	11.98	3	0.76	41
10 Yr (estimated)	12.45	2	1.56	51

Potential Capital Gain Exposure: 29% of assets

Morningstar's Take by Dan Culloton 11-20-06

Dodge & Cox Stock will remain inaccessible until it's unlovable.

Anyone should want this fund. A veteran team manages it with a patient, contrarian style. The fund's advisor is an exemplary steward of fund owners' wealth; it never rolls out trendy funds, keeps fees low, and emphasizes capital preservation as much as capital appreciation. Its record speaks for itself. Performance may speak too well. The fund has taken in a torrent of assets in recent years, even after it closed to new investors in 2004, and is now the third-biggest large-value fund, with nearly $64 billion in assets.

We are frequently asked if this fund will open again. The answer, based on conversations with the fund's managers, is, when you least expect it, expect it. It would take a soul-shaking and asset-depleting drop in the stock market or this fund's relative performance for the fund to take in new money again. In short, the fund would have to get smaller and sentiment about it darker. This isn't surprising from a firm that was founded in the Great Depression.

It's hard for a fund this large to invest successfully without getting in its own way. That the fund has been able to preserve performance so far is testimony to the decision to close all of the firm's equity accounts to new clients, as well as to the fund's approach. It doesn't trade much and often buys when others are selling. For example, the fund added Dell in the second quarter because the managers thought the market had gotten too pessimistic about the computer maker. The fund also has been able to own smaller stocks such as American Power Conversion, which recently agreed to be bought by Schneider Electric.

Taxes may be a chink in this fund's armor. The fund's aftertax returns look good because its pretax returns are so good, but it distributes capital gains like clockwork. In 2006 the fund said it would pay out $6.66, or about 4.5% of its NAV. This fund is still worth owning, though.

Address:	555 California St San Francisco CA 94104 800-621-3979
Web Address:	www.dodgeandcox.com
Inception:	01-04-65
Advisor:	Dodge & Cox
Subadvisor:	None
NTF Plans:	N/A

Minimum Purchase:	Closed	Add: —	IRA: —
Min Auto Inv Plan:	Closed	Add: —	
Sales Fees:	No-load		
Management Fee:	0.50%		
Actual Fees:	Mgt:0.50%	Dist: —	
Expense Projections:	3Yr:$167	5Yr:$291	10Yr:$653
Income Distrib:	Quarterly		

Historical Profile

Return	High
Risk	Average
Rating	★★★★★ Highest

Investment Style: Equity, Stock %

95% 92% 91% 89% 93% 90% 94% 96% 96%

▼ Manager Change
▽ Partial Manager Change

Growth of $10,000
■ Investment Values of Fund
— Investment Values of S&P 500

Performance Quartile (within Category)

1995	1996	1997	1998	1999	2000	2001	2002	2003	2004	2005	2006	History
67.83	79.81	94.57	90.70	100.52	96.67	100.51	88.05	113.78	130.22	137.22	153.46	NAV
33.38	22.27	28.40	5.40	20.21	16.31	9.33	-10.54	32.34	19.17	9.37	18.53	Total Return %
-4.20	-0.69	-4.96	-23.18	-0.83	25.41	21.22	11.56	3.66	8.29	4.46	2.74	+/-S&P 500
-4.98	0.63	-6.78	-10.23	12.86	9.30	14.92	4.98	2.31	2.68	2.32	-3.72	+/-Russ 1000 VI
2.62	1.92	1.89	1.68	1.66	2.18	1.82	1.51	1.85	1.35	1.32	1.56	Income Return %
30.76	20.35	26.51	3.72	18.55	14.13	7.51	-12.05	30.49	17.82	8.05	16.97	Capital Return %
46	21	38	82	4	21	6	6	18	4	16	47	Total Rtn % Rank Cat
1.40	1.29	1.49	1.56	1.48	2.09	1.73	1.51	1.62	1.53	1.70	2.12	Income $
2.52	1.68	6.09	7.42	6.70	17.10	3.20	0.42	0.84	3.65	3.34	6.91	Capital Gains $
0.60	0.59	0.57	0.57	0.55	0.54	0.54	0.54	0.54	0.53	0.52	—	Expense Ratio %
2.07	1.79	1.67	1.63	1.46	2.13	1.80	1.74	1.72	1.32	1.29	—	Income Ratio %
13	10	19	19	18	32	10	13	8	11	12	—	Turnover Rate %
1,228	2,252	4,087	4,355	4,625	5,728	9,396	14,036	29,437	43,266	52,184	64,843	Net Assets $mil

Rating and Risk

Time Period	Load-Adj Return %	Morningstar Rtn vs Cat	Morningstar Risk vs Cat	Morningstar Risk-Adj Rating
1 Yr	18.53			
3 Yr	15.60	High	+Avg	★★★★★
5 Yr	12.84	High	Avg	★★★★★
10 Yr	14.23	High	Avg	★★★★★
Incept	12.33			

Other Measures	Standard Index S&P 500	Best Fit Index MSCI World
Alpha	4.7	1.9
Beta	0.99	0.90
R-Squared	84	86
Standard Deviation	7.46	
Mean	15.60	
Sharpe Ratio	1.56	

Portfolio Analysis 09-30-06

Share change since 06-06 Total Stocks:86	Sector	PE	Tot Ret%	% Assets
⊕ Hewlett-Packard Company	Hardware	19.3	45.21	4.10
Comcast Corporation A	Media	45.2	63.31	3.67
Pfizer Inc.	Health	15.2	15.22	3.32
News CI A	Media	—		2.96
⊕ Time Warner, Inc.	Media	19.6	26.37	2.60
⊕ Chevron Corporation	Energy	9.0	33.76	2.59
⊕ Sony Corporation ADR	Goods	43.2	5.50	2.46
McDonald's Corporation	Consumer	18.9	34.63	2.37
⊕ Matsushita Electric Indu	Ind Mtrls	32.8	4.71	2.29
⊕ Cardinal Health, Inc.	Health	20.8	-5.82	2.27
⊕ Wal-Mart Stores, Inc.	Consumer	16.9	0.13	2.26
Sanofi-Aventis ADR	Health	42.9	7.33	2.25
⊕ Union Pacific Corporatio	Business	17.4	15.87	2.19
FedEx Corporation	Business	17.2	5.40	2.07
⊕ Dow Chemical Company	Ind Mtrls	10.0	-5.44	2.05
HCA, Inc.	Health			1.96
⊕ Citigroup, Inc.	Financial	13.1	19.55	1.93
St. Paul Travelers Compa	Financial	11.6	22.90	1.76
Wachovia Corporation	Financial	12.9	12.02	1.70
Xerox Corporation	Ind Mtrls	13.4	15.70	1.64

Current Investment Style

Value Blnd Growth — Large Mid Small

Market Cap	%
Giant	48.6
Large	41.8
Mid	9.5
Small	0.0
Micro	0.0

Avg $mil: 43,213

Value Measures		Rel Category
Price/Earnings	14.83	1.08
Price/Book	2.20	0.99
Price/Sales	1.12	0.86
Price/Cash Flow	9.38	1.40
Dividend Yield %	1.66	0.71

Growth Measures	%	Rel Category
Long-Term Erngs	10.85	1.05
Book Value	5.03	0.64
Sales	8.17	0.91
Cash Flow	7.14	1.18
Historical Erngs	18.97	1.17

Profitability	%	Rel Category
Return on Equity	15.82	0.88
Return on Assets	7.59	0.77
Net Margin	8.38	0.65

Sector Weightings	% of Stocks	Rel S&P 500	3 Year High	Low
↻ Info	22.12	1.11		
▣ Software	0.78	0.23	1	1
▣ Hardware	9.40	1.02	9	5
▣ Media	10.91	2.88	11	7
▣ Telecom	1.03	0.29	6	1
☞ Service	47.73	1.03		
❤ Health	17.53	1.45	18	11
▣ Consumer	7.21	0.94	7	5
▣ Business	7.56	1.79	9	7
⑤ Financial	15.43	0.69	20	15
⊿ Mfg	30.15	0.89		
▣ Goods	5.91	0.69	8	6
❁ Ind Mtrls	14.49	1.21	15	13
◐ Energy	9.31	0.95	10	8
☡ Utilities	0.44	0.13	4	0

Composition

● Cash	4.4
● Stocks	95.6
● Bonds	0.0
● Other	0.0
Foreign (% of Stock)	16.6

Domini Social Equity

	Ticker	Load	NAV	Yield	Total Assets	Mstar Category
	DSEFX	None	$33.42	0.8%	$1,197 mil	Large Blend

Governance and Management

Stewardship Grade: B

Portfolio Manager(s)

A six-person committee at Kinder, Lydenberg, Domini maintains the Domini 400 Social Index, which has been the basis for this fund's portfolio, with State Street Global Advisors overseeing day-to-day management. Since November 30, 2006, the fund has had five named managers: A three-person team at Wellington Management led by Mammen Chally will manage the portfolio on a day-to-day basis, and Steve Lydenberg and Jeff MacDonagh of Domini Social Investments will oversee the social-screening aspect.

Strategy

This fund has historically tracked the Domini 400 Social Index. The social screens behind this index eliminate companies involved with alcohol, tobacco, firearms, gambling, nuclear power, or weapons contracting, and favor firms with strong records in environmental issues, workplace diversity, and employee relations. Since November 30, 2006, the fund has adhered to the same social criteria while being actively managed by a team at Wellington Management, who pick stocks using quantitative models focused on valuation and momentum factors.

Performance 12-31-06

	1st Qtr	2nd Qtr	3rd Qtr	4th Qtr	Total
2002	-0.04	-12.14	-17.16	9.00	-20.69
2003	-3.56	15.06	3.14	11.08	27.13
2004	1.83	2.04	-3.74	9.24	9.26
2005	-4.81	1.35	3.13	2.54	2.03
2006	3.31	-3.50	6.12	6.41	12.58

Trailing	Total Return%	+/- S&P 500	+/- Russ 1000	%Rank Cat	Growth of $10,000
3 Mo	6.41	-0.29	-0.54	64	10,641
6 Mo	12.93	0.19	0.57	16	11,293
1 Yr	12.58	-3.21	-2.88	74	11,258
3 Yr Avg	7.87	-2.57	-3.11	85	12,552
5 Yr Avg	4.82	-1.37	-2.00	71	12,654
10 Yr Avg	7.60	-0.82	-1.04	56	20,803
15 Yr Avg	9.82	-0.82	-0.98	56	40,759

Tax Analysis	Tax-Adj Rtn%	%Rank Cat	Tax-Cost Rat	%Rank Cat
3 Yr (estimated)	7.55	73	0.30	14
5 Yr (estimated)	4.56	62	0.25	17
10 Yr (estimated)	7.13	36	0.44	15

Potential Capital Gain Exposure: 11% of assets

Historical Profile

Return	Average
Risk	Above Avg
Rating	★★★ Neutral

Investment Style: Equity Stock %

▼ Manager Change
▽ Partial Manager Change

Growth of $10,000
— Investment Values of Fund
— Investment Values of S&P 500

Performance Quartile (within Category)

1995	1996	1997	1998	1999	2000	2001	2002	2003	2004	2005	2006	History
16.11	19.35	26.22	34.40	41.89	34.57	27.37	21.60	27.31	29.54	29.93	33.42	NAV
35.17	21.84	36.02	32.99	22.63	-15.05	-12.76	-20.69	27.13	9.26	2.03	12.58	Total Return %
-2.41	-1.12	2.66	4.41	1.59	-5.95	-0.87	1.41	-1.55	-1.62	-2.88	-3.21	+/-S&P 500
-2.60	-0.61	3.17	5.97	1.72	-7.26	-0.31	0.96	-2.76	-2.14	-4.24	-2.88	+/-Russ 1000
1.25	0.95	0.31	0.06	0.04	0.00	0.14	0.40	0.64	1.08	0.70	0.87	Income Return %
33.92	20.89	35.71	32.93	22.59	-15.05	-12.90	-21.09	26.49	8.18	1.33	11.71	Capital Return %
47	49	7	5	29	95	69	37	56	70	89	74	Total Rtn % Rank Cat
0.15	0.15	0.06	0.02	0.01	0.00	0.05	0.11	0.14	0.29	0.21	0.26	Income $
0.08	0.12	0.03	0.45	0.27	0.98	2.75	0.00	0.00	0.00	0.00	0.00	Capital Gains $
0.90	0.98	0.98	1.17	0.98	0.96	0.93	0.92	0.92	0.94	0.95	0.95	Expense Ratio %
1.38	1.01	0.62	0.07	0.06	-0.05	0.06	0.32	0.63	0.55	1.20	0.74	Income Ratio %
6	5	1	5	8	—	—	—	—	—	9	12	Turnover Rate %
69	115	301	716	1,344	1,329	1,197	1,011	1,258	1,362	1,209	1,147	Net Assets $mil

Rating and Risk

Time Period	Load-Adj Return %	Morningstar Rtn vs Cat	Morningstar Risk vs Cat	Morningstar Risk-Adj Rating
1 Yr	12.58			
3 Yr	7.87	-Avg	Avg	★★
5 Yr	4.82	-Avg	+Avg	★★
10 Yr	7.60	Avg	+Avg	★★★
Incept	10.01			

Other Measures	Standard Index S&P 500	Best Fit Index Russ 1000Gr
Alpha	-2.9	1.3
Beta	1.08	0.88
R-Squared	92	93
Standard Deviation	7.77	
Mean	7.87	
Sharpe Ratio	0.60	

Portfolio Analysis 09-30-06

Share change since 06-06 Total Stocks:400	Sector	PE	Tot Ret%	% Assets
⊖ Microsoft Corporation	Software	23.8	15.83	3.91
⊖ Procter & Gamble Company	Goods	23.9	13.36	3.26
⊖ Johnson & Johnson	Health	17.5	12.45	3.14
⊖ J.P. Morgan Chase & Co.	Financial	13.6	25.60	2.70
⊖ Cisco Systems, Inc.	Hardware	30.1	59.64	2.32
⊖ AT&T, Inc.	Telecom	18.2	51.59	2.10
⊕ Wells Fargo Company	Financial	14.7	16.82	2.02
⊖ Intel Corporation	Hardware	21.0	-17.18	1.96
⊖ Verizon Communications	Telecom	15.9	34.88	1.79
⊖ PepsiCo, Inc.	Goods	21.5	7.86	1.78
⊖ Hewlett-Packard Company	Hardware	19.3	45.21	1.67
⊖ Coca-Cola Company	Goods	21.7	23.10	1.51
⊖ Merck & Co., Inc.	Health	19.1	42.66	1.51
⊖ Wachovia Corporation	Financial	12.9	12.02	1.47
⊖ Amgen, Inc.	Health	29.1	-13.38	1.39
⊖ BellSouth Corporation	Telecom	—	—	1.29
⊖ United Parcel Service, I	Business	19.7	1.76	1.29
⊖ Home Depot, Inc.	Consumer	13.5	1.01	1.24
⊖ Time Warner, Inc.	Media	19.6	26.37	1.23
⊖ Merrill Lynch & Company,	Financial	14.2	39.28	1.15

Current Investment Style

Value Blnd Growth — Large Mid Small

Market Cap	%
Giant	48.8
Large	36.8
Mid	13.0
Small	1.3
Micro	0.1

Avg $mil: 39,272

Value Measures		Rel Category
Price/Earnings	16.61	1.08
Price/Book	2.60	1.02
Price/Sales	1.73	1.24
Price/Cash Flow	5.90	0.70
Dividend Yield %	1.73	0.99

Growth Measures	%	Rel Category
Long-Term Erngs	11.53	0.98
Book Value	9.38	1.04
Sales	9.06	0.93
Cash Flow	8.69	0.84
Historical Erngs	14.94	0.81

Profitability	%	Rel Category
Return on Equity	19.77	1.02
Return on Assets	11.39	1.10
Net Margin	14.86	1.11

Sector Weightings

	% of Stocks	Rel S&P 500	3 Year High Low	
⊙ Info	27.41	1.37		
▣ Software	5.33	1.54	6	5
▣ Hardware	12.64	1.37	15	12
▣ Media	3.27	0.86	6	3
▣ Telecom	6.17	1.76	6	5
⊑ Service	51.67	1.12		
▣ Health	13.84	1.15	14	12
▣ Consumer	10.55	1.38	11	10
▣ Business	4.52	1.07	5	4
▣ Financial	22.76	1.02	25	21
⊞ Mfg	20.93	0.62		
▣ Goods	11.28	1.32	12	11
▣ Ind Mtrls	5.58	0.47	6	5
▣ Energy	3.47	0.35	4	1
▣ Utilities	0.60	0.17	1	1

Composition

● Cash	0.0
● Stocks	100.0
● Bonds	0.0
○ Other	0.0
Foreign (% of Stock)	0.0

Morningstar's Take by David Kathman 12-13-06

We're hopeful about upcoming changes to Domini Social Equity, but the proof will be in the pudding.

In May 2006, Domini Social Investments announced that this fund would get a major overhaul, pending shareholder approval. Since its 1991 inception, this has been an index fund that tracked the Domini 400 Social Index, a socially responsible index similar to the S&P 500. As of November 30, it is now subadvised by Wellington Management, which uses quantitative models to actively manage the portfolio from a universe of stocks that pass Domini's social screens.

Those screens eliminate alcohol, tobacco, gambling, military weapons, and nuclear power stocks, and favor companies friendly to employees, shareholders, and the environment. Because the screens eliminate many energy and industrial stocks, those sectors are significantly underweighted in the Domini 400 Social Index relative to the S&P 500, and technology and telecom stocks are overweighted. Thus, the fund

has outperformed the S&P 500 in tech-led bull markets such as that of the late 1990s, and has underperformed it in recent years, when energy stocks have been the market's main drivers.

The overhaul is designed to bring the fund's sector weightings more in line with those of the S&P 500, and to try adding value from stock-picking. The Wellington team builds the portfolio around an optimized custom benchmark whose sector weightings and other factors are much closer to the S&P 500's than the Domini 400 Social Index's, and it uses valuation and momentum factors to identify the most attractive stocks meeting Domini's criteria.

This plan looks promising, and should help put more focus on Domini's screening criteria, which we've always admired. However, we're still concerned that the fund's expense ratio is rising from 0.95% to 1.15%, which gives the Wellington team a higher hurdle to clear to show that it can really add value.

Address:	536 Broadway New York NY 10012-3915 800-582-6757
Web Address:	www.domini.com
Inception:	06-03-91
Advisor:	Domini Social Investments, LLC
Subadvisor:	Wellington Management Company, LLP
NTF Plans:	Fidelity Retail-NTF, Schwab OneSource

Minimum Purchase:	$2500	Add: $100	IRA: $1500
Min Auto Inv Plan:	$1500	Add: $50	
Sales Fees:	No-load, 0.25%S, 2.00%R		
Management Fee:	0.30%		
Actual Fees:	Mgt:0.30%	Dist:0.25%	
Expense Projections:	3Yr:$374	5Yr:$650	10Yr:$1440
Income Distrib:	Semi-Annually		

MORNINGSTAR® Funds 500

Dreyfus Appreciation

	Ticker	Load	NAV	Yield	Total Assets	Mstar Category
	DGAGX	None	$43.79	1.4%	$4,398 mil	Large Blend

Governance and Management

Stewardship Grade: C

Portfolio Manager(s)

Houston-based Fayez Sarofim & Co. has subadvised this fund for Dreyfus since 1990, but its eponymous leader has been managing money since 1958. An investment committee composed of Fayez Sarofim, Charles Sheedy, Christopher Sarofim, and several others with decades of experience makes portfolio decisions. More than a dozen analysts support the committee, and this number is on the rise.

Strategy

This fund is one of many plays on blue-chip names, but management's preference for companies with proven and well-known brands separates it from the pack. It holds more consumer-goods companies and fewer technology names than the typical large-blend fund. Management likes firms with high-quality earnings, clean balance sheets, and lots of free cash flow. The portfolio is more concentrated in individual stocks than many rivals. Management takes a buy-and-hold approach, which, in turn, translates into strong tax efficiency.

Performance 12-31-06

	1st Qtr	2nd Qtr	3rd Qtr	4th Qtr	Total
2002	2.60	-11.29	-14.34	6.27	-17.14
2003	-4.28	12.96	0.71	10.55	20.39
2004	0.69	1.39	-3.59	7.26	5.57
2005	-0.06	0.72	3.36	0.08	4.14
2006	1.69	0.87	5.87	7.06	16.26

Trailing	Total Return%	+/- S&P 500	+/- Russ 1000	%Rank Cat	Growth of $10,000
3 Mo	7.06	0.36	0.11	31	10,706
6 Mo	13.35	0.61	0.99	12	11,335
1 Yr	16.26	0.47	0.80	16	11,626
3 Yr Avg	8.53	-1.91	-2.45	78	12,783
5 Yr Avg	4.98	-1.21	-1.84	68	12,751
10 Yr Avg	7.86	-0.56	-0.78	47	21,311
15 Yr Avg	9.74	-0.90	-1.06	60	40,316

Tax Analysis	Tax-Adj Rtn%	%Rank Cat	Tax-Cost Rat	%Rank Cat
3 Yr (estimated)	8.00	67	0.49	23
5 Yr (estimated)	4.56	62	0.40	26
10 Yr (estimated)	7.30	30	0.52	19

Potential Capital Gain Exposure: 40% of assets

Historical Profile

Return	Average
Risk	Below Avg
Rating	★★★ Neutral

94% 97% 90% 91% 91% 97% 98% 99% 97%

Investment Style
Equity
Stock %

▼ Manager Change
▽ Partial Manager Change

31.0
25.0 **Growth of $10,000**
20.0 ■ Investment Values of Fund
15.0 — Investment Values of S&P 500
10.0

Performance Quartile (within Category)

1995	1996	1997	1998	1999	2000	2001	2002	2003	2004	2005	2006	History
20.55	25.58	32.38	42.07	45.73	42.94	38.02	31.20	37.14	38.69	39.75	43.79	NAV
37.88	25.67	27.85	30.85	9.97	1.80	-10.75	-17.14	20.39	5.57	4.14	16.26	Total Return %
0.30	2.71	-5.51	2.27	-11.07	10.90	1.14	4.96	-8.29	-5.31	-0.77	0.47	+/-S&P 500
0.11	3.22	-5.00	3.83	-10.94	9.59	1.70	4.51	-9.50	-5.83	-2.13	0.80	+/-Russ 1000
2.21	1.22	1.02	0.70	0.55	0.63	0.71	0.78	1.32	1.40	1.41	1.56	Income Return %
35.67	24.45	26.83	30.15	9.42	1.17	-11.46	-17.92	19.07	4.17	2.73	14.70	Capital Return %
12	14	58	9	84	23	39	15	95	92	72	16	Total Rtn % Rank Cat
0.34	0.25	0.26	0.23	0.23	0.29	0.31	0.30	0.41	0.52	0.54	0.62	Income $
0.03	0.00	0.06	0.07	0.31	3.22	0.00	0.02	0.00	0.00	0.00	1.79	Capital Gains $
0.92	0.91	0.87	0.89	0.87	0.88	0.91	0.97	0.96	0.95	0.92	—	Expense Ratio %
2.28	1.34	0.99	0.75	0.51	0.64	0.72	0.90	1.28	1.40	1.35	—	Income Ratio %
5	5	1	1	12	4	5	2	5	8	7	—	Turnover Rate %
461	877	130	227	232	220	230	338	3,994	4,436	4,472	4,398	Net Assets $mil

Rating and Risk

Time Period	Load-Adj Return %	Morningstar Rtn vs Cat	Morningstar Risk vs Cat	Morningstar Risk-Adj Rating
1 Yr	16.26			
3 Yr	8.53	-Avg	Low	★★
5 Yr	4.98	-Avg	-Avg	★★★
10 Yr	7.86	Avg	-Avg	★★★★
Incept	12.54			

Other Measures	Standard Index S&P 500	Best Fit Index Mstar Large Value
Alpha	0.0	-3.8
Beta	0.74	0.78
R-Squared	70	76
Standard Deviation	6.13	
Mean	8.53	
Sharpe Ratio	0.86	

Portfolio Analysis 10-31-06

Share change since 09-06 Total Stocks:52	Sector	PE	Tot Ret%	% Assets
Altria Group, Inc.	Goods	16.3	19.87	6.51
ExxonMobil Corporation	Energy	11.1	39.07	6.46
General Electric Company	Ind Mtrls	20.0	9.35	4.36
Citigroup, Inc.	Financial	13.1	19.55	4.03
Chevron Corporation	Energy	9.0	33.76	3.98
Procter & Gamble Company	Goods	23.9	13.36	3.75
McGraw-Hill Companies, I	Media	28.5	33.44	3.14
⊖ Coca-Cola Company	Goods	21.7	23.10	2.97
PepsiCo, Inc.	Goods	21.5	7.86	2.96
Johnson & Johnson	Health	17.5	12.45	2.92
Walgreen Company	Consumer	26.6	4.36	2.83
ConocoPhillips	Energy	6.5	26.53	2.67
⊖ Intel Corporation	Hardware	21.0	-17.18	2.60
BP PLC ADR	Energy	10.4	7.94	2.45
News Corporation, Ltd. A	Media	—		2.45
Nestle SA ADR	Goods	21.0	20.91	2.43
Bank of America Corporat	Financial	12.4	20.68	2.21
Merrill Lynch & Company,	Financial	14.2	39.28	2.09
J.P. Morgan Chase & Co.	Financial	13.6	25.60	2.08
American Express Company	Financial	20.9	19.09	1.91

Current Investment Style

Value Blnd Growth — Large Mid Small

	Market Cap	%
	Giant	78.5
	Large	20.1
	Mid	1.5
	Small	0.0
	Micro	0.0
	Avg $mil:	117,041

Value Measures		Rel Category
Price/Earnings	14.76	0.96
Price/Book	3.00	1.17
Price/Sales	1.47	1.05
Price/Cash Flow	10.04	1.19
Dividend Yield %	2.26	1.29

Growth Measures	%	Rel Category
Long-Term Erngs	9.97	0.84
Book Value	11.79	1.31
Sales	14.49	1.50
Cash Flow	14.46	1.40
Historical Erngs	19.73	1.07

Profitability	%	Rel Category
Return on Equity	23.21	1.19
Return on Assets	12.36	1.19
Net Margin	13.86	1.03

Sector Weightings

	% of Stocks	Rel S&P 500	3 Year High	Low
↻ Info	10.58	0.53		
Software	1.61	0.47	3	1
Hardware	2.68	0.29	6	3
Media	6.29	1.66	6	4
Telecom	0.00	0.00	0	0
☞ Service	39.48	0.85		
Health	9.00	0.75	15	9
Consumer	10.15	1.33	10	8
Business	1.87	0.44	2	1
Financial	18.46	0.83	23	17
⊐ Mfg	49.94	1.48		
Goods	22.39	2.62	25	22
Ind Mtrls	7.11	0.60	7	5
Energy	20.44	2.09	21	11
Utilities	0.00	0.00	0	0

Composition

- ● Cash 2.9
- ● Stocks 97.1
- ● Bonds 0.0
- ● Other 0.0
- Foreign 12.4 (% of Stock)

Morningstar's Take by Lawrence Jones 12-20-06

We think Dreyfus Appreciation is as strong as ever.

The investment approach practiced here by managers from subadvisor Fayez Sarofim & Co. gives us confidence and should continue to serve shareholders well over the long haul. A team of highly experienced managers employ a disciplined long-term investment approach that focuses on high-quality, large-cap companies that dominate their industries. Over the past 10 years, for instance, management has averaged a very low 5% portfolio-turnover rate, meaning it will typically hold stocks for more than a decade. This low level of turnover keeps trading costs low and makes the fund one of the more tax-efficient offerings in the large-blend category. Purchasing large, high-quality firms, such as ExxonMobil and Proctor and Gamble, when they trade at reasonable valuations also gives the fund a relatively low level of return volatility.

While it's true that the fund's trailing total returns over the past few years have been disappointing, the fund's performance needs to be situated in a broader context. For instance, when factoring in management's tax-conscious approach, the fund's trailing 10-year return ranks in the category's top third from a tax-adjusted perspective. Likewise, when looking at the Morningstar Investor Return, which is an estimate of how the average investor fared in a fund over a period of time, the fund's returns look even better. Over the trailing 10-year period ending Nov. 30, 2006, the typical investor saw an annualized return of 11.89%, which beats 94% of category rivals. This result is likely due to the fund's low volatility and its solid performance in the bear market of 2000-02.

Finally, with an expense ratio of 0.92%, we're also encouraged by the fund's modest cost. Investors will find the fund's low-turnover, tax-conscious approach to be particularly attractive for taxable accounts.

Address:	200 Park Avenue New York NY 10166 800-645-6561	Minimum Purchase:	$2500	Add: $100	IRA: $750
		Min Auto Inv Plan:	$100	Add: $100	
		Sales Fees:	No-load, 0.25%S	
Web Address:	www.dreyfus.com	Management Fee:	0.55%	
Inception:	01-18-84	Actual Fees:	Mgt:0.55%	Dist:0.25%
Advisor:	The Dreyfus Corporation	Expense Projections:	3Yr:$293	5Yr:$509	10Yr:$1131
Subadvisor:	Fayez Sarofim & Co.	Income Distrib:	Annually	
NTF Plans:	Fidelity Retail-NTF, Schwab OneSource			

Dreyfus Prem Bal Opp J

	Ticker	Load	NAV	Yield	Total Assets	Mstar Category
	THPBX	Closed	$20.28	1.9%	$754 mil	Moderate Allocation

Governance and Management

Stewardship Grade: C

Portfolio Manager(s)

Seasoned. Tom Plumb, principal of the fund's subadvisor, Wisconsin Capital Management, has been part of the management team of this fund since its 1987 inception and became lead manager in 1992. In 2002, David Duchow and Tim O'Brien, comanagers of Dreyfus Premier Blue Chip, were appointed comanagers on this fund.

Strategy

Unlike many of his peers, manager Tom Plumb will look very broadly across the financial markets in search of value. He uses bonds to temper stock-price volatility, but his asset allocation is generally quite aggressive. Plumb buys growth companies that have fallen out of favor. On the bond front, he prefers intermediate-term investment-grade issues. He'll adjust duration (a measure of interest-rate sensitivity) according to his view of the direction of interest rates and will opportunistically scoop up beaten-down bonds.

Historical Profile
Return Average
Risk Above Avg
Rating ★★★ Neutral

| 68% | 64% | 65% | 67% | 67% | 66% | 70% | 72% |

Investment Style
Equity
Stock %

▼ Manager Change
▽ Partial Manager Change

Growth of $10,000
■ Investment Values of Fund
— Investment Values of DJ Mod

31.0 — 25.0 — 20.0 — 15.0 — 10.0

Performance Quartile (within Category)

	1995	1996	1997	1998	1999	2000	2001	2002	2003	2004	2005	2006	History
	13.33	14.84	16.29	17.70	17.67	17.08	17.35	15.47	18.61	19.59	18.85	20.28	NAV
	20.03	23.09	22.54	16.87	8.87	10.21	11.07	-9.39	21.96	7.01	-1.31	9.63	Total Return %
	0.23	12.43	10.64	4.55	-8.46	11.88	13.87	-2.62	-5.42	-5.96	-8.30	-2.67	+/-DJ Mod
	-4.74	11.75	3.34	4.48	-3.98	5.77	10.91	1.15	-2.10	-4.16	-7.31	-0.64	+/-DJ US Mod
	1.91	1.71	0.87	1.16	1.20	1.51	1.51	1.47	1.62	1.11	1.69	2.02	Income Return %
	18.12	21.38	21.67	15.71	7.67	8.70	9.56	-10.86	20.34	5.90	-3.00	7.61	Capital Return %
	93	3	25	29	61	11	2	26	34	79	99	78	Total Rtn % Rank Cat
	0.23	0.23	0.13	0.19	0.21	0.27	0.26	0.26	0.25	0.21	0.33	0.38	Income $
	0.86	1.34	1.71	1.08	1.34	2.08	1.31	0.00	0.00	0.12	0.15	0.00	Capital Gains $
	1.42	1.49	1.45	1.40	1.30	1.25	1.22	1.15	1.10	1.07	0.95	—	Expense Ratio %
	1.84	1.71	1.32	1.04	1.16	1.24	1.42	1.73	1.91	1.90	1.79	—	Income Ratio %
	110	111	135	77	83	67	78	58	79	42	32	—	Turnover Rate %
	—	18	21	37	50	57	60	87	133	234	250	171	Net Assets $mil

Performance 12-31-06

	1st Qtr	2nd Qtr	3rd Qtr	4th Qtr	Total
2002	3.69	-8.45	-12.39	8.95	-9.39
2003	-3.56	15.55	0.41	9.00	21.96
2004	1.40	0.27	-2.33	7.76	7.01
2005	-3.01	1.53	-0.16	0.38	-1.31
2006	3.45	-2.44	3.89	4.56	9.63

Trailing	Total Return%	+/- DJ Mod	+/- DJ US Mod	%Rank Cat	Growth of $10,000
3 Mo	4.56	-1.03	-0.11	72	10,456
6 Mo	8.63	-0.16	0.73	57	10,863
1 Yr	9.63	-2.67	-0.64	78	10,963
3 Yr Avg	5.00	-5.72	-4.12	96	11,576
5 Yr Avg	5.05	-4.97	-2.55	72	12,793
10 Yr Avg	9.34	0.79	0.75	11	24,423
15 Yr Avg	9.52	0.31	0.13	34	39,120

Tax Analysis	Tax-Adj Rtn%	%Rank Cat	Tax-Cost Rat	%Rank Cat
3 Yr (estimated)	4.68	87	0.30	12
5 Yr (estimated)	4.63	57	0.40	19
10 Yr (estimated)	7.87	8	1.34	39

Potential Capital Gain Exposure: 8% of assets

Rating and Risk

Time Period	Load-Adj Return %	Morningstar Rtn vs Cat	Morningstar Risk vs Cat	Morningstar Risk-Adj Rating
1 Yr	9.63			
3 Yr	5.00	Low	Avg	★
5 Yr	5.05	-Avg	High	★★
10 Yr	9.34	+Avg	+Avg	★★★★
Incept	9.75			

Other Measures	Standard Index DJ Mod	Best Fit Index S&P 500
Alpha	-4.0	-3.2
Beta	0.81	0.72
R-Squared	75	82
Standard Deviation	5.54	
Mean	5.00	
Sharpe Ratio	0.33	

Portfolio Analysis 10-31-06

Total Stocks:43				
Share change since 09-30-06	Sectors	P/E Ratio	YTD Return %	% Net Assets
⊖ Microsoft Corporation	Software	23.8	0.23	3.55
⊖ Pfizer Inc.	Health	15.2	1.00	3.12
⊕ Corinthian Colleges, Inc.	Consumer	35.6	-0.81	2.87
⊖ American International Gr	Financial	17.0	-0.18	2.60
⊖ Cardinal Health, Inc.	Health	20.8	-0.43	2.55
⊖ Chevron Corporation	Energy	9.0	-2.83	2.40
⊖ Cabela's, Inc.	Consumer	20.0	-5.68	2.38
ExxonMobil Corporation	Energy	11.1	-5.19	2.37
⊖ J.P. Morgan Chase & Co.	Financial	13.6	-0.02	2.22

Total Fixed-Income:38	Date of Maturity	Amount $000	Value $000	% Net Assets
Cardinal Health 6.75%	02-15-11	10,925	11,458	1.49
GOLDMAN SACHS GROUP	10-01-09	10,000	10,597	1.38
Wal Mart Stores 6.875%	08-10-09	10,000	10,471	1.36
General Elec Cap 6.125%	02-22-11	10,000	10,391	1.35
FHLBA 4.5%	07-12-10	10,300	10,206	1.33
Intl Lease Fin 4.75%	07-01-09	10,015	9,926	1.29
FHLBA 5.25%	09-29-14	10,000	9,884	1.29
AT&T WIRELESS SVCS	03-01-11	8,000	8,779	1.14
FNMA 5%	07-27-15	8,675	8,551	1.11

Equity Style
Style: Blend
Size: Large-Cap

Value Measures		Rel Category
Price/Earnings	15.71	1.03
Price/Book	2.46	1.00
Price/Sales	1.22	0.89
Price/Cash Flow	4.53	0.56
Dividend Yield %	1.86	0.96

Growth Measures	%	Rel Category
Long-Term Erngs	11.65	0.99
Book Value	8.50	0.99
Sales	12.55	1.41
Cash Flow	7.09	0.72
Historical Erngs	14.09	0.79

Market Cap %			
Giant	57.4	Small	9.2
Large	16.5	Micro	2.5
Mid	14.5	Avg $mil:	36,381

Fixed-Income Style
Duration: Short-Term
Quality: High

Avg Eff Duration [1]	2.9 Yrs
Avg Eff Maturity	3.3 Yrs
Avg Credit Quality	AAA
Avg Wtd Coupon	5.84%

[1] figure provided by fund as of 10-31-06

Sector Weightings	% of Stocks	Rel DJ Mod	3 Year High Low
↻ Info	8.63	—	
▣ Software	4.96	—	5 3
▣ Hardware	2.59	—	5 2
⊍ Media	0.00	—	8 0
▪ Telecom	1.08	—	7 1
☰ Service	74.50		
▪ Health	21.20	—	24 18
▪ Consumer	18.14	—	19 5
▪ Business	13.34	—	20 12
▪ Financial	21.82	—	23 14
▫ Mfg	16.86		
▪ Goods	4.09	—	8 4
▪ Ind Mtrls	6.10	—	8 3
▪ Energy	6.67	—	7 4
▪ Utilities	0.00	—	0 0

Composition

	%
● Cash	3.9
● Stocks	71.5
● Bonds	22.7
○ Other	1.9
Foreign (% of Stock)	1.9

Morningstar's Take by Kerry O'Boyle 12-18-06

Dreyfus Premier Balanced Opportunity remains in good hands.

This all-cap balanced fund's recent slump is disappointing, but investors have reason to stick with it. Manager Tom Plumb has been a member of the management team here since 1987, and the fund's lead manager since 1992, so nothing about the investment process has changed from the one that has enabled the fund to outperform nearly 90% of its peers over the past decade. Plumb still follows what he calls a classic growth-at-a-reasonable-price approach that looks for companies trading at a discount to his determination of their enterprise value.

Since the summer of 2004, Plumb has been finding those bargains in mega-cap stocks. Blue-chip names like Microsoft, Pfizer, General Electric, and Coca-Cola dominate the top stock holdings of the portfolio. The fund's average market capitalization is now just over $36 billion, up from $11 billion in 2001.

All of this goes a long way in explaining the fund's recent performance. Despite what many consider to be bargain prices, large-cap stocks have continued to trail small- and mid-cap stocks since 2004. Plumb is sticking with his strategy, however, and in the past few months, bigger companies have begun to show some life. Should the large-cap rally continue, this fund is well poised to recapture some of its past glory.

To be sure, shareholders here have seen the risk involved with this approach. Large stakes in smaller companies, and a shifting multi-cap approach, can make the fund more volatile than more-staid moderate-allocation offerings. Plus, with 70% of assets typically devoted to stocks, the asset mix here is aggressive, as well.

Still, Plumb has proven his mettle over the long haul. We like his long-term approach--evident in the fund's modest turnover--and the way he sticks with his picks during rough spots. We think shareholders here should keep the faith.

Address:	144 Glenn Curtiss Blvd Uniondale, NY 11556-0144 800-554-4611	Minimum Purchase:	Closed
		Min Auto Inv Plan:	Closed
		Sales Fees:	No-load
Web Address:	www.dreyfus.com	Management Fee:	0.80%
Inception:	03-16-87	Actual Fees:	Mgt:0.80%
Advisor:	The Dreyfus Corporation	Expense Projections:	3Yr:$325 5Yr:$563 10Yr:$1248
Subadvisor:	Wisconsin Capital Management	Income Distrib:	Annually
NTF Plans:	Fidelity Retail-NTF		

Add: — | IRA: —
Add: —
Dist: —

M⊖RNINGSTAR® Funds 500

DWS Core Fixed Income Ins

	Ticker	Load	NAV	Yield	SEC Yield	Total Assets	Mstar Category
	MFINX	None	$10.69	4.7%	—	$1,434 mil	Intermediate-Term Bond

Governance and Management

Stewardship Grade:

Portfolio Manager(s)

Gary Bartlett leads a deep and experienced team. Each member specializes in a sector, and they include Christopher Gagnier (corporates: industrials), Tom Flaherty (corporates: banks and financials), Warren Davis (mortgage-backed and similar securities), Dan Taylor (structured securities, including commercial-mortgage and asset-backeds), Tim Vile, and Bill Lissenden. The group is backed by analysts, as well. The group left Deutsche Asset Management for Aberdeen Asset Management late last year, but it continues to manage this fund.

Strategy

The management team thinks the market is too efficient for one to predict the direction of interest rates, so it eschews interest-rate and yield-curve bets altogether. It sticks closely to the positioning of its benchmark--the Lehman Brothers Aggregate Bond Index. Instead, the fund's team focuses on uncovering cheap bonds, and thus, the fund's sector weightings often vary considerably from the index's.

Historical Profile

Return: Above Avg
Risk: Average
Rating: ★★★★ Above Avg

29	30	22	22	18	39	19	28

▼ Manager Change
▽ Partial Manager Change

Growth of $10,000
■ Investment Values of Fund
■ Investment Values of LB Aggr

Investment Style
Fixed Income
Income Rtn %Rank Cat

Performance Quartile (within Category)

1995	1996	1997	1998	1999	2000	2001	2002	2003	2004	2005	2006	History
10.81	10.52	10.71	10.72	10.03	10.51	10.81	11.01	10.95	10.97	10.75	10.69	NAV
17.93	4.49	9.44	7.92	-0.55	12.00	9.33	9.19	4.40	5.28	2.53	4.26	Total Return %
-0.54	0.86	-0.21	-0.77	0.27	0.37	0.89	-1.06	0.30	0.94	0.10	-0.07	+/-LB Aggr
-3.50	1.80	0.01	-2.22	2.33	-0.44	0.51	-3.84	-1.57	-0.02	0.70	0.45	+/-LB 5-10YR
7.24	6.51	6.70	6.22	6.06	6.98	6.45	5.73	4.25	4.61	4.37	4.73	Income Return %
10.69	-2.02	2.74	1.70	-6.61	5.02	2.88	3.46	0.15	0.67	-1.84	-0.47	Capital Return %
52	21	36	38	28	9	12	31	51	12	13	34	Total Rtn % Rank Cat
0.69	0.68	0.68	0.65	0.63	0.68	0.66	0.60	0.46	0.49	0.47	0.50	Income $
0.00	0.07	0.08	0.17	0.00	0.00	0.00	0.16	0.08	0.05	0.02	0.00	Capital Gains $
0.54	0.55	0.55	0.55	0.55	0.54	0.55	0.55	0.55	0.55	0.55	—	Expense Ratio %
6.81	6.52	6.50	6.01	6.08	6.60	6.26	5.60	4.40	4.45	4.29	—	Income Ratio %
182	176	178	122	157	116	161	152	290	190	177	—	Turnover Rate %
507	809	1,124	1,273	1,202	811	793	791	697	605	584	578	Net Assets $mil

Performance 12-31-06

	1st Qtr	2nd Qtr	3rd Qtr	4th Qtr	Total
2002	-0.07	4.01	4.20	0.80	9.19
2003	1.37	2.81	-0.38	0.45	4.40
2004	3.11	-2.22	3.26	1.06	5.28
2005	-0.27	3.00	-0.65	0.45	2.53
2006	-0.55	-0.15	3.76	1.19	4.26

Trailing	Total Return%	+/- LB Aggr	+/- LB 5-10YR	%Rank Cat	Growth of $10,000
3 Mo	1.19	-0.05	0.11	48	10,119
6 Mo	4.99	-0.10	-0.69	36	10,499
1 Yr	4.26	-0.07	0.45	34	10,426
3 Yr Avg	4.00	0.30	0.36	16	11,249
5 Yr Avg	5.09	0.03	-0.83	25	12,818
10 Yr Avg	6.33	0.09	-0.35	10	18,474
15 Yr Avg	—	—	—	—	—

Tax Analysis	Tax-Adj Rtn%	%Rank Cat	Tax-Cost Rat	%Rank Cat
3 Yr (estimated)	2.33	15	1.61	60
5 Yr (estimated)	3.23	24	1.77	62
10 Yr (estimated)	4.00	9	2.19	68

Potential Capital Gain Exposure: -1% of assets

Rating and Risk

Time Period	Load-Adj Return %	Morningstar Rtn vs Cat	Morningstar Risk vs Cat	Morningstar Risk-Adj Rating
1 Yr	4.26			
3 Yr	4.00	+Avg	+Avg	★★★★
5 Yr	5.09	+Avg	Avg	★★★★
10 Yr	6.33	+Avg	Avg	★★★★
Incept	6.89			

Other Measures	Standard Index LB Aggr	Best Fit Index LB Aggr
Alpha	0.3	0.3
Beta	1.00	1.00
R-Squared	99	99
Standard Deviation	3.24	
Mean	4.00	
Sharpe Ratio	0.25	

Morningstar's Take by Paul Herbert 12-01-06

We continue to think DWS Core Fixed Income is an attractive core bond choice.

This fund may not be a household name, but maybe it should be. The fund's managers, all of whom have been working on the fund for nearly a decade, have put up very consistent returns, with less risk than peers, over time.

Part of the fund's success owes to the managers' keen recognition of their strengths and weaknesses. They focus on adding value with individual issue selection rather than on trying to make spot-on interest-rate calls or sector moves. And unlike some peers who will spice up their portfolios with non-U.S. and lower-rated bonds, they stick to those with investment-grade ratings.

That may give the impression of a plain-vanilla fund, but there's more to see if you peel back the onion. The fund's managers seek out security mispricings and have a track record of finding them in less-well-known places. Over time, they've found that collateralized mortgage obligations (CMOs),

which are more difficult to analyze than pass-through securities, can come cheap. They've favored CMOs this year, too. Not only do the securities they prefer represent good values today, but they would also benefit from a pickup in interest-rate volatility.

As mentioned in our last write-up, the managers have had a fairly cautious stance in 2006. Because corporate bonds have looked expensive to them, they've taken a neutral stance on that area and instead favored mortgage-backed bonds. They've left some money on the table in doing so, especially as corporates have fared well during the second half of this year. But favoring certain adjustable-rate mortgage bonds, commercial mortgages, and insurance bonds has helped their cause.

A lingering regulatory issue at the DWS funds' advisor prevents us from backing this fund. Outside of that issue, we see a lot to like here.

Portfolio Analysis 09-30-06

Total Fixed-Income:294	Date of Maturity	Amount $000	Value $000	% Net Assets
US Treasury Bond 6%	02-15-26	52,846	60,463	4.32
US Treasury Note 4.25%	11-15-13	57,248	55,998	4.00
US Treasury Bond 8.125%	08-15-19	17,745	23,401	1.67
Wells Fargo Mbs 2006-Ar2	03-25-36	21,213	21,070	1.50
Bear Stearns Arm Tr 2006	02-25-36	15,416	15,128	1.08
FHLMC CMO 5%	01-15-33	13,771	13,219	0.94
OIL INS	12-29-49	12,040	12,306	0.88
FHLMC CMO 5%	09-15-33	12,670	12,095	0.86
Citigroup Mtg Ln Tr 2006	03-25-36	12,029	12,054	0.86
Wachovia Cmbs 2005-C20 C	07-15-42	12,020	11,859	0.85
Agfirst Farm Cr Bk FRN	12-15-16	10,707	11,749	0.84
Jp Morgan Com Mtg 2005-L	12-15-44	11,772	11,715	0.84
FHLMC CMO 5%	06-15-33	11,250	10,756	0.77
FNMA 5.5%	07-01-24	10,772	10,710	0.76
Hm Ln Tr 2006-Hi4 FRN	09-25-36	10,555	10,555	0.75
Cwabs FRN	10-25-36	10,345	10,455	0.75
Cwabs FRN	10-25-36	10,345	10,382	0.74
FHLMC CMO 5%	06-15-33	10,815	10,380	0.74
FNMA	04-01-36	10,423	10,288	0.73
Wells Fargo Mbs 2006-Ar1	08-25-36	10,255	10,280	0.73

Current Investment Style

Duration: Short Int Long
Quality: High Med Low

¹figure provided by fund

Avg Eff Duration¹	4.5 Yrs
Avg Eff Maturity	7.0 Yrs
Avg Credit Quality	AA
Avg Wtd Coupon	5.54%
Avg Wtd Price	100.99% of par

Coupon Range	% of Bonds	Rel Cat
0% PIK	2.1	0.3
0% to 6%	74.5	1.0
6% to 8%	19.6	0.9
8% to 10%	5.6	1.2
More than 10%	0.2	0.3

1.00=Category Average

Credit Analysis	% bonds 09-30-06		
AAA	76	BB	1
AA	2	B	0
A	5	Below B	0
BBB	13	NR/NA	3

Sector Breakdown — % of assets

US Treasuries	10
TIPS	0
US Agency	0
Mortgage Pass-Throughs	12
Mortgage CMO	41
Mortgage ARM	0
US Corporate	19
Asset-Backed	7
Convertible	0
Municipal	4
Corporate Inflation-Protected	0
Foreign Corporate	1
Foreign Govt	0

Composition			
Cash	5.2	Bonds	94.7
Stocks	0.1	Other	0.0

Special Securities	
Restricted/Illiquid Secs	6
Exotic Mortgage-Backed	0
Emerging-Markets Secs	0
Options/Futures/Warrants	No

Address:	345 Park Avenue New York, NY 10154 800-621-1048
Web Address:	www.dws-scudder.com
Inception:	09-18-92
Advisor:	Deutsche Asset Management Inc.
Subadvisor:	None
NTF Plans:	N/A

Minimum Purchase:	$1000000	Add: $0	IRA: $0
Min Auto Inv Plan:	$0	Add: —
Sales Fees:	No-load, 2.00%R
Management Fee:	0.40% mx./0.36% mn.
Actual Fees:	Mgt:0.40%	Dist:—
Expense Projections:	3Yr:$208	5Yr:$362	10Yr:$810
Income Distrib:	Monthly

E*TRAD Delphi Value Ret

	Ticker	Load	NAV	Yield	Total Assets	Mstar Category
	KDVRX	None	$18.46	0.2%	$141 mil	Mid-Cap Value

Governance and Management

Stewardship Grade: B

Portfolio Manager(s)

Scott Black has successfully run private accounts in the same way for decades. Four analysts help him evaluate the management teams and fundamentals of companies. Black is one of the largest shareholders of the fund. He is also part of the annual Barron's Roundtable and a follower of the Graham and Dodd investment philosophy.

Strategy

Stocks don't get into this fund just because they're cheap. Management doesn't distinguish stocks along "growth" or "value" lines; rather, it looks for great, growing businesses with low valuations and then holds them for a while. It looks for cheap names of any size in any industry but insists on stocks with returns on equity of more than 15%, three- and five-year revenue and earnings-growth rates that beat inflation, and clean balance sheets. Manager Scott Black also aims to keep capital gains distributions low.

Performance 12-31-06

	1st Qtr	2nd Qtr	3rd Qtr	4th Qtr	Total
2002	6.83	-5.47	-13.75	3.75	-9.64
2003	-4.87	17.03	4.83	13.60	32.58
2004	4.56	-1.39	0.92	8.13	12.52
2005	-0.29	1.63	4.41	0.81	6.66
2006	6.99	-0.32	2.44	7.70	17.65

Trailing	Total Return%	+/- S&P 500	+/- Russ MV	%Rank Cat	Growth of $10,000
3 Mo	7.70	1.00	-0.80	58	10,770
6 Mo	10.32	-2.42	-2.01	54	11,032
1 Yr	17.65	1.86	-2.57	26	11,765
3 Yr Avg	12.19	1.75	-6.58	77	14,121
5 Yr Avg	11.08	4.89	-4.80	64	16,911
10 Yr Avg	—	—	—	—	—
15 Yr Avg	—	—	—	—	—

Tax Analysis	Tax-Adj Rtn%	%Rank Cat	Tax-Cost Rat	%Rank Cat
3 Yr (estimated)	11.08	64	0.99	30
5 Yr (estimated)	10.43	43	0.59	18
10 Yr (estimated)	—	—	—	—

Potential Capital Gain Exposure: 47% of assets

Morningstar's Take by John Coumarianos 11-29-06

E*TRADE Delphi Value is better than it looks, but it's still too expensive for us.

The irrepressible Scott Black runs this fund. Black is a dyed-in-the-wool disciple of Warren Buffett. He looks for superior businesses with high returns on invested capital, and tries to snag them at cheap prices. He typically trades little, though he'll sometimes make forays into and out of cyclical stocks as long as they exhibit 15% returns on equity at the peak of their cycles. In contrast to Buffett, he won't typically concentrate his bets very much.

This style has served Black well, helping him post a cumulative return of 116% from January 2001 to October 2006, which represents nearly the life of this fund. However, it has also caused him to look mediocre versus his mid-value peers and the Russell MidCap Value Index, which have had torrid runs since 2000. Part of this underperformance is due to the fund's all-cap nature. Black lets his nose for value lead him anywhere on the market-cap scale he finds cheap, profitable businesses. (The market cap of a stock is the number of shares outstanding multiplied by the price of a share.) He usually holds more mega-cap and small-cap stocks than a pure mid-cap fund would, and the average market cap of the fund has increased to $8 billion from $5 billion over the past four years, while small-cap stocks have soared.

The increased market cap indicates that Black is finding better values among bigger names, potentially setting the fund up for a large-cap rally. Buffett's Berkshire Hathaway has long occupied the top slot in the portfolio, and Black has supplemented it with other profitable financials such as Goldman Sachs, which boasts net margins of more than 20%, and media companies such as McGraw-Hill, which boasts 14% net margins.

Overall, we think Black is a good investor, but he'd have a better chance against more-impressive go-anywhere competitors such as Mutual Shares, Third Avenue Value, and Fairholme if the fund's expenses were lower.

Address:	20 William Street, Suite 310
	Wellesley Hills MA 02481
	800-895-9936
Web Address:	www.kobren.com
Inception:	12-17-98 *
Advisor:	E*trade Asset Management, Inc.
Subadvisor:	Delphi Management Inc
NTF Plans:	Schwab OneSource

Minimum Purchase:	$2500	Add: $250	IRA: $2000
Min Auto Inv Plan:	$2500	Add: $500	
Sales Fees:	No-load, 0.25%S		
Management Fee:	0.85%, 0.15%A		
Actual Fees:	Mgt:0.85%	Dist:0.25%	
Expense Projections:	3Yr:$474	5Yr:$818	10Yr:$1791
Income Distrib:	Annually		

Historical Profile

Return	Average
Risk	Below Avg
Rating	★★★ Neutral

	35%	95%	93%	95%	93%	94%	93%	94%	93%

Investment Style
Equity
Stock %

▼ Manager Change
▽ Partial Manager Change

Growth of $10,000
— Investment Values of Fund
— Investment Values of S&P 500

20.8
16.6
13.0
10.0
6.0

Performance Quartile (within Category)

1995	1996	1997	1998	1999	2000	2001	2002	2003	2004	2005	2006	History
—	—	—	10.12	11.19	13.00	13.18	11.91	15.79	17.22	17.32	18.46	NAV
—	—	—	1.20*	11.30	13.00	1.90	-9.64	32.58	12.52	6.66	17.65	Total Return %
—	—	—	—	-9.74	26.40	13.79	12.46	3.90	1.64	1.75	1.86	+/-S&P 500
—	—	—	—	11.41	-1.88	-0.43	0.00	-5.49	-11.19	-5.99	-2.57	+/-Russ MV
—	—	—	—	0.02	0.00	0.00	0.00	0.00	0.00	0.18	0.24	Income Return %
—	—	—	—	11.28	17.30	1.90	-9.64	32.58	12.52	6.48	17.41	Capital Return %
—	—	—	—	37	65	71	32	63	95	73	26	Total Rtn % Rank Cat
—	—	—	0.00	0.00	0.00	0.00	0.00	0.00	0.00	0.03	0.04	Income $
—	—	—	0.00	0.07	0.12	0.07	0.00	0.00	0.55	1.02	1.88	Capital Gains $
—	—	—	1.75	1.75	1.71	1.64	1.63	1.64	1.58	1.57	—	Expense Ratio %
—	—	—	0.82	0.00	-0.12	-0.12	-0.13	-0.21	-0.28	0.13	—	Income Ratio %
—	—	—	—	17	45	29	23	22	31	22	—	Turnover Rate %
—	—	—	5	31	45	45	44	61	62	66	57	Net Assets $mil

Rating and Risk

Time Period	Load-Adj Return %	Morningstar Rtn vs Cat	Morningstar Risk vs Cat	Morningstar Risk-Adj Rating
1 Yr	17.65			
3 Yr	12.19	-Avg	Avg	★★
5 Yr	11.08	Avg	-Avg	★★★
10 Yr	—	—	—	
Incept	10.78			

Other Measures	Standard Index S&P 500	Best Fit Index Mstar Mid Value
Alpha	0.3	-6.0
Beta	1.21	1.07
R-Squared	75	87
Standard Deviation	9.64	
Mean	12.19	
Sharpe Ratio	0.91	

Portfolio Analysis 11-30-06

Share change since 10-06 Total Stocks:76	Sector	PE	Tot Ret%	% Assets
Berkshire Hathaway Inc.	Financial	13.2	24.89	2.94
⊕ Goldman Sachs Group, Inc	Financial	12.4	57.41	2.11
Lehman Brothers Holdings	Financial	12.2	22.75	1.91
Bear Stearns Companies,	Financial	12.5	42.07	1.83
XTO Energy, Inc.	Energy	9.0	12.16	1.73
Toyota Motor Corporation	Goods	17.9	28.38	1.65
Wells Fargo Company	Financial	14.7	16.82	1.59
Avnet, Inc.	Business	16.5	6.64	1.59
Western Digital Corporat	Hardware	10.4	9.94	1.56
Morgan Stanley	Financial	12.3	45.93	1.55
Whiting Petroleum Corpor	Energy	9.7	16.50	1.53
Seagate Technology	Hardware	23.7	34.47	1.52
Northstar Realty Finance	Financial	13.4	79.48	1.50
Arrow Electronics, Inc.	Business	12.4	-1.50	1.49
Comcast Corporation	Media			1.42
Walt Disney Company	Media	21.0	44.26	1.40
MEMC Electronic Material	Hardware	32.6	76.55	1.39
Citigroup, Inc.	Financial	13.1	19.55	1.37
News Corporation, Ltd. B	Media	22.2	34.75	1.35
Applied Materials	Hardware	19.5	3.89	1.32

Current Investment Style

Market Cap	%
Giant	17.5
Large	23.5
Mid	40.9
Small	16.0
Micro	2.1

Avg $mil: 8,658

Value Measures		Rel Category
Price/Earnings	11.78	0.79
Price/Book	1.89	0.94
Price/Sales	0.97	1.00
Price/Cash Flow	6.17	0.81
Dividend Yield %	1.69	0.94

Growth Measures	%	Rel Category
Long-Term Erngs	11.85	1.07
Book Value	12.91	1.85
Sales	15.58	2.03
Cash Flow	19.61	4.94
Historical Erngs	23.96	1.62

Profitability	%	Rel Category
Return on Equity	16.94	1.17
Return on Assets	10.61	1.44
Net Margin	15.09	1.44

Sector Weightings

Sector Weightings	% of Stocks	Rel S&P 500	3 Year High	Low
Info	16.85	0.84		
Software	0.00	0.00	0	0
Hardware	9.32	1.01	9	2
Media	7.53	1.99	18	8
Telecom	0.00	0.00	0	0
Service	54.20	1.17		
Health	1.22	0.10	2	0
Consumer	8.13	1.06	13	8
Business	9.01	2.13	9	2
Financial	35.84	1.61	37	30
Mfg	28.95	0.86		
Goods	5.55	0.65	9	5
Ind Mtrls	11.89	1.00	15	11
Energy	11.51	1.17	16	8
Utilities	0.00	0.00	0	0

Composition

- Cash 6.9
- Stocks 93.1
- Bonds 0.0
- Other 0.0

Foreign 12.2 (% of Stock)

MORNINGSTAR® Funds 500

Eaton Vance Fltg Rt A

Analyst Pick ✓

	Ticker	Load	NAV	Yield	SEC Yield	Total Assets	Mstar Category
	EVBLX	2.25%	$10.19	6.3%	6.62%	$4,956 mil	Bank Loan

Governance and Management

Stewardship Grade: B

Portfolio Manager(s)

Scott Page and Payson Swaffield have comanaged this fund since its inception in early 2001. (The A shares opened in mid-2003.) Page and Swaffield are quite experienced, having managed Eaton Vance Prime Rate Reserves (a continuously offered closed-end bank-loan fund) since 1996. They have amassed a solid long-term track record.

Strategy

Managers Payson Swaffield and Scott Page invest in senior-secured floating-rate bank loans, the majority of which earn junklike credit ratings. They favor companies with strong cash flows and positive earnings and stay away from those that rely heavily on outside capital to finance their businesses. They also place a big emphasis on diversification by spreading assets widely across issues and industries. Overall, the fund has a slightly more defensive profile than the category norm.

Historical Profile

Return	Low
Risk	Low
Rating	★ Lowest

Investment Style
Fixed Income
Income Rtn %Rank Cat

▼ Manager Change
▽ Partial Manager Change

Growth of $10,000
— Investment Values of Fund
— Investment Values of LB Aggr

Performance Quartile (within Category)

1995	1996	1997	1998	1999	2000	2001	2002	2003	2004	2005	2006	History
—	—	—	—	—	—	—	—	10.17	10.23	10.21	10.19	NAV
—	—	—	—	—	—	—	—	—	3.51	4.38	6.22	Total Return %
—	—	—	—	—	—	—	—	—	-0.83	1.95	1.89	+/-LB Aggr
—	—	—	—	—	—	—	—	—	1.66	2.94	2.00	+/-LB 1-5 YR
—	—	—	—	—	—	—	—	—	2.91	4.58	6.42	Income Return %
—	—	—	—	—	—	—	—	—	0.60	-0.20	-0.20	Capital Return %
—	—	—	—	—	—	—	—	—	87	41	45	Total Rtn % Rank Cat
—	—	—	—	—	—	—	—	0.18	0.29	0.46	0.64	Income $
—	—	—	—	—	—	—	—	0.00	0.00	0.00	0.00	Capital Gains $
—	—	—	—	—	—	—	—	—	1.09	1.05	—	Expense Ratio %
—	—	—	—	—	—	—	—	—	2.81	2.76	—	Income Ratio %
—	—	—	—	—	—	—	—	—	64	67	—	Turnover Rate %
—	—	—	—	—	—	—	—	—	387	1,179	1,852	Net Assets $mil

Performance 12-31-06

	1st Qtr	2nd Qtr	3rd Qtr	4th Qtr	Total
2002	—	—	—	—	—
2003	—	—	1.19	1.11	—*
2004	0.95	0.75	0.63	1.14	3.51
2005	1.13	0.57	1.49	1.13	4.38
2006	1.70	0.93	1.55	1.90	6.22

Trailing	Total Return%	+/- LB Aggr	+/- LB 1-5 YR	%Rank Cat	Growth of $10,000
3 Mo	1.90	0.66	0.89	49	10,190
6 Mo	3.48	-1.61	-0.06	49	10,348
1 Yr	6.22	1.89	2.00	45	10,622
3 Yr Avg	4.70	1.00	2.21	76	11,477
5 Yr Avg	—	—	—	—	—
10 Yr Avg	—	—	—	—	—
15 Yr Avg	—	—	—	—	—

Tax Analysis	Tax-Adj Rtn%	%Rank Cat	Tax-Cost Rat	%Rank Cat
3 Yr (estimated)	2.28	87	1.57	32
5 Yr (estimated)	—	—	—	—
10 Yr (estimated)	—	—	—	—

Potential Capital Gain Exposure: 0% of assets

Rating and Risk

Time Period	Load-Adj Return %	Morningstar Rtn vs Cat	Morningstar Risk vs Cat	Morningstar Risk-Adj Rating
1 Yr	3.83			
3 Yr	3.91	Low	Low	★
5 Yr	—	—	—	—
10 Yr	—	—	—	—
Incept	4.18			

Other Measures	Standard Index LB Aggr	Best Fit Index CSFB Glb HY
Alpha	1.4	1.0
Beta	-0.04	0.07
R-Squared	5	23
Standard Deviation	0.61	
Mean	4.70	
Sharpe Ratio	2.63	

Morningstar's Take by Paul Herbert 12-28-06

Look past Eaton Vance Floating Rate's 1-star Morningstar Rating.

Our star rating doesn't tell this fund's entire story. Bank loans have fared pretty well during the past few years, helped by an improving economy and higher interest rates (because loans' payouts reset at higher levels as market yields increase). With credit miscues playing such small, and decreasing, roles in this picture, funds emphasizing riskier loans have stolen the spotlight. This fund's managers don't play that game, which has hurt its relative results. The silver lining to this cloud has been the most stable performance in the group for the three-year period that ended Nov. 30, 2006, as measured by standard deviation of returns.

An emphasis on steadiness rather than on short-term victories pervades this fund's approach. Managers Scott Page and Payson Swaffield don't think you get adequately compensated over the long haul for taking the risks associated with lower-quality bets. As a result, they favor higher-quality, senior loans, because the fund has the best chance of getting repaid in full by owning them. One of the ways that Page and Swaffield try to ensure that they're avoiding iffy loans is by sticking to larger issuers with ample assets and multiple product lines. And, as deal quality has deteriorated among newer issues in recent months, they've taken smaller positions in these names. Overall, the fund is one of the most diversified offerings by name in the category.

This fund's appeal may not be very evident today. But, we think investors can take some comfort in the strong results of Page/Swaffield-led offerings such as Eaton Vance Senior Floating Rate when the leveraged loan market sank in 2001 and 2002. In a return to such an environment, the fund's relative results will likely improve.

Regardless of particular market conditions, we still like that you can bank on the fund's low costs and skilled managers.

Address:	255 State Street Boston MA 02109 800-225-6265
Web Address:	www.eatonvance.com
Inception:	05-05-03
Advisor:	Eaton Vance Management
Subadvisor:	None
NTF Plans:	DATALynx NTF, Federated Tr NTF

Minimum Purchase:	$1000	Add: $50	IRA: $50
Min Auto Inv Plan:	$0	Add: $50	
Sales Fees:	2.25%L, 1.00%R		
Management Fee:	0.57% mx./0.40% mn.		
Actual Fees:	Mgt:0.68%	Dist: —	
Expense Projections:	3Yr:$552	5Yr:$791	10Yr:$1479
Income Distrib:	Monthly		

Portfolio Analysis 10-31-06

Total Fixed-Income:489	Date of Maturity	Amount $000	Value $000	% Net Assets
Sungard Data Sys FRN	02-11-13	88,224	89,158	1.17
Charter Comm Operating,	04-28-13	81,463	82,257	1.08
Georgia Pacific Corporat	12-20-12	65,639	66,054	0.86
Metro-Goldwyn-Mayer Hold	04-08-12	64,501	63,781	0.84
NRG Energy, Inc.		56,566	56,931	0.75
Nielsen Finance Llc	08-09-13	55,950	56,217	0.74
Community Health Systems	07-05-10	47,978	48,060	0.63
Penn Natl Gaming FRN	10-03-12	47,594	47,903	0.63
Davita FRN	10-05-12	47,517	47,807	0.63
Fidelity Natl Info Solut	03-09-13	44,963	45,119	0.59
Jsg Acquisitions	12-31-14	34,500	44,442	0.58
Insight Midwest Holdings	04-06-14	42,950	43,289	0.57
Huntsman Intl FRN	08-16-12	41,461	42,487	0.56
Graphic Packaging Intl F	08-08-10	40,397	40,913	0.54
Alpha D2 Limited	12-31-07	40,356	40,406	0.53
Rh Donnelley Fin FRN	06-30-10	39,959	39,845	0.52
Iron Mtn FRN	04-02-11	39,669	39,776	0.52
Stile US Acquisition FRN	04-06-13	39,341	38,520	0.50
Cequel Communications LI	11-05-13	37,850	37,826	0.50
Ypso Holding Sa	07-28-14	30,000	37,535	0.49

Current Investment Style

Duration: Short Int Long
Quality: High Med Low

		1 figure provided by fund
Avg Eff Duration[1]	0.1 Yrs	
Avg Eff Maturity	—	
Avg Credit Quality	BB	
Avg Wtd Coupon	0.05%	
Avg Wtd Price	104.04% of par	

Coupon Range	% of Bonds	Rel Cat
0% PIK	99.3	3.0
0% to 6%	99.3	2.0
6% to 8%	0.6	0.0
8% to 10%	0.1	0.0
More than 10%	0.0	0.0

1.00=Category Average

Credit Analysis		% bonds 10-31-06	
AAA	0	BB	58
AA	0	B	26
A	0	Below B	0
BBB	2	NR/NA	14

Sector Breakdown % of assets

US Treasuries	0
TIPS	0
US Agency	0
Mortgage Pass-Throughs	0
Mortgage CMO	0
Mortgage ARM	0
US Corporate	94
Asset-Backed	0
Convertible	0
Municipal	0
Corporate Inflation-Protected	0
Foreign Corporate	1
Foreign Govt	0

Composition

Cash	4.2	Bonds	84.9
Stocks	0.8	Other	10.2

Special Securities

Restricted/Illiquid Secs	Trace
Exotic Mortgage-Backed	0
Emerging-Markets Secs	Trace
Options/Futures/Warrants	No

Eaton Vance Inc Boston A

✔ Analyst Pick

	Ticker	Load	NAV	Yield	SEC Yield	Total Assets	Mstar Category
	EVIBX	4.75%	$6.53	7.3%	5.58%	$1,833 mil	High Yield Bond

Governance and Management

Stewardship Grade: B

Portfolio Manager(s)

Michael Weilheimer has run the fund since 1996. He was joined in January 2000 by Tom Huggins, who was a trader before becoming a portfolio manager. The pair is backed by six analysts who cover several sectors each.

Strategy

Management prefers bonds from issuers that have predictable cash flows. That means the fund has historically been light on cyclical issuers such as steel and paper companies and heavy on media, telecommunications, and cable companies. Management has also historically overweighted B rated bonds. The team has shown a willingness in the past few years, however, to make notable sector and credit-quality shifts to protect the portfolio from volatility and to jump on opportunities with gusto.

Historical Profile

Return	Above Avg
Risk	Average
Rating	★★★★ Above Avg

Investment Style: Fixed Income
Income Rtn %Rank Cat

| 23 | 21 | 21 | 11 | 16 | 10 | 9 | 14 |

▼ Manager Change
▽ Partial Manager Change

Growth of $10,000
— Investment Values of Fund
— Investment Values of LB Aggr

22.6 / 19.0 / 16.0 / 13.0 / 10.0

Performance Quartile (within Category)

1995	1996	1997	1998	1999	2000	2001	2002	2003	2004	2005	2006	History
7.96	8.20	8.70	8.16	8.31	6.87	6.08	5.46	6.45	6.58	6.32	6.53	NAV
15.29	13.74	16.27	2.90	12.19	-7.62	-0.14	-0.41	29.38	10.71	3.61	11.29	Total Return %
-3.18	10.11	6.62	-5.79	13.01	-19.25	-8.58	-10.66	25.28	6.37	1.18	6.96	+/-LB Aggr
-2.10	1.32	3.64	2.32	8.91	-2.41	-5.92	-3.52	1.45	-1.25	1.35	-0.64	+/-CSFB Glb HY
11.28	10.52	9.86	9.50	10.39	10.95	12.11	10.11	10.42	8.47	7.64	7.83	Income Return %
4.01	3.22	6.41	-6.60	1.80	-18.57	-12.25	-10.52	18.96	2.24	-4.03	3.46	Capital Return %
83	32	6	25	4	59	75	46	16	31	18	21	Total Rtn % Rank Cat
0.82	0.80	0.77	0.79	0.81	0.87	0.79	0.59	0.55	0.53	0.49	0.48	Income $
0.00	0.00	0.00	0.00	0.00	0.00	0.00	0.00	0.00	0.00	0.00	0.00	Capital Gains $
1.09	1.07	1.05	1.04	1.01	1.04	1.06	1.07	1.02	1.06	1.06	—	Expense Ratio %
10.50	9.96	9.32	9.22	9.97	10.18	11.28	9.57	9.21	7.93	7.34	—	Income Ratio %
84	81	105	141	132	98	70	—	116	79	71	—	Turnover Rate %
113	154	209	248	385	638	819	832	1,212	1,326	1,192	1,384	Net Assets $mil

Performance 12-31-06

	1st Qtr	2nd Qtr	3rd Qtr	4th Qtr	Total
2002	0.76	-3.46	-2.46	4.96	-0.41
2003	6.00	9.72	3.64	7.34	29.38
2004	1.77	0.23	3.05	5.32	10.71
2005	-1.07	1.79	2.07	0.81	3.61
2006	3.30	0.92	2.86	3.77	11.29

Trailing	Total Return%	+/- LB Aggr	+/- CSFB Glb HY	%Rank Cat	Growth of $10,000
3 Mo	3.77	2.53	-0.68	59	10,377
6 Mo	6.74	1.65	-1.41	75	10,674
1 Yr	11.29	6.96	-0.64	21	11,129
3 Yr Avg	8.48	4.78	-0.14	20	12,766
5 Yr Avg	10.47	5.41	-0.60	18	16,452
10 Yr Avg	7.37	1.13	0.28	11	20,362
15 Yr Avg	9.07	2.57	0.17	7	36,777

Tax Analysis	Tax-Adj Rtn%	%Rank Cat	Tax-Cost Rat	%Rank Cat
3 Yr (estimated)	3.89	65	2.66	67
5 Yr (estimated)	6.11	36	3.01	81
10 Yr (estimated)	3.13	21	3.48	73

Potential Capital Gain Exposure: -5% of assets

Rating and Risk

Time Period	Load-Adj Return %	Morningstar Rtn vs Cat	Morningstar Risk vs Cat	Morningstar Risk-Adj Rating
1 Yr	6.00			
3 Yr	6.73	Avg	-Avg	★★★
5 Yr	9.40	+Avg	Avg	★★★★
10 Yr	6.85	+Avg	Avg	★★★★
Incept	9.20			

Other Measures	Standard Index LB Aggr	Best Fit Index CSFB Glb HY
Alpha	4.9	0.1
Beta	0.21	0.95
R-Squared	4	90
Standard Deviation	3.61	
Mean	8.48	
Sharpe Ratio	1.39	

Morningstar's Take by Lawrence Jones 12-19-06

Even when playing defense, Eaton Vance Income Fund of Boston puts up a mean offense.

This fund's experienced management team, Michael Weilheimer and Tom Huggins, have been moving to a defensive posture here, given how tight spreads (the difference in yield between higher- and lower-rated bonds) are in the high-yield market. However, rather than move assets into the higher-rated strata of the below-investment-grade universe, as many others have done, the team here has used another approach, not liking the added interest-rate risk that comes with higher-quality junk bonds. They instead have focused on purchasing bonds that are more senior in the capital structure (reside at a higher level of legal standing), have placed more emphasis on the bank loan market (currently around 15% of assets), and have moved into some shorter maturity bonds.

Even with these moves, though, performance in 2006 has been strong. And the fund's long-term results impress even more. Over the trailing 10 years, for instance, the fund has bested more than 90% of its high-yield category rivals.

These strong returns, a result of their approach, have not only been a matter of what management has purchased over the years but also about what they've avoided. The team has displayed agility in its avoidance of trouble, most notably in cutting its losses early in the telecom sector collapse of 2000-2001, but it can also effectively work through problem bonds when needed. Of course, keeping out of trouble is the best defense, and to that end management looks to buy the bonds of companies with strong fundamentals. A flexible approach helps out, too, as management can pursue opportunities widely in the high-yield market, including bank debt and convertibles.

A proven approach to high-yield investing, management experience, and its skillful execution make this fund a favorite.

Portfolio Analysis 10-31-06

Total Fixed-Income:269	Date of Maturity	Amount $000	Value $000	% Net Assets
Gsc Hldgs 8%	10-01-12	26,110	27,220	1.48
Nielsen Finance Llc	08-09-13	27,000	27,129	1.47
Intelsat 5.25%	11-01-08	27,120	26,374	1.43
Georgia Pacific Corp	12-23-13	26,000	26,365	1.43
Trump Entmt Resorts Hldg	06-01-15	24,085	23,694	1.28
Insight Comms	02-15-11	20,845	22,044	1.20
Ugs 10%	06-01-12	19,710	21,385	1.16
Universal City Dev Partn	04-01-10	19,730	21,358	1.16
3815688 Cda Inc/Canwest	09-15-12	19,247	19,559	1.06
Cco Hldgs 8.75%	11-15-13	19,005	19,433	1.05
Levi Strauss 12.25%	12-15-12	17,010	19,051	1.03
Rite Aid 144A 6.125%	12-15-08	18,590	18,218	0.99
Ford Motor Cr FRN	11-02-07	17,775	18,026	0.98
Gmac 8%	11-01-31	16,260	17,471	0.95
Orion Pwr Hldgs 12%	05-01-10	14,185	16,171	0.88
Advantage Comms 10.75%	08-15-10	14,835	16,040	0.87
Amsted Inds 144A 10.25%	10-15-11	14,725	15,903	0.86
Equistar Chemicals Lp /	05-01-11	14,675	15,776	0.86
PETROHAWK ENERGY	07-15-13	15,010	15,385	0.83
Nortek 8.5%	09-01-14	15,935	15,298	0.83

Current Investment Style

Duration: Short Int Long
Quality: High Med Low

[1] figure provided by fund

Avg Eff Duration[1]	3.3 Yrs
Avg Eff Maturity	6.3 Yrs
Avg Credit Quality	B
Avg Wtd Coupon	7.79%
Avg Wtd Price	102.75% of par

Coupon Range	% of Bonds	Rel Cat
0% PIK	14.7	2.7
0% to 8%	36.9	0.7
8% to 11%	54.6	1.2
11% to 14%	8.2	1.9
More than 14%	0.3	1.9

1.00=Category Average

Credit Analysis	% bonds 10-31-06		
AAA	9	BB	11
AA	0	B	59
A	0	Below B	15
BBB	2	NR/NA	4

Sector Breakdown

	% of assets
US Treasuries	0
TIPS	0
US Agency	0
Mortgage Pass-Throughs	0
Mortgage CMO	0
Mortgage ARM	0
US Corporate	84
Asset-Backed	0
Convertible	0
Municipal	0
Corporate Inflation-Protected	0
Foreign Corporate	5
Foreign Govt	0

Composition

Cash	10.5	Bonds	87.4
Stocks	0.7	Other	1.4

Special Securities

Restricted/Illiquid Secs	20
Exotic Mortgage-Backed	0
Emerging-Markets Secs	Trace
Options/Futures/Warrants	No

Address:	255 State Street, Boston MA 02109, 800-262-1122
Web Address:	www.eatonvance.com
Inception:	06-15-72
Advisor:	Eaton Vance Management
Subadvisor:	None
NTF Plans:	DATALynx NTF, Federated Tr NTF

Minimum Purchase:	$1000	Add: $50	IRA: $50
Min Auto Inv Plan:	$1000	Add: $50	
Sales Fees:	4.75%L, 1.00%R		
Management Fee:	0.63% mx./0.56% mn.		
Actual Fees:	Mgt:0.63%	Dist: —	
Expense Projections:	3Yr:$796	5Yr:$1032	10Yr:$1708
Income Distrib:	Monthly		

MORNINGSTAR® Funds 500

Eaton Vance Utilities A

Analyst Pick ✓

	Ticker	Load	NAV	Yield	Total Assets	Mstar Category
	EVTMX	5.75%	$13.25	2.5%	$1,377 mil	Specialty-Utilities

Governance and Management

Stewardship Grade: B

Portfolio Manager(s)

Judy Saryan took over management of the fund in March 1999. Saryan is also a comanager on Eaton Vance Tax-Managed Dividend Income and closed-end fund Eaton Vance Tax Advantaged Dividend Income. These other responsibilities require much of her time, but there is a great amount of overlap among the different funds' investable universes.

Strategy

Manager Judy Saryan has paid attention to earnings growth at times, but lately she has concentrated on companies with clean balance sheets, strong cash flow, and dividend growth. She has been more willing to devote a great percentage of the fund to foreign stocks than most rivals. Energy stocks, integrated oil concerns in particular, also play a role here.

Historical Profile
Return High
Risk Average
Rating ★★★★ Highest

												Investment Style
86%	86%	89%	96%	85%	91%	95%	96%	83%				Equity Stock %

▼ Manager Change
▽ Partial Manager Change

Growth of $10,000
— Investment Values of Fund
— Investment Values of S&P 500

Performance Quartile (within Category)

1995	1996	1997	1998	1999	2000	2001	2002	2003	2004	2005	2006	History
9.13	8.77	8.45	10.15	11.65	10.06	7.74	6.58	8.04	9.79	11.48	13.25	NAV
27.52	7.00	16.23	23.79	40.76	6.48	-18.94	-12.50	25.93	25.11	20.24	28.51	Total Return %
-10.06	-15.96	-17.13	-4.79	19.72	15.58	-7.05	9.60	-2.75	14.23	15.33	12.72	+/-S&P 500
-4.46	-2.10	-6.77	4.91	46.78	-44.28	7.33	10.88	-3.46	-5.13	-4.90	11.88	+/-DOWJNS UTIL
5.40	5.85	4.01	2.82	1.62	1.03	1.60	2.52	3.24	2.91	2.79	3.20	Income Return %
22.12	1.15	12.22	20.97	39.14	5.45	-20.54	-15.02	22.69	22.20	17.45	25.31	Capital Return %
50	70	95	34	11	59	32	7	35	36	8	31	Total Rtn % Rank Cat
0.40	0.52	0.33	0.23	0.16	0.12	0.16	0.19	0.21	0.23	0.27	0.36	Income $
0.14	0.45	1.29	0.04	2.26	2.20	0.31	0.00	0.00	0.00	0.00	1.05	Capital Gains $
1.19	1.23	1.13	1.27	1.08	1.08	1.10	1.14	1.15	1.10	1.08	—	Expense Ratio %
4.49	5.59	4.06	2.75	1.33	1.18	1.62	2.99	2.81	2.79	2.35	—	Income Ratio %
103	166	169	78	93	149	169	146	106	59	54	—	Turnover Rate %
457	399	366	409	510	492	361	296	358	489	665	1,057	Net Assets $mil

Performance 12-31-06

	1st Qtr	2nd Qtr	3rd Qtr	4th Qtr	Total
2002	0.76	-7.52	-15.71	11.40	-12.50
2003	-4.27	17.26	0.21	11.94	25.93
2004	4.30	-0.34	5.96	13.60	25.11
2005	3.12	7.24	11.78	-2.73	20.24
2006	4.79	2.78	7.05	11.46	28.51

Trailing	Total Return%	+/- S&P 500	+/- DOWJNS UTIL	%Rank Cat	Growth of $10,000
3 Mo	11.46	4.76	3.98	31	11,146
6 Mo	19.32	6.58	7.17	31	11,932
1 Yr	28.51	12.72	11.88	31	12,851
3 Yr Avg	24.57	14.13	0.70	23	19,330
5 Yr Avg	16.33	10.14	2.82	2	21,304
10 Yr Avg	14.05	5.63	2.90	1	37,235
15 Yr Avg	11.63	0.99	1.94	19	52,085

Tax Analysis	Tax-Adj Rtn%	%Rank Cat	Tax-Cost Rat	%Rank Cat
3 Yr (estimated)	20.53	32	1.32	61
5 Yr (estimated)	13.55	19	1.23	68
10 Yr (estimated)	10.79	8	2.28	100

Potential Capital Gain Exposure: 29% of assets

Rating and Risk

Time Period	Load-Adj Return %	Morningstar Rtn vs Cat	Morningstar Risk vs Cat	Morningstar Risk-Adj Rating
1 Yr	21.12			
3 Yr	22.14	+Avg	Avg	★★★★
5 Yr	14.96	+Avg	-Avg	★★★★
10 Yr	13.38	High	Avg	★★★★★
Incept	13.44			

Other Measures	Standard Index S&P 500	Best Fit Index MSCI Pac xJp
Alpha	14.6	8.5
Beta	0.67	0.55
R-Squared	31	68
Standard Deviation	8.25	
Mean	24.57	
Sharpe Ratio	2.35	

Portfolio Analysis 10-31-06

Share change since 06-06 Total Stocks:84	Sector	PE	Tot Ret%	% Assets
TXU Corporation	Utilities	12.8	11.19	2.92
⊕ AT&T, Inc.	Telecom	18.2	51.59	2.26
⊕ CMS Energy Corporation	Utilities	—	15.09	2.26
⊕ BellSouth Corporation	Telecom	—	—	2.23
⊕ Constellation Energy Gro	Utilities	17.6	22.70	2.14
⊕ NRG Energy, Inc. Trust U	Utilities	11.6	18.87	2.13
⊕ Verizon Communications	Telecom	15.9	34.88	2.08
⊕ Veolia Environnement ADR	Business	34.7	69.38	2.02
⊕ Entergy Corporation	Utilities	19.7	38.40	1.98
Mirant Corporation	Utilities	—	40.31	1.95
FirstEnergy Corporation	Utilities	16.2	27.31	1.94
⊕ International Power plc	Utilities	21.0	83.37	1.91
Telus Corporation	Telecom	28.4	13.70	1.89
Exelon Corporation	Utilities	—	19.79	1.89
Edison International	Utilities	13.0	7.02	1.76
Allegheny Energy, Inc.	Utilities	28.8	45.06	1.68
※ Duke Energy Corporation	Utilities	8.2	30.15	1.67
PG & E Corporation	Utilities	16.4	31.58	1.64
⊕ RWE	Utilities	—	—	1.60
Rogers Communications, I	Telecom	—	41.45	1.58

Current Investment Style

Value Blend Growth — Large/Mid/Small

Market Cap	%
Giant	22.4
Large	50.4
Mid	24.0
Small	3.1
Micro	0.1

Avg $mil: 17,252

Value Measures		Rel Category
Price/Earnings	16.82	1.02
Price/Book	2.32	1.09
Price/Sales	1.43	1.12
Price/Cash Flow	8.59	0.92
Dividend Yield %	2.29	0.74

Growth Measures	%	Rel Category
Long-Term Erngs	9.49	1.08
Book Value	3.66	0.83
Sales	2.63	0.38
Cash Flow	-3.95	NMF
Historical Erngs	9.68	1.11

Profitability	%	Rel Category
Return on Equity	14.33	1.10
Return on Assets	4.06	1.07
Net Margin	8.63	1.05

Industry Weightings	% of Stocks	Rel Cat
Telecom Srv	15.1	1.3
Electric Utls	61.9	1.0
Nat Gas Utls	7.9	0.8
Wireless Srv	6.2	1.5
Energy	4.3	0.5
Media	0.0	0.0
Network Eq	0.0	0.0
Water	0.6	1.0
Other	4.0	1.7

Composition

	%
● Cash	16.3
● Stocks	83.5
● Bonds	0.0
○ Other	0.3
Foreign (% of Stock)	42.9

Morningstar's Take by Katherine Yang 12-19-06

Eaton Vance Utilities' approach and execution serve investors well.

This fund stands out because of manager Judy Saryan's strategy--in particular, her taste for overseas firms. As of Sept. 30, her portfolio held a 39% stake in foreign stock, mainly in Europe. She ventures outside of the U.S. because she likes the stable regulatory environment and cheaper valuations of foreign fare. For example, she has consistently found success for over four years in Fortum, a Finnish utility company, whose stock is up 80% year-to-date as of Dec. 19. She likes the company's low costs and Europe's rising power prices. The fund's high foreign stake is more than twice the category average (16%) and is only exceeded by one rival.

Performance has been impressive under Saryan's watch. The fund has been consistently outperforming its utilities peers since Saryan became manager in March 1999, beating its category and its benchmark (the Dow Jones Utility)

by over 4 and 2 percentage points in annualized returns, respectively. The fund's foreign stake is a big reason for its success, both in the sector rally since 2003 and in utilities' struggles in the 2000-03 bear market.

In 2006, the fund's heavy telecommunications exposure also boosted returns. Giants such as Verizon, AT&T, and Vodafone Group, as well as Canadian operator Telus have been winners for the fund.

The fund's heavy foreign stake could weigh on returns at times, as could its subsector bets. But the fund has been less volatile than its typical category peer, and we're confident in the abilities of Saryan and her team. Additionally, the fund has served investors well, as investor returns have closely match total returns.

Finally, we like the fund's low 1.08% expense ratio. Investors would do well with this Analyst Pick.

Address:	255 State Street United States 800-225-6265	Minimum Purchase:	$1000	Add: $50	IRA: $1000
		Min Auto Inv Plan:	$50	Add: $50	
Web Address:	www.eatonvance.com	Sales Fees:	5.75%L, 0.25%S		
Inception:	12-18-81	Management Fee:	0.75% mx./0.44% mn.		
Advisor:	Boston Management and Research	Actual Fees:	Mgt:0.65% Dist:0.25%		
Subadvisor:	None	Expense Projections:	3Yr:$899 5Yr:$1136 10Yr:$1816		
NTF Plans:	DATALynx NTF, Federated Tr NTF	Income Distrib:	Monthly		

Eaton Vance Wld Health A

	Ticker	Load	NAV	Yield	Total Assets	Mstar Category
	ETHSX	5.75%	$11.31	0.0%	$2,115 mil	Specialty-Health

Governance and Management

Stewardship Grade: C

Portfolio Manager(s)

Sam Isaly, founder of advisor OrbiMed Advisors, has been at the helm since 1989. Sven Borho, Richard Klemm, Geoffrey Hsu, and Trevor Polischuk, who have assisted him for several years, were named comanagers on Jan. 1, 2005. The firm specializes solely in health-care investing, with an unusually strong emphasis on the pharmaceutical and biotech industries.

Strategy

Management invests in pharmaceutical and biotechnology companies from both the United States and overseas. The fund has numerous quirks: an outsized biotech bet, one of the largest foreign stakes among offerings in its category, and a greater propensity for investing in small companies. Unlike many of its peers, the fund has scant exposure to health-care service providers and medical-equipment makers. Manager Sam Isaly tends to hang on to his picks for years, giving the fund a turnover far below the group norm.

Historical Profile

Return	Average
Risk	Average
Rating	★★★ Neutral

Investment Style: Equity Stock %

83% | 78% | 90% | 90% | 86% | 93% | 95% | 98% | 95%

▼ Manager Change
▽ Partial Manager Change

Growth of $10,000
59.0
43.6
■ Investment Values of Fund
32.4
24.0 — Investment Values of S&P 500
17.0
10.0

Performance Quartile (within Category)

	1995	1996	1997	1998	1999	2000	2001	2002	2003	2004	2005	2006	History
	4.01	4.53	4.91	5.83	6.68	11.63	10.33	7.65	9.98	10.66	11.48	11.31	NAV
	61.11	18.25	10.50	23.53	23.98	81.56	-6.63	-25.94	30.46	6.81	7.69	-0.01	Total Return %
	23.53	-4.71	-22.86	-5.05	2.94	90.66	5.26	-3.84	1.78	-4.07	2.78	-15.80	+/-S&P 500
	6.37	-0.41	-26.38	-15.56	28.01	43.72	6.21	-5.13	11.03	2.26	-0.63	-6.89	+/-DJ Hlthcare
	0.00	0.00	0.00	0.00	0.00	0.00	0.00	0.00	0.00	0.00	0.00	0.00	Income Return %
	61.11	18.25	10.50	23.53	23.98	81.56	-6.63	-25.94	30.46	6.81	7.69	-0.01	Capital Return %
	13	21	80	46	82	16	30	54	49	73	66	76	Total Rtn % Rank Cat
	0.00	0.00	0.00	0.00	0.00	0.00	0.00	0.00	0.00	0.00	0.00	0.00	Income $
	0.47	0.20	0.10	0.22	0.47	0.51	0.45	0.00	0.00	0.00	0.00	0.17	Capital Gains $
	2.44	2.21	2.00	1.69	1.63	1.74	1.69	1.67	1.97	1.79	1.56	1.49	Expense Ratio %
	-1.82	-1.81	-1.82	-1.21	-1.11	-1.29	-0.89	-0.90	-1.18	-1.08	-0.70	-0.68	Income Ratio %
	45	66	14	34	41	31	24	38	27	13	13	—	Turnover Rate %
	35	57	92	97	105	592	948	757	1,119	1,298	1,440	1,207	Net Assets $mil

Performance 12-31-06

	1st Qtr	2nd Qtr	3rd Qtr	4th Qtr	Total
2002	-7.36	-15.67	-12.14	7.90	-25.94
2003	0.13	18.93	3.73	5.61	30.46
2004	3.41	0.68	-3.18	5.96	6.81
2005	-10.04	4.90	10.34	3.42	7.69
2006	-0.44	-5.95	4.19	2.49	-0.01

Trailing	Total Return%	+/- S&P 500	+/- DJ Hlthcare	%Rank Cat	Growth of $10,000
3 Mo	2.49	-4.21	0.78	45	10,249
6 Mo	6.78	-5.96	-3.89	69	10,678
1 Yr	-0.01	-15.80	-6.89	76	9,999
3 Yr Avg	4.78	-5.66	-1.80	82	11,504
5 Yr Avg	2.13	-4.06	-0.61	65	11,111
10 Yr Avg	12.29	3.87	2.64	12	31,872
15 Yr Avg	14.23	3.59	4.21	12	73,570

Tax Analysis	Tax-Adj Rtn%	%Rank Cat	Tax-Cost Rat	%Rank Cat
3 Yr (estimated)	2.65	92	0.08	7
5 Yr (estimated)	0.89	74	0.04	3
10 Yr (estimated)	11.08	12	0.49	8

Potential Capital Gain Exposure: 23% of assets

Rating and Risk

Time Period	Load-Adj Return %	Morningstar Rtn vs Cat	Morningstar Risk vs Cat	Morningstar Risk-Adj Rating
1 Yr	-5.76			
3 Yr	2.73	Low	Avg	★
5 Yr	0.93	-Avg	Avg	★★
10 Yr	11.63	+Avg	Avg	★★★★
Incept	14.62			

Other Measures	Standard Index S&P 500	Best Fit Index DJ Hlthcare
Alpha	-3.8	-1.5
Beta	0.82	0.98
R-Squared	30	62
Standard Deviation	10.35	
Mean	4.78	
Sharpe Ratio	0.19	

Portfolio Analysis 10-31-06

Share change since 08-06 Total Stocks:30	Sector	PE	Tot Ret%	% Assets
Novartis	Health	—	—	7.83
Amgen, Inc.	Health	29.1	-13.38	7.04
Genentech, Inc.	Health	48.7	-12.29	6.96
Genzyme Corporation	Health	50.8	-13.00	5.64
Astellas Pharma	Health	—	—	5.33
MedImmune, Inc.	Health	—	-7.57	5.21
Wyeth	Health	17.2	12.88	4.80
Schering-Plough Corporat	Health	36.6	14.63	4.57
Takeda Chemical Industri	Health	—	—	4.51
Vertex Pharmaceuticals	Health	—	35.24	4.10
Gen-Probe, Inc.	Health	46.1	7.34	4.00
Chugai Pharmaceutical	Health	—	—	3.96
Millennium Pharmaceutica	Health	—	12.37	3.91
Pfizer Inc.	Health	15.2	15.22	3.66
Eli Lilly & Company	Health	17.3	-5.16	2.71
Cephalon, Inc.	Health	28.6	8.76	2.44
Biomarin Pharmaceutical,	Health	—	52.04	2.18
OSI Pharmaceuticals, Inc	Health	—	24.75	2.15
Affymetrix, Inc.	Health	72.6	-51.71	2.05
Ligand Pharmaceuticals,	Health	—	-1.79	1.95

Current Investment Style

Value Blnd Growth — Large Mid Small

Market Cap	%
Giant	45.3
Large	16.6
Mid	23.1
Small	14.2
Micro	0.9
Avg $mil:	15,936

Value Measures		Rel Category
Price/Earnings	20.34	0.90
Price/Book	3.92	1.09
Price/Sales	4.75	1.79
Price/Cash Flow	18.20	1.13
Dividend Yield %	0.80	0.95

Growth Measures	%	Rel Category
Long-Term Erngs	13.29	0.91
Book Value	2.53	0.30
Sales	14.62	1.23
Cash Flow	15.84	1.42
Historical Erngs	14.58	0.81

Profitability	%	Rel Category
Return on Equity	9.24	0.77
Return on Assets	0.63	0.16
Net Margin	8.20	0.75

Industry Weightings	% of Stocks	Rel Cat
Biotech	66.5	2.0
Drugs	24.5	0.8
Mgd Care	0.0	0.0
Hospitals	0.0	0.0
Other HC Srv	0.0	0.0
Diagnostics	0.1	0.1
Equipment	3.4	0.3
Good/Srv	5.5	1.5
Other	0.0	0.0

Composition

	%
● Cash	5.4
● Stocks	94.6
● Bonds	0.0
● Other	0.0
Foreign (% of Stock)	23.2

Morningstar's Take by Christopher Davis 12-21-06

Eaton Vance Worldwide Health Sciences hasn't impressed in a while, but we're sticking with it.

No doubt about it, this offering has delivered disappointing results in recent years. The fund's idiosyncratic portfolio, devoted almost exclusively to pharmaceutical and biotech stocks, means it didn't have any exposure to surging managed-care stocks, which stoked the results of many rivals. Had much of the rest of the portfolio been comprised of long-suffering large-cap drug stocks, the source of the fund's underperformance would be clearer. Biotech stocks, though, have historically made up the bulk of its holdings. The fund's biotech-heavy portfolio has been a liability this year, but it should have been a boon in 2003's buoyant market. The industry also rose in 2004 and 2005, though not uniformly. And unfortunately, lead manager Sam Isaly's preference for upstart biotech stocks hasn't panned out as holdings such as NPS Pharmaceuticals suffered big losses.

Given those troubles, some shareholders might worry Isaly and his team have lost their touch. We don't think so. The fund's highly concentrated, offbeat portfolio has often led to stretches of underperformance. Indeed, in the 210 rolling three-year periods since the fund's July 1986 launch, the fund has lagged the health-care category average in 94.

So why do we remain confident in the fund's prospects? Isaly has more than 30 years of experience investing in health care and has been at the helm of this offering for more than two decades. The fund's OrbiMed advisor drug and biotech focus is unique, and the resources the firm devotes to up-and-comers is unrivaled by few of its peers. Moreover, the fund has proved its worth over the long haul, as its fine 10-year record demonstrates.

Isaly's unorthodox approach will try investors' patience at times. But for long-term investors that can wait out the lean times, we continue to regard this fund as a worthwhile investment.

Address:	255 State Street, Boston MA 02109, 800-225-6265
Web Address:	www.eatonvance.com
Inception:	07-26-85
Advisor:	Orbimed Advisors, LLC
Subadvisor:	Orbimed Advisers, Inc.
NTF Plans:	DATALynx NTF, Federated Tr NTF

Minimum Purchase:	$1000	Add: $50	IRA: $50
Min Auto Inv Plan:	$50	Add: $50	
Sales Fees:	5.75%L, 0.25%S, 1.00%R		
Management Fee:	1.26%		
Actual Fees:	Mgt:1.02%	Dist:0.25%	
Expense Projections:	3Yr:$1309	5Yr:$1374	10Yr:$2325
Income Distrib:	Annually		

Morningstar® Funds 500

Excelsior Val & Restruct

	Ticker	Load	NAV	Yield	Total Assets	Mstar Category
	UMBIX	None	$52.54	0.9%	$7,798 mil	Large Value

Governance and Management

Stewardship Grade:

Portfolio Manager(s)

Seasoned. Stock-pickers don't come much more talented than David Williams, who has managed the fund since its 1992 inception. Although he is supported by a pair of portfolio managers (Timothy Evnin and John McDermott, who also manage Excelsior Mid Cap Value & Restructuring) and is backed by U.S. Trust's analyst bench, Williams is the source of most of the fund's investment ideas.

Strategy

Manager David Williams looks for companies that he thinks can improve their bottom lines through reorganizations, consolidations, management turnover, or acquisitions. He isn't afraid to make significant sector bets, and the fund tends to hold some out-of-favor growth companies. He also buys smaller companies than many of his rivals, so the fund's median market cap is a fraction of the category average.

Historical Profile

Return	High
Risk	High
Rating	★★★★ Above Avg

Investment Style: Equity, Stock %

95% 95% 97% 99% 97% 95% 95% 96% 98%

▼ Manager Change
▽ Partial Manager Change

Growth of $10,000
— Investment Values of Fund
— Investment Values of S&P 500

63.2 / 46.4 / 33.8 / 24.0 / 17.0 / 10.0

Performance Quartile (within Category)

1995	1996	1997	1998	1999	2000	2001	2002	2003	2004	2005	2006	History
13.20	15.87	20.82	22.71	32.14	33.82	32.06	24.46	35.86	42.43	46.18	52.54	NAV
38.81	25.05	33.58	10.32	41.98	7.21	-4.96	-23.32	47.78	19.36	9.96	14.88	Total Return %
1.23	2.09	0.22	-18.26	20.94	16.31	6.93	-1.22	19.10	8.48	5.05	-0.91	+/-S&P 500
0.45	3.41	-1.60	-5.31	34.63	0.20	0.63	-7.80	17.75	2.87	2.91	-7.37	+/-Russ 1000 VI
0.98	0.96	0.59	0.55	0.38	1.85	0.24	0.42	0.94	0.94	1.06	1.04	Income Return %
37.83	24.09	32.99	9.77	41.60	5.36	-5.20	-23.74	46.84	18.42	8.90	13.84	Capital Return %
5	13	6	58	1	62	58	84	1	4	12	89	Total Rtn % Rank Cat
0.09	0.12	0.09	0.11	0.09	0.59	0.08	0.13	0.23	0.34	0.45	0.48	Income $
0.24	0.47	0.27	0.14	0.00	0.00	0.00	0.00	0.00	0.00	0.00	0.00	Capital Gains $
0.98	0.91	0.91	0.89	0.93	0.90	1.05	0.94	0.99	0.99	1.07	1.05	Expense Ratio %
0.83	0.88	0.90	0.54	0.59	0.25	-0.54	0.27	0.65	0.78	0.87	1.18	Income Ratio %
82	56	62	30	43	13	15	3	16	4	8	12	Turnover Rate %
58	113	230	597	943	1,731	2,221	1,682	2,827	4,360	5,284	7,447	Net Assets $mil

Performance 12-31-06

	1st Qtr	2nd Qtr	3rd Qtr	4th Qtr	Total
2002	1.78	-12.65	-19.41	7.03	-23.32
2003	-3.27	22.18	4.45	19.71	47.78
2004	4.77	0.77	0.85	12.10	19.36
2005	-2.43	4.91	6.89	0.49	9.96
2006	6.89	-1.35	0.50	8.41	14.88

Trailing	Total Return%	+/- S&P 500	+/- Russ 1000 VI	%Rank Cat	Growth of $10,000
3 Mo	8.41	1.71	0.41	9	10,841
6 Mo	8.95	-3.79	-5.77	96	10,895
1 Yr	14.88	-0.91	-7.37	89	11,488
3 Yr Avg	14.67	4.23	-0.42	12	15,078
5 Yr Avg	11.31	5.12	0.45	7	17,087
10 Yr Avg	13.80	5.38	2.80	1	36,427
15 Yr Avg	—	—	—		

Tax Analysis	Tax-Adj Rtn%	%Rank Cat	Tax-Cost Rat	%Rank Cat
3 Yr (estimated)	14.29	6	0.33	12
5 Yr (estimated)	10.98	5	0.30	16
10 Yr (estimated)	13.43	1	0.33	2

Potential Capital Gain Exposure: 31% of assets

Rating and Risk

Time Period	Load-Adj Return %	Morningstar Rtn vs Cat	Morningstar Risk vs Cat	Morningstar Risk-Adj Rating
1 Yr	14.88			
3 Yr	14.67	+Avg	High	★★★★
5 Yr	11.31	High	High	★★★★
10 Yr	13.80	High	High	★★★★★
Incept	17.07			

Other Measures	Standard Index S&P 500	Best Fit Index S&P Mid 400
Alpha	1.8	1.8
Beta	1.33	0.96
R-Squared	75	89
Standard Deviation	10.51	
Mean	14.67	
Sharpe Ratio	1.05	

Morningstar's Take by Arijit Dutta 12-11-06

Excelsior Value & Restructuring's troubles this year don't deter us.

This fund's multiyear winning streak looks to be in jeopardy in 2006. The fund suffered a 13% loss during a sharp market correction in May and June (easily among the worst losses in the crowded large-value category) over macroeconomic fears, and hasn't quite made up the ground since. The portfolio has significant exposure to sectors and stocks that are especially sensitive to economic slowdowns. For example, the portfolio's 19% stake in energy stocks is almost twice the category average. Also, housing and construction-related names such as Black & Decker and Centex are among the top holdings here.

Veteran lead manager David Williams is not giving in to panic, however. As the portfolio's 12% turnover indicates (the category average is 48%), Williams buys positions after considering the stocks' long-term picture, and sticks with his picks through market turbulence. Although oil prices are

well off their mid-year highs, he thinks energy companies will still generate lavish cash flows even at still-lower prices. Moreover, at current stock valuations, Williams thinks it's cheaper to buy the stocks rather than oil or coal directly. This means mid-size producers such as Consol Energy will remain attractive takeover targets for major energy companies, which would support Williams' "consolidation" theme in this industry. Similarly, in the case of Centex, Williams thinks the stock is trading at cheaper than the assets on the homebuilder's books.

It's true that a deep economic slowdown will undermine Williams' theses. His high-conviction style also leads to massive sector bets, so the toll on the fund can be heavy. Still, Williams has shown an ability to get in at attractive prices, which has led to spectacular upside in the long run. For investors who share Williams' patience, this is a bold but rewarding choice.

Portfolio Analysis 10-31-06

Share change since 09-06 Total Stocks:97

	Sector	PE	Tot Ret%	% Assets
America Movil SA ADR	Telecom	27.7	55.53	3.18
Black & Decker Corporati	Ind Mtrls	12.2	-6.37	2.94
⊕ Harris Corporation	Hardware	24.8	7.57	2.30
Petroleo Brasileiro S.A.	Energy	10.4	51.12	2.27
ConocoPhillips	Energy	6.5	26.53	2.23
Devon Energy Corporation	Energy	9.2	8.06	2.21
Morgan Stanley	Financial	12.3	45.93	2.17
Consol Energy, Inc.	Energy	15.3	-0.68	2.15
Centex Corporation	Consumer	7.2	-21.06	2.12
Union Pacific Corporatio	Business	17.4	15.87	2.02
ACE, Ltd.	Financial	10.6	15.41	1.93
Lehman Brothers Holdings	Financial	12.2	22.75	1.63
Citigroup, Inc.	Financial	13.1	19.55	1.62
Carolina Group	Financial	—	52.24	1.60
Freddie Mac	Financial	23.3	7.06	1.49
United Technologies	Ind Mtrls	17.8	13.65	1.46
Loews Corporation	Financial	14.9	32.04	1.42
Dean Foods Company	Goods	22.0	12.27	1.41
Noble Energy, Inc.	Energy	11.7	22.48	1.41
Empresa Brasileira de Ae	Ind Mtrls	—	8.23	1.40

Current Investment Style

Value Blnd Growth — Large/Mid/Small

Market Cap	%
Giant	20.1
Large	33.2
Mid	33.1
Small	11.8
Micro	1.7

Avg $mil: 12,228

Value Measures		Rel Category
Price/Earnings	13.11	0.95
Price/Book	1.96	0.88
Price/Sales	0.97	0.75
Price/Cash Flow	3.23	0.48
Dividend Yield %	1.85	0.79

Growth Measures	%	Rel Category
Long-Term Erngs	10.83	1.04
Book Value	5.97	0.75
Sales	9.10	1.01
Cash Flow	8.88	1.47
Historical Erngs	23.90	1.48

Profitability	%	Rel Category
Return on Equity	19.66	1.10
Return on Assets	8.76	0.89
Net Margin	12.64	0.98

Sector Weightings

	% of Stocks	Rel S&P 500	3 Year High	Low
Info	12.45	0.62		
Software	0.00	0.00	1	0
Hardware	5.03	0.54	10	5
Media	2.89	0.76	7	4
Telecom	4.53	1.29	5	3
Service	43.08	0.93		
Health	4.89	0.41	5	4
Consumer	5.33	0.70	8	5
Business	6.10	1.44	8	6
Financial	26.76	1.20	27	23
Mfg	44.46	1.32		
Goods	7.98	0.93	14	8
Ind Mtrls	15.74	1.32	16	11
Energy	19.41	1.98	23	8
Utilities	1.33	0.38	4	1

Composition

	%
Cash	0.3
Stocks	98.4
Bonds	0.0
Other	1.3
Foreign (% of Stock)	15.1

Address:	73 Tremont Street, Boston MA 02108, 800-446-1012
Web Address:	www.excelsiorfunds.com
Inception:	12-31-92
Advisor:	US Trust New York Asset Mgt Division
Subadvisor:	None
NTF Plans:	Fidelity Retail-NTF, Schwab OneSource

Minimum Purchase:	$500	Add: $50	IRA: $250
Min Auto Inv Plan:	$50	Add: $50	
Sales Fees:	No-load, 2.00%R		
Management Fee:	0.60%		
Actual Fees:	Mgt:0.60%	Dist: —	
Expense Projections:	3Yr:$334	5Yr:$579	10Yr:$1283
Income Distrib:	Quarterly		

Fairholme

Analyst Pick ✓	**Ticker** FAIRX	**Load** None	**NAV** $28.99	**Yield** 0.8%	**Total Assets** $3,697 mil	**Mstar Category** Mid-Cap Blend	

Governance and Management

Stewardship Grade: A

Portfolio Manager(s)

Bruce Berkowitz started this fund in December 1999 as an outgrowth of his separate-accounts practice. Previously, he worked for Salomon Smith Barney and Lehman Brothers. Larry Pitkowsky was named comanager in early 2002. Keith Trauner is the third member of the investment team.

Strategy

Managers Bruce Berkowitz, Larry Pitkowsky, and Keith Trauner have adopted the principles of legendary value investor Benjamin Graham. Their primary objective is to buy good businesses run by great managers, but they've also had a penchant for buying turnaround stories when they see a big opportunity. Such "special situations" are limited to 25% of the portfolio. The fund's big cash stake preserves value and is a tactical source of funds for new investment opportunities.

Historical Profile

Return	High
Risk	Low
Rating	★★★★ Highest

Investment Style: Equity, Stock %

87% 77% 70% 80% 87% 67% 75%

▼ Manager Change
▽ Partial Manager Change

Growth of $10,000

— Investment Values of Fund
— Investment Values of S&P 500

29.0 / 21.0 / 15.0 / 10.0 / 5.0

Performance Quartile (within Category)

1995	1996	1997	1998	1999	2000	2001	2002	2003	2004	2005	2006	History
—	—	—	—	10.21	14.68	15.47	15.09	18.70	22.77	25.19	28.99	NAV
—	—	—	—	2.20*	46.54	6.18	-1.58	23.96	24.93	13.74	16.72	Total Return %
—	—	—	—	—	55.64	18.07	20.52	-4.72	14.05	8.83	0.93	+/-S&P 500
—	—	—	—	—	29.03	6.79	12.95	-11.66	8.45	1.18	6.40	+/-S&P Mid 400
—	—	—	—	—	0.36	0.20	0.20	0.00	0.32	1.01	0.97	Income Return %
—	—	—	—	—	46.18	5.98	-1.78	23.96	24.61	12.73	15.75	Capital Return %
—	—	—	—	—	1	33	2	95	5	12	21	Total Rtn % Rank Cat
—	—	—	—	0.00	0.04	0.03	0.03	0.00	0.06	0.23	0.24	Income $
—	—	—	—	0.00	0.25	0.09	0.10	0.01	0.53	0.48	0.17	Capital Gains $
—	—	—	—	—	1.00	1.00	1.00	1.00	1.00	1.00	—	Expense Ratio %
—	—	—	—	—	0.46	0.24	0.05	-0.13	0.05	1.55	—	Income Ratio %
—	—	—	—	—	39	29	48	13	23	37	—	Turnover Rate %
—	—	—	—	—	17	26	41	69	235	1,578	3,697	Net Assets $mil

Performance 12-31-06

	1st Qtr	2nd Qtr	3rd Qtr	4th Qtr	Total
2002	4.07	-4.72	-4.95	4.43	-1.58
2003	-6.03	13.82	2.91	12.62	23.96
2004	9.63	-3.71	5.72	11.94	24.93
2005	1.89	3.97	3.45	3.79	13.74
2006	6.35	2.43	-0.95	8.17	16.72

Trailing	Total Return%	+/- S&P 500	+/- S&P Mid 400	%Rank Cat	Growth of $10,000
3 Mo	8.17	1.47	1.18	36	10,817
6 Mo	7.14	-5.60	1.31	65	10,714
1 Yr	16.72	0.93	6.40	21	11,672
3 Yr Avg	18.37	7.93	5.28	5	16,585
5 Yr Avg	15.14	8.95	4.25	5	20,236
10 Yr Avg	—	—	—	—	—
15 Yr Avg	—	—	—	—	—

Tax Analysis	Tax-Adj Rtn%	%Rank Cat	Tax-Cost Rat	%Rank Cat
3 Yr (estimated)	17.75	5	0.52	24
5 Yr (estimated)	14.73	5	0.36	23
10 Yr (estimated)	—	—	—	—

Potential Capital Gain Exposure: 13% of assets

Rating and Risk

Time Period	Load-Adj Return %	Morningstar Rtn vs Cat	Morningstar Risk vs Cat	Morningstar Risk-Adj Rating
1 Yr	16.72			
3 Yr	18.37	High	Low	★★★★★
5 Yr	15.14	High	Low	★★★★★
10 Yr	—	—	—	—
Incept	18.14			

Other Measures	Standard Index S&P 500	Best Fit Index DJ Mod
Alpha	9.3	6.8
Beta	0.68	1.01
R-Squared	34	54
Standard Deviation	7.97	
Mean	18.37	
Sharpe Ratio	1.76	

Portfolio Analysis 08-31-06

Share change since 05-06 Total Stocks:19

	Sector	PE	Tot Ret%	% Assets
⊕ Berkshire Hathaway A	Financial			14.30
⊕ Canadian Natural Resourc	Energy	29.1	7.84	12.19
⊕ EchoStar Communications	Media	29.5	39.92	9.60
⊕ Penn West Energy Trust T	Energy			6.66
⊕ Mohawk Industries, Inc.	Goods	13.0	-13.93	4.74
Sears Holdings Corporati	Consumer	19.5	45.36	3.59
⊕ Leucadia National Corpor	Ind Mtrls	55.4	19.92	3.47
※ Ensign Resource Service	Energy			3.27
IDT	Telecom			2.66
※ Phelps Dodge Corp.	Ind Mtrls	12.7	76.29	2.04
Berkshire Hathaway Inc.	Financial	13.2	24.89	1.92
⊕ Duke Energy Corporation	Utilities	8.2	30.15	1.91
⊖ Annaly Capital Managemen	Financial		32.85	1.23
USA Mobility, Inc.	Telecom	15.1	-1.96	1.00
⊕ Marsh & McLennan Compani	Financial	29.0	-1.16	0.90
IDT Corporation	Telecom		17.04	0.60
JZ Equity Partners	Financial			0.42
HomeFed Corporation	Financial	14.6	-0.74	0.22
White Mountains Insuranc	Financial	15.2	5.27	0.12
Daily Journal Corporatio	Media	24.0	-6.24	0.06

Current Investment Style

Value Blnd Growth — Large Mid Small

Market Cap	%
Giant	26.2
Large	45.8
Mid	23.8
Small	3.4
Micro	0.9

Avg $mil: 11,951

Value Measures		Rel Category
Price/Earnings	9.05	0.56
Price/Book	2.00	0.88
Price/Sales	1.27	1.13
Price/Cash Flow	5.74	0.68
Dividend Yield %	0.58	0.45

Growth Measures	%	Rel Category
Long-Term Erngs	15.29	1.21
Book Value	13.58	1.63
Sales	22.07	2.48
Cash Flow	33.31	3.93
Historical Erngs	41.21	2.30

Profitability	%	Rel Category
Return on Equity	14.93	0.94
Return on Assets	7.50	0.93
Net Margin	14.51	1.33

Sector Weightings

	% of Stocks	Rel S&P 500	3 Year High	Low
⟳ Info	19.62	0.98		
🖥 Software	0.00	0.00	0	0
💻 Hardware	0.00	0.00	0	0
🎙 Media	13.62	3.59	18	3
📶 Telecom	6.00	1.71	30	6
☁ Service	32.01	0.69		
🏥 Health	0.00	0.00	3	0
🏢 Consumer	5.06	0.66	12	0
🏢 Business	0.00	0.00	0	0
💲 Financial	26.95	1.21	52	27
🏭 Mfg	48.36	1.43		
🔧 Goods	6.69	0.78	7	1
⚙ Ind Mtrls	7.77	0.65	24	8
💡 Energy	31.20	3.18	31	5
🔌 Utilities	2.70	0.77	3	0

Composition

	%
● Cash	24.5
● Stocks	75.4
● Bonds	0.0
● Other	0.0
Foreign (% of Stock)	29.9

Morningstar's Take by Todd Trubey 11-17-06

Fairholme Fund has been refuting the efficient market hypothesis since 1999.

The efficient market hypothesis says financial markets reflect all known information and thus are very tough to beat over time. Its corollary is broad diversification. This fund challenges that hypothesis with a condensed all-cap portfolio of 21 stocks and 62% of its assets in the top 10 stocks. Lead manager Bruce Berkowitz looks for stocks where simple math says it's hard to lose money and easy to make it. So far he's been right: The fund's 17.9% annualized return from its Dec. 29, 1999, start through Nov. 16, 2006, tops all but three mid-blend rivals and crushes the S&P 500 Index.

The fund's primary strategy owes largely to Warren Buffett, who buys firms with durable cash flows, brawny balance sheets, and great owner-managers at a big discount to intrinsic value. Berkowitz and crew say that most investors chiefly prize the horse (or firm), but they value the jockey. In judging corporate managers, they seek a long

paper trail proving the creation of shareholder wealth, solid stewardship in tough times, and a habit of setting expectations low and beating them. They think great managers can drive super results even in commodity-type industries. So most Buffettologists avoid the energy sector, but this fund devotes 22% of assets to three such firms.

The fund has two other buckets of investments. First is the fund's 24% cash slice--its largest holding. The cash preserves value and provides liquidity, enabling the managers to pounce when adversity strikes fear in others. The other is a special-situations strategy that aims at firms where quality is lacking but the value proposition is immense. Recently the fund purchased Phelps Dodge, which the managers say just escaped a potentially rotten merger with Inco but has a great balance sheet, huge cash flows, and deep pessimism built into the share price.

This Analyst Pick features good old-fashioned investment in the purest sense.

Address:	51 JFK Parkway	Minimum Purchase:	$2500	Add: $1000 IRA: $1000
	Short Hills NJ 07078	Min Auto Inv Plan:	$2500	Add: $100
	866-202-2263	Sales Fees:	No-load, 2.00%R	
Web Address:	www.fairholmefunds.com	Management Fee:	1.00%, 0.50%A	
Inception:	12-29-99*	Actual Fees:	Mgt:1.00%	Dist: —
Advisor:	Fairholme Capital Management, L.L.C.	Expense Projections:	3Yr:$318	5Yr:$552 10Yr:$1225
Subadvisor:	None	Income Distrib:	Annually	
NTF Plans:	N/A			

Morningstar® Funds 500

FAM Value

	Ticker	Load	NAV	Yield	Total Assets	Mstar Category
	FAMVX	None	$49.65	0.6%	$1,043 mil	Mid-Cap Blend

Governance and Management

Stewardship Grade: A

Portfolio Manager(s)

Thomas Putnam has managed this fund since its inception in January 1987. John Fox joined him in May 2000. In addition to this fund, Putnam also manages FAM Equity-Income. Both have ownership stakes in this offering and its parent, Fenimore Asset Management.

Strategy

The managers look for fundamentally strong companies that are trading at a discount. Good growth records, high margins, and strong balance sheets are important fundamental factors. The fund prefers to invest in industry-leading firms with strong management teams.

Historical Profile

Return	Average
Risk	Low
Rating	★★★ Neutral

Investment Style: Equity, Stock %

86% 88% 88% 91% 92% 91% 80% 85% 87%

▼ Manager Change
▽ Partial Manager Change

Growth of $10,000
— Investment Values of Fund
— Investment Values of S&P 500

31.0 / 24.0 / 17.0 / 10.0

Performance Quartile (within Category)

	1995	1996	1997	1998	1999	2000	2001	2002	2003	2004	2005	2006	History
	24.58	26.53	35.76	34.44	31.35	32.70	36.17	33.69	41.15	46.65	48.00	49.65	NAV
	19.73	11.22	39.06	6.19	-4.84	19.21	15.09	-5.33	24.98	16.86	5.56	8.73	Total Return %
	-17.85	-11.74	5.70	-22.39	-25.88	28.31	26.98	16.77	-3.70	5.98	0.65	-7.06	+/-S&P 500
	-11.20	-8.03	6.81	-12.93	-19.56	1.70	15.70	9.20	-10.64	0.38	-7.00	-1.59	+/-S&P Mid 400
	0.99	0.72	0.28	0.57	0.85	1.16	0.53	0.31	0.28	0.18	0.80	0.65	Income Return %
	18.74	10.50	38.78	5.62	-5.69	18.05	14.56	-5.64	24.70	16.68	4.76	8.08	Capital Return %
	85	85	7	64	94	17	16	8	94	42	80	87	Total Rtn % Rank Cat
	0.21	0.18	0.08	0.20	0.29	0.36	0.17	0.11	0.09	0.07	0.37	0.31	Income $
	0.40	0.63	1.06	3.26	1.09	4.03	1.30	0.44	0.87	1.36	0.87	2.24	Capital Gains $
	1.25	1.27	1.24	1.19	1.23	1.26	1.21	1.21	1.24	1.20	1.18	—	Expense Ratio %
	0.92	0.64	0.25	0.57	0.86	1.08	0.56	0.30	0.26	0.20	0.82	—	Income Ratio %
	10	12	17	16	9	10	18	9	10	14	—	—	Turnover Rate %
	266	254	332	376	373	367	501	470	580	920	1,111	1,043	Net Assets $mil

Performance 12-31-06

	1st Qtr	2nd Qtr	3rd Qtr	4th Qtr	Total
2002	6.75	-5.00	-10.14	3.89	-5.33
2003	-3.15	13.18	2.49	11.25	24.98
2004	6.05	0.55	0.59	8.95	16.86
2005	-1.03	2.77	0.95	2.80	5.56
2006	6.65	-6.17	2.06	6.46	8.73

Trailing	Total Return%	+/- S&P 500	+/- S&P Mid 400	%Rank Cat	Growth of $10,000
3 Mo	6.46	-0.24	-0.53	76	10,646
6 Mo	8.66	-4.08	2.83	53	10,866
1 Yr	8.73	-7.06	-1.59	87	10,873
3 Yr Avg	10.28	-0.16	-2.81	82	13,412
5 Yr Avg	9.68	3.49	-1.21	60	15,872
10 Yr Avg	11.83	3.41	-1.64	50	30,590
15 Yr Avg	11.97	1.33	-1.66	70	54,516

Tax Analysis	Tax-Adj Rtn%	%Rank Cat	Tax-Cost Rat	%Rank Cat
3 Yr (estimated)	9.53	69	0.68	29
5 Yr (estimated)	9.06	53	0.57	34
10 Yr (estimated)	10.70	32	1.01	16

Potential Capital Gain Exposure: 36% of assets

Rating and Risk

Time Period	Load-Adj Return %	Morningstar Rtn vs Cat	Morningstar Risk vs Cat	Morningstar Risk-Adj Rating
1 Yr	8.73			
3 Yr	10.28	-Avg	Low	★★
5 Yr	9.68	Avg	Low	★★★
10 Yr	11.83	Avg	Low	★★★★
Incept	12.36			

Other Measures	Standard Index S&P 500	Best Fit Index Mstar Mid Core
Alpha	0.6	0.4
Beta	0.90	0.59
R-Squared	65	73
Standard Deviation	7.63	
Mean	10.28	
Sharpe Ratio	0.90	

Morningstar's Take by Karen Wallace 11-30-06

We think FAM Value is better than it looks.

You won't see this fund topping any recent leaders' lists; its three-year return falls into the bottom quartile of the mid-blend category. But we don't think management has lost its touch. Managers John Fox and Thomas Putnam are using the same process they always have: They look for firms with strong cash flow and healthy balance sheets. They don't typically invest in companies that take on a lot of debt, and they prefer strong management teams that the managers believe can allocate capital well. Fox and Putnam wait patiently for such stocks to become cheap, which often means buying when a firm is under some sort of cloud. Then they hold on to the stocks for a long time--until their fundamentals have improved. Rather than looking for a quick 20% pop, they want to double their money in about five years, which translates to about a 15% annual growth rate.

Many of the stocks that meet the managers' criteria come from the financials and industrials sectors--those two sectors alone currently comprise more than half of the fund's assets. On the flipside, the fund doesn't typically hold much in the technology or energy sectors, because those firms usually don't meet the managers' criteria for steady growth and reasonable valuations. Those preferences have held the fund back relative to peers in recent years.

Overall, however, we think the steady process is solid. While it may rarely be a category-killer, it has the potential to deliver compelling absolute returns with low volatility. It has risen 12% per year and has one of the lowest standard deviations in the category over the past 10 years.

Prospective investors here should keep in mind that because this fund looks different from its mid-blend peers, it won't move in lock-step with the category. They should also evaluate their portfolio's overall exposure to the fund's favorite sectors before adding this fund to their investment mix.

Address:	118 N Grand St Cobleskill NY 12043 800-932-3271
Web Address:	www.famfunds.com
Inception:	01-02-87
Advisor:	Fenimore Asset Management, Inc.
Subadvisor:	None
NTF Plans:	Fidelity Retail-NTF, Schwab OneSource

Minimum Purchase:	$500	Add: $50	IRA: $100
Min Auto Inv Plan:	$500	Add: $50	
Sales Fees:	No-load		
Management Fee:	1.00% mx./0.95% mn.		
Actual Fees:	Mgt:1.00%	Dist: —	
Expense Projections:	3Yr:$375	5Yr:$649	10Yr:$1432
Income Distrib:	Annually		

Portfolio Analysis 09-30-06

Share change since 06-06 Total Stocks:47	Sector	PE	Tot Ret%	% Assets
Brown & Brown, Inc.	Financial	22.9	-6.98	5.65
⊕ White Mountains Insuranc	Financial	15.2	5.27	5.29
Berkshire Hathaway A	Financial	—	—	3.72
Federated Investors, Inc	Financial	19.0	-6.94	3.49
Kaydon Corporation	Ind Mtrls	19.1	25.23	2.84
International Speedway C	Goods	16.8	6.73	2.53
Markel Corporation	Financial	12.2	51.43	2.50
Liz Claiborne, Inc.	Goods	17.9	22.05	2.47
⊕ CDW Corporation	Business	20.4	23.33	2.44
Vulcan Materials Company	Ind Mtrls	19.8	35.13	2.36
⊕ John Wiley & Sons, Inc.	Media	20.8	-0.40	2.34
⊕ Bed Bath & Beyond, Inc.	Consumer	20.1	5.39	2.31
Ross Stores, Inc.	Consumer	20.6	2.28	2.30
⊕ Zebra Technologies Corpo	Hardware	30.4	-18.81	2.24
Allied Capital Corporati	Financial	8.5	20.62	2.19
Idex Corporation	Ind Mtrls	19.6	16.76	2.18
Meredith Corporation	Media	18.9	9.02	2.17
⊕ Forest City Enterprises,	Financial	—	54.80	2.14
Yum Brands, Inc.	Consumer	20.4	26.76	2.13
Protective Life Corporat	Financial	13.4	10.54	2.12

Current Investment Style

Value Blnd Growth — Large Mid Small

Market Cap	%
Giant	1.3
Large	7.4
Mid	75.2
Small	15.5
Micro	0.7

Avg $mil: 3,498

Value Measures		Rel Category
Price/Earnings	17.46	1.08
Price/Book	2.75	1.22
Price/Sales	1.64	1.46
Price/Cash Flow	12.43	1.47
Dividend Yield %	1.67	1.28

Growth Measures	%	Rel Category
Long-Term Erngs	12.42	0.98
Book Value	10.61	1.28
Sales	10.84	1.22
Cash Flow	6.06	0.72
Historical Erngs	16.60	0.93

Profitability	%	Rel Category
Return on Equity	19.54	1.23
Return on Assets	12.69	1.58
Net Margin	14.76	1.36

Sector Weightings	% of Stocks	Rel S&P 500	3 Year High Low	
⊙ Info	9.88	0.49		
Software	1.33	0.39	2	0
Hardware	2.70	0.29	6	1
Media	5.82	1.54	7	3
Telecom	0.03	0.01	3	0
⊂ Service	63.18	1.37		
Health	5.64	0.47	11	4
Consumer	11.70	1.53	14	11
Business	6.92	1.64	7	0
Financial	38.92	1.75	39	37
⬠ Mfg	26.95	0.80		
Goods	9.73	1.14	12	9
Ind Mtrls	17.22	1.44	20	15
Energy	0.00	0.00	0	0
Utilities	0.00	0.00	0	0

Composition

	%
● Cash	13.2
● Stocks	86.8
● Bonds	0.0
○ Other	0.0
Foreign (% of Stock)	0.0

FBR Small Cap

	Ticker	Load	NAV	Yield	Total Assets	Mstar Category
	FBRVX	None	$53.85	0.0%	$1,049 mil	Mid-Cap Growth

Governance and Management

Stewardship Grade: C

Portfolio Manager(s)

Charles T. Akre has managed this fund since its year-end 1996 inception. Once an employee of the FBR Funds, Akre now subadvises this fund through his private asset management firm, Akre Capital Management. In addition to this fund, Akre also runs some separate accounts and a hedge fund.

Strategy

Manager Charles Akre seeks small-cap companies with sustainable returns on equity of 20% and higher. Company executives must manage their businesses with the shareholder in mind by reinvesting capital and avoiding dilutive options packages. Akre also keeps an eye on valuation, but he'll pay up for companies with higher-quality earnings and healthier balance sheets. He holds fewer than 40 stocks, makes big bets on just a few sectors, and has allowed cash to build at times to about one third of assets.

Historical Profile

Return: High
Risk: Average
Rating: ★★★★★ Highest

		93%	100%	100%	61%	62%	77%	66%	98%	93%

Investment Style
Equity
Stock %

▼ Manager Change
▽ Partial Manager Change

Growth of $10,000
— Investment Values of Fund
— Investment Values of S&P 500

43.6
32.4
24.0
17.0
10.0

Performance Quartile (within Category)

1995	1996	1997	1998	1999	2000	2001	2002	2003	2004	2005	2006	History
—	12.00	16.82	15.75	18.84	16.50	21.71	22.28	32.45	41.81	42.06	53.85	NAV
—	0.00*	44.30	-3.52	19.62	-8.79	32.63	2.63	45.77	30.67	2.31	28.49	Total Return %
—	—	10.94	-32.10	-1.42	0.31	44.52	24.73	17.09	19.79	-2.60	12.70	+/-S&P 500
—	—	21.76	-21.38	-31.67	2.96	52.78	30.04	3.06	15.19	-9.79	17.83	+/-Russ MG
—	—	0.00	0.00	0.00	0.00	0.00	0.00	0.00	0.00	0.00	0.00	Income Return %
—	—	44.30	-3.52	19.62	-8.79	32.63	2.63	45.77	30.67	2.31	28.49	Capital Return %
—	—	2	95	84	62	1	1	11	1	93	1	Total Rtn % Rank Cat
—	0.00	0.00	0.00	0.00	0.00	0.00	0.00	0.00	0.00	0.00	0.00	Income $
—	0.00	0.49	0.43	0.00	0.65	0.17	0.00	0.03	0.57	0.72	0.18	Capital Gains $
—	—	1.65	1.65	1.92	1.95	1.95	1.94	1.60	1.59	1.50	—	Expense Ratio %
—	—	-0.79	-0.81	-1.46	-1.71	-1.34	-1.39	-0.75	-0.75	-0.56	—	Income Ratio %
—	—	—	78	24	3	26	13	16	19	20	—	Turnover Rate %
—	—	10	16	15	9	27	51	348	1,012	810	1,049	Net Assets $mil

Performance 12-31-06

	1st Qtr	2nd Qtr	3rd Qtr	4th Qtr	Total
2002	6.68	-8.03	-6.62	12.02	2.63
2003	2.56	23.15	6.16	8.72	45.77
2004	8.01	1.61	2.61	16.04	30.67
2005	-3.40	6.70	-2.60	1.91	2.31
2006	15.67	-3.76	3.26	11.78	28.49

Trailing	Total Return%	+/- S&P 500	+/- Russ MG	%Rank Cat	Growth of $10,000
3 Mo	11.78	5.08	4.83	4	11,178
6 Mo	15.42	2.68	7.52	1	11,542
1 Yr	28.49	12.70	17.83	1	12,849
3 Yr Avg	19.76	9.32	7.03	1	17,177
5 Yr Avg	20.78	14.59	12.56	1	25,702
10 Yr Avg	17.87	9.45	9.25	1	51,765
15 Yr Avg	—	—	—	—	—

Tax Analysis	Tax-Adj Rtn%	%Rank Cat	Tax-Cost Rat	%Rank Cat
3 Yr (estimated)	19.49	1	0.23	13
5 Yr (estimated)	20.61	1	0.14	11
10 Yr (estimated)	17.44	1	0.36	9

Potential Capital Gain Exposure: 46% of assets

Rating and Risk

Time Period	Load-Adj Return %	Morningstar Rtn vs Cat	Morningstar Risk vs Cat	Morningstar Risk-Adj Rating
1 Yr	28.49			
3 Yr	19.76	High	Avg	★★★★★
5 Yr	20.78	High	Avg	★★★★★
10 Yr	17.87	High	-Avg	★★★★★
Incept	17.87			

Other Measures	Standard Index S&P 500	Best Fit Index DJ Wilshire 4500
Alpha	6.4	5.5
Beta	1.33	0.90
R-Squared	56	68
Standard Deviation	12.11	
Mean	19.76	
Sharpe Ratio	1.29	

Morningstar's Take by Laura Pavlenko Lutton 12-27-06

This fund is reopening, but we'd be aware of its risks.

FBR Small Cap, which has been closed to new investors since October 2004, will accept new accounts as of Jan. 2, 2007. According to FBR, this fund's parent, manager Chuck Akre thinks there are enough investment opportunities available for this offering to warrant reopening. Indeed, when the fund closed, it sported a hefty cash stake and a surging asset base. Akre has since reduced the fund's cash to about 7% of assets, and the fund's assets have stabilized at around $1 billion.

The fund appears capable of managing more assets, but it's worth noting that a potential conflict exists between this fund's current shareholders and its advisor. While shareholders may not be well-served by a flood of new cash, the offering is probably the best opportunity for asset growth among the eight FBR funds. The firm's quirky lineup of funds includes mostly sector offerings, and this relatively diversified fund boasts a peer-beating long-term record and the highest five-star Morningstar rating.

New investors here also should be mindful of this fund's many usual attributes. The fund has always bought small cap stocks--most have market caps of less than $3 billion at the time of purchase--that have good growth prospects and consistently high returns on equity. But as this low-turnover offering has matured, so have its holdings, and the fund's portfolio has resided in the mid-cap row of Morningstar's style box since 2003. Thus, Morningstar recently reassigned the fund to the mid-cap growth category.

The offering is also notable for its concentration. Its 30-odd-stock portfolio sticks mainly to just four sectors. This focused approach has led to some lumpy short-term returns.

In the end, Akre has demonstrated some promising stock-picking skills, and we like the disciplined investment process here. This fund is worth a look.

Address:	1001 19th St North United States 888-888-0025	Minimum Purchase:	$2000	Add: $0	IRA: $1000
		Min Auto Inv Plan:	$500	Add: $50
		Sales Fees:	No-load, 0.22%S, 1.00%R
Web Address:	www.fbrfunds.com/	Management Fee:	0.90%
Inception:	12-31-96*	Actual Fees:	Mgt:0.90%	Dist:0.22%
Advisor:	FBR Fund Advisers Inc.	Expense Projections:	3Yr:$449	5Yr:$779	10Yr:$1710
Subadvisor:	Akre Capital Management, LLC	Income Distrib:	Annually
NTF Plans:	Fidelity Retail-NTF, Schwab OneSource		

Portfolio Analysis 11-30-06

Share change since 10-06 Total Stocks:37

	Sector	PE	Tot Ret%	% Assets
American Tower Corporati	Telecom	—	37.57	15.80
Penn National Gaming	Goods	21.8	26.31	15.40
Markel Corporation	Financial	12.2	51.43	11.62
CarMax, Inc.	Consumer	32.2	93.75	7.03
Pinnacle Entertainment I	Consumer	21.2	34.12	4.86
99 Cents Only Stores	Consumer	—	16.35	3.87
Bally Technologies, Inc.	Consumer	—	43.47	3.19
American Woodmark Corpor	Goods	15.9	69.69	2.89
Simpson Manufacturing	Ind Mtrls	13.5	-12.13	2.84
Monarch Casino & Resort,	Consumer	21.6	5.66	2.37
AES Corporation	Utilities	33.4	39.23	2.37
Global Imaging Systems,	Ind Mtrls	16.4	26.77	2.35
AmeriCredit Corporation	Financial	11.2	-1.80	2.08
Toll Brothers, Inc.	Consumer	6.2	-6.96	1.96
Markwest Hydrocarbon, In	Energy	53.8	150.27	1.70
Hilb Rogal & Hobbs Compa	Financial	17.5	10.67	1.66
Station Casinos Inc.	Consumer	38.6	22.46	1.62
Penn Virginia Corporatio	Energy	13.3	22.81	1.62
D.R. Horton Incorporated	Consumer	6.5	-24.41	1.53
O'Reilly Automotive, Inc	Consumer	20.4	0.16	1.15

Current Investment Style

Value Blnd Growth — Large Mid Small

Market Cap	%
Giant	0.0
Large	19.7
Mid	46.4
Small	26.3
Micro	7.5

Avg $mil: 3,082

Value Measures		Rel Category
Price/Earnings	21.93	1.07
Price/Book	2.41	0.75
Price/Sales	1.28	0.73
Price/Cash Flow	10.89	0.96
Dividend Yield %	0.22	0.35

Growth Measures	%	Rel Category
Long-Term Erngs	15.15	0.93
Book Value	18.68	1.47
Sales	16.20	1.62
Cash Flow	7.02	0.38
Historical Erngs	11.51	0.46

Profitability	%	Rel Category
Return on Equity	15.44	0.86
Return on Assets	7.71	0.82
Net Margin	5.10	0.44

Sector Weightings	% of Stocks	Rel S&P 500	3 Year High	Low
↻ Info	17.21	0.86		
🖥 Software	0.18	0.05	0	0
💻 Hardware	0.00	0.00	0	0
🎙 Media	0.00	0.00	1	0
📱 Telecom	17.03	4.85	19	7
☞ Service	50.55	1.09		
🏥 Health	0.53	0.04	1	0
🏪 Consumer	31.36	4.10	32	24
🏢 Business	1.17	0.28	1	0
💲 Financial	17.49	0.79	35	17
🏭 Mfg	32.24	0.95		
🔧 Goods	20.51	2.40	25	13
⚙ Ind Mtrls	5.59	0.47	7	5
🔥 Energy	3.58	0.37	6	2
💡 Utilities	2.56	0.73	4	2

Composition

		%
●	Cash	6.7
●	Stocks	92.8
●	Bonds	0.0
●	Other	0.5
	Foreign	0.0
	(% of Stock)	

Morningstar® Funds 500

Fidelity

	Ticker	Load	NAV	Yield	Total Assets	Mstar Category
	FFIDX	None	$35.84	0.9%	$7,679 mil	Large Blend

© 2007 Morningstar, Inc. All rights reserved. The information herein is not represented or warranted to be accurate, correct, complete or timely. Past performance is no guarantee of future results. Download your free reports at http://www.morningstar.com/goto/2007Funds500.

Governance and Management

Stewardship Grade: B

Portfolio Manager(s)

John Avery has run this fund since February 2002. He managed Fidelity Advisor Balanced between early 1998 and early 2002, producing subpar results. He did a good job in a shorter stint at Fidelity Advisor Growth & Income, however.

Strategy

Manager John Avery likes to buy firms with management teams that have sensible strategies but trade at a discount to their industry peers. He will also consider poorly managed companies but only if they possess a catalyst and have sufficiently valuable assets to justify their price. He has recently tilted the fund toward economically sensitive fare, so it has often hewed closely to the S&P 500 Index on his watch. But he typically makes few significant sector bets against the benchmark.

Performance 12-31-06

	1st Qtr	2nd Qtr	3rd Qtr	4th Qtr	Total
2002	-1.42	-11.83	-17.00	7.76	-22.25
2003	-2.10	12.65	2.49	12.60	27.26
2004	1.03	1.91	-2.50	7.43	7.84
2005	-1.54	1.40	3.67	3.88	7.52
2006	4.97	-2.34	4.75	5.86	13.67

Trailing	Total Return%	+/- S&P 500	+/- Russ 1000	%Rank Cat	Growth of $10,000
3 Mo	5.86	-0.84	-1.09	78	10,586
6 Mo	10.89	-1.85	-1.47	63	11,089
1 Yr	13.67	-2.12	-1.79	60	11,367
3 Yr Avg	9.64	-0.80	-1.34	59	13,180
5 Yr Avg	5.45	-0.74	-1.37	59	13,039
10 Yr Avg	8.28	-0.14	-0.36	32	22,156
15 Yr Avg	10.78	0.14	-0.02	28	46,443

Tax Analysis	Tax-Adj Rtn%	%Rank Cat	Tax-Cost Rat	%Rank Cat
3 Yr (estimated)	9.23	46	0.37	17
5 Yr (estimated)	5.08	49	0.35	23
10 Yr (estimated)	7.07	37	1.12	51

Potential Capital Gain Exposure: 13% of assets

Morningstar's Take by Greg Carlson 12-28-06

Despite a cheap price tag and an experienced skipper, Fidelity Fund still isn't compelling.

This large-blend fund has a couple of key points in its favor. First, it's run by the experienced John Avery, who's been at the helm for nearly five years, and previously managed Fidelity Advisor Growth & Income and the equity portfolio of Fidelity Advisor Balanced for a combined four years. Furthermore, this fund's 0.56% expense ratio makes it the cheapest of Fidelity's actively managed stock funds and gives it a substantial leg up on many of its numerous rivals.

Yet despite its positive attributes, the fund hasn't delivered the goods on Avery's watch. The fund hasn't especially stood out in either rallies or declines during his tenure. He tends to keep the fund's sector weights closely in line with those of the S&P 500 Index, which the fund has lagged under Avery, and attempts to beat it through stock selection. To his credit, after diverging little from the index for much of his first three years here,

Avery has since made more subsector bets and bought more firms that aren't constituents of the index, such as Swiss consumer goods maker Nestle and electronics maker Amphenol.

While those two picks have been winners, a broad tilt toward faster-growing, pricier companies within sectors has yielded only mixed results. Emphasizing energy service firms like Valero Energy over staid integrated oil giants hurt badly in 2006's third quarter when the commodity's price fell. Stock selection in information technology stocks also held the fund back versus the index in the third quarter of 2006. For the year to date through Dec. 27, the fund returned 14.3% and ranked near the middle of the large-blend pack.

Finally, it's worth noting that a recent filing reveals that Avery's stake in the fund is still substantially less than we would like to see, particularly given his experience and the fund's core mandate. We'd look elsewhere.

Address:	82 Devonshire St Boston MA 02109 800-544-9797
Web Address:	www.fidelity.com
Inception:	04-30-30
Advisor:	Fidelity Management & Research (FMR)
Subadvisor:	Multiple Subadvisors
NTF Plans:	Fidelity Retail-NTF, CommonWealth NTF

Minimum Purchase:	$2500	Add: $250	IRA: $200
Min Auto Inv Plan:	$2500	Add: $100	
Sales Fees:	No-load		
Management Fee:	0.37%		
Actual Fees:	Mgt:0.36%	Dist: —	
Expense Projections:	3Yr:$189	5Yr:$329	10Yr:$738
Income Distrib:	Quarterly		

Historical Profile

Return	Average
Risk	Average
Rating	★★★ Neutral

Investment Style: Equity, Stock %

90% | 93% | 94% | 89% | 93% | 99% | 98% | 99% | 100%

▼ Manager Change
▽ Partial Manager Change

Growth of $10,000
— Investment Values of Fund
— Investment Values of S&P 500

Performance Quartile (within Category)

1995	1996	1997	1998	1999	2000	2001	2002	2003	2004	2005	2006	History
22.61	24.70	29.81	36.69	42.61	32.77	28.88	22.26	28.08	29.88	31.82	35.84	NAV
32.85	19.82	32.06	31.00	24.21	-10.97	-11.22	-22.25	27.26	7.84	7.52	13.67	Total Return %
-4.73	-3.14	-1.30	2.42	3.17	-1.87	0.67	-0.15	-1.42	-3.04	-2.12		+/-S&P 500
-4.92	-2.63	-0.79	3.98	3.30	-3.18	1.23	-0.60	-2.63	-3.56	1.25	-1.79	+/-Russ 1000
2.32	1.70	1.32	1.03	0.82	0.57	0.64	0.73	0.99	1.39	0.97	0.98	Income Return %
30.53	18.12	30.74	29.97	23.39	-11.54	-11.86	-22.98	26.27	6.45	6.55	12.69	Capital Return %
60	67	34	8	24	87	44	52	55	81	28	60	Total Rtn % Rank Cat
0.42	0.37	0.32	0.30	0.29	0.23	0.21	0.21	0.22	0.39	0.29	0.31	Income $
1.40	1.82	2.35	1.81	2.21	5.20	0.00	0.00	0.00	0.00	0.00		Capital Gains $
0.64	0.60	0.59	0.56	0.55	0.56	0.51	0.53	0.61	0.59	0.57	0.56	Expense Ratio %
2.18	1.71	1.34	1.01	0.87	0.57	0.55	0.82	0.93	0.89	1.52	0.87	Income Ratio %
157	150	107	65	71	113	167	155	32	53	74	72	Turnover Rate %
3,214	4,451	6,530	10,563	16,114	15,070	12,452	8,696	10,388	10,812	9,602	7,679	Net Assets $mil

Rating and Risk

Time Period	Load-Adj Return %	Morningstar Rtn vs Cat	Morningstar Risk vs Cat	Morningstar Risk-Adj Rating
1 Yr	13.67			
3 Yr	9.64	Avg	Avg	★★★
5 Yr	5.45	Avg	-Avg	★★★
10 Yr	8.28	Avg	+Avg	★★★
Incept	10.45			

Other Measures	Standard Index S&P 500	Best Fit Index Russ 1000
Alpha	-0.5	-0.7
Beta	0.96	0.93
R-Squared	89	89
Standard Deviation	7.06	
Mean	9.64	
Sharpe Ratio	0.90	

Portfolio Analysis 09-30-06

Share change since 06-06 Total Stocks:131	Sector	PE	Tot Ret%	% Assets
⊕ Bank of America Corporat	Financial	12.4	20.68	3.07
McGraw-Hill Companies, I	Media	28.5	33.44	2.88
Merrill Lynch & Company,	Financial	14.2	39.28	2.86
⊖ Federated Department Sto	Consumer	20.8	16.54	2.72
American Express Company	Financial	20.9	19.09	2.52
Google, Inc.	Business	61.5	11.00	2.26
Honeywell International,	Ind Mtrls	18.6	24.14	2.21
⊖ Staples, Inc.	Consumer	19.6	18.58	2.11
⊕ Monsanto Company	Ind Mtrls	39.8	36.78	2.08
⊕ Wells Fargo Company	Financial	14.7	16.82	2.05
⊖ Johnson & Johnson	Health	17.5	12.45	2.02
⊕ ExxonMobil Corporation	Energy	11.1	39.07	1.96
⊖ Roche Holding	Health	—		1.93
⊖ PepsiCo, Inc.	Goods	21.5	7.86	1.88
⊖ Altria Group, Inc.	Goods	16.3	19.87	1.84
⊖ American International G	Financial	17.0	6.05	1.80
Becton, Dickinson and Co	Health	23.9	18.34	1.73
⊕ Verizon Communications	Telecom	15.9	34.88	1.52
⊖ Qualcomm, Inc.	Hardware	26.6	-11.32	1.50
⊖ Boeing Company	Ind Mtrls	41.2	28.38	1.49

Current Investment Style

Value Blnd Growth — Large Mid Small

Market Cap	%
Giant	52.9
Large	31.6
Mid	14.2
Small	1.0
Micro	0.3
Avg $mil:	41,968

Value Measures		Rel Category
Price/Earnings	17.54	1.14
Price/Book	3.01	1.18
Price/Sales	1.77	1.26
Price/Cash Flow	10.85	1.29
Dividend Yield %	1.56	0.89

Growth Measures	%	Rel Category
Long-Term Erngs	12.25	1.04
Book Value	11.38	1.26
Sales	9.51	0.98
Cash Flow	14.55	1.41
Historical Erngs	20.29	1.10

Profitability	%	Rel Category
Return on Equity	20.54	1.06
Return on Assets	11.50	1.11
Net Margin	13.84	1.03

Sector Weightings	% of Stocks	Rel S&P 500	3 Year High	Low
⟳ Info	21.79	1.09		
🖥 Software	2.17	0.63	4	1
🖳 Hardware	13.14	1.42	13	8
🎙 Media	3.50	0.92	8	3
📶 Telecom	2.98	0.85	5	1
⊄ Service	47.14	1.02		
🏥 Health	12.29	1.02	15	11
🛒 Consumer	7.89	1.03	10	5
📊 Business	3.25	0.77	3	1
💲 Financial	23.71	1.06	24	16
🏭 Mfg	31.08	0.92		
🛠 Goods	9.33	1.09	11	9
⚙ Ind Mtrls	13.94	1.17	22	14
🔋 Energy	7.05	0.72	9	5
🔌 Utilities	0.76	0.22	1	1

Composition

● Cash		0.3
● Stocks		99.6
● Bonds		0.0
● Other		0.1
Foreign (% of Stock)		12.5

Fidelity Adv Small Cap T

	Ticker	Load	NAV	Yield	Total Assets	Mstar Category
	FSCTX	3.50%	$22.14	0.0%	$3,375 mil	Small Growth

Governance and Management

Stewardship Grade: B

Portfolio Manager(s)

Jamie Harmon took over this fund in October 2005. Prior to assuming control here, he generated solid returns at Fidelity Small Cap Retirement from 2000 through 2005 and Fidelity Small Cap Independence from 2001 through 2005. Harmon has long been part of Fidelity's small-cap research team.

Strategy

Manager Jamie Harmon buys a little of every kind of small-cap stock, using a style that he calls aggressive value. That may mean betting on turnarounds, making plays on cheap assets, or buying companies that are trading at discounts to his estimate of their discounted future free cash flows. He also looks for opportunities to trade in and out of a sector to make a quick profit.

Performance 12-31-06

	1st Qtr	2nd Qtr	3rd Qtr	4th Qtr	Total
2002	1.11	-8.19	-18.79	5.60	-20.39
2003	-5.72	21.47	6.52	14.07	39.15
2004	6.87	3.24	-3.95	16.56	23.52
2005	-3.98	5.04	7.30	-0.91	7.24
2006	7.10	-2.30	-0.96	5.82	9.67

Trailing	Total Return%	+/- S&P 500	+/- Russ 2000 Gr	%Rank Cat	Growth of $10,000
3 Mo	5.82	-0.88	-2.95	83	10,582
6 Mo	4.81	-7.93	-2.05	55	10,481
1 Yr	9.67	-6.12	-3.68	54	10,967
3 Yr Avg	13.26	2.82	2.75	18	14,529
5 Yr Avg	9.98	3.79	3.05	18	16,090
10 Yr Avg	—	—	—	—	—
15 Yr Avg	—	—	—	—	—

Tax Analysis	Tax-Adj Rtn%	%Rank Cat	Tax-Cost Rat	%Rank Cat
3 Yr (estimated)	10.48	25	1.29	50
5 Yr (estimated)	8.36	23	0.77	44
10 Yr (estimated)	—	—	—	—

Potential Capital Gain Exposure: 11% of assets

Morningstar's Take by John Coumarianos 12-28-06

We like Fidelity Advisor Small Cap's new manager, but he is running a bulging portfolio.

Jamie Harmon took over this fund for Harry Lange in the fall of 2005, after running Fidelity Small Cap Independence and Fidelity Small Cap Retirement from the spring of 2001, where he outpaced Lange with a tamer portfolio.

Harmon's growth-at-a-reasonable-price style causes his portfolios to straddle the line between small blend and small growth, inviting comparisons to different indexes and peer groups. For his four and one half years on Small Cap Independence, Harmon posted a cumulative return of 52.7%, exactly matching the performance of Morningstar's small-blend category average and smashing growth benchmarks over that time frame. Harmon deserves kudos for keeping up with the small-blend average during a brutal stretch for most growth-leaning strategies such as his.

Harmon is a bottom-up stock-picker, who seeks businesses with good earnings growth prospects trading at reasonable P/E ratios. That fairly expansive approach allows him to invest in untraditional growth areas, as shown in the fund's recent 11% energy stake. Given that exploration and production firms are working increasingly hard, he finds firms that service them very attractive. That's why Universal Compression, which rents compressors to natural-gas firms, is a top holding. Its industry has consolidated over the years, so the firm is getting better prices and has plenty of international opportunities, in Harmon's view.

Harmon wields a large asset base here, but is reasonably conscious of keeping the fund in the small-cap range. Although that will be harder to do for a fund that already sports a $1.7 billion average market cap in a family that doesn't have the most stellar record for shuttering funds on time, ultimately, we like Harmon's experience and endorse this fund for small- and mid-cap exposure.

Address:	82 Devonshire St
	Boston MA 02109
	877-208-0098
Web Address:	www.advisor.fidelity.com
Inception:	09-09-98*
Advisor:	Fidelity Management & Research (FMR)
Subadvisor:	Multiple Subadvisors
NTF Plans:	DATALynx NTF, Federated Tr NTF

Minimum Purchase:	$2500	Add: $100	IRA: $500
Min Auto Inv Plan:	$100	Add: $100	
Sales Fees:	3.50%L, 0.50%S		
Management Fee:	0.72%		
Actual Fees:	Mgt:0.72%	Dist:0.50%	
Expense Projections:	3Yr:$819	5Yr:$1160	10Yr:$2120
Income Distrib:	Annually		

Historical Profile

Return: Above Avg
Risk: Below Avg
Rating: ★★★★ Above Avg

Investment Style: Equity / Stock %

87% 92% 90% 92% 92% 90% 99% 91%

▼ Manager Change
▽ Partial Manager Change

Growth of $10,000
— Investment Values of Fund
— Investment Values of S&P 500

26.8 / 22.8 / 18.0 / 14.0 / 10.0

Performance Quartile (within Category)

	1995	1996	1997	1998	1999	2000	2001	2002	2003	2004	2005	2006	History
NAV	—	—	—	13.88	22.80	18.73	18.00	14.33	19.94	24.63	24.56	22.14	
Total Return %	—	—	—	38.80*	68.46	-17.55	-3.90	-20.39	39.15	23.52	7.24	9.67	
+/-S&P 500	—	—	—		47.42	-8.45	7.99	1.71	10.47	12.64	2.33	-6.12	
+/-Russ 2000 Gr	—	—	—		25.37	4.88	5.33	9.87	-9.39	9.21	3.09	-3.68	
Income Return %	—	—	—		0.00	0.00	0.00	0.00	0.00	0.00	0.00	0.00	
Capital Return %	—	—	—		68.46	-17.55	-3.90	-20.39	39.15	23.52	7.24	9.67	
Total Rtn % Rank Cat	—	—	—		37	85	36	20	69	6	38	54	
Income $	—	—	—	0.00	0.00	0.00	0.00	0.00	0.00	0.00	0.00	0.00	
Capital Gains $	—	—	—	0.00	0.51	0.08	0.00	0.00	0.00	0.00	1.86	4.62	
Expense Ratio %	—	—	—		1.93	1.56	1.53	1.57	1.61	1.59	1.57	—	
Income Ratio %	—	—	—		-0.63	-0.77	-0.80	-0.69	-1.04	-1.23	-1.04	—	
Turnover Rate %	—	—	—		204	62	64	84	40	47	36	—	
Net Assets $mil	—	—	—	100	603	668	669	577	890	1,312	1,525		

Rating and Risk

Time Period	Load-Adj Return %	Morningstar Rtn vs Cat	Morningstar Risk vs Cat	Morningstar Risk-Adj Rating
1 Yr	5.83			
3 Yr	11.92	+Avg	Low	★★★★
5 Yr	9.20	+Avg	-Avg	★★★★
10 Yr	—			
Incept	13.56			

Other Measures	Standard Index S&P 500	Best Fit Index DJ Wilshire 4500
Alpha	-0.9	-2.0
Beta	1.57	1.06
R-Squared	74	88
Standard Deviation	12.50	
Mean	13.26	
Sharpe Ratio	0.80	

Portfolio Analysis 08-31-06

Share change since 05-06 Total Stocks:121

	Sector	PE	Tot Ret%	% Assets
⊕ Alliant Techsystems, Inc	Ind Mtrls	18.2	2.65	2.50
⊕ Belden CDT, Inc.	Hardware	26.9	60.98	2.43
Universal Compression Ho	Energy		51.05	2.06
Mettler-Toledo Internati	Health	22.0	42.84	2.05
⊕ Hilb Rogal & Hobbs Compa	Financial	17.5	10.67	2.00
Sierra Health Services	Health	17.7	-9.86	1.94
⊖ Superior Energy Services	Energy	16.9	55.25	1.91
Lifepoint Hospitals, Inc	Health	14.3	-10.13	1.81
⊕ FTI Consulting, Inc.	Business	20.4	1.64	1.72
✕✕ RadioShack Corporation	Consumer	58.6	-19.05	1.69
Jackson Hewitt Tax Servi	Consumer	24.5	24.30	1.62
⊕ Reinsurance Group of Ame	Financial	12.5	17.46	1.62
Asics	Goods			1.56
✕✕ Fair Isaac, Inc.	Business	25.4	-7.78	1.26
⊕ Aspen Insurance Holdings	Financial	8.3	14.24	1.26
⊕ Global Imaging Systems,	Ind Mtrls	16.4	26.77	1.25
Laidlaw International, I	Ind Mtrls	22.9	34.04	1.24
Aramark Corporation	Consumer	23.9	21.48	1.23
Coventry Health Care, In	Health	15.4	-12.13	1.20
MTN Grp Ltd	Telecom			1.18

Current Investment Style

Value Blnd Growth — Large Mid Small

Market Cap	%
Giant	0.0
Large	1.3
Mid	49.9
Small	41.4
Micro	7.4
Avg $mil: 1,661	

Value Measures		Rel Category
Price/Earnings	15.02	0.71
Price/Book	1.86	0.68
Price/Sales	0.92	0.59
Price/Cash Flow	6.87	0.71
Dividend Yield %	0.84	1.83

Growth Measures	%	Rel Category
Long-Term Erngs	14.06	0.79
Book Value	13.73	1.31
Sales	12.89	1.08
Cash Flow	15.01	0.71
Historical Erngs	18.92	0.78

Profitability	%	Rel Category
Return on Equity	14.61	1.18
Return on Assets	7.38	1.11
Net Margin	8.56	0.99

Sector Weightings	% of Stocks	Rel S&P 500	3 Year High	Low
↻ Info	9.22	0.46		
🖥 Software	2.45	0.71	6	2
💻 Hardware	4.13	0.45	12	4
📺 Media	0.40	0.11	4	0
📞 Telecom	2.24	0.64	6	1
⊂ Service	59.17	1.28		
🏥 Health	20.34	1.69	21	14
🛒 Consumer	10.52	1.38	13	8
💼 Business	11.69	2.76	22	12
💲 Financial	16.62	0.75	17	5
🏭 Mfg	31.60	0.94		
🏠 Goods	6.72	0.79	7	5
🔧 Ind Mtrls	13.60	1.14	17	13
⛽ Energy	11.28	1.15	11	2
💡 Utilities	0.00	0.00	0	0

Composition

- ● Cash 8.9
- ● Stocks 91.1
- ● Bonds 0.0
- ● Other 0.0
- Foreign 10.2 (% of Stock)

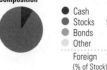

Morningstar® Funds 500

Fidelity Asset Mgr 50%

	Ticker	Load	NAV	Yield	Total Assets	Mstar Category
	FASMX	None	$16.11	2.9%	$9,209 mil	Moderate Allocation

Governance and Management

Stewardship Grade: B

Portfolio Manager(s)

Lead manager Dick Habermann has a long tenure at Fidelity. The 10 underlying equity investment funds are managed by many of the same analysts that head similar Select funds. Matt Conti of Fidelity Focused High Income and Jeff Moore of Fidelity Investment Grade Bond handle the fund's high-yield and investment-grade bond portfolios, respectively.

Strategy

The fund has a neutral allocation mix of 50% stocks, 40% bonds, and 10% cash, and lead manager Dick Habermann only slightly adjusts those weightings based on his economic outlook. The equity portfolio's sector exposure is kept close to the Wilshire 5000 Index and invests in 10 internal funds that are managed by sector analysts. Matt Conti and Jeff Moore use security selection, and not interest-rate bets, to drive returns in the fixed-income portfolio, although the portfolio has historically tilted toward investment-grade issues.

Performance 12-31-06

	1st Qtr	2nd Qtr	3rd Qtr	4th Qtr	Total
2002	0.77	-8.04	-7.39	7.14	-8.05
2003	-1.01	10.91	0.53	6.16	17.18
2004	1.58	-0.25	-1.45	5.55	5.40
2005	-2.22	1.97	1.81	2.48	4.03
2006	2.80	-1.28	3.36	4.08	9.19

Trailing	Total Return%	+/- DJ Mod	+/- DJ US Mod	%Rank Cat	Growth of $10,000
3 Mo	4.08	-1.51	-0.59	85	10,408
6 Mo	7.58	-1.21	-0.32	82	10,758
1 Yr	9.19	-3.11	-1.08	85	10,919
3 Yr Avg	6.18	-4.54	-2.94	89	11,971
5 Yr Avg	5.22	-4.80	-2.38	68	12,897
10 Yr Avg	7.42	-1.13	-1.17	39	20,457
15 Yr Avg	8.79	-0.42	-0.60	51	35,386

Tax Analysis	Tax-Adj Rtn%	%Rank Cat	Tax-Cost Rat	%Rank Cat
3 Yr (estimated)	4.68	87	1.41	71
5 Yr (estimated)	3.92	74	1.24	76
10 Yr (estimated)	5.24	48	2.03	83

Potential Capital Gain Exposure: 6% of assets

Morningstar's Take by Andrew Gogerty 11-14-06

A manager change is a loss for fund shareholders.

In September 2006, Fidelity revamped the naming of its Asset Manager lineup. The funds' names will now indicate their neutral equity weighting. Thus, this fund is now Fidelity Asset Manager 50%.

A more drastic change relates to the fund's equity portfolio. Charles Mangum, manager to Fidelity Dividend Growth, no longer manages this sleeve. Instead, all Asset Manager funds will proportionally invest in 10 internal equity pools reflecting broad market sectors such as health care, energy, and financials. These pools will be headed by many of the same analysts that run similar Fidelity Select funds. Sector allocation will be kept in line with the Wilshire 5000 Index (a broad measure of U.S. equities); the goal is for each manager to outpace his portion of the index through stock selection.

We think this change dampens the fund's appeal. Mangum's consistent style and focus on large caps was a prudent fit for its conservative asset allocation. With the change, it'll hew more closely to its index, and exposure to the health-care and consumer sectors will noticeably decrease, while its weight in industrials and energy will increase. The impact on market cap is unknown, but considering the large-cap orientation of Fidelity's Select funds, we'd expect this portfolio to own a fair number of big companies.

The fund's other attractions, however, remain, including its low costs. And lead manager Dick Habermann continues here; his experience making small asset-allocation shifts away from the fund's neutral positioning of 50% stocks, 40% bonds, and 10% cash to good effect is a plus. Fidelity's army of fixed-income managers and analysts will continue to manage the fund's fixed-income and cash allocation.

The loss of Mangum means this fund isn't as compelling as it once was. It still has appeal but is no longer an Analyst Pick.

Address:	82 Devonshire St Boston MA 02109 800-544-8544
Web Address:	www.fidelity.com
Inception:	12-28-88
Advisor:	Fidelity Management & Research (FMR)
Subadvisor:	Multiple Subadvisors
NTF Plans:	Fidelity Retail-NTF, CommonWealth NTF

Minimum Purchase:	$2500	Add: $250	IRA: $500
Min Auto Inv Plan:	$2500	Add: $100	
Sales Fees:	No-load		
Management Fee:	0.52%		
Actual Fees:	Mgt:0.52%	Dist: —	
Expense Projections:	3Yr:$230	5Yr:$401	10Yr:$894
Income Distrib:	Quarterly		

Historical Profile
Return Average
Risk Average
Rating ★★★ Neutral

| 45% | 56% | 49% | 44% | 40% | 46% | 48% | 41% | 42% |

Investment Style
Equity
Stock %

▼ Manager Change
▽ Partial Manager Change

Growth of $10,000
■ Investment Values of Fund
— Investment Values of DJ Mod

26.8 / 22.0 / 18.0 / 14.0 / 10.0

Performance Quartile (within Category)

1995	1996	1997	1998	1999	2000	2001	2002	2003	2004	2005	2006	History
15.85	16.47	18.35	17.39	18.38	16.82	15.50	13.80	15.76	16.21	16.05	16.11	NAV
18.16	12.73	22.27	16.09	13.59	2.38	-3.93	-8.05	17.18	5.40	4.03	9.19	Total Return %
-1.64	2.07	10.37	3.77	-3.74	4.05	-1.13	-1.28	-10.20	-7.57	-2.96	-3.11	+/-DJ Mod
-6.61	1.39	3.07	3.70	0.74	-2.06	-4.09	2.49	-6.88	-5.77	-1.97	-1.08	+/-DJ US Mod
3.36	3.97	3.75	3.31	3.26	3.58	3.92	3.07	2.78	2.50	2.43	3.13	Income Return %
14.80	8.76	18.52	12.78	10.33	-1.20	-7.85	-11.12	14.40	2.90	1.60	6.06	Capital Return %
98	69	27	35	29	39	39	16	79	91	67	85	Total Rtn % Rank Cat
0.46	0.62	0.61	0.60	0.56	0.65	0.65	0.47	0.38	0.39	0.39	0.50	Income $
0.00	0.75	1.11	3.15	0.74	1.34	0.00	0.00	0.00	0.00	0.41	0.90	Capital Gains $
0.97	0.93	0.78	0.74	0.73	0.71	0.71	0.73	0.74	0.74	0.72	0.71	Expense Ratio %
4.27	3.64	3.39	3.19	3.01	3.32	3.51	3.31	2.82	2.12	2.55	2.79	Income Ratio %
137	131	79	136	104	109	133	129	120	78	32	65	Turnover Rate %
11,165	10,972	12,099	12,879	13,254	12,961	11,924	10,118	11,371	10,955	10,099	9,208	Net Assets $mil

Rating and Risk

Time Period	Load-Adj Return %	Morningstar Rtn vs Cat	Morningstar Risk vs Cat	Morningstar Risk-Adj Rating
1 Yr	9.19			
3 Yr	6.18	-Avg	Low	★★
5 Yr	5.22	-Avg	Avg	★★★
10 Yr	7.42	Avg	Avg	★★★
Incept	9.74			

Other Measures	Standard Index DJ Mod	Best Fit Index Russ 1000
Alpha	-1.6	-1.2
Beta	0.63	0.54
R-Squared	79	86
Standard Deviation	4.21	
Mean	6.18	
Sharpe Ratio	0.70	

Portfolio Analysis 09-30-06

Total Stocks:648 Share change since 06-30-06	Sectors	P/E Ratio	YTD Return %	% Net Assets
⊖ General Electric Company	Ind Mtrls	20.0	0.91	1.05
⊖ American International Gr	Financial	17.0	-0.18	0.81
⊖ Pfizer Inc.	Health	15.2	1.00	0.61
⊖ Johnson & Johnson	Health	17.5	0.74	0.53
⊕ J.P. Morgan Chase & Co.	Financial	13.6	-0.02	0.45
⊕ Bank of America Corporati	Financial	12.4	0.11	0.45
⊕ Wachovia Corporation	Financial	12.9	-0.65	0.42
⊕ Wells Fargo Company	Financial	14.7	-0.17	0.41
⊕ ACE, Ltd.	Financial	10.6	-2.33	0.41

Total Fixed-Income:1692	Date of Maturity	Amount $000	Value $000	% Net Assets
FNMA 5.5%	01-01-34	212,632	209,512	2.00
FNMA 0.05%	10-01-36	197,912	190,165	1.81
US Treasury Note 2%	01-15-14	146,295	157,994	1.51
FNMA 0.06%	05-01-23	107,345	109,564	1.05
US Treasury Note 4.25%	08-15-14	105,203	102,651	0.98
Jpsw Swap Irs 8/10/09 3ml	08-10-09	98,065	98,664	0.94
Lbsp Swap Irs 12/8/08 3ml	12-08-08	64,360	64,893	0.62
Citi Swap Irs 3/06/09 3ml	03-06-09	60,181	60,242	0.57
FNMA 4.5%	07-01-18	59,496	57,480	0.55

Equity Style
Style: Blend
Size: Large-Cap

Value Measures		Rel Category
Price/Earnings	15.67	1.03
Price/Book	2.48	1.00
Price/Sales	1.46	1.07
Price/Cash Flow	9.62	1.19
Dividend Yield %	1.67	0.87

Growth Measures	%	Rel Category
Long-Term Erngs	12.47	1.06
Book Value	10.36	1.20
Sales	6.97	0.78
Cash Flow	11.43	1.16
Historical Erngs	17.15	0.96

Market Cap %			
Giant	38.4	Small	7.0
Large	32.7	Micro	1.1
Mid	20.9	Avg $mil:	22,758

Fixed-Income Style
Duration: —
Quality: —

Avg Eff Duration [1]	—
Avg Eff Maturity	—
Avg Credit Quality	—
Avg Wtd Coupon	3.51%

[1] figure provided by fund

Sector Weightings	% of Stocks	Rel DJ Mod	3 Year High Low
⊙ Info	16.77	—	
Software	1.96	—	7 2
Hardware	10.54	—	11 6
Media	1.11	—	7 1
Telecom	3.16	—	8 3
⊟ Service	50.43	—	
Health	11.65	—	21 12
Consumer	10.55	—	13 9
Business	4.24	—	4 1
Financial	23.99	—	28 22
⊡ Mfg	32.81	—	
Goods	8.67	—	9 4
Ind Mtrls	11.96	—	12 7
Energy	8.86	—	9 5
Utilities	3.32	—	3 0

Composition

	%
● Cash	14.9
● Stocks	42.4
● Bonds	38.9
● Other	3.8
Foreign (% of Stock)	15.3

Fidelity Asset Mgr 70%

	Ticker	Load	NAV	Yield	Total Assets	Mstar Category
	FASGX	None	$16.25	2.4%	$3,177 mil	Moderate Allocation

Governance and Management

Stewardship Grade: B

Portfolio Manager(s)

Lead manager Dick Habermann has a long tenure at Fidelity. The 10 underlying equity-investment funds are managed by many of the same analysts that head similar Fidelity Select funds. Matt Conti of Fidelity Focused High Income and Jeff Moore of Fidelity Investment Grade Bond handle the fund's high-yield and investment-grade bond portfolios, respectively.

Strategy

The fund has a neutral allocation mix of 70% stocks, 25% bonds, and 5% cash, and lead manager Dick Habermann only slightly adjusts those weightings based on his economic outlook. The equity portfolio's sector exposure is kept close to the Wilshire 5000 Index, and the fund invests in 10 internal funds that are managed by sector analysts. Matt Conti and Jeff Moore use security selection, and not interest-rate bets, to drive returns in the fixed-income portfolio, although the portfolio has historically tilted toward investment-grade issues.

Historical Profile

Return	Below Avg
Risk	Above Avg
Rating	★★ Below Avg

Equity weightings: 68% | 71% | 68% | 64% | 60% | 65% | 68% | 62% | 54%

▼ Manager Change
▽ Partial Manager Change

Investment Style
Equity
Stock %

Growth of $10,000
- Investment Values of Fund
- Investment Values of DJ Mod

26.8 — 22.0 — 18.0 — 14.0 — 10.0

Performance Quartile (within Category)

	1995	1996	1997	1998	1999	2000	2001	2002	2003	2004	2005	2006	History
	15.17	16.35	18.48	18.68	19.67	15.91	14.34	11.97	14.28	14.82	15.08	16.25	NAV
	19.95	17.59	26.46	18.08	13.97	-3.55	-7.22	-14.05	21.93	6.05	3.77	10.33	Total Return %
	0.15	6.93	14.56	5.76	-3.36	-1.88	-4.42	-7.28	-5.45	-6.92	-3.22	-1.97	+/-DJ Mod
	-4.82	6.25	7.26	5.69	1.12	-7.99	-7.38	-3.51	-2.13	-5.12	-2.23	0.06	+/-DJ US Mod
	1.79	2.83	2.45	1.89	2.41	2.34	2.64	2.51	2.59	2.24	1.96	2.59	Income Return %
	18.16	14.76	24.01	16.19	11.56	-5.89	-9.86	-16.56	19.34	3.81	1.81	7.74	Capital Return %
	94	19	8	22	28	85	75	72	35	87	70	68	Total Rtn % Rank Cat
	0.23	0.43	0.40	0.35	0.45	0.46	0.42	0.36	0.31	0.32	0.29	0.39	Income $
	0.00	1.07	1.75	2.68	1.10	2.56	0.00	0.00	0.00	0.00	0.01	0.00	Capital Gains $
	1.02	1.01	0.86	0.80	0.80	0.77	0.78	0.81	0.83	0.82	0.80	0.79	Expense Ratio %
	3.16	2.51	2.36	2.49	2.38	2.46	2.62	2.73	2.53	1.77	2.11	2.20	Income Ratio %
	119	138	70	150	101	197	143	101	72	67	37	82	Turnover Rate %
	2,895	3,378	4,663	5,120	5,490	4,827	4,234	3,341	3,774	3,733	3,291	3,177	Net Assets $mil

Performance 12-31-06

	1st Qtr	2nd Qtr	3rd Qtr	4th Qtr	Total
2002	0.84	-11.83	-11.37	9.07	-14.05
2003	-2.17	14.35	0.60	8.35	21.93
2004	1.54	-0.07	-2.69	7.41	6.05
2005	-3.17	1.81	2.26	2.93	3.77
2006	3.85	-2.30	3.40	5.17	10.33

Trailing	Total Return%	+/- DJ Mod	+/- DJ US Mod	%Rank Cat	Growth of $10,000
3 Mo	5.17	-0.42	0.50	45	10,517
6 Mo	8.75	-0.04	0.85	52	10,875
1 Yr	10.33	-1.97	0.06	68	11,033
3 Yr Avg	6.68	-4.04	-2.44	83	12,141
5 Yr Avg	4.94	-5.08	-2.66	75	12,726
10 Yr Avg	6.84	-1.71	-1.75	54	19,379
15 Yr Avg	9.38	0.17	-0.01	38	38,377

Tax Analysis	Tax-Adj Rtn%	%Rank Cat	Tax-Cost Rat	%Rank Cat
3 Yr (estimated)	5.88	70	0.75	36
5 Yr (estimated)	4.12	69	0.78	45
10 Yr (estimated)	4.97	56	1.75	65

Potential Capital Gain Exposure: -4% of assets

Rating and Risk

Time Period	Load-Adj Return %	Morningstar Rtn vs Cat	Morningstar Risk vs Cat	Morningstar Risk-Adj Rating
1 Yr	10.33			
3 Yr	6.68	-Avg	Avg	★★
5 Yr	4.94	-Avg	High	★★
10 Yr	6.84	Avg	High	★★
Incept	9.38			

Other Measures	Standard Index DJ Mod	Best Fit Index Russ 1000
Alpha	-2.4	-2.0
Beta	0.81	0.73
R-Squared	74	89
Standard Deviation	5.55	
Mean	6.68	
Sharpe Ratio	0.62	

Portfolio Analysis 09-30-06

Total Stocks:647 Share change since 06-30-06	Sectors	P/E Ratio	YTD Return %	% Net Assets
⊖ General Electric Company	Ind Mtrls	20.0	0.91	1.36
⊖ American International Gr	Financial	17.0	-0.18	1.04
⊖ Pfizer Inc.	Health	15.2	1.00	0.78
⊖ Johnson & Johnson	Health	17.5	0.74	0.68
⊕ J.P. Morgan Chase & Co.	Financial	13.6	-0.02	0.58
⊕ Bank of America Corporati	Financial	12.4	0.11	0.58
⊕ Wachovia Corporation	Financial	12.9	-0.65	0.54
⊕ Wells Fargo Company	Financial	14.7	-0.17	0.53
⊕ ACE, Ltd.	Financial	10.6	-2.33	0.52

Total Fixed-Income:1692	Date of Maturity	Amount $000	Value $000	% Net Assets
FNMA 5.5%	01-01-34	45,362	44,696	1.24
FNMA 0.05%	10-01-36	42,222	40,569	1.13
US Treasury Note 2%	01-15-14	31,210	33,706	0.94
FNMA 0.06%	05-01-23	22,901	23,374	0.65
US Treasury Note 4.25%	08-15-14	22,444	21,899	0.61
Jpsw Swap Irs 8/10/09 3ml	08-10-09	20,921	21,049	0.59
Lbsp Swap Irs 12/8/08 3ml	12-08-08	13,730	13,844	0.38
Citi Swap Irs 3/06/09 3ml	03-06-09	12,839	12,852	0.36
FNMA 4.5%	07-01-18	12,693	12,262	0.34

Equity Style
Style: Blend
Size: Large-Cap

Value Measures		Rel Category
Price/Earnings	15.67	1.03
Price/Book	2.48	1.00
Price/Sales	1.46	1.07
Price/Cash Flow	9.61	1.19
Dividend Yield %	1.66	0.86

Growth Measures	%	Rel Category
Long-Term Erngs	12.46	1.06
Book Value	10.35	1.20
Sales	6.98	0.79
Cash Flow	11.64	1.18
Historical Erngs	17.23	0.96

Market Cap %			
Giant	38.3	Small	7.0
Large	32.7	Micro	1.1
Mid	20.9	Avg $mil:	22,762

Fixed-Income Style
Duration: —
Quality: —

Avg Eff Duration [1]	—
Avg Eff Maturity	—
Avg Credit Quality	—
Avg Wtd Coupon	3.47%

[1]figure provided by fund

Sector Weightings	% of Stocks	Rel DJ Mod	3 Year High Low
⟳ Info	16.84	—	
🖳 Software	1.96	—	7 2
💻 Hardware	10.60	—	11 5
🎙 Media	1.11	—	7 1
📶 Telecom	3.17	—	8 3
⚙ Service	50.42	—	
🏥 Health	11.67	—	21 12
🛒 Consumer	10.59	—	13 9
🏢 Business	4.26	—	4 1
💲 Financial	23.90	—	27 22
🏭 Mfg	32.74	—	
⚙ Goods	8.59	—	9 3
🔩 Ind Mtrls	11.96	—	12 7
🔋 Energy	8.87	—	9 5
⚡ Utilities	3.32	—	3 0

Composition

- Cash 13.1
- Stocks 54.4
- Bonds 24.1
- Other 8.5
- Foreign 14.7 (% of Stock)

Morningstar's Take by Andrew Gogerty 11-14-06

A manager change is a loss for fund shareholders.

In September 2006, Fidelity revamped the naming of its Asset Manager lineup. The funds' names will now indicate their neutral equity weighting. Thus, this fund is now Fidelity Asset Manager 70%.

A more drastic change, however, relates to the fund's equity portfolio. Charles Mangum, manager to Fidelity Dividend Growth, no longer manages this sleeve. Instead, all Asset Manager funds will proportionally invest in 10 internal equity pools reflecting broad market sectors such as health care, energy, and financials. These pools will be headed by many of the same analysts that run similar Fidelity Select funds. The fund's sector allocation will be kept in line with the Wilshire 5000 Index (a broad measure of U.S. equities); the goal is for each manager to outpace his portion of the index through stock selection.

We think this change dampens the fund's appeal for shareholders. Mangum's consistent style and focus on large-cap stocks was a prudent fit for its somewhat conservative asset allocation. With the change, the fund will hew more closely to its index, and exposure to the health-care and consumer sectors will noticeably decrease, while its weight in industrials and energy will increase. The impact on market cap is unknown as yet, but considering the large-cap orientation of Fidelity's Select funds, we'd expect this portfolio to own a fair number of big companies.

The fund's other attractions remain, including its low costs. And lead manager Dick Habermann continues here; his experience making small asset-allocation shifts away from the neutral positioning of 70% stocks, 25% bonds, and 5% cash to good effect is a plus. Fidelity's army of fixed-income managers and analysts will continue to manage the fixed-income and cash allocation.

The loss of Mangum means this fund isn't as compelling as it once was. It still has appeal, but we would also consider other options.

Address:	82 Devonshire St Boston MA 02109 800-544-8544	Minimum Purchase:	$2500	Add: $250 IRA: $500
		Min Auto Inv Plan:	$2500	Add: $100
Web Address:	www.fidelity.com	Sales Fees:	No-load	
Inception:	12-30-91	Management Fee:	0.57%	
Advisor:	Fidelity Management & Research (FMR)	Actual Fees:	Mgt:0.57%	Dist: —
Subadvisor:	Multiple Subadvisors	Expense Projections:	3Yr:$259	5Yr:$450 10Yr:$1002
NTF Plans:	Fidelity Retail-NTF, CommonWealth NTF	Income Distrib:	Annually	

MORNINGSTAR® Funds 500

Fidelity Asset Mgr 85%

	Ticker	Load	NAV	Yield	Total Assets	Mstar Category
	FAMRX	None	$13.35	1.6%	$485 mil	Large Growth

Governance and Management

Stewardship Grade: B

Portfolio Manager(s)

Lead manager Dick Habermann has been managing money at Fidelity since the early 1970s and has been on board here since the offering's September 1999 inception. The 10 underlying equity-investment funds are managed by many of the same analysts that head similar Fidelity Select funds. Matt Conti and Jeff Moore handle the fund's high-yield and investment-grade bond portfolios, respectively.

Strategy

Lead manager Dick Habermann sets the fund's asset allocation. The fund's neutral stock weighting is 85%, but that equity stake can vary between 60% and 100% based on economic outlook. The equity portfolio's sector exposure is kept close to the Wilshire 5000 Index, and the fund invests in 10 internal funds that are managed by sector analysts. Matt Conti and Jeff Moore use security selection, and not interest-rate bets, to drive returns in the fixed-income portfolio.

Performance 12-31-06

	1st Qtr	2nd Qtr	3rd Qtr	4th Qtr	Total
2002	0.56	-21.16	-20.40	3.08	-34.95
2003	2.60	18.71	9.72	11.25	48.65
2004	3.81	-0.47	-2.74	10.51	11.05
2005	-4.60	1.58	6.66	3.85	7.34
2006	4.30	-2.06	3.65	6.16	12.40

Trailing	Total Return%	+/- S&P 500	+/- Russ 1000Gr	%Rank Cat	Growth of $10,000
3 Mo	6.16	-0.54	0.23	31	10,616
6 Mo	10.03	-2.71	-0.07	26	11,003
1 Yr	12.40	-3.39	3.33	12	11,240
3 Yr Avg	10.24	-0.20	3.37	13	13,397
5 Yr Avg	5.31	-0.88	2.62	17	12,952
10 Yr Avg	—	—	—	—	—
15 Yr Avg	—	—	—	—	—

Tax Analysis	Tax-Adj Rtn%	%Rank Cat	Tax-Cost Rat	%Rank Cat
3 Yr (estimated)	9.89	11	0.32	21
5 Yr (estimated)	5.00	17	0.29	30
10 Yr (estimated)	—	—	—	—

Potential Capital Gain Exposure: -9% of assets

Morningstar's Take by Andrew Gogerty 11-14-06

A manager change is a loss for Fidelity Asset Manager: Aggressive's shareholders.

In September 2006, Fidelity revamped the naming of its Asset Manager lineup. The funds' names will now indicate their neutral equity weighting. Thus, this fund is now Fidelity Asset Manager 85%.

A more drastic change, however, relates to the fund's equity portfolio. Ramin Arani, manager to Fidelity Trend, no longer manages this sleeve. Instead, all Asset Manager funds will proportionately invest in 10 internal equity pools reflecting broad market sectors such as health care, energy, and financials. These pools will be headed by many of the same analysts that run similar Fidelity Select funds. The fund's sector allocation will be kept in line with the Wilshire 5000 Index (a broad measure of U.S. equities); the goal is for each manager to outpace his portion of the index through stock selection.

We think this change damps the fund's appeal

for shareholders. Arani's all-cap style was a prudent fit here, and his other charge has emerged as a brighter spot in Fidelity's lineup. With the change, the fund will hew more closely to its index, and considering the large-cap orientation of Fidelity's Select funds, we'd expect this portfolio to own a fair number of big companies. More importantly, though, is that Arani's experience is lost, and we're yet to see meaningful changes to the firm's culture of steady analyst rotation among sectors.

The fund's other attractions remain, including its low costs. Lead manager Dick Habermann also continues here and has proven experience making asset-allocation shifts. But, in the end, the loss of Arani means this fund isn't as compelling as it once was. It still has appeal, but we would also consider other options.

Address:	82 Devonshire St Boston MA 02109 800-544-8544	Minimum Purchase:	$2500	Add: $250	IRA: $500
		Min Auto Inv Plan:	$2500	Add: $100	
		Sales Fees:	No-load		
Web Address:	www.fidelity.com	Management Fee:	0.57%		
Inception:	09-24-99*	Actual Fees:	Mgt:0.57%	Dist: —	
Advisor:	Fidelity Management & Research (FMR)	Expense Projections:	3Yr:$290	5Yr:$504	10Yr:$1120
Subadvisor:	Multiple Subadvisors	Income Distrib:	Annually		
NTF Plans:	Fidelity Retail-NTF, CommonWealth NTF				

Historical Profile

Return	Above Avg
Risk	Above Avg
Rating	★★★★ Above Avg

Investment Style: Equity Stock %

85% 90% 81% 79% 89% 92% 75% 70%

▽ Manager Change
▽ Partial Manager Change

Growth of $10,000
— Investment Values of Fund
— Investment Values of S&P 500

Performance Quartile (within Category)

	1995	1996	1997	1998	1999	2000	2001	2002	2003	2004	2005	2006	History
	—	—	—	—	11.93	13.03	10.76	6.93	10.24	11.31	12.08	13.35	NAV
	—	—	—	—	20.05*	15.44	-15.72	-34.95	48.65	11.05	7.34	12.40	Total Return %
	—	—	—	—	—	24.54	-3.83	-12.85	19.97	0.17	2.43	-3.39	+/-S&P 500
	—	—	—	—	—	37.86	4.70	-7.07	18.90	4.75	2.08	3.33	+/-Russ 1000Gr
	—	—	—	—	—	1.09	1.69	0.65	0.87	0.59	0.53	1.73	Income Return %
	—	—	—	—	—	14.35	-17.41	-35.60	47.78	10.46	6.81	10.67	Capital Return %
	—	—	—	—	—	2	31	89	3	24	39	12	Total Rtn % Rank Cat
	—	—	—	—	0.02	0.13	0.22	0.07	0.06	0.06	0.06	0.21	Income $
	—	—	—	—	0.05	0.60	0.00	0.00	0.00	0.00	0.00	0.02	Capital Gains $
	—	—	—	—	1.20	0.90	0.85	0.88	1.00	0.91	0.89	0.87	Expense Ratio %
	—	—	—	—	4.06	1.32	1.55	0.87	0.63	0.52	0.53	1.50	Income Ratio %
	—	—	—	—	—	338	255	240	131	86	71	187	Turnover Rate %
	—	—	—	—	43	443	288	148	318	399	418	484	Net Assets $mil

Rating and Risk

Time Period	Load-Adj Return %	Morningstar Rtn vs Cat	Morningstar Risk vs Cat	Morningstar Risk-Adj Rating
1 Yr	12.40			
3 Yr	10.24	+Avg	Avg	★★★★
5 Yr	5.31	+Avg	+Avg	★★★★
10 Yr	—			
Incept	5.86			

Other Measures	Standard Index S&P 500	Best Fit Index Russ MG
Alpha	-1.7	-0.3
Beta	1.25	0.77
R-Squared	84	87
Standard Deviation	9.41	
Mean	10.24	
Sharpe Ratio	0.75	

Portfolio Analysis 09-30-06

Share change since 06-06 Total Stocks:647	Sector	PE	Tot Ret%	% Assets
⊖ S&P 500 Index (Fut)	—	—	—	3.00
⊖ General Electric Company	Ind Mtrls	20.0	9.35	1.60
⊖ American International G	Financial	17.0	6.05	1.23
✕ Dj Eurostoxx 50 (Fut)	—	—	—	1.13
⊕ Pfizer Inc.	Health	15.2	15.22	0.92
⊖ Johnson & Johnson	Health	17.5	12.45	0.80
⊕ FNMA 5.5%		—	—	0.70
⊖ J.P. Morgan Chase & Co.	Financial	13.6	25.60	0.69
⊖ Bank of America Corporat	Financial	12.4	20.68	0.68
⊕ TOPIX Index (Fut)		—	—	0.67
✕ Wachovia Corporation	Financial	12.9	12.02	0.64
✕ FNMA 0.05%		—	—	0.63
⊕ Wells Fargo Company	Financial	14.7	16.82	0.62
⊕ ACE, Ltd.	Financial	10.6	15.41	0.62
⊕ Federated Department Sto	Consumer	20.8	16.54	0.61
⊕ FTSE 100 Index (Fut)		—	—	0.59
✕ Chevron Corporation	Energy	9.0	33.76	0.57
⊕ Roche Holding	Health	—	—	0.54
⊕ US Treasury Note 2%		—	—	0.53
⊕ United Technologies	Ind Mtrls	17.8	13.65	0.53

Current Investment Style

Value Blnd Growth — Large Mid Small

Market Cap	%
Giant	39.5
Large	32.5
Mid	20.2
Small	6.7
Micro	1.2

Avg $mil: 22,751

Value Measures		Rel Category
Price/Earnings	15.65	0.81
Price/Book	2.45	0.74
Price/Sales	1.44	0.74
Price/Cash Flow	9.55	0.84
Dividend Yield %	1.75	1.70

Growth Measures	%	Rel Category
Long-Term Erngs	12.38	0.86
Book Value	10.47	0.90
Sales	6.87	0.59
Cash Flow	11.11	0.66
Historical Erngs	16.23	0.71

Profitability	%	Rel Category
Return on Equity	16.77	0.82
Return on Assets	8.39	0.76
Net Margin	12.36	0.87

Sector Weightings	% of Stocks	Rel S&P 500	3 Year High Low
⟳ Info	15.79	0.79	
Software	1.94	0.56	10 2
Hardware	9.83	1.06	30 9
Media	1.01	0.27	11 1
Telecom	3.01	0.86	7 0
Service	50.48	1.09	
Health	11.45	0.95	20 11
Consumer	10.05	1.31	10 6
Business	4.02	0.95	10 4
Financial	24.96	1.12	25 6
Mfg	33.72	1.00	
Goods	9.60	1.12	10 4
Ind Mtrls	12.05	1.01	12 5
Energy	8.72	0.89	16 5
Utilities	3.35	0.96	3 0

Composition

● Cash	10.4	
● Stocks	70.4	
● Bonds	13.5	
○ Other	5.8	
Foreign	22.3	(% of Stock)

Fidelity Balanced

	Ticker	Load	NAV	Yield	Total Assets	Mstar Category
	FBALX	None	$19.43	2.0%	$22,439 mil	Moderate Allocation

Governance and Management

Stewardship Grade: B

Portfolio Manager(s)

Larry Rakers took over the stock portion of this fund in February 2002 and sibling Advisor Balanced in June 2005. He previously managed Fidelity Convertible Securities, and several Fidelity sector funds. Fixed-income manager George Fischer came on board in March 2004. Fischer began managing government and mortgage-bond offerings for the firm in June 2002 and previously spent six years running various Fidelity municipal-bond funds.

Strategy

Manager Larry Rakers emphasizes moderate valuations and keeps the fund's equity sector weightings in between those of the Russell 3000 Index and the Russell 3000 Value Index. Rakers has shown more of a willingness to hold mid- and small-cap names, and the fund's median market cap falls well below the group average. George Fischer, who recently took over the fixed-income portion, sticks chiefly to high-quality bonds and doesn't make interest-rate bets.

Performance 12-31-06

	1st Qtr	2nd Qtr	3rd Qtr	4th Qtr	Total
2002	2.42	-6.41	-10.89	7.13	-8.49
2003	-1.88	14.94	3.43	9.94	28.24
2004	3.34	-0.52	-0.54	8.50	10.94
2005	-1.01	3.30	5.08	3.00	10.68
2006	4.48	-1.28	2.89	5.21	11.65

Trailing	Total Return%	+/- DJ Mod	+/- DJ US Mod	%Rank Cat	Growth of $10,000
3 Mo	5.21	-0.38	0.54	44	10,521
6 Mo	8.25	-0.54	0.35	70	10,825
1 Yr	11.65	-0.65	1.38	39	11,165
3 Yr Avg	11.09	0.37	1.97	9	13,710
5 Yr Avg	9.98	-0.04	2.38	3	16,090
10 Yr Avg	10.84	2.29	2.25	4	27,988
15 Yr Avg	10.19	0.98	0.80	23	42,868

Tax Analysis	Tax-Adj Rtn%	%Rank Cat	Tax-Cost Rat	%Rank Cat
3 Yr (estimated)	9.70	9	1.25	63
5 Yr (estimated)	8.84	3	1.04	63
10 Yr (estimated)	8.65	4	1.98	81

Potential Capital Gain Exposure: 14% of assets

Morningstar's Take by Andrew Gogerty 11-14-06

Fidelity Balanced remains a strong choice.

Moderate-allocation funds' tendency to move up the market-cap ladder in recent years isn't surprising given the torrid run of mid- and small-cap stocks has led many of these firms to appear overvalued. This fund has followed that path: Its average market cap has risen from approximately $9 billion at the beginning of 2004 to $13.3 billion currently. The fund still has significant exposure to smaller-cap stocks relative to peers, however; the group's average market cap is $28.4 billion.

Although the fund's tilt toward smaller companies proved a performance tailwind in recent years, manager Larry Rakers deserves the lion's share of credit for the fund's success. Since taking over in early 2002, he's been bullish on stocks compared with bonds, and has therefore allocated nearly 70% of assets to equities. In 2006 he has pared that weighting back slightly to 64%, because the stock market's run over the past couple of years, combined with stalling economic indicators

of growth, has made him a bit more cautious. The bond portfolio's management team has also pulled in its reins, redeploying gains on high-yield positions into higher-quality debt and Treasuries, citing that lower-rated debt isn't worth the additional risk at current valuations.

Rakers' success can't be ignored, but investors should temper their expectations. The torrent inflow of new money into the fund in recent years could hamper its ability to take advantage of mid- and small-cap opportunities. Moreover, while Rakers has been moving toward large caps, he admits he missed the rally seen in mega-cap stocks this year. As such, investors should expect that it won't always be on top.

Nonetheless, we like the combination of Rakers' emphasis on moderate valuations and Fidelity's bond research capabilities. Add in the fund's low expenses and Rakers' commitment--he has more than $1 million invested here--and investors have plenty of reason to stay put.

Address:	82 Devonshire Street Boston MA 02109 800-544-6666	Minimum Purchase:	$2500	Add: $250	IRA: $200
		Min Auto Inv Plan:	$100	Add: $100	
		Sales Fees:	No-load		
Web Address:	www.fidelity.com	Management Fee:	0.42%		
Inception:	11-06-86	Actual Fees:	Mgt:0.42%	Dist: —	
Advisor:	Fidelity Management & Research (FMR)	Expense Projections:	3Yr:$205	5Yr:$357	10Yr:$798
Subadvisor:	Multiple Subadvisors	Income Distrib:	Quarterly		
NTF Plans:	Fidelity Retail-NTF, CommonWealth NTF				

Historical Profile

Return High
Risk Above Avg
Rating ★★★★ Highest

57%	60%	55%	53%	55%	61%	66%	67%	61%		

▼ Manager Change
▽ Partial Manager Change

Growth of $10,000
■ Investment Values of Fund
— Investment Values of DJ Mod

31.0
25.0
20.0
15.0
10.0

Performance Quartile (within Category)

1995	1996	1997	1998	1999	2000	2001	2002	2003	2004	2005	2006	History
13.52	14.08	15.27	16.36	15.36	15.19	14.90	13.29	16.75	17.82	18.76	19.43	NAV
14.90	9.34	23.45	20.22	8.86	5.32	2.25	-8.49	28.24	10.94	10.68	11.65	Total Return %
-4.90	-1.32	11.55	7.90	-8.47	6.99	5.05	-1.72	0.86	-2.03	3.69	-0.65	+/-DJ Mod
-9.87	-2.00	4.25	7.83	-3.99	0.88	2.09	2.05	4.18	-0.23	4.68	1.38	+/-DJ US Mod
4.72	4.90	4.07	3.10	2.94	3.18	3.00	2.44	1.97	1.58	1.72	2.21	Income Return %
10.18	4.44	19.38	17.12	5.92	2.14	-0.75	-10.93	26.27	9.36	8.96	9.44	Capital Return %
98	91	19	16	61	9	9	19	6	19	1	39	Total Rtn % Rank Cat
0.57	0.65	0.56	0.46	0.46	0.48	0.45	0.36	0.26	0.26	0.30	0.40	Income $
0.00	0.00	1.46	1.27	1.98	0.49	0.17	0.00	0.00	0.44	0.63	1.04	Capital Gains $
0.90	0.79	0.74	0.67	0.65	0.67	0.64	0.66	0.67	0.66	0.64	0.63	Expense Ratio %
5.33	4.12	3.58	2.97	2.67	2.98	3.05	2.79	2.17	1.63	1.68	2.35	Income Ratio %
269	247	70	135	157	139	115	150	137	99	82	65	Turnover Rate %
4,880	3,919	4,284	5,316	6,123	6,096	7,005	6,550	9,808	12,577	16,603	22,439	Net Assets $mil

Investment Style

Equity
Stock %

Rating and Risk

Time Period	Load-Adj Return %	Morningstar Rtn vs Cat	Morningstar Risk vs Cat	Morningstar Risk-Adj Rating
1 Yr	11.65			
3 Yr	11.09	High	High	★★★★★
5 Yr	9.98	High	+Avg	★★★★★
10 Yr	10.84	High	Avg	★★★★★
Incept	10.71			

Other Measures	Standard Index DJ Mod	Best Fit Index DJ Mod
Alpha	-0.9	-0.9
Beta	1.19	1.19
R-Squared	94	94
Standard Deviation	7.21	
Mean	11.09	
Sharpe Ratio	1.06	

Portfolio Analysis 08-31-06

Total Stocks:576 Share change since 07-31-06	Sectors	P/E Ratio	YTD Return %	% Net Assets
National Oilwell Varco, I	Energy	18.3	-7.11	1.64
General Electric Company	Ind Mtrls	20.0	0.91	1.23
Altria Group, Inc.	Goods	16.3	2.52	1.06
⊕ Bank of America Corporati	Financial	12.4	0.11	1.04
J.P. Morgan Chase & Co.	Financial	13.6	-0.02	1.03
American International Gr	Financial	17.0	-0.18	0.93
Valero Energy Corporation	Energy	6.3	-3.50	0.85
⊕ AT&T, Inc.	Telecom	18.2	-5.43	0.79
Citigroup, Inc.	Financial	13.1	-1.17	0.77

Total Fixed-Income:1504	Date of Maturity	Amount $000	Value $000	% Net Assets
US Treasury Note 4.75%	03-31-11	373,775	374,447	1.76
US Treasury Note 2.375%	04-15-11	339,555	348,601	1.64
FNMA 5%	10-01-33	298,655	286,549	1.35
US Treasury Note 3.75%	05-15-08	288,105	283,063	1.33
US Treasury Note 4.875%	05-31-11	265,000	266,853	1.26
FNMA 4.25%	05-15-09	245,559	240,854	1.13
FNMA 0.04%	02-01-35	222,442	208,193	0.98
Dbsw Swap Irs 6/8/11 3mlv	06-08-11	200,000	202,270	0.95
FNMA 5.5%	06-01-34	196,749	193,336	0.91

Equity Style

Style: Blend
Size: Large-Cap

Value Measures		Rel Category
Price/Earnings	15.48	1.01
Price/Book	2.15	0.87
Price/Sales	1.21	0.88
Price/Cash Flow	5.16	0.64
Dividend Yield %	1.53	0.79

Growth Measures	%	Rel Category
Long-Term Erngs	12.77	1.09
Book Value	10.46	1.21
Sales	9.07	1.02
Cash Flow	11.17	1.13
Historical Erngs	18.80	1.05

Market Cap %			
Giant	26.8	Small	10.7
Large	30.4	Micro	2.5
Mid	29.6	Avg $mil:	13,316

Fixed-Income Style

Duration: —
Quality: —

Avg Eff Duration [1]		—
Avg Eff Maturity		—
Avg Credit Quality		—
Avg Wtd Coupon		3.71%

[1] figure provided by fund

Sector Weightings	% of Stocks	Rel DJ Mod	3 Year High	Low
☎ Info	18.44	—		
Software	2.31	—	2	1
Hardware	9.83	—	13	10
Media	1.67	—	5	2
Telecom	4.63	—	6	4
☞ Service	44.37			
Health	10.77	—	12	10
Consumer	6.12	—	6	6
Business	7.14	—	7	5
Financial	20.34	—	21	17
Mfg	37.19			
Goods	7.20	—	7	5
Ind Mtrls	14.12	—	15	14
Energy	11.81	—	14	10
Utilities	4.06	—	4	2

Composition

- Cash 3.3
- Stocks 61.1
- Bonds 34.6
- Other 0.9
- Foreign 9.7 (% of Stock)

MORNINGSTAR® Funds 500

Fidelity Blue Chip Grth

	Ticker	Load	NAV	Yield	Total Assets	Mstar Category
	FBGRX	None	$44.31	0.5%	$20,650 mil	Large Growth

Governance and Management

Stewardship Grade: B

Portfolio Manager(s)

John McDowell stepped down from this fund in November 2006, after more than a decade at the helm. His comanager Brian Hanson, who joined the fund in 2005, left at the same time to concentrate on other funds he runs. The fund's new manager is Jennifer Uhrig, who has managed Fidelity Advisor Equity Growth since 1997. She is a well-seasoned Fidelity manager, having run Fidelity Mid-Cap Stock for three years and having helmed several sector funds prior to that.

Strategy

Under outgoing management, the fund focused on the market segment suggested by its moniker. Its comanagers each ran separate sleeves of the portfolio, but both looked for giant-cap companies with good short- and long-term earnings-growth prospects. They were more price-conscious than rivals. We have yet to learn how incoming manager Jennifer Uhrig will run the fund. As manager of Fidelity Advisor Growth Equity, she also displayed valuation sensitivity and made occasional sector plays versus her then benchmark, the Russell 3000 Growth Index. This fund's benchmark is the larger-cap Russell 1000 Growth Index.

Performance 12-31-06

	1st Qtr	2nd Qtr	3rd Qtr	4th Qtr	Total
2002	-1.23	-15.70	-16.04	6.84	-25.32
2003	-1.82	13.20	2.44	9.61	24.80
2004	0.98	1.75	-4.52	8.31	6.26
2005	-3.98	1.97	3.35	2.80	4.03
2006	2.34	-5.03	4.26	4.14	5.54

Trailing	Total Return%	+/- S&P 500	+/- Russ 1000Gr	%Rank Cat	Growth of $10,000
3 Mo	4.14	-2.56	-1.79	81	10,414
6 Mo	8.58	-4.16	-1.52	47	10,858
1 Yr	5.54	-10.25	-3.53	65	10,554
3 Yr Avg	5.27	-5.17	-1.60	76	11,666
5 Yr Avg	1.69	-4.50	-1.00	64	10,874
10 Yr Avg	5.61	-2.81	0.17	56	17,260
15 Yr Avg	9.14	-1.50	1.12	33	37,133

Tax Analysis	Tax-Adj Rtn%	%Rank Cat	Tax-Cost Rat	%Rank Cat
3 Yr (estimated)	4.91	72	0.34	23
5 Yr (estimated)	1.40	63	0.29	30
10 Yr (estimated)	4.97	45	0.61	25

Potential Capital Gain Exposure: 17% of assets

Morningstar's Take by Dan Lefkovitz 11-09-06

Our opinion of Fidelity Blue Chip Growth has soured, but not because of its performance.

For years, we've been urging investors to stick with this lagging fund. We've noted that smaller caps have beaten larger caps for several years, and that the steady growers this fund focuses on will eventually come back into favor. And we've noted that this fund had high-quality, experienced managers who stuck to their strategy even as it was deeply out of favor. Their willingness to stand by beleaguered picks is evidenced by a very low turnover rate.

We still think that blue-chip growth is a good place to be in the market, but we're no longer sure this fund is the best way to play its comeback. On November 9, 2006, longtime manager John McDowell retired. His comanager, Brian Hanson, left to concentrate on other charges.

The fund's new skipper is Jennifer Uhrig, who is known from her management of Fidelity Advisor Equity Growth. That large-growth fund's record

under Uhrig is comparable to McDowell's here--essentially in line with the category average (both ran their funds for roughly 10 years). Like here, Advisor Equity Growth's record is dragged down by poor three- and five-year numbers.

But unlike with McDowell on this fund, we can't say that Uhrig was sticking to an out-of-favor style. With the Russell 3000 Growth as her benchmark, Uhrig was able to buy some smaller-cap stocks. We've also noticed that Uhrig has made several seemingly reactive moves recently. She added to energy while the sector was hot and trimmed Microsoft after it plunged. We prefer to see managers go against the grain.

As of this writing, we had yet to learn how Uhrig would be running this fund. Advisor Equity Growth's latest portfolio held many of the same names that this one does, so big changes might not be in the cards. But given Uhrig's track record and our uneasiness over her approach, we can no longer recommend this fund.

Address:	82 Devonshire St Boston MA 02109 800-544-9797
Web Address:	www.fidelity.com
Inception:	12-31-87
Advisor:	Fidelity Management & Research (FMR)
Subadvisor:	Multiple Subadvisors
NTF Plans:	Fidelity Retail-NTF, CommonWealth NTF

Minimum Purchase:	$2500	Add: $250	IRA: $200
Min Auto Inv Plan:	$2500	Add: $100	
Sales Fees:	No-load		
Management Fee:	0.47%		
Actual Fees:	Mgt:0.37%	Dist: —	
Expense Projections:	3Yr:$202	5Yr:$351	10Yr:$786
Income Distrib:	Semi-Annually		

Historical Profile

Return	Average
Risk	Below Avg
Rating	★★★ Neutral

| | 94% | 94% | 97% | 96% | 95% | 97% | 98% | 99% | 98% |

▼ Manager Change
▽ Partial Manager Change

Growth of $10,000
— Investment Values of Fund
— Investment Values of S&P 500

Performance Quartile (within Category)

1995	1996	1997	1998	1999	2000	2001	2002	2003	2004	2005	2006	History
30.77	32.69	39.46	50.39	60.11	51.53	42.94	31.94	39.63	41.71	43.16	44.31	NAV
28.38	15.38	27.02	34.76	24.26	-10.54	-16.55	-25.32	24.80	6.26	4.03	5.54	Total Return %
-9.20	-7.58	-6.34	6.18	3.22	-1.44	-4.66	-3.22	-3.88	-4.62	-0.88	-10.25	+/-S&P 500
-8.80	-7.74	-3.47	-3.95	-8.90	11.88	3.87	2.56	-4.95	-0.04	-1.23	-3.53	+/-Russ 1000Gr
0.48	0.93	0.81	0.25	0.28	0.00	0.12	0.30	0.69	0.99	0.55	0.56	Income Return %
27.90	14.45	26.21	34.51	23.98	-10.54	-16.67	-25.62	24.11	5.27	3.48	4.98	Capital Return %
74	76	45	36	73	44	34	39	71	67	70	65	Total Rtn % Rank Cat
0.12	0.28	0.26	0.10	0.14	0.00	0.06	0.13	0.22	0.39	0.23	0.24	Income $
2.47	2.25	1.75	2.06	2.07	2.52	0.00	0.00	0.00	0.00	0.93		Capital Gains $
1.02	0.95	0.78	0.70	0.70	0.86	0.87	0.74	0.69	0.67	0.64	0.61	Expense Ratio %
0.25	1.10	0.81	0.52	0.32	-0.02	0.01	0.25	0.64	0.48	1.05	0.54	Income Ratio %
182	206	51	49	38	40	46	33	24	23	29	48	Turnover Rate %
7,802	9,570	13,428	19,904	27,876	26,647	21,959	16,682	22,384	23,578	22,312	20,650	Net Assets $mil

Rating and Risk

Time Period	Load-Adj Return %	Morningstar Rtn vs Cat	Morningstar Risk vs Cat	Morningstar Risk-Adj Rating
1 Yr	5.54			
3 Yr	5.27	-Avg	Low	★★★
5 Yr	1.69	Avg	-Avg	★★★
10 Yr	5.61	Avg	-Avg	★★★
Incept	11.98			

Other Measures	Standard Index S&P 500	Best Fit Index Russ 1000Gr
Alpha	-5.3	-1.2
Beta	1.08	0.91
R-Squared	92	97
Standard Deviation	7.77	
Mean	5.27	
Sharpe Ratio	0.29	

Portfolio Analysis 10-31-06

Share change since 07-06 Total Stocks:166

		Sector	PE	Tot Ret%	% Assets
⊖	Johnson & Johnson	Health	17.5	12.45	4.16
⊖	General Electric Company	Ind Mtrls	20.0	9.35	3.92
⊖	Microsoft Corporation	Software	23.8	15.83	3.25
⊖	American International G	Financial	17.0	6.05	3.24
⊕	Wal-Mart Stores, Inc.	Consumer	16.9	0.13	2.55
⊖	Apple Computer, Inc.	Hardware	37.6	18.01	2.20
⊖	Google, Inc.	Business	61.5	11.00	2.06
⊖	UnitedHealth Group, Inc.	Health	20.8	-13.49	1.88
⊕	Wyeth	Health	17.2	12.88	1.88
⊕	Cisco Systems, Inc.	Hardware	30.1	59.64	1.73
⊖	Target Corporation	Consumer	19.3	4.65	1.68
⊕	Schlumberger, Ltd.	Energy	22.3	31.07	1.66
⊖	Altria Group, Inc.	Goods	16.3	19.87	1.55
⊕	Genentech, Inc.	Health	48.7	-12.29	1.55
⊖	Amgen, Inc.	Health	29.1	-13.38	1.54
⊖	PepsiCo, Inc.	Goods	21.5	7.86	1.53
⊕	Merck & Co., Inc.	Health	19.1	42.66	1.50
⊖	American Express Company	Financial	20.9	19.09	1.36
⊖	Avon Products	Goods	31.6	18.45	1.31
⊖	Colgate-Palmolive Compan	Goods	27.6	21.51	1.30

Current Investment Style

Value Blnd Growth — Large Mid Small

Market Cap	%
Giant	53.8
Large	32.5
Mid	12.4
Small	0.9
Micro	0.4

Avg $mil: 48,305

Value Measures		Rel Category
Price/Earnings	19.25	1.00
Price/Book	3.48	1.05
Price/Sales	1.77	0.91
Price/Cash Flow	11.97	1.05
Dividend Yield %	1.17	1.14

Growth Measures	%	Rel Category
Long-Term Erngs	13.55	0.94
Book Value	11.83	1.02
Sales	12.44	1.07
Cash Flow	13.08	0.78
Historical Erngs	18.98	0.83

Profitability	%	Rel Category
Return on Equity	20.83	1.02
Return on Assets	10.77	0.98
Net Margin	13.37	0.94

Investment Style
Equity
Stock %

Sector Weightings	% of Stocks	Rel S&P 500	3 Year High Low
↻ Info	25.63	1.28	
🖥 Software	5.94	1.72	7 5
📱 Hardware	15.24	1.65	18 13
🎙 Media	2.12	0.56	5 2
📞 Telecom	2.33	0.66	2 1
⚙ Service	49.49	1.07	
⚕ Health	24.13	2.00	26 20
🛒 Consumer	10.75	1.41	12 8
💼 Business	5.80	1.37	6 4
💲 Financial	8.81	0.40	14 9
⚒ Mfg	24.86	0.74	
🏭 Goods	8.58	1.00	11 8
⚙ Ind Mtrls	11.09	0.93	12 8
🔋 Energy	5.19	0.53	8 4
💡 Utilities	0.00	0.00	0 0

Composition

● Cash	1.9	
● Stocks	98.1	
● Bonds	0.0	
○ Other	0.0	
Foreign	5.0	
(% of Stock)		

Fidelity Capital & Inc

	Ticker	Load	NAV	Yield	SEC Yield	Total Assets	Mstar Category
	FAGIX	None	$8.89	6.0%	6.01%	$7,483 mil	High Yield Bond

Governance and Management

Stewardship Grade: B

Portfolio Manager(s)

Mark Notkin has managed this fund since July 2003. He has been with Fidelity since 1994, first as a high-yield analyst and more recently as manager of Fidelity's variable annuity high-income product. He is supported by a large team of analysts and research assistants.

Strategy

This fund typically takes on more risk than its average high-yield peer. Management often dabbles in distressed securities and equities while primarily focusing on B rated bonds. The fund's equity stake has ranged as high as 18% of assets, but manager Mark Notkin has trimmed it a bit.

Historical Profile

Return	High
Risk	High
Rating	★★★★ Highest

Investment Style
Fixed Income
Income Rtn %Rank Cat

▼ Manager Change
▽ Partial Manager Change

Growth of $10,000
— Investment Values of Fund
— Investment Values of LB Aggr

Performance Quartile (within Category)

	1995	1996	1997	1998	1999	2000	2001	2002	2003	2004	2005	2006	History
NAV	9.16	9.36	10.01	9.28	9.29	7.73	6.78	6.28	8.06	8.47	8.37	8.89	NAV
	16.74	11.41	14.71	4.77	13.27	-9.43	-4.66	-0.40	39.13	12.57	5.04	13.04	Total Return %
	-1.73	7.78	5.06	-3.92	14.09	-21.06	-13.10	-10.65	35.03	8.23	2.61	8.71	+/-LB Aggr
	-0.65	-1.01	2.08	4.19	9.99	-4.22	-10.44	-3.51	11.20	0.61	2.78	1.11	+/-CSFB Glb HY
	10.58	9.03	7.47	9.91	8.18	8.28	8.21	6.76	10.14	7.15	6.22	6.61	Income Return %
	6.16	2.38	7.24	-5.14	5.09	-17.71	-12.87	-7.16	28.99	5.42	-1.18	6.43	Capital Return %
	65	87	18	10	4	71	92	46	2	10	5	5	Total Rtn % Rank Cat
	0.88	0.80	0.68	0.95	0.72	0.74	0.61	0.44	0.61	0.56	0.51	0.54	Income $
	0.00	0.00	0.00	0.26	0.48	0.00	0.00	0.00	0.00	0.00	0.00	0.00	Capital Gains $
	0.96	0.98	0.86	0.82	0.81	0.82	0.78	0.81	0.83	0.79	0.77	0.77	Expense Ratio %
	7.38	8.03	6.53	7.23	8.84	9.09	9.32	8.48	9.06	7.41	6.61	6.24	Income Ratio %
	78	119	309	179	125	88	132	125	125	113	59	42	Turnover Rate %
	2,322	2,163	2,096	2,196	2,846	2,837	2,875	2,802	4,260	4,912	5,411	7,483	Net Assets $mil

Performance 12-31-06

	1st Qtr	2nd Qtr	3rd Qtr	4th Qtr	Total
2002	-0.17	-10.98	-0.48	12.61	-0.40
2003	11.08	14.73	2.45	6.56	39.13
2004	1.41	-1.04	4.83	6.99	12.57
2005	-0.74	2.52	2.03	1.17	5.04
2006	3.52	-0.05	3.70	5.35	13.04

Trailing	Total Return%	+/- LB Aggr	+/- CSFB Glb HY	%Rank Cat	Growth of $10,000
3 Mo	5.35	4.11	0.90	4	10,535
6 Mo	9.24	4.15	1.09	3	10,924
1 Yr	13.04	8.71	1.11	5	11,304
3 Yr Avg	10.16	6.46	1.54	6	13,368
5 Yr Avg	13.12	8.06	2.05	2	18,522
10 Yr Avg	8.09	1.85	1.00	3	21,770
15 Yr Avg	10.25	3.75	1.35	1	43,219

Tax Analysis	Tax-Adj Rtn%	%Rank Cat	Tax-Cost Rat	%Rank Cat
3 Yr (estimated)	7.72	3	2.21	33
5 Yr (estimated)	10.36	2	2.44	37
10 Yr (estimated)	4.89	2	2.96	23

Potential Capital Gain Exposure: 0% of assets

Rating and Risk

Time Period	Load-Adj Return %	Morningstar Rtn vs Cat	Morningstar Risk vs Cat	Morningstar Risk-Adj Rating
1 Yr	13.04			
3 Yr	10.16	High	High	★★★★★
5 Yr	13.12	High	High	★★★★★
10 Yr	8.09	High	High	★★★★
Incept	10.64			

Other Measures	Standard Index LB Aggr	Best Fit Index CSFB Glb HY
Alpha	6.4	0.4
Beta	0.40	1.20
R-Squared	8	90
Standard Deviation	4.61	
Mean	10.16	
Sharpe Ratio	1.44	

Morningstar's Take by Scott Berry 12-19-06

Fidelity Capital & Income has fired on all cylinders in 2006.

With the economy holding up well, defaults few and far between, and investors comfortable taking on added risk, high-yield funds have certainly had the wind at their backs for much of the year. But good bond-picking by manager Mark Notkin, who held General Motors Acceptance Corporation and who avoided HCA, helped this fund cruise past its average high-yield peer. The fund has received an added boost from its stock holdings, which include cable providers Cablevision Systems and Comcast. Both have returned more than 60% for the year to date through Dec. 18, 2006. Overall, the fund has returned 12.7% over that stretch, while its average high-yield category peer has returned 9.7%.

This fund typically takes on more risk than its average peer, so we expect it to perform better than most during market rallies. But the degree to which it outperformed is surprising, and particularly so given that Notkin has dialed down the fund's risk over the past year. Specifically, he has shifted assets to bank loans, which provide greater security than typical high-yield bonds. He has also been careful to pare down the fund's exposure to subordinated bonds, where he argues some valuations just don't make sense.

We like that Notkin has kept an eye on risk, given that high-yield bonds aren't offering a lot of added yield at the moment. And we think Fidelity's extensive high-yield research capabilities will continue to provide the fund an advantage over the long term. Still, we expect this fund will take its lumps if the stock or bond market stumbles, as it has historically been one of the most volatile funds in the category.

We're disappointed that Notkin has chosen not to invest even a dime of his own money here (Statement of Additional Information, April 30, 2006), but shareholders comfortable with the fund's risk profile have reason to stay the course.

Address:	82 Devonshire St Boston MA 02109 800-544-6666
Web Address:	www.fidelity.com
Inception:	11-01-77
Advisor:	Fidelity Management & Research (FMR)
Subadvisor:	Multiple Subadvisors
NTF Plans:	Fidelity Retail-NTF, CommonWealth NTF

Minimum Purchase:	$2500	Add: $250	IRA: $500
Min Auto Inv Plan:	$2500	Add: $100	
Sales Fees:	No-load, 1.00%R		
Management Fee:	0.57%		
Actual Fees:	Mgt:0.57%	Dist: —	
Expense Projections:	3Yr:$246	5Yr:$428	10Yr:$954
Income Distrib:	Monthly		

Portfolio Analysis 10-31-06

Total Fixed-Income:361	Date of Maturity	Amount $000	Value $000	% Net Assets
Gmac 8%	11-01-31	119,950	127,747	1.86
NTL, Inc.		3,795	102,583	1.49
Cablevision Systems A		2,375	66,001	0.96
Xerox 7.625%	06-15-13	62,845	65,673	0.96
Csc Hldgs 7.625%	07-15-18	64,323	63,358	0.92
Comcast Corporation A		1,530	62,225	0.91
General Mtrs 8.375%	07-15-33	65,595	58,216	0.85
Qwest 8.875%	03-15-12	48,680	53,548	0.78
Georgia Pac 1st Ln Trm B	12-23-12	51,173	51,461	0.75
Lucent Tech 6.45%	03-15-29	57,490	51,454	0.75
Williams Companies, Inc.		2,050	50,082	0.73
Sungard Data Term B	02-10-13	49,439	49,872	0.73
Rogers Communications, I		725	43,391	0.63
Embarq 7.995%	06-01-36	38,658	41,109	0.60
Intelsat 144A 11.25%	06-15-16	37,305	40,569	0.59
Gmac 6.75%	12-01-14	40,130	39,528	0.58
Mgm Mirage 6.625%	07-15-15	40,650	38,516	0.56
Southern Nat Gas 7.35%	02-15-31	35,553	36,931	0.54
Chesapeake Engy 6.5%	08-15-17	38,930	36,594	0.53
News Corporation, Ltd. A		1,752	36,533	0.53

Current Investment Style

Duration: Short Int Long
Quality: High Med Low

1 figure provided by fund

Avg Eff Duration[1]	—
Avg Eff Maturity	8.1 Yrs
Avg Credit Quality	B
Avg Wtd Coupon	6.23%
Avg Wtd Price	99.73% of par

Coupon Range	% of Bonds	Rel Cat
0% PIK	8.4	1.5
0% to 8%	68.7	1.4
8% to 11%	27.1	0.6
11% to 14%	4.0	0.9
More than 14%	0.2	1.5

1.00=Category Average

Credit Analysis	% bonds 10-31-06		
AAA	0	BB	29
AA	0	B	30
A	0	Below B	10
BBB	3	NR/NA	28

Sector Breakdown % of assets

US Treasuries	0
TIPS	0
US Agency	0
Mortgage Pass-Throughs	0
Mortgage CMO	0
Mortgage ARM	0
US Corporate	79
Asset-Backed	0
Convertible	0
Municipal	0
Corporate Inflation-Protected	0
Foreign Corporate	7
Foreign Govt	0

Composition

Cash	10.8	Bonds	66.9
Stocks	14.7	Other	7.6

Special Securities

Restricted/Illiquid Secs	13
Exotic Mortgage-Backed	0
Emerging-Markets Secs	Trace
Options/Futures/Warrants	No

Fidelity Capital Apprec

	Ticker	Load	NAV	Yield	Total Assets	Mstar Category
	FDCAX	None	$27.11	0.4%	$8,699 mil	Large Growth

Governance and Management

Stewardship Grade: B

Portfolio Manager(s)

Longtime manager Harry Lange stepped down from this fund in October 31, 2005 to run Fidelity Magellan. New manager Fergus Shiel is a Fidelity veteran: He ran several of the firm's sector funds and diversified offerings such as Fidelity Fifty and Independence before leaving to start a hedge fund in 2003. Shiel rejoined Fidelity in September 2005. In addition to running this offering, he also serves as manager of Fidelity Advisor Dynamic Capital Appreciation.

Strategy

Under its previous manager, this was decidedly a growth fund, often sporting technology weightings around 40% of assets. Current manager Fergus Shiel uses a more eclectic approach. He mixes value and growth names, as well as smaller and larger stocks. Shiel looks for earnings growth and turnarounds, but also for stocks with P/E ratios he thinks will expand. He has shown a willingness to bet heavily on individual industries, as evidenced by a giant position in the tobacco sector in one of his previous charges. Shiel also trades frequently, so the fund may work best in tax-sheltered accounts.

Performance 12-31-06

	1st Qtr	2nd Qtr	3rd Qtr	4th Qtr	Total
2002	1.36	-12.29	-19.65	10.22	-21.27
2003	1.85	20.69	10.11	12.06	51.68
2004	4.20	-0.51	-3.15	10.81	11.26
2005	-4.65	1.69	7.17	1.81	5.80
2006	8.84	-2.89	0.41	7.22	13.80

Trailing	Total Return%	+/- S&P 500	+/- Russ 1000Gr	%Rank Cat	Growth of $10,000
3 Mo	7.22	0.52	1.29	14	10,722
6 Mo	7.67	-5.07	-2.43	63	10,767
1 Yr	13.80	-1.99	4.73	7	11,380
3 Yr Avg	10.24	-0.20	3.37	13	13,397
5 Yr Avg	9.85	3.66	7.16	1	15,996
10 Yr Avg	10.08	1.66	4.64	5	26,127
15 Yr Avg	12.29	1.65	4.27	6	56,901

Tax Analysis	Tax-Adj Rtn%	%Rank Cat	Tax-Cost Rat	%Rank Cat
3 Yr (estimated)	9.17	16	0.97	62
5 Yr (estimated)	9.21	2	0.58	58
10 Yr (estimated)	8.69	6	1.26	62

Potential Capital Gain Exposure: 16% of assets

Morningstar's Take by Dan Lefkovitz 11-07-06

Against our better judgment, we strongly recommend Fidelity Capital Appreciation.

Morningstar advocates a buy-and-hold approach to investing--both for fund investors and fund managers. As it applies to stock-picking, patience is key. After all, who knows how the market will behave in the short term? Many studies have shown that the best investors buy undervalued securities and hold them until their value is recognized, so we're skeptical of fast-trading portfolio managers. We also get nervous when managers buy stocks not only on the basis of their intrinsic value but also on the view that they'll find market favor.

That's why this fund's manager, Fergus Shiel, raises red flags. When Shiel took over for Harry Lange in November 2005, he told us that he would trade rapidly, didn't have a particular investment style, and would look for stocks poised to become more popular. Sure enough, the fund's annualized turnover rate as of April 2006 was a sky-high 198%,

and the portfolio is a motley assortment of stocks, ranging from mega-cap growth stories like Walt Disney to mid-cap turnaround play AMR to a raft of small-cap names.

We see Shiel as one of the rare investors who can pull off this kind of investing. He steered Fidelity Independence to returns that comfortably beat the S&P 500, as well as the large-blend and large-growth category averages, during his tenure (June 1996 to April 2003). At one point, he had 30% of that fund's assets invested in two tobacco stocks, in which he made a killing. In his one year on the job here, he has beaten 92% of his large-growth peers, thanks to picks like Disney and steel company Allegheny Technology.

Shiel's talent makes this one of our favorite Fidelity funds, but some caution is advised. First, his aggressive bets can sometimes misfire, as Independence's 2001 losses show. Second, Shiel's trading can cause tax headaches, so you might want to hold this fund in a tax-sheltered account.

Address:	82 Devonshire St Boston MA 02109 800-544-6666	Minimum Purchase: Min Auto Inv Plan: Sales Fees:	$2500 $100 No-load	Add: $250 Add: $100	IRA: $200
Web Address: Inception: Advisor: Subadvisor:	www.fidelity.com 11-26-86 Fidelity Management & Research (FMR) Multiple Subadvisors	Management Fee: Actual Fees: Expense Projections: Income Distrib:	0.67% Mgt:0.67% 3Yr:$290 Annually	Dist: — 5Yr:$504	10Yr:$1120
NTF Plans:	Fidelity Retail-NTF, CommonWealth NTF				

Historical Profile

Return High
Risk Above Avg
Rating ★★★★ Above Avg

92%	94%	96%	95%	97%	96%	93%	98%	94%		

▼ Manager Change
▽ Partial Manager Change

Growth of $10,000
■ Investment Values of Fund
— Investment Values of S&P 500

Performance Quartile (within Category)

1995	1996	1997	1998	1999	2000	2001	2002	2003	2004	2005	2006	History
16.78	17.64	19.38	22.07	29.87	22.23	20.55	16.18	24.51	26.03	25.10	27.11	NAV
18.77	15.12	26.52	16.95	45.84	-18.10	-7.56	-21.27	51.68	11.26	5.80	13.80	Total Return %
-18.81	-7.84	-6.84	-11.63	24.80	-9.00	4.33	0.83	23.00	0.38	0.89	-1.99	+/-S&P 500
-18.41	-8.00	-3.97	-21.76	12.68	4.32	12.86	6.61	21.93	4.96	0.54	4.73	+/-Russ 1000Gr
2.61	0.72	0.45	0.52	2.58	0.50	0.00	0.00	0.06	0.04	0.00	0.44	Income Return %
16.16	14.40	26.07	16.43	43.26	-18.60	-7.56	-21.27	51.62	11.22	5.80	13.36	Capital Return %
98	77	48	85	28	72	6	15	2	23	54	7	Total Rtn % Rank Cat
0.40	0.12	0.08	0.10	0.57	0.15	0.00	0.00	0.01	0.01	0.00	0.11	Income $
1.00	1.54	2.85	0.45	1.49	2.13	0.00	0.00	0.00	1.21	2.46	1.34	Capital Gains $
1.06	0.80	0.66	0.67	0.65	0.83	0.91	1.03	0.88	0.91	0.90	—	Expense Ratio %
2.31	1.24	0.43	0.46	0.56	0.15	0.17	-0.35	-0.31	-0.12	-0.05	—	Income Ratio %
87	205	176	121	78	85	120	80	54	72	109	—	Turnover Rate %
1,669	1,642	2,110	2,602	3,686	2,707	2,311	1,796	4,466	6,452	7,316	8,699	Net Assets $mil

Rating and Risk

Time Period	Load-Adj Return %	Morningstar Rtn vs Cat	Morningstar Risk vs Cat	Morningstar Risk-Adj Rating
1 Yr	13.80			
3 Yr	10.24	+Avg	+Avg	★★★★
5 Yr	9.85	High	+Avg	★★★★★
10 Yr	10.08	High	+Avg	★★★★
Incept	12.40			

Other Measures	Standard Index S&P 500	Best Fit Index Russ MG
Alpha	-2.5	-1.5
Beta	1.38	0.91
R-Squared	77	91
Standard Deviation	10.87	
Mean	10.24	
Sharpe Ratio	0.66	

Portfolio Analysis 07-31-06

Share change since 04-06   Total Stocks:149

Share change		Sector	PE	Tot Ret%	% Assets
⊕	Walt Disney Company	Media	21.0	44.26	4.34
⊖	Motorola, Inc.	Hardware	11.8	-8.17	2.94
	Qwest Communications Int	Telecom	—	48.14	2.66
⊕	Abercrombie & Fitch Comp	Consumer	17.5	8.01	2.27
⊕	Whirlpool Corporation	Goods	13.0	1.11	2.21
✿	Altria Group, Inc.	Goods	16.3	19.87	2.06
⊕	Norfolk Southern Corpora	Business	14.0	13.73	2.01
⊖	American Tower Corporati	Telecom	—	37.57	1.94
⊕	Broadcom Corporation	Hardware	39.9	2.79	1.82
⊕	Elan Corporation PLC ADR	Health	—	5.89	1.66
⊕	Biogen Idec, Inc.	Health	NMF	8.64	1.63
⊖	Cameco Corporation	Energy	63.2	28.10	1.54
⊖	Rockwell Automation	Ind Mtrls	17.2	4.77	1.52
⊕	Deere & Company	Ind Mtrls	14.8	42.27	1.51
✿	General Electric Company	Ind Mtrls	20.0	9.35	1.47
⊕	AMR Corporation	Business	—	35.99	1.45
⊕	Reynolds American, Inc.	Goods	15.9	43.87	1.42
⊖	Starbucks Corporation	Consumer	49.3	18.03	1.42
⊕	Wynn Resorts, Ltd.	Consumer	—	82.52	1.38
✿	Johnson & Johnson	Health	17.5	12.45	1.34

Current Investment Style

Value Blnd Growth — Large Mid Small

Market Cap	%
Giant	23.5
Large	35.8
Mid	32.9
Small	6.5
Micro	1.2

Avg $mil: 13,057

Value Measures		Rel Category
Price/Earnings	18.99	0.99
Price/Book	2.75	0.83
Price/Sales	1.08	0.56
Price/Cash Flow	5.29	0.46
Dividend Yield %	1.12	1.09

Growth Measures	%	Rel Category
Long-Term Erngs	13.48	0.94
Book Value	8.09	0.70
Sales	7.13	0.61
Cash Flow	15.28	0.91
Historical Erngs	22.61	0.98

Profitability	%	Rel Category
Return on Equity	17.57	0.86
Return on Assets	7.68	0.70
Net Margin	7.82	0.55

Sector Weightings	% of Stocks	Rel S&P 500	3 Year High Low	
☁ Info	21.14	1.06		
🖥 Software	1.14	0.33	11	0
💻 Hardware	8.80	0.95	29	9
🎬 Media	4.63	1.22	11	5
📞 Telecom	6.57	1.87	7	0
⚙ Service	43.77	0.95		
🏥 Health	10.94	0.91	19	9
🏦 Consumer	13.21	1.73	14	6
📊 Business	15.12	3.57	15	6
💲 Financial	4.50	0.20	11	5
🏭 Mfg	35.08	1.04		
🛒 Goods	13.62	1.59	14	2
⚒ Ind Mtrls	14.10	1.18	14	5
🔋 Energy	7.36	0.75	15	5
💡 Utilities	0.00	0.00	0	0

Composition

		%
●	Cash	6.2
●	Stocks	93.8
●	Bonds	0.0
○	Other	0.0
	Foreign (% of Stock)	7.0

Fidelity Contrafund

	Ticker	Load	NAV	Yield	Total Assets	Mstar Category
	FCNTX	Closed	$65.20	0.5%	$68,565 mil	Large Growth

Governance and Management

Stewardship Grade: B

Portfolio Manager(s)

Will Danoff has been at the helm since September 1990 and is backed by Fidelity's deep research staff. He has adapted his style to the fund's size by holding more large caps, and he has cut the fund's turnover in recent years. He has also run Fidelity Advisor New Insights since its July 2003 inception.

Strategy

Call it forced evolution: As this fund's asset base grew in the 1990s, manager Will Danoff had to move away from mid-caps and small caps and adopt a growth-at-a-reasonable-price philosophy. He continues to own a substantial stake in mid-caps, but it is now dominated by larger fare. It has been more conservative than most of its large-growth rivals in recent years, with big underweightings in racy sectors such as technology. Danoff has reined in the fund's turnover considerably in recent years.

Historical Profile

Return	High
Risk	Low
Rating	★★★★ Highest

90% 94% 91% 89% 90% 94% 89% 90% 89%

Investment Style
Equity
Stock %

▼ Manager Change
▽ Partial Manager Change

Growth of $10,000
— Investment Values of Fund
— Investment Values of S&P 500

42.2
32.4
24.0
17.0
10.0

Performance Quartile (within Category)

1995	1996	1997	1998	1999	2000	2001	2002	2003	2004	2005	2006	History
38.02	42.15	46.63	56.81	60.02	49.18	42.77	38.60	49.35	56.74	64.76	65.20	NAV
36.28	21.94	23.00	31.57	25.03	-6.80	-12.59	-9.63	27.95	15.07	16.23	11.52	Total Return %
-1.30	-1.02	-10.36	2.99	3.99	2.30	-0.70	12.47	-0.73	4.19	11.32	-4.27	+/-S&P 500
-0.90	-1.18	-7.49	-7.14	-8.13	15.62	7.83	18.25	-1.80	8.77	10.97	2.45	+/-Russ 1000Gr
0.30	1.05	0.84	0.64	0.50	0.41	0.45	0.12	0.10	0.09	0.41	0.61	Income Return %
35.98	20.89	22.16	30.93	24.53	-7.21	-13.04	-9.75	27.85	14.98	15.82	10.91	Capital Return %
26	31	66	47	71	30	14	1	51	5	2	14	Total Rtn % Rank Cat
0.09	0.38	0.35	0.30	0.28	0.24	0.22	0.05	0.04	0.05	0.23	0.39	Income $
3.13	3.45	4.56	4.22	10.22	6.62	0.00	0.00	0.00	0.00	0.97	6.49	Capital Gains $
0.96	0.79	0.67	0.61	0.62	0.84	0.91	0.99	0.98	0.92	0.88	—	Expense Ratio %
0.44	1.28	0.91	0.70	0.48	0.45	0.49	0.14	0.01	0.08	0.46	—	Income Ratio %
223	159	144	197	177	166	141	80	67	64	60	—	Turnover Rate %
14,832	23,798	30,809	38,821	46,927	40,220	32,321	27,695	36,051	44,484	60,094	68,565	Net Assets $mil

Performance 12-31-06

	1st Qtr	2nd Qtr	3rd Qtr	4th Qtr	Total
2002	2.88	-3.68	-9.86	1.18	-9.63
2003	-2.15	11.83	5.02	11.34	27.95
2004	3.75	2.36	-0.63	9.04	15.07
2005	0.33	2.95	8.41	3.79	16.23
2006	4.75	-0.77	0.79	6.45	11.52

Trailing	Total Return%	+/- S&P 500	+/- Russ 1000Gr	%Rank Cat	Growth of $10,000
3 Mo	6.45	-0.25	0.52	25	10,645
6 Mo	7.28	-5.46	-2.82	68	10,728
1 Yr	11.52	-4.27	2.45	14	11,152
3 Yr Avg	14.26	3.82	7.39	2	14,917
5 Yr Avg	11.52	5.33	8.83	1	17,249
10 Yr Avg	11.01	2.59	5.57	4	28,420
15 Yr Avg	13.38	2.74	5.36	4	65,773

Tax Analysis	Tax-Adj Rtn%	%Rank Cat	Tax-Cost Rat	%Rank Cat
3 Yr (estimated)	13.50	2	0.67	44
5 Yr (estimated)	11.05	1	0.42	43
10 Yr (estimated)	9.48	4	1.38	69

Potential Capital Gain Exposure: 26% of assets

Rating and Risk

Time Period	Load-Adj Return %	Morningstar Rtn vs Cat	Morningstar Risk vs Cat	Morningstar Risk-Adj Rating
1 Yr	11.52			
3 Yr	14.26	High	Avg	★★★★★
5 Yr	11.52	High	Low	★★★★★
10 Yr	11.01	High	Low	★★★★★
Incept	13.32			

Other Measures	Standard Index S&P 500	Best Fit Index S&P Mid 400
Alpha	3.0	2.7
Beta	1.09	0.81
R-Squared	69	88
Standard Deviation	8.95	
Mean	14.26	
Sharpe Ratio	1.18	

Portfolio Analysis 09-30-06

Share change since 06-06 Total Stocks:423	Sector	PE	Tot Ret%	% Assets
⊕ Google, Inc.	Business	61.5	11.00	3.77
⊕ Berkshire Hathaway Inc.	Financial	—	—	2.40
⊕ Genentech, Inc.	Health	48.7	-12.29	2.37
⊕ Hewlett-Packard Company	Hardware	19.3	45.21	2.14
⊕ Procter & Gamble Company	Goods	23.9	13.36	1.92
⊕ Wells Fargo Company	Financial	14.7	16.82	1.86
⊕ America Movil SA ADR	Telecom	27.7	55.53	1.85
⊕ EnCana Corporation	Energy	11.8	2.55	1.81
⊕ Roche Holding	Health			1.61
⊕ Apple Computer, Inc.	Hardware	37.6	18.01	1.59
⊖ Schlumberger, Ltd.	Energy	22.3	31.07	1.39
⊖ PepsiCo, Inc.	Goods	21.5	7.86	1.38
⊕ Walt Disney Company	Media	21.0	44.26	1.31
⊕ ExxonMobil Corporation	Energy	11.1	39.07	1.22
⊕ Bank of America Corporat	Financial	12.4	20.68	1.09
⊖ American Express Company	Financial	20.9	19.09	0.98
⊖ Valero Energy Corporatio	Energy	6.3	-0.33	0.97
⊕ Metropolitan Life Insura	Financial	16.0	21.67	0.97
⊖ Samsung Electronics	Goods	—	—	0.95
⊕ Danaher Corporation	Ind Mtrls	22.0	30.02	0.95

Current Investment Style

Value Blnd Growth — Large/Mid/Small

Market Cap	%
Giant	48.9
Large	32.1
Mid	15.9
Small	2.9
Micro	0.2

Avg $mil: 33,161

Value Measures		Rel Category
Price/Earnings	17.73	0.92
Price/Book	3.07	0.92
Price/Sales	1.81	0.93
Price/Cash Flow	10.53	0.93
Dividend Yield %	1.25	1.21

Growth Measures	%	Rel Category
Long-Term Erngs	12.75	0.89
Book Value	11.26	0.97
Sales	12.40	1.07
Cash Flow	21.69	1.29
Historical Erngs	22.24	0.97

Profitability	%	Rel Category
Return on Equity	20.62	1.01
Return on Assets	11.44	1.04
Net Margin	14.92	1.05

Sector Weightings	% of Stocks	Rel S&P 500	3 Year High Low
⊙ Info	19.40	0.97	
▣ Software	2.26	0.66	3 2
▣ Hardware	9.07	0.98	10 5
▣ Media	2.68	0.71	4 2
▣ Telecom	5.39	1.54	5 4
⊛ Service	49.30	1.07	
▣ Health	12.08	1.00	17 11
▣ Consumer	5.77	0.75	14 5
▣ Business	8.95	2.12	10 5
▣ Financial	22.50	1.01	23 14
⊟ Mfg	31.30	0.93	
▣ Goods	10.33	1.21	12 7
▣ Ind Mtrls	10.24	0.86	19 10
▣ Energy	9.31	0.95	17 5
▣ Utilities	1.42	0.41	1 0

Composition

	%
● Cash	10.3
● Stocks	89.3
● Bonds	0.0
● Other	0.4
Foreign (% of Stock)	22.0

Morningstar's Take by Greg Carlson 11-10-06

Fidelity Contrafund's size isn't to blame for a subpar 2006, but we expect it to weigh on future returns.

It's been a tough year for this fund. Sure, it's well ahead of its typical large-growth rival for the year to date through Nov. 8, 2006. However, the fund--which previously resided in the large-blend category--trails its benchmark, the S&P 500 Index, by nearly 3 percentage points. (The fund's management fee is adjusted annually based on its three-year performance versus the S&P.)

What has been the source of the fund's underperformance? It's tempting to blame manager Will Danoff's enormous asset load--between this fund and Fidelity Advisor New Insights (both of which closed to new investors earlier this year), as well as variable-annuity accounts, he runs more than $80 billion and has been forced to trade at a much slower pace than he did in the past. However, we'd argue that this year's stumble would have occurred with a far smaller asset base. Danoff, despite this fund's name, isn't a hard-core

contrarian. He prefers companies with substantial profit growth, thus he missed out on much of the rebound by more-staid firms such as drugmaker Pfizer and telecom giants such as AT&T. Although he traded around positions more actively in the past--and often added value, as the fund's superb record attests--he wasn't known for making huge portfolio shifts to capture short-term movements.

That said, Danoff's workload remains a concern. Altering his style--in addition to trading less, he's had to spread the fund's assets across more holdings--may dilute returns, and he'll have difficulty taking substantial stakes in individual stocks that aren't mega-caps. As of June 30, for example, Fidelity owned nearly 15% of the outstanding shares of Marvell Technology and NII Holdings, which both appear in this fund's top 25 holdings and straddle the mid/large-cap line.

Due to Danoff's formidable abilities, we think shareholders should hang on here. But it's difficult to give the fund a strong endorsement.

Address:	82 Devonshire Street Boston MA 02109 800-544-9797	Minimum Purchase:	Closed Add: — IRA: —
		Min Auto Inv Plan:	Closed Add: —
		Sales Fees:	No-load
Web Address:	www.fidelity.com	Management Fee:	0.71%
Inception:	05-17-67	Actual Fees:	Mgt:0.71% Dist: —
Advisor:	Fidelity Management & Research (FMR)	Expense Projections:	3Yr:$290 5Yr:$504 10Yr:$1120
Subadvisor:	Multiple Subadvisors	Income Distrib:	Semi-Annually
NTF Plans:	Fidelity Retail-NTF, CommonWealth NTF		

© 2007 Morningstar, Inc. All rights reserved. The information herein is not represented or warranted to be accurate, correct, complete or timely. Past performance is no guarantee of future results. Download your free reports only at http://www.morningstar.com/goto/2007Funds500.

Fidelity Convertible Sec

	Ticker	Load	NAV	Yield	Total Assets	Mstar Category
	FCVSX	None	$25.33	1.9%	$2,105 mil	Convertibles

Historical Profile

Return	Above Avg
Risk	High
Rating	★★★★ Above Avg

	10%	21%	10%	22%	20%	15%	11%	14%	17%	Investment Style
										Equity Stock %

Growth of $10,000
— Investment Values of Fund
— Investment Values of DJ Mod

Performance Quartile (within Category)

1995	1996	1997	1998	1999	2000	2001	2002	2003	2004	2005	2006	History
16.77	17.56	17.51	18.49	24.28	20.78	19.90	16.34	20.17	21.60	22.46	25.33	NAV
19.38	15.05	14.46	16.28	44.08	7.21	0.50	-13.89	28.32	10.21	5.95	15.13	Total Return %
-0.42	4.39	2.56	3.96	26.75	8.88	3.30	-7.12	0.94	-2.76	-1.04	2.83	+/-DJ Mod
-4.58	2.93	-1.05	4.07	8.09	14.73	3.41	-10.77	5.35	1.90	6.14	3.10	+/-Merrill Lynch Convert
5.03	4.70	4.04	3.60	3.18	2.90	4.55	4.24	4.41	2.85	1.86	2.15	Income Return %
14.35	10.35	10.42	12.68	40.90	4.31	-4.05	-18.13	23.91	7.36	4.09	12.98	Capital Return %
85	59	91	9	18	33	11	96	26	38	26	5	Total Rtn % Rank Cat
0.76	0.77	0.70	0.62	0.58	0.69	0.93	0.83	0.71	0.57	0.40	0.48	Income $
0.76	0.89	1.77	1.16	1.50	4.57	0.02	0.00	0.00	0.02	0.01	0.02	Capital Gains $
0.70	0.83	0.73	0.77	0.82	0.77	0.76	0.85	0.82	0.66	0.69	—	Expense Ratio %
4.59	4.48	3.46	3.21	2.85	2.96	3.40	4.76	4.46	2.26	1.95	—	Income Ratio %
203	175	212	223	246	262	282	138	136	112	81	—	Turnover Rate %
1,046	1,120	1,003	1,036	1,423	1,902	1,829	1,381	1,822	1,885	1,802	2,105	Net Assets $mil

▼ Manager Change
▽ Partial Manager Change

Performance 12-31-06

	1st Qtr	2nd Qtr	3rd Qtr	4th Qtr	Total
2002	-0.70	-9.90	-9.89	6.80	-13.89
2003	2.83	12.15	1.84	9.25	28.32
2004	2.72	0.07	-1.03	8.34	10.21
2005	-3.75	1.93	7.75	0.23	5.95
2006	6.86	0.21	-0.54	8.10	15.13

Trailing	Total Return%	+/- DJ Mod	+/- Merrill Lynch Convert	%Rank Cat	Growth of $10,000
3 Mo	8.10	2.51	3.28	1	10,810
6 Mo	7.52	-1.27	-0.13	29	10,752
1 Yr	15.13	2.83	3.10	5	11,513
3 Yr Avg	10.37	-0.35	3.78	13	13,445
5 Yr Avg	8.24	-1.78	0.63	48	14,857
10 Yr Avg	11.87	3.32	3.26	7	30,700
15 Yr Avg	12.63	3.42	2.73	8	59,540

Tax Analysis	Tax-Adj Rtn%	%Rank Cat	Tax-Cost Rat	%Rank Cat
3 Yr (estimated)	9.50	4	0.79	19
5 Yr (estimated)	7.06	31	1.09	34
10 Yr (estimated)	9.01	7	2.56	94

Potential Capital Gain Exposure: 16% of assets

Rating and Risk

Time Period	Load-Adj Return %	Morningstar Rtn vs Cat	Morningstar Risk vs Cat	Morningstar Risk-Adj Rating
1 Yr	15.13			
3 Yr	10.37	+Avg	+Avg	★★★★
5 Yr	8.24	Avg	+Avg	★★★
10 Yr	11.87	+Avg	High	★★★★
Incept	12.83			

Other Measures	Standard Index DJ Mod	Best Fit Index Merrill Lynch Convert
Alpha	-1.9	2.9
Beta	1.25	1.21
R-Squared	77	81

Standard Deviation	8.40
Mean	10.37
Sharpe Ratio	0.84

Morningstar's Take by Lawrence Jones 12-21-06

We'd like to see more stability at Fidelity Convertible Securities before recommending it.

The frequency of manager change here concerns us. Nine different managers have taken the lead at the fund over the past decade. We find this level of turnover disconcerting, even with Fidelity's deep bench of talent from which to draw replacements, as the changes can lead to inconsistent strategy implementation and returns. This has not been the case thus far, as the fund's sterling record has continued apace regardless of the changes. But we think greater stability would improve the fund's chances of continued success, and we're hopeful that the fund's current manager, Tom Soviero, will stay with this offering for a while.

Soviero comes to the fund with good experience that will aid him in running a convertibles portfolio. He has managed Fidelity Advisor High-Income since June 2000 and Fidelity Leveraged Company Stock since July 2003, delivering impressive results at each. The combination of high-yield bond and equity-investing experience prepares him well.

Since arriving in June 2005, Soviero has made adjustments to the approach typically taken here and significant changes to the portfolio's sector weights. He has, for instance, added to the fund's equity stake (currently 17%), which he plans to keep between 15%-20% of assets, higher than it has been historically. He argues that this will add value for investors. Over the past year, he has reduced the fund's stake in the pharmaceutical and financial sectors, not liking their prospects, while concurrently adding positions in energy, technology, and automakers, areas he invests heavily in elsewhere.

Although an increased equity stake and a shift in sector focus have worked well so far for Soviero, investors should be aware that these changes can court added volatility. And in a fund that already suffers more ups and downs than its typical category rival, in part due to its concentrated portfolio, these changes should not be overlooked.

Portfolio Analysis 08-31-06

Total Fixed-Income:37	Date of Maturity	Amount $000	Value $000	% Net Assets
El Paso Pfd 144A		138	175,678	8.57
Celanese Cv		2,653	73,501	3.58
Halliburton Cv 3.125%	07-15-23	39,400	70,034	3.42
Valero Energy Corporatio		939	53,903	2.63
Tyco Intl Grp S A Cv 3.1	01-15-23	39,900	49,755	2.43
Vishay Intertechnology C	08-01-23	44,930	45,680	2.23
Teekay Shipping Corporat		896	39,640	1.93
Celanese Corporation		2,135	39,476	1.93
Maxtor 2.375%	08-15-12	25,100	35,565	1.73
Flextronics Intl Cv 1%	08-01-10	35,580	35,267	1.72
Quicksilver Res 144A 1.8	11-01-24	24,500	34,952	1.70
Amer Tower 144A Cv 3.25%	08-01-10	11,330	34,002	1.66
General Mtrs Pfd	03-06-32	1,750	32,585	1.59
Amer Express 144A Cv 1.8	12-01-33	31,800	31,840	1.55
Roche Hldgs 144A Cv	07-25-21	30,000	29,514	1.44
Six Flags 4.5%	05-15-15	27,700	29,085	1.42
Fisher Scientific Intl 1	10-01-23	15,600	26,873	1.31
Charter Comms 5.875%	11-16-09	30,840	26,806	1.31
On Semicon	04-15-24	29,500	25,487	1.24
Fluor 1.5%	02-15-24	15,700	24,949	1.22

Investment Style

Avg Eff Maturity	—
Avg Credit Quality	—
Avg Wtd Coupon	2.57%
Avg Wtd Price	131.25% of par

Coupon Range	% of Bonds	Rel Cat
0% PIK	14.6	1.0
0% to 8%	100.0	1.0
8% to 11%	0.0	0.0
11% to 14%	0.0	0.0
More than 14%	0.0	0.0
1.00=Category Average		

Special Securities

Restricted/Illiquid Secs	31
Emerging-Markets Secs	5
Options/Futures/Warrants	No

Composition

Cash	2.0
Stocks	17.1
Bonds	24.5
Convertibles	42.0
Other	14.4

Credit Analysis % bonds 08-31-06

AAA	—	BB	—
AA	—	B	—
A	—	Below B	—
BBB	—	NR/NA	—

Fidelity Disciplined Eq

	Ticker	Load	NAV	Yield	Total Assets	Mstar Category
	FDEQX	None	$29.02	0.6%	$8,143 mil	Large Blend

Governance and Management

Stewardship Grade: B

Portfolio Manager(s)

Keith Quinton started here in October 2006. He has also run Fidelity Tax-Managed Stock since February 2004. He has previous experience managing institutional money for Fidelity.

Strategy

Keith Quinton will employ quantitative models and a final fundamental overlay to try to beat the S&P 500, while sticking close to its sector weightings. The models track dozens of variables that are intended to predict stock-price performance. The models are complex, but they generally favor stocks with strong earnings momentum and reasonable valuations. They also tend to skew toward value and smaller stocks.

Performance 12-31-06

	1st Qtr	2nd Qtr	3rd Qtr	4th Qtr	Total
2002	1.27	-9.65	-14.39	3.98	-18.56
2003	-1.56	13.34	2.29	11.43	27.18
2004	2.55	0.86	-1.83	10.32	12.02
2005	0.44	2.09	5.63	1.81	10.27
2006	4.62	-1.03	3.45	6.98	14.58

Trailing	Total Return%	+/- S&P 500	+/- Russ 1000	%Rank Cat	Growth of $10,000
3 Mo	6.98	0.28	0.03	34	10,698
6 Mo	10.67	-2.07	-1.69	66	11,067
1 Yr	14.58	-1.21	-0.88	45	11,458
3 Yr Avg	12.28	1.84	1.30	14	14,155
5 Yr Avg	7.95	1.76	1.13	16	14,659
10 Yr Avg	9.21	0.79	0.57	16	24,134
15 Yr Avg	10.97	0.33	0.17	24	47,652

Tax Analysis	Tax-Adj Rtn%	%Rank Cat	Tax-Cost Rat	%Rank Cat
3 Yr (estimated)	11.57	13	0.63	29
5 Yr (estimated)	7.49	14	0.43	28
10 Yr (estimated)	7.60	24	1.47	69

Potential Capital Gain Exposure: 15% of assets

Morningstar's Take by John Coumarianos 11-28-06

Fidelity Disciplined Equity's new manager has a decent record elsewhere, but investors shouldn't be happy about the loss of Steven Snider.

Former manager Steven Snider guided this fund to top-quartile large-blend category returns for three of the four full calendar years he was on the fund (2002-05). He generated a cumulative return of 26% from June 1, 2001, through Sept. 30, 2006, versus 15% for the category average and 17% for the S&P 500 Index. Shareholders should be sorry to see him go. Fidelity has a poor record of manager retention, and we wish the firm and this fund's board were able to keep Snider around.

Snider's replacement, Keith Quinton, took over here on Oct. 9, 2006. He has been managing Fidelity Tax-Managed Stock with some success for two years. Quinton has been with Fidelity for a number of years and has run institutional accounts for them, but Snider was a more proven commodity as a retail mutual fund manager.

Quinton will continue to employ a version of

Snider's model-driven strategy, using screens for earnings momentum, price momentum, and valuation. However, he also will use fundamental analysis to complement the model's recommendations, making use of Fidelity's research. He has also indicated that the models tend to skew toward value and smaller-cap stocks. This worked like a charm for Snider, but it could hurt during a mega-cap rally. Also, with $7 billion in the fund, Quinton may not have the flexibility to buy lots of mid-caps, even if the models recommend them.

Quinton has turned around Fidelity Tax-Managed Stock using a similar strategy, and we think he can thrive here. However, we view manager departures such as Snider's as a strike against Fidelity's record as a good steward of capital.

Address:	82 Devonshire St Boston MA 02109 800-544-6666	Minimum Purchase:	$2500	Add: $250	IRA: $200
		Min Auto Inv Plan:	$100	Add: $100	
		Sales Fees:	No-load, 0.75%R		
Web Address:	www.fidelity.com	Management Fee:	0.67%		
Inception:	12-28-88	Actual Fees:	Mgt:0.67%	Dist: —	
Advisor:	Fidelity Management & Research (FMR)	Expense Projections:	3Yr:$293	5Yr:$509	10Yr:$1131
Subadvisor:	Multiple Subadvisors	Income Distrib:	Annually		
NTF Plans:	Fidelity Retail-NTF, CommonWealth NTF				

Historical Profile

Return	Above Avg	
Risk	Below Avg	
Rating	★★★★ Above Avg	

96% 97% 95% 93% 95% 96% 97% 97% 98%

Investment Style Equity Stock %

▼ Manager Change
▽ Partial Manager Change

Growth of $10,000
— Investment Values of Fund
— Investment Values of S&P 500

Performance Quartile (within Category)

1995	1996	1997	1998	1999	2000	2001	2002	2003	2004	2005	2006	History
20.64	22.04	25.86	29.32	30.51	25.82	22.10	17.97	22.74	25.29	27.71	29.02	NAV
29.01	15.11	33.31	21.83	22.41	-3.48	-14.21	-18.56	27.18	12.02	10.27	14.58	Total Return %
-8.57	-7.85	-0.05	-6.75	1.37	5.62	-2.32	3.54	-1.50	1.14	5.36	-1.21	+/-S&P 500
-8.76	-7.34	0.46	-5.19	1.50	4.31	-1.76	3.09	-2.71	0.62	4.00	-0.88	+/-Russ 1000
1.67	1.11	1.13	0.85	0.92	0.52	0.19	0.14	0.61	0.79	0.71	0.69	Income Return %
27.34	14.00	32.18	20.98	21.49	-4.00	-14.40	-18.70	26.57	11.23	9.56	13.89	Capital Return %
79	92	15	53	30	41	80	23	56	27	10	45	Total Rtn % Rank Cat
0.30	0.23	0.25	0.22	0.27	0.16	0.05	0.03	0.11	0.18	0.18	0.19	Income $
2.23	1.49	3.30	1.82	4.90	3.57	0.00	0.00	0.00	0.00	0.00	2.49	Capital Gains $
0.93	0.75	0.64	0.64	0.62	0.79	0.84	1.00	0.90	0.88	0.87	—	Expense Ratio %
1.81	1.22	1.28	1.10	0.80	0.50	0.42	0.16	0.50	0.51	0.79	—	Income Ratio %
221	297	127	125	113	118	101	68	64	42	80	—	Turnover Rate %
2,146	2,099	2,557	3,145	3,614	3,393	2,992	2,752	3,987	4,951	6,104	8,143	Net Assets $mil

Rating and Risk

Time Period	Load-Adj Rtn %	Morningstar Rtn vs Cat	Morningstar Risk vs Cat	Morningstar Risk-Adj Rating
1 Yr	14.58			
3 Yr	12.28	+Avg	+Avg	★★★★
5 Yr	7.95	+Avg	-Avg	★★★★
10 Yr	9.21	+Avg	-Avg	★★★★
Incept	12.88			

Other Measures	Standard Index S&P 500	Best Fit Index Russ 1000
Alpha	0.9	0.5
Beta	1.12	1.09
R-Squared	89	91
Standard Deviation	8.19	
Mean	12.28	
Sharpe Ratio	1.07	

Portfolio Analysis 10-31-06

Share change since 07-06 Total Stocks:160

	Sector	PE	Tot Ret%	% Assets
⊕ J.P. Morgan Chase & Co.	Financial	13.6	25.60	3.72
⊕ Merck & Co., Inc.	Health	19.1	42.66	3.43
⊕ Morgan Stanley	Financial	12.3	45.93	3.21
⊕ IBM	Hardware	17.1	19.77	3.03
⊖ ExxonMobil Corporation	Energy	11.1	39.07	2.91
⊕ Hewlett-Packard Company	Hardware	19.3	45.21	2.80
Citigroup, Inc.	Financial	13.1	19.55	2.27
⊖ J.C. Penney Company, Inc	Consumer	17.3	40.59	2.24
⊕ TXU Corporation	Utilities	12.8	11.19	2.20
⊕ Marathon Oil Corporation	Energy	6.1	54.68	2.13
Bank of America Corporat	Financial	12.4	20.68	1.99
☼ Kohl's Corporation	Consumer	22.6	40.80	1.96
⊕ Johnson & Johnson	Health	17.5	12.45	1.95
⊕ Caterpillar Inc.	Ind Mtrls	11.8	7.86	1.90
Goldman Sachs Group, Inc	Financial	12.4	57.41	1.83
⊕ Allstate Corporation	Financial	8.7	23.38	1.82
⊕ ConocoPhillips	Energy	6.5	26.53	1.78
⊖ Archer Daniels Midland	Ind Mtrls	13.8	31.02	1.60
⊕ CSX Corporation	Business	15.4	37.05	1.54
☼ Xerox Corporation	Ind Mtrls	13.4	15.70	1.53

Current Investment Style

Value Blnd Growth — Large Mid Small

Market Cap	%
Giant	41.3
Large	40.0
Mid	15.7
Small	2.8
Micro	0.2

Avg $mil: 34,202

Value Measures		Rel Category
Price/Earnings	13.35	0.87
Price/Book	2.66	1.04
Price/Sales	1.06	0.76
Price/Cash Flow	6.17	0.73
Dividend Yield %	1.56	0.89

Growth Measures	%	Rel Category
Long-Term Erngs	10.92	0.92
Book Value	9.42	1.04
Sales	8.27	0.85
Cash Flow	12.77	1.24
Historical Erngs	19.39	1.05

Profitability	%	Rel Category
Return on Equity	21.26	1.09
Return on Assets	10.91	1.05
Net Margin	12.54	0.93

Sector Weightings	% of Stocks	Rel S&P 500	3 Year High	Low
☁ Info	17.78	0.89		
🖥 Software	2.17	0.63	5	1
💻 Hardware	10.96	1.19	15	10
🎤 Media	1.05	0.28	4	1
☎ Telecom	3.60	1.03	4	1
⊏ Service	50.09	1.08		
🏥 Health	12.22	1.01	14	9
🛒 Consumer	11.28	1.47	14	8
💼 Business	3.86	0.91	6	2
💲 Financial	22.73	1.02	24	20
⬛ Mfg	32.12	0.95		
🛠 Goods	5.21	0.61	8	4
⚙ Ind Mtrls	14.04	1.18	15	11
⛽ Energy	9.25	0.94	13	7
💡 Utilities	3.62	1.03	4	1

Composition

		%
● Cash		1.3
● Stocks		97.8
● Bonds		0.0
● Other		0.8
Foreign (% of Stock)		2.6

 MORNINGSTAR® Funds 500

Fidelity Discovery

	Ticker	Load	NAV	Yield	Total Assets	Mstar Category
	FDSVX	None	$12.85	0.9%	$448 mil	Large Blend

Governance and Management

Stewardship Grade: B

Portfolio Manager(s)

Adam Hetnarski--who will likely be replaced in the coming months if shareholders approve a change in the fund's benchmark--took the reins here in February 2000, and he has had successful stints at other Fidelity offerings. He put up particularly big numbers during his short stint at Fidelity Export & Multinational. Hetnarski is also a former tech analyst for Fidelity. He manages Fidelity Advisor Destiny II in a similar style.

Strategy

In the fund's current guise, Adam Hetnarski tries to buy companies with rising profits, but his macroeconomic view informs stock selection, and he will make sector shifts based on his short-term expectations. He considers most mid-caps and large caps fair game. Although the fund has a growth bias at times, Hetnarski keeps an eye on valuations and has sometimes bought nontraditional growth fare such as Altria Group and basic-materials stocks. However, the fund's approach may become more growth-oriented.

Historical Profile
Return Average
Risk Average
Rating ★★★ Neutral

Performance Quartile percentages: 87% 93% 97% 80% 89% 90% 99% 96% 92%

▼ Manager Change
▽ Partial Manager Change

Growth of $10,000
— Investment Values of Fund
— Investment Values of S&P 500

Investment Style
Equity
Stock %

History	1995	1996	1997	1998	1999	2000	2001	2002	2003	2004	2005	2006
NAV	—	—	—	11.14	14.91	11.49	10.35	8.67	10.34	11.30	11.41	12.85
Total Return %	—	—	—	—	42.52	-8.35	-9.59	-15.94	19.87	10.62	2.14	13.94
+/-S&P 500	—	—	—	—	21.48	0.75	2.30	6.16	-8.81	-0.26	-2.77	-1.85
+/-Russ 1000	—	—	—	—	21.61	-0.56	2.86	5.71	-10.02	-0.78	-4.13	-1.52
Income Return %	—	—	—	—	0.00	0.00	0.35	0.29	0.58	1.26	1.15	1.06
Capital Return %	—	—	—	—	42.52	-8.35	-9.94	-16.23	19.29	9.36	0.99	12.88
Total Rtn % Rank Cat	—	—	—	—	3	61	31	10	96	46	88	56
Income $	—	—	—	0.00	0.00	0.00	0.04	0.03	0.05	0.13	0.13	0.12
Capital Gains $	—	—	—	0.00	0.72	2.45	0.00	0.00	0.00	0.00	0.00	0.02
Expense Ratio %	—	—	—	1.23	0.87	0.86	0.91	0.99	0.97	0.84	0.81	0.61
Income Ratio %	—	—	—	-0.28	-0.01	-0.08	0.19	0.32	0.43	0.73	1.54	1.04
Turnover Rate %	—	—	—	141	293	291	258	259	367	249	229	184
Net Assets $mil	—	—	—	538	1,374	1,451	1,032	672	655	552	432	448

Performance 12-31-06

	1st Qtr	2nd Qtr	3rd Qtr	4th Qtr	Total
2002	-0.29	-9.59	-15.11	9.86	-15.94
2003	-3.58	12.44	0.64	9.86	19.87
2004	-0.48	0.58	0.79	9.64	10.62
2005	-8.14	3.08	5.24	2.50	2.14
2006	7.19	-5.15	6.77	4.96	13.94

Trailing	Total Return%	+/- S&P 500	+/- Russ 1000	%Rank Cat	Growth of $10,000
3 Mo	4.96	-1.74	-1.99	93	10,496
6 Mo	12.07	-0.67	-0.29	37	11,207
1 Yr	13.94	-1.85	-1.52	56	11,394
3 Yr Avg	8.78	-1.66	-2.20	75	12,872
5 Yr Avg	5.34	-0.85	-1.48	62	12,971
10 Yr Avg	—	—	—	—	—
15 Yr Avg	—	—	—	—	—

Tax Analysis	Tax-Adj Rtn%	%Rank Cat	Tax-Cost Rat	%Rank Cat
3 Yr (estimated)	8.34	62	0.40	19
5 Yr (estimated)	5.02	52	0.30	20
10 Yr (estimated)	—	—	—	—

Potential Capital Gain Exposure: -35% of assets

Rating and Risk

Time Period	Load-Adj Return %	Morningstar Rtn vs Cat	Morningstar Risk vs Cat	Morningstar Risk-Adj Rating
1 Yr	13.94			
3 Yr	8.78	-Avg	+Avg	★★
5 Yr	5.34	Avg	-Avg	★★★
10 Yr	—	—	—	—
Incept	6.14			

Other Measures	Standard Index S&P 500	Best Fit Index Russ 1000
Alpha	-1.1	-1.3
Beta	0.94	0.92
R-Squared	69	70
Standard Deviation	7.86	
Mean	8.78	
Sharpe Ratio	0.71	

Portfolio Analysis 09-30-06

Share change since 06-06 Total Stocks:115

	Sector	PE	Tot Ret%	% Assets
⊕ Microsoft Corporation	Software	23.8	15.83	6.55
⊖ General Electric Company	Ind Mtrls	20.0	9.35	6.25
⊖ American International G	Financial	17.0	6.05	5.30
⊖ Johnson & Johnson	Health	17.5	12.45	4.34
⊖ SLM Corporation	Financial	14.1	-9.76	3.29
⊖ Wyeth	Health	17.2	12.88	2.10
⊖ Roche Holding	Health	—	—	2.00
⊕ Honeywell International,	Ind Mtrls	18.6	24.14	2.00
⊕ Verizon Communications	Telecom	15.9	34.88	1.94
⊖ Ciena Corporation	Hardware	—	33.29	1.93
⊕ Bank of America Corporat	Financial	12.4	20.68	1.90
⊕ EMC Corporation	Hardware	32.7	-3.08	1.71
⊕ Intel Corporation	Hardware	21.0	-17.18	1.56
⊕ Corning Inc.	Hardware	25.5	-4.83	1.55
⊖ Altria Group, Inc.	Goods	16.3	19.87	1.55
⊕ ACE, Ltd.	Financial	10.6	15.41	1.39
⊖ American Tower Corporati	Telecom	—	37.57	1.38
⊖ ExxonMobil Corporation	Energy	11.1	39.07	1.29
⊖ General Dynamics	Ind Mtrls	19.1	32.17	1.24
⊕ Applied Materials	Hardware	19.5	3.89	1.19

Current Investment Style

Value Blnd Growth — Large Mid Small

Market Cap	%
Giant	49.7
Large	32.1
Mid	13.7
Small	3.8
Micro	0.8
Avg $mil:	42,710

Value Measures		Rel Category
Price/Earnings	18.32	1.19
Price/Book	2.69	1.05
Price/Sales	2.28	1.63
Price/Cash Flow	11.20	1.33
Dividend Yield %	1.56	0.89

Growth Measures	%	Rel Category
Long-Term Erngs	12.27	1.04
Book Value	7.33	0.81
Sales	8.12	0.84
Cash Flow	7.57	0.73
Historical Erngs	14.16	0.77

Profitability	%	Rel Category
Return on Equity	15.49	0.80
Return on Assets	9.05	0.87
Net Margin	12.75	0.95

Sector Weightings

	% of Stocks	Rel S&P 500	3 Year High Low
⊙ Info	39.35	1.97	
Software	8.90	2.58	11 4
Hardware	20.65	2.23	21 2
Media	2.95	0.78	16 1
Telecom	6.85	1.95	17 3
⊙ Service	40.02	0.87	
Health	19.55	1.62	28 9
Consumer	3.05	0.40	8 1
Business	0.68	0.16	6 0
Financial	16.74	0.75	19 5
⊙ Mfg	20.66	0.61	
Goods	5.75	0.67	16 6
Ind Mtrls	11.20	0.94	21 9
Energy	2.78	0.28	8 0
Utilities	0.93	0.27	1 0

Composition

● Cash	7.5
● Stocks	91.8
● Bonds	0.0
● Other	0.7
Foreign (% of Stock)	10.1

Morningstar's Take by Greg Carlson 12-28-06

A passel of potential changes cloud Fidelity Discovery's future.

In a recent proxy filing, Fidelity proposed changing this large-blend fund's benchmark from the S&P 500 Index to the Russell 3000 Growth Index for computing the fund's performance fee (which adjusts the base management fee upward when the fund outperforms its benchmark, and vice versa). The firm also wants fundholders to give it the flexibility to change the benchmark without shareholder approval going forward, and to add the word "Growth" to this fund's name. Fidelity has disclosed to Morningstar that if shareholders approve these changes--a highly likely event--manager Adam Hetnarski will likely be replaced with a more growth-oriented skipper. (There are no plans to take Hetnarski off of his other charge, the much larger Fidelity Advisor Destiny II, which he runs in an identical style.)

On one hand, a manager change could prove to be a positive for shareholders. Hetnarski has struggled during his nearly seven-year tenure here; his fast-trading approach and propensity for making big portfolio shifts have paid off at times, but he has often failed to catch short-term anomalies in the market. He was also early in positioning the fund to benefit from a slowing economy, and picks such as UnitedHealth Group and AIG subsequently tumbled. All told, the fund has lagged on his watch. A new manager might better take advantage of the fund's svelte asset base and modest expense ratio.

However, remaking the fund into a growth vehicle isn't necessarily an improvement. Shareholders who purchased the fund as a core holding will likely see their asset allocations thrown off, and those who sell the fund in a taxable account may end up paying capital gains taxes sooner than they planned. Finally, it's not known exactly who would take over the fund. Thus, there's plenty of reason to steer clear of it.

Address:	82 Devonshire St Boston MA 02109 800-544-9797	Minimum Purchase:	$2500	Add: $250	IRA: $200
		Min Auto Inv Plan:	$2500	Add: $100	
Web Address:	www.fidelity.com	Sales Fees:	No-load		
Inception:	04-01-98	Management Fee:	0.56%		
Advisor:	Fidelity Management & Research (FMR)	Actual Fees:	Mgt:0.31%	Dist: —	
Subadvisor:	Multiple Subadvisors	Expense Projections:	3Yr:$218	5Yr:$379	10Yr:$847
		Income Distrib:	Semi-Annually		
NTF Plans:	Fidelity Retail-NTF, CommonWealth NTF				

Fidelity Diversified Int

	Ticker	Load	NAV	Yield	Total Assets	Mstar Category
	FDIVX	Closed	$36.95	0.9%	$47,342 mil	Foreign Large Growth

Governance and Management

Stewardship Grade: B

Portfolio Manager(s)

Bill Bower took over here in 2001, succeeding longtime manager Greg Fraser, who built a stellar record on the offering. Bower had a solid stint at Fidelity International Growth & Income (now Fidelity International Discovery) and has only bolstered this fund's numbers. Bower draws from Fidelity's rich regional research staff as well as a group of global sector analysts based in Boston.

Strategy

Manager Bill Bower runs a sprawling portfolio of more than 350 names, selected with a growth-at-a-reasonable-price approach. He focuses mainly on large-cap stocks but also fishes in small- and mid-cap waters. He isn't afraid to deviate from his benchmark, so the fund sometimes sports small but noticeable stakes in emerging-markets stocks. Although sector weightings tend to move in line with the benchmark, Bower sources his stock ideas broadly, often in line with big picture themes. Fidelity uses fair-value pricing when necessary, and the fund does not hedge its foreign currency exposure.

Performance 12-31-06

	1st Qtr	2nd Qtr	3rd Qtr	4th Qtr	Total
2002	2.46	0.67	-17.17	6.08	-9.37
2003	-5.77	19.73	9.56	15.19	42.38
2004	6.72	-1.83	0.24	13.94	19.66
2005	0.14	0.42	10.83	5.18	17.23
2006	9.65	-1.26	3.07	9.79	22.52

Trailing	Total Return%	+/- MSCI EAFE	+/- MSCI Wd xUS	%Rank Cat	Growth of $10,000
3 Mo	9.80	-0.55	-0.32	78	10,980
6 Mo	13.16	-1.53	-1.06	72	11,316
1 Yr	22.52	-3.82	-3.19	61	12,252
3 Yr Avg	19.78	-0.15	-0.32	23	17,185
5 Yr Avg	17.27	2.29	2.02	6	22,179
10 Yr Avg	13.16	5.45	5.20	6	34,429
15 Yr Avg	12.44	4.58	4.40	1	58,051

Tax Analysis	Tax-Adj Rtn%	%Rank Cat	Tax-Cost Rat	%Rank Cat
3 Yr (estimated)	18.89	20	0.74	45
5 Yr (estimated)	16.63	5	0.55	50
10 Yr (estimated)	12.26	5	0.80	43

Potential Capital Gain Exposure: 30% of assets

Historical Profile

Return	Above Avg	
Risk	Below Avg	
Rating	★★★★ Highest	

| 81% | 88% | 88% | 90% | 88% | 93% | 92% | 96% | 91% |

▽

1995	1996	1997	1998	1999	2000	2001	2002	2003	2004	2005	2006	History
12.69	14.71	16.13	17.72	25.62	21.94	19.08	17.16	24.12	28.64	32.54	36.95	NAV
17.97	20.02	13.72	14.39	50.65	-8.96	-12.99	-9.37	42.38	19.66	17.23	22.52	Total Return %
6.76	13.97	11.94	-5.54	23.62	5.23	8.43	6.57	3.79	-0.59	3.69	-3.82	+/-MSCI EAFE
6.56	13.15	11.45	-4.30	22.67	4.40	8.40	6.43	2.96	-0.72	2.76	-3.19	+/-MSCI Wd xUS
1.95	1.18	1.29	1.43	1.41	2.15	0.05	0.68	1.75	0.62	0.98	1.11	Income Return %
16.02	18.84	12.43	12.96	49.24	-11.11	-13.04	-10.05	40.63	19.04	16.25	21.41	Capital Return %
9	11	18	53	60	9	6	5	14	18	33	61	Total Rtn % Rank Cat
0.22	0.15	0.19	0.23	0.25	0.55	0.01	0.13	0.30	0.15	0.28	0.36	Income $
0.41	0.36	0.41	0.47	0.70	0.81	0.00	0.00	0.00	0.06	0.73	2.51	Capital Gains $
1.12	1.27	1.23	1.19	1.18	1.12	1.16	1.19	1.22	1.12	1.07	—	Expense Ratio %
1.55	1.53	1.49	1.46	0.94	1.62	1.08	0.77	0.96	0.66	1.02	—	Income Ratio %
101	94	81	95	73	94	86	55	51	55	41	—	Turnover Rate %
341	754	1,536	2,157	4,908	6,580	6,379	7,135	13,559	23,420	33,094	47,342	Net Assets $mil

Investment Style

Equity
Stock %

▼ Manager Change
△ Partial Manager Change

Growth of $10,000

— Investment Values of Fund
— Investment Values of MSCI EAFE

43.6
32.4
24.0
17.0
10.0

Performance Quartile (within Category)

Rating and Risk

Time Period	Load-Adj Return %	Morningstar Rtn vs Cat	Morningstar Risk vs Cat	Morningstar Risk-Adj Rating
1 Yr	22.52			
3 Yr	19.78	+Avg	-Avg	★★★★
5 Yr	17.27	High	Low	★★★★★
10 Yr	13.16	+Avg	-Avg	★★★★★
Incept	12.47			

Other Measures	Standard Index MSCI EAFE	Best Fit Index MSCI Wd xUS
Alpha	-1.0	-0.9
Beta	1.06	1.05
R-Squared	95	95
Standard Deviation	10.28	
Mean	19.78	
Sharpe Ratio	1.51	

Portfolio Analysis 10-31-06

Share change since 07-06 Total Stocks:347	Sector	Country	% Assets
⊖ Roche Holding	Health	Switzerland	1.77
⊖ Novartis AG ADR	Health	Switzerland	1.64
⊕ Banco Bilbao Vizcaya Arg	Financial	Spain	1.36
ORIX	Financial	Japan	1.32
⊕ Toyota Motor Corporation	Goods	Japan	1.25
⊕ Tesco	Consumer	U.K.	1.10
⊕ HSBC Holdings PLC ADR	Financial	U.K.	1.07
⊕ Mizuho Financial Grp	Financial	Japan	1.05
⊕ Fiat	Goods	Italy	1.04
⊕ UniCredito Italiano Grp	Financial	Italy	1.03
⊕ Reckitt Benckiser	Goods	U.K.	1.02
⊕ BNP Paribas	Financial	France	1.01
⊕ Nestle	Goods	Switzerland	1.00
⊕ Renault	Goods	France	1.00
⊖ ING Groep NV ADR	Financial	Netherlands	0.98
⊖ UBS AG	Financial	Switzerland	0.97
⊕ Bayer	Ind Mtrls	Germany	0.91
⊕ Canon ADR	Goods	Japan	0.90
⊕ Sumitomo Mitsui Financia	Financial	Japan	0.85
⊖ Reed Elsevier NV ADR	Media	Netherlands	0.84

Current Investment Style

Value Blnd Growth — Large Mid Small

Market Cap	%
Giant	46.1
Large	38.6
Mid	13.7
Small	1.6
Micro	0.0
Avg $mil:	25,072

Value Measures		Rel Category
Price/Earnings	16.68	1.08
Price/Book	2.62	1.00
Price/Sales	1.46	1.04
Price/Cash Flow	9.82	1.01
Dividend Yield %	1.99	0.82

Growth Measures	%	Rel Category
Long-Term Erngs	12.71	0.94
Book Value	9.99	0.91
Sales	6.52	0.75
Cash Flow	12.70	1.04
Historical Erngs	21.95	0.96

Composition

Cash	6.9	Bonds	0.6
Stocks	91.2	Other	1.4
Foreign (% of Stock)			95.4

Sector Weightings

Sector Weightings	% of Stocks	Rel MSCI EAFE	3 Year High	Low
⌖ Info	11.34	0.96		
🖥 Software	1.83	3.27	2	1
💻 Hardware	2.44	0.63	5	2
📺 Media	2.86	1.56	5	2
☎ Telecom	4.21	0.76	8	2
☞ Service	43.73	0.93		
💊 Health	8.86	1.24	14	8
🛒 Consumer	4.13	0.83	6	4
🏢 Business	6.11	1.21	7	4
💲 Financial	24.63	0.82	25	21
⚒ Mfg	44.94	1.10		
🏭 Goods	18.38	1.40	18	15
⚙ Ind Mtrls	16.04	1.04	19	9
⛽ Energy	8.00	1.12	10	8
💡 Utilities	2.52	0.48	3	1

Regional Exposure

	% Stock		% Stock
UK/W. Europe	61	N. America	11
Japan	17	Latn America	2
Asia X Japan	8	Other	1

Country Exposure

	% Stock		% Stock
Japan	17	France	10
U.K.	13	Germany	8
Switzerland	12		

Morningstar's Take by Dan Lefkovitz 12-22-06

Fidelity Diversified International remains a fine core foreign holding, though investors should moderate their expectations.

Like most growth-leaning foreign funds, this closed offering is unlikely to beat the MSCI EAFE Index for 2006. Manager Bill Bower tends to find less growth in the utilities and financials sectors, which have both been hot this year. He has also been relatively light on Europe, where appreciating currencies amplified strong market returns.

The fund remains a winner, though. First of all, its 21.6% gain for the year to date through Dec. 21, 2006, is in line with the foreign-large-growth category and is nothing to sneeze at in absolute terms. Even more impressive is the fund's 17%-plus annualized gain since Bower took over in 2001--a mark that beats 95% of the fund's peers.

Bower's approach is straightforward. He spreads assets diffusely over roughly 350 stocks. He doesn't let the portfolio's sector weightings deviate dramatically from those of the MSCI EAFE Index.

But he will go far afield in search of well-run companies with good midterm earnings prospects. Earnings can either come from internal sources--Bower owns restructuring European auto makers Renault and Fiat--or broad trends. The fund has benefited greatly over the years from luxury goods companies and small alternative energy players. And, though Bower has scaled back on red-hot emerging markets, he has picked several winners among Indian tech companies.

It's important for investors to realize that the fund's recent pace won't persist forever. Foreign markets have benefited from many tailwinds, including currency, that could become headwinds. Also, this fund has swelled in asset size since its October 2004 close. Because Bower buys so many stocks, trades infrequently, and is finding good opportunities among large caps right now, asset growth shouldn't doom this fund. But with $45 billion, it is less nimble than it once was.

Address:	82 Devonshire St, Boston MA 02109, 800-544-9797	Minimum Purchase:	Closed	Add: —	IRA: —
		Min Auto Inv Plan:	Closed	Add: —	
		Sales Fees:	No-load, 1.00%R		
Web Address:	www.fidelity.com	Management Fee:	0.75%		
Inception:	12-27-91	Actual Fees:	Mgt:0.75%	Dist: —	
Advisor:	Fidelity Management & Research (FMR)	Expense Projections:	3Yr:$322	5Yr:$558	10Yr:$1236
Subadvisor:	Multiple Subadvisors	Income Distrib:	Annually		
NTF Plans:	Fidelity Retail-NTF, CommonWealth NTF				

MORNINGSTAR® Funds 500

Fidelity Dividend Growth

Analyst Pick		Ticker	Load	NAV	Yield	Total Assets	Mstar Category
✓		FDGFX	None	$31.68	1.4%	$17,151 mil	Large Blend

Governance and Management

Stewardship Grade: B

Portfolio Manager(s)

Charles Mangum is an experienced Fidelity manager and analyst. He has been on the job here since January 1997 and has built a fine record. He also runs Fidelity Advisor Dividend Growth, and until recently he managed the stock portions of Fidelity Asset Manager 50% and Fidelity Asset Manager 70%. Previously, Mangum, like most Fidelity skippers, ran several sector funds for the firm. His preference for health-care names dates back to his days as a Fidelity analyst in that sector.

Strategy

Charles Mangum is a counterpuncher, and if an area, including technology, has good-enough growth prospects and cheap-enough valuations, he'll give it a look. That said, he tends to prefer companies with relatively stable profit growth. He is patient with his favorite stocks, as the top holdings don't vary much from month to month. Most of the fund's turnover is generated by adjustments to position sizes rather than changes in names.

Performance 12-31-06

	1st Qtr	2nd Qtr	3rd Qtr	4th Qtr	Total
2002	0.81	-15.48	-15.42	10.39	-20.44
2003	-4.84	17.42	0.19	10.19	23.36
2004	1.39	0.61	-4.57	8.71	5.84
2005	-4.25	2.24	2.29	3.36	3.50
2006	4.76	-3.38	7.03	5.85	14.67

Trailing	Total Return%	+/- S&P 500	+/- Russ 1000	%Rank Cat	Growth of $10,000
3 Mo	5.85	-0.85	-1.10	79	10,585
6 Mo	13.30	0.56	0.94	12	11,330
1 Yr	14.67	-1.12	-0.79	43	11,467
3 Yr Avg	7.90	-2.54	-3.08	85	12,562
5 Yr Avg	4.27	-1.92	-2.55	80	12,325
10 Yr Avg	9.68	1.26	1.04	14	25,193
15 Yr Avg	—				

Tax Analysis	Tax-Adj Rtn%	%Rank Cat	Tax-Cost Rat	%Rank Cat
3 Yr (estimated)	7.13	80	0.71	33
5 Yr (estimated)	3.69	79	0.56	37
10 Yr (estimated)	8.15	16	1.39	64

Potential Capital Gain Exposure: 18% of assets

Morningstar's Take by Greg Carlson 12-20-06

Management's leaner asset base gives us one more reason to like Fidelity Dividend Growth.

This fund's manager, Charles Mangum, has a lighter workload these days. As a result of this fund's superb performance early in the bear market (which attracted substantial inflows), as well as Mangum's appointment to run the equity portfolios of Fidelity Asset Manager 70% and Fidelity Asset Manager 50%, he once ran roughly $32 billion. Because Mangum often plows 50% or more of the fund's assets into its top 10 holdings, we called for it to close. Since then, however, this fund and his other charge, Fidelity Advisor Dividend Growth, have seen substantial redemptions, and Mangum was recently taken off the Asset Manager funds. Thus, he now manages a relatively modest $20 billion. Mangum says that drop makes little difference right now, due to his big stake in mega-caps (which have been out of favor for much of the past six years). But when he starts finding smaller fry attractive again--as he did just prior to

the bear market's outset, one reason for the fund's success--he can better focus on his favorites.

Meanwhile, we continue to be impressed with Mangum's stock-picking. He typically favors companies with consistent cash flows, a style that was out of favor from 2003 to 2005--cyclical fare led the post-bear-market rally--but he stuck to his guns, and that stance has modestly paid off. For example, once-beaten-down drugmakers such as Pfizer bounced back amid cost-cutting and increased sales, and AT&T has rallied sharply since its merger with SBC (a top holding here since early 2004). He believes those areas are still undervalued, and he's treading lightly in the red-hot energy sector.

Mangum's contrarian approach has made for extended dry spells, but he's generated fine returns during his nearly 10-year tenure here. This is still one of our favorite large-cap funds.

Address:	82 Devonshire St Boston MA 02109 800-544-9797	Minimum Purchase:	$2500	Add: $250	IRA: $200
		Min Auto Inv Plan:	$2500	Add: $100	
Web Address:	www.fidelity.com	Sales Fees:	No-load		
Inception:	04-27-93	Management Fee:	0.65%		
Advisor:	Fidelity Management & Research (FMR)	Actual Fees:	Mgt:0.36%	Dist: —	
Subadvisor:	Multiple Subadvisors	Expense Projections:	3Yr:$192	5Yr:$335	10Yr:$750
		Income Distrib:	Annually		
NTF Plans:	Fidelity Retail-NTF, CommonWealth NTF				

Historical Profile
Return: Average
Risk: Average
Rating: ★★★ Neutral

	95%	94%	95%	91%	89%	95%	95%	98%	96%

Growth of $10,000
— Investment Values of Fund
— Investment Values of S&P 500

39.4
31.0
24.0
17.0
10.0

Performance Quartile (within Category)

1995	1996	1997	1998	1999	2000	2001	2002	2003	2004	2005	2006	History
15.84	20.09	23.27	28.73	28.99	29.96	28.33	22.32	27.30	28.49	28.79	31.68	NAV
37.53	30.14	27.90	35.85	8.81	12.25	-3.74	-20.44	23.36	5.84	3.50	14.67	Total Return %
-0.05	7.18	-5.46	7.27	-12.23	21.35	8.15	1.66	-5.32	-5.04	-1.41	-1.12	+/-S&P 500
-0.24	7.69	-4.95	8.83	-12.10	20.04	8.71	1.21	-6.53	-5.56	-2.77	-0.79	+/-Russ 1000
0.74	0.58	0.76	0.58	0.50	0.63	0.50	0.78	0.99	1.43	1.09	1.58	Income Return %
36.79	29.56	27.14	35.27	8.31	11.62	-4.24	-21.22	22.37	4.41	2.41	13.09	Capital Return %
14	5	58	3	85	9	14	35	84	91	80	43	Total Rtn % Rank Cat
0.09	0.09	0.15	0.13	0.14	0.18	0.15	0.22	0.22	0.39	0.31	0.45	Income $
1.07	0.37	2.19	2.19	2.14	2.40	0.33	0.00	0.00	0.00	0.38	0.82	Capital Gains $
1.19	0.99	0.92	0.86	0.84	0.74	0.94	0.95	1.02	0.89	0.66	0.59	Expense Ratio %
0.78	0.86	0.99	0.64	0.58	0.52	0.54	0.90	0.94	0.75	1.64	1.21	Income Ratio %
162	129	141	109	104	86	88	81	51	37	26	30	Turnover Rate %
529	2,345	4,480	10,369	12,624	11,781	15,210	13,479	18,171	19,422	16,509	17,151	Net Assets $mil

Rating and Risk

Time Period	Load-Adj Return %	Morningstar Rtn vs Cat	Morningstar Risk vs Cat	Morningstar Risk-Adj Rating
1 Yr	14.67			
3 Yr	7.90	-Avg	Avg	★★
5 Yr	4.27	-Avg	+Avg	★★
10 Yr	9.68	+Avg	Avg	★★★★
Incept	13.60			

Other Measures	Standard Index S&P 500	Best Fit Index S&P 500
Alpha	-1.9	-1.9
Beta	0.94	0.94
R-Squared	84	84
Standard Deviation	7.06	
Mean	7.90	
Sharpe Ratio	0.67	

Portfolio Analysis 10-31-06

Share change since 07-06 Total Stocks:94	Sector	PE	Tot Ret%	% Assets
Cardinal Health, Inc.	Health	20.8	-5.82	7.03
American International G	Financial	17.0	6.05	6.04
⊖ AT&T, Inc.	Telecom	18.2	51.59	5.85
Home Depot, Inc.	Consumer	13.5	1.01	5.15
⊖ Wyeth	Health	17.2	12.88	4.97
⊕ Wal-Mart Stores, Inc.	Consumer	16.9	0.13	4.78
⊕ Clear Channel Communicat	Media	27.4	15.79	4.57
⊖ General Electric Company	Ind Mtrls	20.0	9.35	4.20
⊖ Johnson & Johnson	Health	17.5	12.45	4.11
⊖ Bank of America Corporat	Financial	12.4	20.68	4.04
⊕ IBM	Hardware	17.1	19.77	2.75
Microsoft Corporation	Software	23.8	15.83	2.61
⊕ Hartford Financial Servi	Financial	11.9	10.83	2.28
⊕ CVS Corporation	Consumer	19.7	17.60	2.12
⊕ Wachovia Corporation	Financial	12.9	12.02	1.59
⊕ Cisco Systems, Inc.	Hardware	30.1	59.64	1.42
⊕ Diamond Offshore Drillin	Energy	17.8	17.82	1.42
⊕ GlobalSantaFe Corporatio	Energy	16.3	24.06	1.37
Intel Corporation	Hardware	21.0	-17.18	1.36
⊖ Altria Group, Inc.	Goods	16.3	19.87	1.32

Current Investment Style

Value Blend Growth — Large/Mid/Small

Market Cap	%
Giant	62.9
Large	31.2
Mid	5.9
Small	0.0
Micro	0.0

Avg $mil: 66,923

Value Measures		Rel Category
Price/Earnings	15.00	0.98
Price/Book	2.53	0.99
Price/Sales	1.21	0.86
Price/Cash Flow	10.39	1.23
Dividend Yield %	1.86	1.06

Growth Measures	%	Rel Category
Long-Term Erngs	12.12	1.03
Book Value	9.09	1.01
Sales	11.98	1.24
Cash Flow	6.04	0.59
Historical Erngs	14.16	0.77

Profitability	%	Rel Category
Return on Equity	18.30	0.94
Return on Assets	9.72	0.94
Net Margin	13.29	0.99

Sector Weightings	% of Stocks	Rel S&P 500	3 Year High	Low
☍ Info	27.07	1.35		
Software	4.45	1.29	8	4
Hardware	9.68	1.05	11	5
Media	5.66	1.49	8	5
Telecom	7.28	2.07	8	6
☖ Service	56.51	1.22		
Health	20.58	1.71	23	17
Consumer	14.26	1.86	14	8
Business	0.95	0.22	2	1
Financial	20.72	0.93	28	21
☐ Mfg	16.42	0.49		
Goods	7.28	0.27	7	2
Ind Mtrls	7.68	0.64	10	6
Energy	6.47	0.66	7	4
Utilities	0.00	0.00	1	0

Composition

● Cash	3.4
● Stocks	95.9
● Bonds	0.0
○ Other	0.7
Foreign (% of Stock)	0.5

Fidelity Equity-Inc

	Ticker	Load	NAV	Yield	Total Assets	Mstar Category
	FEQIX	None	$58.55	1.5%	$30,629 mil	Large Value

Governance and Management

Stewardship Grade: B

Portfolio Manager(s)

Stephen Petersen has managed the fund since 1993, and he is supported by Fidelity's considerable research staff. He took on the added responsibility of running Fidelity Puritan's equity portfolio in early 2000. He collaborates with other managers in Fidelity's value group, including Richard Fentin at Fidelity Value and Stephen DuFour of Fidelity Equity-Income II. That group has recently hired a few analysts to focus exclusively on value-oriented stocks, and they also draw from Fidelity's central research pool.

Strategy

Manager Stephen Petersen generally invests in companies with dividend yields greater than the S&P 500 Index's that he feels are undervalued relative to their two- to four-year potential. He spreads the portfolio across more than 200 stocks--mostly giant caps and some foreign names--and dabbles in bonds and convertibles for added income. The portfolio typically emphasizes financials, though Petersen will venture opportunistically into traditional growth areas like hardware and health care. Turnover is low.

Performance 12-31-06

	1st Qtr	2nd Qtr	3rd Qtr	4th Qtr	Total
2002	3.73	-9.80	-19.09	9.42	-17.16
2003	-6.30	17.91	2.85	14.38	29.96
2004	1.75	1.63	-1.42	9.18	11.29
2005	-1.86	0.53	4.01	3.04	5.74
2006	5.21	-0.15	6.15	7.43	19.81

Trailing	Total Return%	+/- S&P 500	+/- Russ 1000 Vl	%Rank Cat	Growth of $10,000
3 Mo	7.43	0.73	-0.57	41	10,743
6 Mo	14.04	1.30	-0.68	28	11,404
1 Yr	19.81	4.02	-2.44	28	11,981
3 Yr Avg	12.13	1.69	-2.96	53	14,098
5 Yr Avg	8.70	2.51	-2.16	42	15,176
10 Yr Avg	9.38	0.96	-1.62	38	24,512
15 Yr Avg	11.97	1.33	-1.06	25	54,516

Tax Analysis	Tax-Adj Rtn%	%Rank Cat	Tax-Cost Rat	%Rank Cat
3 Yr (estimated)	10.71	50	1.27	50
5 Yr (estimated)	7.55	42	1.06	57
10 Yr (estimated)	7.84	34	1.41	42

Potential Capital Gain Exposure: 31% of assets

Morningstar's Take by Dan Lefkovitz 11-15-06

Only over the long term do you come to appreciate Fidelity Equity-Income's low-key charm.

Few managers, at Fidelity or elsewhere, have run their fund as long as Stephen Petersen. He first took the helm here in 1993, whereas the typical manager in the large-value category has been on the job only since 2001.

Though his fund is rarely at the top of the annual performance rankings, Petersen has built a solid long-term record using a patient approach. He is a value investor who gravitates to large-cap companies that are cash rich and well positioned, but out of favor. Then he hangs on and waits for the market to recognize their value. In any given year, some picks might work out and some might not, but the fund's long history validates his stock-picking abilities.

This year has been an unusually good one for the fund. A large energy stake built when the sector was far less in favor has boosted performance in 2006. The fund is also benefiting from Petersen's

telecom purchases of five years ago. (SBC, which became AT&T, and its acquisition target, BellSouth, have been big winners this year.) He has lately been taking profits from the portfolio's holdings in energy and industrials. And he has deployed those assets to areas like health care and technology, which are much less loved. Pfizer and Intel have been two favorites.

Petersen's focus on large caps and low-turnover approach are well suited to this fund. Its asset base, at $30 billion, is large. Petersen also runs the equity sleeve of Fidelity Puritan and a variable annuity, putting his total asset load at roughly $50 billion. The burden of putting this pile to work prevents Petersen from buying much in the way of smaller-cap shares. So while we like this fund for its experienced management, sensible style, and very low fees, we'd advise investors to supplement it with a smaller-cap-focused offering.

Address:	82 Devonshire Street, Boston MA 02109	Minimum Purchase:	$2500	Add: $250	IRA: $200
	800-343-3548	Min Auto Inv Plan:	$0	Add: —	
Web Address:	www.fidelity.com	Sales Fees:	No-load		
Inception:	05-16-66	Management Fee:	0.47%		
Advisor:	Fidelity Management & Research (FMR)	Actual Fees:	Mgt:0.47%	Dist: —	
Subadvisor:	Multiple Subadvisors	Expense Projections:	3Yr:$221	5Yr:$384	10Yr:$859
		Income Distrib:	Quarterly		
NTF Plans:	Fidelity Retail-NTF, CommonWealth NTF				

Historical Profile
Return Average
Risk Average
Rating ★★★ Neutral

	91%	91%	91%	92%	94%	95%	98%	98%	97%

Investment Style
Equity
Stock %

▼ Manager Change
▽ Partial Manager Change

37.0
32.0
25.0 **Growth of $10,000**
20.0 ■ Investment Values of Fund
15.0 — Investment Values of S&P 500
10.0

Performance Quartile (within Category)

1995	1996	1997	1998	1999	2000	2001	2002	2003	2004	2005	2006	History
37.93	42.83	52.41	55.55	53.48	53.43	48.77	39.67	49.75	52.78	52.78	58.55	NAV
31.81	21.02	29.98	12.52	7.15	8.54	-5.02	-17.16	29.96	11.29	5.74	19.81	Total Return %
-5.77	-1.94	-3.38	-16.06	-13.89	17.64	6.87	4.94	1.28	0.41	0.83	4.02	+/-S&P 500
-6.55	-0.62	-5.20	-3.11	-0.20	1.53	0.57	-1.64	-0.07	-5.20	-1.31	-2.44	+/-Russ 1000 Vl
3.18	2.74	2.28	1.64	1.48	1.67	1.44	1.40	1.80	1.65	1.62	1.82	Income Return %
28.63	18.28	27.70	10.88	5.67	6.87	-6.46	-18.56	28.16	9.64	4.12	17.99	Capital Return %
61	35	24	45	42	57	58	45	34	71	48	28	Total Rtn % Rank Cat
0.96	1.02	0.96	0.85	0.81	0.87	0.76	0.68	0.71	0.81	0.84	0.94	Income $
1.36	1.84	2.04	2.39	5.14	3.32	1.18	0.14	0.93	1.66	2.13	3.50	Capital Gains $
0.69	0.67	0.66	0.65	0.66	0.67	0.67	0.67	0.71	0.71	0.69	0.67	Expense Ratio %
3.37	2.86	2.46	1.90	1.54	1.42	1.63	1.41	1.57	1.63	1.56	1.57	Income Ratio %
50	39	30	23	30	26	20	23	23	25	19	19	Turnover Rate %
10,492	14,259	21,178	23,707	22,829	22,353	21,832	17,734	23,520	26,372	26,058	30,629	Net Assets $mil

Rating and Risk

Time Period	Load-Adj Return %	Morningstar Rtn vs Cat	Morningstar Risk vs Cat	Morningstar Risk-Adj Rating
1 Yr	19.81			
3 Yr	12.13	Avg	Avg	★★★
5 Yr	8.70	Avg	Avg	★★★
10 Yr	9.38	Avg	Avg	★★★
Incept	13.18			

Other Measures	Standard Index S&P 500	Best Fit Index S&P 500
Alpha	1.6	1.6
Beta	0.99	0.99
R-Squared	93	93
Standard Deviation	7.10	
Mean	12.13	
Sharpe Ratio	1.21	

Portfolio Analysis 10-31-06

Share change since 07-06 Total Stocks:225	Sector	PE	Tot Ret%	% Assets
⊕ ExxonMobil Corporation	Energy	11.1	39.07	5.16
⊕ Bank of America Corporat	Financial	12.4	20.68	3.31
⊕ American International G	Financial	17.0	6.05	2.64
⊕ Citigroup, Inc.	Financial	13.1	19.55	2.41
⊕ J.P. Morgan Chase & Co.	Financial	13.6	25.60	2.32
⊕ AT&T, Inc.	Telecom	18.2	51.59	2.13
⊕ Pfizer Inc.	Health	15.2	15.22	1.84
⊕ BellSouth Corporation	Telecom	—	—	1.70
⊕ Wachovia Corporation	Financial	12.9	12.02	1.48
⊕ Fannie Mae	Financial	—	24.34	1.46
⊕ General Electric Company	Ind Mtrls	20.0	9.35	1.40
⊕ Chevron Corporation	Energy	9.0	33.76	1.36
⊖ Schlumberger, Ltd.	Energy	22.3	31.07	1.21
⊕ Verizon Communications	Telecom	15.9	34.88	1.18
⊕ Wells Fargo Company	Financial	14.7	16.82	1.18
⊕ Altria Group, Inc.	Goods	16.3	19.87	1.15
⊕ Morgan Stanley	Financial	12.3	45.93	1.15
⊖ Johnson & Johnson	Health	17.5	12.45	1.13
⊕ Wal-Mart Stores, Inc.	Consumer	16.9	0.13	1.11
⊕ Tyco International, Ltd.	Ind Mtrls	15.7	6.83	1.10

Current Investment Style

Value Blnd Growth — Large Mid Small

Market Cap	%
Giant	55.8
Large	31.9
Mid	11.0
Small	1.2
Micro	0.1

Avg $mil: 52,448

Value Measures		Rel Category
Price/Earnings	14.00	1.02
Price/Book	2.33	1.05
Price/Sales	1.36	1.05
Price/Cash Flow	5.27	0.79
Dividend Yield %	2.22	0.95

Growth Measures	%	Rel Category
Long-Term Erngs	10.65	1.03
Book Value	7.02	0.89
Sales	8.74	0.97
Cash Flow	6.73	1.11
Historical Erngs	16.79	1.04

Profitability	%	Rel Category
Return on Equity	18.00	1.00
Return on Assets	9.71	0.99
Net Margin	12.41	0.96

Sector Weightings	% of Stocks	Rel S&P 500	3 Year High Low	
☍ Info	19.95	1.00		
🖥 Software	1.31	0.38	1	1
🖥 Hardware	6.74	0.73	7	4
🔊 Media	5.01	1.32	6	5
📞 Telecom	6.89	1.96	7	5
☎ Service	43.17	0.93		
🏥 Health	7.69	0.64	8	7
🛒 Consumer	4.69	0.61	5	3
💼 Business	2.05	0.48	3	2
💲 Financial	28.74	1.29	31	28
⚒ Mfg	36.87	1.09		
🗑 Goods	7.42	0.87	8	7
⚙ Ind Mtrls	13.12	1.10	17	13
🔥 Energy	12.92	1.32	14	11
💡 Utilities	3.41	0.97	3	3

Composition

		%
● Cash		1.9
● Stocks		96.5
● Bonds		0.5
○ Other		1.1
	Foreign (% of Stock)	5.9

MORNINGSTAR® Funds 500

Fidelity Equity-Inc II

	Ticker	Load	NAV	Yield	Total Assets	Mstar Category
	FEQTX	None	$24.24	1.4%	$11,698 mil	Large Value

Governance and Management

Stewardship Grade: B

Portfolio Manager(s)

In November 2006, Bob Chow took over this fund from Stephen DuFour, who had managed it for nearly seven years. Chow, who has run Fidelity Advisor Equity Income for a decade, will continue to manage that fund. DuFour will remain at Fidelity managing institutional accounts.

Strategy

This fund invests the bulk of its assets in dividend-paying equities and aims to meet or exceed the yield of the S&P 500 Index before fees. New manager Bob Chow will likely use the same approach here as he does at Fidelity Advisor Equity Income; his top 10 holdings are typically dividend-paying behemoths, but he'll hold small positions in more unusual names. We expect the fund to land right in the middle of the large-value style box. He tends to own 200 or more names and trades at a moderate pace.

Historical Profile

Return	Average
Risk	Average
Rating	★★★ Neutral

Investment Style: Equity Stock %

90% 91% 81% 85% 94% 98% 98% 97% 99%

▼ Manager Change
▽ Partial Manager Change

Growth of $10,000
— Investment Values of Fund
— Investment Values of S&P 500

33.0 / 26.0 / 20.0 / 15.0 / 10.0

Performance Quartile (within Category)

1995	1996	1997	1998	1999	2000	2001	2002	2003	2004	2005	2006	History
21.43	23.75	27.01	30.01	27.37	23.86	21.03	17.39	22.78	24.01	22.86	24.24	NAV
26.39	18.71	27.17	22.98	4.37	7.46	-7.16	-15.43	32.60	9.88	4.63	13.73	Total Return %
-11.19	-4.25	-6.19	-5.60	-16.67	16.56	4.73	6.67	3.92	-1.00	-0.28	-2.06	+/-S&P 500
-11.97	-2.93	-8.01	7.35	-2.98	0.45	-1.57	0.09	2.57	-6.61	-2.42	-8.52	+/-Russ 1000 VI
2.10	2.41	1.83	1.25	1.21	1.55	1.40	1.16	1.39	1.65	1.44	1.60	Income Return %
24.29	16.30	25.34	21.73	3.16	5.91	-8.56	-16.59	31.21	8.23	3.19	12.13	Capital Return %
86	61	52	3	52	61	72	30	17	84	63	93	Total Rtn % Rank Cat
0.37	0.51	0.43	0.33	0.36	0.42	0.33	0.24	0.24	0.37	0.34	0.36	Income $
0.55	1.14	2.63	2.65	3.50	4.98	0.79	0.21	0.00	0.61	1.91	1.36	Capital Gains $
0.75	0.72	0.68	0.66	0.64	0.63	0.62	0.63	0.64	0.64	0.62	—	Expense Ratio %
2.37	2.13	1.58	1.20	1.19	1.47	1.49	1.26	1.31	1.56	1.49	—	Income Ratio %
45	46	77	62	71	151	136	135	131	123	143	—	Turnover Rate %
11,977	15,238	16,977	19,454	17,580	13,915	12,212	9,401	12,256	12,915	12,122	11,698	Net Assets $mil

Performance 12-31-06

	1st Qtr	2nd Qtr	3rd Qtr	4th Qtr	Total
2002	2.65	-10.75	-16.41	10.43	-15.43
2003	-4.94	19.60	3.56	12.62	32.60
2004	0.47	0.00	0.18	9.17	9.88
2005	-2.16	0.61	4.17	2.05	4.63
2006	4.52	-2.12	4.42	6.45	13.73

Trailing	Total Return%	+/- S&P 500	+/- Russ 1000 VI	%Rank Cat	Growth of $10,000
3 Mo	6.45	-0.25	-1.55	77	10,645
6 Mo	11.16	-1.58	-3.56	83	11,116
1 Yr	13.73	-2.06	-8.52	93	11,373
3 Yr Avg	9.35	-1.09	-5.74	93	13,075
5 Yr Avg	7.95	1.76	-2.91	56	14,659
10 Yr Avg	9.09	0.67	-1.91	45	23,870
15 Yr Avg	11.66	1.02	-1.37	34	52,296

Tax Analysis	Tax-Adj Rtn%	%Rank Cat	Tax-Cost Rat	%Rank Cat
3 Yr (estimated)	7.76	89	1.45	58
5 Yr (estimated)	6.77	57	1.09	59
10 Yr (estimated)	7.02	49	1.90	71

Potential Capital Gain Exposure: 18% of assets

Rating and Risk

Time Period	Load-Adj Return %	Morningstar Rtn vs Cat	Morningstar Risk vs Cat	Morningstar Risk-Adj Rating
1 Yr	13.73			
3 Yr	9.35	-Avg	Avg	★★
5 Yr	7.95	Avg	+Avg	★★★
10 Yr	9.09	Avg	Avg	★★★
Incept	13.56			

Other Measures	Standard Index S&P 500	Best Fit Index S&P 500
Alpha	-1.1	-1.1
Beta	1.02	1.02
R-Squared	90	90
Standard Deviation	7.44	
Mean	9.35	
Sharpe Ratio	0.81	

Morningstar's Take by Greg Carlson 11-20-06

Despite a change at the top, it's still tough to get excited about Fidelity Equity-Income II.

Stephen DuFour, this large-value fund's manager for six years, was replaced on Nov. 9, 2006, by Bob Chow of Fidelity Advisor Equity Income. DuFour remains at the firm running institutional accounts; Chow will continue to manage his other charge.

We don't think DuFour was a very good fit for this fund. He tended to trade at a rapid pace; portfolio turnover averaged more than 125% during his tenure, a lofty figure given an asset base that often topped $12 billion. DuFour traded around positions, and the fund performed best during volatile stretches for stocks, such as in 2002-03. However, he struggled in other environments; all told, the fund trailed more than two thirds of its rivals on his watch. (It's worth noting that DuFour posted better returns at his other, much smaller charge, Fidelity Advisor Equity Value, where he was able to trade more.)

Chow, on the other hand, plies a strategy that's more amenable to running a large amount of money. At Advisor Equity Income (this fund will presumably be managed identically), he typically holds more than 200 stocks, and doesn't trade very often. His top 10 holdings are nearly always dividend-paying mega-caps, to help fulfill the fund's income mandate. He sometimes makes more unorthodox picks further down the portfolio; for example, his other charge recently held Cisco Systems and Freescale Semiconductor. However, their position sizes are too small to have much impact on the fund's returns. Thus, the fund has nearly always landed in the category's second and third quintiles in calendar years but has barely edged out its typical rival during his tenure.

True, Chow will have the advantage of a lower expense ratio at this fund, which will give him a leg up on peers. But given that he's now running more than twice as much money, we'd expect his style to remain very restrained. Thus, the fund remains an uninspiring choice.

Portfolio Analysis 08-31-06

Share change since 05-06 Total Stocks:91	Sector	PE	Tot Ret%	% Assets
⊖ ExxonMobil Corporation	Energy	11.1	39.07	5.61
⊕ Wal-Mart Stores, Inc.	Consumer	16.9	0.13	5.16
⊕ General Growth Propertie	Financial	—	15.09	4.14
⊕ Bank of America Corporat	Financial	12.4	20.68	3.96
⊖ Citigroup, Inc.	Financial	13.1	19.55	3.07
⊕ AT&T, Inc.	Telecom	18.2	51.59	3.02
⊕ Burlington Northern Sant	Business	15.2	5.52	2.83
⊕ Fannie Mae	Financial	—	24.34	2.78
⊕ Merck & Co., Inc.	Health	19.1	42.66	2.73
⊕ CSX Corporation	Business	15.4	37.05	2.67
⊕ Exelon Corporation	Utilities	—	19.79	2.56
⊕ Hewlett-Packard Company	Hardware	19.3	45.21	2.52
⊕ General Electric Company	Ind Mtrls	20.0	9.35	2.49
Wyeth	Health	17.2	12.88	2.44
⊕ Pfizer Inc.	Health	15.2	15.22	2.05
⊕ Comcast Corporation A	Media	45.2	63.31	1.99
⊖ American International G	Financial	17.0	6.05	1.97
⊖ ConocoPhillips	Energy	6.5	26.53	1.85
☼ Chevron Corporation	Energy	9.0	33.76	1.45
⊕ FMC Corporation	Ind Mtrls	18.5	45.55	1.45

Current Investment Style

Value Blnd Growth — Large Mid Small (Giant cell marked)

Market Cap	%
Giant	59.4
Large	26.5
Mid	12.6
Small	1.6
Micro	0.0

Avg $mil: 48,977

Value Measures		Rel Category
Price/Earnings	13.63	0.99
Price/Book	2.38	1.07
Price/Sales	1.38	1.06
Price/Cash Flow	7.63	1.14
Dividend Yield %	2.20	0.94

Growth Measures	%	Rel Category
Long-Term Erngs	10.79	1.04
Book Value	9.35	1.18
Sales	8.75	0.97
Cash Flow	5.61	0.93
Historical Erngs	17.63	1.09

Profitability	%	Rel Category
Return on Equity	16.53	0.92
Return on Assets	9.41	0.96
Net Margin	13.48	1.04

Sector Weightings	% of Stocks	Rel S&P 500	3 Year High	Low
↻ Info	17.37	0.87		
Software	0.00	0.00	3	0
Hardware	7.71	0.83	12	3
Media	4.90	1.29	8	3
Telecom	4.76	1.36	10	3
ⓖ Service	57.48	1.24		
Health	11.48	0.95	11	5
Consumer	6.64	0.87	9	3
Business	8.88	2.10	9	3
Financial	30.48	1.37	37	25
⌐ Mfg	25.14	0.74		
Goods	4.38	0.51	7	3
Ind Mtrls	5.21	0.44	16	5
Energy	9.86	1.01	14	7
Utilities	5.69	1.63	6	1

Composition

● Cash	0.8	
● Stocks	98.9	
● Bonds	0.1	
○ Other	0.2	
	Foreign	0.5
	(% of Stock)	

Address:	82 Devonshire St Boston MA 02109 800-544-6666
Web Address:	www.fidelity.com
Inception:	08-21-90
Advisor:	Fidelity Management & Research (FMR)
Subadvisor:	Multiple Subadvisors
NTF Plans:	Fidelity Retail-NTF, CommonWealth NTF

Minimum Purchase:	$2500	Add: $250	IRA: $2500
Min Auto Inv Plan:	$2500	Add: $100	
Sales Fees:	No-load		
Management Fee:	0.47%		
Actual Fees:	Mgt:0.47%	Dist: —	
Expense Projections:	3Yr:$218	5Yr:$379	10Yr:$847
Income Distrib:	Quarterly		

Fidelity Europe

	Ticker	Load	NAV	Yield	Total Assets	Mstar Category
	FIEUX	None	$39.36	1.0%	$4,388 mil	Europe Stock

Governance and Management

Stewardship Grade: B

Portfolio Manager(s)

Trygve Toraasen took over for Frederic Gautier on Jan. 9, 2006. Gautier himself had been at the helm only since Aug. 11, 2005, when he succeeded David Baverez. Toraasen started working as an analyst at Fidelity in 1994 and in June 1998 took over Fidelity Nordic, which he continues to manage. He has also run several single-country funds for overseas investors and has run a mid-cap Europe fund (also available overseas) since February 2001. The fund is supported by Fidelity's large European equities operation.

Strategy

Trygve Toraasen will manage the portfolio using a flexible style, looking for companies with unrecognized growth potential or promising restructuring efforts. He also incorporates some top-down analysis into his stock-picking. With growth stocks, he takes a three- to five-year time horizon, and with restructuring companies a shorter period of time. Because Toraasen views the U.K. market as more efficient than continental Europe, he is likely to be underweight the benchmark MSCI Europe's U.K. weighting. Fidelity uses fair-value pricing, and the fund does not hedge its foreign-currency exposure.

Performance 12-31-06

	1st Qtr	2nd Qtr	3rd Qtr	4th Qtr	Total
2002	3.07	-11.87	-28.01	14.00	-25.46
2003	-11.14	29.36	7.98	18.35	46.91
2004	5.56	-0.78	3.37	19.11	28.95
2005	2.02	1.09	10.99	3.24	18.17
2006	11.01	-1.50	3.69	10.42	25.18

Trailing	Total Return%	+/- MSCI EAFE	+/- MSCI Eur	%Rank Cat	Growth of $10,000
3 Mo	10.42	0.07	-1.04	81	11,042
6 Mo	14.49	-0.20	-3.24	93	11,449
1 Yr	25.18	-1.16	-8.54	92	12,518
3 Yr Avg	24.02	4.09	3.09	40	19,075
5 Yr Avg	15.87	0.89	1.00	48	20,886
10 Yr Avg	10.87	3.16	0.40	64	28,063
15 Yr Avg	12.06	4.20	0.70	38	55,177

Tax Analysis	Tax-Adj Rtn%	%Rank Cat	Tax-Cost Rat	%Rank Cat
3 Yr (estimated)	21.88	37	1.73	76
5 Yr (estimated)	14.57	53	1.12	72
10 Yr (estimated)	9.34	68	1.38	42

Potential Capital Gain Exposure: 17% of assets

Historical Profile

Return	Average
Risk	Above Avg
Rating	★★★ Neutral

	90%	95%	92%	95%	94%	96%	95%	96%	96%

▼ Manager Change
▽ Partial Manager Change

38.0
31.0
24.0
17.0

Growth of $10,000
■ Investment Values of Fund
― Investment Values of MSCI EAFE

10.0

Performance Quartile (within Category)

1995	1996	1997	1998	1999	2000	2001	2002	2003	2004	2005	2006	History
22.82	26.61	29.94	33.48	37.47	29.77	24.76	18.32	26.62	34.15	35.97	39.36	NAV
18.84	25.63	22.89	20.77	18.69	-9.14	-16.03	-25.46	46.91	28.95	18.17	25.18	Total Return %
7.63	19.58	21.11	0.84	-8.34	5.05	5.39	-9.52	8.32	8.70	4.63	-1.16	+/-MSCI EAFE
-2.78	4.54	-0.91	-7.73	2.76	-0.74	3.87	-7.08	8.37	8.07	8.75	-8.54	+/-MSCI Eur
0.60	1.05	1.47	0.94	0.54	0.32	0.81	0.57	1.58	0.34	0.88	1.28	Income Return %
18.24	24.58	21.42	19.83	18.15	-9.46	-16.84	-26.03	45.33	28.61	17.29	23.90	Capital Return %
50	47	41	73	78	80	31	97	21	27	21	92	Total Rtn % Rank Cat
0.12	0.24	0.39	0.28	0.18	0.12	0.24	0.14	0.29	0.09	0.30	0.46	Income $
0.81	1.73	2.35	2.25	1.94	4.09	0.00	0.00	0.00	0.08	3.97	5.07	Capital Gains $
1.18	1.27	1.18	1.09	0.89	1.05	0.99	1.13	0.98	1.05	1.07	—	Expense Ratio %
1.12	1.20	1.53	1.15	0.76	0.54	0.45	0.52	1.44	0.32	0.95	—	Income Ratio %
38	45	57	114	106	144	123	127	162	106	99	—	Turnover Rate %
501	773	951	1,623	1,478	1,407	1,153	896	1,476	2,208	2,766	4,388	Net Assets $mil

Investment Style
Equity
Stock %

Rating and Risk

Time Period	Load-Adj Return %	Morningstar Rtn vs Cat	Morningstar Risk vs Cat	Morningstar Risk-Adj Rating
1 Yr	25.18			
3 Yr	24.02	Avg	Avg	★★★
5 Yr	15.87	Avg	+Avg	★★★
10 Yr	10.87	Avg	+Avg	★★★
Incept	11.78			

Other Measures	Standard Index MSCI EAFE	Best Fit Index MSCI Wd xUS
Alpha	1.0	0.9
Beta	1.17	1.16
R-Squared	86	87
Standard Deviation	11.93	
Mean	24.02	
Sharpe Ratio	1.61	

Portfolio Analysis 10-31-06

Share change since 07-06 Total Stocks:83	Sector	Country	% Assets
⊕ BBVA	Financial	Spain	4.67
⊕ Tesco	Consumer	U.K.	3.26
⊕ Banco Santander Central	Financial	Spain	3.20
⊕ HSBC Hldgs	Financial	U.K.	3.11
⊖ Roche Holding	Health	Switzerland	2.84
⊖ BP	Energy	U.K.	2.43
⊖ ING Groep	Financial	Netherlands	2.17
⊖ Novartis	Health	Switzerland	2.07
⊕ AstraZeneca	Health	U.K.	1.87
⊕ Ericsson AB (publ)	Hardware	Sweden	1.72
⊕ Syngenta	Ind Mtrls	Switzerland	1.62
⊕ BMW Grp	Goods	Germany	1.62
⊕ UBS AG	Financial	Switzerland	1.61
⊕ ABB Ltd	Ind Mtrls	Switzerland	1.60
⊕ Societe Generale Grp	Financial	France	1.59
⊕ H&M Hennes & Mauritz	Consumer	Sweden	1.59
⊖ Koninklijke Philips Elec	Goods	Netherlands	1.54
☼ HBOS	Financial	U.K.	1.54
⊕ AXA	Financial	France	1.48
⊕ E.ON	Utilities	Germany	1.47

Current Investment Style

Value Blnd Growth — Large / Mid / Small

Market Cap	%
Giant	63.0
Large	25.4
Mid	11.6
Small	0.0
Micro	0.0

Avg $mil: 47,278

Value Measures		Rel Category
Price/Earnings	14.26	1.11
Price/Book	2.57	1.20
Price/Sales	1.50	1.38
Price/Cash Flow	9.26	1.21
Dividend Yield %	2.96	0.93

Growth Measures	%	Rel Category
Long-Term Erngs	11.98	0.86
Book Value	9.29	1.06
Sales	5.34	0.90
Cash Flow	10.83	1.45
Historical Erngs	21.20	0.97

Composition

Cash	3.9	Bonds	0.0
Stocks	95.8	Other	0.3
Foreign (% of Stock)			100.0

Sector Weightings	% of Stocks	Rel MSCI EAFE	3 Year High	Low
⟳ Info	8.84	0.75		
▣ Software	0.65	1.16	7	1
▣ Hardware	4.81	1.25	5	0
▣ Media	1.06	0.58	13	1
▣ Telecom	2.32	0.42	12	1
☞ Service	54.76	1.16		
▣ Health	10.84	1.52	16	8
▣ Consumer	5.92	1.20	6	0
▣ Business	3.35	0.66	9	3
▣ Financial	34.65	1.15	36	27
▣ Mfg	36.40	0.89		
▣ Goods	18.28	1.39	18	6
▣ Ind Mtrls	8.25	0.53	12	1
▣ Energy	5.93	0.83	15	5
▣ Utilities	3.94	0.75	4	0

Regional Exposure	% Stock		
UK/W. Europe	100	N. America	0
Japan	0	Latn America	0
Asia X Japan	0	Other	0

Country Exposure	% Stock		
U.K.	26	France	11
Switzerland	16	Spain	11
Germany	12		

Morningstar's Take by Dan Lefkovitz 11-15-06

Fidelity Europe doesn't stand out.

Any Europe-stock mutual fund must answer one of two questions. First: Why should an investor own it in addition to a broad foreign fund? Second: Should an investor looking for a Europe fund buy it instead of dirt-cheap Vanguard European Stock Index?

This fund doesn't provide a satisfying enough answer to either question. Under manager Trygve Toraasen, who took charge of the portfolio in January 2006, the fund has focused mostly on Western Europe's largest and most well-known names. No doubt, this is partly because Toraasen is finding value in large caps right now and also because the fund's $4 billion asset base precludes purchasing many smaller-cap stocks. Investors who own a diversified foreign fund, though, are already likely to have exposure to top 10 holdings like Roche, HSBC, and BP.

Nor can we predict with confidence that Toraasen will beat the MSCI Europe Index over the long term. The fund's 20% gain for the year to date through Nov. 14, 2006, while great in absolute terms, trails its benchmark by more than 7 percentage points. And Toraasen's previous experience running Fidelity Nordic and a European mid-cap fund available to overseas investors only goes so far in predicting how he'll fare on this pan-Europe mandate.

Interestingly, this fund was much bolder under a previous manager. David Baverez (2003-05) racked up stellar returns investing in a handful of stocks that included off-the-beaten-path mid-cap and Eastern European names. But after a round of manager changes, this fund has grown more conservative, and Fidelity Europe Capital Appreciation has become the shop's racy Europe option.

Thanks to the fund's strong returns, potential capital gains exposure is high. Investors in taxable accounts should be aware that a significant distribution may come in December.

Address:	82 Devonshire St Boston MA 02109 800-544-9797	Minimum Purchase:	$2500	Add: $250	IRA: $200
		Min Auto Inv Plan:	$100	Add: $100	
		Sales Fees:	No-load, 1.00%R		
Web Address:	www.fidelity.com	Management Fee:	0.84%		
Inception:	10-01-86	Actual Fees:	Mgt:0.84%	Dist: —	
Advisor:	Fidelity Management & Research (FMR)	Expense Projections:	3Yr:$368	5Yr:$638	10Yr:$1409
Subadvisor:	Multiple Subadvisors	Income Distrib:	Annually		
NTF Plans:	Fidelity Retail-NTF, CommonWealth NTF				

MORNINGSTAR® Funds 500

Fidelity Exp & Multinatl

	Ticker	Load	NAV	Yield	Total Assets	Mstar Category
	FEXPX	None	$22.98	0.2%	$4,285 mil	Large Growth

Governance and Management

Stewardship Grade: C

Portfolio Manager(s)

Victor Thay replaced Tim Cohen at the fund's helm on Oct. 31, 2005. Cohen was plucked to run the much larger Fidelity Growth & Income. Thay had mixed results in three years running Fidelity Convertible Securities. He also spent short stints at the helms of Select Natural Gas, Select Home Finance, Select Multimedia, and Advisor Growth & Income. This fund has a history of frequent manager turnover.

Strategy

This fund is supposed to invest mostly in export-oriented American companies, multinationals, and foreign firms that are mostly domestically focused. That leaves plenty of latitude, however, and different managers have interpreted the mandate differently. Victor Thay looks for companies with good cash-generating abilities that have rising incremental returns on capital. Valuation isn't a main concern, but Thay does aim for companies trading cheaply relative to historic ranges or industry norms. He holds around 60 stocks and keeps turnover near 50%. The fund does not hedge foreign-currency exposure.

Historical Profile

Return	High
Risk	Average
Rating	★★★★ Highest

97% 90% 97% 97% 95% 99% 98% 97% 98%

▼ Manager Change
▽ Partial Manager Change

63.2
46.4
33.8 Growth of $10,000
24.0 — Investment Values of Fund
17.0 — Investment Values of S&P 500
10.0

Performance Quartile (within Category)

1995	1996	1997	1998	1999	2000	2001	2002	2003	2004	2005	2006	History
12.72	16.75	17.02	19.88	21.97	16.88	16.97	13.75	18.16	19.64	21.24	22.98	NAV
32.22	38.64	23.69	22.41	41.80	1.48	0.72	-18.66	32.62	13.59	15.29	8.43	Total Return %
-5.36	15.68	-9.67	-6.17	20.76	10.58	12.61	3.44	3.94	2.71	10.38	-7.36	+/-S&P 500
-4.96	15.52	-6.80	-16.30	8.64	23.90	21.14	9.22	2.87	7.29	10.03	-0.64	+/-Russ 1000Gr
0.00	0.00	0.00	0.00	0.25	0.48	0.18	0.29	0.51	0.62	0.31	0.19	Income Return %
32.22	38.64	23.69	22.41	41.55	1.00	0.54	-18.95	32.11	12.97	14.98	8.24	Capital Return %
49	1	62	78	35	10	2	10	22	8	4	35	Total Rtn % Rank Cat
0.00	0.00	0.00	0.00	0.05	0.10	0.03	0.05	0.07	0.11	0.06	0.04	Income $
0.84	0.86	3.79	0.77	4.80	5.21	0.00	0.00	0.00	0.82	1.30	0.01	Capital Gains $
1.22	1.00	0.91	0.88	0.86	0.77	0.81	0.78	0.84	0.83	0.85	0.81	Expense Ratio %
-0.27	-0.39	-0.13	-0.25	0.23	0.38	0.21	0.19	0.60	0.15	0.63	0.30	Income Ratio %
245	313	429	281	265	380	170	228	139	96	68	119	Turnover Rate %
382	397	465	412	514	495	673	675	1,042	1,643	4,173	4,285	Net Assets $mil

Performance 12-31-06

	1st Qtr	2nd Qtr	3rd Qtr	4th Qtr	Total
2002	-0.35	-13.72	-16.79	13.70	-18.66
2003	-2.76	16.68	3.27	13.19	32.62
2004	1.82	3.03	-1.42	9.84	13.59
2005	-1.48	3.26	6.71	6.20	15.29
2006	3.25	-1.69	1.02	5.74	8.43

Trailing	Total Return%	+/- S&P 500	+/- Russ 1000Gr	%Rank Cat	Growth of $10,000
3 Mo	5.74	-0.96	-0.19	43	10,574
6 Mo	6.82	-5.92	-3.28	73	10,682
1 Yr	8.43	-7.36	-0.64	35	10,843
3 Yr Avg	12.40	1.96	5.53	5	14,200
5 Yr Avg	8.90	2.71	6.21	3	15,316
10 Yr Avg	12.89	4.47	7.45	2	33,617
15 Yr Avg	—	—	—		—

Tax Analysis	Tax-Adj Rtn%	%Rank Cat	Tax-Cost Rat	%Rank Cat
3 Yr (estimated)	11.45	6	0.85	55
5 Yr (estimated)	8.28	2	0.57	57
10 Yr (estimated)	9.81	3	2.73	97

Potential Capital Gain Exposure: 18% of assets

Rating and Risk

Time Period	Load-Adj Return %	Morningstar Rtn vs Cat	Morningstar Risk vs Cat	Morningstar Risk-Adj Rating
1 Yr	8.43			
3 Yr	12.40	High	Avg	★★★★★
5 Yr	8.90	High	+Avg	★★★★★
10 Yr	12.89	High	Avg	★★★★★
Incept	16.25			

Other Measures	Standard Index S&P 500	Best Fit Index S&P Mid 400
Alpha	0.4	0.5
Beta	1.23	0.88
R-Squared	73	84
Standard Deviation	9.87	
Mean	12.40	
Sharpe Ratio	0.91	

Portfolio Analysis 08-31-06

Share change since 05-06 Total Stocks:52	Sector	PE	Tot Ret%	% Assets
⊕ Google, Inc.	Business	61.5	11.00	5.05
Bank of America Corporat	Financial	12.4	20.68	4.76
⊕ Johnson & Johnson	Health	17.5	12.45	4.33
⊕ American International G	Financial	17.0	6.05	4.12
⊕ Hewlett-Packard Company	Hardware	19.3	45.21	3.67
⊖ Valero Energy Corporatio	Energy	6.3	-0.33	3.52
⊖ Schlumberger, Ltd.	Energy	22.3	31.07	3.47
⊖ Crown Castle Internation	Telecom	—	20.94	3.23
⊕ Allergan, Inc.	Health	—	11.33	2.94
⊕ Ultra Petroleum Corporat	Energy	30.4	-14.44	2.71
⊖ Honeywell International,	Ind Mtrls	18.6	24.14	2.49
⊖ Canadian Natural Resourc	Energy	29.1	7.84	2.45
⊕ Wells Fargo Company	Financial	14.7	16.82	2.44
⊕ Monsanto Company	Ind Mtrls	39.8	36.78	2.41
⊕ Genentech, Inc.	Health	48.7	-12.29	2.22
Golden West Fin	Financial	—	—	2.16
⊖ Yahoo, Inc.	Media	35.4	-34.81	2.03
⊖ Apple Computer, Inc.	Hardware	37.6	18.01	1.93
⊕ Equinix, Inc.	Business	—	85.53	1.92
⊖ eBay, Inc.	Consumer	40.1	-30.43	1.75

Current Investment Style

Value Blnd Growth — Large Mid Small

Market Cap	%
Giant	45.1
Large	33.9
Mid	17.8
Small	2.4
Micro	0.9

Avg $mil: 30,659

Value Measures		Rel Category
Price/Earnings	17.64	0.92
Price/Book	3.09	0.93
Price/Sales	1.83	0.94
Price/Cash Flow	9.91	0.87
Dividend Yield %	1.00	0.97

Growth Measures	%	Rel Category
Long-Term Erngs	14.37	1.00
Book Value	10.36	0.89
Sales	16.23	1.40
Cash Flow	31.05	1.85
Historical Erngs	27.68	1.20

Profitability	%	Rel Category
Return on Equity	15.75	0.77
Return on Assets	10.84	0.98
Net Margin	12.02	0.84

Sector Weightings	% of Stocks	Rel S&P 500	3 Year High Low	
⟳ Info	16.04	0.80		
Software	0.35	0.10	8	0
Hardware	9.96	1.08	15	6
Media	2.08	0.55	8	1
Telecom	3.65	1.04	4	0
⟳ Service	59.26	1.28		
Health	13.98	1.16	15	8
Consumer	5.44	0.71	15	5
Business	14.06	3.32	14	4
Financial	25.78	1.16	28	20
⟳ Mfg	24.69	0.73		
Goods	3.24	0.38	8	1
Ind Mtrls	6.42	0.54	14	4
Energy	15.03	1.53	17	7
Utilities	0.00	0.00	2	0

Composition

●	Cash	2.2
●	Stocks	97.8
●	Bonds	0.0
○	Other	0.0
	Foreign	15.3
	(% of Stock)	

Morningstar's Take by Dan Lefkovitz 11-15-06

Fidelity Export & Multinational's record is seductive, but we'd resist its charms.

This fund has one of the best long-term records in the large-blend category, hands down. It has trounced the S&P 500 over the trailing three, five, and 10 years and has beaten more than 90% of its peers in each of those periods. This record is a collective effort. Six managers have run the fund since its 1994 inception.

But we can't give a free pass to the fund's current manager, Victor Thay, just because his predecessors put up good numbers. Despite the fund's distinctive name, different managers have taken different tacks here and therefore must be evaluated individually. Thay lacks much of a track record as a diversified equity manager. His longest managerial stint, on Fidelity Convertible Securities, yielded mixed results.

Thay has been at the helm for nearly one year now. His approach is appealing. He invests with conviction, paying little attention to the sector and stock weights of the S&P 500 and building compact portfolios of companies that invest their cash well. He's expressed a desire to take a long-term approach, which strikes us as the best way to take advantage of Fidelity's research capabilities.

It's far too soon to come to a conclusion on Thay, but initial results aren't encouraging. His discipline led the fund into lots of high-priced growth stocks, which is why the portfolio now lands in the large-growth section of the Morningstar Style Box and has a much higher average price-to-earnings ratio than its peers. This has been problematic in 2006. The poor performance of Internet-related stocks such as eBay and Yahoo helps explain why the fund is languishing in the large-blend category's basement. To balance out his growth bias, Thay has added some dividend-paying blue chips such as Johnson & Johnson.

It remains to be seen if this tweak will pay off. For now, investors have more-proven options.

Address:	82 Devonshire St Boston MA 02109 800-544-9797	
Web Address:	www.fidelity.com	
Inception:	10-04-94	
Advisor:	Fidelity Management & Research (FMR)	
Subadvisor:	Multiple Subadvisors	
NTF Plans:	Fidelity Retail-NTF, CommonWealth NTF	

Minimum Purchase:	$2500	Add: $250	IRA: $2500
Min Auto Inv Plan:	$2500	Add: $100	
Sales Fees:	No-load, 0.75%R		
Management Fee:	0.57%		
Actual Fees:	Mgt:0.57%	Dist: —	
Expense Projections:	3Yr:$265	5Yr:$460	10Yr:$1025
Income Distrib:	Semi-Annually		

Fidelity Float Rt Hi Inc

Analyst Pick ✓

Ticker	Load	NAV	Yield	SEC Yield	Total Assets	Mstar Category
FFRHX	None	$9.95	6.2%	6.60%	$4,602 mil	Bank Loan

Governance and Management

Stewardship Grade: B

Portfolio Manager(s)

Christine McConnell leads the effort here and at Fidelity Advisor Floating Rate High Income. She has been with Fidelity since 1987, and she worked as a high-yield bond analyst prior to taking the helm. She is backed by Fidelity's extensive research capabilities and a team of analysts. Fidelity's bank-loan group is part of its larger high-yield investment team.

Strategy

Manager Christine McConnell forms an economic outlook and tries to pick floating-rate bank loans that will perform well in that environment. She focuses on security, collateral, and covenants in an effort to find attractively priced loans. She will also look to take advantage of sector-related opportunities. Of late, for example, she has held large stakes in the telecommunications and cable sectors, arguing that their assets make them more attractive than others. The fund isn't a pure bank-loan play, as it owns a slew of plain-vanilla junk bonds.

Performance 12-31-06

	1st Qtr	2nd Qtr	3rd Qtr	4th Qtr	Total
2002	—	—	—	1.86	1.87 *
2003	1.58	2.39	1.10	1.24	6.47
2004	1.06	0.82	0.99	1.52	4.47
2005	0.87	0.74	1.46	1.10	4.23
2006	1.67	0.69	1.92	1.94	6.37

Trailing	Total Return%	+/- LB Aggr	+/- LB 1-5 YR	%Rank Cat	Growth of $10,000
3 Mo	1.94	0.70	0.93	38	10,194
6 Mo	3.90	-1.19	0.36	21	10,390
1 Yr	6.37	2.04	2.15	35	10,637
3 Yr Avg	5.02	1.32	2.53	56	11,583
5 Yr Avg	—	—	—	—	—
10 Yr Avg	—	—	—	—	—
15 Yr Avg	—	—	—	—	—

Tax Analysis	Tax-Adj Rtn%	%Rank Cat	Tax-Cost Rat	%Rank Cat
3 Yr (estimated)	3.33	50	1.61	42
5 Yr (estimated)	—	—	—	—
10 Yr (estimated)	—	—	—	—

Potential Capital Gain Exposure: 0% of assets

Historical Profile

Return: Below Avg
Risk: Below Avg
Rating: ★★ Below Avg

Investment Style
Fixed Income
Income Rtn %Rank Cat

▼ Manager Change
▽ Partial Manager Change

Growth of $10,000
— Investment Values of Fund
— Investment Values of LB Aggr

Performance Quartile (within Category)

	1995	1996	1997	1998	1999	2000	2001	2002	2003	2004	2005	2006	History
	—	—	—	—	—	—	—	9.58	9.87	9.98	9.95	9.95	NAV
	—	—	—	—	—	—	—	1.87*	6.47	4.47	4.23	6.37	Total Return %
	—	—	—	—	—	—	—	—	2.37	0.13	1.80	2.04	+/-LB Aggr
	—	—	—	—	—	—	—	—	3.12	2.62	2.79	2.15	+/-LB 1-5 YR
	—	—	—	—	—	—	—	—	3.40	3.23	4.53	6.34	Income Return %
	—	—	—	—	—	—	—	—	3.07	1.24	-0.30	0.03	Capital Return %
	—	—	—	—	—	—	—	—	74	59	55	35	Total Rtn % Rank Cat
	—	—	—	—	—	—	—	0.12	0.32	0.31	0.44	0.61	Income $
	—	—	—	—	—	—	—	0.00	0.00	0.01	0.00	0.00	Capital Gains $
	—	—	—	—	—	—	—	0.94	0.86	0.84	0.82	—	Expense Ratio %
	—	—	—	—	—	—	—	3.99	3.27	3.14	4.29	—	Income Ratio %
	—	—	—	—	—	—	—	77	55	61	66	—	Turnover Rate %
	—	—	—	—	—	—	—	65	956	2,162	2,517	3,048	Net Assets $mil

Rating and Risk

Time Period	Load-Adj Return %	Morningstar Rtn vs Cat	Morningstar Risk vs Cat	Morningstar Risk-Adj Rating
1 Yr	6.37			
3 Yr	5.02	-Avg	-Avg	★★
5 Yr	—	—	—	—
10 Yr	—	—	—	—
Incept	5.47			

Other Measures	Standard Index LB Aggr	Best Fit Index CSFB Glb HY
Alpha	1.7	0.9
Beta	0.02	0.15
R-Squared	1	59
Standard Deviation	0.71	
Mean	5.02	
Sharpe Ratio	2.43	

Morningstar's Take by Paul Herbert 12-28-06

Fidelity Floating Rate High Income remains a strong option in its class.

This fund hasn't set the world on fire in recent years, but that's not a good reason to dismiss it. It's true that its 4.87% annualized return for the three-year period that ended Dec. 27, 2006, ranks behind nearly two thirds of the bank-loan group. But though the fund has failed to deliver strong gains, it has treated shareholders to consistent results. The fund has actually delivered some of the smoothest returns in the group, as measured by its low standard deviation of returns, during its history.

Manager Christine McConnell's approach has led to these steady results. Though this offering isn't the strictest in the group when it comes to emphasizing high-quality borrowers, McConnell has tended toward safer fare, stashing about 50% of assets in those rated BB. More than others in the group, however, she concentrates on asset-rich companies. Her thinking is that the fund is likely to be sitting pretty in the event of a reorganization because firms in bankruptcy may have to sell off plants, equipment, or land to make good on their promises. As a result of McConnell's asset-intensive preference, the fund has large stakes in cable, telecom, technology, and utilities firms, which took up more than 25% of assets as of October 2006.

Looking forward, McConnell feels good about loan-market opportunities. Several larger companies have come to market in 2006, and more are expected to do the same in 2007. McConnell likes these trends because these firms tend to have more assets, and they can benefit from other macroeconomic tailwinds such as a weakening dollar. Snapping up these heavies, and maintaining an overall focus on asset coverage should bolster the fund if issuers get sidetracked by earnings woes and defaults pick up.

Add in the fund's low costs and the backing of Fidelity's debt and equity research groups, and you've got the makings of a good holding here.

Address:	82 Devonshire St Boston MA 02109 800-544-4774	
Web Address:	www.advisor.fidelity.com	
Inception:	09-19-02*	
Advisor:	Fidelity Management & Research (FMR)	
Subadvisor:	Multiple Subadvisors	
NTF Plans:	Fidelity Retail-NTF, CommonWealth NTF	

Minimum Purchase:	$2500	Add: $250	IRA: $2500
Min Auto Inv Plan:	$100	Add: $100	
Sales Fees:	No-load, 1.00%R		
Management Fee:	0.67%		
Actual Fees:	Mgt:0.67%	Dist: —	
Expense Projections:	3Yr:$259	5Yr:$450	10Yr:$1002
Income Distrib:	Monthly		

Portfolio Analysis 10-31-06

Total Fixed-Income:262

	Date of Maturity	Amount $000	Value $000	% Net Assets
Charter Comm Op Term B 4	04-28-13	125,000	125,938	2.63
Csc Hldgs Inc Term B 3/2	03-29-13	93,567	93,509	1.95
Nrg Energy Inc Term 2/1/	02-01-13	81,027	81,533	1.70
Georgia Pac 1st Ln Trm B	12-23-12	74,438	74,856	1.56
Sungard Data Term B 2/10	02-10-13	69,103	69,707	1.46
Qwest FRN	06-15-13	56,150	60,429	1.26
Vnu Inc Term 8/09/13	08-09-13	60,000	60,225	1.26
Allied Waste North Amer		59,339	59,339	1.24
Davita FRN	10-05-12	57,858	58,075	1.21
Community Health Term 8/	08-19-11	43,810	43,756	0.91
Celanese Hldg Term 4/6/1	04-06-11	42,644	42,857	0.90
General Growth Term A1 2	02-24-10	40,000	39,700	0.83
Fresenius Medicl Trm B 3	03-31-12	39,810	39,561	0.83
Rogers Wireless FRN	12-15-10	38,450	39,315	0.82
Constellation Term B 6/0	06-05-13	36,492	36,674	0.77
Huntsman Intl Term B 8/1	08-16-12	35,781	35,737	0.75
Directv Hld Llc Term B 4	04-13-13	34,239	34,239	0.72
Crown Castle Op Term B 6	06-01-14	32,918	33,041	0.69
Windstream Corp Term B 7	07-17-13	32,000	32,200	0.67
Lyondell Chem Term 8/13/	08-13-13	32,000	32,120	0.67

Current Investment Style

Duration: Short Int Long
Quality: High Med Low

1 figure provided by fund

Avg Eff Duration[1]	—
Avg Eff Maturity	—
Avg Credit Quality	—
Avg Wtd Coupon	0.41%
Avg Wtd Price	100.59% of par

Coupon Range	% of Bonds	Rel Cat
0% PIK	20.1	0.6
0% to 6%	96.0	1.9
6% to 8%	2.1	0.1
8% to 10%	1.5	0.1
More than 10%	0.5	0.2

1.00=Category Average

Credit Analysis	% bonds 10-31-06		
AAA	—	BB	—
AA	—	B	—
A	—	Below B	—
BBB	—	NR/NA	—

Sector Breakdown	% of assets
US Treasuries	0
TIPS	0
US Agency	0
Mortgage Pass-Throughs	0
Mortgage CMO	0
Mortgage ARM	0
US Corporate	81
Asset-Backed	0
Convertible	0
Municipal	0
Corporate Inflation-Protected	0
Foreign Corporate	2
Foreign Govt	0

Composition			
Cash	16.2	Bonds	77.2
Stocks	0.0	Other	6.5

Special Securities	
Restricted/Illiquid Secs	2
Exotic Mortgage-Backed	0
Emerging-Markets Secs	0
Options/Futures/Warrants	No

MORNINGSTAR® Funds 500

Fidelity Freedom 2010

	Ticker	Load	NAV	Yield	Total Assets	Mstar Category
	FFFCX	None	$14.62	2.5%	$12,269 mil	Target-Date 2000-2014

Governance and Management

Stewardship Grade: B

Portfolio Manager(s)

Ren Cheng and Jonathan Shelon oversee the Fidelity Freedom funds. Cheng has been on board since the October 1996 inception of the first set of Freedom funds, while Shelon was named comanager in March 2005. Shareholders are tapping into the managers of the underlying Fidelity funds, many of whom are quite skilled, as well as Fidelity's strong research capabilities. At times, manager departures and shifts at some of the underlying funds raise concerns about individual funds.

Strategy

This fund aims to be a one-stop solution for retirement savings, using 18 to 23 actively managed Fidelity funds that cover a broad range of areas, such as domestic large-value stocks, foreign large-growth stocks, and high-yield bonds. The fund's asset mix becomes more conservative as 2010 approaches.

Historical Profile
Return High
Risk High
Rating ★★★★★ Highest

	50%	56%	52%	45%	39%	45%	48%	48%	49%

Investment Style
Equity
Stock %

▼ Manager Change
▽ Partial Manager Change

Growth of $10,000
— Investment Values of Fund
— Investment Values of DJ Mod

20.5
17.5
15.0
12.5
10.0

Performance Quartile (within Category)

1995	1996	1997	1998	1999	2000	2001	2002	2003	2004	2005	2006	History
—	10.19	11.69	13.30	14.87	13.84	12.61	11.44	13.02	13.62	14.05	14.62	NAV
—	2.99*	19.27	19.29	19.04	0.67	-4.34	-6.85	17.13	7.24	5.92	9.46	Total Return %
—	—	7.37	6.97	1.71	2.34	-1.54	-0.08	-10.25	-5.73	-1.07	-2.84	+/-DJ Mod
—	—	8.15	6.94	4.57	0.62	-3.41	-5.03	-4.43	-3.38	2.30	1.34	+/-DJ Tgt 2010
—	—	3.65	3.04	3.75	3.20	2.73	2.47	2.46	2.24	2.22	2.74	Income Return %
—	—	15.62	16.25	15.29	-2.53	-7.07	-9.32	14.67	5.00	3.70	6.72	Capital Return %
—	—	1	1	1	60	85	76	19	32	2	32	Total Rtn % Rank Cat
—	0.11	0.37	0.35	0.49	0.46	0.37	0.31	0.28	0.29	0.30	0.38	Income $
—	0.00	0.09	0.28	0.42	0.67	0.27	0.00	0.09	0.05	0.07	0.37	Capital Gains $
—	—	—	—	—	—	—	—	—	—	—	0.62	Expense Ratio %
—	—	—	2.56	2.54	2.82	2.98	3.43	2.84	2.44	2.07	2.48	Income Ratio %
—	—	—	3	20	27	33	16	10	8	4	8	Turnover Rate %
—	—	123	914	1,644	2,313	3,491	4,330	6,787	8,419	12,269	Net Assets $mil

Performance 12-31-06

	1st Qtr	2nd Qtr	3rd Qtr	4th Qtr	Total
2002	0.00	-5.02	-6.05	4.38	-6.85
2003	-0.35	8.62	2.11	5.98	17.13
2004	2.23	-0.62	0.00	5.56	7.24
2005	-1.25	2.17	2.71	2.21	5.92
2006	3.06	-1.43	3.06	4.55	9.46

Trailing	Total Return%	+/- DJ Mod	+/- DJ Tgt 2010	%Rank Cat	Growth of $10,000
3 Mo	4.55	-1.04	1.51	24	10,455
6 Mo	7.74	-1.05	1.92	32	10,774
1 Yr	9.46	-2.84	1.34	32	10,946
3 Yr Avg	7.53	-3.19	0.12	19	12,433
5 Yr Avg	6.29	-3.73	-1.85	35	13,566
10 Yr Avg	8.26	-0.29	0.58	1	22,115
15 Yr Avg	—	—	—	—	—

Tax Analysis	Tax-Adj Rtn%	%Rank Cat	Tax-Cost Rat	%Rank Cat
3 Yr (estimated)	6.46	15	1.00	56
5 Yr (estimated)	5.25	34	0.98	60
10 Yr (estimated)	6.81	1	1.34	1

Potential Capital Gain Exposure: 8% of assets

Rating and Risk

Time Period	Load-Adj Return %	Morningstar Rtn vs Cat	Morningstar Risk vs Cat	Morningstar Risk-Adj Rating
1 Yr	9.46			
3 Yr	7.53	+Avg	+Avg	★★★★
5 Yr	6.29	+Avg	+Avg	★★★★
10 Yr	8.26	High	High	★★★★★
Incept	8.40			

Other Measures	Standard Index S&P 500	Best Fit Index DJ Mod
Alpha	-1.1	-1.1
Beta	0.73	0.73
R-Squared	94	94
Standard Deviation	4.44	
Mean	7.53	
Sharpe Ratio	0.94	

Portfolio Analysis 09-30-06

Total Stocks:0 Share change since 06-30-06	Sectors	P/E Ratio	YTD Return %	% Net Assets
⊕ Fidelity Growth & Income	—	—	—	6.69
⊕ Fidelity Equity-Income	—	—	—	6.19
⊕ Fidelity Blue Chip Growth	—	—	—	6.13
⊕ Fidelity Blue Chip Growth	—	—	—	6.13
⊕ Fidelity Disciplined Equi	—	—	—	6.05
⊕ Fidelity Strategic Real R	—	—	—	5.74
⊕ Fidelity Mid-Cap Stock	—	—	—	3.89
⊕ Fidelity Growth Company	—	—	—	3.86
⊕ Fidelity Europe	—	—	—	3.22

Total Fixed-Income:0	Date of Maturity	Amount $000	Value $000	% Net Assets
Fidelity Investment Grade		191,049	1,411,854	12.51
Fidelity Government Incom		108,121	1,087,701	9.64
Fidelity Intermediate Bon		79,501	817,274	7.24
Fidelity Short-Term Bond		59,959	531,837	4.71
Fidelity High Income		32,020	284,337	2.52
Fidelity Capital & Income		32,903	282,639	2.50

Equity Style
Style: Growth
Size: Large-Cap

Value Measures		Rel Category
Price/Earnings	15.63	1.04
Price/Book	2.53	1.05
Price/Sales	1.30	0.96
Price/Cash Flow	7.63	0.97
Dividend Yield %	1.59	0.80

Growth Measures	%	Rel Category
Long-Term Erngs	12.90	1.10
Book Value	9.65	1.12
Sales	9.83	1.10
Cash Flow	13.31	1.32
Historical Erngs	21.60	1.19

Market Cap %			
Giant	41.0	Small	4.5
Large	33.4	Micro	0.8
Mid	20.3	Avg $mil:	24,663

Fixed-Income Style
Duration: Interm-Term
Quality: High

Avg Eff Duration [1]	4.0 Yrs
Avg Eff Maturity	5.2 Yrs
Avg Credit Quality	AA
Avg Wtd Coupon	3.78%

[1]figure provided by fund as of 09-30-06

Sector Weightings	% of Stocks	Rel DJ Mod	3 Year High Low	
⟳ Info	19.99			
Software	3.22	—	5	3
Hardware	11.31	—	14	11
Media	2.43	—	5	2
Telecom	3.03	—	5	3
⟳ Service	48.61			
Health	15.04	—	15	13
Consumer	9.25	—	9	7
Business	6.28	—	6	4
Financial	18.04	—	20	16
⟳ Mfg	31.39			
Goods	7.60	—	9	6
Ind Mtrls	12.29	—	13	11
Energy	10.17	—	11	6
Utilities	1.33	—	2	1

Composition

● Cash	11.2	
● Stocks	49.5	
● Bonds	37.3	
○ Other	2.0	
Foreign	23.1	(% of Stock)

Morningstar's Take by Greg Carlson 12-20-06

Fidelity Freedom 2010 is a viable choice, but investors can do better.

This fund of funds is designed for investors slated to retire close to 2010. As with other target-date funds, this one is broadly diversified, and its asset allocation gradually grows more conservative over time.

However, this fund boasts distinct advantages over many rivals. First, it's relatively cheap--its 0.62% expense ratio ranks in the bottom quartile among no-load funds in the target-date 2000-2014 category. That's crucial for a fund designed to be held for many years (including the time past its target date). Second, Fidelity's sizable, recently expanded investment staff boasts expertise across a broad range of asset classes and styles. Indeed, the fund holds solid, disparate offerings such as Fidelity Growth Company, Fidelity Diversified International, and Fidelity Investment Grade Bond.

That said, we think this fund could be improved. It recently held 23 funds, which results in substantial overlap--it owns two intermediate-bond funds, three large-growth funds, two foreign large-cap funds, and a set of three regional funds that essentially amounts to a third foreign large-cap fund. What's more, some of those holdings have been middling long-term performers, such as Fidelity Value, or have inexperienced skippers: Three of the fund's holdings are run by managers with less than two years' tenure on diversified funds, and another six have managed their current charges for less than two years.

True, the firm has made some positive tweaks here: It recently dropped yet another large-cap fund, Fidelity Fund, from its portfolio, and has boosted the Freedom funds' planned equity stakes in the first years after their target dates, which should help retirees better battle inflation. What's more, we're fans of Fidelity's bond funds, which play a big role here. But we think investors with access to our Analyst Picks will be better served.

Address:	82 Devonshire St. Boston, MA 02109 800-343-3548	Minimum Purchase:	$2500	Add: $250	IRA: $2500
		Min Auto Inv Plan:	$2500	Add: $100	
		Sales Fees:	No-load		
Web Address:	www.fidelity.com	Management Fee:	0.10%, 0.08%A		
Inception:	10-17-96*	Actual Fees:	Mgt: —	Dist: —	
Advisor:	Strategic Advisers, Inc.	Expense Projections:	3Yr:$205	5Yr:$357	10Yr:$798
Subadvisor:	None	Income Distrib:	Semi-Annually		
NTF Plans:	Fidelity Retail-NTF, CommonWealth NTF				

Fidelity Freedom 2020

	Ticker	Load	NAV	Yield	Total Assets	Mstar Category
	FFFDX	None	$15.53	1.7%	$16,889 mil	Target-Date 2015-2029

Governance and Management

Stewardship Grade: B

Portfolio Manager(s)

Ren Cheng and Jonathan Shelon oversee the Fidelity Freedom funds. Cheng has been on board since the October 1996 inception of the first set of Freedom funds, while Shelon was named comanager in March 2005. Shareholders are tapping into the managers of the underlying Fidelity funds, many of whom are quite skilled, as well as Fidelity's strong research capabilities. At times, manager departures and shifts at some of the underlying funds raise concerns about individual funds.

Strategy

This fund aims to be a one-stop solution for retirement savings, using 18 to 24 actively managed Fidelity funds that cover a broad range of areas, such as domestic large-value stocks, foreign large-growth stocks, and high-yield bonds. The fund's asset mix will become more conservative as 2020 approaches.

Historical Profile
Return: Average
Risk: Above Avg
Rating: ★★★ Neutral

Investment Style: Equity, Stock %

Performance Quartile (within Category)

Investment Values of Fund / **Investment Values of DJ Mod**, Growth of $10,000

	1995	1996	1997	1998	1999	2000	2001	2002	2003	2004	2005	2006	History
	—	10.24	11.93	13.95	16.38	14.56	12.58	10.64	13.02	13.96	14.71	15.53	NAV
	—	3.29*	21.15	21.66	25.31	-3.03	-9.07	-13.71	24.90	9.55	7.75	11.61	Total Return %
	—	—	9.25	9.34	7.98	-1.36	-6.27	-6.94	-2.48	-3.42	0.76	-0.69	+/-DJ Mod
	—	—	6.93	9.56	-0.30	2.11	-2.91	-1.16	-8.39	-5.16	-0.96	-2.67	+/-DJ Tgt 2025
	—	—	3.33	2.37	3.30	2.47	1.83	1.75	2.07	2.01	1.66	1.93	Income Return %
	—	—	17.82	19.29	22.01	-5.50	-10.90	-15.46	22.83	7.54	6.09	9.68	Capital Return %
	—	—	50	1	1	1	100	69	7	34	2	60	Total Rtn % Rank Cat
	—	0.09	0.34	0.28	0.45	0.39	0.26	0.22	0.22	0.26	0.23	0.28	Income $
	—	0.00	0.13	0.27	0.57	0.96	0.43	0.00	0.04	0.04	0.10	0.59	Capital Gains $
	—	—	—	—	—	—	—	—	—	—	—	0.70	Expense Ratio %
	—	—	1.75	1.76	2.03	2.07	2.29	2.03	1.96	1.85	1.79	1.87	Income Ratio %
	—	—	21	15	18	28	16	10	6	3	—	4	Turnover Rate %
	1	84	860	1,560	1,893	2,796	3,735	6,736	9,338	12,265	16,889		Net Assets $mil

Performance 12-31-06

	1st Qtr	2nd Qtr	3rd Qtr	4th Qtr	Total
2002	0.16	-8.59	-11.16	6.09	-13.71
2003	-1.32	12.40	3.32	8.99	24.90
2004	2.46	-1.09	-1.06	8.16	9.55
2005	-1.79	2.17	4.24	3.02	7.75
2006	4.49	-2.13	3.18	5.77	11.61

Trailing	Total Return%	+/- DJ Mod	+/- DJ Tgt 2025	%Rank Cat	Growth of $10,000
3 Mo	5.77	0.18	-0.85	48	10,577
6 Mo	9.13	0.34	-0.76	69	10,913
1 Yr	11.61	-0.69	-2.67	60	11,161
3 Yr Avg	9.63	-1.09	-2.90	23	13,176
5 Yr Avg	7.26	-2.76	-3.42	46	14,197
10 Yr Avg	8.74	0.19	-0.31	1	23,115
15 Yr Avg	—	—	—	—	—

Tax Analysis	Tax-Adj Rtn%	%Rank Cat	Tax-Cost Rat	%Rank Cat
3 Yr (estimated)	8.66	28	0.88	78
5 Yr (estimated)	6.39	43	0.81	91
10 Yr (estimated)	7.41	1	1.22	50

Potential Capital Gain Exposure: 12% of assets

Morningstar's Take by Greg Carlson 12-20-06

Fidelity Freedom 2020 is a worthy holding, but investors with access to better options should seek them out.

This fund of funds is designed for investors with substantial time horizons--those slated to retire close to 2020. As with other target-date funds, this one is broadly diversified, and its asset allocation gradually grows more conservative over time.

This fund, however, boasts distinct advantages over many rivals from other fund shops. First, it's relatively cheap--its 0.70% expense ratio ranks in the bottom quartile among no-load funds in the target-date 2015-2029 category. That's crucial for a fund designed to be held more than a decade. Second, Fidelity's sizable, recently expanded investment staff boasts expertise across a broad range of asset classes and styles. Indeed, the fund holds solid, disparate offerings such as Fidelity Growth Company, Fidelity Diversified International, and Fidelity High Income.

That said, we think this fund, along with Fidelity's other target-date funds, could be improved. It recently held 24 funds, which results in substantial overlap--it owns three large-growth funds, two small-growth funds, two high-yield bond funds, two foreign large-cap funds, and a set of three regional funds that essentially amounts to a third foreign large-cap fund. What's more, some of those holdings have been middling long-term performers, or have inexperienced skippers: Three of the fund's holdings are run by managers with less than two years' tenure on diversified funds, and another six have managed their current charges for less than two years.

True, the firm has made some positive tweaks here: It recently dropped yet another large-cap fund, Fidelity Fund, from its portfolio, and has boosted the Freedom funds' planned equity stakes in the first years after their target dates, which should help retirees better battle inflation. But we think investors with access to our Analyst Picks will be better served.

Address:	82 Devonshire St. Boston, MA 02109 800-343-3548
Web Address:	www.fidelity.com
Inception:	10-17-96 *
Advisor:	Strategic Advisers, Inc.
Subadvisor:	None
NTF Plans:	Fidelity Retail-NTF, CommonWealth NTF

Minimum Purchase:	$2500	Add: $250	IRA: $2500
Min Auto Inv Plan:	$2500	Add: $100	
Sales Fees:	No-load		
Management Fee:	0.10%, 0.08%A		
Actual Fees:	—	Dist: —	
Expense Projections:	3Yr:$233	5Yr:$406	10Yr:$906
Income Distrib:	Semi-Annually		

Rating and Risk

Time Period	Load-Adj Return %	Morningstar Rtn vs Cat	Morningstar Risk vs Cat	Morningstar Risk-Adj Rating
1 Yr	11.61			
3 Yr	9.63	+Avg	+Avg	★★★
5 Yr	7.26	Avg	+Avg	★★★
10 Yr	8.74	—	—	
Incept	8.91			

Other Measures	Standard Index S&P 500	Best Fit Index Russ 1000
Alpha	-1.1	-0.1
Beta	1.02	0.85
R-Squared	93	93
Standard Deviation	6.28	
Mean	9.63	
Sharpe Ratio	0.99	

Portfolio Analysis 09-30-06

Total Stocks:0 Share change since 06-30-06	Sectors	P/E Ratio	YTD Return %	% Net Assets
⊕ Fidelity Growth & Income		—	—	9.13
⊕ Fidelity Equity-Income		—	—	8.41
⊕ Fidelity Blue Chip Growth		—	—	8.36
⊕ Fidelity Blue Chip Growth		—	—	8.36
⊕ Fidelity Disciplined Equi		—	—	8.22
⊕ Fidelity Growth Company		—	—	5.32
⊕ Fidelity Mid-Cap Stock		—	—	5.30
⊕ Fidelity Europe		—	—	4.67
⊕ Fidelity OTC		—	—	4.37

Total Fixed-Income:0	Date of Maturity	Amount $000	Value $000	% Net Assets
Fidelity Investment Grade		166,344	1,229,281	8.08
Fidelity Government Incom		93,670	942,319	6.20
Fidelity Intermediate Bon		68,908	708,373	4.66
Fidelity High Income		64,542	573,131	3.77
Fidelity Capital & Income		62,869	540,047	3.55
Fidelity Short-Term Bond		1,664	14,756	0.10

Equity Style		Fixed-Income Style	
Style: Growth		Duration: Interm-Term	
Size: Large-Cap		Quality: High	

Value Measures		Rel Category
Price/Earnings	15.64	1.05
Price/Book	2.53	1.06
Price/Sales	1.30	1.01
Price/Cash Flow	7.66	1.06
Dividend Yield %	1.59	0.80

Growth Measures	%	Rel Category
Long-Term Erngs	12.91	1.09
Book Value	9.71	1.14
Sales	9.80	1.14
Cash Flow	13.26	1.37
Historical Erngs	21.67	1.23

Avg Eff Duration [1]	4.3 Yrs
Avg Eff Maturity	5.5 Yrs
Avg Credit Quality	AA
Avg Wtd Coupon	4.19%

[1]figure provided by fund as of 09-30-06

Market Cap %
Giant	41.0	Small	4.5
Large	33.4	Micro	0.8
Mid	20.3	Avg $mil:	24,645

Sector Weightings	% of Stocks	Rel DJ Mod	3 Year High	Low
⟳ Info	19.92	—		
▣ Software	3.21	—	5	3
▣ Hardware	11.26	—	13	11
▣ Media	2.44	—	5	2
▣ Telecom	3.01	—	5	3
⊡ Service	48.60			
▣ Health	15.01	—	15	13
▣ Consumer	9.21	—	9	7
▣ Business	6.27	—	6	4
▣ Financial	18.11	—	21	16
⊞ Mfg	31.47			
▣ Goods	7.67	—	9	6
▣ Ind Mtrls	12.32	—	13	11
▣ Energy	10.16	—	11	6
▣ Utilities	1.32	—	2	1

Composition
● Cash	5.0
● Stocks	68.4
● Bonds	25.3
● Other	1.3
Foreign (% of Stock)	23.9

MORNINGSTAR® Funds 500

Fidelity Ginnie Mae

	Ticker	Load	NAV	Yield	SEC Yield	Total Assets	Mstar Category
	FGMNX	None	$10.77	4.8%	5.03%	$3,332 mil	Intermediate Government

Governance and Management

Stewardship Grade: B

Portfolio Manager(s)

William Irving worked as a quantitative fixed-income analyst before taking over this portfolio from Thomas Silvia, who became the head of Fidelity's bond-fund effort in late 2004. He is backed by Fidelity's considerable research capabilities. Irving also took over Fidelity Inflation-Protected Bond in late 2004.

Strategy

This fund plays it relatively safe. Fidelity bond funds don't bet on the direction of interest rates, and this fund is no exception. Manager William Irving tries to add value through coupon selection and by occasionally dipping into adjustable-rate mortgages and CMOs. He also looks for issues likely to prepay at a slower rate than the market expects. The bulk of the fund is made up of plain-vanilla Ginnie Maes, though.

Historical Profile
Return	Above Avg
Risk	Low
Rating	★★★★ Above Avg

Investment Style
Fixed Income
Income Rtn %Rank Cat

▼ Manager Change
▽ Partial Manager Change

Growth of $10,000
- Investment Values of Fund
- Investment Values of LB Aggr

Performance Quartile (within Category)

1995	1996	1997	1998	1999	2000	2001	2002	2003	2004	2005	2006	History
10.89	10.70	10.89	10.89	10.36	10.73	10.86	11.24	11.08	11.08	10.85	10.77	NAV
16.61	4.86	8.70	6.39	1.25	10.74	7.24	8.67	2.20	4.20	2.68	4.13	Total Return %
-1.86	1.23	-0.95	-2.30	2.07	-0.89	-1.20	-1.58	-1.90	-0.14	0.25	-0.20	+/-LB Aggr
-1.73	2.09	-0.89	-3.46	3.48	-2.50	0.01	-2.83	-0.16	0.72	0.03	0.65	+/-LB Govt
7.38	6.57	6.84	6.39	6.25	6.99	6.05	5.09	2.83	4.19	4.62	4.83	Income Return %
9.23	-1.71	1.86	0.00	-5.00	3.75	1.19	3.58	-0.63	0.01	-1.94	-0.70	Capital Return %
49	8	54	83	5	60	34	60	28	8	10	18	Total Rtn % Rank Cat
0.71	0.69	0.71	0.68	0.66	0.70	0.63	0.54	0.31	0.46	0.50	0.51	Income $
0.00	0.00	0.00	0.00	0.00	0.00	0.00	0.00	0.09	0.00	0.02	0.00	Capital Gains $
0.75	0.75	0.75	0.72	0.64	0.63	0.62	0.60	0.57	0.60	0.57	0.45	Expense Ratio %
7.24	6.69	6.75	6.58	6.43	6.67	6.40	5.15	3.25	3.64	4.00	4.61	Income Ratio %
210	107	98	172	73	75	120	327	262	155	160	183	Turnover Rate %
806	793	862	1,093	1,758	1,890	3,901	6,808	4,505	4,036	3,789	3,332	Net Assets $mil

Performance 12-31-06

	1st Qtr	2nd Qtr	3rd Qtr	4th Qtr	Total
2002	1.29	2.99	2.61	1.51	8.67
2003	0.81	0.53	0.69	0.16	2.20
2004	1.79	-0.91	2.34	0.95	4.20
2005	-0.05	2.20	-0.30	0.82	2.68
2006	-0.42	-0.32	3.33	1.52	4.13

Trailing	Total Return%	+/- LB Aggr	+/- LB Govt	%Rank Cat	Growth of $10,000
3 Mo	1.52	0.28	0.68	5	10,152
6 Mo	4.90	-0.19	0.49	16	10,490
1 Yr	4.13	-0.20	0.65	18	10,413
3 Yr Avg	3.66	-0.04	0.46	9	11,139
5 Yr Avg	4.35	-0.71	-0.29	22	12,373
10 Yr Avg	5.57	-0.67	-0.44	22	17,195
15 Yr Avg	5.81	-0.69	-0.49	19	23,329

Tax Analysis	Tax-Adj Rtn%	%Rank Cat	Tax-Cost Rat	%Rank Cat
3 Yr (estimated)	2.04	8	1.56	73
5 Yr (estimated)	2.73	19	1.55	63
10 Yr (estimated)	3.46	22	2.00	76

Potential Capital Gain Exposure: -3% of assets

Rating and Risk

Time Period	Load-Adj Return %	Morningstar Rtn vs Cat	Morningstar Risk vs Cat	Morningstar Risk-Adj Rating
1 Yr	4.13			
3 Yr	3.66	+Avg	-Avg	★★★★
5 Yr	4.35	+Avg	Low	★★★★
10 Yr	5.57	+Avg	Low	★★★★
Incept	7.15			

Other Measures	Standard Index LB Aggr	Best Fit Index LB Mort
Alpha	0.1	-0.4
Beta	0.70	0.92
R-Squared	93	97
Standard Deviation	2.33	
Mean	3.66	
Sharpe Ratio	0.18	

Morningstar's Take by Scott Berry 11-03-06

We like Fidelity Ginnie Mae, but it faces brutally stiff competition.

Expenses play a big role in separating Ginnie Mae fund winners and losers. Demand for Ginnie Maes remains strong and supply is down from peak levels, so there is simply not a lot of opportunity for Ginnie Mae fund managers to add value. Expenses, on the other hand, provide certain funds a head start on others regardless of market conditions. With an expense ratio of just 0.45%, this fund boasts a head start over most competitors. But Vanguard GNMA, which charges just 0.21% per year, is the clear leader when it comes to costs.

We think this fund's management can close at least some of that gap. Ginnie Mae managers don't have a lot of flexibility to add value, but manager Bill Irving looks for opportunities in Fannie Mae and Freddie Mac issues. He will also hold hybrid adjustable-rate mortgages (ARMs), which can be difficult for some managers to analyze because of the prepayment assumptions that must be factored

into their prices. Irving has only been leading the effort here since November 2004, but his work in building Fidelity's prepayment models gives us confidence that he knows the mortgage market better than most. We also like that he's backed by Fidelity's deep fixed-income resources.

We expect the fund's advantages will pay off over the long term, but its near-term results haven't stood out. The fund's adjustable-rate holdings have performed well, thanks in part to Irving's prepayment assumptions. However, the fund's exposure to interest-only securities has hampered results, as liquidity in that area of the market has dried up. For the year to date through Nov. 2, 2006, the fund returned 3.41% and ranked between the Vanguard and T. Rowe Price Ginnie Mae offerings.

We're optimistic about this fund's future prospects, though. We think Fidelity investors looking for a government-bond fund will be well served here.

Portfolio Analysis 10-31-06

Total Fixed-Income:172	Date of Maturity	Amount $000	Value $000	% Net Assets
GNMA 5.5%	10-15-32	841,260	836,688	24.69
Ginnie Mae 5% 30 Year	08-15-33	590,806	576,349	17.00
GNMA 6%	02-15-33	553,303	562,209	16.59
Ginnie Mae 6.5% 30 Year	08-15-35	211,776	217,947	6.43
Ginnie Mae 7% 30 Year	01-15-33	110,740	115,038	3.39
Ginnie Mae 4.5% 30 Year	11-20-33	99,867	96,160	2.84
GNMA 4.5%	04-15-18	82,990	80,485	2.37
GNMA 7.5%	05-15-32	52,403	54,983	1.62
GNMA CMO	03-20-36	49,737	42,869	1.26
GNMA	10-20-32	43,796	42,829	1.26
GNMA	07-20-32	44,000	42,637	1.26
GNMA CMO 4.5%	08-20-35	41,635	40,840	1.20
GNMA 3.75%	01-20-34	36,150	35,589	1.05
FNMA CMO	09-25-35	28,756	28,808	0.85
GNMA CMO 5.5%	04-16-33	25,000	24,267	0.72
GNMA 4%	11-20-33	24,419	23,886	0.70
GNMA	12-20-32	24,682	23,538	0.69
GNMA CMO 5.5%	12-20-33	22,978	22,811	0.67
FHLB 0.06%	01-25-25	20,334	20,215	0.60
FNMA 5.5%	03-01-18	20,059	20,125	0.59

Current Investment Style

Duration: Short Int Long
Quality: High Med Low

1 figure provided by fund

Avg Eff Duration[1]	3.4 Yrs
Avg Eff Maturity	6.0 Yrs
Avg Credit Quality	AAA
Avg Wtd Coupon	3.68%
Avg Wtd Price	98.65% of par

Coupon Range	% of Bonds	Rel Cat
0% PIK	0.3	0
0% to 6%	96.1	1.2
6% to 8%	3.8	0.3
8% to 10%	0.0	0.0
More than 10%	0.0	0.0

1.00=Category Average

Credit Analysis	% bonds 10-31-06		
AAA	99	BB	0
AA	0	B	0
A	0	Below B	0
BBB	0	NR/NA	1

Sector Breakdown
	% of assets
US Treasuries	0
TIPS	0
US Agency	30
Mortgage Pass-Throughs	52
Mortgage CMO	15
Mortgage ARM	0
US Corporate	0
Asset-Backed	0
Convertible	0
Municipal	0
Corporate Inflation-Protected	0
Foreign Corporate	0
Foreign Govt	0

Composition
Cash	2.9	Bonds	97.1
Stocks	0.0	Other	0.0

Special Securities
Restricted/Illiquid Secs	0
Exotic Mortgage-Backed	1
Emerging-Markets Secs	0
Options/Futures/Warrants	No

Address:	82 Devonshire St, Boston MA 02109, 800-544-6666
Web Address:	www.fidelity.com
Inception:	11-08-85
Advisor:	Fidelity Management & Research (FMR)
Subadvisor:	Multiple Subadvisors
NTF Plans:	Fidelity Retail-NTF, CommonWealth NTF

Minimum Purchase:	$2500	Add: $250	IRA: $200
Min Auto Inv Plan:	$2500	Add: $100	
Sales Fees:	No-load		
Management Fee:	0.32%		
Actual Fees:	Mgt:0.32%	Dist: —	
Expense Projections:	3Yr:$144	5Yr:$252	10Yr:$567
Income Distrib:	Monthly		

Fidelity Government Inc

	Analyst Pick	Ticker	Load	NAV	Yield	SEC Yield	Total Assets	Mstar Category
	✓	FGOVX	None	$10.04	4.2%	4.49%	$7,019 mil	Intermediate Government

Governance and Management

Stewardship Grade: B

Portfolio Manager(s)

George Fischer has been in charge here since 2003. Fischer is a veteran of Fidelity's bond group, having had a very successful stint managing several municipal-bond portfolios before taking over here.

Strategy

This fund's strategy involves rotating assets among U.S. Treasury bonds, U.S. agency securities, and mortgage bonds. Management also looks to add value through issue selection and yield-curve allocation. The fund's duration (a measure of interest-rate sensitivity) is tied to a benchmark index, so interest-rate bets don't play a role here.

Historical Profile
Return	Above Avg
Risk	Above Avg
Rating	★★★★ Above Avg

Investment Style: Fixed Income / Income Rtn %Rank Cat

▼ Manager Change
▽ Partial Manager Change

Growth of $10,000
- Investment Values of Fund
- Investment Values of LB Aggr

Performance Quartile (within Category)

1995	1996	1997	1998	1999	2000	2001	2002	2003	2004	2005	2006	History
10.17	9.69	9.91	10.14	9.35	9.87	9.97	10.48	10.22	10.24	10.12	10.04	NAV
18.07	2.08	8.93	8.59	-2.25	12.63	6.72	10.94	2.22	3.60	2.42	3.53	Total Return %
-0.40	-1.55	-0.72	-1.43	-1.41	1.00	-1.72	0.69	-1.88	-0.74	-0.01	-0.80	+/-LB Aggr
-0.27	-0.69	-0.66	-1.26	-0.02	-0.61	-0.51	-0.56	-0.14	0.12	-0.23	0.05	+/-LB Govt
6.88	6.82	6.51	6.23	5.72	6.83	5.72	4.36	3.18	3.05	3.61	4.26	Income Return %
11.19	-4.74	2.42	2.36	-7.97	5.80	1.00	6.58	-0.96	0.55	-1.19	-0.73	Capital Return %
24	69	44	17	63	8	57	11	28	27	20	44	Total Rtn % Rank Cat
0.61	0.67	0.61	0.60	0.56	0.62	0.55	0.43	0.33	0.31	0.36	0.42	Income $
0.00	0.00	0.00	0.00	0.00	0.00	0.00	0.13	0.16	0.03	0.00	0.01	Capital Gains $
0.71	0.71	0.72	0.68	0.67	0.65	0.60	0.68	0.65	0.63	0.58	0.44	Expense Ratio %
6.36	6.52	6.48	5.82	5.91	6.27	5.91	4.50	3.56	3.01	3.21	4.27	Income Ratio %
391	124	199	289	168	131	214	284	253	224	114	108	Turnover Rate %
994	973	1,165	1,583	1,589	1,699	2,402	3,381	3,886	4,478	5,590	5,975	Net Assets $mil

Performance 12-31-06

	1st Qtr	2nd Qtr	3rd Qtr	4th Qtr	Total
2002	-0.35	4.27	6.23	0.50	10.94
2003	0.81	2.29	-0.71	-0.16	2.22
2004	2.80	-2.76	2.86	0.76	3.60
2005	-0.33	2.87	-0.69	0.58	2.42
2006	-0.76	0.08	3.34	0.86	3.53

Trailing	Total Return%	+/- LB Aggr	+/- LB Govt	%Rank Cat	Growth of $10,000
3 Mo	0.86	-0.38	0.02	69	10,086
6 Mo	4.23	-0.86	-0.18	57	10,423
1 Yr	3.53	-0.80	0.05	44	10,353
3 Yr Avg	3.18	-0.52	-0.02	28	10,985
5 Yr Avg	4.49	-0.57	-0.15	15	12,456
10 Yr Avg	5.64	-0.60	-0.37	15	17,309
15 Yr Avg	6.01	-0.49	-0.29	9	24,000

Tax Analysis	Tax-Adj Rtn%	%Rank Cat	Tax-Cost Rat	%Rank Cat
3 Yr (estimated)	1.85	15	1.29	47
5 Yr (estimated)	2.94	11	1.48	56
10 Yr (estimated)	3.62	13	1.91	63

Potential Capital Gain Exposure: -2% of assets

Rating and Risk

Time Period	Load-Adj Return %	Morningstar Rtn vs Cat	Morningstar Risk vs Cat	Morningstar Risk-Adj Rating
1 Yr	3.53			
3 Yr	3.18	+Avg	+Avg	★★★
5 Yr	4.49	+Avg	+Avg	★★★★
10 Yr	5.64	+Avg	+Avg	★★★★
Incept	8.31			

Other Measures	Standard Index LB Aggr	Best Fit Index LB Govt
Alpha	-0.5	0.0
Beta	1.00	0.94
R-Squared	98	99
Standard Deviation	3.31	
Mean	3.18	
Sharpe Ratio	-0.01	

Morningstar's Take by Scott Berry 11-03-06

Fidelity Government Income continues to get the job done.

While some government-bond funds focus on Treasury securities and others focus on mortgages, this one takes a broader approach, holding a mix of Treasury bonds, mortgage securities, and government-agency issues. That approach allows the fund to take advantage of relative value opportunities that may crop up among the different sectors. Recently, for example, the fund has profited from its exposure to hybrid adjustable-rate mortgage securities, which have performed quite well in 2006. The fund's diversified approach has also helped smooth returns. For example, when Ginnie Maes struggled to keep pace with other sectors in 2002, this fund still shone, outperforming nearly 90% of its intermediate-government category peers.

The fund's straightforward approach is supported by its low costs. Its 0.45% expense ratio makes the fund one of the cheapest no-load intermediate-government offerings and allows more return to flow to shareholders without manager George Fischer having to take added risks. Fischer avoids interest-rate bets, for example, keeping the fund's duration (a measure of interest-rate sensitivity) tied to that of a benchmark index.

Low costs, a proven approach, and skilled management add up to a solid long-term record. The fund's three-, five-, and 10-year trailing returns all rank in the category's best quartile. And though the fund's volatility, as measured by standard deviation of returns, checks in a bit higher than the category norm, we think the consistency of the fund's approach and the strength of Fidelity's bond research will continue to keep the portfolio out of too much trouble.

Overall, we think this is a good choice for investors looking to blanket the government-bond market with just one fund.

Portfolio Analysis 10-31-06

Total Fixed-Income: 252

	Date of Maturity	Amount $000	Value $000	% Net Assets
US Treasury Note 2.375%	04-15-11	449,100	458,796	5.82
FNMA 4.75%	12-15-10	323,801	322,229	4.09
US Treasury Note 4.25%	11-15-14	322,185	314,722	3.99
US Treasury Bond 6.125%	08-15-29	253,102	299,708	3.80
US Treasury Note 4.5%	11-15-15	276,800	274,702	3.49
FNMA 0.06%	12-01-23	251,713	249,086	3.16
FNMA 5.125%	04-15-11	210,000	212,033	2.69
Ginnie Mae 6.5% 30 Year	06-15-36	192,542	197,913	2.51
US Treasury Bond 8%	11-15-21	146,794	196,750	2.50
US Treasury Note 4.75%	05-15-14	143,431	144,865	1.84
FNMA 5%	08-01-35	143,857	139,051	1.76
FNMA 3.25%	02-15-09	143,050	138,049	1.75
FNMA 4.625%	01-15-08	121,264	120,634	1.53
Israel St 5.5%	09-18-23	110,500	115,582	1.47
FNMA 0.06%	09-01-13	112,318	112,685	1.43
US Treasury Note 0.875%	04-15-10	105,700	107,199	1.36
FNMA 4.5%	02-01-18	98,038	94,881	1.20
FNMA 0.06%	03-01-26	84,939	86,980	1.10
FNMA 4.5%	10-15-08	81,560	80,983	1.03
US Treasury Note 1.875%	07-15-13	75,000	80,617	1.02

Current Investment Style

Duration: Short / Int / Long
Quality: High / Med / Low

Avg Eff Duration[1]	4.2 Yrs
Avg Eff Maturity	5.6 Yrs
Avg Credit Quality	AAA
Avg Wtd Coupon	3.49%
Avg Wtd Price	101.29% of par

[1] figure provided by fund

Coupon Range	% of Bonds	Rel Cat
0% PIK	6.5	0.8
0% to 6%	87.9	1.1
6% to 8%	12.1	0.8
8% to 10%	0.0	0.0
More than 10%	0.0	0.0

1.00=Category Average

Credit Analysis	% bonds 10-31-06		
AAA	99	BB	0
AA	0	B	0
A	0	Below B	0
BBB	0	NR/NA	1

Sector Breakdown
	% of assets
US Treasuries	18
TIPS	10
US Agency	25
Mortgage Pass-Throughs	18
Mortgage CMO	13
Mortgage ARM	0
US Corporate	3
Asset-Backed	0
Convertible	0
Municipal	0
Corporate Inflation-Protected	0
Foreign Corporate	0
Foreign Govt	0

Composition
Cash	13.9	Bonds	86.0
Stocks	0.0	Other	0.0

Special Securities
Restricted/Illiquid Secs	0
Exotic Mortgage-Backed	2
Emerging-Markets Secs	0
Options/Futures/Warrants	No

Address:	82 Devonshire St Boston MA 02109 800-544-6666	Minimum Purchase:	$2500	Add: $250	IRA: $200
		Min Auto Inv Plan:	$100	Add: $100	
		Sales Fees:	No-load		
Web Address:	www.fidelity.com	Management Fee:	0.32%		
Inception:	04-04-79	Actual Fees:	Mgt:0.32%	Dist: —	
Advisor:	Fidelity Management & Research (FMR)	Expense Projections:	3Yr:$144	5Yr:$252	10Yr:$567
Subadvisor:	Multiple Subadvisors	Income Distrib:	Monthly		
NTF Plans:	Fidelity Retail-NTF, CommonWealth NTF				

MORNINGSTAR® Funds 500

Fidelity Growth & Income

	Ticker	Load	NAV	Yield	Total Assets	Mstar Category
	FGRIX	None	$31.15	0.7%	$30,214 mil	Large Blend

Portfolio Manager(s)

Tim Cohen took control of this portfolio in October 2005. He also ran Fidelity Advisor Diversified Stock from April 2005 to November 2006. Prior to joining this offering, he ran Fidelity Export & Multinational for nearly four years, generating exceptional returns. Cohen previously managed several of Fidelity's Select funds, including Fidelity Select Telecommunications and Fidelity Utilities.

Strategy

Although previous manager Steve Kaye plied a notably risk-averse strategy, this fund looks more eclectic under new manager Tim Cohen. Thus far, he has anchored the portfolio in blue-chip names, due to both valuations and the fund's much larger size. However, on his previous charge he has also delved into cyclical stocks, high-P/E growth securities, and mid-cap names. Owing to this fund's hefty asset base, he'll have more difficulty pulling off the shifts he previously made in bumpy markets, and will have to own more names when he dips down the market-cap ladder.

Performance 12-31-06

	1st Qtr	2nd Qtr	3rd Qtr	4th Qtr	Total
2002	0.83	-10.48	-14.03	5.58	-18.08
2003	-2.27	10.43	0.85	9.33	19.01
2004	1.34	1.11	-0.77	8.03	9.84
2005	-2.46	0.89	2.55	1.78	2.71
2006	4.01	-2.94	2.68	6.80	10.71

Trailing	Total Return%	+/- S&P 500	+/- Russ 1000	%Rank Cat	Growth of $10,000
3 Mo	6.80	0.10	-0.15	39	10,680
6 Mo	9.67	-3.07	-2.69	83	10,967
1 Yr	10.71	-5.08	-4.75	89	11,071
3 Yr Avg	7.69	-2.75	-3.29	87	12,489
5 Yr Avg	4.02	-2.17	-2.80	83	12,178
10 Yr Avg	7.15	-1.27	-1.49	62	19,949
15 Yr Avg	10.42	-0.22	-0.38	37	44,230

Tax Analysis	Tax-Adj Rtn%	%Rank Cat	Tax-Cost Rat	%Rank Cat
3 Yr (estimated)	5.60	92	1.94	82
5 Yr (estimated)	2.63	89	1.34	82
10 Yr (estimated)	5.68	65	1.37	63

Potential Capital Gain Exposure: 17% of assets

Morningstar's Take by Greg Carlson 12-21-06

Its new manager is off to a poor start, but we'd hang on to Fidelity Growth & Income.

Tim Cohen, who replaced veteran Steven Kaye at this fund roughly one year ago, is off to a very rough start. During his brief tenure, the fund has been outpaced by more than 90% of its large-blend rivals, and lags the S&P 500 Index by a wide margin. What's more, Cohen's reshaping of this portfolio has resulted in two substantial capital gains distributions, adding insult to injury for shareholders in taxable accounts.

The fund's poor showing stands in stark contrast to Cohen's stellar four-year stint at a far smaller large-blend offering, Fidelity Export & Multinational. Yet we wouldn't attribute his underperformance here to a dramatically larger asset base. Instead, Cohen's preference for somewhat faster-growing large caps that are more economically sensitive, such as Home Depot, and racier fare such as eBay, has held the fund back as the economy has cooled. When he took over the

fund, he sold behemoths with slower, steadier revenue growth, such as Verizon Communications and Pfizer, which have since rallied sharply.

But although Cohen's misfires (which come on the heels of a bad three-year stretch under Kaye) must be frustrating to long-term shareholders, we think there's good reason to stay the course here. True, the ride may not be a smooth one--Cohen's previous charge was more volatile than most rivals. But he showed a deft touch at Export & Multinational, and we're fans of his counterpunching style: He's added to the fund's stake in Home Depot, and also scooped up other companies that had sold off, including a clutch of homebuilders such as KB Home and semiconductor makers such as Broadcom. He's also putting his money where his mouth is: Since taking over, Cohen has invested more than $1 million into the fund.

Address:	82 Devonshire St Boston MA 02109 800-544-9797
Web Address:	www.fidelity.com
Inception:	12-30-85
Advisor:	Fidelity Management & Research (FMR)
Subadvisor:	Multiple Subadvisors
NTF Plans:	Fidelity Retail-NTF, CommonWealth NTF

Minimum Purchase:	$2500	Add: $250	IRA: $2500
Min Auto Inv Plan:	$2500	Add: $100	
Sales Fees:	No-load		
Management Fee:	0.48%		
Actual Fees:	Mgt:0.47%	Dist: —	
Expense Projections:	3Yr:$221	5Yr:$384	10Yr:$859
Income Distrib:	Quarterly		

Historical Profile

Return	Average
Risk	Low
Rating	★★★ Neutral

| 92% | 92% | 95% | 83% | 88% | 91% | 93% | 98% | 97% |

Investment Style
Equity
Stock %

▼ Manager Change
▽ Partial Manager Change

31.0
25.0 **Growth of $10,000**
20.0 — Investment Values of Fund
15.0 — Investment Values of S&P 500
10.0

Performance Quartile (within Category)

1995	1996	1997	1998	1999	2000	2001	2002	2003	2004	2005	2006	History
27.05	30.73	38.10	45.84	47.16	42.10	37.38	30.31	35.63	38.21	34.40	31.15	NAV
35.38	20.02	30.17	28.31	10.42	-1.98	-9.35	-18.08	19.01	9.84	2.71	10.71	Total Return %
-2.20	-2.94	-3.19	-0.27	-10.62	7.12	2.54	4.02	-9.67	-1.04	-2.20	-5.08	+/-S&P 500
-2.39	-2.43	-2.68	1.29	-10.49	5.81	3.10	3.57	-10.88	-1.56	-3.56	-4.75	+/-Russ 1000
2.31	1.73	1.42	1.04	0.87	0.80	0.93	0.91	1.33	1.56	1.25	0.86	Income Return %
33.07	18.29	28.75	27.27	9.55	-2.78	-10.28	-18.99	17.68	8.28	1.46	9.85	Capital Return %
44	65	46	21	83	35	29	20	97	61	86	89	Total Rtn % Rank Cat
0.48	0.46	0.43	0.39	0.39	0.37	0.39	0.34	0.40	0.55	0.47	0.27	Income $
0.90	1.12	1.36	2.16	2.90	3.91	0.38	0.00	0.00	0.34	4.40	6.08	Capital Gains $
0.77	0.74	0.71	0.68	0.66	0.66	0.66	0.68	0.71	0.69	0.68	0.65	Expense Ratio %
2.21	1.82	1.43	1.02	0.88	0.82	0.94	0.94	1.29	1.13	1.63	0.94	Income Ratio %
67	41	38	32	35	41	46	36	33	30	31	120	Turnover Rate %
14,819	23,896	36,657	48,640	48,528	39,963	34,255	26,269	30,572	32,106	31,082	30,214	Net Assets $mil

Rating and Risk

Time Period	Load-Adj Return %	Morningstar Rtn vs Cat	Morningstar Risk vs Cat	Morningstar Risk-Adj Rating
1 Yr	10.71			
3 Yr	7.69	-Avg	-Avg	★★
5 Yr	4.02	-Avg	Low	★★
10 Yr	7.15	Avg	Low	★★★
Incept	13.11			

Other Measures	Standard Index S&P 500	Best Fit Index Russ 1000
Alpha	-1.9	-2.1
Beta	0.90	0.88
R-Squared	87	88
Standard Deviation	6.63	
Mean	7.69	
Sharpe Ratio	0.67	

Portfolio Analysis 10-31-06

Share change since 07-06 Total Stocks:97

	Sector	PE	Tot Ret%	% Assets
⊕ General Electric Company	Ind Mtrls	20.0	9.35	7.53
⊖ American International G	Financial	17.0	6.05	6.52
⊖ Home Depot, Inc.	Consumer	13.5	1.01	4.85
⊖ Bank of America Corporat	Financial	12.4	20.68	4.58
⊕ Wal-Mart Stores, Inc.	Consumer	16.9	0.13	3.33
⊖ Google, Inc.	Business	61.5	11.00	3.16
⊖ Johnson & Johnson	Health	17.5	12.45	3.06
⊖ Honeywell International,	Ind Mtrls	18.6	24.14	2.67
⊕ eBay, Inc.	Consumer	40.1	-30.43	2.52
⊕ Wachovia Corporation	Financial	12.9	12.02	2.22
⊖ UnitedHealth Group, Inc.	Health	20.8	-13.49	2.09
⊖ ConocoPhillips	Energy	6.5	26.53	1.70
⊖ Schlumberger, Ltd.	Energy	22.3	31.07	1.63
⊕ Apollo Group, Inc. A	Consumer	15.9	-35.54	1.61
⊕ Robert Half Internationa	Business	24.5	-1.17	1.37
⊖ Dell, Inc.	Hardware	18.4	-16.23	1.33
⊕ Hartford Financial Servi	Financial	11.9	10.83	1.29
⊖ Target Corporation	Consumer	19.3	4.65	1.26
⊖ Best Buy Co., Inc.	Consumer	19.8	13.89	1.23
Amgen, Inc.	Health	29.1	-13.38	1.20

Current Investment Style

Value Blnd Growth — Large Mid Small

Market Cap	%
Giant	51.3
Large	29.5
Mid	18.4
Small	0.8
Micro	0.0

Avg $mil: 45,839

Value Measures		Rel Category
Price/Earnings	14.76	0.96
Price/Book	2.64	1.03
Price/Sales	1.46	1.04
Price/Cash Flow	10.37	1.23
Dividend Yield %	1.41	0.81

Growth Measures	%	Rel Category
Long-Term Erngs	12.94	1.09
Book Value	13.95	1.54
Sales	15.71	1.62
Cash Flow	18.34	1.78
Historical Erngs	24.81	1.34

Profitability	%	Rel Category
Return on Equity	19.95	1.03
Return on Assets	10.63	1.02
Net Margin	13.61	1.01

Sector Weightings	% of Stocks	Rel S&P 500	3 Year High Low
⟳ Info	12.11	0.61	
Software	0.86	0.25	6 1
Hardware	9.82	1.06	10 5
Media	1.43	0.38	5 1
Telecom	0.00	0.00	8 0
⟲ Service	59.94	1.30	
Health	13.01	1.08	17 11
Consumer	19.32	2.53	19 8
Business	5.43	1.28	6 4
Financial	22.18	1.00	27 19
⟱ Mfg	27.95	0.83	
Goods	0.78	0.09	10 1
Ind Mtrls	14.11	1.18	14 10
Energy	13.06	1.33	15 6
Utilities	0.00	0.00	2 0

Composition

- ● Cash 2.1
- ● Stocks 97.0
- ● Bonds 0.0
- ○ Other 0.8
- Foreign 10.7 (% of Stock)

Fidelity Growth Company

	Ticker	Load	NAV	Yield	Total Assets	Mstar Category
	FDGRX	Closed	$69.71	0.0%	$30,070 mil	Large Growth

Governance and Management

Stewardship Grade: B

Portfolio Manager(s)

Steve Wymer has managed this fund since 1997 and has been managing portfolios for Fidelity since 1990. He is part of a team that includes other aggressive-growth managers, including Sonu Kalra at Fidelity OTC and John Porter at Fidelity Advisor Growth Opportunities. Like all Fidelity managers, he receives the support of Fidelity's sizable analyst staff.

Strategy

Manager Steve Wymer looks for firms with good growth prospects relative to their valuations. He keeps the lion's share of assets in high-growth stocks from the health-care and technology sectors, but he also makes room for a small crop of turnaround plays. Valuations play a role in his process, but unearthing great growth companies is job one.

Performance 12-31-06

	1st Qtr	2nd Qtr	3rd Qtr	4th Qtr	Total
2002	-6.76	-19.65	-20.54	11.81	-33.45
2003	-0.31	19.31	8.50	9.54	41.36
2004	3.06	2.36	-6.40	13.55	12.12
2005	-5.67	5.60	7.40	6.10	13.50
2006	6.85	-5.75	0.30	8.46	9.56

Trailing	Total Return%	+/- S&P 500	+/- Russ 1000Gr	%Rank Cat	Growth of $10,000
3 Mo	8.46	1.76	2.53	7	10,846
6 Mo	8.79	-3.95	-1.31	43	10,879
1 Yr	9.56	-6.23	0.49	25	10,956
3 Yr Avg	11.72	1.28	4.85	7	13,944
5 Yr Avg	5.58	-0.61	2.89	15	13,119
10 Yr Avg	9.56	1.14	4.12	7	24,918
15 Yr Avg	11.30	0.66	3.28	9	49,823

Tax Analysis	Tax-Adj Rtn%	%Rank Cat	Tax-Cost Rat	%Rank Cat
3 Yr (estimated)	11.70	5	0.02	2
5 Yr (estimated)	5.57	12	0.01	2
10 Yr (estimated)	8.63	7	0.85	40

Potential Capital Gain Exposure: 16% of assets

Morningstar's Take by Greg Carlson 11-03-06

Fidelity Growth Company's risks shouldn't be ignored, but it's a fine holding.

This large-growth fund, which closed to new investors in April 2006, has an aggressive mandate. True, Steve Wymer, who's run the fund for nearly a decade, is taking a more cautious posture these days, in part due to his expectation that economic growth will be muted. After semiconductor stocks sold off sharply this summer, he didn't go on a buying spree like many rivals did.

The fund is positioned defensively only in relation to its past: Its tech weighting is one fifth higher than the category norm, and some of its bigger holdings within the sector are racier names like software maker Red Hat and storage provider Network Appliance. Similarly, the fund's health-care stake--dominated not by giant drug makers, but biotech firms like Celgene, and diagnostics firms--is two thirds higher than its typical rival's. That's because Wymer continues to favor companies with rapid revenue growth.

Although the fund does own a few turnaround stories such as beaten-down retailer Wal-Mart and steadier fare like Pepsi, its price multiples are above average, and its average market capitalization is 60% of the group norm.

We're glad to see that Wymer isn't resorting to a vanilla approach, despite the fund's hefty $28 billion asset base. That bold strategy, combined with deft stockpicking, has resulted in a superb record here during Wymer's tenure. True, the fund has performed admirably in so-so years for stocks, such as 2004 and 2005, but shareholders have benefited most from big returns in 1999 and 2003.

Investors have had to ride out painful losses at times before enjoying those gains; the fund fell nearly 65% from its peak during the bear market. Thus, we think it's critical to take the long-term view here. Shareholders have plenty of reason to hang on to the fund, but it's best used as an aggressive complement in a portfolio.

Address:	82 Devonshire St Boston MA 02109 800-544-6666
Web Address:	www.fidelity.com
Inception:	01-17-83
Advisor:	Fidelity Management & Research (FMR)
Subadvisor:	Multiple Subadvisors
NTF Plans:	Fidelity Retail-NTF, CommonWealth NTF

Minimum Purchase:	Closed	Add: —	IRA: —
Min Auto Inv Plan:	Closed	Add: —	
Sales Fees:	No-load		
Management Fee:	0.72%		
Actual Fees:	Mgt:0.72%	Dist: —	
Expense Projections:	3Yr:$306	5Yr:$531	10Yr:$1178
Income Distrib:	Annually		

Historical Profile

Return	High
Risk	High
Rating	★★★★ Above Avg

94% | 97% | 98% | 98% | 99% | 99% | 100% | 99% | 99%

Investment Style Equity Stock %

▽ Manager Change
▽ Partial Manager Change

Growth of $10,000
— Investment Values of Fund
— Investment Values of S&P 500

59.0
43.6
32.4
24.0
17.0
10.0

Performance Quartile (within Category)

1995	1996	1997	1998	1999	2000	2001	2002	2003	2004	2005	2006	History
36.29	40.46	43.32	51.02	84.30	71.43	53.22	35.42	50.07	56.07	63.63	69.71	NAV
39.61	16.81	18.91	27.23	79.48	-6.32	-25.31	-33.45	41.36	12.12	13.50	9.56	Total Return %
2.03	-6.15	-14.45	-1.35	58.44	2.78	-13.42	-11.35	12.68	1.24	8.59	-6.23	+/-S&P 500
2.43	-6.31	-11.58	-11.48	46.32	16.10	-4.89	-5.57	11.61	5.82	8.24	0.49	+/-Russ 1000Gr
0.59	0.78	0.54	0.21	0.00	0.00	0.00	0.00	0.00	0.14	0.02	0.00	Income Return %
39.02	16.03	18.37	27.02	79.48	-6.32	-25.31	-33.45	41.36	11.98	13.48	9.56	Capital Return %
14	70	82	64	6	28	77	87	6	16	9	25	Total Rtn % Rank Cat
0.16	0.28	0.22	0.09	0.00	0.00	0.00	0.00	0.00	0.07	0.01	0.00	Income $
1.57	1.60	4.35	3.73	6.29	7.50	0.16	0.00	0.00	0.00	0.00	0.00	Capital Gains $
0.95	0.85	0.68	0.63	0.72	0.85	0.95	1.08	0.83	0.82	0.94	—	Expense Ratio %
0.76	0.96	0.54	0.24	-0.11	-0.31	-0.29	-0.38	-0.03	0.15	-0.32	—	Income Ratio %
97	78	93	76	86	69	93	63	47	49	50	—	Turnover Rate %
6,279	9,273	10,509	11,440	24,337	30,397	22,742	14,798	22,609	25,180	27,415	30,070	Net Assets $mil

Rating and Risk

Time Period	Load-Adj Return %	Morningstar Rtn vs Cat	Morningstar Risk vs Cat	Morningstar Risk-Adj Rating
1 Yr	9.56			
3 Yr	11.72	High	+Avg	★★★★★
5 Yr	5.58	+Avg	High	★★★★
10 Yr	9.56	High	High	★★★
Incept	14.24			

Other Measures	Standard Index S&P 500	Best Fit Index Russ MG
Alpha	-1.9	-0.8
Beta	1.50	0.99
R-Squared	75	90
Standard Deviation	11.86	
Mean	11.72	
Sharpe Ratio	0.73	

Portfolio Analysis 08-31-06

Share change since 05-06 Total Stocks:277	Sector	PE	Tot Ret%	% Assets
Google, Inc.	Business	61.5	11.00	5.00
⊖ Celgene Corporation	Health	—	77.56	4.73
⊖ Network Appliance, Inc.	Hardware	56.7	45.48	2.90
⊖ Elan Corporation PLC ADR	Health	—	5.89	2.29
⊖ Apple Computer, Inc.	Hardware	37.6	18.01	2.10
⊕ Monsanto Company	Ind Mtrls	39.8	36.78	2.05
⊕ Wal-Mart Stores, Inc.	Consumer	16.9	0.13	1.79
⊕ Microsoft Corporation	Software	23.8	15.83	1.71
⊕ General Electric Company	Ind Mtrls	20.0	9.35	1.66
⊕ Southwest Airlines, Co.	Business	23.2	-6.65	1.62
⊕ PepsiCo, Inc.	Goods	21.5	7.86	1.61
⊕ Red Hat, Inc.	Software	58.8	-15.63	1.60
⊖ Sepracor, Inc.	Health	NMF	19.34	1.56
Johnson & Johnson	Health	17.5	12.45	1.55
⊕ Salesforce.com, Inc.	Software		13.73	1.39
⊕ Ameriprise Financial, In	Financial	—	—	1.39
⊕ Vertex Pharmaceuticals	Health		35.24	1.37
⊕ US Airways Group, Inc.	Business	—	44.99	1.32
⊖ Qualcomm, Inc.	Hardware	26.6	-11.32	1.29
✿ Nintendo	Goods		—	1.22

Current Investment Style

Value Blnd Growth — Large/Mid/Small

Market Cap	%
Giant	34.3
Large	34.0
Mid	21.7
Small	8.8
Micro	1.3

Avg $mil: 18,226

Value Measures		Rel Category
Price/Earnings	21.78	1.13
Price/Book	3.67	1.11
Price/Sales	1.79	0.92
Price/Cash Flow	9.92	0.87
Dividend Yield %	0.76	0.74

Growth Measures	%	Rel Category
Long-Term Erngs	14.56	1.01
Book Value	7.02	0.61
Sales	8.87	0.76
Cash Flow	14.36	0.86
Historical Erngs	19.27	0.84

Profitability	%	Rel Category
Return on Equity	14.35	0.71
Return on Assets	6.14	0.56
Net Margin	8.99	0.63

Sector Weightings	% of Stocks	Rel S&P 500	3 Year High	Low
⟲ Info	26.16	1.31		
Software	7.02	2.03	9	6
Hardware	16.74	1.81	27	17
Media	1.86	0.49	2	1
Telecom	0.54	0.15	2	0
⟲ Service	51.59	1.12		
Health	29.11	2.41	30	24
Consumer	7.76	1.01	10	5
Business	10.40	2.46	11	6
Financial	4.32	0.19	5	2
⟲ Mfg	22.25	0.66		
Goods	9.04	1.06	9	5
Ind Mtrls	8.85	0.74	9	5
Energy	4.36	0.44	7	3
Utilities	0.00	0.00	0	0

Composition

- Cash 0.7
- Stocks 99.0
- Bonds 0.0
- Other 0.3

Foreign 6.6 (% of Stock)

MORNINGSTAR® Funds 500

Fidelity High Income

	Ticker	Load	NAV	Yield	SEC Yield	Total Assets	Mstar Category
	SPHIX	None	$9.06	6.9%	6.92%	$4,509 mil	High Yield Bond

Governance and Management

Stewardship Grade: B

Portfolio Manager(s)

Fred Hoff took over this portfolio in June 2000 and works with Fidelity's extensive team of research analysts. He started with Fidelity as a high-yield analyst and has managed the high-yield portions of several asset-allocation funds.

Strategy

Manager Fred Hoff invests the bulk of the fund's assets in junk bonds, which offer handsome yields to compensate for their considerable credit risk. Hoff favors companies with strong management that show signs of improving financial situations. He has reined in the fund's risk over the last few years, cutting bonds rated below B and diversifying the portfolio across more issues.

Historical Profile
Return Above Avg
Risk   Average
Rating ★★★★ Above Avg

| 62 | 60 | 98 | 60 | 74 | 26 | 22 | 46 |

Investment Style
Fixed Income
Income Rtn %Rank Cat

▼ Manager Change
▽ Partial Manager Change

Growth of $10,000
— Investment Values of Fund
— Investment Values of LB Aggr

Performance Quartile (within Category)

	1995	1996	1997	1998	1999	2000	2001	2002	2003	2004	2005	2006	History
NAV	12.21	12.54	13.03	12.11	12.00	9.45	8.13	7.60	8.94	9.09	8.78	9.06	NAV
	18.53	14.16	15.92	3.30	8.92	-14.20	1.43	27.48	9.69	3.45	10.74		Total Return %
	0.06	10.53	6.27	-5.39	9.74	-25.83	-13.28	-8.82	23.38	5.35	1.02	6.41	+/-LB Aggr
	1.14	1.74	3.29	2.72	5.64	-8.99	-10.62	-1.68	-0.45	-2.27	1.19	-1.19	+/-CSFB Glb HY
	10.73	9.21	9.33	8.58	8.97	7.27	9.88	8.03	9.38	7.87	6.91	7.40	Income Return %
	7.80	4.95	6.59	-5.28	-0.05	-21.47	-14.72	-6.60	18.10	1.82	-3.46	3.34	Capital Return %
	25	26	8	21	13	91	92	26	29	54	22	32	Total Rtn % Rank Cat
	1.17	1.07	1.11	1.06	1.04	0.84	0.89	0.63	0.69	0.68	0.61	0.63	Income $
	0.12	0.25	0.31	0.30	0.14	0.09	0.00	0.00	0.00	0.00	0.00	0.00	Capital Gains $
	0.80	0.79	0.80	0.80	0.80	0.74	0.74	0.76	0.79	0.77	0.77	0.76	Expense Ratio %
	8.41	8.85	8.51	8.57	9.20	9.85	10.68	10.44	8.82	7.67	7.07	6.97	Income Ratio %
	172	170	102	85	68	50	55	69	81	84	65	40	Turnover Rate %
	1,081	1,717	2,447	2,862	3,262	2,131	1,551	1,741	2,902	3,114	3,355	4,509	Net Assets $mil

Performance 12-31-06

	1st Qtr	2nd Qtr	3rd Qtr	4th Qtr	Total
2002	0.34	-5.89	0.37	7.02	1.43
2003	6.60	9.68	2.73	6.13	27.48
2004	1.30	-0.27	3.23	5.18	9.69
2005	-1.76	2.34	1.41	1.47	3.45
2006	2.78	-0.05	3.49	4.16	10.74

Trailing	Total Return%	+/- LB Aggr	+/- CSFB Glb HY	%Rank Cat	Growth of $10,000
3 Mo	4.16	2.92	-0.29	35	10,416
6 Mo	7.80	2.71	-0.35	31	10,780
1 Yr	10.74	6.41	-1.19	32	11,074
3 Yr Avg	7.91	4.21	-0.71	34	12,566
5 Yr Avg	10.21	5.15	-0.86	21	16,259
10 Yr Avg	5.64	-0.60	-1.45	40	17,309
15 Yr Avg	8.87	2.37	-0.03	12	35,779

Tax Analysis	Tax-Adj Rtn%	%Rank Cat	Tax-Cost Rat	%Rank Cat
3 Yr (estimated)	5.24	27	2.47	53
5 Yr (estimated)	7.28	16	2.66	54
10 Yr (estimated)	2.31	40	3.15	34

Potential Capital Gain Exposure: -17% of assets

Rating and Risk

Time Period	Load-Adj Return %	Morningstar Rtn vs Cat	Morningstar Risk vs Cat	Morningstar Risk-Adj Rating
1 Yr	10.74			
3 Yr	7.91	+Avg	-Avg	★★★★
5 Yr	10.21	+Avg	Avg	★★★★
10 Yr	5.64	Avg	+Avg	★★★
Incept	10.05			

Other Measures	Standard Index LB Aggr	Best Fit Index CSFB Glb HY
Alpha	4.3	-0.3
Beta	0.29	0.93
R-Squared	7	90
Standard Deviation	3.56	
Mean	7.91	
Sharpe Ratio	1.27	

Morningstar's Take by Scott Berry 12-19-06

Fidelity High Income hasn't kept pace with its Fidelity high-yield siblings, but that's just fine with us.

Broker-sold Fidelity Advisor High Income Advantage and no-load Fidelity Capital & Income have blown away most competitors in 2006, this fund included. But both hold larger stakes in equities and smaller stakes in BB rated bonds (the highest credit quality bonds that are still considered junk) than High Income. And with risk being rewarded over the past year, we wouldn't have expected this fund to keep pace with its more aggressive siblings. We would, however, expect the fund to more than keep pace with its average peer, which has a more similar risk profile. And it has, outperforming more than two thirds of its high-yield competitors for the year to date through Dec. 18, thanks in part to good security selection.

Our expectations for this fund stem from manager Fred Hoff's experience, Fidelity's deep research capabilities, and the fund's below-average costs. It took Hoff, who has led the effort here since mid-2000, some time to remake the portfolio into the core high-yield fund it is today from the concentrated portfolio is was under prior management, but the fund's trailing five-year annualized return now ranks in the category's best quartile. And with Fidelity large high-yield research group backing Hoff and below-average expenses providing an ongoing advantage, we expect the fund will enjoy continued success.

Our optimism is tempered a bit, however, by the current state of the high-yield bond market. Junk bonds aren't offering much added yield over Treasury issues and Moody's predicts the default rate will move slowly higher in 2007. That combination could mean rougher sledding for this asset class over the next year or two. That's not to say investors should bail out of high yield, but that they should maintain realistic expectations for this fund and for this asset class.

Portfolio Analysis 10-31-06

Total Fixed-Income:371	Date of Maturity	Amount $000	Value $000	% Net Assets
Intelsat 144A 9.25%	06-15-16	47,470	50,556	1.18
NXP B V / NXP FDG	10-15-15	43,460	43,569	1.01
Gmac 6.75%	12-01-14	43,695	43,040	1.00
FORD MOTOR CR	08-10-11	41,030	42,397	0.99
Sungard Data Term B	02-10-13	37,905	38,237	0.89
SEAGATE TECHNOLOGY HDD H	10-01-16	35,965	35,515	0.83
Ship Fin Intl 8.5%	12-15-13	35,500	34,613	0.80
Georgia Pac 1st Ln Trm B	12-23-12	33,745	33,935	0.79
Xerox Cap Tr I 8%	02-01-27	33,080	33,907	0.79
Sungard Data Sys 9.125%	08-15-13	32,000	33,040	0.77
Houghton Mifflin 9.875%	02-01-13	28,521	30,232	0.70
Toys-R-Us Term	12-09-08	30,000	30,075	0.70
Nrg Engy 7.25%	02-01-14	29,460	29,828	0.69
Nielsen Fin Llc/ Nielsen	08-01-14	28,510	29,685	0.69
PEABODY ENERGY	11-01-16	28,600	29,673	0.69
Rouse 144A 6.75%	05-01-13	28,460	28,779	0.67
Aes 144A 8.75%	05-15-13	26,680	28,614	0.67
Chesapeake Engy 6.5%	08-15-17	30,090	28,285	0.66
Davita Inc Term B	10-05-12	27,368	27,470	0.64
Intelsat 144A 11.25%	06-15-16	23,870	25,959	0.60

Current Investment Style

Duration: Short Int Long
Quality: High Med Low

1 figure provided by fund

		Rel Cat
Avg Eff Duration[1]	—	
Avg Eff Maturity	6.4 Yrs	
Avg Credit Quality	B	
Avg Wtd Coupon	5.90%	
Avg Wtd Price	101.28% of par	

Coupon Range	% of Bonds	Rel Cat
0% PIK	5.0	0.9
0% to 8%	68.9	1.4
8% to 11%	29.4	0.7
11% to 14%	1.5	0.4
More than 14%	0.1	1.1

1.00=Category Average

Credit Analysis		% bonds 10-31-06	
AAA	0	BB	34
AA	0	B	45
A	0	Below B	10
BBB	1	NR/NA	10

Sector Breakdown

	% of assets
US Treasuries	0
TIPS	0
US Agency	0
Mortgage Pass-Throughs	0
Mortgage CMO	0
Mortgage ARM	0
US Corporate	85
Asset-Backed	0
Convertible	0
Municipal	0
Corporate Inflation-Protected	0
Foreign Corporate	6
Foreign Govt	0

Composition

Cash	8.1	Bonds	87.8
Stocks	0.7	Other	3.4

Special Securities

Restricted/Illiquid Secs	22
Exotic Mortgage-Backed	0
Emerging-Markets Secs	Trace
Options/Futures/Warrants	No

Address:	82 Devonshire St Boston MA 02109 800-544-6666	Minimum Purchase:	$2500 Add: $250 IRA: $500
		Min Auto Inv Plan:	$2500 Add: $100
		Sales Fees:	No-load, 1.00%R
Web Address:	www.fidelity.com	Management Fee:	0.57%
Inception:	08-29-90	Actual Fees:	Mgt:0.57% Dist: —
Advisor:	Fidelity Management & Research (FMR)	Expense Projections:	3Yr:$246 5Yr:$428 10Yr:$954
Subadvisor:	Multiple Subadvisors	Income Distrib:	Monthly
NTF Plans:	Fidelity Retail-NTF, CommonWealth NTF		

Fidelity Independence

	Ticker	Load	NAV	Yield	Total Assets	Mstar Category
	FDFFX	None	$21.96	0.5%	$4,707 mil	Large Growth

Governance and Management

Stewardship Grade: B

Portfolio Manager(s)

Jason Weiner left in November 2006 after leading the fund for three plus years. He was replaced by Bob Bertelson, whose last stint as a diversified manager was Fidelity Aggressive Growth from 2000 to 2002, where he posted extremely poor absolute and relative returns. Bertelson has ran multiple other funds during his tenure at the firm, which began in 1991.

Strategy

It's unclear what this fund's new strategy entails. Under its former manager, the fund used bottom-up analysis to identify growing companies trading at reasonable valuations, with a noticeable stake in mid-cap stocks, and pointed sector bets by management.

Historical Profile

Return	High
Risk	Above Avg
Rating	★★★★ Highest

93% 97% 96% 82% 84% 97% 92% 96% 97%

Investment Style
Equity
Stock %

▼ Manager Change
▽ Partial Manager Change

Growth of $10,000
— Investment Values of Fund
— Investment Values of S&P 500

Performance Quartile (within Category)

	1995	1996	1997	1998	1999	2000	2001	2002	2003	2004	2005	2006	History
	18.19	17.29	16.85	20.51	25.85	22.01	15.77	13.07	16.06	17.83	19.65	21.96	NAV
	24.28	8.33	18.54	35.89	47.03	1.70	-27.22	-15.82	23.66	11.65	10.55	12.26	Total Return %
	-13.30	-14.63	-14.82	7.31	25.99	10.80	-15.33	6.28	-5.02	0.77	5.64	-3.53	+/-S&P 500
	-12.90	-14.79	-11.95	-2.82	13.87	24.12	-6.80	12.06	-6.09	5.35	5.29	3.19	+/-Russ 1000Gr
	2.18	1.44	0.75	0.83	0.25	0.31	0.91	1.33	0.77	0.62	0.34	0.51	Income Return %
	22.10	6.89	17.79	35.06	46.78	1.39	-28.13	-17.15	22.89	11.03	10.21	11.75	Capital Return %
	88	97	83	31	26	10	81	6	78	19	19	13	Total Rtn % Rank Cat
	0.35	0.26	0.13	0.14	0.05	0.08	0.20	0.21	0.10	0.10	0.06	0.10	Income $
	1.58	2.15	3.41	2.13	3.66	4.19	0.06	0.00	0.00	0.00	0.00	0.00	Capital Gains $
	0.99	0.70	0.59	0.57	0.58	0.85	0.92	0.97	0.55	0.71	0.72	—	Expense Ratio %
	1.92	1.26	0.66	0.68	0.25	0.19	0.95	1.41	1.00	0.66	0.24	—	Income Ratio %
	108	230	205	266	310	249	187	191	166	119	119	—	Turnover Rate %
	4,072	4,046	3,932	4,946	7,268	8,474	5,486	4,240	4,726	4,705	4,742	4,707	Net Assets $mil

Performance 12-31-06

	1st Qtr	2nd Qtr	3rd Qtr	4th Qtr	Total
2002	5.14	-13.99	-15.78	10.53	-15.82
2003	-5.51	16.92	1.87	9.88	23.66
2004	1.93	2.02	-3.47	11.24	11.65
2005	-3.14	1.85	7.91	3.85	10.55
2006	7.89	-3.16	0.68	6.72	12.26

Trailing	Total Return%	+/- S&P 500	+/- Russ 1000Gr	%Rank Cat	Growth of $10,000
3 Mo	6.72	0.02	0.79	20	10,672
6 Mo	7.45	-5.29	-2.65	66	10,745
1 Yr	12.26	-3.53	3.19	13	11,226
3 Yr Avg	11.49	1.05	4.62	8	13,858
5 Yr Avg	7.60	1.41	4.91	6	14,423
10 Yr Avg	9.72	1.30	4.28	7	25,285
15 Yr Avg	10.71	0.07	2.69	14	46,005

Tax Analysis	Tax-Adj Rtn%	%Rank Cat	Tax-Cost Rat	%Rank Cat
3 Yr (estimated)	11.31	6	0.16	11
5 Yr (estimated)	7.33	6	0.25	26
10 Yr (estimated)	7.48	11	2.04	90

Potential Capital Gain Exposure: -1% of assets

Rating and Risk

Time Period	Load-Adj Return %	Morningstar Rtn vs Cat	Morningstar Risk vs Cat	Morningstar Risk-Adj Rating
1 Yr	12.26			
3 Yr	11.49	High	+Avg	★★★★★
5 Yr	7.60	High	+Avg	★★★★★
10 Yr	9.72	High	+Avg	★★★★
Incept	13.17			

Other Measures	Standard Index S&P 500	Best Fit Index Russ MG
Alpha	-2.0	-0.7
Beta	1.48	0.96
R-Squared	80	92
Standard Deviation	11.36	
Mean	11.49	
Sharpe Ratio	0.74	

Portfolio Analysis 08-31-06

Share change since 05-06 Total Stocks:124	Sector	PE	Tot Ret%	% Assets
⊖ Google, Inc.	Business	61.5	11.00	3.57
⊕ American International G	Financial	17.0	6.05	3.17
⊕ Wells Fargo Company	Financial	14.7	16.82	2.97
⊕ Colgate-Palmolive Compan	Goods	27.6	21.51	2.86
⊕ McDermott International	Energy	23.4	71.02	2.37
✧ ExxonMobil Corporation	Energy	11.1	39.07	1.97
⊕ Biogen Idec, Inc.	Health	NMF	8.64	1.85
⊕ Schlumberger, Ltd.	Energy	22.3	31.07	1.77
✧ AT&T, Inc.	Telecom	18.2	51.59	1.76
⊖ Henry Schein, Inc.	Health	24.0	12.24	1.76
⊖ UnitedHealth Group, Inc.	Health	20.8	-13.49	1.73
⊕ Herbalife, Ltd.	Health	18.1	24.05	1.54
⊕ Prudential Financial, In	Financial	16.1	18.70	1.48
⊕ Sotheby's Holdings, Inc.	Consumer	18.6	70.12	1.25
Ultra Petroleum Corporat	Energy	30.4	-14.44	1.25
Praxair, Inc.	Ind Mtrls	20.8	14.01	1.22
⊕ eBay, Inc.	Consumer	40.1	-30.43	1.22
⊕ Quicksilver Resources, I	Energy	26.3	-12.90	1.19
⊖ Valero Energy Corporatio	Energy	6.3	-0.33	1.18
⊕ Infosys Technologies Ltd	Software	—	—	1.17

Current Investment Style

Value Blnd Growth — Large Mid Small

Market Cap	%
Giant	26.7
Large	30.1
Mid	34.7
Small	8.1
Micro	0.5

Avg $mil: 15,117

Value Measures		Rel Category
Price/Earnings	18.51	0.96
Price/Book	3.08	0.93
Price/Sales	1.95	1.01
Price/Cash Flow	10.48	0.92
Dividend Yield %	1.14	1.11

Growth Measures	%	Rel Category
Long-Term Erngs	14.13	0.98
Book Value	10.91	0.94
Sales	11.30	0.97
Cash Flow	18.38	1.09
Historical Erngs	20.60	0.90

Profitability	%	Rel Category
Return on Equity	21.57	1.06
Return on Assets	10.46	0.95
Net Margin	14.57	1.02

Sector Weightings	% of Stocks	Rel S&P 500	3 Year High	Low
↻ Info	16.42	0.82		
▦ Software	3.89	1.13	10	4
▦ Hardware	7.84	0.85	17	7
▦ Media	0.73	0.19	10	1
▦ Telecom	3.96	1.13	7	2
☎ Service	57.68	1.25		
▦ Health	18.97	1.57	20	9
▦ Consumer	7.78	1.02	12	7
▦ Business	10.11	2.39	14	7
▦ Financial	20.82	0.93	21	6
▦ Mfg	25.88	0.77		
▦ Goods	4.92	0.58	9	4
▦ Ind Mtrls	7.63	0.64	19	8
▦ Energy	11.61	1.18	12	3
▦ Utilities	1.72	0.49	2	0

Composition

● Cash	2.5
● Stocks	97.5
● Bonds	0.0
● Other	0.0
Foreign	11.2
(% of Stock)	

Morningstar's Take by Andrew Gogerty 11-10-06

A manager change is a blow to shareholders and an unfortunate part of the Fidelity culture.

On Nov. 9, Jason Weiner stepped down as manager of Fidelity Independence, Fifty, and Advisor Fifty to take over Advisor Equity Growth and an insurance portfolio within the firm. Bob Bertelson, who in the past has managed Fidelity Aggressive Growth and multiple other funds, succeeds him.

Fund shareholders got the short end of the stick in this deal. Weiner's tenure of three-plus years at the helm here was marked by consistency. He guided the fund to a top-quartile showing in both 2004 and 2005 in the large-growth category and was on pace for a similar showing this year. Weiner put the fund's relatively small asset base--by Fidelity standards--to good use, investing in mid-caps and making small sector calls while employing a moderate growth style.

Bertelson's appointment likely will lead to pointed changes. He has exhibited more of an aggressive-growth style at past offerings, a tilt one could expect to continue here. His record doesn't inspire confidence, however, as Aggressive Growth posted very steep losses, even relative to rival growth funds, during his tenure from 2000 to 2002.

Manager changes at Fidelity have become notorious for their ripple affect on other funds in recent years. A manager departure at one fund often leads to other changes at three, four, or more funds like a sad game of dominos or musical chairs. A common thread with these changes is the poaching of a strong-performing manager to head much larger offerings--Equity Growth and its insurance sibling total more than $13 billion compared with $5.8 billion combined for Weiner's three previous charges. Another driver is the all powerful dollar, as part of a Fidelity portfolio's manager's overall pay compensation is based on assets under management. While these changes are good for the firm and its managers, in this case fund shareholders clearly have lost out.

Address:	82 Devonshire St Boston MA 02109 800-544-6666	Minimum Purchase:	$2500	Add: $250 IRA: $2500
		Min Auto Inv Plan:	$2500	Add: $100
		Sales Fees:	No-load	
Web Address:	www.fidelity.com	Management Fee:	0.55%	
Inception:	03-25-83	Actual Fees:	Mgt:0.55%	Dist: —
Advisor:	Fidelity Management & Research (FMR)	Expense Projections:	3Yr:$246	5Yr:$428 10Yr:$954
Subadvisor:	Multiple Subadvisors	Income Distrib:	Annually	
NTF Plans:	Fidelity Retail-NTF, CommonWealth NTF			

MORNINGSTAR® Funds 500

Fidelity Inflation-Protec

	Ticker	Load	NAV	Yield	SEC Yield	Total Assets	Mstar Category
	FINPX	None	$10.69	2.3%	2.63%	$1,688 mil	Inflation-Protected Bond

Governance and Management

Stewardship Grade: C

Portfolio Manager(s)

William Irving worked as a quantitative fixed-income analyst before taking over this portfolio from Thomas Silvia, who became the head of Fidelity's bond-fund effort, in late 2004. He is backed by Fidelity's considerable research capabilities. Irving also took over Fidelity Ginnie Mae effective Nov. 1, 2004.

Strategy

This fund sticks almost exclusively with U.S. Government Treasury Inflation-Protected Securities. Although management will affix the fund's overall risk characteristics, including interest-rate sensitivity, to that of an index, it will shift among different maturities depending on which of those appear cheap or expensive at a given time. The fund will also buy TIPS through forward contracts and invest the cash needed to back those purchases in ultra-short-term bonds.

Historical Profile
Return	Average
Risk	Above Avg
Rating	★★★ Neutral

Investment Style
Fixed Income
Income Rtn %Rank Cat

▼ Manager Change
▽ Partial Manager Change

Growth of $10,000
— Investment Values of Fund
— Investment Values of LB Aggr

Performance Quartile (within Category)

History	1995	1996	1997	1998	1999	2000	2001	2002	2003	2004	2005	2006
NAV	—	—	—	—	—	—	—	10.63	11.01	11.41	11.00	10.69
Total Return %	—	—	—	—	—	—	—	7.93*	7.76	8.24	2.16	0.23
+/-LB Aggr	—	—	—	—	—	—	—	—	3.66	3.90	-0.27	-4.10
+/-LB US Treas TIPS	—	—	—	—	—	—	—	—	-0.64	-0.22	-0.68	-0.18
Income Return %	—	—	—	—	—	—	—	—	1.69	1.43	1.34	2.23
Capital Return %	—	—	—	—	—	—	—	—	6.07	6.81	0.82	-2.00
Total Rtn % Rank Cat	—	—	—	—	—	—	—	—	37	31	49	27
Income $	—	—	—	—	—	—	—	0.11	0.18	0.16	0.15	0.24
Capital Gains $	—	—	—	—	—	—	—	0.05	0.26	0.34	0.50	0.09
Expense Ratio %	—	—	—	—	—	—	—	—	0.50	0.50	0.50	0.45
Income Ratio %	—	—	—	—	—	—	—	—	4.04	4.04	3.09	4.70
Turnover Rate %	—	—	—	—	—	—	—	—	—	211	117	71
Net Assets $mil	—	—	—	—	—	—	—	—	398	724	1,317	1,344

Performance 12-31-06

	1st Qtr	2nd Qtr	3rd Qtr	4th Qtr	Total
2002	—	—	7.68	0.52	7.93 *
2003	2.51	3.45	0.31	1.29	7.76
2004	4.90	-3.26	4.09	2.47	8.24
2005	-0.49	2.78	-0.12	0.01	2.16
2006	-2.18	0.39	3.41	-1.31	0.23

Trailing	Total Return%	+/- LB Agg	+/- LB US Treas TIPS	%Rank Cat	Growth of $10,000
3 Mo	-1.31	-2.55	0.06	31	9,869
6 Mo	2.06	-3.03	-0.16	25	10,206
1 Yr	0.23	-4.10	-0.18	27	10,023
3 Yr Avg	3.49	-0.21	-0.36	31	11,084
5 Yr Avg	—	—	—	—	—
10 Yr Avg	—	—	—	—	—
15 Yr Avg	—	—	—	—	—

Tax Analysis	Tax-Adj Rtn%	%Rank Cat	Tax-Cost Rat	%Rank Cat
3 Yr (estimated)	1.95	18	1.49	51
5 Yr (estimated)	—	—	—	—
10 Yr (estimated)	—	—	—	—

Potential Capital Gain Exposure: -3% of assets

Rating and Risk

Time Period	Load-Adj Return %	Morningstar Rtn vs Cat	Morningstar Risk vs Cat	Morningstar Risk-Adj Rating
1 Yr	0.23			
3 Yr	3.49	Avg	+Avg	★★★
5 Yr	—	—	—	—
10 Yr	—	—	—	—
Incept	5.78			

Other Measures	Standard Index LB Aggr	Best Fit Index LB Govt
Alpha	-0.3	0.3
Beta	1.40	1.31
R-Squared	77	79
Standard Deviation	5.13	
Mean	3.49	
Sharpe Ratio	0.07	

Morningstar's Take by Paul Herbert 12-21-06

Fidelity Inflation-Protected Bond has some draw, even if it isn't best of breed.

Picking among inflation-protected bond funds isn't easy, because it has become harder for the various offerings to deliver category-beating returns by investing in Treasury Inflation-Protected Securities (TIPS) alone. Since their introduction in 1997, the U.S. Treasury's slate of inflation-protected bonds has become more popular among investors, mainly institutional asset managers, driving their prices up and their yields down.

Last year, Fidelity added a wrinkle to the fund's strategy aimed at helping it handle this problem. Specifically, it started investing a portion of the assets elsewhere. The process is actually a bit more complex than that: With respect to a portion of the portfolio (now around 20% of assets) the fund gains access to TIPS through swaps, which require a minimal outlay relative to buying bonds directly. It invests that sleeve's extra cash in a fund

similar to Analyst Pick Fidelity Ultra-Short Bond. That fund's returns, after the cost of the swaps, helps augment the fund's results.

Lately, that investment has paid off. Manager Bill Irving implemented the strategy with just 10% of assets in September 2005, before kicking it up to 20% in February 2006. This "enhanced cash" portfolio has helped returns considerably as short-term interest rates have climbed to much higher levels. The fund's absolute showing, and those of other funds in the category, hasn't been much to write home about lately. Its slight 12-month return does top two thirds of its category peers'.

In all, we think Fidelity offers a pretty good option here and perhaps an improved one because of its exposure to one of our favorite funds. You likely won't go wrong here, but we prefer a couple of other funds because of features such as lower costs and more experience in this asset class.

Address:	82 Devonshire St Boston MA 02109 800-544-9797
Web Address:	www.fidelity.com
Inception:	06-26-02 *
Advisor:	Fidelity Management & Research (FMR)
Subadvisor:	Multiple Subadvisors
NTF Plans:	Fidelity Retail-NTF, CommonWealth NTF

Minimum Purchase:	$2500	Add: $500	IRA: $2500
Min Auto Inv Plan:	$100	Add: $100	
Sales Fees:	No-load		
Management Fee:	0.43%		
Actual Fees:	Mgt:0.32%	Dist: —	
Expense Projections:	3Yr:$144	5Yr:$252	10Yr:$567
Income Distrib:	Monthly		

Portfolio Analysis 10-31-06

Total Fixed-Income:870	Date of Maturity	Amount $000	Value $000	% Net Assets
US Treasury Note 2%	01-15-14	300,900	323,620	15.45
US Treasury Bond 3.625%	04-15-28	131,150	204,126	9.75
US Treasury Note 1.875%	07-15-13	165,750	178,164	8.51
US Treasury Note 3%	07-15-12	118,885	138,961	6.64
US Treasury Bond 3.875%	04-15-29	81,200	129,645	6.19
US Treasury Bond 2.375%	01-15-25	108,930	119,205	5.69
US Treasury Note	01-15-16	98,500	98,291	4.69
Ustn Tii 3.875%	01-15-09	100,000	96,097	4.59
US Treasury Note 1.625%	01-15-15	69,500	70,186	3.35
Ustn Tii .875%	04-15-10	49,550	50,242	2.40
Ustn Tii 4.25%	01-15-10	44,860	44,470	2.12
Ustn Tii 3.625%	01-15-08	44,750	44,335	2.12
US Treasury Bond 2%	01-15-26	39,500	38,782	1.85
US Treasury Note 2.5%	07-15-16	32,000	32,766	1.56
US TREASURY NOTE	07-15-15	30,000	30,277	1.45
Ustn Tii 3.625% 1/15/08	01-15-08	30,650	29,689	1.42
Ustn Tii 3.875% 1/15/09	01-15-09	20,000	19,200	0.92
US Treasury Note 3.375%	01-15-12	8,700	10,442	0.50
US Treasury Note 3.625%	01-15-08	6,700	8,468	0.40
US Treasury Note 3.875%	01-15-09	5,000	6,349	0.30

Current Investment Style

Duration: Short / Int / Long
Quality: High / Med / Low

1 figure provided by fund

Avg Eff Duration[1]	5.2 Yrs
Avg Eff Maturity	9.9 Yrs
Avg Credit Quality	AAA
Avg Wtd Coupon	2.07%
Avg Wtd Price	113.84% of par

Coupon Range	% of Bonds	Rel Cat
0% PIK	17.5	3.6
0% to 6%	99.8	1.0
6% to 8%	0.2	0.2
8% to 10%	0.0	0.0
More than 10%	0.0	0.0

1.00=Category Average

Credit Analysis	% bonds 10-31-06		
AAA	85	BB	0
AA	3	B	0
A	2	Below B	0
BBB	3	NR/NA	7

Sector Breakdown	% of assets
US Treasuries	0
TIPS	67
US Agency	0
Mortgage Pass-Throughs	0
Mortgage CMO	3
Mortgage ARM	0
US Corporate	15
Asset-Backed	5
Convertible	0
Municipal	0
Corporate Inflation-Protected	0
Foreign Corporate	0
Foreign Govt	0

Composition			
Cash	7.8	Bonds	92.0
Stocks	0.0	Other	0.3

Special Securities	
Restricted/Illiquid Secs	Trace
Exotic Mortgage-Backed	0
Emerging-Markets Secs	0
Options/Futures/Warrants	No

Fidelity Interm Bond

Ticker	**Load**	**NAV**	**Yield**	**SEC Yield**	**Total Assets**	**Mstar Category**
FTHRX	None	$10.26	4.3%	4.84%	$7,817 mil	Intermediate-Term Bond

Governance and Management

Stewardship Grade: B

Portfolio Manager(s)

Ford O'Neil has managed this fund since spring 1998. He works on Fidelity's intermediate-term/aggregate-bond team with a credit analyst, a quantitative analyst, a trader, and one other portfolio manager. O'Neil also manages Fidelity U.S. Bond Index and Fidelity Total Bond.

Strategy

Like all Fidelity bond funds, this offering eschews interest-rate bets. Manager Ford O'Neil ties the fund's duration to that of the Lehman Brothers Intermediate Government/Credit Index. He tries to beat the index with a combination of sector plays, yield-curve positioning, and individual-security selection. The fund's neutral mix is roughly 40% corporate bonds, 40% Treasury bonds, and 20% agency issues.

Historical Profile

Return	Average
Risk	Below Avg
Rating	★★★ Neutral

Investment Style: Fixed Income
Income Rtn %Rank Cat

▼ Manager Change
▽ Partial Manager Change

Growth of $10,000
— Investment Values of Fund
— Investment Values of LB Aggr

Performance Quartile (within Category)

1995	1996	1997	1998	1999	2000	2001	2002	2003	2004	2005	2006	History
10.41	10.08	10.17	10.27	9.76	10.04	10.32	10.73	10.66	10.52	10.29	10.26	NAV
12.81	3.65	7.57	7.32	0.96	9.75	8.83	9.16	4.96	3.20	1.75	4.26	Total Return %
-5.66	0.02	-2.08	-1.37	1.78	-1.88	0.39	-1.09	0.86	-1.14	-0.68	-0.07	+/-LB Aggr
-8.62	0.96	-1.86	-2.82	3.84	-2.69	0.01	-3.87	-1.01	-2.10	-0.08	0.45	+/-LB 5-10YR
6.57	6.53	6.61	6.32	6.06	6.71	6.01	5.05	3.76	3.51	3.88	4.41	Income Return %
6.24	-2.88	0.96	1.00	-5.10	3.04	2.82	4.11	1.20	-0.31	-2.13	-0.15	Capital Return %
97	36	87	56	8	58	16	33	41	78	54	35	Total Rtn % Rank Cat
0.63	0.66	0.65	0.62	0.61	0.64	0.59	0.51	0.39	0.37	0.40	0.44	Income $
0.02	0.03	0.00	0.00	0.00	0.00	0.00	0.00	0.20	0.11	0.01	0.01	Capital Gains $
0.68	0.71	0.69	0.65	0.65	0.65	0.63	0.63	0.64	0.61	0.61	0.44	Expense Ratio %
6.31	6.48	6.46	6.37	6.00	4.93	6.46	5.44	4.47	3.48	3.50	4.96	Income Ratio %
75	169	116	90	108	102	73	78	117	120	74	71	Turnover Rate %
2,821	3,080	3,193	3,444	3,254	3,469	4,808	6,248	6,901	7,184	7,528	7,817	Net Assets $mil

Performance 12-31-06

	1st Qtr	2nd Qtr	3rd Qtr	4th Qtr	Total
2002	-0.01	3.15	3.86	1.91	9.16
2003	1.73	2.88	-0.13	0.41	4.96
2004	2.40	-2.43	2.72	0.57	3.20
2005	-0.77	2.28	-0.37	0.62	1.75
2006	-0.25	0.29	3.12	1.06	4.26

Trailing	Total Return%	+/- LB Aggr	+/- LB 5-10YR	%Rank Cat	Growth of $10,000
3 Mo	1.06	-0.18	-0.02	66	10,106
6 Mo	4.21	-0.88	-1.47	82	10,421
1 Yr	4.26	-0.07	0.45	35	10,426
3 Yr Avg	3.07	-0.63	-0.57	63	10,950
5 Yr Avg	4.64	-0.42	-1.28	46	12,546
10 Yr Avg	5.73	-0.51	-0.95	38	17,458
15 Yr Avg	5.94	-0.56	-1.05	61	23,763

Tax Analysis	Tax-Adj Rtn%	%Rank Cat	Tax-Cost Rat	%Rank Cat
3 Yr (estimated)	1.59	50	1.44	47
5 Yr (estimated)	2.99	37	1.58	48
10 Yr (estimated)	3.64	25	1.98	45

Potential Capital Gain Exposure: -1% of assets

Rating and Risk

Time Period	Load-Adj Return %	Morningstar Rtn vs Cat	Morningstar Risk vs Cat	Morningstar Risk-Adj Rating
1 Yr	4.26			
3 Yr	3.07	Avg	-Avg	★★★
5 Yr	4.64	Avg	-Avg	★★★
10 Yr	5.73	Avg	Low	★★★
Incept	8.38			

Other Measures	Standard Index LB Aggr	Best Fit Index LB 5-10YR
Alpha	-0.5	-0.4
Beta	0.80	0.58
R-Squared	97	98
Standard Deviation	2.65	
Mean	3.07	
Sharpe Ratio	-0.06	

Portfolio Analysis 08-31-06

Total Fixed-Income:1575	Date of Maturity	Amount $000	Value $000	% Net Assets
US Treasury Note 4.25%	08-15-13	300,732	292,415	3.06
US Treasury Note 4.875%	05-15-09	285,550	286,632	3.00
US Treasury Note 2%	01-15-14	249,200	268,712	2.82
Citi Swap Irs 1/20/09 3m	01-20-09	200,000	197,648	2.07
Dbsw Swap Irs 2/28/11	02-28-11	178,160	176,768	1.85
Dbsw Swap Irs 8/29/11 3m	08-29-11	150,000	150,504	1.58
GNMA 0.06%	09-01-36	145,500	148,855	1.56
Lbsp Swap Irs 1/6/09 3ml	01-06-09	150,000	148,380	1.55
FNMA 6.25%	02-01-11	134,795	140,340	1.47
FHLMC 5.25%	07-18-11	132,440	133,629	1.40
US Treasury Note 2%	07-15-14	125,000	132,020	1.38
US Treasury Note 6.5%	02-15-10	120,000	126,741	1.33
Lbsp Swap Irs 12/8/08 3m	12-08-08	125,000	124,173	1.30
FNMA 0.06%	04-01-18	110,989	110,812	1.16
US Treasury Note 0.875%	04-15-10	105,000	106,863	1.12
Jpsw Swap Irs 4/10/11 3m	04-10-11	100,000	101,911	1.07
Ubsd Swap Irs 1/23/09 3m	01-23-09	100,000	98,929	1.04
Lbsp Swap Irs 2/10/10 3m	02-10-10	100,000	96,491	1.01
FNMA 3.25%	08-15-08	92,035	88,883	0.93
US Treasury Note 4.75%	05-15-14	86,990	87,085	0.91

Current Investment Style

Duration: Short Int Long
Quality: High Med Low

	1 figure provided by fund
Avg Eff Duration[1]	3.6 Yrs
Avg Eff Maturity	4.4 Yrs
Avg Credit Quality	AA
Avg Wtd Coupon	3.77%
Avg Wtd Price	99.49% of par

Coupon Range	% of Bonds	Rel Cat
0% PIK	18.2	2.6
0% to 6%	82.0	1.1
6% to 8%	17.0	0.8
8% to 10%	1.0	0.2
More than 10%	0.0	0.0

1.00=Category Average

Credit Analysis		% bonds 08-31-06	
AAA	57	BB	3
AA	7	B	0
A	9	Below B	0
BBB	19	NR/NA	4

Sector Breakdown — % of assets

US Treasuries	15
TIPS	3
US Agency	7
Mortgage Pass-Throughs	11
Mortgage CMO	12
Mortgage ARM	0
US Corporate	28
Asset-Backed	9
Convertible	0
Municipal	0
Corporate Inflation-Protected	0
Foreign Corporate	2
Foreign Govt	0

Composition

Cash	11.1	Bonds	88.5
Stocks	0.0	Other	0.5

Special Securities

Restricted/Illiquid Secs	4
Exotic Mortgage-Backed	1
Emerging-Markets Secs	Trace
Options/Futures/Warrants	No

Morningstar's Take by Scott Berry 12-05-06

Fidelity Intermediate Bond doesn't fit neatly into Morningstar's category system, but that doesn't make it a bad fund.

The fund follows a slightly different path from that of many of its intermediate-term bond category peers. The standard benchmark for an intermediate-bond fund is the Lehman Brothers Aggregate Bond Index, seen by many as the bond world's equivalent to the S&P 500. But this fund's benchmark is the Lehman Brothers Intermediate Government/Credit Index, which typically carries a bit less interest-rate risk and a bit more credit risk than the Aggregate. Those differences apply to this fund as well. Its duration (a measure of interest-rate sensitivity) checks in below the category norm, while its exposure to bonds rated BBB and below checks in above the category average. Overall, those qualities have translated into lower volatility, but also a bit less return than many in the group.

That's a trade-off we're willing to make, though.

And rather than judging the fund based solely on its benchmark, which is a reasonable one, we think quality of management and costs should also be considered. And on both those counts, the fund looks quite good. Manager Ford O'Neil has led the fund past its benchmark over the trailing one-, three-, and five-year periods, and he's backed by Fidelity's extensive bond-research capabilities. Meanwhile, the fund's 0.45% expense ratio provides the fund a built-in head start over its average no-load category peer, which charges 0.73%.

The fund has looked good versus both the index and the category in 2006. Thanks in part to the strong performance of its auto holdings, the fund has bested roughly two thirds of its peers for the year to date through November 20.

The fund's longer-term performance record may not jump off the page, but for investors looking for a relatively tame core bond holding, we think this fund fills the bill quite nicely.

Address:	82 Devonshire St Boston MA 02109 800-544-5555
Web Address:	www.fidelity.com
Inception:	05-23-75
Advisor:	Fidelity Management & Research (FMR)
Subadvisor:	Multiple Subadvisors
NTF Plans:	Fidelity Retail-NTF, CommonWealth NTF

Minimum Purchase:	$2500	Add: $250	IRA: $500
Min Auto Inv Plan:	$2500	Add: $100	
Sales Fees:	No-load		
Management Fee:	0.32%		
Actual Fees:	Mgt:0.32%	Dist: —	
Expense Projections:	3Yr:$144	5Yr:$252	10Yr:$567
Income Distrib:	Monthly		

MORNINGSTAR® Funds 500

Fidelity Interm Muni Inc

Analyst Pick ✓

	Ticker	Load	NAV	Yield	SEC Yield	Total Assets	Mstar Category
	FLTMX	None	$9.97	3.9%	3.53%	$2,058 mil	Muni National Interm

Governance and Management

Stewardship Grade: B

Portfolio Manager(s)

Mark Sommer took over this fund in July 2006. In addition to this fund, Sommer has, since June 2002, managed Fidelity funds focusing on New York, New Jersey, Connecticut, Maryland, and Pennsylvania. Sommer joined Fidelity's fixed-income quantitative research group in 1992 and began managing $4 billion in stable-value assets in 1997.

Strategy

Manager Mark Sommer makes adjustments to the portfolio based on his outlook for the shape of the yield curve and for various sectors of the market. He also tries to find bargains based on a bond's credit quality and structure. No interest-rate bets are made, though, as the fund seeks to generally match the risk and interest-rate sensitivity characteristics of the Lehman Brothers 1-17 Year Muni Index.

Historical Profile
Return: Above Avg
Risk: Average
Rating: ★★★★ Above Avg

Investment Style
Fixed Income
Income Rtn %Rank Cat

▼ Manager Change
▽ Partial Manager Change

Growth of $10,000
— Investment Values of Fund
— Investment Values of LB Muni

Performance Quartile (within Category)

	1995	1996	1997	1998	1999	2000	2001	2002	2003	2004	2005	2006	History
	9.80	9.70	9.94	9.98	9.41	9.78	9.85	10.23	10.21	10.15	9.97	9.97	NAV
	14.84	4.44	8.23	5.89	-1.06	9.26	5.48	9.02	5.30	3.74	2.56	3.97	Total Return %
	-2.62	0.01	-0.96	-0.59	1.00	-2.42	0.35	-0.58	-0.01	-0.74	-0.95	-0.87	+/-LB Muni
	-2.33	-0.10	-1.00	-0.87	0.19	-1.50	0.86	-1.15	-0.40	-0.41	-0.18	-0.74	+/-LB Muni 10YR
	5.67	5.10	5.13	4.88	4.77	5.18	4.79	4.46	4.09	3.94	3.86	3.93	Income Return %
	9.17	-0.66	3.10	1.01	-5.83	4.08	0.69	4.56	1.21	-0.20	-1.30	0.04	Capital Return %
	34	22	35	32	26	53	9	39	10	17	21	31	Total Rtn % Rank Cat
	0.50	0.49	0.49	0.47	0.47	0.48	0.46	0.43	0.41	0.39	0.38	0.38	Income $
	0.00	0.03	0.05	0.06	0.00	0.00	0.00	0.06	0.14	0.04	0.05	0.00	Capital Gains $
	0.56	0.57	0.56	0.55	0.50	0.48	0.49	0.39	0.43	0.43	0.42	—	Expense Ratio %
	5.42	5.25	5.06	4.97	4.58	4.72	5.03	4.60	4.35	4.00	3.89	—	Income Ratio %
									32	31	26	—	Turnover Rate %
	881	941	901	912	1,146	1,061	1,210	1,487	1,752	1,797	1,809	2,023	Net Assets $mil

Performance 12-31-06

	1st Qtr	2nd Qtr	3rd Qtr	4th Qtr	Total
2002	0.58	3.88	4.37	-0.02	9.02
2003	1.20	2.47	0.63	0.91	5.30
2004	1.62	-2.15	3.41	0.89	3.74
2005	-0.54	2.47	-0.04	0.66	2.56
2006	0.15	-0.03	2.94	0.89	3.97

Trailing	Total Return%	+/- LB Muni	+/- LB Muni 10YR	%Rank Cat	Growth of $10,000
3 Mo	0.89	-0.22	-0.03	20	10,089
6 Mo	3.85	-0.70	-0.92	41	10,385
1 Yr	3.97	-0.87	-0.74	31	10,397
3 Yr Avg	3.42	-0.86	-0.44	20	11,061
5 Yr Avg	4.89	-0.64	-0.57	14	12,696
10 Yr Avg	5.20	-0.56	-0.50	13	16,602
15 Yr Avg	5.71	-0.55	-0.57	24	23,001

Tax Analysis	Tax-Adj Rtn%	%Rank Cat	Tax-Cost Rat	%Rank Cat
3 Yr (estimated)	3.37	16	0.05	23
5 Yr (estimated)	4.79	13	0.10	37
10 Yr (estimated)	5.12	7	0.08	35

Potential Capital Gain Exposure: 2% of assets

Rating and Risk

Time Period	Load-Adj Return %	Morningstar Rtn vs Cat	Morningstar Risk vs Cat	Morningstar Risk-Adj Rating
1 Yr	3.97			
3 Yr	3.42	+Avg	Avg	★★★★
5 Yr	4.89	+Avg	Avg	★★★★
10 Yr	5.20	+Avg	Avg	★★★★
Incept	6.18			

Other Measures	Standard Index LB Muni	Best Fit Index LB Muni
Alpha	-0.7	-0.7
Beta	0.90	0.90
R-Squared	99	99
Standard Deviation	2.76	
Mean	3.42	
Sharpe Ratio	0.07	

Morningstar's Take by Scott Berry 12-13-06

We don't think a recent management change at Fidelity Intermediate Municipal Income is cause for concern.

Manager Doug McGinley left this fund to join Fidelity's money market group in July 2006. He was replaced by Mark Sommer, who, like McGinley, has managed a number of Fidelity's municipal-bond funds, including Fidelity New York Municipal, since mid-2002. Sommer's experience and success give us confidence that this fund won't miss a beat. We're also comforted by this fund's history. Sommer will be the fourth manager here in the past seven years, but the fund's proven strategy has remained intact and its results have continued to impress.

The formula for success here is fairly straightforward. Management keeps duration (a measure of interest-rate sensitivity) tied to a benchmark index, while looking to add value through issue selection, sector allocation, and yield-curve positioning (the fund's mix of short- and long-term bonds). That approach limits wild performance swings, while allowing management to take advantage of Fidelity's deep municipal research capabilities. In recent years, for example, this fund and others have profited from Fidelity's ability to identify bonds that are ripe for refunding, a process in which municipalities replace older higher-yielding bonds with new lower-coupon issues.

In addition to Fidelity's strong analytical resources, the fund's low costs provide it a meaningful and sustainable advantage. At 0.43%, the fund ranks among the cheapest no-load intermediate muni funds. The upshot to low costs is that the fund can pay out more yield than most without management having to take on added risk.

Overall, our opinion here hasn't changed. With Sommer well prepared for this assignment and with the fund's advantages still in place, we think this fund remains an excellent choice for municipal-bond investors.

Portfolio Analysis 09-30-06

Total Fixed-Income:714

	Date of Maturity	Amount $000	Value $000	% Net Assets
NEW YORK N Y CITY TRANSI	11-01-28	40,925	45,203	2.15
Gscm Fswp Irs 5/01/10 Bm	05-01-10	23,000	23,252	1.11
California St 5.5%	11-01-33	21,355	23,243	1.11
Citi Fswp Irs 5/01/10 Bm	05-01-10	23,000	23,203	1.10
HILLSBOROUGH CNTY FLA IN	09-01-25	18,000	17,979	0.86
Tobacco Settlement Fing	06-01-16	16,800	17,819	0.85
California St Econ Recov	07-01-14	15,400	16,993	0.81
California St Econ Recov	07-01-15	15,200	16,466	0.78
Reedy Creek Impt Dist 5.	10-01-12	15,125	16,459	0.78
Washington St Pub Pwr Sp	07-01-10	16,000	13,842	0.66
California St 5.5%	04-01-30	10,515	11,520	0.55
Houston Tex Indpt Sch Di	08-15-11	13,740	11,376	0.54
California St Econ Recov	07-01-13	10,300	11,309	0.54
Texas St Tpk Auth 5.75%	08-15-38	10,110	11,076	0.53
California St Econ Recov	07-01-14	9,700	10,738	0.51

Current Investment Style

Duration: Short / Int / Long
Quality: High / Med / Low

¹Avg Eff Duration	5.0 Yrs
Avg Eff Maturity	9.1 Yrs
Avg Credit Quality	AA
Avg Wtd Coupon	4.61%
Avg Wtd Price	103.73% of par

¹figure provided by fund

Credit Analysis % bonds 09-30-06

AAA	63	BB	0
AA	13	B	0
A	16	Below B	0
BBB	7	NR/NA	2

Special Securities

Restricted/Illiquid Secs	0
Options/Futures/Warrants	No

Top 5 States % bonds

TX	15.0	IL	9.8
CA	14.5	WA	6.9
NY	13.3		

Composition

Cash	2.6	Bonds	97.4
Stocks	0.0	Other	0.0

Sector Weightings

	% of Bonds	Rel Cat
General Obligation	37.4	1.01
Utilities	11.0	1.16
Health	8.7	0.97
Water/Waste	7.2	0.79
Housing	0.8	0.16
Education	12.2	0.94
Transportation	9.2	1.74
COP/Lease	2.2	0.90
Industrial	10.5	1.13
Misc Revenue	0.0	—
Demand	0.9	2.26

Address:	82 Devonshire Street, Boston MA 02109, 800-544-9797
Web Address:	www.fidelity.com
Inception:	04-15-77
Advisor:	FMR, Inc.
Subadvisor:	Fidelity Investments Money Mgmt
NTF Plans:	Fidelity Retail-NTF, CommonWealth NTF

Minimum Purchase:	$10000	Add: $1000	IRA: $0
Min Auto Inv Plan:	$10000	Add: $500	
Sales Fees:	No-load, 0.50%R		
Management Fee:	0.31%		
Actual Fees:	Mgt:0.31%	Dist: —	
Expense Projections:	3Yr:$138	5Yr:$241	10Yr:$542
Income Distrib:	Monthly		

Fidelity Interm Govt

	Ticker	Load	NAV	Yield	SEC Yield	Total Assets	Mstar Category
	FSTGX	None	$9.97	4.2%	4.42%	$724 mil	Intermediate Government

Governance and Management

Stewardship Grade: B

Portfolio Manager(s)

Brett Kozlowski is a newcomer, having taken over this fund in October 2006. He's been with Fidelity since 1997 and has relevant experience as a mortgage analyst, so we're confident he can keep this fund on track.

Strategy

This fund follows the standard Fidelity formula. Brett Kozlowski avoids interest-rate bets and keeps the fund's duration (a measure of interest-rate sensitivity) tied to that of the Lehman Brothers Intermediate Government Index. Within this framework, he makes moderate sector bets, moving among mortgage-backed securities, agency bonds, and Treasuries.

Historical Profile

Return	Average
Risk	Average
Rating	★★★ Neutral

Investment Style
Fixed Income
Income Rtn %Rank Cat

▼ Manager Change
▽ Partial Manager Change

Growth of $10,000
— Investment Values of Fund
— Investment Values of LB Aggr

Performance Quartile (within Category)

1995	1996	1997	1998	1999	2000	2001	2002	2003	2004	2005	2006	History
10.00	9.74	9.78	9.85	9.31	9.62	9.81	10.38	10.29	10.24	10.03	9.97	NAV
13.93	4.14	7.69	7.45	0.64	10.33	7.93	10.23	1.92	2.40	1.45	3.64	Total Return %
-4.54	0.51	-1.96	-1.24	1.46	-1.30	-0.51	-0.02	-2.18	-1.94	-0.98	-0.69	+/-LB Aggr
-4.41	1.37	-1.90	-2.40	2.87	-2.91	0.70	-1.27	-0.44	-1.08	-1.20	0.16	+/-LB Govt
6.79	6.74	7.24	6.74	6.27	6.81	5.94	4.27	2.81	2.89	3.53	4.24	Income Return %
7.14	-2.60	0.45	0.71	-5.63	3.52	1.99	5.96	-0.89	-0.49	-2.08	-0.60	Capital Return %
91	18	89	50	15	75	14	22	42	78	73	39	Total Rtn % Rank Cat
0.62	0.65	0.68	0.64	0.60	0.61	0.56	0.41	0.29	0.29	0.36	0.42	Income $
0.00	0.00	0.00	0.00	0.00	0.00	0.00	0.00	0.00	0.00	0.00	0.00	Capital Gains $
0.65	0.62	0.54	0.38	0.53	0.63	0.60	0.59	0.60	0.60	0.57	0.45	Expense Ratio %
7.18	6.89	6.96	6.65	6.58	6.67	6.34	4.63	3.18	2.67	3.23	4.14	Income Ratio %
210	105	105	188	117	66	114	145	229	152	90	97	Turnover Rate %
830	713	758	760	820	766	918	1,367	1,116	941	831	724	Net Assets $mil

Performance 12-31-06

	1st Qtr	2nd Qtr	3rd Qtr	4th Qtr	Total
2002	-0.10	3.96	5.04	1.05	10.23
2003	0.97	1.65	-0.40	-0.30	1.92
2004	2.25	-2.41	2.32	0.29	2.40
2005	-0.80	2.29	-0.44	0.43	1.45
2006	-0.30	0.34	2.73	0.86	3.64

Trailing	Total Return%	+/- LB Aggr	+/- LB Govt	%Rank Cat	Growth of $10,000
3 Mo	0.86	-0.38	0.02	71	10,086
6 Mo	3.61	-1.48	-0.80	90	10,361
1 Yr	3.64	-0.69	0.16	39	10,364
3 Yr Avg	2.49	-1.21	-0.71	64	10,766
5 Yr Avg	3.88	-1.18	-0.76	49	12,096
10 Yr Avg	5.31	-0.93	-0.70	42	16,776
15 Yr Avg	5.46	-1.04	-0.84	57	22,198

Tax Analysis	Tax-Adj Rtn%	%Rank Cat	Tax-Cost Rat	%Rank Cat
3 Yr (estimated)	1.24	48	1.22	40
5 Yr (estimated)	2.59	27	1.24	30
10 Yr (estimated)	3.34	31	1.87	58

Potential Capital Gain Exposure: -6% of assets

Rating and Risk

Time Period	Load-Adj Return %	Morningstar Rtn vs Cat	Morningstar Risk vs Cat	Morningstar Risk-Adj Rating
1 Yr	3.64			
3 Yr	2.49	Avg	Avg	★★★
5 Yr	3.88	Avg	Avg	★★★
10 Yr	5.31	Avg	Avg	★★★
Incept	6.24			

Other Measures	Standard Index LB Aggr	Best Fit Index LB Interm Tr
Alpha	-1.1	0.1
Beta	0.77	0.98
R-Squared	95	99
Standard Deviation	2.57	
Mean	2.49	
Sharpe Ratio	-0.28	

Morningstar's Take by Scott Berry 11-03-06

Despite a management change, we still like what we see at Fidelity Intermediate Government.

George Fischer, who led this fund since mid-2002, was replaced here by Brett Kozlowski in early October 2006. Fischer remains with Fidelity, but has given up some fund management responsibilities for more-administrative duties. Kozlowski has been with Fidelity since 1997, serving most recently as a mortgage analyst and a member of Fidelity's government/mortgage fund management team.

Kozlowski has no relevant fund-management experience, but we're confident that the transition will be a smooth one and that Kozlowski will build on the fund's solid long-term record. That confidence stems from our trust in the fund's strategy and Fidelity's resources, which don't go away with a management change. Like Fischer, Kozlowski won't be looking to make big bets on the overall direction of the market and will be relying on Fidelity's strong analytical resources for support.

And Kozlowski is actually starting off with more primary knowledge about the government and mortgage markets than did Fischer, who made the jump to government-bond funds from municipal-bond funds. We're also encouraged that other management changes in Fidelity's investment-grade bond funds have gone smoothly over the years, including a change at Fidelity Investment Grade Bond.

Finally, we like that Kozlowski doesn't have a huge expense hurdle to jump here. With Fidelity capping expenses at 0.45%, the fund boasts a nice sustainable advantage over its average no-load category peer, which charges 0.66%. That may not seem like much of an advantage, but we think it's meaningful, given the category's often-narrow range of returns.

Overall, we think fund shareholders should stay the course. Management changes often raise red flags, but we see none here.

Portfolio Analysis 10-31-06

Total Fixed-Income:224

	Date of Maturity	Amount $000	Value $000	% Net Assets
US Treasury Note 3.375%	09-15-09	63,842	61,747	7.90
FNMA 4.75%	12-15-10	58,500	58,216	7.45
US Treasury Note 4.375%	12-15-10	45,060	44,724	5.72
US Treasury Note 2.375%	04-15-11	43,000	43,928	5.62
FHLMC 5.25%	07-18-11	42,808	43,470	5.56
US Treasury Note 4.75%	03-31-11	38,000	38,257	4.89
US Treasury Note 4.25%	11-15-14	29,000	28,328	3.62
US Treasury Note 0.875%	04-15-10	24,000	24,340	3.11
US Treasury Note 4.875%	04-30-08	21,246	21,275	2.72
US Treasury Note 4.75%	05-15-14	19,058	19,249	2.46
FNMA 4.625%	10-15-13	19,570	19,190	2.45
FHLBA 5.375%	08-19-11	16,960	17,316	2.21
FNMA 5.5%	01-01-09	12,940	12,979	1.66
FNMA 6.375%	06-15-09	11,870	12,306	1.57
FNMA 5%	09-15-08	11,335	11,351	1.45
Housing Urban Dev 6.06%	08-01-10	10,000	10,132	1.30
US Treasury Note 4.875%	05-15-09	10,000	10,057	1.29
FHLMC 5.125%	04-18-08	10,000	10,023	1.28
FHLMC CMO 4.5%	02-15-23	10,000	9,740	1.25
FHLBA 5.8%	09-02-08	9,595	9,723	1.24

Current Investment Style

Duration: Short Int Long
Quality: High Med Low

¹ figure provided by fund

Avg Eff Duration¹	3.2 Yrs
Avg Eff Maturity	4.1 Yrs
Avg Credit Quality	AAA
Avg Wtd Coupon	3.58%
Avg Wtd Price	100.09% of par

Coupon Range	% of Bonds	Rel Cat
0% PIK	2.5	0.3
0% to 6%	92.8	1.1
6% to 8%	7.1	0.5
8% to 10%	0.0	0.0
More than 10%	0.1	0.1

1.00=Category Average

Credit Analysis	% bonds 10-31-06		
AAA	100	BB	0
AA	0	B	0
A	0	Below B	0
BBB	0	NR/NA	0

Sector Breakdown	% of assets
US Treasuries	30
TIPS	9
US Agency	30
Mortgage Pass-Throughs	10
Mortgage CMO	12
Mortgage ARM	0
US Corporate	2
Asset-Backed	0
Convertible	0
Municipal	0
Corporate Inflation-Protected	0
Foreign Corporate	0
Foreign Govt	0

Composition			
Cash	7.1	Bonds	92.7
Stocks	0.0	Other	0.2

Special Securities	
Restricted/Illiquid Secs	0
Exotic Mortgage-Backed	0
Emerging-Markets Secs	0
Options/Futures/Warrants	No

Address:	82 Devonshire St Boston MA 02109 800-544-6666	Minimum Purchase:	$2500	Add: $250 IRA: $200
		Min Auto Inv Plan:	$100	Add: $100
Web Address:	www.fidelity.com	Sales Fees:	No-load	
Inception:	05-02-88	Management Fee:	0.32%	
Advisor:	Fidelity Management & Research (FMR)	Actual Fees:	Mgt:0.32%	Dist: —
Subadvisor:	Multiple Subadvisors	Expense Projections:	3Yr:$144	5Yr:$252 10Yr:$567
NTF Plans:	Fidelity Retail-NTF, CommonWealth NTF	Income Distrib:	Monthly	

MORNINGSTAR® Funds 500

Fidelity Intl Sm Cp

	Ticker	Load	NAV	Yield	Total Assets	Mstar Category
	FISMX	Closed	$24.93	0.2%	$1,804 mil	Foreign Small/Mid Growth

Governance and Management

Stewardship Grade: B

Portfolio Manager(s)

Ben Paton has been at Fidelity since 1995 and Tokuya Sano since 1993, and both have worked as analysts. Sano has been on board since this fund's 2002 inception, but Paton joined the fund in early 2004. This is the first time that either manager has run a public, U.S.-based fund. In July 2005, Fidelity added a third manager, Wilson Wong. He began his career at Fidelity in 2000 covering Asian stocks, especially utilities, and has run country-specific portfolios. The three managers also run Fidelity Advisor International Small Cap as a clone of this fund.

Strategy

Managers Ben Paton, Tokuya Sano, and Wilson Wong independently run large sleeves of the fund. Paton focuses on European and other non-Asia names. Sano focuses on Japan, and Wong runs the Asia ex-Japan sleeve. The managers apply Fidelity's traditional growth-at-a-reasonable-price investing style to their markets and pay lots of attention to emerging markets. Fidelity uses fair-value pricing on an as-needed basis, and the fund does not hedge foreign currency exposure.

Performance 12-31-06

	1st Qtr	2nd Qtr	3rd Qtr	4th Qtr	Total
2002	—	—	—	10.45	5.70 *
2003	-0.19	26.02	23.06	16.45	80.25
2004	11.62	0.10	-1.34	17.42	29.43
2005	5.67	0.89	14.02	6.50	29.47
2006	13.31	-5.27	-2.56	9.20	14.22

Trailing	Total Return%	+/- MSCI EAFE	+/- MSCI Wd xUS	%Rank Cat	Growth of $10,000
3 Mo	9.20	-1.15	-0.92	92	10,920
6 Mo	6.41	-8.28	-7.81	94	10,641
1 Yr	14.22	-12.12	-11.49	91	11,422
3 Yr Avg	24.16	4.23	4.06	55	19,140
5 Yr Avg	—	—	—	—	—
10 Yr Avg	—	—	—	—	—
15 Yr Avg	—	—	—	—	—

Tax Analysis	Tax-Adj Rtn%	%Rank Cat	Tax-Cost Rat	%Rank Cat
3 Yr (estimated)	21.46	73	2.17	86
5 Yr (estimated)	—	—	—	—
10 Yr (estimated)	—	—	—	—

Potential Capital Gain Exposure: 23% of assets

Morningstar's Take by Dan Lefkovitz 12-22-06

Fidelity International Small Cap's rough year demonstrates its risks.

This high flier, which is closed to new investors, has come down to earth. With 2006 almost in the books, the fund has gained less than 13%, putting it near the bottom of the foreign small/mid growth category. The tough year in relative terms can be blamed in large part on the fund's Japan stake, which is twice as large as the category average. Japanese small caps have had a terrible year. Fidelity Japan Smaller Companies. has lost more than 21% this year.

We've been warning for years that the kind of returns that this fund posted from 2003 to 2005, when it gained an average of 44% per year, were unsustainable. We also warned that this fund was riskier than most peers because it makes big bets on market caps, sectors, and geographic regions. Its three portfolio managers tend to hold a far bigger share of micro-cap stocks that most peers, and micro caps are extremely volatile. Until recently,

they have owned more emerging markets. And they have retained big stakes in both the energy sector and in Japan, even after those two areas ran up considerably. It's no surprise that the fund has been more volatile than its typical peer, measured by standard deviation of returns.

We have other concerns about the fund. Due to its 2003-2005 gains, assets grew rapidly. With more money to put to work, the team has had to buy more stocks (712 at last count, up from 132 in 2002), which dilutes their best ideas. And as the fund has grown bigger, it has lost its pure small-cap focus. Its managers have purchased quite a few large caps for the portfolio. That other Fidelity funds, including Fidelity International Small Cap Opportunities, are competing with this fund for stocks, is also a concern. So is the facts that the managers don't have a long track record. In its brief life, the fund has already seen some manager turnover.

All in all, this is a fund to avoid.

Address:	82 Devonshire St Boston MA 02109 800-544-9797
Web Address:	www.fidelity.com
Inception:	09-18-02 *
Advisor:	Fidelity Management & Research (FMR)
Subadvisor:	Multiple Subadvisors
NTF Plans:	Fidelity Retail-NTF, CommonWealth NTF

Minimum Purchase:	Closed	Add: —	IRA: —
Min Auto Inv Plan:	Closed	Add: —	
Sales Fees:	No-load, 2.00%R		
Management Fee:	0.97%		
Actual Fees:	Mgt:0.97%	Dist: —	
Expense Projections:	3Yr:$406	5Yr:$702	10Yr:$1545
Income Distrib:	Annually		

Historical Profile

Return	Average
Risk	Above Avg
Rating	★★★ Neutral

90%	85%	92%	95%	94%

▼ Manager Change
▽ Partial Manager Change

Investment Style
Equity
Stock %

Growth of $10,000
— Investment Values of Fund
— Investment Values of MSCI EAFE

31.0
24.0
17.0
10.0

Performance Quartile
(within Category)

1995	1996	1997	1998	1999	2000	2001	2002	2003	2004	2005	2006	History
—	—	—	—	—	—	—	10.55	18.67	23.28	26.97	24.93	NAV
—	—	—	—	—	—	—	5.70*	80.25	29.43	29.47	14.22	Total Return %
—	—	—	—	—	—	—		41.66	9.18	15.93	-12.12	+/-MSCI EAFE
—	—	—	—	—	—	—		40.83	9.05	15.00	-11.49	+/-MSCI Wd xUS
—	—	—	—	—	—	—		0.19	0.32	0.60	0.24	Income Return %
—	—	—	—	—	—	—		80.06	29.11	28.87	13.98	Capital Return %
—	—	—	—	—	—	—	7	21	29	91		Total Rtn % Rank Cat
—	—	—	—	—	—	—	0.00	0.02	0.06	0.14	0.07	Income $
—	—	—	—	—	—	—	0.02	0.31	0.77	2.89	5.68	Capital Gains $
—	—	—	—	—	—	—		1.80	1.51	1.28	—	Expense Ratio %
—	—	—	—	—	—	—		-0.56	0.46	0.50	—	Income Ratio %
—	—	—	—	—	—	—		10	84	77	—	Turnover Rate %
—	—	—	—	—	—	—	16	748	1,412	1,688		Net Assets $mil

Rating and Risk

Time Period	Load-Adj Return %	Morningstar Rtn vs Cat	Morningstar Risk vs Cat	Morningstar Risk-Adj Rating
1 Yr	14.22			
3 Yr	24.16	Avg	+Avg	★★★
5 Yr	—	—	—	—
10 Yr	—	—	—	—
Incept	35.25			

Other Measures	Standard Index MSCI EAFE	Best Fit Index MSCI Wd xUS
Alpha	-1.4	-1.4
Beta	1.36	1.34
R-Squared	77	78
Standard Deviation	14.47	
Mean	24.16	
Sharpe Ratio	1.35	

Portfolio Analysis 10-31-06

Share change since 07-06 Total Stocks:653	Sector	Country	% Assets
⊕ Banca Italease	Financial	Italy	2.26
⊕ Gie Icade Tresorerie, Bo	—	France	1.32
⊖ Nissin Kogyo	Ind Mtrls	Japan	1.18
⊖ Steinhoff International	Goods	South Africa	1.11
⊖ Fujikura Ltd	Ind Mtrls	Japan	1.09
☼ CEZ	Utilities	Czech Republic	1.08
☼ Max Petro Plc, London	—	U.K.	1.08
☼ NOK	Goods	Japan	0.98
⊖ Nippon Seiki	Ind Mtrls	Japan	0.92
⊖ International Ferro Meta	Ind Mtrls	U.K.	0.90
⊖ Cambrian Mining	Energy	U.K.	0.81
☼ Fresenius Medical Care	Health	Germany	0.74
⊖ Nihon Dempa Kogyo	Hardware	Japan	0.69
⊖ NGK Spark Plug	Ind Mtrls	Japan	0.68
Modern Times Grp	Media	Sweden	0.67
⊖ Hikari Tsushin	Consumer	Japan	0.67
⊖ Yamada Denki	Consumer	Japan	0.63
121media	—	United States	0.60
⊖ Token	Consumer	Japan	0.60
⊖ Kura		Japan	0.59

Current Investment Style

Value Blnd Growth — Large Mid Small

	Market Cap	%
	Giant	3.4
	Large	16.4
	Mid	36.3
	Small	19.3
	Micro	24.6
	Avg $mil: 1,073	

Value Measures		Rel Category
Price/Earnings	11.93	0.76
Price/Book	2.06	0.85
Price/Sales	0.84	0.76
Price/Cash Flow	7.65	0.98
Dividend Yield %	1.89	0.92

Growth Measures	%	Rel Category
Long-Term Erngs	19.18	0.94
Book Value	11.76	1.25
Sales	10.66	0.85
Cash Flow	8.66	0.58
Historical Erngs	33.59	1.49

Composition

Cash	4.8	Bonds	0.4
Stocks	93.6	Other	1.2
Foreign	(% of Stock)		99.1

Sector Weightings	% of Stocks	Rel MSCI EAFE	3 Year High	Low
⟳ Info	10.32	0.87		
▨ Software	2.07	3.70	5	2
▨ Hardware	5.56	1.44	6	4
▨ Media	1.41	0.77	6	1
▨ Telecom	1.28	0.23	5	1
⟲ Service	33.82	0.72		
▨ Health	5.72	0.80	7	4
▨ Consumer	9.23	1.86	10	7
▨ Business	8.61	1.70	14	9
▨ Financial	10.26	0.34	14	10
⬒ Mfg	55.86	1.36		
▨ Goods	9.47	0.72	13	7
▨ Ind Mtrls	34.16	2.21	36	23
▨ Energy	7.62	1.07	13	4
▨ Utilities	4.61	0.88	5	0

Regional Exposure	% Stock		
UK/W. Europe	41	N. America	4
Japan	33	Latn America	0
Asia X Japan	18	Other	4

Country Exposure	% Stock		
Japan	33	Germany	3
U.K.	24	France	3
Australia	10		

Fidelity Intl Disc

	Ticker	Load	NAV	Yield	Total Assets	Mstar Category
	FIGRX	None	$37.92	1.0%	$9,192 mil	Foreign Large Blend

Governance and Management

Stewardship Grade: B

Portfolio Manager(s)

In October 2004, William Kennedy replaced Penelope Dobkin, who had run the fund since April 2001. Kennedy built a strong record running Fidelity Pacific Basin since 1999. He also managed Fidelity Advisor Japan for two years beginning in 2000 and served as director of equity research in Fidelity's Hong Kong office before that. For a brief period, Kennedy managed the Europe sleeve of a global portfolio, and he also spent a year setting up Fidelity's global research team. He also runs the foreign sleeve of Fidelity Worldwide. He is supported by a deep global research team.

Strategy

Years ago, this fund put a sizable chunk of its assets in bonds, but it's now a pure equity offering. William Kennedy, who took over management in October 2004, keeps the fund's country and sector weightings fairly close to those of the benchmark MSCI EAFE but is wide-ranging in his search for growing stocks at reasonable prices. Kennedy continues to sock a significant share of the portfolio in mid-caps and raised the fund's Asia stake, which is no surprise given his Asia-heavy background. Fidelity uses fair-value pricing on an as-needed basis and doesn't hedge foreign currency exposure.

Performance 12-31-06

	1st Qtr	2nd Qtr	3rd Qtr	4th Qtr	Total
2002	4.74	-0.20	-18.00	5.16	-9.87
2003	-7.85	20.06	10.80	16.92	43.34
2004	5.10	-0.36	-2.71	16.85	19.05
2005	-0.32	1.14	11.43	5.53	18.55
2006	9.76	-1.61	3.42	11.22	24.22

Trailing	Total Return%	+/- MSCI EAFE	+/- MSCI Wd xUS	%Rank Cat	Growth of $10,000
3 Mo	11.22	0.87	1.10	22	11,122
6 Mo	15.03	0.34	0.81	32	11,503
1 Yr	24.22	-2.12	-1.49	59	12,422
3 Yr Avg	20.58	0.65	0.48	17	17,532
5 Yr Avg	17.77	2.79	2.52	4	22,655
10 Yr Avg	11.28	3.57	3.32	6	29,119
15 Yr Avg	10.82	2.96	2.78	13	46,695

Tax Analysis	Tax-Adj Rtn%	%Rank Cat	Tax-Cost Rat	%Rank Cat
3 Yr (estimated)	19.61	15	0.80	43
5 Yr (estimated)	17.10	4	0.57	45
10 Yr (estimated)	10.16	4	1.01	48

Potential Capital Gain Exposure: 24% of assets

Morningstar's Take by Dan Lefkovitz 12-18-06

Don't worry about Fidelity International Discovery's subpar 2006.

Most investors are probably quite satisfied with this fund's 2006 campaign. But those fixated on relative rankings might notice that its 23% gain for the year to date through Dec. 15, 2006, lags both its benchmark, the MSCI EAFE Index, and its foreign large-blend category peers. The fund got tripped up in May and June, when market sentiment turned against risky asset classes like smaller caps and emerging markets. Manager Bill Kennedy had been gradually trimming those stakes. But the fund's remaining European and Japanese smaller caps, as well as stocks in Turkey and South Africa, got hit hard. Though the fund has since recovered, it has not been able to make up lost ground.

Given the 2006 showing, some may be asking whether to buy this fund over its cheaper, index-tracking sibling Fidelity Spartan International Index. We think this fund's case is strong. Kennedy has put up good numbers since taking over the

portfolio in October 2004. His longer track record, on Fidelity Pacific Basin, earned that fund Analyst Pick status. Kennedy is a conservative stock-picker who looks for a combination of growth and value. He has lately gravitated toward developed-market large caps (2006 purchases include UBS and Telefonica) because he thinks they are trading cheaply. And though he is willing to play "themes," such as alternative energy development or rising demand for luxury goods, he is quick to take profits when he thinks prices are rich.

Kennedy maintains a sprawling portfolio, but his willingness to source ideas broadly causes the fund to behave differently than the index. It also gives investors exposure to stocks and countries that many mainstream foreign funds don't offer. In short, this remains a solid core foreign fund and a good alternative to its closed (and swelling) sibling Fidelity Diversified International.

Address:	82 Devonshire St	Minimum Purchase:	$2500	Add: $250	IRA: $200
	Boston MA 02109	Min Auto Inv Plan:	$100	Add: $100	
	800-544-9797	Sales Fees:	No-load, 1.00%R		
Web Address:	www.fidelity.com	Management Fee:	0.79%		
Inception:	12-31-86	Actual Fees:	Mgt:0.79%	Dist: —	
Advisor:	Fidelity Management & Research (FMR)	Expense Projections:	3Yr:$347	5Yr:$601	10Yr:$1329
Subadvisor:	Multiple Subadvisors	Income Distrib:	Annually		
NTF Plans:	Fidelity Retail-NTF, CommonWealth NTF				

Historical Profile

Return	High
Risk	Above Avg
Rating	★★★★ Highest

Investment Style: Equity, Stock %

88% / 90% / 92% / 86% / 87% / 93% / 95% / 96% / 94%

▼ Manager Change
▽ Partial Manager Change

Growth of $10,000
— Investment Values of Fund
— Investment Values of MSCI EAFE

Performance Quartile (within Category)

1995	1996	1997	1998	1999	2000	2001	2002	2003	2004	2005	2006	History
17.95	19.55	19.70	20.91	30.10	22.72	18.76	16.82	23.92	28.20	31.66	37.92	NAV
12.23	12.69	7.12	9.98	53.71	-14.06	-17.43	-9.87	43.34	19.05	18.55	24.22	Total Return %
1.02	6.64	5.34	-9.95	26.68	0.13	3.99	6.07	4.75	-1.20	5.01	-2.12	+/-MSCI EAFE
0.82	5.82	4.85	-8.71	25.73	-0.70	3.96	5.93	3.92	-1.33	4.08	-1.49	+/-MSCI Wd xUS
3.63	1.62	1.89	0.46	1.58	1.69	0.00	0.48	1.07	0.63	1.08	1.19	Income Return %
8.60	11.07	5.23	9.52	52.13	-15.75	-17.43	-10.35	42.27	18.42	17.47	23.03	Capital Return %
39	45	47	73	14	34	12	5	4	28	14	59	Total Rtn % Rank Cat
0.60	0.29	0.37	0.09	0.33	0.51	0.00	0.09	0.18	0.15	0.31	0.38	Income $
0.00	0.37	0.88	0.63	1.50	2.66	0.00	0.00	0.00	0.12	1.40	0.98	Capital Gains $
1.21	1.18	1.14	1.15	1.13	1.10	1.05	1.09	1.12	1.11	1.06	—	Expense Ratio %
2.16	2.98	2.76	2.33	1.62	0.69	0.63	0.91	0.59	1.08	0.92	—	Income Ratio %
						104	81	63	81	87	—	Turnover Rate %
1,273	942	1,080	1,030	871	1,395	1,183	941	907	1,498	2,504	8,974	Net Assets $mil

Rating and Risk

Time Period	Load-Adj Return %	Morningstar Rtn vs Cat	Morningstar Risk vs Cat	Morningstar Risk-Adj Rating
1 Yr	24.22			
3 Yr	20.58	+Avg	+Avg	★★★★
5 Yr	17.77	High	Avg	★★★★★
10 Yr	11.28	High	+Avg	★★★★★
Incept	10.24			

Other Measures	Standard Index MSCI EAFE	Best Fit Index MSCI EAFE
Alpha	-1.6	-1.6
Beta	1.15	1.15
R-Squared	96	96
Standard Deviation	11.14	
Mean	20.58	
Sharpe Ratio	1.46	

Portfolio Analysis 10-31-06

Share change since 07-06 Total Stocks:301

	Sector	Country	% Assets
⊕ Roche Holding	Health	Switzerland	1.53
⊕ UBS AG	Financial	Switzerland	1.39
Novartis	Health	Switzerland	1.37
Nikkei 225 (Fut)	—	—	1.36
⊖ BP PLC ADR	Energy	U.K.	1.29
⊕ Toyota Motor	Goods	Japan	1.29
Total SA	Energy	France	1.24
E.ON	Utilities	Germany	1.14
⊕ Nestle	Goods	Switzerland	1.09
⊕ Allianz	Financial	Germany	1.09
⊕ Mizuho Financial Grp	Financial	Japan	1.04
HSBC Hldgs	Financial	U.K.	1.04
⊕ UniCredito Italiano Grp	Financial	Italy	1.00
BBVA	Financial	Spain	0.98
Royal Dutch Shell	Energy	U.K.	0.87
⊕ BNP Paribas	Financial	France	0.86
Tesco	Consumer	U.K.	0.86
⊕ Canon	Goods	Japan	0.80
⊕ ORIX	Financial	Japan	0.79
Nintendo	Goods	Japan	0.79

Current Investment Style

Value Blnd Growth — Large / Mid / Small

Market Cap	%
Giant	50.4
Large	31.4
Mid	15.2
Small	3.0
Micro	0.0

Avg $mil: 25,637

Value Measures		Rel Category
Price/Earnings	15.97	1.22
Price/Book	2.51	1.16
Price/Sales	1.29	1.11
Price/Cash Flow	8.92	1.07
Dividend Yield %	2.58	0.88

Growth Measures	%	Rel Category
Long-Term Erngs	12.85	1.09
Book Value	9.81	1.07
Sales	7.27	1.11
Cash Flow	10.76	1.30
Historical Erngs	20.94	1.03

Composition

	%		%
Cash	4.0	Bonds	0.0
Stocks	93.8	Other	2.1
Foreign (% of Stock)			99.1

Sector Weightings

	% of Stocks	Rel MSCI EAFE	3 Year High	Low
⊙ Info	9.82	0.83		
🖥 Software	1.12	2.00	2	1
💻 Hardware	2.63	0.68	9	3
🎙 Media	2.50	1.37	6	2
📶 Telecom	3.57	0.64	11	3
⊜ Service	49.19	1.04		
🏥 Health	8.35	1.17	10	7
🛒 Consumer	7.46	1.51	8	6
📋 Business	4.73	0.93	7	4
💲 Financial	28.65	0.95	29	22
🏭 Mfg	41.00	1.00		
🛢 Goods	17.75	1.35	18	11
⚙ Ind Mtrls	11.53	0.75	16	6
🔋 Energy	6.53	0.91	10	7
💡 Utilities	5.19	0.99	5	2

Regional Exposure % Stock

UK/W. Europe	67	N. America	1
Japan	18	Latn America	1
Asia X Japan	12	Other	1

Country Exposure % Stock

Japan	18	Germany	10
U.K.	18	Switzerland	10
France	13		

Morningstar® Funds 500

Fidelity Invt Grade Bond

Ticker FBNDX	**Load** None	**NAV** $7.37	**Yield** 4.5%	**SEC Yield** 4.99%	**Total Assets** $10,981 mil	**Mstar Category** Intermediate-Term Bond

Historical Profile

Return Above Avg
Risk Average
Rating ★★★★ Above Avg

	47	42	35	51	73	78	65	49

Investment Style
Fixed Income
Income Rtn %Rank Cat

▼ Manager Change
▽ Partial Manager Change

Growth of $10,000
— Investment Values of Fund
— Investment Values of LB Aggr

20.5
17.5
15.0
12.5
10.0

Performance Quartile (within Category)

1995	1996	1997	1998	1999	2000	2001	2002	2003	2004	2005	2006	History
7.38	7.12	7.28	7.39	6.89	7.16	7.34	7.57	7.55	7.53	7.37	7.37	NAV
15.51	3.02	8.91	7.94	-1.01	10.84	8.54	9.37	4.67	4.53	2.73	4.82	Total Return %
-2.96	-0.61	-0.74	-0.75	-0.19	-0.79	0.10	-0.88	0.57	0.19	0.30	0.49	+/-LB Aggr
-5.92	0.33	-0.52	-2.20	1.87	-1.60	-0.28	-3.66	-1.30	-0.77	0.90	1.01	+/-LB 5-10YR
7.08	6.53	6.53	5.97	5.92	6.72	5.86	4.43	3.23	3.43	3.97	4.66	Income Return %
8.43	-3.51	2.38	1.97	-6.93	4.12	2.68	4.94	1.44	1.10	-1.24	0.16	Capital Return %
82	61	57	36	41	32	20	27	45	30	7	17	Total Rtn % Rank Cat
0.47	0.47	0.45	0.42	0.43	0.45	0.41	0.32	0.24	0.25	0.29	0.34	Income $
0.03	0.00	0.00	0.03	0.00	0.00	0.01	0.12	0.13	0.10	0.07	0.01	Capital Gains $
0.74	0.75	0.76	0.75	0.71	0.70	0.69	0.64	0.66	0.66	0.63	0.45	Expense Ratio %
6.94	7.00	6.58	6.53	6.12	5.77	6.21	6.31	5.18	3.86	3.16	5.12	Income Ratio %
—	—	—	—	—	—	—	226	230	276	238	69	Turnover Rate %
995	1,246	1,455	1,650	2,191	2,079	2,497	3,702	4,767	5,523	6,283	10,804	Net Assets $mil

Performance 12-31-06

	1st Qtr	2nd Qtr	3rd Qtr	4th Qtr	Total
2002	-0.20	2.83	4.07	2.41	9.37
2003	1.74	2.58	0.01	0.28	4.67
2004	2.59	-2.36	3.25	1.07	4.53
2005	-0.35	2.75	-0.36	0.70	2.73
2006	-0.39	-0.07	3.96	1.30	4.82

Trailing	Total Return%	+/- LB Aggr	+/- LB 5-10YR	%Rank Cat	Growth of $10,000
3 Mo	1.30	0.06	0.22	37	10,130
6 Mo	5.31	0.22	-0.37	20	10,531
1 Yr	4.82	0.49	1.01	17	10,482
3 Yr Avg	4.03	0.33	0.39	15	11,258
5 Yr Avg	5.20	0.14	-0.72	20	12,885
10 Yr Avg	6.08	-0.16	-0.60	21	18,044
15 Yr Avg	6.46	-0.04	-0.53	31	25,574

Tax Analysis	Tax-Adj Rtn%	%Rank Cat	Tax-Cost Rat	%Rank Cat
3 Yr (estimated)	2.58	9	1.39	44
5 Yr (estimated)	3.75	9	1.38	32
10 Yr (estimated)	4.10	8	1.87	34

Potential Capital Gain Exposure: -1% of assets

Rating and Risk

Time Period	Load-Adj Return %	Morningstar Rtn vs Cat	Morningstar Risk vs Cat	Morningstar Risk-Adj Rating
1 Yr	4.82			
3 Yr	4.03	+Avg	Avg	★★★★
5 Yr	5.20	+Avg	Avg	★★★★
10 Yr	6.08	+Avg	-Avg	★★★★
Incept	7.75			

Other Measures	Standard Index LB Aggr	Best Fit Index LB. U.S. Univ. Bd
Alpha	0.3	-0.1
Beta	0.94	0.95
R-Squared	99	99
Standard Deviation	3.07	
Mean	4.03	
Sharpe Ratio	0.25	

Morningstar's Take by Scott Berry 11-28-06

Fidelity Investment Grade Bond faces stiff competition from siblings and peers, but we think it's up to the challenge.

For starters, we think this fund's approach makes its success more repeatable than that of many peers. By focusing on areas where Fidelity's research and resources provide an advantage, such as issue selection and sector allocation, and avoiding areas where Fidelity has no edge, such as broad interest-rate bets, manager Jeff Moore plays to the firm's strengths. His approach keeps the fund's returns from deviating wildly from those of the benchmark Lehman Brothers Aggregate Bond Index, but also allows the fund plenty of opportunity to outperform the index.

And that's just what the fund has done in recent years. The fund's returns have been modest on an absolute basis, but it has outperformed the index in each of the past three calendar years and is on pace to make it four. The fund's returns have also compared favorably with those of its average intermediate-bond category peer, besting more than 80% of its category peers over the trailing three- and five-year periods ending Nov. 26, 2006. In recent months, good issue selection in the corporate sector has paid off, as has exposure to hybrid adjustable-rate mortgages, which will join the Lehman Aggregate index in April 2007. The fund has also held a small slug of junk bonds, which continue to benefit from a stable economy.

The fund's expense ratio has also played a role in its success. Fidelity has effectively capped costs at 0.45%, well below the 0.73% charged by the fund's median no-load category peer. That advantage allows more yield and return to flow to shareholders without Moore having to take on added risk.

Fidelity U.S. Bond Index and Fidelity Total Bond offer good alternatives for those looking to take on a little less or a little more risk, but we think Fidelity's oldest, and largest, bond fund still makes a strong case for itself.

Portfolio Analysis 08-31-06

Total Fixed-Income:1549	Date of Maturity	Amount $000	Value $000	% Net Assets
FNMA 5.5%	08-01-33	852,335	837,732	6.13
FNMA 0.05%	12-01-35	603,668	578,485	4.23
US Treasury Note 2%	01-15-14	500,743	539,950	3.95
FNMA 0.06%	11-01-31	330,879	336,708	2.46
Lbsp Swap Irs 12/8/08 3m	12-08-08	315,000	312,915	2.29
Jpsw Swap Irs 8/10/09 3m	08-10-09	302,645	303,846	2.22
Citi Swap Irs 3/06/09 3m	03-06-09	280,030	283,258	2.07
FNMA 4.5%	03-01-18	282,734	272,338	1.99
US Treasury Note 4.75%	05-15-14	199,025	199,243	1.46
U S Treas Bd Stripped Pr	02-15-15	289,357	194,395	1.42
U S Treas Nt Stripped Pr	02-15-12	241,630	187,935	1.38
Lbsp Swap Irs 8/01/10 3m	08-01-10	140,000	136,639	1.00
GNMA 0.06%	07-15-35	131,091	134,233	0.98
FNMA 6.25%	02-01-11	115,475	120,226	0.88
United Mexican Sts Mtn B	05-20-11	96,235	97,162	0.71
Lbsp Cdx Na Ig	06-20-11	96,800	96,950	0.71
FHLMC 5.875%	03-21-11	90,065	92,443	0.68
U S Treas Nt Stripped Pr	02-15-10	100,000	85,140	0.62
US Treasury Bond 8%	11-15-21	61,152	80,964	0.59
Lbsp Cdx Na Ig 5%	12-20-07	74,500	74,634	0.55

Current Investment Style

Duration
Short Int Long

(style box — Int/Med) Quality High Med Low

1 figure provided by fund

Avg Eff Duration[1]	4.1 Yrs
Avg Eff Maturity	6.0 Yrs
Avg Credit Quality	AA
Avg Wtd Coupon	3.40%
Avg Wtd Price	98.45% of par

Coupon Range	% of Bonds	Rel Cat
0% PIK	21.1	3.0
0% to 6%	86.3	1.2
6% to 8%	13.1	0.6
8% to 10%	0.7	0.1
More than 10%	0.0	0.0

1.00=Category Average

Credit Analysis		% bonds 08-31-06	
AAA	62	BB	3
AA	6	B	1
A	8	Below B	0
BBB	21	NR/NA	0

Sector Breakdown % of assets

US Treasuries	2
TIPS	4
US Agency	7
Mortgage Pass-Throughs	25
Mortgage CMO	16
Mortgage ARM	0
US Corporate	24
Asset-Backed	9
Convertible	0
Municipal	0
Corporate Inflation-Protected	0
Foreign Corporate	2
Foreign Govt	0

Composition

Cash	8.7	Bonds	91.3
Stocks	0.0	Other	0.1

Special Securities

Restricted/Illiquid Secs	4
Exotic Mortgage-Backed	0
Emerging-Markets Secs	Trace
Options/Futures/Warrants	No

Fidelity Leverage Co Stk

	Ticker	Load	NAV	Yield	Total Assets	Mstar Category
	FLVCX	None	$28.97	0.4%	$4,909 mil	Mid-Cap Blend

Governance and Management

Stewardship Grade: B

Portfolio Manager(s)

Fidelity veteran Tom Soviero took charge of this fund in July 2003. He is backed by an experienced team of Fidelity analysts and looks to leverage Fidelity's high-yield and equity research. He has had successful stints at Fidelity High Income and Fidelity Advisor High Income Advantage, which he continues to manage. Soviero was also recently named the manager of Fidelity Convertible Securities.

Strategy

Manager Tom Soviero's strategy revolves around buying what he considers attractively valued stocks that issue high-yield debt or otherwise have leveraged capital structures. However, junk-bond issuers run the risk of not being able to pay back or refinance their debt. In those cases, stock investors can be left with little or nothing. Soviero looks for companies that have a catalyst for improvement, such as a management change, a new product, or a pricing change, and keeps the fund fairly concentrated in his favorite names.

Performance 12-31-06

	1st Qtr	2nd Qtr	3rd Qtr	4th Qtr	Total
2002	-1.96	-18.54	-3.44	27.39	-1.77
2003	4.40	44.06	6.63	22.41	96.31
2004	5.48	2.50	-0.57	15.76	24.46
2005	4.67	1.73	8.31	1.86	17.47
2006	9.68	-0.35	-0.73	8.36	17.57

Trailing	Total Return%	+/- S&P 500	+/- S&P Mid 400	%Rank Cat	Growth of $10,000
3 Mo	8.36	1.66	1.37	32	10,836
6 Mo	7.57	-5.17	1.74	61	10,757
1 Yr	17.57	1.78	7.25	19	11,757
3 Yr Avg	19.79	9.35	6.70	1	17,189
5 Yr Avg	27.08	20.89	16.19	1	33,143
10 Yr Avg	—	—	—	—	—
15 Yr Avg	—	—	—	—	—

Tax Analysis	Tax-Adj Rtn%	%Rank Cat	Tax-Cost Rat	%Rank Cat
3 Yr (estimated)	18.63	3	0.97	41
5 Yr (estimated)	26.21	1	0.68	42
10 Yr (estimated)	—	—	—	—

Potential Capital Gain Exposure: 26% of assets

Historical Profile

Return	High
Risk	High
Rating	★★★★ Highest

Investment Style: Equity Stock %

77% 89% 82% 95% 98% 96%

▼ Manager Change
▽ Partial Manager Change

32.0
27.0
20.0 **Growth of $10,000**
15.0 — Investment Values of Fund
10.0 — Investment Values of S&P 500
6.0

Performance Quartile (within Category)

1995	1996	1997	1998	1999	2000	2001	2002	2003	2004	2005	2006	History
—	—	—	—	—	10.07	10.18	10.00	19.33	22.68	26.02	28.97	NAV
—	—	—	—	—	0.70*	3.23	-1.77	96.31	24.46	17.47	17.57	Total Return %
—	—	—	—	—	—	15.12	20.33	67.63	13.58	12.56	1.78	+/-S&P 500
—	—	—	—	—	—	3.84	12.76	60.69	7.98	4.91	7.25	+/-S&P Mid 400
—	—	—	—	—	—	2.00	0.00	0.00	0.21	0.93	0.47	Income Return %
—	—	—	—	—	—	1.23	-1.77	96.31	24.25	16.54	17.10	Capital Return %
—	—	—	—	—	—	40	3	1	6	5	19	Total Rtn % Rank Cat
—	—	—	—	—	0.00	0.20	0.00	0.00	0.04	0.21	0.12	Income $
—	—	—	—	—	0.00	0.00	0.00	0.27	1.12	0.41	1.40	Capital Gains $
—	—	—	—	—	—	—	0.83	0.93	0.83	0.85	0.85	Expense Ratio %
—	—	—	—	—	—	—	1.12	1.16	0.07	0.23	0.60	Income Ratio %
—	—	—	—	—	—	—	230	203	79	35	23	Turnover Rate %
—	—	—	—	—	—	60	79	1,206	2,142	4,909		Net Assets $mil

Rating and Risk

Time Period	Load-Adj Return %	Morningstar Rtn vs Cat	Morningstar Risk vs Cat	Morningstar Risk-Adj Rating
1 Yr	17.57			
3 Yr	19.79	High	+Avg	★★★★
5 Yr	27.08	High	High	★★★★
10 Yr	—	—	—	
Incept	22.77			

Other Measures	Standard Index S&P 500	Best Fit Index Mstar Small Core
Alpha	5.5	3.9
Beta	1.49	0.90
R-Squared	57	78
Standard Deviation	13.53	
Mean	19.79	
Sharpe Ratio	1.17	

Portfolio Analysis 10-31-06

Share change since 07-06 Total Stocks:160	Sector	PE	Tot Ret%	% Assets
⊕ Service Corporation Inte	Consumer	39.8	26.82	3.14
⊕ Teekay Shipping Corporat	Business	6.3	11.72	2.95
⊖ AES Corporation	Utilities	33.4	39.23	2.70
⊕ Forest Oil Corporation	Energy	16.1	7.07	2.65
General Maritime Corpora	Business	5.0	8.76	2.60
⊕ Atmel Corporation	Hardware	—	95.79	2.54
OMI Corporation	Business	4.2	19.34	2.50
ON Semiconductor Corpora	Hardware	18.7	36.89	2.44
⊕ Chesapeake Energy Corp.	Energy	6.1	-7.14	2.13
Qwest Communications Int	Telecom	—	48.14	2.08
Range Resources Corporat	Energy	16.8	4.62	2.08
⊕ Universal Compression Ho	Energy	—	51.05	2.03
Amkor Technology, Inc.	Hardware	11.4	66.79	1.91
⊕ Flextronics Internationa	Hardware	45.1	9.96	1.89
Celanese Corporation	Ind Mtrls	—	36.48	1.87
Davita, Inc.	Health	21.1	12.32	1.76
CMS Energy Corporation	Utilities	—	15.09	1.49
⊕ Overseas Shipholding Gro	Business	5.5	13.55	1.45
El Paso Corporation	Energy	—	27.07	1.37
⊕ Cenveo, Inc.	Business	21.6	61.09	1.36

Current Investment Style

Value Blnd Growth — Large Mid Small

Market Cap	%
Giant	2.0
Large	20.6
Mid	50.7
Small	24.1
Micro	2.5

Avg $mil: 3,788

Value Measures		Rel Category
Price/Earnings	13.37	0.83
Price/Book	2.03	0.90
Price/Sales	0.85	0.76
Price/Cash Flow	5.61	0.66
Dividend Yield %	1.11	0.85

Growth Measures	%	Rel Category
Long-Term Erngs	13.57	1.07
Book Value	-0.77	NMF
Sales	4.06	0.46
Cash Flow	4.08	0.48
Historical Erngs	25.44	1.42

Profitability	%	Rel Category
Return on Equity	17.53	1.10
Return on Assets	5.85	0.73
Net Margin	10.19	0.94

Sector Weightings

	% of Stocks	Rel S&P 500	3 Year High Low
⌁ Info	24.67	1.23	
▣ Software	1.79	0.52	2 0
▣ Hardware	17.85	1.93	18 3
▣ Media	1.84	0.49	6 1
▣ Telecom	3.19	0.91	17 3
⌘ Service	29.83	0.65	
▨ Health	3.37	0.28	5 3
▨ Consumer	6.88	0.90	9 3
▤ Business	18.54	4.38	24 16
⑂ Financial	1.04	0.05	6 1
▦ Mfg	45.51	1.35	
▨ Goods	3.72	0.44	4 2
▨ Ind Mtrls	11.26	0.94	17 11
▨ Energy	25.01	2.55	27 13
▨ Utilities	5.52	1.58	11 6

Composition

- Cash 2.5
- Stocks 96.3
- Bonds 0.8
- Other 0.5

Foreign 11.9 (% of Stock)

Morningstar's Take by Scott Berry 11-30-06

We like Fidelity Leveraged Company Stock, but think risk-averse investors will be happier elsewhere.

The ups and downs of companies that employ leverage are often magnified. When a company struggles, looming debt payments and bankruptcy fears can punish the stock price, as stockholders are typically left with little or nothing when a company emerges from bankruptcy. On the other hand, leverage allows stockholders to earn big gains when a company is performing well and making good strategic acquisitions.

Two of the fund's stock holdings provide good evidence of such ups and downs. Amkor Technology soared from $5 per share to $13 per share early in 2006, but disappointing earnings and a failure to file a quarterly report on time sent the stock back to $5. It has since rebounded to $10 thanks to good third-quarter earnings. Similarly, Station Casinos saw its stock jump from the high $60s to the low $80s following a strong first quarter, but a

second-quarter slump pushed the stock back to the mid-50s. It has since rebounded to its early-year levels.

A look at the fund's calendar-year returns shows little of that downside risk, but that's because the fund has recovered quickly from the steep losses it has experienced and because of the quirks of the calendar. For example, the fund dropped 25% in one three-month stretch in 2002, before rebounding 27% in that year's fourth quarter. It also lost nearly 30% over a 12-month period from 2001 to 2002.

This fund clearly carries significant risks, but we believe it still has the right manager for the job and the proper support system backing him up. Tom Soviero managed high-yield bond funds before taking over here in mid-2003, so he know the ins and outs of leveraged companies. And he's backed by a deep and talented analyst group, which has helped Fidelity's stable of high-yield funds deliver strong long-term results.

Address:	82 Devonshire St Boston MA 02109 800-544-9797	Minimum Purchase:	$10000 Add: $1000 IRA: $2500
		Min Auto Inv Plan:	$10000 Add: $500
Web Address:	www.fidelity.com	Sales Fees:	No-load, 1.50%R
Inception:	12-19-00*	Management Fee:	0.63%
Advisor:	Fidelity Management & Research (FMR)	Actual Fees:	Mgt:0.62% Dist: —
Subadvisor:	Multiple Subadvisors	Expense Projections:	3Yr:$274 5Yr:$477 10Yr:$1061
		Income Distrib:	Semi-Annually
NTF Plans:	Fidelity Retail-NTF, CommonWealth NTF		

MORNINGSTAR® Funds 500

Fidelity Low-Priced Stk

	Ticker	Load	NAV	Yield	Total Assets	Mstar Category
	FLPSX	Closed	$43.54	0.7%	$39,340 mil	Mid-Cap Blend

Governance and Management

Stewardship Grade: B

Portfolio Manager(s)

Joel Tillinghast has managed this fund since its inception. Not only is he one of the most experienced managers around, he is also one of the best. Tillinghast receives research support from a team of small-cap analysts and from Fidelity's industry analysts, but he does much of the research on his own.

Strategy

This fund focuses on companies with share prices of $35 or less, but that is a marketing gimmick. Manager Joel Tillinghast buys mostly smaller-cap fare with reasonable valuations and solid growth prospects. He spreads the portfolio across many hundreds of holdings. Tillinghast is also willing to devote a substantial chunk of the portfolio to foreign issues and larger-cap stocks and will let cash build if he can't find enough good investment opportunities. The fund closed to new investors on Dec. 31, 2003. It does not hedge foreign-currency exposure.

Historical Profile

Return	High
Risk	Below Avg
Rating	★★★★ Highest

Investment Style: Equity, Stock %

| 89% | 98% | 94% | 80% | 85% | 91% | 86% | 86% | 90% |

▼ Manager Change
▽ Partial Manager Change

Growth of $10,000
— Investment Values of Fund
— Investment Values of S&P 500

Performance Quartile (within Category)

1995	1996	1997	1998	1999	2000	2001	2002	2003	2004	2005	2006	History
18.50	21.35	25.13	22.85	22.64	23.12	27.42	25.17	34.98	40.25	40.84	43.54	NAV
24.89	26.89	26.73	0.53	5.08	18.83	26.71	-6.18	40.85	22.24	8.65	17.76	Total Return %
-12.69	3.93	-6.63	-28.05	-15.96	27.93	38.60	15.92	12.17	11.36	3.74	1.97	+/-S&P 500
-6.04	7.64	-5.52	-18.59	-9.64	1.32	27.32	8.35	5.23	5.76	-3.91	7.44	+/-S&P Mid 400
1.46	1.33	1.34	0.81	0.67	0.75	0.70	0.11	0.08	0.35	0.66	0.84	Income Return %
23.43	25.56	25.39	-0.28	4.41	18.08	26.01	-6.29	40.77	21.89	7.99	16.92	Capital Return %
66	14	54	85	83	20	2	9	25	10	56	18	Total Rtn % Rank Cat
0.23	0.24	0.28	0.20	0.15	0.16	0.16	0.03	0.02	0.12	0.26	0.33	Income $
1.24	1.66	1.58	1.94	1.19	3.43	1.54	0.54	0.44	2.09	2.62	3.78	Capital Gains $
1.11	1.04	1.01	0.95	1.08	0.80	1.00	0.97	1.01	0.97	0.94	0.87	Expense Ratio %
1.31	1.46	1.36	1.10	0.52	0.58	0.92	0.34	0.05	0.15	0.57	0.72	Income Ratio %
65	79	45	47	24	15	44	26	23	28	24	26	Turnover Rate %
3,350	5,664	10,691	9,195	6,646	6,834	12,429	15,104	26,725	35,976	36,721	39,340	Net Assets $mil

Performance 12-31-06

	1st Qtr	2nd Qtr	3rd Qtr	4th Qtr	Total
2002	6.97	-0.27	-16.98	5.93	-6.18
2003	-6.04	21.31	8.50	13.88	40.85
2004	5.86	1.24	0.20	13.83	22.24
2005	-0.97	3.11	4.49	1.83	8.65
2006	8.62	-3.27	2.09	9.78	17.76

Trailing	Total Return%	+/- S&P 500	+/- S&P Mid 400	%Rank Cat	Growth of $10,000
3 Mo	9.78	3.08	2.79	12	10,978
6 Mo	12.08	-0.66	6.25	18	11,208
1 Yr	17.76	1.97	7.44	18	11,776
3 Yr Avg	16.08	5.64	2.99	15	15,641
5 Yr Avg	15.63	9.44	4.74	5	20,671
10 Yr Avg	15.34	6.92	1.87	4	41,668
15 Yr Avg	17.14	6.50	3.51	1	107,295

Tax Analysis	Tax-Adj Rtn%	%Rank Cat	Tax-Cost Rat	%Rank Cat
3 Yr (estimated)	14.54	15	1.33	58
5 Yr (estimated)	14.52	6	0.96	60
10 Yr (estimated)	13.53	3	1.57	43

Potential Capital Gain Exposure: 36% of assets

Rating and Risk

Time Period	Load-Adj Return %	Morningstar Rtn vs Cat	Morningstar Risk vs Cat	Morningstar Risk-Adj Rating
1 Yr	17.76			
3 Yr	16.08	+Avg	Avg	★★★★
5 Yr	15.63	High	Avg	★★★★★
10 Yr	15.34	High	Low	★★★★★
Incept	17.49			

Other Measures	Standard Index S&P 500	Best Fit Index Mstar Small Core
Alpha	2.9	2.3
Beta	1.35	0.76
R-Squared	77	89
Standard Deviation	10.59	
Mean	16.08	
Sharpe Ratio	1.16	

Portfolio Analysis 10-31-06

Share change since 07-06 Total Stocks:836	Sector	PE	Tot Ret%	% Assets
Petroleo Brasileiro S.A.	Energy	10.4	51.12	2.37
⊖ Safeway Inc.	Consumer	20.4	47.22	1.96
⊕ D.R. Horton Incorporated	Consumer	6.5	-24.41	1.96
⊖ Next	Financial	—	—	1.37
Barratt Developments	Business	—	—	1.32
Health Management Associ	Health	19.8	-2.74	1.30
⊖ Oracle Corporation	Software	26.7	40.38	1.23
⊕ Dollar General Corporati	Consumer	17.3	-14.94	1.17
⊕ Hon Hai Precision Indust	Hardware	—	—	1.08
⊕ Bed Bath & Beyond, Inc.	Consumer	20.1	5.39	1.05
⊖ Constellation Brands, In	Goods	18.4	10.64	1.03
PMI Group, Inc.	Financial	10.5	15.39	1.02
⊕ Unumprovident Corporatio	Financial	24.6	-7.25	1.01
⊖ Chesapeake Energy Corp.	Energy	6.1	-7.74	0.91
USG Corporation	Ind Mtrls	—	-15.69	0.86
⊕ Lincare Holdings Inc.	Health	19.3	-4.94	0.86
⊕ Maxim Integrated Product	Hardware	23.1	-14.06	0.84
Pfizer Inc.	Health	15.2	15.22	0.82
⊕ ConocoPhillips	Energy	6.5	26.53	0.80
Metro Inc A	Consumer	—	—	0.80

Current Investment Style

Value Blnd Growth / Large Mid Small

Market Cap	%
Giant	10.6
Large	9.9
Mid	44.8
Small	26.8
Micro	7.9

Avg $mil: 3,332

Value Measures		Rel Category
Price/Earnings	13.12	0.81
Price/Book	1.91	0.85
Price/Sales	0.76	0.68
Price/Cash Flow	6.64	0.79
Dividend Yield %	1.23	0.95

Growth Measures	%	Rel Category
Long-Term Erngs	12.91	1.02
Book Value	11.28	1.36
Sales	11.86	1.33
Cash Flow	9.95	1.17
Historical Erngs	15.99	0.89

Profitability	%	Rel Category
Return on Equity	18.72	1.17
Return on Assets	8.99	1.12
Net Margin	10.66	0.98

Sector Weightings	% of Stocks	Rel S&P 500	3 Year High Low
↻ Info	10.47	0.52	
Software	2.65	0.77	3 1
Hardware	6.54	0.71	7 5
Media	0.77	0.20	2 1
Telecom	0.51	0.15	1 1
⊑ Service	55.30	1.20	
Health	10.37	0.86	14 9
Consumer	20.88	2.73	22 18
Business	9.30	2.20	12 8
Financial	14.75	0.66	19 15
⊔ Mfg	34.22	1.01	
Goods	8.52	1.00	11 8
Ind Mtrls	15.30	1.28	18 15
Energy	10.10	1.03	11 3
Utilities	0.30	0.09	1 0

Composition

	%
● Cash	9.4
● Stocks	90.5
● Bonds	0.0
○ Other	0.1
Foreign	29.3
(% of Stock)	

Morningstar's Take by Dan Lefkovitz 11-21-06

Fidelity Low-Priced Stock continues to defy the odds.

Were this closed fund managed by someone other than Joel Tillinghast, we would have advised investors to sell many years ago. After all, a huge asset base is the enemy of a smaller-cap-focused fund. Tillinghast has more money to put to work ($37 billion) than any other small- or mid-cap manager--more actually than several of his next-largest peers combined. That load prevents him from buying meaningful stakes in illiquid stocks and from getting in and out of many positions in a timely manner.

And yet, Tillinghast has defied the odds. We recently named him one of the greatest stock-fund managers around for his 16-year record here. The fund's returns trounce those of its benchmark (the Russell 2000), its old peer group (the small-blend category), and its new one (mid-blend). Tillinghast has also limited risk. That's thanks to broad diversification, an omnipresent cash stake, and his emphasis on financially solid companies that are trading cheaply.

Some of these features also help Tillinghast cope with the fund's size. He continues to spread assets across hundreds of holdings and trades infrequently. His hunting ground is also larger than most. For years now, Tillinghast has been devoting a hefty chunk of assets (now 29%) to foreign stocks, a big tailwind in recent years. He has also gravitated to larger-cap stocks (thus the category move). Whether that's for liquidity reasons or simply where Tillinghast is finding the best opportunities, the move will serve the fund well if market leadership rotates from small to large. Several recent winners, including Oracle and Pfizer, are larger names.

For an investor starting from scratch, looking to fill a portfolio's smaller-cap slot, a nimbler option might be in order. But shareholders here would do well to keep letting this talented manager work his magic for them.

Address:	82 Devonshire Street Boston MA 02109 800-544-6666	Minimum Purchase:	Closed	Add: —	IRA: —
		Min Auto Inv Plan:	Closed	Add: —	
		Sales Fees:	No-load, 1.50%R		
Web Address:	www.fidelity.com	Management Fee:	0.67%		
Inception:	12-27-89	Actual Fees:	Mgt:0.67%	Dist: —	
Advisor:	Fidelity Management & Research (FMR)	Expense Projections:	3Yr:$281	5Yr:$488	10Yr:$1084
Subadvisor:	Multiple Subadvisors	Income Distrib:	Semi-Annually		
NTF Plans:	Fidelity Retail-NTF, CommonWealth NTF				

Fidelity Magellan

	Ticker	Load	NAV	Yield	Total Assets	Mstar Category
	FMAGX	Closed	$89.52	0.4%	$44,962 mil	Large Growth

Governance and Management

Stewardship Grade: B

Portfolio Manager(s)

Prior to taking over this fund on Oct. 31, 2005, Harry Lange ran Fidelity Capital Appreciation for nearly 10 years and Fidelity Advisor Small Cap for nearly seven years. Lange joined Fidelity as an analyst in 1987, served as a research director in Japan, and managed the firm's technology offerings before moving on to run diversified funds. As manager of one of Fidelity's flagships, Lange is backed by scores of the firm's analysts. He also collaborates with other growth-oriented Fidelity managers, such as Will Danoff and Fergus Shiel.

Strategy

Harry Lange favors fast-growing companies that are benefiting from larger trends. He is valuation-conscious, however, and typically likes to lighten his positions in companies that are trading richly and buy in when they're slumping. Lange invests heavily in traditional growth sectors like tech hardware, but he won't let sector weightings deviate from those of the S&P 500 as much as he did at his previous charge. He holds between 250 and 300 names here and will go overseas for opportunities. Fidelity does not hedge foreign currency exposure.

Performance 12-31-06

	1st Qtr	2nd Qtr	3rd Qtr	4th Qtr	Total
2002	-1.60	-13.72	-16.36	7.51	-23.66
2003	-2.87	14.25	1.48	10.85	24.82
2004	1.42	0.77	-2.77	8.17	7.49
2005	-2.69	1.51	3.55	4.04	6.42
2006	5.98	-3.99	0.32	5.04	7.22

Trailing	Total Return%	+/- S&P 500	+/- Russ 1000Gr	%Rank Cat	Growth of $10,000
3 Mo	5.04	-1.66	-0.89	60	10,504
6 Mo	5.38	-7.36	-4.72	86	10,538
1 Yr	7.22	-8.57	-1.85	48	10,722
3 Yr Avg	7.04	-3.40	0.17	49	12,264
5 Yr Avg	3.17	-3.02	0.48	41	11,689
10 Yr Avg	6.99	-1.43	1.55	35	19,653
15 Yr Avg	9.56	-1.08	1.54	27	39,335

Tax Analysis	Tax-Adj Rtn%	%Rank Cat	Tax-Cost Rat	%Rank Cat
3 Yr (estimated)	5.41	65	1.52	82
5 Yr (estimated)	2.10	53	1.04	84
10 Yr (estimated)	5.73	33	1.18	57

Potential Capital Gain Exposure: 25% of assets

Morningstar's Take by Dan Lefkovitz 12-19-06

Fidelity Magellan looks a lot better compared with its new peers.

We recently moved this closed fund from the large-blend category to the large-growth category. The move reflects manager Harry Lange's growth-oriented approach; Magellan's portfolios have landed squarely in the upper-right-hand corner of the style box since he took the helm on Oct. 31, 2005.

Although Magellan's performance versus its benchmark, the S&P 500, remains abysmal, its record versus its new peer group looks a lot better than it did against the old one. From Lange's start date through Dec. 18, 2006, Magellan has outpaced the typical large-growth fund. The fact that the typical large-growth fund has lagged the typical large-blend fund so badly over the course of his tenure reflects the market's preference for value-oriented stocks.

We stand by our view that it would be a mistake to give up on Magellan now. Lange is one of the most talented growth investors in the business, which is why we designated his former charge, Fidelity Capital Appreciation, a Fund Analyst Pick in the large-growth category. Since taking over this fund, he has remade this portfolio in Capital Appreciation's image. He immediately dumped many of the stodgy names favored by his predecessor, including Bank of America, and bought growth-oriented stocks such as Google and UnitedHealth Group. Lange has also used market volatility to bulk up on the fund's exposure to tech stocks--the portfolio's tech exposure was just shy of 30% of assets as of Sept. 30, 2006. And he was also devoting 28% of assets to foreign stocks, many of them Japanese.

Magellan has seen so many redemptions, its asset base has shrunk from a high of $106 billion in 1999 to $45 billion today. That's still big, but it gives Lange more flexibility than his predecessor had. Investors would do well to sit tight and see what Lange can do in a growth market.

Address:	82 Devonshire St
	Boston MA 02109
	800-544-9797
Web Address:	www.fidelity.com
Inception:	05-02-63
Advisor:	Fidelity Management & Research (FMR)
Subadvisor:	Multiple Subadvisors
NTF Plans:	Fidelity Retail-NTF, CommonWealth NTF

Minimum Purchase:	Closed	Add: —	IRA: —
Min Auto Inv Plan:	Closed	Add: —	
Sales Fees:	No-load		
Management Fee:	0.39%		
Actual Fees:	Mgt:0.39%	Dist: —	
Expense Projections:	3Yr:$189	5Yr:$329	10Yr:$738
Income Distrib:	Semi-Annually		

Historical Profile
Return	Average
Risk	Below Avg
Rating	★★★ Neutral

Investment Style: Equity, Stock %

92% | 91% | 95% | 93% | 93% | 95% | 98% | 96% | 99%

▼ Manager Change
▽ Partial Manager Change

Growth of $10,000
— Investment Values of Fund
— Investment Values of S&P 500

33.0 / 26.0 / 20.0 / 15.0 / 10.0

Performance Quartile (within Category)

1995	1996	1997	1998	1999	2000	2001	2002	2003	2004	2005	2006	History
85.98	80.65	95.27	120.82	136.63	119.30	104.22	78.96	97.74	103.79	106.44	89.52	NAV
36.82	11.69	26.59	33.63	24.05	-9.29	-11.65	-23.66	24.82	7.49	6.42	7.22	Total Return %
-0.76	-11.27	-6.77	5.05	3.01	-0.19	0.24	-1.56	-3.86	1.51	-8.57	Total Return % +/-S&P 500
-0.36	-11.43	-3.90	-5.08	-9.11	13.13	8.77	4.22	-4.93	1.19	1.16	-1.85	+/-Russ 1000Gr
0.88	1.41	1.57	0.72	0.63	0.20	0.39	0.61	0.96	1.27	0.95	0.53	Income Return %
35.94	10.28	25.02	32.91	23.42	-9.49	-12.04	-24.27	23.86	6.22	5.47	6.69	Capital Return %
24	89	47	41	74	41	12	28	71	54	48	48	Total Rtn % Rank Cat
0.59	1.10	1.25	0.67	0.73	0.27	0.46	0.64	0.76	1.24	0.98	0.50	Income $
4.69	12.85	5.21	5.15	11.39	4.69	0.80	0.00	0.00	0.00	3.00	24.66	Capital Gains $
0.96	0.92	0.64	0.61	0.60	0.74	0.88	0.88	0.76	0.70	0.62	0.56	Expense Ratio %
0.39	0.95	1.75	0.77	0.66	0.46	0.29	0.43	0.82	0.83	1.26	0.86	Income Ratio %
120	155	67	34	37	28	17	5	21	13	6	74	Turnover Rate %
53,702	53,989	63,766	83,552	105,939	93,067	79,515	56,751	67,995	63,296	51,181	44,962	Net Assets $mil

Rating and Risk

Time Period	Load-Adj Return %	Morningstar Rtn vs Cat	Morningstar Risk vs Cat	Morningstar Risk-Adj Rating
1 Yr	7.22			
3 Yr	7.04	Avg	-Avg	★★★
5 Yr	3.17	Avg	Avg	★★★
10 Yr	6.99	Avg	-Avg	★★★★
Incept	18.33			

Other Measures	Standard Index S&P 500	Best Fit Index Russ MG
Alpha	-3.4	-2.4
Beta	1.05	0.67
R-Squared	79	89
Standard Deviation	8.14	
Mean	7.04	
Sharpe Ratio	0.48	

Portfolio Analysis 09-30-06

Share change since 06-06 Total Stocks:260	Sector	PE	Tot Ret%	% Assets
⊕ Corning Inc.	Hardware	25.5	-4.83	3.63
⊖ Nokia Corporation ADR	Hardware	18.9	13.44	3.47
Schlumberger, Ltd.	Energy	22.3	31.07	3.22
Johnson & Johnson	Health	17.5	12.45	3.21
American International G	Financial	17.0	6.05	2.83
⊖ UnitedHealth Group, Inc.	Health	20.8	-13.49	2.67
Google, Inc.	Business	61.5	11.00	2.41
⊖ General Electric Company	Ind Mtrls	20.0	9.35	2.35
⊕ Peabody Energy Corporati	Energy	17.3	-1.92	1.92
⊕ Wells Fargo Company	Financial	14.7	16.82	1.84
⊖ Genentech, Inc.	Health	48.7	-12.29	1.82
⊕ Seagate Technology	Hardware	23.7	34.47	1.73
⊕ Samsung Electronics	Goods	—		1.66
⊕ Canadian Natural Resourc	Energy	29.1	7.84	1.50
Allergan, Inc.	Health	—	11.33	1.31
ASML Holding NV	Hardware	31.3	22.66	1.31
Staples, Inc.	Consumer	19.6	18.58	1.18
Merrill Lynch & Company,	Financial	14.2	39.28	1.10
⊕ Burlington Northern Sant	Business	15.2	5.52	1.04
Oracle Corporation	Software	26.7	40.38	1.00

Current Investment Style

Value Blnd Growth — Large / Mid / Small

Market Cap	%
Giant	42.4
Large	33.8
Mid	20.7
Small	2.7
Micro	0.4
Avg $mil:	27,535

Value Measures		Rel Category
Price/Earnings	14.93	0.78
Price/Book	2.93	0.88
Price/Sales	1.83	0.94
Price/Cash Flow	10.69	0.94
Dividend Yield %	1.07	1.04

Growth Measures		Rel Category
Long-Term Erngs	14.19	0.99
Book Value	12.09	1.04
Sales	10.78	0.93
Cash Flow	14.72	0.88
Historical Erngs	8.03	0.35

Profitability	%	Rel Category
Return on Equity	18.96	0.93
Return on Assets	10.24	0.93
Net Margin	13.28	0.93

Sector Weightings	% of Stocks	Rel S&P 500	3 Year High Low	
⌖ Info	26.53	1.33		
Software	4.10	1.19	6	4
Hardware	18.89	2.04	19	10
Media	1.12	0.30	9	1
Telecom	2.42	0.69	3	1
⌖ Service	49.32	1.07		
Health	15.50	1.29	16	11
Consumer	6.97	0.91	11	7
Business	9.30	2.20	10	2
Financial	17.55	0.79	24	17
⌖ Mfg	24.15	0.71		
Goods	4.56	0.53	7	5
Ind Mtrls	10.18	0.85	12	7
Energy	8.56	0.87	12	9
Utilities	0.85	0.24	1	0

Composition

	%
● Cash	1.0
● Stocks	98.8
● Bonds	0.0
● Other	0.2
Foreign (% of Stock)	22.7

Morningstar® Funds 500

Fidelity Mid Cap Value

	Ticker	Load	NAV	Yield	Total Assets	Mstar Category
	FSMVX	None	$16.67	0.5%	$634 mil	Mid-Cap Value

Governance and Management

Stewardship Grade: B

Portfolio Manager(s)

Bruce Dirks took over for Ciaran O'Neill in February 2005 when O'Neill left Fidelity for another firm. This is Dirks' first time running a public mutual fund solo, and he's the third manager in charge of this offering since its November 2001 inception. In addition to this fund, Dirks manages Fidelity Large Cap Value.

Strategy

Manager Bruce Dirks keeps this fund's sector weights within a few percentage points of those in the Russell MidCap Value Index. This move aligns the fund's risk profile with the index's and emphasizes Dirks' stock-picking ability. He takes his cues directly from Fidelity's analysts and several quantitative models.

Historical Profile

Return	Average
Risk	Average
Rating	★★★★ Above Avg

Investment Style: Equity Stock %

97% 99% 98% 99% 99%

▼ Manager Change
▽ Partial Manager Change

Growth of $10,000
— Investment Values of Fund
— Investment Values of S&P 500

17.5
15.0
12.5
10.0
7.0

Performance Quartile (within Category)

	1995	1996	1997	1998	1999	2000	2001	2002	2003	2004	2005	2006	History
NAV	—	—	—	—	—	—	10.59	9.08	12.08	14.35	15.05	16.67	
Total Return %	—	—	—	—	—	—	6.00*	-13.52	33.49	21.87	13.68	14.50	
+/-S&P 500	—	—	—	—	—	—		8.58	4.81	10.99	8.77	-1.29	
+/-Russ MV	—	—	—	—	—	—		-3.88	-4.58	-1.84	1.03	-5.72	
Income Return %	—	—	—	—	—	—		0.76	0.44	0.33	0.67	0.60	
Capital Return %	—	—	—	—	—	—		-14.28	33.05	21.54	13.01	13.90	
Total Rtn % Rank Cat	—	—	—	—	—	—		63	58	25	7	66	
Income $	—	—	—	—	—	—	0.01	0.08	0.04	0.04	0.10	0.09	
Capital Gains $	—	—	—	—	—	—	0.00	0.00	0.00	0.32	1.15	0.45	
Expense Ratio %	—	—	—	—	—	—		1.20	1.18	1.05	0.81		
Income Ratio %	—	—	—	—	—	—		0.59	0.79	0.55	1.08		
Turnover Rate %	—	—	—	—	—	—		68	113	97	207		
Net Assets $mil	—	—	—	—	—	—		15	42	89	143	634	

Performance 12-31-06

	1st Qtr	2nd Qtr	3rd Qtr	4th Qtr	Total
2002	5.57	-3.40	-18.72	4.33	-13.52
2003	-3.41	15.74	4.73	14.03	33.49
2004	5.38	0.63	1.95	12.73	21.87
2005	-0.36	4.99	6.92	1.65	13.68
2006	5.46	0.77	0.95	6.72	14.50

Trailing	Total Return%	+/- S&P 500	+/- Russ MV	%Rank Cat	Growth of $10,000
3 Mo	6.72	0.02	-1.78	79	10,672
6 Mo	7.74	-5.00	-4.59	87	10,774
1 Yr	14.50	-1.29	-5.72	66	11,450
3 Yr Avg	16.63	6.19	-2.14	19	15,865
5 Yr Avg	12.86	6.67	-3.02	35	18,311
10 Yr Avg	—	—	—		
15 Yr Avg	—	—	—		

Tax Analysis	Tax-Adj Rtn%	%Rank Cat	Tax-Cost Rat	%Rank Cat
3 Yr (estimated)	15.36	15	1.09	36
5 Yr (estimated)	12.03	26	0.74	27
10 Yr (estimated)	—		—	

Potential Capital Gain Exposure: 11% of assets

Rating and Risk

Time Period	Load-Adj Return %	Morningstar Rtn vs Cat	Morningstar Risk vs Cat	Morningstar Risk-Adj Rating
1 Yr	14.50			
3 Yr	16.63	+Avg	Avg	★★★★
5 Yr	12.86	Avg	Avg	★★★★
10 Yr	—	—	—	—
Incept	13.82			

Other Measures	Standard Index S&P 500	Best Fit Index Russ MV
Alpha	4.5	-1.9
Beta	1.17	1.00
R-Squared	75	91
Standard Deviation	9.21	
Mean	16.63	
Sharpe Ratio	1.37	

Portfolio Analysis 10-31-06

Share change since 07-06 Total Stocks:108	Sector	PE	Tot Ret%	% Assets
☼ Ameriprise Financial, In	Financial	—	—	1.97
⊕ Safeco Corporation	Financial	8.8	12.89	1.79
⊕ Kroger Company	Consumer	17.5	23.31	1.75
⊖ Edison International	Utilities	13.0	7.02	1.75
⊕ OfficeMax, Inc.	Consumer	—	98.81	1.71
⊕ Radian Group, Inc.	Financial	8.6	-7.86	1.69
⊕ Colonial BancGroup, Inc.	Financial	15.3	11.06	1.69
⊕ PPL Corporation	Utilities	15.2	26.06	1.67
☼ Sunoco, Inc.	Energy	6.9	-19.42	1.64
☼ Sherwin-Williams Company	Goods	15.4	42.73	1.64
⊕ Tesoro Corporation	Energy	6.5	7.51	1.62
⊕ Ann Taylor Stores Corpor	Consumer	16.6	-4.87	1.57
⊕ W.R. Berkley Corporation	Financial	10.3	9.20	1.55
⊕ Dillard's, Inc.	Consumer	14.2	41.62	1.54
⊕ AES Corporation	Utilities	33.4	39.23	1.54
⊕ HCC Insurance Holdings I	Financial	16.5	9.39	1.53
⊕ Cincinnati Financial Cor	Financial	8.1	4.39	1.52
Ambac Financial Group, I	Financial	10.9	16.52	1.50
⊕ Terex Corporation	Ind Mtrls	18.2	117.44	1.44
☼ CSX Corporation	Business	15.4	37.05	1.43

Current Investment Style

Value Blnd Growth — Large Mid Small

Market Cap	%
Giant	0.0
Large	28.3
Mid	69.9
Small	1.8
Micro	0.0

Avg $mil: 6,214

Value Measures		Rel Category
Price/Earnings	14.03	0.95
Price/Book	2.29	1.14
Price/Sales	0.86	0.89
Price/Cash Flow	7.35	0.97
Dividend Yield %	1.19	0.66

Growth Measures	%	Rel Category
Long-Term Erngs	10.93	0.99
Book Value	5.68	0.81
Sales	8.13	1.06
Cash Flow	11.09	2.79
Historical Erngs	23.43	1.59

Profitability	%	Rel Category
Return on Equity	16.97	1.18
Return on Assets	8.99	1.22
Net Margin	10.19	0.97

Sector Weightings	% of Stocks	Rel S&P 500	3 Year High	Low
⟳ Info	8.23	0.41		
▣ Software	0.64	0.19	2	0
▣ Hardware	5.76	0.62	8	2
▣ Media	0.02	0.01	3	0
▣ Telecom	1.81	0.52	2	1
⊂ Service	53.55	1.16		
▣ Health	3.31	0.27	6	3
▣ Consumer	12.56	1.64	14	9
▣ Business	5.08	1.20	8	4
▣ Financial	32.60	1.46	33	28
⊐ Mfg	38.22	1.13		
▣ Goods	6.05	0.71	10	6
▣ Ind Mtrls	13.07	1.09	16	11
▣ Energy	5.40	0.55	8	5
▣ Utilities	13.70	3.91	14	9

Composition

	%
● Cash	1.4
● Stocks	98.6
● Bonds	0.0
● Other	0.0
Foreign (% of Stock)	0.0

Morningstar's Take by Katherine Yang 11-30-06

A sensible strategy gives us confidence in Fidelity Mid Cap Value.

This mid-value fund has a simple and benchmark-focused strategy. Manager Bruce Dirks avoids big sector bets versus the fund's benchmark, the Russell MidCap Value Index, and aims to beat the index through superior stock-picking. Dirks relies on analysts from Pyramis (Fidelity's quantitative branch), as well as Fidelity's recently expanded central research pool of analysts, for ideas.

Dirks uses these quantitative and fundamental inputs to find companies with below-average valuations and the ability to grow sales and earnings--even though they may be struggling over the short term. For example, electric utility Edison International--a top holding for more than a year--trades cheaply relative to its peers because of its prior involvement in the energy trading scandal in California. Dirks believes that, among other factors, the deregulation of energy prices in Illinois,

one of its biggest markets, should boost its stock price.

Dirks' propensity to trade rapidly--turnover has averaged about 200% during his nearly two-year tenure--is a concern. High turnover can decrease tax efficiency and raise trading costs. Indeed, brokerage commissions at this fund have almost doubled since 2004.

Despite the fund's high turnover, we remain optimistic, partly because of its modest expense structure. Its management fee is adjusted annually, based on the fund's three-year performance relative to its benchmark. Additionally, Fidelity caps its expense ratio at 1%, well below the category median.

Dirks has had success applying a similar approach to bigger companies at his other charge, Fidelity Large Cap Value. Although this mid-cap fund has lagged its index under Dirks' management, its solid strategy and modest costs argue in its favor.

Address:	82 Devonshire Street Boston MA 02109 800-343-3548	Minimum Purchase: $2500 Add: $250 IRA: $200
Web Address:	www.fidelity.com	Min Auto Inv Plan: $0 Add: —
Inception:	11-15-01*	Sales Fees: No-load
Advisor:	Fidelity Management & Research (FMR)	Management Fee: 0.50%
Subadvisor:	Multiple Subadvisors	Actual Fees: Mgt:0.50% Dist: —
		Expense Projections: 3Yr:$274 5Yr:$477 10Yr:$1061
NTF Plans:	Fidelity Retail-NTF, CommonWealth NTF	Income Distrib: Semi-Annually

Fidelity Mid-Cap Stock

	Ticker	Load	NAV	Yield	Total Assets	Mstar Category
	FMCSX	Closed	$29.14	0.0%	$12,942 mil	Mid-Cap Growth

Governance and Management

Stewardship Grade: B

Portfolio Manager(s)

Manager Shep Perkins took the helm here in January 2005 after a short, relatively successful stint at Fidelity OTC. Curiously, Steve Calhoun stepped down as comanager in November 2005 after only eight months on the job.

Strategy

Manager Shep Perkins looks for undervalued companies with potential growth driven by an internal catalyst, such as synergies from industry consolidation or dominant niche firms. He anticipates the portfolio will contain approximately 100-150 holdings.

Historical Profile
Return: Above Avg
Risk: Average
Rating: ★★★★ Above Avg

Investment Style
Equity
Stock %

Growth of $10,000
— Investment Values of Fund
— Investment Values of S&P 500

Performance Quartile (within Category)

	1995	1996	1997	1998	1999	2000	2001	2002	2003	2004	2005	2006	History
	13.50	14.64	16.69	17.88	21.87	26.06	22.57	16.26	21.57	23.45	26.57	29.14	NAV
	33.92	18.12	27.08	15.18	39.83	32.07	-12.80	-27.59	33.26	9.05	16.07	14.78	Total Return %
	-3.66	-4.84	-6.28	-13.40	18.79	41.17	-0.91	-5.49	4.58	-1.83	11.16	-1.01	+/-S&P 500
	-0.06	0.64	4.54	-2.68	-11.46	43.82	7.35	-0.18	-9.45	-6.43	3.97	4.12	+/-Russ MG
	0.57	0.23	0.07	0.00	0.06	0.49	0.61	0.40	0.55	0.32	0.17	0.00	Income Return %
	33.35	17.89	27.01	15.18	39.77	31.58	-13.41	-27.99	32.71	8.73	15.90	14.78	Capital Return %
	48	42	22	54	67	2	37	56	64	83	11	12	Total Rtn % Rank Cat
	0.06	0.03	0.01	0.00	0.01	0.10	0.16	0.09	0.09	0.09	0.04	0.00	Income $
	0.74	1.26	1.77	1.28	2.59	2.50	0.00	0.00	0.00	0.00	0.60	1.34	Capital Gains $
	1.22	1.00	0.96	0.86	0.74	0.86	0.87	0.87	0.66	0.65	0.62	0.69	Expense Ratio %
	0.95	1.01	0.17	-0.10	0.08	-0.20	0.79	0.79	0.75	0.34	0.22	-0.03	Income Ratio %
	163	179	155	132	121	205	303	200	120	137	186	74	Turnover Rate %
	1,160	1,695	1,763	1,784	2,286	7,011	6,547	5,132	8,049	9,093	9,949	12,942	Net Assets $mil

Performance 12-31-06

	1st Qtr	2nd Qtr	3rd Qtr	4th Qtr	Total
2002	-0.89	-17.27	-18.40	8.21	-27.59
2003	-2.71	15.74	5.42	12.26	33.26
2004	3.15	-1.03	-3.95	11.22	9.05
2005	-3.58	5.00	9.32	4.87	16.07
2006	13.40	-3.70	0.14	4.96	14.78

Trailing	Total Return%	+/- S&P 500	+/- Russ MG	%Rank Cat	Growth of $10,000
3 Mo	4.96	-1.74	-1.99	80	10,496
6 Mo	5.10	-7.64	-2.80	60	10,510
1 Yr	14.78	-1.01	4.12	12	11,478
3 Yr Avg	13.26	2.82	0.53	22	14,529
5 Yr Avg	6.99	0.80	-1.23	41	14,019
10 Yr Avg	12.70	4.28	4.08	11	33,055
15 Yr Avg	—	—	—		

Tax Analysis	Tax-Adj Rtn%	%Rank Cat	Tax-Cost Rat	%Rank Cat
3 Yr (estimated)	12.68	18	0.51	26
5 Yr (estimated)	6.59	39	0.37	27
10 Yr (estimated)	11.06	10	1.46	54

Potential Capital Gain Exposure: 21% of assets

Morningstar's Take by Andrew Gogerty 12-14-06

Fidelity Mid-Cap Stock has gone two-for-two under new management, but we're standing by our previous concerns.

This mid-growth offering's returns have fluctuated with the market's ebbs and flows this year, but it appears to be on target to close 2006 as it did 2005--beating nearly 90% of its peers. Manager Shep Perkins' decision to increase exposure in areas such as telecom and steel fueled gains, as did strong performance of top holdings Potash Corporation of Saskatchewan and Monsanto Company, which he added to the portfolio shortly after taking over here in early 2005.

Perkins looks to ferret out firms trading below his fair value estimate with a catalyst--such synergies from industry consolidation or niche players with dominant industry position--that he thinks can grow earnings faster than the consensus over the next three years. In 2006, for example, he increased the fund's stake in steel companies to 2% of assets saying that continued overseas demand and potential industry consolidation are catalysts for future earnings growth.

But the fact remains that Perkins stands behind the wheel of a mammoth ship. Fund assets have swelled from $8 billion to nearly $13 billion in the past three years. Fidelity finally closed the doors in April 2006, much later than we would have liked. While the appreciation in Monsanto, Potash, Qwest Communications International, and AT&T have had a small part in the fund's increased weight in large-cap stocks, strong inflows remain the main culprit. The fund's mid-cap stake has fallen to just 53% of assets compared with 81% in 2001. As such, this fund is no longer a pure mid-growth play.

We don't discount Perkins' early success. He has skillfully guided this beast on his watch. But investors should recognize the fund is not as nimble as it once was and that the continued growth in assets will put additional strain on the portfolio.

Address:	82 Devonshire St Boston MA 02109 800-544-5555
Web Address:	www.fidelity.com
Inception:	03-29-94
Advisor:	Fidelity Management & Research (FMR)
Subadvisor:	Multiple Subadvisors
NTF Plans:	Fidelity Retail-NTF, CommonWealth NTF

Minimum Purchase:	Closed	Add: —	IRA: —
Min Auto Inv Plan:	Closed	Add: —	
Sales Fees:	No-load, 0.75%R		
Management Fee:	0.45%		
Actual Fees:	Mgt:0.45%	Dist: —	
Expense Projections:	3Yr:$230	5Yr:$401	10Yr:$894
Income Distrib:	Semi-Annually		

Rating and Risk

Time Period	Load-Adj Return %	Morningstar Rtn vs Cat	Morningstar Risk vs Cat	Morningstar Risk-Adj Rating
1 Yr	14.78			
3 Yr	13.26	+Avg	Avg	★★★★
5 Yr	6.99	Avg	Avg	★★★
10 Yr	12.70	+Avg	-Avg	★★★★
Incept	14.57			

Other Measures	Standard Index S&P 500	Best Fit Index Mstar Mid Growth TR
Alpha	-1.0	-0.2
Beta	1.59	0.98
R-Squared	73	93
Standard Deviation	12.84	
Mean	13.26	
Sharpe Ratio	0.79	

Portfolio Analysis 10-31-06

Share change since 07-06 Total Stocks:168

	Sector	PE	Tot Ret%	% Assets
Qwest Communications Int	Telecom	—	48.14	4.17
NCR Corporation	Hardware	22.6	25.99	2.09
Converse Technology, Inc	Hardware	—	-20.61	2.09
⊕ Omnicare, Inc.	Health	28.5	-32.36	1.83
St. Jude Medical, Inc.	Health	34.9	-27.17	1.80
⊖ Royal Caribbean Cruises,	Consumer	16.0	-6.78	1.52
Humana	Health	21.8	1.80	1.45
⊕ Whirlpool Corporation	Goods	13.0	1.11	1.40
Microchip Technology, In	Hardware	27.2	4.37	1.39
Valero Energy Corporatio	Energy	6.3	-0.33	1.26
⊖ Potash Corporation of Sa	Ind Mtrls	26.0	80.04	1.26
Time Warner Telecom, Inc	Telecom	—	102.34	1.20
⊕ Solectron Corporation	Hardware	26.5	-12.02	1.14
⊕ Flextronics Internationa	Hardware	45.1	9.96	1.12
⊕ E*Trade Financial Corpor	Financial	17.6	7.48	1.11
⊖ Freescale Semiconductor,	Hardware	—	—	1.11
AT&T, Inc.	Telecom	18.2	51.59	1.10
Amphenol Corporation	Hardware	24.9	40.57	1.09
⊖ Circuit City Stores, Inc	Consumer	20.6	-15.56	1.09
Monsanto Company	Ind Mtrls	39.8	36.78	1.07

Current Investment Style

Value Blnd Growth — Large / Mid / Small

Market Cap	%
Giant	2.8
Large	29.2
Mid	54.6
Small	12.2
Micro	1.3

Avg $mil: 6,702

Value Measures		Rel Category
Price/Earnings	19.63	0.96
Price/Book	2.58	0.80
Price/Sales	0.98	0.56
Price/Cash Flow	9.00	0.79
Dividend Yield %	0.62	0.98

Growth Measures	%	Rel Category
Long-Term Erngs	14.67	0.90
Book Value	10.00	0.79
Sales	6.00	0.60
Cash Flow	14.75	0.80
Historical Erngs	25.30	1.01

Profitability	%	Rel Category
Return on Equity	15.32	0.85
Return on Assets	6.83	0.73
Net Margin	8.53	0.73

Sector Weightings	% of Stocks	Rel S&P 500	3 Year High Low	
↻ Info	29.99	1.50		
Software	2.42	0.70	6	2
Hardware	18.50	2.00	23	13
Media	0.00	0.00	6	0
Telecom	9.07	2.58	9	3
Service	38.88	0.84		
Health	13.24	1.10	26	10
Consumer	8.13	1.06	11	5
Business	11.97	2.83	13	7
Financial	5.54	0.25	12	5
Mfg	31.13	0.92		
Goods	5.88	0.69	8	4
Ind Mtrls	14.32	1.20	14	6
Energy	10.29	1.05	13	7
Utilities	0.64	0.18	1	0

Composition

	%
● Cash	2.8
● Stocks	97.2
● Bonds	0.0
○ Other	0.0
Foreign	11.2

(% of Stock)

MORNINGSTAR® Funds 500

Fidelity Mtg Sec

	Ticker	Load	NAV	Yield	SEC Yield	Total Assets	Mstar Category
	FMSFX	None	$11.05	4.8%	5.11%	$1,860 mil	Intermediate-Term Bond

Governance and Management

Stewardship Grade: B

Portfolio Manager(s)

Brett Kozlowski is a newcomer, having taken over this fund in October 2006. He's been with Fidelity since 1997 and has relevant experience as a mortgage analyst, so we're confident he can keep this fund on track.

Strategy

This fund is a bit more adventurous than most government bond funds. Manager Brett Kozlowski buys mostly Ginnie Mae, Fannie Mae, and Freddie Mac issues but also ventures into commercial mortgage-backed securities. Kozlowski looks to add value by rotating the fund's assets among different sectors of the mortgage market and investing in lower- or higher-coupon mortgages, depending on his outlook for the market. The fund's duration (a measure of interest-rate sensitivity) is closely aligned with that of the Lehman Brothers Mortgage-Backed Securities Index.

Performance 12-31-06

	1st Qtr	2nd Qtr	3rd Qtr	4th Qtr	Total
2002	1.18	3.42	2.58	1.66	9.12
2003	1.04	0.97	0.92	0.58	3.55
2004	1.89	-1.07	2.53	1.07	4.45
2005	-0.27	2.31	-0.13	0.57	2.48
2006	-0.12	0.00	3.48	1.43	4.84

Trailing	Total Return%	+/- LB Aggr	+/- LB 5-10YR	%Rank Cat	Growth of $10,000
3 Mo	1.43	0.19	0.35	26	10,143
6 Mo	4.96	-0.13	-0.72	38	10,496
1 Yr	4.84	0.51	1.03	17	10,484
3 Yr Avg	3.92	0.22	0.28	20	11,223
5 Yr Avg	4.86	-0.20	-1.06	34	12,678
10 Yr Avg	5.97	-0.27	-0.71	25	17,858
15 Yr Avg	6.38	-0.12	-0.61	36	25,287

Tax Analysis	Tax-Adj Rtn%	%Rank Cat	Tax-Cost Rat	%Rank Cat
3 Yr (estimated)	2.35	14	1.51	53
5 Yr (estimated)	3.21	25	1.57	47
10 Yr (estimated)	3.78	18	2.07	55

Potential Capital Gain Exposure: -1% of assets

Morningstar's Take by Scott Berry 11-10-06

We still like Fidelity Mortgage Securities, but we're removing it as a Fund Analyst Pick.

George Fischer, who led this fund since mid-2002, was replaced here by Brett Kozlowski in early October 2006. Fischer remains with Fidelity but has given up some fund management responsibilities for more administrative duties. Kozlowski has been with Fidelity since 1997, serving most recently as a mortgage analyst and a member of Fidelity's government/mortgage fund management team.

Kozlowski has no relevant fund management experience, but we're confident that the transition will be a smooth one and that Kozlowski will build on the fund's solid long-term record. That confidence stems from our trust in the fund's strategy and Fidelity's resources, which don't go away with a management change. Many other mortgage-focused funds concentrate exclusively on GNMAs, but this fund has more flexibility to own other mortgage types. We think that flexibility can

be put to good use by Kozlowski, who is backed by Fidelity's strong analytical resources. And Kozlowski is actually starting off with more primary knowledge about the government and mortgage markets than did Fischer.

Finally, we like that Kozlowski doesn't have a huge expense hurdle to jump here. With Fidelity capping expenses at 0.45%, the fund boasts a nice sustainable advantage over its average no-load category peer, which charges 0.73%. That may not seem like much of an advantage, but we think it's meaningful, given the category's often-narrow range of returns.

We think Kozlowski's background will lend itself well here and we think shareholders have reason to stay the course. But we reserve our Analyst Picks for those funds in which we have the utmost confidence. And we'll need to see and hear more from Kozlowski before this fund returns to that level.

Address:	82 Devonshire St
	Boston MA 02109
	800-544-3198
Web Address:	www.fidelity.com
Inception:	12-31-84
Advisor:	Fidelity Management & Research (FMR)
Subadvisor:	Multiple Subadvisors
NTF Plans:	Fidelity Retail-NTF, CommonWealth NTF

Minimum Purchase:	$2500	Add: $250	IRA: $2500
Min Auto Inv Plan:	$2500	Add: $100	
Sales Fees:	No-load		
Management Fee:	0.32%		
Actual Fees:	Mgt:0.32%	Dist: —	
Expense Projections:	3Yr:$144	5Yr:$252	10Yr:$567
Income Distrib:	Monthly		

Historical Profile

Return	Above Avg
Risk	Low
Rating	★★★★ Above Avg

| | 19 | 16 | 18 | 32 | 54 | 93 | 53 | 41 |

▼ Manager Change
▽ Partial Manager Change

Growth of $10,000
■ Investment Values of Fund
— Investment Values of LB Aggr

Performance Quartile (within Category)

1995	1996	1997	1998	1999	2000	2001	2002	2003	2004	2005	2006	History
11.09	10.85	11.01	10.80	10.33	10.74	10.89	11.26	11.22	11.24	11.06	11.05	NAV
17.02	5.43	9.11	5.86	1.89	11.28	7.56	9.12	3.55	4.45	2.48	4.84	Total Return %
-1.45	1.80	-0.54	-2.83	2.71	-0.35	-0.88	-1.13	-0.55	0.11	0.05	0.51	+/-LB Aggr
-4.41	2.74	-0.32	-4.28	4.77	-1.16	-1.26	-3.91	-2.42	-0.85	0.65	1.03	+/-LB 5-10YR
7.70	6.54	6.50	6.46	6.37	7.10	6.16	4.89	2.56	3.72	4.12	4.89	Income Return %
9.32	-1.11	2.61	-0.60	-4.48	4.18	1.40	4.23	0.99	0.73	-1.64	-0.05	Capital Return %
67	9	49	82	3	21	50	33	76	33	15	17	Total Rtn % Rank Cat
0.76	0.70	0.68	0.69	0.67	0.71	0.64	0.52	0.28	0.41	0.45	0.53	Income $
0.10	0.11	0.11	0.15	0.00	0.00	0.00	0.00	0.15	0.06	0.00	0.00	Capital Gains $
0.77	0.73	0.72	0.71	0.70	0.67	0.66	0.63	0.60	0.62	0.55	0.45	Expense Ratio %
7.37	6.75	6.36	6.34	6.29	6.65	6.00	4.76	2.72	3.48	3.91	4.73	Income Ratio %
329	221	149	262	183	99	194	231	356	204	183	232	Turnover Rate %
487	521	484	448	391	377	417	1,339	1,311	1,618	1,764	1,613	Net Assets $mil

Rating and Risk

Time Period	Load-Adj Return %	Morningstar Rtn vs Cat	Morningstar Risk vs Cat	Morningstar Risk-Adj Rating
1 Yr	4.83			
3 Yr	3.92	+Avg	Low	★★★★
5 Yr	4.86	Avg	Low	★★★★
10 Yr	5.97	+Avg	Low	★★★★
Incept	7.83			

Other Measures	Standard Index LB Aggr	Best Fit Index LB Mort
Alpha	0.3	-0.2
Beta	0.73	0.96
R-Squared	95	99
Standard Deviation	2.43	
Mean	3.92	
Sharpe Ratio	0.27	

Portfolio Analysis 08-31-06

Total Fixed-Income:1053	Date of Maturity	Amount $000	Value $000	% Net Assets
FNMA 0.05%	12-01-34	307,543	294,766	11.85
FNMA 5.5%	01-01-34	185,339	182,244	7.32
FHLMC 0.06%	09-01-36	180,290	177,183	7.12
FHLMC 0.05%	07-01-35	125,828	120,703	4.85
FNMA 0.04%	12-01-33	98,152	91,826	3.69
FNMA 5%	04-01-18	92,610	90,899	3.65
FNMA 6%	09-01-32	85,356	85,805	3.45
FNMA 5.5%	01-01-09	85,561	85,437	3.43
FNMA 6.5%	02-01-24	66,289	67,560	2.72
Lbsp Swap Irs 3/06/09 3m	03-06-09	50,000	50,579	2.03
FNMA 0.06%	10-01-08	47,721	48,331	1.94
GNMA 0.06%	12-15-32	45,836	46,973	1.89
FNMA 4.5%	12-01-18	36,672	35,346	1.42
FHLMC 0.06%	11-01-24	31,814	31,462	1.26
FNMA 5.5%	11-01-22	22,228	21,964	0.88
FNMA 0.04%	06-01-18	19,286	18,205	0.73
FHLMC 0.06%	06-01-09	15,286	15,252	0.61
FNMA CMO 5.5%	11-25-32	14,461	14,270	0.57
FHLMC 6.5%	09-01-24	13,242	13,516	0.54
FHLMC 0.08%	01-01-27	10,581	10,991	0.44

Current Investment Style

Duration: Short / Int / Long
Quality: High / Med / Low

1 figure provided by fund

Avg Eff Duration[1]	3.4 Yrs
Avg Eff Maturity	5.0 Yrs
Avg Credit Quality	AAA
Avg Wtd Coupon	2.63%
Avg Wtd Price	98.20% of par

Coupon Range	% of Bonds	Rel Cat
0% PIK	4.3	0.6
0% to 6%	92.9	1.3
6% to 8%	7.1	0.3
8% to 10%	0.0	0.0
More than 10%	0.0	0.0

1.00=Category Average

Credit Analysis		% bonds 08-31-06	
AAA	90	BB	0
AA	3	B	0
A	3	Below B	0
BBB	4	NR/NA	0

Sector Breakdown % of assets

US Treasuries	0
TIPS	0
US Agency	0
Mortgage Pass-Throughs	64
Mortgage CMO	15
Mortgage ARM	0
US Corporate	2
Asset-Backed	5
Convertible	0
Municipal	0
Corporate Inflation-Protected	0
Foreign Corporate	1
Foreign Govt	0

Composition

Cash	11.8	Bonds	88.1
Stocks	0.0	Other	0.1

Special Securities

Restricted/Illiquid Secs	2
Exotic Mortgage-Backed	5
Emerging-Markets Secs	0
Options/Futures/Warrants	No

Investment Style
Fixed Income
Income Rtn %Rank Cat

Fidelity Municipal Income

Analyst Pick ✓

	Ticker	Load	NAV	Yield	SEC Yield	Total Assets	Mstar Category
	FHIGX	None	$12.77	4.1%	3.58%	$4,679 mil	Muni National Long

Governance and Management

Stewardship Grade: B

Portfolio Manager(s)

Christine Thompson took over the fund in 2002, but she has extensive experience as a Fidelity municipal bond fund manager. She is backed by numerous analysts and traders.

Strategy

This fund doesn't make big sweeping bets (it ties its interest-rate sensitivity to that of the Lehman Brothers Municipal Bond Index) and maintains minimal credit risk. Management focuses on yield-curve plays and the structure of the portfolio, such as a bias toward callable or noncallable bonds. The team also uses sophisticated analytics to measure market risk across the portfolio and to keep a close watch on how bonds will respond to different scenarios given their particular tax status or structure.

Performance 12-31-06

	1st Qtr	2nd Qtr	3rd Qtr	4th Qtr	Total
2002	0.92	3.96	5.41	-0.11	10.48
2003	1.32	3.08	-0.07	1.37	5.80
2004	2.10	-2.92	4.20	1.40	4.73
2005	-0.01	3.01	-0.10	0.74	3.66
2006	0.24	-0.05	3.37	1.18	4.78

Trailing	Total Return%	+/- LB Muni	+/- LB Muni 20YR	%Rank Cat	Growth of $10,000
3 Mo	1.18	0.07	-0.25	24	10,118
6 Mo	4.59	0.04	-0.92	31	10,459
1 Yr	4.78	-0.06	-1.08	34	10,478
3 Yr Avg	4.39	0.11	-1.44	21	11,376
5 Yr Avg	5.86	0.33	-0.90	10	13,294
10 Yr Avg	5.88	0.12	-0.70	5	17,707
15 Yr Avg	6.15	-0.11	-0.93	13	24,479

Tax Analysis	Tax-Adj Rtn%	%Rank Cat	Tax-Cost Rat	%Rank Cat
3 Yr (estimated)	4.20	17	0.18	64
5 Yr (estimated)	5.65	9	0.20	63
10 Yr (estimated)	5.75	5	0.12	52

Potential Capital Gain Exposure: 4% of assets

Historical Profile

Return	Above Avg
Risk	Average
Rating	★★★★ Above Avg

	41	36	28	33	31	28	24	28

Growth of $10,000
20.8
18.8
16.4
14.0
12.0
10.0
— Investment Values of Fund
— Investment Values of LB Muni

▼ Manager Change
▽ Partial Manager Change

Performance Quartile (within Category)

1995	1996	1997	1998	1999	2000	2001	2002	2003	2004	2005	2006	History
12.36	12.27	12.68	12.82	11.91	12.70	12.68	13.22	13.18	13.09	12.82	12.77	NAV
16.18	4.95	9.22	6.04	-2.48	12.30	5.00	10.48	5.80	4.73	3.66	4.78	Total Return %
-1.28	0.52	0.03	-0.44	-0.42	0.62	-0.13	0.88	0.49	0.25	0.15	-0.06	+/-LB Muni
-4.79	0.49	-1.62	-0.78	2.20	-2.94	0.13	0.45	-0.53	-1.83	-1.42	-1.08	+/-LB Muni 20YR
6.07	5.38	5.09	4.85	4.75	5.41	4.94	4.84	4.53	4.43	4.28	4.20	Income Return %
10.11	-0.43	4.13	1.19	-7.23	6.89	0.06	5.64	1.27	0.30	-0.62	0.58	Capital Return %
70	8	44	18	6	19	12	5	17	15	26	34	Total Rtn % Rank Cat
0.67	0.65	0.61	0.60	0.60	0.63	0.61	0.60	0.59	0.57	0.55	0.53	Income $
0.00	0.03	0.08	0.01	0.01	0.00	0.04	0.16	0.20	0.13	0.19	0.12	Capital Gains $
0.57	0.56	0.55	0.53	0.49	0.42	0.43	0.46	0.47	0.47	0.45	—	Expense Ratio %
5.69	5.32	4.92	4.75	4.77	4.98	4.80	4.62	4.42	4.36	4.22	—	Income Ratio %
50	53	31	25	28	4	27	23	23	20	25	—	Turnover Rate %
1,794	1,796	2,347	4,639	4,063	4,452	4,514	4,801	4,775	4,619	4,670	4,679	Net Assets $mil

Investment Style

Fixed Income
Income Rtn %Rank Cat

Rating and Risk

Time Period	Load-Adj Return %	Morningstar Rtn vs Cat	Morningstar Risk vs Cat	Morningstar Risk-Adj Rating
1 Yr	4.78			
3 Yr	4.39	+Avg	Avg	★★★★
5 Yr	5.86	+Avg	Avg	★★★★
10 Yr	5.88	High	Avg	★★★★★
Incept	7.01			

Other Measures	Standard Index LB Muni	Best Fit Index LB Muni
Alpha	0.0	0.0
Beta	1.10	1.10
R-Squared	99	99
Standard Deviation	3.37	
Mean	4.39	
Sharpe Ratio	0.34	

Portfolio Analysis 09-30-06

Total Fixed-Income:878

	Date of Maturity	Amount $000	Value $000	% Net Assets
Washington St Pub Pwr Sp	07-01-12	56,550	61,478	1.37
Atlanta Ga Wtr & Wastewt	11-01-43	57,750	60,201	1.34
California St 5.5%	11-01-33	39,600	43,100	0.96
Texas St Tpk Auth 5.5%	08-15-39	37,550	40,527	0.90
Atlanta Ga Wtr & Wastewt	11-01-37	38,395	40,158	0.89
Tobacco Settlement Fing	06-01-15	37,645	39,929	0.89
GOLDEN ST TOB SECURITIZA	06-01-45	35,695	36,633	0.81
North Carolina Cap Facs	07-01-42	34,200	35,731	0.79
Colorado Wtr Res & Pwr D	09-01-43	33,385	35,676	0.79
Massachusetts St Sch Bld	08-15-23	29,965	31,974	0.71
Massachusetts St Sch Bld	08-15-30	30,000	31,714	0.70
Engy Northwest Wash Elec	07-01-16	28,000	31,195	0.69
Texas St Tpk Auth 5.75%	08-15-38	27,550	30,182	0.67
Mercer Cnty N D Pollutn	06-30-13	26,000	29,699	0.66
Metropolitan Pier & Expo	06-15-41	26,420	28,964	0.64

Current Investment Style

Duration: Short Int Long
Quality: High Med Low

¹Avg Eff Duration		6.5 Yrs
Avg Eff Maturity		15.4 Yrs
Avg Credit Quality		AA
Avg Wtd Coupon		4.57%
Avg Wtd Price		103.37% of par

¹figure provided by fund

Credit Analysis   % bonds 09-30-06

AAA	65	BB	0
AA	11	B	0
A	16	Below B	0
BBB	6	NR/NA	2

Top 5 States   % bonds

TX	13.4	CA	12.5
NY	13.2	MA	6.8
IL	12.5		

Composition

Cash	0.1	Bonds	99.9
Stocks	0.0	Other	0.0

Special Securities

Restricted/Illiquid Secs	0
Options/Futures/Warrants	No

Sector Weightings

	% of Bonds	Rel Cat
General Obligation	32.8	1.17
Utilities	14.5	1.39
Health	8.2	0.78
Water/Waste	10.4	1.05
Housing	1.1	0.17
Education	8.5	0.74
Transportation	9.4	1.09
COP/Lease	2.4	1.03
Industrial	11.2	0.93
Misc Revenue	0.0	—
Demand	1.6	3.33

Morningstar's Take by Eric Jacobson 12-21-06

Fidelity Municipal Income is a rejection of much bond-fund mythology.

Many investors prefer to buy individual municipal bonds over funds, and anecdotally, the group has swelled in recent years. The reasons are myriad, but some of the most potent involve return predictability, tax efficiency, and the notion that all municipal bonds are pretty much the same.

The fact is that most investors would be better off with a well-run, low-cost fund, and this one's the poster child. Many believe they'll be safer with a ladder of bonds, bought and held, with none ever sold at a loss. Most funds never lose money over stretches longer than a couple of years, including this one. The Morningstar database boasts more than 140 rolling three-year periods of this fund's returns: It has not had a negative return during any of them. The same is true for rolling five and 10-year periods. In fact the worst three-year performance in the database was a positive 10%.

Some believe such tactics may also produce better after-tax performance, and fear funds that pay out any capital gains. Even with the fairly frequent distributions this one has made, it still boasts some of the best after-tax returns in the municipal-bond national long-term category--and that assumes the highest federal tax rate.

It is a mistake to think all municipal bonds are the same, since so many come with calls and other features that make valuing them extremely tricky. Most managers, including Fidelity's, can add to their returns simply by unloading bonds through brokers onto individual investors who don't adequately factor in those traits.

What has helped produce such stellar pre- and post-tax performance here is meticulous style that involves some of the industry's best risk controls and some of the most comprehensive bond-by-bond analysis around. This fund may not have the highest return at any given moment, but it almost always shines over the long haul, and its management is among the very best around.

Address:	82 Devonshire Street Boston MA 02109 800-544-9797	Minimum Purchase:	$10000	Add: $1000 IRA: $0
		Min Auto Inv Plan:	$10000	Add: $500
Web Address:	www.fidelity.com	Sales Fees:	No-load, 0.50%R	
Inception:	12-01-77	Management Fee:	0.37%	
Advisor:	Fidelity Management & Research (FMR)	Actual Fees:	Mgt:0.38%	Dist: —
Subadvisor:	Multiple Subadvisors	Expense Projections:	3Yr:$151	5Yr:$263 10Yr:$591
		Income Distrib:	Monthly	
NTF Plans:	Fidelity Retail-NTF, CommonWealth NTF			

MORNINGSTAR® Funds 500

Fidelity New Markets Inc

Analyst Pick ✓

Ticker	Load	NAV	Yield	SEC Yield	Total Assets	Mstar Category
FNMIX	None	$14.80	5.7%	5.90%	$2,235 mil	Emerging Markets Bond

Governance and Management

Stewardship Grade: B

Portfolio Manager(s)

John Carlson has managed this fund since 1995 and also oversees Fidelity's emerging-markets equities effort. He previously served as executive director of emerging markets for Lehman Brothers International. Carlson is supported by six analysts, three of whom have been with him throughout his tenure on the fund.

Strategy

John Carlson believes in a good defense. He usually chooses to invest heavily in countries that attract foreign direct investment. He treads lightly on corporate bonds, and he won't invest more than 10% of assets in local currencies or 15% in equities. The fund's country weightings are kept broadly in line with those of the benchmark, J.P. Morgan EMBI Global Index, and Carlson also keeps the fund's duration (a measure of interest-rate sensitivity) to within one year of the index position.

Performance 12-31-06

	1st Qtr	2nd Qtr	3rd Qtr	4th Qtr	Total
2002	7.36	-5.17	-2.42	13.31	12.56
2003	8.03	11.65	2.10	6.47	31.11
2004	3.16	-5.92	9.12	6.24	12.50
2005	-1.24	6.33	4.01	1.72	11.10
2006	3.46	-1.87	6.08	3.89	11.89

Trailing	Total Return%	+/- LB Aggr	+/- Citigroup ESBI-Cap Brady	%Rank Cat	Growth of $10,000
3 Mo	3.89	2.65	-6.53	77	10,389
6 Mo	10.21	5.12	-10.70	71	11,021
1 Yr	11.89	7.56	-12.76	24	11,189
3 Yr Avg	11.83	8.13	-1.80	32	13,985
5 Yr Avg	15.61	10.55	0.92	39	20,653
10 Yr Avg	12.13	5.89	0.12	12	31,421
15 Yr Avg	—	—	—	—	—

Tax Analysis	Tax-Adj Rtn%	%Rank Cat	Tax-Cost Rat	%Rank Cat
3 Yr (estimated)	8.64	36	2.85	79
5 Yr (estimated)	12.40	32	2.78	44
10 Yr (estimated)	8.11	5	3.59	20

Potential Capital Gain Exposure: 6% of assets

Historical Profile

Return	Average
Risk	Below Avg
Rating	★★★ Neutral

| 62 | 58 | 35 | 43 | 47 | 66 | 33 | 46 |

Growth of $10,000
— Investment Values of Fund
— Investment Values of LB Aggr

Performance Quartile (within Category)

1995	1996	1997	1998	1999	2000	2001	2002	2003	2004	2005	2006	History
9.95	12.96	12.97	8.99	11.13	11.39	10.91	11.32	13.90	14.33	14.42	14.80	NAV
7.97	41.39	17.52	-22.38	36.69	14.38	6.64	12.56	31.11	12.50	11.10	11.89	Total Return %
-10.50	37.76	7.87	-31.07	37.51	2.75	-1.80	2.31	27.01	8.16	8.67	7.56	+/-LB Aggr
—	5.88	0.90	-17.08	19.88	1.56	-0.96	3.77	6.79	1.20	5.34	-12.76	+/-Citigroup ESBI-Cap Brady
9.43	9.75	10.81	8.25	11.76	12.20	11.12	8.65	7.23	6.60	6.31	6.16	Income Return %
-1.46	31.64	6.71	-30.63	24.93	2.18	-4.48	3.91	23.88	5.90	4.79	5.73	Capital Return %
78	34	18	54	10	24	66	37	32	47	54	24	Total Rtn % Rank Cat
0.92	0.93	1.32	1.02	1.01	1.30	1.21	0.91	0.79	0.88	0.86	0.86	Income $
0.00	0.00	0.87	0.20	0.00	0.00	0.00	0.00	0.05	0.33	0.56	0.42	Capital Gains $
1.17	1.09	1.08	1.13	1.07	0.99	0.99	1.00	1.00	0.94	0.94	—	Expense Ratio %
9.51	7.68	7.56	10.50	9.88	9.41	11.61	8.48	7.90	6.26	6.12	—	Income Ratio %
306	405	656	488	273	278	259	219	219	237	196	—	Turnover Rate %
174	306	371	207	214	258	293	425	866	1,089	1,734	2,235	Net Assets $mil

Rating and Risk

Time Period	Load-Adj Return %	Morningstar Rtn vs Cat	Morningstar Risk vs Cat	Morningstar Risk-Adj Rating
1 Yr	11.89			
3 Yr	11.83	Avg	-Avg	★★★
5 Yr	15.61	Avg	Avg	★★★
10 Yr	12.13	+Avg	-Avg	★★★★
Incept	13.38			

Other Measures	Standard Index LB Aggr	Best Fit Index Citigroup ESBI-Cap Brady
Alpha	7.6	1.7
Beta	1.44	0.66
R-Squared	48	57
Standard Deviation	6.78	
Mean	11.83	
Sharpe Ratio	1.22	

Portfolio Analysis 09-30-06

Total Fixed-Income:134

	Date of Maturity	Amount $000	Value $000	% Net Assets
Russian Federation FRN	03-31-30	126,298	140,822	6.74
Venezuela Opt (call)	10-19-06	44,080	53,910	2.58
Philippines Rep 9%	02-15-13	45,785	51,508	2.46
Gazstream S A 144A 5.625	07-22-13	37,215	36,936	1.77
Brazil Federative Rep 11	08-17-40	27,965	36,410	1.74
United Mexican Sts Mtn B	08-15-31	27,195	33,926	1.62
Russian Federation 11%	07-24-18	23,437	33,691	1.61
Russian Federation 12.75	06-24-28	18,397	33,023	1.58
Brazil Federative Rep 8.	02-04-25	27,410	32,618	1.56
Brazil Federative Rep 8.	01-20-34	28,215	32,334	1.55
Argentina FRN	08-03-12	34,103	31,493	1.51
Republic Of Turkey 11%	01-14-13	25,930	31,148	1.49
Philippines Rep 9.5%	02-02-30	24,310	29,962	1.43
Republic Of Turkey 11.87	01-15-30	19,635	28,937	1.38
Mexico-United Mexican St	05-15-26	17,480	27,601	1.32
Pemex Project Fdg Master	09-28-49	26,220	26,679	1.28
Brazil Federative Rep 8%	01-15-18	23,470	25,758	1.23
Turkiye Cumhuriyeti 11.7	06-15-10	21,910	25,668	1.23
Philippines Rep 9.875%	01-15-19	20,625	25,420	1.22
United Mexican Sts Mtn B	01-15-17	24,886	24,612	1.18

Current Investment Style

Duration: Short / Int / Long
Quality: High / Med / Low

¹ figure provided by fund

Avg Eff Duration¹	—
Avg Eff Maturity	—
Avg Credit Quality	—
Avg Wtd Coupon	8.24%
Avg Wtd Price	114.43% of par

Coupon Range	% of Bonds	Rel Cat
0% PIK	1.7	0.3
0% to 6%	22.6	0.9
6% to 8%	20.4	0.8
8% to 10%	32.5	0.9
More than 10%	24.5	1.6

1.00=Category Average

Credit Analysis	% bonds 09-30-06		
AAA	—	BB	—
AA	—	B	—
A	—	Below B	—
BBB	—	NR/NA	—

Sector Breakdown — % of assets

US Treasuries	—
TIPS	—
US Agency	—
Mortgage Pass-Throughs	—
Mortgage CMO	—
Mortgage ARM	—
US Corporate	—
Asset-Backed	—
Convertible	—
Municipal	—
Corporate Inflation-Protected	—
Foreign Corporate	—
Foreign Govt	—

Composition			
Cash	6.0	Bonds	89.9
Stocks	0.0	Other	4.1

Special Securities	
Restricted/Illiquid Secs	11
Exotic Mortgage-Backed	0
Emerging-Markets Secs	—
Options/Futures/Warrants	No

Morningstar's Take by Arijit Dutta 12-20-06

Fidelity New Markets' opportunistic style has a lot of appeal, but we'd tread carefully here.

Manager John Carlson has pulled off some nifty moves this year. He added an 8% stake in emerging-markets equities at the start of the year, which performed tremendously until a sharp correction in May. Carlson took timely profits, however, and got completely out of those stock positions before the market turned sour. The correction, which also affected emerging-markets bonds, hurt this fund relatively less, due to some sound country selection. For example, Carlson underweighted Turkey, whose weak macroeconomic position came under an especially severe attack in May through June. On the other hand, the portfolio's overweight in Argentina paid off, due to that country's strong economy. Thus, the fund has performed well in both good times and bad, and has a great record for the year thus far.

This year's run provides a glimpse of the long-term effectiveness of Carlson's approach. He will make unconventional moves when he sees a clear-cut opportunity, but he spreads his bets over a wide range of securities and keeps a keen eye on valuations. For example, he thought that relative to the paltry yields on emerging-country debt (over those available on much safer U.S. Treasuries), stocks offered a much better value. He built his equities stake on numerous small positions, however, and sold them steadily as they climbed. Similarly, the fund pulled ahead this year due to a number of modest bets against the benchmark, such as those in Argentina and Turkey. Over time, these small victories do add up.

We think highly of Carlson and his team, but we continue to be wary of emerging-markets bonds. The category has staged a strong comeback from the historically mild correction earlier in the year, and these funds are set to finish 2006 atop all domestic and foreign fixed-income categories. We would moderate our expectations here, given these rich valuations.

Address:	82 Devonshire Street Boston MA 02109 800-544-9797	Minimum Purchase:	$2500	Add: $250 IRA: $200
		Min Auto Inv Plan:	$2500	Add: $100
Web Address:	www.fidelity.com	Sales Fees:	No-load, 1.00%R	
Inception:	05-04-93	Management Fee:	0.68%	
Advisor:	Fidelity Management & Research (FMR)	Actual Fees:	Mgt:0.67% Dist: —	
Subadvisor:	Multiple Subadvisors	Expense Projections:	3Yr:$300 5Yr:$520 10Yr:$1155	
NTF Plans:	Fidelity Retail-NTF, CommonWealth NTF	Income Distrib:	Monthly	

Fidelity New Millennium

	Ticker	Load	NAV	Yield	Total Assets	Mstar Category
	FMILX	Closed	$29.40	0.0%	$2,360 mil	Mid-Cap Growth

Governance and Management

Stewardship Grade: B

Portfolio Manager(s)

On July 3, 2006, John Roth took over this fund from veteran skipper Neal Miller, who had managed it since its 1992 inception. Roth previously ran several sector funds for the firm, including Fidelity Select Chemicals and Fidelity Select Consumer Industries. He will continue to manage Fidelity Select Multimedia, which he's headed up since May 2004.

Strategy

New skipper John Roth is running this fund far differently than predecessor Neal Miller, who plied a theme-based approach and sought out fast growers. Roth typically buys firms for one of three reasons: They are beating out competitors through innovation, they're able to boost profit growth without relying on industry or macroeconomic conditions, or they've stumbled and he believes he can earn money through a rather quick trade. He'll buy companies of all sizes, but will limit the fund's sector bets against the S&P 500 Index.

Performance 12-31-06

	1st Qtr	2nd Qtr	3rd Qtr	4th Qtr	Total
2002	0.11	-11.89	-15.35	7.32	-19.87
2003	-3.57	18.55	5.97	13.35	37.31
2004	0.86	-2.06	-4.56	10.61	4.28
2005	-4.86	0.20	11.95	3.16	10.10
2006	11.75	-3.67	-2.42	8.08	13.53

Trailing	Total Return%	+/- S&P 500	+/- Russ MG	%Rank Cat	Growth of $10,000
3 Mo	8.08	1.38	1.13	25	10,808
6 Mo	5.46	-7.28	-2.44	55	10,546
1 Yr	13.53	-2.26	2.87	17	11,353
3 Yr Avg	9.23	-1.21	-3.50	69	13,032
5 Yr Avg	7.48	1.29	-0.74	35	14,343
10 Yr Avg	13.87	5.45	5.25	8	36,652
15 Yr Avg	—				

Tax Analysis	Tax-Adj Rtn%	%Rank Cat	Tax-Cost Rat	%Rank Cat
3 Yr (estimated)	7.81	72	1.30	63
5 Yr (estimated)	6.63	38	0.79	55
10 Yr (estimated)	11.71	9	1.90	75

Potential Capital Gain Exposure: 20% of assets

Historical Profile

Return: Above Avg
Risk: Above Avg
Rating: ★★★ Neutral

| 95% | 98% | 93% | 96% | 97% | 98% | 95% | 98% | 99% |

Investment Style
Equity
Stock %

▼ Manager Change
▽ Partial Manager Change

Growth of $10,000
— Investment Values of Fund
— Investment Values of S&P 500

67.4
47.8
33.8
24.0
17.0
10.0

Performance Quartile (within Category)

1995	1996	1997	1998	1999	2000	2001	2002	2003	2004	2005	2006	History
16.96	20.25	22.19	26.27	47.46	34.33	27.63	22.14	30.39	31.69	34.89	29.40	NAV
52.14	23.15	24.63	27.70	108.78	-6.03	-18.15	-19.87	37.31	4.28	10.10	13.53	Total Return %
14.56	0.19	-8.73	-0.88	87.74	3.07	-6.26	2.23	8.63	-6.60	5.19	-2.26	+/-S&P 500
18.16	5.67	2.09	9.84	57.49	5.72	2.00	7.54	-5.40	-11.20	-2.00	2.87	+/-Russ MG
0.00	0.00	0.00	0.00	0.00	0.00	0.00	0.00	0.05	0.00	0.00	0.00	Income Return %
52.14	23.15	24.63	27.70	108.78	-6.03	-18.15	-19.87	37.26	4.28	10.10	13.53	Capital Return %
4	19	31	21	13	55	51	21	40	99	52	17	Total Rtn % Rank Cat
0.00	0.00	0.00	0.00	0.00	0.00	0.00	0.00	0.01	0.00	0.00	0.00	Income $
1.40	0.60	2.89	1.94	6.37	10.11	0.53	0.00	0.00	0.00	10.30		Capital Gains $
1.18	1.03	0.94	0.83	0.93	0.89	0.98	1.02	0.76	0.92	0.80	—	Expense Ratio %
-0.15	-0.17	-0.13	-0.13	-0.36	-0.36	-0.30	-0.38	0.02	-0.18	-0.01	—	Income Ratio %
176	158	142	121	116	97	85	91	97	96	120	—	Turnover Rate %
594	1,253	1,564	1,684	3,772	3,572	2,939	2,616	3,656	3,618	3,478	2,360	Net Assets $mil

Rating and Risk

Time Period	Load-Adj Return %	Morningstar Rtn vs Cat	Morningstar Risk vs Cat	Morningstar Risk-Adj Rating
1 Yr	13.53			
3 Yr	9.23	Avg	+Avg	★★
5 Yr	7.48	Avg	+Avg	★★★
10 Yr	13.87	High	+Avg	★★★
Incept	16.70			

Other Measures	Standard Index S&P 500	Best Fit Index Mstar Mid Growth TR
Alpha	-5.9	-4.8
Beta	1.80	1.10
R-Squared	71	90
Standard Deviation	14.70	
Mean	9.23	
Sharpe Ratio	0.46	

Portfolio Analysis 08-31-06

Share change since 05-06 Total Stocks:262

	Sector	PE	Tot Ret%	% Assets
⊕ Google, Inc.	Business	61.5	11.00	2.94
✕✕ Intel Corporation	Hardware	21.0	-17.18	1.61
✕✕ eBay, Inc.	Consumer	40.1	-30.43	1.37
✕✕ Carter's, Inc.	Goods	29.3	-13.34	1.31
⊕ Brookdale Senior Living,	Health	—	—	1.21
⊖ Moody's Corporation	Financial	32.6	12.95	1.20
✕✕ Noble Energy, Inc.	Energy	11.7	22.48	1.14
✕✕ Wells Fargo Company	Financial	14.7	16.82	1.08
✕✕ Under Armour, Inc. A	Goods	—	—	0.93
⊖ Cameco Corporation	Energy	63.2	28.10	0.89
⊕ Li & Fung Ltd	Goods	—	—	0.88
✕✕ Nestle	Goods	—	—	0.86
✕✕ Berkshire Hathaway A	Financial	—	—	0.82
⊕ Cerner Corporation	Software	37.1	0.10	0.80
✕✕ ConocoPhillips	Energy	6.5	26.53	0.78
✕✕ SCP Pool, Inc.	Goods	21.4	6.25	0.77
✕✕ Merck & Co., Inc.	Health	19.1	42.66	0.77
⊖ Chicago Mercantile Excha	Financial	49.3	39.48	0.76
⊖ ExxonMobil Corporation	Energy	11.1	39.07	0.75
⊖ Gilead Sciences, Inc.	Health	40.6	23.51	0.75

Current Investment Style

Value Blnd Growth — Large Mid Small

Market Cap	%
Giant	21.0
Large	25.9
Mid	34.8
Small	14.5
Micro	3.7

Avg $mil: 9,016

Value Measures		Rel Category
Price/Earnings	18.92	0.92
Price/Book	2.86	0.89
Price/Sales	1.66	0.94
Price/Cash Flow	9.88	0.87
Dividend Yield %	0.92	1.46

Growth Measures	%	Rel Category
Long-Term Erngs	13.98	0.86
Book Value	10.11	0.79
Sales	11.72	1.17
Cash Flow	23.38	1.27
Historical Erngs	23.39	0.94

Profitability	%	Rel Category
Return on Equity	17.13	0.95
Return on Assets	9.67	1.03
Net Margin	12.13	1.04

Sector Weightings

	% of Stocks	Rel S&P 500	3 Year High Low
ⓘ Info	18.28	0.91	
Software	3.05	0.88	10 3
Hardware	11.04	1.19	31 4
Media	2.71	0.72	5 1
Telecom	1.48	0.42	3 0
ⓖ Service	53.66	1.16	
Health	13.52	1.12	23 5
Consumer	9.49	1.24	11 3
Business	11.89	2.81	24 5
Financial	18.76	0.84	19 1
Mfg	28.06	0.83	
Goods	10.95	1.28	11 6
Ind Mtrls	7.42	0.62	26 7
Energy	8.61	0.88	16 7
Utilities	1.08	0.31	2 0

Composition

● Cash	0.6
● Stocks	99.0
● Bonds	0.0
● Other	0.4
Foreign	19.1
(% of Stock)	

Morningstar's Take by Greg Carlson 12-14-06

The jury is out on Fidelity New Millennium's makeover.

This mid-growth fund's new manager, John Roth, has big shoes to fill. His predecessor, Neal Miller, amassed a superb record over a 14-year tenure before retiring in June 2006, and he did so using an atypical, freewheeling approach. Miller developed a knack for identifying trends long before most managers, then chose companies that would benefit from those trends, often with little regard to valuation. Big sector bets were the norm, and the result was a volatile but ultimately rewarding ride.

Roth is applying a flexible, but more restrained strategy--a wise move, as this is his first stint at a diversified fund. He'll buy companies of all sizes, to a greater extent than Miller did, that he believes will either generate high profit growth regardless of economic conditions or take market share from rivals through innovation. Roth will also buy where he thinks he can reap a quick gain due to a stumble. He'll limit the fund's sector bets against its

benchmark, the S&P 500 Index, and he's more valuation-sensitive than Miller, employing a wide variety of metrics. That focus on price has led to a substantially bigger stake in behemoths such as Intel and Wells Fargo, which have lagged smaller fry for years. As a result, the fund has moved into the large-growth part of the Morningstar Style Box. It's worth noting that this closed fund has never been a dedicated midcap offering, thus it could end up changing categories.

We think Roth's strategy makes some sense, and the fund's more-diversified look and lower price multiples should make it less volatile. What's more, he's working with a rather modest asset base, and the fund's expense ratio--which is based in part on its three-year performance against the S&P--is reasonable. That said, Roth's inexperience makes this fund a gamble we don't think investors should take. We'd suggest checking out Fidelity Capital Appreciation, a go-anywhere fund run by a veteran skipper.

Address:	82 Devonshire St Boston MA 02109 800-544-6666	Minimum Purchase:	Closed	Add: —	IRA: —
		Min Auto Inv Plan:	Closed	Add: —	
		Sales Fees:	No-load		
Web Address:	www.fidelity.com	Management Fee:	0.63%		
Inception:	12-28-92	Actual Fees:	Mgt:0.63%	Dist: —	
Advisor:	Fidelity Management & Research (FMR)	Expense Projections:	3Yr:$274	5Yr:$477	10Yr:$1061
Subadvisor:	Multiple Subadvisors	Income Distrib:	Annually		
NTF Plans:	Fidelity Retail-NTF, CommonWealth NTF				

M⊕RNINGSTAR® Funds 500

Fidelity Overseas

	Ticker	Load	NAV	Yield	Total Assets	Mstar Category
	FOSFX	None	$44.80	1.1%	$7,714 mil	Foreign Large Blend

Governance and Management

Stewardship Grade: B

Portfolio Manager(s)

Ian Hart took the reins here on Jan. 1, 2006, succeeding longtime manager Rick Mace. Hart came off a successful stint as manager of Fidelity Europe Capital Appreciation, which he ran from April 2000 through the end of 2005. In the fall of 2005, he also served briefly as an international research director. Hart began his Fidelity career in 1994 as a research analyst, covering European equities out of London. He relies here on Fidelity's analyst network in Boston, London, Hong Kong, and Tokyo, in addition to smaller offices in India, Korea, and Australia.

Strategy

Unlike peers such as Bill Bower (Fidelity Diversified International) and Bill Kennedy (International Discovery), Ian Hart prefers portfolios of about 100 stocks; he'll concentrate assets in top names; and he doesn't follow the MSCI EAFE Index in terms of stock, sector, and country weightings. Hart is a growth-at-a-reasonable-price investor who puts a premium on Fidelity's internal research. He prefers to buy stocks where he thinks that research gives him an edge--often mid-caps or emerging-markets names. Fidelity uses fair value pricing and does not hedge foreign currency exposure.

Performance 12-31-06

	1st Qtr	2nd Qtr	3rd Qtr	4th Qtr	Total
2002	2.19	-4.14	-20.74	3.74	-19.45
2003	-10.00	23.13	11.90	16.37	44.30
2004	5.82	-4.57	-1.58	14.23	13.54
2005	-1.53	-0.17	11.33	9.00	19.29
2006	7.50	-1.01	2.33	10.65	20.49

Trailing	Total Return%	+/- MSCI EAFE	+/- MSCI Wd xUS	%Rank Cat	Growth of $10,000
3 Mo	10.65	0.30	0.53	36	11,065
6 Mo	13.22	-1.47	-1.00	80	11,322
1 Yr	20.49	-5.85	-5.22	91	12,049
3 Yr Avg	17.73	-2.20	-2.37	69	16,318
5 Yr Avg	13.66	-1.32	-1.59	41	18,969
10 Yr Avg	8.25	0.54	0.29	25	22,094
15 Yr Avg	8.55	0.69	0.51	40	34,233

Tax Analysis	Tax-Adj Rtn%	%Rank Cat	Tax-Cost Rat	%Rank Cat
3 Yr (estimated)	16.46	65	1.08	57
5 Yr (estimated)	12.86	38	0.70	55
10 Yr (estimated)	7.14	26	1.03	50

Potential Capital Gain Exposure: 19% of assets

Historical Profile

Return	Above Avg
Risk	High
Rating	★★★ Neutral

											81%	88%	93%	87%	98%	87%	93%	98%	95%

Investment Style
Equity
Stock %

▼ Manager Change
▽ Partial Manager Change

Growth of $10,000
■ Investment Values of Fund
— Investment Values of MSCI EAFE

26.0
22.0
18.0
14.0
10.0

Performance Quartile (within Category)

1995	1996	1997	1998	1999	2000	2001	2002	2003	2004	2005	2006	History
29.07	30.84	32.54	35.98	48.01	34.37	27.42	22.00	31.43	35.38	41.61	44.80	NAV
9.06	13.10	10.92	12.84	42.89	-18.33	-20.22	-19.45	44.30	13.54	19.29	20.49	Total Return %
-2.15	7.05	9.14	-7.09	15.86	-4.14	1.20	-3.51	5.71	-6.71	5.75	-5.85	+/-MSCI EAFE
-2.35	6.23	8.65	-5.85	14.91	-4.97	1.17	-3.65	4.88	-6.84	4.82	-5.22	+/-MSCI Wd xUS
1.25	1.27	1.10	0.61	1.22	1.79	0.00	0.33	1.36	0.60	1.16	1.32	Income Return %
7.81	11.83	9.82	12.23	41.67	-20.12	-20.22	-19.78	42.94	12.94	18.13	19.17	Capital Return %
67	42	25	57	32	67	39	75	2	90	12	91	Total Rtn % Rank Cat
0.34	0.37	0.34	0.20	0.44	0.86	0.00	0.09	0.30	0.19	0.41	0.55	Income $
0.35	1.63	1.34	0.51	2.64	4.12	0.00	0.00	0.00	0.11	0.16	4.64	Capital Gains $
1.05	1.12	1.20	1.24	1.23	1.16	1.12	1.16	1.00	1.01	0.86	—	Expense Ratio %
1.78	1.74	1.28	0.82	1.16	0.55	0.63	0.42	0.75	0.55	1.11	—	Income Ratio %
49	82	68	69	85	132	95	72	104	79	87	—	Turnover Rate %
2,410	3,247	3,705	3,847	5,404	4,653	3,481	2,843	3,961	4,687	5,371	7,714	Net Assets $mil

Rating and Risk

Time Period	Load-Adj Return %	Morningstar Rtn vs Cat	Morningstar Risk vs Cat	Morningstar Risk-Adj Rating
1 Yr	20.49			
3 Yr	17.73	Avg	High	★★
5 Yr	13.66	Avg	High	★★★
10 Yr	8.25	+Avg	+Avg	★★★
Incept	13.45			

Other Measures	Standard Index MSCI EAFE	Best Fit Index MSCI Wd xUS
Alpha	-4.2	-4.2
Beta	1.16	1.15
R-Squared	90	91
Standard Deviation	11.60	
Mean	17.73	
Sharpe Ratio	1.20	

Portfolio Analysis 10-31-06

Share change since 07-06 Total Stocks:111	Sector	Country	% Assets
⊕ Pernod Ricard	Goods	France	4.08
⊕ Reuters Grp	Media	U.K.	3.47
⊕ BAE Systems	Ind Mtrls	U.K.	2.03
⊕ Nintendo	Goods	Japan	1.90
⊖ BBVA	Financial	Spain	1.78
⊕ BHP Billiton	Ind Mtrls	U.K.	1.57
⊕ Lottomatica	Consumer	Italy	1.56
⊕ Credit Suisse Grp	Financial	Switzerland	1.56
⊖ Total SA	Energy	France	1.56
⊖ Bayer	Ind Mtrls	Germany	1.53
⊖ Novartis	Health	Switzerland	1.47
⊖ ING Groep	Financial	Netherlands	1.45
⊖ Neste Oil	Energy	Finland	1.39
⊖ Global Industries, Ltd.	Energy	United States	1.37
☼ Barclays	Financial	U.K.	1.35
⊖ E.ON	Utilities	Germany	1.27
⊕ Satyam Computer	Software	India	1.25
⊖ Johnson & Johnson	Health	United States	1.25
☼ HSBC Holdings PLC ADR	Financial	U.K.	1.21
⊕ Munich Re Grp	Financial	Germany	1.20

Current Investment Style

Value	Blnd	Growth		Market Cap	%
			Large	Giant	42.1
				Large	36.3
			Mid	Mid	19.7
				Small	2.0
			Small	Micro	0.0

Avg $mil: 20,918

Value Measures		Rel Category
Price/Earnings	15.26	1.16
Price/Book	2.30	1.06
Price/Sales	1.15	0.99
Price/Cash Flow	9.80	1.18
Dividend Yield %	2.43	0.83

Growth Measures	%	Rel Category
Long-Term Erngs	13.68	1.16
Book Value	8.75	0.96
Sales	10.06	1.54
Cash Flow	10.49	1.27
Historical Erngs	16.23	0.80

Composition

Cash	4.8	Bonds	0.0
Stocks	95.2	Other	0.0
Foreign (% of Stock)			95.3

Sector Weightings	% of Stocks	Rel MSCI EAFE	3 Year High	Low
ℹ Info	13.84	1.17		
🅂 Software	2.78	4.96	3	1
🅷 Hardware	1.84	0.48	22	1
🄼 Media	6.14	3.36	6	3
🄣 Telecom	3.08	0.55	15	2
🄲 Service	45.62	0.97		
🄷 Health	6.39	0.90	10	6
🄲 Consumer	5.16	1.04	5	3
🄱 Business	3.17	0.63	3	0
🄵 Financial	30.90	1.03	33	24
🄼 Mfg	40.53	0.99		
🄶 Goods	12.66	0.96	14	6
🄸 Ind Mtrls	15.01	0.97	15	5
🄴 Energy	9.95	1.39	23	8
🅄 Utilities	2.91	0.56	9	1

Regional Exposure % Stock

UK/W. Europe	62	N. America	6
Japan	18	Latn America	2
Asia X Japan	9	Other	3

Country Exposure % Stock

U.K.	18	Switzerland	6
Japan	18	Germany	6
France	14		

Morningstar's Take by Dan Lefkovitz 12-18-06

Despite a stumble out of the gate, Fidelity Overseas' new manager holds lots of promise.

With his first year at this fund's helm almost in the books, manager Ian Hart has posted uninspiring returns. Of course, a 20% gain for the year to date through Dec. 15, 2006, is nothing to sneeze at, but compared with the MSCI EAFE Index, the fund's benchmark, or the foreign large-blend category, the fund's peer group, it is lackluster. Both have risen roughly 25%. The fund got tripped up in May, June, and July, when a market pullback punished some of its emerging-markets holdings. And several of Hart's bets in the energy sector did not pan out.

This year's trouble spots demonstrate something about Hart's approach. He is a high conviction manager who takes big bets on both stocks and industries. He will stash a lot of assets in names like Reuters and Pernod Ricard, which are not big constituents of the EAFE Index, and will hold emerging-markets stocks, such as Satyam Computer (India) and Turkiye Garanti Bankasi

(Turkey) that aren't in the index at all. And he plays "themes," such as rising demand for luxury goods or alternative energy development.

Such high conviction investing causes divergent performance. This year, performance diverged the wrong way, but during Hart's five-year stint running Fidelity Europe Capital Appreciation, he delivered great returns. That fund suffered some dry spells, too, but Hart's big bets on stocks, such as Deutsche Borse and various Eastern European names, paid off in spades over the long haul.

Hart's predecessor on this fund took big bets, too. But his favored areas, semiconductors and Japan brokerage houses, gave the fund an aggressive profile, which is why it lost a lot during the bear market. Hart, by contrast, is quite valuation conscious. And his willingness to consider emerging markets and smaller-cap stocks gives investors something different than does an EAFE index fund. It could easily turn out that 2006 was an aberration.

Address:	82 Devonshire St Boston MA 02109 800-544-9797	Minimum Purchase:	$2500	Add: $250	IRA: $200
		Min Auto Inv Plan:	$100	Add: $100	
Web Address:	www.fidelity.com	Sales Fees:	No-load, 1.00%R		
Inception:	12-04-84	Management Fee:	0.69%		
Advisor:	Fidelity Management & Research (FMR)	Actual Fees:	Mgt:0.69%	Dist: —	
Subadvisor:	Multiple Subadvisors	Expense Projections:	3Yr:$318	5Yr:$552	10Yr:$1225
NTF Plans:	Fidelity Retail-NTF, CommonWealth NTF	Income Distrib:	Annually		

Fidelity Pacific Basin

	Ticker	Load	NAV	Yield	Total Assets	Mstar Category
	FPBFX	None	$27.35	0.5%	$1,013 mil	Diversified Pacific/Asia

Governance and Management

Stewardship Grade: B

Portfolio Manager(s)

Dale Nicholls took over this portfolio in October 2004 from Bill Kennedy, who was tapped to manage Fidelity International Discovery. Nicholls has managed Fidelity Advisor Japan since September 2003 and continues to run that fund in addition to this one. Nicholls began working as an analyst in Fidelity's Tokyo office in 1996 and has managed sector funds available only in Japan.

Strategy

Dale Nicholls aims to use Fidelity's research analysts to ferret out ideas. He prefers smaller-cap stocks and is more willing than his predecessor to venture outside of Japan. Nicholls looks for growth potential but also puts a premium on cash flow and the strength of a company's management team. Nicholls will keep the fund's sector allocations within 5 percentage points of the fund's benchmark, the MSCI All Country Pacific Index, but ventures beyond the index for stock ideas. Fidelity uses fair-value pricing on an as-needed basis and does not hedge foreign currency exposure.

Performance 12-31-06

	1st Qtr	2nd Qtr	3rd Qtr	4th Qtr	Total
2002	7.44	-0.47	-12.42	-1.62	-7.87
2003	-7.45	16.17	16.84	10.40	38.69
2004	10.50	-5.73	-4.05	14.14	14.08
2005	-0.15	2.03	14.30	13.81	32.52
2006	8.57	-4.84	0.49	11.89	16.16

Trailing	Total Return%	+/- MSCI EAFE	+/- MSCI Pac	%Rank Cat	Growth of $10,000
3 Mo	11.89	1.54	3.96	9	11,189
6 Mo	12.44	-2.25	4.06	65	11,244
1 Yr	16.16	-10.18	3.96	89	11,616
3 Yr Avg	20.65	0.72	2.79	34	17,562
5 Yr Avg	17.54	2.56	2.03	17	22,435
10 Yr Avg	8.90	1.19	5.70	15	23,457
15 Yr Avg	7.96	0.10	4.74	34	31,546

Tax Analysis	Tax-Adj Rtn%	%Rank Cat	Tax-Cost Rat	%Rank Cat
3 Yr (estimated)	19.63	43	0.85	47
5 Yr (estimated)	16.90	29	0.54	46
10 Yr (estimated)	8.19	1	0.65	29

Potential Capital Gain Exposure: 26% of assets

Historical Profile

Return	Above Avg
Risk	Below Avg
Rating	★★★★ Above Avg

94%　96%　94%　97%　97%　94%　97%　97%　98%

Growth of $10,000
- ■ Investment Values of Fund
- — Investment Values of MSCI EAFE

22.0　18.0　14.0　10.0　6.0

Performance Quartile (within Category)

1995	1996	1997	1998	1999	2000	2001	2002	2003	2004	2005	2006	History
15.20	14.70	12.23	13.22	28.74	17.29	13.85	12.76	17.53	19.77	25.67	27.35	NAV
-6.11	-2.76	-15.10	8.26	119.61	-35.32	-19.90	-7.87	38.69	14.08	32.52	16.16	Total Return %
-17.32	-8.81	-16.88	-11.67	92.58	-21.13	1.52	8.07	0.10	-6.17	18.98	-10.18	+/-MSCI EAFE
-8.89	5.82	10.39	5.85	61.98	-9.54	5.49	1.42	0.21	-4.90	9.88	3.96	+/-MSCI Pac
0.00	0.53	1.70	0.16	1.97	3.90	0.00	0.00	1.25	0.46	0.91	0.62	Income Return %
-6.11	-3.29	-16.80	8.10	117.64	-39.22	-19.90	-7.87	37.44	13.62	31.61	15.54	Capital Return %
100	100	57	9	9	83	58	17	75	89	34	89	Total Rtn % Rank Cat
0.00	0.08	0.25	0.02	0.26	1.12	0.00	0.00	0.16	0.08	0.18	0.16	Income $
0.00	0.00	0.00	0.00	0.23	0.00	0.00	0.00	0.00	0.13	0.32	2.24	Capital Gains $
1.32	1.24	1.31	1.72	1.36	1.22	1.45	1.50	1.17	1.19	1.05	—	Expense Ratio %
0.44	0.30	-0.04	-0.16	-0.24	-0.42	-0.11	-0.15	0.41	0.42	1.09	—	Income Ratio %
65	85	42	57	101	144	123	98	97	145	78	—	Turnover Rate %
469	447	214	227	989	447	331	297	430	497	852	1,013	Net Assets $mil

Rating and Risk

Time Period	Load-Adj Return %	Morningstar Rtn vs Cat	Morningstar Risk vs Cat	Morningstar Risk-Adj Rating
1 Yr	16.16			
3 Yr	20.65	Avg	Avg	★★★
5 Yr	17.54	Avg	-Avg	★★★
10 Yr	8.90	+Avg	-Avg	★★★★
Incept	7.53			

Other Measures	Standard Index MSCI EAFE	Best Fit Index MSCI Pac
Alpha	-1.6	2.7
Beta	1.18	0.99
R-Squared	66	86
Standard Deviation	13.69	
Mean	20.65	
Sharpe Ratio	1.22	

Portfolio Analysis 10-31-06

Share change since 07-06 Total Stocks:265

	Sector	Country	% Assets
⊖ Toyota Motor	Goods	Japan	2.57
⊖ Mizuho Financial Grp	Financial	Japan	1.97
⊖ Sumitomo Mitsui Financia	Financial	Japan	1.75
⊕ NHN	Business	Korea	1.60
⊖ BHP Billiton, Ltd.	Ind Mtrls	Australia	1.38
Natl Australia Bk	Financial	Australia	1.34
⊖ ORIX	Financial	Japan	1.18
⊖ Computershare Ltd	Software	Australia	1.16
⊖ Finl Technolo	—	India	1.09
⊖ Esprit Hldgs Ltd	Consumer	Hong Kong	1.06
⊖ Nippon Electric Glass	Goods	Japan	1.03
⊖ PetroChina	Energy	Hong Kong	0.99
Nissan Motor	Goods	Japan	0.97
⊕ Hon Hai Precision Indust	Hardware	Taiwan	0.97
⊖ T&D Holdings	Financial	Japan	0.96
Mitsubishi Estate	Financial	Japan	0.94
⊕ Rakuten	Consumer	Japan	0.90
⊖ China Life Insurance	Financial	Hong Kong	0.89
⊖ Samsung Electronics	Goods	Korea	0.86
Canon	Goods	Japan	0.79

Current Investment Style

Investment Style
Equity
Stock %

Value	Blnd	Growth		Market Cap	%
			Large	Giant	26.3
				Large	27.3
		Mid		Mid	33.3
			Small	Small	12.0
				Micro	1.1

Avg $mil: 4,178

Value Measures		Rel Category
Price/Earnings	16.39	1.26
Price/Book	2.21	1.12
Price/Sales	1.05	0.92
Price/Cash Flow	6.20	0.73
Dividend Yield %	2.11	1.03

Growth Measures	%	Rel Category
Long-Term Erngs	18.27	1.19
Book Value	11.11	1.10
Sales	13.13	1.50
Cash Flow	14.22	1.26
Historical Erngs	21.51	0.92

Composition

Cash	0.1	Bonds	0.1
Stocks	97.9	Other	1.8
Foreign	(% of Stock)		99.2

Sector Weightings	% of Stocks	Rel MSCI EAFE	3 Year High	Low
☎ Info	11.80	1.00		
Software	3.27	5.84	4	1
Hardware	5.67	1.47	7	1
Media	0.70	0.38	3	0
Telecom	2.16	0.39	8	1
☞ Service	47.10	1.00		
Health	5.05	0.71	7	3
Consumer	8.10	1.64	13	7
Business	11.42	2.25	13	5
Financial	22.53	0.75	26	18
Mfg	41.08	1.00		
Goods	17.73	1.35	25	18
Ind Mtrls	18.86	1.22	22	11
Energy	2.94	0.41	3	0
Utilities	1.55	0.30	2	0

Regional Exposure	% Stock		% Stock
UK/W. Europe	0	N. America	1
Japan	39	Latn America	1
Asia X Japan	60	Other	0

Country Exposure	% Stock		% Stock
Japan	39	Australia	12
Hong Kong	13	Singapore	5
South Korea	12		

Morningstar's Take by Dan Lefkovitz 11-08-06

We like the kind of Asia exposure Fidelity Pacific Basin provides, but we think there are better ways of getting it.

Under manager Dale Nicholls, this fund shows investors a different side of Asia than most competing pan-Asia funds and ETFs on the market. For one thing, Nicholls devotes less than half the portfolio's assets to Japan, currently just 42%. And the type of Japanese companies Nicholls favors tend to be smaller and more domestically focused. The portfolio contains a few big global players--Toyota Motor and Nintendo are in the top 10--but more typical is Stanley Electric, a mid-cap auto light maker. Outside of Japan, Nicholls is similarly all-cap and creative. The portfolio's average market cap, at $4.6 billion, is lower than all but one of its pan-Asia peers.

There's a benefit to Nicholls' approach. Unlike most pan-Asia funds, this one could work well as a complement to many core foreign funds. Those tend to hold nearly one third of their assets in Japanese blue chips and well-known Asia stocks and will thus overlap a lot with most pan-Asia funds.

But Nicholls' approach also courts risk. He's drawn to volatile stocks that can zoom ahead over some time periods but can also head south in a hurry. Note that the fund soared in 2005 and the first quarter of 2006 but has lost money since May 2006, when market favor turned against risk-sensitive fare.

There's also potential for future strategy shifts here. Nicholls' approach differs dramatically from that of his predecessor, Bill Kennedy, who sometimes devoted as much as 70% of assets to Japan and was more conservative in his stock selection. We're concerned that a future manager change might bring another big shift. In any case, this is Nicholls' first pan-Asia fund, and two years isn't enough time to gain confidence in a manager.

We'd suggest investors seeking a wide-ranging pan-Asia fund consider offerings from the Matthews family.

Address:	82 Devonshire St Boston MA 02109 800-544-9797	Minimum Purchase:	$2500 Add: $250 IRA: $200
		Min Auto Inv Plan:	$100 Add: $100
		Sales Fees:	No-load, 1.50%R
Web Address:	www.fidelity.com	Management Fee:	0.76%
Inception:	10-01-86	Actual Fees:	Mgt:0.76% Dist: —
Advisor:	Fidelity Management & Research (FMR)	Expense Projections:	3Yr:$362 5Yr:$628 10Yr:$1386
Subadvisor:	Multiple Subadvisors	Income Distrib:	Annually
NTF Plans:	Fidelity Retail-NTF, CommonWealth NTF		

MORNINGSTAR® Funds 500

Fidelity Puritan

	Ticker	Load	NAV	Yield	Total Assets	Mstar Category
	FPURX	None	$19.97	2.8%	$25,810 mil	Moderate Allocation

Governance and Management

Stewardship Grade: B

Portfolio Manager(s)

Equity manager Stephen Petersen took the helm here in February 2000. He has built a strong record at Fidelity Equity-Income, which he has run since 1993. He also has experience managing gargantuan sums of money--a plus given Puritan's huge asset base. The bond portfolio was overseen by Kevin Grant until he retired in late 2004. Grant is succeeded by George Fischer, an experienced bond manager. As did Grant, Fischer will rely heavily on the rest of Fidelity's bond team in putting together this portfolio.

Strategy

Manager Stephen Petersen tries to ferret out blue chips with above-average dividend yields. That keeps him out of pricey, high-growth plays, but he picks up growth on the cheap where he can. Although Petersen holds some mid-caps, the fund's huge asset base leads him to emphasize the market's giants. Bond manager George Fischer eschews interest-rate bets. He keeps the bulk of the portfolio in high-quality credits, but he does dabble in high-yield debt. The fund typically has 60% to 65% of its assets in stocks, although that figure has ranged higher or lower on occasion.

Performance 12-31-06

	1st Qtr	2nd Qtr	3rd Qtr	4th Qtr	Total
2002	2.21	-5.59	-10.74	6.92	-7.91
2003	-3.16	12.31	1.99	10.17	22.20
2004	2.10	0.38	0.11	6.51	9.28
2005	-1.37	1.24	2.60	2.17	4.67
2006	3.36	-0.10	5.31	5.55	14.78

Trailing	Total Return%	+/- DJ Mod	+/- DJ US Mod	%Rank Cat	Growth of $10,000
3 Mo	5.55	-0.04	0.88	28	10,555
6 Mo	11.16	2.37	3.26	9	11,116
1 Yr	14.78	2.48	4.51	8	11,478
3 Yr Avg	9.50	-1.22	0.38	23	13,129
5 Yr Avg	8.12	-1.90	0.52	11	14,775
10 Yr Avg	8.74	0.19	0.15	16	23,115
15 Yr Avg	10.73	1.52	1.34	12	46,130

Tax Analysis	Tax-Adj Rtn%	%Rank Cat	Tax-Cost Rat	%Rank Cat
3 Yr (estimated)	7.81	30	1.54	78
5 Yr (estimated)	6.63	14	1.38	85
10 Yr (estimated)	6.68	20	1.89	75

Potential Capital Gain Exposure: 18% of assets

Morningstar's Take by Dan Lefkovitz 11-15-06

We think the investors redeeming shares of Fidelity Puritan are making a mistake.

We're puzzled by the outflows that this hybrid fund has seen over the course of 2006. Unlike other heavily redeemed funds, it has not underperformed. Its returns versus the moderate-allocation category look strong for 2006, as well as over the trailing three-year and five-year periods. Perhaps the success of in-house rival Fidelity Balanced has come at this fund's expense.

Whatever the reason, we think investors are making a mistake by selling this fund. Veteran manager Stephen Petersen provides a steady and skillful hand at the rudder. He keeps the portfolio's balance fairly steady at 60% stocks and 40% bonds, and plays it straight on the fixed-income side. He buys high-yield bonds only when they are out of favor (think 2002) and otherwise lets fixed-income specialist George Fischer assemble a high-quality bond portfolio.

Petersen runs the equity portion of the fund as a clone of Fidelity Equity-Income, a large-value fund that he has steered to good returns since 1993. He takes a contrarian approach and is willing to wait for years for the market to recognize the value of his picks. A large energy stake built when the sector was far less in favor has boosted performance in recent years. And the fund is benefiting from Petersen's telecom purchase five years ago. (SBC, which became AT&T, and its acquisition target, Bellsouth, have been big winners this year.) Like many value managers we admire, Petersen has lately gravitated toward "fallen growth" stocks, such as Pfizer and Intel.

Our major concern here is asset bloat. Even after outflows, Petersen runs roughly $50 billion between the stock portion of this fund and Equity-Income. But given his large-cap, low-turnover approach--not to mention the fund's low fees--we think investors here will be rewarded.

Address:	82 Devonshire Street Boston MA 02109 800-544-6666
Web Address:	www.fidelity.com
Inception:	04-16-47
Advisor:	Fidelity Management & Research (FMR)
Subadvisor:	Multiple Subadvisors
NTF Plans:	Fidelity Retail-NTF, CommonWealth NTF

Minimum Purchase:	$2500	Add: $250	IRA: $200
Min Auto Inv Plan:	$2500	Add: $100	
Sales Fees:	No-load		
Management Fee:	0.42%		
Actual Fees:	Mgt:0.42%	Dist: —	
Expense Projections:	3Yr:$199	5Yr:$346	10Yr:$774
Income Distrib:	Quarterly		

Historical Profile

Return	Above Avg
Risk	Average
Rating	★★★★ Above Avg

59%	62%	61%	60%	56%	61%	60%	62%	62%

Growth of $10,000

— Investment Values of Fund
— Investment Values of DJ Mod

▼ Manager Change
▽ Partial Manager Change

Performance Quartile (within Category)

1995	1996	1997	1998	1999	2000	2001	2002	2003	2004	2005	2006	History
17.01	17.24	19.38	20.07	19.03	18.83	17.67	15.79	18.47	18.95	18.73	19.97	NAV
21.46	15.15	22.35	16.59	2.86	7.77	-1.05	-7.91	22.20	9.28	4.67	14.78	Total Return %
1.66	4.49	10.45	4.27	-14.47	9.44	1.75	-1.14	-5.18	-3.69	-2.32	2.48	+/-DJ Mod
-3.31	3.81	3.15	4.20	-9.99	3.33	-1.21	2.63	-1.86	-1.89	-1.33	4.51	+/-DJ US Mod
3.36	3.80	4.03	3.57	3.26	3.28	3.24	2.86	2.89	2.50	2.65	3.24	Income Return %
18.10	11.35	18.32	13.02	-0.40	4.49	-4.29	-10.77	19.31	6.78	2.02	11.54	Capital Return %
88	48	26	30	86	19	19	15	32	44	55	8	Total Rtn % Rank Cat
0.49	0.62	0.68	0.67	0.64	0.61	0.60	0.50	0.45	0.45	0.49	0.59	Income $
0.44	1.54	0.96	1.56	0.97	1.01	0.35	0.00	0.30	0.72	0.59	0.85	Capital Gains $
0.77	0.72	0.66	0.63	0.63	0.64	0.63	0.64	0.66	0.64	0.62	0.62	Expense Ratio %
3.50	3.44	3.69	3.40	3.23	3.24	3.23	3.03	3.03	2.46	2.53	3.97	Income Ratio %
76	139	80	84	80	62	67	79	86	67	75	78	Turnover Rate %
15,628	18,502	22,822	25,682	24,371	21,369	20,315	18,031	21,964	23,935	24,079	25,810	Net Assets $mil

Rating and Risk

Time Period	Load-Adj Return %	Morningstar Rtn vs Cat	Morningstar Risk vs Cat	Morningstar Risk-Adj Rating
1 Yr	14.78			
3 Yr	9.50	+Avg	-Avg	★★★★
5 Yr	8.12	+Avg	Avg	★★★★
10 Yr	8.74	+Avg	Avg	★★★★
Incept	11.76			

Other Measures	Standard Index DJ Mod	Best Fit Index Russ 1000 VI
Alpha	0.6	-1.7
Beta	0.75	0.69
R-Squared	83	93
Standard Deviation	4.88	
Mean	9.50	
Sharpe Ratio	1.25	

Portfolio Analysis 08-31-06

Total Stocks:235 Share change since 07-31-06	Sectors	P/E Ratio	YTD Return %	% Net Assets
⊕ ExxonMobil Corporation	Energy	11.1	-5.19	3.21
Bank of America Corporati	Financial	12.4	0.11	2.19
Citigroup, Inc.	Financial	13.1	-1.17	1.65
American International Gr	Financial	17.0	-0.18	1.64
J.P. Morgan Chase & Co.	Financial	13.6	-0.02	1.55
AT&T, Inc.	Telecom	18.2	-5.43	1.34
BellSouth Corporation	Telecom			1.07
⊕ Pfizer Inc.	Health	15.2	1.00	1.01
General Electric Company	Ind Mtrls	20.0	0.91	0.94

Total Fixed-Income:801	Date of Maturity	Amount $000	Value $000	% Net Assets
US Treasury Note 2.375%	04-15-11	386,570	396,869	1.62
FNMA 5%	04-01-35	384,016	368,173	1.50
US Treasury Note 4.875%	05-31-11	330,000	332,307	1.36
US Treasury Note 4.75%	03-31-11	307,505	308,058	1.26
US Treasury Note 4.25%	11-15-14	174,325	168,619	0.69
FNMA 4.5%	04-01-35	174,692	163,395	0.67
US Treasury Note 2%	01-15-14	150,000	161,745	0.66
US Treasury Note 0.875%	04-15-10	155,335	158,091	0.65
FNMA 0.04%	11-01-19	134,830	129,653	0.53

Equity Style		
Style:	Value	
Size:	Large-Cap	

Value Measures		Rel Category
Price/Earnings	13.50	0.88
Price/Book	2.22	0.90
Price/Sales	1.30	0.95
Price/Cash Flow	5.12	0.63
Dividend Yield %	2.35	1.22

Growth Measures	%	Rel Category
Long-Term Erngs	10.61	0.90
Book Value	6.27	0.73
Sales	8.57	0.97
Cash Flow	7.06	0.72
Historical Erngs	16.85	0.94

Market Cap %			
Giant	54.6	Small	1.2
Large	33.5	Micro	0.1
Mid	10.6	Avg $mil:	48,889

Fixed-Income Style	
Duration:	—
Quality:	—
Avg Eff Duration [1]	—
Avg Eff Maturity	—
Avg Credit Quality	—
Avg Wtd Coupon	4.52%

[1]figure provided by fund

Sector Weightings	% of Stocks	Rel DJ Mod	3 Year High Low
↻ Info	19.59	—	
Software	1.18	—	1 1
Hardware	6.15	—	7 4
Media	5.26	—	6 5
Telecom	7.00	—	7 5
➾ Service	42.84	—	
Health	7.96	—	8 7
Consumer	4.22	—	4 3
Business	1.87	—	3 2
Financial	28.79	—	32 27
Mfg	37.57	—	
Goods	7.87	—	8 7
Ind Mtrls	13.33	—	17 13
Energy	12.96	—	14 12
Utilities	3.41	—	3 3

Composition

● Cash	3.1
● Stocks	61.6
● Bonds	33.2
○ Other	2.1
Foreign (% of Stock)	6.4

Fidelity Real Estate Inv

	Ticker	Load	NAV	Yield	Total Assets	Mstar Category
	FRESX	None	$36.37	1.0%	$8,294 mil	Specialty-Real Estate

Governance and Management

Stewardship Grade: B

Portfolio Manager(s)

The fund enjoys an experienced and deep management team. Manager Steve Buller has been in charge since October 1998 and served as an analyst on the fund before that. He is supported by one half-time and five full-time REIT analysts.

Strategy

This fund tends to favor REITs over real estate operating companies. While doing so, it focuses on large, high-quality REITs with strong earnings and cash flow, and it moves at a relatively moderate pace.

Historical Profile
Return Average
Risk Average
Rating ★★★
Neutral

	92%	88%	88%	86%	92%	95%	96%	99%	98%	Investment Style

Equity
Stock %

▼ Manager Change
▽ Partial Manager Change

63.2
46.4

Growth of $10,000
33.8
24.0 ▬ Investment Values of Fund
17.0 — Investment Values of S&P 500
10.0

Performance Quartile (within Category)

1995	1996	1997	1998	1999	2000	2001	2002	2003	2004	2005	2006	History
13.88	18.03	20.45	15.54	14.70	18.50	18.52	18.39	23.71	29.54	31.16	36.37	NAV
10.92	36.23	21.39	-18.60	-0.97	31.38	9.50	5.77	33.78	34.15	14.87	32.84	Total Return %
-26.66	13.27	-11.97	-47.18	-22.01	40.48	21.39	27.87	5.10	23.27	9.96	17.05	+/-S&P 500
-1.32	-0.81	1.72	-1.60	1.60	0.34	-2.86	2.17	-2.28	1.01	0.87	-3.29	+/-DJ Wilshire REIT
5.49	5.29	4.45	3.86	4.51	5.05	4.31	4.26	2.97	2.90	2.53	1.41	Income Return %
5.43	30.94	16.94	-22.46	-5.48	26.33	5.19	1.51	30.81	31.25	12.34	31.43	Capital Return %
81	47	41	76	22	17	38	29	78	32	23	69	Total Rtn % Rank Cat
0.71	0.72	0.79	0.77	0.69	0.73	0.78	0.77	0.54	0.67	0.73	0.42	Income $
0.00	0.00	0.56	0.41	0.00	0.00	0.89	0.43	0.26	1.34	1.99	4.18	Capital Gains $
1.03	0.95	0.90	0.84	0.86	0.88	0.82	0.79	0.84	0.83	0.82	0.82	Expense Ratio %
5.67	6.28	5.63	4.06	4.23	4.06	4.58	4.54	3.21	3.38	2.52	2.02	Income Ratio %
75	85	55	76	28	32	65	71	32	54	33	61	Turnover Rate %
709	1,722	2,480	1,239	724	1,037	1,245	1,720	2,712	4,557	5,835	8,294	Net Assets $mil

Performance 12-31-06

	1st Qtr	2nd Qtr	3rd Qtr	4th Qtr	Total
2002	7.54	6.08	-8.80	1.66	5.77
2003	1.49	9.94	9.85	9.15	33.78
2004	12.15	-5.38	8.47	16.56	34.15
2005	-5.53	12.64	4.24	3.56	14.87
2006	13.62	-1.33	8.35	9.36	32.84

Trailing	Total Return%	+/- S&P 500	+/- DJ Wilshire REIT	%Rank Cat	Growth of $10,000
3 Mo	9.36	2.66	0.39	59	10,936
6 Mo	18.49	5.75	-0.51	55	11,849
1 Yr	32.84	17.05	-3.29	69	13,284
3 Yr Avg	26.97	16.53	-0.40	38	20,469
5 Yr Avg	23.70	17.51	-0.14	46	28,963
10 Yr Avg	15.09	6.67	-0.20	38	40,773
15 Yr Avg	15.29	4.65	-0.24	57	84,503

Tax Analysis	Tax-Adj Rtn%	%Rank Cat	Tax-Cost Rat	%Rank Cat
3 Yr (estimated)	24.61	30	1.86	40
5 Yr (estimated)	21.58	38	1.71	45
10 Yr (estimated)	12.88	31	1.92	56

Potential Capital Gain Exposure: 32% of assets

Rating and Risk

Time Period	Load-Adj Return %	Morningstar Rtn vs Cat	Morningstar Risk vs Cat	Morningstar Risk-Adj Rating
1 Yr	32.84			
3 Yr	26.97	Avg	Avg	★★★★
5 Yr	23.70	Avg	Avg	★★★
10 Yr	15.09	Avg	Avg	★★★
Incept	13.32			

Other Measures	Standard Index S&P 500	Best Fit Index DJ Wilshire REIT
Alpha	13.2	1.0
Beta	1.28	0.94
R-Squared	31	98
Standard Deviation	15.83	
Mean	26.97	
Sharpe Ratio	1.40	

Morningstar's Take by William Samuel Rocco 12-07-06

Fidelity Real Estate Investment is a strong choice for long-term real-estate exposure, but shareholders have reason to temper their expectations.

This fund has turned in a lackluster showing in 2006. It lags nearly 60% of its peers for the year to date through Dec. 6, 2006. However, that shouldn't shake shareholders' confidence in the fund or in manager Steve Buller's moderate-growth strategy. Indeed, his disciplined approach has contributed to the fund's middling year-to-date returns: Buller has never been one to chase after trendy or pricey growers, and the fund has less exposure to the hot apartment and office subsectors--and to the hottest names in those subsectors--than many of its peers do.

But despite a rather bland showing in 2006 relative to its peers, the fund's results this year don't look too bad when put in context. Its 35.66% year-to-date gain is pretty impressive from an absolute perspective, and it is just 1.1 percentage points behind the category norm. Most importantly, Buller earned superior results with his blue-chip growth-at-a reasonable-price strategy over the long haul and in a variety of market conditions. This fund has outperformed most of its peers in six of his first seven calendar years, including the sluggish real estate markets of 1999 and 2002 as well as the REIT rallies of 2004 and 2005.

The fund's attractions don't end there. Buller has more experience and more analysts than many of his rivals. And the fund's expense ratio is 25 basis points below the median for no-load real estate offerings, which gives it a enduring edge over the competition.

Due to these strengths, the fund remains a good choice for those seeking a conventional REIT vehicle. Such investors need to recognize, however, that real estate funds have enjoyed an exceptional run in recent years and are unlikely to do as well in absolute terms over the next few years as they have over the last few.

Portfolio Analysis 10-31-06

Share change since 07-06 Total Stocks:48	Sector	PE	Tot Ret%	% Assets
⊕ Starwood Hotels & Resort	Consumer	12.9	21.75	8.71
⊖ ProLogis Trust	Financial	33.5	34.02	7.74
⊕ Equity Residential	Financial	NMF	34.64	7.17
⊕ General Growth Propertie	Financial	—	15.09	6.97
⊖ Simon Property Group, In	Financial	58.3	36.98	6.09
⊕ Equity Office Properties	Financial	—	64.28	5.93
⊕ Duke Realty Corporation	Financial	74.7	28.98	5.07
⊖ United Dominion Realty	Financial	—	41.79	4.97
⊕ Vornado Realty Trust	Financial	37.1	51.14	4.29
⊕ Public Storage, Inc.	Financial	46.2	47.46	4.16
⊖ Kimco Realty Corporation	Financial	30.1	44.91	3.96
⊖ Developers Diversified R	Financial	40.5	39.65	3.92
⊕ CBL & Associates Propert	Financial	23.5	14.78	3.31
⊖ Host Hotels & Resorts, I	Financial	51.9	33.95	3.30
⊕ Ventas, Inc.	Financial	32.4	38.19	2.81
⊕ AvalonBay Communities, I	Financial	68.7	49.69	2.59
⊕ Apartment Investment & M	Financial	—	55.18	2.10
⊕ Sovran Self Storage, Inc	Financial	29.1	27.90	1.31
⊖ Inland Real Estate Corpo	Financial	26.4	34.27	1.20
⊕ Alexandria Real Estate E	Financial	43.8	28.54	1.16

Current Investment Style

Value Blnd Growth — Large Mid Small

	Market Cap	%
	Giant	0.9
	Large	57.2
	Mid	34.0
	Small	7.3
	Micro	0.7
	Avg $mil:	8,350

Value Measures		Rel Category
Price/Earnings	18.92	1.00
Price/Book	3.14	1.11
Price/Sales	4.30	1.04
Price/Cash Flow	14.94	0.97
Dividend Yield %	4.04	1.00

Growth Measures	%	Rel Category
Long-Term Erngs	8.59	1.11
Book Value	-0.50	NMF
Sales	10.50	0.96
Cash Flow	10.90	0.94
Historical Erngs	6.95	0.49

Profitability	%	Rel Category
Return on Equity	10.86	0.94
Return on Assets	8.82	0.94
Net Margin	21.97	0.82

Sector Weightings	% of Stocks	Rel S&P 500	3 Year High	Low
↻ Info	0.00	0.00		
📊 Software	0.00	0.00	0	0
💻 Hardware	0.00	0.00	0	0
🎙 Media	0.00	0.00	0	0
☎ Telecom	0.00	0.00	0	0
⚙ Service	100.00	2.16		
🏥 Health	0.07	0.01	0	0
🛒 Consumer	8.90	1.16	10	5
💼 Business	0.00	0.00	0	0
💲 Financial	91.03	4.09	95	89
🏭 Mfg	0.00	0.00		
⚙ Goods	0.00	0.00	0	0
⚙ Ind Mtrls	0.00	0.00	1	0
🔋 Energy	0.00	0.00	0	0
💡 Utilities	0.00	0.00	0	0

Composition

- ● Cash 2.2
- ● Stocks 97.8
- ● Bonds 0.0
- ● Other 0.0
- Foreign 4.1 (% of Stock)

Address:	82 Devonshire Street Boston MA 02109 800-544-6666
Web Address:	www.fidelity.com
Inception:	11-17-86
Advisor:	Fidelity Management & Research (FMR)
Subadvisor:	Multiple Subadvisors
NTF Plans:	Fidelity Retail-NTF, CommonWealth NTF

Minimum Purchase:	$2500	Add: $250	IRA: $500
Min Auto Inv Plan:	$2500	Add: $100	
Sales Fees:	No-load, 0.75%R		
Management Fee:	0.57%		
Actual Fees:	Mgt:0.57%	Dist: —	
Expense Projections:	3Yr:$265	5Yr:$460	10Yr:$1025
Income Distrib:	Quarterly		

MORNINGSTAR® Funds 500

Fidelity Sel Electronics

	Ticker	Load	NAV	Yield	Total Assets	Mstar Category
	FSELX	None	$43.83	0.1%	$2,045 mil	Specialty-Technology

Governance and Management

Stewardship Grade: B

Portfolio Manager(s)

This fund changes managers frequently. Former manager Samuel Peters took the helm here on Feb. 1, 2002, and left in early February 2004. He was replaced by James Morrow. Morrow has served as an analyst at Fidelity since 1998. We suspect Morrow is on his way out, though. He recently took over management of Fidelity Advisor Diversified Stock. Fidelity's large and growing staff of technology analysts should help provide continuity.

Strategy

This offering focuses on electronics manufacturers and distributors. Companies that make semiconductors and semiconductor capital equipment generally figure prominently in its portfolio. Manager James Morrow tries to ascertain the state of the semiconductor cycle we're in. He then allocates assets to subindustries within the sector based on their attractiveness at the current part of the chip cycle, and he tries to buy companies within those subindustries that he thinks offer the best risk/reward prospects.

Performance 12-31-06

	1st Qtr	2nd Qtr	3rd Qtr	4th Qtr	Total
2002	1.99	-32.12	-37.41	14.15	-50.54
2003	1.11	25.16	16.99	16.10	71.89
2004	1.77	-5.58	-18.31	14.90	-9.81
2005	-0.74	4.45	8.02	3.36	15.75
2006	5.95	-9.32	0.69	3.69	0.30

Trailing	Total Return%	+/- S&P 500	+/- ArcaEx Tech 100	%Rank Cat	Growth of $10,000
3 Mo	3.69	-3.01	-1.94	81	10,369
6 Mo	4.40	-8.34	-7.25	93	10,440
1 Yr	0.30	-15.49	-4.38	91	10,030
3 Yr Avg	1.54	-8.90	-6.34	82	10,469
5 Yr Avg	-2.30	-8.49	-7.26	79	8,902
10 Yr Avg	8.32	-0.10	-5.39	30	22,238
15 Yr Avg	16.97	6.33	0.59	10	104,983

Tax Analysis	Tax-Adj Rtn%	%Rank Cat	Tax-Cost Rat	%Rank Cat
3 Yr (estimated)	1.54	79	0.00	1
5 Yr (estimated)	-2.30	78	0.00	1
10 Yr (estimated)	6.37	35	1.80	88

Potential Capital Gain Exposure: -130% of assets

Historical Profile

Return	Average
Risk	Above Avg
Rating	★★ Below Avg

| 92% | 90% | 92% | 92% | 93% | 96% | 98% | 98% | 97% |

▼ Manager Change
▽ Partial Manager Change

95.0
60.0
35.0
10.0

Growth of $10,000
— Investment Values of Fund
— Investment Values of S&P 500

Investment Style
Equity
Stock %

Performance Quartile (within Category)

1995	1996	1997	1998	1999	2000	2001	2002	2003	2004	2005	2006	History
25.74	36.48	30.81	46.56	88.88	57.78	49.27	24.37	41.89	37.78	43.73	43.83	NAV
68.97	41.72	13.72	51.12	106.68	-17.54	-14.73	-50.54	71.89	-9.81	15.75	0.30	Total Return %
31.39	18.76	-19.64	22.54	85.64	-8.44	-2.84	-28.44	43.21	-20.69	10.84	-15.49	+/-S&P 500
21.26	21.69	-6.25	-3.48	-9.72	-1.32	0.86	-17.21	19.75	-21.54	8.39	-4.38	+/-ArcaEx Tech 100
0.00	0.00	0.00	0.00	0.00	0.00	0.00	0.00	0.00	0.00	0.00	0.07	Income Return %
68.97	41.72	13.72	51.12	106.68	-17.54	-14.73	-50.54	71.89	-9.81	15.75	0.23	Capital Return %
1	9	28	52	58	15	13	91	13	95	5	91	Total Rtn % Rank Cat
0.00	0.00	0.00	0.00	0.00	0.00	0.00	0.00	0.00	0.00	0.00	0.03	Income $
5.25	0.00	10.20	0.00	6.62	18.68	0.00	0.00	0.00	0.00	0.00	0.00	Capital Gains $
1.71	1.22	1.29	1.12	1.15	0.98	0.87	0.97	1.06	1.06	0.89	0.88	Expense Ratio %
-0.98	-0.28	-0.54	-0.42	-0.62	-0.46	-0.31	-0.59	-0.78	-0.70	-0.45	-0.17	Income Ratio %
205	366	341	435	160	125	63	57	70	50	119	80	Turnover Rate %
892	1,565	2,302	2,723	6,781	6,350	5,106	2,214	3,932	2,921	2,687	2,045	Net Assets $mil

Rating and Risk

Time Period	Load-Adj Return %	Morningstar Rtn vs Cat	Morningstar Risk vs Cat	Morningstar Risk-Adj Rating
1 Yr	0.30			
3 Yr	1.54	-Avg	+Avg	★★
5 Yr	-2.30	-Avg	+Avg	★★
10 Yr	8.32	+Avg	+Avg	★★
Incept	12.14			

Other Measures	Standard Index S&P 500	Best Fit Index ArcaEx Tech 100
Alpha	-17.3	-6.9
Beta	2.59	1.43
R-Squared	63	79
Standard Deviation	22.44	
Mean	1.54	
Sharpe Ratio	0.04	

Portfolio Analysis 08-31-06

Share change since 05-06 Total Stocks:79	Sector	PE	Tot Ret%	% Assets
⊕ National Semiconductor	Hardware	16.1	-12.17	6.25
⊕ Applied Materials	Hardware	19.5	3.89	6.00
⊖ Intel Corporation	Hardware	21.0	-17.18	5.73
⊕ Maxim Integrated Product	Hardware	23.1	-14.06	5.17
⊖ KLA-Tencor Corporation	Hardware	28.9	1.88	4.78
⊕ Analog Devices, Inc.	Hardware	22.5	-6.66	4.49
⊕ Broadcom Corporation	Hardware	39.9	2.79	4.31
⊕ Marvell Technology Group	Hardware	35.9	-31.57	4.08
⊖ Hon Hai Precision Indust	Hardware	—	—	3.63
⊕ Arrow Electronics, Inc.	Business	12.4	-1.50	3.41
⊖ Linear Technology	Hardware	21.6	-14.44	3.25
⊕ Xilinx, Inc.	Hardware	22.7	-4.28	2.64
✕✕ Lam Research Corporation	Hardware	21.9	41.87	2.37
⊕ ARM Holdings PLC ADR	Hardware	45.1	18.24	2.26
⊖ Samsung Electronics	Goods	—	—	2.25
⊖ Altera Corp.	Hardware	24.8	6.21	2.25
⊕ Texas Instruments, Inc.	Hardware	16.9	-9.82	2.17
✕✕ LG.Philips LCD Company,	Goods	19.7	-29.78	1.76
⊕ CSR	Ind Mtrls	—	—	1.49
⊕ SOITEC	Ind Mtrls	—	—	1.35

Current Investment Style

Value Blnd Growth — Large Mid Small

Market Cap	%
Giant	17.3
Large	20.1
Mid	52.7
Small	7.7
Micro	2.2

Avg $mil: 8,540

Value Measures		Rel Category
Price/Earnings	18.82	0.77
Price/Book	2.87	0.89
Price/Sales	1.77	0.63
Price/Cash Flow	9.31	0.72
Dividend Yield %	0.78	1.77

Growth Measures	%	Rel Category
Long-Term Erngs	16.59	0.97
Book Value	8.51	0.88
Sales	10.78	0.87
Cash Flow	21.94	1.10
Historical Erngs	37.71	1.37

Profitability	%	Rel Category
Return on Equity	15.84	1.01
Return on Assets	11.21	1.21
Net Margin	15.39	1.11

Industry Weightings	% of Stocks	Rel Cat
Software	0.2	0.0
Hardware	2.5	0.2
Networking Eq	0.0	0.0
Semis	62.2	3.5
Semi Equip	24.4	5.0
Comp/Data Sv	0.0	0.0
Telecom	0.0	0.0
Health Care	0.0	0.0
Other	10.8	0.6

Composition

		%
●	Cash	2.7
●	Stocks	97.1
●	Bonds	0.2
○	Other	0.0
	Foreign	24.5

(% of Stock)

Morningstar's Take by Karen Dolan 11-21-06

Fidelity Select Electronics has some major drawbacks.

We've long been troubled by the high level of manager turnover here and at other Select funds. Fortunately, Fidelity's large and growing staff of global tech analysts provides some stability in the face of frequent manager changes. Even so, our concern remains. Fidelity recently announced that manager James Morrow is taking over management of Fidelity Advisor Diversified Stock. He is still running this fund as well as Fidelity Select Technology, but we don't imagine he'll do so for long now that he has a diversified offering to focus on. That just hasn't been Fidelity's pattern.

Stewardship is problematic here, too. We recently noted in the fund's Stewardship Grade that manager James Morrow didn't have any money invested in the fund, and we are unhappy with his overall incentive scheme. Fidelity Select fund managers are rewarded on how their picks perform on a one-year basis in the fund as well as in other

diversified Fidelity funds. That's a poor way to align managers' interests with long-term performance here, in our view. The current bonus plan and frequent manager changes heighten our worry that Fidelity's Select funds are simply used as a training ground for bright talent.

Our bigger issue with this fund, however, is its narrow focus. Semiconductor and semiconductor-equipment companies represent just a slice of the broader tech sector and a miniscule piece of the overall investment universe. And most investors already have exposure to many of the companies that grace its portfolio. Beyond the fact that investors likely have plenty of exposure to chip stocks already, the semiconductor industry is very cyclical as firms contend with vicious competition and intense pricing pressure. For those reasons, we think investors are better off getting exposure to this segment of the market from more diversified offerings.

Address:	82 Devonshire St Boston MA 02109 800-544-9797	Minimum Purchase:	$2500	Add: $250	IRA: $200
		Min Auto Inv Plan:	$2500	Add: $100	
Web Address:	www.fidelity.com	Sales Fees:	No-load, 0.75%R		
Inception:	07-29-85	Management Fee:	0.57%		
Advisor:	Fidelity Management & Research (FMR)	Actual Fees:	Mgt:0.57%	Dist: —	
Subadvisor:	Multiple Subadvisors	Expense Projections:	3Yr:$290	5Yr:$504	10Yr:$1120
NTF Plans:	Fidelity Retail-NTF, CommonWealth NTF	Income Distrib:	Semi-Annually		

Fidelity Sel Energy Serv

	Ticker	Load	NAV	Yield	Total Assets	Mstar Category
	FSESX	None	$67.50	0.0%	$1,384 mil	Specialty-Natural Res

Historical Profile

Return: Above Avg
Risk: High
Rating: ★★ Below Avg

Investment Style
Equity
Stock %

▼ Manager Change
▽ Partial Manager Change

Growth of $10,000
— Investment Values of Fund
— Investment Values of S&P 500

Performance Quartile (within Category)

	1995	1996	1997	1998	1999	2000	2001	2002	2003	2004	2005	2006	History
	15.16	21.73	30.45	14.47	24.91	37.45	29.58	29.38	31.61	42.65	65.74	67.50	NAV
	40.87	49.08	51.87	-49.72	72.15	50.34	-21.01	-0.68	7.59	34.93	54.14	8.64	Total Return %
	3.29	26.12	18.51	-78.30	51.11	59.44	-9.12	21.42	-21.09	24.05	49.23	-7.15	+/-S&P 500
	—	—	34.93	-25.05	44.93	34.53	-5.42	12.58	-26.42	10.36	17.66	-8.18	+/-GS NATR RES
	0.36	0.07	0.00	0.00	0.00	0.00	0.00	0.00	0.00	0.00	0.00	0.00	Income Return %
	40.51	49.01	51.87	-49.72	72.15	50.34	-21.01	-0.68	7.59	34.93	54.14	8.64	Capital Return %
	1	11	1	100	1	13	84	40	100	16	13	70	Total Rtn % Rank Cat
	0.04	0.01	0.00	0.00	0.00	0.00	0.00	0.00	0.00	0.00	0.00	0.00	Income $
	0.48	0.78	1.85	1.71	0.00	0.00	0.00	0.00	0.00	0.00	0.00	4.15	Capital Gains $
	1.79	1.58	1.45	1.22	1.35	1.20	1.12	1.03	1.12	1.13	0.96	0.91	Expense Ratio %
	0.19	0.60	-0.07	-0.35	-0.49	-0.40	0.69	-0.46	-0.68	-0.79	-0.53	-0.21	Income Ratio %
	209	223	167	78	75	69	99	90	64	23	34	58	Turnover Rate %
	254	563	1,133	394	619	624	515	473	369	588	1,467	1,384	Net Assets $mil

Performance 12-31-06

	1st Qtr	2nd Qtr	3rd Qtr	4th Qtr	Total
2002	15.86	-8.84	-16.55	12.70	-0.68
2003	-3.06	9.45	-6.58	8.55	7.59
2004	9.84	4.46	12.54	4.48	34.93
2005	15.05	6.11	23.10	2.56	54.14
2006	12.38	2.34	-12.94	8.50	8.64

Trailing	Total Return%	+/- S&P 500	+/- GS NATR RES	%Rank Cat	Growth of $10,000
3 Mo	8.50	1.80	-1.07	62	10,850
6 Mo	-5.54	-18.28	-8.11	84	9,446
1 Yr	8.64	-7.15	-8.18	70	10,864
3 Yr Avg	31.22	20.78	5.52	18	22,594
5 Yr Avg	19.28	13.09	1.07	51	24,146
10 Yr Avg	14.19	5.77	4.47	28	37,695
15 Yr Avg	16.56	5.92	—	13	99,596

Tax Analysis	Tax-Adj Rtn%	%Rank Cat	Tax-Cost Rat	%Rank Cat
3 Yr (estimated)	30.84	8	0.29	12
5 Yr (estimated)	19.07	42	0.18	11
10 Yr (estimated)	13.60	28	0.52	21

Potential Capital Gain Exposure: 38% of assets

Rating and Risk

Time Period	Load-Adj Return %	Morningstar Rtn vs Cat	Morningstar Risk vs Cat	Morningstar Risk-Adj Rating
1 Yr	8.64			
3 Yr	31.22	+Avg	+Avg	★★★★
5 Yr	19.28	Avg	+Avg	★★
10 Yr	14.19	+Avg	High	★
Incept	11.18			

Other Measures	Standard Index S&P 500	Best Fit Index GS NATR RES
Alpha	18.5	2.7
Beta	1.19	1.12
R-Squared	12	83
Standard Deviation	23.28	
Mean	31.22	
Sharpe Ratio	1.15	

Morningstar's Take by Lawrence Jones 12-21-06

Several factors have made us skeptical of Fidelity Select Energy Service.

This fund has had high levels of manager turnover, seeing five different managers in as many years. We find this level of turnover disconcerting, even with Fidelity's deep bench of talent from which to draw replacements, as the changes can lead to inconsistent strategy implementation and returns. Fidelity suggested it would reform its practice of frequently rotating managers and analysts into new sector funds, but we have yet to see the impact of that policy here. We are, however, encouraged by current manager John Dowd's substantial experience as an energy analyst. Prior to joining Fidelity in 2005, he served as a senior research analyst for Sanford Bernstein, covering the energy sector for several years.

Manager turnover isn't our only worry with this fund, however, as its unusually narrow focus--even for a sector fund--and high level of volatility also concern us. The fund's mandate limits most of its positions to companies that provide services and equipment to energy-sector firms. This limited mandate courts significant sector risk, as the fund's investments have historically been highly sensitive to commodity price fluctuations. For instance, in 1998, as oil prices slid, the fund soaked shareholders with a nearly 50% loss; but in 1999, when prices recovered, the fund posted a 72% gain. The fund's concentrated portfolio, with the top 10 holdings accounting for nearly 56% of net assets, further adds to its potential volatility. That added concentration and added volatility can make the fund a difficult fit for investors' portfolios.

In sum, the fund's narrow focus limits its usefulness as a diversifier, its volatility is extreme even in a turbulent sector, and its management turnover continues to trouble us. We think investors seeking natural-resources exposure can do better elsewhere.

Portfolio Analysis 08-31-06

Share change since 05-06 Total Stocks:63

	Sector	PE	Tot Ret%	% Assets
⊕ National Oilwell Varco,	Energy	18.3	-2.42	8.39
⊖ Noble Corporation	Energy	15.5	8.19	6.51
⊖ GlobalSantaFe Corporatio	Energy	16.3	24.06	6.22
⊖ Diamond Offshore Drillin	Energy	17.8	17.82	5.91
⊖ Schlumberger, Ltd.	Energy	22.3	31.07	5.78
⊕ Halliburton Company	Energy	11.2	1.11	5.56
⊖ Weatherford Internationa	Energy	15.2	16.56	5.50
⊖ Baker Hughes Inc.	Energy	9.9	23.68	4.44
⊖ Transocean, Inc.	Energy	27.1	16.07	3.81
⊕ McDermott International	Energy	23.4	71.02	3.50
⊕ W-H Energy Services, Inc	Energy	13.2	47.19	3.33
⊕ Cooper Cameron Corporati	Energy	21.8	28.14	3.16
⊕ Grant Prideco, Inc.	Energy	15.2	-9.86	2.93
⊖ Pride International, Inc	Energy	17.6	-2.41	2.69
⊖ Smith International, Inc	Energy	17.0	11.59	2.49
⊖ Oceaneering Internationa	Energy	18.4	59.50	2.41
⊖ Ensco International, Inc	Energy	11.0	13.12	2.24
⊖ FMC Technologies, Inc.	Energy	19.7	43.59	1.95
⊕ Helix Energy Solutions G	Energy	10.6	-12.59	1.78
⊖ Veritas DGC, Inc.	Energy	33.8	141.28	1.64

Current Investment Style

Value Blnd Growth — Large Mid Small

Market Cap	%
Giant	5.8
Large	34.5
Mid	47.1
Small	12.5
Micro	0.1
Avg $mil:	7,578

Value Measures		Rel Category
Price/Earnings	15.54	1.24
Price/Book	2.92	1.14
Price/Sales	2.41	1.90
Price/Cash Flow	13.60	1.92
Dividend Yield %	0.33	0.32

Growth Measures	%	Rel Category
Long-Term Erngs	26.65	1.68
Book Value	14.56	1.01
Sales	14.75	0.79
Cash Flow	27.18	0.97
Historical Erngs	61.24	1.33

Profitability	%	Rel Category
Return on Equity	21.37	1.00
Return on Assets	10.77	1.10
Net Margin	16.57	1.08

Industry Weightings	% of Stocks	Rel Cat
Oil & Gas	9.4	0.3
Oil/Gas Products	0.6	0.1
Oil & Gas Srv	88.8	3.0
Pipelines	0.0	0.0
Utilities	0.0	0.0
Hard Commd	0.3	0.0
Soft Commd	0.0	0.0
Misc. Indstrl	0.1	0.0
Other	0.8	0.1

Composition

● Cash	0.0
● Stocks	100.0
● Bonds	0.0
● Other	0.0
Foreign	1.9
(% of Stock)	

Address:	82 Devonshire St Boston MA 02109 800-544-9797	Minimum Purchase:	$2500	Add: $250	IRA: $200
		Min Auto Inv Plan:	$2500	Add: $100	
Web Address:	www.fidelity.com	Sales Fees:	No-load, 0.75%R		
Inception:	12-16-85	Management Fee:	0.58%		
Advisor:	Fidelity Management & Research (FMR)	Actual Fees:	Mgt:0.57%	Dist: —	
Subadvisor:	Multiple Subadvisors	Expense Projections:	3Yr:$287	5Yr:$498	10Yr:$1108
NTF Plans:	Fidelity Retail-NTF, CommonWealth NTF	Income Distrib:	Semi-Annually		

MORNINGSTAR® Funds 500

Fidelity Sel Health Care

	Ticker	Load	NAV	Yield	Total Assets	Mstar Category
	FSPHX	None	$125.06	0.1%	$2,100 mil	Specialty-Health

Governance and Management

Stewardship Grade: B

Portfolio Manager(s)

Matt Sabel took charge of this offering in August 2006, replacing Harlan Carere after his 1.5-year stint at the helm. Sabel remains manager of Fidelity Select Medical Delivery, which he's run since January 2005. Prior to that, he was an analyst for Fidelity for five years, covering managed-care stocks for a year during that stretch. Sabel joins a long parade of managers--this fund's management has turned over frequently.

Strategy

Manager Matt Sabel recently took the helm of this offering, and it's too early to tell what direction the fund is headed. If he takes his predecessor Harlan Carere's lead, investors should expect the fund, which has historically boasted outsized exposure to big pharma, to have less invested in the area going forward. Under Carere, the portfolio grew to more than 270 stocks, up from around 50 when he took charge in March 2005. Should Sabel's tenure at Fidelity Select Medical Delivery be indicative of his approach here, the portfolio will likely remain just as sprawling.

Performance 12-31-06

	1st Qtr	2nd Qtr	3rd Qtr	4th Qtr	Total
2002	-4.00	-12.76	-6.06	4.16	-18.05
2003	-0.08	11.43	-2.55	6.82	15.91
2004	2.17	3.16	-2.99	6.27	8.66
2005	-1.16	7.92	6.21	3.16	16.88
2006	1.83	-5.66	7.23	1.91	4.98

Trailing	Total Return%	+/- S&P 500	+/- DJ Hlthcare	%Rank Cat	Growth of $10,000
3 Mo	1.91	-4.79	0.20	58	10,191
6 Mo	9.28	-3.46	-1.39	29	10,928
1 Yr	4.98	-10.81	-1.90	40	10,498
3 Yr Avg	10.06	-0.38	3.48	21	13,332
5 Yr Avg	4.84	-1.35	2.10	31	12,666
10 Yr Avg	10.22	1.80	0.57	54	26,461
15 Yr Avg	10.67	0.03	0.65	45	45,756

Tax Analysis	Tax-Adj Rtn%	%Rank Cat	Tax-Cost Rat	%Rank Cat
3 Yr (estimated)	8.76	22	1.18	64
5 Yr (estimated)	3.98	31	0.82	64
10 Yr (estimated)	8.58	50	1.49	72

Potential Capital Gain Exposure: 21% of assets

Morningstar's Take by Christopher Davis 12-21-06

With an unseasoned manager and an uncertain future, Fidelity Select Health Care is difficult to recommend.

So much for Fidelity's pledge that it would keep its notoriously short-tenured sector-fund managers at the helm for longer time periods. The managerial musical chairs continue at this offering: With 1.5 years under his belt, Harlan Carere left earlier this month to work as an analyst for some of Fidelity's diversified-fund managers. Carere's replacement is Matt Sabel, who has run Fidelity Select Medical Delivery (which focuses on health-care services stocks) since January 2005. Sabel is the fund's sixth manager in the past six years.

While we were comfortable with Carere's theme-based strategy, his implementation left much to be desired. He dramatically enlarged the size of the portfolio, bringing the number of its holdings to more than 260 as of last May, up from around 60 when he took charge. With Fidelity's analyst ranks growing, we thought it would have

made more sense to use the firm's improving research capabilities to make higher-conviction bets on companies he knows well than to devote more analyst resources to track stocks that have little impact on performance.

We didn't have the opportunity to speak with Sabel, so we're not sure what he has in store for the portfolio. If his tenure at Select Medical Delivery is any indication, we'd be surprised if it took a more-concentrated cast. Despite that fund's limited mandate, Sabel took the 20-stock portfolio he inherited up to 170 holdings by May.

Given Sabel's limited management experience, it's difficult to tell whether he'll succeed. A bigger question, though, is whether Fidelity will even give Sabel sufficient time to succeed. Carere and others have barely been at the helm long enough to build an expertise in the health-care sector, let alone for shareholders to benefit from it. With proven alternatives like Analyst Pick T. Rowe Price Health Sciences, we'd avoid this fund.

Address:	82 Devonshire St	Minimum Purchase:	$2500	Add: $250	IRA: $200
	Boston MA 02109	Min Auto Inv Plan:	$2500	Add: $100	
	800-544-9797	Sales Fees:	No-load, 0.75%R		
Web Address:	www.fidelity.com	Management Fee:	0.57%		
Inception:	07-14-81	Actual Fees:	Mgt:0.57%	Dist: —	
Advisor:	Fidelity Management & Research (FMR)	Expense Projections:	3Yr:$284	5Yr:$493	10Yr:$1096
Subadvisor:	Multiple Subadvisors	Income Distrib:	Semi-Annually		
NTF Plans:	Fidelity Retail-NTF, CommonWealth NTF				

Historical Profile

Return	Average
Risk	Low
Rating	★★★★ Above Avg

92% 92% 94% 92% 92% 99% 99% 99% 97%

▼ Manager Change
▽ Partial Manager Change

Growth of $10,000
— Investment Values of Fund
— Investment Values of S&P 500

Performance Quartile (within Category)

1995	1996	1997	1998	1999	2000	2001	2002	2003	2004	2005	2006	History
97.57	95.40	101.87	136.77	124.82	150.13	127.26	101.98	118.01	128.09	136.09	125.06	NAV
45.86	15.46	31.15	41.28	-2.88	36.65	-15.01	-18.05	15.91	8.66	16.88	4.98	Total Return %
8.28	-7.50	-2.21	12.70	-23.92	45.75	-3.12	4.05	-12.77	-2.22	11.97	-10.81	+/-S&P 500
-8.88	-3.20	-5.73	2.19	1.15	-1.19	-2.17	2.76	-3.52	4.11	8.56	-1.90	+/-DJ Hlthcare
0.84	0.68	0.27	0.19	0.06	0.20	0.09	0.16	0.18	0.11	0.03	0.16	Income Return %
45.02	14.78	30.88	41.09	-2.94	36.45	-15.10	-18.21	15.73	8.55	16.85	4.82	Capital Return %
62	32	16	12	87	76	63	12	93	53	9	40	Total Rtn % Rank Cat
0.59	0.65	0.25	0.19	0.08	0.24	0.13	0.20	0.18	0.13	0.04	0.20	Income $
4.92	15.95	20.73	6.17	7.85	18.63	0.19	2.42	0.00	0.00	13.75	16.99	Capital Gains $
1.36	1.30	1.32	1.18	1.05	1.05	0.97	0.96	0.99	0.99	0.92	0.87	Expense Ratio %
1.08	1.06	0.52	0.31	0.14	0.12	0.21	0.13	0.22	0.12	0.11	-0.12	Income Ratio %
151	54	59	79	66	70	85	90	139	104	32	120	Turnover Rate %
1,449	1,242	1,632	3,032	2,427	3,124	2,511	1,825	1,957	1,970	2,333	2,100	Net Assets $mil

Rating and Risk

Time Period	Load-Adj Return %	Morningstar Rtn vs Cat	Morningstar Risk vs Cat	Morningstar Risk-Adj Rating
1 Yr	4.98			
3 Yr	10.06	+Avg	-Avg	★★★★
5 Yr	4.84	Avg	Low	★★★
10 Yr	10.22	Avg	Low	★★★★
Incept	16.97			

Other Measures	Standard Index S&P 500	Best Fit Index DJ Hlthcare
Alpha	1.9	3.4
Beta	0.69	0.96
R-Squared	31	88
Standard Deviation	8.57	
Mean	10.06	
Sharpe Ratio	0.79	

Portfolio Analysis 08-31-06

Share change since 05-06 Total Stocks:161	Sector	PE	Tot Ret%	% Assets
⊕ Pfizer Inc.	Health	15.2	15.22	9.24
⊖ Johnson & Johnson	Health	17.5	12.45	7.82
⊖ Merck & Co., Inc.	Health	19.1	42.66	5.16
⊕ UnitedHealth Group, Inc.	Health	20.8	-13.49	4.82
⊕ Amgen, Inc.	Health	29.1	-13.38	4.65
⊕ Genentech, Inc.	Health	48.7	-12.29	4.31
⊖ Wyeth	Health	17.2	12.88	3.92
⊕ Allergan, Inc.	Health	—	11.33	2.80
⊕ WellPoint, Inc.	Health	17.2	-1.38	2.79
⊕ Baxter International Inc	Health	24.3	24.81	2.62
⊖ Alcon, Inc.	Health	38.3	-12.60	2.06
⊖ Medtronic, Inc.	Health	23.8	-6.29	1.83
⊕ Schering-Plough Corporat	Health	36.6	14.63	1.83
⊕ Cardinal Health, Inc.	Health	20.8	-5.82	1.70
⊕ Brookdale Senior Living,	Health	—	—	1.68
⊕ Abbott Laboratories	Health	24.3	26.88	1.53
⊕ Boston Scientific Corpor	Health	—	-29.85	1.22
⊕ Bristol-Myers Squibb Com	Health	23.1	19.93	1.17
⊖ Caremark RX, Inc.	Health	23.6	10.90	1.13
⊖ Medco Health Solutions,	Health	28.4	-4.23	1.06

Current Investment Style

Value Blnd Growth — Large Mid Small

Market Cap	%
Giant	47.4
Large	29.4
Mid	16.5
Small	4.9
Micro	1.8

Avg $mil: 29,358

Value Measures		Rel Category
Price/Earnings	19.51	0.86
Price/Book	3.54	0.98
Price/Sales	1.75	0.66
Price/Cash Flow	14.94	0.93
Dividend Yield %	1.17	1.39

Growth Measures	%	Rel Category
Long-Term Erngs	12.92	0.88
Book Value	11.85	1.40
Sales	11.16	0.94
Cash Flow	8.15	0.73
Historical Erngs	11.12	0.62

Profitability	%	Rel Category
Return on Equity	16.62	1.38
Return on Assets	7.43	1.91
Net Margin	12.23	1.12

Industry Weightings	% of Stocks	Rel Cat
Biotech	17.8	0.5
Drugs	45.1	1.5
Mgd Care	13.7	1.2
Hospitals	0.8	0.6
Other HC Srv	1.7	1.1
Diagnostics	0.1	0.1
Equipment	12.9	1.0
Good/Srv	5.3	1.5
Other	2.5	0.8

Composition

● Cash	3.1
● Stocks	96.8
● Bonds	0.0
○ Other	0.1
Foreign	4.3
(% of Stock)	

Investment Style

Equity
Stock %

Fidelity Sel Technology

	Ticker	Load	NAV	Yield	Total Assets	Mstar Category
	FSPTX	None	$67.89	0.0%	$1,724 mil	Specialty-Technology

Governance and Management

Stewardship Grade: C

Portfolio Manager(s)

Like most Fidelity Select funds, this offering has changed managers often and we suspect another change is on the horizon. Manager James Morrow started managing Fidelity Advisor Diversified Stock in November 2006. He is still running this fund for now, but we believe he will eventually shift his responsibilities on this fund to somebody else. Fidelity's new management does say that it wants to have longer-tenured managers on its more prominent sector funds, so we think the next manager could be here longer. Morrow replaced Sonu Kalra here in January 2005.

Strategy

This fund can invest in nearly any type of technology company, giving it broad latitude to emphasize different subsectors. However, its girth prevents it from making rapid, large-scale shifts. Manager James Morrow is a bottom-up stock-picker who tries to buy companies where he thinks the risk/reward prospects are brightest. Thus far, he has displayed a slight contrarian streak, buying eBay when it slumped in early 2005 and sticking with a bet on the then-struggling chip sector. The fund holds roughly 100 names.

Historical Profile

Return	Above Avg
Risk	Above Avg
Rating	★★★ Neutral

87% 88% 94% 92% 89% 99% 100% 95% 94%

Investment Style
Equity
Stock %

▼ Manager Change
▽ Partial Manager Change

Growth of $10,000
— Investment Values of Fund
— Investment Values of S&P 500

117.8
81.4
56.2
38.0
25.4
17.0
10.0

Performance Quartile (within Category)

1995	1996	1997	1998	1999	2000	2001	2002	2003	2004	2005	2006	History
51.31	55.68	45.28	78.86	152.39	88.72	60.60	37.70	60.09	60.19	63.15	67.89	NAV
43.81	15.82	10.33	74.16	131.75	-32.30	-31.70	-37.79	59.39	0.43	4.92	7.51	Total Return %
6.23	-7.14	-23.03	45.58	110.71	-23.20	-19.81	-15.69	30.71	-10.45	0.01	-8.28	+/-S&P 500
-3.90	-4.21	-9.64	19.56	15.35	-16.08	-16.11	-4.46	7.25	-11.30	-2.44	2.83	+/-ArcaEx Tech 100
0.00	0.00	0.00	0.00	0.00	0.00	0.00	0.00	0.00	0.27	0.00	0.00	Income Return %
43.81	15.82	10.33	74.16	131.75	-32.30	-31.70	-37.79	59.39	0.16	4.92	7.51	Capital Return %
75	58	46	12	37	52	38	20	35	70	57	43	Total Rtn % Rank Cat
0.00	0.00	0.00	0.00	0.00	0.00	0.00	0.00	0.00	0.16	0.00	0.00	Income $
8.05	3.68	15.69	0.00	0.00	19.80	20.73	0.00	0.00	0.00	0.00	0.00	Capital Gains $
1.56	1.39	1.44	1.30	1.20	1.04	0.94	1.13	1.22	1.14	0.94	0.93	Expense Ratio %
-0.98	-0.52	-0.72	-0.45	-0.54	-0.34	-0.46	-0.73	-0.86	-0.80	0.20	-0.44	Income Ratio %
102	112	549	556	339	210	136	184	153	127	104	100	Turnover Rate %
401	491	526	1,061	5,209	4,287	2,715	1,459	2,523	2,205	1,868	1,724	Net Assets $mil

Performance 12-31-06

	1st Qtr	2nd Qtr	3rd Qtr	4th Qtr	Total
2002	-7.38	-25.39	-25.48	20.79	-37.79
2003	0.95	25.91	12.17	11.80	59.39
2004	0.28	-0.58	-14.37	17.64	0.43
2005	-7.38	4.59	5.51	2.65	4.92
2006	5.59	-8.49	3.64	7.35	7.51

Trailing	Total Return%	+/- S&P 500	+/- ArcaEx Tech 100	%Rank Cat	Growth of $10,000
3 Mo	7.35	0.65	1.72	36	10,735
6 Mo	11.26	-1.48	-0.39	33	11,126
1 Yr	7.51	-8.28	2.83	43	10,751
3 Yr Avg	4.24	-6.20	-3.64	65	11,327
5 Yr Avg	2.35	-3.84	-2.61	38	11,232
10 Yr Avg	8.75	0.33	-4.96	18	23,136
15 Yr Avg	12.67	2.03	-3.71	50	59,858

Tax Analysis	Tax-Adj Rtn%	%Rank Cat	Tax-Cost Rat	%Rank Cat
3 Yr (estimated)	4.21	61	0.03	8
5 Yr (estimated)	2.33	37	0.02	8
10 Yr (estimated)	6.42	33	2.14	97

Potential Capital Gain Exposure: -144% of assets

Morningstar's Take by Karen Dolan 11-20-06

Fidelity Select Technology is no longer among our top picks.

We hold our Analyst Picks to the absolute highest standards. They must not only boast reasonable expense ratios, topnotch management, and proven strategies, but they also have to be outstanding stewards of investor capital.

Stewardship was the main reason why we removed this fund from our list of favorites in October 2006. All of our picks must have a Stewardship Grade of B or better. This fund's grade recently dropped to a C because we saw that manager James Morrow didn't have much money invested in the fund, and we were unhappy with the way he is compensated. Fidelity Select fund managers receive bonuses based on how their picks perform on a one-year basis in the fund as well as in other diversified Fidelity funds. That's a poor way to align a manager's interests with long-term performance, in our view. The bonus plan structure heightens our worry that Fidelity's Select funds are simply used as a training ground for talent.

We've long been troubled by high manager turnover here and at other Select funds, but that wasn't the key driver to removing it from our picks list. The manager changes have been rather seamless and backed by Fidelity's deeper bench of research analysts. Even so, we're concerned by Fidelity's recent announcement that Morrow is taking over management of Fidelity Advisor Diversified Stock. He is still running this fund, but we don't imagine he'll do so for much longer now that he's assigned to a diversified offering.

We don't see any reason for investors to sell the fund outright. It is still cheap and has access to one of the most-expansive analyst teams around. Fidelity also says it plans to keep managers on Select funds for longer. Meanwhile, the fund remains broadly diversified and more stable than many of its volatile rivals. Though we're less enthused by it, we still think this is one of the better options in a category of few.

Address:	82 Devonshire St Boston MA 02109 800-544-9797
Web Address:	www.fidelity.com
Inception:	07-14-81
Advisor:	Fidelity Management & Research (FMR)
Subadvisor:	Multiple Subadvisors
NTF Plans:	Fidelity Retail-NTF, CommonWealth NTF

Minimum Purchase:	$2500	Add: $250	IRA: $200
Min Auto Inv Plan:	$2500	Add: $100	
Sales Fees:	No-load, 0.75%R		
Management Fee:	0.57%		
Actual Fees:	Mgt:0.57%	Dist: —	
Expense Projections:	3Yr:$306	5Yr:$531	10Yr:$1178
Income Distrib:	Semi-Annually		

Rating and Risk

Time Period	Load-Adj Return %	Morningstar Rtn vs Cat	Morningstar Risk vs Cat	Morningstar Risk-Adj Rating
1 Yr	7.51			
3 Yr	4.24	Avg	Avg	★★★
5 Yr	2.35	Avg	Avg	★★★
10 Yr	8.75	+Avg	+Avg	★★★
Incept	12.99			

Other Measures	Standard Index S&P 500	Best Fit Index ArcaEx Tech 100
Alpha	-12.9	-4.0
Beta	2.21	1.22
R-Squared	72	90
Standard Deviation	17.91	
Mean	4.24	
Sharpe Ratio	0.14	

Portfolio Analysis 08-31-06

Share change since 05-06 Total Stocks:110	Sector	PE	Tot Ret%	% Assets
⊖ Google, Inc.	Business	61.5	11.00	6.51
⊖ Intel Corporation	Hardware	21.0	-17.18	5.78
eBay, Inc.	Consumer	40.1	-30.43	5.05
☀ IBM	Hardware	17.1	19.77	4.52
⊕ National Semiconductor	Hardware	16.1	-12.17	3.23
⊖ Apple Computer, Inc.	Hardware	37.6	18.01	3.07
⊕ Qualcomm, Inc.	Hardware	26.6	-11.32	3.07
⊕ Maxim Integrated Product	Hardware	23.1	-14.06	2.63
⊖ Dell, Inc.	Hardware	18.4	-16.23	2.38
⊖ Hon Hai Precision Indust	Hardware	—	—	2.04
⊕ SolarWorld	Ind Mtrls	—	—	1.96
⊕ Applied Materials	Hardware	19.5	3.89	1.83
⊕ Arrow Electronics, Inc.	Business	12.4	-1.50	1.58
⊖ Samsung Electronics	Goods	—	—	1.53
⊖ First Data Corporation	Business	12.3	9.88	1.49
⊖ Analog Devices, Inc.	Hardware	22.5	-6.66	1.48
⊖ Symantec Corporation	Software	50.9	19.14	1.41
⊕ Marvell Technology Group	Hardware	35.9	-31.57	1.37
⊕ Corning Inc.	Hardware	25.5	-4.83	1.34
KLA-Tencor Corporation	Hardware	28.9	1.88	1.33

Current Investment Style

Value Blnd Growth — Large Mid Small

Market Cap	%
Giant	38.3
Large	21.8
Mid	31.8
Small	6.2
Micro	1.9
Avg $mil:	17,442

Value Measures		Rel Category
Price/Earnings	21.14	0.87
Price/Book	2.83	0.88
Price/Sales	2.08	0.75
Price/Cash Flow	10.61	0.82
Dividend Yield %	0.69	1.57

Growth Measures	%	Rel Category
Long-Term Erngs	16.32	0.95
Book Value	11.23	1.16
Sales	11.89	0.95
Cash Flow	22.34	1.12
Historical Erngs	25.14	0.92

Profitability	%	Rel Category
Return on Equity	18.41	1.17
Return on Assets	11.42	1.23
Net Margin	15.17	1.09

Industry Weightings	% of Stocks	Rel Cat
Software	8.2	0.4
Hardware	19.0	1.7
Networking Eq	3.7	0.5
Semis	27.7	1.5
Semi Equip	7.5	1.5
Comp/Data Sv	12.8	1.4
Telecom	0.9	0.3
Health Care	0.0	0.0
Other	20.2	1.1

Composition

● Cash	5.6	
● Stocks	94.2	
● Bonds	0.2	
○ Other	0.0	
Foreign	17.9	
(% of Stock)		

M⊙**RNINGSTAR® Funds 500**

Fidelity Sh-Int Muni Inc

✓ Analyst Pick

Ticker FSTFX	**Load** None	**NAV** $10.19
Yield 3.0%	**SEC Yield** 3.23%	**Total Assets** $1,518 mil
Mstar Category Muni National Short		

Governance and Management

Stewardship Grade: B

Portfolio Manager(s)

In addition to this fund, Mark Sommer has, since June 2002, managed Fidelity funds focusing on New York, New Jersey, Connecticut, Maryland, and Pennsylvania. Sommer joined Fidelity's fixed-income quantitative research group in 1992 and began managing $4 billion in stable-value assets in 1997. Previously, Sommer was a scientist at Bolt, Beranek & Newman.

Strategy

Manager Mark Sommer does not place bets on the direction of interest rates. Instead, he keeps the fund's duration (a measure of interest-rate sensitivity) tied closely to that of the Lehman Brothers 1-6 Year Muni Index. In trying to add to returns, Sommer tries to find bonds selling at attractive valuations based on state, sector, maturity-spectrum, structure, or individual credit profiles.

Historical Profile
Return Average
Risk Average
Rating ★★★ Neutral

Investment Style: Fixed Income
Income Rtn %Rank Cat

| 41 | 50 | 53 | 43 | 37 | 34 | 24 | 35 |

▼ Manager Change
▽ Partial Manager Change

20.8
18.8
16.4 **Growth of $10,000**
14.0 ▬ Investment Values of Fund
12.0
10.0 ▬ Investment Values of LB Muni

Performance Quartile (within Category)

	1995	1996	1997	1998	1999	2000	2001	2002	2003	2004	2005	2006	History
NAV	10.04	10.00	10.11	10.16	9.93	10.12	10.27	10.52	10.48	10.38	10.20	10.19	NAV
	8.47	3.88	5.45	4.69	1.61	6.20	5.70	6.47	3.01	1.82	1.06	2.96	Total Return %
	-8.99	-0.55	-3.74	-1.79	3.67	-5.48	0.57	-3.13	-2.30	-2.66	-2.45	-1.88	+/-LB Muni
	-0.40	-0.56	-0.03	-0.52	-0.35	-0.03	-0.89	-0.25	0.33	0.04	0.19	-0.09	+/-LB Muni 3YR
	4.48	4.27	4.32	4.18	3.90	4.21	3.98	3.36	2.72	2.60	2.78	3.05	Income Return %
	3.99	-0.39	1.13	0.51	-2.29	1.99	1.72	3.11	0.29	-0.78	-1.72	-0.09	Capital Return %
	25	45	31	39	22	33	2	22	20	13	54	50	Total Rtn % Rank Cat
	0.42	0.42	0.42	0.41	0.39	0.41	0.40	0.34	0.28	0.27	0.28	0.31	Income $
	0.00	0.00	0.00	0.00	0.00	0.00	0.02	0.06	0.07	0.02	0.00	0.00	Capital Gains $
	0.47	0.55	0.54	0.55	0.55	0.55	0.54	0.41	0.45	0.47	0.47	—	Expense Ratio %
	4.45	4.38	4.17	4.25	4.15	3.89	4.02	3.85	3.23	2.69	2.57	—	Income Ratio %
	—	—	—	—	—	—	—	43	38	34	45	—	Turnover Rate %
	913	905	737	699	639	765	958	1,189	1,683	1,839	1,840	1,484	Net Assets $mil

Performance 12-31-06

	1st Qtr	2nd Qtr	3rd Qtr	4th Qtr	Total
2002	0.55	2.73	2.43	0.63	6.47
2003	0.85	1.16	0.86	0.12	3.01
2004	0.91	-1.36	1.92	0.36	1.82
2005	-0.75	1.38	0.01	0.43	1.06
2006	0.14	0.26	1.96	0.57	2.96

Trailing	Total Return%	+/- LB Muni	+/- LB Muni 3YR	%Rank Cat	Growth of $10,000
3 Mo	0.57	-0.54	-0.06	66	10,057
6 Mo	2.54	-2.01	-0.04	22	10,254
1 Yr	2.96	-1.88	-0.09	50	10,296
3 Yr Avg	1.94	-2.34	0.04	41	10,593
5 Yr Avg	3.05	-2.48	0.05	23	11,621
10 Yr Avg	3.88	-1.88	-0.16	14	14,633
15 Yr Avg	4.27	-1.99	-0.18	34	18,724

Tax Analysis	Tax-Adj Rtn%	%Rank Cat	Tax-Cost Rat	%Rank Cat
3 Yr (estimated)	1.93	34	0.01	34
5 Yr (estimated)	2.99	23	0.06	100
10 Yr (estimated)	3.85	17	0.03	34

Potential Capital Gain Exposure: -1% of assets

Rating and Risk

Time Period	Load-Adj Return %	Morningstar Rtn vs Cat	Morningstar Risk vs Cat	Morningstar Risk-Adj Rating
1 Yr	2.96			
3 Yr	1.94	Avg	+Avg	★★★
5 Yr	3.05	Avg	Avg	★★★
10 Yr	3.88	Avg	Avg	★★★
Incept	4.49			

Other Measures	Standard Index LB Muni	Best Fit Index LB Muni 3YR
Alpha	-1.8	0.2
Beta	0.51	1.11
R-Squared	92	96
Standard Deviation	1.65	
Mean	1.94	
Sharpe Ratio	-0.78	

Portfolio Analysis 09-30-06

Total Fixed-Income:431	Date of Maturity	Amount $000	Value $000	% Net Assets
NEW YORK N Y CITY TRANSI	11-01-28	44,300	48,931	3.15
Honolulu Hawaii City & C	10-01-09	26,940	30,225	1.95
New Jersey St Transn Tr	12-15-10	25,000	26,824	1.73
New York N Y 5%	08-01-12	19,770	21,105	1.36
CALIFORNIA ST GO BDS	09-01-10	18,550	19,684	1.27
New Jersey St Tpk Auth 6	01-01-11	17,180	18,830	1.21
Tobacco Settlement Fing	06-01-13	17,500	17,980	1.16
Detroit Mich 5%	04-01-08	14,545	14,855	0.96
Clark Cnty Nev Sch Dist	06-15-09	13,890	14,399	0.93
Jefferson Cnty Ala Swr 5	02-01-33	13,520	14,072	0.91
NEW YORK ST DORM AUTH RE	11-15-23	13,000	13,972	0.90
Chicago III Sch Fin Auth	06-01-09	12,825	13,282	0.86
ILLINOIS EDL FACS AUTH R	03-01-11	12,800	12,733	0.82
OHIO ST GO BDS	03-15-24	12,300	12,144	0.78
Univ Tex Univ Revs 5%	08-15-09	11,255	11,686	0.75

Current Investment Style

Duration Short Int Long
Quality High Med Low

¹Avg Eff Duration	3.0 Yrs
Avg Eff Maturity	4.2 Yrs
Avg Credit Quality	AA
Avg Wtd Coupon	4.57%
Avg Wtd Price	104.27% of par

¹figure provided by fund

Credit Analysis   % bonds 09-30-06

AAA	57	BB	0
AA	18	B	0
A	17	Below B	0
BBB	6	NR/NA	3

Top 5 States   % bonds

NY	17.4	NJ	6.4
TX	12.7	CA	5.7
IL	10.4		

Composition

Cash	2.1	Bonds	97.9
Stocks	0.0	Other	0.0

Special Securities

Restricted/Illiquid Secs	0
Options/Futures/Warrants	No

Sector Weightings

	% of Bonds	Rel Cat
General Obligation	50.7	1.54
Utilities	6.5	0.81
Health	5.1	0.51
Water/Waste	7.8	1.05
Housing	0.0	0.00
Education	14.1	1.64
Transportation	7.1	1.37
COP/Lease	1.1	0.59
Industrial	7.5	0.47
Misc Revenue	0.0	—
Demand	0.0	0.00

Morningstar's Take   by Eric Jacobson 12-21-06

Fidelity Short-Intermediate Municipal Income's recent performance suffers from an odd market and an odd category.

The market itself is odd because we're in a period when short-term bond yields are close to those of long-term bonds. And that situation has arisen in large part because the Federal Reserve has been consistently raising short-term rates since the middle of 2004. That action in and of itself has taken a toll on the returns of short-term bonds, whereas a lack of much inflation fear has concurrently meant that long-term yields have been stable or have even fallen in some cases. So despite this fund's mandate for stability, its sensitivity to the short portion of the maturity spectrum has been a disadvantage lately.

The context of the fund's category hasn't helped its image either. Because there aren't enough ultrashort municipal bond funds (defined as those with durations of a year or less), Morningstar has a single municipal-bond national-short category composed of roughly 44 entrants and covering a broad range of risk. So while the fund's recent 3-year duration makes it appear modest when compared with most municipal bond funds, it stands out at the aggressive end of this group. And while the average rival in this category has a shorter portfolio duration, it also has more concentrated exposure among longer-maturity bonds than this fund. Those two traits have combined to leave it a bit behind as rising short-term yields have hurt funds focusing on those maturities. Alternatively, stable and/or falling long-term yields have benefited funds that have heavily sampled that end of the spectrum.

That explains this fund's recent lethargy, but it's not that critical to its long-term fate. The skill of its manager and the Fidelity team that backs him, a meticulous and measured approach, and a modest expense ratio should prove to be significant advantages. Indeed, they've already earned the fund some terrific five- and 10-year returns.

Address:	82 Devonshire Street Boston MA 02109 800-544-6666
Web Address:	www.fidelity.com
Inception:	12-24-86
Advisor:	Fidelity Management & Research (FMR)
Subadvisor:	Multiple Subadvisors
NTF Plans:	Fidelity Retail-NTF, CommonWealth NTF

Minimum Purchase:	$10000	Add: $1000	IRA: $0
Min Auto Inv Plan:	$10000	Add: $500	
Sales Fees:	No-load, 0.50%R		
Management Fee:	0.37%		
Actual Fees:	Mgt:0.38%	Dist: —	
Expense Projections:	3Yr:$157	5Yr:$274	10Yr:$616
Income Distrib:	Monthly		

Fidelity Sh-Term Bond

Analyst Pick ✓

	Ticker	Load	NAV	Yield	SEC Yield	Total Assets	Mstar Category
	FSHBX	None	$8.87	4.4%	4.94%	$6,929 mil	Short-Term Bond

Governance and Management

Stewardship Grade: B

Portfolio Manager(s)

Andrew Dudley has managed this fund since early 1997. As part of Fidelity's short- to intermediate-term bond team, he works with a credit analyst, a quantitative analyst, a trader, and one other portfolio manager. He has delivered impressive results during his tenure.

Strategy

Like all Fidelity bond funds, this offering doesn't make interest-rate bets. Manager Andrew Dudley ties the portfolio's duration (a measure of interest-rate sensitivity) to that of the Lehman Brothers 1-3 Year Government/Credit Index. He concentrates his efforts on moving among the corporate, Treasury, and mortgage sectors of the bond market, while looking to add value through individual issue selection. Dudley dips into the derivatives market here, but the derivatives don't alter its low-risk profile.

Historical Profile

Return	Above Avg
Risk	Average
Rating	★★★★ Above Avg

												Investment Style
33	38	36	56	39	52	61	39					Fixed Income Income Rtn %Rank Cat

▼ Manager Change
▽ Partial Manager Change

20.5
17.5
15.0
Growth of $10,000
12.5 ■ Investment Values of Fund
10.0 — Investment Values of LB Aggr

Performance Quartile (within Category)

	1995	1996	1997	1998	1999	2000	2001	2002	2003	2004	2005	2006	History
	8.88	8.72	8.70	8.71	8.50	8.62	8.80	8.99	9.04	8.98	8.86	8.87	NAV
	9.82	4.78	6.21	6.15	3.29	7.85	7.63	6.71	3.57	1.86	2.17	4.58	Total Return %
	-8.65	1.15	-3.44	-2.54	4.11	-3.78	-0.81	-3.54	-0.53	-2.48	-0.26	0.25	+/-LB Aggr
	-3.06	0.11	-0.92	-1.48	1.20	-1.06	-1.40	-1.41	0.22	0.01	0.73	0.36	+/-LB 1-5 YR
	4.96	5.93	6.37	6.04	5.77	6.35	5.52	4.47	3.00	2.53	3.52	4.45	Income Return %
	4.86	-1.15	-0.16	0.11	-2.48	1.50	2.11	2.24	0.57	-0.67	-1.35	0.13	Capital Return %
	82	33	63	59	18	45	44	28	22	37	14	18	Total Rtn % Rank Cat
	0.41	0.51	0.54	0.51	0.49	0.53	0.46	0.39	0.27	0.23	0.31	0.39	Income $
	0.13	0.06	0.00	0.00	0.00	0.00	0.00	0.00	0.00	0.00	0.00	0.00	Capital Gains $
	0.69	0.68	0.70	0.70	0.65	0.62	0.58	0.58	0.57	0.57	0.56	0.44	Expense Ratio %
	6.37	6.37	6.41	6.26	5.83	5.96	6.23	4.86	3.88	2.61	2.71	4.48	Income Ratio %
	113	151	104	117	133	126	99	145	80	100	93	55	Turnover Rate %
	1,197	996	875	842	1,333	1,773	3,339	5,195	5,406	5,050	5,244	6,929	Net Assets $mil

Performance 12-31-06

	1st Qtr	2nd Qtr	3rd Qtr	4th Qtr	Total
2002	0.33	1.84	2.57	1.83	6.71
2003	1.26	1.55	0.24	0.47	3.57
2004	1.39	-1.21	1.40	0.29	1.86
2005	-0.15	1.41	0.16	0.74	2.17
2006	0.55	0.72	2.05	1.19	4.58

Trailing	Total Return%	+/- LB Aggr	+/- LB 1-5 YR	%Rank Cat	Growth of $10,000
3 Mo	1.19	-0.05	0.18	25	10,119
6 Mo	3.26	-1.83	-0.28	37	10,326
1 Yr	4.58	0.25	0.36	18	10,458
3 Yr Avg	2.86	-0.84	0.37	17	10,883
5 Yr Avg	3.76	-1.30	-0.01	17	12,027
10 Yr Avg	4.98	-1.26	-0.36	24	16,258
15 Yr Avg	5.08	-1.42	-0.50	32	21,028

Tax Analysis	Tax-Adj Rtn%	%Rank Cat	Tax-Cost Rat	%Rank Cat
3 Yr (estimated)	1.62	13	1.21	54
5 Yr (estimated)	2.45	12	1.26	46
10 Yr (estimated)	3.12	16	1.77	51

Potential Capital Gain Exposure: -1% of assets

Rating and Risk

Time Period	Load-Adj Return %	Morningstar Rtn vs Cat	Morningstar Risk vs Cat	Morningstar Risk-Adj Rating
1 Yr	4.58			
3 Yr	2.86	+Avg	Avg	★★★★
5 Yr	3.76	+Avg	Avg	★★★★
10 Yr	4.98	+Avg	Avg	★★★★
Incept	5.79			

Other Measures	Standard Index LB Aggr	Best Fit Index LB 1-5 YR
Alpha	-0.6	0.1
Beta	0.38	0.68
R-Squared	91	98
Standard Deviation	1.35	
Mean	2.86	
Sharpe Ratio	-0.30	

Morningstar's Take by Scott Berry 12-19-06

Fidelity Short-Term Bond has all the ingredients for continued success.

For starters, the fund's proven, sensible approach plays to Fidelity's strengths. Rather than betting on the overall direction of interest rates, which is a tricky way for even the best managers to consistently add value, manager Andy Dudley attempts to find pockets of value in individual bond issues, sectors, and maturities. In 2006, for example, he found opportunities in commercial mortgage-backed securities and asset-backed securities, which offered much of the yield of corporate bonds without as much credit risk.

Dudley, who has led this fund for roughly 10 years, has an eye for value, as evidenced by the fund's record on his watch. Indeed, the fund has outperformed roughly 80% of its short-term bond peers over the trailing three-, five-, and 10-year periods. And the fund has been remarkably consistent from one year to the next, as it has ranked in the category's best half in each of the

past seven (soon to be eight) calendar years. Most notably, Dudley avoided trouble when corporate bonds slumped in 2002, but scooped up a number of beaten-down corporate issues in time to benefit from a rally in 2003. More recently, he has focused on bonds with good covenants, which should offer some protection from leverage buyout activity.

Capping this fund off is its below-average expense ratio. Fidelity has contractually limited the fund's expense ratio to 0.45%, which places it in the cheapest quartile of no-load short-term bond funds. With returns in the group often tightly bunched, the fund's expense advantage proves invaluable by allowing more yield and return to flow directly to shareholders without Dudley having to take on added risk.

In short, this fund has everything we look for in recommending one fund over another. It remains one of our two short-term bond Analyst Picks.

Portfolio Analysis 08-31-06

Total Fixed-Income:1413	Date of Maturity	Amount $000	Value $000	% Net Assets
US Treasury Note 3.75%	05-15-08	306,903	301,532	3.61
US Treasury Note 3.375%	02-15-08	250,000	244,785	2.93
Euro$ 90 Day Fut Sep 06		1	177,268	2.12
Euro$ 90 Day Fut Dec 07		1	176,905	2.12
Euro$ 90 Day Fut Sep 07		1	176,784	2.11
Euro$ 90 Day Fut Jun 07		1	176,561	2.11
Euro$ 90 Day Fut Mar 07		1	176,300	2.11
Euro$ 90 Day Fut Dec 06		1	176,058	2.11
FHLMC 3.875%	06-15-08	152,291	149,190	1.78
Euro$ 90 Day Fut Mar 08		1	138,407	1.66
FNMA 3.25%	02-15-09	128,000	122,726	1.47
US Treasury Note 4.875%	05-15-09	84,000	84,318	1.01
FNMA 4%	09-02-08	73,170	71,494	0.86
US Treasury Bond 12%	08-15-13	61,275	69,494	0.83
FNMA 0.06%	04-01-18	61,121	61,030	0.73
US Treasury Note 4.375%	11-15-08	55,000	54,555	0.65
FNMA FRN	11-01-35	47,222	46,817	0.56
US Treasury Note 3.875%	01-15-09	36,500	46,672	0.56
FHLMC CMO 3.5%	07-15-22	45,945	45,022	0.54
FNMA CMO 5.5%	02-25-30	41,669	41,724	0.50

Current Investment Style

Duration: Short Int Long

Quality: High Med Low

¹ figure provided by fund

Avg Eff Duration¹	1.7 Yrs
Avg Eff Maturity	2.8 Yrs
Avg Credit Quality	AA
Avg Wtd Coupon	3.42%
Avg Wtd Price	97.59% of par

Coupon Range	% of Bonds	Rel Cat
0% PIK	6.5	0.7
0% to 6%	89.7	1.1
6% to 8%	7.8	0.5
8% to 10%	1.4	0.6
More than 10%	1.2	2.6

1.00=Category Average

Credit Analysis	% bonds 08-31-06		
AAA	59	BB	1
AA	6	B	0
A	12	Below B	0
BBB	18	NR/NA	5

Sector Breakdown % of assets

US Treasuries	11
TIPS	1
US Agency	5
Mortgage Pass-Throughs	10
Mortgage CMO	21
Mortgage ARM	0
US Corporate	16
Asset-Backed	17
Convertible	0
Municipal	0
Corporate Inflation-Protected	0
Foreign Corporate	1
Foreign Govt	0

Composition

Cash	15.3	Bonds	70.0
Stocks	0.0	Other	14.7

Special Securities

Restricted/Illiquid Secs	3
Exotic Mortgage-Backed	1
Emerging-Markets Secs	Trace
Options/Futures/Warrants	No

Address:	82 Devonshire St Boston MA 02109 800-544-9797
Web Address:	www.fidelity.com
Inception:	09-15-86
Advisor:	Fidelity Management & Research (FMR)
Subadvisor:	Multiple Subadvisors
NTF Plans:	Fidelity Retail-NTF, CommonWealth NTF

Minimum Purchase:	$2500	Add: $250	IRA: $500
Min Auto Inv Plan:	$100	Add: $100	
Sales Fees:	No-load		
Management Fee:	0.43%		
Actual Fees:	Mgt:0.32%	Dist: —	
Expense Projections:	3Yr:$144	5Yr:$252	10Yr:$567
Income Distrib:	Monthly		

MORNINGSTAR® Funds 500

Fidelity Small Cap Indep

	Ticker	Load	NAV	Yield	Total Assets	Mstar Category
	FDSCX	None	$21.05	0.2%	$2,775 mil	Small Growth

Governance and Management

Stewardship Grade: B

Portfolio Manager(s)

Richard Thompson has been at Fidelity for nearly a decade, beginning as an associate analyst and working his way up the ranks. He did a stint in London for the firm, where he worked as an analyst and supervised associate analysts. He has a solid analyst background, but only limited experience running a mutual fund. For 16 months Thompson ran a fund in London for foreign investors, and he comanaged Fidelity Small Cap Stock for six months. Fidelity's small-cap team should provide support.

Strategy

This fund applies a growth-at-a-reasonable-price strategy to the small-cap universe. Manager Richard Thompson has worked overseas and will leverage his knowledge of those markets, spicing this fund up with some foreign exposure. Thompson will hew fairly closely to the Russell 2000 Index in terms of sector weightings and will employ Fidelity's favored valuation metrics, such as price/earnings and enterprise value/operating earnings.

Performance 12-31-06

	1st Qtr	2nd Qtr	3rd Qtr	4th Qtr	Total
2002	2.20	-6.58	-13.78	-3.83	-20.83
2003	-2.71	15.30	4.56	15.00	34.89
2004	4.51	-0.11	-2.78	13.31	15.02
2005	-1.17	3.80	7.02	1.07	10.96
2006	10.69	-5.21	-2.33	11.80	14.59

Trailing	Total Return%	+/- S&P 500	+/- Russ 2000 Gr	%Rank Cat	Growth of $10,000
3 Mo	11.80	5.10	3.03	5	11,180
6 Mo	9.20	-3.54	2.34	15	10,920
1 Yr	14.59	-1.20	1.24	22	11,459
3 Yr Avg	13.51	3.07	3.00	15	14,625
5 Yr Avg	9.32	3.13	2.39	24	15,613
10 Yr Avg	8.97	0.55	4.09	43	23,609
15 Yr Avg	—	—	—	—	—

Tax Analysis	Tax-Adj Rtn%	%Rank Cat	Tax-Cost Rat	%Rank Cat
3 Yr (estimated)	11.84	16	1.47	58
5 Yr (estimated)	8.36	23	0.88	51
10 Yr (estimated)	7.93	38	0.95	35

Potential Capital Gain Exposure: 11% of assets

Historical Profile

Return	Above Avg	
Risk	Low	
Rating	★★★★ Above Avg	

Performance Quartile (within Category)

91%	93%	90%	95%	93%	99%	92%	98%	98%		

▼ Manager Change
▽ Partial Manager Change

Growth of $10,000

— Investment Values of Fund
— Investment Values of S&P 500

1995	1996	1997	1998	1999	2000	2001	2002	2003	2004	2005	2006	History
12.39	13.56	15.93	14.19	16.09	16.23	16.80	13.30	17.94	19.72	20.48	21.05	NAV
26.63	13.63	27.25	-7.39	14.10	5.76	6.29	-20.83	34.89	15.02	10.96	14.59	Total Return %
-10.95	-9.33	-6.11	-35.97	-6.94	14.86	18.18	1.27	6.21	4.14	6.05	-1.20	+/-S&P 500
-4.41	2.37	14.30	-8.62	-28.99	28.19	15.52	9.43	-13.65	0.71	6.81	1.24	+/-Russ 2000 Gr
0.77	0.08	0.97	0.19	0.63	0.19	0.00	0.00	0.00	0.00	0.35	0.24	Income Return %
25.86	13.55	26.28	-7.58	13.47	5.57	6.29	-20.83	34.89	15.02	10.61	14.35	Capital Return %
67	69	22	91	88	25	16	21	86	32	16	22	Total Rtn % Rank Cat
0.08	0.01	0.13	0.03	0.09	0.03	0.00	0.00	0.00	0.00	0.07	0.05	Income $
0.77	0.51	1.14	0.62	0.00	0.74	0.44	0.00	0.00	0.89	1.34	2.34	Capital Gains $
0.90	0.99	0.90	0.97	0.82	0.84	0.74	0.91	0.93	0.91	0.75	—	Expense Ratio %
0.40	0.39	0.41	0.63	0.15	0.20	0.66	-0.52	-0.59	-0.49	0.49	—	Income Ratio %
182	192	176	88	173	159	450	290	220	95	61	—	Turnover Rate %
488	538	825	748	612	689	958	841	949	1,093	1,855	2,775	Net Assets $mil

Rating and Risk

Time Period	Load-Adj Return %	Morningstar Rtn vs Cat	Morningstar Risk vs Cat	Morningstar Risk-Adj Rating
1 Yr	14.59			
3 Yr	13.51	+Avg	-Avg	★★★★
5 Yr	9.32	+Avg	Low	★★★★
10 Yr	8.97	Avg	Low	★★★★
Incept	9.89			

Other Measures	Standard Index S&P 500	Best Fit Index Russ 2000 Gr
Alpha	-0.4	4.1
Beta	1.54	0.78
R-Squared	64	87
Standard Deviation	13.24	
Mean	13.51	
Sharpe Ratio	0.78	

Morningstar's Take by John Coumarianos 12-29-06

We'd still stay away from Fidelity Small Cap Independence.

Manager Richard Thompson passed the one-year mark at this small-growth fund in October 2006. Previously, he was an analyst for Fidelity for five years and did a stint in London, where he managed a portfolio for 16 months. He also comanaged Fidelity Small Cap Stock for six months. His experience is limited compared with Jamie Harmon, whose departure from this fund was a loss.

Moreover, this fund, with its girth, is not an easy one for a new manager to cut his teeth on. At $2.7 billion in assets, the fund must accumulate about 5% of a $500 million company's float (the amount of shares outstanding) in order for those shares to constitute 1% of the fund. Although the fund's average market cap dropped a bit by July 2006 to $1.2 billion from $1.4 billion, the fund still has a hefty mid-cap stake relative to its typical category peer. Thompson may find it difficult to trim the fund's mid-cap stake further given this fund's size,

and we'd note that the fund's portfolio centroid (its weighted average of domestic stock holdings) remains on the line between the small-growth and mid-growth squares of Morningstar's style box.

We like the fact that Thompson will utilize his overseas experience. Currently, he has a large position in the Restaurant Group, a U.K. operator of theme-based restaurants designed to compete with more traditional pubs that have dominated Great Britain. Unfortunately, Thompson wasn't successful with another foreign pick, TeleAtlas, a Netherlands-based provider of maps for Global Positioning Systems (GPS). This firm's customers have recently been choosing less-lucrative country-based maps rather than maps of entire continents.

Thompson should also benefit from Fidelity's efforts to beef up its general research staff and its small-cap team. But ultimately we're concerned that Thompson lacks the portfolio management experience needed to run such a large fund well.

Portfolio Analysis 10-31-06

Share change since 07-06 Total Stocks:167

	Sector	PE	Tot Ret%	% Assets
⊕ Medicis Pharmaceuticals	Health	—	10.05	2.42
⊕ Huron Consulting Group,	Business	36.3	89.00	2.15
⊕ Allegheny Technologies C	Ind Mtrls	17.1	152.95	2.10
Fourlis Grp of Companies	Consumer	—	—	1.81
⊖ New River Pharmaceutical	Health	—	110.91	1.80
⊕ ValueClick, Inc.	Business	46.8	30.48	1.54
FLIR Systems, Inc.	Ind Mtrls	28.6	42.54	1.37
⊕ Carpenter Technology Cor	Ind Mtrls	11.7	46.55	1.33
✴ Kanbay International, In	Software	34.2	81.06	1.27
Conceptus, Inc.	Health	—	68.70	1.26
Regal Entertainment Grou	Goods	37.4	19.27	1.24
Digitas, Inc.	Business	27.9	7.11	1.20
Valmont Industries, Inc.	Ind Mtrls	23.9	67.12	1.17
⊕ Corrections Corporation	Business	28.1	50.87	1.16
⊕ Healthways, Inc.	Health	50.4	5.44	1.05
Williams-Sonoma, Inc.	Consumer	17.7	-26.53	1.02
⊕ Goodrich Petroleum Corpo	Energy	31.1	43.86	1.02
⊕ NCR Corporation	Hardware	22.6	25.99	1.02
Alliant Techsystems, Inc	Ind Mtrls	18.2	2.65	1.01
Vail Resorts, Inc.	Consumer	37.2	35.70	0.97

Current Investment Style

Value Blnd Growth — Large Mid Small

Market Cap	%
Giant	0.0
Large	1.4
Mid	38.8
Small	44.8
Micro	15.0

Avg $mil: 1,385

Value Measures		Rel Category
Price/Earnings	18.95	0.90
Price/Book	2.59	0.95
Price/Sales	1.33	0.85
Price/Cash Flow	5.80	0.60
Dividend Yield %	0.86	1.87

Growth Measures	%	Rel Category
Long-Term Erngs	16.89	0.95
Book Value	10.47	1.00
Sales	10.01	0.84
Cash Flow	13.48	0.64
Historical Erngs	13.28	0.55

Profitability	%	Rel Category
Return on Equity	12.25	0.99
Return on Assets	4.71	0.71
Net Margin	7.55	0.87

Sector Weightings	% of Stocks	Rel S&P 500	3 Year High Low
⟳ Info	14.20	0.71	
Software	2.70	0.78	6 2
Hardware	6.90	0.75	8 1
Media	3.22	0.85	3 0
Telecom	1.38	0.39	4 0
⟲ Service	50.26	1.09	
Health	12.46	1.03	19 11
Consumer	13.21	1.73	15 11
Business	14.67	3.47	26 14
Financial	9.92	0.45	30 8
⟰ Mfg	35.52	1.05	
Goods	5.85	0.68	6 4
Ind Mtrls	18.06	1.51	21 5
Energy	11.25	1.15	14 4
Utilities	0.36	0.10	1 0

Composition

		%
●	Cash	1.7
●	Stocks	98.3
●	Bonds	0.0
○	Other	0.0
	Foreign	17.0
	(% of Stock)	

Investment Style	
Equity	
Stock %	

Address:	82 Devonshire St Boston MA 02109 800-544-6666
Web Address:	www.fidelity.com
Inception:	06-28-93
Advisor:	Fidelity Management & Research (FMR)
Subadvisor:	Multiple Subadvisors
NTF Plans:	Fidelity Retail-NTF, CommonWealth NTF

Minimum Purchase:	$2500	Add: $250	IRA: $200
Min Auto Inv Plan:	$100	Add: $100	
Sales Fees:	No-load, 1.50%R		
Management Fee:	0.55%		
Actual Fees:	Mgt:0.55%	Dist: —	
Expense Projections:	3Yr:$274	5Yr:$477	10Yr:$1061
Income Distrib:	Annually		

Fidelity Small Cap Stock

	Ticker	Load	NAV	Yield	Total Assets	Mstar Category
	FSLCX	Closed	$19.01	0.0%	$4,799 mil	Small Blend

Governance and Management

Stewardship Grade: B

Portfolio Manager(s)

Paul Antico, who has been at the helm since the fund's March 1998 inception, returned from a leave of absence on Oct. 3, 2005. He's supported by Fidelity's staff of small-cap analysts and draws on the company's army of industry analysts for additional research. Though small-cap research isn't generally a priority at Fidelity, the firm is taking steps to improve that effort.

Strategy

Manager Paul Antico is a pure bottom-up stock-picker who seeks companies with strong growth prospects but isn't willing to pay the extreme prices that pure growth managers do. He will buy turnaround plays and tends to avoid areas where valuations have run up. Antico spreads his picks across roughly 200 to 235 names and keeps individual stock positions fairly small, limiting the fund's exposure to company-specific risk. Turnover has consistently run about 100% per year.

Historical Profile

Return Average
Risk Average
Rating ★★★ Neutral

Investment Style: Equity / Stock %

87% 89% 88% 87% 92% 95% 84% 91% 91%

▼ Manager Change
▽ Partial Manager Change

Growth of $10,000
— Investment Values of Fund
— Investment Values of S&P 500

Performance Quartile (within Category)

	1995	1996	1997	1998	1999	2000	2001	2002	2003	2004	2005	2006	History
NAV	—	—	—	8.91	12.71	13.51	14.36	11.84	17.10	18.16	18.30	19.01	
Total Return %	—	—	—	-10.69*	42.65	11.84	6.44	-15.73	45.04	14.57	8.09	12.37	
+/-S&P 500	—	—	—		21.61	20.94	18.33	6.37	16.36	3.69	3.18	-3.42	
+/-Russ 2000	—	—	—		21.39	14.86	3.95	4.75	-2.21	-3.76	3.54	-6.00	
Income Return %	—	—	—		0.00	0.32	0.15	0.00	0.00	0.00	0.00	0.00	
Capital Return %	—	—	—		42.65	11.52	6.29	-15.73	45.04	14.57	8.09	12.37	
Total Rtn % Rank Cat	—	—	—	7	52	51	50	42	81	36	75		
Income $	—	—	—	0.02	0.00	0.04	0.02	0.00	0.00	0.00	0.00	0.00	
Capital Gains $	—	—	—	0.00	0.00	0.65	0.00	0.31	0.07	1.33	1.26	1.52	
Expense Ratio %	—	—	—	1.48	0.99	1.13	1.07	1.07	1.10	1.08	1.00	0.93	
Income Ratio %	—	—	—	0.67	0.01	-0.01	0.24	0.24	0.05	-0.34	-0.23	-0.23	
Turnover Rate %	—	—	—	75	170	120	151	132	116	96	99	107	
Net Assets $mil	—	—	—	552	688	1,142	1,354	1,419	2,505	4,159	4,253	4,799	

Performance 12-31-06

	1st Qtr	2nd Qtr	3rd Qtr	4th Qtr	Total
2002	5.08	-7.41	-18.73	6.57	-15.73
2003	-4.81	17.84	10.24	17.30	45.04
2004	4.91	1.86	-4.29	12.01	14.57
2005	-2.86	2.32	6.89	1.74	8.09
2006	14.10	-7.14	-0.72	6.83	12.37

Trailing	Total Return%	+/- S&P 500	+/- Russ 2000	%Rank Cat	Growth of $10,000
3 Mo	6.83	0.13	-2.07	84	10,683
6 Mo	6.06	-6.68	-3.32	71	10,606
1 Yr	12.37	-3.42	-6.00	75	11,237
3 Yr Avg	11.64	1.20	-1.92	76	13,914
5 Yr Avg	11.21	5.02	-0.18	60	17,011
10 Yr Avg	—	—	—	—	—
15 Yr Avg	—	—	—	—	—

Tax Analysis	Tax-Adj Rtn%	%Rank Cat	Tax-Cost Rat	%Rank Cat
3 Yr (estimated)	10.09	66	1.39	41
5 Yr (estimated)	10.17	55	0.94	41
10 Yr (estimated)	—	—	—	—

Potential Capital Gain Exposure: 17% of assets

Rating and Risk

Time Period	Load-Adj Return %	Morningstar Rtn vs Cat	Morningstar Risk vs Cat	Morningstar Risk-Adj Rating
1 Yr	12.37			
3 Yr	11.64	-Avg	Avg	★★
5 Yr	11.21	Avg	Avg	★★★
10 Yr	—			
Incept	11.36			

Other Measures	Standard Index S&P 500	Best Fit Index Russ 2000 Gr
Alpha	-2.1	2.5
Beta	1.53	0.76
R-Squared	70	91
Standard Deviation	12.56	
Mean	11.64	
Sharpe Ratio	0.69	

Morningstar's Take by Greg Carlson 12-19-06

Despite a recent stumble and size concerns, we'd hang on to Fidelity Small Cap Stock.

This fund hasn't looked impressive relative to its small-blend rivals lately--it hasn't cracked the category's top third in a calendar year since 1999. But the fund has faced a stiff headwind over that stretch. Paul Antico, who's run the fund since its 1998 inception, takes a similar stance to some of his colleagues: He's measured against a blend-oriented benchmark--the Russell 2000 Index--but prefers companies with significant earnings growth, and has thus typically tilted the portfolio toward traditional growth areas such as health care and tech. That's held back returns amid value stocks' now-lengthy rally.

2006 provides a case in point. Antico has avoided REITs and utilities--two of the year's best-performing sectors--due to valuation concerns after long runs. He's also steered clear of most of the red-hot energy sector, in part because he's reluctant to make a call on commodity prices. While those decisions can primarily be chalked up to Antico sticking with his approach, he's also made some clear mistakes this year; he ramped up the fund's tech exposure just prior to an early-summer correction.

Nevertheless, we think this fund will look a lot better when growth stocks return to favor--the fund's early years certainly suggest that, and the recent build-out of Fidelity's research staff boosts our confidence.

Of more concern is the extent of Antico's flexibility here. While we were glad to see the fund close to new investors in June 2006, it's still hefty. Due to the fund's size, as well as overlap with some of Fidelity's bigger funds, the firm recently owned at least a 10% stake in 15 of the fund's top 25 holdings, which could hamper Antico's ability to trade them. That said, inflows have slowed to a trickle, and Antico's substantial stake in the fund, as well as its performance-adjusted management fee, provide some comfort. We'd stick around.

Address:	82 Devonshire St Boston MA 02109 800-544-5555
Web Address:	www.fidelity.com
Inception:	03-12-98*
Advisor:	Fidelity Management & Research (FMR)
Subadvisor:	Multiple Subadvisors
NTF Plans:	Fidelity Retail-NTF, CommonWealth NTF

Minimum Purchase:	Closed	Add: —	IRA: —
Min Auto Inv Plan:	Closed	Add: —	
Sales Fees:	No-load, 2.00%R		
Management Fee:	0.69%		
Actual Fees:	Mgt:0.69%	Dist: —	
Expense Projections:	3Yr:$312	5Yr:$542	10Yr:$1201
Income Distrib:	Semi-Annually		

Portfolio Analysis 10-31-06

Share change since 07-06 Total Stocks:203

	Sector	PE	Tot Ret%	% Assets
Children's Place Retail	Consumer	24.3	28.53	4.15
⊕ Cerner Corporation	Software	37.1	0.10	2.67
⊖ Ingram Micro, Inc.	Business	13.3	2.41	2.05
Per-Se Technologies, Inc	Health	63.3	18.92	1.57
⊖ Penn National Gaming	Goods	21.8	26.31	1.29
⊕ Gamestop Corporation A	Goods	33.9	73.19	1.28
⊕ AAR Corporation	Ind Mtrls	26.2	21.88	1.22
Insight Enterprises, Inc	Business	16.7	-3.77	1.20
PRA International	Health	21.4	-10.23	1.19
⊕ Healthways, Inc.	Health	50.4	5.44	1.18
Ness Technologies, Inc.	Business	20.0	32.41	1.10
⊕ Arrow Electronics, Inc.	Business	12.4	-1.50	1.07
Digitas, Inc.	Business	27.9	7.11	1.04
⊕ BE Aerospace	Ind Mtrls	15.3	16.73	0.94
Men's Wearhouse	Consumer	16.6	30.69	0.93
⊖ Gildan Activewear, Inc.	Goods	33.5	8.82	0.93
⊖ TTM Technologies, Inc.	Hardware	10.4	20.53	0.88
⊖ SiRF Technology Holdings	Hardware	95.3	-14.36	0.88
Hyperion Solutions Corpo	Software	34.1	0.34	0.88
⊕ Triumph Group, Inc.	Ind Mtrls	20.7	43.45	0.84

Current Investment Style

Value Blnd Growth — Large/Mid/Small

Market Cap	%
Giant	0.0
Large	0.5
Mid	35.0
Small	42.0
Micro	22.5

Avg $mil: 1,134

Value Measures		Rel Category
Price/Earnings	19.68	1.19
Price/Book	2.19	1.04
Price/Sales	0.97	0.99
Price/Cash Flow	10.12	1.45
Dividend Yield %	0.42	0.39

Growth Measures	%	Rel Category
Long-Term Erngs	17.75	1.27
Book Value	9.04	1.19
Sales	9.76	1.11
Cash Flow	8.71	0.69
Historical Erngs	19.42	1.16

Profitability	%	Rel Category
Return on Equity	9.38	0.73
Return on Assets	4.12	0.58
Net Margin	5.52	0.57

Sector Weightings	% of Stocks	Rel S&P 500	3 Year High	Low
Info	23.18	1.16		
Software	8.24	2.39	10	4
Hardware	14.23	1.54	17	8
Media	0.60	0.16	5	0
Telecom	0.11	0.03	2	0
Service	52.09	1.13		
Health	16.20	1.34	20	13
Consumer	10.74	1.40	14	9
Business	18.88	4.46	22	14
Financial	6.27	0.28	10	5
Mfg	24.74	0.73		
Goods	10.03	1.17	11	4
Ind Mtrls	12.67	1.06	25	11
Energy	2.04	0.21	3	0
Utilities	0.00	0.00	0	0

Composition

	%
Cash	9.0
Stocks	90.8
Bonds	0.0
Other	0.1
Foreign (% of Stock)	17.3

MORNINGSTAR® Funds 500

Fidelity Small Cap Value

	Ticker	Load	NAV	Yield	Total Assets	Mstar Category
	FCPVX	None	$14.00	0.0%	$1,260 mil	Small Blend

Governance and Management

Stewardship Grade: B

Portfolio Manager(s)

On March 14, 2006, Thomas Hense took over this fund from Katherine Lieberman, who had run it since its November 2004 inception. (Lieberman left Fidelity.) Unlike most of the managers who run diversified stock funds for Fidelity, Hense didn't previously helm a sector fund. Instead, he began his career at Fidelity as a high-yield analyst in 1993 and later headed up that group before becoming an equity analyst in 2000. He has since led the small-cap analyst team and has managed small-cap portfolios for institutional clients since 2003.

Strategy

New manager Thomas Hense looks for roughly the same qualities in a company as predecessor Kathy Lieberman: Below-average valuations (relative to industry peers), potentially solid earnings growth, and--when tough times may be ahead--relatively healthy balance sheets. That said, while Lieberman was quite willing to make substantial sector bets, Hense will limit the fund's wagers against the Russell 2000 Value Index. He expects portfolio turnover to average 80% to 100% annually--a shade higher than it was under Lieberman.

Performance 12-31-06

	1st Qtr	2nd Qtr	3rd Qtr	4th Qtr	Total
2002	—	—	—	—	—
2003	—	—	—	—	—*
2004	—	—	—	—	—*
2005	2.42	3.94	6.76	3.48	17.61
2006	13.18	-4.92	-1.35	8.94	15.65

Trailing	Total Return%	+/- S&P 500	+/- Russ 2000	%Rank Cat	Growth of $10,000
3 Mo	8.94	2.24	0.04	25	10,894
6 Mo	7.47	-5.27	-1.91	49	10,747
1 Yr	15.65	-0.14	-2.72	42	11,565
3 Yr Avg	—	—	—	—	—
5 Yr Avg	—	—	—	—	—
10 Yr Avg	—	—	—	—	—
15 Yr Avg	—	—	—	—	—

Tax Analysis	Tax-Adj Rtn%	%Rank Cat	Tax-Cost Rat	%Rank Cat
3 Yr (estimated)	—	—	—	—
5 Yr (estimated)	—	—	—	—
10 Yr (estimated)	—	—	—	—

Potential Capital Gain Exposure: 12% of assets

Morningstar's Take by Greg Carlson 12-20-06

Expect steady performance, not blowout returns, from Fidelity Small Cap Value.

Since Thomas Hense became this fund's manager in March 2006, he's given it a more moderate profile than predecessor Kathy Lieberman did. Lieberman didn't hesitate to make substantial bets against the fund's benchmark, the Russell 2000 Value Index, and found big winners within the energy sector, as well as more growth-oriented areas such as retail. The fund also moved into the small-blend category on her watch. Hense, on the other hand, has attempted to remake the fund into a more traditional value offering, boosting its stake in financials (the index's largest sector weighting), generally limiting the fund's sector bets against the benchmark and, as a result, lowering its price multiples.

Given small-value funds' nearly seven-year run as one of the best-performing diversified domestic fund categories, the timing of Hense's shifts may work against the fund over the next few years if

growth stocks rebound. On the other hand, he's trimmed its exposure to the arguably overheated energy sector and other economically sensitive fare. And although he's avoided most REITs due to concerns about their valuations, he's made savvy picks such as commercial property owner Jones Lang LaSalle, which he liked for its global reach and steady revenues at the time of purchase.

The fund's results during Hense's brief tenure are middling thus far, but he amassed a solid record in his first three years running small-blend-style institutional accounts (which he still manages). Furthermore, this fund's structure gives his tame style a chance to succeed: Its 1.09% expense ratio, which includes an upward adjustment to its management fee due to the fund's early success, is still quite modest. And Hense manages roughly $2.1 billion, which affords him some flexibility here. All told, we think this is a worthy holding.

Address:	82 Devonshire St
	Boston MA 02109
	800-544-5555
Web Address:	www.fidelity.com
Inception:	11-03-04
Advisor:	Fidelity Management & Research (FMR)
Subadvisor:	Multiple Subadvisors
NTF Plans:	Fidelity Retail-NTF, CommonWealth NTF

Minimum Purchase:	$2500	Add: $250	IRA: $500
Min Auto Inv Plan:	$0	Add: —	
Sales Fees:	No-load, 1.50%R		
Management Fee:	0.81%		
Actual Fees:	Mgt:0.81%	Dist: —	
Expense Projections:	3Yr:$347	5Yr:$601	10Yr:$1329
Income Distrib:	Semi-Annually		

Historical Profile
Return
Risk
Rating
Not Rated

Investment Style
Equity
Stock %
95% 96%

▼ Manager Change
▽ Partial Manager Change

Growth of $10,000
— Investment Values of Fund
— Investment Values of S&P 500

Performance Quartile (within Category)

	1995	1996	1997	1998	1999	2000	2001	2002	2003	2004	2005	2006	History
	—	—	—	—	—	—	—	—	—	11.16	12.75	14.00	NAV
	—	—	—	—	—	—	—	—	—	—	17.61	15.65	Total Return %
	—	—	—	—	—	—	—	—	—	—	12.70	-0.14	+/-S&P 500
	—	—	—	—	—	—	—	—	—	—	13.06	-2.72	+/-Russ 2000
	—	—	—	—	—	—	—	—	—	—	0.10	0.00	Income Return %
	—	—	—	—	—	—	—	—	—	—	17.51	15.65	Capital Return %
	—	—	—	—	—	—	—	—	—	—	2	42	Total Rtn % Rank Cat
	—	—	—	—	—	—	—	—	—	0.01	0.01	0.00	Income $
	—	—	—	—	—	—	—	—	—	0.00	0.36	0.68	Capital Gains $
	—	—	—	—	—	—	—	—	—	—	—	1.06	Expense Ratio %
	—	—	—	—	—	—	—	—	—	—	—	0.06	Income Ratio %
	—	—	—	—	—	—	—	—	—	—	—	93	Turnover Rate %
	—	—	—	—	—	—	—	—	—	—	161	1,106	Net Assets $mil

Rating and Risk

Time Period	Load-Adj Return %	Morningstar Rtn vs Cat	Morningstar Risk vs Cat	Morningstar Risk-Adj Rating
1 Yr	15.65			
3 Yr	—	—	—	—
5 Yr	—	—	—	—
10 Yr	—	—	—	—
Incept	21.37			

Other Measures	Standard Index S&P 500	Best Fit Index
Alpha	—	—
Beta	—	—
R-Squared	—	—
Standard Deviation	—	
Mean	—	
Sharpe Ratio	—	

Portfolio Analysis 10-31-06

Share change since 07-06 Total Stocks:160	Sector	PE	Tot Ret%	% Assets
⊕ Tesoro Corporation	Energy	6.5	7.51	2.34
⊕ American Equity Invest L	Financial	10.7	0.23	2.29
⊖ RC2 Corporation	Goods	17.3	23.87	2.27
⊖ Jarden Corporation	Goods	32.0	15.39	2.05
Zenith National Insuranc	Financial	7.4	4.36	2.03
UAP Holding Corporation	Ind Mtrls	24.9	27.68	1.99
⊖ Compass Minerals Interna	Ind Mtrls	26.2	34.51	1.99
⊕ Carpenter Technology Cor	Ind Mtrls	11.7	46.55	1.94
⊕ Boston Private Financial	Financial	18.2	-6.23	1.61
⊖ USI Holdings Corporation	Financial	32.9	11.55	1.61
⊕ IPC Holdings Limited	Financial	10.3	17.68	1.44
⊖ Omnicare, Inc.	Health	28.5	-32.36	1.38
⊖ FTI Consulting, Inc.	Business	20.4	1.64	1.37
⊖ Tektronix Inc.	Hardware	25.0	4.23	1.36
Ingram Micro, Inc.	Business	13.3	2.41	1.33
⊕ Insight Enterprises, Inc	Business	16.7	-3.77	1.29
⊖ Interface, Inc. A	Goods	—	72.99	1.29
Telvent GIT SA	Business	23.3	28.96	1.29
Jones Lang LaSalle, Inc.	Financial	18.6	84.32	1.28
⊕ Intevac, Inc.	Goods	16.2	96.59	1.26

Current Investment Style

Value Blnd Growth — Large / Mid / Small

Market Cap	%
Giant	0.0
Large	0.0
Mid	27.0
Small	57.7
Micro	15.3
Avg $mil:	1,217

Value Measures		Rel Category
Price/Earnings	14.17	0.85
Price/Book	1.73	0.82
Price/Sales	0.75	0.77
Price/Cash Flow	4.98	0.71
Dividend Yield %	0.97	0.91

Growth Measures	%	Rel Category
Long-Term Erngs	13.28	0.95
Book Value	11.78	1.56
Sales	13.02	1.47
Cash Flow	15.80	1.25
Historical Erngs	18.55	1.11

Profitability	%	Rel Category
Return on Equity	11.42	0.89
Return on Assets	6.48	0.91
Net Margin	8.65	0.89

Sector Weightings	% of Stocks	Rel S&P 500	3 Year High Low
⌁ Info	9.68	0.48	
Software	1.72	0.50	— —
Hardware	6.45	0.70	— —
Media	0.00	0.00	— —
Telecom	1.51	0.43	— —
Service	50.30	1.09	
Health	6.26	0.52	— —
Consumer	6.90	0.90	— —
Business	9.48	2.24	— —
Financial	27.66	1.24	— —
Mfg	40.03	1.18	
Goods	11.44	1.34	— —
Ind Mtrls	18.40	1.54	— —
Energy	8.21	0.84	— —
Utilities	1.98	0.57	— —

Composition

● Cash		3.8
● Stocks		96.2
● Bonds		0.0
○ Other		0.0
Foreign (% of Stock)		4.2

Fidelity Small Cap Retire

	Ticker	Load	NAV	Yield	Total Assets	Mstar Category
	FSCRX	None	$16.03	0.0%	$245 mil	Small Blend

Governance and Management

Stewardship Grade: B

Portfolio Manager(s)

Charles Myers has been a member of Fidelity's small-cap research team since 1999. He ran Fidelity Small Cap Growth with Lionel Harris briefly (from April 2005 until March 2006). He will likely walk the line between blend and growth in running this fund, choosing stocks that show good growth characteristics but being mindful of valuation.

Strategy

This fund will invest at least 80% of assets in securities of companies with small market capitalization--those with market capitalizations similar to the companies in the Russell 2000 Index or the Standard & Poor's SmallCap 600 Index. The fund has the ability to venture overseas. Charles Myers will likely hew fairly closely to the Russell 2000 Index and use Fidelity's preferred in-house valuation metrics such as price/earning ratios and enterprise value/operating earnings.

Historical Profile

Return	Below Avg
Risk	Low
Rating	★★ Below Avg

Investment Style: Equity Stock %

83% 93% 94% 98% 92% 98% 98%

▼ Manager Change
▽ Partial Manager Change

Growth of $10,000
— Investment Values of Fund
— Investment Values of S&P 500

18.5
16.0
12.5
10.0
5.0

Performance Quartile (within Category)

	1995	1996	1997	1998	1999	2000	2001	2002	2003	2004	2005	2006	History
	—	—	—	—	—	10.84	13.30	10.27	13.81	15.88	16.34	16.03	NAV
	—	—	—	—	—	8.40*	23.30	-21.04	34.47	14.99	9.17	9.45	Total Return %
	—	—	—	—	—	—	35.19	1.06	5.79	4.11	4.26	-6.34	+/-S&P 500
	—	—	—	—	—	—	20.81	-0.56	-12.78	-3.34	4.62	-8.92	+/-Russ 2000
	—	—	—	—	—	—	0.00	0.00	0.00	0.00	0.25	0.00	Income Return %
	—	—	—	—	—	—	23.30	-21.04	34.47	14.99	8.92	9.45	Capital Return %
	—	—	—	—	—	—	9	78	89	79	27	91	Total Rtn % Rank Cat
	—	—	—	—	—	0.00	0.00	0.00	0.00	0.00	0.04	0.00	Income $
	—	—	—	—	—	0.00	0.06	0.29	0.00	0.00	0.90	1.79	Capital Gains $
	—	—	—	—	—	—	0.93	0.92	0.86	0.99	1.05		Expense Ratio %
	—	—	—	—	—	—	-0.15	-0.48	-0.49	-0.63	-0.29		Income Ratio %
	—	—	—	—	—	—	543	338	242	151	191		Turnover Rate %
	—	—	—	—	—	—	2	25	48	79	121	245	Net Assets $mil

Performance 12-31-06

	1st Qtr	2nd Qtr	3rd Qtr	4th Qtr	Total
2002	2.18	-6.63	-14.02	-3.75	-21.04
2003	-2.82	15.33	4.52	14.80	34.47
2004	4.49	-0.21	-2.71	13.35	14.99
2005	-1.26	3.79	6.88	-0.33	9.17
2006	9.30	-5.43	-0.53	6.44	9.45

Trailing	Total Return%	+/- S&P 500	+/- Russ 2000	%Rank Cat	Growth of $10,000
3 Mo	6.44	-0.26	-2.46	88	10,644
6 Mo	5.88	-6.86	-3.50	73	10,588
1 Yr	9.45	-6.34	-8.92	91	10,945
3 Yr Avg	11.17	0.73	-2.39	82	13,739
5 Yr Avg	7.84	1.65	-3.55	91	14,585
10 Yr Avg	—	—	—	—	—
15 Yr Avg	—	—	—	—	—

Tax Analysis	Tax-Adj Rtn%	%Rank Cat	Tax-Cost Rat	%Rank Cat
3 Yr (estimated)	9.94	67	1.11	31
5 Yr (estimated)	6.94	85	0.83	35
10 Yr (estimated)	—	—	—	—

Potential Capital Gain Exposure: 8% of assets

Rating and Risk

Time Period	Load-Adj Return %	Morningstar Rtn vs Cat	Morningstar Risk vs Cat	Morningstar Risk-Adj Rating
1 Yr	9.45			
3 Yr	11.17	-Avg	-Avg	★★
5 Yr	7.84	-Avg	Low	★★
10 Yr	—			
Incept	11.25			

Other Measures	Standard Index S&P 500	Best Fit Index Russ 2000
Alpha	-1.5	-0.2
Beta	1.37	0.79
R-Squared	63	86
Standard Deviation	11.88	
Mean	11.17	
Sharpe Ratio	0.68	

Morningstar's Take by John Coumarianos 12-29-06

Charles Myers sounds refreshingly different from other Fidelity managers, but he doesn't have a long track record.

Fidelity Small Cap Retirement used to be a retirement account version of Fidelity Small Cap Independence, when Jamie Harmon ran both of them. Harmon left in the spring of 2006 to replace Harry Lange on Fidelity Advisor Small Cap, and the relatively untested Myers took over this fund. Myers ran Fidelity Small Cap Growth with Lionel Harris briefly (from April 2005 through mid-March 2006), where they posted middling returns versus their small-growth peers and slightly trailed the Russell 2000 Growth Index.

Myers has quickly put his stamp on this fund, limiting the number of stocks he owns to 46. He says that he will also seek to keep trading to a minimum. These two characteristics mark a point of departure from the typical Fidelity ethos of jamming tons of stocks into a fund and trading with gusto--either paring and boosting existing positions or shifting in and out of stocks completely. The smaller portfolio is already apparent, though we'll have to wait and see if Myers makes good on his remarks about trading.

Regarding style, Myers appears cut out of the Fidelity growth-at-a-reasonable-price cloth. He seeks businesses that exhibit earnings growth and superior returns on capital, though he's not willing to pay exorbitant prices for them. Consequently, the fund could wind up in the value, blend, or growth parts of the style box at different times.

The fund has struggled a bit so far, as its top holding, institutional pharmacy Omnicare, has been buffeted by charges of Medicaid billing fraud by the Michigan attorney general. Morningstar's equity analysis places the stock in 5-star territory, however, even though we recently lowered its fair value estimate.

It's too early to make a meaningful bet on Myers unless this is the only small-cap fund in your 401(k) plan.

Portfolio Analysis 10-31-06

Share change since 07-06 Total Stocks:46	Sector	PE	Tot Ret%	% Assets
⊕ Domino's Pizza, Inc.	Consumer	16.0	17.90	5.45
Omnicare, Inc.	Health	28.5	-32.36	5.14
⊕ Max Re Capital, Ltd.	Financial	15.4	-3.43	4.92
⊕ Chemed Corporation	Business	25.0	-25.17	4.78
Dollar Financial Corpora	Financial	NMF	132.36	4.37
⊖ Lifetime Brands, Inc.	Goods	18.2	-19.63	4.35
⊕ IPC Holdings Limited	Financial	10.3	17.68	4.11
⊖ Amedisys, Inc.	Health	20.7	3.76	3.85
⊕ J2 Global Communications	Telecom	26.6	27.52	3.57
⊕ Aspen Insurance Holdings	Financial	8.3	14.24	3.19
⊕ Columbus McKinnon Corpor	Ind Mtrls	7.0	-4.37	3.04
⊖ Compass Minerals Interna	Ind Mtrls	26.2	34.51	2.97
⊖ Carpenter Technology Cor	Ind Mtrls	11.7	46.55	2.91
UAP Holding Corporation	Ind Mtrls	24.9	27.68	2.67
☼ Foundation Coal Holdings	Energy	16.1	-15.94	2.60
⊕ Cogent Communications Gr	Telecom	—	195.45	2.55
⊖ Timberland Company	Goods	17.0	-2.98	2.46
Federal Agricultural Mor	Financial	11.1	-8.02	2.44
⊕ Genesco, Inc.	Goods	15.3	-3.84	2.39
⊕ VistaCare, Inc. A	Health	—	-18.80	2.38

Current Investment Style

Value Blnd Growth — Large Mid Small

Market Cap	%
Giant	0.0
Large	0.0
Mid	20.0
Small	59.4
Micro	20.6

Avg $mil: 1,098

Value Measures		Rel Category
Price/Earnings	13.61	0.82
Price/Book	1.59	0.75
Price/Sales	1.07	1.09
Price/Cash Flow	7.34	1.05
Dividend Yield %	1.63	1.52

Growth Measures	%	Rel Category
Long-Term Erngs	15.35	1.10
Book Value	13.13	1.73
Sales	8.24	0.93
Cash Flow	21.25	1.68
Historical Erngs	16.02	0.96

Profitability	%	Rel Category
Return on Equity	7.09	0.55
Return on Assets	4.39	0.61
Net Margin	7.50	0.77

Sector Weightings	% of Stocks	Rel S&P 500	3 Year High Low	
☊ Info	9.33	0.47		
🔲 Software	0.00	0.00	6	0
🖥 Hardware	2.06	0.22	11	1
🎙 Media	1.03	0.27	3	0
📱 Telecom	6.24	1.78	6	0
☕ Service	58.65	1.27		
🏥 Health	15.29	1.27	19	11
🛒 Consumer	9.06	1.18	15	7
📋 Business	10.78	2.55	26	11
💲 Financial	23.52	1.06	29	13
🏭 Mfg	32.01	0.95		
🏭 Goods	9.39	1.10	9	4
⚙ Ind Mtrls	16.43	1.38	16	4
🔥 Energy	6.19	0.63	13	4
💡 Utilities	0.00	0.00	1	0

Composition

		%
●	Cash	2.0
●	Stocks	98.0
●	Bonds	0.0
○	Other	0.0
	Foreign (% of Stock)	1.4

Address:	82 Devonshire St Boston MA 02109 800-962-1375	Minimum Purchase:	$2500	Add: $500	IRA: $2500
		Min Auto Inv Plan:	$2500	Add: $100	
		Sales Fees:	No-load, 1.50%R		
Web Address:	www.fidelity.com	Management Fee:	0.62%		
Inception:	09-26-00*	Actual Fees:	Mgt:0.62%	Dist: —	
Advisor:	Fidelity Management & Research (FMR)	Expense Projections:	3Yr:$337	5Yr:$585	10Yr:$1294
Subadvisor:	Multiple Subadvisors	Income Distrib:	Semi-Annually		
NTF Plans:	Fidelity Retail-NTF, CommonWealth NTF				

MORNINGSTAR® Funds 500

Fidelity Spar 500 Inv

	Analyst Pick	Ticker FSMKX	Load None	NAV $97.97	Yield 1.5%	Total Assets $16,228 mil	Mstar Category Large Blend

Governance and Management

Stewardship Grade: B

Portfolio Manager(s)

Geode Capital Management has served as the subadvisor to this fund and many of Fidelity's other index funds since Aug. 4, 2003.

Strategy

Simple. This fund buys the stocks that make up the S&P 500 Index, as well as index futures, in an attempt to mimic the index's returns.

Historical Profile
Return Average
Risk Average
Rating ★★★ Neutral

	96%	96%	98%	97%	97%	97%	97%	97%	94%

▼ Manager Change
▽ Partial Manager Change

31.0
25.0 **Growth of $10,000**
20.0 ▬ Investment Values of Fund
15.0 ▬ Investment Values of S&P 500
10.0

Performance Quartile (within Category)

1995	1996	1997	1998	1999	2000	2001	2002	2003	2004	2005	2006	History
45.32	53.42	68.50	85.29	100.89	90.76	78.89	60.47	76.60	83.36	86.02	97.97	NAV
37.00	22.60	33.03	28.48	20.65	-9.13	-12.05	-22.17	28.49	10.73	4.86	15.71	Total Return %
-0.58	-0.36	-0.33	-0.10	-0.39	-0.03	-0.16	-0.07	-0.19	-0.15	-0.05	-0.08	+/-S&P 500
-0.77	0.15	0.18	1.46	-0.26	-1.34	0.40	-0.52	-1.40	-0.67	-1.41	0.25	+/-Russ 1000
2.84	2.04	1.84	1.17	1.40	0.96	1.06	1.26	1.69	1.85	1.66	1.76	Income Return %
34.16	20.56	31.19	27.31	19.25	-10.09	-13.11	-23.43	26.80	8.88	3.20	13.95	Capital Return %
23	38	19	19	39	66	54	50	35	43	58	22	Total Rtn % Rank Cat
0.96	0.91	0.97	0.79	1.19	0.97	0.96	0.99	1.02	1.41	1.38	1.51	Income $
0.37	1.05	1.38	1.68	0.70	0.00	0.00	0.00	0.00	0.00	0.00	0.00	Capital Gains $
0.45	0.45	0.44	0.19	0.19	0.19	0.19	0.19	0.19	0.19	0.13	0.10	Expense Ratio %
2.49	2.11	1.82	1.61	1.30	1.21	1.02	1.21	1.62	1.51	1.94	1.77	Income Ratio %
2	5	6	6	4	8	4	4	9	4	4	7	Turnover Rate %
689	1,598	3,870	7,150	10,438	9,572	8,602	6,788	9,825	12,113	7,147	7,902	Net Assets $mil

Performance 12-31-06

	1st Qtr	2nd Qtr	3rd Qtr	4th Qtr	Total
2002	0.24	-13.44	-17.26	8.41	-22.17
2003	-3.19	15.38	2.59	12.12	28.49
2004	1.66	1.68	-1.90	9.21	10.73
2005	-2.15	1.36	3.59	2.06	4.86
2006	4.20	-1.46	5.64	6.67	15.71

Trailing	Total Return%	+/- S&P 500	+/- Russ 1000	%Rank Cat	Growth of $10,000
3 Mo	6.67	-0.03	-0.28	46	10,667
6 Mo	12.69	-0.05	0.33	20	11,269
1 Yr	15.71	-0.08	0.25	22	11,571
3 Yr Avg	10.34	-0.10	-0.64	39	13,434
5 Yr Avg	6.08	-0.11	-0.74	40	13,433
10 Yr Avg	8.27	-0.15	-0.37	32	22,135
15 Yr Avg	10.41	-0.23	-0.39	37	44,170

Tax Analysis	Tax-Adj Rtn%	%Rank Cat	Tax-Cost Rat	%Rank Cat
3 Yr (estimated)	9.71	33	0.57	26
5 Yr (estimated)	5.49	37	0.56	37
10 Yr (estimated)	7.59	25	0.63	25

Potential Capital Gain Exposure: 28% of assets

Rating and Risk

Time Period	Load-Adj Return %	Morningstar Rtn vs Cat	Morningstar Risk vs Cat	Morningstar Risk-Adj Rating
1 Yr	15.71			
3 Yr	10.34	Avg	-Avg	★★★
5 Yr	6.08	Avg	Avg	★★★
10 Yr	8.27	Avg	Avg	★★★
Incept	11.04			

Other Measures	Standard Index S&P 500	Best Fit Index S&P 500
Alpha	-0.1	-0.1
Beta	1.00	1.00
R-Squared	100	100
Standard Deviation	6.92	
Mean	10.34	
Sharpe Ratio	1.00	

Morningstar's Take by Andrew Gogerty 11-06-06

Fidelity Spartan 500 Index is a great choice, but not the only option to anchor a portfolio.

All funds that track the S&P 500 Index have the same goal--to mimic the returns of that venerable benchmark. Therefore, costs are the primary factor in distinguishing between them, and this fund's tiny 0.10% expense ratio gives it a huge head start. Because it has less of an expense drag, this fund's 11.22% gain for the year to date through October 20, 2006, edges out rival offerings from Vanguard, Northern Trust, and T. Rowe Price.

True, E*Trade S&P 500 is cheaper (0.09%), but that's due to a voluntary waiver that isn't guaranteed in the future. We're willing to forego the 0.01% in current savings for this fund's certainty of low costs. (Fees here can't be raised without shareholder approval.) Plus, despite the expense advantage, E*Trade's 11.15% gain this year trails this fund. Credit for that showing goes to Geode Capital Management, this fund's subadvisor and an experienced hand in index management.

That said, quirks in the S&P 500 Index construction make funds that track it vulnerable to competition. At Standard & Poor's, an investment committee makes qualitative decisions regarding constituents in the S&P 500, and it announces changes in advance, giving active managers a chance to profit by trading ahead of the changes. For example, in the week prior to Google's addition to the index in April 2006, the stock jumped 14% as traders bought ahead of index managers, despite no change in news about the company. That means S&P 500 index funds had to pay up for Google simply because it was added to the index. Because of this, we've grown fond of funds that track lesser-known bogies, such as Vanguard Large Cap Index.

But even though it has its quirks, the fund's rock-bottom costs and broad exposure to large-cap stocks make this a solid core holding.

Address:	82 Devonshire St Boston MA 02109 800-544-9797
Web Address:	www.fidelity.com
Inception:	03-06-90
Advisor:	Fidelity Management & Research (FMR)
Subadvisor:	Multiple Subadvisors
NTF Plans:	Fidelity Retail-NTF, CommonWealth NTF

Minimum Purchase:	$10000	Add: $1000	IRA: $10000
Min Auto Inv Plan:	$10000	Add: $500	
Sales Fees:	No-load		
Management Fee:	0.07%		
Actual Fees:	Mgt:0.07%	Dist: —	
Expense Projections:	3Yr:$32	5Yr:$56	10Yr:$128
Income Distrib:	Semi-Annually		

Portfolio Analysis 10-31-06

Share change since 07-06 Total Stocks:500	Sector	PE	Tot Ret%	% Assets
⊕ ExxonMobil Corporation	Energy	11.1	39.07	3.23
⊕ S&P 500 Index (Fut)	—	—	—	2.89
⊕ General Electric Company	Ind Mtrls	20.0	9.35	2.76
⊕ Citigroup, Inc.	Financial	13.1	19.55	1.89
⊕ Microsoft Corporation	Software	23.8	15.83	1.89
⊕ Bank of America Corporat	Financial	12.4	20.68	1.85
⊖ Procter & Gamble Company	Goods	23.9	13.36	1.53
⊕ Johnson & Johnson	Health	17.5	12.45	1.50
⊕ Pfizer Inc.	Health	15.2	15.22	1.48
⊕ American International G	Financial	17.0	6.05	1.33
⊕ Altria Group, Inc.	Goods	16.3	19.87	1.29
⊕ J.P. Morgan Chase & Co.	Financial	13.6	25.60	1.25
⊕ Chevron Corporation	Energy	9.0	33.76	1.12
⊕ Cisco Systems, Inc.	Hardware	30.1	59.64	1.12
⊕ IBM	Hardware	17.1	19.77	1.07
⊖ AT&T, Inc.	Telecom	18.2	51.59	0.99
⊕ Intel Corporation	Hardware	21.0	-17.18	0.94
⊕ Wells Fargo Company	Financial	14.7	16.82	0.93
⊕ Wal-Mart Stores, Inc.	Consumer	16.9	0.13	0.92
⊕ Verizon Communications	Telecom	15.9	34.88	0.82

Current Investment Style

Value Blnd Growth — Large Mid Small

	Market Cap	%
	Giant	51.3
	Large	38.2
	Mid	10.5
	Small	0.0
	Micro	0.0

Avg $mil: 51,900

Value Measures		Rel Category
Price/Earnings	15.55	1.01
Price/Book	2.63	1.03
Price/Sales	1.49	1.06
Price/Cash Flow	7.34	0.87
Dividend Yield %	1.86	1.06

Growth Measures	%	Rel Category
Long-Term Erngs	11.19	0.95
Book Value	8.62	0.95
Sales	9.78	1.01
Cash Flow	9.05	0.88
Historical Erngs	17.17	0.93

Profitability	%	Rel Category
Return on Equity	19.87	1.02
Return on Assets	10.90	1.05
Net Margin	14.07	1.05

Sector Weightings	% of Stocks	Rel S&P 500	3 Year High Low
⟳ Info	20.10	1.01	
🖥 Software	3.51	1.02	5 3
💻 Hardware	9.49	1.03	10 9
📶 Media	3.59	0.95	4 3
📞 Telecom	3.51	1.00	4 3
⟲ Service	46.47	1.01	
🏥 Health	12.38	1.03	14 12
🛒 Consumer	7.79	1.02	9 7
🏢 Business	4.25	1.00	5 4
💲 Financial	22.05	0.99	22 20
🏭 Mfg	33.43	0.99	
🏷 Goods	8.63	1.01	10 8
⚙ Ind Mtrls	11.84	0.99	13 12
🔋 Energy	9.47	0.97	11 6
💡 Utilities	3.49	1.00	3 3

Composition

		%
● Cash		2.8
● Stocks		94.3
● Bonds		0.0
○ Other		2.9
Foreign (% of Stock)		0.0

Fidelity Spar Intl Inv

Analyst Pick ✓	**Ticker** FSIIX	**Load** None

NAV	**Yield**	**Total Assets**	**Mstar Category**
$44.14	1.9%	$3,962 mil	Foreign Large Blend

Governance and Management

Stewardship Grade: B

Portfolio Manager(s)

The fund had been subadvised by Deutsche Asset Management, one of the biggest indexers. But as of mid-January 2003, Fidelity took management duties in-house, giving them to a group known as Geode. In August 2003, Geode Capital Management was spun off and is now a stand-alone firm, but it continues to manage this fund for Fidelity under a subadvisory agreement.

Strategy

The fund is designed to track the performance of the MSCI EAFE Index, a well-established foreign-stock benchmark. Its portfolio consists primarily of large-cap stocks from developed markets. The fund imposes a 1% redemption fee on shares held fewer than 90 days. Fidelity uses fair-value pricing when it deems the situation appropriate. The fund does not hedge its currency exposure.

Performance 12-31-06

	1st Qtr	2nd Qtr	3rd Qtr	4th Qtr	Total
2002	1.06	-2.15	-20.03	6.23	-15.99
2003	-7.75	19.23	7.93	16.53	38.34
2004	4.44	0.63	-0.77	14.93	19.86
2005	-0.41	-0.92	10.46	4.34	13.73
2006	9.15	0.67	4.01	10.39	26.15

Trailing	Total Return%	+/- MSCI EAFE	+/- MSCI Wd xUS	%Rank Cat	Growth of $10,000
3 Mo	10.39	0.04	0.27	43	11,039
6 Mo	14.81	0.12	0.59	39	11,481
1 Yr	26.15	-0.19	0.44	33	12,615
3 Yr Avg	19.81	-0.12	-0.29	28	17,198
5 Yr Avg	14.85	-0.13	-0.40	21	19,983
10 Yr Avg	—	—	—	—	—
15 Yr Avg	—	—	—	—	—

Tax Analysis	Tax-Adj Rtn%	%Rank Cat	Tax-Cost Rat	%Rank Cat
3 Yr (estimated)	18.97	22	0.70	38
5 Yr (estimated)	14.05	20	0.70	55
10 Yr (estimated)	—	—	—	—

Potential Capital Gain Exposure: 19% of assets

Morningstar's Take by Gregg Wolper 12-26-06

Fidelity Spartan International Index is getting more and more competition, but a key trait keeps it near the top of the heap.

The international indexing field, which already had a decent number of choices, keeps growing. A new entrant in the exchange-traded fund arena, WisdomTree, has come out with several new options, including some that target the broad list of developed markets, as this one does. The iShares ETFs that split the MSCI EAFE Index (which this fund aims to track) into value and growth components offer other alternatives. And Vanguard, which (along with iShares MSCI EAFE Index) gives this offering its most prominent EAFE-tracking competition, recently announced that it is bringing out still other funds that will track a different index.

Yet this fund still has an enduring advantage over nearly every rival: its low, low cost. At just 0.10% (10 basis points) per year, its expense ratio is lower than just about every peer, including those offered by Vanguard. In the world of indexing, where managers can't beat their competitors by better stock-picking, a cost advantage, even if it's just 20 or 30 basis points, is a serious matter indeed. True, if the managers weren't adept at accurately tracking their benchmark, that cost gap wouldn't be worth as much, but the team running this fund has shown it can handle that aspect well.

How, then, does this fund (and the other EAFE-trackers, for that matter) stand up against the actively managed competition? Not bad at all. For the year to date through Dec. 22, 2006, it is beating roughly two thirds of its foreign large-blend rivals, and for the trailing five-year stretch, it is ahead of about three fourths of them.

Keep in mind that this fund doesn't have everything: It lacks emerging-markets stocks and small caps. And there are certainly active managers well worth a look. For an index-based core, though, it remains a top choice.

Address:	82 Devonshire St Boston MA 02109 800-544-9797	Minimum Purchase: Min Auto Inv Plan: Sales Fees:	$10000 Add: $1000 IRA: $0 $10000 Add: $500 No-load, 1.00%R
Web Address: Inception: Advisor: Subadvisor:	www.fidelity.com 11-06-97 * Fidelity Management & Research (FMR) Multiple Subadvisors	Management Fee: Actual Fees: Expense Projections: Income Distrib:	0.17% Mgt:0.17% 3Yr:$64 5Yr:$113 10Yr:$235 Semi-Annually
NTF Plans:	Fidelity Retail-NTF, CommonWealth NTF		

Historical Profile

Return	Above Avg
Risk	Average
Rating	★★★★ Above Avg

	Manager Change
▼	Manager Change
▽	Partial Manager Change

Growth of $10,000
— Investment Values of Fund
— Investment Values of MSCI EAFE

Investment Style
Equity
Stock %
76% 63% 84% 87% 86% 86% 86% 92% 90%

Performance Quartile (within Category)

	1995	1996	1997	1998	1999	2000	2001	2002	2003	2004	2005	2006	History
	—	—	24.87	29.50	37.67	31.69	24.44	20.14	27.26	32.02	35.73	44.14	NAV
	—	—	-0.08*	21.16	29.07	-14.90	-21.85	-15.99	38.34	19.86	13.73	26.15	Total Return %
	—	—	—	1.23	2.04	-0.71	-0.43	-0.05	-0.25	-0.39	0.19	-0.19	+/-MSCI EAFE
	—	—	—	2.47	1.09	-1.54	-0.46	-0.19	-1.08	-0.52	-0.74	0.44	+/-MSCI Wd xUS
	—	—	—	1.94	1.29	0.77	1.01	1.60	2.74	2.02	1.88	2.33	Income Return %
	—	—	—	19.22	27.78	-15.67	-22.86	-17.59	35.60	17.84	11.85	23.82	Capital Return %
	—	—	—	9	76	37	51	38	18	18	56	33	Total Rtn % Rank Cat
	—	—	0.06	0.48	0.38	0.29	0.32	0.39	0.55	0.55	0.60	0.83	Income $
	—	—	0.00	0.13	0.00	0.08	0.00	0.00	0.00	0.07	0.07	0.08	Capital Gains $
	—	—	—	0.35	0.36	0.35	0.35	0.35	0.35	0.39	0.47	0.10	Expense Ratio %
	—	—	—	1.43	1.62	1.48	1.53	1.60	1.87	1.99	2.54	Income Ratio %
	—	—	—	2	2	3	2	12	19	31	2	Turnover Rate %
	—	—	21	40	186	349	319	346	455	955	2,833	Net Assets $mil

Rating and Risk

Time Period	Load-Adj Return %	Morningstar Rtn vs Cat	Morningstar Risk vs Cat	Morningstar Risk-Adj Rating
1 Yr	26.15			
3 Yr	19.81	+Avg	-Avg	★★★★
5 Yr	14.85	+Avg	Avg	★★★★
10 Yr	—			
Incept	8.32			

Other Measures	Standard Index MSCI EAFE	Best Fit Index MSCI EAFE
Alpha	-0.1	-0.1
Beta	1.00	1.00
R-Squared	98	98
Standard Deviation	9.54	
Mean	19.81	
Sharpe Ratio	1.63	

Portfolio Analysis 08-31-06

Share change since 05-06 Total Stocks:1164	Sector	Country	% Assets
⊕ BP	Energy	U.K.	1.82
⊕ HSBC Hldgs	Financial	U.K.	1.60
⊕ GlaxoSmithKline	Health	U.K.	1.28
⊕ Toyota Motor	Goods	Japan	1.22
⊕ TOTAL	Energy	France	1.16
⊕ FTSE 100 Index (Fut)	—	—	1.12
⊕ Nestle	Goods	Switzerland	1.08
⊕ Royal Dutch Shell	Energy	U.K.	1.06
⊕ Novartis	Health	Switzerland	1.03
⊕ Roche Holding	Health	Switzerland	1.00
⊕ UBS AG	Financial	Switzerland	0.91
⊕ Mitsubishi UFJ Financial	Financial	Japan	0.91
✳ Dj Eurostoxx 50 Fut	—	—	0.90
⊖ Vodafone Grp	Telecom	U.K.	0.89
⊕ Royal Bank Of Scotland G	Financial	U.K.	0.84
⊕ AstraZeneca	Health	U.K.	0.80
⊕ Royal Dutch Shell	Energy	U.K.	0.77
⊕ Banco Santander Central	Financial	Spain	0.72
⊕ Sanofi-Synthelabo	Health	France	0.71
⊕ BNP Paribas	Financial	France	0.68

Current Investment Style

Value Blnd Growth — Large Mid Small

Market Cap	%
Giant	54.4
Large	32.1
Mid	12.9
Small	0.5
Micro	0.1
Avg $mil:	29,504

Value Measures		Rel Category
Price/Earnings	14.02	1.07
Price/Book	2.04	0.94
Price/Sales	1.07	0.92
Price/Cash Flow	8.19	0.98
Dividend Yield %	3.27	1.12

Growth Measures	%	Rel Category
Long-Term Erngs	11.62	0.98
Book Value	7.26	0.80
Sales	6.40	0.98
Cash Flow	4.37	0.53
Historical Erngs	21.38	1.05

Composition

Cash	5.6	Bonds	0.0
Stocks	90.2	Other	4.2
Foreign	(% of Stock)		98.8

Sector Weightings

	% of Stocks	Rel MSCI EAFE	3 Year High	Low
℃ Info	11.35	0.96		
Software	0.56	1.00	1	1
Hardware	3.85	1.00	5	4
Media	1.85	1.01	3	2
Telecom	5.09	0.91	8	5
ℂ Service	47.27	1.00		
Health	7.80	1.10	9	7
Consumer	4.74	0.96	5	4
Business	4.78	0.94	5	5
Financial	29.95	1.00	30	26
Mfg	41.38	1.01		
Goods	13.21	1.01	15	13
Ind Mtrls	15.34	0.99	15	12
Energy	7.76	1.09	9	6
Utilities	5.07	0.97	5	5

Regional Exposure % Stock

UK/W. Europe	68	N. America	1
Japan	23	Latn America	0
Asia X Japan	8	Other	0

Country Exposure % Stock

U.K.	24	Switzerland	7
Japan	23	Germany	7
France	10		

MORNINGSTAR® Funds 500

Fidelity Spar Tot Mkt Inv

	Ticker	Load	NAV	Yield	Total Assets	Mstar Category
	FSTMX	None	$39.58	1.3%	$6,093 mil	Large Blend

Governance and Management

Stewardship Grade: B

Portfolio Manager(s)

Geode Capital Management took over as subadvisor to this fund and many of Fidelity's other index funds on Aug. 4, 2003.

Strategy

This fund tracks the Dow Jones Wilshire 5000 Index. The fund will own nearly all the large- and mid-cap stocks in that benchmark, but just a representative sample of the thousands of small-cap stocks in that index to limit trading costs. The index's market-cap-based methodology tilts the portfolio decidedly toward large-cap stocks, but its broad exposure covers all sectors of the market.

Historical Profile
Return: Above Avg
Risk: Average
Rating: ★★★★ Above Avg

Investment Style: Equity, Stock %

85% 91% 97% 97% 95% 92% 94% 95% 97%

▼ Manager Change
▽ Partial Manager Change

Growth of $10,000
— Investment Values of Fund
— Investment Values of S&P 500

Performance Quartile (within Category)

	1995	1996	1997	1998	1999	2000	2001	2002	2003	2004	2005	2006	History
	—	—	25.72	31.36	38.13	33.50	29.56	23.05	29.91	33.05	34.66	39.58	NAV
	—	—	3.17*	24.03	23.23	-10.96	-10.79	-20.99	31.24	12.11	6.42	15.73	Total Return %
	—	—	—	-4.55	2.19	-1.86	1.10	1.11	2.56	1.23	1.51	-0.06	+/-S&P 500
	—	—	—	-2.99	2.32	-3.17	1.66	0.66	1.35	0.71	0.15	0.27	+/-Russ 1000
	—	—	—	0.90	0.93	0.79	0.96	1.08	1.39	1.57	1.55	1.50	Income Return %
	—	—	—	23.13	22.30	-11.75	-11.75	-22.07	29.85	10.54	4.87	14.23	Capital Return %
	—	—	—	45	27	87	39	39	17	27	41	22	Total Rtn % Rank Cat
	—	—	0.08	0.23	0.29	0.30	0.32	0.32	0.32	0.47	0.51	0.52	Income $
	—	—	0.00	0.28	0.19	0.18	0.00	0.00	0.00	0.00	0.00	0.00	Capital Gains $
	—	—	—	0.25	0.27	0.26	0.25	0.25	0.25	0.25	0.17	0.10	Expense Ratio %
	—	—	—	1.91	1.40	1.17	0.97	1.15	1.39	1.36	1.73	1.67	Income Ratio %
	—	—	—	7	4	11	8	7	3	3	6	6	Turnover Rate %
	—	—	20	166	756	1,028	1,103	1,033	1,970	2,774	1,955	3,666	Net Assets $mil

Performance 12-31-06

	1st Qtr	2nd Qtr	3rd Qtr	4th Qtr	Total
2002	0.91	-12.59	-16.87	7.74	-20.99
2003	-3.21	16.48	3.63	12.34	31.24
2004	2.54	1.21	-1.90	10.12	12.11
2005	-2.21	2.33	4.06	2.20	6.42
2006	5.45	-1.95	4.42	7.19	15.73

Trailing	Total Return%	+/- S&P 500	+/- Russ 1000	%Rank Cat	Growth of $10,000
3 Mo	7.19	0.49	0.24	28	10,719
6 Mo	11.93	-0.81	-0.43	41	11,193
1 Yr	15.73	-0.06	0.27	22	11,573
3 Yr Avg	11.35	0.91	0.37	23	13,806
5 Yr Avg	7.44	1.25	0.62	21	14,316
10 Yr Avg	—	—	—	—	—
15 Yr Avg	—	—	—	—	—

Tax Analysis	Tax-Adj Rtn%	%Rank Cat	Tax-Cost Rat	%Rank Cat
3 Yr (estimated)	10.80	19	0.49	23
5 Yr (estimated)	6.93	19	0.47	31
10 Yr (estimated)	—	—	—	—

Potential Capital Gain Exposure: 15% of assets

Rating and Risk

Time Period	Load-Adj Return %	Morningstar Rtn vs Cat	Morningstar Risk vs Cat	Morningstar Risk-Adj Rating
1 Yr	15.73			
3 Yr	11.35	+Avg	Avg	★★★★
5 Yr	7.44	+Avg	Avg	★★★★
10 Yr	—			
Incept	6.59			

Other Measures	Standard Index S&P 500	Best Fit Index Russ 1000
Alpha	0.2	-0.2
Beta	1.10	1.07
R-Squared	98	99
Standard Deviation	7.69	
Mean	11.35	
Sharpe Ratio	1.03	

Morningstar's Take by Andrew Gogerty 11-06-06

Investors should temper their expectations for Fidelity Spartan Total Stock Market Index, but we still heartily recommend it.

Exposure to strong-performing small- and mid-cap stocks has fueled this fund's edge over sibling Spartan 500 Index and the large-blend category for the past five years. In 2006, however, the tables have turned, as large-cap stocks have seen renewed life in recent months. Through October 23, Spartan 500's 11.90% year-to-date return edges past this fund's 11.59% gain.

While we're not surprised see a large-cap resurgence, that hardly dims the case for owning this fund. Because it tracks the Dow Jones Wilshire 5000 Total Market Index (a common measure of the entire domestic-stock market), the fund is an appealing one-stop choice for an investor's broad U.S. equity allocation. And even though its sibling fund has recently trumped this offering, we don't expect this fund to be left too far behind. Its benchmark's holdings are ranked by market cap (a

stock's market price times all the shares available for sale). Subadvisor Geode Capital Management stashes a majority of the fund's assets in stocks also found in the S&P 500 Index, and then utilizes sampling to purchase a basket of stocks that replicate the risk/reward characteristics of the Wilshire index's smaller positions.

Not surprisingly, the fund's returns are highly correlated to the S&P 500 Index. According to its R-squared score (a measure of correlation), 97% of its returns can be explained by movements in the S&P 500 Index. As a result, we'd expect the fund's returns to stay in close proximity to Spartan 500's even if large caps continue to build on their recent success, yet its small-cap exposure provides a ballast to returns when smaller fare rule the roost. The fund's rock-bottom 0.10% expense ratio rounds out its appeal. Low fees allow the fund to better track its benchmark, and provide it a sustainable head start over higher-priced total-stock-market index funds.

Portfolio Analysis 08-31-06

Share change since 05-06 Total Stocks:3471	Sector	PE	Tot Ret%	% Assets
⊕ ExxonMobil Corporation	Energy	11.1	39.07	2.70
⊕ General Electric Company	Ind Mtrls	20.0	9.35	2.31
⊕ Citigroup, Inc.	Financial	13.1	19.55	1.60
⊕ Bank of America Corporat	Financial	12.4	20.68	1.52
⊕ Microsoft Corporation	Software	23.8	15.83	1.52
⊕ Procter & Gamble Company	Goods	23.9	13.36	1.33
⊕ Pfizer Inc.	Health	15.2	15.22	1.32
⊕ Johnson & Johnson	Health	17.5	12.45	1.26
⊕ S&P 500 Index (Fut)	—	—	—	1.20
⊕ Altria Group, Inc.	Goods	16.3	19.87	1.13
⊕ J.P. Morgan Chase & Co.	Financial	13.6	25.60	1.03
⊕ Chevron Corporation	Energy	9.0	33.76	0.95
⊕ American International G	Financial	17.0	6.05	0.95
⊕ Cisco Systems, Inc.	Hardware	30.1	59.64	0.88
⊕ IBM	Hardware	17.1	19.77	0.82
⊕ AT&T, Inc.	Telecom	18.2	51.59	0.80
⊕ Wal-Mart Stores, Inc.	Consumer	16.9	0.13	0.76
⊕ Wells Fargo Company	Financial	14.7	16.82	0.75
⊕ Intel Corporation	Hardware	21.0	-17.18	0.74
⊕ PepsiCo, Inc.	Goods	21.5	7.86	0.71

Current Investment Style

Value Blnd Growth — Large Mid Small

Market Cap	%
Giant	40.9
Large	30.8
Mid	19.0
Small	7.6
Micro	1.6
Avg $mil:	25,416

Value Measures		Rel Category
Price/Earnings	15.15	0.99
Price/Book	2.49	0.97
Price/Sales	1.33	0.95
Price/Cash Flow	6.78	0.80
Dividend Yield %	1.85	1.06

Growth Measures	%	Rel Category
Long-Term Erngs	11.51	0.97
Book Value	7.63	0.84
Sales	9.45	0.98
Cash Flow	10.17	0.99
Historical Erngs	16.66	0.90

Profitability	%	Rel Category
Return on Equity	18.16	0.93
Return on Assets	9.92	0.96
Net Margin	13.37	1.00

Sector Weightings	% of Stocks	Rel S&P 500	3 Year High Low
↻ Info	19.01	0.95	
🖥 Software	3.41	0.99	4 3
🖴 Hardware	8.91	0.96	11 9
🎬 Media	3.43	0.91	4 3
📞 Telecom	3.26	0.93	3 3
⊆ Service	47.96	1.04	
🩺 Health	12.57	1.04	13 12
🛒 Consumer	7.70	1.01	10 8
📊 Business	5.26	1.24	6 5
💲 Financial	22.43	1.01	23 21
🏭 Mfg	33.02	0.98	
🛢 Goods	8.03	0.94	9 8
🔩 Ind Mtrls	11.58	0.97	12 10
🔋 Energy	9.79	1.00	10 6
💡 Utilities	3.62	1.03	4 3

Composition

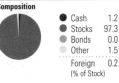

● Cash	1.2	
● Stocks	97.3	
● Bonds	0.0	
○ Other	1.5	
Foreign	0.2	
(% of Stock)		

Address:	82 Devonshire St Boston MA 02109 800-544-9797
Web Address:	www.fidelity.com
Inception:	11-06-97 *
Advisor:	Fidelity Management & Research (FMR)
Subadvisor:	Multiple Subadvisors
NTF Plans:	Fidelity Retail-NTF, CommonWealth NTF

Minimum Purchase:	$10000	Add: $1000	IRA: $0
Min Auto Inv Plan:	$10000	Add: $500	
Sales Fees:	No-load, 0.50%R		
Management Fee:	0.07%		
Actual Fees:	Mgt:0.07%	Dist: —	
Expense Projections:	3Yr:$32	5Yr:$56	10Yr:$128
Income Distrib:	Semi-Annually		

Fidelity Strategic Inc

	Analyst Pick	Ticker	Load	NAV	Yield	SEC Yield	Total Assets	Mstar Category
✓		FSICX	None	$10.64	5.2%	5.44%	$4,220 mil	Multisector Bond

Governance and Management

Stewardship Grade: B

Portfolio Manager(s)

Chris Sharpe and Derek Young took over this portfolio in July 2005. Sharpe joined Fidelity in 2002 as an asset-allocation director, while Young has worked as a portfolio strategist with Fidelity's asset-allocation group since 2003. The fund's issue-selection duties are handled by sector specialists. Mark Notkin handles high yield, Jonathan Kelly covers emerging markets, Andy Weir is responsible for developed-markets debt, and Brett Kozlowski covers the fund's government exposure.

Strategy

Management starts with a neutral asset-allocation mix as a baseline then makes slight adjustments to that mix based on relative valuation and market outlook. The neutral mix is 30% U.S. government issues, 40% U.S. high-yield obligations, 15% developed-markets sovereign debt, and 15% emerging-markets bonds. Chris Sharpe brings more of a long-term strategic allocation view to the portfolio, while Derek Young brings more of a relative-value angle. Fidelity sector specialists handle the fund's issue-selection responsibilities.

Performance 12-31-06

	1st Qtr	2nd Qtr	3rd Qtr	4th Qtr	Total
2002	0.66	0.57	1.98	5.95	9.38
2003	4.51	6.94	1.67	4.39	18.62
2004	1.81	-2.52	4.79	5.23	9.44
2005	-1.09	2.46	0.94	0.81	3.12
2006	1.35	0.32	3.58	2.69	8.15

Trailing	Total Return%	+/- LB Aggr	+/- LB. U.S. Univ. Bd	%Rank Cat	Growth of $10,000
3 Mo	2.69	1.45	1.19	52	10,269
6 Mo	6.37	1.28	0.91	49	10,637
1 Yr	8.15	3.82	3.18	18	10,815
3 Yr Avg	6.87	3.17	2.66	20	12,206
5 Yr Avg	9.63	4.57	3.99	16	15,836
10 Yr Avg	—				
15 Yr Avg	—				

Tax Analysis	Tax-Adj Rtn%	%Rank Cat	Tax-Cost Rat	%Rank Cat
3 Yr (estimated)	4.71	17	2.02	58
5 Yr (estimated)	7.34	13	2.09	44
10 Yr (estimated)	—	—	—	—

Potential Capital Gain Exposure: 4% of assets

Morningstar's Take by Scott Berry 11-30-06

Strong management, a sensible approach, and low costs make Fidelity Strategic Income tough to beat.

When we say management, we're actually referring to the whole Fidelity strategic bond operation, from managers to analysts to research capabilities. Leading the effort are Derek Young and Chris Sharpe, who are responsible for allocating assets across different bond sectors. Young and Sharpe have only been with this fund since mid-2005, but we like that they have been forward looking with their moves, not chasing after returns in high-yield or emerging markets, for example. Young and Sharpe are supported by sector specialists, who are responsible for issue selection, and by the resources of each sector team. Few fund shops can match those resources, which go a long way toward explaining our positive opinion of Fidelity's high-yield, investment-grade, and international-bond groups.

Top-down fund management can be a tricky business, as evidenced by Fidelity's avoidance of interest-rate bets in its investment-grade taxable-bond funds. However, Young and Sharpe have been careful not to let their macro view of the markets overwhelm the bond-picking skills of the sector specialists. Their changes have been more on the margins. For example, they have bulked up on floating-rate bank loans in recent months as a high-yield substitute. And overall, the fund's sector allocations have typically fluctuated just a few percentage points from their neutral allocations.

That approach plays to the fund's research advantage, as well as helping preserve its expense advantage. The fund charges just 0.75%, while its average no-load multisector peer charges 0.89%. That advantage allows more yield and return to flow directly to shareholders without management having to take on added risk.

The fund's exposure to the bond market's riskier segments should not be overlooked, but we think investors have a lot to like here.

Address:	82 Devonshire Street Boston MA 02109 800-544-9797
Web Address:	www.fidelity.com
Inception:	05-05-98 *
Advisor:	Fidelity Management & Research (FMR)
Subadvisor:	Multiple Subadvisors
NTF Plans:	Fidelity Retail-NTF, CommonWealth NTF

Minimum Purchase:	$2500	Add: $250	IRA: $2500
Min Auto Inv Plan:	$2500	Add: $100	
Sales Fees:	No-load		
Management Fee:	0.58%		
Actual Fees:	Mgt:0.58%	Dist: —	
Expense Projections:	3Yr:$243	5Yr:$444	10Yr:$942
Income Distrib:	Monthly		

Historical Profile

Return	Above Avg
Risk	Average
Rating	★★★★ Above Avg

Investment Style
Fixed Income
Income Rtn %Rank Cat

▼ Manager Change
▽ Partial Manager Change

Growth of $10,000
■ Investment Values of Fund
— Investment Values of LB Aggr

Performance Quartile (within Category)

	1995	1996	1997	1998	1999	2000	2001	2002	2003	2004	2005	2006	History
	—	—	—	9.52	9.44	9.13	9.15	9.40	10.50	10.77	10.43	10.64	NAV
	—	—	—	-0.65*	6.35	4.07	6.52	9.38	18.62	9.44	3.12	8.15	Total Return %
	—	—	—		7.17	-7.56	-1.92	-0.87	14.52	5.10	0.69	3.82	+/-LB Aggr
	—	—	—		6.18	-6.75	-1.57	-0.46	12.80	4.47	0.41	3.18	+/-LB. U.S. Univ. Bd
	—	—	—		7.20	7.40	6.36	6.47	6.32	5.41	5.21	5.47	Income Return %
	—	—	—		-0.85	-3.33	0.16	2.91	12.30	4.03	-2.09	2.68	Capital Return %
	—	—	—		16	12	15	25	46	33	31	18	Total Rtn % Rank Cat
	—	—	—	0.39	0.66	0.68	0.56	0.57	0.58	0.55	0.54	0.56	Income $
	—	—	—	0.00	0.00	0.00	0.00	0.00	0.03	0.13	0.12	0.06	Capital Gains $
	—	—	—	1.09	1.10	0.99	0.94	0.84	0.80	0.76	0.75	—	Expense Ratio %
	—	—	—	7.40	7.55	7.94	6.83	6.42	5.64	5.46	5.23	—	Income Ratio %
	—	—	—	97	134	100	178	117	148	94	119	—	Turnover Rate %
	—	—	—	24	41	63	163	771	2,320	3,166	3,444	4,220	Net Assets $mil

Rating and Risk

Time Period	Load-Adj Return %	Morningstar Rtn vs Cat	Morningstar Risk vs Cat	Morningstar Risk-Adj Rating
1 Yr	8.15			
3 Yr	6.87	+Avg	Avg	★★★★
5 Yr	9.63	+Avg	Avg	★★★★
10 Yr	—			
Incept	7.40			

Other Measures	Standard Index LB Aggr	Best Fit Index CSFB Glb HY
Alpha	3.1	-0.5
Beta	0.79	0.78
R-Squared	53	64
Standard Deviation	3.54	
Mean	6.87	
Sharpe Ratio	0.99	

Portfolio Analysis 09-30-06

Total Fixed-Income:608	Date of Maturity	Amount $000	Value $000	% Net Assets
FNMA 4.75%	12-15-10	102,735	102,141	2.51
US Treasury Bond 6.125%	08-15-29	84,100	99,139	2.43
US Treasury Note 3.75%	05-15-08	74,521	73,360	1.80
US Treasury Note 4.25%	08-15-14	69,650	67,960	1.67
US Treasury Note 4.5%	02-15-09	66,000	65,765	1.61
Republic Of Finland	09-15-17	51,100	65,519	1.61
FHLMC 4.125%	10-18-10	63,000	61,225	1.50
US Treasury Note 3.375%	05-15-09	48,146	46,517	1.14
US Treasury Note 4.25%	08-15-15	44,000	42,802	1.05
US Treasury Note 2.375%	04-15-11	40,000	41,047	1.01
US Treasury Note 4.5%	11-15-15	40,200	39,811	0.98
US Treasury Note 4.875%	05-31-11	37,000	37,425	0.92
Russian Federation FRN	03-31-30	33,213	37,032	0.91
US Treasury Note 0.875%	04-15-10	34,500	35,119	0.86
FNMA 4.25%	05-15-09	35,311	34,747	0.85
FNMA 4.875%	04-15-09	34,350	34,306	0.84
Federal Republic Of Germ	06-13-08	25,150	31,701	0.78
Oest Kontrollbank 3.875%	09-15-16	23,700	30,039	0.74
Brazil Federative Rep 11	08-17-40	21,910	28,527	0.70
FNMA 0.06%	05-01-08	27,571	27,625	0.68

Current Investment Style

Duration: Short Int Long
Quality: High Med Low

1 figure provided by fund

Avg Eff Duration[1]	—
Avg Eff Maturity	—
Avg Credit Quality	—
Avg Wtd Coupon	5.52%
Avg Wtd Price	104.63% of par

Coupon Range	% of Bonds	Rel Cat
0% PIK	4.4	0.8
0% to 6%	54.5	1.2
6% to 8%	22.7	0.8
8% to 10%	13.9	0.8
More than 10%	8.8	1.2

1.00=Category Average

Credit Analysis	% bonds 09-30-06		
AAA	—	BB	—
AA	—	B	—
A	—	Below B	—
BBB	—	NR/NA	—

Sector Breakdown

	% of assets
US Treasuries	17
TIPS	1
US Agency	10
Mortgage Pass-Throughs	2
Mortgage CMO	1
Mortgage ARM	0
US Corporate	30
Asset-Backed	0
Convertible	0
Municipal	0
Corporate Inflation-Protected	0
Foreign Corporate	11
Foreign Govt	13

Composition

Cash	14.1	Bonds	79.2
Stocks	0.8	Other	5.8

Special Securities

Restricted/Illiquid Secs	6
Exotic Mortgage-Backed	0
Emerging-Markets Secs	10
Options/Futures/Warrants	No

Ⓜ **Morningstar® Funds 500**

Fidelity Strategic RRet

	Ticker	Load	NAV	Yield	Total Assets	Mstar Category
	FSRRX	None	$10.15	3.3%	$3,654 mil	Conservative Allocation

Governance and Management

Stewardship Grade: B

Portfolio Manager(s)

Chris Sharpe and Derek Young started this fund in September 2005. Sharpe joined Fidelity in 2002 as an asset-allocation director, while Young has worked as a portfolio strategist with Fidelity's asset-allocation group since 2003. The fund's issue-selection duties are handled by sector specialists. Bill Irving handles TIPS, Harley Lank covers floating-rate loans, and Mark Snyderman is responsible for real estate.

Strategy

Management starts with a neutral asset-allocation mix as a baseline, then makes slight adjustments to that mix based on relative valuation and market outlook. The neutral mix is 30% Treasury Inflation-Protected Securities (TIPS), 25% floating-rate loans, 25% commodity-linked notes, and 20% real estate securities. Managers Chris Sharpe and Derek Young rely on Fidelity sector specialists to select individual bond issues.

Performance 12-31-06

	1st Qtr	2nd Qtr	3rd Qtr	4th Qtr	Total
2002	—	—	—	—	—
2003	—	—	—	—	—
2004	—	—	—	—	—
2005	—	—	—	-0.20	— *
2006	-0.30	2.32	0.46	2.35	4.89

Trailing	Total Return%	+/- DJ Mod	+/- DJ 40%	%Rank Cat	Growth of $10,000
3 Mo	2.35	-3.24	-0.69	86	10,235
6 Mo	2.83	-5.96	-3.73	97	10,283
1 Yr	4.89	-7.41	-2.57	94	10,489
3 Yr Avg	—	—	—	—	—
5 Yr Avg	—	—	—	—	—
10 Yr Avg	—	—	—	—	—
15 Yr Avg	—	—	—	—	—

Tax Analysis	Tax-Adj Rtn%	%Rank Cat	Tax-Cost Rat	%Rank Cat
3 Yr (estimated)	—	—	—	—
5 Yr (estimated)	—	—	—	—
10 Yr (estimated)	—	—	—	—

Potential Capital Gain Exposure: 0% of assets

Morningstar's Take by Scott Berry 12-20-06

Fidelity Strategic Real Return has struggled a bit recently, but we like its long-term prospects.

This young fund takes a broader approach to fighting inflation than funds focused on Treasury Inflation-Protected Securities (TIPS). This fund typically holds close to one third of its assets in TIPS (30% of assets as of Oct. 31, 2006), but it also holds floating-rate bank loans (23% of assets), commodity-linked notes (24% of assets), and real-estate-related investments (19% of assets)--the thinking being that those other investment types can provide additional hedges against inflation. There have been arguments for and against real estate as an inflation hedge, but managers Derek Young and Chris Sharpe argue that in a hyperinflationary environment, real estate would link well with inflation.

The fund has looked good versus TIPS funds, which have struggled in 2006 as inflation expectations cooled. But the fund has struggled versus its conservative-allocation category peers,

as commodities and TIPS have weighed on returns at various times during the year. For the year to date through July 31, 2006, the fund ranked just outside the category's top third. However, the fund has since dropped near the very back of the pack for the year to date through Dec. 20, 2006. Young and Sharpe argue that the global-growth story remains intact, so they have maintained the fund's exposure to commodities, while looking to take advantage of opportunities that TIPs may provide.

Young and Sharpe focus on the big picture here, while sector specialists build the portfolio from the ground up. That approach has worked for Fidelity Strategic Income, and given Fidelity's broad research capabilities, we think it can work here as well.

The fund's exposure to commodities and real estate could cause some additional performance hiccups, but we think the fund's sensible approach, reasonable costs, and deep resources all argue in its favor.

Address:	82 Devonshire St. United States 877-208-0098
Web Address:	advisor.fidelity.com
Inception:	09-07-05
Advisor:	Fidelity Management & Research (FMR)
Subadvisor:	Multiple Subadvisors
NTF Plans:	Fidelity Retail-NTF, CommonWealth NTF

Minimum Purchase:	$2500	Add: $250	IRA: $500
Min Auto Inv Plan:	$0	Add: $100	
Sales Fees:	No-load, 0.75%R		
Management Fee:	0.57%		
Actual Fees:	Mgt:0.57%	Dist: —	
Expense Projections:	3Yr:$255	5Yr:$444	10Yr:$990
Income Distrib:	Quarterly		

Historical Profile
Return —
Risk —
Rating Not Rated

Growth of $10,000

■ Investment Values of Fund
— Investment Values of DJ Mod

▼ Manager Change
▽ Partial Manager Change

Investment Style
Equity
Stock %

Performance Quartile (within Category)

	1995	1996	1997	1998	1999	2000	2001	2002	2003	2004	2005	2006	History
NAV	—	—	—	—	—	—	—	—	—	—	10.00	10.15	NAV
	—	—	—	—	—	—	—	—	—	—	—	4.89	Total Return %
	—	—	—	—	—	—	—	—	—	—	—	-7.41	+/-DJ Mod
	—	—	—	—	—	—	—	—	—	—	—	-2.57	+/-DJ 40%
	—	—	—	—	—	—	—	—	—	—	—	3.37	Income Return %
	—	—	—	—	—	—	—	—	—	—	—	1.52	Capital Return %
	—	—	—	—	—	—	—	—	—	—	—	94	Total Rtn % Rank Cat
	—	—	—	—	—	—	—	—	—	—	0.13	0.33	Income $
	—	—	—	—	—	—	—	—	—	—	0.00	0.00	Capital Gains $
	—	—	—	—	—	—	—	—	—	—	—	0.79	Expense Ratio %
	—	—	—	—	—	—	—	—	—	—	—	5.45	Income Ratio %
	—	—	—	—	—	—	—	—	—	—	—	11	Turnover Rate %
	—	—	—	—	—	—	—	—	—	—	—	3,395	Net Assets $mil

Rating and Risk

Time Period	Load-Adj Return %	Morningstar Rtn vs Cat	Morningstar Risk vs Cat	Morningstar Risk-Adj Rating
1 Yr	4.89			
3 Yr	—	—	—	—
5 Yr	—	—	—	—
10 Yr	—	—	—	—
Incept	4.73			

Other Measures	Standard Index DJ Mod	Best Fit Index
Alpha	—	—
Beta	—	—
R-Squared	—	—
Standard Deviation	—	
Mean	—	
Sharpe Ratio	—	

Portfolio Analysis 09-30-06

Total Stocks:69 Share change since 06-30-06	Sectors	P/E Ratio	YTD Return %	% Net Assets
⊕ General Growth Properties	—	—	-0.40	0.21
⊕ Spirit Finance Corporatio	—	23.4	-2.41	0.15
⊕ Annaly Capital Management	—	—	-0.86	0.15
⊕ Equity Residential	—	113.4	-1.71	0.13
⊕ Red Lion Hotels Cap Tr	—	—	—	0.12
⊕ Equity Lifestyle Properti	—	—	-2.02	0.12
⊕ Newcastle Investment Corp	—	12.4	0.26	0.12
⊕ Starwood Hotels & Resorts	—	12.9	-1.71	0.12
⊕ Host Hotels & Resorts, In	—	51.9	-2.69	0.12

Total Fixed-Income:1191	Date of Maturity	Amount $000	Value $000	% Net Assets
US Treasury Bond 2%	01-15-26	93,425	91,850	3.14
US Treasury Bond 2.375%	01-15-25	74,595	81,800	2.80
US Treasury Note 1.875%	07-15-13	67,880	73,234	2.51
US Treasury Note 0.875%	04-15-10	57,905	58,943	2.02
US Treasury Note	01-15-16	58,350	58,413	2.00
US Treasury Note 2%	01-15-14	50,185	54,198	1.85
US Treasury Note 4.25%	01-15-10	40,620	51,943	1.78
US Treasury Note 3.875%	01-15-09	40,150	51,239	1.75
US Treasury Note 3.375%	01-15-12	38,770	46,763	1.60

Equity Style
Style: —
Size: —

Value Measures		Rel Category
Price/Earnings	—	—
Price/Book	—	—
Price/Sales	—	—
Price/Cash Flow	—	—
Dividend Yield %	—	—

Growth Measures	%	Rel Category
Long-Term Erngs	—	—
Book Value	—	—
Sales	—	—
Cash Flow	—	—
Historical Erngs	—	—

Market Cap %
Giant	—	Small	—
Large	—	Micro	—
Mid	—	Avg $mil:	—

Fixed-Income Style
Duration: —
Quality: —

Avg Eff Duration ¹	—
Avg Eff Maturity	—
Avg Credit Quality	—
Avg Wtd Coupon	2.32%

¹figure provided by fund

Sector Weightings	% of Stocks	Rel DJ Mod	3 Year High Low
☌ Info	0.00	—	
▣ Software	—	—	
▣ Hardware	—	—	
▣ Media	—	—	
▣ Telecom	—	—	
☞ Service	0.00	—	
▣ Health	—	—	
▣ Consumer	—	—	
▣ Business	—	—	
▣ Financial	—	—	
⚒ Mfg	0.00	—	
▣ Goods	—	—	
▣ Ind Mtrls	—	—	
▣ Energy	—	—	
▣ Utilities	—	—	

Composition

● Cash	20.1	
● Stocks	3.9	
● Bonds	65.6	
● Other	10.4	
Foreign (% of Stock)	0.0	

Fidelity Tax-Free Bond

Analyst Pick ✓

	Ticker	Load	NAV	Yield	SEC Yield	Total Assets	Mstar Category
	FTABX	None	$10.79	3.9%	3.63%	$504 mil	Muni National Long

Governance and Management

Stewardship Grade: B

Portfolio Manager(s)

Christine Thompson has run this fund since its April 2001 inception, but she has extensive experience as a Fidelity municipal bond fund manager and was named Morningstar's Fixed-Income Manager of the Year for 2003. She's backed by numerous analysts and traders.

Strategy

This fund doesn't make big sweeping bets (it ties its interest-rate sensitivity to that of the three-plus-year, non-AMT Lehman Brothers Municipal Bond Index) and maintains minimal credit risk. Management focuses on yield-curve plays and the structure of the portfolio, such as a bias toward callable or noncallable bonds. The team also uses sophisticated analytics to measure market risk across the portfolio and to keep a close watch on how bonds will respond to different scenarios given their particular tax status or structure.

Performance 12-31-06

	1st Qtr	2nd Qtr	3rd Qtr	4th Qtr	Total
2002	0.93	4.18	5.59	-0.29	10.69
2003	1.31	3.19	0.05	1.52	6.18
2004	2.13	-3.12	4.51	1.39	4.84
2005	-0.17	3.35	-0.22	0.81	3.79
2006	0.13	-0.03	3.50	1.17	4.83

Trailing	Total Return%	+/- LB Muni	+/- LB Muni 20YR	%Rank Cat	Growth of $10,000
3 Mo	1.17	0.06	-0.26	24	10,117
6 Mo	4.72	0.17	-0.79	20	10,472
1 Yr	4.83	-0.01	-1.03	31	10,483
3 Yr Avg	4.48	0.20	-1.35	16	11,405
5 Yr Avg	6.04	0.51	-0.72	6	13,408
10 Yr Avg	—	—	—	—	—
15 Yr Avg	—	—	—	—	—

Tax Analysis	Tax-Adj Rtn%	%Rank Cat	Tax-Cost Rat	%Rank Cat
3 Yr (estimated)	4.43	12	0.05	18
5 Yr (estimated)	5.96	5	0.08	23
10 Yr (estimated)	—			

Potential Capital Gain Exposure: 2% of assets

Historical Profile

Return	High
Risk	High
Rating	★★★★ Above Avg

53	40	38	40

Investment Style
Fixed Income
Income Rtn %Rank Cat

▼ Manager Change
▽ Partial Manager Change

Growth of $10,000
━ Investment Values of Fund
━ Investment Values of LB Muni

14.0
13.0
12.0
11.0
10.0

Performance Quartile (within Category)

	1995	1996	1997	1998	1999	2000	2001	2002	2003	2004	2005	2006	History
	—	—	—	—	—	—	10.08	10.68	10.76	10.80	10.74	10.79	NAV
	—	—	—	—	—	—	4.01*	10.69	6.18	4.84	3.79	4.83	Total Return %
	—	—	—	—	—	—	—	1.09	0.87	0.36	0.28	-0.01	+/-LB Muni
	—	—	—	—	—	—	—	0.66	-0.15	-1.72	-1.29	-1.03	+/-LB Muni 20YR
	—	—	—	—	—	—	—	4.39	4.25	4.14	4.01	4.04	Income Return %
	—	—	—	—	—	—	—	6.30	1.93	0.70	-0.22	0.79	Capital Return %
	—	—	—	—	—	—	—	4	9	13	20	31	Total Rtn % Rank Cat
	—	—	—	—	—	—	0.31	0.43	0.44	0.44	0.42	0.43	Income $
	—	—	—	—	—	—	0.01	0.02	0.12	0.03	0.04	0.03	Capital Gains $
	—	—	—	—	—	—	—	—	—	0.14	0.23	0.17	Expense Ratio %
	—	—	—	—	—	—	—	—	—	4.13	4.14	3.93	Income Ratio %
	—	—	—	—	—	—	—	34	28	28	17	15	Turnover Rate %
	—	—	—	—	—	—	—	150	257	220	253	504	Net Assets $mil

Rating and Risk

Time Period	Load-Adj Return %	Morningstar Rtn vs Cat	Morningstar Risk vs Cat	Morningstar Risk-Adj Rating
1 Yr	4.83			
3 Yr	4.48	+Avg	High	★★★★
5 Yr	6.04	High	High	★★★★
10 Yr	—	—	—	
Incept	5.98			

Other Measures	Standard Index LB Muni	Best Fit Index LB Muni
Alpha	0.0	0.0
Beta	1.18	1.18
R-Squared	99	99
Standard Deviation	3.62	
Mean	4.48	
Sharpe Ratio	0.34	

Morningstar's Take by Eric Jacobson 12-21-06

Fidelity Tax-Free Bond is a potent challenger to the notion of more-personal management.

It's common these days for individuals to buy their own municipal bonds or rely on brokers or asset-management firms to assemble unique portfolios. Sometimes it's about the cachet of personal service, because anecdotally, we know that investors believe they can better protect themselves from risk or earn good returns through one of these methods.

The fact is that most investors would be better off with a well-run, low-cost fund, and for those in the highest tax brackets, it's hard to imagine better choices than this one. On the most basic level, that's because there's much more to buying (or selling) municipal bonds than many realize, and Fidelity boasts one of the best teams in the business. Even among the highest-quality bonds, calls and other structural features make them difficult to value. The lack of a centralized exchange further complicates efforts to know whether a price

is good. Manager Christine Thompson and her colleagues are meticulous, however, in analyzing the thousands of bonds they see in the market. And they are loathe to buy any at a bad price or that don't mesh with their efforts to control risk.

Many investors worry that funds with no maturity are riskier than laddered purchases of individual bonds, but that's an overblown concern. The Morningstar database tracks 31 rolling periods of three-year returns for this fund--none with a loss. The record for sibling fund Fidelity Municipal Income (run nearly the same as this one) goes back much longer (over 140 rolling three-year periods) with the same outcome.

What should ultimately appeal to investors who might otherwise hire private managers, however, is that this fund, which avoids bonds subject to the Alternative Minimum Tax, has produced stellar after-tax returns, and provides world-class management at rock-bottom, institutional-level pricing. It has few real peers.

Address:	82 Devonshire Street Boston MA 02109 800-343-3548
Web Address:	www.fidelity.com
Inception:	04-10-01 *
Advisor:	Fidelity Management & Research (FMR)
Subadvisor:	Multiple Subadvisors
NTF Plans:	Fidelity Retail-NTF, CommonWealth NTF

Minimum Purchase:	$25000	Add: $1000	IRA: $0
Min Auto Inv Plan:	$0	Add: —	
Sales Fees:	No-load		
Management Fee:	0.37%		
Actual Fees:	Mgt:0.37%	Dist: —	
Expense Projections:	3Yr:$160	5Yr:$280	10Yr:$628
Income Distrib:	Monthly		

Portfolio Analysis 10-31-06

Total Fixed-Income:337

	Date of Maturity	Amount $000	Value $000	% Net Assets
GOLDEN ST TOB SECURITIZA	06-01-45	5,200	5,362	1.19
Tobacco Settlement Fing	06-01-21	4,060	4,441	0.98
New York N Y City Transi	08-01-32	4,200	4,408	0.98
GRAND PRAIRIE TEX INDPT	08-01-33	4,000	3,981	0.88
Metropolitan Pier & Expo	06-15-15	5,250	3,742	0.83
Greenville Cnty S C Sch	12-01-33	3,450	3,720	0.82
California St 5.25%	12-01-33	3,300	3,536	0.78
Du Page Cnty Ill Cmnty H	01-01-20	3,175	3,497	0.78
Salt Lake Cnty Utah Hosp	05-15-12	3,100	3,353	0.74
Beech Grove Ind Sch Bldg	07-05-24	2,875	3,323	0.74
NEW YORK N Y CITY TRANSI	11-01-28	3,000	3,311	0.73
SABINE RIVER AUTH TEX PO	05-01-22	3,120	3,282	0.73
CHICAGO ILL PUB BLDG COM	03-01-16	3,000	3,278	0.73
Bolingbrook Ill 5.375%	01-01-38	3,000	3,254	0.72
San Antonio Tex Elec & G	02-01-20	3,000	3,246	0.72

Current Investment Style

Duration: Short Int Long
Quality: High Med Low

¹Avg Eff Duration	6.6 Yrs
Avg Eff Maturity	13.6 Yrs
Avg Credit Quality	AA
Avg Wtd Coupon	4.54%
Avg Wtd Price	105.02% of par

¹figure provided by fund

Credit Analysis % bonds 10-31-06

AAA	63	BB	0
AA	11	B	0
A	17	Below B	0
BBB	7	NR/NA	2

Top 5 States % bonds

TX	17.1	IL	11.0
CA	13.4	IN	4.7
NY	12.1		

Composition

Cash	0.2	Bonds	99.8
Stocks	0.0	Other	0.0

Special Securities

Restricted/Illiquid Secs	0
Options/Futures/Warrants	No

Sector Weightings

	% of Bonds	Rel Cat
General Obligation	41.8	1.49
Utilities	12.3	1.18
Health	6.4	0.62
Water/Waste	7.2	0.73
Housing	0.2	0.04
Education	12.9	1.13
Transportation	4.8	0.55
COP/Lease	2.7	1.13
Industrial	9.9	0.82
Misc Revenue	0.0	—
Demand	1.9	3.88

Morningstar® Funds 500

Fidelity Total Bond

Ticker	Load	NAV	Yield	SEC Yield	Total Assets	Mstar Category
FTBFX	None	$10.45	4.5%	5.06%	$3,065 mil	Intermediate-Term Bond

Governance and Management

Stewardship Grade: B

Portfolio Manager(s)

Ford O'Neil, who also manages Fidelity Intermediate Bond and Fidelity U.S. Bond Index, took over this fund in late 2004. He has had much success managing other funds, so we don't expect performance will slip here. High-yield specialist Eric Mollenhauer, a member of the fund's management team from August 2003 to October 2005, joined O'Neil as the fund's comanager in October 2006.

Strategy

Management follows Fidelity's standard approach here. It looks to add value primarily through issue selection, sector allocation, and yield-curve positioning. Big interest-rate bets are strictly off limits. The fund is broadly diversified across issues and sectors, but, unlike Fidelity Intermediate Bond and Fidelity Investment Grade Bond, it holds stakes in high-yield and emerging-markets bonds. Its benchmark index is the Lehman Brothers U.S. Universal Index.

Historical Profile

Return	High
Risk	Average
Rating	★★★★ Highest

Performance Quartile (within Category)

	1995	1996	1997	1998	1999	2000	2001	2002	2003	2004	2005	2006	History
	—	—	—	—	—	—	—	10.29	10.52	10.63	10.42	10.45	NAV
	—	—	—	—	—	—	—	3.42*	5.87	5.47	2.46	5.12	Total Return %
	—	—	—	—	—	—	—	—	1.77	1.13	0.03	0.79	+/-LB Aggr
	—	—	—	—	—	—	—	—	-0.10	0.17	0.63	1.31	+/-LB 5-10YR
	—	—	—	—	—	—	—	—	3.02	3.52	4.10	4.62	Income Return %
	—	—	—	—	—	—	—	—	2.85	1.95	-1.64	0.50	Capital Return %
	—	—	—	—	—	—	—	—	29	10	15	12	Total Rtn % Rank Cat
	—	—	—	—	—	—	—	0.05	0.31	0.36	0.43	0.47	Income $
	—	—	—	—	—	—	—	0.00	0.06	0.09	0.04	0.02	Capital Gains $
	—	—	—	—	—	—	—	—	0.65	0.65	0.45		Expense Ratio %
	—	—	—	—	—	—	—	—	2.77	3.25	4.95		Income Ratio %
	—	—	—	—	—	—	—	—	336	—	99		Turnover Rate %
	—	—	—	—	—	—	—	45	300	366	3,003		Net Assets $mil

Investment Style Fixed Income
Income Rtn %Rank Cat

▼ Manager Change
▽ Partial Manager Change

Growth of $10,000
— Investment Values of Fund
— Investment Values of LB Aggr

12.4 / 11.5 / 10.7 / 10.0 / 9.0

83 / 62 / 43

Performance 12-31-06

	1st Qtr	2nd Qtr	3rd Qtr	4th Qtr	Total
2002	—	—	—	—	3.42 *
2003	2.09	3.37	-0.04	0.37	5.87
2004	2.53	-2.19	3.52	1.60	5.47
2005	-0.75	2.89	-0.28	0.62	2.46
2006	-0.18	-0.01	3.83	1.44	5.12

Trailing	Total Return%	+/- LB Aggr	+/- LB 5-10YR	%Rank Cat	Growth of $10,000
3 Mo	1.44	0.20	0.36	26	10,144
6 Mo	5.32	0.23	-0.36	20	10,532
1 Yr	5.12	0.79	1.31	12	10,512
3 Yr Avg	4.34	0.64	0.70	9	11,359
5 Yr Avg	—	—	—	—	—
10 Yr Avg	—	—	—	—	—
15 Yr Avg	—	—	—	—	—

Tax Analysis	Tax-Adj Rtn%	%Rank Cat	Tax-Cost Rat	%Rank Cat
3 Yr (estimated)	2.74	7	1.53	54
5 Yr (estimated)	—	—	—	—
10 Yr (estimated)	—	—	—	—

Potential Capital Gain Exposure: 2% of assets

Rating and Risk

Time Period	Load-Adj Return %	Morningstar Rtn vs Cat	Morningstar Risk vs Cat	Morningstar Risk-Adj Rating
1 Yr	5.12			
3 Yr	4.34	High	Avg	★★★★★
5 Yr	—	—	—	—
10 Yr	—	—	—	—
Incept	5.32			

Other Measures	Standard Index LB Aggr	Best Fit Index LB. U.S. Univ. Bd
Alpha	0.7	0.2
Beta	0.93	0.95
R-Squared	97	99
Standard Deviation	3.06	
Mean	4.34	
Sharpe Ratio	0.35	

Morningstar's Take by Scott Berry 11-20-06

Fidelity Total Bond won't always look this good, but we like its long-term prospects.

Fidelity couldn't have timed this fund's launch any better. It opened in October 2002, just as the corporate-bond market was bottoming out. As companies worked to repair balance sheets and pay down debt in late 2002 and 2003, corporate-bond prices soared, providing junk-bond funds a huge lift. This fund is no junk-bond fund, but its exposure to that sector (recently 11% of assets) proved quite beneficial. And though returns have come back to earth more recently, junk bonds have continued to shine relative to other bond types, as default rates have remained low. Meanwhile, the fund has also held a small stake in emerging-markets debt (recently 3% of assets), which has also delivered strong returns in recent years.

These sectors will have their struggles sooner or later, but we think this fund carries sustainable advantages that will help it weather any storm. For starters, Fidelity's bond group is deep and talented.

Fidelity's investment-grade bond group has made great strides over the last decade, building a topnotch operation with strong analytical resources. And both Fidelity's high-yield and emerging-markets groups have strong track records, with Fidelity New Markets Income being a Morningstar Fund Analyst Pick. We expect good issue selection in both areas to keep the fund out of too much trouble.

The fund's low costs also provide it an advantage over most peers. The fund charges just 0.45%, while its average no-load intermediate-category peer charges 0.73%. That difference provides the fund a sizable head start each year. And given the quality of management and resources put to use here, we think the fund is a bargain.

Conservative investors may be turned off by the fund's exposure to the bond market's riskier segments, but we expect the fund to reward long-term investors.

Address:	82 Devonshire St Boston MA 02109 800-343-3548
Web Address:	www.fidelity.com
Inception:	10-15-02*
Advisor:	Fidelity Intl Invest Advisors (U.K.) Ltd
Subadvisor:	Multiple Subadvisors
NTF Plans:	Fidelity Retail-NTF, CommonWealth NTF

Minimum Purchase:	$2500	Add: $250	IRA: $500
Min Auto Inv Plan:	$2500	Add: $500	
Sales Fees:	No-load		
Management Fee:	0.43%		
Actual Fees:	Mgt:0.32%	Dist: —	
Expense Projections:	3Yr:$144	5Yr:$252	10Yr:$567
Income Distrib:	Monthly		

Portfolio Analysis 08-31-06

Total Fixed-Income:1902	Date of Maturity	Amount $000	Value $000	% Net Assets
FNMA 5%	08-01-35	133,989	128,406	4.28
U S Treas Nt Stripped Pr	08-15-10	131,350	109,555	3.65
Dbsw Swap Irs 7/20/10 5.	07-20-10	100,000	101,687	3.39
Dbsw Swap Irs 7/20/09 3m	07-20-09	100,000	101,251	3.38
FNMA 5.5%	12-01-32	100,500	98,765	3.29
US Treasury Note 2%	01-15-14	91,190	98,330	3.28
FNMA 4.5%	05-01-18	85,705	82,584	2.75
US Treasury Note 4.25%	08-15-13	81,769	79,508	2.65
U S Treas Nt Stripped Pr	02-15-12	75,970	59,088	1.97
U S Treas Bd Stripped Pr	02-15-15	78,530	52,758	1.76
FHLMC 6%	05-01-33	40,559	40,629	1.35
FNMA 4.5%	09-01-33	36,801	34,369	1.15
US Treasury Note 4.75%	05-15-14	33,615	33,652	1.12
Dbsw Swap Irs 4/19/09 3m	04-19-09	30,000	30,543	1.02
FNMA 6%	09-01-32	26,461	26,525	0.88
FHLMC 5.875%	03-21-11	25,685	26,363	0.88
FNMA 6.5%	11-01-31	24,247	24,677	0.82
Dbsw Swap Irs 4/07/11 3m	04-07-11	20,000	20,333	0.68
FNMA 6.25%	02-01-11	19,170	19,959	0.67
Wachovia Cmbs 2006-C24 C	03-15-45	16,615	16,738	0.56

Current Investment Style

Duration: Short / Int / Long
Quality: High / Med / Low

¹ figure provided by fund

Avg Eff Duration¹	4.5 Yrs
Avg Eff Maturity	6.9 Yrs
Avg Credit Quality	AA
Avg Wtd Coupon	4.05%
Avg Wtd Price	97.41% of par

Coupon Range	% of Bonds	Rel Cat
0% PIK	24.3	3.5
0% to 6%	82.5	1.1
6% to 8%	14.3	0.7
8% to 10%	2.3	0.5
More than 10%	0.9	1.3

1.00=Category Average

Credit Analysis	% bonds 08-31-06		
AAA	65	BB	5
AA	4	B	5
A	6	Below B	1
BBB	12	NR/NA	5

Sector Breakdown | % of assets

US Treasuries	5
TIPS	4
US Agency	11
Mortgage Pass-Throughs	21
Mortgage CMO	10
Mortgage ARM	0
US Corporate	21
Asset-Backed	8
Convertible	0
Municipal	0
Corporate Inflation-Protected	0
Foreign Corporate	2
Foreign Govt	1

Composition

Cash	16.0	Bonds	82.0
Stocks	0.0	Other	2.0

Special Securities

Restricted/Illiquid Secs	4
Exotic Mortgage-Backed	0
Emerging-Markets Secs	2
Options/Futures/Warrants	No

Fidelity U.S. Bond Index

	Ticker	Load	NAV	Yield	SEC Yield	Total Assets	Mstar Category
	FBIDX	None	$10.86	4.6%	5.02%	$6,479 mil	Intermediate-Term Bond

Governance and Management

Stewardship Grade: B

Portfolio Manager(s)

Ford O'Neil runs this show. He has been with Fidelity since 1990 and has had success at this fund and Fidelity Intermediate Bond, which he has managed since 1998. Management may not play a huge role in most index funds, but O'Neil has managed to squeeze a little extra return out of this portfolio during his tenure.

Strategy

Although this fund is designed to roughly mimic the performance of the Lehman Brothers Aggregate Bond Index, management does have a few tricks up its sleeve. It's impractical to buy all the bonds in the index, so management chooses those that it thinks have more potential than others with similar characteristics. By employing stratified sampling, management seeks to replicate the index's major characteristics, such as duration (a measure of interest-rate sensitivity), maturity, and credit quality, while looking to recoup some of the fund's expense ratio through such research-driven methods as issue selection and sector allocation.

Performance 12-31-06

	1st Qtr	2nd Qtr	3rd Qtr	4th Qtr	Total
2002	0.02	3.51	4.35	2.03	10.22
2003	1.63	2.76	-0.08	0.54	4.91
2004	2.69	-2.56	3.26	1.01	4.36
2005	-0.55	2.91	-0.68	0.60	2.26
2006	-0.55	-0.07	3.85	1.09	4.33

Trailing	Total Return%	+/- LB Aggr	+/- LB 5-10YR	%Rank Cat	Growth of $10,000
3 Mo	1.09	-0.15	0.01	63	10,109
6 Mo	4.98	-0.11	-0.70	37	10,498
1 Yr	4.33	0.00	0.52	31	10,433
3 Yr Avg	3.65	-0.05	0.01	33	11,135
5 Yr Avg	5.18	0.12	-0.74	21	12,873
10 Yr Avg	6.24	0.00	-0.44	13	18,318
15 Yr Avg	6.55	0.05	-0.44	24	25,900

Tax Analysis	Tax-Adj Rtn%	%Rank Cat	Tax-Cost Rat	%Rank Cat
3 Yr (estimated)	2.05	27	1.54	55
5 Yr (estimated)	3.41	18	1.68	55
10 Yr (estimated)	3.99	10	2.12	60

Potential Capital Gain Exposure: -1% of assets

Morningstar's Take by Scott Berry 11-20-06

Fidelity U.S. Bond Index remains a solid choice for investors.

This fund's appeal owes much to the depth of talent and extensive research capabilities of Fidelity's bond group. The Lehman Brothers Aggregate Bond Index is made up of thousands of issues and would be prohibitively expensive to duplicate, so manager Ford O'Neil and Fidelity's bond group have some flexibility to add value with issue selection and yield-curve positioning (the fund's mix of short- and long-term bonds). That flexibility means the fund won't always duplicate the index's returns, but it allows management an opportunity to earn back the fund's expenses and actually outperform the index by a fractional amount on a net basis.

The fund's long-term record provides good evidence of the team's success. In fact, the fund bested the index over the trailing three-, five-, and 10-year periods ending Oct. 31, 2006. The fund enjoyed a particularly strong year in 2003, when good corporate-bond selection helped the fund fully participate in that sector's rally. More recently, O'Neil and company have avoided leveraged-buyout candidates, which typically see their bonds suffer when buyouts are announced or even rumored to be announced. That positioning has paid off, as has the fund's increased exposure to hybrid adjustable-rate mortgages, which will be joining the index April 1.

The fund's costs also provide it an advantage over most peers. The fund charges just 0.31%, while its average no-load category peer charges 0.73%. That built-in head start has proved difficult for most peers to overcome over the long term. That said, the fund's levy is higher than the 0.20% fee for giant Vanguard Total Bond Market Index.

Overall, though, we like what this fund brings to the table. Broad diversification, skilled management, and reasonable costs make this fund a good building block for a diversified investment portfolio.

Address:	82 Devonshire St Boston MA 02109 800-544-5555
Web Address:	www.fidelity.com
Inception:	03-08-90
Advisor:	Fidelity Management & Research (FMR)
Subadvisor:	Multiple Subadvisors
NTF Plans:	Fidelity Retail-NTF, CommonWealth NTF

Minimum Purchase:	$10000	Add: $1000	IRA: $2500
Min Auto Inv Plan:	$0	Add: —	
Sales Fees:	No-load		
Management Fee:	0.32%		
Actual Fees:	Mgt:0.32%		
Expense Projections:	3Yr:$103	5Yr:$180	10Yr:$406
Income Distrib:	Monthly		

Historical Profile

Return	Above Avg
Risk	Average
Rating	★★★★ Above Avg

Investment Style: Fixed Income
Income Rtn %Rank Cat

▼ Manager Change
▽ Partial Manager Change

Growth of $10,000
— Investment Values of Fund
— Investment Values of LB Aggr

Performance Quartile (within Category)

	1995	1996	1997	1998	1999	2000	2001	2002	2003	2004	2005	2006	History
NAV	10.95	10.56	10.79	11.02	10.19	10.59	10.80	11.24	11.19	11.14	10.90	10.86	NAV
Total Return %	18.00	3.39	9.55	8.87	-0.95	11.42	8.08	10.22	4.91	4.36	2.26	4.33	Total Return %
+/-LB Aggr	-0.47	-0.24	-0.10	0.18	-0.13	-0.21	-0.36	-0.03	0.81	0.02	-0.17	0.00	+/-LB Aggr
+/-LB 5-10YR	-3.43	0.70	0.12	-1.27	1.93	-1.02	-0.74	-2.81	-1.06	-0.94	0.43	0.52	+/-LB 5-10YR
Income Return %	7.88	6.93	7.22	6.67	6.25	7.28	6.09	4.87	3.74	3.90	4.09	4.66	Income Return %
Capital Return %	10.12	-3.54	2.33	2.20	-7.20	4.14	1.99	5.35	1.17	0.46	-1.83	-0.33	Capital Return %
Total Rtn % Rank Cat	49	47	31	15	39	19	34	10	41	36	24	31	Total Rtn % Rank Cat
Income $	0.76	0.74	0.74	0.70	0.67	0.72	0.63	0.51	0.41	0.43	0.45	0.50	Income $
Capital Gains $	0.00	0.00	0.00	0.00	0.06	0.00	0.00	0.12	0.18	0.10	0.04	0.00	Capital Gains $
Expense Ratio %	0.32	0.31	0.31	0.32	0.31	0.31	0.31	0.31	0.32	0.32	0.32	0.32	Expense Ratio %
Income Ratio %	7.58	7.11	7.05	6.98	6.35	6.53	6.84	5.54	4.56	3.65	3.73	4.94	Income Ratio %
Turnover Rate %	73	128	65	97	184	133	154	178	204	217	160	82	Turnover Rate %
Net Assets $mil	503	552	665	1,225	1,533	1,785	2,954	4,405	4,765	5,263	5,842	6,479	Net Assets $mil

Rating and Risk

Time Period	Load-Adj Return %	Morningstar Rtn vs Cat	Morningstar Risk vs Cat	Morningstar Risk-Adj Rating
1 Yr	4.33			
3 Yr	3.65	+Avg	+Avg	★★★★
5 Yr	5.18	+Avg	Avg	★★★★
10 Yr	6.24	+Avg	Avg	★★★★
Incept	7.39			

Other Measures	Standard Index LB Aggr	Best Fit Index LB Aggr
Alpha	0.0	0.0
Beta	0.99	0.99
R-Squared	100	100
Standard Deviation	3.22	
Mean	3.65	
Sharpe Ratio	0.13	

Portfolio Analysis 08-31-06

Total Fixed-Income:1283	Date of Maturity	Amount $000	Value $000	% Net Assets
US Treasury Note 4.25%	08-15-13	366,885	356,738	4.65
FNMA 0.05%	07-01-35	319,368	306,175	4.00
FNMA 0.06%	10-01-33	304,527	299,371	3.91
US Treasury Note 6.5%	02-15-10	200,000	211,234	2.76
US Treasury Note 3.375%	10-15-09	215,570	207,318	2.71
US Treasury Note 2%	01-15-14	183,704	198,087	2.58
US Treasury Note 4.875%	05-15-09	196,290	197,034	2.57
FNMA 5%	09-01-18	188,081	184,477	2.41
FNMA 0.06%	11-01-28	154,044	154,442	2.02
FNMA 4.5%	03-01-19	150,610	145,116	1.89
FNMA 3.25%	02-15-09	146,470	140,435	1.83
US Treasury Note 4.75%	05-15-14	123,330	123,465	1.61
FNMA 0.04%	07-01-33	128,124	119,944	1.57
US Treasury Bond 8%	11-15-21	79,717	105,544	1.38
Ubsd Swap Irs 1/23/09 3m	01-23-09	100,000	98,929	1.29
US Treasury Bond 6.25%	05-15-30	65,498	77,569	1.01
FNMA 3.25%	01-15-08	69,435	67,701	0.88
GNMA 0.06%	10-15-32	58,848	60,303	0.79
FNMA 5.5%	11-01-22	58,030	57,343	0.75
Lbsp Swap Irs 12/8/08 3m	12-08-08	55,000	54,636	0.71

Current Investment Style

Duration: Short Int Long
Quality: High Med Low

Avg Eff Duration[1]	4.4 Yrs
Avg Eff Maturity	6.0 Yrs
Avg Credit Quality	AA
Avg Wtd Coupon	3.73%
Avg Wtd Price	100.25% of par

[1] figure provided by fund

Coupon Range	% of Bonds	Rel Cat
0% PIK	5.3	0.8
0% to 6%	80.7	1.1
6% to 8%	18.4	0.9
8% to 10%	0.8	0.2
More than 10%	0.0	0.0

1.00=Category Average

Credit Analysis	% bonds 08-31-06		
AAA	72	BB	1
AA	4	B	0
A	6	Below B	0
BBB	16	NR/NA	1

Sector Breakdown	% of assets
US Treasuries	18
TIPS	3
US Agency	6
Mortgage Pass-Throughs	25
Mortgage CMO	7
Mortgage ARM	0
US Corporate	17
Asset-Backed	5
Convertible	0
Municipal	0
Corporate Inflation-Protected	0
Foreign Corporate	1
Foreign Govt	0

Composition			
Cash	16.9	Bonds	83.1
Stocks	0.0	Other	0.1

Special Securities	
Restricted/Illiquid Secs	3
Exotic Mortgage-Backed	0
Emerging-Markets Secs	Trace
Options/Futures/Warrants	No

MORNINGSTAR® Funds 500

Fidelity Ultra-Short Bd

Analyst Pick ✓

	Ticker	Load	NAV	Yield	SEC Yield	Total Assets	Mstar Category
	FUSFX	None	$10.01	4.9%	5.21%	$1,044 mil	Ultrashort Bond

Governance and Management

Stewardship Grade: B

Portfolio Manager(s)

Manager Andrew Dudley has run this fund since its inception. He has had much success at Fidelity Short-Term Bond, which he still manages, and we expect that success to continue here. Dudley is supported by a team of analysts and Fidelity's extensive research capabilities. Fidelity did Dudley a nice favor in 2005, when it agreed to limit the fund's expense ratio to 0.45%.

Strategy

Manager Andrew Dudley keeps the fund's overall interest-rate risk tied to that of the Lehman Brothers 6-Month Swap Index, which is typically a bit less sensitive to interest-rate changes than the ultrashort category as a whole. The bulk of the fund's assets are invested in asset-backed and mortgage-backed securities, but the fund does hold a small corporate-bond stake. The fund also invests in floating-rate securities.

Historical Profile
Return	Above Avg
Risk	Below Avg
Rating	★★★★ Above Avg

Investment Style Fixed Income
Income Rtn %Rank Cat

▼ Manager Change
▽ Partial Manager Change

Growth of $10,000
— Investment Values of Fund
— Investment Values of LB Aggr

Performance Quartile (within Category)

	1995	1996	1997	1998	1999	2000	2001	2002	2003	2004	2005	2006	History
NAV	—	—	—	—	—	—	—	10.02	10.06	10.04	10.02	10.01	
Total Return %	—	—	—	—	—	—	—	0.94*	1.87	1.32	2.96	4.90	
+/-LB Aggr	—	—	—	—	—	—	—	—	-2.23	-3.02	0.53	0.57	
+/-6 Month CD	—	—	—	—	—	—	—	—	0.70	-0.41	-0.76	-0.33	
Income Return %	—	—	—	—	—	—	—	—	1.47	1.49	3.17	5.00	
Capital Return %	—	—	—	—	—	—	—	—	0.40	-0.17	-0.21	-0.10	
Total Rtn % Rank Cat	—	—	—	—	—	—	—	—	29	49	20	23	
Income $	—	—	—	—	—	—	—	0.07	0.15	0.15	0.31	0.49	
Capital Gains $	—	—	—	—	—	—	—	0.00	0.00	0.00	0.00	0.00	
Expense Ratio %	—	—	—	—	—	—	—	—	0.55	0.55	0.45		
Income Ratio %	—	—	—	—	—	—	—	—	1.77	1.21	4.26		
Turnover Rate %	—	—	—	—	—	—	—	—	—	53	39		
Net Assets $mil	—	—	—	—	—	—	—	80	354	763	1,025		

Performance 12-31-06

	1st Qtr	2nd Qtr	3rd Qtr	4th Qtr	Total
2002	—	—	—	0.68	0.94 *
2003	0.48	0.53	0.37	0.48	1.87
2004	0.54	-0.11	0.46	0.42	1.32
2005	0.48	0.71	0.85	0.89	2.96
2006	1.08	1.09	1.42	1.23	4.90

Trailing	Total Return%	+/- LB Aggr	+/- 6 Month CD	%Rank Cat	Growth of $10,000
3 Mo	1.23	-0.01	-0.07	41	10,123
6 Mo	2.66	-2.43	0.00	47	10,266
1 Yr	4.90	0.57	-0.33	23	10,490
3 Yr Avg	3.05	-0.65	-0.50	24	10,943
5 Yr Avg	—	—	—	—	—
10 Yr Avg	—	—	—	—	—
15 Yr Avg	—	—	—	—	—

Tax Analysis	Tax-Adj Rtn%	%Rank Cat	Tax-Cost Rat	%Rank Cat
3 Yr (estimated)	1.92	16	1.10	47
5 Yr (estimated)	—	—	—	—
10 Yr (estimated)	—	—	—	—

Potential Capital Gain Exposure: 0% of assets

Rating and Risk

Time Period	Load-Adj Return %	Morningstar Rtn vs Cat	Morningstar Risk vs Cat	Morningstar Risk-Adj Rating
1 Yr	4.90			
3 Yr	3.05	+Avg	-Avg	★★★★
5 Yr	—	—	—	—
10 Yr	—	—	—	
Incept	2.76			

Other Measures	Standard Index LB Aggr	Best Fit Index LB 1-5 YR GOVT
Alpha	-0.2	-0.1
Beta	0.06	0.13
R-Squared	44	55
Standard Deviation	0.53	
Mean	3.05	
Sharpe Ratio	-0.66	

Morningstar's Take by Scott Berry 12-19-06

Fidelity Ultra-Short Bond doesn't pack much of a punch, but its low volatility makes it one of our favorites.

This fund is just one step up the risk ladder from a money market mutual fund. Unlike a money market fund, this fund does experience changes to its net asset value (NAV). However, those changes are typically very minor. For the year to date through Oct. 18, 2006, for example, the fund's NAV fluctuated between just $10.01 and $10.03. That stability makes the fund a good option for investors who are looking for an emergency savings fund that may never be tapped but that needs to be safe. It also makes the fund a good option for investors who are saving for a goal that's close at hand, such as a house or other big purchase.

The fund's low volatility owes to its restrained approach. Manager Andrew Dudley keeps the fund's interest-rate risk in line with the Lehman Brothers 6-Month Swap Index, which is typically a bit less sensitive to interest-rate changes than the ultrashort category as a whole. Meanwhile, he looks to identify undervalued bond issues, sectors, and maturities. The fund carries more credit risk than some peers, but Dudley's impressive track record here and at Fidelity Short-Term Bond, and Fidelity's deep research capabilities, make us confident that this fund will continue to deliver consistently good results.

That confidence also stems from the fund's built-in cost advantage. The fund charges 0.45% per year, while its average no-load ultrashort peer charges 0.59%. With the range of returns in the category often quite narrow, that difference can prove most meaningful. The fund is also cheaper than many taxable money market funds, including Schwab Cash Reserves and T. Rowe Price Prime Reserve.

Overall, we think this fund's prudent approach, skilled and experienced management, and below-average costs make it an appealing choice. It remains one of our two ultrashort Analyst Picks.

Address:	82 Devonshire St Boston MA 02109 800-544-6666
Web Address:	www.fidelity.com
Inception:	08-29-02 *
Advisor:	Fidelity Management & Research (FMR)
Subadvisor:	Multiple Subadvisors
NTF Plans:	Fidelity Retail-NTF, CommonWealth NTF

Minimum Purchase:	$2500	Add: $250	IRA: $200
Min Auto Inv Plan:	$100	Add: $100	
Sales Fees:	No-load, 0.25%R		
Management Fee:	0.32%		
Actual Fees:	Mgt:0.32%	Dist: —	
Expense Projections:	3Yr:$144	5Yr:$252	10Yr:$567
Income Distrib:	Monthly		

Portfolio Analysis 10-31-06

Total Fixed-Income:994	Date of Maturity	Amount $000	Value $000	% Net Assets
Euro$ 90 Day Fut Mar 07			26,384	2.43
Euro$ 90 Day Fut Dec 06			26,334	2.42
Euro$ 90 Day Fut Sep 07			24,495	2.25
Euro$ 90 Day Fut Jun 07			24,450	2.25
FNMA CMO	05-25-35	7,425	7,430	0.68
Permanent Fing Plc 2004-	06-10-11	5,490	5,492	0.51
Wells Fargo Mbs 2005-Ar1	06-25-35	4,427	4,335	0.40
Cps Auto Receivables Tr	06-15-16	4,124	4,134	0.38
TELEFONICA EMISONES SA	06-19-09	4,079	4,082	0.38
Gracechurch Mtg Fdg 2005	10-11-41	4,069	4,070	0.37
FNMA 5.5%	11-01-17	3,843	3,857	0.35
Arran Fdg FRN	12-15-10	3,788	3,787	0.35
College Ln FRN	04-25-46	3,782	3,782	0.35
WASHINGTON MUT MASTER NT	09-16-13	3,617	3,617	0.33
Wash Mut Bk Fa Ca Glbl M	05-01-09	3,612	3,615	0.33
Hilton Hotels Pool Tr 20	10-03-15	3,573	3,598	0.33
FHLMC CMO	02-15-32	3,482	3,569	0.33
At&T FRN	05-15-08	3,517	3,519	0.32
Telecom Italia Cap FRN	07-18-11	3,455	3,447	0.32
Rali Series Tr 2006-Qo7	09-25-46	3,435	3,435	0.32

Current Investment Style
Duration: Short Int Long
Quality: High Med Low

1 figure provided by fund

Avg Eff Duration[1]	0.4 Yrs
Avg Eff Maturity	1.8 Yrs
Avg Credit Quality	A
Avg Wtd Coupon	2.22%
Avg Wtd Price	100.02% of par

Coupon Range	% of Bonds	Rel Cat
0% PIK	6.7	0.3
0% to 6%	97.7	1.1
6% to 8%	2.1	0.3
8% to 10%	0.1	0.1
More than 10%	0.0	0.0

1.00=Category Average

Credit Analysis	% bonds 10-31-06		
AAA	39	BB	0
AA	13	B	0
A	14	Below B	0
BBB	20	NR/NA	14

Sector Breakdown	% of assets
US Treasuries	0
TIPS	0
US Agency	0
Mortgage Pass-Throughs	2
Mortgage CMO	19
Mortgage ARM	0
US Corporate	12
Asset-Backed	29
Convertible	0
Municipal	0
Corporate Inflation-Protected	0
Foreign Corporate	1
Foreign Govt	0

Composition			
Cash	36.1	Bonds	63.6
Stocks	0.0	Other	0.3

Special Securities	
Restricted/Illiquid Secs	6
Exotic Mortgage-Backed	0
Emerging-Markets Secs	0
Options/Futures/Warrants	No

Fidelity Value

Ticker	Load	NAV	Yield	Total Assets	Mstar Category
FDVLX	None	$80.60	0.7%	$18,254 mil	Mid-Cap Value

Governance and Management

Stewardship Grade: B

Portfolio Manager(s)

Richard Fentin has been at the helm since 1996 and is backed by Fidelity's deep research staff. He recently relinquished the reins of Fidelity Advisor Value Strategies after a one-year stint, but still manages Fidelity Advisor Value and a variable annuity fund. (He runs those two using the same approach employed here.) A 26-year veteran of the firm, Fentin had a solid record at his previous charge, Fidelity Puritan, which he managed for almost a decade.

Strategy

Manager Richard Fentin looks for stocks that are trading below his estimate of their worth, based on historical valuations, those of industry peers, and current cash flows and earnings; he typically looks at price/sales and price/book ratios as well. That approach has often led to an atypical portfolio. During Fentin's tenure, the fund has often been light on financial stocks relative to its peers. For a number of years, he loaded up on industrial stocks, but he's recently found more value in other corners of the market, such as tech and health care. Assets are spread across nearly 300 names.

Performance 12-31-06

	1st Qtr	2nd Qtr	3rd Qtr	4th Qtr	Total
2002	8.76	-5.62	-19.27	9.53	-9.25
2003	-4.35	17.22	4.94	14.26	34.43
2004	4.96	3.67	0.00	11.39	21.21
2005	0.74	3.72	4.93	4.22	14.27
2006	6.62	-2.84	3.70	7.14	15.09

Trailing	Total Return%	+/- S&P 500	+/- Russ MV	%Rank Cat	Growth of $10,000
3 Mo	7.14	0.44	-1.36	72	10,714
6 Mo	11.11	-1.63	-1.22	35	11,111
1 Yr	15.09	-0.70	-5.13	58	11,509
3 Yr Avg	16.81	6.37	-1.96	16	15,938
5 Yr Avg	14.23	8.04	-1.65	12	19,449
10 Yr Avg	12.00	3.58	-1.65	41	31,058
15 Yr Avg	14.27	3.63	-0.63	18	73,958

Tax Analysis	Tax-Adj Rtn%	%Rank Cat	Tax-Cost Rat	%Rank Cat
3 Yr (estimated)	15.47	14	1.15	39
5 Yr (estimated)	13.34	13	0.78	31
10 Yr (estimated)	10.24	30	1.57	52

Potential Capital Gain Exposure: 20% of assets

Morningstar's Take by Greg Carlson 12-01-06

Fidelity Value is still tough to recommend.

This fund's veteran manager, Rich Fentin, recently had his workload lightened. After managing the $1.7 billion Fidelity Advisor Value Strategies for one year, Fentin was replaced by Matthew Friedman, who was promoted after running several sector funds. So, Fentin's asset load, which weighed in at $18 billion, shrank a bit. However, that reprieve proved temporary: Investors have continued to plow cash into this offering, which now has $17.1 billion. (Fentin also runs Fidelity Advisor Value and a variable annuity fund, which add up to less than $200 million.)

Therefore, the amount of money Fentin must shoehorn into his picks continues to be a concern. True, on some fronts, the fund hasn't shown the telltale signs of asset bloat. It holds roughly the same number of names it did when the fund was much smaller, and its typically low portfolio turnover hasn't declined much. However, the fund has picked up a number of large caps in recent years--Baxter International and Tyco, for example, now reside in its top 10. Granted, the fund's current profile owes partly to Fentin's contrarian approach; smaller fry have led the way for seven years, so he's found large firms more appealing. But nearly half of its assets are stashed in large caps. The most worrisome development is that the fund, along with other siblings, is swamping the shares of some of Fentin's favorites. For example, Fidelity owns nearly 15% of the outstanding shares of National Oilwell Varco and Safeway, which would make it difficult for Fentin to add to his stakes in them because of Fidelity's ownership limits. That issue will only loom larger if investors keep adding to the fund's swollen coffers.

It's unfortunate that we can't endorse this fund--although Fentin's record during his 10-year tenure is rather middling, we've seen fewer ill-timed sector bets and better stock-picking across industries in recent years. But the fund's unchecked growth makes us wary.

Address:	82 Devonshire St Boston MA 02109 800-544-6666
Web Address:	www.fidelity.com
Inception:	12-01-78
Advisor:	Fidelity Management & Research (FMR)
Subadvisor:	Multiple Subadvisors
NTF Plans:	Fidelity Retail-NTF, CommonWealth NTF

Minimum Purchase:	$2500	Add: $250	IRA: $200
Min Auto Inv Plan:	$100	Add: $100	
Sales Fees:	No-load		
Management Fee:	0.46%		
Actual Fees:	Mgt:0.46%	Dist: —	
Expense Projections:	3Yr:$214	5Yr:$373	10Yr:$835
Income Distrib:	Annually		

Historical Profile

Return	Above Avg
Risk	Average
Rating	★★★★ Above Avg

93% 90% 95% 91% 94% 92% 92% 94% 97%

Investment Style
Equity
Stock %

▼ Manager Change
▽ Partial Manager Change

Growth of $10,000
— Investment Values of Fund
— Investment Values of S&P 500

42.2
32.4
24.0
17.0
10.0

Performance Quartile (within Category)

	1995	1996	1997	1998	1999	2000	2001	2002	2003	2004	2005	2006	History
	49.64	51.54	54.04	46.35	43.81	46.35	51.51	46.39	62.07	71.29	75.88	80.60	NAV
	27.13	16.85	21.08	0.18	8.55	8.10	12.25	-9.25	34.43	21.21	14.27	15.09	Total Return %
	-10.45	-6.11	-12.28	-28.40	-12.49	17.20	24.14	12.85	5.75	10.33	9.36	-0.70	+/-S&P 500
	-7.80	-3.41	-13.29	-4.90	8.66	-11.08	9.92	0.39	-3.64	-2.50	1.62	-5.13	+/-Russ MV
	1.18	1.07	0.93	1.02	1.57	2.17	1.10	0.70	0.50	0.26	0.60	0.74	Income Return %
	25.95	15.78	20.15	-0.84	6.98	5.93	11.15	-9.95	33.93	20.95	13.67	14.35	Capital Return %
	50	70	74	52	47	84	30	27	54	29	6	58	Total Rtn % Rank Cat
	0.48	0.53	0.48	0.55	0.73	0.95	0.51	0.36	0.23	0.16	0.43	0.56	Income $
	1.73	5.92	7.95	7.15	5.62	0.00	0.00	0.00	0.05	3.71	5.14	6.09	Capital Gains $
	0.96	0.88	0.66	0.61	0.54	0.48	0.77	0.95	0.98	0.93	0.72	—	Expense Ratio %
	1.58	1.34	1.01	1.06	1.50	1.87	1.29	1.02	0.66	0.37	0.58	—	Income Ratio %
	125	112	56	36	50	48	49	42	40	40	29	—	Turnover Rate %
	5,746	7,080	7,914	5,523	4,383	3,522	5,238	5,092	6,984	10,279	14,328	18,254	Net Assets $mil

Rating and Risk

Time Period	Load-Adj Return %	Morningstar Rtn vs Cat	Morningstar Risk vs Cat	Morningstar Risk-Adj Rating
1 Yr	15.09			
3 Yr	16.81	+Avg	Avg	★★★★
5 Yr	14.23	+Avg	Avg	★★★★
10 Yr	12.00	Avg	Avg	★★★
Incept	14.46			

Other Measures	Standard Index S&P 500	Best Fit Index Mstar Mid Core
Alpha	4.0	3.7
Beta	1.27	0.83
R-Squared	83	92
Standard Deviation	9.54	
Mean	16.81	
Sharpe Ratio	1.35	

Portfolio Analysis 10-31-06

Share change since 07-06 Total Stocks:287	Sector	PE	Tot Ret%	% Assets
⊖ Baxter International Inc	Health	24.3	24.81	1.99
Xerox Corporation	Ind Mtrls	13.4	15.70	1.50
Tyco International, Ltd.	Ind Mtrls	15.7	6.83	1.28
⊖ Safeway Inc.	Consumer	20.4	47.22	1.19
⊖ Symbol Technologies	Hardware	35.6	16.64	1.17
⊕ Avon Products	Goods	31.6	18.45	1.04
⊕ Agilent Technologies, In	Hardware	11.5	11.21	1.03
Flextronics Internationa	Hardware	45.1	9.96	0.97
Ceridian Corporation	Business	23.6	12.60	0.97
Fannie Mae	Financial	—	24.34	0.95
National Oilwell Varco,	Energy	18.3	-2.42	0.88
Schering-Plough Corporat	Health	36.6	14.63	0.85
Owens-Illinois, Inc.	Ind Mtrls	—	-12.31	0.85
⊖ Seagate Technology	Hardware	23.7	34.47	0.84
Carnival Corporation	Goods	18.7	-6.15	0.83
⊕ Masco Corporation	Ind Mtrls	14.8	1.82	0.81
Royal Caribbean Cruises,	Consumer	16.0	-6.78	0.79
OfficeMax, Inc.	Consumer	—	98.81	0.77
⊖ Quest Diagnostics, Inc.	Health	17.4	3.67	0.76
⊕ NCR Corporation	Hardware	22.6	25.99	0.74

Current Investment Style

Value Blnd Growth — Large Mid Small

Market Cap	%
Giant	7.4
Large	35.7
Mid	47.8
Small	8.7
Micro	0.4

Avg $mil: 8,414

Value Measures		Rel Category
Price/Earnings	16.79	1.13
Price/Book	2.19	1.09
Price/Sales	0.97	1.00
Price/Cash Flow	5.86	0.77
Dividend Yield %	1.51	0.84

Growth Measures	%	Rel Category
Long-Term Erngs	12.32	1.12
Book Value	7.72	1.11
Sales	7.29	0.95
Cash Flow	5.18	1.30
Historical Erngs	14.03	0.95

Profitability	%	Rel Category
Return on Equity	14.21	0.98
Return on Assets	6.88	0.93
Net Margin	9.24	0.88

Sector Weightings	% of Stocks	Rel S&P 500	3 Year High Low	
↻ Info	21.19	1.06		
Software	1.75	0.51	3	1
Hardware	11.85	1.28	13	9
Media	3.48	0.92	3	2
Telecom	4.11	1.17	4	3
⊏ Service	45.76	0.99		
Health	12.89	1.07	15	10
Consumer	10.23	1.34	10	7
Business	8.25	1.95	8	7
Financial	14.39	0.65	14	12
⊔ Mfg	33.05	0.98		
Goods	9.39	1.10	10	5
Ind Mtrls	11.56	0.97	21	12
Energy	7.54	0.77	13	8
Utilities	4.56	1.30	6	4

Composition

● Cash	2.9
● Stocks	96.8
● Bonds	0.1
● Other	0.2
Foreign	6.8
(% of Stock)	

MORNINGSTAR® Funds 500

Fidelity Worldwide

	Ticker	Load	NAV	Yield	Total Assets	Mstar Category
	FWWFX	None	$20.11	0.8%	$1,377 mil	World Stock

Portfolio Manager(s)

Jeffrey Feingold took over from Rick Mace as lead manager on Jan. 1, 2006. Feingold also oversees the domestic portion of the portfolio, with Bill Kennedy, who runs Fidelity International Discovery, managing the foreign-stock sleeve. Feingold has been with Fidelity since 1997 and has managed several sector funds, among them, Fidelity Select Defense & Aerospace, Home Finance, Air Transportation, and, most significantly, Financial Services, from October 2001 to April 2004. Both managers are served by a large staff of analysts.

Strategy

Jeffrey Feingold runs the domestic sleeve of this fund in a growth-at-a-reasonable-price style, conscious of keeping sector weighting in line with the domestic index but more willing than his predecessor to buy growthier stocks and mid-cap stocks. He maintains a portfolio of roughly 150 names, about 100 fewer than foreign manager Bill Kennedy, who prefers a sprawling portfolio that includes some emerging-markets and smaller-cap exposure. Feingold will keep assets split evenly between U.S. and foreign stocks. Fidelity does not hedge foreign-currency exposure.

Performance 12-31-06

	1st Qtr	2nd Qtr	3rd Qtr	4th Qtr	Total
2002	2.32	-8.80	-17.69	5.68	-18.83
2003	-6.23	20.92	7.35	13.71	38.41
2004	3.36	-1.06	-2.15	12.18	12.24
2005	-1.75	0.33	8.39	6.29	13.57
2006	5.67	-1.31	3.04	9.27	17.42

Trailing	Total Return%	+/- MSCI EAFE	+/- MSCI World	%Rank Cat	Growth of $10,000
3 Mo	9.27	-1.08	0.90	37	10,927
6 Mo	12.59	-2.10	-0.62	58	11,259
1 Yr	17.42	-8.92	-2.65	69	11,742
3 Yr Avg	14.39	-5.54	-0.29	62	14,968
5 Yr Avg	10.96	-4.02	0.99	48	16,820
10 Yr Avg	8.59	0.88	0.95	50	22,798
15 Yr Avg	10.27	2.41	1.58	50	43,337

Tax Analysis	Tax-Adj Rtn%	%Rank Cat	Tax-Cost Rat	%Rank Cat
3 Yr (estimated)	12.95	65	1.26	67
5 Yr (estimated)	10.07	48	0.80	62
10 Yr (estimated)	7.19	50	1.29	66

Potential Capital Gain Exposure: 20% of assets

Historical Profile

Return	Average
Risk	Average
Rating	★★★ Neutral

82% 92% 90% 88% 96% 95% 96% 98% 98%

▼ Manager Change
▽ Partial Manager Change

Growth of $10,000
— Investment Values of Fund
— Investment Values of MSCI EAFE

26.0 / 22.0 / 18.0 / 14.0 / 10.0

Performance Quartile (within Category)

1995	1996	1997	1998	1999	2000	2001	2002	2003	2004	2005	2006	History
13.44	15.39	15.95	16.53	19.90	15.63	14.66	11.88	16.37	18.25	19.57	20.11	NAV
7.19	18.72	12.08	7.18	30.80	-8.01	-6.21	-18.83	38.41	12.24	13.57	17.42	Total Return %
-4.02	12.67	10.30	-12.75	3.77	6.18	15.21	-2.89	-0.18	-8.01	0.03	-8.92	+/-MSCI EAFE
-13.53	5.24	-3.68	-17.14	5.85	5.18	10.59	1.06	5.30	-2.48	4.08	-2.65	+/-MSCI World
1.18	1.26	0.71	0.63	0.60	2.01	0.00	0.14	0.59	0.61	0.55	0.87	Income Return %
6.01	17.46	11.37	6.55	30.20	-10.02	-6.21	-18.97	37.82	11.63	13.02	16.55	Capital Return %
91	32	66	75	50	48	14	45	31	78	38	69	Total Rtn % Rank Cat
0.15	0.17	0.11	0.10	0.10	0.40	0.00	0.02	0.07	0.10	0.10	0.17	Income $
0.00	0.38	1.16	0.44	1.52	2.25	0.00	0.00	0.00	1.04	2.66	Capital Gains $
1.16	1.18	1.16	1.12	1.07	1.04	1.05	1.20	1.28	1.19	1.01	—	Expense Ratio %
2.05	1.71	1.24	0.91	0.47	0.48	0.29	0.19	0.28	0.29	0.82	—	Income Ratio %
70	49	85	100	164	235	152	120	106	95	93	—	Turnover Rate %
654	926	1,145	1,014	1,125	928	807	642	957	1,169	1,278	1,377	Net Assets $mil

Investment Style
Equity
Stock %

Rating and Risk

Time Period	Load-Adj Return %	Morningstar Rtn vs Cat	Morningstar Risk vs Cat	Morningstar Risk-Adj Rating
1 Yr	17.42			
3 Yr	14.39	Avg	Avg	★★★
5 Yr	10.96	Avg	Avg	★★★
10 Yr	8.59	Avg	Avg	★★★
Incept	8.97			

Other Measures	Standard Index MSCI EAFE	Best Fit Index MSCI World
Alpha	-3.7	-0.3
Beta	0.93	1.12
R-Squared	86	95
Standard Deviation	9.50	
Mean	14.39	
Sharpe Ratio	1.14	

Portfolio Analysis 10-31-06

Share change since 07-06 Total Stocks:401	Sector	Country	% Assets
⊕ ExxonMobil Corporation	Energy	United States	2.04
⊕ Procter & Gamble Company	Goods	United States	1.84
⊕ ABB ADR	Ind Mtrls	Switzerland	1.73
⊖ Merck & Co., Inc.	Health	United States	1.37
⊖ PepsiCo, Inc.	Goods	United States	1.26
⊖ Google, Inc.	Business	United States	1.20
⊕ Apple Computer, Inc.	Hardware	United States	1.17
⊕ General Dynamics	Ind Mtrls	United States	1.10
⊕ Avon Products	Goods	United States	1.10
⊕ State Street Corporation	Financial	United States	1.07
⊖ Northern Trust Corporati	Financial	United States	1.04
⊖ Roche Holding	Health	Switzerland	1.03
⊖ Nintendo	Goods	Japan	1.02
✴ Microsoft Corporation	Software	United States	0.99
⊖ American International G	Financial	United States	0.97
⊕ Federated Department Sto	Consumer	United States	0.95
⊖ Allergan, Inc.	Health	United States	0.95
⊖ Johnson & Johnson	Health	United States	0.91
⊕ J.C. Penney Company, Inc	Consumer	United States	0.87
✴ Time Warner, Inc.	Media	United States	0.86

Current Investment Style

Value Blnd Growth — Large Mid Small

Market Cap	%
Giant	45.5
Large	33.5
Mid	16.7
Small	3.6
Micro	0.8
Avg $mil:	26,678

Value Measures		Rel Category
Price/Earnings	17.36	1.13
Price/Book	2.69	1.13
Price/Sales	1.44	1.10
Price/Cash Flow	9.37	1.08
Dividend Yield %	1.92	0.88

Growth Measures	%	Rel Category
Long-Term Erngs	12.63	1.00
Book Value	10.92	1.22
Sales	8.26	0.99
Cash Flow	9.40	0.96
Historical Erngs	22.19	1.18

Composition

Cash	1.3	Bonds	0.0
Stocks	98.3	Other	0.4
Foreign (% of Stock)			54.8

Sector Weightings	% of Stocks	Rel MSCI EAFE	3 Year High	Low
⌚ Info	13.66	1.16		
▣ Software	2.72	4.86	4	1
▣ Hardware	4.38	1.13	17	4
▣ Media	2.10	1.15	6	1
▣ Telecom	4.46	0.80	9	3
⌗ Service	49.86	1.06		
▣ Health	9.71	1.36	13	10
▣ Consumer	9.15	1.85	11	5
▣ Business	6.50	1.28	8	3
▣ Financial	24.50	0.81	25	20
⌗ Mfg	36.49	0.89		
▣ Goods	13.94	1.06	14	7
▣ Ind Mtrls	11.33	0.73	14	11
▣ Energy	7.15	1.00	11	7
▣ Utilities	4.07	0.78	4	1

Regional Exposure	% Stock		
UK/W. Europe 35	N. America	46	
Japan	10	Latn America	2
Asia X Japan	6	Other	1

Country Exposure	% Stock		
United States 45	Switzerland	7	
Japan	10	France	7
U.K.	9		

Morningstar's Take by Dan Lefkovitz 11-15-06

We have yet to get comfortable with Fidelity Worldwide's flip-flops.

A January 1, 2006, manager change didn't alter this global fund's basic structure. The portfolio is still split roughly in half, with one manager picking foreign stocks and the other domestic.

But the fund has undergone two interesting reversals. For one, the fund's lead manager, who determines the portfolio's overall global allocation, is domestic manager Jeff Feingold. Under the old regime, foreign stock-picker Rick Mace was lead. This is of some concern because Feingold is greener than Mace was. He has shown promise on some sector funds he's run, including Select Financial Services, but he lacks much of a track record as a diversified fund manager.

The other flip-flop pertains to investment approaches. In the past, Rick Mace ran the foreign sleeve in aggressive fashion. He tended to hold 100-150 stocks and would take big bets on certain sectors and regions (he was especially fond of

technology and Asia). Meanwhile, domestic manager Brian Hogan was more cautious. He held more stocks, was more valuation-sensitive, and managed closer to the S&P 500.

These days, there's more caution on the foreign side of the portfolio and more bets being taken on the domestic side. Foreign manager Bill Kennedy maintains a sprawling portfolio, just as he has done (successfully) for the past two years on Fidelity International Discovery and for several years before that on Fidelity Pacific Basin. Feingold has shown himself willing to hold fewer stocks, take bigger positions (almost all the top 20 holdings as of April 30, 2006, were U.S. based), and buy racier stocks than his predecessor. Top-holding Google is a prime example. The fund has lagged so far under its new leadership, but even if it were shooting the lights out, Feingold's inexperience would give us pause. We'd either look to a different global fund or steer investors to separate foreign and domestic offerings.

Address:	82 Devonshire St Boston MA 02109 800-544-9797	Minimum Purchase:	$2500	Add: $250 IRA: $200
		Min Auto Inv Plan:	$100	Add: $100
		Sales Fees:	No-load, 1.00%R	
Web Address:	www.fidelity.com	Management Fee:	0.76%	
Inception:	05-30-90	Actual Fees:	Mgt:0.76%	Dist: —
Advisor:	Fidelity Management & Research (FMR)	Expense Projections:	3Yr:$343	5Yr:$595 10Yr:$1317
Subadvisor:	Multiple Subadvisors	Income Distrib:	Annually	
NTF Plans:	Fidelity Retail-NTF, CommonWealth NTF			

First Eagle Fund of Am Y

	Ticker	Load	NAV	Yield	Total Assets	Mstar Category
	FEAFX	Closed	$25.97	0.0%	$777 mil	Mid-Cap Blend

Governance and Management

Stewardship Grade:

Portfolio Manager(s)

Harold Levy and David Cohen have managed this fund since its 1987 inception. They work with an eight-person analyst team.

Strategy

Comanagers Harold Levy and David Cohen look for companies that are undergoing significant changes and selling for less than the managers' estimates of the companies' future cash flow values. Often, the changes affecting these companies are new management teams, major share repurchases, or elimination of a business segment.

Historical Profile
Return Average
Risk Low
Rating ★★★ Neutral

Investment Style
Equity
Stock %

85% 94% 98% 100% 81% 96% 99% 98% 88%

▼ Manager Change
▽ Partial Manager Change

Growth of $10,000
— Investment Values of Fund
— Investment Values of S&P 500

50.6
43.6
32.4
24.0
17.0
10.0

Performance Quartile (within Category)

	1995	1996	1997	1998	1999	2000	2001	2002	2003	2004	2005	2006	History
	16.96	18.30	19.33	21.43	20.56	20.47	21.58	20.02	23.99	26.06	25.45	25.97	NAV
	36.40	29.34	29.46	20.99	12.09	0.32	8.25	-7.23	22.21	15.91	6.56	15.79	Total Return %
	-1.18	6.38	-3.90	-7.59	-8.95	9.42	20.14	14.87	-6.47	5.03	1.65	0.00	+/-S&P 500
	5.47	10.09	-2.79	1.87	-2.63	-17.19	8.86	7.30	-13.41	-0.57	-6.00	5.47	+/-S&P Mid 400
	0.00	0.00	0.00	0.00	0.00	0.00	0.00	0.00	0.00	0.00	0.00	0.00	Income Return %
	36.40	29.34	29.46	20.99	12.09	0.32	8.25	-7.23	22.21	15.91	6.56	15.79	Capital Return %
	21	8	35	16	64	78	27	10	95	54	74	28	Total Rtn % Rank Cat
	0.00	0.00	0.00	0.00	0.00	0.00	0.00	0.00	0.00	0.00	0.00	0.00	Income $
	0.35	3.13	4.10	1.84	3.29	0.15	0.57	0.00	0.47	1.70	2.34	3.48	Capital Gains $
	1.90	1.80	1.70	1.50	1.40	1.40	1.40	1.51	1.50	1.46	1.43	—	Expense Ratio %
	-0.30	-0.20	-0.30	-0.40	-0.20	-0.20	-0.30	-0.82	-0.79	-0.63	-0.27	—	Income Ratio %
	81	93	98	83	55	55	83	51	44	45	55	—	Turnover Rate %
	136	171	269	457	528	375	422	473	480	654	696	680	Net Assets $mil

Performance 12-31-06

	1st Qtr	2nd Qtr	3rd Qtr	4th Qtr	Total
2002	4.36	-7.10	-7.46	3.41	-7.23
2003	-2.20	8.99	4.08	10.16	22.21
2004	5.71	1.10	-0.66	9.18	15.91
2005	0.08	0.38	3.13	2.85	6.56
2006	5.97	-1.37	3.42	7.12	15.79

Trailing	Total Return%	+/- S&P 500	+/- S&P Mid 400	%Rank Cat	Growth of $10,000
3 Mo	7.12	0.42	0.13	56	10,712
6 Mo	10.78	-1.96	4.95	30	11,078
1 Yr	15.79	0.00	5.47	28	11,579
3 Yr Avg	12.67	2.23	-0.42	49	14,303
5 Yr Avg	10.15	3.96	-0.74	51	16,215
10 Yr Avg	11.95	3.53	-1.52	48	30,920
15 Yr Avg	15.04	4.40	1.41	9	81,796

Tax Analysis	Tax-Adj Rtn%	%Rank Cat	Tax-Cost Rat	%Rank Cat
3 Yr (estimated)	10.86	53	1.61	65
5 Yr (estimated)	9.02	54	1.03	65
10 Yr (estimated)	10.26	38	1.51	38

Potential Capital Gain Exposure: 22% of assets

Rating and Risk

Time Period	Load-Adj Return %	Morningstar Rtn vs Cat	Morningstar Risk vs Cat	Morningstar Risk-Adj Rating
1 Yr	15.79			
3 Yr	12.67	Avg	Low	★★★
5 Yr	10.15	Avg	Low	★★★
10 Yr	11.95	Avg	Low	★★★★
Incept	13.53			

Other Measures	Standard Index S&P 500	Best Fit Index Mstar Mid Core
Alpha	2.5	2.5
Beta	0.93	0.59
R-Squared	82	87
Standard Deviation	7.04	
Mean	12.67	
Sharpe Ratio	1.28	

Portfolio Analysis 10-31-06

Share change since 09-06 Total Stocks:48	Sector	PE	Tot Ret%	% Assets
⊖ Shire PLC ADR	Health	40.2	59.84	4.22
General Dynamics	Ind Mtrls	19.1	32.17	3.97
Dean Foods Company	Goods	22.0	12.27	3.97
Agilent Technologies, In	Hardware	11.5	11.21	3.95
Teekay Shipping Corporat	Business	6.3	11.72	3.72
⊖ DST Systems, Inc.	Business	14.4	4.54	3.66
⊕ Alltel Corp.	Telecom	18.1	19.54	3.62
Autoliv, Inc.	Ind Mtrls	13.6	36.13	3.33
Ball Corporation	Goods	14.3	10.87	3.31
Tyco International, Ltd.	Ind Mtrls	15.7	6.83	3.31
Black & Decker Corporati	Ind Mtrls	12.2	-6.37	3.28
⊖ Constellation Energy Gro	Utilities	17.6	22.70	3.01
UAP Holding Corporation	Ind Mtrls	24.9	27.68	2.87
⊕ American Standard Compan	Consumer	19.3	16.74	2.65
Baxter International Inc	Health	24.3	24.81	2.40
⊖ Valeant Pharmaceuticals	Health	—	-3.43	2.37
Theravance, Inc.	Health	—	37.17	2.18
Edwards Lifesciences Cor	Health	25.7	13.05	2.05
Crown Holdings, Inc.	Goods	—	7.12	2.04
⊖ Grant Prideco, Inc.	Energy	15.2	-9.86	2.00

Current Investment Style

Value Blnd Growth — Large Mid Small

Market Cap | %
Giant | 3.7
Large | 24.2
Mid | 57.2
Small | 14.0
Micro | 0.8

Avg $mil: 5,835

Value Measures		Rel Category
Price/Earnings	18.78	1.17
Price/Book	2.91	1.29
Price/Sales	1.08	0.96
Price/Cash Flow	11.94	1.41
Dividend Yield %	0.99	0.76

Growth Measures	%	Rel Category
Long-Term Erngs	11.99	0.95
Book Value	4.64	0.56
Sales	8.61	0.97
Cash Flow	-10.83	NMF
Historical Erngs	21.50	1.20

Profitability	%	Rel Category
Return on Equity	16.05	1.01
Return on Assets	3.82	0.48
Net Margin	6.44	0.59

Sector Weightings	% of Stocks	Rel S&P 500	3 Year High Low
↻ Info	12.80	0.64	
Software	0.00	0.00	0 0
Hardware	4.47	0.48	11 4
Media	0.23	0.06	1 0
Telecom	8.10	2.31	9 4
⊂ Service	39.33	0.85	
Health	27.73	2.30	35 28
Consumer	3.00	0.39	9 2
Business	8.60	2.03	9 3
Financial	0.00	0.00	1 0
⊔ Mfg	47.89	1.42	
Goods	13.13	1.54	26 10
Ind Mtrls	25.13	2.10	25 14
Energy	6.23	0.64	11 0
Utilities	3.40	0.97	4 0

Composition
● Cash 10.1
● Stocks 88.4
● Bonds 0.0
● Other 1.5
Foreign 9.0
(% of Stock)

Morningstar's Take by Gregg Wolper 11-29-06

First Eagle Fund of America's risk-aversion is an attractive trait that shouldn't be overlooked.

Many investors don't truly mean it when they say they could care less about a fund keeping risks in check and not just getting the highest return possible. They start taking that aspect into account only after their fund tanks. But those who do mean what they say should like this fund. Managers Harold Levy and David Cohen have shown over the years that they take risk control seriously, while still providing solid long-term gains.

The numbers support the point. As measured by standard deviation, for both the trailing five-year and 10-year periods, this fund has been one of the least volatile of any in the mid-blend category. (It's an all-cap portfolio but taken as a whole, it typically has characteristics that land it in mid-blend territory.) During the bear-market period in the early part of this decade, this fund held up far better than most. Although the fund does not usually shine during the strongest rallies, its 10-year and 15-year returns (Levy and Cohen have been in place since 1987) are impressive.

They have achieved this record by owning companies they feel are cheap because investors are overemphasizing the negative factors. Levy says he bought Shire, a drug company, in early 2003 when its stock had plunged after investors panicked over negative news. The managers thought it had great potential though, and it has been a stellar performer ever since (it is a top-five holding and is up 58% in 2006 through Nov. 29). They also bought HealthSouth after its stock tanked when the firm gained notoriety for corporate misbehavior. Levy says he and Cohen like the new management team and its reform plans, and they're sticking with it even though the stock has fallen since their purchase.

With risk-aware, long-tenured managers who are willing to be patient and go against the grain, this fund is worth investigating.

Address:	1345 Avenue of the Americas	Minimum Purchase:	Closed	Add: —	IRA: —
	New York NY 10105	Min Auto Inv Plan:	Closed	Add: —	
	800-334-2143	Sales Fees:	No-load, 0.25%S, 2.00%R		
Web Address:	www.firsteaglefunds.com	Management Fee:	1.00%		
Inception:	04-10-87	Actual Fees:	Mgt:1.00%	Dist:0.25%	
Advisor:	Arnhold and Bleichroeder Advisers, LLC	Expense Projections:	3Yr:$452	5Yr:$782	10Yr:$1713
Subadvisor:	Iridian Asset Management LLC	Income Distrib:	Annually		
NTF Plans:	Fidelity Retail-NTF, Schwab OneSource				

MORNINGSTAR® Funds 500

First Eagle Glbl A

	Ticker	Load	NAV	Yield	Total Assets	Mstar Category
	SGENX	Closed	$45.80	2.5%	$20,089 mil	World Allocation

Governance and Management

Stewardship Grade: A

Portfolio Manager(s)

Manager Charles de Vaulx began working on this fund in 1987 as an analyst, gradually took on more responsibility, and became a full comanager in 1999. (Jean-Marie Eveillard was lead manager from 1979 through 1999 and then co-lead manager with De Vaulx until retiring at the end of 2004.) De Vaulx works with a group of nine in-house analysts. This group also makes the calls for siblings First Eagle Overseas, First Eagle Gold, and First Eagle U.S. Value.

Strategy

This was one of the first funds to take a value approach worldwide, and it is still run according to those precepts. Management errs on the side of caution, favoring securities whose assets and cash flows appear undervalued by the market. Broad diversification also helps reduce risk. The fund invests more in stocks and less in bonds than most category rivals. It favors smaller and midsized stocks but often buys big companies, too. The manager engages in currency hedging; he considers a 50% hedged position against a particular currency to be neutral, but he often veers far away from that level.

Performance 12-31-06

	1st Qtr	2nd Qtr	3rd Qtr	4th Qtr	Total
2002	8.02	-8.17	-8.17	9.18	10.23
2003	-2.13	15.72	8.46	12.05	37.64
2004	5.46	-0.43	2.57	9.89	18.37
2005	2.58	-0.03	8.22	3.54	14.91
2006	7.77	1.30	2.63	7.54	20.50

Trailing	Total Return%	+/- DJ Mod	+/- MSCI World	%Rank Cat	Growth of $10,000
3 Mo	7.54	1.95	-0.83	34	10,754
6 Mo	10.37	1.58	-2.84	40	11,037
1 Yr	20.50	8.20	0.43	33	12,050
3 Yr Avg	17.90	7.18	3.22	10	16,389
5 Yr Avg	19.99	9.97	10.02	3	24,873
10 Yr Avg	14.56	6.01	6.92	1	38,934
15 Yr Avg	14.01	4.80	5.32	1	71,473

Tax Analysis	Tax-Adj Rtn%	%Rank Cat	Tax-Cost Rat	%Rank Cat
3 Yr (estimated)	14.42	20	1.28	48
5 Yr (estimated)	17.31	7	1.22	61
10 Yr (estimated)	11.57	4	2.11	79

Potential Capital Gain Exposure: 23% of assets

Historical Profile

Return High
Risk Average
Rating ★★★★ Highest

	63%	72%	76%	76%	67%	62%	68%	70%	72%

Growth of $10,000
— Investment Values of Fund
— Investment Values of DJ Mod

Performance Quartile (within Category)

1995	1996	1997	1998	1999	2000	2001	2002	2003	2004	2005	2006	History
24.58	26.09	25.45	23.03	24.65	22.29	23.82	25.35	33.32	38.81	42.06	45.80	NAV
15.24	13.64	8.54	-0.26	19.56	9.72	10.21	10.23	37.64	18.37	14.91	20.50	Total Return %
-4.56	2.98	-3.36	-12.58	2.23	11.39	13.01	17.00	10.26	5.40	7.92	8.20	+/-DJ Mod
-5.48	0.16	-7.22	-24.58	-5.39	22.91	27.01	30.12	4.53	3.65	5.42	0.43	+/-MSCI World
3.58	4.43	5.21	4.20	4.65	5.64	2.83	2.06	2.66	1.29	2.18	2.91	Income Return %
11.66	9.21	3.33	-4.46	14.91	4.08	7.38	8.17	34.98	17.08	12.73	17.59	Capital Return %
83	65	86	91	64	29	4	3	3	5	14	33	Total Rtn % Rank Cat
0.81	1.09	1.36	1.07	1.07	1.39	0.63	0.49	0.68	0.43	0.85	1.23	Income $
0.73	0.74	1.47	1.35	1.73	3.19	0.09	0.40	0.85	0.18	1.68	3.63	Capital Gains $
1.26	1.25	1.21	1.19	1.23	1.32	1.40	1.34	1.32	1.24	1.20	—	Expense Ratio %
2.70	3.71	3.08	2.80	2.75	2.68	2.20	2.14	1.91	1.46	1.21	—	Income Ratio %
13	10	13	21	10	12	29	20	7	5	12	—	Turnover Rate %
2,613	3,777	3,998	2,634	1,905	1,651	1,611	1,976	3,738	7,171	10,038	12,249	Net Assets $mil

Investment Style
Equity
Stock %

▼ Manager Change
▽ Partial Manager Change

Rating and Risk

Time Period	Load-Adj Return %	Morningstar Rtn vs Cat	Morningstar Risk vs Cat	Morningstar Risk-Adj Rating
1 Yr	14.48			
3 Yr	15.90	+Avg	Avg	★★★★
5 Yr	18.76	High	Avg	★★★★★
10 Yr	13.97	High	-Avg	★★★★★
Incept	13.02			

Other Measures	Standard Index DJ Mod	Best Fit Index MSCI Wd xUS
Alpha	6.3	3.3
Beta	1.02	0.66
R-Squared	79	88
Standard Deviation	6.73	
Mean	17.90	
Sharpe Ratio	2.03	

Portfolio Analysis 10-31-06

Total Stocks:187
Share change since 09-30-06

	Sectors	P/E Ratio	YTD Return %	% Net Assets
Berkshire Hathaway Inc. A	Financial	—	—	2.67
⊕ Nestle	Goods	—	—	2.63
Sodexho Alliance	Consumer	—	—	2.34
⊕ Costco Wholesale Corporat	Consumer	23.3	1.44	2.27
⊖ Toyota Motor	Goods	—	—	2.12
⊕ Pargesa Holding	Financial	—	—	2.00
Microsoft Corporation	Software	23.8	0.23	1.83
Liberty Interactive A	Media	—	—	1.78
⊖ Johnson & Johnson	Health	17.5	0.74	1.60

Total Fixed-Income:42

	Date of Maturity	Amount $000	Value $000	% Net Assets
US Treasury Note 5.125%	06-30-11	266,593	272,706	1.40
France (Republic Of) 3%	07-25-12	105,397	144,693	0.74
UPC HOLDING B.V.	01-15-14	57,200	71,718	0.37
Malaysia	02-27-09	16,000	45,779	0.24
Upc Hldg B.V. 8.625%	01-15-14	34,750	45,455	0.23
US Treasury Note 4.25%	01-15-10	38,779	40,724	0.21
Singapore (Republic Of) 2	10-01-09	52,947	33,331	0.17
Lear 8.11%	05-15-09	30,742	31,318	0.16

Current Investment Style

Value Blnd Growth

Market Cap	%
Giant	34.5
Large	27.5
Mid	31.4
Small	5.2
Micro	1.4

Avg $mil: 15,389

Value Measures		Rel Category
Price/Earnings	16.73	1.10
Price/Book	2.04	0.90
Price/Sales	1.10	0.85
Price/Cash Flow	9.05	1.18
Dividend Yield %	2.07	0.71

Growth Measures	%	Rel Category
Long-Term Erngs	11.38	1.00
Book Value	7.90	0.96
Sales	8.01	1.24
Cash Flow	4.10	0.62
Historical Erngs	28.82	1.67

Composition

Cash	17.4	Bonds	5.3
Stocks	72.0	Other	5.3
Foreign (% of Stock)			54.8

Sector Weightings	% of Stocks	Rel DJ Mod	3 Year High Low	
⟳ Info	19.97	—		
🖥 Software	3.27	—	4	1
🖴 Hardware	2.31	—	2	0
🎙 Media	11.76	—	12	7
☎ Telecom	2.63	—	3	0
☞ Service	40.64			
🏥 Health	6.70	—	7	3
🛒 Consumer	15.37	—	15	9
🏢 Business	6.89	—	9	7
💲 Financial	11.68	—	13	10
🏭 Mfg	39.40			
🔧 Goods	19.09	—	23	16
⚙ Ind Mtrls	16.01	—	34	15
🔥 Energy	4.09	—	7	3
💡 Utilities	0.21	—	1	0

Regional Exposure % Stock

UK/W. Europe	34	N. America	46
Japan	12	Latn America	1
Asia X Japan	6	Other	1

Country Exposure % Stock

United States	45	Switzerland	9
France	14	South Korea	4
Japan	12		

Morningstar's Take by Gregg Wolper 12-23-06

First Eagle Global is a keeper--partly because it doesn't cause many worries.

This closed fund provides an appropriate home for those who want the growth potential of an equity-heavy allocation fund but don't want to take on a lot of risk. Manager Charles de Vaulx, who has been working on this fund for roughly two decades, has been a dedicated value investor all that time, and that's not going to change. And he trades much less than the norm for the world-allocation category (or just about any other category, for that matter). In fact, the fund's annual turnover rate hasn't been higher than 20% since 2001. Meanwhile, long-term performance is outstanding. And the fund has had a solid 2006 as well, beating roughly three fourths of its world-allocation rivals for the year to date through Dec. 22.

Despite the low turnover, De Vaulx does take action when he spots opportunity. For example, for years he (along with former comanager Jean-Marie Eveillard) shied away from technology stocks--not surprisingly, given the managers' strict value bent. But in 2005 De Vaulx added Microsoft to the fund's top 10, and in 2006 he bought another beaten-down tech name, Intel, which he thought had recovered its stride--and which he noted still holds a huge market share even after some stumbles. Those purchases are two reasons why the fund's U.S. stake, after falling to a record low in 2005 because De Vaulx just couldn't find any compelling choices at the right price, has grown sharply. Yet he retains the cautious streak that's helped this fund contain risk over the years: The fund's cash stake was at 17% at the end of October 2006.

Encouragingly, De Vaulx said in autumn 2006 that many recent purchases, both at home and abroad, are small and midsized. That means the fund's bulk isn't preventing him from mining the realms that played a big role in the fund's earlier success. All told, fundholders should be content here.

Address:	1345 Avenue of the Americas New York NY 10105 800-334-2143	Minimum Purchase:	Closed	Add: —	IRA: —
Web Address:	www.firsteaglefunds.com	Min Auto Inv Plan:	Closed	Add: —	
Inception:	04-28-70	Sales Fees:	5.00%L, 0.25%S, 2.00%R		
Advisor:	Arnhold and Bleichroeder Advisers, LLC	Management Fee:	0.75%		
Subadvisor:	None	Actual Fees:	Mgt:0.75% Dist:0.25%		
		Expense Projections:	3Yr:$862 5Yr:$1127 10Yr:$1882		
NTF Plans:	DATALynx NTF, Federated Tr NTF	Income Distrib:	Annually		

First Eagle Overseas A

	Ticker	Load	NAV	Yield	Total Assets	Mstar Category
	SGOVX	Closed	$25.08	3.2%	$11,362 mil	Foreign Small/Mid Value

Governance and Management

Stewardship Grade: A

Portfolio Manager(s)

Manager Charles de Vaulx has been closely involved with this fund's investment decisions since its 1993 inception. He was named comanager in 1999 alongside Jean-Marie Eveillard, who had been sole manager from inception to that time. De Vaulx became sole manager in January 2005 after Eveillard's retirement. De Vaulx works with a group of nine in-house analysts. He also runs siblings First Eagle Global, First Eagle Gold, and First Eagle U.S. Value. De Vaulx started working with Eveillard as an analyst at First Eagle's predecessor firm, SoGen Asset Management, in 1987.

Strategy

This fund seeks firms of any size (although it has typically favored smaller and midsize companies) that management thinks are cheap relative to the value of their underlying assets or cash flows and have strong positions in their industry. Management also typically owns a small number of bonds and gold-related assets and sometimes holds big cash stakes. The fund charges a 2% redemption fee on shares held fewer than 90 days. It typically hedges some of its currency exposure; it considers a 50% hedged stance to be neutral, but it often goes above or below that.

Performance 12-31-06

	1st Qtr	2nd Qtr	3rd Qtr	4th Qtr	Total
2002	9.32	4.26	-10.51	10.33	12.53
2003	-1.95	16.64	10.72	11.68	41.41
2004	6.60	-0.15	2.95	11.18	21.83
2005	4.00	-0.71	8.90	3.98	16.92
2006	9.29	2.10	2.26	7.18	22.29

Trailing	Total Return%	+/- MSCI EAFE	+/- MSCI Wd xUS	%Rank Cat	Growth of $10,000
3 Mo	7.18	-3.17	-2.94	97	10,718
6 Mo	9.59	-5.10	-4.63	97	10,959
1 Yr	22.29	-4.05	-3.42	79	12,229
3 Yr Avg	20.32	0.39	0.22	71	17,419
5 Yr Avg	22.62	7.64	7.37	20	27,721
10 Yr Avg	15.82	8.11	7.86	28	43,435
15 Yr Avg	—	—	—		—

Tax Analysis	Tax-Adj Rtn%	%Rank Cat	Tax-Cost Rat	%Rank Cat
3 Yr (estimated)	16.32	76	1.66	49
5 Yr (estimated)	19.75	37	1.33	48
10 Yr (estimated)	12.79	46	2.11	91

Potential Capital Gain Exposure: 28% of assets

Morningstar's Take by Gregg Wolper 12-05-06

First Eagle Overseas' cautious approach can both help it and hold it back, but over the long term the benefits tend to win out.

For most of 2006, foreign markets have performed strongly--and the strength of most foreign currencies versus the U.S. dollar provided further gains for U.S.-based funds. So, funds that have been fully invested (and fully exposed to those currencies) have been in the best position to take advantage of the rallies. But although this fund was nearly unhedged (it isn't always that way), it was held back by a large cash stake. For several years, manager Charles de Vaulx has had difficulty finding enough suitable stocks to fill the portfolio, leading to a big cash pile (and the fund's closure in 2004). The cash stake was 24.7% at the end of October 2006, and it's been around that level most of the year. So, the fund's year-to-date return lags more than two thirds of its rivals in the foreign small-/mid-value category through Dec. 4, 2006.

This year's story doesn't end there, though.

Foreign markets sustained sharp losses in the late spring after a long rally, with some emerging markets plunging more than 20% in value in a little more than a month's time. Not surprisingly, this fund held up better than most, and in early July its year-to-date return actually topped two thirds of its peers. Only because of the subsequent sharp rebound has the fund fallen behind again. Should markets struggle for a longer stretch, the benefit of this fund's wariness will be more clear.

Meanwhile, it's not as if shareholders have been starved of gains: The fund is up 20.9% for the year to date. More importantly, fueled by a strategy that finds unloved stocks that typically recover, the fund's trailing five- and 10-year returns each top about three fourths of its category peers. Thus, shareholders need not think they own a cash equivalent, suitable only for bear markets. Instead, they've got one of the better value-oriented options around.

Address:	1345 Avenue of the Americas
	New York NY 10105
	800-334-2143
Web Address:	www.firsteaglefunds.com
Inception:	08-31-93
Advisor:	Arnhold and Bleichroeder Advisers, LLC
Subadvisor:	None
NTF Plans:	DATALynx NTF, Federated Tr NTF

Minimum Purchase:	Closed	Add: —	IRA: —
Min Auto Inv Plan:	Closed	Add: —	
Sales Fees:	5.00%L, 0.25%S, 2.00%R		
Management Fee:	0.75%		
Actual Fees:	Mgt:0.75%	Dist:0.25%	
Expense Projections:	3Yr:$856	5Yr:$1117	10Yr:$1860
Income Distrib:	Annually		

Historical Profile

Return	Average
Risk	Low
Rating	★★★★ Above Avg

| 76% | 84% | 89% | 92% | 74% | 67% | 74% | 66% | 64% |

Investment Style
Equity
Stock %

▼ Manager Change
▽ Partial Manager Change

Growth of $10,000
■ Investment Values of Fund
— Investment Values of MSCI EAFE

50.6
43.6
32.4
24.0
17.0
10.0

Performance Quartile
(within Category)

1995	1996	1997	1998	1999	2000	2001	2002	2003	2004	2005	2006	History
12.46	13.28	12.15	11.19	14.06	11.41	12.02	13.30	18.17	21.77	23.04	25.08	NAV
11.79	14.53	3.02	2.53	33.19	5.68	5.35	12.53	41.41	21.83	16.92	22.29	Total Return %
0.58	8.48	1.24	-17.40	6.16	19.87	26.77	28.47	2.82	1.58	3.38	-4.05	+/-MSCI EAFE
0.38	7.66	0.75	-16.16	5.21	19.04	26.74	28.33	1.99	1.45	2.45	-3.42	+/-MSCI Wd xUS
3.74	4.82	6.21	4.67	1.56	5.41	0.00	1.75	3.57	1.32	3.74	3.78	Income Return %
8.05	9.71	-3.19	-2.14	31.63	0.27	5.35	10.78	37.84	20.51	13.18	18.51	Capital Return %
10	81	37	92	57	6	5	2	87	52	65	79	Total Rtn % Rank Cat
0.44	0.60	0.83	0.57	0.18	0.76	0.00	0.21	0.48	0.24	0.81	0.87	Income $
0.17	0.38	0.69	0.77	0.64	2.64	0.00	0.01	0.14	0.11	1.58	2.20	Capital Gains $
1.40	1.37	1.27	1.22	1.29	1.34	1.50	1.39	1.31	1.25	1.18	—	Expense Ratio %
2.29	3.31	2.28	2.20	2.22	2.10	2.00	0.96	1.23	0.90	1.21	—	Income Ratio %
3	9	15	22	9	17	17	11	3	6	19	—	Turnover Rate %
543	850	964	593	484	388	450	912	2,944	4,267	5,110	5,993	Net Assets $mil

Rating and Risk

Time Period	Load-Adj Return %	Morningstar Rtn vs Cat	Morningstar Risk vs Cat	Morningstar Risk-Adj Rating
1 Yr	16.18			
3 Yr	18.28	Low	Low	★★
5 Yr	21.37	Avg	Low	★★★
10 Yr	15.22	+Avg	Low	★★★★★
Incept	14.69			

Other Measures	Standard Index MSCI EAFE	Best Fit Index MSCI Wd xUS
Alpha	4.3	4.3
Beta	0.74	0.73
R-Squared	85	86
Standard Deviation	7.50	
Mean	20.32	
Sharpe Ratio	2.10	

Portfolio Analysis 10-31-06

Share change since 09-06 Total Stocks:172	Sector	Country	% Assets
⊕ Nestle	Goods	Switzerland	3.03
⊖ Gold Commodity In Ounces	—		2.62
⊖ Toyota Motor	Goods	Japan	2.52
Wendel Investissement	Ind Mtrls	France	2.41
⊖ Sodexho Alliance	Consumer	France	2.40
Pargesa Holding	Financial	Switzerland	2.11
Samsung Electnc	—	Korea	1.94
Tesco	Consumer	U.K.	1.71
Vivendi Universal	Media	France	1.62
⊕ France (Republic Of) 3%	—	France	1.52
Kuehne & Nagel Int'l	Business	Switzerland	1.51
⊕ Shimano	Ind Mtrls	Japan	1.31
⊖ Corporacion Financiera A	Financial	Spain	1.28
Essilor Int'l	Health	France	1.21
L'Oreal	Goods	France	1.07
Aioi Insurance	Financial	Japan	1.01
Ono Pharmaceutical	Health	Japan	1.00
⊖ Vodafone Grp	Telecom	U.K.	0.95
Heineken Holding	Goods	Netherlands	0.95
⊕ Remy Cointreau	Goods	France	0.93

Current Investment Style

Value Blnd Growth — Large/Mid/Small

	Market Cap	%
	Giant	24.8
	Large	21.8
	Mid	38.5
	Small	13.2
	Micro	1.6
	Avg $mil: 7,066	

Value Measures		Rel Category
Price/Earnings	16.58	1.13
Price/Book	1.75	0.88
Price/Sales	1.10	1.24
Price/Cash Flow	8.25	1.31
Dividend Yield %	2.24	0.85

Growth Measures	%	Rel Category
Long-Term Erngs	11.95	0.80
Book Value	9.95	1.29
Sales	5.90	0.80
Cash Flow	2.98	0.33
Historical Erngs	33.70	1.73

Composition

Cash	25.2	Bonds	4.5
Stocks	63.8	Other	6.5
Foreign (% of Stock)			98.2

Sector Weightings

	% of Stocks	Rel MSCI EAFE	3 Year High	Low
☍ Info	11.58	0.98		
🖥 Software	0.66	1.18	1	0
💻 Hardware	0.91	0.24	1	0
📺 Media	6.56	3.58	7	5
☎ Telecom	3.45	0.62	4	0
⊛ Service	34.99	0.74		
🏥 Health	4.56	0.64	5	2
🛒 Consumer	9.75	1.97	11	7
📋 Business	8.29	1.64	10	8
💲 Financial	12.39	0.41	14	11
⬒ Mfg	53.42	1.30		
⚒ Goods	27.84	2.12	30	22
⚙ Ind Mtrls	23.86	1.55	35	23
⛽ Energy	1.72	0.24	4	1
💡 Utilities	0.00	0.00	1	0

Regional Exposure % Stock

UK/W. Europe	58	N. America	4
Japan	22	Latn America	3
Asia X Japan	12	Other	1

Country Exposure % Stock

France	23	U.K.	8
Japan	22	South Korea	6
Switzerland	13		

MORNINGSTAR® Funds 500

Forward Hoover Sm-Cp Eq

	Ticker	Load	NAV	Yield	Total Assets	Mstar Category
	FFSCX	None	$20.47	0.1%	$548 mil	Small Growth

Governance and Management

Stewardship Grade: C

Portfolio Manager(s)

Manager Irene Hoover has headed this offering since its 1998 inception and had done well at her previous charge, Jurika & Voyles Small-Cap Fund.

Strategy

Irene Hoover looks for growth companies trading at realistic price multiples. She utilizes various valuation metrics, preferring a stock's P/E ratio to be less than two thirds of her estimate of the firm's earnings-growth rate. She also looks for catalysts, such as societal themes, management changes, or spin-offs, that are likely to produce higher growth rates.

Historical Profile
Return Above Avg
Risk Below Avg
Rating ★★★★ Above Avg

Investment Style
Equity
Stock %

▼ Manager Change
▽ Partial Manager Change

Growth of $10,000
— Investment Values of Fund
— Investment Values of S&P 500

23.8
19.6
16.0
13.0
10.0

Performance Quartile (within Category)

	1995	1996	1997	1998	1999	2000	2001	2002	2003	2004	2005	2006	History
	—	—	—	11.39	12.19	14.26	14.78	12.05	16.17	18.45	19.40	20.47	NAV
	—	—	—	13.99*	7.03	17.88	4.27	-18.47	36.49	22.77	9.63	9.43	Total Return %
	—	—	—	—	-14.01	26.98	16.16	3.63	7.81	11.89	4.72	-6.36	+/-S&P 500
	—	—	—	—	-36.06	40.31	13.50	11.79	-12.05	8.46	5.48	-3.92	+/-Russ 2000 Gr
	—	—	—	—	0.01	0.00	0.00	0.00	0.00	0.00	0.00	0.09	Income Return %
	—	—	—	—	7.02	17.88	4.27	-18.47	36.49	22.77	9.63	9.34	Capital Return %
	—	—	—	—	94	8	20	12	83	8	22	58	Total Rtn % Rank Cat
	—	—	—	0.01	0.00	0.00	0.00	0.00	0.00	0.00	0.00	0.02	Income $
	—	—	—	0.00	0.00	0.11	0.09	0.00	0.28	1.41	0.82	0.75	Capital Gains $
	—	—	—	1.45	1.45	1.64	1.65	1.85	1.83	1.78	1.73	—	Expense Ratio %
	—	—	—	0.21	-0.54	-1.06	-1.04	-1.34	-1.28	-1.21	-0.96	—	Income Ratio %
	—	—	—	23	134	183	140	147	190	207	181	—	Turnover Rate %
	—	—	—	30	47	97	116	92	128	187	322	408	Net Assets $mil

Performance 12-31-06

	1st Qtr	2nd Qtr	3rd Qtr	4th Qtr	Total
2002	4.74	-9.30	-17.88	4.51	-18.47
2003	-2.57	16.35	8.71	10.75	36.49
2004	5.32	4.52	-1.69	13.44	22.77
2005	-4.17	7.01	5.50	1.33	9.63
2006	14.62	-8.55	-2.36	6.92	9.43

Trailing	Total Return%	+/- S&P 500	+/- Russ 2000 Gr	%Rank Cat	Growth of $10,000
3 Mo	6.92	0.22	-1.85	67	10,692
6 Mo	4.39	-8.35	-2.47	60	10,439
1 Yr	9.43	-6.36	-3.92	58	10,943
3 Yr Avg	13.77	3.33	3.26	13	14,726
5 Yr Avg	10.38	4.19	3.45	16	16,385
10 Yr Avg	—	—	—	—	—
15 Yr Avg	—	—	—	—	—

Tax Analysis	Tax-Adj Rtn%	%Rank Cat	Tax-Cost Rat	%Rank Cat
3 Yr (estimated)	12.79	10	0.86	33
5 Yr (estimated)	9.76	12	0.56	32
10 Yr (estimated)	—	—	—	—

Potential Capital Gain Exposure: 18% of assets

Rating and Risk

Time Period	Load-Adj Return %	Morningstar Rtn vs Cat	Morningstar Risk vs Cat	Morningstar Risk-Adj Rating
1 Yr	9.43			
3 Yr	13.77	+Avg	Avg	★★★★
5 Yr	10.38	+Avg	-Avg	★★★★
10 Yr	—	—	—	—
Incept	11.51			

Other Measures	Standard Index S&P 500	Best Fit Index Russ 2000 Gr
Alpha	-1.1	3.8
Beta	1.69	0.86
R-Squared	67	93
Standard Deviation	14.15	
Mean	13.77	
Sharpe Ratio	0.76	

Morningstar's Take by Marta Norton 12-20-06

Forward Hoover Small Cap Equity's expenses are its fatal flaw.

This fund tries to avoid risk from a variety of different angles. Because manager Irene Hoover knows that small-cap stocks tend to trade less frequently than their larger peers, she begins her process by screening the small-cap universe for stocks with adequate trading volume. (She likes to find stocks trading greater than $1.5 million a day.) Hoover also tries to avoid stocks owned by big institutions. Such investors traffic in big blocks of shares, which further complicates a small-cap stock's liquidity. Hoover then attempts to limit stock-specific risk by searching for companies with low levels of debt and strong, consistent earnings. And by investing in stocks whose valuations underestimate their future earnings, the fund has a margin of safety against falling stock prices.

Its taste for financially healthy companies leads the fund to firms in niche industries that produce recurring revenues. Corrections Corp of America, an owner and operator of prisons, is a good example of this because the company receives a continuous revenue stream from state and Federal governments. Conversely, the fund generally has been light in technology and health care because many small companies in those sectors often have nonexistent or volatile earnings streams.

This strategy has produced strong long-term returns. The fund returned 10.8% over the five-year period ending Dec. 18, 2006. That's higher than the vast majority of its peers, and it's been achieved with below-average volatility as measured by its standard deviation.

Its sensible strategy would make the fund an easy recommendation if it weren't for its excessive expense ratio. Even with a fee waiver, the fund's 1.69% expense ratio is much higher than the 1.26% median for no-load small-cap funds. Given that high expenses significantly reduce what investors earn, we can't recommend the fund.

Portfolio Analysis 11-30-06

Share change since 10-06 Total Stocks:110

	Sector	PE	Tot Ret%	% Assets
⊕ TeleTech Holdings, Inc.	Business	44.5	98.17	1.95
⊕ Manitowoc Company, Inc.	Business	27.2	137.42	1.70
⊕ United Natural Foods, In	Consumer	31.1	36.06	1.52
⊖ The Geo Group, Inc.	Business	58.2	145.44	1.51
Goodrich Petroleum Corpo	Energy	31.1	43.86	1.49
⊖ Waddell & Reed Financial	Financial	62.4	34.04	1.40
⊕ Hibbett Sporting Goods,	Consumer	29.8	7.20	1.39
⊕ AAR Corporation	Ind Mtrls	26.2	21.88	1.38
Urban Outfitters Inc.	Consumer	34.0	-9.01	1.37
Cohen & Steers, Inc.	Financial	—	119.24	1.35
⊖ Corrections Corporation	Business	28.1	50.87	1.32
⊕ Pediatrix Medical Group,	Health	25.0	10.42	1.31
Rackable Systems, Inc.	Hardware	—	—	1.27
Pan American Silver Corp	Ind Mtrls	—	33.67	1.26
Hain Celestial Group, In	Goods	31.3	47.50	1.26
⊖ Avocent Corporation	Hardware	34.7	24.49	1.25
Delta Petroleum Corporat	Energy	NMF	6.39	1.24
⊕ SRA International, Inc.	Business	25.3	-12.44	1.20
⊕ Quicksilver Resources, I	Energy	26.3	-12.90	1.20
Digital Realty Trust, In	Financial	72.5	57.16	1.17

Current Investment Style

Value Blnd Growth — Large Mid Small

Market Cap	%
Giant	0.0
Large	0.0
Mid	34.6
Small	62.8
Micro	2.5

Avg $mil: 1,489

Value Measures		Rel Category
Price/Earnings	20.16	0.96
Price/Book	2.79	1.02
Price/Sales	1.35	0.86
Price/Cash Flow	11.15	1.16
Dividend Yield %	0.85	1.85

Growth Measures	%	Rel Category
Long-Term Erngs	15.64	0.88
Book Value	8.49	0.81
Sales	12.42	1.04
Cash Flow	4.09	0.19
Historical Erngs	18.40	0.76

Profitability	%	Rel Category
Return on Equity	13.82	1.11
Return on Assets	7.44	1.12
Net Margin	7.85	0.91

Sector Weightings

	% of Stocks	Rel S&P 500	3 Year High Low	
⊙ Info	9.77	0.49		
🖳 Software	2.67	0.77	9	1
🖥 Hardware	6.38	0.69	15	3
🎙 Media	0.72	0.19	1	0
📶 Telecom	0.00	0.00	3	0
⚙ Service	54.66	1.18		
🏥 Health	7.69	0.64	16	5
🛒 Consumer	20.72	2.71	24	12
🏢 Business	11.41	2.70	15	4
💲 Financial	14.84	0.67	23	8
⚒ Mfg	35.58	1.05		
🛒 Goods	7.95	0.93	9	1
⚙ Ind Mtrls	12.96	1.09	21	7
🔋 Energy	10.68	1.09	17	5
💡 Utilities	3.99	1.14	4	0

Composition

● Cash	0.0
● Stocks	100.0
● Bonds	0.0
● Other	0.0
Foreign (% of Stock)	2.0

Address:	433 California St. San Francisco CA 94104 800-999-6809
Web Address:	www.forwardfunds.com
Inception:	09-30-98*
Advisor:	Forward Managment, LLC
Subadvisor:	Hoover Investment Management Co., LLC
NTF Plans:	Fidelity Retail-NTF, Schwab OneSource

Minimum Purchase:	$4000	Add: $100	IRA: $4000
Min Auto Inv Plan:	$500	Add: $100	
Sales Fees:	No-load, 0.25%S, 2.00%R		
Management Fee:	1.05% mx./1.00% mn.		
Actual Fees:	Mgt:1.04%	Dist:0.25%	
Expense Projections:	3Yr:$583	5Yr:$1019	10Yr:$2231
Income Distrib:	Annually		

Forward Intl Small Co Inv

	Ticker	Load	NAV	Yield	Total Assets	Mstar Category
	PISRX	None	$18.96	0.2%	$637 mil	Foreign Small/Mid Growth

Governance and Management

Stewardship Grade: B

Portfolio Manager(s)

Aylin Suntay was installed as the new lead manager when Nils Francke and Philippe Sarreau left the team in August 2006 and brought Oliver Knobloch along as another replacement. Michael McLaughlin, who covers Japanese and other Asian stocks, has been on the institutional version of this fund since April 1998. Justin Hill came on at the end of September 2001. Hill covers U.K. small caps.

Strategy

The fund's management team whittles the 10,000-stock international small-cap universe to an "active research list" of 1,500. From there, they run some quantitative analysis, using some proprietary measures, to come up with 250 stocks. The team performs primary research on many of these companies, then chooses 100 stocks to put into the portfolio. Stocks chosen fall into one of four camps: emerging growth, established growth, defensive growth, or cyclical growth.

Performance 12-31-06

	1st Qtr	2nd Qtr	3rd Qtr	4th Qtr	Total
2002	—	1.59	-17.36	2.26	-11.09 *
2003	-4.50	21.63	18.05	17.89	61.64
2004	7.99	-0.45	-0.09	16.89	25.55
2005	4.90	0.22	13.01	6.53	26.57
2006	13.24	-2.10	2.45	14.04	29.51

Trailing	Total Return%	+/- MSCI EAFE	+/- MSCI Wd xUS	%Rank Cat	Growth of $10,000
3 Mo	14.04	3.69	3.92	43	11,404
6 Mo	16.83	2.14	2.61	45	11,683
1 Yr	29.51	3.17	3.80	35	12,951
3 Yr Avg	27.20	7.27	7.10	29	20,581
5 Yr Avg	—	—	—	—	—
10 Yr Avg	—	—	—	—	—
15 Yr Avg	—	—	—	—	—

Tax Analysis	Tax-Adj Rtn%	%Rank Cat	Tax-Cost Rat	%Rank Cat
3 Yr (estimated)	25.87	25	1.05	37
5 Yr (estimated)	—	—	—	—
10 Yr (estimated)	—	—	—	—

Potential Capital Gain Exposure: 17% of assets

Morningstar's Take by Kai Wiecking 12-15-06

Despite a string of good results, we're not quite convinced of this mutual fund.

There's no arguing with the strong numbers subadvisor Pictet, a venerable Swiss asset manager, has put up at Forward International Small Companies since its launch in 2002. The trailing average annual return of 25.6% from its inception on March 4, 2002, through Dec. 4, 2006, is the fifth-best among its 20 rivals in the foreign small/mid-growth category.

But the team has recently lost two important members in Nils Francke and Philippe Sarreau. It is now led by Aylin Suntay, and the team has yet to prove its mettle in more challenging market conditions. While it has consistently been able to add value through individual stock selection, management's record of getting country and sector bets right has been more spotty. Those bets are influenced by a macroeconomic outlook provided by Pictet's economists.

In 2006, the strong gains achieved through able stock-picking have been reduced by what turned out to be an overly optimistic view of the recovery in Japan, where the portfolio maintained a significant overweight while markets went through a severe correction in the summer. At the same time, the fund didn't fully participate in the resurgence in Europe, particularly Germany. The fund's underweighting of the index heavyweight Britain also hurt. But Suntay remains wary of the dominant consumer sector in the U.K., as the housing market there continues to be threatened by rising interest rates.

The recent management turnover has us adopting a wait-and-see attitude here. We may be more inclined to give this fund the benefit of the doubt if it were cheap. But at 1.45%--which includes a temporary fee waiver--expenses here are just average for a no-load option, and with this fund having one of the highest turnover ratios in the group, the total impact of costs might come back to haunt it in leaner times.

Address:	433 California St. San Francisco CA 94104 800-999-6809
Web Address:	www.forwardfunds.com
Inception:	03-04-02 *
Advisor:	Forward Managment, LLC
Subadvisor:	Pictet Asset Management Ltd
NTF Plans:	Fidelity Retail-NTF, Schwab OneSource

Minimum Purchase:	$4000	Add: $100	IRA: $4000
Min Auto Inv Plan:	$500	Add: $100	
Sales Fees:	No-load, 0.25%S, 2.00%R		
Management Fee:	1.00% mx./0.95% mn.		
Actual Fees:	Mgt:1.00%	Dist:0.25%	
Expense Projections:	3Yr:$551	5Yr:$969	10Yr:$2133
Income Distrib:	Annually		

Historical Profile

Return	Average
Risk	Average
Rating	★★★ Neutral

Investment Style
Equity
Stock %

100% 96% 94% 99% 99%

▽ Manager Change
▽ Partial Manager Change

26.8
22.8
18.0 — Growth of $10,000
14.0 ■ Investment Values of Fund
10.0 — Investment Values of MSCI EAFE
7.0

Performance Quartile (within Category)

1995	1996	1997	1998	1999	2000	2001	2002	2003	2004	2005	2006	History
—	—	—	—	—	—	—	6.44	10.39	12.87	15.11	18.96	NAV
—	—	—	—	—	—	—	-11.09*	61.64	25.55	26.57	29.51	Total Return %
—	—	—	—	—	—	—	—	23.05	5.30	13.03	3.17	+/-MSCI EAFE
—	—	—	—	—	—	—	—	22.22	5.17	12.10	3.80	+/-MSCI Wd xUS
—	—	—	—	—	—	—	—	0.30	0.32	0.65	0.29	Income Return %
—	—	—	—	—	—	—	—	61.34	25.23	25.92	29.22	Capital Return %
—	—	—	—	—	—	—	—	22	42	46	35	Total Rtn % Rank Cat
—	—	—	—	—	—	—	0.03	0.02	0.03	0.08	0.04	Income $
—	—	—	—	—	—	—	0.00	0.00	0.14	1.02	0.54	Capital Gains $
—	—	—	—	—	—	—	1.45	1.45	1.46	1.45	—	Expense Ratio %
—	—	—	—	—	—	—	0.27	0.24	0.47	0.82	—	Income Ratio %
—	—	—	—	—	—	—	133	52	175	91	—	Turnover Rate %
—	—	—	—	—	—	—	—	16	6	64	251	Net Assets $mil

Rating and Risk

Time Period	Load-Adj Rtn %	Morningstar Rtn vs Cat	Morningstar Risk vs Cat	Morningstar Risk-Adj Rating
1 Yr	29.51			
3 Yr	27.20	Avg	Avg	★★★
5 Yr	—			
10 Yr	—			
Incept	25.19			

Other Measures	Standard Index MSCI EAFE	Best Fit Index MSCI EAFE
Alpha	1.9	1.9
Beta	1.29	1.29
R-Squared	83	83

Standard Deviation	13.40
Mean	27.20
Sharpe Ratio	1.64

Portfolio Analysis 11-30-06

Share change since 10-06 Total Stocks:128	Sector	Country	% Assets
Geberit	Consumer	Switzerland	1.29
Kingspan Grp	Business	Ireland	1.25
Bco Pastor	Financial	Spain	1.16
Uol Grp	Financial	Singapore	1.14
⊕ Bergman & Beving	Ind Mtrls	Sweden	1.14
Shaftesbury	Financial	U.K.	1.14
Indra Sistemas	Business	Spain	1.13
Biomerieux	Health	France	1.13
Millennium & Copthorne H	Consumer	U.K.	1.13
The Japan General Estate	Financial	Japan	1.12
Andritz	Ind Mtrls	Austria	1.11
SCi Entertainment Grp	Software	U.K.	1.11
Sol Melia	Consumer	Spain	1.10
FBD Hldgs	Financial	Ireland	1.10
Hunting	Ind Mtrls	U.K.	1.09
✲✲ Premiere AG	Media	Germany	1.09
Prime Success Int"l Grp	Goods	Hong Kong	1.08
Ciba Specialty Chemicals	Ind Mtrls	Switzerland	1.08
✲✲ Burren Energy	Energy	U.K.	1.07
A.B.C. Learning Centres	Consumer	Australia	1.07

Current Investment Style

	Market Cap	%
Giant		0.0
Large		0.6
Mid		74.3
Small		24.4
Micro		0.7
Avg $mil:	1,773	

Value Measures		Rel Category
Price/Earnings	16.64	1.06
Price/Book	2.10	0.87
Price/Sales	1.03	0.94
Price/Cash Flow	5.85	0.75
Dividend Yield %	2.35	1.15

Growth Measures	%	Rel Category
Long-Term Erngs	15.61	0.76
Book Value	9.92	1.05
Sales	8.00	0.64
Cash Flow	0.86	0.06
Historical Erngs	22.38	0.99

Composition

Cash	0.1	Bonds	0.0
Stocks	99.4	Other	0.5
Foreign (% of Stock)			99.6

Sector Weightings

Sector Weightings	% of Stocks	Rel MSCI EAFE	3 Year High Low	
☍ Info	6.86	0.58		
▣ Software	1.70	3.04	4	0
▣ Hardware	2.80	0.73	7	2
▣ Media	1.80	0.98	5	0
▣ Telecom	0.56	0.10	5	1
☌ Service	49.62	1.05		
▣ Health	3.70	0.52	7	3
▣ Consumer	11.74	2.37	18	5
▣ Business	16.39	3.23	21	12
▣ Financial	17.79	0.59	22	10
⊔ Mfg	43.51	1.06		
▣ Goods	9.54	0.73	18	8
▣ Ind Mtrls	28.53	1.85	32	20
▣ Energy	1.69	0.24	7	1
▣ Utilities	3.75	0.72	5	0

Regional Exposure % Stock

UK/W. Europe	64	N. America	0
Japan	21	Latn America	1
Asia X Japan	13	Other	1

Country Exposure % Stock

Japan	21	Germany	6
U.K.	17	France	6
Switzerland	7		

M∩RNINGSTAR® Funds 500

FPA Capital

	Analyst Pick	Ticker FPPTX	Load Closed	NAV $41.44	Yield 1.4%	Total Assets $2,207 mil	Mstar Category Small Value

Governance and Management

Stewardship Grade: A

Portfolio Manager(s)

Bob Rodriguez has been at the helm since the fund's 1984 inception. He is assisted by three analysts. Rodriguez also runs fixed-income offering FPA New Income in the same contrarian style he employs here. He was named Morningstar's Fixed-Income Manager of the Year in 2001 for his efforts at that fund.

Strategy

Bob Rodriguez is a dyed-in-the-wool value investor. He looks for companies that are extremely cheap but that also have clean balance sheets, strong cash flows, and dominant market shares. When he can't find stocks inexpensive enough to clear his strict valuation hurdles, he turns to cash or bonds. He invests without regard to where his picks land in the style box, but most tend to be small or mid-cap. This is a compact portfolio--it typically holds no more than 40 stocks--and can concentrate picks in a handful of sectors. Rodriguez trades little, but the fund's tax efficiency is poor.

Performance 12-31-06

	1st Qtr	2nd Qtr	3rd Qtr	4th Qtr	Total
2002	6.72	-2.39	-15.86	9.68	-3.86
2003	-7.45	23.37	7.83	12.52	38.54
2004	5.75	2.39	-1.85	5.97	12.62
2005	3.33	3.90	7.36	1.11	16.53
2006	4.92	-3.60	-0.55	4.81	5.42

Trailing	Total Return%	+/- S&P 500	+/- Russ 2000 VL	%Rank Cat	Growth of $10,000
3 Mo	4.81	-1.89	-4.22	99	10,481
6 Mo	4.23	-8.51	-7.58	95	10,423
1 Yr	5.42	-10.37	-18.06	98	10,542
3 Yr Avg	11.43	0.99	-5.05	85	13,836
5 Yr Avg	13.00	6.81	-2.37	61	18,424
10 Yr Avg	12.69	4.27	-0.58	46	33,026
15 Yr Avg	16.49	5.85	1.29	6	98,703

Tax Analysis	Tax-Adj Rtn%	%Rank Cat	Tax-Cost Rat	%Rank Cat
3 Yr (estimated)	8.20	88	1.14	27
5 Yr (estimated)	10.94	70	0.76	22
10 Yr (estimated)	9.64	74	2.19	98

Potential Capital Gain Exposure: 22% of assets

Morningstar's Take by Christopher Davis 12-22-06

FPA Capital is on the bottom right now, but long-term shareholders are likely to end up on top.

Over the past year, this closed offering has gone from hero to goat. In 2005, it finished the year on the top of the small-value heap thanks to its giant stake in red-hot energy stocks. But in 2006, falling oil and gas prices has hit hard holdings such as Paterson UTI Energy. And with small- and mid-cap value stocks continuing their long rally, the fund's big cash and bond stake has kept it from fully enjoying the party. Blowups like manufactured housing producer Champion Enterprises have also hurt. Winners like Rent-A-Center have helped the fund deliver a 6% return for the year to date through December 20, but that's one of the weakest gains in its category.

Manager Bob Rodriguez isn't one to let short-term underperformance drive his decision making. The long-term picture for energy prices hasn't changed, he argues, given that there's been no major oil discovery in decades. Meanwhile, demand from India, China, and even the U.S. continues apace. As such, he expects his exposure to the sector to remain large for a long time to come. Rodriguez has also ratcheted up his stake in Champion, pointing to its industry leadership and the boost it's getting from Hurricane Katrina rebuilding efforts. Finally, he says he's finding few bargains, and he won't throw his capital at overvalued stocks. Until more stocks meet his criteria, Rodriguez is content to sit on his fund's cash and bond hoard, which stands at nearly one third of assets.

Rodriguez's willingness to stick to his convictions--even when it hurts--is what has made this offering a great long-term success. That means shareholders will have to be patient through relative dry spells in returns, but given Rodriguez's skill and experience, we think shareholders will be rewarded for sticking around.

Address:	11400 W Olympic Blvd Ste 1200
	Los Angeles CA 90064
	800-982-4372
Web Address:	www.FPAFunds.com
Inception:	02-01-68
Advisor:	First Pacific Advisors, Inc.
Subadvisor:	None
NTF Plans:	N/A

Minimum Purchase:	Closed	Add: —	IRA: —
Min Auto Inv Plan:	Closed	Add: —	
Sales Fees:	5.25%L, 2.00%R		
Management Fee:	0.75% mx./0.65% mn.		
Actual Fees:	Mgt:0.65%	Dist: —	
Expense Projections:	3Yr:$776	5Yr:$961	10Yr:$1497
Income Distrib:	Semi-Annually		

Historical Profile

Return	Below Avg
Risk	Average
Rating	★★ Below Avg

Performance Quartile (within Category)

1995	1996	1997	1998	1999	2000	2001	2002	2003	2004	2005	2006	History
27.50	34.01	36.28	31.04	31.02	22.29	28.26	26.86	36.85	39.98	42.88	41.44	NAV
38.39	37.76	17.70	-0.42	14.24	-3.08	38.13	-3.86	38.54	12.62	16.53	5.42	Total Return %
0.81	14.80	-15.66	-29.00	-6.80	6.02	50.02	18.24	9.86	1.74	11.62	-10.37	+/-S&P 500
12.64	16.39	-14.08	6.03	15.73	-25.91	24.11	7.57	-7.49	-9.63	11.82	-18.06	+/-Russ 2000 VL
0.68	1.29	1.27	1.89	0.71	0.49	0.13	0.00	0.07	0.00	0.66	1.49	Income Return %
37.71	36.47	16.43	-2.31	13.53	-3.57	38.00	-3.86	38.47	12.62	15.87	3.93	Capital Return %
3	1	98	20	23	97	3	20	62	98	1	98	Total Rtn % Rank Cat
0.14	0.34	0.42	0.65	0.22	0.14	0.03	0.00	0.02	0.00	0.26	0.63	Income $
0.73	2.60	2.84	4.79	4.03	7.76	2.39	0.33	0.33	1.48	3.39	3.11	Capital Gains $
0.95	0.87	0.84	0.83	0.86	0.86	0.89	0.84	0.87	0.83	0.85	0.83	Expense Ratio %
0.48	1.28	1.27	1.38	1.20	0.35	0.39	0.04	0.00	0.06	0.13	0.83	Income Ratio %
11	21	21	24	19	18	5	23	17	20	16	26	Turnover Rate %
353	568	731	674	539	384	552	616	1,128	1,700	2,122	2,207	Net Assets $mil

Rating and Risk

Time Period	Load-Adj Return %	Morningstar Rtn vs Cat	Morningstar Risk vs Cat	Morningstar Risk-Adj Rating
1 Yr	-0.11			
3 Yr	9.45	Low	Low	★
5 Yr	11.79	-Avg	Avg	★★
10 Yr	12.09	Avg	+Avg	★★
Incept	—			

Other Measures	Standard Index S&P 500	Best Fit Index S&P Mid 400
Alpha	0.6	-0.1
Beta	1.08	0.85
R-Squared	53	76
Standard Deviation	10.08	
Mean	11.43	
Sharpe Ratio	0.80	

Portfolio Analysis 09-30-06

Share change since 06-06 Total Stocks:25	Sector	PE	Tot Ret%	% Assets
⊕ Avnet, Inc.	Business	16.5	6.64	4.97
Ensco International, Inc	Energy	11.0	13.12	4.80
Michaels Stores, Inc.	Consumer	—	—	4.54
⊕ Patterson-UTI Energy, In	Energy	5.7	-28.72	3.94
⊖ Big Lots, Inc.	Consumer	46.2	90.84	3.78
Trinity Industries, Inc.	Ind Mtrls	16.0	20.56	3.77
Charming Shoppes, Inc.	Consumer	17.0	2.89	3.75
Rosetta Res 144A	Energy	—	—	3.59
FHLBA 4.75%	—	—	—	3.52
⊕ Rowan Companies, Inc.	Energy	10.7	-5.59	2.80
Foot Locker, Inc.	Consumer	14.8	-5.67	2.80
US Treasury Note 4.25%	—	—	—	2.70
Arrow Electronics, Inc.	Business	12.4	-1.50	2.43
Zale Corporation	Goods	26.4	12.17	2.31
National Oilwell Varco,	Energy	18.3	-2.42	2.23
Ross Stores, Inc.	Consumer	20.6	2.28	2.13
⊕ Datapath 144A		—	—	2.12
Rent-A-Center, Inc.	Consumer	14.5	56.47	1.80
American Greetings Corpo	Media	27.9	10.23	1.53
Fleetwood Enterprises	Ind Mtrls	—	-35.95	1.46

Current Investment Style

Value Blnd Growth — Large/Mid/Small

Market Cap	%
Giant	0.0
Large	0.0
Mid	78.5
Small	15.6
Micro	6.0
Avg $mil:	2,792

Value Measures		Rel Category
Price/Earnings	12.23	0.80
Price/Book	1.89	1.06
Price/Sales	0.56	0.70
Price/Cash Flow	8.06	1.32
Dividend Yield %	0.62	0.39

Growth Measures	%	Rel Category
Long-Term Erngs	20.77	1.66
Book Value	8.23	1.52
Sales	6.26	0.85
Cash Flow	17.21	2.10
Historical Erngs	22.53	1.98

Profitability	%	Rel Category
Return on Equity	15.48	1.44
Return on Assets	9.13	1.50
Net Margin	9.36	1.03

Sector Weightings	% of Stocks	Rel S&P 500	3 Year High Low	
⌚ Info	2.57	0.13		
🖥 Software	0.00	0.00	0	0
💻 Hardware	0.00	0.00	11	0
🎙 Media	2.57	0.68	3	2
☎ Telecom	0.00	0.00	4	0
☞ Service	52.40	1.13		
🏥 Health	0.89	0.07	1	1
🛒 Consumer	36.27	4.74	36	27
💼 Business	12.46	2.95	12	6
💲 Financial	2.78	0.12	4	1
⚒ Mfg	45.04	1.33		
🏭 Goods	3.89	0.45	9	3
🔧 Ind Mtrls	11.91	1.00	16	11
🔋 Energy	29.24	2.98	32	22
🏢 Utilities	0.00	0.00	0	0

Composition

	%
● Cash	32.3
● Stocks	61.5
● Bonds	6.2
● Other	0.0
Foreign	0.0
(% of Stock)	

Investment Style
Equity
Stock %

▼ Manager Change
▽ Partial Manager Change

Growth of $10,000
— Investment Values of Fund
— Investment Values of S&P 500

Return percentages: 85% 99% 95% 94% 81% 73% 67% 59% 62%

FPA Crescent

	Ticker	Load	NAV	Yield	Total Assets	Mstar Category
	FPACX	Closed	$26.40	1.9%	$1,415 mil	Moderate Allocation

Governance and Management

Stewardship Grade: C

Portfolio Manager(s)

Steven Romick has been the lead manager for this fund since its inception in 1993. Prior to working for First Pacific Advisors, Romick was chairman of Crescent Management and a consulting security analyst for Kaplan, Nathan & Co. Since 2000, Romick has been supported by two savvy investment professionals, Dennis Bryan and Rikard Ekstrand.

Strategy

Unlike the majority of its moderate-allocation peers, this fund's equity portfolio is mostly focused on small companies with dirt-cheap valuations. Manager Steven Romick rarely keeps much more than 20% invested on the bond side, and he buys bonds and convertibles issued primarily by deeply undervalued companies. He'll also take short positions in stocks but does so conservatively and to lower overall portfolio volatility.

Historical Profile

Return	High
Risk	Above Avg
Rating	★★★★ Highest

66% 66% 61% 44% 46% 41% 40% 42% 46%

Investment Style
Equity
Stock %

▼ Manager Change
▽ Partial Manager Change

Growth of $10,000
— Investment Values of Fund
— Investment Values of DJ Mod

40.8
31.0
24.0
17.0
10.0

Performance Quartile (within Category)

	1995	1996	1997	1998	1999	2000	2001	2002	2003	2004	2005	2006	History
	12.03	13.02	15.20	14.82	12.95	12.82	17.19	17.40	21.79	23.55	25.17	26.40	NAV
	26.04	22.88	21.95	2.79	-6.28	3.59	36.14	3.71	26.15	10.21	10.83	12.43	Total Return %
	6.24	12.22	10.05	-9.53	-23.61	5.26	38.94	10.48	-1.23	-2.76	3.84	0.13	+/-DJ Mod
	1.27	11.54	2.75	-9.60	-19.13	-0.85	35.98	14.25	2.09	-0.96	4.83	2.16	+/-DJ US Mod
	3.47	2.93	3.08	3.41	2.49	4.38	1.94	2.52	0.86	0.37	1.43	2.13	Income Return %
	22.57	19.95	18.87	-0.62	-8.77	-0.79	34.20	1.19	25.29	9.84	9.40	10.30	Capital Return %
	51	4	30	96	97	36	1	1	9	30	1	25	Total Rtn % Rank Cat
	0.37	0.34	0.40	0.51	0.35	0.56	0.25	0.43	0.15	0.08	0.34	0.53	Income $
	0.88	1.34	0.26	0.29	0.64	0.00	0.00	0.00	0.37	0.58	0.58	1.34	Capital Gains $
	1.65	1.59	1.57	1.45	1.42	1.49	1.87	1.50	1.54	1.41	1.40	1.39	Expense Ratio %
	2.16	3.35	2.80	3.62	3.67	2.26	2.79	1.73	2.06	0.67	0.57	1.45	Income Ratio %
	101	100	45	18	36	10	37	34	39	20	17	24	Turnover Rate %
	20	37	173	227	84	33	204	209	381	915	1,280	1,415	Net Assets $mil

Performance 12-31-06

	1st Qtr	2nd Qtr	3rd Qtr	4th Qtr	Total
2002	6.52	-0.92	-6.07	4.62	3.71
2003	-2.24	14.64	4.73	7.48	26.15
2004	4.36	1.32	0.44	3.77	10.21
2005	2.68	1.61	5.32	0.86	10.83
2006	5.16	0.57	1.49	4.74	12.43

Trailing	Total Return%	+/- DJ Mod	+/- DJ US Mod	%Rank Cat	Growth of $10,000
3 Mo	4.74	-0.85	0.07	64	10,474
6 Mo	6.30	-2.49	-1.60	94	10,630
1 Yr	12.43	0.13	2.16	25	11,243
3 Yr Avg	11.15	0.43	2.03	9	13,732
5 Yr Avg	12.43	2.41	4.83	1	17,964
10 Yr Avg	11.52	2.97	2.93	3	29,753
15 Yr Avg	—	—	—		—

Tax Analysis	Tax-Adj Rtn%	%Rank Cat	Tax-Cost Rat	%Rank Cat
3 Yr (estimated)	10.21	6	0.85	41
5 Yr (estimated)	11.59	1	0.75	43
10 Yr (estimated)	10.25	2	1.14	25

Potential Capital Gain Exposure: 10% of assets

Rating and Risk

Time Period	Load-Adj Return %	Morningstar Rtn vs Cat	Morningstar Risk vs Cat	Morningstar Risk-Adj Rating
1 Yr	12.43			
3 Yr	11.15	High	+Avg	★★★★★
5 Yr	12.43	High	+Avg	★★★★★
10 Yr	11.52	High	+Avg	★★★★★
Incept	13.02			

Other Measures	Standard Index DJ Mod	Best Fit Index Mstar Small Core
Alpha	1.9	2.5
Beta	0.80	0.39
R-Squared	60	71
Standard Deviation	6.03	
Mean	11.15	
Sharpe Ratio	1.26	

Morningstar's Take by Christopher Davis 12-27-06

This closed fund's wide-ranging hunt for value has made it a standout.

Many prominent value investors argue that some of the best bargains these days can be found among out-of-favor blue chips. You can add FPA Crescent manager Steve Romick, who scooped up shares of Wal-Mart in 2006's second quarter, to that list. Romick also delved into large-cap territory with the addition of ConocoPhillips, one of the big integrated energy companies, and reports adding to his stake more recently as its shares have fallen along with oil prices.

This isn't exactly what you'd expect from Romick. Like his FPA counterparts, his focus historically has been on small and mid-caps. And, actually, it still is: The fund's average market cap clocks in at $4.9 billion, a fraction of the moderate-allocation norm. Romick only ventures up the market-cap spectrum if there's potential for market-beating returns. He also looks across asset classes too: His portfolio includes preferred stocks, as well as government and high-yield bonds. In a departure from his category rivals, which typically hold their stock and bond weightings constant, Romick's asset mix fluctuates depending on where he's finding value. Another quirk: He'll sell pricey stocks short where balance sheets are weak.

A cautious ethic underlies everything Romick does. He assumes that Wal-Mart will increase its earnings just 7% to 8% annually, a fraction of its 13% growth rate over the past five years. And his case for ConocoPhillips doesn't rest on today's high oil prices. Even if oil falls to the upper $30s, he says the stock would still be cheap.

Wal-Mart and Conoco have done little to soak up the fund's cash hoard, which stands at a whopping 47% of assets. Yet in a testament to Romick's abilities, the fund is well ahead of its peers this year. More importantly, though, it's delivered great returns over the long haul. If you own this offering, stick with it.

Address:	11400 W. Olympic Blvd. Los Angeles CA 90064 800-982-4372	Minimum Purchase:	Closed	Add: —	IRA: —
Web Address:	www.fpafunds.com	Min Auto Inv Plan:	Closed	Add: —	
Inception:	06-02-93	Sales Fees:	No-load, 2.00%R	
Advisor:	First Pacific Advisors, Inc.	Management Fee:	1.00%	
Subadvisor:	None	Actual Fees:	Mgt:1.00% Dist: —	
		Expense Projections:	3Yr:$440 5Yr:$761 10Yr:$1669	
NTF Plans:	Fidelity Retail-NTF, Schwab OneSource	Income Distrib:	Semi-Annually	

Portfolio Analysis 09-30-06

Total Stocks:34 Share change since 06-30-06	Sectors	P/E Ratio	YTD Return %	% Net Assets
Ensco International, Inc.	Energy	11.0	-5.05	3.83
⊖ Countrywide	Financial	—	—	3.60
⊕ ConocoPhillips	Energy	6.5	-5.07	3.49
Assurant, Inc.	Financial	12.2	1.45	2.77
⊖ AGCO Corporation	Ind Mtrls	—	-5.69	2.18
Michaels Stores, Inc.	Consumer	—	—	1.74
Magna International	Ind Mtrls	13.1	-4.13	1.72
Patterson-UTI Energy, Inc	Energy	5.7	-6.28	1.60
Rowan Companies, Inc.	Energy	10.7	-6.57	1.55

Total Fixed-Income:13	Date of Maturity	Amount $000	Value $000	% Net Assets
US Treasury Note 4.375%	12-15-10	40,000	39,669	2.67
Goodman Global Hldgs 7.87	12-15-12	15,970	15,172	1.02
US Treasury Note 3.875%	07-15-10	15,000	14,639	0.98
Tenet Healthcare 9.875%	07-01-14	8,000	7,960	0.54
US Treasury Note 3.375%	01-15-12	5,157	5,427	0.37
Reliant Engy 9.25%	07-15-10	5,000	5,163	0.35
Reliant Engy 9.5%	07-15-13	4,750	4,916	0.33
France (Republic Of) 3%	07-25-12	3,303	4,520	0.30
Western Finl Bk Irvine Ca	05-15-12	2,950	3,256	0.22

Equity Style
Style: Value
Size: Mid-Cap

Value Measures		Rel Category
Price/Earnings	11.85	0.78
Price/Book	1.89	0.77
Price/Sales	0.72	0.53
Price/Cash Flow	7.15	0.88
Dividend Yield %	1.55	0.80

Growth Measures	%	Rel Category
Long-Term Erngs	15.90	1.36
Book Value	8.79	1.02
Sales	11.42	1.29
Cash Flow	21.11	2.14
Historical Erngs	17.50	0.98

Market Cap %			
Giant	13.4	Small	12.5
Large	7.7	Micro	0.4
Mid	66.0	Avg $mil:	5,546

Fixed-Income Style
Duration: —
Quality: —

Avg Eff Duration [1]	—
Avg Eff Maturity	—
Avg Credit Quality	—
Avg Wtd Coupon	—

[1] figure provided by fund

Sector Weightings	% of Stocks	Rel DJ Mod	3 Year High Low
↻ Info	3.14		
Software	0.00	—	1 0
Hardware	3.14	—	11 3
Media	0.00	—	0 0
Telecom	0.00	—	3 0
⊂ Service	39.26		
Health	0.00	—	2 0
Consumer	16.93	—	23 13
Business	5.64	—	6 2
Financial	16.69	—	19 13
Mfg	57.61		
Goods	7.87	—	10 3
Ind Mtrls	15.12	—	19 6
Energy	30.80	—	35 29
Utilities	3.82	—	5 1

Composition

● Cash	44.7	
● Stocks	46.4	
● Bonds	7.1	
○ Other	1.9	
Foreign (% of Stock)	23.2	

MORNINGSTAR® Funds 500

FPA New Income

		Ticker	Load	NAV	Yield	SEC Yield	Total Assets	Mstar Category
✔	Analyst Pick	FPNIX	3.50%	$10.85	4.6%	—	$1,850 mil	Intermediate-Term Bond

Governance and Management

Stewardship Grade: A

Portfolio Manager(s)

Management is seasoned and highly decorated. Bob Rodriguez was named Morningstar Fixed-Income Manager of the Year for 2001. He has been at the fund's helm since 1984 and is supported primarily by Tom Atteberry, with whom he shares portfolio management responsibilities. They are assisted by Steven Romick, Steven Geist, and Julian Mann.

Strategy

Unlike many of its intermediate-term bond peers, this fund doesn't pay attention to a broad market index. Instead, management seeks the best values, regardless of sector. That leaves the fund looking less like the norm and more like a contrarian. For example, the fund typically invests more in high yield than most peers, and it has gotten all of its Treasury exposure from inflation-indexed Treasuries since 1998. Management is less willing than many of its peers to take on interest-rate risk, however, especially when yields are low.

Performance 12-31-06

	1st Qtr	2nd Qtr	3rd Qtr	4th Qtr	Total
2002	2.93	2.78	-3.00	1.85	4.52
2003	1.10	2.48	2.36	2.14	8.32
2004	0.80	0.80	0.36	0.63	2.60
2005	0.09	-0.36	0.91	0.92	1.57
2006	0.74	1.20	1.66	1.11	4.79

Trailing	Total Return%	+/- LB Aggr	+/- LB 5-10YR	%Rank Cat	Growth of $10,000
3 Mo	1.11	-0.13	0.03	60	10,111
6 Mo	2.79	-2.30	-2.89	99	10,279
1 Yr	4.79	0.46	0.98	18	10,479
3 Yr Avg	2.98	-0.72	-0.66	67	10,921
5 Yr Avg	4.33	-0.73	-1.59	61	12,361
10 Yr Avg	5.85	-0.39	-0.83	30	17,657
15 Yr Avg	6.81	0.31	-0.18	13	26,864

Tax Analysis	Tax-Adj Rtn%	%Rank Cat	Tax-Cost Rat	%Rank Cat
3 Yr (estimated)	0.27	88	1.46	49
5 Yr (estimated)	1.98	85	1.55	45
10 Yr (estimated)	3.18	57	2.17	65

Potential Capital Gain Exposure: -5% of assets

Historical Profile

Return Average
Risk Low
Rating ★★★ Neutral

| | 1 | 8 | 5 | 25 | 46 | 28 | 63 | 18 |

Investment Style — Fixed Income — Income Rtn %Rank Cat

▼ Manager Change
▽ Partial Manager Change

Growth of $10,000
— Investment Values of Fund
— Investment Values of LB Aggr

Performance Quartile (within Category)

1995	1996	1997	1998	1999	2000	2001	2002	2003	2004	2005	2006	History
11.17	11.09	11.24	10.74	10.30	10.38	10.93	10.88	11.28	11.18	10.84	10.85	NAV
14.36	7.12	8.31	3.86	3.39	9.32	12.33	4.52	8.32	2.60	1.57	4.79	Total Return %
-4.11	3.49	-1.34	-4.83	4.21	-2.31	3.89	-5.73	4.22	-1.74	-0.86	0.46	+/-LB Aggr
-7.07	4.43	-1.12	-6.28	6.27	-3.12	3.51	-8.51	2.35	-2.70	-0.26	0.98	+/-LB 5-10YR
6.60	6.21	6.30	7.71	6.78	7.69	6.30	5.03	4.56	3.50	4.64	4.69	Income Return %
7.76	0.91	2.01	-3.85	-3.39	1.63	6.03	-0.51	3.76	-0.90	-3.07	0.10	Capital Return %
89	3	75	96	2	66	2	95	15	91	62	18	Total Rtn % Rank Cat
0.67	0.67	0.68	0.84	0.71	0.77	0.64	0.54	0.49	0.39	0.51	0.50	Income $
0.00	0.16	0.05	0.08	0.09	0.08	0.07	0.00	0.00	0.00	0.00	0.00	Capital Gains $
0.68	0.63	0.59	0.59	0.60	0.61	0.58	0.58	0.61	0.62	0.61	0.62	Expense Ratio %
6.50	6.44	6.37	6.06	6.43	7.31	6.39	5.06	4.69	3.77	3.69	4.68	Income Ratio %
31	16	69	47	24	21	22	28	52	62	42	60	Turnover Rate %
234	375	563	582	515	486	705	1,088	1,202	2,043	1,698	1,850	Net Assets $mil

Rating and Risk

Time Period	Load-Adj Return %	Morningstar Rtn vs Cat	Morningstar Risk vs Cat	Morningstar Risk-Adj Rating
1 Yr	1.12			
3 Yr	1.76	-Avg	Low	★★
5 Yr	3.59	-Avg	Low	★★
10 Yr	5.47	Avg	Low	★★★
Incept	—			

Other Measures	Standard Index LB Aggr	Best Fit Index CSFB Glb HY
Alpha	-0.3	-0.7
Beta	-0.01	0.07
R-Squared	0	10
Standard Deviation	0.87	
Mean	2.98	
Sharpe Ratio	-0.34	

Morningstar's Take by Christopher Davis 01-03-07

FPA New Income requires its shareholders to think as differently as its idiosyncratic manager, but we think it's worth it.

Underlying manager Bob Rodriguez's approach at this offering is one seemingly simple idea: Don't lose money. This governing principle explains Rodriguez's highly unorthodox portfolio. Most intermediate-term bond funds manage interest-rate risk by keeping duration (a measure of interest-rate sensitivity) aligned with that of a major benchmark, such as the Lehman Brothers Aggregate Bond Index. Not Rodriguez. Indeed, the fund's duration clocks in at an ultralow 0.98 years, versus around 5 years for the Lehman index. Rodriguez also distinguishes himself by his willingness to go on the defensive by building big cash stakes. In September 2005, for instance, the fund's cash stake stood at a whopping 40% of assets. Over the past year, Rodriguez and comanager Tom Atteberry have whittled down that cash hoard considerably, to 18% of assets, as they report

finding better values among short-term bonds. But the pair remains very cautious. They continue to steer almost completely clear of high-yield bonds; they say yields are too low to make their risk worthwhile. Moreover, they are unwilling to take on long-term debt, citing concerns over the prospect of higher inflation thanks to rising energy prices and the U.S. government's worsening fiscal health.

Rodriguez's zeal for capital preservation has paid off again and again. When investors worried about higher interest rates last spring, the fund actually made money while most rivals lost ground, pushing it ahead of its peers for the year. This isn't an isolated incident, either: The fund hasn't suffered a calendar year loss since Rodriguez took charge in 1984.

Rodriguez's willingness to go his own way can hurt at times--his cautiousness backfired in 2004 and 2005--but those who share his long-term focus will find this fund appealing.

Address:	11400 W Olympic Blvd Ste 1200 Los Angeles CA 90064 800-638-3060
Web Address:	www.FPAFunds.com
Inception:	04-01-69
Advisor:	First Pacific Advisors, Inc.
Subadvisor:	None
NTF Plans:	N/A

Minimum Purchase:	$1500	Add: $100	IRA: $100
Min Auto Inv Plan:	$100	Add: $100	
Sales Fees:	3.50%L, 2.00%R		
Management Fee:	0.50%		
Actual Fees:	Mgt:0.50%	Dist: —	
Expense Projections:	3Yr:$539	5Yr:$678	10Yr:$1085
Income Distrib:	Quarterly		

Portfolio Analysis 09-30-06

Total Fixed-Income:76	Date of Maturity	Amount $000	Value $000	% Net Assets
FHLBA 5.25%	06-12-09	135,780	136,902	7.53
FHLBA 4.75%	03-13-09	75,000	74,718	4.11
US Treasury Note 4.25%	10-31-07	51,000	50,633	2.78
FFCB 5.25%	05-04-09	49,630	49,977	2.75
Tennessee Valley Auth 5.	11-13-08	49,362	49,763	2.74
FFCB	07-03-08	25,000	25,203	1.39
FHLBA 5.125%	06-13-08	25,000	25,054	1.38
Qwest Comms Intl 144A FR	02-15-09	24,045	24,497	1.35
Rabobank Nederland Dep M	12-07-07	24,674	24,304	1.34
FAMC 4.25%	07-29-08	23,424	23,107	1.27
Wells Fargo Mbs 2005-2 C	04-25-35	20,033	20,897	1.15
Bayerische Landesbank Gr	04-30-09	21,000	20,675	1.14
France (Republic Of) 3%	07-25-12	14,587	19,964	1.10
Farmer Mac Gtd Nt Tr 144	01-14-11	19,610	19,500	1.07
FHLMC CMO 5%	12-15-34	19,049	18,942	1.04
Metaldyne 11%	06-15-12	19,980	17,932	0.99
Bea Sys Cv 4%	12-15-06	18,000	17,888	0.98
FNMA 6.5%	01-01-36	16,145	16,478	0.91
FHLBA 3.5%	11-03-09	15,000	14,382	0.79
Chase Mortgage Fin CMO 7	01-25-34	13,629	14,309	0.79

Current Investment Style

Duration: Short / Int / Long
Quality: High / Med / Low

¹ figure provided by fund

Avg Eff Duration¹	1.0 Yrs
Avg Eff Maturity	1.5 Yrs
Avg Credit Quality	AAA
Avg Wtd Coupon	5.25%
Avg Wtd Price	100.40% of par

Coupon Range	% of Bonds	Rel Cat
0% PIK	2.8	0.4
0% to 6%	75.1	1.0
6% to 8%	21.8	1.0
8% to 10%	0.4	0.1
More than 10%	2.7	3.8

1.00=Category Average

Credit Analysis	% bonds 09-30-06		
AAA	94	BB	0
AA	1	B	1
A	0	Below B	1
BBB	0	NR/NA	2

Sector Breakdown — % of assets

US Treasuries	3
TIPS	0
US Agency	23
Mortgage Pass-Throughs	8
Mortgage CMO	8
Mortgage ARM	0
US Corporate	6
Asset-Backed	0
Convertible	0
Municipal	0
Corporate Inflation-Protected	0
Foreign Corporate	0
Foreign Govt	1

Composition

Cash	50.3	Bonds	48.0
Stocks	0.0	Other	1.7

Special Securities

Restricted/Illiquid Secs	2
Exotic Mortgage-Backed	0
Emerging-Markets Secs	0
Options/Futures/Warrants	No

FPA Paramount

	Analyst Pick	Ticker	Load	NAV	Yield	Total Assets	Mstar Category
	✓	FPRAX	5.25%	$16.18	0.9%	$620 mil	Mid-Cap Blend

Governance and Management

Stewardship Grade: B

Portfolio Manager(s)

Eric Ende and Steve Geist have been at the helm since March 2000. They have built a fine record at FPA Perennial, which Ende has led since 1995 and Geist has comanaged since 2000.

Strategy

Managers Eric Ende and Steve Geist look for small and midsize companies with strong returns on capital and clean balance sheets trading at a discount to the market's or their own historical price multiples. They hold a compact portfolio consisting of about 30 to 40 names, will concentrate their holdings in a limited number of sectors, and aren't afraid to let the fund's cash stake build if they can't find attractive investment ideas. With big stakes in both fast-growing hardware names and stodgier industrials, the managers' picks span the style box. The pair usually hangs on to holdings for years.

Performance 12-31-06

	1st Qtr	2nd Qtr	3rd Qtr	4th Qtr	Total
2002	6.91	-9.35	-13.62	4.68	-12.37
2003	-8.47	26.48	9.65	11.40	41.41
2004	4.58	3.90	-0.38	7.07	15.89
2005	1.08	0.99	5.63	4.06	12.20
2006	6.35	-5.01	-0.32	4.03	4.76

Trailing	Total Return%	+/- S&P 500	+/- S&P Mid 400	%Rank Cat	Growth of $10,000
3 Mo	4.03	-2.67	-2.96	98	10,403
6 Mo	3.70	-9.04	-2.13	93	10,370
1 Yr	4.76	-11.03	-5.56	98	10,476
3 Yr Avg	10.85	0.41	-2.24	78	13,621
5 Yr Avg	11.04	4.85	0.15	36	16,881
10 Yr Avg	3.28	-5.14	-10.19	96	13,809
15 Yr Avg	7.40	-3.24	-6.23	97	29,179

Tax Analysis	Tax-Adj Rtn%	%Rank Cat	Tax-Cost Rat	%Rank Cat
3 Yr (estimated)	8.75	78	0.12	6
5 Yr (estimated)	9.77	38	0.07	5
10 Yr (estimated)	1.56	96	1.13	21

Potential Capital Gain Exposure: -9% of assets

Morningstar's Take by Christopher Davis 11-28-06

Although it hasn't looked great lately, this Analyst Pick remains a favorite.

This certainly hasn't been a terrific year for FPA Paramount. Despite posting a modest gain thus far, the fund's returns are among the worst in the mid-blend category. An unusually large number of the holdings in its compact portfolio have run into trouble this year, including Plantronics, Zebra Technologies, and Cognex. Managers Eric Ende and Steve Geist viewed the declines as buying opportunities and added to their stakes in the companies. That's exactly what we'd expect from the pair: Ende and Geist don't require rock-bottom price multiples to invest, but they still tend to build positions when they come under fire.

Valuation drives the timing of management's buy and sell decisions, but attractive price tags alone aren't enough. Ende and Geist put the quality of the businesses they're considering front and center. Their watch list consists of companies that boast a long history of high returns on capital, little debt,

and management teams they like. Then they wait for the stocks' price-to-earnings ratios to fall to reasonable levels--typically in the mid- to upper-teens. One recent addition is Copart, an auction house for salvaged automobiles. Because its primary customers are big insurance companies, Ende says the company's nationwide scope gives it barriers to entry. He also points to its high returns on capital, debt-free balance sheet, and ability to integrate acquisitions.

Ultimately, no more than a few dozen companies make management's cut. Once the fund buys, it usually sticks with picks for years. Of course, loyalty to losing picks would be no virtue, but again and again the managers have demonstrated they can spot not only good values but also good businesses with staying power. Over the long haul, that's led to great results here and at sibling FPA Perennial. Thus, we continue to endorse this fund without hesitation.

Address:	11400 W Olympic Blvd Ste 1200 Los Angeles CA 90064 800-982-4372	Minimum Purchase:	$1500	Add: $100 IRA: $100
		Min Auto Inv Plan:	$100	Add: $100
		Sales Fees:	2.00%D	
Web Address:	www.FPAFunds.com	Management Fee:	0.65%	
Inception:	09-08-58	Actual Fees:	Mgt:0.65% Dist: —	
Advisor:	First Pacific Advisors, Inc.	Expense Projections:	3Yr:$794	5Yr:$992 10Yr:$1564
Subadvisor:	None	Income Distrib:	Semi-Annually	
NTF Plans:	N/A			

Historical Profile

Return	Below Avg
Risk	Average
Rating	★★ Below Avg

83%	77%	68%	82%	95%	84%	71%	77%	78%

- ▼ Manager Change
- ▽ Partial Manager Change

Growth of $10,000
- Investment Values of Fund
- Investment Values of S&P 500

Performance Quartile (within Category)

1995	1996	1997	1998	1999	2000	2001	2002	2003	2004	2005	2006	History
14.78	17.63	14.19	9.11	9.19	8.00	9.70	8.50	12.02	13.93	15.58	16.18	NAV
12.66	29.40	-1.76	-24.41	1.65	-10.96	21.67	-12.37	41.41	15.89	12.20	4.76	Total Return %
-24.92	6.44	-35.12	-52.99	-19.39	-1.86	33.56	9.73	12.73	5.01	7.29	-11.03	+/-S&P 500
-18.27	10.15	-34.01	-43.53	-13.07	-28.47	22.28	2.16	5.79	-0.59	-0.36	-5.56	+/-S&P Mid 400
2.12	1.90	1.91	1.81	0.77	1.86	0.40	0.00	0.00	0.00	0.36	0.90	Income Return %
10.54	27.50	-3.67	-26.22	0.88	-12.82	21.27	-12.37	41.41	15.89	11.84	3.86	Capital Return %
98	6	98	99	87	87	6	25	23	55	22	98	Total Rtn % Rank Cat
0.29	0.27	0.31	0.24	0.07	0.17	0.03	0.00	0.00	0.00	0.05	0.14	Income $
1.01	0.91	2.87	1.90	0.00	0.00	0.00	0.00	0.00	0.00	0.00	0.00	Capital Gains $
0.89	0.87	0.86	0.92	1.03	1.17	1.20	1.17	1.15	0.99	0.89	0.85	Expense Ratio %
2.25	1.94	1.84	1.14	0.57	1.22	0.92	-0.34	-0.47	-0.16	0.30	0.89	Income Ratio %
95	131	110	68	21	76	16	14	17	16	13	15	Turnover Rate %
575	692	699	279	148	72	90	80	123	257	399	620	Net Assets $mil

Rating and Risk

Time Period	Load-Adj Return %	Morningstar Rtn vs Cat	Morningstar Risk vs Cat	Morningstar Risk-Adj Rating
1 Yr	-0.74			
3 Yr	8.88	-Avg	-Avg	★★
5 Yr	9.85	Avg	+Avg	★★★
10 Yr	2.72	Low	Avg	★
Incept	—			

Other Measures	Standard Index S&P 500	Best Fit Index Russ 2000 Gr
Alpha	-0.2	3.1
Beta	1.11	0.55
R-Squared	64	83
Standard Deviation	9.51	
Mean	10.85	
Sharpe Ratio	0.79	

Portfolio Analysis 09-30-06

Share change since 06-06 Total Stocks:36	Sector	PE	Tot Ret%	% Assets
⊕ CDW Corporation	Business	20.4	23.33	4.04
⊕ O'Reilly Automotive, Inc	Consumer	20.4	0.16	3.71
⊕ CarMax, Inc.	Consumer	32.2	93.75	3.68
⊕ Charles River Laboratori	Health	—	2.08	3.64
⊕ Cognex Corporation	Hardware	27.3	-19.80	3.35
⊕ Helix Energy Solutions G	—	10.6	-12.59	3.22
⊕ Lincare Holdings Inc.	Health	19.3	-4.94	3.11
⊕ Invitrogen Corporation	Health	29.1	-15.08	3.09
⊖ Zebra Technologies Corpo	Hardware	30.4	-18.81	3.03
⊖ Noble Corporation	Energy	15.5	8.19	3.02
⊕ ScanSource	Ind Mtrls	19.7	11.19	3.00
⊕ Brady Corporation A	Ind Mtrls	17.4	4.55	2.90
⊕ Heartland Express, Inc.	Business	16.9	-0.85	2.77
⊕ HNI Corporation	Goods	17.9	-17.95	2.73
⊖ Carnival Corporation	Goods	18.7	-6.15	2.49
⊕ Plantronics	Hardware	14.3	-24.37	2.40
⊕ Polaris Industries, Inc.	Goods	15.5	-4.10	2.28
⊕ Knight Transportation, I	Business	21.4	-17.31	2.15
⊕ Microchip Technology, In	Hardware	27.2	4.37	2.12
⊕ Idex Corporation	Ind Mtrls	19.6	16.76	2.04

Current Investment Style

Value Blnd Growth		
	Large Mid Small	

Market Cap	%
Giant	0.0
Large	3.2
Mid	65.8
Small	31.0
Micro	0.1
Avg $mil:	2,930

Value Measures		Rel Category
Price/Earnings	17.27	1.07
Price/Book	2.55	1.13
Price/Sales	1.31	1.17
Price/Cash Flow	12.34	1.46
Dividend Yield %	0.89	0.68

Growth Measures	%	Rel Category
Long-Term Erngs	17.30	1.36
Book Value	14.33	1.72
Sales	14.76	1.66
Cash Flow	11.59	1.37
Historical Erngs	19.93	1.11

Profitability	%	Rel Category
Return on Equity	16.48	1.03
Return on Assets	10.40	1.30
Net Margin	11.73	1.08

Sector Weightings	% of Stocks	Rel S&P 500	3 Year High Low
↻ Info	17.60	0.88	
📈 Software	0.00	0.00	0 0
💻 Hardware	17.60	1.90	23 16
🔊 Media	0.00	0.00	0 0
📞 Telecom	0.00	0.00	0 0
⊂ Service	47.78	1.03	
🩺 Health	18.15	1.50	21 14
🛒 Consumer	9.81	1.28	14 10
💼 Business	14.80	3.50	15 3
💲 Financial	5.02	0.23	10 5
⚒ Mfg	34.63	1.02	
🏭 Goods	9.97	1.17	10 4
⚙ Ind Mtrls	19.32	1.62	20 17
🔋 Energy	5.34	0.54	13 5
⚡ Utilities	0.00	0.00	0 0

Composition

		%
● Cash		21.5
● Stocks		78.5
● Bonds		0.0
○ Other		0.0
Foreign		0.0
(% of Stock)		

Investment Style

Equity
Stock %

Franklin Bal Sh Invmt A

	Ticker	Load	NAV	Yield	Total Assets	Mstar Category
	FRBSX	Closed	$66.71	1.2%	$5,201 mil	Mid-Cap Value

Governance and Management

Stewardship Grade: B

Portfolio Manager(s)

Value hound Bruce Baughman has managed this fund since 1990. He has had ups and downs, but he generally has produced competitive returns with relatively low volatility. Baughman is an accountant by training and pays close attention to company balance sheets. He is deliberate and prefers to be fully invested, but he won't compromise his investment style to do so.

Strategy

This fund employs a stricter value discipline than many of its competitors. It requires price/book multiples in the bottom 20% of the universe it tracks and strong corporate governance given that management assumes it will hold on to the stocks in the portfolio for at least five years. That stringent criterion has occasionally forced the fund to hold rather large cash positions, which at times has hindered performance.

Performance 12-31-06

	1st Qtr	2nd Qtr	3rd Qtr	4th Qtr	Total
2002	6.35	-1.15	-13.45	3.35	-5.96
2003	-4.88	13.61	6.06	13.06	29.58
2004	5.36	3.43	1.87	12.87	25.30
2005	0.03	2.93	4.58	2.98	10.90
2006	9.54	-0.74	-0.31	7.34	16.35

Trailing	Total Return%	+/- S&P 500	+/- Russ MV	%Rank Cat	Growth of $10,000
3 Mo	7.34	0.64	-1.16	66	10,734
6 Mo	7.01	-5.73	-5.32	93	10,701
1 Yr	16.35	0.56	-3.87	40	11,635
3 Yr Avg	17.37	6.93	-1.40	12	16,169
5 Yr Avg	14.53	8.34	-1.35	11	19,706
10 Yr Avg	13.16	4.74	-0.49	22	34,429
15 Yr Avg	15.05	4.41	0.15	1	81,903

Tax Analysis	Tax-Adj Rtn%	%Rank Cat	Tax-Cost Rat	%Rank Cat
3 Yr (estimated)	14.06	26	0.89	25
5 Yr (estimated)	12.42	19	0.67	23
10 Yr (estimated)	11.42	15	0.96	24

Potential Capital Gain Exposure: 44% of assets

Historical Profile

Return	Above Avg
Risk	Below Avg
Rating	★★★★ Above Avg

	78%	91%	94%	99%	70%	75%	81%	84%	83%

Investment Style
Equity
Stock %

▼ Manager Change
▽ Partial Manager Change

49.2
42.2
32.4
24.0
17.0

Growth of $10,000
■ Investment Values of Fund
— Investment Values of S&P 500

10.0

Performance Quartile (within Category)

	1995	1996	1997	1998	1999	2000	2001	2002	2003	2004	2005	2006	History
	26.68	28.49	33.54	31.60	30.47	35.67	40.02	37.09	47.57	58.26	61.73	66.71	NAV
	30.05	17.50	25.97	-0.61	-1.53	20.47	17.70	-5.96	29.58	25.30	10.90	16.35	Total Return %
	-7.53	-5.46	-7.39	-29.19	-22.57	29.57	29.59	16.14	0.90	14.42	5.99	0.56	+/-S&P 500
	-4.88	-2.76	-8.40	-5.69	-1.42	1.29	15.37	3.68	-8.49	1.59	-1.75	-3.87	+/-Russ MV
	1.59	1.65	1.67	1.60	1.14	1.19	1.94	0.75	0.45	0.90	0.80	1.43	Income Return %
	28.46	15.85	24.30	-2.21	-2.67	19.28	15.76	-6.71	29.13	24.40	10.10	14.92	Capital Return %
	20	67	48	59	81	54	18	11	76	5	28	40	Total Rtn % Rank Cat
	0.34	0.44	0.47	0.53	0.36	0.36	0.69	0.30	0.17	0.43	0.46	0.88	Income $
	1.06	2.36	1.80	1.16	0.28	0.61	1.17	0.25	0.31	0.91	2.44	4.28	Capital Gains $
	1.17	1.08	1.08	0.93	0.93	1.06	0.96	0.92	1.00	0.91	0.91	—	Expense Ratio %
	1.30	1.69	1.59	1.47	1.19	1.00	2.14	0.63	0.35	0.67	0.57	—	Income Ratio %
	29	35	25	12	18	9	27	11	13	7	4	—	Turnover Rate %
	450	711	1,286	1,517	1,136	1,113	1,778	2,415	3,229	4,219	4,193	4,524	Net Assets $mil

Rating and Risk

Time Period	Load-Adj Return %	Morningstar Rtn vs Cat	Morningstar Risk vs Cat	Morningstar Risk-Adj Rating
1 Yr	9.66			
3 Yr	15.08	Avg	Avg	★★★
5 Yr	13.18	+Avg	-Avg	★★★★
10 Yr	12.50	+Avg	Low	★★★★
Incept	13.87			

Other Measures	Standard Index S&P 500	Best Fit Index Mstar Small Core
Alpha	5.1	3.9
Beta	1.18	0.72
R-Squared	68	93
Standard Deviation	9.75	
Mean	17.37	
Sharpe Ratio	1.37	

Portfolio Analysis 09-30-06

Share change since 06-06 Total Stocks:115

	Sector	PE	Tot Ret%	% Assets
Prudential Financial, In	Financial	16.1	18.70	2.22
Freddie Mac	Financial	23.3	7.06	2.19
CIT Group, Inc.	Financial	11.4	9.45	2.16
Bunge, Ltd.	Goods	21.0	29.46	2.11
⊖ Nucor Corp.	Ind Mtrls	10.3	70.67	1.90
Corn Products Internatio	Goods	22.5	45.73	1.84
Old Republic Internation	Financial	10.6	13.90	1.73
Pulte Homes, Inc.	Consumer	6.7	-15.43	1.67
Dollar Thrifty Automotiv	Consumer	17.0	26.45	1.58
American National Insura	Financial	13.0	0.12	1.51
Sierra Pacific Resources	Utilities	12.2	29.06	1.45
⊖ Trinity Industries, Inc.	Ind Mtrls	16.0	20.56	1.42
⊖ United States Steel Corp	Ind Mtrls	7.4	53.62	1.42
⊕ Monsanto Company	Ind Mtrls	39.8	36.78	1.36
Charming Shoppes, Inc.	Consumer	17.0	2.89	1.27
⊕ Reliance Steel and Alumi	Ind Mtrls	8.2	29.63	1.26
Entergy Corporation	Utilities	19.7	38.40	1.24
Vail Resorts, Inc.	Consumer	37.2	35.70	1.23
Norfolk Southern Corpora	Business	14.0	13.73	1.20
ESCO Technologies, Inc.	Hardware	38.4	2.14	1.15

Current Investment Style

Value Blnd Growth — Large Mid Small

Market Cap	%
Giant	0.9
Large	16.4
Mid	53.4
Small	26.0
Micro	3.4
Avg $mil:	3,504

Value Measures		Rel Category
Price/Earnings	12.03	0.81
Price/Book	1.52	0.76
Price/Sales	0.75	0.77
Price/Cash Flow	2.44	0.32
Dividend Yield %	1.36	0.76

Growth Measures	%	Rel Category
Long-Term Erngs	11.83	1.07
Book Value	4.28	0.61
Sales	5.97	0.78
Cash Flow	0.79	0.20
Historical Erngs	17.50	1.19

Profitability	%	Rel Category
Return on Equity	11.22	0.78
Return on Assets	6.51	0.88
Net Margin	8.93	0.85

Sector Weightings	% of Stocks	Rel S&P 500	3 Year High	Low
⟳ Info	2.31	0.12		
🖥 Software	0.00	0.00	0	0
💻 Hardware	2.31	0.25	2	2
🎙 Media	0.00	0.00	0	0
☎ Telecom	0.00	0.00	0	0
⊂ Service	56.52	1.22		
⚕ Health	1.00	0.08	1	0
🛒 Consumer	15.25	1.99	22	14
🏢 Business	10.49	2.48	13	10
$ Financial	29.78	1.34	30	26
☐ Mfg	41.17	1.22		
🏭 Goods	10.07	1.18	12	9
⚙ Ind Mtrls	20.46	1.71	23	16
⬧ Energy	4.21	0.43	6	4
🔌 Utilities	6.43	1.84	6	5

Composition

● Cash	16.8	
● Stocks	83.1	
● Bonds	0.1	
● Other	0.0	
Foreign	5.8	(% of Stock)

Morningstar's Take by Kerry O'Boyle 11-27-06

Franklin Balance Sheet Investment's deep-value, long-term strategy has proven its worth over time.

This fund's approach sounds so simple it makes one wonder why more funds don't follow its lead. Veteran manager Bruce Baughman seeks out financially sound and well-established companies with very low price/book ratios, and then holds on to them for years. Of course, what seems simple can be complex in its execution. As the fund's name implies, Baughman digs through a firm's balance sheet to come up with his own estimates of book value to determine whether the stock price is indeed cheap. And because he intends to hold on to a stock for more than five years, he spends a great deal of time assessing corporate governance and a firm's ability to increase its book value.

Not surprisingly, that deep-value style seldom delivers the flashy returns that garner headlines. Baughman's penchant for letting cash build when opportunities are scarce can lead to sluggishness during big market rallies. But the fund's long-term

outlook is evident when Baughman points out that whatever is boosting performance most at the present moment is generally something he bought many years ago--as has been the case with steel firms such as Nucor and United States Steel. And over the long haul, the fund's slow and steady approach does stand out among its mid-value rivals.

Although the strategy tends to favor sectors like financials at the expense of technology and biotech, the fund's sector biases haven't resulted in undue volatility (as measured by standard deviation). In fact, the longer the holding period, the lower volatility has been versus the fund's peers during the past decade.

Adding to the fund's appeal are low fees and a timely closing to new investments in 2002--both appropriate features, given that it's one of the largest funds in the group. That gives shareholders more reason to believe that this fine fund can continue to carry on as it has in the past.

Address:	One Franklin Parkway San Mateo CA 94403-1906 800-342-5236	Minimum Purchase:	Closed	Add: —	IRA: —
		Min Auto Inv Plan:	Closed	Add: —	
		Sales Fees:	5.75%L, 0.24%S, 2.00%R		
Web Address:	www.franklintempleton.com	Management Fee:	0.63% mx./0.40% mn., 0.15%A		
Inception:	04-02-90	Actual Fees:	Mgt:0.45% Dist:0.24%		
Advisor:	Franklin Advisory Services, LLC	Expense Projections:	3Yr:$848 5Yr:$1050 10Yr:$1630		
Subadvisor:	None	Income Distrib:	Annually		
NTF Plans:	DATALynx NTF, Federated Tr NTF				

Franklin Fed T/F Inc A

Analyst Pick ✓

Ticker	FKTIX	
Load	4.25%	
NAV	$12.17	
Yield	4.4%	
SEC Yield	3.39%	
Total Assets	$7,294 mil	
Mstar Category	Muni National Long	

Governance and Management

Stewardship Grade: C

Portfolio Manager(s)

Sheila Amoroso is a Franklin veteran and a proven municipal-bond manager. She has been a member of the fund's management team since 1987 and has delivered solid results here and at other Franklin muni offerings. Francisco Rivera, Carrie Higgins, and John Wiley also contribute here.

Strategy

This income-oriented fund follows Franklin's plain-vanilla approach. Its management team, led by Sheila Amoroso, uses a buy-and-hold strategy in an effort to provide a steady stream of income from which the bulk of the fund's total return is derived. Management doesn't make interest-rate bets and avoids potentially volatile derivative securities. And although the fund's duration floats with the market, it typically runs shorter than that of the category as a whole.

Historical Profile

Return	Above Avg
Risk	Low
Rating	★★★★ Above Avg

4	3	7	8	11	12	11	8

▼ Manager Change
▽ Partial Manager Change

Growth of $10,000
- Investment Values of Fund
- Investment Values of LB Muni

Scale: 20.8, 18.8, 16.4, 14.0, 12.0, 10.0

Performance Quartile (within Category)

	1995	1996	1997	1998	1999	2000	2001	2002	2003	2004	2005	2006	History
NAV	12.19	12.01	12.35	12.39	11.39	11.85	11.76	11.98	12.09	12.16	12.11	12.17	
Total Return %	15.10	4.70	8.97	5.94	-2.79	10.14	4.63	7.19	5.84	5.39	4.26	5.08	
+/-LB Muni	-2.36	0.27	-0.22	-0.54	-0.73	-1.54	-0.50	-2.41	0.53	0.91	0.75	0.24	
+/-LB Muni 20YR	-5.87	0.24	-1.87	-0.88	1.89	-5.10	-0.24	-2.84	-0.49	-1.17	-0.82	-0.78	
Income Return %	6.87	6.12	5.98	5.58	5.49	5.90	5.45	5.25	4.85	4.75	4.68	4.53	
Capital Return %	8.23	-1.42	2.99	0.36	-8.28	4.24	-0.82	1.94	0.99	0.64	-0.42	0.55	
Total Rtn % Rank Cat	84	12	50	23	10	70	23	81	16	5	8	21	
Income $	0.75	0.73	0.70	0.67	0.66	0.65	0.63	0.60	0.57	0.56	0.56	0.54	
Capital Gains $	0.00	0.00	0.00	0.00	0.01	0.00	0.00	0.00	0.00	0.00	0.00	0.00	
Expense Ratio %	0.59	0.57	0.58	0.59	0.60	0.60	0.60	0.60	0.61	0.61	0.61	0.61	
Income Ratio %	6.47	6.20	6.00	5.70	5.41	5.64	5.54	5.54	4.98	4.79	4.72	4.33	
Turnover Rate %	20	25	16	15	10	17	10	13	13	7	7	8	
Net Assets $mil	7,211	7,032	7,096	7,189	6,570	6,430	6,576	6,737	6,577	6,303	6,337	6,440	

Performance 12-31-06

	1st Qtr	2nd Qtr	3rd Qtr	4th Qtr	Total
2002	0.70	3.03	3.41	-0.09	7.19
2003	0.97	3.06	-0.31	2.02	5.84
2004	2.33	-2.38	3.59	1.85	5.39
2005	0.75	2.83	-0.25	0.88	4.26
2006	0.44	0.10	3.18	1.31	5.08

Trailing	Total Return%	+/- LB Muni	+/- LB Muni 20YR	%Rank Cat	Growth of $10,000
3 Mo	1.31	0.20	-0.12	9	10,131
6 Mo	4.52	-0.03	-0.99	34	10,452
1 Yr	5.08	0.24	-0.78	21	10,508
3 Yr Avg	4.91	0.63	-0.92	9	11,547
5 Yr Avg	5.55	0.02	-1.21	17	13,101
10 Yr Avg	5.41	-0.35	-1.17	19	16,936
15 Yr Avg	6.00	-0.26	-1.08	23	23,966

Tax Analysis	Tax-Adj Rtn%	%Rank Cat	Tax-Cost Rat	%Rank Cat
3 Yr (estimated)	3.40	44	0.00	1
5 Yr (estimated)	4.63	46	0.00	1
10 Yr (estimated)	4.95	33	0.01	5

Potential Capital Gain Exposure: 5% of assets

Rating and Risk

Time Period	Load-Adj Return %	Morningstar Rtn vs Cat	Morningstar Risk vs Cat	Morningstar Risk-Adj Rating
1 Yr	0.61			
3 Yr	3.40	Avg	-Avg	★★★
5 Yr	4.63	Avg	Low	★★★
10 Yr	4.96	+Avg	Low	★★★★
Incept	7.40			

Other Measures	Standard Index LB Muni	Best Fit Index LB Muni 20YR
Alpha	0.7	-0.3
Beta	0.90	0.78
R-Squared	97	97
Standard Deviation	2.80	
Mean	4.91	
Sharpe Ratio	0.57	

Portfolio Analysis 09-30-06

Total Fixed-Income: 797

	Date of Maturity	Amount $000	Value $000	% Net Assets
Dallas Fort Worth Tex In	11-01-26	85,000	90,761	1.26
North Carolina Eastn Mun	01-01-26	65,350	69,057	0.96
Puerto Rico Comwlth Hwy	07-01-36	62,000	64,270	0.89
New York N Y 6.125%	08-01-25	61,630	63,545	0.88
Denver Colo City & Cnty	10-01-32	47,980	61,044	0.84
Pope Cnty Ark Pollutn Ct	11-01-20	60,500	60,574	0.84
New York N Y City Mun Wt	06-15-33	55,000	59,285	0.82
Golden St Tob Securitiza	06-01-28	50,000	53,120	0.74
Massachusetts St Tpk Aut	01-01-37	52,130	52,965	0.73
California St 5%	02-01-32	49,000	50,520	0.70
San Joaquin Hills Calif	01-15-21	50,000	49,743	0.69
North Carolina Eastn Mun	01-01-23	39,030	46,537	0.64
Denver Colo City & Cnty	11-15-23	43,000	44,184	0.61
Metropolitan Pier & Expo	12-15-28	39,580	41,240	0.57
District Columbia Tob Se	05-15-33	35,000	40,897	0.57

Current Investment Style

¹Avg Eff Duration	—
Avg Eff Maturity	17.2 Yrs
Avg Credit Quality	AA
Avg Wtd Coupon	5.15%
Avg Wtd Price	104.12% of par

¹figure provided by fund

Credit Analysis % bonds 09-30-06

AAA	71	BB	1
AA	9	B	0
A	5	Below B	0
BBB	12	NR/NA	1

Special Securities

Restricted/Illiquid Secs	0
Options/Futures/Warrants	No

Sector Weightings

	% of Bonds	Rel Cat
General Obligation	21.9	0.78
Utilities	12.7	1.22
Health	10.8	1.04
Water/Waste	12.9	1.31
Housing	3.7	0.59
Education	8.5	0.75
Transportation	18.8	2.18
COP/Lease	1.5	0.64
Industrial	8.5	0.70
Misc Revenue	0.0	—
Demand	0.7	1.54

Top 5 States % bonds

NY	11.7	IL	5.1
CA	8.1	FL	4.6
TX	5.2		

Composition

Cash	1.5	Bonds	98.5
Stocks	0.0	Other	0.0

Morningstar's Take by Reginald Laing 12-18-06

Franklin Federal Tax-Free Income is a standout.

With $7.33 billion in assets under management, this is the biggest fund in Morningstar's muni-national long-term category. And Franklin has passed on the cost savings that come with economies of scale: This fund levies a mere 0.61% expense ratio, which is far below the 0.85% median for the category s front-load offerings.

As expenses come directly out of a bond fund's income, this fund's significant expense advantage allows it to offer one of the highest income payouts in the category. To be sure, the fund does hold a modestly bigger stake in higher-yielding midquality issues than its average peer. But the managers never buy bonds rated lower than BBB, and each new holding is thoroughly vetted by Franklin's deep and experienced team of credit analysts.

Lately, though, management thinks midquality bonds aren't paying enough to compensate investors for their added credit risk. For that reason, they've favored taxpayer-backed AAA bonds from states that don't have a lot of muni issuance (for example, Hawaii), as their scarcity value should help their prices hold up on the secondary market. These bonds have maturities in the 25- to 30-year range. That will help maintain this fund's high income return, as longer-dated munis nearly always yield more than shorter-term ones. Finally, because many of these bonds carry call provisions (which allow issuers to repay them and refinance if rates go lower) they tend to have shorter durations (a common measure of interest-rate risk) than noncallable long-term bonds.

Franklin employs a buy-and-hold approach here, so it's likely the fund will hold these bonds until they mature or get called away. That approach isn't flashy, but it has paid off over time. For the trailing 10 years through December 14, 2006, this fund's 5.42% annualized gain beat that of 80% of its peers. And looking forward, we think this fund's low expenses, experienced management, and sensible strategy will lead to similar success.

Address:	One Franklin Parkway, San Mateo CA 94403-1906, 800-342-5236
Web Address:	www.franklintempleton.com
Inception:	10-07-83
Advisor:	Franklin Advisers, Inc.
Subadvisor:	None
NTF Plans:	Fidelity Instl-NTF, Schwab Instl NTF

Minimum Purchase:	$1000, Add: $50, IRA: $0
Min Auto Inv Plan:	$50, Add: $50
Sales Fees:	4.25%L, 0.09%S, 2.00%R
Management Fee:	0.63% mx./0.36% mn., 0.15%A
Actual Fees:	Mgt:0.45% Dist:0.09%
Expense Projections:	3Yr:$612 5Yr:$751 10Yr:$1155
Income Distrib:	Monthly

Morningstar® Funds 500

Franklin Growth A

	Ticker	Load	NAV	Yield	Total Assets	Mstar Category
	FKGRX	5.75%	$41.63	0.3%	$2,566 mil	Large Blend

Governance and Management

Stewardship Grade: B

Portfolio Manager(s)

Jerry Palmieri has run this fund for more than 40 years, making him one of the longest-tenured fund managers around. His stock-picking has been good, but his asset allocation has been mixed. When stocks crashed in 1987, the fund gained more than 19%, and Palmieri was Morningstar's first Manager of the Year. But he kept a third of his money in cash in the late 1990s--missing the bull market's final run--and jumped back into stocks too early in 2002.

Strategy

This fund can own stocks of any size. In practice, though, manager Jerry Palmieri tries to buy industry leaders, skewing the fund toward large-cap stocks. He also has an eye for value, preferring to hold large cash stakes rather than pay inflated prices.

Historical Profile

Return	Below Avg
Risk	Average
Rating	★★★ Neutral

74%　67%　88%　100%　99%　98%　100%　99%　99%

Investment Style
Equity
Stock %

▼ Manager Change
▽ Partial Manager Change

Growth of $10,000
━ Investment Values of Fund
━ Investment Values of S&P 500

Performance Quartile (within Category)

	1995	1996	1997	1998	1999	2000	2001	2002	2003	2004	2005	2006	History
	20.44	23.43	27.09	31.45	34.54	35.03	31.51	23.80	30.44	33.80	36.56	41.63	NAV
	38.40	16.68	18.60	18.52	12.19	7.53	-9.47	-24.35	28.03	11.30	8.36	14.16	Total Return %
	0.82	-6.28	-14.76	-10.06	-8.85	16.63	2.42	-2.25	-0.65	0.42	3.45	-1.63	+/-S&P 500
	0.63	-5.77	-14.25	-8.50	-8.72	15.32	2.98	-2.70	-1.86	-0.10	2.09	-1.30	+/-Russ 1000
	1.09	1.11	1.99	1.62	1.44	1.16	0.44	0.12	0.12	0.26	0.19	0.29	Income Return %
	37.31	15.57	16.61	16.90	10.75	6.37	-9.91	-24.47	27.91	11.04	8.17	13.87	Capital Return %
	10	86	89	63	79	13	30	80	44	35	21	53	Total Rtn % Rank Cat
	0.16	0.23	0.47	0.44	0.45	0.40	0.16	0.04	0.03	0.08	0.06	0.11	Income $
	0.15	0.20	0.24	0.21	0.26	1.67	0.05	0.00	0.00	0.00	0.00	0.00	Capital Gains $
	0.90	0.87	0.89	0.88	0.89	0.93	0.91	0.96	1.06	0.98	0.94	0.91	Expense Ratio %
	1.08	1.16	1.60	1.78	1.19	1.27	0.69	0.24	0.31	0.20	0.40	0.34	Income Ratio %
	1	2	2	1	4	8	—	2	5	2	1	2	Turnover Rate %
	803	1,110	1,509	1,899	2,194	2,139	1,884	1,320	1,608	1,659	1,639	1,806	Net Assets $mil

Performance 12-31-06

	1st Qtr	2nd Qtr	3rd Qtr	4th Qtr	Total
2002	1.27	-15.11	-18.75	8.30	-24.35
2003	-6.01	17.70	2.05	13.40	28.03
2004	-0.39	5.84	-4.71	10.79	11.30
2005	-1.86	0.36	4.63	5.15	8.36
2006	4.79	-1.98	4.13	6.74	14.16

Trailing	Total Return%	+/- S&P 500	+/- Russ 1000	%Rank Cat	Growth of $10,000
3 Mo	6.74	0.04	-0.21	42	10,674
6 Mo	11.15	-1.59	-1.21	58	11,115
1 Yr	14.16	-1.63	-1.30	53	11,416
3 Yr Avg	11.25	0.81	0.27	25	13,769
5 Yr Avg	5.92	-0.27	-0.90	45	13,332
10 Yr Avg	7.43	-0.99	-1.21	58	20,477
15 Yr Avg	9.21	-1.43	-1.59	74	37,492

Tax Analysis	Tax-Adj Rtn%	%Rank Cat	Tax-Cost Rat	%Rank Cat
3 Yr (estimated)	8.99	51	0.07	4
5 Yr (estimated)	4.61	60	0.07	5
10 Yr (estimated)	6.34	54	0.42	14

Potential Capital Gain Exposure: 59% of assets

Rating and Risk

Time Period	Load-Adj Return %	Morningstar Rtn vs Cat	Morningstar Risk vs Cat	Morningstar Risk-Adj Rating
1 Yr	7.60			
3 Yr	9.07	Avg	+Avg	★★
5 Yr	4.68	-Avg	+Avg	★★
10 Yr	6.79	-Avg	-Avg	★★★
Incept	10.47			

Other Measures	Standard Index S&P 500	Best Fit Index Russ 1000Gr
Alpha	0.0	4.2
Beta	1.13	0.95
R-Squared	81	87
Standard Deviation	8.64	
Mean	11.25	
Sharpe Ratio	0.91	

Portfolio Analysis 09-30-06

Share change since 06-06 Total Stocks:99	Sector	PE	Tot Ret%	% Assets
Genentech, Inc.	Health	48.7	-12.29	3.44
Boeing Company	Ind Mtrls	41.2	28.38	3.28
Apple Computer, Inc.	Hardware	37.6	18.01	3.20
General Dynamics	Ind Mtrls	19.1	32.17	2.98
Northrop Grumman Corpora	Ind Mtrls	16.7	14.63	2.83
Amgen, Inc.	Health	29.1	-13.38	2.77
Johnson & Johnson	Health	17.5	12.45	2.69
3M Company	Ind Mtrls	16.7	2.98	2.47
Pfizer Inc.	Health	15.2	15.22	2.36
United Technologies	Ind Mtrls	17.8	13.65	2.11
Computer Sciences Corpor	Business	23.7	5.39	2.04
Textron Incorporated	Ind Mtrls	18.3	23.94	1.91
IBM	Hardware	17.1	19.77	1.91
Allergan, Inc.	Health	—	11.33	1.87
Illinois Tool Works, Inc	Ind Mtrls	15.7	6.69	1.87
Tyco International, Ltd.	Ind Mtrls	15.7	6.83	1.80
Lockheed Martin Corporat	Ind Mtrls	17.3	46.98	1.79
Emerson Electric Company	Ind Mtrls	19.6	20.68	1.74
Hewlett-Packard Company	Hardware	19.3	45.21	1.70
Yahoo, Inc.	Media	35.4	-34.81	1.68

Current Investment Style

Value Blnd Growth — Large/Mid/Small

Market Cap	%
Giant	40.0
Large	39.5
Mid	18.9
Small	1.6
Micro	0.0

Avg $mil: 27,599

Value Measures		Rel Category
Price/Earnings	18.35	1.19
Price/Book	3.19	1.25
Price/Sales	1.24	0.89
Price/Cash Flow	10.52	1.25
Dividend Yield %	1.32	0.75

Growth Measures	%	Rel Category
Long-Term Erngs	12.85	1.09
Book Value	3.84	0.43
Sales	5.12	0.53
Cash Flow	9.40	0.91
Historical Erngs	18.13	0.98

Profitability	%	Rel Category
Return on Equity	19.30	0.99
Return on Assets	9.25	0.89
Net Margin	11.19	0.83

Sector Weightings	% of Stocks	Rel S&P 500	3 Year High Low	
Info	19.68	0.98		
Software	1.52	0.44	2	1
Hardware	13.12	1.42	13	10
Media	5.04	1.33	6	5
Telecom	0.00	0.00	0	0
Service	40.71	0.88		
Health	25.30	2.10	25	22
Consumer	1.24	0.16	3	1
Business	12.83	3.03	15	13
Financial	1.34	0.06	1	0
Mfg	39.62	1.17		
Goods	6.00	0.70	7	5
Ind Mtrls	32.03	2.68	33	30
Energy	1.59	0.16	5	2
Utilities	0.00	0.00	0	0

Composition

	%
● Cash	0.8
● Stocks	99.1
● Bonds	0.0
○ Other	0.1
Foreign	4.0
(% of Stock)	

Morningstar's Take by Kerry O'Boyle 11-02-06

Despite its storied history, we don't think Franklin Growth is the best option for investors going forward.

Manager Jerry Palmieri has been running this fund since March 1965. No, that's not a typo; his more-than-40-year tenure is one of the longest in our database for any fund. But it has been an up-and-down history, as Palmieri's willingness to move into cash when he thinks the market is overdone has had mixed results. It worked like a charm in 1987 when the stock market crashed and the fund ended the year with a nearly 20% gain, but didn't fare as well during the late 1990s when performance lagged over a multiyear period. Although the fund is currently fully invested and has been since 2001, there's no telling when the next asset-allocation call may be coming.

Of greater importance to investors, however, is that an investment made in a cheap S&P 500 Index fund over the past 10- or 15-year period would have outperformed this fund, with lower volatility along

the way. In addition, the fund has taken on a noticeably growthier look in recent years with high-flying stocks such as Yahoo, Apple Computer, and biotech firm Genentech becoming more prominent in the portfolio. Palmieri acknowledges that the fund's flexible mandate allows him to go into almost any area of the market and that he likes to devote 10% to 15% of assets toward what he calls speculative names. As a result, the fund may not fit many investors' idea of a core, large-blend fund.

Granted, we like the fund's buy-and-hold approach--one that hasn't seen annual turnover reach double-digits in more than two decades--and Palmieri's vast experience isn't something that we wish to undervalue. It's just that given the fund's history of trying to time the market, and what we consider its more-aggressive portfolio, we think that in the competitive large-blend field that investors can find better options elsewhere.

Address:	One Franklin Parkway San Mateo CA 94403-1906 800-632-2301	Minimum Purchase: Min Auto Inv Plan: Sales Fees:	$1000 Add: $50 IRA: $250 $50 Add: $50 5.75%L, 0.25%S, 2.00%R
Web Address:	www.franklintempleton.com	Management Fee:	0.63% mx./0.35% mn.
Inception:	03-30-48	Actual Fees:	Mgt:0.46% Dist:0.25%
Advisor:	Franklin Investment Advisory Serv, LLC	Expense Projections:	3Yr:$857 5Yr:$1065 10Yr:$1663
Subadvisor:	None	Income Distrib:	Annually
NTF Plans:	DATALynx NTF, Federated Tr NTF		

Franklin Hi Yld T/F A

	Ticker	Load	NAV	Yield	SEC Yield	Total Assets	Mstar Category
	FRHIX	4.25%	$11.02	4.8%	3.83%	$6,252 mil	High Yield Muni

Governance and Management

Stewardship Grade: C

Portfolio Manager(s)

John Wiley has been manager of this fund since 2000. He is a Franklin veteran with extensive experience managing tax-free money. Sheila Amoroso, John Hopp, Francisco Rivera, and a group of 15 analysts round out the team.

Strategy

This fund follows Franklin's basic buy-and-hold strategy. It avoids interest-rate bets and focuses on income more than on total return. Management looks to add value primarily through issue selection and sector allocation. The fund is more diversified than most high-yield municipal bond funds, but credit risk is a concern, as the fund typically holds 25% to 30% of its assets in nonrated bonds. The fund also holds a few sizable individual positions, which could add to its volatility.

Performance 12-31-06

	1st Qtr	2nd Qtr	3rd Qtr	4th Qtr	Total
2002	0.91	2.31	1.73	0.11	5.15
2003	-0.03	3.79	1.13	2.87	7.99
2004	2.15	-1.42	3.45	2.60	6.88
2005	1.25	3.40	-0.27	0.96	5.45
2006	1.22	0.67	3.37	2.01	7.45

Trailing	Total Return%	+/- LB Muni	+/- LB Muni 10YR	%Rank Cat	Growth of $10,000
3 Mo	2.01	0.90	1.09	15	10,201
6 Mo	5.45	0.90	0.68	24	10,545
1 Yr	7.45	2.61	2.74	30	10,745
3 Yr Avg	6.58	2.30	2.72	41	12,107
5 Yr Avg	6.57	1.04	1.11	39	13,746
10 Yr Avg	5.63	-0.13	-0.07	21	17,293
15 Yr Avg	6.50	0.24	0.22	13	25,718

Tax Analysis	Tax-Adj Rtn%	%Rank Cat	Tax-Cost Rat	%Rank Cat
3 Yr (estimated)	5.07	79	0.00	1
5 Yr (estimated)	5.66	70	0.00	1
10 Yr (estimated)	5.17	49	0.00	1

Potential Capital Gain Exposure: 0% of assets

Historical Profile

Return	Average
Risk	Average
Rating	★★★ Neutral

| | 14 | 10 | 15 | 41 | 34 | 26 | 24 | 26 |

▼ Manager Change
▽ Partial Manager Change

- 20.8
- 18.8
- 16.4 **Growth of $10,000**
- 14.0 — Investment Values of Fund
- 12.0
- 10.0 — Investment Values of LB Muni

Investment Style
Fixed Income
Income Rtn %Rank Cat

Performance Quartile
(within Category)

1995	1996	1997	1998	1999	2000	2001	2002	2003	2004	2005	2006	History
11.26	11.19	11.64	11.51	10.51	10.47	10.49	10.42	10.63	10.75	10.76	11.02	NAV
16.29	6.14	10.58	4.81	-3.21	5.78	5.92	5.15	7.99	6.88	5.45	7.45	Total Return %
-1.17	1.71	1.39	-1.15	-5.90	0.79	-4.45	2.68	2.40	1.94	2.61	+/-LB Muni
-0.88	1.60	1.35	-1.95	-1.96	-4.98	1.30	-5.02	2.29	2.73	2.71	2.74	+/-LB Muni 10YR
7.30	6.70	6.40	5.85	5.78	6.23	5.74	5.84	5.85	5.68	5.39	5.00	Income Return %
8.99	-0.56	4.18	-1.04	-8.99	-0.45	0.18	-0.69	2.14	1.20	0.06	2.45	Capital Return %
41	11	15	79	24	44	19	69	21	27	75	30	Total Rtn % Rank Cat
0.73	0.73	0.70	0.66	0.65	0.64	0.59	0.60	0.59	0.59	0.57	0.53	Income $
0.00	0.00	0.00	0.02	0.00	0.00	0.00	0.00	0.00	0.00	0.00	0.00	Capital Gains $
0.60	0.61	0.62	0.61	0.62	0.61	0.62	0.62	0.62	0.62	0.62	0.63	Expense Ratio %
6.92	6.68	6.41	5.98	5.64	5.92	5.90	5.78	5.69	5.62	5.44	5.11	Income Ratio %
16	9	7	16	19	25	11	10	12	9	9	12	Turnover Rate %
3,694	4,310	5,226	5,897	5,154	4,733	4,605	4,432	4,455	4,597	4,955	5,279	Net Assets $mil

Rating and Risk

Time Period	Load-Adj Return %	Morningstar Rtn vs Cat	Morningstar Risk vs Cat	Morningstar Risk-Adj Rating
1 Yr	2.89			
3 Yr	5.05	-Avg	+Avg	★★
5 Yr	5.65	Avg	Avg	★★★
10 Yr	5.17	Avg	Avg	★★★
Incept	6.94			

Other Measures	Standard Index LB Muni	Best Fit Index LB Muni 20YR
Alpha	2.4	1.5
Beta	0.78	0.68
R-Squared	84	87
Standard Deviation	2.60	
Mean	6.58	
Sharpe Ratio	1.23	

Portfolio Analysis 09-30-06

Total Fixed-Income:669	Date of Maturity	Amount $000	Value $000	% Net Assets
New York N Y City Indl D	08-01-12	74,000	83,616	1.36
New Jersey Econ Dev Auth	09-15-23	79,890	82,587	1.34
Pennsylvania Econ Dev Fi	12-01-36	65,000	69,976	1.14
Farmington N Mex Pollutn	04-01-22	66,125	68,185	1.11
Connecticut St Dev Auth	09-01-28	53,825	56,676	0.92
San Joaquin Hills Calif	01-01-27	139,100	56,064	0.91
San Joaquin Hills Calif	01-01-26	131,900	56,023	0.91
Apache Cnty Ariz Indl De	03-01-37	53,150	53,467	0.87
New York N Y City Indl D	03-01-35	50,000	53,407	0.87
Director St Nev Dept Bus	01-01-40	49,750	51,964	0.85
Indiana Health Fac Fincg	08-01-31	48,500	51,878	0.84
Eagle Cnty Colo Sports &	08-01-19	41,200	43,865	0.71
New Jersey Econ Dev Auth	09-15-19	42,000	43,249	0.70
California St 5%	02-01-33	40,640	42,176	0.69
Henderson Nev Loc Impt D	08-01-18	38,220	40,961	0.67

Current Investment Style

Duration: Short / Int / Long
Quality: High / Med / Low

¹Avg Eff Duration	—
Avg Eff Maturity	18.5 Yrs
Avg Credit Quality	A
Avg Wtd Coupon	5.57%
Avg Wtd Price	101.85% of par

¹figure provided by fund

Credit Analysis % bonds 09-30-06

AAA	36	BB	7
AA	4	B	8
A	5	Below B	1
BBB	19	NR/NA	20

Special Securities

Restricted/Illiquid Secs	0
Options/Futures/Warrants	No

Top 5 States % bonds

CA	18.3	NJ	5.1
NY	10.5	PA	4.4
FL	7.7		

Composition

Cash	1.3	Bonds	98.7
Stocks	0.0	Other	0.0

Sector Weightings

	% of Bonds	Rel Cat
General Obligation	18.2	1.04
Utilities	9.8	1.89
Health	14.8	0.91
Water/Waste	9.4	1.60
Housing	4.5	0.47
Education	3.5	0.61
Transportation	7.7	1.11
COP/Lease	2.3	1.71
Industrial	29.4	0.93
Misc Revenue	0.0	—
Demand	0.6	5.90

Morningstar's Take by Reginald Laing 12-21-06

Franklin High Yield Tax-Free Income is a good choice for muni investors looking for higher income without too much risk.

This fund's appeal begins with its 0.63% expense ratio, which makes it one of the least expensive high-yield municipal bond offerings--load or no load. Expenses come directly out of a bond fund's income, and this fund's low fees allow the managers to maintain one of the more attractive payouts in the category--without having to delve into the riskiest bonds to obtain yield.

Lately, as differences between investment-grade and junk yields have narrowed to historical lows, the managers have been even more circumspect about buying lower-rated bonds that they think are too risky for the amount of income they provide. The fund is not without risks though. It holds modest stakes in volatile tobacco and airline bonds, but its 55.2% stake in bonds rated BBB and below (including nonrated issues) is near its historical low: In June 2004, that stake was 66.1%. It's also lower

than the 68.7% stake its average peer is presently holding in non-investment-grade issues.

Having a higher-quality portfolio means the fund is less likely to suffer credit defaults than its average peer. But it also has held the fund back in the past year, as the market has shown a strong appetite for the lower-quality, higher-yielding bonds that this fund buys somewhat sparingly. However, over longer stretches of time, the fund has enjoyed success. For the trailing 10 years through November 30, 2006, this fund's 5.62% annualized gain tops those of 78% of its peers in Morningstar's high-yield municipal bond category. The fund's conservative nature has held volatility in check too. Its five- and 10-year standard deviations--common measures of volatility--are below the category averages.

We expect this fund to have similar success in the future. Its low fees, as well as its deeply experienced managers and analysts, should make it a long-term winner.

Address:	One Franklin Parkway, San Mateo CA 94403-1906, 800-632-2301
Web Address:	www.franklintempleton.com
Inception:	03-18-86
Advisor:	Franklin Advisers, Inc.
Subadvisor:	None
NTF Plans:	DATALynx NTF, Schwab Instl NTF

Minimum Purchase:	$1000 — Add: $50 — IRA: $0
Min Auto Inv Plan:	$50 — Add: $50
Sales Fees:	4.25%L, 0.10%S, 2.00%R
Management Fee:	0.63% mx./0.36% mn., 0.15%A
Actual Fees:	Mgt:0.46% Dist:0.10%
Expense Projections:	3Yr:$618 5Yr:$761 10Yr:$1178
Income Distrib:	Monthly

M⊙RNINGSTAR® Funds 500

Franklin Income A

	Ticker	Load	NAV	Yield	Total Assets	Mstar Category
	FKINX	4.25%	$2.66	5.3%	$52,245 mil	Conservative Allocation

Governance and Management

Stewardship Grade: C

Portfolio Manager(s)

Charles Johnson and Ed Perks run this fund. Johnson is the chairman of Franklin, while Perks is a seasoned veteran--he's been at the firm for more than a decade.

Strategy

This fund's management takes a value-oriented, contrarian approach to investing. It buys beaten-down blue chips, utilities stocks, and high-yield bonds in an effort to provide shareholders a fat yield and an attractive total return. The team also actively invests across the capital structure of a single issuer (common stock, convertible bonds, traditional debt). Finally, from time to time, the fund will venture into emerging-markets debt as opportunities present themselves.

Performance 12-31-06

	1st Qtr	2nd Qtr	3rd Qtr	4th Qtr	Total
2002	4.42	-5.98	-5.94	7.14	-1.06
2003	1.47	14.24	3.16	9.51	30.96
2004	1.62	-0.44	4.24	6.36	12.17
2005	-1.28	3.63	1.50	-1.91	1.85
2006	4.46	1.88	5.12	6.48	19.12

Trailing	Total Return%	+/- DJ Mod	+/- DJ 40%	%Rank Cat	Growth of $10,000
3 Mo	6.48	0.89	3.44	2	10,648
6 Mo	11.93	3.14	5.37	2	11,193
1 Yr	19.12	6.82	11.66	2	11,912
3 Yr Avg	10.82	0.10	3.78	2	13,610
5 Yr Avg	12.01	1.99	5.28	2	17,631
10 Yr Avg	9.62	1.07	1.92	1	25,055
15 Yr Avg	10.39	1.18	2.27	1	44,050

Tax Analysis	Tax-Adj Rtn%	%Rank Cat	Tax-Cost Rat	%Rank Cat
3 Yr (estimated)	6.71	9	2.31	98
5 Yr (estimated)	8.27	4	2.50	98
10 Yr (estimated)	6.05	8	2.84	100

Potential Capital Gain Exposure: 12% of assets

Morningstar's Take by Andrew Gogerty 11-14-06

Franklin Income wallops the competition by marching to the beat of a different drum.

This conservative-allocation fund doesn't offer the typical mix of blue-chip stocks and high-quality bonds that rivals contain. Manager Ed Perks uses great flexibility to achieve the fund's income-focused mandate. He looks across the market's capital structure for undervalued securities, meaning the portfolio will often hold multiple securities (stocks, bonds, convertibles) from the same firm.

Perks' quest for yield leads to notable biases in the portfolio. For one, the fund often piles into a handful of equity sectors--notably health care and utilities--that have historically produced above-market yields. Perks also will load up on low-quality debt, which increases credit risk. Currently, more than 90% of the fund's fixed-income sleeve is in bonds rated BB or below (including nonrated issues), while its typical peer has just a 12% exposure to these credit tiers.

Finally, Perks will make sizable shifts in the fund's asset allocation based on his view on the two asset classes' valuations.

Over the long term, though, Perks' execution has more than compensated investors for his strategy's risks. The fund's long-term returns are virtually unmatched by its peers. Moreover, the fund's low 0.65% expense ratio siphons off a significantly smaller portion of its income stream, resulting in a plump 6% current yield--one of the category's best--which surely appeals to income-focused investors in or near retirement.

That said, investors should expect bumps along the way. In 2005, the fund's stake in large drugmakers Merck and Pfizer crimped returns while some of its lower-rated bonds defaulted. So investors shouldn't ignore the fund's lopsided equity sector exposure and added credit risk. Still, its low costs and seasoned management should keep it well ahead of the crowd. Investors willing to ride out short-term bumps will do well here.

Address:	One Franklin Parkway
	San Mateo CA 94403-1906
	800-632-2301
Web Address:	www.franklintempleton.com
Inception:	08-31-48
Advisor:	Franklin Advisers, Inc.
Subadvisor:	None
NTF Plans:	Schwab Instl NTF

Minimum Purchase:	$1000	Add: $50	IRA: $250
Min Auto Inv Plan:	$50	Add: $50	
Sales Fees:	4.25%L, 0.15%S, 2.00%R		
Management Fee:	0.63% mx./0.35% mn.		
Actual Fees:	Mgt:0.41%	Dist:0.15%	
Expense Projections:	3Yr:$642	5Yr:$772	10Yr:$1201
Income Distrib:	Monthly		

Historical Profile

Return	High
Risk	High
Rating	★★★★★ Highest

Performance Quartile (within Category)

| 32% | 29% | 31% | 28% | 32% | 38% | 41% | 41% | 42% | Investment Style / Equity / Stock % |

- ▼ Manager Change
- ▽ Partial Manager Change

Growth of $10,000
- — Investment Values of Fund
- — Investment Values of DJ Mod

	1995	1996	1997	1998	1999	2000	2001	2002	2003	2004	2005	2006	History
	2.32	2.36	2.53	2.36	2.15	2.36	2.18	1.99	2.41	2.52	2.40	2.66	NAV
	21.29	10.45	16.85	0.95	-0.74	20.59	0.65	-1.06	30.96	12.17	1.85	19.12	Total Return %
	1.49	-0.21	4.95	-11.37	-18.07	22.26	3.45	5.71	3.58	-0.80	-5.14	6.82	+/-DJ Mod
	3.13	1.56	2.75	-10.78	-8.60	13.80	-2.57	2.96	13.30	3.16	-2.84	11.66	+/-DJ 40%
	8.91	8.04	7.90	7.36	7.91	8.70	7.91	7.69	8.12	6.67	6.14	6.19	Income Return %
	12.38	2.41	8.95	-6.41	-8.65	11.89	-7.26	-8.75	22.84	5.50	-4.29	12.93	Capital Return %
	42	43	15	93	93	1	43	26	1	2	76	2	Total Rtn % Rank Cat
	0.18	0.18	0.18	0.18	0.18	0.18	0.18	0.16	0.16	0.16	0.15	0.14	Income $
	0.03	0.01	0.03	0.01	0.01	0.03	0.02	0.01	0.01	0.01	0.01	0.04	Capital Gains $
	0.71	0.70	0.72	0.72	0.73	0.76	0.73	0.72	0.73	0.68	0.65	0.64	Expense Ratio %
	8.26	8.27	7.45	6.83	7.46	8.01	7.54	6.67	6.63	5.11	5.54	5.61	Income Ratio %
	59	25	16	22	17	24	28	51	48	32	29	28	Turnover Rate %
	6,217	7,082	8,044	7,784	6,285	6,136	6,243	6,521	11,466	17,016	22,276	29,629	Net Assets $mil

Rating and Risk

Time Period	Load-Adj Return %	Morningstar Rtn vs Cat	Morningstar Risk vs Cat	Morningstar Risk-Adj Rating
1 Yr	14.06			
3 Yr	9.23	High	High	★★★★★
5 Yr	11.05	High	High	★★★★★
10 Yr	9.15	High	+Avg	★★★★★
Incept	11.04			

Other Measures	Standard Index DJ Mod	Best Fit Index Russ 1000 VI
Alpha	2.3	0.4
Beta	0.68	0.62
R-Squared	57	61
Standard Deviation	5.38	
Mean	10.82	
Sharpe Ratio	1.36	

Portfolio Analysis 09-30-06

Total Stocks:59 Share change since 06-30-06	Sectors	P/E Ratio	YTD Return %	% Net Assets
Pfizer Inc.	Health	15.2	1.00	2.84
⊖ Merck & Co., Inc.	Health	19.1	1.58	2.50
Bank of America Corporati	Financial	12.4	0.11	2.40
⊕ Public Service Enterprise	Utilities	21.0	-2.09	2.09
FirstEnergy Corporation	Utilities	16.2	-2.16	1.67
⊕ Dominion Resources, Inc.	Utilities	17.8	-2.35	1.63
AT&T, Inc.	Telecom	18.2	-5.43	1.53
Southern Company	Utilities	17.6	-0.87	1.40
Duke Energy Corporation	Utilities	8.2	-2.90	1.34

Total Fixed-Income:533	Date of Maturity	Amount $000	Value $000	% Net Assets
Gmac 6.875%	09-15-11	800,000	796,584	1.70
Cch I 11%	10-01-15	850,000	777,750	1.66
Ford Motor Cr 7.375%	10-28-09	550,000	534,851	1.14
Nortel Networks Cv 4.25%	09-01-08	512,500	490,495	1.05
Ford Mtr 7.45%	07-16-31	600,000	466,500	0.99
Tenet Healthcare 6.375%	12-01-11	515,000	455,131	0.97
Cablevision Sys 8%	04-15-12	440,000	447,700	0.95
General Mtrs 8.375%	07-15-33	510,000	443,700	0.95
Ford Motor Cr 7.375%	02-01-11	450,000	432,314	0.92

Equity Style

Style: Value
Size: Large-Cap

Value Measures		Rel Category
Price/Earnings	14.93	0.99
Price/Book	2.12	0.87
Price/Sales	1.45	1.04
Price/Cash Flow	9.17	1.15
Dividend Yield %	3.47	1.62

Growth Measures	%	Rel Category
Long-Term Erngs	7.58	0.67
Book Value	5.99	0.75
Sales	9.34	1.05
Cash Flow	-5.37	NMF
Historical Erngs	5.75	0.33

Market Cap %			
Giant	42.9	Small	0.0
Large	47.6	Micro	0.0
Mid	9.5	Avg $mil:	38,476

Fixed-Income Style

Duration: Interm-Term
Quality: Low

Avg Eff Duration [1]	4.8 Yrs
Avg Eff Maturity	8.0 Yrs
Avg Credit Quality	BB
Avg Wtd Coupon	6.94%

[1]figure provided by fund as of 09-30-06

Sector Weightings	% of Stocks	Rel DJ Mod	3 Year High Low
Info	7.89	—	
Software	0.00	—	0 0
Hardware	0.00	—	1 0
Media	0.00	—	1 0
Telecom	7.89	—	9 5
Service	30.75		
Health	17.48	—	20 9
Consumer	0.00	—	0 0
Business	0.00	—	0 0
Financial	13.27	—	17 10
Mfg	61.36		
Goods	0.00	—	6 0
Ind Mtrls	5.94	—	6 1
Energy	10.73	—	14 9
Utilities	44.69	—	51 41

Composition

● Cash	2.4
● Stocks	41.9
● Bonds	46.2
● Other	9.5
Foreign (% of Stock)	7.0

Gabelli Asset AAA

	Ticker	Load	NAV	Yield	Total Assets	Mstar Category
	GABAX	None	$47.38	0.6%	$2,527 mil	Mid-Cap Blend

Governance and Management

Stewardship Grade: C

Portfolio Manager(s)

Mario Gabelli has managed this fund since its March 1986 inception. He has clearly demonstrated management acumen, but his total compensation package is excessive ($55 million in 2004), and it's based mostly on assets under management at his firm, rather than individual fund performance.

Strategy

Mario Gabelli first looks for firms trading at less than his estimates of the price a private buyer would pay for them. He buys those with improving fundamentals and clear catalysts that can drive their share prices higher. His style has led him to favor media and communications firms for some time, but industrials and consumer staples are also featured in the portfolio.

Performance 12-31-06

	1st Qtr	2nd Qtr	3rd Qtr	4th Qtr	Total
2002	3.76	-10.06	-15.37	8.55	-14.27
2003	-5.06	17.41	2.41	14.37	30.57
2004	3.06	1.85	-1.68	12.88	16.49
2005	-0.55	2.01	3.28	-0.34	4.42
2006	7.29	0.93	2.94	9.29	21.84

Trailing	Total Return%	+/- S&P 500	+/- S&P Mid 400	%Rank Cat	Growth of $10,000
3 Mo	9.29	2.59	2.30	17	10,929
6 Mo	12.51	-0.23	6.68	15	11,251
1 Yr	21.84	6.05	11.52	8	12,184
3 Yr Avg	14.01	3.57	0.92	31	14,819
5 Yr Avg	10.66	4.47	-0.23	39	16,594
10 Yr Avg	12.81	4.39	-0.66	29	33,379
15 Yr Avg	13.41	2.77	-0.22	33	66,034

Tax Analysis	Tax-Adj Rtn%	%Rank Cat	Tax-Cost Rat	%Rank Cat
3 Yr (estimated)	13.22	24	0.69	30
5 Yr (estimated)	10.13	34	0.48	29
10 Yr (estimated)	11.42	19	1.23	26

Potential Capital Gain Exposure: 54% of assets

Morningstar's Take by Kerry O'Boyle 12-04-06

Investors should ponder getting out of this fund while it's on top.

Gabelli Asset is having an outstanding year. Many sectors that veteran manager Mario Gabelli considers to be the core research competencies of his firm--media, telecom, and industrials--have delivered strong performances. Cable and media stocks have especially stood out after several lackluster years, with merger deals and acquisition talk fueling the rise in a number of stocks. For instance, top-five holding Cablevision has gained more than 80% on the year on news of an offer to take the firm private. In addition, the fund's 9% stake in telecom--more than four times its typical mid-blend rival--has helped, as those stocks have been on fire in 2006.

Despite its recent strong run, we think shareholders have reason to be wary going forward. This fund has the potential to be every bit as cyclical as the industries it favors. It can deliver lackluster returns for years before striking it rich

with a big year like now. Such was the case during the mid-1990s, which culminated in a superb year in 1997. Except now it's unlikely that media and telecom stocks will repeat the returns that they delivered during the tech bubble of the late 1990s. Thus, for this fund to work, it needs a long-term horizon for these cycles to play out.

We can think of few other funds that entail as much manager risk--the potential disruption caused by the departure of its manager--as this one. Mario Gabelli is virtually a one man operation. We've worried before that he might be stretched too thin in running his company and a whole host of funds. Now, the lack of transparency in the day-to-day management of the funds, high analyst turnover, and no clear successor in sight gives us pause about the fund's long-term future.

While likely not an immediate concern, it should cause investors to ask whether the next 10 years will be as good as the previous ones. The bottom line is that we have our doubts.

Address:	One Corporate Center
	Rye NY 10580
	800-422-3554
Web Address:	www.gabelli.com
Inception:	03-03-86
Advisor:	Gabelli Funds, LLC
Subadvisor:	None
NTF Plans:	Fidelity Retail-NTF, Schwab OneSource

Minimum Purchase:	$1000	Add: $0	IRA: $250
Min Auto Inv Plan:	$0	Add: $100	
Sales Fees:	No-load, 0.25%S, 2.00%R		
Management Fee:	1.00%		
Actual Fees:	Mgt:1.00%	Dist:0.25%	
Expense Projections:	3Yr:$434	5Yr:$750	10Yr:$1646
Income Distrib:	Annually		

Historical Profile

Return: Average
Risk: Low
Rating: ★★★★ Above Avg

| 96% | 93% | 92% | 87% | 95% | 99% | 98% | 98% | 99% |

Investment Style
Equity
Stock %

▼ Manager Change
▽ Partial Manager Change

Growth of $10,000
■ Investment Values of Fund
— Investment Values of S&P 500

40.8
31.0
24.0
17.0
10.0

Performance Quartile (within Category)

1995	1996	1997	1998	1999	2000	2001	2002	2003	2004	2005	2006	History
25.75	26.42	31.85	35.47	40.84	33.90	32.97	28.25	36.26	41.45	41.13	47.38	NAV
24.94	13.36	38.07	15.93	28.49	-2.37	0.16	-14.27	30.57	16.49	4.42	21.84	Total Return %
-12.64	-9.60	4.71	-12.65	7.45	6.73	12.05	7.83	1.89	5.61	-0.49	6.05	+/-S&P 500
-5.99	-5.89	5.82	-3.19	13.77	-19.88	0.77	0.26	-5.05	0.01	-8.14	11.52	+/-S&P Mid 400
1.14	0.59	0.26	0.06	0.00	0.75	0.00	0.04	0.11	0.07	0.28	0.75	Income Return %
23.80	12.77	37.81	15.87	28.49	-3.12	0.16	-14.31	30.46	16.42	4.14	21.09	Capital Return %
64	82	8	33	29	82	48	40	77	47	86	8	Total Rtn % Rank Cat
0.25	0.15	0.07	0.02	0.00	0.31	0.00	0.01	0.03	0.03	0.12	0.31	Income $
1.75	2.62	4.54	1.40	4.63	5.57	0.98	0.00	0.59	0.76	2.04	2.44	Capital Gains $
1.33	1.34	1.38	1.36	1.37	1.36	1.36	1.38	1.38	1.38	1.37	—	Expense Ratio %
0.95	0.52	0.22	0.06	-0.10	0.77	0.00	0.04	0.11	0.06	0.29	—	Income Ratio %
26	15	22	21	32	48	15	8	7	7	6	—	Turnover Rate %
1,090	1,082	1,334	1,594	1,994	1,909	1,911	1,683	1,733	2,218	2,254	2,519	Net Assets $mil

Rating and Risk

Time Period	Load-Adj Return %	Morningstar Rtn vs Cat	Morningstar Risk vs Cat	Morningstar Risk-Adj Rating
1 Yr	21.84			
3 Yr	14.01	Avg	Low	★★★★
5 Yr	10.66	Avg	-Avg	★★★
10 Yr	12.81	Avg	Low	★★★★
Incept	14.03			

Other Measures	Standard Index S&P 500	Best Fit Index Mstar Mid Core
Alpha	2.8	2.8
Beta	1.07	0.68
R-Squared	81	84
Standard Deviation	8.21	
Mean	14.01	
Sharpe Ratio	1.26	

Portfolio Analysis 09-30-06

Share change since 06-06 Total Stocks:428

	Sector	PE	Tot Ret%	% Assets
News Corporation, Ltd. A	Media	—	—	4.10
Cablevision Systems A	Media	—	84.55	1.96
⊖ Rogers Communications, I	Telecom	—	41.45	1.73
Deere & Company	Ind Mtrls	14.8	42.27	1.43
Procter & Gamble Company	Goods	23.9	13.36	1.39
ITT Industries, Inc.	Ind Mtrls	37.9	11.45	1.31
DANONE Grp	Goods	—	—	1.27
Time Warner, Inc.	Media	19.6	26.37	1.19
Brown-Forman Corporation	Goods	—	—	1.15
Telephone and Data Syste	Telecom	20.0	52.10	1.08
Archer Daniels Midland	Ind Mtrls	13.8	31.02	1.06
American Express Company	Financial	20.9	19.09	1.02
PepsiCo, Inc.	Goods	21.5	7.86	1.00
Chevron Corporation	Energy	9.0	33.76	0.99
ExxonMobil Corporation	Energy	11.1	39.07	0.99
Diageo PLC ADR	Goods	16.1	40.66	0.98
Genuine Parts Company	Consumer	17.4	11.39	0.97
Liberty Interactive A	Media	—	—	0.97
Idex Corporation	Ind Mtrls	19.6	16.76	0.97
Newmont Mining	Ind Mtrls	27.3	-14.77	0.94

Current Investment Style

Value Blnd Growth — Large Mid Small

Market Cap	%
Giant	22.4
Large	30.4
Mid	30.1
Small	14.1
Micro	3.0
Avg $mil:	10,522

Value Measures		Rel Category
Price/Earnings	16.86	1.05
Price/Book	2.30	1.02
Price/Sales	1.13	1.01
Price/Cash Flow	8.87	1.05
Dividend Yield %	1.55	1.19

Growth Measures	%	Rel Category
Long-Term Erngs	11.58	0.91
Book Value	5.56	0.67
Sales	7.67	0.86
Cash Flow	6.45	0.76
Historical Erngs	18.62	1.04

Profitability	%	Rel Category
Return on Equity	16.28	1.02
Return on Assets	6.66	0.83
Net Margin	8.03	0.74

Sector Weightings	% of Stocks	Rel S&P 500	3 Year High	Low
⊙ Info	30.13	1.51		
Software	0.12	0.03	0	0
Hardware	2.39	0.26	3	2
Media	18.43	4.86	22	18
Telecom	9.19	2.62	11	8
⊂ Service	20.26	0.44		
Health	3.40	0.28	4	3
Consumer	6.21	0.81	10	6
Business	3.51	0.83	4	3
Financial	7.14	0.32	7	6
⊔ Mfg	49.61	1.47		
Goods	18.29	2.14	18	16
Ind Mtrls	22.92	1.92	24	21
Energy	5.71	0.58	7	4
Utilities	2.69	0.77	3	2

Composition

● Cash	0.9
● Stocks	98.7
● Bonds	0.0
● Other	0.5
Foreign	15.9
(% of Stock)	

Morningstar® Funds 500

Gabelli Sm Cp Growth AAA

	Ticker	Load	NAV	Yield	Total Assets	Mstar Category
	GABSX	None	$31.20	0.0%	$755 mil	Small Value

Governance and Management

Stewardship Grade: C

Portfolio Manager(s)

Mario Gabelli has managed this fund since its 1991 inception. He's supported at this fund by a staff of nearly 20 analysts and portfolio managers. Gabelli has amassed strong long-term records at funds such as Gabelli Value, but his total compensation package is excessive ($55 million in 2004), and it's based on assets under management at his firm rather than on fund performance.

Strategy

Mario Gabelli values companies based on his estimates of their future cash flows or on what they might be worth to a potential buyer. He buys companies that trade at discounts to his estimates of their value, show improving fundamentals, and have some catalyst, such as industry consolidation, that will lead the market to recognize their value.

Historical Profile
Return Above Avg
Risk Below Avg
Rating ★★★★ Above Avg

Investment Style Equity Stock %

▼ Manager Change
▽ Partial Manager Change

Growth of $10,000
— Investment Values of Fund
— Investment Values of S&P 500

40.8 / 31.0 / 24.0 / 17.0 / 10.0

Return bar values: 98% 96% 93% 93% 91% 99% 99% 94% 96%

Performance Quartile (within Category)

	1995	1996	1997	1998	1999	2000	2001	2002	2003	2004	2005	2006	History
	18.50	18.53	21.58	21.01	21.43	18.71	19.21	17.93	24.49	28.62	28.25	31.20	NAV
	25.25	11.88	36.47	-0.02	14.21	11.30	4.65	-5.34	37.56	21.68	5.92	19.17	Total Return %
	-12.33	-11.08	3.11	-28.60	-6.83	20.40	16.54	16.76	8.88	10.80	1.01	3.38	+/-S&P 500
	-0.50	-9.49	4.69	6.43	15.70	-11.53	-9.37	6.09	-8.47	-0.57	1.21	-4.31	+/-Russ 2000 VL
	0.00	0.00	0.00	0.00	0.00	0.26	0.07	0.02	0.00	0.00	0.00	0.00	Income Return %
	25.25	11.88	36.47	-0.02	14.21	11.04	4.58	-5.36	37.56	21.68	5.92	19.17	Capital Return %
	37	93	9	19	24	77	91	22	68	45	58	27	Total Rtn % Rank Cat
	0.00	0.00	0.00	0.00	0.00	0.06	0.01	0.00	0.00	0.00	0.00	0.00	Income $
	1.34	2.16	3.66	0.53	2.46	4.73	0.35	0.25	0.17	1.15	2.06	2.45	Capital Gains $
	1.54	1.58	1.62	1.44	1.56	1.49	1.45	1.45	1.45	1.42	1.44	—	Expense Ratio %
	-0.24	-0.42	-0.36	-0.14	-0.34	0.26	0.30	-0.22	-0.22	-0.15	-0.03	—	Income Ratio %
	17	11	14	20	24	47	17	10	4	10	6	—	Turnover Rate %
	229	217	293	321	338	374	440	453	521	703	736	749	Net Assets $mil

Performance 12-31-06

	1st Qtr	2nd Qtr	3rd Qtr	4th Qtr	Total
2002	8.90	-3.25	-15.81	6.71	-5.34
2003	-5.08	18.27	6.66	14.88	37.56
2004	5.19	2.99	-2.45	15.15	21.68
2005	-1.89	3.35	3.27	1.14	5.92
2006	10.23	-2.63	0.26	10.74	19.17

Trailing	Total Return%	+/- S&P 500	+/- Russ 2000 VL	%Rank Cat	Growth of $10,000
3 Mo	10.74	4.04	1.71	9	11,074
6 Mo	11.03	-1.71	-0.78	23	11,103
1 Yr	19.17	3.38	-4.31	27	11,917
3 Yr Avg	15.38	4.94	-1.10	31	15,360
5 Yr Avg	14.87	8.68	-0.50	32	20,000
10 Yr Avg	13.76	5.34	0.49	22	36,299
15 Yr Avg	14.16	3.52	-1.04	53	72,897

Tax Analysis	Tax-Adj Rtn%	%Rank Cat	Tax-Cost Rat	%Rank Cat
3 Yr (estimated)	14.33	15	0.91	21
5 Yr (estimated)	14.13	23	0.64	19
10 Yr (estimated)	12.14	22	1.42	55

Potential Capital Gain Exposure: 46% of assets

Rating and Risk

Time Period	Load-Adj Return %	Morningstar Rtn vs Cat	Morningstar Risk vs Cat	Morningstar Risk-Adj Rating
1 Yr	19.17			
3 Yr	15.38	+Avg	-Avg	★★★★
5 Yr	14.87	Avg	-Avg	★★★★
10 Yr	13.76	+Avg	-Avg	★★★★
Incept	15.52			

Other Measures	Standard Index S&P 500	Best Fit Index Russ 2000
Alpha	2.1	3.8
Beta	1.38	0.76
R-Squared	73	91
Standard Deviation	11.05	
Mean	15.38	
Sharpe Ratio	1.06	

Morningstar's Take by Kerry O'Boyle 12-21-06

Gabelli Small Cap Growth is looking solid right now, but we have doubts about its prospects.

A late surge has propelled this fund from the middle of the pack into the top-third of the small-value category for 2006. Many of the areas of the market that veteran manager Mario Gabelli considers to be the core research competencies of his firm--media, telecom, and industrials--have delivered strong performances. The fund has also benefited from the year's merger and acquisition mania that has seen a number of its holdings taken out at premiums--notably casino-operator Aztar and Sybron Dental. Targeting companies that might be subject to such deals is another specialty of Gabelli, and it's not uncommon to see his funds do well when merger activity is high.

Despite the recent run, though, we think shareholders have reason to be wary. This fund has the potential to be every bit as cyclical as the areas it favors. It can deliver lackluster relative returns for years before striking it rich with a big surge like the one it's enjoying now. It remains to be seen how long the ongoing rally for media and telecom stocks will last or whether strong-performing industrials--which represent a third of fund assets--will continue to thrive. The bottom line: This fund works best over a long time horizon that allows for these cycles to fully play out.

Finally, few funds entail as much manager risk--the potential disruption from the departure of its manager--as this one. Mario Gabelli is virtually a one-man operation. We've worried before about whether he's stretched too thin in running his company and a whole host of funds. The lack of transparency in the day-to-day management of the funds, high analyst turnover, and the absence of a clear successor gives us pause about the fund's long-term future.

While they may not be immediate concerns, these open questions should cause investors to ponder whether the next 10 years will be good as the previous ones.

Portfolio Analysis 09-30-06

Share change since 06-06 Total Stocks:486	Sector	PE	Tot Ret%	% Assets
Thomas & Betts Corporati	Hardware	19.1	12.68	1.82
Clarcor Inc.	Ind Mtrls	21.6	14.81	1.72
Greif Corporation A	Ind Mtrls	27.4	81.72	1.69
RPC, Inc.	Energy	14.9	-3.12	1.62
Cablevision Systems A	Media	—	84.55	1.58
Flowserve Corporation	Ind Mtrls	39.2	27.58	1.31
Franklin Electric Co.	Ind Mtrls	21.3	31.07	1.27
Vimpel-Communications AD	Telecom	25.6	78.50	1.22
Kaman Corporation A	Ind Mtrls	16.7	16.60	1.10
Acuity Brands, Inc.	Ind Mtrls	22.2	66.05	1.07
Sequa Corporation B	Ind Mtrls	—		1.03
Ametek, Inc.	Ind Mtrls	18.9	12.94	1.01
CNA Surety Corporation	Financial	11.8	47.56	1.01
CH Energy Group	Utilities	17.9	20.29	1.00
Republic Services, Inc.	Business	20.7	9.91	0.96
Flowers Foods, Inc.	Goods	23.5	-0.36	0.95
Gaylord Entertainment	Consumer	—	16.84	0.93
Hercules, Inc.	Ind Mtrls	—	70.89	0.92
Rollins, Inc.	Business	27.1	13.52	0.89
Precision Castparts Corp	Ind Mtrls	25.4	51.40	0.86

Current Investment Style

Value Blnd Growth — Large/Mid/Small

Market Cap	%
Giant	0.3
Large	3.8
Mid	26.9
Small	42.4
Micro	26.7

Avg $mil: 1,062

Value Measures		Rel Category
Price/Earnings	17.13	1.11
Price/Book	1.99	1.12
Price/Sales	0.88	1.10
Price/Cash Flow	7.83	1.28
Dividend Yield %	1.20	0.76

Growth Measures	%	Rel Category
Long-Term Erngs	13.94	1.12
Book Value	3.50	0.65
Sales	6.01	0.81
Cash Flow	5.10	0.62
Historical Erngs	14.25	1.25

Profitability	%	Rel Category
Return on Equity	11.04	1.03
Return on Assets	5.12	0.84
Net Margin	5.88	0.65

Sector Weightings	% of Stocks	Rel S&P 500	3 Year High Low	
Info	15.35	0.77		
Software	0.62	0.18	1	0
Hardware	4.67	0.51	5	4
Media	6.64	1.75	13	7
Telecom	3.42	0.97	3	2
Service	30.25	0.65		
Health	7.29	0.60	8	5
Consumer	10.23	1.34	13	10
Business	7.59	1.79	8	6
Financial	5.14	0.23	6	4
Mfg	54.41	1.61		
Goods	9.97	1.17	11	10
Ind Mtrls	36.23	3.03	36	33
Energy	3.49	0.36	4	1
Utilities	4.72	1.35	5	4

Composition

	%
● Cash	3.8
● Stocks	95.8
● Bonds	0.0
○ Other	0.4
Foreign	6.8
(% of Stock)	

Address:	One Corporate Center Rye NY 10580 800-422-3554	Minimum Purchase:	$1000	Add: $0	IRA: $0
		Min Auto Inv Plan:	$0	Add: $100	
		Sales Fees:	No-load, 0.25%S, 2.00%R		
Web Address:	www.gabelli.com	Management Fee:	1.00%		
Inception:	10-22-91	Actual Fees:	Mgt:1.00%	Dist:0.25%	
Advisor:	Gabelli Funds, LLC	Expense Projections:	3Yr:$456	5Yr:$787	10Yr:$1724
Subadvisor:	None	Income Distrib:	Annually		
NTF Plans:	Fidelity Retail-NTF, Schwab OneSource				

GAMCO Growth AAA

	Ticker	Load	NAV	Yield	Total Assets	Mstar Category
	GABGX	None	$30.62	0.0%	$959 mil	Large Growth

Governance and Management

Stewardship Grade: C

Portfolio Manager(s)

Howard Ward has been on the job here since January 1995. He is backed by two analysts dedicated exclusively to this fund, as well as GAMCO's staff of analysts and portfolio managers. He previously managed Scudder Large Company Growth (now DWS Large Company Growth).

Strategy

Manager Howard Ward seeks big, well-known companies trading for less than what he thinks they're worth, based on his estimates of their growth during the next five years. He has recently boosted the number of holdings in the portfolio to more than 90 and tempered some of his sector bets to keep a lid on volatility. He tends to hang on to stocks for the long haul, so the fund's turnover rate is relatively low.

Historical Profile

Return	Average
Risk	Above Avg
Rating	★★★ Neutral

Investment Style: Equity Stock %

99% 99% 99% 100% 100% 100% 100% 99% 99%

▼ Manager Change
▽ Partial Manager Change

Growth of $10,000
— Investment Values of Fund
— Investment Values of S&P 500

40.8
31.0
24.0
17.0
10.0

Performance Quartile (within Category)

1995	1996	1997	1998	1999	2000	2001	2002	2003	2004	2005	2006	History
22.16	24.14	28.63	35.40	46.51	37.79	28.68	18.99	24.95	26.12	28.81	30.62	NAV
32.72	19.42	42.63	29.78	46.25	-10.57	-24.10	-33.79	31.38	4.69	10.30	6.28	Total Return %
-4.86	-3.54	9.27	1.20	25.21	-1.47	-12.21	-11.69	2.70	-6.19	5.39	-9.51	+/-S&P 500
-4.46	-3.70	12.14	-8.93	13.09	11.85	-3.68	-5.91	1.63	-1.61	5.04	-2.79	+/-Russ 1000Gr
0.28	0.11	0.01	0.00	0.00	0.00	0.00	0.00	0.00	0.00	0.00	0.00	Income Return %
32.44	19.31	42.62	29.78	46.25	-10.57	-24.10	-33.79	31.38	4.69	10.30	6.28	Capital Return %
46	51	3	52	27	44	70	88	28	82	20	58	Total Rtn % Rank Cat
0.06	0.02	0.00	0.00	0.00	0.00	0.00	0.00	0.00	0.00	0.00	0.00	Income $
3.90	2.30	5.79	1.75	5.16	3.85	0.00	0.00	0.00	0.00	0.00	0.00	Capital Gains $
1.44	1.43	1.43	1.41	1.37	1.38	1.40	1.43	1.47	1.53	1.49	—	Expense Ratio %
0.22	0.12	-0.23	-0.33	-0.68	-0.63	-0.71	-0.68	-0.60	-0.46	-0.48	—	Income Ratio %
140	88	83	40	52	55	26	30	42	31	39	—	Turnover Rate %
526	623	952	1,864	3,155	3,835	2,958	1,905	1,751	1,452	1,142	958	Net Assets $mil

Performance 12-31-06

	1st Qtr	2nd Qtr	3rd Qtr	4th Qtr	Total
2002	-3.00	-23.69	-15.31	5.62	-33.79
2003	-5.95	18.37	4.16	13.31	31.38
2004	-0.08	-0.08	-3.57	8.74	4.69
2005	-2.49	2.32	6.72	3.60	10.30
2006	3.61	-3.95	1.01	5.73	6.28

Trailing	Total Return%	+/- S&P 500	+/- Russ 1000Gr	%Rank Cat	Growth of $10,000
3 Mo	5.73	-0.97	-0.20	43	10,573
6 Mo	6.80	-5.94	-3.30	74	10,680
1 Yr	6.28	-9.51	-2.79	58	10,628
3 Yr Avg	7.06	-3.38	0.19	48	12,271
5 Yr Avg	1.32	-4.87	-1.37	70	10,678
10 Yr Avg	6.97	-1.45	1.53	35	19,616
15 Yr Avg	8.70	-1.94	0.68	41	34,950

Tax Analysis	Tax-Adj Rtn%	%Rank Cat	Tax-Cost Rat	%Rank Cat
3 Yr (estimated)	7.06	39	0.00	1
5 Yr (estimated)	1.32	65	0.00	1
10 Yr (estimated)	6.03	28	0.88	41

Potential Capital Gain Exposure: -87% of assets

Rating and Risk

Time Period	Load-Adj Return %	Morningstar Rtn vs Cat	Morningstar Risk vs Cat	Morningstar Risk-Adj Rating
1 Yr	6.28			
3 Yr	7.06	Avg	-Avg	★★★
5 Yr	1.32	-Avg	High	★★
10 Yr	6.97	Avg	+Avg	★★★
Incept	11.44			

Other Measures	Standard Index S&P 500	Best Fit Index Russ MG
Alpha	-4.0	-2.8
Beta	1.15	0.71
R-Squared	85	90
Standard Deviation	8.56	
Mean	7.06	
Sharpe Ratio	0.47	

Portfolio Analysis 09-30-06

Share change since 06-06 Total Stocks:141

	Sector	PE	Tot Ret%	% Assets
General Electric Company	Ind Mtrls	20.0	9.35	4.68
⊕ Microsoft Corporation	Software	23.8	15.83	4.42
⊕ Google, Inc.	Business	61.5	11.00	3.17
⊖ Procter & Gamble Company	Goods	23.9	13.36	2.95
⊖ PepsiCo, Inc.	Goods	21.5	7.86	2.87
Citigroup, Inc.	Financial	13.1	19.55	2.85
⊖ Walgreen Company	Consumer	26.6	4.36	1.91
American Express Company	Financial	20.9	19.09	1.81
⊕ Genentech, Inc.	Health	48.7	-12.29	1.65
⊕ Apple Computer, Inc.	Hardware	37.6	18.01	1.58
ITT Industries, Inc.	Ind Mtrls	37.9	11.45	1.58
⊕ Goldman Sachs Group, Inc	Financial	12.4	57.41	1.56
⊕ Alcon, Inc.	Health	38.3	-12.60	1.52
⊖ Amgen, Inc.	Health	29.1	-13.38	1.52
⊕ Cisco Systems, Inc.	Hardware	30.1	59.64	1.52
⊕ Adobe Systems Inc.	Software	48.1	11.26	1.52
⊕ Yahoo, Inc.	Media	35.4	-34.81	1.44
United Technologies	Ind Mtrls	17.8	13.65	1.40
⊕ American International G	Financial	17.0	6.05	1.29
⊕ Stryker Corporation	Health	30.3	24.53	1.27

Current Investment Style

Value Blnd Growth — Large Mid Small

Market Cap	%
Giant	49.1
Large	34.4
Mid	16.6
Small	0.0
Micro	0.0

Avg $mil: 42,394

Value Measures		Rel Category
Price/Earnings	18.83	0.98
Price/Book	3.54	1.07
Price/Sales	2.22	1.14
Price/Cash Flow	12.12	1.07
Dividend Yield %	1.21	1.17

Growth Measures	%	Rel Category
Long-Term Erngs	14.57	1.02
Book Value	11.39	0.98
Sales	12.79	1.10
Cash Flow	15.84	0.94
Historical Erngs	22.95	1.00

Profitability	%	Rel Category
Return on Equity	21.77	1.07
Return on Assets	12.53	1.14
Net Margin	16.46	1.16

Sector Weightings	% of Stocks	Rel S&P 500	3 Year High	Low
⟲ Info	19.95	1.00		
▣ Software	6.53	1.89	8	5
▣ Hardware	9.68	1.05	20	7
▣ Media	3.48	0.92	8	3
▣ Telecom	0.26	0.07	3	0
⊂ Service	48.83	1.06		
▣ Health	13.89	1.15	21	13
▣ Consumer	10.46	1.37	15	10
▣ Business	6.81	1.61	7	0
▣ Financial	17.67	0.79	18	8
⊔ Mfg	31.23	0.92		
▣ Goods	10.69	1.25	11	5
▣ Ind Mtrls	15.25	1.28	17	3
▣ Energy	5.29	0.54	13	5
▣ Utilities	0.00	0.00	0	0

Composition

● Cash	0.9
● Stocks	99.1
● Bonds	0.0
○ Other	0.0
Foreign	6.3
(% of Stock)	

Morningstar's Take by Kerry O'Boyle 11-10-06

We just can't get excited about GAMCO Growth.

Howard Ward is a veteran manager who has run this fund for more than a decade. Although he has shown flashes of stock-picking skill during that period--notably in 1997 and 2005--a number of missteps and portfolio construction shifts have occurred along the way. The most jarring of these happened when Ward concentrated the portfolio in a mere 40 stocks and a handful of sectors in the late-1990s, which were punished severely during the subsequent bear market. Although the fund is once again a well-diversified offering, performance remains spotty.

The fund has been having a tough time in 2006. Ward became defensive early in the year as he trimmed back on technology, retailers, and cyclical industrial stocks in favor of steadier growers with higher yields. He felt that the market was getting ahead of itself despite tepid economic news, and so the fund weathered the early summer stock market correction quite well. However, it has missed out on much of the subsequent rally because Ward had to scramble to trim back on the fund's 13% stake in suddenly sluggish energy stocks--now 6% of assets--and add back to his tech and industrial positions. That points to the difficulty of making top-down market calls--both over the short and long term--if only at the margins, which Ward is still wont to do from time to time.

It doesn't help that the fund is plagued by some of the highest fees in the large-growth category in general--the highest for a fund of its size. The fund's 1.49% annual expense ratio is well above the 1% median for no-load, large-cap funds, with that extra cost serving as a perennial drag on its performance.

Despite the occasional promising sign, we have a tough time getting behind this fund. Those high costs and the fund's past inconsistency make it an iffy prospect for investors going forward.

Address:	One Corporate Center Rye NY 10580-1434 800-422-3554	Minimum Purchase:	$1000	Add: $0 IRA: $250
		Min Auto Inv Plan:	$0	Add: $100
		Sales Fees:	No-load, 0.25%S, 2.00%R	
Web Address:	www.gabelli.com	Management Fee:	1.00%	
Inception:	04-10-87	Actual Fees:	Mgt:1.00%	Dist:0.25%
Advisor:	Gabelli Funds, LLC	Expense Projections:	3Yr:$471	5Yr:$813 10Yr:$1779
Subadvisor:	None	Income Distrib:	Annually	
NTF Plans:	Fidelity Retail-NTF, Schwab OneSource			

MORNINGSTAR® Funds 500

Gateway

	Ticker	Load	NAV	Yield	Total Assets	Mstar Category
	GATEX	None	$27.04	1.8%	$3,330 mil	Long-Short

Governance and Management

Stewardship Grade:

Portfolio Manager(s)

Patrick Rogers has run the fund since 1994. Gateway has one trader and three other portfolio managers who work with Rogers to set its option strategy.

Strategy

The fund makes money by selling index call options. To cover the call options, the fund owns a broadly diversified portfolio of stocks that resemble the S&P 500. When stock prices go up, the fund's ownership of stocks compensates for losses on call options. To protect the fund from large losses in a declining market, management buys index put options.

Historical Profile
Return	Average
Risk	Below Avg
Rating	★★★ Neutral

Investment Style: Equity, Stock %

92% 99% 99% 94% 98% 100% 100% 100% 95%

▼ Manager Change
▽ Partial Manager Change

Growth of $10,000
— Investment Values of Fund
— Investment Values of S&P 500

31.0 / 25.0 / 20.0 / 15.0 / 10.0

Performance Quartile (within Category)

1995	1996	1997	1998	1999	2000	2001	2002	2003	2004	2005	2006	History
16.91	18.48	18.85	21.02	23.67	22.92	21.98	20.76	23.00	24.31	25.00	27.04	NAV
11.04	10.53	12.35	12.26	12.97	6.61	-3.53	-4.86	11.61	6.95	4.66	10.14	Total Return %
-26.54	-12.43	-21.01	-16.32	-8.07	15.71	8.36	17.24	-17.07	-3.93	-0.25	-5.65	+/-S&P 500
-25.76	-11.29	-19.43	-11.88	-7.93	14.07	7.93	16.68	-19.45	-5.00	-1.46	-5.58	+/-Russell3000
1.70	1.20	0.96	0.65	0.35	0.33	0.47	0.69	0.82	1.26	1.83	1.94	Income Return %
9.34	9.33	11.39	11.61	12.62	6.28	-4.00	-5.55	10.79	5.69	2.83	8.20	Capital Return %
100	34	67	34	20	47	80	68	34	22	45	19	Total Rtn % Rank Cat
0.26	0.20	0.18	0.12	0.07	0.08	0.11	0.15	0.17	0.29	0.45	0.48	Income $
0.01	0.00	1.73	0.01	0.00	2.24	0.02	0.00	0.00	0.00	0.00	0.00	Capital Gains $
1.19	1.14	1.07	0.99	0.98	0.98	0.97	0.97	0.97	0.97	0.95	—	Expense Ratio %
1.51	1.18	0.90	0.66	0.37	0.33	0.43	0.66	0.86	1.42	1.87	—	Income Ratio %
5	17	82	12	11	22	18	13	5	71	15	—	Turnover Rate %
176	194	255	464	922	1,492	1,285	1,285	1,406	2,104	2,708	3,330	Net Assets $mil

Performance 12-31-06

	1st Qtr	2nd Qtr	3rd Qtr	4th Qtr	Total
2002	1.36	-6.37	-8.49	9.55	-4.86
2003	-0.82	6.70	1.96	3.44	11.61
2004	1.22	1.59	0.30	3.71	6.95
2005	0.70	1.88	1.60	0.41	4.66
2006	3.24	0.88	3.24	2.43	10.14

Trailing	Total Return%	+/- S&P 500	+/- Russell3000	%Rank Cat	Growth of $10,000
3 Mo	2.43	-4.27	-4.69	38	10,243
6 Mo	5.75	-6.99	-6.34	23	10,575
1 Yr	10.14	-5.65	-5.58	19	11,014
3 Yr Avg	7.23	-3.21	-3.96	22	12,330
5 Yr Avg	5.54	-0.65	-1.63	39	13,094
10 Yr Avg	6.73	-1.69	-1.91	67	19,181
15 Yr Avg	7.12	-3.52	-3.67	100	28,058

Tax Analysis	Tax-Adj Rtn%	%Rank Cat	Tax-Cost Rat	%Rank Cat
3 Yr (estimated)	6.64	18	0.55	39
5 Yr (estimated)	5.07	34	0.45	50
10 Yr (estimated)	6.01	1	0.67	1

Potential Capital Gain Exposure: 14% of assets

Rating and Risk

Time Period	Load-Adj Return %	Morningstar Rtn vs Cat	Morningstar Risk vs Cat	Morningstar Risk-Adj Rating
1 Yr	10.14			
3 Yr	7.23	+Avg	Low	★★★★
5 Yr	5.54	Avg	Avg	★★★
10 Yr	6.73	—	—	—
Incept	9.08			

Other Measures	Standard Index S&P 500	Best Fit Index Russ 1000 VI
Alpha	1.5	-0.2
Beta	0.34	0.36
R-Squared	74	79
Standard Deviation	2.73	
Mean	7.23	
Sharpe Ratio	1.42	

Morningstar's Take by Greg Carlson 12-28-06

Gateway Fund is one of the more appealing options in the long/short category.

This fund employs a patient, sensible strategy. Manager Patrick Rogers owns a basket of large-cap stocks that's expected to closely track the S&P 500 Index while generating a higher yield--thus the fund tends to own bigger stakes than the index in dividend-paying names such as Citigrou, Pfizer and Altria. However, Rogers hedges away most of the stocks' potential capital appreciation by selling call options on the S&P 500 (using the equity portfolio as collateral), which in turn generates income. In order to limit downside risk, he also purchases put options on the index. (The value of these puts rises when the market declines, so they effectively function as shorts.)

Rogers' approach isn't entirely risk-free--the fund's puts are typically 6%-10% below the current level of the S&P, thus the fund can still get hurt when the index drops (witness its 8% loss in 2002's third quarter). But the fund typically provides

significant upside in market rallies--it posted double-digit gains from 1995 through 1999--while limiting volatility. It's generated a respectable 6.7% annualized return over the trailing 10 years.

The fund is also built on a solid foundation. Its expense ratio hasn't declined much in recent years despite significant asset growth, but at 0.95%, it's the cheapest option in the category, and that price tag allows more of the income generated by management's strategy to flow through to shareholders. What's more, the fund is run by an experienced hand--Rogers, a 17-year veteran of Gateway Investment Advisers, has served in the lead role here since 1994, and is supported by three managers and traders. We're also encouraged that Rogers has more than $1 million invested in the fund's shares, which helps signal his conviction in its investment process.

All told, this fund is a good way for cautious investors to gain exposure to the equity markets.

Address:	3805 Edwards Road, Suite 600 Cincinnati OH 45209 800-354-6339
Web Address:	www.gatewayfund.com
Inception:	12-07-77
Advisor:	Gateway Investment Advisers LP
Subadvisor:	None
NTF Plans:	Fidelity Retail-NTF

Minimum Purchase:	$1000	Add: $100	IRA: $500
Min Auto Inv Plan:	$100	Add: $100	
Sales Fees:	No-load, 0.35%S		
Management Fee:	0.92% mx./0.60% mn.		
Actual Fees:	Mgt:0.57%	Dist:0.35%	
Expense Projections:	3Yr:$303	5Yr:$526	10Yr:$1166
Income Distrib:	Annually		

Portfolio Analysis 09-30-06

Share change since 06-06 Total Stocks:321

	Sector	PE	Tot Ret%	% Assets
ExxonMobil Corporation	Energy	11.1	39.07	3.44
⊖ General Electric Company	Ind Mtrls	20.0	9.35	3.09
Bank of America Corporat	Financial	12.4	20.68	2.54
⊕ Wells Fargo Company	Financial	14.7	16.82	2.48
Citigroup, Inc.	Financial	13.1	19.55	2.40
Pfizer Inc.	Health	15.2	15.22	2.08
Microsoft Corporation	Software	23.8	15.83	2.02
Altria Group, Inc.	Goods	16.3	19.87	1.65
J.P. Morgan Chase & Co.	Financial	13.6	25.60	1.56
Johnson & Johnson	Health	17.5	12.45	1.55
Procter & Gamble Company	Goods	23.9	13.36	1.49
⊕ Intel Corporation	Hardware	21.0	-17.18	1.36
Merck & Co., Inc.	Health	19.1	42.66	1.34
AT&T, Inc.	Telecom	18.2	51.59	1.33
Verizon Communications	Telecom	15.9	34.88	1.21
Chevron Corporation	Energy	9.0	33.76	1.15
⊕ Bristol-Myers Squibb Com	Health	23.1	19.93	1.11
American International G	Financial	17.0	6.05	1.06
Lloyds TSB Group PLC ADR	Financial	13.9	43.00	0.99
Wal-Mart Stores, Inc.	Consumer	16.9	0.13	0.96

Current Investment Style

Value Blnd Growth — Large / Mid / Small

Market Cap	%
Giant	57.0
Large	20.6
Mid	18.2
Small	4.1
Micro	0.2

Avg $mil: 42,695

Value Measures		Rel Category
Price/Earnings	15.08	0.98
Price/Book	2.52	1.05
Price/Sales	1.37	1.13
Price/Cash Flow	9.36	1.19
Dividend Yield %	2.77	1.81

Growth Measures	%	Rel Category
Long-Term Erngs	10.29	0.85
Book Value	7.94	1.07
Sales	9.12	0.95
Cash Flow	7.80	0.71
Historical Erngs	14.40	0.75

Profitability	%	Rel Category
Return on Equity	19.41	1.16
Return on Assets	10.65	1.22
Net Margin	14.50	1.24

Sector Weightings	% of Stocks	Rel S&P 500	3 Year High Low
⊙ Info	16.83	0.84	
Software	3.57	1.03	5 3
Hardware	7.80	0.84	12 7
Media	0.99	0.26	4 1
Telecom	4.47	1.27	6 3
⊜ Service	47.82	1.03	
Health	11.73	0.97	14 10
Consumer	6.54	0.85	9 7
Business	3.99	0.94	4 2
Financial	25.56	1.15	26 20
⊔ Mfg	35.35	1.05	
Goods	8.94	1.05	12 9
Ind Mtrls	12.53	1.05	15 12
Energy	8.86	0.90	11 6
Utilities	5.02	1.43	5 3

Composition
- Cash 5.3
- Stocks 94.5
- Bonds 0.0
- Other 0.1
- Foreign 5.1 (% of Stock)

Greenspring

	Ticker	Load	NAV	Yield	Total Assets	Mstar Category
	GRSPX	None	$23.43	2.5%	$244 mil	Moderate Allocation

Governance and Management

Stewardship Grade: B

Portfolio Manager(s)

Seasoned. Chip Carlson has managed this offering since 1987 and also manages separate accounts in the same style. A team approach predominates here, as Carlson is backed by three senior research analysts, including Michael J. Fusting, who has been with the firm for 16 years. The other two analysts each have at least a decade of experience on the fund.

Strategy

This is a unique moderate-allocation fund. It favors deep-value sectors such as financials and energy, and it prefers small caps over the blue chips that populate the portfolios of most of its peers. Additionally, big stakes in convertibles have given this fund one of the highest yields in the group. Cash stakes tend to run high.

Historical Profile

Return	Above Avg
Risk	Above Avg
Rating	★★★★ Above Avg

63% 59% 66% 51% 36% 35% 46% 46% 45%

Investment Style: Equity Stock %

▼ Manager Change
▽ Partial Manager Change

Growth of $10,000
■ Investment Values of Fund
— Investment Values of DJ Mod

Performance Quartile (within Category)

	1995	1996	1997	1998	1999	2000	2001	2002	2003	2004	2005	2006	History
	15.05	17.24	20.04	16.10	15.41	16.98	17.74	15.70	19.96	20.91	21.57	23.43	NAV
	18.74	22.65	23.95	-15.98	2.64	15.64	10.23	-5.99	31.34	8.69	6.57	12.29	Total Return %
	-1.06	11.99	12.05	-28.30	-14.69	17.31	13.03	0.78	3.96	-4.28	-0.42	-0.01	+/-DJ Mod
	-6.03	11.31	4.75	-28.37	-10.21	11.20	10.07	4.55	7.28	-2.48	0.57	2.02	+/-DJ US Mod
	5.14	3.96	4.00	3.78	7.07	5.19	5.73	5.38	3.92	3.29	2.14	2.71	Income Return %
	13.60	18.69	19.95	-19.76	-4.43	10.45	4.50	-11.37	27.42	5.40	4.43	9.58	Capital Return %
	96	5	15	100	87	5	2	6	3	55	22	27	Total Rtn % Rank Cat
	0.68	0.59	0.68	0.75	1.12	0.79	0.96	0.94	0.61	0.65	0.44	0.58	Income $
	0.14	0.56	0.60	0.04	0.00	0.00	0.00	0.00	0.00	0.10	0.25	0.19	Capital Gains $
	1.06	1.04	1.00	1.01	1.08	1.24	1.19	1.19	1.14	1.06	1.16	—	Expense Ratio %
	4.97	3.74	3.10	3.77	6.10	4.83	5.04	5.33	3.44	2.60	2.30	—	Income Ratio %
	65	61	46	72	91	101	89	79	102	35	36	—	Turnover Rate %
	72	91	181	114	61	47	51	51	109	132	157	244	Net Assets $mil

Performance 12-31-06

	1st Qtr	2nd Qtr	3rd Qtr	4th Qtr	Total
2002	7.50	-7.18	-13.46	8.88	-5.99
2003	2.29	11.02	2.56	12.76	31.34
2004	1.45	1.23	0.14	5.68	8.69
2005	-0.76	0.58	6.29	0.45	6.57
2006	7.33	-0.91	0.60	4.96	12.29

Trailing	Total Return%	+/- DJ Mod	+/- DJ US Mod	%Rank Cat	Growth of $10,000
3 Mo	4.96	-0.63	0.29	53	10,496
6 Mo	5.59	-3.20	-2.31	96	10,559
1 Yr	12.29	-0.01	2.02	27	11,229
3 Yr Avg	9.16	-1.56	0.04	28	13,007
5 Yr Avg	9.94	-0.08	2.34	4	16,061
10 Yr Avg	8.15	-0.40	-0.44	26	21,891
15 Yr Avg	10.35	1.14	0.96	20	43,811

Tax Analysis	Tax-Adj Rtn%	%Rank Cat	Tax-Cost Rat	%Rank Cat
3 Yr (estimated)	8.04	25	1.03	51
5 Yr (estimated)	8.51	4	1.30	80
10 Yr (estimated)	6.33	25	1.68	61

Potential Capital Gain Exposure: 16% of assets

Rating and Risk

Time Period	Load-Adj Return %	Morningstar Rtn vs Cat	Morningstar Risk vs Cat	Morningstar Risk-Adj Rating
1 Yr	12.29			
3 Yr	9.16	+Avg	+Avg	★★★★
5 Yr	9.94	High	+Avg	★★★★★
10 Yr	8.15	+Avg	+Avg	★★★
Incept	10.99			

Other Measures	Standard Index DJ Mod	Best Fit Index Russ 2000
Alpha	0.3	2.0
Beta	0.76	0.35
R-Squared	60	72
Standard Deviation	5.79	
Mean	9.16	
Sharpe Ratio	1.00	

Morningstar's Take by John Coumarianos 12-29-06

Greenspring is a good diversifier.

This offbeat fund is composed of small-cap stocks, "busted" convertible bonds, and cash. (Busted convertibles are corporate bonds with options to convert to the underlying stock that have been rendered worthless by the stock's low price.) Over the past few years, this bold tack has allowed the fund to trample its typical peer, which owns a vanilla portfolio of large-cap stocks and high-quality bonds. Small-cap stocks and convertibles have had powerful multiyear runs, putting Greenspring in the right place at the right time.

However, this fund has more going for it than luck, and its results also look good when compared with a custom benchmark that approximates its style. A blended index of Merrill Lynch Convertible Bonds, All Qualities, Index, the Russell 2000 Index, and the Citigroup 3-month Treasury Bill Index in the proportion of 45/45/10 returned 53% cumulatively since the beginning of 2002. The fund returned 58% by contrast. The fund has also experienced lower

volatility than this makeshift benchmark, and it has done a better job of limiting the downside.

Credit for that showing goes to manager Chip Carlson and his lead analyst Mike Fusting, who have added value with solid security selection. Recently, they've purchased convertibles of companies that are delinquent in filing their quarterly financial statements. Carlson thought that software application tester Mercury Interactive had plenty of cash, even though the company failed to file its 2005 annual report in time. The company compensated bondholders with a put option (giving them the right to sell the bond back to the company), and the cash on its balance sheet eventually proved to make it an attractive takeover target for Hewlett-Packard.

Greenspring can struggle when large-caps roar, and it currently has heavy exposure to industrial and energy stocks, making it vulnerable to an economic downturn. Still, it should complement large-cap holdings quite well over the long haul.

Address:	2330 West Joppa Road Suite 110 Lutherville MD 21093 800-576-7498
Web Address:	www.greenspringfund.com
Inception:	07-01-83
Advisor:	Corbyn Investment Management
Subadvisor:	None
NTF Plans:	Fidelity Retail-NTF, Schwab OneSource

Minimum Purchase:	$2000	Add: $100	IRA: $1000
Min Auto Inv Plan:	$1000	Add: $100	
Sales Fees:	No-load, 2.00%R		
Management Fee:	0.75% mx./0.65% mn.		
Actual Fees:	Mgt:0.75%	Dist:—	
Expense Projections:	3Yr:$368	5Yr:$638	10Yr:$1409
Income Distrib:	Annually		

Portfolio Analysis 11-30-06

Total Stocks:43 Share change since 10-31-06	Sectors	P/E Ratio	YTD Return %	% Net Assets
FTI Consulting, Inc.	Business	20.4	-1.11	3.17
Suncor Energy, Inc.	Energy	33.1	-7.43	3.16
NGP Capital Resources Com	Financial	—		2.63
⊕ Horizon Offshore, Inc.	Energy	4.6	-4.97	2.45
KMG America Corporation	Financial	37.3	1.15	2.44
United America Indemnity,	Financial	13.1	-3.12	2.37
Wabash National Corporati	Ind Mtrls	14.8	-1.99	2.21
Energen Corporation	Energy	13.9	-5.20	2.05
USI Holdings Corporation	Financial	32.9	-3.65	1.96

Total Fixed-Income:2	Date of Maturity	Amount $000	Value $000	% Net Assets
Ciena Cv 3.75%	02-01-08	11,502	11,200	4.67
Sepracor Cv 5%	02-15-10	8,715	8,715	3.63
MILLENNIUM PHARMACEUTICAL	01-15-07	8,510	8,521	3.55
Tempur-Pedic 10.25%	08-15-10	7,179	7,789	3.25
Quanta Svcs Cv 4%	07-01-07	7,168	7,096	2.96
Amazon Com Cv 4.75%	02-01-09	6,814	6,712	2.80
Inhale Theraptc Sys Cv 3.	10-17-07	6,706	6,614	2.76
Mercury Interactive Cv 4.	07-01-07	6,278	6,364	2.65
Agere Sys Cv 6.5%	12-15-09	5,622	5,713	2.38

Equity Style

Style: Value
Size: Small-Cap

Value Measures		Rel Category
Price/Earnings	15.31	1.00
Price/Book	1.74	0.70
Price/Sales	0.82	0.60
Price/Cash Flow	7.75	0.96
Dividend Yield %	0.60	0.31

Growth Measures	%	Rel Category
Long-Term Erngs	12.34	1.05
Book Value	-20.38	NMF
Sales	-15.08	NMF
Cash Flow	2.87	0.29
Historical Erngs	18.46	1.03

Market Cap %			
Giant	7.6	Small	28.9
Large	8.0	Micro	39.0
Mid	16.6	Avg $mil:	1,327

Fixed-Income Style

Duration: Short-Term
Quality: Low

Avg Eff Duration [1]	0.8 Yrs
Avg Eff Maturity	1.4 Yrs
Avg Credit Quality	B
Avg Wtd Coupon	4.82%

[1]figure provided by fund as of 11-30-06

Sector Weightings	% of Stocks	Rel DJ Mod	3 Year High	Low
⟳ Info	3.33			
Software	0.00	—	0	0
Hardware	3.33	—	9	3
Media	0.00	—	0	0
Telecom	0.00	—	0	0
⊆ Service	64.06			
Health	2.76	—	7	0
Consumer	5.43	—	7	0
Business	23.39	—	28	21
Financial	32.48	—	39	26
Mfg	32.61			
Goods	0.00	—	3	0
Ind Mtrls	8.92	—	16	9
Energy	20.38	—	25	2
Utilities	3.31	—	8	3

Composition

● Cash	11.4	
● Stocks	45.3	
● Bonds	4.0	
○ Other	39.2	
Foreign	7.0	
(% of Stock)		

Morningstar® Funds 500

Harbor Bond Instl

	Ticker	Load	NAV	Yield	SEC Yield	Total Assets	Mstar Category
	HABDX	None	$11.56	4.4%	4.32%	$2,409 mil	Intermediate-Term Bond

Governance and Management

Stewardship Grade: B

Portfolio Manager(s)

Bill Gross and his extensive team of analysts and traders at PIMCO are considered some of the best in the business. Gross has led this fund since its 1987 inception.

Strategy

This fund makes a series of bets against its benchmark, the Lehman Brothers Aggregate Index. Manager Bill Gross relies on macroeconomic analysis to determine the fund's interest-rate sensitivity (duration--a measure of interest-rate sensitivity--is usually kept between plus or minus 20% of the benchmark) and sector weightings. He also looks out for inefficiencies in the bond market. The fund may also carry exposure to junk debt, emerging-markets issues, foreign bonds, and currencies.

Historical Profile

Return High
Risk Average
Rating ★★★★ Highest

| | 67 | 85 | 93 | 91 | 17 | 93 | 82 | 34 | |

Investment Style
Fixed Income
Income Rtn %Rank Cat

▼ Manager Change
▽ Partial Manager Change

Growth of $10,000
— Investment Values of Fund
— Investment Values of LB Aggr

Performance Quartile (within Category)

1995	1996	1997	1998	1999	2000	2001	2002	2003	2004	2005	2006	History
11.41	11.24	11.37	11.28	10.68	11.23	11.42	11.70	11.83	11.83	11.62	11.56	NAV
19.15	4.94	9.39	9.56	-0.32	11.34	9.03	10.63	5.30	5.47	2.57	3.91	Total Return %
0.68	1.31	-0.26	0.87	0.50	-0.29	0.59	0.38	1.20	1.13	0.14	-0.42	+/-LB Aggr
-2.28	2.25	-0.04	-0.58	2.56	-1.10	0.21	-2.40	-0.67	0.17	0.74	0.10	+/-LB 5-10YR
7.84	6.29	6.04	5.74	5.07	5.34	4.88	5.80	2.59	2.94	4.26	4.42	Income Return %
11.31	-1.35	3.35	3.82	-5.39	6.00	4.15	4.83	2.71	2.53	-1.69	-0.51	Capital Return %
32	14	38	23	23	20	15	7	35	10	11	51	Total Rtn % Rank Cat
0.78	0.70	0.66	0.64	0.56	0.56	0.54	0.65	0.30	0.34	0.50	0.51	Income $
0.00	0.00	0.23	0.51	0.00	0.07	0.27	0.26	0.19	0.30	0.01	0.00	Capital Gains $
0.70	0.70	0.67	0.65	0.61	0.60	0.56	0.58	0.58	0.57	0.58	—	Expense Ratio %
7.11	6.40	6.04	5.41	5.35	6.16	1.64	4.37	3.43	2.21	3.39	—	Income Ratio %
89	193	252	278	271	494	531	293	221	311	333	—	Turnover Rate %
233	288	385	494	618	787	1,006	1,417	1,527	1,613	1,983	2,370	Net Assets $mil

Performance 12-31-06

	1st Qtr	2nd Qtr	3rd Qtr	4th Qtr	Total
2002	1.10	2.97	3.47	2.70	10.63
2003	2.37	2.62	-0.31	0.55	5.30
2004	2.65	-2.04	3.60	1.24	5.47
2005	-0.37	3.01	-0.40	0.35	2.57
2006	-0.42	-0.27	3.76	0.84	3.91

Trailing	Total Return%	+/- LB Aggr	+/- LB 5-10YR	%Rank Cat	Growth of $10,000
3 Mo	0.84	-0.40	-0.24	89	10,084
6 Mo	4.63	-0.46	-1.05	62	10,463
1 Yr	3.91	-0.42	0.10	51	10,391
3 Yr Avg	3.98	0.28	0.34	17	11,242
5 Yr Avg	5.54	0.48	-0.38	12	13,094
10 Yr Avg	6.63	0.39	-0.05	4	19,002
15 Yr Avg	7.11	0.61	0.12	9	28,019

Tax Analysis	Tax-Adj Rtn%	%Rank Cat	Tax-Cost Rat	%Rank Cat
3 Yr (estimated)	2.42	12	1.50	52
5 Yr (estimated)	3.76	9	1.69	56
10 Yr (estimated)	4.33	4	2.16	64

Potential Capital Gain Exposure: -1% of assets

Rating and Risk

Time Period	Load-Adj Return %	Morningstar Rtn vs Cat	Morningstar Risk vs Cat	Morningstar Risk-Adj Rating
1 Yr	3.91			
3 Yr	3.98	+Avg	+Avg	★★★★
5 Yr	5.54	+Avg	Avg	★★★★
10 Yr	6.63	High	Avg	★★★★★
Incept	8.12			

Other Measures	Standard Index LB Aggr	Best Fit Index LB Aggr
Alpha	0.3	0.3
Beta	0.97	0.97
R-Squared	96	96
Standard Deviation	3.20	
Mean	3.98	
Sharpe Ratio	0.23	

Portfolio Analysis 09-30-06

Total Fixed-Income:695	Date of Maturity	Amount $000	Value $000	% Net Assets
EuroDollar (Fut)	12-18-06	1,070,250	1,013,152	15.56
EuroDollar (Fut)	06-18-07	706,750	671,306	10.31
EuroDollar (Fut)	03-19-07	703,000	666,620	10.24
EuroDollar (Fut)	09-17-07	576,750	548,633	8.42
EuroDollar (Fut)	12-17-07	365,250	347,755	5.34
FNMA 5%		196,000	188,388	2.89
FNMA 5.5%	02-01-35	173,748	171,560	2.63
US Treasury Note (Fut)	12-19-06	128,600	138,968	2.13
EuroDollar (Fut)	03-17-08	101,500	96,664	1.48
FNMA 5.5%	05-01-34	77,891	76,979	1.18
US Treasury Bond (Fut)	12-31-06	55,500	58,561	0.90
FNMA 5.5%		44,500	43,846	0.67
US Treasury Bond (Fut)	12-19-06	37,000	41,590	0.64
Libor (Fut)	12-19-06	22,250	39,523	0.61
Chase Cc Master Tr 2002-	06-15-09	35,200	35,238	0.54
Fin Uk 90day Lif (Fut)	09-30-07	18,125	32,182	0.49
Swp097280 Pimco Irs Rec	12-20-16	31,200	30,835	0.47
FNMA 5%	08-01-35	28,139	27,065	0.42
FNMA 5.5%	04-01-34	25,721	25,425	0.39
First Franklin Mtg 2006-	06-25-36	23,023	23,038	0.35

Current Investment Style

Duration
Short Int Long
Quality: High / Med / Low

[1] figure provided by fund

Avg Eff Duration[1]	5.0 Yrs
Avg Eff Maturity	6.5 Yrs
Avg Credit Quality	AA
Avg Wtd Coupon	4.57%
Avg Wtd Price	98.97% of par

Coupon Range	% of Bonds	Rel Cat
0% PIK	8.4	1.2
0% to 6%	96.4	1.3
6% to 8%	3.1	0.1
8% to 10%	0.5	0.1
More than 10%	0.0	0.0

1.00=Category Average

Credit Analysis	% bonds 09-30-06		
AAA	64	BB	7
AA	21	B	0
A	5	Below B	0
BBB	3	NR/NA	0

Sector Breakdown

	% of assets
US Treasuries	1
TIPS	0
US Agency	0
Mortgage Pass-Throughs	17
Mortgage CMO	2
Mortgage ARM	0
US Corporate	4
Asset-Backed	3
Convertible	0
Municipal	0
Corporate Inflation-Protected	0
Foreign Corporate	1
Foreign Govt	0

Composition

Cash	66.0	Bonds	26.3
Stocks	0.0	Other	7.7

Special Securities

Restricted/Illiquid Secs	Trace
Exotic Mortgage-Backed	0
Emerging-Markets Secs	Trace
Options/Futures/Warrants	No

Morningstar's Take by Eric Jacobson 12-06-06

This may not prove to be Harbor Bond's very best year, but it remains one of the market's very best funds.

It certainly hasn't been a bad year. The fund has gained roughly 5.2% through Dec. 5, 2006, putting it just a hair behind its Lehman Brothers Aggregate Bond index benchmark. That has been good enough to place the fund in the top third of its intermediate-term bond category peers. Still, if the fund "only" matches or slightly beats the index by year's end, experience suggests that manager Bill Gross (the PIMCO legend who subadvises this fund for Harbor), who is known for his extremely competitive nature, will not be satisfied.

We don t think investors should be as hard on Gross as he's likely to be on himself. Although Gross manages much more money than he used to, his skills have evolved with that growth, and his results have remained topnotch. The very fact that his dramatic underweighting of credit-sensitive bonds in recent years has only moderately dampened the fund's results is a testament to his ability. Indeed, if the credit markets, which he believes to be richly priced, do eventually sputter, his avoidance will look smart, and should present useful opportunities.

Our favor for this fund goes deeper than Gross himself, though. He has built tremendous capabilities, in both personnel and technology over many years. As a result, PIMCO boasts some of the industry's top professionals, who have some of its best tools at their disposal. That has given Gross a broad pool of ideas from which to draw, helping him to make effective plays on different maturities, mortgages, municipals, non-US, and inflation-indexed bonds to name a few. Meanwhile, he's managed to keep volatility and underlying risk firmly in check.

This fund's combination of modest expenses, a low minimum investment, and world-class management make it among the very best choices available to the average investor.

Address:	One Seagate Toledo OH 43604-1572 800-422-1050	Minimum Purchase:	$1000	Add: $100	IRA: $50000
		Min Auto Inv Plan:	$1000	Add: $100	
		Sales Fees:	No-load		
Web Address:	www.harborfund.com	Management Fee:	0.50%		
Inception:	12-29-87	Actual Fees:	Mgt:0.50%	Dist: —	
Advisor:	Harbor Capital Advisors	Expense Projections:	3Yr:$192	5Yr:$335	10Yr:$750
Subadvisor:	Pacific Investment Management Co., LLC	Income Distrib:	Annually		
NTF Plans:	N/A				

Harbor Capital App Instl

Analyst Pick ✓	**Ticker** HACAX	**Load** None	**NAV** $33.35	**Yield** 0.2%	**Total Assets** $8,750 mil	**Mstar Category** Large Growth

Governance and Management

Stewardship Grade: B

Portfolio Manager(s)

Sig Segalas and his staff at Jennison Associates have run this fund since 1990. The firm, which Segalas cofounded in 1969, focuses on large-growth investing. Unlike many shops, Jennison treats the analyst position as a career-track position, not a steppingstone to a portfolio-management job. The result is a deep, talented analyst staff.

Strategy

This fund buys large-cap firms that are growing revenues faster than the S&P 500 average and that boast traits such as strong R&D and defensible franchises. Manager Sig Segalas also prefers to see strong unit sales growth, which he thinks is key to the sustainability of a firm's growth rate. This is primarily a large-growth fund, but it will hold smaller caps to get exposure to emerging areas, financials, and energy to help offset the risk in other holdings. The fund holds about 60 names, and it generally doesn't buy a new holding without selling an existing one.

Performance 12-31-06

	1st Qtr	2nd Qtr	3rd Qtr	4th Qtr	Total
2002	-2.63	-16.48	-17.50	3.25	-30.73
2003	-2.28	14.63	4.73	11.21	30.47
2004	1.25	1.80	-4.17	10.69	9.34
2005	-5.48	6.13	7.27	5.96	14.02
2006	1.26	-7.32	4.57	4.28	2.33

Trailing	Total Return%	+/- S&P 500	+/- Russ 1000Gr	%Rank Cat	Growth of $10,000
3 Mo	4.28	-2.42	-1.65	78	10,428
6 Mo	9.04	-3.70	-1.06	39	10,904
1 Yr	2.33	-13.46	-6.74	85	10,233
3 Yr Avg	8.46	-1.98	1.59	30	12,759
5 Yr Avg	2.89	-3.30	0.20	45	11,531
10 Yr Avg	7.52	-0.90	2.08	24	20,649
15 Yr Avg	10.29	-0.35	2.27	18	43,455

Tax Analysis	Tax-Adj Rtn%	%Rank Cat	Tax-Cost Rat	%Rank Cat
3 Yr (estimated)	8.37	23	0.08	6
5 Yr (estimated)	2.81	42	0.08	9
10 Yr (estimated)	6.49	21	0.96	45

Potential Capital Gain Exposure: -4% of assets

Morningstar's Take by Kerry O'Boyle 11-08-06

Despite its frustrating showing so far in 2006, we think Analyst Pick Harbor Capital Appreciation has much to offer.

It has been a trying year for manager Sig Segalas. After a standout performance in 2005, the fund has struggled for most of the year as former highfliers such as Whole Foods Market and Genentech have come down to earth. Even the recent surge in large-cap stocks the past few months hasn't fully lifted it out of the red for the year to date through Nov. 3, 2006.

To be sure, veteran investor Segalas is sticking with the approach that made him one of the leading growth managers of the 1990s. He seeks industry leaders with solid balance sheets that are able to generate substantial revenue, rather than earnings growth. Google remains entrenched at the top of the portfolio much as it has since the company went public in August 2004. Segalas thinks the search giant with its expertise and huge research and development spending has raised the cost of

competing with it to such an extent that he has sold struggling rival Yahoo out of the portfolio. The fund has also sold another Internet bellwether in eBay, on what Segalas sees as a major slowdown in the firm's base online auction business.

Segalas is more sanguine about health-care stocks, however, especially foreign pharmaceutical companies Roche and Novartis. Segalas says Roche and Novartis don't have the patent expiration issues of a number of rivals, and they're growing much faster than their U.S.-based counterparts.

Yes, this is an aggressive-growth offering--one that will occasionally stumble. But Segalas has shown a knack for spotting some of the best-run and fastest-growing companies and getting the most out of them. We think this is a fine offering for risk-tolerant investors with a long investing time horizon.

Address:	One Seagate, Toledo OH 43604-1572, 800-422-1050
Web Address:	www.harborfund.com
Inception:	12-29-87
Advisor:	Harbor Capital Advisors
Subadvisor:	Jennison Associates, LLC
NTF Plans:	N/A

Minimum Purchase:	$50000	Add: $100	IRA: $50000
Min Auto Inv Plan:	$50000	Add: $100	
Sales Fees:	No-load		
Management Fee:	0.60%		
Actual Fees:	Mgt:0.60%	Dist: —	
Expense Projections:	3Yr:$218	5Yr:$379	10Yr:$847
Income Distrib:	Annually		

Historical Profile

Return	Above Avg
Risk	Above Avg
Rating	★★★ Neutral

Investment percentages: 97% | 98% | 98% | 99% | 97% | 98% | 99% | 98% | 99%

Growth of $10,000
- Investment Values of Fund
- Investment Values of S&P 500

43.6 / 32.4 / 24.0 / 17.0 / 10.0

▼ Manager Change
▽ Partial Manager Change

Performance Quartile (within Category)

1995	1996	1997	1998	1999	2000	2001	2002	2003	2004	2005	2006	History
22.69	26.33	29.47	37.99	50.65	35.58	29.23	20.21	26.32	28.67	32.66	33.35	NAV
37.82	19.85	31.46	36.80	45.81	-17.00	-17.74	-30.73	30.47	9.34	14.02	2.33	Total Return %
0.24	-3.11	-1.90	8.22	24.77	-7.90	-5.85	-8.63	1.79	-1.54	9.11	-13.46	+/-S&P 500
0.64	-3.27	0.97	-1.91	12.65	5.42	2.68	-2.85	0.72	3.04	8.76	-6.74	+/-Russ 1000Gr
0.15	0.09	0.25	0.22	0.00	0.00	0.11	0.13	0.24	0.42	0.11	0.22	Income Return %
37.67	19.76	31.21	36.58	45.81	-17.00	-17.85	-30.86	30.23	8.92	13.91	2.11	Capital Return %
20	48	22	27	28	69	38	78	34	36	8	85	Total Rtn % Rank Cat
0.03	0.02	0.07	0.07	0.00	0.00	0.04	0.04	0.05	0.11	0.03	0.07	Income $
0.31	0.86	4.85	2.28	4.60	6.17	0.00	0.00	0.00	0.00	0.00	0.00	Capital Gains $
0.75	0.75	0.70	0.68	0.66	0.64	0.66	0.69	0.71	0.67	0.68	—	Expense Ratio %
0.23	0.11	0.23	0.24	-0.05	-0.07	15.59	0.16	0.24	0.09	0.44	—	Income Ratio %
52	74	73	70	68	86	89	76	64	67	69	—	Turnover Rate %
989	1,682	2,906	4,697	7,947	7,786	6,792	4,912	6,607	6,825	7,837	7,939	Net Assets $mil

Rating and Risk

Time Period	Load-Adj Return %	Morningstar Rtn vs Cat	Morningstar Risk vs Cat	Morningstar Risk-Adj Rating
1 Yr	2.33			
3 Yr	8.46	+Avg	+Avg	★★★★
5 Yr	2.89	Avg	+Avg	★★★
10 Yr	7.52	+Avg	+Avg	★★★
Incept	12.60			

Other Measures	Standard Index S&P 500	Best Fit Index Mstar Large Growth
Alpha	-4.2	5.2
Beta	1.39	1.10
R-Squared	78	90
Standard Deviation	10.82	
Mean	8.46	
Sharpe Ratio	0.51	

Portfolio Analysis 09-30-06

Share change since 06-06 Total Stocks:57

	Sector	PE	Tot Ret%	% Assets
⊖ Google, Inc.	Business	61.5	11.00	3.18
⊕ PepsiCo, Inc.	Goods	21.5	7.86	2.79
Adobe Systems Inc.	Software	48.1	11.26	2.75
⊕ Roche Holding AG ADR	Health	34.2	20.41	2.72
⊕ Gilead Sciences, Inc.	Health	40.6	23.51	2.60
⊕ Genentech, Inc.	Health	48.7	-12.29	2.59
⊕ UBS AG	Financial		29.62	2.56
Novartis AG ADR	Health	22.2	11.29	2.53
Walt Disney Company	Media	21.0	44.26	2.51
⊕ General Electric Company	Ind Mtrls	20.0	9.35	2.50
⊕ Apple Computer, Inc.	Hardware	37.6	18.01	2.46
⊕ Federated Department Sto	Consumer	20.8	16.54	2.30
⊕ Cisco Systems, Inc.	Hardware	30.1	59.64	2.30
Alcon, Inc.	Health	38.3	-12.60	2.28
⊕ WellPoint, Inc.	Health	17.2	-1.38	2.25
⊕ Motorola, Inc.	Hardware	11.8	-8.17	2.24
⊕ American International G	Financial	17.0	6.05	2.06
⊖ American Express Company	Financial	20.9	19.09	2.05
⊕ Procter & Gamble Company	Goods	23.9	13.36	2.04
⊕ Microsoft Corporation	Software	23.8	15.83	2.01

Current Investment Style

Value Blnd Growth — Large/Mid/Small

Market Cap	%
Giant	59.0
Large	36.9
Mid	4.2
Small	0.0
Micro	0.0
Avg $mil:	53,098

Value Measures		Rel Category
Price/Earnings	20.88	1.08
Price/Book	3.49	1.05
Price/Sales	2.31	1.19
Price/Cash Flow	13.35	1.17
Dividend Yield %	0.90	0.87

Growth Measures	%	Rel Category
Long-Term Erngs	14.72	1.03
Book Value	14.06	1.21
Sales	14.10	1.22
Cash Flow	21.15	1.26
Historical Erngs	25.38	1.10

Profitability	%	Rel Category
Return on Equity	20.63	1.01
Return on Assets	11.93	1.08
Net Margin	16.07	1.13

Sector Weightings	% of Stocks	Rel S&P 500	3 Year High	Low
↻ Info	30.00	1.50		
Software	7.37	2.14	10	6
Hardware	17.52	1.90	22	17
Media	3.58	0.94	7	2
Telecom	1.53	0.44	2	0
⊂ Service	51.06	1.10		
Health	25.73	2.13	26	18
Consumer	9.17	1.20	18	9
Business	3.22	0.76	6	0
Financial	12.94	0.58	14	9
Mfg	18.94	0.56		
Goods	8.20	0.96	9	4
Ind Mtrls	6.80	0.57	7	2
Energy	3.94	0.40	8	4
Utilities	0.00	0.00	0	0

Composition

● Cash	0.4
● Stocks	98.8
● Bonds	0.0
● Other	0.8
Foreign (% of Stock)	12.7

Mᴏʀɴɪɴɢsᴛᴀʀ® Funds 500

Harbor Intl Growth Inv

| | Analyst Pick | Ticker HIIGX | Load None | NAV $13.57 | Yield 0.0% | Total Assets $616 mil | Mstar Category Foreign Large Growth |

Governance and Management

Stewardship Grade: B

Portfolio Manager(s)

This fund is subadvised by James Gendelman of Marsico Capital Management, who became manager of this fund in March 2004. Since mid-2000, Gendelman has produced consistently topnotch results at Marsico International Opportunities, of which this fund is a virtual clone. He also manages Columbia Marsico International Opportunities. He previously spent 13 years at Goldman Sachs, primarily in a sales and product-development role that focused on launching Goldman's international offerings. He has two dedicated analysts for this fund and ready access to Marsico's other analysts.

Strategy

Manager James Gendelman favors a concentrated format and considers three types of firms for the portfolio: core-growth stocks, aggressive-growth stocks, and firms undergoing life-cycle changes, such as a major restructuring. Like his employer, Tom Marsico, he factors in top-down analysis, though he rigorously researches his picks. He is willing to buy in emerging markets and likes mid-cap names. The fund has a 2% redemption fee on shares held fewer than 60 days, and it uses an outside service to set fair-value prices in certain situations. It rarely hedges foreign currency exposure.

Historical Profile
Return	Average
Risk	Above Avg
Rating	★★★ Neutral

| | 98% | 91% | 94% | 99% | 97% |

Investment Style
Equity
Stock %

▼ Manager Change
▽ Partial Manager Change

Growth of $10,000
— Investment Values of Fund
— Investment Values of MSCI EAFE

22.0
19.0
16.0
13.0
10.0

Performance Quartile (within Category)

	1995	1996	1997	1998	1999	2000	2001	2002	2003	2004	2005	2006	History
NAV	—	—	—	—	—	—	—	6.62	8.37	9.20	10.98	13.57	
Total Return %	—	—	—	—	—	—	—	-1.35*	27.44	10.39	19.47	23.59	
+/-MSCI EAFE	—	—	—	—	—	—	—		-11.15	-9.86	5.93	-2.75	
+/-MSCI Wd xUS	—	—	—	—	—	—	—		-11.98	-9.99	5.00	-2.12	
Income Return %									1.01	0.47	0.12	0.00	
Capital Return %									26.43	9.92	19.35	23.59	
Total Rtn % Rank Cat									88	91	17	48	
Income $								0.03	0.07	0.04	0.01	0.00	
Capital Gains $								0.00	0.00	0.00	0.00	0.00	
Expense Ratio %								1.40	1.40	1.39	1.39	—	
Income Ratio %								0.49	0.32	0.35	—		
Turnover Rate %								116	234	216	183	—	
Net Assets $mil									1	4	9	27	

Performance 12-31-06

	1st Qtr	2nd Qtr	3rd Qtr	4th Qtr	Total
2002	—	—	—	—	-1.35*
2003	-10.73	13.87	11.00	12.94	27.44
2004	2.27	-2.69	-1.80	12.95	10.39
2005	-2.83	-0.67	12.73	9.81	19.47
2006	10.11	-3.06	4.27	11.05	23.59

Trailing	Total Return%	+/- MSCI EAFE	+/- MSCI Wd xUS	%Rank Cat	Growth of $10,000
3 Mo	11.05	0.70	0.93	48	11,105
6 Mo	15.78	1.09	1.56	28	11,578
1 Yr	23.59	-2.75	-2.12	48	12,359
3 Yr Avg	17.69	-2.24	-2.41	50	16,301
5 Yr Avg	—	—	—	—	—
10 Yr Avg	—	—	—	—	—
15 Yr Avg	—	—	—	—	—

Tax Analysis	Tax-Adj Rtn%	%Rank Cat	Tax-Cost Rat	%Rank Cat
3 Yr (estimated)	17.61	31	0.07	6
5 Yr (estimated)	—	—	—	—
10 Yr (estimated)	—	—	—	—

Potential Capital Gain Exposure: -58% of assets

Morningstar's Take by Dan Lefkovitz 12-21-06

A subpar year doesn't alter Harbor International Growth Fund's standing as a Fund Analyst Pick.

In just the second full calendar year that Jim Gendelman of Marsico Capital Management has run this fund, it has recorded a subpar showing. In absolute terms, the fund's 21% gain for the year to date through Dec. 20, 2006, is stellar. But that mark is well behind the benchmark MSCI EAFE Index and the foreign large-growth category average. This might remind longtime shareholders of the fund's travails before Gendelman took over.

Investors shouldn't worry about one poor year in relative terms. Gendelman has a very impressive track record on (the more expensive and less tax-efficient) Marsico International Opportunities, which he has been running since 2000. Gendelman is still a creative growth investor who applies the Marsico approach to overseas markets.

Like Tom Marsico on the domestic side, he looks for companies benefiting from long-term growth trends and chooses his stocks on the basis of rigorous bottom-up research. Gendelman has targeted lodging and gaming companies, just as Marsico has done on the domestic side, and owns Syngenta, an agricultural firm benefiting from alternative energy development. U.S. analog Monsanto is a top holding of Marsico Growth. And Gendelman recently purchased Nestle, partly because, like Marsico holding Procter & Gamble, it is deploying SAP software tools to better run its business.

Gendelman has never paid attention to the stock, sector, or country weightings of EAFE--yet another similarity to Marsico. That can cause the fund to behave quite differently than its peers. In the past, Gendelman's picks among off-index mid-cap and emerging markets names have boosted returns. But this year the fund was held back by being light on utilities and financials, where Gendelman doesn't see growth. If growth stocks come back into favor, this fund should benefit greatly.

Address:	One Seagate Toledo OH 43604-1572 800-422-1050
Web Address:	www.harborfund.com
Inception:	11-01-02*
Advisor:	Harbor Capital Advisors
Subadvisor:	Marsico Capital Management, LLC
NTF Plans:	Fidelity Retail-NTF, Schwab OneSource

Minimum Purchase:	$2500	Add: $100	IRA: $1000
Min Auto Inv Plan:	$2500	Add: $100	
Sales Fees:	No-load, 0.25%S, 2.00%R		
Management Fee:	0.75%		
Actual Fees:	Mgt:0.75%	Dist:0.25%	
Expense Projections:	3Yr:$446	5Yr:$771	10Yr:$1691
Income Distrib:	Annually		

Rating and Risk

Time Period	Load-Adj Return %	Morningstar Rtn vs Cat	Morningstar Risk vs Cat	Morningstar Risk-Adj Rating
1 Yr	23.59			
3 Yr	17.69	Avg	+Avg	★★★
5 Yr	—	—	—	
10 Yr	—	—	—	
Incept	18.93			

Other Measures	Standard Index MSCI EAFE	Best Fit Index MSCI Wd xUS
Alpha	-4.0	-3.9
Beta	1.15	1.13
R-Squared	88	88
Standard Deviation	11.59	
Mean	17.69	
Sharpe Ratio	1.20	

Portfolio Analysis 09-30-06

Share change since 06-06 Total Stocks:53

	Sector	Country	% Assets
⊕ UBS AG	Financial	Switzerland	4.31
⊕ Roche Holding	Health	Switzerland	4.18
⊕ Syngenta	Ind Mtrls	Switzerland	3.94
⊕ Continental	Ind Mtrls	Germany	3.45
⊕ BAE Systems	Ind Mtrls	U.K.	3.24
⊕ Veolia Environnement	Business	France	3.22
⊕ Samsung Electronics	Goods	Korea	2.99
⊕ Diageo	Goods	U.K.	2.94
⊕ America Movil SA ADR	Telecom	Mexico	2.75
☼ Nestle	Goods	Switzerland	2.67
⊕ Lonza Grp	Health	Switzerland	2.56
⊕ DBS Grp Hldgs Ltd	Financial	Singapore	2.55
⊕ LVMH Moet Hennessy L.V.	Goods	France	2.45
⊕ Esprit Hldgs Ltd	Consumer	Hong Kong	2.33
⊕ Cemex SAB de CV ADR	Ind Mtrls	Mexico	2.22
⊕ Reckitt Benckiser	Goods	U.K.	2.19
⊕ Toyota Motor	Goods	Japan	2.08
⊕ Man Grp	Financial	U.K.	2.02
⊕ Ericsson Telephone Compa	Hardware	Sweden	1.99
⊕ Sega Sammy Hldgs	Goods	Japan	1.92

Current Investment Style

Value Blnd Growth — Large Mid Small

Market Cap	%
Giant	43.6
Large	47.4
Mid	9.0
Small	0.0
Micro	0.0
Avg $mil:	23,298

Value Measures		Rel Category
Price/Earnings	16.79	1.09
Price/Book	2.44	0.93
Price/Sales	1.44	1.02
Price/Cash Flow	10.65	1.10
Dividend Yield %	2.37	0.98

Growth Measures	%	Rel Category
Long-Term Erngs	13.54	1.00
Book Value	9.89	0.90
Sales	-2.25	NMF
Cash Flow	2.96	0.24
Historical Erngs	27.04	1.19

Composition

Cash	3.2	Bonds	0.0
Stocks	96.8	Other	0.0
Foreign	(% of Stock)		100.0

Sector Weightings	% of Stocks	Rel MSCI EAFE	3 Year High Low	
⌖ Info	6.19	0.52		
▣ Software	0.00	0.00	3	0
▣ Hardware	3.35	0.87	12	2
▣ Media	0.00	0.00	13	0
▣ Telecom	2.84	0.51	10	3
⌨ Service	51.56	1.09		
▣ Health	9.93	1.39	17	6
▣ Consumer	9.57	1.93	15	7
▣ Business	5.32	1.05	13	4
▣ Financial	26.74	0.89	32	15
▣ Mfg	42.25	1.03		
▣ Goods	19.48	1.48	26	12
▣ Ind Mtrls	19.36	1.25	22	5
▣ Energy	3.41	0.48	9	3
▣ Utilities	0.00	0.00	1	0

Regional Exposure	% Stock		
UK/W. Europe	58	N. America	3
Japan	16	Latn America	7
Asia X Japan	16	Other	0

Country Exposure		% Stock	
Switzerland	20	France	9
Japan	16	Germany	5
U.K.	15		

Harbor Intl Instl

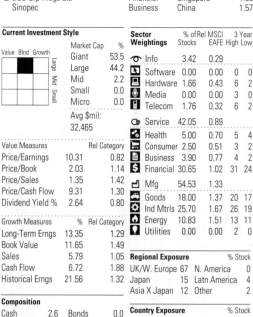

	Analyst Pick	Ticker HAINX	Load None	NAV $62.04	Yield 2.3%	Total Assets $18,546 mil	Mstar Category Foreign Large Value

Governance and Management

Stewardship Grade: B

Portfolio Manager(s)

Hakan Castegren, who has run this fund since its 1987 inception, is the longest-serving manager in the foreign large-value group and was named Morningstar Fund Manager of the Year in 1996. He is supported by four very experienced analysts: Jim LaTorre, Howard Appleby, Jean-Francois Ducrest, and Ted Wendell.

Strategy

Manager Hakan Castegren looks for undervalued large caps that have strong franchises, good restructuring plans, or other reasons to be optimistic about their earnings prospects. In addition, he considers macroeconomic factors and industry themes. He also has a long investment horizon and rarely hedges the fund's currency exposure. The fund has a 2% redemption fee on shares held fewer than 60 days, and it uses an outside service to set fair-value prices in certain situations.

Performance 12-31-06

	1st Qtr	2nd Qtr	3rd Qtr	4th Qtr	Total
2002	6.72	-0.60	-21.25	12.08	-6.38
2003	-9.16	20.74	9.37	17.50	40.95
2004	3.86	-0.31	1.81	11.91	17.97
2005	0.61	-0.58	14.28	5.71	20.84
2006	13.26	-0.98	3.94	13.83	32.69

Trailing	Total Return%	+/- MSCI EAFE	+/- MSCI Wd xUS	%Rank Cat	Growth of $10,000
3 Mo	13.83	3.48	3.71	1	11,383
6 Mo	18.32	3.63	4.10	5	11,832
1 Yr	32.69	6.35	6.98	8	13,269
3 Yr Avg	23.67	3.74	3.57	15	18,914
5 Yr Avg	20.07	5.09	4.82	15	24,956
10 Yr Avg	12.64	4.93	4.68	10	32,880
15 Yr Avg	13.87	6.01	5.83	1	70,168

Tax Analysis	Tax-Adj Rtn%	%Rank Cat	Tax-Cost Rat	%Rank Cat
3 Yr (estimated)	22.52	13	0.93	30
5 Yr (estimated)	19.02	13	0.87	37
10 Yr (estimated)	11.17	12	1.31	34

Potential Capital Gain Exposure: 45% of assets

Morningstar's Take by Kai Wiecking 12-14-06

It doesn't get much better than Harbor International.

This fund has numerous characteristics that make it a standout among foreign options: a skillful, hugely experienced stock-picker at the helm, supported by a strong team (in fact, we're increasingly confident they can pick up the mantle if and when septuagenarian lead manager Hakan Castegren decides to retire); a consistent strategy sporting low turnover; and moderate expenses. The result has been an outstanding track record: The fund's trailing 10-year average annual return of 12.4% through Nov. 30, 2006, ranks within the top 10% of the foreign large-value category.

Unlike many other options in that group, this fund has been able to shine in a variety of market environments. That's because Castegren is quite opportunistic in his definition of value and will happily hang on to his winners as their stock prices rise, provided the factors which initially attracted him are still intact. The benefits of this flexible approach have been evident during the current bull market, which has increasingly blurred the lines between value and growth. Castegren's eclectic portfolio of stocks, composed of leaders of their respective industries, has thrived over the past two years, driven by such diverse picks as Petroleo Brasileiro and Banco Santander Central Hispano, to which they've added in recent months. The Spanish bank continues to exceed expectations both in its domestic market and its Latin American subsidiaries. These two examples point to the smart way in which Castegren has been able to participate in emerging-markets growth. But he's also finding opportunities in more staid areas, such as with new position ASA Abloy, a lock maker in his native Sweden which is building a dominating franchise in many countries across the globe.

Despite its large-cap focus and low turnover, shareholders should continue to expect volatility here. But in the long run, this well-run offering remains a superior pick.

Address:	One Seagate
	Toledo OH 43604-1572
	800-422-1050
Web Address:	www.harborfund.com
Inception:	12-29-87
Advisor:	Harbor Capital Advisors
Subadvisor:	Northern Cross Investments Ltd
NTF Plans:	N/A

Minimum Purchase:	$50000	Add: $100	IRA: $50000
Min Auto Inv Plan:	$50000	Add: $100	
Sales Fees:	No-load, 2.00%R		
Management Fee:	0.75% mx./0.65% mn.		
Actual Fees:	Mgt:0.75%	Dist:—	
Expense Projections:	3Yr:$278	5Yr:$482	10Yr:$1073
Income Distrib:	Annually		

Historical Profile

Return	Above Avg
Risk	High
Rating	★★★★ Above Avg

	1995	1996	1997	1998	1999	2000	2001	2002	2003	2004	2005	2006	History
	92%	91%	92%	92%	88%	93%	94%	94%	94%				
NAV	27.84	32.20	35.86	36.72	41.86	35.09	29.63	26.86	36.79	42.70	49.32	62.04	NAV
	16.06	20.12	15.49	10.36	23.89	-4.97	-12.25	-6.38	40.95	17.97	20.84	32.69	Total Return %
	4.85	14.07	13.71	-9.57	-3.14	9.22	9.17	9.56	2.36	-2.28	7.30	6.35	+/-MSCI EAFE
	4.65	13.25	13.22	-8.33	-4.09	8.39	9.14	9.42	1.53	-2.41	6.37	6.98	+/-MSCI Wd xUS
	1.66	1.50	1.25	1.61	1.77	1.69	0.76	1.13	1.88	1.51	2.41	2.96	Income Return %
	14.40	18.62	14.24	8.75	22.12	-6.66	-13.01	-7.51	39.07	16.46	18.43	29.73	Capital Return %
	30	19	17	66	56	71	34	17	35	88	2	8	Total Rtn % Rank Cat
	0.41	0.42	0.40	0.58	0.65	0.71	0.27	0.34	0.51	0.56	1.03	1.46	Income $
	0.13	0.80	0.90	2.30	2.86	3.79	0.88	0.54	0.56	0.15	1.22	1.88	Capital Gains $
	1.04	0.99	0.97	0.94	0.92	0.92	0.91	0.87	0.89	0.86	0.87	—	Expense Ratio %
	1.53	1.42	1.20	1.27	0.78	1.40	-5.70	1.45	1.83	1.25	1.42	—	Income Ratio %
	14	10	6	14	48	10	7	16	21	12	13	—	Turnover Rate %
	3,460	4,319	5,277	5,374	5,843	4,829	3,655	3,742	6,191	8,542	11,272	17,295	Net Assets $mil

Rating and Risk

Time Period	Load-Adj Return %	Morningstar Rtn vs Cat	Morningstar Risk vs Cat	Morningstar Risk-Adj Rating
1 Yr	32.69			
3 Yr	23.67	+Avg	High	★★★★
5 Yr	20.07	+Avg	High	★★★★
10 Yr	12.64	+Avg	+Avg	★★★★
Incept	15.10			

Other Measures	Standard Index MSCI EAFE	Best Fit Index MSCI Wd xUS
Alpha	1.1	1.1
Beta	1.14	1.13
R-Squared	92	93
Standard Deviation	11.30	
Mean	23.67	
Sharpe Ratio	1.68	

Portfolio Analysis 09-30-06

Share change since 06-06 Total Stocks:76	Sector	Country	% Assets
ABB Ltd	Ind Mtrls	Switzerland	2.61
⊕ Linde	Ind Mtrls	Germany	2.51
BHP Billiton	Ind Mtrls	U.K.	2.32
Petroleo Brasileiro Sa P	Energy	Brazil	2.22
⊕ Novo Nordisk	Health	Denmark	1.99
⊕ Accor	Consumer	France	1.92
Canon	Goods	Japan	1.91
⊕ Investor	Financial	Sweden	1.88
⊕ Diageo	Goods	U.K.	1.87
⊖ Continental	Ind Mtrls	Germany	1.78
⊕ Bco Bradesco Sa	—	Brazil	1.78
☆☆ Banco Santander Central	Financial	Spain	1.76
Axa	Financial	France	1.73
Nestle	Goods	Switzerland	1.73
Richemont (Cie Fin)	Goods	Switzerland	1.72
Holcim	Ind Mtrls	Switzerland	1.72
ORIX	Financial	Japan	1.69
⊕ UBS AG	Financial	Switzerland	1.64
⊕ DBS Grp Hldgs Ltd	Financial	Singapore	1.58
Sinopec	Business	China	1.57

Current Investment Style

Value Blnd Growth — Large/Mid/Small

	Market Cap	%
	Giant	53.5
	Large	44.2
	Mid	2.2
	Small	0.0
	Micro	0.0
	Avg $mil:	32,465

Value Measures		Rel Category
Price/Earnings	10.31	0.82
Price/Book	2.03	1.14
Price/Sales	1.35	1.42
Price/Cash Flow	9.31	1.30
Dividend Yield %	2.64	0.80

Growth Measures	%	Rel Category
Long-Term Erngs	13.35	1.29
Book Value	11.65	1.49
Sales	5.79	1.05
Cash Flow	6.72	1.88
Historical Erngs	21.56	1.32

Composition

Cash	2.6	Bonds	0.0
Stocks	93.8	Other	3.7
Foreign (% of Stock)			100.0

Sector Weightings	% of Stocks	Rel MSCI EAFE	3 Year High Low	
⊙ Info	3.42	0.29		
▣ Software	0.00	0.00	0	0
▣ Hardware	1.66	0.43	6	2
▣ Media	0.00	0.00	3	0
▣ Telecom	1.76	0.32	6	2
⊏ Service	42.05	0.89		
▣ Health	5.00	0.70	5	4
▣ Consumer	2.50	0.51	3	2
▣ Business	3.90	0.77	4	2
⑤ Financial	30.65	1.02	31	24
⊔ Mfg	54.53	1.33		
▣ Goods	18.00	1.37	20	17
❂ Ind Mtrls	25.70	1.67	26	19
▣ Energy	10.83	1.51	13	11
▣ Utilities	0.00	0.00	2	0

Regional Exposure	% Stock		
UK/W. Europe	67	N. America	0
Japan	15	Latn America	4
Asia X Japan	12	Other	2

Country Exposure	% Stock		
U.K.	15	Switzerland	13
Japan	15	Germany	9
France	13		

MORNINGSTAR® Funds 500

Harbor Large Cap Val Inv

	Ticker	Load	NAV	Yield	Total Assets	Mstar Category
	HILVX	None	$19.23	0.7%	$913 mil	Large Value

Governance and Management

Stewardship Grade: B

Portfolio Manager(s)

Armstrong Shaw Associates became the subadvisor on this fund in 2001. The firm has run private accounts since 1984 in the same large-cap value style that it uses here. It tends to hire individuals who have hands-on experience in industries outside of finance. Jeff Shaw is the only named manager here, but he chairs an investment committee of six analyst/managers who all work on the fund.

Strategy

Management seeks out large-cap stocks trading at discounts of 30% or more to the team's estimates of their intrinsic values. To estimate intrinsic value, the team uses discounted cash-flow analysis and analyzes comparable transactions and historic valuations. The less agreement there is between the three methods' values, the greater the discount that the managers demand. The managers keep sector weightings within twice those of the Russell 1000 Value Index's or within 15 percentage points of that index's, whichever is greater.

Performance 12-31-06

	1st Qtr	2nd Qtr	3rd Qtr	4th Qtr	Total
2002	—	—	—	—	-0.36 *
2003	-3.53	15.76	2.62	11.07	27.28
2004	2.72	1.47	-1.34	11.14	14.29
2005	1.41	2.01	1.43	0.06	4.99
2006	2.35	-0.73	5.29	8.09	15.63

Trailing	Total Return%	+/- S&P 500	+/- Russ 1000 Vl	%Rank Cat	Growth of $10,000
3 Mo	8.09	1.39	0.09	16	10,809
6 Mo	13.81	1.07	-0.91	32	11,381
1 Yr	15.63	-0.16	-6.62	82	11,563
3 Yr Avg	11.54	1.10	-3.55	63	13,877
5 Yr Avg	—	—	—	—	—
10 Yr Avg	—	—	—	—	—
15 Yr Avg	—	—	—	—	—

Tax Analysis	Tax-Adj Rtn%	%Rank Cat	Tax-Cost Rat	%Rank Cat
3 Yr (estimated)	11.20	41	0.30	11
5 Yr (estimated)	—	—	—	—
10 Yr (estimated)	—	—	—	—

Potential Capital Gain Exposure: 16% of assets

Historical Profile

Return	Average
Risk	Below Avg
Rating	★★★ Neutral

98%	93%	95%	97%	97%

Investment Style
Equity
Stock %

▼ Manager Change
▽ Partial Manager Change

Growth of $10,000
■ Investment Values of Fund
— Investment Values of S&P 500

Performance Quartile (within Category)

1995	1996	1997	1998	1999	2000	2001	2002	2003	2004	2005	2006	History
—	—	—	—	—	—	—	11.32	14.34	16.30	17.00	19.23	NAV
—	—	—	—	—	—	—	-0.36*	27.28	14.29	4.99	15.63	Total Return %
—	—	—	—	—	—	—	—	-1.40	3.41	0.08	-0.16	+/-S&P 500
—	—	—	—	—	—	—	—	-2.75	-2.20	-2.06	-6.62	+/-Russ 1000 Vl
—	—	—	—	—	—	—	—	0.55	0.60	0.70	0.82	Income Return %
—	—	—	—	—	—	—	—	26.73	13.69	4.29	14.81	Capital Return %
—	—	—	—	—	—	—	—	55	34	58	82	Total Rtn % Rank Cat
—	—	—	—	—	—	—	0.07	0.06	0.09	0.11	0.14	Income $
—	—	—	—	—	—	—	0.00	0.00	0.00	0.00	0.28	Capital Gains $
—	—	—	—	—	—	—	—	1.17	1.10	1.10	—	Expense Ratio %
—	—	—	—	—	—	—	—	0.34	0.68	0.70	—	Income Ratio %
—	—	—	—	—	—	—	35	25	19	24	—	Turnover Rate %
—	—	—	—	—	—	—	7	18	200	300	Net Assets $mil

Rating and Risk

Time Period	Load-Adj Return %	Morningstar Rtn vs Cat	Morningstar Risk vs Cat	Morningstar Risk-Adj Rating
1 Yr	15.63			
3 Yr	11.54	Avg	-Avg	★★★
5 Yr	—	—	—	—
10 Yr	—	—	—	—
Incept	14.15			

Other Measures	Standard Index S&P 500	Best Fit Index Russ 1000 Vl
Alpha	2.1	-1.7
Beta	0.84	0.86
R-Squared	79	80
Standard Deviation	6.52	
Mean	11.54	
Sharpe Ratio	1.22	

Portfolio Analysis 09-30-06

Share change since 06-06 Total Stocks:37	Sector	PE	Tot Ret%	% Assets
⊕ Time Warner, Inc.	Media	19.6	26.37	4.49
⊖ Comcast Corporation	Media	—	—	4.39
⊖ Bank of America Corporat	Financial	12.4	20.68	4.01
⊕ American International G	Financial	17.0	6.05	4.00
⊕ Citigroup, Inc.	Financial	13.1	19.55	3.70
⊖ Morgan Stanley	Financial	12.3	45.93	3.65
⊕ General Electric Company	Ind Mtrls	20.0	9.35	3.63
⊖ Devon Energy Corporation	Energy	9.2	8.06	3.55
⊕ Washington Mutual, Inc.	Financial	13.4	9.62	3.35
⊖ Chevron Corporation	Energy	9.0	33.76	3.35
⊖ Symantec Corporation	Software	50.9	19.14	3.20
⊕ Sprint Nextel Corporatio	Telecom	30.2	-10.44	3.11
Exelon Corporation	Utilities	—	19.79	2.96
⊖ Pitney Bowes Inc.	Ind Mtrls	19.7	12.57	2.94
⊖ Abbott Laboratories	Health	24.3	26.88	2.88
⊕ Xerox Corporation	Ind Mtrls	13.4	15.70	2.85
⊕ Tyco International, Ltd.	Ind Mtrls	15.7	6.83	2.78
⊕ Emerson Electric Company	Ind Mtrls	19.6	20.68	2.56
⊕ ConocoPhillips	Energy	6.5	26.53	2.55
United Technologies	Ind Mtrls	17.8	13.65	2.48

Current Investment Style

Value Blnd Growth — Large Mid Small

Market Cap	%
Giant	48.8
Large	46.1
Mid	5.1
Small	0.0
Micro	0.0
Avg $mil:	52,774

Value Measures		Rel Category
Price/Earnings	13.35	0.97
Price/Book	1.72	0.77
Price/Sales	1.38	1.06
Price/Cash Flow	8.28	1.24
Dividend Yield %	2.02	0.87

Growth Measures	%	Rel Category
Long-Term Erngs	10.58	1.02
Book Value	15.05	1.90
Sales	11.01	1.22
Cash Flow	5.78	0.95
Historical Erngs	15.53	0.96

Profitability	%	Rel Category
Return on Equity	14.02	0.78
Return on Assets	8.35	0.85
Net Margin	11.19	0.86

Sector Weightings	% of Stocks	Rel S&P 500	3 Year High Low	
↻ Info	17.72	0.89		
🖥 Software	3.31	0.96	3	0
🖱 Hardware	2.01	0.22	4	0
📶 Media	9.18	2.42	14	8
📞 Telecom	3.22	0.92	4	0
⚒ Service	47.95	1.04		
🩺 Health	9.29	0.77	13	9
🛒 Consumer	7.86	1.03	14	8
📇 Business	1.84	0.43	6	2
💲 Financial	28.96	1.30	31	24
🏭 Mfg	34.34	1.02		
🏠 Goods	0.00	0.00	1	0
⚙ Ind Mtrls	21.48	1.80	21	15
🔋 Energy	9.79	1.00	10	7
⚡ Utilities	3.07	0.88	6	3

Composition

		%
● Cash		3.4
● Stocks		96.6
● Bonds		0.0
○ Other		0.0
Foreign (% of Stock)		1.5

Morningstar's Take by Kerry O'Boyle 12-27-06

We remain big fans of Harbor Large Cap Value.

This fund hasn't exactly been tearing up the charts lately in terms of performance versus its large-value peers, but we think it has many admirable qualities. Management is experienced. Although only in charge here since September 2001, subadvisor Armstrong Shaw has an impressive two-decade record of managing money in separate accounts using this strategy. The team, led by Jeff Shaw, also invests with a high degree of conviction. The portfolio typically contains fewer than 40 stocks, and the team tends to hold them for years, as shown by the fund's modest turnover.

Shaw looks for solid businesses trading at roughly a 30% discount to their estimate of a firm's intrinsic value, derived using discounted cash-flow models and relative valuation measures. That led to the addition of home supplier Lowe's Companie and software firm Symantec to the portfolio during the summer. Shaw likes Lowe's better than bigger rival Home Depot for its greater growth potential and

better customer experience. He views Symantec's subscription antivirus service as a terrific business, one that he has watched for years and finally was able to buy at an attractive price.

Shaw has admitted that some of the recent performance woes have been the result of poor stock-picking. Despite taking some gains near the top, Shaw lost faith in recently struggling homebuilder Pulte Homes, which he subsequently sold. He points to the difficulty in predicting earnings in the midst of a housing slump, as well as management's lack of candor with fixed and variable costs. Shaw also gave up on and sold Dell, citing increased competition and a longer turnaround than expected.

Still, we think the team here is quite capable. Relative performance has picked up in the past quarter as the market has shifted in favor of larger and higher-quality stocks. Despite the fund's recent rough patch, we think it still merits a look from long-term investors.

Address:	One Seagate Toledo OH 43604-1572 800-422-1050
Web Address:	www.harborfund.com
Inception:	11-01-02*
Advisor:	Harbor Capital Advisors
Subadvisor:	Armstrong Shaw Associates
NTF Plans:	Fidelity Retail-NTF, Schwab OneSource

Minimum Purchase:	$2500	Add: $100	IRA: $1000
Min Auto Inv Plan:	$2500	Add: $100	
Sales Fees:	No-load, 0.25%S		
Management Fee:	0.60%		
Actual Fees:	Mgt:0.60%	Dist:0.25%	
Expense Projections:	3Yr:$350	5Yr:$606	10Yr:$1340
Income Distrib:	Annually		

Harbor Real Return Instl

	Analyst Pick	Ticker	Load	NAV	Yield	SEC Yield	Total Assets	Mstar Category
	✓	HARRX	None	$9.64	3.7%	1.28%	$14 mil	Inflation-Protected Bond

Governance and Management

Stewardship Grade:

Portfolio Manager(s)

John Brynjolfsson, a senior manager at subadvisor PIMCO, has managed this fund since its 2005 inception. He is a member of the PIMCO management team that won Morningstar's Fixed-Income Manager of the Year honors in 1998 and 2000.

Strategy

Manager John Brynjolfsson invests the majority of this fund's assets in TIPS, although he will occasionally venture into corporate and foreign inflation-protected bonds. Because the principal on these bonds is adjusted to keep up with changes in the consumer price index (or some other price index), they provide a unique inflation hedge. He will often buy TIPS through forward contracts, as well, which only require a modest amount of cash to purchase and therefore permit the fund to use the remainder to invest in short-term corporates.

Historical Profile
Return
Risk
Rating — Not Rated

Investment Style
Fixed Income
Income Rtn %Rank Cat

▼ Manager Change
▽ Partial Manager Change

Growth of $10,000
— Investment Values of Fund
— Investment Values of LB Aggr

Performance Quartile (within Category)

	1995	1996	1997	1998	1999	2000	2001	2002	2003	2004	2005	2006	History
	—	—	—	—	—	—	—	—	—	—	10.05	9.64	NAV
	—	—	—	—	—	—	—	—	—	—	—	-0.17	Total Return %
	—	—	—	—	—	—	—	—	—	—	—	-4.50	+/-LB Aggr
	—	—	—	—	—	—	—	—	—	—	—	-0.58	+/-LB US Treas TIPS
	—	—	—	—	—	—	—	—	—	—	—	3.65	Income Return %
	—	—	—	—	—	—	—	—	—	—	—	-3.82	Capital Return %
	—	—	—	—	—	—	—	—	—	—	—	61	Total Rtn % Rank Cat
	—	—	—	—	—	—	—	—	—	—	0.03	0.36	Income $
	—	—	—	—	—	—	—	—	—	—	0.00	0.03	Capital Gains $
	—	—	—	—	—	—	—	—	—	—	—	—	Expense Ratio %
	—	—	—	—	—	—	—	—	—	—	—	—	Income Ratio %
	—	—	—	—	—	—	—	—	—	—	—	—	Turnover Rate %
	—	—	—	—	—	—	—	—	—	—	—	13	Net Assets $mil

Performance 12-31-06

	1st Qtr	2nd Qtr	3rd Qtr	4th Qtr	Total
2002	—	—	—	—	—
2003	—	—	—	—	—
2004	—	—	—	—	—
2005	—	—	—	—	—*
2006	-2.29	0.73	3.39	-1.90	-0.17

Trailing	Total Return%	+/- LB Aggr	+/- LB US Treas TIPS	%Rank Cat	Growth of $10,000
3 Mo	-1.90	-3.14	-0.53	99	9,810
6 Mo	1.42	-3.67	-0.80	90	10,142
1 Yr	-0.17	-4.50	-0.58	61	9,983
3 Yr Avg	—	—	—	—	—
5 Yr Avg	—	—	—	—	—
10 Yr Avg	—	—	—	—	—
15 Yr Avg	—	—	—	—	—

Tax Analysis	Tax-Adj Rtn%	%Rank Cat	Tax-Cost Rat	%Rank Cat
3 Yr (estimated)	—	—	—	—
5 Yr (estimated)	—	—	—	—
10 Yr (estimated)	—	—	—	—

Potential Capital Gain Exposure: % of assets

Rating and Risk

Time Period	Load-Adj Return %	Morningstar Rtn vs Cat	Morningstar Risk vs Cat	Morningstar Risk-Adj Rating
1 Yr	-0.17			
3 Yr	—	—	—	—
5 Yr	—	—	—	—
10 Yr	—	—	—	—
Incept	0.65			

Other Measures	Standard Index LB Aggr	Best Fit Index
Alpha	—	—
Beta	—	—
R-Squared	—	—
Standard Deviation	—	
Mean	—	
Sharpe Ratio	—	

Morningstar's Take by Karen Dolan 12-11-06

Harbor Real Return is still nearly new, but it's already the one to beat.

While this fund has only been around since December 2005 and has fallen behind its category peers in recent months, its long-term picture is bright. We wouldn't usually be nearly as complimentary of such a young offering and, in fact, wouldn't probably even be covering this tiny fund, which has less than $15 million in assets. PIMCO, however, is the fund's subadvisor, and skipper John Brynjolfsson is one of the most knowledgeable, most skilled managers of any who run portfolios of Treasury Inflation-Protected Securities.

Brynjolfsson also runs the highly successful PIMCO Real Return, whose institutional shares have a stellar long-term record but also a minimum investment prohibitive for individual investors. On the other hand, PIMCO's more-affordable share classes are too expensive for our taste and have correspondingly weaker records. Like the proverbial porridge that Goldilocks ate, though, this fund, with its low minimum investment and modest 0.57% annual price tag, is just right.

It's important to note that the fund makes substantial use of off-index plays: It is willing to buy conventional bonds, non-U.S. issues, and currencies, for example. In September, the fund was favoring mortgage-backed bonds and betting on a weaker dollar. Clearly, it is not a plain-vanilla choice and, thus, won't likely appeal to investors seeking sector purity. The modest number of available TIPS issues means few opportunities to otherwise distinguish the fund, though, and Brynjolfsson believes that he can do so with such bets but without taking on undue risk. In fact, PIMCO has a strong firmwide track record of making such unique calls without drastically altering the risk profile of its strategies. Brynjolfsson has had nearly 10 years to successfully do so using this real return strategy, which gives us a great deal of confidence and makes this a nearly perfect choice.

Portfolio Analysis 09-30-06

Total Fixed-Income:19	Date of Maturity	Amount $000	Value $000	% Net Assets
US TREASURY NOTE	07-15-15	4,518	4,377	21.46
US Treasury Note 0.875%	04-15-10	4,298	4,075	19.98
US Treasury Note 3%	07-15-12	1,698	1,762	8.64
US Treasury Bond 2%	01-15-26	1,640	1,574	7.72
FNMA 6%		1,100	1,105	5.42
US Treasury Note 4.25%	01-15-10	786	832	4.08
FNMA 5.5%		600	591	2.90
Fixed Inf Eur R 2.26125%	07-14-11	400	507	2.49
US Treasury Note 2.375%	04-15-11	410	411	2.01
US Treasury Bond 3.875%	04-15-29	309	400	1.96
US Treasury Note 3.625%	01-15-08	378	381	1.87
Swp098767 Pimco Irs Rec	06-15-09	200	373	1.83
US Treasury Bond 3.625%	04-15-28	252	312	1.53
US Treasury Note 3.5%	01-15-11	234	245	1.20
US Treasury Note	01-15-16	205	200	0.98
US Treasury Note 3.875%	01-15-09	186	192	0.94
US Treasury Note 1.875%	07-15-13	166	162	0.79
US Treasury Note 2.5%	07-15-16	101	103	0.50
US Treasury Bond 4.5%	02-15-36	100	96	0.47

Current Investment Style

Duration: Short Int Long
Quality: High Med Low

1 figure provided by fund

Avg Eff Duration[1]	7.2 Yrs
Avg Eff Maturity	10.6 Yrs
Avg Credit Quality	AAA
Avg Wtd Coupon	2.46%
Avg Wtd Price	99.40% of par

Coupon Range	% of Bonds	Rel Cat
0% PIK	0.6	0.1
0% to 6%	100.0	1.0
6% to 8%	0.0	0.0
8% to 10%	0.0	0.0
More than 10%	0.0	0.0

1.00=Category Average

Credit Analysis	% bonds 09-30-06		
AAA	100	BB	0
AA	0	B	0
A	0	Below B	0
BBB	0	NR/NA	0

Sector Breakdown	% of assets
US Treasuries	0
TIPS	77
US Agency	0
Mortgage Pass-Throughs	9
Mortgage CMO	0
Mortgage ARM	0
US Corporate	0
Asset-Backed	0
Convertible	0
Municipal	0
Corporate Inflation-Protected	0
Foreign Corporate	0
Foreign Govt	0

Composition			
Cash	13.2	Bonds	86.8
Stocks	0.0	Other	0.0

Special Securities	
Restricted/Illiquid Secs	0
Exotic Mortgage-Backed	0
Emerging-Markets Secs	0
Options/Futures/Warrants	No

Address:	One Seagate Toledo OH 43604-1572 800-422-1050	Minimum Purchase:	$1000	Add: $0 IRA: $0
		Min Auto Inv Plan:	$1000	Add: —
		Sales Fees:	No-load	
Web Address:	www.harborfund.com	Management Fee:	0.50%	
Inception:	12-01-05	Actual Fees:	Mgt:0.50%	Dist: —
Advisor:	Harbor Capital Advisors	Expense Projections:	3Yr:$343	5Yr:$595 10Yr:$1317
Subadvisor:	Pacific Investment Management Co., LLC	Income Distrib:	Quarterly	
NTF Plans:	N/A			

MORNINGSTAR® Funds 500

Homestead Value

	Ticker	Load	NAV	Yield	Total Assets	Mstar Category
	HOVLX	None	$35.94	1.5%	$610 mil	Large Value

Portfolio Manager(s)

Management is very experienced. Industry veterans Stuart Teach and Peter Morris have both been managing this fund since its inception in November 1990. Mark Ashton joined them in 1999.

Strategy

Management seeks out companies that have hit hard times but that it thinks are fundamentally strong. Typically, management has shied away from investing in the volatile, and often pricey, technology sector, instead favoring more-value-oriented areas, such as financials and consumer durables. A buy-and-hold approach is gospel here: The fund's turnover rate typically stays less than 20%.

Historical Profile

Return	Above Avg
Risk	Below Avg
Rating	★★★★ Above Avg

Investment Style: Equity Stock %

94% 99% 100% 92% 95% 98% 94% 92% 91%

▼ Manager Change
▽ Partial Manager Change

Growth of $10,000
— Investment Values of Fund
— Investment Values of S&P 500

31.0
24.0
17.0
10.0

Performance Quartile (within Category)

	1995	1996	1997	1998	1999	2000	2001	2002	2003	2004	2005	2006	History
NAV	18.44	20.99	25.50	26.50	23.53	25.38	25.50	22.24	27.52	30.44	32.78	35.94	NAV
	33.78	17.94	26.70	8.31	-3.21	9.64	5.90	-11.56	26.16	14.71	10.94	17.82	Total Return %
	-3.80	-5.02	-6.66	-20.27	-24.25	18.74	17.79	10.54	-2.52	3.83	6.03	2.03	+/-S&P 500
	-4.58	-3.70	-8.48	-7.32	-10.56	2.63	11.49	3.96	-3.87	-1.78	3.89	-4.43	+/-Russ 1000 VI
	2.82	2.10	1.76	1.57	1.56	1.65	1.30	1.29	1.66	1.28	1.37	1.75	Income Return %
	30.96	15.84	24.94	6.74	-4.77	7.99	4.60	-12.85	24.50	13.43	9.57	16.07	Capital Return %
	41	69	57	74	89	51	13	7	67	30	6	56	Total Rtn % Rank Cat
	0.41	0.39	0.37	0.40	0.41	0.39	0.33	0.33	0.37	0.35	0.42	0.57	Income $
	0.53	0.36	0.71	0.72	1.74	0.00	1.05	0.00	0.14	0.76	0.56	2.09	Capital Gains $
	0.84	0.73	0.79	0.72	0.74	0.85	0.85	0.83	0.84	0.82	0.76	—	Expense Ratio %
	2.50	2.08	1.59	1.52	1.47	1.58	1.26	1.35	1.54	1.23	1.33	—	Income Ratio %
	10	5	6	10	17	18	19	29	12	8	8	—	Turnover Rate %
	148	232	367	446	376	335	320	275	262	390	458	610	Net Assets $mil

Performance 12-31-06

	1st Qtr	2nd Qtr	3rd Qtr	4th Qtr	Total
2002	4.43	-4.75	-16.53	6.53	-11.56
2003	-7.64	18.32	0.87	14.46	26.16
2004	1.53	4.27	-0.03	8.39	14.71
2005	-0.30	3.75	5.15	2.00	10.94
2006	6.19	1.64	2.68	6.31	17.82

Trailing	Total Return%	+/- S&P 500	+/- Russ 1000 VI	%Rank Cat	Growth of $10,000
3 Mo	6.31	-0.39	-1.69	82	10,631
6 Mo	9.16	-3.58	-5.56	95	10,916
1 Yr	17.82	2.03	-4.43	56	11,782
3 Yr Avg	14.46	4.02	-0.63	14	14,996
5 Yr Avg	10.84	4.65	-0.02	10	16,729
10 Yr Avg	9.94	1.52	-1.06	27	25,796
15 Yr Avg	12.09	1.45	-0.94	21	55,399

Tax Analysis	Tax-Adj Rtn%	%Rank Cat	Tax-Cost Rat	%Rank Cat
3 Yr (estimated)	13.43	11	0.90	35
5 Yr (estimated)	10.00	8	0.76	41
10 Yr (estimated)	8.82	15	1.02	21

Potential Capital Gain Exposure: 39% of assets

Rating and Risk

Time Period	Load-Adj Return %	Morningstar Rtn vs Cat	Morningstar Risk vs Cat	Morningstar Risk-Adj Rating
1 Yr	17.82			
3 Yr	14.46	+Avg	-Avg	★★★★
5 Yr	10.84	+Avg	-Avg	★★★★
10 Yr	9.94	+Avg	Avg	★★★★
Incept	12.34			

Other Measures	Standard Index S&P 500	Best Fit Index MSCI World
Alpha	5.0	2.4
Beta	0.80	0.75
R-Squared	71	78
Standard Deviation	6.55	
Mean	14.46	
Sharpe Ratio	1.62	

Portfolio Analysis 09-30-06

Share change since 06-06 Total Stocks:44	Sector	PE	Tot Ret%	% Assets
⊕ Bristol-Myers Squibb Com	Health	23.1	19.93	3.55
Marathon Oil Corporation	Energy	6.1	54.68	3.49
Abbott Laboratories	Health	24.3	26.88	3.33
J.P. Morgan Chase & Co.	Financial	13.6	25.60	3.25
⊕ Schering-Plough Corporat	Health	36.6	14.63	3.22
⊖ Dow Chemical Company	Ind Mtrls	10.0	-5.44	3.17
⊕ Tyco International, Ltd.	Ind Mtrls	15.7	6.83	3.17
⊕ GlaxoSmithKline PLC ADR	Health	17.6	7.95	3.03
⊕ Southwest Airlines, Co.	Business	23.2	-6.65	2.93
Citigroup, Inc.	Financial	13.1	19.55	2.90
Parker Hannifin Corporat	Ind Mtrls	13.2	18.00	2.82
⊕ Fifth Third Bancorp	Financial	15.4	12.99	2.81
Flowserve Corporation	Ind Mtrls	39.2	27.58	2.52
Genworth Financial, Inc.	Financial	12.9	-0.17	2.49
Questar Corporation	Energy	16.0	11.02	2.46
Bemis Company, Inc.	Goods	20.8	24.90	2.45
Genuine Parts Company	Consumer	17.4	11.39	2.34
ConocoPhillips	Energy	6.5	26.53	2.31
⊖ Chevron Corporation	Energy	9.0	33.76	2.23
Hca	Health	—	—	2.23

Current Investment Style

Value Blnd Growth — Large Mid Small

Market Cap	%
Giant	28.5
Large	35.4
Mid	33.0
Small	3.1
Micro	0.0
Avg $mil:	22,173

Value Measures		Rel Category
Price/Earnings	13.52	0.98
Price/Book	2.15	0.97
Price/Sales	1.03	0.79
Price/Cash Flow	7.69	1.15
Dividend Yield %	2.23	0.96

Growth Measures	%	Rel Category
Long-Term Erngs	10.57	1.02
Book Value	6.72	0.85
Sales	9.39	1.04
Cash Flow	6.76	1.12
Historical Erngs	18.74	1.16

Profitability	%	Rel Category
Return on Equity	18.82	1.05
Return on Assets	9.49	0.97
Net Margin	10.96	0.85

Sector Weightings	% of Stocks	Rel S&P 500	3 Year High Low	
⟳ Info	3.80	0.19		
▣ Software	0.00	0.00	0	0
▣ Hardware	3.80	0.41	4	1
▣ Media	0.00	0.00	0	0
▣ Telecom	0.00	0.00	0	0
⟲ Service	53.66	1.16		
▣ Health	18.82	1.56	19	12
▣ Consumer	4.74	0.62	11	5
▣ Business	3.98	0.94	7	4
▣ Financial	26.12	1.17	28	22
⟱ Mfg	42.54	1.26		
▣ Goods	8.06	0.94	10	8
▣ Ind Mtrls	19.41	1.63	19	14
▣ Energy	15.07	1.54	24	15
▣ Utilities	0.00	0.00	0	0

Composition

	%
● Cash	9.2
● Stocks	90.8
● Bonds	0.0
● Other	0.0
Foreign (% of Stock)	3.4

Morningstar's Take by Lawrence Jones 12-21-06

We think seasoned management and a low price tag make Homestead Value a compelling choice.

We're impressed with this fund's veteran management team. Stuart Teach and Peter Morris bring a lot of experience to the table here. Both managers have been running the fund since its late-1990 inception, giving them nearly 16 years of experience with the same approach and mandate--longer tenure than the vast majority of managers in the large-value category. They also have a lengthy track record running pension money for electrical utility companies. Mark Ashton, who joined the team in 1999, spent 14 years at Capital Research (advisor to the American funds).

Management has consistently practiced a flexible, and long-term, value-based approach at the fund. The managers look for fundamentally strong companies whose stock prices have been beaten down in the short run but that still retain positive long-term prospects. They will look for favorable measures on fundamental valuation metrics, such as price/earnings and price/book, yet their process doesn't involve overly rigid screening. Management will concentrate the portfolio in roughly 40-60 holdings, including a sizable stake in mid-cap companies, giving the fund's portfolio a considerably lower average market cap than is typical in the category.

While portfolio concentration and a focus on mid-caps can lead to added volatility, we haven't seen that here. The fund's volatility has been modest, and it has tended to fare well in turbulent markets. Investors should note, however, the fund's high level of mid-cap exposure (currently 33%) could make it a difficult fit for portfolios already heavy in mid-caps.

Finally, the fund's modest cost adds to its appeal. The fund's expense ratio, at 0.76%, is well below median for a no-load fund in the category. Add in the fund's experienced management and flexible approach, and we think this fund is an appealing choice in a crowded category.

Address:	4301 Wilson Blvd Arlington VA 22203 800-258-3030	Minimum Purchase:	$500	Add: $0	IRA: $200
		Min Auto Inv Plan:	$0	Add: —	
		Sales Fees:	No-load, 2.00%R		
Web Address:	www.homesteadfunds.com	Management Fee:	0.65% mx./0.40% mn.		
Inception:	11-19-90	Actual Fees:	Mgt:0.56%	Dist: —	
Advisor:	RE Advisers Corporation	Expense Projections:	3Yr:$243	5Yr:$422	10Yr:$942
Subadvisor:	None	Income Distrib:	Semi-Annually		
NTF Plans:	TD Waterhouse Ins NT				

 **Funds 500**

239

Hussman Strategic Growth

	Ticker	Load	NAV	Yield	Total Assets	Mstar Category
	HSGFX	None	$15.64	0.8%	$2,843 mil	Long-Short

Governance and Management

Stewardship Grade: A

Portfolio Manager(s)

John Hussman launched this fund in July 2000. He holds a doctorate in economics and taught in that field before starting this fund. Although Hussman receives the advice of key personnel on the fund's board of trustees and at Hussman Econometrics, this fund depends heavily on Hussman himself, leaving the fund exposed to manager risk. He invests all of his liquid assets (outside of cash and money market accounts) in his two funds.

Strategy

This fund employs a distinctive strategy. Manager John Hussman analyzes price trends and trading volume as well as valuation measures to assess the general market climate and the attractiveness of individual stocks. Depending on his market assessment, Hussman may use S&P 100 and Russell 2000 Index put and call options to hedge the portfolio. He can also simulate 150% market exposure when the climate is very favorable by purchasing a limited amount of call options on individual stocks. It's worth noting that the fund may not go net short; its most bearish position is fully hedged.

Performance 12-31-06

	1st Qtr	2nd Qtr	3rd Qtr	4th Qtr	Total
2002	8.46	3.01	1.95	0.11	14.02
2003	-1.97	11.20	3.41	7.42	21.08
2004	4.05	-0.31	-2.39	3.87	5.16
2005	1.69	1.79	3.40	-1.23	5.71
2006	1.66	1.19	0.37	0.25	3.51

Trailing	Total Return%	+/- S&P 500	+/- Russell3000	%Rank Cat	Growth of $10,000
3 Mo	0.25	-6.45	-6.87	85	10,025
6 Mo	0.63	-12.11	-11.46	79	10,063
1 Yr	3.51	-12.28	-12.21	84	10,351
3 Yr Avg	4.79	-5.65	-6.40	45	11,507
5 Yr Avg	9.70	3.51	2.53	7	15,887
10 Yr Avg	—	—	—	—	—
15 Yr Avg	—	—	—	—	—

Tax Analysis	Tax-Adj Rtn%	%Rank Cat	Tax-Cost Rat	%Rank Cat
3 Yr (estimated)	3.51	43	1.22	69
5 Yr (estimated)	8.46	11	1.13	64
10 Yr (estimated)	—	—	—	—

Potential Capital Gain Exposure: 2% of assets

Morningstar's Take by Sonya Morris 12-07-06

Consistency is Hussman Strategic Growth's strong suit.

This isn't your typical mutual fund. Manager John Hussman supplements a diversified portfolio of stocks with options hedges to adjust the fund's overall equity exposure to correspond with his assessment of market conditions, which is informed by a variety of statistical models. Because of its distinctive approach, this fund can often behave quite differently from the broader market. For example, since it has been bearishly positioned for the past few years, it hasn't fully participated in the market's advance, so its three-year trailing return lags the DJ Wilshire 5000 Index, a proxy for the broad market. However, the fund looks much better when judged over longer time spans. Its five-year gain of 9.4% through Dec. 6, 2006, surpasses the index's 5.8% result. And it has produced those results with remarkable consistency. It is one of the least-volatile equity funds available, and it has never generated a negative return over any rolling

12-month period.

All due credit goes to Hussman for those results: He devised and executes the fund's strategy, and also conducts most of the research and trading. However, that hints at a noteworthy risk. This is essentially a one-man show. Hussman handles all managerial duties and most analytical chores for both this offering and his other charge, Hussman Strategic Total Return. That's undoubtedly a heavy load.

On the other hand, because Hussman doesn't have to appease shareholders or partners, he can run his shop as he sees fit, and he has chosen to do so in a shareholder-friendly manner. He has steadily lowered the fund's expense ratio as assets have risen, and he provides extensive shareholder communication on the fund's Web site. Plus, he invests substantially all of his personal assets in his funds. Even though it's not risk-free, we think this fund is a fine choice for a supplemental holding.

Address:	5136 Dorsey Hall Drive, Ellicott City, MD 21042, 800-487-7626
Web Address:	www.hussmanfunds.com
Inception:	07-24-00*
Advisor:	Hussman Econometrics Advisors, Inc
Subadvisor:	None
NTF Plans:	N/A

Minimum Purchase:	$1000	Add: $100	IRA: $500
Min Auto Inv Plan:	$1000	Add: $100	
Sales Fees:	No-load, 1.50%R		
Management Fee:	1.00% mx./0.90% mn.		
Actual Fees:	Mgt:0.97%	Dist: —	
Expense Projections:	3Yr:$356	5Yr:$617	10Yr:$1363
Income Distrib:	Annually		

Historical Profile

Return	Above Avg
Risk	Average
Rating	★★★★ Above Avg

Investment Style: Equity, Stock %

89% 89% 95% 93% 92% 91%

▼ Manager Change
▽ Partial Manager Change

Growth of $10,000
— Investment Values of Fund
— Investment Values of S&P 500

19.6
16.6
13.0
10.0
5.0

Performance Quartile (within Category)

	1995	1996	1997	1998	1999	2000	2001	2002	2003	2004	2005	2006	History
NAV	—	—	—	—	—	11.64	11.94	12.66	15.32	15.36	15.68	15.64	NAV
Total Return %	—	—	—	—	—	16.40*	14.67	14.02	21.08	5.16	5.71	3.51	Total Return %
+/-S&P 500	—	—	—	—	—		26.56	36.12	-7.60	-5.72	0.80	-12.28	+/-S&P 500
+/-Russell3000	—	—	—	—	—		26.13	35.56	-9.98	-6.79	-0.41	-12.21	+/-Russell3000
Income Return %	—	—	—	—	—		0.00	0.00	0.00	0.21	0.36	0.85	Income Return %
Capital Return %	—	—	—	—	—		14.67	14.02	21.08	4.95	5.35	2.66	Capital Return %
Total Rtn % Rank Cat	—	—	—	—	—	8	20	23	26	36	84		Total Rtn % Rank Cat
Income $	—	—	—	—	—	0.00	0.00	0.00	0.00	0.03	0.05	0.13	Income $
Capital Gains $	—	—	—	—	—	0.00	1.35	0.93	0.01	0.71	0.50	0.46	Capital Gains $
Expense Ratio %	—	—	—	—	—			1.99	1.99	1.45	1.34	1.14	Expense Ratio %
Income Ratio %	—	—	—	—	—			-0.53	-0.81	-0.15	-0.39	0.63	Income Ratio %
Turnover Rate %	—	—	—	—	—			55	199	123	66	63	Turnover Rate %
Net Assets $mil	—	—	—	—	—		14	44	443	771	1,470	2,843	Net Assets $mil

Rating and Risk

Time Period	Load-Adj Return %	Morningstar Rtn vs Cat	Morningstar Risk vs Cat	Morningstar Risk-Adj Rating
1 Yr	3.51			
3 Yr	4.79	Avg	-Avg	★★★
5 Yr	9.70	+Avg	Avg	★★★★
10 Yr	—	—	—	
Incept	12.39			

Other Measures	Standard Index S&P 500	Best Fit Index MSCI Eur
Alpha	-0.3	-2.7
Beta	0.27	0.26
R-Squared	20	35
Standard Deviation	4.13	
Mean	4.79	
Sharpe Ratio	0.37	

Portfolio Analysis 09-30-06

Share change since 06-06 Total Stocks:161

	Sector	PE	Tot Ret%	% Assets
⊕ PepsiCo, Inc.	Goods	21.5	7.86	2.05
⊕ Home Depot, Inc.	Consumer	13.5	1.01	1.93
Computer Sciences Corpor	Business	23.7	5.39	1.85
⊕ Applera Corporation	Health	39.9	38.90	1.82
⊕ Coca-Cola Company	Goods	21.7	23.10	1.75
⊕ Waste Management, Inc.	Business	16.6	24.21	1.72
⊕ Campbell Soup Company	Goods	21.3	33.40	1.72
ExxonMobil Corporation	Energy	11.1	39.07	1.68
⊕ GlaxoSmithKline PLC ADR	Health	17.6	7.95	1.67
⊕ Nike, Inc. B	Goods	19.2	15.84	1.65
⊖ Pfizer Inc.	Health	15.2	15.22	1.60
⊕ Deere & Company	Ind Mtrls	14.8	42.27	1.58
⊕ Colgate-Palmolive Compan	Goods	27.6	21.51	1.56
⊕ Nokia Corporation ADR	Hardware	18.9	15.84	1.54
⊖ Johnson & Johnson	Health	17.5	12.45	1.53
ConocoPhillips	Energy	6.5	26.53	1.50
Novartis AG ADR	Health	22.2	11.29	1.37
⊕ SanDisk Corporation	Hardware	24.2	-31.50	1.34
⊖ McDonald's Corporation	Consumer	18.9	34.63	1.23
Verizon Communications	Telecom	15.9	34.88	1.16

Current Investment Style

Value Blnd Growth — Large Mid Small

Market Cap	%
Giant	36.8
Large	29.2
Mid	27.4
Small	6.4
Micro	0.3

Avg $mil: 22,428

Value Measures		Rel Category
Price/Earnings	15.02	0.97
Price/Book	2.77	1.15
Price/Sales	1.20	0.99
Price/Cash Flow	7.83	1.00
Dividend Yield %	1.66	1.08

Growth Measures	%	Rel Category
Long-Term Erngs	10.79	0.89
Book Value	11.19	1.51
Sales	13.00	1.36
Cash Flow	12.65	1.15
Historical Erngs	20.53	1.07

Profitability	%	Rel Category
Return on Equity	22.71	1.36
Return on Assets	10.11	1.16
Net Margin	11.56	0.99

Sector Weightings	% of Stocks	Rel S&P 500	3 Year High Low	
↻ Info	22.94	1.15		
Software	4.10	1.19	7	2
Hardware	12.16	1.32	12	5
Media	2.08	0.55	5	1
Telecom	4.60	1.31	5	2
Service	36.23	0.78		
Health	17.57	1.46	28	18
Consumer	7.49	0.98	23	7
Business	8.10	1.91	8	2
Financial	3.07	0.14	5	1
Mfg	40.84	1.21		
Goods	21.06	2.46	21	13
Ind Mtrls	11.53	0.97	14	4
Energy	8.10	0.83	13	6
Utilities	0.15	0.04	1	0

Composition

● Cash	8.4
● Stocks	90.7
● Bonds	0.0
○ Other	1.0
Foreign (% of Stock)	14.2

Morningstar® Funds 500

Janus

	Ticker	Load	NAV	Yield	Total Assets	Mstar Category
	JANSX	None	$28.14	0.3%	$11,496 mil	Large Growth

Governance and Management

Stewardship Grade: C

Portfolio Manager(s)

Manager David Corkins took over this fund on Feb. 1, 2006. Former manager Blaine Rollins stepped down after several years of lackluster results. Corkins posted a strong record in previous stints managing Janus Growth & Income and Janus Mercury. Rollins now runs Janus Triton, a small- and mid-cap growth fund.

Strategy

Manager David Corkins seeks to strike a balance between risk and reward. He won't load up on individual stocks or sectors and stresses valuation, strong free cash flows, and high returns on invested capital in his stock-picking. Corkins also likes management teams that have a shareholder orientation. He relies heavily on Janus' team of shared research analysts to contribute thoughts here.

Performance 12-31-06

	1st Qtr	2nd Qtr	3rd Qtr	4th Qtr	Total
2002	-0.08	-16.23	-15.06	1.89	-27.56
2003	-1.85	14.12	3.96	13.11	31.71
2004	-2.51	4.98	-7.08	10.08	4.69
2005	-2.77	0.50	4.62	1.70	3.98
2006	5.48	-4.60	4.28	5.39	10.59

Trailing	Total Return%	+/- S&P 500	+/- Russ 1000Gr	%Rank Cat	Growth of $10,000
3 Mo	5.39	-1.31	-0.54	51	10,539
6 Mo	9.90	-2.84	-0.20	28	10,990
1 Yr	10.59	-5.20	1.52	18	11,059
3 Yr Avg	6.38	-4.06	-0.49	59	12,039
5 Yr Avg	2.81	-3.38	0.12	47	11,486
10 Yr Avg	6.12	-2.30	0.68	48	18,112
15 Yr Avg	8.26	-2.38	0.24	51	32,887

Tax Analysis	Tax-Adj Rtn%	%Rank Cat	Tax-Cost Rat	%Rank Cat
3 Yr (estimated)	6.33	50	0.05	4
5 Yr (estimated)	2.78	42	0.03	4
10 Yr (estimated)	5.01	45	1.05	49

Potential Capital Gain Exposure: -27% of assets

Morningstar's Take by Karen Dolan 11-12-06

We like Janus Fund's measured, more-moderate approach.

Manager David Corkins may be new to this fund, but he isn't new to Janus or to portfolio management. And this isn't the first time that Corkins has shaken up a portfolio. Corkins took the helm here in January 2006 after a three-year stint managing Janus Mercury. Prior to that, Corkins successfully managed Janus Growth & Income.

Much as he did at Mercury, Corkins has made some meaningful changes here. He is focusing the fund's attention in some ways and broadening it in others. For example, he reduced the number of holdings in the portfolio from 120 to 90 and ditched the previous manager's strategy of keeping a large number of tiny positions. Meanwhile, he actually broadened the portfolio by focusing less on the top 10 stocks. He is also relying more heavily on Janus' central pool of research analysts and consequently increased the proportion of the portfolio invested in their recommended stocks. With these moves,

Corkins has set the fund up to be more dependent on individual stocks and less reliant on big industry or stock bets.

The fund's newfound balance extends to the types of companies it favors, too. It has a good balance of aggressive-growth picks and more moderate firms. For instance, the portfolio is home to some traditional growth fare such as pharmaceutical outfit Roche Holding and chipmaker Texas Instruments. Yet Corkins gets just as excited about results that come from improving internal operations, as is the case with Procter & Gamble; Corkins thinks that P&G's ability to further improve its already-stellar operational efficiency is underappreciated.

We think Corkins' changes have made this fund more reliable without hurting its chances to shine. The fund doesn't need to make huge bets to get ahead. Its cheap expense ratio gives it a leg up, and we think its stock-specific focus can carry it the rest of the way past its peers.

Address:	151 Detroit Street		Minimum Purchase:	$2500	Add: $100	IRA: $1000
	Denver CO 80206		Min Auto Inv Plan:	$500	Add: $100	
	800-525-0020		Sales Fees:	No-load		
Web Address:	www.janus.com		Management Fee:	0.64%		
Inception:	02-05-70		Actual Fees:	Mgt:0.64%	Dist: —	
Advisor:	Janus		Expense Projections:	3Yr:$281	5Yr:$488	10Yr:$1084
Subadvisor:	None		Income Distrib:	Annually		
NTF Plans:	Fidelity Retail-NTF, Schwab OneSource					

Historical Profile

Return	Average
Risk	Average
Rating	★★★ Neutral

Investment Style: Equity, Stock %

96% · 96% · 95% · 99% · 99% · 99% · 98% · 97% · 95%

Growth of $10,000
— Investment Values of Fund
— Investment Values of S&P 500

38.0 / 31.0 / 24.0 / 17.0 / 10.0

▼ Manager Change
▽ Partial Manager Change

Performance Quartile (within Category)

1995	1996	1997	1998	1999	2000	2001	2002	2003	2004	2005	2006	History
23.04	24.45	24.90	33.65	44.05	33.29	24.60	17.82	23.47	24.57	25.53	28.14	NAV
29.43	19.61	22.72	38.89	47.13	-14.91	-26.10	-27.56	31.71	4.69	3.98	10.59	Total Return %
-8.15	-3.35	-10.64	10.31	26.09	-5.81	-14.21	-5.46	3.03	-6.19	-0.93	-5.20	+/-S&P 500
-7.75	-3.51	-7.77	0.18	13.97	7.51	-5.68	0.32	1.96	-1.61	-1.28	1.52	+/-Russ 1000Gr
4.13	0.91	0.95	0.34	0.00	1.26	0.00	0.00	0.00	0.00	0.07	0.37	Income Return %
25.30	18.70	21.77	38.55	47.13	-16.17	-26.10	-27.56	31.71	4.69	3.91	10.22	Capital Return %
67	49	69	21	25	61	79	55	27	82	71	18	Total Rtn % Rank Cat
0.78	0.21	0.23	0.08	0.00	0.55	0.00	0.00	0.00	0.00	0.02	0.10	Income $
0.49	2.92	4.75	0.82	5.22	3.84	0.00	0.00	0.00	0.00	0.00	0.00	Capital Gains $
0.86	0.85	0.86	0.87	0.84	0.84	0.83	0.84	0.89	0.90	0.87	—	Expense Ratio %
1.25	0.91	0.85	0.00	-0.14	-0.19	-0.16	-0.24	-0.17	-0.17	0.07	—	Income Ratio %
118	104	132	70	63	65	51	27	22	21	78	—	Turnover Rate %
12,466	15,890	19,200	25,491	42,330	39,174	25,622	15,426	17,123	13,604	11,239	11,422	Net Assets $mil

Rating and Risk

Time Period	Load-Adj Return %	Morningstar Rtn vs Cat	Morningstar Risk vs Cat	Morningstar Risk-Adj Rating
1 Yr	10.59			
3 Yr	6.38	Avg	Avg	★★★
5 Yr	2.81	Avg	Avg	★★★
10 Yr	6.12	Avg	Avg	★★★
Incept	13.76			

Other Measures	Standard Index S&P 500	Best Fit Index Russ 1000Gr
Alpha	-5.0	-0.4
Beta	1.20	1.00
R-Squared	83	87
Standard Deviation	9.10	
Mean	6.38	
Sharpe Ratio	0.37	

Portfolio Analysis 11-30-06

Share change since 10-06 Total Stocks:96	Sector	PE	Tot Ret%	% Assets
Boeing Company	Ind Mtrls	41.2	28.38	3.52
Procter & Gamble Company	Goods	23.9	13.36	3.28
J.P. Morgan Chase & Co.	Financial	13.6	25.60	3.11
ExxonMobil Corporation	Energy	11.1	39.07	3.04
Roche Holding	Health	—	—	2.80
General Electric Company	Ind Mtrls	20.0	9.35	2.72
Yahoo, Inc.	Media	35.4	-34.81	2.31
⊕ UBS AG	Financial	—	29.62	1.97
NRG Energy, Inc. Trust U	Utilities	11.6	18.87	1.95
⊕ Texas Instruments, Inc.	Hardware	16.9	-9.82	1.77
⊕ Coventry Health Care, In	Health	15.4	-12.13	1.69
Apple Computer, Inc.	Hardware	37.6	18.01	1.64
Precision Castparts Corp	Ind Mtrls	25.4	51.40	1.64
EMC Corporation	Hardware	32.7	-3.08	1.61
Electronic Arts, Inc.	Software	91.2	-3.73	1.60
Nordstrom, Inc.	Consumer	21.9	33.35	1.45
Fannie Mae	Financial	—	24.34	1.44
⊖ Merck & Co., Inc.	Health	19.1	42.66	1.42
Advanced Micro Devices	Hardware	18.5	-33.50	1.40
Merrill Lynch & Company,	Financial	14.2	39.28	1.39

Current Investment Style

Value Blnd Growth — Large Mid Small

Market Cap	%
Giant	43.0
Large	40.7
Mid	15.9
Small	0.5
Micro	0.0

Avg $mil: 37,293

Value Measures		Rel Category
Price/Earnings	18.84	0.98
Price/Book	3.21	0.97
Price/Sales	1.81	0.93
Price/Cash Flow	10.55	0.93
Dividend Yield %	1.26	1.22

Growth Measures	%	Rel Category
Long-Term Erngs	13.52	0.94
Book Value	11.28	0.97
Sales	12.69	1.09
Cash Flow	17.55	1.05
Historical Erngs	23.75	1.03

Profitability	%	Rel Category
Return on Equity	19.29	0.95
Return on Assets	10.22	0.93
Net Margin	13.09	0.92

Sector Weightings	% of Stocks	Rel S&P 500	3 Year High Low	
☁ Info	21.06	1.05		
🖥 Software	5.27	1.53	8	0
💻 Hardware	10.40	1.13	23	10
📺 Media	2.42	0.64	19	2
📞 Telecom	2.97	0.85	3	0
⚙ Service	44.21	0.96		
🏥 Health	13.61	1.13	21	6
🛒 Consumer	10.46	1.37	19	7
🏢 Business	5.85	1.38	9	3
💲 Financial	14.29	0.64	14	3
🏭 Mfg	34.73	1.03		
⚙ Goods	8.81	1.03	11	4
⚙ Ind Mtrls	16.05	1.34	17	11
🔋 Energy	5.86	0.60	9	0
🔌 Utilities	4.01	1.15	4	0

Composition

	%
● Cash	3.7
● Stocks	95.4
● Bonds	0.0
○ Other	0.9
Foreign (% of Stock)	17.6

Janus Balanced

	Ticker	Load	NAV	Yield	Total Assets	Mstar Category
	JABAX	None	$24.41	1.8%	$2,517 mil	Moderate Allocation

Governance and Management

Stewardship Grade: B

Portfolio Manager(s)

Marc Pinto guides the stock selection, while Gibson Smith picks bonds. They collaborate on asset-allocation decisions. Pinto has run a separate account for Janus since 1997. Smith runs both Janus Short-Term Bond and Janus High-Yield. They took over from Karen Reidy, who retired in May 2005.

Strategy

Comanager Marc Pinto is using a conservative growth strategy to guide the stock portion of the fund. He wants to own firms with good business models and strong competitive positions and looks at returns on invested capital and profit margins for supporting evidence. Comanager Gibson Smith won't focus on making interest-rate bets, preferring to concentrate on credit analysis. The fund shouldn't vary by more than 5 percentage points from a 60/40 split between stocks and bonds.

Performance 12-31-06

	1st Qtr	2nd Qtr	3rd Qtr	4th Qtr	Total
2002	0.92	-4.16	-5.32	2.04	-6.56
2003	-0.84	7.08	0.37	6.72	13.74
2004	2.01	0.20	0.07	6.28	8.71
2005	-1.60	2.93	2.76	3.53	7.75
2006	3.96	-2.17	4.23	4.29	10.56

Trailing	Total Return%	+/- DJ Mod	+/- DJ US Mod	%Rank Cat	Growth of $10,000
3 Mo	4.29	-1.30	-0.38	79	10,429
6 Mo	8.71	-0.08	0.81	54	10,871
1 Yr	10.56	-1.74	0.29	63	11,056
3 Yr Avg	9.00	-1.72	-0.12	31	12,950
5 Yr Avg	6.60	-3.42	-1.00	36	13,765
10 Yr Avg	9.70	1.15	1.11	9	25,239
15 Yr Avg	—	—	—	—	—

Tax Analysis	Tax-Adj Rtn%	%Rank Cat	Tax-Cost Rat	%Rank Cat
3 Yr (estimated)	8.29	22	0.65	30
5 Yr (estimated)	5.83	28	0.72	41
10 Yr (estimated)	8.31	5	1.27	34

Potential Capital Gain Exposure: 13% of assets

Morningstar's Take by Kai Wiecking 12-26-06

Janus Balanced is a decent choice for investors seeking a predictable option.

This fund is run in two separate sleeves, with both the equity and fixed-income allocation hovering in a tight range, within 5 percentage points of a 60/40 split. The stock portfolio, run by Marc Pinto, is focused on large-cap growth stocks, while the bond portfolio, run by Gibson Smith, tends to be rather conservative. Smith keeps the bulk of the bond assets committed to investment-grade, domestic securities, and he makes just moderate bets on the direction of interest rates.

Pinto and Smith have only been at the helm here since May 2005, so it is still somewhat early for an assessment on how well their styles work together. But so far, they have complemented each other well, as Smith's staid bonds have provided support when Pinto's growth stocks have been flagging, and vice versa. The fund's year-to-date return of 4.9% through Sept. 24, 2006, is only average when compared with its peers in the moderate-allocation

category. But as most of the fund's rivals have a higher allocation to stocks, which have rallied for most of the year, that's hardly surprising.

After getting strong performance from the fund's technology holdings, including chipmaker Advanced Micro Devices, Pinto has taken profits in that sector. Meanwhile, Smith has been raising the fund's overall allocation to bonds and gradually extending the fund's sensitivity to interest rates. The added rate sensitivity paid off until very recently, when bond yields started rising again. Regardless of such short-term considerations, the fund's newly competitive expense ratio significantly enhances its appeal. After lowering its price tag to 0.79% in 2005 despite outflows, this offering now lands in the cheapest quartile for no-load moderate-allocation funds.

Provided this price reduction proves to be lasting, we think this fund is a sensible choice for those seeking a core investment that doesn't require much upkeep.

Address:	151 Detroit Street Denver CO 80206 800-525-0020
Web Address:	www.janus.com
Inception:	09-01-92
Advisor:	Janus
Subadvisor:	None
NTF Plans:	Fidelity Retail-NTF, Schwab OneSource

Minimum Purchase:	$2500	Add: $100	IRA: $1000
Min Auto Inv Plan:	$500	Add: $100	
Sales Fees:	No-load		
Management Fee:	0.55%		
Actual Fees:	Mgt:0.55%	Dist: —	
Expense Projections:	3Yr:$255	5Yr:$444	10Yr:$990
Income Distrib:	Quarterly		

Historical Profile

Return	Above Avg
Risk	Below Avg
Rating	★★★★ Above Avg

Investment Style: Equity, Stock %

| 38% | 41% | 45% | 45% | 41% | 58% | 63% | 62% | 59% |

▼ Manager Change
▽ Partial Manager Change

Growth of $10,000
— Investment Values of Fund
— Investment Values of DJ Mod

Performance Quartile (within Category)

1995	1996	1997	1998	1999	2000	2001	2002	2003	2004	2005	2006	History
13.72	14.14	15.33	19.61	23.39	21.24	19.63	17.88	19.94	21.25	22.48	24.41	NAV
27.32	15.30	21.81	31.20	23.51	-2.16	-5.04	-6.56	13.74	8.71	7.75	10.56	Total Return %
7.52	4.64	9.91	18.88	6.18	-0.49	-2.24	0.21	-13.64	-4.26	0.76	-1.74	+/-DJ Mod
2.55	3.96	2.61	18.81	10.66	-6.60	-5.20	3.98	-10.32	-2.46	1.75	0.29	+/-DJ US Mod
9.26	1.91	2.54	2.32	2.35	4.17	2.52	2.42	2.09	2.06	1.90	1.91	Income Return %
18.06	13.39	19.27	28.88	21.16	-6.33	-7.56	-8.98	11.65	6.65	5.85	8.65	Capital Return %
38	45	30	2	6	71	53	96	53	9	63	Total Rtn % Rank Cat
1.06	0.26	0.36	0.35	0.46	0.96	0.53	0.47	0.37	0.41	0.40	0.43	Income $
0.00	1.41	1.49	0.11	0.32	0.69	0.00	0.00	0.00	0.00	0.00	0.00	Capital Gains $
1.32	1.21	1.10	1.03	0.91	0.85	0.83	0.84	0.88	0.87	0.79	—	Expense Ratio %
2.52	2.35	2.63	2.34	2.37	2.92	2.79	2.44	2.00	1.82	1.93	—	Income Ratio %
185	151	139	73	64	87	117	88	73	45	47	—	Turnover Rate %
139	220	389	1,137	3,420	4,739	4,472	3,902	3,750	2,901	2,569	2,499	Net Assets $mil

Rating and Risk

Time Period	Load-Adj Return %	Morningstar Rtn vs Cat	Morningstar Risk vs Cat	Morningstar Risk-Adj Rating
1 Yr	10.56			
3 Yr	9.00	+Avg	Avg	★★★★
5 Yr	6.60	Avg	Low	★★★
10 Yr	9.70	+Avg	Avg	★★★★
Incept	11.25			

Other Measures	Standard Index DJ Mod	Best Fit Index Mstar Mid Core
Alpha	-0.2	0.6
Beta	0.81	0.45
R-Squared	82	90
Standard Deviation	5.27	
Mean	9.00	
Sharpe Ratio	1.06	

Portfolio Analysis 11-30-06

Total Stocks:53 Share change since 10-31-06	Sectors	P/E Ratio	YTD Return %	% Net Assets
Merrill Lynch & Company,	Financial	14.2	0.76	3.49
Roche Holding	Health	—	—	3.23
J.P. Morgan Chase & Co.	Financial	13.6	-0.02	2.72
General Electric Company	Ind Mtrls	20.0	0.91	2.62
ExxonMobil Corporation	Energy	11.1	-5.19	2.32
Procter & Gamble Company	Goods	23.9	-0.98	1.90
⊕ Altria Group, Inc.	Goods	16.3	2.52	1.87
Canadian National Railway	Business	18.6	-1.12	1.86
Reckitt Benckiser	Goods	—	—	1.68

Total Fixed-Income:85	Date of Maturity	Amount $000	Value $000	% Net Assets
US Treasury Note 4.875%	05-31-08	55,941	56,085	2.24
US Treasury Bond 4.5%	02-15-36	42,135	41,717	1.67
US Treasury Note 5.125%	05-15-16	34,573	36,307	1.45
US Treasury Note 4.5%	11-15-10	28,215	28,265	1.13
US Treasury Note 4.875%	08-15-16	27,266	28,123	1.12
US TREASURY NOTE	07-15-15	25,735	25,162	1.01
US Treasury Note 4%	04-15-10	25,079	24,717	0.99
US Treasury Note 4.5%	02-15-09	24,069	24,031	0.96
US Treasury Note 4.875%	04-30-11	21,343	21,705	0.87

Equity Style

Style: Growth
Size: Large-Cap

Value Measures		Rel Category
Price/Earnings	17.38	1.14
Price/Book	2.70	1.09
Price/Sales	2.07	1.51
Price/Cash Flow	9.80	1.21
Dividend Yield %	1.49	0.77

Growth Measures	%	Rel Category
Long-Term Erngs	12.18	1.04
Book Value	12.01	1.39
Sales	11.89	1.34
Cash Flow	15.28	1.55
Historical Erngs	20.94	1.17

Market Cap %			
Giant	59.7	Small	0.0
Large	38.9	Micro	0.0
Mid	1.4	Avg $mil:	60,522

Fixed-Income Style

Duration: Interm-Term
Quality: High

Avg Eff Duration [1]	4.2 Yrs
Avg Eff Maturity	5.9 Yrs
Avg Credit Quality	AA
Avg Wtd Coupon	4.67%

[1]figure provided by fund as of 11-30-06

Sector Weightings	% of Stocks	Rel DJ Mod	3 Year High Low
⌖ Info	12.18	—	
Software	1.81	—	4 0
Hardware	7.88	—	15 8
Media	2.49	—	12 2
Telecom	0.00	—	0 0
⌨ Service	52.35		
Health	16.40	—	20 7
Consumer	10.06	—	18 8
Business	7.63	—	9 3
Financial	18.26	—	22 11
Mfg	35.47		
Goods	15.65	—	16 8
Ind Mtrls	11.89	—	16 11
Energy	7.93	—	12 4
Utilities	0.00	—	0 0

Composition

	%
● Cash	5.0
● Stocks	58.6
● Bonds	35.6
○ Other	0.9
Foreign (% of Stock)	31.5

MORNINGSTAR® Funds 500

Janus Contrarian

Ticker	**Load**	**NAV**	**Yield**	**Total Assets**	**Mstar Category**
JSVAX	None	$16.83	1.9%	$4,286 mil	Large Blend

Governance and Management

Stewardship Grade: C

Portfolio Manager(s)

David Decker has been on board since the fund's inception in February 2000. Decker started his career at Janus in 1992 as a research analyst. The fund's comanager, Matthew Ankrum, left the fund in spring 2006, less than two years after taking the portfolio-management job.

Strategy

David Decker looks for stocks with what he considers to be asymmetrical risk profiles, or a higher probability of upside and a smaller probability of limited downside. He likes companies with strong free cash flow, accelerating returns on invested capital, and savvy management. Decker often buys these companies when controversy takes a swipe at their stock prices, making them temporarily cheap in his eyes. He looks across the market-cap spectrum and overseas for his ideas.

Performance 12-31-06

	1st Qtr	2nd Qtr	3rd Qtr	4th Qtr	Total
2002	4.97	-14.51	-17.33	2.85	-23.70
2003	-2.41	24.67	8.96	15.60	53.26
2004	4.34	-0.97	-0.18	18.87	22.61
2005	-2.79	2.95	13.28	2.33	16.02
2006	10.50	-4.72	5.40	12.27	24.58

Trailing	Total Return%	+/- S&P 500	+/- Russ 1000	%Rank Cat	Growth of $10,000
3 Mo	12.27	5.57	5.32	1	11,227
6 Mo	18.33	5.59	5.97	1	11,833
1 Yr	24.58	8.79	9.12	1	12,458
3 Yr Avg	21.01	10.57	10.03	1	17,720
5 Yr Avg	15.69	9.50	8.87	1	20,724
10 Yr Avg	—	—	—	—	—
15 Yr Avg	—	—	—	—	—

Tax Analysis	Tax-Adj Rtn%	%Rank Cat	Tax-Cost Rat	%Rank Cat
3 Yr (estimated)	20.07	1	0.78	36
5 Yr (estimated)	15.14	1	0.48	31
10 Yr (estimated)	—	—	—	—

Potential Capital Gain Exposure: 29% of assets

Morningstar's Take by Andrew Gogerty 11-06-06

If investors take the time to understand it, Janus Contrarian is a solid choice.

Manager David Decker doesn't necessarily fit the large-blend manager mold. He looks globally and across the market-cap spectrum for companies that are undervalued based on his estimate of future earnings potential and that have the ability to increase their returns on invested capital. Glass maker Owens-Illinois, for example, garners a top spot in the portfolio because Decker believes the market sell-off due to rising fuel costs was overdone and that investors are looking past the company's success in improving margins and returns on capital.

This clearly indicates Decker is doing more than just buying anything that others don't (as its moniker might suggest), and the fund isn't always at odds with the markets. The fund's 38% stake in foreign stocks and a sizable chunk in mid-caps have been a boon in recent years, as these areas--India especially, which is one of his favorites--have

outpaced large-cap domestic equities. These tilts have continued the fund's early success, and its trailing returns stand among the category's best.

The fund's distinctive characteristics combined with a top-heavy portfolio mean the offering will hit bumps from time to time, but overall its disciplined process makes it an intriguing choice. Decker's stock selection has been generally spot-on over time, and his focus on returns on invested capital rather than generic stock-price multiples is a step aside from the norm. In 2006, for example, Decker significantly added to the fund's stake in Florida land-owner St. Joe because his analysis indicates the firm's acreage value alone is not reflected in the stock price.

Investors comfortable with the fund's risks due to its somewhat atypical portfolio should give it a look. It could certainly serve as an investor's core fund, but those building a more-compartmentalized portfolio ought to use it in a supporting role.

Address:	151 Detroit Street Denver CO 80206 800-525-0020	
Web Address:	www.janus.com	
Inception:	02-29-00*	
Advisor:	Janus Capital Management LLC	
Subadvisor:	None	
NTF Plans:	Fidelity Retail-NTF, Schwab OneSource	

Minimum Purchase:	$2500	Add: $100	IRA: $1000
Min Auto Inv Plan:	$500	Add: $100	
Sales Fees:	No-load		
Management Fee:	0.64%		
Actual Fees:	Mgt:0.64%	Dist: —	
Expense Projections:	3Yr:$296	5Yr:$515	10Yr:$1143
Income Distrib:	Annually		

Historical Profile

Return	High
Risk	High
Rating	★★★★ Highest

Investment Style: Equity / Stock %

98% 98% 96% 98% 97% 99% 99%

Growth of $10,000
— Investment Values of Fund
— Investment Values of S&P 500

18.0
15.5
12.5
10.0
6.0

▼ Manager Change
▽ Partial Manager Change

Performance Quartile (within Category)

	1995	1996	1997	1998	1999	2000	2001	2002	2003	2004	2005	2006	History
	—	—	—	—	—	10.52	9.26	7.06	10.82	13.24	15.14	16.83	NAV
	—	—	—	—	—	7.75*	-11.74	-23.70	53.26	22.61	16.02	24.58	Total Return %
	—	—	—	—	—	0.15	-1.60	24.58	11.73	11.11	8.79	+/-S&P 500
	—	—	—	—	—	0.71	-2.05	23.37	11.21	9.75	9.12	+/-Russ 1000
	—	—	—	—	—	0.23	0.06	0.00	0.24	0.28	2.35	Income Return %
	—	—	—	—	—	-11.97	-23.76	53.26	22.37	15.74	22.23	Capital Return %
	—	—	—	—	—	49	75	1	1	2	1	Total Rtn % Rank Cat
	—	—	—	—	—	0.25	0.02	0.01	0.00	0.03	0.04	0.36	Income $
	—	—	—	—	—	0.00	0.00	0.00	0.00	0.00	0.18	1.66	Capital Gains $
	—	—	—	—	—	0.99	0.91	0.98	1.01	0.98	0.93	—	Expense Ratio %
	—	—	—	—	—	0.14	0.29	0.03	-0.17	0.07	0.45	—	Income Ratio %
	—	—	—	—	—	72	77	60	44	30	42	—	Turnover Rate %
	—	—	—	—	—	2,940	2,079	1,267	2,618	2,775	3,161	4,286	Net Assets $mil

Rating and Risk

Time Period	Load-Adj Return %	Morningstar Rtn vs Cat	Morningstar Risk vs Cat	Morningstar Risk-Adj Rating
1 Yr	24.58			
3 Yr	21.01	High	High	★★★★★
5 Yr	15.69	High	High	★★★★★
10 Yr	—	—	—	
Incept	10.43			

Other Measures	Standard Index S&P 500	Best Fit Index MSCI World
Alpha	6.8	3.7
Beta	1.41	1.31
R-Squared	67	83
Standard Deviation	11.88	
Mean	21.01	
Sharpe Ratio	1.41	

Portfolio Analysis 11-30-06

Share change since 10-06 Total Stocks:57	Sector	PE	Tot Ret%	% Assets
⊕ St. Joe Corporation	Financial	75.4	-19.32	6.05
Liberty Global, Inc. A	Media	14.6	29.56	6.00
Ceridian Corporation	Business	23.6	12.60	4.83
⊕ Owens-Illinois, Inc.	Ind Mtrls	—	-12.31	4.78
⊕ Coventry Health Care, In	Health	15.4	-12.13	4.48
ICICI Bank, Ltd. ADR	Financial	30.9	47.20	3.44
CapitaLand Ltd	Financial	—	—	3.23
NRG Energy, Inc. Trust U	Utilities	11.6	18.87	3.18
Reliance Industries Ltd	Ind Mtrls	—	—	2.89
Cemex SAB de CV ADR	Ind Mtrls	11.1	14.21	2.73
Tyco International, Ltd.	Ind Mtrls	15.7	6.83	2.58
Station Casinos Inc.	Consumer	38.6	22.46	2.55
Merrill Lynch & Company,	Financial	14.2	39.28	2.25
Kinder Morgan Management	Energy	50.1	8.12	2.23
⊖ SK	Energy	—	—	2.17
Masco Corporation	Ind Mtrls	14.8	1.82	2.17
National Thermal Power	Energy	—	—	2.01
J.P. Morgan Chase & Co.	Financial	13.6	25.60	1.96
Plum Creek Timber Compan	Financial	22.8	15.65	1.89
CA, Inc.	Software	NMF	-19.10	1.85

Current Investment Style

Value Blnd Growth / Large Mid Small

Market Cap	%
Giant	27.2
Large	24.6
Mid	47.2
Small	0.4
Micro	0.5

Avg $mil: 11,537

Value Measures		Rel Category
Price/Earnings	18.05	1.17
Price/Book	2.43	0.95
Price/Sales	1.18	0.84
Price/Cash Flow	6.06	0.72
Dividend Yield %	1.86	1.06

Growth Measures	%	Rel Category
Long-Term Erngs	11.34	0.96
Book Value	9.75	1.08
Sales	14.23	1.47
Cash Flow	21.93	2.13
Historical Erngs	14.54	0.79

Profitability	%	Rel Category
Return on Equity	19.15	0.99
Return on Assets	9.80	0.94
Net Margin	12.88	0.96

Sector Weightings	% of Stocks	Rel S&P 500	3 Year High Low	
↻ Info	11.13	0.56		
Software	1.88	0.54	8	2
Hardware	0.00	0.00	7	0
Media	9.25	2.44	19	7
Telecom	0.00	0.00	1	0
⊆ Service	49.16	1.06		
Health	5.99	0.50	6	0
Consumer	4.20	0.55	8	3
Business	6.96	1.65	9	6
Financial	32.01	1.44	32	15
Mfg	39.70	1.17		
Goods	4.33	0.51	10	4
Ind Mtrls	21.86	1.83	23	18
Energy	9.13	0.93	14	7
Utilities	4.38	1.25	4	1

Composition

● Cash	1.0
● Stocks	99.0
● Bonds	0.0
○ Other	0.0
Foreign (% of Stock)	37.7

Janus Enterprise

	Ticker	Load	NAV	Yield	Total Assets	Mstar Category
	JAENX	None	$47.45	0.0%	$1,801 mil	Mid-Cap Growth

Governance and Management

Stewardship Grade: B

Portfolio Manager(s)

Jonathan Coleman became the manager of this fund at the start of February 2002. Previously, he comanaged Janus Venture and served as an assistant manager on Janus Fund. He is helped here by an assistant portfolio manager, Brian Demain.

Strategy

Jonathan Coleman toned down the fund's aggressiveness since coming aboard. He searches for fast-growing companies with management teams he likes that also have dominant market share in their industries. Unlike his predecessor, Coleman invests in some decidedly stodgy sectors, such as industrials. He also limits the fund's largest position sizes to about 3.5% of assets.

Historical Profile

Return: Above Avg
Risk: Average
Rating: ★★★ Neutral

98% 97% 96% 97% 86% 99% 99% 98% 97%

Investment Style
Equity
Stock %

▼ Manager Change
▽ Partial Manager Change

Growth of $10,000
— Investment Values of Fund
— Investment Values of S&P 500

59.0
43.6
32.4
24.0
17.0
10.0

Performance Quartile (within Category)

1995	1996	1997	1998	1999	2000	2001	2002	2003	2004	2005	2006	History
27.44	29.34	30.48	36.22	76.67	53.27	32.00	22.95	31.17	37.62	41.91	47.45	NAV
27.25	11.65	10.82	33.75	121.90	-30.52	-39.93	-28.28	35.82	20.69	11.40	13.22	Total Return %
-10.33	-11.31	-22.54	5.17	100.86	-21.42	-28.04	-6.18	7.14	9.81	6.49	-2.57	+/-S&P 500
-6.73	-5.83	-11.72	15.89	70.61	-18.77	-19.78	-0.87	-6.89	5.21	-0.70	2.56	+/-Russ MG
7.13	0.00	0.00	0.00	0.00	0.00	0.00	0.00	0.00	0.00	0.00	0.00	Income Return %
20.12	11.65	10.82	33.75	121.90	-30.52	-39.93	-28.28	35.82	20.69	11.40	13.22	Capital Return %
77	76	89	12	9	94	95	62	50	8	42	20	Total Rtn % Rank Cat
1.64	0.00	0.00	0.00	0.00	0.00	0.00	0.00	0.00	0.00	0.00	0.00	Income $
0.16	1.28	1.96	4.30	3.33	0.00	0.00	0.00	0.00	0.00	0.00	0.00	Capital Gains $
1.23	1.12	1.04	1.08	0.95	0.88	0.90	0.90	1.02	1.03	0.95	—	Expense Ratio %
0.02	-0.78	-0.61	-0.67	-0.67	-0.65	-0.55	-0.43	-0.46	-0.46	-0.30	—	Income Ratio %
194	93	111	134	98	80	85	64	32	27	28	—	Turnover Rate %
499	722	573	728	4,435	6,267	3,209	1,626	1,884	1,835	1,792	1,776	Net Assets $mil

Performance 12-31-06

	1st Qtr	2nd Qtr	3rd Qtr	4th Qtr	Total
2002	-9.09	-11.65	-13.00	2.64	-28.28
2003	0.04	16.59	4.63	11.28	35.82
2004	5.33	3.75	-3.82	14.84	20.69
2005	-2.61	2.87	7.40	3.53	11.40
2006	7.90	-5.17	3.06	7.38	13.22

Trailing	Total Return%	+/- S&P 500	+/- Russ MG	%Rank Cat	Growth of $10,000
3 Mo	7.38	0.68	0.43	37	10,738
6 Mo	10.66	-2.08	2.76	11	11,066
1 Yr	13.22	-2.57	2.56	20	11,322
3 Yr Avg	15.04	4.60	2.31	11	15,225
5 Yr Avg	8.20	2.01	-0.02	28	14,830
10 Yr Avg	7.37	-1.05	-1.25	66	20,362
15 Yr Avg	—				

Tax Analysis	Tax-Adj Rtn%	%Rank Cat	Tax-Cost Rat	%Rank Cat
3 Yr (estimated)	15.04	7	0.00	1
5 Yr (estimated)	8.20	21	0.00	1
10 Yr (estimated)	6.82	48	0.51	12

Potential Capital Gain Exposure: -197% of assets

Rating and Risk

Time Period	Load-Adj Return %	Morningstar Rtn vs Cat	Morningstar Risk vs Cat	Morningstar Risk-Adj Rating
1 Yr	13.22			
3 Yr	15.04	High	-Avg	★★★★★
5 Yr	8.20	+Avg	-Avg	★★★★
10 Yr	7.37	Avg	+Avg	★★
Incept	11.45			

Other Measures	Standard Index S&P 500	Best Fit Index Russ MG
Alpha	1.3	2.5
Beta	1.45	0.95
R-Squared	81	95
Standard Deviation	11.08	
Mean	15.04	
Sharpe Ratio	1.03	

Portfolio Analysis 11-30-06

Share change since 10-06 Total Stocks:101	Sector	PE	Tot Ret%	% Assets
⊖ Lamar Advertising Compan	Business	—	41.75	3.47
EOG Resources	Energy	10.1	-14.62	3.14
⊖ Potash Corporation of Sa	Ind Mtrls	26.0	80.04	3.11
T Rowe Price Group	Financial	26.1	23.27	2.74
Celgene Corporation	Health	—	77.56	2.69
Ball Corporation	Goods	14.3	10.87	2.58
Berkshire Hathaway Inc.	Financial	13.2	24.89	1.96
Chicago Mercantile Excha	Financial	49.3	39.48	1.85
Coventry Health Care, In	Health	15.4	-12.13	1.74
⊕ Owens-Illinois, Inc.	Ind Mtrls	—	-12.31	1.63
Crown Castle Internation	Telecom	—	20.94	1.59
Staples, Inc.	Consumer	19.6	18.58	1.59
Cypress Semiconductor Co	Hardware	—	18.39	1.53
Dade Behring Holdings, I	Health	26.3	-2.13	1.48
Ryanair Holdings PLC ADR	Business	36.6	45.56	1.45
Respironics Inc.	Health	26.8	1.83	1.36
Apple Computer, Inc.	Hardware	37.6	18.01	1.31
Moody's Corporation	Financial	32.6	12.95	1.31
⊕ Ametek, Inc.	Ind Mtrls	18.9	12.94	1.30
Assurant, Inc.	Financial	12.2	28.01	1.30

Current Investment Style

Value Blnd Growth — Large Mid Small

Market Cap	%
Giant	4.4
Large	28.6
Mid	60.1
Small	6.9
Micro	0.0

Avg $mil: 6,539

Value Measures		Rel Category
Price/Earnings	22.08	1.08
Price/Book	3.68	1.15
Price/Sales	2.08	1.18
Price/Cash Flow	12.59	1.10
Dividend Yield %	0.54	0.86

Growth Measures	%	Rel Category
Long-Term Erngs	17.23	1.06
Book Value	7.38	0.58
Sales	13.22	1.32
Cash Flow	16.03	0.87
Historical Erngs	28.86	1.16

Profitability	%	Rel Category
Return on Equity	17.68	0.98
Return on Assets	10.01	1.07
Net Margin	11.97	1.03

Sector Weightings

	% of Stocks	Rel S&P 500	3 Year High Low	
⌖ Info	16.52	0.83		
Software	3.16	0.92	6	3
Hardware	8.77	0.95	13	8
Media	1.28	0.34	5	1
Telecom	3.31	0.94	5	1
⌂ Service	62.12	1.34		
Health	16.90	1.40	20	15
Consumer	12.75	1.67	18	8
Business	16.50	3.90	18	14
Financial	15.97	0.72	16	8
Mfg	21.35	0.63		
Goods	5.25	0.61	12	5
Ind Mtrls	10.22	0.86	10	2
Energy	5.33	0.54	8	5
Utilities	0.55	0.16	1	0

Composition

● Cash	1.7	
● Stocks	96.9	
● Bonds	0.0	
○ Other	1.5	
Foreign	8.3	(% of Stock)

Morningstar's Take by Andrew Gogerty 12-13-06

We like what Janus Enterprise brings to the table.

This mid-growth fund's risk/reward profile has received an upgrade since manager Jonathan Coleman took the helm in February 2002. Not only does the fund's 10.5% annualized gain during his tenure through Dec. 12, 2006, top the category by 2 percentage points, the fund is on track to land in the top half for the fourth straight year. Meanwhile, volatility of returns (measured by standard deviation) has been below the group average.

Returns are nice, but it's the fund's tempered, eclectic profile under Coleman that appeals to us for the long term. Steady growers such as T. Rowe Price Group, the mutual fund company, and highfliers such as biotech maven Celgene rub elbows alongside glass-maker Owens-Illinois, a potential turnaround. But don't mistake this portfolio as haphazard. Coleman's decisions are matched up against stiff criteria such as improving returns on invested capital, healthy margins, solid balance sheets, and relatively reasonable

valuations. He tends to look past earnings-per-share (a common metric of growth managers), saying that returns on capital are a better indication of a firm's ability to build shareholder value. He also limits positions to approximately 3.5% of assets and has thus far kept turnover near 30% (implying a holding period of more than three years).

We like the menu here but are keeping a watchful eye on Coleman's plate. In addition to his duties here he remains one of the firm's co-chief investment officers. That title comes with extra duties not required of other managers, but he has ample incentive to keep his eye clearly on the ball. Coleman has more than $1 million invested here and has indicated that he has not sold any part of his investment during his tenure.

The fund's bottom-quartile costs round out its appeal. It continues to be one of the more well-rounded offerings in an often-hairy corner of the market. Investors should give it a look.

Address:	151 Detroit Street Denver CO 80206 800-525-0020	Minimum Purchase:	$2500	Add: $100	IRA: $1000
		Min Auto Inv Plan:	$500	Add: $100	
		Sales Fees:	No-load		
Web Address:	www.janus.com	Management Fee:	0.64%		
Inception:	09-01-92	Actual Fees:	Mgt:0.64%	Dist: —	
Advisor:	Janus Capital Management LLC	Expense Projections:	3Yr:$306	5Yr:$531	10Yr:$1178
Subadvisor:	None	Income Distrib:	Annually		
NTF Plans:	Fidelity Retail-NTF, Schwab OneSource				

 MORNINGSTAR® Funds 500

Janus Fundamental Equity

	Ticker	Load	NAV	Yield	Total Assets	Mstar Category
	JAEIX	None	$25.91	0.4%	$1,045 mil	Large Blend

Governance and Management

Stewardship Grade: C

Portfolio Manager(s)

Manager Min Sohn took over for Karen Reidy in May 2005 after Reidy retired from managing money. Sohn has run Janus Growth & Income since January 2004. Before becoming a manager, Sohn was Janus' top analyst.

Strategy

Because he is a former analyst, manager Min Sohn can be expected to pay a great deal of attention to the discounted cash-flow models that Janus analysts bring in for review. Sohn has shown an early preference for companies with substantial cash flows. Sohn has tended to hold more stocks that are highly rated by Janus' analysts. We don't expect large sector bets here, but Sohn has not established a lengthy track record.

Historical Profile
Return High
Risk Average
Rating ★★★★ Highest

Investment Style: Equity — Stock %

53% 64% 76% 85% 88% 99% 98% 94% 97%

▼ Manager Change
▽ Partial Manager Change

Growth of $10,000
— Investment Values of Fund
— Investment Values of S&P 500

32.0
25.0
20.0
15.0
10.0

Performance Quartile (within Category)

	1995	1996	1997	1998	1999	2000	2001	2002	2003	2004	2005	2006	History
NAV	—	11.08	13.54	18.72	25.14	20.63	17.98	14.63	17.97	20.36	23.62	25.91	NAV
Total Return %	—	15.59*	31.08	40.05	38.50	-7.16	-12.11	-18.02	23.27	13.77	16.36	10.28	Total Return %
+/-S&P 500	—	—	-2.28	11.47	17.46	1.94	-0.22	4.08	-5.41	2.89	11.45	-5.51	+/-S&P 500
+/-Russ 1000	—	—	-1.77	13.03	17.59	0.63	0.34	3.63	-6.62	2.37	10.09	-5.18	+/-Russ 1000
Income Return %	—	—	0.61	0.41	0.83	3.35	0.73	0.62	0.43	0.46	0.35	0.49	Income Return %
Capital Return %	—	—	30.47	39.64	37.67	-10.51	-12.84	-18.64	22.84	13.31	16.01	9.79	Capital Return %
Total Rtn % Rank Cat	—	—	41	2	5	54	55	19	84	14	1	91	Total Rtn % Rank Cat
Income $	—	0.06	0.07	0.06	0.15	0.84	0.15	0.11	0.06	0.08	0.07	0.11	Income $
Capital Gains $	—	0.42	0.88	0.18	0.58	1.85	0.00	0.00	0.00	0.00	0.00	0.03	Capital Gains $
Expense Ratio %	—	—	1.71	1.45	1.21	1.01	0.93	0.93	0.89	0.96	0.97	—	Expense Ratio %
Income Ratio %	—	—	3.09	0.62	0.41	0.81	0.65	0.85	0.66	0.40	0.24	—	Income Ratio %
Turnover Rate %	—	—	325	180	101	81	116	115	115	77	58	—	Turnover Rate %
Net Assets $mil	—	—	29	89	349	948	964	817	698	706	660	1,045	Net Assets $mil

Performance 12-31-06

	1st Qtr	2nd Qtr	3rd Qtr	4th Qtr	Total
2002	2.89	-9.62	-15.25	4.03	-18.02
2003	-2.87	11.19	1.46	12.50	23.27
2004	1.56	3.18	-1.38	10.10	13.77
2005	-1.96	3.91	10.37	3.50	16.36
2006	6.52	-3.22	2.09	4.78	10.28

Trailing	Total Return%	+/- S&P 500	+/- Russ 1000	%Rank Cat	Growth of $10,000
3 Mo	4.78	-1.92	-2.17	94	10,478
6 Mo	6.97	-5.77	-5.39	95	10,697
1 Yr	10.28	-5.51	-5.18	91	11,028
3 Yr Avg	13.44	3.00	2.46	7	14,598
5 Yr Avg	8.09	1.90	1.27	15	14,755
10 Yr Avg	11.84	3.42	3.20	5	30,618
15 Yr Avg	—				

Tax Analysis	Tax-Adj Rtn%	%Rank Cat	Tax-Cost Rat	%Rank Cat
3 Yr (estimated)	13.29	4	0.13	6
5 Yr (estimated)	7.91	12	0.17	11
10 Yr (estimated)	10.94	3	0.80	34

Potential Capital Gain Exposure: 16% of assets

Morningstar's Take by Andrew Gogerty 11-06-06

Janus Fundamental Equity has started strong under its new manager but remains a work in progress.

In June 2006, Janus changed this fund's name to Fundamental Equity and also added the Russell 1000 Growth Index as a secondary benchmark to the current S&P 500 Index.

We think these changes are appropriate given the fund's profile under manager Min Sohn, but we're careful to point out that nothing fundamentally has changed inside his research process. Sohn spent six years as a Janus equity analyst and leverages his experience with the firm's forecasting models to evaluate the analysts' best research ideas. His primary focus is on stocks with strong, sustainable cash flows, from company-specific growth drivers. Sohn has the flexibility to show conviction in picks when appropriate. Also, he looks to keep the fund diversified across sectors, but the fund's sector weights could deviate from those in the S&P 500 by 10 percentage points, which would be sizable.

Sohn has gotten off to a quick start. Since taking over, the fund's 31% cumulative gain through Oct. 29, 2006, is 10 percentage points better than the large-blend category norm. A pointed move into energy stocks has fueled the fund's early gains on his watch, as did picks in the technology and hardware sectors.

But we'd caution investors to temper their expectations. Sohn is early in his tenure here, having only run his other charge, sibling Growth & Income, since 2004. His tenure has coincided with a broad market upswing, and he's yet to be stress-tested during a market downturn. Also, the fund's above-average volatility has been masked by Sohn's success and could lead to a bumpy ride when the market is sliding.

Overall, we have a favorable impression of Sohn, as his stock theses appear to be clearly defined and well researched. As such, this fund merits attention from investors, but we wouldn't overestimate its future success.

Address:	151 Detroit Street Denver CO 80206 800-525-0020
Web Address:	www.janus.com
Inception:	06-28-96*
Advisor:	Janus Capital Management LLC
Subadvisor:	None
NTF Plans:	Fidelity Retail-NTF, Schwab OneSource

Minimum Purchase:	$2500	Add: $100	IRA: $1000
Min Auto Inv Plan:	$500	Add: $100	
Sales Fees:	No-load		
Management Fee:	0.60%		
Actual Fees:	Mgt:0.60%	Dist: —	
Expense Projections:	3Yr:$287	5Yr:$498	10Yr:$1108
Income Distrib:	Annually		

Rating and Risk

Time Period	Load-Adj Return %	Morningstar Rtn vs Cat	Morningstar Risk vs Cat	Morningstar Risk-Adj Rating
1 Yr	10.28			
3 Yr	13.44	High	High	★★★★★
5 Yr	8.09	+Avg	-Avg	★★★★
10 Yr	11.84	High	Avg	★★★★★
Incept	12.78			

Other Measures	Standard Index S&P 500	Best Fit Index Russ MG
Alpha	1.8	2.6
Beta	1.16	0.76
R-Squared	73	87
Standard Deviation	9.31	
Mean	13.44	
Sharpe Ratio	1.06	

Portfolio Analysis 11-30-06

Share change since 10-06 Total Stocks:58

	Sector	PE	Tot Ret%	% Assets
General Electric Company	Ind Mtrls	20.0	9.35	4.07
J.P. Morgan Chase & Co.	Financial	13.6	25.60	3.97
Merrill Lynch & Company,	Financial	14.2	39.28	3.82
Citigroup, Inc.	Financial	13.1	19.55	3.43
Roche Holding	Health	—		2.95
Merck & Co., Inc.	Health	19.1	42.66	2.87
Hess Corporation	Ind Mtrls	7.8	19.01	2.81
Yahoo, Inc.	Media	35.4	-34.81	2.66
Suncor Energy, Inc.	Energy	33.1	25.42	2.57
Fannie Mae	Financial	—	24.34	2.56
EMC Corporation	Hardware	32.7	-3.08	2.50
Valero Energy Corporatio	Energy	6.3	-0.33	2.43
Advanced Micro Devices	Hardware	18.5	-33.50	2.42
Federated Department Sto	Consumer	20.8	16.54	2.33
Procter & Gamble Company	Goods	23.9	13.36	2.28
Adobe Systems Inc.	Software	48.1	11.26	2.13
Coventry Health Care, In	Health	15.4	-12.13	2.12
ExxonMobil Corporation	Energy	11.1	39.07	2.10
Commerce Bancorp, Inc.	Financial	23.6	3.89	2.10
⊕ CVS Corporation	Consumer	19.7	17.60	2.07

Current Investment Style

Value Blend Growth — Large Mid Small

Market Cap	%
Giant	47.7
Large	38.4
Mid	12.0
Small	1.8
Micro	0.1
Avg $mil:	39,785

Value Measures		Rel Category
Price/Earnings	15.80	1.03
Price/Book	2.58	1.01
Price/Sales	1.52	1.09
Price/Cash Flow	8.20	0.97
Dividend Yield %	1.27	0.73

Growth Measures	%	Rel Category
Long-Term Erngs	11.74	0.99
Book Value	14.65	1.62
Sales	13.20	1.36
Cash Flow	20.76	2.01
Historical Erngs	24.27	1.31

Profitability	%	Rel Category
Return on Equity	18.83	0.97
Return on Assets	10.01	0.96
Net Margin	12.95	0.96

Sector Weightings	% of Stocks	Rel S&P 500	3 Year High Low
Info	20.76	1.04	
Software	6.46	1.87	10 0
Hardware	11.56	1.25	15 7
Media	2.74	0.72	10 2
Telecom	0.00	0.00	1 0
Service	45.34	0.98	
Health	12.12	1.00	18 7
Consumer	10.62	1.39	17 6
Business	4.69	1.11	7 3
Financial	17.91	0.80	22 9
Mfg	33.88	1.00	
Goods	5.79	0.68	11 6
Ind Mtrls	13.07	1.09	20 8
Energy	15.02	1.53	19 4
Utilities	0.00	0.00	1 0

Composition

●	Cash	2.9
●	Stocks	97.1
●	Bonds	0.0
●	Other	0.0
	Foreign	15.5
	(% of Stock)	

Janus Global Life Sci

	Ticker	Load	NAV	Yield	Total Assets	Mstar Category
	JAGLX	None	$19.66	0.0%	$948 mil	Specialty-Health

Governance and Management

Stewardship Grade: C

Portfolio Manager(s)

Tom Malley has been running the fund since its January 1999 inception. Previously, he served as an assistant portfolio manager on Janus Mercury. Andy Acker, who has worked as an analyst on the fund since 1999, was promoted to assistant portfolio manager in early 2006. The duo is supported by four dedicated health-care analysts.

Strategy

Manager Tom Malley searches across the globe and market-cap spectrum for fast-growing health-care names that are undervalued based on current and future cash-flow analysis. But he remains willing to pay up for his picks, even though he has toned things down a bit in recent years. Although the fund still invests in aggressive areas such as biotechnology, the fund's assets are more diversified across other industries than they have been in the past.

Performance 12-31-06

	1st Qtr	2nd Qtr	3rd Qtr	4th Qtr	Total
2002	-6.03	-14.54	-9.43	-3.91	-30.11
2003	2.04	10.14	3.70	9.36	27.44
2004	7.80	2.67	-4.16	8.37	14.95
2005	-4.17	7.66	7.00	0.96	11.45
2006	5.39	-6.34	1.77	-2.38	-1.95

Trailing	Total Return%	+/- S&P 500	+/- DJ Hlthcare	%Rank Cat	Growth of $10,000
3 Mo	-2.38	-9.08	-4.09	100	9,762
6 Mo	-0.66	-13.40	-11.33	100	9,934
1 Yr	-1.95	-17.74	-8.83	89	9,805
3 Yr Avg	7.90	-2.54	1.32	40	12,562
5 Yr Avg	2.27	-3.92	-0.47	64	11,188
10 Yr Avg	—	—	—	—	—
15 Yr Avg	—	—	—	—	—

Tax Analysis	Tax-Adj Rtn%	%Rank Cat	Tax-Cost Rat	%Rank Cat
3 Yr (estimated)	7.90	28	0.00	1
5 Yr (estimated)	2.27	53	0.00	1
10 Yr (estimated)	—	—	—	—

Potential Capital Gain Exposure: -70% of assets

Morningstar's Take by Andrew Gogerty 11-06-06

A change in focus has continued to pay off for investors at Janus Global Life Sciences, but we still wouldn't necessarily buy it.

It's been roughly three years since skipper Tom Malley overhauled his investment strategy at this fund, and so far the results have been encouraging. The fund's 11.1% annualized gain for the three years ending Nov. 2, 2006, is better than 75% of its health-care peers, while volatility has been in line with the group norm.

What's more, we think the fund's new diversified, long-term-focused process will continue to benefit shareholders. The fund's past aggressive, biotech-heavy, fast-trading profile has been replaced with a more fundamental investment philosophy that focuses on cash-flow generation, returns on equity, and sustainable competitive advantages. Switzerland-based drugmaker Roche Holding, for example, occupies a top spot because Malley believes that its current drugs haven't fully penetrated the market, and this potential for further

cash-flow growth isn't being fully valued. Malley thinks the stock could do even better if drugs in the research phase are successful.

This change in focus has appeal, but there are still risks. Although the fund is more diversified, biotech stocks--which can be more volatile--still hold 35% of the fund's assets. Moreover, Malley isn't afraid to let top picks soak up a significant chunk of assets (currently more than a third), which increases stock-specific risk on top of the already-compact portfolio.

And while these issues don't drown the case for owning the fund, slotting this or any health-care offering in an overall portfolio can be difficult. Granted, fund expenses are low, but many large-cap offerings--especially growth-oriented funds that most investors already own--probably contain a significant stake in this sector. So, the diversification benefits are likely to be minimal, and this offering can't seek shelter in another sector when health care falls from favor.

Address:	151 Detroit Street
	Denver CO 80206
	800-525-0020
Web Address:	www.janus.com
Inception:	12-31-98*
Advisor:	Janus Capital Management LLC
Subadvisor:	None
NTF Plans:	Fidelity Retail-NTF, Schwab OneSource

Minimum Purchase:	$2500	Add: $100	IRA: $1000
Min Auto Inv Plan:	$500	Add: $100	
Sales Fees:	No-load, 2.00%R		
Management Fee:	0.64%		
Actual Fees:	Mgt:0.64%	Dist: —	
Expense Projections:	3Yr:$309	5Yr:$536	10Yr:$1190
Income Distrib:	Annually		

Historical Profile

Return Average
Risk Average
Rating ★★★ Neutral

| 93% | 87% | 89% | 99% | 99% | 99% | 99% | 95% |

Investment Style
Equity
Stock %

▼ Manager Change
▽ Partial Manager Change

Growth of $10,000
— Investment Values of Fund
— Investment Values of S&P 500

22.8
18.0
14.0
10.0
6.0

Performance Quartile (within Category)

1995	1996	1997	1998	1999	2000	2001	2002	2003	2004	2005	2006	History
—	—	—	10.00	16.10	21.45	17.57	12.28	15.65	17.99	20.05	19.66	NAV
—	—	—	0.00*	61.00	33.34	-18.09	-30.11	27.44	14.95	11.45	-1.95	Total Return %
—	—	—	—	39.96	42.44	-6.20	-8.01	-1.24	4.07	6.54	-17.74	+/-S&P 500
—	—	—	—	65.03	-4.50	-5.25	-9.30	8.01	10.40	3.13	-8.83	+/-DJ Hlthcare
—	—	—	—	0.00	0.10	0.00	0.00	0.00	0.00	0.00	0.00	Income Return %
—	—	—	—	61.00	33.24	-18.09	-30.11	27.44	14.95	11.45	-1.95	Capital Return %
—	—	—	—	11	84	74	71	68	12	34	89	Total Rtn % Rank Cat
—	—	—	0.00	0.00	0.02	0.00	0.00	0.00	0.00	0.00	0.00	Income $
—	—	—	0.00	0.00	0.00	0.00	0.00	0.00	0.00	0.00	0.00	Capital Gains $
—	—	—	—	1.19	0.94	0.91	0.88	0.98	1.01	—	—	Expense Ratio %
—	—	—	—	-0.41	0.14	0.32	-0.42	-0.28	-0.52	—	—	Income Ratio %
—	—	—	—	235	147	84	73	135	78	—	—	Turnover Rate %
—	—	—	—	601	3,992	2,418	1,278	1,273	1,265	948	—	Net Assets $mil

Rating and Risk

Time Period	Load-Adj Return %	Morningstar Rtn vs Cat	Morningstar Risk vs Cat	Morningstar Risk-Adj Rating
1 Yr	-1.95			
3 Yr	7.90	Avg	Avg	★★★
5 Yr	2.27	Avg	Avg	★★★
10 Yr	—	—	—	
Incept	8.83			

Other Measures	Standard Index S&P 500	Best Fit Index DJ Hlthcare
Alpha	-0.8	1.7
Beta	0.82	0.92
R-Squared	29	53
Standard Deviation	10.51	
Mean	7.90	
Sharpe Ratio	0.47	

Portfolio Analysis 11-30-06

Share change since 10-06 Total Stocks:54	Sector	PE	Tot Ret%	% Assets
Roche Holding	Health	—	—	4.37
⊕ Nuvelo, Inc.	Health	—	-50.68	3.76
⊕ Alexion Pharmaceuticals,	Health	—	99.46	3.44
Merck & Co., Inc.	Health	19.1	42.66	3.43
Celgene Corporation	Health	—	77.56	3.43
United Therapeutics Corp	Health	28.5	-21.34	3.41
CVS Corporation	Consumer	19.7	17.60	2.84
Gilead Sciences, Inc.	Health	40.6	23.51	2.66
⊖ Coventry Health Care, In	Health	15.4	-12.13	2.63
Manor Care, Inc.	Health	24.6	19.65	2.52
Novartis	Health	—	—	2.47
⊖ Advanced Magnetics, Inc.	Health	—	438.99	2.29
⊖ Cardinal Health, Inc.	Health	20.8	-5.82	2.10
⊕ Hospira, Inc.	Health	25.4	-21.51	2.09
⊖ WellPoint, Inc.	Health	17.2	-1.38	2.04
⊖ Caremark RX, Inc.	Health	23.6	10.90	1.98
Healthsouth Corporation	Health	—	-7.55	1.92
Syngenta	Ind Mtrls	—	—	1.85
⊖ Cubist Pharmaceuticals,	Health	—	-14.74	1.83
STADA Arzneimittel	Health	—	—	1.77

Current Investment Style

Value Blnd Growth — Large Mid Small

	Market Cap	%
	Giant	21.2
	Large	31.2
	Mid	21.6
	Small	23.8
	Micro	2.1
	Avg $mil:	9,619

Value Measures		Rel Category
Price/Earnings	21.18	0.93
Price/Book	3.45	0.96
Price/Sales	1.87	0.70
Price/Cash Flow	15.03	0.93
Dividend Yield %	0.73	0.87

Growth Measures	%	Rel Category
Long-Term Erngs	14.68	1.00
Book Value	14.83	1.75
Sales	11.06	0.93
Cash Flow	0.60	0.05
Historical Erngs	13.59	0.76

Profitability	%	Rel Category
Return on Equity	9.04	0.75
Return on Assets	0.78	0.20
Net Margin	9.77	0.89

Industry Weightings	% of Stocks	Rel Cat
Biotech	35.9	1.1
Drugs	19.0	0.6
Mgd Care	17.3	1.6
Hospitals	0.0	0.0
Other HC Srv	7.2	4.8
Diagnostics	4.2	3.2
Equipment	8.2	0.6
Good/Srv	4.1	1.1
Other	4.0	1.3

Composition

● Cash		0.0
● Stocks		95.4
● Bonds		0.0
● Other		4.6
Foreign		16.7
(% of Stock)		

MORNINGSTAR® Funds 500

Janus Global Opps

	Ticker	Load	NAV	Yield	Total Assets	Mstar Category
	JGVAX	None	$14.07	0.6%	$152 mil	World Stock

Governance and Management

Stewardship Grade: C

Portfolio Manager(s)

Jason Yee has been head of this fund since its inception in mid-2001. However, in July 2004, Janus placed him in charge of international flagship Janus Worldwide as well. He cut his teeth as an analyst at Janus from 1992 until 1996, after which he left the firm to work at a small money-management shop in Denver. He returned to Janus in 2000. Gregory Kolb, a longtime analyst at Janus, was named as comanager on the fund in May 2005.

Strategy

Jason Yee won't buy stocks unless he can get them cheap. He likes to grab a company when its stock is trading at a noticeable discount to his estimate of the firm's worth. This isn't bottom-of-the-barrel value investing, though: Yee also wants companies that boast strong free cash flows and impressive franchises. The fund invests across the globe and across market caps, but the portfolio is usually quite concentrated.

Performance 12-31-06

	1st Qtr	2nd Qtr	3rd Qtr	4th Qtr	Total
2002	8.32	-4.83	-21.31	3.65	-15.92
2003	-12.05	22.21	12.98	13.99	38.41
2004	5.17	3.54	-5.72	12.33	15.33
2005	-0.84	-2.90	4.60	3.35	4.07
2006	3.40	-3.02	2.31	8.39	11.19

Trailing	Total Return%	+/- MSCI EAFE	+/- MSCI World	%Rank Cat	Growth of $10,000
3 Mo	8.39	-1.96	0.02	54	10,839
6 Mo	10.89	-3.80	-2.32	82	11,089
1 Yr	11.19	-15.15	-8.88	97	11,119
3 Yr Avg	10.10	-9.83	-4.58	94	13,346
5 Yr Avg	9.21	-5.77	-0.76	59	15,535
10 Yr Avg	—	—	—	—	—
15 Yr Avg	—	—	—	—	—

Tax Analysis	Tax-Adj Rtn%	%Rank Cat	Tax-Cost Rat	%Rank Cat
3 Yr (estimated)	9.16	94	0.85	47
5 Yr (estimated)	8.59	60	0.57	45
10 Yr (estimated)	—	—	—	—

Potential Capital Gain Exposure: 18% of assets

Morningstar's Take by Karen Dolan 12-12-06

Janus Global Opportunities hasn't lost its touch.

In mid-2004, manager Jason Yee's responsibilities expanded beyond this fund. He became Janus' international CIO and took the helm of Janus Worldwide. Around that same time, the fund's relative performance began to slump. While Yee now splits his time between this fund and his other responsibilities, we think the fund has gotten stronger in some ways. Yee's broader role led him to think more about Janus' resources and bolster the supporting team. He recently gave up his CIO duties, but the fund is now armed with a deeper analyst bench as a result of his broader role.

The fund benefits from the research Yee is doing for Worldwide, too. Many of his favorite ideas show up in both portfolios. This fund differs mainly because it only holds 30 or so stocks and can own some smaller firms.

Yee's additional responsibilities opened the door for comanager Gregory Kolb to assume a bigger role here. Kolb is generating a lot of the new ideas and

has a say on what stocks make it into the portfolio. Kolb's role on this fund seems likely to continue to grow.

The driving philosophy is still the same; Yee and Kolb both look for high-quality companies trading at compelling valuations. They favor firms that don't have to spend a lot of money to make money and thus see a big proportion of their sales translate into earnings. That has led the fund to battered tech fare and kept it away from rallying emerging-markets and energy stocks, which have been the keys to its underperformance. The fund's unique leanings could pull it ahead in a hurry, especially if hot emerging markets and energy stocks cool down.

The fund has undoubtedly missed the boat on some strong-performing corners of the market in recent years, but we like its current positioning and have faith in Yee's strategy. That said, we are watching how Yee's and Kolb's roles evolve and what that means for investors here.

Address:	151 Detroit Street
	Denver CO 80206
	800-525-0020
Web Address:	www.janus.com
Inception:	06-29-01 *
Advisor:	Janus
Subadvisor:	None
NTF Plans:	Fidelity Retail-NTF, Schwab OneSource

Minimum Purchase:	$2500	Add: $100	IRA: $1000
Min Auto Inv Plan:	$500	Add: $100	
Sales Fees:	No-load, 2.00%R		
Management Fee:	0.64%		
Actual Fees:	Mgt:0.64%	Dist: —	
Expense Projections:	3Yr:$328	5Yr:$569	10Yr:$1259
Income Distrib:	Annually		

Historical Profile
Return: Average
Risk: Above Avg
Rating: ★★★ Neutral

	87%	88%	88%	87%	97%	98%

Investment Style
Equity
Stock %

▼ Manager Change
▽ Partial Manager Change

Growth of $10,000
— Investment Values of Fund
— Investment Values of MSCI EAFE

17.2
14.4
12.0
10.0
7.0

Performance Quartile (within Category)

	1995	1996	1997	1998	1999	2000	2001	2002	2003	2004	2005	2006	History
NAV	—	—	—	—	—	—	10.70	8.96	12.37	14.24	14.71	14.07	
Total Return %	—	—	—	—	—	—	7.29*	-15.92	38.41	15.33	4.07	11.19	
+/-MSCI EAFE	—	—	—	—	—	—	—	0.02	-0.18	-4.92	-9.47	-15.15	
+/-MSCI World	—	—	—	—	—	—	—	3.97	5.30	0.61	-5.42	-8.88	
Income Return %	—	—	—	—	—	—	—	0.34	0.35	0.21	0.78	0.63	
Capital Return %	—	—	—	—	—	—	—	-16.26	38.06	15.12	3.29	10.56	
Total Rtn % Rank Cat	—	—	—	—	—	—	—	25	30	49	95	97	
Income $	—	—	—	—	—	—	0.02	0.04	0.03	0.03	0.11	0.09	
Capital Gains $	—	—	—	—	—	—	0.01	0.00	0.00	0.00	0.00	2.22	
Expense Ratio %	—	—	—	—	—	—	—	1.50	1.16	1.16	1.09	—	
Income Ratio %	—	—	—	—	—	—	—	0.64	0.40	0.27	0.24	—	
Turnover Rate %	—	—	—	—	—	—	—	—	84	31	37	—	
Net Assets $mil	—	—	—	—	—	—	96	150	153	230	152		

Rating and Risk

Time Period	Load-Adj Return %	Morningstar Rtn vs Cat	Morningstar Risk vs Cat	Morningstar Risk-Adj Rating
1 Yr	11.19			
3 Yr	10.10	-Avg	Avg	★★
5 Yr	9.21	Avg	+Avg	★★★
10 Yr	—	—	—	—
Incept	9.72			

Other Measures	Standard Index MSCI EAFE	Best Fit Index Mstar Mid Core
Alpha	-4.4	-0.6
Beta	0.72	0.68
R-Squared	54	66
Standard Deviation	9.25	
Mean	10.10	
Sharpe Ratio	0.74	

Portfolio Analysis 11-30-06

Share change since 10-06 Total Stocks:26	Sector	Country	% Assets
Dell, Inc.	Hardware	United States	8.85
IAC/InterActiveCorp	Consumer	United States	6.11
Willis Group Holdings, L	Financial	Bermuda	5.98
Tyco International, Ltd.	Ind Mtrls	United States	5.64
Esprit Hldgs Ltd	Consumer	Hong Kong	5.28
Liberty Global, Inc. A	Media	United States	4.73
⊖ British Sky Broadcasting	Media	U.K.	4.66
J.P. Morgan Chase & Co.	Financial	United States	4.41
Koninklijke Philips Elec	Goods	Netherlands	4.34
NIPPONKOA Insurance	Financial	Japan	4.22
Metro AG Grp	Consumer	Germany	3.84
Tenma	Ind Mtrls	Japan	3.78
Expedia, Inc.	Consumer	United States	3.59
NewAlliance Bancshares,	Financial	United States	3.54
Amazon.com, Inc.	Consumer	United States	3.46
Apollo Group, Inc. A	Consumer	United States	3.33
Treehouse Foods, Inc.	Goods	United States	3.23
Nissin Healthcare Food S	Consumer	Japan	3.08
Patterson Companies, Inc	Health	United States	2.95
Syngenta	Ind Mtrls	Switzerland	2.32

Current Investment Style

Value Blnd Growth — Large Mid Small

Market Cap	%
Giant	30.2
Large	33.2
Mid	25.9
Small	10.8
Micro	0.0

Avg $mil: 13,200

Value Measures		Rel Category
Price/Earnings	18.39	1.20
Price/Book	1.96	0.82
Price/Sales	1.18	0.90
Price/Cash Flow	9.16	1.06
Dividend Yield %	1.83	0.84

Growth Measures	%	Rel Category
Long-Term Erngs	13.16	1.04
Book Value	2.55	0.28
Sales	7.65	0.92
Cash Flow	8.02	0.82
Historical Erngs	19.29	1.03

Composition

Cash	2.0	Bonds	0.0
Stocks	98.0	Other	0.0
Foreign (% of Stock)			47.0

Sector Weightings

Sector Weightings	% Stocks	Rel MSCI EAFE	3 Year High	Low
⟳ Info	22.89	1.94		
Software	0.00	0.00	3	0
Hardware	9.03	2.34	9	0
Media	11.90	6.50	24	11
Telecom	1.96	0.35	5	0
⟳ Service	57.42	1.22		
Health	3.01	0.42	18	3
Consumer	29.27	5.91	29	4
Business	0.00	0.00	14	0
Financial	25.14	0.84	28	15
⟳ Mfg	19.69	0.48		
Goods	7.72	0.59	16	7
Ind Mtrls	11.97	0.78	20	12
Energy	0.00	0.00	0	0
Utilities	0.00	0.00	1	0

Regional Exposure % Stock

UK/W. Europe	21	N. America	53
Japan	14	Latn America	6
Asia X Japan	5	Other	1

Country Exposure % Stock

United States	53	Bermuda	6
Japan	14	Hong Kong	5
U.K.	8		

Janus Growth & Income

	Ticker	Load	NAV	Yield	Total Assets	Mstar Category
	JAGIX	None	$38.26	1.4%	$6,955 mil	Large Growth

Governance and Management

Stewardship Grade: C

Portfolio Manager(s)

Minyoung Sohn replaced former manager David Corkins in January 2004. This is Sohn's first assignment as a portfolio manager after being an analyst at Janus since 1998. He also runs Janus Fundamental Equity in a similar style, but without the income goal.

Strategy

Minyoung Sohn looks to buy and hold companies with strong balance sheets that can deliver higher earnings or cash-flow growth than Wall Street expects. Turnover is about half the category average, and the fund has generally been more diversified than many of Janus' other growth offerings. Sohn will also allocate up to 15% of fund assets to structured notes that are designed to act like covered calls, with the goal being higher income.

Performance 12-31-06

	1st Qtr	2nd Qtr	3rd Qtr	4th Qtr	Total
2002	-0.23	-10.45	-16.37	5.05	-21.51
2003	-1.89	11.29	1.63	12.32	24.65
2004	1.56	0.95	-3.14	12.67	11.89
2005	-1.43	2.92	8.83	1.87	12.48
2006	5.71	-4.12	1.60	4.70	7.82

Trailing	Total Return%	+/- S&P 500	+/- Russ 1000Gr	%Rank Cat	Growth of $10,000
3 Mo	4.70	-2.00	-1.23	69	10,470
6 Mo	6.38	-6.36	-3.72	78	10,638
1 Yr	7.82	-7.97	-1.25	41	10,782
3 Yr Avg	10.71	0.27	3.84	10	13,569
5 Yr Avg	5.83	-0.36	3.14	13	13,275
10 Yr Avg	10.71	2.29	5.27	4	27,661
15 Yr Avg	11.45	0.81	3.43	9	50,839

Tax Analysis	Tax-Adj Rtn%	%Rank Cat	Tax-Cost Rat	%Rank Cat
3 Yr (estimated)	10.39	8	0.29	19
5 Yr (estimated)	5.54	13	0.27	28
10 Yr (estimated)	9.81	4	0.81	37

Potential Capital Gain Exposure: 18% of assets

Morningstar's Take by Andrew Gogerty 11-09-06

Janus Growth & Income continues its success under new management, but concerns remain.

Current manager Minyoung Sohn cut his teeth as a Janus equity analyst for six years before taking the reins here in January 2004. As a result, he has considerable knowledge of the firm's cash flow forecasting models and leverages his experience to evaluate the analysts' best research ideas. His primary focus is on stocks with strong, sustainable cash flows, from company-specific growth drivers. Sohn has the flexibility to show conviction in picks when appropriate. Also, he looks to keep the fund diversified across sectors, but the fund's sector weights could deviate from those in the S&P 500 by more than 10 percentage points at times, which would be sizable.

Sohn has gotten off to a quick start. The fund's 32% cumulative gain during his tenure through October 2006 is 11 percentage points better than the large-growth category norm. Sohn's deliberate move into energy stocks fueled his early success, as

did picks in the technology and hardware sectors.

That said, investors should take note of the fund's 8% stake in structured notes designed to act like covered calls. Sohn's goal with these instruments is to generate current income by selling a part of a stock's upside potential. The income acts as a cushion against dips in the stock price and allows the fund to book a gain when the stock price is flat. But, because these calls have finite lives, Sohn and his analysts must also estimate a price target over a specific time period. His success here has been mixed, and miscues have in part weighed on fund returns compared with his other charge, Janus Fundamental Equity, where he utilizes the same equity research process but not the notes.

Overall, though, Sohn's stock theses appear to be clearly defined and well researched. As such, this fund merits attention from investors, but we're watching his execution in delivering a higher income stream for investors.

Address:	151 Detroit Street	Minimum Purchase:	$2500	Add: $100	IRA: $1000
	Denver CO 80206	Min Auto Inv Plan:	$500	Add: $100	
	800-525-0020	Sales Fees:	No-load		
Web Address:	www.janus.com	Management Fee:	0.62%		
Inception:	05-15-91	Actual Fees:	Mgt:0.62%	Dist: —	
Advisor:	Janus Capital Management LLC	Expense Projections:	3Yr:$281	5Yr:$488	10Yr:$1084
Subadvisor:	None	Income Distrib:	Quarterly		
NTF Plans:	Fidelity Retail-NTF, Schwab OneSource				

Historical Profile
Return High
Risk Below Avg
Rating ★★★★ Highest

Investment Style
Equity
Stock %

78% 83% 80% 79% 75% 96% 96% 90% 90%

▼ Manager Change
▽ Partial Manager Change

Growth of $10,000

— Investment Values of Fund
— Investment Values of S&P 500

42.2
32.4
24.0
17.0
10.0

Performance Quartile (within Category)

1995	1996	1997	1998	1999	2000	2001	2002	2003	2004	2005	2006	History
16.67	19.05	23.15	29.10	41.94	35.35	29.97	23.34	28.91	32.19	36.01	38.26	NAV
36.35	26.03	34.66	34.87	51.18	-11.41	-14.36	-21.51	24.65	11.89	12.48	7.82	Total Return %
-1.23	3.07	1.30	6.29	30.14	-2.31	-2.47	0.59	-4.03	1.01	7.57	-7.97	+/-S&P 500
-0.83	2.91	4.17	-3.84	18.02	11.01	6.06	6.37	-5.10	5.59	7.22	-1.25	+/-Russ 1000Gr
7.33	0.58	0.37	0.34	0.34	0.55	0.85	0.65	0.68	0.52	0.58	1.52	Income Return %
29.02	25.45	34.29	34.53	50.84	-11.96	-15.21	-22.16	23.97	11.37	11.90	6.30	Capital Return %
25	11	9	34	19	47	39	16	73	18	12	41	Total Rtn % Rank Cat
1.01	0.10	0.07	0.08	0.10	0.23	0.30	0.20	0.16	0.15	0.19	0.54	Income $
1.23	1.89	2.38	2.02	1.84	1.62	0.00	0.00	0.00	0.00	0.00	0.00	Capital Gains $
1.17	1.03	0.96	0.96	0.90	0.88	0.86	0.88	0.91	0.92	0.87	—	Expense Ratio %
1.11	0.70	0.30	0.33	0.37	0.49	0.96	0.73	0.67	0.24	0.68	—	Income Ratio %
195	153	127	95	43	41	59	—	50	41	38	—	Turnover Rate %
632	1,101	2,005	3,504	7,493	8,349	7,148	5,277	5,977	5,616	6,241	6,797	Net Assets $mil

Rating and Risk

Time Period	Load-Adj Return %	Morningstar Rtn vs Cat	Morningstar Risk vs Cat	Morningstar Risk-Adj Rating
1 Yr	7.82			
3 Yr	10.71	High	Avg	★★★★★
5 Yr	5.83	+Avg	-Avg	★★★★
10 Yr	10.71	High	-Avg	★★★★★
Incept	13.22			

Other Measures	Standard Index S&P 500	Best Fit Index Russ MG
Alpha	-1.0	-0.3
Beta	1.22	0.82
R-Squared	69	86
Standard Deviation	10.10	
Mean	10.71	
Sharpe Ratio	0.74	

Portfolio Analysis 11-30-06

Share change since 10-06 Total Stocks:66

	Sector	PE	Tot Ret%	% Assets
Advanced Micro Devices	Hardware	18.5	-33.50	3.73
General Electric Company	Ind Mtrls	20.0	9.35	3.54
Suncor Energy, Inc.	Energy	33.1	25.42	3.12
Yahoo, Inc.	Media	35.4	-34.81	2.85
EMC Corporation	Hardware	32.7	-3.08	2.84
EnCana Corporation	Energy	11.8	2.55	2.84
Roche Holding	Health			2.72
Procter & Gamble Company	Goods	23.9	13.36	2.55
Citigroup, Inc.	Financial	13.1	19.55	2.54
ExxonMobil Corporation	Energy	11.1	39.07	2.47
J.P. Morgan Chase & Co.	Financial	13.6	25.60	2.14
Fannie Mae	Financial	—	24.34	2.10
Samsung Electnc GDR 144A	Goods			2.07
⊕ CVS Corporation	Consumer	19.7	17.60	1.92
Hess Corporation	Ind Mtrls	7.8	19.01	1.83
Rockwell Automation	Ind Mtrls	17.2	4.77	1.82
Sanofi-Synthelabo	Health			1.80
Boeing Company	Ind Mtrls	41.2	28.38	1.75
British Sky Broadcasting	Media			1.74
Dell, Inc.	Hardware	18.4	-16.23	1.65

Current Investment Style

Value Blnd Growth — Large Mid Small

Market Cap	%
Giant	44.4
Large	35.2
Mid	17.9
Small	2.3
Micro	0.3

Avg $mil: 29,648

Value Measures		Rel Category
Price/Earnings	16.71	0.87
Price/Book	3.01	0.91
Price/Sales	1.68	0.87
Price/Cash Flow	8.60	0.76
Dividend Yield %	1.20	1.17

Growth Measures	%	Rel Category
Long-Term Erngs	12.04	0.84
Book Value	13.42	1.16
Sales	12.81	1.10
Cash Flow	18.86	1.12
Historical Erngs	23.08	1.00

Profitability	%	Rel Category
Return on Equity	20.76	1.02
Return on Assets	9.64	0.88
Net Margin	11.88	0.83

Sector Weightings	% of Stocks	Rel S&P 500	3 Year High	Low
⟳ Info	25.70	1.29		
▣ Software	2.21	0.64	8	2
▣ Hardware	15.14	1.64	17	12
▣ Media	6.80	1.79	13	5
▣ Telecom	1.55	0.44	2	0
⟐ Service	35.54	0.77		
▣ Health	9.28	0.77	16	9
▣ Consumer	11.90	1.56	12	4
▣ Business	3.76	0.89	4	1
▣ Financial	10.60	0.48	19	8
⟐ Mfg	38.78	1.15		
▣ Goods	9.78	1.14	15	9
▣ Ind Mtrls	13.45	1.13	13	8
▣ Energy	15.55	1.59	19	6
▣ Utilities	0.00	0.00	0	0

Composition

- ● Cash 1.7
- ● Stocks 90.4
- ● Bonds 0.0
- ● Other 7.9
- Foreign 27.8 (% of Stock)

MORNINGSTAR® Funds 500

Janus High-Yield

Ticker	Load	NAV	Yield	SEC Yield	Total Assets	Mstar Category
JAHYX	None	$9.83	7.3%	7.45%	$522 mil	High Yield Bond

Governance and Management

Stewardship Grade: C

Portfolio Manager(s)

Gibson Smith joined the fund in December 2003. He has been with Janus since 2001 and has worked as an assistant portfolio manager on Janus Flexible Bond and as a portfolio manager on Janus Short-Term Bond. He is supported by 11 analysts.

Strategy

This fund's profile has changed a bit under its current manager. Former manager Sandy Rufenacht was quite willing to hold large cash stakes, while Gibson Smith, who took over the fund in late 2003, plans to stay more fully invested. Smith has also trimmed the fund's exposure to the gaming sector, which was a favorite of Rufenacht's. Overall, the fund still looks a bit more conservative than its average peer, but not as conservative as it was with Rufenacht at the helm.

Performance 12-31-06

	1st Qtr	2nd Qtr	3rd Qtr	4th Qtr	Total
2002	2.31	-1.54	-1.60	3.46	2.56
2003	4.02	4.83	1.64	4.74	16.08
2004	1.53	-0.43	4.51	3.57	9.42
2005	-1.63	2.70	0.69	1.04	2.77
2006	2.68	0.30	3.60	4.13	11.10

Trailing	Total Return%	+/- LB Aggr	+/- CSFB Glb HY	%Rank Cat	Growth of $10,000
3 Mo	4.13	2.89	-0.32	37	10,413
6 Mo	7.87	2.78	-0.28	28	10,787
1 Yr	11.10	6.77	-0.83	25	11,110
3 Yr Avg	7.70	4.00	-0.92	38	12,492
5 Yr Avg	8.26	3.20	-2.81	60	14,871
10 Yr Avg	6.97	0.73	-0.12	16	19,616
15 Yr Avg	—				

Tax Analysis	Tax-Adj Rtn%	%Rank Cat	Tax-Cost Rat	%Rank Cat
3 Yr (estimated)	5.10	30	2.41	48
5 Yr (estimated)	5.60	52	2.46	39
10 Yr (estimated)	3.76	11	3.00	26

Potential Capital Gain Exposure: -2% of assets

Morningstar's Take by Kai Wiecking 12-06-06

Janus High-Yield makes a case for itself, but investors need to keep its risk in mind.

Lead manager Gibson Smith just celebrated his third anniversary at the helm of this fund. The fund's trailing average annual return of 7.8% over that period through December 5, 2006, ranks slightly ahead of its typical rival in the high-yield bond category. Recent results have placed even better in a tightly bunched field, a feat aided by a decline in expenses: At 0.87%, this offering's price tag is now in line with the typical no-load option in the group. And with asset outflows slowing to a halt, we hope costs will go down further here.

Smith's deft issue selection is what mostly drove performance in 2006. Top holding Acco Brands, an office supplies company, delivered the balance sheet improvements it had promised and rallied strongly. Smith also captured much of the strong rebound in General Motors and Ford, but has recently taken profits and shifted into more defensive health-care names. With spreads (the

yield differential between various credit ratings) at very tight levels, Smith has begun to generally reduce exposure to CCC rated bonds in favor of B rated issues. Still, shareholders should be aware that the bull market in junk bonds is beginning to look a tad long in the tooth by some measures, and the fund could easily suffer in a recessionary scenario.

We're encouraged that Janus has allowed Smith to ramp up hiring, and his team of analysts has now grown to 11 members. Smith is adamant that risk management is a major consideration for each of them.

All told, we like the course this fund has taken under Smith, and expect his credit-selection abilities to continue delivering good returns in the long run. But with risk arguably exceeding potential rewards in the junk-bond market going into 2007, now might be a good time for shareholders to check whether this fund plays a bigger role in their overall portfolios than they originally intended.

Address:	151 Detroit Street Denver CO 80206 800-525-0020
Web Address:	www.janus.com
Inception:	12-29-95*
Advisor:	Janus
Subadvisor:	None
NTF Plans:	Fidelity Retail-NTF, Schwab OneSource

Minimum Purchase:	$2500	Add: $100	IRA: $1000
Min Auto Inv Plan:	$500	Add: $100	
Sales Fees:	No-load, 2.00%R		
Management Fee:	0.65% mx./0.55% mn.		
Actual Fees:	Mgt:0.60%	Dist: —	
Expense Projections:	3Yr:$281	5Yr:$488	10Yr:$1084
Income Distrib:	Monthly		

Historical Profile

Return: Above Avg
Risk: Low
Rating: ★★★★ Above Avg

	1995	1996	1997	1998	1999	2000	2001	2002	2003	2004	2005	2006	History
	10.00	11.23	11.39	10.61	10.28	9.69	9.37	8.97	9.71	9.92	9.53	9.83	NAV
	0.00*	23.99	15.47	0.97	5.54	2.49	4.59	2.56	16.08	9.42	2.77	11.10	Total Return %
	—	20.36	5.82	-7.72	6.36	-9.14	-3.85	-7.69	11.98	5.08	0.34	6.77	+/-LB Aggr
	—	11.57	2.84	0.39	2.26	7.70	-1.19	-0.55	-11.85	-2.54	0.51	-0.83	+/-CSFB Glb HY
	—	10.11	8.80	8.21	8.76	8.57	8.08	6.95	7.51	7.08	6.78	7.78	Income Return %
	—	13.88	6.67	-7.24	-3.22	-6.08	-3.49	-4.39	8.57	2.34	-4.01	3.32	Capital Return %
	—	1	11	46	40	6	40	15	93	59	41	25	Total Rtn % Rank Cat
	0.00	0.97	0.95	0.90	0.89	0.85	0.76	0.63	0.65	0.67	0.65	0.72	Income $
	0.00	0.11	0.56	0.40	0.00	0.00	0.00	0.00	0.00	0.00	0.00	0.00	Capital Gains $
	—	1.00	1.00	0.96	1.00	1.00	0.99	0.96	0.95	0.96	0.87	—	Expense Ratio %
	—	9.00	8.45	7.85	8.48	8.43	8.04	7.02	6.90	6.96	6.65	—	Income Ratio %
	—	324	404	336	310	295	358	161	203	133	102	—	Turnover Rate %
	—	238	357	295	275	301	433	668	666	563	509	532	Net Assets $mil

Rating and Risk

Time Period	Load-Adj Return %	Morningstar Rtn vs Cat	Morningstar Risk vs Cat	Morningstar Risk-Adj Rating
1 Yr	11.10			
3 Yr	7.70	Avg	-Avg	★★★
5 Yr	8.26	Avg	Low	★★★
10 Yr	6.97	+Avg	Low	★★★★
Incept	8.41			

Other Measures	Standard Index LB Aggr	Best Fit Index CSFB Glb HY
Alpha	4.1	-0.6
Beta	0.43	0.95
R-Squared	15	91
Standard Deviation	3.63	
Mean	7.70	
Sharpe Ratio	1.19	

Portfolio Analysis 11-30-06

Total Fixed-Income:243	Date of Maturity	Amount $000	Value $000	% Net Assets
Gmac 8%	11-01-31	7,307	8,190	1.56
Hca 144A 9.25%	11-15-16	7,375	7,698	1.46
Trump Entmt Resorts Hldg	06-01-15	7,683	7,625	1.45
Acco Brands 7.625%	08-15-15	7,704	7,560	1.44
Healthsouth 144A 10.75%	06-15-16	6,171	6,572	1.25
Goodyear Tire & Rubr 9%	07-01-15	5,478	5,601	1.06
General Mtrs 7.125%	07-15-13	5,830	5,407	1.03
Primedia 8.875%	05-15-11	5,298	5,219	0.99
Virgin Riv Casino 9%	01-15-12	5,018	5,194	0.99
Charter Comms Oper 144A	04-30-12	4,948	5,084	0.97
Lyondell Chem 11.125%	07-15-12	4,652	5,036	0.96
Centennial Communctns 10	01-01-13	4,717	4,929	0.94
Visant Hldg 8.75%	12-01-13	4,720	4,844	0.92
Gmac 7.75%	01-19-10	4,598	4,814	0.92
Qwest 8.875%	03-15-12	4,310	4,800	0.91
Mission Engy Hldg 13.5%	07-15-08	4,119	4,572	0.87
Ford Mtr Cr FRN	04-15-12	4,189	4,434	0.84
Cch I 11%	10-01-15	4,256	4,171	0.79
Ford Motor Cr 6.625%	06-16-08	4,150	4,127	0.78
Gmac 6.75%	12-01-14	4,000	4,102	0.78

Current Investment Style

Duration: Short Int Long

¹ figure provided by fund

Avg Eff Duration¹	3.9 Yrs
Avg Eff Maturity	6.7 Yrs
Avg Credit Quality	B
Avg Wtd Coupon	8.37%
Avg Wtd Price	101.18% of par

Coupon Range	% of Bonds	Rel Cat
0% PIK	3.3	0.6
0% to 8%	40.0	0.8
8% to 11%	53.0	1.2
11% to 14%	7.0	1.6
More than 14%	0.0	0.0

1.00=Category Average

Credit Analysis	% bonds 11-30-06		
AAA	0	BB	27
AA	0	B	58
A	0	Below B	12
BBB	2	NR/NA	1

Sector Breakdown	% of assets
US Treasuries	0
TIPS	0
US Agency	0
Mortgage Pass-Throughs	0
Mortgage CMO	0
Mortgage ARM	0
US Corporate	91
Asset-Backed	0
Convertible	0
Municipal	0
Corporate Inflation-Protected	0
Foreign Corporate	2
Foreign Govt	0

Composition			
Cash	6.4	Bonds	89.3
Stocks	0.1	Other	4.1

Special Securities	
Restricted/Illiquid Secs	17
Exotic Mortgage-Backed	0
Emerging-Markets Secs	Trace
Options/Futures/Warrants	No

Janus Mid Cap Val Inv

		Ticker	Load	NAV	Yield	Total Assets	Mstar Category
✓ Analyst Pick		JMCVX	None	$23.81	3.0%	$6,489 mil	Mid-Cap Value

Governance and Management

Stewardship Grade: B

Portfolio Manager(s)

Tom Perkins of Perkins, Wolf, McDonnell & Company has run this fund since its August 1998 inception. He was joined by comanager Jeff Kautz, who had been an analyst at the Chicago-based firm since 1997, in February 2002. In sum, the firm employs four portfolio managers and eight analysts. The firm is 30% owned by Janus, which has the option to buy an additional 14% annually. Bonuses for investment personnel are predicated on firm profitability.

Strategy

The managers hunt for stocks trading at or near their historic lows. In particular, they look for turnaround stories with strong cash flow, little to no debt, and proven management. The portfolio typically contains 120 to 150 stocks, and individual positions are generally capped at about 3% of assets.

Historical Profile

Return	Average
Risk	Average
Rating	★★★ Neutral

Investment Style: Equity, Stock %

Quartile %	79%	91%	93%	84%	88%	90%	84%	89%	93%

Growth of $10,000
— Investment Values of Fund
— Investment Values of S&P 500

▼ Manager Change
▽ Partial Manager Change

Performance Quartile (within Category)

	1995	1996	1997	1998	1999	2000	2001	2002	2003	2004	2005	2006	History
NAV	—	—	—	11.38	12.51	14.39	16.96	14.71	20.39	22.09	22.32	23.81	NAV
Total Return %	—	—	—	14.40*	21.56	27.34	20.52	-13.09	39.33	18.36	10.36	15.25	Total Return %
+/-S&P 500	—	—	—	0.52	36.44	32.41	9.01	10.65	7.48	5.45	-0.54	+/-S&P 500	
+/-Russ MV	—	—	—	21.67	8.16	18.19	-3.45	1.26	-5.35	-2.29	-4.97	+/-Russ MV	
Income Return %	—	—	—	0.39	0.80	0.20	0.18	0.70	0.41	3.94	3.31	Income Return %	
Capital Return %	—	—	—	21.17	26.54	20.32	-13.27	38.63	17.95	6.42	11.94	Capital Return %	
Total Rtn % Rank Cat	—	—	—	13	32	7	59	26	54	35	56	Total Rtn % Rank Cat	
Income $	—	—	—	0.06	0.04	0.10	0.03	0.03	0.10	0.08	0.87	0.74	Income $
Capital Gains $	—	—	—	0.00	1.24	1.36	0.35	0.00	0.00	1.93	1.20	1.19	Capital Gains $
Expense Ratio %	—	—	—	1.68	1.62	1.59	1.22	1.15	1.08	0.94	—	Expense Ratio %	
Income Ratio %	—	—	—	-2.30	0.54	0.72	0.78	0.20	0.45	0.56	—	Income Ratio %	
Turnover Rate %	—	—	—	—	154	129	116	65	97	91	—	Turnover Rate %	
Net Assets $mil	—	—	—	23	25	51	265	948	1,747	3,453	5,382	Net Assets $mil	

NAV values: 39.4, 32.4, 24.0, 17.0, 10.0

Performance 12-31-06

	1st Qtr	2nd Qtr	3rd Qtr	4th Qtr	Total
2002	5.54	-6.98	-17.66	7.51	-13.09
2003	-2.99	17.17	6.52	15.08	39.33
2004	5.30	3.03	-0.90	10.10	18.36
2005	0.23	2.66	4.80	2.34	10.36
2006	5.33	-1.23	2.67	7.90	15.25

Trailing	Total Return%	+/- S&P 500	+/- Russ MV	%Rank Cat	Growth of $10,000
3 Mo	7.90	1.20	-0.60	53	10,790
6 Mo	10.78	-1.96	-1.55	43	11,078
1 Yr	15.25	-0.54	-4.97	56	11,525
3 Yr Avg	14.61	4.17	-4.16	48	15,055
5 Yr Avg	12.76	6.57	-3.12	37	18,230
10 Yr Avg	—	—	—	—	—
15 Yr Avg	—	—	—	—	—

Tax Analysis	Tax-Adj Rtn%	%Rank Cat	Tax-Cost Rat	%Rank Cat
3 Yr (estimated)	12.49	45	1.85	67
5 Yr (estimated)	11.45	33	1.16	57
10 Yr (estimated)	—	—	—	—

Potential Capital Gain Exposure: 15% of assets

Morningstar's Take by Laura Pavlenko Lutton 12-01-06

We remain fans of Janus Mid Cap Value's prudent approach.

A few aspects of this fund's strategy suggest it's one of the gutsier members of the mid-value category. For one, the fund has long walked the line between the value and blend sections of the Morningstar Style Box. This results from management's relative-value approach and affinity for some stocks that traditionally are considered growth fare, such as those in the health-care sector. Such investment traits can lead to returns that are at times out of sync with the mid-value category norms. Indeed, the fund has trailed the Russell MidCap Value Index during periods when growth stocks have performed particularly poorly.

That said, this fund's managers, Tom Perkins and Jeff Kautz, pay considerable attention to asset preservation and downside risk. Low valuation isn't enough to attract these investors. They also require low debt levels, strong cash flows, and proven operations. They're particularly cautious when it comes to regulated, capital-intensive businesses, such as utilities, an area where the fund treads lightly. The fund also owns fewer tech stocks because the team is wary of many of the pricey, volatile companies that populate that sector.

Over time, this approach has worked well. Since the fund's 1998 inception, it has lost money in just one calendar year, and its long-term record versus the mid-value category average is strong amid reasonable volatility.

This fund remains a category favorite, but we're paying closer attention to its ballooning asset base. All told, Perkins and Kautz run more than $7 billion in this style. We've seen management teams successfully handle such sums, and we think the managers' personal investments in the fund will encourage them to call for the offering's closure should its asset base become unwieldy. That said, the fund is in uncharted waters, and we'll be watching for signs that management is in over its head.

Address:	151 Detroit Street Denver CO 80206 800-525-0020
Web Address:	www.janus.com
Inception:	08-12-98*
Advisor:	Janus
Subadvisor:	Perkins, Wolf, McDonnell and Co, LLC
NTF Plans:	Fidelity Retail-NTF, Schwab OneSource

Minimum Purchase:	$2500	Add: $100	IRA: $1000
Min Auto Inv Plan:	$500	Add: $100	
Sales Fees:	No-load		
Management Fee:	0.64%		
Actual Fees:	Mgt:0.64%	Dist: —	
Expense Projections:	3Yr:$296	5Yr:$515	10Yr:$1143
Income Distrib:	Annually		

Rating and Risk

Time Period	Load-Adj Return %	Morningstar Rtn vs Cat	Morningstar Risk vs Cat	Morningstar Risk-Adj Rating
1 Yr	15.25			
3 Yr	14.61	Avg	-Avg	★★★
5 Yr	12.76	Avg	Avg	★★★
10 Yr	—	—	—	—
Incept	17.58			

Other Measures	Standard Index S&P 500	Best Fit Index Mstar Mid Core
Alpha	3.2	2.9
Beta	1.10	0.72
R-Squared	83	94
Standard Deviation	8.26	
Mean	14.61	
Sharpe Ratio	1.31	

Portfolio Analysis 11-30-06

Share change since 10-06 Total Stocks:146	Sector	PE	Tot Ret%	% Assets
⊖ Alliancebernstein Holdin	Financial	20.8	50.15	2.55
Berkshire Hathaway Inc.	Financial	13.2	24.89	1.60
Old Republic Internation	Financial	10.6	13.90	1.45
⊕ Forest Oil Corporation	Energy	16.1	7.07	1.32
Newfield Exploration Com	Energy	12.7	-8.23	1.31
SunTrust Banks, Inc.	Financial	14.1	19.81	1.26
Synovus Financial Corp.	Financial	17.0	17.31	1.21
⊕ Legg Mason	Financial	25.1	-19.99	1.18
⊕ Diebold Incorporated	Hardware	45.0	25.12	1.17
⊕ URS Corporation	Business	18.8	13.93	1.16
⊖ Mercantile Bankshares Co	Financial	20.2	27.85	1.13
⊕ Bank of Hawaii Corporati	Financial	15.6	7.82	1.12
⊕ International Flavors &	Ind Mtrls	23.0	49.66	1.09
⊕ Kinder Morgan Energy Par	Energy	33.7	7.30	1.09
⊖ DPL Incorporated	Utilities	20.6	10.87	1.08
Pitney Bowes Inc.	Ind Mtrls	19.7	12.57	1.07
⊕ Genuine Parts Company	Consumer	17.4	11.39	1.05
⊖ ProLogis Trust	Financial	33.5	34.02	1.05
☼ Southwest Airlines, Co.	Business	23.2	-6.65	0.97
Ball Corporation	Goods	14.3	10.87	0.96

Current Investment Style

Value Blnd Growth — Large/Mid/Small (Mid-Large shaded)

Market Cap	%
Giant	5.4
Large	24.6
Mid	65.1
Small	4.8
Micro	0.0

Avg $mil: 6,962

Value Measures		Rel Category
Price/Earnings	16.87	1.14
Price/Book	2.08	1.03
Price/Sales	1.21	1.25
Price/Cash Flow	9.23	1.22
Dividend Yield %	1.79	0.99

Growth Measures	%	Rel Category
Long-Term Erngs	11.63	1.05
Book Value	11.11	1.59
Sales	10.06	1.31
Cash Flow	7.57	1.91
Historical Erngs	15.68	1.06

Profitability	%	Rel Category
Return on Equity	15.69	1.09
Return on Assets	9.22	1.25
Net Margin	13.78	1.31

Sector Weightings	% of Stocks	Rel S&P 500	3 Year High	Low
↻ Info	9.91	0.50		
Software	1.43	0.41	4	1
Hardware	5.67	0.61	7	4
Media	1.06	0.28	5	1
Telecom	1.75	0.50	4	1
⊆ Service	55.98	1.21		
Health	11.08	0.92	13	10
Consumer	8.16	1.07	13	7
Business	9.89	2.34	12	6
Financial	26.85	1.21	27	21
⊔ Mfg	34.10	1.01		
Goods	4.96	0.58	7	3
Ind Mtrls	14.80	1.24	17	11
Energy	12.45	1.27	18	11
Utilities	1.89	0.54	3	0

Composition

	%
● Cash	7.2
● Stocks	92.9
● Bonds	0.0
○ Other	0.0
Foreign (% of Stock)	1.2

Janus Orion

	Ticker	Load	NAV	Yield	Total Assets	Mstar Category
	JORNX	None	$9.86	0.2%	$3,323 mil	Mid-Cap Growth

Governance and Management

Stewardship Grade: C

Portfolio Manager(s)

Ron Sachs has managed this fund since its 2000 inception. Previously, he served as assistant manager on Janus Enterprise. Before joining Janus in 1996, Sachs was a consultant at Bain & Company. In March 2005, Sachs began running Janus Triton, but he gave up that responsibility in February 2006.

Strategy

This offering will go just about anywhere in its search for promising investments, from small caps to blue chips. The portfolio only holds a few dozen names, making for a fairly aggressive offering. Sachs looks for companies with pricing power that are growing as well as capable of generating high free cash flow. Owning a collection of great businesses is of prime importance.

Historical Profile
Return Above Avg
Risk Average
Rating ★★★★ Above Avg

				96%	77%	86%	95%	93%	87%	85%

Investment Style
Equity
Stock %

▼ Manager Change
▽ Partial Manager Change

Growth of $10,000
— Investment Values of Fund
— Investment Values of S&P 500

Performance Quartile (within Category)

1995	1996	1997	1998	1999	2000	2001	2002	2003	2004	2005	2006	History
—	—	—	—	—	7.01	5.98	4.20	6.04	6.94	8.33	9.86	NAV
—	—	—	—	—	-29.69*	-14.69	-29.77	43.81	14.90	20.93	18.64	Total Return %
—	—	—	—	—	—	-2.80	-7.67	15.13	4.02	16.02	2.85	+/-S&P 500
—	—	—	—	—	—	5.46	-2.36	1.10	-0.58	8.83	7.98	+/-Russ MG
—	—	—	—	—	—	0.00	0.00	0.00	0.00	0.90	0.28	Income Return %
—	—	—	—	—	—	-14.69	-29.77	43.81	14.90	20.03	18.36	Capital Return %
—	—	—	—	—	—	43	70	16	43	3	4	Total Rtn % Rank Cat
—	—	—	—	—	0.02	0.00	0.00	0.00	0.00	0.06	0.02	Income $
—	—	—	—	—	0.00	0.00	0.00	0.00	0.00	0.06	0.00	Capital Gains $
—	—	—	—	—	—	1.12	1.03	1.04	1.08	1.08	—	Expense Ratio %
—	—	—	—	—	—	0.82	-0.06	-0.30	-0.43	-0.05	—	Income Ratio %
—	—	—	—	—	—	35	206	161	72	69	—	Turnover Rate %
—	—	—	—	—	—	879	688	391	541	568	3,323	Net Assets $mil

Performance 12-31-06

	1st Qtr	2nd Qtr	3rd Qtr	4th Qtr	Total
2002	-2.01	-16.21	-16.70	2.69	-29.77
2003	-3.10	23.59	4.17	15.27	43.81
2004	5.13	4.25	-3.70	11.22	14.90
2005	0.14	4.32	11.31	4.00	20.93
2006	11.04	-3.03	0.22	9.93	18.64

Trailing	Total Return%	+/- S&P 500	+/- Russ MG	%Rank Cat	Growth of $10,000
3 Mo	9.93	3.23	2.98	10	10,993
6 Mo	10.17	-2.57	2.27	12	11,017
1 Yr	18.64	2.85	7.98	4	11,864
3 Yr Avg	18.13	7.69	5.40	2	16,485
5 Yr Avg	10.74	4.55	2.52	10	16,654
10 Yr Avg	—	—	—	—	—
15 Yr Avg	—	—	—	—	—

Tax Analysis	Tax-Adj Rtn%	%Rank Cat	Tax-Cost Rat	%Rank Cat
3 Yr (estimated)	18.00	1	0.11	6
5 Yr (estimated)	10.66	7	0.07	6
10 Yr (estimated)	—	—	—	—

Potential Capital Gain Exposure: 1% of assets

Rating and Risk

Time Period	Load-Adj Return %	Morningstar Rtn vs Cat	Morningstar Risk vs Cat	Morningstar Risk-Adj Rating
1 Yr	18.64			
3 Yr	18.13	High	Avg	★★★★★
5 Yr	10.74	+Avg	Avg	★★★★
10 Yr	—			
Incept	-0.02			

Other Measures	Standard Index S&P 500	Best Fit index S&P Mid 400
Alpha	3.7	3.8
Beta	1.51	1.08
R-Squared	74	86
Standard Deviation	12.10	
Mean	18.13	
Sharpe Ratio	1.18	

Morningstar's Take by Karen Dolan 12-14-06

Newcomers to Janus Orion are in good hands.

In November 2006, Janus Olympus merged into this fund. That added a little more than $2 billion to this fund's $1.1 billion asset base. Like Orion, Olympus was a multi-cap growth fund and used the same central research team. Olympus was more willing to own high-priced stocks under longtime manager Clair Young's watch. Orion, on the other hand, is edgy in its own way because it focuses on fewer holdings and has a sizable overseas stake. Despite their prior differences, we think the combination makes sense because both funds have similar uses in the context of a portfolio.

We also like the merger because we think highly of manager Ron Sachs and would rather have him focus his attention on one fund. He adds value here by favoring companies that have solid growth potential that other investors have yet to appreciate. By scooping up such opportunities before their growth is apparent, Sachs is often able to buy shares at a reasonable price.

His attention to valuation has kept the fund out of some stocks such as Internet search giant Google, for example. Sachs likes Google's business, but its valuation has been too high for him all along, so he's not disappointed that he hasn't owned it. Sachs would rather own other stocks that better fit his growth and valuation criteria. For instance, Sachs is very optimistic about top holding Dade Behring. While other investors are worried about the short-term issues surrounding Dade's new medical-device technology aimed at big hospitals, Sachs thinks the firm will experience healthy growth from it in the long run.

Sachs' patience with picks such as Dade has paid off handsomely over time. With the exception of some hiccups during the bear market, the fund has outperformed peers consistently under his watch. The fund's cheap expense ratio further supports its case. All things considered, this is a strong contender.

Address:	151 Detroit Street Denver CO 80206 800-525-0020	Minimum Purchase:	$2500 Add: $100 IRA: $1000
		Min Auto Inv Plan:	$500 Add: $100
		Sales Fees:	No-load
Web Address:	www.janus.com	Management Fee:	0.64%
Inception:	06-30-00*	Actual Fees:	Mgt:0.64% Dist: —
Advisor:	Janus	Expense Projections:	3Yr:$325 5Yr:$563 10Yr:$1245
Subadvisor:	None	Income Distrib:	Annually
NTF Plans:	Fidelity Retail-NTF, Schwab OneSource		

Portfolio Analysis 11-30-06

Share change since 10-06 Total Stocks:70	Sector	PE	Tot Ret%	% Assets
⊕ Dade Behring Holdings, I	Health	26.3	-2.13	6.14
ABB Ltd	Ind Mtrls	—	—	5.09
Celgene Corporation	Health	—	77.56	4.81
CapitalSource, Inc.	Financial	15.7	32.16	4.47
⊕ Campari	Goods	—	—	3.54
Roche Holding	Health			3.43
America Movil SA ADR	Telecom	27.7	55.53	3.29
Apple Computer, Inc.	Hardware	37.6	18.01	3.04
⊕ Yahoo, Inc.	Media	35.4	-34.81	2.93
VistaPrint, Ltd.	Business			2.62
Trimble Navigation Ltd.	Hardware	29.7	42.94	2.59
Nordstrom, Inc.	Consumer	21.9	33.35	2.53
FedEx Corporation	Business	17.2	5.40	2.13
⊕ Crown Castle Internation	Telecom	—	20.94	2.04
Chicago Mercantile Excha	Financial	49.3	39.48	1.98
Potash Corporation of Sa	Ind Mtrls	26.0	80.04	1.95
⊕ Whole Foods Market, Inc.	Consumer	32.8	-37.19	1.93
National Financial Partn	Financial	28.4	-15.12	1.79
⊕ Qualcomm, Inc.	Hardware	26.6	-11.32	1.68
Intuitive Surgical, Inc.	Health	35.2	-18.22	1.42

Current Investment Style

Value Blnd Growth — Large Mid Small

Market Cap	%
Giant	20.2
Large	30.3
Mid	39.0
Small	9.8
Micro	0.6

Avg $mil: 11,046

Value Measures		Rel Category
Price/Earnings	24.80	1.21
Price/Book	4.26	1.33
Price/Sales	2.77	1.57
Price/Cash Flow	16.70	1.46
Dividend Yield %	0.53	0.84

Growth Measures	%	Rel Category
Long-Term Erngs	19.06	1.17
Book Value	7.33	0.58
Sales	12.51	1.25
Cash Flow	19.81	1.07
Historical Erngs	38.32	1.53

Profitability	%	Rel Category
Return on Equity	16.09	0.90
Return on Assets	8.96	0.96
Net Margin	12.51	1.08

Sector Weightings	% of Stocks	Rel S&P 500	3 Year High Low	
↻ Info	23.85	1.19		
📊 Software	1.11	0.32	3	0
💻 Hardware	10.49	1.14	13	1
🎬 Media	3.47	0.92	11	2
📞 Telecom	8.78	2.50	9	0
⊆ Service	60.71	1.31		
🏥 Health	21.25	1.76	27	8
🛒 Consumer	9.41	1.23	15	5
📋 Business	13.40	3.17	16	6
💲 Financial	16.65	0.75	24	16
⚒ Mfg	15.43	0.46		
⚙ Goods	5.18	0.61	25	1
🔧 Ind Mtrls	10.25	0.86	16	4
💡 Energy	0.00	0.00	7	0
💡 Utilities	0.00	0.00	0	0

Composition

		%
● Cash		14.6
● Stocks		84.5
● Bonds		0.0
○ Other		0.9
Foreign		28.4
(% of Stock)		

Janus Overseas

	Ticker	Load	NAV	Yield	Total Assets	Mstar Category
	JAOSX	None	$46.30	1.2%	$5,932 mil	Foreign Large Growth

Governance and Management

Stewardship Grade: B

Portfolio Manager(s)

Brent Lynn was installed as lead manager here following Helen Young Hayes' departure in mid-2003. Before taking sole control, Lynn served as comanager with Hayes beginning in December 2000, having been an analyst with Janus since 1991. Analyst Garth Yettick is an associate portfolio manager on the fund.

Strategy

Manager Brent Lynn scours the world for the fastest-growing companies. He emphasizes experienced management and high returns on capital. The fund often ends up concentrated by region, sector, or both. Price multiples for the portfolio have been on the high side at times, and its stake in emerging markets has far exceeded that of its peers. Janus recently implemented new systems to improve its fair-value pricing methods to deter market-timers.

Performance 12-31-06

	1st Qtr	2nd Qtr	3rd Qtr	4th Qtr	Total
2002	-0.39	-10.48	-18.23	4.40	-23.89
2003	-10.33	18.67	10.69	16.13	36.79
2004	11.23	-10.92	2.34	16.93	18.58
2005	0.41	1.56	18.88	9.20	32.39
2006	19.89	-2.12	6.61	17.67	47.21

Trailing	Total Return%	+/- MSCI EAFE	+/- MSCI Wd xUS	%Rank Cat	Growth of $10,000
3 Mo	17.67	7.32	7.55	1	11,767
6 Mo	25.45	10.76	11.23	1	12,545
1 Yr	47.21	20.87	21.50	1	14,721
3 Yr Avg	32.21	12.28	12.11	1	23,110
5 Yr Avg	19.19	4.21	3.94	1	24,055
10 Yr Avg	14.42	6.71	6.46	2	38,461
15 Yr Avg	—	—	—		

Tax Analysis	Tax-Adj Rtn%	%Rank Cat	Tax-Cost Rat	%Rank Cat
3 Yr (estimated)	31.74	1	0.36	28
5 Yr (estimated)	18.74	1	0.38	36
10 Yr (estimated)	13.66	2	0.66	30

Potential Capital Gain Exposure: 28% of assets

Historical Profile

Return	High	
Risk	High	
Rating	★★★★★ Highest	

90% | 90% | 85% | 83% | 90% | 97% | 97% | 97% | 97%

▽ Manager Change
▽ Partial Manager Change

61.8
45.0
— Growth of $10,000
32.4
24.0 — Investment Values of Fund
17.0 — Investment Values of MSCI EAFE
10.0

Performance Quartile (within Category)

1995	1996	1997	1998	1999	2000	2001	2002	2003	2004	2005	2006	History
12.05	15.22	17.39	20.08	37.20	26.54	20.30	15.29	20.66	24.26	31.83	46.30	NAV
22.05	28.83	18.23	16.03	86.07	-18.57	-23.11	-23.89	36.79	18.58	32.39	47.21	Total Return %
10.84	22.78	16.45	-3.90	59.04	-4.38	-1.69	-7.95	-1.80	-1.67	18.85	20.87	+/-MSCI EAFE
10.64	21.96	15.96	-2.66	58.09	-5.21	-1.72	-8.09	-2.63	-1.80	17.92	21.50	+/-MSCI Wd xUS
1.65	0.35	0.63	0.56	0.00	2.12	0.38	0.80	1.59	1.10	1.15	1.73	Income Return %
20.40	28.48	17.60	15.47	86.07	-20.69	-23.49	-24.69	35.20	17.48	31.24	45.48	Capital Return %
6	7	13	40	10	50	46	83	35	24	1	1	Total Rtn % Rank Cat
0.17	0.04	0.10	0.10	0.00	0.79	0.10	0.16	0.24	0.23	0.28	0.55	Income $
0.05	0.26	0.50	0.00	0.14	3.06	0.00	0.00	0.00	0.00	0.00	0.00	Capital Gains $
1.73	1.23	1.01	0.96	0.91	0.88	0.85	0.89	0.94	0.93	0.89	—	Expense Ratio %
0.36	0.73	0.81	0.58	-0.03	0.22	0.77	0.69	1.21	0.72	0.88	—	Income Ratio %
188	71	72	105	92	62	65	63	104	58	57	—	Turnover Rate %
129	955	3,241	4,329	8,765	8,157	5,278	3,092	2,768	2,331	3,007	6,371	Net Assets $mil

Rating and Risk

Time Period	Load-Adj Return %	Morningstar Rtn vs Cat	Morningstar Risk vs Cat	Morningstar Risk-Adj Rating
1 Yr	47.21			
3 Yr	32.21	High	High	★★★★★
5 Yr	19.19	High	High	★★★★★
10 Yr	14.42	High	High	★★★★
Incept	15.31			

Other Measures	Standard Index MSCI EAFE	Best Fit Index MSCI EmrMkt
Alpha	3.4	8.0
Beta	1.47	0.81
R-Squared	77	80
Standard Deviation	15.92	
Mean	32.21	
Sharpe Ratio	1.66	

Portfolio Analysis 11-30-06

Share change since 10-06 Total Stocks:72	Sector	Country	% Assets
Potash Corporation of Sa	Ind Mtrls	Canada	5.51
Reliance Industries Ltd	Ind Mtrls	India	4.93
Li & Fung Ltd	Goods	Hong Kong	4.88
Companhia Vale Do Rio Do	Ind Mtrls	Brazil	3.91
China Overseas Land & In	Financial	Hong Kong	3.17
Bunge, Ltd.	Goods	United States	2.81
The Tata Iron & Steel	Ind Mtrls	India	2.75
Sony	Goods	Japan	2.51
⊕ Nabors Industries, Ltd.	Energy	United States	2.48
Samsung Electronics	Goods	Korea	2.37
Melco International Deve	Consumer	Hong Kong	2.37
⊕ ARM Hldgs	Hardware	U.K.	2.30
⊕ Publishing & Broadcastin	Media	Australia	2.07
Esprit Hldgs Ltd	Consumer	Hong Kong	2.05
Mitsubishi Securities	Financial	Japan	1.81
Mitsubishi Estate	Financial	Japan	1.74
ASML Holding	Hardware	Netherlands	1.73
IG Grp Hldgs	Financial	U.K.	1.73
Technip	Energy	France	1.70
Logitech Int'l	Hardware	Switzerland	1.58

Current Investment Style

Value Blnd Growth — Large Mid Small

Market Cap	%
Giant	21.1
Large	41.4
Mid	34.8
Small	2.5
Micro	0.2
Avg $mil:	8,837

Value Measures		Rel Category
Price/Earnings	18.83	1.22
Price/Book	2.98	1.14
Price/Sales	1.77	1.26
Price/Cash Flow	12.76	1.32
Dividend Yield %	1.52	0.63

Growth Measures	%	Rel Category
Long-Term Erngs	19.56	1.44
Book Value	16.57	1.51
Sales	11.99	1.38
Cash Flow	4.97	0.41
Historical Erngs	26.18	1.15

Composition

Cash	1.1	Bonds	0.0
Stocks	97.1	Other	1.8
Foreign (% of Stock)			90.9

Sector Weightings

	% of Stocks	Rel MSCI EAFE	3 Year High	Low
↻ Info	13.53	1.14		
🖥 Software	1.12	2.00	5	1
💾 Hardware	8.46	2.19	13	7
📺 Media	2.89	1.58	6	1
☎ Telecom	1.06	0.19	2	0
⊂ Service	34.73	0.74		
🏥 Health	4.10	0.58	5	1
🛒 Consumer	10.05	2.03	12	4
💼 Business	4.05	0.80	6	0
$ Financial	16.53	0.55	28	16
🏭 Mfg	51.74	1.26		
📦 Goods	15.90	1.21	25	12
⚙ Ind Mtrls	26.79	1.74	27	17
🔋 Energy	9.05	1.27	10	3
💡 Utilities	0.00	0.00	1	0

Regional Exposure		% Stock
UK/W. Europe	18	N. America 17
Japan	9	Latn America 15
Asia X Japan	39	Other 2

Country Exposure		% Stock
Hong Kong	15	United States 9
Brazil	14	Japan 9
India	12	

Morningstar's Take by Karen Dolan 11-13-06

Janus Overseas' boldness isn't a deal breaker, but it can make the fund tough to use.

This fund has looked like a cross between a diversified international fund and one that focuses exclusively on emerging markets under manager Brent Lynn's watch. At the end of September 2006, the fund held 41% of assets in emerging-markets stocks, which dwarfs the 10% stake that's typical of its category rivals.

While the fund's large emerging-markets stake adds to its risks, Lynn is comfortable with it because he has selected each holding for its own fundamental strengths and growth prospects. He is willing to consider broad themes driving an entire industry, too. For example, the fund currently owns several Indian and Brazilian firms involved in sugar production. Lynn is convinced that the supply/demand imbalance for sugar will only worsen and therefore boost the prices that sugar cane producers can levy.

Yet, downturns in emerging-markets stocks aren't always driven by poor fundamentals. So, stocks with otherwise healthy financials are vulnerable to broader market moves affecting specific countries or regions. And with most of the fund's emerging-markets positions in Brazil and India, it is particularly exposed to big moves in those two countries. What's more, emerging markets have rallied strongly during the past three years, and higher valuations warrant more caution.

To Lynn's credit, he latched on to emerging markets at precisely the right time and has locked in gains by trimming winners along the way.

To make room for its eclectic picks, Lynn has had to park fewer assets in Europe and Japan, making the fund unfit as a core foreign holding. We're also uneasy because Lynn hasn't been tested by a prolonged downturn in emerging markets. Still, we think Lynn's success thus far owes to a sound approach and good execution. This fund is worthwhile for investors comfortable with the risks it takes.

Address:	151 Detroit Street Denver CO 80206 800-525-0020	Minimum Purchase:	$2500	Add: $100	IRA: $1000
		Min Auto Inv Plan:	$500	Add: $100	
		Sales Fees:	No-load, 2.00%R		
Web Address:	www.janus.com	Management Fee:	0.64%		
Inception:	05-02-94	Actual Fees:	Mgt:0.64%	Dist: —	
Advisor:	Janus	Expense Projections:	3Yr:$287	5Yr:$498	10Yr:$1108
Subadvisor:	None	Income Distrib:	Annually		
NTF Plans:	Fidelity Retail-NTF, Schwab OneSource				

252

Morningstar® Funds 500

Janus Research

	Ticker	Load	NAV	Yield	Total Assets	Mstar Category
	JAMRX	None	$24.95	0.1%	$3,929 mil	Large Growth

Governance and Management

Stewardship Grade: C

Portfolio Manager(s)

Jim Goff, Janus' director of research, is the named portfolio manager here, but he largely serves in an administrative role. The fund's future rests in the hands of its equity analysts, who make decisions within the framework of their sector teams. Janus has made considerable investments in its analyst staff in recent years, improving the fund's chances of working.

Strategy

This fund is now a showcase for Janus' analysts. With the fund staying sector neutral to the Russell 1000 Growth Index, the only way for it to forge ahead will be if the individual analysts consistently make good decisions with the stocks on their coverage lists. With about 120 stocks in the portfolio, it should remain a diversified core-growth option.

Historical Profile

Return Above Avg
Risk Average
Rating ★★★ Neutral

	88%	95%	86%	93%	94%	98%	100%	99%	98%

Investment Style
Equity
Stock %

▼ Manager Change
▽ Partial Manager Change

Growth of $10,000
— Investment Values of Fund
— Investment Values of S&P 500

59.0
43.6
32.4
24.0
17.0
10.0

Performance Quartile (within Category)

1995	1996	1997	1998	1999	2000	2001	2002	2003	2004	2005	2006	History
16.04	16.52	16.50	24.11	43.81	29.67	20.79	14.76	19.50	21.57	22.98	24.95	NAV
33.01	17.67	11.88	58.41	96.23	-22.75	-29.78	-29.00	32.11	10.77	6.82	8.65	Total Return %
-4.57	-5.29	-21.48	29.83	75.19	-13.65	-17.89	-6.90	3.43	-0.11	1.91	-7.14	+/-S&P 500
-4.17	-5.45	-18.61	19.70	63.07	-0.33	-9.36	-1.12	2.36	4.47	1.56	-0.42	+/-Russ 1000Gr
12.91	0.47	0.25	0.00	0.00	3.80	0.15	0.00	0.00	0.15	0.29	0.08	Income Return %
20.10	17.20	11.63	58.41	96.23	-26.55	-29.93	-29.00	32.11	10.62	6.53	8.57	Capital Return %
42	64	96	4	8	85	87	65	24	26	45	34	Total Rtn % Rank Cat
1.76	0.08	0.04	0.00	0.00	1.66	0.04	0.00	0.00	0.03	0.06	0.02	Income $
0.30	2.28	1.90	2.01	3.27	2.78	0.00	0.00	0.00	0.00	0.00	0.00	Capital Gains $
1.12	1.00	0.96	0.97	0.91	0.88	0.88	0.92	0.95	0.97	0.92	—	Expense Ratio %
0.50	0.45	0.21	-0.33	-0.39	0.08	0.16	-0.07	-0.31	-0.26	0.42	—	Income Ratio %
201	177	157	105	89	71	83	97	54	43	38	—	Turnover Rate %
1,596	2,061	1,911	3,112	13,543	13,345	8,438	4,879	5,366	4,694	4,590	3,888	Net Assets $mil

Performance 12-31-06

	1st Qtr	2nd Qtr	3rd Qtr	4th Qtr	Total
2002	-5.34	-18.80	-12.39	5.43	-29.00
2003	-1.08	15.55	1.84	13.50	32.11
2004	2.56	0.45	-4.58	12.68	10.77
2005	-3.85	1.21	6.00	3.56	6.82
2006	3.83	-5.57	4.39	6.16	8.65

Trailing	Total Return%	+/- S&P 500	+/- Russ 1000Gr	%Rank Cat	Growth of $10,000
3 Mo	6.16	-0.54	0.23	31	10,616
6 Mo	10.82	-1.92	0.72	15	11,082
1 Yr	8.65	-7.14	-0.42	34	10,865
3 Yr Avg	8.74	-1.70	1.87	26	12,858
5 Yr Avg	3.82	-2.37	1.13	32	12,062
10 Yr Avg	8.57	0.15	3.13	12	22,756
15 Yr Avg	—	—	—		—

Tax Analysis	Tax-Adj Rtn%	%Rank Cat	Tax-Cost Rat	%Rank Cat
3 Yr (estimated)	8.68	20	0.06	4
5 Yr (estimated)	3.78	27	0.04	5
10 Yr (estimated)	7.30	13	1.17	56

Potential Capital Gain Exposure: -117% of assets

Rating and Risk

Time Period	Load-Adj Return %	Morningstar Rtn vs Cat	Morningstar Risk vs Cat	Morningstar Risk-Adj Rating
1 Yr	8.65			
3 Yr	8.74	+Avg	Avg	★★★★
5 Yr	3.82	Avg	Avg	★★★
10 Yr	8.57	+Avg	+Avg	★★★
Incept	12.41			

Other Measures	Standard Index S&P 500	Best Fit Index Russ MG
Alpha	-3.2	-1.9
Beta	1.26	0.79
R-Squared	82	88
Standard Deviation	9.62	
Mean	8.74	
Sharpe Ratio	0.59	

Morningstar's Take by Andrew Gogerty 11-09-06

Janus Mercury's upcoming name change aside, we need to see more here before giving the fund a heartier recommendation.

At the end of December 2006, this fund will be renamed Janus Research. (At the same time, the offering now known as Janus Research will be renamed Global Research and look to keep a minimum 40% stake in foreign stocks).

This change makes sense because the fund was handed over to the firm's equity analyst staff in February 2006 after its former manager, David Corkins, stepped down to manage the firm's flagship Janus Fund. Janus' analyst staff is divided into eight broad teams, and sector and industry analysts must typically convince their team members on their picks before they are included in the portfolio. The goal is to outperform the Russell 1000 Growth Index through stock selection, as the fund will remain sector neutral to this benchmark. Jim Goff, the firm's director of research, oversees the analysts but takes a hands-off approach with

regard to stock decisions and is primarily responsible for monitoring fund trading and the quarterly sector rebalancing to the index.

To their credit, the analyst staff hit the ground running with the current Research (soon to be Global Research), posting strong returns at the firm's first analyst-driven fund since February 2005. In addition, Janus has bulked up its analyst staff in recent years and refined its research approach to provide more in-depth analysis than in the past. In addition, the fund's diversification will help mitigate miscues here--only a handful of stocks consume more than 2% of assets.

But, we remain cautious. There is a clear difference between producing quality equity analysis and translating that effort to effective portfolio construction. Until we see convincing evidence that the analyst staff as a whole can make this transition in their own subportfolios, we're inclined to stick with our favorites among the firm's manager-driven funds.

Portfolio Analysis 11-30-06

Share change since 10-06 Total Stocks:110	Sector	PE	Tot Ret%	% Assets
General Electric Company	Ind Mtrls	20.0	9.35	2.29
Apple Computer, Inc.	Hardware	37.6	18.01	1.75
NVR, Inc.	Consumer	6.2	-8.12	1.74
⊕ Owens-Illinois, Inc.	Ind Mtrls	—	-12.31	1.60
Qualcomm, Inc.	Hardware	26.6	-11.32	1.42
Precision Castparts Corp	Ind Mtrls	25.4	51.40	1.41
EMC Corporation	Hardware	32.7	-3.08	1.40
Sysco Corporation	Consumer	25.2	20.96	1.38
⊕ Coventry Health Care, In	Health	15.4	-12.13	1.32
Corning Inc.	Hardware	25.5	-4.83	1.31
Companhia Vale Do Rio Do	Ind Mtrls	13.6	47.78	1.31
Boeing Company	Ind Mtrls	41.2	28.38	1.30
Electronic Arts, Inc.	Software	91.2	-3.73	1.30
Cypress Semiconductor Co	Hardware	—	18.39	1.28
⊖ Roche Holding	Health			1.26
Tyco International, Ltd.	Ind Mtrls	15.7	6.83	1.24
Texas Instruments, Inc.	Hardware	16.9	-9.82	1.22
⊕ CapitaLand Ltd	Financial			1.22
Altria Group, Inc.	Goods	16.3	19.87	1.22
United Parcel Service, I	Business	19.7	1.76	1.21

Current Investment Style

Value Blnd Growth — Large/Mid/Small

Market Cap	%
Giant	27.8
Large	32.1
Mid	34.7
Small	5.5
Micro	0.0
Avg $mil:	16,068

Value Measures		Rel Category
Price/Earnings	18.87	0.98
Price/Book	3.09	0.93
Price/Sales	1.47	0.76
Price/Cash Flow	10.33	0.91
Dividend Yield %	1.12	1.09

Growth Measures	%	Rel Category
Long-Term Erngs	13.52	0.94
Book Value	12.38	1.07
Sales	12.83	1.11
Cash Flow	14.51	0.86
Historical Erngs	18.91	0.82

Profitability	%	Rel Category
Return on Equity	18.49	0.91
Return on Assets	9.67	0.88
Net Margin	11.90	0.84

Sector Weightings	% of Stocks	Rel S&P 500	3 Year High	Low
↻ Info	22.34	1.12		
Software	5.07	1.47	9	4
Hardware	12.76	1.38	13	9
Media	3.29	0.87	21	3
Telecom	1.22	0.35	1	0
⊈ Service	46.93	1.02		
Health	16.01	1.33	21	13
Consumer	14.95	1.95	16	6
Business	7.17	1.70	11	4
Financial	8.80	0.40	18	7
Mfg	30.73	0.91		
Goods	12.68	1.48	14	6
Ind Mtrls	13.68	1.15	14	7
Energy	3.43	0.35	8	1
Utilities	0.94	0.27	2	0

Composition

	%
● Cash	0.9
● Stocks	97.5
● Bonds	0.0
● Other	1.5
Foreign	21.4
(% of Stock)	

Address:	151 Detroit Street Denver CO 80206 800-525-0020
Web Address:	www.janus.com
Inception:	05-03-93
Advisor:	Janus Capital Management LLC
Subadvisor:	None
NTF Plans:	Fidelity Retail-NTF, Schwab OneSource

Minimum Purchase:	$2500	Add: $100	IRA: $1000
Min Auto Inv Plan:	$500	Add: $100	
Sales Fees:	No-load		
Management Fee:	0.64%		
Actual Fees:	Mgt:0.64%	Dist: —	
Expense Projections:	3Yr:$296	5Yr:$515	10Yr:$1143
Income Distrib:	Annually		

 Morningstar Funds 500

253

Janus Sm Cap Val Instl

	Ticker	Load	NAV	Yield	Total Assets	Mstar Category
	JSIVX	Closed	$26.16	4.9%	$2,015 mil	Small Value

Portfolio Manager(s)

After more than a decade of running funds for an insurance company, manager Bob Perkins cofounded his own investment company in 1980 and started this fund in 1985. His son Todd serves on the team as comanager. Their firm is 30% owned by Janus, which has the option to buy an additional 14% annually. Bonuses for investment personnel are predicated on firm profitability.

Strategy

Managers Bob and Todd Perkins favor stocks that trade at or near their historic lows. They insist that picks sport traits such as strong cash flow and debt-free balance sheets. The Perkins think that such a profile suggests that company management can turn things around within four to six quarters. They have a soft spot for high dividend yields, but they also build positions in fallen growth stocks. The portfolio typically contains 65 to 70 stocks, and individual positions are generally capped at about 3.5% of assets, although the portfolio has lately been more diverse.

Performance 12-31-06

	1st Qtr	2nd Qtr	3rd Qtr	4th Qtr	Total
2002	7.03	-5.48	-22.47	7.94	-15.33
2003	-4.69	16.97	7.16	14.83	37.18
2004	4.63	1.54	-0.67	7.83	13.80
2005	-0.23	3.18	4.50	1.46	9.14
2006	6.37	-4.47	2.96	7.60	12.57

Trailing	Total Return%	+/- S&P 500	+/- Russ 2000 VL	%Rank Cat	Growth of $10,000
3 Mo	7.60	0.90	-1.43	69	10,760
6 Mo	10.79	-1.95	-1.02	24	11,079
1 Yr	12.57	-3.22	-10.91	79	11,257
3 Yr Avg	11.82	1.38	-4.66	82	13,982
5 Yr Avg	10.18	3.99	-5.19	94	16,237
10 Yr Avg	14.47	6.05	1.20	12	38,629
15 Yr Avg	15.85	5.21	0.65	12	90,874

Tax Analysis	Tax-Adj Rtn%	%Rank Cat	Tax-Cost Rat	%Rank Cat
3 Yr (estimated)	8.53	86	2.94	90
5 Yr (estimated)	7.98	94	2.00	82
10 Yr (estimated)	12.07	23	2.10	90

Potential Capital Gain Exposure: 14% of assets

Historical Profile

Return	Average
Risk	Below Avg
Rating	★★★ Neutral

84% 91% 93% 89% 88% 88% 82% 85% 92%

59.0
43.6
32.4
24.0
17.0
10.0

Growth of $10,000
■ Investment Values of Fund
— Investment Values of S&P 500

▼ Manager Change
▽ Partial Manager Change

Performance Quartile (within Category)

1995	1996	1997	1998	1999	2000	2001	2002	2003	2004	2005	2006	History
14.57	16.48	19.94	19.32	21.67	25.47	28.15	22.81	31.09	29.98	27.95	26.16	NAV
26.09	25.60	33.06	1.83	14.69	27.16	20.42	-15.33	37.18	13.80	9.14	12.57	Total Return %
-11.49	2.64	-0.30	-26.75	-6.35	36.26	32.31	6.77	8.50	2.92	4.23	-3.22	+/-S&P 500
0.34	4.23	1.28	8.28	16.18	4.33	6.40	-3.90	-8.85	-8.45	4.43	-10.91	+/-Russ 2000 VL
0.71	0.72	1.54	0.74	1.25	1.78	0.96	0.23	0.86	1.25	3.50	5.29	Income Return %
25.38	24.88	31.52	1.09	13.44	25.38	19.46	-15.56	36.32	12.55	5.64	7.28	Capital Return %
32	32	24	14	21	18	25	82	72	95	17	79	Total Rtn % Rank Cat
0.09	0.11	0.23	0.14	0.24	0.39	0.24	0.07	0.20	0.39	1.05	1.48	Income $
1.41	1.72	1.73	0.81	0.23	1.60	2.25	0.96	0.00	4.96	3.76	3.86	Capital Gains $
1.64	1.48	1.33	1.19	1.01	0.88	0.84	0.82	0.82	0.81	0.79	—	Expense Ratio %
0.64	0.69	0.63	1.26	1.69	1.99	1.26	0.53	0.91	1.12	1.05	—	Income Ratio %
90	69	81	69	66	72	47	39	60	50	44	—	Turnover Rate %
32	36	61	144	525	1,003	1,517	1,282	1,559	1,454	1,200	876	Net Assets $mil

Rating and Risk

Time Period	Load-Adj Return %	Morningstar Rtn vs Cat	Morningstar Risk vs Cat	Morningstar Risk-Adj Rating
1 Yr	12.57			
3 Yr	11.82	-Avg	Low	★★
5 Yr	10.18	-Avg	-Avg	★★
10 Yr	14.47	+Avg	Avg	★★★★
Incept	13.87			

Other Measures	Standard Index S&P 500	Best Fit Index Mstar Small Value
Alpha	0.3	-0.9
Beta	1.16	0.74
R-Squared	73	91
Standard Deviation	9.32	
Mean	11.82	
Sharpe Ratio	0.90	

Portfolio Analysis 11-30-06

Share change since 10-06 Total Stocks:102	Sector	PE	Tot Ret%	% Assets
Old Republic Internation	Financial	10.6	13.90	2.52
Lubrizol Corporation	Ind Mtrls	16.6	18.17	2.47
⊕ UAP Holding Corporation	Ind Mtrls	24.9	27.68	2.42
Casey's General Stores,	Consumer	20.9	-4.26	2.35
Waddell & Reed Financial	Financial	62.4	34.04	2.29
⊖ Laidlaw International, I	Ind Mtrls	22.9	34.04	2.17
Kansas City Southern, In	Business	16.3	18.63	2.15
⊖ Wolverine World Wide	Goods	19.8	28.51	1.88
Forest Oil Corporation	Energy	16.1	7.07	1.77
⊖ Ferro Corporation	Ind Mtrls	56.0	13.73	1.76
F.N.B. Corporation	Financial	19.4	11.30	1.69
⊖ Perrigo Company	Health	22.5	17.27	1.67
St. Mary Land & Explorat	Energy	11.5	0.33	1.59
⊖ Kaydon Corporation	Ind Mtrls	19.1	25.23	1.59
⊖ MacDermid Incorporated	Ind Mtrls	20.4	23.18	1.54
⊕ Albany International Cor	Ind Mtrls	15.1	-8.01	1.47
Inergy LP	Energy	65.2	24.43	1.47
First Financial Bancorp	Financial	27.5	-1.38	1.44
Steris Corporation	Health	27.6	1.31	1.42
First Charter Corporatio	Financial	27.9	6.51	1.38

Current Investment Style

Value Blnd Growth — Large Mid Small

Market Cap	%
Giant	0.0
Large	0.0
Mid	28.0
Small	61.3
Micro	10.8

Avg $mil: 1,264

Value Measures		Rel Category
Price/Earnings	18.80	1.22
Price/Book	1.63	0.92
Price/Sales	0.99	1.24
Price/Cash Flow	7.62	1.25
Dividend Yield %	1.59	1.01

Growth Measures	%	Rel Category
Long-Term Erngs	11.37	0.91
Book Value	7.96	1.47
Sales	-10.80	NMF
Cash Flow	6.23	0.76
Historical Erngs	8.95	0.79

Profitability	%	Rel Category
Return on Equity	10.22	0.95
Return on Assets	6.01	0.99
Net Margin	9.35	1.03

Sector Weightings	% of Stocks	Rel S&P 500	3 Year High	Low
ⓘ Info	12.30	0.62		
Software	2.13	0.62	5	2
Hardware	6.33	0.69	6	3
Media	3.84	1.01	4	0
Telecom	0.00	0.00	1	0
Service	47.08	1.02		
Health	6.88	0.57	15	7
Consumer	6.23	0.81	10	6
Business	9.93	2.35	10	4
Financial	24.04	1.08	33	22
Mfg	40.63	1.20		
Goods	4.31	0.50	10	2
Ind Mtrls	23.94	2.01	26	14
Energy	12.15	1.24	18	9
Utilities	0.23	0.07	4	0

Composition

● Cash		7.9
● Stocks		92.1
● Bonds		0.0
● Other		0.0
Foreign		1.3
(% of Stock)		

Morningstar's Take by Reginald Laing 12-21-06

Janus Small Cap Value has been out of step with its peer group. That could be a good thing if small-value stocks cool off.

Management here hasn't lost its touch. True, this fund (which is closed to new investors) has looked lackluster of late: For the trailing three years through Dec. 20, 2006, its 12.3% annualized return--while respectable in absolute terms--lagged those of 80% of its peers in Morningstar's small-value category. But managers Bob and Todd Perkins' conservatism explains much of that underperformance.

During a good portion of the recent small-value rally, management kept more than 10% of the portfolio in cash. (It was as high as18.2% in October 2005.) The team also has kept the portfolio's exposure to hot-performing industries limited. For instance, the managers have deemed most REITs too richly valued relative to the amount of cash they generate. Although long a portfolio favorite, REITs now account for roughly 2% of

assets (versus 9.7% for the Russell 2000 Value Index, a common small-value benchmark). That has hurt, as REITs have continued to run up in value, buoyed by the attractive rental income that gets passed on to REIT shareholders.

Lately, management has found opportunities among beaten-down tech companies, such as network switch maker Foundry Networks and business software company Hyperion Solutions, when they sold off sharply in early 2006. As Foundry's share value has come back, the Perkinses have trimmed the position, which is typical of their circumspect approach.

That strict valuation discipline--buying stocks as they get cheaper, trimming when they approach a target price--should preserve capital when small-value stocks finally stumble. Moreover, the Perkinses have proved their mettle as stock-pickers, over many years and in a variety of markets. That's why investors selling this fund are making a mistake.

Address:	151 Detroit Street Denver CO 80206 800-525-3713	Minimum Purchase:	Closed	Add: —	IRA: —
Web Address:	www.janus.com	Min Auto Inv Plan:	Closed	Add: —
Inception:	02-14-85	Sales Fees:	No-load
Advisor:	Janus	Management Fee:	0.72%
Subadvisor:	Perkins, Wolf, McDonnell and Co, LLC	Actual Fees:	Mgt:0.72%	Dist: —
		Expense Projections:	3Yr:$306	5Yr:$531	10Yr:$1178
NTF Plans:	Federated Tr NTF	Income Distrib:	Annually

Janus Twenty

	Ticker	Load	NAV	Yield	Total Assets	Mstar Category
	JAVLX	Closed	$54.62	0.6%	$9,870 mil	Large Growth

Governance and Management

Stewardship Grade: C

Portfolio Manager(s)

Before assuming control of this fund in mid-1997, Scott Schoelzel managed Janus Olympus and Dreyfus Founders Growth. He runs Janus Adviser Forty--a large-growth fund run in a similar but slightly less concentrated fashion.

Strategy

Manager Scott Schoelzel has typically sought fast-growing firms that dominate their industries. During the bear market, however, the fund focused less on aggressive-growth firms and now boasts a more diversified portfolio, including both financial-services and energy stocks at times. That characteristic, to some extent, has continued even as the markets have performed better, but aggressive names have also become top positions. As the name of the fund indicates, it is typically concentrated in 25 to 35 stocks, and Schoelzel isn't afraid to make large individual stock bets. He is also willing to hold a substantial cash position.

Historical Profile
Return: High
Risk: Above Avg
Rating: ★★★★ Highest

	79%	89%	99%	78%	77%	95%	96%	92%	100%

Investment Style
Equity
Stock %

Growth of $10,000
— Investment Values of Fund
— Investment Values of S&P 500

63.2 / 46.4 / 33.8 / 24.0 / 17.0 / 10.0

▼ Manager Change
▽ Partial Manager Change

Performance Quartile (within Category)

1995	1996	1997	1998	1999	2000	2001	2002	2003	2004	2005	2006	History
25.67	27.47	30.99	53.30	83.43	54.80	38.46	29.01	36.17	44.80	48.92	54.62	NAV
36.22	27.85	29.70	73.39	64.90	-32.42	-29.20	-24.02	25.31	23.89	9.42	12.30	Total Return %
-1.36	4.89	-3.66	44.81	43.86	-23.32	-17.31	-1.92	-3.37	13.01	4.51	-3.49	+/-S&P 500
-0.96	4.73	-0.79	34.68	31.74	-10.00	-8.78	3.86	-4.44	17.59	4.16	3.23	+/-Russ 1000Gr
10.04	0.71	0.36	0.45	0.35	0.00	0.61	0.56	0.60	0.03	0.22	0.66	Income Return %
26.18	27.14	29.34	72.94	64.55	-32.42	-29.81	-24.58	24.71	23.86	9.20	11.64	Capital Return %
26	7	33	1	10	97	86	31	67	1	24	13	Total Rtn % Rank Cat
2.28	0.18	0.10	0.14	0.19	0.00	0.34	0.21	0.17	0.01	0.10	0.32	Income $
2.99	5.32	4.46	0.30	4.08	1.75	0.00	0.00	0.00	0.00	0.00	0.00	Capital Gains $
0.99	0.92	0.91	0.91	0.87	0.85	0.84	0.83	0.88	0.89	0.86	—	Expense Ratio %
0.62	0.67	0.33	0.39	0.40	-0.13	0.63	0.56	0.52	0.06	0.21	—	Income Ratio %
147	137	123	54	40	27	50	53	44	14	44	—	Turnover Rate %
3,057	4,071	6,004	15,797	36,909	24,253	15,082	9,476	9,886	10,082	9,755	9,789	Net Assets $mil

Performance 12-31-06

	1st Qtr	2nd Qtr	3rd Qtr	4th Qtr	Total
2002	-5.72	-11.58	-11.67	3.18	-24.02
2003	-0.52	12.86	1.20	10.29	25.31
2004	5.53	3.62	0.33	12.93	23.89
2005	-7.19	6.42	9.29	1.36	9.42
2006	2.98	-2.06	1.60	9.59	12.30

Trailing	Total Return%	+/- S&P 500	+/- Russ 1000Gr	%Rank Cat	Growth of $10,000
3 Mo	9.59	2.89	3.66	4	10,959
6 Mo	11.34	-1.40	1.24	11	11,134
1 Yr	12.30	-3.49	3.23	13	11,230
3 Yr Avg	15.04	4.60	8.17	1	15,225
5 Yr Avg	7.71	1.52	5.02	6	14,497
10 Yr Avg	9.91	1.49	4.47	6	25,726
15 Yr Avg	10.39	-0.25	2.37	17	44,050

Tax Analysis	Tax-Adj Rtn%	%Rank Cat	Tax-Cost Rat	%Rank Cat
3 Yr (estimated)	14.93	1	0.10	7
5 Yr (estimated)	7.55	5	0.15	16
10 Yr (estimated)	9.16	5	0.68	29

Potential Capital Gain Exposure: 11% of assets

Rating and Risk

Time Period	Load-Adj Return %	Morningstar Rtn vs Cat	Morningstar Risk vs Cat	Morningstar Risk-Adj Rating
1 Yr	12.30			
3 Yr	15.04	High	+Avg	★★★★★
5 Yr	7.71	High	Avg	★★★★★
10 Yr	9.91	High	+Avg	★★★★
Incept	13.39			

Other Measures	Standard Index S&P 500	Best Fit Index DJ Wilshire 4500
Alpha	2.5	2.3
Beta	1.28	0.81
R-Squared	63	66
Standard Deviation	11.02	
Mean	15.04	
Sharpe Ratio	1.04	

Morningstar's Take by Karen Dolan 11-06-06

Boldness is Janus Twenty's friend and foe.

Manager Scott Schoelzel takes an all-or-nothing approach to investing. He only wants to hear Janus analysts' most passionate ideas, he challenges the thesis on every stock, and he does a lot of digging on his own. That level of diligence gives him the confidence he needs to make big bets here.

Schoelzel's boldness is apparent in a number of ways. His favorite picks tend to soak up considerable assets and often crowd in certain sectors. The fund's top holding as of Sept. 30, 2006, ConocoPhillips, took up 6.0% of assets; past holdings have consumed up to 15% of the fund's portfolio. Likewise, few stocks take small billing: Only four of the fund's 37 September holdings amounted to less than a 1% position, and those stocks were moving in or out of the portfolio.

The fund's bets vary in nature. Sometimes Schoelzel gravitates toward an entire industry; other times he focuses on specific firms. The fund has been moving away from energy--where it has

had a huge stake since early 2005--and toward other corners, such as agriculture. He says that firms such as Potash Corporation of Saskatchewan will benefit from supply-and-demand imbalances for fertilizer ingredients, and they're relatively early in that cycle.

Such boldness has drawbacks, and they can be major. The fund's focused nature and unique positioning can take investors for a ride, both on the upside and downside. In the early 2000s, it got hammered when tech and telecom stocks dove. It lost 66.7% of its value from the peak of the bull market in April 2000 to the bottom of the bear market in October 2002. We don't think the fund will repeat that because of its broadened research effort and newfound attention to risk, but it is still more susceptible to bumps than most rivals. Even so, investors willing to stomach its volatility can be well served by this fund's conviction. Its seasoned manager, improved infrastructure, and low expenses make it worth holding on to.

Address:	151 Detroit Street Denver CO 80206 800-525-0020
Web Address:	www.janus.com
Inception:	04-30-85
Advisor:	Janus
Subadvisor:	None
NTF Plans:	Fidelity Retail-NTF, Schwab OneSource

Minimum Purchase:	Closed	Add: —	IRA: —
Min Auto Inv Plan:	Closed	Add: —	
Sales Fees:	No-load		
Management Fee:	0.64%		
Actual Fees:	Mgt:0.64%	Dist: —	
Expense Projections:	3Yr:$274	5Yr:$477	10Yr:$1061
Income Distrib:	Annually		

Portfolio Analysis 11-30-06

Share change since 10-06 Total Stocks:37	Sector	PE	Tot Ret%	% Assets
Celgene Corporation	Health	—	77.56	5.41
Roche Holding	Health	—	—	4.99
⊖ ConocoPhillips	Energy	6.5	26.53	4.89
Google, Inc.	Business	61.5	11.00	4.82
Wells Fargo Company	Financial	14.7	16.82	4.54
⊕ Potash Corporation of Sa	Ind Mtrls	26.0	80.04	4.07
Harrah's Entertainment,	Consumer	43.4	18.55	4.07
Goldman Sachs Group, Inc	Financial	12.4	57.41	3.97
Research in Motion, Ltd.	Hardware	72.5	93.58	3.88
Gilead Sciences, Inc.	Health	40.6	23.51	3.81
Electronic Arts, Inc.	Software	91.2	-3.73	3.70
Syngenta	Ind Mtrls	—	—	3.68
Procter & Gamble Company	Goods	23.9	13.36	3.62
⊕ Apple Computer, Inc.	Hardware	37.6	18.01	3.62
Genentech, Inc.	Health	48.7	-12.29	3.07
Occidental Petroleum Cor	Energy	8.0	24.32	3.03
⊕ Merrill Lynch & Company,	Financial	14.2	39.28	2.85
Alcon, Inc.	Health	38.3	-12.60	2.53
⊕ Lehman Brothers Holdings	Financial	12.2	22.75	2.53
⊖ Apache Corporation	Energy	7.8	-2.30	2.42

Current Investment Style

Value Blnd Growth — Large Mid Small

Market Cap	%
Giant	44.5
Large	50.9
Mid	4.6
Small	0.0
Micro	0.0

Avg $mil: 39,582

Value Measures		Rel Category
Price/Earnings	17.48	0.91
Price/Book	3.12	0.94
Price/Sales	1.82	0.94
Price/Cash Flow	11.84	1.04
Dividend Yield %	1.08	1.05

Growth Measures	%	Rel Category
Long-Term Erngs	11.97	0.83
Book Value	15.15	1.31
Sales	14.96	1.29
Cash Flow	19.08	1.14
Historical Erngs	32.21	1.40

Profitability	%	Rel Category
Return on Equity	18.27	0.90
Return on Assets	11.26	1.02
Net Margin	15.32	1.08

Sector Weightings	% of Stocks	Rel S&P 500	3 Year High	Low
⟳ Info	12.64	0.63		
Software	3.71	1.08	10	3
Hardware	8.93	0.97	9	4
Media	0.00	0.00	4	0
Telecom	0.00	0.00	3	0
⟳ Service	47.74	1.03		
Health	21.50	1.78	32	21
Consumer	5.59	0.73	25	6
Business	4.83	1.14	5	0
Financial	15.82	0.71	21	8
⟳ Mfg	39.62	1.17		
Goods	6.64	0.78	10	6
Ind Mtrls	17.32	1.45	17	0
Energy	15.66	1.60	32	0
Utilities	0.00	0.00	1	0

Composition

● Cash		0.3
● Stocks		99.7
● Bonds		0.0
● Other		0.0
Foreign (% of Stock)		21.7

Janus Venture

	Ticker	Load	NAV	Yield	Total Assets	Mstar Category
	JAVTX	Closed	$62.45	0.0%	$1,471 mil	Small Growth

Governance and Management

Stewardship Grade: C

Portfolio Manager(s)

Will Bales has been on board since 1997. Former comanager Jonathan Coleman stepped down in late 2000 to head other Janus funds. A team of five dedicated small-cap analysts within Janus' 40-plus analyst staff assists Bales on this offering.

Strategy

Manager Will Bales follows the typical Janus approach. He looks for well-managed, fast-growing companies with improving returns on invested capital. This once led to a very aggressive portfolio stuffed full of high P/E stocks, but now consistency in earnings and valuation is more important.

Historical Profile
Return	Above Avg
Risk	Above Avg
Rating	★★★★ Above Avg

Investment Style bands: 76% 94% 93% 94% 98% 98% 99% 99% 99%

Investment Style
Equity
Stock %

▼ Manager Change
▽ Partial Manager Change

Growth of $10,000
— Investment Values of Fund
— Investment Values of S&P 500

Scale: 50.6 / 43.6 / 32.4 / 24.0 / 17.0 / 10.0

Performance Quartile (within Category)

1995	1996	1997	1998	1999	2000	2001	2002	2003	2004	2005	2006	History
54.10	53.06	50.05	57.14	121.67	49.94	43.98	32.00	49.84	58.59	56.58	62.45	NAV
26.46	8.02	12.61	23.22	140.71	-45.77	-11.93	-27.24	55.75	17.56	1.55	23.58	Total Return %
-11.12	-14.94	-20.75	-5.36	119.67	-36.67	-0.04	-5.14	27.07	6.68	-3.36	7.79	+/-S&P 500
-4.58	-3.24	-0.34	21.99	97.62	-23.34	-2.70	3.02	7.21	3.25	-2.60	10.23	+/-Russ 2000 Gr
7.41	0.00	0.14	0.01	0.00	0.00	0.00	0.00	0.00	0.00	0.00	0.00	Income Return %
19.05	8.02	12.47	23.21	140.71	-45.77	-11.93	-27.24	55.75	17.56	1.55	23.58	Capital Return %
68	86	70	6	7	99	56	49	16	19	84	2	Total Rtn % Rank Cat
3.61	0.00	0.07	0.00	0.00	0.00	0.00	0.00	0.00	0.00	0.00	0.00	Income $
3.85	5.28	9.29	4.41	14.26	16.38	0.00	0.00	0.00	0.00	2.93	7.49	Capital Gains $
0.91	0.88	0.92	0.94	0.92	0.86	0.86	0.87	0.93	0.90	0.87	—	Expense Ratio %
0.29	-0.33	0.11	-0.29	-0.55	-0.35	-0.36	-0.73	-0.67	-0.74	-0.64	—	Income Ratio %
113	136	146	90	104	87	70	90	75	61	63	—	Turnover Rate %
1,790	1,705	1,234	1,246	2,876	1,487	1,175	743	1,408	1,477	1,319	1,466	Net Assets $mil

Performance 12-31-06

	1st Qtr	2nd Qtr	3rd Qtr	4th Qtr	Total
2002	-1.43	-11.03	-20.79	4.75	-27.24
2003	-4.44	26.81	11.22	15.56	55.75
2004	3.51	1.71	-6.33	19.21	17.56
2005	-5.44	3.72	3.20	0.34	1.55
2006	16.30	-8.12	0.68	14.87	23.58

Trailing	Total Return%	+/- S&P 500	+/- Russ 2000 Gr	%Rank Cat	Growth of $10,000
3 Mo	14.87	8.17	6.10	1	11,487
6 Mo	15.65	2.91	8.79	1	11,565
1 Yr	23.58	7.79	10.23	2	12,358
3 Yr Avg	13.84	3.40	3.33	12	14,753
5 Yr Avg	10.83	4.64	3.90	12	16,722
10 Yr Avg	10.31	1.89	5.43	30	26,678
15 Yr Avg	10.55	-0.09	3.45	34	45,017

Tax Analysis	Tax-Adj Rtn%	%Rank Cat	Tax-Cost Rat	%Rank Cat
3 Yr (estimated)	12.95	9	0.78	30
5 Yr (estimated)	10.31	9	0.47	26
10 Yr (estimated)	8.49	33	1.65	69

Potential Capital Gain Exposure: 29% of assets

Rating and Risk

Time Period	Load-Adj Return %	Morningstar Rtn vs Cat	Morningstar Risk vs Cat	Morningstar Risk-Adj Rating
1 Yr	23.58			
3 Yr	13.84	+Avg	+Avg	★★★★
5 Yr	10.83	+Avg	+Avg	★★★★
10 Yr	10.31	Avg	+Avg	★★★
Incept	13.72			

Other Measures	Standard Index S&P 500	Best Fit Index Russ 2000 Gr
Alpha	-2.2	3.5
Beta	1.90	0.94
R-Squared	68	88
Standard Deviation	15.88	
Mean	13.84	
Sharpe Ratio	0.70	

Portfolio Analysis 11-30-06

Share change since 10-06 Total Stocks:110

	Sector	PE	Tot Ret%	% Assets
⊖ Ultimate Software Group,	Software	NMF	21.97	2.83
VistaPrint, Ltd.	Business	—	—	2.58
Equinix, Inc.	Business	—	85.53	2.55
Jarden Corporation	Goods	32.0	15.39	2.50
Submarino	Consumer	—	—	2.49
World Fuel Services Corp	Energy	22.4	32.34	2.43
CoStar Group, Inc.	Business	NMF	24.07	2.42
Omnicell, Inc.	Hardware	62.1	55.90	2.40
All Amer Latina	Business	—	—	2.33
International Securities	Financial	—	70.81	2.18
Lions Gate Entertainment	Media	43.3	39.71	2.17
Talx Corporation	Business	28.7	-9.28	2.09
Marvel Enterprises, Inc.	Media	34.5	64.29	2.06
Radiation Therapy Servic	Health	25.1	-10.73	1.90
ValueVision Media, Inc.	Consumer	—	4.29	1.72
Advisory Board Company	Business	41.0	12.31	1.71
Orient-Express Hotels, L	Consumer	50.0	50.53	1.65
⊖ Infocrossing, Inc.	Business	NMF	89.32	1.65
SiRF Technology Holdings	Hardware	95.3	-14.36	1.52
⊖ American Reprographics C	Business	—	31.09	1.39

Current Investment Style

Value Blnd Growth — Large Mid Small

Market Cap	%
Giant	0.0
Large	0.0
Mid	24.2
Small	52.0
Micro	23.7

Avg $mil: 920

Value Measures		Rel Category
Price/Earnings	28.73	1.37
Price/Book	3.16	1.16
Price/Sales	1.16	0.74
Price/Cash Flow	14.91	1.55
Dividend Yield %	0.04	0.09

Growth Measures	%	Rel Category
Long-Term Erngs	23.66	1.33
Book Value	11.08	1.06
Sales	29.46	2.48
Cash Flow	23.04	1.09
Historical Erngs	15.10	0.62

Profitability	%	Rel Category
Return on Equity	12.40	1.00
Return on Assets	5.56	0.83
Net Margin	6.88	0.79

Sector Weightings
	% of Stocks	Rel S&P 500	3 Year High Low
↻ Info	19.53	0.98	
Software	5.32	1.54	11 5
Hardware	7.76	0.84	15 4
Media	5.16	1.36	6 0
Telecom	1.29	0.37	3 1
☞ Service	65.20	1.41	
Health	12.68	1.05	19 11
Consumer	11.62	1.52	17 9
Business	37.37	8.83	37 22
Financial	3.53	0.16	16 3
Mfg	15.26	0.45	
Goods	6.77	0.79	10 5
Ind Mtrls	3.65	0.31	5 1
Energy	4.84	0.49	8 2
Utilities	0.00	0.00	0 0

Composition
● Cash	0.4	
● Stocks	99.3	
○ Bonds	0.0	
○ Other	0.3	
Foreign	11.9 (% of Stock)	

Morningstar's Take by Andrew Gogerty 12-20-06

We'd stick with Janus Venture.

True, the fact that the fund is one of the top-performing small-growth offerings in 2006 makes our opinion seem obvious. Strong stock selection in multiple sectors has fueled gains. Witness gains from firms such as online printer VistaPrint, media moguls Lions Gate and Marvel Enterprises, and software firm Ultimate Software. Winning has been nothing new for this closed fund, however. Not only do its three- and five-year returns rank near the top, but it's outperformed the category in four of the past five years.

There's more here than just outsized returns, though. Manager Will Bales hunts for companies with strong growth prospects and the ability to generate high returns that trade at decent valuations. In mid-2006 he scooped up VistaPrint because of its low-cost structure and first-mover status for smaller businesses' printing needs. Payroll processor Ultimate Software was added as the firm changed to a subscription model--which

has allowed it to increase market share among smaller employers. But unlike the late 1990s and early 2000s, valuation now plays a key role. Bales has begun paring back the fund's stake in Ultimate because the stock was pushing up against his fair value estimate. In general, he looks to begin trimming positions as they get within 10% of his price target.

The fund's modest turnover and low costs further its appeal, but investors should remain cognizant of the risks. Bales' approach hasn't made the fund a standout during market corrections, and even with a more-diversified portfolio--compared with the late 1990s--investors should be prepared for a choppy ride from time to time.

Overall, though, these risks don't overwhelm the case for staying put. Bales' tenure, and its rock-bottom costs argue strongly in its favor, and he's slowing proving that he can provide competitive long-term returns within the fund's more-diversified format.

Address:	151 Detroit Street Denver CO 80206 800-525-0020	Minimum Purchase:	Closed Add: — IRA: —
		Min Auto Inv Plan:	Closed Add: —
		Sales Fees:	No-load
Web Address:	www.janus.com	Management Fee:	0.64%
Inception:	04-30-85	Actual Fees:	Mgt:0.64%
Advisor:	Janus Capital Management LLC	Expense Projections:	3Yr:$278 5Yr:$482 10Yr:$1073
Subadvisor:	None	Income Distrib:	Annually
NTF Plans:	Fidelity Retail-NTF, Schwab OneSource		

MORNINGSTAR® Funds 500

Janus Worldwide

	Ticker	Load	NAV	Yield	Total Assets	Mstar Category
	JAWWX	None	$50.46	1.3%	$4,542 mil	World Stock

Governance and Management

Stewardship Grade: C

Portfolio Manager(s)

In July 2004, Jason Yee replaced Laurence Chang as manager of the fund. Yee, who also manages Janus Global Opportunities, cut his teeth as an analyst at Janus from 1992 until 1996. He left the firm to work at a small money-management shop in Denver but returned to Janus in 2000. He served as CIO of Janus' international division for two years before the CIO role was consolidated from four people to two.

Strategy

Jason Yee will not buy stocks unless he can get them at a bargain. He likes to grab a company when it's selling at a noticeable discount to his estimate of the stock's worth. This is not bottom-of-the-barrel value investing, though: Yee also wants companies that boast strong free cash flows and impressive franchises. At another fund, he has invested across the globe and across market caps, but that was with a much smaller asset base. It's unlikely he will have as much flexibility here. He aims to hold a portfolio of between 40 and 70 names with minimal exposure to emerging markets.

Performance 12-31-06

	1st Qtr	2nd Qtr	3rd Qtr	4th Qtr	Total
2002	-0.89	-12.57	-17.56	3.56	-26.01
2003	-8.37	16.34	3.01	13.14	24.23
2004	5.51	-8.39	-2.09	11.52	5.54
2005	-0.63	-2.48	5.36	3.66	5.84
2006	4.85	-3.54	5.04	10.98	17.90

Trailing	Total Return%	+/- MSCI EAFE	+/- MSCI World	%Rank Cat	Growth of $10,000
3 Mo	10.98	0.63	2.61	17	11,098
6 Mo	16.58	1.89	3.37	6	11,658
1 Yr	17.90	-8.44	-2.17	64	11,790
3 Yr Avg	9.61	-10.32	-5.07	95	13,169
5 Yr Avg	3.89	-11.09	-6.08	95	12,102
10 Yr Avg	6.82	-0.89	-0.82	73	19,343
15 Yr Avg	10.25	2.39	1.56	55	43,219

Tax Analysis	Tax-Adj Rtn%	%Rank Cat	Tax-Cost Rat	%Rank Cat
3 Yr (estimated)	9.21	93	0.36	22
5 Yr (estimated)	3.52	95	0.36	30
10 Yr (estimated)	6.09	68	0.68	20

Potential Capital Gain Exposure: -98% of assets

Historical Profile

Return Below Avg
Risk Average
Rating ★★ Below Avg

Investment Style: Equity, Stock %

Quartile bar chart percentages: 87% 91% 90% 85% 85% 99% 92% 98% 100%

▼ Manager Change
▽ Partial Manager Change

Growth of $10,000
— Investment Values of Fund
— Investment Values of MSCI EAFE

Performance Quartile (within Category)

	1995	1996	1997	1998	1999	2000	2001	2002	2003	2004	2005	2006	History
NAV	28.40	33.69	37.78	47.36	76.43	56.86	43.84	32.13	39.54	41.41	43.34	50.46	
Total Return %	21.90	26.40	20.48	25.87	64.37	-16.87	-22.88	-26.01	24.23	5.54	5.84	17.90	
+/-MSCI EAFE	10.69	20.35	18.70	5.94	37.34	-2.68	-1.46	-10.07	-14.36	-14.71	-7.70	-8.44	
+/-MSCI World	1.18	12.92	4.72	1.55	39.42	-3.68	-6.08	-6.12	-8.88	-9.18	-3.65	-2.17	
Income Return %	1.07	0.54	0.58	0.51	0.06	0.99	0.02	0.70	1.12	0.79	1.19	1.48	
Capital Return %	20.83	25.86	19.90	25.36	64.31	-17.86	-22.90	-26.71	23.11	4.75	4.65	16.42	
Total Rtn % Rank Cat	27	4	28	19	18	80	75	87	93	96	90	64	
Income $	0.26	0.15	0.20	0.19	0.03	0.75	0.01	0.31	0.36	0.31	0.49	0.64	
Capital Gains $	1.07	2.04	2.60	0.00	1.28	6.17	0.00	0.00	0.00	0.00	0.00	0.00	
Expense Ratio %	1.23	1.01	0.95	0.92	0.88	0.86	0.85	0.86	0.92	0.92	0.85	—	
Income Ratio %	0.99	0.73	0.65	0.47	0.07	0.13	0.53	0.62	0.99	0.61	0.90	—	
Turnover Rate %	142	80	79	86	68	58	78	73	108	120	33	—	
Net Assets $mil	1,975	5,046	10,568	16,323	33,803	33,144	21,679	12,815	10,961	7,043	4,991	4,503	

Rating and Risk

Time Period	Load-Adj Return %	Morningstar Rtn vs Cat	Morningstar Risk vs Cat	Morningstar Risk-Adj Rating
1 Yr	17.90			
3 Yr	9.61	Low	Avg	★
5 Yr	3.89	Low	Avg	★
10 Yr	6.82	-Avg	Avg	★★
Incept	11.34			

Other Measures	Standard Index MSCI EAFE	Best Fit Index DJ Mod
Alpha	-5.6	-3.1
Beta	0.77	1.33
R-Squared	61	70
Standard Deviation	9.41	
Mean	9.61	
Sharpe Ratio	0.69	

Portfolio Analysis 11-30-06

Share change since 10-06 Total Stocks:66

	Sector	Country	% Assets
⊖ Dell, Inc.	Hardware	United States	6.03
⊖ British Sky Broadcasting	Media	U.K.	5.06
⊖ Willis Group Holdings, L	Financial	Bermuda	4.44
⊖ IAC/InterActiveCorp	Consumer	United States	3.87
⊖ Tyco International, Ltd.	Ind Mtrls	United States	3.67
⊖ Yahoo, Inc.	Media	United States	3.62
⊖ Esprit Hldgs Ltd	Consumer	Hong Kong	3.58
⊖ Koninklijke Philips Elec	Goods	Netherlands	3.51
⊖ J.P. Morgan Chase & Co.	Financial	United States	3.45
⊖ Cisco Systems, Inc.	Hardware	United States	3.38
⊖ Amazon.com, Inc.	Consumer	United States	2.56
⊖ Potash Corporation of Sa	Ind Mtrls	Canada	2.46
⊖ Millea Hldgs	Financial	Japan	2.46
⊖ Berkshire Hathaway Inc.	Financial	United States	2.42
⊖ Burberry Grp	Consumer	U.K.	2.03
⊖ Vodafone Grp	Telecom	U.K.	1.94
⊖ Walt Disney Company	Media	United States	1.91
⊖ Expedia, Inc.	Consumer	United States	1.87
⊖ eBay, Inc.	Consumer	United States	1.83
⊖ Syngenta	Ind Mtrls	Switzerland	1.68

Current Investment Style

Value Blnd Growth — Large Mid Small

Market Cap	%
Giant	43.7
Large	38.7
Mid	17.6
Small	0.0
Micro	0.0
Avg $mil:	28,365

Value Measures		Rel Category
Price/Earnings	17.80	1.16
Price/Book	2.30	0.96
Price/Sales	1.49	1.14
Price/Cash Flow	9.72	1.12
Dividend Yield %	1.65	0.76

Growth Measures	%	Rel Category
Long-Term Erngs	13.33	1.05
Book Value	7.72	0.86
Sales	12.87	1.54
Cash Flow	13.45	1.37
Historical Erngs	23.78	1.27

Composition			
Cash	0.3	Bonds	0.0
Stocks	99.7	Other	0.0
Foreign (% of Stock)			47.5

Sector Weightings	% of Stocks	Rel MSCI EAFE	3 Year High	3 Year Low
↻ Info	28.65	2.42		
▣ Software	0.57	1.02	3	0
▣ Hardware	12.52	3.24	13	0
▣ Media	12.58	6.87	21	5
▣ Telecom	2.98	0.54	4	1
☞ Service	49.82	1.05		
▣ Health	4.60	0.65	14	5
▣ Consumer	22.75	4.60	23	3
▣ Business	2.65	0.52	11	2
▣ Financial	19.82	0.66	26	16
↥ Mfg	21.53	0.53		
▣ Goods	11.09	0.85	25	11
▣ Ind Mtrls	10.44	0.68	23	10
▣ Energy	0.00	0.00	9	0
▣ Utilities	0.00	0.00	0	0

Regional Exposure	% Stock		
UK/W. Europe	25	N. America	55
Japan	7	Latn America	5
Asia X Japan	8	Other	0

Country Exposure	% Stock		
United States	52	Bermuda	4
U.K.	12	Hong Kong	4
Japan	7		

Morningstar's Take by Karen Dolan 12-12-06

Janus Worldwide is on firm footing, but the market has yet to agree.

This fund's relative performance has stunk under new manager Jason Yee's lead. It has gained an annualized 13.2% since he took over in July 2004 through November, 30 2006. That's great in absolute terms, but the fund's average peer has gained of 16.9% over the same stretch.

We think better days lie ahead for the fund, though. Yee applies a fundamentally sound approach. He looks for high-quality companies trading at compelling valuations. He favors firms that don't have to spend a lot of money to make money and thus see a big proportion of their sales translate into earnings. That has led him to battered media stocks, out-of-favor tech fare and suffering homebuilders more recently. What's more, it has kept the fund away from rallying emerging markets and energy stocks. The fund has indeed missed out on some strong-performing markets, but its unique leanings could pull it ahead in a hurry, especially if

emerging markets and energy stocks cool down.

Things have yet to turn around for the fund, though. In fact, several of Yee's picks have continued to plummet since being added to the portfolio. That has been the case with computer maker Dell and Internet travel engine Expedia, for example. Yee hasn't compromised his philosophy to chase what's worked and ditch what hasn't; he is showing confidence in his team's research and patiently sticking with his highest-conviction picks.

Yee has made changes to more than just the portfolio in the past two years. A brief stint as International CIO forced him to think more broadly about Janus' resources and strengthen the team. Janus has since consolidated the CIO roles, so Yee is back to focusing solely on this strategy.

The fund has undoubtedly missed the boat on some strong-performing corners of the market, but we're optimistic about its future. Worldwide's strategy, current positioning, revamped team, and cheap expense ratio make it compelling.

Address:	151 Detroit Street Denver CO 80206 800-525-0020
Web Address:	www.janus.com
Inception:	05-15-91
Advisor:	Janus
Subadvisor:	None
NTF Plans:	Fidelity Retail-NTF, Schwab OneSource

Minimum Purchase:	$2500	Add: $100	IRA: $1000
Min Auto Inv Plan:	$500	Add: $100	
Sales Fees:	No-load, 2.00%R		
Management Fee:	0.60%		
Actual Fees:	Mgt:0.60%	Dist: —	
Expense Projections:	3Yr:$271	5Yr:$471	10Yr:$1049
Income Distrib:	Annually		

Jensen J

	Ticker	Load	NAV	Yield	Total Assets	Mstar Category
	JENSX	None	$26.93	0.8%	$2,310 mil	Large Growth

Governance and Management

Stewardship Grade: A

Portfolio Manager(s)

Although fund founder Val Jensen stepped down in early March 2004, the fund has long been run by a team. Gary Hibler has been on board since the fund's 1992 inception, and will retire in February 2007. Robert Zagunis joined the team in 1993, Robert Millen joined in 2000, and Eric Schoenstein was promoted from analyst to manager in 2004. Also, Robert McIver, who joined the firm as an analyst in September 2004, was recently promoted to manager. They are supported by two analysts: Winfield Evans, hired in 2004, and Kurt Havnaer, who joined in 2005.

Strategy

This fund's management team screens nearly 10,000 publicly traded companies for those that have delivered returns on equity of at least 15% in each of the past 10 years. That whittles the pool of candidates down to 100 to 125 names. The managers then analyze those companies to determine which ones have the best prospects, and they buy those trading at discounts of at least 40% to their estimate of intrinsic value. Although turnover is low, management will sell a holding that doesn't deliver an ROE of at least 15% or that has diminished growth prospects.

Performance 12-31-06

	1st Qtr	2nd Qtr	3rd Qtr	4th Qtr	Total
2002	3.30	-12.43	-8.65	7.74	-10.97
2003	-5.40	9.70	1.22	10.49	16.06
2004	1.01	3.11	-5.05	7.19	6.01
2005	-1.42	-1.49	0.51	1.01	-1.40
2006	2.55	-1.25	6.30	5.90	14.01

Trailing	Total Return%	+/- S&P 500	+/- Russ 1000Gr	%Rank Cat	Growth of $10,000
3 Mo	5.90	-0.80	-0.03	39	10,590
6 Mo	12.58	-0.16	2.48	5	11,258
1 Yr	14.01	-1.78	4.94	6	11,401
3 Yr Avg	6.02	-4.42	-0.85	65	11,917
5 Yr Avg	4.25	-1.94	1.56	26	12,313
10 Yr Avg	9.49	1.07	4.05	7	24,760
15 Yr Avg	—	—	—		

Tax Analysis	Tax-Adj Rtn%	%Rank Cat	Tax-Cost Rat	%Rank Cat
3 Yr (estimated)	5.73	60	0.27	18
5 Yr (estimated)	4.00	25	0.24	25
10 Yr (estimated)	8.92	6	0.52	19

Potential Capital Gain Exposure: 24% of assets

Morningstar's Take by Greg Carlson 11-10-06

Jensen Fund's forward-looking approach is paying off this year, but it's only for patient investors.

Gary Hibler, one of this large-growth fund's managers since its 1992 inception, will retire on Feb. 15, 2007. But there's no need for concern; Hibler's replacement, Rob McIver, was hired back in 2004. McIver and three other managers--including 13-year veteran Robert Zagunis--will continue to run the fund, and they're supported by two analysts. Thus, the fund will have a deeper investment team after Hibler's departure than it has had for much of its history.

This long-term thinking extends to the team's strategy. It only buys firms that have generated 15% returns on equity for 10 years straight and that the team expects to maintain a competitive advantage--thus driving profits higher--over the long haul. While the stocks of those firms aren't always in favor, the team has demonstrated a knack for buying them at opportune times and sticking with them to reap the benefits. (Single-digit

portfolio turnover isn't unusual here.) For example, top holding McGraw-Hill, a publisher and financial-services provider, has doubled in value since a mid-2003 purchase, while medical-device maker Stryker has more than tripled since the team scooped up its shares in 1999. Those two stocks have also posted solid gains this year, powering the fund to a top-decile showing thus far in 2006. It's worth noting that, despite the fund's poor performance in most stock rallies (and resiliency in bear markets), this year's fine showing comes in a year of double-digit market gains.

We don't know whether the fund's most significant recent purchase--Microsoft--will prove similarly successful, but the team is buying in alongside esteemed value investors such as Marty Whitman and Davis Selected Advisors.

All told, the fund's modest costs and superb risk/reward profile make it an attractive choice for those who can ride out stretches of poor relative returns.

Address:	2130 Pacwest Center Portland OR 97204-3721 800-992-4144
Web Address:	www.jenseninvestment.com
Inception:	08-03-92
Advisor:	Jensen Investment Management Inc.
Subadvisor:	None
NTF Plans:	Fidelity Retail-NTF, Schwab OneSource

Minimum Purchase:	$2500	Add: $100	IRA: $2500
Min Auto Inv Plan:	$100	Add: $100	
Sales Fees:	No-load, 0.25%S		
Management Fee:	0.50%		
Actual Fees:	Mgt:0.50%	Dist:0.25%	
Expense Projections:	3Yr:$271	5Yr:$471	10Yr:$1049
Income Distrib:	Quarterly		

Historical Profile

Return	Above Avg
Risk	Low
Rating	★★★★ Above Avg

| 99% | 92% | 86% | 93% | 98% | 99% | 99% | 99% | 98% |

Investment Style Equity Stock %

▼ Manager Change
▽ Partial Manager Change

Growth of $10,000
■ Investment Values of Fund
— Investment Values of S&P 500

Performance Quartile (within Category)

1995	1996	1997	1998	1999	2000	2001	2002	2003	2004	2005	2006	History
11.26	13.49	16.14	18.61	21.67	22.70	22.62	20.07	23.13	24.35	23.82	26.93	NAV
27.61	21.06	22.99	16.70	16.71	20.04	0.03	-10.97	16.06	6.01	-1.40	14.01	Total Return %
-9.97	-1.90	-10.37	-11.88	-4.33	29.14	11.92	11.12	-12.62	-4.87	-6.31	-1.78	+/-S&P 500
-9.57	-2.06	-7.50	-22.01	-16.45	42.46	20.45	16.91	-13.69	-0.29	-6.66	4.94	+/-Russ 1000Gr
1.80	1.15	0.58	1.31	0.25	0.41	0.34	0.31	0.75	0.71	0.77	0.89	Income Return %
25.81	19.91	22.41	15.39	16.46	19.63	-0.31	-11.28	15.31	5.30	-2.17	13.12	Capital Return %
77	39	66	85	86	1	2	2	99	70	97	6	Total Rtn % Rank Cat
0.16	0.13	0.08	0.21	0.05	0.08	0.08	0.07	0.15	0.16	0.19	0.21	Income $
0.00	0.00	0.37	0.00	0.00	3.07	0.00	0.00	0.00	0.00	0.00	0.00	Capital Gains $
1.20	1.20	1.32	1.02	0.96	0.94	0.95	1.00	0.90	0.88	0.85	0.85	Expense Ratio %
1.48	1.23	0.61	1.44	0.27	0.31	0.45	0.23	0.62	0.71	0.77	0.85	Income Ratio %
11	48	24	21	14	32	4	1	7	5	9	10	Turnover Rate %
11	13	18	23	27	40	118	1,051	1,718	2,547	2,275	1,833	Net Assets $mil

Rating and Risk

Time Period	Load-Adj Return %	Morningstar Rtn vs Cat	Morningstar Risk vs Cat	Morningstar Risk-Adj Rating
1 Yr	14.01			
3 Yr	6.02	Avg	Low	★★★
5 Yr	4.25	+Avg	Low	★★★★
10 Yr	9.49	High	Low	★★★★★
Incept	9.18			

Other Measures	Standard Index S&P 500	Best Fit Index Mstar Large Core TR
Alpha	-1.8	-2.9
Beta	0.67	0.76
R-Squared	59	70
Standard Deviation	6.00	
Mean	6.02	
Sharpe Ratio	0.48	

Portfolio Analysis 09-30-06

Share change since 06-06 Total Stocks:25	Sector	PE	Tot Ret%	% Assets
⊖ McGraw-Hill Companies, I	Media	28.5	33.44	5.47
⊖ Stryker Corporation	Health	30.3	24.53	5.24
⊖ Procter & Gamble Company	Goods	23.9	13.36	5.13
⊖ Emerson Electric Company	Ind Mtrls	19.6	20.68	5.03
⊖ Omnicom Group, Inc.	Business	21.4	24.14	5.02
⊖ General Electric Company	Ind Mtrls	20.0	9.35	4.95
⊖ T Rowe Price Group	Financial	26.1	23.27	4.73
⊖ Abbott Laboratories	Health	24.3	26.88	4.72
⊖ Johnson & Johnson	Health	17.5	12.45	4.54
⊖ 3M Company	Ind Mtrls	16.7	2.98	4.36
⊖ Automatic Data Processin	Business	24.9	9.11	4.31
⊖ Colgate-Palmolive Compan	Goods	27.6	21.51	4.12
⊖ PepsiCo, Inc.	Goods	21.5	7.86	4.07
⊖ Sysco Corporation	Consumer	25.2	20.96	3.97
⊖ Equifax, Inc.	Business	19.1	7.27	3.79
⊖ Medtronic, Inc.	Health	23.8	-6.29	3.71
⊖ Patterson Companies, Inc	Health	24.7	6.32	3.70
✵ Microsoft Corporation	Software	23.8	15.83	3.63
⊖ Ecolab, Inc.	Ind Mtrls	32.2	25.88	3.26
⊕ Wells Fargo Company	Financial	14.7	16.82	2.99

Current Investment Style

	Market Cap	%
Value Blnd Growth (Large Mid Small)	Giant	40.7
	Large	43.7
	Mid	15.6
	Small	0.0
	Micro	0.0
	Avg $mil:	36,001

Value Measures		Rel Category
Price/Earnings	20.20	1.05
Price/Book	4.52	1.36
Price/Sales	2.29	1.18
Price/Cash Flow	15.53	1.36
Dividend Yield %	1.61	1.56

Growth Measures	%	Rel Category
Long-Term Erngs	12.15	0.85
Book Value	11.59	1.00
Sales	9.84	0.85
Cash Flow	7.02	0.42
Historical Erngs	12.65	0.55

Profitability	%	Rel Category
Return on Equity	26.57	1.31
Return on Assets	12.23	1.11
Net Margin	14.81	1.04

Sector Weightings	% of Stocks	Rel S&P 500	3 Year High Low	
⟳ Info	9.24	0.46		
▤ Software	3.68	1.07	4	0
▣ Hardware	0.00	0.00	0	0
🎙 Media	5.56	1.47	9	5
📶 Telecom	0.00	0.00	0	0
⬤ Service	55.36	1.20		
⚕ Health	22.24	1.84	31	22
🛒 Consumer	6.47	0.85	6	0
📋 Business	18.80	4.44	23	15
$ Financial	7.85	0.35	13	5
⬢ Mfg	35.40	1.05		
⚙ Goods	17.51	2.05	21	17
⚙ Ind Mtrls	17.89	1.50	19	14
⛽ Energy	0.00	0.00	0	0
💡 Utilities	0.00	0.00	0	0

Composition

● Cash		1.6
● Stocks		98.5
● Bonds		0.0
○ Other		0.0
Foreign (% of Stock)		0.0

MORNINGSTAR® Funds 500

JPMorgan U.S. Real Est A

	Ticker	Load	NAV	Yield	Total Assets	Mstar Category
Analyst Pick	SUSIX	5.25%	$22.62	1.2%	$950 mil	Specialty-Real Estate

Governance and Management

Stewardship Grade:

Portfolio Manager(s)

Security Capital Research & Management is the fund's advisor. In September 2003, Bank One agreed to acquire Security Capital from GE Real Estate. Bank One then merged with J.P. Morgan Chase in 2004. Security Capital expects to remain autonomous, though. Ken Statz, Kevin Bedell, and Anthony Manno have been at the helm since the fund's late-1996 inception. Before that, they spent many years in the real estate industry. Comanager David Rosenbaum has been with Security Capital since 1997, focusing on preferred securities.

Strategy

Management uses a valuation matrix, which includes a discounted cash-flow model and NAVs to set price targets on its universe of stocks. Management selects those with the best rate-of-return prospects given current prices relative to the targets. The portfolio typically holds 20 to 25 stocks, and its top 10 holdings generally account for more than half of its assets.

Performance 12-31-06

	1st Qtr	2nd Qtr	3rd Qtr	4th Qtr	Total
2002	7.48	1.62	-9.56	0.81	-0.43
2003	1.31	11.62	9.84	8.71	35.02
2004	11.36	-2.28	7.26	17.21	36.81
2005	-6.60	13.56	3.85	5.11	15.77
2006	16.19	-0.04	7.46	9.13	36.21

Trailing	Total Return%	+/- S&P 500	+/- DJ Wilshire REIT	%Rank Cat	Growth of $10,000
3 Mo	9.13	2.43	0.16	68	10,913
6 Mo	17.28	4.54	-1.72	82	11,728
1 Yr	36.21	20.42	0.08	26	13,621
3 Yr Avg	29.22	18.78	1.85	11	21,577
5 Yr Avg	23.74	17.55	-0.10	46	29,010
10 Yr Avg	—	—	—		
15 Yr Avg	—	—	—		

Tax Analysis	Tax-Adj Rtn%	%Rank Cat	Tax-Cost Rat	%Rank Cat
3 Yr (estimated)	23.92	38	2.36	58
5 Yr (estimated)	19.72	68	2.20	67
10 Yr (estimated)	—	—	—	—

Potential Capital Gain Exposure: 33% of assets

Morningstar's Take by John Coumarianos 12-28-06

JP Morgan U.S. Real Estate is no stranger to success, but we'd keep expectations in check.

The experienced management team at Security Capital Research and Management runs the fund by placing larger bets on fewer stocks than many of its peers. It currently holds 25 stocks, and hasn't held more than 30 in the past five years. Concentration like this can lead to high returns, but it can also court volatility. However, the fund has notched a 25% annualized gain for the past five years through Nov. 30, 2006, edging past the real estate category average by about a percentage point per year and keeping pace with the DJ Wilshire Real Estate Securities Index. The fund's worst-month and worst-quarter performances (13% and 10% losses, respectively) over this period of time are in line with the peer group and benchmark norms.

The managers' emphasis on valuation has helped damp volatility. They model businesses' cash flows for five years, applying different discount rates (the rate the expected returns must exceed), according to their understanding of each business's risks to arrive at a valuation. Additionally, the team simply avoids situations when it can't assess the discount rate.

This approach has led to success with apartment and office REITs lately. Apartment owner/operators Avalon Bay and Equity Residential have surged on anticipation of rent increases as high home prices discourage prospective owners. Equity Office Properties also benefited from rent increases, and then in November, the firm agreed to a private-equity buyout at a healthy premium.

We think this team's concentrated approach should continue to do well relative to those of its peers, but we caution investors to temper their expectations for real estate. Those who have enjoyed the category's multiyear run should consider trimming their stake; those who are getting started should begin slowly and add on dips.

Address:	245 Park Avenue New York, NY 10167 800-480-4111	Minimum Purchase:	$1000	Add: $25	IRA: $0
		Min Auto Inv Plan:	$100	Add: $100	
		Sales Fees:	5.25%L, 0.25%S		
Web Address:	www.jpmorganfunds.com	Management Fee:	0.60%		
Inception:	04-23-97*	Actual Fees:	Mgt:0.60%	Dist:0.25%	
Advisor:	Security Capital Research & Mgmt Inc	Expense Projections:	3Yr:$900	5Yr:$1181	10Yr:$1981
Subadvisor:	None	Income Distrib:	Quarterly		
NTF Plans:	Schwab OneSource, DATALynx NTF				

Historical Profile

Return: Average
Risk: Average
Rating: ★★★ Neutral

| | | | 93% | 87% | 90% | 92% | 100% | 98% | 98% | 97% | 98% |

Investment Style
Equity
Stock %

▼ Manager Change
▽ Partial Manager Change

Growth of $10,000
— Investment Values of Fund
— Investment Values of S&P 500

Values shown: 40.8 / 31.0 / 24.0 / 17.0 / 10.0

Performance Quartile (within Category)

1995	1996	1997	1998	1999	2000	2001	2002	2003	2004	2005	2006	History
—	—	11.95	9.82	9.37	12.14	12.16	11.27	14.46	17.82	19.19	22.62	NAV
—	—	3.80*	-11.94	0.58	35.84	7.04	-0.43	35.02	36.81	15.77	36.21	Total Return %
—	—	—	-40.52	-20.46	44.94	18.93	21.67	6.34	25.93	10.86	20.42	+/-S&P 500
—	—	—	5.06	3.15	4.80	-5.32	-4.03	-1.04	3.67	1.77	0.08	+/-DJ Wilshire REIT
—	—	—	4.02	5.33	5.75	4.78	4.72	5.40	3.73	2.49	1.71	Income Return %
—	—	—	-15.96	-4.75	30.09	2.26	-5.15	29.62	33.08	13.28	34.50	Capital Return %
—	—	—	8	15	1	76	91	64	14	12	26	Total Rtn % Rank Cat
—	—	0.52	0.46	0.51	0.53	0.57	0.56	0.60	0.53	0.43	0.32	Income $
—	—	0.48	0.29	0.00	0.00	0.24	0.29	0.07	1.35	0.97	3.14	Capital Gains $
—	—	—	0.94	1.00	1.20	1.35	1.24	1.21	1.18	1.31	—	Expense Ratio %
—	—	—	4.08	4.75	4.18	5.02	4.96	3.41	2.59	1.74	—	Income Ratio %
—	—	—	104	109	50	91	91	75	67	49	—	Turnover Rate %
—	—	10	117	91	46	116	160	205	298	304	432	Net Assets $mil

Rating and Risk

Time Period	Load-Adj Return %	Morningstar Rtn vs Cat	Morningstar Risk vs Cat	Morningstar Risk-Adj Rating
1 Yr	29.06			
3 Yr	26.91	Avg	Avg	★★★
5 Yr	22.41	Avg	Avg	★★★
10 Yr	—	—	—	—
Incept	16.99			

Other Measures	Standard Index S&P 500	Best Fit Index DJ Wilshire REIT
Alpha	15.5	2.7
Beta	1.21	0.94
R-Squared	27	98
Standard Deviation	15.87	
Mean	29.22	
Sharpe Ratio	1.51	

Portfolio Analysis 11-30-06

Share change since 10-06 Total Stocks:25	Sector	PE	Tot Ret%	% Assets
⊕ Simon Property Group, In	Financial	58.3	36.98	6.04
⊕ AvalonBay Communities, I	Financial	68.7	49.69	6.03
⊖ Equity Office Properties	Financial	—	64.28	5.86
Starwood Hotels & Resort	Consumer	12.9	21.75	5.52
⊕ Public Storage, Inc.	Financial	46.2	47.46	4.99
⊕ Archstone-Smith Trust	Financial	59.0	43.93	4.86
Corporate Office Propert	Financial	NMF	45.78	4.70
⊕ Equity Residential	Financial	NMF	34.64	4.67
⊖ ProLogis Trust	Financial	33.5	34.02	4.55
⊖ Camden Property Trust	Financial	32.0	32.17	4.10
⊕ Douglas Emmett, Inc.	Financial	—	—	3.96
SL Green Realty Corporat	Financial	57.8	77.73	3.90
⊕ Macerich Company	Financial	—	33.91	3.77
⊕ Federal Realty Investmen	Financial	53.5	44.88	3.56
⊖ Mack-Cali Realty Corpora	Financial	34.0	24.56	3.51
☼ Health Care Property	Financial	34.6	53.18	3.36
Post Properties, Inc.	Financial	NMF	18.95	3.19
⊕ Brandywine Realty Trust	Financial	—	24.09	3.18
⊕ Strategic Hotel & Resort	Financial	10.6	10.59	3.02
⊕ AMB Property Corporation	Financial	29.8	23.30	2.95

Current Investment Style

Value Blnd Growth — Large/Mid/Small

Market Cap	%
Giant	0.0
Large	37.4
Mid	56.7
Small	6.0
Micro	0.0

Avg $mil: 6,436

Value Measures		Rel Category
Price/Earnings	21.74	1.15
Price/Book	3.42	1.20
Price/Sales	5.31	1.28
Price/Cash Flow	20.76	1.34
Dividend Yield %	3.32	0.82

Growth Measures	%	Rel Category
Long-Term Erngs	7.48	0.97
Book Value	-0.70	NMF
Sales	12.16	1.11
Cash Flow	0.28	0.02
Historical Erngs	6.83	0.48

Profitability	%	Rel Category
Return on Equity	11.12	0.97
Return on Assets	9.70	1.04
Net Margin	22.88	0.85

Sector Weightings	% of Stocks	Rel S&P 500	3 Year High Low	
⟳ Info	0.00	0.00		
▣ Software	0.00	0.00	0	0
▣ Hardware	0.00	0.00	0	0
▣ Media	0.00	0.00	0	0
▣ Telecom	0.00	0.00	0	0
⟳ Service	100.00	2.16		
▣ Health	0.00	0.00	0	0
▣ Consumer	5.65	0.74	9	5
▣ Business	0.00	0.00	0	0
▣ Financial	94.35	4.24	95	91
⟳ Mfg	0.00	0.00		
▣ Goods	0.00	0.00	0	0
▣ Ind Mtrls	0.00	0.00	0	0
▣ Energy	0.00	0.00	0	0
▣ Utilities	0.00	0.00	0	0

Composition

		%
●	Cash	2.4
●	Stocks	97.7
●	Bonds	0.0
○	Other	0.0
	Foreign	0.0
	(% of Stock)	

Julius Baer Intl Eq II A

	Ticker	Load	NAV	Yield	Total Assets	Mstar Category
	JETAX	None	$15.09	0.2%	$3,807 mil	Foreign Large Blend

Governance and Management

Stewardship Grade: C

Portfolio Manager(s)

Rudolph-Riad Younes and Richard Pell have worked for Bank Julius Baer and other firms in various investment-related capacities for many years. They have run the successful Julius Baer International Equity since the spring of 1995 and have a team of five analysts. Although they work together, Younes handles the day-to-day management while Pell focuses more on providing broader strategic oversight. They were named Morningstar's International-Stock Managers of the Year for 2002.

Strategy

The managers consider sector selection and the outlook for the U.S. economy more than most peers, but they also perform intensive company analysis. They incorporate growth and value factors but exclude companies below $2.5 billion in market cap. They are willing to hold significant cash stakes. Individual stock positions typically are small. The fund's weightings can diverge sharply from those of the MSCI EAFE Index. It occasionally hedges its exposure to foreign currencies. It has a 2% short-term redemption fee and sometimes uses fair-value pricing.

Performance 12-31-06

	1st Qtr	2nd Qtr	3rd Qtr	4th Qtr	Total
2002	—	—	—	—	—
2003	—	—	—	—	—
2004	—	—	—	—	—
2005	—	—	13.33	2.79	—*
2006	11.61	-1.67	3.86	12.85	28.62

Trailing	Total Return%	+/- MSCI EAFE	+/- MSCI Wd xUS	%Rank Cat	Growth of $10,000
3 Mo	12.85	2.50	2.73	8	11,285
6 Mo	17.20	2.51	2.98	8	11,720
1 Yr	28.62	2.28	2.91	11	12,862
3 Yr Avg	—	—	—	—	—
5 Yr Avg	—	—	—	—	—
10 Yr Avg	—	—	—	—	—
15 Yr Avg	—	—	—	—	—

Tax Analysis	Tax-Adj Rtn%	%Rank Cat	Tax-Cost Rat	%Rank Cat
3 Yr (estimated)	—	—	—	—
5 Yr (estimated)	—	—	—	—
10 Yr (estimated)	—	—	—	—

Potential Capital Gain Exposure: 17% of assets

Morningstar's Take by Gregg Wolper 12-22-06

Julius Baer International Equity II has the right idea.

This fund, which came out in May 2005, is managed by Rudolph-Riad Younes and Richard Pell, who have amassed a superb record over more than a decade running now-closed Julius Baer International Equity Fund. This fund is very similar; the only difference is that it doesn't own companies below $2.5 billion in market capitalization. Younes says the funds now have about 80% to 85% of their portfolios in common, and a glance at their top holdings and sector and country weightings shows them to be very similar. The slight differences--essentially the roughly 5% small-cap stake of the older fund--do mean returns are not identical. The distinction favored the older fund over the trailing 12-month period through Dec. 21, 2006: Julius Baer International Equity has a 31.2% gain over that stretch, while Julius Baer International Equity II's return is 29.0%. However, it's important to note that even the latter's gain

lands in the top decile of the foreign large-blend category.

Several factors account for that excellent showing. For one thing, this fund has been very light in Japan, a weak market in 2006. Also, Younes says, some of the portfolio's biggest gains owed to takeover bids for its port and airport holdings, a key theme of the managers in recent years. Other notable winners were Indian and Italian banks and an unusually high stake in Russia, among the world's strongest markets in 2006.

With this fund's high emerging-markets weighting and willingness to flout the indexes, it may seem a risky play. And while there's an element of that, Younes and Pell do try to offset the risks by keeping individual position sizes very small and investing in a wide variety of themes, not just two or three. Their long record on the older fund indicates that they've found the right balance.

Address:	615 E. Michigan Street LC-3 Milwaukee WI 53202 800-387-6977	Minimum Purchase:	$1000	Add: $1000 IRA: $100
		Min Auto Inv Plan:	$100	Add: $100
		Sales Fees:	No-load, 0.25%S, 2.00%R	
Web Address:	www.us-funds.juliusbaer.com	Management Fee:	0.90%, 0.25%A	
Inception:	05-04-05	Actual Fees:	Mgt:0.90%	Dist:0.25%
Advisor:	Julius Baer Securities Inc.	Expense Projections:	3Yr:$576	5Yr:$1045 10Yr:$2340
Subadvisor:	None	Income Distrib:	Annually	
NTF Plans:	Fidelity Retail-NTF, Schwab OneSource			

Historical Profile
Return
Risk
Rating
Not Rated

81% 83%

15.0
14.0
13.0
12.0
11.0
10.0

Growth of $10,000
■ Investment Values of Fund
— Investment Values of MSCI EAFE

Investment Style
Equity
Stock %

▼ Manager Change
▽ Partial Manager Change

Performance Quartile (within Category)

1995	1996	1997	1998	1999	2000	2001	2002	2003	2004	2005	2006	History
—	—	—	—	—	—	—	—	—	—	11.80	15.09	NAV
—	—	—	—	—	—	—	—	—	—	—	28.62	Total Return %
—	—	—	—	—	—	—	—	—	—	—	2.28	+/-MSCI EAFE
—	—	—	—	—	—	—	—	—	—	—	2.91	+/-MSCI Wd xUS
—	—	—	—	—	—	—	—	—	—	—	0.29	Income Return %
—	—	—	—	—	—	—	—	—	—	—	28.33	Capital Return %
—	—	—	—	—	—	—	—	—	—	—	11	Total Rtn % Rank Cat
—	—	—	—	—	—	—	—	—	—	0.00	0.03	Income $
—	—	—	—	—	—	—	—	—	—	0.00	0.05	Capital Gains $
—	—	—	—	—	—	—	—	—	—	—	—	Expense Ratio %
—	—	—	—	—	—	—	—	—	—	—	—	Income Ratio %
—	—	—	—	—	—	—	—	—	—	—	—	Turnover Rate %
—	—	—	—	—	—	—	—	—	—	—	864	Net Assets $mil

Rating and Risk

Time Period	Load-Adj Return %	Morningstar Rtn vs Cat	Morningstar Risk vs Cat	Morningstar Risk-Adj Rating
1 Yr	28.62			
3 Yr	—	—	—	—
5 Yr	—	—	—	—
10 Yr	—	—	—	—
Incept	28.59			

Other Measures	Standard Index MSCI EAFE	Best Fit Index
Alpha	—	—
Beta	—	—
R-Squared	—	—
Standard Deviation	—	
Mean	—	
Sharpe Ratio	—	

Portfolio Analysis 10-31-06

Share change since 07-06 Total Stocks:309

	Sector	Country	% Assets
⊕ Pko Bk Polski S.A.	Financial	Poland	1.45
⊕ Total SA	Energy	France	1.33
⊕ Komercni banka	Financial	Czech Republic	1.29
⊕ Fraport	Business	Germany	1.28
⊕ OTP Bank	Financial	Hungary	1.26
⊕ Almancora Comm.VA	Financial	Belgium	1.24
⊕ Vodafone Grp	Telecom	U.K.	1.24
⊕ Bank Pekao	Financial	Poland	1.19
⊕ Nestle	Goods	Switzerland	1.19
⊕ Lafarge	Ind Mtrls	France	1.09
⊕ LVMH Moet Hennessy L.V.	Goods	France	0.96
⊕ Holcim	Ind Mtrls	Switzerland	0.96
⊕ GlaxoSmithKline	Health	U.K.	0.91
⊕ Novartis	Health	Switzerland	0.90
⊕ Deutsche Post	Business	Germany	0.86
⊖ Diageo	Goods	U.K.	0.85
⊕ Consulta (Ci)		U.K.	0.84
⊕ ING Groep	Financial	Netherlands	0.76
⊕ Air Liquide	Ind Mtrls	France	0.76
⊕ Commerzbank Grp	Financial	Germany	0.75

Current Investment Style

Value Blnd Growth — Large Mid Small

Market Cap	%
Giant	33.4
Large	42.7
Mid	23.9
Small	0.0
Micro	0.0
Avg $mil:	19,885

Value Measures		Rel Category
Price/Earnings	15.47	1.18
Price/Book	2.36	1.09
Price/Sales	1.54	1.33
Price/Cash Flow	9.60	1.15
Dividend Yield %	2.88	0.99

Growth Measures	%	Rel Category
Long-Term Erngs	12.55	1.06
Book Value	0.77	0.08
Sales	6.27	0.96
Cash Flow	5.10	0.62
Historical Erngs	22.20	1.09

Composition

Cash	13.3	Bonds	0.0
Stocks	83.3	Other	3.4
Foreign (% of Stock)			99.6

Sector Weightings

		% of Stocks	Rel MSCI EAFE	3 Year High Low
☁ Info	12.44	1.05		
🔲 Software	0.20	0.36	—	—
🔲 Hardware	1.48	0.38	—	—
🔲 Media	3.45	1.89	—	—
🔲 Telecom	7.31	1.31	—	—
☁ Service	52.98	1.12		
🔲 Health	7.25	1.02	—	—
🔲 Consumer	3.82	0.77	—	—
🔲 Business	8.46	1.67	—	—
🔲 Financial	33.45	1.11	—	—
☁ Mfg	34.58	0.84		
🔲 Goods	13.51	1.03	—	—
🔲 Ind Mtrls	14.37	0.93	—	—
🔲 Energy	4.73	0.66	—	—
🔲 Utilities	1.97	0.38	—	—

Regional Exposure

	% Stock		% Stock
UK/W. Europe	66	N. America	2
Japan	9	Latn America	2
Asia X Japan	6	Other	15

Country Exposure

	% Stock		% Stock
France	12	Japan	9
U.K.	11	Switzerland	8
Germany	9		

MORNINGSTAR® Funds 500

Julius Baer Intl Eqty A

	Ticker	Load	NAV	Yield	Total Assets	Mstar Category
	BJBIX	Closed	$42.23	0.6%	$21,724 mil	Foreign Large Blend

Governance and Management

Stewardship Grade: C

Portfolio Manager(s)

Rudolph-Riad Younes and Richard Pell have worked for Bank Julius Baer and other firms in various investment-related capacities for many years. They've been running this fund since the spring of 1995 and have a team of about five analysts. Although they work together, Younes handles the day-to-day management, while Pell focuses more on providing broader strategic oversight. They were named Morningstar's International Fund Managers of the Year for 2002.

Strategy

The managers consider sector selection and the outlook for the U.S. economy more than most peers but also perform intensive company analysis. This strategy incorporates growth and value factors and all sizes of companies, though small caps are not plentiful in the portfolio. Individual stock positions are typically less than 3% of assets. The fund's weightings can diverge sharply from those of the MSCI EAFE Index. It occasionally hedges some of its foreign-currency exposure. It has a 2% short-term redemption fee and sometimes uses fair-value pricing.

Performance 12-31-06

	1st Qtr	2nd Qtr	3rd Qtr	4th Qtr	Total
2002	4.32	0.69	-13.08	5.59	-3.60
2003	-7.14	15.82	7.91	17.11	35.92
2004	6.30	-3.02	1.50	17.75	23.22
2005	0.25	-0.41	13.88	2.95	17.05
2006	12.95	-1.15	4.04	13.41	31.75

Trailing	Total Return%	+/- MSCI EAFE	+/- MSCI Wd xUS	%Rank Cat	Growth of $10,000
3 Mo	13.41	3.06	3.29	5	11,341
6 Mo	18.00	3.31	3.78	6	11,800
1 Yr	31.75	5.41	6.04	3	13,175
3 Yr Avg	23.86	3.93	3.76	3	19,002
5 Yr Avg	20.02	5.04	4.77	2	24,904
10 Yr Avg	16.99	9.28	9.03	1	48,027
15 Yr Avg	—	—	—	—	—

Tax Analysis	Tax-Adj Rtn%	%Rank Cat	Tax-Cost Rat	%Rank Cat
3 Yr (estimated)	22.22	4	1.32	69
5 Yr (estimated)	18.81	3	1.01	77
10 Yr (estimated)	16.01	1	0.84	35

Potential Capital Gain Exposure: 32% of assets

Morningstar's Take by Gregg Wolper 12-22-06

Like a sports dynasty, Julius Baer International Equity dominates its field by making key adjustments while keeping its core and philosophy intact.

Certain things stay the same here. Managers Rudolph-Riad Younes and Richard Pell have stuck with their uncommon approach regardless of the market climate. They take into account global and local macroeconomic trends more than most rivals, don't care if the portfolio differs sharply from the MSCI EAFE Index, and keep individual position sizes low. Some important aspects of the portfolio don't alter much, either. Most notably, for many years the fund has devoted significant assets to Central and Eastern Europe, and the Japan stake has been much lower than the norm.

However, the managers do make critical changes when they deem them necessary. For example, for several years they've had far more assets in Turkey--the stake had grown all the way to 6% by early 2006--than practically any other

fund. Those stocks provided spectacular gains. Yet Younes says they cut the stake to just 2% in the spring of 2006, because they were concerned that Turkey's government was becoming complacent in its financial policies, and they didn't want to get greedy after such a huge gain. Turkey's market plunged soon thereafter. Younes says they didn't go back in, either (the stake is now 1%)--a sound move, since Turkey is the rare emerging market that continued to struggle after the June slide.

This approach has given the fund the best trailing 10-year record of the roughly 90 foreign large-blend funds with records that long. And a burgeoning asset base--it now has more than $21 billion--hasn't slowed it down. For the year to date through Dec. 21, 2006, its 30% gain is also one of the group's highest.

This fund thus remains one of the best in the international realm. It is closed to new investors, but a similar sibling, Julius Baer International Equity II, is open.

Address:	615 E. Michigan Street LC-3 Milwaukee WI 53202 800-387-6977	Minimum Purchase:	Closed	Add: —	IRA: —
		Min Auto Inv Plan:	Closed	Add: —	
		Sales Fees:	No-load, 0.25%S, 2.00%R		
Web Address:	www.us-funds.juliusbaer.com	Management Fee:	0.90% mx./0.85% mn., 0.25%A		
Inception:	10-04-93	Actual Fees:	Mgt:0.89%	Dist:0.25%	
Advisor:	Julius Baer Securities Inc.	Expense Projections:	3Yr:$418	5Yr:$723	10Yr:$1590
Subadvisor:	None	Income Distrib:	Annually		
NTF Plans:	Fidelity Retail-NTF, Schwab OneSource				

Historical Profile

Return	High
Risk	Above Avg
Rating	★★★★ Highest

	84%	93%	83%	89%	76%	71%	87%	92%	84%	

Growth of $10,000
■ Investment Values of Fund
— Investment Values of MSCI EAFE

Performance Quartile (within Category)

1995	1996	1997	1998	1999	2000	2001	2002	2003	2004	2005	2006	History
10.29	12.07	13.77	17.11	27.91	25.67	20.81	19.74	26.50	31.61	35.44	42.23	NAV
-0.19	17.66	15.33	27.07	76.58	-8.02	-18.93	-3.60	35.92	23.22	17.05	31.75	Total Return %
-11.40	11.61	13.55	7.14	49.55	6.17	2.49	12.34	-2.67	2.97	3.51	5.41	+/-MSCI EAFE
-11.60	10.79	13.06	8.38	48.60	5.34	2.46	12.20	-3.50	2.84	2.58	6.04	+/-MSCI Wd xUS
0.00	0.36	1.24	0.00	0.37	0.01	0.00	1.52	1.65	1.71	0.00	0.79	Income Return %
-0.19	17.30	14.09	27.07	76.21	-8.03	-18.93	-5.12	34.27	21.51	17.05	30.96	Capital Return %
100	18	8	2	1	11	28	1	31	4	19	3	Total Rtn % Rank Cat
0.00	0.04	0.15	0.00	0.06	0.00	0.00	0.32	0.33	0.45	0.00	0.28	Income $
0.00	0.00	0.00	0.39	1.76	0.00	0.00	0.00	0.00	0.58	1.57	4.17	Capital Gains $
2.67	2.37	1.79	1.87	1.96	1.37	1.40	1.43	1.31	1.32	1.31	—	Expense Ratio %
-0.63	-0.58	0.00	-0.15	-0.48	0.32	0.36	0.49	0.83	0.58	1.09	—	Income Ratio %
116	67	94	134	73	72	89	93	114	100	57	—	Turnover Rate %
10	22	47	73	105	240	305	742	2,207	4,761	7,547	9,791	Net Assets $mil

Rating and Risk

Time Period	Load-Adj Return %	Morningstar Rtn vs Cat	Morningstar Risk vs Cat	Morningstar Risk-Adj Rating
1 Yr	31.75			
3 Yr	23.86	High	High	★★★★★
5 Yr	20.02	High	-Avg	★★★★★
10 Yr	16.99	High	High	★★★★★
Incept	12.68			

Other Measures	Standard Index MSCI EAFE	Best Fit Index MSCI Wd xUS
Alpha	0.2	0.2
Beta	1.22	1.20
R-Squared	93	93
Standard Deviation	11.93	
Mean	23.86	
Sharpe Ratio	1.60	

Portfolio Analysis 10-31-06

Share change since 07-06 Total Stocks:466

		Sector	Country	% Assets
⊖	Pko Bk Polski S.A.	Financial	Poland	1.41
⊖	Total SA	Energy	France	1.39
	Komercni banka	Financial	Czech Republic	1.25
⊕	Vodafone Grp	Telecom	U.K.	1.19
	Nestle	Goods	Switzerland	1.19
⊖	OTP Bank	Financial	Hungary	1.12
⊖	Bank Pekao	Financial	Poland	1.06
⊖	Lafarge	Ind Mtrls	France	1.06
	Fraport	Business	Germany	0.99
⊖	KBC Bank & Insurance	Financial	Belgium	0.97
	Novartis	Health	Switzerland	0.94
	GlaxoSmithKline	Health	U.K.	0.92
⊕	Consulta (Ci)	—	U.K.	0.87
⊖	Diageo	Goods	U.K.	0.85
	LVMH Moet Hennessy L.V.	Goods	France	0.84
⊕	Holcim	Ind Mtrls	Switzerland	0.79
⊖	UniCredito Italiano Grp	Financial	Italy	0.77
	ING Groep	Financial	Netherlands	0.76
	Bk Vontobel Ag	—	Switzerland	0.75
⊖	Roche Holding	Health	Switzerland	0.74

Current Investment Style

Value Blnd Growth / Large Mid Small

Market Cap	%
Giant	33.1
Large	38.2
Mid	22.9
Small	4.7
Micro	1.1
Avg $mil:	16,237

Value Measures		Rel Category
Price/Earnings	14.53	1.11
Price/Book	2.25	1.04
Price/Sales	1.32	1.14
Price/Cash Flow	8.06	0.97
Dividend Yield %	2.84	0.97

Growth Measures	%	Rel Category
Long-Term Erngs	12.47	1.06
Book Value	-7.17	NMF
Sales	6.89	1.05
Cash Flow	7.49	0.91
Historical Erngs	22.88	1.13

Composition

Cash	11.6	Bonds	0.3
Stocks	83.5	Other	4.6
Foreign (% of Stock)			99.7

Sector Weightings	% of Stocks	Rel MSCI EAFE	3 Year High	Low
⌖ Info	11.26	0.95		
Software	0.21	0.37	0	0
Hardware	1.59	0.41	6	1
Media	3.00	1.64	6	2
Telecom	6.46	1.16	11	4
⊆ Service	54.27	1.15		
Health	7.63	1.07	11	5
Consumer	4.00	0.81	5	3
Business	9.26	1.83	10	4
Financial	33.38	1.11	38	28
Mfg	34.46	0.84		
Goods	13.66	1.04	17	12
Ind Mtrls	14.00	0.91	14	5
Energy	5.00	0.70	13	5
Utilities	1.80	0.34	5	1

Regional Exposure	% Stock		
UK/W. Europe 65	N. America		1
Japan 9	Latn America		2
Asia X Japan 6	Other		17

Country Exposure	% Stock		
France	11	Germany	9
U.K.	11	Switzerland	7
Japan	9		

Kalmar Gr Val Sm Cp

	Ticker	Load	NAV	Yield	Total Assets	Mstar Category
	KGSCX	None	$16.81	0.0%	$435 mil	Small Growth

Governance and Management

Stewardship Grade:

Portfolio Manager(s)

Ford Draper Jr. established Kalmar Investments in 1982, using this same strategy to manage separate accounts. Nine team members provide investment research. The three most senior members of the investment team all have more than 20 years of industry experience and at least 10 at Kalmar.

Strategy

Management invests in established, well-managed companies with above-average revenue and earnings growth, and it likes to buy them when they are cheap. This results in a portfolio of stocks that are reasonably priced relative to their earnings-growth rates. Management often can't find the growth it seeks in financial-services stocks, and its desire for profitability can limit its tech exposure.

Performance 12-31-06

	1st Qtr	2nd Qtr	3rd Qtr	4th Qtr	Total
2002	1.16	-5.19	-18.68	7.03	-16.53
2003	-3.24	18.64	10.07	13.59	43.54
2004	4.39	1.68	-6.68	13.88	12.81
2005	-3.83	2.70	5.32	1.19	5.25
2006	10.83	-7.97	0.24	3.84	6.17

Trailing	Total Return%	+/- S&P 500	+/- Russ 2000 Gr	%Rank Cat	Growth of $10,000
3 Mo	3.84	-2.86	-4.93	97	10,384
6 Mo	4.09	-8.65	-2.77	64	10,409
1 Yr	6.17	-9.62	-7.18	79	10,617
3 Yr Avg	8.02	-2.42	-2.49	69	12,604
5 Yr Avg	8.60	2.41	1.67	31	15,106
10 Yr Avg	—	—	—	—	—
15 Yr Avg	—	—	—	—	—

Tax Analysis	Tax-Adj Rtn%	%Rank Cat	Tax-Cost Rat	%Rank Cat
3 Yr (estimated)	7.47	59	0.51	18
5 Yr (estimated)	8.11	26	0.45	25
10 Yr (estimated)	—	—	—	—

Potential Capital Gain Exposure: 31% of assets

Morningstar's Take by Dan Culloton 11-27-06

This fund makes sense, but it would make more if it were cheaper.

Kalmar Growth-with-Value Small Cap has a clunky name but a well-drilled process. Lead manager Ford Draper Jr. and his decent-size research staff beat the bushes for stocks capable of growing at least 15% per year but either aren't on or have fallen off the rest of Wall Street's radar screens. Draper and his team rely primarily on their own gumshoeing and a smidgeon of top-down and third-party analysis to find reasonably priced stocks that can deliver the growth.

For many funds, that means dipping into core or value stocks that may not have a lot of expansion potential. But this fund hasn t sacrificed growth for valuations. All of the portfolio's average growth measures, such as earnings and book value, are in line or above those of the typical small growth fund. And it has been able to find companies that dominate potentially profitable niches, such as Concur Technologies, the largest provider of

corporate expense management software.

The management has practiced this brand of investing for a long time. He has led this fund for nearly 10 years and managed separate accounts in the same style for almost 25 years. Long-term returns on those accounts are competitive, if not spectacular, on an absolute basis.

The fund's focus on ferreting out financially sound companies has helped limit the fund's risk, at least relative to its usually variable category. On an absolute basis, this fund can be rough. It's capable of falling by double digits in as short a span as three months. Still, average measures of volatility, such as standard deviation, are lower, however, than the fund's peer group average.

This does look like a sensible fund for the long term, but it would be nice if its expense ratio, which is higher than the median for no-load small cap funds, was lower.

Address:	Barley Mill House, 3701 Kennett Pike Greenville, DE 19807 800-282-2319
Web Address:	www.kalmarinvestments.com
Inception:	04-11-97 *
Advisor:	Kalmar Investment Advisers
Subadvisor:	None
NTF Plans:	Schwab OneSource

Minimum Purchase:	$10000	Add: $0	IRA: $1000
Min Auto Inv Plan:	$10000	Add: $100	
Sales Fees:	No-load, 2.00%R		
Management Fee:	1.00%		
Actual Fees:	Mgt:1.00%	Dist: —	
Expense Projections:	3Yr:$409	5Yr:$708	10Yr:$1556
Income Distrib:	Annually		

Historical Profile
Return: Average
Risk: Below Avg
Rating: ★★★ Neutral

	90%	97%	88%	95%	90%	93%	97%	90%	99%

Investment Style
Equity
Stock %

▼ Manager Change
▽ Partial Manager Change

Growth of $10,000
— Investment Values of Fund
— Investment Values of S&P 500

22.6
19.0
16.0
13.0
10.0

Performance Quartile (within Category)

1995	1996	1997	1998	1999	2000	2001	2002	2003	2004	2005	2006	History
—	—	13.70	12.65	13.41	12.95	12.95	10.81	14.80	16.17	16.53	16.81	NAV
—	—	47.53*	-7.66	6.01	15.70	0.00	-16.53	43.54	12.81	5.25	6.17	Total Return %
—	—	—	-36.24	-15.03	24.80	11.89	5.57	14.86	1.93	0.34	-9.62	+/-S&P 500
—	—	—	-8.89	-37.08	38.13	9.23	13.73	-5.00	-1.50	1.10	-7.18	+/-Russ 2000 Gr
—	—	—	0.00	0.00	0.00	0.00	0.00	0.00	0.00	0.00	0.00	Income Return %
—	—	—	-7.66	6.01	15.70	0.00	-16.53	43.54	12.81	5.25	6.17	Capital Return %
—	—	—	91	95	10	27	8	54	46	57	79	Total Rtn % Rank Cat
—	—	0.00	0.00	0.00	0.00	0.00	0.00	0.00	0.00	0.00	0.00	Income $
—	—	0.92	0.00	0.00	2.59	0.00	0.00	0.72	0.53	0.49	0.75	Capital Gains $
—	—	1.25	1.24	1.25	1.22	1.23	1.23	1.26	1.27	1.29	—	Expense Ratio %
—	—	-0.51	-0.52	-0.78	-0.82	-0.96	-1.03	-1.03	-0.90	-0.79	—	Income Ratio %
—	—	—	27	52	64	47	41	46	23	30	—	Turnover Rate %
—	—	227	222	195	196	207	217	270	372	415	435	Net Assets $mil

Rating and Risk

Time Period	Load-Adj Return %	Morningstar Rtn vs Cat	Morningstar Risk vs Cat	Morningstar Risk-Adj Rating
1 Yr	6.17			
3 Yr	8.02	Avg	-Avg	★★★
5 Yr	8.60	Avg	-Avg	★★★
10 Yr	—	—	—	—
Incept	9.99			

Other Measures	Standard Index S&P 500	Best Fit Index Russ 2000 Gr
Alpha	-6.1	-1.1
Beta	1.64	0.80
R-Squared	73	94
Standard Deviation	13.08	
Mean	8.02	
Sharpe Ratio	0.41	

Portfolio Analysis 10-31-06

Share change since 09-06 Total Stocks:97	Sector	PE	Tot Ret%	% Assets
Avocent Corporation	Hardware	34.7	24.49	2.69
Albemarle Corporation	Ind Mtrls	30.2	89.76	2.36
MSC Industrial Direct Co	Business	21.6	-1.47	2.20
Coldwater Creek	Consumer	36.0	20.47	2.20
Corrections Corporation	Business	28.1	50.87	2.17
Ultra Petroleum Corporat	Energy	30.4	-14.44	2.02
⊕ Cooper Companies	Health	35.7	-13.14	2.00
Mobile Mini	Ind Mtrls	25.4	13.67	1.91
PSS World Medical, Inc.	Health	27.7	31.60	1.85
ATMI, Inc.	Hardware	30.1	9.15	1.84
⊕ Parallel Petroleum Corpo	Energy	23.8	3.29	1.78
Laureate Education, Inc.	Consumer	27.1	-7.39	1.77
Respironics Inc.	Health	26.8	1.83	1.69
⊖ Insight Enterprises, Inc	Business	16.7	-3.77	1.68
Rogers Corporation	Ind Mtrls	23.2	50.97	1.65
Chicago Bridge & Iron Co	Business	87.7	8.97	1.54
Alliance Data Systems Co	Business	29.1	75.48	1.52
Covance, Inc.	Health	28.4	21.34	1.50
SRA International, Inc.	Business	25.3	-12.44	1.48
Polycom, Inc.	Hardware	50.6	102.03	1.47

Current Investment Style

Value Blnd Growth — Large/Mid/Small

	Market Cap	%
	Giant	0.0
	Large	0.0
	Mid	38.7
	Small	51.8
	Micro	9.6
	Avg $mil:	1,521

Value Measures		Rel Category
Price/Earnings	23.34	1.11
Price/Book	2.54	0.93
Price/Sales	1.47	0.94
Price/Cash Flow	12.44	1.29
Dividend Yield %	0.17	0.37

Growth Measures	%	Rel Category
Long-Term Erngs	19.46	1.10
Book Value	11.71	1.12
Sales	11.85	1.00
Cash Flow	20.78	0.98
Historical Erngs	20.22	0.83

Profitability	%	Rel Category
Return on Equity	10.67	0.86
Return on Assets	6.39	0.96
Net Margin	8.81	1.02

Sector Weightings	% of Stocks	Rel S&P 500	3 Year High	Low
⊕ Info	22.04	1.10		
Software	5.24	1.52	5	1
Hardware	15.48	1.68	15	11
Media	0.00	0.00	1	0
Telecom	1.32	0.38	1	0
⊙ Service	51.46	1.11		
Health	13.82	1.15	18	13
Consumer	14.51	1.90	23	14
Business	22.08	5.22	27	20
Financial	1.05	0.05	1	0
⊟ Mfg	26.50	0.78		
Goods	6.24	0.73	7	1
Ind Mtrls	9.21	0.77	15	9
Energy	11.05	1.13	12	7
Utilities	0.00	0.00	0	0

Composition

● Cash	0.0
● Stocks	99.2
● Bonds	0.0
● Other	0.8
Foreign (% of Stock)	6.2

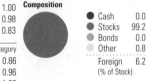
Morningstar® Funds 500

Legg Mason Opp Prim

	Ticker	Load	NAV	Yield	Total Assets	Mstar Category
	LMOPX	1.00%d	$18.94	0.0%	$6,772 mil	Mid-Cap Growth

Governance and Management

Stewardship Grade: B

Portfolio Manager(s)

Bill Miller is widely regarded as one of the most accomplished fund managers in the business. His Legg Mason Value Trust has beaten the S&P 500 in each of the past 15 calendar years. With more than a decade at that fund's helm, he brings a wealth of experience to this offering.

Strategy

Bill Miller has free rein here. Although he seeks companies that are trading at discounts to his estimates of their intrinsic values, that often includes names that others might consider expensive. The fund typically holds between 20 and 40 positions, and it invests in both debt and equity instruments. Miller can also take short positions here, although it's getting too big to short individual stocks.

Historical Profile
Return Above Avg
Risk High
Rating ★★★★ Above Avg

Performance Quartile (within Category)

| | 85% | 84% | 76% | 94% | 93% | 91% | 90% | Investment Style Equity Stock % |

▼ Manager Change
▽ Partial Manager Change

Growth of $10,000
— Investment Values of Fund
— Investment Values of S&P 500

	1995	1996	1997	1998	1999	2000	2001	2002	2003	2004	2005	2006	History
NAV	—	—	—	—	10.00	9.65	9.80	8.23	13.77	15.67	16.72	18.94	NAV
	—	—	—	—	0.00*	-1.68	1.94	-15.52	67.95	13.80	6.70	13.41	Total Return %
	—	—	—	—	—	7.42	13.83	6.58	39.27	2.92	1.79	-2.38	+/-S&P 500
	—	—	—	—	—	10.07	22.09	11.89	25.24	-1.68	-5.40	2.75	+/-Russ MG
	—	—	—	—	—	0.40	0.37	0.51	0.61	0.00	0.00	0.00	Income Return %
	—	—	—	—	—	-2.08	1.57	-16.03	67.34	13.80	6.70	13.41	Capital Return %
	—	—	—	—	—	49	9	10	1	51	76	18	Total Rtn % Rank Cat
	—	—	—	—	0.00	0.04	0.04	0.05	0.05	0.00	0.00	0.00	Income $
	—	—	—	—	0.00	0.14	0.00	0.00	0.00	0.00	0.00	0.02	Capital Gains $
	—	—	—	—	1.99	1.98	1.89	1.94	1.90	1.87	—	—	Expense Ratio %
	—	—	—	—	—	0.63	-0.45	0.99	0.00	-0.66	—	—	Income Ratio %
	—	—	—	—	—	—	26	60	44	27	13	—	Turnover Rate %
	—	—	—	—	—	1,112	1,714	1,414	2,756	3,599	4,724	Net Assets $mil

Performance 12-31-06

	1st Qtr	2nd Qtr	3rd Qtr	4th Qtr	Total
2002	7.04	-18.78	-18.31	18.96	-15.52
2003	3.89	38.29	5.84	10.45	67.95
2004	3.70	3.57	-9.80	17.47	13.80
2005	-7.98	4.51	10.09	0.78	6.70
2006	10.29	-8.53	-1.72	14.39	13.41

Trailing	Total Return%	+/- S&P 500	+/- Russ MG	%Rank Cat	Growth of $10,000
3 Mo	14.39	7.69	7.44	1	11,439
6 Mo	12.42	-0.32	4.52	4	11,242
1 Yr	13.41	-2.38	2.75	18	11,341
3 Yr Avg	11.25	0.81	-1.48	44	13,769
5 Yr Avg	14.33	8.14	6.11	2	19,534
10 Yr Avg	—	—	—		—
15 Yr Avg	—	—	—		—

Tax Analysis	Tax-Adj Rtn%	%Rank Cat	Tax-Cost Rat	%Rank Cat
3 Yr (estimated)	11.25	31	0.00	1
5 Yr (estimated)	14.25	1	0.07	6
10 Yr (estimated)	—	—	—	—

Potential Capital Gain Exposure: 34% of assets

Rating and Risk

Time Period	Load-Adj Return %	Morningstar Rtn vs Cat	Morningstar Risk vs Cat	Morningstar Risk-Adj Rating
1 Yr	12.41			
3 Yr	11.25	Avg	High	★★★
5 Yr	14.33	High	High	★★★★★
10 Yr	—	—	—	—
Incept	10.07			

Other Measures	Standard Index S&P 500	Best Fit Index Russ MG
Alpha	-7.3	-5.4
Beta	2.36	1.54
R-Squared	74	87
Standard Deviation	18.78	
Mean	11.25	
Sharpe Ratio	0.49	

Morningstar's Take by Greg Carlson 12-05-06

Legg Mason Opportunity is leaving its famous sibling in the dust, but it plays to a more limited audience.

This mid-growth fund, a more freewheeling vehicle for superstar manager Bill Miller than his bigger charge, Legg Mason Value, has soared 18% as the market has rallied in the past three months--that's nearly double the gain of Value. The fund's spike is a result of its bold approach. While both funds sport concentrated portfolios, Miller owns primarily large caps at Value; he's free at this smaller fund to buy the equity and debt of firms of all sizes and engage in short selling. Some of the shakier firms that Miller won't hold in Value, such as AK Steel and telecom concern Level 3 Communications, have driven this fund's recent vault from the category's bottom quartile to the top third. What's more, the fund has outpaced its sibling by an annualized 7.3% since its December 1999 inception.

That said, we wouldn't suggest this fund as an alternative to Value, which lags far behind the S&P 500 Index this year after beating the benchmark for a remarkable 15 consecutive years. This fund's inception roughly coincided with the start of smaller stocks' rally, giving it a huge edge. Furthermore, the fund is much more volatile.

There are other caveats to keep in mind here. The fund's asset base is nearing $7 billion, limiting Miller's ability to short-sell and to buy less-liquid names. What's more, about a fourth of its portfolio overlaps with Value and similarly managed separate accounts totaling more than $40 billion. Thus, Legg Mason owns huge stakes in firms like top five holding Amazon.com, limiting Miller's ability to buy more. Finally, due to a 1% 12b-1 fee, the fund's expense ratio is a lofty 2.08%. We think only investors who get financial advice included in that price tag should pay it.

But despite our concerns, this fund still has tremendous potential, thanks to Miller's prodigious talent. It's best used in moderate doses, though.

Address:	100 Light Street Baltimore MD 21202 800-822-5544
Web Address:	www.leggmason.com
Inception:	12-30-99*
Advisor:	LMM LLC
Subadvisor:	Legg Mason Capital Management, Inc.
NTF Plans:	N/A

Minimum Purchase:	$1000	Add: $100	IRA: $1000
Min Auto Inv Plan:	$50	Add: $50	
Sales Fees:	1.00%D, 1.00%S		
Management Fee:	1.00% mx./0.75% mn.		
Actual Fees:	Mgt:0.76%	Dist:1.00%	
Expense Projections:	3Yr:$652	5Yr:$1119	10Yr:$2410
Income Distrib:	Annually		

Portfolio Analysis 09-30-06

Share change since 06-06 Total Stocks:47	Sector	PE	Tot Ret%	% Assets
NII Holdings, Inc.	Telecom	45.9	47.53	7.01
United States Steel Corp	Ind Mtrls	7.4	53.62	5.85
Tyco International, Ltd.	Ind Mtrls	15.7	6.83	4.73
⊕ Mittal Steel Company NV	Ind Mtrls	8.2	62.46	4.31
⊕ Amazon.com, Inc.	Consumer	55.1	-16.31	3.62
IAC/InterActiveCorp	Consumer	40.6	31.26	3.24
Level 3 Communications,	Telecom	—	95.12	3.02
Level 3 Comms 10%		—	—	2.87
Netflix, Inc.	Consumer	22.1	-4.44	2.75
Jarden Corporation	Goods	32.0	15.39	2.65
⊕ Ryland Group, Inc.	Consumer	5.7	-23.60	2.64
⊕ Cleveland-Cliffs Inc.	Ind Mtrls	9.6	10.65	2.64
AES Corporation	Utilities	33.4	39.23	2.63
⊕ Sprint Nextel Corporatio	Telecom	30.2	-10.44	2.62
AMR Corporation	Business		35.99	2.42
Sepracor, Inc.	Health	NMF	19.34	2.11
⊕ Yahoo, Inc.	Media	35.4	-34.81	2.04
Pulte Homes, Inc.	Consumer	6.7	-15.43	1.80
NetEase.com, Inc. ADR	Business	94.6	33.12	1.79
VeriSign, Inc.	Software	55.5	9.82	1.79

Current Investment Style

Value Blnd Growth — Large Mid Small

Market Cap	%
Giant	5.3
Large	22.3
Mid	54.8
Small	14.9
Micro	2.7

Avg $mil: 6,105

Value Measures		Rel Category
Price/Earnings	13.25	0.65
Price/Book	1.64	0.51
Price/Sales	0.59	0.34
Price/Cash Flow	5.59	0.49
Dividend Yield %	0.81	1.29

Growth Measures	%	Rel Category
Long-Term Erngs	13.71	0.84
Book Value	9.58	0.75
Sales	-7.07	NMF
Cash Flow	13.94	0.75
Historical Erngs	29.33	1.17

Profitability	%	Rel Category
Return on Equity	17.06	0.95
Return on Assets	5.83	0.62
Net Margin	7.19	0.62

Sector Weightings	% of Stocks	Rel S&P 500	3 Year High Low	
↗ Info	24.95	1.25		
Software	4.05	1.17	6	4
Hardware	1.96	0.21	2	0
Media	4.70	1.24	7	5
Telecom	14.24	4.06	15	10
☞ Service	41.75	0.90		
Health	3.17	0.26	9	3
Consumer	26.32	3.44	31	14
Business	7.92	1.87	16	8
Financial	4.34	0.19	22	4
↓ Mfg	33.31	0.99		
Goods	6.19	0.72	7	3
Ind Mtrls	24.16	2.02	24	9
Energy	0.00	0.00	1	0
Utilities	2.96	0.85	3	2

Composition

Composition	%
● Cash	0.1
● Stocks	89.9
● Bonds	5.8
● Other	4.1
Foreign (% of Stock)	8.7

Legg Mason P Aggr Grow A

	Ticker	Load	NAV	Yield	Total Assets	Mstar Category
	SHRAX	5.75%	$115.66	0.0%	$10,812 mil	Large Growth

Governance and Management

Stewardship Grade: D

Portfolio Manager(s)

Very seasoned. Richie Freeman is one of the longest-tenured managers in the large-growth group, having managed this fund since its 1983 inception.

Strategy

Manager Richie Freeman looks for dynamic small- and mid-cap companies that are growing their earnings by 20% per year. Once he finds a stock he likes, Freeman sticks with it: The fund's turnover is among the lowest in the large-growth category. Given Freeman's buy-and-hold strategy and the success of his long-held picks, the fund's average market cap falls into large-cap territory.

Historical Profile

Return	Above Avg
Risk	Above Avg
Rating	★★★★ Above Avg

94% 91% 87% 90% 93% 94% 99% 99% 99%

Investment Style
Equity
Stock %

▼ Manager Change
▽ Partial Manager Change

Growth of $10,000
50.6
43.6
— Investment Values of Fund
32.4
24.0
17.0 — Investment Values of S&P 500
10.0

Performance Quartile (within Category)

1995	1996	1997	1998	1999	2000	2001	2002	2003	2004	2005	2006	History
31.48	31.52	38.56	51.09	82.78	98.61	93.68	63.00	86.04	95.17	107.11	115.66	NAV
35.73	2.72	28.44	35.08	63.74	19.12	-5.00	-32.75	36.57	10.61	12.55	7.98	Total Return %
-1.85	-20.24	-4.92	6.50	42.70	28.22	6.89	-10.65	7.89	-0.27	7.64	-7.81	+/-S&P 500
-1.45	-20.40	-2.05	-3.63	30.58	41.54	15.42	-4.87	6.82	4.31	7.29	-1.09	+/-Russ 1000Gr
0.00	0.00	0.00	0.00	0.00	0.00	0.00	0.00	0.00	0.00	0.00	0.00	Income Return %
35.73	2.72	28.44	35.08	63.74	19.12	-5.00	-32.75	36.57	10.61	12.55	7.98	Capital Return %
28	98	39	34	11	1	4	85	13	27	12	39	Total Rtn % Rank Cat
0.00	0.00	0.00	0.00	0.00	0.00	0.00	0.00	0.00	0.00	0.00	0.00	Income $
2.88	0.81	1.96	0.88	0.72	0.00	0.00	0.00	0.00	0.00	0.00	0.00	Capital Gains $
1.37	1.30	1.21	1.21	1.18	1.14	1.17	1.21	1.22	1.19	1.21	1.13	Expense Ratio %
-1.05	-0.97	-0.93	-0.97	-0.89	-0.66	-0.80	-0.88	-0.86	-0.82	-0.69	-0.59	Income Ratio %
44	13	6	7	8	1	—	1	1	5	2	1	Turnover Rate %
294	269	340	472	956	1,728	2,211	1,854	2,788	3,425	4,006	4,560	Net Assets $mil

Performance 12-31-06

	1st Qtr	2nd Qtr	3rd Qtr	4th Qtr	Total
2002	-5.90	-25.52	-12.63	9.83	-32.75
2003	2.19	17.04	3.09	10.76	36.57
2004	5.00	-1.27	-1.65	8.49	10.61
2005	-4.51	2.64	11.64	2.85	12.55
2006	4.72	-4.58	3.92	3.98	7.98

Trailing	Total Return%	+/- S&P 500	+/- Russ 1000Gr	%Rank Cat	Growth of $10,000
3 Mo	3.98	-2.72	-1.95	84	10,398
6 Mo	8.06	-4.68	-2.04	56	10,806
1 Yr	7.98	-7.81	-1.09	39	10,798
3 Yr Avg	10.36	-0.08	3.49	12	13,441
5 Yr Avg	4.31	-1.88	1.62	26	12,349
10 Yr Avg	14.78	6.36	9.34	1	39,688
15 Yr Avg	13.55	2.91	5.53	2	67,268

Tax Analysis	Tax-Adj Rtn%	%Rank Cat	Tax-Cost Rat	%Rank Cat
3 Yr (estimated)	8.21	24	0.00	1
5 Yr (estimated)	3.08	37	0.00	1
10 Yr (estimated)	13.93	1	0.15	5

Potential Capital Gain Exposure: 38% of assets

Morningstar's Take by Annie Sorich 11-06-06

Legg Mason Partners Aggressive Growth continues to be one of our favorites.

Manager Richie Freeman has more than proven his worth at this offering. During his 23-year tenure, his low-turnover, high-conviction approach has delivered superior results. For example, the fund's annualized trailing 10-year returns land it at the top of the large-growth category through Nov. 6, 2006.

Longtime shareholders may notice a gaping hole in the portfolio, however: Former top-10 holding Chiron, which the fund had owned since 1986, was acquired by Novartis in April 2006. Now that the fund is owned by Legg Mason instead of banking conglomerate Citigroup, Freeman was able to successfully lobby with other investors for a higher acquisition price for Chiron. While Freeman doesn't consider himself a shareholder activist, his actions would have been difficult to execute while the fund was under Citigroup, because of the potential for conflict of interest with the firm's large investment-banking arm.

Freeman's longtime ownership of Chiron brings to light a strength of the fund's strategy--his knack for recognizing influential companies in their early stages of growth, buying them, and holding on unless a serious fundamental change occurs--or as in this case, an acquisition. We don't know of many other managers who still own stocks that they bought 23 years ago as Freeman has with Forest Laboratories. While most of the portfolio's performance can be explained by its top 25 to 30 holdings, the remaining 50 or so stocks are potentially the next Intel or Genentech--other stocks the fund has owned for decades.

Our one concern is the fund's fees. Even though assets are 10 times greater than 10 years ago, expenses have not budged. Given this fund's size, it should cost less, not more, to administer, and we think it should be considerably cheaper.

Still, we heartily recommend this unique offering and its fine manager.

Address:	125 Broad Street New York NY 10004 800-451-2010
Web Address:	www.leggmason.com
Inception:	10-24-83
Advisor:	Legg Mason Partners Fund Advisor, LLC
Subadvisor:	Clearbridge Advisers, LLC
NTF Plans:	DATALynx NTF, Fidelity Instl-NTF

Minimum Purchase:	$500	Add: $50	IRA: $250
Min Auto Inv Plan:	$25	Add: $25	
Sales Fees:	5.75%L, 0.25%S		
Management Fee:	0.75% mx.,0.65% mn.		
Actual Fees:	Mgt:0.69%	Dist:0.25%	
Expense Projections:	3Yr:$908	5Yr:$1152	10Yr:$1849
Income Distrib:	Annually		

Rating and Risk

Time Period	Load-Adj Return %	Morningstar Rtn vs Cat	Morningstar Risk vs Cat	Morningstar Risk-Adj Rating
1 Yr	1.77			
3 Yr	8.21	+Avg	Avg	★★★
5 Yr	3.08	Avg	+Avg	★★★
10 Yr	14.10	High	+Avg	★★★★★
Incept	13.67			

Other Measures	Standard Index S&P 500	Best Fit Index Merrill Lynch Convert
Alpha	-1.8	2.2
Beta	1.29	1.49
R-Squared	72	78

Standard Deviation	10.44
Mean	10.36
Sharpe Ratio	0.69

Portfolio Analysis 09-30-06

Share change since 06-06 Total Stocks:83	Sector	PE	Tot Ret%	% Assets
Lehman Brothers Holdings	Financial	12.2	22.75	9.52
UnitedHealth Group, Inc.	Health	20.8	-13.49	8.02
Anadarko Petroleum Corp.	Energy	5.2	-7.44	6.37
Weatherford Internationa	Energy	15.2	16.56	5.11
Amgen, Inc.	Health	29.1	-13.38	4.65
Genzyme Corporation	Health	50.8	-13.00	4.52
Comcast	Media			4.05
Tyco International, Ltd.	Ind Mtrls	15.7	6.83	4.02
Forest Laboratories, Inc	Health	22.5	24.39	3.87
Biogen Idec, Inc.	Health	NMF	8.64	3.42
Time Warner, Inc.	Media	19.6	26.37	3.31
Merrill Lynch & Company,	Financial	14.2	39.28	3.29
L-3 Communications Holdi	Hardware	20.9	11.04	2.38
Micron Technology, Inc.	Hardware	24.1	4.88	2.33
Cablevision Systems A	Media	—	84.55	2.15
SanDisk Corporation	Hardware	24.2	-31.50	2.05
Grant Prideco, Inc.	Energy	15.2	-9.86	1.86
Motorola, Inc.	Hardware	11.8	-8.17	1.79
Walt Disney Company	Media	21.0	44.26	1.63
Broadcom Corporation	Hardware	39.9	2.79	1.45

Current Investment Style

Value Blnd Growth — Large Mid Small

Market Cap	%
Giant	33.7
Large	41.5
Mid	18.3
Small	5.5
Micro	1.1
Avg $mil:	20,198

Value Measures		Rel Category
Price/Earnings	16.13	0.84
Price/Book	2.33	0.70
Price/Sales	2.22	1.14
Price/Cash Flow	10.19	0.90
Dividend Yield %	0.78	0.76

Growth Measures	%	Rel Category
Long-Term Erngs	14.15	0.99
Book Value	9.11	0.79
Sales	15.44	1.33
Cash Flow	17.78	1.06
Historical Erngs	28.18	1.23

Profitability	%	Rel Category
Return on Equity	15.12	0.74
Return on Assets	8.51	0.77
Net Margin	14.95	1.05

Sector Weightings	% of Stocks	Rel S&P 500	3 Year High	Low
⌖ Info	31.92	1.60		
Software	1.54	0.45	2	1
Hardware	14.85	1.61	15	12
Media	15.52	4.09	16	12
Telecom	0.01	0.00	3	0
⌥ Service	49.60	1.07		
Health	33.15	2.75	45	32
Consumer	0.49	0.06	1	0
Business	0.06	0.01	1	0
Financial	15.90	0.71	16	12
Mfg	18.48	0.55		
Goods	0.03	0.00	0	0
Ind Mtrls	4.08	0.34	4	3
Energy	14.37	1.47	17	6
Utilities	0.00	0.00	0	0

Composition

● Cash	0.9
● Stocks	99.1
● Bonds	0.0
● Other	0.0
Foreign	1.0
(% of Stock)	

MCRNINGSTAR® Funds 500

Legg Mason Spec Invt Pr

Ticker LMASX	**Load** None	**NAV** $38.92	**Yield** 0.0%	**Total Assets** $3,694 mil	**Mstar Category** Mid-Cap Blend

Governance and Management

Stewardship Grade: B

Portfolio Manager(s)

The firm hired Sam Peters from Fidelity in April 2005 to comanage the fund with Miller, with the idea that he would start running it solo in 2006. In accordance with that plan, Peters was named sole manager in January 2006. Peters has one dedicated analyst, also from Fidelity, and access to the firm's analyst pool of more than a dozen researchers.

Strategy

The fund focuses on companies that manager Sam Peters thinks are trading cheaply relative to their prospects, based on qualitative research and estimates of the present value of their future free cash flows. Peters, like his colleagues at Legg Mason, is willing to make fairly optimistic assumptions about growth, however, and the fund will hold more-expensive names than many value offerings. The fund has featured exceptionally large individual positions from time to time, and the volatile technology and telecom sectors have occasionally played prominent roles in the portfolio.

Performance 12-31-06

	1st Qtr	2nd Qtr	3rd Qtr	4th Qtr	Total
2002	5.90	-15.01	-10.61	13.44	-8.74
2003	-1.18	29.17	6.50	13.55	54.36
2004	3.53	3.43	-7.49	14.13	13.05
2005	-5.46	4.65	5.35	3.95	8.34
2006	7.15	-9.43	1.59	9.33	7.80

Trailing	Total Return%	+/- S&P 500	+/- S&P Mid 400	%Rank Cat	Growth of $10,000
3 Mo	9.33	2.63	2.34	16	10,933
6 Mo	11.07	-1.67	5.24	26	11,107
1 Yr	7.80	-7.99	-2.52	91	10,780
3 Yr Avg	9.71	-0.73	-3.38	88	13,205
5 Yr Avg	13.21	7.02	2.32	13	18,596
10 Yr Avg	13.07	4.65	-0.40	25	34,157
15 Yr Avg	13.52	2.88	-0.11	30	67,002

Tax Analysis	Tax-Adj Rtn%	%Rank Cat	Tax-Cost Rat	%Rank Cat
3 Yr (estimated)	7.50	87	2.01	78
5 Yr (estimated)	11.58	20	1.44	83
10 Yr (estimated)	11.35	22	1.52	39

Potential Capital Gain Exposure: 24% of assets

Morningstar's Take by Greg Carlson 11-22-06

Despite a stretch of poor returns, we think Legg Mason Special is headed in the right direction.

This fund has struggled mightily of late: A respectable absolute return of 7% nevertheless leaves the fund behind more than 90% of its mid-blend rivals for the year to date through Nov. 21, 2006.

The fund's poor showing began at roughly the same time that manager Sam Peters, who had joined Legg Mason in early 2005, took sole control of the fund from legendary skipper Bill Miller, but we wouldn't judge Peters harshly at this point. Like Miller and the rest of the firm's managers, Peters isn't likely to dump stocks at the first sign of trouble; he prefers to hang on if his long-term investment thesis remains intact. His steadfastness has proved costly this year, as inherited stakes in Amazon.com and online travel site Expedia have tanked. But Peters believes that both stocks--also favorites of Miller--are too cheap, given the firms' competitive advantages, so he's sticking with

them.

Despite those legacy positions, it's worth noting that Peters has remade the fund to his liking and has given it more of a pure mid-cap focus. Relying in part on his experience running tech and health-care sector funds for Fidelity (where he worked prior to joining Legg Mason), he's boosted this fund's stakes in those sectors. We like those moves for two reasons. First, Peters' track record at Fidelity was solid, which gives us a measure of confidence in his picks. Second, it reduces the fund's overlap with Miller's funds, Legg Mason Value and Legg Mason Opportunity, which currently own huge stakes in some firms--thus, Peters should have more flexibility to move in and out of his holdings.

All told, it's too soon to pound the table for this fund, but it certainly holds promise. Because it comes with a 1% 12b-1 fee, however, only investors who get good financial advice in the bargain should pay the fund's lofty price tag.

Address:	100 Light St Baltimore MD 21202 888-425-6432	Minimum Purchase:	$1000	Add: $100 IRA: $1000
		Min Auto Inv Plan:	$1000	Add: $50
		Sales Fees:	No-load, 1.00%S	
Web Address:	www.leggmason.com	Management Fee:	0.70% mx./0.65% mn.	
Inception:	12-30-85	Actual Fees:	Mgt:0.68%	Dist:1.00%
Advisor:	Legg Mason Capital Management, Inc.	Expense Projections:	3Yr:$554	5Yr:$954 10Yr:$2073
Subadvisor:	None	Income Distrib:	Annually	
NTF Plans:	DATALynx NTF, TD Waterhouse Ins NT			

Historical Profile

Return	Above Avg
Risk	High
Rating	★★★ Neutral

	93%	92%	95%	96%	90%	97%	99%	100%	100%

Investment Style Equity Stock %

▼ Manager Change
▽ Partial Manager Change

Growth of $10,000
■ Investment Values of Fund
— Investment Values of S&P 500

43.6
32.4
24.0
17.0
10.0

Performance Quartile (within Category)

1995	1996	1997	1998	1999	2000	2001	2002	2003	2004	2005	2006	History
22.81	27.83	32.27	36.70	40.15	33.94	33.73	29.63	44.49	46.48	44.59	38.92	NAV
22.50	28.65	22.12	23.31	35.54	-12.00	2.26	-8.74	54.36	13.05	8.34	7.80	Total Return %
-15.08	5.69	-11.24	-5.27	14.50	-2.90	14.15	13.36	25.68	2.17	3.43	-7.99	+/-S&P 500
-8.43	9.40	-10.13	4.19	20.82	-29.51	2.87	5.79	18.74	-3.43	-4.22	-2.52	+/-S&P Mid 400
0.16	0.00	0.00	0.00	0.00	0.00	0.00	0.00	0.00	0.00	0.00	0.00	Income Return %
22.34	28.65	22.12	23.31	35.54	-12.00	2.26	-8.74	54.36	13.05	8.34	7.80	Capital Return %
79	9	70	11	20	90	42	13	11	82	60	91	Total Rtn % Rank Cat
0.03	0.00	0.00	0.00	0.00	0.00	0.00	0.00	0.00	0.00	0.00	0.00	Income $
0.44	1.41	1.49	2.66	8.04	1.52	1.00	1.20	1.22	3.69	5.77	8.68	Capital Gains $
1.93	1.96	1.92	1.86	1.84	1.80	1.79	1.79	1.83	1.78	1.76	1.76	Expense Ratio %
-0.20	0.00	-0.90	-1.10	-1.00	-1.20	-0.90	-1.00	-0.90	-1.30	-1.37	-1.39	Income Ratio %
28	36	29	30	48	29	37	36	18	15	18	38	Turnover Rate %
713	964	1,367	1,730	2,567	2,281	2,242	2,020	3,226	3,627	3,552	3,354	Net Assets $mil

Rating and Risk

Time Period	Load-Adj Return %	Morningstar Rtn vs Cat	Morningstar Risk vs Cat	Morningstar Risk-Adj Rating
1 Yr	7.80			
3 Yr	9.71	-Avg	High	★
5 Yr	13.21	+Avg	+Avg	★★★
10 Yr	13.07	+Avg	High	★★★
Incept	13.50			

Other Measures	Standard Index S&P 500	Best Fit Index DJ Wilshire 4500
Alpha	-5.2	-6.4
Beta	1.76	1.19
R-Squared	70	84
Standard Deviation	14.48	
Mean	9.71	
Sharpe Ratio	0.49	

Portfolio Analysis 09-30-06

Share change since 06-06 Total Stocks:44	Sector	PE	Tot Ret%	% Assets
⊕ Amazon.com, Inc.	Consumer	55.1	-16.31	5.35
Level 3 Communications,	Telecom	—	95.12	4.90
⊕ Medicis Pharmaceuticals	Health	—	10.05	4.67
Sprint Nextel Corporatio	Telecom	30.2	-10.44	4.09
United States Steel Corp	Ind Mtrls	7.4	53.62	4.00
CNET Networks, Inc.	Media	52.5	-38.12	3.99
Investors Financial Serv	Financial	17.9	16.09	3.94
NII Holdings, Inc.	Telecom	45.9	47.53	3.62
⊖ Bear Stearns Companies,	Financial	12.5	42.07	3.11
⊖ Expedia, Inc.	Consumer	—	-12.44	3.04
⊕ Ambac Financial Group, I	Financial	10.9	16.52	2.98
⊖ AutoZone, Inc.	Consumer	15.3	25.95	2.95
WellPoint, Inc.	Health	17.2	-1.38	2.78
Shire PLC ADR	Health	40.2	59.84	2.74
Activision	Software		25.47	2.72
Montpelier Re Holdings,	Financial	9.3	0.14	2.70
⊖ Advanced Medical Optics,	Health	17.5	-15.79	2.52
⊕ Juniper Networks, Inc.	Hardware	34.3	-15.07	2.49
Accenture, Ltd.	Business	22.0	29.32	2.41
Sears Holdings Corporati	Consumer	19.5	45.36	2.35

Current Investment Style

Value Blnd Growth — Large/Mid/Small

Market Cap	%
Giant	0.0
Large	24.5
Mid	56.3
Small	18.1
Micro	1.1
Avg $mil:	5,849

Value Measures		Rel Category
Price/Earnings	15.71	0.98
Price/Book	1.65	0.73
Price/Sales	1.25	1.12
Price/Cash Flow	9.47	1.12
Dividend Yield %	0.36	0.28

Growth Measures	%	Rel Category
Long-Term Erngs	13.82	1.09
Book Value	19.49	2.34
Sales	13.54	1.52
Cash Flow	4.54	0.54
Historical Erngs	24.68	1.38

Profitability	%	Rel Category
Return on Equity	16.03	1.01
Return on Assets	2.88	0.36
Net Margin	5.36	0.49

Sector Weightings	% of Stocks	Rel S&P 500	3 Year High Low
↻ Info	29.98	1.50	
▨ Software	6.43	1.86	6 2
▨ Hardware	5.39	0.58	5 0
▨ Media	5.38	1.42	8 5
▨ Telecom	12.78	3.64	16 12
⊕ Service	62.35	1.35	
▨ Health	21.39	1.77	22 16
▨ Consumer	20.44	2.67	25 16
▨ Business	4.52	1.07	17 5
▨ Financial	16.00	0.72	20 15
⊔ Mfg	7.67	0.23	
▨ Goods	1.54	0.18	8 1
▨ Ind Mtrls	6.13	0.51	6 0
▨ Energy	0.00	0.00	0 0
▨ Utilities	0.00	0.00	0 0

Composition

● Cash	0.2
● Stocks	99.8
● Bonds	0.0
○ Other	0.0
Foreign (% of Stock)	5.9

Legg Mason Value Prim

	Ticker	Load	NAV	Yield	Total Assets	Mstar Category
	LMVTX	None	$72.72	0.0%	$20,784 mil	Large Blend

Governance and Management

Stewardship Grade: B

Portfolio Manager(s)

Longtime manager Bill Miller has vastly outperformed his average peer and the S&P 500 Index during his tenure. Assistant manager Nancy Dennin, who focused mostly on administrative tasks, stepped down in September 2004. Many of her duties are now handled by Mary Chris Gay, who was named as a comanager here in March 2006. In 2004, the firm hired a new research director, Ira Malis, and a chief strategist, Michael Mauboussin, and it has bulked up its analyst team.

Strategy

Bill Miller looks for companies that are trading cheaply relative to his estimates of what they are worth. This often leads him to beaten-down turnaround plays. Unlike many value managers, however, Miller is willing to make fairly optimistic assumptions about growth, and he doesn't shy away from owning companies in traditional growth sectors. In this portfolio, pricey Internet stocks rub elbows with bargain-priced financials and turnaround plays. Miller will also let favored names run, allowing top positions to soak up a large percentage of assets.

Performance 12-31-06

	1st Qtr	2nd Qtr	3rd Qtr	4th Qtr	Total
2002	-3.66	-13.73	-13.96	13.38	-18.92
2003	-2.91	25.48	3.54	13.79	43.53
2004	-1.22	4.59	-5.80	15.04	11.96
2005	-5.95	3.52	2.00	6.05	5.32
2006	0.64	-5.67	1.58	9.77	5.85

Trailing	Total Return%	+/- S&P 500	+/- Russ 1000	%Rank Cat	Growth of $10,000
3 Mo	9.77	3.07	2.82	3	10,977
6 Mo	11.50	-1.24	-0.86	51	11,150
1 Yr	5.85	-9.94	-9.61	99	10,585
3 Yr Avg	7.67	-2.77	-3.31	87	12,482
5 Yr Avg	7.75	1.56	0.93	17	14,524
10 Yr Avg	12.14	3.72	3.50	4	31,449
15 Yr Avg	14.58	3.94	3.78	3	77,025

Tax Analysis	Tax-Adj Rtn%	%Rank Cat	Tax-Cost Rat	%Rank Cat
3 Yr (estimated)	7.67	72	0.00	1
5 Yr (estimated)	7.75	13	0.00	1
10 Yr (estimated)	11.36	2	0.70	29

Potential Capital Gain Exposure: 37% of assets

Morningstar's Take by Greg Carlson 01-01-07

Legg Mason Value finally had a bad year. So what?

The streak is finally over. After beating the S&P 500 Index in every calendar year since 1991, this fund fell far short in 2006, lagging the benchmark by 9.9 percentage points. But lost in the uproar over its poor showing is the fact that the fund has always been quite volatile--as we have pointed out before, it has lagged the index over numerous 12-month periods in the past, sometimes by very substantial margins.

Meanwhile, we're as impressed as ever with lead manager Bill Miller's focus on long-term fundamentals and analytical ability. True, he's made (and admitted to) mistakes in recent years, such as his avoidance of energy and other commodity-related stocks, as well as a poorly timed bet on homebuilders such as Pulte Homes--he bought them after they dipped in late 2005, but they proceeded to fall much further in 2006. As usual, though, Miller and his team aren't chasing their tails. They believe that commodity prices are still

well above the cost of production; thus, future margins are likely to be lower. They've also dug into builders' balance sheets and grilled management, and are convinced of the value of the firms' land holdings (which some argue could depreciate). Miller is also sticking with the Internet names that weighed heavily on returns in 2006, such as Amazon, Yahoo, and eBay.

To be sure, Miller faces a couple of significant challenges here. A longstanding one is the lofty expense ratio of the Primary shares, which have the majority of the fund's assets and sport a 1% 12b-1 fee. Furthermore, he runs a very large pool of money; as a result, Legg Mason owns very large stakes in some of Miller's favorites, thus he might have difficulty buying more shares. Asset size could also hamper his ability to scoop up smaller firms.

That said, the fund remains a very attractive choice. We suggest investors adopt Miller's philosophy and tune out the short-term noise.

Address:	100 Light St
	Baltimore MD 21203
	888-425-6432
Web Address:	www.leggmason.com
Inception:	04-16-82
Advisor:	Legg Mason Capital Management, Inc.
Subadvisor:	None
NTF Plans:	DATALynx NTF, TD Waterhouse Ins NT

Minimum Purchase:	$1000	Add: $100	IRA: $1000
Min Auto Inv Plan:	$1000	Add: $50	
Sales Fees:	No-load, 0.95%S		
Management Fee:	0.70% mx./0.65% mn.		
Actual Fees:	Mgt:0.66%	Dist:0.95%	
Expense Projections:	3Yr:$530	5Yr:$913	10Yr:$1987
Income Distrib:	Annually		

Historical Profile

Return	Above Avg
Risk	High
Rating	★★★ Neutral

Investment Style: Equity

| 93% | 99% | 99% | 99% | 100% | 98% | 100% | 100% | 98% | | | Stock % |

Growth of $10,000
— Investment Values of Fund
— Investment Values of S&P 500

▼ Manager Change
▽ Partial Manager Change

Performance Quartile (within Category)

1995	1996	1997	1998	1999	2000	2001	2002	2003	2004	2005	2006	History
25.19	32.99	42.74	61.58	75.27	55.44	50.06	40.59	58.26	65.23	68.70	72.72	NAV
40.76	38.43	37.05	48.04	26.71	-7.14	-9.29	-18.92	43.53	11.96	5.32	5.85	Total Return %
3.18	15.47	3.69	19.46	5.67	1.96	2.60	3.18	14.85	1.08	0.41	-9.94	+/-S&P 500
2.99	15.98	4.20	21.02	5.80	0.65	3.16	2.73	13.64	0.56	-0.95	-9.61	+/-Russ 1000
0.93	0.66	0.11	0.00	0.00	0.00	0.00	0.00	0.00	0.00	0.00	0.00	Income Return %
39.83	37.77	36.94	48.04	26.71	-7.14	-9.29	-18.92	43.53	11.96	5.32	5.85	Capital Return %
5	2	5	1	17	54	28	25	2	28	54	99	Total Rtn % Rank Cat
0.17	0.16	0.04	0.00	0.00	0.00	0.00	0.00	0.00	0.00	0.00	0.00	Income $
1.24	1.53	2.32	1.41	2.46	14.47	0.26	0.00	0.00	0.00	0.00	0.00	Capital Gains $
1.81	1.82	1.77	1.73	1.69	1.68	1.69	1.68	1.72	1.70	1.68	1.68	Expense Ratio %
0.50	0.80	0.40	-0.10	-0.40	-0.60	-0.50	-0.50	-0.40	-0.60	0.77	-0.83	Income Ratio %
20	20	10	13	20	27	24	25	4	9	13		Turnover Rate %
1,340	1,976	3,683	8,079	12,540	10,597	9,788	7,218	10,738	11,947	11,898	11,713	Net Assets $mil

Rating and Risk

Time Period	Load-Adj Return %	Morningstar Rtn vs Cat	Morningstar Risk vs Cat	Morningstar Risk-Adj Rating
1 Yr	5.85			
3 Yr	7.67	-Avg	High	★
5 Yr	7.75	+Avg	High	★★★
10 Yr	12.14	High	High	★★★★
Incept	16.04			

Other Measures	Standard Index S&P 500	Best Fit Index Russ 1000Gr
Alpha	-5.7	-0.1
Beta	1.52	1.32
R-Squared	76	86
Standard Deviation	12.00	
Mean	7.67	
Sharpe Ratio	0.41	

Portfolio Analysis 09-30-06

Share change since 06-06 Total Stocks:41	Sector	PE	Tot Ret%	% Assets
AES Corporation	Utilities	33.4	39.23	5.41
Tyco International, Ltd.	Ind Mtrls	15.7	6.83	5.19
⊖ Qwest Communications Int	Telecom	—	48.14	4.99
⊕ Sprint Nextel Corporatio	Telecom	30.2	-10.44	4.86
UnitedHealth Group, Inc.	Health	20.8	-13.49	4.55
J.P. Morgan Chase & Co.	Financial	13.6	25.60	4.55
Google, Inc.	Business	61.5	11.00	4.14
Sears Holdings Corporati	Consumer	19.5	45.36	3.99
⊕ Amazon.com, Inc.	Consumer	55.1	-16.31	3.89
⊕ Aetna, Inc.	Health	14.1	-8.34	3.26
⊕ Countrywide Financial Co	Financial	9.8	26.22	3.07
DirecTV, Inc.	Media	26.5	76.63	2.91
Citigroup, Inc.	Financial	13.1	19.55	2.69
IAC/InterActiveCorp	Consumer	40.6	31.26	2.67
Eastman Kodak Company	Goods	—	12.58	2.65
⊕ eBay, Inc.	Consumer	40.1	-30.43	2.63
⊕ Yahoo, Inc.	Media	35.4	-34.81	2.50
⊕ American International G	Financial	17.0	6.05	2.27
Time Warner, Inc.	Media	19.6	26.37	2.25
⊕ Home Depot, Inc.	Consumer	13.5	1.01	2.24

Current Investment Style

Value Blend Growth — Large Mid Small

	Market Cap	%
	Giant	37.7
	Large	48.7
	Mid	13.6
	Small	0.0
	Micro	0.0
	Avg $mil: 33,810	

Value Measures		Rel Category
Price/Earnings	16.72	1.09
Price/Book	1.54	0.60
Price/Sales	1.10	0.79
Price/Cash Flow	8.09	0.96
Dividend Yield %	1.16	0.66

Growth Measures	%	Rel Category
Long-Term Erngs	13.29	1.12
Book Value	12.33	1.37
Sales	12.03	1.24
Cash Flow	13.19	1.28
Historical Erngs	22.53	1.22

Profitability	%	Rel Category
Return on Equity	15.84	0.81
Return on Assets	7.14	0.69
Net Margin	9.61	0.72

Sector Weightings	% of Stocks	Rel S&P 500	3 Year High	Low
↻ Info	28.55	1.43		
Software	3.28	0.95	5	2
Hardware	7.47	0.81	7	3
Media	7.79	2.06	8	6
Telecom	10.01	2.85	11	10
☞ Service	55.04	1.19		
Health	12.12	1.00	17	12
Consumer	21.57	2.82	23	19
Business	6.32	1.49	8	6
Financial	15.03	0.67	23	14
↳ Mfg	16.41	0.49		
Goods	3.59	0.42	4	3
Ind Mtrls	7.32	0.61	7	5
Energy	0.00	0.00	0	0
Utilities	5.50	1.57	6	3

Composition

● Cash	1.6
● Stocks	98.4
● Bonds	0.0
○ Other	0.0
Foreign (% of Stock)	1.5

MORNINGSTAR® Funds 500

LKCM Small Cap Equity Ins

	Ticker	Load	NAV	Yield	Total Assets	Mstar Category
	LKSCX	None	$21.98	0.0%	$628 mil	Small Blend

Governance and Management

Stewardship Grade: A

Portfolio Manager(s)

Luther King founded Luther King Capital Management in 1979 and has managed this fund since its 1994 inception. Steve Purvis has comanaged the fund since January 1998, serving as the firm's director of research before that. They are supported by a team of 25 investment professionals, three of whom are dedicated small-cap analysts.

Strategy

Managers Luther King and Steve Purvis look for companies they'd like to own outright. This means that their holdings tend to have a unique niche or product, high returns on capital, and a strong balance sheet. They consider valuation important and will trim a stock if it's getting too expensive, but they won't buy a stock just because it's cheap. Although they consider themselves primarily bottom-up managers, they do use macroeconomic forecasts to help shape the portfolio.

Performance 12-31-06

	1st Qtr	2nd Qtr	3rd Qtr	4th Qtr	Total
2002	7.98	-4.29	-15.67	1.21	-11.79
2003	-4.92	16.15	8.14	12.80	34.71
2004	4.35	7.60	-1.82	10.75	22.09
2005	-1.12	4.38	7.95	2.69	14.42
2006	15.91	-6.74	0.13	6.23	14.98

Trailing	Total Return%	+/- S&P 500	+/- Russ 2000	%Rank Cat	Growth of $10,000
3 Mo	6.23	-0.47	-2.67	90	10,623
6 Mo	6.37	-6.37	-3.01	67	10,637
1 Yr	14.98	-0.81	-3.39	48	11,498
3 Yr Avg	17.11	6.67	3.55	12	16,061
5 Yr Avg	13.80	7.61	2.41	22	19,086
10 Yr Avg	11.91	3.49	2.47	39	30,810
15 Yr Avg	—	—	—		—

Tax Analysis	Tax-Adj Rtn%	%Rank Cat	Tax-Cost Rat	%Rank Cat
3 Yr (estimated)	15.15	12	1.67	51
5 Yr (estimated)	12.48	24	1.16	53
10 Yr (estimated)	10.20	39	1.53	53

Potential Capital Gain Exposure: 20% of assets

Historical Profile

Return	Above Avg	
Risk	Below Avg	
Rating	★★★★ Above Avg	

83% 79% 79% 86% 88% 95% 95% 95% 94%

Investment Style
Equity
Stock %

▼ Manager Change
▽ Partial Manager Change

Growth of $10,000
— Investment Values of Fund
— Investment Values of S&P 500

43.6
32.4
24.0
17.0
10.0

Performance Quartile (within Category)

1995	1996	1997	1998	1999	2000	2001	2002	2003	2004	2005	2006	History
13.84	16.20	16.89	15.72	18.08	17.00	17.29	15.24	19.54	21.46	21.12	21.98	NAV
33.23	26.95	23.07	-6.26	16.83	11.37	7.50	-11.79	34.71	22.09	14.42	14.98	Total Return %
-4.35	3.99	-10.29	-34.84	-4.21	20.47	19.39	10.31	6.03	11.21	9.51	-0.81	+/-S&P 500
4.78	10.46	0.71	-3.71	-4.43	14.39	5.01	8.69	-12.54	3.76	9.87	-3.39	+/-Russ 2000
1.33	0.49	0.45	0.39	0.18	0.28	0.44	0.03	0.00	0.00	0.00	0.00	Income Return %
31.90	26.46	22.62	-6.65	16.65	11.09	7.06	-11.82	34.71	22.09	14.42	14.98	Capital Return %
20	25	71	56	41	57	45	23	88	23	8	48	Total Rtn % Rank Cat
0.14	0.07	0.07	0.07	0.03	0.05	0.07	0.01	0.00	0.00	0.00	0.00	Income $
0.00	1.02	2.64	0.05	0.25	3.10	0.92	0.01	1.00	2.40	3.46	2.32	Capital Gains $
1.00	1.00	0.95	0.91	0.90	0.93	0.92	0.94	0.97	0.96	0.99	—	Expense Ratio %
1.15	0.39	0.22	0.35	0.16	0.32	0.46	-0.19	-0.45	-0.38	-0.23	—	Income Ratio %
53	66	34	35	48	79	62	52	43	53	56	—	Turnover Rate %
123	199	255	246	230	211	221	207	267	344	370	607	Net Assets $mil

Rating and Risk

Time Period	Load-Adj Return %	Morningstar Rtn vs Cat	Morningstar Risk vs Cat	Morningstar Risk-Adj Rating
1 Yr	14.98			
3 Yr	17.11	+Avg	Avg	★★★★
5 Yr	13.80	+Avg	-Avg	★★★★
10 Yr	11.91	Avg	-Avg	★★★★
Incept	14.60			

Other Measures	Standard Index S&P 500	Best Fit Index Mstar Small Core
Alpha	2.5	0.9
Beta	1.57	0.96
R-Squared	64	87
Standard Deviation	13.47	
Mean	17.11	
Sharpe Ratio	1.00	

Morningstar's Take by David Kathman 12-05-06

LKCM Small Cap Equity's low-key, steady approach has a lot to recommend it.

This fund has been an oasis of stability in the often volatile small-cap space. Managers Steve Purvis and Luther King look for small-cap stocks with high returns on capital, strong balance sheets, and reasonable valuations. Purvis and King evaluate stocks from a long-term perspective, and most of the holdings are relatively stable niche businesses that they wouldn't mind owning outright. Overly speculative stocks aren't welcome here.

Yet this isn't a value portfolio. Stability is key, and good growth prospects are also important to the managers. The portfolio's average valuations and earnings growth are slightly above the small-blend average. Many of its top holdings lean toward the growth area of the Morningstar Style Box despite reasonable P/E ratios; these include varied names such as Cash America International, Tempur-Pedic International, and PSS World Medical, all of which posted good gains in 2006.

This combination of growth and value factors has kept the fund in the small-blend category and has led to remarkably steady results. Since its 1994 inception, the fund has comfortably beaten its category and the Russell 2000 Index while staying on a very even keel. Only twice has it ever lost money in a calendar year, and the one time it ranked in the category's bottom quartile, in 2003, it still gained 35%--its highest single-year gain.

The fund has navigated the choppy market of the past few years very well, with top-quartile finishes in 2002, 2004, and 2005. It was on pace for another category-beating year throughout most of 2006 but fell to the middle of the pack late in the year when speculative stocks rallied, leaving many of this fund's tamer holdings behind.

This fund's asset base has grown considerably in the past year, but it's still well less than $1 billion, very reasonable for a small-cap fund. Given the number of good small-cap funds that are closed, this open fund remains an attractive option.

Portfolio Analysis 09-30-06

Share change since 06-06 Total Stocks:94	Sector	PE	Tot Ret%	% Assets
⊕ Cash America Internation	Financial	24.8	102.85	1.78
⊕ Mobile Mini	Ind Mtrls	25.4	13.67	1.72
⊕ Anixter International	Ind Mtrls	12.6	38.80	1.64
⊕ Nuance Communications, I	Software	—	50.20	1.57
⊕ PSS World Medical, Inc.	Health	27.7	31.60	1.56
⊕ Franklin Electric Co.	Ind Mtrls	21.3	31.07	1.49
⊕ Emcor Group, Inc.	Business	26.9	68.37	1.45
⊕ Rent-A-Center, Inc.	Consumer	14.5	56.47	1.43
⊕ Reddy Ice Holdings, Inc.	Goods	—	—	1.37
⊕ Tempur-Pedic Internation	Consumer	16.8	77.91	1.34
⊕ Ladish Company, Inc.	Ind Mtrls	19.9	65.91	1.34
⊕ Ness Technologies, Inc.	Business	20.0	32.41	1.33
⊕ Forward Air Corporation	Business	19.5	-20.42	1.32
⊕ Perrigo Company	Health	22.5	17.27	1.32
⊕ Glacier Bancorp, Inc.	Financial	20.2	24.57	1.30
⊕ Argonaut Group, Inc.	Financial	14.7	6.38	1.25
⊕ First State Bancorporati	Financial	18.6	4.47	1.24
⊕ Raven Industries, Inc.	Hardware	19.0	-5.98	1.24
⊕ Cabot Oil & Gas Corporat	Energy	8.3	34.90	1.23
⊕ Parametric Technology Co	Software	38.1	18.16	1.23

Current Investment Style

Value Blnd Growth

Market Cap	%
Giant	0.0
Large	0.0
Mid	21.1
Small	60.3
Micro	18.6

Avg $mil: 1,054

Value Measures		Rel Category
Price/Earnings	17.40	1.05
Price/Book	2.23	1.06
Price/Sales	1.03	1.05
Price/Cash Flow	6.69	0.96
Dividend Yield %	0.34	0.32

Growth Measures	%	Rel Category
Long-Term Erngs	15.79	1.13
Book Value	8.42	1.11
Sales	6.02	0.68
Cash Flow	13.28	1.05
Historical Erngs	21.64	1.30

Profitability	%	Rel Category
Return on Equity	11.13	0.86
Return on Assets	6.64	0.93
Net Margin	8.26	0.85

Sector Weightings	% of Stocks	Rel S&P 500	3 Year High Low
☎ Info	16.13	0.81	
🖥 Software	6.42	1.86	8 4
💻 Hardware	5.76	0.62	8 4
🎙 Media	1.79	0.47	3 1
📶 Telecom	2.16	0.62	3 1
🛎 Service	51.42	1.11	
⚕ Health	8.96	0.74	13 6
🛒 Consumer	13.82	1.81	24 11
📋 Business	10.01	2.37	17 6
💲 Financial	18.63	0.84	19 12
🏭 Mfg	32.45	0.96	
🔧 Goods	5.37	0.63	7 5
⚙ Ind Mtrls	16.65	1.39	19 15
🔥 Energy	10.43	1.06	14 7
💡 Utilities	0.00	0.00	0 0

Composition

● Cash	6.5
● Stocks	93.5
● Bonds	0.0
● Other	0.0
Foreign (% of Stock)	1.4

Address:	301 Commerce Fort Worth TX 76102 800-688-5526	
Web Address:	www.lkcm.com	
Inception:	07-14-94	
Advisor:	Luther King Capital Mgmt Corporation	
Subadvisor:	None	
NTF Plans:	N/A	

Minimum Purchase:	$10000	Add: $1000 IRA: $0
Min Auto Inv Plan:	$10000	Add: $100
Sales Fees:	No-load, 1.00%R	
Management Fee:	0.75%	
Actual Fees:	Mgt:0.75%	Dist: —
Expense Projections:	3Yr:$315	5Yr:$547 10Yr:$1213
Income Distrib:	Annually	

Longleaf Partners

	Ticker	Load	NAV	Yield	Total Assets	Mstar Category
	LLPFX	Closed	$34.86	0.4%	$10,833 mil	Large Blend

Governance and Management

Stewardship Grade: A

Portfolio Manager(s)

Mason Hawkins and Staley Cates have been at the helm since 1987 and 1994, respectively. John Buford was named comanager in 1999 but stepped down at the close of 2005 to enter a seminary. The firm has brought in three analysts since 1997, and the most experienced of the three should be ready by now to step up and cover the companies Buford followed. The team members keep all of their own invested assets in this fund and its siblings.

Strategy

This fund takes value seriously. Its comanagers look for companies that trade at discounts of 40% or more to the team's estimates of their intrinsic value, using discounted cash-flow analysis, asset values, or sales of comparable firms to determine the latter. The managers place much importance on the ability of a company's management to run the business on an operational level and to effectively allocate capital. They aren't afraid to take sizable positions, and the fund typically holds 20-25 names. The turnover rate is typically very low.

Historical Profile

Return	Above Avg
Risk	Average
Rating	★★★★ Above Avg

Investment Style: Equity, Stock %

96% 98% 100% 83% 83% 85% 79% 97% 93%

▼ Manager Change
▽ Partial Manager Change

Growth of $10,000
— Investment Values of Fund
— Investment Values of S&P 500

42.2 / 32.4 / 24.0 / 17.0 / 10.0

Performance Quartile (within Category)

1995	1996	1997	1998	1999	2000	2001	2002	2003	2004	2005	2006	History
21.15	22.85	25.98	24.39	20.49	22.71	24.51	22.24	29.98	31.32	30.97	34.86	NAV
27.48	21.02	28.25	14.28	2.18	20.60	10.34	-8.34	34.80	7.14	3.62	21.63	Total Return %
-10.10	-1.94	-5.11	-14.30	-18.86	29.70	22.23	13.76	6.12	-3.74	-1.29	5.84	+/-S&P 500
-10.29	-1.43	-4.60	-12.74	-18.73	28.39	22.79	13.31	4.91	-4.26	-2.65	6.17	+/-Russ 1000
1.40	1.81	0.94	1.15	1.42	0.80	0.87	0.35	0.00	0.50	0.96	0.50	Income Return %
26.08	19.21	27.31	13.13	0.76	19.80	9.47	-8.69	34.80	6.64	2.66	21.13	Capital Return %
86	57	57	76	94	2	3	2	9	86	79	2	Total Rtn % Rank Cat
0.24	0.38	0.21	0.25	0.29	0.15	0.20	0.09	0.00	0.15	0.29	0.14	Income $
0.44	2.38	3.11	4.81	4.23	1.72	0.33	0.14	0.00	0.63	1.18	2.64	Capital Gains $
1.01	0.95	0.94	0.93	0.92	0.93	0.94	0.91	0.91	0.90	0.91	—	Expense Ratio %
1.45	1.61	0.81	1.12	1.16	0.75	0.89	0.17	0.32	0.28	0.95	—	Income Ratio %
13	33	38	44	50	20	18	20	7	13	7	—	Turnover Rate %
1,876	2,300	2,605	3,688	3,631	3,757	4,535	5,052	7,669	8,999	8,676	10,833	Net Assets $mil

Performance 12-31-06

	1st Qtr	2nd Qtr	3rd Qtr	4th Qtr	Total
2002	7.10	-8.15	-12.36	6.32	-8.34
2003	-1.03	16.67	3.97	12.28	34.80
2004	1.20	1.85	-2.98	7.14	7.14
2005	-1.09	0.00	3.87	0.85	3.62
2006	10.36	-1.26	3.53	7.81	21.63

Trailing	Total Return%	+/- S&P 500	+/- Russ 1000	%Rank Cat	Growth of $10,000
3 Mo	7.81	1.11	0.86	15	10,781
6 Mo	11.62	-1.12	-0.74	49	11,162
1 Yr	21.63	5.84	6.17	2	12,163
3 Yr Avg	10.53	0.09	-0.45	34	13,503
5 Yr Avg	10.78	4.59	3.96	3	16,684
10 Yr Avg	12.77	4.35	4.13	3	33,261
15 Yr Avg	15.09	4.45	4.29	1	82,331

Tax Analysis	Tax-Adj Rtn%	%Rank Cat	Tax-Cost Rat	%Rank Cat
3 Yr (estimated)	9.54	37	0.90	41
5 Yr (estimated)	10.12	3	0.60	39
10 Yr (estimated)	10.97	3	1.60	75

Potential Capital Gain Exposure: 31% of assets

Rating and Risk

Time Period	Load-Adj Return %	Morningstar Rtn vs Cat	Morningstar Risk vs Cat	Morningstar Risk-Adj Rating
1 Yr	21.63			
3 Yr	10.53	Avg	+Avg	★★★
5 Yr	10.78	High	-Avg	★★★★★
10 Yr	12.77	High	Avg	★★★★★
Incept	14.25			

Other Measures	Standard Index S&P 500	Best Fit Index Russ 2000 Gr
Alpha	0.6	3.6
Beta	0.94	0.44
R-Squared	59	69

Standard Deviation	8.52
Mean	10.53
Sharpe Ratio	0.85

Morningstar's Take by Gregg Wolper 11-11-06

Three words explain how Longleaf Partners earned its stellar 2006 rank: smarts, guts, and patience.

Investors shouldn't get carried away with lists of yearly leaders. Many chart-toppers focus on narrow, risky fields such as a single emerging market. But we know those funds do get noticed, so it's instructive to see how this fund won its spot on the list.

For the year to date through Nov. 10, 2006, this closed fund has amassed a 20.9% return, best in the large-blend category (save for a tiny offering with just $8 million in assets). One reason: General Motors, at 4.5% of assets in the June portfolio, is up an astounding 84%. DirecTV and Comcast, with similar amounts of assets, have each gained about 55%. Level 3 Communications, Walt Disney, and Yum Brands have also scored huge gains.

The diversity of that list proves the fund doesn't focus on one sector. Note, too, that most of those firms were extremely out of favor just a short time ago. What sets this fund apart are the ability of Mason Hawkins and Staley Cates to identify seemingly weak firms that are in fact primed for recovery, and their willingness to buy when sentiment about them is dire and hold on even as others remain convinced the stocks are dogs.

One key stock, top holding Dell, has not been a 2006 winner. In fact, it has performed poorly since they bought it in 2005. But Hawkins and Cates tell Morningstar that Dell scores exceptionally well on all three of their main criteria: business and financial fundamentals, management ability and commitment, and price versus estimated value. So, they bought more when the price sank. In other words, their approach remains firmly intact.

Don't forget: This fund's concentrated structure and fondness for out-of-favor stocks can lead to poor calendar-year rankings as well as chart-topping ones. However, its long-term results have been outstanding. It should continue to shine well into the future.

Portfolio Analysis 09-30-06

Share change since 06-06 Total Stocks:25

	Sector	PE	Tot Ret%	% Assets
⊕ Dell, Inc.	Hardware	18.4	-16.23	9.42
Liberty Capital A	Media	—		6.99
DirecTV, Inc.	Media	26.5	76.63	5.53
NIPPONKOA Insurance	Financial	—		5.13
Aon Corp.	Financial	19.6	-0.07	5.00
⊖ Yum Brands, Inc.	Consumer	20.4	26.76	4.92
Walt Disney Company	Media	21.0	44.26	4.83
General Motors Corporati	Goods	—	63.96	4.78
Comcast Corporation	Media	—		4.76
⊕ Cemex SAB de CV ADR	Ind Mtrls	11.1	14.21	4.68
⊕ Sprint Nextel Corporatio	Telecom	30.2	-10.44	4.59
⊖ Vivendi Universal	Media	—		4.56
FedEx Corporation	Business	17.2	5.40	4.38
Level 3 Communications,	Telecom	—	95.12	4.37
⊖ Koninklijke Philips Elec	Goods	—		4.18
⊕ Chesapeake Energy Corp.	Energy	6.1	-7.74	4.14
Level 3 Comms 10%	—	—		4.00
Pioneer Natural Resource	Energy	11.4	-22.11	3.47
Telephone and Data Syste	Telecom	—		2.34
☼ eBay, Inc.	Consumer	40.1	-30.43	1.41

Current Investment Style

Value Blnd Growth — Large / Mid / Small

Market Cap	%
Giant	33.4
Large	50.2
Mid	16.4
Small	0.0
Micro	0.0

Avg $mil: 20,526

Value Measures		Rel Category
Price/Earnings	16.65	1.08
Price/Book	1.51	0.59
Price/Sales	0.71	0.51
Price/Cash Flow	7.09	0.84
Dividend Yield %	1.31	0.75

Growth Measures	%	Rel Category
Long-Term Erngs	12.05	1.02
Book Value	9.43	1.04
Sales	-0.29	NMF
Cash Flow	11.48	1.11
Historical Erngs	28.75	1.55

Profitability	%	Rel Category
Return on Equity	22.56	1.16
Return on Assets	5.99	0.58
Net Margin	5.06	0.38

Sector Weightings	% of Stocks	Rel S&P 500	3 Year High Low
⊙ Info	54.17	2.71	
Software	1.45	0.42	1 0
Hardware	10.11	1.09	10 0
Media	29.79	7.86	36 28
Telecom	12.82	3.65	13 6
⊂ Service	22.36	0.48	
Health	0.00	0.00	0 0
Consumer	6.79	0.89	15 5
Business	4.70	1.11	12 5
Financial	10.87	0.49	17 11
⊔ Mfg	23.47	0.69	
Goods	10.29	1.26	18 10
Ind Mtrls	5.02	0.42	8 0
Energy	8.16	0.83	8 4
Utilities	0.00	0.00	0 0

Composition

● Cash	2.8
● Stocks	93.2
● Bonds	4.0
● Other	0.0
Foreign	20.6
(% of Stock)	

Address:	6410 Poplar Ave, Suite 900 Memphis, TN 38119 800-445-9469
Web Address:	www.longleafpartners.com
Inception:	04-08-87
Advisor:	Southeastern Asset Management Inc.
Subadvisor:	None
NTF Plans:	N/A

Minimum Purchase:	Closed	Add: —	IRA: —
Min Auto Inv Plan:	Closed	Add: —	
Sales Fees:	No-load		
Management Fee:	1.00% mx./0.75% mn., 0.10%A		
Actual Fees:	Mgt:0.76%	Dist: —	
Expense Projections:	3Yr:$290	5Yr:$504	10Yr:$1120
Income Distrib:	Annually		

 MORNINGSTAR® Funds 500

Longleaf Partners Intl

	Ticker	Load	NAV	Yield	Total Assets	Mstar Category
	LLINX	None	$18.91	0.1%	$3,435 mil	Foreign Large Value

Governance and Management

Stewardship Grade: B

Portfolio Manager(s)

Comanagers Mason Hawkins, Staley Cates, and Andrew McDermott have run this fund since its inception. Hawkins and Cates are veteran managers of Longleaf Partners' domestic offerings. McDermott is based in London and Japan, which allows the team to keep close tabs on its Asian holdings. One of the team's analysts, Jim Thompson, works out of London and provides research for the fund's U.K. and European holdings.

Strategy

This fund's managers buy only companies that trade at discounts of 40% or more to the managers' estimates of their intrinsic values. They also pay scant attention to country and sector weightings. The fund holds 20 to 30 names and eschews pricey sectors. Although it carries substantial issue- and country-specific risk, its limited valuation risk and tendency to hold cash can help moderate volatility. The managers hedge back into the U.S. dollar the economic (or earnings) exposure of the fund's holdings to foreign currency.

Historical Profile

Return	Low	
Risk	Average	
Rating	★	
	Lowest	

Quartile bars: 78% | 99% | 96% | 100% | 95% | 84% | 85% | 88% | 94%

Investment Style
Equity
Stock %

▼ Manager Change
▽ Partial Manager Change

Growth of $10,000
— Investment Values of Fund
— Investment Values of MSCI EAFE

26.0
20.0
15.0
10.0

Performance Quartile (within Category)

	1995	1996	1997	1998	1999	2000	2001	2002	2003	2004	2005	2006	History
NAV	—	—	—	9.97	12.02	12.06	12.34	9.97	14.11	15.55	17.36	18.91	
Total Return %	—	—	—	9.02*	24.37	25.93	10.47	-16.52	41.52	10.21	12.88	17.07	
+/-MSCI EAFE	—	—	—	-2.66	40.12	31.89	-0.58	2.93	-10.04	-0.66	-9.27		
+/-MSCI Wd xUS	—	—	—	-3.61	39.29	31.86	-0.72	2.10	-10.17	-1.59	-8.64		
Income Return %	—	—	—	0.57	3.80	1.15	0.00	0.00	0.00	0.00	0.09		
Capital Return %	—	—	—	23.80	22.13	9.32	-16.52	41.52	10.21	12.88	16.98		
Total Rtn % Rank Cat	—	—	—	55	1	1	79	33	100	54	96		
Income $	—	—	0.01	0.06	0.38	0.13	0.00	0.00	0.00	0.00	0.01		
Capital Gains $	—	—	0.00	0.33	2.63	0.85	0.32	0.00	0.00	0.19	1.35		
Expense Ratio %	—	—	—	1.75	1.75	1.79	1.82	1.80	1.68	1.66	—		
Income Ratio %	—	—	—	0.10	0.60	3.36	1.17	-0.68	-0.68	-0.57	—		
Turnover Rate %	—	—	—	—	50	69	32	16	10	19	—		
Net Assets $mil	—	—	—	75	294	403	834	1,016	1,924	2,580	3,435		

Performance 12-31-06

	1st Qtr	2nd Qtr	3rd Qtr	4th Qtr	Total
2002	3.57	-5.32	-19.59	5.88	-16.52
2003	-11.84	30.72	10.97	10.67	41.52
2004	6.52	-0.20	-4.67	8.74	10.21
2005	2.32	-0.82	8.05	2.95	12.88
2006	5.47	-1.69	4.72	7.82	17.07

Trailing	Total Return%	+/- MSCI EAFE	+/- MSCI Wd xUS	%Rank Cat	Growth of $10,000
3 Mo	7.82	-2.53	-2.30	93	10,782
6 Mo	12.91	-1.78	-1.31	75	11,291
1 Yr	17.07	-9.27	-8.64	96	11,707
3 Yr Avg	13.35	-6.58	-6.75	100	14,563
5 Yr Avg	11.47	-3.51	-3.78	100	17,210
10 Yr Avg	—				
15 Yr Avg	—				

Tax Analysis	Tax-Adj Rtn%	%Rank Cat	Tax-Cost Rat	%Rank Cat
3 Yr (estimated)	12.87	96	0.42	6
5 Yr (estimated)	10.98	95	0.44	11
10 Yr (estimated)	—			

Potential Capital Gain Exposure: 32% of assets

Rating and Risk

Time Period	Load-Adj Return %	Morningstar Rtn vs Cat	Morningstar Risk vs Cat	Morningstar Risk-Adj Rating
1 Yr	17.07			
3 Yr	13.35	Low	Low	★
5 Yr	11.47	Low	+Avg	★
10 Yr	—			
Incept	15.48			

Other Measures	Standard Index MSCI EAFE	Best Fit Index MSCI World
Alpha	0.9	1.9
Beta	0.56	0.72
R-Squared	45	49
Standard Deviation	7.95	
Mean	13.35	
Sharpe Ratio	1.23	

Morningstar's Take by Gregg Wolper 12-18-06

Longleaf Partners International can be a fine choice--but only for certain investors.

Run by the same shareholder-friendly shop that has made Longleaf Partners and Longleaf Partners Small-Cap outstanding long-term performers, this fund has much to recommend it. As they do with its siblings, its managers look for a small number of businesses in which they feel the utmost confidence. When they find such stocks, they own them for a long, long time, and they buy only at deeply discounted prices. The managers are very experienced.

Given that pedigree and solid strategy, this fund merits attention. However, it has some traits that would put off certain investors. First, this is not an all-foreign fund. Comanagers Mason Hawkins and Staley Cates (the third is Andrew McDermott) say that they feel an obligation to fund shareholders to include their team's absolute best ideas and opportunities in the portfolio even if some may be based in the United States. One reason: They don't consider a U.S.-based company to be off-limits if they determine the bulk of its intrinsic value--not its straight revenue or earnings--is derived abroad. That explains why the fund's top holding is Dell, with more than 8% of assets, and why it owns other companies generally considered U.S. stocks. Second, even aside from that, the fund's weightings--and returns--will differ markedly from those of indexes, because the managers don't pay any attention to them. Third, with so many of its stocks allotted a large percentage of assets, short-term performance can be affected negatively by weak showings of just a few. Finally, unlike most rivals, this fund hedges most currency exposure back into the dollar.

Investors willing to accept those traits should look closely here. And they shouldn't be put off by the fund's low 2006 rank, which owes greatly to that hedging (the dollar has posted double-digit losses against European currencies) and the decline in Dell's price.

Address:	6410 Poplar Ave, Suite 900 Memphis, TN 38119 800-445-9469
Web Address:	www.longleafpartners.com
Inception:	10-26-98*
Advisor:	Southeastern Asset Management Intl.
Subadvisor:	None
NTF Plans:	N/A

Minimum Purchase:	$10000	Add: $0	IRA: $10000
Min Auto Inv Plan:	$10000	Add: $100	
Sales Fees:	No-load		
Management Fee:	1.50% mx./1.25% mn., 0.10%A		
Actual Fees:	Mgt:1.49%	Dist: —	
Expense Projections:	3Yr:$517	5Yr:$892	10Yr:$1944
Income Distrib:	Annually		

Portfolio Analysis 09-30-06

Share change since 06-06 Total Stocks:21	Sector	Country	% Assets
⊕ Dell, Inc.	Hardware	United States	8.45
NIPPONKOA Insurance	Financial	Japan	7.40
Olympus	Health	Japan	6.13
Renault	Goods	France	5.95
Nestle	Goods	Switzerland	5.32
⊕ Cemex SAB de CV ADR	Ind Mtrls	Mexico	5.07
Vivendi Universal	Media	France	4.94
⊕ Millea Hldgs	Financial	Japan	4.92
News Corporation, Ltd. B	Media	United States	4.86
Cheung Kong (hldgs) Ltd	Financial	Hong Kong	4.79
Molson Coors Brewing Com	Goods	United States	4.68
British Sky Broadcasting	Media	U.K.	4.57
Willis Group Holdings, L	Financial	Bermuda	4.43
⊕ Yum Brands, Inc.	Consumer	United States	4.33
Fairfax Financial Hldgs	Financial	Canada	3.84
KDDI	Telecom	Japan	3.48
⊖ Philips Electronics NV A	Goods	Netherlands	3.46
NTT DoCoMo	Telecom	Japan	2.09
✴ Ingersoll-Rand Company,	Ind Mtrls	United States	2.01
⊖ Koninklijke Philips Elec	Goods	Netherlands	1.69

Current Investment Style

Value Blnd Growth — Large/Mid/Small

	Market Cap	%
	Giant	49.8
	Large	35.6
	Mid	14.6
	Small	0.0
	Micro	0.0
	Avg $mil:	20,322

Value Measures		Rel Category
Price/Earnings	1.26	0.10
Price/Book	1.70	0.96
Price/Sales	1.06	1.12
Price/Cash Flow	8.72	1.22
Dividend Yield %	1.79	0.55

Growth Measures	%	Rel Category
Long-Term Erngs	9.76	0.95
Book Value	7.51	0.96
Sales	0.42	0.08
Cash Flow	-0.74	NMF
Historical Erngs	30.79	1.88

Composition

Cash	6.5	Bonds	0.0
Stocks	93.5	Other	0.0
Foreign (% of Stock)			74.0

Sector Weightings	% of Stocks	Rel MSCI EAFE	3 Year High Low	
⊙ Info	31.53	2.67		
Software	0.00	0.00	0	0
Hardware	9.04	2.34	9	0
Media	16.54	9.04	31	17
Telecom	5.95	1.07	11	6
⊑ Service	38.34	0.81		
Health	6.56	0.92	7	0
Consumer	4.63	0.94	6	4
Business	0.00	0.00	8	0
Financial	27.15	0.90	31	23
Mfg	30.14	0.74		
Goods	22.57	1.72	34	23
Ind Mtrls	7.57	0.49	8	0
Energy	0.00	0.00	0	0
Utilities	0.00	0.00	0	0

Regional Exposure		% Stock
UK/W. Europe 28	N. America	31
Japan 26	Latn America	10
Asia X Japan 5	Other	0

Country Exposure		% Stock
United States 26	Switzerland	6
Japan 26	Netherlands	6
France 12		

Longleaf Partners Sm-Cap

Analyst Pick

Ticker	Load	NAV	Yield	Total Assets	Mstar Category
LLSCX	Closed	$30.12	1.7%	$3,258 mil	Small Value

Governance and Management

Stewardship Grade: A

Portfolio Manager(s)

Staley Cates and Mason Hawkins have comanaged this fund since 1991. John Buford was named comanager in 1999 but left the firm at the end of 2005. Hawkins and Cates rely on a group of in-house analysts. The managers and analysts, along with all employees of advisor Southeastern Asset Management, are required to keep all of their own invested assets in Longleaf Partners funds.

Strategy

This fund's comanagers buy small-cap companies trading at discounts of 40% or more to the team's estimates of their intrinsic values. To arrive at these values, the team uses several methods. Much of the time, it projects future free cash flow out eight years, assuming very low growth after that period, then discounts the terminal value and flows back to the present. The team also looks for firms selling at steep discounts to the difference between their net assets or the sales prices of comparable businesses. Management takes sizable positions, and the fund typically holds just 20 to 30 names.

Performance 12-31-06

	1st Qtr	2nd Qtr	3rd Qtr	4th Qtr	Total
2002	11.16	-4.52	-16.30	8.36	-3.74
2003	-4.97	26.50	4.46	14.55	43.85
2004	1.53	3.62	-1.95	11.27	14.78
2005	2.18	2.33	1.51	4.35	10.75
2006	5.55	-2.17	8.42	9.27	22.33

Trailing	Total Return%	+/- S&P 500	+/- Russ 2000 VL	%Rank Cat	Growth of $10,000
3 Mo	9.27	2.57	0.24	27	10,927
6 Mo	18.47	5.73	6.66	1	11,847
1 Yr	22.33	6.54	-1.15	8	12,233
3 Yr Avg	15.85	5.41	-0.63	24	15,548
5 Yr Avg	16.58	10.39	1.21	11	21,534
10 Yr Avg	14.51	6.09	1.24	9	38,764
15 Yr Avg	14.84	4.20	-0.36	18	79,689

Tax Analysis	Tax-Adj Rtn%	%Rank Cat	Tax-Cost Rat	%Rank Cat
3 Yr (estimated)	13.27	32	2.23	71
5 Yr (estimated)	14.67	17	1.64	70
10 Yr (estimated)	12.56	15	1.70	75

Potential Capital Gain Exposure: 25% of assets

Morningstar's Take by Gregg Wolper 12-26-06

Longleaf Partners Small Cap provides an excellent showcase for its managers' skills.

Managers Mason Hawkins and Staley Cates have used a disciplined and focused value strategy for years both here and at Longleaf Partners Fund. With this fund targeting smaller fare that is less well known to investors, and having been closed to new buyers for years, it is well-positioned to put that approach to best advantage. And it has done so, both in 2006 and over time. For the trailing 10-year period, this fund lands in the top decile of the small-value category, and that's also where it stands for the year to date through Dec. 22, 2006.

This year's biggest winners help explain how the managers' strategy works. Like many of their picks, top holding Level 3 Communications was deeply out of favor on Wall Street for years, but they held on to their stakes (in both bonds and stock) even as it hurt performance at times--and they even added some more stock in early 2006. The stock position was 8% of assets at the end of September,

highlighting another key trait here: The managers put a lot of money in the companies they like. Level 3's stock is up nearly 100% in 2006. Similarly, Fairfax Financial was a drag on returns early this year, but management kept the faith, and after a sharp rebound, it's now up 41% for 2006. And sometimes they don't have to wait long: Hawkins and Cates say they bought cement firm Texas Industries (for the second time) in mid-2006 because they had great confidence in its management and its business. The stock, which had fallen sharply before they bought, immediately went on a tear.

With the managers' willingness to buy firms with some type of cloud over them, and to invest heavily in them, this fund can significantly lag its rivals at times. But patient, long-term shareholders should be rewarded well, as they have been to date.

Address:	6410 Poplar Ave, Suite 900
	Memphis, TN 38119
	800-445-9469
Web Address:	www.longleafpartners.com
Inception:	12-28-88
Advisor:	Southeastern Asset Management Inc.
Subadvisor:	None
NTF Plans:	N/A

Minimum Purchase:	Closed	Add: —	IRA: —
Min Auto Inv Plan:	Closed	Add: —	
Sales Fees:	No-load		
Management Fee:	1.00% mx./0.75% mn., 0.10%A		
Actual Fees:	Mgt:0.79%	Dist: —	
Expense Projections:	3Yr:$296	5Yr:$515	10Yr:$1143
Income Distrib:	Annually		

Historical Profile

Return	Above Avg
Risk	Low
Rating	★★★★★ Highest

	94%	99%	100%	93%	78%	87%	58%	84%	91%

Investment Style
Equity
Stock %

▼ Manager Change
▽ Partial Manager Change

Growth of $10,000
■ Investment Values of Fund
— Investment Values of S&P 500

59.0
43.6
32.4
24.0
17.0
10.0

Performance Quartile (within Category)

1995	1996	1997	1998	1999	2000	2001	2002	2003	2004	2005	2006	History
14.46	17.86	22.18	21.95	20.20	22.62	21.68	20.33	28.81	29.85	27.02	30.12	NAV
18.57	30.64	29.04	12.71	4.05	12.80	5.45	-3.74	43.85	14.78	10.75	22.33	Total Return %
-19.01	7.68	-4.32	-15.87	-16.99	21.90	17.34	18.36	15.17	3.90	5.84	6.54	+/-S&P 500
-7.18	9.27	-2.74	19.16	5.54	-10.03	-8.57	7.69	-2.18	-7.47	6.04	-1.15	+/-Russ 2000 VL
0.89	0.16	1.01	0.84	0.40	0.24	1.15	2.42	2.14	1.61	2.29	2.22	Income Return %
17.68	30.48	28.03	11.87	3.65	12.56	4.30	-6.16	41.71	13.17	8.46	20.11	Capital Return %
80	9	63	1	48	73	88	19	32	93	8	8	Total Rtn % Rank Cat
0.12	0.02	0.18	0.17	0.08	0.05	0.24	0.53	0.44	0.43	0.57	0.56	Income $
1.17	1.00	0.69	2.77	2.54	0.11	1.84	0.02	0.00	2.70	5.27	2.33	Capital Gains $
1.30	1.23	1.09	1.01	0.97	0.98	0.96	0.95	0.95	0.93	0.93	—	Expense Ratio %
0.84	0.18	1.18	0.87	0.38	0.24	1.14	2.43	1.89	1.52	2.21	—	Income Ratio %
33	28	17	53	47	22	40	17	4	31	17	—	Turnover Rate %
136	252	915	1,351	1,431	1,477	1,635	1,914	2,365	2,674	2,538	3,258	Net Assets $mil

Rating and Risk

Time Period	Load-Adj Return %	Morningstar Rtn vs Cat	Morningstar Risk vs Cat	Morningstar Risk-Adj Rating
1 Yr	22.33			
3 Yr	15.85	+Avg	Low	★★★★
5 Yr	16.58	+Avg	-Avg	★★★★
10 Yr	14.51	+Avg	Low	★★★★★
Incept	13.27			

Other Measures	Standard Index S&P 500	Best Fit Index Mstar Small Core
Alpha	4.2	4.1
Beta	1.12	0.60
R-Squared	71	74
Standard Deviation	9.16	
Mean	15.85	
Sharpe Ratio	1.32	

Portfolio Analysis 09-30-06

Share change since 06-06   Total Stocks:25

	Sector	PE	Tot Ret%	% Assets
⊕ Level 3 Communications,	Telecom	—	95.12	8.04
⊕ Wendy's International	Consumer	20.7	30.52	7.68
Olympus	Health	—	—	5.66
Discovery Holding Compan	Media	—	—	5.39
✭ Texas Industries, Inc.	Ind Mtrls	18.0	29.57	5.28
⊕ Service Corporation Inte	Consumer	39.8	26.82	5.04
⊕ Pioneer Natural Resource	Energy	11.4	-22.11	4.73
Hilb Rogal & Hobbs Compa	Financial	17.5	10.67	4.70
Jacuzzi Brands, Inc.	Ind Mtrls	22.1	47.98	4.56
Everest Re Group, Ltd.	Financial	—	-1.62	4.34
IHOP Corp.	Consumer	21.9	14.62	4.32
⊕ Potlatch	Ind Mtrls	14.8	27.61	4.29
Molson Coors Brewing Com	Goods	22.5	16.31	4.27
⊕ Ruddick Corporation	Consumer	17.7	32.72	3.93
⊖ Level 3 Comms 144A 11.5%	—	—	—	3.87
Fairfax Financial Hldgs	Financial	—	38.46	3.59
PepsiAmericas, Inc.	Goods	16.1	-7.76	3.51
Willis Group Holdings, L	Financial	17.0	10.34	2.99
✭ Del Monte Foods Company	Goods	19.0	7.31	2.09
⊕ Vail Resorts, Inc.	Consumer	37.2	35.70	1.52

Current Investment Style

Value Blnd Growth — Large Mid Small

Market Cap	%
Giant	0.0
Large	7.5
Mid	59.3
Small	33.1
Micro	0.0
Avg $mil:	3,019

Value Measures		Rel Category
Price/Earnings	17.60	1.14
Price/Book	1.87	1.05
Price/Sales	1.04	1.30
Price/Cash Flow	9.22	1.51
Dividend Yield %	0.91	0.58

Growth Measures	%	Rel Category
Long-Term Erngs	9.95	0.80
Book Value	1.76	0.32
Sales	1.67	0.23
Cash Flow	-3.56	NMF
Historical Erngs	9.19	0.81

Profitability	%	Rel Category
Return on Equity	7.66	0.71
Return on Assets	2.95	0.48
Net Margin	3.86	0.43

Sector Weightings	% of Stocks	Rel S&P 500	3 Year High Low
↻ Info	17.56	0.88	
🖥 Software	0.00	0.00	0 0
🖥 Hardware	0.00	0.00	8 0
🎙 Media	7.11	1.88	17 7
☎ Telecom	10.45	2.98	10 3
⚙ Service	50.90	1.10	
🏥 Health	6.21	0.51	7 0
🛒 Consumer	24.65	3.22	26 16
💼 Business	0.83	0.20	1 0
💲 Financial	19.21	0.86	28 18
🏭 Mfg	31.52	0.93	
🔩 Goods	10.82	1.27	27 11
⚙ Ind Mtrls	15.51	1.30	20 7
🔥 Energy	5.19	0.53	7 0
💡 Utilities	0.00	0.00	0 0

Composition

	%
● Cash	4.5
● Stocks	91.2
● Bonds	3.9
● Other	0.5
Foreign (% of Stock)	14.6

MORNINGSTAR® Funds 500

Loomis Sayles Bond Ret

	Ticker	Load	NAV	Yield	SEC Yield	Total Assets	Mstar Category
	LSBRX	None	$14.25	5.2%	5.10%	$8,730 mil	Multisector Bond

Governance and Management

Stewardship Grade: B

Portfolio Manager(s)

Dan Fuss has managed this fund since 1991 and is widely acknowledged to be one of the best in the business. Kathleen Gaffney joined him in 1997 and works on several other Loomis Sayles bond portfolios.

Strategy

This fund is about as aggressive as bond funds come. Comanagers Dan Fuss and Kathleen Gaffney typically keep close to one third of assets in a mix of domestic junk bonds and emerging-markets credits. Their strategy resembles that of a value-biased stock manager, and they often load up on bonds in out-of-favor sectors.

Historical Profile
Return High
Risk Above Avg
Rating ★★★★ Highest

Investment Style
Fixed Income
Income Rtn %Rank Cat

▼ Manager Change
▽ Partial Manager Change

Growth of $10,000
■ Investment Values of Fund
— Investment Values of LB Aggr

Performance Quartile (within Category)

	1995	1996	1997	1998	1999	2000	2001	2002	2003	2004	2005	2006	History
	—	12.38	12.82	11.95	11.52	11.06	10.43	10.99	13.31	13.80	13.53	14.25	NAV
	—	12.36*	12.36	4.51	4.23	4.09	2.29	13.18	28.83	11.02	4.01	10.99	Total Return %
	—	—	2.71	-4.18	5.05	-7.54	-6.15	2.93	24.73	6.68	1.58	6.66	+/-LB Aggr
	—	—	2.58	-2.80	4.06	-6.73	-5.80	3.34	23.01	6.05	1.30	6.02	+/-LB. U.S. Univ. Bd
	—	—	6.88	7.37	7.99	8.22	8.11	7.51	7.19	7.11	5.98	5.54	Income Return %
	—	—	5.48	-2.86	-3.76	-4.13	-5.82	5.67	21.64	3.91	-1.97	5.45	Capital Return %
	—	—	7	21	36	11	76	10	11	12	13	6	Total Rtn % Rank Cat
	—	0.00	0.83	0.92	0.93	0.92	0.87	0.76	0.77	0.92	0.81	0.73	Income $
	—	0.00	0.22	0.52	0.00	0.00	0.00	0.00	0.00	0.00	0.00	0.00	Capital Gains $
	—	—	1.00	1.00	1.00	1.00	1.00	1.00	1.00	1.00	1.00	1.00	Expense Ratio %
	—	—	7.09	7.13	7.90	8.10	8.28	7.15	6.35	5.24	4.64	4.99	Income Ratio %
	—	42	41	24	33	17	20	22	35	42	22	26	Turnover Rate %
	—	—	33	56	61	79	63	71	180	344	900	3,157	Net Assets $mil

Performance 12-31-06

	1st Qtr	2nd Qtr	3rd Qtr	4th Qtr	Total
2002	1.32	3.19	0.06	8.19	13.18
2003	6.69	11.04	1.87	6.75	28.83
2004	2.24	-3.59	6.60	5.66	11.02
2005	-1.01	2.31	2.04	0.65	4.01
2006	2.52	0.48	4.92	2.69	10.99

Trailing	Total Return%	+/- LB Aggr	+/-LB. U.S. Univ. Bd	%Rank Cat	Growth of $10,000
3 Mo	2.69	1.45	1.19	53	10,269
6 Mo	7.75	2.66	2.29	13	10,775
1 Yr	10.99	6.66	6.02	6	11,099
3 Yr Avg	8.62	4.92	4.41	4	12,815
5 Yr Avg	13.32	8.26	7.68	7	18,687
10 Yr Avg	9.31	3.07	2.91	5	24,356
15 Yr Avg	—				

Tax Analysis	Tax-Adj Rtn%	%Rank Cat	Tax-Cost Rat	%Rank Cat
3 Yr (estimated)	6.38	3	2.06	63
5 Yr (estimated)	10.82	6	2.21	56
10 Yr (estimated)	6.33	4	2.73	62

Potential Capital Gain Exposure: 4% of assets

Rating and Risk

Time Period	Load-Adj Return %	Morningstar Rtn vs Cat	Morningstar Risk vs Cat	Morningstar Risk-Adj Rating
1 Yr	10.99			
3 Yr	8.62	High	+Avg	★★★★★
5 Yr	13.32	High	+Avg	★★★★★
10 Yr	9.31	High	+Avg	★★★★★
Incept	9.31			

Other Measures	Standard Index LB Aggr	Best Fit Index DJ Mod
Alpha	4.8	1.2
Beta	0.92	0.56
R-Squared	42	50
Standard Deviation	4.67	
Mean	8.62	
Sharpe Ratio	1.12	

Morningstar's Take by Paul Herbert 11-21-06

We don't advocate trying Loomis Sayles Bond's approach at home.

This fund practices a bold strategy. Managers Dan Fuss and Kathleen Gaffney search for bargains, hoping to benefit when others' short-term pessimism obscures good fundamental value. Usually, and lately, they have found these mispriced ideas in lower-quality corporate bonds and non-U.S. (including emerging-markets) issues. The result is a portfolio that takes on a great deal of credit and currency risk. The managers' preference for longer-dated issues adds an extra dose of interest-rate sensitivity to the mix. The fund's duration (a measure of interest-rate sensitivity) stood at 6.5 years recently, while the typical multisector fund's sat at about 4.6 years.

It isn't every day that we get behind a fund that is so assertive, but backing this fund makes sense. First, Loomis Sayles has given the managers the tools to make the fund work. The shop emphasizes bond-picking, and boasts a nearly 40-person-strong credit analyst effort and a 12-member global-bond team. We also like that Fuss, who has stashed more than $1 million in three separate Loomis funds, has an established record, having led the effort here since the fund's inception in 1991.

Overall, we think Fuss' experience and support will help the fund deliver the goods over time, something that it hasn't had any trouble doing so far. It owns a stellar, peer- and benchmark-beating long-term record. And its showing so far in 2006 indicates that little has changed. Since the Federal Reserve paused in its rate-raising regime in June, the long-dated Treasury bonds that the managers picked up earlier in the year have rallied. Supermarket and auto picks in the high-yield space have also aided its results.

The risk here is that the fund will encounter trouble when lower-quality bonds stumble, as it did during stretches of 1998-2001. Investors who can hang on through such periods of bumpy returns should be happy here, though.

Address:	399 Boylston Street Boston MA 02116 800-633-3330
Web Address:	www.loomissayles.com
Inception:	12-31-96 *
Advisor:	Loomis Sayles & Company, LP
Subadvisor:	None
NTF Plans:	Fidelity Retail-NTF, Schwab OneSource

Minimum Purchase:	$2500	Add: $50	IRA: $2500
Min Auto Inv Plan:	$2500	Add: $50	
Sales Fees:	No-load, 0.25%S, 2.00%R		
Management Fee:	0.60% mx./0.50% mn.		
Actual Fees:	Mgt:0.59%	Dist:0.25%	
Expense Projections:	3Yr:$336	5Yr:$588	10Yr:$1310
Income Distrib:	Quarterly		

Portfolio Analysis 09-30-06

Total Fixed-Income:287	Date of Maturity	Amount $000	Value $000	% Net Assets
US Treasury Bond 5.375%	02-15-31	430,825	465,325	6.72
Canada Govt 2.75%	12-01-07	366,130	322,974	4.67
Canada Govt 4.25%	09-01-08	221,710	199,524	2.88
TELEFONICA EMISONES SA	06-20-36	174,550	184,207	2.66
Gen Elec Cap 6.5%	09-28-15	240,358	153,364	2.22
Inter Amer Dev Bk 6%	12-15-17	184,525	117,102	1.69
Mexico (United Mexican S	12-07-23	1,150,900	99,953	1.44
Mexico (United Mexican S	12-20-12	1,050,000	99,279	1.43
Inter-American Developme	05-11-09	297,000	94,934	1.37
FNMA 2.29%	02-19-09	145,900	89,335	1.29
Verizon Global Fdg 5.85%	09-15-35	87,716	82,642	1.19
Albertsons 7.45%	08-01-29	88,220	81,715	1.18
Georgia Pac 7.75%	11-15-29	78,125	75,000	1.08
Sth Africa(Rep Of) 13%	08-31-11	500,585	73,409	1.06
Barclays Financial Llc	02-22-10	2,816,000	71,664	1.04
Jpm Chase Brl	05-10-10	241,667	69,943	1.01
Manitoba Prov Cda 5.75%	06-02-08	74,125	68,076	0.98
ONTARIO PROV CDA	03-08-08	70,975	63,282	0.91
Bristol Myers Squibb Cv	09-15-23	62,700	62,813	0.91
British Columbia Prov Cd	06-09-08	66,745	61,546	0.89

Current Investment Style

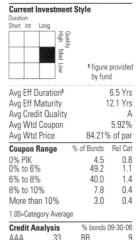

Duration Short Int Long / Quality High Med Low

1 figure provided by fund

Avg Eff Duration[1]	6.5 Yrs
Avg Eff Maturity	12.1 Yrs
Avg Credit Quality	A
Avg Wtd Coupon	5.92%
Avg Wtd Price	84.21% of par

Coupon Range	% of Bonds	Rel Cat
0% PIK	4.5	0.8
0% to 6%	49.2	1.1
6% to 8%	40.0	1.4
8% to 10%	7.8	0.4
More than 10%	3.0	0.4

1.00=Category Average

Credit Analysis	% bonds 09-30-06		
AAA	33	BB	9
AA	9	B	15
A	7	Below B	4
BBB	19	NR/NA	2

Sector Breakdown	% of assets
US Treasuries	8
TIPS	0
US Agency	0
Mortgage Pass-Throughs	1
Mortgage CMO	0
Mortgage ARM	0
US Corporate	53
Asset-Backed	2
Convertible	0
Municipal	0
Corporate Inflation-Protected	0
Foreign Corporate	4
Foreign Govt	18

Composition			
Cash	11.2	Bonds	79.4
Stocks	0.9	Other	8.5

Special Securities	
Restricted/Illiquid Secs	4
Exotic Mortgage-Backed	0
Emerging-Markets Secs	7
Options/Futures/Warrants	No

Loomis Sayles GlbBd Ret

	Analyst Pick	Ticker	Load	NAV	Yield	SEC Yield	Total Assets	Mstar Category
		LSGLX	None	$15.28	2.7%	3.34%	$1,316 mil	World Bond

Governance and Management

Stewardship Grade: B

Portfolio Manager(s)

Kenneth Buntrock and David Rolley have run this offering since John DeBeer stepped aside in 2000. Each has been with Loomis Sayles for at least nine years, though, and the fund's strategy has been consistent since its inception.

Strategy

Managers Kenneth Buntrock and David Rolley and their team look for government and corporate bonds with the best return potential in developed and emerging markets. They see a benefit to holding foreign currencies when they are undervalued. They keep an eye on the characteristics of the Lehman Brothers Global Aggregate, but they won't necessarily hew close to it.

Historical Profile

Return	Above Avg
Risk	Average
Rating	★★★★ Above Avg

42 39 65 100 26 63 80 40

19.2
16.4
14.0
12.0 — Investment Values of Fund
10.0 — Investment Values of LB Aggr

Growth of $10,000

Performance Quartile (within Category)

1995	1996	1997	1998	1999	2000	2001	2002	2003	2004	2005	2006	History
—	—	11.83	12.10	11.47	10.76	11.27	12.93	15.05	15.99	14.53	15.28	NAV
—	—	2.05*	10.33	3.58	-0.98	4.74	20.22	20.99	9.48	-4.60	7.98	Total Return %
—	—	1.64	4.40	-12.61	-3.70	9.97	16.89	5.14	-7.03	3.65	+/-LB Aggr
—	—		-7.46	8.65	1.65	8.28	-1.77	2.47	-2.66	4.60	1.04	+/-SB Wld Govt
—	—		5.63	5.51	4.98	0.00	5.42	4.55	2.87	4.06	2.82	Income Return %
—	—		4.70	-1.93	-5.96	4.74	14.80	16.44	6.61	-8.66	5.16	Capital Return %
—	—		39	14	73	28	23	11	50	50	14	Total Rtn % Rank Cat
—	—	0.78	0.67	0.64	0.57	0.00	0.61	0.59	0.43	0.65	0.41	Income $
—	—	0.00	0.29	0.43	0.00	0.00	0.00	0.00	0.05	0.08	0.00	Capital Gains $
—	—	1.15	1.15	1.15	1.15	1.15	1.00	1.15	1.04	1.00	1.00	Expense Ratio %
—	—	5.60	5.77	6.08	6.41	6.42	7.51	4.69	2.88	2.57	2.93	Income Ratio %
—	—	75	—	42	17	58	65	107	61	63	77	Turnover Rate %
—	—	5	6	8	12	10	13	114	558	500	609	Net Assets $mil

Performance 12-31-06

	1st Qtr	2nd Qtr	3rd Qtr	4th Qtr	Total
2002	0.53	9.18	2.02	7.36	20.22
2003	4.87	7.67	1.58	5.49	20.99
2004	2.06	-3.32	4.11	6.58	9.48
2005	-2.38	-0.58	-0.58	-1.14	-4.60
2006	0.83	2.25	2.07	2.61	7.98

Trailing	Total Return%	+/- LB Aggr	+/- SB Wld Govt	%Rank Cat	Growth of $10,000
3 Mo	2.61	1.37	0.52	27	10,261
6 Mo	4.74	-0.35	1.75	21	10,474
1 Yr	7.98	3.65	1.04	14	10,798
3 Yr Avg	4.09	0.39	1.21	35	11,278
5 Yr Avg	10.40	5.34	0.90	14	16,400
10 Yr Avg	—	—	—	—	—
15 Yr Avg	—	—	—	—	—

Tax Analysis	Tax-Adj Rtn%	%Rank Cat	Tax-Cost Rat	%Rank Cat
3 Yr (estimated)	2.88	24	1.16	14
5 Yr (estimated)	8.95	10	1.31	15
10 Yr (estimated)	—	—	—	—

Potential Capital Gain Exposure: -1% of assets

Rating and Risk

Time Period	Load-Adj Return %	Morningstar Rtn vs Cat	Morningstar Risk vs Cat	Morningstar Risk-Adj Rating
1 Yr	7.98			
3 Yr	4.09	+Avg	Avg	★★★★
5 Yr	10.40	+Avg	Avg	★★★★
10 Yr	—	—	—	—
Incept	—	—	—	—

Other Measures	Standard Index LB Aggr	Best Fit Index SB Wld Govt
Alpha	0.5	1.0
Beta	0.86	0.66
R-Squared	32	91
Standard Deviation	4.94	
Mean	4.09	
Sharpe Ratio	0.18	

Morningstar's Take by Lawrence Jones 12-21-06

Loomis Sayles Global Bond is one of our favorites.

In late August 2006 we announced that this fund had been added to our Fund Analyst Picks, reflecting our opinion that several factors make it a standout in the world-bond category. An important element is skilled and experience management. Managers Kenneth Buntrock and David Rolley have 32 years and 26 years of investment experience, respectively. Both have been at the helm of this fund for the past six years, and both have significant prior experience in international investing and economic analysis. A team of six dedicated analysts, with an average of 15 years experience, supports management. Overall, we feel the fund is in good hands with seasoned managers and ample support.

The strategy that management uses here seeks to maximize total return through both a macro-level global economic analysis, to help determine country and currency selection as well as interest-rate positioning, and careful analysis of individual securities, using the value-based bond-picking approach Loomis Sayles is famous for. The managers will take varying degrees of currency risk, depending on their market outlook, which separates the fund from many in the category that will be either always hedged or unhedged.

Despite having a tough year in 2005, as the dollar strengthened unexpectedly and hurt the fund's absolute return that year, the team has shown considerable skill in navigating difficult international-currency markets. Lately, management has found non-Japan Asia region sovereign debt attractive due to strongly growing economies, relatively undervalued local currencies, and more-compelling real yields than can be found in Japanese bonds. So far, the move has paid off.

The fund's nondollar bonds and junk-rated emerging-markets debt court some credit risk, and result in added volatility, but we're confident management will continue to deliver good long-term results here.

Portfolio Analysis 10-31-06

Total Fixed-Income:167	Date of Maturity	Amount $000	Value $000	% Net Assets
Munchener Hypothekenbank	01-16-12	31,180	42,021	3.48
Depfa Acs Bk 0.75%	09-22-08	4,450,001	38,093	3.15
Belgium (Kingdom Of) 3.7	03-28-09	25,295	32,339	2.68
Spain (Kingdom Of) 3.6%	01-31-09	24,415	31,113	2.58
Sweden (Kingdom Of) 5.25	03-15-11	184,365	27,191	2.25
Belgium (Kingdom Of) 5.5	09-28-17	17,665	25,949	2.15
US Treasury Note 4.875%	08-15-16	23,530	24,019	1.99
Kfw Intl Fin 2.05%	09-21-09	2,671,000	23,579	1.95
FHLMC 5%	07-01-35	24,294	23,484	1.94
Koenigreich Norwegen 5%	05-15-15	142,280	22,986	1.90
Oesterreichische Kontrol	03-22-10	2,530,000	22,236	1.84
FNMA 5.5%	12-01-35	22,142	21,894	1.81
NETHERLANDS (KINGDOM OF)	01-15-28	12,995	20,448	1.69
FNMA 1.75%	03-26-08	2,310,000	20,062	1.66
Ireland (Republic Of) 4.	04-18-16	14,545	19,805	1.64
Kreditanstalt Fur Wieder	10-11-10	15,925	19,448	1.61
United Kingdom (Governme	03-07-25	9,100	18,935	1.57
Norway (Kingdom Of) 5.5%	05-15-09	115,805	18,344	1.52
United Kingdom (Governme	03-07-12	7,820	15,105	1.25
Germany (Federal Republi	01-04-37	10,740	14,096	1.17

Current Investment Style

Duration: Short Int Long
Quality: High Med Low

	1 figure provided by fund
Avg Eff Duration[1]	4.6 Yrs
Avg Eff Maturity	6.5 Yrs
Avg Credit Quality	AA
Avg Wtd Coupon	4.60%
Avg Wtd Price	87.66% of par

Coupon Range	% of Bonds	Rel Cat
0% PIK	4.5	1.2
0% to 6%	79.7	1.0
6% to 8%	16.4	1.3
8% to 10%	1.6	0.4
More than 10%	2.3	1.0

1.00=Category Average

Credit Analysis	% bonds 10-31-06		
AAA	60	BB	5
AA	15	B	5
A	4	Below B	0
BBB	11	NR/NA	0

Sector Breakdown — % of assets

US Treasuries	—
TIPS	—
US Agency	—
Mortgage Pass-Throughs	—
Mortgage CMO	—
Mortgage ARM	—
US Corporate	—
Asset-Backed	—
Convertible	—
Municipal	—
Corporate Inflation-Protected	—
Foreign Corporate	—
Foreign Govt	—

Composition

Cash	9.1	Bonds	86.7
Stocks	0.0	Other	4.3

Special Securities

Restricted/Illiquid Secs	2
Exotic Mortgage-Backed	0
Emerging-Markets Secs	—
Options/Futures/Warrants	No

Address:	399 Boylston Street, Boston MA 02116, 800-633-3330
Web Address:	www.loomissayles.com
Inception:	01-01-97*
Advisor:	Loomis Sayles & Company, LP
Subadvisor:	None
NTF Plans:	Fidelity Retail-NTF, Schwab OneSource

Minimum Purchase:	$2500	Add: $50	IRA: $2500
Min Auto Inv Plan:	$2500	Add: $50	
Sales Fees:	No-load, 0.25%S		
Management Fee:	0.60% mx./0.50% mn.		
Actual Fees:	Mgt:0.59%	Dist:0.25%	
Expense Projections:	3Yr:$331	5Yr:$579	10Yr:$1289
Income Distrib:	Annually		

Lord Abbett Affiliated A

	Ticker	Load	NAV	Yield	Total Assets	Mstar Category
	LAFFX	5.75%	$15.28	1.2%	$21,201 mil	Large Value

Governance and Management

Stewardship Grade: B

Portfolio Manager(s)

Eli Salzmann has worked on the fund since 1997 and took over as lead manager in 1998. He is assisted by comanagers Stan Dinsky and Ken Fuller, as well as a team of six analysts dedicated to this offering.

Strategy

Eli Salzmann and other senior Lord Abbett managers hunt for companies that are cheap relative to their normalized earnings and possess a catalyst for growth. They also use company-specific analysis to gauge the strength of an industry: Looking for inflection points, they will overweight certain sectors, based in part on their view of macroeconomic conditions.

Historical Profile

Return Average
Risk Average
Rating ★★★ Neutral

Investment Style: Equity, Stock %

▼ Manager Change
▽ Partial Manager Change

Growth of $10,000
— Investment Values of Fund
— Investment Values of S&P 500

Performance Quartile (within Category)

	1995	1996	1997	1998	1999	2000	2001	2002	2003	2004	2005	2006	History
	11.59	12.58	13.97	14.74	15.20	15.76	13.69	10.53	13.55	14.78	14.05	15.28	NAV
	31.70	20.14	25.16	14.42	16.88	15.76	-7.94	-18.79	30.89	12.60	3.33	17.61	Total Return %
	-5.88	-2.82	-8.20	-14.16	-4.16	24.34	3.95	3.31	2.21	1.72	-1.58	1.82	+/-S&P 500
	-6.66	-1.50	-10.02	-1.21	9.53	8.23	-2.35	-3.27	0.86	-3.89	-3.72	-4.64	+/-Russ 1000 VI
	3.08	2.64	2.44	1.74	1.66	1.61	1.54	1.51	1.91	1.49	1.37	1.44	Income Return %
	28.62	17.50	22.72	12.68	15.22	13.63	-9.48	-20.30	28.98	11.11	1.96	16.17	Capital Return %
	62	48	72	35	7	23	77	54	28	56	79	59	Total Rtn % Rank Cat
	0.30	0.30	0.30	0.24	0.24	0.24	0.24	0.21	0.20	0.20	0.20	0.20	Income $
	1.19	1.03	1.39	0.95	1.76	1.39	0.57	0.41	0.00	0.25	1.02	1.00	Capital Gains $
	0.63	0.66	0.65	0.63	0.74	0.79	0.79	0.85	0.84	0.83	0.83	—	Expense Ratio %
	2.90	2.61	2.15	1.64	1.36	1.62	1.28	1.08	1.17	0.92	1.26	—	Income Ratio %
	54	47	46	56	62	52	77	60	43	33	49	—	Turnover Rate %
	5,307	6,292	7,730	8,594	9,704	10,658	10,292	8,883	12,600	15,002	14,837	16,421	Net Assets $mil

Performance 12-31-06

	1st Qtr	2nd Qtr	3rd Qtr	4th Qtr	Total
2002	3.15	-10.96	-19.74	10.16	-18.79
2003	-5.46	18.25	2.90	13.78	30.89
2004	2.47	1.10	-1.93	10.82	12.60
2005	-2.61	-0.49	4.22	2.30	3.33
2006	5.88	-0.47	5.85	5.44	17.61

Trailing	Total Return%	+/- S&P 500	+/- Russ 1000 VI	%Rank Cat	Growth of $10,000
3 Mo	5.44	-1.26	-2.56	92	10,544
6 Mo	11.60	-1.14	-3.12	75	11,160
1 Yr	17.61	1.82	-4.64	59	11,761
3 Yr Avg	11.02	0.58	-4.07	72	13,684
5 Yr Avg	7.78	1.59	-3.08	59	14,544
10 Yr Avg	9.95	1.53	-1.05	26	25,820
15 Yr Avg	11.91	1.27	-1.12	27	54,080

Tax Analysis	Tax-Adj Rtn%	%Rank Cat	Tax-Cost Rat	%Rank Cat
3 Yr (estimated)	7.43	92	1.30	52
5 Yr (estimated)	5.26	84	1.17	63
10 Yr (estimated)	7.43	43	1.71	61

Potential Capital Gain Exposure: 21% of assets

Rating and Risk

Time Period	Load-Adj Return %	Morningstar Rtn vs Cat	Morningstar Risk vs Cat	Morningstar Risk-Adj Rating
1 Yr	10.84			
3 Yr	8.85	-Avg	Avg	★★
5 Yr	6.51	-Avg	+Avg	★★
10 Yr	9.30	Avg	Avg	★★★
Incept	—			

Other Measures	Standard Index S&P 500	Best Fit Index MSCI World
Alpha	0.8	-2.1
Beta	0.96	0.89
R-Squared	83	88
Standard Deviation	7.34	
Mean	11.02	
Sharpe Ratio	1.04	

Portfolio Analysis 09-30-06

Share change since 08-06 Total Stocks:101	Sector	PE	Tot Ret%	% Assets
ExxonMobil Corporation	Energy	11.1	39.07	5.26
Procter & Gamble Company	Goods	23.9	13.36	3.98
⊖ Kraft Foods, Inc.	Goods	18.0	30.52	2.72
Wyeth	Health	17.2	12.88	2.61
AT&T, Inc.	Telecom	18.2	51.59	2.61
⊕ Novartis AG ADR	Health	22.2	11.29	2.59
Pfizer Inc.	Health	15.2	15.22	2.41
⊕ General Electric Company	Ind Mtrls	20.0	9.35	2.41
⊕ Citigroup, Inc.	Financial	13.1	19.55	2.36
Bank of America Corporat	Financial	12.4	20.68	2.13
Kroger Company	Consumer	17.5	23.31	2.00
Comcast Corporation	Media	—	—	1.89
⊖ Schlumberger, Ltd.	Energy	22.3	31.07	1.83
J.P. Morgan Chase & Co.	Financial	13.6	25.60	1.78
Baxter International Inc	Health	24.3	24.81	1.75
Kimberly-Clark Corporati	Goods	22.7	17.55	1.67
Diageo PLC ADR	Goods	16.1	40.66	1.61
⊖ Campbell Soup Company	Goods	21.3	33.40	1.61
⊖ Emerson Electric Company	Ind Mtrls	19.6	20.68	1.60
Barrick Gold Corporation	Ind Mtrls	40.2	10.95	1.58

Current Investment Style

Value Blnd Growth — Large / Mid / Small

Market Cap	%
Giant	51.5
Large	42.4
Mid	6.2
Small	0.0
Micro	0.0

Avg $mil: 53,819

Value Measures		Rel Category
Price/Earnings	15.65	1.14
Price/Book	2.48	1.12
Price/Sales	1.47	1.13
Price/Cash Flow	6.15	0.92
Dividend Yield %	2.26	0.97

Growth Measures	%	Rel Category
Long-Term Erngs	9.93	0.96
Book Value	8.58	1.08
Sales	8.61	0.96
Cash Flow	1.84	0.30
Historical Erngs	12.03	0.74

Profitability	%	Rel Category
Return on Equity	18.16	1.01
Return on Assets	8.58	0.88
Net Margin	11.59	0.89

Sector Weightings	% of Stocks	Rel S&P 500	3 Year High Low
↻ Info	8.25	0.41	
Software	0.12	0.03	2 0
Hardware	1.96	0.21	10 2
Media	2.07	0.55	10 2
Telecom	4.10	1.17	5 3
⊏ Service	42.79	0.93	
Health	17.06	1.41	18 8
Consumer	4.25	0.56	5 3
Business	4.20	0.99	7 3
Financial	17.28	0.78	18 11
Mfg	48.96	1.45	
Goods	17.64	2.06	18 9
Ind Mtrls	17.08	1.43	26 17
Energy	8.32	0.85	11 8
Utilities	5.92	1.69	6 1

Composition

● Cash	0.0	
● Stocks	99.9	
● Bonds	0.0	
● Other	0.1	
Foreign	11.0	(% of Stock)

Morningstar's Take by Greg Carlson 12-28-06

Lord Abbett Affiliated has lately suffered for its managers' convictions, but it remains a fine core holding.

This fund had a so-so 2006 and has looked downright sluggish relative to its large-value peers in recent months. That's primarily due to its atypical look; while many of the fund's rivals have big stakes in financials and have been scooping up formerly popular tech names such as Microsoft (both sectors have rallied lately), lead manager Eli Salzmann and his team are somewhat skeptical of those areas. In particular, the team--which buys companies that sell at a discount to their average long-term profits and possess an attribute that should boost earnings--believes that the margins of many banks are unsustainably high, and has instead taken sizable positions in insurers such as Aflac. As such, the fund's financials weighting is just over half the group norm.

Within tech, management is wary of firms that have had difficulty adapting to a changing competitive landscape, such as Microsoft (which it sold in April after the extent of that firm's spending to battle online foes became evident) and Dell, which has lost a significant portion of the PC market to Hewlett Packard, the fund's only sizable tech holding. It's also worth noting that the team's tendency to discount companies with far-above-normal profits has resulted in only a light stake in the energy sector, which has staged a huge rally in recent years.

But although Salzmann and company's somewhat contrarian tack has lately weighed on returns, we think it bodes well for the fund's long-term prospects. Building a hefty position in out-of-favor, stable-growth names such as drug maker Wyeth and consumer staples providers like Procter & Gamble should serve the fund well as the rally by cyclical fare fades. Our confidence in the fund is also bolstered by the experience and depth of its team, as well as a reasonable 0.83% expense ratio.

Address:	90 Hudson Street Jersey City NJ 07302 800-821-5129	Minimum Purchase:	$250 Add: $0 IRA: $250
		Min Auto Inv Plan:	$250 Add: $50
		Sales Fees:	5.75%L, 0.35%S
Web Address:	www.lordabbett.com	Management Fee:	0.50% mx./0.30% mn., 0.04%A
Inception:	05-01-34	Actual Fees:	Mgt:0.30% Dist:0.35%
Advisor:	Lord, Abbett & Co. LLC	Expense Projections:	3Yr:$822 5Yr:$1004 10Yr:$1530
Subadvisor:	None	Income Distrib:	Quarterly
NTF Plans:	Federated Tr NTF, Fidelity Instl-NTF		

MainStay ICAP Equity I

	Ticker	Load	NAV	Yield	Total Assets	Mstar Category
	ICAEX	None	$45.03	1.3%	$1,009 mil	Large Value

Governance and Management

Stewardship Grade: A

Portfolio Manager(s)

Team leader Rob Lyon, who is ICAP's president and chief investment officer, has run the fund since its inception. Prior to joining ICAP in 1988, Lyon served as director of research at Fred Alger Management. Jerrold Senser, Gary Maurer, Tom Wenzel, and others on the ICAP team are all very experienced. They draw on research produced by several sector-specific analysts. ICAP has a big presence in institutional money management.

Strategy

The fund's managers begin with a universe of 400 large-cap stocks and 50 mostly European ADRs. They then buy the 40 to 50 stocks with the best mix of attractive valuations, consistent or improving earnings, and catalysts for growth over the next 12 to 18 months. Catalysts can include a product launch, a management change, or a change in the macroeconomic environment. The fund's sector weightings have shifted quite dramatically at times. Management will sell a stock if it reaches a predetermined price target.

Performance 12-31-06

	1st Qtr	2nd Qtr	3rd Qtr	4th Qtr	Total
2002	-0.26	-10.15	-19.67	4.65	-24.66
2003	-1.05	13.16	1.47	13.38	28.83
2004	3.08	0.32	-1.05	8.80	11.33
2005	0.79	1.96	7.03	0.84	10.91
2006	6.54	-0.17	4.94	7.67	20.17

Trailing	Total Return%	+/- S&P 500	+/- Russ 1000 VI	%Rank Cat	Growth of $10,000
3 Mo	7.67	0.97	-0.33	31	10,767
6 Mo	12.99	0.25	-1.73	47	11,299
1 Yr	20.17	4.38	-2.08	23	12,017
3 Yr Avg	14.06	3.62	-1.03	18	14,839
5 Yr Avg	7.57	1.38	-3.29	64	14,403
10 Yr Avg	9.95	1.53	-1.05	26	25,820
15 Yr Avg	—	—	—		—

Tax Analysis	Tax-Adj Rtn%	%Rank Cat	Tax-Cost Rat	%Rank Cat
3 Yr (estimated)	11.63	32	2.13	83
5 Yr (estimated)	6.07	70	1.39	73
10 Yr (estimated)	8.48	20	1.34	38

Potential Capital Gain Exposure: 22% of assets

Morningstar's Take by Andrew Gogerty 11-14-06

Thus far, it's business as usual for ICAP, and that's a good thing for shareholders.

In June 2006, Institutional Capital sold its business to New York Life Investment Management and subsequently merged its ICAP funds into NYLIM's MainStay fund family. Initially, we expressed concern that fund family mergers have a checkered past. While our concerns remain valid, they appear to be just that--concerns. In the first few months, the merger seems to be a seamless transition, as key managers Rob Lyon and Jerry Senser, along with their investment team, continue to execute their unique style of buying undervalued large-cap stocks relative to the market, yet also considering macroeconomic factors when determining short-term growth catalysts.

In recent years the fund's exposure to cyclical and energy stocks has been a significant tailwind as has its exposure to China and India's growth. Coming into this year the firm has put on the brakes somewhat, trimming the fund's cyclical stakes in

Caterpillar and United States Steel. These gains have been redeployed into more-diversified players like General Electric and Honeywell International, which Lyon believes will hold up better amid his forecast for a slower pace of economic growth. He's also added back consumer exposure through Intercontinental Hotels amid declining gas prices.

These moves have paid off thus far and continue the fund's long-standing success, but investors should note that sector and macro calls can backfire, and the fund is willing to hold a greater stake in foreign names than many of its peers. Also, because Lyon and his team typically look out just 12 to 18 months in evaluating their picks, turnover here is relatively high and increases the chance of taxable distributions. But those concerns don't damp the case for owning it. Lyon's history of execution and experience, the fund's reasonable costs, and the firm's history of treating shareholders right is why we like this fund, and those traits are still intact.

Address:	51 Madison Avenue Chicago IL 60606 800-624-6782
Web Address:	www.icapfunds.com
Inception:	12-30-94
Advisor:	Institutional Capital Corp
Subadvisor:	None
NTF Plans:	Schwab OneSource

Minimum Purchase:	$0	Add: $0	IRA: $0
Min Auto Inv Plan:	$0	Add: $250	
Sales Fees:	No-load		
Management Fee:	0.80%		
Actual Fees:	Mgt:0.80%	Dist: —	
Expense Projections:	3Yr:$263	5Yr:$468	10Yr:$1059
Income Distrib:	Quarterly		

Historical Profile

Return	Above Avg
Risk	Average
Rating	★★★ Neutral

	89%	92%	94%	95%	94%	99%	98%	99%	100%

Investment Style
Equity
Stock %

▼ Manager Change
▽ Partial Manager Change

Growth of $10,000
— Investment Values of Fund
— Investment Values of S&P 500

Performance Quartile (within Category)

1995	1996	1997	1998	1999	2000	2001	2002	2003	2004	2005	2006	History
26.03	31.16	35.12	38.63	43.14	43.66	43.01	32.07	40.89	44.01	41.17	45.03	NAV
38.85	26.26	29.08	11.42	16.28	7.86	-0.61	-24.66	28.83	11.33	10.91	20.17	Total Return %
1.27	3.30	-4.28	-17.16	-4.76	16.96	11.28	-2.56	0.15	0.45	6.00	4.38	+/-S&P 500
0.49	4.62	-6.10	-4.21	8.93	0.85	4.98	-9.14	-1.20	-5.16	3.86	-2.08	+/-Russ 1000 VI
1.40	1.15	1.22	1.43	1.33	1.13	0.85	0.85	1.16	1.76	1.47	1.54	Income Return %
37.45	25.11	27.86	9.99	14.95	6.73	-1.46	-25.51	27.67	9.57	9.44	18.63	Capital Return %
5	9	32	52	10	60	33	90	41	71	6	23	Total Rtn % Rank Cat
0.28	0.30	0.38	0.50	0.51	0.48	0.37	0.36	0.37	0.72	0.64	0.63	Income $
1.42	1.37	4.60	0.00	1.24	2.35	0.00	0.00	0.00	0.76	7.01	3.74	Capital Gains $
0.80	0.80	0.80	0.80	0.80	0.80	0.80	0.80	0.80	0.80	0.80	—	Expense Ratio %
1.49	1.15	1.06	1.39	1.22	1.13	0.87	0.96	1.03	1.63	1.37	—	Income Ratio %
105	125	121	133	118	116	87	85	97	74	86	—	Turnover Rate %
47	149	371	717	960	1,050	1,189	877	1,079	948	812	1,001	Net Assets $mil

Rating and Risk

Time Period	Load-Adj Return %	Morningstar Rtn vs Cat	Morningstar Risk vs Cat	Morningstar Risk-Adj Rating
1 Yr	20.17			
3 Yr	14.06	+Avg	Avg	★★★★
5 Yr	7.57	Avg	Avg	★★★
10 Yr	9.95	+Avg	Avg	★★★
Incept	13.41			

Other Measures	Standard Index S&P 500	Best Fit Index Russ 1000 VI
Alpha	4.0	-0.5
Beta	0.90	0.96
R-Squared	81	89
Standard Deviation	6.93	
Mean	14.06	
Sharpe Ratio	1.49	

Portfolio Analysis 10-31-06

Share change since 09-06 Total Stocks:45	Sector	PE	Tot Ret%	% Assets
⊕ ExxonMobil Corporation	Energy	11.1	39.07	4.90
⊕ Bank of America Corporat	Financial	12.4	20.68	4.79
⊖ Citigroup, Inc.	Financial	13.1	19.55	4.52
⊖ McDonald's Corporation	Consumer	18.9	34.63	3.58
⊖ BellSouth Corporation	Telecom	—		3.49
⊕ Altria Group, Inc.	Goods	16.3	19.87	3.42
⊕ J.P. Morgan Chase & Co.	Financial	13.6	25.60	3.31
⊕ American International G	Financial	17.0	6.05	3.26
⊕ Novartis AG ADR	Health	22.2	11.29	3.19
⊕ Wells Fargo Company	Financial	14.7	16.82	3.12
⊕ General Electric Company	Ind Mtrls	20.0	9.35	3.10
⊖ Wal-Mart Stores, Inc.	Consumer	16.9	0.13	3.03
⊕ Entergy Corporation	Utilities	19.7	38.40	2.86
⊕ Honeywell International,	Ind Mtrls	18.6	24.14	2.82
⊕ PepsiCo, Inc.	Goods	21.5	7.86	2.78
⊖ Baxter International Inc	Health	24.3	24.81	2.73
⊕ Dominion Resources, Inc.	Utilities	17.8	12.56	2.59
⊕ Motorola, Inc.	Hardware	11.8	-8.17	2.29
⊕ Total SA ADR	Energy	10.6	19.24	2.28
⊕ Sprint Nextel Corporatio	Telecom	30.2	-10.44	2.25

Current Investment Style

Value Blnd Growth — Large Mid Small

Market Cap	%
Giant	57.9
Large	37.6
Mid	4.5
Small	0.0
Micro	0.0

Avg $mil: 73,537

Value Measures		Rel Category
Price/Earnings	14.43	1.05
Price/Book	2.31	1.04
Price/Sales	1.58	1.22
Price/Cash Flow	10.32	1.54
Dividend Yield %	2.24	0.96

Growth Measures	%	Rel Category
Long-Term Erngs	10.49	1.01
Book Value	7.83	0.99
Sales	7.66	0.85
Cash Flow	4.33	0.71
Historical Erngs	18.32	1.13

Profitability	%	Rel Category
Return on Equity	19.71	1.10
Return on Assets	10.90	1.11
Net Margin	14.16	1.09

Sector Weightings	% of Stocks	Rel S&P 500	3 Year High	Low
↻ Info	13.58	0.68		
🖬 Software	0.00	0.00	3	0
🖥 Hardware	6.96	0.75	8	4
🎤 Media	0.88	0.23	10	0
📶 Telecom	5.74	1.64	6	2
🛎 Service	47.41	1.03		
🏥 Health	9.41	0.78	11	7
🛒 Consumer	9.28	1.21	9	4
🏢 Business	2.75	0.65	10	3
💵 Financial	25.97	1.17	29	22
🏭 Mfg	39.02	1.15		
🏷 Goods	7.18	0.84	10	6
⚙ Ind Mtrls	13.85	1.16	15	4
🔋 Energy	10.99	1.12	15	10
💡 Utilities	7.00	2.00	8	2

Composition

● Cash		0.0
● Stocks		100.0
● Bonds		0.0
● Other		0.0
Foreign (% of Stock)		11.1

Mᴏʀɴɪɴɢsᴛᴀʀ® Funds 500

MainStay ICAP Intl I

	Analyst Pick	Ticker	Load	NAV	Yield	Total Assets	Mstar Category
	✓	ICEUX	None	$39.10	2.6%	$596 mil	Foreign Large Value

Governance and Management

Stewardship Grade: A

Portfolio Manager(s)

Rob Lyon, Jerry Senser, and Matt Pickering won Morningstar's International Fund Manager of the Year award in 2005. Lyon has been the lead manager here since the fund's 1997 inception. Senser was named comanager in 2003 and along with Lynon comanages the domestic ICAP Equity and Fund Analyst Pick ICAP Select Equity. Pickering left the firm in October 2006 to join crosstown rival Harris Associates. ICAP's team of roughly two dozen sector analysts compare foreign stocks with their domestic counterparts.

Strategy

Like its siblings, this fund homes in on undervalued stocks with catalysts for growth. Management favors a concentrated portfolio of large developed-market multinationals, but it is not guided by the popular MSCI EAFE Index. The firm uses top-down analysis, in addition to company-level research. The fund also sports a high turnover rate, which comes less from churning stocks than from trading around positions in an attempt to add value. ICAP does not hedge its foreign-currency exposure.

Performance 12-31-06

	1st Qtr	2nd Qtr	3rd Qtr	4th Qtr	Total
2002	-1.21	-0.82	-23.77	9.29	-18.37
2003	-6.87	21.04	4.10	20.88	41.85
2004	1.24	3.30	3.71	16.98	26.87
2005	0.23	-0.33	13.17	5.39	19.15
2006	8.42	1.72	2.36	10.11	24.30

Trailing	Total Return%	+/- MSCI EAFE	+/- MSCI Wd xUS	%Rank Cat	Growth of $10,000
3 Mo	10.11	-0.24	-0.01	42	11,011
6 Mo	12.71	-1.98	-1.51	82	11,271
1 Yr	24.30	-2.04	-1.41	71	12,430
3 Yr Avg	23.40	3.47	3.30	17	18,791
5 Yr Avg	16.82	1.84	1.57	41	21,756
10 Yr Avg	—	—	—	—	—
15 Yr Avg	—	—	—	—	—

Tax Analysis	Tax-Adj Rtn%	%Rank Cat	Tax-Cost Rat	%Rank Cat
3 Yr (estimated)	21.60	19	1.46	58
5 Yr (estimated)	15.48	37	1.15	60
10 Yr (estimated)	—	—	—	—

Potential Capital Gain Exposure: 16% of assets

Morningstar's Take by Andrew Gogerty 12-08-06

Changes at MainStay ICAP International in 2006 don't change our high opinion of it.

In June 2006, Institutional Capital, winner of Morningstar's International Manager of the Year Award for 2005, sold its business to New York Life Investment Management and subsequently merged its ICAP funds into NYLIM's MainStay fund family. In addition, manager Matt Pickering departed in October to join crosstown rival Harris Associates (manager of the Oakmark Funds).

Initially, we expressed concern about the MainStay sale, as fund family mergers have a checkered history at best. Our concerns remain valid, but the merger appears to be seamless thus far. Key managers Rob Lyon and Jerry Senser, and their investment team continue to execute their unique style of buying undervalued large-cap stocks relative to the market, yet also considering macroeconomic factors when determining short-term growth catalysts.

Moreover, we're not overly worried about

Pickering's departure. Lyon and Senser's experience in guiding this offering remains, and we don't anticipate a disruption in the research effort. Tom Wetzel, the firm's seasoned director of research, is stepping in to cover financials on a global basis (Pickering's specialty was European financials) with current analyst Rob Stoll.

Nor are we concerned that the fund has fallen to the back of the pack in 2006 (though its absolute return of 22% through December 13 is great). The fund's exposure to Japan and a handful of European telecom stocks--key drivers of performance in recent years--have held back returns. But one year in no way dampens the case for owning it. Lyon has demonstrated a sound knack for mixing macro tilts and sound fundamental research to identify undervalued stocks with internal catalysts to ignite growth over the next 12 to 18 months. Moreover, the fund's reasonable costs and the firm's history of shareholder friendliness are still intact.

Address:	51 Madison Avenue Chicago IL 60606 800-624-6782	
Web Address:	www.icapfunds.com	
Inception:	12-31-97*	
Advisor:	Institutional Capital Corp	
Subadvisor:	None	
NTF Plans:	Schwab OneSource	

Minimum Purchase:	$0	Add: $0	IRA: $0
Min Auto Inv Plan:	$0	Add: $250	
Sales Fees:	No-load, 2.00%R		
Management Fee:	0.80%		
Actual Fees:	Mgt:0.80%	Dist: —	
Expense Projections:	3Yr:$270	5Yr:$489	10Yr:$1119
Income Distrib:	Annually		

Historical Profile

Return	Above Avg
Risk	Above Avg
Rating	★★★★ Above Avg

| | | 100% | 97% | 98% | 90% | 97% | 93% | 81% | 93% | 100% | |

Investment Style
Equity
Stock %

▼ Manager Change
▽ Partial Manager Change

26.8
22.8
18.0 **Growth of $10,000**
14.0 ■ Investment Values of Fund
— Investment Values of MSCI EAFE
10.0

Performance Quartile (within Category)

1995	1996	1997	1998	1999	2000	2001	2002	2003	2004	2005	2006	History
—	—	20.00	24.32	27.91	24.19	21.69	17.45	24.20	30.18	32.89	39.10	NAV
—	—	0.00*	27.40	22.03	-4.81	-8.95	-18.37	41.85	26.87	19.15	24.30	Total Return %
—	—	—	7.47	-5.00	9.38	12.47	-2.43	3.26	6.62	5.61	-2.04	+/-MSCI EAFE
—	—	—	8.71	-5.95	8.55	12.44	-2.57	2.43	6.49	4.68	-1.41	+/-MSCI Wd xUS
—	—	—	1.88	1.83	1.40	0.84	1.35	2.39	1.24	1.80	3.14	Income Return %
—	—	—	25.52	20.20	-6.21	-9.79	-19.72	39.46	25.63	17.35	21.16	Capital Return %
—	—	—	1	64	70	14	96	30	11	9	71	Total Rtn % Rank Cat
—	—	0.00	0.37	0.44	0.37	0.20	0.29	0.41	0.30	0.54	1.03	Income $
—	—	0.00	0.73	1.22	2.04	0.13	0.00	0.00	0.18	2.50	0.70	Capital Gains $
—	—	—	1.00	1.00	0.80	0.95	0.80	0.80	0.80	0.80	—	Expense Ratio %
—	—	—	1.69	1.71	1.53	0.72	1.48	1.89	1.23	2.05	—	Income Ratio %
—	—	—	272	245	370	267	276	218	122	139	—	Turnover Rate %
—	—	28	32	33	21	18	45	93	154	568		Net Assets $mil

Rating and Risk

Time Period	Load-Adj Return %	Morningstar Rtn vs Cat	Morningstar Risk vs Cat	Morningstar Risk-Adj Rating
1 Yr	24.30			
3 Yr	23.40	+Avg	+Avg	★★★★
5 Yr	16.82	Avg	+Avg	★★★
10 Yr	—			
Incept	12.69			

Other Measures	Standard Index MSCI EAFE	Best Fit Index MSCI EASExJ
Alpha	2.9	1.9
Beta	1.01	0.99
R-Squared	87	89
Standard Deviation	10.19	
Mean	23.40	
Sharpe Ratio	1.82	

Portfoiio Analysis 10-31-06

Share change since 09-06 Total Stocks:43	Sector	Country	% Assets
⊖ Total SA ADR	Energy	France	4.81
⊖ InterContinental Hotels	Consumer	U.K.	4.09
⊖ Allianz	Financial	Germany	3.90
⊖ Mizuho Financial Grp	Financial	Japan	3.76
⊕ Nestle SA ADR	Goods	Switzerland	3.62
⊕ Vivendi Universal	Media	France	3.56
⊖ Barclays	Financial	U.K.	3.26
⊖ Novartis AG ADR	Health	Switzerland	3.15
⊖ Credit Suisse Group ADR	Financial	Switzerland	3.13
⊖ UBS AG	Financial	Switzerland	3.00
⊖ Toyota Motor Corporation	Goods	Japan	2.72
⊕ BP PLC ADR	Energy	U.K.	2.71
✵ Deutsche Bank AG	Financial	Germany	2.66
⊖ Diageo	Goods	U.K.	2.62
⊖ Imperial Chemical Indust	Ind Mtrls	U.K.	2.52
⊖ ING Groep NV ADR	Financial	Netherlands	2.50
⊖ SABMiller	Goods	U.K.	2.42
⊖ UniCredito Italiano Grp	Financial	Italy	2.41
⊖ EDP Electricidade de Por	Utilities	Portugal	2.33
⊕ Central Japan Railway	Business	Japan	2.29

Current Investment Style

Value Blnd Growth — Large Mid Small

Market Cap	%
Giant	75.4
Large	16.9
Mid	7.7
Small	0.0
Micro	0.0

Avg $mil: 48,089

Value Measures		Rel Category
Price/Earnings	10.65	0.85
Price/Book	2.22	1.25
Price/Sales	1.57	1.65
Price/Cash Flow	6.31	0.88
Dividend Yield %	2.48	0.76

Growth Measures	%	Rel Category
Long-Term Erngs	14.37	1.39
Book Value	9.93	1.27
Sales	2.14	0.39
Cash Flow	4.33	1.21
Historical Erngs	35.57	2.17

Composition

Cash	0.0	Bonds	0.0
Stocks	100.0	Other	0.0
Foreign	(% of Stock)		100.0

Sector Weightings	% of Stocks	Rel MSCI EAFE	3 Year High	Low
⊙ Info	9.85	0.83		
🖥 Software	0.00	0.00	0	0
💾 Hardware	2.19	0.57	7	0
📺 Media	5.85	3.20	7	0
📞 Telecom	1.81	0.32	8	1
🅖 Service	48.47	1.03		
🏥 Health	9.09	1.28	16	6
🛒 Consumer	4.13	0.83	9	0
🏢 Business	6.77	1.34	7	0
💲 Financial	28.48	0.95	34	19
🔧 Mfg	41.68	1.02		
🏭 Goods	15.30	1.17	20	8
⚙ Ind Mtrls	13.02	0.84	19	0
🔋 Energy	9.19	1.29	20	9
💡 Utilities	4.17	0.80	10	2

Regional Exposure	% Stock		
UK/W. Europe 76	N. America	0	
Japan 20	Latn America	0	
Asia X Japan 4	Other	0	

Country Exposure	% Stock		
U.K.	23	France	12
Japan	20	Germany	11
Switzerland	15		

MainStay ICAP Sel Eq I

✔ Analyst Pick	**Ticker** ICSLX	**Load** None	**NAV** $41.62	**Yield** 1.2%	**Total Assets** $1,535 mil	**Mstar Category** Large Value

Governance and Management

Stewardship Grade: A

Portfolio Manager(s)

Team leader Rob Lyon, who is ICAP's president and chief investment officer, has run the fund since its inception. Prior to joining ICAP in 1988, Lyon served as director of research at Fred Alger Management. Jerrold Senser, Gary Maurer, Tom Wenzel, and others on the ICAP team are all very experienced. They draw on research produced by several sector-specific analysts. ICAP has a big presence in institutional money management.

Strategy

The fund's managers begin with a universe of 400 large-cap stocks and 50 mostly European ADRs. They then buy around 30 stocks with the best mix of attractive valuations, consistent or improving earnings, and catalysts for growth over the next 12 to 18 months. Catalysts can include a product launch, a management change, or a change in the macroeconomic environment. The fund's sector weightings have shifted quite dramatically at times. Management will sell a stock if it reaches a predetermined price target.

Performance 12-31-06

	1st Qtr	2nd Qtr	3rd Qtr	4th Qtr	Total
2002	-1.87	-8.39	-19.06	3.71	-24.53
2003	1.67	15.53	3.00	16.27	40.68
2004	5.46	1.39	-0.42	10.80	17.98
2005	1.54	1.34	5.66	0.46	9.22
2006	7.08	-0.71	4.58	8.46	20.60

Trailing	Total Return%	+/- S&P 500	+/- Russ 1000 VI	%Rank Cat	Growth of $10,000
3 Mo	8.46	1.76	0.46	8	10,846
6 Mo	13.43	0.69	-1.29	38	11,343
1 Yr	20.60	4.81	-1.65	19	12,060
3 Yr Avg	15.83	5.39	0.74	5	15,540
5 Yr Avg	10.53	4.34	-0.33	12	16,497
10 Yr Avg	—	—	—	—	—
15 Yr Avg	—	—	—	—	—

Tax Analysis	Tax-Adj Rtn%	%Rank Cat	Tax-Cost Rat	%Rank Cat
3 Yr (estimated)	14.69	4	0.98	39
5 Yr (estimated)	9.75	10	0.71	38
10 Yr (estimated)	—	—	—	—

Potential Capital Gain Exposure: 19% of assets

Morningstar's Take by Andrew Gogerty 11-14-06

It's business as usual for Mainstay ICAP Select Equity, and that's a good thing for shareholders.

In June 2006, Institutional Capital sold its business to New York Life Investment Management and subsequently merged its ICAP funds into NYLIM's MainStay fund family. Initially, we expressed concern, as fund family mergers have a checkered past. While our concerns remain valid, they appear to be just that--concerns. In the first few months, the merger seems to be a seamless transition, as key managers Rob Lyon and Jerry Senser, along with their investment team, continue to execute their unique style of buying undervalued large-cap stocks relative to the market, yet also considering macroeconomic factors when determining short-term growth catalysts.

In recent years, the fund's exposure to cyclical and energy stocks has been a significant tailwind, as has its exposure to China and India's growth. Coming into this year, however, the firm has put the brakes on somewhat, trimming the fund's cyclical stakes in Caterpillar and United States Steel. These gains have been redeployed into more diversified players such as General Electric and Honeywell International, which Lyon believes will hold up better amid his forecast for a slower pace of economic growth. He's also added back consumer exposure through Intercontinental Hotels Group amid declining gas prices.

These moves have paid off and continue the fund's long-standing success, but investors should note that sector and macro calls can backfire, and the fund is willing to hold a greater stake in foreign names than many of its peers. Also, because Lyon and his team typically look out just 12 to 18 months in evaluating their picks, turnover here is relatively high, increasing the chance of taxable distributions. But those concerns don't damp the case for owning it. Lyon's history of execution, the fund's reasonable costs, and the firm's history of treating shareholders right is why we like this fund, and those traits are still intact.

Address:	51 Madison Avenue Chicago IL 60606 800-624-6782	Minimum Purchase: Min Auto Inv Plan: Sales Fees:	$0 $0 No-load
Web Address:	www.icapfunds.com	Management Fee:	0.80%
Inception:	12-31-97 *	Actual Fees:	Mgt:0.80%
Advisor:	Institutional Capital Corp	Expense Projections:	3Yr:$263
Subadvisor:	None	Income Distrib:	Quarterly
NTF Plans:	Schwab OneSource		

Add: $0 IRA: $0
Add: —
Dist: —
5Yr:$468 10Yr:$1059

Historical Profile

Return	Above Avg	
Risk	Average	
Rating	★★★★ Above Avg	

▼ Manager Change
▽ Partial Manager Change

Growth of $10,000
■ Investment Values of Fund
— Investment Values of S&P 500

Investment Style
Equity
Stock %

82% 94% 96% 91% 97% 94% 98% 99% 100%

Performance Quartile (within Category)

1995	1996	1997	1998	1999	2000	2001	2002	2003	2004	2005	2006	History
—	—	20.00	22.77	27.91	29.50	28.50	21.36	29.79	34.35	36.17	41.62	NAV
—	—	0.00*	15.33	27.17	9.49	-1.59	-24.53	40.68	17.98	9.22	20.60	Total Return %
—	—	—	-13.25	6.13	18.59	10.30	-2.43	12.00	7.10	4.31	4.81	+/-S&P 500
—	—	—	-0.30	19.82	2.48	4.00	-9.01	10.65	1.49	2.17	-1.65	+/-Russ 1000 VI
—	—	—	1.45	1.70	1.15	0.53	0.56	0.99	1.90	1.33	1.44	Income Return %
—	—	—	13.88	25.47	8.34	-2.12	-25.09	39.69	16.08	7.89	19.16	Capital Return %
—	—	—	28	2	52	38	90	5	8	17	19	Total Rtn % Rank Cat
—	—	0.00	0.29	0.39	0.32	0.15	0.16	0.21	0.56	0.45	0.52	Income $
—	—	0.00	0.00	0.63	0.72	0.37	0.00	0.00	0.20	0.88	1.44	Capital Gains $
—	—	—	0.80	0.80	0.80	0.80	0.80	0.80	0.80	0.80	—	Expense Ratio %
—	—	—	1.82	1.63	1.24	0.54	0.64	0.88	2.18	1.37	—	Income Ratio %
—	—	—	250	375	400	309	358	317	198	—	—	Turnover Rate %
—	—	—	10	24	38	54	38	80	281	637	1,516	Net Assets $mil

Rating and Risk

Time Period	Load-Adj Return %	Morningstar Rtn vs Cat	Morningstar Risk vs Cat	Morningstar Risk-Adj Rating
1 Yr	20.60			
3 Yr	15.83	High	+Avg	★★★★★
5 Yr	10.53	+Avg	Avg	★★★★
10 Yr	—			
Incept	11.24			

Other Measures	Standard Index S&P 500	Best Fit Index Russ 1000 VI
Alpha	5.1	0.1
Beta	0.96	1.05
R-Squared	76	87
Standard Deviation	7.58	
Mean	15.83	
Sharpe Ratio	1.56	

Portfolio Analysis 10-31-06

Share change since 09-06 Total Stocks:30	Sector	PE	Tot Ret%	% Assets
⊕ Novartis AG ADR	Health	22.2	11.29	5.56
⊕ ExxonMobil Corporation	Energy	11.1	39.07	5.08
⊕ General Electric Company	Ind Mtrls	20.0	9.35	4.97
⊕ St. Paul Travelers Compa	Financial	11.6	22.90	4.93
⊕ McDonald's Corporation	Consumer	18.9	34.63	4.81
⊕ Altria Group, Inc.	Goods	16.3	19.87	4.80
⊕ American International G	Financial	17.0	6.05	4.78
⊕ Bank of America Corporat	Financial	12.4	20.68	4.75
⊕ Citigroup, Inc.	Financial	13.1	19.55	4.75
⊕ J.P. Morgan Chase & Co.	Financial	13.6	25.60	4.61
⊕ Wal-Mart Stores, Inc.	Consumer	16.9	0.13	4.28
⊕ Dominion Resources, Inc.	Utilities	17.8	12.56	4.18
⊕ Baxter International Inc	Health	24.3	24.81	4.03
⊕ Hewlett-Packard Company	Hardware	19.3	45.21	3.59
⊖ Honeywell International,	Ind Mtrls	18.6	24.14	3.57
⊕ Hess Corporation	Ind Mtrls	7.8	19.01	2.92
⊕ CSX Corporation	Business	15.4	37.05	2.87
⊖ Entergy Corporation	Utilities	19.7	38.40	2.86
⊖ Aon Corp.	Financial	19.6	-0.07	2.85
⊕ Intercontinental Hotels	Consumer	13.8	74.87	2.47

Current Investment Style

Value Blnd Growth — Large Mid Small

Market Cap	%
Giant	53.5
Large	37.2
Mid	9.4
Small	0.0
Micro	0.0
Avg $mil:	70,457

Value Measures		Rel Category
Price/Earnings	13.96	1.02
Price/Book	2.54	1.14
Price/Sales	1.41	1.08
Price/Cash Flow	11.27	1.68
Dividend Yield %	2.24	0.96

Growth Measures	%	Rel Category
Long-Term Erngs	10.34	1.00
Book Value	4.61	0.58
Sales	7.14	0.79
Cash Flow	4.16	0.69
Historical Erngs	16.73	1.04

Profitability	%	Rel Category
Return on Equity	19.54	1.09
Return on Assets	10.26	1.05
Net Margin	12.77	0.99

Sector Weightings	% of Stocks	Rel S&P 500	3 Year High Low
☁ Info	6.96	0.35	
Software	0.00	0.00	7 0
Hardware	6.96	0.75	9 0
Media	0.00	0.00	13 0
Telecom	0.00	0.00	5 0
☁ Service	55.88	1.21	
Health	13.06	1.08	13 4
Consumer	13.29	1.74	13 2
Business	2.87	0.68	17 3
Financial	26.66	1.20	31 19
☁ Mfg	37.17	1.10	
Goods	4.80	0.56	13 3
Ind Mtrls	15.69	1.31	22 3
Energy	9.64	0.98	17 9
Utilities	7.04	2.01	10 4

Composition

● Cash	0.0
● Stocks	100.0
● Bonds	0.0
○ Other	0.0
Foreign	14.1
(% of Stock)	

MORNINGSTAR® Funds 500

MainStay MAP I

	Ticker	Load	NAV	Yield	Total Assets	Mstar Category
	MUBFX	None	$37.54	0.5%	$1,568 mil	Large Blend

Governance and Management

Stewardship Grade:

Portfolio Manager(s)

The portfolio was split between Markston International and Jennison Associates until June 2006, when managers from ICAP took over the Jennison portion of the fund. The Markston managers--Michael Mullarkey, Roger Lob, and Chris Mullarkey--each independently manage pieces of their half of the fund. The ICAP managers, Robert Lyon and Jerrold Senser, are both veteran managers who have helped deliver a strong long-term record at ICAP Equity, a large-cap value fund.

Strategy

This fund owns small, medium, and large companies. One subadvisor, Markston, looks closely at insider transactions, management changes, and stock buybacks in assembling the portfolio. It also considers the effects of broad themes in the economy. The result is an eclectic mix of value and growth names. Meanwhile, the ICAP managers stick mainly with large-cap value stocks that have promising growth prospects over the coming 12 to 18 months.

Historical Profile
Return High
Risk Average
Rating ★★★★ Highest

94%	96%	96%	79%	88%	90%	91%	94%	96%		

Investment Style
Equity
Stock %

▼ Manager Change
▽ Partial Manager Change

57.6
43.6
32.4 **Growth of $10,000**
24.0 ■ Investment Values of Fund
17.0 — Investment Values of S&P 500
10.0

Performance Quartile (within Category)

	1995	1996	1997	1998	1999	2000	2001	2002	2003	2004	2005	2006	History
NAV	19.36	20.66	22.73	24.58	26.25	27.31	27.75	22.03	30.56	34.20	35.06	37.54	NAV
	32.62	24.02	28.35	24.25	12.18	16.88	2.36	-19.81	38.72	16.29	8.93	16.44	Total Return %
	-4.96	1.06	-5.01	-4.33	-8.86	25.98	14.25	2.29	10.04	5.41	4.02	0.65	+/-S&P 500
	-5.15	1.57	-4.50	-2.77	-8.73	24.67	14.81	1.84	8.83	4.89	2.66	0.98	+/-Russ 1000
	2.62	1.98	1.41	1.57	0.45	0.11	0.24	0.59	0.00	0.00	0.21	0.58	Income Return %
	30.00	22.04	26.94	22.68	11.73	16.77	2.12	-20.40	38.72	16.29	8.72	15.86	Capital Return %
	62	20	56	44	79	6	30	5	5	18	15	Total Rtn % Rank Cat
	0.43	0.36	0.29	0.33	0.11	0.03	0.07	0.16	0.00	0.00	0.07	0.19	Income $
	2.21	2.86	3.41	2.96	1.14	3.16	0.14	0.06	0.00	1.31	2.13	3.06	Capital Gains $
	0.81	0.74	0.82	0.70	0.88	1.00	1.00	1.08	1.10	0.99	0.95	—	Expense Ratio %
	2.30	1.82	1.18	1.10	0.39	0.37	0.62	0.88	0.08	0.31	0.69	—	Income Ratio %
	39	53	58	41	32	40	19	77	61	64	56	—	Turnover Rate %
	60	73	94	57	63	69	97	123	208	307	338	372	Net Assets $mil

Performance 12-31-06

	1st Qtr	2nd Qtr	3rd Qtr	4th Qtr	Total
2002	1.48	-10.67	-15.77	5.02	-19.81
2003	-3.04	20.27	4.40	13.94	38.72
2004	3.99	2.08	-0.99	10.64	16.29
2005	-1.05	1.36	6.30	2.17	8.93
2006	6.82	-1.63	2.77	7.83	16.44

Trailing	Total Return%	+/- S&P 500	+/- Russ 1000	%Rank Cat	Growth of $10,000
3 Mo	7.83	1.13	0.88	15	10,783
6 Mo	10.81	-1.93	-1.55	64	11,081
1 Yr	16.44	0.65	0.98	15	11,644
3 Yr Avg	13.83	3.39	2.85	6	14,749
5 Yr Avg	10.41	4.22	3.59	4	16,407
10 Yr Avg	13.38	4.96	4.74	2	35,105
15 Yr Avg	14.00	3.36	3.20	5	71,379

Tax Analysis	Tax-Adj Rtn%	%Rank Cat	Tax-Cost Rat	%Rank Cat
3 Yr (estimated)	12.44	8	1.22	56
5 Yr (estimated)	9.52	4	0.81	53
10 Yr (estimated)	11.63	2	1.54	73

Potential Capital Gain Exposure: 22% of assets

Rating and Risk

Time Period	Load-Adj Return %	Morningstar Rtn vs Cat	Morningstar Risk vs Cat	Morningstar Risk-Adj Rating
1 Yr	16.44			
3 Yr	13.83	High	+Avg	★★★★★
5 Yr	10.41	High	+Avg	★★★★★
10 Yr	13.38	High	-Avg	★★★★★
Incept	11.65			

Other Measures	Standard Index S&P 500	Best Fit Index Russ 1000
Alpha	2.1	1.7
Beta	1.16	1.12
R-Squared	88	89
Standard Deviation	8.48	
Mean	13.83	
Sharpe Ratio	1.20	

Morningstar's Take by Andrew Gunter 12-28-06

MainStay MAP is playing in a different sandbox, and that presents new concerns.

In our last analysis, we covered this fund's manager shuffle in detail. To summarize, its board of directors fired subadvisor Jennison Associates in June 2006 and replaced it with Institutional Capital Management. The board retained this fund's other longtime subadvisor, Markston International.

ICAP's hiring comes as this portfolio has endured significant shift causing it to move recently from the mid-blend to the large-blend category. When Jennison came aboard in late 2002, the fund's average market cap was roughly $5 billion. Every year since, the subadvisors' inclination for undervalued large caps drove the portfolio's average market cap higher. Today, its $36.7 billion mark equals that of its typical large-blend competitor, so those who bought this fund for mid-cap exposure should consider alternatives.

Looking forward, this fund won't behave like the typical large-blend offering. That's because the addition of two experienced ICAP managers, Jerrold Senser and Rob Lyon, only reinforces the value tilt this portfolio already had. They're accustomed to managing two large-value funds for ICAP, and they started here by adding mega-cap value stock Altria. It already held General Electric, Wal-Mart, ExxonMobil, and the nation's three largest banks within its top 10 positions. While many of these are high-quality stocks, they'll cause the fund to significantly trail the large-blend category when growth-oriented fare returns to favor. Such holdings may give it a nicer cushion than its rivals, however, in a sharp market decline.

Even so, we're unsure of this fund's future. Its subadvisors must prove themselves against a new, venerable set of actively managed funds, and its 1.32% expense ratio on A shares looks steep compared with the typical broker-sold fund's 1.13% price tag. So, until this fund proves itself against the fierce competition of its new category, we'd look elsewhere.

Portfolio Analysis 11-30-06

Share change since 10-06 Total Stocks:226

	Sector	PE	Tot Ret%	% Assets
⊕ General Electric Company	Ind Mtrls	20.0	9.35	3.60
⊕ Citigroup, Inc.	Financial	13.1	19.55	3.16
⊕ McDonald's Corporation	Consumer	18.9	34.63	2.76
⊕ Novartis AG ADR	Health	22.2	11.29	2.74
⊖ St. Paul Travelers Compa	Financial	11.6	22.90	2.69
⊕ J.P. Morgan Chase & Co.	Financial	13.6	25.60	2.55
⊕ American International G	Financial	17.0	6.05	2.44
⊕ Bank of America Corporat	Financial	12.4	20.68	2.38
⊖ ExxonMobil Corporation	Energy	11.1	39.07	2.28
⊖ Altria Group, Inc.	Goods	16.3	19.87	2.25
Duke Energy Corporation	Utilities	8.2	30.15	2.19
⊕ Dominion Resources, Inc.	Utilities	17.8	12.56	2.18
⊕ Wal-Mart Stores, Inc.	Consumer	16.9	0.13	2.10
⊕ Hess Corporation	Ind Mtrls	7.8	19.01	1.97
Morgan Stanley	Financial	12.3	45.93	1.91
⊖ Baxter International Inc	Health	24.3	24.81	1.82
⊖ Hewlett-Packard Company	Hardware	19.3	45.21	1.70
⊕ Textron Incorporated	Ind Mtrls	18.3	23.94	1.69
Metropolitan Life Insura	Financial	16.0	21.67	1.64
⊕ CSX Corporation	Business	15.4	37.05	1.61

Current Investment Style

Value Blend Growth — Large Mid Small

Market Cap	%
Giant	40.9
Large	43.6
Mid	11.7
Small	3.2
Micro	0.7
Avg $mil:	38,198

Value Measures		Rel Category
Price/Earnings	15.14	0.99
Price/Book	2.37	0.93
Price/Sales	1.42	1.01
Price/Cash Flow	8.79	1.04
Dividend Yield %	1.81	1.03

Growth Measures	%	Rel Category
Long-Term Erngs	11.02	0.93
Book Value	5.82	0.64
Sales	4.08	0.42
Cash Flow	3.83	0.37
Historical Erngs	20.19	1.09

Profitability	%	Rel Category
Return on Equity	17.45	0.90
Return on Assets	9.77	0.94
Net Margin	12.56	0.94

Sector Weightings	% of Stocks	Rel S&P 500	3 Year High Low	
↻ Info	8.54	0.43		
▣ Software	1.65	0.48	6	3
▣ Hardware	5.68	0.61	8	5
▣ Media	0.83	0.22	7	1
▣ Telecom	0.38	0.11	2	0
⊟ Service	52.86	1.14		
▣ Health	10.41	0.86	14	9
▣ Consumer	9.57	1.25	10	5
▣ Business	6.60	1.56	11	4
▣ Financial	26.28	1.18	27	17
⊔ Mfg	38.60	1.14		
▣ Goods	3.06	0.36	3	1
▣ Ind Mtrls	18.41	1.54	22	15
▣ Energy	9.83	1.00	15	8
▣ Utilities	7.30	2.09	8	2

Composition

● Cash		3.5
● Stocks		96.2
● Bonds		0.0
○ Other		0.3
Foreign (% of Stock)		7.2

Address:	169 Lackawanna Ave. Parsippany, NJ 07054 800-624-6782	Minimum Purchase:	$5000000	Add: $0 IRA: $5000000
		Min Auto Inv Plan:	$0	Add: —
Web Address:	www.mainstayfunds.com	Sales Fees:	No-load	
Inception:	01-21-71	Management Fee:	0.75% mx./0.70% mn.	
Advisor:	New York Life Investment Management LLC	Actual Fees:	Mgt:0.74%	Dist: —
Subadvisor:	Institutional Capital LLC	Expense Projections:	3Yr:$303 5Yr:$525	10Yr:$1166
NTF Plans:	N/A	Income Distrib:	Quarterly	

Mairs & Power Balanced

	Ticker	Load	NAV	Yield	Total Assets	Mstar Category
	MAPOX	None	$63.06	2.9%	$141 mil	Moderate Allocation

Governance and Management

Stewardship Grade: B

Portfolio Manager(s)

Bill Frels is the president and treasurer of Mairs & Power Inc. and has been the lead manager on this offering since July 1992. He has comanaged the better-known Mairs & Power Growth since December 1999 and took sole charge of that offering in June 2004. Ronald Kaliebe was added as a comanager of the fund in January 2006.

Strategy

Manager Bill Frels buys what he knows. On the stock side, he looks for well-managed companies with strong market shares in their industries, most of which are located in or around the firm's home state of Minnesota. He tends to run a concentrated portfolio of only 45 names, and once he adds a stock to the fund, it usually stays; the rate of turnover is microscopic. Frels also runs the conservative but flexible fixed-income portfolio, which focuses on government-agency bonds and short-term corporates. Overall, he strives for a roughly 60/40 asset mix of equities to bonds.

Performance 12-31-06

	1st Qtr	2nd Qtr	3rd Qtr	4th Qtr	Total
2002	3.02	-6.00	-9.36	6.62	-6.42
2003	-0.83	11.81	1.28	8.32	21.65
2004	3.50	1.87	-0.04	6.29	12.02
2005	-0.69	1.42	1.46	2.22	4.47
2006	5.73	-0.66	2.46	4.16	12.10

Trailing	Total Return%	+/- DJ Mod	+/- DJ US Mod	%Rank Cat	Growth of $10,000
3 Mo	4.16	-1.43	-0.51	83	10,416
6 Mo	6.72	-2.07	-1.18	92	10,672
1 Yr	12.10	-0.20	1.83	29	11,210
3 Yr Avg	9.47	-1.25	0.35	23	13,119
5 Yr Avg	8.35	-1.67	0.75	9	14,933
10 Yr Avg	10.14	1.59	1.55	7	26,269
15 Yr Avg	10.76	1.55	1.37	11	46,317

Tax Analysis	Tax-Adj Rtn%	%Rank Cat	Tax-Cost Rat	%Rank Cat
3 Yr (estimated)	8.25	23	1.11	55
5 Yr (estimated)	7.15	9	1.11	68
10 Yr (estimated)	8.66	4	1.34	39

Potential Capital Gain Exposure: 27% of assets

Morningstar's Take by Kerry O'Boyle 12-11-06

Mairs & Power Balanced quietly keeps posting stellar results.

This offering is something of a hidden gem in the mutual fund world. While sibling Mairs & Power Growth has generated enough attention to build assets to more than $2.6 billion, this offering has remained largely unnoticed despite its fine record. Granted, the fund is only currently accessible to investors in 22 states and the District of Columbia. But the firm does respond to investor demand, and the number of states where it is offered has grown in recent years. Indeed, the Growth fund was once limited in its availability as well, but is now open in all 50 states.

This offering is well worth the look. Manager Bill Frels heads an investment committee that employs a similar stock-picking process here as at the Growth fund. The main difference is that this fund has more of a quality large-cap and dividend focus than its sibling, reflecting the more conservative goals of a balanced fund. The fixed-income portfolio

is also appropriately mild--investing in short-term corporate bonds and government-backed agencies for decent yields and low interest-rate risk--and the asset mix is typically a modest 60% to 65% in equities, with the rest in bonds and cash.

That moderate approach has helped the fund to outpace most of its rivals in 2006. A nearly 30% stake in industrial stocks--twice that of the typical moderate-allocation fund--boosted returns early in the year. The fund's value bias is also working in its favor, as value-oriented stocks of all sizes have done well thus far this year.

But it's management's conviction in its holdings that impresses us the most. Turnover in this concentrated portfolio of 46 stocks and roughly 100 bonds tends to be minimal. That kind of patient, long-term commitment minimizes trading costs and aids tax efficiency, while also allowing the firm's research effort to bear fruit.

We heartily recommend this fund.

Address:	332 Minnesota St Ste W-1520 St Paul MN 55101 800-304-7404	Minimum Purchase:	$2500	Add: $100	IRA: $1000
		Min Auto Inv Plan:	$0	Add: $100	
		Sales Fees:	No-load		
Web Address:	www.mairsandpower.com	Management Fee:	0.60%		
Inception:	03-17-61	Actual Fees:	Mgt:0.60%	Dist: —	
Advisor:	Mairs & Power Inc	Expense Projections:	3Yr:$269	5Yr:$468	10Yr:$1040
Subadvisor:	None	Income Distrib:	Quarterly		
NTF Plans:	Schwab Instl NTF				

Historical Profile

Return	Above Avg
Risk	Average
Rating	★★★★ Above Avg

1995	1996	1997	1998	1999	2000	2001	2002	2003	2004	2005	2006	History
32.70	36.84	45.52	50.05	50.13	51.86	49.71	45.09	53.21	57.66	58.42	63.06	NAV
30.06	17.91	28.04	14.15	4.60	16.55	-1.27	-6.42	21.65	12.02	4.47	12.10	Total Return %
10.26	7.25	16.14	1.83	-12.73	18.22	1.53	0.35	-5.73	-0.95	-2.52	-0.20	+/-DJ Mod
5.29	6.57	8.84	1.76	-8.25	12.11	-1.43	4.12	-2.41	0.85	-1.53	1.83	+/-DJ US Mod
3.94	3.40	3.25	2.75	2.81	3.19	2.83	2.95	3.21	2.89	2.79	3.13	Income Return %
26.12	14.51	24.79	11.40	1.79	13.36	-4.10	-9.37	18.44	9.13	1.68	8.97	Capital Return %
17	17	6	47	80	4	21	8	37	11	59	29	Total Rtn % Rank Cat
1.02	1.10	1.19	1.24	1.39	1.58	1.45	1.45	1.43	1.52	1.59	1.81	Income $
0.28	0.54	0.35	0.60	0.81	4.92	0.00	0.00	0.08	0.35	0.19	0.56	Capital Gains $
1.12	1.08	0.92	0.91	0.88	0.93	0.95	0.99	0.94	0.92	0.84	—	Expense Ratio %
3.47	3.16	2.81	2.69	2.70	2.81	2.89	3.11	3.01	2.86	2.84	—	Income Ratio %
4	8	5	12	13	12	16	11	7	9	13	—	Turnover Rate %
17	21	29	38	41	41	42	43	64	91	118	141	Net Assets $mil

Rating and Risk

Time Period	Load-Adj Return %	Morningstar Rtn vs Cat	Morningstar Risk vs Cat	Morningstar Risk-Adj Rating
1 Yr	12.10			
3 Yr	9.47	+Avg	-Avg	★★★★
5 Yr	8.35	+Avg	Avg	★★★★
10 Yr	10.14	High	Avg	★★★★★
Incept	10.13			

Other Measures	Standard Index DJ Mod	Best Fit Index Mstar Mid Core
Alpha	1.0	1.7
Beta	0.70	0.39
R-Squared	73	80
Standard Deviation	4.78	
Mean	9.47	
Sharpe Ratio	1.25	

Portfolio Analysis 09-30-06

Total Stocks:46 Share change since 06-30-06	Sectors	P/E Ratio	YTD Return %	% Net Assets
⊕ 3M Company	Ind Mtrls	16.7	-0.44	3.26
Emerson Electric Company	Ind Mtrls	19.6	-0.41	3.05
⊕ Wells Fargo Company	Financial	14.7	-0.17	2.85
⊕ H.B. Fuller Company	Ind Mtrls	19.1	2.48	2.52
Valspar Corporation	Goods	16.6	2.10	2.47
Graco Incorporated	Ind Mtrls	18.8	0.13	2.20
Pfizer Inc.	Health	15.2	1.00	1.89
Schlumberger, Ltd.	Energy	22.3	-7.11	1.84
Merrill Lynch & Company,	Financial	14.2	0.76	1.80

Total Fixed-Income:116	Date of Maturity	Amount $000	Value $000	% Net Assets
FNMA 6%	04-20-20	1,000	995	0.74
FNMA 5.75%	07-07-20	1,000	980	0.73
Toro 7.8%	06-15-27	500	569	0.42
Wyeth 6.45%	02-01-24	500	532	0.39
Supervalu 7.875%	08-01-09	500	518	0.38
Provident Cos 7%	07-15-18	500	514	0.38
Farmers Exchange Cap 144A	07-15-28	500	512	0.38
General Elec Cap 6.35%	05-12-18	500	511	0.38
FFCB 6.05%	04-18-16	500	502	0.37

Equity Style			Fixed-Income Style	
Style: Value			Duration: —	
Size: Large-Cap			Quality: —	

Value Measures		Rel Category
Price/Earnings	14.75	0.97
Price/Book	2.76	1.12
Price/Sales	1.34	0.98
Price/Cash Flow	10.81	1.33
Dividend Yield %	2.25	1.17

Avg Eff Duration [1]	—
Avg Eff Maturity	—
Avg Credit Quality	—
Avg Wtd Coupon	6.14%

[1] figure provided by fund

Growth Measures	%	Rel Category
Long-Term Erngs	10.53	0.90
Book Value	7.10	0.82
Sales	9.32	1.05
Cash Flow	8.78	0.89
Historical Erngs	15.76	0.88

Market Cap %			
Giant	46.0	Small	8.3
Large	23.4	Micro	0.3
Mid	21.9	Avg $mil:	26,123

Sector Weightings	% of Stocks	Rel DJ Mod	3 Year High	Low
↻ Info	5.02	—		
Software	0.00	—	0	0
Hardware	3.48	—	4	3
Media	0.00	—	0	0
Telecom	1.54	—	3	1
☞ Service	40.66			
Health	13.24	—	15	12
Consumer	3.83	—	4	1
Business	2.98	—	5	3
Financial	20.61	—	23	20
Mfg	54.33			
Goods	14.18	—	18	14
Ind Mtrls	28.06	—	30	22
Energy	11.11	—	12	10
Utilities	0.98	—	2	1

Composition

		%
● Cash		3.1
● Stocks		62.7
● Bonds		33.8
○ Other		0.4
Foreign		1.9
(% of Stock)		

MO**RNINGSTAR** Funds 500

Mairs & Power Growth

	Ticker	Load	NAV	Yield	Total Assets	Mstar Category
	MPGFX	None	$77.10	1.2%	$2,694 mil	Large Blend

Governance and Management

Stewardship Grade: B

Portfolio Manager(s)

William Frels succeeded longtime manager George Mairs III in June 2004. Frels has been a comanager here since December 1999 and has delivered strong results at Mairs & Power Balanced since 1992. Mark Henneman was named as a comanager on the fund in January 2006.

Strategy

Manager Bill Frels and the investment team at Mairs & Power buy what they know. They look for well-managed companies with strong market share in their industries, and they keep the portfolio in about 35 companies, most of which are located in or around the firm's home state, Minnesota. Once a stock is added to the fund, it usually stays. The turnover rate is microscopic.

Historical Profile

Return	High
Risk	Below Avg
Rating	★★★★ Highest

Investment Style: Equity, Stock %

100% 100% 100% 98% 98% 97% 98% 98%

▼ Manager Change
▽ Partial Manager Change

Growth of $10,000
— Investment Values of Fund
— Investment Values of S&P 500

59.0 / 43.6 / 32.4 / 24.0 / 17.0 / 10.0

Performance Quartile (within Category)

1995	1996	1997	1998	1999	2000	2001	2002	2003	2004	2005	2006	History
28.02	34.74	43.34	46.34	46.45	53.41	54.36	49.26	60.90	70.33	71.69	77.10	NAV
47.70	27.76	28.68	9.36	7.16	26.48	6.48	-8.12	26.33	17.99	4.37	10.24	Total Return %
10.12	4.80	-4.68	-19.22	-13.88	35.58	18.37	13.98	-2.35	7.11	-0.54	-5.55	+/-S&P 500
9.93	5.31	-4.17	-17.66	-13.75	34.27	18.93	13.53	-3.56	6.59	-1.90	-5.22	+/-Russ 1000
1.43	1.27	1.13	0.83	1.01	1.18	0.96	0.83	1.08	1.12	1.11	1.30	Income Return %
46.27	26.49	27.55	8.53	6.15	25.30	5.52	-8.95	25.25	16.87	3.26	8.94	Capital Return %
1	7	54	89	89	1	4	2	65	2	69	91	Total Rtn % Rank Cat
0.28	0.36	0.39	0.36	0.47	0.54	0.51	0.45	0.53	0.68	0.78	0.93	Income $
0.76	0.70	0.96	0.68	2.74	4.82	2.00	0.24	0.77	0.82	0.93	0.99	Capital Gains $
0.99	0.89	0.84	0.82	0.79	0.78	0.76	0.78	0.75	0.73	0.70	—	Expense Ratio %
1.00	1.18	0.98	0.97	0.83	1.06	0.97	0.93	1.05	1.12	1.15	—	Income Ratio %
4	3	5	2	6	15	4	1	2	3	3	—	Turnover Rate %
71	150	413	555	547	582	677	850	1,307	2,056	2,523	2,694	Net Assets $mil

Performance 12-31-06

	1st Qtr	2nd Qtr	3rd Qtr	4th Qtr	Total
2002	6.75	-8.38	-12.84	7.77	-8.12
2003	-2.56	13.43	3.34	10.60	26.33
2004	4.88	5.17	-2.89	10.17	17.99
2005	-2.36	1.44	0.55	4.80	4.37
2006	5.11	-2.46	1.68	5.76	10.24

Trailing	Total Return%	+/- S&P 500	+/- Russ 1000	%Rank Cat	Growth of $10,000
3 Mo	5.76	-0.94	-1.19	81	10,576
6 Mo	7.53	-5.21	-4.83	94	10,753
1 Yr	10.24	-5.55	-5.22	91	11,024
3 Yr Avg	10.73	0.29	-0.25	32	13,577
5 Yr Avg	9.52	3.33	2.70	7	15,757
10 Yr Avg	12.33	3.91	3.69	3	31,986
15 Yr Avg	14.66	4.02	3.86	2	77,836

Tax Analysis	Tax-Adj Rtn%	%Rank Cat	Tax-Cost Rat	%Rank Cat
3 Yr (estimated)	10.01	29	0.65	30
5 Yr (estimated)	8.89	6	0.58	38
10 Yr (estimated)	11.33	3	0.89	39

Potential Capital Gain Exposure: 32% of assets

Rating and Risk

Time Period	Load-Adj Return %	Morningstar Rtn vs Cat	Morningstar Risk vs Cat	Morningstar Risk-Adj Rating
1 Yr	10.24			
3 Yr	10.73	+Avg	Avg	★★★★
5 Yr	9.52	High	Low	★★★★★
10 Yr	12.33	High	-Avg	★★★★★
Incept	12.03			

Other Measures	Standard Index S&P 500	Best Fit Index Russ 1000Gr
Alpha	1.2	4.4
Beta	0.87	0.76
R-Squared	67	77
Standard Deviation	7.25	
Mean	10.73	
Sharpe Ratio	1.00	

Morningstar's Take by Kerry O'Boyle 11-01-06

We think Mairs & Power Growth has the right stuff.

Sometimes investing doesn't have to be as complicated as some would make it out to be. Take this fine multicap fund, for example. Manager Bill Frels heads an investment committee that buys companies whose businesses and managements they know quite well--those mostly located in and around Mairs & Power's own base in the Twin Cities area of Minnesota and the rest of the Midwest. They hold on to stocks for years, if not decades, as turnover here rarely climbs into double digits annually. That low turnover also aids tax efficiency for those in taxable accounts. Plus, the fund is cheap at 0.70% in yearly expenses, allowing shareholders to keep even more of the portfolio's returns than would its typical peer.

This patient, long-term focused approach is reflected in recent moves at the fund. Frels trimmed back on industrial materials supplier Graco after a big runup in the stock during the first half of the

year, taking some profits and moving the stock down in the portfolio a bit. But he still likes the firm, and he thinks everything is on track. Although medical-device companies St. Jude Medical and Medtronic have been punished by an industrywide slump in defibrillator sales due to a major recall by a competitor--hurting fund performance this year--Frels has added to the fund's stake in each. He thinks that the defibrillator market will recover, and in the meantime both stocks are quite cheap.

To be sure, a sizable stake in strong performing small- and mid-cap stocks has provided a tailwind to the fund the past several years versus purer large-cap options. The fund will likely lag its large-blend category peers should mega-cap stocks stage a rally, as they did in 1998 and 1999.

Still, over the long haul we think this fund's many appealing qualities outweigh such short-term considerations. We think investors can be well served making this fund a core holding in their portfolio.

Address:	332 Minnesota St Ste W-1520 St Paul MN 55101 800-304-7404
Web Address:	www.mairsandpower.com
Inception:	11-07-58
Advisor:	Mairs & Power Inc
Subadvisor:	None
NTF Plans:	N/A

Minimum Purchase:	$2500	Add: $100	IRA: $1000
Min Auto Inv Plan:	$2500	Add: $100	
Sales Fees:	No-load		
Management Fee:	0.60%		
Actual Fees:	Mgt:0.60%	Dist: —	
Expense Projections:	3Yr:$225	5Yr:$391	10Yr:$873
Income Distrib:	Semi-Annually		

Portfolio Analysis 09-30-06

Share change since 06-06 Total Stocks:42	Sector	PE	Tot Ret%	% Assets
⊕ Wells Fargo Company	Financial	14.7	16.82	4.56
⊕ Target Corporation	Consumer	19.3	4.65	4.18
Emerson Electric Company	Ind Mtrls	19.6	20.68	4.13
⊕ 3M Company	Ind Mtrls	16.7	2.98	4.04
⊕ Medtronic, Inc.	Health	23.8	-6.29	3.82
Valspar Corporation	Goods	16.6	13.94	3.61
⊖ Ecolab, Inc.	Ind Mtrls	32.2	25.88	3.54
⊖ US Bancorp	Financial	13.9	26.29	3.50
Johnson & Johnson	Health	17.5	12.45	3.42
General Mills, Inc.	Goods	19.1	19.94	3.42
⊖ Donaldson Company, Inc.	Business	21.3	10.22	3.28
General Electric Company	Ind Mtrls	20.0	9.35	3.24
⊕ Graco Incorporated	Ind Mtrls	18.8	10.11	3.17
⊕ H.B. Fuller Company	Ind Mtrls	19.1	62.81	3.14
⊖ TCF Financial Corporatio	Financial	13.7	4.67	3.13
Toro Company	Ind Mtrls	16.2	7.44	2.86
Bemis Company, Inc.	Goods	20.3	24.90	2.81
⊕ Pfizer Inc.	Health	15.2	15.22	2.80
Baxter International Inc	Health	24.3	24.81	2.73
⊕ Honeywell International,	Ind Mtrls	18.6	24.14	2.71

Current Investment Style

Value Blnd Growth — Large / Mid / Small

Market Cap	%
Giant	27.7
Large	24.8
Mid	34.5
Small	12.5
Micro	0.5

Avg $mil: 13,690

Value Measures		Rel Category
Price/Earnings	16.87	1.10
Price/Book	3.03	1.18
Price/Sales	1.40	1.00
Price/Cash Flow	12.36	1.46
Dividend Yield %	1.84	1.05

Growth Measures	%	Rel Category
Long-Term Erngs	11.62	0.98
Book Value	7.22	0.80
Sales	6.71	0.69
Cash Flow	7.11	0.69
Historical Erngs	12.23	0.66

Profitability	%	Rel Category
Return on Equity	19.28	0.99
Return on Assets	11.12	1.07
Net Margin	13.29	0.99

Sector Weightings	% of Stocks	Rel S&P 500	3 Year High Low
⊙ Info	4.03	0.20	
Software	0.45	0.13	0 0
Hardware	3.36	0.36	4 1
Media	0.00	0.00	0 0
Telecom	0.22	0.06	1 0
☞ Service	51.79	1.12	
Health	17.32	1.44	21 16
Consumer	7.03	0.92	9 7
Business	10.03	2.37	12 10
Financial	17.41	0.78	18 16
Mfg	44.17	1.31	
Goods	12.69	1.48	15 12
Ind Mtrls	31.48	2.64	33 26
Energy	0.00	0.00	0 0
Utilities	0.00	0.00	0 0

Composition

	%
● Cash	2.2
● Stocks	97.8
● Bonds	0.0
○ Other	0.0
Foreign	0.0
(% of Stock)	

Managers Fremont Bond

	Ticker	Load	NAV	Yield	SEC Yield	Total Assets	Mstar Category
	MBDFX	None	$10.23	4.7%	4.43%	$1,172 mil	Intermediate-Term Bond

Governance and Management

Stewardship Grade: C

Portfolio Manager(s)

Bill Gross and his extensive team of analysts and traders at PIMCO are considered some of the best in the business. Gross has led this fund since its 1993 inception.

Strategy

This fund typically makes a series of bets against its benchmark, the Lehman Brothers Aggregate Index. Bill Gross relies on macroeconomic analysis to determine the fund's interest-rate sensitivity (duration usually stays within 20% of the index) and sector weightings, which can include high-yield, foreign bonds, and currency exposure.

Historical Profile
Return High
Risk Above Avg
Rating ★★★★ Highest

| 3 | 45 | 4 | 44 | 88 | 73 | 91 | 67 |

Investment Style
Fixed Income
Income Rtn %Rank Cat

▼ Manager Change
▽ Partial Manager Change

Growth of $10,000
— Investment Values of Fund
— Investment Values of LB Aggr

Performance Quartile (within Category)

1995	1996	1997	1998	1999	2000	2001	2002	2003	2004	2005	2006	History
10.14	9.95	10.13	10.22	9.51	9.97	10.10	10.41	10.48	10.46	10.37	10.23	NAV
21.25	5.22	9.72	10.00	-1.24	12.77	9.77	9.78	5.32	5.33	2.98	3.47	Total Return %
2.78	1.59	0.07	1.31	-0.42	1.14	1.33	-0.47	1.22	0.99	0.55	-0.86	+/-LB Aggr
-0.18	2.53	0.29	-0.14	1.64	0.33	0.95	-3.25	-0.65	0.03	1.15	-0.34	+/-LB 5-10YR
7.66	6.99	6.86	7.23	5.87	7.72	5.95	3.90	3.42	2.46	3.60	4.76	Income Return %
13.59	-1.77	2.86	2.77	-7.11	5.05	3.82	5.88	1.90	2.87	-0.62	-1.29	Capital Return %
12	10	25	2	50	5	7	19	35	11	5	76	Total Rtn % Rank Cat
0.68	0.69	0.66	0.71	0.58	0.71	0.57	0.39	0.35	0.25	0.37	0.48	Income $
0.22	0.00	0.09	0.18	0.00	0.00	0.25	0.27	0.13	0.32	0.02	0.00	Capital Gains $
0.60	0.68	0.61	0.60	0.60	0.62	0.57	0.59	0.61	0.60	0.60	—	Expense Ratio %
6.69	6.82	6.40	5.92	6.01	6.44	4.90	3.75	2.81	2.24	3.43	—	Income Ratio %
21	154	191	256	298	195	160	81	85	113	392	—	Turnover Rate %
93	73	109	216	175	298	783	1,228	851	879	1,007	1,172	Net Assets $mil

Performance 12-31-06

	1st Qtr	2nd Qtr	3rd Qtr	4th Qtr	Total
2002	0.42	2.47	4.00	2.59	9.78
2003	2.05	2.82	-0.32	0.71	5.32
2004	2.94	-2.48	3.66	1.22	5.33
2005	-0.37	3.37	-0.37	0.40	2.98
2006	-0.40	-0.34	3.74	0.59	3.47

Trailing	Total Return%	+/- LB Aggr	+/- LB 5-10YR	%Rank Cat	Growth of $10,000
3 Mo	0.59	-0.65	-0.49	97	10,059
6 Mo	4.28	-0.81	-1.40	80	10,428
1 Yr	3.47	-0.86	-0.34	76	10,347
3 Yr Avg	3.91	0.21	0.27	21	11,219
5 Yr Avg	5.34	0.28	-0.58	17	12,971
10 Yr Avg	6.71	0.47	0.03	4	19,145
15 Yr Avg	—	—	—	—	—

Tax Analysis	Tax-Adj Rtn%	%Rank Cat	Tax-Cost Rat	%Rank Cat
3 Yr (estimated)	2.35	14	1.50	52
5 Yr (estimated)	3.61	12	1.64	52
10 Yr (estimated)	4.34	4	2.22	71

Potential Capital Gain Exposure: -1% of assets

Rating and Risk

Time Period	Load-Adj Return %	Morningstar Rtn vs Cat	Morningstar Risk vs Cat	Morningstar Risk-Adj Rating
1 Yr	3.47			
3 Yr	3.91	+Avg	+Avg	★★★★
5 Yr	5.34	+Avg	+Avg	★★★★
10 Yr	6.71	High	+Avg	★★★★★
Incept	6.76			

Other Measures	Standard Index LB Aggr	Best Fit Index LB Aggr
Alpha	0.2	0.2
Beta	1.01	1.01
R-Squared	96	96
Standard Deviation	3.33	
Mean	3.91	
Sharpe Ratio	0.21	

Morningstar's Take by Eric Jacobson 12-06-06

Managers Fremont Bond can keep its head held high.

It certainly hasn't been a bad year here. The fund has gained roughly 5% through Dec. 5, 2006, putting it slightly behind its Lehman Brothers Aggregate Bond index benchmark. That has been good enough to place the fund in the top half of its intermediate-term bond category peers. Still, if the fund "only" matches or slightly beats the index by year's end, experience suggests that Bill Gross (the PIMCO legend who subadvises the portfolio for the Managers Funds), who is known for his competitive nature, will not be satisfied.

We don't think investors should be as hard on Gross as he's likely to be on himself. Although Gross manages much more money than he used to, his skills have evolved with that growth, and his results have remained topnotch. The very fact that his dramatic underweighting of credit-sensitive bonds in recent years has only moderately dampened the fund's results is a testament to his ability. Indeed, if the credit markets, which he believes to be richly priced, do eventually sputter, his avoidance will look smart, and should present useful opportunities.

Our favor for this fund goes deeper than Gross himself, though. He has built tremendous capabilities, in both personnel and technology over many years. As a result, PIMCO boasts some of the industry's top professionals, who have some of its best tools at their disposal. That has given Gross a broad pool of ideas from which to draw, helping him to make effective plays on different maturities, mortgages, municipals, non-US, and inflation-indexed bonds to name a few. Meanwhile, he's managed to keep volatility and underlying risk firmly in check.

Near-clone Harbor Bond is a smidge cheaper and has a slightly lower minimum investment, but this fund still scores well on both counts, making it among the very best choices available to the average investor.

Portfolio Analysis 11-30-06

Total Fixed-Income:530	Date of Maturity	Amount $000	Value $000	% Net Assets
EuroDollar (Fut)		17	2,341,699	59.69
FNMA 5.5%	12-01-35	100,500	100,154	2.55
US Treasury Bond (Fut)			53,393	1.36
US Treasury Note	11-30-08	42,300	42,320	1.08
FNMA 5.5%	02-01-35	41,306	41,238	1.05
90 Day Sterling Future D			29,556	0.75
Usd Interest Rate Swap R		28,200	28,234	0.72
US Treasury Note	11-30-11	21,600	21,661	0.55
FNMA 5%	12-01-33	22,000	21,498	0.55
90 Day Sterling Future S			20,473	0.52
FHLMC CMO 6.5%	08-15-31	16,022	16,604	0.42
FNMA 5.5%	04-01-34	16,551	16,533	0.42
3m Euro Euribor Future M			15,937	0.41
FNMA 5.5%	05-01-35	15,662	15,618	0.40
FNMA 5.5%	04-01-35	14,721	14,679	0.37
FNMA 5%	03-01-36	14,871	14,537	0.37
Gbp Interest Rate Swap R		7,100	13,852	0.35
FNMA 5.5%	03-01-35	13,420	13,382	0.34
Dnb Nor Bk Asa 144A FRN	10-13-09	13,100	13,105	0.33
US Treasury Bond 2%	01-15-26	12,576	12,320	0.31

Current Investment Style

Duration Short Int Long

Quality High Med Low

1 figure provided by fund

Avg Eff Duration[1]	5.3 Yrs
Avg Eff Maturity	6.8 Yrs
Avg Credit Quality	AAA
Avg Wtd Coupon	4.60%
Avg Wtd Price	100.73% of par

Coupon Range	% of Bonds	Rel Cat
0% PIK	13.3	1.9
0% to 6%	91.9	1.3
6% to 8%	7.8	0.4
8% to 10%	0.2	0.0
More than 10%	0.0	0.0

1.00=Category Average

Credit Analysis	% bonds 11-30-06		
AAA	80	BB	1
AA	8	B	1
A	5	Below B	0
BBB	3	NR/NA	1

Sector Breakdown	% of assets
US Treasuries	2
TIPS	0
US Agency	0
Mortgage Pass-Throughs	13
Mortgage CMO	2
Mortgage ARM	0
US Corporate	6
Asset-Backed	1
Convertible	0
Municipal	0
Corporate Inflation-Protected	0
Foreign Corporate	0
Foreign Govt	0

Composition			
Cash	71.1	Bonds	24.9
Stocks	0.0	Other	4.0

Special Securities	
Restricted/Illiquid Secs	1
Exotic Mortgage-Backed	0
Emerging-Markets Secs	Trace
Options/Futures/Warrants	No

Address:	800 Connecticut Avenue Norwalk, CT 06854 800-548-4539	Minimum Purchase:	$2000	Add: $100	IRA: $1000
		Min Auto Inv Plan:	$100	Add: $100	
Web Address:	www.managersfunds.com	Sales Fees:	No-load		
Inception:	04-30-93	Management Fee:	0.40%		
Advisor:	Managers Investment Group LLC	Actual Fees:	Mgt:0.40%	Dist: —	
Subadvisor:	Pacific Investment Management Co., LLC	Expense Projections:	3Yr:$212	5Yr:$375	10Yr:$850
NTF Plans:	ETrade No Load ETF, Vanguard NTF	Income Distrib:	Monthly		

Morningstar® Funds 500

Managers Fremont Mic-Cap

	Ticker	Load	NAV	Yield	Total Assets	Mstar Category
	MMCFX	Closed	$35.63	0.0%	$310 mil	Small Growth

Governance and Management

Stewardship Grade:

Portfolio Manager(s)

This management team, which has run this fund since its 1994 inception, has three senior members. Bob Kern handles semiconductor and services stocks. David Kern covers health care and software. Greg Weaver, who joined in 1997, handles communications and networking stocks. Three analysts round out the team.

Strategy

Lead manager Bob Kern and his team look to invest in companies with innovative products that can grab market share or dominate an underserved niche. He is willing to invest before companies have a proven track record of success as long as the potential payoff is high enough. With that framework, he projects a firm's enterprise value as a guide to valuation. The team of three senior investment managers takes responsibility for certain sectors, with an emphasis on tech, health-care, and consumer-oriented stocks.

Historical Profile
Return	Average
Risk	Above Avg
Rating	★★★ Neutral

82% 71% 80% 78% 86% 87% 87% 91% 90%

Investment Style
Equity
Stock %

▼ Manager Change
▽ Partial Manager Change

Growth of $10,000
— Investment Values of Fund
— Investment Values of S&P 500

73.0
66.0
47.8
33.8
24.0
17.0
10.0

Performance Quartile (within Category)

1995	1996	1997	1998	1999	2000	2001	2002	2003	2004	2005	2006	History
15.10	21.50	20.28	20.86	39.35	26.87	28.29	18.98	29.73	32.64	31.74	35.63	NAV
54.04	48.70	6.99	2.86	129.50	-10.62	5.28	-32.91	56.64	9.79	-2.76	12.26	Total Return %
16.46	25.74	-26.37	-25.72	108.46	-1.52	17.17	-10.81	27.96	-1.09	-7.67	-3.53	+/-S&P 500
23.00	37.44	-5.96	1.63	86.41	11.81	14.51	-2.65	8.10	-4.52	-6.91	-1.09	+/-Russ 2000 Gr
0.00	0.00	0.00	0.00	0.00	0.06	0.00	0.00	0.00	0.00	0.00	0.00	Income Return %
54.04	48.70	6.99	2.86	129.50	-10.68	5.28	-32.91	56.64	9.79	-2.76	12.26	Capital Return %
8	3	87	53	11	63	18	75	14	64	95	36	Total Rtn % Rank Cat
0.00	0.00	0.00	0.00	0.00	0.02	0.00	0.00	0.00	0.00	0.00	0.00	Income $
0.50	0.92	2.76	0.00	5.86	9.23	0.00	0.00	0.00	0.00	0.00	0.00	Capital Gains $
2.04	1.96	1.88	1.94	1.82	1.57	1.60	1.61	1.64	1.62	1.56	—	Expense Ratio %
-0.67	-0.51	-0.67	-1.22	-0.97	0.06	-0.47	-1.33	-1.47	-1.41	-1.11	—	Income Ratio %
144	81	125	170	164	117	93	68	105	83	68	—	Turnover Rate %
10	143	167	165	574	628	712	406	603	544	405	310	Net Assets $mil

Performance 12-31-06

	1st Qtr	2nd Qtr	3rd Qtr	4th Qtr	Total
2002	-2.69	-19.91	-18.64	5.80	-32.91
2003	-1.90	27.71	8.12	15.64	56.64
2004	1.68	-3.31	-4.89	17.41	9.79
2005	-10.42	2.12	5.73	0.54	-2.76
2006	13.80	-8.50	-1.48	9.43	12.26

Trailing	Total Return%	+/- S&P 500	+/- Russ 2000 Gr	%Rank Cat	Growth of $10,000
3 Mo	9.43	2.73	0.66	22	10,943
6 Mo	7.81	-4.93	0.95	25	10,781
1 Yr	12.26	-3.53	-1.09	36	11,226
3 Yr Avg	6.22	-4.22	-4.29	83	11,984
5 Yr Avg	4.72	-1.47	-2.21	66	12,594
10 Yr Avg	11.59	3.17	6.71	20	29,940
15 Yr Avg	—				

Tax Analysis	Tax-Adj Rtn%	%Rank Cat	Tax-Cost Rat	%Rank Cat
3 Yr (estimated)	6.22	73	0.00	1
5 Yr (estimated)	4.72	58	0.00	1
10 Yr (estimated)	9.45	24	1.92	80

Potential Capital Gain Exposure: 7% of assets

Rating and Risk

Time Period	Load-Adj Return %	Morningstar Rtn vs Cat	Morningstar Risk vs Cat	Morningstar Risk-Adj Rating
1 Yr	12.26			
3 Yr	6.22	-Avg	+Avg	★★
5 Yr	4.72	Avg	+Avg	★★
10 Yr	11.59	+Avg	+Avg	★★★
Incept	16.78			

Other Measures	Standard Index S&P 500	Best Fit Index Russ 2000 Gr
Alpha	-10.6	-4.1
Beta	2.14	1.05
R-Squared	69	88
Standard Deviation	17.70	
Mean	6.22	
Sharpe Ratio	0.25	

Portfolio Analysis 10-31-06

Share change since 09-06 Total Stocks:82	Sector	PE	Tot Ret%	% Assets
⊖ Equinix, Inc.	Business	—	85.53	5.02
ATMI, Inc.	Hardware	30.1	9.15	4.29
⊕ FEI Company	Hardware	—	37.56	3.15
AudioCodes, Ltd.	Hardware	31.6	-15.59	2.74
⊖ Conceptus, Inc.	Health	—	68.70	2.47
Omnicell, Inc.	Hardware	62.1	55.90	2.45
⊖ Regeneration Technologie	Health	—	-17.76	2.39
Power Integrations, Inc.	Hardware	—	-1.51	2.32
Eclipsys Corporation	Software	—	8.61	2.06
TVI Corporation	Ind Mtrls	18.6	-41.25	1.97
⊖ NeoPharm, Inc.	Health	—	-84.52	1.89
⊖ Exfo Electro-Optical Eng	Hardware	47.6	24.89	1.82
Techwell, Inc.	Hardware	—	—	1.69
⊖ Cogent Communications Gr	Telecom	—	195.45	1.69
Terayon Communications S	Hardware	—	-3.46	1.62
eCollege.com	Business	58.3	-13.20	1.62
⊖ Anaren, Inc.	Hardware	27.1	13.63	1.36
⊖ Internap Network Service	Business	—	361.86	1.35
Flow International Corpo	Ind Mtrls	73.3	30.88	1.30
⊕ CalAmp Corporation	Hardware	—	-19.54	1.30

Current Investment Style

Value Blnd Growth — Large/Mid/Small

Market Cap	%
Giant	0.0
Large	0.0
Mid	5.6
Small	28.9
Micro	65.6
Avg $mil:	344

Value Measures		Rel Category
Price/Earnings	28.75	1.37
Price/Book	2.16	0.79
Price/Sales	2.08	1.32
Price/Cash Flow	11.93	1.24
Dividend Yield %	0.04	0.09

Growth Measures	%	Rel Category
Long-Term Erngs	22.07	1.24
Book Value	-2.47	NMF
Sales	-1.40	NMF
Cash Flow	12.96	0.61
Historical Erngs	11.58	0.48

Profitability	%	Rel Category
Return on Equity	-6.05	NMF
Return on Assets	-3.57	NMF
Net Margin	-2.72	NMF

Sector Weightings
	% of Stocks	Rel S&P 500	3 Year High Low
⟳ Info	53.25	2.66	
Software	10.44	3.03	14 7
Hardware	36.86	3.99	37 22
Media	3.16	0.83	3 0
Telecom	2.79	0.79	3 0
⟲ Service	35.43	0.77	
Health	13.74	1.14	22 14
Consumer	3.05	0.40	19 3
Business	17.25	4.08	19 13
Financial	1.39	0.06	3 0
⊣ Mfg	11.32	0.34	
Goods	1.36	0.16	6 0
Ind Mtrls	9.96	0.83	12 3
Energy	0.00	0.00	0 0
Utilities	0.00	0.00	0 0

Composition
● Cash	9.9
● Stocks	90.1
● Bonds	0.0
● Other	0.0
Foreign	7.0
(% of Stock)	

Morningstar's Take by Greg Carlson 12-22-06

In order to reap the rewards offered by Managers Fremont Micro-Cap, investors have to stay on an even keel.

Lead manager Bob Kern and his team ply a distinctive, bold approach. They invest in the market's smallest companies, which tend to have very volatile stock prices. What's more, they focus on companies that have innovative products and services--these firms, which the team often finds within the tech and health-care sectors, are often richly valued and sometimes have yet to turn a profit. Thus, when a product fails to live up to expectations, the company's stock is often severely punished. For example, the fund recently owned NeoPharm, a biotech firm that saw a promising cancer drug in development perform poorly in trials--the stock then dropped more than 80% in one day. (To its credit, the team had already trimmed this position after the stock had rallied; it sold the rest of the stake following the bad news.)

Of course, the fund's tiny holdings are capable of surprisingly good results, too, and they're highly sought after when the economy is on the upswing--witness the fund's huge gains in 1999 and 2003. All told, Kern and company have delivered the goods here over the long term--the fund has outpaced more than 85% of its small-growth rivals over the past decade.

Unfortunately, the fund's investor returns--which take into account cash flows in and out of the fund--are far lower. While the fund gained an annualized 12.4% for the 10 years ending Oct. 31, 2006, shareholders earned just 4.5% annualized. That's because they tended to jump into the fund after a period of hot performance and flee at the end of tough stretches. We'd hesitate to blame that phenomenon on management, which has made its aggressive strategy plain. But it underlines the fact that investors should limit the fund to a small portion of their portfolio and rebalance to maintain their weighting through good times and bad.

Address:	800 Connecticut Avenue Norwalk, CT 06854 800-548-4539	Minimum Purchase:	Closed	Add: — IRA: —
		Min Auto Inv Plan:	Closed	Add: —
Web Address:	www.managersfunds.com	Sales Fees:	No-load	
Inception:	06-30-94	Management Fee:	1.00%	
Advisor:	Managers Investment Group LLC	Actual Fees:	Mgt:1.00%	Dist: —
Subadvisor:	Kern Capital Management LLC	Expense Projections:	3Yr:$483	5Yr:$834 10Yr:$1824
		Income Distrib:	Annually	
NTF Plans:	Fidelity Retail-NTF, Schwab OneSource			

MORNINGSTAR® Funds 500

Managers Special Equity M

	Ticker	Load	NAV	Yield	Total Assets	Mstar Category
	MGSEX	None	$83.59	0.0%	$3,209 mil	Small Blend

Governance and Management

Stewardship Grade: C

Portfolio Manager(s)

Tom Hoffman, director of research for Managers Funds, oversees six subadvisors: Andy Knuth of Westport Select Cap joined in 1985, while Bob Kern of Managers Fremont Micro-Cap joined in 1997. A team from Skyline Special Equities was hired in 2000. Donald Smith of Donald Smith & Co. joined in 2002, Veredus Capital Management, which also runs ABN AMRO/Veredus Aggressive Growth, was hired in January 2005 to replace Essex Investment Management, and Smith Asset Management joined in May 2006.

Strategy

Six subadvisors run this fund: Andy Knuth of Westport buys modestly priced firms with solid growth prospects. Bob Kern of Kern Capital Management favors micro-cap firms with innovative products. A team from Skyline Asset Management seeks small companies that trade at cheap prices yet possess strong earnings-growth potential. Deep-value manager Donald Smith & Co. buys stocks with very low price/book ratios. Veredus favors firms that beat analysts' earnings estimates and have rising stock prices. Smith Asset Management also plies a momentum-oriented strategy, but is more valuation-sensitive.

Performance 12-31-06

	1st Qtr	2nd Qtr	3rd Qtr	4th Qtr	Total
2002	0.96	-10.21	-19.67	7.14	-21.98
2003	-6.37	20.73	9.57	15.05	42.50
2004	4.08	0.83	-3.96	14.28	15.19
2005	-3.58	1.66	3.55	2.46	4.00
2006	10.28	-4.66	-1.80	8.59	12.12

Trailing	Total Return%	+/- S&P 500	+/- Russ 2000	%Rank Cat	Growth of $10,000
3 Mo	8.59	1.89	-0.31	36	10,859
6 Mo	6.64	-6.10	-2.74	62	10,664
1 Yr	12.12	-3.67	-6.25	76	11,212
3 Yr Avg	10.33	-0.11	-3.23	89	13,430
5 Yr Avg	8.35	2.16	-3.04	87	14,933
10 Yr Avg	9.90	1.48	0.46	77	25,703
15 Yr Avg	12.35	1.71	0.88	64	57,358

Tax Analysis	Tax-Adj Rtn%	%Rank Cat	Tax-Cost Rat	%Rank Cat
3 Yr (estimated)	9.13	75	1.09	30
5 Yr (estimated)	7.64	80	0.66	27
10 Yr (estimated)	8.90	60	0.91	18

Potential Capital Gain Exposure: 21% of assets

Morningstar's Take by Greg Carlson 12-22-06

Managers Special Equity will likely look better in its new category in the coming years, but we wouldn't stick around.

This fund recently migrated from our small-growth category to small-blend. The fund had migrated to the latter part of the Morningstar Style Box since the late 2003 firing of one of its subadvisors, Gary Pilgrim, who preferred fast-growing fare at very rich prices. The category change makes sense--the fund was designed as a core small-cap holding and has long used the Russell 2000 Index as its benchmark, not a growth-oriented bogy. What's more, since Pilgrim's departure, the fund's returns have been more closely correlated with the typical small-blend fund.

Because growth stocks have lagged value stocks in recent years, the fund's category change has driven its return rankings sharply downward. We think the fund is better than its current rankings indicate, but it's still difficult to recommend.

Granted, it employs six subadvisors, some of whom sport sterling long-term records. However, we're not completely sold on a couple of other managers, particularly the momentum-oriented team that also runs Aston/Veredus Aggressive Growth. It's also worth noting that Managers has added to the fund's subadvisor ranks over time to handle asset growth--as such, Andy Knuth (of Westport Select Cap), who's worked on the fund since 1985, runs a far smaller slice of it than he did a few years ago.

The biggest reason to avoid this fund is its expense ratio, which has risen to 1.4% in recent years despite substantial asset growth (prior to a recent spate of redemptions). Managers has increasingly shifted the cost of its presence on discount brokerages' no-transaction-fee platforms to shareholders, and thus the fund is now more expensive than its typical no-load rival, despite a $3.3 billion asset base. Although the fund's relative returns will likely improve when growth stocks return to favor, we'd steer clear.

Address:	800 Connecticut Avenue Norwalk, CT 06854 800-548-4539	Minimum Purchase:	$2000	Add: $100	IRA: $1000
		Min Auto Inv Plan:	$100	Add: $100	
		Sales Fees:	No-load		
Web Address:	www.managersfunds.com	Management Fee:	0.90%		
Inception:	06-01-84	Actual Fees:	Mgt:0.90%	Dist: —	
Advisor:	Managers Investment Group LLC	Expense Projections:	3Yr:$454	5Yr:$784	10Yr:$1715
Subadvisor:	Multiple Subadvisors	Income Distrib:	Annually		
NTF Plans:	Fidelity Retail-NTF, Schwab OneSource				

Historical Profile

Return	Below Avg
Risk	Average
Rating	★★ Below Avg

92%	93%	90%	90%	90%	90%	93%	93%	91%

Investment Style: Equity / Stock %

Growth of $10,000
— Investment Values of Fund
— Investment Values of S&P 500

Performance Quartile (within Category)

1995	1996	1997	1998	1999	2000	2001	2002	2003	2004	2005	2006	History
43.34	50.95	61.17	61.22	91.42	76.80	70.60	55.08	78.49	90.41	86.77	83.59	NAV
33.94	24.75	24.45	0.20	54.11	-2.56	-8.07	-21.98	42.50	15.19	4.00	12.12	Total Return %
-3.64	1.79	-8.91	-28.38	33.07	6.54	3.82	0.12	13.82	4.31	-0.91	-3.67	+/-S&P 500
5.49	8.26	2.09	2.75	32.85	0.46	-10.56	-1.50	-4.75	-3.14	-0.55	-6.25	+/-Russ 2000
0.00	0.00	0.14	0.00	0.00	0.00	0.00	0.00	0.00	0.00	0.00	0.00	Income Return %
33.94	24.75	24.31	0.20	54.11	-2.56	-8.07	-21.98	42.50	15.19	4.00	12.12	Capital Return %
17	38	60	20	5	90	93	81	52	77	75	76	Total Rtn % Rank Cat
0.00	0.00	0.07	0.00	0.00	0.00	0.00	0.00	0.00	0.00	0.00	0.00	Income $
5.66	3.07	2.07	0.07	2.82	11.77	0.00	0.00	0.00	0.00	7.28	13.56	Capital Gains $
1.44	1.43	1.35	1.34	1.31	1.26	1.29	1.31	1.43	1.40	1.40	—	Expense Ratio %
-0.16	-0.10	0.17	-0.26	-0.47	-0.16	-0.27	-0.56	-0.72	-0.69	-0.60	—	Income Ratio %
65	56	49	64	89	69	62	67	64	68	80	—	Turnover Rate %
118	271	720	957	1,545	2,125	2,312	2,016	3,290	3,428	3,004	2,634	Net Assets $mil

Rating and Risk

Time Period	Load-Adj Return %	Morningstar Rtn vs Cat	Morningstar Risk vs Cat	Morningstar Risk-Adj Rating
1 Yr	12.12			
3 Yr	10.33	-Avg	Avg	★★
5 Yr	8.35	-Avg	Avg	★★
10 Yr	9.90	-Avg	+Avg	★★
Incept	13.65			

Other Measures	Standard Index S&P 500	Best Fit Index Russ 2000 Gr
Alpha	-4.2	1.0
Beta	1.67	0.81
R-Squared	77	95
Standard Deviation	13.02	
Mean	10.33	
Sharpe Ratio	0.58	

Portfolio Analysis 11-30-06

Share change since 10-06 Total Stocks:355	Sector	PE	Tot Ret%	% Assets
MI Developments Inc. A	Financial	—	—	1.78
ITT Educational Services	Consumer	26.8	12.59	1.67
Reliant Energy, Inc.	Utilities	—	37.69	1.55
AK Steel Holding Corpora	Ind Mtrls	87.4	112.58	1.53
Air France-KLM ADR	Business	11.2	96.86	1.17
⊕ Spansion, Inc. A	Hardware	—	—	1.16
Visteon Corporation	Ind Mtrls	0.8	35.46	1.09
⊖ Dillard's, Inc.	Consumer	14.2	41.62	0.91
Ross Stores, Inc.	Consumer	20.6	2.28	0.89
⊕ ATMI, Inc.	Hardware	30.1	9.15	0.89
⊖ Tech Data Corporation	Business	—	-4.39	0.89
Downey Financial Corpora	Financial	10.1	6.76	0.88
⊖ Equinix, Inc.	Business	—	85.53	0.88
Semiconductor Manufactur	Hardware	—	-4.73	0.85
Pogo Producing Company	Energy	4.7	-2.16	0.79
⊕ Omnicell, Inc.	Hardware	62.1	55.90	0.78
Alaska Air Group, Inc.	Business	—	10.58	0.78
IMS Health, Inc.	Health	17.4	10.77	0.70
Trident Microsystems Inc	Hardware	92.0	1.00	0.66
Saks, Inc.	Consumer	25.4	63.34	0.65

Current Investment Style

Value Blnd Growth — Large Mid Small

Market Cap	%
Giant	0.0
Large	1.3
Mid	36.7
Small	51.9
Micro	10.2
Avg $mil:	1,485

Value Measures		Rel Category
Price/Earnings	19.25	1.16
Price/Book	2.27	1.08
Price/Sales	0.87	0.89
Price/Cash Flow	8.68	1.24
Dividend Yield %	0.52	0.49

Growth Measures	%	Rel Category
Long-Term Erngs	14.17	1.02
Book Value	3.56	0.47
Sales	-6.10	NMF
Cash Flow	2.82	0.22
Historical Erngs	14.25	0.85

Profitability	%	Rel Category
Return on Equity	10.90	0.85
Return on Assets	5.92	0.83
Net Margin	7.05	0.73

Sector Weightings	% of Stocks	Rel S&P 500	3 Year High	Low
⊙ Info	23.39	1.17		
🖳 Software	4.95	1.43	6	3
🖥 Hardware	15.95	1.73	16	8
🎙 Media	0.26	0.07	3	0
📶 Telecom	2.23	0.64	3	0
⌨ Service	54.62	1.18		
🩺 Health	8.42	0.70	11	6
🛒 Consumer	13.73	1.79	21	13
💼 Business	17.78	4.20	18	12
💲 Financial	14.69	0.66	18	13
🏭 Mfg	22.00	0.65		
🛢 Goods	2.21	0.26	5	1
⚙ Ind Mtrls	14.61	1.22	21	14
🔥 Energy	2.57	0.26	4	2
💡 Utilities	2.61	0.75	4	2

Composition

	%
● Cash	8.7
● Stocks	91.0
● Bonds	0.0
● Other	0.3
Foreign (% of Stock)	6.4

Manager Change ▼
Partial Manager Change ▽

MORNINGSTAR® Funds 500

Marsico 21st Century

	Ticker	Load	NAV	Yield	Total Assets	Mstar Category
	MXXIX	None	$15.23	0.9%	$1,276 mil	Large Growth

Governance and Management

Stewardship Grade: B

Portfolio Manager(s)

Cory Gilchrist has been with Marsico Capital Management since May 2000, working in various capacities but primarily in the shop's successful International Opportunities. Prior to Marsico, Gilchrist worked at Invista Capital Management, serving on a team that managed international-equity funds. The firms founder, Tom Marsico, contributes significantly here as do the firm's 16 analysts and international skipper, James Gendelman.

Strategy

As is the case with the other Marsico funds, manager Cory Gilchrist uses macroeconomic themes to determine the portfolio's overall positioning. From there, he focuses largely on three types of companies: rapidly growing firms that are hitting on all cylinders, steadier-growth companies, and otherwise-promising companies that have suffered short-term setbacks. Unlike Marsico's other U.S.-stock funds, however, this one buys stocks of any market capitalization.

Performance 12-31-06

	1st Qtr	2nd Qtr	3rd Qtr	4th Qtr	Total
2002	2.04	-0.40	-12.68	0.92	-10.45
2003	-0.91	22.17	9.39	12.36	48.79
2004	4.48	-0.10	-0.49	17.75	22.30
2005	-6.83	1.61	6.16	7.31	7.84
2006	11.27	-2.64	-1.00	10.62	18.65

Trailing	Total Return%	+/- S&P 500	+/- Russ 1000Gr	%Rank Cat	Growth of $10,000
3 Mo	10.62	3.92	4.69	2	11,062
6 Mo	9.52	-3.22	-0.58	33	10,952
1 Yr	18.65	2.86	9.58	1	11,865
3 Yr Avg	16.10	5.66	9.23	1	15,649
5 Yr Avg	15.83	9.64	13.14	1	20,850
10 Yr Avg	—	—	—	—	—
15 Yr Avg	—	—	—	—	—

Tax Analysis	Tax-Adj Rtn%	%Rank Cat	Tax-Cost Rat	%Rank Cat
3 Yr (estimated)	15.98	1	0.10	7
5 Yr (estimated)	15.76	1	0.06	7
10 Yr (estimated)	—	—	—	—

Potential Capital Gain Exposure: 14% of assets

Morningstar's Take by Karen Dolan 11-12-06

Marsico 21st Century is enjoying the fruits of its flexibility.

This fund invests on many of the same broad economic themes and stock-specific considerations that characterize Marsico Capital Management's style. Yet unlike the firm's large-cap-focused funds--Marsico Focus and Marsico Growth--this one can buy stocks of any size. Manager Cory Gilchrist and firm founder Tom Marsico have been on the mark with their big-picture thoughts this year, but this fund has met far better results than the firm's large-cap-only offerings. Its 13.8% return for the year-to-date through Nov. 10, 2006, puts it ahead of 98% of other large-cap growth funds while Marsico Focus has only gained 3.0% and lags the majority of the peer group.

The fund's success has boiled down to specific stocks. Shareholders here have benefited from picks on the smaller end of the market-cap spectrum and the fact that the fund didn't stake as much on stocks that have pulled down Marsico

Focus and Growth; for example, though the fund holds sizable positions in UnitedHealth and Genentech, it owns meaningfully less than its larger-cap siblings and has thus avoided the extent of their downside this year. On top of that, many of the fund's big winners have been smaller companies such as kids' clothing retailer Gymboree and cable company Cablevision Systems.

This fund will hit rough patches of its own. It will likely struggle during mega-cap-dominated markets and its focus on fewer stocks and sectors leaves it susceptible to big dips in specific holdings and industries. What's more, the fund's flexibility adds another variable that could work against it. If it is off the mark with its top-down, bottom-up, or market-cap calls, it will lag. Gilchrist has proved skillful at managing those variables, making this a good way to access the firm's top-down maneuvering and excellent stock-picking skills. It is especially appealing because of its small asset base, given the size of Marsico's other charges.

Address:	1200 17th St	Minimum Purchase:	$2500	Add: $100	IRA: $1000
	Denver CO 80202	Min Auto Inv Plan:	$1000	Add: $50	
	888-860-8686	Sales Fees:	No-load, 0.25%S, 2.00%R		
Web Address:	www.marsicofunds.com	Management Fee:	0.85%		
Inception:	02-01-00*	Actual Fees:	Mgt:0.85%	Dist:0.25%	
Advisor:	Marsico Capital Management, LLC	Expense Projections:	3Yr:$431	5Yr:$745	10Yr:$1635
Subadvisor:	None	Income Distrib:	Annually		
NTF Plans:	Fidelity Retail-NTF, Schwab OneSource				

Historical Profile

Return	High
Risk	Above Avg
Rating	★★★★★ Highest

Investment Values of Fund
Investment Values of S&P 500

Growth of $10,000

10.0

6.0

4.0

▼ Manager Change
▽ Partial Manager Change

96%	94%	95%	100%	99%	95%	92%	

Performance Quartile (within Category)

1995	1996	1997	1998	1999	2000	2001	2002	2003	2004	2005	2006	History
—	—	—	—	—	9.19	7.37	6.60	9.82	12.01	12.95	15.23	NAV
—	—	—	—	—	-8.10*	-19.80	-10.45	48.79	22.30	7.84	18.65	Total Return %
—	—	—	—	—	-7.91	11.65	20.11	11.42	2.93	2.86	+/-S&P 500
—	—	—	—	—	0.62	17.43	19.04	16.00	2.58	9.58	+/-Russ 1000Gr
—	—	—	—	—	0.00	0.00	0.00	0.00	0.02	1.04	Income Return %
—	—	—	—	—	-19.80	-10.45	48.79	22.30	7.82	17.61	Capital Return %
—	—	—	—	—		51	2	3	1	36	1	Total Rtn % Rank Cat
—	—	—	—	—	0.00	0.00	0.00	0.00	0.00	0.00	0.13	Income $
—	—	—	—	—	0.00	0.00	0.00	0.00	0.00	0.00	0.00	Capital Gains $
—	—	—	—	—	1.50	1.50	1.60	1.55	1.50	1.39	1.33	Expense Ratio %
—	—	—	—	—	-0.92	-0.76	-0.99	-1.05	-0.48	-0.19	0.20	Income Ratio %
—	—	—	—	—	267	399	388	236	191	175	136	Turnover Rate %
—	—	—	—	—	99	69	54	162	323	428	1,276	Net Assets $mil

Rating and Risk

Time Period	Load-Adj Return %	Morningstar Rtn vs Cat	Morningstar Risk vs Cat	Morningstar Risk-Adj Rating
1 Yr	18.65			
3 Yr	16.10	High	+Avg	★★★★★
5 Yr	15.83	High	+Avg	★★★★★
10 Yr	—	—	—	—
Incept	6.41			

Other Measures	Standard Index S&P 500	Best Fit Index DJ Wilshire 4500
Alpha	2.2	1.4
Beta	1.48	0.98
R-Squared	69	80
Standard Deviation	12.24	
Mean	16.10	
Sharpe Ratio	1.03	

Portfolio Analysis 11-30-06

Share change since 10-06 Total Stocks:43	Sector	PE	Tot Ret%	% Assets
⊕ Station Casinos Inc.	Consumer	38.6	22.46	4.80
⊕ Las Vegas Sands, Inc.	Consumer	75.7	126.70	4.34
⊕ UnitedHealth Group, Inc.	Health	20.8	-13.49	4.01
⊕ Amylin Pharmaceuticals	Health	—	-9.64	3.68
Cisco Systems, Inc.	Hardware	30.1	59.64	3.33
⊕ Saks, Inc.	Consumer	25.4	63.34	3.21
Wynn Resorts, Ltd.	Consumer	—	82.52	3.08
⊕ CB Richard Ellis Group,	Financial	30.3	69.24	3.03
Comcast Corporation A	Media	45.2	63.31	2.99
⊖ UBS AG	Financial	—	29.62	2.98
St. Joe Corporation	Financial	75.4	-19.32	2.98
⊕ Goldman Sachs Group, Inc	Financial	12.4	57.41	2.93
⊕ Heineken Holding	Goods	—	—	2.81
Burlington Northern Sant	Business	15.2	5.52	2.74
⊖ Nordstrom, Inc.	Consumer	21.9	33.35	2.73
⊕ KKR Financial Corporatio	Financial	—	—	2.72
Genzyme Corporation	Health	50.8	-13.00	2.57
⊖ General Dynamics	Ind Mtrls	19.1	32.17	2.49
Wells Fargo Company	Financial	14.7	16.82	2.41
United Technologies	Ind Mtrls	17.8	13.65	2.19

Current Investment Style

Value Blnd Growth — Large Mid Small

Market Cap	%
Giant	31.2
Large	27.5
Mid	36.5
Small	3.7
Micro	1.1
Avg $mil:	15,994

Value Measures		Rel Category
Price/Earnings	22.09	1.15
Price/Book	3.10	0.93
Price/Sales	1.23	0.63
Price/Cash Flow	12.13	1.07
Dividend Yield %	0.75	0.73

Growth Measures	%	Rel Category
Long-Term Ergns	14.07	0.98
Book Value	9.51	0.82
Sales	11.19	0.96
Cash Flow	11.61	0.69
Historical Ergns	21.30	0.93

Profitability	%	Rel Category
Return on Equity	15.31	0.75
Return on Assets	8.09	0.73
Net Margin	10.06	0.71

Sector Weightings	% of Stocks	Rel S&P 500	3 Year High	Low
↻ Info	9.07	0.45		
🖥 Software	0.00	0.00	5	0
💻 Hardware	3.64	0.39	14	1
🎙 Media	5.43	1.43	8	0
📶 Telecom	0.00	0.00	3	0
⊂ Service	75.57	1.64		
🏥 Health	15.34	1.27	23	6
🛒 Consumer	21.70	2.84	26	8
🏢 Business	5.47	1.29	17	0
💲 Financial	33.06	1.48	39	23
⊡ Mfg	15.37	0.45		
🔧 Goods	3.07	0.36	22	2
⚙ Ind Mtrls	8.24	0.69	18	0
🔋 Energy	1.84	0.19	7	0
💡 Utilities	2.22	0.63	2	0

Composition

- ● Cash 8.2
- ● Stocks 91.8
- ● Bonds 0.0
- ● Other 0.0

Foreign 16.3
(% of Stock)

Marsico Focus

	Ticker	Load	NAV	Yield	Total Assets	Mstar Category
	MFOCX	None	$19.29	0.1%	$4,944 mil	Large Growth

Governance and Management

Stewardship Grade: B

Portfolio Manager(s)

Tom Marsico started his own investment-management shop in 1997, after several years at two other growth-oriented shops, Fred Alger Management and Janus Capital. Marsico has a staff of 16 analysts and five traders. Two other portfolio managers at Marsico Capital Management also chip in. Marsico is also a large shareholder in each of the four funds the shop offers. More than 70% of the fund's board is independent; all the independent trustees have money invested in the fund.

Strategy

Manager Tom Marsico combines top-down analysis with bottom-up stock-picking. He fills the bulk of the portfolio with steady-growth stocks that he intends to hold for the long haul, but he has owned more-explosive growth names. He also reserves a portion of the portfolio for relatively inexpensive firms that stand to benefit from a catalyst. Marsico limits the portfolio to a small number of stocks, typically about 25 to 30.

Performance 12-31-06

	1st Qtr	2nd Qtr	3rd Qtr	4th Qtr	Total
2002	4.49	-3.45	-14.87	-3.00	-16.69
2003	-0.09	14.22	4.33	10.23	31.24
2004	1.01	-1.93	0.68	12.00	11.70
2005	-4.27	2.96	6.60	4.41	9.69
2006	4.28	-4.58	0.33	8.78	8.60

Trailing	Total Return%	+/- S&P 500	+/- Russ 1000Gr	%Rank Cat	Growth of $10,000
3 Mo	8.78	2.08	2.85	5	10,878
6 Mo	9.14	-3.60	-0.96	37	10,914
1 Yr	8.60	-7.19	-0.47	34	10,860
3 Yr Avg	9.99	-0.45	3.12	14	13,306
5 Yr Avg	7.79	1.60	5.10	6	14,551
10 Yr Avg	—	—	—		—
15 Yr Avg	—	—	—		—

Tax Analysis	Tax-Adj Rtn%	%Rank Cat	Tax-Cost Rat	%Rank Cat
3 Yr (estimated)	9.85	12	0.13	9
5 Yr (estimated)	7.71	4	0.07	8
10 Yr (estimated)	—	—	—	—

Potential Capital Gain Exposure: 25% of assets

Historical Profile

Return High
Risk Below Avg
Rating ★★★★ Highest

	88%	96%	95%	99%	96%	100%	100%	94%	95%

Growth of $10,000
— Investment Values of Fund
— Investment Values of S&P 500

22.6
19.6
16.0
13.0
10.0

Performance Quartile (within Category)

1995	1996	1997	1998	1999	2000	2001	2002	2003	2004	2005	2006	History
—	—	10.00	15.13	23.45	17.23	13.60	11.33	14.87	16.61	18.22	19.29	NAV
—	—	0.00*	51.30	55.27	-17.91	-20.81	-16.69	31.24	11.70	9.69	8.60	Total Return %
—	—	—	22.72	34.23	-8.81	-8.92	5.41	2.56	0.82	4.78	-7.19	+/-S&P 500
—	—	—	12.59	22.11	4.51	-0.39	11.19	1.49	5.40	4.43	-0.47	+/-Russ 1000Gr
—	—	—	0.00	0.00	0.00	0.00	0.00	0.00	0.00	0.00	0.11	Income Return %
—	—	—	51.30	55.27	-17.91	-20.81	-16.69	31.24	11.70	9.69	8.49	Capital Return %
—	—	—	6	15	71	56	7	29	19	23	34	Total Rtn % Rank Cat
—	—	0.00	0.00	0.00	0.00	0.00	0.00	0.00	0.00	0.00	0.02	Income $
—	—	0.00	0.00	0.04	1.96	0.04	0.00	0.00	0.00	0.00	0.47	Capital Gains $
—	—	—	1.56	1.31	1.27	1.30	1.35	1.34	1.30	—		Expense Ratio %
—	—	—	-0.27	-0.43	-0.69	-0.36	-0.68	-0.59	-0.36	—		Income Ratio %
—	—	—	170	173	176	127	117	90	84	—		Turnover Rate %
—	—	2	1,204	3,257	2,325	1,401	1,349	2,641	3,237	4,944		Net Assets $mil

Rating and Risk

Time Period	Load-Adj Return %	Morningstar Rtn vs Cat	Morningstar Risk vs Cat	Morningstar Risk-Adj Rating
1 Yr	8.60			
3 Yr	9.99	+Avg	Avg	★★★★
5 Yr	7.79	High	-Avg	★★★★★
10 Yr	—	—	—	
Incept	9.28			

Other Measures	Standard Index S&P 500	Best Fit Index Mstar Mid Core
Alpha	-1.5	-1.6
Beta	1.19	0.76
R-Squared	71	77
Standard Deviation	9.70	
Mean	9.99	
Sharpe Ratio	0.70	

Portfolio Analysis 11-30-06

Share change since 10-06 Total Stocks:32

	Sector	PE	Tot Ret%	% Assets
UnitedHealth Group, Inc.	Health	20.8	-13.49	7.43
Goldman Sachs Group, Inc	Financial	12.4	57.41	5.77
Genentech, Inc.	Health	48.7	-12.29	5.18
⊖ UBS AG	Financial	—	29.62	4.71
⊕ Toyota Motor Corporation	Goods	17.9	28.38	4.65
Burlington Northern Sant	Business	15.2	5.52	4.26
Comcast Corporation A	Media	45.2	63.31	4.19
FedEx Corporation	Business	17.2	5.40	4.18
Procter & Gamble Company	Goods	23.9	13.36	4.10
⊕ Las Vegas Sands, Inc.	Consumer	75.7	126.70	3.71
Cisco Systems, Inc.	Hardware	30.1	59.64	3.52
⊕ Indl And Commrcl Bk Of C	Financial	—	—	3.40
MGM Mirage, Inc.	Consumer	32.0	56.40	3.36
Lehman Brothers Holdings	Financial	12.2	22.75	3.17
Monsanto Company	Ind Mtrls	39.8	36.78	3.16
Lowe's Companies Inc.	Consumer	15.6	-6.05	3.02
Lockheed Martin Corporat	Ind Mtrls	17.3	46.98	3.00
Wynn Resorts, Ltd.	Consumer	—	82.52	2.97
Wells Fargo Company	Financial	14.7	16.82	2.77
PepsiCo, Inc.	Goods	21.5	7.86	2.70

Current Investment Style

Value Blnd Growth — Large Mid Small

Market Cap	%
Giant	53.1
Large	40.2
Mid	6.7
Small	0.0
Micro	0.0

Avg $mil: 52,640

Value Measures		Rel Category
Price/Earnings	19.06	0.99
Price/Book	3.21	0.97
Price/Sales	1.98	1.02
Price/Cash Flow	14.79	1.30
Dividend Yield %	0.84	0.82

Growth Measures	%	Rel Category
Long-Term Erngs	14.60	1.02
Book Value	13.24	1.14
Sales	15.44	1.33
Cash Flow	13.00	0.77
Historical Erngs	27.84	1.21

Profitability	%	Rel Category
Return on Equity	18.49	0.91
Return on Assets	9.18	0.83
Net Margin	12.50	0.88

Sector Weightings

	% of Stocks	Rel S&P 500	3 Year High	Low
⊙ Info	8.13	0.41		
Software	0.00	0.00	6	0
Hardware	3.71	0.40	19	4
Media	4.42	1.17	5	0
Telecom	0.00	0.00	2	0
⊙ Service	67.85	1.47		
Health	15.08	1.25	33	15
Consumer	21.52	2.81	24	8
Business	8.90	2.10	12	2
Financial	22.35	1.00	24	16
⊙ Mfg	24.02	0.71		
Goods	12.08	1.41	14	4
Ind Mtrls	9.11	0.76	11	4
Energy	2.83	0.29	7	0
Utilities	0.00	0.00	4	0

Composition

● Cash	5.2
● Stocks	94.8
● Bonds	0.0
○ Other	0.0
Foreign (% of Stock)	14.9

Morningstar's Take by Karen Dolan 11-08-06

Marsico Focus is down, but it's not out.

This fund isn't having a good year. Such periods have been the exception rather than the rule during manager Tom Marsico's long tenure using this focused style. Prior to starting his own firm, he successfully managed Janus Twenty from March 1988 to August 1997. When looking at rolling returns for both funds during his tenure--where for each figure, an earlier month drops off as a later month is tacked on--Marsico has outpaced the average large-cap growth fund in 150 out of 209 one-year periods, or 72% of the time.

All funds hit rough patches from time to time, and that's what we think is going on here. The fund has had its fair share of stock disappointments recently. UnitedHealth Group was the fund's top holding coming into 2006. Its stock price plummeted when allegations about options backdating surfaced early in the year. Marsico and his team of analysts have researched several layers of management and think the current issues don't affect UnitedHealth's long-term value. Marsico has used the controversy as a buying opportunity. Other picks such as Lowe's Companies and Genentech have also hurt returns in 2006.

The fund's recent performance begs the question of whether the fund's size is hampering returns. As of Sept. 30, 2006, Marsico was running $60 billion between this style and a slightly more diversified version. That puts him in uncharted territory. To deal with the girth, Marsico has expanded the analyst team, hired more traders, and cut back on the amount of time he spends talking to clients about the funds. He also says that the team's research is uncovering more ideas abroad, thus expanding the fund's universe. We'll continue to watch for signs that assets may be getting in the way, but we don't think Marsico would compromise performance to grow; filings show that he has more than $1 million invested here, and we believe his total commitment is much higher than that. This remains a favorite.

Address:	1200 17th St Denver CO 80202 888-860-8686	Minimum Purchase:	$2500 Add: $100 IRA: $1000
		Min Auto Inv Plan:	$1000 Add: $50
		Sales Fees:	No-load, 0.25%S, 2.00%R
Web Address:	www.marsicofunds.com	Management Fee:	0.85% mx./0.75% mn.
Inception:	12-31-97 *	Actual Fees:	Mgt:0.85% Dist:0.25%
Advisor:	Marsico Capital Management, LLC	Expense Projections:	3Yr:$397 5Yr:$686 10Yr:$1511
Subadvisor:	None	Income Distrib:	Annually
NTF Plans:	Fidelity Retail-NTF, Schwab OneSource		

MORNINGSTAR® Funds 500

Marsico Growth

	Ticker	Load	NAV	Yield	Total Assets	Mstar Category
	MGRIX	None	$20.09	0.0%	$2,714 mil	Large Growth

Governance and Management

Stewardship Grade: B

Portfolio Manager(s)

Tom Marsico started his own investment-management shop in 1997, after several years at two other growth-oriented shops, Fred Alger Management and Janus Capital. Marsico has a staff of 16 analysts and five traders. Two other portfolio managers at Marsico Capital Management also chip in. Marsico is also a large shareholder in each of the four funds the shop offers. More than 70% of the fund's board is independent; all the independent trustees have money invested in the fund.

Strategy

Manager Tom Marsico combines top-down analysis with bottom-up stock-picking to build this portfolio. He holds about 10 to 25 more names here than at Marsico Focus, but the fund is still quite concentrated. Marsico primarily buys growth stocks, but he'll also look at cheaper names that he thinks have a catalyst for a turnaround. The fund doesn't end up looking much like its rivals or bogy.

Performance 12-31-06

	1st Qtr	2nd Qtr	3rd Qtr	4th Qtr	Total
2002	3.84	-4.79	-14.53	-1.52	-16.79
2003	-0.85	15.00	5.62	9.58	31.97
2004	2.66	-0.69	1.33	10.72	14.38
2005	-4.30	3.49	3.43	4.20	6.74
2006	3.34	-4.47	0.00	7.95	6.58

Trailing	Total Return%	+/- S&P 500	+/- Russ 1000Gr	%Rank Cat	Growth of $10,000
3 Mo	7.95	1.25	2.02	8	10,795
6 Mo	7.95	-4.79	-2.15	58	10,795
1 Yr	6.58	-9.21	-2.49	55	10,658
3 Yr Avg	9.17	-1.27	2.30	22	13,011
5 Yr Avg	7.40	1.21	4.71	7	14,290
10 Yr Avg	—	—	—	—	—
15 Yr Avg	—	—	—	—	—

Tax Analysis	Tax-Adj Rtn%	%Rank Cat	Tax-Cost Rat	%Rank Cat
3 Yr (estimated)	9.17	16	0.00	1
5 Yr (estimated)	7.40	5	0.00	1
10 Yr (estimated)	—	—	—	—

Potential Capital Gain Exposure: 22% of assets

Morningstar's Take by Karen Dolan 11-08-06

Marsico Growth has appeal, but there's a cheaper way to access its strategy.

This fund hasn't shone in 2006. Such periods have been the exception rather than the rule for manager Tom Marsico, though. Prior to starting his own firm, he managed Janus Twenty from March 1988 to August 1997. When looking at rolling returns for that fund and this one--where for each figure, an earlier month drops off as a later month is tacked on--Marsico has outpaced the average large-cap growth fund 74% of the time.

All funds hit rough patches from time to time, and that's what we think is going on here. The fund has had its fair share of stock disappointments recently. UnitedHealth Group was the fund's top holding coming into 2006. Its stock price plummeted when allegations about options backdating surfaced early in the year. Marsico and his team of analysts have researched several layers of management at the firm and think the current issues don't affect its long-term value. Marsico has

used the controversy as a buying opportunity. Other picks such as Lowe's Companies and Genentech have also hurt returns in 2006.

The fund's recent performance begs the question of whether the fund's size is hampering returns. As of Sept. 30, 2006, Marsico was running $60 billion between this style and a more focused version. That puts him in uncharted territory. To deal with the girth, Marsico has expanded the analyst team, hired more traders, and cut back on the amount of time he spends talking to clients about the funds. He also says that the team's research is uncovering more ideas abroad, thus expanding the fund's universe. We'll continue to watch for signs that assets are getting in the way, but we don't think Marsico would compromise performance to grow; filings show that he has more than $1 million invested here, and we believe his commitment is much higher than that. We like this strategy, but Analyst Pick USAA Aggressive Growth is a cheaper way to own it.

Address:	1200 17th St
	Denver CO 80202
	888-860-8686
Web Address:	www.marsicofunds.com
Inception:	12-31-97 *
Advisor:	Marsico Capital Management, LLC
Subadvisor:	None
NTF Plans:	Fidelity Retail-NTF, Schwab OneSource

Minimum Purchase:	$2500	Add: $100	IRA: $1000
Min Auto Inv Plan:	$1000	Add: $50	
Sales Fees:	No-load, 0.25%S, 2.00%R		
Management Fee:	0.85% mx./0.75% mn.		
Actual Fees:	Mgt:0.85%	Dist:0.25%	
Expense Projections:	3Yr:$400	5Yr:$692	10Yr:$1523
Income Distrib:	Annually		

Historical Profile
Return High
Risk Below Avg
Rating ★★★★ Highest

	87%	90%	99%	93%	99%	100%	100%	98%	100%

Growth of $10,000
- Investment Values of Fund
- Investment Values of S&P 500

▼ Manager Change
▽ Partial Manager Change

Investment Style
Equity
Stock %

Performance Quartile (within Category)

1995	1996	1997	1998	1999	2000	2001	2002	2003	2004	2005	2006	History
—	—	10.00	14.34	21.86	17.67	14.06	11.70	15.44	17.66	18.85	20.09	NAV
—	—	0.00*	43.40	53.31	-15.85	-20.33	-16.79	31.97	14.38	6.74	6.58	Total Return %
—	—	—	14.82	32.27	-6.75	-8.44	5.31	3.29	3.50	1.83	-9.21	+/-S&P 500
—	—	—	4.69	20.15	6.57	0.09	11.09	2.22	8.08	1.48	-2.49	+/-Russ 1000Gr
—	—	—	0.00	0.00	0.00	0.00	0.00	0.00	0.00	0.00	0.00	Income Return %
—	—	—	43.40	53.31	-15.85	-20.33	-16.79	31.97	14.38	6.74	6.58	Capital Return %
—	—	—	13	16	64	53	8	25	7	45	55	Total Rtn % Rank Cat
—	—	0.00	0.00	0.00	0.00	0.00	0.00	0.00	0.00	0.00	0.00	Income $
—	—	0.00	0.00	0.11	0.70	0.02	0.00	0.00	0.00	0.00	0.00	Capital Gains $
—	—	—	1.51	1.43	1.30	1.33	1.37	1.38	1.30	1.26	—	Expense Ratio %
—	—	—	-0.14	-0.46	-0.55	-0.53	-0.49	-0.62	-0.34	-0.14	—	Income Ratio %
—	—	—	141	137	137	120	111	91	73	73	—	Turnover Rate %
—	—	18	374	1,048	830	604	622	1,019	1,637	2,245	2,714	Net Assets $mil

Rating and Risk

Time Period	Load-Adj Return %	Morningstar Rtn vs Cat	Morningstar Risk vs Cat	Morningstar Risk-Adj Rating
1 Yr	6.58			
3 Yr	9.17	+Avg	Avg	★★★★
5 Yr	7.40	High	-Avg	★★★★★
10 Yr	—	—	—	
Incept	8.63			

Other Measures	Standard Index S&P 500	Best Fit Index DJ Wilshire 4500
Alpha	-1.9	-2.3
Beta	1.13	0.73
R-Squared	75	81
Standard Deviation	8.98	
Mean	9.17	
Sharpe Ratio	0.66	

Portfolio Analysis 11-30-06

Share change since 10-06 Total Stocks:44	Sector	PE	Tot Ret%	% Assets
⊕ UnitedHealth Group, Inc.	Health	20.8	-13.49	6.97
Goldman Sachs Group, Inc	Financial	12.4	57.41	5.85
Genentech, Inc.	Health	48.7	-12.29	4.74
⊖ UBS AG	Financial	—	29.62	4.33
Comcast Corporation A	Media	45.2	63.31	4.25
Procter & Gamble Company	Goods	23.9	13.36	4.17
Burlington Northern Sant	Business	15.2	5.52	3.63
FedEx Corporation	Business	17.2	5.40	3.30
Lehman Brothers Holdings	Financial	12.2	22.75	3.15
General Dynamics	Ind Mtrls	19.1	32.17	3.04
Toyota Motor Corporation	Goods	17.9	28.38	3.01
Lockheed Martin Corporat	Ind Mtrls	17.3	46.98	3.01
⊕ Las Vegas Sands, Inc.	Consumer	75.7	126.70	2.88
Wells Fargo Company	Financial	14.7	16.82	2.77
Wynn Resorts, Ltd.	Consumer	—	82.52	2.58
Lowe's Companies Inc.	Consumer	15.6	-6.05	2.50
MGM Mirage, Inc.	Consumer	32.0	56.40	2.48
Monsanto Company	Ind Mtrls	39.8	36.78	2.41
Cisco Systems, Inc.	Hardware	30.1	59.64	2.39
⊕ Schlumberger, Ltd.	Energy	22.3	31.07	2.37

Current Investment Style

Market Cap	%
Giant	49.6
Large	40.5
Mid	9.8
Small	0.0
Micro	0.0

Avg $mil: 45,533

Value Measures		Rel Category
Price/Earnings	18.76	0.97
Price/Book	3.11	0.94
Price/Sales	1.72	0.89
Price/Cash Flow	13.05	1.15
Dividend Yield %	0.94	0.91

Growth Measures	%	Rel Category
Long-Term Erngs	14.23	0.99
Book Value	12.83	1.11
Sales	13.32	1.15
Cash Flow	14.50	0.86
Historical Erngs	25.64	1.11

Profitability	%	Rel Category
Return on Equity	18.66	0.92
Return on Assets	8.75	0.79
Net Margin	11.17	0.78

Sector Weightings	% of Stocks	Rel S&P 500	3 Year High Low
⌖ Info	10.18	0.51	
Software	0.00	0.00	5 0
Hardware	3.36	0.36	20 3
Media	4.26	1.12	5 0
Telecom	2.56	0.73	3 0
☰ Service	64.78	1.40	
Health	14.48	1.20	31 14
Consumer	21.28	2.78	26 11
Business	9.10	2.15	10 2
Financial	19.92	0.89	21 13
⊔ Mfg	25.02	0.74	
Goods	9.12	1.07	15 4
Ind Mtrls	13.02	1.09	14 9
Energy	2.38	0.24	7 0
Utilities	0.50	0.14	2 0

Composition

● Cash	0.2	
● Stocks	99.8	
● Bonds	0.0	
○ Other	0.0	
	Foreign	14.8
	(% of Stock)	

 M⋆RNINGSTAR® Funds 500

Marsico Intl Opp

	Ticker	Load	NAV	Yield	Total Assets	Mstar Category
	MIOFX	None	$16.91	0.2%	$679 mil	Foreign Large Growth

Governance and Management

Stewardship Grade: B

Portfolio Manager(s)

James Gendelman has run this fund since its 2001 inception. He previously spent 13 years at Goldman Sachs, primarily in a sales and product-development role that focused on launching Goldman's international offerings. He also runs Harbor International Growth and Columbia Marsico International Opportunities as clones of this fund. He has two analysts working closely with him on this fund but has ready access to Marsico's other analysts, who increasingly search for good ideas globally.

Strategy

Like other Marsico funds, this offering is run in a fairly concentrated format and can lean toward fast-growing firms. James Gendelman considers three types of firms for the portfolio: core-growth stocks, aggressive-growth stocks, and firms undergoing life-cycle changes, such as a major restructuring. Like his employer, Tom Marsico, he factors in top-down analysis, though he rigorously researches his picks. He is willing to buy in emerging markets and likes mid-cap names. The fund has a redemption fee to deter market-timers. It rarely hedges foreign currency exposure.

Performance 12-31-06

	1st Qtr	2nd Qtr	3rd Qtr	4th Qtr	Total
2002	4.96	1.21	-16.17	3.57	-7.76
2003	-6.21	20.74	7.06	16.72	41.52
2004	8.19	-2.88	-1.39	12.98	17.06
2005	-2.91	-0.60	12.17	10.07	19.14
2006	9.99	-3.07	4.36	11.41	23.95

Trailing	Total Return%	+/- MSCI EAFE	+/- MSCI Wd xUS	%Rank Cat	Growth of $10,000
3 Mo	11.41	1.06	1.29	38	11,141
6 Mo	16.26	1.57	2.04	21	11,626
1 Yr	23.95	-2.39	-1.76	41	12,395
3 Yr Avg	20.01	0.08	-0.09	20	17,284
5 Yr Avg	17.68	2.70	2.43	5	22,569
10 Yr Avg	—	—	—		
15 Yr Avg	—	—	—		

Tax Analysis	Tax-Adj Rtn%	%Rank Cat	Tax-Cost Rat	%Rank Cat
3 Yr (estimated)	19.58	14	0.36	28
5 Yr (estimated)	17.42	3	0.22	21
10 Yr (estimated)	—			

Potential Capital Gain Exposure: 21% of assets

Historical Profile

Return High
Risk Average
Rating ★★★★ Highest

	74%	94%	86%	99%	98%	97%	98%

Performance Quartile (within Category)

	1995	1996	1997	1998	1999	2000	2001	2002	2003	2004	2005	2006	History
	—	—	—	—	—	9.33	7.86	7.25	10.26	12.01	14.21	16.91	NAV
	—	—	—	—	—	-3.52*	-15.65	-7.76	41.52	17.06	19.14	23.95	Total Return %
	—	—	—	—	—		5.77	8.18	2.93	-3.19	5.60	-2.39	+/-MSCI EAFE
	—	—	—	—	—		5.74	8.04	2.10	-3.32	4.67	-1.76	+/-MSCI Wd xUS
	—	—	—	—	—		0.10	0.00	0.00	0.00	0.81	0.24	Income Return %
	—	—	—	—	—		-15.75	-7.76	41.52	17.06	18.33	23.71	Capital Return %
	—	—	—	—	—		16	1	18	34	18	41	Total Rtn % Rank Cat
	—	—	—	—	—	0.04	0.01	0.00	0.00	0.00	0.00	0.03	Income $
	—	—	—	—	—	0.27	0.00	0.00	0.00	0.00	0.00	0.65	Capital Gains $
	—	—	—	—	—		1.60	1.60	1.60	1.68	1.60	—	Expense Ratio %
	—	—	—	—	—		0.33	0.05	-0.25	0.18	0.07	—	Income Ratio %
	—	—	—	—	—		190	543	192	211	105	—	Turnover Rate %
	—	—	—	—	—		14	21	38	147	679		Net Assets $mil

Rating and Risk

Time Period	Load-Adj Return %	Morningstar Rtn vs Cat	Morningstar Risk vs Cat	Morningstar Risk-Adj Rating
1 Yr	23.95			
3 Yr	20.01	+Avg	+Avg	★★★★
5 Yr	17.68	High	Avg	★★★★★
10 Yr	—	—	—	—
Incept	9.80			

Other Measures	Standard Index MSCI EAFE	Best Fit Index MSCI EAFE
Alpha	-1.9	-1.9
Beta	1.14	1.14
R-Squared	88	88
Standard Deviation	11.48	
Mean	20.01	
Sharpe Ratio	1.38	

Portfolio Analysis 11-30-06

Share change since 10-06 Total Stocks:52	Sector	Country	% Assets
⊖ Roche Holding	Health	Switzerland	4.03
⊖ UBS AG	Financial	Switzerland	3.91
⊕ America Movil SA ADR	Telecom	Mexico	3.29
⊕ BAE Systems	Ind Mtrls	U.K.	3.19
⊕ Continental	Ind Mtrls	Germany	3.07
⊕ Toyota Motor	Goods	Japan	3.03
⊕ Syngenta	Ind Mtrls	Switzerland	3.03
⊕ Esprit Hldgs Ltd	Consumer	Hong Kong	2.96
⊕ Nestle	Goods	Switzerland	2.95
⊕ Ericsson Telephone Compa	Hardware	Sweden	2.94
⊕ Samsung Electronics	Goods	Korea	2.90
⊖ Lonza Grp	Health	Switzerland	2.73
Cemex SAB de CV ADR	Ind Mtrls	Mexico	2.71
⊖ Veolia Environnement	Business	France	2.69
⊕ Erste Bank	Financial	Austria	2.61
⊕ Man Grp	Financial	U.K.	2.52
Macquarie Bank Ltd	Financial	Australia	2.52
⊖ Diageo	Goods	U.K.	2.52
⊕ Indl And Commrcl Bk Of C	Financial	China	2.15
⊕ Unibanco Uniao de Bancos	Financial	Brazil	2.07

Current Investment Style

Value Blnd Growth		Market Cap	%
	Large	Giant	47.5
	Mid	Large	46.7
	Small	Mid	5.8
		Small	0.0
		Micro	0.0

Avg $mil: 28,666

Value Measures		Rel Category
Price/Earnings	16.82	1.09
Price/Book	2.94	1.12
Price/Sales	1.61	1.14
Price/Cash Flow	10.88	1.12
Dividend Yield %	2.22	0.91

Growth Measures	%	Rel Category
Long-Term Erngs	13.32	0.98
Book Value	11.26	1.02
Sales	-0.97	NMF
Cash Flow	5.87	0.48
Historical Erngs	25.99	1.14

Composition

Cash	2.5	Bonds	0.0
Stocks	97.5	Other	0.0
Foreign (% of Stock)			100.0

Sector Weightings	% of Stocks	Rel MSCI EAFE	3 Year High	Low
↻ Info	10.22	0.86		
🖥 Software	0.00	0.00	3	0
💻 Hardware	5.31	1.38	12	2
🎙 Media	0.00	0.00	13	0
📞 Telecom	4.91	0.88	10	2
🏢 Service	51.66	1.09		
🩺 Health	10.05	1.41	18	6
🛒 Consumer	8.82	1.78	14	5
📊 Business	5.34	1.05	14	3
💲 Financial	27.45	0.91	31	14
🏭 Mfg	38.11	0.93		
🏠 Goods	17.86	1.36	30	14
⚙ Ind Mtrls	17.91	1.16	24	2
🔋 Energy	2.34	0.33	10	2
💡 Utilities	0.00	0.00	2	0

Regional Exposure		% Stock
UK/W. Europe	55	N. America 3
Japan	11	Latn America 9
Asia X Japan	21	Other 1

Country Exposure		% Stock
Switzerland	19	France 7
U.K.	14	Mexico 7
Japan	11	

Morningstar's Take by Dan Lefkovitz 12-21-06

Marsico International Opportunities has a promising future.

This fund has had an uncharacteristically poor year. In absolute terms, its 21.31% gain for the year to date through Dec. 20, 2006, looks great. But the fund lags its benchmark, the MSCI EAFE Index, by 4.5 percentage points and lands in the bottom half of the foreign large-growth category.

Investors shouldn't worry about one poor year in relative terms. This is the same fund that has beaten 96% of its peers over the trailing five-year period. All the reasons that we made a cheaper and more tax-efficient version of the fund, Harbor International Growth, a Fund Analyst Pick, are still in place.

Manager Jim Gendelman is still a creative growth investor who applies the Marsico approach to overseas markets. Like Tom Marsico on the domestic side, he looks for companies benefiting from long-term growth trends and chooses his companies on the basis of rigorous bottom-up

research. Gendelman has targeted lodging and gaming companies, just as Marsico has done on the domestic side, and owns Syngenta, an agricultural firm benefiting from alternative energy development. U.S. analog Monsanto is a top holding of Marsico Growth. And Gendelman recently purchased Nestle partly because, like Marsico holding Procter & Gamble, it is deploying SAP software tools to better run its business.

Gendelman has never paid much attention to the stock, sector, or country weightings of the MSCI EAFE Index--yet another similarity to Marsico. That can cause the fund to behave quite differently than its peers. In the past, Gendelman's picks among off-index mid-cap and emerging-markets names have boosted returns. But this year the fund was held back by being light on utilities and financials, where Gendelman doesn't see growth. If growth stocks come back into favor, this fund should be well positioned.

Address:	1200 17th St Denver CO 80202 888-860-8686	Minimum Purchase:	$2500	Add: $100	IRA: $1000
		Min Auto Inv Plan:	$1000	Add: $50	
		Sales Fees:	No-load, 0.25%S, 2.00%R		
Web Address:	www.marsicofunds.com	Management Fee:	0.85%		
Inception:	06-30-00 *	Actual Fees:	Mgt:0.85%	Dist:0.25%	
Advisor:	Marsico Capital Management, LLC	Expense Projections:	3Yr:$505	5Yr:$871	10Yr:$1900
Subadvisor:	None	Income Distrib:	Annually		
NTF Plans:	Fidelity Retail-NTF, Schwab OneSource				

MORNINGSTAR® Funds 500

Masters' Select Equity

	Ticker	Load	NAV	Yield	Total Assets	Mstar Category
	MSEFX	None	$15.69	0.0%	$863 mil	Large Blend

Governance and Management

Stewardship Grade: A

Portfolio Manager(s)

Christopher Davis and Ken Feinberg of Davis NY Venture, as well as Craig Blum and Stephen Burlingame of TCW Select Equities, each invest 20% of assets in large-cap stocks. Mason Hawkins of Longleaf Partners and Bill Miller of Legg Mason Value each devote 20% of assets to stocks of all sizes. Dick Weiss of Wells Fargo Advantage Common Stock and Bill D'Alonzo of Brandywine both put 10% of the fund into small- and mid-cap names.

Strategy

Litman/Gregory Fund Advisors selects six equity subadvisors to run this fund. These managers pick their best stocks, up to 15 each, to include in the portfolio. Although each subadvisor makes big bets on individual positions, the overall fund isn't too concentrated.

Historical Profile
Return: Above Avg
Risk: High
Rating: ★★★ Neutral

Investment Style: Equity, Stock %

94% 94% 96% 94% 92% 96% 93% 98% 96%

▼ Manager Change
▽ Partial Manager Change

Growth of $10,000
— Investment Values of Fund
— Investment Values of S&P 500

22.6 / 19.0 / 16.0 / 13.0 / 10.0

Performance Quartile (within Category)

	1995	1996	1997	1998	1999	2000	2001	2002	2003	2004	2005	2006	History
	—	10.00	11.84	13.57	14.38	12.98	12.59	10.19	13.44	15.26	15.24	15.69	NAV
	—	0.00*	29.11	14.90	26.45	3.17	-2.55	-19.06	31.89	13.54	4.96	9.34	Total Return %
	—	—	-4.25	-13.68	5.41	12.27	9.34	3.04	3.21	2.66	0.05	-6.45	+/-S&P 500
	—	—	-3.74	-12.12	5.54	10.96	9.90	2.59	2.00	2.14	-1.31	-6.12	+/-Russ 1000
	—	—	0.31	0.27	0.12	0.00	0.00	0.00	0.00	0.00	0.00	0.00	Income Return %
	—	—	28.80	14.63	26.33	3.17	-2.55	-19.06	31.89	13.54	4.96	9.34	Capital Return %
	—	—	52	74	18	20	10	25	15	15	57	95	Total Rtn % Rank Cat
	—	0.00	0.03	0.03	0.02	0.00	0.00	0.00	0.00	0.00	0.00	0.00	Income $
	—	0.00	1.05	0.00	2.68	1.76	0.06	0.00	0.00	0.00	0.75	0.98	Capital Gains $
	—	—	1.47	1.38	1.26	1.24	1.26	1.25	1.23	1.22	1.19	—	Expense Ratio %
	—	—	0.12	0.30	-0.12	-0.35	-0.36	-0.30	-0.39	-0.46	-0.14	—	Income Ratio %
	—	—	145	135	116	130	95	94	84	39	46	—	Turnover Rate %
	—	—	297	406	449	469	508	431	610	855	892	863	Net Assets $mil

Performance 12-31-06

	1st Qtr	2nd Qtr	3rd Qtr	4th Qtr	Total
2002	-0.87	-11.30	-14.00	7.04	-19.06
2003	-5.50	18.38	4.91	12.37	31.89
2004	3.50	2.88	-3.77	10.82	13.54
2005	-5.18	0.97	5.27	4.14	4.96
2006	4.20	-4.09	0.53	8.84	9.34

Trailing	Total Return%	+/- S&P 500	+/- Russ 1000	%Rank Cat	Growth of $10,000
3 Mo	8.84	2.14	1.89	6	10,884
6 Mo	9.41	-3.33	-2.95	86	10,941
1 Yr	9.34	-6.45	-6.12	95	10,934
3 Yr Avg	9.22	-1.22	-1.76	67	13,029
5 Yr Avg	6.82	0.63	0.00	28	13,908
10 Yr Avg	10.12	1.70	1.48	11	26,222
15 Yr Avg	—	—	—	—	—

Tax Analysis	Tax-Adj Rtn%	%Rank Cat	Tax-Cost Rat	%Rank Cat
3 Yr (estimated)	8.54	58	0.62	29
5 Yr (estimated)	6.42	24	0.37	24
10 Yr (estimated)	8.64	12	1.34	62

Potential Capital Gain Exposure: 24% of assets

Rating and Risk

Time Period	Load-Adj Return %	Morningstar Rtn vs Cat	Morningstar Risk vs Cat	Morningstar Risk-Adj Rating
1 Yr	9.34			
3 Yr	9.22	Avg	High	★★
5 Yr	6.82	+Avg	High	★★★
10 Yr	10.12	+Avg	+Avg	★★★★
Incept	10.13			

Other Measures	Standard Index S&P 500	Best Fit Index Russ MG
Alpha	-4.3	-2.7
Beta	1.51	0.96
R-Squared	82	89
Standard Deviation	11.47	
Mean	9.22	
Sharpe Ratio	0.55	

Morningstar's Take by Greg Carlson 12-28-06

Investors should disregard Masters' Select Equity's recent struggles.

This large-blend fund has stunk it up in 2006--it lags more than 90% of its peers for the year to date through Dec. 27, 2006. That shouldn't be too surprising. Although its assets are spread among six proven subadvisors plying distinct strategies, the fund still courts short-term risk. Each manager supplies just nine to 15 stocks, so the fund is far from broadly diversified; it recently held 78 stocks. What's more, because two of the managers, Dick Weiss of Wells Capital and Bill D'Alonzo of Friess Associates, focus primarily on small caps, the fund owns a bigger slug of such volatile names than its typical peer. Finally, many of the subadvisors, including Bill Miller of Legg Mason Value and Mason Hawkins of Longleaf Partners, ply an eclectic style, so the fund bears little resemblance to the S&P 500 Index (the most common benchmark for large-blend funds). For example, this fund recently didn't own any of the eight largest constituents of the index, including such behemoths as General Electric and Microsoft.

It's worth noting that the stocks that have weighed most heavily on the fund's returns this year are favored by more than one of its managers, at least at the funds they manage for their own firms. (Litman/Gregory, the fund's advisor, doesn't disclose who's responsible for which stocks in the fund.) Struggling computer maker Dell, for example, is owned by all four subadvisors who buy large caps, and both Bill Miller and the managers of TCW Select Equities own retailer Amazon and insurer Progressive, which have both struggled in 2006. That type of consensus gives us more confidence that these picks will eventually pay off.

Despite its misfires, this remains one of our favorite large-cap funds. It's delivered excellent returns over the long haul, and a stellar manager roster and shareholder-friendly advisor make it a fine choice.

Portfolio Analysis 09-30-06

Share change since 06-06 Total Stocks:78

	Sector	PE	Tot Ret%	% Assets
⊖ Tyco International, Ltd.	Ind Mtrls	15.7	6.83	4.50
J.P. Morgan Chase & Co.	Financial	13.6	25.60	3.86
⊕ Google, Inc.	Business	61.5	11.00	3.44
EOG Resources	Energy	10.1	-14.62	3.38
⊖ Amazon.com, Inc.	Consumer	55.1	-16.31	2.87
DirecTV, Inc.	Media	26.5	76.63	2.32
⊕ Countrywide Financial Co	Financial	9.8	26.22	2.32
⊖ American International G	Financial	17.0	6.05	2.11
Progressive Corporation	Financial	12.4	-16.93	2.09
Level 3 Communications,	Telecom		95.12	2.09
✸ Sprint Nextel Corporatio	Telecom	30.2	-10.44	2.08
⊕ Cemex SAB de CV ADR	Ind Mtrls	11.1	14.21	2.06
Aon Corp.	Financial	19.6	-0.07	1.94
FedEx Corporation	Business	17.2	5.40	1.90
Dell, Inc.	Hardware	18.4	-16.23	1.89
⊕ ConocoPhillips	Energy	6.5	26.53	1.88
American Express Company	Financial	20.9	19.09	1.88
Capital One Financial Co	Financial	10.4	-10.97	1.86
Comcast	Media			1.82
Walt Disney Company	Media	21.0	44.26	1.82

Current Investment Style

Value Blnd Growth — Large Mid Small

Market Cap	%
Giant	34.5
Large	31.1
Mid	22.0
Small	10.1
Micro	2.4
Avg $mil: 16,771	

Value Measures		Rel Category
Price/Earnings	15.79	1.03
Price/Book	1.85	0.72
Price/Sales	1.07	0.76
Price/Cash Flow	8.93	1.06
Dividend Yield %	1.12	0.64

Growth Measures	%	Rel Category
Long-Term Erngs	12.97	1.10
Book Value	6.07	0.67
Sales	5.81	0.60
Cash Flow	15.75	1.53
Historical Erngs	23.94	1.29

Profitability	%	Rel Category
Return on Equity	17.24	0.89
Return on Assets	9.23	0.89
Net Margin	11.34	0.85

Sector Weightings	% of Stocks	Rel S&P 500	3 Year High Low	
↻ Info	25.09	1.26		
Software	3.80	1.10	4	0
Hardware	6.83	0.74	9	7
Media	10.08	2.66	14	9
Telecom	4.38	1.25	4	1
⊊ Service	50.49	1.09		
Health	5.95	0.49	6	4
Consumer	11.42	1.49	19	11
Business	8.27	1.96	10	5
Financial	24.85	1.12	26	24
Mfg	24.42	0.72		
Goods	7.27	0.85	11	7
Ind Mtrls	9.39	0.79	11	6
Energy	7.76	0.79	9	3
Utilities	0.00	0.00	0	0

Composition

		%
● Cash		2.8
● Stocks		96.1
● Bonds		0.0
● Other		0.1
Foreign (% of Stock)		5.2

Address:	2020 E. Financial Way Glendora CA 91741 800-960-0188
Web Address:	www.mastersselect.com
Inception:	12-31-96*
Advisor:	Litman Gregory Fund Advisors LLC
Subadvisor:	Multiple Subadvisors
NTF Plans:	N/A

Minimum Purchase:	$5000	Add: $250	IRA: $1000
Min Auto Inv Plan:	$2500	Add: $250	
Sales Fees:	No-load, 2.00%R		
Management Fee:	1.10% mx./1.00% mn., 0.10%A		
Actual Fees:	Mgt:1.09%	Dist: —	
Expense Projections:	3Yr:$378	5Yr:$654	10Yr:$1443
Income Distrib:	Annually		

Masters' Select Small Co

Analyst Pick ✔

	Ticker	Load	NAV	Yield	Total Assets	Mstar Category
	MSSFX	None	$14.86	0.0%	$269 mil	Small Growth

Governance and Management

Stewardship Grade: A

Portfolio Manager(s)

Five managers with experience running small-cap funds call the shots here. Former Morningstar Fund Manager of the Year Bob Rodriguez of FPA Capital leads a strong roster that also includes John Rogers of Ariel Fund, Bill D'Alonzo of Brandywine, and Dick Weiss of Wells Fargo Advantage Common Stock. Most of the team from a fifth subadvisor, Copper Rock Capital Partners, previously managed State Street Research Emerging Growth, and the firm, led by Tucker Walsh and Michael Malouf, now runs Old Mutual Emerging Growth.

Strategy

Litman/Gregory Advisors divvies up assets among five subadvisors, and each picks eight to 15 stocks according to his own investing style. Broadly speaking, Bob Rodriguez and John Rogers are value managers; Bill D'Alonzo, Michael Malouf, and Tucker Walsh favor growth stocks; and Dick Weiss falls in between, but all have the flexibility to invest in stocks that don't neatly fall into one bucket or the other. Litman/Gregory isn't dogmatic about the fund's market-cap limits, so there will be a number of smaller mid-caps here.

Performance 12-31-06

	1st Qtr	2nd Qtr	3rd Qtr	4th Qtr	Total
2002	—	—	—	—	—
2003	—	—	8.00	10.34	—*
2004	8.23	4.55	-0.07	7.03	21.01
2005	-2.67	3.64	6.30	-1.80	5.29
2006	10.92	-6.27	-1.23	6.80	9.68

Trailing	Total Return%	+/- S&P 500	+/- Russ 2000 Gr	%Rank Cat	Growth of $10,000
3 Mo	6.80	0.10	-1.97	69	10,680
6 Mo	5.49	-7.25	-1.37	46	10,549
1 Yr	9.68	-6.11	-3.67	54	10,968
3 Yr Avg	11.80	1.36	1.29	26	13,974
5 Yr Avg	—	—	—	—	—
10 Yr Avg	—	—	—	—	—
15 Yr Avg	—	—	—	—	—

Tax Analysis	Tax-Adj Rtn%	%Rank Cat	Tax-Cost Rat	%Rank Cat
3 Yr (estimated)	10.93	21	0.78	30
5 Yr (estimated)	—	—	—	—
10 Yr (estimated)	—	—	—	—

Potential Capital Gain Exposure: 14% of assets

Morningstar's Take by Greg Carlson 12-21-06

It hasn't delivered on its tremendous potential thus far, but Masters' Select Smaller Companies is a fine holding.

This small-growth fund is designed to be a core small-cap holding. To that end, it employs five subadvisors whose investing styles range from deep value to aggressive growth. Yet despite the quality of its manager lineup--three of the five subadvisors run Analyst Picks--the fund has failed to beat its benchmark, the Russell 2000 Index, since its mid-2003 inception.

Despite the fund's unsatisfying record, however, we're not too concerned. Much of its weakness owes to a poor 2006--the fund trails the index by 8 percentage points for the year to date through December 20, 2006. That in turn is primarily the result of a healthy contrarian streak among the fund's managers. Value stocks have led growth stocks by a wide margin since the market's early 2000 peak, so this fund's portfolio has increasingly tilted toward the latter. It's dramatically

underweighted in financial stocks, particularly REITs, relative to the index, and holds a hefty stake in tech stocks. That positioning has weighed on returns, as traditional value haunts like REITs and utilities have continued to lead the market. And in the one hot sector where the fund did own a substantial stake--energy--its service-oriented stocks, likely contributed by Bob Rodriguez of FPA Capital, have largely underperformed.

We think investors who take a patient approach with this fund will ultimately be rewarded. It will likely outpace its benchmark when growth finally returns to favor, and its subadvisors' almost uniformly excellent long-term records provide a measure of comfort. Furthermore, the funds' advisor, Litman/Gregory, has put the fund in a position to succeed by committing to closing it at a small size (thus giving the subadvisors flexibility), yet charging a modest expense ratio.

Address:	2020 E. Financial Way
	Glendora CA 91741
	800-960-0188
Web Address:	www.mastersselect.com
Inception:	06-30-03
Advisor:	Litman Gregory Fund Advisors LLC
Subadvisor:	Multiple Subadvisors
NTF Plans:	N/A

Minimum Purchase:	$5000	Add: $250	IRA: $1000
Min Auto Inv Plan:	$2500	Add: $250	
Sales Fees:	No-load, 2.00%R		
Management Fee:	1.14%		
Actual Fees:	Mgt:1.14%	Dist: —	
Expense Projections:	3Yr:$421	5Yr:$729	10Yr:$1601
Income Distrib:	Annually		

Historical Profile

Return	Above Avg
Risk	Below Avg
Rating	★★★★ Above Avg

Investment Style: Equity, Stock %

90% 85% 86% 91%

▼ Manager Change
▽ Partial Manager Change

Growth of $10,000
— Investment Values of Fund
— Investment Values of S&P 500

Performance Quartile (within Category)

	1995	1996	1997	1998	1999	2000	2001	2002	2003	2004	2005	2006	History
NAV	—	—	—	—	—	—	—	—	11.79	13.84	14.10	14.86	
Total Return %	—	—	—	—	—	—	—	—	21.01	5.29	9.68		
+/-S&P 500	—	—	—	—	—	—	—	—	10.13	0.38	-6.11		
+/-Russ 2000 Gr	—	—	—	—	—	—	—	—	6.70	1.14	-3.67		
Income Return %	—	—	—	—	—	—	—	—	0.00	0.00	0.00		
Capital Return %	—	—	—	—	—	—	—	—	21.01	5.29	9.68		
Total Rtn % Rank Cat	—	—	—	—	—	—	—	—	12	56	54		
Income $	—	—	—	—	—	—	—	0.00	0.00	0.00	0.00		
Capital Gains $	—	—	—	—	—	—	—	0.13	0.43	0.47	0.62		
Expense Ratio %	—	—	—	—	—	—	—	—	1.65	1.40	—		
Income Ratio %	—	—	—	—	—	—	—	—	-1.33	-1.07	—		
Turnover Rate %	—	—	—	—	—	—	—	—	—	149	—		
Net Assets $mil	—	—	—	—	—	—	—	—	51	162	269		

Rating and Risk

Time Period	Load-Adj Return %	Morningstar Rtn vs Cat	Morningstar Risk vs Cat	Morningstar Risk-Adj Rating
1 Yr	9.68			
3 Yr	11.80	+Avg	-Avg	★★★★
5 Yr	—	—	—	—
10 Yr	—	—	—	—
Incept	15.67			

Other Measures	Standard Index S&P 500	Best Fit Index Russ 2000 Gr
Alpha	-1.3	2.6
Beta	1.44	0.77
R-Squared	59	88
Standard Deviation	12.81	
Mean	11.80	
Sharpe Ratio	0.68	

Portfolio Analysis 09-30-06

Share change since 06-06 Total Stocks:67

	Sector	PE	Tot Ret%	% Assets
⊖ Magma Design Automation,	Hardware	—	6.18	2.28
⊖ BearingPoint, Inc.	Business	—	0.13	2.23
⊖ Epicor Software Corporat	Software	27.1	-4.39	2.16
⊖ Heartland Payment System	Software	—		2.10
⊕ Hewitt Associates, Inc.	Business	—	-8.07	2.03
⊖ Janus Capital Group, Inc	Financial	42.2	16.13	2.01
⊖ Parametric Technology Co	Software	38.1	18.16	2.00
CapitalSource, Inc.	Financial	15.7	32.16	1.99
⊖ Respironics Inc.	Health	26.8	1.83	1.98
Hub Group, Inc. A	Business	25.2	55.87	1.97
Foot Locker, Inc.	Consumer	14.8	-5.67	1.89
✿ BE Aerospace	Ind Mtrls	15.3	16.73	1.84
National Oilwell Varco,	Energy	18.3	-2.42	1.83
⊕ Avnet, Inc.	Business	16.5	6.64	1.83
⊕ Interline Brands, Inc.	Consumer	25.2	-1.23	1.83
Ariba, Inc.	Software	—	5.31	1.81
Washington Group Interna	Business	22.6	12.88	1.73
Albany International Cor	Ind Mtrls	15.1	-8.01	1.69
Vasco Data Security Inte	Software	51.9	20.18	1.68
✿ Rackable Systems, Inc.	Hardware	—		1.67

Current Investment Style

Value Blnd Growth — Large Mid Small

Market Cap	%
Giant	0.0
Large	0.0
Mid	36.6
Small	48.6
Micro	14.7

Avg $mil: 1,290

Value Measures		Rel Category
Price/Earnings	17.84	0.85
Price/Book	2.03	0.74
Price/Sales	0.90	0.57
Price/Cash Flow	8.73	0.90
Dividend Yield %	0.17	0.37

Growth Measures	%	Rel Category
Long-Term Erngs	16.77	0.94
Book Value	4.18	0.40
Sales	6.85	0.58
Cash Flow	9.46	0.45
Historical Erngs	8.84	0.36

Profitability	%	Rel Category
Return on Equity	9.09	0.73
Return on Assets	5.82	0.87
Net Margin	6.20	0.72

Sector Weightings

	% of Stocks	Rel S&P 500	3 Year High Low
↻ Info	24.34	1.22	
Software	11.58	3.36	16 5
Hardware	8.58	0.93	11 3
Media	3.38	0.89	7 3
Telecom	0.80	0.23	1 0
Service	54.03	1.17	
Health	10.98	0.91	14 3
Consumer	16.85	2.20	17 15
Business	14.81	3.50	19 9
Financial	11.39	0.51	12 8
Mfg	21.63	0.64	
Goods	0.00	0.00	6 0
Ind Mtrls	12.23	1.02	20 7
Energy	9.40	0.96	18 9
Utilities	0.00	0.00	0 0

Composition

	%
● Cash	8.6
● Stocks	91.4
● Bonds	0.0
● Other	0.0
Foreign (% of Stock)	1.7

Morningstar® Funds 500

Masters' Select Value

	Ticker	Load	NAV	Yield	Total Assets	Mstar Category
	MSVFX	None	$16.34	0.3%	$367 mil	Large Blend

Governance and Management

Stewardship Grade: A

Portfolio Manager(s)

This fund's group of managers is, for the most part, a value all-star team. Mason Hawkins of Longleaf Partners, Bill Miller of Legg Mason Value, and Bill Nygren of Oakmark Select each run one fourth of the fund. The other 25% is run by Franklin Mutual Advisers, which runs Mutual Shares, but Michael Embler recently replaced lead skipper David Winters, who left to start his own firm, Wintergreen Advisers.

Strategy

Litman/Gregory Advisors has selected four value managers to run different portions of this fund. Each picks eight to 15 favorite stocks to include in the portfolio. Because all four are value managers and look for companies trading at a discount to their intrinsic or transaction value, it is likely that some picks will overlap. Due to the fund's small asset base, investors might expect it to hold more mid- and small-cap stocks than the managers hold elsewhere.

Performance 12-31-06

	1st Qtr	2nd Qtr	3rd Qtr	4th Qtr	Total
2002	3.15	-10.94	-12.57	6.86	-14.17
2003	-7.34	22.99	4.03	11.69	32.42
2004	4.70	0.15	0.88	8.44	14.70
2005	-3.49	1.25	3.50	2.95	4.13
2006	6.10	-3.68	3.15	10.78	16.77

Trailing	Total Return%	+/- S&P 500	+/- Russ 1000	%Rank Cat	Growth of $10,000
3 Mo	10.78	4.08	3.83	2	11,078
6 Mo	14.27	1.53	1.91	7	11,427
1 Yr	16.77	0.98	1.31	12	11,677
3 Yr Avg	11.73	1.29	0.75	19	13,948
5 Yr Avg	9.65	3.46	2.83	7	15,851
10 Yr Avg	—	—	—	—	—
15 Yr Avg	—	—	—	—	—

Tax Analysis	Tax-Adj Rtn%	%Rank Cat	Tax-Cost Rat	%Rank Cat
3 Yr (estimated)	11.04	17	0.62	29
5 Yr (estimated)	9.25	5	0.36	24
10 Yr (estimated)	—	—	—	—

Potential Capital Gain Exposure: 26% of assets

Morningstar's Take by Greg Carlson 12-28-06

Masters' Select Value's recent rebound might prove short-lived, but its long-term prospects are bright.

This fund is ending the year on a high note. Over the trailing three months ending Dec. 27, 2006, the fund returned 11.7% and outperformed nearly all of its large-blend category peers.

It had been rougher sledding here. In fact, from the start of 2005 through Oct. 13, 2006, the fund lagged nearly 90% of its rivals. Such a poor showing might come as a surprise, given the high quality of the fund's subadvisor lineup and the fact that its assets are spread among four managers with distinct approaches: Bill Miller of Legg Mason Value, Mason Hawkins of Longleaf Partners, Michael Embler of Mutual Shares, and Bill Nygren of Oakmark Select. However, because each subadvisor supplies just eight to 15 picks to the portfolio, this fund is far from broadly diversified; it holds only 49 stocks, and its sector weightings often bear little resemblance to the group norm. Thus, it's been more volatile than its typical rival.

Although the fund's managers hardly operate in lockstep, a common theme has emerged at their individual charges--once-richly priced firms in traditional growth sectors such as technology, telecom, and media are now more attractive than typical value haunts like financials and energy. For example, in their own funds, each of the four managers have held beaten-down computer maker Dell, three of the four have held Sprint Nextel, and each one has owned media giants such as Liberty Interactive and Walt Disney. (Sprint, Liberty, and Disney are also in this fund.) Until very recently, most of these stocks lagged far behind cyclical fare. In the past several months, however, investors have flocked to companies with steadier revenue streams, and the fund has outpaced most rivals.

There's no way of knowing whether the fund's recent outperformance will continue, but its superb manager lineup and shareholder-friendly advisor make it a fine choice.

Address:	2020 E. Financial Way	Minimum Purchase:	$5000	Add: $250	IRA: $1000
	Glendora CA 91741	Min Auto Inv Plan:	$2500	Add: $250	
	800-960-0188	Sales Fees:	No-load, 2.00%R		
Web Address:	www.mastersselect.com	Management Fee:	1.10%		
Inception:	06-30-00*	Actual Fees:	Mgt:1.10%	Dist: —	
Advisor:	Litman Gregory Fund Advisors LLC	Expense Projections:	3Yr:$391	5Yr:$679	10Yr:$1498
Subadvisor:	Multiple Subadvisors	Income Distrib:	Annually		
NTF Plans:	N/A				

Historical Profile
Return High
Risk Above Avg
Rating ★★★★ Highest

90%	88%	91%	80%	93%	95%

▼ Manager Change
▽ Partial Manager Change

Growth of $10,000
— Investment Values of Fund
— Investment Values of S&P 500

Performance Quartile (within Category)

1995	1996	1997	1998	1999	2000	2001	2002	2003	2004	2005	2006	History
—	—	—	—	—	10.45	11.43	9.81	12.99	14.90	14.60	16.34	NAV
—	—	—	—	—	4.50*	9.64	-14.17	32.42	14.70	4.13	16.77	Total Return %
—	—	—	—	—	—	21.53	7.93	3.74	3.82	-0.78	0.98	+/-S&P 500
—	—	—	—	—	—	22.09	7.48	2.53	3.30	-2.14	1.31	+/-Russ 1000
—	—	—	—	—	—	0.01	0.00	0.00	0.00	0.40	0.29	Income Return %
—	—	—	—	—	—	9.63	-14.17	32.42	14.70	3.73	16.48	Capital Return %
—	—	—	—	—	—	3	6	13	9	73	12	Total Rtn % Rank Cat
—	—	—	—	—	0.00	0.00	0.00	0.00	0.00	0.06	0.04	Income $
—	—	—	—	—	0.00	0.03	0.00	0.00	0.00	0.84	0.66	Capital Gains $
—	—	—	—	—	—	1.35	1.29	1.28	1.23	1.21	—	Expense Ratio %
—	—	—	—	—	—	-0.04	0.55	0.35	0.20	0.26	—	Income Ratio %
—	—	—	—	—	—	33	54	22	29	30	—	Turnover Rate %
—	—	—	—	—	56	160	138	181	306	338	367	Net Assets $mil

Rating and Risk

Time Period	Load-Adj Return %	Morningstar Rtn vs Cat	Morningstar Risk vs Cat	Morningstar Risk-Adj Rating
1 Yr	16.77			
3 Yr	11.73	+Avg	+Avg	★★★★
5 Yr	9.65	High	+Avg	★★★★★
10 Yr	—	—	—	—
Incept	9.61			

Other Measures	Standard Index S&P 500	Best Fit Index Mstar Mid Core
Alpha	0.1	0.0
Beta	1.17	0.76
R-Squared	78	85
Standard Deviation	9.14	
Mean	11.73	
Sharpe Ratio	0.91	

Portfolio Analysis 09-30-06

Share change since 06-06 Total Stocks:49

	Sector	PE	Tot Ret%	% Assets
⊖ Tyco International, Ltd.	Ind Mtrls	15.7	6.83	4.57
⊖ Dell, Inc.	Hardware	18.4	-16.23	4.23
⊕ Sprint Nextel Corporatio	Telecom	30.2	-10.44	3.77
⊖ Home Depot, Inc.	Consumer	13.5	1.01	3.29
☼ KT&G	Goods	—	—	2.97
⊖ Liberty Interactive A	Media	—	—	2.92
DirecTV, Inc.	Media	26.5	76.63	2.74
⊕ Cemex SAB de CV ADR	Ind Mtrls	11.1	14.21	2.45
J.P. Morgan Chase & Co.	Financial	13.6	25.60	2.43
Imperial Tobacco Grp	Goods	—	—	2.42
Walt Disney Company	Media	21.0	44.26	2.33
Capital One Financial Co	Financial	10.4	-10.97	2.33
Berkshire Hathaway Inc.	Financial	13.2	24.89	2.25
Level 3 Communications,	Telecom	—	95.12	2.22
General Motors Corporati	Goods	—	63.96	2.19
⊖ Orkla	Ind Mtrls	—	—	2.17
☼ Yahoo, Inc.	Media	35.4	-34.81	2.09
⊖ News Cl A	Media	—	—	2.08
IAC/InterActiveCorp	Consumer	40.6	31.26	2.04
⊕ Eastman Kodak Company	Goods	—	12.58	1.99

Current Investment Style

Value Blnd Growth — Large/Mid/Small

Market Cap	%
Giant	36.7
Large	38.5
Mid	24.8
Small	0.0
Micro	0.0

Avg $mil: 24,271

Value Measures		Rel Category
Price/Earnings	15.65	1.02
Price/Book	1.61	0.63
Price/Sales	0.96	0.69
Price/Cash Flow	10.00	1.18
Dividend Yield %	1.53	0.87

Growth Measures	%	Rel Category
Long-Term Erngs	12.17	1.03
Book Value	6.70	0.74
Sales	4.70	0.49
Cash Flow	5.34	0.52
Historical Erngs	24.18	1.31

Profitability	%	Rel Category
Return on Equity	16.90	0.87
Return on Assets	7.06	0.68
Net Margin	7.35	0.55

Sector Weightings	% of Stocks	Rel S&P 500	3 Year High Low
⟳ Info	37.26	1.86	
Software	0.00	0.00	0 0
Hardware	6.21	0.67	7 0
Media	20.62	5.44	21 11
Telecom	10.43	2.97	10 5
☖ Service	37.69	0.82	
Health	0.97	0.08	2 0
Consumer	15.51	2.03	21 16
Business	7.67	1.81	13 7
Financial	13.54	0.61	28 13
⊔ Mfg	25.05	0.74	
Goods	12.02	1.41	18 11
Ind Mtrls	13.03	1.09	14 9
Energy	0.00	0.00	2 0
Utilities	0.00	0.00	2 0

Composition

- ● Cash 2.1
- ● Stocks 95.5
- ● Bonds 1.3
- ○ Other 1.1
- Foreign 18.4 (% of Stock)

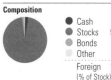

Masters' Select Intl

| | Analyst Pick | Ticker MSILX | Load Closed | NAV $18.74 | Yield 1.9% | Total Assets $1,725 mil | Mstar Category Foreign Large Blend |

Governance and Management

Stewardship Grade: A

Portfolio Manager(s)

There have been a few changes over time, but this fund continues to sport an impressive roster of managers: Oakmark International's David Herro; Ted Tyson, formerly of American Century and Harbor International Growth; Bill Fries of Thornburg International Value; Jim Gendelman of Marsico International; and Amit Wadhwaney of Third Avenue International. Each runs between 15% and 24% of the portfolio.

Strategy

The five managers follow diverse styles, with each contributing eight to 15 stock picks to the portfolio. Advisor Litman/Gregory has been diligent in fighting market-timers. Years ago, it implemented a 2% redemption fee on shares held less than six months; it has turned away substantial amounts of money from platforms that wanted permission not to enforce the redemption fee; and it has always been aggressive about finding and getting rid of market-timers. The firm, which has used fair-value pricing for specific securities for some time, is also researching the possibility of using broader fair-value pricing.

Performance 12-31-06

	1st Qtr	2nd Qtr	3rd Qtr	4th Qtr	Total
2002	5.99	-2.64	-20.80	4.82	-14.33
2003	-10.28	23.65	7.58	16.35	38.86
2004	4.32	-4.14	-0.07	14.44	14.37
2005	0.83	2.11	14.15	5.26	23.70
2006	8.18	-0.26	3.55	10.63	23.61

Trailing	Total Return%	+/- MSCI EAFE	+/- MSCI Wd xUS	%Rank Cat	Growth of $10,000
3 Mo	10.63	0.28	0.51	36	11,063
6 Mo	14.56	-0.13	0.34	45	11,456
1 Yr	23.61	-2.73	-2.10	67	12,361
3 Yr Avg	20.48	0.55	0.38	18	17,488
5 Yr Avg	15.78	0.80	0.53	12	20,805
10 Yr Avg	—	—	—	—	—
15 Yr Avg	—	—	—	—	—

Tax Analysis	Tax-Adj Rtn%	%Rank Cat	Tax-Cost Rat	%Rank Cat
3 Yr (estimated)	17.91	41	2.13	90
5 Yr (estimated)	14.25	18	1.32	95
10 Yr (estimated)	—	—	—	—

Potential Capital Gain Exposure: 20% of assets

Morningstar's Take by William Samuel Rocco 12-14-06

This closed mutual fund's subpar returns in 2006 aren't surprising or alarming.

Masters Select International lags three fourths of its foreign large-blend rivals for the year to date through December 13. This multimanager fund's cash stake, which has averaged slightly more than 6% in 2006, has slowed returns a bit in this year's strong rally, and some of its sector and country biases have taken a modest toll on its performance. But selected individual holdings have done the most harm. The Canadian paper company Abitibi Consolidated dropped sharply after its early 2006 purchase and did real damage before it was sold. Additionally, Thomson, a French supplier of technology to the media and entertainment industries that has also been sold, hurt as well.

Shareholders shouldn't be shocked by this. The fund's country, sector, and market-cap weights usually differ significantly from the category norms, because all five of its managers have distinctive tastes and readily look beyond the usual foreign-stock suspects for opportunities. Individual holdings tend to matter more here than elsewhere, because Litman/Gregory limits each manager to eight to 15 picks and the fund's portfolio is more compact than most of its peers' as a result. It's also only to be expected that the fund's portfolio biases will be out of step with the world's markets at times and that some of its individual picks will sting on occasion.

Shareholders shouldn't be worried, either. The fund boasts impressive three-year, five-year and since-inception returns, because its portfolio biases have done more good than harm overall and the managers' stock selection has generally been quite good. All five of its managers have had a lot of success elsewhere, which is further evidence of their talents. And the fund has relatively low costs, which give it an ongoing edge.

This closed mutual fund remains a distinctive and distinguished core international holding.

Address:	2020 E. Financial Way Glendora CA 91741 800-960-0188	Minimum Purchase:	Closed	Add: — IRA: —
		Min Auto Inv Plan:	Closed	Add: —
		Sales Fees:	No-load, 2.00%R	
Web Address:	www.mastersselect.com	Management Fee:	1.10% mx./1.00% mn., 0.10%A	
Inception:	12-01-97*	Actual Fees:	Mgt:1.08% Dist: —	
Advisor:	Litman Gregory Fund Advisors LLC	Expense Projections:	3Yr:$381 5Yr:$668 10Yr:$1489	
Subadvisor:	Multiple Subadvisors	Income Distrib:	Annually	
NTF Plans:	N/A			

Historical Profile

Return	Above Avg
Risk	Above Avg
Rating	★★★★ Above Avg

▼ Manager Change
▽ Partial Manager Change

Growth of $10,000
— Investment Values of Fund
— Investment Values of MSCI EAFE

Performance Quartile (within Category)

1995	1996	1997	1998	1999	2000	2001	2002	2003	2004	2005	2006	History
—	—	9.88	10.95	18.67	15.31	12.53	10.70	14.83	16.89	17.48	18.74	NAV
—	—	-1.20*	11.74	75.01	-5.01	-17.94	-14.33	38.86	14.37	23.70	23.61	Total Return %
—	—	—	-8.19	47.98	9.18	3.48	1.61	0.27	-5.88	10.16	-2.73	+/-MSCI EAFE
—	—	—	-6.95	47.03	8.35	3.45	1.47	-0.56	-6.01	9.23	-2.10	+/-MSCI Wd xUS
—	—	—	0.89	0.31	0.25	0.22	0.27	0.25	0.47	2.04	2.34	Income Return %
—	—	—	10.85	74.70	-5.26	-18.16	-14.60	38.61	13.90	21.66	21.27	Capital Return %
—	—	—	63	2	7	15	25	15	85	4	67	Total Rtn % Rank Cat
—	—	0.00	0.09	0.03	0.05	0.03	0.03	0.03	0.07	0.29	0.41	Income $
—	—	0.00	0.00	0.38	2.34	0.00	0.00	0.00	0.00	2.92	2.38	Capital Gains $
—	—	1.77	1.55	1.29	1.18	1.19	1.13	1.10	1.09	1.08	—	Expense Ratio %
—	—	0.42	0.87	0.01	0.47	0.52	0.47	0.69	0.76	1.17	—	Income Ratio %
—	—	—	74	100	149	174	141	110	88	160	—	Turnover Rate %
—	—	46	95	218	276	278	336	732	1,137	1,429	1,725	Net Assets $mil

Rating and Risk

Time Period	Load-Adj Return %	Morningstar Rtn vs Cat	Morningstar Risk vs Cat	Morningstar Risk-Adj Rating
1 Yr	23.61			
3 Yr	20.48	+Avg	+Avg	★★★★
5 Yr	15.78	+Avg	+Avg	★★★★
10 Yr	—			
Incept	13.40			

Other Measures	Standard Index MSCI EAFE	Best Fit Index MSCI Wd xUS
Alpha	-0.1	-0.1
Beta	1.05	1.04
R-Squared	85	86
Standard Deviation	10.72	
Mean	20.48	
Sharpe Ratio	1.51	

Portfolio Analysis 09-30-06

Share change since 06-06 Total Stocks:68	Sector	Country	% Assets
⊕ UBS AG	Financial	Switzerland	3.62
⊖ Roche Holding	Health	Switzerland	3.19
⊖ STADA Arzneimittel	Health	Germany	3.07
⊕ HSBC Hldgs	Financial	Hong Kong	2.84
⊕ NII Holdings, Inc.	Telecom	United States	2.53
⊖ America Movil SA ADR	Telecom	Mexico	2.50
Inditex Grp	Goods	Spain	2.39
⊕ Hong Kong Exchanges & Cl	Financial	Hong Kong	2.24
⊕ Serono	Health	Switzerland	2.14
BMW Grp	Goods	Germany	2.13
⊕ Hellenic Org. of Footbal	Consumer	Greece	2.08
☼ Adidas-Salomon	Goods	Germany	1.97
China Merchants Hldgs (I	Ind Mtrls	Hong Kong	1.93
☼ Canadian Natural Resourc	Energy	Canada	1.86
British Sky Broadcasting	Media	U.K.	1.83
☼ Alstom	Ind Mtrls	France	1.78
Southern Copper Corporat	Ind Mtrls	Peru	1.73
Nestle	Goods	Switzerland	1.70
SK Telecom	Telecom	Korea	1.67
⊖ Ppr Sa, Paris	Consumer	France	1.63

Current Investment Style

	Market Cap	%
	Giant	27.1
	Large	44.4
	Mid	25.1
	Small	3.4
	Micro	0.0
	Avg $mil:	12,835

Value Measures		Rel Category
Price/Earnings	17.06	1.30
Price/Book	2.24	1.03
Price/Sales	1.27	1.09
Price/Cash Flow	8.27	0.99
Dividend Yield %	2.95	1.01

Growth Measures	%	Rel Category
Long-Term Erngs	13.03	1.10
Book Value	5.35	0.59
Sales	6.23	0.95
Cash Flow	5.28	0.64
Historical Erngs	30.73	1.51

Composition

Cash	7.0	Bonds	0.0
Stocks	93.0	Other	0.0
Foreign (% of Stock)			97.3

Sector Weightings	% of Stocks	Rel MSCI EAFE	3 Year High	Low
⊕ Info	14.64	1.24		
Software	0.00	0.00	1	0
Hardware	2.69	0.70	5	1
Media	1.97	1.08	10	2
Telecom	9.98	1.79	11	3
Service	49.89	1.06		
Health	15.83	2.22	19	4
Consumer	12.08	2.44	16	8
Business	1.67	0.33	5	1
Financial	20.31	0.67	21	14
Mfg	35.49	0.87		
Goods	16.54	1.26	21	13
Ind Mtrls	13.18	0.85	14	6
Energy	4.01	0.56	16	4
Utilities	1.76	0.34	2	0

Regional Exposure	% Stock		
UK/W. Europe	51	N. America	7
Japan	12	Latn America	8
Asia X Japan	20	Other	2

Country Exposure	% Stock		
Switzerland	14	Japan	12
U.K.	13	Germany	8
Hong Kong	12		

MORNINGSTAR® Funds 500

Matrix Advisors Value

	Ticker	Load	NAV	Yield	Total Assets	Mstar Category
	MAVFX	None	$57.50	0.8%	$197 mil	Large Blend

Portfolio Manager(s)

David Katz has led the management team here since Matrix inherited the fund from Management Asset Corporation in July 1996. Katz is backed by two research analysts and two of the firm's partners, Steve Roukis and Jordan Posner. Five partners sit on the firm's investment committee.

Strategy

This fund's flexible mandate allows it to buy both large- and small-capitalization names. Manager David Katz looks for stocks that sell at a discount of one third or more to their intrinsic values, but he's willing to delve deeply into pricey sectors such as technology. He sets sell targets and sticks to them, but he often repurchases favorites if they temporarily slip.

Historical Profile

Return	Above Avg
Risk	High
Rating	★★★ Neutral

Investment Style: Equity, Stock %

Quartile bar values: 94% 96% 84% 98% 99% 96% 100% 99% 95%

▼ Manager Change
▽ Partial Manager Change

Growth of $10,000
— Investment Values of Fund
— Investment Values of S&P 500

Performance Quartile (within Category)

	1995	1996	1997	1998	1999	2000	2001	2002	2003	2004	2005	2006	History
	—	26.33	30.86	30.94	40.77	43.11	47.23	37.22	53.59	54.41	52.69	57.50	NAV
	—	9.93*	17.85	2.90	32.85	7.96	12.35	-20.74	44.59	3.90	0.90	16.31	Total Return %
	—	—	-15.51	-25.68	11.81	17.06	24.24	1.36	15.91	-6.98	-4.01	0.52	+/-S&P 500
	—	—	-15.00	-24.12	11.94	15.75	24.80	0.91	14.70	-7.50	-5.37	0.85	+/-Russ 1000
	—	—	0.65	0.30	0.00	0.37	0.35	0.18	0.57	0.79	0.63	0.93	Income Return %
	—	—	17.20	2.60	32.85	7.59	12.00	-20.92	44.02	3.11	0.27	15.38	Capital Return %
	—	—	92	98	9	13	3	37	2	97	94	16	Total Rtn % Rank Cat
	0.33	0.17	0.09	0.00	0.15	0.15	0.08	0.21	0.42	0.34	0.49		Income $
	0.00	0.00	0.00	0.70	0.32	0.78	1.03	0.14	0.00	0.81	1.82	3.16	Capital Gains $
	—	—	1.42	1.23	1.25	0.99	0.99	0.99	0.99	0.99	0.99	0.99	Expense Ratio %
	—	—	0.44	0.45	0.10	0.31	0.60	0.29	0.54	0.51	0.99	0.60	Income Ratio %
	—	—	129	68	33	40	55	45	30	17	18	28	Turnover Rate %
	8	9	9	13	30	51	67	225	294	194	197		Net Assets $mil

Performance 12-31-06

	1st Qtr	2nd Qtr	3rd Qtr	4th Qtr	Total
2002	1.91	-14.52	-20.30	14.16	-20.74
2003	-4.67	25.14	4.64	15.84	44.59
2004	1.04	-0.24	-7.07	10.91	3.90
2005	-3.31	-1.27	1.46	4.17	0.90
2006	2.45	-3.87	7.77	9.59	16.31

Trailing	Total Return%	+/- S&P 500	+/- Russ 1000	%Rank Cat	Growth of $10,000
3 Mo	9.59	2.89	2.64	4	10,959
6 Mo	18.10	5.36	5.74	2	11,810
1 Yr	16.31	0.52	0.85	16	11,631
3 Yr Avg	6.83	-3.61	-4.15	93	12,192
5 Yr Avg	6.92	0.73	0.10	26	13,973
10 Yr Avg	10.57	2.15	1.93	9	27,313
15 Yr Avg	—	—	—	—	—

Tax Analysis	Tax-Adj Rtn%	%Rank Cat	Tax-Cost Rat	%Rank Cat
3 Yr (estimated)	5.83	90	0.94	43
5 Yr (estimated)	6.25	26	0.63	41
10 Yr (estimated)	10.00	7	0.52	19

Potential Capital Gain Exposure: 24% of assets

Rating and Risk

Time Period	Load-Adj Return %	Morningstar Rtn vs Cat	Morningstar Risk vs Cat	Morningstar Risk-Adj Rating
1 Yr	16.31			
3 Yr	6.83	-Avg	High	★
5 Yr	6.92	+Avg	High	★★
10 Yr	10.57	High	High	★★★★
Incept	11.02			

Other Measures	Standard Index S&P 500	Best Fit Index S&P 500
Alpha	-5.1	-5.1
Beta	1.28	1.28
R-Squared	83	83
Standard Deviation	9.74	
Mean	6.83	
Sharpe Ratio	0.40	

Morningstar's Take by Andrew Gunter 12-11-06

Matrix Advisors Value's strategy hasn't changed one bit, which is good news for investors.

This fund has faced several headwinds of late. Manager David Katz's concentrated portfolio leans heavily on the media and financial sectors' corporations, while notably underweighting energy positions relative to many large-blend category rivals. This preference, along with an emphasis on mega-cap stocks, drove bottom-decile returns here in 2004, 2005, and early 2006. During much of that time, energy stocks soared while mega-caps lagged the broader market.

Even so, Katz isn't one to scuttle his struggling picks. He uses a rigorous, multiscreen process to find healthy companies trading at large discounts to his estimate of their intrinsic values, so typically that leads to about 30 picks in which he has lots of confidence. He'll only sell a stock when it reaches his fair value estimate or if company fundamentals deteriorate. That explains why the portfolio's turnover dropped to less than 20% annually in 2004

and 2005 as its stocks struggled. Katz saw no fundamental deterioration in the fund's stocks, so he held on.

Part of Katz's confidence, too, comes from buying companies he believes will lead their sectors' return to favor. A great example is sixth-largest holding Microsoft, an underperformer he started buying in early 2004. The company's fortress-like balance sheet and cheap valuation were good reasons to buy it originally, but now Katz eagerly awaits its release of Windows Vista. He believes Vista's launch will boost corporate spending not just on Microsoft applications, but across other technology-related industries as well.

We urge shareholders here to show the same type of patience as Katz shows with his stocks. After all, investors who held on through this fund's previous dry spell, in 1997-98, then saw five straight years of category-topping returns.

Portfolio Analysis 11-30-06

Share change since 10-06 Total Stocks:32	Sector	PE	Tot Ret%	% Assets
⊖ Symbol Technologies	Hardware	35.6	16.64	3.85
⊕ Dollar General Corporati	Consumer	17.3	-14.94	3.80
Time Warner, Inc.	Media	19.6	26.37	3.75
⊕ Novellus Systems, Inc.	Hardware	35.3	42.70	3.62
⊕ Wal-Mart Stores, Inc.	Consumer	16.9	0.13	3.59
First Data Corporation	Business	12.3	9.88	3.54
Microsoft Corporation	Software	23.8	15.83	3.52
MedImmune, Inc.	Health	—	-7.57	3.44
⊕ General Electric Company	Ind Mtrls	20.0	9.35	3.43
Chevron Corporation	Energy	9.0	33.76	3.38
American International G	Financial	17.0	6.05	3.36
⊕ Vishay Intertechnology	Hardware	18.2	-1.60	3.34
⊕ Gap, Inc.	Consumer	19.5	12.45	3.28
⊕ Wyeth	Health	17.2	12.88	3.26
⊕ Pfizer Inc.	Health	15.2	15.22	3.25
Comcast Corporation	Media			3.22
⊕ Citigroup, Inc.	Financial	13.1	19.55	3.17
Tyco International, Ltd.	Ind Mtrls	15.7	6.83	3.09
Bank of America Corporat	Financial	12.4	20.68	3.08
Morgan Stanley	Financial	12.3	45.93	3.05

Current Investment Style

Value Blnd Growth — Large Mid Small

Market Cap	%
Giant	57.0
Large	18.0
Mid	25.0
Small	0.0
Micro	0.0

Avg $mil: 43,601

Value Measures		Rel Category
Price/Earnings	16.35	1.06
Price/Book	2.41	0.94
Price/Sales	1.54	1.10
Price/Cash Flow	11.71	1.39
Dividend Yield %	1.67	0.95

Growth Measures	%	Rel Category
Long-Term Erngs	11.42	0.97
Book Value	6.27	0.69
Sales	11.13	1.15
Cash Flow	1.49	0.14
Historical Erngs	14.61	0.79

Profitability	%	Rel Category
Return on Equity	15.02	0.77
Return on Assets	9.99	0.96
Net Margin	11.35	0.85

Sector Weightings	% of Stocks	Rel S&P 500	3 Year High	Low
⟲ Info	28.08	1.40		
Software	3.71	1.08	4	0
Hardware	17.03	1.84	21	15
Media	7.34	1.94	10	3
Telecom	0.00	0.00	0	0
⟲ Service	58.36	1.26		
Health	17.16	1.42	24	12
Consumer	14.37	1.88	14	8
Business	5.80	1.37	6	1
Financial	21.03	0.94	31	21
⟲ Mfg	13.58	0.40		
Goods	0.00	0.00	4	0
Ind Mtrls	8.91	0.75	11	7
Energy	4.67	0.48	6	2
Utilities	0.00	0.00	0	0

Composition

	%
● Cash	5.0
● Stocks	95.0
● Bonds	0.0
● Other	0.0
Foreign (% of Stock)	2.3

Address:	2020 East Financial Way, Suite 100 Glendora CA 91741 866-209-1965	Minimum Purchase:	$1000	Add: $100	IRA: $500
		Min Auto Inv Plan:	$500	Add: $100	
		Sales Fees:	No-load, 1.00%R		
Web Address:	www.matrixadvisorsvaluefund.com	Management Fee:	1.00%		
Inception:	07-01-96*	Actual Fees:	Mgt:1.00%	Dist: —	
Advisor:	Matrix Asset Advisors, Inc.	Expense Projections:	3Yr:$350	5Yr:$606	10Yr:$1340
Subadvisor:	None	Income Distrib:	Annually		
NTF Plans:	Fidelity Retail-NTF, Schwab OneSource				

Matthews Pacific Tiger

Analyst Pick ✓

	Ticker	Load	NAV	Yield	Total Assets	Mstar Category
	MAPTX	Closed	$23.71	0.9%	$3,201 mil	Pacific/Asia ex-Japan Stk

Governance and Management

Stewardship Grade: A

Portfolio Manager(s)

Lead manager Mark Headley, who has one of the broadest resumes of any Asia manager, also serves as the lead manager of Matthews Japan and Matthews Asia Pacific. Comanager Richard Gao, who served as a foreign-exchange trader and assistant manager for Bank of China before joining Matthews in 1997, also serves as the lead manager of Matthews China. Headley and Gao are supported by their firm's three other managers as well as its four analysts.

Strategy

Mark Headley and Richard Gao focus on firms with robust long-term earnings prospects and moderate valuations. They pay attention to all of emerging Asia, consider companies of all sizes, and are not afraid to run a compact portfolio. To combat market-timing, the fund levies a 2% redemption fee on shares held 90 days or fewer, and it uses fair-value pricing whenever necessary.

Historical Profile
Return Above Avg
Risk Average
Rating ★★★★ Above Avg

Investment Style: Equity Stock %

98% 98% 98% 100% 100% 100% 100% 100% 100%

▼ Manager Change
▽ Partial Manager Change

Growth of $10,000
■ Investment Values of Fund
— Investment Values of MSCI EAFE

Performance Quartile (within Category)

1995	1996	1997	1998	1999	2000	2001	2002	2003	2004	2005	2006	History
9.76	12.12	7.15	6.84	12.32	8.20	8.81	8.24	13.15	15.90	19.27	23.71	NAV
3.06	24.18	-40.89	-2.86	83.01	-24.00	7.91	-6.47	60.15	23.34	22.51	27.22	Total Return %
-8.15	18.13	-42.67	-22.79	55.98	-9.81	29.33	9.47	21.56	3.09	8.97	0.88	+/-MSCI EAFE
-3.78	14.85	4.72	4.31	23.59	13.88	12.05	4.58	19.38	9.11	4.65	-1.25	+/-MSCIAC FExJ
0.00	0.00	0.05	0.20	2.77	3.35	0.13	0.00	0.54	0.73	0.76	1.19	Income Return %
3.06	24.18	-40.94	-3.06	80.24	-27.35	7.78	-6.47	59.61	22.61	21.75	26.03	Capital Return %
52	20	82	13	25	48	16	24	29	3	31	84	Total Rtn % Rank Cat
0.00	0.00	0.01	0.01	0.19	0.41	0.01	0.00	0.04	0.10	0.12	0.23	Income $
0.00	0.00	0.02	0.06	0.00	0.84	0.03	0.00	0.00	0.21	0.09	0.56	Capital Gains $
2.17	1.90	1.90	1.90	1.90	1.81	1.90	1.79	1.75	1.48	1.31	—	Expense Ratio %
0.36	0.32	0.27	0.30	3.35	1.56	0.67	-0.17	1.04	0.95	1.10	—	Income Ratio %
93	125	71	73	99	52	64	57	28	15	3	—	Turnover Rate %
3	33	37	52	119	71	87	107	456	855	2,032	3,201	Net Assets $mil

Performance 12-31-06

	1st Qtr	2nd Qtr	3rd Qtr	4th Qtr	Total
2002	10.10	-2.06	-18.84	6.87	-6.47
2003	-7.65	25.10	20.80	14.75	60.15
2004	4.64	-4.94	6.65	16.27	23.34
2005	-0.06	3.21	12.44	5.63	22.51
2006	7.84	-3.51	7.93	13.28	27.22

Trailing	Total Return%	+/- MSCI EAFE	+/- MSCIAC FExJ	%Rank Cat	Growth of $10,000
3 Mo	13.28	2.93	-2.12	86	11,328
6 Mo	22.27	7.58	1.05	85	12,227
1 Yr	27.22	0.88	-1.25	84	12,722
3 Yr Avg	24.34	4.41	4.30	49	19,224
5 Yr Avg	23.55	8.57	6.84	23	28,788
10 Yr Avg	9.51	1.80	9.14	21	24,805
15 Yr Avg	—	—	—		—

Tax Analysis	Tax-Adj Rtn%	%Rank Cat	Tax-Cost Rat	%Rank Cat
3 Yr (estimated)	23.71	38	0.51	54
5 Yr (estimated)	23.15	20	0.32	38
10 Yr (estimated)	8.84	23	0.61	71

Potential Capital Gain Exposure: 31% of assets

Rating and Risk

Time Period	Load-Adj Return %	Morningstar Rtn vs Cat	Morningstar Risk vs Cat	Morningstar Risk-Adj Rating
1 Yr	27.22			
3 Yr	24.34	Avg	-Avg	★★★★
5 Yr	23.55	+Avg	Avg	★★★★
10 Yr	9.51	+Avg	+Avg	★★★★
Incept	9.38			

Other Measures	Standard Index MSCI EAFE	Best Fit Index MSCIAC FExJ
Alpha	0.6	5.3
Beta	1.23	0.89
R-Squared	69	89
Standard Deviation	13.97	
Mean	24.34	
Sharpe Ratio	1.42	

Portfolio Analysis 09-30-06

Share change since 06-06 Total Stocks:65	Sector	Country	% Assets
⊖ Lenovo Grp Ltd	Hardware	Hong Kong	3.77
Advcd Info Serv	Telecom	Thailand	3.63
⊖ Dah Sing Financial Grp	Financial	Hong Kong	3.12
Hana Financial Group	Financial	Korea	3.04
Taiwan Semiconductor Mfg	Hardware	Taiwan	2.99
Swire Pacific	Ind Mtrls	Hong Kong	2.88
DBS Grp Hldgs Ltd	Financial	Singapore	2.72
Hang Lung Grp Ltd	Financial	Hong Kong	2.67
Bangkok Bk	Financial	Thailand	2.60
Fraser & Neave Ltd	Ind Mtrls	Singapore	2.55
Amorepacific	—	Korea	2.45
Cipla Ltd	Health	India	2.30
⊕ NHN	Business	Korea	2.26
President Chain Store	Consumer	Taiwan	2.20
SK Telecom	Telecom	Korea	2.19
Hite Brewery	Goods	Korea	2.17
⊕ Infosys Technologies Ltd	Software	India	2.14
Television Broadcasts Lt	Media	Hong Kong	1.93
Shangri-La Asia Ltd	Consumer	Hong Kong	1.89
Hyflux Ltd	Utilities	Singapore	1.89

Current Investment Style

Value Blnd Growth — Large/Mid/Small

	Market Cap	%
	Giant	28.2
	Large	40.3
	Mid	30.6
	Small	1.0
	Micro	0.0
	Avg $mil:	4,973

Value Measures		Rel Category
Price/Earnings	16.01	1.16
Price/Book	2.53	1.14
Price/Sales	1.08	0.78
Price/Cash Flow	4.66	0.66
Dividend Yield %	2.96	1.01

Growth Measures	%	Rel Category
Long-Term Erngs	16.54	1.02
Book Value	8.77	0.77
Sales	28.24	1.38
Cash Flow	29.79	1.71
Historical Erngs	8.76	0.40

Composition

Cash	0.0	Bonds	0.0
Stocks	100.0	Other	0.0
Foreign (% of Stock)			100.0

Sector Weightings

	% of Stocks	Rel MSCI EAFE	3 Year High	Low
↻ Info	24.92	2.11		
🖳 Software	2.22	3.96	2	1
💻 Hardware	9.48	2.46	13	5
🎬 Media	2.42	1.32	4	2
📞 Telecom	10.80	1.94	13	7
☞ Service	55.10	1.17		
🏥 Health	6.70	0.94	7	2
🛒 Consumer	9.11	1.84	10	6
🏢 Business	11.50	2.27	12	5
💲 Financial	27.79	0.92	30	23
🏭 Mfg	19.96	0.49		
🏗 Goods	10.51	0.80	20	11
⚙ Ind Mtrls	7.49	0.49	9	7
🔋 Energy	0.00	0.00	0	0
💡 Utilities	1.96	0.37	4	2

Regional Exposure % Stock

UK/W. Europe	0	N. America	0
Japan	0	Latn America	0
Asia X Japan	100	Other	0

Country Exposure % Stock

Hong Kong	34	Singapore	12
South Korea	23	Thailand	6
India	12		

Morningstar's Take by William Samuel Rocco 11-08-06

Shareholders should take Matthews Pacific Tiger's 2006 struggles in stride.

This closed fund has been a relatively sluggish performer this year. Its 0% energy weight has been part of the problem. Indeed, though some Asia oil stocks did cool off in late summer, most have earned robust gains in 2006, and PetroChina, which is popular with the fund's rivals, is up more than 40% since January 1. The fund has also been slowed by a few longtime and sizable holdings, including Lenovo Group, which is in the red for 2006 despite surging in recent months. Consequently, the fund trails 78% of its rivals for the year to date through November 8.

Shareholders shouldn't be too bothered by these results, though. Even the best offerings slump now and then. The 18% the fund has gained so far in 2006 is more than respectable in absolute terms. And the fund's managers are patient and focused growth investors who've always had trouble finding energy stocks that meet their standards. Thus, it

should come as no surprise that the managers have stuck with some holdings that have struggled but remain fundamentally strong in their view, or that a big rally in Asia oil stocks would slow the fund.

Meanwhile, the managers have executed their strategy well in most rallies, and at other times, so the fund has superior long-term gains. And the fund's strengths don't end there: Its all-cap orientation and broad country range make it a better diversifier than most of its rivals, while its low costs give it an ongoing advantage.

This closed fund remains one of its category's best. But shareholders should note that it and its peers are unlikely to do as well over the next few years as they have over the last few. And if they own the fund in a taxable account and are considering adding to their stakes, they should note that the fund is sitting on a lot of potential capital gains exposure and, thus, could make a distribution this year.

Address:	Four Embarcadero Center San Francisco, CA 94111 800-789-2742	Minimum Purchase:	Closed	Add: —	IRA: —
		Min Auto Inv Plan:	Closed	Add: —	
		Sales Fees:	No-load, 2.00%R		
Web Address:	www.matthewsfunds.com	Management Fee:	0.75% mx./0.65% mn., 0.25%A		
Inception:	09-12-94	Actual Fees:	Mgt:0.75% Dist: —		
Advisor:	Matthews International Capital Mgt LLC	Expense Projections:	3Yr:$415 5Yr:$718 10Yr:$1579		
Subadvisor:	None	Income Distrib:	Annually		
NTF Plans:	Fidelity Retail-NTF, Schwab OneSource				

Merger

	Ticker	Load	NAV	Yield	Total Assets	Mstar Category
	MERFX	None	$15.62	0.7%	$1,526 mil	Long-Short

Governance and Management

Stewardship Grade: A

Portfolio Manager(s)

No retail mutual fund manager has been doing merger arbitrage exclusively longer than comanagers Fred Green and Bonnie Smith. They have been at the fund's helm since its inception in 1989. Their firm, Westchester Capital Management, has been doing merger arbitrage for private and institutional accounts since 1980. Four other portfolio managers and traders support Green and Smith.

Strategy

This fund uses a merger-arbitrage strategy, buying the stock of acquisition targets and occasionally shorting the acquirer's stock. If the deal closes, the fund makes money. The fund can also invest in corporate reorganizations, and in certain circumstances, it will use options and invest in corporate bonds. The offering's fixed-income positions are usually small, though. Before investing, management researchs the strategic rationale behind the merger. It shoots for a 10% to 15% gain on its investments.

Historical Profile
Return Below Avg
Risk Below Avg
Rating ★★ Below Avg

	94%	93%	93%	47%	52%	64%	74%	90%	93%	Investment Style

Equity
Stock %

▼ Manager Change
▽ Partial Manager Change

Growth of $10,000
■ Investment Values of Fund
— Investment Values of S&P 500

Performance Quartile (within Category)

1995	1996	1997	1998	1999	2000	2001	2002	2003	2004	2005	2006	History
14.13	14.11	14.15	13.58	14.72	15.52	14.77	13.73	15.21	15.42	14.67	15.62	NAV
14.15	9.95	11.65	5.35	17.39	17.58	2.01	-5.67	11.04	2.71	0.81	10.98	Total Return %
-23.43	-13.01	-21.71	-23.23	-3.65	26.68	13.90	16.43	-17.64	-8.17	-4.10	-4.81	+/-S&P 500
-22.65	-11.87	-20.13	-18.79	-3.51	25.04	13.47	15.87	-20.02	-9.24	-5.31	-4.74	+/-Russell3000
0.58	1.32	0.21	1.56	0.54	0.93	1.35	1.37	0.26	0.01	0.06	0.76	Income Return %
13.57	8.63	11.44	3.79	16.85	16.65	0.66	-7.04	10.78	2.70	0.75	10.22	Capital Return %
67	67	100	67	7	24	68	71	36	71	69	18	Total Rtn % Rank Cat
0.08	0.19	0.03	0.22	0.07	0.14	0.21	0.20	0.04	0.00	0.01	0.11	Income $
0.83	1.24	1.58	1.10	1.15	1.65	0.85	0.00	0.00	0.20	0.87	0.55	Capital Gains $
1.41	1.36	1.36	1.33	1.38	1.34	1.34	1.38	1.37	1.37	1.36	2.08	Expense Ratio %
0.57	1.36	0.13	1.36	0.54	1.57	2.23	1.36	0.34	-0.68	-0.35	0.43	Income Ratio %
290	277	271	355	387	419	384	258	309	257	312	369	Turnover Rate %
246	474	436	346	635	1,042	980	823	1,345	1,651	1,260	1,526	Net Assets $mil

Performance 12-31-06

	1st Qtr	2nd Qtr	3rd Qtr	4th Qtr	Total
2002	-0.74	-5.87	-2.46	3.51	-5.67
2003	0.29	5.08	2.56	2.73	11.04
2004	1.64	-0.97	-1.37	3.46	2.71
2005	-0.45	0.91	1.87	-1.49	0.81
2006	4.09	2.29	2.11	2.07	10.98

Trailing	Total Return%	+/- S&P 500	+/- Russell3000	%Rank Cat	Growth of $10,000
3 Mo	2.07	-4.63	-5.05	58	10,207
6 Mo	4.23	-8.51	-7.86	37	10,423
1 Yr	10.98	-4.81	-4.74	18	11,098
3 Yr Avg	4.74	-5.70	-6.45	48	11,490
5 Yr Avg	3.78	-2.41	-3.39	74	12,038
10 Yr Avg	7.14	-1.28	-1.50	34	19,930
15 Yr Avg	8.33	-2.31	-2.46	34	33,207

Tax Analysis	Tax-Adj Rtn%	%Rank Cat	Tax-Cost Rat	%Rank Cat
3 Yr (estimated)	3.40	49	1.28	72
5 Yr (estimated)	2.84	53	0.91	57
10 Yr (estimated)	5.02	75	1.98	67

Potential Capital Gain Exposure: -2% of assets

Rating and Risk

Time Period	Load-Adj Return %	Morningstar Rtn vs Cat	Morningstar Risk vs Cat	Morningstar Risk-Adj Rating
1 Yr	10.98			
3 Yr	4.74	Avg	-Avg	★★★
5 Yr	3.78	-Avg	-Avg	★★
10 Yr	7.14	—	—	
Incept	8.33			

Other Measures	Standard Index S&P 500	Best Fit Index Merrill Lynch Convert
Alpha	-0.5	0.3
Beta	0.28	0.35
R-Squared	35	44
Standard Deviation	3.40	
Mean	4.74	
Sharpe Ratio	0.45	

Portfolio Analysis 09-30-06

Share change since 06-06 Total Stocks:56	Sector	PE	Tot Ret%	% Assets
⊕ Price Communications Cor	Telecom	—	42.92	5.55
✵ Freescale Semiconductor,	Hardware	—	—	4.08
✵ Mercury Interactive Corp	Software	—	—	3.89
⊖ Kinder Morgan, Inc.	Energy	20.8	19.22	3.58
✵ Veritas DGC, Inc.	Energy	33.8	141.28	3.11
✵ BellSouth Corporation	Telecom	—	—	3.10
⊕ Golden West Fin	Financial	—	—	3.06
⊕ Univision Communications	Media	43.5	20.52	2.98
✵ HCA, Inc.	Health	—	—	2.88
⊕ North Fork Bancorporatio	Financial	—	—	2.66
⊕ Constellation Energy Gro	Utilities	17.6	22.70	2.63
✵ Serono	Health	—	—	2.51
✵ Ati Tech	Hardware	—	—	2.42
⊕ Fidelity National Financ	Financial	—	—	2.41
⊕ Petco Animal Suppl	Consumer	—	—	2.30
✵ Energy Partners, Ltd.	Energy	32.0	12.07	2.30
✵ Delta and Pine Land Comp	Ind Mtrls	75.0	79.15	2.27
✵ Reckson Associates Realt	Financial	46.0	31.78	2.24
✵ AmerUs Group Company	Financial	—	—	2.23
⊕ Maverick Tube	Ind Mtrls	—	—	2.12

Current Investment Style

Value Blnd Growth — Large/Mid/Small

Market Cap	%
Giant	5.6
Large	28.2
Mid	40.3
Small	24.8
Micro	1.0

Avg $mil: 5,017

Value Measures		Rel Category
Price/Earnings	18.95	1.23
Price/Book	2.58	1.07
Price/Sales	1.62	1.34
Price/Cash Flow	7.05	0.90
Dividend Yield %	2.55	1.67

Growth Measures	%	Rel Category
Long-Term Erngs	10.94	0.90
Book Value	5.30	0.71
Sales	11.27	1.18
Cash Flow	6.70	0.61
Historical Erngs	21.38	1.11

Profitability	%	Rel Category
Return on Equity	13.25	0.79
Return on Assets	6.21	0.71
Net Margin	14.39	1.23

Sector Weightings	% of Stocks	Rel S&P 500	3 Year High Low
☎ Info	29.39	1.47	
🖥 Software	5.37	1.56	7 0
💾 Hardware	8.48	0.92	8 0
🎤 Media	4.23	1.12	12 3
📶 Telecom	11.31	3.22	21 6
☁ Service	40.78	0.88	
⚕ Health	6.69	0.55	21 5
🛒 Consumer	6.40	0.84	22 4
💼 Business	0.66	0.16	10 1
💲 Financial	27.03	1.21	27 7
🏭 Mfg	29.84	0.88	
⚙ Goods	1.81	0.21	16 1
⚙ Ind Mtrls	8.88	0.74	15 1
🔥 Energy	12.63	1.29	17 0
💡 Utilities	6.52	1.86	10 0

Composition

	%
● Cash	4.3
● Stocks	93.3
● Bonds	0.9
○ Other	1.5
Foreign (% of Stock)	14.4

Morningstar's Take by Dan Culloton 11-20-06

Merger Fund is adding to its game.

This fund sticks out in the long-short category. Unlike many funds in the group, it doesn't try to balance its short positions with those it holds for the long term. Neither does it base its shorts on some bottom-up or top-down assessment of stock valuations or attractiveness. Rather, it tries to capture the spread between the share price of firms that are about to be acquired and their proposed purchase prices. It does this by buying the shares of the target companies of deals the managers like and sometimes shorting the stocks of the acquiring firm. This minimizes the risk of stock fluctuations, leaving the fund and its shareholders exposed only to the risk that the transactions don't close.

Consequently, the key to making this strategy--which aims to produce consistent positive returns with low volatility--work over the long term is the ability to pick the right mergers and acquisitions. The management team has a longer record of evaluating and selecting arbitrage opportunities than any of its peers in the tiny subset of open-end funds that employ strategies like this. Furthermore, it hasn't rested on its laurels. This year it has implemented new quantitative tools to, among other things, help the managers compare their own estimate of the probability of a deal's success with what the market thinks might happen. The new systems haven't supplanted management's qualitative research into the strategic rationale and financial structure of transactions--which Fred Green and Bonnie Smith have practiced for more than two decades--but the tools have helped them pick exit and entry points and hedge individual investments.

Assessing deal risk is essential for this fund because it is often drawn to situations that are fraught with regulatory and competitive complications, such as German utility E.ON's bid for Spanish power company Endesa. So it's encouraging an established fund is still honing its competitive edge.

Address:	100 Summit Lake Drive Valhalla, NY 10595 800-343-8959	Minimum Purchase:	$2000	Add: $0	IRA: $2000
		Min Auto Inv Plan:	$2000	Add: $100	
		Sales Fees:	No-load, 0.22%S, 2.00%R		
Web Address:		Management Fee:	1.00%		
Inception:	01-31-89	Actual Fees:	Mgt:1.00%	Dist:0.22%	
Advisor:	Westchester Capital Management Inc	Expense Projections:	3Yr:$557	5Yr:$959	10Yr:$2084
Subadvisor:	None	Income Distrib:	Annually		
NTF Plans:	Fidelity Retail-NTF, Schwab OneSource				

Meridian Growth

	Ticker	Load	NAV	Yield	Total Assets	Mstar Category
	MERDX	None	$39.24	0.0%	$1,867 mil	Mid-Cap Growth

Governance and Management

Stewardship Grade: B

Portfolio Manager(s)

Rick Aster has been at the helm since the fund's 1984 inception. He is the founder of the fund's advisor, Aster Investment Management Company. In mid-2005, Aster brought aboard a former Brandywine analyst, Talal Qatato, to assist him with stock-picking.

Strategy

This fund takes a kinder, gentler approach to growth investing. Manager Rick Aster looks for small- and mid-cap names growing their earnings at least 15% a year. He won't pay up for that growth, however, which gives the fund price multiples below the mid-growth averages. Aster employs a buy-and-hold style and won't necessarily dump picks that have drifted into large-cap territory. He keeps a compact portfolio of about 50 holdings and often concentrates his picks in a handful of sectors.

Performance 12-31-06

	1st Qtr	2nd Qtr	3rd Qtr	4th Qtr	Total
2002	1.60	-3.90	-18.51	3.28	-17.82
2003	-2.00	20.96	7.48	16.09	47.90
2004	5.78	1.26	-3.76	11.04	14.47
2005	-5.16	1.27	0.28	4.16	0.33
2006	10.31	-4.46	4.70	4.96	15.81

Trailing	Total Return%	+/- S&P 500	+/- Russ MG	%Rank Cat	Growth of $10,000
3 Mo	4.96	-1.74	-1.99	80	10,496
6 Mo	9.89	-2.85	1.99	13	10,989
1 Yr	15.81	0.02	5.15	10	11,581
3 Yr Avg	9.97	-0.47	-2.76	60	13,299
5 Yr Avg	10.08	3.89	1.86	13	16,164
10 Yr Avg	12.73	4.31	4.11	10	33,143
15 Yr Avg	12.59	1.95	2.46	9	59,224

Tax Analysis	Tax-Adj Rtn%	%Rank Cat	Tax-Cost Rat	%Rank Cat
3 Yr (estimated)	9.26	55	0.65	34
5 Yr (estimated)	9.39	12	0.63	45
10 Yr (estimated)	10.54	12	1.94	77

Potential Capital Gain Exposure: 22% of assets

Morningstar's Take by Christopher Davis 12-14-06

Meridian Growth is back in the saddle, but it might not be able to gallop as quickly.

After badly lagging its rivals in 2005, this offering has been strutting its stuff in 2006. Winners like Las Vegas Sands and Granite Construction have propelled the fund to a 17% gain for the year to date through Dec. 13, a top-decile showing in the mid-growth category.

Investors shouldn't expect this fund to move with the crowd. Aster is willing to build big weightings in individual sectors, which gives the fund an idiosyncratic look relative to its rivals. He's also a stickler for steady earnings growth. So, when highly volatile areas, such as energy in 2005 or technology in the late 1990s, lead the way, the fund is likely to look relatively slow. Moreover, Aster pays more attention to valuation than most mid-growth managers. That's another reason he stayed away from tech in the late 1990s.

It's worth noting that even when the fund has lagged, it's usually managed to deliver decent returns in absolute terms. And thanks to Aster's risk-conscious strategy, the fund has held on to those gains in difficult environments. That mix has led to fine long-term returns.

The fund could have trouble keeping up that act thanks to its growing size. With $1.9 billion in assets, it's not unreasonably large, and it's true that Aster's low-turnover, contrarian approach makes it easier to handle asset growth. And while the fund's market cap has risen, other signs of asset bloat, such as a less concentrated portfolio, haven't materialized. What worries us that Meridian Value, also led by Aster, slowed down considerably when its assets grew tremendously in the early 2000s. Adding to our concerns is Aster's unwillingness to close Value to new investors.

But even if the fund isn't what it was, what it still could be remains appealing. In addition to Aster's skill and sensible strategy, the fund's low 0.84% expense ratio gives him a real edge. We still think this fund can beat the competition.

Address:	60 E Sir Francis Drake Blvd
	Larkspur CA 94939
	800-446-6662
Web Address:	www.meridianfund.com
Inception:	08-01-84
Advisor:	Aster Investment Management CO Inc
Subadvisor:	None
NTF Plans:	N/A

Minimum Purchase:	$1000	Add: $50	IRA: $1000
Min Auto Inv Plan:	$1000	Add: $50	
Sales Fees:	No-load, 2.00%R		
Management Fee:	1.00% mx./0.75% mn.		
Actual Fees:	Mgt:0.76%	Dist: —	
Expense Projections:	3Yr:$271	5Yr:$471	10Yr:$1049
Income Distrib:	Annually		

Historical Profile

Return	Above Avg
Risk	Below Avg
Rating	★★★★ Above Avg

88% 100% 100% 100% 95% 98% 98% 99% 98%

Investment Style: Equity, Stock %

- ▼ Manager Change
- ▽ Partial Manager Change

Growth of $10,000
- Investment Values of Fund
- Investment Values of S&P 500

Performance Quartile (within Category)

1995	1996	1997	1998	1999	2000	2001	2002	2003	2004	2005	2006	History
29.90	30.08	30.73	24.29	25.40	28.06	28.79	22.98	33.03	37.24	36.57	39.24	NAV
22.43	11.19	19.23	3.09	13.33	28.20	14.76	-17.82	47.90	14.47	0.33	15.81	Total Return %
-15.15	-11.77	-14.13	-25.49	-7.71	37.30	26.65	4.28	19.22	3.59	-4.58	0.02	+/-S&P 500
-11.55	-6.29	-3.31	-14.77	-37.96	39.95	34.91	9.59	5.19	-1.01	-11.77	5.15	+/-Russ MG
1.23	1.26	1.11	0.46	0.62	9.85	0.00	0.20	1.00	0.00	0.00	0.03	Income Return %
21.20	9.93	18.12	2.63	12.71	18.35	14.76	-18.02	46.90	14.47	0.33	15.78	Capital Return %
92	77	56	84	89	5	2	16	7	46	98	10	Total Rtn % Rank Cat
0.31	0.36	0.32	0.14	0.15	2.44	0.00	0.06	0.23	0.00	0.00	0.01	Income $
0.54	2.76	4.81	6.50	1.78	1.86	2.84	0.61	0.69	0.56	0.80	3.12	Capital Gains $
1.06	0.96	0.96	0.95	1.01	1.09	1.04	1.06	0.95	0.88	0.86	0.85	Expense Ratio %
1.18	0.99	1.23	0.76	0.49	0.31	-0.26	1.18	-0.47	-0.21	-0.21	-0.03	Income Ratio %
29	34	37	38	1	28	42	26	27	19	32	29	Turnover Rate %
375	378	332	231	138	152	208	317	482	1,252	1,704	1,867	Net Assets $mil

Rating and Risk

Time Period	Load-Adj Return %	Morningstar Rtn vs Cat	Morningstar Risk vs Cat	Morningstar Risk-Adj Rating
1 Yr	15.81			
3 Yr	9.97	Avg	-Avg	★★★
5 Yr	10.08	+Avg	Avg	★★★★
10 Yr	12.73	+Avg	Low	★★★★★
Incept	13.97			

Other Measures	Standard Index S&P 500	Best Fit Index DJ Wilshire 4500
Alpha	-3.0	-3.4
Beta	1.42	0.91
R-Squared	82	88
Standard Deviation	10.80	
Mean	9.97	
Sharpe Ratio	0.64	

Portfolio Analysis 09-30-06

Share change since 06-06 Total Stocks:46

	Sector	PE	Tot Ret%	% Assets
⊖ American Tower Corporati	Telecom	—	37.57	3.28
Willis Group Holdings, L	Financial	17.0	10.34	2.85
⊕ DENTSPLY International,	Health	30.2	11.74	2.67
Edwards Lifesciences Cor	Health	25.7	13.05	2.63
⊖ Affiliated Managers Grou	Financial	32.5	31.00	2.60
⊖ T Rowe Price Group	Financial	26.1	23.27	2.60
⊕ Royal Caribbean Cruises,	Consumer	16.0	-6.78	2.60
⊕ C.R. Bard, Inc.	Health	26.7	26.81	2.58
⊖ Davita, Inc.	Health	21.1	12.32	2.58
⊕ Diebold Incorporated	Hardware	45.0	25.12	2.53
Laboratory Corporation o	Health	24.3	36.44	2.51
⊕ Cerner Corporation	Software	37.1	0.10	2.47
⊕ Mercury General Corporat	Financial	13.8	-6.10	2.44
Las Vegas Sands, Inc.	Consumer	75.7	126.70	2.41
⊕ Bed Bath & Beyond, Inc.	Consumer	20.1	5.39	2.40
⊕ Airgas, Inc.	Ind Mtrls	21.8	24.06	2.39
⊕ CSG Systems Internationa	Software	23.3	19.76	2.35
Republic Services, Inc.	Business	20.7	9.91	2.33
Allied Waste Industries	Business	25.6	40.62	2.30
Advent Software, Inc.	Software	76.0	21.94	2.25

Current Investment Style

Value Blnd Growth — Large / Mid / Small

Market Cap	%
Giant	0.0
Large	11.8
Mid	58.4
Small	29.8
Micro	0.0

Avg $mil: 3,379

Value Measures		Rel Category
Price/Earnings	19.92	0.97
Price/Book	2.65	0.83
Price/Sales	1.38	0.78
Price/Cash Flow	9.46	0.83
Dividend Yield %	0.85	1.35

Growth Measures	%	Rel Category
Long-Term Erngs	13.72	0.84
Book Value	7.66	0.60
Sales	9.29	0.93
Cash Flow	9.37	0.51
Historical Erngs	11.50	0.46

Profitability	%	Rel Category
Return on Equity	15.29	0.85
Return on Assets	8.43	0.90
Net Margin	8.97	0.77

Sector Weightings	% of Stocks	Rel S&P 500	3 Year High Low
⟳ Info	19.89	0.99	
Software	10.98	3.18	11 2
Hardware	5.58	0.60	21 3
Media	0.00	0.00	0 0
Telecom	3.33	0.95	3 2
⟳ Service	67.77	1.47	
Health	15.33	1.27	20 14
Consumer	24.19	3.16	26 19
Business	12.35	2.92	17 9
Financial	15.90	0.71	18 10
⟳ Mfg	12.35	0.37	
Goods	5.83	0.68	8 1
Ind Mtrls	6.52	0.55	7 2
Energy	0.00	0.00	0 0
Utilities	0.00	0.00	0 0

Composition

- Cash 1.7
- Stocks 98.3
- Bonds 0.0
- Other 0.0
- Foreign 4.9 (% of Stock)

MORNINGSTAR® Funds 500

Meridian Value

	Ticker	Load	NAV	Yield	Total Assets	Mstar Category
	MVALX	None	$35.60	1.0%	$1,753 mil	Mid-Cap Blend

Governance and Management

Stewardship Grade: C

Portfolio Manager(s)

Lead manager Rick Aster founded the fund in February 1994 and is the architect of its strategy. Aster provides broad oversight and has the final say on which stocks enter the portfolio. Jamie England took over the fund's day-to-day management responsibilities in January 2004 after a two-year stint as analyst under his predecessor. Larry Cordisco joined in 2003 as an analyst after three years at Bank of America. In January 2004, Meridian hired Jim O'Connor, a recent MBA graduate and sell-side analyst, as another analyst.

Strategy

This fund's strategy, devised by lead manager and fund founder Rick Aster in 1994, is to screen for companies that have had two or three disappointing quarters in a row on the grounds that such firms are often punished too harshly. Day-to-day manager Jamie England and two analysts then whittle down the list by looking for companies with attractive valuations poised for a turnaround. The fund employs a multi-cap approach, though with mid and large caps now dominating the portfolio, as the fund's market cap has marched upwards in recent years.

Historical Profile

Return	Above Avg
Risk	Below Avg
Rating	★★★★ Above Avg

Investment Style: Equity, Stock %

Growth of $10,000
— Investment Values of Fund
— Investment Values of S&P 500

▼ Manager Change
▽ Partial Manager Change

Performance Quartile (within Category)

1995	1996	1997	1998	1999	2000	2001	2002	2003	2004	2005	2006	History
11.91	14.85	15.86	18.32	22.69	29.11	32.42	28.09	37.84	38.09	34.63	35.60	NAV
23.80	32.29	21.37	18.94	38.28	37.14	11.70	-13.36	34.71	15.10	2.92	18.67	Total Return %
-13.78	9.33	-11.99	-9.64	17.24	46.24	23.59	8.74	6.03	4.22	-1.99	2.88	+/-S&P 500
-7.13	13.04	-10.88	-0.18	23.56	19.63	12.31	1.17	-0.91	-1.38	-9.64	8.35	+/-S&P Mid 400
0.00	4.85	2.23	0.00	3.73	4.84	0.13	0.00	0.00	0.75	0.83	1.17	Income Return %
23.80	27.44	19.14	18.94	34.55	32.30	11.57	-13.36	34.71	14.35	2.09	17.50	Capital Return %
73	4	72	23	14	3	20	33	48	64	91	16	Total Rtn % Rank Cat
0.00	0.58	0.33	0.00	0.68	1.09	0.04	0.00	0.00	0.28	0.32	0.41	Income $
0.00	0.27	1.90	0.47	1.68	0.68	0.04	0.00	0.00	5.11	4.28	5.09	Capital Gains $
2.78	2.55	2.51	2.16	1.63	1.41	1.10	1.12	1.11	1.09	1.08	1.09	Expense Ratio %
-0.58	-1.36	-1.96	-1.35	-0.65	0.39	0.60	-0.22	-0.12	0.01	0.48	0.49	Income Ratio %
77	125	144	133	124	86	77	54	60	81	59	58	Turnover Rate %
1	5	9	18	35	286	1,135	1,185	1,508	2,134	1,903	1,753	Net Assets $mil

Performance 12-31-06

	1st Qtr	2nd Qtr	3rd Qtr	4th Qtr	Total
2002	0.62	-6.99	-14.83	8.71	-13.36
2003	-1.64	14.55	5.21	13.63	34.71
2004	5.60	0.98	-3.52	11.88	15.10
2005	-1.76	1.84	1.97	0.88	2.92
2006	9.56	-4.74	5.17	8.11	18.67

Trailing	Total Return%	+/- S&P 500	+/- S&P Mid 400	%Rank Cat	Growth of $10,000
3 Mo	8.11	1.41	1.12	37	10,811
6 Mo	13.71	0.97	7.88	11	11,371
1 Yr	18.67	2.88	8.35	16	11,867
3 Yr Avg	12.02	1.58	-1.07	63	14,057
5 Yr Avg	10.41	4.22	-0.48	44	16,407
10 Yr Avg	17.50	9.08	4.03	1	50,162
15 Yr Avg	—				

Tax Analysis	Tax-Adj Rtn%	%Rank Cat	Tax-Cost Rat	%Rank Cat
3 Yr (estimated)	9.66	67	2.11	80
5 Yr (estimated)	9.01	54	1.27	75
10 Yr (estimated)	15.63	1	1.59	44

Potential Capital Gain Exposure: 16% of assets

Rating and Risk

Time Period	Load-Adj Return %	Morningstar Rtn vs Cat	Morningstar Risk vs Cat	Morningstar Risk-Adj Rating
1 Yr	18.67			
3 Yr	12.02	Avg	Avg	★★★
5 Yr	10.41	Avg	-Avg	★★★
10 Yr	17.50	High	-Avg	★★★★★
Incept	17.40			

Other Measures	Standard Index S&P 500	Best Fit Index Russ MV
Alpha	-0.3	-6.5
Beta	1.29	1.05
R-Squared	80	87
Standard Deviation	9.90	
Mean	12.02	
Sharpe Ratio	0.88	

Morningstar's Take by Christopher Davis 11-30-06

Meridian Value has looked good lately, but we wouldn't jump in yet.

Finally. That's what longtime shareholders of this mid-blend fund must be saying. The offering posted lackluster relative results in 2004 and 2005, after Jamie England took day-to-day control of the portfolio. The fund's early returns were a departure from the consistently good results it had delivered under its prior manager. But England has been on-the-mark in 2006. Many of his picks, including Manitowoc and Equity Residential, have posted handsome gains.

So what's England doing differently? He hasn't changed the strategy designed by fund founder Rick Aster. He looks for companies that have suffered successive quarters of earnings disappointments but are poised for a turnaround. This approach didn't work well in 2004 and 2005, England says, because high-quality companies meeting his criteria were tough to come by when earnings were up sharply nearly across the board. That's plausible,

but he initially handled the difficult environment poorly by delving into slower-growing firms with deeper-seated problems, including Eastman Kodak. But England and Aster eventually responded sensibly, slimming the portfolio to better reflect their best ideas.

To be sure, there's further cause for optimism. England worked as an analyst for a couple of years under his predecessor, so he presumably played a part in the fund's past success. Moreover, the fund's strategy makes sense. Because investors often overpunish companies that post disappointing results, there's potential for outsized gain. It's not for nothing that the fund's 10-year return is among the fund world's best.

Ultimately, though, our endorsement of this fund hinges not just on the soundness of its strategy but the quality of its execution. Given the mixed results England has generated since taking charge, we're not confident in his abilities. Therefore, we'd recommend looking elsewhere.

Address:	60 E Sir Francis Drake Blvd Larkspur CA 94939 800-446-6662	Minimum Purchase: Min Auto Inv Plan: Sales Fees:	$1000 $1000 No-load, 2.00%R	Add: $50 IRA: $1000 Add: $50
Web Address:	www.meridianfund.com	Management Fee:	1.00%	
Inception:	02-10-94	Actual Fees:	Mgt:1.00%	Dist: —
Advisor:	Aster Investment Management CO Inc	Expense Projections:	3Yr:$347	5Yr:$601 10Yr:$1329
Subadvisor:	None	Income Distrib:	Annually	
NTF Plans:	N/A			

Portfolio Analysis 09-30-06

Share change since 06-06 Total Stocks:63

	Sector	PE	Tot Ret%	% Assets
⊖ Newell Rubbermaid, Inc.	Goods	19.2	25.66	3.11
⊖ J.P. Morgan Chase & Co.	Financial	13.6	25.60	3.10
⊖ Baxter International Inc	Health	24.3	24.81	2.92
⊖ Waste Management, Inc.	Business	16.6	24.21	2.90
⊕ Pactiv Corporation	Goods	18.9	62.23	2.82
Equity Residential	Financial	NMF	34.64	2.66
Apartment Investment & M	Financial	—	55.18	2.66
⊕ Allied Waste Industries	Business	25.6	40.62	2.62
⊕ Willis Group Holdings, L	Financial	17.0	10.34	2.54
⊖ Safeway Inc.	Consumer	20.4	47.22	2.53
⊖ Nokia Corporation ADR	Hardware	18.9	13.44	2.36
⊕ Anheuser-Busch Companies	Goods	18.8	17.41	2.31
⊖ Schering-Plough Corporat	Health	36.6	14.63	2.24
☆ Alltel Corp.	Telecom	18.1	19.54	2.21
BE Aerospace	Ind Mtrls	15.3	16.73	2.10
⊕ International Flavors &	Ind Mtrls	23.0	49.66	2.08
⊕ Sysco Corporation	Consumer	25.2	20.96	2.06
⊕ Regions Financial Corpor	Financial	13.6	14.92	1.93
⊕ Diebold Incorporated	Hardware	45.0	25.12	1.91
⊖ Symbol Technologies	Hardware	35.6	16.64	1.82

Current Investment Style

Value Blnd Growth — Large Mid Small

Market Cap	%
Giant	7.7
Large	26.8
Mid	53.1
Small	11.5
Micro	0.8
Avg $mil:	7,092

Value Measures		Rel Category
Price/Earnings	18.33	1.14
Price/Book	2.22	0.98
Price/Sales	1.05	0.94
Price/Cash Flow	10.40	1.23
Dividend Yield %	1.98	1.52

Growth Measures	%	Rel Category
Long-Term Erngs	12.03	0.95
Book Value	3.57	0.43
Sales	4.85	0.54
Cash Flow	-5.69	NMF
Historical Erngs	5.58	0.31

Profitability	%	Rel Category
Return on Equity	13.45	0.84
Return on Assets	6.76	0.84
Net Margin	9.21	0.85

Sector Weightings	% of Stocks	Rel S&P 500	3 Year High Low	
↻ Info	17.71	0.89		
Software	0.00	0.00	6	0
Hardware	13.59	1.47	18	7
Media	1.87	0.49	9	2
Telecom	2.25	0.64	2	0
☞ Service	50.52	1.09		
Health	10.80	0.90	19	4
Consumer	9.76	1.28	11	7
Business	8.42	1.99	14	8
Financial	21.54	0.97	22	8
Mfg	31.77	0.94		
Goods	13.42	1.57	15	6
Ind Mtrls	8.32	0.70	15	7
Energy	6.29	0.64	10	6
Utilities	3.74	1.07	4	0

Composition

● Cash	1.8
● Stocks	98.2
● Bonds	0.0
● Other	0.0
Foreign (% of Stock)	9.1

Metro West Low Dur M

	Ticker	Load	NAV	Yield	SEC Yield	Total Assets	Mstar Category
	MWLDX	None	$9.45	4.6%	4.64%	$1,500 mil	Short-Term Bond

Governance and Management

Stewardship Grade: A

Portfolio Manager(s)

The fund's management team, which includes Tad Rivelle, Laird Landmann, and Stephen Kane, has put up good numbers here since the fund's inception in 1997. Prior to founding Metropolitan West, the team had a strong record with Hotchkis and Wiley in the mid-1990s. David Lippman joined the group in 2001.

Strategy

Managers Tad Rivelle, Laird Landmann, Stephen Kane, and David Lippman don't typically make big macroeconomic bets but instead try to boost returns by identifying undervalued corners of the bond market. The fund's duration is kept within one year of the Merrill Lynch 1-3 Year U.S. Treasury Index's. The fund typically takes on more issue-specific and credit risk than its average category peer, although its limit on new purchases has been reduced to 2.5% of assets.

Performance 12-31-06

	1st Qtr	2nd Qtr	3rd Qtr	4th Qtr	Total
2002	0.33	-2.43	-0.92	2.70	-0.39
2003	0.83	2.78	0.85	1.38	5.95
2004	1.64	-1.24	1.41	1.45	3.28
2005	0.40	0.96	0.65	0.68	2.72
2006	1.04	0.83	2.08	2.10	6.19

Trailing	Total Return%	+/- LB Aggr	+/- LB 1-5 YR	%Rank Cat	Growth of $10,000
3 Mo	2.10	0.86	1.09	3	10,210
6 Mo	4.23	-0.86	0.69	8	10,423
1 Yr	6.19	1.86	1.97	2	10,619
3 Yr Avg	4.05	0.35	1.56	3	11,265
5 Yr Avg	3.52	-1.54	-0.25	27	11,888
10 Yr Avg	—	—	—	—	—
15 Yr Avg	—	—	—	—	—

Tax Analysis	Tax-Adj Rtn%	%Rank Cat	Tax-Cost Rat	%Rank Cat
3 Yr (estimated)	2.55	3	1.44	75
5 Yr (estimated)	1.85	40	1.61	82
10 Yr (estimated)	—	—	—	—

Potential Capital Gain Exposure: -2% of assets

Morningstar's Take by Paul Herbert 12-28-06

This fund just keeps on rolling.

At this late stage of 2006, it's looking like Metropolitan West Low Duration will deliver a return that ranks in the short-term bond category's best 5% for the fourth straight calendar year. Its success this year has sprung from several sources. Unlike some rivals, management has the flexibility to invest a portion of the fund's assets in corporate bonds rated below BBB. Stakes in short-term paper from GMAC and Ford Motor Credit, which were downgraded to junk status in 2005, have helped the fund's lot, as these bonds have notched heady gains this year. Plus, positions in mortgage- and asset-backed securities rated AAA have added to the fund's yield. Finally, a one-time settlement payment relating to the fund's former position in Worldcom debt gave it a boost. In all, the fund has returned 6.26% for the year to date through Dec. 27.

Investors shouldn't expect the fund to put up annual gains that large every year. Management

doesn't think valuations for lower-quality bonds, either for corporate debt or for asset-backed securities, correctly reflect their risks. Therefore it has been favoring higher-quality bonds across the board, and taking other defensive measures such as diversifying the fund across more names. As a result, the fund's results could be less outstanding on an absolute basis going forward.

Some other features should allow the fund to make rivals envious, though. Its management team has a solid long-term track record, which led us to recognize it as our Fixed-Income Fund Manager of the Year in 2005. Plus, while the fund has grown in recent years, it has retained a number of distinctive and misunderstood holdings that should help it along. A final built-in edge is that management's expense hurdle is just 0.58% of assets.

Its past history shows that this fund isn't a shrinking violet, so those who prize stability over all else may want to look elsewhere. For others, though, this fund has plenty of appeal.

Address:	11766 Wilshire Blvd Los Angeles CA 90025 800-241-4671
Web Address:	www.mwamllc.com
Inception:	03-31-97 *
Advisor:	Metropolitan West Attest Mangement LLC
Subadvisor:	None
NTF Plans:	Fidelity Retail-NTF, Schwab OneSource

Minimum Purchase:	$5000	Add: $0	IRA: $1000
Min Auto Inv Plan:	$100	Add: $100	
Sales Fees:	No-load, 0.19%S		
Management Fee:	0.30%		
Actual Fees:	Mgt:0.30%	Dist:0.19%	
Expense Projections:	3Yr:$190	5Yr:$333	10Yr:$748
Income Distrib:	Monthly		

Historical Profile

Return	Above Avg	
Risk	Above Avg	
Rating	★★★★ Above Avg	

Investment Style	Fixed Income Income Rtn %Rank Cat

▼ Manager Change
▽ Partial Manager Change

Growth of $10,000

— Investment Values of Fund
— Investment Values of LB Aggr

Performance Quartile (within Category)

1995	1996	1997	1998	1999	2000	2001	2002	2003	2004	2005	2006	History
—	—	10.17	10.16	10.02	9.91	9.98	9.41	9.50	9.43	9.32	9.45	NAV
—	—	6.83*	6.64	6.23	7.32	7.60	-0.39	5.95	3.28	2.72	6.19	Total Return %
—	—	—	-2.05	7.05	-4.31	-0.84	-10.64	1.85	-1.06	0.29	1.86	+/-LB Aggr
—	—	—	-0.99	4.14	-1.59	-1.43	-8.51	2.60	1.43	1.28	1.97	+/-LB 1-5 YR
—	—	—	6.65	7.19	8.43	6.94	5.41	4.96	4.02	3.91	4.74	Income Return %
—	—	—	-0.01	-0.96	-1.11	0.66	-5.80	0.99	-0.74	-1.19	1.45	Capital Return %
—	—	—	38	1	64	46	99	4	7	4	2	Total Rtn % Rank Cat
—	—	0.49	0.66	0.71	0.81	0.67	0.53	0.46	0.37	0.36	0.43	Income $
—	—	0.01	0.01	0.05	0.00	0.00	0.00	0.00	0.00	0.00	0.00	Capital Gains $
—	—	—	0.58	0.58	0.58	0.58	0.58	0.58	0.58	0.58	0.58	Expense Ratio %
—	—	—	6.72	6.61	7.22	8.08	6.21	5.40	4.47	3.75	4.01	Income Ratio %
—	—	—	73	126	53	26	65	94	108	96		Turnover Rate %
—	—	78	210	338	140	333	327	320	325	327	813	Net Assets $mil

Rating and Risk

Time Period	Load-Adj Return %	Morningstar Rtn vs Cat	Morningstar Risk vs Cat	Morningstar Risk-Adj Rating
1 Yr	6.19			
3 Yr	4.05	High	Avg	★★★★★
5 Yr	3.52	+Avg	+Avg	★★★★
10 Yr	—			
Incept	5.34			

Other Measures	Standard Index LB Aggr	Best Fit Index LB. U.S. Univ. Bd
Alpha	0.7	0.5
Beta	0.26	0.27
R-Squared	38	42
Standard Deviation	1.41	
Mean	4.05	
Sharpe Ratio	0.57	

Portfolio Analysis 06-30-06

Total Fixed-Income:175	Date of Maturity	Amount $000	Value $000	% Net Assets
US Treasury Note 3.125%	09-15-08	114,898	111,149	11.08
Gecc Cp 07/13/06	07-14-10	23,225	23,183	2.31
FNMA CMO 4%	02-25-10	20,740	14,738	1.47
Residential Asset Sec 20	05-25-32	23,414	13,600	1.36
Gmac FRN	12-01-14	12,798	12,500	1.25
Terwin Mtg Tr 2006-4sl F	03-26-41	12,500	12,123	1.21
Terwin Mtg Tr 4.75%	12-26-36	12,100	11,767	1.17
Chase Mortgage Fin Tr 20	12-25-35	12,175	11,474	1.14
Nomura Asset Alt Ln 2006	01-25-36	14,000	11,329	1.13
First Franklin Mtg 2005-	03-25-35	11,038	11,062	1.10
FHLBA 4.25%	09-26-08	10,910	10,759	1.07
Ford Motor Cr 144A FRN	06-15-11	10,541	10,669	1.06
FNMA FRN	07-01-34	19,072	10,587	1.06
Cwheq Revolving Heq 2005	02-15-36	14,000	10,465	1.04
FHLMC FRN	05-01-34	17,500	10,352	1.03
FNMA FRN	12-01-35	11,350	10,200	1.00
FHLBA 4.375%	10-03-08	9,850	9,730	0.97
FHLMC FRN	08-01-34	17,561	9,605	0.96
Hm Equity Mtg Tr 2006-1	05-25-36	11,750	9,580	0.96
Keycorp Instl Cap B 8.25	12-15-26	9,000	9,473	0.94

Current Investment Style

Duration: Short Int Long
Quality: High Med Low

1 figure provided by fund

Avg Eff Duration[1]	1.8 Yrs
Avg Eff Maturity	2.6 Yrs
Avg Credit Quality	AA
Avg Wtd Coupon	4.12%
Avg Wtd Price	82.33% of par

Coupon Range	% of Bonds	Rel Cat
0% PIK	18.6	2.1
0% to 6%	78.6	1.0
6% to 8%	11.7	0.7
8% to 10%	8.6	3.7
More than 10%	1.1	2.3

1.00=Category Average

Credit Analysis	% bonds 06-30-06		
AAA	59	BB	6
AA	15	B	1
A	11	Below B	0
BBB	8	NR/NA	0

Sector Breakdown	% of assets
US Treasuries	11
TIPS	0
US Agency	6
Mortgage Pass-Throughs	10
Mortgage CMO	14
Mortgage ARM	0
US Corporate	23
Asset-Backed	20
Convertible	0
Municipal	0
Corporate Inflation-Protected	0
Foreign Corporate	0
Foreign Govt	0

Composition			
Cash	16.1	Bonds	83.5
Stocks	0.0	Other	0.4

Special Securities	
Restricted/Illiquid Secs	9
Exotic Mortgage-Backed	0
Emerging-Markets Secs	0
Options/Futures/Warrants	No

MORNINGSTAR® Funds 500

Metro West Total Ret

Analyst Pick ✓

	Ticker	Load	NAV	Yield	SEC Yield	Total Assets	Mstar Category
	MWTRX	None	$9.73	5.0%	4.94%	$2,123 mil	Intermediate-Term Bond

Governance and Management

Stewardship Grade: B

Portfolio Manager(s)

The fund's management team of Stephen Kane, Laird Landmann, and Tad Rivelle delivered solid returns at Hotchkis & Wiley and PIMCO before starting this fund in 1997. David Lippman joined the team in 2001. The team has also had success with Metropolitan West Low Duration Bond, which follows a similar approach to this fund but carries less interest-rate risk.

Strategy

This fund attempts to outperform its peers through duration bets, yield-curve adjustments, sector rotation, and issue selection. Management argues that there are issue- and sector-level inefficiencies in the bond market because information is not always widely disseminated. In recent years, that has meant above-average stakes in corporate bonds and asset-backed securities. Management is not shy about holding large positions or taking on credit risk, although the fund follows a policy of putting no more than 2.5% of assets in a single purchase.

Historical Profile

Return	Above Avg
Risk	Above Avg
Rating	★★★★ Above Avg

Investment Style: Fixed Income — Income Rtn %Rank Cat

▼ Manager Change
▽ Partial Manager Change

Growth of $10,000
— Investment Values of Fund
— Investment Values of LB Aggr

Performance Quartile (within Category)

	1995	1996	1997	1998	1999	2000	2001	2002	2003	2004	2005	2006	History
NAV	—	—	10.51	10.65	10.05	10.11	10.15	9.30	9.92	9.82	9.57	9.73	
Total Return %	—	—	11.88*	9.96	1.72	10.18	9.18	-0.95	13.88	5.15	3.10	7.03	
+/-LB Aggr	—	—		1.27	2.54	-1.45	0.74	-11.20	9.78	0.81	0.67	2.70	
+/-LB 5-10YR	—	—		-0.18	4.60	-2.26	0.36	-13.98	7.91	-0.15	1.27	3.22	
Income Return %	—	—		7.10	7.42	9.48	7.81	7.17	6.96	6.15	5.73	5.25	
Capital Return %	—	—		2.86	-5.70	0.70	1.37	-8.12	6.92	-1.00	-2.63	1.78	
Total Rtn % Rank Cat	—	—		2	4	50	13	99	2	14	4	3	
Income $	—	—	0.54	0.72	0.76	0.91	0.76	0.70	0.63	0.59	0.55	0.49	
Capital Gains $	—	—	0.11	0.15	0.01	0.00	0.10	0.04	0.00	0.00	0.00	0.00	
Expense Ratio %	—	—		0.65	0.65	0.65	0.65	0.65	0.65	0.65	0.65	0.65	
Income Ratio %	—	—		7.39	6.92	7.68	9.16	7.14	7.40	5.62	6.02	5.49	
Turnover Rate %	—	—		—	136	128	205	78	90	165	180	174	
Net Assets $mil	—	—	15	83	187	278	621	568	483	453	503	882	

Performance 12-31-06

	1st Qtr	2nd Qtr	3rd Qtr	4th Qtr	Total
2002	-0.21	-2.82	-2.30	4.54	-0.95
2003	1.66	6.49	1.77	3.36	13.88
2004	2.80	-2.68	2.81	2.23	5.15
2005	0.13	2.44	0.28	0.23	3.10
2006	0.07	0.36	3.67	2.80	7.03

Trailing	Total Return%	+/- LB Aggr	+/- LB 5-10YR	%Rank Cat	Growth of $10,000
3 Mo	2.80	1.56	1.72	3	10,280
6 Mo	6.57	1.48	0.89	5	10,657
1 Yr	7.03	2.70	3.22	3	10,703
3 Yr Avg	5.08	1.38	1.44	3	11,603
5 Yr Avg	5.53	0.47	-0.39	13	13,088
10 Yr Avg	—	—	—	—	—
15 Yr Avg	—	—	—	—	—

Tax Analysis	Tax-Adj Rtn%	%Rank Cat	Tax-Cost Rat	%Rank Cat
3 Yr (estimated)	3.04	4	1.94	83
5 Yr (estimated)	3.21	26	2.20	89
10 Yr (estimated)	—	—	—	—

Potential Capital Gain Exposure: -4% of assets

Morningstar's Take by Eric Jacobson 12-07-06

Metropolitan West Total Return Bond is like a Dachshund whose knifelike teeth allow it to scrap with Pit Bulls.

The practice of bond investing has evolved over the past 20 years, making it increasingly difficult for small managers. The explosion of complex derivatives, mortgage- and asset-backed structures, to name a few, has meant that those hoping to compete have had to invest millions of dollars in managerial expertise, information gathering, and analysis. Although numerous mid- and smaller sized firms remain in business, the most successful have carved a niche or two in which to specialize so that they can remain competitive. By contrast, large sums invested across multiple sectors have gravitated to a handful of giant firms such as PIMCO, BlackRock, and Western Asset Management, which employ hundreds of professionals across numerous specialties.

Met West never got the memo. Its founders grew up at PIMCO and planned their business to cover the breadth of taxable bonds. From early days, meanwhile, they've employed more analysts and managers than most peers their size. Even after an unprecedented market tumble among investment-grade credits left the firm smarting in 2002, Met West continued to expand, adding to its expertise in high yield.

Today, the firm has a modest $18 billion under management, and boasts depth and expertise across sectors with an investment staff of 25. That mix means that each contribution has the potential for meaningful impact on returns, and this fund's results are proof of concept. Over the past few years, portfolio-level interest-rate and maturity calls, mortgages, asset-backeds and corporates have all taken turns as the main drivers of success during given periods. The fund's recent returns are topnotch, and despite the 2002 trouble, its long-term gains have been stellar.

Those factors help explain why we named the fund's skippers Manager of the Year in 2005.

Address:	11766 Wilshire Blvd Los Angeles CA 90025 800-241-4671
Web Address:	www.mwamllc.com
Inception:	03-31-97 *
Advisor:	Metropolitan West Attest Mangement LLC
Subadvisor:	None
NTF Plans:	Fidelity Retail-NTF, Schwab OneSource

Minimum Purchase:	$5000	Add: $0	IRA: $1000
Min Auto Inv Plan:	$100	Add: $100	
Sales Fees:	No-load, 0.21%S		
Management Fee:	0.35%		
Actual Fees:	Mgt:0.35%	Dist:0.21%	
Expense Projections:	3Yr:$212	5Yr:$371	10Yr:$833
Income Distrib:	Monthly		

Rating and Risk

Time Period	Load-Adj Return %	Morningstar Rtn vs Cat	Morningstar Risk vs Cat	Morningstar Risk-Adj Rating
1 Yr	7.03			
3 Yr	5.08	High	-Avg	★★★★★
5 Yr	5.53	+Avg	High	★★★★
10 Yr	—			
Incept	7.20			

Other Measures	Standard Index LB Aggr	Best Fit Index LB. U.S. Univ. Bd
Alpha	1.4	1.0
Beta	0.75	0.79
R-Squared	75	79
Standard Deviation	2.87	
Mean	5.08	
Sharpe Ratio	0.63	

Portfolio Analysis 06-30-06

Total Fixed-Income:206	Date of Maturity	Amount $000	Value $000	% Net Assets
US Treasury Note 4.875%	04-30-11	276,128	273,399	16.37
U S Treas Nt Stripped Pr	08-15-09	98,140	83,833	5.02
US Treasury Bond 6.125%	11-15-27	68,676	75,903	4.54
US Treasury Note 4.875%	02-15-12	73,995	73,209	4.38
US Treasury Note 4.25%	11-15-14	71,622	67,381	4.03
Adjustable Rate Mtg 2005	11-25-35	25,925	23,708	1.42
FNMA 4.5%	07-26-40	25,740	23,327	1.40
Jp Morgan Mtg Tr 2006-A3	05-25-36	23,500	23,111	1.38
Gmac FRN	12-01-14	22,996	22,318	1.34
Terwin Mtg Tr 2006-4sl F	10-02-14	23,030	22,249	1.33
US Treasury Bond 8.125%	08-15-19	17,125	21,686	1.30
Abs FRN	08-15-33	21,415	21,618	1.29
Ford Motor Cr 7%	10-01-13	22,370	19,279	1.15
FHLMC FRN	05-01-34	31,644	19,002	1.14
Cwheq Revolving Heq 2005	02-15-36	25,000	18,644	1.12
FNMA 5.5%	02-01-34	25,153	17,493	1.05
Citigroup Mtg Ln Tr FRN	05-25-34	19,094	17,249	1.03
Chase Mortgage Fin Tr 20	12-25-35	18,315	17,180	1.03
FNMA 6%	03-01-33	19,871	17,158	1.03
Cwalt CMO	08-25-35	19,720	17,119	1.02

Current Investment Style

Duration: Short Int Long — (Int / High Quality selected)
Quality: High Med Low

1 figure provided by fund

Avg Eff Duration [1]	4.7 Yrs
Avg Eff Maturity	6.5 Yrs
Avg Credit Quality	AA
Avg Wtd Coupon	5.12%
Avg Wtd Price	89.37% of par

Coupon Range	% of Bonds	Rel Cat
0% PIK	11.8	1.7
0% to 6%	67.9	0.9
6% to 8%	21.6	1.0
8% to 10%	8.4	1.8
More than 10%	2.1	3.0

1.00=Category Average

Credit Analysis	% bonds 06-30-06		
AAA	68	BB	5
AA	5	B	4
A	7	Below B	1
BBB	9	NR/NA	0

Sector Breakdown	% of assets
US Treasuries	32
TIPS	0
US Agency	5
Mortgage Pass-Throughs	12
Mortgage CMO	15
Mortgage ARM	0
US Corporate	18
Asset-Backed	14
Convertible	0
Municipal	0
Corporate Inflation-Protected	0
Foreign Corporate	0
Foreign Govt	1

Composition			
Cash	4.0	Bonds	93.8
Stocks	0.0	Other	2.2

Special Securities	
Restricted/Illiquid Secs	8
Exotic Mortgage-Backed	1
Emerging-Markets Secs	0
Options/Futures/Warrants	No

MFS Total Return A

	Ticker	Load	NAV	Yield	Total Assets	Mstar Category
	MSFRX	5.75%	$16.18	2.4%	$11,560 mil	Moderate Allocation

Governance and Management

Stewardship Grade: C

Portfolio Manager(s)

Brooks Taylor took over as lead manager on Jan. 1, 2005, relieving David Calabro, who had been on board here since 1995 and retired from MFS at the end of February 2005. Taylor had been running Calabro's sleeve of this offering since February 2004. Beyond Taylor, there are five other equity managers, several of whom are very experienced, picking value stocks for the fund. Michael Roberge took the reins of the fund's fixed-income subportfolio in 2002 and is assisted by Bill Douglas and Richard Hawkins, who joined the fund in October 2005.

Strategy

This fund maintains a 60/40 mix between stocks and bonds. The equity portion is made up of value stocks selling at discounts to the S&P 500 or to industry peers. The bond portfolio generally has a strong bias toward investment-grade corporate issues and largely eschews big duration and credit plays. Overall, this is a plain-vanilla balanced fund.

Historical Profile

Return	Average
Risk	Low
Rating	★★★ Neutral

Investment Style: Equity, Stock %

47% 55% 58% 55% 50% 58% 59% 59% 60%

▼ Manager Change
▽ Partial Manager Change

Growth of $10,000
— Investment Values of Fund
— Investment Values of DJ Mod

30.8
26.8
22.0
18.0
14.0
10.0

Performance Quartile (within Category)

	1995	1996	1997	1998	1999	2000	2001	2002	2003	2004	2005	2006	History
NAV	14.41	14.79	15.82	14.96	13.88	15.41	14.48	13.27	15.10	16.00	15.37	16.18	NAV
Total Return %	26.91	14.61	20.67	11.92	2.31	19.03	-0.63	-5.56	16.85	11.37	3.29	11.56	Total Return %
+/-DJ Mod	7.11	3.95	8.77	-0.40	-15.02	20.70	2.17	1.21	-10.53	-1.60	-3.70	-0.74	+/-DJ Mod
+/-DJ US Mod	2.14	3.27	1.47	-0.47	-10.54	14.59	-0.79	4.98	-7.21	0.20	-2.71	1.29	+/-DJ US Mod
Income Return %	5.21	4.38	4.10	3.88	3.25	3.49	3.13	2.91	2.79	2.61	2.73	2.68	Income Return %
Capital Return %	21.70	10.23	16.57	8.04	-0.94	15.54	-3.76	-8.47	14.06	8.76	0.56	8.88	Capital Return %
Total Rtn % Rank Cat	43	49	41	60	87	3	18	6	82	15	78	40	Total Rtn % Rank Cat
Income $	0.63	0.62	0.59	0.60	0.48	0.47	0.47	0.42	0.37	0.39	0.43	0.41	Income $
Capital Gains $	0.66	1.06	1.37	2.07	0.94	0.55	0.35	0.00	0.00	0.39	0.71	0.54	Capital Gains $
Expense Ratio %	0.87	0.91	0.93	0.90	0.89	0.90	0.88	0.92	0.90	0.89	0.91	0.90	Expense Ratio %
Income Ratio %	4.82	4.35	3.84	3.44	3.45	3.36	3.09	2.84	2.45	2.37	2.43	2.56	Income Ratio %
Turnover Rate %	102	140	143	126	151	112	96	86	71	65	50	48	Turnover Rate %
Net Assets $mil	2,356	2,707	3,263	3,811	3,629	3,795	4,541	4,772	6,205	6,845	7,282	7,337	Net Assets $mil

Performance 12-31-06

	1st Qtr	2nd Qtr	3rd Qtr	4th Qtr	Total
2002	2.48	-4.06	-8.20	4.62	-5.56
2003	-2.55	10.21	1.18	7.52	16.85
2004	2.38	0.16	1.48	7.02	11.37
2005	-0.74	1.74	1.52	0.75	3.29
2006	2.36	-0.56	4.49	4.88	11.56

Trailing	Total Return%	+/- DJ Mod	+/- DJ US Mod	%Rank Cat	Growth of $10,000
3 Mo	4.88	-0.71	0.21	56	10,488
6 Mo	9.60	0.81	1.70	29	10,960
1 Yr	11.56	-0.74	1.29	40	11,156
3 Yr Avg	8.67	-2.05	-0.45	39	12,833
5 Yr Avg	7.21	-2.81	-0.39	22	14,164
10 Yr Avg	8.75	0.20	0.16	15	23,136
15 Yr Avg	9.96	0.75	0.57	29	41,545

Tax Analysis	Tax-Adj Rtn%	%Rank Cat	Tax-Cost Rat	%Rank Cat
3 Yr (estimated)	4.99	83	1.46	74
5 Yr (estimated)	4.58	58	1.28	79
10 Yr (estimated)	5.82	34	2.12	87

Potential Capital Gain Exposure: 13% of assets

Rating and Risk

Time Period	Load-Adj Return %	Morningstar Rtn vs Cat	Morningstar Risk vs Cat	Morningstar Risk-Adj Rating
1 Yr	5.14			
3 Yr	6.55	-Avg	Low	★★
5 Yr	5.94	Avg	-Avg	★★★
10 Yr	8.11	+Avg	Low	★★★★
Incept	10.86			

Other Measures	Standard Index	Best Fit Index
	DJ Mod	Russ 1000 Vl
Alpha	0.4	-1.4
Beta	0.66	0.59
R-Squared	83	86
Standard Deviation	4.31	
Mean	8.67	
Sharpe Ratio	1.21	

Portfolio Analysis 10-31-06

Total Stocks:206 Share change since 09-30-06	Sectors	P/E Ratio	YTD Return %	% Net Assets
⊖ Bank of America Corporati	Financial	12.4	0.11	2.34
⊖ Altria Group, Inc.	Goods	16.3	2.52	1.69
⊖ ExxonMobil Corporation	Energy	11.1	-5.19	1.54
⊕ Citigroup, Inc.	Financial	13.1	-1.17	1.31
⊖ J.P. Morgan Chase & Co.	Financial	13.6	-0.02	1.27
⊖ FPL Group	Utilities	17.7	-0.29	1.21
⊖ Johnson & Johnson	Health	17.5	0.74	1.21
Mellon Financial Corporat	Financial	20.4	0.64	1.14
⊕ Lockheed Martin Corporati	Ind Mtrls	17.3	1.76	1.09

Total Fixed-Income:583	Date of Maturity	Amount $000	Value $000	% Net Assets
US Treasury Note 5.625%	05-15-08	262,276	272,452	2.37
US Treasury Note 4.75%	11-15-08	154,763	158,328	1.38
US Treasury Bond 6%	02-15-26	116,011	134,616	1.17
US Treasury Note 6.5%	02-15-10	96,429	103,272	0.90
US Treasury Note 5%	02-15-11	90,600	93,199	0.81
US Treasury Bond 5.375%	02-15-31	77,449	84,969	0.74
US Treasury Note 4.25%	01-15-10	43,028	45,714	0.40
US Treasury Note 2%	01-15-14	46,080	45,184	0.39
US Treasury Note 4.25%	11-15-13	35,234	35,225	0.31

Equity Style
Style: Value
Size: Large-Cap

Value Measures		Rel Category
Price/Earnings	13.97	0.91
Price/Book	2.29	0.93
Price/Sales	1.30	0.95
Price/Cash Flow	6.43	0.79
Dividend Yield %	2.15	1.11

Growth Measures	%	Rel Category
Long-Term Erngs	10.65	0.91
Book Value	5.55	0.64
Sales	7.67	0.86
Cash Flow	4.06	0.41
Historical Erngs	17.91	1.00

Market Cap %			
Giant	39.3	Small	1.1
Large	42.1	Micro	0.0
Mid	17.5	Avg $mil:	33,782

Fixed-Income Style
Duration: Interm-Term
Quality: High

Avg Eff Duration [1]	4.7 Yrs
Avg Eff Maturity	16.8 Yrs
Avg Credit Quality	AA
Avg Wtd Coupon	5.58%

[1]figure provided by fund as of 10-31-06

Sector Weightings	% of Stocks	Rel DJ Mod	3 Year High Low	
⟳ Info	11.84			
Software	1.95	—	4	2
Hardware	3.07	—	5	2
Media	2.71	—	7	2
Telecom	4.11	—	8	4
☞ Service	46.01			
Health	8.96	—	11	8
Consumer	3.79	—	5	2
Business	2.74	—	3	2
Financial	30.52	—	31	26
⊐ Mfg	42.14			
Goods	8.81	—	9	7
Ind Mtrls	17.26	—	18	14
Energy	10.17	—	13	10
Utilities	5.90	—	6	4

Composition

● Cash	1.8	
● Stocks	60.3	
● Bonds	37.7	
● Other	0.2	
	Foreign	6.2
	(% of Stock)	

Morningstar's Take by Laura Pavlenko Lutton 12-21-06

Some subtle shifts in personnel and strategy don't alter MFS Total Return's main pros and cons.

This team-managed moderate-allocation offering has gone through more than a half-dozen management changes since year-end 2003. The latest changes were the May 2006 addition of Nevin Chitkara, a former analyst and new comanager of MFS Value, and the June 2006 arrival of Jonathan Sage. Sage replaced veteran Constantinos Mokas, who left MFS after a string of poor returns in the mid-cap portfolio he managed.

This management shuffle has resulted in a few changes to the fund's strategy. For one, the tiny convertibles portfolio that Mokas ran has been liquidated because it didn't meaningfully diversify this hybrid portfolio. Also, Sage is using a mostly quantitative-based strategy to choose mid-cap stocks for the portfolio. (Mokas based his picks on fundamental research.)

None of these recent changes--management or strategy--significantly impact our outlook on this offering. To be sure, we wish the management team was more stable, and that the strategy was so sound that it didn't need tweaking on the margin. But this fund's fate still rests squarely on the shoulders of some experienced investors, namely Steve Gorham, Ken Enright, and MFS' fixed-income managers, led here by Mike Roberge. Their focus on plain-vanilla large-value stocks and high-quality bonds has led to strong relative and absolute returns in recent years, when both of these emphases were favored by the market. Other pluses include this fund's higher yield, which helps smooth returns, and its relatively low 0.91% expense ratio.

In all, this fund has been reasonably successful, but we'd point out that it probably won't look so hot when growth stocks outpace value or when riskier bonds are in style. But those comfortable with this fund's market risk have found a decent offering.

Address:	500 Boylston St Boston MA 02116 800-225-2606	Minimum Purchase:	$1000 Add: $0 IRA: $250
		Min Auto Inv Plan:	$50 Add: $50
		Sales Fees:	5.75%L, 0.35%S
Web Address:	www.mfs.com	Management Fee:	0.35% mx./0.34% mn.
Inception:	10-06-70	Actual Fees:	Mgt:0.34% Dist:0.35%
Advisor:	MFS Investment Management	Expense Projections:	3Yr:$848 5Yr:$1050 10Yr:$1630
Subadvisor:	None	Income Distrib:	Monthly
NTF Plans:	DATALynx NTF, Federated Tr NTF		

Morningstar® Funds 500

Morgan Stan Ins US R/E A

	Analyst Pick	Ticker	Load	NAV	Yield	Total Assets	Mstar Category
		MSUSX	None	$28.23	1.5%	$1,904 mil	Specialty-Real Estate

Governance and Management

Stewardship Grade:

Portfolio Manager(s)

Manager Ted Bigman has been managing REIT money since the mid-1980s. Former comanager Doug Funke, who had comanaged the fund since 1999, left the firm in mid-2004. Bigman also runs Morgan Stanley Real Estate using an identical strategy.

Strategy

This fund targets companies that trade at discounts to the managers' assessment of underlying asset values. Management is willing to load up in specific subsectors when it uncovers large discrepancies between stock prices and intrinsic values. The fund generally focuses on the largest, most-liquid REITs and on residential, retail, and commercial properties. The fund tends to emphasize offices and apartments while carrying minimal exposure to smaller subsectors such as health care.

Performance 12-31-06

	1st Qtr	2nd Qtr	3rd Qtr	4th Qtr	Total
2002	7.79	2.78	-10.05	0.53	0.18
2003	0.96	13.07	11.11	8.49	37.61
2004	11.55	-4.11	9.16	17.56	37.28
2005	-5.56	14.76	3.90	4.49	17.66
2006	14.35	0.76	8.70	10.87	38.85

Trailing	Total Return%	+/- S&P 500	+/- DJ Wilshire REIT	%Rank Cat	Growth of $10,000
3 Mo	10.87	4.17	1.90	22	11,087
6 Mo	20.51	7.77	1.51	18	12,051
1 Yr	38.85	23.06	2.72	10	13,885
3 Yr Avg	30.90	20.46	3.53	2	22,429
5 Yr Avg	25.33	19.14	1.49	17	30,923
10 Yr Avg	17.06	8.64	1.77	3	48,315
15 Yr Avg	—	—	—		

Tax Analysis	Tax-Adj Rtn%	%Rank Cat	Tax-Cost Rat	%Rank Cat
3 Yr (estimated)	28.03	5	2.19	50
5 Yr (estimated)	22.81	18	2.01	57
10 Yr (estimated)	14.18	7	2.46	84

Potential Capital Gain Exposure: 43% of assets

Morningstar's Take by John Coumarianos 12-28-06

We like Morgan Stanley Institutional U.S. Real Estate's focus on quality, but real estate's best days may be behind it.

This fund is having another banner year in 2006, as its year-to-date record sits in the top decile of the real estate category. More importantly, its three-, five-, and 10-year returns are equally impressive.

Veteran manager Ted Bigman owes much of this success to his strict value investment process. He prefers an asset approach to valuation, though to calculate net asset value, Bigman incorporates some forecasts of a business's future cash flows. Still, the manager and his team of six analysts are not anxious to stretch their ability to predict cash-flow growth far into the future.

This approach has translated into an emphasis on high-quality properties. Prominent holdings include Brookfield Properties and Boston Properties, both of which own office buildings in cities with constrained supply such as New York and Boston.

Also, high-end apartment owner AvalonBay Communities is a top pick.

Additionally, Bigman's bet on hotels, such as Starwood Hotels & Resorts Worldwide, Host Hotels & Resorts, and Hilton Hotels, have panned out nicely in 2006's second half after a slow start. Bigman has believed that these stocks have been trading below their replacement cost, and he sees little supply in the near future, especially given high construction costs and the lack of available prime locations. Although Starwood has been a favorite, Bigman increased the general hotel bet throughout 2005, illustrating his willingness to buy what's out of favor.

We think this fund's emphasis on quality should help it relative to its peers in the event of a downturn in real estate, but we caution investors to be mindful of the sector's multiyear run. Those who've had real estate exposure should consider trimming gains, while those who haven't should consider building it slowly instead of all at once.

Address:	1221 Avenue of the Americas New York NY 10020 800-548-7786	Minimum Purchase:	$500000	Add: $1000	IRA: $0
		Min Auto Inv Plan:	$0	Add: —	
		Sales Fees:	No-load, 2.00%R		
Web Address:	www.morganstanley.com/im	Management Fee:	0.80% mx./0.70% mn., 0.08%A		
Inception:	02-24-95*	Actual Fees:	Mgt:0.76%	Dist:—	
Advisor:	Morgan Stanley Investment Mgt Inc.	Expense Projections:	3Yr:$284	5Yr:$493	10Yr:$1096
Subadvisor:	None	Income Distrib:	Annually		
NTF Plans:	N/A				

Historical Profile

Return	High
Risk	Below Avg
Rating	★★★★ Highest

Investment Style: Equity / Stock %

	90%	89%	93%	92%	92%	96%	98%	99%	98%

▼ Manager Change
▽ Partial Manager Change

94.0
67.4
47.8

Growth of $10,000
— Investment Values of Fund
— Investment Values of S&P 500

33.8
24.0
17.0
10.0

Performance Quartile (within Category)

	1995	1996	1997	1998	1999	2000	2001	2002	2003	2004	2005	2006	History
NAV	11.42	14.41	15.38	12.71	11.84	14.50	14.63	13.55	17.92	23.21	23.41	28.23	
Total Return %	21.07*	39.56	27.62	-12.29	-1.48	29.65	9.27	0.18	37.61	37.28	17.66	38.85	
+/-S&P 500	16.60	-5.74	-40.87	-22.52	38.75	21.16	22.28	8.93	26.40	12.75	23.06		
+/-DJ Wilshire REIT	—	2.52	7.95	4.71	1.09	-1.39	-3.09	-3.42	1.55	4.14	3.66	2.72	
Income Return %		3.44	3.04	3.26	5.28	4.83	4.04	3.61	3.58	2.38	1.96	2.13	
Capital Return %		36.12	24.58	-15.55	-6.76	24.82	5.23	-3.43	34.03	34.90	15.70	36.72	
Total Rtn % Rank Cat	—	13	5	13	27	30	41	89	35	12	1	10	
Income $	0.24	0.39	0.43	0.49	0.66	0.56	0.57	0.52	0.48	0.42	0.44	0.49	
Capital Gains $	0.43	1.01	2.42	0.33	0.04	0.23	0.61	0.60	0.18	0.86	3.38	3.54	
Expense Ratio %	1.00	1.00	1.00	1.00	1.00	1.00	1.00	0.99	1.00	0.97	0.89	—	
Income Ratio %	4.04	3.08	2.72	3.33	6.52	4.13	4.19	3.49	3.08	2.02	1.87	—	
Turnover Rate %		171	135	117	47	31	33	47	17	21	33	—	
Net Assets $mil	69	210	361	259	311	585	662	—	897	1,103	1,209	1,636	

Rating and Risk

Time Period	Load-Adj Return %	Morningstar Rtn vs Cat	Morningstar Risk vs Cat	Morningstar Risk-Adj Rating
1 Yr	38.85			
3 Yr	30.90	High	-Avg	★★★★★
5 Yr	25.33	+Avg	-Avg	★★★★
10 Yr	17.06	High	-Avg	★★★★★
Incept	19.38			

Other Measures	Standard Index S&P 500	Best Fit Index DJ Wilshire REIT
Alpha	16.7	5.2
Beta	1.20	0.88
R-Squared	31	98
Standard Deviation	14.95	
Mean	30.90	
Sharpe Ratio	1.68	

Portfolio Analysis 09-30-06

Share change since 06-06 Total Stocks:50

	Sector	PE	Tot Ret%	% Assets
Simon Property Group, In	Financial	58.3	36.98	9.36
Starwood Hotels & Resort	Consumer	12.9	21.75	5.73
Boston Properties, Inc.	Financial	14.9	62.75	5.59
Host Hotels & Resorts, I	Financial	51.9	33.95	5.50
Equity Office Properties	Financial		64.28	4.78
Equity Residential	Financial	NMF	34.64	4.72
Public Storage, Inc.	Financial	46.2	47.46	4.70
Brookfield Properties Co	Financial	56.4	36.73	4.54
AvalonBay Communities, I	Financial	68.7	49.69	4.53
Hilton Hotels Corporatio	Consumer	29.9	45.62	3.82
Archstone-Smith Trust	Financial	59.0	43.93	3.77
Regency Centers Corporat	Financial	55.7	37.58	3.01
Vornado Realty Trust	Financial	37.1	51.14	2.85
Macerich Company	Financial	—	33.91	2.72
Essex Property Trust	Financial	NMF	44.29	2.53
Federal Realty Investmen	Financial	53.5	44.88	2.50
AMB Property Corporation	Financial	29.8	23.30	2.18
Mack-Cali Realty Corpora	Financial	34.0	24.56	2.02
Brandywine Realty Trust	Financial	—	24.09	1.88
General Growth Propertie	Financial		15.09	1.79

Current Investment Style

Value Blnd Growth — Large / Mid / Small

Market Cap	%
Giant	0.0
Large	56.3
Mid	36.0
Small	5.0
Micro	2.7
Avg $mil:	7,267

Value Measures		Rel Category
Price/Earnings	19.84	1.05
Price/Book	3.34	1.18
Price/Sales	3.88	0.93
Price/Cash Flow	17.88	1.16
Dividend Yield %	3.40	0.84

Growth Measures	%	Rel Category
Long-Term Erngs	7.63	0.99
Book Value	-3.44	NMF
Sales	5.13	0.47
Cash Flow	-9.76	NMF
Historical Erngs	5.39	0.38

Profitability	%	Rel Category
Return on Equity	12.13	1.05
Return on Assets	9.73	1.04
Net Margin	23.55	0.88

Sector Weightings	% of Stocks	Rel S&P 500	3 Year High	Low
Info	0.00	0.00		
Software	0.00	0.00	0	0
Hardware	0.00	0.00	0	0
Media	0.00	0.00	0	0
Telecom	0.00	0.00	0	0
Service	99.99	2.16		
Health	0.96	0.08	1	0
Consumer	11.77	1.54	12	7
Business	0.00	0.00	0	0
Financial	87.26	3.92	93	87
Mfg	0.00	0.00		
Goods	0.00	0.00	0	0
Ind Mtrls	0.00	0.00	0	0
Energy	0.00	0.00	0	0
Utilities	0.00	0.00	0	0

Composition

Cash	1.5	
Stocks	98.1	
Bonds	0.0	
Other	0.4	
Foreign	6.4	(% of Stock)

Muhlenkamp

	Ticker	Load	NAV	Yield	Total Assets	Mstar Category
	MUHLX	None	$87.15	0.8%	$2,883 mil	Large Value

Governance and Management

Stewardship Grade:

Portfolio Manager(s)

Ron Muhlenkamp founded Muhlenkamp & Co. in 1977 to manage private accounts for individuals and institutions. He launched this fund in 1988 and is backed by four research analysts.

Strategy

This fund's picks are derived from a combination of macroeconomic analysis and bottom-up individual stock assessment. Manager Ron Muhlenkamp will give the fund more or less cyclical exposure depending on his outlook for GDP growth, interest rates, and other top-down factors. Returns on equity and valuations drive the stock selection. The fund is managed in a low-turnover, tax-efficient manner.

Historical Profile
Return — Above Avg
Risk — High
Rating — ★★★ Neutral

	89%	97%	96%	97%	95%	94%	96%	99%	100%

Investment Style
Equity
Stock %

▼ Manager Change
▽ Partial Manager Change

Growth of $10,000
— Investment Values of Fund
— Investment Values of S&P 500

Performance Quartile (within Category)

1995	1996	1997	1998	1999	2000	2001	2002	2003	2004	2005	2006	History
21.26	27.52	36.55	37.65	41.11	48.98	53.56	42.89	63.51	78.97	84.44	87.15	NAV
32.96	29.98	33.30	3.22	11.40	25.30	9.35	-19.92	48.08	24.51	7.88	4.08	Total Return %
-4.62	7.02	-0.06	-25.36	-9.64	34.40	21.24	2.18	19.40	13.63	2.97	-11.71	+/-S&P 500
-5.40	8.34	-1.88	-12.41	4.05	18.29	14.94	-4.40	18.05	8.02	0.83	-18.17	+/-Russ 1000 VI
1.23	0.53	0.47	0.21	0.00	0.00	0.00	0.00	0.17	0.96	0.87		Income Return %
31.73	29.45	32.83	3.01	11.40	25.30	9.35	-19.92	48.08	24.34	6.92	3.21	Capital Return %
50	2	6	86	24	6	6	66	1	1	26	99	Total Rtn % Rank Cat
0.20	0.11	0.13	0.08	0.00	0.00	0.00	0.00	0.00	0.11	0.76	0.74	Income $
0.12	0.00	0.00	0.00	0.80	2.33	0.00	0.00	0.00	0.00	0.00		Capital Gains $
1.35	1.56	1.33	1.32	1.38	1.28	1.17	1.17	1.18	1.14	1.06	—	Expense Ratio %
1.10	0.58	0.53	0.21	-0.26	-0.20	-0.14	-0.10	-0.04	0.16	1.02	—	Income Ratio %
23	17	14	27	14	32	11	11	9	7	6	—	Turnover Rate %
24	42	125	195	177	266	539	601	1,157	1,985	3,083	2,883	Net Assets $mil

Performance 12-31-06

	1st Qtr	2nd Qtr	3rd Qtr	4th Qtr	Total
2002	6.16	-10.64	-21.53	7.57	-19.92
2003	-4.90	27.51	5.17	16.11	48.08
2004	5.57	0.21	1.59	15.85	24.51
2005	-2.57	6.19	3.79	0.47	7.88
2006	1.82	-5.47	-0.69	8.88	4.08

Trailing	Total Return%	+/- S&P 500	+/- Russ 1000 VI	%Rank Cat	Growth of $10,000
3 Mo	8.88	2.18	0.88	5	10,888
6 Mo	8.13	-4.61	-6.59	98	10,813
1 Yr	4.08	-11.71	-18.17	99	10,408
3 Yr Avg	11.82	1.38	-3.27	59	13,982
5 Yr Avg	10.64	4.45	-0.22	11	16,579
10 Yr Avg	13.29	4.87	2.29	2	34,827
15 Yr Avg	14.52	3.88	1.49	3	76,422

Tax Analysis	Tax-Adj Rtn%	%Rank Cat	Tax-Cost Rat	%Rank Cat
3 Yr (estimated)	11.57	33	0.22	9
5 Yr (estimated)	10.49	7	0.14	8
10 Yr (estimated)	13.03	1	0.23	1

Potential Capital Gain Exposure: 31% of assets

Rating and Risk

Time Period	Load-Adj Return %	Morningstar Rtn vs Cat	Morningstar Risk vs Cat	Morningstar Risk-Adj Rating
1 Yr	4.08			
3 Yr	11.82	Avg	High	★★
5 Yr	10.64	+Avg	High	★★★
10 Yr	13.29	High	High	★★★★
Incept	14.00			

Other Measures	Standard Index S&P 500	Best Fit Index Mstar Mid Value
Alpha	-1.6	-9.5
Beta	1.47	1.31
R-Squared	72	85
Standard Deviation	11.84	
Mean	11.82	
Sharpe Ratio	0.73	

Portfolio Analysis 09-30-06

Share change since 06-06 Total Stocks:63	Sector	PE	Tot Ret%	% Assets
⊕ Cemex SAB de CV ADR	Ind Mtrls	11.1	14.21	4.89
Allstate Corporation	Financial	8.7	23.38	4.81
Merrill Lynch & Company,	Financial	14.2	39.28	4.40
⊕ UnitedHealth Group, Inc.	Health	20.8	-13.49	4.13
⊕ Johnson & Johnson	Health	17.5	12.45	4.10
American International G	Financial	17.0	6.05	3.99
Capital One Financial Co	Financial	10.4	-10.97	3.95
Citigroup, Inc.	Financial	13.1	19.55	3.89
Countrywide Financial Co	Financial	9.8	26.22	3.86
ConocoPhillips	Energy	6.5	26.53	3.48
Anadarko Petroleum Corp.	Energy	5.2	-7.44	3.46
Altria Group, Inc.	Goods	16.3	19.87	3.34
Nabors Industries, Ltd.	Energy	9.0	-21.37	3.26
⊕ Caterpillar Inc.	Ind Mtrls	11.8	7.86	3.00
Devon Energy Corporation	Energy	9.2	8.06	2.92
Pfizer Inc.	Health	15.2	15.22	2.84
⊕ BHP Billiton, Ltd. ADR	Ind Mtrls	10.8	21.15	2.76
NVR, Inc.	Consumer	6.2	-8.12	2.68
⊖ Centex Corporation	Consumer	7.2	-21.06	2.47
Patterson-UTI Energy, In	Energy	5.7	-28.72	2.32

Current Investment Style

Value Blnd Growth — Large Mid Small

	Market Cap	%
	Giant	39.0
	Large	25.7
	Mid	26.5
	Small	7.8
	Micro	1.1
	Avg $mil:	21,347

Value Measures		Rel Category
Price/Earnings	9.65	0.70
Price/Book	1.94	0.87
Price/Sales	0.94	0.72
Price/Cash Flow	6.53	0.97
Dividend Yield %	1.57	0.67

Growth Measures	%	Rel Category
Long-Term Erngs	12.44	1.20
Book Value	16.12	2.04
Sales	17.33	1.93
Cash Flow	19.81	3.27
Historical Erngs	26.73	1.66

Profitability	%	Rel Category
Return on Equity	22.24	1.24
Return on Assets	13.15	1.34
Net Margin	14.64	1.13

Sector Weightings	% of Stocks	Rel S&P 500	3 Year High Low	
☎ Info	0.68	0.03		
Software	0.02	0.01	0	0
Hardware	0.41	0.04	5	0
Media	0.00	0.00	0	0
Telecom	0.25	0.07	4	0
☞ Service	54.12	1.17		
Health	11.18	0.93	11	4
Consumer	11.02	1.44	19	11
Business	1.95	0.46	3	2
Financial	29.97	1.35	30	26
⚒ Mfg	45.20	1.34		
Goods	8.19	0.96	12	8
Ind Mtrls	19.75	1.65	20	13
Energy	17.12	1.75	18	9
Utilities	0.14	0.04	3	0

Composition

● Cash	0.1	
● Stocks	99.9	
● Bonds	0.0	
○ Other	0.0	
Foreign	8.0	(% of Stock)

Morningstar's Take by Greg Carlson 12-28-06

It's gut-check time for shareholders of Muhlenkamp Fund.

This fund's risks came to the fore in a big way in 2006. Veteran manager Ron Muhlenkamp has long employed a bold strategy; he makes long-term calls on the direction of the economy and tilts the portfolio accordingly. He uses fundamental analysis to pick companies of all sizes, but they tend to cluster within a few preferred sectors. For much of the past five years, based on his call for solid economic growth, the fund has held hefty stakes in energy firms, mortgage lenders, and homebuilders--that approach paid off in spades, with the exception of 2002's selloff. Now, however, the fund has been hit hard by the same bet: Housing-related stocks such as NVR are still down for the year despite rebounding since July, and energy stocks tanked in the third quarter as the economy showed signs of cooling. All told, this offering has returned just 4.6% for the year to date through Dec. 27, 2006, making it one of the worst performers in the large-value category. (The fund recently moved to this group from mid-value.)

Despite the fund's struggles, however, Muhlenkamp isn't backing off--after their recent selloff, he now believes cyclical fare is cheap and that the economy will continue to grow rather than slipping into recession. If he's wrong, we'd expect more poor performance, at least over the short term. True, Muhlenkamp isn't betting the entire fund on this viewpoint. Over the past several years, he's added steadier, out-of-favor mega-caps to the portfolio such as drugmakers Johnson & Johnson and Pfizer, as well as troubled insurer American International Group. (These moves precipitated the fund's category change.) But the fund's fortunes still rest primarily with the direction of the economy.

We think there's plenty of reason to stay the course here--Muhlenkamp's reasoning is solid, and his long-term record is superb. But investors have to be patient to endure the fund's swoons.

Address:	5000 Stonewood, Suite 300 Wexford PA 15090 800-860-3863
Web Address:	www.muhlenkamp.com
Inception:	11-17-88
Advisor:	Muhlenkamp & CO Inc
Subadvisor:	None
NTF Plans:	Fidelity Retail-NTF, Schwab OneSource

Minimum Purchase:	$1500	Add: $50	IRA: $1500
Min Auto Inv Plan:	$200	Add: $50	
Sales Fees:	No-load, 2.00%R		
Management Fee:	1.00% mx./0.90% mn.		
Actual Fees:	Mgt:0.94%	Dist:—	
Expense Projections:	3Yr:$337	5Yr:$585	10Yr:$1294
Income Distrib:	Annually		

Morningstar® Funds 500

Mutual Beacon A

	Ticker	Load	NAV	Yield	Total Assets	Mstar Category
	TEBIX	5.75%	$16.61	1.3%	$7,132 mil	Large Value

Governance and Management

Stewardship Grade: C

Portfolio Manager(s)

Michael Embler took the reins in May 2005 after longtime manager David Winters left the firm. Embler led the distressed debt team at Mutual Series before taking over here and currently serves as the firm's CIO. He is joined by Chuck Lahr, who specializes in financial-services stocks and has been the assistant manager since January 2005.

Strategy

This fund tries to sniff out bargains among unloved and downtrodden companies. In addition to equity investments in traditional value areas, such as industrials and financials, it also buys distressed credits. Companies undergoing turnarounds and restructurings are common in the portfolio, and the managers will actively try to influence companies to improve their businesses. The fund often carries an ample cash cushion and invests a large portion of its portfolio in foreign securities.

Performance 12-31-06

	1st Qtr	2nd Qtr	3rd Qtr	4th Qtr	Total
2002	2.92	-5.85	-10.83	2.52	-11.41
2003	-3.11	14.21	3.72	12.38	28.99
2004	3.63	-0.53	1.16	9.46	14.13
2005	0.32	2.52	4.27	1.55	8.89
2006	7.25	-0.60	4.56	8.23	20.65

Trailing	Total Return%	+/- S&P 500	+/- Russ 1000 Vl	%Rank Cat	Growth of $10,000
3 Mo	8.23	1.53	0.23	13	10,823
6 Mo	13.16	0.42	-1.56	44	11,316
1 Yr	20.65	4.86	-1.60	19	12,065
3 Yr Avg	14.46	4.02	-0.63	14	14,996
5 Yr Avg	11.37	5.18	0.51	7	17,133
10 Yr Avg	11.62	3.20	0.62	7	30,021
15 Yr Avg	—	—	—	—	—

Tax Analysis	Tax-Adj Rtn%	%Rank Cat	Tax-Cost Rat	%Rank Cat
3 Yr (estimated)	10.38	55	1.64	65
5 Yr (estimated)	8.70	21	1.24	67
10 Yr (estimated)	8.71	17	2.04	78

Potential Capital Gain Exposure: 26% of assets

Historical Profile

Return	Above Avg	
Risk	Low	
Rating	★★★★ Above Avg	

84% 86% 78% 72% 68% 66% 75% 85% 86%

▼ Manager Change
▽ Partial Manager Change

Growth of $10,000
— Investment Values of Fund
— Investment Values of S&P 500

26.8
22.0
18.0
14.0
10.0

Performance Quartile (within Category)

1995	1996	1997	1998	1999	2000	2001	2002	2003	2004	2005	2006	History
—	12.98	14.09	13.09	13.81	13.34	13.01	11.27	14.33	15.87	15.44	16.61	NAV
—	6.32*	22.52	2.02	16.40	13.89	5.78	-11.41	28.99	14.13	8.89	20.65	Total Return %
—	—	-10.84	-26.56	-4.64	22.99	17.67	10.69	0.31	3.25	3.98	4.86	+/-S&P 500
—	—	-12.66	-13.61	9.05	6.88	11.37	4.11	-1.04	-2.36	1.84	-1.60	+/-Russ 1000 Vl
—	—	3.95	2.89	1.63	2.89	1.16	1.23	1.69	2.26	1.56	1.57	Income Return %
—	—	18.57	-0.87	14.77	11.00	4.62	-12.64	27.30	11.87	7.33	19.08	Capital Return %
—	—	89	87	9	27	13	7	41	36	19	19	Total Rtn % Rank Cat
—	0.33	0.51	0.40	0.21	0.39	0.15	0.16	0.19	0.32	0.25	0.24	Income $
—	0.75	1.26	0.87	1.19	1.86	0.94	0.11	0.00	0.15	1.59	1.70	Capital Gains $
—	—	1.09	1.11	1.13	1.16	1.14	1.15	1.21	1.18	1.17	—	Expense Ratio %
—	—	1.58	1.89	1.18	1.20	1.12	1.53	1.13	1.64	1.58	—	Income Ratio %
—	67	55	65	68	62	55	52	50	29	35	—	Turnover Rate %
—	97	751	950	761	759	979	922	1,304	1,466	1,637	2,180	Net Assets $mil

Rating and Risk

Time Period	Load-Adj Return %	Morningstar Rtn vs Cat	Morningstar Risk vs Cat	Morningstar Risk-Adj Rating
1 Yr	13.71			
3 Yr	12.22	Avg	-Avg	★★★
5 Yr	10.06	+Avg	Low	★★★★
10 Yr	10.97	+Avg	Low	★★★★★
Incept	11.45			

Other Measures	Standard Index S&P 500	Best Fit Index Russ MV
Alpha	5.2	1.3
Beta	0.77	0.64
R-Squared	69	79
Standard Deviation	6.42	
Mean	14.46	
Sharpe Ratio	1.66	

Portfolio Analysis 09-30-06

Share change since 06-06 Total Stocks:109

	Sector	PE	Tot Ret%	% Assets
White Mountains Insuranc	Financial	15.2	5.27	2.87
Weyerhaeuser Company	Ind Mtrls	—	10.21	2.48
⊕ Altria Group, Inc.	Goods	16.3	19.87	2.16
Verizon Communications	Telecom	15.9	34.88	1.95
⊖ News Cl A	Media	—	—	1.91
⊕ Tyco International, Ltd.	Ind Mtrls	15.7	6.83	1.89
Altadis	Goods	—	—	1.88
Fortis	Financial	—	—	1.84
Berkshire Hathaway Inc.	Financial	13.2	24.89	1.84
⊕ Pfizer Inc.	Health	15.2	15.22	1.65
Orkla	Ind Mtrls	—	—	1.65
Florida East Coast Indus	Business	38.4	41.38	1.58
NTL, Inc.	Telecom	—	6.08	1.51
British American Tobacco	Goods	—	—	1.47
⊕ KT&G	Goods	—	—	1.47
Microsoft Corporation	Software	23.8	15.83	1.35
AGCO Corporation	Ind Mtrls	—	86.72	1.32
Imperial Tobacco Grp	Goods	—	—	1.25
BellSouth Corporation	Telecom	—	—	1.23
Washington Post Company	Media	21.8	-1.53	1.18

Current Investment Style

Value Blnd Growth | Large Mid Small

Market Cap	%
Giant	36.9
Large	33.0
Mid	27.4
Small	2.2
Micro	0.4

Avg $mil: 21,314

Value Measures		Rel Category
Price/Earnings	14.34	1.04
Price/Book	1.89	0.85
Price/Sales	1.26	0.97
Price/Cash Flow	10.17	1.52
Dividend Yield %	2.87	1.23

Growth Measures	%	Rel Category
Long-Term Erngs	10.34	1.00
Book Value	6.08	0.77
Sales	6.23	0.69
Cash Flow	-2.39	NMF
Historical Erngs	10.81	0.67

Profitability	%	Rel Category
Return on Equity	15.07	0.84
Return on Assets	6.08	0.62
Net Margin	11.58	0.89

Sector Weightings	% of Stocks	Rel S&P 500	3 Year High	Low
↻ Info	20.83	1.04		
⬚ Software	1.57	0.46	2	0
⬚ Hardware	2.84	0.31	3	0
⬚ Media	9.26	2.44	11	9
⬚ Telecom	7.16	2.04	7	3
⬚ Service	43.70	0.95		
⬚ Health	7.13	0.59	7	4
⬚ Consumer	1.40	0.18	2	1
⬚ Business	2.94	0.70	4	2
⬚ Financial	32.23	1.45	32	24
⬚ Mfg	35.48	1.05		
⬚ Goods	19.47	2.28	28	19
⬚ Ind Mtrls	12.31	1.03	19	12
⬚ Energy	0.52	0.05	6	1
⬚ Utilities	3.18	0.91	3	1

Composition

	%
● Cash	7.6
● Stocks	85.8
● Bonds	1.3
● Other	5.3
Foreign (% of Stock)	37.2

Morningstar's Take by John Coumarianos 12-28-06

The foray into fallen growth stocks continues for Mutual Beacon.

Like all the Mutual Series funds, this venerable value hound tends to avoid large companies that are closely followed by the analyst community. Instead, managers Michael Embler and Charles Lahr shop the bargain bins for unknown, unloved, neglected, and obscure stocks that have a greater chance of being mispriced.

Lately, however, they have found some battered well-known stocks to buy. In addition to beefing up their positions in Microsoft and Pfizer, they recently picked up embattled computer maker Dell . Although it's known as a technology company, Dell is a manufacturing business with management and operational clouds hanging over it, according to the managers. They think competition has impaired the business somewhat but not to the extent that the stock's current price implies, making it a classic Mutual Series situation of exploiting what the managers interpret as a market overreaction.

This interest in unloved and battered stocks has helped the fund pick up shares that have little downside, placing it among those in its group with the lowest volatility (measured by standard deviation of returns) for the past five years. We think this helps investors stick around and enjoy the fund's returns. Indeed, it has posted a 70.9% cumulative gain for the past five years through Nov. 30, 2006 versus a 49.8% return for the large-value category average.

This fund's recent emphasis on larger stocks has moved it into the large-value segment of the Morningstar Style Box from the mid-value segment. However, with one third of the assets of its sibling Mutual Shares, it remains more nimble. Its penchant for the unloved means that it won't always hold the very-highest-quality businesses and that it will often lag in growth rallies. Still, we think the fund is poised to capture a return to favor of steady-Eddie large-cap stocks. We also think it's a fine go-anywhere value fund for the long haul.

Address:	101 John F Kennedy Pkwy Short Hills NJ 07078 800-342-5236
Web Address:	www.franklintempleton.com
Inception:	11-01-96*
Advisor:	Franklin Mutual Advisers, LLC
Subadvisor:	None
NTF Plans:	DATALynx NTF, Federated Tr NTF

Minimum Purchase:	$1000	Add: $50	IRA: $250
Min Auto Inv Plan:	$50	Add: $50	
Sales Fees:	5.75%L, 0.33%S, 2.00%R		
Management Fee:	0.60% mx./0.54% mn., 0.15%A		
Actual Fees:	Mgt:0.60% Dist:0.33%		
Expense Projections:	3Yr:$940	5Yr:$1207	10Yr:$1967
Income Distrib:	Semi-Annually		

Mutual Discovery A

	Ticker	Load	NAV	Yield	Total Assets	Mstar Category
	TEDIX	5.75%	$30.15	1.8%	$12,836 mil	World Stock

Governance and Management

Stewardship Grade: C

Portfolio Manager(s)

Longtime manager David Winters left Franklin Mutual Advisers on May 10, 2005. Assistant portfolio manager David Segal remains at this fund. He is joined by Anne Gudefin, who has managed Mutual Qualified since December 2003.

Strategy

The managers hunt for bargain-basement stocks of all sizes, particularly in Europe and the United States. They also look to buy the debt of distressed companies and are active participants on creditors' committees as these firms restructure. Historically the managers hedged all foreign-currency exposure back into the dollar, but they have recently been removing some of the hedge on a tactical basis.

Historical Profile

Return	Above Avg
Risk	Low
Rating	★★★★ Above Avg

Investment Style: Equity Stock %

Stock %: 80% 85% 68% 75% 71% 75% 87% 87% 83%

▼ Manager Change
▽ Partial Manager Change

Growth of $10,000
■ Investment Values of Fund
— Investment Values of MSCI EAFE

Performance Quartile (within Category)

1995	1996	1997	1998	1999	2000	2001	2002	2003	2004	2005	2006	History
—	17.16	18.83	17.19	21.00	18.83	18.08	16.06	20.66	24.08	26.04	30.15	NAV
—	4.86*	22.47	-2.37	26.38	12.26	0.86	-9.39	31.13	18.98	15.29	23.02	Total Return %
—	—	20.69	-22.30	-0.65	26.45	22.28	6.55	-7.46	-1.27	1.75	-3.32	+/-MSCI EAFE
—	—	6.71	-26.69	1.43	25.45	17.66	10.50	-1.98	4.26	5.80	2.95	+/-MSCI World
—	—	4.53	2.25	2.07	2.70	1.51	1.43	2.35	2.30	1.53	2.17	Income Return %
—	—	17.94	-4.62	24.31	9.56	-0.65	-10.82	28.78	16.68	13.76	20.85	Capital Return %
—	—	20	92	63	4	4	10	68	17	22	18	Total Rtn % Rank Cat
—	0.28	0.77	0.42	0.35	0.55	0.28	0.26	0.38	0.47	0.37	0.56	Income $
—	1.07	1.36	0.81	0.32	4.04	0.62	0.08	0.00	0.00	1.34	1.23	Capital Gains $
—	—	1.33	1.35	1.38	1.37	1.37	1.39	1.46	1.42	1.39	—	Expense Ratio %
—	—	1.39	1.46	0.98	1.30	1.57	1.53	1.20	1.52	1.07	—	Income Ratio %
—	80	58	84	88	75	59	41	46	34	26	—	Turnover Rate %
—	68	698	863	845	880	913	927	1,438	2,108	3,545	6,125	Net Assets $mil

Performance 12-31-06

	1st Qtr	2nd Qtr	3rd Qtr	4th Qtr	Total
2002	4.59	-3.88	-10.69	0.92	-9.39
2003	-3.92	15.46	4.80	12.79	31.13
2004	3.97	0.04	2.25	11.87	18.98
2005	1.00	3.46	6.64	3.47	15.29
2006	9.83	-1.56	4.52	8.85	23.02

Trailing	Total Return%	+/- MSCI EAFE	+/- MSCI World	%Rank Cat	Growth of $10,000
3 Mo	8.85	-1.50	0.48	45	10,885
6 Mo	13.78	-0.91	0.57	33	11,378
1 Yr	23.02	-3.32	2.95	18	12,302
3 Yr Avg	19.05	-0.88	4.37	13	16,873
5 Yr Avg	14.93	-0.05	4.96	14	20,052
10 Yr Avg	13.12	5.41	5.48	9	34,308
15 Yr Avg	—	—	—		—

Tax Analysis	Tax-Adj Rtn%	%Rank Cat	Tax-Cost Rat	%Rank Cat
3 Yr (estimated)	15.43	35	1.11	60
5 Yr (estimated)	12.49	24	0.96	74
10 Yr (estimated)	10.41	15	1.81	91

Potential Capital Gain Exposure: 26% of assets

Rating and Risk

Time Period	Load-Adj Return %	Morningstar Rtn vs Cat	Morningstar Risk vs Cat	Morningstar Risk-Adj Rating
1 Yr	15.94			
3 Yr	16.73	+Avg	Low	★★★★
5 Yr	13.58	+Avg	Low	★★★★
10 Yr	12.45	+Avg	Low	★★★★★
Incept	12.77			

Other Measures	Standard Index MSCI EAFE	Best Fit Index MSCI World
Alpha	4.1	6.7
Beta	0.67	0.80
R-Squared	76	81
Standard Deviation	7.31	
Mean	19.05	
Sharpe Ratio	2.01	

Morningstar's Take by John Coumarianos 12-28-06

Mutual Discovery can help its shareholders in nearly any market conditions.

This fund is the most flexible of all the Mutual Series funds. More than just a deep-value shop hunting for cheap stocks, Mutual Series engages in merger arbitrage, bankruptcies, and other restructurings, including private financings. The shop will also put pressure on management teams that it thinks aren't acting in the best interests of shareholders. Mutual Discovery will employ all of these tactics on a global basis.

Recently, with narrow yield spreads (the difference between yields on high-quality and low-quality bonds), managers Anne Gudefin and David Segal have been hunting the globe for cheap stocks and opportunities where they can encourage change. New holdings include Scandinavian fishery Pan Fish, which the managers think is undervalued and provides a product that is enjoying increasing demand. Gudefin and Segal are also high on Japanese banks such as Sumitomo Mitsui.

Sumitomo has higher exposure to small-business lending and mortgage growth, which the managers think are in nascent-growth phases. Also, they believe Japan is in a part of the credit cycle that allows them to anticipate book value growth of 10%-20% per year.

Activist positions include forestry-business Weyerhaeuser, which recently sold its paper business to Domtar. Completion of the purchase has also allowed management to embark on a share-repurchase plan. Gudefin and Segal think the shares have been under undue pressure from a slowing housing market but favor the company's long-term cash-generation abilities. Additionally, Gudefin has been elected to the corporate assembly of Nordic consumer-goods company Orkla. Mutual Series has been able to influence the sale of the conglomerate's media assets and encourage a share-repurchase plan.

This fund is loath to pay up for stocks, and it may not look great when the markets are roaring.

Portfolio Analysis 09-30-06

Share change since 06-06 Total Stocks:175	Sector	Country	% Assets
⊕ KT&G	Goods	Korea	2.44
British American Tobacco	Goods	U.K.	2.40
Orkla	Ind Mtrls	Norway	2.08
Imperial Tobacco Grp	Goods	U.K.	1.84
Weyerhaeuser Company	Ind Mtrls	United States	1.61
Carrefour	Consumer	France	1.37
Carlsberg	Goods	Denmark	1.35
Altadis	Goods	Spain	1.29
⊖ Pernod Ricard	Goods	France	1.27
Mitsubishi UFJ Financial	Financial	Japan	1.22
Anglo American	Ind Mtrls	U.K.	1.20
⊕ Time Warner, Inc.	Media	United States	1.15
Linde	Ind Mtrls	Germany	1.14
Potlatch Corp.	Financial	United States	1.14
⊕ THE LINK REAL ESTATE INV	Financial	Hong Kong	1.11
Sumitomo Mitsui Financia	Financial	Japan	1.11
CSM	Goods	Netherlands	1.10
Florida East Coast Indus	Business	United States	1.04
Fortis	Financial	Belgium	1.04
Euronext	Financial	Netherlands	1.02

Current Investment Style

Value Blnd Growth — Large Mid Small

Market Cap	%
Giant	32.8
Large	33.8
Mid	30.0
Small	3.1
Micro	0.4
Avg $mil:	14,397

Value Measures		Rel Category
Price/Earnings	13.41	0.87
Price/Book	1.95	0.82
Price/Sales	1.21	0.92
Price/Cash Flow	10.42	1.20
Dividend Yield %	2.47	1.14

Growth Measures	%	Rel Category
Long-Term Erngs	13.34	1.05
Book Value	9.09	1.01
Sales	5.26	0.63
Cash Flow	-0.68	NMF
Historical Erngs	17.85	0.95

Composition

Cash	12.1	Bonds	0.9
Stocks	83.3	Other	3.6
Foreign (% of Stock)			73.2

Sector Weightings	% of Stocks	Rel MSCI EAFE	3 Year High	Low
☎ Info	10.82	0.92		
🖥 Software	1.02	1.82	1	0
💻 Hardware	2.37	0.61	2	0
🎤 Media	4.00	2.19	6	3
📱 Telecom	3.43	0.62	7	2
☞ Service	38.03	0.81		
🏥 Health	3.81	0.54	4	3
🛒 Consumer	3.89	0.79	4	1
🏢 Business	4.22	0.83	5	3
💲 Financial	26.11	0.87	26	16
🔧 Mfg	51.15	1.25		
🏭 Goods	26.39	2.01	35	26
⚙ Ind Mtrls	17.94	1.16	22	18
🔋 Energy	3.16	0.44	5	3
💡 Utilities	3.66	0.70	4	0

Regional Exposure	% Stock		
UK/W. Europe 49	N. America		30
Japan 5	Latn America		1
Asia X Japan 15	Other		0

Country Exposure	% Stock		
United States 27	South Korea		7
France 10	Germany		6
U.K. 10			

Address:	101 John F Kennedy Pkwy Short Hills NJ 07078 800-342-5236	Minimum Purchase:	$1000	Add: $50 IRA: $250
		Min Auto Inv Plan:	$50	Add: $50
		Sales Fees:	5.75%L, 0.35%S, 2.00%R	
Web Address:	www.franklintempleton.com	Management Fee:	0.80% mx./0.73% mn., 0.15%A	
Inception:	11-01-96*	Actual Fees:	Mgt:0.79% Dist:0.35%	
Advisor:	Franklin Mutual Advisers, LLC	Expense Projections:	3Yr:$998 5Yr:$1307 10Yr:$2179	
Subadvisor:	None	Income Distrib:	Semi-Annually	
NTF Plans:	DATALynx NTF, Federated Tr NTF			

Morningstar® Funds 500

Mutual European A

	Ticker	Load	NAV	Yield	Total Assets	Mstar Category
	TEMIX	5.75%	$24.19	2.3%	$2,363 mil	Europe Stock

Governance and Management

Stewardship Grade: C

Portfolio Manager(s)

Longtime manager David Winters left Franklin Mutual Advisers on May 10, 2005. Philippe Brugere-Trelat, who had served as Winters' comanager since late 2004, took the reins. Brugere-Trelat worked at Mutual Series from 1984 to 1994, then on hedge funds--his entire career spent applying a value approach to European markets. He is supported here by Charles Lahr, a foreign financials specialist who also runs Mutual Financial Services. Shop CEO Peter Langerman, several analysts, and portfolio managers of the shop's other funds contribute, as well.

Strategy

The managers look for shares of companies selling at a discount to intrinsic value, and they put a premium on free cash-flow generation and corporate management that uses that cash to benefit shareholders. Unlike many Europe-stock offerings, this fund pays no heed to the benchmark MSCI Europe Index, in terms of stock, sector, and country weighting. It has been fond of smaller European markets and mid-caps. It normally hedges much or all of its foreign-currency exposure (currently 80%) to reduce volatility. The managers also buy distressed debt and will dabble in arbitrage plays.

Performance 12-31-06

	1st Qtr	2nd Qtr	3rd Qtr	4th Qtr	Total
2002	7.64	-1.39	-13.52	0.17	-8.05
2003	-4.52	16.29	6.07	12.36	32.34
2004	3.98	1.65	1.96	12.49	21.23
2005	1.03	2.56	7.71	5.34	17.56
2006	11.29	-2.04	6.45	9.39	26.96

Trailing	Total Return%	+/- MSCI EAFE	+/- MSCI Eur	%Rank Cat	Growth of $10,000
3 Mo	9.39	-0.96	-2.07	92	10,939
6 Mo	16.45	1.76	-1.28	63	11,645
1 Yr	26.96	0.62	-6.76	88	12,696
3 Yr Avg	21.85	1.92	0.92	43	18,092
5 Yr Avg	17.10	2.12	2.23	40	22,018
10 Yr Avg	16.09	8.38	5.62	14	44,458
15 Yr Avg	—				

Tax Analysis	Tax-Adj Rtn%	%Rank Cat	Tax-Cost Rat	%Rank Cat
3 Yr (estimated)	17.45	76	1.69	74
5 Yr (estimated)	14.15	58	1.36	77
10 Yr (estimated)	12.85	29	2.22	79

Potential Capital Gain Exposure: 33% of assets

Morningstar's Take by Dan Lefkovitz 11-15-06

Recent moves illustrate why Mutual European, despite sluggish relative returns, is a long-term winner.

Value investors look at market volatility as an opportunity. So it's no surprise that lead manager Philippe Brugere-Trelat put some of the fund's cash stake to work during European market turbulence in the second and third quarters of 2006. He bought Philips Electronics during a market sell-off in May 2006 on the view that the company's transition from making semiconductors to medical devices and household products will unlock shareholder value. He also added to top-10 positions Siemens and Fortis.

But the fund's cash stake, even when it's small, acts as a drag when markets are running. That helps explain why the fund's record for the trailing three-year period, while great in absolute terms, looks mediocre compared with its benchmark, the MSCI Europe Index, and subpar versus the Europe-stock peer group. The fund has also been

hurt by its currency hedge. When European currencies appreciate against the dollar, as they have been doing, the fund suffers.

Investors who can accept that the hedge can sometimes hurt have been rewarded over the long term. For the trailing 10-year period, the fund has beaten the index and the peer group by wide margins. And in years like 2005, when the dollar appreciates, the fund can look great on a relative basis. More importantly, the fund preserves capital much better than most in down years.

We also like the team here. Brugere-Trelat has been investing in Europe for 20 years, including stints at Mutual Series and at a hedge fund. Comanager Charles Lahr, who also runs Mutual Financial Services, brings specialized knowledge to bear. And Peter Langerman has served as a steadying influence since returning to head up Mutual Series in 2005. We only wish that Brugere-Trelat committed more personal money to the fund.

Address:	101 John F Kennedy Pkwy Short Hills NJ 07078 800-342-5236
Web Address:	www.franklintempleton.com
Inception:	11-01-96*
Advisor:	Franklin Mutual Advisers, LLC
Subadvisor:	None
NTF Plans:	DATALynx NTF, Federated Tr NTF

Minimum Purchase:	$1000	Add: $50	IRA: $250
Min Auto Inv Plan:	$50	Add: $50	
Sales Fees:	5.75%L, 0.33%S, 2.00%R		
Management Fee:	0.80% mx./0.73% mn., 0.15%A		
Actual Fees:	Mgt:0.79%	Dist:0.33%	
Expense Projections:	3Yr:$987	5Yr:$1287	10Yr:$2137
Income Distrib:	Semi-Annually		

Historical Profile

Return	Above Avg
Risk	Low
Rating	★★★★ Above Avg

Investment Style: Equity, Stock %

85% 94% 81% 69% 72% 81% 83% 89% 87%

▼ Manager Change
▽ Partial Manager Change

39.4
32.4
24.0 — **Growth of $10,000**
17.0 — Investment Values of Fund
 — Investment Values of MSCI EAFE
10.0

Performance Quartile (within Category)

1995	1996	1997	1998	1999	2000	2001	2002	2003	2004	2005	2006	History
—	11.38	12.57	12.47	16.75	15.36	14.27	12.83	16.58	19.50	20.99	24.19	NAV
—	5.41*	22.70	4.07	46.05	14.07	-5.05	-8.05	32.34	21.23	17.56	26.96	Total Return %
—	—	20.92	-15.86	19.02	28.26	16.37	7.89	-6.25	0.98	4.02	0.62	+/-MSCI EAFE
—	—	-1.10	-24.43	30.12	22.47	14.85	10.33	-6.20	0.35	8.14	-6.76	+/-MSCI Eur
—	—	7.13	2.41	3.64	2.92	1.80	1.46	2.95	3.29	2.51	2.87	Income Return %
—	—	15.57	1.66	42.41	11.15	-6.85	-9.51	29.39	17.94	15.05	24.09	Capital Return %
—	46	83	19	3	7	33	72	36	25	88		Total Rtn % Rank Cat
0.05	0.81	0.30	0.45	0.48	0.28	0.21	0.38	0.54	0.49	0.59		Income $
0.02	0.56	0.36	0.89	3.16	0.04	0.10	0.00	0.02	1.43	1.75		Capital Gains $
—	—	1.37	1.40	1.39	1.38	1.40	1.40	1.43	1.42	—		Expense Ratio %
—	—	1.84	1.68	1.36	1.56	1.88	1.53	1.84	1.75	—		Income Ratio %
—	—	—	98	98	127	112	52	30	52	33		Turnover Rate %
—	17	93	171	177	233	256	304	417	545	962		Net Assets $mil

Rating and Risk

Time Period	Load-Adj Return %	Morningstar Rtn vs Cat	Morningstar Risk vs Cat	Morningstar Risk-Adj Rating
1 Yr	19.66			
3 Yr	19.47	Avg	Low	★★★
5 Yr	15.72	Avg	Low	★★★
10 Yr	15.41	+Avg	Low	★★★★
Incept	15.74			

Other Measures	Standard Index MSCI EAFE	Best Fit Index MSCI World
Alpha	6.0	7.5
Beta	0.71	0.88
R-Squared	76	78
Standard Deviation	7.69	
Mean	21.85	
Sharpe Ratio	2.23	

Portfolio Analysis 09-30-06

Share change since 06-06 Total Stocks:84	Sector	Country	% Assets
⊖ Orkla	Ind Mtrls	Norway	2.86
⊖ British American Tobacco	Goods	U.K.	2.78
Nestle	Goods	Switzerland	2.63
⊕ Anglo American	Ind Mtrls	U.K.	2.62
Imperial Tobacco Grp	Goods	U.K.	2.59
Fortis	Financial	Belgium	2.35
Altadis	Goods	Spain	2.35
Siemens	Hardware	Germany	2.27
Bnp Paribas	—	France	2.20
DANONE Grp	Goods	France	2.07
⊕ Linde	Ind Mtrls	Germany	2.05
Carrefour	Consumer	France	2.02
NTL, Inc.	Telecom	U.K.	1.89
⊕ Suez	Utilities	France	1.74
⊕ RWE	Utilities	Germany	1.73
⊕ E.ON	Utilities	Germany	1.65
⊕ Koninklijke Philips Elec	Goods	Netherlands	1.63
Svenska Handelsbanken	Financial	Sweden	1.56
⊖ Pernod Ricard	Goods	France	1.46
⊖ Carlsberg	Goods	Denmark	1.36

Current Investment Style

Value Blnd Growth — Large Mid Small

	Market Cap	%
	Giant	35.4
	Large	32.6
	Mid	26.2
	Small	4.7
	Micro	1.1
	Avg $mil:	16,374

Value Measures		Rel Category
Price/Earnings	13.41	1.05
Price/Book	2.12	0.99
Price/Sales	1.01	0.93
Price/Cash Flow	9.46	1.23
Dividend Yield %	3.31	1.04

Growth Measures	%	Rel Category
Long-Term Erngs	12.07	0.87
Book Value	11.83	1.35
Sales	5.57	0.94
Cash Flow	1.63	0.22
Historical Erngs	19.57	0.89

Composition

Cash	9.1	Bonds	0.0
Stocks	86.9	Other	4.0
Foreign (% of Stock)			95.9

Sector Weightings	% of Stocks	Rel MSCI EAFE	3 Year High	Low
☁ Info	10.16	0.86		
▣ Software	0.00	0.00	0	0
▣ Hardware	2.96	0.77	3	0
◑ Media	2.18	1.19	2	1
▤ Telecom	5.02	0.90	10	2
☞ Service	31.66	0.67		
▤ Health	2.80	0.39	3	1
▤ Consumer	4.02	0.81	5	2
S Business	5.57	1.34	8	4
S Financial	18.07	0.60	22	18
⊐ Mfg	58.18	1.42		
◲ Goods	27.23	2.08	38	25
✿ Ind Mtrls	18.21	1.18	22	15
◳ Energy	5.75	0.80	6	3
▽ Utilities	6.99	1.33	7	0

Regional Exposure

	% Stock		
UK/W. Europe	96	N. America	4
Japan	0	Latn America	0
Asia X Japan	0	Other	0

Country Exposure

	% Stock		
France	19	Netherlands	10
Germany	15	Norway	8
U.K.	15		

Mutual Qualified A

	Ticker	Load	NAV	Yield	Total Assets	Mstar Category
	TEQIX	5.75%	$21.76	1.5%	$5,692 mil	Large Value

Governance and Management

Stewardship Grade: C

Portfolio Manager(s)

Manager Ray Garea left this fund at the end of July 2001. Jeff Diamond replaced him but left in December 2003. Anne Gudefin, an expert in European securities and the fund's assistant manager under Diamond, is the lead manager. Shawn Tumulty, who leads the firm's distressed-debt team, is the assistant manager. Several other managers have departed the Mutual Series complex in recent years.

Strategy

This deep-value offering hunts for bargains amid the market's rubble. Its management uses methods such as discounted cash-flow and sum-of-the-parts analysis to identify firms that it thinks are undervalued. In addition to domestic equities, management is also fond of foreign conglomerates, distressed credits, and merger-arbitrage plays. The fund usually holds 130 to 150 equity positions and will have significant cash positions when management can't find securities that meet its criteria.

Performance 12-31-06

	1st Qtr	2nd Qtr	3rd Qtr	4th Qtr	Total
2002	3.41	-6.26	-12.32	2.37	-13.00
2003	-2.80	14.63	3.44	12.78	29.99
2004	3.37	-0.35	2.08	10.58	16.27
2005	-0.41	3.62	4.75	2.55	10.85
2006	7.56	-1.01	3.77	7.65	18.94

Trailing	Total Return%	+/- S&P 500	+/- Russ 1000 VI	%Rank Cat	Growth of $10,000
3 Mo	7.65	0.95	-0.35	32	10,765
6 Mo	11.70	-1.04	-3.02	72	11,170
1 Yr	18.94	3.15	-3.31	40	11,894
3 Yr Avg	15.30	4.86	0.21	7	15,328
5 Yr Avg	11.63	5.44	0.77	6	17,334
10 Yr Avg	11.63	3.21	0.63	7	30,048
15 Yr Avg	—	—	—	—	—

Tax Analysis	Tax-Adj Rtn%	%Rank Cat	Tax-Cost Rat	%Rank Cat
3 Yr (estimated)	11.31	39	1.54	61
5 Yr (estimated)	8.99	17	1.21	65
10 Yr (estimated)	8.85	14	1.91	72

Potential Capital Gain Exposure: 33% of assets

Morningstar's Take by John Coumarianos 11-20-06

Mutual Qualified looks better in its new surroundings.

Mutual Qualified had performed poorly relative to its mid-value peers recently. However, this fund hasn't traditionally adhered to a particular square of Morningstar's Style Box: As a result of heavier investment in large-cap stocks over the past few years, the fund moved to the the large-value category as of Dec. 1. Though the fund didn't stand out relative to its mid-cap focused peers, in its new category it lands in the top quartile over all long-term trailing periods.

This is a go-anywhere fund, and we think it has made all the right moves. The average market capitalization (the price of a share multiplied by shares outstanding) of stocks in the fund has moved from $6 billion to nearly $12 billion over the past four years, putting it somewhere in between a mid-cap fund and a large-cap fund at a time when mid-caps have dominated their larger brethren. This fund did just fine by holding more mid-caps four

years ago, and we think it's doing the right thing again by holding more large-caps now. Besides profiting from smaller names, the fund also has had consistently high foreign exposure during a time when overseas markets have outperformed. The fund currently has 39% of the portfolio in Europe stocks, and 12% devoted to the stocks of Asian companies.

Managers Anne Gudefin and Shawn Tumulty don't necessarily view their portfolio in terms of these allocations, however. They prefer to let the search for cheap stocks, distressed debt, and merger-arbitrage opportunities take them where it may. Right now, they continue to hold a slew of cheap tobacco stocks such as Korea Tobacco and Ginseng, and Altria in addition to forestry company Weyerhaeuser, which they've encouraged to restructure.

This fund could lag if growth stocks take off in a big way, but it remains a terrific option for the value side of a portfolio.

Address:	101 John F Kennedy Pkwy Short Hills NJ 07078 800-342-5236
Web Address:	www.franklintempleton.com
Inception:	11-01-96*
Advisor:	Franklin Mutual Advisers, LLC
Subadvisor:	None
NTF Plans:	DATALynx NTF, Federated Tr NTF

Minimum Purchase:	$1000	Add: $50	IRA: $250
Min Auto Inv Plan:	$50	Add: $50	
Sales Fees:	5.75%L, 0.35%S, 2.00%R		
Management Fee:	0.60% mx./0.54% mn., 0.15%A		
Actual Fees:	Mgt:0.60%	Dist:0.35%	
Expense Projections:	3Yr:$934	5Yr:$1197	10Yr:$1946
Income Distrib:	Semi-Annually		

Historical Profile

Return	Above Avg
Risk	Low
Rating	★★★★ Above Avg

Investment Style: Equity Stock %
85% 87% 76% 74% 64% 65% 79% 90% 83%

▼ Manager Change
▽ Partial Manager Change

Growth of $10,000
■ Investment Values of Fund
— Investment Values of S&P 500

Performance Quartile (within Category)

	1995	1996	1997	1998	1999	2000	2001	2002	2003	2004	2005	2006	History
NAV	—	16.23	18.14	16.42	16.87	16.56	16.44	13.91	17.80	19.41	19.71	21.76	
Total Return %	—	6.21*	24.44	0.15	13.27	13.81	7.85	-13.00	29.99	16.27	10.85	18.94	
+/-S&P 500	—	—	-8.92	-28.43	-7.77	22.91	19.74	9.10	1.31	5.39	5.94	3.15	
+/-Russ 1000 VI	—	—	-10.74	-15.48	5.92	6.80	13.44	2.52	-0.04	-0.22	3.80	-3.31	
Income Return %	—	—	3.74	2.16	1.42	3.00	0.84	1.29	1.89	1.82	1.82	1.72	
Capital Return %	—	—	20.70	-2.01	11.85	10.81	7.01	-14.29	28.10	14.45	9.03	17.22	
Total Rtn % Rank Cat	—	—	77	89	18	28	8	14	33	18	7	40	
Income $	—	0.41	0.60	0.39	0.23	0.49	0.14	0.21	0.26	0.32	0.35	0.33	
Capital Gains $	—	0.82	1.40	1.33	1.48	1.98	1.27	0.22	0.00	0.93	1.44	1.30	
Expense Ratio %	—	—	1.11	1.11	1.11	1.13	1.14	1.15	1.20	1.17	1.16	—	
Income Ratio %	—	—	1.48	1.66	0.97	1.08	0.94	1.46	0.99	1.66	1.69	—	
Turnover Rate %	—	65	53	67	60	55	53	51	50	38	21	—	
Net Assets $mil	—	55	452	571	474	444	485	454	627	696	800	993	

Rating and Risk

Time Period	Load-Adj Return %	Morningstar Rtn vs Cat	Morningstar Risk vs Cat	Morningstar Risk-Adj Rating
1 Yr	12.10			
3 Yr	13.05	+Avg	Avg	★★★★
5 Yr	10.32	+Avg	Low	★★★★
10 Yr	10.97	+Avg	Low	★★★★★
Incept	11.44			

Other Measures	Standard Index S&P 500	Best Fit Index Russ MV
Alpha	5.5	1.0
Beta	0.84	0.71
R-Squared	72	86
Standard Deviation	6.81	
Mean	15.30	
Sharpe Ratio	1.67	

Portfolio Analysis 09-30-06

Share change since 06-06 Total Stocks:132

	Sector	PE	Tot Ret%	% Assets
⊕ KT&G	Goods	—	—	3.44
White Mountains Insuranc	Financial	15.2	5.27	3.20
Weyerhaeuser Company	Ind Mtrls	—	10.21	2.41
Altadis	Goods	—	—	2.17
DANONE Grp	Goods	—	—	2.03
Orkla	Ind Mtrls	—	—	2.01
Generale de Sante (GDS)	Health	—	—	1.95
British American Tobacco	Goods	—	—	1.95
⊖ Pernod Ricard	Goods	—	—	1.88
⊕ Reynolds American, Inc.	Goods	15.9	43.87	1.55
Sovereign Bancorp, Inc.	Financial	23.8	25.01	1.54
NTL, Inc.	Telecom	—	6.08	1.52
Carrefour	Consumer	—	—	1.51
Florida East Coast Indus	Business	38.4	41.38	1.48
Mitsubishi UFJ Financial	Financial	—	—	1.33
KONE	Business	—	—	1.28
⊕ Altria Group, Inc.	Goods	16.3	19.87	1.21
⊕ Time Warner, Inc.	Media	19.6	26.37	1.17
✵ KKR Financial Corporatio	Financial	—	—	1.16
CSM	Goods	—	—	1.11

Current Investment Style

Value Blnd Growth — Large Mid Small

Market Cap	%
Giant	27.4
Large	30.8
Mid	30.2
Small	8.0
Micro	3.6
Avg $mil:	11,898

Value Measures		Rel Category
Price/Earnings	13.89	1.01
Price/Book	1.90	0.86
Price/Sales	0.96	0.74
Price/Cash Flow	9.76	1.46
Dividend Yield %	2.27	0.97

Growth Measures	%	Rel Category
Long-Term Erngs	10.83	1.04
Book Value	8.84	1.12
Sales	4.70	0.52
Cash Flow	-0.44	NMF
Historical Erngs	2.38	0.15

Profitability	%	Rel Category
Return on Equity	15.17	0.85
Return on Assets	6.47	0.66
Net Margin	11.06	0.85

Sector Weightings	% of Stocks	Rel S&P 500	3 Year High	Low
♋ Info	11.57	0.58		
Software	0.81	0.23	1	0
Hardware	2.29	0.25	2	0
Media	4.27	1.13	9	4
Telecom	4.20	1.20	6	2
☛ Service	45.56	0.99		
Health	7.44	0.62	8	7
Consumer	4.66	0.61	5	4
Business	5.07	1.20	7	5
Financial	28.39	1.27	34	27
Mfg	42.87	1.27		
Goods	24.13	2.82	25	17
Ind Mtrls	12.98	1.09	17	12
Energy	4.32	0.44	5	3
Utilities	1.44	0.41	2	1

Composition

		%
●	Cash	10.1
●	Stocks	83.5
●	Bonds	1.3
●	Other	5.1
	Foreign	53.2
	(% of Stock)	

MORNINGSTAR® Funds 500

Mutual Shares A

	Ticker	Load	NAV	Yield	Total Assets	Mstar Category
	TESIX	5.75%	$25.91	1.6%	$21,597 mil	Large Value

Governance and Management

Stewardship Grade: C

Portfolio Manager(s)

Longtime manager David Winters left Franklin Mutual Advisers in May 2005 to start his own firm. Assistant portfolio manager Deborah Turner remains and is joined by Peter Langerman and David Segal. Langerman is a Mutual Series veteran who returned after several years as director of New Jersey's Division of Investment. Langerman served as a portfolio manager and CEO of the firm before departing in 2002.

Strategy

This deep-value fund tries to ferret out gems among the market's rubble. Its management uses a variety of methods to value companies, including discounted cash-flow and sum-of-the-parts analyses. That has led it, in addition to domestic equities, into a stack of mispriced foreign conglomerates and distressed credits. The fund holds about 125 stocks and frequents the financials and industrials arenas.

Performance 12-31-06

	1st Qtr	2nd Qtr	3rd Qtr	4th Qtr	Total
2002	2.43	-5.98	-10.18	2.66	-11.20
2003	-2.26	12.82	2.45	11.70	26.18
2004	3.21	0.04	0.56	9.31	13.50
2005	0.17	2.25	4.52	2.72	9.98
2006	6.30	-0.95	3.88	7.87	17.98

Trailing	Total Return%	+/- S&P 500	+/- Russ 1000 Vl	%Rank Cat	Growth of $10,000
3 Mo	7.87	1.17	-0.13	24	10,787
6 Mo	12.05	-0.69	-2.67	66	11,205
1 Yr	17.98	2.19	-4.27	54	11,798
3 Yr Avg	13.77	3.33	-1.32	22	14,726
5 Yr Avg	10.54	4.35	-0.32	12	16,504
10 Yr Avg	11.10	2.68	0.10	10	28,651
15 Yr Avg	—	—	—	—	—

Tax Analysis	Tax-Adj Rtn%	%Rank Cat	Tax-Cost Rat	%Rank Cat
3 Yr (estimated)	10.17	58	1.24	49
5 Yr (estimated)	8.16	31	0.98	53
10 Yr (estimated)	8.43	21	1.82	67

Potential Capital Gain Exposure: 21% of assets

Historical Profile

Return	Above Avg
Risk	Low
Rating	★★★★ Above Avg

Investment Style: Equity, Stock %

77% 81% 77% 71% 59% 64% 70% 80% 84%

▼ Manager Change
▽ Partial Manager Change

Growth of $10,000
— Investment Values of Fund
— Investment Values of S&P 500

26.0 22.0 18.0 14.0 10.0

Performance Quartile (within Category)

1995	1996	1997	1998	1999	2000	2001	2002	2003	2004	2005	2006	History
—	18.56	21.26	19.49	20.38	19.73	19.37	16.78	20.89	22.94	23.81	25.91	NAV
—	6.66*	26.01	0.01	14.63	13.42	5.94	-11.20	26.18	13.50	9.98	17.98	Total Return %
—	—	-7.35	-28.57	-6.41	22.52	17.83	10.90	-2.50	2.62	5.07	2.19	+/-S&P 500
—	—	-9.17	-15.62	7.28	6.41	11.53	4.32	-3.85	-2.99	2.93	-4.27	+/-Russ 1000 Vl
—	—	2.69	2.19	1.78	3.19	0.92	1.02	1.57	1.55	1.45	1.90	Income Return %
—	—	23.32	-2.18	12.85	10.23	5.02	-12.22	24.61	11.95	8.53	16.08	Capital Return %
—	—	64	90	15	31	13	6	67	44	12	54	Total Rtn % Rank Cat
—	0.47	0.49	0.46	0.34	0.63	0.18	0.19	0.26	0.32	0.33	0.45	Income $
—	1.16	1.58	1.29	1.58	2.51	1.35	0.26	0.00	0.42	1.09	1.67	Capital Gains $
—	—	1.07	1.08	1.10	1.11	1.12	1.14	1.19	1.16	1.11	—	Expense Ratio %
—	—	1.58	1.78	1.23	1.34	1.05	1.44	0.93	1.27	1.64	—	Income Ratio %
—	58	50	69	66	63	53	51	55	33	22	—	Turnover Rate %
—	77	1,038	1,515	1,365	1,285	1,579	1,551	2,337	2,946	4,217	6,757	Net Assets $mil

Rating and Risk

Time Period	Load-Adj Return %	Morningstar Rtn vs Cat	Morningstar Risk vs Cat	Morningstar Risk-Adj Rating
1 Yr	11.19			
3 Yr	11.55	Avg	Low	★★★
5 Yr	9.23	+Avg	Low	★★★★
10 Yr	10.44	+Avg	Low	★★★★★
Incept	10.97			

Other Measures	Standard Index S&P 500	Best Fit Index MSCI World
Alpha	4.7	2.3
Beta	0.75	0.71
R-Squared	75	85
Standard Deviation	5.95	
Mean	13.77	
Sharpe Ratio	1.68	

Morningstar's Take by John Coumarianos 12-28-06

The foray into fallen growth stocks continues for Mutual Shares.

Like all the Mutual Series funds, this venerable value hound tends to avoid large companies that are closely followed by the analyst community. Instead, managers Peter Langerman, Deborah Turner, and David Segal shop the bargain bins for unknown, unloved, neglected, and obscure stocks that have a greater chance of being mispriced.

Lately, however, they have found some battered well-known stocks to buy. In addition to beefing up their positions in Microsoft and Pfizer, they recently picked up embattled computer maker Dell. Although it's known as a technology company, Dell is a manufacturing business with management and operational clouds hanging over it, according to the managers. They think competition has impaired the business somewhat but not to the extent that the stock's current price implies, making it a classic Mutual Series situation of exploiting what the managers interpret as a market overreaction.

This interest in unloved and battered stocks has helped the fund pick up shares that have little downside, placing it among those in its group with the lowest volatility (measured by standard deviation of returns) for the past five years. We think this helps investors stick around and enjoy the fund's returns. Indeed, it has posted a 65.5% cumulative gain for the past five years through Nov. 30, 2006 versus a 49.8% return for the large-value category average.

This fund's recent emphasis on larger capitalization has moved its average market capitalization from $8 billion to $22 billion over the past few years, and it has taken full advantage of its ability to roam overseas. This flexibility makes it less style-pure than some prefer, but it's also the cause of its fine performance. Also, its willingness to hold cash means that it will often lag in growth rallies. Still, we think the fund is poised to capture a return to favor of steady-Eddie large-cap stocks and remains an excellent choice for the long haul.

Address:	101 John F Kennedy Pkwy
	Short Hills NJ 07078
	800-342-5236
Web Address:	www.franklintempleton.com
Inception:	11-01-96*
Advisor:	Franklin Mutual Advisers, LLC
Subadvisor:	None
NTF Plans:	DATALynx NTF, Federated Tr NTF

Minimum Purchase:	$1000	Add: $50	IRA: $250
Min Auto Inv Plan:	$50	Add: $50	
Sales Fees:	5.75%L, 0.35%S, 2.00%R		
Management Fee:	0.60% mx./0.51% mn., 0.15%A		
Actual Fees:	Mgt:0.57%	Dist:0.35%	
Expense Projections:	3Yr:$922	5Yr:$1177	10Yr:$1903
Income Distrib:	Semi-Annually		

Portfolio Analysis 09-30-06

Share change since 06-06 Total Stocks:144	Sector	PE	Tot Ret%	% Assets
Berkshire Hathaway Inc.	Financial	13.2	24.89	2.37
Weyerhaeuser Company	Ind Mtrls	—	10.21	2.07
White Mountains Insuranc	Financial	15.2	5.27	1.83
⊕ Verizon Communications	Telecom	15.9	34.88	1.75
British American Tobacco	Goods	—	—	1.64
Tyco International, Ltd.	Ind Mtrls	15.7	6.83	1.61
Altadis	Goods	—	—	1.60
Fortis	Financial	—	—	1.56
Orkla	Ind Mtrls	—	—	1.52
Pfizer Inc.	Health	15.2	15.22	1.51
⊕ International Paper Co.	Ind Mtrls	—	4.51	1.50
News Cl A	Media	—	—	1.48
⊕ BellSouth Corporation	Telecom	—	—	1.48
⊕ Altria Group, Inc.	Goods	16.3	19.87	1.44
⊕ Reynolds American, Inc.	Goods	15.9	43.87	1.43
Time Warner, Inc.	Media	19.6	26.37	1.21
Florida East Coast Indus	Business	38.4	41.38	1.19
⊖ Pernod Ricard	Goods	—	—	1.17
Imperial Tobacco Grp	Goods	—	—	1.15
Nestle	Goods	—	—	1.13

Current Investment Style

Value Blnd Growth — Large Mid Small

Market Cap	%
Giant	36.7
Large	36.2
Mid	24.1
Small	3.0
Micro	0.0
Avg $mil:	22,274

Value Measures		Rel Category
Price/Earnings	14.18	1.03
Price/Book	1.93	0.87
Price/Sales	1.14	0.88
Price/Cash Flow	9.14	1.36
Dividend Yield %	2.50	1.07

Growth Measures	%	Rel Category
Long-Term Ergns	9.76	0.94
Book Value	7.71	0.97
Sales	6.57	0.73
Cash Flow	-0.08	NMF
Historical Ergns	15.59	0.97

Profitability	%	Rel Category
Return on Equity	16.01	0.89
Return on Assets	6.33	0.65
Net Margin	11.10	0.86

Sector Weightings	% of Stocks	Rel S&P 500	3 Year High Low
☊ Info	21.88	1.09	
▨ Software	1.58	0.46	2 0
▨ Hardware	4.49	0.49	4 0
▨ Media	8.55	2.26	9 8
▨ Telecom	7.26	2.07	7 3
☞ Service	42.51	0.92	
▨ Health	5.81	0.48	7 5
▨ Consumer	2.75	0.36	3 1
▨ Business	2.79	0.66	5 3
▨ Financial	31.16	1.40	31 26
▨ Mfg	35.62	1.05	
▨ Goods	16.68	1.95	28 17
▨ Ind Mtrls	13.18	1.10	17 12
▨ Energy	3.16	0.32	7 3
▨ Utilities	2.60	0.74	3 0

Composition

● Cash	11.6
● Stocks	83.9
● Bonds	1.0
○ Other	3.5
Foreign (% of Stock)	36.3

N/I Numeric Inv Sm CapVI

Ticker	**Load**	**NAV**	**Yield**	**Total Assets**	**Mstar Category**	
NISVX	Closed	$17.36	0.8%	$240 mil	Small Value	

Governance and Management

Stewardship Grade: B

Portfolio Manager(s)

All Numeric funds are team-managed, but Daniel Taylor took over in 2005 as lead manager along with longtime skipper Arup Datta, who focuses on N/I's large-cap and mid-cap strategies but serves as an overseer here. Taylor also took the helm of N/I Numeric Investors Emerging Growth and N/I Numeric Investors Growth. Taylor had previously comanaged those offerings since 2001 and joined the firm in 1999. He's assisted by Dennis Suvorov, who joined the firm as an analyst in 2001. They are supported by Numeric CIO Langdon Wheeler and three research analysts.

Strategy

Four quantitative models are used to build this broadly diversified portfolio. Management takes most of its cues from the shop's fair-value model, which focuses on companies trading at a discount to their industry peers and that carry a relatively low price/cash-flow ratio. The other models identify companies that avoid accounting gimmicks, boast increasing earnings or price momentum, and are not magnets for short-sellers. The fund's sector weightings mimic those of the Russell 2000 Value Index. Portfolio turnover is high but may moderate as the earnings-trend model is used more sparingly.

Performance 12-31-06

	1st Qtr	2nd Qtr	3rd Qtr	4th Qtr	Total
2002	16.70	2.68	-17.02	2.02	1.44
2003	-2.28	22.36	6.65	17.25	49.52
2004	7.03	-0.54	1.01	15.13	23.80
2005	-2.85	5.28	4.66	1.27	8.41
2006	11.32	-1.22	0.48	8.45	19.82

Trailing	Total Return%	+/- S&P 500	+/- Russ 2000 VL	%Rank Cat	Growth of $10,000
3 Mo	8.45	1.75	-0.58	51	10,845
6 Mo	8.98	-3.76	-2.83	42	10,898
1 Yr	19.82	4.03	-3.66	21	11,982
3 Yr Avg	17.16	6.72	0.68	7	16,082
5 Yr Avg	19.52	13.33	4.15	1	24,390
10 Yr Avg	—	—	—	—	—
15 Yr Avg	—	—	—	—	—

Tax Analysis	Tax-Adj Rtn%	%Rank Cat	Tax-Cost Rat	%Rank Cat
3 Yr (estimated)	10.34	75	5.82	100
5 Yr (estimated)	13.67	29	4.89	100
10 Yr (estimated)	—	—	—	—

Potential Capital Gain Exposure: 8% of assets

Morningstar's Take by Greg Carlson 12-21-06

It's falling short of its goal in 2006, but N/I Numeric Investors Small Cap Value's shareholders own a superb fund.

It's not apparent at first glance, but this fund is having an off year. It aims to outpace the Russell 2000 Value Index, but the fund is lagging the benchmark by more than 3 percentage points for the year to date through Dec. 19, 2006. That said, the index has been very difficult to beat this year--only eight of the fund's 126 small-value rivals have managed that feat thus far. Despite lagging the index, this fund resides in the category's top quintile.

The benchmark's dominance is likely due to the fact that the same, low-price-multiple areas that have led the market for years (particularly REITs) have continued to rally in 2006. Meanwhile, many actively managed funds have shied away, including this one, which employs quantitative stock-picking models. Although the fund is kept sector-neutral relative to the index, it has more leeway on subsector weightings.

Despite a subpar year, this fund owns an enviable long-term record against both its rivals and the benchmark. Its results attest to the efficacy of Numeric's models, as well as the willingness of its sizable team to make improvements. Lead manager Dan Taylor, a seven-year Numeric veteran, is backed by three other portfolio managers, as well as two analysts (all of whom support the firm's other three mutual funds as well). In addition, an eight-person central research team develops new factors for the models.

We also derive confidence from Numeric's generally shareholder-friendly actions: It closed this fund at a small size, and its performance-adjusted management fee is heavily tilted in favor of investors. We don't think its recent absolute returns--20% annualized over the past five years--are sustainable, and the team's fast-trading approach means it's best kept in a tax-deferred account. But it's a fine holding.

Address:	400 Bellevue Pkwy Ste 100 Wilmington DE 19809 800-686-3742	
Web Address:	www.numeric.com	
Inception:	11-30-98*	
Advisor:	Numeric Investors LLC	
Subadvisor:	None	
NTF Plans:	N/A	

Minimum Purchase:	Closed	Add: —	IRA: —
Min Auto Inv Plan:	Closed	Add: —	
Sales Fees:	No-load, 2.00%R		
Management Fee:	1.35%		
Actual Fees:	Mgt:1.35%	Dist: —	
Expense Projections:	3Yr:$610	5Yr:$1054	10Yr:$2289
Income Distrib:	Annually		

Historical Profile

Return	High
Risk	Average
Rating	★★★★★ Highest

Investment Style: Equity Stock %

95% / 96% / 97% / 96% / 99% / 96% / 99% / 98%

▼ Manager Change
▽ Partial Manager Change

Growth of $10,000
— Investment Values of Fund
— Investment Values of S&P 500

39.4 / 32.4 / 24.0 / 17.0 / 10.0

Performance Quartile (within Category)

	1995	1996	1997	1998	1999	2000	2001	2002	2003	2004	2005	2006	History
	—	—	—	12.37	10.83	14.52	15.69	14.46	19.19	19.30	16.88	17.36	NAV
	—	—	—	3.08*	-0.63	35.61	27.89	1.44	49.52	23.80	8.41	19.82	Total Return %
	—	—	—	—	-21.67	44.71	39.78	23.54	20.84	12.92	3.50	4.03	+/-S&P 500
	—	—	—	—	0.86	12.78	13.87	12.87	3.49	1.55	3.70	-3.66	+/-Russ 2000 VL
	—	—	—	—	0.79	1.32	0.12	0.00	0.64	0.43	0.89	1.02	Income Return %
	—	—	—	—	-1.42	34.29	27.77	1.44	48.88	23.37	7.52	18.80	Capital Return %
	—	—	—	—	63	4	12	4	22	19	26	21	Total Rtn % Rank Cat
	—	—	—	0.00	0.10	0.14	0.02	0.00	0.09	0.08	0.15	0.17	Income $
	—	—	—	0.00	1.32	0.00	2.58	1.41	2.24	3.76	3.71	2.59	Capital Gains $
	—	—	—	—	1.00	1.00	1.67	1.73	1.55	0.92	0.99	0.54	Expense Ratio %
	—	—	—	—	1.15	1.35	0.17	-0.35	0.33	0.45	0.43	0.87	Income Ratio %
	—	—	—	—	—	—	256	277	276	268	367	349	242	Turnover Rate %
	—	—	—	—	11	20	46	114	198	258	222	240	Net Assets $mil

Rating and Risk

Time Period	Load-Adj Return %	Morningstar Rtn vs Cat	Morningstar Risk vs Cat	Morningstar Risk-Adj Rating
1 Yr	19.82			
3 Yr	17.16	High	+Avg	★★★★
5 Yr	19.52	High	Avg	★★★★★
10 Yr	—			
Incept	19.88			

Other Measures	Standard Index S&P 500	Best Fit Index Russ 2000 VL
Alpha	2.6	0.9
Beta	1.56	0.98
R-Squared	73	94
Standard Deviation	12.54	
Mean	17.16	
Sharpe Ratio	1.08	

Portfolio Analysis 10-31-06

Share change since 09-06 Total Stocks:233	Sector	PE	Tot Ret%	% Assets
⊖ Zenith National Insuranc	Financial	7.4	4.36	1.52
⊖ PS Business Parks, Inc.	Financial	99.3	46.55	1.42
⊕ Commerce Group, Inc.	Financial	8.2	7.44	1.36
⊖ Cash America Internation	Financial	24.8	102.85	1.34
⊖ Felcor Lodging Trust, In	Financial	—	31.79	1.33
⊖ CBL & Associates Propert	Financial	23.5	14.78	1.27
⊕ Fair Isaac, Inc.	Business	25.4	-7.78	1.26
⊖ Parkway Properties, Inc.	Financial	52.6	34.46	1.25
⊕ Spirit Finance Corporati	Financial	23.4	18.22	1.25
⊖ J.M. Smucker Co.	Goods	19.5	12.99	1.21
⊖ FreightCar America, Inc.	Ind Mtrls	—	15.62	1.17
⊕ Penn Virginia Corporatio	Energy	13.3	22.81	1.17
⊕ Entertainment Properties	Financial	23.1	51.98	1.16
⊕ RPM International, Inc.	Goods	—	24.55	1.14
⊕ General Maritime Corpora	Business	5.0	8.76	1.13
⊖ St. Mary Land & Explorat	Energy	11.5	0.33	1.13
✸ American Axle & Mfg Hold	Ind Mtrls	16.7	7.35	1.11
⊕ OMI Corporation	Business	4.2	19.34	1.10
⊕ Celanese Corporation	Ind Mtrls	—	36.48	1.10
⊕ Overseas Shipholding Gro	Business	5.5	13.55	1.09

Current Investment Style

Value Blnd Growth — Large Mid Small

Market Cap	%
Giant	0.0
Large	0.0
Mid	33.2
Small	54.3
Micro	12.4

Avg $mil: 1,279

Value Measures		Rel Category
Price/Earnings	12.32	0.80
Price/Book	1.87	1.05
Price/Sales	0.91	1.14
Price/Cash Flow	5.83	0.95
Dividend Yield %	1.31	0.83

Growth Measures	%	Rel Category
Long-Term Erngs	11.55	0.93
Book Value	5.05	0.93
Sales	10.33	1.40
Cash Flow	10.56	1.29
Historical Erngs	8.02	0.70

Profitability	%	Rel Category
Return on Equity	13.95	1.30
Return on Assets	7.87	1.29
Net Margin	12.17	1.34

Sector Weightings	% of Stocks	Rel S&P 500	3 Year High Low	
⟳ Info	11.55	0.58		
⬛ Software	2.34	0.68	5	0
⬛ Hardware	6.58	0.71	8	1
⬛ Media	1.00	0.26	2	0
⬛ Telecom	1.63	0.46	4	0
⟳ Service	61.58	1.33		
⬛ Health	6.73	0.56	7	3
⬛ Consumer	9.03	1.18	13	7
⬛ Business	11.39	2.69	14	7
⬛ Financial	34.43	1.55	36	30
⟳ Mfg	26.86	0.79		
⬛ Goods	6.12	0.72	9	3
⬛ Ind Mtrls	9.76	0.82	18	8
⬛ Energy	6.08	0.62	10	4
⬛ Utilities	4.90	1.40	6	2

Composition	
● Cash	1.8
● Stocks	98.2
● Bonds	0.0
○ Other	0.0
Foreign (% of Stock)	1.3

Mᴏʀɴɪɴɢsᴛᴀʀ® Funds 500

Neuberger Ber Genesis Inv

		Ticker	Load	NAV	Yield	Total Assets	Mstar Category
		NBGNX	Closed	$33.36	1.3%	$10,397 mil	Small Blend

Governance and Management

Stewardship Grade: B

Portfolio Manager(s)

Judy Vale has managed this fund since February 1994, and comanager Bob D'Alelio joined her in August 1997. In December 2005, Gordon Bowyer and Brett Reiner were promoted to associate portfolio managers after serving as dedicated analysts under Vale and D'Alelio for several years. The team can also draw on ideas from Neuberger Berman's shared analyst team.

Strategy

A four-person management team led by Judy Vale and Bob D'Alelio tries to own companies that dominate a competitive niche, generate good free cash flow, and are able to grow internally regardless of what the economy does. They try to keep the portfolio's P/E ratio below that of the Russell 2000, though they'll pay up more for stocks in faster-growing industries. They can't buy stocks with market caps above $1.5 billion, but many of the stocks in the portfolio have grown bigger than that due to price appreciation.

Performance 12-31-06

	1st Qtr	2nd Qtr	3rd Qtr	4th Qtr	Total
2002	7.77	-5.02	-8.60	3.73	-2.96
2003	-3.36	13.53	6.17	13.07	31.70
2004	5.18	4.52	-1.37	9.54	18.76
2005	2.78	4.37	9.12	-0.59	16.37
2006	6.51	-4.17	-1.12	6.34	7.31

Trailing	Total Return%	+/- S&P 500	+/- Russ 2000	%Rank Cat	Growth of $10,000
3 Mo	6.34	-0.36	-2.56	89	10,634
6 Mo	5.15	-7.59	-4.23	83	10,515
1 Yr	7.31	-8.48	-11.06	95	10,731
3 Yr Avg	14.04	3.60	0.48	39	14,831
5 Yr Avg	13.64	7.45	2.25	24	18,952
10 Yr Avg	13.91	5.49	4.47	21	36,781
15 Yr Avg	14.73	4.09	3.26	18	78,552

Tax Analysis	Tax-Adj Rtn%	%Rank Cat	Tax-Cost Rat	%Rank Cat
3 Yr (estimated)	13.13	29	0.80	20
5 Yr (estimated)	13.08	21	0.49	17
10 Yr (estimated)	13.17	15	0.65	13

Potential Capital Gain Exposure: 36% of assets

Morningstar's Take by David Kathman 12-13-06

Don't give up on Neuberger Berman Genesis.

This has been a fund of extremes over the past few years. As of mid-December 2006, its year-to-date returns were stuck in the bottom 10% of the small-blend category, and it was trailing the Russell 2000 benchmark by a wide margin. In 2005, by contrast, it ranked in the category's top 5%, and it trounced the Russell 2000. The fund is no stranger to such ups and downs; it also landed in the category's bottom decile in 2003, and in the category's top decile in 2000 and 2002.

It might be tempting to conclude from these roller-coaster results that this is a volatile fund, but in fact the opposite is the case. The portfolio's standard deviation has been among the lowest in the small-blend category over the trailing three, five, and 10 years, and its annual turnover has averaged less than 20%. It's actually a remarkably stable fund in a volatile peer group, which is why its results relative to that peer group have varied so much from year to year.

Lead managers Judy Vale and Bob D'Alelio have been with the fund since 1994 and 1997, and during that time they've followed a very consistent strategy that looks for small niche leaders that generate good free cash flow and aren't too cyclical. Though the managers won't buy stocks with market caps above $1.5 billion, they often keep winners for years, which is why more than half the portfolio is now in mid-caps. They've maintained bets in areas where they see long-term value, notably energy, health care, and niche defense stocks.

The fund's $10 billion asset base is large for either a small-cap or a mid-cap fund, but those assets have been shrinking over the past year, and we're not too worried. The fund's very low turnover has allowed the managers to handle the asset base quite well, and a soft close in December 2001 has also helped. Overall, this fund remains an attractive way for skittish investors to get small- and mid-cap exposure without much volatility.

Address:	605 Third Ave 2nd FL New York NY 10158-0006 800-877-9700
Web Address:	www.nb.com
Inception:	09-27-88
Advisor:	Neuberger Berman Management Inc.
Subadvisor:	Neuberger Berman, LLC
NTF Plans:	Schwab OneSource

Minimum Purchase:	Closed	Add: —	IRA: —
Min Auto Inv Plan:	Closed	Add: —	
Sales Fees:	No-load		
Management Fee:	0.92%, 0.26%A		
Actual Fees:	Mgt:0.92%	Dist:—	
Expense Projections:	3Yr:$328	5Yr:$569	10Yr:$1259
Income Distrib:	Annually		

Historical Profile

Return	Above Avg
Risk	Low
Rating	★★★★ Above Avg

93%	92%	93%	95%	93%	94%	94%	97%	94%

Investment Style
Equity
Stock %

- ▼ Manager Change
- ▽ Partial Manager Change

Growth of $10,000
— Investment Values of Fund
— Investment Values of S&P 500

Performance Quartile (within Category)

1995	1996	1997	1998	1999	2000	2001	2002	2003	2004	2005	2006	History
9.38	12.03	16.03	14.44	14.94	18.67	20.33	19.66	25.88	29.84	33.97	33.36	NAV
27.31	29.86	34.89	-6.95	4.04	32.51	12.11	-2.96	31.70	18.76	16.37	7.31	Total Return %
-10.27	6.90	1.53	-35.53	-17.00	41.61	24.00	19.14	3.02	7.88	11.46	-8.48	+/-S&P 500
-1.14	13.37	12.53	-4.40	-17.22	35.53	9.62	17.52	-15.55	0.43	11.82	-11.06	+/-Russ 2000
0.00	0.00	0.00	0.75	0.55	0.00	0.00	0.00	0.00	0.00	0.00	1.37	Income Return %
27.31	29.86	34.89	-7.70	3.49	32.51	12.11	-2.96	31.70	18.76	16.37	5.94	Capital Return %
49	16	19	64	72	6	32	4	94	52	5	95	Total Rtn % Rank Cat
0.00	0.00	0.00	0.12	0.08	0.00	0.00	0.00	0.00	0.00	0.00	0.46	Income $
0.55	0.15	0.19	0.34	0.34	1.04	0.58	0.07	0.01	0.89	0.77	2.67	Capital Gains $
1.35	1.28	1.16	1.11	1.17	1.21	1.11	1.10	1.08	1.05	1.04	1.02	Expense Ratio %
-0.16	-0.18	-0.08	0.72	0.61	-0.02	-0.07	-0.05	-0.31	-0.38	-0.25	-0.15	Income Ratio %
37	21	18	18	33		19	19	17	23	11	19	Turnover Rate %
119	299	1,246	1,195	736	841	1,061	1,054	1,301	1,539	1,907	1,844	Net Assets $mil

Rating and Risk

Time Period	Load-Adj Return %	Morningstar Rtn vs Cat	Morningstar Risk vs Cat	Morningstar Risk-Adj Rating
1 Yr	7.31			
3 Yr	14.04	Avg	Low	★★★★
5 Yr	13.64	+Avg	Low	★★★★
10 Yr	13.91	+Avg	Low	★★★★
Incept	14.20			

Other Measures	Standard Index S&P 500	Best Fit Index S&P Mid 400
Alpha	2.6	1.8
Beta	1.14	0.91
R-Squared	53	77
Standard Deviation	10.65	
Mean	14.04	
Sharpe Ratio	0.98	

Portfolio Analysis 10-31-06

Share change since 09-06 Total Stocks:125

	Sector	PE	Tot Ret%	% Assets
⊖ XTO Energy, Inc.	Energy	9.0	12.16	2.99
⊖ National Oilwell Varco,	Energy	18.3	-2.42	2.65
⊖ Church & Dwight Company,	Goods	22.2	30.00	2.60
⊖ Alberto Culver Company	Goods	10.4	19.16	2.53
⊖ Henry Schein, Inc.	Health	24.0	12.24	2.01
⊖ Mentor Corporation	Health	52.4	7.70	2.00
⊖ Southwestern Energy Comp	Energy	32.6	-2.48	1.95
⊖ Denbury Resources, Inc.	Energy	16.0	21.99	1.75
⊖ AptarGroup, Inc.	Goods	21.1	14.89	1.73
⊖ Clarcor Inc.	Ind Mtrls	21.6	14.81	1.71
⊖ Zebra Technologies Corpo	Hardware	30.4	-18.81	1.67
⊖ Alliant Techsystems, Inc	Ind Mtrls	18.2	2.65	1.66
⊖ Idexx Laboratories	Health	30.4	10.17	1.59
⊖ Pharmaceutical Product D	Health	24.3	4.26	1.58
⊖ Brady Corporation A	Ind Mtrls	17.4	4.55	1.48
⊖ Helix Energy Solutions G	Energy	10.6	-12.59	1.44
⊖ Joy Global, Inc.	Ind Mtrls	15.1	22.11	1.42
⊖ Roper Industries, Inc.	Ind Mtrls	24.8	27.83	1.42
⊖ Matthews International C	Ind Mtrls	20.0	8.68	1.36
⊖ DRS Technologies, Inc.	Ind Mtrls	19.7	2.71	1.34

Current Investment Style

Value Blnd Growth — Large Mid Small

Market Cap	%
Giant	0.0
Large	4.3
Mid	60.3
Small	33.4
Micro	2.0
Avg $mil:	2,388

Value Measures		Rel Category
Price/Earnings	18.93	1.14
Price/Book	2.85	1.35
Price/Sales	1.85	1.89
Price/Cash Flow	10.36	1.48
Dividend Yield %	0.69	0.64

Growth Measures	%	Rel Category
Long-Term Erngs	16.36	1.17
Book Value	18.03	2.38
Sales	15.27	1.73
Cash Flow	20.52	1.62
Historical Erngs	20.94	1.25

Profitability	%	Rel Category
Return on Equity	18.62	1.44
Return on Assets	10.46	1.46
Net Margin	15.75	1.63

Sector Weightings	% of Stocks	Rel S&P 500	3 Year High	Low
↻ Info	6.55	0.33		
🖥 Software	2.76	0.80	3	2
💻 Hardware	3.22	0.35	8	3
📺 Media	0.57	0.15	1	0
📱 Telecom	0.00	0.00	0	0
⊂ Service	41.96	0.91		
❤ Health	20.99	1.74	24	20
🛒 Consumer	3.48	0.45	8	3
📋 Business	7.35	1.74	11	7
💲 Financial	10.14	0.46	16	9
🏭 Mfg	51.48	1.52		
⚙ Goods	7.68	0.90	9	6
🔧 Ind Mtrls	22.20	1.86	23	15
🔋 Energy	21.27	2.17	26	12
💡 Utilities	0.33	0.09	0	0

Composition

- Cash 5.5
- Stocks 94.5
- Bonds 0.0
- Other 0.0
- Foreign 5.7 (% of Stock)

Neuberger Ber Intl Inv

	Ticker	Load	NAV	Yield	Total Assets	Mstar Category
	NBISX	Closed	$24.48	1.1%	$1,631 mil	Foreign Small/Mid Growth

Governance and Management

Stewardship Grade: B

Portfolio Manager(s)

Lead manager Benjamin Segal joined the fund (as comanager) in 2000. In late 2005, Milu Komer, who has worked with Segal on the fund as an analyst for about five years, was promoted to comanager. Segal and Komer work with a team of three analysts who focus specifically on this fund (two of them have been on the team for at least four years) and also consult research from Neuberger Berman's research department and outside sources.

Strategy

The fund uses an all-cap approach. Its manager favors steadily growing firms, based on both revenue and earnings growth, but is equally concerned about the quality of company management and valuations. He also looks for high returns on capital. The managers try to reduce the overall portfolio's risk level by keeping individual positions small. Currency hedging is used infrequently. The fund has used FTInteractive for fair-value pricing since mid-2004.

Performance 12-31-06

	1st Qtr	2nd Qtr	3rd Qtr	4th Qtr	Total
2002	1.22	0.52	-17.94	4.08	-13.10
2003	-6.96	20.48	8.63	17.68	43.30
2004	8.19	2.50	2.18	15.02	30.33
2005	3.79	1.11	14.35	3.39	23.96
2006	11.12	-1.16	1.39	12.42	25.18

Trailing	Total Return%	+/- MSCI EAFE	+/- MSCI Wd xUS	%Rank Cat	Growth of $10,000
3 Mo	12.42	2.07	2.30	72	11,242
6 Mo	13.98	-0.71	-0.24	69	11,398
1 Yr	25.18	-1.16	-0.53	67	12,518
3 Yr Avg	26.46	6.53	6.36	38	20,224
5 Yr Avg	20.29	5.31	5.04	55	25,185
10 Yr Avg	11.42	3.71	3.46	90	29,487
15 Yr Avg	—	—	—	—	—

Tax Analysis	Tax-Adj Rtn%	%Rank Cat	Tax-Cost Rat	%Rank Cat
3 Yr (estimated)	25.08	32	1.09	38
5 Yr (estimated)	19.37	48	0.76	60
10 Yr (estimated)	10.39	83	0.92	40

Potential Capital Gain Exposure: 21% of assets

Morningstar's Take by Gregg Wolper 12-23-06

There's good reason to like Neuberger Berman International, even though its performance rankings don't stand out.

For the trailing five-year period through Dec. 22, 2006 (which covers lead manager Benjamin Segal's tenure), this fund ranks around the middle of the foreign small/mid-growth category. The story is much the same for 2006: Its year-to-date return lags nearly two thirds of that group.

But this is not the mediocre offering those numbers might imply. In fact, it is an all-cap portfolio, and until 2006, smaller stocks have outperformed, often by wide margins. That handicapped this fund in its category rankings, for most others in this group are dedicated primarily to small caps. (This fund's average market cap is the category's highest.) Though it had some impact this year, the discrepancy wasn't as large. Some stock- and sector-specific factors did hold the fund back, such as an underweighting in the utilities sector, which Segal doesn't like because he sees it as a low-growth, highly regulated area.

Viewed as an all-cap offering, the fund's rankings look better. Its 2006 return would land in the top half of the foreign large-growth or foreign large-blend categories, and its longer-term results also would rank much higher. And the fund's five-year returns trounce the MSCI EAFE Index (its benchmark) by more than 5 percentage points on an annualized basis.

Moreover, the fund's strategy is appealing. With substantial holdings in all sizes of companies, about 10% of assets in emerging markets, and a reasonable balance between growth and value leanings, the fund provides exposure to a broad swath of the international markets (aside from utilities). It doesn't mimic indexes and owns plenty of stocks generally overlooked by peers. In addition, its expense ratio has been falling sharply. All in all, current shareholders (the fund is closed to new investors) own a solid fund.

Address:	605 Third Ave 2nd FL New York NY 10158-0006 800-877-9700
Web Address:	www.nb.com
Inception:	06-15-94
Advisor:	Neuberger Berman Management Inc.
Subadvisor:	Neuberger Berman, LLC
NTF Plans:	Schwab OneSource

Minimum Purchase:	Closed	Add: —	IRA: —
Min Auto Inv Plan:	Closed	Add: —
Sales Fees:	No-load, 2.00%R
Management Fee:	1.06%, 0.26%A
Actual Fees:	Mgt:1.06%	Dist: —
Expense Projections:	3Yr:$400	5Yr:$692	10Yr:$1523
Income Distrib:	Annually

Historical Profile

Return	Average
Risk	Below Avg
Rating	★★★ Neutral

Investment Style: Equity, Stock %

Growth of $10,000
- Investment Values of Fund
- Investment Values of MSCI EAFE

▼ Manager Change
▽ Partial Manager Change

	1995	1996	1997	1998	1999	2000	2001	2002	2003	2004	2005	2006	History
	10.64	13.14	14.47	14.80	24.31	14.04	11.45	9.92	14.05	18.20	21.67	24.48	NAV
	7.88	23.69	11.21	2.35	65.86	-24.36	-18.01	-13.10	43.30	30.33	23.96	25.18	Total Return %
	-3.33	17.64	9.43	-17.58	38.83	-10.17	3.41	2.84	4.71	10.08	10.42	-1.16	+/-MSCI EAFE
	-3.53	16.82	8.94	-16.34	37.88	-11.00	3.38	2.70	3.88	9.95	9.49	-0.53	+/-MSCI Wd xUS
	0.40	0.19	0.00	0.00	0.07	0.00	0.14	0.26	1.60	0.76	0.70	1.33	Income Return %
	7.48	23.50	11.21	2.35	65.79	-24.36	-18.15	-13.36	41.70	29.57	23.26	23.85	Capital Return %
	50	25	60	100	61	84	23	43	83	13	58	67	Total Rtn % Rank Cat
	0.04	0.02	0.00	0.00	0.01	0.00	0.02	0.03	0.16	0.11	0.13	0.29	Income $
	0.00	0.00	0.14	0.01	0.21	4.32	0.04	0.00	0.00	0.00	0.75	2.33	Capital Gains $
	1.70	1.70	1.70	1.71	1.61	1.43	1.56	1.69	1.70	1.57	1.39	1.25	Expense Ratio %
	0.73	0.24	-0.02	-0.24	-0.43	-0.33	0.33	0.31	1.00	0.68	0.82	1.19	Income Ratio %
	41	45	37	46	94	—	61	63	90	72	38	48	Turnover Rate %
	33	73	112	127	192	137	90	70	103	246	688	765	Net Assets $mil

Performance Quartile (within Category)

Rating and Risk

Time Period	Load-Adj Return %	Morningstar Rtn vs Cat	Morningstar Risk vs Cat	Morningstar Risk-Adj Rating
1 Yr	25.18			
3 Yr	26.46	Avg	-Avg	★★★
5 Yr	20.29	Avg	-Avg	★★★
10 Yr	11.42	-Avg	-Avg	★★
Incept	11.47			

Other Measures	Standard Index MSCI EAFE	Best Fit Index MSCI Wd xUS
Alpha	2.8	2.8
Beta	1.18	1.17
R-Squared	85	86
Standard Deviation	12.07	
Mean	26.46	
Sharpe Ratio	1.76	

Portfolio Analysis 11-30-06

Share change since 10-06 Total Stocks:93

	Sector	Country	% Assets
⊖ Anglo Irish Bank	Financial	Ireland	3.11
⊖ Porsche	Goods	Germany	2.39
⊖ Punch Taverns	Consumer	U.K.	2.27
⊕ CRH (UK)	—	Ireland	2.27
Vodafone Grp	Telecom	U.K.	2.26
Burren Energy	Energy	U.K.	2.19
Barclays	Financial	U.K.	2.00
InBev	Goods	Belgium	1.98
⊖ Redrow	Consumer	U.K.	1.91
Woodside Petroleum Ltd	Energy	Australia	1.79
Canadian Natural Res	Energy	Canada	1.71
FCC	—	Japan	1.69
Nissan Motor	Goods	Japan	1.66
Talisman Energy	Energy	—	1.63
William Hill	Consumer	U.K.	1.63
⊕ Suncor Energy	Energy	Canada	1.62
Hardman Resources Ltd	Energy	Australia	1.60
Companhia Vale Do Rio Do	Ind Mtrls	Brazil	1.57
Petroleo Brasileiro S.A.	Energy	Brazil	1.55
⊕ MacDonald Dettwiler and	Software	Canada	1.54

Current Investment Style

Value Blnd Growth — Large Mid Small

Market Cap	%
Giant	24.2
Large	22.7
Mid	38.6
Small	14.4
Micro	0.0

Avg $mil: 6,962

Value Measures		Rel Category
Price/Earnings	14.04	0.90
Price/Book	2.18	0.90
Price/Sales	1.10	1.00
Price/Cash Flow	6.75	0.86
Dividend Yield %	2.30	1.12

Growth Measures	%	Rel Category
Long-Term Erngs	11.62	0.57
Book Value	8.91	0.94
Sales	16.97	1.35
Cash Flow	23.03	1.53
Historical Erngs	8.10	0.36

Composition

Cash	4.8	Bonds	0.0
Stocks	92.3	Other	2.9
Foreign (% of Stock)			100.0

Sector Weightings

	% of Stocks	Rel MSCI EAFE	3 Year High	Low
↻ Info	9.97	0.84		
🖥 Software	1.85	3.30	2	0
💻 Hardware	2.77	0.72	4	1
🎙 Media	0.00	0.00	4	0
📶 Telecom	5.35	0.96	10	3
⚙ Service	35.27	0.75		
🏥 Health	2.86	0.40	7	1
🛒 Consumer	9.47	1.91	13	8
💼 Business	5.45	1.07	13	5
💲 Financial	17.49	0.58	26	13
🏭 Mfg	54.75	1.34		
🏗 Goods	10.90	0.83	14	9
⚒ Ind Mtrls	18.87	1.22	21	12
⛽ Energy	24.98	3.49	28	8
💡 Utilities	0.00	0.00	2	0

Regional Exposure

	% Stock		% Stock
UK/W. Europe	61	N. America	8
Japan	15	Latn America	6
Asia X Japan	11	Other	0

Country Exposure

	% Stock		% Stock
U.K.	19	Germany	9
Japan	15	Canada	8
Ireland	9		

MORNINGSTAR® Funds 500

Neuberger Ber Fasciano In

Ticker NBFSX	**Load** None	**NAV** $42.14	**Yield** 0.0%	**Total Assets** $495 mil	**Mstar Category** Small Growth	

Governance and Management

Stewardship Grade: B

Portfolio Manager(s)

Seasoned. Michael Fasciano started this offering on his own back in 1987. He sold his firm to Neuberger Berman, which is now part of Lehman Brothers, in January 2001 and is backed by that firm's research staff. He has two dedicated analysts, both hired in 2005.

Strategy

Manager Michael Fasciano seeks companies with clean balance sheets and the ability to increase earnings by 15% to 25% a year, but he also requires stocks in the portfolio to have reasonable valuations. He will buy only stocks with market caps of less than $1.5 billion, but he will let them grow to $3 billion in size before he sells them. The fund's turnover tends to be fairly low, as Fasciano typically has a three- to five-year time horizon for each of his picks.

Performance 12-31-06

	1st Qtr	2nd Qtr	3rd Qtr	4th Qtr	Total
2002	10.44	-5.49	-13.19	0.79	-8.67
2003	-8.02	19.46	4.16	13.34	29.72
2004	3.13	2.71	-1.35	7.70	12.55
2005	-4.97	2.28	4.82	0.69	2.60
2006	9.44	-5.91	-3.89	5.96	4.86

Trailing	Total Return%	+/- S&P 500	+/- Russ 2000 Gr	%Rank Cat	Growth of $10,000
3 Mo	5.96	-0.74	-2.81	82	10,596
6 Mo	1.83	-10.91	-5.03	87	10,183
1 Yr	4.86	-10.93	-8.49	87	10,486
3 Yr Avg	6.59	-3.85	-3.92	80	12,110
5 Yr Avg	7.48	1.29	0.55	40	14,343
10 Yr Avg	7.74	-0.68	2.86	54	21,075
15 Yr Avg	10.07	-0.57	2.97	42	42,173

Tax Analysis	Tax-Adj Rtn%	%Rank Cat	Tax-Cost Rat	%Rank Cat
3 Yr (estimated)	5.85	76	0.69	26
5 Yr (estimated)	7.03	36	0.42	23
10 Yr (estimated)	7.14	44	0.56	12

Potential Capital Gain Exposure: 23% of assets

Morningstar's Take by David Kathman 12-19-06

Neuberger Berman Fasciano has more to offer than its recent performance might suggest.

This fund has had another tough year in 2006. As of Dec. 19, it trailed 89% of its peers in the small-growth category for the year to date, on track for its third year out of the past four in the category's bottom quartile. Those numbers are certainly not pretty, but they're also not unexpected given the fund's strategy, and they don't change our positive view of the fund for patient, long-term investors.

One thing we like about this offering is manager Michael Fasciano, who has been running the fund for nearly 20 years and has much of his wealth invested in it. He has been using the same approach that whole time--looking for small-cap stocks that will double their earnings in the next three to five years, but which are also reasonably priced and fiscally responsible. He likes to see low debt, high returns on equity, and high insider ownership, and he tends to hang on to stocks he

likes for years, resulting in low turnover.

This has not been a recipe for success in the small-cap market of the past few years, when speculative stocks in hot industries have raced past the relatively staid stocks that Fasciano prefers. This fund hasn't completely missed out; a number of energy stocks such as Tetra Technologies (now the portfolio's top holding) have done very well, as have some industrials such as specialty chemical firm Rockwood Holdings. But the fund's media holdings got hammered in 2006, leading Fasciano to sell some of them, and many of its other holdings have posted only middling returns.

On the plus side, this fund has been extremely stable, with one of the lowest standard deviations in the small-growth category. It has lost money only once in the past 15 years--in 2002, when it outperformed 99% of its peers. It's definitely not for those who want an aggressive small-cap fund, but cautious investors with a long-term view should find a lot to like here.

Address:	605 Third Ave 2nd FL New York NY 10158-0006 800-877-9700
Web Address:	www.nb.com
Inception:	11-10-88
Advisor:	Neuberger Berman Management Inc.
Subadvisor:	Neuberger Berman, LLC
NTF Plans:	Fidelity Retail-NTF, Schwab OneSource

Minimum Purchase:	$1000	Add: $100	IRA: $250
Min Auto Inv Plan:	$100	Add: $100	
Sales Fees:	No-load		
Management Fee:	1.00%, 0.15%A		
Actual Fees:	Mgt:1.00%	Dist: —	
Expense Projections:	3Yr:$384	5Yr:$665	10Yr:$1466
Income Distrib:	Annually		

Historical Profile

Return	Average
Risk	Low
Rating	★★★ Neutral

| 50% | 83% | 100% | 99% | 96% | 91% | 92% | 89% | 93% |

Investment Style
Equity
Stock %

▼ Manager Change
▽ Partial Manager Change

Growth of $10,000
■ Investment Values of Fund
— Investment Values of S&P 500

Performance Quartile (within Category)

1995	1996	1997	1998	1999	2000	2001	2002	2003	2004	2005	2006	History
21.18	26.20	30.31	31.19	32.72	32.98	33.33	30.44	39.29	42.86	42.39	42.14	NAV
31.12	26.54	21.51	7.19	6.16	1.70	4.46	-8.67	29.72	12.55	2.60	4.86	Total Return %
-6.46	3.58	-11.85	-21.39	-14.88	10.80	16.35	13.43	1.04	1.67	-2.31	-10.93	+/-S&P 500
0.08	15.28	8.56	5.96	-36.93	24.13	13.69	21.59	-18.82	-1.76	-1.55	-8.49	+/-Russ 2000 Gr
0.00	0.00	0.00	0.10	1.25	0.90	0.00	0.00	0.00	0.00	0.00	0.00	Income Return %
31.12	26.54	21.51	7.09	4.91	0.80	4.46	-8.67	29.72	12.55	2.60	4.86	Capital Return %
59	15	33	39	95	33	19	1	96	47	81	87	Total Rtn % Rank Cat
0.00	0.00	0.00	0.03	0.39	0.29	0.00	0.00	0.00	0.00	0.00	0.00	Income $
1.34	0.59	1.49	1.25	0.40	1.08	0.00	0.19	1.34	1.61	2.31		Capital Gains $
1.70	1.50	1.40	1.30	1.20	1.20	1.58	1.36	1.24	1.22	1.20	1.20	Expense Ratio %
-0.60	-0.30	-0.40	0.24	1.80	0.80	-1.03	-0.48	-0.36	-0.52	-0.13	-0.28	Income Ratio %
38	46	41	50	20	29	4	24	24	17	22	39	Turnover Rate %
24	34	56	233	398	237	199	214	318	456	520	465	Net Assets $mil

Rating and Risk

Time Period	Load-Adj Return %	Morningstar Rtn vs Cat	Morningstar Risk vs Cat	Morningstar Risk-Adj Rating
1 Yr	4.86			
3 Yr	6.59	-Avg	Low	★★
5 Yr	7.48	Avg	Low	★★★
10 Yr	7.74	Avg	Low	★★★★
Incept	11.31			

Other Measures	Standard Index S&P 500	Best Fit Index Russ 2000 Gr
Alpha	-5.2	-1.6
Beta	1.28	0.66
R-Squared	63	89
Standard Deviation	11.07	
Mean	6.59	
Sharpe Ratio	0.34	

Portfolio Analysis 10-31-06

Share change since 09-06 Total Stocks:76	Sector	PE	Tot Ret%	% Assets
Tetra Technologies, Inc.	Energy	18.9	67.63	2.71
Bucyrus International, I	Ind Mtrls	20.2	47.92	2.43
Wintrust Financial Corpo	Financial	16.1	-12.04	2.39
Idex Corporation	Ind Mtrls	19.6	16.76	2.30
J2 Global Communications	Telecom	26.6	27.52	2.13
Rollins, Inc.	Business	27.1	13.52	2.02
⊖ Landstar System, Inc.	Business	18.1	-8.30	2.02
Meredith Corporation	Media	18.9	9.02	1.92
⊖ Young Innovations, Inc.	Health	19.4	-1.83	1.88
K-V Pharmaceutical Compa	Health	24.5	15.44	1.87
Actuant Corporation A	Ind Mtrls	15.6	-14.47	1.86
Middleby Corporation	Ind Mtrls	24.1	21.01	1.82
Steak n Shake Company	Consumer	16.5	3.84	1.69
⊖ ScanSource	Ind Mtrls	19.7	11.19	1.67
Central Garden & Pet Com	Ind Mtrls	16.0	5.40	1.64
Hub Group, Inc. A	Business	25.2	55.87	1.63
Clarcor Inc.	Ind Mtrls	21.6	14.81	1.60
International Speedway C	Goods	16.8	6.73	1.58
Landauer, Inc.	Business	26.9	18.22	1.57
Ritchie Bros. Auctioneer	Consumer	34.7	28.67	1.50

Current Investment Style

Value Blnd Growth — Large Mid Small

Market Cap	%
Giant	0.0
Large	0.0
Mid	14.5
Small	68.2
Micro	17.3
Avg $mil:	1,067

Value Measures		Rel Category
Price/Earnings	18.53	0.88
Price/Book	2.55	0.93
Price/Sales	1.42	0.90
Price/Cash Flow	10.87	1.13
Dividend Yield %	0.86	1.87

Growth Measures	%	Rel Category
Long-Term Erngs	15.75	0.89
Book Value	15.11	1.44
Sales	14.22	1.20
Cash Flow	13.10	0.62
Historical Erngs	18.01	0.74

Profitability	%	Rel Category
Return on Equity	18.09	1.46
Return on Assets	11.22	1.68
Net Margin	11.99	1.38

Sector Weightings

	% of Stocks	Rel S&P 500	3 Year High	Low
⟳ Info	8.06	0.40		
🖳 Software	0.55	0.16	2	0
💻 Hardware	1.98	0.21	5	2
🎬 Media	3.24	0.85	13	3
📶 Telecom	2.29	0.65	2	0
⟳ Service	55.16	1.19		
🏥 Health	11.11	0.92	15	9
🛒 Consumer	8.18	1.07	12	7
📋 Business	24.22	5.73	24	15
💲 Financial	11.65	0.52	15	10
⟳ Mfg	36.79	1.09		
🏭 Goods	3.80	0.44	5	3
⚙ Ind Mtrls	26.21	2.20	27	19
🔋 Energy	6.78	0.69	7	2
💡 Utilities	0.00	0.00	0	0

Composition

● Cash	7.1
● Stocks	92.9
● Bonds	0.0
○ Other	0.0
Foreign (% of Stock)	1.6

Neuberger Ber Part Inv

Ticker NPRTX	**Load** None	**NAV** $31.05	**Yield** 0.6%	**Total Assets** $4,102 mil	**Mstar Category** Large Blend

Governance and Management

Stewardship Grade: C

Portfolio Manager(s)

Basu Mullick has been a member of the management team here since 1998 and took over for Bob Gendelman as lead manager in October 2000. He served as a portfolio manager at Ark Asset Management from 1993 to 1998.

Strategy

This fund's manager, Basu Mullick, buys financially strong, industry-leading companies whose stocks are out of favor. He won't buy any stock with a P/E ratio that is higher than its industry average, and he uses historical price multiples to spot stocks that are suffering from temporary market weakness relative to their growth prospects. However, he will hang on to stocks after they've recovered as long as their basic strengths are still intact, so the fund's overall valuations land squarely in blend territory.

Performance 12-31-06

	1st Qtr	2nd Qtr	3rd Qtr	4th Qtr	Total
2002	2.69	-12.55	-21.32	6.39	-24.82
2003	-1.79	20.37	1.19	13.59	35.87
2004	5.85	-0.36	0.54	12.42	19.21
2005	1.99	5.31	8.09	1.62	17.99
2006	4.96	-3.67	0.53	11.37	13.19

Trailing	Total Return%	+/- S&P 500	+/- Russ 1000	%Rank Cat	Growth of $10,000
3 Mo	11.37	4.67	4.42	1	11,137
6 Mo	11.96	-0.78	-0.40	40	11,196
1 Yr	13.19	-2.60	-2.27	67	11,319
3 Yr Avg	16.77	6.33	5.79	1	15,922
5 Yr Avg	10.21	4.02	3.39	5	16,259
10 Yr Avg	8.91	0.49	0.27	19	23,479
15 Yr Avg	11.89	1.25	1.09	14	53,935

Tax Analysis	Tax-Adj Rtn%	%Rank Cat	Tax-Cost Rat	%Rank Cat
3 Yr (estimated)	16.12	1	0.56	26
5 Yr (estimated)	9.83	3	0.34	22
10 Yr (estimated)	7.34	30	1.44	67

Potential Capital Gain Exposure: 23% of assets

Morningstar's Take by David Kathman 12-13-06

A few bumps in the road haven't dimmed the long-term appeal of Neuberger Berman Partners.

After several years of blowing away the competition, this fund has finally slowed down a bit. Its returns ranked in the top 10% of the large-blend category each year from 2003 through 2005. But in 2006, it spent most of the year near the bottom of the category rankings before a late rally pulled it up to the middle of the pack. We're not too concerned, though; we've been saying for years that this fund is prone to occasional dry spells, but it still looks like a long-term winner.

The core of manager Basu Mullick's strategy involves finding stocks that are reasonably priced but still have high potential growth rates and returns on equity. He doesn't just pay lip service to these ideas; this fund's valuations are significantly lower than the S&P 500's, and its growth rates are significantly higher. Mullick also has a lot of conviction in his picks, making big bets on sectors or industries he likes. Over the past few years, big

stakes in energy and housing stocks have been the main drivers behind the fund's great returns, but they also caused the fund to fall to earth in 2006 when those sectors took major hits.

Mullick didn't back down in the face of these short-term troubles. He still likes the coal stocks that are a big part of his energy stake, and thinks supply constraints will keep oil and natural-gas prices high. He has added to beaten-down homebuilders because he thinks that demographic trends will keep the housing market strong and that the recent downturn has been a "blip" resulting from speculators exiting the market.

This confidence proved well placed when housing stocks rallied strongly in the fourth quarter, leading the fund's recovery. There's still some short-term uncertainty here, but the fund's long-term results have been impressive enough that we're willing to give Mullick the benefit of the doubt. Investors with the patience to ride out the slow periods should still be rewarded.

Address:	605 Third Ave 2nd FL New York NY 10158-0006 800-877-9700	Minimum Purchase:	$1000 Add: $100 IRA: $250
		Min Auto Inv Plan:	$100 Add: $100
		Sales Fees:	No-load
Web Address:	www.nb.com	Management Fee:	0.71%, 0.26%A
Inception:	01-20-75	Actual Fees:	Mgt:0.71% Dist: —
Advisor:	Neuberger Berman Management Inc.	Expense Projections:	3Yr:$262 5Yr:$455 10Yr:$1014
Subadvisor:	Neuberger Berman, LLC	Income Distrib:	Annually
NTF Plans:	Schwab OneSource		

Historical Profile

Return	High
Risk	High
Rating	★★★★ Highest

Investment Style: Equity, Stock %

Investment style percentages: 91% 92% 96% 99% 97% 98% 98% 97% 99%

▼ Manager Change
▽ Partial Manager Change

Growth of $10,000
■ Investment Values of Fund
— Investment Values of S&P 500

Performance Quartile (within Category)

	1995	1996	1997	1998	1999	2000	2001	2002	2003	2004	2005	2006	History
NAV	22.14	25.19	26.30	25.50	24.00	21.93	20.79	15.60	21.19	25.09	28.05	31.05	NAV
	35.21	26.49	29.23	6.28	7.80	0.57	-3.02	-24.82	35.87	19.21	17.99	13.19	Total Return %
	-2.37	3.53	-4.13	-22.30	-13.24	9.67	8.87	-2.72	7.19	8.33	13.08	-2.60	+/-S&P 500
	-2.56	4.04	-3.62	-20.74	-13.11	8.36	9.43	-3.17	5.98	7.81	11.72	-2.27	+/-Russ 1000
	1.08	0.99	0.75	0.00	1.14	0.71	0.36	0.14	0.04	0.80	1.07	0.69	Income Return %
	34.13	25.50	28.48	6.28	6.66	-0.14	-3.38	-24.96	35.83	18.41	16.92	12.50	Capital Return %
	46	12	51	94	87	26	12	83	7	1	1	67	Total Rtn % Rank Cat
	0.20	0.22	0.19	0.00	0.29	0.17	0.08	0.03	0.01	0.17	0.27	0.19	Income $
	2.70	2.61	5.84	2.41	3.10	1.93	0.38	0.00	0.00	0.00	1.31	0.51	Capital Gains $
	0.83	0.84	0.81	0.80	0.82	0.84	0.84	0.87	0.90	0.87	0.85	0.82	Expense Ratio %
	0.83	0.93	0.72	0.79	0.94	0.60	0.35	0.16	0.08	0.76	0.83	0.84	Income Ratio %
	98	96	77	109	132	95	73	53	65	67	61	33	Turnover Rate %
	1,657	2,218	3,230	3,250	2,668	1,991	1,666	1,083	1,327	1,475	2,112	2,248	Net Assets $mil

Rating and Risk

Time Period	Load-Adj Return %	Morningstar Rtn vs Cat	Morningstar Risk vs Cat	Morningstar Risk-Adj Rating
1 Yr	13.19			
3 Yr	16.77	High	High	★★★★★
5 Yr	10.21	High	High	★★★★★
10 Yr	8.91	+Avg	+Avg	★★★★
Incept	15.13			

Other Measures	Standard Index S&P 500	Best Fit Index S&P Mid 400
Alpha	3.4	2.9
Beta	1.39	1.05
R-Squared	65	85
Standard Deviation	11.81	
Mean	16.77	
Sharpe Ratio	1.10	

Portfolio Analysis 11-30-06

Share change since 10-06 Total Stocks:71	Sector	PE	Tot Ret%	% Assets
Terex Corporation	Ind Mtrls	18.2	117.44	2.50
⊕ KB Home	Consumer	4.6	-28.06	2.22
⊖ D.R. Horton Incorporated	Consumer	6.5	-24.41	2.18
Berkshire Hathaway Inc.	Financial	13.2	24.89	2.17
American International G	Financial	17.0	6.05	2.11
Goldman Sachs Group, Inc	Financial	12.4	57.41	2.09
⊕ TXU Corporation	Utilities	12.8	11.19	2.09
⊖ Phelps Dodge Corp.	Ind Mtrls	12.7	76.29	2.07
⊕ NVR, Inc.	Consumer	6.2	-8.12	2.00
⊕ Joy Global, Inc.	Ind Mtrls	15.1	22.11	1.97
⊖ Shire PLC ADR	Health	40.2	59.84	1.95
Centex Corporation	Consumer	7.2	-21.06	1.95
Lennar Corporation	Consumer	5.8	-12.94	1.94
Canadian Natural Resourc	Energy	29.1	7.84	1.92
Arch Coal, Inc.	Energy	27.4	-24.01	1.90
UnitedHealth Group, Inc.	Health	20.8	-13.49	1.89
Aetna, Inc.	Health	14.1	-8.34	1.86
Countrywide Financial Co	Financial	9.8	26.22	1.82
Peabody Energy Corporati	Energy	17.3	-1.48	1.68
⊕ Chicago Bridge & Iron Co	Business	87.7	8.97	1.67

Current Investment Style

Value Blnd Growth — Large/Mid/Small (Large Mid style box)

Market Cap	%
Giant	22.2
Large	38.3
Mid	38.2
Small	1.3
Micro	0.0

Avg $mil: 17,556

Value Measures		Rel Category
Price/Earnings	13.11	0.85
Price/Book	2.30	0.90
Price/Sales	1.03	0.74
Price/Cash Flow	9.37	1.11
Dividend Yield %	1.29	0.74

Growth Measures	%	Rel Category
Long-Term Erngs	14.16	1.20
Book Value	17.83	1.97
Sales	17.30	1.79
Cash Flow	15.87	1.54
Historical Erngs	26.96	1.46

Profitability	%	Rel Category
Return on Equity	21.77	1.12
Return on Assets	10.77	1.04
Net Margin	13.30	0.99

Sector Weightings	% of Stocks	Rel S&P 500	3 Year High	Low
⊙ Info	11.54	0.58		
Software	6.57	1.90	7	3
Hardware	4.97	0.54	9	2
Media	0.00	0.00	6	0
Telecom	0.00	0.00	1	0
⊑ Service	45.42	0.98		
Health	13.78	1.14	14	8
Consumer	16.73	2.19	22	11
Business	3.19	0.75	12	3
Financial	11.72	0.53	28	11
Mfg	43.04	1.27		
Goods	2.28	0.27	5	1
Ind Mtrls	14.05	1.18	14	9
Energy	21.52	2.20	26	4
Utilities	5.09	1.48	6	0

Composition

● Cash	0.9
● Stocks	99.1
● Bonds	0.0
● Other	0.0
Foreign (% of Stock)	12.7

Nicholas

	Ticker	Load	NAV	Yield	Total Assets	Mstar Category
	NICSX	None	$58.38	1.3%	$2,349 mil	Large Blend

Portfolio Manager(s)

Albert O. Nicholas founded this fund in 1969 and has run it ever since. He also manages Nicholas Equity Income and Nicholas High Income. His son, David, joined him at the helm of this fund in 1996, but David does not participate in day-to-day management of the offering. A small group of analysts assists with stock research.

Strategy

Lead manager Ab Nicholas emphasizes steady growers selling at good prices and tends to favor financials and health-care issues. Specifically, he looks for stocks trading at a lower P/E than the average stock in the S&P 500. He will also play the contrarian card at times, which could weigh on returns should these companies not turn around.

Historical Profile

Return	Below Avg
Risk	Below Avg
Rating	★★★ Neutral

Investment Style: Equity Stock %

▼ Manager Change
▽ Partial Manager Change

Growth of $10,000
— Investment Values of Fund
— Investment Values of S&P 500

Performance Quartile (within Category)

	1995	1996	1997	1998	1999	2000	2001	2002	2003	2004	2005	2006	History
	60.03	65.94	83.80	85.82	81.15	61.45	54.47	42.41	54.47	60.42	58.20	58.38	NAV
	35.40	19.78	37.01	13.12	1.70	-1.47	-10.98	-21.85	28.66	11.80	5.60	9.34	Total Return %
	-2.18	-3.18	3.65	-15.46	-19.34	7.63	0.91	0.25	-0.02	0.92	0.69	-6.45	+/-S&P 500
	-2.37	-2.67	4.16	-13.90	-19.21	6.32	1.47	-0.20	-1.23	0.40	-0.67	-6.12	+/-Russ 1000
	1.32	0.69	0.59	0.72	0.38	0.26	0.38	0.29	0.21	0.12	0.42	1.43	Income Return %
	34.08	19.09	36.42	12.40	1.32	-1.73	-11.36	-22.14	28.45	11.68	5.18	7.91	Capital Return %
	44	67	5	81	94	33	41	46	33	29	51	94	Total Rtn % Rank Cat
	0.62	0.40	0.38	0.59	0.31	0.19	0.24	0.16	0.09	0.07	0.25	0.82	Income $
	4.04	5.33	5.78	8.27	5.94	19.25	0.00	0.00	0.00	0.41	5.32	4.33	Capital Gains $
	0.77	0.74	0.72	0.71	0.71	0.73	0.72	0.73	0.75	0.73	0.75	0.77	Expense Ratio %
	1.34	0.87	0.61	0.44	0.58	0.46	0.30	0.22	0.38	0.17	0.17	0.41	Income Ratio %
	30	26	15	17	25	40	41	39	33	18	21	32	Turnover Rate %
	3,505	3,984	5,257	5,823	5,154	4,088	3,140	2,139	2,452	2,504	2,552	2,349	Net Assets $mil

Performance 12-31-06

	1st Qtr	2nd Qtr	3rd Qtr	4th Qtr	Total
2002	-1.34	-12.04	-10.70	0.85	-21.85
2003	-4.81	17.81	2.25	12.20	28.66
2004	3.07	1.14	-2.10	9.55	11.80
2005	-0.61	4.89	0.95	0.35	5.60
2006	5.65	-4.37	2.32	5.76	9.34

Trailing	Total Return%	+/- S&P 500	+/- Russ 1000	%Rank Cat	Growth of $10,000
3 Mo	5.76	-0.94	-1.19	81	10,576
6 Mo	8.22	-4.52	-4.14	93	10,822
1 Yr	9.34	-6.45	-6.12	94	10,934
3 Yr Avg	8.88	-1.56	-2.10	74	12,908
5 Yr Avg	5.36	-0.83	-1.46	61	12,983
10 Yr Avg	6.02	-2.40	-2.62	81	17,942
15 Yr Avg	8.44	-2.20	-2.36	85	33,717

Tax Analysis	Tax-Adj Rtn%	%Rank Cat	Tax-Cost Rat	%Rank Cat
3 Yr (estimated)	7.83	70	0.96	44
5 Yr (estimated)	4.70	59	0.63	41
10 Yr (estimated)	4.61	83	1.33	61

Potential Capital Gain Exposure: 44% of assets

Rating and Risk

Time Period	Load-Adj Return %	Morningstar Rtn vs Cat	Morningstar Risk vs Cat	Morningstar Risk-Adj Rating
1 Yr	9.34			
3 Yr	8.88	-Avg	Avg	★★★
5 Yr	5.36	Avg	-Avg	★★★
10 Yr	6.02	-Avg	-Avg	★★
Incept	11.87			

Other Measures	Standard Index S&P 500	Best Fit Index Russ 1000
Alpha	-0.5	-0.8
Beta	0.87	0.85
R-Squared	73	75
Standard Deviation	6.98	
Mean	8.88	
Sharpe Ratio	0.80	

Morningstar's Take by Andrew Gogerty 12-18-06

We're tempering our expectations for Nicholas.

Namesake manager Ab Nicholas begins his investment search by screening for stocks with price/earnings ratios that are lower than the average stock in the S&P 500 Index--regardless of market cap or industry. From there, he focuses on recurring earnings, and not projected cash flow like many of the fund's large-blend peers, and narrows his universe to those with histories of solid earnings growth.

This stance gives the fund's portfolio and total-return profiles certain biases. Nicholas' appetite for consistent earnings tilts the fund decidedly toward service stocks. Health-care, financial, business, and consumer-services stocks soak up nearly 70% of assets, while it's practically void of the more cyclical technology and telecom companies. Predictably, the fund's returns held up well during the bear market and at the beginning of its rebound in 2003, but its lack of exposure to technology and cyclical industrials caused the fund's returns to lag in the late 1990s and thus far in 2006, respectively. Moreover, the fund's all-cap nature kept it on the sidelines relative to its peers in recent months as large caps have emerged after a long stretch of underperformance.

Still, this fund does have appeal. Its 0.77% expense ratio is one of the cheapest levies for an actively managed no-load fund, providing a small head start over its peers each year. Moreover, while its sector tilts invite volatility, Nicholas has delivered a relatively smooth ride for investors. The fund's volatility of returns (as measured by standard deviation) is less than the group norm.

Overall, we'd caution investors to temper their expectations. If the market turns decidedly to large caps, this fund's persistent all-cap style will likely weigh on returns. In addition, there is no dearth of all-weather choices in this crowded category, so investors should shop around. But, Nicholas' commitment to his approach and the fund's rock-bottom costs give it certain appeal.

Portfolio Analysis 12-31-06

Share change since 11-06 Total Stocks:59

	Sector	PE	Tot Ret%	% Assets
Berkshire Hathaway Inc.	Financial	—	—	6.88
⊖ Affiliated Managers Grou	Financial	32.5	31.00	6.21
Marshall & Ilsley Corp.	Financial	15.2	14.38	4.21
FedEx Corporation	Business	17.2	5.40	3.24
Thermo Fisher Scientific	Health	37.4	50.32	3.18
Davita, Inc.	Health	21.1	12.32	3.03
W.R. Berkley Corporation	Financial	10.3	9.20	2.98
O'Reilly Automotive, Inc	Consumer	20.4	0.16	2.80
Constellation Brands, In	Goods	18.4	10.64	2.79
⊖ Kinder Morgan Management	Energy	50.1	8.12	2.64
Fortune Brands, Inc.	Goods	17.1	11.58	2.55
Tyco International, Ltd.	Ind Mtrls	15.7	6.83	2.53
⊕ Yum Brands, Inc.	Consumer	20.4	26.76	2.38
WellPoint, Inc.	Health	17.2	-1.38	2.35
Walgreen Company	Consumer	26.6	4.36	2.35
⊕ Capital One Financial Co	Financial	10.4	-10.97	2.24
Cardinal Health, Inc.	Health	20.8	-5.82	2.20
⊕ Oshkosh Truck Corporatio	Ind Mtrls	17.1	9.47	2.19
⊕ Wal-Mart Stores, Inc.	Consumer	16.9	0.13	2.16
Medtronic, Inc.	Health	23.8	-6.29	2.13

Current Investment Style

Value Blnd Growth — Large/Mid/Small

Market Cap	%
Giant	16.3
Large	32.0
Mid	45.1
Small	5.3
Micro	1.3

Avg $mil: 10,463

Value Measures		Rel Category
Price/Earnings	16.38	1.07
Price/Book	2.43	0.95
Price/Sales	1.18	0.84
Price/Cash Flow	9.56	1.13
Dividend Yield %	1.15	0.66

Growth Measures	%	Rel Category
Long-Term Erngs	12.62	1.07
Book Value	10.22	1.13
Sales	14.15	1.46
Cash Flow	11.30	1.09
Historical Erngs	18.42	1.00

Profitability	%	Rel Category
Return on Equity	17.70	0.91
Return on Assets	9.38	0.90
Net Margin	10.88	0.81

Sector Weightings

	% of Stocks	Rel S&P 500	3 Year High Low
⟳ Info	2.69	0.13	
🖅 Software	0.85	0.25	1 0
🖳 Hardware	0.38	0.04	0 0
🎙 Media	1.21	0.32	7 0
📱 Telecom	0.25	0.07	0 0
⌗ Service	67.71	1.47	
🩺 Health	13.93	1.16	35 14
🛒 Consumer	14.01	1.83	20 13
💼 Business	8.97	2.12	9 6
💲 Financial	30.80	1.38	32 25
⌨ Mfg	29.60	0.88	
🛢 Goods	8.40	0.98	11 4
⚙ Ind Mtrls	10.38	0.87	10 2
🔋 Energy	10.74	1.10	15 2
💡 Utilities	0.08	0.02	0 0

Composition

- Cash 2.9
- Stocks 97.0
- Bonds 0.1
- Other 0.0

Foreign 3.7 (% of Stock)

Nicholas II I

	Ticker	Load	NAV	Yield	Total Assets	Mstar Category
	NCTWX	None	$22.93	0.3%	$541 mil	Mid-Cap Growth

Governance and Management

Stewardship Grade: A

Portfolio Manager(s)

David Nicholas has managed this fund since March 1993. He also manages Nicholas Limited Edition and, along with his father (firm founder Ab Nicholas), comanages the firm's flagship Nicholas Fund. A small group of analysts assist with stock research.

Strategy

This fund is more conservative than many in the mid-cap growth category. Manager David Nicholas applies a growth-at-a-reasonable-price strategy, seeking fast-growing companies generally trading less than 20 times their future earnings or 1.5 times their growth rate. The fund favors steady growers and typically has relatively small exposure to the technology and cyclical industrial sectors.

Historical Profile

Return	Below Avg
Risk	Low
Rating	★★★ Neutral

Investment Style: Equity Stock %

99% 100% 100% 100% 100% 96% 97% 96% 96%

▼ Manager Change
▽ Partial Manager Change

Growth of $10,000

■ Investment Values of Fund
— Investment Values of S&P 500

31.0 25.0 20.0 15.0 10.0

Performance Quartile (within Category)

1995	1996	1997	1998	1999	2000	2001	2002	2003	2004	2005	2006	History
28.73	30.99	36.94	36.03	35.96	21.34	20.09	16.01	21.34	22.98	22.20	22.93	NAV
28.55	19.38	37.01	9.24	1.17	-2.09	-3.11	-20.31	33.30	12.03	5.94	8.25	Total Return %
-9.03	-3.58	3.65	-19.34	-19.87	7.01	8.78	1.79	4.62	1.15	1.03	-7.54	+/-S&P 500
-5.43	1.90	14.47	-8.62	-50.12	9.66	17.04	7.10	-9.41	-3.45	-6.16	-2.41	+/-Russ MG
1.11	0.77	0.22	0.36	0.03	0.00	0.00	0.00	0.00	0.00	0.09	0.29	Income Return %
27.44	18.61	36.79	8.88	1.14	-2.09	-3.11	-20.31	33.30	12.03	5.85	7.96	Capital Return %
71	32	3	71	99	49	14	24	64	64	79	53	Total Rtn % Rank Cat
0.27	0.22	0.07	0.13	0.01	0.00	0.00	0.00	0.00	0.00	0.02	0.06	Income $
2.40	3.02	5.24	4.00	0.47	13.12	0.58	0.00	0.00	0.91	2.13	1.05	Capital Gains $
0.66	0.62	0.61	0.59	0.61	0.62	0.62	0.65	0.65	0.63	0.70	0.67	Expense Ratio %
0.68	0.29	0.23	0.33	0.03	0.02	-0.03	-0.12	-0.06	-0.04	0.02	0.19	Income Ratio %
20	24	30	20	21	65	50	47	26	15	21	17	Turnover Rate %
693	784	1,025	1,109	941	690	578	417	522	557	565	541	Net Assets $mil

Performance 12-31-06

	1st Qtr	2nd Qtr	3rd Qtr	4th Qtr	Total
2002	-2.29	-11.61	-11.59	4.37	-20.31
2003	-2.56	15.32	5.45	12.50	33.30
2004	4.45	1.84	-3.61	9.26	12.03
2005	-2.96	3.36	1.95	3.60	5.94
2006	6.67	-5.45	3.22	3.99	8.25

Trailing	Total Return%	+/- S&P 500	+/- Russ MG	%Rank Cat	Growth of $10,000
3 Mo	3.99	-2.71	-2.96	90	10,399
6 Mo	7.33	-5.41	-0.57	31	10,733
1 Yr	8.25	-7.54	-2.41	53	10,825
3 Yr Avg	8.71	-1.73	-4.02	74	12,847
5 Yr Avg	6.42	0.23	-1.80	50	13,649
10 Yr Avg	6.96	-1.46	-1.66	69	19,598
15 Yr Avg	8.79	-1.85	-1.34	59	35,386

Tax Analysis	Tax-Adj Rtn%	%Rank Cat	Tax-Cost Rat	%Rank Cat
3 Yr (estimated)	7.77	73	0.86	43
5 Yr (estimated)	5.86	50	0.53	38
10 Yr (estimated)	5.17	70	1.67	63

Potential Capital Gain Exposure: 37% of assets

Rating and Risk

Time Period	Load-Adj Return %	Morningstar Rtn vs Cat	Morningstar Risk vs Cat	Morningstar Risk-Adj Rating
1 Yr	8.25			
3 Yr	8.71	-Avg	Low	★★★
5 Yr	6.42	Avg	Low	★★★
10 Yr	6.96	-Avg	Low	★★★
Incept	11.42			

Other Measures	Standard Index S&P 500	Best Fit Index Russ MG
Alpha	-2.4	-1.2
Beta	1.13	0.71
R-Squared	81	88
Standard Deviation	8.60	
Mean	8.71	
Sharpe Ratio	0.64	

Portfolio Analysis 12-31-06

Share change since 11-06 Total Stocks:87

	Sector	PE	Tot Ret%	% Assets
Fiserv, Inc.	Business	19.6	21.15	2.96
Willis Group Holdings, L	Financial	17.0	10.34	2.25
CDW Corporation	Business	20.4	23.33	2.07
Marshall & Ilsley Corp.	Financial	15.2	14.38	2.04
O'Reilly Automotive, Inc	Consumer	20.4	0.16	1.89
Bemis Company, Inc.	Goods	20.3	24.90	1.83
Respironics Inc.	Health	26.8	1.83	1.77
Microchip Technology, In	Hardware	27.2	4.37	1.74
Cintas Corporation	Business	20.1	-2.62	1.74
Davita, Inc.	Health	21.1	12.32	1.70
Nationwide Financial Ser	Financial	11.3	25.62	1.69
Liberty Global, Inc.	Media	—	—	1.57
IAC/InterActiveCorp	Consumer	40.6	31.26	1.55
QLogic Corporation	Hardware	31.5	34.85	1.54
Manpower, Inc.	Business	20.7	62.53	1.52
PetSmart Inc.	Consumer	23.0	12.99	1.52
Hormel Foods Corporation	Goods	18.7	16.09	1.48
Harris Corporation	Hardware	24.8	7.57	1.48
St. Jude Medical, Inc.	Health	34.9	-27.17	1.42
Biomet, Inc.	Health	25.2	13.93	1.41

Current Investment Style

Value Blnd Growth — Large Mid Small

Market Cap	%
Giant	2.2
Large	26.0
Mid	70.2
Small	1.6
Micro	0.0

Avg $mil: 7,029

Value Measures		Rel Category
Price/Earnings	19.98	0.97
Price/Book	2.91	0.91
Price/Sales	1.75	0.99
Price/Cash Flow	13.00	1.14
Dividend Yield %	0.86	1.37

Growth Measures	%	Rel Category
Long-Term Erngs	15.28	0.94
Book Value	8.63	0.68
Sales	13.82	1.38
Cash Flow	14.51	0.79
Historical Erngs	19.18	0.77

Profitability	%	Rel Category
Return on Equity	17.45	0.97
Return on Assets	10.74	1.15
Net Margin	12.17	1.05

Sector Weightings	% of Stocks	Rel S&P 500	3 Year High Low	
ⓘ Info	18.62	0.93		
🗎 Software	0.99	0.29	1	0
🖥 Hardware	13.28	1.44	15	9
🎙 Media	4.35	1.15	6	4
📶 Telecom	0.00	0.00	0	0
☞ Service	64.83	1.40		
⚕ Health	19.71	1.63	22	18
🛒 Consumer	14.32	1.87	23	12
💼 Business	16.23	3.84	21	15
💲 Financial	14.57	0.65	16	12
🏭 Mfg	16.56	0.49		
🔧 Goods	4.49	0.53	7	4
⚙ Ind Mtrls	5.47	0.46	6	1
🔥 Energy	6.60	0.67	7	3
Ω Utilities	0.00	0.00	0	0

Composition

	%
● Cash	4.4
● Stocks	95.6
● Bonds	0.0
○ Other	0.0
Foreign	3.4
(% of Stock)	

Morningstar's Take by Andrew Gogerty 12-07-06

Nicholas II has appeal, but we don't consider it a standout.

This is one of the steadier offerings within the often wild mid-growth category. Manager David Nicholas, who has guided this fund for over a decade, tends to shun riskier highfliers in favor of slower but steady growth stories such as data processor Fiserv and billboard company Lamar Advertising that trade at reasonable valuations.

This stance gives the fund's portfolio certain biases. Nicholas' appetite for consistent earnings tilts the fund decidedly toward services stocks. Health-care, financial, and consumer-services stocks soak up 46% of assets, while the fund maintains a modest 14% stake in technology stocks and is practically devoid of industrial companies. Predictably, the fund's returns held up well during the bear market and at the beginning of its rebound in 2003, but its light exposure to technology and cyclical industrials caused its relative returns to lag in the late 1990s and in recent years. Overall, its long-term record lands in the category's middle third.

Still, what Nicholas' picks tend to have in common are solid balance sheets and steady earnings growth from defensible margins. In addition, he will take gains off the table early rather than expose the fund to heightened volatility. This combination has provided a smooth ride for investors, as volatility (measured by standard deviation of returns) has been below that of the fund's peers.

Overall, those looking to dip a toe in the mid-growth pool might find the fund's conservative profile appealing, but we'd definitely shop around. Nicholas' research doesn't reveal any glaring flaws, but at the same time his process hasn't shown a knack for beating his peers over the long term, either. Investors desiring mid-growth exposure can certainly do worse, but we'd suggest choosing one of our Analyst Picks.

Address:	700 North Water Street Milwaukee WI 53202 800-544-6547	Minimum Purchase:	$100000	Add: $100	IRA: $0
Web Address:	www.nicholasfunds.com	Min Auto Inv Plan:	$100000	Add: $50	
Inception:	10-17-83	Sales Fees:	No-load		
Advisor:	Nicholas Company, Inc.	Management Fee:	0.75% mx./0.50% mn.		
Subadvisor:	None	Actual Fees:	Mgt:0.54%	Dist: —	
NTF Plans:	N/A	Expense Projections:	3Yr:$224	5Yr:$390	10Yr:$871
		Income Distrib:	Annually		

Morningstar® Funds 500

Northeast Investors

Analyst Pick ✓

	Ticker	Load	NAV	Yield	SEC Yield	Total Assets	Mstar Category
	NTHEX	None	$7.76	6.8%	—	$1,373 mil	High Yield Bond

Governance and Management

Stewardship Grade: A

Portfolio Manager(s)

Bruce Monrad and Ernest Monrad have extensive experience. Ernest Monrad has been with the fund since 1960, and Bruce Monrad since 1989. As the fund's long-term performance shows, they have done quite well. Both invest heavily in the fund themselves, so their interests are aligned with those of the fund's shareholders.

Strategy

Managers Bruce Monrad and Ernest Monrad hold a core of domestic high-yield bonds, but they will dabble in emerging-markets debt and individual stocks, and can also use leverage in an effort to boost returns. Sector allocations and issue selection often determine the fund's relative performance. In 2001 and 2002, for example, the fund's avoidance of the telecommunications and cable sectors helped it avoid a number of high-profile blowups.

Performance 12-31-06

	1st Qtr	2nd Qtr	3rd Qtr	4th Qtr	Total
2002	5.79	1.14	-5.69	2.30	3.23
2003	0.59	5.07	2.14	5.92	14.35
2004	4.07	1.25	2.95	5.44	14.38
2005	-0.15	-0.11	1.84	0.63	2.23
2006	4.08	2.11	1.32	4.12	12.10

Trailing	Total Return%	+/- LB Aggr	+/- CSFB Glb HY	%Rank Cat	Growth of $10,000
3 Mo	4.12	2.88	-0.33	38	10,412
6 Mo	5.49	0.40	-2.66	96	10,549
1 Yr	12.10	7.77	0.17	12	11,210
3 Yr Avg	9.44	5.74	0.82	10	13,108
5 Yr Avg	9.12	4.06	-1.95	38	15,471
10 Yr Avg	5.65	-0.59	-1.44	39	17,326
15 Yr Avg	8.96	2.46	0.06	10	36,225

Tax Analysis	Tax-Adj Rtn%	%Rank Cat	Tax-Cost Rat	%Rank Cat
3 Yr (estimated)	6.63	8	2.57	60
5 Yr (estimated)	6.12	35	2.75	61
10 Yr (estimated)	2.13	45	3.33	57

Potential Capital Gain Exposure: -41% of assets

Morningstar's Take by Scott Berry 12-12-06

Analyst Pick Northeast Investors Trust is putting the finishing touches on a fine year, but it could face rougher sledding in 2007.

This fund got a boost in 2006 from decisions made in 2005. It was then that managers Bruce and Ernest Monrad starting picking up senior bonds of highly leveraged companies. Not all the Monrads' picks have paid off, as bankrupt auto suppliers Dura and Collins and Aikman have weighed on results. However, Delphi, Calpine, and Foamex have pushed higher in 2006. Add in good performance from the entertainment sector and certain individual equities, including J.P. Morgan Chase, and the fund is closing in on a 12% return for the year. That places the fund ahead of 90% of its high-yield peers for the year through Dec. 11, 2006.

But we've heard from a number of high-yield managers, including Bruce Monrad, that high-yield opportunities are getting harder to find. And indeed yields on high-yield bonds have crept closer to Treasury yields lately, dampening the compensation that high-yield investors receive for taking on added risk. The Monrads haven't seen a need to bulk up on cash yet, arguing that short-term bonds have offered enough value to keep them happy. But without a lot of yield in the market and with defaults possibly creeping higher in 2007, double-digit returns will be hard to come by.

We continue to like this fund, though. The Monrads have more experience than anyone in the group, so they aren't likely to get caught off guard too often. And though they have missed their mark on occasion with individual issues, they have delivered good results overall. That success also owes to the fund's low costs, which provide the fund a built-in advantage over its average no-load category peer.

The fund's risks should not be overlooked--It takes on plenty of credit risk and the Monrads will employ leverage to enhance returns. Overall, though, we think this fund has a lot to recommend it.

Address:	150 Federal Street
	Boston MA 02110
	800-225-6704
Web Address:	www.northeastinvestors.com
Inception:	08-01-50
Advisor:	Northeast Investors Trust
Subadvisor:	None
NTF Plans:	N/A

Minimum Purchase:	$1000	Add: $0	IRA: $500
Min Auto Inv Plan:	$1000	Add: $50	
Sales Fees:	No-load		
Management Fee:	0.50%		
Actual Fees:	Mgt:0.50%	Dist: —	
Expense Projections:	3Yr:$233	5Yr:$406	10Yr:$906
Income Distrib:	Quarterly		

Historical Profile

Return	Average
Risk	Below Avg
Rating	★★★ Neutral

| | 46 | 18 | 13 | 31 | 57 | 46 | 24 | 5 |

Investment Style Fixed Income
Income Rtn %Rank Cat

▼ Manager Change
▽ Partial Manager Change

Growth of $10,000
■ Investment Values of Fund
— Investment Values of LB Aggr

Performance Quartile (within Category)

	1995	1996	1997	1998	1999	2000	2001	2002	2003	2004	2005	2006	History
NAV	10.16	11.12	11.65	10.47	9.77	8.17	7.43	7.05	7.41	7.87	7.42	7.76	
Total Return %	17.27	20.16	13.89	-0.25	3.50	-6.05	1.33	3.23	14.35	14.38	2.23	12.10	
+/-LB Aggr	-1.20	16.53	4.24	-8.94	4.32	-17.68	-7.11	-7.02	10.25	10.04	-0.20	7.77	
+/-CSFB Glb HY	-0.12	7.74	1.26	-0.83	0.22	-0.84	-4.45	0.12	-13.58	2.42	-0.03	0.17	
Income Return %	10.76	10.20	8.91	8.86	10.56	11.32	11.08	8.61	8.79	7.77	8.05	7.33	
Capital Return %	6.51	9.96	4.98	-9.11	-7.06	-17.37	-9.75	-5.38	5.56	6.61	-5.82	4.77	
Total Rtn % Rank Cat	55	6	30	60	59	41	68	12	96	6	57	12	
Income $	0.99	1.00	0.96	1.00	1.06	1.06	0.87	0.62	0.60	0.56	0.62	0.53	
Capital Gains $	0.00	0.00	0.00	0.18	0.00	0.00	0.00	0.00	0.00	0.00	0.00	0.00	
Expense Ratio %	1.02	0.66	0.64	0.61	0.61	0.61	0.65	0.70	0.65	0.67	0.73	1.23	
Income Ratio %	9.77	9.41	8.65	8.73	9.99	10.84	11.10	8.61	7.97	7.92	6.62	6.60	
Turnover Rate %	41	32	33	64	27	4	22	18	13	40	45	16	
Net Assets $mil	805	1,355	2,161	2,314	1,854	1,318	1,292	1,730	1,761	1,565	1,573	1,373	

Rating and Risk

Time Period	Load-Adj Return %	Morningstar Rtn vs Cat	Morningstar Risk vs Cat	Morningstar Risk-Adj Rating
1 Yr	12.10			
3 Yr	9.44	+Avg	-Avg	★★★★★
5 Yr	9.12	Avg	-Avg	★★★
10 Yr	5.65	Avg	-Avg	★★★
Incept	5.88			

Other Measures	Standard Index LB Aggr	Best Fit Index CSFB Glb HY
Alpha	5.9	1.9
Beta	0.03	0.78
R-Squared	0	67
Standard Deviation	3.42	
Mean	9.44	
Sharpe Ratio	1.70	

Portfolio Analysis 06-30-06

Total Fixed-Income:83	Date of Maturity	Amount $000	Value $000	% Net Assets
Trump Entmt Resorts Hldg	06-01-15	69,914	67,205	4.64
Midwest Generation 8.75%	05-01-34	50,000	53,000	3.66
Charter Comms Oper 144A	04-30-12	40,000	39,800	2.75
Orion Pwr Hldgs 12%	05-01-10	29,000	32,770	2.26
Anr Pipe 8.875%	03-15-10	29,630	31,297	2.16
DELPHI		36,950	30,669	2.12
Dura Oper 8.625%	04-15-12	35,310	30,014	2.07
Us West Comms 5.625%	11-15-08	30,127	29,374	2.03
Park Pl Entmt 8.875%	09-15-08	26,000	27,300	1.88
Interpublic Grp Cos 7.25	08-15-11	29,900	27,134	1.87
Cinemark	03-15-14	34,000	26,350	1.82
Tekni-Plex 144A 8.75%	11-15-13	27,500	26,125	1.80
Calpine 144A 8.5%	07-15-10	27,000	25,954	1.79
Trw Automotive Acquisiti	02-15-13	23,540	25,717	1.77
Pliant 11.125%	09-01-09	25,000	24,065	1.66
Chubb Corporation		445	22,192	1.53
Calpine 144A 8.75%	07-15-13	23,000	22,109	1.52
Lyondell Chem 11.125%	07-15-12	20,000	21,700	1.50
Polymer Group, Inc. A		843	21,474	1.48
Husky Oil FRN	08-15-28	20,000	21,030	1.45

Current Investment Style

Duration: Short Int Long
Quality: High Med Low

¹ figure provided by fund

Avg Eff Duration¹	—
Avg Eff Maturity	—
Avg Credit Quality	—
Avg Wtd Coupon	8.21%
Avg Wtd Price	211.27% of par

Coupon Range	% of Bonds	Rel Cat
0% PIK	6.5	1.2
0% to 8%	32.7	0.6
8% to 11%	58.0	1.3
11% to 14%	9.4	2.2
More than 14%	0.0	0.0

1.00=Category Average

Credit Analysis	% bonds 06-30-06		
AAA	—	BB	—
AA	—	B	—
A	—	Below B	—
BBB	—	NR/NA	—

Sector Breakdown | % of assets

US Treasuries	0
TIPS	0
US Agency	0
Mortgage Pass-Throughs	0
Mortgage CMO	0
Mortgage ARM	0
US Corporate	83
Asset-Backed	2
Convertible	0
Municipal	0
Corporate Inflation-Protected	0
Foreign Corporate	2
Foreign Govt	1

Composition

| Cash | 11.1 | Bonds | 78.4 |
| Stocks | 9.4 | Other | 1.2 |

Special Securities

Restricted/Illiquid Secs	12
Exotic Mortgage-Backed	0
Emerging-Markets Secs	0
Options/Futures/Warrants	No

Northern Technology

	Ticker	Load	NAV	Yield	Total Assets	Mstar Category
	NTCHX	None	$12.26	0.0%	$165 mil	Specialty-Technology

Governance and Management

Stewardship Grade: C

Portfolio Manager(s)

In July 2006, longtime manager George Gilbert retired from Northern Trust Investments, leaving Matthew Peron in charge of this fund. Prior to joining Northern in late 2005, Peron worked as a portfolio manager and analyst at Lincoln Capital and Alliance Capital. Deborah Koch, who lends her expertise in small- and mid-cap names to the process here, has been a comanager since mid-2004.

Strategy

Management focuses on companies with strong positions in large and growing markets. Big companies have typically dominated the portfolio, but this team decided in early 2006 to start looking at smaller firms with niche dominance. At the same time, the fund started to invest outside of technology, and investors should expect roughly 20% of the assets to go to health-care stocks.

Performance 12-31-06

	1st Qtr	2nd Qtr	3rd Qtr	4th Qtr	Total
2002	-8.02	-24.15	-24.37	12.46	-40.66
2003	-0.13	22.33	11.39	13.90	55.00
2004	0.44	0.95	-9.89	12.79	3.05
2005	-11.34	4.01	4.40	2.17	-1.63
2006	5.16	-9.17	5.23	4.97	5.51

Trailing	Total Return%	+/- S&P 500	+/- ArcaEx Tech 100	%Rank Cat	Growth of $10,000
3 Mo	4.97	-1.73	-0.66	62	10,497
6 Mo	10.45	-2.29	-1.20	43	11,045
1 Yr	5.51	-10.28	0.83	61	10,551
3 Yr Avg	2.27	-8.17	-5.61	77	10,697
5 Yr Avg	-0.33	-6.52	-5.29	61	9,836
10 Yr Avg	7.11	-1.31	-6.60	35	19,875
15 Yr Avg	—	—	—		—

Tax Analysis	Tax-Adj Rtn%	%Rank Cat	Tax-Cost Rat	%Rank Cat
3 Yr (estimated)	2.26	74	0.01	3
5 Yr (estimated)	-0.33	58	0.00	1
10 Yr (estimated)	5.11	51	1.87	91

Potential Capital Gain Exposure: -606% of assets

Morningstar's Take by Reginald Laing 12-22-06

Strategy and manager changes make us leery of Northern Technology.

In July 2006, longtime manager George Gilbert retired from Northern Trust Investments, this fund's advisor. Matthew Peron, who joined Northern and this fund's management team in late 2005, has taken over as lead manager. Deb Koch remains a comanager, a post she's held since July 2004.

Even before Peron took the helm, he made some changes to the strategy here. He introduced a quant screen that helps management sift through a larger investment universe. Before, the fund leaned toward blue-chip tech companies, but the quant model has allowed management to delve into smaller, less well-known companies, such as Meridian Bioscience, a biotech firm with a $636 million market cap. Overall, the portfolio's average weighted market cap has gone down from $24.22 billion in September 2004 to $10.98 billion in September 2006. (The typical tech fund's average market cap was $12.72 billion in September 2004

and $12.19 billion in September 2006.) The fund also has broadened its definition of tech. The managers now buy companies from traditionally non-tech industries, such as defense contractor Lockheed Martin. Koch and Peron like Lockheed's improving balance sheet and profit margins, and they consider it a tech stock, as the firm develops sophisticated weapon systems for the military.

We have mixed feelings about the changes here. Owning companies from other sectors has diversified the portfolio and should temper volatility, but it makes the fund less of a pure technology play--which might make it more closely resemble investors' core-growth holdings. Also, smaller-cap companies historically have been less stable than bigger, more-diversified firms, and it's somewhat worrying that the fund is taking on the risk of owning smaller stocks at the same time that it's breaking in a new management team. Until Koch and Peron prove their ability to execute the revamped strategy, we'd seek other options.

Address:	50 South LaSalle Street Chicago, IL 60607 800-595-9111	Minimum Purchase:	$2500	Add: $50	IRA: $500
		Min Auto Inv Plan:	$250	Add: $50	
		Sales Fees:	No-load		
Web Address:	www.northernfunds.com	Management Fee:	1.00%		
Inception:	04-01-96*	Actual Fees:	Mgt:1.00%	Dist: —	
Advisor:	Northern Trust Investment, N.a.	Expense Projections:	3Yr:$421	5Yr:$729	10Yr:$1601
Subadvisor:	None	Income Distrib:	Annually		
NTF Plans:	Fidelity Retail-NTF, Schwab OneSource				

Historical Profile

Return	Average
Risk	Average
Rating	★★★ Neutral

Investment Style: Equity, Stock %

97% | 98% | 88% | 99% | 98% | 99% | 99% | 100% | 100%

▽ Manager Change
▽ Partial Manager Change

Growth of $10,000
— Investment Values of Fund
— Investment Values of S&P 500

Performance Quartile (within Category)

	1995	1996	1997	1998	1999	2000	2001	2002	2003	2004	2005	2006	History
	—	13.11	14.35	25.58	51.76	19.03	12.47	7.40	11.47	11.82	11.62	12.26	NAV
	—	32.53*	16.68	83.02	134.48	-38.43	-34.47	-40.66	55.00	3.05	-1.63	5.51	Total Return %
	—	—	-16.68	54.44	113.44	-29.33	-22.58	-18.56	26.32	-7.83	-6.54	-10.28	+/-S&P 500
	—	—	-3.29	28.42	18.08	-22.21	-18.88	-7.33	2.86	-8.68	-8.99	0.83	+/-ArcaEx Tech 100
	—	—	0.00	0.00	0.00	0.00	0.00	0.00	0.00	0.00	0.06	0.00	Income Return %
	—	—	16.68	83.02	134.48	-38.43	-34.47	-40.66	55.00	3.05	-1.69	5.51	Capital Return %
	—	—	19	8	34	86	47	40	50	55	94	61	Total Rtn % Rank Cat
	—	0.00	0.00	0.00	0.00	0.00	0.00	0.00	0.00	0.00	0.01	0.00	Income $
	—	0.15	0.90	0.67	5.74	12.51	0.00	0.00	0.00	0.00	0.00	0.00	Capital Gains $
	—	—	1.25	1.25	1.23	1.25	1.25	1.25	1.25	1.25	1.25	1.25	Expense Ratio %
	—	—	-0.75	-0.96	-0.87	-1.05	-0.74	-0.96	-0.90	-0.92	-0.69	-0.54	Income Ratio %
	—	—	68	75	61	156	180	76	62	61	30	76	Turnover Rate %
	—	34	81	228	1,810	1,195	609	288	423	325	220	165	Net Assets $mil

Rating and Risk

Time Period	Load-Adj Return %	Morningstar Rtn vs Cat	Morningstar Risk vs Cat	Morningstar Risk-Adj Rating
1 Yr	5.51			
3 Yr	2.27	-Avg	-Avg	★★
5 Yr	-0.33	Avg	-Avg	★★★
10 Yr	7.11	Avg	Avg	★★★
Incept	9.43			

Other Measures	Standard Index S&P 500	Best Fit Index ArcaEx Tech 100
Alpha	-13.3	-5.4
Beta	1.93	1.05
R-Squared	75	91
Standard Deviation	15.38	
Mean	2.27	
Sharpe Ratio	0.01	

Portfolio Analysis 09-30-06

Share change since 06-06 Total Stocks:80

	Sector	PE	Tot Ret%	% Assets
Cisco Systems, Inc.	Hardware	30.1	59.64	3.74
⊖ Hewlett-Packard Company	Hardware	19.3	45.21	3.43
Lam Research Corporation	Hardware	21.9	41.87	3.10
⊖ Nokia Corporation ADR	Hardware	18.9	13.44	3.08
⊕ Lockheed Martin Corporat	Ind Mtrls	17.3	46.98	2.97
⊖ Motorola, Inc.	Hardware	11.8	-8.17	2.90
Raytheon Company	Ind Mtrls	19.1	34.19	2.66
⊖ Coherent, Inc.	Hardware	28.2	6.37	2.57
Texas Instruments, Inc.	Hardware	16.9	-9.82	2.42
⊖ Biogen Idec, Inc.	Health	NMF	8.64	2.00
⊖ IBM	Hardware	17.1	19.77	1.79
⊕ Microsoft Corporation	Software	23.8	15.83	1.75
⊖ Accenture, Ltd.	Business	22.0	29.32	1.75
Electronic Data Systems	Business	35.3	15.50	1.72
Boeing Company	Ind Mtrls	41.2	28.38	1.60
⊖ Gilead Sciences, Inc.	Health	40.6	23.51	1.59
Applera Corporation	Health	39.9	38.90	1.55
⊕ Veritas DGC, Inc.	Energy	33.8	141.28	1.52
Micron Technology, Inc.	Hardware	24.1	4.88	1.52
⊖ BMC Software, Inc.	Software	39.5	57.15	1.50

Current Investment Style

Value Blnd Growth — Large Mid Small

Market Cap	%
Giant	25.2
Large	23.4
Mid	35.5
Small	15.9
Micro	0.0

Avg $mil: 10,983

Value Measures		Rel Category
Price/Earnings	20.38	0.84
Price/Book	3.15	0.98
Price/Sales	2.07	0.74
Price/Cash Flow	10.69	0.82
Dividend Yield %	0.44	1.00

Growth Measures	%	Rel Category
Long-Term Erngs	14.67	0.86
Book Value	2.86	0.30
Sales	7.51	0.60
Cash Flow	20.74	1.04
Historical Erngs	21.89	0.80

Profitability	%	Rel Category
Return on Equity	18.08	1.15
Return on Assets	9.52	1.02
Net Margin	12.93	0.93

Industry Weightings	% of Stocks	Rel Cat
Software	17.0	0.8
Hardware	11.1	1.0
Networking Eq	7.7	1.0
Semis	12.9	0.7
Semi Equip	4.4	0.9
Comp/Data Sv	6.7	0.7
Telecom	0.6	0.2
Health Care	10.3	2.1
Other	29.3	1.6

Composition

● Cash	0.0	
● Stocks	100.0	
● Bonds	0.0	
● Other	0.0	
Foreign	6.8	(% of Stock)

MORNINGSTAR® Funds 500

Oak Value

	Ticker	Load	NAV	Yield	Total Assets	Mstar Category
	OAKVX	None	$28.16	0.3%	$162 mil	Large Blend

Governance and Management

Stewardship Grade:

Portfolio Manager(s)

Comanager and chief investment officer David Carr is a founder of Oak Value Capital Management and has been a manager of the fund since its inception in 1993. Larry Coats joined the advisor in 1994 and became a comanager in 2003 after several years on the investment committee. Former comanager Matt Sauer left the firm in May 2006. Christy Phillips, who joined Oak Value in 2003, serves as director of research, and along with the two managers, is on the investment committee. The firm also has four analysts, all of whom have joined the advisor in the past two or three years.

Strategy

The managers look for companies with understandable business models, sustainable cash flows, and strong management teams. But it won't buy such a company unless it's selling at a discount to the team's estimate of its intrinsic value. They typically keep only 20 to 25 stocks in the portfolio and hold on to them for a long time.

Historical Profile
Return	Average
Risk	Above Avg
Rating	★★ Below Avg

Investment Style: Equity Stock %

97% | 95% | 95% | 100% | 100% | 98% | 95% | 94% | 99%

▼ Manager Change
▽ Partial Manager Change

Growth of $10,000
— Investment Values of Fund
— Investment Values of S&P 500

31.0
25.0
20.0
15.0
10.0

Performance Quartile (within Category)

1995	1996	1997	1998	1999	2000	2001	2002	2003	2004	2005	2006	History
14.06	17.49	23.19	27.29	25.52	29.49	29.08	21.55	28.47	30.74	30.08	28.16	NAV
28.84	28.99	37.70	18.93	-3.12	18.17	-0.47	-24.34	32.11	7.97	-1.37	14.18	Total Return %
-8.74	6.03	4.34	-9.65	-24.16	27.27	11.42	-2.24	3.43	-2.91	-6.28	-1.61	+/-S&P 500
-8.93	6.54	4.85	-8.09	-24.03	25.96	11.98	-2.69	2.22	-3.43	-7.64	-1.28	+/-Russ 1000
0.00	0.00	0.00	0.41	0.29	0.11	0.00	0.00	0.00	0.00	0.00	0.37	Income Return %
28.84	28.99	37.70	18.52	-3.41	18.06	-0.47	-24.34	32.11	7.97	-1.37	13.81	Capital Return %
80	6	3	61	97	5	8	80	14	81	97	53	Total Rtn % Rank Cat
0.00	0.00	0.00	0.09	0.08	0.03	0.00	0.00	0.00	0.00	0.00	0.11	Income $
0.10	0.63	0.81	0.19	0.91	0.55	0.27	0.52	0.00	0.00	0.24	5.75	Capital Gains $
1.89	1.90	1.59	1.22	1.10	1.13	1.22	1.23	1.36	1.25	1.25	1.29	Expense Ratio %
-0.53	-0.43	-0.16	0.41	0.27	0.28	-0.12	-0.36	-0.33	-0.52	-0.39	0.24	Income Ratio %
104	58	22	15	38	22	52	63	28	24	29	29	Turnover Rate %
13	29	140	561	470	329	320	220	250	262	238	162	Net Assets $mil

Performance 12-31-06

	1st Qtr	2nd Qtr	3rd Qtr	4th Qtr	Total
2002	0.93	-13.31	-16.65	3.76	-24.34
2003	-5.89	26.13	0.82	10.39	32.11
2004	2.77	-0.82	-2.52	8.66	7.97
2005	-0.62	0.88	-0.88	-0.75	-1.37
2006	-0.53	0.49	7.29	6.47	14.18

Trailing	Total Return%	+/- S&P 500	+/- Russ 1000	%Rank Cat	Growth of $10,000
3 Mo	6.47	-0.23	-0.48	61	10,647
6 Mo	14.23	1.49	1.87	7	11,423
1 Yr	14.18	-1.61	-1.28	53	11,418
3 Yr Avg	6.74	-3.70	-4.24	94	12,161
5 Yr Avg	3.98	-2.21	-2.84	84	12,155
10 Yr Avg	8.53	0.11	-0.11	27	22,672
15 Yr Avg	—	—	—		—

Tax Analysis	Tax-Adj Rtn%	%Rank Cat	Tax-Cost Rat	%Rank Cat
3 Yr (estimated)	5.63	92	1.04	48
5 Yr (estimated)	3.24	84	0.71	46
10 Yr (estimated)	7.86	19	0.62	25

Potential Capital Gain Exposure: 34% of assets

Rating and Risk

Time Period	Load-Adj Return %	Morningstar Rtn vs Cat	Morningstar Risk vs Cat	Morningstar Risk-Adj Rating
1 Yr	14.18			
3 Yr	6.74	Low	Avg	★
5 Yr	3.98	-Avg	+Avg	★★
10 Yr	8.53	+Avg	+Avg	★★★
Incept	11.44			

Other Measures	Standard Index S&P 500	Best Fit Index Mstar Large Core TR
Alpha	-2.4	-3.1
Beta	0.85	0.90
R-Squared	68	69
Standard Deviation	7.13	
Mean	6.74	
Sharpe Ratio	0.50	

Morningstar's Take by Gregg Wolper 11-24-06

Oak Value has appeal, but know its structure and strategy before buying in.

Managers David Carr and Larry Coats use a careful approach that relies on intensive company research, and the fund's low turnover rate makes clear that they're willing to stick with their picks even when most investors are negative. An example is Comcast, which hurt the fund in 2005 but rebounded strongly in 2006. (They then sold it.) They have long tenures at their small advisory firm, which concentrates on just one strategy and keeps its focus on investing rather than marketing. Meanwhile, the fund's trailing three-year record is weak, but its 10-year return ranks in the large-blend category's top quartile.

It's important for potential investors to be aware of what this fund is and isn't. For example, although its name, many holdings (most notably, top-holding Berkshire Hathaway, which gets 9% of assets), and key elements of its strategy are value oriented, it's not a strict-value fund. Its portfolio typically lands in the large-blend style box, which is why we place it in that category. Its managers tell Morningstar that they will only buy stocks trading at a substantial discount to what they consider their worth, but they also must clearly see the growth potential for a company. Another factor to note is the fund's concentration. It has just 20 to 25 holdings; currently 11 get more than 5% of assets each. That magnifies both the positive and negative impact of each stock.

The fund also can be completely out of hot areas. That largely explains its poor 2005 results: The managers tend to avoid energy firms because they feel their fortunes depend too much on unpredictable commodity prices. So funds that did own those rallying stocks shot far ahead of this one, but that trait too should not deter investors. All told, this small fund deserves more attention.

Portfolio Analysis 09-30-06

Share change since 06-06 Total Stocks:23

	Sector	PE	Tot Ret%	% Assets
⊖ Praxair, Inc.	Ind Mtrls	20.8	14.01	6.87
⊖ Berkshire Hathaway A	Financial			5.79
⊖ E.W. Scripps Company	Media	33.1	5.05	5.68
⊖ Aflac, Inc.	Financial	15.2	0.30	5.47
⊖ Harley-Davidson, Inc.	Goods	18.5	38.81	5.46
⊖ Willis Group Holdings, L	Financial	17.0	10.34	5.34
⊖ Time Warner, Inc.	Media	19.6	26.37	5.28
⊖ Constellation Brands, In	Goods	18.4	10.64	5.22
⊖ United Technologies	Ind Mtrls	17.8	13.65	5.11
⊖ Cadbury Schweppes PLC AD	Goods	17.3	14.72	5.04
⊖ Equifax, Inc.	Business	19.1	7.27	5.00
⊖ Oracle Corporation	Software	26.7	40.38	4.62
⊖ Tyco International, Ltd.	Ind Mtrls	15.7	6.83	4.26
☼ American Express Company	Financial	20.9	19.09	4.16
⊖ IMS Health, Inc.	Health	17.4	10.77	3.94
⊕ E.I. du Pont de Nemours	Ind Mtrls	18.4	18.64	3.68
⊖ Masco Corporation	Ind Mtrls	14.8	1.82	3.58
⊖ Berkshire Hathaway Inc.	Financial	13.2	24.89	3.02
☼ eBay, Inc.	Consumer	40.1	-30.43	2.71
⊖ Johnson & Johnson	Health	17.5	12.45	2.64

Current Investment Style

Value Blend Growth — Large Mid Small

Market Cap	%
Giant	31.3
Large	38.1
Mid	28.7
Small	1.9
Micro	0.0

Avg $mil: 21,461

Value Measures		Rel Category
Price/Earnings	17.54	1.14
Price/Book	2.94	1.15
Price/Sales	1.96	1.40
Price/Cash Flow	11.52	1.36
Dividend Yield %	1.24	0.71

Growth Measures	%	Rel Category
Long-Term Erngs	12.14	1.03
Book Value	5.36	0.59
Sales	10.63	1.10
Cash Flow	7.47	0.72
Historical Erngs	13.96	0.75

Profitability	%	Rel Category
Return on Equity	21.63	1.11
Return on Assets	11.88	1.14
Net Margin	12.56	0.94

Sector Weightings	% of Stocks	Rel S&P 500	3 Year High	Low
↻ Info	20.21	1.01		
🖩 Software	4.68	1.36	5	0
💻 Hardware	0.00	0.00	3	0
🎥 Media	15.53	4.10	26	16
📶 Telecom	0.00	0.00	0	0
⊈ Service	38.56	0.83		
🩺 Health	6.67	0.55	7	0
🛒 Consumer	2.74	0.36	8	0
💼 Business	5.06	1.20	24	5
💲 Financial	24.09	1.08	29	19
⌐ Mfg	41.21	1.22		
🏭 Goods	17.40	2.04	27	17
⚙ Ind Mtrls	23.81	1.99	24	0
🔥 Energy	0.00	0.00	0	0
💡 Utilities	0.00	0.00	0	0

Composition
	%
● Cash	1.3
● Stocks	98.7
● Bonds	0.0
● Other	0.0
Foreign	10.5
(% of Stock)	

Address:	3100 Tower Blvd Durham NC 27707 800-622-2474	Minimum Purchase:	$2500	Add: $100 IRA: $1000
		Min Auto Inv Plan:	$2500	Add: $100
Web Address:	www.oakvaluefund.com	Sales Fees:	No-load, 2.00%R	
Inception:	01-18-93	Management Fee:	0.90% 0.10%A	
Advisor:	Oak Value Capital Management, Inc	Actual Fees:	Mgt:0.90%	Dist: —
Subadvisor:	None	Expense Projections:	3Yr:$409	5Yr:$708 10Yr:$1556
		Income Distrib:	Semi-Annually	
NTF Plans:	Fidelity Retail-NTF, Schwab OneSource			

Oakmark Equity & Inc I

	Ticker	Load	NAV	Yield	Total Assets	Mstar Category
	OAKBX	None	$25.88	1.8%	$11,607 mil	Moderate Allocation

Governance and Management

Stewardship Grade: B

Portfolio Manager(s)

Clyde McGregor has managed the fund since its inception and is a large shareholder in the fund. Edward Studzinski joined him in March 2000. McGregor became an analyst with Harris Associates, the fund's advisor, in the early 1980s, and Studzinski joined Harris as an analyst in 1995. McGregor and Studzinski make decisions related to the bond portfolio themselves and can cull ideas from Harris' teams of analysts.

Strategy

Management keeps the fund's stock/bond mix close to 60/40, but bottom-up stock-picking drives the fund's asset allocation. On the stock side, the managers target value stocks, with an emphasis on cash-rich companies, and they keep the portfolio concentrated. On the bond side, they invest most of the fund's assets in Treasuries, while holding small positions in corporate, high-yield, and non-U.S. government bonds.

Performance 12-31-06

	1st Qtr	2nd Qtr	3rd Qtr	4th Qtr	Total
2002	4.19	-3.19	-8.57	6.12	-2.14
2003	-2.28	13.20	2.01	9.19	23.21
2004	4.18	1.87	-1.07	5.11	10.36
2005	-0.64	2.83	5.83	0.44	8.60
2006	2.00	1.57	2.36	4.50	10.82

Trailing	Total Return%	+/- DJ Mod	+/- DJ US Mod	%Rank Cat	Growth of $10,000
3 Mo	4.50	-1.09	-0.17	73	10,450
6 Mo	6.96	-1.83	-0.94	90	10,696
1 Yr	10.82	-1.48	0.55	57	11,082
3 Yr Avg	9.92	-0.80	0.80	18	13,281
5 Yr Avg	9.88	-0.14	2.28	4	16,017
10 Yr Avg	13.27	4.72	4.68	1	34,766
15 Yr Avg	—	—	—		

Tax Analysis	Tax-Adj Rtn%	%Rank Cat	Tax-Cost Rat	%Rank Cat
3 Yr (estimated)	8.98	15	0.86	42
5 Yr (estimated)	9.14	2	0.67	38
10 Yr (estimated)	12.01	1	1.11	23

Potential Capital Gain Exposure: 17% of assets

Morningstar's Take by Paul Herbert 12-21-06

Oakmark Equity & Income continues to show its nonconformist streak.

Unlike the bulk of balanced funds, this one doesn't have an equity portfolio that looks like one of its advisors' large-blend funds or a bond portfolio geared around the Lehman Brothers Aggregate Bond Index. Managers Clyde McGregor and Ed Studzinski, who are responsible for picking securities for both asset classes, focus on finding inexpensive stocks across the market-cap spectrum and building a portfolio of bonds that will offer a nice combination of yield and price stability.

The managers also have been charting their own course as of late. A great many value-oriented managers, including the bosses of Oakmark and Oakmark Select, have been finding more opportunities in mega-cap stocks during recent years. McGregor and Studzinski haven't taken that step to the same extent though. McGregor says they find large caps "generically" attractive. But the duo thinks its real advantage is in understanding

firms better than other managers do, and that's harder when you're looking at the most-researched firms. Judging by their purchases and sales during the first nine months of 2006, the managers have been net sellers of stocks, including big companies such as Morgan Stanley. In the fund's bond portfolio, they've also taken the unusual step of buying short-term Canadian government bonds, which offer lower yields than similar U.S. Treasury fare because our northern neighbor has a solid credit picture.

Such moves and other uncommon decisions could end up working against the fund. (For instance, it continues to own a number of energy stocks, which could stumble after rallying in recent years.) In all, though, we like that the managers are sticking to the decision-making processes that have worked over the long term. As long as they continue to own solid, well-run businesses at cheap prices and hold on to them for the long term, this closed fund will remain a strong bet.

Address:	Two N Lasalle St Ste 500
	Chicago, IL 60602
	800-625-6275
Web Address:	www.oakmark.com
Inception:	11-01-95*
Advisor:	Harris Associates LP
Subadvisor:	None
NTF Plans:	Fidelity Retail-NTF, Schwab OneSource

Minimum Purchase:	$1000	Add: $100	IRA: $1000
Min Auto Inv Plan:	$500	Add: $100	
Sales Fees:	No-load, 2.00%R		
Management Fee:	0.75% mx./0.60% mn.		
Actual Fees:	Mgt:0.72%	Dist: —	
Expense Projections:	3Yr:$284	5Yr:$493	10Yr:$1096
Income Distrib:	Semi-Annually		

Historical Profile

Return	High
Risk	Below Avg
Rating	★★★★ Highest

| | 59% | 60% | 61% | 59% |

Investment Style
Equity
Stock %

▼ Manager Change
▽ Partial Manager Change

Growth of $10,000
■ Investment Values of Fund
— Investment Values of DJ Mod

31.0
24.0
17.0
10.0

Performance Quartile (within Category)

	1995	1996	1997	1998	1999	2000	2001	2002	2003	2004	2005	2006	History
NAV	10.24	11.55	13.76	15.03	14.40	15.96	18.63	17.99	22.02	23.50	24.98	25.88	NAV
	2.40*	15.29	26.56	12.38	7.90	19.89	18.01	-2.14	23.21	10.36	8.60	10.82	Total Return %
	—	4.63	14.66	0.06	-9.43	21.56	20.81	4.63	-4.17	-2.61	1.61	-1.48	+/-DJ Mod
	—	3.95	7.36	-0.01	-4.95	15.45	17.85	8.40	-0.85	-0.81	2.60	0.55	+/-DJ US Mod
	—	1.17	2.04	1.54	3.00	1.69	0.97	1.30	0.77	0.91	1.45	2.01	Income Return %
	—	14.12	24.52	10.84	4.90	18.20	17.04	-3.44	22.44	9.45	7.15	8.81	Capital Return %
	—	46	7	57	67	2	1	2	25	26	5	57	Total Rtn % Rank Cat
	0.00	0.12	0.24	0.21	0.45	0.24	0.15	0.24	0.14	0.20	0.34	0.50	Income $
	0.00	0.13	0.59	0.20	1.36	1.00	0.04	0.00	0.00	0.59	0.20	1.31	Capital Gains $
	—	—	2.50	1.50	1.31	1.18	1.24	0.98	0.96	0.93	0.92	0.86	Expense Ratio %
	—	—	1.21	2.38	2.39	2.65	3.04	2.07	1.71	1.07	0.78	1.88	Income Ratio %
	—	—	66	53	46	81	87	124	73	48	72	81	Turnover Rate %
	—	6	15	41	59	58	75	1,099	2,614	5,172	8,129	10,851	Net Assets $mil

Rating and Risk

Time Period	Load-Adj Return %	Morningstar Rtn vs Cat	Morningstar Risk vs Cat	Morningstar Risk-Adj Rating
1 Yr	10.82			
3 Yr	9.92	+Avg	-Avg	★★★★
5 Yr	9.88	High	Avg	★★★★★
10 Yr	13.27	High	-Avg	★★★★★
Incept	13.48			

Other Measures	Standard Index DJ Mod	Best Fit Index MSCI Wd xUS
Alpha	2.3	0.6
Beta	0.57	0.37
R-Squared	54	60
Standard Deviation	4.55	
Mean	9.92	
Sharpe Ratio	1.41	

Portfolio Analysis 11-30-06

Total Stocks:42 Share change since 10-31-06	Sectors	P/E Ratio	YTD Return %	% Net Assets
XTO Energy, Inc.	Energy	9.0	-2.55	4.66
General Dynamics	Ind Mtrls	19.1	4.91	3.06
Nestle SA ADR	Goods	21.0	-2.53	3.00
EnCana Corporation	Energy	11.8	-1.18	2.96
⊕ Caremark RX, Inc.	Health	23.6	-0.82	2.93
Diageo PLC ADR	Goods	16.1	-2.70	2.76
ConocoPhillips	Energy	6.5	-5.07	2.64
EchoStar Communications C	Media	29.5	2.42	2.59
Safeco Corporation	Financial	8.8	-0.25	2.11

Total Fixed-Income:14	Date of Maturity	Amount $000	Value $000	% Net Assets
US Treasury Note 4.875%	02-15-12	500,000	510,684	4.45
US Treasury Note 4.875%	05-15-09	500,000	503,887	4.39
US Treasury Note 5.125%	06-30-08	500,000	503,321	4.39
US Treasury Note 4.875%	08-15-16	375,000	386,792	3.37
US Treasury Note 5.125%	06-30-11	250,000	256,914	2.24
US Treasury Note 4.875%	05-31-11	250,000	254,326	2.22
US Treasury Note 4.75%	03-31-11	250,000	252,881	2.20
US Treasury Note 4.5%	02-15-16	250,000	250,703	2.18
US Treasury Note 4.75%	11-15-08	250,000	250,674	2.18

Equity Style
Style: Blend
Size: Large-Cap

Value Measures		Rel Category
Price/Earnings	15.25	1.00
Price/Book	2.45	0.99
Price/Sales	1.19	0.87
Price/Cash Flow	8.04	0.99
Dividend Yield %	1.07	0.55

Growth Measures	%	Rel Category
Long-Term Erngs	12.42	1.06
Book Value	11.01	1.28
Sales	15.31	1.72
Cash Flow	18.65	1.89
Historical Erngs	25.15	1.41

Market Cap %			
Giant	25.3	Small	3.0
Large	40.7	Micro	0.2
Mid	30.8	Avg $mil:	17,737

Fixed-Income Style
Duration: Short-Term
Quality: High

Avg Eff Duration [1]	3.2 Yrs
Avg Eff Maturity	3.7 Yrs
Avg Credit Quality	AAA
Avg Wtd Coupon	3.14%

[1]figure provided by fund as of 11-30-06

Sector Weightings	% of Stocks	Rel DJ Mod	3 Year High Low
⊙ Info	16.40	—	
Software	0.82	—	5 1
Hardware	0.64	—	1 0
Media	14.94	—	17 1
Telecom	0.00	—	0 0
☞ Service	32.35	—	
Health	12.63	—	27 9
Consumer	6.42	—	11 6
Business	2.99	—	15 3
Financial	10.31	—	12 5
Mfg	51.23	—	
Goods	18.92	—	20 8
Ind Mtrls	13.18	—	18 13
Energy	19.13	—	24 10
Utilities	0.00	—	0 0

Composition

● Cash	8.5	
● Stocks	58.9	
● Bonds	32.6	
○ Other	0.0	
Foreign	16.8	(% of Stock)

MORNINGSTAR® Funds 500

Oakmark Global I

	Analyst Pick	Ticker OAKGX	Load None	NAV $25.28	Yield 1.1%	Total Assets $2,634 mil	Mstar Category World Stock

Governance and Management

Stewardship Grade: A

Portfolio Manager(s)

After six years, Michael Welsh stepped down from his comanager role on Sept. 30, 2005. He has been replaced by Rob Taylor, who has been part of Oakmark's international team for more than a decade. Taylor is supported by David Herro (lead manager of Oakmark International and Oakmark International Small Cap), Chad Clark (comanager of International Small Cap), and five analysts. Clyde McGregor, comanager of Oakmark Equity & Income, replaced Greg Jackson as the fund's domestic manager in 2003 and is supported by a talented pool of U.S. analysts.

Strategy

This fund's managers buy stocks that trade at discounts to their estimates of the stocks' intrinsic value. The managers take an all-cap approach; they aren't afraid to build big positions in individual names, sectors, and countries; and they run a focused portfolio. The managers don't normally hedge their foreign currency risk, but they will do so when a currency they own differs significantly from their estimate of its fair value.

Performance 12-31-06

	1st Qtr	2nd Qtr	3rd Qtr	4th Qtr	Total
2002	10.86	-6.60	-17.70	14.87	-2.11
2003	-10.55	33.51	9.55	13.88	48.98
2004	3.89	1.40	-2.86	13.00	15.63
2005	0.60	0.64	8.29	3.29	13.23
2006	6.86	0.80	5.58	9.19	24.18

Trailing	Total Return%	+/- MSCI EAFE	+/- MSCI World	%Rank Cat	Growth of $10,000
3 Mo	9.19	-1.16	0.82	38	10,919
6 Mo	15.28	0.59	2.07	15	11,528
1 Yr	24.18	-2.16	4.11	13	12,418
3 Yr Avg	17.59	-2.34	2.91	31	16,260
5 Yr Avg	18.85	3.87	8.88	1	23,714
10 Yr Avg	—	—	—	—	—
15 Yr Avg	—	—	—	—	—

Tax Analysis	Tax-Adj Rtn%	%Rank Cat	Tax-Cost Rat	%Rank Cat
3 Yr (estimated)	16.16	28	1.22	65
5 Yr (estimated)	17.97	1	0.74	57
10 Yr (estimated)	—	—	—	—

Potential Capital Gain Exposure: 22% of assets

Morningstar's Take by William Samuel Rocco 12-26-06

Oakmark Global has more than its share of strengths, but that doesn't mean it can prosper every year.

The management team is seasoned and deep here. Clyde McGregor, who has run the domestic portion of this fund since late 2003, has been at the helm of thriving Oakmark Equity & Income for more than a decade. Robert Taylor has only been in charge of the foreign portion of this fund for a little more than one year, but he has 12 years of investment experience at Harris Associates (the advisor to the Oakmark Funds). And both managers have lots of analytical support.

This fund's strategy is proven and distinctive. McGregor and Taylor focus on names that are trading at significant discounts to their intrinsic values, go wherever the best bargains are, and readily buy stocks in bunches, just like other Oakmark managers have done to produce winning results at their charges. And this all-cap fund thus normally sports a relative concentrated portfolio

with atypical geographic exposure, sectors weights, and stock holdings for a world-stock offering.

The family strategy has served this fund well throughout its life. This fund has posted a top-quartile 23% gain in 2006, as a diverse mix of McGregor and Taylor picks have paid off. And it has outgained all other world-stock funds since opening in 1999, because stock selection has generally been quite good here.

All this is encouraging--and we remain bullish about the long-term here--but interested investors should be sure they approach this fund with their eyes wide open. The world's stock markets have enjoyed exceptionally favorable conditions in recent years; this fund's all-cap orientation has been helpful during most of its life, and its willingness to concentrate holdings and other bold traits court risk. This means that the next few years are unlikely to be as good as the last few and that there will be some rough spells here.

Historical Profile

Return	High
Risk	Above Avg
Rating	★★★★ Highest

Investment Style: Equity / Stock %

	91%	92%	90%	97%	91%	97%	99%	98%

▼ Manager Change
▽ Partial Manager Change

Growth of $10,000
■ Investment Values of Fund
— Investment Values of MSCI EAFE

Performance Quartile (within Category)

1995	1996	1997	1998	1999	2000	2001	2002	2003	2004	2005	2006	History
—	—	—	—	9.97	11.31	13.26	12.98	19.28	21.81	23.47	25.28	NAV
—	—	—	—	-0.20*	15.84	20.05	-2.11	48.98	15.63	13.23	24.18	Total Return %
—	—	—	—	—	30.03	41.47	13.83	10.39	-4.62	-0.31	-2.16	+/-MSCI EAFE
—	—	—	—	—	29.03	36.85	17.78	15.87	0.91	3.74	4.11	+/-MSCI World
—	—	—	—	—	1.75	0.02	0.00	0.01	0.54	1.21	1.34	Income Return %
—	—	—	—	—	14.09	20.03	-2.11	48.97	15.09	12.02	22.84	Capital Return %
—	—	—	—	—	3	1	3	11	47	40	13	Total Rtn % Rank Cat
—	—	—	—	0.01	0.17	0.00	0.00	0.00	0.10	0.26	0.31	Income $
—	—	—	—	0.00	0.05	0.29	0.00	0.05	0.37	0.97	3.54	Capital Gains $
—	—	—	—	—	1.75	1.75	1.75	1.55	1.28	1.26	1.18	Expense Ratio %
—	—	—	—	—	0.98	0.54	0.00	-0.01	0.00	0.47	1.18	Income Ratio %
—	—	—	—	—	—	147	114	86	42	16	41	Turnover Rate %
—	—	—	—	31	28	76	230	1,168	1,535	2,548		Net Assets $mil

Rating and Risk

Time Period	Load-Adj Return %	Morningstar Rtn vs Cat	Morningstar Risk vs Cat	Morningstar Risk-Adj Rating
1 Yr	24.18			
3 Yr	17.59	+Avg	-Avg	★★★★
5 Yr	18.85	High	High	★★★★★
10 Yr	—	—	—	—
Incept	17.44			

Other Measures	Standard Index MSCI EAFE	Best Fit Index MSCI World
Alpha	1.2	2.7
Beta	0.79	0.99
R-Squared	83	87
Standard Deviation	8.19	
Mean	17.59	
Sharpe Ratio	1.65	

Portfolio Analysis 11-30-06

Share change since 10-06 Total Stocks:52	Sector	Country	% Assets
Vodafone Grp	Telecom	U.K.	3.22
Snap-on, Inc.	Ind Mtrls	United States	3.21
Harley-Davidson, Inc.	Goods	United States	3.19
Credit Suisse Grp	Financial	Switzerland	3.12
GlaxoSmithKline	Health	U.K.	3.12
Oracle Corporation	Software	United States	3.06
DaimlerChrysler AG	Goods	Germany	3.05
Julius Baer Holding Ltd	Financial	Switzerland	2.98
XTO Energy, Inc.	Energy	United States	2.93
⊕ ROHM	Hardware	Japan	2.92
Diageo	Goods	U.K.	2.88
SK Telecom	Telecom	Korea	2.70
Square Enix	Software	Japan	2.63
Laboratory Corporation o	Health	United States	2.50
Bank of Ireland	Financial	Ireland	2.50
Tyco International, Ltd.	Ind Mtrls	United States	2.48
BMW Grp	Goods	Germany	2.26
⊕ Intel Corporation	Hardware	United States	2.22
⊖ Nestle	Goods	Switzerland	2.14
Neopost	Ind Mtrls	France	2.10

Current Investment Style

	Market Cap	%
	Giant	42.4
	Large	28.3
	Mid	25.7
	Small	3.5
	Micro	0.0
	Avg $mil:	19,649

Value Measures		Rel Category
Price/Earnings	16.81	1.09
Price/Book	2.38	1.00
Price/Sales	1.50	1.15
Price/Cash Flow	9.21	1.06
Dividend Yield %	2.48	1.14

Growth Measures	%	Rel Category
Long-Term Erngs	10.62	0.84
Book Value	0.89	0.10
Sales	5.65	0.68
Cash Flow	4.83	0.49
Historical Erngs	12.71	0.68

Composition			
Cash	2.1	Bonds	0.0
Stocks	97.9	Other	0.0
Foreign	(% of Stock)		56.2

Sector Weightings	% of Stocks	Rel MSCI EAFE	3 Year High	Low
☍ Info	34.14	2.89		
Software	5.82	10.39	6	0
Hardware	7.00	1.81	7	0
Media	13.43	7.34	15	6
Telecom	7.89	1.42	10	2
☂ Service	31.80	0.67		
Health	11.91	1.67	20	10
Consumer	0.00	0.00	3	0
Business	8.32	1.64	21	4
Financial	11.57	0.38	19	8
☐ Mfg	34.06	0.83		
Goods	20.62	1.57	21	14
Ind Mtrls	10.44	0.68	16	10
Energy	3.00	0.42	6	2
Utilities	0.00	0.00	0	0

Regional Exposure		% Stock
UK/W. Europe 39	N. America	44
Japan 12	Latn America	1
Asia X Japan 5	Other	0

Country Exposure		% Stock
United States 44	Japan	12
Switzerland 13	Germany	5
U.K. 12		

Address:	Two N Lasalle St Ste 500 Chicago, IL 60602 800-625-6275
Web Address:	www.oakmark.com
Inception:	08-04-99*
Advisor:	Harris Associates LP
Subadvisor:	None
NTF Plans:	Fidelity Retail-NTF, Schwab OneSource

Minimum Purchase:	$1000	Add: $100	IRA: $1000
Min Auto Inv Plan:	$500	Add: $100	
Sales Fees:	No-load, 2.00%R		
Management Fee:	1.00% mx./0.90% mn.		
Actual Fees:	Mgt:0.98%	Dist: —	
Expense Projections:	3Yr:$381	5Yr:$660	10Yr:$1455
Income Distrib:	Annually		

Oakmark I

Analyst Pick	✓
Ticker	OAKMX
Load	None
NAV	$45.92
Yield	0.9%
Total Assets	$5,984 mil
Mstar Category	Large Blend

Governance and Management

Stewardship Grade: B

Portfolio Manager(s)

Bill Nygren has worked for Harris Associates, advisor to the Oakmark funds, for two decades. He makes the final decisions about the portfolio, and he has also run Oakmark Select with aplomb. Comanager Kevin Grant, a former analyst at the firm, has run the fund with Nygren since March 2000, when former manager Robert Sanborn was pushed out.

Strategy

This traditionally was one of the purest value funds around, but manager Bill Nygren has found more fallen growth stocks that meet his valuation criteria. He buys stocks that are trading at discounts to their estimated private market values. To estimate companies' intrinsic values, Nygren and his colleagues use discounted cash-flow analysis and look at comparable transactions, among many other factors. The fund has migrated from its former mid-cap home into large-cap territory, as many of Nygren's recent purchases have fallen into the latter area.

Historical Profile

Return	Above Avg
Risk	Below Avg
Rating	★★★★ Above Avg

Investment Style: Equity, Stock %
87% 89% 91% 90% 94% 91% 91% 94% 94%

▼ Manager Change
▽ Partial Manager Change

31.0 — Growth of $10,000
25.0 ■ Investment Values of Fund
20.0 — Investment Values of S&P 500
15.0
10.0

Performance Quartile (within Category)

	1995	1996	1997	1998	1999	2000	2001	2002	2003	2004	2005	2006	History
NAV	29.75	32.35	40.41	35.82	27.20	29.99	35.27	30.08	37.54	41.77	40.88	45.92	
Total Return %	34.42	16.21	32.59	3.73	-10.47	11.78	18.29	-14.41	25.30	11.73	-1.31	18.26	
+/-S&P 500	-3.16	-6.75	-0.77	-24.85	-31.51	20.88	30.18	7.69	-3.38	0.85	-6.22	2.47	
+/-Russ 1000	-3.35	-6.24	-0.26	-23.29	-31.38	19.57	30.74	7.24	-4.59	0.33	-7.58	2.80	
Income Return %	1.24	1.16	1.24	1.21	0.73	1.42	0.66	0.32	0.47	0.45	0.83	1.06	
Capital Return %	33.18	15.05	31.35	2.52	-11.20	10.36	17.63	-14.73	24.83	11.28	-2.14	17.20	
Total Rtn % Rank Cat	51	89	27	97	99	9	1	6	70	30	97	6	
Income $	0.28	0.34	0.40	0.44	0.26	0.39	0.20	0.11	0.14	0.17	0.35	0.43	
Capital Gains $	0.84	1.87	1.98	5.63	4.73	0.00	0.00	0.00	0.00	0.00	0.00	2.00	
Expense Ratio %	1.17	1.18	1.08	1.08	1.11	1.21	1.15	1.17	1.14	1.05	1.03	1.05	
Income Ratio %	1.27	1.13	1.19	1.22	1.02	1.42	0.73	0.38	0.48	0.47	0.79	0.94	
Turnover Rate %	18	24	—	43	13	50	57	44	21	19	16	9	
Net Assets $mil	3,302	4,195	7,301	7,668	3,818	2,206	3,644	3,789	5,509	7,156	6,102	5,947	

Performance 12-31-06

	1st Qtr	2nd Qtr	3rd Qtr	4th Qtr	Total
2002	4.17	-8.36	-16.60	7.51	-14.41
2003	-4.09	16.95	0.33	11.35	25.30
2004	1.44	2.23	-0.64	8.44	11.73
2005	-2.20	0.22	-0.46	1.16	-1.31
2006	3.82	-0.35	5.56	8.30	18.26

Trailing	Total Return%	+/- S&P 500	+/- Russ 1000	%Rank Cat	Growth of $10,000
3 Mo	8.30	1.60	1.35	9	10,830
6 Mo	14.32	1.58	1.96	6	11,432
1 Yr	18.26	2.47	2.80	6	11,826
3 Yr Avg	9.25	-1.19	-1.73	66	13,040
5 Yr Avg	6.94	0.75	0.12	26	13,986
10 Yr Avg	8.58	0.16	-0.06	26	22,777
15 Yr Avg	14.00	3.36	3.20	4	71,379

Tax Analysis	Tax-Adj Rtn%	%Rank Cat	Tax-Cost Rat	%Rank Cat
3 Yr (estimated)	8.75	55	0.46	21
5 Yr (estimated)	6.59	22	0.33	22
10 Yr (estimated)	7.37	29	1.11	50

Potential Capital Gain Exposure: 32% of assets

Rating and Risk

Time Period	Load-Adj Return %	Morningstar Rtn vs Cat	Morningstar Risk vs Cat	Morningstar Risk-Adj Rating
1 Yr	18.26			
3 Yr	9.25	Avg	Low	★★★
5 Yr	6.94	+Avg	-Avg	★★★★
10 Yr	8.58	+Avg	Avg	★★★★
Incept	15.57			

Other Measures	Standard Index S&P 500	Best Fit Index Mstar Large Core TR
Alpha	0.4	-0.4
Beta	0.78	0.84
R-Squared	77	81
Standard Deviation	6.14	
Mean	9.25	
Sharpe Ratio	0.96	

Portfolio Analysis 11-30-06

Share change since 10-06 Total Stocks:54	Sector	PE	Tot Ret%	% Assets
McDonald's Corporation	Consumer	18.9	34.63	3.01
Washington Mutual, Inc.	Financial	13.4	9.62	2.98
Yum Brands, Inc.	Consumer	20.4	26.76	2.82
Harley-Davidson, Inc.	Goods	18.5	38.81	2.62
Time Warner, Inc.	Media	19.6	26.37	2.53
Limited Brands, Inc.	Consumer	14.5	32.47	2.48
Baxter International Inc	Health	24.3	24.81	2.19
Kohl's Corporation	Consumer	22.6	40.80	2.18
H & R Block, Inc.	Consumer	25.3	-3.95	2.17
⊕ Intel Corporation	Hardware	21.0	-17.18	2.13
Raytheon Company	Ind Mtrls	19.1	34.19	2.11
J.P. Morgan Chase & Co.	Financial	13.6	25.60	2.11
⊕ Viacom, Inc. B	Media	—	—	2.05
InBev	Goods	—	—	2.05
⊕ Texas Instruments, Inc.	Hardware	16.9	-9.82	2.04
⊕ Home Depot, Inc.	Consumer	13.5	1.01	2.04
Black & Decker Corporati	Ind Mtrls	12.2	-6.37	2.03
Citigroup, Inc.	Financial	13.1	19.55	2.01
Pulte Homes, Inc.	Consumer	6.7	-15.43	2.00
US Bancorp	Financial	13.9	26.29	1.96

Current Investment Style

Value Blnd Growth — Large Mid Small

Market Cap	%
Giant	32.6
Large	58.4
Mid	8.9
Small	0.0
Micro	0.0

Avg $mil: 33,308

Value Measures		Rel Category
Price/Earnings	17.05	1.11
Price/Book	2.84	1.11
Price/Sales	1.54	1.10
Price/Cash Flow	12.52	1.48
Dividend Yield %	1.78	1.02

Growth Measures	%	Rel Category
Long-Term Erngs	11.50	0.97
Book Value	6.66	0.74
Sales	11.23	1.16
Cash Flow	2.13	0.21
Historical Erngs	16.49	0.89

Profitability	%	Rel Category
Return on Equity	21.28	1.09
Return on Assets	10.39	1.00
Net Margin	12.03	0.90

Sector Weightings

	% of Stocks	Rel S&P 500	3 Year High Low
◔ Info	25.26	1.26	
🖥 Software	0.00	0.00	0 0
💻 Hardware	10.32	1.12	10 1
📺 Media	14.94	3.94	20 11
📞 Telecom	0.00	0.00	2 0
⚙ Service	46.73	1.01	
🏥 Health	9.53	0.79	13 6
🛒 Consumer	21.47	2.81	22 17
💼 Business	2.22	0.52	8 2
💲 Financial	13.51	0.61	16 14
🏭 Mfg	28.02	0.83	
🏠 Goods	16.00	1.87	18 15
⚙ Ind Mtrls	10.57	0.89	11 9
🔋 Energy	1.45	0.15	5 1
💡 Utilities	0.00	0.00	0 0

Composition

	%
● Cash	5.7
● Stocks	94.3
● Bonds	0.0
○ Other	0.0
Foreign	3.9
(% of Stock)	

Morningstar's Take by Paul Herbert 12-29-06

Oakmark Fund is moving a little to the right.

This fund joined the large-blend category at the beginning of December 2006. It isn't unusual for funds run by truly bottom-up managers like this fund's bosses to move around our style box. Consider that its new category siblings Longleaf Partners and Selected American Shares have resided in other groups in recent years.

And those who have been watching the fund's buying habits shouldn't be surprised by these moves. Its comanagers have spied value in beaten-down growth areas, including media, pharmaceutical, and select technology stocks. Despite the fact that many stocks in these areas have shown steady earnings growth throughout the past half decade, they have been shunned by investors. The fund has suffered for holding some of these stocks, but as we've mentioned in the past, we think that this emphasis on higher-quality stocks will ultimately be rewarded. The work of Morningstar's equity analysts supports the claim

that large-cap firms with solid competitive edges look attractive today.

Some of the fund's large-growth selections started paying off in 2006. In particular, the fund benefited from rises in the prices of its media-distribution and drug stocks. Consumer-oriented picks, including Harley Davidson and Kohl's, also pitched in.

Investors shouldn't take the fund's migration towards growth areas to mean that it has abandoned traditional value areas. The managers continue to find value in financial-services stocks, including Washington Mutual. Though the press has taken some swipes at the company, management continues to favor it for its retail-banking strength and increasing dividend

Overall, we think this fund has what it takes to succeed. Its willingness to stand out on a limb gives it quite a bit of appeal. Furthermore, experienced managers, reasonable fees, and good stewardship are all marks in its favor.

Address:	Two N Lasalle St Ste 500 Chicago, IL 60602 800-625-6275	Minimum Purchase:	$1000 Add: $100 IRA: $1000
		Min Auto Inv Plan:	$500 Add: $100
		Sales Fees:	No-load, 2.00%R
Web Address:	www.oakmark.com	Management Fee:	1.00% mx./0.65% mn.
Inception:	08-05-91	Actual Fees:	Mgt:0.86% Dist: —
Advisor:	Harris Associates LP	Expense Projections:	3Yr:$328 5Yr:$569 10Yr:$1259
Subadvisor:	None	Income Distrib:	Annually
NTF Plans:	Fidelity Retail-NTF, Schwab OneSource		

Morningstar® Funds 500

Expand Your Investing Horizons with These Other Morningstar Annuals!

Morningstar® ETFs 150™

We've improved and expanded this essential ETF research tool. We now cover 150 ETFs and provide the Morningstar Rating for every ETF. Plus, you'll find nearly 100 additional pages of helpful editorial guidance. Articles help you determine which ETFs will give you optimal exposure to the part of the market you're looking to track. They explain how to avoid common ETF-investing mistakes. You'll find out how to blend ETFs into your existing portfolio and much more!

▶ Exclusive! Best time to buy or sell
▶ Nearly 100 pages of "how-to" guidance

January 2007. Softbound. 8 1/2" x 11". Approx. 235 pages. $35 (plus $4.95 S&H).

Morningstar® Stocks 500™

If you want to add stocks to your portfolio, this popular annual is a must-have. Follow our analysts' guidance on widely held stocks. Each report page contains the Morningstar Rating for stocks, a fair value estimate, Consider Buying/Selling prices, historical data, written analysis by a Morningstar stock analyst—everything you expect from Morningstar.

▶ Buy/sell guidance in every report
▶ Morningstar's picks for 2007

January 2007. Softbound. 8 1/2" x 11". Approx. 600 pages. $35 (plus $4.95 S&H).

Examine both annuals risk-free for 30 days.

Additional Reports Available Free!
Order either book now and gain access to additional Morningstar ETF Reports or Morningstar Stock Reports of your choice. Access up to 50 of our 1,800 Stock Reports or all of our ETF Reports any time in 2007—you decide when!

To order, call toll-free 866-608-9570
Mention code AMS-INS-7A

MORNINGSTAR®

Get Fresh Fund Ideas All Year Long—Free

Access updated analysis and research on up to 50 online fund reports any time in 2007. It's fast, easy, and completely free to you.

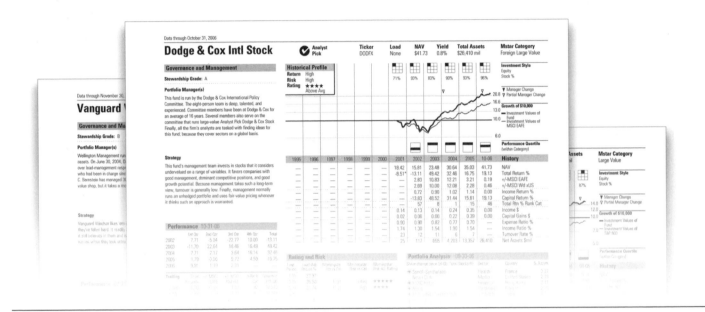

Thank you for purchasing *Morningstar Funds 500*. In addition to the reports contained here, you have free access to 50 more of our 2,000 Fund Reports at any time during 2007. You decide when and what Fund Reports you want to download!

Note that you will be asked to register if you are not already registered for one of Morningstar's online services. This process takes only a minute, does not require a credit card, and is absolutely free.

Online mutual fund information includes:

▶ Up-to-date financial data, including performance info

▶ The latest Morningstar Ratings for funds

▶ Portfolio holdings and anaylsis

▶ Manager profiles

▶ Fresh Analyst Reports

▶ And more!

When you're ready to access your free Fund Reports, visit this Web address:

www.morningstar.com/goto/2007Funds500

Thank You for Choosing Morningstar!

Oakmark International I

	Ticker	Load	NAV	Yield	Total Assets	Mstar Category
	OAKIX	None	$25.45	1.5%	$8,598 mil	Foreign Large Value

Governance and Management

Stewardship Grade: B

Portfolio Manager(s)

David Herro has been at the helm of this fund since it opened in late 1992. Herro, who serves as Harris Associates' CIO of International Equities, has run Oakmark International Small Cap for 11 years. He's supported by seven investment professionals here, including 12-year Harris veteran Rob Taylor (who is a comanager of Oakmark Global) and 11-year Harris veteran Chad Clark (who is a comanager of Oakmark International Small Cap).

Strategy

The manager invests in stocks that trade at discounts of at least 40% to his estimates of intrinsic value. He readily considers fallen growth stocks (which can push the fund into the blend or growth areas of the Morningstar Style Box). He also readily considers emerging-markets and smaller-cap names, and the fund's sector and country weightings often look quite different from its peers'. The manager doesn't usually hedge his currency risk, but he will do so when a currency he owns differs significantly from his estimate of its fair value. To combat market-timers, the fund has a 2% redemption fee.

Performance 12-31-06

	1st Qtr	2nd Qtr	3rd Qtr	4th Qtr	Total
2002	11.46	-2.23	-22.93	8.99	-8.46
2003	-11.72	25.43	7.70	15.75	38.04
2004	3.61	1.82	-0.16	13.07	19.09
2005	2.13	-0.05	9.04	2.52	14.12
2006	10.17	2.90	5.09	9.62	30.60

Trailing	Total Return%	+/- MSCI EAFE	+/- MSCI Wd xUS	%Rank Cat	Growth of $10,000
3 Mo	9.62	-0.73	-0.50	65	10,962
6 Mo	15.21	0.52	0.99	42	11,521
1 Yr	30.60	4.26	4.89	15	13,060
3 Yr Avg	21.08	1.15	0.98	35	17,751
5 Yr Avg	17.53	2.55	2.28	32	22,426
10 Yr Avg	12.36	4.65	4.40	12	32,071
15 Yr Avg	—	—	—	—	—

Tax Analysis	Tax-Adj Rtn%	%Rank Cat	Tax-Cost Rat	%Rank Cat
3 Yr (estimated)	19.32	36	1.45	57
5 Yr (estimated)	16.37	29	0.99	50
10 Yr (estimated)	10.36	13	1.78	85

Potential Capital Gain Exposure: -15% of assets

Historical Profile

Return Above Avg
Risk Above Avg
Rating ★★★ Neutral

		97%	96%	96%	95%	92%	95%	96%	96%	95%

Investment Style
Equity
Stock %

▼ Manager Change
▽ Partial Manager Change

Growth of $10,000

━ Investment Values of Fund
━ Investment Values of MSCI EAFE

38.0
31.0
24.0
17.0
10.0

Performance Quartile (within Category)

1995	1996	1997	1998	1999	2000	2001	2002	2003	2004	2005	2006	History
12.38	15.68	12.83	10.91	14.70	15.46	14.49	13.14	18.02	21.13	22.52	25.45	NAV
8.32	28.02	3.33	-7.00	39.47	12.50	-5.13	-8.46	38.04	19.09	14.12	30.60	Total Return %
-2.89	21.97	1.55	-26.93	12.44	26.69	16.29	7.48	-0.55	-1.16	0.58	4.26	+/-MSCI EAFE
-3.09	21.15	1.06	-25.69	11.49	25.86	16.26	7.34	-1.38	-1.29	-0.35	4.89	+/-MSCI Wd xUS
0.00	1.31	3.67	1.90	4.46	3.45	1.07	0.87	0.83	1.48	2.81	1.97	Income Return %
8.32	26.71	-0.34	-8.90	35.01	9.05	-6.20	-9.33	37.21	17.61	11.31	28.63	Capital Return %
92	1	79	100	17	2	5	26	57	77	40	15	Total Rtn % Rank Cat
0.00	0.16	0.58	0.24	0.49	0.51	0.16	0.13	0.11	0.27	0.59	0.44	Income $
1.04	0.00	2.86	0.78	0.00	0.50	0.00	0.00	0.00	0.05	1.04	3.48	Capital Gains $
1.40	1.32	1.26	1.32	1.29	1.30	1.30	1.31	1.25	1.20	1.11	1.10	Expense Ratio %
1.40	1.45	2.09	1.95	1.94	1.87	1.40	1.34	1.03	1.40	1.32	1.80	Income Ratio %
27	42	61	43	54	64	58	24	34	21	14	—	Turnover Rate %
786	1,233	1,238	797	785	818	964	1,656	3,509	4,677	5,816	8,005	Net Assets $mil

Rating and Risk

Time Period	Load-Adj Return %	Morningstar Rtn vs Cat	Morningstar Risk vs Cat	Morningstar Risk-Adj Rating
1 Yr	30.60			
3 Yr	21.08	Avg	Low	★★★
5 Yr	17.53	Avg	+Avg	★★★
10 Yr	12.36	+Avg	High	★★★
Incept	13.71			

Other Measures	Standard Index MSCI EAFE	Best Fit Index MSCI EAFE
Alpha	3.6	3.6
Beta	0.82	0.82
R-Squared	88	88
Standard Deviation	8.33	
Mean	21.08	
Sharpe Ratio	1.98	

Portfolio Analysis 11-30-06

Share change since 10-06 Total Stocks:60

		Sector	Country	% Assets
⊕	GlaxoSmithKline	Health	U.K.	3.70
	DaimlerChrysler AG	Goods	Germany	3.68
⊕	UBS AG	Financial	Switzerland	3.25
	ChinaTrust Financial Hld	Financial	Taiwan	3.14
	British Sky Broadcasting	Media	U.K.	3.08
⊖	Credit Suisse Grp	Financial	Switzerland	2.99
⊕	SK Telecom	Telecom	Korea	2.97
⊖	Signet Grp	Goods	U.K.	2.95
	Adecco	Business	Switzerland	2.90
⊕	Daiwa Securities Grp	Financial	Japan	2.89
	Diageo	Goods	U.K.	2.85
⊕	ROHM	Hardware	Japan	2.71
⊕	Novartis	Health	Switzerland	2.45
⊕	Lloyds TSB Grp	Financial	U.K.	2.36
	Nestle	Goods	Switzerland	2.36
	BMW Grp	Goods	Germany	2.35
	Compass Grp	Consumer	U.K.	2.25
⊖	Bank of Ireland	Financial	Ireland	2.20
⊖	Vodafone Grp	Telecom	U.K.	2.16
	Cadbury Schweppes	Goods	U.K.	2.09

Current Investment Style

Value Blnd Growth — Large / Mid / Small

	Market Cap	%
	Giant	44.0
	Large	32.9
	Mid	21.8
	Small	1.4
	Micro	0.0
	Avg $mil:	21,014

Value Measures		Rel Category
Price/Earnings	14.56	1.16
Price/Book	2.18	1.22
Price/Sales	1.18	1.24
Price/Cash Flow	8.14	1.14
Dividend Yield %	3.05	0.93

Growth Measures	%	Rel Category
Long-Term Erngs	9.24	0.90
Book Value	6.42	0.82
Sales	3.57	0.65
Cash Flow	2.93	0.82
Historical Erngs	15.14	0.92

Composition

Cash	4.6	Bonds	0.0
Stocks	95.4	Other	0.0
Foreign	(% of Stock)		99.6

Sector Weightings

Sector Weightings	% of Stocks	Rel MSCI EAFE	3 Year High	3 Year Low
⟳ Info	23.06	1.95		
🖥 Software	0.00	0.00	0	0
💾 Hardware	3.83	0.99	4	0
🎙 Media	11.73	6.41	12	4
📞 Telecom	7.50	1.35	11	3
⚙ Service	44.37	0.94		
🏥 Health	9.19	1.29	16	9
🛒 Consumer	3.59	0.73	4	0
💼 Business	6.21	1.22	9	6
💲 Financial	25.38	0.84	27	19
🏭 Mfg	32.57	0.80		
🏬 Goods	25.16	1.92	30	23
⚙ Ind Mtrls	7.11	0.46	16	7
🔋 Energy	0.30	0.04	2	0
💡 Utilities	0.00	0.00	0	0

Regional Exposure

	% Stock		% Stock
UK/W. Europe	73	N. America	0
Japan	14	Latn America	1
Asia X Japan	12	Other	0

Country Exposure

	% Stock		% Stock
U.K.	29	Germany	10
Switzerland	19	France	8
Japan	14		

Morningstar's Take by William Samuel Rocco 12-07-06

Oakmark International is a good long-term holding for foreign-value fans.

This fund has all the fundamentals necessary to be a good core international holding. Oakmark is a fundholder-friendly shop. David Herro is a seasoned veteran--he has the third-longest tenure of the 77 foreign large-value managers--and he has a lot of his own money invested here. This fund favors larger caps from larger markets, and Herro relies on a sound stock-selection strategy that has worked well on several other Oakmark offerings.

Herro has executed the family strategy, which focuses on stocks that are trading at substantial discounts to their intrinsic values, quite well here overall. The fund has gained 5 percentage points more than the foreign large-value norm of 23% for the year to date through Dec. 7, as a number of Herro's picks have prospered, including top-10 and longtime holding Diageo, which is up 37% since Jan. 1 as its free cash flow has improved. The fund has posted strong absolute and relative returns over the trailing three-, five-, and 10-year periods because Herro's stock selection has been on target much more often than not.

All this is encouraging--and we believe that this fund has considerable merit as a core foreign holding--but interested investors should be sure to consider three factors before climbing aboard. First, the hefty absolute gains that this and other foreign large-value funds have posted in recent years aren't sustainable indefinitely. Second, the fund is riskier than many of its rivals, because Herro runs a relatively compact portfolio of names, isn't afraid to load up on individual sectors and countries, and is more comfortable pursuing smaller-cap and emerging-markets bargains than most of his peers. Third, this fund is expected to make a substantial capital gains distribution later this month.

Address:	Two N Lasalle St Ste 500 Chicago, IL 60602 800-625-6275	Minimum Purchase:	$1000 Add: $100 IRA: $1000
		Min Auto Inv Plan:	$500 Add: $100
		Sales Fees:	No-load, 2.00%R
Web Address:	www.oakmark.com	Management Fee:	1.00% mx./0.82% mn.
Inception:	09-30-92	Actual Fees:	Mgt:0.91% Dist: —
Advisor:	Harris Associates LP	Expense Projections:	3Yr:$353 5Yr:$612 10Yr:$1352
Subadvisor:	None	Income Distrib:	Annually
NTF Plans:	Fidelity Retail-NTF, Schwab OneSource		

Oakmark Intl Small Cap I

	Ticker	Load	NAV	Yield	Total Assets	Mstar Category
	OAKEX	Closed	$22.89	2.1%	$1,396 mil	Foreign Small/Mid Value

Governance and Management

Stewardship Grade: B

Portfolio Manager(s)

David Herro has been at the helm since the fund opened in November 1995. Chad Clark, a longtime analyst on the fund, has been his comanager since early 2005. There currently are six other analysts on the firm's international team, including 12-year Harris veteran Rob Taylor.

Strategy

The managers invest in stocks trading at discounts of at least 40% of the estimates of their intrinsic values. They sell stocks that get within 10% of their estimates. The fund often carries a large emerging-markets stake, and it has an unusual portfolio makeup. The managers don't normally hedge currency risk, but they will when a currency they own differs significantly from their estimate of its fair value. The fund has a 2% redemption fee on shares held for fewer than three months. A pricing committee meets when conditions warrant, putting fair-value pricing into effect.

Performance 12-31-06

	1st Qtr	2nd Qtr	3rd Qtr	4th Qtr	Total
2002	10.19	2.51	-22.25	8.04	-5.12
2003	-12.24	29.18	14.12	17.81	52.41
2004	6.54	2.92	3.69	13.41	28.95
2005	5.44	-2.65	10.85	6.58	21.26
2006	11.86	-0.58	8.42	11.89	34.90

Trailing	Total Return%	+/- MSCI EAFE	+/- MSCI Wd xUS	%Rank Cat	Growth of $10,000
3 Mo	11.89	1.54	1.77	63	11,189
6 Mo	21.30	6.61	7.08	1	12,130
1 Yr	34.90	8.56	9.19	3	13,490
3 Yr Avg	28.25	8.32	8.15	12	21,095
5 Yr Avg	24.99	10.01	9.74	14	30,505
10 Yr Avg	15.50	7.79	7.54	37	42,249
15 Yr Avg	—				

Tax Analysis	Tax-Adj Rtn%	%Rank Cat	Tax-Cost Rat	%Rank Cat
3 Yr (estimated)	25.14	20	2.42	62
5 Yr (estimated)	22.89	13	1.68	63
10 Yr (estimated)	13.40	39	1.82	82

Potential Capital Gain Exposure: 27% of assets

Historical Profile

Return	Above Avg
Risk	Average
Rating	★★★★ Above Avg

Growth of $10,000
- Investment Values of Fund
- Investment Values of MSCI EAFE

Investment Style: Equity, Stock %

	1995	1996	1997	1998	1999	2000	2001	2002	2003	2004	2005	2006	History
		94%	89%	96%	93%	96%	94%	93%	98%	93%			
NAV	9.63	11.59	8.09	8.62	12.50	10.55	11.58	10.62	16.06	20.03	19.98	22.89	NAV
Total Return %	-3.70*	25.01	-19.91	9.20	53.77	-8.86	12.98	-5.12	52.41	28.95	21.26	34.90	Total Return %
+/-MSCI EAFE	—	18.96	-21.69	-10.73	26.74	5.33	34.40	10.82	13.82	8.70	7.72	8.56	+/-MSCI EAFE
+/-MSCI Wd xUS	—	18.14	-22.18	-9.49	25.79	4.50	34.37	10.68	12.99	8.57	6.79	9.19	+/-MSCI Wd xUS
Income Return %	—	0.81	0.48	2.53	1.32	2.72	1.52	0.79	1.10	1.69	3.52	2.83	Income Return %
Capital Return %	—	24.20	-20.39	6.67	52.45	-11.58	11.46	-5.91	51.31	27.26	17.74	32.07	Capital Return %
Total Rtn % Rank Cat		1	86	41	43	47	1	56	42	44	28	3	Total Rtn % Rank Cat
Income $	0.00	0.08	0.06	0.20	0.11	0.34	0.16	0.09	0.12	0.27	0.70	0.56	Income $
Capital Gains $	0.00	0.36	1.34	0.00	0.59	0.49	0.14	0.27	0.00	0.38	3.54	3.43	Capital Gains $
Expense Ratio %		2.50	1.93	1.96	1.79	1.76	1.74	1.64	1.57	1.49	1.41	—	Expense Ratio %
Income Ratio %		0.65	1.23	2.17	2.31	1.98	1.83	1.28	0.99	0.72	0.96	—	Income Ratio %
Turnover Rate %		—	27	63	69	126	40	49	42	30	29	47	Turnover Rate %
Net Assets $mil	7	47	50	56	129	84	190	368	598	862	1,042	1,396	Net Assets $mil

Performance Quartile (within Category)

Rating and Risk

Time Period	Load-Adj Return %	Morningstar Rtn vs Cat	Morningstar Risk vs Cat	Morningstar Risk-Adj Rating
1 Yr	34.90			
3 Yr	28.25	+Avg	-Avg	★★★★
5 Yr	24.99	+Avg	+Avg	★★★★
10 Yr	15.50	+Avg	Avg	★★★★
Incept	15.68			

Other Measures	Standard Index MSCI EAFE	Best Fit Index MSCI EASExJ
Alpha	9.1	8.2
Beta	0.86	0.85
R-Squared	67	70
Standard Deviation	9.91	
Mean	28.25	
Sharpe Ratio	2.27	

Portfolio Analysis 11-30-06

Share change since 10-06 Total Stocks:59

	Sector	Country	% Assets
Tandberg	Goods	Norway	3.66
MLP	Financial	Germany	3.59
⊖ JJB Sports	Consumer	U.K.	3.39
Benfield Grp Ltd	Business	U.K.	3.34
Julius Baer Holding Ltd	Financial	Switzerland	3.31
Sogecable	Media	Spain	3.30
⊖ Square Enix	Software	Japan	3.19
Daekyo	Consumer	Korea	2.92
Media Prima	Media	Malaysia	2.58
Carpetright	Consumer	U.K.	2.51
Kongsberg Automotive Hld	Ind Mtrls	Norway	2.39
Morse	Business	U.K.	2.38
Bulgari	Goods	Italy	2.36
⊕ Baycorp Advantage Ltd	Financial	Australia	2.06
Vitec Grp	Goods	U.K.	2.05
Neopost	Ind Mtrls	France	2.05
⊖ Intrum Justitia	Business	Sweden	2.03
⊕ Lotte Confectionery	Goods	Korea	2.02
Schindler Holding Ltd	Ind Mtrls	Switzerland	2.01
Domino Printing Sciences	Business	U.K.	1.94

Current Investment Style

Value Blnd Growth — Large Mid Small

Market Cap	%
Giant	0.0
Large	7.0
Mid	41.2
Small	43.9
Micro	7.8

Avg $mil: 1,268

Value Measures		Rel Category
Price/Earnings	16.64	1.13
Price/Book	2.34	1.17
Price/Sales	1.17	1.31
Price/Cash Flow	9.13	1.45
Dividend Yield %	3.79	1.44

Growth Measures	%	Rel Category
Long-Term Erngs	12.18	0.82
Book Value	-0.84	NMF
Sales	0.49	0.07
Cash Flow	-0.15	NMF
Historical Erngs	2.90	0.15

Composition

	%		%
Cash	7.4	Bonds	0.0
Stocks	92.6	Other	0.0
Foreign (% of Stock)	98.9		

Sector Weightings	% of Stocks	Rel MSCI EAFE	3 Year High Low	
⊙ Info	18.11	1.53		
Software	4.71	8.41	6	1
Hardware	1.47	0.38	4	0
Media	11.93	6.52	12	4
Telecom	0.00	0.00	0	0
⊙ Service	43.65	0.92		
Health	4.11	0.58	6	3
Consumer	9.93	2.21	15	2
Business	14.56	2.87	23	14
Financial	14.05	0.47	16	11
⊙ Mfg	38.24	0.93		
Goods	17.24	1.31	17	7
Ind Mtrls	21.00	1.36	34	21
Energy	0.00	0.00	0	0
Utilities	0.00	0.00	0	0

Regional Exposure		% Stock	
UK/W. Europe	66	N. America	1
Japan	9	Latn America	2
Asia X Japan	21	Other	1

Country Exposure		% Stock	
U.K.	23	Germany	8
Switzerland	11	South Korea	7
Japan	9		

Morningstar's Take by William Samuel Rocco 12-07-06

This closed mutual fund has much more than its strong gains going for it, but it's certainly not immune to rough spells.

Oakmark International Small Cap boasts superior short-term and long-term returns. It's the third-best foreign small/mid-cap value fund (and it's up 31%) for the year to date through Dec. 7, thanks to several winning picks. Indeed, Tandberg, a Norwegian maker of video-conferencing equipment that's a top 10 holding here, has rebounded sharply after some late-2005 earnings misses because new management has come in and executed everything well. The fund also sports superior three-, five-, and 10-year gains, as David Herro has delivered the goods in variety of market climates.

Meanwhile, this fund is an even better portfolio diversifier than most foreign small/mid-cap value offerings. It closed to new investors back in mid-2002, when it had only around $400 million in assets. Thus, Herro has faced less asset pressure than many of his peers, and he's still able to run a

fairly compact portfolio and focus on the lower end of the market-cap spectrum. In fact, the fund's average market cap remains less than half the category norm. It relies on the same frugal discipline as its Oakmark siblings, so it's also more value oriented than many of its peers.

Additionally, because Oakmark is also a fundholder-friendly shop, this fund remains a terrific complement to most foreign large-growth and foreign large-blend funds. Shareholders should remember that the managers' practice of running a compact portfolio and willingness to load up on bargains in particular sectors or markets have backfired on occasion in the past and are likely to do so again at some point in the future. They should also note that the big absolute gains this fund and its peers have posted in recent years aren't sustainable forever, and this fund is expected to make a sizable capital-gains distribution later this month.

Address:	Two N Lasalle St Ste 500	Minimum Purchase:	Closed Add: — IRA: —
	Chicago, IL 60602	Min Auto Inv Plan:	Closed Add: —
	800-625-6275	Sales Fees:	No-load, 2.00%R
Web Address:	www.oakmark.com	Management Fee:	1.25% mx./1.05% mn.
Inception:	11-01-95 *	Actual Fees:	Mgt:1.17% Dist: —
Advisor:	Harris Associates LP	Expense Projections:	3Yr:$446 5Yr:$771 10Yr:$1691
Subadvisor:	None	Income Distrib:	Annually
NTF Plans:	Fidelity Retail-NTF, Schwab OneSource		

MORNINGSTAR® Funds 500

Oakmark Select I

	Ticker	Load	NAV	Yield	Total Assets	Mstar Category
	OAKLX	None	$33.48	1.1%	$6,116 mil	Large Blend

Governance and Management

Stewardship Grade: B

Portfolio Manager(s)

Lead manager Bill Nygren has two decades of investment experience, including a stint as research director for Harris Associates, the advisor to the Oakmark Funds. He also serves as lead manager of Oakmark Fund. Comanager Henry Berghoef is also experienced but plays a subordinate role. Berghoef is the director of research for Harris Associates.

Strategy

Management looks for companies trading at significant discounts to what a rational businessperson would pay for them. Although there is no question that Bill Nygren is a value manager, he has historically been willing to invest in nontraditional value areas, including biotechnology. The portfolio is very concentrated, typically holding only 15 to 20 stocks. Top positions usually approach 10% of net assets but at times have reached 15% or more of assets.

Performance 12-31-06

	1st Qtr	2nd Qtr	3rd Qtr	4th Qtr	Total
2002	2.53	-8.09	-15.58	10.02	-12.47
2003	-0.50	16.20	0.04	11.53	29.00
2004	2.45	-1.53	1.00	7.69	9.73
2005	0.12	-0.27	0.42	4.56	4.84
2006	2.52	-0.77	3.02	8.39	13.60

Trailing	Total Return%	+/- S&P 500	+/- Russ 1000	%Rank Cat	Growth of $10,000
3 Mo	8.39	1.69	1.44	8	10,839
6 Mo	11.66	-1.08	-0.70	48	11,166
1 Yr	13.60	-2.19	-1.86	61	11,360
3 Yr Avg	9.33	-1.11	-1.65	65	13,068
5 Yr Avg	8.09	1.90	1.27	15	14,755
10 Yr Avg	17.05	8.63	8.41	1	48,274
15 Yr Avg	—	—	—	—	—

Tax Analysis	Tax-Adj Rtn%	%Rank Cat	Tax-Cost Rat	%Rank Cat
3 Yr (estimated)	8.21	64	1.02	47
5 Yr (estimated)	7.39	15	0.65	42
10 Yr (estimated)	15.87	1	1.01	45

Potential Capital Gain Exposure: 33% of assets

Morningstar's Take by Paul Herbert 12-29-06

A category change for Oakmark Select makes sense, but it doesn't affect its long-term story.

We moved this fund from the large-value to the large-blend category at the beginning of December 2006. This is the second time that we have reclassified it in recent years--recall that its home was the mid-value group from its inception 10 years ago until late 2004. It isn't uncommon for funds run by truly bottom-up managers like this fund's bosses to move around our style box.

Plus, the category change is consistent with the way that comanager Bill Nygren has talked about the fund's evolution in recent years. Nygren and comanager Henry Berghoef have seen appeal in big-cap growth stocks, which isn't surprising given that investors have been giving them short shrift during the past several years. Take the fund's stakes in tech behemoths Intel and Dell as examples. Some large-cap growth stocks, including these two, haven't performed well, and help to explain the fund's tepid results lately. As we've

mentioned in the past, though, we think that this emphasis on large-growth stocks will be rewarded. The work of Morningstar's equity analysts supports the claim that large-cap firms with solid competitive advantages look attractive today. And, while the resurgence has been brief, it's worth pointing out that these stocks have fared better in recent months.

The fund continues to emphasize against-the-grain value picks, too. As a headline example, it continues to highlight Washington Mutual. Though there has been negative press about the company in recent weeks, the managers like its retail-banking approach, as well as its growing dividend and cheap valuation.

In all, we're confident that this fund will be a winner. In addition to the points mentioned above, its experienced managers, reasonable fees, and good stewardship are all marks in its favor.

Address:	Two N Lasalle St Ste 500 Chicago, IL 60602 800-625-6275	Minimum Purchase: $1000 Add: $100 IRA: $1000
		Min Auto Inv Plan: $500 Add: $100
		Sales Fees: No-load, 2.00%R
Web Address:	www.oakmark.com	Management Fee: 1.00% mx./0.73% mn.
Inception:	11-01-96*	Actual Fees: Mgt:0.85% Dist: —
Advisor:	Harris Associates LP	Expense Projections: 3Yr:$318 5Yr:$552 10Yr:$1225
Subadvisor:	None	Income Distrib: Annually
NTF Plans:	Fidelity Retail-NTF, Schwab OneSource	

Historical Profile

Return	Above Avg
Risk	Above Avg
Rating	★★★★ Above Avg

88%	100%	90%	92%	93%	91%	92%	91%	95%

Investment Style Equity, Stock %

▼ Manager Change
▽ Partial Manager Change

Growth of $10,000
■ Investment Values of Fund
— Investment Values of S&P 500

Performance Quartile (within Category)

1995	1996	1997	1998	1999	2000	2001	2002	2003	2004	2005	2006	History
—	11.42	17.52	19.54	18.42	21.65	27.24	23.82	30.62	33.35	32.90	33.48	NAV
—	14.20*	55.02	16.21	14.49	25.81	26.06	-12.47	29.00	9.73	4.84	13.60	Total Return %
—	—	21.66	-12.37	-6.55	34.91	37.95	9.63	0.32	-1.15	-0.07	-2.19	+/-S&P 500
—	—	22.17	-10.81	-6.42	33.60	38.51	9.18	-0.89	-1.67	-1.43	-1.86	+/-Russ 1000
—	—	0.00	0.28	1.01	0.47	0.23	0.08	0.43	0.79	0.88	1.19	Income Return %
—	—	55.02	15.93	13.48	25.34	25.83	-12.55	28.57	8.94	3.96	12.41	Capital Return %
—	—	1	69	74	1	1	4	30	62	59	61	Total Rtn % Rank Cat
—	0.00	0.00	0.05	0.20	0.09	0.05	0.02	0.10	0.24	0.29	0.39	Income $
—	0.00	0.17	0.71	3.72	1.36	0.05	0.26	0.09	1.79	3.53		Capital Gains $
—	—	1.12	1.22	1.16	1.17	1.08	1.07	1.02	1.00	0.99		Expense Ratio %
—	—	-0.11	0.17	0.98	0.76	0.26	0.09	0.23	0.50	1.08		Income Ratio %
—	—	—	56	67	69	21	32	20	14	22		Turnover Rate %
—	50	982	1,298	1,581	2,102	4,684	4,080	5,631	5,734	6,051		Net Assets $mil

Rating and Risk

Time Period	Load-Adj Return %	Morningstar Rtn vs Cat	Morningstar Risk vs Cat	Morningstar Risk-Adj Rating
1 Yr	13.60			
3 Yr	9.33	Avg	+Avg	★★★
5 Yr	8.09	+Avg	+Avg	★★★★
10 Yr	17.05	High	+Avg	★★★★★
Incept	18.29			

Other Measures	Standard Index S&P 500	Best Fit Index Mstar Mid Core
Alpha	0.0	0.0
Beta	0.86	0.55
R-Squared	57	61
Standard Deviation	7.86	
Mean	9.33	
Sharpe Ratio	0.77	

Portfolio Analysis 09-30-06

Share change since 06-06 Total Stocks:21	Sector	PE	Tot Ret%	% Assets
⊖ Washington Mutual, Inc.	Financial	13.4	9.62	14.92
Yum Brands, Inc.	Consumer	20.4	26.76	7.58
H & R Block, Inc.	Consumer	25.3	-3.95	5.71
McDonald's Corporation	Consumer	18.9	34.63	5.46
First Data Corporation	Business	12.3	9.88	5.02
Time Warner, Inc.	Media	19.6	26.37	4.76
Liberty Interactive A	Media	—	—	4.53
⊖ J.P. Morgan Chase & Co.	Financial	13.6	25.60	4.40
⊕ Intel Corporation	Hardware	21.0	-17.18	4.38
Xerox Corporation	Ind Mtrls	13.4	15.70	4.36
⊖ Dun & Bradstreet Corpora	Business	23.1	23.64	4.19
Limited Brands, Inc.	Consumer	14.5	32.47	4.19
Viacom, Inc. B	Media	—	—	3.78
IMS Health, Inc.	Business	17.4	10.77	3.77
⊖ Bristol-Myers Squibb Com	Health	23.1	19.93	3.60
Dell, Inc.	Hardware	18.4	-16.23	3.50
⊖ Pulte Homes, Inc.	Consumer	6.7	12.45	2.83
⊖ Gap, Inc.	Consumer	19.5	12.45	2.76
Discovery Holding Compan	Media	—	—	2.66
⊖ Mattel, Inc.	Goods	15.8	47.48	2.37

Current Investment Style

Value Blnd Growth — Large/Mid/Small

Market Cap	%
Giant	22.7
Large	50.3
Mid	27.0
Small	0.0
Micro	0.0

Avg $mil: 24,692

Value Measures		Rel Category
Price/Earnings	16.48	1.07
Price/Book	2.36	0.92
Price/Sales	1.75	1.25
Price/Cash Flow	16.04	1.90
Dividend Yield %	2.01	1.15

Growth Measures	%	Rel Category
Long-Term Erngs	11.02	0.93
Book Value	8.52	0.94
Sales	8.34	0.86
Cash Flow	-1.69	NMF
Historical Erngs	12.73	0.69

Profitability	%	Rel Category
Return on Equity	23.67	1.22
Return on Assets	10.47	1.01
Net Margin	13.01	0.97

Sector Weightings	% of Stocks	Rel S&P 500	3 Year High Low
↻ Info	24.82	1.24	
⬚ Software	0.00	0.00	0 0
⬚ Hardware	8.28	0.90	8 0
⬚ Media	16.54	4.36	19 8
⬚ Telecom	0.00	0.00	4 0
⬚ Service	68.11	1.47	
⬚ Health	3.79	0.31	7 3
⬚ Consumer	29.99	3.92	31 27
⬚ Business	14.02	3.31	20 14
⬚ Financial	20.31	0.91	22 19
⬚ Mfg	7.07	0.21	
⬚ Goods	2.49	0.29	8 2
⬚ Ind Mtrls	4.58	0.38	5 4
⬚ Energy	0.00	0.00	5 0
⬚ Utilities	0.00	0.00	0 0

Composition

		%
● Cash		4.9
● Stocks		95.1
● Bonds		0.0
○ Other		0.0
Foreign (% of Stock)		0.0

Oppenheimer Develop MktA ✔ Analyst Pick

	Ticker	Load	NAV	Yield	Total Assets	Mstar Category
	ODMAX	5.75%	$41.21	1.1%	$10,305 mil	Diversified Emerging Mkts

Governance and Management

Stewardship Grade: B

Portfolio Manager(s)

Mark Madden, who ran Pioneer Emerging Markets from mid-1994 through mid-2004, joined longtime manager Rajeev Bhaman as a comanager in August 2004. Bhaman transitioned off this fund on Dec. 1, 2004, and Madden took sole control of the portfolio. Madden is supported by two dedicated investment professionals: Marco Spinar and Sam Polyak (who worked with Madden for several years at Pioneer and joined Oppenheimer as emerging markets research director in September 2005). Madden also has another 14 international experts to call on.

Strategy

Manager Mark Madden favors good businesses that are reasonably priced and growing nicely. He likes them to have superior products and operate in businesses with barriers to entry. He goes wherever the best opportunities are and lets his country and sector weights fall where they may. He also considers smaller firms as readily as larger ones. Thus, the fund's portfolio tends to stand out. The fund has a 2% redemption fee on shares held fewer than 30 days and uses fair-value pricing in certain circumstances.

Performance 12-31-06

	1st Qtr	2nd Qtr	3rd Qtr	4th Qtr	Total
2002	14.01	-5.61	-18.82	12.65	-1.60
2003	-8.39	25.87	17.05	22.43	65.24
2004	3.78	-4.68	10.50	21.66	33.00
2005	1.34	6.86	18.17	10.36	41.23
2006	10.68	-9.48	6.54	17.28	25.19

Trailing	Total Return%	+/- MSCI EAFE	+/- MSCI EmrMkt	%Rank Cat	Growth of $10,000
3 Mo	17.28	6.93	0.00	54	11,728
6 Mo	24.95	10.26	2.86	30	12,495
1 Yr	25.19	-1.15	-3.99	97	12,519
3 Yr Avg	32.98	13.05	5.72	8	23,516
5 Yr Avg	30.76	15.78	7.24	8	38,227
10 Yr Avg	19.07	11.36	12.34	1	57,283
15 Yr Avg	—	—	—		

Tax Analysis	Tax-Adj Rtn%	%Rank Cat	Tax-Cost Rat	%Rank Cat
3 Yr (estimated)	28.77	32	1.23	50
5 Yr (estimated)	27.84	12	1.07	59
10 Yr (estimated)	17.27	2	0.92	74

Potential Capital Gain Exposure: 30% of assets

Historical Profile

Return	Above Avg
Risk	Average
Rating	★★★★ Above Avg

		89%	93%		80%	84%	78%	91%	93%	99%

Growth of $10,000

— Investment Values of Fund
— Investment Values of MSCI EAFE

▼ Manager Change
▽ Partial Manager Change

54.8 / 47.8 / 33.8 / 24.0 / 17.0 / 10.0

Performance Quartile (within Category)

1995	1996	1997	1998	1999	2000	2001	2002	2003	2004	2005	2006	History
—	10.15	11.01	8.70	15.72	14.30	13.28	12.87	20.61	26.88	36.33	41.21	NAV
—	1.50*	14.09	-19.36	82.29	-5.26	-5.73	-1.60	65.24	33.00	41.23	25.19	Total Return %
—	—	12.31	-39.29	55.26	8.93	15.69	14.34	26.65	12.75	27.69	-1.15	+/-MSCI EAFE
—	—	27.54	8.31	18.20	26.64	-1.05	6.37	13.65	10.55	10.92	-3.99	+/-MSCI EmrMkt
—	—	0.88	0.91	1.43	1.25	1.38	1.48	4.80	1.79	1.69	1.39	Income Return %
—	—	13.21	-20.27	80.86	-6.51	-7.11	-3.08	60.44	31.21	39.54	23.80	Capital Return %
—	—	2	15	23	1	71	21	16	5	4	97	Total Rtn % Rank Cat
—	0.00	0.09	0.10	0.12	0.20	0.20	0.20	0.62	0.37	0.45	0.51	Income $
—	0.00	0.46	0.07	0.00	0.39	0.00	0.00	0.00	0.13	1.11	3.65	Capital Gains $
—	—	1.94	2.18	2.37	1.96	1.69	1.77	1.76	1.52	1.43	1.37	Expense Ratio %
—	—	1.45	0.87	1.11	1.56	1.76	1.91	1.42	1.64	2.01	1.11	Income Ratio %
—	—	27	78	37	22	16	10	6	15	28	65	Turnover Rate %
—	7	33	27	62	131	196	342	859	2,410	5,970	8,193	Net Assets $mil

Rating and Risk

Time Period	Load-Adj Return %	Morningstar Rtn vs Cat	Morningstar Risk vs Cat	Morningstar Risk-Adj Rating
1 Yr	17.99			
3 Yr	30.38	Avg	-Avg	★★★
5 Yr	29.22	+Avg	+Avg	★★★★
10 Yr	18.36	High	Avg	★★★★★
Incept	18.31			

Other Measures	Standard Index MSCI EAFE	Best Fit Index MSCI EmrMkt
Alpha	3.6	6.7
Beta	1.51	0.90
R-Squared	74	91
Standard Deviation	16.55	
Mean	32.98	
Sharpe Ratio	1.63	

Portfolio Analysis 08-31-06

Share change since 05-06 Total Stocks:191	Sector	Country	% Assets
⊕ Petroleo Brasileiro S.A.	Energy	Brazil	3.45
⊖ America Movil SA ADR	Telecom	Mexico	2.06
⊕ Hon Hai Precision Indust	Hardware	Taiwan	1.61
Anglo American Platinum	Ind Mtrls	South Africa	1.60
Anglogold Ashanti, Ltd.	Ind Mtrls	South Africa	1.54
⊖ Samsung Electronics	Goods	Korea	1.50
⊖ Surgutneftegaz	Energy	Russia	1.46
⊕ Infosys Technologies Ltd	Software	India	1.35
⊕ All Amer Latina	Business	Brazil	1.29
Orascom Telecom Hldgs (S	—	Egypt	1.25
☼ Taiwan Semiconductor Man	Hardware	Taiwan	1.25
Housing Development Fina	Financial	India	1.23
⊖ Telekomunikasi Indonesia	Telecom	Indonesia	1.17
⊕ United Microelect	Hardware	Taiwan	1.13
⊖ Reliance Industries Ltd	Ind Mtrls	India	1.13
Indonesian Satellite	Telecom	Indonesia	1.12
Larsen & Toubro Ltd	Ind Mtrls	India	1.11
⊕ Tata Consultancy Service	Business	India	1.08
⊕ Humax	Goods	Korea	1.06
⊖ Sadia	Ind Mtrls	Brazil	1.03

Current Investment Style

Value Blnd Growth		Market Cap	%
	Large	Giant	32.0
	Mid	Large	34.7
	Small	Mid	25.0
		Small	7.7
		Micro	0.5

Avg $mil: 7,346

Value Measures		Rel Category
Price/Earnings	13.14	1.01
Price/Book	1.86	0.85
Price/Sales	0.70	0.64
Price/Cash Flow	5.46	0.82
Dividend Yield %	3.00	0.91

Growth Measures	%	Rel Category
Long-Term Erngs	16.39	1.06
Book Value	7.29	0.73
Sales	17.71	1.12
Cash Flow	20.83	1.88
Historical Erngs	7.00	0.39

Composition

Cash	0.3	Bonds	0.0
Stocks	98.9	Other	0.9
Foreign (% of Stock)			98.2

Sector Weightings

		% of Stocks	Rel MSCI EAFE	3 Year High	Low
↻ Info	18.86		1.60		
🖳 Software	2.81		5.02	4	1
💻 Hardware	8.02		2.08	9	0
🎬 Media	0.22		0.12	7	0
📶 Telecom	7.81		1.40	12	1
⊕ Service	32.82		0.69		
🏥 Health	2.24		0.31	5	2
🛒 Consumer	5.53		1.12	12	5
💼 Business	7.94		1.57	9	5
💲 Financial	17.11		0.57	26	17
🏭 Mfg	48.32		1.18		
🏗 Goods	15.59		1.19	17	14
🔧 Ind Mtrls	18.09		1.17	18	10
⛽ Energy	13.91		1.95	14	4
💡 Utilities	0.73		0.14	2	1

Regional Exposure % Stock

UK/W. Europe	3	N. America	3
Japan	0	Latn America	22
Asia X Japan	52	Other	20

Country Exposure % Stock

Brazil	15	South Korea	12
India	15	South Africa	7
Taiwan	13		

Morningstar's Take by William Samuel Rocco 11-06-06

We're not too worried about Oppenheimer Developing Markets' 2006 woes.

This fund is lagging this year. It was slowed by the sizable inflows it received as the world's emerging markets surged early in 2006. Its big position in India and oversized stakes in less-popular and higher-risk markets such as Turkey stung when most developing markets tanked in late spring. Manager Mark Madden's decisions to avoid oil producers and to favor consumer names have also hurt. As a result, the fund is mired in its category's worst decile for the year to date.

These results, though frustrating, should be put in perspective. Oppenheimer has addressed the inflow issue: It raised the minimum initial investment to $50,000 last spring, and the fund is now out of reach for most new investors. Madden, who came on board as a comanager in August 2004 and took sole control a few months later, always goes wherever the best opportunities are and lets his country and sector weights fall where they may,

so the contrarian traits that have been burdensome this year are central to his style.

Meanwhile, there are ample grounds for long-term optimism here. The fund thrived in the few months Madden ran it with Rajeev Bhaman. It posted top-decile gains in the 2005 rally, as its contrarianism paid off. And the fund has comfortably outpaced its average peer on Madden's watch. What's more, the fund earned excellent results with its current strategy before Madden came on board, and he posted good results at his former charge, Pioneer Emerging Markets, with a similar approach.

The fund remains a good long-term emerging-markets play despite its 2006 woes. That said, taxable investors who want to add to their stake--or who can gain access--should note that Oppenheimer expects the fund to make a significant capital gains distribution later this year.

Address:	6803 South Tucson Way Centennial CO 80112-3924 800-225-5677	Minimum Purchase:	$50000	Add: $50 IRA: $1000
		Min Auto Inv Plan:	$1000	Add: $50
		Sales Fees:	5.75%L, 0.24%S, 2.00%R	
Web Address:	www.oppenheimerfunds.com	Management Fee:	1.00% mx./0.75% mn.	
Inception:	11-18-96 *	Actual Fees:	Mgt:0.85% Dist:0.24%	
Advisor:	OppenheimerFunds, Inc.	Expense Projections:	3Yr:$987 5Yr:$1287 10Yr:$2137	
Subadvisor:	None	Income Distrib:	Annually	
NTF Plans:	DATALynx NTF, Federated Tr NTF			

Morningstar® Funds 500

Oppenheimer Glob A

		Analyst Pick	Ticker	Load	NAV	Yield	Total Assets	Mstar Category
	✓		OPPAX	5.75%	$73.51	0.7%	$17,153 mil	World Stock

Governance and Management

Stewardship Grade: B

Portfolio Manager(s)

Rajeev Bhaman became this fund's sole portfolio manager in October 2005. Bhaman ran Oppenheimer Developing Markets from late 1996 to 2004 and compiled a stellar record. In August 2004, this fund's longtime manager, Bill Wilby, chose Bhaman as his successor, and the two comanaged this fund for more than a year. Bhaman is supported by two generalist analysts, Justin Leverenz and Rezo Kanovich, and collaborates extensively with such long-tenured and successful Oppenheimer global managers as Frank Jennings (Global Opportunities) and George Evans (International Growth).

Strategy

Like his predecessor, Bill Wilby, manager Rajeev Bhaman employs a theme-based strategy focusing on companies most likely to benefit from mass affluence, new technologies, restructuring, and aging. (The themes form the acronym MANTRA.) He is inclined to use less macroeconomic analysis than did Wilby, but he is similarly long-term-oriented and fond of buying on bad news--when prices are cheap. Like Wilby, he keeps position sizes small. Oppenheimer uses fair-value pricing selectively to deter market-timers, and the fund's foreign-currency exposure is unhedged.

Performance 12-31-06

	1st Qtr	2nd Qtr	3rd Qtr	4th Qtr	Total
2002	1.52	-9.19	-18.18	2.81	-22.45
2003	-7.89	21.09	9.65	16.99	43.07
2004	4.31	-1.06	-0.96	16.10	18.67
2005	-3.42	2.91	9.54	4.56	13.83
2006	7.41	-3.45	4.34	8.48	17.38

Trailing	Total Return%	+/- MSCI EAFE	+/- MSCI World	%Rank Cat	Growth of $10,000
3 Mo	8.48	-1.87	0.11	52	10,848
6 Mo	13.19	-1.50	-0.02	45	11,319
1 Yr	17.38	-8.96	-2.69	70	11,738
3 Yr Avg	16.61	-3.32	1.93	37	15,857
5 Yr Avg	11.96	-3.02	1.99	40	17,592
10 Yr Avg	13.39	5.68	5.75	7	35,136
15 Yr Avg	12.31	4.45	3.62	19	57,053

Tax Analysis	Tax-Adj Rtn%	%Rank Cat	Tax-Cost Rat	%Rank Cat
3 Yr (estimated)	13.57	57	0.66	39
5 Yr (estimated)	10.15	48	0.44	36
10 Yr (estimated)	11.14	11	1.40	69

Potential Capital Gain Exposure: 34% of assets

Morningstar's Take by Dan Lefkovitz 11-15-06

The contrarian in us loves Oppenheimer Global.

Take a look at this venerable world-stock fund's portfolio and you'll find several out-of-favor names. Key holdings, most notably eBay, have had a rough go of it in 2006, contributing to uncharacteristically middling returns.

But we're not worried. Manager Rajeev Bhaman is furthering the fund's long tradition of zigging when the market zags. Since becoming the fund's sole portfolio manager in October 2005, Bhaman has taken profits in hot stocks such as energy concern EnCana and has gravitated toward developed-markets blue chips, among them beaten-up technology shares such as Ericsson and Microsoft. His predecessor, Bill Wilby, made lots of money for investors by taking a contrarian approach to tech, selling on strength (1999 and early 2000) and buying on weakness (2002).

No doubt, Wilby's departure raised concerns. But the transition to Bhaman was handled in exemplary fashion, with the two running the fund together for more than a year. And Bhaman is a highly experienced manager who posted stellar returns on his previous charge, Oppenheimer Developing Markets. He took a patient approach on that fund and was comfortable with a portfolio that looked different even if that led to short-term underperformance. That attitude has clearly carried over. That Bhaman collaborates with a team of talented and highly experienced colleagues is another plus. So is the fund's reasonable expense ratio.

Investors should note, though, that the fund's asset base has grown quite a bit over the years, meaning that it's not as nimble as it once was. With $20 billion to put to work across the strategy, Bhaman would have a hard time if he ever wanted to put half the fund's assets into mid-caps, as Wilby did in 1999. So, while we think this fund is good enough for investors to build their portfolios around, we'd recommend supplementing it with a smaller-cap-focused offering.

Address:	6803 South Tucson Way Centennial CO 80112-3924 800-225-5677
Web Address:	www.oppenheimerfunds.com
Inception:	12-22-69
Advisor:	OppenheimerFunds, Inc.
Subadvisor:	None
NTF Plans:	DATALynx NTF, Federated Tr NTF

Minimum Purchase:	$1000	Add: $50	IRA: $500
Min Auto Inv Plan:	$500	Add: $50	
Sales Fees:	5.75%L, 0.24%S, 2.00%R		
Management Fee:	0.80% mx./0.56% mn.		
Actual Fees:	Mgt:0.63%	Dist:0.24%	
Expense Projections:	3Yr:$900	5Yr:$1139	10Yr:$1823
Income Distrib:	Annually		

Historical Profile

Return	Above Avg
Risk	Average
Rating	★★★★ Above Avg

Investment Style Equity Stock %

▼ Manager Change
▽ Partial Manager Change

Growth of $10,000
■ Investment Values of Fund
— Investment Values of MSCI EAFE

Performance Quartile (within Category)

	1995	1996	1997	1998	1999	2000	2001	2002	2003	2004	2005	2006	History
	34.89	39.03	41.00	42.60	62.55	52.98	46.73	36.24	51.50	60.77	66.70	73.51	NAV
	16.58	17.52	21.82	12.71	58.48	4.06	-11.80	-22.45	43.07	18.67	13.83	17.38	Total Return %
	5.37	11.47	20.04	-7.22	31.45	18.25	9.62	-6.51	4.48	-1.58	0.29	-8.96	+/-MSCI EAFE
	-4.14	4.04	6.06	-11.61	33.53	17.25	5.00	-2.56	9.96	3.95	4.34	-2.69	+/-MSCI World
	0.75	1.52	2.12	0.95	0.84	0.00	0.00	0.00	0.92	0.66	0.71	0.80	Income Return %
	15.83	16.00	19.70	11.76	57.64	4.06	-11.80	-22.45	42.15	18.01	13.12	16.58	Capital Return %
	60	36	23	58	28	12	29	75	19	20	33	70	Total Rtn % Rank Cat
	0.24	0.53	0.83	0.39	0.36	0.00	0.00	0.00	0.34	0.34	0.43	0.54	Income $
	2.05	1.38	5.75	2.99	4.12	11.96	0.00	0.00	0.00	0.00	2.02	4.21	Capital Gains $
	1.20	1.17	1.13	1.14	1.16	1.08	1.12	1.23	1.23	1.15	1.12	1.08	Expense Ratio %
	0.90	0.62	0.74	0.96	0.37	0.41	0.42	0.18	0.59	0.48	0.66	0.61	Income Ratio %
	84	103	66	65	68	62	36	27	46	22	29	23	Turnover Rate %
	2,183	2,610	3,239	3,428	5,206	6,154	5,807	4,681	6,651	9,721	10,991	13,131	Net Assets $mil

Rating and Risk

Time Period	Load-Adj Return %	Morningstar Rtn vs Cat	Morningstar Risk vs Cat	Morningstar Risk-Adj Rating
1 Yr	10.63			
3 Yr	14.33	Avg	Avg	★★★
5 Yr	10.64	Avg	Avg	★★★
10 Yr	12.72	High	Avg	★★★★
Incept	12.89			

Other Measures	Standard Index MSCI EAFE	Best Fit Index MSCI World
Alpha	-2.4	-1.1
Beta	0.98	1.28
R-Squared	79	90
Standard Deviation	10.36	
Mean	16.61	
Sharpe Ratio	1.24	

Portfolio Analysis 09-30-06

Share change since 06-06 Total Stocks:143

		Sector	Country	% Assets
	Ericsson AB (publ)	Hardware	Sweden	3.32
⊖	Vodafone Grp	Telecom	U.K.	1.98
	Microsoft Corporation	Software	United States	1.79
	H&M Hennes & Mauritz	Consumer	Sweden	1.75
	Sanofi-Synthelabo	Health	France	1.60
	Royal Bank Of Scotland G	Financial	U.K.	1.54
⊖	Reckitt Benckiser	Goods	U.K.	1.53
⊕	eBay, Inc.	Consumer	United States	1.48
⊕	Advanced Micro Devices	Hardware	United States	1.45
	Carnival Corporation	Goods	United States	1.32
	Roche Holding	Health	Switzerland	1.31
⊕	Infosys Technologies Ltd	Software	India	1.27
⊕	Adobe Systems Inc.	Software	United States	1.25
	Morgan Stanley	Financial	United States	1.25
	Credit Suisse Grp	Financial	Switzerland	1.22
	LVMH Moet Hennessy L.V.	Goods	France	1.22
⊖	Corning Inc.	Hardware	United States	1.21
⊕	Automatic Data Processin	Business	United States	1.20
	Siemens	Hardware	Germany	1.19
	Koninklijke Philips Elec	Goods	Netherlands	1.18

Current Investment Style

Value Blnd Growth — Large/Mid/Small

Market Cap	%
Giant	47.0
Large	40.9
Mid	10.3
Small	1.6
Micro	0.2

Avg $mil: 28,655

Value Measures		Rel Category
Price/Earnings	15.12	0.98
Price/Book	2.48	1.04
Price/Sales	1.71	1.31
Price/Cash Flow	10.16	1.17
Dividend Yield %	2.11	0.97

Growth Measures	%	Rel Category
Long-Term Erngs	12.23	0.96
Book Value	7.90	0.88
Sales	9.27	1.11
Cash Flow	9.61	0.98
Historical Erngs	25.00	1.33

Composition

Cash	0.5	Bonds	0.0
Stocks	99.4	Other	0.1
Foreign (% of Stock)			60.5

Sector Weightings

		% of Stocks	Rel MSCI EAFE	3 Year High	Low
⟳	Info	29.97	2.54		
	Software	7.05	12.59	8	5
	Hardware	14.39	3.73	14	11
	Media	4.20	2.30	9	4
	Telecom	4.33	0.78	9	4
☞	Service	37.00	0.78		
	Health	12.20	1.71	16	12
	Consumer	6.90	1.39	8	5
	Business	2.57	0.51	3	2
	Financial	15.33	0.51	19	14
⊔	Mfg	33.04	0.81		
	Goods	19.83	1.51	20	11
	Ind Mtrls	6.57	0.43	7	3
	Energy	6.64	0.93	10	6
	Utilities	0.00	0.00	1	0

Regional Exposure % Stock

UK/W. Europe	37	N. America	41
Japan	11	Latn America	4
Asia X Japan	7	Other	0

Country Exposure % Stock

United States	40	France	7
U.K.	13	Sweden	6
Japan	11		

Oppenheimer Glob Oppor A

	Ticker	Load	NAV	Yield	Total Assets	Mstar Category
	OPGIX	5.75%	$35.93	0.3%	$4,666 mil	World Stock

Governance and Management

Stewardship Grade: B

Portfolio Manager(s)

Frank Jennings has built a terrific record since coming on board in October 1995. Jennings came to Oppenheimer from Mitchell Hutchins Asset Management, where he was managing director of global equities. Before that he managed money at AIG Global Investors and also served as an international economist at Prudential (he has a doctorate in economics). In August 2004, Jennings named Randy Dishmon his assistant manager. Dishmon has a background in technology and has been an analyst on Oppenheimer's global equity team since June 2001.

Strategy

This fund's portfolio can run the gamut of stocks and bonds, U.S. and foreign equities, and large caps and small caps. Manager Frank Jennings and assistant manager Randy Dishmon are long-term investors, and stock-picking is informed by various themes that form the acronym MANTRA: mass affluence, new technologies, restructuring, and aging. Asset allocation, however, can be informed by calls on the market and macro factors. Oppenheimer uses fair-value pricing. Jennings and Dishmon are not currently hedging foreign-currency exposure but will do so opportunistically.

Performance 12-31-06

	1st Qtr	2nd Qtr	3rd Qtr	4th Qtr	Total
2002	-0.40	-10.44	-25.26	9.52	-26.99
2003	-9.15	29.14	15.45	16.10	57.25
2004	10.82	-0.74	-7.21	27.25	29.88
2005	-7.46	5.07	8.23	11.59	17.43
2006	14.37	-7.69	2.15	2.92	11.00

Trailing	Total Return%	+/- MSCI EAFE	+/- MSCI World	%Rank Cat	Growth of $10,000
3 Mo	2.92	-7.43	-5.45	98	10,292
6 Mo	5.14	-9.55	-8.07	98	10,514
1 Yr	11.00	-15.34	-9.07	97	11,100
3 Yr Avg	19.19	-0.74	4.51	13	16,932
5 Yr Avg	14.22	-0.76	4.25	18	19,441
10 Yr Avg	15.45	7.74	7.81	1	42,067
15 Yr Avg	13.96	6.10	5.27	1	71,005

Tax Analysis	Tax-Adj Rtn%	%Rank Cat	Tax-Cost Rat	%Rank Cat
3 Yr (estimated)	15.10	39	1.51	79
5 Yr (estimated)	11.74	31	1.00	75
10 Yr (estimated)	12.93	2	1.60	81

Potential Capital Gain Exposure: 11% of assets

Morningstar's Take by Dan Lefkovitz 11-15-06

Oppenheimer Global Opportunities is a great way to give your portfolio some zest.

In past analyses, we've described this global fund as "unique," "quirky," even "a pretty sporty vehicle." What we mean is that longtime manager Frank Jennings and assistant manager Randy Dishmon don't play by the same rules as most peers. They aren't too worried about "diversification," as their willingness to tilt the portfolio heavily toward certain stocks and sectors demonstrates. And they make asset-allocation calls, shifting into bonds or cash based on market conditions. Yet another tendency that sets them apart is their occasional macro bets, such as hedging currencies when they see opportunity.

Such practices typically make us nervous, as they are hard to get right consistently and can be a recipe for volatility. It's no surprise, therefore, that the fund has been the most volatile in the world-stock category over the past 10 years (aside from one even quirkier offering) or that it lost a

bundle in 2001 and 2002.

But long-time investors will be the first to point out that the fund also has the category's number one 10-year record. Jennings' knack for nailing macro calls, such as hedging the euro in 2004, makes us less nervous about his current bet on long-dated U.S. Treasuries. More important for the fund's returns, his topnotch stock-picking, demonstrated on former holdings like National Semiconductor and Sirius Satellite Radio, invites confidence regarding top holding Advanced Micro Devices as well as a slug of small-cap biotech names such as Telik. AMD has boosted returns in the past, but its recent struggles have caused the fund to lag in 2006, even though the managers made a timely move into cash and bonds before a market pullback in May.

Quirkiness and volatility mean that we wouldn't build a portfolio around this fund. But as a supplementary offering designed to provide some pop, it has our enthusiastic recommendation.

Address:	6803 South Tucson Way Centennial CO 80112-3924 800-225-5677	Minimum Purchase: Min Auto Inv Plan: Sales Fees:	$1000 $500 5.75%L, 0.25%S, 2.00%R	Add: $50 IRA: $500 Add: $50
Web Address:	www.oppenheimerfunds.com	Management Fee:	0.80% mx./0.63% mn.	
Inception:	10-22-90	Actual Fees:	Mgt:0.69% Dist:0.25%	
Advisor:	OppenheimerFunds, Inc.	Expense Projections:	3Yr:$915	5Yr:$1165 10Yr:$1878
Subadvisor:	None	Income Distrib:	Annually	
NTF Plans:	DATALynx NTF, Federated Tr NTF			

Historical Profile

Return	Above Avg
Risk	High
Rating	★★★ Neutral

84% 68% 83% 80% 94% 95% 98% 97% 86%

▽

Growth of $10,000
— Investment Values of Fund
— Investment Values of MSCI EAFE

59.0
43.6
32.4
24.0
17.0
10.0

▼ Manager Change
▽ Partial Manager Change

Performance Quartile (within Category)

1995	1996	1997	1998	1999	2000	2001	2002	2003	2004	2005	2006	History
14.60	15.00	17.44	16.64	29.12	27.04	22.59	16.28	25.60	33.25	36.94	35.93	NAV
17.37	15.31	28.25	12.83	86.57	-4.23	-16.32	-26.99	57.25	29.88	17.43	11.00	Total Return %
6.16	9.26	26.47	-7.10	59.54	9.96	5.10	-11.05	18.66	9.63	3.89	-15.34	+/-MSCI EAFE
-3.35	1.83	12.49	-11.49	61.62	8.96	0.48	-7.10	24.14	15.16	7.94	-9.07	+/-MSCI World
2.99	2.77	4.36	2.31	2.30	0.18	0.07	1.02	0.00	0.00	2.12	0.32	Income Return %
14.38	12.54	23.89	10.52	84.27	-4.41	-16.39	-28.01	57.25	29.88	15.31	10.68	Capital Return %
57	55	2	58	6	29	50	89	1	1	12	97	Total Rtn % Rank Cat
0.40	0.40	0.65	0.40	0.38	0.05	0.02	0.23	0.00	0.00	0.70	0.12	Income $
0.83	1.38	1.07	2.56	1.32	0.81	0.00	0.00	0.00	1.31	5.10		Capital Gains $
1.63	1.52	1.43	1.36	1.33	1.20	1.22	1.40	1.36	1.19	1.16	1.13	Expense Ratio %
3.09	2.65	2.47	1.62	2.51	0.72	0.38	-0.17	-0.48	-0.20	0.32	0.62	Income Ratio %
135	208	90	117	98	48	53	39	61	52	107	96	Turnover Rate %
109	124	187	257	789	1,540	1,353	916	1,329	2,027	2,327	3,121	Net Assets $mil

Rating and Risk

Time Period	Load-Adj Return %	Morningstar Rtn vs Cat	Morningstar Risk vs Cat	Morningstar Risk-Adj Rating
1 Yr	4.62			
3 Yr	16.86	+Avg	High	★★★
5 Yr	12.87	+Avg	High	★★★
10 Yr	14.77	High	High	★★★★
Incept	13.47			

Other Measures	Standard Index MSCI EAFE	Best Fit Index Mstar Mid Growth TR
Alpha	-6.0	3.3
Beta	1.40	1.19
R-Squared	61	79
Standard Deviation	16.95	
Mean	19.19	
Sharpe Ratio	0.93	

Portfolio Analysis 09-30-06

Share change since 06-06 Total Stocks:75

		Sector	Country	% Assets
⊕ Advanced Micro Devices		Hardware	United States	11.60
☼ US Treasury Bond 4.5%		—	United States	4.26
Telik, Inc.		Health	United States	3.95
Nektar Therapeutics, Inc		Health	United States	3.84
Oakley, Inc.		Goods	United States	2.58
☼ US Treasury Bond 5.375%		—	United States	2.40
Bombardier Inc Subordina		Ind Mtrls	Canada	2.36
☼ US Treasury Bond 5.25%		—	United States	2.35
☼ US Treasury Bond 5.25%		—	United States	2.35
⊕ Saks, Inc.		Consumer	United States	2.30
Cree, Inc.		Hardware	United States	2.24
☼ US Treasury Note 4.5%		—	United States	2.20
⊕ Interpublic Group of Com		Business	United States	1.98
⊖ Continental Airlines, In		Business	United States	1.89
Electrocomponents		Business	U.K.	1.62
⊕ Rite Aid Corporation		Consumer	United States	1.61
☼ Nomura Hldgs		Financial	Japan	1.57
⊖ AMR Corporation		Business	United States	1.54
Iberdrola		Utilities	Spain	1.49
NicOx		Health	France	1.48

Current Investment Style

Value Blnd Growth — Large / Mid / Small

Market Cap	%
Giant	12.7
Large	29.3
Mid	24.5
Small	29.4
Micro	4.2

Avg $mil: 4,515

Value Measures		Rel Category
Price/Earnings	19.28	1.25
Price/Book	2.92	1.22
Price/Sales	0.97	0.74
Price/Cash Flow	8.20	0.95
Dividend Yield %	0.92	0.42

Growth Measures	%	Rel Category
Long-Term Erngs	14.29	1.13
Book Value	0.30	0.03
Sales	1.61	0.19
Cash Flow	9.66	0.98
Historical Erngs	21.09	1.13

Composition

Cash	0.5	Bonds	13.6
Stocks	85.9	Other	0.0
Foreign (% of Stock)			41.2

Investment Style
Equity
Stock %

Sector Weightings	% of Stocks	Rel MSCI EAFE	3 Year High	Low
↻ Info	23.30	1.97		
🖥 Software	1.56	2.79	4	0
💻 Hardware	21.51	5.57	31	9
🎙 Media	0.23	0.13	11	0
☎ Telecom	0.00	0.00	3	0
⊆ Service	50.81	1.08		
❤ Health	23.28	3.27	32	19
🛒 Consumer	9.03	1.82	9	3
💼 Business	9.77	1.93	16	3
$ Financial	8.73	0.29	16	5
⊞ Mfg	25.90	0.63		
🏭 Goods	12.00	0.91	16	11
⚙ Ind Mtrls	12.15	0.79	16	2
🔋 Energy	0.00	0.00	3	0
💡 Utilities	1.75	0.33	2	0

Regional Exposure	% Stock		
UK/W. Europe	30	N. America	62
Japan	8	Latn America	0
Asia X Japan	1	Other	0

Country Exposure	% Stock		
United States	59	France	6
Japan	8	Switzerland	5
U.K.	7		

Morningstar® Funds 500

Oppenheimer Intl Grth A

	Ticker	Load	NAV	Yield	Total Assets	Mstar Category
	OIGAX	5.75%	$27.86	0.8%	$1,921 mil	Foreign Large Growth

Governance and Management

Stewardship Grade: B

Portfolio Manager(s)

George Evans has been the fund's manager since its inception in March 1996 and has managed international accounts at Oppenheimer Funds since 1991. When Bill Wilby, longtime manager of Oppenheimer Global, stepped down, Evans assumed more management duties on Oppenheimer's global equity team. That team boasts several experienced and talented investors, including Frank Jennings, Rajeev Bhaman, and Mark Madden.

Strategy

George Evans looks for growth stocks that fit into four investment themes, which form the acronym M.A.N.T.R.A: Mass Affluence, New Technology, Restructuring, and Aging. Evans favors companies with good three- to five-year growth prospects. He's willing to dip into small- and mid-cap names and emerging markets. When stocks appreciate, he is more willing to trim than sell, so the portfolio contains some richly priced names. Evans generally doesn't hedge currencies. Oppenheimer levies redemption fees and uses fair-value pricing on an as-needed basis.

Performance 12-31-06

	1st Qtr	2nd Qtr	3rd Qtr	4th Qtr	Total
2002	1.86	-7.04	-28.21	7.84	-26.70
2003	-14.19	35.01	10.20	20.01	53.20
2004	3.87	-2.74	-0.90	16.32	16.46
2005	-1.52	-0.74	11.93	4.26	14.08
2006	10.62	-2.17	5.16	13.89	29.61

Trailing	Total Return%	+/- MSCI EAFE	+/- MSCI Wd xUS	%Rank Cat	Growth of $10,000
3 Mo	13.89	3.54	3.77	10	11,389
6 Mo	19.77	5.08	5.55	7	11,977
1 Yr	29.61	3.27	3.90	6	12,961
3 Yr Avg	19.86	-0.07	-0.24	22	17,220
5 Yr Avg	14.10	-0.88	-1.15	32	19,339
10 Yr Avg	10.87	3.16	2.91	11	28,063
15 Yr Avg	—	—	—	—	—

Tax Analysis	Tax-Adj Rtn%	%Rank Cat	Tax-Cost Rat	%Rank Cat
3 Yr (estimated)	17.23	37	0.25	20
5 Yr (estimated)	12.40	40	0.32	31
10 Yr (estimated)	9.57	10	0.59	25

Potential Capital Gain Exposure: 26% of assets

Morningstar's Take by Dan Lefkovitz 12-20-06

Oppenheimer International Growth may not always look this good, but it's still a terrific long-term holding.

This Fund Analyst Pick has been firing on all cylinders in 2006. Longtime manager George Evans has posted a near-30% gain for the year to date through mid-December. This will likely be one of the few foreign large-growth funds to beat the benchmark MSCI EAFE Index in 2006 (value funds have fared better). Evans' winners include NicOx, a French drug discovery firm, Aalberts Industries, a Dutch maker of drink dispensers, and ABB, a Swiss company benefiting from renewed investment in energy infrastructure.

These stocks demonstrate two key pillars of Evans' approach: flexibility and patience. The three winners come from a range of industries, including a traditional growth area (health care) and a nontraditional one (industrials). NicOx is a small cap, Aalberts a mid-cap, and ABB a large cap, which helps explain why this portfolio's average

market cap of $12 billion is roughly half that of its typical peer. And though ABB has only been in the portfolio since June 2005, the other two names are longtime holdings. Evans bought Aalberts in 2002 and NicOx upon its 1998 IPO. Not surprisingly, the fund's most recent turnover ratio (26%) was one of the category's lowest.

Owning this fund requires that investors take a similarly long-term view. Evans' picks don't work out every year, which is why annual return rankings have been bumpy. Smaller caps invite volatility. So does a significant emerging-markets stake (roughly 10% of assets), and Evans' willingness to hang on to stocks even as their price appreciates. It is also unlikely that foreign funds will sustain such lofty returns, which have been driven in large part by the depreciation of the dollar.

But for investors looking to access the best of overseas markets, the fund holds lots of appeal. Evans is proven, the portfolio is unique, and Oppenheimer's global equities group is topnotch.

Address:	6803 South Tucson Way Centennial CO 80112-3924 800-225-5677	Minimum Purchase:	$1000 Add: $50 IRA: $500
		Min Auto Inv Plan:	$500 Add: $50
		Sales Fees:	5.75%L, 0.24%S, 2.00%R
Web Address:	www.oppenheimerfunds.com	Management Fee:	0.80% mx./0.67% mn.
Inception:	03-25-96 *	Actual Fees:	Mgt:0.76% Dist:0.24%
Advisor:	OppenheimerFunds, Inc.	Expense Projections:	3Yr:$1022 5Yr:$1347 10Yr:$2264
Subadvisor:	None	Income Distrib:	Annually
NTF Plans:	DATALynx NTF, Federated Tr NTF		

Historical Profile

Return	Above Avg
Risk	High
Rating	★★★ Neutral

Investment Style	
Equity	
Stock %	

89% 91% 77% 84% 85% 93% 98% 98% 99%

▼ Manager Change
▽ Partial Manager Change

Growth of $10,000
— Investment Values of Fund
— Investment Values of MSCI EAFE

Performance Quartile (within Category)

1995	1996	1997	1998	1999	2000	2001	2002	2003	2004	2005	2006	History
—	11.91	14.41	14.41	22.88	19.71	15.05	10.92	16.52	19.12	21.66	27.86	NAV
—	19.10*	22.86	6.37	60.42	-9.58	-23.42	-26.70	53.20	16.46	14.08	29.61	Total Return %
—	—	21.08	-13.56	33.39	4.61	-2.00	-10.76	14.61	-3.79	0.54	3.27	+/-MSCI EAFE
—	—	20.59	-12.32	32.44	3.78	-2.03	-10.90	13.78	-3.92	-0.39	3.90	+/-MSCI Wd xUS
—	—	0.00	0.89	0.00	0.00	0.22	0.74	1.84	0.70	0.79	0.97	Income Return %
—	—	22.86	5.48	60.42	-9.58	-23.64	-27.44	51.36	15.76	13.29	28.64	Capital Return %
—	—	2	87	34	15	51	92	1	44	55	6	Total Rtn % Rank Cat
—	0.00	0.00	0.13	0.00	0.00	0.04	0.11	0.20	0.12	0.15	0.21	Income $
—	0.00	0.22	0.76	0.21	0.94	0.00	0.00	0.20	0.00	0.00	—	Capital Gains $
—	—	—	1.78	1.40	1.55	1.38	1.42	1.56	1.42	1.43	—	Expense Ratio %
—	—	—	-0.36	0.44	-0.15	0.22	0.62	0.62	0.18	0.22	—	Income Ratio %
—	—	—	64	82	75	61	33	46	61	37	—	Turnover Rate %
—	—	20	133	186	267	542	548	341	528	736	1,179	Net Assets $mil

Rating and Risk

Time Period	Load-Adj Return %	Morningstar Rtn vs Cat	Morningstar Risk vs Cat	Morningstar Risk-Adj Rating
1 Yr	22.16			
3 Yr	17.52	Avg	Avg	★★★
5 Yr	12.76	Avg	High	★★★
10 Yr	10.22	+Avg	High	★★★
Incept	11.25			

Other Measures	Standard Index MSCI EAFE	Best Fit Index MSCI EAFE
Alpha	-1.9	-1.9
Beta	1.13	1.13
R-Squared	91	91
Standard Deviation	11.26	
Mean	19.86	
Sharpe Ratio	1.40	

Portfolio Analysis 08-31-06

Share change since 05-06 Total Stocks:143	Sector	Country	% Assets
⊖ ABB Ltd	Ind Mtrls	Switzerland	2.38
⊕ Capita Grp	Business	U.K.	2.20
⊖ Ericsson AB (publ)	Hardware	Sweden	2.17
⊖ Continental	Ind Mtrls	Germany	2.14
⊖ Aalberts Industries	Ind Mtrls	Netherlands	2.10
⊕ William Demant Holding	Health	Denmark	2.10
⊖ Anglo Irish Bank	Financial	Ireland	1.84
⊖ Collins Stewart Tullet	Financial	U.K.	1.80
⊖ Mitsubishi UFJ Financial	Financial	Japan	1.78
⊖ Technip	Energy	France	1.70
⊖ Royal Bank Of Scotland G	Financial	U.K.	1.42
❈ Embraer-Empresa Brasilei	Ind Mtrls	Brazil	1.40
⊖ Sumitomo Realty & Develo	Financial	Japan	1.37
⊖ Impala Platinum Hldgs Lt	Ind Mtrls	South Africa	1.37
❈ TOTAL	Energy	France	1.24
⊕ Canon	Goods	Japan	1.16
⊖ Tandberg	Goods	Norway	1.13
NicOx	Health	France	1.11
⊕ Infosys Technologies Ltd	Software	India	1.09
⊕ Wolseley	Ind Mtrls	U.K.	1.06

Current Investment Style

Value Blnd Growth — Large/Mid/Small

Market Cap	%
Giant	29.8
Large	37.6
Mid	25.0
Small	6.0
Micro	1.6

Avg $mil: 12,556

Value Measures		Rel Category
Price/Earnings	16.84	1.09
Price/Book	2.76	1.05
Price/Sales	1.39	0.99
Price/Cash Flow	9.98	1.03
Dividend Yield %	2.31	0.95

Growth Measures	%	Rel Category
Long-Term Erngs	13.58	1.00
Book Value	9.31	0.85
Sales	9.75	1.12
Cash Flow	9.44	0.77
Historical Erngs	21.07	0.92

Composition

Cash	0.7	Bonds	0.0
Stocks	98.6	Other	0.6
Foreign (% of Stock)			98.6

Sector Weightings	% of Stocks	Rel MSCI EAFE	3 Year High Low	
↻ Info	13.30	1.13		
Software	2.51	4.48	3	2
Hardware	5.30	1.37	11	5
Media	3.98	2.17	8	4
Telecom	1.51	0.27	7	2
☞ Service	43.86	0.93		
Health	11.61	1.63	18	12
Consumer	4.15	0.84	6	4
Business	10.42	2.06	10	6
Financial	17.68	0.59	21	15
⊓ Mfg	42.84	1.05		
Goods	19.67	1.50	20	14
Ind Mtrls	17.59	1.14	18	7
Energy	5.58	0.78	7	1
Utilities	0.00	0.00	1	0

Regional Exposure	% Stock		
UK/W. Europe	68	N. America	1
Japan	17	Latn America	3
Asia X Japan	8	Other	3

Country Exposure	% Stock		
U.K.	20	Switzerland	9
Japan	17	Germany	7
France	12		

Oppenheimer Main Street A

Ticker	Load	NAV	Yield	Total Assets	Mstar Category
MSIGX	5.75%	$40.66	0.9%	$11,821 mil	Large Blend

Governance and Management

Stewardship Grade: B

Portfolio Manager(s)

Lead manager Nikos Monoyios worked for more than 20 years with this fund's original manager, Chuck Albers, first at Guardian Park Avenue and then here until Albers' retirement at the end of 2003. Marc Reinganum is a former finance professor who has been the team's director of quantitative research since September 2002 and became comanager upon Albers' retirement. Monoyios also comanages Oppenheimer Main Street Opportunity.

Strategy

Managers Nikos Monoyios and Marc Reinganum use bottom-up quantitative models to look for stocks that rank highly on a combination of quality, valuation, momentum, and other factors such as stock buybacks and mergers. They also use top-down models that lead them to adjust the fund's market capitalization and other macro factors, but they won't make huge sector bets. Individual stock positions are no more than 0.60% above or below their weightings in the benchmark.

Performance 12-31-06

	1st Qtr	2nd Qtr	3rd Qtr	4th Qtr	Total
2002	1.23	-8.78	-16.49	4.50	-19.42
2003	-3.31	14.00	3.04	11.77	26.95
2004	2.01	0.57	-1.99	8.79	9.39
2005	-1.97	1.41	4.11	2.17	5.74
2006	5.04	-1.92	4.68	6.56	14.91

Trailing	Total Return%	+/- S&P 500	+/- Russ 1000	%Rank Cat	Growth of $10,000
3 Mo	6.56	-0.14	-0.39	54	10,656
6 Mo	11.55	-1.19	-0.81	50	11,155
1 Yr	14.91	-0.88	-0.55	40	11,491
3 Yr Avg	9.95	-0.49	-1.03	50	13,292
5 Yr Avg	6.34	0.15	-0.48	34	13,598
10 Yr Avg	7.60	-0.82	-1.04	55	20,803
15 Yr Avg	12.04	1.40	1.24	13	55,030

Tax Analysis	Tax-Adj Rtn%	%Rank Cat	Tax-Cost Rat	%Rank Cat
3 Yr (estimated)	7.21	79	0.55	25
5 Yr (estimated)	4.64	60	0.42	28
10 Yr (estimated)	6.03	59	0.87	38

Potential Capital Gain Exposure: 23% of assets

Morningstar's Take by David Kathman 12-13-06

Oppenheimer Main Street will never dazzle, but it's not without charms for the right kind of investor.

As quantitative stock funds go, this one sports an impressive pedigree. The quantitative models underlying it ultimately date back to 1972 and the Guardian Park Avenue fund, where the team started before moving to this fund in 1998. Lead manager Nikos Monoyios has been part of the team since the late 1970s, and comanager Marc Reinganum is a former finance professor who advised the team for a decade before joining it in 2002.

The goal here is to outperform the S&P 500 Index over time while keeping volatility low. The models incorporate big-picture macro factors as well as bottom-up fundamentals, including quality, valuation, and momentum factors. Those models are always being revised to reflect changing market conditions; most recently, the team expanded its "January effect" model to emphasize riskier stocks during the entire fourth and first quarters.

Returns have been OK but not spectacular since the current managers took over, mixing stretches of outperformance with occasional stumbles but edging past the S&P 500 overall. The fund navigated the bear market very well in 2001-02, for example, but a big move into mega-cap stocks in early 2004 proved premature. However, the fund's continued overweighting in mega-caps finally started to pay off in 2006 as blue chips began to awaken from their slumber.

The fund has had more consistent success in controlling risk. It has been less volatile, in terms of standard deviation, than 85% of its large-blend peers, and when it has trailed the category, it has always done so by modest amounts. There's something to be said for such stability in the whipsaw market of recent years.

This can be a decent core fund, as long as investors know what they're getting into. It's never going to be a category leader, but its experienced team and general stability should hold some appeal for cautious investors.

Historical Profile

Return	Below Avg
Risk	Below Avg
Rating	★★★ Neutral

Investment Style: Equity, Stock %

Quartile row (top): 94% 91% 96% 96% 98% 99% 99% 100% 99%

▼ Manager Change
▽ Partial Manager Change

Growth of $10,000
— Investment Values of Fund
— Investment Values of S&P 500

Performance Quartile (within Category)

	1995	1996	1997	1998	1999	2000	2001	2002	2003	2004	2005	2006	History
	26.89	28.74	33.39	39.91	42.00	36.43	32.50	26.00	32.80	35.46	37.13	40.66	NAV
	30.77	15.70	26.59	25.19	17.12	-7.94	-10.46	-19.42	26.95	9.39	5.74	14.91	Total Return %
	-6.81	-7.26	-6.77	-3.39	-3.92	1.16	1.43	2.68	-1.73	-1.49	0.83	-0.88	+/-S&P 500
	-7.00	-6.75	-6.26	-1.83	-3.79	-0.15	1.99	2.23	-2.94	-2.01	-0.53	-0.55	+/-Russ 1000
	2.04	1.50	1.40	0.75	0.08	0.28	0.18	0.59	0.77	1.26	1.04	1.02	Income Return %
	28.73	14.20	25.19	24.44	17.04	-8.22	-10.64	-20.01	26.18	8.13	4.70	13.89	Capital Return %
	72	90	63	41	65	58	36	28	58	68	50	40	Total Rtn % Rank Cat
	0.43	0.40	0.40	0.25	0.03	0.12	0.07	0.19	0.20	0.41	0.37	0.38	Income $
	0.08	1.98	2.50	1.50	4.48	2.10	0.05	0.00	0.00	0.00	0.00	1.59	Capital Gains $
	1.07	0.99	0.94	0.90	0.91	0.90	0.86	0.99	0.97	0.93	0.92	0.92	Expense Ratio %
	2.31	1.55	1.29	0.83	0.50	0.54	0.47	0.52	0.87	0.75	1.36	0.93	Income Ratio %
	101	93	62	81	72	73	76	78	94	76	79	84	Turnover Rate %
	2,466	3,590	4,849	6,525	8,694	7,953	7,426	6,042	7,549	7,997	7,900	8,188	Net Assets $mil

Rating and Risk

Time Period	Load-Adj Return %	Morningstar Rtn vs Cat	Morningstar Risk vs Cat	Morningstar Risk-Adj Rating
1 Yr	8.30			
3 Yr	7.80	-Avg	-Avg	★★
5 Yr	5.08	Avg	-Avg	★★★
10 Yr	6.96	-Avg	-Avg	★★★
Incept	13.49			

Other Measures	Standard Index S&P 500	Best Fit Index S&P 500
Alpha	-0.4	-0.4
Beta	0.99	0.99
R-Squared	97	97
Standard Deviation	6.94	
Mean	9.95	
Sharpe Ratio	0.95	

Portfolio Analysis 08-31-06

Share change since 05-06 Total Stocks:420

	Sector	PE	Tot Ret%	% Assets
⊕ ExxonMobil Corporation	Energy	11.1	39.07	3.83
⊕ General Electric Company	Ind Mtrls	20.0	9.35	2.72
⊕ Bank of America Corporat	Financial	12.4	20.68	2.39
⊕ Citigroup, Inc.	Financial	13.1	19.55	2.33
⊖ Microsoft Corporation	Software	23.8	15.83	2.00
⊖ Chevron Corporation	Energy	9.0	33.76	1.63
⊕ Johnson & Johnson	Health	17.5	12.45	1.61
⊖ J.P. Morgan Chase & Co.	Financial	13.6	25.60	1.58
⊕ Altria Group, Inc.	Goods	16.3	19.87	1.47
⊕ Pfizer Inc.	Health	15.2	15.22	1.43
⊕ Hewlett-Packard Company	Hardware	19.3	45.21	1.39
⊖ ConocoPhillips	Energy	6.5	26.53	1.29
⊖ Cisco Systems, Inc.	Hardware	30.1	59.64	1.28
⊖ Merck & Co., Inc.	Health	19.1	42.66	1.23
⊕ PepsiCo, Inc.	Goods	21.5	7.86	1.15
⊖ Wachovia Corporation	Financial	12.9	12.02	1.10
⊕ Procter & Gamble Company	Goods	23.9	13.36	1.09
⊕ IBM	Hardware	17.1	19.77	1.07
⊖ UnitedHealth Group, Inc.	Health	20.8	-13.49	1.07
⊕ Coca-Cola Company	Goods	21.7	23.10	1.02

Current Investment Style

Value Blnd Growth — Large/Mid/Small

Market Cap	%
Giant	53.6
Large	38.6
Mid	6.8
Small	1.0
Micro	0.0

Avg $mil: 49,520

Value Measures		Rel Category
Price/Earnings	13.78	0.90
Price/Book	2.55	1.00
Price/Sales	1.32	0.94
Price/Cash Flow	8.19	0.97
Dividend Yield %	1.91	1.09

Growth Measures	%	Rel Category
Long-Term Erngs	10.82	0.92
Book Value	7.81	0.86
Sales	10.94	1.13
Cash Flow	15.97	1.55
Historical Erngs	19.82	1.07

Profitability	%	Rel Category
Return on Equity	21.58	1.11
Return on Assets	11.67	1.12
Net Margin	14.50	1.08

Sector Weightings

	% of Stocks	Rel S&P 500	3 Year High	3 Year Low
⌖ Info	19.02	0.95		
Software	3.57	1.03	5	3
Hardware	10.22	1.11	13	9
Media	2.58	0.68	5	2
Telecom	2.65	0.75	5	2
⌖ Service	45.34	0.98		
Health	12.24	1.01	14	11
Consumer	5.80	0.76	12	6
Business	4.42	1.04	4	1
Financial	22.88	1.03	26	20
⌖ Mfg	35.66	1.06		
Goods	7.32	0.86	10	6
Ind Mtrls	14.54	1.22	15	8
Energy	12.41	1.27	14	8
Utilities	1.39	0.40	4	0

Composition

● Cash	0.5	
● Stocks	99.0	
● Bonds	0.0	
○ Other	0.5	
Foreign	0.5	(% of Stock)

Address:	6803 South Tucson Way
	Centennial CO 80112-3924
	800-225-5677
Web Address:	www.oppenheimerfunds.com
Inception:	02-03-88
Advisor:	OppenheimerFunds, Inc.
Subadvisor:	None
NTF Plans:	DATALynx NTF, Federated Tr NTF

Minimum Purchase:	$1000	Add: $50	IRA: $500
Min Auto Inv Plan:	$500	Add: $50	
Sales Fees:	5.75%L, 0.24%S		
Management Fee:	0.65% mx./0.45% mn.		
Actual Fees:	Mgt:0.46%	Dist:0.24%	
Expense Projections:	3Yr:$853	5Yr:$1057	10Yr:$1646
Income Distrib:	Annually		

 Morningstar® Funds 500

Osterweis

	Ticker	Load	NAV	Yield	Total Assets	Mstar Category
	OSTFX	None	$26.48	0.7%	$301 mil	Mid-Cap Blend

Governance and Management

Stewardship Grade:

Portfolio Manager(s)

Veteran investor John Osterweis leads a team of four other managers. He's managed the fund since its 1993 inception, as well as institutional accounts in the same style at his eponymously named firm since 1983. Matthew K. Berler, Stephen P. Moore, Michael R. Hughes, and Alexander "Sasha" Kovriga round out the team. Their investment industry experience ranges from a few years (Kovriga) to nearly two decades (Berler) and includes stints at firms like American Funds advisor Capital Research (Moore) and Merrill Lynch (Hughes). It's a solid squad.

Strategy

John Osterweis and his team follow the cash. When analyzing a stock, they use five questions as their points of departure: Does it generate cash? Does it have good managers? Does it have a defensible niche? What is its catalyst? What is its ultimate growth potential? From there the fund assembles a fairly concentrated portfolio of stocks from across the market-cap and style spectrum, and waits. Osterweis and his squad are patient with their picks, so turnover is low.

Performance 12-31-06

	1st Qtr	2nd Qtr	3rd Qtr	4th Qtr	Total
2002	3.02	-9.94	-9.30	4.99	-11.67
2003	-0.24	12.60	3.78	14.19	33.13
2004	5.96	-0.04	0.63	10.41	17.68
2005	0.76	3.38	3.65	1.03	9.08
2006	4.24	-3.59	3.53	7.03	11.36

Trailing	Total Return%	+/- S&P 500	+/- S&P Mid 400	%Rank Cat	Growth of $10,000
3 Mo	7.03	0.33	0.04	58	10,703
6 Mo	10.81	-1.93	4.98	30	11,081
1 Yr	11.36	-4.43	1.04	62	11,136
3 Yr Avg	12.65	2.21	-0.44	49	14,295
5 Yr Avg	10.95	4.76	0.06	38	16,813
10 Yr Avg	15.28	6.86	1.81	5	41,451
15 Yr Avg	—	—	—		—

Tax Analysis	Tax-Adj Rtn%	%Rank Cat	Tax-Cost Rat	%Rank Cat
3 Yr (estimated)	11.35	42	1.15	50
5 Yr (estimated)	10.07	35	0.79	50
10 Yr (estimated)	13.70	2	1.37	34

Potential Capital Gain Exposure: 15% of assets

Morningstar's Take by Dan Culloton 11-17-06

Don't ostracize Osterweis.

It's rare to find a fund with a consistent long-term record under one manager that still has a small asset base. This fund has both. John Osterweis has led this fund's management team since its inception 13 years ago. The fund has beaten both the mid-cap blend category average and broad stock market, as defined by the Morningstar U.S. Market Index, in that time, but it has not gathered a lot of assets. At nearly $300 million in assets, it's smaller than the typical mid-cap blend fund and should still have room to grow without affecting the managers' strategy. Capacity is important because this fund has shown a penchant for small-cap stocks. It can't get too large if it wants to stay nimble enough to continue satisfying that appetite.

It still has a lot of headroom in absolute terms, though, and the fund may have more than many of its peers because of its wide-ranging, patient, contrarian style. The managers invest across the

market-cap spectrum and even overseas (13% of the portfolio was in foreign stocks like Nestle at the end of the third quarter). They also often gravitate to out-of-favor stocks such as baby clothes maker Carter's, whose shares have slipped since acquiring rival Oshkosh. The portfolio is compact and sticks with picks through turmoil. For example, it has held onto contact lens maker Bausch & Lomb as it's fallen due to a product recall and delayed financial statements. The managers think Carter's can improve the Oshkosh brand and that the worst may be over for Bausch & Lomb.

Such picks could take time to pay off, which makes this fund's ride bumpy at times. Still, trading less than its peers and buying when others are selling should help the fund handle asset growth, should it ever come. And it should. The fund has made its high conviction approach work over time with less volatility than its rivals or the broad market. Expenses could be lower, but this fund still has a lot to offer patient investors.

Address:	615 East Michigan Street Milwaukee, WI 53202 800-700-3316
Web Address:	www.osterweis.com
Inception:	10-01-93
Advisor:	Osterweis Capital Management Inc
Subadvisor:	None
NTF Plans:	N/A

Minimum Purchase:	$5000	Add: $500	IRA: $1500
Min Auto Inv Plan:	$250	Add: $250	
Sales Fees:	No-load, 2.00%R		
Management Fee:	1.00%		
Actual Fees:	Mgt:1.00%	Dist: —	
Expense Projections:	3Yr:$400	5Yr:$692	10Yr:$1523
Income Distrib:	Annually		

Historical Profile
Return	Above Avg
Risk	Low
Rating	★★★★ Above Avg

| | 88% | 91% | 76% | 72% | 67% | 82% | 84% | 88% | 89% | |

Investment Style
Equity
Stock %

▼ Manager Change
▽ Partial Manager Change

Growth of $10,000
— Investment Values of Fund
— Investment Values of S&P 500

50.6
43.6
32.4
24.0
17.0
10.0

Performance Quartile (within Category)

1995	1996	1997	1998	1999	2000	2001	2002	2003	2004	2005	2006	History
11.24	12.83	14.89	15.94	24.51	21.63	19.23	16.94	22.32	24.98	25.93	26.48	NAV
14.78	16.11	28.25	18.62	67.41	7.38	-9.84	-11.67	33.13	17.68	9.08	11.36	Total Return %
-22.80	-6.85	-5.11	-9.96	46.37	16.48	2.05	10.43	4.45	6.80	4.17	-4.43	+/-S&P 500
-16.15	-3.14	-4.00	-0.50	52.69	-10.13	-9.23	2.86	-2.49	1.20	-3.48	1.04	+/-S&P Mid 400
1.93	0.72	0.37	0.00	0.00	0.04	0.23	0.25	1.34	1.51	0.58	0.77	Income Return %
12.85	15.39	27.88	18.62	67.41	7.34	-10.07	-11.92	31.79	16.17	8.50	10.59	Capital Return %
97	70	39	25	4	64	87	22	61	33	53	62	Total Rtn % Rank Cat
0.19	0.08	0.05	0.00	0.00	0.01	0.05	0.05	0.23	0.34	0.15	0.20	Income $
0.00	0.13	1.47	1.60	1.98	4.53	0.21	0.00	0.94	1.18	2.22		Capital Gains $
1.74	1.75	1.75	1.75	1.75	1.57	1.45	1.43	1.41	1.36	1.32	1.26	Expense Ratio %
3.32	1.49	0.63	0.13	-0.27	-0.48	0.37	0.33	1.23	1.08	0.89	0.79	Income Ratio %
29	57	41	26	31	39	32	49	34	58	38	30	Turnover Rate %
16	17	20	21	42	50	57	71	111	155	230	301	Net Assets $mil

Rating and Risk

Time Period	Load-Adj Return %	Morningstar Rtn vs Cat	Morningstar Risk vs Cat	Morningstar Risk-Adj Rating
1 Yr	11.36			
3 Yr	12.65	Avg	Low	★★★
5 Yr	10.95	Avg	Low	★★★★
10 Yr	15.28	High	-Avg	★★★★★
Incept	14.04			

Other Measures	Standard Index S&P 500	Best Fit Index DJ Wilshire 4500
Alpha	2.4	1.9
Beta	0.94	0.63
R-Squared	72	85
Standard Deviation	7.58	
Mean	12.65	
Sharpe Ratio	1.19	

Portfolio Analysis 09-30-06

Share change since 06-06 Total Stocks:41	Sector	PE	Tot Ret%	% Assets
⊕ Charles River Laboratori	Health	—	2.08	3.55
Crown Holdings, Inc.	Goods	—	7.12	3.26
⊕ SLM Corporation	Financial	14.1	-9.76	3.24
⊗ Nestle	Goods	—	—	3.09
Johnson & Johnson	Health	17.5	12.45	3.07
⊗ Annaly Capital Managemen	Financial	—	32.85	3.04
Pitney Bowes Inc.	Ind Mtrls	19.7	12.57	3.02
⊕ Ares Capital Corporation	Financial	11.8	30.55	3.02
⊕ Costco Wholesale Corpora	Consumer	23.3	7.90	3.00
⊗ FPL Group	Utilities	17.7	35.49	2.99
⊕ Genworth Financial, Inc.	Financial	12.9	-0.17	2.99
⊕ Websense, Inc.	Software	30.0	-30.44	2.94
Southern Union Company	Energy	—	20.09	2.86
⊕ R. H. Donnelley Corporat	Business	—	1.82	2.85
Invitrogen Corporation	Health	29.1	-15.08	2.74
Avery Dennison Corp.	Ind Mtrls	22.0	26.06	2.66
Manor Care, Inc.	Health	24.6	19.65	2.50
Service Corporation Inte	Consumer	39.8	26.82	2.37
Lamar Advertising Compan	Business	—	41.75	2.33
Azimut Hldg	Financial	—	—	2.33

Current Investment Style

Value Blnd Growth — Large Mid Small

Market Cap	%
Giant	12.3
Large	16.3
Mid	52.8
Small	17.8
Micro	0.8

Avg $mil: 5,401

Value Measures		Rel Category
Price/Earnings	19.00	1.18
Price/Book	1.91	0.85
Price/Sales	1.40	1.25
Price/Cash Flow	9.13	1.08
Dividend Yield %	2.57	1.98

Growth Measures	%	Rel Category
Long-Term Erngs	11.95	0.94
Book Value	7.12	0.86
Sales	7.67	0.86
Cash Flow	1.53	0.18
Historical Erngs	9.05	0.51

Profitability	%	Rel Category
Return on Equity	13.53	0.85
Return on Assets	6.16	0.77
Net Margin	11.09	1.02

Sector Weightings	% of Stocks	Rel S&P 500	3 Year High Low	
⟳ Info	12.10	0.61		
Software	4.88	1.41	5	0
Hardware	1.64	0.18	9	2
Media	4.04	1.07	14	4
Telecom	1.54	0.44	6	2
⟲ Service	56.54	1.22		
Health	22.22	1.84	23	17
Consumer	7.25	0.95	19	7
Business	9.47	2.24	10	5
Financial	17.60	0.79	19	7
⟱ Mfg	31.35	0.93		
Goods	13.30	1.56	17	9
Ind Mtrls	6.38	0.53	11	6
Energy	5.81	0.59	11	5
Utilities	5.86	1.67	6	0

Composition

	%
● Cash	9.4
● Stocks	89.2
● Bonds	0.0
○ Other	1.4
Foreign (% of Stock)	13.0

Pax World Balanced

	Analyst Pick	Ticker PAXWX	Load None	NAV $24.53	Yield 1.5%	Total Assets $2,204 mil	Mstar Category Moderate Allocation

Governance and Management

Stewardship Grade: B

Portfolio Manager(s)

Chris Brown has more than a decade of experience as an investment professional, and he has run this fund skillfully since taking the wheel in early 1998. He is supported by one analyst/assistant manager, one research assistant, and one trader in Portsmouth, N.H.

Strategy

This moderate-allocation fund has a 55% to 75% equity range and a 25% to 45% bond range. On the stock side, it tends to favor services, retail, health-care, and tech stocks, which readily pass environmental and other screens. Manager Chris Brown amplifies those tendencies with growth-oriented stock selection. He favors domestic blue chips but readily considers mid-cap and international names. On the bond side, he favors agency, mortgage-backed, and corporate credits, and he tends to keep interest-rate risk modest.

Performance 12-31-06

	1st Qtr	2nd Qtr	3rd Qtr	4th Qtr	Total
2002	0.70	-6.08	-8.87	5.75	-8.86
2003	-1.12	8.17	1.93	7.57	17.27
2004	2.51	1.56	0.05	8.86	13.39
2005	-1.59	2.10	4.37	0.49	5.39
2006	4.44	-1.50	2.68	4.81	10.71

Trailing	Total Return%	+/- DJ Mod	+/- DJ US Mod	%Rank Cat	Growth of $10,000
3 Mo	4.81	-0.78	0.14	60	10,481
6 Mo	7.62	-1.17	-0.28	82	10,762
1 Yr	10.71	-1.59	0.44	59	11,071
3 Yr Avg	9.78	-0.94	0.66	21	13,230
5 Yr Avg	7.17	-2.85	-0.43	23	14,137
10 Yr Avg	9.52	0.97	0.93	10	24,828
15 Yr Avg	8.95	-0.26	-0.44	46	36,175

Tax Analysis	Tax-Adj Rtn%	%Rank Cat	Tax-Cost Rat	%Rank Cat
3 Yr (estimated)	8.92	15	0.78	37
5 Yr (estimated)	6.44	18	0.68	38
10 Yr (estimated)	8.08	7	1.31	37

Potential Capital Gain Exposure: 19% of assets

Morningstar's Take by William Samuel Rocco 12-27-06

Pax World Balanced remains a terrific choice for SRI fans.

This fund's and its siblings' shareholders recently voted to give Pax World Management the freedom to modify its zero-tolerance screens in the areas of alcohol and gambling, to update its diversity and environmental criteria, and to add other screens. Time will tell exactly how the revised screening process will affect this fund and its siblings, of course, but there are three reasons for SRI fans to be sanguine about these developments: Pax has proven its commitment to socially responsible investing, the adjustments make sense on their face, and they're the first such modifications in this fund's 35-year history.

Additionally, SRI fans who are interested in this fund shouldn't be the least bit concerned that the acquisition of Citizens Advisors by Pax World Management that was announced a few months ago is not being pursued at this time. The merger and resulting reorganization of the two firm's fund lineups were unlikely to have had a significant impact on this fund had it gone through, and the lack of a deal certainly doesn't hurt this offering in anyway.

Meanwhile, this fund still has three advantages over the SRI competition. First, Chris Brown is one of the longer-serving SRI managers. Second, his strategy is both wide-ranging and sound. Besides investing in U.S. blue-chip stocks and U.S. agency, corporate, and mortgage-backed bonds, he pays considerable attention to overseas equities, devotes a significant portion of the portfolio to mid-cap stocks, and even considers foreign bonds. Thus, this fund is much more diversified than most of its SRI rivals and can be used as a stand-alone fund and a core holding. Third, Brown has earned good long-term results with his strategy relative to its category peers and SRI rivals.

SRI fans who ignore this fund will likely do so at their own peril.

Address:	222 State Street Portsmouth NH 03801-3852 800-372-7827
Web Address:	www.paxworld.com
Inception:	11-30-71
Advisor:	Pax World Management Corp.
Subadvisor:	None
NTF Plans:	Fidelity Retail-NTF, Schwab OneSource

Minimum Purchase:	$250	Add: $50	IRA: $0
Min Auto Inv Plan:	$250	Add: $50	
Sales Fees:	No-load, 0.25%S		
Management Fee:	0.75% mx./0.50% mn.		
Actual Fees:	Mgt:0.50%	Dist:0.25%	
Expense Projections:	3Yr:$306	5Yr:$531	10Yr:$1178
Income Distrib:	Semi-Annually		

Historical Profile

Return	Above Avg
Risk	Below Avg
Rating	★★★★ Above Avg

	64%	66%	58%	56%	60%	70%	71%	66%	68%

Investment Style: Equity / Stock %

- ▼ Manager Change
- ▽ Partial Manager Change

Growth of $10,000
- ■ Investment Values of Fund
- — Investment Values of DJ Mod

31.0 / 25.0 / 20.0 / 15.0 / 10.0

Performance Quartile (within Category)

1995	1996	1997	1998	1999	2000	2001	2002	2003	2004	2005	2006	History
16.33	16.56	18.52	21.64	23.40	22.41	19.91	17.82	20.68	23.22	23.65	24.53	NAV
29.19	10.36	25.12	24.62	17.23	5.66	-9.09	-8.86	17.27	13.39	5.39	10.71	Total Return %
9.39	-0.30	13.22	12.30	-0.10	7.33	-6.29	-2.09	-10.11	0.42	-1.60	-1.59	+/-DJ Mod
4.42	-0.98	5.92	12.23	4.38	1.22	-9.25	1.68	-6.79	2.22	-0.61	0.44	+/-DJ US Mod
5.97	3.40	3.06	2.54	2.13	2.26	2.12	1.65	1.16	1.06	1.22	1.64	Income Return %
23.22	6.96	22.06	22.08	15.10	3.40	-11.21	-10.51	16.11	12.33	4.17	9.07	Capital Return %
21	88	11	8	16	28	86	21	78	5	41	59	Total Rtn % Rank Cat
0.79	0.55	0.50	0.47	0.46	0.53	0.47	0.33	0.21	0.22	0.28	0.39	Income $
0.14	0.89	1.65	0.88	1.41	1.75	0.00	0.00	0.00	0.00	0.54	1.25	Capital Gains $
0.97	0.89	0.91	0.95	0.89	0.96	0.93	0.95	0.99	0.95	0.96	—	Expense Ratio %
3.44	3.24	2.67	2.33	2.05	2.14	2.27	1.74	1.09	1.07	1.32	—	Income Ratio %
28	35	14	29	21	26	38	37	19	33	22	—	Turnover Rate %
477	518	629	838	1,070	1,228	1,162	1,035	1,226	1,465	1,928	2,204	Net Assets $mil

Rating and Risk

Time Period	Load-Adj Return %	Morningstar Rtn vs Cat	Morningstar Risk vs Cat	Morningstar Risk-Adj Rating
1 Yr	10.71			
3 Yr	9.78	+Avg	+Avg	★★★★
5 Yr	7.17	+Avg	-Avg	★★★★
10 Yr	9.52	+Avg	-Avg	★★★★
Incept	—			

Other Measures	Standard Index DJ Mod	Best Fit Index Mstar Mid Core
Alpha	-0.6	0.6
Beta	0.96	0.52
R-Squared	88	90
Standard Deviation	6.00	
Mean	9.78	
Sharpe Ratio	1.05	

Portfolio Analysis 09-30-06

Total Stocks:103 Share change since 06-30-06	Sectors	P/E Ratio	YTD Return %	% Net Assets
⊖ America Movil SA ADR	Telecom	27.7	-1.04	1.87
⊕ Cemex SAB de CV ADR	Ind Mtrls	11.1	-1.71	1.61
⊕ Cisco Systems, Inc.	Hardware	30.1	4.76	1.59
Amgen, Inc.	Health	29.1	3.84	1.53
CVS Corporation	Consumer	19.7	1.42	1.41
⊕ Staples, Inc.	Consumer	19.6	-3.60	1.39
⊕ Baker Hughes Inc.	Energy	9.9	-8.69	1.38
⊕ Ensco International, Inc.	Energy	11.0	-5.05	1.36
Procter & Gamble Company	Goods	23.9	-0.98	1.25

Total Fixed-Income:184	Date of Maturity	Amount $000	Value $000	% Net Assets
Cit Grp 5.5%	11-30-07	10,000	10,030	0.48
FNMA 5%	03-02-15	10,000	9,861	0.47
Bristol Myers Squibb 5.75	10-01-11	8,400	8,566	0.41
FNMA FRN	02-17-09	7,324	7,105	0.34
FHLMC 4.125%	08-19-08	7,000	6,887	0.33
FFCB 4.95%	05-09-12	7,000	6,878	0.33
FHLBA 3.25%	05-12-09	6,000	5,986	0.28
FHLBA 4.875%	11-15-11	6,000	5,977	0.28
FNMA FRN	03-01-35	5,938	5,974	0.28

Equity Style
Style: Growth
Size: Large-Cap

Value Measures		Rel Category
Price/Earnings	16.88	1.10
Price/Book	2.80	1.13
Price/Sales	1.42	1.04
Price/Cash Flow	10.06	1.24
Dividend Yield %	1.08	0.56

Growth Measures	%	Rel Category
Long-Term Erngs	13.68	1.17
Book Value	13.51	1.57
Sales	12.39	1.40
Cash Flow	13.51	1.37
Historical Erngs	20.85	1.17

Market Cap %			
Giant	30.7	Small	2.9
Large	33.6	Micro	0.4
Mid	32.5	Avg $mil:	17,372

Fixed-Income Style
Duration: —
Quality: —

Avg Eff Duration [1]	—
Avg Eff Maturity	—
Avg Credit Quality	—
Avg Wtd Coupon	4.50%

[1]figure provided by fund

Sector Weightings	% of Stocks	Rel DJ Mod	3 Year High Low
↻ Info	23.60	—	
Software	7.08	—	9 5
Hardware	9.24	—	10 6
Media	0.00	—	8 0
Telecom	7.28	—	8 4
⊆ Service	41.14		
Health	15.48	—	20 15
Consumer	6.69	—	13 5
Business	12.50	—	13 7
Financial	6.47	—	9 4
⊠ Mfg	35.26		
Goods	15.06	—	15 9
Ind Mtrls	6.04	—	9 4
Energy	11.77	—	13 6
Utilities	2.39	—	6 2

Composition
- Cash 5.8
- Stocks 68.4
- Bonds 25.1
- Other 0.7
- Foreign 22.2 (% of Stock)

MORNINGSTAR® Funds 500

Payden Core Bond

	Ticker	Load	NAV	Yield	SEC Yield	Total Assets	Mstar Category
	PYCBX	None	$10.13	4.7%	—	$878 mil	Intermediate-Term Bond

Governance and Management

Stewardship Grade: A

Portfolio Manager(s)

Lead manager Brian Matthews works with a roster of sector specialists, each of whom leads a team of analysts.

Strategy

This fund benchmarks itself against the Lehman Brothers Aggregate Bond Index, and it sticks to investment-grade sectors. Duration (a measure of interest-rate sensitivity) is typically kept within six months of the bogy's, with plus or minus one year being about as extreme as it gets. Diversification and issue selection are cornerstones of the fund's approach.

Historical Profile

Return	Average
Risk	Above Avg
Rating	★★★ Neutral

31	29	23	65	71	78	49	42

Investment Style
Fixed Income
Income Rtn %Rank Cat

▼ Manager Change
▽ Partial Manager Change

Growth of $10,000
— Investment Values of Fund
— Investment Values of LB Aggr

Performance Quartile (within Category)

1995	1996	1997	1998	1999	2000	2001	2002	2003	2004	2005	2006	History
10.23	9.76	9.97	10.07	9.25	9.54	9.91	10.59	10.60	10.61	10.38	10.13	NAV
19.71	1.75	9.00	8.07	-2.28	10.33	9.55	11.52	4.03	4.51	1.93	2.21	Total Return %
1.24	-1.88	-0.65	-0.62	-1.46	-1.30	1.11	1.27	-0.07	0.17	-0.50	-2.12	+/-LB Aggr
-1.72	-0.94	-0.43	-2.07	0.60	-2.11	0.73	-1.51	-1.94	-0.79	0.10	-1.60	+/-LB 5-10YR
6.39	6.31	6.20	6.17	6.07	6.98	5.60	4.49	3.24	3.82	4.11	4.63	Income Return %
13.32	-4.56	2.80	1.90	-8.35	3.35	3.95	7.03	0.79	0.69	-2.18	-2.42	Capital Return %
26	89	52	35	72	45	9	2	61	32	43	99	Total Rtn % Rank Cat
0.56	0.63	0.59	0.60	0.59	0.63	0.52	0.44	0.34	0.40	0.43	0.47	Income $
0.00	0.00	0.05	0.08	0.00	0.00	0.00	0.00	0.07	0.06	0.04	0.00	Capital Gains $
0.45	0.45	0.45	0.44	0.50	0.50	0.50	0.55	0.51	0.44	0.45	—	Expense Ratio %
6.20	6.41	6.03	6.12	6.06	6.59	5.63	4.50	3.21	3.75	3.48	—	Income Ratio %
252	197	317	156	67	161	787	582	303	164	210	—	Turnover Rate %
31	37	119	244	153	86	155	284	488	583	640	878	Net Assets $mil

Performance 12-31-06

	1st Qtr	2nd Qtr	3rd Qtr	4th Qtr	Total
2002	0.09	4.40	5.16	1.50	11.52
2003	1.33	2.96	-0.58	0.29	4.03
2004	3.15	-2.72	3.12	1.00	4.51
2005	-1.42	2.61	-0.40	1.17	1.93
2006	-0.78	-0.64	3.42	0.25	2.21

Trailing	Total Return%	+/- LB Aggr	+/- LB 5-10YR	%Rank Cat	Growth of $10,000
3 Mo	0.25	-0.99	-0.83	99	10,025
6 Mo	3.67	-1.42	-2.01	95	10,367
1 Yr	2.21	-2.12	-1.60	99	10,221
3 Yr Avg	2.88	-0.82	-0.76	72	10,889
5 Yr Avg	4.78	-0.28	-1.14	39	12,630
10 Yr Avg	5.80	-0.44	-0.88	34	17,573
15 Yr Avg	—	—	—	—	—

Tax Analysis	Tax-Adj Rtn%	%Rank Cat	Tax-Cost Rat	%Rank Cat
3 Yr (estimated)	1.34	61	1.50	52
5 Yr (estimated)	3.23	24	1.48	40
10 Yr (estimated)	3.73	20	1.96	43

Potential Capital Gain Exposure: -3% of assets

Rating and Risk

Time Period	Load-Adj Return %	Morningstar Rtn vs Cat	Morningstar Risk vs Cat	Morningstar Risk-Adj Rating
1 Yr	2.21			
3 Yr	2.88	Avg	High	★★★
5 Yr	4.78	Avg	+Avg	★★★
10 Yr	5.80	Avg	+Avg	★★★
Incept	5.64			

Other Measures	Standard Index LB Aggr	Best Fit Index LB. U.S. Univ. Bd
Alpha	-0.8	-1.4
Beta	1.07	1.10
R-Squared	93	94
Standard Deviation	3.60	
Mean	2.88	
Sharpe Ratio	-0.09	

Morningstar's Take by Kai Wiecking 12-01-06

Payden Core Bond is going through a rough spot, but we still find it appealing for the long run.

This fund is a suitable fixed-income portfolio anchor, but only for those investors who can tolerate significant levels of volatility. That's because lead manager Brian Matthews applies a very active investment strategy here, which entails significant variations to the fund's sector exposures and credit risk, and smaller variations to the fund's interest-rate risk. This all indicates that Matthews is managing this offering for total return rather than income.

And he's done reasonably well with that approach. The fund's trailing five-year average annual return of 4.9% ranks ahead of 71% of its rivals in the very competitive intermediate-term bond category. These numbers would look better if it wasn't for the fund's struggles in 2006 thus far.

Matthews and his team have actually been adopting a very defensive stance in terms of credit quality throughout the year. But since hedge funds and foreign investors in particular are still indiscriminate in their hunt for yield, their risk appetites continue to depress spreads (the yield differential between high-grade bonds and lesser securities). Matthews' shifting away from corporate bonds and into treasuries thus caused the fund to lag most of its peers. The manager is unrepentant, though, as he is unwilling to incur the additional risk for such puny yield rewards given the softening economic environment.

Based on all the aforementioned considerations alone, we'd be hesitant to give this offering our nod. But we haven't yet mentioned one very important factor speaking in its favor: low expenses. At 0.45%, its price tag is considerably cheaper than the 0.73% assessed by its typical no-load peer. This, and the fact that we have confidence in Matthews' ability to deliver over a full market cycle, makes it easier for us to recommend this fund for risk-tolerant long-term investors.

Address:	333 S Grand Ave Los Angeles CA 90071 800-572-9336	
Web Address:	www.payden.com	
Inception:	12-31-93	
Advisor:	Payden & Rygel	
Subadvisor:	None	
NTF Plans:	Schwab OneSource	

Minimum Purchase:	$5000	Add: $1000	IRA: $2000
Min Auto Inv Plan:	$5000	Add: $1000	
Sales Fees:	No-load		
Management Fee:	0.28% mx./0.25% mn.		
Actual Fees:	Mgt:0.28%	Dist: —	
Expense Projections:	3Yr:$153	5Yr:$270	10Yr:$612
Income Distrib:	Monthly		

Portfolio Analysis 10-31-06

Total Fixed-Income:121	Date of Maturity	Amount $000	Value $000	% Net Assets
FNMA 6%	11-01-35	99,660	100,251	8.39
FNMA 5.5%	11-01-35	98,679	97,507	8.16
US Treasury Note 3.125%	10-15-08	83,140	80,733	6.75
US Treasury Note 4.5%	11-15-15	56,563	56,134	4.70
US Treasury Note 4.875%	08-15-16	45,942	46,897	3.92
US Treasury Note 4.25%	08-15-13	40,589	39,802	3.33
G2sf 5.5% 30yr Tba	11-01-36	32,341	32,098	2.69
FNMA 5%	09-01-33	28,146	27,243	2.28
Amer Express Credit 2006	08-15-11	20,800	20,800	1.74
US Treasury Bond 6.125%	11-15-27	17,010	19,979	1.67
FNMA 5.87%	06-01-36	19,500	19,695	1.65
US Treasury Note 3.875%	09-15-10	19,018	18,548	1.55
FNMA 5%	11-01-35	18,390	17,752	1.49
FNMA 5.5%	04-01-34	16,073	15,927	1.33
US Treasury Bond 6.25%	08-15-23	13,160	15,315	1.28
Volkswagen Cr Ownr Tr 20	07-20-10	13,500	13,500	1.13
US Treasury Bond 6%	02-15-26	11,743	13,477	1.13
Jp Morgan Com Mtg 2006-L	04-15-45	12,160	12,750	1.07
Germany (Federal Republi	01-04-37	9,510	12,480	1.04
Lb-Ubs Cmbs 2005-C2 CMO	04-15-30	12,390	12,274	1.03

Current Investment Style

Duration: Short Int Long
Quality: High Med Low

[1] figure provided by fund

Avg Eff Duration[1]	5.1 Yrs
Avg Eff Maturity	7.0 Yrs
Avg Credit Quality	AAA
Avg Wtd Coupon	4.55%
Avg Wtd Price	99.98% of par

Coupon Range	% of Bonds	Rel Cat
0% PIK	6.6	0.9
0% to 6%	94.3	1.3
6% to 8%	5.3	0.2
8% to 10%	0.3	0.1
More than 10%	0.0	0.0

1.00=Category Average

Credit Analysis		% bonds 10-31-06
AAA	94	
AA	2	
A	3	
BBB	2	
BB		0
B		0
Below B		0
NR/NA		0

Sector Breakdown	% of assets
US Treasuries	26
TIPS	0
US Agency	3
Mortgage Pass-Throughs	26
Mortgage CMO	19
Mortgage ARM	0
US Corporate	5
Asset-Backed	11
Convertible	0
Municipal	0
Corporate Inflation-Protected	0
Foreign Corporate	0
Foreign Govt	1

Composition			
Cash	9.4	Bonds	90.5
Stocks	0.0	Other	0.1

Special Securities	
Restricted/Illiquid Secs	0
Exotic Mortgage-Backed	0
Emerging-Markets Secs	Trace
Options/Futures/Warrants	No

Payden Limited Maturity

✓ Analyst Pick

	Ticker	Load	NAV	Yield	SEC Yield	Total Assets	Mstar Category
	PYLMX	None	$9.87	4.3%	4.63%	$165 mil	Ultrashort Bond

Governance and Management

Stewardship Grade: A

Portfolio Manager(s)

Payden & Rygel uses a team approach to managing its funds, but this portfolio falls under the main responsibility of James Sarni, who has been at the helm here since 1994 and is also overall head of the short strategies team. He was joined by assistant manager Colleen Ambrose in February 2006.

Strategy

This fund works the quiet end of the ultrashort category and keeps its duration between about one third and three fourths of a year. It sticks mostly with high-quality securities and spreads its assets among several sectors, including mortgages, asset-backeds, corporates, and government bonds.

Historical Profile

Return	Average
Risk	Below Avg
Rating	★★★ Neutral

Investment Style: Fixed Income
Income Rtn %Rank Cat

▼ Manager Change
▽ Partial Manager Change

Growth of $10,000
— Investment Values of Fund
— Investment Values of LB Aggr

Performance Quartile (within Category)

1995	1996	1997	1998	1999	2000	2001	2002	2003	2004	2005	2006	History
10.07	10.05	10.05	10.06	9.95	10.02	10.06	10.02	9.96	9.90	9.86	9.87	NAV
7.08	5.16	5.53	5.82	4.67	7.01	6.22	2.39	1.20	1.09	2.54	4.51	Total Return %
-11.39	1.53	-4.12	-2.87	5.49	-4.62	-2.22	-7.86	-2.90	-3.25	0.11	0.18	+/-LB Aggr
1.10	-0.30	-0.19	0.38	-0.79	0.43	2.59	0.58	0.03	-0.64	-1.18	-0.72	+/-6 Month CD
5.96	5.35	5.53	5.72	5.79	6.27	5.26	2.79	1.80	1.70	2.95	4.41	Income Return %
1.12	-0.19	0.00	0.10	-1.12	0.74	0.96	-0.40	-0.60	-0.61	-0.41	0.10	Capital Return %
72	86	91	20	36	32	28	71	74	60	40	59	Total Rtn % Rank Cat
0.58	0.53	0.54	0.56	0.57	0.61	0.52	0.28	0.18	0.17	0.29	0.43	Income $
0.00	0.00	0.00	0.00	0.00	0.00	0.05	0.00	0.00	0.00	0.00	0.00	Capital Gains $
0.33	0.30	0.30	0.29	0.38	0.40	0.40	0.40	0.40	0.40	0.40	—	Expense Ratio %
5.59	5.45	5.52	5.58	5.56	6.04	5.50	2.76	1.60	1.42	2.50	—	Income Ratio %
166	217	135	91	60	103	112	115	91	84	99	—	Turnover Rate %
16	53	138	115	90	167	187	205	298	359	234	165	Net Assets $mil

Performance 12-31-06

	1st Qtr	2nd Qtr	3rd Qtr	4th Qtr	Total
2002	0.39	0.84	0.68	0.46	2.39
2003	0.42	0.47	0.13	0.17	1.20
2004	0.47	-0.12	0.42	0.31	1.09
2005	0.49	0.58	0.67	0.78	2.54
2006	0.95	1.09	1.24	1.15	4.51

Trailing	Total Return%	+/- LB Aggr	+/- 6 Month CD	%Rank Cat	Growth of $10,000
3 Mo	1.15	-0.09	-0.15	64	10,115
6 Mo	2.41	-2.68	-0.25	83	10,241
1 Yr	4.51	0.18	-0.72	59	10,451
3 Yr Avg	2.71	-0.99	-0.84	56	10,835
5 Yr Avg	2.34	-2.72	-0.38	77	11,226
10 Yr Avg	4.08	-2.16	0.05	61	14,917
15 Yr Avg	—	—	—	—	—

Tax Analysis	Tax-Adj Rtn%	%Rank Cat	Tax-Cost Rat	%Rank Cat
3 Yr (estimated)	1.64	36	1.04	37
5 Yr (estimated)	1.36	49	0.96	24
10 Yr (estimated)	2.43	54	1.59	39

Potential Capital Gain Exposure: -3% of assets

Rating and Risk

Time Period	Load-Adj Return %	Morningstar Rtn vs Cat	Morningstar Risk vs Cat	Morningstar Risk-Adj Rating
1 Yr	4.51			
3 Yr	2.71	Avg	-Avg	★★★
5 Yr	2.34	-Avg	Low	★★
10 Yr	4.08	Avg	-Avg	★★★
Incept	4.37			

Other Measures	Standard Index LB Aggr	Best Fit Index LB 1-5 YR
Alpha	-0.6	-0.5
Beta	0.06	0.12
R-Squared	53	60
Standard Deviation	0.50	
Mean	2.71	
Sharpe Ratio	-1.91	

Morningstar's Take by Kai Wiecking 12-19-06

Payden Limited is a sensible alternative to money-market funds.

This fund is somewhat hard to categorize. Its risk-return profile places it somewhere between "aggressive" money market funds and the more defensive ultrashort bond funds. What investors can expect here is for the fund to outperform money market funds over the long term, but due to its somewhat greater sensitivity to changes in interest rates, it can lag them during periods of rising rates. And the fund will generally look mediocre in terms of return when compared with its category peers, but it offers lower volatility than most rivals.

This asset class is neither terribly exciting nor rewarding, but that's not its purpose. The investors who seek out this option use it to park monies that are meant to be safe, often in order to balance risk elsewhere in a portfolio or to simply save for a short-term goal. However, some investors use the asset class as a parking space for market-timing purposes. And that may explain why this fund has

seen significant outflows over the past 18 months. Thankfully for remaining shareholders, expenses remained stubbornly low at 0.40%, less than 75% of its no-load peers in the group. Moderate expenses are crucial to the long-term viability of bond funds, especially in such a low-return subsector as ultrashort bonds.

But Payden's experienced management team, led by Jim Sarni, often adds value through active management, too. In recent months, the team has increased the portfolio's sensitivity to interest rates as it expect a significant slowing of the economy. The move has paid off thus far. As always, the bulk of assets remains invested in safe AAA rated paper, but Sarni maintains a significant exposure to several BBB rated floating-rate corporate bonds, mostly from the automobile sector, to provide some added yield.

All told, this fund with its seasoned skipper and moderate price tag is still a good option for conservative investors.

Address:	333 S Grand Ave
	Los Angeles CA 90071
	800-572-9336
Web Address:	www.payden.com
Inception:	04-29-94
Advisor:	Payden & Rygel
Subadvisor:	None
NTF Plans:	Schwab OneSource

Minimum Purchase:	$5000	Add: $1000	IRA: $2000
Min Auto Inv Plan:	$2500	Add: $250	
Sales Fees:	No-load		
Management Fee:	0.28% mx./0.25% mn., 0.06%A		
Actual Fees:	Mgt:0.28%	Dist: —	
Expense Projections:	3Yr:$150	5Yr:$270	10Yr:$619
Income Distrib:	Monthly		

Portfolio Analysis 10-31-06

Total Fixed-Income:62	Date of Maturity	Amount $000	Value $000	% Net Assets
Gmacm Heq Ln Tr 2005-He3	02-25-36	5,800	5,806	3.49
FNMA FRN	11-01-35	5,240	5,397	3.25
Whole Auto Ln Tr 2003-1	03-15-10	5,316	5,289	3.18
Chase Man Auto Owner Tr	02-15-10	4,627	4,567	2.75
Structured Asset Mtg 200	05-25-36	4,418	4,449	2.68
Wamu Mtg Cert 2006-Ar13	05-25-46	4,382	4,370	2.63
Daimlerchrysler Mstr Tr	04-15-10	4,200	4,201	2.53
Bear Stearns Alt-A 2006-	03-25-36	4,168	4,189	2.52
FHLMC FRN	02-01-34	4,144	4,149	2.50
Gs Auto Ln Tr 2003-1 2.7	06-15-10	4,116	4,102	2.47
Wamu Mtg Cert 2006-Ar4 C	05-25-46	4,025	4,028	2.42
Structured Asset Mtg 200	12-25-35	3,780	3,847	2.31
Structured Asset Mtg 200	02-25-36	3,522	3,589	2.16
FNMA FRN	02-01-36	3,468	3,572	2.15
Puma Global Tr 2004-S-1	08-09-35	3,225	3,231	1.94
First Franklin Mtg 2004-	01-25-35	3,158	3,164	1.90
Arkle Master Issuer FRN	08-17-11	3,000	3,000	1.80
World Omni Auto Tr 2003-	11-15-10	2,917	2,876	1.73
ORACLE	01-13-09	2,740	2,744	1.65
Usaa Auto Ln Grantor Tr	02-15-10	2,667	2,663	1.60

Current Investment Style

Duration: Short Int Long
Quality: High Med Low

1 figure provided by fund

Avg Eff Duration[1]	0.6 Yrs
Avg Eff Maturity	1.5 Yrs
Avg Credit Quality	AA
Avg Wtd Coupon	2.76%
Avg Wtd Price	100.24% of par

Coupon Range	% of Bonds	Rel Cat
0% PIK	29.5	1.3
0% to 6%	98.3	1.1
6% to 8%	1.7	0.2
8% to 10%	0.0	0.0
More than 10%	0.0	0.0

1.00=Category Average

Credit Analysis	% bonds 10-31-06		
AAA	73	BB	0
AA	1	B	0
A	8	Below B	0
BBB	18	NR/NA	0

Sector Breakdown | % of assets

US Treasuries	0
TIPS	0
US Agency	0
Mortgage Pass-Throughs	10
Mortgage CMO	24
Mortgage ARM	0
US Corporate	13
Asset-Backed	33
Convertible	0
Municipal	0
Corporate Inflation-Protected	0
Foreign Corporate	0
Foreign Govt	2

Composition

| Cash | 18.4 | Bonds | 81.6 |
| Stocks | 0.0 | Other | 0.0 |

Special Securities

Restricted/Illiquid Secs	1
Exotic Mortgage-Backed	0
Emerging-Markets Secs	Trace
Options/Futures/Warrants	No

MORNINGSTAR® Funds 500

PIMCO CommRealRetStrD

	Ticker	Load	NAV	Yield	Total Assets	Mstar Category
	PCRDX	None	$13.88	2.8%	$13,369 mil	Specialty-Natural Res

Governance and Management

Stewardship Grade: B

Portfolio Manager(s)

Manager John Brynjolfsson has managed this fund since inception. He has also managed PIMCO Real Return since 1997. That fund mostly invests in TIPS. He is a member of the PIMCO management team that won Morningstar's Fixed-Income Manager of the Year honors in 1998 and 2000.

Strategy

In contrast to most natural-resources funds that invest in the stocks of companies that produce commodities, this fund invests in derivative instruments that seek to replicate the performance of the Dow Jones-AIG Commodity Index. Because the fund can gain full exposure to the index with only a portion of assets, the remaining assets are invested in TIPS. Through the investment in TIPS, the managers hope to recoup the expenses of running the fund and even hope to best the index. An IRS ruling has changed the way this fund gains its exposure to commodities and TIPS, but the end result is the same for investors.

Performance 12-31-06

	1st Qtr	2nd Qtr	3rd Qtr	4th Qtr	Total
2002	—	—	—	—	8.40 *
2003	3.98	5.47	4.70	12.45	29.12
2004	16.59	-7.43	10.16	-2.65	15.75
2005	11.16	-3.10	16.26	-4.25	19.91
2006	-5.68	5.14	-4.92	2.38	-3.46

Trailing	Total Return%	+/- S&P 500	+/- GS NATR RES	%Rank Cat	Growth of $10,000
3 Mo	2.38	-4.32	-7.19	89	10,238
6 Mo	-2.65	-15.39	-5.22	72	9,735
1 Yr	-3.46	-19.25	-20.28	89	9,654
3 Yr Avg	10.25	-0.19	-15.45	90	13,401
5 Yr Avg	—	—	—	—	—
10 Yr Avg	—	—	—	—	—
15 Yr Avg	—	—	—	—	—

Tax Analysis	Tax-Adj Rtn%	%Rank Cat	Tax-Cost Rat	%Rank Cat
3 Yr (estimated)	6.86	90	3.07	86
5 Yr (estimated)	—	—	—	—
10 Yr (estimated)	—	—	—	—

Potential Capital Gain Exposure: -3% of assets

Morningstar's Take by Karen Dolan 11-13-06

We applaud PIMCO CommodityRealReturn's recent transition, but competition threatens its appeal.

In December 2005, the IRS banned commodity funds from using a special derivative contract called a swap. So, this fund and others like it had to find another method for getting exposure to commodities. PIMCO's transition was seamless. By May 2006, the fund had moved 95% of its assets into structured notes spread between 18 different issuers. Many of the fund's rivals have had a harder time making the switch. We're glad that PIMCO has effectively dealt with the disruption and moved on without any noticeable effect on shareholders.

This fund is still our favorite choice for commodity exposure within the mutual fund universe, but it is getting competition from some innovative new securities, Barclay's iPath exchange-traded-notes. The ETNs are better for taxable accounts and charge meaningfully less than this fund's 1.24% levy.

Even so, this fund still has some differentiating

qualities. It uses a clever mix of derivatives to secure 100% exposure to the returns of the Dow Jones AIG Commodity Total Return Index and another 100% exposure to a portfolio of Treasury Inflation-Protected Securities. The fund's TIPS portion is modeled after Analyst Pick PIMCO Real Return.

TIPS have stung over short stretches, though. For example, the fund lost 5.7% of its value in the first quarter 2006 while the DJAIGCI lost only 2.4% over the same stretch. The return difference is primarily attributable to its TIPS exposure, but we think PIMCO's bond expertise will add value over time.

More generally, we think investors should tread carefully with commodities right now. Raw good prices are notoriously volatile, so chasing recent returns might be a bad idea. For those willing to stick with a small helping for a long time, however, we think this fund can function as a strong diversifier in a tax-sheltered account.

Address:	840 Newport Center Drive Newport Beach CA 92660 800-426-0107
Web Address:	www.allianzinvestors.com
Inception:	11-29-02 *
Advisor:	Allianz Global Investors Fund Mgmt LLC
Subadvisor:	Research Affiliates, LLC
NTF Plans:	Fidelity Retail-NTF, Schwab OneSource

Minimum Purchase:	$5000	Add: $100	IRA: $0
Min Auto Inv Plan:	$0	Add:	
Sales Fees:	No-load, 0.25%S, 2.00%R		
Management Fee:	0.49%, 0.75%A		
Actual Fees:	Mgt:0.49%	Dist:0.25%	
Expense Projections:	3Yr:$393	5Yr:$681	10Yr:$1500
Income Distrib:	Quarterly		

Historical Profile

Return	Low
Risk	Low
Rating	★ Lowest

Growth of $10,000
— Investment Values of Fund
— Investment Values of S&P 500

Performance Quartile (within Category)

	1995	1996	1997	1998	1999	2000	2001	2002	2003	2004	2005	2006	History
	—	—	—	—	—	—	—	11.57	13.63	14.79	14.78	13.88	NAV
	—	—	—	—	—	—	—	8.40*	29.12	15.75	19.91	-3.46	Total Return %
	—	—	—	—	—	—	—	0.44	4.87	15.00	-19.25	+/-S&P 500
	—	—	—	—	—	—	—	-4.89	-8.82	-16.57	-20.28	+/-GS NATR RES
	—	—	—	—	—	—	—	10.18	5.97	20.11	2.62	Income Return %
	—	—	—	—	—	—	—	18.94	9.78	-0.20	-6.08	Capital Return %
	—	—	—	—	—	—	—	53	92	90	89	Total Rtn % Rank Cat
	—	—	—	—	—	—	0.76	1.16	0.79	2.85	0.39	Income $
	—	—	—	—	—	—	0.00	0.14	0.18	0.07	0.00	Capital Gains $
	—	—	—	—	—	—	—	—	1.24	1.24	1.24	Expense Ratio %
	—	—	—	—	—	—	—	—	-62.62	39.03	3.69	Income Ratio %
	—	—	—	—	—	—	—	—	492	290	292	Turnover Rate %
	—	—	—	—	—	—	—	193	759	1,241	Net Assets $mil

Rating and Risk

Time Period	Load-Adj Return %	Morningstar Rtn vs Cat	Morningstar Risk vs Cat	Morningstar Risk-Adj Rating
1 Yr	-3.46			
3 Yr	10.25	Low	Low	★
5 Yr	—	—	—	—
10 Yr	—	—	—	—
Incept	16.63			

Other Measures	Standard Index S&P 500	Best Fit Index GS NATR RES
Alpha	7.7	-4.2
Beta	0.03	0.56
R-Squared	0	43
Standard Deviation	16.17	
Mean	10.25	
Sharpe Ratio	0.48	

Portfolio Analysis 09-30-06

Share change since 06-06 Total Stocks:0	Sector	PE	Tot Ret%	% Assets
⊖ US Treasury Bond 2.375%	—	—		5.70
⊕ US Treasury Note 0.875%	—	—		5.33
⊖ US Treasury Note 3%	—	—		4.83
⊖ US Treasury Bond 3.625%	—	—		4.26
⊕ US Treasury Note 3.625%	—	—		3.73
⊕ US TREASURY NOTE	—	—		3.70
✄ US Treasury Note (Fut)	—	—		3.48
⊕ US Treasury Note 3.875%	—	—		3.29
⊖ US Treasury Note 2%	—	—		3.22
⊕ EuroDollar (Fut)	—	—		2.77
⊖ US Treasury Note 2%	—	—		2.66
✄ US Treasury Note (Fut)	—	—		2.63
⊕ US Treasury Note 1.875%	—	—		2.12
⊕ US Treasury Note 3.5%	—	—		2.09
⊕ US Treasury Bond 2%	—	—		1.92
⊖ US Treasury Note 4.25%	—	—		1.90
⊕ FNMA 5.5%	—	—		1.77
✄ Pimo Cayman Cmdty Fd Ltd	—	—		1.60
⊖ US Treasury Note 3.875%	—	—		1.44
⊕ US Treasury Note 2.375%	—	—		1.35

Current Investment Style

Value Blnd Growth — Large Mid Small

Market Cap	%
Giant	—
Large	—
Mid	—
Small	—
Micro	—
Avg $mil:	

Value Measures		Rel Category
Price/Earnings	—	—
Price/Book	—	—
Price/Sales	—	—
Price/Cash Flow	—	—
Dividend Yield %	—	—

Growth Measures	%	Rel Category
Long-Term Erngs	—	—
Book Value	—	—
Sales	—	—
Cash Flow	—	—
Historical Erngs	—	—

Profitability	%	Rel Category
Return on Equity	—	—
Return on Assets	—	—
Net Margin	—	—

Industry Weightings	% of Stocks	Rel Cat
Oil & Gas	—	—
Oil/Gas Products	—	—
Oil & Gas Srv	—	—
Pipelines	—	—
Utilities	—	—
Hard Commd	—	—
Soft Commd	—	—
Misc. Indstrl	—	—
Other	—	—

Composition

● Cash	28.4
● Stocks	0.0
● Bonds	61.3
● Other	10.3
Foreign (% of Stock)	0.0

Investment Style

Equity
Stock %

▼ Manager Change
▽ Partial Manager Change

PIMCO Emerg Mkts Bd D

Analyst Pick ✓

Ticker PEMDX	**Load** None	**NAV** $11.05	**Yield** 5.0%	**SEC Yield** 4.59%	**Total Assets** $2,580 mil	**Mstar Category** Emerging Markets Bond

Governance and Management

Stewardship Grade: B

Portfolio Manager(s)

Longtime manager Mohamed El-Erian left in early 2006, and his assistant Michael Gomez has succeeded him. Gomez has assisted here since 2003, and before joining PIMCO, he traded emerging-markets bonds for Goldman Sachs. Prior to that, he advised the Colombian government's department of public credit. Gomez has tremendous resources at his disposal, including two comanagers in Munich, one in Singapore, and four in PIMCO's California office. Macroeconomic direction for the fund's investment-grade credits is also provided by PIMCO analysts.

Strategy

Unlike some of its large peers, this fund isn't afraid to completely avoid countries with debt that comprises a good deal of the market. Management sometimes overweights countries it favors and attempts to hedge such moves by shorting the bonds of neighboring countries that it believes to be relatively weak. In addition to shorting bonds (effectively betting that they will decline in value), the fund also utilizes derivatives, including credit-default swaps.

Performance 12-31-06

	1st Qtr	2nd Qtr	3rd Qtr	4th Qtr	Total
2002	7.26	-6.97	-3.64	16.92	12.40
2003	10.37	10.34	2.60	5.68	32.04
2004	3.13	-6.32	9.50	5.67	11.79
2005	-1.52	6.85	3.85	1.84	11.29
2006	1.12	-2.04	6.20	3.94	9.35

Trailing	Total Return%	+/- LB Agg	+/- Citigroup ESBI-Cap Brady	%Rank Cat	Growth of $10,000
3 Mo	3.94	2.70	-6.48	76	10,394
6 Mo	10.39	5.30	-10.52	68	11,039
1 Yr	9.35	5.02	-15.30	78	10,935
3 Yr Avg	10.80	7.10	-2.83	66	13,603
5 Yr Avg	15.09	10.03	0.40	56	20,192
10 Yr Avg	—	—	—	—	—
15 Yr Avg	—	—	—	—	—

Tax Analysis	Tax-Adj Rtn%	%Rank Cat	Tax-Cost Rat	%Rank Cat
3 Yr (estimated)	7.82	57	2.69	59
5 Yr (estimated)	11.28	57	3.31	79
10 Yr (estimated)	—	—	—	—

Potential Capital Gain Exposure: 6% of assets

Morningstar's Take by Arijit Dutta 12-21-06

It hasn't been a great year overall for PIMCO Emerging Markets Bond, but it has shown off a key strength.

Emerging-markets bonds, which have rallied tremendously for the past several years, continued their winning ways through 2006. Things did get rocky in May, however, as investors worldwide fled risky assets. During the May-June correction, this fund fared better than just about all category rivals. The portfolio's relatively higher quality (it only has a 2% stake in bonds rated B or below, while the category average is 23%) gave it some protection as many of the riskiest bonds got hit the hardest. Lead manager Michael Gomez's decision to raise cash and stay out of countries like Turkey that have uncertain macroeconomic outlooks also proved beneficial in the correction.

The fund hasn't participated as much on the upside, but we think managing risk is crucial in this asset class. Developing countries' creditworthiness can swing very quickly, which makes their bonds rather volatile. Moreover, the category's multiyear rally has led to historically low yields, so investors aren't getting paid as much for taking on the credit risk. PIMCO managers have been especially cautious, however, and have shunned dubious issues, including significant benchmark components such as Turkey. Gomez has instead stuck with longer-term debt in countries with solid financial positions, such as Brazil and Russia. Gomez claims they offer much better values, though those bonds haven't rallied as hard as many smaller, riskier issues in recent years.

Management's disciplined approach makes this fund a solid choice. We wouldn't rush into any emerging-markets bond fund at this point: The category's multiyear romp has led to historically rich valuations. For long-term investors, however, this fund's ability to not follow the herd can be rewarding.

Address:	840 Newport Center Drive Newport Beach CA 92660 800-426-0107
Web Address:	www.allianzinvestors.com
Inception:	03-31-00 *
Advisor:	Allianz Global Investors Fund Mgmt LLC
Subadvisor:	Research Affiliates, LLC
NTF Plans:	Fidelity Retail-NTF, Schwab OneSource

Minimum Purchase:	$5000	Add: $100	IRA: $2500
Min Auto Inv Plan:	$0	Add: —	
Sales Fees:	No-load, 0.25%S, 2.00%R		
Management Fee:	0.45%, 0.55%A		
Actual Fees:	Mgt:0.45%	Dist:0.25%	
Expense Projections:	3Yr:$397	5Yr:$686	10Yr:$1511
Income Distrib:	Monthly		

Historical Profile

Return	Average
Risk	Above Avg
Rating	★★★ Neutral

▼ Manager Change
▽ Partial Manager Change

— Growth of $10,000
— Investment Values of Fund
— Investment Values of LB Aggr

Performance Quartile (within Category)

Investment Style Fixed Income Income Rtn %Rank Cat

1995	1996	1997	1998	1999	2000	2001	2002	2003	2004	2005	2006	History
—	—	—	—	—	8.21	9.10	9.25	10.51	10.86	11.16	11.05	NAV
—	—	—	—	—	7.58*	27.79	12.40	32.04	11.79	11.29	9.35	Total Return %
—	—	—	—	—	—	19.35	2.15	27.94	7.45	8.86	5.02	+/-LB Aggr
—	—	—	—	—	—	20.19	3.61	7.72	0.49	5.53	-15.30	+/-Citigroup ESBI-Cap Brady
—	—	—	—	—	—	9.97	7.57	6.06	4.29	5.15	5.37	Income Return %
—	—	—	—	—	—	17.82	4.83	25.98	7.50	6.14	3.98	Capital Return %
—	—	—	—	—	—	6	40	22	60	48	78	Total Rtn % Rank Cat
—	—	—	—	—	0.61	0.78	0.66	0.54	0.44	0.55	0.58	Income $
—	—	—	—	—	0.40	0.50	0.25	1.08	0.40	0.34	0.54	Capital Gains $
—	—	—	—	—	—	1.33	1.25	1.27	1.25	1.25	1.25	Expense Ratio %
—	—	—	—	—	—	9.33	7.05	7.02	4.57	3.85	4.96	Income Ratio %
—	—	—	—	—	328	902	617	388	461	415	280	Turnover Rate %
—	—	—	—	—	5	33	161	190	245	216		Net Assets $mil

Rating and Risk

Time Period	Load-Adj Return %	Morningstar Rtn vs Cat	Morningstar Risk vs Cat	Morningstar Risk-Adj Rating
1 Yr	9.35			
3 Yr	10.80	Avg	+Avg	★★★
5 Yr	15.09	Avg	+Avg	★★★
10 Yr	—			
Incept	16.32			

Other Measures	Standard Index LB Aggr	Best Fit Index LB. U.S. Univ. Bd
Alpha	6.5	5.5
Beta	1.81	1.93
R-Squared	61	67
Standard Deviation	7.56	
Mean	10.80	
Sharpe Ratio	0.98	

Portfolio Analysis 09-30-06

Total Fixed-Income:148	Date of Maturity	Amount $000	Value $000	% Net Assets
US Treasury Note (Fut)	12-29-06	785,400	828,720	20.06
EuroDollar (Fut)	09-15-08	240,750	229,170	5.55
EuroDollar (Fut)	06-15-09	235,750	224,163	5.43
US Treasury Note (Fut)	12-19-06	136,700	147,721	3.58
EuroDollar (Fut)	12-17-07	118,750	113,062	2.74
Russian Federation FRN	03-31-30	99,606	111,409	2.70
Brazil Federative Rep 11	08-17-40	68,276	89,015	2.15
Brazil Federative Rep 10	07-14-14	65,230	82,125	1.99
Gazprom 9.625%	03-01-13	62,930	74,679	1.81
Brazil Federative Rep 8.	01-20-34	50,480	58,178	1.41
Brazil Federative Rep 10	05-15-27	42,810	57,558	1.39
Pemex Proj Fdg Master Tr	02-01-22	40,033	48,180	1.17
Republic Of Ecuador 4%	08-15-30	51,475	47,614	1.15
Republic Of Venezuela 14	12-09-20	42,450	38,099	0.92
US Treasury Note 3.625%	05-15-13	39,500	37,334	0.90
Argentina FRN	08-03-12	51,635	36,377	0.88
Venezuela (Republic Of)	08-07-10	33,550	32,627	0.79
Colombia Rep 8.25%	12-22-14	29,030	32,194	0.78
Pemex Proj Fdg Master Tr	12-15-15	32,900	32,184	0.78
United Mexican Sts Mtn B	09-24-22	26,180	31,416	0.76

Current Investment Style

Duration: Short Int Long
Quality: High Med Low

1 figure provided by fund

Avg Eff Duration[1]	6.7 Yrs
Avg Eff Maturity	12.0 Yrs
Avg Credit Quality	BBB
Avg Wtd Coupon	7.74%
Avg Wtd Price	113.29% of par

Coupon Range	% of Bonds	Rel Cat
0% PIK	1.0	0.2
0% to 6%	28.0	1.1
6% to 8%	22.8	0.9
8% to 10%	30.5	0.9
More than 10%	18.6	1.2

1.00=Category Average

Credit Analysis	% bonds 09-30-06		
AAA	6	BB	47
AA	0	B	2
A	3	Below B	0
BBB	42	NR/NA	0

Sector Breakdown

	% of assets
US Treasuries	—
TIPS	—
US Agency	—
Mortgage Pass-Throughs	—
Mortgage CMO	—
Mortgage ARM	—
US Corporate	—
Asset-Backed	—
Convertible	—
Municipal	—
Corporate Inflation-Protected	—
Foreign Corporate	—
Foreign Govt	—

Composition

Cash	29.9	Bonds	45.7
Stocks	0.0	Other	24.4

Special Securities

Restricted/Illiquid Secs	6
Exotic Mortgage-Backed	0
Emerging-Markets Secs	
Options/Futures/Warrants	No

MORNINGSTAR® Funds 500

PIMCO For Bd USD-Hdgd D

✓ Analyst Pick

	Ticker	Load	NAV	Yield	SEC Yield	Total Assets	Mstar Category
	PFODX	None	$10.18	2.8%	3.14%	$2,469 mil	World Bond

Governance and Management

Stewardship Grade: B

Portfolio Manager(s)

Sudi Mariappa leads PIMCO's global portfolio management. Mariappa came to PIMCO in 2000 from Merrill Lynch. He also manages Analyst Pick PIMCO Foreign Bond (Unhedged). He is backed by PIMCO's impressive global team, which consists of 19 portfolio managers in several locations worldwide. The team also has access to 42 analysts.

Strategy

Management invests the bulk of its assets overseas, primarily in government-issued bonds. It hedges most of its currency exposure back into the dollar, so the fund offers little in the way of currency diversification. Although management may make sizable bets if valuations look particularly attractive, it builds positions gradually as its macroeconomic views change.

Historical Profile

Return Average
Risk Low
Rating ★★★ Neutral

	42	55	39	60	88	88	85

Investment Style
Fixed Income
Income Rtn %Rank Cat

Growth of $10,000
■ Investment Values of Fund
— Investment Values of LB Aggr

Performance Quartile (within Category)

1995	1996	1997	1998	1999	2000	2001	2002	2003	2004	2005	2006	History
—	—	—	10.57	9.97	10.10	10.46	10.58	10.39	10.47	10.42	10.18	NAV
—	—	—	4.82*	1.11	9.38	8.48	7.24	3.10	6.17	5.24	2.48	Total Return %
—	—	—	—	1.93	-2.25	0.04	-3.01	-1.00	1.83	2.81	-1.85	+/-LB Aggr
—	—	—	—	6.18	12.01	12.02	-14.75	-15.42	-5.97	14.44	-4.46	+/-SB Wld Govt
—	—	—	—	5.44	5.76	4.62	3.57	2.92	2.37	2.53	2.81	Income Return %
—	—	—	—	-4.33	3.62	3.86	3.67	0.18	3.80	2.71	-0.33	Capital Return %
—	—	—	—	22	16	9	78	92	74	6	85	Total Rtn % Rank Cat
—	—	—	0.42	0.56	0.56	0.46	0.37	0.30	0.24	0.26	0.29	Income $
—	—	—	0.35	0.15	0.21	0.02	0.25	0.21	0.31	0.33	0.21	Capital Gains $
—	—	—	—	0.95	1.16	0.99	0.95	0.95	0.96	0.95	0.95	Expense Ratio %
—	—	—	—	4.82	5.77	5.26	4.09	3.31	2.52	2.44	2.95	Income Ratio %
—	—	—	280	376	330	417	434	589	711	477	571	Turnover Rate %
—	—	—	5	9	19	45	112	157	206	285	227	Net Assets $mil

Performance 12-31-06

	1st Qtr	2nd Qtr	3rd Qtr	4th Qtr	Total
2002	0.22	2.19	1.94	2.72	7.24
2003	1.99	1.34	-0.40	0.15	3.10
2004	1.89	-0.41	1.65	2.94	6.17
2005	1.33	2.71	0.38	0.74	5.24
2006	-0.49	0.09	2.57	0.32	2.48

Trailing	Total Return%	+/- LB Aggr	+/- SB Wld Govt	%Rank Cat	Growth of $10,000
3 Mo	0.32	-0.92	-1.77	91	10,032
6 Mo	2.90	-2.19	-0.09	59	10,290
1 Yr	2.48	-1.85	-4.46	85	10,248
3 Yr Avg	4.62	0.92	1.74	23	11,451
5 Yr Avg	4.83	-0.23	-4.67	83	12,660
10 Yr Avg	—	—	—	—	—
15 Yr Avg	—	—	—	—	—

Tax Analysis	Tax-Adj Rtn%	%Rank Cat	Tax-Cost Rat	%Rank Cat
3 Yr (estimated)	2.87	26	1.67	55
5 Yr (estimated)	3.04	83	1.71	49
10 Yr (estimated)	—	—	—	—

Potential Capital Gain Exposure: 2% of assets

Rating and Risk

Time Period	Load-Adj Return %	Morningstar Rtn vs Cat	Morningstar Risk vs Cat	Morningstar Risk-Adj Rating
1 Yr	2.48			
3 Yr	4.62	+Avg	Low	★★★★
5 Yr	4.83	-Avg	Low	★★
10 Yr	—	—	—	—
Incept	5.47			

Other Measures	Standard Index LB Aggr	Best Fit Index LB LTGvtBd
Alpha	1.1	0.9
Beta	0.40	0.18
R-Squared	39	44
Standard Deviation	1.98	
Mean	4.62	
Sharpe Ratio	0.63	

Morningstar's Take by Arijit Dutta 12-22-06

PIMCO Foreign Bond (U.S. Dollar-Hedged) is still a solid core choice.

The currency market turned its back on this fund in 2006, but we've still seen hints of the strength here. Following its surprise revival last year, the dollar has resumed its decline in 2006, not giving this fund much of a chance against the world-bond category. (Most portfolios in this group are unhedged.) But the fund did stay true to form when markets corrected during a month-long period in May and June. The portfolio's minimal exposure to lower-rated bonds and an overall AAA average credit-quality allowed the fund to post a modest gain during the correction while most rivals lost money. Moreover, though the portfolio's higher quality and lack of emerging-markets exposure have not been favorable for the year to date (risky assets have staged a comeback since June), it remains ahead of most hedged rivals.

Instead of taking much risk on the credit-quality side, management seeks to get ahead through decisive bets in large, stable markets. For example, the portfolio's 35% combined stake in euro-area behemoths France and Germany is well more than twice the category average. Though those markets have in general underperformed other major countries, management's preference for longer-maturity bonds has benefited the portfolio. (Interest rates have risen faster in short-term bonds due to rate hikes by European authorities.) Management has also maintained a strong, contrarian preference for short-term Japanese bonds, due to its faith in the yen's fundamental strength. While that bet has yet to pay off, management says it will persist. (Though the portfolio's overall currency exposure is hedged back to the dollar, it will still benefit if the yen rises in value relative to other currencies.)

This isn't the right vehicle for those seeking non-dollar exposure, but management's quality- and valuation-conscious approach should continue to serve other investors well.

Portfolio Analysis 09-30-06

Total Fixed-Income:303	Date of Maturity	Amount $000	Value $000	% Net Assets
EuroDollar (Fut)	06-18-07	692,250	657,534	13.99
EuroDollar (Fut)	09-17-07	250,250	238,050	5.06
EuroDollar (Fut)	12-18-06	198,500	187,910	4.00
Germany (Federal Republi	07-04-27	95,560	165,239	3.52
France (Republic Of) 4%	10-25-14	111,700	144,706	3.08
EuroDollar (Fut)	09-15-08	143,750	136,836	2.91
Japan	03-20-11	—	109,741	2.33
Federal Republic Of Germ	07-04-14	81,490	107,305	2.28
FNMA 6%		88,000	88,413	1.88
Germany (Federal Republi	01-04-14	63,452	83,412	1.77
FNMA 6.5%		76,000	77,401	1.65
EuroDollar (Fut)	12-15-08	78,000	74,217	1.58
EuroDollar (Fut)	03-16-09	78,000	74,194	1.58
EuroDollar (Fut)	06-15-09	78,000	74,166	1.58
Japan (Government Of) 1.	06-20-14	8,010,000	68,502	1.46
EuroDollar (Fut)	03-17-08	65,750	62,617	1.33
EuroDollar (Fut)	06-16-08	65,750	62,607	1.33
EuroDollar (Fut)	12-17-07	65,750	62,601	1.33
Germany (Federal Republi	01-04-28	39,370	62,062	1.32
Japan (Government Of) 2.	06-20-35	7,380,000	60,810	1.29

Current Investment Style

Duration: Short Int Long
Quality: High Med Low

¹ figure provided by fund

Avg Eff Duration¹	6.2 Yrs
Avg Eff Maturity	9.1 Yrs
Avg Credit Quality	AA
Avg Wtd Coupon	4.54%
Avg Wtd Price	103.39% of par

Coupon Range	% of Bonds	Rel Cat
0% PIK	2.8	0.7
0% to 6%	79.6	1.0
6% to 8%	17.2	1.3
8% to 10%	3.3	0.7
More than 10%	0.0	0.0

1.00=Category Average

Credit Analysis		% bonds 09-30-06	
AAA	68	BB	3
AA	23	B	0
A	1	Below B	0
BBB	5	NR/NA	0

Sector Breakdown % of assets

US Treasuries	
TIPS	
US Agency	
Mortgage Pass-Throughs	
Mortgage CMO	
Mortgage ARM	
US Corporate	
Asset-Backed	
Convertible	
Municipal	
Corporate Inflation-Protected	
Foreign Corporate	
Foreign Govt	

Composition

Cash	44.3	Bonds	53.2
Stocks	0.0	Other	2.5

Special Securities

Restricted/Illiquid Secs	2
Exotic Mortgage-Backed	0
Emerging-Markets Secs	—
Options/Futures/Warrants	No

Address:	840 Newport Center Drive Newport Beach CA 92660 800-426-0107	Minimum Purchase: $5000 Add: $100 IRA: $2500
		Min Auto Inv Plan: $1000 Add: $50
Web Address:	www.allianzinvestors.com	Sales Fees: No-load, 0.25%S, 2.00%R
Inception:	04-08-98 *	Management Fee: 0.25% 0.45%A
Advisor:	Allianz Global Investors Fund Mgmt LLC	Actual Fees: Mgt:0.25% Dist:0.25%
Subadvisor:	Research Affiliates, LLC	Expense Projections: 3Yr:$302 5Yr:$525 10Yr:$1165
		Income Distrib: Monthly
NTF Plans:	Fidelity Retail-NTF, Schwab OneSource	

MORNINGSTAR® Funds 500

PIMCO For Bd (Unhdgd) D

	Ticker	Load	NAV	Yield	SEC Yield	Total Assets	Mstar Category
	PFBDX	None	$10.18	2.9%	3.33%	$2,198 mil	World Bond

Governance and Management

Stewardship Grade: B

Portfolio Manager(s)

Sudi Mariappa leads PIMCO's global portfolio management. Mariappa came to PIMCO in 2000 from Merrill Lynch. He also manages Analyst Pick PIMCO Foreign Bond (U.S. Dollar-Hedged). He is backed by PIMCO's impressive global team, which consists of 19 portfolio managers in several locations worldwide. The team also has access to 42 analysts.

Strategy

Management invests the bulk of its assets overseas, primarily in government-issued bonds. It doesn't hedge its currency exposure back into the dollar, which means the fund offers a lot of currency diversification. Although management may make sizable bets if valuations look particularly attractive, it builds positions gradually as its macroeconomic views change.

Performance 12-31-06

	1st Qtr	2nd Qtr	3rd Qtr	4th Qtr	Total
2002	—	—	—	—	—
2003	—	—	—	—	—
2004	—	—	2.67	10.46	—*
2005	-3.30	-2.83	-1.26	-2.43	-9.47
2006	0.24	3.73	0.31	1.79	6.17

Trailing	Total Return%	+/- LB Aggr	+/- SB Wld Govt	%Rank Cat	Growth of $10,000
3 Mo	1.79	0.55	-0.30	58	10,179
6 Mo	2.10	-2.99	-0.89	89	10,210
1 Yr	6.17	1.84	-0.77	36	10,617
3 Yr Avg	—	—	—	—	—
5 Yr Avg	—	—	—	—	—
10 Yr Avg	—	—	—	—	—
15 Yr Avg	—	—	—	—	—

Tax Analysis	Tax-Adj Rtn%	%Rank Cat	Tax-Cost Rat	%Rank Cat
3 Yr (estimated)	—	—	—	—
5 Yr (estimated)	—	—	—	—
10 Yr (estimated)	—	—	—	—

Potential Capital Gain Exposure: 0% of assets

Morningstar's Take by Arijit Dutta 12-22-06

PIMCO Foreign Bond (Unhedged) is a sensible way to get currency exposure.

This fund continues to post impressive results. While it has benefited from a declining dollar, the fund's 7% return in 2006 puts it ahead of a big majority of unhedged rivals as well. The results look even stronger considering the portfolio's conservative bent: It offers one of the highest-quality portfolios in the category, with virtually no stakes in high-yield and emerging-markets bonds. That stance hasn't been helpful this year (barring a month-long correction in May and June when investors fled risky assets).

Instead of taking much risk on the credit-quality side, management seeks to get ahead through decisive bets in large, stable markets. For example, the portfolio's 30% combined stake in euro-area behemoths France and Germany is almost twice the category average. Though those markets have in general underperformed other major countries, management's preference for longer-maturity bonds

has benefited the portfolio. (Interest rates have risen faster in short-term bonds due to rate hikes by European authorities.) Management has maintained an even stronger, contrarian preference for short-term Japanese bonds, due to its faith in the yen's fundamental strength. (The portfolio's 34% current exposure to yen-denominated securities is more than four times the category average.) While that bet has yet to pay off, management says it will persist.

We'd keep in mind the added volatility that comes with unhedged portfolios. For example, measured by standard deviation, this fund is likely to be more than twice as volatile as its hedged version, PIMCO Foreign Bond (U.S. Dollar-Hedged). That said, management's quality- and valuation-conscious approach should continue to shelter investors from risk in the long run. Meanwhile, the fund should serve as a great way to diversify heavily dollar-denominated portfolios.

Address:	840 Newport Center Drive Newport Beach CA 92660 800-426-0107
Web Address:	www.allianzinvestors.com
Inception:	04-30-04
Advisor:	Allianz Global Investors Fund Mgmt LLC
Subadvisor:	Research Affiliates, LLC
NTF Plans:	Fidelity Retail-NTF, Schwab OneSource

Minimum Purchase:	$5000	Add: $100	IRA: $2500
Min Auto Inv Plan:	$0	Add: —	
Sales Fees:	No-load, 0.25%S, 2.00%R		
Management Fee:	0.25%, 0.45%A		
Actual Fees:	Mgt:0.25%	Dist:0.25%	
Expense Projections:	3Yr:$303	5Yr:$525	10Yr:$1166
Income Distrib:	Monthly		

Historical Profile

Return —
Risk —
Rating — Not Rated

Growth of $10,000
■ Investment Values of Fund
— Investment Values of LB Aggr

Performance Quartile (within Category)

1995	1996	1997	1998	1999	2000	2001	2002	2003	2004	2005	2006	History
—	—	—	—	—	—	—	—	—	11.25	9.94	10.18	NAV
—	—	—	—	—	—	—	—	—	—	-9.47	6.17	Total Return %
—	—	—	—	—	—	—	—	—	—	-11.90	1.84	+/-LB Aggr
—	—	—	—	—	—	—	—	—	—	-0.27	-0.77	+/-SB Wld Govt
—	—	—	—	—	—	—	—	—	—	2.28	3.06	Income Return %
—	—	—	—	—	—	—	—	—	—	-11.75	3.11	Capital Return %
—	—	—	—	—	—	—	—	—	—	87	36	Total Rtn % Rank Cat
—	—	—	—	—	—	—	—	—	0.09	0.25	0.30	Income $
—	—	—	—	—	—	—	—	—	0.11	0.00	0.07	Capital Gains $
—	—	—	—	—	—	—	—	—	—	—	0.95	Expense Ratio %
—	—	—	—	—	—	—	—	—	—	—	2.95	Income Ratio %
—	—	—	—	—	—	—	—	—	—	—	480	Turnover Rate %
—	—	—	—	—	—	—	—	—	—	55	140	Net Assets $mil

Rating and Risk

Time Period	Load-Adj Return %	Morningstar Rtn vs Cat	Morningstar Risk vs Cat	Morningstar Risk-Adj Rating
1 Yr	6.17			
3 Yr	—	—	—	—
5 Yr	—	—	—	—
10 Yr	—	—	—	—
Incept	3.68			

Other Measures	Standard Index LB Aggr	Best Fit Index
Alpha	—	—
Beta	—	—
R-Squared	—	—
Standard Deviation	—	
Mean	—	
Sharpe Ratio	—	

Portfolio Analysis 09-30-06

Total Fixed-Income:303	Date of Maturity	Amount $000	Value $000	% Net Assets
EuroDollar (Fut)	06-18-07	290,750	276,169	8.23
EuroDollar (Fut)	09-17-07	161,000	153,151	4.56
France (Republic Of) 4%	10-25-14	92,900	120,351	3.59
EuroDollar (Fut)	12-18-06	113,000	106,971	3.19
Federal Republic Of Germ	07-04-14	69,000	90,858	2.71
FNMA 5.5%	05-01-34	67,174	66,387	1.98
Germany (Federal Republi	01-04-28	41,700	65,735	1.96
Spain (Kingdom Of) 4.4%	01-31-15	42,000	55,863	1.66
Japan (Government Of) 2.	09-20-35	6,210,001	53,264	1.59
Germany (Federal Republi	01-04-15	39,000	49,713	1.48
FNMA 6%		45,000	45,211	1.35
Japan	03-20-11	5,150,001	44,466	1.32
EuroDollar (Fut)	09-15-08	44,250	42,122	1.25
EuroDollar (Fut)	12-15-08	44,250	42,104	1.25
EuroDollar (Fut)	03-16-09	44,250	42,091	1.25
EuroDollar (Fut)	06-15-09	44,250	42,075	1.25
Germany (Federal Republi	01-04-30	22,640	38,745	1.15
Germany (Federal Republi	01-04-14	27,340	35,940	1.07
Japan (Government Of) 1.	06-20-14	3,970,000	33,952	1.01
Japan	03-20-15	3,850,000	32,474	0.97

Current Investment Style

Duration: Short Int Long
Quality: High Med Low

1 figure provided by fund

Avg Eff Duration[1]	5.9 Yrs
Avg Eff Maturity	8.8 Yrs
Avg Credit Quality	AAA
Avg Wtd Coupon	4.41%
Avg Wtd Price	102.21% of par

Coupon Range	% of Bonds	Rel Cat
0% PIK	3.0	0.8
0% to 6%	91.1	1.1
6% to 8%	6.4	0.5
8% to 10%	2.5	0.6
More than 10%	0.0	0.0

1.00=Category Average

Credit Analysis	% bonds 09-30-06		
AAA	75	BB	2
AA	16	B	0
A	2	Below B	0
BBB	5	NR/NA	0

Sector Breakdown	% of assets
US Treasuries	—
TIPS	—
US Agency	—
Mortgage Pass-Throughs	—
Mortgage CMO	—
Mortgage ARM	—
US Corporate	—
Asset-Backed	—
Convertible	—
Municipal	—
Corporate Inflation-Protected	—
Foreign Corporate	—
Foreign Govt	—

Composition			
Cash	45.7	Bonds	51.9
Stocks	0.0	Other	2.4

Special Securities	
Restricted/Illiquid Secs	1
Exotic Mortgage-Backed	0
Emerging-Markets Secs	—
Options/Futures/Warrants	No

MORNINGSTAR® Funds 500

PIMCO High-Yield D

	Ticker	Load	NAV	Yield	SEC Yield	Total Assets	Mstar Category
	PHYDX	None	$9.89	6.7%	6.49%	$7,322 mil	High Yield Bond

Governance and Management

Stewardship Grade: B

Portfolio Manager(s)

Lead manager Ray Kennedy has been with PIMCO since 1996 and became comanager of this fund in early 2002. He worked alongside veteran manager Ben Trosky for several years and took over this offering when Trosky retired at the end of 2002.

Strategy

Unlike most high-yield funds, which concentrate on single B issues, this portfolio emphasizes slightly higher-quality BBs and has even been known to stash 30% or more in the investment-grade arena. Furthermore, it casts a wider net than most, sometimes holding small weightings in mortgage-backed securities or just about anything else that looks particularly attractive. It generally buys no bonds rated below B.

Historical Profile
Return: Average
Risk: Above Avg
Rating: ★★★ Neutral

Investment Style
Fixed Income
Income Rtn %Rank Cat

▼ Manager Change
▽ Partial Manager Change

Growth of $10,000
— Investment Values of Fund
— Investment Values of LB Aggr

Performance Quartile (within Category)

	1995	1996	1997	1998	1999	2000	2001	2002	2003	2004	2005	2006	History
NAV	—	—	—	11.31	10.68	9.71	9.36	8.52	9.77	9.97	9.72	9.89	
Total Return %	—	—	—	2.72*	2.41	-0.88	4.60	-1.22	23.21	9.01	4.21	9.00	
+/-LB Aggr	—	—	—		3.23	-12.51	-3.84	-11.47	19.11	4.67	1.78	4.67	
+/-CSFB Glb HY	—	—	—		-0.87	4.33	-1.18	-4.33	-4.72	-2.95	1.95	-2.93	
Income Return %	—	—	—		8.19	8.53	8.45	7.84	8.08	6.76	6.73	7.06	
Capital Return %	—	—	—		-5.78	-9.41	-3.85	-9.06	15.13	2.25	-2.52	1.94	
Total Rtn % Rank Cat	—	—	—		75	14	40	56	57	68	10	76	
Income $	—	—	—	0.67	0.89	0.88	0.79	0.71	0.67	0.64	0.65	0.67	
Capital Gains $	—	—	—	0.00	0.00	0.00	0.00	0.00	0.00	0.00	0.00	0.01	
Expense Ratio %	—	—	—		0.90			0.90	0.90	0.90	0.90	0.90	
Income Ratio %	—	—	—					15.06	7.86	8.20	6.85	6.83	
Turnover Rate %	—	—	—	37	39	39	53	96	129	105	62	105	
Net Assets $mil	—	—	—	4	22	24	88	189	488	427	457	425	

Performance 12-31-06

	1st Qtr	2nd Qtr	3rd Qtr	4th Qtr	Total
2002	0.02	-5.01	-4.39	8.74	-1.22
2003	6.51	8.10	1.44	5.49	23.21
2004	0.81	-1.22	5.14	4.12	9.01
2005	-1.17	3.21	1.03	1.12	4.21
2006	2.38	-0.92	3.70	3.62	9.00

Trailing	Total Return%	+/- LB Aggr	+/- CSFB Glb HY	%Rank Cat	Growth of $10,000
3 Mo	3.62	2.38	-0.83	70	10,362
6 Mo	7.45	2.36	-0.70	50	10,745
1 Yr	9.00	4.67	-2.93	76	10,900
3 Yr Avg	7.38	3.68	-1.24	49	12,381
5 Yr Avg	8.55	3.49	-2.52	52	15,071
10 Yr Avg	—	—	—	—	—
15 Yr Avg	—	—	—	—	—

Tax Analysis	Tax-Adj Rtn%	%Rank Cat	Tax-Cost Rat	%Rank Cat
3 Yr (estimated)	4.93	34	2.28	38
5 Yr (estimated)	5.85	43	2.49	41
10 Yr (estimated)	—	—	—	—

Potential Capital Gain Exposure: 0% of assets

Rating and Risk

Time Period	Load-Adj Return %	Morningstar Rtn vs Cat	Morningstar Risk vs Cat	Morningstar Risk-Adj Rating
1 Yr	9.00			
3 Yr	7.38	Avg	Avg	★★★
5 Yr	8.55	Avg	+Avg	★★★
10 Yr	—	—	—	
Incept	5.86			

Other Measures	Standard Index LB Aggr	Best Fit Index CSFB Glb HY
Alpha	3.7	-0.9
Beta	0.58	0.96
R-Squared	26	85
Standard Deviation	3.76	
Mean	7.38	
Sharpe Ratio	1.06	

Morningstar's Take by John Coumarianos 12-19-06

When people remember why they call high-yield bonds "junk" again, you'll be happy that you own PIMCO High Yield.

This fund plays it about as conservatively as a junk-bond fund can. It tends to own a lot of corporate bonds in the BB range (the highest or safest level of high-yield bonds, which are thought to have potential problems paying interest and/or principal). So this fund will often sport a slightly higher yield than a high-quality intermediate-term bond fund, and carry a bit more risk. However, it will often generate less yield than its high-yield competitors that reach down deeper into the dumpster of junk bonds.

Lately, investors have been rewarded for taking on more risk, causing this fund to lag its peers. For 2006 through mid-December, the fund is trailing 76% of its high-yield competitors, and it's middling for the three- and five-year periods as well. It is worth noting, however, that in 2000, when junk bonds faltered, the fund lost just 1%, landing in the

top quintile of its category.

Part of what's driving narrower spreads (the difference in yield between higher-quality and lower-quality bonds) and making it pay to own riskier bonds is the recent spate of mergers and takeovers. Lower-quality bondholders generally have the protection of a provision forcing an acquiring entity to pay them out at an attractive sum. The higher-quality bonds that manager Ray Kennedy typically favors sometimes lack this provision, which can be valuable in healthy economic times when merger and takeover activity may be high.

So, Kennedy's gently moved into lower-quality bonds, though it doesn't make sense to say he's compromising his process. Some of the fund's top performers have been auto bonds, which he thinks provide the asset protection he requires. Although the current climate is not the best for Kennedy's conservative style, we think long-term investors will appreciate his ability to avoid disaster.

Portfolio Analysis 09-30-06

Total Fixed-Income: 348

	Date of Maturity	Amount $000	Value $000	% Net Assets
EuroDollar (Fut)	12-17-07	1,132,500	1,078,253	10.30
EuroDollar (Fut)	03-17-08	864,250	823,068	7.86
EuroDollar (Fut)	09-15-08	397,250	378,142	3.61
EuroDollar (Fut)	12-15-08	397,250	377,983	3.61
US Treasury Note (Fut)	12-19-06	302,500	326,889	3.12
EuroDollar (Fut)	06-16-08	340,500	324,224	3.10
Ford Motor Cr 7.375%	02-01-11	144,244	138,575	1.32
Qwest Comms Intl 7.5%	02-15-14	129,549	130,521	1.25
Wynn Las Vegas 6.625%	12-01-14	100,000	97,500	0.93
Williams Cos 7.875%	09-01-21	91,028	95,579	0.91
Midwest Gen Engy 2000 8.	01-02-16	77,682	82,586	0.79
Cco Hldgs 8.75%	11-15-13	73,080	73,902	0.71
Csc Hldgs 7.625%	04-01-11	65,005	67,036	0.64
Pseg Engy Hldgs 8.5%	06-15-11	65,000	66,292	0.63
Nrg Engy 7.375%	02-01-16	66,465	66,216	0.63
Gmac 7.25%	03-02-11	56,209	56,583	0.54
Allied Waste North Amer	03-15-15	56,251	56,110	0.54
EuroDollar (Fut)	03-16-09	58,000	55,170	0.53
Allied Waste North Amer	04-15-13	52,771	54,222	0.52
Aes Ironwood 8.857%	11-30-25	48,801	54,169	0.52

Current Investment Style

Duration: Short Int Long
Quality: High Med Low

1 figure provided by fund

Avg Eff Duration[1]	4.8 Yrs
Avg Eff Maturity	7.4 Yrs
Avg Credit Quality	BB
Avg Wtd Coupon	7.94%
Avg Wtd Price	101.90% of par

Coupon Range	% of Bonds	Rel Cat
0% PIK	0.3	0.1
0% to 8%	61.2	1.2
8% to 11%	38.0	0.8
11% to 14%	0.8	0.2
More than 14%	0.0	0.0

1.00=Category Average

Credit Analysis	% bonds 09-30-06		
AAA	8	BB	39
AA	0	B	45
A	0	Below B	3
BBB	5	NR/NA	0

Sector Breakdown
% of assets

US Treasuries	0
TIPS	0
US Agency	0
Mortgage Pass-Throughs	0
Mortgage CMO	0
Mortgage ARM	0
US Corporate	54
Asset-Backed	2
Convertible	0
Municipal	0
Corporate Inflation-Protected	0
Foreign Corporate	6
Foreign Govt	0

Composition

Cash	34.9	Bonds	57.8
Stocks	0.0	Other	7.3

Special Securities

Restricted/Illiquid Secs	6
Exotic Mortgage-Backed	0
Emerging-Markets Secs	Trace
Options/Futures/Warrants	No

Address:	840 Newport Center Drive, Newport Beach CA 92660, 800-426-0107
Web Address:	www.allianzinvestors.com
Inception:	04-08-98*
Advisor:	Allianz Global Investors Fund Mgmt LLC
Subadvisor:	Research Affiliates, LLC
NTF Plans:	Fidelity Retail-NTF, Schwab OneSource

Minimum Purchase:	$5000	Add: $100	IRA: $2500
Min Auto Inv Plan:	$0	Add: —	
Sales Fees:	No-load, 0.25%S, 2.00%R		
Management Fee:	0.25%, 0.40%A		
Actual Fees:	Mgt:0.25%	Dist:0.25%	
Expense Projections:	3Yr:$287	5Yr:$498	10Yr:$1108
Income Distrib:	Monthly		

PIMCO Low Duration D

Ticker	Load	NAV	Yield	SEC Yield	Total Assets	Mstar Category
PLDDX	None	$9.91	4.2%	4.27%	$10,716 mil	Short-Term Bond

Governance and Management

Stewardship Grade: B

Portfolio Manager(s)

Bill Gross has led this fund since its 1987 inception. He and his team at PIMCO won Morningstar's 1998 and 2000 Fixed-Income Manager of the Year honors.

Strategy

This fund sticks primarily to short-term bonds, investing in a mix of corporates, mortgage-backed securities (with short durations), and Treasuries. Manager Bill Gross makes occasional adjustments to the fund's duration, but he doesn't stray far from that of the Merrill Lynch U.S. Treasury 1-3 Year Index. He will also occasionally dabble in lower-quality bonds.

Historical Profile
Return: Average
Risk: Average
Rating: ★★★ Neutral

26	18	35	71	79	88	69	

Investment Style
Fixed Income
Income Rtn %Rank Cat

▼ Manager Change
▽ Partial Manager Change

16.0
14.0 **Growth of $10,000**
12.0 — Investment Values of Fund
10.0 — Investment Values of LB Aggr

Performance Quartile (within Category)

1995	1996	1997	1998	1999	2000	2001	2002	2003	2004	2005	2006	History
—	—	—	10.17	9.84	9.90	10.07	10.27	10.24	10.20	9.99	9.91	NAV
—	—	—	5.03*	2.63	7.36	7.67	7.32	2.60	2.06	1.22	3.43	Total Return %
—	—	—		3.45	-4.27	-0.77	-2.93	-1.50	-2.28	-1.21	-0.90	+/-LB Aggr
—	—	—		0.54	-1.55	-1.36	-0.80	-0.75	0.21	-0.22	-0.79	+/-LB 1-5 YR
—	—	—		5.95	6.69	5.80	3.87	2.46	1.81	2.95	4.22	Income Return %
—	—	—		-3.32	0.67	1.87	3.45	0.14	0.25	-1.73	-0.79	Capital Return %
—	—	—		43	63	43	19	47	28	65	79	Total Rtn % Rank Cat
—	—	—	0.46	0.59	0.64	0.56	0.38	0.25	0.18	0.30	0.41	Income $
—	—	—	0.06	0.00	0.00	0.01	0.14	0.05	0.06	0.04	0.00	Capital Gains $
—	—	—	0.75	0.75	0.75	0.75	0.75	0.75	0.75	0.75	0.75	Expense Ratio %
—	—	—		—	6.11	6.23	4.59	2.98	1.67	1.77	3.25	Income Ratio %
—	—	—		309	245	82	348	569	218	247	278	68	Turnover Rate %
—	—	—	3	9	17	82	327	610	704	588	458	Net Assets $mil

Performance 12-31-06

	1st Qtr	2nd Qtr	3rd Qtr	4th Qtr	Total
2002	0.92	2.28	1.98	1.95	7.32
2003	1.27	1.28	-0.09	0.14	2.60
2004	1.08	-0.73	1.23	0.47	2.06
2005	-0.38	1.11	0.02	0.48	1.22
2006	0.08	0.31	2.27	0.74	3.43

Trailing	Total Return%	+/- LB Aggr	+/- LB 1-5 YR	%Rank Cat	Growth of $10,000
3 Mo	0.74	-0.50	-0.27	94	10,074
6 Mo	3.03	-2.06	-0.51	56	10,303
1 Yr	3.43	-0.90	-0.79	79	10,343
3 Yr Avg	2.23	-1.47	-0.26	57	10,684
5 Yr Avg	3.30	-1.76	-0.47	40	11,763
10 Yr Avg	—	—	—	—	—
15 Yr Avg	—	—	—	—	—

Tax Analysis	Tax-Adj Rtn%	%Rank Cat	Tax-Cost Rat	%Rank Cat
3 Yr (estimated)	1.10	44	1.11	45
5 Yr (estimated)	2.02	28	1.24	44
10 Yr (estimated)	—	—	—	—

Potential Capital Gain Exposure: -4% of assets

Morningstar's Take by Arijit Dutta 01-01-07

We love many--but not all--things about PIMCO Low Duration.

The fund's institutional share class has an enviable record. It has very seldom finished a calendar year in anywhere but the short-term bond category's best half over the past 10 years. Its trailing returns of five years or longer place in the category's best quartile, and volatility has been modest.

A number of traits distinguish this offering from the competition, starting with advisor PIMCO and legendary manager Bill Gross. The firm boasts a legion of talented managers and analysts, as well as an infrastructure designed to make the best use of Gross' insights. Those capabilities give Gross and this fund the flexibility to invest across a wide variety of sectors to generate extra return. For example, the fund has ventured modestly into a wide range of areas, including mortgage-backed securities, corporate bonds, and even emerging-markets debt.

Generally speaking, we would be wary of most funds with that much flexibility, as those that venture that far out often do so simply to pump up their yields. This fund pays a lot of attention to risk, however. This past year, Gross has reduced the portfolio's corporate and emerging-markets stakes, owing to rich valuations in those sectors. Overall, the current portfolio is less exposed to credit risk than most rivals. While that stance hasn't allowed the fund to shine this year, we think the caution is warranted.

While that's plenty of reason for us to recommend the fund, our enthusiasm is damped when it comes to its retail share class. Even with PIMCO's acumen, the returns of short-term bond portfolios are too low and tightly packed to overcome such high expense burdens. Indeed, returns of the fund's retail share class lag those of its institutional sibling by a considerable margin. Thus, we'd look for alternatives to the fund's more costly shares.

Address:	840 Newport Center Drive Newport Beach CA 92660 800-426-0107
Web Address:	www.allianzinvestors.com
Inception:	04-08-98*
Advisor:	Allianz Global Investors Fund Mgmt LLC
Subadvisor:	Research Affiliates, LLC
NTF Plans:	Fidelity Retail-NTF, Schwab OneSource

Minimum Purchase:	$5000	Add: $100	IRA: $2500
Min Auto Inv Plan:	$1000	Add: $50	
Sales Fees:	No-load, 0.25%S, 2.00%R		
Management Fee:	0.25%, 0.25%A		
Actual Fees:	Mgt:0.25%	Dist:0.25%	
Expense Projections:	3Yr:$239	5Yr:$417	10Yr:$930
Income Distrib:	Monthly		

Rating and Risk

Time Period	Load-Adj Return %	Morningstar Rtn vs Cat	Morningstar Risk vs Cat	Morningstar Risk-Adj Rating
1 Yr	3.43			
3 Yr	2.23	Avg	Avg	★★★
5 Yr	3.30	Avg	Avg	★★★
10 Yr	—	—	—	—
Incept	4.48			

Other Measures	Standard Index LB Aggr	Best Fit Index LB 1-5 YR
Alpha	-1.2	-0.5
Beta	0.39	0.68
R-Squared	84	86
Standard Deviation	1.39	
Mean	2.23	
Sharpe Ratio	-0.72	

Portfolio Analysis 09-30-06

Total Fixed-Income:2024	Date of Maturity	Amount $000	Value $000	% Net Assets
EuroDollar (Fut)	03-19-07	6,008,751	5,697,798	16.71
EuroDollar (Fut)	12-18-06	5,569,001	5,271,894	15.46
EuroDollar (Fut)	06-18-07	4,882,251	4,637,406	13.60
EuroDollar (Fut)	12-17-07	4,402,251	4,191,382	12.29
EuroDollar (Fut)	09-17-07	3,067,000	2,917,483	8.56
Banc Amer Fdg 2005-D CMO	05-25-35	305,888	298,291	0.87
FHLMC FRN	08-01-35	117,631	115,905	0.34
Gsr Mtg Tr 2005-Ar6 CMO	09-25-35	115,943	114,410	0.34
Bear Stearns Arm Tr 2005	10-25-35	109,663	108,201	0.32
Dg Fdg Tr Pfd 144A		10	101,256	0.30
FNMA 5.5%	02-01-35	96,357	95,144	0.28
Bear Stearns Arm Tr 2005	10-25-35	91,627	89,578	0.26
FNMA 5.5%		89,500	88,185	0.26
FHLMC FRN	06-01-35	69,905	68,449	0.20
Amer Hm Mtg 2004-3 CMO 4	10-25-34	67,700	66,433	0.19
Bear Stearns Arm Tr 2005	10-25-35	67,827	66,201	0.19
FHLMC CMO 5%	07-15-24	65,647	65,329	0.19
EuroDollar (Fut)	03-17-08	68,500	65,236	0.19
FNMA 5%		66,000	64,651	0.19
Amer Hm Mtg 2004-4 CMO 4	02-25-45	65,358	64,012	0.19

Current Investment Style

Duration: Short Int Long
Quality: High Med Low

¹figure provided by fund

Avg Eff Duration¹	2.7 Yrs
Avg Eff Maturity	—
Avg Credit Quality	AAA
Avg Wtd Coupon	4.02%
Avg Wtd Price	99.12% of par

Coupon Range	% of Bonds	Rel Cat
0% PIK	18.6	2.1
0% to 6%	95.0	1.2
6% to 8%	4.7	0.3
8% to 10%	0.3	0.1
More than 10%	0.0	0.0

1.00=Category Average

Credit Analysis	% bonds 09-30-06		
AAA	89	BB	1
AA	3	B	0
A	4	Below B	0
BBB	3	NR/NA	0

Sector Breakdown	% of assets
US Treasuries	0
TIPS	0
US Agency	0
Mortgage Pass-Throughs	7
Mortgage CMO	5
Mortgage ARM	0
US Corporate	4
Asset-Backed	2
Convertible	0
Municipal	0
Corporate Inflation-Protected	0
Foreign Corporate	0
Foreign Govt	0

Composition			
Cash	81.6	Bonds	18.0
Stocks	0.0	Other	0.4

Special Securities	
Restricted/Illiquid Secs	Trace
Exotic Mortgage-Backed	0
Emerging-Markets Secs	Trace
Options/Futures/Warrants	No

MORNINGSTAR® Funds 500

PIMCO Real Ret D

Ticker	Load	NAV	Yield	SEC Yield	Total Assets	Mstar Category
PRRDX	None	$10.65	3.1%	3.86%	$13,149 mil	Inflation-Protected Bond

Governance and Management

Stewardship Grade: B

Portfolio Manager(s)

John Brynjolfsson has managed this fund since its 1997 inception. He is a member of the PIMCO management team that won Morningstar's Fixed-Income Manager of the Year honors in 1998 and 2000.

Strategy

Manager John Brynjolfsson invests the majority of this fund's assets in TIPS, although he will occasionally venture into corporate and foreign inflation-indexed bonds. Because the principal on these bonds is adjusted to keep up with changes in the consumer price index (or some other price index), they provide a unique inflation hedge. He will often buy TIPS through forward contracts, as well, which only require a modest amount of cash to purchase and therefore permit the fund to use the remainder to invest in short-term corporates.

Performance 12-31-06

	1st Qtr	2nd Qtr	3rd Qtr	4th Qtr	Total
2002	1.28	6.11	7.58	0.80	16.54
2003	2.09	3.69	0.63	1.41	8.02
2004	5.13	-3.07	3.74	2.83	8.71
2005	-0.39	2.78	0.06	-0.27	2.18
2006	-2.17	0.47	3.26	-1.64	-0.17

Trailing	Total Return%	+/- LB AggUS	+/- LB Treas TIPS	%Rank Cat	Growth of $10,000
3 Mo	-1.64	-2.88	-0.27	87	9,836
6 Mo	1.57	-3.52	-0.65	80	10,157
1 Yr	-0.17	-4.50	-0.58	60	9,983
3 Yr Avg	3.50	-0.20	-0.35	27	11,087
5 Yr Avg	6.90	1.84	-0.29	43	13,960
10 Yr Avg	—	—	—	—	—
15 Yr Avg	—	—	—	—	—

Tax Analysis	Tax-Adj Rtn%	%Rank Cat	Tax-Cost Rat	%Rank Cat
3 Yr (estimated)	1.71	35	1.73	79
5 Yr (estimated)	4.91	25	1.86	46
10 Yr (estimated)	—	—	—	—

Potential Capital Gain Exposure: -5% of assets

Morningstar's Take by Eric Jacobson 12-12-06

PIMCO Real Return offers the possibility of taking some of the edge off the TIPS market.

Many investors prefer to have sector purity in their portfolios. If one values that above all else, this probably isn't the right fund. Skipper John Brynjolfsson isn't constrained to the limited universe of available U.S. Treasury Inflation-Protected Bonds. So, while many rivals maintain generic portfolios and deliver a fairly equivalent set of results, this one has flexibility to buy conventional bonds, non-U.S. issues, currency, and a variety of derivative tools such as swaps, options, and futures to make the portfolio look as Brynjolfsson wants it.

But while that might look like a big red warning flag in the hands of most managers, it's a level of freedom we think Brynjolfsson and PIMCO have earned. A big reason is that we don't believe the freedom has been abused. While the fund does take non-TIPS positions, they tend to be modest and with the intent of not sharply changing the

portfolio's risk profile. PIMCO tracks a plethora of characteristics and is constantly working to better analyze the underlying risks of its fund. That this fund's performance is highly correlated to the Lehman Brothers TIPS Index and that its volatility has been close in line with its peers isn't proof of the fund's risk profile but helps support the notion that it is in sync with the category.

The point of Brynjolfsson's efforts is to try to add extra value above and beyond what can be earned from the homogenous TIPS market but also to help mitigate its risks when the market appears rich or likely to underperform that of conventional bonds. It's for that reason that he may sometimes hold lots of TIPS but short the Treasury market a bit or, as he's currently doing, take on some exposure to nondollar currencies.

These efforts have met with much success, earning the fund's institutional shares a fantastic record. We're not as sanguine about the fund's pricier lettered share classes, though.

Address:	840 Newport Center Drive Newport Beach CA 92660 800-426-0107
Web Address:	www.allianzinvestors.com
Inception:	04-08-98*
Advisor:	Allianz Global Investors Fund Mgmt LLC
Subadvisor:	Research Affiliates, LLC
NTF Plans:	Fidelity Retail-NTF, Schwab OneSource

Minimum Purchase:	$5000	Add: $100	IRA: $0
Min Auto Inv Plan:	$0	Add: —	
Sales Fees:	No-load, 0.25%S, 2.00%R		
Management Fee:	0.25%, 0.65%A		
Actual Fees:	Mgt:0.25% Dist:0.25%		
Expense Projections:	3Yr:$287	5Yr:$498	10Yr:$1108
Income Distrib:	Monthly		

Historical Profile

Return Average
Risk Above Avg
Rating ★★★ Neutral

| | 23 | 23 | 19 | 57 | 38 | 39 | 67 |

Investment Style
Fixed Income
Income Rtn %Rank Cat

▼ Manager Change
∇ Partial Manager Change

Growth of $10,000
— Investment Values of Fund
— Investment Values of LB Aggr

18.0
16.0
14.0
12.0
10.0

Performance Quartile (within Category)

1995	1996	1997	1998	1999	2000	2001	2002	2003	2004	2005	2006	History
—	—	—	9.77	9.63	10.03	10.18	11.26	11.25	11.49	11.08	10.65	NAV
—	—	—	4.07*	5.29	13.02	8.24	16.54	8.02	8.71	2.18	-0.17	Total Return %
—	—	—	—	6.11	1.39	-0.20	6.29	3.92	4.37	-0.25	-4.50	+/-LB Aggr
—	—	—	—	2.89	-0.15	0.35	-0.03	-0.38	0.25	-0.66	-0.58	+/-LB US Treas TIPS
—	—	—	—	6.64	7.83	5.86	4.24	3.51	3.59	4.49	3.08	Income Return %
—	—	—	—	-1.35	5.19	2.38	12.30	4.51	5.12	-2.31	-3.25	Capital Return %
—	—	—	—	—	12	34	28	29	25	9	48 60	Total Rtn % Rank Cat
—	—	—	0.39	0.63	0.73	0.57	0.42	0.39	0.40	0.51	0.34	Income $
—	—	—	0.00	0.02	0.08	0.10	0.15	0.51	0.32	0.15	0.08	Capital Gains $
—	—	—	—	—	—	0.92	0.93	0.94	0.90	0.91	0.90 0.90	Expense Ratio %
—	—	—	—	—	6.44	7.14	3.10	4.04	3.04	4.37	Income Ratio %
—	—	—	160	967	154	253	202	237	191	308	388	Turnover Rate %
—	—	—	—	7	37	375	733	788	1,070	979	Net Assets $mil

Rating and Risk

Time Period	Load-Adj Return %	Morningstar Rtn vs Cat	Morningstar Risk vs Cat	Morningstar Risk-Adj Rating
1 Yr	-0.17			
3 Yr	3.50	Avg	+Avg	★★★
5 Yr	6.90	Avg	High	★★★
10 Yr	—	—	—	
Incept	7.44			

Other Measures	Standard Index LB Aggr	Best Fit Index LB Govt
Alpha	-0.3	0.4
Beta	1.36	1.27
R-Squared	73	74
Standard Deviation	5.13	
Mean	3.50	
Sharpe Ratio	0.07	

Portfolio Analysis 09-30-06

Total Fixed-Income:295

	Date of Maturity	Amount $000	Value $000	% Net Assets
US Treasury Note 3%	07-15-12	1,567,417	1,626,747	6.63
US Treasury Bond 3.625%	04-15-28	1,065,372	1,320,605	5.38
US Treasury Bond 2.375%	01-15-25	1,266,953	1,287,740	5.25
US Treasury Note 2%	01-15-14	1,258,519	1,234,873	5.03
US Treasury Bond 3.875%	04-15-29	923,626	1,193,714	4.87
US Treasury Note 3.625%	01-15-08	1,143,775	1,153,292	4.70
US Treasury Note 0.875%	04-15-10	1,212,858	1,149,704	4.69
US Treasury Note (Fut)	12-29-06	952,900	1,005,458	4.10
US Treasury Note (Fut)	12-19-06	879,500	950,410	3.87
US Treasury Note 4.25%	01-15-10	816,104	863,413	3.52
US Treasury Note 3.5%	01-15-11	799,164	837,312	3.41
US Treasury Note 1.875%	07-15-13	835,321	813,950	3.32
US TREASURY NOTE	07-15-15	766,670	742,592	3.03
EuroDollar (Fut)	12-17-07	657,250	625,768	2.55
US Treasury Bond 2%	01-15-26	638,145	612,221	2.50
US Treasury Note 3.875%	01-15-09	528,478	543,817	2.22
US Treasury Note 2%	07-15-14	546,473	535,758	2.18
FNMA 5.5%		462,600	455,805	1.86
US Treasury Note 4.875%	04-30-11	350,000	354,006	1.44
US Treasury Note 1.625%	01-15-15	365,729	347,986	1.42

Current Investment Style

Duration: Short Int Long
Quality: High Med Low

1 figure provided by fund

Avg Eff Duration[1]	7.0 Yrs
Avg Eff Maturity	10.5 Yrs
Avg Credit Quality	AAA
Avg Wtd Coupon	3.01%
Avg Wtd Price	104.28% of par

Coupon Range	% of Bonds	Rel Cat
0% PIK	2.5	0.5
0% to 6%	98.7	1.0
6% to 8%	1.0	1.2
8% to 10%	0.3	1.1
More than 10%	0.0	0.0

1.00=Category Average

Credit Analysis	% bonds 09-30-06		
AAA	95	BB	1
AA	0	B	1
A	1	Below B	0
BBB	2	NR/NA	0

Sector Breakdown | % of assets

US Treasuries	3
TIPS	66
US Agency	0
Mortgage Pass-Throughs	3
Mortgage CMO	1
Mortgage ARM	0
US Corporate	2
Asset-Backed	1
Convertible	0
Municipal	0
Corporate Inflation-Protected	0
Foreign Corporate	0
Foreign Govt	0

Composition

Cash	21.1	Bonds	69.9
Stocks	0.0	Other	9.0

Special Securities

Restricted/Illiquid Secs	Trace
Exotic Mortgage-Backed	0
Emerging-Markets Secs	Trace
Options/Futures/Warrants	No

PIMCO Total Ret D

	Ticker	Load	NAV	Yield	SEC Yield	Total Assets	Mstar Category
	PTTDX	None	$10.38	4.4%	4.48%	$100,110 mil	Intermediate-Term Bond

Governance and Management

Stewardship Grade: B

Portfolio Manager(s)

Bill Gross and PIMCO's extensive team of analysts and traders, who jointly received Morningstar's Fixed-Income Manager of the Year honors in 1998 and 2000, are widely acknowledged to be among the best in the business.

Strategy

Manager Bill Gross couples PIMCO's long-term macroeconomic outlook with its take on short-term cyclical factors to determine this fund's sector weightings and duration. Although Gross will focus heavily on certain sectors, he doesn't make huge interest-rate bets against the Lehman Brothers Aggregate Index. (Such plays are typically plus or minus 20% of the index's duration--a measure of interest-rate sensitivity.) However, he will occasionally invest in nonindex sectors of the market, such as high-yield, developed-markets international, and emerging-markets debt.

Historical Profile

Return	Above Avg
Risk	Above Avg
Rating	★★★★ Above Avg

Investment Style
Fixed Income
Income Rtn %Rank Cat

62	48	69	75	81	95	76

▼ Manager Change
▽ Partial Manager Change

16.0
14.0 **Growth of $10,000**
12.0 ▬ Investment Values of Fund
10.0 ▬ Investment Values of LB Aggr

Performance Quartile (within Category)

1995	1996	1997	1998	1999	2000	2001	2002	2003	2004	2005	2006	History
—	—	—	10.54	9.90	10.39	10.46	10.67	10.71	10.67	10.50	10.38	NAV
—	—	—	7.26*	-0.61	11.73	9.14	9.86	5.19	4.81	2.56	3.66	Total Return %
—	—	—	0.21	0.10	0.70	-0.39	1.09	0.47	0.13	-0.67	+/-LB Aggr
—	—	—	2.27	-0.71	0.32	-3.17	-0.78	-0.49	0.73	-0.15	+/-LB 5-10YR
—	—	—		5.60	6.54	5.54	4.35	3.11	2.09	3.39	4.43	Income Return %
—	—	—		-6.21	5.19	3.60	5.51	2.08	2.72	-0.83	-0.77	Capital Return %
—	—	—			30	14	14	18	37	22	12	67	Total Rtn % Rank Cat
—	—	—	0.46	0.57	0.63	0.56	0.44	0.33	0.22	0.36	0.46	Income $
—	—	—	0.42	0.00	0.00	0.30	0.35	0.18	0.33	0.08	0.04	Capital Gains $
—	—	—		0.75		0.75	0.75	0.75	0.75	0.75	0.75	Expense Ratio %
—	—	—				6.24	4.73	3.77	2.40	2.10	3.78	Income Ratio %
—	—	—	206	154	223	448	445	234	273	470	325	Turnover Rate %
—	—	—	14	64	174	530	1,323	1,703	2,208	3,106	3,722	Net Assets $mil

Performance 12-31-06

	1st Qtr	2nd Qtr	3rd Qtr	4th Qtr	Total
2002	0.57	3.25	3.35	2.37	9.86
2003	1.96	2.74	-0.26	0.67	5.19
2004	2.62	-2.26	3.16	1.30	4.81
2005	-0.38	3.13	-0.57	0.40	2.56
2006	-0.61	-0.37	3.80	0.84	3.66

Trailing	Total Return%	+/- LB Aggr	+/- LB 5-10YR	%Rank Cat	Growth of $10,000
3 Mo	0.84	-0.40	-0.24	89	10,084
6 Mo	4.68	-0.41	-1.00	58	10,468
1 Yr	3.66	-0.67	-0.15	67	10,366
3 Yr Avg	3.67	-0.03	0.03	31	11,142
5 Yr Avg	5.19	0.13	-0.73	21	12,879
10 Yr Avg	—	—	—	—	—
15 Yr Avg	—	—	—	—	—

Tax Analysis	Tax-Adj Rtn%	%Rank Cat	Tax-Cost Rat	%Rank Cat
3 Yr (estimated)	2.14	22	1.48	50
5 Yr (estimated)	3.37	19	1.73	59
10 Yr (estimated)	—		—	

Potential Capital Gain Exposure: -1% of assets

Rating and Risk

Time Period	Load-Adj Return %	Morningstar Rtn vs Cat	Morningstar Risk vs Cat	Morningstar Risk-Adj Rating
1 Yr	3.66			
3 Yr	3.67	+Avg	Avg	★★★★
5 Yr	5.19	+Avg	+Avg	★★★★
10 Yr	—	—	—	
Incept	6.08			

Other Measures	Standard Index LB Aggr	Best Fit Index LB Aggr
Alpha	0.0	0.0
Beta	0.97	0.97
R-Squared	97	97
Standard Deviation	3.18	
Mean	3.67	
Sharpe Ratio	0.14	

Morningstar's Take by Eric Jacobson 12-06-06

Don't be fooled; PIMCO Total Return remains an able competitor.

Having recently crossed the $100 billion mark (across share classes), this fund has become even more of a target than usual. To be sure, skipper Bill Gross has always drawn the scrutiny of pundits and rivals. But the fund's growing asset base has given those detractors new fuel for their fires. The main complaints assail the fund's inability to capitalize on smaller bond issues (corporates, in particular), and a sense that it's now more index-like.

In fact, Gross can make few waves in this fund with individual security bets. And while that is less true for most of PIMCO's "smaller" funds, this one indeed relies mostly on "macro" sector selection to drive its returns today.

That essential truth does not make this fund undesirable. Gross has evolved with the size of his business, and has proven his ability to manage huge sums well. Although his critics point to low recent weightings in corporate bonds as proof that

he is hamstrung by size (the implication being that his distaste for richly priced corporates is a fiction), we find such arguments unconvincing. Gross has supported his position with sound arguments. And though it's clearly difficult for him to move around a lot of money in corporate bonds, PIMCO is a leader in the use of derivative tools. The size of the market for credit derivatives suggests that if and when he decides to get more exposure, the fund will have meaningful ways to do so.

The suggestion that this fund has become an index tracker is also premature. The range of bond sector returns has been tight in recent years, playing against Gross' strengths. Yet he has still managed to top the Lehman Brothers Aggregate--and his category peers--by meaningful margins, without taking on much credit risk. The fund's short- and long-term returns remain stellar, and we continue to believe its institutional shares are an excellent choice for the core portion of a bond portfolio.

Address:	840 Newport Center Drive Newport Beach CA 92660 800-426-0107	
Web Address:	www.allianzinvestors.com	
Inception:	04-08-98*	
Advisor:	Allianz Global Investors Fund Mgmt LLC	
Subadvisor:	Research Affiliates, LLC	
NTF Plans:	Fidelity Retail-NTF, Schwab OneSource	

Minimum Purchase:	$5000	Add: $100	IRA: $2500
Min Auto Inv Plan:	$1000	Add: $50	
Sales Fees:	No-load, 0.25%S, 2.00%R		
Management Fee:	0.25%, 0.25%A		
Actual Fees:	Mgt:0.25%	Dist:0.25%	
Expense Projections:	3Yr:$239	5Yr:$417	10Yr:$930
Income Distrib:	Monthly		

Portfolio Analysis 09-30-06

Total Fixed-Income:11883	Date of Maturity	Amount $000	Value $000	% Net Assets
EuroDollar (Fut)	03-19-07	—	—	13.54
EuroDollar (Fut)	06-18-07	—	—	12.37
EuroDollar (Fut)	12-17-07	—	—	10.58
EuroDollar (Fut)	09-17-07	—	—	10.42
EuroDollar (Fut)	12-18-06	—	—	10.28
EuroDollar (Fut)	03-17-08	—	—	3.70
FNMA 5%		6,500,500	6,254,124	2.10
FNMA 5.5%		5,437,401	5,357,535	1.80
FNMA 5.5%	05-01-34	2,043,409	2,019,484	0.68
FNMA 5.5%	01-01-36	1,965,266	1,937,755	0.65
US Treasury Note (Fut)	12-29-06	1,438,100	1,517,420	0.51
FNMA 5.5%	11-01-34	1,370,971	1,353,710	0.45
EuroDollar (Fut)	06-16-08	1,312,000	1,249,286	0.42
FNMA 5.5%	09-01-34	1,143,893	1,129,491	0.38
US Treasury Note 4.5%	09-30-11	1,000,000	996,485	0.33
FNMA 5.5%	01-01-35	877,503	866,455	0.29
US Treasury Note (Fut)	12-19-06	763,900	825,489	0.28
EuroDollar (Fut)	09-15-08	826,750	786,983	0.26
US Treasury Bond 2.375%	01-15-25	756,561	768,973	0.26
FNMA 5.5%	02-01-35	610,901	603,210	0.20

Current Investment Style

Duration: Short Int Long
Quality: High Med Low

1 figure provided by fund

Avg Eff Duration[1]	5.5 Yrs
Avg Eff Maturity	7.0 Yrs
Avg Credit Quality	AA
Avg Wtd Coupon	4.51%
Avg Wtd Price	99.55% of par

Coupon Range	% of Bonds	Rel Cat
0% PIK	14.0	2.0
0% to 6%	92.9	1.3
6% to 8%	5.8	0.3
8% to 10%	1.1	0.2
More than 10%	0.1	0.2

1.00=Category Average

Credit Analysis	% bonds 09-30-06		
AAA	77	BB	1
AA	8	B	2
A	5	Below B	0
BBB	7	NR/NA	0

Sector Breakdown % of assets

US Treasuries	1
TIPS	0
US Agency	0
Mortgage Pass-Throughs	16
Mortgage CMO	2
Mortgage ARM	0
US Corporate	5
Asset-Backed	1
Convertible	0
Municipal	0
Corporate Inflation-Protected	0
Foreign Corporate	0
Foreign Govt	0

Composition

Cash	72.9	Bonds	25.8
Stocks	0.0	Other	1.3

Special Securities

Restricted/Illiquid Secs	Trace
Exotic Mortgage-Backed	0
Emerging-Markets Secs	Trace
Options/Futures/Warrants	No

MORNINGSTAR® Funds 500

Pioneer A

	Ticker	Load	NAV	Yield	Total Assets	Mstar Category
	PIODX	5.75%	$48.10	0.8%	$7,902 mil	Large Blend

Governance and Management

Stewardship Grade: B

Portfolio Manager(s)

John Carey is a veteran manager and has been with Pioneer since 1979. He has been running the show here since 1986. In 2001, he was joined by assistant portfolio manager Walter Hunnewell. Carey has also put up solid numbers at his other charge, Pioneer Equity-Income.

Strategy

John Carey uses a patient, growth-at-a-reasonable-price approach. He looks for blue-chip companies that have been beaten down, but have some catalyst for increased earnings. Along with healthy operating margins, Carey favors firms whose rates of return on equity surpass those of industry peers. He sticks with what he buys, too, as the fund has one of the category's lowest turnover rates.

Performance   12-31-06

	1st Qtr	2nd Qtr	3rd Qtr	4th Qtr	Total
2002	3.40	-12.24	-18.18	7.40	-20.26
2003	-5.99	14.45	2.69	12.75	24.58
2004	0.48	1.55	-0.26	9.69	11.63
2005	-1.07	0.14	4.68	2.60	6.39
2006	4.88	-0.21	5.45	5.45	16.39

Trailing	Total Return%	+/- S&P 500	+/- Russ 1000	%Rank Cat	Growth of $10,000
3 Mo	5.45	-1.25	-1.50	86	10,545
6 Mo	11.21	-1.53	-1.15	57	11,121
1 Yr	16.39	0.60	0.93	15	11,639
3 Yr Avg	11.40	0.96	0.42	22	13,825
5 Yr Avg	6.55	0.36	-0.27	31	13,733
10 Yr Avg	9.70	1.28	1.06	14	25,239
15 Yr Avg	11.24	0.60	0.44	22	49,421

Tax Analysis	Tax-Adj Rtn%	%Rank Cat	Tax-Cost Rat	%Rank Cat
3 Yr (estimated)	8.61	57	0.56	26
5 Yr (estimated)	4.82	57	0.45	29
10 Yr (estimated)	8.22	15	0.76	32

Potential Capital Gain Exposure: 43% of assets

Morningstar's Take   by Annie Sorich 12-18-06

Pioneer Fund makes for a solid core holding.

Things are looking bright at Pioneer's flagship offering. Its 17.5% gain for the year to date through December 15, 2006, is just outside the top decile among large-blend funds. Several of the fund's top holdings such as T. Rowe Price, AT&T, and BellSouth have boosted performance, as has an underweight position in the energy sector--which has started to see signs of a slowdown.

The fund's recent showing at the top of the category is somewhat unusual. True, it's more adventurous than manager John Carey's other charge, Pioneer Equity-Income, which means it has a better opportunity for more-exciting returns than its sibling. But overall steady, not spectacular, long-term returns are more likely compared with peers, considering the fund's patient, growth-at-a-reasonable-price approach. Carey keeps sector allocations within 5% of the S&P 500 Index and individual position sizes fairly small. In addition, his strategy seeks companies with steady dividend yields, which tends to provide a downside cushion. Indeed, the fund has historically been less volatile than its typical peer, as evident by its low standard deviation.

While standout performance like this year's may be rare, the fund's approach makes it an attractive long-term holding. Carey has proven his stock-picking abilities in his 20 years at the helm, which is more time than most large-blend funds have been in existence. His tenure speaks to the resilience of the strategy, which hasn't changed much since its inception in 1928.

If there's a drawback to the fund, it's that it will likely lag its peers that make more concentrated bets when the market is driven by one industry or sector. But the fund's reasonable expense ratio, which is lower than 75% of its broker-sold large-cap peers, gives it an automatic head start against the competition. We think this fund's tried and true approach makes for a fine choice at the center of a portfolio.

Address:	60 State St., 13th Floor Boston MA 02109 800-225-6292
Web Address:	www.pioneerinvestments.com
Inception:	02-10-28
Advisor:	Pioneer Investment Management, Inc.
Subadvisor:	None
NTF Plans:	DATALynx NTF, Federated Tr NTF

Minimum Purchase:	$1000	Add: $100	IRA: $250
Min Auto Inv Plan:	$0	Add: —	
Sales Fees:	5.75%L, 0.25%S		
Management Fee:	0.60%		
Actual Fees:	Mgt:0.57%	Dist:0.25%	
Expense Projections:	3Yr:$899	5Yr:$1136	10Yr:$1816
Income Distrib:	Quarterly		

Historical Profile

Return	Average
Risk	Average
Rating	★★★ Neutral

| | 99% | 99% | 100% | 100% | 99% | 99% | 100% | 100% | 98% | Investment Style Equity Stock % |

▼ Manager Change
▽ Partial Manager Change

Growth of $10,000
— Investment Values of Fund
— Investment Values of S&P 500

Performance Quartile (within Category)

1995	1996	1997	1998	1999	2000	2001	2002	2003	2004	2005	2006	History
24.36	26.89	34.95	43.33	47.60	44.26	38.87	30.76	38.00	42.06	44.21	48.10	NAV
26.64	19.70	38.47	29.09	15.54	0.12	-11.13	-20.26	24.58	11.63	6.39	16.39	Total Return %
-10.94	-3.26	5.11	0.51	-5.50	9.22	0.76	1.84	-4.10	0.75	1.48	0.60	+/-S&P 500
-11.13	-2.75	5.62	2.07	-5.37	7.91	1.32	1.39	-5.31	0.23	0.12	0.93	+/-Russ 1000
2.30	1.54	1.15	0.59	0.40	0.26	0.37	0.66	0.92	0.89	0.93	1.00	Income Return %
24.34	18.16	37.32	28.50	15.14	-0.14	-11.50	-20.92	23.66	10.74	5.46	15.39	Capital Return %
88	68	3	14	70	27	42	34	76	31	41	15	Total Rtn % Rank Cat
0.49	0.37	0.31	0.20	0.17	0.12	0.16	0.26	0.28	0.34	0.39	0.43	Income $
2.09	1.82	1.89	1.49	2.22	3.24	0.30	0.00	0.00	0.00	0.14	2.83	Capital Gains $
0.94	0.99	1.03	1.08	1.09	1.11	1.13	1.11	1.09	1.06	1.08	—	Expense Ratio %
2.02	1.42	0.93	0.53	0.40	0.31	0.44	0.76	0.86	0.90	0.88	—	Income Ratio %
31	25	17	9	10	20	6	7	6	14	13	—	Turnover Rate %
2,446	2,896	3,992	5,395	6,637	6,644	6,146	4,586	5,371	5,627	5,650	6,682	Net Assets $mil

Rating and Risk

Time Period	Load-Adj Return %	Morningstar Rtn vs Cat	Morningstar Risk vs Cat	Morningstar Risk-Adj Rating
1 Yr	9.70			
3 Yr	9.22	Avg	Avg	★★★
5 Yr	5.29	Avg	Avg	★★★
10 Yr	9.05	+Avg	-Avg	★★★★
Incept	12.42			

Other Measures	Standard Index S&P 500	Best Fit Index S&P 500
Alpha	1.0	1.0
Beta	0.98	0.98
R-Squared	94	94
Standard Deviation	6.99	
Mean	11.40	
Sharpe Ratio	1.13	

Portfolio Analysis   10-31-06

Share change since 09-06 Total Stocks:121	Sector	PE	Tot Ret%	% Assets
McGraw-Hill Companies, I	Media	28.5	33.44	2.64
Chevron Corporation	Energy	9.0	33.76	2.30
Norfolk Southern Corpora	Business	14.0	13.73	2.18
BellSouth Corporation	Telecom	—	—	1.76
Target Corporation	Consumer	19.3	4.65	1.73
Chubb Corporation	Financial	8.8	10.53	1.59
Walgreen Company	Consumer	26.6	4.36	1.59
John Wiley & Sons, Inc.	Media	20.8	-0.40	1.57
⊖ AT&T, Inc.	Telecom	18.2	51.59	1.56
PACCAR, Inc.	Ind Mtrls	11.5	46.88	1.55
ExxonMobil Corporation	Energy	11.1	39.07	1.51
Deere & Company	Ind Mtrls	14.8	42.27	1.46
Inco Ltd.	Ind Mtrls	10.3	69.87	1.46
United Technologies	Ind Mtrls	17.8	13.65	1.40
Becton, Dickinson and Co	Health	23.9	18.34	1.38
National City Corporatio	Financial	12.0	13.67	1.36
Hewlett-Packard Company	Hardware	18.9	45.21	1.35
Johnson Controls, Inc.	Ind Mtrls	16.2	19.64	1.34
PepsiCo, Inc.	Goods	21.5	7.86	1.33
State Street Corporation	Financial	22.4	23.22	1.32

Current Investment Style

Value Blnd Growth — Large Mid Small

Market Cap	%
Giant	36.8
Large	53.2
Mid	10.1
Small	0.0
Micro	0.0

Avg $mil: 35,649

Value Measures		Rel Category
Price/Earnings	15.41	1.00
Price/Book	2.88	1.13
Price/Sales	1.42	1.01
Price/Cash Flow	9.01	1.07
Dividend Yield %	1.82	1.04

Growth Measures	%	Rel Category
Long-Term Erngs	11.15	0.94
Book Value	10.34	1.15
Sales	10.86	1.12
Cash Flow	10.00	0.97
Historical Erngs	18.17	0.98

Profitability	%	Rel Category
Return on Equity	22.30	1.15
Return on Assets	11.18	1.08
Net Margin	13.90	1.04

Sector Weightings	% of Stocks	Rel S&P 500	3 Year High Low	
ⓘ Info	20.55	1.03		
Software	1.62	0.47	4	2
Hardware	9.08	0.98	13	8
Media	5.45	1.44	6	5
Telecom	4.40	1.25	5	3
Ⓖ Service	44.29	0.96		
Health	13.50	1.12	14	10
Consumer	8.36	1.09	9	6
Business	6.40	1.51	8	6
Financial	16.03	0.72	19	15
Ⓜ Mfg	35.16	1.04		
Goods	9.25	1.08	12	9
Ind Mtrls	16.68	1.40	17	14
Energy	7.90	0.81	10	7
Utilities	1.33	0.38	2	1

Composition

● Cash	1.6
● Stocks	98.4
○ Bonds	0.0
○ Other	0.0
	Foreign	7.1
	(% of Stock)	

Pioneer High Yield A

	Ticker	Load	NAV	Yield	SEC Yield	Total Assets	Mstar Category
	TAHYX	4.50%	$10.82	4.8%	4.47%	$4,737 mil	High Yield Bond

Governance and Management

Stewardship Grade: C

Portfolio Manager(s)

Margie Patel has run this fund since its inception in 1998. The fund started out at Marty Whitman's Third Avenue Management shop as Third Avenue High Yield but was sold to Pioneer in early 2000. Patel works with a team of 18 Pioneer equity analysts. She also runs Pioneer Equity Opportunity.

Strategy

This high-yield bond fund typically owns a large chunk of convertible bonds. Manager Margie Patel often favors convertibles, arguing that they provide the fund exposure to sectors of the market that typically don't issue a lot of high-yield fare. They also provide added total-return potential and added liquidity. She has trimmed the fund's convertible stake in recent months and has added a significant equity stake, but they still play a role here. In the high-yield market, Patel prefers to invest in stable companies and has largely avoided the telecom sector.

Historical Profile

Return: Below Avg
Risk: Above Avg
Rating: ★★ Below Avg

Investment Style: Fixed Income
Income Rtn %Rank Cat

▼ Manager Change
▽ Partial Manager Change

Growth of $10,000
— Investment Values of Fund
— Investment Values of LB Aggr

Performance Quartile (within Category)

	1995	1996	1997	1998	1999	2000	2001	2002	2003	2004	2005	2006	History
NAV	—	—	—	8.89	10.39	10.35	10.98	9.70	11.94	11.61	10.74	10.82	
Total Return %	—	—	—	-6.69*	27.09	12.81	16.74	-2.70	32.13	6.75	2.35	10.60	
+/-LB Aggr	—	—	—	—	27.91	1.18	8.30	-12.95	28.03	2.41	-0.08	6.27	
+/-CSFB Glb HY	—	—	—	—	23.81	18.02	10.96	-5.81	4.20	-5.21	0.09	-1.33	
Income Return %	—	—	—	—	7.88	10.49	10.52	9.34	8.14	6.44	5.36	5.18	
Capital Return %	—	—	—	—	19.21	2.32	6.22	-12.04	23.99	0.31	-3.01	5.42	
Total Rtn % Rank Cat	—	—	—	—	1	2	2	68	7	96	54	35	
Income $	—	—	—	—	0.44	0.68	1.04	1.04	0.98	0.76	0.74	0.60	0.54
Capital Gains $	—	—	—	—	0.00	0.15	0.34	0.04	0.00	0.01	0.35	0.52	0.49
Expense Ratio %	—	—	—	—	1.90	1.90	0.95	0.96	1.10	1.06	1.02	1.06	
Income Ratio %	—	—	—	—	6.22	7.31	8.96	9.54	9.13	7.30	5.63	5.30	
Turnover Rate %	—	—	—	—	38	38	57	24	29	38	44	24	
Net Assets $mil	—	—	—	—	8	9	61	572	1,505	3,614	3,642	2,511	2,151

Performance 12-31-06

	1st Qtr	2nd Qtr	3rd Qtr	4th Qtr	Total
2002	2.42	-3.77	-8.98	8.45	-2.70
2003	8.01	9.79	3.14	8.03	32.13
2004	2.76	-2.50	2.94	3.50	6.75
2005	-2.17	1.47	3.06	0.04	2.35
2006	3.31	-0.88	2.67	5.20	10.60

Trailing	Total Return%	+/- LB Aggr	+/- CSFB Glb HY	%Rank Cat	Growth of $10,000
3 Mo	5.20	3.96	0.75	5	10,520
6 Mo	8.00	2.91	-0.15	22	10,800
1 Yr	10.60	6.27	-1.33	35	11,060
3 Yr Avg	6.51	2.81	-2.11	76	12,083
5 Yr Avg	9.21	4.15	-1.86	37	15,535
10 Yr Avg	—	—	—	—	—
15 Yr Avg	—	—	—	—	—

Tax Analysis	Tax-Adj Rtn%	%Rank Cat	Tax-Cost Rat	%Rank Cat
3 Yr (estimated)	2.82	89	1.97	18
5 Yr (estimated)	5.61	51	2.40	35
10 Yr (estimated)	—	—	—	—

Potential Capital Gain Exposure: 4% of assets

Rating and Risk

Time Period	Load-Adj Return %	Morningstar Rtn vs Cat	Morningstar Risk vs Cat	Morningstar Risk-Adj Rating
1 Yr	5.62			
3 Yr	4.89	Low	High	★
5 Yr	8.21	Avg	+Avg	★★★
10 Yr	—	—	—	
Incept	9.92			

Other Measures	Standard Index LB Aggr	Best Fit Index DJ Mod
Alpha	3.0	-2.1
Beta	0.48	0.74
R-Squared	10	73
Standard Deviation	5.15	
Mean	6.51	
Sharpe Ratio	0.63	

Morningstar's Take by Lawrence Jones 12-17-06

After struggling a bit in recent years, Pioneer High Yield is back on its game.

This fund's manager, Margie Patel, likes to go her own way, and that's a good thing. When she began the fund, Patel developed an approach to high-yield investing very different from that of other category rivals. She focuses on total return, not solely on delivering outsized yield, and she runs the fund with a value-orientation, a contrarian style, and a broad set of investment options (true to its Third Avenue origin). For instance, convertible bonds have long played an important role in the process here, supplementing traditional high-yield fare. Patel also pays attention to industry valuation, attempting to position the portfolio in undervalued areas of the market. Just as important, however, has been Patel's deft skill in adapting to changes in the market.

One such change recently presented a challenge to the fund. From April 2004 to April 2005, hedge funds running convertible arbitrage strategies caused volatility and losses in that market sector, causing the fund to struggle. Patel quickly recognized the need for added flexibility in the fund's mandate, and the fund board agreed to allow her to place up to 18% of portfolio assets directly into equities. This flexibility has worked to the fund's advantage in 2006, as the portfolio's increased equity portion has performed strongly. Moreover, Patel has shown talent in running an equity fund, Pioneer Equity Opportunity, giving us confidence with the increasing role stocks play in the fund. Currently, the portfolio holds 64% of assets in high-yield bonds and roughly 17% in each other segment, convertibles and equities.

The fund's unusual makeup may make it less suitable for those seeking a traditional high-yield fund. And the fund does take its share of risk, both in terms of credit risk, and the potential volatility of an equity-heavy portfolio. That said, we've long thought Patel handled risk well, making the fund a solid option for more adventurous bond investors.

Address:	60 State Street 13th Floor Boston MA 02109 800-225-6292
Web Address:	www.pioneerinvestments.com
Inception:	02-12-98 *
Advisor:	Pioneer Investment Management, Inc.
Subadvisor:	None
NTF Plans:	DATALynx NTF, Federated Tr NTF

Minimum Purchase:	$1000	Add: $100	IRA: $250
Min Auto Inv Plan:	$1000	Add: $200	
Sales Fees:	4.50%L, 0.25%S		
Management Fee:	0.70% mx./0.30% mn.		
Actual Fees:	Mgt:0.61%	Dist:0.25%	
Expense Projections:	3Yr:$772	5Yr:$1008	10Yr:$1686
Income Distrib:	Monthly		

Portfolio Analysis 09-30-06

Total Fixed-Income:74	Date of Maturity	Amount $000	Value $000	% Net Assets
Freeport-Mcmoran Copper	01-01-19	140	175,906	3.65
Interpublic Grp Cos 7.25	08-15-11	149,820	143,827	2.98
MILLENNIUM CHEMICALS	11-15-23	70,120	138,662	2.88
Tesoro	11-01-15	137,375	132,223	2.74
Drs Tech 6.875%	11-01-13	132,588	130,931	2.72
Valeant Pharmaceuticals	12-15-11	137,000	129,123	2.68
Bowater 6.5%	06-15-13	144,490	128,235	2.66
Forest City Enterprises	06-01-15	121,745	124,180	2.58
Vertex Pharmaceuticals		3,373	113,495	2.35
Crescent Real Estate Equ	04-15-09	99,535	103,019	2.14
Interpublic Grp Cos Cv 4	03-15-23	95,523	100,419	2.08
Mueller Inds 6%	11-01-14	99,943	91,947	1.91
Allegheny Engy Sply 144A	04-15-12	79,130	86,252	1.79
Novelis 7.25%	02-15-15	79,903	75,908	1.57
Forest City Enterprises	02-01-17	78,700	73,978	1.53
Jlg Inds 8.375%	06-15-12	67,705	70,413	1.46
Roper Inds Cv 1.4813%	01-15-34	116,442	68,555	1.42
Bowater Cda Fin 7.95%	11-15-11	71,660	68,435	1.42
GEORGIA GULF	10-15-20	68,326	67,297	1.40
GEORGIA GULF	10-15-20	66,874	66,409	1.38

Current Investment Style

Duration: Short Int Long
Quality: High Med Low

1 figure provided by fund

Avg Eff Duration¹	4.7 Yrs
Avg Eff Maturity	6.3 Yrs
Avg Credit Quality	B
Avg Wtd Coupon	6.93%
Avg Wtd Price	104.53% of par

Coupon Range	% of Bonds	Rel Cat
0% PIK	0.0	0.0
0% to 8%	74.1	1.5
8% to 11%	25.9	0.6
11% to 14%	0.0	0.0
More than 14%	0.0	0.0

1.00=Category Average

Credit Analysis	% bonds 09-30-06		
AAA	0	BB	37
AA	0	B	47
A	0	Below B	3
BBB	6	NR/NA	8

Sector Breakdown | % of assets

US Treasuries	0
TIPS	0
US Agency	0
Mortgage Pass-Throughs	0
Mortgage CMO	0
Mortgage ARM	0
US Corporate	88
Asset-Backed	0
Convertible	0
Municipal	0
Corporate Inflation-Protected	0
Foreign Corporate	10
Foreign Govt	0

Composition

Cash	1.6	Bonds	64.1
Stocks	15.8	Other	18.5

Special Securities

Restricted/Illiquid Secs	9
Exotic Mortgage-Backed	0
Emerging-Markets Secs	0
Options/Futures/Warrants	No

Morningstar® Funds 500

Polaris Global Value

	Ticker	Load	NAV	Yield	Total Assets	Mstar Category
	PGVFX	None	$19.98	0.8%	$602 mil	World Stock

Governance and Management

Stewardship Grade:

Portfolio Manager(s)

Bernard R. Horn Jr., has managed this fund since its 1998 inception. He works with a small team of investment professionals at Polaris Capital Management (this fund's subadvisor), including assistant manager Sumanta Biswas. Horn is president and chief investment officer of Polaris Capital, which he founded in 1995 (though Horn had been managing accounts in a similar style to this fund since 1980). Horn also manages Quant Foreign Value.

Strategy

Management uses a quantitative model to rank 24,000 stocks around the world, with free cash flow the most crucial element. The model doesn't make macroeconomic predictions, but currency risk and other country-specific elements are factored in; companies based in a country with volatile currencies must meet a higher hurdle. Of several hundred companies that pass management's standards, which have a strong valuation component, about 75 are picked based on fundamental research, including evaluation of company executives, and are then equal-weighted. The fund does not hedge its currency exposure.

Performance 12-31-06

	1st Qtr	2nd Qtr	3rd Qtr	4th Qtr	Total
2002	17.98	-1.27	-16.40	6.61	3.82
2003	-6.27	24.42	9.92	14.72	47.06
2004	7.97	0.46	1.23	12.60	23.63
2005	0.95	-0.27	7.32	2.30	10.52
2006	9.63	-1.13	2.96	11.62	24.57

Trailing	Total Return%	+/- MSCI EAFE	+/- MSCI World	%Rank Cat	Growth of $10,000
3 Mo	11.62	1.27	3.25	10	11,162
6 Mo	14.92	0.23	1.71	17	11,492
1 Yr	24.57	-1.77	4.50	11	12,457
3 Yr Avg	19.40	-0.53	4.72	11	17,022
5 Yr Avg	21.05	6.07	11.08	1	25,991
10 Yr Avg	—	—	—	—	—
15 Yr Avg	—	—	—	—	—

Tax Analysis	Tax-Adj Rtn%	%Rank Cat	Tax-Cost Rat	%Rank Cat
3 Yr (estimated)	19.06	7	0.28	19
5 Yr (estimated)	20.71	1	0.28	23
10 Yr (estimated)	—	—	—	—

Potential Capital Gain Exposure: 23% of assets

Morningstar's Take by Gregg Wolper 12-20-06

Polaris Global Value carves its own path, and more investors might want to tag along.

As he has with all-foreign Quant Foreign Value, lead manager Bernard Horn has succeeded with this world-stock offering because he follows his own ideas wherever they lead him, rather than following the crowd or the indexes. For example, at the end of 2006's third quarter, this fund had about 13% of assets in Scandinavia, while the MSCI World Index had just 2.5% there (and most peers a similarly paltry amount). Conversely, this fund had much less than the index's weighting in the United States. Horn says there simply are better opportunities outside the U.S. and have been for some time. And besides the regional weights, many individual stocks in this portfolio don't show up in any other manager's fund to the same degree, if at all.

These choices often draw upon Horn's views on large trends. For example, in recent years, he's been convinced that global trade flows will be strong for a long time, so he's bought lesser-known stocks he thinks will benefit. Yet Horn is careful not to bet the farm on his ideas. Despite his eagerness to take advantage of those growing levels of global trade, he says he purposely balanced his tilt toward that theme with some spring 2006 purchases of a number of Japanese companies that focus on the domestic market rather than depending on global trade patterns.

This technique has worked wonders in 2006 as well as over the long term. Horn says this year his Japanese buys provided strong gains, as did a wide variety of other holdings. The fund is in the world-stock category's top quartile for the year to date through Dec. 19, 2006--and it is beating every other fund in that group for the trailing five-year period.

An excellent record and appealing strategy have attracted some attention, but not that much: This fund has less than $600 million in assets. It makes sense to take a look here.

Address:	Two Portland Square
	Portland, ME 04101
	888-263-5594
Web Address:	www.polariscapital.com
Inception:	06-01-98*
Advisor:	Polaris Capital Management Inc
Subadvisor:	None
NTF Plans:	DATALynx NTF

Minimum Purchase:	$2500	Add: $250	IRA: $2000
Min Auto Inv Plan:	$2000	Add: $250	
Sales Fees:	No-load, 1.00%R		
Management Fee:	1.00%		
Actual Fees:	Mgt:1.00%	Dist: —	
Expense Projections:	3Yr:$412	5Yr:$713	10Yr:$1568
Income Distrib:	Annually		

Historical Profile

Return High
Risk Average
Rating ★★★★ Highest

| 98% | 98% | 91% | 92% | 91% | 96% | 97% |

Investment Style
Equity
Stock %

▼ Manager Change
▽ Partial Manager Change

Growth of $10,000
— Investment Values of Fund
— Investment Values of MSCI EAFE

Values scale: 22.0 / 18.0 / 14.0 / 10.0 / 6.0

Performance Quartile (within Category)

	1995	1996	1997	1998	1999	2000	2001	2002	2003	2004	2005	2006	History
	—	—	—	8.24	8.92	7.93	8.01	8.30	12.04	14.80	16.20	19.98	NAV
	—	—	—	-15.74*	16.50	-5.82	2.21	3.82	47.06	23.63	10.52	24.57	Total Return %
	—	—	—	—	-10.53	8.37	23.63	19.76	8.47	3.38	-3.02	-1.77	+/-MSCI EAFE
	—	—	—	—	-8.45	7.37	19.01	23.71	13.95	8.91	1.03	4.50	+/-MSCI World
	—	—	—	—	3.96	0.28	1.20	0.19	0.41	0.68	1.06	0.97	Income Return %
	—	—	—	—	12.54	-6.10	1.01	3.63	46.65	22.95	9.46	23.60	Capital Return %
	—	—	—	—	85	37	2	3	15	6	60	11	Total Rtn % Rank Cat
	—	—	—	0.04	0.31	0.02	0.10	0.02	0.03	0.08	0.16	0.16	Income $
	—	—	—	0.14	0.34	0.43	0.00	0.00	0.13	0.00	0.00	0.04	Capital Gains $
	—	—	—	—	1.75	1.75	1.75	1.75	1.75	1.75	1.48	—	Expense Ratio %
	—	—	—	—	0.63	0.70	0.74	-0.18	0.52	0.73	—	—	Income Ratio %
	—	—	—	—	51	38	34	40	26	15	—	—	Turnover Rate %
	—	—	—	—	—	17	17	23	36	142	602	—	Net Assets $mil

Rating and Risk

Time Period	Load-Adj Return %	Morningstar Rtn vs Cat	Morningstar Risk vs Cat	Morningstar Risk-Adj Rating
1 Yr	24.57			
3 Yr	19.40	High	Avg	★★★★★
5 Yr	21.05	High	Avg	★★★★★
10 Yr	—	—	—	
Incept	11.04			

Other Measures	Standard Index MSCI EAFE	Best Fit Index MSCI World
Alpha	1.1	4.5
Beta	0.90	1.07
R-Squared	84	89
Standard Deviation	9.32	
Mean	19.40	
Sharpe Ratio	1.62	

Portfolio Analysis 09-30-06

Share change since 06-06 Total Stocks:82

	Sector	Country	% Assets
Ameris Bancorp	Financial	United States	1.53
⊕ KONE	Business	Finland	1.45
⊕ Continental	Ind Mtrls	Germany	1.44
UnitedHealth Group, Inc.	Health	United States	1.42
⊕ Meiji Dairies	Goods	Japan	1.42
⊕ Adesa, Inc.	Consumer	United States	1.39
⊕ SK Telecom	Telecom	Korea	1.37
⊕ YIT	Business	Finland	1.37
⊕ Toro Company	Ind Mtrls	United States	1.37
⊕ Camillo Eitzen & Co.	Business	Norway	1.37
Verizon Communications	Telecom	United States	1.37
⊕ Persimmon	Consumer	U.K.	1.36
FPL Group	Utilities	United States	1.36
⊕ International Bancshares	Financial	United States	1.35
Ford Motor Company	Goods	United States	1.34
⊕ Sovereign Bancorp, Inc.	Financial	United States	1.34
⊕ National City Corporatio	Financial	United States	1.33
Solvay	Ind Mtrls	Belgium	1.33
Bellway	Consumer	U.K.	1.33
Iino Kaiun Kaisha Ltd	Business	Japan	1.33

Current Investment Style

Value Blnd Growth — Large/Mid/Small

Market Cap	%
Giant	16.1
Large	33.5
Mid	32.6
Small	10.6
Micro	7.2

Avg $mil: 6,085

Value Measures		Rel Category
Price/Earnings	10.55	0.69
Price/Book	1.70	0.71
Price/Sales	0.78	0.60
Price/Cash Flow	5.56	0.64
Dividend Yield %	2.64	1.22

Growth Measures	%	Rel Category
Long-Term Erngs	10.12	0.80
Book Value	11.15	1.24
Sales	5.75	0.69
Cash Flow	0.37	0.04
Historical Erngs	15.27	0.82

Composition

Cash	3.0	Bonds	0.0
Stocks	97.0	Other	0.0
Foreign (% of Stock)			64.6

Sector Weightings	% of Stocks	Rel MSCI EAFE	3 Year High	Low
⚙ Info	5.46	0.46		
🖥 Software	0.00	0.00	0	0
💾 Hardware	0.00	0.00	5	0
📺 Media	0.00	0.00	0	0
📞 Telecom	5.46	0.98	6	1
🗘 Service	47.63	1.01		
❤ Health	2.75	0.39	8	3
🛒 Consumer	10.88	2.20	11	7
💼 Business	11.01	2.17	12	7
💲 Financial	22.99	0.76	26	20
🏭 Mfg	46.91	1.15		
🏠 Goods	9.85	0.75	12	9
⚙ Ind Mtrls	29.77	1.93	30	22
⚡ Energy	3.34	0.47	6	3
💡 Utilities	3.95	0.75	9	4

Regional Exposure	% Stock		
UK/W. Europe	39	N. America	37
Japan	13	Latn America	1
Asia X Japan	5	Other	5

Country Exposure	% Stock		
United States	35	Finland	7
Japan	13	France	5
U.K.	9		

Presidio

	Ticker	Load	NAV	Yield	Total Assets	Mstar Category
	PRSDX	None	$13.64	0.0%	$52 mil	Small Blend

Governance and Management

Stewardship Grade:

Portfolio Manager(s)

Kevin O'Boyle launched this offering in May 2005. Prior to that, he led Meridian Value from June 1995 through December 2004, where he built a terrific long-term record. The founder of advisor KCO Investments, O'Boyle's shop is essentially a one-man operation. In addition to fund management duties, O'Boyle handles administrative and compliance duties and is chairman of the fund's board of directors.

Strategy

Manager Kevin O'Boyle screens for companies that have suffered several quarters of disappointing earnings on the grounds that such stocks are unduly punished for their troubles. He then looks for firms operating in growing markets with strong returns on capital and solid balance sheets. O'Boyle emphasizes small caps though his strategy allows him to roam the market-cap spectrum. The portfolio is relatively compact, with 40 to 50 holdings.

Historical Profile
Return
Risk
Rating   Not Rated

Investment Style
Equity
Stock %

77%   85%

▼ Manager Change
▽ Partial Manager Change

13.5
12.8
12.1
11.4
10.7
10.0

Growth of $10,000
— Investment Values of Fund
— Investment Values of S&P 500

Performance Quartile
(within Category)

	1995	1996	1997	1998	1999	2000	2001	2002	2003	2004	2005	2006	History
	—	—	—	—	—	—	—	—	—	—	11.80	13.64	NAV
	—	—	—	—	—	—	—	—	—	—	—	15.59	Total Return %
	—	—	—	—	—	—	—	—	—	—	—	-0.20	+/-S&P 500
	—	—	—	—	—	—	—	—	—	—	—	-2.78	+/-Russ 2000
	—	—	—	—	—	—	—	—	—	—	—	0.00	Income Return %
	—	—	—	—	—	—	—	—	—	—	—	15.59	Capital Return %
	—	—	—	—	—	—	—	—	—	—	—	43	Total Rtn % Rank Cat
	—	—	—	—	—	—	—	—	—	—	0.00	0.00	Income $
	—	—	—	—	—	—	—	—	—	—	0.00	0.00	Capital Gains $
	—	—	—	—	—	—	—	—	—	—	—	1.50	Expense Ratio %
	—	—	—	—	—	—	—	—	—	—	—	-0.59	Income Ratio %
	—	—	—	—	—	—	—	—	—	—	—	29	Turnover Rate %
	—	—	—	—	—	—	—	—	—	—	—	52	Net Assets $mil

Performance 12-31-06

	1st Qtr	2nd Qtr	3rd Qtr	4th Qtr	Total
2002	—	—	—	—	—
2003	—	—	—	—	—
2004	—	—	—	—	—
2005	—	—	7.16	5.08	—*
2006	8.56	-5.15	2.30	9.73	15.59

Trailing	Total Return%	+/- S&P 500	+/- Russ 2000	%Rank Cat	Growth of $10,000
3 Mo	9.73	3.03	0.83	15	10,973
6 Mo	12.26	-0.48	2.88	7	11,226
1 Yr	15.59	-0.20	-2.78	43	11,559
3 Yr Avg	—	—	—	—	—
5 Yr Avg	—	—	—	—	—
10 Yr Avg	—	—	—	—	—
15 Yr Avg	—	—	—	—	—

Tax Analysis	Tax-Adj Rtn%	%Rank Cat	Tax-Cost Rat	%Rank Cat
3 Yr (estimated)	—	—	—	—
5 Yr (estimated)	—	—	—	—
10 Yr (estimated)	—	—	—	—

Potential Capital Gain Exposure: 12% of assets

Rating and Risk

Time Period	Load-Adj Return %	Morningstar Rtn vs Cat	Morningstar Risk vs Cat	Morningstar Risk-Adj Rating
1 Yr	15.59			
3 Yr	—	—	—	—
5 Yr	—	—	—	—
10 Yr	—	—	—	—
Incept	20.54			

Other Measures	Standard Index S&P 500	Best Fit Index
Alpha	—	—
Beta	—	—
R-Squared	—	—
Standard Deviation	—	
Mean	—	
Sharpe Ratio	—	

Morningstar's Take by Christopher Davis 12-27-06

There's more to Presidio than its recent success.

After appearing sluggish earlier in the year, this offering has shown renewed vigor. Many of manager Kevin O'Boyle's picks, including Zoll Medical Corporation and American Power Conversion, have rallied sharply, propelling the fund to a 16% return for the year to date, a percentage point ahead of the typical small-blend offering.

Can this young fund keep up this act? Ordinarily, we'd be skeptical. After all, the fund is less than two years old, and it's a lot easier to deliver good returns when there's not much in the way of assets (they stand at just $50 million). O'Boyle, however, is much more experienced than his tenure here suggests. He led Meridian Value from 1994 through 2003 with aplomb, and his success continued even as assets ballooned past the $1 billion mark. Moreover, O'Boyle also isn't doing things much differently here, either. He looks for out-of-favor companies that have suffered several quarters of earnings disappointments, just as he did at Meridian.

Of course, many successful managers have floundered when they try to strike out on their own. Often that's because they don't have same access to quality research. But at Meridian, O'Boyle did all of the research during most of his tenure. We also like that the fund's slim asset base allows O'Boyle to invest heavily in smaller names--a benefit he had before Meridian Value got too big.

What can go wrong here? Asset bloat is nowhere near a concern now, but we'd like O'Boyle to say if and at what level he'd close the fund. Also, this is a one-man show--O'Boyle handles many of the fund's administrative duties in addition to portfolio management. That's a distraction most rivals don't have to deal with. Those caveats aside, we think this offering is well worth considering.

Disclosure: Manager Kevin O'Boyle is the brother of Morningstar fund analyst Kerry O'Boyle.

Portfolio Analysis 07-31-06

Share change since 04-06 Total Stocks:53

	Sector	PE	Tot Ret%	% Assets
Playtex Products	Goods	77.9	5.27	2.76
⊕ Cardinal Health, Inc.	Health	20.8	-5.82	2.59
News Corporation, Ltd. B	Media	22.2	34.75	2.59
⊕ Reynolds & Reynolds Comp	Software	—	—	2.51
⊖ Omnicell, Inc.	Hardware	62.1	55.90	2.46
⊕ Zoll Medical Corporation	Health	74.1	131.20	2.45
⊕ UAP Holding Corporation	Ind Mtrls	24.9	27.68	2.39
⊕ Electronic Data Systems	Business	35.3	15.50	2.38
Ikon Office Solutions, I	Ind Mtrls	20.7	59.10	2.37
☼ Helen Of Troy	Goods			2.28
⊕ FTI Consulting, Inc.	Business	20.4	1.64	2.27
☼ Marsh & McLennan Compani	Financial	29.0	-1.16	2.23
⊕ Ensco International, Inc	Energy	11.0	13.12	2.16
Treehouse Foods, Inc.	Goods			2.12
Neenah Paper, Inc.	Ind Mtrls	24.0	27.74	2.12
⊕ Newmont Mining	Ind Mtrls	27.3	-14.77	2.01
⊕ American Power Conversio	Ind Mtrls	58.9	41.75	1.96
Newell Rubbermaid, Inc.	Goods	19.2	25.66	1.95
⊕ streetTRACKS Gold Shares	—			1.89
⊕ Modtech Holdings, Inc.	Business		-47.00	1.87

Current Investment Style

Value Blnd Growth (Large Mid Small)

Market Cap	%
Giant	3.1
Large	11.2
Mid	23.7
Small	26.7
Micro	35.2

Avg $mil: 1,323

Value Measures		Rel Category
Price/Earnings	20.35	1.23
Price/Book	2.29	1.09
Price/Sales	0.93	0.95
Price/Cash Flow	12.32	1.77
Dividend Yield %	0.47	0.44

Growth Measures	%	Rel Category
Long-Term Erngs	15.33	1.10
Book Value	4.58	0.61
Sales	7.73	0.88
Cash Flow	-7.51	NMF
Historical Erngs	-4.24	NMF

Profitability	%	Rel Category
Return on Equity	6.41	0.50
Return on Assets	3.56	0.50
Net Margin	4.59	0.47

Sector Weightings	% of Stocks	Rel S&P 500	3 Year High Low
☁ Info	19.56	0.98	
Software	6.65	1.93	— —
Hardware	9.85	1.07	— —
Media	3.06	0.81	— —
Telecom	0.00	0.00	— —
☞ Service	46.32	1.00	
Health	17.54	1.45	— —
Consumer	10.44	1.36	— —
Business	12.27	2.90	— —
Financial	6.07	0.27	— —
☐ Mfg	34.13	1.01	
Goods	12.31	1.44	— —
Ind Mtrls	17.21	1.44	— —
Energy	4.61	0.47	— —
Utilities	0.00	0.00	— —

Composition

● Cash	13.5
● Stocks	84.6
● Bonds	0.0
● Other	1.9
Foreign	0.0
(% of Stock)	

Address:	726 Lake Street San Francisco CA 94118 800-595-3166	Minimum Purchase:	$10000	Add: $100	IRA: $3000
		Min Auto Inv Plan:	$5000	Add: $100	
		Sales Fees:	No-load, 2.00%R		
Web Address:	www.presidiofunds.com	Management Fee:	1.00%		
Inception:	05-03-05	Actual Fees:	Mgt:1.00%	Dist: —	
Advisor:	Kco Investments, Inc.	Expense Projections:	3Yr:$474	5Yr:$818	10Yr:$1791
Subadvisor:	None	Income Distrib:	Annually		
NTF Plans:	N/A				

M⊙RNINGSTAR® Funds 500

PRIMECAP Odyssey Agg Gr ✓ Analyst Pick

	Ticker	Load	NAV	Yield	Total Assets	Mstar Category
	POAGX	None	$14.34	0.0%	$159 mil	Mid-Cap Growth

Governance and Management

Stewardship Grade: ....

Portfolio Manager(s)

The fund's four active skippers--Howard Schow, Theo Kolokotrones, Joel Fried, and Alfred Mordecai--employ an unusual team structure, with each independently managing a portion of the fund's assets. Their strong record at Vanguard Primecap and Vanguard Capital Opportunity speaks for itself. They were named Morningstar's Domestic-Stock Managers of the Year for 2003. They're backed by nine analysts, plus two other portfolio managers (Mitchell Milias and Dave Van Slooten) who don't work directly on this fund.

Strategy

This fund's strategy is very similar to the one that its manager employs at Vanguard Capital Opportunity. Here, as there, management follows a contrarian-growth approach. It looks for swiftly growing firms but likes to buy its stocks on the cheap, when they're out of favor. The fund often has outsized sector weightings because many of the managers' favorites are clustered in a few industries. Smaller stocks play a bigger role here, however, given this fund's small asset base.

Historical Profile
Return ——
Risk ——
Rating Not Rated

Investment Style: Equity, Stock %

93% 93% 85%

▼ Manager Change
▽ Partial Manager Change

Growth of $10,000
— Investment Values of Fund
— Investment Values of S&P 500

Performance Quartile (within Category)

History	1995	1996	1997	1998	1999	2000	2001	2002	2003	2004	2005	2006
NAV	—	—	—	—	—	—	—	—	—	11.08	11.96	14.34
Total Return %	—	—	—	—	—	—	—	—	—	—	7.94	21.57
+/-S&P 500	—	—	—	—	—	—	—	—	—	—	3.03	5.78
+/-Russ MG	—	—	—	—	—	—	—	—	—	—	-4.16	10.91
Income Return %	—	—	—	—	—	—	—	—	—	—	0.00	0.00
Capital Return %	—	—	—	—	—	—	—	—	—	—	7.94	21.57
Total Rtn % Rank Cat	—	—	—	—	—	—	—	—	—	—	68	1
Income $	—	—	—	—	—	—	—	—	—	0.00	0.00	0.00
Capital Gains $	—	—	—	—	—	—	—	—	—	0.00	0.00	0.20
Expense Ratio %	—	—	—	—	—	—	—	—	—	—	—	—
Income Ratio %	—	—	—	—	—	—	—	—	—	—	—	—
Turnover Rate %	—	—	—	—	—	—	—	—	—	—	—	—
Net Assets $mil	—	—	—	—	—	—	—	—	—	—	12	159

Performance 12-31-06

	1st Qtr	2nd Qtr	3rd Qtr	4th Qtr	Total
2002	—	—	—	—	—
2003	—	—	—	—	—
2004	—	—	—	—	—*
2005	-5.51	0.86	7.95	4.91	7.94
2006	9.20	-2.68	3.86	10.15	21.57

Trailing	Total Return%	+/- S&P 500	+/- Russ MG	%Rank Cat	Growth of $10,000
3 Mo	10.15	3.45	3.20	9	11,015
6 Mo	14.40	1.66	6.50	1	11,440
1 Yr	21.57	5.78	10.91	1	12,157
3 Yr Avg	—	—	—	—	—
5 Yr Avg	—	—	—	—	—
10 Yr Avg	—	—	—	—	—
15 Yr Avg	—	—	—	—	—

Tax Analysis	Tax-Adj Rtn%	%Rank Cat	Tax-Cost Rat	%Rank Cat
3 Yr (estimated)	—	—	—	—
5 Yr (estimated)	—	—	—	—
10 Yr (estimated)	—	—	—	—

Potential Capital Gain Exposure: 12% of assets

Rating and Risk

Time Period	Load-Adj Return %	Morningstar Rtn vs Cat	Morningstar Risk vs Cat	Morningstar Risk-Adj Rating
1 Yr	21.57			
3 Yr	—	—	—	—
5 Yr	—	—	—	—
10 Yr	—	—	—	—
Incept	18.89			

Other Measures	Standard Index S&P 500	Best Fit Index
Alpha	—	—
Beta	—	—
R-Squared	—	—
Standard Deviation	—	
Mean	—	
Sharpe Ratio	—	

Morningstar's Take by David Kathman 12-12-06

Primecap Odyssey Aggressive Growth has a lot of good things going for it.

After struggling a bit in 2005, its first full year of existence, this fund has had a banner year in 2006. As of December 11, it had gained 23.8% for the year to date, which put it in the top 3% of mid-cap growth funds and trounced the 18.2% return of its older and larger cousin, Vanguard Capital Opportunity. We don't expect the fund to do quite so well every year, but it's shaping up as a fine alternative to the closed Capital Opportunity.

Both funds are managed by the highly successful Primecap team using the same low-turnover, contrarian-growth strategy found in all the team's funds; however, in these funds there's a greater emphasis on smaller, faster-growing stocks. While both funds are in the mid-cap growth category, this fund's average market cap is about one quarter the size of Capital Opportunity's. That's because Capital Opportunity's $9.5 billion asset base has led it to become top-heavy with highly liquid large caps,

while this fund's $150 million in assets allows it to focus more on small- and mid-caps.

Thus, in this fund, it's easier for the managers to build up positions in small stocks they find especially promising. Both funds have overweightings in health care and tech stocks because that's where the managers are seeing the best opportunities. However, this fund's top 10 holdings include several small stocks not in Capital Opportunity's top 50, such as small-cap genomics firm Affymetrix and micro-cap software firm Stratasys.

That greater emphasis on small caps is one reason this fund has beaten Capital Opportunity in 2006, though that emphasis will also make it more volatile over time. And while this fund is open to new investors, its expense ratio is higher than Capital Opportunity's rock-bottom 0.51%. However, that ratio came down from 1.25% to 1.03% in the fund's most recent semi-annual report, and is likely to fall below 1% in the near future.

Address:	225 South Lake Avenue, Suite 400 Pasadena CA 91101-3005 800-729-2307
Web Address:	www.odysseyfunds.com
Inception:	11-01-04
Advisor:	PRIMECAP Management Co.
Subadvisor:	None
NTF Plans:	N/A

Minimum Purchase:	$2000	Add: $150	IRA: $1000
Min Auto Inv Plan:	$2000	Add: $150	
Sales Fees:	No-load, 2.00%R		
Management Fee:	0.60% mx./0.55% mn.		
Actual Fees:	Mgt:0.60%	Dist: —	
Expense Projections:	3Yr:$458	5Yr:$876	10Yr:$2041
Income Distrib:	Annually		

Portfolio Analysis 09-30-06

Share change since 06-06 Total Stocks:80	Sector	PE	Tot Ret%	% Assets
⊕ Affymetrix, Inc.	Health	72.6	-51.71	3.31
⊕ ASML Holding NV	Hardware	31.3	22.66	3.28
Sepracor, Inc.	Health	NMF	19.34	2.53
⊕ Stratasys	Software	32.4	25.59	2.41
⊕ Cymer, Inc.	Hardware	19.9	23.77	2.40
⊕ FormFactor, Inc.	Hardware	34.3	52.48	2.25
⊕ Yahoo, Inc.	Media	35.4	-34.81	2.24
⊕ Boston Scientific Corpor	Health	—	-29.85	2.23
Avocent Corporation	Hardware	34.7	24.49	2.14
⊕ Roche Holding	Health	—	—	2.03
Conceptus, Inc.	Health	—	68.70	1.97
⊕ Avid Technology, Inc.	Software	56.0	-31.96	1.93
⊕ NVIDIA Corporation	Hardware	33.4	102.46	1.91
⊕ AMR Corporation	Business	—	35.99	1.87
⊕ Possis Medical, Inc.	Health	NMF	35.18	1.84
☼ Medarex, Inc.	Health	—	6.79	1.78
⊕ Alaska Air Group, Inc.	Business	—	10.58	1.64
⊕ Abiomed, Inc.	Health	—	52.60	1.57
⊕ KLA-Tencor Corporation	Hardware	28.9	1.88	1.49
⊕ Altera Corp.	Hardware	24.8	6.21	1.47

Current Investment Style

Value Blnd Growth — Large Mid Small

Market Cap	%
Giant	2.4
Large	20.9
Mid	27.6
Small	28.7
Micro	20.4

Avg $mil: 2,639

Value Measures		Rel Category
Price/Earnings	23.73	1.16
Price/Book	2.53	0.79
Price/Sales	1.77	1.01
Price/Cash Flow	11.72	1.03
Dividend Yield %	0.21	0.33

Growth Measures	%	Rel Category
Long-Term Erngs	17.15	1.06
Book Value	7.36	0.58
Sales	5.24	0.52
Cash Flow	-3.65	NMF
Historical Erngs	2.24	0.09

Profitability	%	Rel Category
Return on Equity	4.17	0.23
Return on Assets	2.36	0.25
Net Margin	5.66	0.49

Sector Weightings	% of Stocks	Rel S&P 500	3 Year High Low
⊙ Info	45.21	2.26	
Software	14.52	4.21	22 13
Hardware	25.85	2.80	26 23
Media	3.30	0.87	4 0
Telecom	1.54	0.44	2 0
⊂ Service	41.97	0.91	
Health	25.50	2.11	27 16
Consumer	4.38	0.57	5 3
Business	8.84	2.09	13 8
Financial	3.25	0.15	3 1
Mfg	12.82	0.38	
Goods	2.56	0.30	7 2
Ind Mtrls	7.80	0.65	9 7
Energy	2.46	0.25	11 2
Utilities	0.00	0.00	0 0

Composition

	%
● Cash	15.0
● Stocks	85.0
● Bonds	0.0
○ Other	0.0
Foreign (% of Stock)	9.1

PRIMECAP Odyssey Growth

	Ticker	Load	NAV	Yield	Total Assets	Mstar Category
	POGRX	None	$13.90	0.1%	$254 mil	Large Growth

Governance and Management

Stewardship Grade:

Portfolio Manager(s)

The fund's five managers--Howard Schow, Mitchell Milias, Theo Kolokotrones, Joel Fried, and Alfred Mordecai--employ an unusual management structure. Each manages a percentage of assets independently, sharing ideas but making autonomous buy-and-sell decisions. All have considerable experience. They are backed by eight analysts.

Strategy

This fund's contrarian-growth strategy is modeled after the one that management utilizes at Vanguard Primecap and Vanguard Primecap Core. The managers look for swiftly growing firms, but they like to buy them when they're out of favor. They're particularly fond of companies with high unit growth. The fund often has outsized sector weightings because many of the managers' favorites are clustered in particular industries, such as hardware. This fund's smaller asset base allows it to feature mid-cap stocks more prominently.

Historical Profile
Return
Risk
Rating   Not Rated

Investment Style
Equity
Stock %

92% 91% 88%

▼ Manager Change
▽ Partial Manager Change

Growth of $10,000
■ Investment Values of Fund
— Investment Values of S&P 500

13.0
12.0
11.0
10.0

Performance Quartile (within Category)

History	1995	1996	1997	1998	1999	2000	2001	2002	2003	2004	2005	2006
NAV	—	—	—	—	—	—	—	—	—	10.96	12.24	13.90
Total Return %	—	—	—	—	—	—	—	—	—	—	11.75	14.85
+/-S&P 500	—	—	—	—	—	—	—	—	—	—	6.84	-0.94
+/-Russ 1000Gr	—	—	—	—	—	—	—	—	—	—	6.49	5.78
Income Return %	—	—	—	—	—	—	—	—	—	—	0.00	0.16
Capital Return %	—	—	—	—	—	—	—	—	—	—	11.75	14.69
Total Rtn % Rank Cat	—	—	—	—	—	—	—	—	—	—	14	5
Income $	—	—	—	—	—	—	—	—	—	0.00	0.00	0.02
Capital Gains $	—	—	—	—	—	—	—	—	—	0.00	0.01	0.14
Expense Ratio %	—	—	—	—	—	—	—	—	—	—	—	—
Income Ratio %	—	—	—	—	—	—	—	—	—	—	—	—
Turnover Rate %	—	—	—	—	—	—	—	—	—	—	—	—
Net Assets $mil	—	—	—	—	—	—	—	—	—	—	10	254

Performance 12-31-06

	1st Qtr	2nd Qtr	3rd Qtr	4th Qtr	Total
2002	—	—	—	—	—
2003	—	—	—	—	—
2004	—	—	—	—	—*
2005	-2.92	3.95	4.97	5.49	11.75
2006	7.43	-2.66	3.44	6.17	14.85

Trailing	Total Return%	+/- S&P 500	+/- Russ 1000Gr	%Rank Cat	Growth of $10,000
3 Mo	6.17	-0.53	0.24	31	10,617
6 Mo	9.82	-2.92	-0.28	29	10,982
1 Yr	14.85	-0.94	5.78	5	11,485
3 Yr Avg	—	—	—	—	—
5 Yr Avg	—	—	—	—	—
10 Yr Avg	—	—	—	—	—
15 Yr Avg	—	—	—	—	—

Tax Analysis	Tax-Adj Rtn%	%Rank Cat	Tax-Cost Rat	%Rank Cat
3 Yr (estimated)	—	—	—	—
5 Yr (estimated)	—	—	—	—
10 Yr (estimated)	—	—	—	—

Potential Capital Gain Exposure: 10% of assets

Morningstar's Take by David Kathman 11-08-06

Primecap Odyssey Growth is worth a look, especially now that it's getting cheaper.

This is one of three Primecap Odyssey funds launched in late 2004, all of which are managed by the well-known Vanguard Primecap team, but sold directly by Primecap Management rather than Vanguard. Of the other two, Primecap Odyssey Stock is a large-cap, growth-leaning core fund very similar to Vanguard Primecap, while Primecap Odyssey Aggressive Growth is a more aggressive small- and mid-cap offering. This fund occupies a middle ground. It's in the large-growth category like its sibling Odyssey Stock, but it holds about 50% more mid-caps and has a notably growthier profile.

The Primecap team has put together one of the best long-term records in the business and runs this fund in the same basic way as all its others. Each of the five named managers separately runs a sleeve of the portfolio, though all of them use a contrarian-growth approach. They tend to hang on to stocks for the long term, so that turnover is very

low (9% for this fund in 2005).

This fund, like the other Primecap Odyssey funds, has a much smaller asset base than the team's Vanguard funds, so the managers can more easily build up positions in stocks they like (or reduce those they don't). Thus, Eli Lilly is a top holding across all the team's large-cap funds, but this fund's top 10 also includes some smaller, more-aggressive health-care names that the managers find promising, such as Affymetrix and Sepracor.

With Vanguard Primecap closed, this fund is one of several options for new investors wanting access to that stellar management team. It's probably most similar to Vanguard Primecap Core, which is heavier in large caps but cheaper, at 0.72% of assets versus this fund's 1.25% expense ratio. However, this fund's annualized expense ratio was only 0.86% in the most recent semiannual report, a positive step for an already attractive fund.

Rating and Risk

Time Period	Load-Adj Return %	Morningstar Rtn vs Cat	Morningstar Risk vs Cat	Morningstar Risk-Adj Rating
1 Yr	14.85			
3 Yr	—	—	—	—
5 Yr	—	—	—	—
10 Yr	—	—	—	—
Incept	17.09			

Other Measures	Standard Index S&P 500	Best Fit Index
Alpha	—	—
Beta	—	—
R-Squared	—	—
Standard Deviation	—	
Mean	—	
Sharpe Ratio	—	

Portfolio Analysis 09-30-06

Share change since 06-06 Total Stocks:111	Sector	PE	Tot Ret%	% Assets
⊕ Medtronic, Inc.	Health	23.8	-6.29	3.02
⊕ Eli Lilly & Company	Health	17.3	-5.16	3.00
⊕ ASML Holding NV	Hardware	31.3	22.66	2.31
⊕ Novartis AG ADR	Health	22.2	11.29	2.28
⊕ Affymetrix, Inc.	Health	72.6	-51.71	2.02
Sepracor, Inc.	Health	NMF	19.34	2.02
⊕ Southwest Airlines, Co.	Business	23.2	-6.65	1.99
⊕ Sony Corporation ADR	Goods	43.2	5.50	1.98
⊕ Intuit	Software	20.9	14.48	1.93
⊕ Bed Bath & Beyond, Inc.	Consumer	20.1	5.39	1.88
⊕ Possis Medical, Inc.	Health	NMF	35.18	1.80
⊕ Amgen, Inc.	Health	29.1	-13.38	1.76
Roche Holding	Health			1.53
⊕ Avery Dennison Corp.	Ind Mtrls	22.0	26.06	1.52
⊕ GlaxoSmithKline PLC ADR	Health	17.6	7.95	1.48
Oracle Corporation	Software	26.7	40.38	1.46
⊕ Avid Technology, Inc.	Software	56.0	-31.96	1.43
⊕ Yahoo, Inc.	Media	35.4	-34.81	1.41
⊕ Boston Scientific Corpor	Health		-29.85	1.37
⊕ AMR Corporation	Business		35.99	1.33

Current Investment Style

Market Cap	%
Giant	30.7
Large	33.1
Mid	22.0
Small	11.7
Micro	2.5

Avg $mil: 15,108

Value Measures		Rel Category
Price/Earnings	20.45	1.06
Price/Book	2.65	0.80
Price/Sales	1.83	0.94
Price/Cash Flow	11.09	0.97
Dividend Yield %	0.67	0.65

Growth Measures	%	Rel Category
Long-Term Erngs	14.76	1.03
Book Value	13.22	1.14
Sales	10.75	0.93
Cash Flow	12.91	0.77
Historical Erngs	12.70	0.55

Profitability	%	Rel Category
Return on Equity	18.26	0.90
Return on Assets	8.89	0.81
Net Margin	12.33	0.87

Sector Weightings	% of Stocks	Rel S&P 500	3 Year High Low
⟳ Info	34.40	1.72	
Software	10.35	3.00	11 6
Hardware	19.17	2.07	21 18
Media	3.98	1.05	7 3
Telecom	0.90	0.26	1 1
⚙ Service	50.12	1.08	
Health	28.83	2.39	32 27
Consumer	7.59	0.99	8 5
Business	7.75	1.83	8 7
Financial	5.95	0.27	7 5
⊡ Mfg	15.49	0.46	
Goods	4.48	0.52	4 2
Ind Mtrls	5.68	0.48	8 6
Energy	5.33	0.54	12 5
Utilities	0.00	0.00	0 0

Composition

Composition	%
● Cash	12.2
● Stocks	87.8
● Bonds	0.0
● Other	0.0
Foreign (% of Stock)	13.7

Address:	225 South Lake Avenue, Suite 400 Pasadena CA 91101-3005 800-729-2307	Minimum Purchase:	$2000	Add: $150	IRA: $1000
		Min Auto Inv Plan:	$2000	Add: $150	
		Sales Fees:	No-load, 2.00%R		
Web Address:	www.odysseyfunds.com	Management Fee:	0.60% mx./0.55% mn.		
Inception:	11-01-04	Actual Fees:	Mgt:0.60%	Dist:—	
Advisor:	PRIMECAP Management Co.	Expense Projections:	3Yr:$455	5Yr:$866	10Yr:$2013
Subadvisor:	None	Income Distrib:	Annually		
NTF Plans:	N/A				

MORNINGSTAR® Funds 500

Putnam Fund for Gr&Inc A

	Ticker	Load	NAV	Yield	Total Assets	Mstar Category
	PGRWX	5.25%	$20.00	1.0%	$15,262 mil	Large Value

Governance and Management

Stewardship Grade: B

Portfolio Manager(s)

Joshua Brooks and Eric Harthun are this fund's primary managers. Brooks, a manager here since August 2005, was chief investment officer for value investing at Delaware Investments before joining Putnam in 2003. In addition to running this fund, Brooks is also Putnam's CIO for large-cap investing. Harthun has worked on this fund since May 2006; previously, he was comanager of Putnam Small Cap Value. The fund's third manager, David King, also runs the successful Putnam New Value and has been a manager here since 1993.

Strategy

The fund's three managers follow a plain-vanilla investing style. They look for fundamentally strong blue-chip companies that are trading below the managers' estimates of their fair values. Additionally, they pay ample attention to diversification and stick with larger-cap names.

Historical Profile

Return	Low
Risk	Average
Rating	★★ Below Avg

96% 99% 98% 96% 95% 99% 98% 98% 99%

▼ Manager Change
▽ Partial Manager Change

31.0
25.0 — **Growth of $10,000**
20.0 — Investment Values of Fund
15.0 — Investment Values of S&P 500
10.0

Investment Style
Equity
Stock %

Performance Quartile (within Category)

1995	1996	1997	1998	1999	2000	2001	2002	2003	2004	2005	2006	History
16.19	18.02	19.54	20.49	18.75	19.53	17.72	14.14	17.70	19.40	19.73	20.00	NAV
36.54	21.81	24.16	15.18	1.26	7.94	-6.37	-19.13	27.22	10.97	5.15	15.82	Total Return %
-1.04	-1.15	-9.20	-13.40	-19.78	17.04	5.52	2.97	-1.46	0.09	0.24	0.03	+/-S&P 500
-1.82	0.17	-11.02	-0.45	-6.09	0.93	-0.78	-3.61	-2.81	-5.52	-1.90	-6.43	+/-Russ 1000 Vl
3.18	2.59	2.57	1.88	1.99	1.35	1.44	1.19	1.80	1.30	1.35	1.12	Income Return %
33.36	19.22	21.59	13.30	-0.73	6.59	-7.81	-20.32	25.42	9.67	3.80	14.70	Capital Return %
18	25	80	29	66	60	67	58	56	74	55	80	Total Rtn % Rank Cat
0.40	0.42	0.46	0.37	0.41	0.25	0.28	0.21	0.25	0.23	0.26	0.22	Income $
0.72	1.24	2.38	1.60	1.64	0.42	0.30	0.00	0.00	0.00	0.40	2.58	Capital Gains $
0.89	0.92	0.86	0.84	0.79	0.81	0.82	0.86	0.90	0.92	0.89	—	Expense Ratio %
3.20	2.59	1.95	1.27	1.32	1.38	1.14	1.33	1.53	1.25	1.23	—	Income Ratio %
58	41	64	79	50	52	37	30	33	29	53	—	Turnover Rate %
8,611	12,305	17,298	20,760	21,090	20,229	19,023	14,196	14,702	12,739	11,834	12,031	Net Assets $mil

Performance 12-31-06

	1st Qtr	2nd Qtr	3rd Qtr	4th Qtr	Total
2002	2.71	-11.59	-18.60	9.40	-19.13
2003	-5.65	18.13	0.70	13.36	27.22
2004	2.42	1.16	-1.54	8.77	10.97
2005	-1.25	1.41	2.95	1.98	5.15
2006	3.88	-1.00	4.84	7.42	15.82

Trailing	Total Return%	+/- S&P 500	+/- Russ 1000 Vl	%Rank Cat	Growth of $10,000
3 Mo	7.42	0.72	-0.58	42	10,742
6 Mo	12.62	-0.12	-2.10	56	11,262
1 Yr	15.82	0.03	-6.43	80	11,582
3 Yr Avg	10.56	0.12	-4.53	79	13,514
5 Yr Avg	6.81	0.62	-4.05	78	13,901
10 Yr Avg	7.36	-1.06	-3.64	77	20,343
15 Yr Avg	10.24	-0.40	-2.79	67	43,161

Tax Analysis	Tax-Adj Rtn%	%Rank Cat	Tax-Cost Rat	%Rank Cat
3 Yr (estimated)	7.35	92	1.14	45
5 Yr (estimated)	4.72	91	0.90	48
10 Yr (estimated)	5.18	86	1.50	47

Potential Capital Gain Exposure: 21% of assets

Rating and Risk

Time Period	Load-Adj Return %	Morningstar Rtn vs Cat	Morningstar Risk vs Cat	Morningstar Risk-Adj Rating
1 Yr	9.74			
3 Yr	8.59	Low	Avg	★★
5 Yr	5.67	Low	Avg	★★
10 Yr	6.78	-Avg	Avg	★★
Incept	7.87			

Other Measures	Standard Index S&P 500	Best Fit Index S&P 500
Alpha	0.4	0.4
Beta	0.96	0.96
R-Squared	93	93
Standard Deviation	6.87	
Mean	10.56	
Sharpe Ratio	1.04	

Morningstar's Take by Reginald Laing 12-22-06

Investors should avoid Putnam Fund for Growth & Income for now.

In May 2006, two manager firings led to the appointment of Eric Harthun, who will comanage the fund alongside Josh Brooks, Putnam's deputy head of investments. (Dave King will continue to run a 15% sleeve of the overall portfolio in an identical manner to his other charge, Putnam New Value.) Harthun was a logical choice: He previously comanaged Putnam Small Cap Value, which delivered strong returns during his time there. Moreover, he has prior experience with large-value investing. Before joining Putnam, he worked with the team that manages the well-regarded Robeco Boston Partners Large Cap Value. That experience has added relevance here, as Robeco Boston Partners conducts a similar mix of fundamental and quantitative analysis to the one employed at this Putnam fund.

The fund has undergone a minor change since Harthun joined the team: The number of holdings has increased modestly, which should lower the fund's stock-specific risk. But spreading bets across more names doesn't mean this fund is less bold. Harthun and Brooks took advantage of the May 2006 market sell-off to add to holdings that were hit particularly hard. For instance, they raised their stakes in homebuilder stocks such as Lennar and Toll Brothers, both of which are now trading at discounts to what Morningstar equity analysts deem their fair values.

This contrarian approach has merit, and in general we're encouraged by recent developments at this laggard fund. However, now is definitely not the time to buy it. First, the managers still have to prove themselves before we consider endorsing the fund. Of more immediate concern is that Putnam's parent company, Marsh & McLennan, recently announced that the fund company is likely for sale. A potential change at the advisor level makes this fund's future uncertain. For these reasons, we'd avoid it for now.

Address:	One Post Office Sq Boston MA 02109 800-225-1581
Web Address:	www.putnaminvestments.com
Inception:	11-06-57
Advisor:	Putnam Investment Management Co.
Subadvisor:	None
NTF Plans:	Federated Tr NTF, Fidelity Instl-NTF

Minimum Purchase:	$500	Add: $50	IRA: $500
Min Auto Inv Plan:	$500	Add: $25	
Sales Fees:	5.25%L, 0.25%S, 1.00%R		
Management Fee:	0.65% mx./0.32% mn.		
Actual Fees:	Mgt:0.44%	Dist:0.25%	
Expense Projections:	3Yr:$794	5Yr:$992	10Yr:$1564
Income Distrib:	Quarterly		

Portfolio Analysis 09-30-06

Share change since 06-06 Total Stocks:135	Sector	PE	Tot Ret%	% Assets
⊕ Citigroup, Inc.	Financial	13.1	19.55	4.92
⊖ Bank of America Corporat	Financial	12.4	20.68	3.96
⊖ ExxonMobil Corporation	Energy	11.1	39.07	2.87
⊖ American International G	Financial	17.0	6.05	2.71
⊖ Pfizer Inc.	Health	15.2	15.22	2.28
⊕ Morgan Stanley	Financial	12.3	45.93	2.00
⊖ Berkshire Hathaway Inc.	Financial	13.2	24.89	2.00
⊖ Tyco International, Ltd.	Ind Mtrls	15.7	6.83	1.93
⊕ Capital One Financial Co	Financial	10.4	-10.97	1.89
⊖ US Bancorp	Financial	13.9	26.29	1.78
⊕ Countrywide Financial Co	Financial	9.8	26.22	1.71
⊖ Home Depot, Inc.	Consumer	13.5	1.01	1.61
⊖ Bear Stearns Companies,	Financial	12.5	42.07	1.60
⊕ Verizon Communications	Telecom	15.9	34.88	1.53
⊕ Goldman Sachs Group, Inc	Financial	12.4	57.41	1.46
⊕ Sprint Nextel Corporatio	Telecom	30.2	-10.44	1.43
⊕ 3M Company	Ind Mtrls	16.7	2.98	1.42
☼ AT&T, Inc.	Telecom	18.2	51.59	1.42
⊖ Lockheed Martin Corporat	Ind Mtrls	17.3	46.98	1.40
⊖ PG & E Corporation	Utilities	16.4	31.58	1.35

Current Investment Style

Value Blnd Growth — Large Mid Small

	Market Cap	%
	Giant	40.9
	Large	38.9
	Mid	20.2
	Small	0.0
	Micro	0.0
	Avg $mil:	35,346

Value Measures		Rel Category
Price/Earnings	12.85	0.94
Price/Book	1.94	0.87
Price/Sales	1.12	0.86
Price/Cash Flow	4.31	0.64
Dividend Yield %	2.03	0.87

Growth Measures	%	Rel Category
Long-Term Erngs	11.14	1.07
Book Value	12.42	1.57
Sales	8.25	0.92
Cash Flow	8.04	1.33
Historical Erngs	15.70	0.97

Profitability	%	Rel Category
Return on Equity	16.75	0.93
Return on Assets	10.39	1.06
Net Margin	13.00	1.00

Sector Weightings	% of Stocks	Rel S&P 500	3 Year High	Low
⊙ Info	13.38	0.67		
🖥 Software	3.02	0.88	3	0
💻 Hardware	5.87	0.64	6	4
📺 Media	0.00	0.00	3	0
📱 Telecom	4.49	1.28	4	1
⊕ Service	56.91	1.23		
🏥 Health	7.93	0.66	13	8
🛒 Consumer	9.52	1.24	10	6
📋 Business	3.07	0.73	3	2
💲 Financial	36.39	1.63	36	27
🏭 Mfg	29.70	0.88		
🔧 Goods	6.29	0.74	10	5
⚙ Ind Mtrls	15.35	1.29	20	15
🔋 Energy	5.73	0.58	12	6
💡 Utilities	2.33	0.67	5	2

Composition

● Cash	0.7	
● Stocks	99.3	
● Bonds	0.0	
● Other	0.0	
Foreign (% of Stock)	0.7	

Rainier Sm/Mid Cap

	Ticker	Load	NAV	Yield	Total Assets	Mstar Category
	RIMSX	Closed	$36.67	0.0%	$3,928 mil	Mid-Cap Growth

Governance and Management

Stewardship Grade:

Portfolio Manager(s)

Jim Margard, Peter Musser, and Mark Dawson have all managed the fund for about over 10 years. Daniel Brewer and Mark Broughton are more recent additions to the management team. All are principals in Rainier Investment Management, so we wouldn't expect to see much turnover.

Strategy

The fund's portfolio consists of stocks that have higher-than-average growth projections but that trade at average P/E ratios. Its sector weights are kept close to the Russell 2500 Index's. To make sure it can liquidate positions, management limits each to seven days of trading volume.

Historical Profile

Return High
Risk Average
Rating ★★★★ Highest

| | 97% | 100% | 98% | 98% | 98% | 100% | 100% | 100% | 100% |

Investment Style
Equity
Stock %

Growth of $10,000
— Investment Values of Fund
— Investment Values of S&P 500

50.6 / 43.6 / 32.4 / 24.0 / 17.0 / 10.0

▼ Manager Change
▽ Partial Manager Change

Performance Quartile (within Category)

1995	1996	1997	1998	1999	2000	2001	2002	2003	2004	2005	2006	History
16.94	18.78	22.45	22.19	26.11	23.92	21.93	17.54	25.65	29.04	33.15	36.67	NAV
47.48	22.56	32.23	2.97	17.67	17.67	-3.92	-20.02	46.24	17.36	17.53	14.67	Total Return %
9.90	-0.40	-1.13	-25.61	-3.37	16.12	7.97	2.08	17.56	6.48	12.62	-1.12	+/-S&P 500
13.50	5.08	9.69	-14.89	-33.62	18.77	16.23	7.39	3.53	1.88	5.43	4.01	+/-Russ MG
0.53	0.34	0.01	0.01	0.00	0.00	0.00	0.00	0.00	0.00	0.00	0.00	Income Return %
46.95	22.22	32.22	2.96	17.67	7.02	-3.92	-20.02	46.24	17.36	17.53	14.67	Capital Return %
11	21	9	85	86	33	16	22	10	22	6	12	Total Rtn % Rank Cat
0.07	0.06	0.00	0.00	0.00	0.00	0.00	0.00	0.00	0.00	0.00	0.00	Income $
1.16	1.77	2.31	0.85	0.00	3.87	1.02	0.00	0.00	1.05	0.99	1.36	Capital Gains $
1.48	1.48	1.40	1.26	1.25	1.25	1.24	1.26	1.32	1.28	1.25	1.21	Expense Ratio %
1.04	0.66	0.27	-0.06	-0.04	-0.24	-0.26	-0.42	-0.55	-0.59	-0.40	-0.38	Income Ratio %
	151	131	107	144	199	166	162	141	134	115	94	Turnover Rate %
54	125	353	542	438	445	308	167	258	539	1,545	2,735	Net Assets $mil

Performance 12-31-06

	1st Qtr	2nd Qtr	3rd Qtr	4th Qtr	Total
2002	1.41	-8.86	-17.22	4.53	-20.02
2003	-2.11	21.84	6.36	15.28	46.24
2004	4.99	1.15	-3.12	14.07	17.36
2005	-0.07	2.31	11.55	3.05	17.53
2006	13.97	-4.29	-2.88	8.24	14.67

Trailing	Total Return%	+/- S&P 500	+/- Russ MG	%Rank Cat	Growth of $10,000
3 Mo	8.24	1.54	1.29	23	10,824
6 Mo	5.13	-7.61	-2.77	60	10,513
1 Yr	14.67	-1.12	4.01	12	11,467
3 Yr Avg	16.51	6.07	3.78	5	15,816
5 Yr Avg	13.09	6.90	4.87	4	18,498
10 Yr Avg	11.79	3.37	3.17	13	30,481
15 Yr Avg	—	—	—	—	—

Tax Analysis	Tax-Adj Rtn%	%Rank Cat	Tax-Cost Rat	%Rank Cat
3 Yr (estimated)	15.76	4	0.64	33
5 Yr (estimated)	12.65	3	0.39	29
10 Yr (estimated)	10.26	13	1.37	49

Potential Capital Gain Exposure: 14% of assets

Rating and Risk

Time Period	Load-Adj Return %	Morningstar Rtn vs Cat	Morningstar Risk vs Cat	Morningstar Risk-Adj Rating
1 Yr	14.67			
3 Yr	16.51	High	High	★★★★★
5 Yr	13.09	High	+Avg	★★★★★
10 Yr	11.79	+Avg	-Avg	★★★★
Incept	14.98			

Other Measures	Standard Index S&P 500	Best Fit Index S&P Mid 400
Alpha	0.9	0.2
Beta	1.76	1.35
R-Squared	67	89
Standard Deviation	14.76	
Mean	16.51	
Sharpe Ratio	0.90	

Morningstar's Take by Andrew Gunter 12-06-06

Rainier Small/Mid Cap Equity's strong 2006 showing comes as no surprise.

This fund boasts a seasoned management team, led by Jim Margard, that also runs Rainier's two other growth-oriented funds. Margard's six-person team combines fundamental research with quantitative models as it seeks stocks with the greatest potential for positive earnings revisions. The strategy isn't groundbreaking, but the Rainier team has fine-tuned it over many years to make it powerful.

Rainier buys stocks using a growth-at-a-reasonable-price approach, but doesn't sell just because stocks appreciate quickly. Margard's team constantly reevaluates current holdings, and it will hold on to strong performers. For example, top-five stock Sotheby's Holdings has appreciated more than 65% this year, but Rainier continues to buy more of it. According to Margard, the Rainier team's expectations for Sotheby's future earnings have nearly doubled this year, even after

entering 2006 with much optimism for the company.

Still, at the portfolio level, this fund has a tempered risk/reward profile. Rainier's team will make sector bets, but only in small doses. That drives participation in surprise rallies, though moderation tends to prevent strong outperformance in them. In addition, the managers here own plenty of stocks (roughly 125) and limit position sizes to reduce any stock-specific risk. Over the long term, these measures have benefited shareholders: The fund's cautious approach posted bottom-half returns in 1998 and 1999, but in the trailing five years ended Dec. 5, 2006, it beat 97% of its mid-growth rivals.

This fund is a fine choice for exposure to small- and mid-size growth companies. It's true to its name and owns plenty of both, so investors should watch out for portfolio overlap with pure small-cap and mid-cap funds.

Portfolio Analysis 09-30-06

Share change since 06-06 Total Stocks:127

	Sector	PE	Tot Ret%	% Assets
⊕ Precision Castparts Corp	Ind Mtrls	25.4	51.40	2.42
⊕ Diamond Offshore Drillin	Energy	17.8	17.82	2.36
⊕ Joy Global, Inc.	Ind Mtrls	15.1	22.11	2.06
⊕ Noble Corporation	Energy	15.5	8.19	2.00
⊕ Arch Capital Group, Ltd.	Financial	18.2	23.49	1.92
⊖ Sotheby's Holdings, Inc.	Consumer	18.6	70.12	1.90
⊕ Northern Trust Corporati	Financial	20.9	19.11	1.67
⊕ Sunstone Hotel Investors	Financial	49.9	4.97	1.64
⊕ Lazard, Ltd.	Financial	—	—	1.62
⊕ Endo Pharmaceutical Hold	Health	17.7	-8.86	1.62
⊕ Herman Miller, Inc.	Goods	23.7	30.34	1.58
⊕ Host Hotels & Resorts, I	Financial	51.9	33.95	1.55
⊕ Wesco International, Inc	Ind Mtrls	17.8	37.63	1.45
⊕ Assurant, Inc.	Financial	12.2	28.01	1.44
⊕ Alliance Data Systems Co	Business	29.1	75.48	1.42
⊕ RTI International Metals	Ind Mtrls	27.8	106.11	1.41
⊕ McDermott International	Energy	23.4	71.02	1.35
⊕ Thomas & Betts Corporati	Hardware	19.1	12.68	1.31
⊕ Cytyc Corporation	Health	27.2	0.25	1.31
⊕ PPL Corporation	Utilities	15.2	26.06	1.29

Current Investment Style

Value Blnd Growth — Large Mid Small

Market Cap	%
Giant	1.3
Large	9.9
Mid	49.9
Small	34.3
Micro	4.7
Avg $mil: 2,918	

Value Measures		Rel Category
Price/Earnings	18.14	0.88
Price/Book	3.07	0.96
Price/Sales	1.72	0.98
Price/Cash Flow	9.25	0.81
Dividend Yield %	0.85	1.35

Growth Measures	%	Rel Category
Long-Term Erngs	17.30	1.06
Book Value	12.56	0.99
Sales	15.65	1.57
Cash Flow	24.85	1.35
Historical Erngs	25.70	1.03

Profitability	%	Rel Category
Return on Equity	16.41	0.91
Return on Assets	8.75	0.93
Net Margin	11.75	1.01

Sector Weightings	% of Stocks	Rel S&P 500	3 Year High	Low
↻ Info	17.23	0.86		
🖥 Software	4.76	1.38	10	4
🖥 Hardware	10.80	1.17	13	7
🎙 Media	0.81	0.21	2	0
📶 Telecom	0.86	0.25	5	1
☁ Service	50.27	1.09		
🩺 Health	13.84	1.15	16	9
🛒 Consumer	6.88	0.90	11	4
🏢 Business	9.37	2.22	14	9
💲 Financial	20.18	0.91	20	15
⛏ Mfg	32.50	0.96		
🔩 Goods	7.72	0.90	8	3
⚙ Ind Mtrls	11.24	0.94	17	11
🔋 Energy	11.48	1.17	13	6
💡 Utilities	2.06	0.59	3	0

Composition

● Cash	0.0
● Stocks	100.0
● Bonds	0.0
● Other	0.0
Foreign (% of Stock)	5.0

Address:	601 Union Street Suite 2801 Seattle WA 98101 800-248-6314	
Web Address:	www.rainierfunds.com	
Inception:	05-10-94	
Advisor:	Rainier Investment Management, Inc.	
Subadvisor:	None	
NTF Plans:	Fidelity Retail-NTF, Schwab OneSource	

Minimum Purchase:	Closed	Add: —	IRA: —
Min Auto Inv Plan:	Closed	Add: —	
Sales Fees:	No-load, 0.25%S		
Management Fee:	0.85%, 0.10%A		
Actual Fees:	Mgt:0.85%	Dist:0.25%	
Expense Projections:	3Yr:$384	5Yr:$665	10Yr:$1466
Income Distrib:	Annually		

Mᴏʀɴɪɴɢsᴛᴀʀ® Funds 500

Robeco BostPtn SmCpII Inv

Ticker BPSCX	**Load** Closed	**NAV** $21.40
Yield 0.1%	**Total Assets** $344 mil	**Mstar Category** Small Value

Governance and Management

Stewardship Grade: C

Portfolio Manager(s)

David Dabora has run this fund since its mid-1998 inception. He has four small-cap analysts and more than a dozen other analysts working with him. Dabora has a six-figure investment in this fund and also invests in the portfolio's individual holdings. Assistant portfolio managers George Gumpert and Christopher Hart replaced Harry Rosenbluth at year-end 2005. They do not have authority to buy and sell stocks in the portfolio.

Strategy

Lead manager David Dabora focuses on fundamentally sound firms that are trading at discounts to their intrinsic values and that have catalysts for improvement, such as a new CEO or restructuring plan. He's quite risk-conscious, so he invests in more than 100 issues, keeps individual holdings small, and invests across the industry spectrum. The fund's cheapskate tendencies do sometimes result in sector concentration, though.

Historical Profile
Return Average
Risk Above Avg
Rating ★★★ Neutral

Investment Style
Equity
Stock %

95% | 97% | 98% | 97% | 100% | 100% | 97% | 96%

▼ Manager Change
▽ Partial Manager Change

Growth of $10,000
— Investment Values of Fund
— Investment Values of S&P 500

Performance Quartile (within Category)

	1995	1996	1997	1998	1999	2000	2001	2002	2003	2004	2005	2006	History
	—	—	—	8.16	8.67	12.21	17.79	14.95	22.65	23.31	21.73	21.40	NAV
	—	—	—	-18.40*	6.25	44.41	47.49	-15.94	52.90	16.47	7.54	15.66	Total Return %
	—	—	—	—	-14.79	53.51	59.38	6.16	24.22	5.59	2.63	-0.13	+/-S&P 500
	—	—	—	—	7.74	21.58	33.47	-4.51	6.87	-5.78	2.83	-7.82	+/-Russ 2000 VL
	—	—	—	—	0.00	0.00	0.00	0.00	0.00	0.00	0.03	0.08	Income Return %
	—	—	—	—	6.25	44.41	47.49	-15.94	52.90	16.47	7.51	15.58	Capital Return %
	—	—	—	—	37	1	1	86	14	90	39	58	Total Rtn % Rank Cat
	—	—	—	0.00	0.00	0.00	0.00	0.00	0.00	0.00	0.01	0.02	Income $
	—	—	—	0.00	0.00	0.00	0.29	0.21	0.00	0.20	3.02	3.35	Capital Gains $
	—	—	—	—	1.80	1.77	1.80	1.79	1.80	1.74	1.78	1.77	Expense Ratio %
	—	—	—	—	-0.42	-0.40	-0.54	-1.00	-0.77	-0.77	-0.64	-0.58	Income Ratio %
	—	—	—	—	87	162	36	119	73	47	38	34	Turnover Rate %
	—	—	—	—	1	382	205	316	346	276	229		Net Assets $mil

Performance 12-31-06

	1st Qtr	2nd Qtr	3rd Qtr	4th Qtr	Total
2002	6.46	-2.59	-21.19	2.85	-15.94
2003	-5.82	29.19	8.91	15.39	52.90
2004	8.57	-1.22	-4.61	13.86	16.47
2005	-3.30	4.44	4.25	2.15	7.54
2006	7.92	-4.48	1.43	10.62	15.66

Trailing	Total Return%	+/- S&P 500	+/- Russ 2000 VL	%Rank Cat	Growth of $10,000
3 Mo	10.62	3.92	1.59	10	11,062
6 Mo	12.20	-0.54	0.39	11	11,220
1 Yr	15.66	-0.13	-7.82	58	11,566
3 Yr Avg	13.15	2.71	-3.33	69	14,487
5 Yr Avg	13.24	7.05	-2.13	56	18,621
10 Yr Avg	—	—	—		
15 Yr Avg	—	—	—		

Tax Analysis	Tax-Adj Rtn%	%Rank Cat	Tax-Cost Rat	%Rank Cat
3 Yr (estimated)	10.47	74	2.37	73
5 Yr (estimated)	11.57	60	1.47	59
10 Yr (estimated)	—		—	

Potential Capital Gain Exposure: 23% of assets

Morningstar's Take by Todd Trubey 12-15-06

Robeco Boston Partners Small Cap Value Fund's investors should focus more on solid fundamentals than poor trailing returns.

Those who have purchased shares of this closed fund should realize that very little has changed since they bought in. David Dabora has run the fund since its mid-1998 inception. He still seeks out cheap small-cap firms with high-quality businesses that are on the upswing. The only key change is that the fund's portfolio has grown from about 100 holdings to nearly 200 as assets have grown off a tiny base. Even that's true-to-form, as Dabora likes to distribute assets fairly evenly across holdings.

The fund probably looks different to investors, though, as super early returns have soured. From its June 30, 1998, inception through the end of 2003, its 17% annual gain topped all but three small-value rivals. From Jan. 1, 2004, through Dec. 14, 2006, though, it trails over 70% of peers. The most obvious cause for the slump is that Dabora's emphasis on sustainability has caused him to

largely avoid energy stocks, which ran red hot from 2004 through mid-2006. Less obviously, the current rally has been tough on many valuation-conscious managers who prefer robust businesses.

Investors have been selling the fund, perhaps with bad reasoning and timing. The fund has, as of its Sept. 30, 2006, portfolio, an attractive profile. Its return on equity and return on assets are higher than the Russell 2000 and Russell 2000 Value indexes. And yet the fund's aggregate price/book and price/earnings ratios are lower than the bogies'. That means that the portfolio generates better business results than most small caps, and yet it's cheaper. And for those who insist on measuring a fund via returns, we'd point to this: As quality fare has come back into favor, the fund's 10.8% gain from Sept. 14, 2006, through Dec. 14 tops 80% of rivals.

We continue to wish that the fund were cheaper, but for current investors, we think the best idea here is to stay put.

Address:	400 Bellevue Pkwy Wilmington DE 19809 888-261-4073	Minimum Purchase:	Closed Add: — IRA: —
		Min Auto Inv Plan:	Closed Add: —
		Sales Fees:	No-load, 0.25%S, 1.00%R
Web Address:	www.robecoinvest.com	Management Fee:	1.25%
Inception:	06-30-98*	Actual Fees:	Mgt:1.25% Dist:0.25%
Advisor:	Boston Partners Asset Management LLC	Expense Projections:	3Yr:$563 5Yr:$970 10Yr:$2105
Subadvisor:	None	Income Distrib:	Annually
NTF Plans:	Fidelity Retail-NTF, Schwab OneSource		

Rating and Risk

Time Period	Load-Adj Return %	Morningstar Rtn vs Cat	Morningstar Risk vs Cat	Morningstar Risk-Adj Rating
1 Yr	15.66			
3 Yr	13.15	Avg	Avg	★★★
5 Yr	13.24	Avg	+Avg	★★★
10 Yr	—	—	—	
Incept	15.63			

Other Measures	Standard Index S&P 500	Best Fit Index DJ Wilshire 4500
Alpha	-0.1	-1.2
Beta	1.42	0.97
R-Squared	71	89
Standard Deviation	11.56	
Mean	13.15	
Sharpe Ratio	0.85	

Portfolio Analysis 09-30-06

Share change since 06-06 Total Stocks:185

		Sector	PE	Tot Ret%	% Assets
⊖	Platinum Underwriters Ho	Financial	21.1	0.68	2.02
⊖	Assured Guaranty, Ltd.	Financial	12.9	5.35	1.73
⊖	IPC Holdings Limited	Financial	10.3	17.68	1.56
⊖	Sealy Corporation	Consumer			1.46
⊕	UAP Holding Corporation	Ind Mtrls	24.9	27.68	1.46
⊖	Oxford Industries, Inc.	Goods	17.0	-8.01	1.36
⊕	Silgan Holdings, Inc.	Goods	17.5	23.12	1.32
⊖	Trammell Crow Company	Financial			1.25
⊖	Technitrol, Inc.	Ind Mtrls	19.2	41.82	1.22
⊖	Kindred Healthcare, Inc.	Health	14.4	-1.98	1.19
⊖	Watson Wyatt Worldwide,	Business	19.9	63.12	1.13
⊖	Winnebago Industries	Ind Mtrls	23.1	0.10	1.10
⊖	Acuity Brands, Inc.	Ind Mtrls	22.2	66.05	1.10
⊖	RBC Bearings, Inc.	Ind Mtrls		—	1.08
⊖	Gevity HR, Inc.	Business	18.3	-6.59	1.07
⊖	Max Re Capital, Ltd.	Financial	15.4	-3.43	1.03
⊖	Scholastic Corporation	Media	34.5	25.71	1.02
⊖	Insight Enterprises, Inc	Business	16.7	-3.77	1.00
⊖	Navigators Group	Financial	11.3	10.48	0.98
⊖	Tempur-Pedic Internation	Consumer	16.8	77.91	0.98

Current Investment Style

Value Blnd Growth — Large Mid Small

Market Cap	%
Giant	0.0
Large	0.0
Mid	10.2
Small	68.3
Micro	21.4
Avg $mil: 852	

Value Measures		Rel Category
Price/Earnings	15.00	0.98
Price/Book	1.55	0.87
Price/Sales	0.66	0.82
Price/Cash Flow	5.12	0.84
Dividend Yield %	1.88	1.19

Growth Measures	%	Rel Category
Long-Term Erngs	13.00	1.04
Book Value	7.87	1.45
Sales	9.78	1.32
Cash Flow	16.38	2.00
Historical Erngs	6.48	0.57

Profitability	%	Rel Category
Return on Equity	11.18	1.04
Return on Assets	4.76	0.78
Net Margin	7.84	0.87

Sector Weightings	% of Stocks	Rel S&P 500	3 Year High	Low
↗ Info	6.84	0.34		
🖥 Software	0.24	0.07	1	0
💻 Hardware	3.24	0.35	3	1
📶 Media	2.33	0.61	3	1
☎ Telecom	1.03	0.29	3	1
🛎 Service	61.10	1.32		
🏥 Health	8.51	0.71	13	8
🛒 Consumer	11.02	1.44	12	9
💼 Business	16.13	3.81	20	16
💲 Financial	25.44	1.14	33	25
🏭 Mfg	32.07	0.95		
🔧 Goods	10.28	1.20	10	7
⚙ Ind Mtrls	17.85	1.49	18	8
💡 Energy	3.94	0.40	5	2
💡 Utilities	0.00	0.00	2	0

Composition

●	Cash	4.4
●	Stocks	95.6
●	Bonds	0.0
○	Other	0.0
	Foreign	3.0
	(% of Stock)	

Robeco WPG Core Bond

	Ticker	Load	NAV	Yield	SEC Yield	Total Assets	Mstar Category
	WPGCX	None	$10.53	4.1%	—	$170 mil	Intermediate-Term Bond

Governance and Management

Stewardship Grade: B

Portfolio Manager(s)

Dan Vandivort took over this fund early in 1995 and was joined by comanager Sid Bakst in 1998. A team of sector specialists conducts its own trading, and three credit analysts round out the team. Advisor Weiss, Peck & Greer has divested some businesses in recent months, which has led to some changes to its investment team during the past few months. While such changes bear watching, they do not directly impact this fund.

Strategy

New name, same game. This fund added the "Robeco" part of its moniker in the first half of 2005. Lead manager Dan Vandivort doesn't make interest-rate bets and doesn't take on much credit risk. He keeps the portfolio's duration--a measure of interest-rate sensitivity--within 5% of that of the Lehman Brothers Aggregate Index. The fund rotates among the Treasury, mortgage, agency, and corporate sectors of the market and also concentrates on individual security selection and yield-curve positioning.

Performance 12-31-06

	1st Qtr	2nd Qtr	3rd Qtr	4th Qtr	Total
2002	-0.30	3.88	4.75	2.17	10.85
2003	1.76	2.83	-0.10	0.48	5.04
2004	2.72	-2.65	3.27	1.06	4.38
2005	-0.38	2.65	-0.59	0.45	2.11
2006	-0.69	-0.37	3.55	1.04	3.12

Trailing	Total Return%	+/- LB Aggr	+/- LB 5-10YR	%Rank Cat	Growth of $10,000
3 Mo	1.04	-0.20	-0.04	68	10,104
6 Mo	4.65	-0.44	-1.03	60	10,465
1 Yr	3.12	-1.21	-0.69	88	10,312
3 Yr Avg	3.20	-0.50	-0.44	56	10,991
5 Yr Avg	5.06	0.00	-0.86	26	12,799
10 Yr Avg	6.21	-0.03	-0.47	14	18,266
15 Yr Avg	5.70	-0.80	-1.29	75	22,968

Tax Analysis	Tax-Adj Rtn%	%Rank Cat	Tax-Cost Rat	%Rank Cat
3 Yr (estimated)	1.92	34	1.24	33
5 Yr (estimated)	3.75	9	1.25	22
10 Yr (estimated)	4.31	4	1.79	25

Potential Capital Gain Exposure: -4% of assets

Morningstar's Take by Paul Herbert 11-26-06

Robeco WPG Core Bond isn't having its finest moment, but we're sticking with it.

For the first time in years, this fund has had a tough time keeping up with the pack in 2006. Its trademark caution has stood in its way--the fund does not own lower-quality or non-U.S. bonds, which have typically fared well, for instance. Perhaps more notable is that a couple of tactical moves have worked against it as well. Becoming very bearish on corporate bonds for a portion of the year hurt, as these issues held up better than average, despite their richer valuations and higher event risk. (We suggested that this tactic could nick the fund in our last Analyst Report.) And a foray into TIPs during the third quarter backfired, as inflation concerns have been relatively subdued.

Although they still remain concerned about inflation, the managers are changing their stance on corporate bonds. While they had been expecting companies' bondholder-unfriendly behavior to broadly hurt the sector, the negative effects of these activities have been confined to individual firms. The managers have therefore waded back into the corporate pond, targeting issuers and areas with less event risk, such as banks and financials. They've also added to commercial mortgage- and asset-backed securities, which have competitive yields and less risk.

The bad execution is irksome, but we're willing to cut the managers some slack. First, although the initial move to drastically underweight corporate bonds didn't work out, management's main rationale was avoiding losses, something that conservative investors will appreciate. Second, adding select corporates and structured securities will boost the fund's income payout, which should appease income fans. Third, the fund hasn't underperformed by much--its year-to-date gain as of Nov. 24 lags the typical intermediate fund's by less than 0.50%. Finally, the fund's experienced managers, careful approach, and low fees continue to serve as long-term edges.

Address:	400 Bellevue Pkwy Wilmington DE 19809 888-261-4073
Web Address:	www.robecoinvest.com
Inception:	02-20-86
Advisor:	Weiss, Peck & Greer, LLC
Subadvisor:	None
NTF Plans:	N/A

Minimum Purchase:	$50000	Add: $5000	IRA: $2500
Min Auto Inv Plan:	$5000	Add: $100	
Sales Fees:	No-load, 2.00%R		
Management Fee:	0.45%		
Actual Fees:	Mgt:0.45%	Dist: —	
Expense Projections:	3Yr:$208	5Yr:$385	10Yr:$900
Income Distrib:	Monthly		

Historical Profile

Return	Above Avg
Risk	Above Avg
Rating	★★★★ Above Avg

Growth of $10,000

- Investment Values of Fund
- Investment Values of LB Aggr

Investment Style: Fixed Income, Income Rtn %Rank Cat

▼ Manager Change
▽ Partial Manager Change

Performance Quartile (within Category)

1995	1996	1997	1998	1999	2000	2001	2002	2003	2004	2005	2006	History
9.38	9.19	9.34	9.64	9.07	9.40	9.80	10.44	10.66	10.81	10.64	10.53	NAV
13.26	3.85	7.37	9.26	-0.12	10.66	9.61	10.85	5.04	4.38	2.11	3.12	Total Return %
-5.21	0.22	-2.28	0.57	0.70	-0.97	1.17	0.60	0.94	0.04	-0.32	-1.21	+/-LB Aggr
-8.17	1.16	-2.06	-0.88	2.76	-1.78	0.79	-2.18	-0.93	-0.92	0.28	-0.69	+/-LB 5-10YR
6.87	5.86	5.66	5.97	5.94	6.79	5.29	4.15	2.91	2.94	3.71	4.14	Income Return %
6.39	-2.01	1.71	3.29	-6.06	3.87	4.32	6.70	2.13	1.44	-1.60	-1.02	Capital Return %
94	31	91	7	19	37	8	5	39	35	32	88	Total Rtn % Rank Cat
0.59	0.54	0.51	0.54	0.56	0.60	0.49	0.40	0.30	0.31	0.39	0.43	Income $
0.00	0.00	0.00	0.00	0.00	0.00	0.00	0.00	0.00	0.00	0.00	0.00	Capital Gains $
0.82	0.81	0.86	0.50	0.50	0.50	0.50	0.50	0.45	0.43	0.44	0.43	Expense Ratio %
6.52	5.87	5.56	5.71	5.98	6.58	5.04	4.02	2.81	2.90	3.52	4.29	Income Ratio %
375	333	330	685	531	448	432	539	562	806	603	296	Turnover Rate %
172	128	108	139	137	114	124	105	145	154	159	170	Net Assets $mil

Rating and Risk

Time Period	Load-Adj Return %	Morningstar Rtn vs Cat	Morningstar Risk vs Cat	Morningstar Risk-Adj Rating
1 Yr	3.12			
3 Yr	3.20	Avg	+Avg	★★★
5 Yr	5.06	+Avg	+Avg	★★★★
10 Yr	6.21	+Avg	Avg	★★★★
Incept	6.84			

Other Measures	Standard Index LB Aggr	Best Fit Index LB Aggr
Alpha	-0.4	-0.4
Beta	1.00	1.00
R-Squared	99	99
Standard Deviation	3.24	
Mean	3.20	
Sharpe Ratio	0.03	

Portfolio Analysis 10-31-06

Total Fixed-Income:154	Date of Maturity	Amount $000	Value $000	% Net Assets
FNMA 5%	11-15-36	10,880	10,503	4.65
FNMA 5%	11-15-21	8,470	8,340	3.70
US Treasury Note 4.5%	02-15-09	8,220	8,192	3.63
FNMA 5.5%	11-15-36	7,170	7,085	3.14
FNMA 6%	11-15-36	6,115	6,151	2.73
US Treasury Note 2.5%	07-15-16	4,370	4,475	1.98
US Treasury Note	01-15-16	4,275	4,266	1.89
FNMA 5.5%	07-01-34	4,047	4,000	1.77
US Treasury Note 2.375%	04-15-11	3,495	3,571	1.58
US Treasury Note 4.875%	08-15-16	3,185	3,251	1.44
US Treasury Note 4.875%	08-31-08	3,025	3,032	1.34
FHLMC 6%	01-01-36	2,949	2,969	1.32
US Treasury Note 4.875%	05-15-09	2,495	2,509	1.11
FHLMC 5.5%	09-01-19	2,359	2,361	1.05
Wells Fargo Mbs 2005-Ar1	10-25-35	2,360	2,336	1.04
Honda Auto Recv 2006-3 5	04-15-12	1,850	1,857	0.82
NISSAN AUTO RECV 2006-C	04-15-10	1,840	1,853	0.82
FHLMC 6.5%	10-01-36	1,720	1,754	0.78
Gsr Mtg Tr 2005-Ar6 CMO	09-25-35	1,760	1,737	0.77
Soundview Hm Ln 2006-Opt	07-25-36	1,733	1,733	0.77

Current Investment Style

Duration: Short Int Long
Quality: High Med Low

1 figure provided by fund

Avg Eff Duration[1]	5.0 Yrs
Avg Eff Maturity	15.3 Yrs
Avg Credit Quality	AAA
Avg Wtd Coupon	4.77%
Avg Wtd Price	100.02% of par

Coupon Range	% of Bonds	Rel Cat
0% PIK	6.1	0.9
0% to 6%	86.5	1.2
6% to 8%	13.3	0.6
8% to 10%	0.3	0.1
More than 10%	0.0	0.0

1.00=Category Average

Credit Analysis	% bonds 10-31-06		
AAA	76	BB	0
AA	4	B	0
A	14	Below B	0
BBB	6	NR/NA	0

Sector Breakdown	% of assets
US Treasuries	15
TIPS	0
US Agency	3
Mortgage Pass-Throughs	20
Mortgage CMO	12
Mortgage ARM	0
US Corporate	20
Asset-Backed	12
Convertible	0
Municipal	0
Corporate Inflation-Protected	0
Foreign Corporate	2
Foreign Govt	0

Composition			
Cash	16.1	Bonds	83.6
Stocks	0.0	Other	0.4

Special Securities	
Restricted/Illiquid Secs	5
Exotic Mortgage-Backed	0
Emerging-Markets Secs	Trace
Options/Futures/Warrants	No

MORNINGSTAR® Funds 500

Royce Opportunity Inv

	Ticker	Load	NAV	Yield	Total Assets	Mstar Category
	RYPNX	None	$13.04	0.0%	$2,064 mil	Small Value

Governance and Management

Stewardship Grade: B

Portfolio Manager(s)

Buzz Zaino has managed this fund since April 1998. Zaino brings his own brand of value to this fund after a 17-year stint with Lehman Brothers and a tour with Trust Company of the West. Zaino added William Hench, an accountant with sell-side experience, as an assistant portfolio manager in 2004.

Strategy

Manager Buzz Zaino looks for stocks that fit into one of four categories: undervalued asset plays, turnaround stories, undervalued growth, and interrupted earnings. In each area, Zaino's holdings must meet his quantitative definition of a value stock based on P/E or price/sales ratios. This fund is loaded with micro-cap stocks. Position sizes typically don't exceed 1% of assets.

Historical Profile

Return	Above Avg
Risk	High
Rating	★★★★ Above Avg

Investment Style: Equity Stock %

▼ Manager Change
▽ Partial Manager Change

Growth of $10,000
— Investment Values of Fund
— Investment Values of S&P 500

Performance Quartile (within Category)

	1995	1996	1997	1998	1999	2000	2001	2002	2003	2004	2005	2006	History
	—	5.26	5.92	6.02	7.19	7.78	9.01	7.37	12.14	13.31	12.29	13.04	NAV
	—	5.20*	20.83	4.91	32.34	19.85	17.32	-17.01	72.87	17.51	4.76	18.76	Total Return %
	—	—	-12.53	-23.67	11.30	28.95	29.21	5.09	44.19	6.63	-0.15	2.97	+/-S&P 500
	—	—	-10.95	11.36	33.83	-2.98	3.30	-5.58	26.84	-4.74	0.05	-4.72	+/-Russ 2000 VL
	—	—	1.52	0.00	0.00	0.00	0.00	0.00	0.00	0.00	0.00	0.00	Income Return %
	—	—	19.31	4.91	32.34	19.85	17.32	-17.01	72.87	17.51	4.76	18.76	Capital Return %
	—	—	91	5	7	50	42	88	2	81	68	33	Total Rtn % Rank Cat
	—	0.00	0.08	0.00	0.00	0.00	0.00	0.00	0.00	0.00	0.00	0.00	Income $
	—	0.00	0.36	0.18	0.74	0.81	0.11	0.11	0.58	0.93	1.67	1.56	Capital Gains $
	—	—	—	0.99	1.25	1.46	1.24	1.19	1.17	1.15	1.14	—	Expense Ratio %
	—	—	—	1.23	-0.16	-0.07	0.00	-0.19	-0.49	-0.65	-0.55	—	Income Ratio %
	—	—	—	77	120	122	56	44	46	55	47	—	Turnover Rate %
	—	—	18	22	33	60	297	526	636	1,310	1,678	1,808	Net Assets $mil

Return 92% 97% 95% 93% 95% 93% 93% 94% 92%

43.6 / 32.4 / 24.0 / 17.0 / 10.0

Performance 12-31-06

	1st Qtr	2nd Qtr	3rd Qtr	4th Qtr	Total
2002	10.10	-5.95	-27.76	10.94	-17.01
2003	-6.11	31.94	16.43	19.86	72.87
2004	6.01	1.01	-4.46	14.86	17.51
2005	-4.36	1.10	6.14	2.08	4.76
2006	16.68	-5.93	-0.07	8.27	18.76

Trailing	Total Return%	+/- S&P 500	+/- Russ 2000 VL	%Rank Cat	Growth of $10,000
3 Mo	8.27	1.57	-0.76	56	10,827
6 Mo	8.19	-4.55	-3.62	53	10,819
1 Yr	18.76	2.97	-4.72	33	11,876
3 Yr Avg	13.50	3.06	-2.98	62	14,621
5 Yr Avg	15.97	9.78	0.60	19	20,976
10 Yr Avg	17.34	8.92	4.07	1	49,484
15 Yr Avg	—	—	—		—

Tax Analysis	Tax-Adj Rtn%	%Rank Cat	Tax-Cost Rat	%Rank Cat
3 Yr (estimated)	11.67	56	1.61	46
5 Yr (estimated)	14.41	20	1.35	52
10 Yr (estimated)	15.43	1	1.63	70

Potential Capital Gain Exposure: 19% of assets

Rating and Risk

Time Period	Load-Adj Return %	Morningstar Rtn vs Cat	Morningstar Risk vs Cat	Morningstar Risk-Adj Rating
1 Yr	18.76			
3 Yr	13.50	Avg	High	★★
5 Yr	15.97	+Avg	High	★★★
10 Yr	17.34	High	High	★★★★★
Incept	17.72			

Other Measures	Standard Index S&P 500	Best Fit Index Russ 2000
Alpha	-2.6	-0.6
Beta	1.90	1.07
R-Squared	73	95
Standard Deviation	15.23	
Mean	13.50	
Sharpe Ratio	0.70	

Morningstar's Take by John Coumarianos 12-28-06

This fund is not for the faint of heart, but it should continue to reward patient investors.

Royce Opportunity is one of the most volatile funds in the small-value category, but it also sports one of the best long-term records. Both the volatility and performance result from manager Buzz Zaino's distinct value approach. Zaino buys micro-cap stocks that fall into one of four categories--unrecognized asset values, turnarounds, undervalued growth, and interrupted earnings. Nearly all of his stocks have warts of one kind or another, and Zaino tries to choose those whose warts are temporary or can be eliminated.

For example, upscale home furnishings retailer Restoration Hardware is under a cloud because of its significant debt and questions about the strength of the housing market. Still, Zaino thinks the business has improved dramatically over the past few years, as the firm has evolved from trying to sell lots of quirky items to being a more traditional retailer of upscale furnishings. He also is

impressed with the company's ability to make inroads with contractors and establish itself as a one-stop source for a wide variety of items.

Besides small retailers, Zaino is high on many steel companies. Despite the commodity nature of the business, he sees sustainable increased worldwide demand. The fund has enjoyed great success with Oregon Steel, which has received a buyout offer from Russian steel and mining company Evraz. Zaino will carefully monitor his steel companies' prices as they move higher than their historical price/earnings ratio ranges of seven or eight to nearly 10. His view is that their growth justifies the higher multiples, and he will try to use volatility to add to his positions when they decline.

Risks abound in this portfolio, but Zaino takes small positions that mitigate blowups. Additionally, his experience in the micro-cap realm gives us the confidence to recommend this fund as a great complement to large-cap holdings in a long-term portfolio.

Portfolio Analysis 09-30-06

Share change since 06-06 Total Stocks:273

	Sector	PE	Tot Ret%	% Assets
⊖ Carpenter Technology Cor	Ind Mtrls	11.7	46.55	0.94
⊖ Gerber Scientific, Inc.	Software	28.3	31.24	0.87
⊖ Robbins & Myers, Inc.	Ind Mtrls	—	127.64	0.85
⊕ Park Electrochemical Cor	Hardware	13.9	3.89	0.76
⊕ Landry's Restaurants, In	Consumer	13.7	13.41	0.72
⊕ Scholastic Corporation	Media	34.5	25.71	0.71
⊖ Dillard's, Inc.	Consumer	14.2	41.62	0.70
⊕ Analogic Corporation	Health	—	18.20	0.69
⊕ Spartech Corporation	Ind Mtrls	27.6	22.01	0.69
⊖ Flow International Corpo	Ind Mtrls	73.3	30.88	0.69
⊕ Benchmark Electronics	Hardware	16.1	8.65	0.68
⊕ Circor International, In	Ind Mtrls	24.6	44.10	0.66
⊕ Keane, Inc.	Business	22.0	8.17	0.66
⊕ Cypress Semiconductor Co	Hardware	—	18.39	0.65
⊕ Epicor Software Corporat	Software	27.1	-4.39	0.64
⊕ Barnes Group, Inc.	Ind Mtrls	14.9	35.19	0.64
⊕ C-COR Incorporated	Hardware	—	129.22	0.63
☆ Parametric Technology Co	Software	38.1	18.16	0.63
⊕ Maxwell Technologies, In	Hardware	—	-1.55	0.61
⊖ Varian, Inc.	Health	28.7	12.57	0.61

Current Investment Style

Value Blnd Growth — Large Mid Small

Market Cap	%
Giant	0.0
Large	0.0
Mid	12.2
Small	38.0
Micro	49.8
Avg $mil:	528

Value Measures		Rel Category
Price/Earnings	17.62	1.15
Price/Book	1.58	0.89
Price/Sales	0.65	0.81
Price/Cash Flow	3.67	0.60
Dividend Yield %	0.51	0.32

Growth Measures	%	Rel Category
Long-Term Erngs	15.44	1.24
Book Value	-1.42	NMF
Sales	3.14	0.42
Cash Flow	13.27	1.62
Historical Erngs	0.69	0.06

Profitability	%	Rel Category
Return on Equity	4.13	0.38
Return on Assets	1.47	0.24
Net Margin	1.31	0.14

Sector Weightings	% of Stocks	Rel S&P 500	3 Year High	Low
↻ Info	39.28	1.96		
Software	8.14	2.36	8	5
Hardware	26.14	2.83	29	21
Media	2.72	0.72	5	2
Telecom	2.28	0.65	2	1
⊂ Service	26.45	0.57		
Health	4.69	0.39	5	2
Consumer	7.39	0.97	9	7
Business	10.96	2.59	12	10
Financial	3.41	0.15	5	2
⊔ Mfg	34.27	1.01		
Goods	5.97	0.70	6	4
Ind Mtrls	26.50	2.22	33	27
Energy	1.80	0.18	5	1
Utilities	0.00	0.00	0	0

Composition

	%
● Cash	7.6
● Stocks	92.4
● Bonds	0.0
● Other	0.0
Foreign (% of Stock)	1.6

Address:	1414 Ave of the Americas New York NY 10019 800-221-4268
Web Address:	www.roycefunds.com
Inception:	11-19-96*
Advisor:	Royce & Associates, LLC.
Subadvisor:	None
NTF Plans:	ETrade No Load ETF

Minimum Purchase:	$2000	Add: $50	IRA: $1000
Min Auto Inv Plan:	$1000	Add: $100	
Sales Fees:	No-load, 1.00%R		
Management Fee:	1.00% mx./0.85% mn.		
Actual Fees:	Mgt:1.00%	Dist: —	
Expense Projections:	3Yr:$362	5Yr:$628	10Yr:$1386
Income Distrib:	Annually		

Royce Premier Inv

	Ticker	Load	NAV	Yield	Total Assets	Mstar Category
	RYPRX	Closed	$17.66	0.4%	$4,530 mil	Small Blend

Governance and Management

Stewardship Grade: B

Portfolio Manager(s)

Chuck Royce is one of the best and most experienced small-value managers in the business. He has managed Pennsylvania Mutual for nearly 30 years and has earned a reputation for low-risk investing. Whitney George is a force at the firm, guiding Royce Micro-Cap and Royce Low-Priced Stock with strong results. As of spring 2006, Lauren Romeo assists; she tends to specialize in higher-quality stocks.

Strategy

This Royce offering has comfortably sat in the small-blend category for more than five years, although it does have a hefty weighting in smaller mid-caps. Chuck Royce and comanager Whitney George have been more willing to pay up for well-positioned companies in this concentrated portfolio. It is focused on the larger companies in the small-cap arena.

Historical Profile

Return Above Avg
Risk Low
Rating ★★★★ Above Avg

91% 91% 89% 87% 91% 82% 85% 88% 91%

Investment Style
Equity
Stock %

▼ Manager Change
▽ Partial Manager Change

Growth of $10,000
— Investment Values of Fund
— Investment Values of S&P 500

42.2
32.4
24.0
17.0
10.0

Performance Quartile (within Category)

	1995	1996	1997	1998	1999	2000	2001	2002	2003	2004	2005	2006	History
	7.12	7.81	8.70	9.14	9.56	9.83	10.54	9.39	12.90	15.12	16.86	17.66	NAV
	17.81	18.13	18.41	6.74	11.49	17.12	9.61	-7.75	38.74	22.82	17.07	8.81	Total Return %
	-19.77	-4.83	-14.95	-21.84	-9.55	26.22	21.50	14.35	10.06	11.94	12.16	-6.98	+/-S&P 500
	-10.64	1.64	-3.95	9.29	-9.77	20.14	7.12	12.73	-8.51	4.49	12.52	-9.56	+/-Russ 2000
	1.42	1.40	1.13	0.57	0.11	0.31	0.00	0.00	0.00	0.00	0.00	0.43	Income Return %
	16.39	16.73	17.28	6.17	11.38	16.81	9.61	-7.75	38.74	22.82	17.07	8.38	Capital Return %
	83	76	86	7	53	32	39	11	67	18	4	93	Total Rtn % Rank Cat
	0.09	0.10	0.09	0.05	0.01	0.03	0.00	0.00	0.00	0.00	0.00	0.07	Income $
	0.42	0.49	0.46	0.09	0.58	1.27	0.23	0.34	0.13	0.71	0.84	0.63	Capital Gains $
	1.25	1.25	1.24	1.23	1.23	1.20	1.19	1.17	1.16	1.14	1.13	—	Expense Ratio %
	1.48	1.25	1.20	0.55	0.11	0.34	-0.04	-0.40	-0.29	-0.43	-0.09	—	Income Ratio %
	39	34	18	46	48	40	41	33	26	24	20	—	Turnover Rate %
	302	317	534	572	568	674	799	854	1,772	2,974	3,382	3,737	Net Assets $mil

Performance 12-31-06

	1st Qtr	2nd Qtr	3rd Qtr	4th Qtr	Total
2002	6.07	-6.62	-12.55	6.49	-7.75
2003	-4.05	18.42	7.50	13.58	38.74
2004	7.91	4.67	0.34	8.37	22.82
2005	-2.58	2.44	10.54	6.12	17.07
2006	11.15	-5.55	-2.26	6.04	8.81

Trailing	Total Return%	+/- S&P 500	+/- Russ 2000	%Rank Cat	Growth of $10,000
3 Mo	6.04	-0.66	-2.86	93	10,604
6 Mo	3.64	-9.10	-5.74	92	10,364
1 Yr	8.81	-6.98	-9.56	93	10,881
3 Yr Avg	16.09	5.65	2.53	16	15,645
5 Yr Avg	14.90	8.71	3.51	17	20,026
10 Yr Avg	13.73	5.31	4.29	24	36,203
15 Yr Avg	14.04	3.40	2.57	25	71,756

Tax Analysis	Tax-Adj Rtn%	%Rank Cat	Tax-Cost Rat	%Rank Cat
3 Yr (estimated)	15.28	11	0.70	15
5 Yr (estimated)	14.19	15	0.62	25
10 Yr (estimated)	12.60	21	0.99	21

Potential Capital Gain Exposure: 31% of assets

Rating and Risk

Time Period	Load-Adj Return %	Morningstar Rtn vs Cat	Morningstar Risk vs Cat	Morningstar Risk-Adj Rating
1 Yr	8.81			
3 Yr	16.09	+Avg	-Avg	★★★★
5 Yr	14.90	+Avg	Low	★★★★
10 Yr	13.73	+Avg	Low	★★★★
Incept	14.04			

Other Measures	Standard Index S&P 500	Best Fit Index Mstar Small Core
Alpha	3.3	1.4
Beta	1.32	0.84
R-Squared	55	84
Standard Deviation	12.11	
Mean	16.09	
Sharpe Ratio	1.03	

Morningstar's Take by Todd Trubey 12-11-06

Don't give up on Royce Premier.

As noted in our last analysis, this fund's rather poor 2006 campaign isn't alarming. It remains in the small-blend category but now resides in the mid-growth square of the Morningstar Style Box. So while its 10.6% gain through December 8 trails 90% of category rivals, that's average in the mid-growth category.

A structural constraint here is slightly more bothersome. Comanagers Chuck Royce and Whitney George only put high-confidence picks in the $500 million to $2.5 billion market-cap range into this compact portfolio. The fund thrives when holdings rise well into mid-cap territory; the skippers sell only based on declining business fundamentals or on valuation. When the process works, a stock like Polo Ralph Lauren can gain over 40% and reach an $8.4 billion market cap as it did this year and stay put here. Still, one of Royce's key plays is to load up on favorite stocks that drop. And this year he did get to rebuild a position in Florida Rock, which fell below $2.5 billion. Had Florida Rock's market cap remained above $2.5 billion, the fund couldn't have added to it no matter how attractive it was.

Putting that aside, the financials area nicely illustrates the fund's process. The comanagers note that the fund has a fairly light 9% stake because there haven't been a lot of blowups in the sector that would lead them to pounce. Still, they did add Knight Capital to the fund after gaining confidence in the firm while it resided in other Royce funds. The trading firm's stock plummeted in the bear market while the managers here say the firm dealt with several shortcomings. They argue it then got efficient, cut head count sharply, and prepared smartly for the surge in algorithmic trading. George believes it has plenty of room to grow and expand profit margins.

This former Analyst Pick lost that honor largely because of a heavy asset base. But we still think the closed fund has a sensible strategy and good risk/reward ratio for its current owners.

Portfolio Analysis 09-30-06

Share change since 06-06 Total Stocks:59

	Sector	PE	Tot Ret%	% Assets
Lincoln Electric Holding	Ind Mtrls	16.8	54.47	3.43
Ipsco	Ind Mtrls	7.4	13.97	3.34
Thor Industries, Inc.	Ind Mtrls	15.2	10.47	2.78
Ensign Resource Service	Energy	—	—	2.68
Endo Pharmaceutical Hold	Health	17.7	-8.86	2.66
⊕ Unit Corporation	Energy	6.8	-11.96	2.57
⊕ Florida Rock Industries	Ind Mtrls	14.0	-11.07	2.52
⊕ Simpson Manufacturing	Ind Mtrls	13.5	-12.13	2.31
TSX Grp	Financial	—	—	2.28
Ritchie Bros. Auctioneer	Consumer	34.7	28.67	2.16
Winnebago Industries	Ind Mtrls	23.1	0.10	2.15
Trican Well Service Ltd	Energy	—	—	2.02
Alleghany Corporation	Financial	12.4	30.59	2.01
EGL, Inc.	Business	24.1	-20.74	1.98
⊕ Timberland Company	Goods	17.0	-2.98	1.96
⊕ Knight Capital Group, In	Business	14.3	93.83	1.94
⊕ Meridian Gold, Inc.	Ind Mtrls	—	27.07	1.92
Polo Ralph Lauren Corpor	Goods	25.5	38.77	1.87
Arkansas Best Corporatio	Business	10.4	-16.42	1.86
Pan American Silver Corp	Ind Mtrls	—	33.67	1.82

Current Investment Style

Value Blnd Growth — Large/Mid/Small

	Market Cap	%
	Giant	0.0
	Large	5.2
	Mid	58.5
	Small	36.3
	Micro	0.0
	Avg $mil:	1,973

Value Measures		Rel Category
Price/Earnings	15.09	0.91
Price/Book	2.56	1.21
Price/Sales	1.33	1.36
Price/Cash Flow	8.83	1.27
Dividend Yield %	0.81	0.76

Growth Measures	%	Rel Category
Long-Term Erngs	14.08	1.01
Book Value	11.56	1.53
Sales	14.83	1.68
Cash Flow	24.90	1.96
Historical Erngs	27.52	1.65

Profitability	%	Rel Category
Return on Equity	16.31	1.27
Return on Assets	9.84	1.38
Net Margin	11.76	1.21

Sector Weightings	% of Stocks	Rel S&P 500	3 Year High	Low
☎ Info	10.24	0.51		
🖥 Software	0.89	0.26	1	1
🖥 Hardware	8.50	0.92	9	5
📶 Media	0.00	0.00	1	0
📞 Telecom	0.85	0.24	2	1
⊙ Service	42.19	0.91		
🏥 Health	11.12	0.92	17	10
🛒 Consumer	9.47	1.24	9	7
📋 Business	12.24	2.89	13	10
💲 Financial	9.36	0.42	11	9
🏭 Mfg	47.57	1.41		
🏭 Goods	7.78	0.91	8	6
⚙ Ind Mtrls	30.82	2.58	33	27
🔥 Energy	8.97	0.92	14	8
⚡ Utilities	0.00	0.00	0	0

Composition

	%
● Cash	9.3
● Stocks	90.7
● Bonds	0.0
○ Other	0.0
Foreign (% of Stock)	20.9

Address:	1414 Ave of the Americas New York NY 10019 800-221-4268	Minimum Purchase:	Closed	Add: — IRA: —
		Min Auto Inv Plan:	Closed	Add: —
Web Address:	www.roycefunds.com	Sales Fees:	No-load, 1.00%R	
Inception:	12-31-91	Management Fee:	1.00% mx./0.85% mn.	
Advisor:	Royce & Associates, LLC.	Actual Fees:	Mgt:0.98%	Dist: —
Subadvisor:	None	Expense Projections:	3Yr:$359 5Yr:$622	10Yr:$1375
NTF Plans:	DATALynx NTF, ETrade No Load ETF	Income Distrib:	Annually	

MORNINGSTAR® Funds 500

Royce Special Equity Inv

Analyst Pick ✓

	Ticker	Load	NAV	Yield	Total Assets	Mstar Category
	RYSEX	None	$19.72	0.5%	$605 mil	Small Value

Governance and Management

Stewardship Grade: A

Portfolio Manager(s)

Charlie Dreifus, a senior portfolio manager at Royce Associates, runs the show, pouring over balance sheets and conducting nearly all of the fund's bottom-up research. Dreifus worked at Lazard Freres and Oppenheimer for about 30 years, managing money using an approach similar to the one he now employs.

Strategy

Eschewing sector considerations, manager Charlie Dreifus zeroes in on stocks trading at a steep discount to his estimate of intrinsic value, regardless of industry. A balance-sheet skeptic, Dreifus insists on crystal-clear financial reporting from potential picks and has a strong preference for companies with high returns on invested capital and plenty of cash on hand.

Performance 12-31-06

	1st Qtr	2nd Qtr	3rd Qtr	4th Qtr	Total
2002	15.20	3.72	-9.00	6.06	15.32
2003	-4.21	12.39	4.70	13.25	27.64
2004	5.40	3.27	-3.02	7.91	13.91
2005	-2.35	0.05	-2.30	3.72	-0.99
2006	8.98	-3.68	2.29	6.16	14.00

Trailing	Total Return%	+/- S&P 500	+/- Russ 2000 VL	%Rank Cat	Growth of $10,000
3 Mo	6.16	-0.54	-2.87	90	10,616
6 Mo	8.60	-4.14	-3.21	48	10,860
1 Yr	14.00	-1.79	-9.48	67	11,400
3 Yr Avg	8.74	-1.70	-7.74	95	12,858
5 Yr Avg	13.61	7.42	-1.76	52	18,927
10 Yr Avg	—	—	—	—	—
15 Yr Avg	—	—	—	—	—

Tax Analysis	Tax-Adj Rtn%	%Rank Cat	Tax-Cost Rat	%Rank Cat
3 Yr (estimated)	7.65	89	1.00	23
5 Yr (estimated)	12.82	38	0.70	21
10 Yr (estimated)	—	—	—	—

Potential Capital Gain Exposure: 34% of assets

Morningstar's Take by Todd Trubey 12-14-06

Royce Special Equity is one of our favorite conservative equity funds, but its charms are hidden in plain view.

This unusual Analyst Pick is unlikely to entice the typical investor. If the vast majority of funds are hamburgers, this one is sushi. It's very high quality, a delicacy to those who appreciate it--but just raw fish to all too many.

Its greatest challenge in attracting the masses is its apparently poor return profile. It's 14.5% gain in 2006 (through Dec. 12) trails over 60% of small-value category members, and over its lifetime its 10.9% annualized return is just a bit above average. As we're fond of noting, though, it's been great when investors need returns the most--it gained 15% in 2002 when the typical rival lost 10%. Plus, it's been very stable--only four of 135 category peers have a lower five-year standard deviation (a statistical measure of volatility).

The portfolio is the expression of Manager Charlie Dreifus's skeptical, picky philosophy of investing. Trained in old-school accounting, Dreifus spurns any firm whose filings suggest even a whiff of aggressive record-keeping. A conservative when it comes to valuation, he uses stingy merger and acquisition methods to judge a firm's intrinsic value. Finally, he yearns for steady, persistent growth and avoids rosy forecasts and risky business models.

To our minds, the result is a very durable fund that you can count on long term. The portfolio's overall return-on-equity--a good measurement of firm quality--is 15.5%, which lands in its category's top decile. The fund's book-value growth, a conservative measure of business strength, is nearly double the category average.

This fund closed to new investors after assets surged in 2002 and 2003 on the heels of its bear-market performance. It reopened this year, but given fine returns elsewhere, few investors have bought it. We encourage you to diverge from the crowd if a low-key small-cap fund entices.

Address:	1414 Ave of the Americas New York NY 10019 800-221-4268	Minimum Purchase:	$2000	Add: $50 IRA: $1000
		Min Auto Inv Plan:	$1000	Add: $100
		Sales Fees:	No-load, 1.00%R	
Web Address:	www.roycefunds.com	Management Fee:	1.00% mx./0.85% mn.	
Inception:	05-01-98*	Actual Fees:	Mgt:1.00% Dist:—	
Advisor:	Royce & Associates, LLC.	Expense Projections:	3Yr:$362 5Yr:$628 10Yr:$1386	
Subadvisor:	None	Income Distrib:	Annually	
NTF Plans:	ETrade No Load ETF, Pershing NTF			

Historical Profile

Return	Below Avg
Risk	Low
Rating	★★ Below Avg

96%	96%	92%	92%	84%	82%	88%	95%	97%

▼ Manager Change
▽ Partial Manager Change

- 22.6
- 19.6
- 16.0 **Growth of $10,000**
- 13.0 ━ Investment Values of Fund
- 10.0 ━ Investment Values of S&P 500
- 7.0

Performance Quartile (within Category)

1995	1996	1997	1998	1999	2000	2001	2002	2003	2004	2005	2006	History
—	—	—	9.30	8.31	9.55	12.37	14.24	17.97	19.61	18.70	19.72	NAV
—	—	—	-6.84*	-9.64	16.30	30.75	15.32	27.64	13.91	-0.99	14.00	Total Return %
—	—	—	—	-30.68	25.40	42.64	37.42	-1.04	3.03	-5.90	-1.79	+/-S&P 500
—	—	—	—	-8.15	-6.53	16.73	26.75	-18.39	-8.34	-5.70	-9.48	+/-Russ 2000 VL
—	—	—	—	1.02	1.32	1.17	0.20	0.32	1.02	1.10	0.60	Income Return %
—	—	—	—	-10.66	14.98	29.58	15.12	27.32	12.89	-2.09	13.40	Capital Return %
—	—	—	—	91	60	6	1	96	95	91	67	Total Rtn % Rank Cat
—	—	—	0.02	0.10	0.11	0.11	0.03	0.05	0.18	0.22	0.11	Income $
—	—	—	0.00	0.00	0.00	0.00	0.00	0.15	0.67	0.50	1.51	Capital Gains $
—	—	—	—	1.49	1.49	1.49	1.20	1.19	1.15	—		Expense Ratio %
—	—	—	—	0.96	1.38	0.87	0.27	0.35	1.02	—		Income Ratio %
—	—	—	—	—	91	57	61	124	41	22	17	Turnover Rate %
—	—	—	3	3	3	6	394	748	857	438		Net Assets $mil

Rating and Risk

Time Period	Load-Adj Return %	Morningstar Rtn vs Cat	Morningstar Risk vs Cat	Morningstar Risk-Adj Rating
1 Yr	14.00			
3 Yr	8.74	Low	-Avg	★
5 Yr	13.61	Avg	Low	★★★
10 Yr	—			
Incept	10.75			

Other Measures	Standard Index S&P 500	Best Fit Index Mstar Small Core
Alpha	-2.6	-3.9
Beta	1.20	0.73
R-Squared	58	79
Standard Deviation	10.85	
Mean	8.74	
Sharpe Ratio	0.53	

Portfolio Analysis 09-30-06

Share change since 06-06 Total Stocks:59

	Sector	PE	Tot Ret%	% Assets
National Presto Industri	Goods	21.8	41.62	5.06
⊖ Lancaster Colony Corpora	Goods	17.7	22.65	4.21
⊖ Bio-Rad Laboratories Inc	Health	22.0	26.10	4.16
Claire's Stores, Inc.	Consumer	19.2	14.94	4.00
⊖ Rofin-Sinar Technologies	Ind Mtrls	19.7	39.08	3.78
Lawson Products, Inc.	Ind Mtrls	20.4	23.40	3.66
Carpenter Technology Cor	Ind Mtrls	11.7	46.55	3.18
Hilb Rogal & Hobbs Compa	Financial	15.1	10.67	2.99
⊖ Genlyte Group Inc.	Ind Mtrls	15.1	45.81	2.97
CSS Industries, Inc.	Media	17.0	16.93	2.84
Cascade Corporation	Ind Mtrls	15.7	14.68	2.68
⊕ Insteel Industries, Inc.	Ind Mtrls	9.1	115.94	2.46
⊖ Lone Star Technologies	Ind Mtrls	8.7	-6.29	2.36
Arden Group, Inc. A	Consumer	18.6	37.34	2.31
⊖ Arkansas Best Corporatio	Business	10.4	-16.42	2.20
Deb Shops, Inc.	Consumer	15.7	-9.60	2.13
⊖ Bandag A	Ind Mtrls	—	—	2.06
⊖ Jack In The Box, Inc.	Consumer	19.8	74.75	2.05
⊕ Standex International Co	Ind Mtrls	17.0	11.73	2.02
⊕ Global Imaging Systems,	Ind Mtrls	16.4	26.77	1.97

Current Investment Style

Value Blnd Growth — Large Mid Small

Market Cap	%
Giant	0.0
Large	0.0
Mid	18.9
Small	43.9
Micro	37.2
Avg $mil:	743

Value Measures		Rel Category
Price/Earnings	14.08	0.92
Price/Book	2.05	1.15
Price/Sales	0.93	1.16
Price/Cash Flow	7.90	1.29
Dividend Yield %	1.19	0.75

Growth Measures	%	Rel Category
Long-Term Erngs	12.20	0.98
Book Value	10.36	1.91
Sales	9.53	1.29
Cash Flow	9.43	1.15
Historical Erngs	17.74	1.56

Profitability	%	Rel Category
Return on Equity	15.56	1.45
Return on Assets	9.89	1.62
Net Margin	7.95	0.88

Sector Weightings

	% of Stocks	Rel S&P 500	3 Year High	Low
⟳ Info	5.68	0.28		
🖥 Software	0.00	0.00	0	0
🖥 Hardware	2.72	0.29	3	0
🎬 Media	2.96	0.78	3	2
📱 Telecom	0.00	0.00	0	0
⟳ Service	32.12	0.70		
⚕ Health	7.50	0.62	8	4
🛒 Consumer	15.98	2.09	27	16
📋 Business	5.53	1.31	10	6
💲 Financial	3.11	0.14	3	2
⚒ Mfg	62.20	1.84		
⚙ Goods	17.44	2.04	28	17
🔧 Ind Mtrls	44.76	3.75	45	23
🔋 Energy	0.00	0.00	4	0
💡 Utilities	0.00	0.00	0	0

Composition

● Cash	2.7	
● Stocks	97.3	
● Bonds	0.0	
○ Other	0.0	
Foreign	0.0	(% of Stock)

Royce Total Return Inv

	Ticker	Load	NAV	Yield	Total Assets	Mstar Category
	RYTRX	None	$13.75	1.1%	$6,003 mil	Small Value

Governance and Management

Stewardship Grade: B

Portfolio Manager(s)

Consistent. Chuck Royce has run this fund since its 1993 inception. He has been chief investment officer with Royce Funds for 28 years. Jay Kaplan and George Necakov were recently named comanagers on the fund.

Strategy

An emphasis on dividend-paying stocks is just one of the ways this fund maintains its low-risk profile. Chuck Royce thinks the dividend provides a cushion during market downturns. Although the fund spreads its bets across many holdings, it does not seek diversification across all industries. Financials and industrial stocks have been its favorites.

Historical Profile

Return	Average
Risk	Low
Rating	★★★★ Above Avg

| 76% | 83% | 96% | 90% | 90% | 81% | 82% | 85% | 91% |

Investment Style
Equity
Stock %

▽ Manager Change
▽ Partial Manager Change

Growth of $10,000
— Investment Values of Fund
— Investment Values of S&P 500

49.2
42.2
32.4
24.0
17.0
10.0

Performance Quartile (within Category)

	1995	1996	1997	1998	1999	2000	2001	2002	2003	2004	2005	2006	History
	5.76	6.29	7.52	7.56	7.15	7.77	8.59	8.37	10.69	12.26	12.60	13.75	NAV
	26.86	25.48	23.70	4.75	1.55	19.43	14.78	-1.60	29.99	17.52	8.23	14.54	Total Return %
	-10.72	2.52	-9.66	-23.83	-19.49	28.53	26.67	20.50	1.31	6.64	3.32	-1.25	+/-S&P 500
	1.11	4.11	-8.08	11.20	3.04	-3.40	0.76	9.83	-16.04	-4.73	3.52	-8.94	+/-Russ 2000 VL
	2.54	2.78	1.78	1.99	2.13	2.11	1.36	0.88	1.11	1.11	1.02	1.24	Income Return %
	24.32	22.70	21.92	2.76	-0.58	17.32	13.42	-2.48	28.88	16.41	7.21	13.30	Capital Return %
	26	34	79	7	54	52	54	12	93	81	28	63	Total Rtn % Rank Cat
	0.13	0.16	0.11	0.15	0.16	0.15	0.11	0.09	0.09	0.12	0.13	0.16	Income $
	0.60	0.73	0.15	0.16	0.35	0.57	0.21	0.01	0.08	0.17	0.55	0.52	Capital Gains $
	1.67	1.25	1.25	1.25	1.25	1.25	1.24	1.20	1.18	1.15	1.12	—	Expense Ratio %
	2.42	2.50	3.15	2.75	2.32	2.08	1.14	1.01	1.27	1.08	1.13	—	Income Ratio %
	68	111	26	66	39	24	24	22	20	22	24	—	Turnover Rate %
	3	6	121	244	249	277	511	980	2,285	3,738	4,257	4,438	Net Assets $mil

Performance 12-31-06

	1st Qtr	2nd Qtr	3rd Qtr	4th Qtr	Total
2002	9.14	-3.37	-11.86	5.85	-1.60
2003	-4.30	16.00	4.86	11.66	29.99
2004	4.31	1.98	0.09	10.37	17.52
2005	-1.06	2.56	4.28	2.28	8.23
2006	9.37	-3.48	1.22	7.20	14.54

Trailing	Total Return%	+/- S&P 500	+/- Russ 2000 VL	%Rank Cat	Growth of $10,000
3 Mo	7.20	0.50	-1.83	80	10,720
6 Mo	8.50	-4.24	-3.31	48	10,850
1 Yr	14.54	-1.25	-8.94	63	11,454
3 Yr Avg	13.36	2.92	-3.12	65	14,567
5 Yr Avg	13.25	7.06	-2.12	56	18,629
10 Yr Avg	12.89	4.47	-0.38	41	33,617
15 Yr Avg	—	—	—	—	—

Tax Analysis	Tax-Adj Rtn%	%Rank Cat	Tax-Cost Rat	%Rank Cat
3 Yr (estimated)	12.39	45	0.86	18
5 Yr (estimated)	12.46	45	0.70	21
10 Yr (estimated)	11.54	32	1.20	40

Potential Capital Gain Exposure: 29% of assets

Rating and Risk

Time Period	Load-Adj Return %	Morningstar Rtn vs Cat	Morningstar Risk vs Cat	Morningstar Risk-Adj Rating
1 Yr	14.54			
3 Yr	13.36	Avg	Low	★★★
5 Yr	13.25	Avg	Low	★★★
10 Yr	12.89	Avg	Low	★★★★
Incept	14.16			

Other Measures	Standard Index S&P 500	Best Fit Index Mstar Small Core
Alpha	1.6	0.6
Beta	1.18	0.70
R-Squared	75	97
Standard Deviation	9.34	
Mean	13.36	
Sharpe Ratio	1.05	

Morningstar's Take by John Coumarianos 01-02-07

How big can Royce Total Return get and still be effective?

This fund remains the most conservative offering of a value-oriented shop that has specialized in small- and micro-cap stocks. Thanks to the small-cap rally of recent years, investors have piled into many Royce funds, and this one's portfolio has swelled from just under $1 billion in assets in 2002 to $6 billion in 2006. This is now the largest actively managed fund in the small-value category. It is double the size of Longleaf Partners Small-Cap and nearly triple the size of FPA Capital and Artisan Small Cap Value. These smaller funds are among our favorites, and they are all closed.

In accord with the increase in assets, the average market cap (the price of a stock multiplied by the number of shares outstanding) of the fund's portfolio has gone from nearly $1 billion to nearly $1.7 billion over the past four years, as it has become difficult to invest in the smallest stocks. Manager Chuck Royce has to purchase more than 10% of a $500 million company for the position to occupy 1% of the portfolio, making it easier to stick to larger stocks.

In addition to going up the cap scale to accommodate the fund's girth, Royce also has broadened the portfolio. At last count, the fund owned 450 stocks, up from 150 holdings in 2000, when its asset base was a fraction of what it is now. We're concerned that Royce can't have the same conviction in 450 stocks as he did in 150.

We don't think the fund's girth is responsible for its lackluster relative performance over the past five years. This fund is designed to provide stability in rough markets, with its emphasis on companies that pay dividends and post steady profits. Its 86% cumulative return for the past five years through December 2006 is terrific on an absolute basis. Also, its low volatility and bodes well for a time when small caps no longer rule the roost.

All told, we still like this fund, but its size ultimately may void its good qualities.

Address:	1414 Ave of the Americas New York NY 10019 800-221-4268
Web Address:	www.roycefunds.com
Inception:	12-15-93
Advisor:	Royce & Associates, LLC.
Subadvisor:	None
NTF Plans:	DATALynx NTF, ETrade No Load ETF

Minimum Purchase:	$2000	Add: $50	IRA: $1000
Min Auto Inv Plan:	$1000	Add: $100	
Sales Fees:	No-load, 1.00%R		
Management Fee:	1.00% mx./0.85% mn.		
Actual Fees:	Mgt:0.96%	Dist: —	
Expense Projections:	3Yr:$356	5Yr:$617	10Yr:$1363
Income Distrib:	Quarterly		

Portfolio Analysis 09-30-06

Share change since 03-06 Total Stocks:420	Sector	PE	Tot Ret%	% Assets
⊕ Alliancebernstein Holdin	—	20.8	50.15	2.07
US Treasury Note 3.25%	—	—	—	1.75
⊕ Canada Govt 4.25%	—	—	—	0.81
Nuveen Investments, Inc.	Financial	23.9	24.13	0.79
TSX Grp	Financial	—	—	0.76
SEI Investments Company	Business	26.8	61.73	0.73
⊕ Cabot Corporation	Ind Mtrls	—	23.97	0.68
⊕ T Rowe Price Group	Financial	26.1	23.27	0.64
⊕ Leucadia National Corpor	Ind Mtrls	55.4	19.92	0.63
Federated Investors, Inc	Financial	19.0	-6.94	0.62
Ritchie Bros. Auctioneer	Consumer	34.7	28.67	0.62
Clarcor Inc.	Ind Mtrls	21.6	14.81	0.59
⊕ Lincoln Electric Holding	Ind Mtrls	16.8	54.47	0.58
⊖ Whitney Holding Corporat	Financial	17.5	22.11	0.57
⊕ Brady Corporation A	Ind Mtrls	17.4	4.55	0.56
⊕ Woodward Governor Compan	Ind Mtrls	19.6	40.18	0.56
⊕ Brown & Brown, Inc.	Financial	22.9	-6.98	0.54
⊕ Franklin Electric Co.	Ind Mtrls	21.3	31.07	0.52
⊖ Seacor Holdings, Inc.	Energy	8.9	45.58	0.52
⊕ Erie Indemnity Company A	Financial	18.4	12.01	0.51

Current Investment Style

Value Blnd Growth — Large Mid Small

Market Cap	%
Giant	0.0
Large	3.3
Mid	47.3
Small	38.6
Micro	10.8

Avg $mil: 1,665

Value Measures		Rel Category
Price/Earnings	14.52	0.94
Price/Book	2.13	1.20
Price/Sales	1.05	1.31
Price/Cash Flow	8.22	1.34
Dividend Yield %	1.96	1.24

Growth Measures	%	Rel Category
Long-Term Erngs	12.13	0.97
Book Value	6.60	1.22
Sales	10.60	1.43
Cash Flow	11.47	1.40
Historical Erngs	13.51	1.19

Profitability	%	Rel Category
Return on Equity	15.78	1.47
Return on Assets	9.53	1.56
Net Margin	12.70	1.40

Sector Weightings

	% of Stocks	Rel S&P 500	3 Year High Low	
⊙ Info	5.25	0.26		
🖥 Software	0.70	0.20	1	0
🖥 Hardware	2.96	0.32	4	3
🎙 Media	0.73	0.19	1	1
📶 Telecom	0.86	0.25	1	0
⊙ Service	51.73	1.12		
🏥 Health	5.43	0.45	6	5
🛒 Consumer	7.52	0.98	9	7
📋 Business	10.76	2.54	12	10
💲 Financial	28.02	1.26	28	23
⊙ Mfg	43.02	1.27		
🏭 Goods	9.96	1.16	10	9
⚙ Ind Mtrls	22.98	1.92	27	21
🔥 Energy	6.91	0.71	9	7
💡 Utilities	3.17	0.91	3	3

Composition

	%
● Cash	4.3
● Stocks	91.2
● Bonds	3.6
● Other	0.8
Foreign (% of Stock)	8.6

M⊙RNINGSTAR® Funds 500

Royce Value Service

	Ticker	Load	NAV	Yield	Total Assets	Mstar Category
	RYVFX	None	$11.06	0.1%	$470 mil	Small Blend

Governance and Management

Stewardship Grade:

Portfolio Manager(s)

Whitney George and Jay Kaplan comanage the fund. George is one of Royce's most seasoned portfolio managers, playing key roles at the successful Royce Micro-Cap, Royce Low-Priced Stock, and Royce Premier funds. Kaplan arrived at Royce in 2000 after managing a small-cap fund for Prudential for five years.

Strategy

Royce's overall approach includes finding firms that have strong balance sheets, solid growth prospects, and good valuations. Here the plan is to hold about 60 such stocks in the $500 million to $5 billion market-cap range. To date, though, the fund hasn't invested heavily in mid-caps, an area Royce has not traditionally ventured into much.

Historical Profile

Return	Above Avg
Risk	High
Rating	★★★★ Above Avg

Investment Style: Equity, Stock %

87% 81% 89% 93%

▼ Manager Change
▽ Partial Manager Change

Growth of $10,000
— Investment Values of Fund
— Investment Values of S&P 500

22.0 / 18.0 / 14.0 / 10.0 / 6.0

Performance Quartile (within Category)

1995	1996	1997	1998	1999	2000	2001	2002	2003	2004	2005	2006	History
—	—	—	—	—	—	5.89	4.35	6.56	8.39	9.67	11.06	NAV
—	—	—	—	—	—	19.20*	-23.51	54.32	30.94	17.23	16.76	Total Return %
—	—	—	—	—	—	-1.41	25.64	20.06	12.32	0.97	+/-S&P 500
—	—	—	—	—	—	-3.03	7.07	12.61	12.68	-1.61	+/-Russ 2000
—	—	—	—	—	—	0.00	0.00	0.00	0.00	0.17	Income Return %
—	—	—	—	—	—	-23.51	54.32	30.94	17.23	16.59	Capital Return %
—	—	—	—	—	—	87	9	2	3	29	Total Rtn % Rank Cat
—	—	—	—	—	0.00	0.00	0.00	0.00	0.00	0.02	Income $
—	—	—	—	—	0.07	0.16	0.15	0.19	0.16	0.22	Capital Gains $
—	—	—	—	—	—	1.49	1.49	1.49	—	Expense Ratio %
—	—	—	—	—	—	-0.06	-0.73	-0.77	—	Income Ratio %
—	—	—	—	—	—	181	83	—	Turnover Rate %
167	167	146	142	—	—	1	1	4	38	452	Net Assets $mil

Performance 12-31-06

	1st Qtr	2nd Qtr	3rd Qtr	4th Qtr	Total
2002	-0.34	-16.52	-21.02	16.41	-23.51
2003	2.07	22.07	9.78	12.82	54.32
2004	9.91	3.33	2.42	12.58	30.94
2005	-0.60	2.64	7.71	6.67	17.23
2006	12.93	-5.86	-2.14	12.23	16.76

Trailing	Total Return%	+/- S&P 500	+/- Russ 2000	%Rank Cat	Growth of $10,000
3 Mo	12.23	5.53	3.33	5	11,223
6 Mo	9.83	-2.91	0.45	19	10,983
1 Yr	16.76	0.97	-1.61	29	11,676
3 Yr Avg	21.47	11.03	7.91	3	17,923
5 Yr Avg	16.17	9.98	4.78	11	21,158
10 Yr Avg	—	—	—		—
15 Yr Avg	—	—	—		—

Tax Analysis	Tax-Adj Rtn%	%Rank Cat	Tax-Cost Rat	%Rank Cat
3 Yr (estimated)	20.82	3	0.54	11
5 Yr (estimated)	15.30	8	0.75	32
10 Yr (estimated)	—	—	—	—

Potential Capital Gain Exposure: 10% of assets

Rating and Risk

Time Period	Load-Adj Return %	Morningstar Rtn vs Cat	Morningstar Risk vs Cat	Morningstar Risk-Adj Rating
1 Yr	16.76			
3 Yr	21.47	High	+Avg	★★★★★
5 Yr	16.17	+Avg	High	★★★★
10 Yr	—	—	—	—
Incept	18.15			

Other Measures	Standard Index S&P 500	Best Fit Index Mstar Small Core
Alpha	6.4	4.6
Beta	1.56	0.96
R-Squared	61	86
Standard Deviation	13.60	
Mean	21.47	
Sharpe Ratio	1.27	

Morningstar's Take by John Coumarianos 01-03-07

Royce Value is likely to become Royce's first mid-cap fund; we think it's a winner regardless of categorization.

This fund buys companies in the $500 million to $5 billion range, making it the Royce fund that is the likeliest candidate to become a mid-cap fund at some point. Royce Premier, by contrast, owns companies with up to $2.5 billion in market capitalization (the amount it would take to own all the shares of a business).

This fund can own larger businesses, but managers Whitney George and Jay Kaplan still employ the same Royce process: They scrutinize companies' balance sheets, making sure that the still-smallish firms they own aren't burdened with potentially crushing debt. Like other Royce managers, they buy businesses they think are facing temporary problems. Heavy debt loads could make otherwise temporary problems permanent. Studying the balance sheet also gives an indication of how much money the business has to spend to

achieve its returns. Management views return on assets as the salient measure of profitability.

Florida Rock is a business that fits the bill. Providing concrete products in the Southeast, the company has been the beneficiary of development in the region. A recent sell-off due to fears of a slowing housing market gave the fund the opportunity to add shares. Kaplan notes that commercial real estate and road construction remain very strong.

Although George and Kaplan are fundamentally oriented investors, they aren't afraid to let macroeconomic factors influence them. For example, they own significant positions in precious metals mining companies, such as Silver Standard Resources and Meridian Gold, as they think the dollar will remain weak. Metals and mining stocks have a way of turning fast, but we think George and Kaplan are up to the task of navigating these and the market's other waters. This supporting player is a keeper.

Portfolio Analysis 09-30-06

Share change since 06-06 Total Stocks:64

	Sector	PE	Tot Ret%	% Assets
⊕ Florida Rock Industries	Ind Mtrls	14.0	-11.07	2.97
⊕ Ipsco	Ind Mtrls	7.4	13.97	2.75
⊕ RC2 Corporation	Goods	17.3	23.87	2.61
⊕ Unit Corporation	Energy	6.8	-11.96	2.54
⊕ Cimarex Energy Company	Energy	6.4	-14.79	2.39
⊕ Applebee's International	Consumer	21.9	10.16	2.38
⊕ Simpson Manufacturing	Ind Mtrls	13.5	-12.13	2.37
⊕ Netgear, Inc.	Hardware	27.4	36.36	2.35
⊕ Silver Standard Resource	Ind Mtrls	—	100.39	2.19
⊕ Agnico-Eagle Mines	Ind Mtrls	90.6	108.95	2.18
⊕ Arkansas Best Corporatio	Business	10.4	-16.42	2.14
⊕ CDW Corporation	Business	20.4	23.33	2.04
⊕ Meridian Gold, Inc.	Ind Mtrls	—	27.07	2.01
St. Mary Land & Explorat	Energy	11.5	0.33	1.93
⊕ Knight Capital Group, In	Business	14.3	93.83	1.92
⊕ Thor Industries, Inc.	Ind Mtrls	15.2	10.47	1.91
⊕ Korn/Ferry International	Business	16.8	22.85	1.90
⊕ Heidrick & Struggles Int	Business	23.2	32.17	1.89
Pan American Silver Corp	Ind Mtrls	—	33.67	1.80
⊕ International Speedway C	Goods	16.8	6.73	1.77

Current Investment Style

Value Blnd Growth — Large Mid Small

	Market Cap	%
	Giant	0.0
	Large	4.6
	Mid	50.5
	Small	43.7
	Micro	1.1
	Avg $mil:	1,687

Value Measures		Rel Category
Price/Earnings	13.92	0.84
Price/Book	2.33	1.10
Price/Sales	1.20	1.22
Price/Cash Flow	8.23	1.18
Dividend Yield %	0.66	0.62

Growth Measures	%	Rel Category
Long-Term Erngs	13.67	0.98
Book Value	15.91	2.10
Sales	15.88	1.80
Cash Flow	21.39	1.69
Historical Erngs	28.19	1.69

Profitability	%	Rel Category
Return on Equity	15.97	1.24
Return on Assets	10.26	1.43
Net Margin	11.85	1.22

Sector Weightings

	% of Stocks	Rel S&P 500	3 Year High	Low
⊙ Info	6.35	0.32		
Software	1.42	0.41	7	1
Hardware	4.93	0.53	11	4
Media	0.00	0.00	0	0
Telecom	0.00	0.00	3	0
⊙ Service	35.44	0.77		
Health	3.19	0.26	11	3
Consumer	11.26	1.47	16	7
Business	17.57	4.15	18	5
Financial	3.42	0.15	17	3
⊙ Mfg	58.23	1.72		
Goods	11.85	1.39	15	10
Ind Mtrls	32.61	2.73	33	18
Energy	13.77	1.41	21	12
Utilities	0.00	0.00	2	0

Composition

● Cash	7.2
● Stocks	92.8
● Bonds	0.0
● Other	0.0
Foreign	18.0
(% of Stock)	

Address:	1414 Ave of the Americas New York NY 10019 800-221-4268
Web Address:	www.roycefunds.com
Inception:	06-14-01 *
Advisor:	Royce & Associates, LLC.
Subadvisor:	None
NTF Plans:	Fidelity Retail-NTF, Schwab OneSource

Minimum Purchase:	$2000	Add: $50	IRA: $1000
Min Auto Inv Plan:	$1000	Add: $100	
Sales Fees:	No-load, 0.25%S, 1.00%R		
Management Fee:	1.00% mx./0.85% mn.		
Actual Fees:	Mgt:1.00%	Dist:0.25%	
Expense Projections:	3Yr:$479	5Yr:$830	10Yr:$1820
Income Distrib:	Annually		

MORNINGSTAR® Funds 500

RS Diversified Growth A

	Ticker	Load	NAV	Yield	Total Assets	Mstar Category
	RSDGX	4.75%	$24.13	0.0%	$216 mil	Small Growth

Governance and Management

Stewardship Grade: D

Portfolio Manager(s)

After managing this offering since its 1996 inception, John Wallace stepped down to focus on other RS funds. John Seabern, who came aboard in October 1997, remains at the helm.

Strategy

Manager John Seabern looks for rapidly growing firms boasting strong earnings momentum that they think can at least double in price over the next two years. He favors companies with growth catalysts, such as new products or management. Although the managers' process is bottom-up, they will load up on fast-moving sectors such as technology if the bulk of the opportunities are there. They trade around positions frequently, giving the fund extremely high turnover. To limit stock-specific risk, they keep individual positions small and trim stocks that fall more than 15% below the fund's cost.

Performance 12-31-06

	1st Qtr	2nd Qtr	3rd Qtr	4th Qtr	Total
2002	-8.30	-19.50	-24.93	9.85	-39.12
2003	-10.24	36.03	11.45	16.04	57.91
2004	1.34	-2.07	-9.78	13.34	1.48
2005	-7.89	2.20	8.01	-3.21	-1.59
2006	8.78	-7.62	-3.74	11.71	8.06

Trailing	Total Return%	+/- S&P 500	+/- Russ 2000 Gr	%Rank Cat	Growth of $10,000
3 Mo	11.71	5.01	2.94	5	11,171
6 Mo	7.53	-5.21	0.67	27	10,753
1 Yr	8.06	-7.73	-5.29	68	10,806
3 Yr Avg	2.57	-7.87	-7.94	96	10,791
5 Yr Avg	0.74	-5.45	-6.19	91	10,376
10 Yr Avg	11.27	2.85	6.39	23	29,092
15 Yr Avg	—				

Tax Analysis	Tax-Adj Rtn%	%Rank Cat	Tax-Cost Rat	%Rank Cat
3 Yr (estimated)	0.92	96	0.00	1
5 Yr (estimated)	-0.24	94	0.00	1
10 Yr (estimated)	9.10	28	1.47	58

Potential Capital Gain Exposure: -51% of assets

Morningstar's Take by Christopher Davis 12-27-06

Despite its virtues, it's tough to make a compelling case for RS Diversified Growth.

This offering has some appealing attributes. Manager John Seabern is very experienced: Next year will mark his 10th at the helm. He also has the benefit of veteran analysts at his disposal. Moreover, the fund boasts a demonstrated ability to reap enormous gains in up markets, as its 58% gain in 2003 and triple-digit return in 1999 make amply clear.

So what's the problem? We're dismayed by the fund's ongoing difficulty controlling risk on the downside. After its harrowing fall in the bear market--it slid nearly 70% from March 2000 through October 2002--Seabern and former comanager John Wallace took steps to limit volatility, moderating the fund's sector bets and reducing its exposure to less-liquid names. They also tightened their sell discipline. When a stock falls 15% from its cost, they're quick to pull the trigger to stem further losses. Seabern, who assumed sole control of the portfolio in early 2005, hasn't altered the thrust of this approach, although he says he's increasingly emphasized firms that can also generate stable cash flows over longer periods.

However, those measures haven't had enough of an impact. Between January and April 2005, for instance, weak tech picks dragged the fund to a 15% loss (4 percentage points more than the small-growth average), contributing to its bottom-decile showing for the year. The fund has also struggled in 2006's topsy-turvy market. As stocks have slid over the past few months, the fund has dropped nearly 20% and is down 8% for the year to date through Aug. 9, 2006, placing it just outside its group's bottom decile.

Another fly in the ointment is the fund's lofty--and rising--expense ratio. At 1.63% annually, it's far more costly than the typical no-load small-cap fund, making it even tougher for Seabern to compete with his rivals. All told, we'd take a pass on this fund.

Address:	388 Market Street San Francisco CA 94111 800-766-3863	Minimum Purchase:	$5000	Add: $100	IRA: $1000
		Min Auto Inv Plan:	$1000	Add: $100	
		Sales Fees:	4.75%L, 0.25%S		
Web Address:	www.rsim.com	Management Fee:	1.00%		
Inception:	08-01-96*	Actual Fees:	Mgt:1.00%	Dist:0.25%	
Advisor:	RS Investment Management Co LLC	Expense Projections:	3Yr:$980	5Yr:$1347	10Yr:$2377
Subadvisor:	None	Income Distrib:	Annually		
NTF Plans:	Schwab OneSource				

Historical Profile

Return	Below Avg
Risk	Above Avg
Rating	★★ Below Avg

| 94% | 97% | 98% | 95% | 98% | 100% | 98% | 100% | 94% |

Investment Style
Equity
Stock %

▼ Manager Change
▽ Partial Manager Change

Growth of $10,000

— Investment Values of Fund
— Investment Values of S&P 500

59.0
43.6
32.4
24.0
17.0
10.0

Performance Quartile (within Category)

1995	1996	1997	1998	1999	2000	2001	2002	2003	2004	2005	2006	History
—	12.42	14.04	15.89	32.99	22.83	23.26	14.16	22.36	22.69	22.33	24.13	NAV
—	24.20*	29.45	16.28	150.21	-26.91	1.88	-39.12	57.91	1.48	-1.59	8.06	Total Return %
—	—	-3.91	-12.30	129.17	-17.81	13.77	-17.02	29.23	-9.40	-6.50	-7.73	+/-S&P 500
—	—	16.50	15.05	107.12	-4.48	11.11	-8.86	9.37	-12.83	-5.74	-5.29	+/-Russ 2000 Gr
—	—	0.00	0.00	0.00	0.00	0.00	0.00	0.00	0.00	0.00	0.00	Income Return %
—	—	29.45	16.28	150.21	-26.91	1.88	-39.12	57.91	1.48	-1.59	8.06	Capital Return %
—	—	16	18	3	95	23	84	14	93	94	68	Total Rtn % Rank Cat
—	0.00	0.00	0.00	0.00	0.00	0.00	0.00	0.00	0.00	0.00	0.00	Income $
—	0.00	1.93	0.39	5.48	1.23	0.00	0.00	0.00	0.00	0.00	0.00	Capital Gains $
—	—	2.28	1.94	1.89	1.84	1.51	1.52	1.50	1.48	1.58	—	Expense Ratio %
—	—	-1.05	-1.20	-1.29	-1.40	-1.01	-1.03	-1.11	-0.92	-1.23	—	Income Ratio %
—	—	—	370	403	473	383	255	223	305	230	—	Turnover Rate %
—	60	80	69	305	523	852	572	1,098	956	216	Net Assets $mil

Rating and Risk

Time Period	Load-Adj Return %	Morningstar Rtn vs Cat	Morningstar Risk vs Cat	Morningstar Risk-Adj Rating
1 Yr	2.93			
3 Yr	0.92	Low	+Avg	★
5 Yr	-0.24	Low	+Avg	★
10 Yr	10.73	+Avg	+Avg	★★★
Incept	12.60			

Other Measures	Standard Index S&P 500	Best Fit Index Russ 2000 Gr
Alpha	-13.1	-7.3
Beta	1.98	1.00
R-Squared	67	91
Standard Deviation	16.61	
Mean	2.57	
Sharpe Ratio	0.04	

Portfolio Analysis 09-30-06

Share change since 06-06 Total Stocks:95	Sector	PE	Tot Ret%	% Assets
⊕ Build-A-Bear Workshop, I	Consumer	21.4	-5.47	2.15
⊕ NutriSystem, Inc.	Goods	33.2	75.99	2.05
⊖ Trizetto Group, Inc.	Software	60.3	8.12	1.83
⊖ Cache, Inc.	Consumer	31.9	45.73	1.77
⊕ PolyMedica Corporation	Health	29.4	22.59	1.74
⊖ Cymer, Inc.	Hardware	19.9	23.77	1.72
⊕ Equinix, Inc.	Business	—	85.53	1.68
✕ Atheros Communications,	Hardware	38.9	64.00	1.53
✕ Kyphon, Inc.	Health	56.5	-1.05	1.42
✕ WebEx Communications, In	Software	36.5	61.30	1.41
⊖ California Pizza Kitchen	Consumer	32.2	4.19	1.38
⊖ FactSet Research Systems	Business	33.8	37.91	1.36
⊖ Affiliated Managers Grou	Financial	32.5	31.00	1.35
⊖ Cogent Communications Gr	Telecom	—	195.45	1.34
⊖ FTI Consulting, Inc.	Business	20.4	1.64	1.34
⊖ Iconix Brand Group, Inc.	Goods	42.7	90.29	1.31
⊖ Viasys Healthcare, Inc.	Health	29.9	8.25	1.29
⊖ InPhonic, Inc.	Telecom	—	27.62	1.29
⊕ Pinnacle Entertainment I	Consumer	21.2	34.12	1.27
⊖ Oregon Steel Mills, Inc.	Ind Mtrls	14.0	112.14	1.27

Current Investment Style

Value Blnd Growth — Large/Mid/Small

Market Cap	%
Giant	0.0
Large	0.0
Mid	20.5
Small	47.6
Micro	32.0

Avg $mil: 846

Value Measures		Rel Category
Price/Earnings	19.24	0.92
Price/Book	3.26	1.19
Price/Sales	1.82	1.16
Price/Cash Flow	8.78	0.91
Dividend Yield %	0.05	0.11

Growth Measures	%	Rel Category
Long-Term Erngs	19.31	1.09
Book Value	-0.89	NMF
Sales	-0.49	NMF
Cash Flow	11.94	0.56
Historical Erngs	24.43	1.01

Profitability	%	Rel Category
Return on Equity	8.79	0.71
Return on Assets	4.95	0.74
Net Margin	6.13	0.71

Sector Weightings	% of Stocks	Rel S&P 500	3 Year High Low	
↻ Info	30.74	1.54		
🖳 Software	10.48	3.04	14	7
🖥 Hardware	15.43	1.67	20	12
🎙 Media	0.00	0.00	2	0
📶 Telecom	4.83	1.38	8	2
☞ Service	52.71	1.14		
🩺 Health	13.73	1.14	19	12
🛒 Consumer	10.94	1.43	12	5
💲 Business	19.02	4.50	21	10
💲 Financial	9.02	0.41	12	5
⌐ Mfg	16.55	0.49		
🏭 Goods	3.68	0.43	5	2
✿ Ind Mtrls	6.93	0.58	10	1
🔥 Energy	5.94	0.61	9	6
💡 Utilities	0.00	0.00	1	0

Composition

		%
● Cash		5.8
● Stocks		94.2
● Bonds		0.0
● Other		0.0
Foreign (% of Stock)		7.1

Morningstar® Funds 500

RS Emerging Growth A

	Ticker	Load	NAV	Yield	Total Assets	Mstar Category
	RSEGX	4.75%	$35.66	0.0%	$743 mil	Small Growth

Governance and Management

Stewardship Grade: D

Portfolio Manager(s)

Jim Callinan was named Morningstar's 1999 Domestic Stock Fund Manager of the Year. He has delivered strong results since taking the helm in 1996, and he also blew past the competition during an earlier stint at Putnam OTC Emerging Growth. He's supported by a team of analysts, including Wendell Laidley, a software analyst formerly of First Boston, and Greg Miliotes, a health-care analyst formerly of Robertson Stephens.

Strategy

Jim Callinan and his team of analysts look for companies growing revenues or earnings at 20% or better per year. Among those, the team prefers firms with proprietary advantages that give them an edge over their rivals, strong management teams, and high or improving margins. The fund often puts more than half of its assets into the technology sector. It typically holds well more than 100 names, and individual position sizes are relatively small.

Historical Profile

Return	Below Avg
Risk	Above Avg
Rating	★★ Below Avg

Investment Style: Equity Stock %

	100%	100%	86%	100%	96%	98%	96%	97%	97%

▼ Manager Change
▽ Partial Manager Change

Growth of $10,000
— Investment Values of Fund
— Investment Values of S&P 500

77.2
53.4
36.6
25.4
17.0
10.0

Performance Quartile (within Category)

1995	1996	1997	1998	1999	2000	2001	2002	2003	2004	2005	2006	History
19.21	20.07	18.71	22.95	60.67	44.02	32.00	19.15	28.10	32.36	32.58	35.66	NAV
20.31	21.53	18.54	28.02	182.56	-25.04	-27.31	-40.16	46.74	15.16	0.68	9.45	Total Return %
-17.27	-1.43	-14.82	-0.56	161.52	-15.94	-15.42	-18.06	18.06	4.28	-4.23	-6.34	+/-S&P 500
-10.73	10.27	5.59	26.79	139.47	-2.61	-18.08	-9.90	-1.80	0.85	-3.47	-3.90	+/-Russ 2000 Gr
0.00	0.00	0.00	0.00	0.00	0.00	0.00	0.00	0.00	0.00	0.00	0.00	Income Return %
20.31	21.53	18.54	28.02	182.56	-25.04	-27.31	-40.16	46.74	15.16	0.68	9.45	Capital Return %
84	34	47	3	2	93	86	88	39	30	87	57	Total Rtn % Rank Cat
0.00	0.00	0.00	0.00	0.00	0.00	0.00	0.00	0.00	0.00	0.00	0.00	Income $
1.58	3.19	5.02	0.88	3.31	1.44	0.00	0.00	0.00	0.00	0.00	0.00	Capital Gains $
1.64	1.60	1.50	1.47	1.51	1.29	1.37	1.53	1.49	1.59	1.54	—	Expense Ratio %
-0.99	-0.83	-0.68	-1.03	-1.19	-0.82	-0.79	-1.35	-1.39	-1.47	-1.32	—	Income Ratio %
147	270	462	291	177	157	148	166	190	156	95	—	Turnover Rate %
159	210	249	394	3,577	3,869	2,498	1,310	1,636	1,411	935	743	Net Assets $mil

Performance 12-31-06

	1st Qtr	2nd Qtr	3rd Qtr	4th Qtr	Total
2002	-9.16	-21.33	-22.61	8.19	-40.16
2003	-3.50	24.13	10.64	10.72	46.74
2004	5.55	-1.08	-5.56	16.78	15.16
2005	-8.56	4.02	4.13	1.65	0.68
2006	11.30	-7.42	-1.70	8.06	9.45

Trailing	Total Return%	+/- S&P 500	+/- Russ 2000 Gr	%Rank Cat	Growth of $10,000
3 Mo	8.06	1.36	-0.71	49	10,806
6 Mo	6.23	-6.51	-0.63	38	10,623
1 Yr	9.45	-6.34	-3.90	57	10,945
3 Yr Avg	8.27	-2.17	-2.24	66	12,692
5 Yr Avg	2.19	-4.00	-4.74	83	11,144
10 Yr Avg	10.04	1.62	5.16	33	26,032
15 Yr Avg	10.20	-0.44	3.10	39	42,926

Tax Analysis	Tax-Adj Rtn%	%Rank Cat	Tax-Cost Rat	%Rank Cat
3 Yr (estimated)	6.52	70	0.00	1
5 Yr (estimated)	1.20	87	0.00	1
10 Yr (estimated)	8.03	37	1.35	50

Potential Capital Gain Exposure: 11% of assets

Rating and Risk

Time Period	Load-Adj Return %	Morningstar Rtn vs Cat	Morningstar Risk vs Cat	Morningstar Risk-Adj Rating
1 Yr	4.25			
3 Yr	6.52	-Avg	+Avg	★★
5 Yr	1.20	-Avg	+Avg	★★
10 Yr	9.51	Avg	High	★★
Incept	15.16			

Other Measures	Standard Index S&P 500	Best Fit Index Mstar Small Growth
Alpha	-7.7	-1.1
Beta	1.97	0.97
R-Squared	69	94
Standard Deviation	16.21	
Mean	8.27	
Sharpe Ratio	0.37	

Morningstar's Take by Christopher Davis 12-27-06

We were wrong about RS Emerging Growth.

The case for our endorsement of this offering during and after its harrowing fall in the bear market rested on three pillars. For one, we thought manager Jim Callinan's experience and the substantial analyst support at his disposal gave the fund a competitive advantage. Second, we liked that Callinan has stuck with his strategy of seeking fast-growing stocks in emerging sectors of the economy through thick and thin. Finally, we believed he would trounce the competition if his highly aggressive strategy returned to favor.

Our faith in Callinan's abilities has diminished, however. While he rode the tech and Internet wave with aplomb in the late 1990s, he's had difficulty ferreting out winners in both areas in recent years, as in 2005, when picks like Infospace and Overstock.com helped limit the fund to a slim 1% return--a bottom-quartile showing in the small-growth category. Callinan has also run into trouble elsewhere. In 2005, the fund was also stymied by biotech holdings such as Rigel and Alexion, which stumbled badly after the release of disappointing clinical data. Even in 2003, when tech and biotech stocks were up big, the fund merely matched the small-growth average, albeit with a healthy 47% return.

Should our assessment of Callinan's talents prove too pessimistic, we still think the inherent risks of his strategy aren't worth the potential rewards. His preference for emerging firms and his willingness to pay up for them has led to enormous losses that are difficult to recoup, even over longer periods. Indeed, those who bought this fund at its March 2000 peak would still be down nearly 60%. Because Callinan, unlike other RS growth managers, took few steps after the bear market to lessen volatility, the risks remain great.

We acknowledge the fund's potential for gain, but given its extreme risks and our deteriorating confidence in management, we can no longer recommend it.

Portfolio Analysis 09-30-06

Share change since 06-06 Total Stocks:118

Sector	PE	Tot Ret%	% Assets
⊖ Digital River, Inc. — Business	38.3	87.59	1.95
⊕ Kyphon, Inc. — Health	56.5	-1.05	1.91
⊕ Atheros Communications, — Hardware	38.9	64.00	1.70
Portfolio Recovery Assoc — Business	17.3	0.54	1.68
⊖ LifeCell Corporation — Health	45.6	26.79	1.61
⊖ Akamai Technologies, Inc — Software	26.0	166.53	1.61
⊕ PolyMedica Corporation — Health	29.4	22.59	1.56
Affiliated Managers Grou — Financial	32.5	31.00	1.54
⊕ Silicon Image, Inc. — Hardware	39.1	40.24	1.50
⊕ Equinix, Inc. — Business	—	85.53	1.49
⊕ Time Warner Telecom, Inc — Telecom	—	102.34	1.48
⊕ Vital Images, Inc. — Health	67.4	33.08	1.47
⊕ Investment Technology Gr — Financial	20.4	20.99	1.47
⊕ Coldwater Creek — Consumer	36.0	20.47	1.39
⊖ aQuantive, Inc. — Business	45.9	-2.30	1.33
⊕ Allscripts Healthcare So — Software	NMF	101.42	1.31
⊕ Navigators Group — Financial	11.3	10.48	1.27
optionsXpress Holdings, — Financial	—	-6.86	1.22
⊕ THQ, Inc. — Software	81.9	36.35	1.21
⊕ MicroStrategy, Inc. — Business	26.5	37.91	1.20

Current Investment Style

Value Blnd Growth — Large Mid Small

Market Cap	%
Giant	0.0
Large	0.0
Mid	24.3
Small	61.9
Micro	13.7
Avg $mil:	1,160

Value Measures		Rel Category
Price/Earnings	25.44	1.21
Price/Book	3.85	1.41
Price/Sales	2.81	1.79
Price/Cash Flow	12.92	1.34
Dividend Yield %	0.10	0.22

Growth Measures	%	Rel Category
Long-Term Erngs	21.10	1.19
Book Value	7.18	0.69
Sales	19.58	1.65
Cash Flow	27.60	1.30
Historical Erngs	21.67	0.89

Profitability	%	Rel Category
Return on Equity	12.95	1.04
Return on Assets	8.89	1.33
Net Margin	10.83	1.25

Sector Weightings	% of Stocks	Rel S&P 500	3 Year High Low	
⌖ Info	29.42	1.47		
Software	11.98	3.47	12	7
Hardware	14.33	1.55	21	14
Media	0.44	0.12	2	0
Telecom	2.67	0.76	4	2
⌾ Service	60.04	1.30		
Health	22.04	1.83	25	19
Consumer	10.40	1.36	15	10
Business	16.23	3.84	21	12
Financial	11.37	0.51	11	7
⌂ Mfg	10.55	0.31		
Goods	5.42	0.63	6	0
Ind Mtrls	1.70	0.14	4	1
Energy	3.43	0.35	7	1
Utilities	0.00	0.00	1	0

Composition

● Cash	2.9
● Stocks	97.1
● Bonds	0.0
● Other	0.0
Foreign	7.0
(% of Stock)	

Address:	388 Market Street San Francisco CA 94111 800-766-3863	Minimum Purchase:	$5000 Add: $100 IRA: $1000
		Min Auto Inv Plan:	$1000 Add: $100
		Sales Fees:	4.75%L, 0.25%S
Web Address:	www.rsim.com	Management Fee:	0.95%
Inception:	11-30-87	Actual Fees:	Mgt:0.95% Dist:0.25%
Advisor:	RS Investment Management Co LLC	Expense Projections:	3Yr:$953 5Yr:$1299 10Yr:$2272
Subadvisor:	None	Income Distrib:	Annually
NTF Plans:	Schwab OneSource		

RS MidCap Opport A

	Ticker	Load	NAV	Yield	Total Assets	Mstar Category
	RSMOX	4.75%	$14.17	0.0%	$268 mil	Mid-Cap Growth

Governance and Management

Stewardship Grade: C

Portfolio Manager(s)

John Wallace has one of the better long-term records of any manager. He fared extremely well at Oppenheimer Total Return and Oppenheimer Main Street Growth & Income from 1990 through 1995 and had great success at RS Diversified Growth in the late 1990s.

Strategy

Manager John Wallace seeks fast-growing companies with strong earnings growth that he thinks can double in price within 18 months. He sets upside price targets on his buys and starts selling stocks when they get within 10% of those targets. He's also quick to trim names that drop more than 15% below the fund's cost. The fund's price multiples are below the category average, and Wallace spreads his picks across roughly 80-100 names. The fund's turnover is extremely high.

Performance 12-31-06

	1st Qtr	2nd Qtr	3rd Qtr	4th Qtr	Total
2002	-4.23	-14.63	-15.54	6.57	-26.41
2003	1.51	19.30	7.81	13.75	48.49
2004	3.78	0.98	-2.99	10.53	12.36
2005	-3.12	2.63	7.93	2.07	9.52
2006	9.89	-4.57	-0.71	5.10	9.43

Trailing	Total Return%	+/- S&P 500	+/- Russ MG	%Rank Cat	Growth of $10,000
3 Mo	5.10	-1.60	-1.85	78	10,510
6 Mo	4.35	-8.39	-3.55	68	10,435
1 Yr	4.35	-6.36	-1.23	44	10,943
3 Yr Avg	10.43	-0.01	-2.30	56	13,467
5 Yr Avg	8.03	1.84	-0.19	30	14,714
10 Yr Avg	9.73	1.31	1.11	31	25,308
15 Yr Avg	—	—	—		—

Tax Analysis	Tax-Adj Rtn%	%Rank Cat	Tax-Cost Rat	%Rank Cat
3 Yr (estimated)	8.50	64	0.14	8
5 Yr (estimated)	6.89	34	0.09	8
10 Yr (estimated)	6.20	58	2.75	95

Potential Capital Gain Exposure: 11% of assets

Morningstar's Take by Christopher Davis 12-14-06

RS MidCap Opportunities sticks its neck out, but it does so sensibly.

Manager John Wallace certainly is no wallflower. He wants fast-growing companies whose stocks can double in price in 18 months, and he'll delve heavily in areas where he thinks earnings growth will be the strongest. Wallace will invest wherever he can find growth, but these days his biggest bet is on technology, the most traditional of growth sectors. He says corporate balance sheets are flush with cash, and in a slowing economy, he thinks companies will buy technology to jump-start growth. Wallace ratcheted up his stake in the sector on weakness in the summer, adding holdings such as BEA Systems and Integrated Device Technology. The fund's combined hardware and software weightings now account for 29% of its stock holdings, versus 17% for the typical mid-growth offering.

One might expect such boldness to lead to a lot of volatility. The fund certainly isn't immune to steep losses--it dropped 11% from May through July 2006, for instance--but volatility (as measured by standard deviation) hasn't been any worse than the mid-growth average. In part, that's because Wallace keeps the position sizes small, limiting the impact of an errant stock pick. He also avoids excessive valuation risk by quickly trimming winners when they reach his upside targets. On the flip side, he's also quick to limit losses. If a stock falls 15% below what he paid for it, he's out.

Wallace's approach leads to a lot of turnover (last year it clocked in at 207%), which could make the fund a headache for investors in taxable accounts. It also requires investors to weather substantial losses to make their investment worthwhile. Those that can will find a seasoned, successful investor in Wallace. This fund isn't exactly cheap, but its annual expense ratio fell recently from 1.49% to 1.34%, further heightening its appeal.

Address:	388 Market Street San Francisco CA 94111 800-766-3863	Minimum Purchase: Min Auto Inv Plan: Sales Fees: Management Fee: Actual Fees: Expense Projections: Income Distrib:	$5000 $1000 4.75%L, 0.25%S 0.85% Mgt:0.85% 3Yr:$892 Annually	Add: $100 Add: $100 Dist:0.25% 5Yr:$1205	IRA: $1000 10Yr:$2094
Web Address: Inception: Advisor: Subadvisor:	www.rsim.com 07-12-95 * RS Investment Management Co LLC None				
NTF Plans:	Schwab OneSource				

Historical Profile

Return	Average
Risk	Average
Rating	★★★ Neutral

| | 77% | 96% | 89% | 87% | 91% | 91% | 96% | 96% | 96% |

▼ Manager Change
▽ Partial Manager Change

— Growth of $10,000
■ Investment Values of Fund
— Investment Values of S&P 500

Investment Style
Equity
Stock %

Performance Quartile (within Category)

1995	1996	1997	1998	1999	2000	2001	2002	2003	2004	2005	2006	History
11.24	13.62	13.52	14.04	15.92	11.65	9.92	7.30	10.84	12.18	13.34	14.17	NAV
12.40*	24.16	22.39	11.65	56.12	-6.28	-14.01	-26.41	48.49	12.36	9.52	9.43	Total Return %
—	1.20	-10.97	-16.93	35.08	2.82	-2.12	-4.31	19.81	1.48	4.61	-6.36	+/-S&P 500
—	6.68	-0.15	-6.21	4.83	5.47	6.14	1.00	5.78	-3.12	-2.58	-1.23	+/-Russ MG
—	0.18	0.28	1.43	0.33	0.12	0.85	0.00	0.00	0.00	0.00	0.00	Income Return %
—	23.98	22.11	10.22	55.79	-6.40	-14.86	-26.41	48.49	12.36	9.52	9.43	Capital Return %
—	15	41	65	46	55	42	50	7	61	58	44	Total Rtn % Rank Cat
0.00	0.02	0.04	0.19	0.05	0.02	0.10	0.00	0.00	0.00	0.00	0.00	Income $
0.00	0.32	3.04	0.77	5.06	3.14	0.00	0.00	0.00	0.00	0.00	0.44	Capital Gains $
—	1.71	1.30	1.30	1.59	1.39	1.47	1.53	1.53	1.49	1.34	—	Expense Ratio %
—	0.18	0.45	1.00	0.31	-0.14	0.87	-0.60	-0.76	-0.88	-0.77	—	Income Ratio %
—	212	236	212	408	542	409	401	253	184	207	—	Turnover Rate %
136	310	298	184	227	198	156	89	141	209	219	268	Net Assets $mil

Rating and Risk

Time Period	Load-Adj Return %	Morningstar Rtn vs Cat	Morningstar Risk vs Cat	Morningstar Risk-Adj Rating
1 Yr	4.24			
3 Yr	8.65	-Avg	+Avg	★★
5 Yr	6.99	Avg	+Avg	★★★
10 Yr	9.20	Avg	-Avg	★★★
Incept	11.15			

Other Measures	Standard Index S&P 500	Best Fit Index Mstar Mid Growth TR
Alpha	-3.6	-3.1
Beta	1.60	1.02
R-Squared	67	91
Standard Deviation	13.50	
Mean	10.43	
Sharpe Ratio	0.56	

Portfolio Analysis 09-30-06

Share change since 06-06 Total Stocks:81

	Sector	PE	Tot Ret%	% Assets
⊕ Palm, Inc.	Hardware	4.7	-11.38	1.98
⊕ Mueller Water Products,	Ind Mtrls	—		1.96
⊕ Netflix, Inc.	Consumer	22.1	-4.44	1.75
⊕ Cymer, Inc.	Hardware	19.9	23.77	1.68
⊕ Boyd Gaming Corporation	Consumer	32.8	-3.73	1.62
⊕ Sunrise Senior Living, I	Health	18.5	-8.87	1.62
⊕ Tellabs, Inc.	Hardware	18.0	-5.87	1.60
⊕ Trident Microsystems Inc	Hardware	92.0	1.00	1.56
✵ NutriSystem, Inc.	Goods	33.2	75.99	1.55
✵ Checkfree Corporation	Software	30.2	-12.51	1.48
⊖ Ciena Corporation	Hardware	—	33.29	1.45
⊖ People's Bank	Financial	45.5	47.71	1.41
⊖ bebe stores, inc.	Consumer	19.5	42.46	1.38
✵ Alliance Data Systems Co	Business	29.1	75.48	1.38
⊖ Gemstar-TV Guide Interna	Goods	65.0	53.64	1.37
⊖ Novellus Systems, Inc.	Hardware	35.3	42.70	1.36
⊕ Scientific Games Corpora	Consumer	40.4	10.81	1.34
✵ Celgene Corporation	Health	—	77.56	1.33
⊖ InterDigital Communicati	Hardware	7.5	83.13	1.31
⊖ Cephalon, Inc.	Health	28.6	8.76	1.30

Current Investment Style

Value Blnd Growth — Large Mid Small

Market Cap	%
Giant	1.3
Large	14.1
Mid	62.9
Small	20.7
Micro	1.1

Avg $mil: 4,194

Value Measures		Rel Category
Price/Earnings	21.86	1.07
Price/Book	3.27	1.02
Price/Sales	1.82	1.03
Price/Cash Flow	9.44	0.83
Dividend Yield %	0.37	0.59

Growth Measures	%	Rel Category
Long-Term Erngs	16.01	0.99
Book Value	8.20	0.64
Sales	5.86	0.59
Cash Flow	18.46	1.00
Historical Erngs	24.32	0.97

Profitability	%	Rel Category
Return on Equity	17.72	0.99
Return on Assets	9.21	0.98
Net Margin	10.93	0.94

Sector Weightings	% of Stocks	Rel S&P 500	3 Year High Low	
↻ Info	30.42	1.52		
🖥 Software	8.42	2.44	8	2
💻 Hardware	20.90	2.26	22	17
🎬 Media	1.10	0.29	3	1
📞 Telecom	0.00	0.00	6	0
☞ Service	49.43	1.07		
🏥 Health	16.91	1.40	22	13
🛒 Consumer	12.44	1.63	17	8
🏢 Business	7.06	1.67	13	4
💲 Financial	13.02	0.58	15	7
🏭 Mfg	20.16	0.60		
🛢 Goods	8.12	0.95	8	3
⚙ Ind Mtrls	5.63	0.47	12	3
🔋 Energy	5.43	0.55	15	5
💡 Utilities	0.98	0.28	6	0

Composition

● Cash	3.8	
● Stocks	96.2	
● Bonds	0.0	
● Other	0.0	
Foreign	1.1	
(% of Stock)		

M∂RNINGSTAR® Funds 500

RS Value A

	Ticker	Load	NAV	Yield	Total Assets	Mstar Category
	RSVAX	4.75%	$27.43	1.1%	$2,001 mil	Mid-Cap Blend

Governance and Management

Stewardship Grade: C

Portfolio Manager(s)

Andrew Pilara has managed the fund since September 1998. Two former analysts on the fund, David Kelley and Joe Wolf, were named comanagers in early 2004. Mackenzie Davis became a comanager in October 2006, though he's been an analyst for the fund since 2004. Wolf has worked on the fund since 2001. Kelley has worked on the fund since 2002.

Strategy

The fund uses a value-based style to find out-of-favor companies that the managers think are worth more than the market suggests. The team looks for companies that are cheap and that earn or are on their way to earning a cash return on capital that exceeds their cost of capital. The managers have at times concentrated the fund in commodities-based industries such as energy and precious metals, but they've made an effort recently to keep the fund better diversified across sectors.

Performance 12-31-06

	1st Qtr	2nd Qtr	3rd Qtr	4th Qtr	Total
2002	2.27	5.51	-8.70	2.91	1.38
2003	6.82	16.97	13.42	17.13	65.98
2004	6.28	-1.11	4.80	17.39	29.31
2005	0.82	4.19	5.50	0.77	11.67
2006	4.52	-0.39	2.93	8.59	16.37

Trailing	Total Return%	+/- S&P 500	+/- S&P Mid 400	%Rank Cat	Growth of $10,000
3 Mo	8.59	1.89	1.60	27	10,859
6 Mo	11.77	-0.97	5.94	22	11,177
1 Yr	16.37	0.58	6.05	24	11,637
3 Yr Avg	18.89	8.45	5.80	4	16,805
5 Yr Avg	23.11	16.92	12.22	3	28,279
10 Yr Avg	6.50	-1.92	-6.97	93	18,771
15 Yr Avg	—	—	—	—	—

Tax Analysis	Tax-Adj Rtn%	%Rank Cat	Tax-Cost Rat	%Rank Cat
3 Yr (estimated)	16.63	8	0.30	14
5 Yr (estimated)	21.70	3	0.18	11
10 Yr (estimated)	5.71	87	0.26	4

Potential Capital Gain Exposure: 18% of assets

Historical Profile

Return Average
Risk Average
Rating ★★★ Neutral

88%	99%	92%	84%	90%	83%	86%	87%	82%

▼ Manager Change
▽ Partial Manager Change

Growth of $10,000
— Investment Values of Fund
— Investment Values of S&P 500

Investment Style
Equity
Stock %

Performance Quartile (within Category)

1995	1996	1997	1998	1999	2000	2001	2002	2003	2004	2005	2006	History
13.78	16.57	11.61	7.23	10.00	11.03	10.12	10.26	17.03	21.99	24.55	27.43	NAV
30.86	21.68	-29.51	-32.69	38.31	10.30	-8.25	1.38	65.98	29.31	11.67	16.37	Total Return %
-6.72	-1.28	-62.87	-61.27	17.27	19.40	3.64	23.48	37.30	18.43	6.76	0.58	+/-S&P 500
-0.07	2.43	-61.76	-51.81	23.59	-7.21	-7.64	15.91	30.36	12.83	-0.89	6.05	+/-S&P Mid 400
0.00	0.00	0.30	0.00	0.00	0.00	0.00	0.00	0.00	0.18	0.03	1.27	Income Return %
30.86	21.68	-29.81	-32.69	38.31	10.30	-8.25	1.38	65.98	29.13	11.64	15.10	Capital Return %
36	37	100	100	14	55	81	1	5	1	31	24	Total Rtn % Rank Cat
0.00	0.00	0.05	0.00	0.00	0.00	0.00	0.00	0.00	0.03	0.01	0.31	Income $
0.00	0.20	0.03	0.58	0.00	0.00	0.00	0.00	0.00	0.00	0.00	0.83	Capital Gains $
2.54	2.46	2.48	2.83	2.17	2.22	2.22	1.67	1.54	1.49	1.39	—	Expense Ratio %
-0.20	-0.02	0.01	-0.80	-1.17	0.19	-0.59	-0.40	0.54	0.65	-0.15	—	Income Ratio %
79	44	36	39	86	117	131	125	129	147	83	—	Turnover Rate %
508	1,063	403	126	116	92	67	57	373	625	1,570	2,001	Net Assets $mil

Rating and Risk

Time Period	Load-Adj Return %	Morningstar Rtn vs Cat	Morningstar Risk vs Cat	Morningstar Risk-Adj Rating
1 Yr	10.84			
3 Yr	16.98	+Avg	Avg	★★★★
5 Yr	21.92	High	-Avg	★★★★★
10 Yr	5.99	Low	Avg	★
Incept	8.50			

Other Measures	Standard Index S&P 500	Best Fit Index Mstar Mid Value
Alpha	6.9	-0.4
Beta	1.12	1.09
R-Squared	54	78
Standard Deviation	10.35	
Mean	18.89	
Sharpe Ratio	1.42	

Portfolio Analysis 09-30-06

Share change since 06-06 Total Stocks:47	Sector	PE	Tot Ret%	% Assets
⊕ Corrections Corporation	Business	28.1	50.87	4.62
Kkr Private Equity	—	—	—	3.27
Brookfield Asset Managem	Financial	25.7	46.00	2.87
Comcast Corporation A	Media	45.2	63.31	2.86
⊕ Talisman Energy, Inc.	Energy	13.8	-2.90	2.79
⊕ Scientific Games Corpora	Consumer	40.4	10.81	2.78
⊕ NCR Corporation	Hardware	22.6	25.99	2.70
Symantec Corporation	Software	50.9	19.14	2.66
MI Developments	Financial	—	—	2.65
☼ AP ALTERNATIVE ASSETS L.		—	—	2.61
Liberty Global	Media	—	—	2.53
PPL Corporation	Utilities	15.2	26.06	2.49
⊕ Peabody Energy Corporati	Energy	17.3	-1.48	2.43
Amvescap PLC ADR	Financial	44.2	62.99	2.31
⊕ Allegheny Technologies C	Ind Mtrls	17.1	152.95	2.24
Triad Hospitals, Inc.	Health	15.5	6.63	2.05
Ameriprise Financial, In	Financial	—	—	2.01
Federated Investors, Inc	Financial	19.0	-6.94	2.01
⊕ Viacom, Inc. B	Media	—	—	1.96
Ambac Financial Group, I	Financial	10.9	16.52	1.96

Current Investment Style

Value Blnd Growth — Large Mid Small

Market Cap	%
Giant	7.9
Large	33.1
Mid	56.7
Small	2.3
Micro	0.0

Avg $mil: 8,079

Value Measures		Rel Category
Price/Earnings	18.56	1.15
Price/Book	2.12	0.94
Price/Sales	1.56	1.39
Price/Cash Flow	7.37	0.87
Dividend Yield %	0.85	0.65

Growth Measures	%	Rel Category
Long-Term Erngs	12.82	1.01
Book Value	10.25	1.23
Sales	7.76	0.87
Cash Flow	24.57	2.90
Historical Erngs	31.00	1.73

Profitability	%	Rel Category
Return on Equity	15.05	0.94
Return on Assets	7.15	0.89
Net Margin	10.82	1.00

Sector Weightings	% of Stocks	Rel S&P 500	3 Year High	Low
↻ Info	30.29	1.52		
⬚ Software	5.42	1.57	6	0
⬚ Hardware	4.09	0.44	8	0
⬚ Media	20.78	5.48	21	10
⬚ Telecom	0.00	0.00	4	0
⬚ Service	51.43	1.11		
⬚ Health	6.20	0.51	24	5
⬚ Consumer	5.42	0.71	23	1
⬚ Business	9.93	2.35	13	3
⬚ Financial	29.88	1.34	35	7
⬚ Mfg	18.27	0.54		
⬚ Goods	0.00	0.00	6	0
⬚ Ind Mtrls	8.47	0.71	23	7
⬚ Energy	6.64	0.68	12	7
⬚ Utilities	3.16	0.90	5	0

Composition

	%
● Cash	14.7
● Stocks	82.0
● Bonds	0.0
● Other	3.3
Foreign (% of Stock)	21.9

Morningstar's Take by Christopher Davis 11-29-06

RS Value's appeal continues to grow.

Lead manager Andy Pilara has been bulking up this fund's already formidable roster of portfolio managers and analysts. He says his goal is to add depth, not breadth, to his team. The new additions are seasoned; recent hire Earl Schliemer, for instance, had eight years of experience as a financials analyst at RCM Global Investors before coming aboard. Schliemer joins Robert Harris, a colleague from RCM, as a second analyst covering financials. Ken Settles, another new analyst, focuses on the industrials and energy sectors along with recently named comanager Mackenzie Davis. In total, nine managers and analysts lead this offering and siblings RS Partners and RS Large Cap Value.

Many fund shops add to their analyst staffs so they can follow more companies. Pilara, however, wants to use his growing analytical heft to better understand the stocks already held in this compact portfolio. Pilara and his crew apply rigorous criteria in vetting potential picks. No name makes the cut unless they think it can earn a high enough return on invested capital to top its costs of capital. They also want a hefty margin of safety--generally, they're looking for stocks trading at a 50% discount to what they think they're worth.

Investors who command such steep discounts often restrict themselves to deep-value stocks, but that's not the case here. The portfolio now straddles the growth and blend columns of the Morningstar Style Box. Indeed, one recent addition is Yahoo, which Pilara likes for its high returns on capital and cheap price tag.

Pilara and his team have executed their strategy with aplomb, as the fund's long-term record attests. A concentrated portfolio and offbeat sector weightings court volatility, but management's experience and its exacting standards give us confidence.

Address:	388 Market Street San Francisco CA 94111 800-766-3863	Minimum Purchase:	$5000	Add: $100	IRA: $1000
		Min Auto Inv Plan:	$1000	Add: $100	
		Sales Fees:	4.75%L, 0.25%S		
Web Address:	www.rsim.com	Management Fee:	0.85%		
Inception:	06-30-93	Actual Fees:	Mgt:0.85%	Dist:0.25%	
Advisor:	RS Investment Management Co LLC	Expense Projections:	3Yr:$907	5Yr:$1221	10Yr:$2109
Subadvisor:	None	Income Distrib:	Annually		
NTF Plans:	Schwab OneSource				

Schneider Small Cap Val

Analyst Pick ✓

Ticker	Load	NAV	Yield	Total Assets	Mstar Category
SCMVX	Closed	$21.66	0.8%	$118 mil	Small Value

Governance and Management

Stewardship Grade: A

Portfolio Manager(s)

Arnie Schneider III founded Schneider Capital Management in 1996 and launched this fund in 1998. Six analysts focus on specific industries and assist Schneider, who pulls the trigger on the portfolio. This team is also responsible for Schneider Value, which employs a similar strategy but focuses on larger companies. Before founding the firm, Schneider worked as an analyst and later led a value team for Wellington Management Company.

Strategy

This research-driven fund favors companies with market caps between $500 million and $1.8 billion. Arnie Schneider III and his team use fundamental research to identify struggling companies as well as industries in a rough patch. He often invests in companies going through management changes, strategy shifts, or cost cuts. Schneider doesn't pay attention to any benchmarks, but he does pay attention to valuation. He sets target prices based on bottom-up analysis, and only the stocks with the deepest discounts make it into the portfolio.

Performance 12-31-06

	1st Qtr	2nd Qtr	3rd Qtr	4th Qtr	Total
2002	10.75	-2.22	-28.86	10.53	-14.85
2003	-7.88	35.71	21.56	35.59	106.05
2004	6.06	2.60	-1.05	18.17	27.23
2005	-4.24	3.88	9.04	1.25	9.82
2006	14.35	-5.22	0.49	11.17	21.08

Trailing	Total Return%	+/- S&P 500	+/- Russ 2000 VL	%Rank Cat	Growth of $10,000
3 Mo	11.17	4.47	2.14	7	11,117
6 Mo	11.71	-1.03	-0.10	15	11,171
1 Yr	21.08	5.29	-2.40	14	12,108
3 Yr Avg	19.16	8.72	2.68	2	16,920
5 Yr Avg	24.31	18.12	8.94	1	29,685
10 Yr Avg	—	—	—		
15 Yr Avg	—	—	—		

Tax Analysis	Tax-Adj Rtn%	%Rank Cat	Tax-Cost Rat	%Rank Cat
3 Yr (estimated)	13.61	23	4.66	98
5 Yr (estimated)	20.34	1	3.19	98
10 Yr (estimated)	—		—	

Potential Capital Gain Exposure: 12% of assets

Morningstar's Take by Karen Dolan 12-20-06

Strong performance hasn't left Schneider Small-Cap Value any less nimble.

Small-cap value funds' stellar absolute returns have captured investors' attention. New assets combined with market appreciation has left many funds bloated. Yet, this fund has been shielded from an unwieldy asset base because manager Arnie Schneider has been extremely disciplined about letting new money in the door. Aside from a brief opening in 2006, he stopped taking new investors in 2002. In total, Schneider is managing a mere $540 million in this style.

Flexibility is key to Schneider's approach because he frequently adds to or trims from positions as stock prices move around. He looks for companies or entire industries that are operating well below normal earnings levels. He aims to buy them when prospects look dim and hang on until earnings bounce back to more-normal levels. Typically, such firms only have one line of business and are rather cyclical in nature. Schneider doesn't

get hung up on management quality and balance-sheet strength either, which gives the fund a lower-quality bent. He does require a price low enough to compensate for the risk that things may never get better. Still, the fund's troubled holdings can sting returns when high-quality or growth stocks lead the way over battered ones.

The current market environment, not asset size, has made Schneider's job more challenging. Earnings for many firms and most industries are nearing historical highs, not lows, so the universe of underperformers has shrunk. Still, Schneider is coming up with new ideas, and unlike many of his rivals, this fund's small asset base gives him the flexibility to execute them.

Small-cap value stocks will eventually cool down, so investors need to be prepared for performance to moderate. Even so, we think this fund can play an important role in a diversified portfolio and is better-equipped than most of its peers to face a range of market conditions.

Address:	460 East Swedesford Road, Suite 1080 Wayne, PA 19087 888-520-3277	
Web Address:	www.schneidercap.com	
Inception:	09-02-98*	
Advisor:	Schneider Capital Management	
Subadvisor:	None	
NTF Plans:	N/A	

Minimum Purchase:	Closed	Add: —	IRA: —
Min Auto Inv Plan:	Closed	Add: —	
Sales Fees:	No-load, 1.75%R		
Management Fee:	1.00%		
Actual Fees:	Mgt:1.00%	Dist: —	
Expense Projections:	3Yr:$479	5Yr:$871	10Yr:$1969
Income Distrib:	Annually		

Historical Profile

Return	High
Risk	High
Rating	★★★★★ Highest

Investment Style: Equity, Stock %

Growth of $10,000
— Investment Values of Fund
— Investment Values of S&P 500

▼ Manager Change
▽ Partial Manager Change

Performance Quartile (within Category)

	1995	1996	1997	1998	1999	2000	2001	2002	2003	2004	2005	2006	History
	—	—	—	12.33	15.53	15.14	17.12	14.47	27.91	23.14	20.76	21.66	NAV
	—	—	—	24.71*	47.07	17.20	19.37	-14.85	106.05	27.23	9.82	21.08	Total Return %
	—	—	—	—	26.03	26.30	31.26	7.25	77.37	16.35	4.91	5.29	+/-S&P 500
	—	—	—	—	48.56	-5.63	5.35	-3.42	60.02	4.98	5.11	-2.40	+/-Russ 2000 VL
	—	—	—	—	0.00	0.52	0.43	0.18	0.78	0.00	0.00	0.95	Income Return %
	—	—	—	—	47.07	16.68	18.94	-15.03	105.27	27.23	9.82	20.13	Capital Return %
	—	—	—	—	—	3	59	31	79	1	3	14	Total Rtn % Rank Cat
	—	—	—	0.13	0.00	0.08	0.07	0.03	0.11	0.00	0.00	0.20	Income $
	—	—	—	0.00	2.48	2.80	0.84	0.08	1.69	12.06	4.69	3.28	Capital Gains $
	—	—	—	—	—	—	1.10	1.10	1.10	1.10	1.10	1.10	Expense Ratio %
	—	—	—	—	—	—	0.44	0.71	0.34	0.53	-0.49	0.29	Income Ratio %
	—	—	—	—	—	—	85	79	102	85	111	91	Turnover Rate %
	—	—	—	—	15	21	40	40	56	56	118		Net Assets $mil

Rating and Risk

Time Period	Load-Adj Return %	Morningstar Rtn vs Cat	Morningstar Risk vs Cat	Morningstar Risk-Adj Rating
1 Yr	21.08			
3 Yr	19.16	High	High	★★★★★
5 Yr	24.31	High	High	★★★★★
10 Yr	—	—	—	
Incept	27.61			

Other Measures	Standard Index S&P 500	Best Fit Index Mstar Small Value
Alpha	3.0	1.2
Beta	1.79	1.14
R-Squared	69	85
Standard Deviation	14.79	
Mean	19.16	
Sharpe Ratio	1.05	

Portfolio Analysis 09-30-06

Share change since 06-06 Total Stocks:84	Sector	PE	Tot Ret%	% Assets
⊖ American Home Mortgage I	Financial	9.4	20.59	5.09
⊕ First BanCorp	Financial	—	-21.03	4.59
⊕ Reliant Energy, Inc.	Utilities	—	37.69	4.32
⊕ Anworth Mortgage Asset C	Financial	—	31.52	4.18
⊖ BE Aerospace	Ind Mtrls	15.3	16.73	2.81
⊖ ASM International, NV	Hardware	—	24.51	2.70
⊖ BE Semiconductor Industr	Hardware	—	—	2.66
⊕ AAR Corporation	Ind Mtrls	26.2	21.88	2.62
⊕ W Holding Company	Financial	13.2	-25.46	2.48
⊕ Hudson Highland Group, I	Business	90.9	-3.92	2.38
⊕ Take-Two Interactive Sof	Software	—	0.34	2.36
Navistar International	Ind Mtrls	—	16.81	2.11
MI Developments Inc. A	Financial	—	—	2.09
⊕ WCI Communities, Inc.	Consumer	6.6	-28.57	2.08
AGCO Corporation	Ind Mtrls	—	86.72	2.04
☼ Orient-Express Hotels, L	Consumer	50.0	50.53	1.80
Internet Capital Group,	Business	6.9	24.82	1.62
Deerfield Triarc Capital	Financial	—	—	1.52
⊕ Fleetwood Enterprises	Ind Mtrls	—	-35.95	1.35
⊖ Proassurance Corporation	Financial	13.9	2.63	1.34

Current Investment Style

Value Blnd Growth — Large Mid Small

Market Cap	%
Giant	0.0
Large	0.9
Mid	17.8
Small	56.5
Micro	24.8
Avg $mil:	915

Value Measures		Rel Category
Price/Earnings	13.16	0.86
Price/Book	1.35	0.76
Price/Sales	0.41	0.51
Price/Cash Flow	6.00	0.98
Dividend Yield %	2.48	1.57

Growth Measures	%	Rel Category
Long-Term Erngs	12.26	0.98
Book Value	2.53	0.47
Sales	4.86	0.66
Cash Flow	-4.50	NMF
Historical Erngs	0.79	0.07

Profitability	%	Rel Category
Return on Equity	3.89	0.36
Return on Assets	3.12	0.51
Net Margin	5.10	0.56

Sector Weightings	% of Stocks	Rel S&P 500	3 Year High Low	
↻ Info	14.09	0.70		
🖥 Software	3.70	1.07	4	0
💻 Hardware	9.44	1.02	14	9
🎙 Media	0.94	0.25	1	0
📞 Telecom	0.01	0.00	1	0
⊂ Service	56.75	1.23		
❤ Health	2.05	0.17	2	0
🛒 Consumer	8.95	1.17	12	7
🏢 Business	13.58	3.21	15	7
$ Financial	32.17	1.44	32	13
⚒ Mfg	29.15	0.86		
⚙ Goods	4.50	0.53	7	5
⚙ Ind Mtrls	19.01	1.59	38	19
🔋 Energy	0.88	0.09	5	0
💡 Utilities	4.76	1.36	8	4

Composition

● Cash	5.2
● Stocks	94.8
● Bonds	0.0
○ Other	0.0
Foreign	20.1
(% of Stock)	

MORNINGSTAR® Funds 500

Schneider Value

	Ticker	Load	NAV	Yield	Total Assets	Mstar Category
	SCMLX	None	$22.78	0.3%	$218 mil	Large Value

Governance and Management

Stewardship Grade: A

Portfolio Manager(s)

Arnie Schneider III founded Schneider Capital Management in 1996 and launched this fund in 2002. Six analysts focus on specific industries and assist Schneider, who pulls the trigger on the portfolio. This team is also responsible for Schneider Small Cap Value, which employs a similar strategy but focuses on small-cap companies. Before founding the firm, Schneider worked as an analyst and later led a value team for Wellington Management Company.

Strategy

This research-driven fund favors companies with market caps of more than $1.2 billion. Arnie Schneider III and his team use fundamental research to identify both struggling companies and industries in a rough patch. He often invests in companies going through management changes, strategy shifts, or cost cuts. Schneider doesn't pay attention to any benchmarks, but he does pay close attention to valuation. He sets target prices based on bottom-up analysis, and only the stocks with the deepest discounts make it into the portfolio.

Performance 12-31-06

	1st Qtr	2nd Qtr	3rd Qtr	4th Qtr	Total
2002	—	—	—	12.37	—*
2003	-3.93	22.75	9.38	22.37	57.85
2004	6.83	4.36	-1.74	13.86	24.72
2005	-2.15	1.94	3.06	1.58	4.43
2006	6.18	2.13	3.80	9.57	23.34

Trailing	Total Return%	+/- S&P 500	+/- Russ 1000 VI	%Rank Cat	Growth of $10,000
3 Mo	9.57	2.87	1.57	3	10,957
6 Mo	13.73	0.99	-0.99	34	11,373
1 Yr	23.34	7.55	1.09	3	12,334
3 Yr Avg	17.12	6.68	2.03	1	16,065
5 Yr Avg	—	—	—	—	—
10 Yr Avg	—	—	—	—	—
15 Yr Avg	—	—	—	—	—

Tax Analysis	Tax-Adj Rtn%	%Rank Cat	Tax-Cost Rat	%Rank Cat
3 Yr (estimated)	15.51	2	1.37	54
5 Yr (estimated)	—	—	—	—
10 Yr (estimated)	—	—	—	—

Potential Capital Gain Exposure: 13% of assets

Historical Profile

Return High
Risk High
Rating ★★★★ Highest

								98%	100%	92%	92%	Investment Style Equity Stock %

▼ Manager Change
▽ Partial Manager Change

Growth of $10,000
■ Investment Values of Fund
— Investment Values of S&P 500

Performance Quartile (within Category)

1995	1996	1997	1998	1999	2000	2001	2002	2003	2004	2005	2006	History
—	—	—	—	—	—	—	11.21	16.98	20.01	19.41	22.78	NAV
—	—	—	—	—	—	—	—	57.85	24.72	4.43	23.34	Total Return %
—	—	—	—	—	—	—	—	29.17	13.84	-0.48	7.55	+/-S&P 500
—	—	—	—	—	—	—	—	27.82	8.23	-2.62	1.09	+/-Russ 1000 VI
—	—	—	—	—	—	—	0.03	0.50	0.32	0.42	0.43	Income Return %
—	—	—	—	—	—	—	0.00	57.35	24.40	4.01	22.91	Capital Return %
—	—	—	—	—	—	—	1	1	66	3		Total Rtn % Rank Cat
—	—	—	—	—	—	—	0.03	0.06	0.05	0.08	0.08	Income $
—	—	—	—	—	—	—	0.00	0.62	1.09	1.40	1.08	Capital Gains $
—	—	—	—	—	—	—	—	0.85	0.85	0.85	Expense Ratio %
—	—	—	—	—	—	—	—	0.72	0.35	0.69	Income Ratio %
—	—	—	—	—	—	—	—	98	117	105	Turnover Rate %
—	—	—	—	—	—	—	4	18	57	218	Net Assets $mil

Rating and Risk

Time Period	Load-Adj Return %	Morningstar Rtn vs Cat	Morningstar Risk vs Cat	Morningstar Risk-Adj Rating
1 Yr	23.34			
3 Yr	17.12	High	High	★★★★★
5 Yr	—	—	—	—
10 Yr	—	—	—	—
Incept	27.92			

Other Measures	Standard Index S&P 500	Best Fit Index Russ MV
Alpha	4.1	-2.3
Beta	1.30	1.07
R-Squared	73	81
Standard Deviation	10.46	
Mean	17.12	
Sharpe Ratio	1.26	

Portfolio Analysis 09-30-06

Share change since 06-06 Total Stocks:55	Sector	PE	Tot Ret%	% Assets
⊕ Reliant Energy, Inc.	Utilities	—	37.69	5.72
⊕ Fannie Mae	Financial	—	24.34	4.96
⊕ Countrywide Financial Co	Financial	9.8	26.22	4.61
⊕ Hilton Hotels Corporatio	Consumer	29.9	45.62	4.53
⊕ J.P. Morgan Chase & Co.	Financial	13.6	25.60	4.13
⊕ CSX Corporation	Business	15.4	37.05	3.69
⊕ North Fork Bancorporatio	Financial	—	—	3.24
⊕ iShares Russell 1000 Val	—	—	—	2.93
⊕ Tyco International, Ltd.	Ind Mtrls	15.7	6.83	2.81
⊕ Dell, Inc.	Hardware	18.4	-16.23	2.65
⊕ Annaly Capital Managemen	Financial	—	32.85	2.60
⊕ Genworth Financial, Inc.	Financial	12.9	-0.17	2.54
⊕ Navistar International	Ind Mtrls	—	16.81	2.46
✳ Massey Energy Company	Energy	—	-38.29	2.36
⊕ AU Optronics Corporation	Hardware	16.3	-4.63	2.33
⊖ Boeing Company	Ind Mtrls	41.2	28.38	2.20
✳ Centex Corporation	Consumer	7.2	-21.06	2.01
⊕ XM Satellite Radio Holdi	Media	—	-46.92	1.96
⊕ Omnicare, Inc.	Health	28.5	-32.36	1.83
⊕ Triad Hospitals, Inc.	Health	15.5	6.63	1.69

Current Investment Style

Value Blnd Growth — Large Mid Small

Market Cap	%
Giant	21.2
Large	28.7
Mid	41.5
Small	8.6
Micro	0.0
Avg $mil:	11,028

Value Measures		Rel Category
Price/Earnings	13.69	1.00
Price/Book	1.60	0.72
Price/Sales	0.71	0.55
Price/Cash Flow	5.78	0.86
Dividend Yield %	1.61	0.69

Growth Measures	%	Rel Category
Long-Term Erngs	12.08	1.16
Book Value	5.33	0.67
Sales	4.71	0.52
Cash Flow	10.20	1.68
Historical Erngs	15.75	0.98

Profitability	%	Rel Category
Return on Equity	9.41	0.52
Return on Assets	4.14	0.42
Net Margin	8.28	0.64

Sector Weightings	% of Stocks	Rel S&P 500	3 Year High Low	
⟲ Info	18.96	0.95		
Software	0.57	0.17	1	0
Hardware	8.59	0.93	11	5
Media	7.36	1.94	7	3
Telecom	2.44	0.70	8	1
⟲ Service	50.65	1.10		
Health	4.56	0.38	5	3
Consumer	10.14	1.33	10	5
Business	6.17	1.46	13	6
Financial	29.78	1.34	30	7
⟲ Mfg	30.39	0.90		
Goods	4.04	0.47	10	4
Ind Mtrls	16.96	1.42	33	17
Energy	2.99	0.31	4	0
Utilities	6.40	1.83	8	5

Composition

● Cash	6.3	
● Stocks	91.9	
● Bonds	0.0	
○ Other	1.8	
Foreign (% of Stock)	6.5	

Morningstar's Take by Karen Dolan 11-15-06

Schneider Value isn't a one-trick pony.

Manager Arnie Schneider's ability to recognize when specific companies or entire industries are operating well below normal earnings levels is unmatched. However, the current market environment makes his job much more difficult; earnings for many firms and most industries are nearing historical highs, not lows. So the universe of battered underperformers has shrunk.

That's not to suggest that Schneider isn't finding anything new. In fact, he is. For example, he has added several financial firms that are experiencing depressed results due to the softening housing market and flattened yield curve. Examples include mortgage originator, Countrywide Financial and REIT Annaly Capital Management, which borrows money at short-term rates and invests in longer-term mortgage-related securities. Schneider also has bought some battered home builders, keying in on those that are cutting costs to deal with the current downturn.

Troubled companies can be tough to navigate because a turnaround may take a long time or never happen. Schneider has done a good job assessing that risk and ensuring that the price is low enough to compensate. For example, he bought convertible preferred shares of General Motors early in 2006. At the time, the share price was factoring in a two-thirds chance that GM would go bankrupt. Schneider thought the actual risk was far less than that and scooped up shares. He was right: The market's fears about GM's bankruptcy risk have indeed abated, leading to a boost in performance here.

Schneider's approach has been hugely successful, but the fund does harbor risks investors need to be comfortable with. Its deep value style will not always strike the market's fancy and may cause it to lag when high-quality companies or growth stocks lead the way over battered ones. But we don't see that as a risk for patient long-term investors. This is a stellar choice.

Address:	460 East Swedesford Road, Suite 1080 Wayne, PA 19087 888-520-3277
Web Address:	www.schneidercap.com
Inception:	09-30-02
Advisor:	Schneider Capital Management
Subadvisor:	None
NTF Plans:	N/A

Minimum Purchase:	$20000	Add: $2500	IRA: $20000
Min Auto Inv Plan:	$20000	Add: $2500	
Sales Fees:	No-load, 1.00%R		
Management Fee:	0.70%		
Actual Fees:	Mgt:0.70%	Dist: —	
Expense Projections:	3Yr:$385	5Yr:$705	10Yr:$1611
Income Distrib:	Annually		

Schwab YieldPlus Inv

	Ticker	Load	NAV	Yield	SEC Yield	Total Assets	Mstar Category
	SWYPX	None	$9.69	5.0%	5.51%	$10,199 mil	Ultrashort Bond

Governance and Management

Stewardship Grade:

Portfolio Manager(s)

Kimon Daifotis has been running this fund since its October 1999 inception. He joined the firm in 1997 after a five-year stint working at Lehman Brothers. He was joined by comanagers Matthew Hastings in late 2004 and more recently by Steven Hung and Andrew Tikovsky. The quartet picks bonds from 13 taxable credit analysts, who also support other Schwab funds.

Strategy

Manager Kimon Daifotis keeps the fund's overall interest-rate risk between three months and one year, which should help stabilize the fund's NAV. Assets are invested across a wide range of sectors and asset types, including asset-backed and mortgage-backed securities, corporate bonds, and U.S. Treasuries. He also keeps the fund very diversified across issuers to further minimize credit risk.

Historical Profile

Return	High	
Risk	Average	
Rating	★★★★★ Highest	

Investment Style: Fixed Income
Income Rtn %Rank Cat

▼ Manager Change
▽ Partial Manager Change

Growth of $10,000
— Investment Values of Fund
— Investment Values of LB Aggr

Performance Quartile (within Category)

	1995	1996	1997	1998	1999	2000	2001	2002	2003	2004	2005	2006	History
	—	—	—	—	9.99	9.86	9.88	9.73	9.72	9.69	9.66	9.69	NAV
	—	—	—	—	1.55*	5.72	5.89	2.66	2.90	2.22	3.35	5.41	Total Return %
	—	—	—	—	—	-5.91	-2.55	-7.59	-1.20	-2.12	0.92	1.08	+/-LB Aggr
	—	—	—	—	—	-0.86	2.26	0.85	1.73	0.49	-0.37	0.18	+/-6 Month CD
	—	—	—	—	—	7.07	5.72	4.21	3.00	2.53	3.66	5.13	Income Return %
	—	—	—	—	—	-1.35	0.17	-1.55	-0.10	-0.31	-0.31	0.28	Capital Return %
	—	—	—	—	—	93	47	60	4	9	9	6	Total Rtn % Rank Cat
	—	—	—	—	0.16	0.68	0.55	0.41	0.29	0.24	0.35	0.48	Income $
	—	—	—	—	0.00	0.00	0.00	0.00	0.00	0.00	0.00	0.00	Capital Gains $
	—	—	—	—	—	0.55	—	0.55	0.56	0.60	0.59	0.58	Expense Ratio %
	—	—	—	—	—	6.72	—	4.36	3.08	2.43	3.00	4.62	Income Ratio %
	—	—	—	—	—	81	106	42	109	89	76	54	Turnover Rate %
	—	—	—	—	32	64	293	370	422	745	727	1,022	Net Assets $mil

Performance 12-31-06

	1st Qtr	2nd Qtr	3rd Qtr	4th Qtr	Total
2002	0.65	0.76	0.12	1.11	2.66
2003	0.87	0.76	0.29	0.95	2.90
2004	0.69	0.17	0.86	0.48	2.22
2005	0.71	0.76	0.90	0.93	3.35
2006	1.14	1.21	1.46	1.50	5.41

Trailing	Total Return%	+/- LB Aggr	+/- 6 Month CD	%Rank Cat	Growth of $10,000
3 Mo	1.50	0.26	0.20	8	10,150
6 Mo	2.98	-2.11	0.32	13	10,298
1 Yr	5.41	1.08	0.18	6	10,541
3 Yr Avg	3.65	-0.05	0.10	6	11,135
5 Yr Avg	3.30	-1.76	0.58	5	11,763
10 Yr Avg	—	—	—		—
15 Yr Avg	—	—	—		—

Tax Analysis	Tax-Adj Rtn%	%Rank Cat	Tax-Cost Rat	%Rank Cat
3 Yr (estimated)	2.32	2	1.28	73
5 Yr (estimated)	1.96	3	1.30	74
10 Yr (estimated)	—		—	

Potential Capital Gain Exposure: -1% of assets

Rating and Risk

Time Period	Load-Adj Return %	Morningstar Rtn vs Cat	Morningstar Risk vs Cat	Morningstar Risk-Adj Rating
1 Yr	5.41			
3 Yr	3.65	High	-Avg	★★★★★
5 Yr	3.30	High	Avg	★★★★★
10 Yr	—			
Incept	4.09			

Other Measures	Standard Index LB Aggr	Best Fit Index LB Muni 3YR
Alpha	0.3	0.6
Beta	0.05	0.14
R-Squared	30	46
Standard Deviation	0.47	
Mean	3.65	
Sharpe Ratio	1.28	

Morningstar's Take by Bridget Hughes 12-28-06

Schwab YieldPlus looks like a category killer. And it almost is.

This offering has proved itself a fine ultrashort-bond fund. Its 3.33% annualized five-year return through Dec. 27, 2006, lands near the very top of the category, and it has easily outperformed its average rival since its 1999 inception, while it hasn't been any more volatile than its typical peer. Particularly important for an ultrashort-bond fund considering many investors use such instruments for cash management, its net asset value has remained fairly steady, varying by just six cents over the past four-plus years. Its information ratio, which gauges how well the management team has balanced risk and return compared with a benchmark, is also superior.

Behind this strong performance is an impressive operation. The fund is home to a fairly complex portfolio, complete with hundreds of securities. In some respects, it has to be: The fund has grown to easily the category's largest, with around $10 billion in assets. But lead manager Kim Daifotis says the diffuse portfolio is also key to maintaining diversification (and low volatility), and he and his team have always searched high and low for mispriced securities. Schwab also recently hired another portfolio manager specializing in structured bonds, including asset-backed securities and mortgage-backed securities, and Daifotis says another portfolio manager will likely be added. Meanwhile, this being one of Schwab's largest offerings, a slew of industry analysts (13) spend the majority of their time working on this portfolio.

While there's no guarantee that the fund will continue to top the charts, we think the odds are in its favor. Our one beef continues to be the fund's expense ratio--we'd like to see it come down further considering the fund's asset size. On the other hand, it's certainly not expensive; its 0.59% expense ratio is below average for no-load ultrashort funds geared toward individual investors.

Address:	101 Montgomery St San Francisco CA 94104 800-407-0256
Web Address:	www.schwab.com
Inception:	10-01-99*
Advisor:	Charles Schwab Investment Mgt, Inc.
Subadvisor:	None
NTF Plans:	Schwab Instl NTF

Minimum Purchase:	$2500	Add: $100	IRA: $1000
Min Auto Inv Plan:	$2500	Add: $100	
Sales Fees:	No-load		
Management Fee:	0.35% mx./0.30% mn.		
Actual Fees:	Mgt:0.30%	Dist:—	
Expense Projections:	3Yr:$186	5Yr:$324	10Yr:$726
Income Distrib:	Monthly		

Portfolio Analysis 08-31-06

Total Fixed-Income:418	Date of Maturity	Amount $000	Value $000	% Net Assets
Jp Morgan Alt Ln Tr 2006	09-25-36	177,200	177,526	2.14
Slm Stud Ln Tr 2005-5 FR	10-25-21	157,250	156,677	1.89
Rbs Cap Tr Iv FRN	09-29-49	155,765	156,620	1.89
Residential Asset 2005-A	06-25-35	110,160	110,278	1.33
Jp Morgan Mtg Tr 2006-A2	04-25-36	96,627	95,540	1.15
Banc Amer Fdg 2006-2 CMO	03-25-36	95,573	95,399	1.15
Chase Mortgage Fin CMO 5	02-25-19	96,674	95,169	1.15
D R Horton 8.5%	04-15-12	90,093	94,464	1.14
Daimler-Benz North Amerc	09-10-07	90,158	90,453	1.09
FHLMC FRN	06-01-36	86,200	87,296	1.05
FNMA Pfd		1,723	86,054	1.04
Cwalt CMO 6%	04-25-36	84,111	84,555	1.02
Toll Brothers 8.25%	02-01-11	73,615	75,087	0.91
Bear Stearns Arm Tr 2004	07-25-34	75,973	73,480	0.89
Cwalt CMO 5.5%	02-25-36	68,455	67,931	0.82
Slm Stud Ln Tr 2003-9 FR	03-15-19	64,924	65,258	0.79
Axa-Uap FRN	12-29-49	64,600	64,619	0.78
Residential Asset Sec 20	04-25-36	64,707	64,359	0.78
Residential Accredit 200	12-25-17	63,430	62,934	0.76
ABBEY NATL PLC	10-29-49	62,057	62,230	0.75

Current Investment Style

Duration: Short Int Long
Quality: High Med Low

¹figure provided by fund

Avg Eff Duration¹	0.7 Yrs
Avg Eff Maturity	1.3 Yrs
Avg Credit Quality	A
Avg Wtd Coupon	4.27%
Avg Wtd Price	100.73% of par

Coupon Range	% of Bonds	Rel Cat
0% PIK	19.9	0.9
0% to 6%	78.7	0.9
6% to 8%	7.4	0.9
8% to 10%	13.2	6.6
More than 10%	0.7	3.7

1.00=Category Average

Credit Analysis		% bonds 08-31-06	
AAA	34	BB	9
AA	14	B	1
A	19	Below B	1
BBB	16	NR/NA	7

Sector Breakdown	% of assets
US Treasuries	0
TIPS	0
US Agency	0
Mortgage Pass-Throughs	3
Mortgage CMO	26
Mortgage ARM	0
US Corporate	36
Asset-Backed	17
Convertible	0
Municipal	0
Corporate Inflation-Protected	0
Foreign Corporate	4
Foreign Govt	0

Composition			
Cash	12.6	Bonds	84.4
Stocks	0.0	Other	3.0

Special Securities	
Restricted/Illiquid Secs	9
Exotic Mortgage-Backed	0
Emerging-Markets Secs	0
Options/Futures/Warrants	No

MORNINGSTAR® Funds 500

Selected American S

Analyst Pick ✓

	Ticker	Load	NAV	Yield	Total Assets	Mstar Category
	SLASX	None	$46.06	0.6%	$11,924 mil	Large Blend

Governance and Management

Stewardship Grade: A

Portfolio Manager(s)

Comanager Chris Davis has been a comanager on this fund since 1995, and he plans to stick around--the Davis family owns the firm and invests heavily in the funds. Comanager Ken Feinberg began as a financial-stock analyst with the firm in 1994 and became comanager in 1998. Other employees are also significant owners, and the bonus plan here is set up with an eye toward long-term outperformance.

Strategy

Management tries to buy great companies whose shares are temporarily depressed, estimating a firm's intrinsic value based on managers' own earnings analysis, which tries to assess a firm's true cash earnings. They then look at those earnings relative to a return on adjusted invested capital. The idea is to figure out how well the company has historically allocated its capital.

Historical Profile
Return High
Risk Below Avg
Rating ★★★★★ Highest

	89%	96%	86%	90%	85%	94%	97%	97%	96%	Investment Style Equity Stock %

▼ Manager Change
△ Partial Manager Change

Growth of $10,000
— Investment Values of Fund
— Investment Values of S&P 500

Performance Quartile (within Category)

1995	1996	1997	1998	1999	2000	2001	2002	2003	2004	2005	2006	History
17.68	21.53	27.18	31.16	35.80	35.33	30.99	25.51	33.17	36.87	40.24	46.06	NAV
38.09	30.74	37.25	16.27	20.32	9.33	-11.17	-17.06	30.90	11.97	9.90	15.19	Total Return %
0.51	7.78	3.89	-12.31	-0.72	18.43	0.72	5.04	2.22	1.09	4.99	-0.60	+/-S&P 500
0.32	8.29	4.40	-10.75	-0.59	17.12	1.28	4.59	1.01	0.57	3.63	-0.27	+/-Russ 1000
1.69	1.03	0.95	0.55	0.48	0.38	0.41	0.65	0.79	0.77	0.76	0.71	Income Return %
36.40	29.71	36.30	15.72	19.84	8.95	-11.58	-17.71	30.11	11.20	9.14	14.48	Capital Return %
10	5	4	69	44	12	43	15	19	28	11	35	Total Rtn % Rank Cat
0.22	0.18	0.20	0.15	0.15	0.14	0.14	0.20	0.20	0.26	0.28	0.29	Income $
0.15	1.30	2.03	0.26	1.44	3.46	0.24	0.00	0.01	0.01	0.00	0.00	Capital Gains $
1.09	1.03	0.96	0.94	0.93	0.92	0.94	0.93	0.93	0.92	0.90	—	Expense Ratio %
1.42	0.87	0.62	0.52	0.24	0.52	0.45	0.61	0.80	0.76	0.81	—	Income Ratio %
27	29	26	20	21	22	20	19	8	3	4	—	Turnover Rate %
925	1,378	2,218	2,905	3,703	5,703	5,563	4,353	5,976	6,664	7,975	7,518	Net Assets $mil

Performance 12-31-06

	1st Qtr	2nd Qtr	3rd Qtr	4th Qtr	Total
2002	-0.97	-9.78	-13.22	6.96	-17.06
2003	-5.21	17.74	2.32	14.63	30.90
2004	3.80	0.46	-0.98	8.44	11.97
2005	0.03	1.33	4.17	4.08	9.90
2006	2.98	0.36	3.53	7.65	15.19

Trailing	Total Return%	+/- S&P 500	+/- Russ 1000	%Rank Cat	Growth of $10,000
3 Mo	7.65	0.95	0.70	19	10,765
6 Mo	11.45	-1.29	-0.91	51	11,145
1 Yr	15.19	-0.60	-0.27	35	11,519
3 Yr Avg	12.33	1.89	1.35	14	14,174
5 Yr Avg	9.00	2.81	2.18	10	15,386
10 Yr Avg	11.12	2.70	2.48	7	28,703
15 Yr Avg	12.16	1.52	1.36	11	55,920

Tax Analysis	Tax-Adj Rtn%	%Rank Cat	Tax-Cost Rat	%Rank Cat
3 Yr (estimated)	12.17	9	0.14	7
5 Yr (estimated)	8.83	7	0.16	11
10 Yr (estimated)	10.33	5	0.71	29

Potential Capital Gain Exposure: 43% of assets

Morningstar's Take by Kerry O'Boyle 11-01-06

Consistency and excellence have been the hallmarks of Selected American Shares.

This fine fund remains among the cream of the crop of actively managed large-blend funds. Managers Chris Davis and Ken Feinberg don't wed themselves to any particular valuation metric; instead, they seek well-managed firms trading at a discount to their estimate of its intrinsic value. This holistic approach is heavily reliant upon digging through balance sheets to root out the sustainability of future cash flows as well as company management's ability to deploy future capital effectively.

That can be a challenge. One of the portfolio's laggards this year has been Sprint Nextel. Despite the firm's proven track record of absorbing acquisitions in the past, management has taken a number of missteps since the two entities merged at the end of 2004. Davis and Feinberg have pared their estimates of the firm, but continue to hold on as they don't view the stock as overpriced. Overall,

the fund has slipped a bit thus far in 2006 relative to past years, and now trails a majority of its category peers.

Nonetheless, we continue to like management's long-term outlook and thoughtful approach. Annual turnover at the fund remains well below the category median of 58%, reflecting the managers' conviction in their research and the fund's holdings. Davis and Feinberg are constantly looking at the market from different angles. For instance, they trimmed back on struggling Avon Products, putting those assets to work in rival Procter & Gamble--the theme being that revitalized industry leaders such as McDonald's and Hewlett-Packard have regained their dominance after sorting through short-term problems. They saw P&G as the next in line to stage such a comeback when the fund bought it at depressed prices during 2006.

Despite a slightly off year, the fund's long-term focus, reasonable fees, and shareholder-friendly practices make it an offering worth owning.

Address:	2949 E. Elvira Road Tucson AZ 85706 800-243-1575	Minimum Purchase:	$1000 Add: $25 IRA: $1000
		Min Auto Inv Plan:	$25 Add: $25
		Sales Fees:	No-load, 0.25%S
Web Address:	www.selectedfunds.com	Management Fee:	0.65% mx./0.49% mn.
Inception:	02-28-33	Actual Fees:	Mgt:0.54% Dist:0.25%
Advisor:	Davis Selected Advisers LP	Expense Projections:	3Yr:$287 5Yr:$498 10Yr:$1108
Subadvisor:	Davis Selected Advisers - NY, Inc.	Income Distrib:	Annually
NTF Plans:	Schwab OneSource		

Rating and Risk

Time Period	Load-Adj Return %	Morningstar Rtn vs Cat	Morningstar Risk vs Cat	Morningstar Risk-Adj Rating
1 Yr	15.19			
3 Yr	12.33	+Avg	Low	★★★★
5 Yr	9.00	High	-Avg	★★★★★
10 Yr	11.12	High	Avg	★★★★★
Incept	—			

Other Measures	Standard Index S&P 500	Best Fit Index S&P 500
Alpha	3.0	3.0
Beta	0.80	0.81
R-Squared	82	82
Standard Deviation	6.16	
Mean	12.33	
Sharpe Ratio	1.42	

Portfolio Analysis 09-30-06

Share change since 06-06 Total Stocks:74	Sector	PE	Tot Ret%	% Assets
American Express Company	Financial	20.9	19.09	4.46
Altria Group, Inc.	Goods	16.3	19.87	4.36
⊕ American International G	Financial	17.0	6.05	4.35
J.P. Morgan Chase & Co.	Financial	13.6	25.60	4.25
⊕ Tyco International, Ltd.	Ind Mtrls	15.7	6.83	4.10
⊕ ConocoPhillips	Energy	6.5	26.53	3.95
Costco Wholesale Corpora	Consumer	23.3	7.90	3.63
⊖ Golden West Fin	Financial	—	—	3.27
Comcast Corporation	Media	—	—	3.14
Berkshire Hathaway Inc.	Financial	—	—	3.03
⊕ HSBC Hldgs	Financial	—	—	2.89
⊕ Wells Fargo Company	Financial	14.7	16.82	2.69
Progressive Corporation	Financial	12.4	-16.93	2.26
⊕ Occidental Petroleum Cor	Energy	8.0	24.32	2.21
Microsoft Corporation	Software	23.8	15.83	2.15
Devon Energy Corporation	Energy	9.2	8.06	2.12
Citigroup, Inc.	Financial	13.1	19.55	2.11
⊕ Wal-Mart Stores, Inc.	Consumer	16.9	0.13	2.04
Loews Corporation	Financial	14.9	32.04	2.01
Sealed Air Corporation	Goods	22.8	16.85	1.93

Current Investment Style

Value Blnd Growth — Large Mid Small

	Market Cap	%
	Giant	50.0
	Large	36.9
	Mid	13.1
	Small	0.0
	Micro	0.0

Avg $mil: 40,333

Value Measures		Rel Category
Price/Earnings	13.76	0.90
Price/Book	2.21	0.86
Price/Sales	1.23	0.88
Price/Cash Flow	8.26	0.98
Dividend Yield %	2.00	1.14

Growth Measures	%	Rel Category
Long-Term Erngs	11.11	0.94
Book Value	9.36	1.04
Sales	11.00	1.14
Cash Flow	14.31	1.39
Historical Erngs	18.54	1.00

Profitability	%	Rel Category
Return on Equity	19.82	1.02
Return on Assets	12.38	1.19
Net Margin	13.99	1.04

Sector Weightings	% of Stocks	Rel S&P 500	3 Year High	Low
☎ Info	12.63	0.63		
Software	2.24	0.65	2	1
Hardware	1.51	0.16	3	2
Media	6.74	1.78	7	3
Telecom	2.14	0.61	2	0
☞ Service	56.29	1.22		
Health	2.40	0.20	5	2
Consumer	9.54	1.25	10	5
Business	3.68	0.87	5	4
Financial	40.67	1.83	56	39
☐ Mfg	31.07	0.92		
Goods	13.02	1.52	13	10
Ind Mtrls	6.65	0.56	7	5
Energy	11.40	1.16	12	6
Utilities	0.00	0.00	0	0

Composition

● Cash	3.8
● Stocks	95.9
● Bonds	0.3
○ Other	0.0
Foreign	10.2
(% of Stock)	

Selected Special Shares S

Analyst Pick ✓

	Ticker	Load	NAV	Yield	Total Assets	Mstar Category
	SLSSX	None	$13.98	0.8%	$150 mil	Mid-Cap Blend

Governance and Management

Stewardship Grade: A

Portfolio Manager(s)

Team managed. Although Morningstar's 2005 Fund Managers of the Year--Chris Davis and Ken Feinberg--are listed as managers, this fund consists of the best ideas of Davis Selected Advisors' full team of sector analysts. Davis aids in determining the level of assets allotted to each analyst, and Feinberg runs a roughly 10% sleeve of the fund, but the day-to-day oversight comes from analysts Chip Tucker and Danton Goei.

Strategy

This fund consists of the best ideas of the firm's team of sector analysts. In their role as sector specialists, many encounter small- and mid-sized companies--as well as international stocks--that don't always make it into firm's larger portfolios, and thus are candidates for this fund. Unlike other analyst-driven offerings, however, this one does not endeavor to be sector-neutral. Assets are allocated to the analysts with the most compelling ideas, and the level of assets devoted to each can shift over time.

Historical Profile

Return	Average
Risk	Average
Rating	★★★ Neutral

Investment Style: Equity, Stock %

97% | 100% | 72% | 98% | 94% | 97% | 98% | 98% | 98%

▼ Manager Change
▽ Partial Manager Change

Growth of $10,000
— Investment Values of Fund
— Investment Values of S&P 500

Scale: 33.0, 26.0, 20.0, 15.0, 10.0

Performance Quartile (within Category)

	1995	1996	1997	1998	1999	2000	2001	2002	2003	2004	2005	2006	History
	10.80	10.89	13.03	14.76	16.17	13.68	10.50	8.61	11.70	12.44	12.47	13.98	NAV
	34.24	11.86	26.90	24.52	16.83	-1.10	-14.41	-17.62	41.40	11.34	8.45	17.74	Total Return %
	-3.34	-11.10	-6.46	-4.06	-4.21	8.00	-2.52	4.48	12.72	0.46	3.54	1.95	+/-S&P 500
	3.31	-7.39	-5.35	5.40	2.11	-18.61	-13.80	-3.09	5.78	-5.14	-4.11	7.42	+/-S&P Mid 400
	0.00	0.00	0.00	0.00	0.00	0.00	0.00	0.00	0.00	1.24	1.00	0.89	Income Return %
	34.24	11.86	26.90	24.52	16.83	-1.10	-14.41	-17.62	41.40	10.10	7.45	16.85	Capital Return %
	23	84	49	8	49	79	92	62	24	90	59	18	Total Rtn % Rank Cat
	0.00	0.00	0.00	0.00	0.00	0.00	0.00	0.00	0.00	0.15	0.13	0.11	Income $
	1.26	1.18	0.62	1.32	0.97	2.24	1.21	0.04	0.47	0.43	0.89	0.57	Capital Gains $
	1.48	1.33	1.28	1.25	1.17	1.15	1.15	1.17	1.21	1.17	1.12	—	Expense Ratio %
	-0.58	-0.66	-0.61	-0.58	-0.59	-0.25	-0.20	-0.46	-0.39	0.37	0.11	—	Income Ratio %
	127	98	51	41	44	35	117	46	46	30	53	—	Turnover Rate %
	60	62	75	94	107	97	73	60	96	91	68	55	Net Assets $mil

Performance 12-31-06

	1st Qtr	2nd Qtr	3rd Qtr	4th Qtr	Total
2002	4.67	-11.28	-19.08	9.64	-17.62
2003	-5.34	23.31	6.77	13.46	41.40
2004	3.93	-0.90	-3.40	11.91	11.34
2005	-0.24	1.45	4.69	2.36	8.45
2006	8.58	-2.66	3.64	7.48	17.74

Trailing	Total Return%	+/- S&P 500	+/- S&P Mid 400	%Rank Cat	Growth of $10,000
3 Mo	7.48	0.78	0.49	51	10,748
6 Mo	11.39	-1.35	5.56	24	11,139
1 Yr	17.74	1.95	7.42	18	11,774
3 Yr Avg	12.44	2.00	-0.65	53	14,216
5 Yr Avg	10.61	4.42	-0.28	41	16,557
10 Yr Avg	9.97	1.55	-3.50	74	25,867
15 Yr Avg	10.63	-0.01	-3.00	85	45,509

Tax Analysis	Tax-Adj Rtn%	%Rank Cat	Tax-Cost Rat	%Rank Cat
3 Yr (estimated)	11.33	43	0.99	42
5 Yr (estimated)	9.72	40	0.80	51
10 Yr (estimated)	8.45	69	1.38	36

Potential Capital Gain Exposure: 42% of assets

Rating and Risk

Time Period	Load-Adj Return %	Morningstar Rtn vs Cat	Morningstar Risk vs Cat	Morningstar Risk-Adj Rating
1 Yr	17.74			
3 Yr	12.44	Avg	Avg	★★★
5 Yr	10.61	Avg	+Avg	★★★
10 Yr	9.97	-Avg	Avg	★★
Incept	—			

Other Measures	Standard Index S&P 500	Best Fit Index Russ MG
Alpha	0.1	1.4
Beta	1.28	0.80
R-Squared	80	87
Standard Deviation	9.86	
Mean	12.44	
Sharpe Ratio	0.92	

Portfolio Analysis 09-30-06

Share change since 06-06 Total Stocks:72	Sector	PE	Tot Ret%	% Assets
⊕ Garmin, Ltd.	Hardware	28.2	69.45	3.61
Markel Corporation	Financial	12.2	51.43	3.34
Molex, Inc. A	Hardware	—	—	3.13
Harley-Davidson, Inc.	Goods	18.5	38.81	3.02
⊕ Netflix, Inc.	Consumer	22.1	-4.44	2.92
Lagardere SCA	Media	—	—	2.89
Hunter Douglas Grp	Goods	—	—	2.75
E*Trade Financial Corpor	Financial	17.6	7.48	2.74
Tiffany & Co.	Goods	22.0	3.58	2.40
Expedia, Inc.	Consumer	—	-12.44	2.36
Golden West Fin	Financial	—	—	2.28
Microsoft Corporation	Software	23.8	15.83	2.24
⊕ Ambac Financial Group, I	Financial	10.9	16.52	2.24
Brown & Brown, Inc.	Financial	22.9	-6.98	2.23
⊕ Transocean, Inc.	Energy	27.1	16.07	2.12
⊖ Zimmer Holdings, Inc.	Health	24.5	16.22	2.09
Pargesa Holding	Financial	—	—	2.01
⊕ NTL, Inc.	Telecom	—	6.08	1.89
⊖ Idexx Laboratories	Health	30.4	10.17	1.86
Commerce Bancorp, Inc.	Financial	23.6	3.89	1.85

Current Investment Style

Value Blnd Growth — Large / Mid / Small (Mid position)

Market Cap	%
Giant	5.4
Large	36.0
Mid	51.7
Small	4.4
Micro	2.5

Avg $mil: 8,391

Value Measures		Rel Category
Price/Earnings	16.46	1.02
Price/Book	2.10	0.93
Price/Sales	1.27	1.13
Price/Cash Flow	9.65	1.14
Dividend Yield %	1.15	0.88

Growth Measures	%	Rel Category
Long-Term Erngs	13.93	1.10
Book Value	15.77	1.90
Sales	11.29	1.27
Cash Flow	9.84	1.16
Historical Erngs	16.03	0.90

Profitability	%	Rel Category
Return on Equity	17.66	1.11
Return on Assets	10.32	1.29
Net Margin	13.81	1.27

Sector Weightings

	% of Stocks	Rel S&P 500	3 Year High	3 Year Low
⊙ Info	22.81	1.14		
Software	2.99	0.87	5	1
Hardware	9.91	1.07	14	6
Media	4.24	1.12	7	4
Telecom	5.67	1.62	6	1
⊕ Service	55.31	1.20		
Health	6.42	0.53	9	6
Consumer	16.10	2.10	22	15
Business	5.17	1.22	10	4
Financial	27.62	1.24	28	12
⊟ Mfg	21.88	0.65		
Goods	13.27	1.55	14	11
Ind Mtrls	6.43	0.54	16	6
Energy	2.18	0.22	6	2
Utilities	0.00	0.00	6	0

Composition

● Cash	0.9
● Stocks	97.7
● Bonds	1.4
● Other	0.0
Foreign	17.9
(% of Stock)	

Morningstar's Take by Kerry O'Boyle 12-01-06

A strong research culture earns Selected Special a spot as an Analyst Pick in the mid-blend category.

Though best known for its large-cap funds, Davis Selected Advisors also runs this fine analyst-driven all-cap offering. The thinking here is that in covering their respective sectors, the firm's analysts encounter a number of excellent smaller-sized and international companies that don't necessarily fit the profile of the bigger funds. Instead of letting that research go to waste, the analysts have the opportunity to run their own pot of assets and put those ideas to work here.

This fund's design sets it apart from the scores of mostly unexceptional analyst-driven funds from other advisors. These rivals tie their analyst-run portfolios' sector weightings to a benchmark's, which can be troublesome if the analysts are forced to own full weightings in a sector without a lot of attractive stocks. (Or, inversely, if they're charged with holding few stocks in a very appealing area just to mimic the index's stance.) Here, assets are allocated to analysts with the most compelling ideas. The process isn't completely bottom-up, though. Although noted manager Chris Davis doesn't run a sleeve of this fund himself, he's active in the allocation of assets among the analysts.

Still, the fund might not be a good fit for investors that already own its bigger sibling. Roughly a third of the holdings (and accounting for varying position sizes, about 20% of assets) do overlap with Selected American. In addition, given that this fund and load clone Davis Growth Opportunity are much smaller than their large-cap siblings, the analysts' incentives are heavily weighted toward their work on the large-cap funds.

Overall, though, the firm's history of rooting out great businesses at attractive prices is in full force here. We think the firm's shareholder-friendly culture and proven stock-picking ability warrant its inclusion as a top choice.

Address:	2949 E. Elvira Road Tucson AZ 85706 800-243-1575	Minimum Purchase:	$1000 Add: $25 IRA: $1000
		Min Auto Inv Plan:	$25 Add: $25
Web Address:	www.selectedfunds.com	Sales Fees:	No-load, 0.25%S
Inception:	05-01-39	Management Fee:	0.70% mx./0.60% mn.
Advisor:	Davis Selected Advisers LP	Actual Fees:	Mgt:0.69% Dist:0.25%
Subadvisor:	Davis Selected Advisers - NY, Inc.	Expense Projections:	3Yr:$368 5Yr:$638 10Yr:$1409
		Income Distrib:	Annually
NTF Plans:	Schwab OneSource		

MORNINGSTAR® Funds 500

Sequoia

	Ticker	Load	NAV	Yield	Total Assets	Mstar Category
	SEQUX	Closed	$152.75	0.0%	$3,631 mil	Large Blend

Governance and Management

Stewardship Grade:

Portfolio Manager(s)

Bob Goldfarb has comanaged the fund, first with Bill Ruane and now with David Poppe, since 1998. Before that, Goldfarb had been part of the fund's value-oriented stock-picking process for more than 30 years. Poppe was named comanager on Nov. 25, 2005, following the death of Ruane. He spent five years at the fund previously, and was Ruane and Goldfarb's choice to become the next comanager. Eleven analysts support Goldfarb and Poppe.

Strategy

Manager Bob Goldfarb isn't afraid to play favorites. The fund typically holds anywhere between 10 and 20 stocks. When its high standards aren't met, it holds as much as 30% of assets in Treasuries. Companies with top-quality management, long-lasting competitive advantages, and simple businesses qualify for entry into the portfolio.

Historical Profile
Return Above Avg
Risk   Below Avg
Rating ★★★★ Above Avg

Investment Style: Equity Stock %

80% 78% 75% 80% 81% 82% 91% 93% 100%

▼ Manager Change
△ Partial Manager Change

Growth of $10,000
— Investment Values of Fund
— Investment Values of S&P 500

42.2 / 32.4 / 24.0 / 17.0 / 10.0

Performance Quartile (within Category)

	1995	1996	1997	1998	1999	2000	2001	2002	2003	2004	2005	2006	History
	78.13	88.44	125.63	160.70	127.27	122.09	130.24	126.63	147.61	154.27	155.45	152.75	NAV
	41.38	21.74	43.20	35.25	-16.54	20.06	10.52	-2.64	17.12	4.66	7.78	8.34	Total Return %
	3.80	-1.22	9.84	6.67	-37.58	29.16	22.41	19.46	-11.56	-6.22	2.87	-7.45	+/-S&P 500
	3.61	-0.71	10.35	8.23	-37.45	27.85	22.97	19.01	-12.77	-6.74	1.51	-7.12	+/-Russ 1000
	0.56	0.48	0.12	0.29	0.55	1.31	0.81	0.01	0.00	0.00	0.00	0.00	Income Return %
	40.82	21.26	43.08	34.96	-17.09	18.75	9.71	-2.65	17.12	4.66	7.78	8.34	Capital Return %
	4	50	2	3	99	3	3	1	99	95	25	97	Total Rtn % Rank Cat
	0.31	0.38	0.11	0.37	0.86	1.66	0.97	0.01	0.00	0.00	0.00	0.00	Income $
	0.08	6.10	0.88	8.02	6.59	28.51	3.38	0.16	0.61	0.21	10.64	15.60	Capital Gains $
	1.00	1.00	1.00	1.00	1.00	1.00	1.00	1.00	1.00	1.00	1.00	—	Expense Ratio %
	0.50	0.40	0.10	0.30	0.60	1.20	0.80	-0.30	-0.50	-0.40	-0.50	—	Income Ratio %
	15	23	8	21	12	36	7	3	6	8	—	Turnover Rate %
	2,186	2,581	3,673	5,002	3,898	3,944	3,925	4,372	—	—	3,586	3,631	Net Assets $mil

Performance 12-31-06

	1st Qtr	2nd Qtr	3rd Qtr	4th Qtr	Total
2002	0.96	-2.54	-2.76	1.74	-2.64
2003	-7.42	11.73	2.57	10.39	17.12
2004	6.00	-2.64	-2.33	3.83	4.66
2005	-1.00	0.45	-0.57	9.02	7.78
2006	2.65	-1.82	3.97	3.40	8.34

Trailing	Total Return%	+/- S&P 500	+/- Russ 1000	%Rank Cat	Growth of $10,000
3 Mo	3.40	-3.30	-3.55	99	10,340
6 Mo	7.50	-5.24	-4.86	94	10,750
1 Yr	8.34	-7.45	-7.12	97	10,834
3 Yr Avg	6.91	-3.53	-4.07	93	12,220
5 Yr Avg	6.86	0.67	0.04	27	13,934
10 Yr Avg	11.57	3.15	2.93	6	29,886
15 Yr Avg	13.22	2.58	2.42	7	64,394

Tax Analysis	Tax-Adj Rtn%	%Rank Cat	Tax-Cost Rat	%Rank Cat
3 Yr (estimated)	6.06	88	0.80	37
5 Yr (estimated)	6.32	25	0.51	33
10 Yr (estimated)	10.42	5	1.03	46

Potential Capital Gain Exposure: 72% of assets

Rating and Risk

Time Period	Load-Adj Return %	Morningstar Rtn vs Cat	Morningstar Risk vs Cat	Morningstar Risk-Adj Rating
1 Yr	8.34			
3 Yr	6.91	-Avg	Avg	★★
5 Yr	6.86	+Avg	Low	★★★★
10 Yr	11.57	High	Avg	★★★★★
Incept	15.66			

Other Measures	Standard Index S&P 500	Best Fit Index Russ 1000Gr
Alpha	0.2	1.9
Beta	0.50	0.49
R-Squared	23	32
Standard Deviation	7.22	
Mean	6.91	
Sharpe Ratio	0.52	

Morningstar's Take by John Coumarianos 12-28-06

We think Sequoia is a coiled spring.

Much as Warren Buffett gradually altered his investment style from buying fair companies at great prices to buying great companies at fair prices, so has this fund. In fact, Sequoia has a whopping 29% of its assets in Buffett's Berkshire Hathaway. As a result of following Buffett's lead, the fund's centroid is now in the large-growth section of the Morningstar Style Box.

Managers Bob Goldfarb and David Poppe rarely keep significant parts of the fund in cash, as the late Bill Ruane did when he and Goldfarb shared management duties. Many investors prefer to sell mediocre businesses when they reach fair value, but hold superior businesses indefinitely. That is because businesses with sustainable returns on invested capital are rare, and when investors think they've snagged one at a good price, they avoid selling it for fear of not finding a suitable replacement. Therefore, the fund may not have as steady a profile as it used to, such as when it

trounced its competitors from 2000 through 2002 while holding as much as 23% of its assets in cash.

Although a large position in auto insurer Progressive has hurt the fund this year, as the business made investments in claim service, we think the fund's highly profitable growth stocks should serve it well. Among the fund's profitable holdings that have suffered from neglect in recent years is Berkshire Hathaway itself. The firm has been under a cloud from hurricane losses and uncertainty regarding its cash position. However, Morningstar equity analysts think the stock is undervalued. Additionally, top holdings Expeditors International and fastener maker Fastenal have garnered "wide moat" ratings from Morningstar analysts for their sustainable profitability; both stocks are trading in 5-star territory.

We think it's only a matter for time before this fine core holding enjoys another surge.

Portfolio Analysis 09-30-06

Share change since 06-06 Total Stocks:22

	Sector	PE	Tot Ret%	% Assets
⊖ Berkshire Hathaway Inc.	Financial			29.26
Progressive Corporation	Financial	12.4	-16.93	15.62
⊖ Mohawk Industries, Inc.	Goods	13.0	-13.93	7.31
⊕ TJX Companies	Consumer	16.9	24.05	6.41
⊕ Bed Bath & Beyond, Inc.	Consumer	20.1	5.39	5.73
Fastenal Company	Business	27.8	-7.37	4.69
Idexx Laboratories	Health	30.4	10.17	4.18
Expeditors International	Business	34.4	20.54	4.01
⊕ Target Corporation	Consumer	19.3	4.65	3.66
Wal-Mart Stores, Inc.	Consumer	16.9	0.13	3.49
Porsche	Goods	—	—	2.95
Walgreen Company	Consumer	26.6	4.36	2.82
Brown & Brown, Inc.	Financial	22.9	-6.98	2.65
O'Reilly Automotive, Inc	Consumer	20.4	0.16	1.69
☼ Lowe's Companies Inc.	Consumer	15.6	-6.05	1.55
Tiffany & Co.	Goods	22.0	3.58	1.14
☼ Apollo Group, Inc. A	Consumer	15.9	-35.54	1.08
MasterCard Incorporated	Business	—	—	0.79
Danaher Corporation	Ind Mtrls	22.0	30.02	0.79
Patterson Companies, Inc	Health	24.7	6.32	0.12

Current Investment Style

Value Blnd Growth — Large Mid Small

Market Cap	%
Giant	5.0
Large	56.0
Mid	39.1
Small	0.0
Micro	0.0

Avg $mil: 13,074

Value Measures		Rel Category
Price/Earnings	16.82	1.09
Price/Book	3.25	1.27
Price/Sales	1.17	0.84
Price/Cash Flow	11.50	1.36
Dividend Yield %	0.47	0.27

Growth Measures	%	Rel Category
Long-Term Erngs	12.67	1.07
Book Value	17.21	1.91
Sales	14.63	1.51
Cash Flow	23.44	2.27
Historical Erngs	16.27	0.88

Profitability	%	Rel Category
Return on Equity	22.58	1.16
Return on Assets	14.19	1.37
Net Margin	8.34	0.62

Sector Weightings	% of Stocks	Rel S&P 500	3 Year High Low
♱ Info	0.00	0.00	
Software	0.00	0.00	0 0
Hardware	0.00	0.00	0 0
Media	0.00	0.00	0 0
Telecom	0.00	0.00	0 0
☞ Service	87.82	1.90	
Health	4.30	0.36	4 1
Consumer	26.49	3.46	26 11
Business	9.49	2.24	10 7
Financial	47.54	2.13	68 48
Mfg	12.19	0.36	
Goods	11.40	1.33	14 11
Ind Mtrls	0.79	0.07	1 1
Energy	0.00	0.00	0 0
Utilities	0.00	0.00	0 0

Composition
- Cash 0.0
- Stocks 100.0
- Bonds 0.0
- Other 0.0
- Foreign 3.0 (% of Stock)

Address:	767 Fifth Ave New York NY 10153-4798 800-686-6884	Minimum Purchase:	Closed	Add: —	IRA: —
		Min Auto Inv Plan:	Closed	Add: —	
		Sales Fees:	No-load		
Web Address:	www.sequoiafund.com	Management Fee:	1.00%		
Inception:	07-15-70	Actual Fees:	Mgt:1.00%	Dist: —	
Advisor:	Ruane, Cunniff & Goldfarb Inc	Expense Projections:	3Yr:$325	5Yr:$566	10Yr:$1257
Subadvisor:	None	Income Distrib:	Annually		
NTF Plans:	N/A				

Skyline Spec Equities

	Ticker	Load	NAV	Yield	Total Assets	Mstar Category
	SKSEX	None	$25.99	0.0%	$589 mil	Small Value

Governance and Management

Stewardship Grade: B

Portfolio Manager(s)

Mike Maloney, a comanager since March 2001, was named lead manager in December 2004 when former lead manager Bill Dutton stepped down. Maloney is assisted by the fund's two comanagers, Bill Fiedler and Mark Odegard. The team conducts its own research, assisted by three analysts and Dutton.

Strategy

This fund's managers look for small companies that are trading at significant discounts to the overall market and that enjoy strong earnings prospects. They set target prices for every purchase and sell holdings that meet those targets. Although the fund used to concentrate almost exclusively on consumer, financial, and industrial issues, it began paying more attention to tech, energy, and real estate names in early 2000.

Performance 12-31-06

	1st Qtr	2nd Qtr	3rd Qtr	4th Qtr	Total
2002	11.87	-1.39	-20.91	6.27	-7.29
2003	-6.23	21.93	7.21	14.79	40.71
2004	6.08	-0.98	-0.99	12.13	16.61
2005	-1.19	3.67	5.59	2.51	10.89
2006	12.70	-3.87	0.83	8.67	18.71

Trailing	Total Return%	+/- S&P 500	+/- Russ 2000 VL	%Rank Cat	Growth of $10,000
3 Mo	8.67	1.97	-0.36	43	10,867
6 Mo	9.57	-3.17	-2.24	34	10,957
1 Yr	18.71	2.92	-4.77	34	11,871
3 Yr Avg	15.35	4.91	-1.13	33	15,348
5 Yr Avg	14.90	8.71	-0.47	31	20,026
10 Yr Avg	11.94	3.52	-1.33	59	30,892
15 Yr Avg	14.80	4.16	-0.40	24	79,274

Tax Analysis	Tax-Adj Rtn%	%Rank Cat	Tax-Cost Rat	%Rank Cat
3 Yr (estimated)	12.04	50	2.87	89
5 Yr (estimated)	12.65	41	1.96	81
10 Yr (estimated)	10.34	57	1.43	57

Potential Capital Gain Exposure: 18% of assets

Historical Profile

Return Above Avg
Risk Average
Rating ★★★ Neutral

	94%	95%	95%	94%	100%	93%	96%	99%	90%

Investment Style
Equity
Stock %

▼ Manager Change
▽ Partial Manager Change

Growth of $10,000

— Investment Values of Fund
— Investment Values of S&P 500

40.8
31.0
24.0
17.0
10.0

Performance Quartile (within Category)

1995	1996	1997	1998	1999	2000	2001	2002	2003	2004	2005	2006	History
16.79	18.16	21.66	19.78	15.90	19.75	22.50	20.86	27.78	28.64	25.43	25.99	NAV
13.82	30.37	35.43	-7.17	-13.29	24.21	13.92	-7.29	40.71	16.61	10.89	18.71	Total Return %
-23.76	7.41	2.07	-35.75	-34.33	33.31	25.81	14.81	12.03	5.73	5.98	2.92	+/-S&P 500
-11.93	9.00	3.65	-0.72	-11.80	1.38	-0.10	4.14	-5.32	-5.64	6.18	-4.77	+/-Russ 2000 VL
0.00	0.00	0.00	0.00	0.00	0.00	0.00	0.00	0.00	0.00	0.00	0.00	Income Return %
13.82	30.37	35.43	-7.17	-13.29	24.21	13.92	-7.29	40.71	16.61	10.89	18.71	Capital Return %
91	11	12	64	100	26	59	35	51	89	7	34	Total Rtn % Rank Cat
0.00	0.00	0.00	0.00	0.00	0.00	0.00	0.00	0.00	0.00	0.00	0.00	Income $
1.00	3.61	2.89	0.32	1.23	0.00	0.00	0.00	1.56	3.69	6.42	4.21	Capital Gains $
1.51	1.51	1.48	1.47	1.48	1.51	1.49	1.48	1.48	1.47	1.47	—	Expense Ratio %
0.35	-0.32	-0.41	-0.50	-0.32	-0.32	-0.16	-0.26	-0.26	-0.47	-0.39	—	Income Ratio %
71	130	62	68	223	92	93	81	527	47	49	—	Turnover Rate %
175	219	467	446	223	287	374	383	527	567	519	589	Net Assets $mil

Rating and Risk

Time Period	Load-Adj Return %	Morningstar Rtn vs Cat	Morningstar Risk vs Cat	Morningstar Risk-Adj Rating
1 Yr	18.71			
3 Yr	15.35	+Avg	Avg	★★★★
5 Yr	14.90	+Avg	Avg	★★★
10 Yr	11.94	Avg	Avg	★★★
Incept	14.42			

Other Measures	Standard Index S&P 500	Best Fit Index Mstar Small Core
Alpha	1.9	0.6
Beta	1.42	0.84
R-Squared	69	90
Standard Deviation	11.74	
Mean	15.35	
Sharpe Ratio	1.01	

Portfolio Analysis 11-30-06

Share change since 10-06 Total Stocks:64	Sector	PE	Tot Ret%	% Assets
⊕ Cytec Industries	Ind Mtrls	20.0	19.52	3.03
iStar Financial, Inc.	Financial	18.6	44.44	2.96
⊕ Reinsurance Group of Ame	Financial	12.5	17.46	2.76
⊕ Centene Corporation	Health	—	-6.54	2.66
⊕ Crane Company	Ind Mtrls	14.0	5.37	2.54
⊕ NCI Building Systems	Ind Mtrls	16.5	21.82	2.45
⊕ Heidrick & Struggles Int	Business	23.2	32.17	2.36
Adesa, Inc.	Consumer	19.1	15.06	2.25
⊕ Toro Company	Ind Mtrls	16.2	7.44	2.13
⊕ MCG Capital Corporation	Financial	11.3	54.30	2.12
⊕ Hanover Insurance Group,	Financial	26.9	17.57	1.97
⊕ Navigant Consulting	Business	22.4	-10.10	1.87
⊕ Electronics for Imaging,	Hardware	27.7	-0.11	1.86
Scotts Miracle-Gro Compa	Ind Mtrls	21.6	15.43	1.85
SMART Modular Technologi	Hardware	—	—	1.82
⊕ Perot Systems Corporatio	Business	26.6	15.91	1.81
⊕ Prosperity Bancshares, I	Financial	18.6	21.60	1.79
⊕ Jos A. Bank Clothiers	Consumer	15.3	-15.49	1.78
⊕ Parametric Technology Co	Software	38.1	18.16	1.77
⊕ Aspen Insurance Holdings	Financial	8.3	14.24	1.77

Current Investment Style

Value Blnd Growth — Large Mid Small

Market Cap	%
Giant	0.0
Large	0.0
Mid	35.0
Small	49.9
Micro	15.1
Avg $mil: 1,329	

Value Measures		Rel Category
Price/Earnings	14.69	0.96
Price/Book	1.93	1.08
Price/Sales	0.90	1.13
Price/Cash Flow	7.62	1.25
Dividend Yield %	1.44	0.91

Growth Measures	%	Rel Category
Long-Term Erngs	12.84	1.03
Book Value	6.59	1.22
Sales	9.84	1.33
Cash Flow	2.32	0.28
Historical Erngs	8.57	0.75

Profitability	%	Rel Category
Return on Equity	10.42	0.97
Return on Assets	6.06	0.99
Net Margin	8.44	0.93

Sector Weightings	% of Stocks	Rel S&P 500	3 Year High Low	
⊙ Info	21.04	1.05		
📊 Software	1.98	0.57	4	0
💻 Hardware	17.48	1.89	18	3
📱 Media	0.00	0.00	1	0
📞 Telecom	1.58	0.45	2	0
⊆ Service	56.85	1.23		
🏥 Health	2.97	0.25	6	1
🛒 Consumer	11.70	1.53	12	7
📋 Business	13.00	3.07	18	12
💲 Financial	29.18	1.31	31	22
🏭 Mfg	22.12	0.65		
🚗 Goods	0.00	0.00	6	0
⚙ Ind Mtrls	20.20	1.69	37	20
⛽ Energy	1.92	0.20	3	2
💡 Utilities	0.00	0.00	0	0

Composition

	%
● Cash	10.3
● Stocks	89.7
● Bonds	0.0
○ Other	0.0
Foreign	1.3
(% of Stock)	

Morningstar's Take by Karen Wallace 01-04-07

Skyline Special Equities' appeal lies in its straightforward approach.

Managers Bill Fiedler, Mike Maloney, and Mark Odegard start by screening for stocks with market caps of $2 billion or less and trading at prices more than 20% below their historical P/E ratio. Then they focus on fundamentals to find companies with good growth prospects, attractive balance sheets, and shareholder-focused management teams. When a stock reaches a market multiple, the team sells it and redeploys the assets into new ideas.

That approach has recently led the managers to technology stocks. The fund's tech exposure is now nearly double the weighting of the typical small-value fund and the Russell 2000 Value Index. While one could assume that exposure would invite streaky performance, the managers' valuation consciousness, which has actually prompted the fund's shift to technology, has thus far kept a lid on volatility. In addition, although they aren't afraid to invest with conviction in particular sectors, the portfolio as a whole tends to be well diversified across sectors and individual issues rarely soak up more than 3% of assets.

Many of the team's technology picks worked well in 2006. For instance, it picked up shares of semiconductor firm SMART Modular Technologies in early 2006 after the company's IPO generated little interest. The managers thought it was a solid business that was selling cheap at 10 times earnings. The stock had a nice rise in the fourth quarter and finished the year with roughly a 50% gain.

Overall, results have been good. The fund's standard deviation is well below the small-value category median, and three- and five-year results land comfortably in the top half of the category. One quibble we have is that the fund's expense ratio, which at 1.47%, is about 25 basis points above the median for no-load small-cap offerings. Overall, it's a decent choice in a category where many cheaper and well run funds are closed.

Address:	311 South Wacker Drive Chicago IL 60606 800-828-2759	Minimum Purchase:	$1000	Add: $100	IRA: $1000
		Min Auto Inv Plan:	$1000	Add: $50	
		Sales Fees:	No-load, 2.00%R		
Web Address:	www.skylinelp.com	Management Fee:	1.40% mx./1.15% mn.		
Inception:	04-23-87	Actual Fees:	Mgt:1.46%	Dist: —	
Advisor:	Skyline Asset Management, LP	Expense Projections:	3Yr:$465	5Yr:$803	10Yr:$1757
Subadvisor:	None	Income Distrib:	Annually		
NTF Plans:	Fidelity Retail-NTF, Schwab OneSource				

MORNINGSTAR® Funds 500

Sound Shore

	Analyst Pick	Ticker SSHFX	Load None	NAV $39.19	Yield 0.5%	Total Assets $2,880 mil	Mstar Category Large Value

Governance and Management

Stewardship Grade: A

Portfolio Manager(s)

Managers Harry Burn and Gibbs Kane founded their firm in 1978 and have led this fund since its inception in May 1985. John DeGulis, an analyst here since 1995, was named a comanager of the fund in 2003. They work with a group of three in-house analysts. The firm's profit-sharing plan is invested in the fund.

Strategy

Management seeks beaten-down stocks with solid fundamentals. It screens a universe of 1,250 U.S. equities to identify stocks trading at large discounts to their historic price multiples. Once it has narrowed the list, the team scrutinizes a firm's competitive position by speaking with company management, competitors, and customers. The team then prepares detailed financial and valuation models. The result is a portfolio of 40 or so mid- and large-cap companies.

Performance 12-31-06

	1st Qtr	2nd Qtr	3rd Qtr	4th Qtr	Total
2002	2.49	-10.23	-16.36	9.90	-15.43
2003	-6.94	21.73	2.81	13.11	31.74
2004	3.55	1.46	0.09	9.69	15.34
2005	-2.92	1.75	8.11	0.00	6.80
2006	3.19	-1.60	7.01	7.27	16.56

Trailing	Total Return%	+/- S&P 500	+/- Russ 1000 Vl	%Rank Cat	Growth of $10,000
3 Mo	7.27	0.57	-0.73	49	10,727
6 Mo	14.79	2.05	0.07	16	11,479
1 Yr	16.56	0.77	-5.69	71	11,656
3 Yr Avg	12.82	2.38	-2.27	38	14,360
5 Yr Avg	9.85	3.66	-1.01	20	15,996
10 Yr Avg	10.51	2.09	-0.49	18	27,165
15 Yr Avg	13.17	2.53	0.14	10	63,969

Tax Analysis	Tax-Adj Rtn%	%Rank Cat	Tax-Cost Rat	%Rank Cat
3 Yr (estimated)	11.52	34	1.15	46
5 Yr (estimated)	8.99	17	0.78	42
10 Yr (estimated)	9.62	7	0.81	11

Potential Capital Gain Exposure: 10% of assets

Morningstar's Take by Gregg Wolper 12-11-06

Sound Shore Fund's credentials as a strong core holding remain intact.

Those investors making adjustments to their portfolio--or deciding to start one--around the new year should give serious consideration to using this one as an anchor. The fund has many of the attributes one looks for. Two of its managers have been in place for 21 years (the third became a manager in 2003 after eight years as an analyst here). They use a sound value-based strategy that they don't alter regardless of the passing trends of the marketplace. They haven't come out with hot new funds. The expense ratio is reasonable. And performance has been more than respectable. For the trailing 10-year period through November 2006 and the trailing five-year stretch through December 8, 2006, the fund lands in the top quartile of the large-value category and has beaten the S&P 500 Index by substantial margins.

So, there's no reason to become concerned over the fund's less-than-impressive 2006 ranking. For the year-to-date through December 8, it's in the bottom quartile with a return of 14.6%. One stock-specific problem in particular has hurt: a top holding, Boston Scientific, is down 32% this year because, among other things, investors did not view its takeover of Guidant favorably. Another large position, Sprint Nextel, is down about 9% for the year to date.

Investors should note that while the managers definitely use a value-based strategy, that doesn't mean they exclude sectors commonly seen as the home of growth stocks. Most notably, they're not averse to technology-related companies. In fact, Symantec and Freescale Semiconductor (which was taken over) were the best contributors in 2006's third quarter.

One final note: Although this fund has attracted attention in recent years, it is still a reasonable size--another reason to look here.

Address:	Two Portland Square	Minimum Purchase:	$10000	Add: $0	IRA: $2000
	Portland ME 04101-4049	Min Auto Inv Plan:	$10000	Add: $50	
	800-551-1980	Sales Fees:	No-load		
Web Address:	www.soundshorefund.com	Management Fee:	0.75%		
Inception:	05-03-85	Actual Fees:	Mgt:0.75%	Dist: —	
Advisor:	Sound Shore Management Inc	Expense Projections:	3Yr:$296	5Yr:$515	10Yr:$1143
Subadvisor:	None	Income Distrib:	Semi-Annually		
NTF Plans:	Fidelity Retail-NTF, Schwab OneSource				

Historical Profile

Return	Above Avg
Risk	Above Avg
Rating	★★★★ Above Avg

| 97% | 98% | 93% | 95% | 97% | 94% | 95% | 93% | 96% |

▼ Manager Change
▽ Partial Manager Change

40.8
31.0
24.0
17.0
10.0

Growth of $10,000
■ Investment Values of Fund
— Investment Values of S&P 500

Performance Quartile (within Category)

1995	1996	1997	1998	1999	2000	2001	2002	2003	2004	2005	2006	History
18.16	21.71	28.57	29.62	29.47	33.70	30.58	25.81	33.51	36.70	36.63	39.19	NAV
29.87	33.27	36.40	4.40	0.05	20.18	-0.81	-15.43	31.74	15.34	6.80	16.56	Total Return %
-7.71	10.31	3.04	-24.18	-20.99	29.28	11.08	6.67	3.06	4.46	1.89	0.77	+/-S&P 500
-8.49	11.63	1.22	-11.23	-7.30	13.17	4.78	0.09	1.71	-1.15	-0.25	-5.69	+/-Russ 1000 Vl
1.38	0.70	0.57	0.73	0.57	0.48	0.30	0.17	0.20	0.30	0.18	0.57	Income Return %
28.49	32.57	35.83	3.67	-0.52	19.70	-1.11	-15.60	31.54	15.04	6.62	15.99	Capital Return %
71	1	2	85	73	13	33	30	21	24	34	71	Total Rtn % Rank Cat
0.21	0.13	0.12	0.21	0.17	0.14	0.10	0.05	0.05	0.10	0.07	0.21	Income $
1.67	2.35	0.89	0.00	0.00	1.56	2.76	0.00	0.44	1.85	2.51	3.30	Capital Gains $
1.15	1.15	1.08	0.99	0.98	0.98	0.98	0.98	0.98	0.98	0.98	—	Expense Ratio %
1.41	0.70	0.62	0.77	0.50	0.44	0.32	0.17	0.18	0.33	0.20	—	Income Ratio %
53	69	53	44	41	98	104	72	62	50	62	—	Turnover Rate %
68	131	1,304	1,965	1,184	1,052	1,047	759	1,016	1,698	2,265	2,880	Net Assets $mil

Rating and Risk

Time Period	Load-Adj Return %	Morningstar Rtn vs Cat	Morningstar Risk vs Cat	Morningstar Risk-Adj Rating
1 Yr	16.56			
3 Yr	12.82	Avg	+Avg	★★★
5 Yr	9.85	+Avg	+Avg	★★★★
10 Yr	10.51	+Avg	+Avg	★★★★
Incept	13.29			

Other Measures	Standard Index S&P 500	Best Fit Index S&P 500
Alpha	2.0	2.0
Beta	1.04	1.04
R-Squared	81	81
Standard Deviation	7.90	
Mean	12.82	
Sharpe Ratio	1.17	

Portfolio Analysis 09-30-06

Share change since 06-06 Total Stocks:39	Sector	PE	Tot Ret%	% Assets
⊕ Time Warner, Inc.	Media	19.6	26.37	4.11
⊕ Boston Scientific Corpor	Health	—	-29.85	3.77
⊕ Symantec Corporation	Software	50.9	19.14	3.52
⊕ Sprint Nextel Corporatio	Telecom	30.2	-10.44	3.48
⊕ Kinetic Concepts, Inc.	Health	15.5	-0.53	3.27
⊕ Berkshire Hathaway Inc.	Financial	—		3.25
Walt Disney Company	Media	21.0	44.26	3.17
⊖ Baxter International Inc	Health	24.3	24.81	3.16
⊕ Unilever NV	Goods	16.9	25.03	3.02
⊖ Bank of America Corporat	Financial	12.4	20.68	3.01
US Bancorp	Financial	13.9	26.29	2.92
⊖ Freescale Semiconductor,	Hardware	—		2.78
⊕ Motorola, Inc.	Hardware	11.8	-8.17	2.64
⊕ Interpublic Group of Com	Business	—	26.84	2.58
⊖ Lyondell Chemical Compan	Energy	10.1	11.52	2.56
⊕ Honda Motor ADR	Goods	13.5	39.19	2.54
⊕ Pfizer Inc.	Health	15.2	15.22	2.53
⊕ Aetna, Inc.	Health	14.1	-8.34	2.51
⊖ Royal Dutch Shell PLC AD	Energy	8.7	19.33	2.51
⊕ Liberty Capital A	Media	—		2.49

Current Investment Style

Value Blnd Growth — Large Mid Small

Market Cap	%
Giant	33.8
Large	44.9
Mid	21.4
Small	0.0
Micro	0.0
Avg $mil:	24,552

Value Measures		Rel Category
Price/Earnings	14.50	1.06
Price/Book	1.61	0.73
Price/Sales	1.21	0.93
Price/Cash Flow	7.27	1.09
Dividend Yield %	1.34	0.58

Growth Measures	%	Rel Category
Long-Term Erngs	11.38	1.10
Book Value	9.96	1.26
Sales	9.83	1.09
Cash Flow	8.97	1.48
Historical Erngs	13.87	0.86

Profitability	%	Rel Category
Return on Equity	12.89	0.72
Return on Assets	6.55	0.67
Net Margin	5.57	0.43

Sector Weightings	% of Stocks	Rel S&P 500	3 Year High Low	
↻ Info	30.19	1.51		
🖥 Software	3.66	1.06	4	0
💻 Hardware	10.37	1.12	12	5
🎤 Media	12.54	3.31	13	6
📱 Telecom	3.62	1.03	5	0
⊂ Service	50.49	1.09		
🏥 Health	20.43	1.69	21	14
🛒 Consumer	0.00	0.00	5	0
💼 Business	9.09	2.15	13	4
💲 Financial	20.97	0.94	29	21
⚒ Mfg	19.31	0.57		
🔩 Goods	5.80	0.68	6	2
⚙ Ind Mtrls	2.04	0.17	15	2
🔋 Energy	9.14	0.93	16	8
💡 Utilities	2.33	0.67	2	0

Composition

● Cash	4.1
● Stocks	95.9
● Bonds	0.0
○ Other	0.0
Foreign (% of Stock)	10.9

SSgA Emerging Markets

	Ticker	Load	NAV	Yield	Total Assets	Mstar Category
	SSEMX	None	$23.43	1.4%	$2,531 mil	Diversified Emerging Mkts

Governance and Management

Stewardship Grade: B

Portfolio Manager(s)

The fund has a strong management team. Brad Aham came on board as an analyst in the mid-1990s, has served as lead manager since 1999, and is supported by a deep and experienced team of investment professionals

Strategy

This fund's managers employ a quantitative strategy to screen companies and regions for reasonable price multiples and strong earnings forecasts. While doing so, they pay ample attention to diversification. The fund levies a 2% redemption fee on shares held for less than six months.

Historical Profile

Return Above Avg
Risk Average
Rating ★★★★ Above Avg

	88%	87%	82%	83%	77%	83%	89%	86%	82%	Investment Style
										Equity Stock %

▼ Manager Change
▽ Partial Manager Change

Growth of $10,000
— Investment Values of Fund
— Investment Values of MSCI EAFE

26.0 / 20.0 / 15.0 / 10.0 / 6.0

Performance Quartile (within Category)

1995	1996	1997	1998	1999	2000	2001	2002	2003	2004	2005	2006	History
9.70	10.98	9.69	7.86	12.67	8.81	8.85	8.37	12.60	15.01	18.77	23.43	NAV
-7.89	14.88	-8.81	-15.94	64.81	-29.97	0.45	-5.03	53.97	24.67	37.28	33.46	Total Return %
-19.10	8.83	-10.59	-35.87	37.78	-15.78	21.87	10.91	15.38	4.42	23.74	7.12	+/-MSCI EAFE
-0.98	10.95	4.64	11.73	0.72	1.93	5.13	2.94	2.38	2.22	6.97	4.28	+/-MSCI EmrMkt
1.11	1.11	1.38	2.81	2.93	0.53	0.00	0.38	3.06	1.52	3.21	1.78	Income Return %
-9.00	13.77	-10.19	-18.75	61.88	-30.50	0.45	-5.41	50.91	23.15	34.07	31.68	Capital Return %
83	36	77	4	56	43	18	42	52	45	20	36	Total Rtn % Rank Cat
0.12	0.11	0.15	0.27	0.23	0.07	0.00	0.03	0.26	0.19	0.48	0.33	Income $
0.10	0.06	0.26	0.00	0.00	0.00	0.00	0.00	0.00	0.41	1.09	1.11	Capital Gains $
1.50	1.28	1.25	1.25	1.25	1.25	1.25	1.25	1.25	1.25	1.25	1.25	Expense Ratio %
1.74	1.10	1.07	1.85	1.78	0.89	1.48	0.98	1.59	1.44	1.64	1.29	Income Ratio %
20	4	15	39	40	56	50	92	88	64	53	37	Turnover Rate %
81	148	255	236	414	318	375	374	645	871	1,402	1,739	Net Assets $mil

Performance 12-31-06

	1st Qtr	2nd Qtr	3rd Qtr	4th Qtr	Total
2002	12.54	-6.73	-15.93	7.62	-5.03
2003	-5.73	21.29	14.63	17.48	53.97
2004	9.46	-10.44	8.91	16.78	24.67
2005	2.93	4.34	18.42	7.94	37.28
2006	14.38	-4.66	3.66	18.05	33.46

Trailing	Total Return%	+/- MSCI EAFE	+/- MSCI EmrMkt	%Rank Cat	Growth of $10,000
3 Mo	18.05	7.70	0.77	33	11,805
6 Mo	22.38	7.69	0.29	73	12,238
1 Yr	33.46	7.12	4.28	36	13,346
3 Yr Avg	31.70	11.77	4.44	23	22,843
5 Yr Avg	27.28	12.30	3.76	31	33,404
10 Yr Avg	11.49	3.79	4.76	19	29,673
15 Yr Avg	—	—	—	—	—

Tax Analysis	Tax-Adj Rtn%	%Rank Cat	Tax-Cost Rat	%Rank Cat
3 Yr (estimated)	29.80	19	1.44	57
5 Yr (estimated)	25.94	31	1.05	57
10 Yr (estimated)	10.53	23	0.86	72

Potential Capital Gain Exposure: 37% of assets

Rating and Risk

Time Period	Load-Adj Return %	Morningstar Rtn vs Cat	Morningstar Risk vs Cat	Morningstar Risk-Adj Rating
1 Yr	33.46			
3 Yr	31.70	+Avg	+Avg	★★★★
5 Yr	27.28	Avg	Avg	★★★
10 Yr	11.49	+Avg	Avg	★★★★
Incept	10.03			

Other Measures	Standard Index MSCI EAFE	Best Fit Index MSCI EmrMkt
Alpha	-0.1	2.7
Beta	1.70	1.04
R-Squared	75	98
Standard Deviation	18.46	
Mean	31.70	
Sharpe Ratio	1.43	

Morningstar's Take by William Samuel Rocco 11-08-06

SSgA Emerging Markets is an attractive emerging-markets vehicle, but the strong pace it has set in recent years can only be sustained for so long.

This fund starts off with several advantages over its peers. It has one of the lowest expense ratios in its group and thus enjoys a major long-term edge. A seasoned team that has experienced a mix of market climates is in charge here--lead manager Brad Aham has been a key part of the team since the fund opened in 1993--while some emerging-markets managers have yet to face a sustained downturn. The team uses a quantitative-driven, blue-chip strategy that pays considerable attention to valuations and diversification. Such an approach makes a lot of sense given the dangers that come with focusing on the developing world and gives the fund a fighting chance in all sorts of conditions.

Overall, the team has executed its fairly conservative strategy well. The fund has generally posted solid returns in rallies. It has posted competitive gains thus far in 2006, thanks to its moderate overweightings in Indonesia and Russia and the team's stock selection in China and Brazil. The fund has also tended to hold up fairly well in sell-offs, due to its diversification and other reserved traits. And its consistent results add up to strong long-term returns.

These strengths really count, and the fund is a good long-term emerging-markets option. But it's important to understand that valuations and other factors prevent all funds from soaring for too long and that this and other emerging-markets funds are unlikely to do as well over the next few years as they have over the last few. It's also crucial to recognize that the fund is quite volatile in absolute terms, even though it's less daring than many of its rivals. It, in fact, has lost 15% or more in 13 rolling three-month periods in the last decade, and it remains capable of sharp declines.

Address:	2 International Place Boston, MA 02110 800-647-7327
Web Address:	www.ssgafunds.com
Inception:	03-01-94
Advisor:	SSgA Funds Management Inc
Subadvisor:	None
NTF Plans:	Fidelity Retail-NTF

Minimum Purchase:	$1000	Add: $1000	IRA: $250
Min Auto Inv Plan:	$1000	Add: $100	
Sales Fees:	No-load, 0.11%S, 2.00%R		
Management Fee:	0.75%		
Actual Fees:	Mgt:0.75%	Dist:0.11%	
Expense Projections:	3Yr:$403	5Yr:$699	10Yr:$1543
Income Distrib:	Annually		

Portfolio Analysis 11-30-06

Share change since 10-06 Total Stocks:273

	Sector	Country	% Assets
⊕ Gazprom OAO (ADR)	Energy	U.K.	4.50
⊕ Samsung Electronics	Goods	Korea	3.23
⊕ Petroleo Brasileiro S.A.	Energy	Brazil	2.83
⊕ Lukoil ADR	Energy	Russia	2.60
⊕ China Mobile	Telecom	Hong Kong	2.21
⊕ Companhia Vale Do Rio Do	Ind Mtrls	Brazil	1.68
⊕ PetroChina	Energy	Hong Kong	1.32
⊕ POSCO	Ind Mtrls	Korea	1.30
⊕ Kookmin Bank	Financial	Korea	1.20
⊕ Telekomunikasi Indonesia	Telecom	Indonesia	1.17
Taiwan Semiconductor Mfg	Hardware	Taiwan	1.11
⊕ America Movil SA ADR	Telecom	Mexico	1.03
⊕ MMC Norilsk Nickel ADR	Ind Mtrls	Russia	0.96
Sasol Ltd	Energy	South Africa	0.94
Tenaris SA ADR	Ind Mtrls	Luxembourg	0.90
Indl And Commrcl Bk Of C	Financial	China	0.88
Samsung Electnc	—	Korea	0.87
⊕ Bco Itau Hldg F	—	Brazil	0.84
⊕ China Life Insurance	Financial	Hong Kong	0.81
Hon Hai Precision Indust	Hardware	Taiwan	0.80

Current Investment Style

Value Blnd Growth — Large Mid Small

Market Cap	%
Giant	43.9
Large	32.4
Mid	20.7
Small	2.5
Micro	0.5
Avg $mil:	14,764

Value Measures		Rel Category
Price/Earnings	13.09	1.01
Price/Book	2.29	1.05
Price/Sales	1.20	1.09
Price/Cash Flow	6.52	0.98
Dividend Yield %	3.14	0.95

Growth Measures	%	Rel Category
Long-Term Erngs	14.62	0.94
Book Value	16.61	1.66
Sales	14.19	0.90
Cash Flow	14.44	1.31
Historical Erngs	27.04	1.51

Composition			
Cash	10.2	Bonds	0.3
Stocks	81.7	Other	7.8
Foreign (% of Stock)			99.9

Sector Weightings	% of Stocks	Rel MSCI EAFE	3 Year High	Low
↻ Info	20.64	1.75		
🖳 Software	0.40	0.71	1	0
🖥 Hardware	4.96	1.28	8	4
🎙 Media	1.32	0.72	2	1
📶 Telecom	13.96	2.51	16	11
⊖ Service	29.39	0.62		
🩺 Health	1.14	0.16	3	1
🛒 Consumer	4.16	0.84	5	3
🏢 Business	5.24	1.03	6	4
💲 Financial	18.85	0.63	19	16
🏭 Mfg	49.99	1.22		
🔩 Goods	7.92	0.60	19	8
🛠 Ind Mtrls	19.57	1.27	22	16
🔥 Energy	21.64	3.03	24	10
💡 Utilities	0.86	0.16	3	1

Regional Exposure	% Stock		
UK/W. Europe	8	N. America	0
Japan	0	Latn America	20
Asia X Japan	49	Other	23

Country Exposure	% Stock		
South Korea	17	South Africa	10
Brazil	13	Taiwan	8
Hong Kong	11		

MORNINGSTAR® Funds 500

SSgA Yield Plus

	Ticker	Load	NAV	Yield	SEC Yield	Total Assets	Mstar Category
	SSYPX	None	$9.94	5.0%	—	$203 mil	Ultrashort Bond

Governance and Management

Stewardship Grade: C

Portfolio Manager(s)

Frank Gianatasio has taken over lead manager responsibilities from Mike O'Hara, who became this fund's lead manager in February 2003. Also, Robert Pickett has replaced Julio Fuentes as comanager here, and four analysts contribute to the group.

Strategy

Former lead manager Mike O'Hara shifted the portfolio from a focus on corporate bonds to asset-backed securities, and with Frank Gianatasio taking charge here the focus and strategy will remain the same. Gianatasio keeps duration extremely short and aims to pick up yield through issue selection and sector allocation. He keeps a chunk of the portfolio in credit card-backed bonds for the sake of liquidity. But the kick mostly comes through mortgage-backed securities. He emphasizes high-quality bonds and pays a good deal of attention to risk controls.

Historical Profile

Return	Below Avg
Risk	Low
Rating	★★ Below Avg

Investment Style
Fixed Income
Income Rtn %Rank Cat

▼ Manager Change
▽ Partial Manager Change

Growth of $10,000
— Investment Values of Fund
— Investment Values of LB Aggr

Performance Quartile (within Category)

	1995	1996	1997	1998	1999	2000	2001	2002	2003	2004	2005	2006	History
	10.01	10.00	9.99	9.90	9.91	9.94	9.96	9.93	9.94	9.96	9.95	9.94	NAV
	6.56	5.49	5.54	4.83	5.52	6.69	4.53	1.35	1.14	1.53	3.10	5.02	Total Return %
	-11.91	1.86	-4.11	-3.86	6.34	-4.94	-3.91	-8.90	-2.96	-2.81	0.67	0.69	+/-LB Aggr
	0.58	0.03	-0.18	-0.61	0.06	0.11	0.90	-0.46	-0.03	-0.20	-0.62	-0.21	+/-6 Month CD
	6.05	5.59	5.65	5.76	5.43	6.37	4.33	1.65	1.04	1.33	3.20	5.13	Income Return %
	0.51	-0.10	-0.11	-0.93	0.09	0.32	0.20	-0.30	0.10	0.20	-0.10	-0.11	Capital Return %
	82	70	88	58	5	66	86	85	77	37	16	17	Total Rtn % Rank Cat
	0.59	0.55	0.55	0.56	0.52	0.61	0.42	0.16	0.10	0.13	0.31	0.50	Income $
	0.00	0.00	0.00	0.00	0.00	0.00	0.00	0.00	0.00	0.00	0.00	0.00	Capital Gains $
	0.38	0.36	0.38	0.41	0.41	0.42	0.48	0.53	0.58	0.57	0.56	0.59	Expense Ratio %
	5.64	5.59	5.42	5.66	5.29	5.90	5.31	2.17	1.18	1.08	2.40	4.71	Income Ratio %
	200	97	92	249	167	162	86	80	71	32	25	68	Turnover Rate %
	1,381	1,002	704	788	542	258	215	262	267	265	168	203	Net Assets $mil

Performance 12-31-06

	1st Qtr	2nd Qtr	3rd Qtr	4th Qtr	Total
2002	0.28	0.35	0.40	0.32	1.35
2003	0.27	0.46	0.24	0.17	1.14
2004	0.44	0.27	0.34	0.47	1.53
2005	0.50	0.81	0.78	0.97	3.10
2006	1.00	1.33	1.36	1.24	5.02

Trailing	Total Return%	+/- LB Aggr	+/- 6 Month CD	%Rank Cat	Growth of $10,000
3 Mo	1.24	0.00	-0.06	40	10,124
6 Mo	2.61	-2.48	-0.05	55	10,261
1 Yr	5.02	0.69	-0.21	17	10,502
3 Yr Avg	3.21	-0.49	-0.34	15	10,994
5 Yr Avg	2.42	-2.64	-0.30	67	11,270
10 Yr Avg	3.91	-2.33	-0.12	79	14,675
15 Yr Avg	—	—	—		

Tax Analysis	Tax-Adj Rtn%	%Rank Cat	Tax-Cost Rat	%Rank Cat
3 Yr (estimated)	2.08	7	1.09	45
5 Yr (estimated)	1.54	22	0.86	10
10 Yr (estimated)	2.37	59	1.48	16

Potential Capital Gain Exposure: -2% of assets

Rating and Risk

Time Period	Load-Adj Return %	Morningstar Rtn vs Cat	Morningstar Risk vs Cat	Morningstar Risk-Adj Rating
1 Yr	5.02			
3 Yr	3.21	+Avg	Low	★★★★
5 Yr	2.42	-Avg	Low	★★
10 Yr	3.91	-Avg	Low	★★
Incept	4.18			

Other Measures	Standard Index LB Aggr	Best Fit Index Citigroup ESBI-Cap Brady
Alpha	-0.1	0.0
Beta	0.01	-0.01
R-Squared	1	4
Standard Deviation	0.47	
Mean	3.21	
Sharpe Ratio	-0.26	

Morningstar's Take by Lawrence Jones 12-21-06

SSgA Yield Plus is attractive, if a bit expensive.

This fund's manager, Frank Gianatasio, has the resources needed to do well. His efforts are supported by comanager Robert Pickett, an SSgA veteran who heads up asset allocation and global high-grade credit departments, and four research analysts, including a recently added asset-backed sector specialist. Mike O'Hara, this fund's former manager, oversees the active global fixed-income group now. Overall, we're pleased with the team's level of experience with residential mortgage and asset-backed securities, the type of investments that form the core of the portfolio here.

Since the time O'Hara ran the fund, the approach here has been to keep the fund's duration (a measure of interest-rate sensitivity) among the shortest in the ultrashort-bond category. The goal is to protect the fund during periods of rising rates and to keep principal stable. Gianatasio accomplishes this by investing in high-quality mortgage- and asset-backed securities, where he

believes the marketplace still displays inefficiencies that can be exploited. Other segments of the portfolio are kept in credit card asset-backed issues, for liquidity purposes, or in foreign issues. In fact, one of the fund's most successful positions has been in mortgage-backed bonds from Australia and the United Kingdom (around 20% of assets), which provide the fund with business cycle diversification.

As a result of this approach, recent performance at the fund has been strong. The defensive duration position here and purchasing a significant amount of floating-rate notes helped performance as rates spiked in the last few years. Longer-term performance is mixed; the fund tends to outperform during periods of rising rates, as we have seen recently.

While we like many aspects of the fund, we have been disappointed by its increasing cost. Were costs to come down, we would find the fund more attractive.

Portfolio Analysis 11-30-06

Total Fixed-Income:83	Date of Maturity	Amount $000	Value $000	% Net Assets
Ge Busn Ln Tr 2004-1 CMO	05-15-32	7,736	7,739	3.73
Smhl Global Fd No 3 FRN	12-01-28	5,473	5,482	2.64
Novastar Heq Ln Tr 2005-	01-25-36	5,000	5,023	2.42
Hm Equity Mtg Inabs 2005	03-25-36	5,000	5,020	2.42
Structured Asset Inv 200	04-25-33	5,000	5,003	2.41
Granite Master Issuer 14	12-20-54	5,000	5,003	2.41
Permanent Fing Plc 2004-	06-10-11	5,000	5,003	2.41
Natl City Ccmt 2002-1 FR	01-15-09	5,000	5,001	2.41
Residential Accredit Loa	12-25-36	5,000	5,000	2.41
Gsamp Tr 2006-Fm1 FRN	04-25-36	5,000	5,000	2.41
C-Bass Abs FRN	12-25-35	4,783	4,784	2.30
Permanent Fing Plc 2004-	03-10-09	4,500	4,500	2.17
Argent Secs FRN	04-25-34	4,000	4,051	1.95
Slm Private St Ln Tr 200	03-15-22	4,000	4,048	1.95
Gsamp Tr 2005-He6 FRN	11-25-35	4,000	4,018	1.94
New Century Heq Tr 2006-	05-25-36	4,000	4,007	1.93
Securitized Asset Rec 20	05-25-36	4,000	4,003	1.93
Ace Secs Heq 2005-He6 FR	10-25-36	4,000	4,001	1.93
Structured Asset Sec 200	04-25-36	4,000	3,984	1.92
Structured Asset Inv 200	12-25-34	3,811	3,833	1.85

Current Investment Style

Duration: Short Int Long
Quality: High Med Low

¹ figure provided by fund

Avg Eff Duration¹	0.0 Yrs
Avg Eff Maturity	—
Avg Credit Quality	AA
Avg Wtd Coupon	3.34%
Avg Wtd Price	98.93% of par

Coupon Range	% of Bonds	Rel Cat
0% PIK	0.0	0.0
0% to 6%	100.0	1.1
6% to 8%	0.0	0.0
8% to 10%	0.0	0.0
More than 10%	0.0	0.0

1.00=Category Average

Credit Analysis	% bonds 11-30-06		
AAA	42	BB	0
AA	31	B	0
A	11	Below B	0
BBB	1	NR/NA	14

Sector Breakdown — % of assets

US Treasuries	0
TIPS	0
US Agency	0
Mortgage Pass-Throughs	2
Mortgage CMO	18
Mortgage ARM	0
US Corporate	5
Asset-Backed	68
Convertible	0
Municipal	0
Corporate Inflation-Protected	0
Foreign Corporate	7
Foreign Govt	0

Composition

Cash	0.1	Bonds	99.9
Stocks	0.0	Other	0.0

Special Securities

Restricted/Illiquid Secs	7
Exotic Mortgage-Backed	1
Emerging-Markets Secs	0
Options/Futures/Warrants	No

Address:	2 International Place, Boston, MA 02110, 800-647-7327	Minimum Purchase:	$1000 Add: $100 IRA: $250
		Min Auto Inv Plan:	$1000 Add: $100
		Sales Fees:	No-load, 0.09%S
Web Address:	www.ssgafunds.com	Management Fee:	0.25%
Inception:	11-09-92	Actual Fees:	Mgt:0.25% Dist:0.09%
Advisor:	SSgA Funds Management Inc	Expense Projections:	3Yr:$189 5Yr:$329 10Yr:$738
Subadvisor:	None	Income Distrib:	Monthly
NTF Plans:	Fidelity Retail-NTF, Schwab OneSource		

T. Rowe Price Balanced

	Ticker	Load	NAV	Yield	Total Assets	Mstar Category
	RPBAX	None	$21.29	2.4%	$2,929 mil	Moderate Allocation

Governance and Management

Stewardship Grade: A

Portfolio Manager(s)

Rich Whitney has steered this fund since 1991. He runs the domestic-stock portfolio, which tends to closely resemble those of T. Rowe's large-cap offerings. Ned Notzon, who has long run the fund's investment-grade bond portfolio, was recently named comanager; he and Whitney also set the fund's security mix. Ray Mills, who runs T. Rowe Price International Growth & Income, manages the fund's slice of foreign stocks. Meanwhile, Mark Vaselkiv of T. Rowe Price High-Yield also plies his specialty here.

Strategy

The fund strives to be a one-stop shop for investors. It offers a relatively stock-heavy neutral allocation of 65% equities and 35% bonds/cash. Comanager Rich Whitney relies heavily on T. Rowe's other managers and analysts to assemble the domestic-stock portfolio, employing the firm's trademark growth-at-a-reasonable-price approach. He and the fund's other skipper, fixed-income expert Ned Notzon, add spice by placing 12% to 15% of assets in foreign stocks and up to 8% in high-yield bonds. The managers also keep the fund well diversified among issues and sectors.

Performance 12-31-06

	1st Qtr	2nd Qtr	3rd Qtr	4th Qtr	Total
2002	1.32	-5.40	-9.66	5.62	-8.54
2003	-1.94	11.64	1.97	9.02	21.71
2004	2.01	-0.10	1.08	7.10	10.32
2005	-0.90	1.61	3.25	1.50	5.52
2006	2.98	-0.39	4.91	5.68	13.73

Trailing	Total Return%	+/- DJ Mod	+/- DJ US Mod	%Rank Cat	Growth of $10,000
3 Mo	5.68	0.09	1.01	24	10,568
6 Mo	10.87	2.08	2.97	12	11,087
1 Yr	13.73	1.43	3.46	15	11,373
3 Yr Avg	9.81	-0.91	0.69	20	13,241
5 Yr Avg	8.06	-1.96	0.46	12	14,734
10 Yr Avg	8.19	-0.36	-0.40	24	21,972
15 Yr Avg	9.23	0.02	-0.16	41	37,595

Tax Analysis	Tax-Adj Rtn%	%Rank Cat	Tax-Cost Rat	%Rank Cat
3 Yr (estimated)	8.52	19	1.17	58
5 Yr (estimated)	6.87	12	1.10	67
10 Yr (estimated)	6.83	18	1.26	33

Potential Capital Gain Exposure: 2% of assets

Morningstar's Take by Greg Carlson 12-28-06

T. Rowe Price Balanced Fund doesn't always make the best use of its resources, but it's a solid choice.

This tame fund has several moving parts. Ned Notzon sets its asset allocation and runs the investment-grade bond sleeve; Ray Mills of T. Rowe Price International Growth & Income manages the foreign-stock portfolio; Mark Vaselkiv of T. Rowe Price High-Yield handles lower-rated bonds; and Rich Whitney (who sits on the firm's asset allocation committee with Notzon) steers the domestic-stock sleeve. While T. Rowe Price is known for its generally moderate investment approach, and Notzon won't make big shifts in this fund's overall security mix, Mills, Notzon, and Vaselkiv each have a significant amount of latitude to steer their underlying portfolios into the most attractively valued stocks or bonds.

Whitney, on the other hand, takes a more-constrained tack: He keeps the sector weightings of the domestic-stock slice in line with the S&P 500 Index's, and attempts to beat it by

selecting the best firms in each sector. While that strategy helps fulfill his goal of delivering predictable returns, we're not sure it's the best way to use T. Rowe's talented analyst staff, which has often helped steer managers away from overvalued sectors (such as tech at the bull market's peak). For example, this fund's stake in energy and industrials stocks, which have staged a strong three-year rally, still roughly matches both the S&P's and the moderate-allocation group norm, despite Whitney's concerns about valuations.

That said, the fund holds a lot of appeal. Whitney has modestly outpaced the S&P over the long haul, and the fund's diverse asset mix helps reduce its correlation to broad market indexes (despite a hefty stake in large-cap stocks). What's more, all of the fund's managers boast a wealth of experience, and a low 0.69% expense ratio gives it a sustained advantage over rivals.

Address:	100 East Pratt Street Baltimore MD 21202 800-638-5660	Minimum Purchase:	$2500	Add: $100	IRA: $1000
		Min Auto Inv Plan:	$50	Add: $50	
		Sales Fees:	No-load		
Web Address:	www.troweprice.com	Management Fee:	0.46%		
Inception:	12-29-39	Actual Fees:	Mgt:0.46%	Dist: —	
Advisor:	T. Rowe Price Associates, Inc.	Expense Projections:	3Yr:$227	5Yr:$395	10Yr:$883
Subadvisor:	None	Income Distrib:	Quarterly		
NTF Plans:	N/A				

Historical Profile

Return: Above Avg
Risk: Below Avg
Rating: ★★★★ Above Avg

		59%	64%	59%	60%	59%	65%	65%	65%	64%

▼ Manager Change
▽ Partial Manager Change

Growth of $10,000
■ Investment Values of Fund
— Investment Values of DJ Mod

Performance Quartile (within Category)

1995	1996	1997	1998	1999	2000	2001	2002	2003	2004	2005	2006	History
13.22	14.48	16.54	18.59	19.69	19.17	17.49	15.51	18.41	19.70	19.77	21.29	NAV
24.88	14.57	18.97	15.97	10.27	2.09	-3.98	-8.54	21.71	10.32	5.52	13.73	Total Return %
5.08	3.91	7.07	3.65	-7.06	3.76	-1.18	-1.77	-5.67	-2.65	-1.47	1.43	+/-DJ Mod
0.11	3.23	-0.23	3.58	-2.58	-2.35	-4.14	2.00	-2.35	-0.85	-0.48	3.46	+/-DJ US Mod
4.30	3.84	3.71	3.18	2.94	2.72	2.79	2.72	2.73	2.52	2.53	2.73	Income Return %
20.58	10.73	15.26	12.79	7.33	-0.63	-6.77	-11.26	18.98	7.80	2.99	11.00	Capital Return %
63	50	58	37	54	41	40	20	37	27	39	15	Total Rtn % Rank Cat
0.47	0.50	0.53	0.52	0.54	0.53	0.52	0.47	0.42	0.46	0.49	0.53	Income $
0.17	0.13	0.12	0.04	0.23	0.40	0.38	0.03	0.00	0.12	0.50	0.60	Capital Gains $
0.95	0.87	0.81	0.78	0.79	0.79	0.83	0.79	0.78	0.71	0.69	—	Expense Ratio %
3.87	3.70	3.36	3.04	2.80	2.75	2.84	2.88	2.50	2.49	2.49	—	Income Ratio %
13	22	16	12	21	17	36	49	38	23	27	—	Turnover Rate %
608	876	1,219	1,650	2,091	1,896	1,791	1,582	2,049	2,333	2,525	2,929	Net Assets $mil

Rating and Risk

Time Period	Load-Adj Return %	Morningstar Rtn vs Cat	Morningstar Risk vs Cat	Morningstar Risk-Adj Rating
1 Yr	13.73			
3 Yr	9.81	+Avg	-Avg	★★★★
5 Yr	8.06	+Avg	Avg	★★★★
10 Yr	8.19	+Avg	-Avg	★★★★
Incept	10.06			

Other Measures	Standard Index DJ Mod	Best Fit Index Russ 1000 Vl
Alpha	0.8	-1.2
Beta	0.77	0.68
R-Squared	91	92
Standard Deviation	4.78	
Mean	9.81	
Sharpe Ratio	1.33	

Portfolio Analysis 09-30-06

Total Stocks:341 Share change since 06-30-06	Sectors	P/E Ratio	YTD Return %	% Net Assets
General Electric Company	Ind Mtrls	20.0	0.91	2.03
ExxonMobil Corporation	Energy	11.1	-5.19	1.71
Citigroup, Inc.	Financial	13.1	-1.17	1.33
Microsoft Corporation	Software	23.8	0.23	1.07
Bank of America Corporati	Financial	12.4	0.11	1.01
American International Gr	Financial	17.0	-0.18	0.93
Procter & Gamble Company	Goods	23.9	-0.98	0.87
UnitedHealth Group, Inc.	Health	20.8	-0.76	0.72
Wal-Mart Stores, Inc.	Consumer	16.9	1.78	0.67

Total Fixed-Income:581	Date of Maturity	Amount $000	Value $000	% Net Assets
T. Rowe Price Instl High		9,256	93,394	3.40
US Treasury Note 3.75%	05-15-08	48,000	47,250	1.72
US Treasury Note 3.375%	02-15-08	30,900	30,316	1.10
US Treasury Bond 8.125%	08-15-19	20,700	27,298	0.99
US Treasury Bond 6.25%	08-15-23	20,720	24,055	0.88
FHLMC 6.625%	09-15-09	22,500	23,554	0.86
US Treasury Note 4%	03-15-10	23,375	22,933	0.84
US Treasury Note 4.375%	08-15-12	22,700	22,466	0.82
US Treasury Bond 6.5%	11-15-26	16,000	19,385	0.71

Equity Style
Style: Blend
Size: Large-Cap

Value Measures		Rel Category
Price/Earnings	14.83	0.97
Price/Book	2.49	1.01
Price/Sales	1.33	0.97
Price/Cash Flow	7.99	0.99
Dividend Yield %	2.35	1.22

Growth Measures	%	Rel Category
Long-Term Erngs	11.50	0.98
Book Value	9.39	1.09
Sales	10.13	1.14
Cash Flow	7.62	0.77
Historical Erngs	18.84	1.05

Market Cap %			
Giant	53.8	Small	0.0
Large	36.2	Micro	0.0
Mid	9.9	Avg $mil:	46,595

Fixed-Income Style
Duration: Interm-Term
Quality: High

Avg Eff Duration [1]	5.0 Yrs
Avg Eff Maturity	7.5 Yrs
Avg Credit Quality	AA
Avg Wtd Coupon	5.70%

[1] figure provided by fund as of 09-30-06

Sector Weightings	% of Stocks	Rel DJ Mod	3 Year High Low
Info	17.94		
Software	3.59	—	4 3
Hardware	6.47	—	8 6
Media	3.52	—	4 3
Telecom	4.36	—	4 4
Service	46.09		
Health	10.75	—	11 10
Consumer	6.97	—	8 7
Business	5.19	—	6 4
Financial	23.18	—	23 21
Mfg	35.97		
Goods	8.08	—	9 8
Ind Mtrls	14.09	—	16 14
Energy	9.49	—	11 7
Utilities	4.31	—	4 3

Composition

● Cash	1.6	
● Stocks	64.1	
● Bonds	34.1	
○ Other	0.3	
Foreign	26.6	(% of Stock)

Investment Style
Equity
Stock %

MORNINGSTAR® Funds 500

T. Rowe Price BlChpGr

	Ticker	Load	NAV	Yield	Total Assets	Mstar Category
	TRBCX	None	$35.73	0.4%	$9,769 mil	Large Growth

Governance and Management

Stewardship Grade: B

Portfolio Manager(s)

Larry Puglia has been at the helm since the fund's June 1993 inception. T. Rowe Price's deep bench of analysts assists him.

Strategy

Manager Larry Puglia seeks stocks with sustainable earnings growth, strong management, and leading market positions. Although the fund lands in the large-growth category, the portfolio is well diversified, split between lower-priced financials and growth-oriented tech and health-care stocks. Puglia pays close attention to valuation, which makes the fund one of its group's more-temperate options. Turnover here is modest.

Historical Profile

Return	Above Avg
Risk	Below Avg
Rating	★★★★ Above Avg

Investment Style: Equity Stock %

95% 96% 95% 98% 100% 100% 98% 99% 100%

▼ Manager Change
▽ Partial Manager Change

Growth of $10,000
■ Investment Values of Fund
— Investment Values of S&P 500

Performance Quartile (within Category)

1995	1996	1997	1998	1999	2000	2001	2002	2003	2004	2005	2006	History
15.09	19.06	24.17	30.60	36.34	33.85	28.97	21.95	28.45	30.92	32.68	35.73	NAV
37.90	27.75	27.56	28.84	20.00	-2.53	-14.42	-24.23	29.75	9.25	5.95	9.73	Total Return %
0.32	4.79	-5.80	0.26	-1.04	6.57	-2.53	-2.13	1.07	-1.63	1.04	-6.06	+/-S&P 500
0.72	4.63	-2.93	-9.87	-13.16	19.89	6.00	3.65	0.00	2.95	0.69	0.66	+/-Russ 1000Gr
1.35	0.93	0.63	0.46	0.10	0.00	0.00	0.00	0.14	0.56	0.26	0.40	Income Return %
36.55	26.82	26.93	28.38	19.90	-2.53	-14.42	-24.23	29.61	8.69	5.69	9.33	Capital Return %
19	7	41	57	83	18	24	32	39	38	52	24	Total Rtn % Rank Cat
0.15	0.14	0.12	0.11	0.03	0.00	0.00	0.00	0.03	0.16	0.08	0.13	Income $
0.08	0.08	0.02	0.39	0.33	1.62	0.00	0.00	0.00	0.00	0.00	0.00	Capital Gains $
1.25	1.12	0.95	0.91	0.91	0.91	0.96	0.96	0.95	0.88	0.85	—	Expense Ratio %
1.27	0.87	0.86	0.43	0.10	-0.09	-0.06	0.00	0.10	0.56	0.28	—	Income Ratio %
38	26	24	34	41	51	48	46	33	32	44	—	Turnover Rate %
146	540	2,345	4,330	6,709	7,113	6,242	4,482	6,317	7,290	7,998	8,861	Net Assets $mil

Performance 12-31-06

	1st Qtr	2nd Qtr	3rd Qtr	4th Qtr	Total
2002	-1.28	-15.80	-15.41	7.76	-24.23
2003	-1.28	15.51	1.92	11.65	29.75
2004	1.86	1.04	-3.07	9.52	9.25
2005	-5.14	3.65	3.42	4.19	5.95
2006	2.94	-3.98	4.64	6.09	9.73

Trailing	Total Return%	+/- S&P 500	+/- Russ 1000Gr	%Rank Cat	Growth of $10,000
3 Mo	6.09	-0.61	0.16	33	10,609
6 Mo	11.02	-1.72	0.92	13	11,102
1 Yr	9.73	-6.06	0.66	24	10,973
3 Yr Avg	8.29	-2.15	1.42	32	12,699
5 Yr Avg	4.54	-1.65	1.85	24	12,486
10 Yr Avg	7.46	-0.96	2.02	25	20,534
15 Yr Avg	—				

Tax Analysis	Tax-Adj Rtn%	%Rank Cat	Tax-Cost Rat	%Rank Cat
3 Yr (estimated)	8.15	25	0.13	9
5 Yr (estimated)	4.45	20	0.09	10
10 Yr (estimated)	7.23	14	0.21	8

Potential Capital Gain Exposure: 21% of assets

Rating and Risk

Time Period	Load-Adj Return %	Morningstar Rtn vs Cat	Morningstar Risk vs Cat	Morningstar Risk-Adj Rating
1 Yr	9.73			
3 Yr	8.29	+Avg	-Avg	★★★★
5 Yr	4.54	+Avg	Avg	★★★★
10 Yr	7.46	+Avg	-Avg	★★★★
Incept	11.15			

Other Measures	Standard Index S&P 500	Best Fit Index Russ 1000Gr
Alpha	-2.8	1.5
Beta	1.14	0.95
R-Squared	89	94
Standard Deviation	8.29	
Mean	8.29	
Sharpe Ratio	0.62	

Morningstar's Take by Christopher Davis 11-07-06

Choose your sides wisely, but this is one sibling rivalry where it's easy to come out ahead.

T. Rowe Price's large-growth stable is an embarrassment of riches. There's this offering,T. Rowe Price Blue Chip Growth, and its siblings, T. Rowe Price Growth Stock and New America Growth. The latter is a Fund Analyst Pick in its category and has appeal beyond this fund (and Growth Stock, too, for that matter). With a relatively svelte $800 million asset base, New America Growth manager Joe Milano has more flexibility to traverse the market-cap spectrum. While we expect that fund to top its competitors, its more-aggressive strategy and larger weighting in mid-caps mean it's not for everyone. Moreover, this offering is no slouch. Manager Larry Puglia has been at the helm since its 1993 inception. He's delivered fine results over the long haul: The fund's long-term returns rank in the large-growth category's top quartile.

This offering actually has a lot more in common with Growth Stock. Like that fund's Bob Smith, Puglia employs a valuation-conscious strategy, emphasizes larger names, and keeps his portfolio well diversified. There are important differences. Consistent with his blue-chip mandate, Puglia is more apt to favor the largest of the large caps. He also keeps a smaller slice of his portfolio overseas. Growth Stock's foreign weighting accounts for 16% of assets, versus 7% for this fund.

So which fund to choose? For those who want a more consistent dose of mega-caps and don't need more foreign exposure, this offering makes sense. For others, Growth Stock is a marginally better choice. Smith's done a bit better job of stemming losses in tough markets and posting gains in good environments, giving his fund a better long-term record. His fund is also modestly cheaper.

That's not to diminish this fund's worth. We think it's still a fine option. Shareholders don't need to switch, especially if they'd have a tax bill for doing so.

Portfolio Analysis 09-30-06

Share change since 06-06 Total Stocks:120

Sector	PE	Tot Ret%	% Assets
⊕ General Electric Company — Ind Mtrls	20.0	9.35	3.96
Microsoft Corporation — Software	23.8	15.83	2.59
Danaher Corporation — Ind Mtrls	22.0	30.02	2.52
⊕ UnitedHealth Group, Inc. — Health	20.8	-13.49	2.36
⊕ Schlumberger, Ltd. — Energy	22.3	31.07	2.06
⊕ Google, Inc. — Business	61.5	11.00	1.93
⊖ State Street Corporation — Financial	22.4	23.22	1.80
⊕ Cisco Systems, Inc. — Hardware	30.1	59.64	1.77
American International G — Financial	17.0	6.05	1.71
⊕ Kohl's Corporation — Consumer	22.6	40.80	1.70
⊖ Citigroup, Inc. — Financial	13.1	19.55	1.64
⊕ Amgen, Inc. — Health	29.1	-13.38	1.57
⊕ American Express Company — Financial	20.9	19.09	1.54
Procter & Gamble Company — Goods	23.9	13.36	1.54
⊖ Caremark RX, Inc. — Health	23.6	10.90	1.53
⊖ Wal-Mart Stores, Inc. — Consumer	16.9	0.13	1.52
⊕ UBS AG — Financial	—	29.62	1.43
⊕ Franklin Resources — Financial	23.6	17.79	1.41
⊕ Smith International, Inc — Energy	17.0	11.59	1.39
⊕ Gilead Sciences, Inc. — Health	40.6	23.51	1.33

Current Investment Style

Value Blnd Growth — Large Mid Small

Market Cap	%
Giant	45.4
Large	44.2
Mid	10.4
Small	0.0
Micro	0.0

Avg $mil: 43,522

Value Measures		Rel Category
Price/Earnings	19.16	0.99
Price/Book	3.24	0.98
Price/Sales	2.04	1.05
Price/Cash Flow	12.42	1.09
Dividend Yield %	1.02	0.99

Growth Measures	%	Rel Category
Long-Term Erngs	14.62	1.02
Book Value	11.16	0.96
Sales	13.75	1.19
Cash Flow	14.32	0.85
Historical Erngs	22.09	0.96

Profitability	%	Rel Category
Return on Equity	20.40	1.00
Return on Assets	11.96	1.09
Net Margin	15.54	1.09

Sector Weightings

	% of Stocks	Rel S&P 500	3 Year High	Low
↻ Info	23.09	1.16		
▣ Software	4.66	1.35	7	4
▣ Hardware	12.77	1.38	13	10
◉ Media	2.40	0.63	7	2
☎ Telecom	3.26	0.93	3	2
☞ Service	55.86	1.21		
⚕ Health	19.87	1.65	20	15
▤ Consumer	10.22	1.34	12	10
🏢 Business	4.39	1.04	6	4
💲 Financial	21.38	0.96	23	20
🗗 Mfg	21.05	0.62		
▤ Goods	3.56	0.42	5	3
⚙ Ind Mtrls	10.48	0.88	11	8
◊ Energy	7.01	0.72	8	3
◊ Utilities	0.00	0.00	0	0

Composition

● Cash	0.0
● Stocks	100.0
● Bonds	0.0
● Other	0.0
Foreign	7.1
(% of Stock)	

Address:	100 East Pratt Street
	Baltimore MD 21202
	800-638-5660
Web Address:	www.troweprice.com
Inception:	06-30-93
Advisor:	T. Rowe Price Associates, Inc.
Subadvisor:	None
NTF Plans:	N/A

Minimum Purchase:	$2500	Add: $100	IRA: $1000
Min Auto Inv Plan:	$50	Add: $50	
Sales Fees:	No-load		
Management Fee:	0.61%		
Actual Fees:	Mgt:0.61%	Dist: —	
Expense Projections:	3Yr:$271	5Yr:$471	10Yr:$1049
Income Distrib:	Annually		

T. Rowe Price Cap Apprec

	Ticker	Load	NAV	Yield	Total Assets	Mstar Category
	PRWCX	None	$20.62	2.2%	$9,367 mil	Moderate Allocation

Governance and Management

Stewardship Grade: B

Portfolio Manager(s)

Steve Boesel took the reins here in September 2001 but retired in June 2006. He's been replaced by Jeff Arricale and David Giroux, analysts at T. Rowe for four and seven years, respectively. The duo has covered financial services and industrial stocks, two of the most-prominent sectors in the portfolio. However, neither Arricale nor Giroux has managed a retail fund before, with the exception of their slices of T. Rowe Price Capital Opportunity, an analyst-run fund.

Strategy

Steve Boesel, who took over here in August 2001, was recently replaced by analysts Jeff Arricale and David Giroux; the duo will retain his approach. Like Boesel, they fill 60%-65% of the portfolio with stocks they think have been overly punished by the market. They favor names with relatively high yields and cheap valuations. They also prefer to own a double-digit stake in convertible bonds, focusing on those that are trading far from their conversion premium. Finally, the fund isn't an enthusiastic investor in traditional fixed income; the duo would rather hold cash.

Performance 12-31-06

	1st Qtr	2nd Qtr	3rd Qtr	4th Qtr	Total
2002	7.72	-4.57	-7.91	6.20	0.54
2003	-2.89	13.04	1.99	12.06	25.47
2004	2.91	2.17	1.74	7.78	15.29
2005	-0.41	1.39	3.76	1.99	6.85
2006	3.99	-0.86	4.88	5.94	14.54

Trailing	Total Return%	+/- DJ Mod	+/- DJ US Mod	%Rank Cat	Growth of $10,000
3 Mo	5.94	0.35	1.27	16	10,594
6 Mo	11.11	2.32	3.21	10	11,111
1 Yr	14.54	2.24	4.27	9	11,454
3 Yr Avg	12.16	1.44	3.04	4	14,110
5 Yr Avg	12.22	2.20	4.62	1	17,797
10 Yr Avg	12.18	3.63	3.59	2	31,561
15 Yr Avg	12.60	3.39	3.21	2	59,303

Tax Analysis	Tax-Adj Rtn%	%Rank Cat	Tax-Cost Rat	%Rank Cat
3 Yr (estimated)	10.76	4	1.25	63
5 Yr (estimated)	11.01	1	1.08	66
10 Yr (estimated)	9.85	2	2.08	85

Potential Capital Gain Exposure: 14% of assets

Historical Profile

Return High
Risk Average
Rating ★★★★ Highest

49%	54%	58%	60%	59%	64%	62%	66%	62%

Investment Style
Equity
Stock %

▼ Manager Change
▽ Partial Manager Change

39.4
31.0
24.0
17.0

Growth of $10,000
— Investment Values of Fund
— Investment Values of DJ Mod

10.0

Performance Quartile (within Category)

1995	1996	1997	1998	1999	2000	2001	2002	2003	2004	2005	2006	History
13.67	14.47	14.71	13.22	12.51	13.95	14.64	14.21	17.50	19.49	20.06	20.62	NAV
22.57	16.82	16.20	5.77	7.07	22.17	10.26	0.54	25.47	15.29	6.85	14.54	Total Return %
2.77	6.16	4.30	-6.55	-10.26	23.84	13.06	7.31	-1.91	2.32	-0.14	2.24	+/-DJ Mod
-2.20	5.48	-3.00	-6.62	-5.78	17.73	10.10	11.08	1.41	4.12	0.85	4.27	+/-DJ US Mod
3.64	4.39	3.46	3.40	3.78	3.60	2.72	1.91	1.83	1.66	1.54	2.49	Income Return %
18.93	12.43	12.74	2.37	3.29	18.57	7.54	-1.37	23.64	13.63	5.31	12.05	Capital Return %
81	24	82	91	72	1	2	1	12	2	18	9	Total Rtn % Rank Cat
0.44	0.60	0.50	0.50	0.50	0.45	0.38	0.28	0.26	0.29	0.30	0.50	Income $
0.72	0.90	1.58	1.82	1.13	0.82	0.35	0.23	0.06	0.39	0.47	1.86	Capital Gains $
0.97	0.76	0.66	0.62	0.88	0.87	0.86	0.85	0.83	0.78	0.76	—	Expense Ratio %
3.28	4.07	3.17	3.04	3.44	3.22	2.85	2.39	1.85	1.84	1.66	—	Income Ratio %
47	44	48	53	42	32	25	18	18	18	12	—	Turnover Rate %
864	960	1,060	1,004	856	914	1,405	1,853	2,937	4,952	7,384	9,317	Net Assets $mil

Rating and Risk

Time Period	Load-Adj Return %	Morningstar Rtn vs Cat	Morningstar Risk vs Cat	Morningstar Risk-Adj Rating
1 Yr	14.54			
3 Yr	12.16	High	Avg	★★★★★
5 Yr	12.22	High	Avg	★★★★★
10 Yr	12.18	High	-Avg	★★★★★
Incept	12.90			

Other Measures	Standard Index DJ Mod	Best Fit Index Russ 1000 Vl
Alpha	2.3	-0.3
Beta	0.86	0.78
R-Squared	79	86
Standard Deviation	5.70	
Mean	12.16	
Sharpe Ratio	1.49	

Portfolio Analysis 09-30-06

Total Stocks:70 Share change since 06-30-06	Sectors	P/E Ratio	YTD Return %	% Net Assets
Microsoft Corporation	Software	23.8	0.23	2.95
⊕ Tyco International, Ltd.	Ind Mtrls	15.7	1.55	2.62
⊕ Marsh & McLennan Companie	Financial	29.0	1.24	2.46
⊕ Murphy Oil Corporation	Energy	12.8	-6.21	2.19
⊕ General Electric Company	Ind Mtrls	20.0	0.91	2.04
⊕ American International Gr	Financial	17.0	-0.18	2.04
⊕ Intel Corporation	Hardware	21.0	3.75	1.96
Wyeth	Health	17.2	0.90	1.63
Coca-Cola Company	Goods	21.7	0.66	1.47

Total Fixed-Income:9	Date of Maturity	Amount $000	Value $000	% Net Assets
Nextel Comms 7.375%	08-01-15	94,903	98,420	1.17
Liberty Media 3.25%	03-15-31	102,120	82,375	0.98
US Treasury Note 4.875%	05-15-09	81,175	81,644	0.97
US Treasury Note 4.875%	05-31-08	81,175	81,327	0.97
Roche Hldgs 144A Cv	07-25-21	84,888	78,127	0.93
Newell Finl Tr I Cv		1,609	75,597	0.90
Lucent Tech Cv 2.75%	06-15-25	74,795	74,945	0.89
General Mls Cv	10-28-22	78,952	58,424	0.70
Echostar Comms New Cv 5.7	05-15-08	56,751	57,133	0.68

Equity Style
Style: Value
Size: Large-Cap

Value Measures		Rel Category
Price/Earnings	15.54	1.02
Price/Book	2.07	0.84
Price/Sales	1.39	1.01
Price/Cash Flow	10.02	1.24
Dividend Yield %	2.29	1.19

Growth Measures	%	Rel Category
Long-Term Erngs	11.45	0.98
Book Value	8.13	0.94
Sales	9.33	1.05
Cash Flow	2.02	0.20
Historical Erngs	18.27	1.02

Market Cap %			
Giant	44.4	Small	1.1
Large	40.9	Micro	0.0
Mid	13.7	Avg $mil:	37,210

Fixed-Income Style
Duration: —
Quality: —

Avg Eff Duration [1]	—
Avg Eff Maturity	—
Avg Credit Quality	—
Avg Wtd Coupon	3.56%

[1]figure provided by fund

Sector Weightings	% of Stocks	Rel DJ Mod	3 Year High Low
↻ Info	22.81		
Software	4.73	—	5 5
Hardware	4.56	—	5 1
Media	7.38	—	8 6
Telecom	6.14	—	6 4
Service	41.68		
Health	10.10	—	12 8
Consumer	4.78	—	9 4
Business	1.93	—	6 2
Financial	24.87	—	25 14
Mfg	35.52		
Goods	7.86	—	9 5
Ind Mtrls	18.03	—	23 15
Energy	5.95	—	13 4
Utilities	3.68	—	10 4

Composition

● Cash	18.9
● Stocks	62.2
● Bonds	5.5
● Other	13.5
Foreign (% of Stock)	4.1

Morningstar's Take by Greg Carlson 12-28-06

Despite a management change in mid-2006, we're comfortable recommending T. Rowe Price Capital Appreciation.

Stephen Boesel, this fund's manager for five years, retired on June 30, 2006. His replacements, Jeff Arricale and David Giroux, haven't run a fund before, but they're well prepared for their roles: They were tapped for this assignment roughly two years ago and spent the intervening period visiting companies within the fund's equity portfolio and learning the intricacies of the convertible-bond market. (They took over this fund's converts sleeve, which generally comprises 10%-20% of its assets, in January.)

The new managers' smooth transition not only gives us confidence in their readiness to run this fund but also makes it more likely that shareholders won't see a jarring change in style here. Arricale and Giroux are intimately familiar with the fund's historical profile--a relatively low-risk, value-oriented equity portfolio combined with

stakes in convertible and traditional bonds, as well as cash, to further mute volatility. That approach has generated superb results through the tenures of Boesel and previous skipper Rich Howard: The fund has outpaced all but a few of its moderate-allocation peers over the past decade. And thus far, it has continued to deliver under Arricale and Giroux. For the year to date through Dec. 27, the fund returned 14.93%, while its average moderate allocation peer returned 11.63%.

True, the fund's value tilt has given it a boost in recent years, but we think management's healthy contrarian tack should serve it well. For example, Boesel, working in concert with Arricale and Giroux, bulked up on out-of-favor, mega-cap growth names such as Microsoft and Home Depot while trimming the economically sensitive fare that once dominated the fund. The fund's modest 0.76% expense ratio further burnishes its appeal. All told, this fund is a fine choice.

Address:	100 East Pratt Street Baltimore MD 21202 800-638-5660	Minimum Purchase:	$2500	Add: $100	IRA: $1000
		Min Auto Inv Plan:	$50	Add: $50	
		Sales Fees:	No-load		
Web Address:	www.troweprice.com	Management Fee:	0.61%		
Inception:	06-30-86	Actual Fees:	Mgt:0.61%	Dist: —	
Advisor:	T. Rowe Price Associates, Inc.	Expense Projections:	3Yr:$243	5Yr:$422	10Yr:$942
Subadvisor:	None	Income Distrib:	Annually		
NTF Plans:	N/A				

Morningstar® Funds 500

T. Rowe Price Div Growth

	Ticker	Load	NAV	Yield	Total Assets	Mstar Category
	PRDGX	None	$25.36	1.3%	$872 mil	Large Blend

Governance and Management

Stewardship Grade: A

Portfolio Manager(s)

Tom Huber replaced Bill Stromberg as the fund's day-to-day manager in March 2000. Huber has been an analyst at T. Rowe Price since 1994. A seven-member advisory committee, including Stromberg, works on the fund.

Strategy

Manager Tom Huber looks for reasonably priced stocks of companies that deliver increasing dividends. He is drawn to market leaders with high returns on equity and capital. Although Huber's focus on stocks with increasing dividends gives the fund a value bent, the fund's broad-based portfolio places it in the large-blend camp. Like many T. Rowe managers, Huber moves cautiously and keeps turnover low.

Performance 12-31-06

	1st Qtr	2nd Qtr	3rd Qtr	4th Qtr	Total
2002	2.41	-11.10	-16.41	7.13	-18.47
2003	-4.66	15.49	1.96	11.49	25.17
2004	1.35	1.38	-0.71	9.67	11.90
2005	-1.96	1.02	2.17	2.13	3.35
2006	4.83	-1.14	5.16	6.85	16.45

Trailing	Total Return%	+/- S&P 500	+/- Russ 1000	%Rank Cat	Growth of $10,000
3 Mo	6.85	0.15	-0.10	38	10,685
6 Mo	12.36	-0.38	-0.10	31	11,236
1 Yr	16.45	0.66	0.99	14	11,645
3 Yr Avg	10.43	-0.01	-0.55	36	13,467
5 Yr Avg	6.57	0.38	-0.25	31	13,746
10 Yr Avg	7.86	-0.56	-0.78	48	21,311
15 Yr Avg	—	—	—	—	—

Tax Analysis	Tax-Adj Rtn%	%Rank Cat	Tax-Cost Rat	%Rank Cat
3 Yr (estimated)	9.62	35	0.73	34
5 Yr (estimated)	5.91	31	0.62	40
10 Yr (estimated)	6.85	42	0.94	42

Potential Capital Gain Exposure: 33% of assets

Historical Profile

Return	Average
Risk	Below Avg
Rating	★★★★ Above Avg

Manager Change ▼
Partial Manager Change ▽

Growth of $10,000
— Investment Values of Fund
— Investment Values of S&P 500

Investment Style
Equity
Stock %

81% 85% 87% 93% 94% 97% 98% 97% 96%

Performance Quartile (within Category)

1995	1996	1997	1998	1999	2000	2001	2002	2003	2004	2005	2006	History
13.81	16.37	20.13	22.01	20.21	21.88	20.79	16.76	20.72	22.92	22.78	25.36	NAV
31.75	25.36	30.77	15.04	-2.82	10.06	-3.64	-18.47	25.17	11.90	3.35	16.45	Total Return %
-5.83	2.40	-2.59	-13.54	-23.86	19.16	8.25	3.63	-3.51	1.02	-1.56	0.66	+/-S&P 500
-6.02	2.91	-2.08	-11.98	-23.73	17.85	8.81	3.18	-4.72	0.50	-2.92	0.99	+/-Russ 1000
3.30	2.66	2.73	2.33	2.07	1.45	1.29	0.97	1.38	1.21	1.14	1.56	Income Return %
28.45	22.70	28.04	12.71	-4.89	8.61	-4.93	-19.44	23.79	10.69	2.21	14.89	Capital Return %
65	15	43	73	97	11	13	22	72	29	81	14	Total Rtn % Rank Cat
0.36	0.36	0.44	0.46	0.45	0.29	0.28	0.20	0.23	0.25	0.26	0.35	Income $
0.33	0.51	0.75	0.63	0.72	0.05	0.00	0.00	0.00	0.00	0.65	0.77	Capital Gains $
1.10	1.10	0.80	0.77	0.77	0.81	0.82	0.83	0.83	0.78	0.75	—	Expense Ratio %
2.92	2.53	2.42	2.26	2.01	1.43	1.31	1.08	1.25	1.21	1.09	—	Income Ratio %
56	43	39	37	38	36	35	20	17	17	23	—	Turnover Rate %
85	209	747	1,338	1,028	751	692	531	695	755	773	872	Net Assets $mil

Rating and Risk

Time Period	Load-Adj Return %	Morningstar Rtn vs Cat	Morningstar Risk vs Cat	Morningstar Risk-Adj Rating
1 Yr	16.45			
3 Yr	10.43	Avg	-Avg	★★★★
5 Yr	6.57	+Avg	-Avg	★★★★
10 Yr	7.86	Avg	Low	★★★★
Incept	10.97			

Other Measures	Standard Index S&P 500	Best Fit Index S&P 500
Alpha	0.5	0.5
Beta	0.92	0.92
R-Squared	96	96
Standard Deviation	6.50	
Mean	10.43	
Sharpe Ratio	1.08	

Portfolio Analysis 09-30-06

Share change since 06-06 Total Stocks:110

	Sector	PE	Tot Ret%	% Assets
ExxonMobil Corporation	Energy	11.1	39.07	2.68
Citigroup, Inc.	Financial	13.1	19.55	2.44
⊕ General Electric Company	Ind Mtrls	20.0	9.35	2.10
⊕ Microsoft Corporation	Software	23.8	15.83	1.78
⊖ TELUS Corporation Non Vo	Telecom	28.4	13.70	1.68
⊕ UBS AG	Financial	—	29.62	1.65
State Street Corporation	Financial	22.4	23.22	1.53
⊕ Wells Fargo Company	Financial	14.7	16.82	1.51
Total SA ADR	Energy	10.6	19.24	1.50
Pfizer Inc.	Health	15.2	15.22	1.48
⊕ Target Corporation	Consumer	19.3	4.65	1.41
Wyeth	Health	17.2	12.88	1.40
⊕ Baker Hughes Inc.	Energy	9.9	23.68	1.40
Chevron Corporation	Energy	9.0	33.76	1.35
Time Warner, Inc.	Media	19.6	26.37	1.34
Roper Industries, Inc.	Ind Mtrls	24.8	27.83	1.33
PepsiCo, Inc.	Goods	21.5	7.86	1.28
US Bancorp	Financial	13.9	26.29	1.26
Morgan Stanley	Financial	12.3	45.93	1.25
American Express Company	Financial	20.9	19.09	1.21

Current Investment Style

Value Blnd Growth — Large Mid Small

Market Cap	%
Giant	42.2
Large	39.0
Mid	18.8
Small	0.0
Micro	0.0
Avg $mil:	36,151

Value Measures		Rel Category
Price/Earnings	16.15	1.05
Price/Book	2.86	1.12
Price/Sales	1.65	1.18
Price/Cash Flow	10.57	1.25
Dividend Yield %	2.02	1.15

Growth Measures	%	Rel Category
Long-Term Erngs	11.75	0.99
Book Value	5.61	0.62
Sales	11.01	1.14
Cash Flow	5.23	0.51
Historical Erngs	18.47	1.00

Profitability	%	Rel Category
Return on Equity	20.39	1.05
Return on Assets	11.02	1.06
Net Margin	12.87	0.96

Sector Weightings

	% of Stocks	Rel S&P 500	3 Year High Low
⊙ Info	17.64	0.88	
Software	2.09	0.61	2 2
Hardware	5.24	0.57	6 5
Media	5.62	1.48	7 6
Telecom	4.69	1.34	6 4
⊑ Service	50.33	1.09	
Health	11.66	0.97	12 9
Consumer	7.59	0.99	9 7
Business	6.85	1.62	9 7
Financial	24.23	1.09	26 22
⊡ Mfg	32.04	0.95	
Goods	7.00	0.82	8 7
Ind Mtrls	13.50	1.13	14 11
Energy	9.42	0.96	10 7
Utilities	2.12	0.61	2 1

Composition

	%
● Cash	3.2
● Stocks	96.3
● Bonds	0.0
● Other	0.6
Foreign	9.4
(% of Stock)	

Morningstar's Take by Christopher Davis 12-28-06

It seems the times are finally catching up with T. Rowe Price Dividend Growth's strategy.

In corporate boardrooms, dividends have become increasingly cool. In the wake of tax law changes in 2003 that put dividend income on equal footing with capital gains, many companies ratcheted up their payouts or instituted dividends for the first time. After initially greeting this development with a yawn, investors appear to have begun to come around recently. In 2006, that's lent a boost to this offering, which focuses on companies increasing their dividends. Savvy stock-picking has also helped this year. Winning energy and industrials picks, such as Baker Hughes and Lockheed Martin, helped propel the fund to the large-blend category's top quartile for the year to date through Oct. 30.

These days, manager Tom Huber has been reducing the fund's exposure to cyclical names like Lockheed Martin (he actually sold Lockheed in 2006's second quarter). With the economy slowing, Huber wants to give the portfolio a more defensive cast. He's been boosting the fund's exposure to consumer staples and health-care stocks such as Coca-Cola and Caremark RX. Huber points to Coke's above-average dividend, discounted valuation relative to other staples stocks, and ample free cash flow. Meanwhile, Huber says pharmacy-benefits manager Caremark has been capitalizing on increasing use of generic, mail-order, and specialty drugs and has been returning this cash to shareholders with share repurchases and a recently instituted dividend.

Of course, not all of Huber's picks will pan out, but we think the odds are good that he'll get most things right over time. Since coming aboard in March 2000, he's been able to post strong results in both difficult and sunnier environments. The fund's moderate 0.74% annual price tag also gives him a real edge. For investors seeking an all-weather core holding, this fund continues to hold appeal.

Address:	100 East Pratt Street	Minimum Purchase:	$2500	Add: $100 IRA: $1000
	Baltimore MD 21202	Min Auto Inv Plan:	$50	Add: $50
	800-638-5660	Sales Fees:	No-load	
Web Address:	www.troweprice.com	Management Fee:	0.52%	
Inception:	12-31-92	Actual Fees:	Mgt:0.51%	Dist: —
Advisor:	T. Rowe Price Associates, Inc.	Expense Projections:	3Yr:$249	5Yr:$433 10Yr:$966
Subadvisor:	None	Income Distrib:	Quarterly	
NTF Plans:	N/A			

T. Rowe Price Emg Mkt St

Analyst Pick ✓

Ticker	Load	NAV	Yield	Total Assets	Mstar Category
PRMSX	None	$32.41	0.7%	$2,622 mil	Diversified Emerging Mkts

Governance and Management

Stewardship Grade: B

Portfolio Manager(s)

This fund is run by a deep and experienced team of managers based in London and various emerging markets. Lead manager Chris Alderson has been in charge since the fund's 1995 inception and has the final say on buys and sells. Comanagers Mark Edwards, Frances Dydasco, and Gonzalo Pangaro contribute ideas based on the regional emerging-markets portfolios they also run.

Strategy

Chris Alderson and his comanagers hunt for companies that have strong earnings growth and are leaders in their industries. They're not averse to accumulating substantial stakes in growth industries, but they build them slowly and avoid the raciest issues. Management will typically not hedge currency risk.

Historical Profile
Return	Above Avg
Risk	Above Avg
Rating	★★★★ Above Avg

Performance Quartile (within Category)

| | 87% | 86% | 87% | 93% | 88% | 82% | 91% | 90% | 92% | **Investment Style** Equity Stock % |

▼ Manager Change
▽ Partial Manager Change

Growth of $10,000
— Investment Values of Fund
— Investment Values of MSCI EAFE

32.4 / 24.0 / 17.0 / 10.0

1995	1996	1997	1998	1999	2000	2001	2002	2003	2004	2005	2006	History
10.76	11.69	11.68	8.28	15.52	11.43	10.77	10.22	15.47	19.41	25.68	32.41	NAV
7.70*	11.82	1.23	-28.75	87.44	-26.35	-5.69	-4.92	52.30	26.98	38.77	32.01	Total Return %
—	5.77	-0.55	-48.68	60.41	-12.16	15.73	11.02	13.71	6.73	25.23	5.67	+/-MSCI EAFE
—	7.89	14.68	-1.08	23.35	5.55	-1.01	3.05	0.71	4.53	8.46	2.83	+/-MSCI EmrMkt
—	0.37	0.00	0.34	0.00	0.00	0.00	0.19	0.88	0.26	0.93	0.93	Income Return %
—	11.45	1.23	-29.09	87.44	-26.35	-5.78	-5.11	51.42	26.72	37.84	31.08	Capital Return %
—	57	39	59	17	22	70	41	62	22	14	52	Total Rtn % Rank Cat
0.01	0.04	0.00	0.04	0.00	0.00	0.01	0.02	0.09	0.04	0.18	0.24	Income $
0.00	0.30	0.15	0.00	0.00	0.00	0.00	0.00	0.00	0.18	1.05	1.20	Capital Gains $
1.75	1.75	1.75	1.75	1.75	1.50	1.58	1.51	1.43	1.33	1.27	—	Expense Ratio %
0.54	0.44	0.21	0.46	-0.14	-0.12	0.19	0.41	1.12	1.08	1.23	—	Income Ratio %
—	42	84	54	59	56	70	70	66	70	53	—	Turnover Rate %
17	73	124	72	124	152	155	170	439	753	1,554	2,622	Net Assets $mil

Performance 12-31-06

	1st Qtr	2nd Qtr	3rd Qtr	4th Qtr	Total
2002	11.14	-7.60	-15.73	9.87	-4.92
2003	-7.93	22.85	13.93	18.18	52.30
2004	9.63	-8.96	6.80	19.13	26.98
2005	1.70	6.08	20.63	6.63	38.77
2006	11.53	-7.75	7.15	19.75	32.01

Trailing	Total Return%	+/- MSCI EAFE	+/- MSCI EmrMkt	%Rank Cat	Growth of $10,000
3 Mo	19.75	9.40	2.47	18	11,975
6 Mo	28.32	13.63	6.23	7	12,832
1 Yr	32.01	5.67	2.83	52	13,201
3 Yr Avg	32.50	12.57	5.24	11	23,262
5 Yr Avg	27.49	12.51	3.97	26	33,681
10 Yr Avg	12.20	4.49	5.47	12	31,618
15 Yr Avg	—	—	—	—	—

Tax Analysis	Tax-Adj Rtn%	%Rank Cat	Tax-Cost Rat	%Rank Cat
3 Yr (estimated)	31.45	9	0.79	32
5 Yr (estimated)	26.81	19	0.53	32
10 Yr (estimated)	11.85	8	0.31	15

Potential Capital Gain Exposure: 36% of assets

Rating and Risk

Time Period	Load-Adj Return %	Morningstar Rtn vs Cat	Morningstar Risk vs Cat	Morningstar Risk-Adj Rating
1 Yr	32.01			
3 Yr	32.50	+Avg	+Avg	★★★★
5 Yr	27.49	+Avg	Avg	★★★
10 Yr	12.20	+Avg	High	★★★★
Incept	12.05			

Other Measures	Standard Index MSCI EAFE	Best Fit Index MSCI EmrMkt
Alpha	0.8	3.8
Beta	1.68	1.02
R-Squared	76	97
Standard Deviation	18.24	
Mean	32.50	
Sharpe Ratio	1.48	

Morningstar's Take by Arijit Dutta 12-12-06

T. Rowe Price Emerging Markets should resume its winning ways.

After two straight years of thumping the competition, this fund is taking a bit of breather in 2006. Until very recently, prominent holdings in the technology hardware sector like Samsung Electronics and Hon Hai Precision Industry didn't do much for the portfolio. (Hardware remains the worst-performing sector this year, despite gains in recent months.) Also, the portfolio's modest overweightings in Turkey and South Africa (both are lagging badly in 2006) have held it back.

Management's thinking behind these positions reveals an important facet of its strategy, however. The goal here is to seek attractive trade-offs between growth and valuations. Though lead manager Chris Alderson doesn't see explosive growth ahead for giant hardware companies like Samsung and Taiwan Semiconductor, he's still drawn to their cheap valuations. Indeed, the portfolio's average market cap has almost doubled over the past year, as Alderson and team have found pockets of value among the bigger emerging-markets companies. On the other hand, management is still convinced of the growth opportunities ahead for its holdings in Turkey and South Africa, so it has stayed the course despite macroeconomic worries that have dogged those countries.

This balanced approach has served shareholders here very well over the long run, and the fund retains its key strengths. Several experienced managers, who all run successful regional portfolios for T. Rowe, contribute ideas here. This management setup is a nice way to compare ideas across far-flung emerging markets. The fund's 1.27% expense ratio is also just about the best deal retail investors can get in this category. Low expenses can give an especially noticeable edge if red-hot emerging markets slow to a more modest pace in the future.

Address:	100 East Pratt Street Baltimore MD 21202 800-638-5660
Web Address:	www.troweprice.com
Inception:	03-31-95*
Advisor:	T. Rowe Price International, Inc
Subadvisor:	None
NTF Plans:	N/A

Minimum Purchase:	$2500	Add: $100	IRA: $1000
Min Auto Inv Plan:	$2500	Add: $50	
Sales Fees:	No-load, 2.00%R		
Management Fee:	1.06%		
Actual Fees:	Mgt:1.06%	Dist: —	
Expense Projections:	3Yr:$403	5Yr:$697	10Yr:$1534
Income Distrib:	Annually		

Portfolio Analysis 09-30-06

Share change since 06-06 Total Stocks:133	Sector	Country	% Assets
⊖ America Movil SA ADR	Telecom	Mexico	3.51
⊖ Samsung Electronics	Goods	Korea	3.36
⊖ Petroleo Brasileiro S.A.	Energy	Brazil	2.52
Kookmin Bank	Financial	Korea	2.12
⊕ Hon Hai Precision Indust	Hardware	Taiwan	2.07
⊕ Bco Itau Hldg F	—	Brazil	1.90
Gazprom OAO (ADR)	Energy	U.K.	1.73
Lukoil ADR	Energy	Russia	1.64
Orascom Telecom Hldgs (S	—	Egypt	1.54
⊖ Petroleo Brasileiro S.A.	Energy	Brazil	1.53
Naspers Ltd	Media	South Africa	1.50
Savings Bank of the Russ	Financial	Russia	1.43
Woori Finance Hldgs	Financial	Korea	1.31
⊖ Grupo Financiero Banorte	Financial	Mexico	1.28
Housing Development Fina	Financial	India	1.26
Bharti Televentures Ltd	Telecom	India	1.26
⊕ MediaTek	Hardware	Taiwan	1.25
⊖ Companhia Vale Do Rio Do	Ind Mtrls	Brazil	1.20
⊖ Wal-Mart de Mexico	Consumer	Mexico	1.18
⊖ Taiwan Semiconductor Mfg	Hardware	Taiwan	1.16

Current Investment Style

Value Blnd Growth — Large Mid Small

Market Cap	%
Giant	39.5
Large	31.5
Mid	21.5
Small	7.4
Micro	0.0

Avg $mil: 9,898

Value Measures		Rel Category
Price/Earnings	14.03	1.08
Price/Book	1.96	0.90
Price/Sales	1.30	1.18
Price/Cash Flow	7.37	1.11
Dividend Yield %	2.05	0.62

Growth Measures	%	Rel Category
Long-Term Erngs	15.96	1.03
Book Value	9.68	0.97
Sales	20.40	1.29
Cash Flow	21.00	1.90
Historical Erngs	11.70	0.66

Composition

Cash	3.1	Bonds	0.0
Stocks	92.4	Other	4.5
Foreign (% of Stock)			99.6

Sector Weightings	% of Stocks	Rel MSCI EAFE	3 Year High	Low
↻ Info	25.90	2.19		
🖥 Software	0.77	1.38	2	1
💻 Hardware	9.76	2.53	10	2
🎙 Media	6.27	3.43	7	5
📱 Telecom	9.10	1.63	18	9
☞ Service	40.37	0.85		
🏥 Health	0.00	0.00	2	0
🏢 Consumer	10.79	2.18	11	3
💼 Business	5.71	1.13	6	3
💲 Financial	23.87	0.79	30	19
🏭 Mfg	33.74	0.82		
⚙ Goods	10.08	0.77	17	10
⚙ Ind Mtrls	8.60	0.56	17	9
🔋 Energy	14.26	1.99	17	8
💡 Utilities	0.80	0.15	2	0

Regional Exposure % Stock
UK/W. Europe	6	N. America	0
Japan	0	Latn America	22
Asia X Japan	46	Other	26

Country Exposure % Stock
South Korea	15	Mexico	9
Taiwan	12	South Africa	9
Brazil	12		

Morningstar® Funds 500

T. Rowe Price Eq Inc

Analyst Pick ✓	**Ticker** PRFDX	**Load** None	**NAV** $29.55	**Yield** 1.6%	**Total Assets** $23,617 mil	**Mstar Category** Large Value

Governance and Management

Stewardship Grade: A

Portfolio Manager(s)

Seasoned. Brian Rogers has managed this offering since its 1985 inception. He is backed by T. Rowe Price's deep bench of analysts. In January 2004, Rogers became T. Rowe Price's chief investment officer. He says he invests a large portion of his assets in the fund.

Strategy

This offering employs a true-blue approach to value investing. Longtime manager Brian Rogers strives to keep the fund's yield at least 25% higher than that of the S&P 500 Index, and he looks for companies trading cheaply relative to their historic price multiples. This strategy often leads him to load up on traditional value sectors, such as energy and industrial cyclicals, although he is willing to delve into growth-oriented areas such as health care, technology, and telecom when the price is right.

Historical Profile
Return Above Avg
Risk Below Avg
Rating ★★★★ Above Avg

Growth of $10,000
■ Investment Values of Fund
— Investment Values of S&P 500

Investment Style
Equity
Stock %

▼ Manager Change
▽ Partial Manager Change

	93%	93%	92%	94%	96%	96%	94%	95%	95%

Performance Quartile (within Category)

1995	1996	1997	1998	1999	2000	2001	2002	2003	2004	2005	2006	History
20.01	22.54	26.07	26.32	24.81	24.67	23.65	19.79	24.16	26.59	25.92	29.55	NAV
33.35	20.40	28.82	9.23	3.82	13.12	1.64	-13.04	25.78	15.05	4.26	19.14	Total Return %
-4.23	-2.56	-4.54	-19.35	-17.22	22.22	13.53	9.06	-2.90	4.17	-0.65	3.35	+/-S&P 500
-5.01	-1.24	-6.36	-6.40	-3.53	6.11	7.23	2.48	-4.25	-1.44	-2.79	-3.11	+/-Russ 1000 Vl
4.15	3.30	2.99	2.40	2.04	2.12	1.49	1.54	1.99	1.76	1.75	1.91	Income Return %
29.20	17.10	25.83	6.83	1.78	11.00	0.15	-14.58	23.79	13.29	2.51	17.23	Capital Return %
46	43	35	68	55	32	24	14	71	26	68	38	Total Rtn % Rank Cat
0.65	0.65	0.66	0.61	0.53	0.51	0.36	0.36	0.39	0.42	0.46	0.49	Income $
0.54	0.84	2.14	1.49	1.97	2.64	1.01	0.45	0.27	0.72	1.33	0.79	Capital Gains $
0.85	0.81	0.79	0.77	0.77	0.78	0.80	0.79	0.78	0.74	0.71	—	Expense Ratio %
3.69	3.08	2.67	2.26	1.95	2.01	1.53	1.72	1.80	1.69	1.73	—	Income Ratio %
21	25	24	23	22	22	17	15	12	16	21	—	Turnover Rate %
5,215	7,818	12,771	13,495	12,321	10,187	10,128	8,954	12,167	15,947	17,878	21,061	Net Assets $mil

Performance 12-31-06

	1st Qtr	2nd Qtr	3rd Qtr	4th Qtr	Total
2002	4.62	-7.93	-17.33	9.21	-13.04
2003	-6.02	16.82	1.49	12.90	25.78
2004	1.91	2.59	0.72	9.25	15.05
2005	-0.62	0.34	2.88	1.63	4.26
2006	5.36	-0.29	5.57	7.42	19.14

Trailing	Total Return%	+/- S&P 500	+/- Russ 1000 Vl	%Rank Cat	Growth of $10,000
3 Mo	7.42	0.72	-0.58	42	10,742
6 Mo	13.40	0.66	-1.32	38	11,340
1 Yr	19.14	3.35	-3.11	38	11,914
3 Yr Avg	12.64	2.20	-2.45	42	14,292
5 Yr Avg	9.35	3.16	-1.51	29	15,635
10 Yr Avg	10.13	1.71	-0.87	23	26,246
15 Yr Avg	12.40	1.76	-0.63	15	57,742

Tax Analysis	Tax-Adj Rtn%	%Rank Cat	Tax-Cost Rat	%Rank Cat
3 Yr (estimated)	11.30	39	1.19	47
5 Yr (estimated)	8.14	31	1.11	60
10 Yr (estimated)	8.19	27	1.76	64

Potential Capital Gain Exposure: 25% of assets

Rating and Risk

Time Period	Load-Adj Return %	Morningstar Rtn vs Cat	Morningstar Risk vs Cat	Morningstar Risk-Adj Rating
1 Yr	19.14			
3 Yr	12.64	Avg	-Avg	★★★
5 Yr	9.35	+Avg	Avg	★★★★
10 Yr	10.13	+Avg	-Avg	★★★★
Incept	13.33			

Other Measures	Standard Index S&P 500	Best Fit Index S&P 500
Alpha	2.8	2.8
Beta	0.88	0.88
R-Squared	92	92
Standard Deviation	6.32	
Mean	12.64	
Sharpe Ratio	1.42	

Portfolio Analysis 09-30-06

Share change since 06-06 Total Stocks:119	Sector	PE	Tot Ret%	% Assets
⊕ General Electric Company	Ind Mtrls	20.0	9.35	2.90
⊖ J.P. Morgan Chase & Co.	Financial	13.6	25.60	2.57
⊖ ExxonMobil Corporation	Energy	11.1	39.07	1.88
⊖ Chevron Corporation	Energy	9.0	33.76	1.85
⊖ AT&T, Inc.	Telecom	18.2	51.59	1.79
⊖ Microsoft Corporation	Software	23.8	15.83	1.75
⊖ Morgan Stanley	Financial	12.3	45.93	1.63
⊖ Merck & Co., Inc.	Health	19.1	42.66	1.63
⊖ International Paper Co.	Ind Mtrls		4.51	1.57
⊕ Marsh & McLennan Compani	Financial	29.0	-1.16	1.54
⊖ Royal Dutch Shell PLC AD	Energy	8.7	19.33	1.44
⊖ Union Pacific Corporatio	Business	17.4	15.87	1.33
⊖ Tribune Company	Media	16.0	4.15	1.31
⊖ Honeywell International,	Ind Mtrls	18.6	24.14	1.31
⊖ Pfizer Inc.	Health	15.2	15.22	1.30
⊖ American International G	Financial	17.0	6.05	1.29
⊖ Colgate-Palmolive Compan	Goods	27.6	21.51	1.28
⊖ Time Warner, Inc.	Media	19.6	26.37	1.25
⊖ Eli Lilly & Company	Health	17.3	-5.16	1.17
⊖ Wyeth	Health	17.2	12.88	1.14

Current Investment Style

Value Blnd Growth — Large Mid Small

Market Cap	%
Giant	43.6
Large	38.2
Mid	18.1
Small	0.0
Micro	0.0
Avg $mil:	37,857

Value Measures		Rel Category
Price/Earnings	15.44	1.12
Price/Book	2.36	1.06
Price/Sales	1.39	1.07
Price/Cash Flow	9.58	1.43
Dividend Yield %	2.38	1.02

Growth Measures	%	Rel Category
Long-Term Erngs	10.07	0.97
Book Value	4.11	0.52
Sales	6.81	0.76
Cash Flow	-0.88	NMF
Historical Erngs	11.65	0.72

Profitability	%	Rel Category
Return on Equity	18.25	1.02
Return on Assets	8.65	0.88
Net Margin	10.71	0.83

Sector Weightings	% of Stocks	Rel S&P 500	3 Year High	Low
⌖ Info	20.76	1.04		
📊 Software	1.83	0.53	2	1
💻 Hardware	5.53	0.60	7	3
🎙 Media	7.69	2.03	9	8
📱 Telecom	5.71	1.63	6	6
☞ Service	36.92	0.80		
🏥 Health	11.10	0.92	11	9
🛒 Consumer	4.37	0.57	6	3
📋 Business	2.70	0.64	4	3
💲 Financial	18.75	0.84	20	19
🏭 Mfg	42.31	1.25		
Goods	12.14	1.42	15	11
Ind Mtrls	16.15	1.35	16	13
Energy	8.46	0.86	11	8
Utilities	5.56	1.59	6	4

Composition

● Cash	4.4
● Stocks	95.3
● Bonds	0.0
● Other	0.3
Foreign (% of Stock)	3.9

Morningstar's Take by Christopher Davis 12-21-06

Going against the grain has borne fruit for T. Rowe Price Equity-Income.

This fund's manager, Brian Rogers, zigs when most other investors zag. For instance, he scooped up shares of Hewlett-Packard in the depths of the 2000 to 2002 slump. Over the past two years, though, investors have enthusiastically bid up shares of HP as it cut costs and made inroads against its chief rival, Dell. Dell has since gone from hero to goat, making it cheap enough to get Rogers' attention. He thinks the odds of a Dell turnaround are higher than HP continuing its success, so he sold the latter and bought the former earlier this year. Similarly, he swapped American Express with insurer American International Group and H&R Block, arguing the stocks are better values within the financials sector.

Rogers' contrarian instincts typically have paid off for shareholders--although it often has required some patience. In 2002, for example, he scooped up shares of beaten-down drugmaker Merck and

began boosting his stake further in 2004 after the stock tanked following the company's decision to stop marketing its blockbuster drug Vioxx. Over the past year, Merck has rallied nicely. Rogers' 2002 foray into beaten-down telecom names, such as AT&T and Qwest Communications International, has started to pay off more recently as well.

To be sure, not everything has gone the fund's way lately. Rogers' ongoing bet on media names like Viacom and New York Times has detracted from returns. But the fund has still managed to stay modestly ahead of its large-value rivals this year. And even though we don't know for sure if his media picks will pan out, it's more important that Rogers gets most things right over the long haul. His two decade-plus record of success leads us to think he can. The big advantages he has--low costs and a strong analytical staff--bolsters our confidence.

Simply put, this offering is still a topnotch choice for large-value exposure.

Address:	100 East Pratt Street Baltimore MD 21202 800-638-5660	Minimum Purchase:	$2500 Add: $100 IRA: $1000
		Min Auto Inv Plan:	$50 Add: $50
		Sales Fees:	No-load
Web Address:	www.troweprice.com	Management Fee:	0.56%
Inception:	10-31-85	Actual Fees:	Mgt:0.56% Dist: —
Advisor:	T. Rowe Price Associates, Inc.	Expense Projections:	3Yr:$227 5Yr:$395 10Yr:$883
Subadvisor:	None	Income Distrib:	Quarterly
NTF Plans:	N/A		

T. Rowe Price Fincl Svcs

Ticker	Load	NAV	Yield	Total Assets	Mstar Category
PRISX	None	$21.38	1.8%	$445 mil	Specialty-Financial

Governance and Management

Stewardship Grade: B

Portfolio Manager(s)

Michael Holton is a longtime T. Rowe Price analyst who specialized in financial-services issues for a couple of years before becoming this fund's manager in November 2002. He receives the support of several analysts. Holton invests in this fund through his firm's 401(k) plan.

Strategy

Like his predecessor, Anna Dopkin, manager Michael Holton seeks well-established companies with strong management, above-average earnings-growth rates, and strong market share. The fund's various managers have also invested with a long-term view, which has kept turnover low. Holton makes notable subsector bets, emphasizing stocks in industries where he sees considerable upside. The portfolio is fairly concentrated with about 50 stocks.

Historical Profile

Return	Above Avg
Risk	Average
Rating	★★★★ Above Avg

Investment Style: Equity, Stock %

97% 96% 88% 86% 100% 99% 99% 100% 95%

▼ Manager Change
▽ Partial Manager Change

Growth of $10,000
— Investment Values of Fund
— Investment Values of S&P 500

31.0
24.0
17.0
10.0

Performance Quartile (within Category)

	1995	1996	1997	1998	1999	2000	2001	2002	2003	2004	2005	2006	History
	—	11.31	15.56	16.82	16.12	21.38	18.84	16.75	21.86	23.50	21.14	21.38	NAV
	—	13.40*	41.44	11.55	1.70	36.76	-3.13	-10.10	35.08	13.42	5.10	15.98	Total Return %
	—	—	8.08	-17.03	-19.34	45.86	8.76	12.00	6.40	2.54	0.19	0.19	+/-S&P 500
	—	—	-7.50	4.04	0.18	9.82	3.25	2.25	2.85	0.03	-1.36	-3.44	+/-DJ Finance
	—	—	0.88	1.03	0.59	0.56	0.70	0.69	1.37	0.78	1.36	2.03	Income Return %
	—	—	40.56	10.52	1.11	36.20	-3.83	-10.79	33.71	12.64	3.74	13.95	Capital Return %
	—	—	78	39	26	11	35	40	34	44	66	67	Total Rtn % Rank Cat
	—	0.03	0.10	0.16	0.10	0.09	0.15	0.13	0.23	0.17	0.32	0.43	Income $
	—	0.00	0.33	0.34	0.85	0.55	1.68	0.06	0.51	1.10	3.28	2.70	Capital Gains $
	—	1.25	1.25	1.19	1.14	1.00	0.97	1.00	0.97	0.93	0.93	—	Expense Ratio %
	—	1.71	1.15	0.94	0.50	0.69	0.69	0.80	1.16	0.77	1.21	—	Income Ratio %
	—	6	46	47	37	33	55	50	51	35	56	—	Turnover Rate %
	—	30	177	224	159	337	309	265	371	412	394	445	Net Assets $mil

Performance 12-31-06

	1st Qtr	2nd Qtr	3rd Qtr	4th Qtr	Total
2002	4.46	-5.49	-15.54	7.81	-10.10
2003	-6.81	21.59	4.90	13.64	35.08
2004	2.88	-1.78	-0.54	12.85	13.42
2005	-4.98	0.54	3.30	6.51	5.10
2006	5.72	-1.39	4.04	6.93	15.98

Trailing	Total Return%	+/- S&P 500	+/- DJ Finance	%Rank Cat	Growth of $10,000
3 Mo	6.93	0.23	-0.04	50	10,693
6 Mo	11.25	-1.49	-3.67	71	11,125
1 Yr	15.98	0.19	-3.44	67	11,598
3 Yr Avg	11.40	0.96	-1.57	62	13,825
5 Yr Avg	10.92	4.73	0.11	34	16,790
10 Yr Avg	13.57	5.15	1.14	17	35,697
15 Yr Avg	—	—	—	—	—

Tax Analysis	Tax-Adj Rtn%	%Rank Cat	Tax-Cost Rat	%Rank Cat
3 Yr (estimated)	9.06	62	2.10	72
5 Yr (estimated)	9.25	38	1.51	64
10 Yr (estimated)	11.97	13	1.41	59

Potential Capital Gain Exposure: 14% of assets

Rating and Risk

Time Period	Load-Adj Return %	Morningstar Rtn vs Cat	Morningstar Risk vs Cat	Morningstar Risk-Adj Rating
1 Yr	15.98			
3 Yr	11.40	Avg	Avg	★★★
5 Yr	10.92	Avg	+Avg	★★★
10 Yr	13.57	+Avg	Avg	★★★★
Incept	14.61			

Other Measures	Standard Index S&P 500	Best Fit Index DJ Finance
Alpha	0.6	-0.9
Beta	1.06	0.96
R-Squared	68	81
Standard Deviation	8.86	
Mean	11.40	
Sharpe Ratio	0.91	

Morningstar's Take by Laura Pavlenko Lutton 12-21-06

T. Rowe Price Financial Services is playing defense, which may prove prudent.

Manager Michael Holton's approach doesn't seem that unusual in one sense, but from another point of view he is one of the bolder diversified-financials fund managers. He scans the financial-services sector for stocks he thinks look undervalued based on the companies' expected earnings growth, which can be heavily influenced by the larger macroeconomic environment. That's pretty standard, but Holton's willingness to make sizable industry and subsector bets isn't. If he finds a number of companies from one area that meet his criteria, he isn't afraid to load up.

In recent years, Holton had been particularly bullish on companies with considerable exposure to capital markets, including investment banks, trust banks, and brokers. But he has grown less optimistic about those firms' prospects, particularly given that the share prices have done well in recent years and earnings growth may be more difficult should economic growth slow. Thus, Holton has trimmed the fund's exposure to stocks such as Goldman Sachs and State Street.

In place of those market-sensitive stocks, Holton has been bulking up on banks. This move bucks conventional wisdom in the sector: Most investors think bank earnings will be pinched by higher interest rates and weaker loan repayment rates. But Holton points out that bank stocks have underperformed the sector norms in recent years, and he thinks they will rise as investors anticipate falling interest rates and a steeper yield curve. Since the start of 2006, he's increased the fund's stake in U.S. banks dramatically, from less than 10% to about 40% of assets today. Large, newer positions include US Bancorp and TCF Financial.

Most managers have a tough time getting such moves right, but over his almost four years at this offering, Holton has been correct more often than not. He has delivered peer- and market-beating returns amid reasonable volatility.

Portfolio Analysis 09-30-06

Share change since 06-06 Total Stocks:37

	Sector	PE	Tot Ret%	% Assets
J.P. Morgan Chase & Co.	Financial	13.6	25.60	5.71
US Bancorp	Financial	13.9	26.29	5.30
⊕ Wells Fargo Company	Financial	14.7	16.82	5.24
⊕ TCF Financial Corporatio	Financial	13.7	4.67	4.94
⊕ SunTrust Banks, Inc.	Financial	14.1	19.81	4.74
⊕ Citigroup, Inc.	Financial	13.1	19.55	4.71
Fifth Third Bancorp	Financial	15.4	12.99	4.44
✲ Bank of America Corporat	Financial	12.4	20.68	4.40
⊕ Capital One Financial Co	Financial	10.4	-10.97	4.34
⊕ UBS AG	Financial	—	29.62	4.31
H & R Block, Inc.	Consumer	25.3	-3.95	4.27
✲ XL Capital, Ltd.	Financial	—	9.35	4.16
⊕ Synovus Financial Corp.	Financial	17.0	17.31	3.78
Compass Bancshares, Inc.	Financial	17.2	27.16	3.49
✲ General Electric Company	Ind Mtrls	20.0	9.35	3.46
⊖ First Horizon National C	Financial	16.8	13.71	3.04
CapitalSource, Inc.	Financial	15.7	32.16	3.04
Axis Capital Holdings, L	Financial	5.9	8.78	2.90
Lincoln National Corp.	Financial	12.9	28.58	2.82
Stifel Financial Corp.	Financial	39.7	4.36	2.34

Current Investment Style

Value Blnd Growth — Large / Mid / Small

Market Cap	%
Giant	36.5
Large	27.1
Mid	34.0
Small	0.0
Micro	2.5
Avg $mil:	23,429

Value Measures		Rel Category
Price/Earnings	12.47	0.94
Price/Book	1.95	1.02
Price/Sales	2.11	0.92
Price/Cash Flow	6.10	0.96
Dividend Yield %	2.99	1.19

Growth Measures	%	Rel Category
Long-Term Erngs	11.04	0.98
Book Value	9.00	0.98
Sales	8.51	1.00
Cash Flow	2.09	0.09
Historical Erngs	23.91	1.70

Profitability	%	Rel Category
Return on Equity	15.09	0.98
Return on Assets	11.80	0.97
Net Margin	19.45	0.94

Industry Weightings	% of Stocks	Rel Cat
Intl Banks	17.3	1.0
Banks	40.8	1.9
Real Estate	3.5	1.2
Sec Mgmt	6.1	0.5
S & Ls	0.0	0.0
Prop & Reins	12.9	0.8
Life Ins	4.4	0.8
Misc. Ins	0.2	0.1
Other	14.8	1.1

Composition

		%
●	Cash	5.3
●	Stocks	94.7
●	Bonds	0.0
○	Other	0.0
	Foreign	9.2

(% of Stock)

Address:	100 East Pratt Street, Baltimore MD 21202, 800-638-5660	Minimum Purchase:	$2500 Add: $100 IRA: $1000
Web Address:	www.troweprice.com	Min Auto Inv Plan:	$50 Add: $50
Inception:	09-30-96 *	Sales Fees:	No-load
Advisor:	T. Rowe Price Associates, Inc.	Management Fee:	0.66%
Subadvisor:	None	Actual Fees:	Mgt:0.66% Dist: —
NTF Plans:	N/A	Expense Projections:	3Yr:$296 5Yr:$515 10Yr:$1143
		Income Distrib:	Annually

MORNINGSTAR® Funds 500

T. Rowe Price Glob Stock

Analyst Pick ✓

	Ticker	Load	NAV	Yield	Total Assets	Mstar Category
	PRGSX	None	$22.64	0.4%	$426 mil	World Stock

Governance and Management

Stewardship Grade: A

Portfolio Manager(s)

Manager Rob Gensler started in April 2005, replacing Bob Smith and Dean Tenerelli. Gensler has left great records at his previous charges, T. Rowe Price Media & Telecom and T. Rowe Price Global Technology. He joined T. Rowe as a telecom analyst in 1995. He has significant personal investments in this fund.

Strategy

Rob Gensler, manager since April 2005, has charted a bold new course for the fund. Gensler runs a more concentrated, more growth-oriented portfolio. He also ventures more into emerging-markets and small-cap fare. This is all part of Gensler's go-anywhere approach. He looks for companies with sustainable competitive edges and will get them where he can. He will pay up for such companies on occasion, so the portfolio can look pricier than most peers'. Gensler is constantly looking for better stock opportunities, so the portfolio's turnover is also high.

Historical Profile

Return Average
Risk Average
Rating ★★★★ Above Avg

Investment Style: Equity Stock %

93% 87% 91% 94% 97% 97% 97% 94% 98%

▼ Manager Change
▽ Partial Manager Change

Growth of $10,000
— Investment Values of Fund
— Investment Values of MSCI EAFE

26.8 22.8 18.0 14.0 10.0

Performance Quartile (within Category)

	1995	1996	1997	1998	1999	2000	2001	2002	2003	2004	2005	2006	History
	10.00	11.76	12.72	15.00	18.72	16.43	13.78	10.89	14.11	16.06	19.37	22.64	NAV
	0.00*	20.01	13.23	22.50	28.76	-7.99	-15.39	-20.75	30.05	14.40	22.74	22.50	Total Return %
	—	13.96	11.45	2.57	1.73	6.20	6.03	-4.81	-8.54	-5.85	9.20	-3.84	+/-MSCI EAFE
	—	6.53	-2.53	-1.82	3.81	5.20	1.41	-0.86	-3.06	-0.32	13.25	2.43	+/-MSCI World
	—	0.60	0.51	0.79	0.40	0.11	0.73	0.22	0.37	0.57	0.12	0.46	Income Return %
	—	19.41	12.72	21.71	28.36	-8.10	-16.12	-20.97	29.68	13.83	22.62	22.04	Capital Return %
	—	23	60	25	56	47	45	60	71	58	2	20	Total Rtn % Rank Cat
	0.00	0.06	0.06	0.10	0.06	0.02	0.12	0.03	0.04	0.08	0.02	0.09	Income $
	0.00	0.18	0.53	0.45	0.49	0.79	0.00	0.00	0.00	0.01	0.32	0.99	Capital Gains $
	—	—	1.30	1.30	1.20	1.20	1.20	1.20	1.20	1.20	1.20	—	Expense Ratio %
	—	—	0.88	0.68	0.76	0.76	0.15	0.89	0.20	0.42	0.22	—	Income Ratio %
	—	—	50	42	47	38	72	52	48	39	72	—	Turnover Rate %
	—	17	34	49	90	99	99	77	63	82	86	425	Net Assets $mil

Performance 12-31-06

	1st Qtr	2nd Qtr	3rd Qtr	4th Qtr	Total
2002	-0.29	-9.83	-18.56	8.23	-20.75
2003	-5.42	16.99	3.82	13.21	30.05
2004	2.48	0.48	-1.79	13.12	14.40
2005	-3.55	5.75	11.66	7.78	22.74
2006	7.43	-3.03	4.86	12.14	22.50

Trailing	Total Return%	+/- MSCI EAFE	+/- MSCI World	%Rank Cat	Growth of $10,000
3 Mo	12.14	1.79	3.77	7	11,214
6 Mo	17.59	2.90	4.38	1	11,759
1 Yr	22.50	-3.84	2.43	20	12,250
3 Yr Avg	19.82	-0.11	5.14	8	17,202
5 Yr Avg	12.13	-2.85	2.16	37	17,726
10 Yr Avg	9.44	1.73	1.80	37	24,647
15 Yr Avg	—	—	—	—	—

Tax Analysis	Tax-Adj Rtn%	%Rank Cat	Tax-Cost Rat	%Rank Cat
3 Yr (estimated)	19.12	6	0.58	34
5 Yr (estimated)	11.69	31	0.39	32
10 Yr (estimated)	8.68	30	0.69	21

Potential Capital Gain Exposure: 18% of assets

Rating and Risk

Time Period	Load-Adj Return %	Morningstar Rtn vs Cat	Morningstar Risk vs Cat	Morningstar Risk-Adj Rating
1 Yr	22.50			
3 Yr	19.82	High	+Avg	★★★★★
5 Yr	12.13	Avg	Avg	★★★★
10 Yr	9.44	Avg	Avg	★★★
Incept	10.36			

Other Measures	Standard Index MSCI EAFE	Best Fit Index MSCI World
Alpha	0.9	4.0
Beta	0.94	1.16
R-Squared	72	85
Standard Deviation	10.50	
Mean	19.82	
Sharpe Ratio	1.49	

Morningstar's Take by Arijit Dutta 12-20-06

T. Rowe Price Global Stock's daring style still earns our nod.

This fund has come back from some tough challenges this year. Investors fled risky assets like emerging-markets and small-cap stocks during a month-long correction in May and June. This caused especially sharp pain here. The portfolio's 20% emerging-markets stake at the time was almost triple the world-stock category average, and its $16 billion average market cap is significantly less than the group norm. As a result, the fund's 15% loss during the downturn was among the category's very worst. The fund came roaring back in recent months, however, on the coattails of some of those emerging-markets stocks, due to a great stock selection in the United States.

Manager Rob Gensler earns kudos for taking the fund's mid-year setback in stride. He didn't see that many of his emerging-markets holdings had lost their long-term appeal, so in some cases he actually bought more when the markets plunged. For

example, Gensler is especially enthusiastic about the spread of wireless telephony in emerging countries. Thus, he bought more of America Movil and Bharti Televentures when they tumbled (both have surged back since June). Several of his top U.S. holdings, such as Goldman Sachs and Juniper Networks, have also staged spectacular rallies since their mid-year woes. In Goldman Sachs' case, for example, Gensler held on because of his conviction that the company is very well positioned to benefit from long-term industry trends, such as growth in derivative securities.

We think Gensler's approach makes the best use of the fund's broad, global mandate. He buys companies he thinks are on the right end of the competitive forces in any industry and doesn't mind if such stocks happen to be small or in emerging markets. Moreover, Gensler's capacity to not be swayed by market sentiment also inspires confidence in his analysis. This is a great one-stop choice.

Address:	100 East Pratt Street Baltimore MD 21202 800-638-5660
Web Address:	www.troweprice.com
Inception:	12-29-95 *
Advisor:	T. Rowe Price International, Inc
Subadvisor:	None
NTF Plans:	N/A

Minimum Purchase:	$2500	Add: $100	IRA: $1000
Min Auto Inv Plan:	$2500	Add: $50	
Sales Fees:	No-load, 2.00%R		
Management Fee:	0.66%		
Actual Fees:	Mgt:0.66%	Dist: —	
Expense Projections:	3Yr:$335	5Yr:$619	10Yr:$1430
Income Distrib:	Annually		

Portfolio Analysis 09-30-06

Share change since 06-06 Total Stocks:73

	Sector	Country	% Assets
⊕ American Tower Corporati	Telecom	United States	4.81
⊕ Monster Worldwide, Inc.	Business	United States	3.28
⊕ Juniper Networks, Inc.	Hardware	United States	2.91
Bharti Televentures Ltd	Telecom	India	2.54
⊕ Sumitomo Mitsui Financia	Financial	Japan	2.31
America Movil SA ADR	Telecom	Mexico	2.30
⊕ Goldman Sachs Group, Inc	Financial	United States	2.13
⊕ UBS AG	Financial	Switzerland	2.10
⊕ Murphy Oil Corporation	Energy	United States	2.02
✲ Aetna, Inc.	Health	United States	1.79
⊕ Wynn Resorts, Ltd.	Consumer	United States	1.79
⊕ Cephalon, Inc.	Health	United States	1.72
BCA ROMANA DE DEZV	Financial	—	1.71
⊕ TD Ameritrade Holding Co	Financial	United States	1.65
✲ EGYPTIAN	—	Egypt	1.65
Erste Bank	Financial	Austria	1.64
Tencent Hldgs	Telecom	Hong Kong	1.55
⊕ Smith International, Inc	Energy	United States	1.53
⊕ Google, Inc.	Business	United States	1.53
⊕ Roche Holding	Health	Switzerland	1.52

Current Investment Style

Value Blnd Growth — Large/Mid/Small

Market Cap	%
Giant	31.4
Large	32.9
Mid	33.2
Small	1.9
Micro	0.6

Avg $mil: 15,561

Value Measures		Rel Category
Price/Earnings	18.26	1.19
Price/Book	2.54	1.06
Price/Sales	1.97	1.50
Price/Cash Flow	10.72	1.24
Dividend Yield %	1.05	0.48

Growth Measures	%	Rel Category
Long-Term Erngs	15.34	1.21
Book Value	17.33	1.93
Sales	13.52	1.62
Cash Flow	29.14	2.97
Historical Erngs	31.41	1.68

Composition

Cash	0.5	Bonds	0.0
Stocks	98.1	Other	1.4
Foreign	(% of Stock)		51.3

Sector Weightings

	% of Stocks	Rel MSCI EAFE	3 Year High	Low
⊙ Info	22.71	1.92		
▣ Software	0.65	1.16	4	0
▣ Hardware	4.55	1.18	10	5
▣ Media	3.08	1.68	8	2
▣ Telecom	14.43	2.59	17	3
⊕ Service	55.58	1.18		
▣ Health	12.68	1.78	15	10
▣ Consumer	7.14	1.44	12	2
▣ Business	8.48	1.67	8	4
▣ Financial	27.28	0.91	29	24
▣ Mfg	21.71	0.53		
▣ Goods	3.33	0.25	11	1
▣ Ind Mtrls	7.63	0.49	11	5
▣ Energy	10.75	1.50	13	4
▣ Utilities	0.00	0.00	1	0

Regional Exposure

	% Stock		% Stock
UK/W. Europe	27	N. America	49
Japan	4	Latn America	6
Asia X Japan	9	Other	5

Country Exposure

	% Stock		% Stock
United States	49	U.K.	4
Switzerland	7	Japan	4
France	5		

T. Rowe Price Glob Tech

	Ticker	Load	NAV	Yield	Total Assets	Mstar Category
	PRGTX	None	$6.71	0.0%	$138 mil	Specialty-Technology

Governance and Management

Stewardship Grade: B

Portfolio Manager(s)

Jeff Rottinghaus replaced Rob Gensler (who had led the charge here since January 2002) in May 2006. Prior to joining T. Rowe Price as a tech analyst in 2001, Rottinghaus ran a tech-consulting business for several years. Currently, he also runs the technology sleeve of T. Rowe Price New Horizons and T. Rowe Price Developing Tech. He has the support of a sizable worldwide staff of technology and related analysts.

Strategy

This fund offers a broad mix of technology, telecommunication-services, and media stocks. In addition, management devotes a significant chunk of assets to foreign stocks. Like at most T. Rowe funds, the approach here is mindful of valuations. However, manager Jeff Rottinghaus puts more emphasis on companies' ability to improve their positions within their industries.

Performance 12-31-06

	1st Qtr	2nd Qtr	3rd Qtr	4th Qtr	Total
2002	-5.05	-19.73	-24.03	21.09	-29.89
2003	-1.20	20.36	9.60	14.98	49.85
2004	3.21	3.88	-10.47	14.82	10.22
2005	-6.55	7.20	7.44	3.04	10.91
2006	5.08	-7.49	4.89	7.88	10.00

Trailing	Total Return%	+/- S&P 500	+/- ArcaEx Tech 100	%Rank Cat	Growth of $10,000
3 Mo	7.88	1.18	2.25	33	10,788
6 Mo	13.15	0.41	1.50	24	11,315
1 Yr	10.00	-5.79	5.32	23	11,000
3 Yr Avg	10.38	-0.06	2.50	14	13,448
5 Yr Avg	7.15	0.96	2.19	4	14,124
10 Yr Avg	—	—	—		—
15 Yr Avg	—	—	—		—

Tax Analysis	Tax-Adj Rtn%	%Rank Cat	Tax-Cost Rat	%Rank Cat
3 Yr (estimated)	10.38	12	0.00	1
5 Yr (estimated)	7.15	3	0.00	1
10 Yr (estimated)	—			

Potential Capital Gain Exposure: -38% of assets

Morningstar's Take by Arijit Dutta 12-26-06

We're encouraged to see T. Rowe Price Global Technology maintaining its stride.

New manager Jeff Rottinghaus has dealt with some tough challenges since taking charge in May. The portfolio's 16% stake in emerging-markets stocks (which is well more than twice the tech category average) left it especially vulnerable when such stocks plunged sharply in later spring. Also, top holdings Yahoo and Juniper Networks, while struggling all year, dropped alarmingly after Rottinghaus took over. Still, the fund has stayed ahead of the competition for the year. Emerging markets recovered since June. Success at some of the portfolio's smaller holdings such as Dutch navigation equipment maker TomTom have also had a meaningful impact, due to the relatively compact portfolio.

Short-term performance is indeed fleeting, but we appreciate the poise Rottinghaus has shown in this tough environment. For example, take Satyam Computer Services and Infosys Technologies, the portfolio's major holdings in the emerging Indian market. Rottinghaus concedes that after years of strong performance, Indian tech stocks have considerable valuation risk. He continues to hold them and, in fact, bought more during the correction because, in his view, these companies are very strongly positioned against the worldwide competition in computer software (both stocks have rebounded since the correction). He has also stuck with Yahoo and Juniper because he believes those stocks' short-term woes don't undermine the companies' ability to compete effectively.

Thus, we think Rottinghaus displays some of the same characteristics that we liked in the fund's previous manager. He won't get swayed by market sentiment if his analysis still reveals strengths in a company, and he strikes a nice balance between growth and valuation. While Rottinghaus is still untested in a leadership role, what we have seen so far bodes well for the fund.

Address:	100 East Pratt Street
	Baltimore MD 21202
	800-638-5660
Web Address:	www.troweprice.com
Inception:	09-29-00*
Advisor:	T. Rowe Price Associates, Inc.
Subadvisor:	None
NTF Plans:	Federated Tr NTF

Minimum Purchase:	$2500	Add: $100	IRA: $1000
Min Auto Inv Plan:	$50	Add: $50	
Sales Fees:	No-load		
Management Fee:	0.76%		
Actual Fees:	Mgt:0.76%	Dist: —	
Expense Projections:	3Yr:$474	5Yr:$818	10Yr:$1791
Income Distrib:	Annually		

Historical Profile

Return	High
Risk	Below Avg
Rating	★★★★ Highest

| 96% | 91% | 98% | 95% | 92% | 95% |

▼ Manager Change
▽ Partial Manager Change

10.0
6.0 — Growth of $10,000
4.0
2.0

— Investment Values of Fund
— Investment Values of S&P 500

Performance Quartile (within Category)

1995	1996	1997	1998	1999	2000	2001	2002	2003	2004	2005	2006	History
—	—	—	—	—	7.43	4.75	3.33	4.99	5.50	6.10	6.71	NAV
—	—	—	—	—	-25.70*	-36.07	-29.89	49.85	10.22	10.91	10.00	Total Return %
—	—	—	—	—	—	-24.18	-7.79	21.17	-0.66	6.00	-5.79	+/-S&P 500
—	—	—	—	—	—	-20.48	3.44	-2.29	-1.51	3.55	5.32	+/-ArcaEx Tech 100
—	—	—	—	—	—	0.00	0.00	0.00	0.00	0.00	0.00	Income Return %
—	—	—	—	—	—	-36.07	-29.89	49.85	10.22	10.91	10.00	Capital Return %
—	—	—	—	—	—	53	7	63	28	18	23	Total Rtn % Rank Cat
—	—	—	—	—	0.00	0.00	0.00	0.00	0.00	0.00	0.00	Income $
—	—	—	—	—	0.00	0.00	0.00	0.00	0.00	0.00	0.00	Capital Gains $
—	—	—	—	—	—	—	1.50	1.50	1.50	1.50	—	Expense Ratio %
—	—	—	—	—	—	—	-1.08	-1.15	-1.17	-0.45	—	Income Ratio %
—	—	—	—	—	—	32	189	211	151	137	—	Turnover Rate %
—	—	—	—	—	—	131	84	55	85	92	138	Net Assets $mil

Rating and Risk

Time Period	Load-Adj Return %	Morningstar Rtn vs Cat	Morningstar Risk vs Cat	Morningstar Risk-Adj Rating
1 Yr	10.00			
3 Yr	10.38	+Avg	-Avg	★★★★
5 Yr	7.15	High	-Avg	★★★★★
10 Yr	—	—	—	
Incept	-6.18			

Other Measures	Standard Index S&P 500	Best Fit Index ArcaEx Tech 100
Alpha	-4.9	2.4
Beta	1.84	1.04
R-Squared	65	85
Standard Deviation	15.64	
Mean	10.38	
Sharpe Ratio	0.50	

Portfolio Analysis 09-30-06

Share change since 06-06 Total Stocks:62	Sector	PE	Tot Ret%	% Assets
⊖ Microsoft Corporation	Software	23.8	15.83	5.58
⊖ Samsung Electnc	—	—	—	3.71
Symbol Technologies	Hardware	35.6	16.64	2.95
⊕ Yahoo, Inc.	Media	35.4	-34.81	2.59
⊕ Juniper Networks, Inc.	Hardware	34.3	-15.07	2.53
⊕ Taiwan Semiconductor Man	Hardware	18.9	18.75	2.42
⊕ Adobe Systems Inc.	Software	48.1	11.26	2.38
Maxim Integrated Product	Hardware	23.1	-14.06	2.34
American Tower Corporati	Telecom		37.57	2.32
⊖ CD Networks		—	—	2.28
⊕ Google, Inc.	Business	61.5	11.00	2.23
⊕ Cisco Systems, Inc.	Hardware	30.1	59.64	2.19
⊕ Infosys Technologies Ltd	Software		—	2.08
Corning Inc.	Hardware	25.5	-4.83	2.03
⊖ Satyam Computer	Software		—	2.02
⊕ Red Hat, Inc.	Software	58.8	-15.63	1.92
⊖ Hoya	Goods		—	1.90
⊖ Nokia	Hardware		—	1.89
⊕ TomTom	Software		—	1.88
⊖ Salesforce.com, Inc.	Software		13.73	1.85

Current Investment Style

Value Blnd Growth — Large/Mid/Small

Market Cap	%
Giant	27.7
Large	26.5
Mid	35.9
Small	8.4
Micro	1.5

Avg $mil: 10,897

Value Measures		Rel Category
Price/Earnings	25.33	1.04
Price/Book	3.22	1.00
Price/Sales	3.06	1.10
Price/Cash Flow	14.43	1.11
Dividend Yield %	0.81	1.84

Growth Measures	%	Rel Category
Long-Term Erngs	19.45	1.13
Book Value	12.68	1.32
Sales	14.74	1.18
Cash Flow	12.31	0.62
Historical Erngs	26.67	0.97

Profitability	%	Rel Category
Return on Equity	18.28	1.17
Return on Assets	12.12	1.30
Net Margin	16.29	1.17

Industry Weightings	% of Stocks	Rel Cat
Software	28.3	1.3
Hardware	6.3	0.6
Networking Eq	10.8	1.4
Semis	16.3	0.9
Semi Equip	5.0	1.0
Comp/Data Sv	9.9	1.1
Telecom	3.7	1.3
Health Care	0.0	0.0
Other	19.8	1.1

Composition

Composition	%
● Cash	1.5
● Stocks	94.8
● Bonds	0.0
● Other	3.7
Foreign (% of Stock)	33.5

Morningstar® Funds 500

T. Rowe Price GNMA

	Ticker	Load	NAV	Yield	SEC Yield	Total Assets	Mstar Category
	PRGMX	None	$9.37	5.0%	4.77%	$1,259 mil	Intermediate Government

Governance and Management

Stewardship Grade: B

Portfolio Manager(s)

Connie Bavely joined this fund in October 2000 and has delivered solid results during her tenure. She also contributes on T. Rowe Price New Income, a more diversified offering that looks to best the Lehman Brothers Aggregate Bond Index.

Strategy

Manager Connie Bavely searches for inefficiencies in the GNMA market, looking for situations in which investors have made faulty assumptions about the likely prepayment of certain bonds. She also tries to add value when rates are falling by selectively investing in GNMA CMOs and project loans. She will also venture into Treasuries when opportunities present themselves. For example, at times the fund has dipped into Treasury Inflation-Protected Securities.

Performance 12-31-06

	1st Qtr	2nd Qtr	3rd Qtr	4th Qtr	Total
2002	0.91	3.56	3.12	1.18	9.03
2003	0.89	0.84	0.00	0.60	2.36
2004	1.58	-1.13	2.27	1.05	3.80
2005	-0.07	1.75	0.05	0.98	2.74
2006	-0.17	-0.69	3.45	1.26	3.86

Trailing	Total Return%	+/- LB Aggr	+/- LB Govt	%Rank Cat	Growth of $10,000
3 Mo	1.26	0.02	0.42	24	10,126
6 Mo	4.76	-0.33	0.35	23	10,476
1 Yr	3.86	-0.47	0.38	28	10,386
3 Yr Avg	3.47	-0.23	0.27	16	11,078
5 Yr Avg	4.33	-0.73	-0.31	22	12,361
10 Yr Avg	5.61	-0.63	-0.40	17	17,260
15 Yr Avg	5.80	-0.70	-0.50	22	23,296

Tax Analysis	Tax-Adj Rtn%	%Rank Cat	Tax-Cost Rat	%Rank Cat
3 Yr (estimated)	1.79	18	1.62	79
5 Yr (estimated)	2.68	21	1.58	67
10 Yr (estimated)	3.45	23	2.05	82

Potential Capital Gain Exposure: -2% of assets

Morningstar's Take by Arijit Dutta 12-11-06

T. Rowe Price GNMA has given itself a better chance to compete.

A prospectus change in June this year allows this fund to invest in nongovernment securities. While the portfolio will still devote 80% of its assets to Ginnie Maes, manager Connie Bavely has some convincing reasons for the recent expansion of the fund's mandate. Valuations of Ginnie Mae securities have looked stretched after the superb year they had in 2005, so Bavely appreciates the room to seek better bargains elsewhere. Moreover, cash flows of certain nongovernment issues, such as commercial mortgage-backed securities (CMBS), react differently than Ginnie Maes to changes in interest rates. Thus, the change adds flexibility and diversification here.

Even more important, this plays nicely into the fund's security-selection-based strategy. T. Rowe bond managers don't make large bets on the direction of interest rates, and rely instead on identifying mispriced securities. For example,

Bavely has favored 15-year mortgages in recent years, which offer good values due to their relatively illiquid status, and carry less interest-rate risk to boot. Also, Bavely looks out for mortgage pools that offer more transparency regarding their underlying loans, which gives her a better shot at valuing them correctly.

It's tough to succeed on security selection alone because individual securities in this asset class have very similar characteristics, but Bavely has done a solid job. The fund's record under her management is better than most mortgage-focused rivals', including some eligible options with sharply lower expenses. The one notable exception is Vanguard GNMA, whose rock-bottom expenses have proved too big an edge. (T. Rowe has indeed beaten Vanguard before expenses.)

T. Rowe is not quite the best option based on expenses. Bavely has shown, however, that she can keep the fund in contention due to her team's detailed approach.

Address:	100 East Pratt Street Baltimore MD 21202 800-638-5660
Web Address:	www.troweprice.com
Inception:	11-26-85
Advisor:	T. Rowe Price Associates, Inc.
Subadvisor:	None
NTF Plans:	N/A

Minimum Purchase:	$2500	Add: $100	IRA: $1000
Min Auto Inv Plan:	$50	Add: $50	
Sales Fees:	No-load		
Management Fee:	0.46%		
Actual Fees:	Mgt:0.46%	Dist: —	
Expense Projections:	3Yr:$211	5Yr:$368	10Yr:$822
Income Distrib:	Monthly		

Historical Profile

Return	Above Avg
Risk	Below Avg
Rating	★★★★ Above Avg

Growth of $10,000
— Investment Values of Fund
— Investment Values of LB Aggr

Performance Quartile (within Category)

1995	1996	1997	1998	1999	2000	2001	2002	2003	2004	2005	2006	History
9.74	9.37	9.58	9.57	8.99	9.34	9.48	9.89	9.73	9.66	9.48	9.37	NAV
17.81	3.12	9.48	6.56	0.21	10.94	7.69	9.03	2.36	3.80	2.74	3.86	Total Return %
-0.66	-0.51	-0.17	-2.13	1.03	-0.69	-0.75	-1.22	-1.74	-0.54	0.31	-0.47	+/-LB Aggr
-0.53	0.35	-0.11	-3.29	2.44	-2.30	0.46	-2.47	0.00	0.32	0.09	0.38	+/-LB Govt
7.87	6.90	7.11	6.68	6.45	6.83	6.20	4.61	4.00	4.53	4.63	5.00	Income Return %
9.94	-3.78	2.37	-0.12	-6.24	4.11	1.49	4.42	-1.64	-0.73	-1.89	-1.14	Capital Return %
27	44	16	77	26	55	19	49	23	18	8	28	Total Rtn % Rank Cat
0.68	0.65	0.65	0.62	0.60	0.60	0.56	0.43	0.39	0.43	0.44	0.46	Income $
0.00	0.00	0.00	0.00	0.00	0.00	0.00	0.00	0.00	0.00	0.00	0.00	Capital Gains $
0.76	0.74	0.74	0.70	0.71	0.71	0.70	0.70	0.70	0.69	0.67	0.66	Expense Ratio %
7.50	7.04	6.98	6.67	6.36	6.61	6.39	3.68	3.68	3.23	3.90	4.14	Income Ratio %
121	114	116	121	87	64	71	386	386	302	167	135	Turnover Rate %
896	928	1,063	1,146	1,089	1,091	1,139	1,408	1,315	1,356	1,262	1,259	Net Assets $mil

Rating and Risk

Time Period	Load-Adj Return %	Morningstar Rtn vs Cat	Morningstar Risk vs Cat	Morningstar Risk-Adj Rating
1 Yr	3.86			
3 Yr	3.47	+Avg	-Avg	★★★★
5 Yr	4.33	+Avg	-Avg	★★★★
10 Yr	5.61	+Avg	-Avg	★★★★
Incept	6.84			

Other Measures	Standard Index LB Aggr	Best Fit Index LB Mort
Alpha	-0.1	-0.6
Beta	0.66	0.87
R-Squared	91	96
Standard Deviation	2.24	
Mean	3.47	
Sharpe Ratio	0.10	

Portfolio Analysis 09-30-06

Total Fixed-Income:2504	Date of Maturity	Amount $000	Value $000	% Net Assets
GNMA 6%	11-20-33	44,720	45,192	3.61
US Treasury Note 4.25%	11-15-13	35,100	34,332	2.74
GNMA 5.5%	02-20-34	34,554	34,256	2.74
GNMA 5%	10-20-33	31,565	30,652	2.45
GNMA 5.5%	07-15-33	29,244	29,083	2.33
GNMA 5.5%	12-20-33	28,628	28,381	2.27
GNMA 5%	08-20-33	28,192	27,376	2.19
GNMA CMO 5.5%	05-20-31	26,199	26,371	2.11
GNMA	10-20-30	25,651	25,636	2.05
GNMA 5.5%	07-20-35	25,568	25,324	2.02
GNMA 6%	01-20-35	24,051	24,297	1.94
GNMA 5.5%	01-15-35	22,424	22,272	1.78
GNMA 6%	07-15-34	21,200	21,482	1.72
GNMA 5%	09-15-33	19,404	18,891	1.51
GNMA 6%	09-20-34	18,683	18,874	1.51
GNMA 5%	07-20-33	18,604	18,066	1.44
GNMA 5.5%	06-15-35	16,769	16,650	1.33
GNMA 6%	08-20-34	16,142	16,308	1.30
GNMA 6%	04-15-34	15,805	16,012	1.28
Lb-Ubs Cmbs 2006-C1 CMO	02-15-31	15,500	15,267	1.22

Current Investment Style

Duration: Short Int Long
Quality: High Med Low

¹ figure provided by fund

Avg Eff Duration¹	3.8 Yrs
Avg Eff Maturity	6.1 Yrs
Avg Credit Quality	AAA
Avg Wtd Coupon	5.69%
Avg Wtd Price	100.21% of par

Coupon Range	% of Bonds	Rel Cat
0% PIK	0.4	0.0
0% to 6%	80.8	1.0
6% to 8%	18.4	1.2
8% to 10%	0.6	0.3
More than 10%	0.2	0.2

1.00=Category Average

Credit Analysis		% bonds 09-30-06	
AAA	100	BB	0
AA	0	B	0
A	0	Below B	0
BBB	0	NR/NA	0

Sector Breakdown	% of assets
US Treasuries	4
TIPS	0
US Agency	0
Mortgage Pass-Throughs	80
Mortgage CMO	14
Mortgage ARM	0
US Corporate	1
Asset-Backed	0
Convertible	0
Municipal	0
Corporate Inflation-Protected	0
Foreign Corporate	0
Foreign Govt	0

Composition			
Cash	1.7	Bonds	98.3
Stocks	0.0	Other	0.0

Special Securities	
Restricted/Illiquid Secs	Trace
Exotic Mortgage-Backed	0
Emerging-Markets Secs	0
Options/Futures/Warrants	No

Investment Style
Fixed Income
Income Rtn %Rank Cat

▼ Manager Change
▽ Partial Manager Change

T. Rowe Price Grth & Inc

	Ticker	Load	NAV	Yield	Total Assets	Mstar Category
	PRGIX	None	$22.14	1.3%	$1,675 mil	Large Blend

Governance and Management

Stewardship Grade: A

Portfolio Manager(s)

Anna Dopkin took over management of this fund from Robert Sharps in October 2002. Dopkin has been a T. Rowe Price analyst covering the financial-services sector for six years, and she managed T. Rowe Price Financial Services for nearly three years, becoming sole manager in December 2000. Under her guidance, that fund performed well enough to warrant inclusion in our Fund Analyst Picks list for the financials category. Dopkin is backed by more than 30 analysts on this fund.

Strategy

In the past, this fund emphasized stocks with sizable yields and histories of growing dividends. Nowadays, management is focusing on reasonably priced companies with high ROEs and earnings growth. It includes both growth and value stocks in the portfolio, as opposed to its previous value orientation. The goal is also to have a dividend yield higher than that of the S&P 500.

Performance 12-31-06

	1st Qtr	2nd Qtr	3rd Qtr	4th Qtr	Total
2002	-0.43	-14.19	-17.93	8.60	-23.84
2003	-4.62	15.91	1.70	14.04	28.22
2004	1.29	0.96	-1.40	9.91	10.82
2005	-3.08	0.79	2.33	2.64	2.60
2006	4.11	-2.13	4.77	7.20	14.44

Trailing	Total Return%	+/- S&P 500	+/- Russ 1000	%Rank Cat	Growth of $10,000
3 Mo	7.20	0.50	0.25	28	10,720
6 Mo	12.31	-0.43	-0.05	32	11,231
1 Yr	14.44	-1.35	-1.02	48	11,444
3 Yr Avg	9.17	-1.27	-1.81	67	13,011
5 Yr Avg	4.91	-1.28	-1.91	69	12,708
10 Yr Avg	6.68	-1.74	-1.96	72	19,091
15 Yr Avg	9.84	-0.80	-0.96	56	40,870

Tax Analysis	Tax-Adj Rtn%	%Rank Cat	Tax-Cost Rat	%Rank Cat
3 Yr (estimated)	7.44	75	1.58	71
5 Yr (estimated)	3.73	78	1.12	71
10 Yr (estimated)	5.04	77	1.54	73

Potential Capital Gain Exposure: 24% of assets

Morningstar's Take by Karen Wallace 11-06-06

T. Rowe Price Growth & Income has been living up to its potential lately.

Manager Anna Dopkin looks for reasonably priced stocks that can grow steadily. Not afraid to go against the grain, she has favored high-quality blue-chip stocks such as Microsoft and Coca-Cola for several years now, believing that the market was not recognizing the value of fundamentals such as solid balance sheets and steady cash flows. The fund suffered for Dopkin's conviction in 2005, when investors seemed to have an unquenchable thirst for risk; smaller caps and cyclicals led the way, while steady, profitable blue chips looked sluggish for the most part. But Dopkin stuck with these firms, believing that their stocks would return to favor.

As we mentioned in our last Analyst Report, the fund was in a good position to benefit when blue chips returned to the market's favor. And though it may be too soon to say for certain, the tide now seems to be turning in that direction. Slower GDP growth and a sluggish housing market indicate that the economy is slowing down, and high-quality, large-cap names often outperform in this type of environment. Indeed, the blue-chip-heavy Dow Jones Industrial Average has mounted a comeback over the past three months. And this fund has returned 8.6% over that stretch to place in the top quartile of the crowded and competitive large-blend category. While it's important not to place too much emphasis on a time period as short as three months, we're encouraged by recent performance.

And overall, we think this fund has three elements that argue heavily in its favor. First, Dopkin's long-term adherence to her sensible investment strategy makes this fund a good core holding. Second, the fund's focus on steady-growing firms helps lead to below-average volatility (as measured by standard deviation). And finally, low fees provide the fund a long-term advantage over peers.

Address:	100 East Pratt Street
	Baltimore MD 21202
	800-638-5660
Web Address:	www.troweprice.com
Inception:	12-21-82
Advisor:	T. Rowe Price Associates, Inc.
Subadvisor:	None
NTF Plans:	N/A

Minimum Purchase:	$2500	Add: $100	IRA: $1000
Min Auto Inv Plan:	$50	Add: $50	
Sales Fees:	No-load		
Management Fee:	0.56%		
Actual Fees:	Mgt:0.56%	Dist: —	
Expense Projections:	3Yr:$243	5Yr:$422	10Yr:$942
Income Distrib:	Quarterly		

Historical Profile

Return	Below Avg
Risk	Average
Rating	★★★ Neutral

| | 91% | 94% | 84% | 96% | 96% | 98% | 98% | 98% | 92% |

			Investment Style
			Equity
			Stock %

▼ Manager Change
▽ Partial Manager Change

Growth of $10,000
■ Investment Values of Fund
— Investment Values of S&P 500

Performance Quartile (within Category)

1995	1996	1997	1998	1999	2000	2001	2002	2003	2004	2005	2006	History
19.18	22.63	26.36	26.25	24.44	24.44	22.82	17.11	21.72	22.51	20.62	22.14	NAV
30.92	25.64	23.53	9.96	3.78	8.97	-2.17	-23.84	28.22	10.82	2.60	14.44	Total Return %
-6.66	2.68	-9.83	-18.62	-17.26	18.07	9.72	-1.74	-0.46	-0.06	-2.31	-1.35	+/-S&P 500
-6.85	3.19	-9.32	-17.06	-17.13	16.76	10.28	-2.19	-1.67	-0.58	-3.67	-1.02	+/-Russ 1000
3.85	2.69	2.50	2.08	1.96	1.40	1.09	0.71	1.11	1.20	1.04	1.43	Income Return %
27.07	22.95	21.03	7.88	1.82	7.57	-3.26	-24.55	27.11	9.62	1.56	13.01	Capital Return %
71	15	79	89	93	12	10	77	39	41	86	48	Total Rtn % Rank Cat
0.59	0.51	0.56	0.53	0.51	0.34	0.26	0.16	0.19	0.26	0.23	0.29	Income $
0.60	0.90	0.97	2.13	2.25	1.83	0.78	0.15	0.00	1.27	2.24	1.12	Capital Gains $
0.84	0.82	0.78	0.77	0.77	0.77	0.81	0.81	0.82	0.78	0.76	—	Expense Ratio %
3.31	2.53	2.22	2.03	1.78	1.35	1.08	0.84	1.02	1.15	0.98	—	Income Ratio %
26	14	16	20	20	80	66	45	41	36	52	—	Turnover Rate %
1,748	2,489	3,447	3,563	3,440	2,989	2,394	1,675	1,970	1,904	1,741	1,675	Net Assets $mil

Rating and Risk

Time Period	Load-Adj Return %	Morningstar Rtn vs Cat	Morningstar Risk vs Cat	Morningstar Risk-Adj Rating
1 Yr	14.44			
3 Yr	9.17	Avg	Avg	★★★
5 Yr	4.91	-Avg	+Avg	★★
10 Yr	6.68	-Avg	-Avg	★★★
Incept	10.84			

Other Measures	Standard Index S&P 500	Best Fit Index Russ 1000
Alpha	-1.1	-1.4
Beta	1.00	0.97
R-Squared	95	95
Standard Deviation	7.10	
Mean	9.17	
Sharpe Ratio	0.83	

Portfolio Analysis 09-30-06

Share change since 06-06 Total Stocks:109	Sector	PE	Tot Ret%	% Assets
General Electric Company	Ind Mtrls	20.0	9.35	3.69
Citigroup, Inc.	Financial	13.1	19.55	2.68
Microsoft Corporation	Software	23.8	15.83	2.15
Marsh & McLennan Compani	Financial	29.0	-1.16	1.79
ExxonMobil Corporation	Energy	11.1	39.07	1.70
Intel Corporation	Hardware	21.0	-17.18	1.39
⊕ Avon Products	Goods	31.6	18.45	1.39
Schlumberger, Ltd.	Energy	22.3	31.07	1.38
⊕ Entergy Corporation	Utilities	19.7	38.40	1.38
Coca-Cola Company	Goods	21.7	23.10	1.38
Baker Hughes Inc.	Energy	9.9	23.68	1.33
⊕ American Tower Corporati	Telecom		37.57	1.33
Fifth Third Bancorp	Financial	15.4	12.99	1.32
Equity Residential	Financial	NMF	34.64	1.31
Bed Bath & Beyond, Inc.	Consumer	20.1	5.39	1.26
⊖ Honeywell International,	Ind Mtrls	18.6	24.14	1.22
⊖ Legg Mason	Financial	25.1	-19.99	1.17
Wal-Mart Stores, Inc.	Consumer	16.9	0.13	1.15
NiSource, Inc.	Utilities	21.8	20.51	1.13
⊕ Juniper Networks, Inc.	Hardware	34.3	-15.07	1.11

Current Investment Style

Value Blnd Growth — Large / Mid / Small

Market Cap	%
Giant	35.1
Large	45.7
Mid	19.2
Small	0.0
Micro	0.0
Avg $mil:	31,767

Value Measures		Rel Category
Price/Earnings	16.38	1.07
Price/Book	2.59	1.01
Price/Sales	1.70	1.21
Price/Cash Flow	5.49	0.65
Dividend Yield %	1.90	1.09

Growth Measures	%	Rel Category
Long-Term Erngs	11.85	1.00
Book Value	9.31	1.03
Sales	10.96	1.13
Cash Flow	5.48	0.53
Historical Erngs	17.99	0.97

Profitability	%	Rel Category
Return on Equity	20.00	1.03
Return on Assets	10.44	1.01
Net Margin	13.38	1.00

Sector Weightings	% of Stocks	Rel S&P 500	3 Year High Low	
↻ Info	19.20	0.96		
Software	4.03	1.17	5	3
Hardware	9.08	0.98	13	8
Media	2.65	0.70	8	3
Telecom	3.44	0.98	3	1
⊂ Service	45.87	0.99		
Health	8.53	0.71	11	9
Consumer	8.91	1.16	10	6
Business	3.49	0.83	6	3
Financial	24.94	1.12	26	22
Mfg	34.94	1.03		
Goods	7.29	0.85	8	5
Ind Mtrls	10.86	0.91	15	8
Energy	10.65	1.09	11	7
Utilities	6.14	1.75	6	2

Composition

	%
● Cash	7.3
● Stocks	92.1
● Bonds	0.0
● Other	0.7
Foreign	7.6
(% of Stock)	

MORNINGSTAR® Funds 500

T. Rowe Price Gr Stk

	Ticker	Load	NAV	Yield	Total Assets	Mstar Category
	PRGFX	None	$31.63	0.6%	$18,921 mil	Large Growth

Governance and Management

Stewardship Grade: A

Portfolio Manager(s)

Bob Smith has been at the helm of this offering since 1997. He is supported by T. Rowe Price's deep analyst bench domestically and overseas. Until recently, Smith comanaged T. Rowe Price Global Stock, explaining his penchant for investing a bit of this fund's portfolio overseas.

Strategy

Manager Bob Smith uses a growth-at-a-reasonable-price approach, paying particular attention to financially sound companies with strong management teams and ample free cash flows. His growth leanings push the fund into the large-growth camp, but the fund is more diversified by sector than its typical peer. Smith also pays more attention to foreign blue chips than most of his rivals do: The fund often has 10%-15% of assets invested abroad, considerably above the category norm.

Performance 12-31-06

	1st Qtr	2nd Qtr	3rd Qtr	4th Qtr	Total
2002	-1.41	-14.97	-15.15	8.25	-23.00
2003	-1.61	16.36	2.59	11.74	31.23
2004	1.52	1.01	-3.17	11.02	10.24
2005	-4.69	3.70	3.49	4.18	6.56
2006	3.94	-3.01	5.97	6.75	14.05

Trailing	Total Return%	+/- S&P 500	+/- Russ 1000Gr	%Rank Cat	Growth of $10,000
3 Mo	6.75	0.05	0.82	19	10,675
6 Mo	13.13	0.39	3.03	4	11,313
1 Yr	14.05	-1.74	4.98	6	11,405
3 Yr Avg	10.24	-0.20	3.37	13	13,397
5 Yr Avg	6.25	0.06	3.56	11	13,541
10 Yr Avg	9.20	0.78	3.76	8	24,112
15 Yr Avg	10.95	0.31	2.93	13	47,524

Tax Analysis	Tax-Adj Rtn%	%Rank Cat	Tax-Cost Rat	%Rank Cat
3 Yr (estimated)	9.97	11	0.24	16
5 Yr (estimated)	6.05	10	0.19	20
10 Yr (estimated)	7.56	11	1.50	75

Potential Capital Gain Exposure: 22% of assets

Morningstar's Take by Christopher Davis 11-13-06

T. Rowe Price Growth Stock has staying power.

This offering continues to roll along nicely. Whereas most large-growth funds have garnered modest gains in 2006, this offering is up 10% for the year to date through Nov. 10, 2006, placing in the category's top decile. The fund's exposure to strong-performing energy and industrials stocks has been modest, but manager Bob Smith's picks in both sectors, such as Schlumberger and BHP Billiton, have been big winners.

To be sure, not everything has come up roses. UnitedHealth Group, the fund's biggest winner in 2005, has been trouble lately. The stock has slumped in 2006 amid allegations the company wrongly backdated options for its former chief executive. UnitedHealth, along with other managed-care holdings WellPoint and Humana, were also dogged by worries that the pricing environment for the industry was becoming less favorable. Smith thinks investors have overreacted, and he's been boosting his managed-care stake.

Again and again, Smith's willingness to go against the grain has paved the way for the fund's success. Reflecting his price-conscious ethos, he shied away from racy tech and telecom fare in the late 1990s, leading to peer-beating returns in the bear market. But he delved in when the sectors bottomed in 2002, helping fuel the fund's handsome gains in 2003. Smith also began to build his managed-care weighting in 2004 when the industry was much less popular, which has hurt a bit this year but overall has given the fund a big boost.

All told, we like what we see here. Smith is a seasoned investor--he's been here since 1997--and we're impressed by what he has accomplished, delivering strong results in a diversity of environments. He gets an added edge from T. Rowe's deep crew of analysts and the fund's modest 0.70% expense ratio. If you're looking for a core growth offering, this fund remains a fine choice.

Address:	100 East Pratt Street	Minimum Purchase:	$2500	Add: $100	IRA: $1000
	Baltimore MD 21202	Min Auto Inv Plan:	$50	Add: $50	
	800-638-5660	Sales Fees:	No-load		
Web Address:	www.troweprice.com	Management Fee:	0.56%		
Inception:	04-11-50	Actual Fees:	Mgt:0.56%	Dist: —	
Advisor:	T. Rowe Price Associates, Inc.	Expense Projections:	3Yr:$230	5Yr:$401	10Yr:$894
Subadvisor:	None	Income Distrib:	Quarterly		
NTF Plans:	N/A				

Historical Profile

Return	Above Avg
Risk	Below Avg
Rating	★★★★ Highest

Investment Style: Equity Stock %

93% | 96% | 93% | 95% | 99% | 97% | 97% | 96% | 97%

▼ Manager Change
▽ Partial Manager Change

- 36.0 / 31.0
- 25.0 Growth of $10,000
- 20.0 ■ Investment Values of Fund
- 15.0 — Investment Values of S&P 500
- 10.0

Performance Quartile (within Category)

1995	1996	1997	1998	1999	2000	2001	2002	2003	2004	2005	2006	History
23.35	26.18	28.99	32.07	33.27	27.20	24.18	18.58	24.33	26.67	28.40	31.63	NAV
30.97	21.70	26.57	27.41	22.15	0.27	-9.79	-23.00	31.23	10.24	6.56	14.05	Total Return %
-6.61	-1.26	-6.79	-1.17	1.11	9.37	2.10	-0.90	2.55	-0.64	1.65	-1.74	+/-S&P 500
-6.21	-1.42	-3.92	-11.30	-11.01	22.69	10.63	4.88	1.48	3.94	1.30	4.98	+/-Russ 1000Gr
1.23	0.81	0.76	0.86	0.31	0.21	0.29	0.17	0.27	0.62	0.07	0.67	Income Return %
29.74	20.89	25.81	26.55	21.84	0.06	-10.08	-23.17	30.96	9.62	6.49	13.38	Capital Return %
56	33	48	63	79	12	8	23	29	28	47	6	Total Rtn % Rank Cat
0.23	0.19	0.20	0.25	0.10	0.07	0.08	0.04	0.05	0.15	0.02	0.19	Income $
0.97	2.06	3.87	4.27	5.42	6.28	0.27	0.00	0.00	0.00	0.00	0.57	Capital Gains $
0.80	0.77	0.75	0.74	0.74	0.73	0.77	0.77	0.76	0.74	0.72	—	Expense Ratio %
1.09	0.74	0.75	0.67	0.31	0.20	0.34	0.23	0.29	0.72	0.42	—	Income Ratio %
42	49	41	55	56	74	64	47	35	31	36	—	Turnover Rate %
2,762	3,431	3,988	5,041	5,672	5,428	4,685	3,728	5,645	8,174	11,149	15,941	Net Assets $mil

Rating and Risk

Time Period	Load-Adj Return %	Morningstar Rtn vs Cat	Morningstar Risk vs Cat	Morningstar Risk-Adj Rating
1 Yr	14.05			
3 Yr	10.24	+Avg	-Avg	★★★★★
5 Yr	6.25	+Avg	Avg	★★★★
10 Yr	9.20	+Avg	-Avg	★★★★★
Incept	9.42			

Other Measures	Standard Index S&P 500	Best Fit Index Russ 1000Gr
Alpha	-1.1	3.3
Beta	1.15	0.96
R-Squared	91	94
Standard Deviation	8.35	
Mean	10.24	
Sharpe Ratio	0.83	

Portfolio Analysis 09-30-06

Share change since 06-06 Total Stocks:121	Sector	PE	Tot Ret%	% Assets
⊕ General Electric Company	Ind Mtrls	20.0	9.35	4.10
⊕ UnitedHealth Group, Inc.	Health	20.8	-13.49	2.44
⊕ UBS AG	Financial		29.62	2.18
⊕ Schlumberger, Ltd.	Energy	22.3	31.07	1.90
⊖ Wal-Mart Stores, Inc.	Consumer	16.9	0.13	1.79
⊖ Microsoft Corporation	Software	23.8	15.83	1.69
⊕ American Express Company	Financial	20.9	19.09	1.66
⊕ Accenture, Ltd.	Business	22.0	29.32	1.66
⊕ SLM Corporation	Financial	14.1	-9.76	1.63
Citigroup, Inc.	Financial	13.1	19.55	1.62
⊖ Kohl's Corporation	Consumer	22.6	40.80	1.60
⊖ American International G	Financial	17.0	6.05	1.59
⊖ Danaher Corporation	Ind Mtrls	22.0	30.02	1.58
⊖ Caremark RX, Inc.	Health	23.6	10.90	1.53
⊕ Amgen, Inc.	Health	29.1	-13.38	1.45
⊕ Google, Inc.	Business	61.5	11.00	1.34
⊕ Automatic Data Processin	Business	24.9	9.11	1.22
⊕ Yahoo, Inc.	Media	35.4	-34.81	1.21
☼ TOTAL	Energy		—	1.17
⊕ State Street Corporation	Financial	22.4	23.22	1.14

Current Investment Style

Value Blnd Growth — Large Mid Small

Market Cap	%
Giant	44.4
Large	44.8
Mid	10.9
Small	0.0
Micro	0.0

Avg $mil: 40,325

Value Measures		Rel Category
Price/Earnings	18.17	0.94
Price/Book	3.16	0.95
Price/Sales	1.88	0.97
Price/Cash Flow	11.77	1.03
Dividend Yield %	1.17	1.14

Growth Measures	%	Rel Category
Long-Term Erngs	14.71	1.03
Book Value	12.72	1.10
Sales	13.60	1.17
Cash Flow	14.39	0.86
Historical Erngs	24.28	1.06

Profitability	%	Rel Category
Return on Equity	21.15	1.04
Return on Assets	11.37	1.03
Net Margin	15.16	1.06

Sector Weightings	% of Stocks	Rel S&P 500	3 Year High Low
ⓘ Info	23.64	1.18	
🖥 Software	4.59	1.33	8 5
💻 Hardware	10.43	1.13	12 8
🎤 Media	4.29	1.13	10 4
📱 Telecom	4.33	1.23	4 3
🔧 Service	56.01	1.21	
🩺 Health	18.14	1.50	18 13
🛒 Consumer	11.14	1.46	15 11
💼 Business	5.92	1.40	7 6
💲 Financial	20.81	0.93	21 18
🏭 Mfg	20.36	0.60	
🛠 Goods	5.04	0.59	6 4
⚙ Ind Mtrls	8.99	0.75	10 6
🔥 Energy	6.33	0.65	6 4
💡 Utilities	0.00	0.00	0 0

Composition

● Cash	2.8	
● Stocks	97.3	
● Bonds	0.0	
● Other	0.0	
Foreign	15.3	(% of Stock)

T. Rowe Price Health Sci

Ticker PRHSX	**Load** None	**NAV** $26.13	**Yield** 0.0%

Total Assets $1,716 mil   **Mstar Category** Specialty-Health

✔ **Analyst Pick**

Governance and Management

Stewardship Grade: A

Portfolio Manager(s)

Kris Jenner, a physician by training, has been at the fund's helm since February 2000. Prior to that, he served as T. Rowe Price's biotechnology analyst for two years. Four analysts support Jenner in running the portfolio. Jenner says he keeps his entire retirement account invested in this offering.

Strategy

Kris Jenner emphasizes smaller-cap pharmaceutical and biotech stocks, which he thinks have the brightest long-term growth prospects in the health-care sector. Recognizing that such names are often quite volatile, Jenner has also given the fund considerable exposure to big-cap drugmakers and health-care service companies. Even so, with a hefty biotech stake and a market cap far below the category average, the fund is more adventuresome than most diversified health-care offerings.

Performance 12-31-06

	1st Qtr	2nd Qtr	3rd Qtr	4th Qtr	Total
2002	-5.88	-16.93	-9.24	1.82	-27.74
2003	4.34	18.43	1.90	9.90	37.49
2004	8.62	2.31	-4.24	8.86	15.84
2005	-9.65	7.76	11.64	4.45	13.53
2006	5.31	-6.02	4.55	5.90	9.58

Trailing	Total Return%	+/- S&P 500	+/- DJ Hlthcare	%Rank Cat	Growth of $10,000
3 Mo	5.90	-0.80	4.19	8	10,590
6 Mo	10.73	-2.01	0.06	9	11,073
1 Yr	9.58	-6.21	2.70	17	10,958
3 Yr Avg	12.95	2.51	6.37	8	14,410
5 Yr Avg	7.44	1.25	4.70	19	14,316
10 Yr Avg	12.45	4.03	2.80	8	32,329
15 Yr Avg	—	—	—	—	—

Tax Analysis	Tax-Adj Rtn%	%Rank Cat	Tax-Cost Rat	%Rank Cat
3 Yr (estimated)	12.23	7	0.64	36
5 Yr (estimated)	7.03	14	0.38	34
10 Yr (estimated)	11.21	9	1.10	64

Potential Capital Gain Exposure: 27% of assets

Morningstar's Take by Christopher Davis 12-21-06

T. Rowe Price Health Sciences continues to demonstrate its appeal.

Although its returns haven't exactly jumped off the page in 2006, this offering has continued to outpace the competition. That's despite the fact the stars haven't exactly been aligned with its relatively bold approach. Investors fled from wild-and-woolly biotech to steady-Eddie pharmaceuticals in the second quarter, but reflecting manager Kris Jenner's preference for faster-growing names, the fund's stake in large-cap drug stocks is modest. Instead, Jenner keeps an outsized slice of his portfolio in biotechnology stocks (at about 40% of assets, the fund's weighting is considerably above the health-care category norm), which should have taken a heavy toll on returns. Jenner's ongoing bet on HMOs should have hurt, too, amid mounting concerns over slower premium growth, rising costs, and allegations of improper issuance of stock options at industry bellwether UnitedHealth Group.

The fund has certainly felt the sting from

faltering managed-care holdings like UnitedHealth and Cigna. But Jenner has averted the worst of the biotech storm with good stock-picking. Top-holding Gilead Sciences, for instance, is up nicely thanks to the ongoing strength of its HIV-drug franchise. Smaller-cap biotech names like Vertex Pharmaceuticals have also turned in handsome gains, pushing the fund to the health-care category's top quartile, albeit with a modest 3% return.

What's impressed us most about Jenner is his ability to deliver the goods in different types of markets. The fund held its ground in adverse environments for its style, as it did this year as well as in 2001 and 2002. But it has also excelled in better times--witness the double-digit gains it's enjoyed in recent years. In addition to Jenner's skill, the fund gets an added edge from moderate costs. This remains a top-flight choice for health-care exposure.

Address:	100 East Pratt Street Baltimore MD 21202 800-638-5660	Minimum Purchase:	$2500 Add: $100 IRA: $1000
Web Address:	www.troweprice.com	Min Auto Inv Plan:	$50 Add: $50
Inception:	12-29-95*	Sales Fees:	No-load
Advisor:	T. Rowe Price Associates, Inc.	Management Fee:	0.66%
Subadvisor:	None	Actual Fees:	Mgt:0.66% Dist: —
		Expense Projections:	3Yr:$290 5Yr:$504 10Yr:$1120
NTF Plans:	N/A	Income Distrib:	Annually

MORNINGSTAR® Funds 500

Historical Profile

Return	Above Avg
Risk	Above Avg
Rating	★★★★ Above Avg

Investment Style: Equity, Stock %

92% 95% 94% 98% 99% 98% 96% 99% 99%

▼ Manager Change
▽ Partial Manager Change

Growth of $10,000
━ Investment Values of Fund
─ Investment Values of S&P 500

31.0 24.0 17.0 10.0

Performance Quartile (within Category)

1995	1996	1997	1998	1999	2000	2001	2002	2003	2004	2005	2006	History
10.00	12.27	13.66	16.01	15.93	21.70	20.08	14.51	19.95	23.11	25.07	26.13	NAV
0.00*	26.75	19.41	22.37	7.97	52.19	-5.97	-27.74	37.49	15.84	13.53	9.58	Total Return %
—	3.79	-13.95	-6.21	-13.07	61.29	5.92	-5.64	8.81	4.96	8.62	-6.21	+/-S&P 500
—	8.09	-17.47	-16.72	12.00	14.35	6.87	-6.93	18.06	11.29	5.21	2.70	+/-DJ Hlthcare
—	0.00	0.00	0.00	0.00	0.00	0.00	0.00	0.00	0.00	0.00	0.00	Income Return %
—	26.75	19.41	22.37	7.97	52.19	-5.97	-27.74	37.49	15.84	13.53	9.58	Capital Return %
—	1	61	51	54	50	29	63	21	8	22	17	Total Rtn % Rank Cat
0.00	0.00	0.00	0.00	0.00	0.00	0.00	0.00	0.00	0.00	0.00	0.00	Income $
0.00	0.40	0.97	0.66	1.26	2.48	0.31	0.00	0.00	0.00	1.16	1.34	Capital Gains $
—	—	1.35	1.18	1.16	1.11	0.98	1.02	1.04	1.00	0.93	—	Expense Ratio %
—	—	-0.32	-0.21	-0.25	-0.25	-0.22	-0.60	-0.64	-0.64	-0.58	—	Income Ratio %
—	—	133	104	86	82	111	75	63	45	44	—	Turnover Rate %
—	—	194	271	317	303	972	961	678	1,028	1,331	1,716	Net Assets $mil

Rating and Risk

Time Period	Load-Adj Return %	Morningstar Rtn vs Cat	Morningstar Risk vs Cat	Morningstar Risk-Adj Rating
1 Yr	9.58			
3 Yr	12.95	High	+Avg	★★★★
5 Yr	7.44	+Avg	Avg	★★★★
10 Yr	12.45	+Avg	+Avg	★★★
Incept	13.67			

Other Measures	Standard Index S&P 500	Best Fit Index Merrill Lynch Convert
Alpha	2.1	5.0
Beta	1.09	1.38
R-Squared	40	52
Standard Deviation	11.83	
Mean	12.95	
Sharpe Ratio	0.82	

Portfolio Analysis 09-30-06

Share change since 06-06 Total Stocks:167	Sector	PE	Tot Ret%	% Assets
⊖ Gilead Sciences, Inc.	Health	40.6	23.51	4.65
⊖ Cephalon, Inc.	Health	28.6	8.76	3.71
⊖ Genentech, Inc.	Health	48.7	-12.29	3.33
⊖ Amgen, Inc.	Health	29.1	-13.38	2.90
UnitedHealth Group, Inc.	Health	20.8	-13.49	2.74
⊕ Roche Holding	Health	—	—	2.24
⊕ WellPoint, Inc.	Health	17.2	-1.38	2.20
⊕ Sepracor, Inc.	Health	NMF	19.34	2.11
⊕ OSI Pharmaceuticals, Inc	Health	—	24.75	1.86
⊖ Medicines	Health	—	81.78	1.83
⊖ Cigna Corporation	Health	13.3	17.89	1.75
Wyeth	Health	17.2	12.88	1.68
⊕ Elan Corporation PLC ADR	Health	—	5.89	1.62
⊕ Aetna, Inc.	Health	14.1	-8.34	1.43
⊖ Davita, Inc.	Health	21.1	12.32	1.41
⊖ Caremark RX, Inc.	Health	23.6	10.90	1.36
⊖ Amylin Pharmaceuticals	Health	—	-9.64	1.33
⊕ Novartis AG ADR	Health	22.2	11.29	1.23
⊕ Vertex Pharmaceuticals	Health	—	35.24	1.22
⊕ Myogen, Inc.	Health	—	—	1.20

Current Investment Style

Value Blnd Growth — Large/Mid/Small

Market Cap	%
Giant	20.1
Large	26.4
Mid	30.1
Small	18.2
Micro	5.3
Avg $mil:	8,193

Value Measures		Rel Category
Price/Earnings	23.15	1.02
Price/Book	3.40	0.94
Price/Sales	2.01	0.76
Price/Cash Flow	15.25	0.95
Dividend Yield %	0.45	0.54

Growth Measures	%	Rel Category
Long-Term Erngs	15.46	1.05
Book Value	9.75	1.15
Sales	15.32	1.28
Cash Flow	10.66	0.96
Historical Erngs	18.29	1.02

Profitability	%	Rel Category
Return on Equity	9.58	0.80
Return on Assets	0.55	0.14
Net Margin	6.53	0.60

Industry Weightings	% of Stocks	Rel Cat
Biotech	43.1	1.3
Drugs	14.9	0.5
Mgd Care	18.0	1.6
Hospitals	2.5	2.1
Other HC Srv	2.0	1.4
Diagnostics	1.7	1.3
Equipment	10.2	0.8
Good/Srv	3.8	1.1
Other	3.8	1.3

Composition

● Cash		0.1
● Stocks		99.3
● Bonds		0.0
● Other		0.6
Foreign		15.3
(% of Stock)		

T. Rowe Price Hi-Yld

✓ Analyst Pick		

	Ticker	Load	NAV	Yield	SEC Yield	Total Assets	Mstar Category
	PRHYX	Closed	$7.04	7.3%	6.94%	$4,802 mil	High Yield Bond

Governance and Management

Stewardship Grade: A

Portfolio Manager(s)

Mark Vaselkiv took over this fund in 1996, and it has performed very well on his watch. He is backed by a 15-member team that includes analysts and traders. The team works closely with T. Rowe Price's equity-research staff.

Strategy

Manager Mark Vaselkiv keeps this fund well diversified, which reduces its issue-specific risk. Vaselkiv also tends to favor less-speculative bonds than many of his peers, although he has the flexibility to dip into beaten-down issues and sectors. In 2003, for example, he increased the fund's exposure to CCC rated issues, which gave the fund a lift during the market's rally. More recently, he has shifted back into BB and B rated issues.

Historical Profile

Return	Above Avg
Risk	Below Avg
Rating	★★★★ Above Avg

36	48	45	48	36	24	18	18

Growth of $10,000
— Investment Values of Fund
— Investment Values of LB Aggr

Investment Style
Fixed Income
Income Rtn %Rank Cat

▼ Manager Change
▽ Partial Manager Change

Performance Quartile (within Category)

1995	1996	1997	1998	1999	2000	2001	2002	2003	2004	2005	2006	History
8.19	8.34	8.74	8.36	7.94	6.94	6.67	6.27	7.06	7.20	6.91	7.04	NAV
15.77	11.58	14.46	4.46	4.18	-3.25	6.10	3.08	22.53	10.33	3.41	9.75	Total Return %
-2.70	7.95	4.81	-4.23	5.00	-14.88	-2.34	-7.17	18.43	5.99	0.98	5.42	+/-LB Aggr
-1.62	-0.84	1.83	3.88	0.90	1.96	0.32	-0.03	-5.40	-1.63	1.15	-2.18	+/-CSFB Glb HY
9.99	9.58	9.45	9.08	9.47	10.03	10.32	9.24	9.44	8.00	7.53	7.73	Income Return %
5.78	2.00	5.01	-4.62	-5.29	-13.28	-4.22	-6.16	13.09	2.33	-4.12	2.02	Capital Return %
80	82	21	11	52	22	22	12	64	38	23	55	Total Rtn % Rank Cat
0.74	0.75	0.76	0.76	0.76	0.76	0.59	0.57	0.54	0.52	0.52	Income $
0.00	0.00	0.00	0.00	0.00	0.00	0.00	0.00	0.01	0.00	0.00	Capital Gains $
0.88	0.85	0.84	0.81	0.82	0.83	0.82	0.83	0.81	0.78	0.77	0.77	Expense Ratio %
9.27	8.89	9.15	8.78	8.93	9.60	10.16	9.56	9.09	8.07	7.18	7.29	Income Ratio %
74	100	111	130	96	76	80	71	60	74	67	65	Turnover Rate %
1,227	1,325	1,572	1,704	1,682	1,447	1,577	1,940	3,197	3,486	3,158	3,809	Net Assets $mil

Performance 12-31-06

	1st Qtr	2nd Qtr	3rd Qtr	4th Qtr	Total
2002	2.32	-2.76	-1.02	4.67	3.08
2003	5.44	7.36	2.28	5.84	22.53
2004	1.75	-0.43	4.19	4.51	10.33
2005	-1.15	1.75	1.92	0.88	3.41
2006	2.37	-0.18	3.52	3.75	9.75

Trailing	Total Return%	+/- LB Aggr	+/- CSFB Glb HY	%Rank Cat	Growth of $10,000
3 Mo	3.75	2.51	-0.70	62	10,375
6 Mo	7.40	2.31	-0.75	52	10,740
1 Yr	9.75	5.42	-2.18	55	10,975
3 Yr Avg	7.79	4.09	-0.83	36	12,524
5 Yr Avg	9.60	4.54	-1.47	29	15,814
10 Yr Avg	7.30	1.06	0.21	12	20,230
15 Yr Avg	8.41	1.91	-0.49	16	33,577

Tax Analysis	Tax-Adj Rtn%	%Rank Cat	Tax-Cost Rat	%Rank Cat
3 Yr (estimated)	4.96	33	2.63	65
5 Yr (estimated)	6.48	29	2.85	69
10 Yr (estimated)	3.82	8	3.24	45

Potential Capital Gain Exposure: -5% of assets

Rating and Risk

Time Period	Load-Adj Return %	Morningstar Rtn vs Cat	Morningstar Risk vs Cat	Morningstar Risk-Adj Rating
1 Yr	9.75			
3 Yr	7.79	Avg	-Avg	★★★★
5 Yr	9.60	+Avg	-Avg	★★★★
10 Yr	7.30	+Avg	-Avg	★★★★
Incept	8.96			

Other Measures	Standard Index LB Aggr	Best Fit Index CSFB Glb HY
Alpha	4.2	-0.5
Beta	0.31	0.94
R-Squared	9	95

Standard Deviation	3.47
Mean	7.79
Sharpe Ratio	1.26

Morningstar's Take by Arijit Dutta 12-18-06

T. Rowe Price High Yield has had a lackluster year, but its case remains solid as ever.

This fund hasn't quite made the best of the ongoing junk-bond rally in 2006. Manager Mark Vaselkiv has taken a somewhat guarded approach lately, as indicated by the portfolio's relatively light stake in the lowest-rated bonds. Markets haven't rewarded that stance, however, since riskier fare has especially thrived in the boom. Vaselkiv has also passed up on a number of private-equity debt issues (firms that sell such debt use the proceeds to buy out public companies) that have tremendously appreciated. Those misses have meant a middling-at-best showing for the fund this year.

Vaselkiv's approach actually makes sense in this environment. He hasn't been overly conservative, but Vaselkiv has avoided sectors where he has seen signs of market excess. For example, bonds issued by several retailers that were taken private this year have thrived. Vaselkiv has stayed away, however, since deeply indebted retailers tend to fare very badly when economic conditions worsen. Instead, he has bought debt in companies that have relatively stable cash flows, such as Yellow Pages publisher R. H. Donnelley. Conditions in the high-yield market have indeed been benign for several years now, causing many lenders to rush in. We appreciate that Vaselkiv is being more circumspect.

His calculated approach has served shareholders very well in past market downturns. For example, the fund escaped the high-yield market's meltdowns in 2000 and 2002, thanks in part to Vaselkiv's avoidance of high-flying telecom issues that subsequently went bust. Even this year, the fund held up far better than its rivals when markets ran into a spot of trouble during a month-long period in May and June. Vaselkiv's ability to navigate this risky asset class has delivered plenty of upside in the long run, without exposing investors to undue risk.

Portfolio Analysis 09-30-06

Total Fixed-Income:388

	Date of Maturity	Amount $000	Value $000	% Net Assets
Gmac 8%	11-01-31	89,675	94,383	2.10
Ford Mtr Cr FRN	04-15-12	60,625	63,504	1.41
Windstream 144A 8.625%	08-01-16	53,850	57,620	1.28
Nrg Engy 7.375%	02-01-16	45,750	45,407	1.01
Mirant North Amer 7.375%	12-31-13	41,200	41,200	0.92
R H Donnelley 8.875%	01-15-16	40,650	40,955	0.91
Nextel Comms 6.875%	10-31-13	37,704	38,470	0.85
Gsc Hldgs 8%	10-01-12	37,125	38,146	0.85
Rogers Wireless 8%	12-15-12	33,325	35,533	0.79
Host Marriott L P 6.75%	06-01-16	34,780	34,258	0.76
Nordic Tel 144A 8.875%	05-01-16	32,100	33,825	0.75
Chesapeake Engy 6.5%	08-15-17	32,655	30,532	0.68
QWEST	10-01-14	29,375	30,366	0.67
Educ Mgmt 144A 10.25%	06-01-16	28,275	28,982	0.64
Bombardier 144A 6.75%	05-01-12	30,175	28,817	0.64
Sungard Data Sys 9.125%	08-15-13	26,475	27,435	0.61
Sierra Pac Res New 8.625	03-15-14	25,070	27,170	0.60
Cinemark	03-15-14	29,755	23,804	0.53
Charter Commun Bank Debt	04-28-13	23,500	23,618	0.52
General Mtrs Pfd	03-06-32	1,167	23,480	0.52

Current Investment Style

Duration: Short Int Long
Quality: High Med Low

1 figure provided by fund

Avg Eff Duration[1]	4.4 Yrs
Avg Eff Maturity	7.6 Yrs
Avg Credit Quality	B
Avg Wtd Coupon	7.94%
Avg Wtd Price	101.97% of par

Coupon Range	% of Bonds	Rel Cat
0% PIK	5.4	1.0
0% to 8%	50.0	1.0
8% to 11%	44.0	1.0
11% to 14%	6.0	1.4
More than 14%	0.0	0.0

1.00=Category Average

Credit Analysis	% bonds 09-30-06		
AAA	0	BB	32
AA	0	B	57
A	0	Below B	5
BBB	2	NR/NA	4

Sector Breakdown	% of assets
US Treasuries	0
TIPS	0
US Agency	0
Mortgage Pass-Throughs	0
Mortgage CMO	0
Mortgage ARM	0
US Corporate	88
Asset-Backed	0
Convertible	0
Municipal	0
Corporate Inflation-Protected	0
Foreign Corporate	8
Foreign Govt	0

Composition			
Cash	3.5	Bonds	88.3
Stocks	2.0	Other	6.1

Special Securities	
Restricted/Illiquid Secs	16
Exotic Mortgage-Backed	0
Emerging-Markets Secs	0
Options/Futures/Warrants	No

Address:	100 East Pratt Street Baltimore MD 21202 800-638-5660
Web Address:	www.troweprice.com
Inception:	12-31-84
Advisor:	T. Rowe Price Associates, Inc.
Subadvisor:	None
NTF Plans:	Federated Tr NTF

Minimum Purchase:	Closed	Add: —	IRA: —
Min Auto Inv Plan:	Closed	Add: —	
Sales Fees:	No-load, 1.00%R		
Management Fee:	0.61%		
Actual Fees:	Mgt:0.61%	Dist: —	
Expense Projections:	3Yr:$246	5Yr:$428	10Yr:$954
Income Distrib:	Monthly		

T. Rowe Price Intl Bd

	Analyst Pick	Ticker	Load	NAV	Yield	SEC Yield	Total Assets	Mstar Category
	✓	RPIBX	None	$9.69	3.2%	3.62%	$2,145 mil	World Bond

Governance and Management

Stewardship Grade: B

Portfolio Manager(s)

Ian Kelson is the lead manager at this fund, backed by comanagers Chris Rothery and Mike Conelius. Kelson joined T. Rowe Price in 2000 as head of fixed-income investment. Rothery has been with the fund since 1994; Conelius has been around since 1995. The three also manage T. Rowe Price Emerging Markets Bond, which has a solid long-term record.

Strategy

This fund provides investors with diversification from U.S. markets. The managers establish duration positioning and country exposure relative to the Lehman Brothers Global Aggregate Ex-USD Bond Index. The fund will venture into emerging markets and high-yield corporate debt, but management stashes the bulk of its assets in government bonds from developed countries.

Historical Profile

Return	Average
Risk	Above Avg
Rating	★★★ Neutral

Investment Style: Fixed Income
Income Rtn %Rank Cat

▼ Manager Change
▽ Partial Manager Change

Growth of $10,000
— Investment Values of Fund
— Investment Values of LB Aggr

Performance Quartile (within Category)

1995	1996	1997	1998	1999	2000	2001	2002	2003	2004	2005	2006	History
10.46	10.46	9.58	10.46	9.16	8.47	7.86	9.29	10.25	10.69	9.40	9.69	NAV
20.31	7.14	-3.17	15.03	-7.86	-3.13	-3.41	21.80	18.78	11.41	-8.18	7.55	Total Return %
1.84	3.51	-12.82	6.34	-7.04	-14.76	-11.85	11.55	14.68	7.07	-10.61	3.22	+/-LB Aggr
0.76	3.06	1.09	-2.76	-2.79	-0.50	0.13	-0.19	0.26	-0.73	1.02	0.61	+/-SB Wld Govt
6.86	5.92	5.16	5.47	3.76	4.39	3.90	3.25	2.78	2.50	2.55	3.44	Income Return %
13.45	1.22	-8.33	9.56	-11.62	-7.52	-7.31	18.55	16.00	8.91	-10.73	4.11	Capital Return %
35	69	85	16	86	83	83	10	24	19	77	20	Total Rtn % Rank Cat
0.62	0.60	0.53	0.51	0.38	0.39	0.32	0.25	0.25	0.25	0.26	0.32	Income $
0.12	0.11	0.02	0.00	0.11	0.00	0.00	0.00	0.00	0.44	0.17	0.09	Capital Gains $
0.90	0.87	0.86	0.88	0.90	0.91	0.95	0.93	0.91	0.88	0.86	—	Expense Ratio %
6.10	5.86	5.38	5.19	3.93	4.76	3.98	3.01	2.58	2.46	2.67	—	Income Ratio %
237	234	156	129	95	161	108	114	39	70	104	—	Turnover Rate %
1,016	969	826	926	779	753	762	1,058	1,303	1,658	1,595	2,025	Net Assets $mil

Performance 12-31-06

	1st Qtr	2nd Qtr	3rd Qtr	4th Qtr	Total
2002	-1.89	13.56	2.72	6.44	21.80
2003	3.65	5.05	2.76	6.16	18.78
2004	1.41	-3.23	2.96	10.25	11.41
2005	-3.27	-2.50	-0.42	-2.23	-8.18
2006	0.47	3.10	0.88	2.92	7.55

Trailing	Total Return%	+/- LB Aggr	+/- SB Wld Govt	%Rank Cat	Growth of $10,000
3 Mo	2.92	1.68	0.83	23	10,292
6 Mo	3.83	-1.26	0.84	34	10,383
1 Yr	7.55	3.22	0.61	20	10,755
3 Yr Avg	3.23	-0.47	0.35	54	11,001
5 Yr Avg	9.74	4.68	0.24	20	15,916
10 Yr Avg	4.33	-1.91	-0.37	71	15,279
15 Yr Avg	5.94	-0.56	-0.41	67	23,763

Tax Analysis	Tax-Adj Rtn%	%Rank Cat	Tax-Cost Rat	%Rank Cat
3 Yr (estimated)	1.51	53	1.67	55
5 Yr (estimated)	7.84	17	1.73	50
10 Yr (estimated)	2.45	68	1.80	31

Potential Capital Gain Exposure: 4% of assets

Morningstar's Take by Arijit Dutta 12-22-06

T. Rowe Price International Bond is a bold and effective choice.

This fund is among the spicier offerings in its group. While most world-bond peers stick mainly with large, developed countries, management here looks more freely for valuation and return opportunities in markets beyond. For example, earlier this year, the portfolio's small stakes in emerging markets such as Turkey and Brazil added up to a sizable total stake of 9%, nearly twice the category average.

That approach courts volatility. Emerging markets rallied on to start the year, allowing the fund to solidly lead the pack. However, investors fled risky assets during a month-long period in May and June due to various macroeconomic worries, causing sharp losses here.

Management handled the problems with poise, however. Lead manager Ian Kelson thought investors panicked unduly during the correction, overlooking the pockets of strength in emerging markets. For example, Kelson added to the portfolio's stake in Brazil during the sell-off because he continued to see all-round economic strength and sound policy in that country. True, the sharp uptick in Turkey's inflation outlook (which caused the bonds to experience an especially deep correction) did catch the fund by surprise. But Kelson held on, encouraged by the Turkish authorities' prompt response to the inflation threat.

We think Kelson and team can manage the risks here. They have shown conviction in their analysis by not selling amid the market frenzy. Also, we continue to see signs that management will heed valuations. For example, Kelson has reduced the portfolio's positions in Brazil and Turkey after emerging-markets bonds resumed their rally following the May-June hiccup.

Overall, we think this is a useful fund for those looking to diversify domestic fixed-income assets.

Address:	100 East Pratt Street Baltimore MD 21202 800-638-5660
Web Address:	www.troweprice.com
Inception:	09-10-86
Advisor:	T. Rowe Price Associates, Inc.
Subadvisor:	None
NTF Plans:	N/A

Minimum Purchase:	$2500	Add: $100	IRA: $1000
Min Auto Inv Plan:	$50	Add: $50	
Sales Fees:	No-load, 2.00%R		
Management Fee:	0.66%		
Actual Fees:	Mgt:0.66%	Dist: —	
Expense Projections:	3Yr:$274	5Yr:$477	10Yr:$1061
Income Distrib:	Monthly		

Rating and Risk

Time Period	Load-Adj Return %	Morningstar Rtn vs Cat	Morningstar Risk vs Cat	Morningstar Risk-Adj Rating
1 Yr	7.55			
3 Yr	3.23	Avg	+Avg	★★★
5 Yr	9.74	+Avg	+Avg	★★★★
10 Yr	4.33	-Avg	+Avg	★★
Incept	7.31			

Other Measures	Standard Index LB Aggr	Best Fit Index SB Wld Govt
Alpha	-0.2	0.3
Beta	0.88	0.94
R-Squared	18	98
Standard Deviation	6.73	
Mean	3.23	
Sharpe Ratio	0.03	

Portfolio Analysis 09-30-06

Total Fixed-Income:150	Date of Maturity	Amount $000	Value $000	% Net Assets
United Kingdom (Governme	03-07-11	55,195	101,361	5.05
Germany (Federal Republi	07-04-10	73,300	98,256	4.90
Poland (Republic Of) 6%	11-24-10	166,375	54,363	2.71
United Kingdom (Governme	06-07-32	22,820	43,332	2.16
Germany (Federal Republi	01-04-37	33,400	43,108	2.15
Netherlands (Kingdom Of)	07-15-08	33,000	43,034	2.15
Japan (Government Of) 1.	03-21-11	4,934,901	42,463	2.12
Spain (Kingdom Of) 6%	01-31-08	32,164	42,044	2.10
Italy (Republic Of) 6%	11-01-07	31,788	41,337	2.06
Japan(Govt) Frn Bds 10ju	10-18-12	4,890,082	41,131	2.05
France(Govt Of) 5.75%	10-25-32	23,794	38,993	1.94
Japan (Government Of) 1.	12-20-13	4,293,250	36,137	1.80
Belgium (Kingdom Of) 4.2	09-28-13	23,850	31,317	1.56
France (Republic Of) 5.5	04-25-29	19,749	30,878	1.54
Kreditanstalt Fur Wieder	12-07-10	16,246	30,071	1.50
France (Republic Of) 4.7	10-25-12	20,900	28,074	1.40
Japan (Government Of) 1.	03-20-25	3,042,050	24,943	1.24
Japan (Government Of) 1%	12-20-12	2,973,950	24,784	1.24
France (Republic Of) 4%	10-25-14	18,900	24,488	1.22
Japan 50%	06-10-15	2,920,920	23,640	1.18

Current Investment Style

Duration: Short Int Long
Quality: High Med Low

1 figure provided by fund

Avg Eff Duration[1]	4.9 Yrs
Avg Eff Maturity	7.8 Yrs
Avg Credit Quality	AA
Avg Wtd Coupon	4.97%
Avg Wtd Price	102.26% of par

Coupon Range	% of Bonds	Rel Cat
0% PIK	0.0	0.0
0% to 6%	87.5	1.1
6% to 8%	6.7	0.5
8% to 10%	3.0	0.7
More than 10%	2.8	1.2

1.00=Category Average

Credit Analysis		% bonds 09-30-06	
AAA	57	BB	4
AA	13	B	0
A	22	Below B	0
BBB	5	NR/NA	0

Sector Breakdown % of assets

US Treasuries	—
TIPS	—
US Agency	—
Mortgage Pass-Throughs	—
Mortgage CMO	—
Mortgage ARM	—
US Corporate	—
Asset-Backed	—
Convertible	—
Municipal	—
Corporate Inflation-Protected	—
Foreign Corporate	—
Foreign Govt	—

Composition

Cash	22.1	Bonds	75.2
Stocks	0.0	Other	2.8

Special Securities

Restricted/Illiquid Secs	Trace
Exotic Mortgage-Backed	0
Emerging-Markets Secs	0
Options/Futures/Warrants	No

MORNINGSTAR® Funds 500

T. Rowe Price Intl Disc

	Ticker	Load	NAV	Yield	Total Assets	Mstar Category
	PRIDX	None	$47.48	0.6%	$2,311 mil	Foreign Small/Mid Growth

Governance and Management

Stewardship Grade: B

Portfolio Manager(s)

Justin Thomson ran small-cap money for LGT Asset Management for several years before taking the helm at this fund in June 1998. Comanagers Mark Edwards and Frances Dydasco are experienced Asia investors, and Campbell Gunn specializes in Japan. The comanagers also run their own regional funds at T. Rowe Price.

Strategy

Manager Justin Thomson focuses on firms with market caps between $250 million and $3 billion that enjoy rapid earnings growth, robust sales growth, and strong returns on equity. Thomson likes to focus on countries that have favorable regulations that promote new businesses and give them a fighting chance against large corporations. The firm has frequently employed fair-value pricing in an effort to limit any potential damage to long-term shareholders from short-term fund traders.

Performance 12-31-06

	1st Qtr	2nd Qtr	3rd Qtr	4th Qtr	Total
2002	-1.30	-2.85	-18.05	6.57	-16.27
2003	-3.49	25.03	18.27	15.82	65.29
2004	8.60	0.59	-0.45	13.80	23.76
2005	2.30	0.03	16.38	7.38	27.89
2006	14.17	-3.88	3.86	12.00	27.65

Trailing	Total Return%	+/- MSCI EAFE	+/- MSCI Wd xUS	%Rank Cat	Growth of $10,000
3 Mo	12.00	1.65	1.88	78	11,200
6 Mo	16.31	1.62	2.09	52	11,631
1 Yr	27.65	1.31	1.94	45	12,765
3 Yr Avg	26.42	6.49	6.32	39	20,204
5 Yr Avg	22.83	7.85	7.58	30	27,959
10 Yr Avg	16.33	8.62	8.37	20	45,386
15 Yr Avg	12.96	5.10	4.92	1	62,211

Tax Analysis	Tax-Adj Rtn%	%Rank Cat	Tax-Cost Rat	%Rank Cat
3 Yr (estimated)	25.33	30	0.86	32
5 Yr (estimated)	22.15	29	0.55	40
10 Yr (estimated)	14.77	9	1.34	60

Potential Capital Gain Exposure: 26% of assets

Morningstar's Take by Arijit Dutta 12-21-06

T. Rowe Price International Discovery has its risks, but it is in capable hands.

Even by foreign small- and mid-growth standards, this is an aggressive fund. The portfolio's average market cap of $1 billion is half the category average, which shows management's focus on the smallest companies in the world. Moreover, management's emphasis on "hidden gem" small-growth stocks often leads to significant portfolio stakes in far-flung emerging markets. For example, the portfolio had a 10% stake in India as of March this year, while the typical rival owns almost nothing in that country (management has since cut the stake to 4%). Smaller stocks are inherently volatile, and emerging markets have substantial macroeconomic risks, so this clearly isn't a fund for conservative investors.

That said, the fund has a decent record of keeping volatility in check. Most recently, the fund survived the sharp market correction in May to June of this year, when riskier assets such as small-cap

and emerging-markets stocks took especially severe pounding. To be sure, the fund's 19% loss during that month-long period was no picnic. However, it still lost less than a significant majority of rivals. Management took timely profits in stocks that looked especially richly valued, such as those in India and in Europe's telecom sector. Its decision to raise cash further helped limit the damage. Management's good sense in easing off the gas pedal takes some edge off the fund's aggressive style.

Thus, we think this is a worthwhile small-cap vehicle. Sudden, big losses come with the territory, but the fund has delivered great returns in prosperous markets to compensate. It is also encouraging that T. Rowe has recently decided to add two new analysts in the near future. This will strengthen the hand of an already experienced management team. We would not expect the fund to keep up its scorching pace of recent years, but it should prove to be a useful long-run holding.

Address:	100 East Pratt Street
	Baltimore MD 21202
	800-638-5660
Web Address:	www.troweprice.com
Inception:	12-30-88
Advisor:	T. Rowe Price International, Inc
Subadvisor:	T.rowe Price Global Investment Svs Ltd
NTF Plans:	N/A

Minimum Purchase:	$2500	Add: $100	IRA: $1000
Min Auto Inv Plan:	$2500	Add: $50	
Sales Fees:	No-load, 2.00%R		
Management Fee:	1.06%		
Actual Fees:	Mgt:1.06%	Dist: —	
Expense Projections:	3Yr:$406	5Yr:$702	10Yr:$1545
Income Distrib:	Annually		

Historical Profile

Return	Average
Risk	Average
Rating	★★★ Neutral

Historical (%)	96%	90%	89%	95%	92%	96%	92%	96%	93%

Investment Style
Equity
Stock %

▼ Manager Change
▽ Partial Manager Change

Growth of $10,000
■ Investment Values of Fund
— Investment Values of MSCI EAFE

43.6 / 32.4 / 24.0 / 17.0 / 10.0

Performance Quartile (within Category)

	1995	1996	1997	1998	1999	2000	2001	2002	2003	2004	2005	2006	History
	14.36	16.22	15.05	15.65	36.77	25.45	19.18	16.06	26.40	32.63	41.36	47.48	NAV
	-4.36	13.87	-5.67	6.12	155.03	-15.60	-24.64	-16.27	65.29	23.76	27.89	27.65	Total Return %
	-15.57	7.82	-7.45	-13.81	128.00	-1.41	-3.22	-0.33	26.70	3.51	14.35	1.31	+/-MSCI EAFE
	-15.77	7.00	-7.94	-12.57	127.05	-2.24	-3.25	-0.47	25.87	3.38	13.42	1.94	+/-MSCI Wd xUS
	0.66	0.49	0.00	0.07	0.00	0.00	0.00	0.00	0.50	0.04	0.46	0.75	Income Return %
	-5.02	13.38	-5.67	6.05	155.03	-15.60	-24.64	-16.27	64.79	23.72	27.43	26.90	Capital Return %
	100	100	80	90	1	60	65	61	15	55	42	45	Total Rtn % Rank Cat
	0.10	0.07	0.00	0.01	0.00	0.00	0.00	0.00	0.08	0.01	0.15	0.31	Income $
	0.02	0.06	0.25	0.30	2.81	5.83	0.00	0.00	0.06	0.03	0.21	4.91	Capital Gains $
	1.50	1.45	1.41	1.47	1.42	1.27	1.38	1.44	1.41	1.32	1.28	—	Expense Ratio %
	0.55	0.40	0.13	0.25	-0.17	0.15	0.25	0.06	0.46	0.28	0.54	—	Income Ratio %
	44	52	73	34	98	81	59	94	116	106	85	—	Turnover Rate %
	303	322	228	193	687	765	486	370	705	1,002	1,502	2,311	Net Assets $mil

Rating and Risk

Time Period	Load-Adj Return %	Morningstar Rtn vs Cat	Morningstar Risk vs Cat	Morningstar Risk-Adj Rating
1 Yr	27.65			
3 Yr	26.42	Avg	Avg	★★★
5 Yr	22.83	Avg	Avg	★★★
10 Yr	16.33	Avg	Avg	★★★
Incept	12.68			

Other Measures	Standard Index MSCI EAFE	Best Fit Index MSCI EAFE
Alpha	2.9	2.9
Beta	1.18	1.18
R-Squared	81	81
Standard Deviation	12.35	
Mean	26.42	
Sharpe Ratio	1.72	

Portfolio Analysis 09-30-06

Share change since 06-06 Total Stocks:218

	Sector	Country	% Assets
Finl Technolo		India	1.57
⊕ SOITEC	Ind Mtrls	France	1.46
⊕ Wacker Chemie	—	Germany	1.40
Phonak Holding Ltd	Health	Switzerland	1.12
IG Grp Hldgs	—	U.K.	1.00
Wiener Staedtische Allge	Financial	Austria	0.95
Geberit	Consumer	Switzerland	0.92
EFG International	—	Switzerland	0.89
✵ Prologis European Proper	—	Luxembourg	0.87
⊕ Benfield Grp Ltd	Business	U.K.	0.86
Germanos	Telecom	Greece	0.84
UCB Grp	Health	Belgium	0.80
⊕ Guala Closures	Goods	Italy	0.75
Wincor Nixdorf	Hardware	Germany	0.73
⊕ ICAP	Financial	U.K.	0.73
GRIFOLS, SA, BARCELONA	—	Spain	0.73
✵ Haseko	Consumer	Japan	0.73
⊕ NHK Spring	Ind Mtrls	Japan	0.72
⊖ H&R Wasag	Ind Mtrls	Germany	0.71
⊕ Otsuka	Business	Japan	0.71

Current Investment Style

	Market Cap	%
Value Blnd Growth	Giant	0.0
	Large	2.3
	Mid	59.3
	Small	28.5
	Micro	9.9
	Avg $mil:	1,192

Value Measures		Rel Category
Price/Earnings	17.52	1.12
Price/Book	2.44	1.01
Price/Sales	1.07	0.97
Price/Cash Flow	6.59	0.84
Dividend Yield %	1.80	0.88

Growth Measures	%	Rel Category
Long-Term Erngs	17.17	0.84
Book Value	9.57	1.01
Sales	10.75	0.86
Cash Flow	-3.32	NMF
Historical Erngs	17.63	0.78

Composition

Cash	5.3	Bonds	0.0
Stocks	93.2	Other	1.5
Foreign (% of Stock)			98.9

Sector Weightings	% of Stocks	Rel MSCI EAFE	3 Year High Low	
↻ Info	12.66	1.07		
Software	2.53	4.52	6	2
Hardware	3.59	0.93	5	2
Media	3.35	1.83	4	2
Telecom	3.19	0.57	5	2
☞ Service	54.39	1.15		
Health	10.29	1.45	11	6
Consumer	14.71	2.97	16	11
Business	17.50	3.45	18	14
Financial	11.89	0.40	16	12
↤ Mfg	32.95	0.80		
Goods	9.75	0.74	16	8
Ind Mtrls	17.93	1.16	20	17
Energy	4.10	0.57	6	2
Utilities	1.17	0.22	1	0

Regional Exposure % Stock

UK/W. Europe	53	N. America	1
Japan	20	Latn America	0
Asia X Japan	24	Other	2

Country Exposure % Stock

Japan	20	Switzerland	6
U.K.	17	Hong Kong	6
Germany	8		

T. Rowe Price Intl Stk

	Ticker	Load	NAV	Yield	Total Assets	Mstar Category
	PRITX	None	$16.83	1.1%	$6,921 mil	Foreign Large Growth

Governance and Management

Stewardship Grade: B

Portfolio Manager(s)

A team of experienced T. Rowe Price professionals runs this fund. It includes Mark Bickford-Smith, the lead manager, and comanagers David J.L. Warren and Dean Tenerelli. Bickford-Smith is also responsible for stock selection in developed Asia outside Japan and emerging markets. Warren has similar responsibility for Japan, as does Tenerelli for Europe. Bickford-Smith and Warren have each been here for more than a decade, while Tenerelli joined the team in March 2005.

Strategy

Management focuses on large caps with good earnings growth and moderate prices. Management goes with a diversified portfolio, as it mixes companies with strong growth prospects with stocks that have more defensive characteristics. Turnover has historically been quite low, though in the future management expects to move at a somewhat faster pace in replacing worn out or broken stock ideas. T. Rowe Price applies fair-value pricing to the fund.

Performance 12-31-06

	1st Qtr	2nd Qtr	3rd Qtr	4th Qtr	Total
2002	1.27	-4.94	-21.64	8.47	-18.18
2003	-10.14	19.92	6.17	14.74	31.28
2004	3.74	-2.01	-1.97	14.29	13.89
2005	-0.62	-1.32	12.22	5.65	16.27
2006	7.37	-3.34	3.45	11.07	19.26

Trailing	Total Return%	+/- MSCI EAFE	+/- MSCI Wd xUS	%Rank Cat	Growth of $10,000
3 Mo	11.07	0.72	0.95	47	11,107
6 Mo	14.91	0.22	0.69	42	11,491
1 Yr	19.26	-7.08	-6.45	83	11,926
3 Yr Avg	16.45	-3.48	-3.65	67	15,791
5 Yr Avg	11.15	-3.83	-4.10	66	16,965
10 Yr Avg	5.82	-1.89	-2.14	69	17,607
15 Yr Avg	7.73	-0.13	-0.31	45	30,553

Tax Analysis	Tax-Adj Rtn%	%Rank Cat	Tax-Cost Rat	%Rank Cat
3 Yr (estimated)	15.71	60	0.64	42
5 Yr (estimated)	10.50	59	0.58	52
10 Yr (estimated)	4.79	68	0.97	62

Potential Capital Gain Exposure: 29% of assets

Morningstar's Take by Arijit Dutta 12-20-06

T. Rowe Price International Stock isn't a standout option yet, but it has its quiet strengths.

This fund's long-term record is at least middling, but it has taken some tough blows in 2006. While the portfolio's overweighting in Japan is modest (a 24% stake, compared with the foreign large-growth category average of 18%), that market's severe underperformance this year has taken its toll. Also, some specific stocks have suffered badly. For example, Japanese consumer-lender Aiful has blown up amidst allegations of overly aggressive lending practices. Turkish bank Turkiye Bankasi is another holding that has flopped due to that country's macroeconomic problems. As a result, the fund's 18% year-to-date return, while decent in absolute terms, doesn't come close to matching those posted by a vast majority of rivals.

While management has clearly made some mistakes lately, we wouldn't write off this fund. Over the past year and a half, it has undergone some changes that we think give the fund a better

chance to compete. Lead manager Mark Bickford-Smith points to a more growth-oriented, compact portfolio than in years past, which should lead to less benchmark-like returns. Indeed, the fund recently moved from our foreign large-blend to our foreign large-growth category, and the number of portfolio holdings has declined from 185 to 123 since the end of 2004. Some recent purchases also highlight these changes. Stocks like Swedish construction-equipment renter Atlas Copco and National Bank of Greece are smaller companies, with faster growth prospects than index heavyweights.

We think the fund stands a good chance of making this work. It hasn't abandoned its focus on developed-market large-cap, steady-growth names, so the fund still passes muster as a core holding. Yet, management has made efforts to distinguish and add more punch to the portfolio, which should improve performance. It is also the cheapest actively managed retail offering in the category.

Address:	100 East Pratt Street	Minimum Purchase:	$2500	Add: $100	IRA: $1000
	Baltimore MD 21202	Min Auto Inv Plan:	$2500	Add: $50	
	800-638-5660	Sales Fees:	No-load, 2.00%R		
Web Address:	www.troweprice.com	Management Fee:	0.66%		
Inception:	05-09-80	Actual Fees:	Mgt:0.66%	Dist: —	
Advisor:	T. Rowe Price International, Inc	Expense Projections:	3Yr:$284	5Yr:$493	10Yr:$1096
Subadvisor:	T. Rowe Price Global Investment Services	Income Distrib:	Annually		
NTF Plans:	N/A				

Historical Profile

Return	Below Avg
Risk	Average
Rating	★★ Below Avg

Investment Style: Equity, Stock %

Investment Style percentages: 94% 94% 92% 96% 96% 97% 97% 99% 98%

▼ Manager Change
▽ Partial Manager Change

Growth of $10,000
— Investment Values of Fund
— Investment Values of MSCI EAFE

Performance Quartile (within Category)

1995	1996	1997	1998	1999	2000	2001	2002	2003	2004	2005	2006	History
12.23	13.80	13.42	14.99	19.03	14.52	10.99	8.88	11.49	12.93	14.79	16.83	NAV
11.39	15.99	2.70	16.14	34.60	-17.09	-22.02	-18.18	31.28	13.89	16.27	19.26	Total Return %
0.18	9.94	0.92	-3.79	7.57	-2.90	-0.60	-2.24	-7.31	-6.36	2.73	-7.08	+/-MSCI EAFE
-0.02	9.12	0.43	-2.55	6.62	-3.73	-0.63	-2.38	-8.14	-6.49	1.80	-6.45	+/-MSCI Wd xUS
1.59	1.47	1.45	1.64	0.87	0.47	2.07	1.00	1.46	1.31	1.55	1.35	Income Return %
9.80	14.52	1.25	14.50	33.73	-17.56	-24.09	-19.18	29.82	12.58	14.72	17.91	Capital Return %
34	29	73	38	82	49	38	43	68	68	41	83	Total Rtn % Rank Cat
0.18	0.18	0.20	0.22	0.13	0.09	0.30	0.11	0.13	0.15	0.20	0.20	Income $
0.20	0.20	0.55	0.35	0.91	1.18	0.03	0.00	0.03	0.00	0.04	0.60	Capital Gains $
0.91	0.88	0.85	0.85	0.85	0.84	0.90	0.92	0.95	0.92	0.89	—	Expense Ratio %
1.56	1.58	1.33	1.50	1.05	0.55	2.14	0.96	1.39	1.22	1.47	—	Income Ratio %
18	12	16	12	18	38	17	24	25	28	63	—	Turnover Rate %
6,703	9,341	9,721	10,142	12,674	9,735	6,507	4,434	5,208	5,221	5,763	6,851	Net Assets $mil

Rating and Risk

Time Period	Load-Adj Return %	Morningstar Rtn vs Cat	Morningstar Risk vs Cat	Morningstar Risk-Adj Rating
1 Yr	19.26			
3 Yr	16.45	-Avg	Avg	★★
5 Yr	11.15	Avg	Avg	★★★
10 Yr	5.82	-Avg	-Avg	★★
Incept	11.33			

Other Measures	Standard Index MSCI EAFE	Best Fit Index MSCI EAFE
Alpha	-4.1	-4.1
Beta	1.08	1.08
R-Squared	95	95
Standard Deviation	10.50	
Mean	16.45	
Sharpe Ratio	1.21	

Portfolio Analysis 09-30-06

Share change since 06-06 Total Stocks:123

Share change		Sector	Country	% Assets
	Sumitomo Mitsui Financia	Financial	Japan	1.93
⊖	Royal Dutch Shell	Energy	U.K.	1.87
⊕	UBS AG	Financial	Switzerland	1.77
	Novartis	Health	Switzerland	1.75
	LVMH Moet Hennessy L.V.	Goods	France	1.60
⊖	Erste Bank	Financial	Austria	1.59
	Swiss Life Hldgs	Financial	Switzerland	1.58
⊖	UniCredito Italiano Grp	Financial	Italy	1.58
✲✲	Telefonica	Telecom	Spain	1.51
	Petroleo Brasileiro S.A.	Energy	Brazil	1.47
	ASSALOY	Ind Mtrls	Sweden	1.46
⊕	Hellenic Telecommunicati	Telecom	Greece	1.36
	Mitsui Fudosan	Financial	Japan	1.32
⊕	AXA	Financial	France	1.31
✲✲	National Bank of Greece	Financial	Greece	1.31
✲✲	Accor	Consumer	France	1.28
⊕	Pernod Ricard	Goods	France	1.27
	Capitalia Gruppo Bancari	Financial	Italy	1.24
⊖	AMVESCAP	Financial	U.K.	1.22
✲✲	TOTAL	Energy	France	1.20

Current Investment Style

Value Blnd Growth — Large/Mid/Small

	Market Cap	%
	Giant	40.4
	Large	41.9
	Mid	17.6
	Small	0.0
	Micro	0.0
	Avg $mil:	21,461

Value Measures		Rel Category
Price/Earnings	14.39	0.93
Price/Book	2.29	0.87
Price/Sales	1.36	0.96
Price/Cash Flow	9.24	0.95
Dividend Yield %	2.32	0.95

Growth Measures	%	Rel Category
Long-Term Erngs	12.96	0.96
Book Value	10.53	0.96
Sales	7.55	0.87
Cash Flow	12.36	1.01
Historical Erngs	23.49	1.03

Composition

Cash	1.4	Bonds	0.0
Stocks	98.3	Other	0.3
Foreign	(% of Stock)		100.0

Sector Weightings

Sector Weightings	% of Stocks	Rel MSCI EAFE	3 Year High	Low
⌖ Info	12.17	1.03		
📊 Software	0.00	0.00	1	0
💻 Hardware	2.81	0.73	5	1
🎙 Media	1.48	0.81	6	1
📶 Telecom	7.88	1.41	11	8
☞ Service	55.74	1.18		
🩺 Health	6.60	0.93	10	6
Consumer	6.02	1.22	8	3
🏢 Business	7.85	1.55	8	5
💲 Financial	35.27	1.17	38	23
⬜ Mfg	32.09	0.78		
🏭 Goods	14.02	1.07	17	14
⚙ Ind Mtrls	10.52	0.68	13	6
⬛ Energy	7.24	1.01	10	7
⚡ Utilities	0.31	0.06	2	0

Regional Exposure

	% Stock		
UK/W. Europe	62	N. America	1
Japan	24	Latn America	5
Asia X Japan	8	Other	0

Country Exposure

	% Stock		
Japan	24	Italy	8
U.K.	11	Spain	6
France	10		

MORNINGSTAR® Funds 500

T. Rowe Price Latin Amer

Analyst Pick ✓	**Ticker** PRLAX	**Load** None	**NAV** $37.74	**Yield** 0.8%	**Total Assets** $2,222 mil	**Mstar Category** Latin America Stock

Governance and Management

Stewardship Grade: B

Portfolio Manager(s)

Gonzalo Pangaro replaced Benedict Thomas as manager at the end of January 2004. Pangaro had worked with Thomas as comanager from March 2000 through December 2002. Pangaro has the support of three analysts who work exclusively on Latin American stocks and an analyst covering global telecommunications--an important sector in Latin America.

Strategy

Management anchors the portfolio in reasonably priced blue chips that it thinks will improve earnings year after year. At the same time, management actively scans the growing list of new stocks in the region that focus on consumer demand, business infrastructure, and other expanding areas. The fund will build big positions in individual growth industries such as telecom, but management does this and everything else at a moderate pace. Turnover is well below average here.

Performance 12-31-06

	1st Qtr	2nd Qtr	3rd Qtr	4th Qtr	Total
2002	10.91	-18.58	-21.26	15.18	-18.10
2003	-2.13	22.04	9.81	20.40	57.92
2004	7.61	-7.47	14.69	21.15	38.35
2005	3.70	12.15	30.78	5.23	60.05
2006	16.94	-0.17	6.22	21.96	51.24

Trailing	Total Return%	+/- MSCI EAFE	+/- MSCI EMF LA	%Rank Cat	Growth of $10,000
3 Mo	21.96	11.61	0.83	34	12,196
6 Mo	29.55	14.86	3.05	14	12,955
1 Yr	51.24	24.90	11.90	1	15,124
3 Yr Avg	49.61	29.68	10.00	1	33,487
5 Yr Avg	34.07	19.09	6.20	15	43,317
10 Yr Avg	17.94	10.23	5.25	1	52,073
15 Yr Avg	—	—	—		—

Tax Analysis	Tax-Adj Rtn%	%Rank Cat	Tax-Cost Rat	%Rank Cat
3 Yr (estimated)	49.04	1	0.38	15
5 Yr (estimated)	33.62	12	0.34	27
10 Yr (estimated)	17.38	1	0.47	34

Potential Capital Gain Exposure: 43% of assets

Morningstar's Take by Arijit Dutta 12-11-06

T. Rowe Price Latin America has an effective strategy, but we'd use the fund cautiously.

This fund continues to make the most of the massive rally in Latin American stocks. Manager Gonzalo Pangaro lightened the portfolio's industrial materials stake earlier this year as booming commodity prices drove those stocks to lofty valuations. This helped the fund survive the sharp market correction in May and June that took an especially heavy toll on commodity stocks. Since June, as markets have rebounded, the portfolio's top holdings such as Brazilian retailer Lojas Renner and airliner Tam Sa have outshone. As a result, the fund has stayed ahead of all mutual fund and ETF options in this small category, further bolstering its stellar long-term record.

Pangaro's stock selection has been key. Latin America is a narrow market, with just two dominant countries (Brazil and Mexico) and a few commodity stocks that soak up a major portion of equity assets. Still, Pangaro has done a great job of diversifying

the portfolio by focusing on the growing role of business and consumer services companies in the region's maturing economies. For example, Tam Sa has benefited from improved air-travel infrastructure, and from greater demand in both its cargo and passenger segments. Similarly, Lojas Renner has thrived, as rising purchasing power among consumers helped popularize department stores in Brazil. Pangaro's string of winning calls in less widely followed stocks and his willingness to buy significant stakes in them bodes well for the fund's chances of continued success.

We would keep our expectations in check, however. Latin America cannot continue to deliver the monster returns of the past several years. (For example, the fund has averaged 51% over the past three years.) Gut-wrenching volatility also continues to haunt the region's markets, which suggests diversified emerging markets or broad foreign offerings as better alternatives for most investors.

Address:	100 East Pratt Street Baltimore MD 21202 800-638-5660	Minimum Purchase:	$2500 Add: $100 IRA: $1000
		Min Auto Inv Plan:	$2500 Add: $50
		Sales Fees:	No-load, 2.00%R
Web Address:	www.troweprice.com	Management Fee:	1.06%
Inception:	12-29-93	Actual Fees:	Mgt:1.06% Dist: —
Advisor:	T. Rowe Price International, Inc	Expense Projections:	3Yr:$409 5Yr:$708 10Yr:$1556
Subadvisor:	None	Income Distrib:	Annually
NTF Plans:	N/A		

Historical Profile

Return	Above Avg
Risk	Below Avg
Rating	★★★★ Above Avg

74% 77% 79% 66% 66% 55% 84% 88% 92%

Investment Style Equity Stock %

▼ Manager Change
▽ Partial Manager Change

46.4
33.8
24.0
17.0
10.0

Growth of $10,000
— Investment Values of Fund
— Investment Values of MSCI EAFE

Performance Quartile (within Category)

1995	1996	1997	1998	1999	2000	2001	2002	2003	2004	2005	2006	History
6.81	8.26	10.77	6.81	10.81	9.56	9.17	7.51	11.69	15.95	25.32	37.74	NAV
-18.70	23.35	31.88	-35.43	59.38	-11.20	-0.23	-18.10	57.92	38.35	60.05	51.24	Total Return %
-29.91	17.30	30.10	-55.36	32.35	2.99	21.19	-2.16	19.33	18.10	46.51	24.90	+/-MSCI EAFE
-3.67	4.48	3.54	2.63	3.90	7.18	4.01	6.69	-9.14	3.58	15.13	11.90	+/-MSCI EMF LA
0.71	1.62	1.45	1.30	0.59	0.37	1.57	0.00	2.13	1.80	1.25	1.22	Income Return %
-19.41	21.73	30.43	-36.73	58.79	-11.57	-1.80	-18.10	55.79	36.55	58.80	50.02	Capital Return %
40	100	17	17	40	1	1	1	71	57	1	1	Total Rtn % Rank Cat
0.06	0.11	0.12	0.14	0.04	0.04	0.15	0.00	0.16	0.21	0.20	0.31	Income $
0.00	0.03	0.00	0.00	0.00	0.00	0.20	0.00	0.00	0.00	0.01	0.23	Capital Gains $
1.82	1.66	1.47	1.53	1.62	1.46	1.49	1.53	1.55	1.41	1.29	—	Expense Ratio %
0.76	1.29	1.30	1.35	1.05	0.42	1.40	1.88	1.55	2.22	1.55	—	Income Ratio %
19	22	33	19	43	28	30	27	35	18	—	—	Turnover Rate %
150	211	433	182	268	207	177	129	201	310	1,085	2,222	Net Assets $mil

Rating and Risk

Time Period	Load-Adj Return %	Morningstar Rtn vs Cat	Morningstar Risk vs Cat	Morningstar Risk-Adj Rating
1 Yr	51.24			
3 Yr	49.61	+Avg	Avg	★★★★
5 Yr	34.07	+Avg	-Avg	★★★★
10 Yr	17.94	—		
Incept	12.09			

Other Measures	Standard Index MSCI EAFE	Best Fit Index MSCI EMF LA
Alpha	11.0	7.2
Beta	1.88	1.00
R-Squared	61	98
Standard Deviation	22.74	
Mean	49.61	
Sharpe Ratio	1.77	

Portfolio Analysis 09-30-06

Share change since 06-06 Total Stocks:39

	Sector	Country	% Assets
America Movil SA ADR	Telecom	Mexico	11.33
⊖ Petroleo Brasileiro S.A.	Energy	Brazil	8.33
⊕ Petroleo Brasileiro S.A.	Energy	Brazil	7.07
⊕ Bco Itau Hldg F		Brazil	5.70
⊕ Companhia Vale Do Rio Do	Ind Mtrls	Brazil	5.21
Wal-Mart de Mexico	Consumer	Mexico	4.76
Banco Bradesco	Financial	Brazil	4.53
⊕ Cemex SAB de CV ADR	Ind Mtrls	Mexico	3.60
⊖ Companhia Vale Do Rio Do	Ind Mtrls	Brazil	3.43
⊕ Grupo Financiero Banorte	Financial	Mexico	3.36
Grupo Televisa SA ADR	Media	Mexico	3.24
Urbi Desarrollos Urbanos	—	Mexico	3.10
⊕ Tenaris SA ADR	Ind Mtrls	Luxembourg	3.07
⊖ Tam Sa	Business	Brazil	2.90
Lojas Renner	Consumer	Brazil	2.77
⊕ Energias do Brasil	Utilities	Brazil	2.63
⊖ Natura Cosmeticos		Brazil	2.02
⊖ Controladora Comercial M	Consumer	Mexico	1.94
⊕ Banco Santander-Chile AD	Financial	Chile	1.93
Tele Norte Leste Partici	Telecom	Brazil	1.72

Current Investment Style

	Market Cap	%
	Giant	58.1
	Large	19.9
	Mid	19.1
	Small	2.5
	Micro	0.4
	Avg $mil:	16,755

Value Measures		Rel Category
Price/Earnings	15.80	0.97
Price/Book	1.09	0.43
Price/Sales	1.26	0.76
Price/Cash Flow	4.12	0.33
Dividend Yield %	2.11	0.52

Growth Measures	%	Rel Category
Long-Term Erngs	15.78	0.87
Book Value	9.73	4.12
Sales	16.74	0.77
Cash Flow	30.61	1.83
Historical Erngs	17.53	0.89

Composition

Cash	0.8	Bonds	0.0
Stocks	92.1	Other	7.1
Foreign (% of Stock)			100.0

Sector Weightings	% of Stocks	Rel MSCI EAFE	3 Year High	Low
⟳ Info	19.21	1.63		
Software	0.00	0.00	0	0
Hardware	0.00	0.00	0	0
Media	3.82	2.09	6	4
Telecom	15.39	2.76	29	14
⟲ Service	33.91	0.72		
Health	0.00	0.00	1	0
Consumer	13.08	2.64	13	9
Business	6.82	1.35	7	2
Financial	14.01	0.47	14	4
⟱ Mfg	46.88	1.15		
Goods	2.70	0.21	9	2
Ind Mtrls	21.44	1.39	29	21
Energy	18.16	2.54	21	16
Utilities	4.58	0.87	5	1

Regional Exposure		% Stock
UK/W. Europe	5	N. America	0
Japan	0	Latn America	95
Asia X Japan	0	Other	0

Country Exposure		% Stock
Brazil	53	Chile	3
Mexico	37	Colombia	2
Luxembourg	4		

T. Rowe Price Med & Tele

Analyst Pick ✓

	Ticker	Load	NAV	Yield	Total Assets	Mstar Category
	PRMTX	None	$43.18	0.0%	$1,456 mil	Specialty-Communications

Governance and Management

Stewardship Grade: B

Portfolio Manager(s)

Rob Bartolo and Henry Ellenbogen took over for Rob Gensler in April 2005. They have experience on this offering, having served as analysts under Gensler and will maintain his attention to valuation and subsector diversification.

Strategy

The managers seek to buy communications- and media-related companies positioned to benefit from secular trends. They look for firms trading at discounts to comparable industry peers, but they will pay more for those they think are dominant. The duo will follow in previous manager Rob Gensler's footsteps by maintaining subsector diversification and looking abroad for opportunities.

Performance 12-31-06

	1st Qtr	2nd Qtr	3rd Qtr	4th Qtr	Total
2002	-10.92	-23.18	-10.37	16.75	-28.39
2003	-2.49	27.01	5.82	19.04	55.99
2004	6.31	3.76	-3.22	18.31	26.30
2005	-4.29	7.50	9.40	4.97	18.15
2006	8.31	-0.63	5.95	12.74	28.55

Trailing	Total Return%	+/- S&P 500	+/- DJ Telecom	%Rank Cat	Growth of $10,000
3 Mo	12.74	6.04	4.19	22	11,274
6 Mo	19.45	6.71	-0.34	35	11,945
1 Yr	28.55	12.76	-8.28	14	12,855
3 Yr Avg	24.25	13.81	8.29	1	19,182
5 Yr Avg	16.47	10.28	14.63	1	21,432
10 Yr Avg	17.44	9.02	13.71	1	49,907
15 Yr Avg	—	—	—	—	—

Tax Analysis	Tax-Adj Rtn%	%Rank Cat	Tax-Cost Rat	%Rank Cat
3 Yr (estimated)	24.25	1	0.00	1
5 Yr (estimated)	16.47	1	0.00	1
10 Yr (estimated)	15.81	1	1.39	87

Potential Capital Gain Exposure: 30% of assets

Morningstar's Take by Andrew Gogerty 11-06-06

T. Rowe Price Media & Telecom is an Analyst Pick, but we still wouldn't load up on it.

Comanagers Henry Ellenbogen and Rob Bartolo prefer companies poised to benefit from secular trends. For example, they say top-holding American Tower's asset base and strict zoning requirements for new construction will allow it to benefit from increased demand for cell tower space as the industry shifts to more wireless communication. The duo will also invest outside the U.S. in emerging opportunities. Canadian wireless firms Telus and Rogers Communications are two of their best ideas right now because Bartolo says lack of price competition, low penetration in the marketplace, and a favorable regulatory environment will drive future growth.

This eclectic portfolio and management's willingness to stray from industry benchmarks have certainly paid off. In 2006, for example, the fund has had little exposure to the strong-performing regional bell companies (particularly AT&T and BellSouth), yet its execution within other industries has helped it to post another strong gain. Its 19.9% gain through Nov. 2, 2006, places in the group's best quartile and builds upon the new team's strong start in 2005.

Still, we wouldn't go overboard. Some of the fund's holdings carry a fair amount of price risk. Bartolo and Ellenbogen focus on long-term growth prospects, meaning some holdings may look rich based on current-year earnings. Investors should also expect some bumps in the short term because the managers are more willing than their predecessor to hold stocks through rough near-term news. Having nearly half the fund's assets in its top 10 holdings also courts considerable risk of a blowup among the management's best ideas.

But these concerns aren't unusual among telecom funds. Their narrow focus often adds little to a diversified portfolio. Still, investors wanting exposure in this category should look here first.

Address:	100 East Pratt Street Baltimore MD 21202 800-638-5660
Web Address:	www.troweprice.com
Inception:	10-13-93
Advisor:	T. Rowe Price Associates, Inc.
Subadvisor:	None
NTF Plans:	N/A

Minimum Purchase:	$2500	Add: $100	IRA: $1000
Min Auto Inv Plan:	$50	Add: $50	
Sales Fees:	No-load		
Management Fee:	0.66%		
Actual Fees:	Mgt:0.66%	Dist: —	
Expense Projections:	3Yr:$293	5Yr:$509	10Yr:$1131
Income Distrib:	Annually		

Historical Profile

Return	High
Risk	Average
Rating	★★★★ Highest

92% 88% 83% 93% 98% 97% 100% 98% 99%

Investment Style
Equity
Stock %

▽ Manager Change
▽ Partial Manager Change

67.4
47.8
33.8
24.0
17.0
10.0

Growth of $10,000
— Investment Values of Fund
— Investment Values of S&P 500

Performance Quartile (within Category)

	1995	1996	1997	1998	1999	2000	2001	2002	2003	2004	2005	2006	History
NAV	17.99	15.22	17.40	22.54	39.99	21.65	20.15	14.43	22.51	28.43	33.59	43.18	NAV
Total Return %	43.29	1.78	28.05	35.14	93.09	-25.11	-6.93	-28.39	55.99	26.30	18.15	28.55	Total Return %
+/-S&P 500	5.71	-21.18	-5.31	6.56	72.05	-16.01	4.96	-6.29	27.31	15.42	13.24	12.76	+/-S&P 500
+/-DJ Telecom	2.60	1.74	-12.59	-16.68	74.68	15.16	5.84	6.16	48.66	7.60	22.15	-8.28	+/-DJ Telecom
Income Return %	0.52	0.00	0.00	0.00	0.00	0.93	0.00	0.00	0.00	0.00	0.00	0.00	Income Return %
Capital Return %	42.77	1.78	28.05	35.14	93.09	-26.04	-6.93	-28.39	55.99	26.30	18.15	28.55	Capital Return %
Total Rtn % Rank Cat	1	87	50	56	8	22	4	7	38	9	6	14	Total Rtn % Rank Cat
Income $	0.07	0.00	0.00	0.00	0.00	0.37	0.00	0.00	0.00	0.00	0.00	0.00	Income $
Capital Gains $	1.13	3.09	2.05	0.86	3.22	8.60	0.00	0.00	0.00	0.00	0.00	0.00	Capital Gains $
Expense Ratio %	1.25	1.22	1.21	1.03	0.93	0.94	1.08	1.15	1.10	0.96	0.92	—	Expense Ratio %
Income Ratio %	-0.25	-0.55	-0.06	-0.38	-0.24	1.07	-0.39	-0.31	-0.51	-0.30	-0.13	—	Income Ratio %
Turnover Rate %	119	103	39	49	58	198	241	185	124	108	78	—	Turnover Rate %
Net Assets $mil	269	223	134	246	930	798	675	421	665	877	1,035	1,456	Net Assets $mil

Rating and Risk

Time Period	Load-Adj Return %	Morningstar Rtn vs Cat	Morningstar Risk vs Cat	Morningstar Risk-Adj Rating
1 Yr	28.55			
3 Yr	24.25	High	-Avg	★★★★★
5 Yr	16.47	High	-Avg	★★★★★
10 Yr	17.44	+Avg	Avg	★★★★
Incept	15.90			

Other Measures	Standard Index S&P 500	Best Fit Index Russ MG
Alpha	8.3	9.8
Beta	1.59	1.02
R-Squared	79	89
Standard Deviation	12.30	
Mean	24.25	
Sharpe Ratio	1.58	

Portfolio Analysis 09-30-06

Share change since 06-06 Total Stocks:77

	Sector	PE	Tot Ret%	% Assets
American Tower Corporati	Telecom	—	37.57	8.03
TELUS Corporation Non Vo	Telecom	28.4	13.70	7.05
Crown Castle Internation	Telecom	—	20.94	5.80
Rogers Communications, I	Telecom	—	41.45	5.59
Lamar Advertising Compan	Business	—	41.75	5.41
⊖ America Movil SA ADR	Telecom	27.7	55.53	4.07
⊕ International Game Tech.	Consumer	34.3	52.07	4.03
⊕ EchoStar Communications	Media	29.5	39.92	3.76
Google, Inc.	Business	61.5	11.00	3.62
Bharti Televentures Ltd	Telecom	—	—	3.36
⊖ Wynn Resorts, Ltd.	Consumer	—	82.52	2.65
⊕ Grupo Televisa SA ADR	Media	80.8	35.28	2.14
⊕ Time Warner Telecom, Inc	Telecom	—	102.34	2.11
☆ Leap Wireless Internatio	Telecom	81.7	57.00	2.05
⊕ SBA Communications Corpo	Telecom	—	53.63	1.61
⊖ Yahoo, Inc.	Media	35.4	-34.81	1.45
⊖ Viacom, Inc. B	Media	—	—	1.35
NAVTEQ Corporation	Business	35.5	-20.29	1.35
⊕ Amazon.com, Inc.	Consumer	55.1	-16.31	1.35
Hutchison Telecom Intl	Telecom	—	—	1.31

Current Investment Style

Value Blnd Growth — Large/Mid/Small

Market Cap	%
Giant	13.4
Large	43.5
Mid	34.9
Small	7.4
Micro	0.7

Avg $mil: 9,545

Value Measures		Rel Category
Price/Earnings	35.85	1.74
Price/Book	3.23	1.72
Price/Sales	3.23	1.67
Price/Cash Flow	12.14	1.48
Dividend Yield %	0.67	0.36

Growth Measures	%	Rel Category
Long-Term Erngs	20.63	1.51
Book Value	4.33	0.31
Sales	7.88	0.98
Cash Flow	24.54	2.32
Historical Erngs	43.58	1.72

Profitability	%	Rel Category
Return on Equity	9.01	0.73
Return on Assets	4.77	0.82
Net Margin	5.16	0.61

Industry Weightings	% of Stocks	Rel Cat
Telecom Srv	5.4	0.2
Wireless Srv	31.7	1.2
Network Eq	2.7	0.2
Semis	1.6	0.6
Big Media	7.6	1.9
Cable TV	6.4	2.9
Other Media	3.0	1.4
Soft/Hardwr	2.9	1.0
Other	38.8	4.4

Composition

	%
● Cash	1.0
● Stocks	99.0
● Bonds	0.0
● Other	0.0
Foreign	34.8
(% of Stock)	

MORNINGSTAR® Funds 500

T. Rowe Price Mid Gr

	Ticker	Load	NAV	Yield	Total Assets	Mstar Category
	RPMGX	Closed	$53.69	0.1%	$15,319 mil	Mid-Cap Growth

Governance and Management

Stewardship Grade: B

Portfolio Manager(s)

Brian Berghuis has run this offering since its June 1992 inception. He is assisted by comanager John Wakeman, and the two draw ideas from T. Rowe's deep analyst bench.

Strategy

Manager Brian Berghuis looks for companies with sound business models that are growing rapidly. But unlike some other mid-growth managers, he pays close attention to valuations: The fund's average P/E is well below that of its typical rival. He also keeps the fund well-diversified across sectors and does not let individual positions in the portfolio become too significant.

Historical Profile

Return	Above Avg
Risk	Below Avg
Rating	★★★★ Above Avg

	92%	92%	96%	94%	95%	94%	96%	97%	96%

Investment Style
Equity
Stock %

▼ Manager Change
▽ Partial Manager Change

Growth of $10,000
— Investment Values of Fund
— Investment Values of S&P 500

43.6 / 32.4 / 24.0 / 17.0 / 10.0

Performance Quartile (within Category)

1995	1996	1997	1998	1999	2000	2001	2002	2003	2004	2005	2006	History
20.13	24.43	28.60	34.08	40.13	39.79	39.40	31.04	42.90	49.88	54.14	53.69	NAV
40.95	24.84	18.33	22.00	23.78	7.43	-0.98	-21.22	38.21	18.39	14.82	6.79	Total Return %
3.37	1.88	-15.03	-6.58	2.74	16.53	10.91	0.88	9.53	7.51	9.91	-9.00	+/-S&P 500
6.97	7.36	-4.21	4.14	-27.51	19.18	19.17	6.19	-4.50	2.91	2.72	-3.87	+/-Russ MG
0.00	0.00	0.00	0.00	0.00	0.00	0.00	0.00	0.00	0.00	0.00	0.15	Income Return %
40.95	24.84	18.33	22.00	23.78	7.43	-0.98	-21.22	38.21	18.39	14.82	6.64	Capital Return %
20	10	59	31	82	31	11	29	34	15	16	65	Total Rtn % Rank Cat
0.00	0.00	0.00	0.00	0.00	0.00	0.00	0.00	0.00	0.00	0.00	0.08	Income $
0.79	0.69	0.30	0.73	1.88	3.27	0.00	0.00	0.00	0.90	3.15	4.07	Capital Gains $
1.25	1.04	0.95	0.91	0.87	0.86	0.89	0.88	0.87	0.83	0.80	—	Expense Ratio %
-0.01	-0.11	-0.14	-0.14	-0.09	-0.09	-0.35	-0.50	-0.44	-0.39	-0.12	—	Income Ratio %
58	38	43	47	53	54	43	36	30	30	29	—	Turnover Rate %
264	1,021	1,839	3,310	5,243	6,589	6,739	5,713	9,869	12,651	15,187	14,609	Net Assets $mil

Performance 12-31-06

	1st Qtr	2nd Qtr	3rd Qtr	4th Qtr	Total
2002	0.53	-10.96	-18.88	8.49	-21.22
2003	-1.32	19.62	4.20	12.36	38.21
2004	3.36	4.22	-2.14	12.32	18.39
2005	-2.25	4.12	8.17	4.28	14.82
2006	6.22	-4.69	-0.05	5.54	6.79

Trailing	Total Return%	+/- S&P 500	+/- Russ MG	%Rank Cat	Growth of $10,000
3 Mo	5.54	-1.16	-1.41	70	10,554
6 Mo	5.49	-7.25	-2.41	55	10,549
1 Yr	6.79	-9.00	-3.87	65	10,679
3 Yr Avg	13.23	2.79	0.50	23	14,517
5 Yr Avg	9.59	3.40	1.37	16	15,807
10 Yr Avg	11.63	3.21	3.01	14	30,048
15 Yr Avg	—	—	—	—	—

Tax Analysis	Tax-Adj Rtn%	%Rank Cat	Tax-Cost Rat	%Rank Cat
3 Yr (estimated)	12.33	20	0.79	40
5 Yr (estimated)	9.07	15	0.47	33
10 Yr (estimated)	10.97	10	0.59	15

Potential Capital Gain Exposure: 32% of assets

Rating and Risk

Time Period	Load-Adj Return %	Morningstar Rtn vs Cat	Morningstar Risk vs Cat	Morningstar Risk-Adj Rating
1 Yr	6.79			
3 Yr	13.23	+Avg	Low	★★★★
5 Yr	9.59	+Avg	-Avg	★★★★
10 Yr	11.63	+Avg	-Avg	★★★★
Incept	15.75			

Other Measures	Standard Index S&P 500	Best Fit Index Russ MG
Alpha	0.8	1.5
Beta	1.29	0.87
R-Squared	74	93

Standard Deviation	10.21
Mean	13.23
Sharpe Ratio	0.96

Portfolio Analysis 09-30-06

Share change since 06-06 Total Stocks:152

	Sector	PE	Tot Ret%	% Assets
Roper Industries, Inc.	Ind Mtrls	24.8	27.83	1.55
Crown Castle Internation	Telecom	—	20.94	1.47
Rockwell Collins, Inc.	Ind Mtrls	23.7	37.70	1.37
Manor Care, Inc.	Health	24.6	19.65	1.34
EOG Resources	Energy	10.1	-14.62	1.31
Cephalon, Inc.	Health	28.6	8.76	1.29
Lamar Advertising Compan	Business	—	41.75	1.29
BJ Services Company	Energy	10.6	-19.55	1.26
DST Systems, Inc.	Business	14.4	4.54	1.19
Manpower, Inc.	Business	20.7	62.53	1.18
American Tower Corporati	Telecom	—	37.57	1.17
XTO Energy, Inc.	Energy	9.0	12.16	1.15
Smith International, Inc	Energy	17.0	11.59	1.15
Rogers Communications, I	Telecom	—	41.45	1.15
MedImmune, Inc.	Health	—	-7.57	1.14
International Game Tech.	Consumer	34.3	52.07	1.13
Ametek, Inc.	Ind Mtrls	18.9	12.94	1.12
⊖ Southwest Airlines, Co.	Business	23.2	-6.65	1.07
⊕ Amazon.com, Inc.	Consumer	55.1	-16.31	1.03
Assurant, Inc.	Financial	12.2	28.01	1.03

Current Investment Style

Value Blnd Growth — Large Mid Small

Market Cap	%
Giant	0.0
Large	19.0
Mid	71.8
Small	9.1
Micro	0.1

Avg $mil: 5,256

Value Measures		Rel Category
Price/Earnings	20.70	1.01
Price/Book	3.07	0.96
Price/Sales	1.79	1.02
Price/Cash Flow	11.53	1.01
Dividend Yield %	0.55	0.87

Growth Measures	%	Rel Category
Long-Term Erngs	16.55	1.02
Book Value	12.38	0.97
Sales	14.48	1.45
Cash Flow	17.18	0.93
Historical Erngs	26.66	1.07

Profitability	%	Rel Category
Return on Equity	16.00	0.89
Return on Assets	7.13	0.76
Net Margin	9.59	0.82

Sector Weightings	% of Stocks	Rel S&P 500	3 Year High	Low
ⓘ Info	27.67	1.38		
🖥 Software	6.13	1.78	7	6
💻 Hardware	12.73	1.38	13	9
🎙 Media	2.43	0.64	5	2
📶 Telecom	6.38	1.82	6	3
ⓢ Service	51.79	1.12		
🏥 Health	18.58	1.54	20	18
🛒 Consumer	10.96	1.43	13	10
💼 Business	14.95	3.53	18	13
💲 Financial	7.30	0.33	10	7
Mfg	20.55	0.61		
🏠 Goods	1.74	0.20	3	2
⚙ Ind Mtrls	9.77	0.82	12	10
🔥 Energy	9.04	0.92	10	7
💡 Utilities	0.00	0.00	0	0

Composition

		%
●	Cash	3.8
●	Stocks	96.2
●	Bonds	0.0
○	Other	0.0
	Foreign	6.1
	(% of Stock)	

Morningstar's Take by Karen Wallace 12-18-06

A slow year for T. Rowe Price Mid Cap Growth isn't cause for alarm.

The fact that this closed fund is on pace to finish 2006 in the mid-cap growth category's bottom third might be jarring to some investors, especially given manager Brian Berghuis's long-term record of beating his peers. But we think investors should put this year's relative return in perspective. First, and most importantly for shareholders, the fund's 7.4% return through Dec. 19, 2006, is fairly solid in absolute terms. And secondly, Berghuis is taking the same sensible tack he always has.

Berghuis tends to run the portfolio with a quality bias, and that has held the fund back this year as the market has rewarded lower-quality, more-speculative fare. He favors companies with solid management teams, a sound strategy, solid balance sheets, and strong cash flows. Although many category peers claim to do the same, Berghuis sets himself apart by taking a contrarian view at times, which often leads him away from the more overvalued areas of the market and toward those that are unloved. For instance, he has been adding to the fund's overweight in technology for some time now, believing that tech firms such as electronics manufacturing services provider Jabil Circuit would benefit from a pickup in business spending. Unfortunately, that scenario has not yet played out, while options backdating scandals have taken their toll on many tech firms' share prices this year. Berghuis is still optimistic that tech firms present a good growth opportunity at a good value, however, and the fund still has plenty of exposure there.

In general, we think there's a lot to like here. Berghuis's consistently applied valuation-conscious approach will not always put the fund in the market's sweet spot, but it has led to an impressive long-term record here with below-average volatility. We think it will remain tough to beat.

Address:	100 East Pratt Street Baltimore MD 21202 800-638-5660	Minimum Purchase:	Closed Add: — IRA: —
		Min Auto Inv Plan:	Closed Add: —
		Sales Fees:	No-load
Web Address:	www.troweprice.com	Management Fee:	0.66%
Inception:	06-30-92	Actual Fees:	Mgt:0.66% Dist: —
Advisor:	T. Rowe Price Associates, Inc.	Expense Projections:	3Yr:$255 5Yr:$444 10Yr:$990
Subadvisor:	None	Income Distrib:	Annually
NTF Plans:	N/A		

T. Rowe Price Mid Val

Analyst Pick	Ticker	Load	NAV	Yield	Total Assets	Mstar Category
	TRMCX	Closed	$25.42	0.9%	$7,467 mil	Mid-Cap Value

Governance and Management

Stewardship Grade: B

Portfolio Manager(s)

Prior to taking charge in January 2001, Dave Wallack was the fund's natural-resources stock analyst. He has also been on its investment committee, which oversees and supervises the portfolio manager, since the fund's 1996 inception. Wallack is assisted by T. Rowe's large analyst staff.

Strategy

Manager Dave Wallack looks for reasonably priced companies with experienced management teams that are market leaders in their industries. He is also drawn to firms with the financial flexibility to invest in new products and acquire companies. And he likes firms that posses value drivers, such as divestitures of underperforming businesses and stock buybacks. As is typical of T. Rowe Price managers, Wallack keeps the portfolio broadly diversified, with relatively small positions in his top holdings.

Historical Profile

Return	High
Risk	Below Avg
Rating	★★★★ Highest

Investment Style: Equity, Stock %

95% 93% 90% 90% 94% 94% 91% 90% 90%

▼ Manager Change
▽ Partial Manager Change

Growth of $10,000
— Investment Values of Fund
— Investment Values of S&P 500

Performance Quartile (within Category)

	1995	1996	1997	1998	1999	2000	2001	2002	2003	2004	2005	2006	History
	—	11.56	14.47	13.66	13.37	15.64	16.40	15.00	20.34	22.99	23.38	25.42	NAV
	—	16.30*	27.11	1.39	3.52	22.75	14.36	-7.38	39.00	20.56	7.73	20.24	Total Return %
	—	—	-6.25	-27.19	-17.52	31.85	26.25	14.72	10.32	9.68	2.82	4.45	+/-S&P 500
	—	—	-7.26	-3.69	3.63	3.57	12.03	2.26	0.93	-3.15	-4.92	0.02	+/-Russ MV
	—	—	0.69	1.31	1.68	1.27	0.83	0.73	0.87	0.49	0.70	1.07	Income Return %
	—	—	26.42	0.08	1.84	21.48	13.53	-8.11	38.13	20.07	7.03	19.17	Capital Return %
	—	—	43	50	59	48	25	14	27	38	65	12	Total Rtn % Rank Cat
	—	0.07	0.08	0.19	0.23	0.17	0.13	0.12	0.13	0.10	0.16	0.25	Income $
	—	0.00	0.14	0.76	0.51	0.56	1.31	0.07	0.36	1.40	1.24	2.44	Capital Gains $
	—	—	1.25	1.25	1.08	1.04	0.99	0.98	0.96	0.91	0.84	—	Expense Ratio %
	—	—	2.10	1.18	1.24	1.60	1.33	0.95	0.98	0.91	0.63	—	Income Ratio %
	—	—	4	16	32	27	32	58	51	50	50	—	Turnover Rate %
	—	49	218	221	212	282	503	991	1,867	4,541	6,518		Net Assets $mil

Performance 12-31-06

	1st Qtr	2nd Qtr	3rd Qtr	4th Qtr	Total
2002	10.12	-6.48	-17.29	8.74	-7.38
2003	-5.87	20.18	4.83	17.20	39.00
2004	4.62	3.05	0.32	11.46	20.56
2005	-1.96	2.48	3.07	4.02	7.73
2006	5.99	-1.01	5.30	8.83	20.24

Trailing	Total Return%	+/- S&P 500	+/- Russ MV	%Rank Cat	Growth of $10,000
3 Mo	8.83	2.13	0.33	28	10,883
6 Mo	14.60	1.86	2.27	4	11,460
1 Yr	20.24	4.45	0.02	12	12,024
3 Yr Avg	16.02	5.58	-2.75	26	15,617
5 Yr Avg	14.99	8.80	-0.89	7	20,105
10 Yr Avg	14.18	5.76	0.53	8	37,662
15 Yr Avg	—	—	—	—	—

Tax Analysis	Tax-Adj Rtn%	%Rank Cat	Tax-Cost Rat	%Rank Cat
3 Yr (estimated)	14.09	25	1.66	57
5 Yr (estimated)	13.59	10	1.22	60
10 Yr (estimated)	12.58	4	1.40	45

Potential Capital Gain Exposure: 18% of assets

Rating and Risk

Time Period	Load-Adj Return %	Morningstar Rtn vs Cat	Morningstar Risk vs Cat	Morningstar Risk-Adj Rating
1 Yr	20.24			
3 Yr	16.02	+Avg	-Avg	★★★★
5 Yr	14.99	High	Avg	★★★★★
10 Yr	14.18	High	-Avg	★★★★★
Incept	15.09			

Other Measures	Standard Index S&P 500	Best Fit Index Russ 1000
Alpha	3.9	3.5
Beta	1.18	1.14
R-Squared	89	90
Standard Deviation	8.56	
Mean	16.02	
Sharpe Ratio	1.42	

Morningstar's Take by Christopher Davis 11-30-06

T. Rowe Price Mid-Cap Value's recent success points to its long-term attractions.

It has been a fine year for this closed offering. Up nearly 18% through Nov. 29, 2006, the fund ranks in the mid-value category's top quartile. Its broad list of winners this year includes tech, industrials, and energy holdings such as software firm Intuit, tractor king Deere & Company, and Diamond Offshore Drilling. Manager Dave Wallack keeps his portfolio well diversified across sectors and individual holdings, so good performance is rarely attributable to getting just a few big calls right. Yet Wallack hasn't diversified the fund into blandness. The portfolio's 11% media stake is 3.7 times the category norm, for instance.

Many of this year's top picks illustrate Wallack's trademark approach. He's drawn to beaten-down companies in industries that have been out of favor for years. For example, Wallack began ramping up his stake in energy stocks like Diamond Offshore beginning in 2002. The industry had suffered years

of underinvestment and was consolidating. Plus, he thought oil prices would rise amid a favorable supply/demand dynamic. As that thesis came to fruition, shareholders benefited handsomely.

Investing in turnaround stories is tricky business, but Wallack has done so with aplomb. He's delivered terrific long-term returns with consistency. Indeed, the fund has beaten its peers in two thirds of the 59 trailing one-year periods since Wallack took charge in January 2001.

To be sure, the picture isn't perfect here. Although the fund hasn't show signs of bloat, its $7.1 billion asset base bears close watching. Moreover, Wallack, whose investment stands between $100,000 and $500,000, could stand to make a bigger commitment to the fund.

Still, we think highly of Wallack's abilities, and the fund's modest price tag gives him an added edge. If you bought this fund before it closed, stick with it.

Address:	100 East Pratt Street Baltimore MD 21202 800-638-5660	Minimum Purchase:	Closed	Add: — IRA: —
		Min Auto Inv Plan:	Closed	Add: —
		Sales Fees:	No-load	
Web Address:	www.troweprice.com	Management Fee:	0.66%	
Inception:	06-28-96*	Actual Fees:	Mgt:0.66%	Dist: —
Advisor:	T. Rowe Price Associates, Inc.	Expense Projections:	3Yr:$262	5Yr:$455 10Yr:$1014
Subadvisor:	None	Income Distrib:	Annually	
NTF Plans:	N/A			

Portfolio Analysis 09-30-06

Share change since 06-06 Total Stocks:115	Sector	PE	Tot Ret%	% Assets
⊕ Marsh & McLennan Compani	Financial	29.0	-1.16	2.66
⊕ Murphy Oil Corporation	Energy	12.8	-4.82	1.76
⊕ Nalco Holding Company	Ind Mtrls	33.9	15.53	1.64
Mattel, Inc.	Goods	15.8	47.48	1.63
⊕ Intuit	Software	20.9	14.48	1.60
⊕ TECO Energy	Utilities	14.4	5.12	1.55
⊖ Universal Health Service	Health	23.6	19.31	1.54
NiSource, Inc.	Utilities	21.8	20.51	1.48
⊕ International Paper Co.	Ind Mtrls		4.51	1.48
⊕ Tribune Company	Media	16.0	4.15	1.44
⊕ Molex Cl A	Hardware	—	—	1.39
⊕ Sara Lee Corporation	Goods	22.6	10.03	1.34
⊕ Pinnacle West Capital	Utilities	21.9	27.04	1.32
☼ ConAgra Foods, Inc.	Goods	36.7	38.10	1.31
⊕ Willis Group Holdings, L	Financial	17.0	10.34	1.26
⊕ Clorox Company	Goods	21.7	14.90	1.25
⊕ Sun Microsystems, Inc.	Hardware	—	29.36	1.24
Synovus Financial Corp.	Financial	17.0	17.31	1.24
⊕ Telephone and Data Syste	Telecom	20.0	52.10	1.24
⊕ H & R Block, Inc.	Consumer	25.3	-3.95	1.22

Current Investment Style

Value Blnd Growth — Large Mid Small

Market Cap	%
Giant	0.0
Large	31.5
Mid	62.8
Small	5.7
Micro	0.1

Avg $mil: 6,149

Value Measures		Rel Category
Price/Earnings	17.71	1.19
Price/Book	2.10	1.04
Price/Sales	1.16	1.20
Price/Cash Flow	9.70	1.28
Dividend Yield %	1.75	0.97

Growth Measures	%	Rel Category
Long-Term Erngs	10.97	0.99
Book Value	3.38	0.48
Sales	6.39	0.83
Cash Flow	-0.84	NMF
Historical Erngs	9.04	0.61

Profitability	%	Rel Category
Return on Equity	11.92	0.83
Return on Assets	5.96	0.81
Net Margin	7.50	0.72

Sector Weightings	% of Stocks	Rel S&P 500	3 Year High	Low
♾ Info	21.87	1.09		
Software	3.46	1.00	5	3
Hardware	6.45	0.70	6	4
Media	10.48	2.77	11	9
Telecom	1.48	0.42	4	1
⊆ Service	46.52	1.01		
Health	9.00	0.75	10	8
Consumer	8.92	1.17	9	5
Business	6.04	1.43	10	6
Financial	22.56	1.01	25	18
⊡ Mfg	31.60	0.94		
Goods	8.82	1.03	9	4
Ind Mtrls	11.36	0.95	12	9
Energy	2.98	0.30	11	3
Utilities	8.44	2.41	10	7

Composition

		%
●	Cash	7.8
●	Stocks	90.2
●	Bonds	0.0
○	Other	2.0
	Foreign (% of Stock)	4.6

T. Rowe Price New Amer

Analyst Pick ✓

	Ticker	Load	NAV	Yield	Total Assets	Mstar Category
	PRWAX	None	$31.38	0.0%	$811 mil	Large Growth

Governance and Management

Stewardship Grade: B

Portfolio Manager(s)

Joseph Milano took the reins here in July 2002 from interim manager Robert Smith. In May 2002, Smith had replaced Marc Baylin, who oversaw the fund's transition to a pure large-growth fund in 2000. Baylin took over for Jack LaPorte, who had managed the fund since its 1985 inception. There is some continuity here, though; Baylin and Milano both worked on the fund as analysts for several years.

Strategy

Before 2000, this fund avoided technology and stayed in services industries such as telecommunications, retail, and financials. The fund's mandate changed to growth in 2000, however, opening it up to tech. It looks for low-debt, high-growth companies trading at discounts to historical price multiples and future cash flows. Manager Joe Milano says that his primary areas of interest are IT services, technology, media, retail, and health care, although he's been willing to look for ideas just about anywhere.

Performance 12-31-06

	1st Qtr	2nd Qtr	3rd Qtr	4th Qtr	Total
2002	-4.37	-17.07	-18.75	10.91	-28.54
2003	-0.86	18.24	3.09	11.89	35.22
2004	2.72	2.48	-3.89	9.81	11.10
2005	-4.44	2.72	2.18	4.03	4.35
2006	3.36	-4.67	3.22	5.45	7.24

Trailing	Total Return%	+/- S&P 500	+/- Russ 1000Gr	%Rank Cat	Growth of $10,000
3 Mo	5.45	-1.25	-0.48	50	10,545
6 Mo	8.84	-3.90	-1.26	42	10,884
1 Yr	7.24	-8.55	-1.83	47	10,724
3 Yr Avg	7.52	-2.92	0.65	42	12,430
5 Yr Avg	3.74	-2.45	1.05	33	12,015
10 Yr Avg	4.31	-4.11	-1.13	76	15,250
15 Yr Avg	7.96	-2.68	-0.06	59	31,546

Tax Analysis	Tax-Adj Rtn%	%Rank Cat	Tax-Cost Rat	%Rank Cat
3 Yr (estimated)	6.43	49	1.01	65
5 Yr (estimated)	3.10	37	0.62	62
10 Yr (estimated)	3.06	75	1.20	58

Potential Capital Gain Exposure: 19% of assets

Morningstar's Take by Karen Wallace 11-15-06

T. Rowe Price New America Growth isn't a typical large-growth fund, and that's why we like it.

Manager Joe Milano seeks companies that operate in large markets, are growing market share, and have high profit margins and strong balance sheets. Although many peers focus on the same fundamentals, what makes this fund unique is Milano's skillful execution.

For one, Milano doesn't hesitate to venture into areas less traveled by his peers. The fund has a small asset base relative to many category peers, and Milano makes good use of the flexibility that affords him. Milano keeps a higher percentage of the portfolio in mid-cap names (nearly 45%), and he will look outside of traditional growth areas to unearth stocks that are not widely owned by category peers. For example, he recently bought Fastenal, a company that sells fasteners like nuts and bolts, used in construction and industrial applications. Milano was impressed by the firm's management team and its sales growth, and he

believes that non-residential construction may be in the early years of a multiyear expansion and Fastenal is in a good position to benefit.

We also admire Milano's patience and attention to valuations. Unlike some category peers who will head for the exits at early signs of trouble, Milano takes a long-term view when he values a company; he'll buy into a stock when its price is sagging, and then he'll hold on through lean times if he expects that its prospects are bright. For example, he has added to the fund's position in eBay this year as the stock has lost 25% of its value because he feels that the market is overly pessimistic about the company's slowing growth.

That's not to say that Milano won't make the occasional bad stock pick, or that the fund won't have a bad year relative to its category--the fact that it charts its own course almost guarantees that it will. But we think Milano's deft approach, combined with the fund's reasonable fees, add up to an attractive long-term investment.

Address:	100 East Pratt Street Baltimore MD 21202 800-638-5660	Minimum Purchase:	$2500	Add: $100	IRA: $1000
		Min Auto Inv Plan:	$50	Add: $50	
		Sales Fees:	No-load		
Web Address:	www.troweprice.com	Management Fee:	0.66%		
Inception:	09-30-85	Actual Fees:	Mgt:0.66%	Dist: —	
Advisor:	T. Rowe Price Associates, Inc.	Expense Projections:	3Yr:$290	5Yr:$504	10Yr:$1120
Subadvisor:	None	Income Distrib:	Annually		
NTF Plans:	N/A				

Historical Profile

Return	Average
Risk	Average
Rating	★★★ Neutral

▼ Manager Change
▽ Partial Manager Change

Investment Style: Equity, Stock %

99% 91% 94% 92% 100% 99% 97% 100% 100%

Growth of $10,000
■ Investment Values of Fund
— Investment Values of S&P 500

Performance Quartile (within Category)

	1995	1996	1997	1998	1999	2000	2001	2002	2003	2004	2005	2006	History
	34.91	38.37	44.19	47.79	48.06	35.77	30.87	22.06	29.83	33.14	31.88	31.38	NAV
	44.31	20.01	21.10	17.89	12.76	-10.53	-11.89	-28.54	35.22	11.10	4.35	7.24	Total Return %
	6.73	-2.95	-12.26	-10.69	-8.28	-1.43	0.00	-6.44	6.54	0.22	-0.56	-8.55	+/-S&P 500
	7.13	-3.11	-9.39	-20.82	-20.40	11.89	8.53	-0.66	5.47	4.80	-0.91	-1.83	+/-Russ 1000Gr
	0.00	0.00	0.00	0.00	0.00	0.00	0.00	0.00	0.00	0.00	0.00	0.00	Income Return %
	44.31	20.01	21.10	17.89	12.76	-10.53	-11.89	-28.54	35.22	11.10	4.35	7.24	Capital Return %
	8	46	74	83	92	44	12	60	15	23	67	47	Total Rtn % Rank Cat
	0.00	0.00	0.00	0.00	0.00	0.00	0.00	0.00	0.00	0.00	0.00	0.00	Income $
	1.75	3.49	2.20	3.84	5.40	7.52	0.64	0.00	0.00	0.00	2.75	2.83	Capital Gains $
	1.07	1.01	0.96	0.95	0.94	0.93	0.99	0.99	0.98	0.92	0.91	—	Expense Ratio %
	-0.46	-0.39	-0.34	-0.49	-0.43	-0.33	-0.36	-0.42	-0.34	-0.07	-0.16	—	Income Ratio %
	56	37	43	46	40	81	52	61	62	51	53	—	Turnover Rate %
	1,028	1,440	1,758	2,064	1,826	1,519	1,183	761	921	952	866	809	Net Assets $mil

Rating and Risk

Time Period	Load-Adj Return %	Morningstar Rtn vs Cat	Morningstar Risk vs Cat	Morningstar Risk-Adj Rating
1 Yr	7.24			
3 Yr	7.52	Avg	Avg	★★★
5 Yr	3.74	Avg	+Avg	★★★
10 Yr	4.31	-Avg	Avg	★★
Incept	10.91			

Other Measures	Standard Index S&P 500	Best Fit Index Russ 1000Gr
Alpha	-3.7	0.5
Beta	1.17	1.04
R-Squared	78	92
Standard Deviation	9.10	
Mean	7.52	
Sharpe Ratio	0.49	

Portfolio Analysis 09-30-06

Share change since 06-06 Total Stocks:98	Sector	PE	Tot Ret%	% Assets
⊖ Cisco Systems, Inc.	Hardware	30.1	59.64	2.49
⊖ Smith International, Inc	Energy	17.0	11.59	2.15
⊖ Microsoft Corporation	Software	23.8	15.83	1.93
⊕ eBay, Inc.	Consumer	40.1	-30.43	1.90
⊕ Fastenal Company	Business	27.8	-7.37	1.80
⊖ Iron Mountain, Inc.	Business	44.8	-2.09	1.72
⊕ Harman International Ind	Goods	26.4	2.16	1.70
⊖ Home Depot, Inc.	Consumer	13.5	1.01	1.69
⊖ St. Jude Medical, Inc.	Health	34.9	-27.17	1.69
⊕ Yahoo, Inc.	Media	35.4	-34.81	1.66
⊖ General Electric Company	Ind Mtrls	20.0	9.35	1.64
⊖ Amgen, Inc.	Health	29.1	-13.38	1.64
⊖ Adobe Systems Inc.	Software	48.1	11.26	1.62
⊖ Sysco Corporation	Consumer	25.2	20.96	1.58
⊖ Amdocs Ltd.	Software	28.6	40.91	1.57
⊖ General Dynamics	Ind Mtrls	19.1	32.17	1.55
⊕ Getty Images, Inc.	Business	19.5	-52.03	1.52
⊕ PetSmart Inc.	Consumer	23.0	12.99	1.50
Symantec Corporation	Software	50.9	19.14	1.49
⊕ American Tower Corporati	Telecom	—	37.57	1.47

Current Investment Style

Value Blnd Growth — Large/Mid/Small

Market Cap	%
Giant	19.8
Large	34.0
Mid	44.8
Small	1.2
Micro	0.1

Avg $mil: 14,577

Value Measures		Rel Category
Price/Earnings	20.88	1.08
Price/Book	3.20	0.96
Price/Sales	1.94	1.00
Price/Cash Flow	12.61	1.11
Dividend Yield %	0.73	0.71

Growth Measures	%	Rel Category
Long-Term Erngs	15.98	1.11
Book Value	16.11	1.39
Sales	14.66	1.26
Cash Flow	19.08	1.14
Historical Erngs	22.20	0.97

Profitability	%	Rel Category
Return on Equity	18.40	0.91
Return on Assets	9.93	0.90
Net Margin	12.55	0.88

Sector Weightings	% of Stocks	Rel S&P 500	3 Year High	Low
⟳ Info	27.51	1.38		
Software	8.44	2.45	9	7
Hardware	12.63	1.37	15	10
Media	4.97	1.31	6	4
Telecom	1.47	0.42	3	1
⟳ Service	55.18	1.19		
Health	18.98	1.57	20	15
Consumer	11.98	1.57	18	12
Business	17.78	4.20	19	15
Financial	6.44	0.29	12	6
⟳ Mfg	17.31	0.51		
Goods	3.55	0.42	5	1
Ind Mtrls	7.82	0.65	8	3
Energy	5.94	0.61	6	4
Utilities	0.00	0.00	0	0

Composition

● Cash	0.3
● Stocks	99.7
● Bonds	0.0
○ Other	0.0
Foreign	2.5
(% of Stock)	

T. Rowe Price New Asia

Analyst Pick ✓	**Ticker** PRASX	**Load** None	**NAV** $14.21	**Yield** 1.3%	**Total Assets** $2,252 mil	**Mstar Category** Pacific/Asia ex-Japan Stk

Governance and Management

Stewardship Grade: B

Portfolio Manager(s)

After comanager Mark Edwards moved to London in June 2006 to focus exclusively on T. Rowe's broad emerging-markets portfolio, his former comanager Frances Dydasco is now the sole lead manager. Dydasco has managed here since 1996. T. Rowe has eight Asia ex-Japan analysts and is looking to hire a few more, including a senior person to head the regional research desk.

Strategy

The fund uses a moderate growth strategy, favoring industry leaders with strong earnings prospects and reasonable prices. Management prefers companies that can grow through cycles or benefit from enduring trends in their domestic economies. Management is willing to significantly overweight countries abundant in such stocks.

Performance 12-31-06

	1st Qtr	2nd Qtr	3rd Qtr	4th Qtr	Total
2002	9.50	-3.09	-17.60	3.66	-9.36
2003	-8.05	20.43	20.03	15.52	53.54
2004	5.99	-9.87	6.64	16.41	18.60
2005	1.79	4.21	13.15	5.34	26.43
2006	12.43	-8.20	8.93	21.08	36.12

Trailing	Total Return%	+/- MSCI EAFE	+/- MSCIAC FExJ	%Rank Cat	Growth of $10,000
3 Mo	21.08	10.73	5.68	46	12,108
6 Mo	31.89	17.20	10.67	35	13,189
1 Yr	36.12	9.78	7.65	62	13,612
3 Yr Avg	26.85	6.92	6.81	23	20,411
5 Yr Avg	23.22	8.24	6.51	29	28,406
10 Yr Avg	7.05	-0.66	6.68	38	19,764
15 Yr Avg	9.20	1.34	3.45	1	37,440

Tax Analysis	Tax-Adj Rtn%	%Rank Cat	Tax-Cost Rat	%Rank Cat
3 Yr (estimated)	25.17	21	1.32	81
5 Yr (estimated)	22.10	37	0.91	80
10 Yr (estimated)	6.41	34	0.60	68

Potential Capital Gain Exposure: 31% of assets

Morningstar's Take by Arijit Dutta 11-09-06

T. Rowe Price New Asia continues to do the right things.

This fund has seen a few changes and enhancements this year. It switched from its former two-manager structure in May, when longtime comanager Frances Dydasco became the sole skipper. Dydasco says the change will result in a more compact portfolio now that the fund no longer has two separate sleeves (the portfolio has indeed shrunk to 116 stocks currently, down from the 150-odd names it had earlier this year). She is also looking to boost the already sizable analyst ranks here. The fund's research bench recently added an experienced India analyst, and more hires are in the offing.

These changes play nicely into the fund's strategy and bolster its existing strengths. This is easily one of the more distinct portfolios in the Pacific/Asia ex-Japan category. The portfolio's average market cap is less than half the category average, and it tends to have large stakes in

smaller markets in the region. (For example, its 26% stake in India is more than triple the category norm.) It takes widespread research to pick winners from among lesser-known stocks, so we're glad to see additions to the team here. We also applaud Dydasco for showing more conviction because a slimmer portfolio naturally packs more punch, and extracts more mileage from the sound research.

Thus, the fund remains one of this narrow category's most viable choices. Single-country China and India offerings have dominated the fray this year, making even this fund's generous 21% year-to-date return look pale by comparison. The fund's flavorful, yet relatively diversified approach gives it a much better chance over the long run, however. Moreover, the fund's expenses continue to dip lower, cementing its claim as the best mutual fund bargain in the category for retail investors. We'd use the fund sparingly though, given this category's multiyear romp.

Address:	100 East Pratt Street Baltimore MD 21202 800-638-5660
Web Address:	www.troweprice.com
Inception:	09-28-90
Advisor:	T. Rowe Price International, Inc
Subadvisor:	None
NTF Plans:	N/A

Minimum Purchase:	$2500	Add: $100	IRA: $1000
Min Auto Inv Plan:	$2500	Add: $50	
Sales Fees:	No-load, 2.00%R		
Management Fee:	0.81%		
Actual Fees:	Mgt:0.81%	Dist:—	
Expense Projections:	3Yr:$334	5Yr:$579	10Yr:$1283
Income Distrib:	Annually		

Historical Profile
Return Above Avg
Risk Average
Rating ★★★★ Above Avg

	93%	91%	94%	95%	96%	93%	93%	92%	96%

Investment Style
Equity
Stock %

▼ Manager Change
▽ Partial Manager Change

Growth of $10,000
— Investment Values of Fund
— Investment Values of MSCI EAFE

22.0
18.0
14.0
10.0
5.0

Performance Quartile (within Category)

1995	1996	1997	1998	1999	2000	2001	2002	2003	2004	2005	2006	History
8.22	9.26	5.74	5.01	9.97	6.90	6.21	5.59	8.51	10.04	11.83	14.21	NAV
3.75	13.51	-37.13	-11.11	99.88	-30.79	-10.00	-9.36	53.54	18.60	26.43	36.12	Total Return %
-7.46	7.46	-38.91	-31.04	72.85	-16.60	11.42	6.58	14.95	-1.65	12.89	9.78	+/-MSCI EAFE
-3.09	4.18	8.48	-3.94	40.46	7.09	-5.86	1.69	12.77	4.37	8.57	7.65	+/-MSCIAC FExJ
1.12	0.73	0.86	1.57	0.80	0.00	0.00	0.64	1.07	0.00	1.20	1.78	Income Return %
2.63	12.78	-37.99	-12.68	99.08	-30.79	-10.00	-10.00	52.47	18.60	25.23	34.34	Capital Return %
38	68	69	51	11	74	68	31	39	8	21	62	Total Rtn % Rank Cat
0.09	0.06	0.08	0.09	0.04	0.00	0.00	0.04	0.06	0.00	0.12	0.21	Income $
0.00	0.01	0.04	0.00	0.00	0.00	0.00	0.00	0.01	0.05	0.72	1.59	Capital Gains $
1.15	1.11	1.10	1.29	1.21	1.08	1.22	1.17	1.17	1.09	1.05	—	Expense Ratio %
0.97	0.66	0.76	2.33	0.87	0.41	0.49	0.53	1.06	1.12	1.38	—	Income Ratio %
64	42	42	68	70	52	49	72	72	72	56	—	Turnover Rate %
1,880	2,182	782	622	1,375	800	639	543	885	997	1,442	2,252	Net Assets $mil

Rating and Risk

Time Period	Load-Adj Return %	Morningstar Rtn vs Cat	Morningstar Risk vs Cat	Morningstar Risk-Adj Rating
1 Yr	36.12			
3 Yr	26.85	+Avg	Avg	★★★★
5 Yr	23.22	+Avg	+Avg	★★★★
10 Yr	7.05	Avg	Avg	★★★
Incept	9.75			

Other Measures	Standard Index MSCI EAFE	Best Fit Index MSCIAC FExJ
Alpha	1.6	5.9
Beta	1.31	0.99
R-Squared	62	87
Standard Deviation	15.81	
Mean	26.85	
Sharpe Ratio	1.40	

Portfolio Analysis 09-30-06

Share change since 06-06 Total Stocks:117

	Sector	Country	% Assets
Finl Technolo	—	India	3.13
Kookmin Bank	Financial	Korea	2.97
Sun Hung Kai Properties	Financial	Hong Kong	2.10
Ping An Insurance Grp Co	Financial	Hong Kong	2.05
⊕ Cathay Finl Hldg	Financial	Taiwan	1.72
Glaxosmithkline Pharmace	Health	India	1.66
Kangwon Land	Consumer	Korea	1.54
China Life Insurance	Financial	Hong Kong	1.50
PetroChina	Energy	Hong Kong	1.46
IJM	Business	Malaysia	1.41
Suzlon Engy	Ind Mtrls	India	1.40
JCG Hldgs Ltd	Financial	Hong Kong	1.40
Sun Tv		India	1.34
Housing Development Fina	Financial	India	1.28
Bharti Televentures Ltd	Telecom	India	1.28
Lotte Shopping	—	Korea	1.27
Kumgang Korea Chemical	—	Korea	1.24
⊕ Exide Industries Ltd	Hardware	India	1.23
LG Card	Financial	Korea	1.22
Olam International	Consumer	Singapore	1.21

Current Investment Style

Value Blnd Growth — Large/Mid/Small

Market Cap	%
Giant	22.0
Large	36.8
Mid	36.0
Small	5.2
Micro	0.0

Avg $mil: 3,494

Value Measures		Rel Category
Price/Earnings	16.16	1.17
Price/Book	1.76	0.80
Price/Sales	1.31	0.95
Price/Cash Flow	7.16	1.01
Dividend Yield %	2.57	0.87

Growth Measures	%	Rel Category
Long-Term Erngs	15.74	0.97
Book Value	6.01	0.53
Sales	16.84	0.83
Cash Flow	12.12	0.70
Historical Erngs	9.72	0.44

Composition

Cash	3.2	Bonds	0.0
Stocks	96.1	Other	0.7
Foreign (% of Stock)			99.4

Sector Weightings	% of Stocks	Rel MSCI EAFE	3 Year High Low	
⊕ Info	15.32	1.30		
Software	0.00	0.00	3	0
Hardware	2.28	0.59	10	2
Media	5.60	3.06	6	3
Telecom	7.44	1.34	11	6
⊖ Service	58.53	1.24		
Health	2.95	0.41	4	1
Consumer	9.14	1.85	10	4
Business	13.98	2.76	14	6
Financial	32.46	1.08	32	20
Mfg	26.14	0.64		
Goods	11.09	0.85	23	11
Ind Mtrls	7.86	0.51	13	5
Energy	3.41	0.48	7	2
Utilities	3.78	0.72	4	0

Regional Exposure		% Stock
UK/W. Europe	1	N. America 1
Japan	0	Latn America 0
Asia X Japan	98	Other 0

Country Exposure		% Stock
India	26	Taiwan 9
Hong Kong	20	Singapore 8
South Korea	19	

Morningstar® Funds 500

T. Rowe Price New Era

	Ticker	Load	NAV	Yield	Total Assets	Mstar Category
	PRNEX	None	$46.00	1.2%	$4,473 mil	Specialty-Natural Res

Governance and Management

Stewardship Grade: A

Portfolio Manager(s)

Charlie Ober has called the shots since 1997 and was an analyst on the fund from 1980 to 1997. He leads a four-member team that follows natural-resources stocks.

Strategy

Veteran manager Charlie Ober looks for companies selling below his estimates of their private-market values. The fund has typically limited its energy exposure to less than 60% of assets, but management will now permit the portfolio's energy stake to increase to 80%. The remainder of the portfolio is diversified across other natural-resources subsectors and includes nonresource names that management expects to do well during inflationary periods.

Historical Profile
Return: Average
Risk: Low
Rating: ★★★★ Above Avg

96%	96%	97%	96%	99%	94%	93%	92%	97%		

Investment Style
Equity
Stock %

▼ Manager Change
▽ Partial Manager Change

Growth of $10,000
▬ Investment Values of Fund
▬ Investment Values of S&P 500

43.6
32.4
24.0
17.0
10.0

Performance Quartile (within Category)

1995	1996	1997	1998	1999	2000	2001	2002	2003	2004	2005	2006	History
22.65	26.06	25.95	19.78	21.80	24.30	22.24	20.63	27.22	33.68	41.10	46.00	NAV
20.76	24.25	10.96	-9.88	21.22	20.37	-4.35	-6.34	33.20	30.09	29.88	17.00	Total Return %
-16.82	1.29	-22.40	-38.46	0.18	29.47	7.54	15.76	4.52	19.21	24.97	1.21	+/-S&P 500
—	—	-5.98	14.79	-6.00	4.56	11.24	6.92	-0.81	5.52	-6.60	0.18	+/-GS NATR RES
2.38	1.68	1.42	1.54	1.52	1.33	1.11	0.90	1.21	0.84	1.10	1.39	Income Return %
18.38	22.57	9.54	-11.42	19.70	19.04	-5.46	-7.24	31.99	29.25	28.78	15.61	Capital Return %
62	69	28	3	83	66	26	57	31	34	72	34	Total Rtn % Rank Cat
0.48	0.38	0.37	0.40	0.30	0.29	0.27	0.20	0.25	0.23	0.37	0.57	Income $
1.20	1.71	2.54	3.17	1.82	1.51	0.68	0.00	0.00	1.46	2.32	1.55	Capital Gains $
0.79	0.76	0.74	0.75	0.74	0.72	0.72	0.72	0.72	0.69	0.68	—	Expense Ratio %
2.00	1.53	1.33	1.27	1.29	1.29	1.11	1.03	1.13	0.87	1.02	—	Income Ratio %
23	29	28	23	32	29	18	11	18	19	36	—	Turnover Rate %
1,090	1,468	1,493	997	1,082	1,195	1,070	985	1,334	2,161	3,763	4,473	Net Assets $mil

Performance 12-31-06

	1st Qtr	2nd Qtr	3rd Qtr	4th Qtr	Total
2002	9.80	-3.56	-17.20	6.82	-6.34
2003	-2.76	10.57	4.42	18.65	33.20
2004	4.96	3.19	12.21	7.04	30.09
2005	7.60	2.43	15.60	1.94	29.88
2006	9.68	3.35	-7.15	11.16	17.00

Trailing	Total Return%	+/- S&P 500	+/- GS NATR RES	%Rank Cat	Growth of $10,000
3 Mo	11.16	4.46	1.59	24	11,116
6 Mo	3.21	-9.53	0.64	31	10,321
1 Yr	17.00	1.21	0.18	34	11,700
3 Yr Avg	25.50	15.06	-0.20	67	19,767
5 Yr Avg	19.79	13.60	1.58	44	24,666
10 Yr Avg	13.16	4.74	3.44	38	34,429
15 Yr Avg	13.17	2.53	—	50	63,969

Tax Analysis	Tax-Adj Rtn%	%Rank Cat	Tax-Cost Rat	%Rank Cat
3 Yr (estimated)	24.20	54	1.04	28
5 Yr (estimated)	18.87	46	0.77	33
10 Yr (estimated)	11.35	52	1.60	86

Potential Capital Gain Exposure: 42% of assets

Rating and Risk

Time Period	Load-Adj Return %	Morningstar Rtn vs Cat	Morningstar Risk vs Cat	Morningstar Risk-Adj Rating
1 Yr	17.00			
3 Yr	25.50	Avg	-Avg	★★★
5 Yr	19.79	Avg	Low	★★★
10 Yr	13.16	Avg	Low	★★★★
Incept	—			

Other Measures	Standard Index S&P 500	Best Fit Index GS NATR RES
Alpha	12.8	2.5
Beta	1.18	0.86
R-Squared	23	94
Standard Deviation	16.87	
Mean	25.50	
Sharpe Ratio	1.25	

Morningstar's Take by Lawrence Jones 12-21-06

Several factors make T. Rowe Price New Era look appealing.

Manager Charlie Ober has been with the fund a long time. Ober started here as an analyst in 1980, and became the fund's sole manager in 1997. In addition to the energy industry, he has covered the forest products and paper, chemical, and metals and mining industries over the years. Now, as he approaches a decade as lead of this offering (making him one of the most experienced managers in the natural-resources category), he has the help of four analysts in this work. We're encouraged by Ober's experience, which is particularly important in a volatile category like this one, since it provides him with valuable perspective when navigating through different market cycles.

In addition to Ober's experience, we like his approach at the fund. Whereas many funds in the category hold huge positions in energy stocks, management here will keep the portfolio more broadly diversified. Depending on his market outlook for the sector, Ober will usually hold between 40% and 60% of the portfolio in energy stocks. Currently, however, the fund is at 65% (compared with the category's 71% average stake), illustrating Ober's positive view on energy. Additionally, Ober practices a low-turnover, long-term strategy here that focuses on the giant-cap integrated oil companies. Low turnover not only keeps trading costs down, it also makes the fund more tax-efficient than others. Also, holding giant industry leaders serves as ballast in a segment of the market known for turbulence.

While this restrained approach can hold the fund back when the energy sector soars, as it has in recent years, investors trade sky-high returns for increased stability. In fact, the fund holds the lowest volatility levels in the category for the trailing five and 10-year periods.

Overall, we think the fund's experienced management, moderate approach, and relatively low volatility, argue in its favor.

Address:	100 East Pratt Street
	Baltimore MD 21202
	800-638-5660
Web Address:	www.troweprice.com
Inception:	01-20-69
Advisor:	T. Rowe Price Associates, Inc.
Subadvisor:	None
NTF Plans:	N/A

Minimum Purchase:	$2500	Add: $100	IRA: $1000
Min Auto Inv Plan:	$50	Add: $50	
Sales Fees:	No-load		
Management Fee:	0.56%		
Actual Fees:	Mgt:0.56%	Dist: —	
Expense Projections:	3Yr:$218	5Yr:$379	10Yr:$847
Income Distrib:	Annually		

Portfolio Analysis 09-30-06

Share change since 06-06 Total Stocks:92	Sector	PE	Tot Ret%	% Assets
⊕ Schlumberger, Ltd.	Energy	22.3	31.07	3.54
⊕ ExxonMobil Corporation	Energy	11.1	39.07	3.28
⊕ Cooper Cameron Corporati	Energy	21.8	28.14	3.15
Royal Dutch Shell PLC AD	Energy	8.7	19.33	3.08
⊕ ConocoPhillips	Energy	6.5	26.53	2.64
⊕ Baker Hughes Inc.	Energy	9.9	23.68	2.56
⊕ Diamond Offshore Drillin	Energy	17.8	17.82	2.49
⊕ Total SA ADR	Energy	10.6	19.24	2.42
⊕ Canadian Natural Resourc	Energy	29.1	7.84	2.39
⊕ Murphy Oil Corporation	Energy	12.8	-4.82	2.25
⊕ Smith International, Inc	Energy	17.0	11.59	2.24
⊕ BHP Billiton Ltd	Ind Mtrls	—	—	2.22
⊕ BP PLC ADR	Energy	10.4	7.94	2.06
⊕ Transocean, Inc.	Energy	27.1	16.07	2.02
⊕ Statoil	Energy			2.00
⊕ BJ Services Company	Energy	10.6	-19.55	1.80
⊕ Teck Cominco Limited B	Ind Mtrls	10.9	40.45	1.70
⊕ Devon Energy Corporation	Energy	9.2	8.06	1.65
⊕ Rio Tinto	Ind Mtrls	—	—	1.53
⊕ International Paper Co.	Ind Mtrls		4.51	1.51

Current Investment Style

Value Blnd Growth — Large Mid Small

Market Cap	%
Giant	31.4
Large	30.5
Mid	33.8
Small	4.3
Micro	0.0

Avg $mil: 19,146

Value Measures		Rel Category
Price/Earnings	12.93	1.03
Price/Book	2.55	0.99
Price/Sales	1.14	0.90
Price/Cash Flow	7.48	1.06
Dividend Yield %	1.48	1.42

Growth Measures	%	Rel Category
Long-Term Erngs	15.45	0.98
Book Value	9.28	0.64
Sales	16.13	0.86
Cash Flow	26.50	0.95
Historical Erngs	38.39	0.83

Profitability	%	Rel Category
Return on Equity	21.29	0.99
Return on Assets	9.89	1.01
Net Margin	14.61	0.95

Industry Weightings

	% of Stocks	Rel Cat
Oil & Gas	24.8	0.8
Oil/Gas Products	6.9	0.7
Oil & Gas Srv	30.4	1.0
Pipelines	1.7	1.7
Utilities	4.7	4.4
Hard Commd	5.1	0.6
Soft Commd	5.6	2.5
Misc. Indstrl	9.1	1.2
Other	11.7	1.4

Composition

● Cash	2.5
● Stocks	97.5
● Bonds	0.0
○ Other	0.0
Foreign	32.1
(% of Stock)	

T. Rowe Price New Horiz

	Ticker	Load	NAV	Yield	Total Assets	Mstar Category
	PRNHX	None	$32.29	0.0%	$6,998 mil	Small Growth

Governance and Management

Stewardship Grade: B

Portfolio Manager(s)

Stability has been the name of the game at this fund. Jack Laporte has run it since 1987. T. Rowe Price's staff of 30 to 35 sector analysts also contributes ideas.

Strategy

Jack Laporte scours the small-cap universe for companies with strong and predictable earnings growth and then typically lets his winners run. With nearly 300 names and broad industry diversification, this fund covers more territory than most peers.

Historical Profile

Return	Above Avg
Risk	Average
Rating	★★★★ Above Avg

96% 95% 94% 98% 98% 99% 97% 96% 99%

Investment Style
Equity
Stock %

▼ Manager Change
▽ Partial Manager Change

Growth of $10,000
— Investment Values of Fund
— Investment Values of S&P 500

38.0 31.0 24.0 17.0 10.0

Performance Quartile (within Category)

1995	1996	1997	1998	1999	2000	2001	2002	2003	2004	2005	2006	History
20.50	21.77	23.30	23.34	27.53	23.89	22.63	16.61	24.80	29.24	31.74	32.29	NAV
55.44	17.03	9.77	6.25	32.52	-1.86	-2.84	-26.60	49.31	17.90	11.90	7.39	Total Return %
17.86	-5.93	-23.59	-22.33	11.48	7.24	9.05	-4.50	20.63	7.02	6.99	-8.40	+/-S&P 500
24.40	5.77	-3.18	5.02	-10.57	20.57	6.39	3.66	0.77	3.59	7.75	-5.96	+/-Russ 2000 Gr
0.00	0.00	0.00	0.00	0.00	0.00	0.00	0.00	0.00	0.00	0.00	0.00	Income Return %
55.44	17.03	9.77	6.25	32.52	-1.86	-2.84	-26.60	49.31	17.90	11.90	7.39	Capital Return %
7	55	80	42	71	43	32	46	29	18	12	73	Total Rtn % Rank Cat
0.00	0.00	0.00	0.00	0.00	0.00	0.00	0.00	0.00	0.00	0.00	0.00	Income $
2.41	2.19	0.58	1.27	3.02	3.14	0.56	0.00	0.00	0.00	1.00	1.79	Capital Gains $
0.90	0.90	0.88	0.89	0.90	0.88	0.91	0.92	0.91	0.87	0.84	—	Expense Ratio %
-0.23	-0.41	-0.57	-0.65	-0.66	-0.51	-0.77	-0.81	-0.75	-0.67	-0.47	—	Income Ratio %
56	41	45	41	45	47	27	24	29	25	24	—	Turnover Rate %
2,855	4,363	5,104	5,228	6,022	6,122	5,583	3,359	4,960	5,831	6,552	6,998	Net Assets $mil

Performance 12-31-06

	1st Qtr	2nd Qtr	3rd Qtr	4th Qtr	Total
2002	-1.50	-15.48	-19.16	9.06	-26.60
2003	-1.57	24.53	6.58	14.29	49.31
2004	7.66	-0.30	-4.06	14.49	17.90
2005	-2.09	5.41	5.67	2.60	11.90
2006	11.66	-8.83	-0.68	6.22	7.39

Trailing	Total Return%	+/- S&P 500	+/- Russ 2000 Gr	%Rank Cat	Growth of $10,000
3 Mo	6.22	-0.48	-2.55	77	10,622
6 Mo	5.50	-7.24	-1.36	45	10,550
1 Yr	7.39	-8.40	-5.96	73	10,739
3 Yr Avg	12.32	1.88	1.81	23	14,170
5 Yr Avg	9.20	3.01	2.27	25	15,528
10 Yr Avg	8.63	0.21	3.75	49	22,882
15 Yr Avg	12.22	1.58	5.12	6	56,371

Tax Analysis	Tax-Adj Rtn%	%Rank Cat	Tax-Cost Rat	%Rank Cat
3 Yr (estimated)	11.83	17	0.44	16
5 Yr (estimated)	8.92	18	0.26	13
10 Yr (estimated)	7.63	41	0.92	33

Potential Capital Gain Exposure: 41% of assets

Rating and Risk

Time Period	Load-Adj Return %	Morningstar Rtn vs Cat	Morningstar Risk vs Cat	Morningstar Risk-Adj Rating
1 Yr	7.39			
3 Yr	12.32	+Avg	-Avg	★★★★
5 Yr	9.20	+Avg	Avg	★★★★
10 Yr	8.63	Avg	Avg	★★★
Incept	11.43			

Other Measures	Standard Index S&P 500	Best Fit Index Mstar Small Growth
Alpha	-2.1	3.5
Beta	1.63	0.78
R-Squared	72	94
Standard Deviation	13.12	
Mean	12.32	
Sharpe Ratio	0.71	

Morningstar's Take by Karen Wallace 12-27-06

T. Rowe Price New Horizons has a lot to recommend it, but one detractor.

This fund has an experienced and talented manager calling the shots, not to mention a proven and repeatable strategy and reasonable fees. Manager Jack Laporte buys small-cap companies early in their life cycles that he thinks can grow for many years, have adequate capital to fund their growth, and have strong management teams. Then he holds on to them. For example, he picked up shares of homebuilder Toll Brothers nearly 10 years ago. Initially, it was just 0.1% of the portfolio, but it has grown to 1.5% of assets as the stock has appreciated. Despite its long-term success, Toll Brothers has been one of the reasons this fund has struggled in 2006. The stock has lost nearly 9% as the housing market has slowed.

Even though the fund's process is solid, we worry about its growing size. The $7 billion-in-assets fund is many times the size of the typical small-growth fund. Funds with small asset bases that fish in small-cap waters have an advantage because they can more easily trade less-liquid small-cap stocks without influencing their share prices as much.

The fund, however, has traits that allay our concerns. Laporte trades less. The fund's turnover is about one fifth of its average rival. Laporte also has demonstrated that he can run a large fund with a lot of holdings for a long time—it's been among the largest options in its peer group for nearly 10 years. And Laporte hasn't suddenly changed his strategy by increasing the number of holdings in the portfolio or moving into mid-caps to compensate for huge inflows. Still, it's worth watching for signs of asset bloat.

Overall, despite the size concerns, we think this is a good fund. It has distinguished itself in three ways that are meaningful to shareholders: Returns are consistently above-average, volatility has been moderate, and costs are well below average.

Portfolio Analysis 09-30-06

Share change since 06-06 Total Stocks:280

	Sector	PE	Tot Ret%	% Assets
⊖ NII Holdings, Inc.	Telecom	45.9	47.53	3.37
Henry Schein, Inc.	Health	24.0	12.24	2.83
Davita, Inc.	Health	21.1	12.32	2.18
O'Reilly Automotive, Inc	Consumer	20.4	0.16	1.77
⊖ Apollo Group, Inc. A	Consumer	15.9	-35.54	1.57
Coventry Health Care, In	Health	15.4	-12.13	1.49
Toll Brothers, Inc.	Consumer	6.2	-6.96	1.47
Oshkosh Truck Corporatio	Ind Mtrls	17.1	9.47	1.41
Roper Industries, Inc.	Ind Mtrls	24.8	27.83	1.35
⊕ Laureate Education, Inc.	Consumer	27.1	-7.39	1.26
FMC Technologies, Inc.	Energy	19.7	43.59	1.21
⊕ Corporate Executive Boar	Business	46.2	-0.97	1.18
Actuant Corporation A	Ind Mtrls	15.6	-14.47	1.13
FactSet Research Systems	Business	33.8	37.91	1.11
⊕ Panera Bread Company, In	Consumer	31.9	-14.88	1.10
Grant Prideco, Inc.	Energy	15.2	-9.86	0.92
Crown Castle Internation	Telecom	—	20.94	0.91
Integrated Device Techno	Hardware	—	17.45	0.88
Mobile Mini	Ind Mtrls	25.4	13.67	0.88
Christopher & Banks Corp	Consumer	18.4	0.22	0.87

Current Investment Style

Value Blnd Growth — Large Mid Small

Market Cap	%
Giant	0.0
Large	0.8
Mid	46.2
Small	44.8
Micro	8.1

Avg $mil: 1,867

Value Measures		Rel Category
Price/Earnings	19.79	0.94
Price/Book	2.57	0.94
Price/Sales	1.63	1.04
Price/Cash Flow	10.42	1.08
Dividend Yield %	0.26	0.57

Growth Measures	%	Rel Category
Long-Term Erngs	17.09	0.96
Book Value	14.97	1.43
Sales	17.43	1.47
Cash Flow	25.16	1.19
Historical Erngs	26.52	1.09

Profitability	%	Rel Category
Return on Equity	13.11	1.06
Return on Assets	5.99	0.90
Net Margin	8.34	0.96

Sector Weightings

	% of Stocks	Rel S&P 500	3 Year High Low
↻ Info	21.03	1.05	
☐ Software	6.48	1.88	9 6
☐ Hardware	7.95	0.86	9 8
☐ Media	1.08	0.28	3 1
☐ Telecom	5.52	1.57	6 4
☞ Service	60.34	1.31	
☐ Health	20.11	1.67	21 18
☐ Consumer	17.43	2.28	24 17
☐ Business	15.00	3.55	15 9
☐ Financial	7.80	0.35	10 7
⊔ Mfg	18.64	0.55	
☐ Goods	1.46	0.17	2 1
☐ Ind Mtrls	10.16	0.85	10 7
☐ Energy	7.02	0.72	8 5
☐ Utilities	0.00	0.00	0 0

Composition

● Cash	0.9	
● Stocks	99.0	
● Bonds	0.0	
○ Other	0.1	
Foreign (% of Stock)	0.9	

Address:	100 East Pratt Street Baltimore MD 21202 800-638-5660	Minimum Purchase:	$2500	Add: $100	IRA: $1000
		Min Auto Inv Plan:	$50	Add: $50	
		Sales Fees:	No-load		
Web Address:	www.troweprice.com	Management Fee:	0.66%		
Inception:	06-03-60	Actual Fees:	Mgt:0.66%	Dist: —	
Advisor:	T. Rowe Price Associates, Inc.	Expense Projections:	3Yr:$268	5Yr:$466	10Yr:$1037
Subadvisor:	None	Income Distrib:	Annually		
NTF Plans:	N/A				

MORNINGSTAR® Funds 500

T. Rowe Price New Inc

	Ticker	Load	NAV	Yield	SEC Yield	Total Assets	Mstar Category
	PRCIX	None	$8.92	4.6%	4.55%	$4,476 mil	Intermediate-Term Bond

Governance and Management

Stewardship Grade: B

Portfolio Manager(s)

Dan Shackelford was named lead manager of this fund in December 2002, but he has been a member of the fund's management team since January 2000. Sector specialists Connie Bavely, Brian Brennan, and David Tiberii support Shackelford in advisory roles.

Strategy

This fund looks to outperform the Lehman Brothers Aggregate Bond Index. It holds a mix of corporate bonds, Treasury bonds, mortgage-related issues, and nondollar bonds. Manager Dan Shackelford makes adjustments to the fund's sector weightings and duration depending on relative valuations and his economic outlook. The fund's duration, however, tends to stay within 10% of the index's. Shackelford relies heavily on sector specialists for the fund's issue selection.

Historical Profile

Return	Average
Risk	Average
Rating	★★★★ Above Avg

Investment Style Fixed Income
Income Rtn %Rank Cat

▼ Manager Change
▽ Partial Manager Change

Growth of $10,000
— Investment Values of Fund
— Investment Values of LB Aggr

Performance Quartile (within Category)

1995	1996	1997	1998	1999	2000	2001	2002	2003	2004	2005	2006	History
9.28	8.89	9.07	8.81	8.16	8.50	8.68	8.89	9.05	9.11	8.97	8.92	NAV
18.36	2.39	9.32	5.04	-1.58	11.13	8.15	7.48	5.61	4.60	2.85	4.13	Total Return %
-0.11	-1.24	-0.33	-3.65	-0.76	-0.50	-0.29	-2.77	1.51	0.26	0.42	-0.20	+/-LB Aggr
-3.07	-0.30	-0.11	-5.10	1.30	-1.31	-0.67	-5.55	-0.36	-0.70	1.02	0.32	+/-LB 5-10YR
7.44	6.57	6.69	6.43	5.98	6.74	6.03	4.97	3.80	3.79	4.20	4.65	Income Return %
10.92	-4.18	2.63	-1.39	-7.56	4.39	2.12	2.51	1.81	0.81	-1.35	-0.52	Capital Return %
42	78	40	89	58	24	31	72	32	28	6	40	Total Rtn % Rank Cat
0.61	0.59	0.58	0.57	0.51	0.53	0.50	0.42	0.33	0.34	0.38	0.41	Income $
0.00	0.00	0.04	0.14	0.00	0.00	0.00	0.00	0.01	0.02	0.00	0.00	Capital Gains $
0.78	0.75	0.74	0.71	0.72	0.73	0.73	0.72	0.71	0.71	0.69	0.67	Expense Ratio %
6.95	6.66	6.65	6.31	6.16	6.32	6.30	5.38	4.23	3.56	3.85	4.23	Income Ratio %
54	36	87	147	94	84	112	222	221	219	136	105	Turnover Rate %
1,668	1,688	1,945	2,103	1,795	1,715	1,803	2,018	2,297	2,866	3,519	4,465	Net Assets $mil

Performance 12-31-06

	1st Qtr	2nd Qtr	3rd Qtr	4th Qtr	Total
2002	0.02	2.68	2.90	1.71	7.48
2003	2.02	3.18	-0.34	0.67	5.61
2004	2.41	-2.36	3.21	1.36	4.60
2005	-0.36	3.06	-0.50	0.66	2.85
2006	-0.82	-0.30	3.86	1.39	4.13

Trailing	Total Return%	+/- LB Aggr	+/- LB 5-10YR	%Rank Cat	Growth of $10,000
3 Mo	1.39	0.15	0.31	29	10,139
6 Mo	5.31	0.22	-0.37	20	10,531
1 Yr	4.13	-0.20	0.32	40	10,413
3 Yr Avg	3.86	0.16	0.22	22	11,203
5 Yr Avg	4.92	-0.14	-1.00	32	12,714
10 Yr Avg	5.62	-0.62	-1.06	44	17,277
15 Yr Avg	5.84	-0.66	-1.15	69	23,429

Tax Analysis	Tax-Adj Rtn%	%Rank Cat	Tax-Cost Rat	%Rank Cat
3 Yr (estimated)	2.32	16	1.48	50
5 Yr (estimated)	3.34	21	1.51	42
10 Yr (estimated)	3.50	35	2.01	48

Potential Capital Gain Exposure: 0% of assets

Rating and Risk

Time Period	Load-Adj Return %	Morningstar Rtn vs Cat	Morningstar Risk vs Cat	Morningstar Risk-Adj Rating
1 Yr	4.13			
3 Yr	3.86	+Avg	Avg	★★★★
5 Yr	4.92	Avg	Avg	★★★★
10 Yr	5.62	Avg	Avg	★★★
Incept	7.87			

Other Measures	Standard Index LB Aggr	Best Fit Index LB Aggr
Alpha	0.2	0.2
Beta	0.96	0.96
R-Squared	99	99
Standard Deviation	3.14	
Mean	3.86	
Sharpe Ratio	0.20	

Morningstar's Take by Arijit Dutta 11-30-06

We continue to see consistency and sound judgment at T. Rowe Price New Income.

This fund has reversed its difficulties from earlier this year, thanks to management's calculated moves. Concerns about rising interest rates deepened toward the middle of 2006, which hurt this portfolio because of its much heavier exposure to longer-dated bonds (relative to intermediate-term bond category peers). Manager Dan Shackelford held on to T. Rowe's firmwide forecast of lower long-term rates, however. Since July, markets have indeed come around to that view. Also, while the portfolio's underweighting in high-yield issues has held it back, Shackelford's decision to maintain a modest presence in emerging markets (mainly through highly rated countries such as Mexico and Poland) has contributed handsomely. The fund has now pulled slightly ahead of the category for the year.

The fund's flexible mandate and Shackelford's thoughtful execution should continue to prove an effective mix. Shackelford has considerable freedom here to incorporate the expertise of other T. Rowe bond managers, which leads to a diversified portfolio covering a broad range of assets. This gives him added opportunities to add value, such as foreign and high-yield bonds in recent years. Shackelford is valuation-conscious, however, which is reassuring because some of the portfolio's more offbeat stakes can be risky. For example, he reduced the portfolio's corporate and high-yield exposure last year because those bonds looked richly priced. Moreover, Shackelford minimizes security-specific risk by spreading assets over a large number of individual bonds.

We must say, though, this isn't quite the cheapest option in the category. The fund is up against some seasoned rivals, and returns fall in a rather narrow range in this bitterly contested category, so costs matter a lot. Still, the fund's diversified approach and sound management make it a viable choice.

Portfolio Analysis 09-30-06

Total Fixed-Income:1154	Date of Maturity	Amount $000	Value $000	% Net Assets
FNMA 6%	02-01-34	87,040	87,715	2.11
US Treasury Note 4.25%	11-15-14	82,190	80,161	1.93
US Treasury Note 5.125%	05-15-16	51,671	53,584	1.29
FNMA 5.5%	01-01-36	51,263	50,517	1.22
FHLMC 5.125%	07-15-12	47,748	48,212	1.16
US Treasury Note 4.25%	11-15-13	45,460	44,466	1.07
FNMA 5.5%	06-01-33	44,084	43,621	1.05
US Treasury Note 2%	07-15-14	40,961	40,148	0.97
US Treasury Bond 7.5%	11-15-16	31,290	38,325	0.92
Poland (Republic Of) 5%	10-24-13	118,100	36,699	0.88
FHLMC 5%	11-01-35	36,989	35,588	0.86
FNMA 6.5%		33,400	33,995	0.82
US Treasury Bond 6.5%	11-15-26	26,870	32,555	0.78
FNMA 5.5%	04-01-34	32,156	31,798	0.77
10 Year Int Rate Swap	09-12-16	31,150	31,447	0.76
US Treasury Note 4.875%	02-15-12	30,950	31,385	0.76
Mexico (United Mexican S	12-19-13	347,800	31,296	0.75
FHLMC 5.5%	12-01-18	29,653	29,713	0.72
US Treasury Bond 8.5%	02-15-20	21,165	28,837	0.69
FHLMC CMO 4.5%	03-15-16	29,183	28,497	0.69

Current Investment Style

Duration: Short Int Long
Quality: High Med Low

1 figure provided by fund

Avg Eff Duration[1]	4.7 Yrs
Avg Eff Maturity	7.3 Yrs
Avg Credit Quality	AA
Avg Wtd Coupon	5.30%
Avg Wtd Price	98.97% of par

Coupon Range	% of Bonds	Rel Cat
0% PIK	3.8	0.5
0% to 6%	77.5	1.1
6% to 8%	19.3	0.9
8% to 10%	3.1	0.7
More than 10%	0.0	0.0

1.00=Category Average

Credit Analysis		% bonds 09-30-06	
AAA	73	BB	1
AA	3	B	1
A	9	Below B	0
BBB	12	NR/NA	0

Sector Breakdown % of assets

US Treasuries	13
TIPS	0
US Agency	5
Mortgage Pass-Throughs	30
Mortgage CMO	15
Mortgage ARM	0
US Corporate	22
Asset-Backed	5
Convertible	0
Municipal	0
Corporate Inflation-Protected	0
Foreign Corporate	1
Foreign Govt	2

Composition

Cash	6.5	Bonds	91.5
Stocks	0.4	Other	1.6

Special Securities

Restricted/Illiquid Secs	4
Exotic Mortgage-Backed	0
Emerging-Markets Secs	3
Options/Futures/Warrants	No

Address:	100 East Pratt Street Baltimore MD 21202 800-638-5660
Web Address:	www.troweprice.com
Inception:	10-15-73
Advisor:	T. Rowe Price Associates, Inc.
Subadvisor:	None
NTF Plans:	N/A

Minimum Purchase:	$2500	Add: $100	IRA: $1000
Min Auto Inv Plan:	$50	Add: $50	
Sales Fees:	No-load		
Management Fee:	0.46%		
Actual Fees:	Mgt:0.46%	Dist: —	
Expense Projections:	3Yr:$214	5Yr:$373	10Yr:$835
Income Distrib:	Monthly		

T. Rowe Price Pers Inc

Ticker	**Load**	**NAV**	**Yield**	**Total Assets**	**Mstar Category**
PRSIX	None	$15.84	2.9%	$605 mil	Conservative Allocation

Governance and Management

Stewardship Grade: B

Portfolio Manager(s)

Lead manager Ned Notzon, who sets the fund's security mix, fills the same role at four other T. Rowe Price funds and runs the investment-grade bond slice of T. Rowe Price Balanced. The managers of this fund's subportfolios include Larry Puglia of T. Rowe Price Blue Chip Growth, Stephen Boesel of T. Rowe Price Capital Appreciation, Greg McCrickard of T. Rowe Price Small-Cap Stock, Ray Mills of T. Rowe Price International Growth & Income, Daniel Shackelford of T. Rowe Price New Income, and Mark Vaselkiv of T. Rowe Price High-Yield.

Strategy

The fund is designed to provide one-stop exposure to most asset classes. Each stock or bond component mirrors one of T. Rowe Price's offerings. The stock portfolio, which typically consumes 35% to 45% of the fund's assets, is divided among large-growth, large-value, small-cap, and international components. The fund's bond stake includes domestic investment-grade and high-yield issues, and sometimes international bonds. An investment committee headed by lead manager Ned Notzon determines the fund's asset allocation.

Performance 12-31-06

	1st Qtr	2nd Qtr	3rd Qtr	4th Qtr	Total
2002	1.33	-2.79	-5.97	4.32	-3.37
2003	-0.59	9.20	1.95	7.15	18.58
2004	2.45	0.00	1.14	6.10	9.95
2005	-1.28	2.06	2.57	1.79	5.19
2006	2.52	-0.90	3.58	4.19	9.64

Trailing	Total Return%	+/- DJ Mod	+/- DJ 40%	%Rank Cat	Growth of $10,000
3 Mo	4.19	-1.40	1.15	21	10,419
6 Mo	7.92	-0.87	1.36	19	10,792
1 Yr	9.64	-2.66	2.18	21	10,964
3 Yr Avg	8.24	-2.48	1.20	10	12,681
5 Yr Avg	7.76	-2.26	1.03	8	14,531
10 Yr Avg	7.74	-0.81	0.04	9	21,075
15 Yr Avg	—	—	—		—

Tax Analysis	Tax-Adj Rtn%	%Rank Cat	Tax-Cost Rat	%Rank Cat
3 Yr (estimated)	7.10	6	1.05	53
5 Yr (estimated)	6.63	7	1.05	44
10 Yr (estimated)	6.18	6	1.45	32

Potential Capital Gain Exposure: 13% of assets

Morningstar's Take by Christopher Davis 11-20-06

T. Rowe Price Personal Strategy Income is a good way to keep things simple.

This offering is designed to provide all-in-one exposure to stocks and bonds. To that end, lead manager Ned Notzon and his committee spread the portfolio broadly across asset classes, typically keeping around 40% of assets in stocks and the remainder in bonds. They delegate security-selection duties to other T. Rowe Price managers. The large-growth slice of the portfolio, for instance, is a clone of T. Rowe Price Blue Chip Growth. But the committee oversees the fund's overall asset allocation and adjusts it to reflect where it's finding the most-attractive values.

The committee has given the fund an increasingly growth-oriented cast in recent years. The group likes to tilt the portfolio toward areas that have been out of favor, and given their long-running losing streak, large-growth stocks fit the bill. Believing such names look relatively cheap, it has been pushing more money toward Blue Chip

Growth's Larry Puglia. That's why the fund has moved from the large-blend slot of our style box (where it typically resides) into large-growth territory.

While that bet has yet to pay off, the committee has gotten it right more often than not. Indeed, its earlier calls, including its decision to ratchet up the fund's equity stake beginning in late 2002, have added value on the margins over the years. Yet what will make or break the fund is the quality of its holdings. Fortunately, with managers like Puglia, not to mention T. Rowe Price Small-Cap Stock's Greg McCrickard and T. Rowe Price High Yield's Mark Vaselkiv, we think the fund is in capable hands.

This offering holds special appeal for income-oriented investors willing to stomach a bit more volatility or for younger retirees. Rivals like Fidelity Asset Manager 20% and Vanguard LifeStrategy Income keep much less of their portfolios in stocks.

Address:	100 East Pratt Street Baltimore MD 21202 800-638-5660	Minimum Purchase:	$2500	Add: $100 IRA: $1000
		Min Auto Inv Plan:	$50	Add: $50
		Sales Fees:	No-load	
Web Address:	www.troweprice.com	Management Fee:	0.46%	
Inception:	07-29-94	Actual Fees:	Mgt:0.46%	Dist: —
Advisor:	T. Rowe Price Associates, Inc.	Expense Projections:	3Yr:$255	5Yr:$444 10Yr:$990
Subadvisor:	None	Income Distrib:	Quarterly	
NTF Plans:	N/A			

Historical Profile

Return	Above Avg
Risk	Above Avg
Rating	★★★★ Above Avg

Growth of $10,000
— Investment Values of Fund
— Investment Values of DJ Mod

38%	43%	40%	39%	43%	44%	46%	47%	44%			

	Manager Change			
	Partial Manager Change			

Performance Quartile (within Category)

1995	1996	1997	1998	1999	2000	2001	2002	2003	2004	2005	2006	History
11.70	11.56	12.45	13.27	13.03	13.18	12.81	12.00	13.87	14.84	15.07	15.84	NAV
24.71	11.79	15.01	11.50	5.17	6.59	0.95	-3.37	18.58	9.95	5.19	9.64	Total Return %
4.91	1.13	3.11	-0.82	-12.16	8.26	3.75	3.40	-8.80	-3.02	-1.80	-2.66	+/-DJ Mod
6.55	2.90	0.91	-0.23	-2.69	-0.20	-2.27	0.65	0.92	0.94	0.50	2.18	+/-DJ 40%
4.95	4.16	4.66	4.00	4.05	4.13	3.69	3.00	2.69	2.55	2.38	3.09	Income Return %
19.76	7.63	10.35	7.50	1.12	2.46	-2.74	-6.37	15.89	7.40	2.81	6.55	Capital Return %
16	25	30	34	47	17	37	53	13	6	10	21	Total Rtn % Rank Cat
0.48	0.47	0.53	0.49	0.53	0.53	0.48	0.38	0.32	0.35	0.35	0.46	Income $
0.10	0.98	0.28	0.10	0.37	0.16	0.00	0.00	0.01	0.04	0.18	0.20	Capital Gains $
0.95	0.95	0.95	0.95	0.90	0.90	0.90	1.02	0.80	0.71	0.76	0.78	Expense Ratio %
4.71	4.31	4.38	4.13	3.91	4.06	4.04	2.54	2.89	2.36	2.45	2.68	Income Ratio %
50	34	45	31	49	45	80	116	109	98	84	53	Turnover Rate %
26	33	66	213	206	228	251	259	341	371	483	605	Net Assets $mil

Rating and Risk

Time Period	Load-Adj Return %	Morningstar Rtn vs Cat	Morningstar Risk vs Cat	Morningstar Risk-Adj Rating
1 Yr	9.64			
3 Yr	8.24	+Avg	+Avg	★★★★
5 Yr	7.76	High	+Avg	★★★★★
10 Yr	7.74	+Avg	Avg	★★★★
Incept	9.14			

Other Measures	Standard Index DJ Mod	Best Fit Index DJ Mod
Alpha	0.0	0.0
Beta	0.67	0.67
R-Squared	94	94
Standard Deviation	4.05	
Mean	8.24	
Sharpe Ratio	1.19	

Portfolio Analysis 09-30-06

Total Stocks:656 Share change since 06-30-06	Sectors	P/E Ratio	YTD Return %	% Net Assets
⊕ General Electric Company	Ind Mtrls	20.0	0.91	1.14
⊕ Microsoft Corporation	Software	23.8	0.23	0.98
American International Gr	Financial	17.0	-0.18	0.67
⊕ First Data Corporation	Business	12.3	-0.59	0.57
⊖ Corning Inc.	Hardware	25.5	-0.37	0.51
⊖ Merck & Co., Inc.	Health	19.1	1.58	0.50
Danaher Corporation	Ind Mtrls	22.0	-1.04	0.50
⊕ CVS Corporation	Consumer	19.7	1.42	0.48
UnitedHealth Group, Inc.	Health	20.8	-0.76	0.48

Total Fixed-Income:459	Date of Maturity	Amount $000	Value $000	% Net Assets
T. Rowe Price Instl High		2,959	29,853	5.23
US Treasury Note 4.875%	02-15-12	9,515	9,649	1.69
US Treasury Note 4.25%	11-15-13	8,730	8,539	1.50
US Treasury Note 5%	08-15-11	8,270	8,430	1.48
US Treasury Note 4.875%	08-31-08	5,000	5,013	0.88
FNMA 5%	08-01-35	3,951	3,798	0.67
FNMA 6%	02-01-34	2,887	2,910	0.51
Canada Govt 5.25%	06-01-12	2,775	2,656	0.47
Federal Republic Of Germa	04-09-10	1,800	2,258	0.40

Equity Style
Style: Growth
Size: Large-Cap

Value Measures		Rel Category
Price/Earnings	16.50	1.10
Price/Book	2.75	1.13
Price/Sales	1.51	1.09
Price/Cash Flow	10.41	1.31
Dividend Yield %	1.76	0.82

Growth Measures	%	Rel Category
Long-Term Erngs	13.20	1.17
Book Value	9.50	1.19
Sales	10.12	1.14
Cash Flow	11.65	1.29
Historical Erngs	18.38	1.06

Market Cap %			
Giant	40.4	Small	3.6
Large	43.0	Micro	0.7
Mid	12.3	Avg $mil:	30,978

Fixed-Income Style
Duration: Interm-Term
Quality: High

Avg Eff Duration [1]	4.6 Yrs
Avg Eff Maturity	7.3 Yrs
Avg Credit Quality	AA
Avg Wtd Coupon	5.33%

[1]figure provided by fund as of 09-30-06

Sector Weightings	% of Stocks	Rel DJ Mod	3 Year High Low
⌁ Info	18.05	—	
Software	3.59	—	4 3
Hardware	9.08	—	9 6
Media	2.75	—	5 3
Telecom	2.63	—	4 2
⌂ Service	51.81		
Health	14.69	—	15 11
Consumer	8.45	—	10 8
Business	6.70	—	8 6
Financial	21.97	—	22 20
Mfg	30.16		
Goods	6.81	—	10 7
Ind Mtrls	14.06	—	16 12
Energy	7.14	—	8 7
Utilities	2.15	—	3 2

Composition

● Cash	15.4
● Stocks	43.7
● Bonds	40.3
○ Other	0.5
Foreign (% of Stock)	19.5

MORNINGSTAR® Funds 500

T. Rowe Price Real Est

	Ticker	Load	NAV	Yield	Total Assets	Mstar Category
✓ Analyst Pick	TRREX	None	$25.33	2.4%	$2,380 mil	Specialty-Real Estate

Governance and Management

Stewardship Grade: A

Portfolio Manager(s)

David Lee has managed this fund since its October 1997 inception. Lee had been T. Rowe Price's real estate analyst prior to that. In 2005, the fund added its first dedicated analyst. T. Rowe's hotel analyst adds some expertise.

Strategy

Manager David Lee uses a large-cap, low-turnover strategy. With the Wilshire Real Estate Securities Index as its benchmark, the fund will own both REITs and REOCs (real estate operating companies). Ideal candidates for the fund will have proven management teams that are in the process of repositioning or redeveloping their assets.

Historical Profile

Return	Above Avg
Risk	Average
Rating	★★★★ Above Avg

Quartile bars: 97% 93% 93% 93% 89% 98% 98% 95% 92%

Investment Style
Equity
Stock %

▼ Manager Change
▽ Partial Manager Change

Growth of $10,000
— Investment Values of Fund
— Investment Values of S&P 500

31.0 / 24.0 / 17.0 / 10.0

Performance Quartile (within Category)

	1995	1996	1997	1998	1999	2000	2001	2002	2003	2004	2005	2006	History
	—	—	10.69	8.68	8.11	10.19	10.54	10.62	13.65	17.90	19.49	25.33	NAV
	—	—	7.82*	-14.86	-1.23	31.92	8.87	5.38	34.84	36.82	14.54	36.75	Total Return %
	—	—	—	-43.44	-22.27	41.02	20.76	27.48	6.16	25.94	9.63	20.96	+/-S&P 500
	—	—	—	2.14	1.34	0.88	-3.49	1.78	-1.22	3.68	0.54	0.62	+/-DJ Wilshire REIT
	—	—	—	4.18	5.28	5.30	5.30	4.72	5.66	4.46	3.98	3.23	Income Return %
	—	—	—	-19.04	-6.51	26.02	3.57	0.66	29.18	32.36	10.56	33.52	Capital Return %
	—	—	—	32	25	13	45	33	68	13	28	19	Total Rtn % Rank Cat
	—	—	0.09	0.44	0.45	0.47	0.53	0.49	0.59	0.60	0.70	0.62	Income $
	—	—	0.00	0.00	0.00	0.00	0.00	0.00	0.00	0.07	0.24	0.60	Capital Gains $
	—	—	—	1.00	1.00	1.00	1.00	1.00	1.00	0.90	0.85	—	Expense Ratio %
	—	—	—	4.07	4.22	4.61	4.09	4.07	3.49	2.74	1.86	—	Income Ratio %
	—	—	—	57	27	19	37	10	4	8	18	—	Turnover Rate %
	—	—	7	28	25	54	69	132	290	640	944	2,326	Net Assets $mil

Performance 12-31-06

	1st Qtr	2nd Qtr	3rd Qtr	4th Qtr	Total
2002	8.45	3.97	-7.78	1.35	5.38
2003	1.78	11.04	9.90	8.57	34.84
2004	12.11	-3.71	8.18	17.15	36.82
2005	-6.91	14.41	3.83	3.58	14.54
2006	16.14	-0.38	8.36	9.07	36.75

Trailing	Total Return%	+/- S&P 500	+/- DJ Wilshire REIT	%Rank Cat	Growth of $10,000
3 Mo	9.07	2.37	0.10	70	10,907
6 Mo	18.20	5.46	-0.80	63	11,820
1 Yr	36.75	20.96	0.62	19	13,675
3 Yr Avg	28.93	18.49	1.56	13	21,432
5 Yr Avg	24.95	18.76	1.11	23	30,457
10 Yr Avg	—	—	—	—	—
15 Yr Avg	—	—	—	—	—

Tax Analysis	Tax-Adj Rtn%	%Rank Cat	Tax-Cost Rat	%Rank Cat
3 Yr (estimated)	27.12	8	1.40	20
5 Yr (estimated)	23.06	17	1.51	32
10 Yr (estimated)	—	—	—	—

Potential Capital Gain Exposure: 28% of assets

Morningstar's Take by John Coumarianos 12-29-06

An unusual move pays off for this Analyst Pick.

David Lee has successfully managed T. Rowe Price Real Estate since its inception in late 1997. Lee seeks sector and geographic diversification from his holdings. His flexibility allows him to use either funds from operations (FFO) or net asset value (NAV) in valuing properties. He can buy either REITs (real estate investment trusts) or REOCs (real estate operating companies) but has tended to prefer REITs, which provide greater yield. Indeed, the fund's 2.35% trailing 12-month yield has been among the highest in the category, especially after removing real estate funds that buy the bonds and preferred issues of REITs.

Lee doesn't typically get too fancy, but he recently purchased a convertible bond of Equity Office Properties Trust before chairman and real estate legend Sam Zell agreed to a buyout. Lee thought the convertible gave him a better risk-reward profile than the common stock because of its high yield, limited downside, and attractive covenant provisions. (The bonds of REITs often have enticing covenants, which provide for handsome payouts to holders in the event of an ownership change.) When a consortium of investors led by the Blackstone Group bid for Equity Office in late November, Lee's bet paid off.

Lee's flexibility is one of the attractions of this fund. However, we should note that businesses tend to issue convertible bonds when they deem their stock price rich, and REITs have enjoyed a multiyear period of powerful returns. The convertible allows issuers to pay less interest than they would on a plain bond in exchange for an option to purchase stock that may well be worthless if the stock doesn't rise more.

We think investors contemplating adding this fine fund to their portfolios can avoid filling out their entire allocation with their first purchase. Those who've enjoyed the multiyear run in the category might consider whether their allocations now represent too large a piece of their portfolios.

Address:	100 East Pratt Street Baltimore MD 21202 800-638-5660
Web Address:	www.troweprice.com
Inception:	10-31-97*
Advisor:	T. Rowe Price Associates, Inc.
Subadvisor:	None
NTF Plans:	N/A

Minimum Purchase:	$2500	Add: $100	IRA: $1000
Min Auto Inv Plan:	$50	Add: $50	
Sales Fees:	No-load, 1.00%R		
Management Fee:	0.61%		
Actual Fees:	Mgt:0.61%	Dist: —	
Expense Projections:	3Yr:$271	5Yr:$471	10Yr:$1049
Income Distrib:	Quarterly		

Rating and Risk

Time Period	Load-Adj Return %	Morningstar Rtn vs Cat	Morningstar Risk vs Cat	Morningstar Risk-Adj Rating
1 Yr	36.75			
3 Yr	28.93	+Avg	Avg	★★★★
5 Yr	24.95	+Avg	Avg	★★★★
10 Yr	—	—	—	—
Incept	16.22			

Other Measures	Standard Index S&P 500	Best Fit Index DJ Wilshire REIT
Alpha	15.2	2.4
Beta	1.23	0.94
R-Squared	28	99
Standard Deviation	15.86	
Mean	28.93	
Sharpe Ratio	1.50	

Portfolio Analysis 09-30-06

Share change since 06-06 Total Stocks:43	Sector	PE	Tot Ret%	% Assets
⊕ Simon Property Group, In	Financial	58.3	36.98	5.83
⊕ Equity Residential	Financial	NMF	34.64	3.98
⊕ Archstone-Smith Trust	Financial	59.0	43.93	3.83
⊕ Eop Oper 144A 4%	—	—	—	3.76
⊕ ProLogis Trust	Financial	33.5	34.02	3.60
⊕ Macerich Company	Financial	—	33.91	3.42
⊕ Vornado Realty Trust	Financial	37.1	51.14	3.36
⊕ Boston Properties, Inc.	Financial	14.9	62.75	3.34
⊕ Host Hotels & Resorts, I	Financial	51.9	33.95	3.34
⊕ AMB Property Corporation	Financial	29.8	23.30	3.21
⊕ General Growth Propertie	Financial	—	15.09	2.87
⊕ Reckson Associates Realt	Financial	46.0	31.78	2.74
⊕ SL Green Realty Corporat	Financial	57.8	77.73	2.50
⊕ Mack-Cali Realty Corpora	Financial	34.0	24.56	2.37
⊕ New Plan Excel Realty Tr	Financial	30.7	22.91	2.34
⊕ EastGroup Properties, In	Financial	58.8	23.45	2.30
⊕ Brookfield Properties Co	Financial	56.4	36.73	2.28
⊕ Kimco Realty Corporation	Financial	30.1	44.91	2.17
⊕ Regency Centers Corporat	Financial	55.7	37.58	2.14
⊕ Duke Realty Corporation	Financial	74.7	28.98	2.14

Current Investment Style

Value Blnd Growth — Large/Mid/Small

Market Cap	%
Giant	0.0
Large	36.8
Mid	52.5
Small	10.7
Micro	0.0
Avg $mil:	5,795

Value Measures		Rel Category
Price/Earnings	18.87	1.00
Price/Book	3.32	1.17
Price/Sales	5.10	1.23
Price/Cash Flow	17.70	1.14
Dividend Yield %	3.62	0.90

Growth Measures	%	Rel Category
Long-Term Erngs	7.13	0.92
Book Value	0.14	0.29
Sales	10.26	0.94
Cash Flow	-2.06	NMF
Historical Erngs	3.80	0.27

Profitability	%	Rel Category
Return on Equity	11.92	1.04
Return on Assets	10.49	1.12
Net Margin	27.20	1.01

Sector Weightings	% of Stocks	Rel S&P 500	3 Year High	Low
↻ Info	0.00	0.00		
🗔 Software	0.00	0.00	0	0
🖥 Hardware	0.00	0.00	0	0
🎙 Media	0.00	0.00	0	0
📶 Telecom	0.00	0.00	0	0
⊂ Service	100.00	2.16		
🏥 Health	0.00	0.00	0	0
🛒 Consumer	1.32	0.17	5	1
📋 Business	0.00	0.00	0	0
💲 Financial	98.68	4.43	99	94
↳ Mfg	0.00	0.00		
🏭 Goods	0.00	0.00	0	0
⚙ Ind Mtrls	0.00	0.00	1	0
🔋 Energy	0.00	0.00	0	0
💡 Utilities	0.00	0.00	0	0

Composition

		%
●	Cash	2.7
●	Stocks	92.2
●	Bonds	4.6
○	Other	0.5
	Foreign (% of Stock)	2.5

T. Rowe Price Rtmt 2015

Analyst Pick ✓

Ticker TRRGX	**Load** None	**NAV** $12.37	**Yield** 1.8%	**Total Assets** $1,867 mil	**Mstar Category** Target-Date 2015-2029

Governance and Management

Stewardship Grade: B

Portfolio Manager(s)

Jerome Clark oversees the T. Rowe Price retirement-fund series. He joined the firm in 1992 as a quantitative analyst on the fixed-income side and eventually rose to run some of the shop's U.S. government-bond funds. Clark is currently a vice president with the firm and also manages the T. Rowe Price College Savings Plan portfolios and institutional asset-allocation offerings.

Strategy

This fund of funds provides a shifting mix of stocks and bonds to investors retiring in or around 2015. The fund's asset allocation follows a predetermined "glide path" and becomes more conservative as it approaches its target date and for 30 years beyond. But although it does increase its allocation to bonds and cash, this offering's large equity allocation is more aggressive than that of its typical retirement-focused peer. The fund is also unique in that it maintains a relatively hefty equity weighting 30 years into retirement.

Performance 12-31-06

	1st Qtr	2nd Qtr	3rd Qtr	4th Qtr	Total
2002	—	—	—	—	—
2003	—	—	—	—	—
2004	—	0.80	-0.20	8.72	—*
2005	-1.77	1.90	3.81	2.68	6.69
2006	4.37	-1.54	4.25	6.16	13.73

Trailing	Total Return%	+/- DJ Mod	+/- DJ Tgt 2025	%Rank Cat	Growth of $10,000
3 Mo	6.16	0.57	-0.46	40	10,616
6 Mo	10.67	1.88	0.78	35	11,067
1 Yr	13.73	1.43	-0.55	25	11,373
3 Yr Avg	—	—	—	—	—
5 Yr Avg	—	—	—	—	—
10 Yr Avg	—	—	—	—	—
15 Yr Avg	—	—	—	—	—

Tax Analysis	Tax-Adj Rtn%	%Rank Cat	Tax-Cost Rat	%Rank Cat
3 Yr (estimated)	—	—	—	—
5 Yr (estimated)	—	—	—	—
10 Yr (estimated)	—	—	—	—

Potential Capital Gain Exposure: 9% of assets

Historical Profile
Return
Risk
Rating — Not Rated

Investment Style: Equity, Stock %

72% 70% 70%

▼ Manager Change
▽ Partial Manager Change

Growth of $10,000
— Investment Values of Fund
— Investment Values of DJ Mod

13.0 / 12.0 / 11.0 / 10.0

Performance Quartile (within Category)

	1995	1996	1997	1998	1999	2000	2001	2002	2003	2004	2005	2006	History
	—	—	—	—	—	—	—	—	—	10.74	11.22	12.37	NAV
	—	—	—	—	—	—	—	—	—	—	6.69	13.73	Total Return %
	—	—	—	—	—	—	—	—	—	—	-0.30	1.43	+/-DJ Mod
	—	—	—	—	—	—	—	—	—	—	-2.02	-0.55	+/-DJ Tgt 2025
	—	—	—	—	—	—	—	—	—	—	1.58	2.05	Income Return %
	—	—	—	—	—	—	—	—	—	—	5.11	11.68	Capital Return %
	—	—	—	—	—	—	—	—	—	—	21	25	Total Rtn % Rank Cat
	—	—	—	—	—	—	—	—	—	0.11	0.17	0.23	Income $
	—	—	—	—	—	—	—	—	—	0.02	0.07	0.16	Capital Gains $
	—	—	—	—	—	—	—	—	—	—	—	0.69	Expense Ratio %
	—	—	—	—	—	—	—	—	—	—	1.31	1.99	Income Ratio %
	—	—	—	—	—	—	—	—	—	—	1	11	Turnover Rate %
	—	—	—	—	—	—	—	—	—	—	344	1,867	Net Assets $mil

Rating and Risk

Time Period	Load-Adj Return %	Morningstar Rtn vs Cat	Morningstar Risk vs Cat	Morningstar Risk-Adj Rating
1 Yr	13.73			
3 Yr	—	—	—	—
5 Yr	—	—	—	—
10 Yr	—	—	—	—
Incept	10.24			

Other Measures	Standard Index S&P 500	Best Fit Index
Alpha	—	—
Beta	—	—
R-Squared	—	—
Standard Deviation	—	
Mean	—	
Sharpe Ratio	—	

Portfolio Analysis 09-30-06

Total Stocks:0 Share change since 06-30-06	Sectors	P/E Ratio	YTD Return %	% Net Assets
⊕ T. Rowe Price Equity Inde	—	—	—	22.63
⊕ T. Rowe Price Growth Stoc	—	—	—	15.45
⊕ T. Rowe Price Value	—	—	—	11.58
⊕ T. Rowe Price Internation	—	—	—	5.75
⊕ T. Rowe Price Intl Gr & I	—	—	—	5.05
⊕ T. Rowe Price Mid-Cap Gro	—	—	—	4.10
⊕ T. Rowe Price Mid-Cap Val	—	—	—	3.24
⊖ T. Rowe Price Small-Cap S	—	—	—	2.74
⊕ T. Rowe Price Small-Cap V	—	—	—	1.30

Total Fixed-Income:0	Date of Maturity	Amount $000	Value $000	% Net Assets
T. Rowe Price New Income		27,665	246,221	15.80
T. Rowe Price High-Yield		17,455	120,613	7.74

Morningstar's Take by Karen Wallace 12-27-06

T. Rowe Price Retirement 2015 is one of the best--and most aggressive--options for one-stop retirement investing.

Manager Jerome Clark oversees the T. Rowe Price Retirement funds, which are made up of well-compiled mixes of reasonably priced T. Rowe Price funds. This fund, which is geared toward investors with approximately 10 years until retirement, has close to 70% of assets in stocks, and about a fifth of that total is devoted to foreign stocks. Many of the underlying funds in the portfolio are topnotch options, and investors can get access to many funds through this channel that are otherwise closed to new investors, such as T. Rowe Price Small-Cap Value and T. Rowe Price Mid-Cap Growth. Rounding out the portfolio are allocations to bonds (21%) and cash (4%).

As the retirement date approaches, the portfolios begin to roll down to a more conservative allocation. Unlike target-date funds offered by other fund shops, however, the T. Rowe Price Retirement series funds do not reach a static mix at their retirement dates; rather, they continue to roll down to a more conservative allocation 30 years past the retirement date. At that time, the minimum stock exposure (around 20%) is reached.

Prospective investors should be aware that a higher allocation to equities means this fund is more aggressive, and theoretically more volatile, than most of its Target-Date 2015-2029 peers. And because the fund continues to reallocate to bonds and cash for a longer period of time than peers, it will always have a comparatively higher equity allocation, and it will always be more aggressive. We believe that the allocation makes sense for many investors, because an investor may live for many years past his or her retirement date and would still have a long time horizon to invest.

If the idea of owning a single fund that is diversified across asset classes and automatically rebalanced appeals to you, this is one of the best options available.

Address:	100 East Pratt Street Baltimore MD 21202 800-492-7670
Web Address:	www.troweprice.com
Inception:	02-27-04
Advisor:	T. Rowe Price Associates, Inc.
Subadvisor:	None
NTF Plans:	N/A

Minimum Purchase:	$2500	Add: $100	IRA: $1000
Min Auto Inv Plan:	$2500	Add: $50	
Sales Fees:	No-load		
Management Fee:	0.00%		
Actual Fees:	Mgt:0.00%	Dist: —	
Expense Projections:	3Yr:$221	5Yr:$384	10Yr:$859
Income Distrib:	Annually		

Equity Style
Style: Blend
Size: Large-Cap

Value Measures		Rel Category
Price/Earnings	16.02	1.08
Price/Book	2.51	1.05
Price/Sales	1.39	1.08
Price/Cash Flow	8.61	1.19
Dividend Yield %	1.79	0.90

Growth Measures	%	Rel Category
Long-Term Erngs	12.30	1.04
Book Value	8.52	1.00
Sales	9.67	1.12
Cash Flow	8.94	0.92
Historical Erngs	18.15	1.03

Market Cap %			
Giant	38.9	Small	4.4
Large	36.2	Micro	0.9
Mid	19.6	Avg $mil:	24,927

Fixed-Income Style
Duration: Interm-Term
Quality: Medium

Avg Eff Duration [1]	4.6 Yrs
Avg Eff Maturity	7.4 Yrs
Avg Credit Quality	A
Avg Wtd Coupon	6.16%

[1]figure provided by fund as of 09-30-06

Sector Weightings	% of Stocks	Rel DJ Mod	3 Year High Low
↻ Info	19.55	—	
🖥 Software	3.37	—	4 3
🖥 Hardware	8.00	—	9 7
🎙 Media	4.28	—	6 4
☎ Telecom	3.90	—	4 4
⊏ Service	49.90		
🏥 Health	12.52	—	13 11
🛒 Consumer	8.39	—	10 8
🏢 Business	6.25	—	7 6
💲 Financial	22.74	—	23 21
🏭 Mfg	30.54		
⚙ Goods	8.22	—	9 8
🔧 Ind Mtrls	11.76	—	13 12
🔥 Energy	8.29	—	9 7
💡 Utilities	2.27	—	3 2

Composition

	%
● Cash	4.1
● Stocks	70.4
● Bonds	21.3
● Other	4.2
Foreign (% of Stock)	20.3

MORNINGSTAR® Funds 500

T. Rowe Price SciTech

	Ticker	Load	NAV	Yield	Total Assets	Mstar Category
	PRSCX	None	$20.96	0.0%	$3,284 mil	Specialty-Technology

Governance and Management

Stewardship Grade: A

Portfolio Manager(s)

Longtime manager Chip Morris stepped down from this fund in January 2002. Michael Sola, who has been with T. Rowe since 1995, replaced Morris. Sola is a one-time networking and software analyst who has also managed T. Rowe Price Developing Technologies since its August 2000 inception.

Strategy

Manager Mike Sola aims to provide broad exposure to technology with less volatility than most tech funds. The idea is to outperform with stock picks rather than industry bets. He typically holds 75-85 names to reduce issue-specific risk and will favor industry leaders over racier fare. Sola is also well aware of the limitations that the fund's large asset base imposes on him. In addition to keeping him away from outsized industry bets (which are hard to unwind quickly at a fund of this size), he favors blue chips and keeps turnover relatively low for a tech fund.

Performance 12-31-06

	1st Qtr	2nd Qtr	3rd Qtr	4th Qtr	Total
2002	-7.17	-27.75	-26.23	20.10	-40.58
2003	1.05	20.70	8.31	14.49	51.25
2004	-2.66	2.73	-11.33	14.58	1.60
2005	-6.28	3.30	5.30	0.51	2.46
2006	4.91	-9.99	5.14	7.87	7.10

Trailing	Total Return%	+/- S&P 500	+/- ArcaEx Tech 100	%Rank Cat	Growth of $10,000
3 Mo	7.87	1.17	2.24	34	10,787
6 Mo	13.42	0.68	1.77	23	11,342
1 Yr	7.10	-8.69	2.42	47	10,710
3 Yr Avg	3.69	-6.75	-4.19	68	11,148
5 Yr Avg	0.04	-6.15	-4.92	57	10,020
10 Yr Avg	1.22	-7.20	-12.49	91	11,289
15 Yr Avg	8.55	-2.09	-7.83	70	34,233

Tax Analysis	Tax-Adj Rtn%	%Rank Cat	Tax-Cost Rat	%Rank Cat
3 Yr (estimated)	3.69	63	0.00	1
5 Yr (estimated)	0.04	55	0.00	1
10 Yr (estimated)	0.14	88	1.07	60

Potential Capital Gain Exposure: -170% of assets

Historical Profile

Return	Below Avg	
Risk	Average	
Rating	★★★	Neutral

96% 96% 96% 95% 95% 98% 94% 98% 94%

59.0
43.6
32.4 **Growth of $10,000**
24.0 ■ Investment Values of Fund
17.0 ― Investment Values of S&P 500
10.0

Performance Quartile (within Category)

1995	1996	1997	1998	1999	2000	2001	2002	2003	2004	2005	2006	History
29.12	29.71	27.26	37.67	63.71	35.57	20.92	12.43	18.80	19.10	19.57	20.96	NAV
55.53	14.23	1.71	42.35	100.99	-34.19	-41.19	-40.58	51.25	1.60	2.46	7.10	Total Return %
17.95	-8.73	-31.65	13.77	79.95	-25.09	-29.30	-18.48	22.57	-9.28	-2.45	-8.69	+/-S&P 500
7.82	-5.80	-18.26	-12.25	-15.41	-17.97	-25.60	-7.25	-0.89	-10.13	-4.90	2.42	+/-ArcaEx Tech 100
0.00	0.00	0.00	0.00	0.00	0.00	0.00	0.00	0.00	0.00	0.00	0.00	Income Return %
55.53	14.23	1.71	42.35	100.99	-34.19	-41.19	-40.58	51.25	1.60	2.46	7.10	Capital Return %
20	67	97	74	63	58	66	39	57	62	73	47	Total Rtn % Rank Cat
0.00	0.00	0.00	0.00	0.00	0.00	0.00	0.00	0.00	0.00	0.00	0.00	Income $
4.54	3.60	2.87	0.99	10.72	7.28	0.00	0.00	0.00	0.00	0.00	0.00	Capital Gains $
1.01	0.97	0.94	0.94	0.87	0.86	1.00	1.11	1.09	1.01	1.00	—	Expense Ratio %
-0.15	-0.33	-0.44	-0.61	-0.26	-0.55	-0.73	-0.87	-0.73	-0.15	-0.45	—	Income Ratio %
130	126	134	109	128	134	144	61	48	55	59	—	Turnover Rate %
2,285	3,292	3,538	4,696	12,271	8,892	5,209	2,839	4,391	3,911	3,228	2,825	Net Assets $mil

Investment Style
Equity
Stock %

▼ Manager Change
▽ Partial Manager Change

Rating and Risk

Time Period	Load-Adj Return %	Morningstar Rtn vs Cat	Morningstar Risk vs Cat	Morningstar Risk-Adj Rating
1 Yr	7.10			
3 Yr	3.69	Avg	-Avg	★★★
5 Yr	0.04	Avg	Avg	★★★
10 Yr	1.22	Low	Avg	★★
Incept	10.60			

Other Measures	Standard Index S&P 500	Best Fit Index ArcaEx Tech 100
Alpha	-11.3	-4.0
Beta	1.85	1.05
R-Squared	64	85
Standard Deviation	15.89	
Mean	3.69	
Sharpe Ratio	0.10	

Portfolio Analysis 09-30-06

Share change since 06-06 Total Stocks:62	Sector	PE	Tot Ret%	% Assets
⊖ Cisco Systems, Inc.	Hardware	30.1	59.64	4.27
⊖ Yahoo, Inc.	Media	35.4	-34.81	4.15
⊖ Juniper Networks, Inc.	Hardware	34.3	-15.07	4.08
⊖ Samsung Electronics	Goods	—	—	3.69
⊖ Xilinx, Inc.	Hardware	22.7	-4.28	3.39
Analog Devices, Inc.	Hardware	22.5	-6.66	3.38
⊖ Nokia Corporation ADR	Hardware	18.9	13.44	3.23
⊕ eBay, Inc.	Consumer	40.1	-30.43	2.93
⊕ Maxim Integrated Product	Hardware	23.1	-14.06	2.86
⊕ Google, Inc.	Business	61.5	11.00	2.84
⊖ Qualcomm, Inc.	Hardware	26.6	-11.32	2.68
⊖ EMC Corporation	Hardware	32.7	-3.08	2.56
⊖ Microsoft Corporation	Software	23.8	15.83	2.51
⊕ Apple Computer, Inc.	Hardware	37.6	18.01	2.34
Corning Inc.	Hardware	25.5	-4.83	2.24
⊕ Marvell Technology Group	Hardware	35.9	-31.57	2.16
⊖ Adobe Systems Inc.	Software	48.1	11.26	2.03
⊕ VeriSign, Inc.	Software	55.5	9.82	1.99
⊖ Red Hat, Inc.	Software	58.8	-15.63	1.90
⊖ Cognos Inc.	Software	33.2	22.33	1.74

Current Investment Style

Value Blnd Growth — Large Mid Small

Market Cap	%
Giant	31.9
Large	28.3
Mid	37.1
Small	2.6
Micro	0.0
Avg $mil:	19,075

Value Measures		Rel Category
Price/Earnings	24.77	1.02
Price/Book	3.11	0.96
Price/Sales	2.57	0.92
Price/Cash Flow	12.15	0.94
Dividend Yield %	0.71	1.61

Growth Measures	%	Rel Category
Long-Term Erngs	18.55	1.08
Book Value	14.45	1.50
Sales	14.71	1.18
Cash Flow	17.93	0.90
Historical Erngs	21.73	0.79

Profitability	%	Rel Category
Return on Equity	17.46	1.11
Return on Assets	11.34	1.22
Net Margin	17.53	1.26

Industry Weightings	% of Stocks	Rel Cat
Software	20.1	0.9
Hardware	11.9	1.0
Networking Eq	14.1	1.9
Semis	26.1	1.5
Semi Equip	1.2	0.2
Comp/Data Sv	5.5	0.6
Telecom	0.6	0.2
Health Care	0.0	0.0
Other	20.6	1.1

Composition

● Cash	5.2
● Stocks	94.2
● Bonds	0.0
● Other	0.6
Foreign	21.0
(% of Stock)	

Morningstar's Take by Karen Wallace 11-13-06

T. Rowe Price Science and Technology takes a sane approach to a volatile sector.

Manager Michael Sola tries to control volatility by investing in industry leaders rather than speculative firms, spreading his bets across many stocks and keeping the portfolio broadly diversified among industries. He also pays attention to valuations, and isn't afraid to go against the grain. For example, Sola reduced the fund's positions in semiconductor stocks Intel and Microchip Technology early in 2006 after a strong finish to 2005. He allocated the money to Internet portals such as Yahoo and Google, and online auctioneer eBay, believing that they were attractively priced after the market sold them off. Sola thinks the growing trend toward online advertising and e-commerce will benefit these stocks.

Those bets have hurt the fund this year--Yahoo and eBay have each lost more than a quarter of their value for the year to date through November 10. Also, its mega-cap bias has stung the fund in

relative terms over the past several years as smaller, more speculative firms have outperformed. We think that the fund will look better on a relative basis when blue chips come back into favor.

All told, this fund is a good choice in a racy category. We like Sola's contrarian investing style, and the fund's diversification has led to a smoother ride than peers have delivered--the fund's volatility in terms of standard deviation is much lower than the category median. And at 1.00%, its expenses are reasonable.

One thing for prospective investors to keep in mind, however, is that you might not need this fund at all. Although it is less volatile than peers, any fund that focuses on the technology sector is risky. Also, if you own a large-cap fund, you may already have plenty of exposure to many stocks in this portfolio, such as Microsoft, Cisco Systems, Dell, and Google. (If you own an S&P 500 Index fund, for instance, you own all these stocks already.)

Address:	100 East Pratt Street Baltimore MD 21202 800-638-5660	Minimum Purchase:	$2500	Add: $100	IRA: $1000
		Min Auto Inv Plan:	$50	Add: $50	
		Sales Fees:	No-load		
Web Address:	www.troweprice.com	Management Fee:	0.66%		
Inception:	09-30-87	Actual Fees:	Mgt:0.66%	Dist: —	
Advisor:	T. Rowe Price Associates, Inc.	Expense Projections:	3Yr:$318	5Yr:$552	10Yr:$1225
Subadvisor:	Rcm Capital Management LLC	Income Distrib:	Annually		
NTF Plans:	N/A				

T. Rowe Price Sm Stk

	Ticker	Load	NAV	Yield	Total Assets	Mstar Category
	OTCFX	Closed	$34.23	0.1%	$7,698 mil	Small Blend

Governance and Management

Stewardship Grade: B

Portfolio Manager(s)

Greg McCrickard has managed this offering since September 1992. Before becoming the fund's manager, he worked as an analyst at T. Rowe Price for six years. McCrickard is assisted by T. Rowe's large analyst staff, most notably the fund's longtime analyst Curt Organt.

Strategy

Manager Greg McCrickard divides this portfolio into two sections. The first half is composed of value issues, for which he uses discounted cash-flow analysis to help identify cheap stocks. With the other half of the portfolio, McCrickard concentrates on out-of-favor growth stocks. McCrickard is a buy-and-hold manager: The fund's turnover is lower than average. He is very conscious of the portfolio's average market cap; he aims to keep it in line with that of the Russell 2000 Index.

Historical Profile

Return	Average
Risk	Below Avg
Rating	★★★ Neutral

90% 91% 91% 91% 95% 92% 91% 91% 94%

Growth of $10,000
- Investment Values of Fund
- Investment Values of S&P 500

42.2 / 32.4 / 24.0 / 17.0 / 10.0

Investment Style: Equity, Stock %

▼ Manager Change ▽ Partial Manager Change

Performance Quartile (within Category)

1995	1996	1997	1998	1999	2000	2001	2002	2003	2004	2005	2006	History
16.32	18.07	22.20	20.79	22.80	23.87	25.34	21.50	27.98	31.82	32.81	34.23	NAV
33.85	21.05	28.81	-3.46	14.66	16.49	6.81	-14.21	32.35	18.77	8.44	12.78	Total Return %
-3.73	-1.91	-4.55	-32.04	-6.38	25.59	18.70	7.89	3.67	7.89	3.53	-3.01	+/-S&P 500
5.40	4.56	6.45	-0.91	-6.60	19.51	4.32	6.27	-14.90	0.44	3.89	-5.59	+/-Russ 2000
0.87	0.55	0.22	0.45	0.38	0.61	0.42	0.04	0.00	0.00	0.00	0.06	Income Return %
32.98	20.50	28.59	-3.91	14.28	15.88	6.39	-14.25	32.35	18.77	8.44	12.72	Capital Return %
18	53	34	41	46	35	48	34	93	52	33	72	Total Rtn % Rank Cat
0.12	0.09	0.04	0.10	0.08	0.14	0.10	0.01	0.00	0.00	0.00	0.02	Income $
2.01	1.58	1.01	0.50	0.89	2.46	0.05	0.23	0.46	1.39	1.73	2.73	Capital Gains $
1.11	1.07	1.02	1.01	0.96	0.94	0.98	0.96	0.96	0.94	0.92	—	Expense Ratio %
0.74	0.56	0.33	0.46	0.47	0.63	0.45	0.04	-0.10	-0.17	-0.11	—	Income Ratio %
58	31	23	26	42	33	17	15	16	18	20	—	Turnover Rate %
279	416	816	1,153	1,740	2,255	3,158	3,298	4,937	6,371	6,926	7,069	Net Assets $mil

Performance 12-31-06

	1st Qtr	2nd Qtr	3rd Qtr	4th Qtr	Total
2002	4.18	-6.78	-17.55	7.15	-14.21
2003	-4.84	16.57	4.95	13.68	32.35
2004	4.75	2.32	-1.53	12.54	18.77
2005	-3.43	2.51	6.06	3.28	8.44
2006	11.16	-4.85	-0.03	6.66	12.78

Trailing	Total Return%	+/- S&P 500	+/- Russ 2000	%Rank Cat	Growth of $10,000
3 Mo	6.66	-0.04	-2.24	86	10,666
6 Mo	6.63	-6.11	-2.75	62	10,663
1 Yr	12.78	-3.01	-5.59	72	11,278
3 Yr Avg	13.25	2.81	-0.31	53	14,525
5 Yr Avg	10.52	4.33	-0.87	70	16,489
10 Yr Avg	11.34	2.92	1.90	52	29,276
15 Yr Avg	13.17	2.53	1.70	43	63,969

Tax Analysis	Tax-Adj Rtn%	%Rank Cat	Tax-Cost Rat	%Rank Cat
3 Yr (estimated)	12.16	40	0.96	25
5 Yr (estimated)	9.76	61	0.69	29
10 Yr (estimated)	10.27	37	0.96	20

Potential Capital Gain Exposure: 30% of assets

Morningstar's Take by Karen Wallace 01-02-07

Investors in closed T. Rowe Price Small-Cap Stock should sit tight.

Although this fund's 12.8% return in 2006 was solid in absolute terms, it looks less impressive compared with its typical small-blend peer's gain. We're not too concerned about its relative underperformance, however, as a big reason for its lackluster category standing is manager Greg McCrickard's consistent and moderate approach.

McCrickard's quality bias and contrarian approach have led him away from the speculative fare that has dominated the market this year. McCrickard and longtime analyst Curt Organt look for attractively priced small-cap companies that are financially sound and well positioned in their respective markets. They pay close attention to companies that have some sort of catalyst that would cause the stock's price to rise, such as a new, talented management team or a promising new product. For example, during 2006 McCrickard established a position in pharmaceutical company

Medicis after competitive threats depressed the share price. McCrickard believes Medicis is poised to gain significant market share as it gears up to market its new product, Reloxin, which, if approved, will provide stiff competition to Allergan's Botox.

In addition to careful stock selection, McCrickard also mitigates volatility in a number of other ways here. For one, the overall portfolio is a blend of growthy firms and more staid value picks, which helps it stay afloat in a variety of market conditions. In addition, the fund is well diversified among industries, and individual positions rarely soak up more than 1.5% of assets.

Although the fund's moderate risk profile means it will rarely shoot to the top of the pack, it has done a decent job of generating consistently solid returns over the long haul. And although its asset base, at $7.7 billion, is larger than we'd like to see, we are pleased that the fund closed to new investors in 2004 to stem the tide of inflows.

Address:	100 East Pratt Street			
	Baltimore MD 21202			
	800-638-5660			
Web Address:	www.troweprice.com			
Inception:	06-01-56			
Advisor:	T. Rowe Price Associates, Inc.			
Subadvisor:	None			
NTF Plans:	N/A			

Minimum Purchase:	Closed	Add: —	IRA: —
Min Auto Inv Plan:	Closed	Add: —	
Sales Fees:	No-load		
Management Fee:	0.76%		
Actual Fees:	Mgt:0.76%	Dist: —	
Expense Projections:	3Yr:$293	5Yr:$509	10Yr:$1131
Income Distrib:	Annually		

Rating and Risk

Time Period	Load-Adj Return %	Morningstar Rtn vs Cat	Morningstar Risk vs Cat	Morningstar Risk-Adj Rating
1 Yr	12.78			
3 Yr	13.25	Avg	-Avg	★★★
5 Yr	10.52	-Avg	-Avg	★★★
10 Yr	11.34	Avg	-Avg	★★★
Incept	13.62			

Other Measures	Standard Index S&P 500	Best Fit Index Mstar Small Core
Alpha	-0.3	-1.5
Beta	1.46	0.86
R-Squared	75	96
Standard Deviation	11.57	
Mean	13.25	
Sharpe Ratio	0.86	

Portfolio Analysis 09-30-06

Share change since 06-06 Total Stocks:312	Sector	PE	Tot Ret%	% Assets
Sunrise Senior Living, I	Health	18.5	-8.87	1.10
ResMed, Inc.	Health	40.1	28.48	1.08
Toro Company	Ind Mtrls	16.2	7.44	1.02
Seacor Holdings, Inc.	Energy	8.9	45.58	1.00
Harsco Corporation	Ind Mtrls	16.3	14.65	0.97
⊖ Ann Taylor Stores Corpor	Consumer	16.6	-4.87	0.95
A.O. Smith Corporation	Ind Mtrls	15.3	8.72	0.93
Harbor Florida Bancshare	Financial	—	—	0.89
⊖ FMC Technologies, Inc.	Energy	19.7	43.59	0.87
Jack Henry & Associates	Business	22.0	13.31	0.87
Ohio Casualty Corporatio	Financial	8.6	6.59	0.87
Henry Schein, Inc.	Health	24.0	12.24	0.86
Armor Holdings, Inc.	Ind Mtrls	15.3	28.61	0.83
Westamerica Bancorporati	Financial	15.3	-2.10	0.81
Airgas, Inc.	Ind Mtrls	21.8	24.06	0.79
Chittenden Corporation	Financial	16.4	13.44	0.78
⊕ Teledyne Technologies, I	Ind Mtrls	19.7	37.90	0.76
⊕ Baldor Electric Company	Ind Mtrls	22.5	33.18	0.75
Affiliated Managers Grou	Financial	32.5	31.00	0.74
FactSet Research Systems	Business	33.8	37.91	0.72

Current Investment Style

Value Blnd Growth — Large Mid Small

Market Cap	%
Giant	0.0
Large	0.0
Mid	27.3
Small	61.4
Micro	11.3
Avg $mil:	1,265

Value Measures		Rel Category
Price/Earnings	19.24	1.16
Price/Book	2.21	1.05
Price/Sales	1.23	1.26
Price/Cash Flow	7.61	1.09
Dividend Yield %	0.82	0.77

Growth Measures	%	Rel Category
Long-Term Erngs	14.48	1.04
Book Value	9.03	1.19
Sales	13.36	1.51
Cash Flow	18.31	1.44
Historical Erngs	16.55	0.99

Profitability	%	Rel Category
Return on Equity	10.74	0.83
Return on Assets	5.57	0.78
Net Margin	9.30	0.96

Sector Weightings	% of Stocks	Rel S&P 500	3 Year High	Low
Info	15.45	0.77		
Software	5.22	1.51	7	5
Hardware	8.15	0.88	10	8
Media	1.29	0.34	1	1
Telecom	0.79	0.23	1	0
Service	56.85	1.23		
Health	14.30	1.19	14	10
Consumer	11.38	1.49	12	9
Business	11.17	2.64	15	11
Financial	20.00	0.90	20	17
Mfg	27.70	0.82		
Goods	2.92	0.34	5	3
Ind Mtrls	16.73	1.40	17	15
Energy	5.64	0.58	8	6
Utilities	2.41	0.69	2	0

Composition

- Cash 6.2
- Stocks 93.8
- Bonds 0.0
- Other 0.0
- Foreign 1.8 (% of Stock)

MORNINGSTAR® Funds 500

T. Rowe Price Sm Val

	Ticker	Load	NAV	Yield	Total Assets	Mstar Category
	PRSVX	Closed	$41.21	0.6%	$6,201 mil	Small Blend

Governance and Management

Stewardship Grade: B

Portfolio Manager(s)

Manager Preston Athey has been managing director of this fund's investment-advisory committee since 1991. He has been managing investments at the company since 1982. He taps T. Rowe's large analyst staff for research.

Strategy

This fund is as straightforward as its name. Manager Preston Athey tends to look at much smaller stocks than do his peers, and he buys stocks that are trading cheaply based on value measures appropriate to their particular industries. Athey lets his winners run, keeping turnover very low, but he'll generally finance new acquisitions by selling stakes in companies that have run up in terms of market capitalization and valuation.

Historical Profile

Return	Above Avg
Risk	Low
Rating	★★★★ Above Avg

Investment Values of Fund
Investment Values of S&P 500

Growth of $10,000

	1995	1996	1997	1998	1999	2000	2001	2002	2003	2004	2005	2006	History
	94%	90%	90%	90%	93%	92%	90%	91%	90%				
NAV	16.53	19.56	23.40	18.97	17.62	19.14	22.66	21.94	29.39	35.68	36.91	41.21	NAV
	29.29	24.61	27.92	-12.47	1.19	19.77	21.94	-1.76	36.43	25.69	8.74	16.24	Total Return %
	-8.29	1.65	-5.44	-41.05	-19.85	28.87	33.83	20.34	7.75	14.81	3.83	0.45	+/-S&P 500
	0.84	8.12	5.56	-9.92	-20.07	22.79	19.45	18.72	-10.82	7.36	4.19	-2.13	+/-Russ 2000
	1.34	1.39	1.02	1.07	0.90	1.14	0.89	0.62	0.55	0.54	0.48	0.73	Income Return %
	27.95	23.22	26.90	-13.54	0.29	18.63	21.05	-2.38	35.88	25.15	8.26	15.51	Capital Return %
	36	40	42	86	79	25	11	3	81	10	32	35	Total Rtn % Rank Cat
	0.18	0.23	0.20	0.25	0.17	0.20	0.17	0.14	0.12	0.16	0.17	0.27	Income $
	0.61	0.80	1.39	1.20	1.35	1.68	0.48	0.18	0.41	1.08	1.76	1.41	Capital Gains $
	0.98	0.94	0.87	0.87	0.92	0.90	0.89	0.89	0.88	0.86	0.84	—	Expense Ratio %
	1.59	1.28	1.01	1.02	0.84	1.06	0.88	0.66	0.48	0.53	0.52	—	Income Ratio %
	18	15	15	17	7	14	17	12	10	9	12	—	Turnover Rate %
	936	1,410	2,088	1,632	1,262	1,361	2,012	2,395	3,295	4,462	4,719	5,455	Net Assets $mil

Performance Quartile (within Category)

Performance 12-31-06

	1st Qtr	2nd Qtr	3rd Qtr	4th Qtr	Total
2002	10.72	-0.20	-17.05	7.18	-1.76
2003	-4.15	17.59	6.63	13.51	36.43
2004	6.80	3.41	1.23	12.42	25.69
2005	-2.75	3.52	7.15	0.80	8.74
2006	14.82	-4.03	-2.31	7.99	16.24

Trailing	Total Return%	+/- S&P 500	+/- Russ 2000	%Rank Cat	Growth of $10,000
3 Mo	7.99	1.29	-0.91	53	10,799
6 Mo	5.49	-7.25	-3.89	77	10,549
1 Yr	16.24	0.45	-2.13	35	11,624
3 Yr Avg	16.68	6.24	3.12	13	15,885
5 Yr Avg	16.32	10.13	4.93	9	21,295
10 Yr Avg	13.42	5.00	3.98	28	35,229
15 Yr Avg	15.19	4.55	3.72	15	83,411

Tax Analysis	Tax-Adj Rtn%	%Rank Cat	Tax-Cost Rat	%Rank Cat
3 Yr (estimated)	15.79	9	0.76	18
5 Yr (estimated)	15.59	6	0.63	25
10 Yr (estimated)	12.11	25	1.15	34

Potential Capital Gain Exposure: 46% of assets

Rating and Risk

Time Period	Load-Adj Return %	Morningstar Rtn vs Cat	Morningstar Risk vs Cat	Morningstar Risk-Adj Rating
1 Yr	16.24			
3 Yr	16.68	+Avg	-Avg	★★★★
5 Yr	16.32	High	Low	★★★★★
10 Yr	13.42	+Avg	Low	★★★★
Incept	13.99			

Other Measures	Standard Index S&P 500	Best Fit Index Mstar Small Core
Alpha	3.3	1.3
Beta	1.39	0.89
R-Squared	63	95
Standard Deviation	11.99	
Mean	16.68	
Sharpe Ratio	1.08	

Portfolio Analysis 09-30-06

Share change since 06-06 Total Stocks:288

	Sector	PE	Tot Ret%	% Assets
Landstar System, Inc.	Business	18.1	-8.30	1.88
Kilroy Realty Corporatio	Financial	NMF	29.67	1.69
Tetra Technologies, Inc.	Energy	18.9	67.63	1.64
⊕ JLG Industries, Inc.	Ind Mtrls	—	—	1.55
Proassurance Corporation	Financial	13.9	2.63	1.31
Carpenter Technology Cor	Ind Mtrls	11.7	46.55	1.29
East West Bancorp, Inc.	Financial	16.0	-2.42	1.23
Texas Regional Bancshare	Financial	—	—	1.09
Raven Industries, Inc.	Hardware	19.0	-5.98	1.09
Dollar Thrifty Automotiv	Consumer	17.0	26.45	0.97
Whiting Petroleum Corpor	Energy	9.7	16.50	0.96
Trammell Crow Company	Financial	—	—	0.95
First Republic Bank	Financial	18.8	7.05	0.91
Penn Virginia Corporatio	Energy	13.3	22.81	0.91
⊝ Aaron Rents, Inc.	Consumer	22.5	36.83	0.83
Markel Corporation	Financial	12.2	51.43	0.82
⊕ Genesee & Wyoming, Inc.	Business	8.3	4.82	0.81
Owens & Minor, Inc.	Health	21.6	15.80	0.79
iShares Russell 2000 Val		—	—	0.79
Rare Hospitality Interna	Consumer	27.4	8.36	0.79

Current Investment Style

Value Blnd Growth — Large Mid Small

	Market Cap	%
	Giant	0.0
	Large	0.0
	Mid	18.5
	Small	56.6
	Micro	24.9
	Avg $mil: 877	

Value Measures		Rel Category
Price/Earnings	16.39	0.99
Price/Book	2.00	0.95
Price/Sales	0.97	0.99
Price/Cash Flow	6.55	0.94
Dividend Yield %	1.16	1.08

Growth Measures	%	Rel Category
Long-Term Erngs	13.60	0.98
Book Value	8.68	1.15
Sales	9.98	1.13
Cash Flow	8.80	0.69
Historical Erngs	16.61	0.99

Profitability	%	Rel Category
Return on Equity	12.29	0.95
Return on Assets	7.25	1.01
Net Margin	10.13	1.05

Sector Weightings	% of Stocks	Rel S&P 500	3 Year High Low	
☎ Info	9.78	0.49		
🖳 Software	2.46	0.71	3	2
🖥 Hardware	5.77	0.62	6	5
🎬 Media	1.22	0.32	3	1
📶 Telecom	0.33	0.09	0	0
🔁 Service	53.93	1.17		
🏥 Health	5.17	0.43	6	5
🛒 Consumer	10.88	1.42	12	11
🏢 Business	13.94	3.30	15	12
💲 Financial	23.94	1.07	25	22
🏭 Mfg	36.29	1.07		
🛢 Goods	3.51	0.41	4	3
⚙ Ind Mtrls	20.46	1.71	22	20
🔋 Energy	8.70	0.89	10	6
🔌 Utilities	3.62	1.03	4	2

Composition

	%
● Cash	7.7
● Stocks	90.3
● Bonds	0.8
● Other	1.3
Foreign (% of Stock)	3.6

Morningstar's Take by Karen Wallace 12-28-06

We like this closed fund for its steady approach.

Longtime manager Preston Athey doesn't take a gutsy line of attack at T. Rowe Price Small Cap Value. Rather, he controls risk in a number of ways. For one, he looks for steady-growing companies with good fundamentals such as strong cash flows and responsible management teams, and he's careful not to overpay for stocks. In addition, this fund holds more stocks than its typical small-blend category rival, and assets here are less concentrated in the fund's top 10 holdings than is the case at its typical peer, which makes for a smoother ride.

We also admire Athey's low-turnover approach. He tends to hold on to this fund's winners much longer than most small-cap managers do. Rather than be a slave to size and valuation concerns alone, he will hold on to a stock if he feels it still has significant upside. For example, he was impressed by insurer Brown & Brown's management team, so he held on to the stock long after it evolved from small-cap to mid-cap, value to growth. Athey finally sold the shares 12 years later for 20 times the price he paid.

One potential concern here is the fund's size: At $6 billion, its asset base is very large for a fund that invests in small-cap fare. But our size concerns are allayed somewhat by the fact that Athey doesn't trade as much as his peers do, and also because the fund is so well diversified across issues.

Overall, what this fund's steady and dependable process lacks in excitement, it more than makes up for with its compelling risk-adjusted returns. Simply put, this fund has outperformed the typical small-blend fund over all standard trailing time periods, while taking on considerably less risk, as measured by standard deviation. Low expenses also give it an advantage over rivals. We think this fund will continue to outperform its peers on a relative basis, even if small caps takes a back seat to larger fare going forward.

Address:	100 East Pratt Street Baltimore MD 21202 800-638-5660
Web Address:	www.troweprice.com
Inception:	06-30-88
Advisor:	T. Rowe Price Associates, Inc.
Subadvisor:	None
NTF Plans:	N/A

Minimum Purchase:	Closed	Add: —	IRA: —
Min Auto Inv Plan:	Closed	Add: —	
Sales Fees:	No-load, 1.00%R		
Management Fee:	0.66%		
Actual Fees:	Mgt:0.66%	Dist: —	
Expense Projections:	3Yr:$268	5Yr:$466	10Yr:$1037
Income Distrib:	Annually		

T. Rowe Price Spect Grth

Ticker	Load	NAV	Yield	Total Assets	Mstar Category
PRSGX	None	$20.40	0.8%	$3,525 mil	Large Blend

Governance and Management

Stewardship Grade: B

Portfolio Manager(s)

A five-member committee meets once a month to steer this fund. The committee is led by Ned Notzon and includes fund managers Brian Rogers (who's also T. Rowe Price's CIO), Jack Laporte, Steve Boesel, and Mary Miller.

Strategy

Diversification is the name of the game here. This fund invests in nine T. Rowe Price funds that range from small to large cap, value to growth, and domestic to international. It overweights areas of the market that are undervalued and skimps on those that look expensive.

Historical Profile

Return High
Risk Above Avg
Rating ★★★★★ Highest

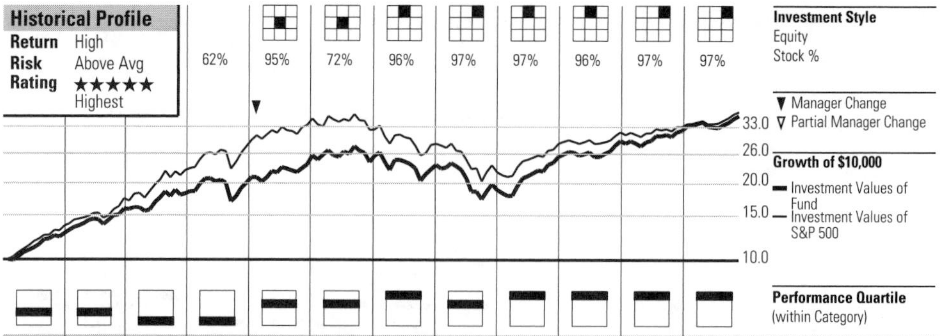

62%
95%
72%
96%
97%
97%
96%
97%
97%
Investment Style
Equity
Stock %
▼ Manager Change
▽ Partial Manager Change
33.0
26.0
20.0
15.0
10.0
Growth of $10,000
Investment Values of Fund
Investment Values of S&P 500
Performance Quartile
(within Category)

1995	1996	1997	1998	1999	2000	2001	2002	2003	2004	2005	2006	History
13.49	15.13	15.93	16.45	17.71	15.72	14.04	11.13	14.80	16.87	18.22	20.40	NAV
29.96	20.53	17.40	13.62	21.20	-0.11	-7.83	-19.66	34.09	15.16	9.47	16.37	Total Return %
-7.62	-2.43	-15.96	-14.96	0.16	8.99	4.06	2.44	5.41	4.28	4.56	0.58	+/-S&P 500
-7.81	-1.92	-15.45	-13.40	0.29	7.68	4.62	1.99	4.20	3.76	3.20	0.91	+/-Russ 1000
1.89	1.48	1.32	1.13	1.03	0.68	1.02	0.57	0.90	0.81	0.83	0.93	Income Return %
28.07	19.05	16.08	12.49	20.17	-0.79	-8.85	-20.23	33.19	14.35	8.64	15.44	Capital Return %
75	61	93	79	34	28	23	30	10	7	14	16	Total Rtn % Rank Cat
0.21	0.20	0.20	0.18	0.17	0.12	0.16	0.08	0.10	0.12	0.14	0.17	Income $
0.76	0.93	1.60	1.37	1.91	1.85	0.28	0.07	0.02	0.05	0.11	0.63	Capital Gains $
—	—	—	—	—	—	—	—	—	—	—	0.86	Expense Ratio %
1.81	1.58	1.26	1.09	0.85	0.70	1.05	0.68	0.75	0.81	0.75	—	Income Ratio %
7	3	20	18	20	12	6	4	2	18	10	—	Turnover Rate %
1,358	2,104	2,605	2,768	3,031	2,889	2,373	1,739	2,237	2,605	2,855	3,525	Net Assets $mil

Performance 12-31-06

	1st Qtr	2nd Qtr	3rd Qtr	4th Qtr	Total
2002	1.64	-12.54	-16.83	8.67	-19.66
2003	-4.94	18.81	4.22	13.93	34.09
2004	3.85	0.33	-1.23	11.91	15.16
2005	-2.19	2.42	5.50	3.58	9.47
2006	6.48	-3.09	4.36	8.06	16.37

Trailing	Total Return%	+/- S&P 500	+/- Russ 1000	%Rank Cat	Growth of $10,000
3 Mo	8.07	1.37	1.12	12	10,807
6 Mo	12.78	0.04	0.42	18	11,278
1 Yr	16.37	0.58	0.91	16	11,637
3 Yr Avg	13.63	3.19	2.65	6	14,672
5 Yr Avg	9.59	3.40	2.77	7	15,807
10 Yr Avg	8.93	0.51	0.29	18	23,522
15 Yr Avg	11.10	0.46	0.30	22	48,497

Tax Analysis	Tax-Adj Rtn%	%Rank Cat	Tax-Cost Rat	%Rank Cat
3 Yr (estimated)	13.03	5	0.53	25
5 Yr (estimated)	9.09	6	0.46	30
10 Yr (estimated)	7.53	27	1.29	59

Potential Capital Gain Exposure: 33% of assets

Rating and Risk

Time Period	Load-Adj Return %	Morningstar Rtn vs Cat	Morningstar Risk vs Cat	Morningstar Risk-Adj Rating
1 Yr	16.37			
3 Yr	13.63	High	+Avg	★★★★★
5 Yr	9.59	High	+Avg	★★★★★
10 Yr	8.93	+Avg	Avg	★★★★
Incept	11.07			

Other Measures	Standard Index S&P 500	Best Fit Index Russ 1000
Alpha	1.7	1.4
Beta	1.18	1.15
R-Squared	93	94
Standard Deviation	8.43	
Mean	13.63	
Sharpe Ratio	1.19	

Portfolio Analysis 09-30-06

Share change since 06-06 Total Stocks:0	Sector	PE	Tot Ret%	% Assets
⊕ T. Rowe Price Growth Sto	—	—	—	19.11
⊕ T. Rowe Price Blue Chip	—	—	—	18.05
⊖ MF T. Rowe Price Equity-	—	—	—	13.33
⊕ T. Rowe Price Value	—	—	—	13.31
⊖ T. Rowe Price New Horizo	—	—	—	12.17
⊕ T. Rowe Price Internatio	—	—	—	8.87
⊕ T. Rowe Price Intl Gr &	—	—	—	6.93
⊕ T. Rowe Price Mid-Cap Va	—	—	—	5.44
⊕ T. Rowe Price Emerging M	—	—	—	2.80

Morningstar's Take by Christopher Davis 11-20-06

T. Rowe Price Spectrum Growth is a good way to make life simpler.

This offering provides all-in-one exposure to stocks. To that end, lead manager Ned Notzon and his committee spread the portfolio broadly across market caps and investment styles. They do so by investing the fund's assets in nine T. Rowe funds, including T. Rowe Price Equity Income and New Horizons. The committee's job is to oversee the fund's overall asset allocation and adjust it to reflect where it's finding the most-attractive values.

The committee has given the fund an increasingly growth-oriented cast in recent years. The group likes to tilt the portfolio toward areas that have been out of favor, and given their long-running laggard ways, large-growth stocks fit the bill. Believing such names look relatively cheap, it has been pushing more money toward T. Rowe Price Growth Stock and Blue Chip Growth. That's why the fund has nudged into the large-growth slot of the Morningstar Style Box. (Typically, it's resided in large-blend territory.)

While that bet has yet to pay off, the committee has gotten such moves right more often than not. Indeed, its earlier calls, such as its decision to ratchet up its small-cap weighting in 2002 and 2003, have boosted returns over the years. Still, its strength is in the quality of its holdings. With managers like Equity Income's Brian Rogers and Growth Stock's Bob Smith, we think the fund is in capable hands.

The fund gets an added edge from moderate costs. All of the funds it invests in charge below-average costs relative to their category rivals, and it levies no additional fees on top of those of its underlying holdings. This is a fine choice for those that can stomach the volatility of an all-stock portfolio. But one-stop shop T. Rowe Price Personal Strategy Growth keeps 20% of its holdings in bonds, making it an alternative for long-term investors who want a bit less volatility.

Address:	100 East Pratt Street Baltimore MD 21202 800-638-5660
Web Address:	www.troweprice.com
Inception:	06-29-90
Advisor:	T. Rowe Price Associates, Inc.
Subadvisor:	None
NTF Plans:	N/A

Minimum Purchase:	$2500	Add: $100	IRA: $1000
Min Auto Inv Plan:	$50	Add: $50	
Sales Fees:	No-load		
Management Fee:	0.00%		
Actual Fees:	Mgt:0.00%	Dist: —	
Expense Projections:	3Yr:$265	5Yr:$460	10Yr:$1025
Income Distrib:	Annually		

Current Investment Style

Value Blnd Growth — Large Mid Small

Market Cap	%
Giant	36.5
Large	35.8
Mid	20.5
Small	6.2
Micro	1.0
Avg $mil: 21,600	

Value Measures		Rel Category
Price/Earnings	16.74	1.09
Price/Book	2.56	1.00
Price/Sales	1.49	1.06
Price/Cash Flow	10.23	1.21
Dividend Yield %	1.64	0.94

Growth Measures	%	Rel Category
Long-Term Erngs	12.99	1.10
Book Value	8.60	0.95
Sales	10.26	1.06
Cash Flow	8.68	0.84
Historical Erngs	17.52	0.95

Profitability	%	Rel Category
Return on Equity	18.55	0.95
Return on Assets	8.97	0.86
Net Margin	12.55	0.94

Sector Weightings	% of Stocks	Rel S&P 500	3 Year High	3 Year Low
Info	20.43	1.02		
Software	3.33	0.97	4	3
Hardware	7.92	0.86	8	6
Media	4.55	1.20	7	5
Telecom	4.63	1.32	5	4
Service	50.90	1.10		
Health	13.80	1.14	14	12
Consumer	9.18	1.20	11	9
Business	6.25	1.48	7	6
Financial	21.67	0.97	22	19
Mfg	28.66	0.85		
Goods	7.70	0.90	8	8
Ind Mtrls	11.57	0.97	12	10
Energy	7.55	0.77	8	7
Utilities	1.84	0.53	2	2

Composition

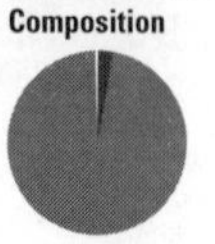

Cash	2.6
Stocks	96.8
Bonds	0.0
Other	0.6
Foreign (% of Stock)	24.9

T. Rowe Price Spect Inc

Analyst Pick ✓

	Ticker	Load	NAV	Yield	SEC Yield	Total Assets	Mstar Category
	RPSIX	None	$12.19	4.5%	4.38%	$4,314 mil	Multisector Bond

Governance and Management

Stewardship Grade: A

Portfolio Manager(s)

Ned Notzon has been at the helm since late 1998. He serves on an investment team that meets once a month to determine the fund's allocations to various sectors of the market. While he is looking to add value by shifting assets from fund to fund, his portfolio adjustments tend to be quite small.

Strategy

The fund can invest in up to nine other T. Rowe Price funds to gain exposure to virtually all sectors of the bond market. The idea is to beat the returns of the Lehman Brothers Aggregate Index without adding volatility. Included among the holdings is a small stake in stock fund T. Rowe Price Equity-Income. Manager Ned Notzon and his team will slightly adjust the fund's holdings if they see a sector as particularly under- or overvalued.

Performance 12-31-06

	1st Qtr	2nd Qtr	3rd Qtr	4th Qtr	Total
2002	1.14	1.51	0.13	4.05	6.96
2003	2.09	6.52	1.02	4.65	14.96
2004	2.02	-1.23	2.79	4.33	8.05
2005	-0.77	1.47	0.72	0.67	2.09
2006	1.26	0.13	3.67	3.11	8.38

Trailing	Total Return%	+/- LB Aggr	+/- LB. U.S. Univ. Bd	%Rank Cat	Growth of $10,000
3 Mo	3.11	1.87	1.61	28	10,311
6 Mo	6.90	1.81	1.44	36	10,690
1 Yr	8.38	4.05	3.41	15	10,838
3 Yr Avg	6.14	2.44	1.93	43	11,957
5 Yr Avg	8.01	2.95	2.37	60	14,700
10 Yr Avg	7.06	0.82	0.66	18	19,782
15 Yr Avg	7.65	1.15	0.94	27	30,214

Tax Analysis	Tax-Adj Rtn%	%Rank Cat	Tax-Cost Rat	%Rank Cat
3 Yr (estimated)	4.41	24	1.63	19
5 Yr (estimated)	6.17	38	1.70	10
10 Yr (estimated)	4.76	13	2.15	11

Potential Capital Gain Exposure: 6% of assets

Morningstar's Take by Arijit Dutta 11-30-06

T. Rowe Price Spectrum Income has several of its many cylinders firing right now, but its long-term case also remains solid.

This fund of funds' 2006 run is impressive on multiple counts. Though it has significantly less exposure to high-yield bonds, the year's undisputed leader among fixed-income categories, the fund has an impressive lead in its multisector-bond peer group. Manager Ned Notzon, who has directed asset allocation here since 1998, points to strength in several underlying T. Rowe funds. For example, T. Rowe's foreign-bond, emerging-markets bond, and mortgage-bond funds are all having a strong 2006.

The fund's structure is indeed its best feature, though Notzon makes important contributions in asset allocation as well. This is a convenient vehicle for gaining broad exposure to the entire gamut of fixed-income investments, from Treasuries to foreign bonds. Moreover, just about all the underlying T. Rowe funds have solid long-term records in their respective categories. At the same time, Notzon allocates assets across the funds based on valuations, which can lead to strong performance over time without added risk. For example, the portfolio had significantly higher stakes in foreign and high-yield bonds a couple of years ago. Notzon has gradually taken profits in those areas, and raised stakes in T. Rowe's mortgage and equity-income funds.

Results have been pleasing. While the fund doesn't tend to blow the competition away in any given year (2006 is an exception), its overall record under Notzon is quite strong. Also, as we'd predict at a diversified offering such as this one, volatility has been remarkably low. For example, currency movements will often keep domestic- and foreign-bond markets going separate ways, which damps the portfolio's volatility.

The fund has yet another attractive structural advantage. T. Rowe doesn't charge additional fees here other than those on the underlying funds, making it the category's cheapest no-load offering.

Address:	100 East Pratt Street Baltimore MD 21202 800-638-5660
Web Address:	www.troweprice.com
Inception:	06-29-90
Advisor:	T. Rowe Price Associates, Inc.
Subadvisor:	None
NTF Plans:	N/A

Minimum Purchase:	$2500	Add: $100	IRA: $1000
Min Auto Inv Plan:	$50	Add: $50	
Sales Fees:	No-load		
Management Fee:	0.00%		
Actual Fees:	Mgt:0.00%	Dist: —	
Expense Projections:	3Yr:$227	5Yr:$395	10Yr:$883
Income Distrib:	Monthly		

Historical Profile

Return	Average
Risk	Below Avg
Rating	★★★ Neutral

Investment Style: Fixed Income, Income Rtn %Rank Cat

▼ Manager Change
▽ Partial Manager Change

Growth of $10,000
— Investment Values of Fund
— Investment Values of LB Aggr

Performance Quartile (within Category)

1995	1996	1997	1998	1999	2000	2001	2002	2003	2004	2005	2006	History
11.24	11.20	11.66	11.50	10.71	10.77	10.59	10.76	11.77	12.09	11.79	12.19	NAV
19.42	7.65	12.19	6.58	0.26	7.41	4.50	6.96	14.96	8.05	2.09	8.38	Total Return %
0.95	4.02	2.54	-2.11	1.08	-4.22	-3.94	-3.29	10.86	3.71	-0.34	4.05	+/-LB Aggr
0.95	3.20	2.41	-0.73	0.09	-3.41	-3.59	-2.88	9.14	3.08	-0.62	3.41	+/-LB. U.S. Univ. Bd
7.32	6.55	6.53	6.40	6.17	6.73	6.06	5.28	4.77	4.26	4.19	4.71	Income Return %
12.10	1.10	5.66	0.18	-5.91	0.68	-1.56	1.68	10.19	3.79	-2.10	3.67	Capital Return %
26	94	8	3	82	2	48	47	69	66	55	15	Total Rtn % Rank Cat
0.72	0.71	0.71	0.72	0.69	0.70	0.64	0.55	0.50	0.49	0.50	0.54	Income $
0.06	0.15	0.15	0.18	0.13	0.06	0.02	0.00	0.06	0.11	0.05	0.02	Capital Gains $
—	—	—	—	—	—	—	—	—	—	—	0.73	Expense Ratio %
6.43	6.46	6.21	6.22	5.95	6.03	1.05	5.17	4.47	4.18	4.03	—	Income Ratio %
20	18	14	13	19	19	6	14	4	8	40	—	Turnover Rate %
987	1,356	2,022	2,574	2,548	2,471	2,465	2,713	3,533	4,489	3,895	4,314	Net Assets $mil

Rating and Risk

Time Period	Load-Adj Return %	Morningstar Rtn vs Cat	Morningstar Risk vs Cat	Morningstar Risk-Adj Rating
1 Yr	8.38			
3 Yr	6.14	Avg	-Avg	★★★
5 Yr	8.01	Avg	-Avg	★★★
10 Yr	7.06	+Avg	-Avg	★★★★
Incept	8.27			

Other Measures	Standard Index LB Aggr	Best Fit Index DJ Mod
Alpha	2.5	0.1
Beta	0.62	0.38
R-Squared	51	61
Standard Deviation	2.85	
Mean	6.14	
Sharpe Ratio	0.98	

Portfolio Analysis 09-30-06

Total Fixed-Income:0	Date of Maturity	Amount $000	Value $000	% Net Assets
T. Rowe Price New Income		100,428	893,810	21.77
T. Rowe Price High-Yield		112,689	778,683	18.96
MF T. Rowe Price Equity-		25,759	728,985	17.75
T. Rowe Price GNMA		55,970	524,443	12.77
Price T Rowe Intl Bond		50,514	479,886	11.69
T. Rowe Price Short-Term		56,014	262,705	6.40
T. Rowe Price U.S. Treas		10,651	123,237	3.00
T Rowe Price Emerging Ma		7,813	107,116	2.61
T. Rowe Price Corporate		9,490	91,005	2.22

Current Investment Style

Duration: Short Int Long
Quality: High Med Low

¹ figure provided by fund

Avg Eff Duration¹	4.3 Yrs
Avg Eff Maturity	7.0 Yrs
Avg Credit Quality	A
Avg Wtd Coupon	6.15%
Avg Wtd Price	101.13% of par

Coupon Range	% of Bonds	Rel Cat
0% PIK	3.5	0.6
0% to 6%	55.8	1.2
6% to 8%	27.9	0.9
8% to 10%	12.2	0.7
More than 10%	4.1	0.6

1.00=Category Average

Credit Analysis		% bonds 09-30-06	
AAA	56	BB	8
AA	3	B	13
A	7	Below B	3
BBB	8	NR/NA	3

Sector Breakdown	% of assets
US Treasuries	9
TIPS	0
US Agency	2
Mortgage Pass-Throughs	26
Mortgage CMO	9
Mortgage ARM	0
US Corporate	35
Asset-Backed	3
Convertible	0
Municipal	0
Corporate Inflation-Protected	0
Foreign Corporate	3
Foreign Govt	1

Composition			
Cash	7.9	Bonds	59.0
Stocks	17.3	Other	15.8

Special Securities	
Restricted/Illiquid Secs	5
Exotic Mortgage-Backed	0
Emerging-Markets Secs	Trace
Options/Futures/Warrants	No

T. Rowe Price T/F Inc

	Ticker	Load	NAV	Yield	SEC Yield	Total Assets	Mstar Category
	PRTAX	None	$10.05	4.4%	3.56%	$1,817 mil	Muni National Long

Governance and Management

Stewardship Grade: A

Portfolio Manager(s)

Mary Miller was named T. Rowe Price's director of fixed income in 2004 but has no plans to leave this fund, which she has managed with much success since early 1997. She is backed by a team of eight analysts.

Strategy

Manager Mary Miller maintains a cautious stance but seeks out pockets of opportunity. She doesn't venture far from the duration of an internally selected peer group, though she will make modest adjustments depending on her view on the direction of market yields. Miller usually focuses on higher-rated bonds but will park some assets in midrated bonds when they offer compelling yields. Miller avoids bonds that are subject to the alternative minimum tax.

Historical Profile

Return	Above Avg	
Risk	Below Avg	
Rating	★★★★ Above Avg	

Growth of $10,000
— Investment Values of Fund
— Investment Values of LB Muni

Performance Quartile (within Category)

1995	1996	1997	1998	1999	2000	2001	2002	2003	2004	2005	2006	History
9.80	9.59	9.94	9.97	9.09	9.68	9.62	10.02	10.07	10.06	9.99	10.05	NAV
17.69	3.26	9.32	5.96	-3.91	12.29	4.38	9.23	5.11	4.31	3.70	5.14	Total Return %
0.23	-1.17	0.13	-0.52	-1.85	0.61	-0.75	-0.37	-0.20	-0.17	0.19	0.30	+/-LB Muni
-3.28	-1.20	-1.52	-0.86	0.77	-2.95	-0.49	-0.80	-1.22	-2.25	-1.38	-0.72	+/-LB Muni 20YR
6.07	5.36	5.53	5.23	5.07	5.57	5.07	4.98	4.58	4.39	4.41	4.50	Income Return %
11.62	-2.10	3.79	0.73	-8.98	6.72	-0.69	4.25	0.53	-0.08	-0.71	0.64	Capital Return %
37	56	38	21	34	20	29	31	38	32	24	20	Total Rtn % Rank Cat
0.52	0.51	0.52	0.51	0.49	0.49	0.48	0.47	0.45	0.43	0.44	0.44	Income $
0.00	0.00	0.00	0.04	0.01	0.00	0.00	0.00	0.00	0.00	0.00	0.00	Capital Gains $
0.59	0.58	0.57	0.55	0.55	0.55	0.54	0.54	0.55	0.54	0.54	0.53	Expense Ratio %
5.80	5.49	5.41	5.31	5.06	5.24	5.25	4.95	4.78	4.47	4.33	4.37	Income Ratio %
49	49	41	36	34	44	29	28	24	27	30	31	Turnover Rate %
1,397	1,345	1,385	1,481	1,328	1,396	1,328	1,401	1,488	1,451	1,467	1,482	Net Assets $mil

Performance 12-31-06

	1st Qtr	2nd Qtr	3rd Qtr	4th Qtr	Total
2002	0.90	3.32	4.69	0.09	9.23
2003	1.04	2.44	0.03	1.52	5.11
2004	1.57	-2.10	3.66	1.20	4.31
2005	-0.05	3.02	-0.09	0.80	3.70
2006	0.39	-0.00	3.48	1.21	5.14

Trailing	Total Return%	+/- LB Muni	+/- LB Muni 20YR	%Rank Cat	Growth of $10,000
3 Mo	1.21	0.10	-0.22	19	10,121
6 Mo	4.73	0.18	-0.78	19	10,473
1 Yr	5.14	0.30	-0.72	20	10,514
3 Yr Avg	4.38	0.10	-1.45	21	11,372
5 Yr Avg	5.48	-0.05	-1.28	20	13,057
10 Yr Avg	5.47	-0.29	-1.11	17	17,033
15 Yr Avg	6.05	-0.21	-1.03	22	24,136

Tax Analysis	Tax-Adj Rtn%	%Rank Cat	Tax-Cost Rat	%Rank Cat
3 Yr (estimated)	4.38	14	0.00	1
5 Yr (estimated)	5.48	14	0.00	1
10 Yr (estimated)	5.46	11	0.01	5

Potential Capital Gain Exposure: 6% of assets

Rating and Risk

Time Period	Load-Adj Return %	Morningstar Rtn vs Cat	Morningstar Risk vs Cat	Morningstar Risk-Adj Rating
1 Yr	5.14			
3 Yr	4.38	+Avg	-Avg	★★★★
5 Yr	5.48	+Avg	-Avg	★★★★
10 Yr	5.47	+Avg	-Avg	★★★★
Incept	6.65			

Other Measures	Standard Index LB Muni	Best Fit Index LB Muni NY
Alpha	0.1	0.3
Beta	0.98	1.01
R-Squared	99	99
Standard Deviation	3.04	
Mean	4.38	
Sharpe Ratio	0.37	

Morningstar's Take by Scott Berry 12-20-06

This fund doesn't have a standing reservation in the municipal national long-term category's best half, but it sure seems that way.

T. Rowe Price Tax-Free Income hasn't held large stakes in the strong-performing yet riskier areas of the municipal market, but an allocation to long-term bonds and good performance from the fund's hospital holdings have worked in its favor at various times during the year. For the year to date through Dec. 18, 2006, the fund returned 5.28%, putting on pace to outperform its average rival for the 10th year in a row.

The fund's consistency owes to its steady approach, experienced management, and reasonable costs. Manager Mary Miller, who has led the effort here for nearly 10 years, will make slight adjustments to the fund's interest-rate sensitivity, sector allocations, and yield-curve positioning (the fund's mix of short- and long-term bonds), but her moves are measured such that any wrong move isn't likely to do much damage to the fund's long-term record. And getting them right more often than not has allowed the fund to perform relatively well in different market environments. Small interest-rate moves helped the fund best its average peer during a favorable bond market in 1998, for example, but also during a tougher market in 1999. More recently, the fund's forays into California have paid off, as the state has worked to put its fiscal house in order.

All the while, the fund's expense ratio continues to work in its favor. This fund isn't the cheapest no-load muni offering, but its 0.53% expense ratio provides it a slight sustainable advantage over its average no-load long-term muni peer. That advantage is partially reflected in the fund's consistently above-average yield.

Investors shouldn't expect this fund to top the charts year in and year out, but for those looking for a steady and proven municipal-bond fund, this one fills the bill.

Portfolio Analysis 09-30-06

Total Fixed-Income:336	Date of Maturity	Amount $000	Value $000	% Net Assets
Burlington Kans Pollutio	06-01-31	21,525	23,043	1.28
Triborough Brdg & Tunl A	01-01-17	18,275	20,470	1.13
Medical Univ S C Hosp Au	08-15-31	17,830	18,631	1.03
New York N Y City Transi	02-01-29	16,640	17,710	0.98
Massachusetts St 5.25%	08-01-28	15,000	17,283	0.96
Liberty N Y Dev 5.25%	10-01-35	15,000	17,105	0.95
TENNESSEE ENERGY ACQUISI	09-01-18	15,000	16,628	0.92
New Hampshire St Busn Fi	05-01-21	14,500	15,747	0.87
Washington St 5.7%	10-01-15	14,000	15,744	0.87
California St Pub Wks Br	06-01-28	14,810	15,651	0.87
Puerto Rico Comwlth Govt	12-01-10	14,960	15,612	0.87
Illinois Fin Auth 5.5%	08-15-43	12,750	13,916	0.77
District Columbia 5.125%	06-01-17	12,720	13,673	0.76
New York N Y City Mun Wt	06-15-37	13,000	13,627	0.76
Metropolitan Transn Auth	07-01-21	12,750	13,287	0.74

Current Investment Style

Duration: Short Int Long
Quality: High Med Low

¹Avg Eff Duration	5.8 Yrs
Avg Eff Maturity	14.2 Yrs
Avg Credit Quality	AA
Avg Wtd Coupon	5.46%
Avg Wtd Price	106.70% of par

¹figure provided by fund

Credit Analysis % bonds 09-30-06

AAA	46	BB	2
AA	20	B	1
A	19	Below B	0
BBB	8	NR/NA	3

Top 5 States % bonds

NY	15.7	TX	5.7
CA	12.6	IL	5.0
MA	5.8		

Composition

Cash	1.2	Bonds	98.8
Stocks	0.0	Other	0.0

Special Securities

Restricted/Illiquid Secs	0
Options/Futures/Warrants	No

Sector Weightings

	% of Bonds	Rel Cat
General Obligation	27.5	0.98
Utilities	18.1	0.74
Health	15.6	1.50
Water/Waste	9.9	1.00
Housing	3.4	0.54
Education	8.2	0.72
Transportation	3.6	0.42
COP/Lease	3.2	1.36
Industrial	10.5	0.87
Misc Revenue	0.0	—
Demand	0.0	0.00

Address:	100 East Pratt Street Baltimore MD 21202 800-225-5132	Minimum Purchase:	$2500	Add: $100	IRA: $1000
		Min Auto Inv Plan:	$2500	Add: $50	
		Sales Fees:	No-load		
Web Address:	www.troweprice.com	Management Fee:	0.46%		
Inception:	10-26-76	Actual Fees:	Mgt:0.46%	Dist: —	
Advisor:	T. Rowe Price Associates, Inc.	Expense Projections:	3Yr:$170	5Yr:$296	10Yr:$665
Subadvisor:	None	Income Distrib:	Monthly		
NTF Plans:	N/A				

MORNINGSTAR® Funds 500

T. Rowe Price T/F Sh-Int

	Ticker	Load	NAV	Yield	SEC Yield	Total Assets	Mstar Category
✓ Analyst Pick	PRFSX	None	$5.34	3.2%	3.21%	$490 mil	Muni National Short

Governance and Management

Stewardship Grade: B

Portfolio Manager(s)

Charlie Hill has been with this fund since 1993 and has had much success. He is backed by the firm's strong credit-research department. He also managed T. Rowe Price Tax-Free Intermediate--which was recently merged into T. Rowe Price Summit Municipal Intermediate Fund--and two of T. Rowe Price's single-state municipal-bond funds.

Strategy

Manager Charlie Hill generally keeps interest rate and credit risk under wraps. Duration (a measure of interest-rate sensitivity) stays close to its benchmark index, and most of the fund's assets are stashed in credits rated AA or higher. But that doesn't mean Hill can't hunt for opportunity. He believes the best way to outperform over time is to avoid big duration bets and to seek out incrementally higher-yielding bonds. By prospectus, he can fill up to 5% of assets with lower-rated or nonrated issues.

Historical Profile

Return	Above Avg
Risk	Above Avg
Rating	★★★★ Above Avg

Investment Style: Fixed Income
Income Rtn %Rank Cat

| 39 | 34 | 37 | 34 | 20 | 14 | 17 | 31 |

▼ Manager Change
▽ Partial Manager Change

Growth of $10,000
— Investment Values of Fund
— Investment Values of LB Muni

20.8
18.8
16.4
14.0
12.0
10.0

Performance Quartile (within Category)

	1995	1996	1997	1998	1999	2000	2001	2002	2003	2004	2005	2006	History
	5.36	5.34	5.36	5.38	5.21	5.33	5.42	5.53	5.50	5.44	5.34	5.34	NAV
	8.11	4.01	5.31	4.97	0.99	6.76	5.81	6.16	2.78	1.60	0.97	3.26	Total Return %
	-9.35	-0.42	-3.88	-1.51	3.05	-4.92	0.68	-3.44	-2.53	-2.88	-2.54	-1.58	+/-LB Muni
	-0.76	-0.43	-0.17	-0.24	-0.97	0.53	-0.78	-0.56	0.10	-0.18	0.10	0.21	+/-LB Muni 3YR
	4.58	4.37	4.33	4.21	4.04	4.38	4.12	3.71	3.14	2.69	2.82	3.25	Income Return %
	3.53	-0.36	0.98	0.76	-3.05	2.38	1.69	2.45	-0.36	-1.09	-1.85	0.01	Capital Return %
	33	34	36	14	39	11	1	33	29	23	62	30	Total Rtn % Rank Cat
	0.23	0.23	0.23	0.22	0.21	0.22	0.22	0.20	0.17	0.15	0.15	0.17	Income $
	0.00	0.00	0.03	0.02	0.01	0.00	0.00	0.02	0.01	0.00	0.00	0.00	Capital Gains $
	0.59	0.57	0.56	0.54	0.53	0.53	0.53	0.52	0.52	0.51	0.51	0.51	Expense Ratio %
	4.19	4.39	4.30	4.23	4.06	4.07	4.27	3.92	3.54	3.03	2.66	2.88	Income Ratio %
	93	70	84	77	40	41	41	30	30	42	27	30	Turnover Rate %
	451	439	439	458	417	405	447	560	582	571	513	490	Net Assets $mil

Performance 12-31-06

	1st Qtr	2nd Qtr	3rd Qtr	4th Qtr	Total
2002	0.37	2.62	2.19	0.86	6.16
2003	0.44	1.34	0.59	0.39	2.78
2004	0.68	-1.34	1.78	0.48	1.60
2005	-0.82	1.45	-0.01	0.36	0.97
2006	0.20	0.22	2.16	0.65	3.26

Trailing	Total Return%	+/- LB Muni	+/- LB Muni 3YR	%Rank Cat	Growth of $10,000
3 Mo	0.65	-0.46	0.02	51	10,065
6 Mo	2.83	-1.72	0.25	6	10,283
1 Yr	3.26	-1.58	0.21	30	10,326
3 Yr Avg	1.94	-2.34	0.04	42	10,593
5 Yr Avg	2.94	-2.59	-0.06	29	11,559
10 Yr Avg	3.84	-1.92	-0.20	25	14,576
15 Yr Avg	4.20	-2.06	-0.25	53	18,536

Tax Analysis	Tax-Adj Rtn%	%Rank Cat	Tax-Cost Rat	%Rank Cat
3 Yr (estimated)	1.94	33	0.00	1
5 Yr (estimated)	2.91	26	0.03	50
10 Yr (estimated)	3.80	22	0.04	50

Potential Capital Gain Exposure: 0% of assets

Rating and Risk

Time Period	Load-Adj Return %	Morningstar Rtn vs Cat	Morningstar Risk vs Cat	Morningstar Risk-Adj Rating
1 Yr	3.26			
3 Yr	1.94	+Avg	+Avg	★★★★
5 Yr	2.94	+Avg	+Avg	★★★
10 Yr	3.84	+Avg	Avg	★★★★
Incept	5.02			

Other Measures	Standard Index LB Muni	Best Fit Index LB Muni 10YR
Alpha	-1.9	-1.6
Beta	0.55	0.47
R-Squared	90	91
Standard Deviation	1.80	
Mean	1.94	
Sharpe Ratio	-0.72	

Morningstar's Take by Scott Berry 12-20-06

T. Rowe Price Tax-Free Short-Intermediate faces brutally stiff competition, but it remains one of our favorites.

This fund faces off in the muni-national short-term category with no-load giants Vanguard Limited-Term Tax-Exempt and Fidelity Short-Intermediate Municipal Income. It actually has less than one third the assets of the Fidelity fund and less than one tenth the assets of the Vanguard fund, but it competes well with both. In fact, each fund's three-, five-, and 10-year trailing average returns (through Nov. 30, 2006) are each separated by just 0.07 percentage points or less.

The fund's costs put it at a bit of a disadvantage to its Vanguard rival, but skilled management and a little added credit risk have helped the fund basically earn back that difference over time. Manager Charlie Hill has been with T. Rowe Price since 1991 and has led the effort here since 1995. And in his 10-plus years at the fund, he has made a number of timely adjustments to the fund's portfolio

mix. The fund's light exposure to airline bonds worked in its favor in 2002, for example, while a shift into California bonds paid off in 2004. Meanwhile, the added yield provided by the fund's above-average stake in A rated bonds has helped boost its overall returns.

In recent months, Hill has positioned the fund to benefit from a more favorable bond market environment. He argued in September that fundamentals, such as a housing slowdown and lower inflationary pressures, were turning in the market's favor. That positioning has paid off thus far, as bond prices have generally moved higher since the Federal Reserve kept its target rate unchanged in August.

Overall, we continue to like this fund. Hill's experience, the fund's proven approach, and a reasonable expense ratio make it an easy fund to recommend.

Portfolio Analysis 09-30-06

Total Fixed-Income:139	Date of Maturity	Amount $000	Value $000	% Net Assets
South Carolina Transn In	10-01-30	15,000	15,944	3.24
Georgia St Rd & Twy Auth	06-01-09	13,500	14,001	2.84
TENNESSEE ENERGY ACQUISI	09-01-12	10,000	10,607	2.15
New Jersey St Transn Tr	06-15-16	10,085	10,462	2.12
California St 5%	03-01-14	8,500	9,190	1.87
New York St Urban Dev 5.	01-01-21	8,820	9,113	1.85
Puerto Rico Pub Fin 5.25	08-01-31	8,350	8,971	1.82
Maryland St Dept Transn	02-01-09	7,370	7,700	1.56
Jefferson Cnty Ala Swr	02-01-40	6,405	6,955	1.41
Maryland St Health & Hig	07-01-30	6,000	6,717	1.36
Puerto Rico Pub Fin 5.5%	08-01-29	6,000	6,551	1.33
Northeast Md Waste Disp	04-01-11	6,000	6,429	1.30
New York N Y City Transi	11-01-11	6,000	6,402	1.30
San Antonio Tex 5%	08-01-10	5,745	6,034	1.22
Pennsylvania St 5.25%	02-01-12	5,300	5,726	1.16

Current Investment Style

Duration: Short Int Long
Quality: High Med Low

¹Avg Eff Duration	3.2 Yrs
Avg Eff Maturity	4.0 Yrs
Avg Credit Quality	AA
Avg Wtd Coupon	5.26%
Avg Wtd Price	105.42% of par

¹figure provided by fund

Credit Analysis   % bonds 09-30-06

AAA	49	BB	0
AA	28	B	0
A	18	Below B	0
BBB	4	NR/NA	2

Special Securities

Restricted/Illiquid Secs	0
Options/Futures/Warrants	No

Top 5 States   % bonds

NY	14.0	VA	6.9
MD	7.3	TX	6.3
CA	7.0		

Composition

Cash	2.2	Bonds	97.8
Stocks	0.0	Other	0.0

Sector Weightings

	% of Bonds	Rel Cat
General Obligation	28.1	0.85
Utilities	15.1	1.87
Health	4.0	0.40
Water/Waste	10.5	1.41
Housing	1.6	0.17
Education	6.5	0.76
Transportation	18.2	3.50
COP/Lease	1.9	1.03
Industrial	11.1	0.68
Misc Revenue	0.0	—
Demand	3.2	4.66

Address:	100 East Pratt Street Baltimore MD 21202 800-225-5132
Web Address:	www.troweprice.com
Inception:	12-23-83
Advisor:	T. Rowe Price Associates, Inc.
Subadvisor:	None
NTF Plans:	N/A

Minimum Purchase:	$2500	Add: $100	IRA: $1000
Min Auto Inv Plan:	$2500	Add: $50	
Sales Fees:	No-load		
Management Fee:	0.41%		
Actual Fees:	Mgt:0.41%	Dist: —	
Expense Projections:	3Yr:$164	5Yr:$285	10Yr:$640
Income Distrib:	Monthly		

T. Rowe Price T/F Hi-Yld

	Analyst Pick	Ticker	Load	NAV	Yield	SEC Yield	Total Assets	Mstar Category
		PRFHX	None	$12.14	4.8%	4.01%	$1,566 mil	High Yield Muni

Governance and Management

Stewardship Grade: B

Portfolio Manager(s)

Jim Murphy leads the effort here. He joined T. Rowe Price from Prudential in early 2001 and has led the fund since that time. He is supported by a team of seven credit analysts.

Strategy

This fund hunts for opportunity on two fronts. First, its credit-research department ferrets out good yield in lower-quality credits. The fund typically keeps significantly more than half of its assets in such bonds. It also makes occasional, slight changes to duration (a measure of interest-rate sensitivity) to take advantage of management's interest-rate outlook. To damp risk, the fund spreads assets across more than 300 issues.

Historical Profile

Return	Average
Risk	Average
Rating	★★★ Neutral

Investment Style: Fixed Income / Income Rtn %Rank Cat

▼ Manager Change
▽ Partial Manager Change

Growth of $10,000
— Investment Values of Fund
— Investment Values of LB Muni

Performance Quartile (within Category)

	1995	1996	1997	1998	1999	2000	2001	2002	2003	2004	2005	2006	History
	12.24	12.12	12.62	12.57	11.30	11.52	11.39	11.46	11.64	11.79	11.93	12.14	NAV
	16.60	4.98	10.17	5.55	-5.10	8.14	4.66	6.38	7.10	6.64	6.26	6.88	Total Return %
	-0.86	0.55	0.98	-0.93	-3.04	-3.54	-0.47	-3.22	1.79	2.16	2.75	2.04	+/-LB Muni
	-0.57	0.44	0.94	-1.21	-3.85	-2.62	0.04	-3.79	1.40	2.49	3.52	2.17	+/-LB Muni 10YR
	6.69	5.88	5.88	5.48	5.32	6.09	5.89	5.76	5.46	5.29	5.06	4.97	Income Return %
	9.91	-0.90	4.29	0.07	-10.42	2.05	-1.23	0.62	1.64	1.35	1.20	1.91	Capital Return %
	38	32	22	30	66	7	50	39	32	36	48	42	Total Rtn % Rank Cat
	0.73	0.70	0.69	0.68	0.65	0.67	0.66	0.64	0.61	0.60	0.58	0.58	Income $
	0.00	0.00	0.00	0.06	0.00	0.00	0.00	0.00	0.00	0.00	0.00	0.01	Capital Gains $
	0.79	0.75	0.74	0.72	0.71	0.71	0.72	0.71	0.71	0.71	0.70	0.70	Expense Ratio %
	6.29	6.07	5.86	5.59	5.28	5.54	5.89	5.72	5.56	5.33	5.12	4.91	Income Ratio %
	60	39	37	24	39	57	15	33	31	26	23	20	Turnover Rate %
	983	1,033	1,200	1,345	1,132	1,084	1,089	1,119	1,136	1,218	1,380	1,566	Net Assets $mil

Performance 12-31-06

	1st Qtr	2nd Qtr	3rd Qtr	4th Qtr	Total
2002	1.23	2.39	2.45	0.18	6.38
2003	0.81	3.19	0.63	2.31	7.10
2004	2.25	-1.01	3.32	1.97	6.64
2005	1.22	3.12	0.74	1.06	6.26
2006	1.30	0.57	3.25	1.60	6.88

Trailing	Total Return%	+/- LB Muni	+/- LB Muni 10YR	%Rank Cat	Growth of $10,000
3 Mo	1.60	0.49	0.68	53	10,160
6 Mo	4.90	0.35	0.13	48	10,490
1 Yr	6.88	2.04	2.17	42	10,688
3 Yr Avg	6.59	2.31	2.73	39	12,110
5 Yr Avg	6.65	1.12	1.19	35	13,798
10 Yr Avg	5.59	-0.17	-0.11	24	17,228
15 Yr Avg	6.29	0.03	0.01	38	24,968

Tax Analysis	Tax-Adj Rtn%	%Rank Cat	Tax-Cost Rat	%Rank Cat
3 Yr (estimated)	6.58	29	0.01	25
5 Yr (estimated)	6.64	30	0.01	50
10 Yr (estimated)	5.58	22	0.01	17

Potential Capital Gain Exposure: 2% of assets

Rating and Risk

Time Period	Load-Adj Return %	Morningstar Rtn vs Cat	Morningstar Risk vs Cat	Morningstar Risk-Adj Rating
1 Yr	6.88			
3 Yr	6.59	+Avg	-Avg	★★★★
5 Yr	6.65	Avg	-Avg	★★★
10 Yr	5.59	Avg	Avg	★★★
Incept	7.72			

Other Measures	Standard Index LB Muni	Best Fit Index LB Muni 20YR
Alpha	2.5	1.7
Beta	0.70	0.61
R-Squared	93	93
Standard Deviation	2.22	
Mean	6.59	
Sharpe Ratio	1.43	

Portfolio Analysis 09-30-06

Total Fixed-Income:461	Date of Maturity	Amount $000	Value $000	% Net Assets
California St 5.5%	11-01-33	15,640	17,176	1.12
Mississippi Busn Fin 5.9	05-01-22	14,325	14,398	0.94
New York N Y City Indl D	03-01-15	13,500	14,356	0.94
Oklahoma Dev Fin Auth 8%	02-01-32	11,690	12,858	0.84
Mashantucket Western Peq	09-01-36	12,285	12,780	0.83
North Carolina Eastn Mun	01-01-26	10,125	11,020	0.72
California St 5.25%	11-01-16	10,000	10,906	0.71
Oregon St Dept Administr	11-01-20	10,000	10,703	0.70
Mohegan Tribe Indians Co	01-01-31	10,000	10,653	0.70
New York N Y 5%	04-01-23	10,000	10,560	0.69
Sacramento Calif City Fi	01-01-30	10,000	10,443	0.68
California St 5%	02-01-33	10,000	10,379	0.68
Wisconsin Hsg & Econ Dev	03-01-36	10,110	10,164	0.66
Golden St Tob Securitiza	06-01-33	9,100	10,104	0.66
Tobacco Settlement Auth	06-01-38	9,675	9,941	0.65

Current Investment Style

¹Avg Eff Duration	5.3 Yrs
Avg Eff Maturity	18.7 Yrs
Avg Credit Quality	BBB
Avg Wtd Coupon	5.93%
Avg Wtd Price	104.77% of par

¹figure provided by fund

Credit Analysis	% bonds 09-30-06		
AAA	12	BB	7
AA	5	B	3
A	15	Below B	2
BBB	25	NR/NA	32

Top 5 States	% bonds		
CA	12.1	TX	5.8
NY	8.9	MD	5.5
IL	7.4		

Composition			
Cash	0.5	Bonds	99.5
Stocks	0.0	Other	0.0

Special Securities	
Restricted/Illiquid Secs	1
Options/Futures/Warrants	No

Sector Weightings	% of Bonds	Rel Cat
General Obligation	17.2	0.99
Utilities	9.1	1.77
Health	12.0	0.74
Water/Waste	9.9	1.69
Housing	10.3	1.09
Education	2.8	0.49
Transportation	2.0	0.28
COP/Lease	1.2	0.94
Industrial	35.0	1.11
Misc Revenue	0.0	—
Demand	0.4	4.30

Morningstar's Take by Scott Berry 12-22-06

We're sticking with T. Rowe Price Tax-Free High Yield.

We like this fund for its prudent and consistent approach. With the yield difference between low-quality municipal bonds and high-quality issues at historically, and arguably unsustainably low levels, manager Jim Murphy has been careful not to stretch for yield. Rather than loading up on lower-rated bonds that aren't offering adequate compensation for their added risk, he has found opportunities in bonds with structures that are out of favor, such as callable zero-coupon bonds for example. He has also leveraged the work of T. Rowe Price's taxable-high-yield group to find opportunities in corporate-backed municipals. Specifically, the fund has owned municipal issues backed by Ford and Stone Container, which have both performed well.

We expect Murphy's approach will ultimately pay off when the market faces some rougher sledding, and avoiding losers becomes just as important as picking winners. But it has left the fund looking somewhat pedestrian in recent years. While large stakes in tobacco bonds and airline bonds, two of the market's most volatile segments, have juiced the returns of some competitors, this fund's diversification has held it back a bit. For the trailing one-, three-, and five-year periods ending Dec. 20, 2006, the fund ranked just outside the high-yield muni category's top third.

Still, we're encouraged that the fund has remained competitive in recent years. And we expect the fund's advantages will continue to pay off over the long term. Those advantages include good analytical resources that stretch across the high-yield universe from taxable bonds to tax-free issues, below-average costs, and experienced management.

Overall, we remain confident in this fund's approach and in its management. It remains our only high-yield muni Fund Analyst Pick.

Address:	100 East Pratt Street	Minimum Purchase:	$2500 Add: $100 IRA: $1000
	Baltimore MD 21202	Min Auto Inv Plan:	$2500 Add: $50
	800-225-5132	Sales Fees:	No-load
Web Address:	www.troweprice.com	Management Fee:	0.61%
Inception:	03-01-85	Actual Fees:	Mgt:0.61% Dist: —
Advisor:	T. Rowe Price Associates, Inc.	Expense Projections:	3Yr:$224 5Yr:$390 10Yr:$871
Subadvisor:	None	Income Distrib:	Monthly
NTF Plans:	N/A		

MORNINGSTAR® Funds 500

T. Rowe Price US Try L/T

	Ticker	Load	NAV	Yield	SEC Yield	Total Assets	Mstar Category
	PRULX	None	$11.37	4.5%	3.82%	$293 mil	Long Government

Governance and Management

Stewardship Grade: B

Portfolio Manager(s)

Although his 2003 appointment marks the first mutual fund management assignment for new skipper Brian Brennan, he brings 16 years of experience to the table. Much of that time was spent managing fixed-income assets in separate accounts. And although he now has prime responsibility for this portfolio, Brennan will continue to receive support from colleagues Cheryl Mickel, Connie Bavely, Alan Levenson, and Dan Shackelford.

Strategy

Management stores at least 85% of assets in Treasuries. Although the rest of the portfolio is typically composed of GNMA mortgages, management will also hold other bonds that are fully backed by the U.S. government. The fund's duration (a measure of interest-rate sensitivity) is typically kept within a range of 9.0 to 11.0 years, though it generally hews close to the midpoint. As such, the fund can be subject to dramatic fluctuations when interest rates change. In general, though, the bulk of management effort is spent on yield-curve and government-subsector selections.

Performance 12-31-06

	1st Qtr	2nd Qtr	3rd Qtr	4th Qtr	Total
2002	-1.33	5.46	10.53	0.10	15.13
2003	1.09	4.13	-2.50	-0.52	2.10
2004	4.25	-4.44	5.13	1.01	5.79
2005	0.39	6.68	-2.49	0.95	5.42
2006	-3.81	-1.34	6.22	0.25	1.07

Trailing	Total Return%	+/- LB Aggr	+/- LB LTGvtBd	%Rank Cat	Growth of $10,000
3 Mo	0.25	-0.99	-0.32	42	10,025
6 Mo	6.49	1.40	-0.60	64	10,649
1 Yr	1.07	-3.26	-0.99	47	10,107
3 Yr Avg	4.07	0.37	-1.44	60	11,271
5 Yr Avg	5.79	0.73	-1.32	73	13,250
10 Yr Avg	6.78	0.54	-0.97	55	19,271
15 Yr Avg	6.91	0.41	-1.17	75	27,244

Tax Analysis	Tax-Adj Rtn%	%Rank Cat	Tax-Cost Rat	%Rank Cat
3 Yr (estimated)	2.35	67	1.65	69
5 Yr (estimated)	3.90	79	1.79	67
10 Yr (estimated)	4.61	50	2.03	55

Potential Capital Gain Exposure: 3% of assets

Historical Profile

Return	Average
Risk	Below Avg
Rating	★★★ Neutral

	1995	1996	1997	1998	1999	2000	2001	2002	2003	2004	2005	2006	History
	11.36	10.43	11.27	11.98	10.22	11.50	11.29	12.28	11.74	11.86	11.88	11.37	NAV
	28.60	-2.37	14.73	12.82	-8.75	19.11	3.39	15.13	2.10	5.79	5.42	1.07	Total Return %
	10.13	-6.00	5.08	4.13	-7.93	7.48	-5.05	4.88	-2.00	1.45	2.99	-3.26	+/-LB Aggr
	-2.30	-1.53	-0.39	-0.59	-0.02	-1.18	-0.95	-1.86	-0.51	-2.15	-1.19	-0.99	+/-LB LTGvtBd
	7.20	5.77	6.25	5.72	5.34	6.21	5.30	5.16	4.45	4.47	4.59	4.42	Income Return %
	21.40	-8.14	8.48	7.10	-14.09	12.90	-1.91	9.97	-2.35	1.32	0.83	-3.35	Capital Return %
	50	60	55	67	50	68	42	82	54	84	58	47	Total Rtn % Rank Cat
	0.66	0.64	0.63	0.63	0.62	0.62	0.60	0.57	0.53	0.51	0.53	0.51	Income $
	0.00	0.00	0.00	0.07	0.11	0.00	0.00	0.10	0.26	0.03	0.08	0.11	Capital Gains $
	0.80	0.80	0.80	0.67	0.66	0.64	0.63	0.66	0.68	0.67	0.67	0.63	Expense Ratio %
	7.05	6.05	6.22	5.71	5.30	5.89	5.51	5.13	4.54	4.31	4.26	4.45	Income Ratio %
	99	60	68	81	74	22	31	49	66	52	55	26	Turnover Rate %
	71	73	207	310	324	315	306	297	245	232	225	293	Net Assets $mil

Rating and Risk

Time Period	Load-Adj Return %	Morningstar Rtn vs Cat	Morningstar Risk vs Cat	Morningstar Risk-Adj Rating
1 Yr	1.07			
3 Yr	4.07	Avg	-Avg	★★★
5 Yr	5.79	-Avg	-Avg	★★★
10 Yr	6.78	Avg	-Avg	★★★
Incept	7.56			

Other Measures	Standard Index LB Aggr	Best Fit Index LB Long Tr
Alpha	0.1	-1.0
Beta	2.02	0.90
R-Squared	93	99
Standard Deviation	6.82	
Mean	4.07	
Sharpe Ratio	0.15	

Portfolio Analysis 09-30-06

Total Fixed-Income:114	Date of Maturity	Amount $000	Value $000	% Net Assets
US Treasury Bond 7.125%	02-15-23	32,557	40,895	15.12
US Treasury Bond 5.375%	02-15-31	31,388	33,909	12.53
US Treasury Bond 8.875%	02-15-19	24,476	33,792	12.49
US Treasury Bond 7.625%	02-15-25	18,075	24,144	8.92
US Treasury Bond 6%	02-15-26	19,084	21,836	8.07
US Treasury Bond 7.875%	02-15-21	14,828	19,487	7.20
US Treasury Bond 6.25%	05-15-30	12,639	15,190	5.61
US Treasury Bond 6.125%	08-15-29	10,184	12,006	4.44
US Treasury Bond 4.5%	02-15-36	11,125	10,659	3.94
US Treasury Bond 8.875%	08-15-17	5,000	6,754	2.50
GNMA 7%	12-20-32	5,709	5,871	2.17
US Treasury Note 2%	07-15-14	5,200	5,097	1.88
US Treasury Bond 5.5%	08-15-28	2,819	3,072	1.14
US Treasury Bond 6.375%	08-15-27	2,100	2,521	0.93
US Treasury Note 5.125%	05-15-16	2,300	2,385	0.88
GNMA 6.5%		2,300	2,358	0.87
US Treasury Bond 2%	01-15-26	2,435	2,335	0.86
GNMA 5.5%	04-20-36	2,328	2,306	0.85
US Treasury Note 4.5%	11-15-15	2,080	2,060	0.76
US Treasury Note 4%	03-15-10	2,000	1,962	0.73

Current Investment Style

Duration: Short Int Long
Quality: High Med Low

¹ figure provided by fund

Avg Eff Duration¹	10.5 Yrs
Avg Eff Maturity	16.7 Yrs
Avg Credit Quality	AAA
Avg Wtd Coupon	6.65%
Avg Wtd Price	119.56% of par

Coupon Range	% of Bonds	Rel Cat
0% PIK	0.0	0.0
0% to 6%	37.0	0.5
6% to 8%	47.2	3.2
8% to 10%	15.7	2.9
More than 10%	0.0	0.1

1.00=Category Average

Credit Analysis	% bonds 09-30-06		
AAA	100	BB	0
AA	0	B	0
A	0	Below B	0
BBB	0	NR/NA	0

Sector Breakdown	% of assets
US Treasuries	88
TIPS	0
US Agency	0
Mortgage Pass-Throughs	8
Mortgage CMO	2
Mortgage ARM	0
US Corporate	0
Asset-Backed	0
Convertible	0
Municipal	0
Corporate Inflation-Protected	0
Foreign Corporate	0
Foreign Govt	0

Composition			
Cash	2.9	Bonds	97.1
Stocks	0.0	Other	0.0

Special Securities	
Restricted/Illiquid Secs	0
Exotic Mortgage-Backed	0
Emerging-Markets Secs	0
Options/Futures/Warrants	No

Morningstar's Take by Marta Norton 12-19-06

T. Rowe Price U.S. Treasury Long-Term's performance won't grab the limelight, but we like its steady approach.

This fund got off to a rocky start this year. With interest rates on the rise, funds such as this one, with most of its assets devoted to long-term Treasuries, have taken hits. In fact, the fund had trouble posting positive returns from January through May. Things have changed of late, though. Economic data have suggested a slowing economy, and the Federal Reserve stopped raising interest rates in August. That's helped the fund climb out of its hole to post a 2.07% gain for the year to date period ending Dec. 18, 2006.

The fund also grabbed a few extra percentage points with a timely move out of Treasury Inflation-Protected Securities and into Ginnie Maes. In August, manager Brian Brennan cut the fund's allocation to TIPs from roughly 4.5% to around 2.5% in order to avoid the seasonal slump that TIPs generally experience at the tail end of the summer.

This also helped the fund avoid the negative impact declining energy prices had on the TIPs market. Brennan increased the fund's Ginnie Mae stake to approximately 10% because he believed they looked attractively priced compared with other agency bonds.

Still, the fund's gains lag those of many of its long-term peers. That's because, while it focuses on long-term bonds, it generally doesn't stretch as far out on the yield curve as some of its rivals. Although that limits its potential for peer-beating returns, we're not bothered by the fund's more moderate approach because it offers investors a smoother ride. The fund's standard deviation (a measure of return volatility) checks in below that of its average peer over the short and long term.

We think this fund's approach makes sense, and its below category-median expenses add to its appeal. Investors interested in a long-term government-bond fund should like what they find here.

Address:	100 East Pratt Street Baltimore MD 21202 800-638-5660
Web Address:	www.troweprice.com
Inception:	09-29-89
Advisor:	T. Rowe Price Associates, Inc.
Subadvisor:	None
NTF Plans:	N/A

Minimum Purchase:	$2500	Add: $100	IRA: $1000
Min Auto Inv Plan:	$50	Add: $50	
Sales Fees:	No-load		
Management Fee:	0.37%		
Actual Fees:	Mgt:0.31%	Dist: —	
Expense Projections:	3Yr:$202	5Yr:$351	10Yr:$786
Income Distrib:	Monthly		

T. Rowe Price Value

	Ticker	Load	NAV	Yield	Total Assets	Mstar Category
	TRVLX	None	$27.05	1.0%	$6,357 mil	Large Value

Governance and Management

Stewardship Grade: B

Portfolio Manager(s)

John Linehan took charge on March 31, 2003. He joined T. Rowe Price in 1998 as an analyst covering the paper, energy, and airline industries and has been a member of the fund's investment committee since 2001. Linehan has also helped Brian Rogers and Steve Boesel run the firm's institutional large-value accounts since 1999.

Strategy

Like his predecessor Brian Rogers, manager John Linehan seeks stocks that appear cheap relative to historical standards. But unlike Rogers, who was apt to own firms with shakier fundamentals, Linehan favors high-quality names. And because he runs the fund as a pure large-value portfolio, its average market cap should continue to rise. Linehan also devotes a small slice of the portfolio to overseas names in hopes of exploiting valuation disparities that often arise between U.S. companies and their foreign counterparts.

Historical Profile

Return	Above Avg
Risk	Above Avg
Rating	★★★★ Above Avg

95% 93% 93% 95% 97% 96% 93% 93% 94%

Investment Style
Equity
Stock %

▼ Manager Change
▽ Partial Manager Change

Growth of $10,000
— Investment Values of Fund
— Investment Values of S&P 500

40.8
31.0
24.0
17.0
10.0

Performance Quartile (within Category)

1995	1996	1997	1998	1999	2000	2001	2002	2003	2004	2005	2006	History
13.21	15.76	18.24	18.31	17.50	19.15	18.88	15.56	20.01	22.90	23.38	27.05	NAV
39.85	28.51	29.25	6.85	19.75	15.75	1.60	-16.58	30.00	15.36	6.30	19.75	Total Return %
2.27	5.55	-4.11	-21.73	-11.88	24.85	13.49	5.52	1.32	4.48	1.39	3.96	+/-S&P 500
1.49	6.87	-5.93	-8.78	1.81	8.74	7.19	-1.06	-0.03	-1.13	-0.75	-2.50	+/-Russ 1000 VI
2.56	2.00	1.35	1.12	1.19	1.31	0.89	0.79	1.29	0.90	1.09	1.15	Income Return %
37.29	26.51	27.90	5.73	7.97	14.44	0.71	-17.37	28.71	14.46	5.21	18.60	Capital Return %
3	5	30	78	31	22	24	40	33	23	40	29	Total Rtn % Rank Cat
0.26	0.26	0.21	0.20	0.21	0.23	0.17	0.15	0.20	0.18	0.25	0.27	Income $
0.82	0.91	1.83	0.96	2.20	0.84	0.40	0.04	0.01	0.00	0.72	0.68	Capital Gains $
1.10	1.10	1.05	0.98	0.92	0.91	0.94	0.95	0.97	0.93	0.90	—	Expense Ratio %
2.03	1.71	1.26	1.06	1.14	1.38	0.93	1.01	1.06	1.10	1.14	—	Income Ratio %
90	68	67	72	68	56	42	30	31	17	19	—	Turnover Rate %
47	198	546	775	851	989	1,322	1,140	1,480	2,463	3,279	5,226	Net Assets $mil

Performance 12-31-06

	1st Qtr	2nd Qtr	3rd Qtr	4th Qtr	Total
2002	4.98	-11.05	-18.66	9.82	-16.58
2003	-7.20	17.80	3.82	14.54	30.00
2004	1.65	3.24	-0.62	10.61	15.36
2005	-0.96	1.06	2.71	3.41	6.30
2006	5.86	-0.44	5.36	7.85	19.75

Trailing	Total Return%	+/- S&P 500	+/- Russ 1000 VI	%Rank Cat	Growth of $10,000
3 Mo	7.85	1.15	-0.15	24	10,785
6 Mo	13.63	0.89	-1.09	35	11,363
1 Yr	19.75	3.96	-2.50	29	11,975
3 Yr Avg	13.66	3.22	-1.43	23	14,683
5 Yr Avg	9.75	3.56	-1.11	21	15,923
10 Yr Avg	10.94	2.52	-0.06	12	28,241
15 Yr Avg	—	—	—	—	—

Tax Analysis	Tax-Adj Rtn%	%Rank Cat	Tax-Cost Rat	%Rank Cat
3 Yr (estimated)	12.92	14	0.65	25
5 Yr (estimated)	9.14	15	0.56	30
10 Yr (estimated)	9.30	10	1.48	46

Potential Capital Gain Exposure: 19% of assets

Rating and Risk

Time Period	Load-Adj Return %	Morningstar Rtn vs Cat	Morningstar Risk vs Cat	Morningstar Risk-Adj Rating
1 Yr	19.75			
3 Yr	13.66	+Avg	Avg	★★★★
5 Yr	9.75	+Avg	+Avg	★★★★
10 Yr	10.94	+Avg	+Avg	★★★★
Incept	14.46			

Other Measures	Standard Index S&P 500	Best Fit Index S&P 500
Alpha	3.3	3.3
Beta	0.95	0.95
R-Squared	92	92
Standard Deviation	6.84	
Mean	13.66	
Sharpe Ratio	1.46	

Morningstar's Take by Christopher Davis 11-20-06

T. Rowe Price Value's cautious, patient approach underlies its appeal.

These days, manager John Linehan says he favors stocks in "growth purgatory." These are the one-time darlings of growth investors that have fallen from favor in recent years. One example is Microsoft, which is historically cheap and poised to benefit from its new Vista operating system. Linehan expects the launch to trigger a round of PC upgrades, lending a boost to other beaten-down growth holdings such as Intel and Dell.

Linehan's early-2006 purchase of the latter is illustrative of his approach. He regards the PC maker as more of a manufacturing than a tech company and worries its direct-sales model won't be as advantageous in the future as it was in the past. Because Dell doesn't have the staying power of favorites like Microsoft or Coca-Cola, Linehan has been reluctant to make it a big position. Still, he says the stock is inexpensive, especially given his expectation the company can grow earnings at a

15% annual rate. And although an earnings restatement may be in the offing (Dell recently delayed release of its earnings), Linehan argues it won't affect the company's long-term value.

Linehan's strategy allows him to look beyond issues like these that could affect stock prices in the short run but not over the long haul. Instead, he's more focused on what will happen over the next three to five years, which we think gives him an edge. With most investors fixated on quarterly earnings, Linehan's long-term orientation gives the fund a better shot at distinguishing itself from the crowd. He's certainly done so since his March 2003 start, outpacing the typical large-value fund by more than 2 percentage points annually.

Admittedly, Linehan's track record here isn't long, but he's been comanaging T. Rowe Price Institutional Large Value for six years with success. He also benefits from strong analytical resources and moderate expenses. This is a fine large-value option.

Address:	100 East Pratt Street Baltimore MD 21202 800-638-5660
Web Address:	www.troweprice.com
Inception:	09-30-94
Advisor:	T. Rowe Price Associates, Inc.
Subadvisor:	None
NTF Plans:	N/A

Minimum Purchase:	$2500	Add: $100	IRA: $1000
Min Auto Inv Plan:	$50	Add: $50	
Sales Fees:	No-load		
Management Fee:	0.66%		
Actual Fees:	Mgt:0.66%	Dist: —	
Expense Projections:	3Yr:$287	5Yr:$498	10Yr:$1108
Income Distrib:	Annually		

Portfolio Analysis 09-30-06

Share change since 06-06 Total Stocks:115

Sector	PE	Tot Ret%	% Assets
⊕ General Electric Company	Ind Mtrls	20.0	9.35	2.78
⊕ Microsoft Corporation	Software	23.8	15.83	1.85
⊕ Total SA ADR	Energy	10.6	19.24	1.68
⊕ Tyco International, Ltd.	Ind Mtrls	15.7	6.83	1.59
⊕ Coca-Cola Company	Goods	21.7	23.10	1.48
⊕ International Paper Co.	Ind Mtrls	—	4.51	1.42
⊕ Marsh & McLennan Compani	Financial	29.0	-1.16	1.37
⊕ Johnson & Johnson	Health	17.5	12.45	1.36
⊕ Intel Corporation	Hardware	21.0	-17.18	1.31
Schlumberger, Ltd.	Energy	22.3	31.07	1.25
J.P. Morgan Chase & Co.	Financial	13.6	25.60	1.23
⊕ Hartford Financial Servi	Financial	11.9	10.83	1.23
⊕ Time Warner, Inc.	Media	19.6	26.37	1.22
⊕ Murphy Oil Corporation	Energy	12.8	-4.82	1.21
⊕ First Horizon National C	Financial	16.8	13.71	1.16
⊕ Fifth Third Bancorp	Financial	15.4	12.99	1.15
⊕ E.I. du Pont de Nemours	Ind Mtrls	18.4	18.64	1.14
Morgan Stanley	Financial	12.3	45.93	1.13
⊕ Anheuser-Busch Companies	Goods	18.8	17.41	1.13
TJX Companies	Consumer	16.9	24.05	1.11

Current Investment Style

Value Blnd Growth — Large Mid Small

Market Cap	%
Giant	41.0
Large	41.6
Mid	16.7
Small	0.6
Micro	0.0
Avg $mil:	33,198

Value Measures		Rel Category
Price/Earnings	15.76	1.15
Price/Book	2.40	1.08
Price/Sales	1.26	0.97
Price/Cash Flow	9.54	1.42
Dividend Yield %	2.23	0.96

Growth Measures	%	Rel Category
Long-Term Erngs	10.99	1.06
Book Value	4.15	0.52
Sales	7.12	0.79
Cash Flow	2.88	0.48
Historical Erngs	14.30	0.89

Profitability	%	Rel Category
Return on Equity	18.89	1.05
Return on Assets	9.30	0.95
Net Margin	10.29	0.79

Sector Weightings	% of Stocks	Rel S&P 500	3 Year High	Low
⊙ Info	20.66	1.03		
Software	2.60	0.75	3	2
Hardware	6.60	0.71	7	3
Media	9.07	2.39	11	9
Telecom	2.39	0.68	4	2
⊆ Service	41.17	0.89		
Health	9.65	0.80	10	8
Consumer	7.80	1.02	8	5
Business	2.91	0.69	5	3
Financial	20.81	0.93	23	21
Mfg	38.16	1.13		
Goods	4.43	1.13	10	10
Ind Mtrls	13.62	1.14	20	14
Energy	9.04	0.92	10	8
Utilities	3.30	0.94	3	3

Composition

	%
● Cash	4.7
● Stocks	94.0
● Bonds	0.0
● Other	1.3
Foreign (% of Stock)	8.2

Mᴏʀɴɪɴɢsᴛᴀʀ® Funds 500

TCW Dividend Focused I

	Ticker	Load	NAV	Yield	Total Assets	Mstar Category
	TGDFX	None	$13.30	1.7%	$1,473 mil	Large Value

Governance and Management

Portfolio Manager(s)

Diane Jaffee has more than 20 years of investment experience. She took over as lead portfolio manager of this fund in 2001, although she has been on the fund's management team since 1995.

Strategy

Manager Diane Jaffee looks for relative-value opportunities that are poised for growth. She places added emphasis on stocks that pay higher-than-average dividends but will take positions in companies that pay no dividend if their valuation and growth prospects justify it. Jaffee is willing to hold both mid- and large-cap stocks.

Historical Profile

Return
Risk
Rating   Not Rated

| | 93% | 91% | 91% |

Investment Style
Equity
Stock %

▼ Manager Change
▽ Partial Manager Change

Growth of $10,000
— Investment Values of Fund
— Investment Values of S&P 500

12.1
11.4
10.7
10.0
9.0

Performance Quartile
(within Category)

	1995	1996	1997	1998	1999	2000	2001	2002	2003	2004	2005	2006	History
	—	—	—	—	—	—	—	—	—	11.45	11.61	13.30	NAV
	—	—	—	—	—	—	—	—	—	—	3.26	18.45	Total Return %
	—	—	—	—	—	—	—	—	—	—	-1.65	2.66	+/-S&P 500
	—	—	—	—	—	—	—	—	—	—	-3.79	-3.80	+/-Russ 1000 VI
	—	—	—	—	—	—	—	—	—	—	1.48	1.97	Income Return %
	—	—	—	—	—	—	—	—	—	—	1.78	16.48	Capital Return %
	—	—	—	—	—	—	—	—	—	—	80	48	Total Rtn % Rank Cat
	—	—	—	—	—	—	—	—	—	0.06	0.17	0.23	Income $
	—	—	—	—	—	—	—	—	—	0.08	0.04	0.21	Capital Gains $
	—	—	—	—	—	—	—	—	—	—	1.02	0.87	Expense Ratio %
	—	—	—	—	—	—	—	—	—	—	1.37	1.81	Income Ratio %
	—	—	—	—	—	—	—	—	—	44	32	25	Turnover Rate %
	—	—	—	—	—	—	—	—	—	6	92	167	Net Assets $mil

Performance 12-31-06

	1st Qtr	2nd Qtr	3rd Qtr	4th Qtr	Total
2002	—	—	—	—	—
2003	—	—	—	—	—
2004	—	—	—	—	—*
2005	-0.87	1.50	2.10	0.52	3.26
2006	4.29	0.25	6.35	6.53	18.45

Trailing	Total Return%	+/- S&P 500	+/- Russ 1000 VI	%Rank Cat	Growth of $10,000
3 Mo	6.53	-0.17	-1.47	75	10,653
6 Mo	13.29	0.55	-1.43	41	11,329
1 Yr	18.45	2.66	-3.80	48	11,845
3 Yr Avg	—	—	—	—	—
5 Yr Avg	—	—	—	—	—
10 Yr Avg	—	—	—	—	—
15 Yr Avg	—	—	—	—	—

Tax Analysis	Tax-Adj Rtn%	%Rank Cat	Tax-Cost Rat	%Rank Cat
3 Yr (estimated)	—	—	—	—
5 Yr (estimated)	—	—	—	—
10 Yr (estimated)	—	—	—	—

Potential Capital Gain Exposure: 11% of assets

Rating and Risk

Time Period	Load-Adj Return %	Morningstar Rtn vs Cat	Morningstar Risk vs Cat	Morningstar Risk-Adj Rating
1 Yr	18.45			
3 Yr	—	—	—	—
5 Yr	—	—	—	—
10 Yr	—	—	—	—
Incept	14.42			

Other Measures	Standard Index S&P 500	Best Fit Index
Alpha	—	—
Beta	—	—
R-Squared	—	—
Standard Deviation	—	
Mean	—	
Sharpe Ratio	—	

Portfolio Analysis 11-30-06

Share change since 10-06 Total Stocks:55	Sector	PE	Tot Ret%	% Assets
⊕ AT&T, Inc.	Telecom	18.2	51.59	3.05
J.P. Morgan Chase & Co.	Financial	13.6	25.60	2.99
Merrill Lynch & Company,	Financial	14.2	39.28	2.69
Citigroup, Inc.	Financial	13.1	19.55	2.61
⊕ Chevron Corporation	Energy	9.0	33.76	2.60
Nokia Corporation ADR	Hardware	18.9	13.44	2.48
Packaging Corporation of	Goods	43.0	0.73	2.38
CSX Corporation	Business	15.4	37.05	2.38
St. Paul Travelers Compa	Financial	11.6	22.90	2.38
Kraft Foods, Inc.	Goods	18.0	30.52	2.33
ConocoPhillips	Energy	6.5	26.53	2.25
Hewlett-Packard Company	Hardware	19.3	45.21	2.23
⊕ Pfizer Inc.	Health	15.2	15.22	2.16
⊕ E.I. du Pont de Nemours	Ind Mtrls	18.4	18.64	2.16
⊕ Regal Entertainment Grou	Goods	37.4	19.27	2.08
Intel Corporation	Hardware	21.0	-17.18	2.08
American Electric Power	Utilities	18.4	19.58	1.99
⊕ BCE Inc.	Telecom	14.3	19.09	1.96
⊖ Wyeth	Health	17.2	12.88	1.85
IBM	Hardware	17.1	19.77	1.85

Current Investment Style

Value Blnd Growth — Large Mid Small

Market Cap	%
Giant	40.4
Large	40.2
Mid	18.9
Small	0.5
Micro	0.0

Avg $mil: 29,696

Value Measures		Rel Category
Price/Earnings	14.56	1.06
Price/Book	2.23	1.00
Price/Sales	1.17	0.90
Price/Cash Flow	8.53	1.27
Dividend Yield %	2.70	1.16

Growth Measures	%	Rel Category
Long-Term Erngs	9.96	0.96
Book Value	4.43	0.56
Sales	5.59	0.62
Cash Flow	0.07	0.01
Historical Erngs	13.29	0.82

Profitability	%	Rel Category
Return on Equity	14.77	0.82
Return on Assets	7.30	0.74
Net Margin	9.41	0.73

Sector Weightings	% of Stocks	Rel S&P 500	3 Year High Low
⌖ Info	25.60	1.28	
🖥 Software	0.00	0.00	6 0
🖳 Hardware	11.69	1.27	13 4
🎤 Media	4.15	1.09	6 2
📶 Telecom	9.76	2.78	10 2
☞ Service	41.83	0.91	
🏥 Health	9.89	0.82	11 2
🛒 Consumer	1.73	0.23	10 2
🏢 Business	8.85	2.09	9 3
💲 Financial	21.36	0.96	28 21
⚒ Mfg	32.57	0.96	
🏭 Goods	16.67	1.95	18 11
⚙ Ind Mtrls	7.81	0.65	20 7
🔥 Energy	5.90	0.60	8 2
💡 Utilities	2.19	0.63	5 2

Composition

		%
●	Cash	9.1
●	Stocks	90.9
●	Bonds	0.0
●	Other	0.0
	Foreign	6.6
	(% of Stock)	

Morningstar's Take by Reginald Laing 12-22-06

TCW Dividend Focused is a good choice for a core holding.

As its name suggests, this fund emphasizes--though doesn't confine itself to--stocks that pay an attractive dividend. Manager Diane Jaffee also looks for companies that appear cheap based on several valuation criteria and have a catalyst that will help them unlock their unrealized value. Top-five holding J.P. Morgan Chase is one such company. A product of two large mergers, the banking giant has had difficulty integrating the legacy firms' overlapping businesses. For that reason and others, the market has punished the stock, giving it price/earnings, price/book, and price/sales ratios below those of its typical industry peer. That makes it a compelling value to Jaffee. Moreover, the company pays a dividend nearly twice that of the average stock in the S&P 500, and boasts a talented CEO, who Jaffee believes will cut costs and turn the company and its stock around.

Jaffee will also invest up to 20% of assets in non-dividend-paying stocks, such as cable company Comcast. As with J.P. Morgan, Jaffee thinks it has a strong management team intent on cutting costs and improving profit margins.

This flexible total-return approach gives the fund a higher income payout than its typical large-value peer and should also help it when more growth-oriented stocks lead the market. While this is a fairly straightforward strategy, a lot still depends on Jaffee. Happily for investors here, she has proven her ability to execute it over the decade in which she's been on the fund's management team. For the trailing 10 years through Nov. 30, 2006, the older N share class's 11.4% annualized return ranked the fund ahead of 93% of its large-value peers.

Of course, past performance doesn't guarantee future returns, but we feel comfortable with Jaffee's approach and experience. This fund is a solid choice.

Address:	865 South Figueroa Street Los Angeles CA 90017 800-386-3829	Minimum Purchase:	$2000	Add: $250	IRA: $500
		Min Auto Inv Plan:	$2000	Add: $100	
		Sales Fees:	No-load		
Web Address:	www.tcw.com	Management Fee:	0.75%		
Inception:	11-01-04	Actual Fees:	Mgt:0.75%	Dist: —	
Advisor:	TCW Investment Management Co.	Expense Projections:	3Yr:$325	5Yr:$563	10Yr:$1248
Subadvisor:	None	Income Distrib:	Quarterly		
NTF Plans:	N/A				

TCW Opportunity I

	Ticker	Load	NAV	Yield	Total Assets	Mstar Category
	TGOIX	None	$14.72	0.0%	$131 mil	Small Blend

Governance and Management

Stewardship Grade: C

Portfolio Manager(s)

Manager Diane Jaffee has been on board since November 1995. She has six dedicated analysts assisting her with stock selection. Before becoming a money manager, Jaffee had worked as a research analyst since 1982, and she is a seasoned stock-picker. Former comanager William Church departed this offering in 2003 to run a hedge fund for TCW.

Strategy

Manager Diane Jaffee and her team screen for stocks that look cheap based on a variety of metrics, including price/earnings, price/cash flow, and price/book ratios. The team also looks for companies that are trading at discounts to their private market values. If a stock looks cheap based on any of these criteria, the managers follow up with more fundamental research, looking for some catalyst for growth, such as a new management team or product line. All new positions account for 0.25% of assets when they're added to the portfolio.

Performance 12-31-06

	1st Qtr	2nd Qtr	3rd Qtr	4th Qtr	Total
2002	10.95	-5.28	-19.65	-1.25	-16.62
2003	-4.72	23.82	9.18	16.77	50.40
2004	5.32	0.66	-1.89	9.50	13.89
2005	-3.47	3.30	2.90	2.84	5.52
2006	13.75	-7.12	-2.58	8.26	11.44

Trailing	Total Return%	+/- S&P 500	+/- Russ 2000	%Rank Cat	Growth of $10,000
3 Mo	8.26	1.56	-0.64	46	10,826
6 Mo	5.47	-7.27	-3.91	78	10,547
1 Yr	11.44	-4.35	-6.93	80	11,144
3 Yr Avg	10.23	-0.21	-3.33	90	13,394
5 Yr Avg	10.93	4.74	-0.46	65	16,798
10 Yr Avg	10.58	2.16	1.14	62	27,338
15 Yr Avg	—	—	—	—	—

Tax Analysis	Tax-Adj Rtn%	%Rank Cat	Tax-Cost Rat	%Rank Cat
3 Yr (estimated)	9.25	73	0.89	23
5 Yr (estimated)	10.31	52	0.56	21
10 Yr (estimated)	9.33	55	1.13	32

Potential Capital Gain Exposure: 25% of assets

Morningstar's Take by Reginald Laing 12-29-06

TCW Opportunity is a reasonable option.

Manager Diane Jaffee looks for companies that are trading at lower valuations than the typical stock in the fund's Russell 2000 benchmark. But she'll only take a position in such a depressed stock if she thinks the company has a catalyst for getting out of its rut in the coming years. Health-food grocer Wild Oats is one example. Jaffee deems the stock cheap because its price/sales ratio has been below that of its fellow retailers for some time. However, Jaffee thinks the company's attempt to refurbish its stores and brand name and improve its inventory system through adopting new technology will significantly increase its share value.

Wild Oats has been in the portfolio since mid-2001, and the fund's turnover rate has hovered around 50% in recent years (which indicates a two-year average holding period). That's well below the category average, and Jaffee's patience not only gives her stock picks more time to pay off; it keeps trading costs in check and boosts the fund's

tax efficiency.

Of course, investors here probably haven't focused on tax efficiency in recent years--but rather, on the fund's underwhelming relative returns. They shouldn't lose faith yet, however, as Jaffee's longer-term record is solid--albeit with a misstep as comanager in 1998, when an errant bet on energy stocks hurt the fund. (Since then, Jaffee has limited the fund's sector risk, which should prevent similar setbacks in the future.) Like small-blend sibling TCW Value Added, this fund lately has been hurt by its exposure to semiconductor-related stocks, which have suffered from a multiyear cyclical slump. If that industry turns around, though, expect this fund to look a lot better than it has.

Jaffee is an experienced manager plying a sensible strategy. And while the fund isn't among the cheapest in the category, its expense ratio is at least below the median for similar no-load funds. All in all, it's a decent option.

Address:	865 South Figueroa Street Los Angeles CA 90017 800-386-3829
Web Address:	www.tcw.com
Inception:	05-09-94
Advisor:	TCW Investment Management Co.
Subadvisor:	None
NTF Plans:	N/A

Minimum Purchase:	$2000	Add: $250	IRA: $500
Min Auto Inv Plan:	$2000	Add: $100	
Sales Fees:	No-load		
Management Fee:	0.90%		
Actual Fees:	Mgt:0.90%	Dist: —	
Expense Projections:	3Yr:$393	5Yr:$681	10Yr:$1500
Income Distrib:	Annually		

Historical Profile

Return	Average
Risk	Above Avg
Rating	★★ Below Avg

- ▼ Manager Change
- ▽ Partial Manager Change

Growth of $10,000
- ■ Investment Values of Fund
- — Investment Values of S&P 500

Performance Quartile (within Category)

	1995	1996	1997	1998	1999	2000	2001	2002	2003	2004	2005	2006	History
	7.81	8.58	7.81	5.85	7.57	10.24	10.41	8.68	12.97	13.83	13.96	14.72	NAV
	15.88	25.64	11.72	-25.10	29.40	39.48	7.81	-16.62	50.40	13.89	5.52	11.44	Total Return %
	-21.70	2.68	-21.64	-53.68	8.36	48.58	19.70	5.48	21.72	3.01	0.61	-4.35	+/-S&P 500
	-12.57	9.15	-10.64	-22.55	8.14	42.50	5.32	3.86	3.15	-4.44	0.97	-6.93	+/-Russ 2000
	0.00	0.00	0.00	0.00	0.00	0.00	0.00	0.00	0.00	0.00	0.00	0.00	Income Return %
	15.88	25.64	11.72	-25.10	29.40	39.48	7.81	-16.62	50.40	13.89	5.52	11.44	Capital Return %
	89	32	93	97	20	1	44	55	16	86	62	80	Total Rtn % Rank Cat
	0.00	0.00	0.00	0.00	0.00	0.00	0.00	0.00	0.00	0.00	0.00	0.00	Income $
	0.18	1.19	1.70	0.00	0.00	0.00	0.29	0.61	0.00	0.08	0.92	0.63	0.83	Capital Gains $
	1.03	1.01	1.02	1.14	1.27	1.30	1.27	1.15	1.40	1.31	1.24	1.16	Expense Ratio %
	0.11	-0.07	-0.19	-0.34	-0.35	-0.21	-0.35	-0.27	-0.41	-0.48	-0.22	-0.10	Income Ratio %
	148	182	159	124	150	164	111	42	56	52	45	49	Turnover Rate %
	20	42	52	18	10	11	10	15	27	32	32	35	Net Assets $mil

Rating and Risk

Time Period	Load-Adj Return %	Morningstar Rtn vs Cat	Morningstar Risk vs Cat	Morningstar Risk-Adj Rating
1 Yr	11.44			
3 Yr	10.23	-Avg	+Avg	★★
5 Yr	10.93	Avg	+Avg	★★★
10 Yr	10.58	Avg	+Avg	★★
Incept	11.83			

Other Measures	Standard Index S&P 500	Best Fit Index Russ 2000
Alpha	-4.6	-3.0
Beta	1.74	1.01
R-Squared	66	92
Standard Deviation	14.65	
Mean	10.23	
Sharpe Ratio	0.52	

Portfolio Analysis 11-30-06

Share change since 10-06 Total Stocks:106

	Sector	PE	Tot Ret%	% Assets
⊖ Arena Pharmaceuticals, I	Health	—	-9.15	3.06
Mattson Technology	Hardware	32.9	-7.36	2.93
Eclipsys Corporation	Software	—	8.61	2.61
⊕ Hain Celestial Group, In	Goods	31.3	47.50	2.33
Wabtec	Ind Mtrls	18.2	13.08	2.24
Thoratec Laboratories Co	Health	NMF	-15.03	2.14
⊕ BearingPoint, Inc.	Business	—	0.13	2.03
⊕ Bank Mutual Corporation	Financial	34.2	17.08	1.89
⊕ Wild Oats Markets, Inc.	Consumer	30.0	19.04	1.81
Lindsay Manufacturing Co	Ind Mtrls	40.0	71.33	1.77
Shaw Group	Ind Mtrls	47.7	15.16	1.76
GrafTech International,	Ind Mtrls	—	11.25	1.63
⊕ Avista Corporation	Utilities	15.2	46.53	1.60
⊕ 3Com Corporation	Hardware	—	14.17	1.50
⊕ AGCO Corporation	Ind Mtrls	—	86.72	1.48
Equity Inns	Financial	—	24.12	1.44
⊕ Ikon Office Solutions, I	Ind Mtrls	20.7	59.10	1.44
⊕ Blockbuster, Inc.	Consumer	—	41.07	1.43
Donegal Group, Inc. A	Financial	—		1.41
⊕ Dynegy, Inc.	Utilities	—	49.59	1.41

Current Investment Style

Value Blnd Growth — Large Mid Small

Market Cap	%
Giant	0.0
Large	0.0
Mid	20.6
Small	55.1
Micro	24.3

Avg $mil: 937

Value Measures		Rel Category
Price/Earnings	21.45	1.29
Price/Book	1.84	0.87
Price/Sales	0.83	0.85
Price/Cash Flow	6.73	0.96
Dividend Yield %	0.59	0.55

Growth Measures	%	Rel Category
Long-Term Erngs	14.39	1.03
Book Value	-3.21	NMF
Sales	3.04	0.34
Cash Flow	6.95	0.55
Historical Erngs	-2.04	NMF

Profitability	%	Rel Category
Return on Equity	0.35	0.03
Return on Assets	0.38	0.05
Net Margin	3.15	0.33

Sector Weightings	% of Stocks	Rel S&P 500	3 Year High Low	
↻ Info	20.53	1.03		
🖥 Software	3.60	1.04	11	4
🖥 Hardware	12.95	1.40	13	8
🎙 Media	1.86	0.49	4	1
📶 Telecom	2.12	0.60	3	1
☰ Service	45.19	0.98		
🏥 Health	12.25	1.02	16	12
🛒 Consumer	8.90	1.16	12	7
📋 Business	8.77	2.07	10	3
💲 Financial	15.27	0.69	17	11
⚒ Mfg	34.27	1.01		
⚙ Goods	7.25	0.85	8	4
⚙ Ind Mtrls	20.66	1.73	27	19
🔥 Energy	2.79	0.28	8	2
💡 Utilities	3.57	1.02	4	1

Composition

		%
●	Cash	0.9
●	Stocks	99.1
●	Bonds	0.0
○	Other	0.0
	Foreign	0.3
	(% of Stock)	

MORNINGSTAR® Funds 500

TCW Select Equities I

	Ticker	Load	NAV	Yield	Total Assets	Mstar Category
	TGCEX	None	$19.10	0.0%	$3,536 mil	Large Growth

Governance and Management

Stewardship Grade: C

Portfolio Manager(s)

Longtime manager Glen Bickerstaff turned over day-to-day management duties to Craig Blum and Stephen Burlingame in January 2005. Bickerstaff will, however, continue to be involved in a supervisory role at the fund. Blum and Burlingame have worked closely with Bickerstaff since 2002 but gathered just one year of portfolio management experience before they took the helm.

Strategy

Comanagers Craig Blum and Stephen Burlingame use a combination of top-down and bottom-up analysis. They first look for major secular trends and then focus on businesses that they think will benefit. Management also wants to see companies with unique business models or market niches and favor those with lots of free cash flow. They stick with their holdings over the long haul, so the fund's turnover is fairly low.

Historical Profile

Return	Average
Risk	High
Rating	★★ Below Avg

98%	100%	100%	100%	100%	99%	98%	99%	100%

▽ ... ▽ ▽ ▽

▼ Manager Change
▽ Partial Manager Change

40.8
31.0
24.0
17.0
10.0

Growth of $10,000
■ Investment Values of Fund
— Investment Values of S&P 500

Performance Quartile (within Category)

Investment Style
Equity
Stock %

1995	1996	1997	1998	1999	2000	2001	2002	2003	2004	2005	2006	History
13.77	16.39	14.22	16.91	23.19	20.52	16.57	11.54	17.34	19.58	20.31	19.10	NAV
26.45	20.59	22.70	37.97	42.95	-6.21	-19.25	-30.36	50.26	12.92	3.73	-5.12	Total Return %
-11.13	-2.37	-10.66	9.39	21.91	2.89	-7.36	-8.26	21.58	2.04	-1.18	-20.91	+/-S&P 500
-10.73	-2.53	-7.79	-0.74	9.79	16.21	1.17	-2.48	20.51	6.62	-1.53	-14.19	+/-Russ 1000Gr
0.47	0.15	0.00	0.00	0.00	0.00	0.00	0.00	0.00	0.00	0.00	0.00	Income Return %
25.98	20.44	22.70	37.97	42.95	-6.21	-19.25	-30.36	50.26	12.92	3.73	-5.12	Capital Return %
81	42	69	24	33	28	48	75	2	10	73	98	Total Rtn % Rank Cat
0.05	0.02	0.00	0.00	0.00	0.00	0.00	0.00	0.00	0.00	0.00	0.00	Income $
0.00	0.20	5.76	2.45	0.92	1.32	0.00	0.00	0.00	0.00	0.00	0.17	Capital Gains $
0.85	0.82	0.83	0.86	0.88	0.85	0.87	0.86	0.89	0.86	0.90	0.89	Expense Ratio %
0.48	0.18	0.08	-0.14	-0.39	-0.31	-0.52	-0.56	-0.56	-0.55	-0.59	-0.44	Income Ratio %
54	40	39	104	48	52	12	3	22	14	16	39	Turnover Rate %
190	232	117	222	310	572	1,139	992	2,096	2,799	3,313	2,648	Net Assets $mil

Performance 12-31-06

	1st Qtr	2nd Qtr	3rd Qtr	4th Qtr	Total
2002	-0.66	-21.93	-19.22	11.18	-30.36
2003	4.51	20.07	7.53	11.37	50.26
2004	-0.12	7.16	-5.44	11.57	12.92
2005	-9.86	3.74	5.35	5.29	3.73
2006	-1.82	-5.32	-1.96	4.11	-5.12

Trailing	Total Return%	+/- S&P 500	+/- Russ 1000Gr	%Rank Cat	Growth of $10,000
3 Mo	4.11	-2.59	-1.82	82	10,411
6 Mo	2.07	-10.67	-8.03	97	10,207
1 Yr	-5.12	-20.91	-14.19	98	9,488
3 Yr Avg	3.58	-6.86	-3.29	91	11,113
5 Yr Avg	3.07	-3.12	0.38	42	11,632
10 Yr Avg	7.86	-0.56	2.42	21	21,311
15 Yr Avg	—	—	—	—	—

Tax Analysis	Tax-Adj Rtn%	%Rank Cat	Tax-Cost Rat	%Rank Cat
3 Yr (estimated)	3.54	86	0.04	3
5 Yr (estimated)	3.04	38	0.03	4
10 Yr (estimated)	6.56	21	1.21	59

Potential Capital Gain Exposure: 16% of assets

Rating and Risk

Time Period	Load-Adj Return %	Morningstar Rtn vs Cat	Morningstar Risk vs Cat	Morningstar Risk-Adj Rating
1 Yr	-5.12			
3 Yr	3.58	-Avg	High	★
5 Yr	3.07	Avg	High	★★
10 Yr	7.86	+Avg	+Avg	★★★
Incept	9.68			

Other Measures	Standard Index S&P 500	Best Fit Index Mstar Large Growth
Alpha	-10.1	0.9
Beta	1.63	1.39
R-Squared	62	83
Standard Deviation	14.14	
Mean	3.58	
Sharpe Ratio	0.09	

Portfolio Analysis 11-30-06

Share change since 10-06 Total Stocks:30	Sector	PE	Tot Ret%	% Assets
⊖ Google, Inc.	Business	61.5	11.00	8.33
⊕ Qualcomm, Inc.	Hardware	26.6	-11.32	6.99
Schlumberger, Ltd.	Energy	22.3	31.07	6.65
⊖ Network Appliance, Inc.	Hardware	56.7	45.48	6.57
⊖ Progressive Corporation	Financial	12.4	-16.93	6.11
⊕ SLM Corporation	Financial	14.1	-9.76	5.46
⊖ Amazon.com, Inc.	Consumer	55.1	-16.31	5.12
⊖ Genentech, Inc.	Health	48.7	-12.29	4.92
⊖ Countrywide Financial Co	Financial	9.8	26.22	4.84
⊖ eBay, Inc.	Consumer	40.1	-30.43	4.35
⊖ Commerce Bancorp, Inc.	Financial	23.6	3.89	3.34
⊖ Salesforce.com, Inc.	Software	—	13.73	3.23
⊖ Pulte Homes, Inc.	Consumer	6.7	-15.43	3.17
⊖ Genzyme Corporation	Health	50.8	-13.00	3.09
⊖ Varian Medical Systems,	Health	26.8	-5.50	3.05
⊖ General Electric Company	Ind Mtrls	20.0	9.35	2.99
⊖ Zimmer Holdings, Inc.	Health	24.5	16.22	2.81
⊖ Expeditors International	Business	34.4	20.54	2.60
⊖ WellPoint, Inc.	Health	17.2	-1.38	2.39
⊖ Amgen, Inc.	Health	29.1	-13.38	2.14

Current Investment Style

Value Blnd Growth — Large Mid Small

Market Cap	%
Giant	36.5
Large	44.4
Mid	19.1
Small	0.0
Micro	0.0

Avg $mil: 30,588

Value Measures		Rel Category
Price/Earnings	22.12	1.15
Price/Book	3.40	1.02
Price/Sales	2.51	1.29
Price/Cash Flow	15.60	1.37
Dividend Yield %	0.63	0.61

Growth Measures	%	Rel Category
Long-Term Erngs	15.73	1.10
Book Value	17.93	1.55
Sales	19.04	1.64
Cash Flow	15.44	0.92
Historical Erngs	25.32	1.10

Profitability	%	Rel Category
Return on Equity	23.31	1.15
Return on Assets	13.73	1.25
Net Margin	17.10	1.20

Sector Weightings	% of Stocks	Rel S&P 500	3 Year High	Low
↻ Info	24.80	1.24		
Software	7.08	2.05	9	0
Hardware	16.26	1.76	31	15
Media	1.46	0.39	15	1
Telecom	0.00	0.00	0	0
☞ Service	65.54	1.42		
Health	18.45	1.53	20	8
Consumer	14.33	1.87	26	14
Business	11.24	2.66	11	0
Financial	21.52	0.97	25	14
↳ Mfg	9.66	0.29		
Goods	0.00	0.00	2	0
Ind Mtrls	3.00	0.25	3	2
Energy	6.66	0.68	7	0
Utilities	0.00	0.00	0	0

Composition

		%
●	Cash	0.2
●	Stocks	99.8
●	Bonds	0.0
●	Other	0.0
	Foreign	0.0
	(% of Stock)	

Morningstar's Take by Reginald Laing 11-13-06

TCW Select Equities has looked bad lately, but that might add to its appeal.

This fund has never been appropriate for timid investors, and its recent performance demonstrates why. For the trailing 12 months through Nov. 10, 2006, its 6.4% loss trails the returns of 98% of its peers in Morningstar's large-growth category. Big positions in auto insurer Progressive and online auction house eBay have hurt, as have losses in other top holdings.

High volatility is a risk inherent in running a concentrated portfolio (this fund's top individual holding will at times take up more than 10% of assets). But managers Steve Burlingame and Craig Blum tend to stand by their picks, as this fund's low portfolio turnover indicates. With the exception of eBay and Dell, which the managers have lightened up on, the portfolio has remained largely the same over the past year. And if you thought--as we did--that this fund had appeal a year ago, then debatably it's more attractive now, as several of its top holdings are a good deal cheaper than they were then.

One beleaguered pick--which Blum and Burlingame have added to in recent months--is wireless-equipment maker Qualcomm. The stock has declined significantly in 2006 due to a legal dispute with handset maker Nokia over royalty payments. But the managers' thesis remains the same: They think the company's digital television network, which will bring video to wireless phones that use Qualcomm technology, is alone worth a good portion of the stock's market capitalization. They seem to be getting a good price: Qualcomm is trading at a meaningful discount to what a Morningstar equity analyst considers its fair value.

Because of its high-growth tilt and large bets on individual stocks, this fund will be volatile. Over time, though, we think Blum and Burlingame will compensate investors for the risks they take. This remains a solid option.

Address:	865 South Figueroa Street Los Angeles CA 90017 800-386-3829	Minimum Purchase:	$2000	Add: $250	IRA: $500
		Min Auto Inv Plan:	$2000	Add: $100	
		Sales Fees:	No-load		
Web Address:	www.tcw.com	Management Fee:	0.75%		
Inception:	03-01-93	Actual Fees:	Mgt:0.75%	Dist: —	
Advisor:	TCW Investment Management Co.	Expense Projections:	3Yr:$287	5Yr:$498	10Yr:$1108
Subadvisor:	None	Income Distrib:	Annually		
NTF Plans:	N/A				

TCW Total Return Bond I

Analyst Pick ✓

Ticker	Load	NAV	Yield	SEC Yield	Total Assets	Mstar Category
TGLMX	None	$9.47	4.8%	4.96%	$537 mil	Intermediate-Term Bond

Governance and Management

Stewardship Grade: B

Portfolio Manager(s)

Jeffrey Gundlach, who has primary responsibility for this portfolio, has been managing it since its 1993 inception. He has been with TCW since 1985. He is supported by TCW CIO Philip Barach.

Strategy

Management keeps this mortgage-backed securities fund's duration (a measure of interest-rate sensitivity) between the (shorter) Lehman Brothers Mortgage Backed Securities Index and the Lehman Brothers Aggregate Bond Index, which is the benchmark for most core bond funds. That is intended to help keep the fund competitive with both basic government mortgage funds and intermediate-term bond portfolios. In that pursuit, the fund buys lots of out-of-index sectors such as CMOs, private-label CMOs, ARMs, and inverse floaters.

Historical Profile

Return	High
Risk	Below Avg
Rating	★★★★ Highest

Investment Style
Fixed Income
Income Rtn %Rank Cat

▼ Manager Change
▽ Partial Manager Change

Growth of $10,000
— Investment Values of Fund
— Investment Values of LB Aggr

Performance Quartile (within Category)

	1995	1996	1997	1998	1999	2000	2001	2002	2003	2004	2005	2006	History
	9.79	9.56	9.84	9.58	8.84	9.39	9.65	9.96	9.58	9.61	9.44	9.47	NAV
	20.80	5.08	11.93	7.23	-0.46	13.58	9.41	11.04	3.06	5.19	3.36	5.27	Total Return %
	2.33	1.45	2.28	-1.46	0.36	1.95	0.97	0.79	-1.04	0.85	0.93	0.94	+/-LB Aggr
	-0.63	2.39	2.50	-2.91	2.42	1.14	0.59	-1.99	-2.91	-0.11	1.53	1.46	+/-LB 5-10YR
	8.24	7.34	8.27	10.04	7.54	7.00	6.58	7.72	6.99	4.85	5.17	4.90	Income Return %
	12.56	-2.26	3.66	-2.81	-8.00	6.58	2.83	3.32	-3.93	0.34	-1.81	0.37	Capital Return %
	15	12	2	59	26	1	11	3	86	13	3	11	Total Rtn % Rank Cat
	0.69	0.70	0.76	0.95	0.70	0.60	0.60	0.72	0.68	0.45	0.48	0.45	Income $
	0.00	0.00	0.05	0.00	0.00	0.00	0.00	0.00	0.00	0.00	0.00	0.00	Capital Gains $
	0.68	0.68	0.67	0.70	0.69	0.77	0.74	0.70	0.51	0.44	0.44	0.44	Expense Ratio %
	7.88	7.15	7.77	8.52	6.62	6.63	6.31	7.78	5.76	4.73	5.12	4.86	Income Ratio %
	24	39	16	28	28	8	11	26	60	33	24	22	Turnover Rate %
	77	114	78	92	90	83	79	127	144	176	237	374	Net Assets $mil

Performance 12-31-06

	1st Qtr	2nd Qtr	3rd Qtr	4th Qtr	Total
2002	0.98	3.93	4.22	1.52	11.04
2003	1.01	1.19	0.20	0.63	3.06
2004	2.67	-2.01	3.39	1.12	5.19
2005	-0.40	2.78	-0.03	0.99	3.36
2006	-0.29	0.19	3.86	1.46	5.27

Trailing	Total Return%	+/- LB Aggr	+/- LB 5-10YR	%Rank Cat	Growth of $10,000
3 Mo	1.46	0.22	0.38	24	10,146
6 Mo	5.38	0.29	-0.30	18	10,538
1 Yr	5.27	0.94	1.46	11	10,527
3 Yr Avg	4.60	0.90	0.96	6	11,444
5 Yr Avg	5.55	0.49	-0.37	12	13,101
10 Yr Avg	6.88	0.64	0.20	2	19,452
15 Yr Avg	—	—	—	—	—

Tax Analysis	Tax-Adj Rtn%	%Rank Cat	Tax-Cost Rat	%Rank Cat
3 Yr (estimated)	2.86	5	1.66	63
5 Yr (estimated)	3.40	18	2.04	82
10 Yr (estimated)	4.20	5	2.51	92

Potential Capital Gain Exposure: 0% of assets

Rating and Risk

Time Period	Load-Adj Return %	Morningstar Rtn vs Cat	Morningstar Risk vs Cat	Morningstar Risk-Adj Rating
1 Yr	5.27			
3 Yr	4.60	High	-Avg	★★★★★
5 Yr	5.55	+Avg	Low	★★★★★
10 Yr	6.88	High	-Avg	★★★★★
Incept	6.67			

Other Measures	Standard Index LB Aggr	Best Fit Index LB 5-10YR
Alpha	0.9	1.1
Beta	0.83	0.61
R-Squared	95	97
Standard Deviation	2.78	
Mean	4.60	
Sharpe Ratio	0.48	

Morningstar's Take by Eric Jacobson 12-07-06

If you think alchemy is impossible, watching TCW Galileo Total Return for a few years might just make you a believer.

Okay, lead manager Jeffrey Gundlach isn't actually turning lead into gold. What he does, however, is still pretty impressive. Every security choice comes with trade-offs. With Treasuries one enjoys protection from credit risk as well as predictability of performance: Even when they're volatile, the price action of Treasury bonds is relatively easy to model in relation to the rest of the market. Government-agency backed mortgages offer similar protection from credit risk, but the prepayment risk they court is so significant--and can so drastically alter a mortgage security's expected performance--that they frequently offer as much income as midquality corporate bonds.

The Holy Grail of bond investing is to short-circuit those kinds of relationships and enjoy higher returns than Treasuries without the ill effects that risk-taking can bring. That's quite difficult, though, as credit-focused investors almost always have to endure some stretch of trouble. And while many smart managers believe mortgages are perennially underpriced and therefore an excellent alternative, they aren't for the meek. Because homeowners have an open-ended option to refinance at any time, analyzing and valuing mortgages is as difficult a task as almost any in the bond market.

Gundlach and his team excel in such work. By mixing and matching quirky mortgage securities such as ARMs, CMOs, and their various derivatives--and ably managing their risks--they have made this portfolio much more predictable than many plain-vanilla mortgage funds, while earning returns that beat most diversified core bond funds. A decision to cut fees a few years ago has helped meaningfully, and the fund's trailing returns are fantastic. In other hands this could be a risky choice, but Gundlach has proved himself here. This portfolio is a terrific option.

Address:	865 South Figueroa Street
	Los Angeles CA 90017
	800-386-3829
Web Address:	www.tcw.com
Inception:	06-18-93
Advisor:	TCW Investment Management Co.
Subadvisor:	None
NTF Plans:	N/A

Minimum Purchase:	$2000	Add: $250	IRA: $500
Min Auto Inv Plan:	$2000	Add: $100	
Sales Fees:	No-load		
Management Fee:	0.50%		
Actual Fees:	Mgt:0.50%	Dist: —	
Expense Projections:	3Yr:$205	5Yr:$357	10Yr:$798
Income Distrib:	Monthly		

Portfolio Analysis 11-30-06

Total Fixed-Income:111	Date of Maturity	Amount $000	Value $000	% Net Assets
FHLMC CMO 5%	06-15-32	23,697	23,274	4.43
Cwalt CMO	01-25-36	17,936	18,120	3.45
FNMA FRN	10-01-35	16,644	16,404	3.12
FHLMC CMO 4.5%	07-15-23	16,502	15,982	3.04
FHLMC 6%	02-15-36	14,925	15,191	2.89
FHLMC CMO 4.5%	10-15-34	15,638	15,127	2.88
FNMA	08-25-33	13,669	13,202	2.51
FHLMC CMO 4.25%	01-15-23	13,084	12,667	2.41
FNMA CMO 4%	10-25-18	12,949	12,521	2.38
FNMA CMO 4%	07-25-17	12,656	12,276	2.34
FHLMC CMO 4.25%	06-15-32	11,894	11,550	2.20
FHLMC CMO 4.25%	06-15-19	11,892	11,545	2.20
FHLMC CMO 5%	07-15-31	11,004	10,702	2.04
Residential Accredit 200	06-25-35	10,093	10,091	1.92
FNMA CMO 5.5%	08-25-35	10,340	9,848	1.87
FHLMC CMO 4.5%	03-15-19	10,010	9,611	1.83
FNMA CMO 4.5%	08-25-24	10,000	9,284	1.77
FNMA CMO	10-25-35	9,500	9,134	1.74
FNMA CMO 4.25%	03-25-33	9,564	9,095	1.73
GNMA	05-20-33	8,606	8,454	1.61

Current Investment Style

Duration: Short / Int / Long

			High Quality
	■		Med
			Low

¹ figure provided by fund

Avg Eff Duration¹	5.2 Yrs
Avg Eff Maturity	6.7 Yrs
Avg Credit Quality	AAA
Avg Wtd Coupon	4.28%
Avg Wtd Price	96.49% of par

Coupon Range	% of Bonds	Rel Cat
0% PIK	14.9	2.1
0% to 6%	94.4	1.3
6% to 8%	4.0	0.2
8% to 10%	1.5	0.3
More than 10%	0.1	0.1

1.00=Category Average

Credit Analysis	% bonds 11-30-06		
AAA	97	BB	0
AA	0	B	0
A	0	Below B	0
BBB	0	NR/NA	3

Sector Breakdown — % of assets

US Treasuries	0
TIPS	0
US Agency	0
Mortgage Pass-Throughs	15
Mortgage CMO	81
Mortgage ARM	0
US Corporate	0
Asset-Backed	0
Convertible	0
Municipal	0
Corporate Inflation-Protected	0
Foreign Corporate	0
Foreign Govt	0

Composition

Cash	4.0	Bonds	96.0
Stocks	0.0	Other	0.0

Special Securities

Restricted/Illiquid Secs	0
Exotic Mortgage-Backed	3
Emerging-Markets Secs	0
Options/Futures/Warrants	No

MORNINGSTAR® Funds 500

TCW Value Added I

	Ticker	Load	NAV	Yield	Total Assets	Mstar Category
	TGSVX	None	$12.99	0.0%	$29 mil	Small Blend

Governance and Management

Stewardship Grade: C

Portfolio Manager(s)

Experienced. Nicholas Galluccio and Susan Suvall have been running money together for 20 years. They are also in charge of TCW Value Opportunities, which they run in a similar style. They have delivered strong results at that offering since its inception in 1997. Five analysts assist Galluccio and Suvall.

Strategy

Managers Nicholas Galluccio and Susan Suvall break up the portfolio into four categories: companies trading below liquidation value, turnaround stories, busted-growth stocks, and emerging-growth stocks. Like many money managers, they want to see high free cash flow and a strong balance sheet. They often delve into nontraditional value sectors, such as technology. They are committed to keeping the portfolio in the small-cap space and will sell a holding if its market cap gets too high.

Historical Profile
Return Low
Risk High
Rating ★ Lowest

Investment Style
Equity
Stock %

100% / 100% / 96% / 99% / 100% / 99%

▼ Manager Change
▽ Partial Manager Change

15.5
12.5 **Growth of $10,000**
10.0 ▬ Investment Values of Fund
— Investment Values of S&P 500
5.0

Performance Quartile (within Category)

	1995	1996	1997	1998	1999	2000	2001	2002	2003	2004	2005	2006	History
	—	—	—	—	—	10.87	13.03	9.05	14.70	13.88	12.68	12.99	NAV
	—	—	—	—	—	11.14*	20.14	-30.54	63.76	4.50	-1.76	18.21	Total Return %
	—	—	—	—	—	—	32.03	-8.44	35.06	-6.38	-6.67	2.42	+/-S&P 500
	—	—	—	—	—	—	17.65	-10.06	16.51	-13.83	-6.31	-0.16	+/-Russ 2000
	—	—	—	—	—	—	0.26	0.00	0.00	0.00	0.00	0.00	Income Return %
	—	—	—	—	—	—	19.88	-30.54	63.76	4.50	-1.76	18.21	Capital Return %
	—	—	—	—	—	—	14	95	3	98	95	16	Total Rtn % Rank Cat
	—	—	—	—	—	0.00	0.03	0.00	0.00	0.00	0.00	0.00	Income $
	—	—	—	—	—	0.24	0.00	0.00	0.12	1.46	0.96	1.98	Capital Gains $
	—	—	—	—	—	—	1.55	1.58	1.56	1.61	1.50	—	Expense Ratio %
	—	—	—	—	—	—	0.00	-0.85	-1.14	-1.16	-0.91	—	Income Ratio %
	—	—	—	—	—	—	32	77	72	68	72	—	Turnover Rate %
	—	—	—	—	—	—	1	11	22	39	39	29	Net Assets $mil

Performance 12-31-06

	1st Qtr	2nd Qtr	3rd Qtr	4th Qtr	Total
2002	9.75	-17.62	-32.34	13.55	-30.54
2003	-6.63	28.28	14.76	19.13	63.76
2004	2.31	1.00	-11.13	13.79	4.50
2005	-6.34	1.00	1.68	2.14	-1.76
2006	14.20	-6.35	2.14	8.23	18.21

Trailing	Total Return%	+/- S&P 500	+/- Russ 2000	%Rank Cat	Growth of $10,000
3 Mo	8.23	1.53	-0.67	47	10,823
6 Mo	10.54	-2.20	1.16	15	11,054
1 Yr	18.21	2.42	-0.16	16	11,821
3 Yr Avg	6.67	-3.77	-6.89	97	12,137
5 Yr Avg	6.66	0.47	-4.73	94	13,804
10 Yr Avg	—	—	—	—	—
15 Yr Avg	—	—	—	—	—

Tax Analysis	Tax-Adj Rtn%	%Rank Cat	Tax-Cost Rat	%Rank Cat
3 Yr (estimated)	4.55	97	1.99	62
5 Yr (estimated)	5.32	95	1.26	57
10 Yr (estimated)	—	—	—	—

Potential Capital Gain Exposure: 11% of assets

Rating and Risk

Time Period	Load-Adj Return %	Morningstar Rtn vs Cat	Morningstar Risk vs Cat	Morningstar Risk-Adj Rating
1 Yr	18.21			
3 Yr	6.67	Low	High	★
5 Yr	6.66	Low	High	★
10 Yr	—	—	—	
Incept	9.79			

Other Measures	Standard Index S&P 500	Best Fit Index Russ 2000
Alpha	-10.7	-7.5
Beta	2.20	1.15
R-Squared	81	92
Standard Deviation	16.78	
Mean	6.67	
Sharpe Ratio	0.28	

Portfolio Analysis 11-30-06

Share change since 10-06 Total Stocks:218	Sector	PE	Tot Ret%	% Assets
⊖ Novellus Systems, Inc.	Hardware	35.3	42.70	1.23
⊖ SafeNet, Inc.	Software	—	-25.70	1.20
⊖ Kemet Corporation	Hardware	—	3.25	1.09
⊖ Vishay Intertechnology	Hardware	18.2	-1.60	1.06
⊖ Entegris, Inc.	Hardware	89.9	14.86	1.03
⊖ Brooks Automation, Inc.	Hardware	40.3	14.92	1.03
⊖ Pacific Sunwear	Consumer	18.9	-21.43	0.98
⊖ Monaco Coach Corporation	Ind Mtrls	NMF	8.52	0.96
⊖ RadioShack Corporation	Consumer	58.6	-19.05	0.95
⊖ International Rectifier	Hardware	24.0	20.78	0.94
⊖ Astoria Financial Corpor	Financial	15.1	6.02	0.90
⊖ Lattice Semiconductor	Hardware	—	50.00	0.89
⊖ Ferro Corporation	Ind Mtrls	56.0	13.73	0.89
⊖ Pilgrim's Pride Corporat	Goods	—	-10.93	0.86
⊖ Macrovision Corporation	Software	66.5	68.92	0.85
⊖ Insituform Technologies	Business	37.3	33.51	0.84
⊖ Hexcel Corporation	Ind Mtrls	7.6	-3.55	0.83
⊖ LTX Corporation	Hardware	27.1	24.44	0.82
⊖ Aspen Insurance Holdings	Financial	8.3	14.24	0.82
⊕ Verigy Ltd.	Hardware	—	—	0.82

Current Investment Style

Value Blnd Growth — Large/Mid/Small

Market Cap	%
Giant	0.0
Large	0.0
Mid	16.8
Small	51.9
Micro	31.4

Avg $mil: 820

Value Measures		Rel Category
Price/Earnings	19.37	1.17
Price/Book	1.62	0.77
Price/Sales	0.85	0.87
Price/Cash Flow	7.97	1.14
Dividend Yield %	0.63	0.59

Growth Measures	%	Rel Category
Long-Term Erngs	15.00	1.08
Book Value	5.30	0.70
Sales	-4.82	NMF
Cash Flow	3.00	0.24
Historical Erngs	2.59	0.15

Profitability	%	Rel Category
Return on Equity	6.75	0.52
Return on Assets	3.89	0.54
Net Margin	5.68	0.59

Sector Weightings

	% of Stocks	Rel S&P 500	3 Year High	Low
↻ Info	38.43	1.92		
Software	4.85	1.41	7	4
Hardware	31.89	3.45	36	27
Media	1.02	0.27	3	1
Telecom	0.67	0.19	1	0
⊂ Service	32.71	0.71		
Health	5.96	0.49	8	4
Consumer	10.35	1.35	13	9
Business	7.27	1.72	10	7
Financial	9.13	0.41	10	4
⊔ Mfg	28.86	0.85		
Goods	7.99	0.93	8	4
Ind Mtrls	17.93	1.50	21	16
Energy	2.94	0.30	7	1
Utilities	0.00	0.00	0	0

Composition

● Cash	1.1
● Stocks	98.9
● Bonds	0.0
○ Other	0.0
Foreign	1.4
(% of Stock)	

Morningstar's Take by Reginald Laing 12-29-06

TCW Value Added has appeal, but it would have more if it were cheaper.

Managers Nick Galluccio and Susan Suvall, who have run money in this style since the mid-1980s, look for companies that fall into any of several value categories--such as firms with undervalued assets, turnaround stories, and tiny emerging-growth companies that have had temporary setbacks. Teen retailer Pacific Sunwear is a company management thinks is turning itself around. Its sales have suffered from high energy prices, and its stock now trades at a low multiple relative to the cash flow it generates. Galluccio and Suvall think gas prices will ease pressure on the consumer, and that Pacific's new management team can easily fix a merchandising problem and hence unlock shareholder value.

The managers here aren't afraid to add to their high-conviction picks as they fall in price (as they recently did with Pacific). Their willingness to play the contrarian can lead to lean years--such as 2004

and 2005, when this fund's bet on struggling semiconductor stocks dragged on returns. But when their bets pay off, they tend to do so in spades, as they did in 2006 when a number of holdings were acquired at nice premiums.

This fund's record of highly volatile returns may make it tough to stick with, but investors should be rewarded in the long run. For the trailing 10 years through Nov. 30, 2006, this fund's older separate-account clone delivered a 13.9% annualized gross return, which outstripped the 12.4% gross return of the typical small-blend peer. If you consider that many small-blend funds haven't survived, that record looks even better.

But the separate account's record is gross of fees, and this fund carries a hefty 1.62% expense ratio (1.26% is the median for similar funds). The fund has two of the most experienced small-cap managers, but that levy is a high hurdle for anyone to clear. We'd like the board to give retail investors a better deal before we fully endorse the fund.

Address:	865 South Figueroa Street Los Angeles CA 90017 800-386-3829	Minimum Purchase:	$2000	Add: $250	IRA: $500
		Min Auto Inv Plan:	$2000	Add: $100	
		Sales Fees:	No-load		
Web Address:	www.tcw.com	Management Fee:	1.00%		
Inception:	06-14-00*	Actual Fees:	Mgt:1.00%	Dist: —	
Advisor:	TCW Investment Management Co.	Expense Projections:	3Yr:$542	5Yr:$933	10Yr:$2030
Subadvisor:	None	Income Distrib:	Annually		
NTF Plans:	N/A				

TCW Value Opportunities I

Analyst Pick	**Ticker** TGVOX	**Load** None	**NAV** $22.62	**Yield** 0.3%	**Total Assets** $969 mil	**Mstar Category** Mid-Cap Blend

Governance and Management

Stewardship Grade: B

Portfolio Manager(s)

Experienced. Susan Suvall and Nicholas Galluccio have managed portfolios together at TCW since 1985. Suvall and Galluccio have run this fund since its inception in 1997 and are also responsible for small-cap sibling TCW Value Added. Four dedicated analysts assist with stock research and selection.

Strategy

Comanagers Susan Suvall and Nicholas Galluccio start with quantitative screens, looking at a firm's projected earnings over the next two years. They break up the portfolio into three categories: companies trading below liquidation value, turnaround stories, and busted-growth stocks. Like many money managers, they want to see high free cash flows and strong balance sheets. They often delve into nontraditional value sectors such as technology and keep the portfolio fairly concentrated with approximately 55-60 holdings.

Performance 12-31-06

	1st Qtr	2nd Qtr	3rd Qtr	4th Qtr	Total
2002	3.18	-16.60	-25.69	13.76	-27.25
2003	-3.13	22.05	10.30	14.25	48.98
2004	5.43	2.09	-9.05	13.10	10.72
2005	0.45	-0.67	3.59	2.84	6.30
2006	8.63	-3.43	3.16	4.32	12.90

Trailing	Total Return%	+/- S&P 500	+/- S&P Mid 400	%Rank Cat	Growth of $10,000
3 Mo	4.32	-2.38	-2.67	97	10,432
6 Mo	7.62	-5.12	1.79	61	10,762
1 Yr	12.90	-2.89	2.58	52	11,290
3 Yr Avg	9.94	-0.50	-3.15	86	13,288
5 Yr Avg	7.57	1.38	-3.32	86	14,403
10 Yr Avg	—	—	—	—	—
15 Yr Avg	—	—	—	—	—

Tax Analysis	Tax-Adj Rtn%	%Rank Cat	Tax-Cost Rat	%Rank Cat
3 Yr (estimated)	8.59	79	1.23	53
5 Yr (estimated)	6.77	80	0.74	46
10 Yr (estimated)	—	—	—	—

Potential Capital Gain Exposure: 19% of assets

Morningstar's Take by Laura Pavlenko Lutton 12-04-06

TCW Value Opportunities is a fine choice for those who understand its risks.

This fund finds itself in unusual territory in 2006: the middle of the mid-blend category pack. For the year to date through December 1, the fund has gained about 12%, which is strong in absolute turns but mediocre relative to its typical peer. Normally, this fund runs near the top or the bottom of its category, turning in peer-beating returns when more-speculative stocks are running (the case in 2003) and struggling in recent years when value stocks have ruled the roost.

This volatility isn't too surprising given the fund's strategy. Managers Susan Suvall and Nicholas Galluccio buy broken growth stocks that most of their peers won't touch. The managers often invest in firms with operational problems, but otherwise have strong balance sheets and established products. For example, the pair recently picked up shares of Gap, the struggling retailer, because they like the company's improved balance sheet and

new merchandising experts. They think the stock will appreciate should the company report that its sales are improving or it's being sold.

In addition to taking on considerable stock-specific risk, Suvall and Galluccio also court sector-specific risk because they're not afraid to pile into areas where numerous stocks meet their investment criteria. A favorite sector of late is hardware, which soaked up 30% of the fund's assets at last count. (The typical mid-blend fund keeps about 5% of its assets in that sector.)

This fund's volatility may be a turnoff to some investors, but we think Suvall and Galluccio are two of the most skilled and thoughtful managers in the category. Over the long term, their picks have delivered, and we think this offering is particularly well positioned for a sustained growth rally, the likes of which we haven't seen since the late 1990s. The fund's low fees are icing on the cake.

Historical Profile

Return	Below Avg
Risk	Above Avg
Rating	★ Lowest

Investment Style: Equity / Stock %

Percentages across top: 95% | 100% | 100% | 100% | 100% | 94% | 97% | 100% | 100%

▼ Manager Change
▽ Partial Manager Change

Growth of $10,000
— Investment Values of Fund
— Investment Values of S&P 500

Performance Quartile (within Category)

	1995	1996	1997	1998	1999	2000	2001	2002	2003	2004	2005	2006	History
NAV	—	—	10.01	10.04	11.28	14.24	18.86	13.72	20.44	22.33	22.01	22.62	
Total Return %	—	—	-1.46*	0.30	25.06	38.26	33.65	-27.25	48.98	10.72	6.30	12.90	
+/-S&P 500	—	—	—	-28.28	4.02	47.36	45.54	-5.15	20.30	-0.16	1.39	-2.89	
+/-S&P Mid 400	—	—	—	-18.82	10.34	20.75	34.26	-12.72	13.36	-5.76	-6.26	2.58	
Income Return %	—	—	—	0.00	0.00	0.55	0.00	0.00	0.00	0.00	0.18	0.35	
Capital Return %	—	—	—	0.30	25.06	37.71	33.65	-27.25	48.98	10.72	6.12	12.55	
Total Rtn % Rank Cat	—	—	—	86	35	3	1	91	13	91	76	52	
Income $	—	—	0.01	0.00	0.00	0.06	0.00	0.00	0.00	0.00	0.04	0.08	
Capital Gains $	—	—	0.00	0.00	1.21	1.24	0.16	0.00	0.00	0.30	1.69	2.15	
Expense Ratio %	—	—	—	—	1.16	1.18	1.15	1.02	0.95	0.98	0.93	—	
Income Ratio %	—	—	—	—	0.05	-0.10	0.41	-0.04	-0.34	-0.24	-0.14	—	
Turnover Rate %	—	—	—	—	—	140	137	76	85	54	46	—	
Net Assets $mil	—	—	—	28	32	72	520	294	659	902	770		

Rating and Risk

Time Period	Load-Adj Return %	Morningstar Rtn vs Cat	Morningstar Risk vs Cat	Morningstar Risk-Adj Rating
1 Yr	12.90			
3 Yr	9.94	-Avg	+Avg	★★
5 Yr	7.57	-Avg	+Avg	★
10 Yr	—			
Incept	13.88			

Other Measures	Standard Index S&P 500	Best Fit Index Russ MG
Alpha	-3.3	-2.0
Beta	1.47	0.94
R-Squared	76	86
Standard Deviation	11.55	
Mean	9.94	
Sharpe Ratio	0.60	

Portfolio Analysis 11-30-06

Share change since 10-06 Total Stocks:59

	Sector	PE	Tot Ret%	% Assets
Analog Devices, Inc.	Hardware	22.5	-6.66	2.89
Teradyne, Inc.	Hardware	18.0	2.68	2.48
Thermo Fisher Scientific	Health	37.4	50.32	2.42
Regis Corporation	Consumer	16.4	2.96	2.30
Federated Department Sto	Consumer	20.8	16.54	2.24
Federated Investors, Inc	Financial	19.0	-6.94	2.19
People's Bank	Financial	45.5	47.71	2.16
Cheesecake Factory, Inc.	Consumer	23.9	-34.21	2.15
Bausch & Lomb Inc.	Health	—	-22.57	2.14
LSI Logic Corporation	Hardware	NMF	12.50	2.11
Arthur J. Gallagher & Co	Financial	25.1	-0.04	2.10
Vishay Intertechnology	Hardware	18.2	-1.60	2.08
Novellus Systems, Inc.	Hardware	35.3	42.70	2.06
Diebold Incorporated	Hardware	45.0	25.12	2.06
Sun Microsystems, Inc.	Hardware	—	29.36	2.03
International Flavors &	Ind Mtrls	23.0	49.66	2.02
SPX Corporation	Ind Mtrls	27.9	36.11	2.00
Marshall & Ilsley Corp.	Financial	15.2	14.38	1.99
KLA-Tencor Corporation	Hardware	28.9	1.88	1.99
Murphy Oil Corporation	Energy	12.8	-4.82	1.96

Current Investment Style

Value Blnd Growth — Large Mid Small

Market Cap	%
Giant	0.0
Large	14.3
Mid	74.2
Small	11.5
Micro	0.0
Avg $mil:	4,632

Value Measures		Rel Category
Price/Earnings	19.08	1.19
Price/Book	2.04	0.90
Price/Sales	1.34	1.20
Price/Cash Flow	10.92	1.29
Dividend Yield %	1.04	0.80

Growth Measures	%	Rel Category
Long-Term Erngs	13.15	1.04
Book Value	9.97	1.20
Sales	8.21	0.92
Cash Flow	-0.56	NMF
Historical Erngs	12.30	0.69

Profitability	%	Rel Category
Return on Equity	12.05	0.76
Return on Assets	7.37	0.92
Net Margin	9.13	0.84

Sector Weightings	% of Stocks	Rel S&P 500	3 Year High	Low
Info	33.95	1.70		
Software	2.47	0.72	6	0
Hardware	31.48	3.41	33	20
Media	0.00	0.00	6	0
Telecom	0.00	0.00	0	0
Service	42.31	0.92		
Health	15.73	1.30	19	13
Consumer	8.51	1.11	15	5
Business	1.45	0.34	13	1
Financial	16.62	0.75	17	8
Mfg	23.74	0.70		
Goods	4.73	0.55	7	4
Ind Mtrls	14.46	1.21	15	8
Energy	4.55	0.46	9	2
Utilities	0.00	0.00	0	0

Composition

Cash	0.1
Stocks	99.9
Bonds	0.0
Other	0.0
Foreign (% of Stock)	3.7

Address:	865 South Figueroa Street Los Angeles CA 90017 800-386-3829	Minimum Purchase:	$2000	Add: $250 IRA: $500
		Min Auto Inv Plan:	$2000	Add: $100
		Sales Fees:	No-load	
Web Address:	www.tcw.com	Management Fee:	0.80%	
Inception:	11-03-97 *	Actual Fees:	Mgt:0.80%	Dist: —
Advisor:	TCW Investment Management Co.	Expense Projections:	3Yr:$293	5Yr:$509 10Yr:$1131
Subadvisor:	None	Income Distrib:	Annually	
NTF Plans:	N/A			

412

© 2007 Morningstar, Inc. All rights reserved. The information herein is not represented or warranted to be accurate, correct, complete or timely.
Past performance is no guarantee of future results. Download your free reports at http://www.morningstar.com/goto/2007Funds500.

MORNINGSTAR® Funds 500

Templeton Devel Mkts A

	Ticker	Load	NAV	Yield	Total Assets	Mstar Category
	TEDMX	5.75%	$28.28	1.8%	$5,949 mil	Diversified Emerging Mkts

Governance and Management

Stewardship Grade: C

Portfolio Manager(s)

Lead manager Mark Mobius is a veteran of emerging-markets investing. He has been running this fund since 1991 and has run a similar closed-end fund, Templeton Emerging Markets, since 1987. Mobius is supported by comanagers Tom Wu and Dennis Lim and a large analyst staff that is spread across the globe.

Strategy

Mark Mobius, Tom Wu, and Dennis Lim are buy-and-hold investors who focus on firms that appear cheap relative to their assets or relative to their long-term earnings. They are willing to make significant sector and country bets at times. The analytical team for their emerging-markets group works separately from the staff of Templeton's other foreign and world-stock funds.

Historical Profile
Return	Below Avg
Risk	Below Avg
Rating	★★★ Neutral

Investment Style: Equity / Stock %

Quartile percentages: 91% 87% 81% 88% 92% 92% 99% 96% 98%

▼ Manager Change
▽ Partial Manager Change

Growth of $10,000
— Investment Values of Fund
— Investment Values of MSCI EAFE

Values shown: 23.6, 18.0, 14.0, 10.0, 6.0

Performance Quartile (within Category)

	1995	1996	1997	1998	1999	2000	2001	2002	2003	2004	2005	2006	History
	13.01	15.40	12.94	10.30	15.61	10.59	9.88	10.00	14.99	18.52	23.42	28.28	NAV
	0.36	22.51	-9.41	-18.72	51.55	-31.85	-5.76	1.68	53.14	25.45	28.19	28.29	Total Return %
	-10.85	16.46	-11.19	-38.65	24.52	-17.66	15.66	17.62	14.55	5.20	14.65	1.95	+/-MSCI EAFE
	7.27	18.58	4.04	8.95	-12.54	0.05	-1.08	9.65	1.55	3.00	-2.12	-0.89	+/-MSCI EmrMkt
	1.50	1.35	1.01	1.48	0.00	0.40	0.97	0.50	2.53	1.71	1.57	2.28	Income Return %
	-1.14	21.16	-10.42	-20.20	51.55	-32.25	-6.73	1.18	50.61	23.74	26.62	26.01	Capital Return %
	45	17	81	11	90	62	72	10	57	37	73	79	Total Rtn % Rank Cat
	0.20	0.18	0.16	0.19	0.00	0.06	0.10	0.05	0.25	0.26	0.29	0.53	Income $
	0.25	0.34	0.84	0.05	0.00	0.00	0.00	0.00	0.00	0.00	0.00	1.17	Capital Gains $
	2.10	2.03	1.96	2.11	2.02	2.09	2.09	2.24	2.17	2.03	1.97	—	Expense Ratio %
	1.66	1.16	0.99	1.40	0.45	0.56	0.56	0.96	1.85	1.12	1.36	—	Income Ratio %
	10	12	30	38	46	69	61	49	49	59	35	—	Turnover Rate %
	2,148	3,307	3,457	2,182	2,955	1,540	1,228	1,174	1,880	2,306	3,428	4,904	Net Assets $mil

Performance 12-31-06

	1st Qtr	2nd Qtr	3rd Qtr	4th Qtr	Total
2002	11.44	-3.65	-12.88	8.70	1.68
2003	-5.19	20.81	12.19	19.17	53.14
2004	6.50	-5.05	7.25	15.67	25.45
2005	2.57	3.71	13.50	6.17	28.19
2006	11.29	-4.63	4.13	16.08	28.29

Trailing	Total Return%	+/- MSCI EAFE	+/- MSCI EmrMkt	%Rank Cat	Growth of $10,000
3 Mo	16.08	5.73	-1.20	75	11,608
6 Mo	20.88	6.19	-1.21	91	12,088
1 Yr	28.29	1.95	-0.89	79	12,829
3 Yr Avg	27.31	7.38	0.05	72	20,634
5 Yr Avg	26.29	11.31	2.77	47	32,125
10 Yr Avg	8.70	0.99	1.97	63	23,030
15 Yr Avg	9.82	1.96	1.83	1	40,759

Tax Analysis	Tax-Adj Rtn%	%Rank Cat	Tax-Cost Rat	%Rank Cat
3 Yr (estimated)	23.87	79	0.76	31
5 Yr (estimated)	24.01	60	0.63	37
10 Yr (estimated)	7.38	78	0.63	56

Potential Capital Gain Exposure: 31% of assets

Rating and Risk

Time Period	Load-Adj Return %	Morningstar Rtn vs Cat	Morningstar Risk vs Cat	Morningstar Risk-Adj Rating
1 Yr	20.92			
3 Yr	24.82	Low	Low	★
5 Yr	24.80	-Avg	Low	★★★
10 Yr	8.06	-Avg	-Avg	★★★
Incept	9.27			

Other Measures	Standard Index MSCI EAFE	Best Fit Index MSCI EmrMkt
Alpha	0.3	3.0
Beta	1.42	0.85
R-Squared	77	97
Standard Deviation	15.20	
Mean	27.31	
Sharpe Ratio	1.47	

Portfolio Analysis 06-30-06

Share change since 03-06 Total Stocks:148

	Sector	Country	% Assets
⊕ Samsung Electronics	Goods	Korea	5.05
⊕ Lukoil ADR	Energy	Russia	3.68
⊕ PetroChina	Energy	Hong Kong	3.55
⊕ Petroleo Brasileiro S.A.	Energy	Brazil	3.52
⊕ Remgro Ltd	Ind Mtrls	South Africa	2.14
⊕ Anglo American	Ind Mtrls	U.K.	2.05
⊕ Companhia Vale Do Rio Do	Ind Mtrls	Brazil	1.89
⊕ Taiwan Semiconductor Mfg	Hardware	Taiwan	1.87
China Mobile	Telecom	Hong Kong	1.72
⊕ CNOOC Ltd	Energy	Hong Kong	1.62
⊕ Mega Finl Hldg	Financial	Taiwan	1.62
⊕ Old Mutual	Financial	U.K.	1.60
⊕ Turkish Petroleum Refine	Energy	Turkey	1.56
⊖ Banco Bradesco S.A. (ADR)	Financial	Brazil	1.51
⊕ Mining & Metallurgical N	Ind Mtrls	Russia	1.44
⊕ Aluminum Corp of China	Ind Mtrls	Hong Kong	1.40
⊕ Hana Financial Group	Financial	Korea	1.32
⊕ HSBC Hldgs	Financial	Hong Kong	1.29
⊕ Mol Magyar Olaj- Es Gazi	Energy	Hungary	1.28
⊕ Nedbank Grp	Financial	South Africa	1.26

Current Investment Style

Value Blnd Growth — Large/Mid/Small

Market Cap	%
Giant	36.1
Large	39.2
Mid	21.4
Small	3.0
Micro	0.3

Avg $mil: 11,430

Value Measures		Rel Category
Price/Earnings	10.09	0.78
Price/Book	1.65	0.76
Price/Sales	0.75	0.68
Price/Cash Flow	4.22	0.64
Dividend Yield %	3.94	1.20

Growth Measures	%	Rel Category
Long-Term Erngs	12.95	0.84
Book Value	8.10	0.81
Sales	16.30	1.03
Cash Flow	11.81	1.07
Historical Erngs	8.86	0.50

Composition

Cash	1.0	Bonds	0.0
Stocks	97.9	Other	1.1
Foreign (% of Stock)			99.6

Sector Weightings	% of Stocks	Rel MSCI EAFE	3 Year High Low	
⌚ Info	14.10	1.19		
▣ Software	0.40	0.71	0	0
▣ Hardware	3.98	1.03	4	2
▣ Media	0.00	0.00	1	0
▣ Telecom	9.72	1.75	18	10
⊡ Service	34.13	0.72		
▣ Health	1.57	0.22	2	1
▣ Consumer	5.89	1.19	6	6
▣ Business	7.31	1.44	8	5
▣ Financial	19.36	0.64	20	11
⊡ Mfg	51.75	1.26		
▣ Goods	12.87	0.98	24	13
▣ Ind Mtrls	16.35	1.06	25	16
▣ Energy	20.45	2.86	20	8
▣ Utilities	2.08	0.40	3	2

Regional Exposure	% Stock		
UK/W. Europe	7	N. America	0
Japan	0	Latn America	13
Asia X Japan	54	Other	26

Country Exposure	% Stock		
South Korea	17	Brazil	10
Hong Kong	15	Turkey	7
Taiwan	12		

Morningstar's Take by Arijit Dutta 12-12-06

Templeton Developing Markets' merits don't quite cover its flaws.

This fund has much to offer when it comes to strategy, research, and management. Templeton has a vast analyst staff devoted to emerging markets who take a long-term view of a company's earnings prospects when rating stocks. This allows management to wade into areas that less-patient or less-detailed investors may be fleeing. For example, management has steadily added to the portfolio's energy holdings on weakness this year. (Since May, commodities stocks and emerging markets in general have suffered bouts of sharp volatility.) Lead manager Mark Mobius, a 19-year veteran at Templeton, says the supply of oil and gasoline will remain tight for years to come, which should keep prices high enough for energy companies to generate copious cash flows.

The approach is not designed to show immediate results, but it should reward patient investors. For example, energy stocks haven't made up the lost ground, and management continues to avoid raging markets like India that don't offer nearly the discounts analysts here seek. Still, by avoiding potentially rich valuations and by seeking pockets of opportunity, the fund makes the best of this rather volatile asset class.

We stop shy of a wholehearted recommendation, however. Our main concern is the sheer bulk of assets management runs here (including institutional accounts, management is in charge of well more than $30 billion in emerging-markets assets) limits the fund's potential. Templeton has launched sister offerings over the past year to take advantage of the team's research abilities in select emerging-markets and smaller-cap stocks. Management admits that this flagship offering is too large to take meaningful positions in most of the team's brightest ideas in those areas. Also, while the fund's expense ratio has inched lower, it remains much higher than some very eligible rivals.

Address:	500 East Broward Blvd Ste 2100 Fort Lauderdale FL 33394-3091 800-342-5236	Minimum Purchase:	$1000 Add: $50 IRA: $250
		Min Auto Inv Plan:	$50 Add: $50
		Sales Fees:	5.75%L, 0.34%S, 2.00%R
Web Address:	www.franklintempleton.com	Management Fee:	1.25% mx./1.00% mn., 0.15%A
Inception:	10-16-91	Actual Fees:	Mgt:1.21% Dist:0.34%
Advisor:	Templeton Asset Management Ltd.	Expense Projections:	3Yr:$1158 5Yr:$1576 10Yr:$2739
Subadvisor:	None	Income Distrib:	Semi-Annually
NTF Plans:	DATALynx NTF, Federated Tr NTF		

Templeton Foreign A

	Ticker	Load	NAV	Yield	Total Assets	Mstar Category
	TEMFX	5.75%	$13.64	2.0%	$18,203 mil	Foreign Large Value

Governance and Management

Stewardship Grade: C

Portfolio Manager(s)

Jeff Everett has been with Templeton since 1989. He took over this fund from longtime manager Mark Holowesko at the beginning of 2001 and also manages Templeton World. He is supported by a team of 35 analysts located in seven offices worldwide. He is supported by Templeton managers Murdo Murchison and Lisa Myers.

Strategy

This fund favors firms that are trading cheaply relative to their assets, cash flow, and earnings potential. The managers dip freely into emerging markets and make large sector and country bets. They're devoted enough to their deep-value discipline to weather dry spells; for example, the fund badly lagged the category average in 1998. The managers generally don't hedge currencies. Templeton imposes a 2% redemption fee on shares held fewer than 30 days.

Performance 12-31-06

	1st Qtr	2nd Qtr	3rd Qtr	4th Qtr	Total
2002	4.65	-0.52	-16.41	4.97	-8.64
2003	-9.27	17.77	9.23	11.81	30.51
2004	4.04	-1.36	0.92	14.07	18.14
2005	-0.24	-0.57	9.43	1.93	10.63
2006	6.47	-0.30	3.05	9.64	19.93

Trailing	Total Return%	+/- MSCI EAFE	+/- MSCI Wd xUS	%Rank Cat	Growth of $10,000
3 Mo	9.64	-0.71	-0.48	64	10,964
6 Mo	12.98	-1.71	-1.24	73	11,298
1 Yr	19.93	-6.41	-5.78	90	11,993
3 Yr Avg	16.16	-3.77	-3.94	90	15,674
5 Yr Avg	13.32	-1.66	-1.93	85	18,687
10 Yr Avg	8.88	1.17	0.92	85	23,414
15 Yr Avg	10.07	2.21	2.03	82	42,173

Tax Analysis	Tax-Adj Rtn%	%Rank Cat	Tax-Cost Rat	%Rank Cat
3 Yr (estimated)	12.27	98	1.42	55
5 Yr (estimated)	10.74	95	1.12	59
10 Yr (estimated)	6.56	92	1.55	69

Potential Capital Gain Exposure: 29% of assets

Historical Profile

Return Low
Risk Below Avg
Rating ★ Lowest

91%	82%	84%	83%	74%	80%	83%	87%	92%

Investment Style
Equity
Stock %

▼ Manager Change
▽ Partial Manager Change

Growth of $10,000
— Investment Values of Fund
— Investment Values of MSCI EAFE

26.8
22.0
18.0
14.0
10.0

Performance Quartile (within Category)

1995	1996	1997	1998	1999	2000	2001	2002	2003	2004	2005	2006	History
9.18	10.36	9.95	8.39	11.22	10.34	9.25	8.31	10.64	12.30	12.68	13.64	NAV
11.15	18.00	6.65	-4.89	39.21	-3.67	-7.92	-8.64	30.51	18.14	10.63	19.93	Total Return %
-0.06	11.95	4.87	-24.82	12.18	10.52	13.50	7.30	-8.08	-2.11	-2.91	-6.41	+/-MSCI EAFE
-0.26	11.13	4.38	-23.58	11.23	9.69	13.47	7.16	-8.91	-2.24	-3.84	-5.78	+/-MSCI Wd xUS
2.87	3.02	3.15	2.61	3.77	2.06	2.45	1.51	2.31	2.14	1.73	2.42	Income Return %
8.28	14.98	3.50	-7.50	35.44	-5.73	-10.37	-10.15	28.20	16.00	8.90	17.51	Capital Return %
70	41	58	94	19	55	10	28	90	86	75	90	Total Rtn % Rank Cat
0.25	0.28	0.32	0.26	0.31	0.23	0.25	0.14	0.19	0.23	0.21	0.30	Income $
0.36	0.18	0.85	0.77	0.09	0.21	0.00	0.00	0.00	0.02	0.67	1.18	Capital Gains $
1.15	1.12	1.08	1.12	1.13	1.15	1.18	1.16	1.22	1.23	1.15	1.16	Expense Ratio %
2.81	3.09	3.28	2.79	2.92	2.14	2.54	1.63	1.79	1.58	1.71	2.09	Income Ratio %
22	16	37	38	26	45	21	34	33	25	34	26	Turnover Rate %
7,312	11,082	14,014	10,862	13,170	10,743	8,748	8,115	12,040	15,182	15,471	13,922	Net Assets $mil

Rating and Risk

Time Period	Load-Adj Return %	Morningstar Rtn vs Cat	Morningstar Risk vs Cat	Morningstar Risk-Adj Rating
1 Yr	13.03			
3 Yr	13.89	Low	-Avg	★
5 Yr	11.99	Low	Low	★
10 Yr	8.24	Low	Avg	★
Incept	13.34			

Other Measures	Standard Index MSCI EAFE	Best Fit Index MSCI EAFE
Alpha	-2.5	-2.5
Beta	0.95	0.95
R-Squared	96	96
Standard Deviation	9.19	
Mean	16.16	
Sharpe Ratio	1.34	

Portfolio Analysis 09-30-06

Share change since 06-06 Total Stocks:128	Sector	Country	% Assets
Cheung Kong (hldgs) Ltd	Financial	Hong Kong	3.06
⊕ Sumitomo Mitsui Financia	Financial	Japan	2.89
⊕ Sanofi-Synthelabo	Health	France	2.46
⊕ GlaxoSmithKline	Health	U.K.	2.40
ING Groep	Financial	Netherlands	2.22
British Sky Broadcasting	Media	U.K.	2.16
Samsung Electronics	Goods	Korea	1.92
ACE, Ltd.	Financial	United States	1.92
Kkr Private Equity	—	United States	1.69
⊕ BP	Energy	U.K.	1.64
⊖ AMVESCAP	Financial	U.K.	1.59
Mitsubishi UFJ Financial	Financial	Japan	1.58
⊕ Pearson	Media	U.K.	1.58
⊕ Siemens	Hardware	Germany	1.57
UPM-Kymmene	Ind Mtrls	Finland	1.51
UniCredito Italiano Grp	Financial	Italy	1.49
Hutchison Whampoa Ltd	Telecom	Hong Kong	1.49
⊕ Reliance Industries Ltd	Ind Mtrls	India	1.49
Repsol YPF	Energy	Spain	1.37
France Telecom	Telecom	France	1.36

Current Investment Style

Value Blnd Growth — Large Mid Small

Market Cap	%
Giant	50.5
Large	39.2
Mid	10.3
Small	0.0
Micro	0.1
Avg $mil:	24,374

Value Measures		Rel Category
Price/Earnings	13.21	1.05
Price/Book	1.74	0.98
Price/Sales	1.07	1.13
Price/Cash Flow	7.23	1.01
Dividend Yield %	3.80	1.16

Growth Measures	%	Rel Category
Long-Term Erngs	11.01	1.07
Book Value	7.83	1.00
Sales	8.66	1.58
Cash Flow	3.24	0.91
Historical Erngs	15.55	0.95

Composition

Cash	4.1	Bonds	1.1
Stocks	92.4	Other	2.4
Foreign (% of Stock)			95.7

Sector Weightings	% of Stocks	Rel MSCI EAFE	3 Year High	Low
⟳ Info	26.32	2.23		
▦ Software	1.03	1.84	2	1
▦ Hardware	4.46	1.16	4	2
▦ Media	5.22	2.85	7	3
▦ Telecom	15.61	2.80	16	10
▭ Service	46.12	0.98		
▦ Health	7.50	1.05	8	6
▦ Consumer	3.57	0.72	4	1
▦ Business	6.04	1.19	6	4
▦ Financial	29.01	0.96	29	22
▦ Mfg	27.57	0.67		
▦ Goods	6.02	0.46	12	6
▦ Ind Mtrls	10.15	0.66	19	10
▦ Energy	8.43	1.18	11	7
▦ Utilities	2.97	0.57	7	2

Regional Exposure

	% Stock		% Stock
UK/W. Europe	48	N. America	6
Japan	13	Latn America	4
Asia X Japan	28	Other	1

Country Exposure

	% Stock		% Stock
U.K.	23	South Korea	6
Japan	13	France	6
Hong Kong	10		

Morningstar's Take by Arijit Dutta 12-13-06

Templeton Foreign doesn't have much to brag about right now, but that should change.

This fund has found it especially tough matching the pace of most foreign large-value rivals in 2006. The portfolio's sharp underweight in Europe (its 26% stake is merely half the category average) is largely to blame. Longtime manager Jeff Everett has instead found stocks more to his liking in non-Japan Asian markets like Hong Kong, South Korea, and Taiwan. Those markets haven't performed nearly as well as European stocks in dollar terms, however, as the euro and the British pound have posted strong gains versus other currencies. Although the fund is lagging badly in 2006 as a result, it's worth pointing out that its 17% annualized three-year return is strong in absolute terms (the category average is 19%).

More important, we think Everett's process is as sound as ever and will help revive relative performance here. As is the tradition at Templeton, Everett avoids stocks that are richly valued based on their long-term earnings potential, which has ruled out many hot areas. For example, the portfolio doesn't own many of the raging European electric-utility companies. Instead, Everett says top holding France Telecom is a great value in this environment. That stock has badly underperformed for several years, driving its dividend yield to attractive levels. Everett uses the same logic to find undervalued gems in any sector. For example, he likes several financial stocks in Asia that haven't generated nearly as much market euphoria as European banks have.

Markets worldwide have rallied strongly for several years now, so we think it makes a lot of sense to tease out the few remaining pockets of value. The fund should stage a comeback on back of such picks. Also, Everett's aversion of lofty valuations should allow the fund to hold up well if foreign markets were to correct, as was the case in May and June this year. This remains a soundly managed, low-cost core choice.

Address:	500 East Broward Blvd Ste 2100 Fort Lauderdale FL 33394-3091 800-632-2301
Web Address:	www.franklintempleton.com
Inception:	10-05-82
Advisor:	Templeton Global Advisors Limited
Subadvisor:	None
NTF Plans:	DATALynx NTF, Federated Tr NTF

Minimum Purchase:	$1000	Add: $50	IRA: $250
Min Auto Inv Plan:	$50	Add: $50	
Sales Fees:	5.75%L, 0.25%S, 2.00%R		
Management Fee:	0.63% mx./0.51% mn., 0.15%A		
Actual Fees:	Mgt:0.59%	Dist:0.25%	
Expense Projections:	3Yr:$922	5Yr:$1177	10Yr:$1903
Income Distrib:	Annually		

Morningstar® Funds 500

Templeton Growth A

	Ticker	Load	NAV	Yield	Total Assets	Mstar Category
	TEPLX	5.75%	$25.66	1.8%	$35,790 mil	World Stock

Governance and Management

Stewardship Grade: C

Portfolio Manager(s)

Murdo Murchison replaced lead manager Mark Holowesko in January 2001. He has managed Templeton's offshore portfolios since 1993. Murchison is supported by comanager Jeff Everett.

Strategy

This fund favors firms whose stocks are cheap, relative to their underlying assets, cash flow, and earnings potential. Templeton analysts take a long-term view, which can often be significantly different than prevailing market sentiment. Management has shown patience in allowing stocks to reach their long-term potential. The fund may invest in emerging markets, and its manager doesn't hedge currencies. To deter market-timers, Templeton imposes a 2% redemption fee on all shares held fewer than 30 days.

Performance 12-31-06

	1st Qtr	2nd Qtr	3rd Qtr	4th Qtr	Total
2002	3.50	-1.56	-16.96	6.99	-9.48
2003	-7.47	20.22	4.97	13.78	32.85
2004	3.05	1.46	-0.32	12.27	17.00
2005	0.31	-0.35	6.21	1.87	8.15
2006	5.54	0.83	5.69	8.31	21.81

Trailing	Total Return%	+/- MSCI EAFE	+/- MSCI World	%Rank Cat	Growth of $10,000
3 Mo	8.31	-2.04	-0.06	56	10,831
6 Mo	14.47	-0.22	1.26	22	11,447
1 Yr	21.81	-4.53	1.74	28	12,181
3 Yr Avg	15.51	-4.42	0.83	48	15,412
5 Yr Avg	13.14	-1.84	3.17	28	18,539
10 Yr Avg	10.85	3.14	3.21	24	28,013
15 Yr Avg	12.23	4.37	3.54	23	56,446

Tax Analysis	Tax-Adj Rtn%	%Rank Cat	Tax-Cost Rat	%Rank Cat
3 Yr (estimated)	11.56	81	1.49	78
5 Yr (estimated)	10.43	44	1.23	87
10 Yr (estimated)	8.09	37	1.91	94

Potential Capital Gain Exposure: 22% of assets

Historical Profile

Return	Average
Risk	Below Avg
Rating	★★★★ Above Avg

Investment Style
Equity
Stock %

▼ Manager Change
▽ Partial Manager Change

Growth of $10,000
— Investment Values of Fund
— Investment Values of MSCI EAFE

Performance Quartile (within Category)

1995	1996	1997	1998	1999	2000	2001	2002	2003	2004	2005	2006	History
17.35	19.54	19.40	16.37	19.96	18.39	18.00	15.93	20.67	22.89	22.94	25.66	NAV
19.83	20.55	16.18	-2.48	30.44	1.74	0.54	-9.48	32.85	17.00	8.15	21.81	Total Return %
8.62	14.50	14.40	-22.41	3.41	15.93	21.96	6.46	-5.74	-3.25	-5.39	-4.53	+/-MSCI EAFE
-0.89	7.07	0.42	-26.80	5.49	14.93	17.34	10.41	-0.26	2.28	-1.34	1.74	+/-MSCI World
2.75	2.83	2.87	2.09	3.30	1.87	2.20	2.00	2.85	2.03	1.81	2.15	Income Return %
17.08	17.72	13.31	-4.57	27.14	-0.13	-1.66	-11.48	30.00	14.97	6.34	19.66	Capital Return %
40	20	44	93	51	16	5	11	60	37	74	28	Total Rtn % Rank Cat
0.44	0.49	0.54	0.41	0.53	0.37	0.40	0.36	0.45	0.42	0.41	0.49	Income $
1.61	0.81	2.88	2.04	0.69	1.42	0.06	0.00	0.78	1.32	1.68		Capital Gains $
1.12	1.09	1.08	1.08	1.12	1.11	1.15	1.10	1.13	1.10	1.06	1.05	Expense Ratio %
2.40	2.87	2.81	2.53	2.60	1.83	2.11	1.85	2.05	1.75	1.61	1.82	Income Ratio %
35	20	42	48	32	51	24	56	32	25	20	35	Turnover Rate %
7,308	9,614	12,660	12,238	14,413	12,795	12,108	11,049	15,024	18,461	21,753	27,121	Net Assets $mil

Rating and Risk

Time Period	Load-Adj Return %	Morningstar Rtn vs Cat	Morningstar Risk vs Cat	Morningstar Risk-Adj Rating
1 Yr	14.81			
3 Yr	13.25	-Avg	-Avg	★★★
5 Yr	11.80	Avg	-Avg	★★★★
10 Yr	10.20	Avg	-Avg	★★★★
Incept	13.93			

Other Measures	Standard Index MSCI EAFE	Best Fit Index MSCI EASExJ
Alpha	-0.4	-1.1
Beta	0.77	0.76
R-Squared	88	91
Standard Deviation	7.76	
Mean	15.51	
Sharpe Ratio	1.50	

Portfolio Analysis 09-30-06

Share change since 06-06 Total Stocks:97

	Sector	Country	% Assets
Microsoft Corporation	Software	United States	2.30
Tyco International, Ltd.	Ind Mtrls	United States	2.27
News CI A	Media	United States	2.23
American International G	Financial	United States	2.06
Merck & Co., Inc.	Health	United States	1.96
Pfizer Inc.	Health	United States	1.94
Siemens	Hardware	Germany	1.90
Royal Bank Of Scotland G	Financial	U.K.	1.77
⊕ Viacom, Inc. B	Media	United States	1.74
BMW Grp	Goods	Germany	1.67
GlaxoSmithKline	Health	U.K.	1.58
Reed Elsevier	Media	Netherlands	1.56
⊕ Time Warner, Inc.	Media	United States	1.49
⊕ Oracle Corporation	Software	United States	1.49
⊖ Royal Dutch Shell	Energy	U.K.	1.48
⊕ Seagate Technology	Hardware	United States	1.44
Vodafone Grp	Telecom	U.K.	1.43
HSBC Hldgs	Financial	U.K.	1.42
⊖ Nestle	Goods	Switzerland	1.41
BP	Energy	U.K.	1.34

Current Investment Style

Value Blnd Growth — Large Mid Small

Market Cap	%
Giant	47.3
Large	40.5
Mid	12.2
Small	0.0
Micro	0.0
Avg $mil:	34,178

Value Measures		Rel Category
Price/Earnings	15.12	0.98
Price/Book	2.11	0.88
Price/Sales	1.07	0.82
Price/Cash Flow	7.91	0.91
Dividend Yield %	2.57	1.18

Growth Measures	%	Rel Category
Long-Term Erngs	10.75	0.85
Book Value	3.69	0.41
Sales	5.09	0.61
Cash Flow	-0.49	NMF
Historical Erngs	6.74	0.36

Composition

Cash	5.9	Bonds	0.0
Stocks	94.1	Other	0.0
Foreign (% of Stock)			56.2

Sector Weightings	% of Stocks	Rel MSCI EAFE	3 Year High	Low
↻ Info	27.16	2.30		
▤ Software	4.61	8.23	5	1
▤ Hardware	4.63	1.20	5	2
▥ Media	12.46	6.81	12	4
▤ Telecom	5.46	0.98	13	5
⊝ Service	42.59	0.90		
▤ Health	14.15	1.99	16	12
▤ Consumer	4.42	0.89	6	3
▤ Business	4.30	0.85	7	3
▤ Financial	19.72	0.66	20	11
▤ Mfg	30.26	0.74		
▤ Goods	12.06	0.92	14	11
▤ Ind Mtrls	9.53	0.62	18	10
▤ Energy	6.26	0.88	9	6
▤ Utilities	2.41	0.46	7	2

Regional Exposure % Stock

UK/W. Europe	43	N. America	45
Japan	6	Latn America	2
Asia X Japan	5	Other	0

Country Exposure % Stock

United States	44	Japan	6
U.K.	17	Switzerland	5
Germany	6		

Morningstar's Take by Arijit Dutta 12-20-06

Templeton Growth's patient, thoughtful style continues to impress us.

This world-stock fund has made some interesting moves over the past year and a half. Manager Murdo Murchison has increasingly found better valuations among large-cap stocks and in the United States, which have been two of the most out-of-favor slices of the market in recent years. As a result, several mega-caps like News Corporation, Merck, and Comcast have come into the portfolio. Since the start of 2005, the portfolio's U.S. stake has more than doubled to 44%, and its average market cap has risen from $21 billion to $34 billion currently. The portfolio's turnover has remained in the 20% range (the world-stock category average is 72%), which highlights the slow and steady pace of change that Murchison prefers.

Results have been slow to come, but the fund has reaped some benefits this year. After languishing last year, Merck has posted a 42% gain in 2006, as investors have finally focused on the drugmaker's improved lineup of new medicines, rather than on its legal woes, which, Templeton analysts have argued, Merck can survive due to its strong balance sheet. News Corporation and Comcast have also surged this year, rewarding Murchison's patience through their double-digit losses in 2005. He singled them out in the much-berated media sector last year due to their capable managements and improved operations. Volatile areas like small caps and other speculative fare remain in the lead, but this portfolio has still fared well with its slant toward large, cash-rich companies.

The fund's recent success has shown yet again the benefits of Murchison's style. He won't chase the market's hot pockets, which limits the fund's downside. Murchison relies instead on companies whose prospects aren't nearly as dim as the market believes, so the stocks can deliver substantial gains for patient investors. This should continue to be a winning recipe.

Address:	500 East Broward Blvd Ste 2100 Fort Lauderdale FL 33394-3091 800-632-2301	Minimum Purchase:	$1000 Add: $50 IRA: $250
		Min Auto Inv Plan:	$50 Add: $50
		Sales Fees:	5.75%L, 0.25%S, 2.00%R
Web Address:	www.franklintempleton.com	Management Fee:	0.63% mx./0.51% mn., 0.15%A
Inception:	11-29-54	Actual Fees:	Mgt:0.57% Dist:0.25%
Advisor:	Templeton Global Advisors Limited	Expense Projections:	3Yr:$890 5Yr:$1121 10Yr:$1784
Subadvisor:	None	Income Distrib:	Annually
NTF Plans:	DATALynx NTF, Federated Tr NTF		

Templeton World A

	Ticker	Load	NAV	Yield	Total Assets	Mstar Category
	TEMWX	5.75%	$19.42	1.6%	$9,757 mil	World Stock

Governance and Management

Stewardship Grade: C

Portfolio Manager(s)

Jeff Everett, a Templeton manager since 1996, is well versed in the company gospel. He assisted former manager Mark Holowesko for seven years. He uses Templeton's extensive team of analysts and the firm's centralized buy list. Managers here generally don't hedge currencies. To deter market-timers, Franklin Templeton imposes a 2% redemption fee on shares held fewer than 30 days.

Strategy

Like its siblings, this fund generally favors cheap stocks. Templeton analysts discount long-term cash flows of a company to arrive at a fair valuation. Management may take on significant stakes in undervalued sectors and is willing to commit as much as 25% of assets to emerging markets. The fund also holds on to stocks for the long haul, shunning calls to follow market trends.

Historical Profile

Return	Average
Risk	Average
Rating	★★★ Neutral

Investment Style
Equity
Stock %

▼ Manager Change
▽ Partial Manager Change

Growth of $10,000
— Investment Values of Fund
— Investment Values of MSCI EAFE

Performance Quartile (within Category)

1995	1996	1997	1998	1999	2000	2001	2002	2003	2004	2005	2006	History
14.91	16.55	16.82	15.93	18.69	16.48	14.86	12.89	16.87	17.75	17.74	19.42	NAV
21.55	21.45	19.23	6.01	28.12	-3.99	-8.10	-12.15	33.38	15.63	11.67	20.89	Total Return %
10.34	15.40	17.45	-13.92	1.09	10.20	13.32	3.79	-5.21	-4.62	-1.87	-5.45	+/-MSCI EAFE
0.83	7.97	3.47	-18.31	3.17	9.20	8.70	7.74	0.27	0.91	2.18	0.82	+/-MSCI World
2.64	2.93	2.73	2.14	2.42	1.46	1.62	1.10	2.32	1.93	1.52	1.96	Income Return %
18.91	18.52	16.50	3.87	25.70	-5.45	-9.72	-13.25	31.06	13.70	10.15	18.93	Capital Return %
28	18	32	76	58	29	17	17	57	47	51	39	Total Rtn % Rank Cat
0.37	0.43	0.44	0.36	0.38	0.27	0.27	0.16	0.30	0.32	0.27	0.34	Income $
1.88	1.04	2.60	1.39	1.09	1.15	0.00	0.00	0.00	1.25	1.70	1.60	Capital Gains $
1.04	1.05	1.03	1.03	1.04	1.04	1.07	1.09	1.08	1.11	1.11	1.06	Expense Ratio %
1.67	2.18	2.66	2.58	2.34	1.99	1.52	1.79	1.15	1.40	1.32	1.49	Income Ratio %
31	34	22	39	43	36	47	25	45	44	38	35	Turnover Rate %
5,020	5,988	7,160	8,682	8,724	9,957	8,448	7,060	5,744	7,110	7,786	9,247	Net Assets $mil

Investment Style panels: 88% 81% 89% 92% 93% 95%

Performance 12-31-06

	1st Qtr	2nd Qtr	3rd Qtr	4th Qtr	Total
2002	3.30	-3.00	-18.07	7.01	-12.15
2003	-8.77	19.81	7.59	13.41	33.38
2004	4.15	-1.20	-0.98	13.48	15.63
2005	0.00	1.13	8.64	1.64	11.67
2006	5.47	0.27	5.33	8.53	20.89

Trailing	Total Return%	+/- MSCI EAFE	+/- MSCI World	%Rank Cat	Growth of $10,000
3 Mo	8.53	-1.82	0.16	51	10,853
6 Mo	14.32	-0.37	1.11	23	11,432
1 Yr	20.89	-5.45	0.82	39	12,089
3 Yr Avg	16.00	-3.93	1.32	42	15,609
5 Yr Avg	12.84	-2.14	2.87	30	18,294
10 Yr Avg	10.08	2.37	2.44	32	26,127
15 Yr Avg	11.86	4.00	3.17	28	53,718

Tax Analysis	Tax-Adj Rtn%	%Rank Cat	Tax-Cost Rat	%Rank Cat
3 Yr (estimated)	11.63	80	1.85	87
5 Yr (estimated)	10.01	49	1.35	90
10 Yr (estimated)	7.49	45	1.77	89

Potential Capital Gain Exposure: 27% of assets

Rating and Risk

Time Period	Load-Adj Return %	Morningstar Rtn vs Cat	Morningstar Risk vs Cat	Morningstar Risk-Adj Rating
1 Yr	13.94			
3 Yr	13.73	Avg	Avg	★★★
5 Yr	11.51	Avg	Avg	★★★
10 Yr	9.43	Avg	Avg	★★★
Incept	13.91			

Other Measures	Standard Index MSCI EAFE	Best Fit Index MSCI World
Alpha	-2.1	1.5
Beta	0.92	1.07
R-Squared	88	92
Standard Deviation	9.24	
Mean	16.00	
Sharpe Ratio	1.32	

Portfolio Analysis 09-30-06

Share change since 06-06 Total Stocks:108

	Sector	Country	% Assets
Cheung Kong (hldgs) Ltd	Financial	Hong Kong	3.58
⊕ Microsoft Corporation	Software	United States	2.77
News Cl A	Media	United States	2.41
Merrill Lynch & Company,	Financial	United States	2.41
Comcast	Media	United States	2.38
DirecTV, Inc.	Media	United States	2.36
J.P. Morgan Chase & Co.	Financial	United States	2.25
⊕ Sumitomo Mitsui Financia	Financial	Japan	1.86
⊕ Sanofi-Synthelabo	Health	France	1.78
Samsung Electronics	Goods	Korea	1.74
ACE, Ltd.	Financial	United States	1.63
⊕ GlaxoSmithKline	Health	U.K.	1.62
Kkr Private Equity	—	United States	1.57
British Sky Broadcasting	Media	U.K.	1.50
⊕ BP	Energy	U.K.	1.47
Pearson	Media	U.K.	1.45
UPM-Kymmene	Ind Mtrls	Finland	1.39
⊕ Time Warner, Inc.	Media	United States	1.35
Fannie Mae	Financial	United States	1.35
⊕ Tenet Healthcare Corpora	Health	United States	1.34

Current Investment Style

Value Blnd Growth — Large Mid Small

	Market Cap	%
	Giant	51.5
	Large	34.4
	Mid	14.0
	Small	0.1
	Micro	0.0
	Avg $mil:	30,075

Value Measures		Rel Category
Price/Earnings	14.24	0.93
Price/Book	1.91	0.80
Price/Sales	1.13	0.86
Price/Cash Flow	7.05	0.82
Dividend Yield %	2.70	1.24

Growth Measures	%	Rel Category
Long-Term Erngs	11.24	0.89
Book Value	5.19	0.58
Sales	7.08	0.85
Cash Flow	4.12	0.42
Historical Erngs	16.54	0.88

Composition

Cash	1.8	Bonds	0.4
Stocks	95.2	Other	2.6
Foreign	(% of Stock)		59.7

Sector Weightings	% of Stocks	Rel MSCI EAFE	3 Year High	Low
⊙ Info	32.56	2.75		
🖹 Software	6.32	11.29	6	3
🖥 Hardware	3.93	1.02	4	1
🎤 Media	14.30	7.81	14	2
📶 Telecom	8.01	1.44	10	7
⊂ Service	44.75	0.95		
🩺 Health	8.91	1.25	14	8
🛒 Consumer	2.80	0.57	5	1
💼 Business	6.41	1.26	7	4
💲 Financial	26.63	0.89	29	24
⚒ Mfg	22.69	0.55		
🏭 Goods	6.79	0.52	10	7
⚙ Ind Mtrls	7.20	0.47	13	7
🔋 Energy	7.02	0.98	12	7
💡 Utilities	1.68	0.32	5	2

Regional Exposure	% Stock		
UK/W. Europe 33		N. America	40
Japan 9		Latn America	1
Asia X Japan 17		Other	0

Country Exposure	% Stock		
United States 40		Hong Kong	6
U.K. 18		South Korea	4
Japan 9			

Morningstar's Take by Arijit Dutta 12-20-06

Templeton World continues to sow the seeds of future success.

This world-stock fund's slow, incremental changes over the past year and a half have started to add up. The portfolio's U.S. stake has risen from 24% at the start of 2005 to 40% currently, through purchases like News Corporation, Comcast, and Microsoft. These large companies have also driven up the portfolio's average market cap from $19 billion at the end of 2004 to $30 billion now. Rather than make a top-down call on the United States or on blue-chip stocks, however, manager Jeff Everett has based these choices on the bottom-up work of Templeton analysts. According to the analysts' calculations, an increasing number of large U.S. companies have been selling very cheaply, relative to their assets and business prospects.

These moves have paid off in 2006. After patiently weathering tough, double-digit losses for both News Corporation and Comcast in 2005, Everett has seen those companies surge this year.

Markets have finally started to recognize their strong leadership and abundant cash flows, rather than brood over competition-related fears that have gripped the media sector in recent years. Overall, risky areas such as small caps and other speculative fare remain in the lead, but the fund has fared well on the portfolio's large, cash-rich companies.

The long-term case for the fund also rests on its patient, thoughtful style. Like other Templeton managers, Everett prefers stocks from deeply unloved areas of the market and is willing to wait for them to deliver a sizable upside. Another example is Microsoft, which remains a sluggish stock, but Everett points to the company's new and able leadership for his continued conviction that the business has solid growth ahead. At the same time, he says Microsoft's huge cash horde means there is limited downside in the stock.

The fund strikes a balance between risk and reward, and therefore remains a solid core choice.

Address:	500 East Broward Blvd Ste 2100 Fort Lauderdale FL 33394-3091 800-632-2301
Web Address:	www.franklintempleton.com
Inception:	01-17-78
Advisor:	Templeton Global Advisors Limited
Subadvisor:	None
NTF Plans:	DATALynx NTF, Federated Tr NTF

Minimum Purchase:	$1000 Add: $50 IRA: $250
Min Auto Inv Plan:	$50 Add: $50
Sales Fees:	5.75%L, 0.24%S, 2.00%R
Management Fee:	0.63% mx./0.54% mn., 0.15%A
Actual Fees:	Mgt:0.61% Dist:0.24%
Expense Projections:	3Yr:$893 5Yr:$1126 10Yr:$1795
Income Distrib:	Annually

MORNINGSTAR® Funds 500

Third Avenue Intl Value

	Ticker	Load	NAV	Yield	Total Assets	Mstar Category
	TAVIX	Closed	$21.94	4.6%	$2,373 mil	Foreign Small/Mid Value

Governance and Management

Stewardship Grade: B

Portfolio Manager(s)

Amit Wadhwaney has been the fund's skipper since its inception. Before this, Wadhwaney hadn't run a retail mutual fund. But he has considerable experience at Third Avenue, having been a senior analyst for many years in support of the firm's domestic charges (including Third Avenue Value and Third Avenue Small-Cap Value). He's supported primarily by senior research analyst Jakub Rehor and research analyst Matthew Fine. He also draws on the firm's other managers and analysts for ideas and research support.

Strategy

Amit Wadhwaney is a value hound. He looks for companies that trade at big discounts to their private or liquidation values, scrutinizing each firm's balance sheet to get a fix on the sum of its parts. Although he has targeted small caps, he views the fund as an all-cap offering and will venture into larger fare. He pays no heed to benchmarks, so sector bets are common, and the portfolio is more focused than the norm. He won't hedge companies with U.S. dollar revenues or costs, but he will hedge other firms when he thinks their currencies are materially overvalued relative to the U.S. dollar.

Performance 12-31-06

	1st Qtr	2nd Qtr	3rd Qtr	4th Qtr	Total
2002	1.60	2.46	-10.09	3.77	-2.87
2003	-0.21	16.86	12.64	17.75	54.68
2004	7.13	0.00	7.81	10.58	27.70
2005	4.83	1.14	7.53	3.50	18.00
2006	9.17	-0.82	1.13	6.97	17.13

Trailing	Total Return%	+/- MSCI EAFE	+/- MSCI Wd xUS	%Rank Cat	Growth of $10,000
3 Mo	6.97	-3.38	-3.15	100	10,697
6 Mo	8.19	-6.50	-6.03	100	10,819
1 Yr	17.13	-9.21	-8.58	98	11,713
3 Yr Avg	20.85	0.92	0.75	65	17,650
5 Yr Avg	21.54	6.56	6.29	34	26,521
10 Yr Avg	—	—	—	—	—
15 Yr Avg	—	—	—	—	—

Tax Analysis	Tax-Adj Rtn%	%Rank Cat	Tax-Cost Rat	%Rank Cat
3 Yr (estimated)	19.25	54	1.32	35
5 Yr (estimated)	20.31	34	1.01	33
10 Yr (estimated)	—	—	—	—

Potential Capital Gain Exposure: 16% of assets

Historical Profile

Return Average
Risk Low
Rating ★★★ Neutral

	87%	85%	62%	64%	73%

Investment Style
Equity
Stock %

▼ Manager Change
▽ Partial Manager Change

22.8
18.0 **Growth of $10,000**
14.0 ▬ Investment Values of Fund
10.0 — Investment Values of MSCI EAFE
7.0

Performance Quartile (within Category)

1995	1996	1997	1998	1999	2000	2001	2002	2003	2004	2005	2006	History
—	—	—	—	—	—	10.00	9.63	14.59	18.41	21.16	21.94	NAV
—	—	—	—	—	—	0.00*	-2.87	54.68	27.70	18.00	17.13	Total Return %
—	—	—	—	—	—	—	13.07	16.09	7.45	4.46	-9.21	+/-MSCI EAFE
—	—	—	—	—	—	—	12.93	15.26	7.32	3.53	-8.58	+/-MSCI Wd xUS
—	—	—	—	—	—	—	0.82	3.08	1.51	2.49	5.12	Income Return %
—	—	—	—	—	—	—	-3.69	51.60	26.19	15.51	12.01	Capital Return %
—	—	—	—	—	—	—	26	28	45	58	98	Total Rtn % Rank Cat
—	—	—	—	—	—	0.00	0.08	0.30	0.22	0.46	1.08	Income $
—	—	—	—	—	—	0.00	0.00	0.00	0.00	0.10	1.74	Capital Gains $
—	—	—	—	—	—	—	—	1.75	1.75	1.75	—	Expense Ratio %
—	—	—	—	—	—	—	—	0.34	0.52	0.58	—	Income Ratio %
—	—	—	—	—	—	—	—	26	4	11	—	Turnover Rate %
—	—	—	—	—	—	—	26	140	667	2,373		Net Assets $mil

Rating and Risk

Time Period	Load-Adj Return %	Morningstar Rtn vs Cat	Morningstar Risk vs Cat	Morningstar Risk-Adj Rating
1 Yr	17.13			
3 Yr	20.85	Avg	Low	★★★
5 Yr	21.54	Avg	Low	★★★
10 Yr	—	—	—	—
Incept	21.54			

Other Measures	Standard Index MSCI EAFE	Best Fit Index MSCI Wd xUS
Alpha	4.8	4.7
Beta	0.73	0.73
R-Squared	70	72
Standard Deviation	8.16	
Mean	20.85	
Sharpe Ratio	1.97	

Portfolio Analysis 10-31-06

Share change since 07-06 Total Stocks:58	Sector	Country	% Assets
⊕ Catalyst Paper Corporati	Ind Mtrls	Canada	4.75
⊕ BIL International Ltd	Financial	Singapore	4.22
⊕ Telecom Corp. of New Zea	Telecom	New Zealand	3.56
Saskatchewan Wheat Pool	Ind Mtrls	Canada	2.88
Nippon Sheet Glass	Ind Mtrls	Japan	2.62
Guoco Grp Ltd	Financial	Hong Kong	2.59
⊕ Brit Insurance Hldgs	Financial	U.K.	2.56
Aker Kvaerner	Business	Norway	2.55
⊕ Hutchison Whampoa Ltd	Telecom	Hong Kong	2.51
Nationale Portefeuille (	Financial	Belgium	2.34
Zinifex	Ind Mtrls	Australia	2.34
⊕ Canfor Corporation	Ind Mtrls	Canada	2.21
WBL	Hardware	Singapore	2.19
⊕ Netia Hldgs	Telecom	Poland	2.17
Seino Transportation	Business	Japan	2.05
Dundee Precious Metals I	Ind Mtrls	Canada	1.78
⊖ Subsea 7	Business	Cayman Islands	1.53
Toll Nz	Business	New Zealand	1.49
Futaba	Hardware	Japan	1.49
Nichicon	Hardware	Japan	1.43

Current Investment Style

Value Blnd Growth — Large / Mid / Small

Market Cap	%
Giant	3.8
Large	15.5
Mid	52.0
Small	26.1
Micro	2.6
Avg $mil: 1,617	

Value Measures		Rel Category
Price/Earnings	13.11	0.89
Price/Book	1.16	0.58
Price/Sales	0.51	0.57
Price/Cash Flow	7.58	1.21
Dividend Yield %	2.42	0.92

Growth Measures	%	Rel Category
Long-Term Erngs	17.21	1.15
Book Value	-0.70	NMF
Sales	12.13	1.64
Cash Flow	4.83	0.53
Historical Erngs	56.53	2.90

Composition

Cash	26.2	Bonds	0.0
Stocks	73.2	Other	0.6
Foreign (% of Stock)			100.0

Sector Weightings	% of Stocks	Rel MSCI EAFE	3 Year High	Low
↻ Info	21.74	1.84		
🖥 Software	0.56	1.00	5	1
💾 Hardware	8.33	2.16	9	0
🎤 Media	1.56	0.85	5	2
📶 Telecom	11.29	2.03	11	6
☞ Service	47.44	1.00		
🏥 Health	0.00	0.00	0	0
🛒 Consumer	0.00	0.00	6	0
🏢 Business	19.65	3.88	28	14
💲 Financial	27.79	0.92	32	20
⛭ Mfg	30.82	0.75		
🏭 Goods	1.12	0.09	3	1
⚙ Ind Mtrls	27.92	1.81	28	15
🔋 Energy	1.78	0.25	12	2
🔌 Utilities	0.00	0.00	0	0

Regional Exposure	% Stock		
UK/W. Europe 21	N. America	18	
Japan 17	Latn America	5	
Asia X Japan 37	Other	2	

Country Exposure		% Stock	
Canada	18	Hong Kong	10
Japan	17	New Zealand	9
Singapore	10		

Morningstar's Take by William Samuel Rocco 12-16-06

Third Avenue International Value is one of the most distinctive overseas mutual funds around.

There are only a limited number of foreign small/mid-value funds to begin with, and this one, which is closed to new investors, stands out from the others. Amit Wadhwaney searches far and wide for issues that meet his strict value criteria, buys stocks in bunches, and is unconcerned about index and peer-group weights. Thus, the fund's country and sector exposures tend to be unusual, as its oversized stakes in Singapore, Canada, and New Zealand and its zero to tiny stakes in health care, consumer goods, and utilities attest.

The fund's atypical traits don't end there. Wadhwaney holds cash whenever he can't find enough good bargains, and cash has hovered around 30% during much of 2006. He readily buys unpopular and unknown names. Seven of the fund's top 10 holdings as of July 31, 2006, in fact, are owned in significant amounts by very few if any other international funds. And unlike the vast majority of fund managers and shops, he and his firm are willing to own big portions of individual companies and to get directly involved with them. (Third Avenue recently made a successful tender offer for Catalyst Paper, and it now owns 38% of the company--through various separate accounts and funds--and Wadhwaney sits on the board.)

This distinctive style certainly comes with real company-specific and other risks. It also has led to poor relative returns this year, as the cash and exposure to Catalyst and other paper companies has hurt. But we're bullish about the fund's long-term prospects for several reasons. Its strict value standards and often sizable cash stake mute risk, and it has been less volatile than most of its peers so far. Wadhwaney has posted solid results every year but this one, and the fund has outpaced its typical peer by a small margin since opening. And the other Third Avenue managers have earned good risk-adjusted returns while applying the family strategy to their universes.

Address:	622 Third Avenue New York NY 10017 800-443-1021	Minimum Purchase:	Closed	Add: —	IRA: —
		Min Auto Inv Plan:	Closed	Add: —	
Web Address:	www.thirdavenuefunds.com	Sales Fees:	No-load, 2.00%R		
Inception:	12-31-01 *	Management Fee:	1.25%		
Advisor:	Third Avenue Management LLC	Actual Fees:	Mgt:1.25%	Dist: —	
Subadvisor:	None	Expense Projections:	3Yr:$483	5Yr:$834	10Yr:$1824
NTF Plans:	Fidelity Retail-NTF	Income Distrib:	Annually		

Third Avenue RealEst Val

	Analyst Pick ✓	Ticker TAREX	Load None	NAV $34.64	Yield 2.4%	Total Assets $3,262 mil	Mstar Category Specialty-Real Estate

Governance and Management

Stewardship Grade: B

Portfolio Manager(s)

Lead manager Mike Winer has run this fund since its 1998 inception. He has extensive real estate industry experience, including stints in development and distressed situations. He's supported by senior analyst Jason Wolf, who joined the fund in April 2004 with an impressive and varied resume in the real estate industry. A second analyst joined the team in September 2006.

Strategy

Like other Third Avenue offerings, this one seeks companies that trade at a discount to management's estimate of net asset value. The manager favors REOCs over REITs because the former can reinvest cash flow back into the business for growth. The fund often stashes more than 60% of assets in its top 10 holdings, which means it's among the most concentrated in the category.

Historical Profile

Return	Below Avg
Risk	Low
Rating	★★★ Neutral

76% 93% 82% 86% 85% 95% 73% 89% 95%

▼ Manager Change
▽ Partial Manager Change

43.6
32.4
24.0
17.0

Growth of $10,000
— Investment Values of Fund
— Investment Values of S&P 500

10.0

Performance Quartile (within Category)

	1995	1996	1997	1998	1999	2000	2001	2002	2003	2004	2005	2006	History
	—	—	—	10.65	10.89	13.68	15.78	15.96	21.38	26.96	29.36	34.64	NAV
	—	—	—	7.47*	5.17	30.91	18.20	4.24	37.34	28.16	14.38	30.16	Total Return %
	—	—	—	—	-15.87	40.01	30.09	26.34	8.66	17.28	9.47	14.37	+/-S&P 500
	—	—	—	—	7.74	-0.13	5.84	0.64	1.28	-4.98	0.38	-5.97	+/-DJ Wilshire REIT
	—	—	—	—	2.37	2.49	1.37	1.12	2.83	0.84	1.65	3.04	Income Return %
	—	—	—	—	2.80	28.42	16.83	3.12	34.51	27.32	12.73	27.12	Capital Return %
	—	—	—	—	2	22	6	44	41	85	30	81	Total Rtn % Rank Cat
	—	—	—	0.10	0.25	0.27	0.19	0.18	0.45	0.18	0.44	0.89	Income $
	—	—	—	0.00	0.06	0.29	0.20	0.30	0.08	0.26	1.03	2.63	Capital Gains $
	—	—	—	—	1.87	1.87	1.50	1.50	1.22	1.19	1.15	—	Expense Ratio %
	—	—	—	—	3.20	3.20	3.89	2.79	0.93	3.51	0.47	—	Income Ratio %
	—	—	—	—	5	5	23	20	19	11	8	—	Turnover Rate %
	—	—	—	—	3	10	27	77	346	787	2,029	3,262	Net Assets $mil

Performance 12-31-06

	1st Qtr	2nd Qtr	3rd Qtr	4th Qtr	Total
2002	5.96	2.09	-6.50	3.06	4.24
2003	-0.13	15.24	6.04	12.53	37.34
2004	8.23	-0.78	7.01	11.52	28.16
2005	1.19	8.43	0.85	3.37	14.38
2006	10.46	-1.48	8.89	9.85	30.16

Trailing	Total Return%	+/- S&P 500	+/- DJ Wilshire REIT	%Rank Cat	Growth of $10,000
3 Mo	9.85	3.15	0.88	41	10,985
6 Mo	19.61	6.87	0.61	27	11,961
1 Yr	30.16	14.37	-5.97	81	13,016
3 Yr Avg	24.03	13.59	-3.34	68	19,080
5 Yr Avg	22.26	16.07	-1.58	68	27,316
10 Yr Avg	—	—	—	—	—
15 Yr Avg	—	—	—	—	—

Tax Analysis	Tax-Adj Rtn%	%Rank Cat	Tax-Cost Rat	%Rank Cat
3 Yr (estimated)	22.59	54	1.16	11
5 Yr (estimated)	20.98	54	1.05	10
10 Yr (estimated)	—	—	—	—

Potential Capital Gain Exposure: 36% of assets

Rating and Risk

Time Period	Load-Adj Return %	Morningstar Rtn vs Cat	Morningstar Risk vs Cat	Morningstar Risk-Adj Rating
1 Yr	30.16			
3 Yr	24.03	-Avg	Low	★★★
5 Yr	22.26	-Avg	Low	★★★
10 Yr	—	—	—	—
Incept	20.77			

Other Measures	Standard Index S&P 500	Best Fit Index DJ Wilshire REIT
Alpha	12.9	8.2
Beta	0.86	0.47
R-Squared	43	78
Standard Deviation	9.00	
Mean	24.03	
Sharpe Ratio	2.11	

Portfolio Analysis 10-31-06

Share change since 07-06 Total Stocks:50

	Sector	PE	Tot Ret%	% Assets
Forest City Enterprises,	Financial	—	54.80	12.90
⊖ ProLogis Trust	Financial	33.5	34.02	9.18
St. Joe Corporation	Financial	75.4	-19.32	9.11
Brookfield Asset Managem	Financial	25.7	46.00	8.18
⊖ Vornado Realty Trust	Financial	37.1	51.14	4.97
British Land	Financial	—	—	3.86
Henderson Land Developme	Financial	—	—	2.88
Liberty Int'l	Financial	—	—	2.81
⊖ Brookfield Properties Co	Financial	56.4	36.73	2.71
⊖ Trammell Crow Company	Financial	—	—	2.57
⊖ PS Business Parks, Inc.	Financial	99.3	46.55	2.53
UNITE Grp	Financial	—	—	2.46
Derwent Valley Hldgs	Financial	—	—	2.35
⊕ Wharf (Hldgs) Ltd	Ind Mtrls	—	—	2.02
Acadia Realty Trust	Financial	36.8	28.74	1.96
Quintain Estates & Devel	Financial	—	—	1.94
Sears Holdings Corporati	Consumer	19.5	45.36	1.59
Hang Lung Properties Ltd	Financial	—	—	1.58
American Financial Realt	Financial	—	3.69	1.53
Jer Investors Trust, Inc	Financial	—	—	1.35

Current Investment Style

Value Blnd Growth — Large Mid Small

Market Cap	%
Giant	0.0
Large	42.2
Mid	32.0
Small	17.7
Micro	8.1
Avg $mil:	4,575

Value Measures		Rel Category
Price/Earnings	22.15	1.17
Price/Book	2.10	0.74
Price/Sales	3.33	0.80
Price/Cash Flow	15.82	1.02
Dividend Yield %	1.96	0.49

Growth Measures	%	Rel Category
Long-Term Erngs	13.36	1.73
Book Value	7.82	15.96
Sales	18.05	1.65
Cash Flow	-4.04	NMF
Historical Erngs	67.95	4.82

Profitability	%	Rel Category
Return on Equity	16.01	1.39
Return on Assets	9.94	1.06
Net Margin	29.48	1.10

Sector Weightings	% of Stocks	Rel S&P 500	3 Year High Low
↻ Info	0.00	0.00	
Software	0.00	0.00	0 0
Hardware	0.00	0.00	0 0
Media	0.00	0.00	0 0
Telecom	0.00	0.00	0 0
⊄ Service	96.96	2.10	
Health	0.00	0.00	0 0
Consumer	4.65	0.61	7 3
Business	0.00	0.00	1 0
Financial	92.31	4.15	92 84
凸 Mfg	3.03	0.09	
Goods	0.00	0.00	0 0
Ind Mtrls	3.03	0.25	9 1
Energy	0.00	0.00	0 0
Utilities	0.00	0.00	0 0

Composition

		%
●	Cash	3.3
●	Stocks	95.5
●	Bonds	0.3
○	Other	0.9
	Foreign (% of Stock)	37.7

Morningstar's Take by William Samuel Rocco 12-07-06

Third Avenue Real Estate Value is a category standout.

This fund never follows the real estate crowd. Mike Winer doesn't concentrate on REITs like most of his counterparts do. He prefers real estate operating companies (REOCs). He also pays significant attention to atypical real estate investments, such as retailers with major property holdings, that most of his peers ignore. The fund had only about 26% of its assets in REITs as of Sept. 30, 2006, while most of its peers have the vast majority of their assets in such securities.

This fund distinguishes itself from its peers in many other ways. Winer readily considers smaller-cap and overseas issues that meet his safe and cheap criteria, so the fund's average market cap is well below the group norm and its foreign stake is well above the category average. And like his Third Avenue peers, Winer believes in issue concentration, moves at a measured pace, and lets cash build when he can't find enough compelling

bargains.

This distinctive discipline does have its drawbacks. The emphasis on REOCs and other non-REITs keeps the fund's yield well below the group average. And the wide-ranging deep-value style can slow the fund in long REIT-led rallies, while its issue focus exposes it to stock-specific risk. The fund is lagging this year for both reasons.

But the pros far outweigh the cons here. The fund has been far less volatile than most of its rivals, thanks to its strict value standards and diversification across various types of real estate investments. And it has handily outpaced its average peer since opening in late 1998, as Winer's security selection has generally been quite good.

This fund makes a great long-term holding for real estate fans, as long as they're not seeking income and understand it won't escape when its hot category eventually cools off (though it is likely to hold up better than the norm).

Address:	622 Third Avenue New York NY 10017 800-443-1021	Minimum Purchase:	$10000 Add: $1000 IRA: $2500
		Min Auto Inv Plan:	$10000 Add: $200
		Sales Fees:	No-load, 1.00%R
Web Address:	www.thirdavenuefunds.com	Management Fee:	0.90%
Inception:	09-17-98*	Actual Fees:	Mgt:0.90% Dist: —
Advisor:	Third Avenue Management LLC	Expense Projections:	3Yr:$362 5Yr:$628 10Yr:$1386
Subadvisor:	None	Income Distrib:	Annually
NTF Plans:	Fidelity Retail-NTF		

M🟊RNINGSTAR® Funds 500

Third Avenue Sm-Cap Val

		Ticker	Load	NAV	Yield	Total Assets	Mstar Category
✔ Analyst Pick		TASCX	Closed	$25.83	1.6%	$2,415 mil	Small Blend

Governance and Management

Stewardship Grade: A

Portfolio Manager(s)

Curtis Jensen became this fund's sole manager when comanager Marty Whitman stepped down in mid-2001. Jensen has been on the fund since its inception, however, and shares Whitman's commitment to value investing. Whitman remains at the firm, and Jensen continues to work closely with him. The firm has lost two distressed debt analysts in recent years, but it has replaced them.

Strategy

Curtis Jensen does things a bit differently at this fund than firm founder Marty Whitman does at sibling Third Avenue Value. He still tries to invest in companies with strong balance sheets at less than half of what he thinks they're worth. This usually means purchasing companies at a significant discount to net asset value, or less than 10 times peak earnings. Like Whitman, Jensen uses a tax-efficient, buy-and-hold strategy. But at this fund, he focuses mostly on small caps and runs a somewhat more concentrated portfolio. Also, unlike Third Avenue Value, this fund does not usually buy distressed debt.

Performance 12-31-06

	1st Qtr	2nd Qtr	3rd Qtr	4th Qtr	Total
2002	5.99	-3.68	-20.46	9.75	-10.89
2003	-5.24	18.60	10.37	12.13	39.08
2004	5.87	3.73	0.97	9.37	21.27
2005	1.55	2.36	5.46	1.35	11.09
2006	5.93	-0.89	0.35	5.77	11.43

Trailing	Total Return%	+/- S&P 500	+/- Russ 2000	%Rank Cat	Growth of $10,000
3 Mo	5.77	-0.93	-3.13	95	10,577
6 Mo	6.14	-6.60	-3.24	69	10,614
1 Yr	11.43	-4.36	-6.94	80	11,143
3 Yr Avg	14.50	4.06	0.94	29	15,011
5 Yr Avg	13.22	7.03	1.83	27	18,604
10 Yr Avg	—	—	—		
15 Yr Avg	—	—	—		

Tax Analysis	Tax-Adj Rtn%	%Rank Cat	Tax-Cost Rat	%Rank Cat
3 Yr (estimated)	13.72	23	0.68	15
5 Yr (estimated)	12.63	23	0.52	19
10 Yr (estimated)	—	—	—	—

Potential Capital Gain Exposure: 22% of assets

Morningstar's Take by Kerry O'Boyle 12-21-06

It's been a frustrating year for Third Avenue Small-Cap Value.

Flush with cash, this fund saw a prime buying opportunity in the midst of an early-summer stock market correction in 2006. Although manager Curtis Jensen was able to deploy some of that 40% cash stake to new ideas, he wasn't able to put enough of it to work. Jensen had the misfortune of watching prices run away from him as a strong rally took hold in August and continued for much of the rest of the year. What bargains there were had gone, and Jensen said that the fundamentals didn't justify chasing the higher prices. The fund's cash remains at a still-high 25%, boosted somewhat by four more of the fund's holdings--comprising 4.5% of assets--that disappeared through mergers and acquisitions during the second half of the year.

Obviously, a 25% slug of cash amid a strong market rally hasn't been a boon to performance. The absence from the portfolio of high-flying REITs and resurgent utility stocks hasn't helped either. All

told, the fund is on track to turn in its worst performance relative to its small-blend peers in a calendar year since its 1997 inception.

Despite the recent setback, this remains one of our favorite small-cap funds. Jensen is part of the topnotch deep-value team at Third Avenue that has a knack for rooting out bargains. Indeed, this opportunism was on display as the fund partook of a couple of merger-arbitrage deals in Andrew and Andrx (now part of Watson Pharmaceuticals). Though such short-term plays are unusual for the fund, this allowed Jensen to put some of the cash to work for a return better than money markets'. Plus, he was able to build up some new positions in the portfolio during the second half of the year in Cimarex Energy and Catalyst Paper.

This small-blend Analyst Pick has proven its mettle. We think it will be better able to handle all that cash now that it's closed, and continue to serve shareholders well over the long haul.

Address:	622 Third Avenue New York NY 10017 800-443-1021
Web Address:	www.thirdavenuefunds.com
Inception:	04-01-97 *
Advisor:	Third Avenue Management LLC
Subadvisor:	None
NTF Plans:	Federated Tr NTF, Pershing NTF

Minimum Purchase:	Closed	Add: —	IRA: —
Min Auto Inv Plan:	Closed	Add: —	
Sales Fees:	No-load, 1.00%R		
Management Fee:	0.90%		
Actual Fees:	Mgt:0.90%	Dist: —	
Expense Projections:	3Yr:$359	5Yr:$622	10Yr:$1375
Income Distrib:	Annually		

Historical Profile

Return	Above Avg
Risk	Low
Rating	★★★★ Above Avg

		94%	96%	72%	100%	86%	88%	76%	69%	77%

▼ Manager Change
▽ Partial Manager Change

Growth of $10,000
— Investment Values of Fund
— Investment Values of S&P 500

Performance Quartile (within Category)

1995	1996	1997	1998	1999	2000	2001	2002	2003	2004	2005	2006	History
—	—	11.64	11.23	12.40	13.59	15.37	13.56	18.75	22.57	24.45	25.83	NAV
—	—	17.02*	-2.77	11.29	17.18	15.26	-10.89	39.08	21.27	11.09	11.43	Total Return %
—	—	—	-31.35	-9.75	26.28	27.15	11.21	10.40	10.39	6.18	-4.36	+/-S&P 500
—	—	—	-0.22	-9.97	20.20	12.77	9.59	-8.17	2.94	6.54	-6.94	+/-Russ 2000
—	—	—	0.76	0.87	1.71	0.86	0.90	0.18	0.49	1.34	1.75	Income Return %
—	—	—	-3.53	10.42	15.47	14.40	-11.79	38.90	20.78	9.75	9.68	Capital Return %
—	—	—	36	54	31	24	20	65	32	17	80	Total Rtn % Rank Cat
—	—	0.06	0.09	0.10	0.21	0.12	0.14	0.03	0.09	0.30	0.43	Income $
—	—	0.00	0.00	0.00	0.69	0.17	0.00	0.08	0.08	0.33	0.99	Capital Gains $
—	—	—	1.65	1.28	1.28	1.30	1.23	1.17	1.17	1.14	—	Expense Ratio %
—	—	—	1.44	0.72	0.72	1.43	1.16	1.03	0.21	0.28	—	Income Ratio %
—	—	—		6	10	19	18	19	22	10	—	Turnover Rate %
—	—	—	106	144	127	141	364	395	602	1,134	2,415	Net Assets $mil

Rating and Risk

Time Period	Load-Adj Return %	Morningstar Rtn vs Cat	Morningstar Risk vs Cat	Morningstar Risk-Adj Rating
1 Yr	11.43			
3 Yr	14.50	+Avg	Low	★★★★
5 Yr	13.22	+Avg	Low	★★★★
10 Yr	—			
Incept	12.61			

Other Measures	Standard Index S&P 500	Best Fit Index Mstar Small Core
Alpha	3.1	2.1
Beta	1.11	0.66
R-Squared	69	88
Standard Deviation	9.15	
Mean	14.50	
Sharpe Ratio	1.18	

Portfolio Analysis 10-31-06

Share change since 07-06 Total Stocks:82	Sector	PE	Tot Ret%	% Assets
⊕ Pogo Producing Company	Energy	4.7	-2.16	2.83
Brookfield Asset Managem	Financial	25.7	46.00	2.70
⊕ Cimarex Energy Company	Energy	6.4	-14.79	2.68
Whiting Petroleum Corpor	Energy	9.7	16.50	2.33
St. Joe Corporation	Financial	75.4	-19.32	2.27
Bandag, Inc.	Ind Mtrls	26.3	22.04	2.13
CommScope, Inc.	Hardware	17.5	51.42	1.95
K-Swiss, Inc. A	Goods	13.8	-4.60	1.92
Comstock Resources, Inc.	Energy	12.2	1.80	1.90
St. Mary Land & Explorat	Energy	11.5	0.33	1.88
Forest City Enterprises,	Financial	—	54.80	1.78
⊕ Deltic Timber Corporatio	Ind Mtrls	45.9	8.18	1.65
⊕ National Western Life In	Financial	11.3	11.40	1.54
⊕ Canfor Corporation	Ind Mtrls	—	—	1.44
✿ Catalyst Paper Corporati	Ind Mtrls	—	—	1.43
Agrium, Inc.	Ind Mtrls	14.6	43.83	1.42
TimberWest Forest	Ind Mtrls	—	—	1.34
E-L Financial Corporatio	Financial	—	—	1.33
Synopsys	Software	—	33.25	1.28
Alexander & Baldwin	Business	21.0	-16.50	1.25

Current Investment Style

Value Blnd Growth — Large Mid Small

	Market Cap	%
	Giant	0.0
	Large	6.0
	Mid	41.7
	Small	38.7
	Micro	13.7
	Avg $mil: 1,670	

Value Measures		Rel Category
Price/Earnings	14.10	0.85
Price/Book	1.59	0.75
Price/Sales	1.10	1.12
Price/Cash Flow	6.38	0.91
Dividend Yield %	1.42	1.33

Growth Measures	%	Rel Category
Long-Term Erngs	9.11	0.65
Book Value	6.41	0.85
Sales	11.22	1.27
Cash Flow	8.99	0.71
Historical Erngs	19.87	1.19

Profitability	%	Rel Category
Return on Equity	12.88	1.00
Return on Assets	7.66	1.07
Net Margin	13.51	1.39

Sector Weightings	% of Stocks	Rel S&P 500	3 Year High Low
⟳ Info	19.12	0.96	
Software	3.44	1.00	4 0
Hardware	13.08	1.42	25 13
Media	1.01	0.27	1 0
Telecom	1.59	0.45	2 0
⊂ Service	32.75	0.71	
Health	1.73	0.14	5 2
Consumer	7.18	0.94	9 5
Business	4.07	0.96	4 2
Financial	19.77	0.89	31 19
⊔ Mfg	48.14	1.42	
Goods	5.86	0.69	6 2
Ind Mtrls	22.62	1.89	30 23
Energy	19.66	2.01	20 2
Utilities	0.00	0.00	1 0

Composition

	%
● Cash	22.7
● Stocks	77.3
● Bonds	0.0
○ Other	0.0
Foreign (% of Stock)	17.0

Third Avenue Value

	Ticker	Load	NAV	Yield	Total Assets	Mstar Category
	TAVFX	None	$59.46	5.4%	$9,725 mil	Mid-Cap Blend

Governance and Management

Stewardship Grade: A

Portfolio Manager(s)

Marty Whitman is a premier value manager and is an expert in bankruptcies and distressed securities. He has been managing mutual funds since 1986 and is supported by a staff of 11 analysts and portfolio managers.

Strategy

Manager Marty Whitman sniffs out bargains among beaten-down and unloved companies. He tries to buy asset plays at discounts of at least 20% to NAV and earnings-driven companies at no more than 10 times peak earnings. Although he wants to buy cheap companies, he also wants them to be safe. The strength of a company's balance sheet is thus a key factor in his investment decisions. Whitman also keeps a notable percentage of the fund's assets in distressed debt--and lately international stocks. He uses a buy-and-hold style and manages the fund with a watchful eye on tax efficiency.

Performance 12-31-06

	1st Qtr	2nd Qtr	3rd Qtr	4th Qtr	Total
2002	6.07	-7.40	-19.40	7.14	-15.19
2003	-4.63	18.55	9.75	10.47	37.09
2004	8.95	2.21	1.26	12.27	26.60
2005	5.13	1.86	7.12	1.57	16.50
2006	6.74	-1.21	2.80	5.81	14.69

Trailing	Total Return%	+/- S&P 500	+/- S&P Mid 400	%Rank Cat	Growth of $10,000
3 Mo	5.81	-0.89	-1.18	88	10,581
6 Mo	8.78	-3.96	2.95	52	10,878
1 Yr	14.69	-1.10	4.37	36	11,469
3 Yr Avg	19.15	8.71	6.06	3	16,915
5 Yr Avg	14.49	8.30	3.60	6	19,672
10 Yr Avg	13.50	5.08	0.03	17	35,478
15 Yr Avg	15.26	4.62	1.63	6	84,174

Tax Analysis	Tax-Adj Rtn%	%Rank Cat	Tax-Cost Rat	%Rank Cat
3 Yr (estimated)	17.46	6	1.42	61
5 Yr (estimated)	13.33	8	1.01	63
10 Yr (estimated)	12.24	12	1.11	19

Potential Capital Gain Exposure: 26% of assets

Historical Profile

Return High
Risk Below Avg
Rating ★★★★ Highest

90%	97%	84%	81%	78%	84%	71%	70%	74%

Investment Style
Equity
Stock %

▼ Manager Change
▽ Partial Manager Change

50.6
43.6 Growth of $10,000
32.4
24.0 — Investment Values of Fund
17.0 — Investment Values of S&P 500
10.0

Performance Quartile (within Category)

1995	1996	1997	1998	1999	2000	2001	2002	2003	2004	2005	2006	History
21.80	25.86	31.46	32.29	35.99	36.22	36.43	30.47	41.45	51.70	54.78	59.46	NAV
31.73	21.92	23.87	3.92	12.82	20.76	2.82	-15.19	37.09	26.60	16.50	14.69	Total Return %
-5.85	-1.04	-9.49	-24.66	-8.22	29.86	14.71	6.91	8.41	15.72	11.59	-1.10	+/-S&P 500
0.80	2.67	-8.38	-15.20	-1.90	3.25	3.43	-0.66	1.47	10.12	3.94	4.37	+/-S&P Mid 400
2.39	2.63	1.59	1.28	0.00	2.10	1.70	1.08	1.03	1.87	3.11	5.92	Income Return %
29.34	19.29	22.28	2.64	12.82	18.66	1.12	-16.27	36.06	24.73	13.39	8.77	Capital Return %
33	36	66	73	62	11	41	51	38	3	7	36	Total Rtn % Rank Cat
0.41	0.57	0.41	0.40	0.00	0.68	0.62	0.39	0.32	0.78	1.61	3.24	Income $
0.15	0.14	0.16	0.00	0.42	6.16	0.19	0.04	0.00	0.00	3.87	0.10	Capital Gains $
1.25	1.21	1.13	1.08	1.10	1.09	1.07	1.07	1.11	1.12	1.10	1.08	Expense Ratio %
2.24	2.67	2.10	1.44	1.27	1.41	1.31	0.90	1.23	0.34	0.77	2.83	Income Ratio %
15	14	10	24	5	30	21	19	11	8	16	7	Turnover Rate %
329	645	1,676	1,600	1,379	1,940	2,654	2,233	3,098	4,321	6,891	9,725	Net Assets $mil

Rating and Risk

Time Period	Load-Adj Return %	Morningstar Rtn vs Cat	Morningstar Risk vs Cat	Morningstar Risk-Adj Rating
1 Yr	14.69			
3 Yr	19.15	High	Low	★★★★★
5 Yr	14.49	High	Avg	★★★★★
10 Yr	13.50	+Avg	Low	★★★★★
Incept	16.79			

Other Measures	Standard Index S&P 500	Best Fit Index DJ Mod
Alpha	8.9	6.5
Beta	0.83	1.15
R-Squared	50	70
Standard Deviation	8.00	
Mean	19.15	
Sharpe Ratio	1.83	

Portfolio Analysis 10-31-06

Share change since 07-06 Total Stocks:92

	Sector	PE	Tot Ret%	% Assets
Toyota Industries	Goods	—	—	7.04
⊕ Cheung Kong (hldgs) Ltd	Financial	—	—	6.31
St. Joe Corporation	Financial	75.4	-19.32	3.67
Henderson Land Developme	Financial	—	—	3.29
Brookfield Asset Managem	Financial	25.7	46.00	3.28
⊕ Nabors Industries, Ltd.	Energy	9.0	-21.37	3.15
Forest City Enterprises,	Financial	—	54.80	2.99
Investor	Financial	—	—	2.66
Posco ADR	Ind Mtrls	6.4	66.98	2.65
MBIA Incorporated	Financial	12.0	23.87	2.42
⊕ Millea Holdings, Inc. AD	Financial	22.5	5.20	2.22
Covanta Holding Corporat	Business	33.8	46.35	2.01
Mellon Financial Corpora	Financial	20.4	25.99	1.89
Tejon Ranch Corporation	Ind Mtrls	—	39.88	1.86
AVX Corporation	Hardware	19.4	3.10	1.60
Mitsui Sumitomo Insuranc	Financial	—	—	1.52
Legg Mason	Financial	25.1	-19.99	1.47
⊕ Wheelock &	Consumer	—	—	1.29
Hutchison Whampoa Ltd	Telecom	—	—	1.27
Trammell Crow Company	Financial	—	—	1.18

Current Investment Style

Value Blnd Growth — Large Mid Small

Market Cap	%
Giant	22.5
Large	37.0
Mid	32.0
Small	6.6
Micro	1.9

Avg $mil: 9,315

Value Measures		Rel Category
Price/Earnings	17.23	1.07
Price/Book	1.45	0.64
Price/Sales	1.96	1.75
Price/Cash Flow	9.22	1.09
Dividend Yield %	1.36	1.05

Growth Measures	%	Rel Category
Long-Term Erngs	15.34	1.21
Book Value	12.92	1.55
Sales	11.96	1.34
Cash Flow	26.70	3.15
Historical Erngs	42.86	2.40

Profitability	%	Rel Category
Return on Equity	14.07	0.88
Return on Assets	8.72	1.09
Net Margin	23.62	2.17

Sector Weightings	% of Stocks	Rel S&P 500	3 Year High Low	
↻ Info	6.90	0.35		
🖩 Software	0.88	0.26	1	0
🖥 Hardware	4.28	0.46	8	4
🎬 Media	0.00	0.00	0	0
📱 Telecom	1.74	0.50	3	2
⚙ Service	66.99	1.45		
🏥 Health	2.55	0.21	3	2
🛒 Consumer	2.26	0.30	12	0
📋 Business	3.98	0.94	5	2
💲 Financial	58.20	2.61	61	47
🏭 Mfg	26.11	0.77		
🛢 Goods	9.66	1.13	11	9
⚙ Ind Mtrls	9.32	0.78	18	9
💡 Energy	5.96	0.61	6	2
⚡ Utilities	1.17	0.33	1	0

Composition

		%
● Cash		23.5
● Stocks		74.0
● Bonds		1.6
● Other		0.9
Foreign		51.9
(% of Stock)		

Morningstar's Take by Kerry O'Boyle 11-30-06

Shareholders here face another year-end tax bite, but it's largely a result of the fund's history of success.

The good news for Third Avenue Value is that manager Marty Whitman's six-year investment in USG has paid off in a big way. The firm emerged from bankruptcy in June 2006 after five long years, providing the fund a windfall from its stake in senior secured notes that have converted to common stock. The bad news is that all of those earnings are being treated as ordinary income, not capital gains, for tax purposes. Thus, for the second year in a row, shareholders are facing a sizable taxable distribution (scheduled to take place on December 19) amounting to an estimated $3.41 a share, or more than 5% of the fund's net asset value. The unavoidable tax hit comes despite efforts to run the fund in a tax-efficient manner.

Whitman's ability to identify and invest in the distressed debt of companies on the cheap is a key part of the fund's strategy. Although individually not big pieces of the portfolio, such investments can have a big impact. For example, the fund's stake in Kmart (now part of Sears Holdings)--which emerged from Chapter 11 in 2004--delivered huge gains. They can also blow up. Whitman is calling his investment in auto supplier Collins & Aikman in April 2005 a likely wipeout, and is not optimistic about the prospects of a rebound.

Despite such hits and misses, volatility at the fund has traditionally been modest relative to its peers. The fund's enormous stake in financial stocks, especially holdings with real estate exposure comprising about 25% of fund assets, would also appear to court risk. But Whitman's tried-and-true bottom-up security selection, which emphasizes "safe and cheap," and a long investment horizon have overcome most obstacles.

Although this go-anywhere value maven may not appeal to style purists, Whitman has proven himself to be an exceptional manager capable of delivering outsized returns.

Address:	622 Third Avenue New York NY 10017 800-443-1021	Minimum Purchase:	$10000	Add: $1000	IRA: $2500
		Min Auto Inv Plan:	$10000	Add: $200	
		Sales Fees:	No-load, 1.00%R		
Web Address:	www.thirdavenuefunds.com	Management Fee:	0.90%		
Inception:	11-01-90	Actual Fees:	Mgt:0.90%	Dist: —	
Advisor:	Third Avenue Management LLC	Expense Projections:	3Yr:$350	5Yr:$606	10Yr:$1340
Subadvisor:	None	Income Distrib:	Annually		
NTF Plans:	Fidelity Retail-NTF, Schwab OneSource				

M∢RNINGSTAR® Funds 500

Thompson Plumb Growth

	Ticker	Load	NAV	Yield	Total Assets	Mstar Category
	THPGX	None	$48.95	0.7%	$761 mil	Large Blend

Governance and Management

Stewardship Grade:

Portfolio Manager(s)

Thompson Investment Management was established after the dissolution of Thompson Plumb in 2004. Firm founder John W. Thompson still consults on this fund, but his son, John C. Thompson, is the day-to-day manager. They are supported by four analysts.

Strategy

The managers like to buy companies that are reasonably priced relative to historical earnings growth, but potential picks must also generate large amounts of cash and have strong balance sheets. They are willing to exploit the fund's all-cap mandate and will include smaller-cap stocks in the portfolio when they find attractive values. They will also make significant sector bets.

Historical Profile
Return: Average
Risk: High
Rating: ★★★ Neutral

Investment Style: Equity, Stock %
96% 99% 99% 100% 100% 100% 100% 100%

▼ Manager Change
▽ Partial Manager Change

Growth of $10,000
— Investment Values of Fund
— Investment Values of S&P 500

49.2 / 42.2 / 32.4 / 24.0 / 17.0 / 10.0

Performance Quartile (within Category)

1995	1996	1997	1998	1999	2000	2001	2002	2003	2004	2005	2006	History
24.54	30.17	36.44	39.35	40.27	40.78	44.31	34.91	45.89	46.78	44.28	48.95	NAV
30.49	33.05	32.37	18.41	6.44	25.68	19.13	-20.42	31.86	4.14	-2.41	14.96	Total Return %
-7.09	10.09	-0.99	-10.17	-14.60	34.78	31.02	1.68	3.18	-6.74	-7.32	-0.83	+/-S&P 500
-7.28	10.60	-0.48	-8.61	-14.47	33.47	31.58	1.23	1.97	-7.26	-8.68	-0.50	+/-Russ 1000
0.00	0.00	0.00	0.00	0.00	0.00	0.06	0.56	0.40	0.96	0.58	0.77	Income Return %
30.49	33.05	32.37	18.41	6.44	25.68	19.07	-20.98	31.46	3.18	-2.99	14.19	Capital Return %
73	4	30	63	91	1	1	34	15	97	99	39	Total Rtn % Rank Cat
0.00	0.00	0.00	0.00	0.00	0.00	0.02	0.25	0.14	0.44	0.27	0.34	Income $
0.55	2.47	3.36	3.50	1.56	9.35	4.03	0.11	0.00	0.55	1.12	1.62	Capital Gains $
2.00	1.58	1.52	1.41	1.32	1.29	1.20	1.11	1.07	1.05	1.08	—	Expense Ratio %
-0.31	-0.27	-0.41	-0.19	-0.34	-0.09	0.11	0.68	0.47	1.12	0.50	—	Income Ratio %
87	102	78	67	79	64	63	74	41	29	20	—	Turnover Rate %
13	24	47	72	78	85	328	512	1,000	1,525	985	761	Net Assets $mil

Performance 12-31-06

	1st Qtr	2nd Qtr	3rd Qtr	4th Qtr	Total
2002	2.30	-17.65	-18.94	16.53	-20.42
2003	-7.36	23.81	0.85	14.00	31.86
2004	1.26	2.58	-7.41	8.27	4.14
2005	-4.62	0.16	0.49	1.65	-2.41
2006	2.12	-2.59	7.79	7.22	14.96

Trailing	Total Return%	+/- S&P 500	+/- Russ 1000	%Rank Cat	Growth of $10,000
3 Mo	7.22	0.52	0.27	27	10,722
6 Mo	15.56	2.82	3.20	4	11,556
1 Yr	14.96	-0.83	-0.50	39	11,496
3 Yr Avg	5.32	-5.12	-5.66	98	11,682
5 Yr Avg	4.16	-2.03	-2.66	81	12,260
10 Yr Avg	11.84	3.42	3.20	5	30,618
15 Yr Avg	—				

Tax Analysis	Tax-Adj Rtn%	%Rank Cat	Tax-Cost Rat	%Rank Cat
3 Yr (estimated)	4.63	96	0.66	30
5 Yr (estimated)	3.66	79	0.48	31
10 Yr (estimated)	10.06	6	1.59	75

Potential Capital Gain Exposure: 17% of assets

Rating and Risk

Time Period	Load-Adj Return %	Morningstar Rtn vs Cat	Morningstar Risk vs Cat	Morningstar Risk-Adj Rating
1 Yr	14.96			
3 Yr	5.32	Low	Avg	★
5 Yr	4.16	-Avg	High	★
10 Yr	11.84	High	High	★★★★★
Incept	12.33			

Other Measures	Standard Index S&P 500	Best Fit Index S&P 500
Alpha	-4.1	-4.1
Beta	0.92	0.92
R-Squared	71	71
Standard Deviation	7.55	
Mean	5.32	
Sharpe Ratio	0.30	

Morningstar's Take by Andrew Gogerty 11-06-06

Now might be the time to give Thompson Plumb Growth a look.

We're not surprised by the resurgence seen in large-cap stocks in recent months given their long period of underperformance. In fact, many market observers have been calling for this trend for some time, and some believe we're finally at its beginning. This fund was in a perfect spot to take advantage: Its 13% gain for the three months through Oct. 26, 2006, tops nearly the entire large-blend category and has pulled the fund's year-to-date returns to within 1% of the S&P 500 Index's.

We're not overemphasizing the fund's recent, short-term success, but we do think this early change along with its portfolio's profile make a compelling argument. Manager John C. Thompson looks to buy stocks with histories of plush cash flow, healthy balance sheets, and strong, recurring returns on equity. This profile tilts the portfolio toward large-cap stocks with strong market

positions or distinct competitive advantages. Thompson believes companies meeting these hurdles are trading at lower premiums to lesser-quality firms than in the past. Industry leaders Microsoft and American International Group, for example, have above-average earnings-growth expectations compared with the index, yet trade at below-market P/E ratios. Overall, 75% of the fund's assets are in stocks trading below Morningstar equity analysts' fair value estimates, suggesting good returns to come.

Should the market take time to return to high-quality, large-cap stocks, however, Thompson will be willing to wait. The fund's 30% average turnover for the past three years is well below the 67% category average, and he's coupled this patience with conviction in his best ideas--more than 50% of assets reside in the top 10 holdings. True, this combination invites volatility, but the fund's long-term record argues for investors to be tolerant of shorter-term gyrations.

Portfolio Analysis 09-30-06

Share change since 06-06 Total Stocks:46

	Sector	PE	Tot Ret%	% Assets
⊖ Fannie Mae	Financial	—	24.34	9.06
⊖ Microsoft Corporation	Software	23.8	15.83	6.34
⊖ Pfizer Inc.	Health	15.2	15.22	5.77
⊖ American International G	Financial	17.0	6.05	5.20
⊖ Viacom, Inc. B	Media	—	—	5.08
⊖ Coca-Cola Company	Goods	21.7	23.10	4.76
⊖ Tyco International, Ltd.	Ind Mtrls	15.7	6.83	4.76
⊖ ExxonMobil Corporation	Energy	11.1	39.07	4.51
⊖ Chevron Corporation	Energy	9.0	33.76	4.50
⊖ Freddie Mac	Financial	23.3	7.06	3.95
⊖ Time Warner, Inc.	Media	19.6	26.37	3.80
⊖ First Data Corporation	Business	12.3	9.88	3.25
⊖ Amgen, Inc.	Health	29.1	-13.38	3.22
⊖ Wal-Mart Stores, Inc.	Consumer	16.9	0.13	3.19
⊖ Fifth Third Bancorp	Financial	15.4	12.99	3.05
⊖ Morgan Stanley	Financial	12.3	45.93	3.05
⊖ Berkshire Hathaway Inc.	Financial	13.2	24.89	2.42
⊖ IMS Health, Inc.	Health	17.4	10.77	2.06
⊖ Cardinal Health, Inc.	Health	20.8	-5.82	1.89
⊖ Citigroup, Inc.	Financial	13.1	19.55	1.82

Current Investment Style

Value Blnd Growth — Large Mid Small

Market Cap	%
Giant	69.1
Large	23.3
Mid	7.5
Small	0.2
Micro	0.0

Avg $mil: 70,634

Value Measures		Rel Category
Price/Earnings	13.69	0.89
Price/Book	2.69	1.05
Price/Sales	1.59	1.14
Price/Cash Flow	2.10	0.25
Dividend Yield %	1.96	1.12

Growth Measures	%	Rel Category
Long-Term Erngs	11.59	0.98
Book Value	2.69	0.30
Sales	11.59	1.20
Cash Flow	6.85	0.66
Historical Erngs	16.06	0.87

Profitability	%	Rel Category
Return on Equity	19.75	1.02
Return on Assets	11.24	1.08
Net Margin	14.45	1.08

Sector Weightings	% of Stocks	Rel S&P 500	3 Year High Low
⟲ Info	23.49	1.18	
▣ Software	6.52	1.89	7 5
▣ Hardware	6.49	0.70	6 2
▣ Media	10.48	2.77	14 10
▣ Telecom	0.00	0.00	0 0
☞ Service	55.44	1.20	
▣ Health	14.91	1.24	23 10
▣ Consumer	7.49	0.98	7 4
▣ Business	4.03	0.95	10 4
▣ Financial	29.01	1.30	32 22
⊔ Mfg	21.07	0.62	
▣ Goods	5.81	0.68	10 6
▣ Ind Mtrls	6.09	0.51	7 4
▣ Energy	9.17	0.94	11 2
▣ Utilities	0.00	0.00	0 0

Composition

	%
● Cash	0.0
● Stocks	100.0
● Bonds	0.0
○ Other	0.0
Foreign (% of Stock)	0.7

Address:	1200 John Q. Hammons Drive Madison WI 53717 800-999-0887
Web Address:	www.thompsonplumb.com
Inception:	02-10-92
Advisor:	Thompson Investment Management, LLC
Subadvisor:	None
NTF Plans:	Fidelity Retail-NTF

Minimum Purchase:	$2500	Add: $100	IRA: $2000
Min Auto Inv Plan:	$2500	Add: $50	
Sales Fees:	No-load		
Management Fee:	1.00% mx./0.90% mn.		
Actual Fees:	Mgt:0.91%	Dist:—	
Expense Projections:	3Yr:$347	5Yr:$601	10Yr:$1329
Income Distrib:	Annually		

Thornburg Intl Value A

	Ticker	Load	NAV	Yield	Total Assets	Mstar Category
	TGVAX	4.50%	$28.48	1.0%	$9,916 mil	Foreign Large Blend

Governance and Management

Stewardship Grade: A

Portfolio Manager(s)

William Fries, who also runs highly successful Thornburg Value, has been at the helm of this fund since its mid-1998 inception. Longtime team member Wendy Trevisani and Lei Wang became Fries' comanagers Feb. 1, 2006. They're supported by a strong team of investment professionals.

Strategy

William Fries and his comanager will invest across the market: growth and value, mid- to large-cap, and developed- and emerging-markets stocks. They devote 40% or so of the portfolio to large-value stocks that pay dividends, primarily in the financial and consumer sectors. They invest another 40% or so to blue-chip growth stocks selling below their earnings prospects. And they devote the rest to rapid growers that are becoming industry or market leaders. The portfolio holds between 50 and 60 stocks. The managers readily add to picks that have slipped and will hold on to winners.

Performance 12-31-06

	1st Qtr	2nd Qtr	3rd Qtr	4th Qtr	Total
2002	6.71	-3.45	-16.86	4.55	-10.45
2003	-9.42	20.98	9.85	16.32	40.02
2004	4.95	-1.66	1.28	12.64	17.73
2005	-0.02	1.49	10.70	4.75	17.68
2006	9.85	0.02	3.65	10.31	25.62

Trailing	Total Return%	+/- MSCI EAFE	+/- MSCI Wd xUS	%Rank Cat	Growth of $10,000
3 Mo	10.31	-0.04	0.19	45	11,031
6 Mo	14.34	-0.35	0.12	52	11,434
1 Yr	25.62	-0.72	-0.09	40	12,562
3 Yr Avg	20.29	0.36	0.19	21	17,406
5 Yr Avg	16.89	1.91	1.64	7	21,822
10 Yr Avg	—	—	—	—	—
15 Yr Avg	—	—	—	—	—

Tax Analysis	Tax-Adj Rtn%	%Rank Cat	Tax-Cost Rat	%Rank Cat
3 Yr (estimated)	17.90	42	0.46	25
5 Yr (estimated)	15.49	9	0.28	22
10 Yr (estimated)	—	—	—	—

Potential Capital Gain Exposure: 24% of assets

Morningstar's Take by William Samuel Rocco 12-26-06

This wide-ranging mutual fund has real appeal.

Thornburg International Value provides broader exposure than most foreign large blend offerings. Bill Fries, Wendy Trevisani, and Lei Wang pursue three different types of opportunities: consistent earners such as top name Roche Holding, basic-value stocks like number-three holding UBS, and emerging-franchise issues such as number-four holding America Movil. While doing so, the managers invest across the sector spectrum, consider mid-caps, and pay lots of attention to emerging-markets issues.

Meanwhile, Fries and his comanagers have executed this far-reaching strategy quite well here overall. They've delivered only average gains in 2006, as their telecom and other good picks have been offset by Teva Pharmaceutical and a few other poor-performing stocks. But they produced superior results in six of the fund's first seven years--and solid gains in the other one--so the three-year, five-year, and since-inception returns are all excellent here.

The fund also boasts a strong management team. Fries, who has been at the helm since the fund opened in 1998, has more than 30 years of experience as an investment professional and was named Morningstar's International Manager of the Year in 2003. Trevisani and Wang, who became comanagers on the fund in February 2006 after working closely with Fries for some time, are seasoned. And the three managers have ample support.

These traits make the fund a terrific option for investors seeking a wide-ranging or stand-alone foreign holding. But such investors should recognize that the managers taste for emerging-markets stocks and practice of running a compact portfolio of 50 to 60 names come with risks. And they should note that this and most other foreign funds have posted exceptional absolute gains over the past few years and are unlikely to gain as much over the next few.

Address:	119 E Marcy St Santa Fe NM 87501 800-847-0200
Web Address:	www.thornburg.com
Inception:	05-28-98*
Advisor:	Thornburg Investment Management Inc.
Subadvisor:	None
NTF Plans:	DATALynx NTF, Federated Tr NTF

Minimum Purchase:	$5000	Add: $100	IRA: $2000
Min Auto Inv Plan:	$5000	Add: $100	
Sales Fees:	4.50%L, 0.25%S, 1.00%R		
Management Fee:	0.88% mx./0.68% mn.		
Actual Fees:	Mgt:0.77%	Dist:0.25%	
Expense Projections:	3Yr:$885	5Yr:$1201	10Yr:$2097
Income Distrib:	Quarterly		

Historical Profile

Return: Above Avg
Risk: Below Avg
Rating: ★★★★ Above Avg

Equity ownership %: 85% 81% 81% 84% 94% 95% 94% 96%

Investment Style Equity Stock %

▼ Manager Change
▽ Partial Manager Change

Growth of $10,000
■ Investment Values of Fund
— Investment Values of MSCI EAFE

Values on chart: 23.6 / 18.0 / 14.0 / 10.0 / 6.0

Performance Quartile (within Category)

	1995	1996	1997	1998	1999	2000	2001	2002	2003	2004	2005	2006	History
NAV	—	—	—	10.80	17.29	15.63	13.87	12.42	17.39	20.40	23.46	28.48	
Total Return %	—	—	—	-9.32*	63.40	-1.57	-10.53	-10.45	40.02	17.73	17.68	25.62	
+/-MSCI EAFE	—	—	—		36.37	12.62	10.89	5.49	1.43	-2.52	4.14	-0.72	
+/-MSCI Wd xUS	—	—	—		35.42	11.79	10.86	5.35	0.60	-2.65	3.21	-0.09	
Income Return %	—	—	—		2.75	8.33	0.78	0.00	0.00	0.41	0.59	1.21	
Capital Return %	—	—	—		60.65	-9.90	-11.31	-10.45	40.02	17.32	17.09	24.41	
Total Rtn % Rank Cat	—	—	—		3	2	3	7	11	44	15	40	
Income $	—	—	—	0.03	0.30	1.41	0.12	0.00	0.00	0.07	0.12	0.28	
Capital Gains $	—	—	—	0.00	0.00	0.00	0.00	0.00	0.00	0.00	0.40	0.65	
Expense Ratio %	—	—	—			1.63	1.53	1.54	1.57	1.59	1.49	1.33	
Income Ratio %	—	—	—			1.07	2.61	0.22	0.19	0.44	0.88	1.25	
Turnover Rate %	—	—	—			58	86	61	28	58	36	37	
Net Assets $mil	—	—	—	39	79	68	78	299	944	4,605			

Rating and Risk

Time Period	Load-Adj Return %	Morningstar Rtn vs Cat	Morningstar Risk vs Cat	Morningstar Risk-Adj Rating
1 Yr	19.96			
3 Yr	18.45	Avg	Avg	★★★
5 Yr	15.82	+Avg	-Avg	★★★★
10 Yr	—			
Incept	12.34			

Other Measures	Standard Index MSCI EAFE	Best Fit Index MSCI Wd xUS
Alpha	0.7	0.7
Beta	0.98	0.97
R-Squared	91	91
Standard Deviation	9.75	
Mean	20.29	
Sharpe Ratio	1.64	

Portfolio Analysis 11-30-06

Share change since 10-06 Total Stocks:53

	Sector	Country	% Assets
Roche Holding	Health	Switzerland	3.01
Rogers Comms CI B	Telecom	Canada	2.80
UBS AG	Financial	Switzerland	2.70
America Movil SA ADR	Telecom	Mexico	2.63
⊕ Sinopec	Business	China	2.48
Eni	Energy	Italy	2.42
⊕ Teva Pharmaceutical Indu	Health	Israel	2.38
⊕ CHINA MERCHANTS BANK	Financial	China	2.32
France Telecom	Telecom	France	2.25
⊕ Reckitt Benckiser	Goods	U.K.	2.22
⊕ China Merchants Hldgs (I	Ind Mtrls	Hong Kong	2.21
⊕ Swiss Re	Financial	Switzerland	2.16
Barclays	Financial	U.K.	2.14
Canadian Natural Res	Energy	Canada	2.11
Hong Kong Exchanges & CI	Financial	Hong Kong	2.10
LVMH Moet Hennessy L.V.	Goods	France	2.03
Wal-Mart de Mexico	Consumer	Mexico	2.02
Amdocs Ltd.	Software	United States	1.99
Toyota Motor	Goods	Japan	1.96
☼ China Mobile	Telecom	Hong Kong	1.94

Current Investment Style

Value Blnd Growth — Large / Mid / Small

Market Cap	%
Giant	50.6
Large	41.5
Mid	7.9
Small	0.0
Micro	0.0
Avg $mil:	30,864

Value Measures		Rel Category
Price/Earnings	16.85	1.28
Price/Book	2.74	1.26
Price/Sales	1.44	1.24
Price/Cash Flow	10.06	1.21
Dividend Yield %	2.31	0.79

Growth Measures	%	Rel Category
Long-Term Erngs	13.63	1.16
Book Value	11.17	1.22
Sales	9.62	1.47
Cash Flow	8.88	1.08
Historical Erngs	23.00	1.13

Composition

Cash	2.9	Bonds	0.0
Stocks	96.1	Other	1.0
Foreign (% of Stock)			96.4

Sector Weightings	% of Stocks	Rel MSCI EAFE	3 Year High Low	
↻ Info	15.36	1.30		
Software	3.35	5.98	6	0
Hardware	0.00	0.00	4	0
Media	0.00	0.00	9	0
Telecom	12.01	2.16	14	7
⊂ Service	46.65	0.99		
Health	10.00	1.40	16	5
Consumer	8.42	1.70	17	5
Business	5.88	1.16	7	2
Financial	22.35	0.74	28	18
◻ Mfg	37.98	0.93		
Goods	19.65	1.50	22	12
Ind Mtrls	10.85	0.70	11	5
Energy	7.48	1.05	11	5
Utilities	0.00	0.00	3	0

Regional Exposure % Stock

UK/W. Europe	52	N. America	9
Japan	13	Latn America	6
Asia X Japan	17	Other	3

Country Exposure % Stock

U.K.	18	France	9
Japan	13	Hong Kong	8
Switzerland	12		

Morningstar® Funds 500

Thornburg Value A

	Ticker	Load	NAV	Yield	Total Assets	Mstar Category
	TVAFX	4.50%	$39.29	0.8%	$3,365 mil	Large Blend

Governance and Management

Stewardship Grade: B

Portfolio Manager(s)

William Fries, who is also the lead manager of highly successful Thornburg International Value, has been at the helm of this fund since its 1995 inception. Longtime team members Connor Browne and Edward Maran were named Fries' comanagers on Feb. 1, 2006. They have seven other equity specialists at Thornburg to draw on for support.

Strategy

William Fries and his comanagers divide holdings into three groups: basic value (stocks selling below their earnings power), consistent earners (blue-chip stocks selling below their historical price multiples), and emerging franchises (rapidly growing companies establishing leadership in their industries). The final group occupies a smaller portion of this fund's assets than the other two. The managers aren't afraid to load up on stocks in particular sectors and keep the portfolio concentrated, holding between 40 and 50 stocks.

Historical Profile

Return	Above Avg
Risk	Above Avg
Rating	★★★★ Above Avg

82% 94% 93% 95% 93% 95% 94% 94% 91%

Stock %

Investment Style
Equity

▼ Manager Change
▽ Partial Manager Change

Growth of $10,000
— Investment Values of Fund
— Investment Values of S&P 500

38.0
31.0
24.0
17.0
10.0

Performance Quartile (within Category)

	1995	1996	1997	1998	1999	2000	2001	2002	2003	2004	2005	2006	History
	11.83	15.59	19.24	23.36	31.37	31.40	28.73	21.59	29.10	30.88	33.58	39.29	NAV
	-0.53*	37.82	33.70	22.25	37.44	3.96	-8.11	-24.85	34.99	7.20	9.54	21.95	Total Return %
	—	14.86	0.34	-6.33	16.40	13.06	3.78	-2.75	6.31	-3.68	4.63	6.16	+/-S&P 500
	—	15.37	0.85	-4.77	16.53	11.75	4.34	-3.20	5.10	-4.20	3.27	6.49	+/-Russ 1000
	—	2.43	1.18	0.77	1.06	3.26	0.40	0.00	0.19	1.05	0.74	0.97	Income Return %
	—	35.39	32.52	21.48	36.38	0.70	-8.51	-24.85	34.80	6.15	8.80	20.98	Capital Return %
	7	2	13	52	6	18	23	83	9	86	13	2	Total Rtn % Rank Cat
	0.05	0.28	0.18	0.15	0.25	1.01	0.13	0.00	0.04	0.30	0.23	0.32	Income $
	0.00	0.37	1.35	0.00	0.39	0.25	0.00	0.00	0.00	0.00	0.00	1.30	Capital Gains $
	—	1.55	1.61	1.61	1.44	1.38	1.37	1.40	1.43	1.37	1.40	1.34	Expense Ratio %
	—	2.48	1.35	0.96	0.62	2.31	0.07	0.00	0.66	0.69	1.05	1.02	Income Ratio %
	—	60	79	100	63	72	72	76	83	69	59	51	Turnover Rate %
	7	15	80	234	506	936	1,233	793	1,051	1,084	980	1,307	Net Assets $mil

Performance 12-31-06

	1st Qtr	2nd Qtr	3rd Qtr	4th Qtr	Total
2002	-1.57	-12.62	-16.11	4.15	-24.85
2003	-1.48	21.39	1.98	10.69	34.99
2004	2.23	-2.41	-2.55	10.26	7.20
2005	-1.64	2.66	5.71	2.63	9.54
2006	6.77	-1.19	6.79	8.24	21.95

Trailing	Total Return%	+/- S&P 500	+/- Russ 1000	%Rank Cat	Growth of $10,000
3 Mo	8.24	1.54	1.29	10	10,824
6 Mo	15.60	2.86	3.24	4	11,560
1 Yr	21.95	6.16	6.49	2	12,195
3 Yr Avg	12.72	2.28	1.74	11	14,322
5 Yr Avg	7.76	1.57	0.94	17	14,531
10 Yr Avg	12.04	3.62	3.40	4	31,170
15 Yr Avg	—	—	—	—	—

Tax Analysis	Tax-Adj Rtn%	%Rank Cat	Tax-Cost Rat	%Rank Cat
3 Yr (estimated)	10.48	22	0.47	22
5 Yr (estimated)	6.45	23	0.30	20
10 Yr (estimated)	10.79	4	0.66	27

Potential Capital Gain Exposure: 19% of assets

Rating and Risk

Time Period	Load-Adj Return %	Morningstar Rtn vs Cat	Morningstar Risk vs Cat	Morningstar Risk-Adj Rating
1 Yr	16.47			
3 Yr	11.00	+Avg	+Avg	★★★★
5 Yr	6.77	+Avg	+Avg	★★★★
10 Yr	11.53	High	+Avg	★★★★★
Incept	13.32			

Other Measures	Standard Index S&P 500	Best Fit Index Russ 1000
Alpha	1.3	0.9
Beta	1.12	1.10
R-Squared	87	89
Standard Deviation	8.37	
Mean	12.72	
Sharpe Ratio	1.11	

Portfolio Analysis 11-30-06

Share change since 10-06 Total Stocks:44	Sector	PE	Tot Ret%	% Assets
ExxonMobil Corporation	Energy	11.1	39.07	3.19
Microsoft Corporation	Software	23.8	15.83	2.91
American International G	Financial	17.0	6.05	2.71
Las Vegas Sands, Inc.	Consumer	75.7	126.70	2.70
American Tower Corporati	Telecom	—	37.57	2.54
General Electric Company	Ind Mtrls	20.0	9.35	2.53
⊕ Citigroup, Inc.	Financial	13.1	19.55	2.51
WellPoint, Inc.	Health	17.2	-1.38	2.48
Chevron Corporation	Energy	9.0	33.76	2.47
Target Corporation	Consumer	19.3	4.65	2.45
☼ Alcoa, Inc.	Ind Mtrls	12.0	3.49	2.43
Pfizer Inc.	Health	15.2	15.22	2.40
JetBlue Airways Corporat	Business	—	-7.67	2.38
NYSE Group	Financial	—	94.40	2.37
☼ Thermo Fisher Scientific	Health	37.4	50.32	2.35
Apache Corporation	Energy	7.8	-2.30	2.30
Oracle Corporation	Software	26.7	40.38	2.28
⊕ HSBC Hldgs	Financial	—	—	2.25
⊖ Southern Copper Corporat	Ind Mtrls	8.5	79.47	2.21
ConocoPhillips	Energy	6.5	26.53	2.16

Current Investment Style

Value Blnd Growth — Large Mid Small

Market Cap	%
Giant	45.2
Large	33.1
Mid	18.0
Small	3.7
Micro	0.0

Avg $mil: 37,829

Value Measures		Rel Category
Price/Earnings	17.64	1.15
Price/Book	2.58	1.01
Price/Sales	1.21	0.86
Price/Cash Flow	10.34	1.23
Dividend Yield %	1.29	0.74

Growth Measures	%	Rel Category
Long-Term Erngs	11.91	1.01
Book Value	8.67	0.96
Sales	7.40	0.76
Cash Flow	-7.99	NMF
Historical Erngs	22.95	1.24

Profitability	%	Rel Category
Return on Equity	19.39	1.00
Return on Assets	9.07	0.87
Net Margin	12.27	0.91

Sector Weightings	% of Stocks	Rel S&P 500	3 Year High	Low
☊ Info	29.22	1.46		
Software	7.48	2.17	9	3
Hardware	6.18	0.67	8	2
Media	4.57	1.21	13	5
Telecom	10.99	3.13	12	5
⌖ Service	44.15	0.96		
Health	10.62	0.88	22	11
Consumer	9.38	1.23	10	4
Business	8.37	1.98	10	4
Financial	15.78	0.71	35	14
⌂ Mfg	26.63	0.79		
Goods	2.00	0.23	6	0
Ind Mtrls	11.38	0.95	11	2
Energy	11.11	1.13	14	5
Utilities	2.14	0.61	2	0

Composition

	%
● Cash	5.1
● Stocks	91.1
● Bonds	1.4
○ Other	2.4
Foreign (% of Stock)	11.0

Morningstar's Take by William Samuel Rocco 11-06-06

Thornburg Value is an exceptional large-blend offering, but that doesn't mean it can thrive every year.

This fund has a strong management team. Bill Fries, who has been at the helm since the fund opened in late 1995, has a longer tenure than 90% of his large-blend peers. Ed Maran and Connor Browne became comanagers on the fund in early 2006 after working closely with Fries for several years. Fries, Maran, and Browne have seven other stock specialists at Thornburg to draw upon for support.

The three managers use a distinctive style that should appeal to investors who believe in giving managers real latitude while picking stocks. They pursue emerging-franchise stocks, fundamentally sound large-value names, and attractively priced blue-chip growth stocks that are the bread and butter of many of their peers. Indeed, they established a position in JetBlue Airways this summer (due to its prospects, plans, and price), and

the fund is one of the few large-blend funds with a sizable position in the stock. They consider overseas opportunities much more readily than most of their peers do and run a focused portfolio of 40 to 50 names, so all of their picks really count.

The managers have executed this strategy well this year and in the past. The fund leads the large-blend category with a 17% gain for the year to date, due to a variety of good picks. It boasts terrific long-term returns, as the stock selection has generally been good here.

All this is encouraging, and we remain confident about the fund's long-term prospects. But investors should be sure they understand that no offering can prosper every year and that the fund's issue concentration will sometimes cause it short-term pain (as its bottom-quartile 2002 and 2004 results attest). They should also note that Thornburg expects the fund to make a small capital gains distribution later this year.

Address:	119 E Marcy St Santa Fe NM 87501 800-847-0200	Minimum Purchase:	$5000 Add: $100 IRA: $2000
		Min Auto Inv Plan:	$5000 Add: $100
		Sales Fees:	4.50%L, 0.25%S, 1.00%R
Web Address:	www.thornburg.com	Management Fee:	0.88% mx./0.68% mn., 0.12%A
Inception:	10-02-95*	Actual Fees:	Mgt:0.80% Dist:0.25%
Advisor:	Thornburg Investment Management Inc.	Expense Projections:	3Yr:$873 5Yr:$1181 10Yr:$2054
Subadvisor:	None	Income Distrib:	Quarterly
NTF Plans:	DATALynx NTF, Federated Tr NTF		

Torray

	Ticker	Load	NAV	Yield	Total Assets	Mstar Category
	TORYX	None	$41.57	0.2%	$1,199 mil	Large Blend

Governance and Management

Stewardship Grade:

Portfolio Manager(s)

Comanagers Bob Torray and Doug Eby have plenty of experience and a great record. Torray founded his own firm in 1972, and he has guided the fund since its late-1990 inception. Eby came aboard in January 1992. They are supported by four analysts. Both are personally invested in the fund to a substantial degree.

Strategy

The managers jump into companies when they trade at fire-sale prices and then hang on for the long haul. A buy-and-hold style leads them mostly to larger companies that they think have sustainable competitive advantages. The fund tends to concentrate more assets in individual holdings than its peers do, and it also takes sizable sector positions. The fund is run in a tax-efficient manner.

Historical Profile

Return	Average
Risk	Average
Rating	★★★ Neutral

100%	100%	97%	99%	98%	98%	100%	97%	95%

Investment Style
Equity
Stock %

▼ Manager Change
▽ Partial Manager Change

Growth of $10,000
— Investment Values of Fund
— Investment Values of S&P 500

40.8
31.0
24.0
17.0
10.0

Performance Quartile (within Category)

1995	1996	1997	1998	1999	2000	2001	2002	2003	2004	2005	2006	History
20.11	25.22	33.85	36.48	44.31	39.79	37.53	32.24	39.98	41.08	39.02	41.57	NAV
50.37	29.09	37.12	8.19	24.03	-3.38	-0.52	-13.04	25.19	6.90	2.08	13.74	Total Return %
12.79	6.13	3.76	-20.39	2.99	5.72	11.37	9.06	-3.49	-3.98	-2.83	-2.05	+/-S&P 500
12.60	6.64	4.27	-18.83	3.12	4.41	11.93	8.61	-4.70	-4.50	-4.19	-1.72	+/-Russ 1000
1.56	0.93	0.52	0.41	0.20	0.58	0.47	0.55	1.07	0.53	0.39	0.23	Income Return %
48.81	28.16	36.60	7.78	23.83	-3.96	-0.99	-13.59	24.12	6.37	1.69	13.51	Capital Return %
1	6	5	91	25	40	8	5	71	87	89	59	Total Rtn % Rank Cat
0.21	0.19	0.13	0.14	0.07	0.25	0.18	0.21	0.34	0.21	0.16	0.09	Income $
0.32	0.53	0.58	0.54	0.79	2.80	1.76	0.21	0.00	1.38	2.69	2.61	Capital Gains $
1.25	1.25	1.13	1.09	1.07	1.06	1.07	1.07	1.11	1.08	1.07	—	Expense Ratio %
1.31	0.87	0.47	0.42	0.18	0.64	0.45	0.58	0.62	0.41	0.34	—	Income Ratio %
23	21	12	26	33	45	38	23	37	27	33	—	Turnover Rate %
51	117	609	1,461	1,896	1,822	1,641	1,368	1,655	1,735	1,331	1,199	Net Assets $mil

Performance 12-31-06

	1st Qtr	2nd Qtr	3rd Qtr	4th Qtr	Total
2002	6.66	-13.53	-13.77	9.35	-13.04
2003	-3.75	16.73	0.81	10.53	25.19
2004	1.44	1.00	-2.66	7.19	6.90
2005	-3.93	0.12	3.39	2.65	2.08
2006	4.84	-4.17	6.14	6.66	13.74

Trailing	Total Return%	+/- S&P 500	+/- Russ 1000	%Rank Cat	Growth of $10,000
3 Mo	6.66	-0.04	-0.29	46	10,666
6 Mo	13.22	0.48	0.86	13	11,322
1 Yr	13.74	-2.05	-1.72	59	11,374
3 Yr Avg	7.46	-2.98	-3.52	89	12,409
5 Yr Avg	6.20	0.01	-0.62	37	13,509
10 Yr Avg	9.10	0.68	0.46	17	23,892
15 Yr Avg	12.84	2.20	2.04	9	61,227

Tax Analysis	Tax-Adj Rtn%	%Rank Cat	Tax-Cost Rat	%Rank Cat
3 Yr (estimated)	6.43	86	0.96	44
5 Yr (estimated)	5.44	38	0.72	47
10 Yr (estimated)	8.30	14	0.73	31

Potential Capital Gain Exposure: 26% of assets

Rating and Risk

Time Period	Load-Adj Return %	Morningstar Rtn vs Cat	Morningstar Risk vs Cat	Morningstar Risk-Adj Rating
1 Yr	13.74			
3 Yr	7.46	-Avg	Avg	★★
5 Yr	6.20	Avg	Avg	★★★
10 Yr	9.10	+Avg	+Avg	★★★★
Incept	13.23			

Other Measures	Standard Index S&P 500	Best Fit Index S&P 500
Alpha	-2.8	-2.8
Beta	1.01	1.01
R-Squared	84	84
Standard Deviation	7.68	
Mean	7.46	
Sharpe Ratio	0.56	

Portfolio Analysis 09-30-06

Share change since 06-06 Total Stocks:40	Sector	PE	Tot Ret%	% Assets
Level 3 Comms 10%	—	—	—	4.99
Eli Lilly & Company	Health	17.3	-5.16	4.85
⊖ Amgen, Inc.	Health	29.1	-13.38	4.81
Markel Corporation	Financial	12.2	51.43	4.77
Cardinal Health, Inc.	Health	20.8	-5.82	4.51
⊕ Applied Materials	Hardware	19.5	3.89	4.27
Fairfax Financial Holdin	Financial	—	38.46	4.18
Medtronic, Inc.	Health	23.8	-6.29	4.12
Ambac Financial Group, I	Financial	10.9	16.52	4.06
⊖ Abbott Laboratories	Health	24.3	26.88	3.71
☆ EMC Corporation	Hardware	32.7	-3.08	3.32
⊕ Intel Corporation	Hardware	21.0	-17.18	3.25
⊕ J.P. Morgan Chase & Co.	Financial	13.6	25.60	2.96
⊖ First Data Corporation	Business	12.3	9.88	2.87
⊖ Illinois Tool Works, Inc	Ind Mtrls	15.7	6.69	2.86
☆ Haemonetics Corporation	Health	21.4	-7.86	2.84
⊕ Tribune Company	Media	16.0	4.15	2.77
⊕ Marsh & McLennan Compani	Financial	29.0	-1.16	2.63
⊖ Goldman Sachs Group, Inc	Financial	12.4	57.41	2.45
⊖ Automatic Data Processin	Business	24.9	9.11	2.40

Current Investment Style

Value Blnd Growth — Large Mid Small

Market Cap	%
Giant	35.7
Large	36.5
Mid	19.6
Small	8.2
Micro	0.0

Avg $mil: 21,406

Value Measures		Rel Category
Price/Earnings	15.67	1.02
Price/Book	2.26	0.88
Price/Sales	1.43	1.02
Price/Cash Flow	11.82	1.40
Dividend Yield %	1.14	0.65

Growth Measures	%	Rel Category
Long-Term Erngs	12.72	1.08
Book Value	3.31	0.37
Sales	8.06	0.83
Cash Flow	-3.82	NMF
Historical Erngs	11.73	0.63

Profitability	%	Rel Category
Return on Equity	15.91	0.82
Return on Assets	10.11	0.97
Net Margin	14.36	1.07

Sector Weightings	% of Stocks	Rel S&P 500	3 Year High	Low
↻ Info	20.16	1.01		
Software	0.00	0.00	0	0
Hardware	11.43	1.24	11	1
Media	7.01	1.85	17	7
Telecom	1.72	0.49	3	0
Service	66.30	1.43		
Health	28.40	2.35	28	14
Consumer	2.51	0.33	4	0
Business	5.56	1.31	12	6
Financial	29.83	1.34	30	25
Mfg	13.53	0.40		
Goods	1.06	0.12	9	1
Ind Mtrls	12.47	1.04	22	12
Energy	0.00	0.00	0	0
Utilities	0.00	0.00	1	0

Composition

● Cash	0.2	
● Stocks	94.8	
● Bonds	5.0	
○ Other	0.0	
Foreign (% of Stock)	4.4	

Morningstar's Take by Todd Trubey 11-03-06

Don't give up on Torray Fund.

Many investors hope they're like Warren Buffett, but comanagers Bob Torray and Doug Eby are similar enough to merit comparison. They're focused investors who see risk not as market sensitivity but as the danger of owning a bad business. Like Buffett, their top goal is to buy good, dependable firms, and their second is to get a reasonable price. Their current media holdings illustrate their approach. They say that newspaper firms like Gannett are largely seen as a "melting ice cubes," but for now, the cash flows are plush and the stocks are cheap on that basis. They recently bought Time Warner, arguing that the stock price doesn't account for increasing assets--yet.

No investor, though, is a clone of Buffett, and one key difference for Torray and Eby is their willingness to invest in technology firms. They call recent purchase EMC a poster child of their approach. They say it's a top-quartile business that recently sold at a bottom-quartile price. When the

digital-storage titan's quarterly earnings number disappointed Wall Street in April 2006, the shares sank from $14 to below $10 in three months. This fund's skippers say the shortfall came because the firm temporarily couldn't meet customer demand and had made a savvy acquisition. Their analysis, though, points to why Buffett would stay away: Prices constantly drop in digital storage, even as demand continually rises. That balance isn't precarious, but Buffett prefers less tricky stuff.

It's crucial to grasp that this investing style swings in and out of favor. Indeed, from Jan. 1, 2003, through Oct. 31, 2006, the fund's 11.0% annualized return badly lags the S&P 500 Index's 14.5% gain. But many Buffett-style investments have suffered lately; Berkshire Hathaway has only gained 10.7% annually over that stretch. Long term, this fund has delivered rich rewards. Its 13% annualized gain since its late 1990 inception tops 90% of large-blend category peers.

Investors can expect a bright future here.

Address:	6610 Rockledge Drive Bethesda, MD 20817 800-626-9769	Minimum Purchase:	$10000	Add: $500	IRA: $10000
		Min Auto Inv Plan:	$500	Add: $500	
		Sales Fees:	No-load		
Web Address:	www.torray.com	Management Fee:	1.00%		
Inception:	12-18-90	Actual Fees:	Mgt:1.00%	Dist: —	
Advisor:	Torray LLC	Expense Projections:	3Yr:$340	5Yr:$590	10Yr:$1306
Subadvisor:	None	Income Distrib:	Quarterly		
NTF Plans:	Schwab OneSource				

MORNINGSTAR® Funds 500

Touchstn Dvrsf S/C Val Z

	Ticker	Load	NAV	Yield	Total Assets	Mstar Category
	TCSVX	None	$19.24	0.0%	$262 mil	Small Value

Governance and Management

Stewardship Grade:

Portfolio Manager(s)

Lawrence Creatura and Mike Jones have been at the helm since the fund's 1996 inception. Jones also comanages Touchstone Value Opportunities, which has posted mixed results in recent years. They are assisted by seven industry analysts, most of whom have been with subadvisor Clover Capital Management for more than a decade. Management and analysts receive bonus compensation quarterly, based on their performance over the past quarter, 12 months, and three years. To our dismay, the bonus plan is short-term focused in orientation, weighting the quarterly and 12-month periods most heavily.

Strategy

Managers Lawrence Creatura and Mike Jones favor a big-picture approach, evaluating economic conditions and industry trends before analyzing individual stocks. The pair focuses on small stocks because they think those are often the market's most undervalued issues. The fund's market cap tends to be below the category average, although it has risen as assets have grown. Creatura and Jones have also been willing to make large sector bets on occasion. The managers will venture into more-growth-oriented sectors such as health care and technology when they are cheap enough.

Performance 12-31-06

	1st Qtr	2nd Qtr	3rd Qtr	4th Qtr	Total
2002	6.99	-6.19	-22.37	1.70	-20.75
2003	-10.32	24.85	11.22	16.69	45.32
2004	6.95	2.38	-3.30	13.47	20.14
2005	-3.93	2.59	3.99	0.56	3.06
2006	13.49	-4.13	-0.87	7.39	15.83

Trailing	Total Return%	+/- S&P 500	+/- Russ 2000 VL	%Rank Cat	Growth of $10,000
3 Mo	7.39	0.69	-1.64	77	10,739
6 Mo	6.45	-6.29	-5.36	79	10,645
1 Yr	15.83	0.04	-7.65	56	11,583
3 Yr Avg	12.77	2.33	-3.71	73	14,341
5 Yr Avg	10.56	4.37	-4.81	89	16,519
10 Yr Avg	13.51	5.09	0.24	26	35,509
15 Yr Avg	—	—	—		

Tax Analysis	Tax-Adj Rtn%	%Rank Cat	Tax-Cost Rat	%Rank Cat
3 Yr (estimated)	9.78	78	2.65	82
5 Yr (estimated)	8.76	90	1.63	70
10 Yr (estimated)	11.81	25	1.50	66

Potential Capital Gain Exposure: 7% of assets

Historical Profile

Return Average
Risk Above Avg
Rating ★★ Below Avg

		97%	93%	100%	89%	99%	95%	99%	100%	99%

Investment Style
Equity
Stock %

▼ Manager Change
▽ Partial Manager Change

Growth of $10,000
— Investment Values of Fund
— Investment Values of S&P 500

38.0
31.0
24.0
17.0
10.0

Performance Quartile (within Category)

1995	1996	1997	1998	1999	2000	2001	2002	2003	2004	2005	2006	History
—	12.11	12.80	12.79	15.26	15.39	19.55	15.45	22.44	26.96	23.27	19.24	NAV
—	22.72*	15.47	2.01	29.57	10.59	27.42	-20.75	45.32	20.14	3.06	15.83	Total Return %
—	—	-17.89	-26.57	8.53	19.69	39.31	1.35	16.64	9.26	-1.85	0.04	+/-S&P 500
—	—	-16.31	8.46	31.06	-12.24	13.40	-9.32	-0.71	-2.11	-1.65	-7.65	+/-Russ 2000 VL
—	—	0.00	0.00	0.00	0.00	0.36	0.26	0.05	0.00	0.00	0.00	Income Return %
—	—	15.47	2.01	29.57	10.59	27.06	-21.01	45.27	20.14	3.06	15.83	Capital Return %
—	—	100	13	8	78	13	98	30	58	79	56	Total Rtn % Rank Cat
—	0.03	0.00	0.00	0.00	0.00	0.05	0.05	0.01	0.00	0.00	0.00	Income $
—	0.13	1.17	0.25	1.24	1.39	0.00	0.00	0.00	0.00	4.53	7.79	Capital Gains $
—	—	1.40	1.40	1.40	1.40	1.40	1.28	1.26	1.27	1.22	—	Expense Ratio %
—	—	-0.03	-0.64	-0.50	-0.10	-0.11	0.37	0.31	0.08	-0.09	—	Income Ratio %
—	—	14	59	70	80	142	120	38	52	61	—	Turnover Rate %
—	6	15	17	20	37	412	503	480	592	262		Net Assets $mil

Rating and Risk

Time Period	Load-Adj Return %	Morningstar Rtn vs Cat	Morningstar Risk vs Cat	Morningstar Risk-Adj Rating
1 Yr	15.83			
3 Yr	12.77	-Avg	Avg	★★
5 Yr	10.56	-Avg	+Avg	★
10 Yr	13.51	+Avg	+Avg	★★★
Incept	14.55			

Other Measures	Standard Index S&P 500	Best Fit Index Russ 2000
Alpha	-1.0	0.6
Beta	1.51	0.85
R-Squared	72	95
Standard Deviation	12.19	
Mean	12.77	
Sharpe Ratio	0.78	

Portfolio Analysis 09-30-06

Share change since 08-06 Total Stocks:155	Sector	PE	Tot Ret%	% Assets
⊖ Felcor Lodging Trust, In	Financial	—	31.79	2.14
⊖ Phillips-Van Heusen Corp	Goods	20.7	55.45	1.44
⊖ Mid-America Apartment Co	Financial	—	23.26	1.22
⊖ Avista Corporation	Utilities	15.2	46.53	1.22
⊖ Fairchild Semiconductor	Hardware	92.0	-0.59	1.12
⊖ PFF Bancorp, Inc.	Financial	15.4	15.38	1.12
⊖ Advanta B	Financial	16.2	37.83	1.09
⊖ OM Group, Inc.	Ind Mtrls	8.2	141.37	1.06
⊖ Carolina Group	Financial	—	52.24	1.05
⊖ Wolverine World Wide	Goods	19.8	28.51	1.05
⊖ First Midwest Bancorp	Financial	17.0	13.70	0.93
⊖ Dollar Thrifty Automotiv	Consumer	17.0	26.45	0.93
⊖ Domino's Pizza, Inc.	Consumer	16.0	17.90	0.91
⊖ Hot Topic, Inc.	Consumer	32.4	-6.39	0.91
⊖ Sterling Bancshares, Inc	Financial	20.1	28.52	0.89
⊖ West Coast Bancorp	Financial	18.5	32.97	0.89
⊖ Prosperity Bancshares, I	Financial	18.6	21.60	0.88
⊖ H.B. Fuller Company	Ind Mtrls	19.1	62.81	0.87
⊖ Rent-A-Center, Inc.	Consumer	14.5	56.47	0.86
⊖ Flowserve Corporation	Ind Mtrls	39.2	27.58	0.86

Current Investment Style

Value Blnd Growth — Large Mid Small

Market Cap	%
Giant	0.0
Large	0.0
Mid	32.1
Small	54.0
Micro	14.0

Avg $mil: 1,218

Value Measures		Rel Category
Price/Earnings	15.81	1.03
Price/Book	2.04	1.15
Price/Sales	0.84	1.05
Price/Cash Flow	6.00	0.98
Dividend Yield %	1.17	0.74

Growth Measures	%	Rel Category
Long-Term Erngs	12.04	0.96
Book Value	3.64	0.67
Sales	9.06	1.22
Cash Flow	15.98	1.95
Historical Erngs	12.97	1.14

Profitability	%	Rel Category
Return on Equity	9.62	0.89
Return on Assets	6.11	1.00
Net Margin	9.74	1.08

Sector Weightings

	% of Stocks	Rel S&P 500	3 Year High	Low
⟳ Info	12.68	0.63		
Software	3.71	1.08	4	2
Hardware	7.85	0.85	9	4
Media	0.00	0.00	3	0
Telecom	1.12	0.32	1	0
⟐ Service	57.59	1.25		
Health	4.32	0.36	9	4
Consumer	11.01	1.44	13	8
Business	8.33	1.97	13	8
Financial	33.93	1.52	35	26
⟐ Mfg	29.73	0.88		
Goods	8.45	0.99	9	5
Ind Mtrls	11.78	0.99	16	9
Energy	3.48	0.36	8	3
Utilities	6.02	1.72	9	5

Composition

● Cash	0.3
● Stocks	98.9
● Bonds	0.0
● Other	0.8
Foreign	0.8
(% of Stock)	

Morningstar's Take by Christopher Davis 12-28-06

Touchstone Diversified Small Cap Value's name is new, but it's the same uninspiring choice.

This offering, formerly named Constellation Clover Small Cap Value, is still run by subadvisor Clover Capital and managers Lawrence Creatura, Mike Jones, and Stephen Gutch. But the fund is now sold under the marketing umbrella of Touchstone Investments. Touchstone sells mainly through advisors, so it closed this no-load share class to new investors, making it available only through load-bearing channels. The new broker-sold share classes aren't cheap. At 1.57% annually, the annual expense ratio for this fund's A-shares is well above the levy charged by the typical small cap fund with front loads.

The fund's appeal wouldn't be all that great, though, even with a lower price tag. Our chief criticism of it has long been its history of high volatility and erratic returns. Management has attempted to address this concern in recent years, reining in sector bets and limiting position sizes to 2% of assets or less. It also has used risk-monitoring software to spot unintended bets, such as overexposure to high-volatility stocks. Management's efforts have reduced volatility: The fund's three-year standard deviation (a measure of volatility) is now average, relative to the small-value norm.

Yet management's risk-reduction efforts haven't kept the fund out of the category's cellar: Last year, it ranked in the bottom quartile with a meager 3% gain. It's fared better in 2006 in absolute terms (it's up 15% through December 27), but a wayward technology bet has kept it in the middle of the pack.

True, the fund boasts some favorable attributes, such as its experienced management and excellent 10-year record. However, its past successes were early on in the fund's history, when its asset base was smaller and stake in higher-returning micro-caps was higher. All in all, this offering is an unappealing package.

Address:	1205 Westlakes Drive Berwyn, PA 19312 800-543-0407	Minimum Purchase:	$2500	Add: $50	IRA: $2000
		Min Auto Inv Plan:	$100	Add: $50	
Web Address:	www.constellationfundsgroup.com	Sales Fees:	No-load		
Inception:	02-28-96 *	Management Fee:	0.85%		
Advisor:	Touchstone Advisors Inc	Actual Fees:	Mgt:0.85%	Dist: —	
Subadvisor:	Clover Capital Management Inc	Expense Projections:	3Yr:$417	5Yr:$723	10Yr:$1589
		Income Distrib:	Quarterly		
NTF Plans:	Fidelity Retail-NTF, Schwab OneSource				

Touchstn Snds Cp Sel Gr Z

Ticker	Load	NAV	Yield	Total Assets	Mstar Category
PTSGX	None	$7.77	0.0%	$570 mil	Large Growth

Governance and Management

Stewardship Grade:

Portfolio Manager(s)

This fund is managed by Sands Capital Management, which is well regarded in institutional circles. Sands, which has one large-cap growth strategy, has a 10-person investment staff, including the fund's three named managers--Frank Sands Sr., the firm's chief investment officer, Frank Sands Jr., the firm's director of research, and David Levanson, a senior portfolio manager and research analyst. Levanson, who has completed stints at State Street Research & Management and MFS Investments, has primary oversight responsibilities for the fund.

Strategy

The goal here is to own growing companies for the long haul. However, unlike many rivals, management tries to be conscious of valuations. This doesn't mean that the fund won't own richly priced stocks--it will when management thinks a firm's growth prospects are good enough to justify a high valuation--but it should keep the fund away from purely speculative fare. Finally, because turnover is low, we expect tax efficiency to be pretty good.

Historical Profile

Return	Average
Risk	Above Avg
Rating	★★★ Neutral

		99%	99%	100%	98%	96%	98%	98%		

▽ ▽

▼ Manager Change
▽ Partial Manager Change

Growth of $10,000
- — Investment Values of Fund
- — Investment Values of S&P 500

10.0
6.0
4.0

Performance Quartile (within Category)

1995	1996	1997	1998	1999	2000	2001	2002	2003	2004	2005	2006	History
—	—	—	—	—	7.63	6.47	4.65	6.37	7.58	8.31	7.77	NAV
—	—	—	—	—	-23.67*	-15.20	-28.13	36.99	19.00	9.63	-6.50	Total Return %
—	—	—	—	—		-3.31	-6.03	8.31	8.12	4.72	-22.29	+/-S&P 500
—	—	—	—	—		5.22	-0.25	7.24	12.70	4.37	-15.57	+/-Russ 1000Gr
—	—	—	—	—		0.00	0.00	0.00	0.00	0.00	0.00	Income Return %
—	—	—	—	—		-15.20	-28.13	36.99	19.00	9.63	-6.50	Capital Return %
—	—	—	—	—		28	58	12	1	23	99	Total Rtn % Rank Cat
—	—	—	—	—		0.00	0.00	0.00	0.00	0.00	0.00	Income $
—	—	—	—	—		0.00	0.00	0.00	0.00	0.00	0.00	Capital Gains $
—	—	—	—	—			1.16	1.17	1.20	—		Expense Ratio %
—	—	—	—	—			-0.69	-0.81	-0.95	—		Income Ratio %
—	—	—	—	—			37	24	28	11	—	Turnover Rate %
—	—	—	—	—		45	44	30	47	74	380	Net Assets $mil

Performance 12-31-06

	1st Qtr	2nd Qtr	3rd Qtr	4th Qtr	Total
2002	-2.78	-15.90	-18.15	7.39	-28.13
2003	3.66	14.52	6.70	8.15	36.99
2004	6.12	4.88	-4.09	11.47	19.00
2005	-9.10	7.55	5.26	6.54	9.63
2006	-1.93	-7.98	0.93	2.64	-6.50

Trailing	Total Return%	+/- S&P 500	+/- Russ 1000Gr	%Rank Cat	Growth of $10,000
3 Mo	2.64	-4.06	-3.29	98	10,264
6 Mo	3.60	-9.14	-6.50	94	10,360
1 Yr	-6.50	-22.29	-15.57	99	9,350
3 Yr Avg	6.85	-3.59	-0.02	51	12,199
5 Yr Avg	3.73	-2.46	1.04	33	12,009
10 Yr Avg	—	—	—	—	—
15 Yr Avg	—	—	—	—	—

Tax Analysis	Tax-Adj Rtn%	%Rank Cat	Tax-Cost Rat	%Rank Cat
3 Yr (estimated)	6.85	42	0.00	1
5 Yr (estimated)	3.73	28	0.00	1
10 Yr (estimated)	—	—	—	—

Potential Capital Gain Exposure: -1% of assets

Morningstar's Take by Reginald Laing 12-22-06

This renamed fund's underperformance might make it more attractive, not less.

As a result of Touchstone Investments' recent acquisition of Constellation Investment Management, this fund has been renamed Touchstone Sands Capital Select Growth. Its subadvisor, Sands Capital Management, remains the same, though.

That Sands is staying in place is a good thing. The firm is well respected in the institutional realm, and this fund's separate-account clone has one of the best long-term records among large-growth portfolios in our database. Recent performance hasn't been stellar, though: For the trailing 12 months through Dec. 21, 2006, the retail fund's 8.3% loss trailed the returns of nearly all its peers.

Because of this fund's concentration in 25 to 30 stocks, as well as its willingness to pay up for aggressive-growth companies, it will have setbacks when one or two holdings disappoint market expectations for earnings or revenue growth. That's

been the case lately, with top holdings such as online auctioneer eBay and generic drugmaker Teva Pharmaceuticals posting steep losses in 2006. But they remain top holdings in this low-turnover fund; indeed, they may be more attractive now, as they're a good deal cheaper.

Beyond the losses from individual holdings, though, this fund's style has also been out of favor for some time, as value stocks have far outpaced the high-growth firms the portfolio specializes in. But if that situation reverses itself, and fallen growth stocks like Teva return to market prominence, look for this fund to surge.

Our reservation about this fund is its high expense ratio. At 1.36%, it's well above the 1.0% median for similar no-load offerings. The 0.86% management fee here seems reasonable enough, and we hope Touchstone finds a way to trim administrative costs once its acquisition of Constellation is complete. A lower expense ratio would make this fund even more appealing.

Rating and Risk

Time Period	Load-Adj Return %	Morningstar Rtn vs Cat	Morningstar Risk vs Cat	Morningstar Risk-Adj Rating
1 Yr	-6.50			
3 Yr	6.85	Avg	+Avg	★★★
5 Yr	3.73	Avg	+Avg	★★★
10 Yr	—	—	—	
Incept	-3.87			

Other Measures	Standard Index S&P 500	Best Fit Index Mstar Large Growth
Alpha	-5.1	3.8
Beta	1.31	1.13
R-Squared	58	78
Standard Deviation	11.74	
Mean	6.85	
Sharpe Ratio	0.35	

Portfolio Analysis 09-30-06

Share change since 08-06 Total Stocks:25

	Sector	PE	Tot Ret%	% Assets
⊕ Google, Inc.	Business	61.5	11.00	9.76
⊕ Starbucks Corporation	Consumer	49.3	18.03	8.01
⊕ Genentech, Inc.	Health	48.7	-12.29	6.76
⊕ Genzyme Corporation	Health	50.8	-13.00	5.11
⊕ Chicago Mercantile Excha	Financial	49.3	39.48	5.04
⊕ Allergan, Inc.	Health	—	11.33	4.92
⊕ Apple Computer, Inc.	Hardware	37.6	18.01	4.54
⊕ Teva Pharmaceutical Indu	Health	20.7	-27.22	4.39
⊕ eBay, Inc.	Consumer	40.1	-30.43	4.35
⊕ Lowe's Companies Inc.	Consumer	15.6	-6.05	4.33
⊕ Apollo Group, Inc. A	Consumer	15.9	-35.54	4.08
⊕ Moody's Corporation	Business	32.6	12.95	3.95
⊕ America Movil SA ADR	Telecom	27.7	55.53	3.65
⊕ Qualcomm, Inc.	Hardware	26.6	-11.32	3.54
⊕ Walgreen Company	Consumer	26.6	4.36	3.36
⊕ Varian Medical Systems,	Health	26.8	-5.50	3.12
⊕ Yahoo, Inc.	Media	35.4	-34.81	2.91
⊕ IntercontinentalExchange	Financial	—	—	2.88
⊕ Schlumberger, Ltd.	Energy	22.3	31.07	2.70
⊕ Red Hat, Inc.	Software	58.8	-15.63	2.13

Current Investment Style

Value Blnd Growth — Large Mid Small

Market Cap	%
Giant	31.6
Large	51.2
Mid	17.3
Small	0.0
Micro	0.0

Avg $mil: 28,294

Value Measures		Rel Category
Price/Earnings	30.23	1.57
Price/Book	5.65	1.70
Price/Sales	3.76	1.94
Price/Cash Flow	18.33	1.61
Dividend Yield %	0.21	0.20

Growth Measures	%	Rel Category
Long-Term Erngs	20.72	1.44
Book Value	18.56	1.60
Sales	22.09	1.90
Cash Flow	31.46	1.87
Historical Erngs	44.47	1.93

Profitability	%	Rel Category
Return on Equity	19.75	0.97
Return on Assets	13.76	1.25
Net Margin	17.04	1.20

Sector Weightings	% of Stocks	Rel S&P 500	3 Year High	Low
↻ Info	17.11	0.86		
Software	2.17	0.63	6	1
Hardware	8.24	0.89	15	7
Media	2.97	0.78	4	0
Telecom	3.73	1.06	4	0
☞ Service	80.14	1.73		
Health	32.07	2.66	37	23
Consumer	24.63	3.22	39	25
Business	15.36	3.63	15	2
Financial	8.08	0.36	10	5
Mfg	2.75	0.08		
Goods	0.00	0.00	8	0
Ind Mtrls	0.00	0.00	0	0
Energy	2.75	0.28	3	0
Utilities	0.00	0.00	0	0

Composition

● Cash	0.8	
● Stocks	98.0	
● Bonds	0.0	
● Other	1.2	
Foreign (% of Stock)	8.2	

Address:	1205 Westlakes Drive Berwyn, PA 19312 800-543-0407		
Web Address:	www.constellationfundsgroup.com		
Inception:	08-11-00*		
Advisor:	Touchstone Advisors Inc		
Subadvisor:	Sands Capital Management, LLC		
NTF Plans:	Fidelity Retail-NTF, Schwab OneSource		

Minimum Purchase:	$2500	Add: $50	IRA: $2000
Min Auto Inv Plan:	$100	Add: $50	
Sales Fees:	No-load, 0.25%S		
Management Fee:	0.85%		
Actual Fees:	Mgt:0.85%	Dist:0.25%	
Expense Projections:	3Yr:$447	5Yr:$778	10Yr:$1716
Income Distrib:	Quarterly		

MORNINGSTAR® Funds 500

Turner Midcap Growth

	Ticker	Load	NAV	Yield	Total Assets	Mstar Category
	TMGFX	None	$29.21	0.0%	$1,131 mil	Mid-Cap Growth

Governance and Management

Stewardship Grade: B

Portfolio Manager(s)

Lead manager Chris McHugh has run the fund successfully since its 1996 inception. He started as an analyst with Turner Investment Partners in 1990 and has been a member of its technology sector team since then. Longtime analysts Tara Hedlund and Jason Schrotberger came aboard as comanagers in September 2006. A group of sector-focused analysts contribute ideas to this and other Turner funds.

Strategy

Like other Turner funds, this one hunts for stocks that exhibit accelerating earnings growth and positive price trends. Management will pay a premium for its high-momentum picks. That leads it to high-P/E stocks with sometimes stratospheric growth rates. It's pretty finicky about staying in mid-cap territory, and it keeps its sector weightings in line with the Russell Midcap Growth Index's.

Historical Profile
Return: Above Avg
Risk: Above Avg
Rating: ★★★ Neutral

Investment Style: Equity, Stock %

97% | 96% | 99% | 96% | 99% | 99% | 100% | 98% | 100%

▼ Manager Change
▽ Partial Manager Change

Growth of $10,000
— Investment Values of Fund
— Investment Values of S&P 500

43.6 / 32.4 / 24.0 / 17.0 / 10.0

Performance Quartile (within Category)

1995	1996	1997	1998	1999	2000	2001	2002	2003	2004	2005	2006	History
—	10.22	13.84	17.51	36.45	30.59	21.91	14.71	22.00	24.43	27.37	29.21	NAV
—	3.33*	40.56	26.52	125.45	-8.00	-28.38	-32.86	49.56	11.05	12.03	6.72	Total Return %
—	—	7.20	-2.06	104.41	1.10	-16.49	-10.76	20.88	0.17	7.12	-9.07	+/-S&P 500
—	—	18.02	8.66	74.16	3.75	-8.23	-5.45	6.85	-4.43	-0.07	-3.94	+/-Russ MG
—	—	0.00	0.00	0.00	0.00	0.00	0.00	0.00	0.00	0.00	0.00	Income Return %
—	—	40.56	26.52	125.45	-8.00	-28.38	-32.86	49.56	11.05	12.03	6.72	Capital Return %
—	—	3	23	7	61	80	84	5	71	35	65	Total Rtn % Rank Cat
—	0.00	0.00	0.00	0.00	0.00	0.00	0.00	0.00	0.00	0.00	0.00	Income $
—	0.11	0.50	0.00	2.70	3.07	0.00	0.00	0.00	0.00	0.00	0.00	Capital Gains $
—	—	—	1.25	1.23	1.03	1.03	1.04	1.05	1.15	1.16	—	Expense Ratio %
—	—	—	-0.62	-0.79	-0.58	-0.72	-0.77	-0.81	-0.87	-0.84	—	Income Ratio %
—	—	—	—	304	291	307	335	260	209	167	—	Turnover Rate %
—	—	2	13	35	333	937	749	652	877	998	1,125	Net Assets $mil

Performance 12-31-06

	1st Qtr	2nd Qtr	3rd Qtr	4th Qtr	Total
2002	-3.83	-19.55	-18.70	6.75	-32.86
2003	1.09	19.44	10.02	12.59	49.56
2004	3.23	-0.22	-7.37	16.39	11.05
2005	-2.54	3.49	7.10	3.71	12.03
2006	11.76	-6.73	-3.15	5.72	6.72

Trailing	Total Return%	+/- S&P 500	+/- Russ MG	%Rank Cat	Growth of $10,000
3 Mo	5.72	-0.98	-1.23	68	10,572
6 Mo	2.38	-10.36	-5.52	83	10,238
1 Yr	6.72	-9.07	-3.94	65	10,672
3 Yr Avg	9.91	-0.53	-2.82	61	13,277
5 Yr Avg	5.92	-0.27	-2.30	56	13,332
10 Yr Avg	13.42	5.00	4.80	9	35,229
15 Yr Avg	—	—	—		—

Tax Analysis	Tax-Adj Rtn%	%Rank Cat	Tax-Cost Rat	%Rank Cat
3 Yr (estimated)	9.91	48	0.00	1
5 Yr (estimated)	5.92	49	0.00	1
10 Yr (estimated)	12.51	6	0.80	25

Potential Capital Gain Exposure: -17% of assets

Rating and Risk

Time Period	Load-Adj Return %	Morningstar Rtn vs Cat	Morningstar Risk vs Cat	Morningstar Risk-Adj Rating
1 Yr	6.72			
3 Yr	9.91	Avg	+Avg	★★★
5 Yr	5.92	Avg	+Avg	★★
10 Yr	13.42	+Avg	+Avg	★★★
Incept	13.44			

Other Measures	Standard Index S&P 500	Best Fit Index Mstar Mid Growth TR
Alpha	-5.1	-4.5
Beta	1.78	1.12
R-Squared	70	96
Standard Deviation	14.52	
Mean	9.91	
Sharpe Ratio	0.50	

Portfolio Analysis 12-31-06

Share change since 11-06 Total Stocks:103	Sector	PE	Tot Ret%	% Assets
Coach, Inc.	Goods	32.1	28.85	2.68
International Game Tech.	Consumer	34.3	52.07	2.67
NII Holdings, Inc.	Telecom	45.9	47.53	2.59
KLA-Tencor Corporation	Hardware	28.9	1.88	1.83
Precision Castparts Corp	Ind Mtrls	25.4	51.40	1.80
Hilton Hotels Corporatio	Consumer	29.9	45.62	1.80
Celgene Corporation	Health	—	77.56	1.78
⊖ NVIDIA Corporation	Hardware	33.4	102.46	1.75
⊕ F5 Networks, Inc.	Hardware	49.5	29.76	1.74
NutriSystem, Inc.	Goods	33.2	75.99	1.64
Wynn Resorts, Ltd.	Consumer	—	82.52	1.61
⊖ Allergan, Inc.	Health	—	11.33	1.54
American Tower Corporati	Telecom	—	37.57	1.51
⊖ Akamai Technologies, Inc	Software	26.0	166.53	1.50
T Rowe Price Group	Financial	26.1	23.27	1.47
⊕ Range Resources Corporat	Energy	16.8	4.62	1.43
Thermo Fisher Scientific	Health	37.4	50.32	1.38
Polo Ralph Lauren Corpor	Goods	25.5	38.77	1.36
IntercontinentalExchange	Financial	—	—	1.34
⊕ Salesforce.com, Inc.	Software	—	13.73	1.33

Current Investment Style

Value Blnd Growth — Large / Mid / Small

Market Cap	%
Giant	0.0
Large	26.9
Mid	66.6
Small	6.5
Micro	0.0

Avg $mil: 6,176

Value Measures		Rel Category
Price/Earnings	26.37	1.29
Price/Book	3.96	1.23
Price/Sales	2.33	1.32
Price/Cash Flow	14.27	1.25
Dividend Yield %	0.34	0.54

Growth Measures	%	Rel Category
Long-Term Erngs	17.91	1.10
Book Value	13.18	1.04
Sales	11.72	1.17
Cash Flow	19.23	1.04
Historical Erngs	25.23	1.01

Profitability	%	Rel Category
Return on Equity	18.05	1.01
Return on Assets	9.37	1.00
Net Margin	12.12	1.04

Sector Weightings	% of Stocks	Rel S&P 500	3 Year High Low
Info	26.50	1.33	
Software	5.58	1.62	9 2
Hardware	15.37	1.66	22 11
Media	0.00	0.00	4 0
Telecom	5.55	1.58	7 0
Service	44.81	0.97	
Health	15.54	1.29	23 15
Consumer	9.48	1.24	17 9
Business	9.88	2.34	14 8
Financial	9.91	0.44	12 6
Mfg	28.69	0.85	
Goods	12.98	1.52	13 4
Ind Mtrls	7.47	0.63	12 4
Energy	8.24	0.84	13 3
Utilities	0.00	0.00	1 0

Composition

Cash	0.0	
Stocks	100.0	
Bonds	0.0	
Other	0.0	
Foreign (% of Stock)	2.8	

Morningstar's Take by Brian Smith 12-05-06

Turner Midcap Growth is a worthwhile fund but should only play a supporting role.

This high-flying growth fund looks for companies whose earnings are poised to take off. If earnings drive share prices, then superior earnings should ultimately result in higher share prices--much higher in some cases. Lead manager Chris McHugh will gladly pay a rich price if he feels that a company's growth prospects stand head and shoulders above its peers and above what is expected by the market. Nutri/System is a good example. The company has broadened its customer base by using well-known celebrities Dan Marino and Don Shula to market its weight loss products to men and retirees. Revenues have doubled, earnings have tripled, and the company's share price is up a whopping 92% in 2006 through early December.

Of course, not every holding pans out as well as Nutri/System. When anticipated earnings growth fails to materialize, underlying share prices often get hammered. Thus, the earnings momentum sought here makes the fund very volatile. It soared during the late 1990s but plummeted during the subsequent bear market. McHugh and his team attempt to dampen risk by owning about 120 stocks, as well as hewing closely to the sector allocation of the Russell Midcap Growth Index.

In addition to above-average volatility, the strategy can be costly. Overall fund expenses are in line with peers, but triple-digit annual turnover pushes up trading costs and potentially generates a lot of short-term taxable gains.

We do like the funds investment approach and McHugh's consistency with adhering to it. Long-term performance during his tenure has been solid. (The fund's middling three- and five-year returns are more a reflection of the fact that aggressive growth stocks have been in the doghouse for most of this decade.) Investors looking for a dedicated mid-cap fund to complement value-oriented funds will find it here, but we'd be prepared for bumps along the way.

Address:	1235 Westlakes Drive, Suite 350 Berwyn PA 19312 800-224-6312
Web Address:	www.turnerinvestments.com
Inception:	10-01-96*
Advisor:	Turner Investment Partners, Inc.
Subadvisor:	None
NTF Plans:	Fidelity Retail-NTF, Schwab OneSource

Minimum Purchase:	$2500	Add: $50	IRA: $2000
Min Auto Inv Plan:	$100	Add: $50	
Sales Fees:	No-load		
Management Fee:	0.75%, 0.15%A		
Actual Fees:	Mgt:0.75%	Dist: —	
Expense Projections:	3Yr:$381	5Yr:$660	10Yr:$1455
Income Distrib:	Annually		

Turner Small Cap Growth

	Ticker	Load	NAV	Yield	Total Assets	Mstar Category
	TSCEX	Closed	$28.76	0.0%	$283 mil	Small Growth

Governance and Management

Stewardship Grade: A

Portfolio Manager(s)

Prior to his arrival at Turner, Bill McVail ran BlackRock Small Cap Growth successfully for nearly five years. His specialty at Turner is the consumer-discretionary sector. Chris McHugh, Jason Schrotberger, and Frank Sustersic also serve as members of the fund's management team. Turner's employee retirement plan is among the largest owners of several of its funds.

Strategy

Manager Bill McVail looks at earnings momentum and technical factors to pick rapidly growing companies. He doesn't ignore valuation, but it clearly takes a backseat. As risky as that seems, he also requires strong fundamentals, limits individual positions to 2% of assets, and keeps the fund sector-neutral with respect to the Russell 2000 Growth Index.

Historical Profile

Return	Average
Risk	Above Avg
Rating	★★★ Neutral

Investment Style Percentages: 100% | 96% | 100% | 100% | 97% | 97% | 98% | 98% | 95%

Investment Style
Equity
Stock %

Growth of $10,000
— Investment Values of Fund
— Investment Values of S&P 500

64.6 / 46.4 / 33.8 / 24.0 / 17.0 / 10.0

▼ Manager Change
▽ Partial Manager Change

Performance Quartile (within Category)

1995	1996	1997	1998	1999	2000	2001	2002	2003	2004	2005	2006	History
17.37	21.86	24.62	26.72	41.49	24.73	20.07	13.44	21.42	23.97	25.37	28.76	NAV
68.16	28.85	14.97	8.53	85.04	-14.38	-18.84	-33.03	59.38	11.90	5.84	13.36	Total Return %
30.58	5.89	-18.39	-20.05	64.00	-5.28	-6.95	-10.93	30.70	1.02	0.93	-2.43	+/-S&P 500
37.12	17.59	2.02	7.30	41.95	8.05	-9.61	-2.77	10.84	-2.41	1.69	0.01	+/-Russ 2000 Gr
0.00	0.00	0.00	0.00	0.00	0.00	0.00	0.00	0.00	0.00	0.00	0.00	Income Return %
68.16	28.85	14.97	8.53	85.04	-14.38	-18.84	-33.03	59.38	11.90	5.84	13.36	Capital Return %
1	10	62	34	24	75	78	75	13	51	50	27	Total Rtn % Rank Cat
0.00	0.00	0.00	0.00	0.00	0.00	0.00	0.00	0.00	0.00	0.00	0.00	Income $
1.04	0.51	0.48	0.00	7.18	10.47	0.00	0.00	0.00	0.00	0.00	0.00	Capital Gains $
1.25	1.25	1.24	1.25	1.25	1.25	1.25	1.25	1.25	1.25	1.25	1.25	Expense Ratio %
-0.68	-0.88	-0.84	-0.99	-0.98	-0.94	-0.96	-0.99	-0.79	-0.95	-0.91	-0.79	Income Ratio %
183	149	131	168	224	203	176	188	188	151	153	154	Turnover Rate %
17	74	153	189	379	368	286	147	228	264	262	283	Net Assets $mil

Performance 12-31-06

	1st Qtr	2nd Qtr	3rd Qtr	4th Qtr	Total
2002	-3.59	-17.42	-21.03	6.50	-33.03
2003	-3.05	27.78	13.39	13.45	59.38
2004	3.41	0.95	-4.61	12.38	11.90
2005	-7.30	3.83	6.98	2.80	5.84
2006	17.11	-8.08	-4.14	9.85	13.36

Trailing	Total Return%	+/- S&P 500	+/- Russ 2000 Gr	%Rank Cat	Growth of $10,000
3 Mo	9.85	3.15	1.08	16	10,985
6 Mo	5.31	-7.43	-1.55	48	10,531
1 Yr	13.36	-2.43	0.01	27	11,336
3 Yr Avg	10.32	-0.12	-0.19	38	13,426
5 Yr Avg	7.46	1.27	0.53	40	14,330
10 Yr Avg	8.68	0.26	3.80	48	22,988
15 Yr Avg	—	—	—	—	—

Tax Analysis	Tax-Adj Rtn%	%Rank Cat	Tax-Cost Rat	%Rank Cat
3 Yr (estimated)	10.32	26	0.00	1
5 Yr (estimated)	7.46	32	0.00	1
10 Yr (estimated)	6.83	49	1.70	71

Potential Capital Gain Exposure: -15% of assets

Rating and Risk

Time Period	Load-Adj Return %	Morningstar Rtn vs Cat	Morningstar Risk vs Cat	Morningstar Risk-Adj Rating
1 Yr	13.36			
3 Yr	10.32	Avg	+Avg	★★★
5 Yr	7.46	Avg	+Avg	★★★
10 Yr	8.68	Avg	+Avg	★★
Incept	14.08			

Other Measures	Standard Index S&P 500	Best Fit Index Russ 2000 Gr
Alpha	-5.7	-0.2
Beta	1.95	1.02
R-Squared	67	96
Standard Deviation	16.41	
Mean	10.32	
Sharpe Ratio	0.48	

Morningstar's Take by Paul Herbert 12-21-06

This fund is volatile, but in all it's a good choice for more-assertive investors.

For confirmation of the ups and downs that this fund can experience, you don't have to look any further than its 2006 showing. It shot out of the gate during the first quarter, but gave back the lion's share of those gains during the subsequent two quarters. Small-cap stocks, including some of the same ones that helped propel the fund early on, took it on the chin. Yet it's rebounded nicely of late, returning more than 8% so far during the quarter (through December 20) as small cap stocks have rallied. Strong security selection has helped amplify returns. Our analysis has shown that the top 10 holdings (as of the end of November) have returned an average of 26% during the same timeframe, with high-flying New River Pharmaceuticals up an incredible 155%.

These kinds of showings are common for funds like this one. Manager Bill McVail and his colleagues look for companies with steep earnings trajectories. Their stocks frequently deliver outstanding gains early in their lives, as investors catch on that their businesses are improving. During the 1990s, this fund shot the lights out as small, growing firms rallied. But such stocks often command lofty prices, and usually get taken down hard when uncertainty enters the picture.

McVail and his team know these tendencies well, and take steps such as selling stocks at the first hint of trouble and picking up those that have beaten expectations but haven't yet seen their prices jump. Plus, the firm has helped the managers out by closing the fund to new investors so they can keep fishing in small-cap waters and keeping the fund's costs relatively low.

These factors combine to smooth out the rough edges inherent in the fund's approach. Still, it's only appropriate for folks who can tolerate some bumps in the road.

Portfolio Analysis 12-31-06

Share change since 11-06 Total Stocks:116

Sector		PE	Tot Ret%	% Assets
Varian Semiconductor Equ	Hardware	27.6	55.43	1.90
Psychiatric Solutions, I	Health	43.7	27.75	1.72
Polycom, Inc.	Hardware	50.6	102.03	1.55
West Pharmaceutical Serv	Goods	28.8	107.69	1.53
New River Pharmaceutical	Health	—	110.91	1.36
Administaff, Inc.	Business	26.0	2.61	1.30
aQuantive, Inc.	Business	45.9	-2.30	1.26
Digital River, Inc.	Business	38.3	87.59	1.22
Cymer, Inc.	Hardware	19.9	23.77	1.21
Time Warner Telecom, Inc	Telecom	—	102.34	1.18
United Natural Foods, In	Consumer	31.1	36.06	1.18
Medicis Pharmaceuticals	Health	—	10.05	1.18
⊕ Cenveo, Inc.	Business	21.6	61.09	1.16
Phillips-Van Heusen Corp	Goods	20.7	55.45	1.16
WMS Industries, Inc.	Consumer	38.0	38.94	1.16
⊕ Iconix Brand Group, Inc.	Goods	42.7	90.29	1.13
⊕ VistaPrint, Ltd.	Business	—	—	1.13
Comtech Group, Inc.	Ind Mtrls	44.6	192.92	1.12
Guess ?, Inc.	Goods	29.8	78.17	1.12
Under Armour, Inc. A	Goods	—	—	1.08

Current Investment Style

Value Blnd Growth — Large Mid Small

	%
Market Cap	
Giant	0.0
Large	0.0
Mid	32.4
Small	64.2
Micro	3.4
Avg $mil:	1,449

Value Measures		Rel Category
Price/Earnings	25.19	1.20
Price/Book	3.70	1.36
Price/Sales	1.73	1.10
Price/Cash Flow	8.69	0.90
Dividend Yield %	0.51	1.11

Growth Measures	%	Rel Category
Long-Term Erngs	18.57	1.05
Book Value	6.22	0.59
Sales	9.09	0.76
Cash Flow	28.82	1.36
Historical Erngs	22.09	0.91

Profitability	%	Rel Category
Return on Equity	12.80	1.03
Return on Assets	6.31	0.95
Net Margin	7.47	0.86

Sector Weightings

	% of Stocks	Rel S&P 500	3 Year High	Low
↻ Info	19.74	0.99		
🖥 Software	6.06	1.76	13	3
💻 Hardware	11.12	1.20	19	11
🎬 Media	0.00	0.00	2	0
📞 Telecom	2.56	0.73	5	1
⊕ Service	53.11	1.15		
🏥 Health	17.13	1.42	23	16
🛒 Consumer	8.24	1.08	15	7
📋 Business	18.60	4.40	19	9
💲 Financial	9.14	0.41	12	8
⚒ Mfg	27.14	0.80		
🏭 Goods	9.79	1.15	10	1
🔧 Ind Mtrls	12.28	1.03	13	9
🔥 Energy	5.07	0.52	8	2
💡 Utilities	0.00	0.00	1	0

Composition

	%
● Cash	4.5
● Stocks	94.8
● Bonds	0.0
● Other	0.7
Foreign	3.7
(% of Stock)	

Address:	1235 Westlakes Drive, Suite 350 Berwyn PA 19312 800-224-6312
Web Address:	www.turnerinvestments.com
Inception:	02-07-94
Advisor:	Turner Investment Partners, Inc.
Subadvisor:	None
NTF Plans:	Fidelity Retail-NTF, Schwab OneSource

Minimum Purchase:	Closed	Add: —	IRA: —
Min Auto Inv Plan:	Closed	Add: —	
Sales Fees:	No-load		
Management Fee:	1.00%, 0.15%A		
Actual Fees:	Mgt:1.00%	Dist: —	
Expense Projections:	3Yr:$456	5Yr:$787	10Yr:$1724
Income Distrib:	Annually		

MORNINGSTAR® Funds 500

Tweedy, Browne American

	Ticker	Load	NAV	Yield	Total Assets	Mstar Category
	TWEBX	Closed	$24.33	1.0%	$531 mil	Mid-Cap Value

Governance and Management

Stewardship Grade: A

Portfolio Manager(s)

Longtime managers William Browne, Christopher Browne, and John Spears are old-school value investors who follow the disciplines of Ben Graham and Warren Buffett. They also manage the respected Tweedy, Browne Global Value. The three, along with many other Tweedy, Browne personnel, have sizable personal investments in the funds.

Strategy

The fund's managers buy stocks that are trading at discounts to their assessments of companies' private-market values. They also look for stocks with insider buying, citing empirical studies that show such stocks outperform. Management buys stocks of all sizes including megacaps, so the portfolio tends to have one of the largest average market caps in the mid-value category.

Performance 12-31-06

	1st Qtr	2nd Qtr	3rd Qtr	4th Qtr	Total
2002	2.82	-5.36	-17.42	5.88	-14.91
2003	-4.73	11.39	4.55	11.08	23.24
2004	2.14	0.29	-1.06	7.98	9.42
2005	-2.76	1.26	2.40	1.46	2.30
2006	2.10	0.04	5.31	3.77	11.62

Trailing	Total Return%	+/- S&P 500	+/- Russ MV	%Rank Cat	Growth of $10,000
3 Mo	3.77	-2.93	-4.73	99	10,377
6 Mo	9.28	-3.46	-3.05	68	10,928
1 Yr	11.62	-4.17	-8.60	88	11,162
3 Yr Avg	7.71	-2.73	-11.06	95	12,496
5 Yr Avg	5.55	-0.64	-10.33	98	13,101
10 Yr Avg	8.81	0.39	-4.84	81	23,264
15 Yr Avg	—	—	—		—

Tax Analysis	Tax-Adj Rtn%	%Rank Cat	Tax-Cost Rat	%Rank Cat
3 Yr (estimated)	6.36	92	1.25	45
5 Yr (estimated)	4.60	97	0.90	38
10 Yr (estimated)	7.82	71	0.91	19

Potential Capital Gain Exposure: 47% of assets

Morningstar's Take by Arijit Dutta 11-30-06

A change at Tweedy, Browne American Value should improve its prospects.

As of Dec. 11, this fund's new ceiling on foreign holdings will be 50% of assets, up from its previous limit of 20%. Management says it wants to raise stakes in existing foreign names and buy a large-cap foreign stock or two, but hasn't been able to do so because the portfolio has been pushing up against the 20% barrier for a number of years. That said, management doesn't foresee going much beyond 20%, so U.S. stocks will still compose the lion's share of this portfolio.

The change should alleviate a key concern here. Although the fund closed last year, management hasn't found enough attractively priced stocks to soak up the portfolio's large cash stake (as of September 2006, it had a 12% cash stake, while the mid-value category average is 5%). With added flexibility to invest more overseas, management should be able to put the cash to work. That could help performance, because holding cash has held

the fund back in generally strong equity markets.

Indeed, performance has also lagged due to other reasons. The portfolio is loaded with stable, cash-rich financials and has minimal exposure to more economically sensitive areas like industrial materials and energy. That stance has not been favorable at all for the past several years.

We would not overlook the potential benefits of the fund's approach however. Management's top priority is to not lose money, so it sticks to companies with solid balance sheets that it can own for years and only buys them when the stock price affords a wide margin of safety. This valuation-conscious, low-turnover approach continues to protect investors' capital in times of market distress (most recently, the fund held up better than just about all rivals during the market correction in May and June of this year). Thus, the fund's case as a risk-averse option is still solid, and we'd keep in mind that market conditions won't always be against it.

Address:	350 Park Ave New York NY 10022 800-432-4789	Minimum Purchase:	Closed	Add: —	IRA: —
		Min Auto Inv Plan:	Closed	Add: —	
		Sales Fees:	No-load		
Web Address:	www.tweedy.com	Management Fee:	1.25%		
Inception:	12-08-93	Actual Fees:	Mgt:1.25%	Dist: —	
Advisor:	Tweedy, Browne Company LLC	Expense Projections:	3Yr:$431	5Yr:$745	10Yr:$1635
Subadvisor:	None	Income Distrib:	Annually		
NTF Plans:	N/A				

Historical Profile

Return	Below Avg
Risk	Low
Rating	★★ Below Avg

	86%	91%	91%	95%	95%	95%	88%	90%	87%

Investment Style
Equity
Stock %

▼ Manager Change
▽ Partial Manager Change

Growth of $10,000
— Investment Values of Fund
— Investment Values of S&P 500

Performance Quartile (within Category)

1995	1996	1997	1998	1999	2000	2001	2002	2003	2004	2005	2006	History
13.25	15.64	21.11	22.74	22.37	24.42	23.42	19.45	23.87	25.37	23.77	24.33	NAV
36.21	22.45	38.87	9.59	2.00	14.45	-0.08	-14.91	23.24	9.42	2.30	11.62	Total Return %
-1.37	-0.51	5.51	-18.99	-19.04	23.55	11.81	7.19	-5.44	-1.46	-2.61	-4.17	+/-S&P 500
1.28	2.19	4.50	4.51	2.11	-4.73	-2.41	-5.27	-14.83	-14.29	-10.35	-8.60	+/-Russ MV
1.08	1.29	1.07	0.67	1.21	0.46	0.33	0.43	0.51	1.63	1.30	1.14	Income Return %
35.13	21.16	37.80	8.92	0.79	13.99	-0.41	-15.34	22.73	7.79	1.00	10.48	Capital Return %
7	38	1	21	63	74	75	74	94	98	89	88	Total Rtn % Rank Cat
0.11	0.17	0.17	0.14	0.28	0.10	0.08	0.10	0.10	0.39	0.33	0.27	Income $
0.02	0.42	0.43	0.25	0.53	1.08	0.90	0.37	0.00	0.36	1.86	1.94	Capital Gains $
1.74	1.39	1.39	1.39	1.39	1.37	1.36	1.36	1.36	1.38	1.37	1.36	Expense Ratio %
1.25	1.13	0.92	0.69	0.55	1.13	0.40	0.23	0.59	1.09	1.30	1.08	Income Ratio %
4	9	16	6	16	19	10	6	8	3	4	9	Turnover Rate %
168	278	721	1,160	1,026	956	977	717	751	715	577	531	Net Assets $mil

Rating and Risk

Time Period	Load-Adj Return %	Morningstar Rtn vs Cat	Morningstar Risk vs Cat	Morningstar Risk-Adj Rating
1 Yr	11.62			
3 Yr	7.71	Low	Low	★
5 Yr	5.55	Low	Low	★
10 Yr	8.81	-Avg	Low	★★★
Incept	10.84			

Other Measures	Standard Index S&P 500	Best Fit Index S&P 500
Alpha	-1.1	-1.1
Beta	0.78	0.78
R-Squared	84	84
Standard Deviation	5.88	
Mean	7.71	
Sharpe Ratio	0.75	

Portfolio Analysis 09-30-06

Share change since 06-06 Total Stocks:40	Sector	PE	Tot Ret%	% Assets
Nestle SA ADR	Goods	21.0	20.91	5.47
Transatlantic Holdings,	Financial	12.6	-6.80	4.84
Heineken Holding	Goods	—	—	4.46
Comcast	Media	—	—	4.39
⊕ Wells Fargo Company	Financial	14.7	16.82	4.19
PNC Financial Services G	Financial	8.7	23.60	4.14
Diageo PLC ADR	Goods	16.1	40.66	3.66
American International G	Financial	17.0	6.05	3.63
American Express Company	Financial	20.9	19.09	3.53
Federated Investors, Inc	Financial	19.0	-6.94	3.44
Freddie Mac	Financial	23.3	7.06	3.32
National Western Life In	Financial	11.3	11.40	3.21
Pfizer Inc.	Health	15.2	15.22	3.12
MBIA Incorporated	Financial	12.0	23.87	3.09
⊖ Torchmark Corporation	Financial	12.9	15.60	2.99
⊕ Wal-Mart Stores, Inc.	Consumer	16.9	0.13	2.55
American National Insura	Financial	13.0	0.12	2.36
Bank of America Corporat	Financial	12.4	20.68	2.13
⊕ ABN AMRO Holding NV ADR	Financial	10.5	28.85	2.12
Great American Financial	Financial	19.0	16.70	1.90

Current Investment Style

Value Blnd Growth — Large Mid Small

Market Cap	%
Giant	42.2
Large	17.3
Mid	28.2
Small	7.7
Micro	4.6

Avg $mil: 18,377

Value Measures		Rel Category
Price/Earnings	11.29	0.76
Price/Book	1.87	0.93
Price/Sales	1.55	1.60
Price/Cash Flow	1.45	0.19
Dividend Yield %	1.91	1.06

Growth Measures	%	Rel Category
Long-Term Erngs	10.57	0.96
Book Value	5.17	0.74
Sales	5.96	0.78
Cash Flow	6.53	1.64
Historical Erngs	7.94	0.54

Profitability	%	Rel Category
Return on Equity	18.97	1.31
Return on Assets	12.41	1.69
Net Margin	14.64	1.40

Sector Weightings	% of Stocks	Rel S&P 500	3 Year High Low	
⟳ Info	7.22	0.36		
Software	0.00	0.00	0	0
Hardware	0.00	0.00	0	0
Media	6.38	1.68	8	6
Telecom	0.84	0.24	1	0
⟳ Service	67.60	1.46		
Health	7.41	0.61	12	5
Consumer	3.51	0.46	4	1
Business	1.66	0.39	9	2
Financial	55.02	2.47	61	48
⟳ Mfg	25.18	0.75		
Goods	19.55	2.29	20	12
Ind Mtrls	5.50	0.46	8	4
Energy	0.13	0.01	0	0
Utilities	0.00	0.00	0	0

Composition

		%
● Cash		11.9
● Stocks		86.6
● Bonds		0.0
○ Other		1.5
Foreign		23.7
(% of Stock)		

Tweedy, Browne Glob Val

	Ticker	Load	NAV	Yield	Total Assets	Mstar Category
	TBGVX	Closed	$30.93	1.4%	$7,897 mil	Foreign Small/Mid Value

Governance and Management

Stewardship Grade: A

Portfolio Manager(s)

The fund has been around since 1993, and lead managers Christopher Browne, William Browne, and John Spears are experienced investors. They also run Tweedy, Browne American Value, a similar U.S.-focused offering. The managers have lots of their own money invested here.

Strategy

Like its sibling Tweedy, Browne American Value, this fund looks for stocks that are cheaper than the private market values the fund's managers assign them. The fund often ends up concentrated in admittedly wide-ranging financials, industrial-cyclicals, and service industries. To dampen volatility, the team hedges virtually all of its currency exposure back into the U.S. dollar. The managers tend to shop across the market-cap spectrum for their picks, but they usually stay away from emerging markets because they find it difficult to hedge their developing-markets currency exposure.

Historical Profile

Return: Below Avg
Risk: Low
Rating: ★★★ Neutral

| 93% | 89% | 90% | 87% | 86% | 87% | 85% | 80% | 85% |

Investment Style
Equity
Stock %

▼ Manager Change
▽ Partial Manager Change

Growth of $10,000
— Investment Values of Fund
— Investment Values of MSCI EAFE

38.0
31.0
24.0
17.0
10.0

Performance Quartile (within Category)

1995	1996	1997	1998	1999	2000	2001	2002	2003	2004	2005	2006	History
12.95	14.45	16.39	16.82	20.21	19.98	18.53	15.81	19.55	23.19	26.40	30.93	NAV
10.70	20.23	22.96	10.99	25.28	12.39	-4.67	-12.14	24.93	20.01	15.42	20.14	Total Return %
-0.51	14.18	21.18	-8.94	-1.75	26.58	16.75	3.80	-13.66	-0.24	1.88	-6.20	+/-MSCI EAFE
-0.71	13.36	20.69	-7.70	-2.70	25.75	16.72	3.66	-14.49	-0.37	0.95	-5.57	+/-MSCI Wd xUS
0.00	4.27	6.03	2.31	1.54	1.02	0.92	1.08	1.27	1.39	1.57	1.64	Income Return %
10.70	15.96	16.93	8.68	23.74	11.37	-5.59	-13.22	23.66	18.62	13.85	18.50	Capital Return %
28	25	1	37	73	1	14	66	100	66	70	88	Total Rtn % Rank Cat
0.00	0.55	0.87	0.38	0.26	0.21	0.18	0.20	0.20	0.27	0.37	0.43	Income $
0.20	0.57	0.49	0.99	0.59	2.52	0.33	0.27	0.00	0.00	0.00	0.35	Capital Gains $
1.65	1.60	1.58	1.42	1.41	1.38	1.38	1.37	1.37	1.39	1.39	1.38	Expense Ratio %
1.08	1.15	0.73	1.05	1.26	1.10	1.06	1.22	1.17	1.08	1.41	1.33	Income Ratio %
16	17	20	16	23	18	12	7	8	8	13	6	Turnover Rate %
802	1,211	1,985	2,492	3,142	3,564	3,834	4,132	4,899	6,144	7,429	7,897	Net Assets $mil

Performance 12-31-06

	1st Qtr	2nd Qtr	3rd Qtr	4th Qtr	Total
2002	6.80	-5.81	-16.47	4.57	-12.14
2003	-8.67	14.40	8.41	10.28	24.93
2004	8.59	3.06	-0.27	7.53	20.01
2005	3.84	2.45	5.67	2.67	15.42
2006	8.18	-2.87	5.73	8.14	20.14

Trailing	Total Return%	+/- MSCI EAFE	+/- MSCI Wd xUS	%Rank Cat	Growth of $10,000
3 Mo	8.14	-2.21	-1.98	94	10,814
6 Mo	14.33	-0.36	0.11	80	11,433
1 Yr	20.14	-6.20	-5.57	88	12,014
3 Yr Avg	18.50	-1.43	-1.60	85	16,640
5 Yr Avg	12.80	-2.18	-2.45	100	18,262
10 Yr Avg	12.84	5.13	4.88	59	33,468
15 Yr Avg	—	—	—		

Tax Analysis	Tax-Adj Rtn%	%Rank Cat	Tax-Cost Rat	%Rank Cat
3 Yr (estimated)	17.90	65	0.51	22
5 Yr (estimated)	12.19	96	0.54	24
10 Yr (estimated)	11.40	54	1.28	55

Potential Capital Gain Exposure: 47% of assets

Rating and Risk

Time Period	Load-Adj Return %	Morningstar Rtn vs Cat	Morningstar Risk vs Cat	Morningstar Risk-Adj Rating
1 Yr	20.14			
3 Yr	18.50	-Avg	Low	★★
5 Yr	12.80	Low	Low	★
10 Yr	12.84	Avg	Low	★★★★
Incept	13.20			

Other Measures	Standard Index MSCI EAFE	Best Fit Index MSCI World
Alpha	6.5	8.1
Beta	0.49	0.60
R-Squared	45	51
Standard Deviation	6.92	
Mean	18.50	
Sharpe Ratio	2.03	

Morningstar's Take by Arijit Dutta 12-18-06

Tweedy, Browne Global Value's strengths are hard to see right now, but we appreciate them.

Markets remain unfavorable to this closed fund. The dollar has suffered big declines this year against major foreign currencies like the euro and the British pound, which hasn't given this hedged portofolio much of a chance. Due to the portfolio's all-cap nature, its average market cap of $10 billion is more than three times the foreign small-mid value norm, which also continues to be a drag (smaller stocks have maintained their multiyear leadership in 2006). A generally declining dollar and the tremendous rally in small-cap stocks over the past several years have indeed taken their toll on this fund's record. Still, it's worth pointing out that the fund has very healthy absolute returns, even through this tough stretch, and its long-term record is still decent.

Meanwhile, management continues to stick to its long-standing, contrarian ways. The strong, multiyear worldwide rally has caused valuations to rise to the point where the pickings are slim, so management has held sizable cash (the portfolio's current 13% cash stake is almost triple the category average). Management has remained alert to individual stock opportunities, however. For example, it made giant insurer American International Group a top holding last year after the stock plummeted due to regulatory concerns (the stock has rebounded nicely from its lows). Management also says this year's collapse in the Japanese small-cap arena has afforded it some nice bargains.

We take heart from management's efforts to find deeply underappreciated stocks in this market. That approach has not only long been the source of a strong upside here, but it has also protected the fund in broad market slumps. For example, the fund held up better than just about all of its rivals during this year's sharp correction in May and June.

We'd hold on to this fund.

Address:	350 Park Ave New York NY 10022 800-432-4789	Minimum Purchase:	Closed	Add: —	IRA: —
		Min Auto Inv Plan:	Closed	Add: —	
		Sales Fees:	No-load, 2.00%R		
Web Address:	www.tweedy.com	Management Fee:	1.25%		
Inception:	06-15-93	Actual Fees:	Mgt:1.25%	Dist: —	
Advisor:	Tweedy, Browne Company LLC	Expense Projections:	3Yr:$437	5Yr:$755	10Yr:$1657
Subadvisor:	None	Income Distrib:	Annually		
NTF Plans:	N/A				

Portfolio Analysis 09-30-06

Share change since 06-06 Total Stocks:143

	Sector	Country	% Assets
Nestle	Goods	Switzerland	3.90
⊕ ABN AMRO Holding	Financial	Netherlands	3.44
American International G	Financial	United States	3.15
KONE	Business	Finland	3.02
CNP Assurances	Financial	France	2.89
Axel Springer Verlag	Media	Germany	2.88
Heineken Holding	Goods	Netherlands	2.76
KBC Bank & Insurance	Financial	Belgium	2.22
Volkswagen	Goods	Germany	2.17
Sanofi-Synthelabo	Health	France	2.08
Jardine Strategic Hldgs	Consumer	Singapore	2.03
Diageo	Goods	U.K.	1.82
Novartis	Health	Switzerland	1.77
Heineken	Goods	Netherlands	1.69
Barclays	Financial	U.K.	1.67
Sika	Business	Switzerland	1.61
Akzo Nobel	Ind Mtrls	Netherlands	1.56
⊕ MEDIASET	Media	Italy	1.49
Telegraaf Media Groep Nv	—	Netherlands	1.46
Altadis	Goods	Spain	1.38

Current Investment Style

Value Blnd Growth — Large Mid Small

Market Cap	%
Giant	31.4
Large	30.1
Mid	25.0
Small	11.1
Micro	2.4

Avg $mil: 10,366

Value Measures		Rel Category
Price/Earnings	14.49	0.98
Price/Book	1.79	0.90
Price/Sales	0.92	1.03
Price/Cash Flow	7.24	1.15
Dividend Yield %	3.26	1.24

Growth Measures	%	Rel Category
Long-Term Erngs	9.73	0.65
Book Value	8.58	1.11
Sales	5.47	0.74
Cash Flow	-0.91	NMF
Historical Erngs	12.65	0.65

Composition

Cash	13.5	Bonds	0.0
Stocks	84.7	Other	1.8
Foreign	(% of Stock)		91.8

Sector Weightings

		% of Stocks	Rel MSCI EAFE	3 Year High	Low
⟳ Info		14.29	1.21		
▣ Software		0.00	0.00	0	0
▣ Hardware		0.77	0.20	2	1
▣ Media		13.01	7.11	20	13
▣ Telecom		0.51	0.09	1	0
⟲ Service		46.55	0.99		
▣ Health		8.38	1.18	15	8
▣ Consumer		3.99	0.81	4	2
▣ Business		10.59	2.09	11	6
▣ Financial		23.59	0.78	24	17
▤ Mfg		39.16	0.96		
▣ Goods		27.79	2.12	28	20
▣ Ind Mtrls		10.26	0.66	16	10
▣ Energy		0.01	0.00	0	0
▣ Utilities		1.10	0.21	1	0

Regional Exposure

	% Stock		% Stock
UK/W. Europe	74	N. America	10
Japan	5	Latn America	2
Asia X Japan	9	Other	0

Country Exposure

	% Stock		% Stock
Netherlands	18	United States	8
Switzerland	16	Germany	8
U.K.	10		

MORNINGSTAR® Funds 500

UMB Scout International

	Ticker	Load	NAV	Yield	Total Assets	Mstar Category
	UMBWX	None	$32.66	1.0%	$3,019 mil	Foreign Large Blend

Performance 12-31-06

	1st Qtr	2nd Qtr	3rd Qtr	4th Qtr	Total
2002	-0.32	-4.08	-17.60	6.81	-15.85
2003	-4.11	15.07	5.74	14.07	33.10
2004	4.52	-0.21	-0.33	13.53	18.02
2005	1.66	1.34	12.66	3.02	19.58
2006	7.93	-1.52	3.36	10.62	21.51

Trailing	Total Return%	+/- MSCI EAFE	+/- MSCI Wd xUS	%Rank Cat	Growth of $10,000
3 Mo	10.62	0.27	0.50	37	11,062
6 Mo	14.33	-0.36	0.11	53	11,433
1 Yr	21.51	-4.83	-4.20	86	12,151
3 Yr Avg	19.70	-0.23	-0.40	30	17,151
5 Yr Avg	13.94	-1.04	-1.31	36	19,204
10 Yr Avg	11.16	3.45	3.20	7	28,806
15 Yr Avg	—	—	—		—

Tax Analysis	Tax-Adj Rtn%	%Rank Cat	Tax-Cost Rat	%Rank Cat
3 Yr (estimated)	19.04	21	0.55	30
5 Yr (estimated)	13.44	28	0.44	35
10 Yr (estimated)	10.51	2	0.58	15

Potential Capital Gain Exposure: 27% of assets

Historical Profile

Return	Above Avg
Risk	Below Avg
Rating	★★★★ Above Avg

	73%	85%	80%	85%	85%	94%	95%	90%

Investment Style
Equity
Stock %

▼ Manager Change
▽ Partial Manager Change

Growth of $10,000
— Investment Values of Fund
— Investment Values of MSCI EAFE

Performance Quartile (within Category)

1995	1996	1997	1998	1999	2000	2001	2002	2003	2004	2005	2006	History
12.08	13.94	16.02	18.56	23.77	21.24	18.67	15.58	20.58	24.10	28.26	32.66	NAV
14.66	18.35	18.35	17.96	31.43	-8.17	-11.00	-15.85	33.10	18.02	19.58	21.51	Total Return %
3.45	12.30	16.57	-1.97	4.40	6.02	10.42	0.09	-5.49	-2.23	6.04	-4.83	+/-MSCI EAFE
3.25	11.48	16.08	-0.73	3.45	5.19	10.39	-0.05	-6.32	-2.36	5.11	-4.20	+/-MSCI Wd xUS
2.04	1.92	1.75	1.97	1.16	0.20	1.08	0.73	0.87	0.83	0.94	1.17	Income Return %
12.62	16.43	16.60	15.99	30.27	-8.37	-12.08	-16.58	32.23	17.19	18.64	20.34	Capital Return %
14	16	1	26	63	12	4	37	47	41	12	86	Total Rtn % Rank Cat
0.22	0.23	0.24	0.31	0.21	0.05	0.23	0.14	0.14	0.17	0.23	0.33	Income $
0.12	0.11	0.22	0.02	0.36	0.56	0.01	0.00	0.00	0.00	0.30	1.30	Capital Gains $
0.85	0.85	0.86	0.87	0.86	0.91	1.12	1.12	1.14	1.10	1.04	1.03	Expense Ratio %
1.97	2.40	1.93	2.01	1.69	1.29	1.04	0.77	1.16	0.87	1.10	1.08	Income Ratio %
27	5	18	3	8	8	11	13	12	12	19	23	Turnover Rate %
24	41	57	108	268	307	358	354	593	1,023	1,820	3,019	Net Assets $mil

Rating and Risk

Time Period	Load-Adj Return %	Morningstar Rtn vs Cat	Morningstar Risk vs Cat	Morningstar Risk-Adj Rating
1 Yr	21.51			
3 Yr	19.70	+Avg	+Avg	★★★★
5 Yr	13.94	Avg	-Avg	★★★
10 Yr	11.16	High	Low	★★★★★
Incept	11.58			

Other Measures	Standard Index MSCI EAFE	Best Fit Index MSCI Wd xUS
Alpha	-1.0	-1.0
Beta	1.06	1.05
R-Squared	93	94
Standard Deviation	10.36	
Mean	19.70	
Sharpe Ratio	1.49	

Portfolio Analysis 09-30-06

Share change since 06-06 Total Stocks:84	Sector	Country	% Assets
⊕ Canon ADR	Goods	Japan	2.26
Allianz SE ADR	Financial	Germany	1.71
Aegon NV ADR	Financial	Netherlands	1.71
Samsung Electnc GDR 144A	Goods	Korea	1.55
ABB ADR	Ind Mtrls	Switzerland	1.52
Tesco PLC (ADR)	Consumer	U.K.	1.46
Luxottica Group S.p.A. A	Health	Italy	1.45
Imperial Chemical Indust	Ind Mtrls	U.K.	1.44
Mettler-Toledo Internati	Health	United States	1.41
⊕ Scottish Power PLC ADR	Utilities	U.K.	1.41
Ericsson Telephone Compa	Hardware	Sweden	1.41
Australia & New Zealand	Financial	Australia	1.40
Takeda Chemical Industri	Health	Japan	1.39
⊕ Teva Pharmaceutical Indu	Health	Israel	1.39
Henkel	Ind Mtrls	Germany	1.35
Companhia de Bebidas das	Goods	Brazil	1.33
Taiwan Semiconductor Man	Hardware	Taiwan	1.31
⊕ Sanofi-Aventis ADR	Health	France	1.31
Cosmote Mobile Telecomm.	Telecom	Greece	1.29
Sampo	Financial	Finland	1.27

Current Investment Style

Value Blnd Growth — Large Mid Small

	Market Cap	%
	Giant	47.6
	Large	36.8
	Mid	15.6
	Small	0.0
	Micro	0.0
	Avg $mil:	26,403

Value Measures		Rel Category
Price/Earnings	17.86	1.36
Price/Book	3.05	1.41
Price/Sales	1.66	1.43
Price/Cash Flow	12.16	1.46
Dividend Yield %	1.92	0.66

Growth Measures	%	Rel Category
Long-Term Erngs	10.91	0.92
Book Value	9.53	1.04
Sales	10.83	1.65
Cash Flow	8.30	1.00
Historical Erngs	22.60	1.11

Composition			
Cash	10.0	Bonds	0.0
Stocks	90.0	Other	0.0
Foreign (% of Stock)			97.3

Sector Weightings	% of Stocks	Rel MSCI EAFE	3 Year High	Low
↻ Info	11.12	0.94		
Software	1.16	2.07	2	1
Hardware	4.81	1.25	11	5
Media	0.00	0.00	1	0
Telecom	5.15	0.92	10	5
☞ Service	46.10	0.98		
Health	19.20	2.70	19	9
Consumer	6.15	1.24	9	3
Business	4.03	0.79	5	2
Financial	16.72	0.56	17	6
⚒ Mfg	42.79	1.05		
Goods	18.77	1.43	19	14
Ind Mtrls	15.30	0.99	27	15
Energy	6.24	0.87	17	6
Utilities	2.48	0.47	3	1

Regional Exposure   % Stock

UK/W. Europe	59	N. America	7
Japan	18	Latn America	5
Asia X Japan	9	Other	2

Country Exposure   % Stock

Japan	18	Germany	8
U.K.	17	Canada	4
Switzerland	8		

Morningstar's Take by Gregg Wolper 12-09-06

If you're looking for core foreign exposure, consider UMB Scout WorldWide.

This fund can supply just about everything investors typically look for in their primary international funds. Its portfolio tends to land in the large-blend area of the Morningstar Style Box, meaning that it doesn't tilt too far toward either the value or growth sides of the spectrum (though certain value- or growth-oriented funds could serve as a core holding), and it stays away from potentially more-volatile small stocks. It has moderate exposure to emerging-markets stocks, and manager James Moffett also taps into the growth of those markets through companies in Europe or Japan with strong sales there. In addition, he limits risk by keeping individual position sizes low.

There are other attractions as well. Moffett is experienced, having run this fund in the same manner since its 1993 inception. And it comes with a reasonable expense ratio. Moffett further reins in expenses by trading infrequently, thus minimizing commission costs (which don't show up in the expense ratio). The record shows all this fits together well. For the trailing 10-year period through the end of November 2006, it topped more than 90% of its large-blend category rivals.

This year hasn't been stellar in relative terms, however. Though the fund has amassed a 19.4% gain for the year to date through Dec. 8, 2006, that lags about four fifths of the category. Moffett explains that although he thought an expected slowdown in the U.S. and Chinese economies would hurt materials stocks, he didn't act quickly enough to shift into consumer-oriented firms such as recent purchase British American Tobacco. And earlier in the year, an overweighting in energy (cut to neutral weight in midyear) dented returns when energy prices fell.

Given the fund's history, though, investors shouldn't be too concerned over its 2006 ranking. It remains a solid option.

Undiscovered Mg BehGrlns

Ticker UBRLX	**Load** None	**NAV** $24.06	**Yield** 0.0%	**Total Assets** $117 mil	**Mstar Category** Mid-Cap Growth

Governance and Management

Stewardship Grade: D

Portfolio Manager(s)

Day-to-day manager Fred Stanske has been at the wheel since this fund's inception and has run separate-account money in the same style since 1996. Russ Fuller is founder and president of Fuller & Thaler, the fund's advisor. Fuller and the firm's other namesake, Richard Thaler, have been leading figures in the growing field of behavioral-finance research. The firm manages roughly $2.5 billion in assets.

Strategy

This fund's guiding principle is that investors are slow to react to earnings improvements. Management buys small- and mid-cap stocks that posted earnings surprises without being followed by as much of a rise in prices as the changes warranted. Fred Stanske only considers firms at which there has been a large earnings surprise propelled by sustainable factors, such as market-share gains. And he observes a strict sell discipline, fully liquidating stocks as soon as results fail to top expectations. Stanske pays no heed to benchmarks or valuations. Thus, the fund often has large sector bets.

Performance 12-31-06

	1st Qtr	2nd Qtr	3rd Qtr	4th Qtr	Total
2002	1.51	-10.28	-14.12	5.54	-17.45
2003	1.35	26.51	13.33	8.37	57.47
2004	3.18	0.10	-9.34	17.79	10.30
2005	-3.48	2.32	6.44	0.70	5.86
2006	9.55	-9.63	-3.89	9.31	4.02

Trailing	Total Return%	+/- S&P 500	+/- Russ MG	%Rank Cat	Growth of $10,000
3 Mo	9.31	2.61	2.36	11	10,931
6 Mo	5.07	-7.67	-2.83	61	10,507
1 Yr	4.02	-11.77	-6.64	84	10,402
3 Yr Avg	6.69	-3.75	-6.04	90	12,144
5 Yr Avg	9.56	3.37	1.34	16	15,786
10 Yr Avg	—	—	—	—	—
15 Yr Avg	—	—	—	—	—

Tax Analysis	Tax-Adj Rtn%	%Rank Cat	Tax-Cost Rat	%Rank Cat
3 Yr (estimated)	6.69	82	0.00	1
5 Yr (estimated)	9.56	11	0.00	1
10 Yr (estimated)	—	—	—	—

Potential Capital Gain Exposure: -12% of assets

Morningstar's Take by Arijit Dutta 12-11-06

Undiscovered Managers Behavioral Growth is more capable than its recent record indicates.

This fund is nearing its third straight year of subpar returns, although there could be some relief ahead. Even by mid-growth category standards, the portfolio tends to favor technology and health-care stocks (its 30% technology weight is almost twice the category average, for example), which are the two sectors with the worst three-year returns. Also, manager Fred Stanske hasn't followed many of his peers as they have taken sizable stakes in recent years in materials and energy stocks, which have been winning areas. The fund has shown signs of life in recent months, however. Energy stocks have slowed since mid-year, and although tech stocks are yet to outperform in general, some of the portfolio's holdings have shot ahead. For example, top-holding specialty electronic chip-maker NVIDIA has almost doubled since July.

That stock is in fact a great example of the potency of the strategy here. Stanske bought NVIDIA in late 2004 after the company beat Wall Street earnings estimates by a wide margin. The chipmaker has continued to surpass market expectations due to its expansion in the fast-growing market for portable video-player and video-game components. Thus, Stanske has held on (he sells when the Street's estimates start to catch up with a business' higher earnings, typically well before peers who focus on earnings momentum alone). Companies will often beat expectations when they have new products that boost earnings, so this strategy is a viable way to cash in on a company's growth spurt.

We think the fund can bounce back. Indeed, despite the toll the lagging performance in recent years has taken, Stanske's record here since he took charge in 1997 is still decent. Our main gripe here is accessibility, however. The fund's institutional shares require a minimum investment of $3 million, and its retail share class is too expensive.

Address:	700 North Pearl Street Dallas, TX 75201 800-480-4111
Web Address:	www.jpmorganfunds.com
Inception:	12-29-97 *
Advisor:	JP Morgan Investment Management, Inc.
Subadvisor:	Fuller & Thaler Asset Management Inc
NTF Plans:	ETrade No Load ETF

Minimum Purchase:	$3000000	Add: $0	IRA: $0
Min Auto Inv Plan:	$0	Add: —	
Sales Fees:	No-load		
Management Fee:	0.95%, 0.15%A		
Actual Fees:	Mgt:0.95%	Dist: —	
Expense Projections:	3Yr:$435	5Yr:$761	10Yr:$1681
Income Distrib:	Annually		

Historical Profile

Return	Average
Risk	High
Rating	★★★ Neutral

	1995	1996	1997	1998	1999	2000	2001	2002	2003	2004	2005	2006	History
			12.86	17.13	28.38	19.64	15.24	12.58	19.81	21.85	23.13	24.06	NAV
			2.88*	33.20	65.67	-26.77	-22.40	-17.45	57.47	10.30	5.86	4.02	Total Return %
				4.62	44.63	-17.67	-10.51	4.65	28.79	-0.58	0.95	-11.77	+/-S&P 500
				15.34	14.38	-15.02	-2.25	9.96	14.76	-5.18	-6.24	-6.64	+/-Russ MG
				0.00	0.00	0.00	0.00	0.00	0.00	0.00	0.00	0.00	Income Return %
				33.20	65.67	-26.77	-22.40	-17.45	57.47	10.30	5.86	4.02	Capital Return %
				13	38	92	64	15	2	76	80	84	Total Rtn % Rank Cat
			0.00	0.00	0.00	0.00	0.00	0.00	0.00	0.00	0.00	0.00	Income $
			0.00	0.00	0.00	1.14	0.00	0.00	0.00	0.00	0.00	0.00	Capital Gains $
				1.30	1.30	1.30	1.30	1.30	1.30	1.30	1.30	1.30	Expense Ratio %
				-0.35	-0.72	-0.97	-1.16	-1.16	-0.97	-1.14	-1.03	-0.99	Income Ratio %
					72	90	97	94	129	161	92	97	Turnover Rate %
			23	165	159	96	60	112	143	132	103	Net Assets $mil

Rating and Risk

Time Period	Load-Adj Return %	Morningstar Rtn vs Cat	Morningstar Risk vs Cat	Morningstar Risk-Adj Rating
1 Yr	4.02			
3 Yr	6.69	-Avg	High	★
5 Yr	9.56	+Avg	High	★★★★
10 Yr	—			
Incept	8.22			

Other Measures	Standard Index S&P 500	Best Fit Index Mstar Mid Growth TR
Alpha	-10.3	-9.3
Beta	2.17	1.35
R-Squared	69	90
Standard Deviation	18.00	
Mean	6.69	
Sharpe Ratio	0.27	

Portfolio Analysis 11-30-06

Share change since 10-06 Total Stocks:45	Sector	PE	Tot Ret%	% Assets
⊖ NVIDIA Corporation	Hardware	33.4	102.46	4.05
⊖ Intuitive Surgical, Inc.	Health	35.2	-18.22	3.52
⊖ Priceline.com, Inc.	Consumer	10.8	95.39	2.99
⊖ THQ, Inc.	Software	81.9	36.35	2.98
⊖ GATX Corporation	Consumer	—	22.62	2.97
⊖ Gen-Probe, Inc.	Health	46.1	7.34	2.75
⊖ Brocade Communications S	Software	51.6	101.72	2.65
⊖ OfficeMax, Inc.	Consumer	—	98.81	2.52
⊖ ValueClick, Inc.	Business	46.8	30.48	2.50
⊖ MicroStrategy, Inc.	Business	26.5	37.91	2.41
⊖ NutriSystem, Inc.	Goods	33.2	75.99	2.39
⊖ Thomas & Betts Corporati	Hardware	19.1	12.68	2.31
⊖ Church & Dwight Company,	Goods	22.2	30.00	2.22
⊖ Leap Wireless Internatio	Telecom	81.7	57.00	2.20
⊖ Amerigroup Corporation	Health	21.6	84.43	2.20
⊖ WellCare Health Plans, I	Health	30.9	68.67	2.19
⊖ RealNetworks, Inc.	Business	5.5	40.98	2.18
⊖ NBTY, Inc.	Health	27.0	155.82	2.17
⊖ TIBCO Software, Inc.	Software	33.0	26.37	2.15
⊖ Dade Behring Holdings, I	Health	26.3	-2.13	2.15

Current Investment Style

Value Blnd Growth — Large Mid Small

	Market Cap	%
	Giant	0.0
	Large	4.7
	Mid	52.3
	Small	43.0
	Micro	0.0
	Avg $mil:	2,138

Value Measures		Rel Category
Price/Earnings	23.17	1.13
Price/Book	3.03	0.94
Price/Sales	1.79	1.02
Price/Cash Flow	2.41	0.21
Dividend Yield %	0.12	0.19

Growth Measures	%	Rel Category
Long-Term Erngs	18.36	1.13
Book Value	11.14	0.88
Sales	7.17	0.72
Cash Flow	33.07	1.79
Historical Erngs	43.60	1.75

Profitability	%	Rel Category
Return on Equity	15.03	0.84
Return on Assets	9.70	1.04
Net Margin	10.68	0.92

Sector Weightings	% of Stocks	Rel S&P 500	3 Year High Low	
☊ Info	32.02	1.60		
Software	7.77	2.25	19	7
Hardware	20.01	2.17	37	17
Media	0.00	0.00	1	0
Telecom	4.24	1.21	8	1
⊑ Service	58.99	1.28		
Health	26.05	2.16	26	12
Consumer	22.13	2.89	25	11
Business	10.81	2.56	14	3
Financial	0.00	0.00	2	0
⊡ Mfg	8.99	0.27		
Goods	6.13	0.72	14	2
Ind Mtrls	1.79	0.15	10	0
Energy	1.07	0.11	2	0
Utilities	0.00	0.00	0	0

Composition

● Cash	0.2	
● Stocks	99.8	
● Bonds	0.0	
● Other	0.0	
Foreign	0.0	
(% of Stock)		

MORNINGSTAR® Funds 500

USAA Aggressive Growth

		Analyst Pick	Ticker USAUX	Load None	NAV $33.01	Yield 0.0%	Total Assets $1,182 mil	Mstar Category Large Growth

Governance and Management

Stewardship Grade: B

Portfolio Manager(s)

USAA enlisted Tom Marsico to subadvise this offering in June 2002. Marsico also runs Marsico Focus and Marsico Growth. He has built terrific records at those offerings and at prior charges. Sixteen analysts assist him, and two other portfolio managers pitch in as well.

Strategy

Subadvisor Tom Marsico, who took over this portfolio in mid-2002, combines top-down macroeconomic analysis with bottom-up stock-picking. He fills the bulk of the portfolio with steady-growth stocks that he intends to hold for the long haul, but he also has owned more-explosive growth names in tech and telecom. He reserves a portion of the portfolio for relatively inexpensive firms that stand to benefit from a catalyst. Here, he'll typically own about 40-50 stocks. Marsico isn't seduced by a benchmark, so the fund often looks quite different from its peers or bogy.

Performance 12-31-06

	1st Qtr	2nd Qtr	3rd Qtr	4th Qtr	Total
2002	-5.02	-14.78	-12.44	-2.08	-30.60
2003	1.21	13.39	4.76	8.79	30.79
2004	2.05	-0.53	0.15	11.18	13.03
2005	-4.62	4.70	3.29	3.95	7.23
2006	2.97	-4.40	-0.32	7.39	5.37

Trailing	Total Return%	+/- S&P 500	+/- Russ 1000Gr	%Rank Cat	Growth of $10,000
3 Mo	7.39	0.69	1.46	12	10,739
6 Mo	7.04	-5.70	-3.06	71	10,704
1 Yr	5.37	-10.42	-3.70	67	10,537
3 Yr Avg	8.49	-1.95	1.62	29	12,769
5 Yr Avg	3.00	-3.19	0.31	43	11,593
10 Yr Avg	4.50	-3.92	-0.94	73	15,530
15 Yr Avg	6.76	-3.88	-1.26	82	26,676

Tax Analysis	Tax-Adj Rtn%	%Rank Cat	Tax-Cost Rat	%Rank Cat
3 Yr (estimated)	8.48	22	0.01	1
5 Yr (estimated)	2.99	39	0.01	2
10 Yr (estimated)	3.77	64	0.70	30

Potential Capital Gain Exposure: 12% of assets

Morningstar's Take by Karen Dolan 11-08-06

USAA Aggressive Growth is down, but it's not out.

This fund hasn't shone in 2006. Such periods have been the exception rather than the rule during manager Tom Marsico's long tenure using this style, though. Prior to starting his own firm, he managed Janus Twenty from March 1988 to August 1997. When looking at rolling returns--where for each figure, an earlier month drops off as a later month is tacked on--for that fund and Marsico Growth (which this fund is modeled after), Marsico has outpaced the average large-cap growth fund 74% of the time.

All funds hit rough patches from time to time, and that's what we think is going on here. The fund has had its fair share of stock disappointments recently. UnitedHealth Group was the fund's top holding coming into 2006. Its stock price plummeted when allegations about options backdating surfaced early in the year. Marsico and his team of analysts have researched several layers of management at the firm and think the current

issues don't affect its long-term value. Marsico has used the controversy as a buying opportunity. Other picks such as Lowe's Companies and Genentech have also hurt returns in 2006.

The fund's recent performance begs the question of whether the fund's size is hampering returns. As of Sept. 30, 2006, Marsico was running $60 billion between this style and a more focused version. That puts him in uncharted territory. To deal with the girth, Marsico has expanded the analyst team, hired more traders, and cut back on the amount of time he spends talking to clients about the funds. He also says that the team's research is uncovering more ideas abroad, thus expanding the fund's universe. We'll continue to watch for signs that assets are getting in the way, but we don't think Marsico would compromise performance to grow; filings show that he has more than $1 million invested in this strategy, and we believe his total commitment is much higher than that. This remains a favorite.

Address:	9800 Fredericksburg Road San Antonio TX 78288-0227 800-531-8448	Minimum Purchase:	$3000	Add: $50	IRA: $250
		Min Auto Inv Plan:	$0	Add: $50	
		Sales Fees:	No-load		
Web Address:	www.usaa.com	Management Fee:	0.50% mx./0.33% mn.		
Inception:	07-29-81	Actual Fees:	Mgt:0.50%	Dist: —	
Advisor:	USAA Investment Management Company	Expense Projections:	3Yr:$337	5Yr:$585	10Yr:$1294
Subadvisor:	Marsico Capital Management, LLC	Income Distrib:	Annually		
NTF Plans:	Pershing NTF, TD Waterhouse Ins NT				

Historical Profile

Return	Average
Risk	Average
Rating	★★★ Neutral

	98%	97%	99%	97%	97%	96%	100%	96%	93%

Investment Style
Equity
Stock %

▼ Manager Change
▽ Partial Manager Change

- 59.0
- 43.6
- 32.4 **Growth of $10,000**
- 24.0 ■ Investment Values of Fund
- 17.0 — Investment Values of S&P 500
- 10.0

Performance Quartile (within Category)

1995	1996	1997	1998	1999	2000	2001	2002	2003	2004	2005	2006	History
26.09	29.81	29.73	30.69	55.15	42.78	28.50	19.78	25.87	29.24	31.34	33.01	NAV
50.42	16.47	7.56	22.22	91.09	-19.95	-33.38	-30.60	30.79	13.03	7.23	5.37	Total Return %
12.84	-6.49	-25.80	-6.36	70.05	-10.85	-21.49	-8.50	2.11	2.15	2.32	-10.42	+/-S&P 500
13.24	-6.65	-22.93	-16.49	57.93	2.47	-12.96	-2.72	1.04	6.73	1.97	-3.70	+/-Russ 1000Gr
0.00	0.00	0.00	0.00	0.00	0.00	0.00	0.00	0.00	0.04	0.04		Income Return %
50.42	16.47	7.56	22.22	91.09	-19.95	-33.38	-30.60	30.79	13.03	7.19	5.33	Capital Return %
2	72	98	78	5	79	93	77	32	10	40	67	Total Rtn % Rank Cat
0.00	0.00	0.00	0.00	0.00	0.00	0.00	0.00	0.00	0.01	0.01		Income $
1.61	0.57	2.34	3.99	2.31	1.87	0.00	0.00	0.00	0.00	0.00		Capital Gains $
0.86	0.74	0.74	0.71	0.72	0.60	0.66	0.99	1.16	1.03	1.02	0.99	Expense Ratio %
-0.28	-0.42	-0.47	-0.38	-0.55	-0.42	-0.52	-0.77	-0.44	-0.07	0.05	-0.04	Income Ratio %
138	44	57	83	35	33	23	170	110	88	71	65	Turnover Rate %
443	716	732	833	1,658	1,588	1,037	694	936	1,076	1,145	1,182	Net Assets $mil

Rating and Risk

Time Period	Load-Adj Return %	Morningstar Rtn vs Cat	Morningstar Risk vs Cat	Morningstar Risk-Adj Rating
1 Yr	5.37			
3 Yr	8.49	+Avg	Avg	★★★★
5 Yr	3.00	Avg	-Avg	★★★
10 Yr	4.50	-Avg	High	★
Incept	9.37			

Other Measures	Standard Index S&P 500	Best Fit Index DJ Wilshire 4500
Alpha	-2.6	-3.0
Beta	1.15	0.74
R-Squared	74	80
Standard Deviation	9.13	
Mean	8.49	
Sharpe Ratio	0.59	

Portfolio Analysis 10-31-06

Share change since 07-06 Total Stocks:43	Sector	PE	Tot Ret%	% Assets
UnitedHealth Group, Inc.	Health	20.8	-13.49	6.37
Genentech, Inc.	Health	48.7	-12.29	5.48
⊕ Goldman Sachs Group, Inc	Financial	12.4	57.41	4.37
⊕ Comcast Corporation A	Media	45.2	63.31	4.35
Procter & Gamble Company	Goods	23.9	13.36	4.31
⊕ UBS AG	Financial	—	29.62	4.02
Burlington Northern Sant	Business	15.2	5.52	3.40
⊖ Lehman Brothers Holdings	Financial	12.2	22.75	3.35
⊖ FedEx Corporation	Business	17.2	5.40	3.15
☼ Toyota Motor Corporation	Goods	17.9	28.38	2.98
General Dynamics	Ind Mtrls	19.1	32.17	2.86
⊖ Lowe's Companies Inc.	Consumer	15.6	-6.05	2.54
Yum Brands, Inc.	Consumer	20.4	26.76	2.47
Union Pacific Corporatio	Business	17.4	15.87	2.35
⊖ MGM Mirage, Inc.	Consumer	32.0	56.40	2.30
⊕ Monsanto Company	Ind Mtrls	39.8	36.78	2.23
⊕ Las Vegas Sands, Inc.	Consumer	75.7	126.70	2.19
Amylin Pharmaceuticals	Health	—	-9.64	2.18
⊕ Wells Fargo Company	Financial	14.7	16.82	2.17
⊖ Schlumberger, Ltd.	Energy	22.3	31.07	2.17

Current Investment Style

Value Blnd Growth		Market Cap	%
	Large Mid Small	Giant	48.0
		Large	43.0
		Mid	9.0
		Small	0.0
		Micro	0.0
		Avg $mil: 44,003	

Value Measures		Rel Category
Price/Earnings	17.98	0.93
Price/Book	3.08	0.93
Price/Sales	1.83	0.94
Price/Cash Flow	12.83	1.13
Dividend Yield %	0.91	0.88

Growth Measures	%	Rel Category
Long-Term Erngs	14.41	1.00
Book Value	11.64	1.00
Sales	12.72	1.10
Cash Flow	13.45	0.80
Historical Erngs	25.38	1.10

Profitability	%	Rel Category
Return on Equity	18.13	0.89
Return on Assets	8.73	0.79
Net Margin	9.92	0.70

Sector Weightings	% of Stocks	Rel S&P 500	3 Year High Low	
⟳ Info	11.64	0.58		
🖥 Software	0.00	0.00	6	0
🖳 Hardware	4.83	0.52	18	4
🎙 Media	4.70	1.24	5	0
Telecom	2.11	0.60	2	0
⟲ Service	65.61	1.42		
Health	16.82	1.39	32	17
Consumer	19.63	2.57	23	8
Business	19.53	2.28	10	2
Financial	19.53	0.88	22	14
⟘ Mfg	22.76	0.67		
Goods	9.88	1.16	15	4
Ind Mtrls	10.53	0.88	14	9
Energy	2.35	0.24	7	0
Utilities	0.00	0.00	1	0

Composition

	%
● Cash	7.5
● Stocks	92.5
● Bonds	0.0
● Other	0.0
Foreign	14.4
(% of Stock)	

USAA Income

	Ticker	Load	NAV	Yield	SEC Yield	Total Assets	Mstar Category
	USAIX	None	$12.11	4.8%	4.93%	$1,803 mil	Intermediate-Term Bond

Governance and Management

Stewardship Grade: B

Portfolio Manager(s)

Margaret Didi Weinblatt has been at the helm since February 2000. She also manages USAA GNMA, which she took over in May 2002. Before joining the fund, she was a comanager at Neuberger Berman Limited Maturity Bond from 1986 to 1995.

Strategy

Like its typical peer, this offering invests across the major sectors of the taxable-bond market, usually holding a mix of Treasuries, agency bonds, mortgage-backed securities, and corporate debt. The fund will hold a handful of preferred stocks and REITs, though. Further, management doesn't strictly manage the portfolio's duration (a measure of interest-rate sensitivity) against an index, preferring to look instead to a self-selected peer group.

Historical Profile

Return	Above Avg
Risk	Above Avg
Rating	★★★★ Above Avg

Investment Style: Fixed Income
Income Rtn %Rank Cat

▼ Manager Change
▽ Partial Manager Change

Growth of $10,000
— Investment Values of Fund
— Investment Values of LB Aggr

Performance Quartile (within Category)

History	1995	1996	1997	1998	1999	2000	2001	2002	2003	2004	2005	2006
NAV	13.00	12.31	12.78	12.56	11.30	11.96	12.06	12.40	12.42	12.42	12.20	12.11
Total Return %	24.47	1.33	11.05	8.75	-3.85	13.34	7.58	8.63	4.91	4.52	2.96	4.16
+/-LB Aggr	6.00	-2.30	1.40	0.06	-3.03	1.71	-0.86	-1.62	0.81	0.18	0.53	-0.17
+/-LB 5-10YR	3.04	-1.36	1.62	-1.39	-0.97	0.90	-1.24	-4.40	-1.06	-0.78	1.13	0.35
Income Return %	7.75	6.59	6.98	6.80	6.27	7.26	6.82	5.68	4.74	4.49	4.78	4.86
Capital Return %	16.72	-5.26	4.07	1.95	-10.12	6.08	0.76	2.95	0.17	0.03	-1.82	-0.70
Total Rtn % Rank Cat	2	95	6	17	93	2	49	47	41	31	5	39
Income $	0.84	0.83	0.83	0.84	0.76	0.79	0.79	0.67	0.58	0.55	0.58	0.58
Capital Gains $	0.00	0.00	0.00	0.46	0.03	0.00	0.00	0.00	0.00	0.00	0.00	0.00
Expense Ratio %	0.41	0.40	0.39	0.38	0.38	0.42	0.41	0.55	0.50	0.52	0.55	0.59
Income Ratio %	7.27	6.64	6.76	6.62	6.31	6.78	6.63	5.89	4.79	4.36	4.38	4.81
Turnover Rate %	31	81	58	47	54	25	43	60	61	28	24	36
Net Assets $mil	1,893	1,928	1,722	1,769	1,319	1,339	1,547	1,736	1,757	1,753	1,807	1,803

Performance 12-31-06

	1st Qtr	2nd Qtr	3rd Qtr	4th Qtr	Total
2002	-0.37	3.28	4.38	1.14	8.63
2003	1.51	3.04	-0.35	0.65	4.91
2004	2.64	-2.60	3.29	1.22	4.52
2005	-0.12	2.85	-0.32	0.55	2.96
2006	-0.59	-0.25	3.74	1.25	4.16

Trailing	Total Return%	+/- LB Aggr	+/- LB 5-10YR	%Rank Cat	Growth of $10,000
3 Mo	1.25	0.01	0.17	43	10,125
6 Mo	5.03	-0.06	-0.65	33	10,503
1 Yr	4.16	-0.17	0.35	39	10,416
3 Yr Avg	3.88	0.18	0.24	22	11,210
5 Yr Avg	5.02	-0.04	-0.90	27	12,775
10 Yr Avg	6.11	-0.13	-0.57	18	18,095
15 Yr Avg	6.51	0.01	-0.48	28	25,755

Tax Analysis	Tax-Adj Rtn%	%Rank Cat	Tax-Cost Rat	%Rank Cat
3 Yr (estimated)	2.20	20	1.62	60
5 Yr (estimated)	3.23	24	1.70	57
10 Yr (estimated)	3.71	21	2.26	75

Potential Capital Gain Exposure: -1% of assets

Rating and Risk

Time Period	Load-Adj Return %	Morningstar Rtn vs Cat	Morningstar Risk vs Cat	Morningstar Risk-Adj Rating
1 Yr	4.16			
3 Yr	3.88	+Avg	+Avg	★★★★
5 Yr	5.02	+Avg	+Avg	★★★★
10 Yr	6.11	+Avg	+Avg	★★★★
Incept	8.93			

Other Measures	Standard Index LB Aggr	Best Fit Index LB Aggr
Alpha	0.2	0.2
Beta	0.98	0.98
R-Squared	99	99
Standard Deviation	3.20	
Mean	3.88	
Sharpe Ratio	0.20	

Morningstar's Take by Kai Wiecking 11-20-06

There's much to like at USAA Income.

This fund's appeal has much to do with its skilled manager. Didi Weinblatt has fashioned this previously uninspiring offering into one of the better available options in the intermediate-term bond category since taking the reins in early 2000.

Weinblatt tends to favor midquality bonds for their added yield and return potential--more than 40% of the fund's assets were recently invested in bonds rated A or BBB, for example. And following a recent prospectus change, Weinblatt can allocate up to 10 percent of assets to junk bonds. But she is a cautious risk-taker, and only intends to use this flexibility when the yield offered by a company with improving fundamentals warrants the additional risk. In the current market, she has only been able to find one such bond, USG. Newly rid of its asbestos liabilities, the company is emerging from bankruptcy.

The bulk of Weinblatt's recent buying has been in the commercial mortgage-backed sector, focusing on longer-dated, AAA rated bonds. She bought these securities with the proceeds from maturing shorter-term paper, thereby intentionally increasing the portfolio's sensibility to interest rates. That move worked very well in the third quarter, when long-term rates moved lower.

Due to its fairly aggressive credit profile, the fund's payouts consistently range toward the top of the category. But its overall performance is competitive, too: The fund's trailing average five-year annual return of 4.8% through November 17, 2006, beats that of 64% of its category peers. The continuing increase in expenses is a reflection of performance fees kicking in. But at 0.59%, the fund's price tag remains well below average.

All told, we continue to like this fund for its seasoned manager, good diversification, and moderate cost. This offering's above-average volatility makes it unsuitable for conservative investors or those with a short time horizon. For everyone else, this is a fine option.

Portfolio Analysis 10-31-06

Total Fixed-Income:215

	Date of Maturity	Amount $000	Value $000	% Net Assets
US Treasury Bond 5.25%	11-15-28	45,771	48,642	2.71
US Treasury Note 4%	02-15-15	43,000	41,251	2.30
US Treasury Note 4%	02-15-14	38,000	36,620	2.04
US Treasury Bond 2.375%	01-15-25	32,450	32,858	1.83
FNMA 6%	05-01-36	29,368	29,559	1.64
FNMA 5%	06-01-33	30,294	29,336	1.63
FHLMC 5.5%	04-01-36	28,986	28,680	1.60
Household Fin 6.375%	10-15-11	25,200	26,470	1.47
Lombardy Region 5.804%	10-25-32	25,000	25,956	1.44
FNMA 6%	06-01-36	24,329	24,487	1.36
FNMA 5.5%	04-01-36	23,903	23,642	1.32
Phillips Pete 8.75%	05-25-10	21,000	23,443	1.30
FHLMC 5%	01-01-21	23,154	22,802	1.27
FNMA 5.5%	09-01-35	22,953	22,703	1.26
FHLMC 5.5%	11-01-20	21,563	21,591	1.20
Landesbank Baden-Wurttem	04-01-12	20,000	21,074	1.17
Prologis Pfd		345	20,089	1.12
Citibank Ccmt 2003-A4 FR	03-20-09	20,000	20,019	1.11
FNMA 5.5%	01-01-36	19,268	19,059	1.06
New Jersey St Tpk Auth 4	01-01-16	19,000	18,015	1.00

Current Investment Style

Duration: Short Int Long
Quality: High Med Low

¹ figure provided by fund

Avg Eff Duration¹	4.6 Yrs
Avg Eff Maturity	6.6 Yrs
Avg Credit Quality	AA
Avg Wtd Coupon	5.40%
Avg Wtd Price	101.08% of par

Coupon Range	% of Bonds	Rel Cat
0% PIK	1.5	0.2
0% to 6%	71.2	1.0
6% to 8%	24.8	1.1
8% to 10%	4.0	0.9
More than 10%	0.0	0.0

1.00=Category Average

Credit Analysis	% bonds 10-31-06		
AAA	50	BB	0
AA	10	B	0
A	20	Below B	0
BBB	20	NR/NA	0

Sector Breakdown

	% of assets
US Treasuries	9
TIPS	2
US Agency	1
Mortgage Pass-Throughs	22
Mortgage CMO	9
Mortgage ARM	0
US Corporate	41
Asset-Backed	6
Convertible	0
Municipal	3
Corporate Inflation-Protected	0
Foreign Corporate	2
Foreign Govt	1

Composition

Cash	4.8	Bonds	87.3
Stocks	0.0	Other	8.0

Special Securities

Restricted/Illiquid Secs	11
Exotic Mortgage-Backed	0
Emerging-Markets Secs	Trace
Options/Futures/Warrants	No

Address:	9800 Fredericksburg Road San Antonio TX 78288-0227 800-531-8448
Web Address:	www.usaa.com
Inception:	03-04-74
Advisor:	USAA Investment Management Company
Subadvisor:	None
NTF Plans:	Pershing NTF, TD Waterhouse Ins NT

Minimum Purchase:	$3000	Add: $50	IRA: $250	
Min Auto Inv Plan:	$0	Add: $20		
Sales Fees:	No-load			
Management Fee:	0.24%			
Actual Fees:	Mgt:0.26%	Dist: —		
Expense Projections:	3Yr:$189	5Yr:$329	10Yr:$738	
Income Distrib:	Monthly			

USAA Tax Ex Interm-Term

Analyst Pick	**Ticker** USATX	**Load** None	**NAV** $13.20	**Yield** 4.2%	**SEC Yield** 3.57%	**Total Assets** $2,775 mil	**Mstar Category** Muni National Interm	

Governance and Management

Stewardship Grade: B

Portfolio Manager(s)

Cliff Gladson has been at the helm since 1993. He has also run USAA Tax Exempt Short-Term for nearly as long and took charge of USAA NY Bond Fund in 1999. Gladson named Regina Shafer comanager in June 2003. Shafer has been a fixed-income analyst for USAA since 1995 and has run several of the firm's muni money market funds since 1999. Gladson says he's grooming Shafer as his successor.

Strategy

Manager Cliff Gladson employs an income-oriented approach, giving this fund one of the muni-national intermediate-term bond category's plumpest yields. Though Gladson favors securities with healthy yields, he won't buy longer-duration or lower-quality credits unless he believes they are undervalued. In the past, he has been more adventuresome on duration and credit quality than his typical rival, but he has given the portfolio an increasingly conservative cast in recent years.

Performance 12-31-06

	1st Qtr	2nd Qtr	3rd Qtr	4th Qtr	Total
2002	0.69	2.96	3.61	0.26	7.69
2003	1.25	2.00	0.37	1.46	5.18
2004	1.39	-1.52	3.39	1.01	4.27
2005	-0.33	2.81	-0.15	0.76	3.09
2006	0.28	-0.10	3.43	0.94	4.59

Trailing	Total Return%	+/- LB Muni	+/- LB Muni 10YR	%Rank Cat	Growth of $10,000
3 Mo	0.94	-0.17	0.02	13	10,094
6 Mo	4.40	-0.15	-0.37	12	10,440
1 Yr	4.59	-0.25	-0.12	11	10,459
3 Yr Avg	3.98	-0.30	0.12	9	11,242
5 Yr Avg	4.95	-0.58	-0.51	13	12,732
10 Yr Avg	5.28	-0.48	-0.42	9	16,729
15 Yr Avg	5.81	-0.45	-0.47	14	23,329

Tax Analysis	Tax-Adj Rtn%	%Rank Cat	Tax-Cost Rat	%Rank Cat
3 Yr (estimated)	3.96	7	0.02	10
5 Yr (estimated)	4.94	11	0.01	4
10 Yr (estimated)	5.27	5	0.01	5

Potential Capital Gain Exposure: 3% of assets

Morningstar's Take by Kai Wiecking 12-21-06

USAA Tax Exempt Intermediate-Term remains an excellent choice.

This fund's expense ratio isn't as low as it used to be. As recently as 2001, this fund made do with 0.36%, even though the asset level at the time was slightly lower than it is today. However, it still provides the fund nice advantage over most competitors in the muni national intermediate category. The fund's expense ratio now checks in at 0.55% versus 0.65% for its typical no-load rival.

Expenses are an important consideration, especially in a category with such tightly bunched returns as this. But despite the reduced cost edge, veteran manager Cliff Gladson continues to guide the fund past most of his peers. The fund's average annual return of 5.5% since Cliff Gladson took over through Dec. 20, 2006, outpaced 91% of its competitors. That's an edge of only 0.6 percentage points over its typical rival, but thanks to the effects of compounding, it has translated to 14.6 percentage points of extra return.

The way Gladson has achieved this is by patiently adding small increments of return rather than making big bets on the market. In recent months, for example, Gladson has very gradually and moderately extended the fund's duration (a measure of sensitivity to interest rates), as he thinks rates have peaked. He also has cautiously added some BBB rated bonds when spreads (the interest-rate differential between highly rated bonds and lower-grade securities) widened somewhat in May and June. But while Gladson often takes on more credit risk than some of his peers, he refrains from using leverage to boost yields. And while the fund is vulnerable to occasional bouts of volatility, its performance swings are typically in line with what's normal for the group.

All told, we continue to recommend this fund for its skillful management and consistently attractive payouts--provided the trend of rising expenses has come to a halt.

Historical Profile
Return High
Risk Below Avg
Rating ★★★★ Highest

2	1	2	3	4	4	5	9

Investment Style
Fixed Income
Income Rtn %Rank Cat

▼ Manager Change
▽ Partial Manager Change

20.8
18.8
16.4 **Growth of $10,000**
14.0 — Investment Values of Fund
12.0
10.0 — Investment Values of LB Muni

Performance Quartile (within Category)

1995	1996	1997	1998	1999	2000	2001	2002	2003	2004	2005	2006	History
13.08	12.92	13.38	13.50	12.47	12.97	13.00	13.33	13.38	13.34	13.17	13.20	NAV
15.07	4.49	9.39	6.32	-2.56	9.83	5.55	7.69	5.18	4.27	3.09	4.59	Total Return %
-2.39	0.06	0.20	-0.16	-0.50	-1.85	0.42	-1.91	-0.13	-0.21	-0.42	-0.25	+/-LB Muni
-2.10	-0.05	0.16	-0.44	-1.31	-0.93	0.93	-2.48	-0.52	0.12	0.35	-0.12	+/-LB Muni 10YR
6.07	5.67	5.69	5.40	5.28	5.66	5.35	5.09	4.78	4.39	4.22	4.31	Income Return %
9.00	-1.18	3.70	0.92	-7.84	4.17	0.20	2.60	0.40	-0.12	-1.13	0.28	Capital Return %
30	15	3	12	60	40	8	76	13	8	10	11	Total Rtn % Rank Cat
0.71	0.72	0.72	0.71	0.70	0.69	0.68	0.65	0.62	0.58	0.55	0.56	Income $
0.00	0.00	0.00	0.00	0.00	0.00	0.00	0.00	0.02	0.02	0.02	0.00	Capital Gains $
0.40	0.38	0.37	0.37	0.36	0.36	0.36	0.45	0.49	0.51	0.55	0.55	Expense Ratio %
5.63	5.54	5.65	5.42	5.21	5.39	5.41	5.06	4.86	4.58	4.28	4.15	Income Ratio %
72	28	23	8	12	10	9	12	15	23	21	22	Turnover Rate %
1,673	1,711	1,936	2,252	2,147	2,230	2,397	2,564	2,601	2,676	2,783	2,775	Net Assets $mil

Rating and Risk

Time Period	Load-Adj Return %	Morningstar Rtn vs Cat	Morningstar Risk vs Cat	Morningstar Risk-Adj Rating
1 Yr	4.59			
3 Yr	3.98	High	Avg	★★★★★
5 Yr	4.95	High	-Avg	★★★★★
10 Yr	5.28	High	-Avg	★★★★★
Incept	7.63			

Other Measures	Standard Index LB Muni	Best Fit Index LB Muni NY
Alpha	-0.2	-0.1
Beta	0.94	0.96
R-Squared	98	98
Standard Deviation	2.90	
Mean	3.98	
Sharpe Ratio	0.25	

Portfolio Analysis 09-30-06

Total Fixed-Income:541	Date of Maturity	Amount $000	Value $000	% Net Assets
NORTHERN TOB SECURITIZAT	06-01-23	40,000	40,031	1.47
Brazos River Auth 5.375%	04-01-19	32,925	33,828	1.24
Washington D C Conventio	10-01-18	30,000	30,970	1.14
New York N Y 5.5%	08-01-15	26,625	29,030	1.07
Dickinson Cnty Mich Econ	11-01-18	25,000	25,444	0.93
Chicago Ill Brd Ed	12-01-13	29,925	22,753	0.84
California St 5%	12-01-15	20,000	21,594	0.79
Mississippi Hosp Equip &	12-01-15	19,850	21,035	0.77
Los Angeles Calif Dept W	07-01-25	20,000	20,761	0.76
Indiana St Fin Auth 4.55	12-01-24	20,000	20,124	0.74
Tobacco Securitization A	06-01-25	19,500	19,850	0.73
Port Corpus Christi Tex	04-01-18	19,050	19,669	0.72
Cohasset Minn Pollutn Ct	07-01-22	18,015	18,349	0.67
Plano Tex Indpt Sch Dist	02-15-19	17,475	18,302	0.67
METROPOLITAN TRANSN AUTH	11-15-24	16,565	17,655	0.65

Current Investment Style

Duration Short Int Long

Quality High Med Low

¹Avg Eff Duration	5.0 Yrs
Avg Eff Maturity	9.2 Yrs
Avg Credit Quality	AA
Avg Wtd Coupon	4.66%
Avg Wtd Price	102.94% of par

¹figure provided by fund

Credit Analysis % bonds 09-30-06

AAA	51	BB	0
AA	16	B	0
A	13	Below B	1
BBB	19	NR/NA	0

Special Securities

Restricted/Illiquid Secs	0
Options/Futures/Warrants	No

Sector Weightings

	% of Bonds	Rel Cat
General Obligation	26.9	0.73
Utilities	11.2	1.19
Health	16.1	1.80
Water/Waste	4.2	0.45
Housing	5.3	1.02
Education	13.8	1.06
Transportation	4.8	0.91
COP/Lease	3.4	1.37
Industrial	14.2	1.53
Misc Revenue	0.0	—
Demand	0.1	0.31

Top 5 States % bonds

TX	15.6	IL	8.0
NY	12.3	FL	5.5
CA	11.5		

Composition

Cash	1.8	Bonds	98.1
Stocks	0.0	Other	0.1

Address:	9800 Fredericksburg Road San Antonio TX 78288-0227 800-531-8448
Web Address:	www.usaa.com
Inception:	03-19-82
Advisor:	USAA Investment Management Company
Subadvisor:	None
NTF Plans:	Pershing NTF, TD Waterhouse Ins NT

Minimum Purchase:	$3000	Add: $50	IRA: $0
Min Auto Inv Plan:	$0	Add: —	
Sales Fees:	No-load		
Management Fee:	0.33%		
Actual Fees:	Mgt:0.33%	Dist: —	
Expense Projections:	3Yr:$176	5Yr:$307	10Yr:$689
Income Distrib:	Monthly		

USAA Tax Ex Long-Term

Ticker	Load	NAV	Yield	SEC Yield	Total Assets	Mstar Category
USTEX	None	$13.96	4.4%	3.63%	$2,418 mil	Muni National Long

Governance and Management

Stewardship Grade: B

Portfolio Manager(s)

Bob Pariseau took the reins in November 1999. He has also run USAA California Bond and USAA Virginia Bond since 1995. Pariseau and colleague Cliff Gladson lead a team of three veteran muni-bond analysts. Pariseau keeps more than one third of his assets invested in this and other USAA funds.

Strategy

Although manager Bob Pariseau has tempered the fund's income focus, he isn't afraid to make some relatively bold moves to boost yield. He has brought the fund's credit profile more closely in line with the category average, but he still takes on a bit more credit risk than his typical peer. Although he sticks with investment-grade debt, Pariseau often finds bargains in issues rated A and BBB.

Historical Profile

Return High
Risk Average
Rating ★★★★ Highest

Investment Style
Fixed Income
Income Rtn %Rank Cat

▼ Manager Change
▽ Partial Manager Change

Growth of $10,000
— Investment Values of Fund
— Investment Values of LB Muni

Performance Quartile (within Category)

	1995	1996	1997	1998	1999	2000	2001	2002	2003	2004	2005	2006	History
	13.63	13.42	13.99	14.04	12.60	13.33	13.18	13.76	14.05	14.18	14.06	13.96	NAV
	18.58	4.47	10.38	5.97	-5.00	12.11	4.33	9.71	7.02	5.60	3.82	4.76	Total Return %
	1.12	0.04	1.19	-0.51	-2.94	0.43	-0.80	0.11	1.71	1.12	0.31	-0.08	+/-LB Muni
	-2.39	0.01	-0.46	-0.85	-0.32	-3.13	-0.54	-0.32	0.69	-0.96	-1.26	-1.10	+/-LB Muni 20YR
	6.77	5.94	5.96	5.62	5.58	6.06	5.53	5.20	4.84	4.61	4.46	4.46	Income Return %
	11.81	-1.47	4.42	0.35	-10.58	6.05	-1.20	4.51	2.18	0.99	-0.64	0.29	Capital Return %
	25	16	10	21	59	25	31	19	4	4	18	37	Total Rtn % Rank Cat
	0.80	0.79	0.78	0.77	0.76	0.74	0.72	0.67	0.65	0.63	0.62	0.61	Income $
	0.00	0.00	0.00	0.00	0.00	0.00	0.00	0.00	0.00	0.03	0.14	Capital Gains $
	0.38	0.37	0.37	0.36	0.36	0.36	0.36	0.45	0.54	0.56	0.56	0.55	Expense Ratio %
	6.23	5.99	5.95	5.65	5.44	5.77	5.72	5.25	4.90	4.63	4.50	4.38	Income Ratio %
	163	53	41	35	30	29	47	40	29	23	17	26	Turnover Rate %
	1,910	1,873	2,002	2,173	1,910	2,071	2,075	2,229	2,238	2,282	2,376	2,418	Net Assets $mil

Performance 12-31-06

	1st Qtr	2nd Qtr	3rd Qtr	4th Qtr	Total
2002	0.73	3.59	5.30	-0.16	9.71
2003	1.71	2.78	0.33	2.04	7.02
2004	1.70	-2.05	4.31	1.64	5.60
2005	-0.13	3.33	-0.08	0.69	3.82
2006	0.24	-0.33	3.56	1.24	4.76

Trailing	Total Return%	+/- LB Muni	+/- LB Muni 20YR	%Rank Cat	Growth of $10,000
3 Mo	1.24	0.13	-0.19	14	10,124
6 Mo	4.84	0.29	-0.67	15	10,484
1 Yr	4.76	-0.08	-1.10	37	10,476
3 Yr Avg	4.72	0.44	-1.11	11	11,484
5 Yr Avg	6.16	0.63	-0.60	5	13,484
10 Yr Avg	5.77	0.01	-0.81	7	17,524
15 Yr Avg	6.14	-0.12	-0.94	14	24,445

Tax Analysis	Tax-Adj Rtn%	%Rank Cat	Tax-Cost Rat	%Rank Cat
3 Yr (estimated)	4.66	9	0.06	22
5 Yr (estimated)	6.12	4	0.04	15
10 Yr (estimated)	5.75	5	0.02	9

Potential Capital Gain Exposure: 6% of assets

Rating and Risk

Time Period	Load-Adj Return %	Morningstar Rtn vs Cat	Morningstar Risk vs Cat	Morningstar Risk-Adj Rating
1 Yr	4.76			
3 Yr	4.72	High	+Avg	★★★★★
5 Yr	6.16	High	Avg	★★★★★
10 Yr	5.77	High	Avg	★★★★★
Incept	8.52			

Other Measures	Standard Index LB Muni	Best Fit Index LB Muni NY
Alpha	0.3	0.5
Beta	1.12	1.15
R-Squared	98	98
Standard Deviation	3.45	
Mean	4.72	
Sharpe Ratio	0.42	

Portfolio Analysis 09-30-06

Total Fixed-Income:292	Date of Maturity	Amount $000	Value $000	% Net Assets
Mashantucket Western Peq	09-01-27	64,950	66,602	2.80
Regl Transn Auth 6.5%	07-01-30	37,550	50,003	2.11
Michigan St Hosp Fin Aut	11-15-26	43,000	46,587	1.96
District Columbia 5.5%	06-01-29	37,580	39,517	1.66
South Carolina Jobs-Econ	11-15-26	30,000	32,855	1.38
New Jersey St Tpk Auth 5	01-01-27	30,020	31,779	1.34
Dallas Tex Indpt Sch Dis	08-15-32	29,670	30,386	1.28
Maine St Tpk Auth 5.75%	07-01-28	27,750	30,095	1.27
Univ Med Ctr 5%	07-01-35	28,500	29,106	1.23
Regl Transn Auth 5.75%	06-01-20	23,980	28,295	1.19
TEXAS ST VETS LD BRD VET	08-01-35	23,985	26,558	1.12
Illinois Fin Auth 5%	11-15-31	24,535	25,556	1.08
New York N Y G.O. Bds 5.	05-15-30	22,740	24,705	1.04
New York St Dorm Auth 6%	08-15-16	21,500	24,641	1.04
Bell Cnty Tex Health Fac	07-01-19	19,500	23,741	1.00

Current Investment Style

¹Avg Eff Duration	5.5 Yrs
Avg Eff Maturity	16.7 Yrs
Avg Credit Quality	AA
Avg Wtd Coupon	5.16%
Avg Wtd Price	105.19% of par

¹figure provided by fund

Credit Analysis	% bonds 09-30-06		
AAA	53	BB	0
AA	15	B	0
A	16	Below B	1
BBB	15	NR/NA	0

Top 5 States	% bonds		
TX	18.9	CA	4.8
NY	13.1	FL	4.1
IL	9.1		

Composition			
Cash	0.1	Bonds	99.9
Stocks	0.0	Other	0.0

Special Securities

Restricted/Illiquid Secs	Trace
Options/Futures/Warrants	No

Sector Weightings	% of Bonds	Rel Cat
General Obligation	36.9	1.31
Utilities	1.0	0.10
Health	23.1	2.22
Water/Waste	7.3	0.74
Housing	1.7	0.27
Education	9.7	0.85
Transportation	6.1	0.70
COP/Lease	1.0	0.42
Industrial	13.0	1.08
Misc Revenue	0.0	—
Demand	0.3	0.58

Morningstar's Take by Kai Wiecking 12-26-06

With the succession issue handled, we continue to think highly of USAA Tax Exempt Long-Term.

The strong points far outweigh the areas of concern at this fund. For starters, manager Bob Pariseau's track record speaks for itself: For each of the trailing one-, three-, and five-year periods through Aug. 27, 2006, this fund's returns comfortably rank within the top 15% for the muni-national long-term category. Yet its volatility, as measured by standard deviation of returns, checks in near the category midpoint.

We like the fund's balanced approach and the fact that Pariseau is openly addressing the succession issue here. John Bonnell has rejoined USAA after stints at Strong and Oppenheimer. Pariseau will train Bonnell to eventually take over from him. The two managers will continue to employ the same approach that has brought the fund success in recent years. USAA's ability to attract and retain talent--not a given in light of the firm's relatively remote San Antonio location--thus seems to be intact.

The fund's success also owes much to USAA's long-established investment approach. Pariseau focuses primarily on generating income through issue selection, but he does make moderate bets on the direction of interest rates. Throughout this year, for example, he has slightly extended the fund's duration (a measure of interest-rate sensitivity), as he banked on a halt to the Fed's campaign of raising rates, which has since materialized. But Pariseau carefully monitors risk, and he is now growing a bit more cautious, as he deems the muni-bond market to be fully valued following its extended run. And unlike some competitors, he foregoes derivatives and leverage as potential yield boosters.

Overall, we think Pariseau's experience and prudence combined with solid credit research make this a good choice for muni investors.

Address:	9800 Fredericksburg Road San Antonio TX 78288-0227 800-531-8448	Minimum Purchase:	$3000	Add: $50	IRA: $0
		Min Auto Inv Plan:	$0	Add: —	
		Sales Fees:	No-load		
Web Address:	www.usaa.com	Management Fee:	0.34%		
Inception:	03-19-82	Actual Fees:	Mgt:0.33%	Dist: —	
Advisor:	USAA Investment Management Company	Expense Projections:	3Yr:$176	5Yr:$307	10Yr:$689
Subadvisor:	None	Income Distrib:	Monthly		
NTF Plans:	Pershing NTF, TD Waterhouse Ins NT				

MORNINGSTAR® Funds 500

USAA Tax Ex Short-Term

	Analyst Pick ✓	Ticker USSTX	Load None	NAV $10.61	Yield 3.6%	SEC Yield 3.43%	Total Assets $1,086 mil	Mstar Category Muni National Short

Governance and Management

Stewardship Grade: B

Portfolio Manager(s)

Clifford Gladson has a good record at this fund and at USAA Tax Exempt Intermediate-Term. Gladson named Regina Shafer comanager in June 2003 and says he's grooming her as his successor. Shafer has been a fixed-income analyst for USAA since 1995 and has run several of the firm's muni money market funds since 1999. Three veteran analysts assist, and fellow muni manager Bob Pariseau completes the team.

Strategy

Less is more at this fund. Manager Clifford Gladson maintains a short and steady duration and keeps trading to a minimum. Gladson eschews explicit interest-rate bets and searches for income instead. He looks for the most income he can find for the duration risk, often in lower-rated investment-grade bonds.

Performance 12-31-06

	1st Qtr	2nd Qtr	3rd Qtr	4th Qtr	Total
2002	0.51	1.97	1.95	0.45	4.97
2003	0.93	1.09	0.47	0.45	2.97
2004	0.70	-0.85	1.28	0.40	1.52
2005	-0.07	0.97	0.42	0.44	1.78
2006	0.57	0.53	1.58	0.82	3.54

Trailing	Total Return%	+/- LB Muni	+/- LB Muni 3YR	%Rank Cat	Growth of $10,000
3 Mo	0.82	-0.29	0.19	20	10,082
6 Mo	2.42	-2.13	-0.16	29	10,242
1 Yr	3.54	-1.30	0.49	16	10,354
3 Yr Avg	2.27	-2.01	0.37	18	10,697
5 Yr Avg	2.95	-2.58	-0.05	27	11,565
10 Yr Avg	3.84	-1.92	-0.20	23	14,576
15 Yr Avg	4.21	-2.05	-0.24	47	18,563

Tax Analysis	Tax-Adj Rtn%	%Rank Cat	Tax-Cost Rat	%Rank Cat
3 Yr (estimated)	2.27	14	0.00	1
5 Yr (estimated)	2.95	25	0.00	1
10 Yr (estimated)	3.84	19	0.00	1

Potential Capital Gain Exposure: 0% of assets

Morningstar's Take by Kai Wiecking 12-26-06

Shareholders in USAA Tax Exempt Short-Term will be delighted to hear that there's not much to report here.

That's because lead manager Cliff Gladson is successfully continuing what he's been doing ever since taking the helm at this offering 12 years ago--straightforward buy-and-hold investing with no gimmicks attached. Gladson doesn't use derivatives or make big bets on the direction of interest rates, both of which can result in wild performance swings. Instead, he focuses his efforts on generating the highest-possible income without taking on undue risk. Sure, the bulk of the portfolio is usually invested in midgrade bonds rather than AAA rated bonds. But USAA's deep and talented muni-research bench makes it one of the few shops that can be trusted to keep close tabs on the individual risks of each holding. The fact that volatility here is below average for the muni-national short-term category is an indication of its ability to avoid pitfalls.

A closer look at the fund's track record reveals that it fell short of the group average in only one of the past 11 years. Consequently, its trailing 10-year average return of 3.9% through November 30, 2006, beats that of 78% of its rivals in the group.

In early 2006, Gladson gradually increased the portfolio's sensitivity to interest rates, as he correctly deemed that the Fed's rate-raising campaign was nearing its end. He's now scouring the market for attractively valued A and BB rated issues, but the scarcity of supply has limited his capacity to act. Investors need not worry that Gladson has suddenly turned into a big risk-taker; all this activity is more or less at the margin. Overall, the portfolio remains diversified at all levels.

All told, this offering with its experienced and sober management remains a solid option for self-directed muni investors looking for good income without a lot of interest-rate risk.

Address:	9800 Fredericksburg Road San Antonio TX 78288-0227 800-531-8448
Web Address:	www.usaa.com
Inception:	03-19-82
Advisor:	USAA Investment Management Company
Subadvisor:	None
NTF Plans:	Pershing NTF, TD Waterhouse Ins NT

Minimum Purchase:	$3000	Add: $50	IRA: $0
Min Auto Inv Plan:	$0	Add: —	
Sales Fees:	No-load		
Management Fee:	0.33%		
Actual Fees:	Mgt:0.33%	Dist: —	
Expense Projections:	3Yr:$176	5Yr:$307	10Yr:$689
Income Distrib:	Monthly		

Historical Profile

Return	Above Avg
Risk	Average
Rating	★★★★ Above Avg

Investment Style
Fixed Income
Income Rtn %Rank Cat

▼ Manager Change
▽ Partial Manager Change

Growth of $10,000
■ Investment Values of Fund
— Investment Values of LB Muni

Performance Quartile (within Category)

1995	1996	1997	1998	1999	2000	2001	2002	2003	2004	2005	2006	History
10.65	10.62	10.74	10.77	10.47	10.60	10.69	10.85	10.87	10.76	10.62	10.61	NAV
8.11	4.44	5.86	5.02	1.78	6.03	5.10	4.97	2.97	1.52	1.78	3.54	Total Return %
-9.35	0.01	-3.33	-1.46	3.84	-5.65	-0.03	-4.63	-2.34	-2.96	-1.73	-1.30	+/-LB Muni
-0.76	0.00	0.38	-0.19	-0.18	-0.20	-1.49	-1.75	0.29	-0.26	0.91	0.49	+/-LB Muni 3YR
4.96	4.70	4.69	4.73	4.63	4.74	4.25	3.45	2.79	2.54	3.09	3.63	Income Return %
3.15	-0.26	1.17	0.29	-2.85	1.29	0.85	1.52	0.18	-1.02	-1.31	-0.09	Capital Return %
30	15	23	12	18	36	39	57	21	30	21	16	Total Rtn % Rank Cat
0.50	0.49	0.49	0.50	0.49	0.49	0.44	0.36	0.30	0.27	0.33	0.38	Income $
0.00	0.00	0.00	0.00	0.00	0.00	0.00	0.00	0.00	0.00	0.00	0.00	Capital Gains $
0.42	0.42	0.41	0.39	0.38	0.38	0.38	0.46	0.54	0.56	0.55	0.56	Expense Ratio %
4.50	4.73	4.60	4.57	4.55	4.48	4.60	3.90	3.25	2.60	2.60	3.22	Income Ratio %
103	36	28	8	7	19	19	20	14	22	8	24	Turnover Rate %
777	786	937	1,005	988	1,003	1,122	1,226	1,367	1,319	1,177	1,086	Net Assets $mil

Rating and Risk

Time Period	Load-Adj Return %	Morningstar Rtn vs Cat	Morningstar Risk vs Cat	Morningstar Risk-Adj Rating
1 Yr	3.54			
3 Yr	2.27	+Avg	Avg	★★★★
5 Yr	2.95	Avg	Avg	★★★★
10 Yr	3.84	+Avg	Avg	★★★★
Incept	5.38			

Other Measures	Standard Index LB Muni	Best Fit Index LB Muni 3YR
Alpha	-1.3	-0.1
Beta	0.30	0.64
R-Squared	88	93
Standard Deviation	1.00	
Mean	2.27	
Sharpe Ratio	-0.99	

Portfolio Analysis 09-30-06

Total Fixed-Income:199

	Date of Maturity	Amount $000	Value $000	% Net Assets
Mcintosh Ala Indl Dev Br	07-01-28	46,550	46,550	4.10
NEW YORK ST URBAN DEV	01-01-17	34,475	36,832	3.24
Amer Falls Idaho Reservo	02-01-25	19,885	19,885	1.75
HILLSBOROUGH CNTY FLA IN	05-15-18	19,390	19,403	1.71
BRAZOS RIV TEX HBR NAV D	05-15-33	19,000	19,098	1.68
JORDANELLE SPL SVC DIST	06-20-09	18,470	18,566	1.63
Chesapeake Va Indl Dev A	03-01-13	18,665	18,367	1.62
New York N Y City Indl D	05-01-29	17,967	17,967	1.58
Chicago Ill Brd Ed	12-01-09	20,000	17,799	1.57
New York St Dorm Auth 5.	07-01-32	15,000	16,373	1.44
LINCOLN CNTY WYO POLLUTN		15,000	14,632	1.29
Michigan St Strategic Fd	12-01-08	14,200	14,200	1.25
SWEETWATER CNTY WYO POLL	12-01-14	14,000	13,771	1.21
Massachusetts St 5.5%	06-01-08	12,575	12,970	1.14
Maricopa Cnty Ariz Indl	01-01-39	12,405	12,405	1.09

Current Investment Style

Duration: Short Int Long
Quality: High Med Low

¹Avg Eff Duration	1.9 Yrs
Avg Eff Maturity	2.3 Yrs
Avg Credit Quality	A
Avg Wtd Coupon	3.47%
Avg Wtd Price	100.52% of par

¹figure provided by fund

Credit Analysis	% bonds 09-30-06		
AAA	20	BB	0
AA	20	B	0
A	29	Below B	3
BBB	28	NR/NA	0

Special Securities	
Restricted/Illiquid Secs	0
Options/Futures/Warrants	No

Top 5 States	% bonds		
NY	16.6	FL	6.5
TX	9.6	WY	6.3
CA	6.8		

Composition			
Cash	12.7	Bonds	87.3
Stocks	0.0	Other	0.0

Sector Weightings	% of Bonds	Rel Cat
General Obligation	26.6	0.81
Utilities	2.5	0.31
Health	12.8	1.28
Water/Waste	0.0	0.00
Housing	6.3	0.69
Education	11.0	1.28
Transportation	1.1	0.20
COP/Lease	4.5	2.47
Industrial	35.2	2.18
Misc Revenue	0.0	—
Demand	0.0	0.00

Van Kampen Comstock A

	Ticker	Load	NAV	Yield	Total Assets	Mstar Category
	ACSTX	5.75%	$19.25	1.9%	$19,859 mil	Large Value

Governance and Management

Stewardship Grade: C

Portfolio Manager(s)

Robert Baker has been at the helm since July 1994. He's assisted by two comanagers: Jason Leder since 1995 and Kevin Holt since 1999.

Strategy

Managers here like to take advantage of troubled situations. They use a bottom-up contrarian approach and have varied valuation criteria for stock selection to dive headfirst into some extremely beaten-down issues. Investors should expect some big sector bets and should be willing to wait through periods of underperformance, as managers often move early.

Historical Profile

Return	Average
Risk	Above Avg
Rating	★★★ Neutral

92% 91% 89% 83% 95% 92% 90% 92% 92%

▼ Manager Change
▽ Partial Manager Change

Growth of $10,000
— Investment Values of Fund
— Investment Values of S&P 500

42.2
32.4
24.0
17.0
10.0

Performance Quartile (within Category)

	1995	1996	1997	1998	1999	2000	2001	2002	2003	2004	2005	2006	History
	14.54	14.78	16.20	16.39	14.80	17.23	15.68	12.34	15.95	18.51	17.81	19.25	NAV
	36.15	22.34	29.92	20.12	2.38	31.91	-1.79	-19.59	30.98	17.57	4.19	16.06	Total Return %
	-1.43	-0.62	-3.44	-8.46	-18.66	41.01	10.10	2.51	2.30	6.69	-0.72	0.27	+/-S&P 500
	-2.21	0.70	-5.26	4.49	-4.97	24.90	3.80	-4.07	0.95	1.08	-2.86	-6.19	+/-Russ 1000 VI
	2.23	1.81	1.74	1.80	1.81	2.19	1.34	1.09	1.50	1.39	1.75	2.19	Income Return %
	33.92	20.53	28.18	18.32	0.57	29.72	-3.13	-20.68	29.48	16.18	2.44	13.87	Capital Return %
	22	20	24	8	62	2	39	62	28	11	69	76	Total Rtn % Rank Cat
	0.27	0.26	0.25	0.28	0.29	0.31	0.23	0.17	0.18	0.22	0.32	0.38	Income $
	1.96	2.59	2.57	2.67	1.65	1.65	1.00	0.14	0.00	0.00	1.16	0.95	Capital Gains $
	0.96	1.00	0.94	0.91	0.89	0.93	0.87	0.89	0.90	0.84	0.80	—	Expense Ratio %
	1.82	1.71	1.71	1.59	1.73	2.10	1.30	1.33	1.40	1.47	1.77	—	Income Ratio %
	151	176	114	102	72	89	62	52	40	34	30	—	Turnover Rate %
	1,078	1,241	1,532	1,756	1,797	2,509	3,797	4,195	6,734	10,592	12,065	13,715	Net Assets $mil

Performance 12-31-06

	1st Qtr	2nd Qtr	3rd Qtr	4th Qtr	Total
2002	3.49	-13.96	-19.33	11.95	-19.59
2003	-4.53	18.45	3.44	11.97	30.98
2004	3.43	1.57	2.27	9.43	17.57
2005	-1.26	0.28	1.33	3.84	4.19
2006	2.90	0.83	5.48	6.05	16.06

Trailing	Total Return%	+/- S&P 500	+/- Russ 1000 VI	%Rank Cat	Growth of $10,000
3 Mo	6.05	-0.65	-1.95	87	10,605
6 Mo	11.87	-0.87	-2.85	69	11,187
1 Yr	16.06	0.27	-6.19	76	11,606
3 Yr Avg	12.45	2.01	-2.64	46	14,219
5 Yr Avg	8.41	2.22	-2.45	47	14,974
10 Yr Avg	11.98	3.56	0.98	4	31,003
15 Yr Avg	12.41	1.77	-0.62	15	57,819

Tax Analysis	Tax-Adj Rtn%	%Rank Cat	Tax-Cost Rat	%Rank Cat
3 Yr (estimated)	8.90	78	1.22	48
5 Yr (estimated)	6.09	69	0.97	52
10 Yr (estimated)	8.57	19	2.47	90

Potential Capital Gain Exposure: 15% of assets

Rating and Risk

Time Period	Load-Adj Return %	Morningstar Rtn vs Cat	Morningstar Risk vs Cat	Morningstar Risk-Adj Rating
1 Yr	9.39			
3 Yr	10.25	-Avg	-Avg	★★
5 Yr	7.13	Avg	+Avg	★★
10 Yr	11.32	+Avg	+Avg	★★★★
Incept	12.06			

Other Measures	Standard Index S&P 500	Best Fit Index Mstar Large Core TR
Alpha	3.1	2.4
Beta	0.80	0.86
R-Squared	76	78
Standard Deviation	6.35	
Mean	12.45	
Sharpe Ratio	1.38	

Portfolio Analysis 09-30-06

Share change since 06-06 Total Stocks:83	Sector	PE	Tot Ret%	% Assets
⊕ Freddie Mac	Financial	23.3	7.06	3.85
⊖ Verizon Communications	Telecom	15.9	34.88	3.62
⊖ International Paper Co.	Ind Mtrls		4.51	3.60
Bank of America Corporat	Financial	12.4	20.68	3.46
⊕ Citigroup, Inc.	Financial	13.1	19.55	3.36
⊖ AT&T, Inc.	Telecom	18.2	51.59	3.05
⊖ GlaxoSmithKline PLC ADR	Health	17.6	7.95	2.78
⊕ Bristol-Myers Squibb Com	Health	23.1	19.93	2.45
⊕ E.I. du Pont de Nemours	Ind Mtrls	18.4	18.64	2.27
⊕ Wal-Mart Stores, Inc.	Consumer	16.9	0.13	2.13
⊕ Alcoa, Inc.	Ind Mtrls	12.0	3.49	2.05
⊕ Wachovia Corporation	Financial	12.9	12.02	1.98
⊕ Comcast Corporation A	Media	45.2	63.31	1.89
⊕ Kimberly-Clark Corporati	Goods	22.7	17.55	1.85
⊕ Schering-Plough Corporat	Health	36.6	14.63	1.80
⊕ Wells Fargo Company	Financial	14.7	16.82	1.75
⊖ Clear Channel Communicat	Media	27.4	15.79	1.70
⊕ Wyeth	Health	17.2	12.88	1.68
⊕ Time Warner, Inc.	Media	19.6	26.37	1.68
⊕ Pfizer Inc.	Health	15.2	15.22	1.68

Current Investment Style

Value Blnd Growth — Large Mid Small

Market Cap	%
Giant	57.6
Large	39.1
Mid	3.0
Small	0.2
Micro	0.1

Avg $mil: 60,608

Value Measures		Rel Category
Price/Earnings	15.27	1.11
Price/Book	2.09	0.94
Price/Sales	1.70	1.31
Price/Cash Flow	1.74	0.26
Dividend Yield %	2.50	1.07

Growth Measures	%	Rel Category
Long-Term Erngs	9.95	0.96
Book Value	5.56	0.70
Sales	6.06	0.67
Cash Flow	-2.95	NMF
Historical Erngs	9.24	0.57

Profitability	%	Rel Category
Return on Equity	18.22	1.02
Return on Assets	9.24	0.94
Net Margin	12.82	0.99

Sector Weightings	% of Stocks	Rel S&P 500	3 Year High	Low
⊙ Info	26.86	1.34		
🖥 Software	0.88	0.26	1	0
💻 Hardware	0.54	0.59	5	3
🎤 Media	11.20	2.96	11	4
📱 Telecom	9.29	2.65	12	8
🔧 Service	51.69	1.12		
🏥 Health	18.26	1.51	18	12
🛒 Consumer	3.13	0.41	6	3
📋 Business	1.37	0.32	2	1
💲 Financial	28.93	1.30	29	21
🏭 Mfg	21.45	0.63		
🛢 Goods	9.87	1.15	12	7
⚙ Ind Mtrls	10.03	0.84	14	10
🔥 Energy	0.62	0.06	16	1
💡 Utilities	0.93	0.27	6	1

Composition

	%
● Cash	8.4
● Stocks	91.6
● Bonds	0.0
● Other	0.0
Foreign (% of Stock)	9.6

Morningstar's Take by Marta Norton 12-19-06

Van Kampen Comstock runs well over the long haul, even though it hits a few bumps along the way.

This fund uses a strict contrarian approach. Managers Bob Baker, Jason Leder, and Kevin Holt look for stocks trading below the value of their underlying assets. And when they find the right opportunity, they'll load up for the long haul. For instance, the fund has had more than 8% of its assets in media stocks since mid-2005 and has had an unusually high telecom stake since late 2003.

There are some downsides to this approach. For one, buying and holding lots of out-of-favor stocks spells volatility. In fact, as of Nov. 30, 2006, the fund's five- and 10-year standard deviations (a measure of return volatility) were above those of the average large-value peer. That's because the fund often makes its moves early. That can lead to poor returns over the short term, as stocks can languish before rebounding. Over the past few years, for example, the fund has moved into larger caps, such as Anheuser-Busch, because they fell to

attractive valuations during the long small-cap rally. The behemoths initially dragged on the fund's performance, but lately they've shown signs of life. Anheuser-Busch was up 14.7% for the year-to-date period ending Dec. 18, 2006.

We think the long-term rewards for calls like that one far outweigh the short-term costs. Granted, contrarian bets are hard to get right, but this management team has experience on its side. Baker has been running this strategy since 1994, and while the fund has made some missteps along the way (it was blindsided along with many other funds by accounting scandals at WorldCom and Qwest in 2002), it has amassed a fine long-term record. Over the 10-year period ending December 18, its 11.7% gain made it a top-decile performer.

Low expenses are another incentive to invest here. The fund's 0.80% expense ratio is below those of most of its peers, and allows investors to put more of their money to work. Those willing to wait for their reward have a good option here.

Address:	1221 Avenue Of The Americas New York, NY 10020 800-847-2424	
Web Address:	www.vankampen.com	
Inception:	10-07-68	
Advisor:	Van Kampen Asset Management, Inc.	
Subadvisor:	None	
NTF Plans:	Federated Tr NTF, Fidelity Instl-NTF	

Minimum Purchase:	$0	Add: $25	IRA: $500
Min Auto Inv Plan:	$25	Add: $25	
Sales Fees:	5.75%L, 0.25%S, 2.00%R		
Management Fee:	0.50% mx./0.35% mn.		
Actual Fees:	Mgt:0.37%	Dist:0.25%	
Expense Projections:	3Yr:$816	5Yr:$994	10Yr:$1508
Income Distrib:	Quarterly		

Morningstar® Funds 500

Van Kampen Eq and Inc A

	Ticker	Load	NAV	Yield	Total Assets	Mstar Category
	ACEIX	5.75%	$9.12	2.1%	$18,465 mil	Moderate Allocation

Governance and Management

Stewardship Grade: C

Portfolio Manager(s)

Lead manager James Gilligan has been at the helm since January 1990. James Roeder, Vincent Vizachero, and Tom Bastian joined him as comanagers in May 1999, April 2002, and May 2003, respectively. David Armstrong, David Horowitz, and Stefania Perrucci have overseen the straight bond portion of the fund since mid-to-late 2005. All in all, this is an experienced and skilled management group.

Strategy

This fund usually devotes 55%-65% of assets to stocks, 25%-35% to convertible and straight bonds, and 5%-10% to cash. (Weightings will vary, depending on manager Jim Gilligan's assessment of relative valuation and market cycles.) The fixed-income portion serves to provide stability and current income; dramatic credit and interest-rate bets aren't part of the strategy. Management prefers convertibles, when reasonably priced, to straight debt. The stock portion of the fund is devoted primarily to temporarily out-of-favor firms with strong cash flows.

Historical Profile

Return	Above Avg
Risk	Average
Rating	★★★★ Above Avg

Investment Style: Equity, Stock %

60% 62% 60% 57% 57% 63% 65% 58% 59%

▼ Manager Change
▽ Partial Manager Change

Growth of $10,000
— Investment Values of Fund
— Investment Values of DJ Mod

38.0 / 31.0 / 24.0 / 17.0 / 10.0

Performance Quartile (within Category)

1995	1996	1997	1998	1999	2000	2001	2002	2003	2004	2005	2006	History
6.31	6.74	7.24	7.82	7.64	8.07	7.46	6.62	7.90	8.62	8.68	9.12	NAV
32.60	15.55	24.13	16.99	9.95	20.19	-2.23	-8.32	22.16	11.77	7.81	12.53	Total Return %
12.80	4.89	12.23	4.67	-7.38	21.86	0.57	-1.55	-5.22	-1.20	0.82	0.23	+/-DJ Mod
7.83	4.21	4.93	4.60	-2.90	15.75	-2.39	2.22	-1.90	0.60	1.81	2.26	+/-DJ US Mod
3.69	2.51	2.55	2.46	2.38	2.70	2.56	2.29	2.56	2.34	2.11	2.36	Income Return %
28.91	13.04	21.58	14.53	7.57	17.49	-4.79	-10.61	19.60	9.43	5.70	10.17	Capital Return %
8	42	15	29	55	2	24	18	33	13	8	24	Total Rtn % Rank Cat
0.19	0.16	0.17	0.18	0.18	0.20	0.20	0.17	0.17	0.18	0.18	0.20	Income $
0.32	0.37	0.92	0.45	0.74	0.86	0.21	0.07	0.00	0.01	0.42	0.42	Capital Gains $
0.95	0.97	0.86	0.85	0.82	0.82	0.82	0.82	0.83	0.80	0.78	—	Expense Ratio %
3.43	2.50	2.09	2.31	2.43	2.62	2.60	2.34	2.18	1.97	1.98	—	Income Ratio %
92	99	86	61	81	85	92	53	49	42	38	—	Turnover Rate %
357	472	638	819	1,068	1,636	2,261	2,833	5,192	7,741	10,372	12,620	Net Assets $mil

Performance 12-31-06

	1st Qtr	2nd Qtr	3rd Qtr	4th Qtr	Total
2002	3.20	-5.52	-11.22	5.91	-8.32
2003	-2.70	12.83	1.69	9.42	22.16
2004	2.05	0.65	0.77	7.98	11.77
2005	-0.40	2.32	4.61	1.13	7.81
2006	2.26	0.01	5.00	4.80	12.53

Trailing	Total Return%	+/- DJ Mod	+/- DJ US Mod	%Rank Cat	Growth of $10,000
3 Mo	4.80	-0.79	0.13	60	10,480
6 Mo	10.04	1.25	2.14	22	11,004
1 Yr	12.53	0.23	2.26	24	11,253
3 Yr Avg	10.69	-0.03	1.57	12	13,562
5 Yr Avg	8.72	-1.30	1.12	8	15,190
10 Yr Avg	11.04	2.49	2.45	3	28,497
15 Yr Avg	12.03	2.82	2.64	4	54,956

Tax Analysis	Tax-Adj Rtn%	%Rank Cat	Tax-Cost Rat	%Rank Cat
3 Yr (estimated)	7.14	45	1.27	64
5 Yr (estimated)	6.21	21	1.14	70
10 Yr (estimated)	8.17	6	2.00	81

Potential Capital Gain Exposure: 7% of assets

Rating and Risk

Time Period	Load-Adj Return %	Morningstar Rtn vs Cat	Morningstar Risk vs Cat	Morningstar Risk-Adj Rating
1 Yr	6.06			
3 Yr	8.52	Avg	-Avg	★★★
5 Yr	7.44	+Avg	Avg	★★★★
10 Yr	10.38	High	Avg	★★★★★
Incept	11.00			

Other Measures	Standard Index DJ Mod	Best Fit Index Russ 1000 VI
Alpha	2.1	-0.2
Beta	0.70	0.66
R-Squared	75	86
Standard Deviation	4.78	
Mean	10.69	
Sharpe Ratio	1.49	

Portfolio Analysis 09-30-06

Total Stocks:81 Share change since 06-30-06	Sectors	P/E Ratio	YTD Return %	% Net Assets
J.P. Morgan Chase & Co.	Financial	13.6	-0.02	2.19
⊖ Bayer AG ADR	Ind Mtrls	19.1	-1.63	1.92
⊕ Citigroup, Inc.	Financial	13.1	-1.17	1.84
General Electric Company	Ind Mtrls	20.0	0.91	1.55
⊕ Verizon Communications	Telecom	15.9	-0.07	1.52
⊕ Eli Lilly & Company	Health	17.3	-0.58	1.48
⊕ Freddie Mac	Financial	23.3	-2.90	1.48
⊕ Symantec Corporation	Software	50.9	2.54	1.47
⊕ Schering-Plough Corporati	Health	36.6	-0.89	1.43

Total Fixed-Income:200	Date of Maturity	Amount $000	Value $000	% Net Assets
US Treasury Note 4.5%	02-28-11	256,900	256,017	1.44
US Treasury Note 4.75%	11-15-08	184,000	184,309	1.04
US Treasury Note 4%	02-15-14	175,000	168,321	0.95
US Treasury Note 6.5%	02-15-10	133,000	140,757	0.79
US Treasury Note 3%	11-15-07	125,000	122,500	0.69
US Treasury Bond 6.375%	08-15-27	96,750	116,176	0.65
US Treasury Note 3.875%	02-15-13	119,075	114,410	0.64
US Treasury Bond 7.625%	02-15-25	75,000	100,201	0.56
QWEST COMMUNICATIONS INTL	11-15-25	56,901	92,891	0.52

Equity Style
Style: Value
Size: Large-Cap

Value Measures		Rel Category
Price/Earnings	15.35	1.00
Price/Book	1.91	0.77
Price/Sales	1.60	1.17
Price/Cash Flow	2.50	0.31
Dividend Yield %	2.17	1.12

Growth Measures	%	Rel Category
Long-Term Erngs	10.11	0.86
Book Value	7.74	0.90
Sales	6.95	0.78
Cash Flow	2.46	0.25
Historical Erngs	14.45	0.81

Market Cap %		
Giant	51.2	Small 0.0
Large	46.9	Micro 0.0
Mid	1.9	Avg $mil: 53,771

Fixed-Income Style
Duration: —
Quality: —

Avg Eff Duration [1]	—
Avg Eff Maturity	—
Avg Credit Quality	—
Avg Wtd Coupon	4.10%

[1]figure provided by fund

Sector Weightings	% of Stocks	Rel DJ Mod	3 Year High Low
Info	20.70	—	
Software	2.50	—	3 1
Hardware	5.08	—	7 2
Media	6.70	—	8 6
Telecom	6.42	—	6 3
Service	50.11		
Health	18.70	—	20 11
Consumer	4.55	—	6 3
Business	0.00	—	8 0
Financial	26.86	—	27 21
Mfg	29.18		
Goods	9.04	—	10 8
Ind Mtrls	10.86	—	13 10
Energy	5.67	—	14 6
Utilities	3.61	—	5 3

Composition

	%
● Cash	8.8
● Stocks	58.7
● Bonds	19.3
● Other	13.3
Foreign (% of Stock)	16.8

Morningstar's Take by Marta Norton 12-19-06

Van Kampen Equity and Income remains a top choice.

This fund relies heavily on management's ability to tear apart financial statements. Skipper Jim Gilligan and his team first screen for large-cap stocks that look cheap on a historical basis according to metrics such as price to normalized earnings (they don't want to be misled by unsustainable earnings blips). They then dig into the financials, looking for improving revenues, falling costs, stable cash flow, and strong returns on capital. They also look for companies that stand to benefit from industry consolidation or new management. But given that much of their process revolves around companies' financials, it helps that Gilligan and many of his team members have CPAs. Their accounting backgrounds make them especially adept at this process.

The fund also uses this strategy to select convertible bonds, which, as of Nov. 30, 2006, claimed about 15.5% of its portfolio. Gilligan uses the hybrid securities that have stock and bond characteristics when he likes a company and thinks it's cheap, but isn't sure if it can turn itself around. That's the case with Eastman Kodak. He likes the company's price, but isn't sure if it'll be able to morph from a film company to a digital one.

The fund also invests in bonds. Gilligan decides how much to allocate here, but David Armstrong, David Horowitz, and Stefania Perrucci take care of actual security selection. They generally don't make interest-rate bets and usually stick to AAA bonds. As of Nov. 30, 2006, fixed-income claimed about 17.7% of the fund's assets.

The fund's contrarian approach has made it a top-performing moderate-allocation fund. We do worry that Gilligan and members of his team are overextended, though. They run $30 billion in a similar style for eight different Morgan Stanley funds, which limits their flexibility. Still, the fund's low turnover helps ease our concerns. Its low expenses are also hard to pass up.

Address:	1221 Avenue Of The Americas New York, NY 10020 800-847-2424	Minimum Purchase:	$0 Add: $0 IRA: $500
		Min Auto Inv Plan:	$25 Add: $25
		Sales Fees:	5.75%L, 0.25%S, 2.00%R
Web Address:	www.vankampen.com	Management Fee:	0.50% mx./0.35% mn.
Inception:	08-03-60	Actual Fees:	Mgt:0.35% Dist:0.25%
Advisor:	Van Kampen Asset Management, Inc.	Expense Projections:	3Yr:$810 5Yr:$983 10Yr:$1486
Subadvisor:	None	Income Distrib:	Quarterly
NTF Plans:	Federated Tr NTF, Fidelity Instl-NTF		

Van Kampen Growth & IncA

	Ticker	Load	NAV	Yield	Total Assets	Mstar Category
	ACGIX	5.75%	$22.08	1.4%	$10,418 mil	Large Value

Governance and Management

Stewardship Grade: C

Portfolio Manager(s)

James Gilligan is the constant at this fund; he has been at the helm since 1990. James Roeder, Vincent Vizachero, and Tom Bastian joined him as comanagers in May 1999, April 2002, and May 2003, respectively. This group also manages Van Kampen Equity and Income and Morgan Stanley Balanced Growth. While Van Kampen and parent firm Morgan Stanley have suffered from portfolio manager turnover, we don't think that's a concern here: Gilligan is too valuable to be allowed to leave.

Strategy

Lead manager James Gilligan looks for beaten-down companies with a catalyst for change. Requiring signs of near-term improvements helps keep the fund from picking up value traps. But Gilligan isn't afraid to make significant sector bets if he sees attractive opportunities. The portfolio usually contains between 80 and 100 names.

Historical Profile
Return Average
Risk Below Avg
Rating ★★★ Neutral

87%	90%	86%	91%	92%	95%	95%	92%	91%

Investment Style
Equity
Stock %

▼ Manager Change
▽ Partial Manager Change

Growth of $10,000
■ Investment Values of Fund
— Investment Values of S&P 500

40.8
31.0
24.0
17.0
10.0

Performance Quartile (within Category)

1995	1996	1997	1998	1999	2000	2001	2002	2003	2004	2005	2006	History
14.21	15.39	16.62	18.33	17.74	18.73	17.01	14.29	18.04	20.19	20.54	22.08	NAV
35.67	18.05	24.49	18.44	12.70	19.02	-6.06	-14.71	27.57	13.94	9.87	16.01	Total Return %
-1.91	-4.91	-8.87	-10.14	-8.34	28.12	5.83	7.39	-1.11	3.06	4.96	0.22	+/-S&P 500
-2.69	-3.59	-10.69	2.81	5.35	12.01	-0.47	0.81	-2.46	-2.55	2.82	-6.24	+/-Russ 1000 VI
2.40	1.70	1.50	1.20	1.04	1.13	1.09	1.05	1.17	1.28	1.30	1.64	Income Return %
33.27	16.35	22.99	17.24	11.66	17.89	-7.15	-15.76	26.40	12.66	8.57	14.37	Capital Return %
25	68	77	10	19	14	66	25	53	39	13	77	Total Rtn % Rank Cat
0.27	0.24	0.23	0.20	0.19	0.20	0.20	0.18	0.17	0.23	0.26	0.33	Income $
0.90	1.09	2.25	1.11	2.63	2.12	0.37	0.07	0.00	0.11	1.38	1.34	Capital Gains $
1.15	1.04	0.94	0.92	0.88	0.88	0.82	0.85	0.86	0.81	0.80	—	Expense Ratio %
2.24	1.68	1.33	1.13	1.11	1.23	1.29	1.05	1.24	1.25	1.27	—	Income Ratio %
108	110	94	76	93	97	115	66	61	45	43	—	Turnover Rate %
399	580	778	929	1,018	1,365	1,744	2,071	3,647	5,728	6,539	7,875	Net Assets $mil

Performance 12-31-06

	1st Qtr	2nd Qtr	3rd Qtr	4th Qtr	Total
2002	4.64	-8.49	-17.70	8.21	-14.71
2003	-4.99	16.19	2.37	12.89	27.57
2004	1.76	1.47	0.31	10.01	13.94
2005	-0.09	2.39	5.72	1.60	9.87
2006	2.90	0.01	5.94	6.41	16.01

Trailing	Total Return%	+/- S&P 500	+/- Russ 1000 VI	%Rank Cat	Growth of $10,000
3 Mo	6.41	-0.29	-1.59	78	10,641
6 Mo	12.73	-0.01	-1.99	54	11,273
1 Yr	16.01	0.22	-6.24	77	11,601
3 Yr Avg	13.25	2.81	-1.84	30	14,525
5 Yr Avg	9.58	3.39	-1.28	24	15,800
10 Yr Avg	11.37	2.95	0.37	9	29,355
15 Yr Avg	12.55	1.91	-0.48	13	58,909

Tax Analysis	Tax-Adj Rtn%	%Rank Cat	Tax-Cost Rat	%Rank Cat
3 Yr (estimated)	9.73	66	1.17	46
5 Yr (estimated)	7.34	45	0.88	47
10 Yr (estimated)	8.81	15	1.72	62

Potential Capital Gain Exposure: 19% of assets

Rating and Risk

Time Period	Load-Adj Return %	Morningstar Rtn vs Cat	Morningstar Risk vs Cat	Morningstar Risk-Adj Rating
1 Yr	9.34			
3 Yr	11.03	-Avg	-Avg	★★★
5 Yr	8.29	Avg	-Avg	★★★
10 Yr	10.71	+Avg	-Avg	★★★★
Incept	10.00			

Other Measures	Standard Index S&P 500	Best Fit Index Russ 1000 VI
Alpha	3.8	0.0
Beta	0.81	0.85
R-Squared	81	84
Standard Deviation	6.26	
Mean	13.25	
Sharpe Ratio	1.52	

Morningstar's Take by Marta Norton 12-19-06

Van Kampen Growth and Income makes value investing look easy.

Like many of its peers, this fund's management likes troubled companies it thinks will make a comeback. Lead manager Jim Gilligan and his team first screen for stocks with historically cheap price-to-normalized earnings. (That means they smooth earnings to get rid of temporary blips.) That's a commonly used metric, but this team often looks back 10 to 15 years to get an idea of earnings' trends and cycles. It then digs into the financials, looking for climbing revenues, falling costs, and the like. It also looks for industry consolidation or new leadership. But since managers are most interested in the financials, it helps that Gilligan and many members of his team are CPAs.

There are some strong points here. Since the fund is price-sensitive and evaluates earnings over long historical cycles, it often anticipates market rallies and makes big, long-term bets there. At the end of 2001, for instance, the managers loaded up on oil companies they thought were cheap and likely to rebound. By 2003 the fund had as much as 17% in energy. That didn't pay off immediately, but in 2003 and 2004, oil and gas stocks gained 122.1% and 89.5%, respectively.

The team's valuation sensitivity also means it is quick to pare back when stock prices grow speculative. Doing so sometimes leaves money on the table (energy prices continued to rise after the fund began cutting its stake there in mid-2005), but it also helps the fund avoid painful corrections.

These calls are hard to make, and management doesn't always get it right. Experience helps, though. Gilligan has been here since 1990 and has racked up a strong long-term record over that time.

Our only real concern here is asset bloat. Gilligan and his team run $30 billion in eight separate Morgan Stanley funds. That's a lot of money to put to work. But their large-cap, low-turnover approach helps ease our concerns. This fund remains a compelling (and cheap) buy.

Portfolio Analysis 09-30-06

Share change since 06-06 Total Stocks:77	Sector	PE	Tot Ret%	% Assets
⊕ J.P. Morgan Chase & Co.	Financial	13.6	25.60	3.47
⊖ Bayer AG ADR	Ind Mtrls	19.1	31.11	2.92
⊕ Citigroup, Inc.	Financial	13.1	19.55	2.84
⊕ General Electric Company	Ind Mtrls	20.0	9.35	2.58
⊕ Time Warner, Inc.	Media	19.6	26.37	2.38
⊕ Schering-Plough Corporat	Health	36.6	14.63	2.32
⊕ Verizon Communications	Telecom	15.9	34.88	2.31
⊕ Eli Lilly & Company	Health	17.3	-5.16	2.27
⊕ Freddie Mac	Financial	23.3	7.06	2.26
⊕ Symantec Corporation	Software	50.9	19.14	2.23
⊕ Abbott Laboratories	Health	24.3	26.88	2.15
⊕ Roche Holding AG ADR	Health	34.2	20.41	2.08
⊕ Sprint Nextel Corporatio	Telecom	30.2	-10.44	2.05
⊕ Marsh & McLennan Compani	Financial	29.0	-1.16	1.98
⊕ St. Paul Travelers Compa	Financial	11.6	22.90	1.90
⊖ Merrill Lynch & Company,	Financial	14.2	39.28	1.80
⊖ Bristol-Myers Squibb Com	Health	23.1	19.93	1.71
⊕ Wal-Mart Stores, Inc.	Consumer	16.9	0.13	1.63
⊕ Coca-Cola Company	Goods	21.7	23.10	1.60
⊕ Siemens Aktiengesellscha	Hardware	24.2	17.26	1.58

Current Investment Style

Value Blnd Growth — Large Mid Small

Market Cap	%
Giant	52.3
Large	45.8
Mid	1.9
Small	0.0
Micro	0.0

Avg $mil: 54,758

Value Measures		Rel Category
Price/Earnings	15.31	1.12
Price/Book	1.91	0.86
Price/Sales	1.65	1.27
Price/Cash Flow	2.53	0.38
Dividend Yield %	2.17	0.93

Growth Measures	%	Rel Category
Long-Term Erngs	10.08	0.97
Book Value	7.55	0.95
Sales	6.90	0.77
Cash Flow	2.04	0.34
Historical Erngs	14.55	0.90

Profitability	%	Rel Category
Return on Equity	16.99	0.95
Return on Assets	8.69	0.89
Net Margin	12.23	0.94

Sector Weightings	% of Stocks	Rel S&P 500	3 Year High	Low
☎ Info	21.04	1.05		
Software	2.45	0.71	2	1
Hardware	5.36	0.58	7	2
Media	6.93	1.83	8	6
Telecom	6.30	1.79	6	3
☞ Service	49.33	1.07		
Health	18.14	1.50	19	11
Consumer	4.57	0.60	6	3
Business	0.00	0.00	8	0
Financial	26.62	1.20	27	21
Mfg	29.64	0.88		
Goods	9.47	1.11	10	7
Ind Mtrls	11.24	0.94	14	11
Energy	5.08	0.52	14	5
Utilities	3.85	1.10	5	3

Composition

		%
●	Cash	9.1
●	Stocks	90.9
●	Bonds	0.0
●	Other	0.0
	Foreign (% of Stock)	17.0

Address:	1221 Avenue Of The Americas New York NY 10020 800-421-5666
Web Address:	www.vankampen.com
Inception:	08-01-46
Advisor:	Van Kampen Asset Management, Inc.
Subadvisor:	None
NTF Plans:	Federated Tr NTF, Fidelity Instl-NTF

Minimum Purchase:	$0	Add: $0	IRA: $0
Min Auto Inv Plan:	$25	Add: $25	
Sales Fees:	5.75%L, 0.25%S, 2.00%R		
Management Fee:	0.50% mx./0.35% mn.		
Actual Fees:	Mgt:0.35%	Dist:0.25%	
Expense Projections:	3Yr:$816	5Yr:$994	10Yr:$1508
Income Distrib:	Quarterly		

MORNINGSTAR® Funds 500

Vanguard 500 Index

Analyst Pick ✓	**Ticker** VFINX	**Load** None	**NAV** $130.59	**Yield** 1.6%	**Total Assets** $118,479 mil	**Mstar Category** Large Blend

Governance and Management

Stewardship Grade: B

Portfolio Manager(s)

In the spring of 2005, this fund's former manager, Gus Sauter, formally handed this offering's reins to Michael Buek. Sauter has been reducing his involvement in the daily management of individual funds since becoming the firm's chief investment officer in 2003. Buek has worked closely with Sauter on this fund since 1991 and has been with Vanguard since 1987.

Strategy

The core of this fund's strategy is simple: It buys and holds the stocks that make up the S&P 500 Index. Manager Michael Buek attempts to add value on the margins by opportunistically buying futures contracts, among other techniques, and he actively tries to reduce trading costs.

Performance 12-31-06

	1st Qtr	2nd Qtr	3rd Qtr	4th Qtr	Total
2002	0.24	-13.43	-17.22	8.39	-22.15
2003	-3.19	15.39	2.60	12.12	28.50
2004	1.66	1.68	-1.91	9.21	10.74
2005	-2.16	1.32	3.58	2.05	4.77
2006	4.18	-1.48	5.62	6.67	15.64

Trailing	Total Return%	+/- S&P 500	+/- Russ 1000	%Rank Cat	Growth of $10,000
3 Mo	6.67	-0.03	-0.28	46	10,667
6 Mo	12.66	-0.08	0.30	21	11,266
1 Yr	15.64	-0.15	0.18	24	11,564
3 Yr Avg	10.30	-0.14	-0.68	40	13,419
5 Yr Avg	6.07	-0.12	-0.75	40	13,427
10 Yr Avg	8.34	-0.08	-0.30	31	22,279
15 Yr Avg	10.54	-0.10	-0.26	32	44,956

Tax Analysis	Tax-Adj Rtn%	%Rank Cat	Tax-Cost Rat	%Rank Cat
3 Yr (estimated)	9.95	30	0.32	15
5 Yr (estimated)	5.69	34	0.36	24
10 Yr (estimated)	7.83	20	0.47	16

Potential Capital Gain Exposure: 36% of assets

Morningstar's Take by Dan Culloton 11-20-06

Vanguard 500 Index is still standing.

This fund has taken some hits recently. Rivals and observers have attacked its benchmark index, the S&P 500, as flawed because it overemphasizes pricey stocks by ranking its constituents by their market capitalizations. Observers, Morningstar included, also have noted that traders front-running changes to the S&P 500 can increase transaction costs and erode the returns of funds tracking the index. And recently, more investors have been selling this fund than buying it.

Despite these legitimate concerns, this fund remains a competitive core holding. Its index's construction methodology isn't perfect, but it's still a simple, low-turnover way to track the market. Furthermore, new alternative schemes, such as ranking stocks by dividends, cash flow, book value, or sales, have short real-world track records. The fundamental indexes' back-tested results look great, but they have been influenced by a market that in recent years has favored smaller, more

value-oriented stocks.

Managers of this fund and other S&P 500 funds concede the sheer number of funds and amount of money tracking the index can increase the costs of tracking the benchmark; yet managers also maintain they can mitigate those impact costs with savvy trading. Indeed, the fund's returns are within hundredths of a percent of those of cheaper rivals that track the same index, which shows the fund is controlling costs and tracking error.

The outflows may be a contrarian indicator. People have been heading for the exits when this fund looks attractive on a fundamental basis. Many of the fund's stocks were at or below Morningstar equity analysts' fair value estimates in November 2006. The S&P 500 jumped in 2006, but several of its top holdings, including Microsoft, Johnson & Johnson, and Wal-Mart, still look attractively valued, according to Morningstar stock analysts.

This fund isn't finished yet.

Address:	PO Box 2600 Valley Forge PA 19482 800-523-1188
Web Address:	www.vanguard.com
Inception:	08-31-76
Advisor:	Vanguard Advisers, Inc.
Subadvisor:	None
NTF Plans:	Vanguard NTF

Minimum Purchase:	$3000	Add: $100	IRA: $3000
Min Auto Inv Plan:	$3000	Add: $50	
Sales Fees:	No-load		
Management Fee:	0.16%		
Actual Fees:	Mgt:0.16%	Dist: —	
Expense Projections:	3Yr:$58	5Yr:$101	10Yr:$230
Income Distrib:	Quarterly		

Historical Profile
Return	Average
Risk	Average
Rating	★★★ Neutral

98% 99% 99% 98% 99% 99% 100% 100% 100%

Investment Style
Equity
Stock %

Growth of $10,000
— Investment Values of Fund
— Investment Values of S&P 500

31.0
25.0
20.0
15.0
10.0

▼ Manager Change
▽ Partial Manager Change

Performance Quartile (within Category)

1995	1996	1997	1998	1999	2000	2001	2002	2003	2004	2005	2006	History
57.60	69.17	90.07	113.95	135.33	121.86	105.89	81.15	102.67	111.64	114.92	130.59	NAV
37.45	22.88	33.19	28.62	21.07	-9.06	-12.02	-22.15	28.50	10.74	4.77	15.64	Total Return %
-0.13	-0.08	-0.17	0.04	0.03	0.04	-0.13	-0.05	-0.18	-0.14	-0.14	-0.15	+/-S&P 500
-0.32	0.43	0.34	1.60	0.16	-1.27	0.43	-0.50	-1.39	-0.66	-1.50	0.18	+/-Russ 1000
2.86	2.24	1.92	1.49	1.25	0.96	1.05	1.29	1.77	1.91	1.79	1.87	Income Return %
34.59	20.64	31.27	27.13	19.82	-10.02	-13.07	-23.44	26.73	8.83	2.98	13.77	Capital Return %
16	31	16	17	35	65	53	50	34	42	60	24	Total Rtn % Rank Cat
1.22	1.28	1.32	1.33	1.41	1.30	1.28	1.36	1.43	1.95	1.98	2.14	Income $
0.13	0.25	0.59	0.42	1.00	0.00	0.00	0.00	0.00	0.00	0.00	0.00	Capital Gains $
0.20	0.20	0.19	0.18	0.18	0.18	0.18	0.18	0.18	0.18	0.18	—	Expense Ratio %
2.38	2.04	1.66	1.35	1.13	0.98	1.14	1.43	1.61	1.86	1.75	—	Income Ratio %
4	5	5	6	6	9	4	7	2	3	7	—	Turnover Rate %
17,372	30,332	49,358	74,229	104,652	88,240	73,151	56,224	75,342	84,167	69,375	72,013	Net Assets $mil

Rating and Risk

Time Period	Load-Adj Return %	Morningstar Rtn vs Cat	Morningstar Risk vs Cat	Morningstar Risk-Adj Rating
1 Yr	15.64			
3 Yr	10.30	Avg	-Avg	★★★
5 Yr	6.07	Avg	Avg	★★★
10 Yr	8.34	Avg	Avg	★★★
Incept	12.23			

Other Measures	Standard Index S&P 500	Best Fit Index S&P 500
Alpha	-0.1	-0.1
Beta	1.00	1.00
R-Squared	100	100
Standard Deviation	6.91	
Mean	10.30	
Sharpe Ratio	1.00	

Portfolio Analysis 09-30-06

Share change since 06-06 Total Stocks:509	Sector	PE	Tot Ret%	% Assets
⊖ ExxonMobil Corporation	Energy	11.1	39.07	3.31
⊖ General Electric Company	Ind Mtrls	20.0	9.35	3.03
⊖ Citigroup, Inc.	Financial	13.1	19.55	2.04
⊖ Bank of America Corporat	Financial	12.4	20.68	2.01
⊖ Microsoft Corporation	Software	23.8	15.83	1.96
⊖ Pfizer Inc.	Health	15.2	15.22	1.72
⊖ Procter & Gamble Company	Goods	23.9	13.36	1.63
⊖ Johnson & Johnson	Health	17.5	12.45	1.58
⊖ American International G	Financial	17.0	6.05	1.43
⊖ J.P. Morgan Chase & Co.	Financial	13.6	25.60	1.35
⊕ Altria Group, Inc.	Goods	16.3	19.87	1.33
⊖ Chevron Corporation	Energy	9.0	33.76	1.18
⊖ Cisco Systems, Inc.	Hardware	30.1	59.64	1.17
⊖ AT&T, Inc.	Telecom	18.2	51.59	1.05
⊖ IBM	Hardware	17.1	19.77	1.01
⊖ Wells Fargo Company	Financial	14.7	16.82	1.01
⊖ Wal-Mart Stores, Inc.	Consumer	16.9	0.13	1.01
⊖ Intel Corporation	Hardware	21.0	-17.18	0.99
⊖ Verizon Communications	Telecom	15.9	34.88	0.89
⊖ PepsiCo, Inc.	Goods	21.5	7.86	0.89

Current Investment Style

Value Blend Growth — Large Mid Small

Market Cap	%
Giant	51.2
Large	38.0
Mid	10.7
Small	0.1
Micro	0.0

Avg $mil: 50,558

Value Measures		Rel Category
Price/Earnings	15.18	0.99
Price/Book	2.56	1.00
Price/Sales	1.44	1.03
Price/Cash Flow	7.11	0.84
Dividend Yield %	1.92	1.10

Growth Measures	%	Rel Category
Long-Term Erngs	11.17	0.95
Book Value	8.61	0.95
Sales	9.77	1.01
Cash Flow	9.11	0.88
Historical Erngs	17.21	0.93

Profitability	%	Rel Category
Return on Equity	19.63	1.01
Return on Assets	10.79	1.04
Net Margin	14.04	1.05

Sector Weightings

Sector Weightings	% of Stocks	Rel S&P 500	3 Year High	Low
⊙ Info	19.98	1.00		
🖥 Software	3.49	1.01	5	3
🖥 Hardware	9.53	1.03	11	9
🎙 Media	3.46	0.91	4	3
☎ Telecom	3.50	1.00	4	3
⊂ Service	46.76	1.01		
🏥 Health	12.71	1.05	13	12
🛒 Consumer	7.72	1.01	9	8
💼 Business	4.06	0.96	5	4
$ Financial	22.27	1.00	22	20
Mfg	33.25	0.98		
🏭 Goods	8.64	1.01	10	8
⚙ Ind Mtrls	11.89	1.00	13	12
🛢 Energy	9.32	0.95	10	6
💡 Utilities	3.40	0.97	4	3

Composition
● Cash	0.1	
● Stocks	99.8	
● Bonds	0.0	
● Other	0.0	
Foreign	0.0	(% of Stock)

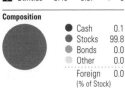

Vanguard Asset Alloc

	Ticker	Load	NAV	Yield	Total Assets	Mstar Category
	VAAPX	None	$28.78	2.0%	$12,656 mil	Moderate Allocation

Governance and Management

Stewardship Grade: B

Portfolio Manager(s)

Tom Loeb, the chairman and CEO of Mellon Capital, has run this fund since its 1988 inception. He has been with Mellon since its founding in 1983, and he had more than one decade of investment-management experience before that. William Fouse, who originally designed the fund's quantitative model in the early 1970s and served as Loeb's comanager for 16 years, gave up his management responsibilities on the fund in mid-2004. Loeb is supported by a big team of portfolio managers, analysts, and traders.

Strategy

Unlike many moderate-allocation offerings, this fund doesn't keep a fairly static asset mix. Instead, management frequently shifts the fund's asset mix based on a quantitative model designed to gauge the relative attractiveness of stocks, bonds, and cash, and it can invest the entire portfolio in a single asset class. The stock segment tracks the S&P 500, while the bond segment tracks the Lehman Brothers Long Term Treasury Index. Management sometimes uses futures to get some of its stock and bond equity exposure; these instruments register as cash in Morningstar's composition section.

Performance 12-31-06

	1st Qtr	2nd Qtr	3rd Qtr	4th Qtr	Total
2002	-0.09	-8.40	-15.57	9.51	-15.38
2003	-3.32	15.29	3.09	10.02	26.42
2004	2.39	0.09	0.00	8.39	11.09
2005	-1.79	1.29	3.51	1.98	5.00
2006	4.15	-1.00	5.57	6.60	16.02

Trailing	Total Return%	+/- DJ Mod	+/- DJ US Mod	%Rank Cat	Growth of $10,000
3 Mo	6.60	1.01	1.93	7	10,660
6 Mo	12.54	3.75	4.64	3	11,254
1 Yr	16.02	3.72	5.75	5	11,602
3 Yr Avg	10.61	-0.11	1.49	13	13,533
5 Yr Avg	7.68	-2.34	0.08	16	14,477
10 Yr Avg	9.22	0.67	0.63	11	24,156
15 Yr Avg	10.45	1.24	1.06	15	44,411

Tax Analysis	Tax-Adj Rtn%	%Rank Cat	Tax-Cost Rat	%Rank Cat
3 Yr (estimated)	10.18	6	0.39	17
5 Yr (estimated)	7.21	9	0.44	22
10 Yr (estimated)	7.81	8	1.29	35

Potential Capital Gain Exposure: 28% of assets

Historical Profile

Return	Above Avg
Risk	Above Avg
Rating	★★★★ Above Avg

Investment Style: Equity, Stock %

47% 40% 44% 54% 63% 70% 83% 81% 82%

▼ Manager Change
▽ Partial Manager Change

31.0
25.0 — Growth of $10,000
20.0 — Investment Values of Fund
15.0 — Investment Values of DJ Mod
10.0

Performance Quartile (within Category)

1995	1996	1997	1998	1999	2000	2001	2002	2003	2004	2005	2006	History
17.05	17.94	21.05	24.38	23.80	23.67	21.81	18.08	22.56	24.56	25.33	28.78	NAV
35.46	15.73	27.32	25.40	5.21	4.91	-5.30	-15.38	26.42	11.09	5.00	16.02	Total Return %
15.66	5.07	15.42	13.08	-12.12	6.58	-2.50	-8.61	-0.96	-1.88	-1.99	3.72	+/-DJ Mod
10.69	4.39	8.12	13.01	-7.64	0.47	-5.46	-4.84	2.36	-0.08	-1.00	5.75	+/-DJ US Mod
4.92	4.26	4.15	3.63	3.64	4.33	2.59	1.82	1.55	2.14	1.84	2.26	Income Return %
30.54	11.47	23.17	21.77	1.57	0.58	-7.89	-17.20	24.87	8.95	3.16	13.76	Capital Return %
4	40	6	7	78	31	57	79	9	17	48	5	Total Rtn % Rank Cat
0.66	0.72	0.74	0.76	0.88	1.02	0.61	0.40	0.28	0.48	0.45	0.57	Income $
0.61	1.05	1.01	1.18	0.96	0.27	0.00	0.00	0.00	0.00	0.00	0.00	Capital Gains $
0.49	0.47	0.49	0.49	0.49	0.44	0.44	0.42	0.43	0.38	0.38	0.41	Expense Ratio %
4.41	4.17	3.96	3.80	3.49	4.18	3.16	2.19	1.34	1.79	1.98	2.01	Income Ratio %
34	47	10	60	11	29	77	54	43	34	6	16	Turnover Rate %
1,791	2,597	4,099	6,974	8,597	8,889	7,750	6,513	8,445	9,724	9,350	10,635	Net Assets $mil

Rating and Risk

Time Period	Load-Adj Return %	Morningstar Rtn vs Cat	Morningstar Risk vs Cat	Morningstar Risk-Adj Rating
1 Yr	16.02			
3 Yr	10.61	+Avg	+Avg	★★★★
5 Yr	7.68	+Avg	High	★★★★
10 Yr	9.22	+Avg	+Avg	★★★★
Incept	11.57			

Other Measures	Standard Index DJ Mod	Best Fit Index S&P 500
Alpha	0.0	0.7
Beta	0.99	0.92
R-Squared	82	97
Standard Deviation	6.47	
Mean	10.61	
Sharpe Ratio	1.11	

Portfolio Analysis 09-30-06

Total Stocks:500

Share change since 06-30-06	Sectors	P/E Ratio	YTD Return %	% Net Assets
⊖ ExxonMobil Corporation	Energy	11.1	-5.19	2.71
⊕ General Electric Company	Ind Mtrls	20.0	0.91	2.47
Citigroup, Inc.	Financial	13.1	-1.17	1.66
⊖ Bank of America Corporati	Financial	12.4	0.11	1.65
⊖ Microsoft Corporation	Software	23.8	0.23	1.60
Pfizer Inc.	Health	15.2	1.00	1.40
⊖ Procter & Gamble Company	Goods	23.9	-0.98	1.34
⊖ Johnson & Johnson	Health	17.5	0.74	1.29
⊕ American International Gr	Financial	17.0	-0.18	1.16

Total Fixed-Income:0	Date of Maturity	Amount $000	Value $000	% Net Assets

Morningstar's Take by John Coumarianos 11-28-06

Vanguard Asset Allocation continues to make the right moves.

This fund began the second quarter of 2006 with 100% equity exposure. On May 24, after having shed some stock exposure, it took advantage of a market downturn to move the portfolio from 90% stocks back to 100% stocks. These moves have allowed the fund to squeeze out another victory over the S&P 500 Index through the first three quarters of 2006. The fund has also succeeded over the past decade, with a 10-year trailing return of 9.24%, versus 8.64% for the index.

Beating the S&P is no mean feat for this fund. Its equity sleeve is tethered to the S&P 500, and its bond portfolio tracks the Lehman Brothers Long Term Treasury Index, so by definition, it can't surpass its benchmark when stocks are outperforming bonds. And like all index funds, it must overcome its expense burden, though that job is made easier by its modest 0.38% price tag. The fact that the fund has bested its benchmark over

the long haul is testament to its quantitative approach. The fund's models, overseen by veteran manager Thomas Loeb, have skillfully calibrated the fund's exposure to stocks and bonds over time.

The fund's main risks are in being fully invested in stocks when the market is falling and underexposed to stocks when the market is rising. For example, as a result of sitting in bonds and cash, the fund posted a meager 5% return in 1999 when the S&P 500 surged 21%. Although the market ultimately vindicated the valuation models, investors had to endure a year of pain before things began to pan out during the bear market (2000-02), when bond exposure proved to be a huge boon.

This fund has been successful, but it won't allow investors to keep tight control of their asset allocations. Therefore, we think it is best used as a substitute for an S&P 500 fund or a large-cap core holding.

Address:	P.O. Box 2600 Valley Forge PA 19482 800-997-2798
Web Address:	www.vanguard.com
Inception:	11-03-88
Advisor:	Mellon Capital Management Corporation
Subadvisor:	None
NTF Plans:	Vanguard NTF

Minimum Purchase:	$3000	Add: $100	IRA: $3000
Min Auto Inv Plan:	$3000	Add: $50	
Sales Fees:	No-load		
Management Fee:	0.37%		
Actual Fees:	Mgt:0.36%	Dist: —	
Expense Projections:	3Yr:$122	5Yr:$213	10Yr:$480
Income Distrib:	Semi-Annually		

Equity Style
Style: Blend
Size: Large-Cap

Value Measures		Rel Category
Price/Earnings	15.19	0.99
Price/Book	2.56	1.04
Price/Sales	1.44	1.05
Price/Cash Flow	7.14	0.88
Dividend Yield %	1.92	0.99

Growth Measures	%	Rel Category
Long-Term Erngs	11.17	0.95
Book Value	8.63	1.00
Sales	9.80	1.10
Cash Flow	9.12	0.92
Historical Erngs	17.24	0.96

Market Cap %

Giant	51.2	Small	0.1
Large	38.0	Micro	0.0
Mid	10.8	Avg $mil:	50,541

Fixed-Income Style
Duration: —
Quality: —

Avg Eff Duration [1]	—
Avg Eff Maturity	—
Avg Credit Quality	—
Avg Wtd Coupon	—

[1]figure provided by fund

Sector Weightings	% of Stocks	Rel DJ Mod	3 Year High Low
Info	20.05	—	
Software	3.51	—	4 3
Hardware	9.55	—	11 9
Media	3.50	—	4 3
Telecom	3.49	—	4 3
Service	46.74		
Health	12.73	—	13 12
Consumer	7.74	—	9 8
Business	4.06	—	5 4
Financial	22.21	—	22 20
Mfg	33.20		
Goods	8.62	—	10 8
Ind Mtrls	11.88	—	13 11
Energy	9.34	—	10 6
Utilities	3.36	—	4 3

Composition

● Cash	18.4	
● Stocks	81.6	
● Bonds	0.0	
● Other	0.0	
Foreign	0.0	(% of Stock)

MORNINGSTAR® Funds 500

Vanguard Bal Idx

	Ticker	Load	NAV	Yield	Total Assets	Mstar Category
	VBINX	None	$21.36	2.8%	$8,855 mil	Moderate Allocation

Governance and Management

Stewardship Grade: B

Portfolio Manager(s)

In 2005, Vanguard announced that Gus Sauter will no longer run this fund's equity sleeve. Since assuming the role of CIO, Sauter has gradually scaled back his involvement with individual funds. The daily management of this fund now falls to Michael Perre, who has been with Vanguard since 1999. It's a similar story on the bond side. Chris Alwine, the former bond skipper, recently assumed a new role overseeing Vanguard's bond analysts. So he has handed over managerial duties to Gregory Davis, who has also been at Vanguard since 1999.

Strategy

This fund, which is passively managed, is split 60/40 between stocks and bonds. The equity stake currently tracks the Wilshire 5000 Index, although it's slated to switch to the MSCI US Broad Market Index by the end of 2005. The new MSCI bogy will cover much of the same ground that the Wilshire index does, spanning virtually all U.S. stocks. The bond stake mirrors the Lehman Brothers Aggregate Index, a proxy for all U.S. investment-grade taxable bonds.

Performance 12-31-06

	1st Qtr	2nd Qtr	3rd Qtr	4th Qtr	Total
2002	0.67	-6.55	-8.58	5.20	-9.52
2003	-1.28	10.75	2.13	7.35	19.87
2004	2.63	-0.21	0.22	6.52	9.33
2005	-1.64	2.63	2.12	1.52	4.65
2006	2.98	-1.27	4.23	4.77	11.02

Trailing	Total Return%	+/- DJ Mod	+/- DJ US Mod	%Rank Cat	Growth of $10,000
3 Mo	4.77	-0.82	0.10	62	10,477
6 Mo	9.20	0.41	1.30	39	10,920
1 Yr	11.02	-1.28	0.75	52	11,102
3 Yr Avg	8.30	-2.42	-0.82	48	12,702
5 Yr Avg	6.62	-3.40	-0.98	36	13,778
10 Yr Avg	7.92	-0.63	-0.67	31	21,430
15 Yr Avg	—	—	—	—	—

Tax Analysis	Tax-Adj Rtn%	%Rank Cat	Tax-Cost Rat	%Rank Cat
3 Yr (estimated)	7.47	38	0.77	37
5 Yr (estimated)	5.71	30	0.85	50
10 Yr (estimated)	6.65	21	1.18	27

Potential Capital Gain Exposure: 21% of assets

Morningstar's Take by Reginald Laing 12-22-06

Vanguard Balanced Index remains a strong choice.

For the trailing three years through Dec. 21, 2006, this fund's 8.8% annualized gain is only middling in Morningstar's moderate-allocation category. To be sure, that's a short performance period on which to judge this fund (over the past 10 years, it has outpaced more than two thirds of its peers). But it's instructive to know why this fund has been only average recently, since it shows how investors may wish to supplement this solid core offering.

The fund will only be as good as the indexes it follows. Its 60% equity portion tracks the MSCI US Broad Market Index, which represents the entire domestic stock market. That leaves out foreign equities, and lately, their absence has hurt. Most funds in the category have at least some international exposure, and a buoyant world stock market (the MSCI EAFE, a widely followed foreign-stock index, has far outpaced the S&P 500 in recent years) has helped the relative returns of

many of this fund's peers in recent years.

For the 40% bond stake, the fund tracks the Lehman Brothers Aggregate Bond Index, a bogy for the U.S. investment-grade bond market. That excludes the entire market for both high-yield and foreign bonds. High-yield issues also have rallied and helped this fund's peers, the majority of which take on some exposure to bonds rated below investment grade.

In short, given its relatively plain-vanilla approach to balanced investing, one can't expect this offering to outperform its more flexible peers. And its recent unremarkable showing emphasizes the fact that this fund isn't a one-stop shop. We don't advocate jumping headlong into a foreign-stock fund at this time, given the rally that asset class has recently enjoyed, but we think it's important for investors to include some foreign exposure in their long-term asset-allocation plans. Meanwhile, this fund can ably serve as a solid domestic core holding.

Address:	P O Box 2600 Valley Forge PA 19482 800-997-2798	Minimum Purchase:	$3000	Add: $100	IRA: $3000
		Min Auto Inv Plan:	$3000	Add: $50	
Web Address:	www.vanguard.com	Sales Fees:	No-load		
Inception:	11-09-92	Management Fee:	0.17%		
Advisor:	Vanguard Advisers, Inc.	Actual Fees:	Mgt:0.17%	Dist: —	
Subadvisor:	None	Expense Projections:	3Yr:$64	5Yr:$113	10Yr:$255
NTF Plans:	Vanguard NTF	Income Distrib:	Quarterly		

Historical Profile

Return	Average
Risk	Average
Rating	★★★★ Above Avg

| | 58% | 59% | 58% | 59% | 58% | 60% | 60% | 60% | 60% |

▼ Manager Change
△ Partial Manager Change

Growth of $10,000
— Investment Values of Fund
— Investment Values of DJ Mod

Performance Quartile (within Category)

1995	1996	1997	1998	1999	2000	2001	2002	2003	2004	2005	2006	History
12.77	13.92	16.29	18.48	20.22	19.08	17.86	15.65	18.27	19.45	19.81	21.36	NAV
28.64	13.95	22.24	17.85	13.61	-2.04	-3.02	-9.52	19.87	9.33	4.65	11.02	Total Return %
8.84	3.29	10.34	5.53	-3.72	-0.37	-0.22	-2.75	-7.51	-3.64	-2.34	-1.28	+/-DJ Mod
3.87	2.61	3.04	5.46	0.76	-6.48	-3.18	1.02	-4.19	-1.84	-1.35	0.75	+/-DJ US Mod
4.41	3.89	3.87	3.36	3.19	3.24	3.17	2.95	2.91	2.76	2.75	3.06	Income Return %
24.23	10.06	18.37	14.49	10.42	-5.28	-6.19	-12.47	16.96	6.57	1.90	7.96	Capital Return %
25	57	27	25	29	70	30	27	51	43	55	52	Total Rtn % Rank Cat
0.45	0.49	0.53	0.54	0.58	0.65	0.60	0.52	0.45	0.50	0.53	0.60	Income $
0.05	0.12	0.14	0.14	0.14	0.10	0.03	0.00	0.00	0.00	0.00	0.00	Capital Gains $
0.20	0.20	0.20	0.21	0.22	0.22	0.22	0.22	0.22	0.20	0.20	—	Expense Ratio %
3.85	3.69	3.56	3.29	3.18	3.30	3.26	3.14	2.68	2.66	2.69	—	Income Ratio %
16	37	18	25	29	28	33	40	27	26	31	—	Turnover Rate %
590	826	1,260	2,004	3,128	3,586	3,117	2,990	3,895	4,674	4,098	3,926	Net Assets $mil

Rating and Risk

Time Period	Load-Adj Return %	Morningstar Rtn vs Cat	Morningstar Risk vs Cat	Morningstar Risk-Adj Rating
1 Yr	11.02			
3 Yr	8.30	Avg	-Avg	★★★
5 Yr	6.62	Avg	-Avg	★★★
10 Yr	7.92	Avg	Avg	★★★★
Incept	9.32			

Other Measures	Standard Index DJ Mod	Best Fit Index Russ 1000
Alpha	-0.7	0.0
Beta	0.78	0.65
R-Squared	89	92
Standard Deviation	4.86	
Mean	8.30	
Sharpe Ratio	1.01	

Portfolio Analysis 09-30-06

Total Stocks:3641 Share change since 06-30-06	Sectors	P/E Ratio	YTD Return %	% Net Assets
⊕ ExxonMobil Corporation	Energy	11.1	-5.19	1.62
⊕ General Electric Company	Ind Mtrls	20.0	0.91	1.47
⊕ Citigroup, Inc.	Financial	13.1	-1.17	0.99
⊕ Bank of America Corporati	Financial	12.4	0.11	0.98
⊖ Microsoft Corporation	Software	23.8	0.23	0.97
⊕ Pfizer Inc.	Health	15.2	1.00	0.83
⊕ Procter & Gamble Company	Goods	23.9	-0.98	0.81
⊕ Johnson & Johnson	Health	17.5	0.74	0.77
⊕ J.P. Morgan Chase & Co.	Financial	13.6	-0.02	0.65

Total Fixed-Income:3421	Date of Maturity	Amount $000	Value $000	% Net Assets
US Treasury Note 3.875%	05-15-10	52,775	51,522	0.59
US Treasury Bond 7.25%	05-15-16	42,240	50,635	0.58
US Treasury Note 4.375%	01-31-08	47,575	47,292	0.54
US Treasury Note 3.875%	05-15-09	46,762	45,893	0.52
US Treasury Bond 8.75%	05-15-17	27,275	36,416	0.42
Discover Card Mstr Tr I 2	10-15-07	33,000	33,045	0.38
US Treasury Note 4%	02-15-14	32,920	31,650	0.36
US Treasury Note 3.375%	02-15-08	31,850	31,248	0.36
FHLMC 5.25%	05-21-09	26,000	26,223	0.30

Equity Style		Fixed-Income Style	
Style: Blend		Duration: Interm-Term	
Size: Large-Cap		Quality: High	

Value Measures		Rel Category
Price/Earnings	15.48	1.01
Price/Book	2.49	1.01
Price/Sales	1.37	1.00
Price/Cash Flow	7.19	0.89
Dividend Yield %	1.81	0.94

Avg Eff Duration [1]	4.8 Yrs
Avg Eff Maturity	7.2 Yrs
Avg Credit Quality	AAA
Avg Wtd Coupon	5.35%

[1]figure provided by fund as of 09-30-06

Growth Measures	%	Rel Category
Long-Term Erngs	11.50	0.98
Book Value	8.24	0.96
Sales	9.28	1.05
Cash Flow	9.63	0.98
Historical Erngs	16.89	0.94

Market Cap %			
Giant	41.0	Small	6.2
Large	31.3	Micro	2.1
Mid	19.5	Avg $mil:	26,825

Sector Weightings	% of Stocks	Rel DJ Mod	3 Year High	Low
℧ Info	19.46	—		
🖳 Software	3.59	—	4	3
🖥 Hardware	9.14	—	10	9
📺 Media	3.42	—	5	3
📞 Telecom	3.31	—	3	3
☎ Service	48.46			
⚕ Health	12.61	—	13	12
🛒 Consumer	8.08	—	10	8
🏢 Business	5.37	—	6	5
💲 Financial	22.40	—	23	20
Ⓜ Mfg	32.08			
🏭 Goods	7.93	—	9	8
⚙ Ind Mtrls	11.60	—	12	10
🔋 Energy	9.05	—	10	6
💡 Utilities	3.50	—	4	3

Composition

- Cash 0.5
- Stocks 60.1
- Bonds 39.4
- Other 0.0
- Foreign 0.1 (% of Stock)

Vanguard FTSE Soc Idx Inv

	Ticker	Load	NAV	Yield	Total Assets	Mstar Category
	VFTSX	None	$9.21	1.3%	$570 mil	Large Growth

Governance and Management

Stewardship Grade: B

Portfolio Manager(s)

Michael Perre, of Vanguard's indexing team, recently took over day-to-day management of this fund from the firm's index guru, Gus Sauter, who had run the fund since its May 2000 launch. The social screening behind the fund's new bogy, the FTSE4Good U.S. Select Index, is conducted by a team from FTSE Group, a provider of global indexes.

Strategy

This offering began tracking a different benchmark in December 2005. Instead of the Calvert Social Index, constructed by the largest purveyor of socially conscious funds, it now follows the FTSE4Good U.S. Select Index, which was created especially for this fund. However, the social screens for the two benchmarks are quite similar: They exclude alcoholic-beverage and tobacco makers, as well as firms with unfair or unsafe labor practices and poor environmental records. Those criteria have typically led to a pronounced growth tilt at this fund.

Performance 12-31-06

	1st Qtr	2nd Qtr	3rd Qtr	4th Qtr	Total
2002	-1.68	-15.20	-17.62	10.31	-24.24
2003	-2.58	16.23	3.03	11.81	30.45
2004	1.20	1.71	-4.01	9.58	8.27
2005	-4.99	2.10	3.34	3.84	4.10
2006	3.39	-2.46	5.77	6.02	13.09

Trailing	Total Return%	+/- S&P 500	+/- Russ 1000Gr	%Rank Cat	Growth of $10,000
3 Mo	6.02	-0.68	0.09	35	10,602
6 Mo	12.13	-0.61	2.03	7	11,213
1 Yr	13.09	-2.70	4.02	9	11,309
3 Yr Avg	8.42	-2.02	1.55	31	12,745
5 Yr Avg	4.73	-1.46	2.04	22	12,600
10 Yr Avg	—	—	—	—	—
15 Yr Avg	—	—	—	—	—

Tax Analysis	Tax-Adj Rtn%	%Rank Cat	Tax-Cost Rat	%Rank Cat
3 Yr (estimated)	8.21	24	0.19	13
5 Yr (estimated)	4.49	20	0.23	24
10 Yr (estimated)	—	—	—	—

Potential Capital Gain Exposure: 13% of assets

Historical Profile

Return	Above Avg
Risk	Average
Rating	★★★★ Above Avg

Investment Style: Equity, Stock %

98% 99% 99% 99% 99% 98% 100%

▼ Manager Change
▽ Partial Manager Change

Growth of $10,000
— Investment Values of Fund
— Investment Values of S&P 500

10.0
7.0
5.0

Performance Quartile (within Category)

	1995	1996	1997	1998	1999	2000	2001	2002	2003	2004	2005	2006	History
	—	—	—	—	—	9.09	7.76	5.82	7.52	8.02	8.25	9.21	NAV
	—	—	—	—	—	—	-14.08	-24.24	30.45	8.27	4.10	13.09	Total Return %
	—	—	—	—	—	—	-2.19	-2.14	1.77	-2.61	-0.81	-2.70	+/-S&P 500
	—	—	—	—	—	—	6.34	3.64	0.70	1.97	-1.16	4.02	+/-Russ 1000Gr
	—	—	—	—	—	—	0.55	0.77	1.20	1.60	1.25	1.45	Income Return %
	—	—	—	—	—	—	-14.63	-25.01	29.25	6.67	2.85	11.64	Capital Return %
	—	—	—	—	—	—	22	32	34	48	69	9	Total Rtn % Rank Cat
	—	—	—	—	—	0.03	0.05	0.06	0.07	0.12	0.10	0.12	Income $
	—	—	—	—	—	0.01	0.00	0.00	0.00	0.00	0.00	0.00	Capital Gains $
	—	—	—	—	—	0.25	0.25	0.25	0.25	0.25	0.25	0.25	Expense Ratio %
	—	—	—	—	—	0.98	0.70	0.82	1.18	1.17	1.74	1.41	Income Ratio %
	—	—	—	—	—	3	10	18	14	8	12	51	Turnover Rate %
	—	—	—	—	—	62	99	98	203	332	389	472	Net Assets $mil

Rating and Risk

Time Period	Load-Adj Return %	Morningstar Rtn vs Cat	Morningstar Risk vs Cat	Morningstar Risk-Adj Rating
1 Yr	13.09			
3 Yr	8.42	+Avg	-Avg	★★★★
5 Yr	4.73	+Avg	Avg	★★★★
10 Yr	—	—	—	—
Incept	-0.23			

Other Measures	Standard Index S&P 500	Best Fit Index S&P 500
Alpha	-2.7	-2.7
Beta	1.14	1.14
R-Squared	93	93
Standard Deviation	8.14	
Mean	8.42	
Sharpe Ratio	0.64	

Portfolio Analysis 09-30-06

Share change since 06-06 Total Stocks:455

	Sector	PE	Tot Ret%	% Assets
⊕ Bank of America Corporat	Financial	12.4	20.68	3.66
⊕ American International G	Financial	17.0	6.05	2.60
⊕ J.P. Morgan Chase & Co.	Financial	13.6	25.60	2.44
⊕ AT&T, Inc.	Telecom	18.2	51.59	1.89
⊕ Wells Fargo Company	Financial	14.7	16.82	1.81
⊕ Intel Corporation	Hardware	21.0	-17.18	1.79
⊕ Google, Inc.	Business	61.5	11.00	1.38
⊕ Merck & Co., Inc.	Health	19.1	42.66	1.36
⊕ Wachovia Corporation	Financial	12.9	12.02	1.33
⊕ Amgen, Inc.	Health	29.1	-13.38	1.26
⊕ Morgan Stanley	Financial	12.3	45.93	1.17
⊕ BellSouth Corporation	Telecom	—	—	1.16
⊕ Home Depot, Inc.	Consumer	13.5	1.01	1.12
⊕ Comcast Corporation A	Media	45.2	63.31	1.12
⊕ Abbott Laboratories	Health	24.3	26.88	1.11
⊕ Goldman Sachs Group, Inc	Financial	12.4	57.41	1.10
⊕ Schlumberger, Ltd.	Energy	22.3	31.07	1.09
⊕ Merrill Lynch & Company,	Financial	14.2	39.28	1.03
⊕ American Express Company	Financial	20.9	19.09	1.02
⊕ UnitedHealth Group, Inc.	Health	20.8	-13.49	1.00

Current Investment Style

Value Blnd Growth — Large Mid Small

Market Cap	%
Giant	37.0
Large	42.1
Mid	20.8
Small	0.1
Micro	0.0

Avg $mil: 29,894

Value Measures		Rel Category
Price/Earnings	15.90	0.83
Price/Book	2.34	0.70
Price/Sales	1.65	0.85
Price/Cash Flow	5.75	0.51
Dividend Yield %	1.66	1.61

Growth Measures	%	Rel Category
Long-Term Erngs	12.30	0.86
Book Value	9.25	0.80
Sales	10.12	0.87
Cash Flow	10.60	0.63
Historical Erngs	15.29	0.66

Profitability	%	Rel Category
Return on Equity	17.43	0.86
Return on Assets	11.05	1.00
Net Margin	14.92	1.05

Sector Weightings	% of Stocks	Rel S&P 500	3 Year High	Low
⟳ Info	18.06	0.90		
Software	2.02	0.59	6	2
Hardware	6.21	0.67	17	6
Media	4.90	1.29	5	4
Telecom	4.93	1.40	5	3
☞ Service	72.69	1.57		
Health	16.28	1.35	18	15
Consumer	11.39	1.49	12	8
Business	5.88	1.39	7	5
Financial	39.14	1.76	39	25
⎍ Mfg	9.26	0.27		
Goods	3.32	0.39	7	3
Ind Mtrls	2.85	0.24	5	3
Energy	2.89	0.29	3	1
Utilities	0.20	0.06	1	0

Composition

● Cash	0.0
● Stocks	100.0
● Bonds	0.0
○ Other	0.0
Foreign	0.2

(% of Stock)

Morningstar's Take by Greg Carlson 11-13-06

We wouldn't fret much about Vanguard FTSE Social Index's quirkier profile.

Since this socially screened fund switched benchmarks in December 2005, it's undergone substantial changes. The constituents of its former bogy, the Calvert Social Index--constructed by SRI fund shop Calvert--had to pass a wide array of social screens. But even though its new benchmark, the FTSE4Good U.S. Select Index, uses similarly stringent standards, its composition is quite different. For example, while the Calvert index--which is still tracked by the more-expensive Calvert Social Index--sports a 22% stake in tech stocks (compared with the S&P 500's 12%), the FTSE index has a massive, 38% weighting in financial stocks (the S&P's stake is 21%). Thus, the fund's fortunes are now tied to that sector's. What's more, while the Calvert index excluded 12 of the S&P's 25 largest constituents, the FTSE index shuns 18 of those names, so a rally by the very largest companies could leave this fund on the outside looking in.

As a result of the transition to the new index, the fund's portfolio turnover for the fiscal year ended August 2006 was 51%, nearly triple its previous high. That activity almost certainly boosted the trading commissions paid out by the fund (2006 figures aren't yet available).

But despite these concerns, we still think this is one of the most attractive socially conscious choices around. The fund's outsized financials stake includes a diverse mix of businesses, including banks, insurers, brokerages and asset managers, thus limiting risk. Furthermore, we're confident in the decision-making of Vanguard's crack indexing team. For example, the team took tax consequences into account before making the change--the fund isn't expected to make any taxable distributions this year. Finally, its rock-bottom 0.25% expense ratio gives it a big advantage over its often-pricey socially conscious rivals.

Address:	PO Box 2600 Valley Forge PA 19482 800-997-2798	Minimum Purchase:	$3000	Add: $100 IRA: $3000
		Min Auto Inv Plan:	$3000	Add: $50
		Sales Fees:	No-load	
Web Address:	www.vanguard.com	Management Fee:	0.19%	
Inception:	05-31-00	Actual Fees:	Mgt:0.19%	Dist: —
Advisor:	Vanguard Advisers, Inc.	Expense Projections:	3Yr:$80	5Yr:$141 10Yr:$318
Subadvisor:	None	Income Distrib:	Annually	
NTF Plans:	Vanguard NTF			

MORNINGSTAR® Funds 500

Vanguard Cap Opp

Analyst Pick ✓	**Ticker** VHCOX	**Load** Closed
NAV $36.68	**Yield** 0.2%	**Total Assets** $9,329 mil
Mstar Category Mid-Cap Growth		

Governance and Management

Stewardship Grade: B

Portfolio Manager(s)

The fund's four managers--Howard Schow, Theo Kolokotrones, Joel Fried, and Al Mordecai--employ an unusual team structure. Although they share ideas, each independently manages a portion of the fund's assets. Their strong record at Vanguard Primecap speaks for itself. They were named Morningstar's Domestic-Stock Managers of the Year for 2003.

Strategy

The fund's managers follow a contrarian-growth approach. They look for swiftly growing firms but like to buy their stocks on the cheap when they're out of favor. The fund often has outsized sector weightings because many of the managers' favorites are clustered in a few industries.

Historical Profile

Return	High
Risk	Average
Rating	★★★★ Highest

Investment Style: Equity, Stock %

87% 82% 94% 91% 94% 93% 96% 97% 98%

▼ Manager Change
▽ Partial Manager Change

Growth of $10,000
— Investment Values of Fund
— Investment Values of S&P 500

43.6 / 32.4 / 24.0 / 17.0 / 10.0

Performance Quartile (within Category)

	1995	1996	1997	1998	1999	2000	2001	2002	2003	2004	2005	2006	History
NAV	9.82	11.13	10.20	12.49	24.02	26.22	23.61	17.00	25.41	30.77	33.03	36.68	NAV
	-1.79*	13.41	-7.93	31.98	97.77	18.04	-9.68	-27.94	49.55	21.65	8.27	16.78	Total Return %
	—	-9.55	-41.29	3.40	76.73	27.14	2.21	-5.84	20.87	10.77	3.36	0.99	+/-S&P 500
	—	-4.07	-30.47	14.12	46.48	29.79	10.47	-0.53	6.84	6.17	-3.83	6.12	+/-Russ MG
	—	0.07	0.40	0.15	0.28	0.67	0.27	0.06	0.08	0.28	0.18	0.21	Income Return %
	—	13.34	-8.33	31.83	97.49	17.37	-9.95	-28.00	49.47	21.37	8.09	16.57	Capital Return %
	—	71	98	15	17	14	27	59	5	4	67	8	Total Rtn % Rank Cat
	0.03	0.01	0.05	0.02	0.04	0.16	0.07	0.01	0.01	0.07	0.06	0.07	Income $
	0.00	0.00	0.00	0.90	0.59	1.92	0.00	0.00	0.00	0.07	0.23	1.86	Capital Gains $
	0.47	0.50	0.49	0.94	0.75	0.62	0.60	0.58	0.59	0.52	0.51	0.49	Expense Ratio %
	1.29	0.11	0.27	0.18	0.31	0.64	0.28	0.07	0.05	0.06	0.33	0.15	Income Ratio %
		128	195	103	22	15	20	14	14	10	12	11	Turnover Rate %
	81	117	63	206	2,367	5,056	4,846	3,275	5,455	6,962	5,203	5,268	Net Assets $mil

Performance 12-31-06

	1st Qtr	2nd Qtr	3rd Qtr	4th Qtr	Total
2002	-1.52	-20.73	-18.29	12.97	-27.94
2003	-2.59	23.25	8.72	14.57	49.55
2004	7.67	3.47	-3.78	13.48	21.65
2005	-4.91	3.76	5.14	4.37	8.27
2006	9.90	-6.09	5.93	6.82	16.78

Trailing	Total Return%	+/- S&P 500	+/- Russ MG	%Rank Cat	Growth of $10,000
3 Mo	6.82	0.12	-0.13	51	10,682
6 Mo	13.14	0.40	5.24	3	11,314
1 Yr	16.78	0.99	6.12	8	11,678
3 Yr Avg	15.43	4.99	2.70	9	15,380
5 Yr Avg	10.63	4.44	2.41	11	16,572
10 Yr Avg	15.56	7.14	6.94	3	42,469
15 Yr Avg	—	—	—	—	—

Tax Analysis	Tax-Adj Rtn%	%Rank Cat	Tax-Cost Rat	%Rank Cat
3 Yr (estimated)	15.04	7	0.34	17
5 Yr (estimated)	10.40	8	0.21	15
10 Yr (estimated)	14.75	4	0.70	19

Potential Capital Gain Exposure: 37% of assets

Rating and Risk

Time Period	Load-Adj Return %	Morningstar Rtn vs Cat	Morningstar Risk vs Cat	Morningstar Risk-Adj Rating
1 Yr	16.78			
3 Yr	15.43	High	+Avg	★★★★★
5 Yr	10.63	+Avg	+Avg	★★★★
10 Yr	15.56	High	Avg	★★★★★
Incept	14.63			

Other Measures	Standard Index S&P 500	Best Fit Index Russ MG
Alpha	0.6	1.8
Beta	1.64	1.08
R-Squared	73	87
Standard Deviation	13.17	
Mean	15.43	
Sharpe Ratio	0.92	

Portfolio Analysis 09-30-06

Share change since 06-06   Total Stocks:120

	Sector	PE	Tot Ret%	% Assets
⊖ Research in Motion, Ltd.	Hardware	72.5	93.58	4.36
⊖ Corning Inc.	Hardware	25.5	-4.83	3.77
⊖ Symantec Corporation	Software	50.9	19.14	3.17
⊕ FedEx Corporation	Business	17.2	5.40	3.14
⊕ NVIDIA Corporation	Hardware	33.4	102.46	3.04
⊖ Applera Corporation	Health	39.9	38.90	2.92
Biogen Idec, Inc.	Health	NMF	8.64	2.86
⊕ ASML Holding NV	Hardware	31.3	22.66	2.62
⊕ Monsanto Company	Ind Mtrls	39.8	36.78	2.55
Pfizer Inc.	Health	15.2	15.22	2.45
⊖ DirecTV, Inc.	Media	26.5	76.63	2.25
Novartis AG ADR	Health	22.2	11.29	2.08
⊖ Micron Technology, Inc.	Hardware	24.1	4.88	2.04
Thomas & Betts Corporati	Hardware	19.1	12.68	2.04
TJX Companies	Consumer	16.9	24.05	1.64
⊖ THQ, Inc.	Software	81.9	36.35	1.63
Murphy Oil Corporation	Energy	12.8	-4.82	1.56
Comverse Technology, Inc	Hardware	—	-20.61	1.55
Men's Wearhouse	Consumer	16.6	30.69	1.51
Nordstrom, Inc.	Consumer	21.9	33.35	1.49

Current Investment Style

Value Blnd Growth — Large Mid Small

Market Cap	%
Giant	13.4
Large	41.3
Mid	31.6
Small	13.3
Micro	0.3

Avg $mil: 11,365

Value Measures		Rel Category
Price/Earnings	19.98	0.97
Price/Book	2.34	0.73
Price/Sales	1.69	0.96
Price/Cash Flow	10.53	0.92
Dividend Yield %	0.52	0.83

Growth Measures	%	Rel Category
Long-Term Erngs	13.83	0.85
Book Value	13.73	1.08
Sales	12.15	1.22
Cash Flow	16.28	0.88
Historical Erngs	18.71	0.75

Profitability	%	Rel Category
Return on Equity	14.13	0.79
Return on Assets	7.91	0.84
Net Margin	10.03	0.86

Sector Weightings	% of Stocks	Rel S&P 500	3 Year High	Low
◔ Info	48.05	2.40		
🖥 Software	12.40	3.59	12	9
💻 Hardware	31.04	3.36	31	26
📡 Media	3.09	0.82	4	2
☎ Telecom	1.52	0.43	3	2
⊂ Service	39.35	0.85		
🩺 Health	20.08	1.67	23	19
🛒 Consumer	11.83	1.55	13	11
💼 Business	5.87	1.39	8	6
$ Financial	1.57	0.07	2	1
🏭 Mfg	12.58	0.37		
🛢 Goods	1.56	0.18	2	1
⚙ Ind Mtrls	4.93	0.41	6	4
🔥 Energy	6.09	0.62	11	6
💡 Utilities	0.00	0.00	0	0

Composition

● Cash	2.3	
● Stocks	97.7	
● Bonds	0.0	
○ Other	0.0	
Foreign	11.7	(% of Stock)

Morningstar's Take by David Kathman 12-11-06

Vanguard Capital Opportunity continues to justify our high opinion of it.

This fund features one of the best long-term records in the mid-cap growth category, and it has shown few signs of slowing down despite its $9.5 billion asset base. In 2005 it trailed its category for only the second time since the topnotch Primecap team took over the fund in early 1998, but in 2006 it has come roaring back after a slow start, ranking in the category's top 10% for the year to date through mid-December.

The fund's recent success has been all the more impressive given that about half of the portfolio is now in large caps, mostly large-growth stocks, which have been one of the market's toughest areas. The managers have kept big overweights in technology and health care because that's where they're seeing the most long-term value, regardless of what the market thinks now. While some of the fund's larger tech stocks have continued to tread water, others have started to show signs of life,

and top-10 holdings Research in Motion and NVIDIA have contributed to the fund's resurgence by going on a tear in the second half of 2006.

The fund's health-care stocks have been a similarly mixed bag, with mid-caps such as Applera outperforming larger stocks, but the managers remain enthusiastic about the latter. They think the market has greatly overreacted to high-profile problems at big pharma and medical-device companies, so they've added to such stocks as Medtronic and have stayed with top-20 holdings Pfizer and Novartis.

That long-term perspective and willingness to go against the grain have been major factors in the success of the Primecap team over the past 20 years. They're also among the most attractive features of this fund, although a low 0.51% expense ratio certainly doesn't hurt either. The fund has been closed to new investors since early 2004, but those who already own it should definitely hang on to this Analyst Pick.

Address:	P O Box 2600 Valley Forge PA 19482 800-997-2798	Minimum Purchase:	Closed Add: — IRA: —
		Min Auto Inv Plan:	Closed Add: —
		Sales Fees:	No-load, 1.00%R
Web Address:	www.vanguard.com	Management Fee:	0.50% mx./0.15% mn.
Inception:	08-14-95 *	Actual Fees:	Mgt:0.49% Dist: —
Advisor:	PRIMECAP Management Co.	Expense Projections:	3Yr:$164 5Yr:$285 10Yr:$640
Subadvisor:	None	Income Distrib:	Annually
NTF Plans:	Vanguard NTF		

Vanguard Capital Value

	Ticker	Load	NAV	Yield	Total Assets	Mstar Category
	VCVLX	None	$12.68	0.9%	$500 mil	Large Value

Governance and Management

Stewardship Grade: B

Portfolio Manager(s)

David Fassnacht, who has been on board here since 2001, took over lead manager responsibilities for this fund in June 2004, when Charles Freeman retired. Before assuming control, Fassnacht worked as an assistant portfolio manager on this fund and Vanguard Windsor. He is backed by a highly experienced team at Wellington Management.

Strategy

This fund is a diehard and opportunistic value hunter. Its managers favor stocks that have fallen hard and may hold sizable positions in individual names or sectors. While doing so, they look across the market-cap spectrum. In recent years, management has gravitated toward beaten-down growth stocks.

Historical Profile

Return	Average
Risk	High
Rating	★★ Below Avg

Investment Style
Equity
Stock %

83% 98% 96% 100% 100% 98%

▽ (Partial Manager Change)

14.0
12.0
10.0

6.0

▼ Manager Change
▽ Partial Manager Change

Growth of $10,000
■ Investment Values of Fund
— Investment Values of S&P 500

Performance Quartile (within Category)

	1995	1996	1997	1998	1999	2000	2001	2002	2003	2004	2005	2006	History
NAV	—	—	—	—	—	—	10.26	7.31	10.30	11.75	11.67	12.68	
Total Return %	—	—	—	—	—	—	2.60*	-28.07	41.74	15.38	4.21	18.90	
+/-S&P 500	—	—	—	—	—	—	—	-5.97	13.06	4.50	-0.70	3.11	
+/-Russ 1000 VI	—	—	—	—	—	—	—	-12.55	11.71	-1.11	-2.84	-3.35	
Income Return %	—	—	—	—	—	—	—	0.68	0.82	1.26	0.85	1.11	
Capital Return %	—	—	—	—	—	—	—	-28.75	40.92	14.12	3.36	17.79	
Total Rtn % Rank Cat	—	—	—	—	—	—	—	98	4	23	69	41	
Income $	—	—	—	—	—	—	0.00	0.07	0.06	0.13	0.10	0.13	
Capital Gains $	—	—	—	—	—	—	0.00	0.00	0.00	0.00	0.48	1.07	
Expense Ratio %	—	—	—	—	—	—	—	0.54	0.53	0.53	0.60		
Income Ratio %	—	—	—	—	—	—	—	0.77	0.82	0.95	1.02		
Turnover Rate %	—	—	—	—	—	—	—	40	40	40	47		
Net Assets $mil	—	—	—	—	—	—	—	91	199	377	449	500	

Performance 12-31-06

	1st Qtr	2nd Qtr	3rd Qtr	4th Qtr	Total
2002	-2.63	-18.82	-17.63	10.48	-28.07
2003	-4.24	22.14	5.85	14.48	41.74
2004	2.62	0.66	-2.07	14.05	15.38
2005	-2.04	1.22	-0.09	5.19	4.21
2006	5.66	-2.11	2.73	11.90	18.90

Trailing	Total Return%	+/- S&P 500	+/- Russ 1000 VI	%Rank Cat	Growth of $10,000
3 Mo	11.90	5.20	3.90	1	11,190
6 Mo	14.96	2.22	0.24	13	11,496
1 Yr	18.90	3.11	-3.35	41	11,890
3 Yr Avg	12.65	2.21	-2.44	41	14,295
5 Yr Avg	7.82	1.63	-3.04	58	14,571
10 Yr Avg	—	—	—	—	—
15 Yr Avg	—	—	—	—	—

Tax Analysis	Tax-Adj Rtn%	%Rank Cat	Tax-Cost Rat	%Rank Cat
3 Yr (estimated)	11.77	30	0.78	31
5 Yr (estimated)	7.22	47	0.56	30
10 Yr (estimated)	—	—	—	—

Potential Capital Gain Exposure: 18% of assets

Morningstar's Take by Dan Culloton 11-20-06

Vanguard Capital Value deserves a long leash.

This fund offers investors an undiluted shot of its manager's cross-grain style. Accordingly, it occasionally looks out of favor itself as its manager David Fassnacht moves against the crowd in search of opportunity. This is why the fund has lagged most of its large-value peers since the start of 2005 (though the fund gained some steam in the final quarter of 2006). The fund shaved its energy exposure as those stocks ran up and moved into one-time growth darlings, whose share prices have languished even as they have remained profitable. This fund also is prone to look different than its category rivals because it has more leeway to buy mid- and small-cap stocks.

Over time, however, Fassnacht's contrarian instincts should serve this fund well. His purchase of traditional growth stocks, such as broadband networking gear maker Cisco Systems and cable television firm Comcast, look prescient. And smaller picks, such as Canadian income trust Cinram

International, show Fassnacht has the courage to delve into obscure situations. He says the maker of DVDs for Hollywood studios is misunderstood and has been unfairly punished due to concerns about movie downloading and because a collapsing hedge fund--Amaranth--was trying to unload a large position in the company earlier in the year. Fassnacht thinks the market will notice Cinram's large free-cash-flow yield when the dust settles.

Such calls may not work out soon or ever, which is why this fund is not for everyone. You have to be willing to put up with bouts of underperformance and ugly stocks if you want to invest here. Still, it's hard to beat the market and your peers by trying to look like them, and Fassnacht is an experienced investor who has shown an ability to make his nonconformist style work elsewhere, such as at the more diversified Vanguard Windsor.

This can be a valuable holding for risk tolerant investors looking for a truly actively managed value fund.

Address:	P.O. Box 2600 Valley Forge PA 19482 800-997-2798	Minimum Purchase:	$3000	Add: $100 IRA: $3000
		Min Auto Inv Plan:	$3000	Add: $50
		Sales Fees:	No-load	
Web Address:	www.vanguard.com	Management Fee:	0.56%	
Inception:	12-17-01*	Actual Fees:	Mgt:0.56%	Dist: —
Advisor:	Wellington Management Company, LLP	Expense Projections:	3Yr:$189	5Yr:$329 10Yr:$738
Subadvisor:	None	Income Distrib:	Annually	
NTF Plans:	Vanguard NTF			

Rating and Risk

Time Period	Load-Adj Return %	Morningstar Rtn vs Cat	Morningstar Risk vs Cat	Morningstar Risk-Adj Rating
1 Yr	18.90			
3 Yr	12.65	Avg	High	★★★
5 Yr	7.82	Avg	High	★★
10 Yr	—	—	—	
Incept	8.31			

Other Measures	Standard Index S&P 500	Best Fit Index Russ 1000
Alpha	0.0	-0.4
Beta	1.32	1.29
R-Squared	84	85
Standard Deviation	9.97	
Mean	12.65	
Sharpe Ratio	0.93	

Portfolio Analysis 09-30-06

Share change since 06-06 Total Stocks:75	Sector	PE	Tot Ret%	% Assets
⊕ Cisco Systems, Inc.	Hardware	30.1	59.64	6.49
⊕ Cinram International Inc	Media	—		4.13
⊖ Comcast Corporation	Media	—		3.60
Wyeth	Health	17.2	12.88	3.47
Sanofi-Aventis ADR	Health	42.9	7.33	3.21
Tyco International, Ltd.	Ind Mtrls	15.7	6.83	2.95
⊖ Bank of America Corporat	Financial	12.4	20.68	2.89
⊕ R. H. Donnelley Corporat	Business	—	1.82	2.71
American Axle & Mfg Hold	Ind Mtrls	16.7	7.35	2.60
Microsoft Corporation	Software	23.8	15.83	2.43
⊕ UAL Corporation	Business	—		2.41
⊕ Cooper Companies	Health	35.7	-13.14	2.38
Sprint Nextel Corporatio	Telecom	30.2	-10.44	2.34
Goodrich Corporation	Ind Mtrls	12.9	12.95	2.29
⊖ Citigroup, Inc.	Financial	13.1	19.55	2.25
Cytec Industries	Ind Mtrls	20.0	19.52	2.02
ACE, Ltd.	Financial	10.6	15.41	2.01
Foot Locker, Inc.	Consumer	14.8	-5.67	1.95
Fairchild Semiconductor	Hardware	92.0	-0.59	1.61
⊖ Alcoa, Inc.	Ind Mtrls	12.0	3.49	1.58

Current Investment Style

Value Blnd Growth — Large Mid Small

Market Cap	%
Giant	33.5
Large	19.0
Mid	36.0
Small	10.6
Micro	0.9

Avg $mil: 13,574

Value Measures		Rel Category
Price/Earnings	14.58	1.06
Price/Book	1.58	0.71
Price/Sales	0.68	0.52
Price/Cash Flow	4.93	0.74
Dividend Yield %	1.92	0.82

Growth Measures	%	Rel Category
Long-Term Erngs	11.15	1.07
Book Value	12.51	1.58
Sales	4.64	0.52
Cash Flow	3.66	0.60
Historical Erngs	8.22	0.51

Profitability	%	Rel Category
Return on Equity	13.78	0.77
Return on Assets	5.11	0.52
Net Margin	9.11	0.70

Sector Weightings	% of Stocks	Rel S&P 500	3 Year High	Low
↻ Info	33.13	1.66		
🖬 Software	3.38	0.98	3	1
🖳 Hardware	14.02	1.52	15	8
🎙 Media	12.16	3.21	12	6
📶 Telecom	3.57	1.02	4	0
⊆ Service	39.96	0.86		
🏥 Health	16.14	1.34	16	12
🛒 Consumer	2.76	0.36	9	3
📈 Business	7.75	1.83	8	3
💲 Financial	13.31	0.60	28	13
⬒ Mfg	26.89	0.80		
🏭 Goods	2.50	0.29	6	1
⬡ Ind Mtrls	21.67	1.81	22	15
🔋 Energy	2.72	0.28	5	2
💡 Utilities	0.00	0.00	0	0

Composition

● Cash	1.6	
● Stocks	98.4	
● Bonds	0.0	
● Other	0.0	
Foreign	15.3	
(% of Stock)		

Morningstar® Funds 500

Vanguard Convertible Sec

	Ticker	Load	NAV	Yield	Total Assets	Mstar Category
	VCVSX	None	$13.64	3.1%	$719 mil	Convertibles

Governance and Management

Stewardship Grade: B

Portfolio Manager(s)

In 1996 manager Larry Keele cofounded this fund's subadvisor, Oaktree Capital Management. The shop specializes in convertibles, high-yield bonds, and distressed debt. He took on this fund in November 1996, and Andrew Watts has assisted him since then. Stu Spangler and Steve Prado also serve as analysts on the fund.

Strategy

Manager Larry Keele invests only in convertible bonds. He likes to make sure a convertible security has a solid structure and an attractive price before his group runs the issuing firm through a gauntlet of credit analysis. Upside potential for the stock is the last piece of analysis. Keele avoids convertible preferreds, equitylike converts, and "busted" converts, which results in a portfolio of nearly 100% balanced convertible bonds.

Performance 12-31-06

	1st Qtr	2nd Qtr	3rd Qtr	4th Qtr	Total
2002	-3.41	-4.61	-6.64	5.39	-9.35
2003	2.50	10.76	4.98	10.40	31.58
2004	4.54	-2.25	-0.38	5.30	7.20
2005	-4.06	0.79	5.28	4.71	6.60
2006	8.28	-2.83	3.16	4.05	12.94

Trailing	Total Return%	+/- DJ Mod	+/- Merrill Lynch Convert	%Rank Cat	Growth of $10,000
3 Mo	4.05	-1.54	-0.77	71	10,405
6 Mo	7.34	-1.45	-0.31	32	10,734
1 Yr	12.94	0.64	0.91	20	11,294
3 Yr Avg	8.88	-1.84	2.29	26	12,908
5 Yr Avg	9.01	-1.01	1.40	27	15,393
10 Yr Avg	9.02	0.47	0.41	28	23,717
15 Yr Avg	9.82	0.61	-0.08	43	40,759

Tax Analysis	Tax-Adj Rtn%	%Rank Cat	Tax-Cost Rat	%Rank Cat
3 Yr (estimated)	6.76	27	1.95	78
5 Yr (estimated)	7.12	29	1.73	80
10 Yr (estimated)	6.44	32	2.37	85

Potential Capital Gain Exposure: 5% of assets

Morningstar's Take by Kerry O'Boyle 12-11-06

Vanguard Convertible Securities is one of our favorites.

A strategy focused entirely on middle-of-the-road converts has served this pure-play convertible fund well. While a number of convertible mutual funds favor either equity strategies that concentrate on a convert's underlying stock or credit approaches that emphasize yield and the defensive qualities of converts, this fund plays it straight. That balance has paid off since the spring of 2005, when a correction in the convertible market crushed valuations. Since that time the fund has benefited from a rebound in convertibles and largely avoided the stock market correction in early summer 2006 that punished many of its rivals.

Granted, performance at the fund hasn't always looked as good as the past 12 months, and likely won't continue to look as good over the next. But manager Larry Keele of subadviser Oaktree Capital Management is a convertible veteran who has built

the firm he cofounded largely around investing in distressed debt, high-yield, and convertible securities. The fund represents the appealing balance between upside potential and downside protection that convertibles have to offer.

Currently, Keele is pleased with the variety of new issues coming out, and that the convert market has returned to normal state--which he characterized as a good mix of under-, over-, and fairly-valued issues--after the choppiness of the past few years. He's recently added converts from SanDisk and Gilead Sciences to the portfolio. Plus, two separate converts from Teva Pharmaceutical add up to a top-10 holding. Keele thinks the firm's stock is undervalued, and likes the short maturities, solid credit, and call protection found in the converts.

Although clearly enjoying a great run at the moment, we think this Analyst Pick is a terrific long-term holding as well, and enthusiastically recommend it to new and existing investors.

Address:	PO Box 2600 V26 Valley Forge PA 19482 800-662-7447	Minimum Purchase:	$10000	Add: $100	IRA: $10000
		Min Auto Inv Plan:	$10000	Add: $50	
		Sales Fees:	No-load, 1.00%R		
Web Address:	www.vanguard.com	Management Fee:	0.92%		
Inception:	06-17-86	Actual Fees:	Mgt:0.83%	Dist: —	
Advisor:	Oaktree Capital Management, LLC	Expense Projections:	3Yr:$274	5Yr:$477	10Yr:$1061
Subadvisor:	None	Income Distrib:	Quarterly		
NTF Plans:	Vanguard NTF				

Historical Profile

Return	Average
Risk	Above Avg
Rating	★★★★ Above Avg

Investment Style: Equity, Stock %

▼ Manager Change
▽ Partial Manager Change

Growth of $10,000
— Investment Values of Fund
— Investment Values of DJ Mod

Performance Quartile (within Category)

	1995	1996	1997	1998	1999	2000	2001	2002	2003	2004	2005	2006	History
NAV	11.62	11.63	11.82	11.34	13.46	12.96	12.00	10.41	13.23	13.29	13.40	13.64	NAV
	16.74	15.44	16.39	0.56	30.36	4.21	-3.09	-9.35	31.58	7.20	6.60	12.94	Total Return %
	-3.06	4.78	4.49	-11.76	13.03	5.88	-0.29	-2.58	4.20	-5.77	-0.39	0.64	+/-DJ Mod
	-7.22	3.32	0.88	-11.65	-5.63	11.73	-0.18	-6.23	8.61	-1.11	6.79	0.91	+/-Merrill Lynch Convert
	5.21	4.10	4.72	4.64	4.48	4.29	4.24	3.98	4.09	2.90	2.43	3.47	Income Return %
	11.53	11.34	11.67	-4.08	25.88	-0.08	-7.33	-13.33	27.49	4.30	4.17	9.47	Capital Return %
	95	56	76	57	33	44	28	76	17	73	16	20	Total Rtn % Rank Cat
	0.54	0.47	0.54	0.54	0.50	0.57	0.54	0.47	0.42	0.38	0.32	0.46	Income $
	0.14	1.29	1.12	0.00	0.70	0.51	0.00	0.00	0.00	0.50	0.43	1.02	Capital Gains $
	0.75	0.69	0.67	0.73	0.55	0.56	0.71	0.95	0.84	0.68	0.86	—	Expense Ratio %
	4.63	3.43	4.29	4.36	4.30	4.19	4.21	4.27	3.82	2.94	2.18	—	Income Ratio %
	46	97	182	186	162	182	156	118	127	123	86	—	Turnover Rate %
	168	166	187	178	197	345	303	286	874	941	558	719	Net Assets $mil

Rating and Risk

Time Period	Load-Adj Return %	Morningstar Rtn vs Cat	Morningstar Risk vs Cat	Morningstar Risk-Adj Rating
1 Yr	12.94			
3 Yr	8.88	Avg	Avg	★★★★
5 Yr	9.01	+Avg	Avg	★★★★
10 Yr	9.02	Avg	+Avg	★★★
Incept	9.10			

Other Measures	Standard Index DJ Mod	Best Fit Index Merrill Lynch Convert
Alpha	-1.9	1.9
Beta	1.04	1.09
R-Squared	71	86
Standard Deviation	7.32	
Mean	8.88	
Sharpe Ratio	0.77	

Portfolio Analysis 09-30-06

Total Fixed-Income:48	Date of Maturity	Amount $000	Value $000	% Net Assets
Fisher Scientific Intl 3	03-01-24	18,725	21,791	3.20
Gilead Sciences 144A Cv	05-01-11	20,170	21,380	3.14
Manor Care 144A 2.125%	08-01-35	13,995	17,161	2.52
Wyeth Cv FRN	01-15-24	15,705	17,109	2.51
Chesapeake Engy Cv		147	15,164	2.23
Genzyme 1.25%	12-01-23	13,520	14,804	2.17
Lsi Logic Cv 4%	05-15-10	14,055	14,090	2.07
Rf Microdevices Cv 1.5%	07-01-10	12,135	14,031	2.06
INTERPUBLIC GROUP COS	03-15-23	13,220	13,898	2.04
L-3 Comms 3%	08-01-35	13,610	13,848	2.03
Amdocs Cv 0.5%	03-15-24	12,975	13,802	2.03
Teva Pharma Fin Ii 0.5%	02-01-24	12,480	13,151	1.93
NABORS INDS	06-15-23	12,310	12,833	1.88
MEDIMMUNE	07-15-11	11,570	12,510	1.84
HILTON HOTELS	04-15-23	9,265	12,114	1.78
Symantec 144A Cv 0.75%	06-15-11	9,605	11,682	1.72
Electnc Data Sys New Cv	07-15-23	11,300	11,371	1.67
Allergan 144A Cv 1.5%	04-01-26	10,665	11,225	1.65
Andrew Cv 3.25%	08-15-13	11,390	11,119	1.63
ITRON	08-01-26	9,690	10,938	1.61

Investment Style	
Avg Eff Maturity	4.8 Yrs
Avg Credit Quality	BB
Avg Wtd Coupon	2.33%
Avg Wtd Price	107.09% of par

Coupon Range	% of Bonds	Rel Cat
0% PIK	5.9	0.4
0% to 8%	100.0	1.0
8% to 11%	0.0	0.0
11% to 14%	0.0	0.0
More than 14%	0.0	0.0
1.00=Category Average		

Special Securities	
Restricted/Illiquid Secs	25
Emerging-Markets Secs	0
Options/Futures/Warrants	No

Credit Analysis	% bonds 09-30-06		
AAA	0	BB	20
AA	0	B	20
A	8	Below B	5
BBB	15	NR/NA	32

Composition	
Cash	1.7
Stocks	0.0
Bonds	44.3
Convertibles	48.3
Other	5.7

Vanguard Dev Mkts Idx

	Ticker	Load	NAV	Yield	Total Assets	Mstar Category
	VDMIX	None	$12.58	2.4%	$2,856 mil	Foreign Large Blend

Governance and Management

Stewardship Grade: B

Portfolio Manager(s)

The fund is made up of two component Vanguard funds. Vanguard indexing expert Gus Sauter managed those until 2005, when other Vanguard individuals stepped forward and took day-to-day responsibility for them. However, Sauter, now chief investment officer at Vanguard, still has oversight of the funds.

Strategy

This is a passively managed fund of funds that invests all of its assets in Vanguard European Stock Index and Vanguard Pacific Stock Index, with the majority going to the Europe fund. Its goal is to track the performance of the MSCI EAFE Index. It has minimal exposure to emerging markets. It does not hedge its foreign-currency exposure. The fund imposes a 2% redemption fee on shares redeemed within two months after purchase.

Performance 12-31-06

	1st Qtr	2nd Qtr	3rd Qtr	4th Qtr	Total
2002	1.01	-2.28	-19.83	6.52	-15.70
2003	-8.19	19.35	8.11	17.00	38.61
2004	4.35	0.49	-0.49	15.23	20.25
2005	-0.22	-1.31	10.93	3.75	13.34
2006	9.30	0.81	4.00	10.11	26.18

Trailing	Total Return%	+/- MSCI EAFE	+/- MSCI Wd xUS	%Rank Cat	Growth of $10,000
3 Mo	10.11	-0.24	-0.01	56	11,011
6 Mo	14.52	-0.17	0.30	46	11,452
1 Yr	26.18	-0.16	0.47	32	12,618
3 Yr Avg	19.81	-0.12	-0.29	28	17,198
5 Yr Avg	14.98	0.00	-0.27	20	20,096
10 Yr Avg	—	—	—	—	—
15 Yr Avg	—	—	—	—	—

Tax Analysis	Tax-Adj Rtn%	%Rank Cat	Tax-Cost Rat	%Rank Cat
3 Yr (estimated)	19.13	21	0.57	31
5 Yr (estimated)	14.32	17	0.57	45
10 Yr (estimated)	—	—	—	—

Potential Capital Gain Exposure: 31% of assets

Historical Profile

Return	Above Avg
Risk	Average
Rating	★★★★ Above Avg

1995	1996	1997	1998	1999	2000	2001	2002	2003	2004	2005	2006	History
—	—	—	—	—	9.07	6.95	5.74	7.81	9.20	10.21	12.58	NAV
—	—	—	—	—	-7.79*	-22.04	-15.70	38.61	20.25	13.34	26.18	Total Return %
—	—	—	—	—	—	-0.62	0.24	0.02	0.00	-0.20	-0.16	+/-MSCI EAFE
—	—	—	—	—	—	-0.65	0.10	-0.81	-0.13	-1.13	0.47	+/-MSCI Wd xUS
—	—	—	—	—	—	1.32	1.67	2.49	2.43	2.38	2.93	Income Return %
—	—	—	—	—	—	-23.36	-17.37	36.12	17.82	10.96	23.25	Capital Return %
—	—	—	—	—	—	55	36	17	14	64	32	Total Rtn % Rank Cat
—	—	—	—	—	0.15	0.12	0.12	0.14	0.19	0.22	0.30	Income $
—	—	—	—	—	0.00	0.00	0.00	0.00	0.00	0.00	0.01	Capital Gains $
—	—	—	—	—	—	—	—	—	—	—	0.29	Expense Ratio %
—	—	—	—	—	—	1.66	0.04	1.30	1.48	1.52	—	Income Ratio %
—	—	—	—	—	—	8	3	5	7	4	—	Turnover Rate %
—	—	—	—	—	99	189	399	734	1,198	2,856		Net Assets $mil

Rating and Risk

Time Period	Load-Adj Return %	Morningstar Rtn vs Cat	Morningstar Risk vs Cat	Morningstar Risk-Adj Rating
1 Yr	26.18			
3 Yr	19.81	+Avg	-Avg	★★★★
5 Yr	14.98	+Avg	Avg	★★★★
10 Yr	—	—	—	—
Incept	5.69			

Other Measures	Standard Index MSCI EAFE	Best Fit Index MSCI EAFE
Alpha	-0.1	-0.1
Beta	1.00	1.00
R-Squared	99	99
Standard Deviation	9.51	
Mean	19.81	
Sharpe Ratio	1.63	

Portfolio Analysis 09-30-06

Share change since 06-06 Total Stocks:0	Sector	Country	% Assets
⊕ Vanguard European Stock	—	United States	68.43
⊕ Vanguard Pacific Stock I	—	United States	31.50

Morningstar's Take by Gregg Wolper 12-27-06

Vanguard Developed Markets Index has plenty of competition and probably can't keep up its current pace--but it can serve you quite well nonetheless.

In recent years the international-indexing field has become crowded. Besides the popular exchange-traded iShares MSCI EAFE Index--which tracks the same benchmark as this fund--the younger iShares that track the value or growth components of that index allow investors more choice. A new player, WisdomTree, has come out with international index-tracking ETFs. Fidelity Spartan International Index was already a tough competitor, with an expense ratio of just 0.10% a year. (This fund's 2006 expense ratio was 0.27%.) Now Vanguard itself (which already offers a fund that adds an emerging-markets stake to the holdings in this fund) has announced it's coming out with a new fund tracking a different index entirely.

Still, it's hard to find much fault with this fund. It provides diversified exposure to large companies from the biggest markets, and it has Vanguard's experienced index-trackers at the helm. Its cost is extremely low compared with actively managed international funds. Even that cost disadvantage versus the Fidelity rival shouldn't be overrated. If you already own this fund, it may not be worth the potential tax hit to switch, and if you're a Vanguard-only type, the convenience may well outweigh the rather small gains of owning the Fidelity fund instead. In fact, because indexing is not an exact science and fair-value pricing disparities come into play, the Fidelity fund won't always come out ahead: For example, for the year to date through Dec. 26, 2006, this fund tops its Fidelity rival, 25.6% to 24.8%.

Just keep in mind, though, that a 25% one-year gain is too much to expect on a regular basis from an EAFE fund. Foreign markets and currencies won't always be this strong. That said, this fund can serve you well.

Address:	PO Box 2600 Valley Forge PA 19482 800-997-2798
Web Address:	www.vanguard.com
Inception:	05-08-00*
Advisor:	Vanguard Advisers, Inc.
Subadvisor:	None
NTF Plans:	Vanguard NTF

Minimum Purchase:	$3000	Add: $100	IRA: $3000
Min Auto Inv Plan:	$3000	Add: $50	
Sales Fees:	No-load, 2.00%R		
Management Fee:	0.00%		
Actual Fees:	—	Dist: —	
Expense Projections:	3Yr:$93	5Yr:$163	10Yr:$368
Income Distrib:	Annually		

Current Investment Style

	Value	Blnd	Growth		Market Cap	%
Large					Giant	55.5
Mid					Large	31.6
Small					Mid	12.4
					Small	0.4
					Micro	0.1
					Avg $mil: 28,961	

Value Measures		Rel Category
Price/Earnings	10.09	0.77
Price/Book	2.01	0.93
Price/Sales	1.04	0.90
Price/Cash Flow	8.11	0.97
Dividend Yield %	3.15	1.08

Growth Measures	%	Rel Category
Long-Term Erngs	11.07	0.94
Book Value	7.85	0.86
Sales	5.96	0.91
Cash Flow	4.33	0.52
Historical Erngs	9.79	0.48

Composition

Cash	0.7	Bonds	0.0
Stocks	97.8	Other	1.5
Foreign (% of Stock)			100.0

Sector Weightings	% of Stocks	Rel MSCI EAFE	3 Year High	Low
☁ Info	11.62	0.98		
🖥 Software	0.59	1.05	1	1
💻 Hardware	3.85	1.00	5	4
🎬 Media	1.89	1.03	2	2
📶 Telecom	5.29	0.95	9	5
☎ Service	48.15	1.02		
🏥 Health	7.81	1.10	9	8
🛒 Consumer	5.09	1.03	5	4
📋 Business	4.89	0.96	5	5
💲 Financial	30.36	1.01	30	25
🏭 Mfg	40.24	0.98		
⚙ Goods	12.78	0.97	15	13
🔧 Ind Mtrls	15.05	0.98	16	12
💡 Energy	7.55	1.06	9	8
⚡ Utilities	4.86	0.93	5	4

Regional Exposure	% Stock
UK/W. Europe 68	N. America 0
Japan 24	Latn America 0
Asia X Japan 8	Other 0

Country Exposure	% Stock
U.K. 24	Switzerland 7
Japan 24	Germany 7
France 10	

Investment Style
Equity
Stock %

Growth of $10,000
— Investment Values of Fund
— Investment Values of MSCI EAFE

Performance Quartile (within Category)

MORNINGSTAR® Funds 500

Vanguard Dividend Growth

	Ticker	Load	NAV	Yield	Total Assets	Mstar Category
	VDIGX	None	$14.57	1.8%	$1,217 mil	Large Value

Portfolio Manager(s)

In February 2006 Donald Kilbride assumed control of this fund after its former manager, Minerva Butler, left Wellington Management, the fund's advisor. Although this is Kilbride's first solo stint running a fund, he served as backup manager on Vanguard Wellington for two and a half years. Prior to joining Wellington in 2002, Kilbride was director of research at a Boston-based hedge fund.

Strategy

Like his predecessor, manager Donald Kilbride gravitates to financially sound industry leaders that generate enough free cash flow to grow dividends. Although the vast majority of portfolio holdings pay dividends, the fund can stash up to 10% of assets in nondividend payers that management thinks have the potential to pay dividends in the future. Kilbride is price-conscious and prefers to purchase stocks when they are trading at historically low valuations. He is a long-term investor, and turnover should be well below average.

Performance 12-31-06

	1st Qtr	2nd Qtr	3rd Qtr	4th Qtr	Total
2002	3.12	-9.13	-18.74	0.91	-23.16
2003	-5.46	17.79	2.37	13.33	29.20
2004	2.06	1.32	-0.44	7.83	11.02
2005	-1.15	0.08	3.28	2.02	4.23
2006	5.23	-0.90	6.94	7.22	19.58

Trailing	Total Return%	+/- S&P 500	+/- Russ 1000 Vl	%Rank Cat	Growth of $10,000
3 Mo	7.22	0.52	-0.78	51	10,722
6 Mo	14.66	1.92	-0.06	18	11,466
1 Yr	19.58	3.79	-2.67	31	11,958
3 Yr Avg	11.43	0.99	-3.66	66	13,836
5 Yr Avg	6.56	0.37	-4.30	82	13,740
10 Yr Avg	6.87	-1.55	-4.13	85	19,434
15 Yr Avg	—	—	—		

Tax Analysis	Tax-Adj Rtn%	%Rank Cat	Tax-Cost Rat	%Rank Cat
3 Yr (estimated)	11.12	42	0.28	11
5 Yr (estimated)	6.01	71	0.52	28
10 Yr (estimated)	5.30	82	1.47	46

Potential Capital Gain Exposure: 17% of assets

Morningstar's Take by Dan Culloton 11-20-06

The best is yet to come for Vanguard Dividend Growth.

This fund has seen some changes in recent years, and until this year, spotty performance. About four years ago, it switched from being a utilities-sector fund to a more diversified, dividend-focused fund. Then earlier this year, a new manager took over. All the while it spent more time behind its average large-value peer than in front of it. These are all red flags, but if you consider this offering's fundamentals, there is more reason to be optimistic than worried.

First, the strategy is sound. The fund looks for stocks that have a proven ability and willingness to increase their dividends over time and that are trading at reasonable prices. That guides the fund to established companies with strong free cash flow and dependable business models.

Second, manager Donald Kilbride is more impressive than his short tenure implies. He worked as a backup manager on Vanguard Wellington and

is supported by a large staff of analysts. Kilbride also has put his stamp on the fund, taking a somewhat bolder approach to the offering's strategy. The fund still goes after dividend-paying stocks with the financial wherewithal and willingness to increase their payouts, but Kilbride has trimmed the portfolio from about 70 holdings to around 60, which should give his favorite positions more impact. Lately those have included fallen growth stocks such as medical device maker Medtronic, which Kilbride says can bounce back from product recalls and has committed to paying out 20% of its previous year's earnings.

Last, the fund's relative performance should improve if more growth-oriented, large-cap stocks take over market leadership from smaller, more value-oriented ones. Not only does this fund's blue-chip portfolio have a higher average market cap than its peers, but a significant portion of its holdings are trading below Morningstar equity analysts' fair value estimates. This one's solid.

Address:	PO Box 2600 Valley Forge, PA 19482 800-997-2798	Minimum Purchase:	$3000	Add: $100 IRA: $3000
		Min Auto Inv Plan:	$3000	Add: $50
Web Address:	www.vanguard.com	Sales Fees:	No-load	
Inception:	05-15-92	Management Fee:	0.35%	
Advisor:	Wellington Management Company, LLP	Actual Fees:	Mgt:0.34%	Dist: —
Subadvisor:	None	Expense Projections:	3Yr:$119	5Yr:$208 10Yr:$468
NTF Plans:	Vanguard NTF	Income Distrib:	Semi-Annually	

Historical Profile

Return	Below Avg
Risk	Below Avg
Rating	★★ Below Avg

| 84% | 88% | 95% | 95% | 96% | 97% | 98% | 100% | 98% |

Investment Style
Equity
Stock %

▼ Manager Change
▽ Partial Manager Change

31.0
25.0 **Growth of $10,000**
20.0 ■ Investment Values of Fund
15.0 ── Investment Values of S&P 500
10.0

Performance Quartile (within Category)

1995	1996	1997	1998	1999	2000	2001	2002	2003	2004	2005	2006	History
12.68	12.74	14.98	16.54	14.33	15.66	11.88	8.79	11.15	12.15	12.42	14.57	NAV
34.03	5.28	25.09	21.83	-2.96	18.77	-19.45	-23.16	29.20	11.02	4.23	19.58	Total Return %
-3.55	-17.68	-8.27	-6.75	-24.00	27.87	-7.56	-1.06	0.52	0.14	-0.68	3.79	+/-S&P 500
-4.33	-16.36	-10.09	6.20	-10.31	11.76	-13.86	-7.64	-0.83	-5.47	-2.82	-2.67	+/-Russ 1000 Vl
5.74	4.49	4.79	4.02	3.17	3.83	2.44	3.24	2.17	1.98	1.99	2.10	Income Return %
28.29	0.79	20.30	17.81	-6.13	14.94	-21.89	-26.40	27.03	9.04	2.24	17.48	Capital Return %
38	98	73	5	88	15	97	84	39	73	68	31	Total Rtn % Rank Cat
0.56	0.56	0.60	0.59	0.51	0.53	0.37	0.38	0.19	0.22	0.24	0.26	Income $
0.00	0.02	0.26	1.01	1.20	0.73	0.41	0.00	0.00	0.00	0.00	0.00	Capital Gains $
0.50	0.41	0.40	0.44	0.38	0.38	0.35	0.37	0.34	0.40	0.36	0.37	Expense Ratio %
5.43	4.88	4.63	4.30	3.51	3.13	2.76	2.85	3.57	1.84	2.04	1.85	Income Ratio %
35	35	38	41	55	47	48	27	104	23	20	16	Turnover Rate %
758	659	685	951	841	954	706	555	783	984	984	1,217	Net Assets $mil

Rating and Risk

Time Period	Load-Adj Return %	Morningstar Rtn vs Cat	Morningstar Risk vs Cat	Morningstar Risk-Adj Rating
1 Yr	19.58			
3 Yr	11.43	Avg	Low	★★★
5 Yr	6.56	-Avg	Avg	★★
10 Yr	6.87	-Avg	-Avg	★★
Incept	8.36			

Other Measures	Standard Index S&P 500	Best Fit Index S&P 500
Alpha	2.1	2.1
Beta	0.82	0.82
R-Squared	88	88
Standard Deviation	6.11	
Mean	11.43	
Sharpe Ratio	1.30	

Portfolio Analysis 09-30-06

Share change since 06-06 Total Stocks:62	Sector	PE	Tot Ret%	% Assets
⊕ ExxonMobil Corporation	Energy	11.1	39.07	3.36
⊕ Total SA ADR	Energy	10.6	19.24	2.92
Chevron Corporation	Energy	9.0	33.76	2.68
⊕ Medtronic, Inc.	Health	23.8	-4.26	2.66
Bank of America Corporat	Financial	12.4	20.68	2.60
⊖ General Electric Company	Ind Mtrls	20.0	9.35	2.60
⊖ Microsoft Corporation	Software	23.8	15.83	2.51
⊕ Eli Lilly & Company	Health	17.3	-5.16	2.46
Citigroup, Inc.	Financial	13.1	19.55	2.37
⊕ Schering-Plough Corporat	Health	36.6	14.63	2.31
⊕ Cardinal Health, Inc.	Health	20.8	-5.82	2.29
⊕ Nike, Inc. B	Goods	19.2	15.84	2.21
CBS, Inc. B	Media	—	33.16	2.04
⊕ Gap, Inc.	Consumer	19.5	12.45	2.00
American International G	Financial	17.0	6.05	1.99
⊕ Wal-Mart Stores, Inc.	Consumer	16.9	0.13	1.91
Altria Group, Inc.	Goods	16.3	19.87	1.88
ACE, Ltd.	Financial	10.6	15.41	1.86
AstraZeneca PLC ADR	Health	18.7	13.28	1.85
Lockheed Martin Corporat	Ind Mtrls	17.3	46.98	1.84

Current Investment Style

Value Blnd Growth — Large/Mid/Small

Market Cap	%
Giant	58.4
Large	39.0
Mid	2.6
Small	0.0
Micro	0.0

Avg $mil: 63,317

Value Measures		Rel Category
Price/Earnings	15.23	1.11
Price/Book	2.91	1.31
Price/Sales	1.26	0.97
Price/Cash Flow	9.76	1.46
Dividend Yield %	2.13	0.91

Growth Measures	%	Rel Category
Long-Term Erngs	10.68	1.03
Book Value	2.65	0.33
Sales	10.73	1.19
Cash Flow	5.89	0.97
Historical Erngs	15.26	0.94

Profitability	%	Rel Category
Return on Equity	20.24	1.13
Return on Assets	9.83	1.00
Net Margin	10.63	0.82

Sector Weightings	% of Stocks	Rel S&P 500	3 Year High	Low
⌖ Info	15.86	0.79		
📊 Software	2.57	0.74	4	3
🖥 Hardware	5.51	0.60	8	6
🔊 Media	5.25	1.39	7	3
📱 Telecom	2.53	0.72	4	2
☁ Service	43.72	0.95		
🏥 Health	16.47	1.37	16	12
🛒 Consumer	10.73	1.40	11	6
💼 Business	3.60	0.85	4	1
$ Financial	12.92	0.58	20	12
⌂ Mfg	40.43	1.20		
🏭 Goods	12.43	1.45	12	9
⚙ Ind Mtrls	15.30	1.28	24	15
🔋 Energy	10.69	1.09	11	6
💡 Utilities	2.01	0.57	4	2

Composition

- ● Cash 2.2
- ● Stocks 97.8
- ● Bonds 0.0
- ○ Other 0.0
- Foreign 6.2 (% of Stock)

Vanguard Em Mkt Idx

	Ticker	Load	NAV	Yield	Total Assets	Mstar Category
	VEIEX	None	$24.21	1.6%	$10,817 mil	Diversified Emerging Mkts

Governance and Management

Stewardship Grade: B

Portfolio Manager(s)

Vanguard's Duane F. Kelly has been a manager of this fund since its 1994 inception. For much of that time he worked closely with Gus Sauter, Vanguard indexing chief, but Sauter has been reducing his involvement in the daily management of individual funds since becoming the firm's chief investment officer in 2003.

Strategy

This fund tracks the MSCI Emerging Markets Index. Until August 2006, it tracked a customized version of the MSCI Emerging Markets Free Index, which emphasizes the most-liquid emerging markets with the fewest barriers to foreign investment. That approach gave it heavy exposure to the major emerging markets but excluded a few markets, such as Russia, that now are included. In an effort to combat market-timing, the fund has a short-term redemption fee of 2% and also uses fair-value pricing on occasion. It does not hedge its currency exposure.

Historical Profile

Return	Average
Risk	Average
Rating	★★★ Neutral

84% 85% 84% 85% 82% 88% 95% 94% 94%

Growth of $10,000
— Investment Values of Fund
— Investment Values of MSCI EAFE

Performance Quartile (within Category)

	1995	1996	1997	1998	1999	2000	2001	2002	2003	2004	2005	2006	History
	10.75	12.28	9.98	7.91	12.50	8.84	8.37	7.63	11.85	14.68	19.07	24.21	NAV
	0.56	15.83	-16.82	-18.12	61.57	-27.56	-7.43	-7.43	57.65	26.12	32.05	29.07	Total Return %
	-10.65	9.78	-18.60	-38.05	34.54	-13.37	18.54	8.51	19.06	5.87	18.51	2.73	+/-MSCI EAFE
	7.47	11.90	-3.37	9.55	-2.52	4.34	1.80	0.54	6.06	3.67	1.74	-0.11	+/-MSCI EmrMkt
	1.66	1.58	1.87	2.61	3.41	1.75	2.38	1.46	2.25	2.19	2.15	2.08	Income Return %
	-1.10	14.25	-18.69	-20.73	58.16	-29.31	-5.26	-8.89	55.40	23.93	29.90	26.99	Capital Return %
	42	34	92	9	68	28	46	65	31	30	52	75	Total Rtn % Rank Cat
	0.18	0.17	0.23	0.26	0.27	0.22	0.21	0.12	0.17	0.26	0.32	0.40	Income $
	0.00	0.00	0.00	0.00	0.00	0.00	0.00	0.00	0.00	0.00	0.00	0.00	Capital Gains $
	0.60	0.60	0.57	0.61	0.58	0.59	0.57	0.57	0.53	0.48	0.45	0.42	Expense Ratio %
	2.00	1.69	1.96	2.99	2.55	1.51	1.67	1.67	2.26	2.44	2.48	2.20	Income Ratio %
	3	1	19	22	22	40	23	65	16	11	15	26	Turnover Rate %
	234	637	681	577	1,138	1,019	801	896	1,873	3,140	6,018	8,109	Net Assets $mil

Performance 12-31-06

	1st Qtr	2nd Qtr	3rd Qtr	4th Qtr	Total
2002	10.39	-8.33	-17.12	10.37	-7.43
2003	-5.64	22.50	14.74	18.86	57.65
2004	7.85	-8.76	7.98	18.71	26.12
2005	1.43	3.69	17.23	7.10	32.05
2006	11.22	-4.57	4.00	16.93	29.07

Trailing	Total Return%	+/- MSCI EAFE	+/- MSCI EmrMkt	%Rank Cat	Growth of $10,000
3 Mo	16.93	6.58	-0.35	64	11,693
6 Mo	21.61	6.92	-0.48	81	12,161
1 Yr	29.07	2.73	-0.11	75	12,907
3 Yr Avg	29.06	9.13	1.80	51	21,497
5 Yr Avg	25.69	10.71	2.17	56	31,369
10 Yr Avg	9.28	1.57	2.55	57	24,289
15 Yr Avg	—	—	—		

Tax Analysis	Tax-Adj Rtn%	%Rank Cat	Tax-Cost Rat	%Rank Cat
3 Yr (estimated)	28.28	38	0.43	18
5 Yr (estimated)	25.01	48	0.44	27
10 Yr (estimated)	8.44	61	0.71	61

Potential Capital Gain Exposure: 34% of assets

Rating and Risk

Time Period	Load-Adj Return %	Morningstar Rtn vs Cat	Morningstar Risk vs Cat	Morningstar Risk-Adj Rating
1 Yr	28.43			
3 Yr	28.84	Avg	Avg	★★★
5 Yr	25.56	Avg	Avg	★★★
10 Yr	9.22	Avg	Avg	★★★
Incept	9.32			

Other Measures	Standard Index MSCI EAFE	Best Fit Index MSCI EmrMkt
Alpha	-1.7	1.4
Beta	1.66	1.00
R-Squared	78	99
Standard Deviation	17.72	
Mean	29.06	
Sharpe Ratio	1.36	

Portfolio Analysis 09-30-06

Share change since 06-06	Total Stocks:803	Sector	Country	% Assets
✿ GAZ OAO		Goods	Russia	5.19
⊕ Samsung Electronics		Goods	Korea	3.94
✿ America Movil S.A. de C.		Telecom	Mexico	1.84
✿ Lukoil ADR		Energy	Russia	1.78
⊖ Taiwan Semiconductor Mfg		Hardware	Taiwan	1.77
⊖ China Mobile		Telecom	Hong Kong	1.77
⊕ Petroleo Brasileiro Sa P		Energy	Brazil	1.41
⊕ Kookmin Bank		Financial	Korea	1.27
⊕ Hon Hai Precision Indust		Hardware	Taiwan	1.22
⊖ Teva Pharmaceutical Indu		Health	Israel	1.21
⊖ Petroleo Brasileiro		Energy	Brazil	1.15
⊕ PetroChina		Energy	Hong Kong	1.03
⊕ CEMEX		Financial	Mexico	0.98
⊖ Sasol Ltd		Energy	South Africa	0.97
⊕ Infosys Technologies Ltd		Software	India	0.89
⊖ Cia Vale Rio Doce			Brazil	0.86
⊕ POSCO		Ind Mtrls	Korea	0.82
⊖ Reliance Industries Ltd		Ind Mtrls	India	0.81
✿ Surgutneftegaz		Energy	Russia	0.77
⊖ Bco Itau Hldg F			Brazil	0.77

Current Investment Style

Value Blnd Growth — Large Mid Small

Market Cap	%
Giant	37.2
Large	35.9
Mid	17.4
Small	9.1
Micro	0.4

Avg $mil: 8,934

Value Measures		Rel Category
Price/Earnings	12.62	0.97
Price/Book	1.93	0.89
Price/Sales	1.02	0.93
Price/Cash Flow	5.52	0.83
Dividend Yield %	3.98	1.21

Growth Measures	%	Rel Category
Long-Term Erngs	14.26	0.92
Book Value	11.56	1.16
Sales	15.16	0.96
Cash Flow	11.00	0.99
Historical Erngs	16.31	0.91

Composition

Cash	0.4	Bonds	0.3
Stocks	94.1	Other	5.1
Foreign (% of Stock)			99.5

Sector Weightings	% of Stocks	Rel MSCI EAFE	3 Year High	Low
⊙ Info	21.19	1.79		
▣ Software	1.58	2.82	2	2
▣ Hardware	7.57	1.96	10	5
▣ Media	1.28	0.70	2	1
▣ Telecom	10.76	1.93	13	11
⊂ Service	30.33	0.64		
▣ Health	2.36	0.33	4	2
▣ Consumer	3.87	0.78	4	3
▣ Business	4.96	0.98	6	4
▣ Financial	19.14	0.64	21	16
◰ Mfg	48.47	1.18		
▣ Goods	18.39	1.40	18	14
▣ Ind Mtrls	16.08	1.04	24	16
▣ Energy	11.16	1.56	11	8
▣ Utilities	2.84	0.54	3	2

Regional Exposure		% Stock
UK/W. Europe 0	N. America	0
Japan 0	Latn America	18
Asia X Japan 55	Other	27

Country Exposure		% Stock
South Korea 18	Hong Kong	9
Taiwan 14	South Africa	8
Russia 11		

Morningstar's Take by Gregg Wolper 11-13-06

The new-look Vanguard Emerging Markets Stock Index has some new risks, but don t let that alone discourage you.

For years this fund followed a custom-made version of MSCI's Emerging Markets Free Index. The Free index excluded some countries in which trading was difficult, and Vanguard's version put a few more on that list. Over time, as many countries' markets matured--at least in terms of trading--both the Free index and Vanguard's version added countries in, until only one major difference between the fund and what's now the MSCI Emerging Markets Index remained: Russia. That changed in August 2006, when Vanguard announced it would dispense with its customized benchmark, and the fund would begin to track the MSCI index itself.

That decision has had important consequences. In recent years, Russia's market capitalization has soared, powered by high energy prices and by global investors' search for new destinations. As a result, the fund's Russia stake jumped from 0% in June 2006 to 10.4% at the end of September, making it the third-biggest country weighting in the portfolio. Energy giant Gazprom was the number-one holding, with Lukoil in the fifth slot.

So, is this fund more appealing now? On one hand, its new portfolio is a more accurate reflection of the way active emerging-markets managers invest these days; Russian companies are common in such funds. On the other hand, Russia is also more volatile than some more-mature emerging markets, and its pronounced energy tilt makes it vulnerable to declines in oil and gas prices.

All told, therefore, this fund still offers a cheap, straightforward play on emerging markets and is more representative than it used to be. But it does carry new risks as well--on top of the risks it already contained as an emerging-markets fund that has ridden a long rally in most such markets.

Address:	PO Box 2600 Valley Forge PA 19482 800-662-7447	Minimum Purchase:	$3000	Add: $100	IRA: $3000
		Min Auto Inv Plan:	$3000	Add: $50	
		Sales Fees:	No-load, 0.50%R		
Web Address:	www.vanguard.com	Management Fee:	0.24%		
Inception:	05-04-94	Actual Fees:	Mgt:0.24%	Dist: —	
Advisor:	The Vanguard Group, Inc.	Expense Projections:	3Yr:$241	5Yr:$346	10Yr:$655
Subadvisor:	None	Income Distrib:	Annually		
NTF Plans:	Vanguard NTF				

MORNINGSTAR® Funds 500

Vanguard Energy

	Ticker	Load	NAV	Yield	Total Assets	Mstar Category
	VGENX	None	$64.63	1.6%	$10,332 mil	Specialty-Natural Res

Governance and Management

Stewardship Grade: B

Portfolio Manager(s)

Karl Bandtel of Wellington Management manages the vast majority of this fund's assets. A long-time team member here, Bandtel assumed the lead at the end of 2002. He is supported by a team of analysts, many of whom have been with the firm for several years. A tiny sliver of the fund's assets are managed by Vanguard Quantitative Equity Group, which uses computer models to pick stocks. QEG runs at least a portion of six other Vanguard offerings and is the sole manager of Vanguard Strategic Equity.

Strategy

This pure energy fund has stakes in most subsectors, but it emphasizes large, integrated oil companies. Wellington Management, which runs the lion's share of the fund, tends to hang on to its picks for the long haul, seizing stocks it thinks are attractively valued, often because bad news or a weak earnings report has prompted a sell-off. Vanguard's quantitative-equity group runs a smaller portion of the portfolio, using a computer model to pick stocks based on factors such as valuation and improving fundamentals.

Performance 12-31-06

	1st Qtr	2nd Qtr	3rd Qtr	4th Qtr	Total
2002	11.84	-4.40	-13.83	7.86	-0.62
2003	0.99	11.69	1.64	16.70	33.80
2004	7.31	7.13	10.80	7.28	36.65
2005	14.50	7.16	22.01	-3.41	44.60
2006	11.43	4.54	-7.38	10.92	19.68

Trailing	Total Return%	+/- S&P 500	+/- GS NATR RES	%Rank Cat	Growth of $10,000
3 Mo	10.92	4.22	1.35	26	11,092
6 Mo	2.74	-10.00	0.17	35	10,274
1 Yr	19.68	3.89	2.86	22	11,968
3 Yr Avg	33.23	22.79	7.53	12	23,649
5 Yr Avg	25.75	19.56	7.54	19	31,444
10 Yr Avg	16.53	8.11	6.81	10	46,172
15 Yr Avg	16.78	6.14	—	7	102,454

Tax Analysis	Tax-Adj Rtn%	%Rank Cat	Tax-Cost Rat	%Rank Cat
3 Yr (estimated)	32.36	3	0.65	20
5 Yr (estimated)	24.57	21	0.94	50
10 Yr (estimated)	15.08	8	1.24	45

Potential Capital Gain Exposure: 53% of assets

Morningstar's Take by Lawrence Jones 12-21-06

Vanguard Energy is a compelling option in this subsector of the natural-resources category.

One factor that distinguishes this fund within the category is its investment approach. Managers Jim Bevilacqua and Karl Bandtel, of esteemed subadvisor Wellington Management, practice a low turnover, long-term strategy here that focuses on the giant-cap integrated oil companies. With an average portfolio turnover rate of less than 20% over the past few years, this fund's long-term orientation stands in sharp relief to the nearly 140% turnover that is currently typical in the category. Low turnover not only keeps trading costs down, it also makes the fund more tax-efficient than others. Also, giant industry leaders, such as ExxonMobile, Chevron, and Total SA, serve as ballast in a segment of the market known for turbulence.

A segment of the portfolio is run in a different style, however. Comanagers Joel Dickson and James Troyer, of Vanguard's Quantitative Equity Group, dip further down the market-cap ladder than will their peers at Wellington. Additionally, as the process at QEG involves quantitative models that focus on valuation, earnings prospects, and investor sentiment, it may tend to load different stocks into the portfolio at different times than would the Wellington group. This could be a concern depending on how the two portfolio segments act in concert. It's not a pressing worry at the moment, as Vanguard's portion of the portfolio only amounts to a bit over 10% of assets, but it bears monitoring, because Vanguard is absorbing all new inflows, which continue to come in at a healthy clip.

We remain fans of this fund, but shareholders shouldn't expect the energy rally to continue forever. And should it end, the fund's performance is likely to suffer. Investors should therefore keep expectations in check, resist chasing returns, and limit the fund to a modest portion of their portfolios.

Address:	PO Box 2600 Valley Forge, PA 19482 800-997-2798	Minimum Purchase:	$25000	Add: $100	IRA: $25000
		Min Auto Inv Plan:	$25000	Add: $50	
		Sales Fees:	No-load, 1.00%R		
Web Address:	www.vanguard.com	Management Fee:	0.15% mx./0.05% mn.		
Inception:	05-23-84	Actual Fees:	Mgt:0.25%	Dist: —	
Advisor:	Vanguard Advisers, Inc.	Expense Projections:	3Yr:$90	5Yr:$157	10Yr:$356
Subadvisor:	None	Income Distrib:	Annually		
NTF Plans:	Vanguard NTF				

Historical Profile

Return	High
Risk	Average
Rating	★★★★★ Highest

Performance Quartile (within Category)

1995	1996	1997	1998	1999	2000	2001	2002	2003	2004	2005	2006	History
97%	96%	96%	97%	95%	91%	93%	91%	93%				
17.31	22.54	24.14	18.42	21.92	28.07	25.29	23.20	29.85	40.00	56.05	64.63	NAV
25.32	34.00	14.89	-20.53	20.98	36.43	-2.55	-0.62	33.80	36.65	44.60	19.68	Total Return %
-12.26	11.04	-18.47	-49.11	-0.06	45.53	9.34	21.48	5.12	25.77	39.69	3.89	+/-S&P 500
—	—	-2.05	4.14	-6.24	20.62	13.04	12.64	-0.21	12.08	8.12	2.86	+/-GS NATR RES
1.96	1.39	1.43	1.45	1.93	1.64	1.43	1.44	1.68	1.77	1.86	1.84	Income Return %
23.36	32.61	13.46	-21.98	19.05	34.79	-3.98	-2.06	32.12	34.88	42.74	17.84	Capital Return %
21	38	19	50	85	34	17	38	30	11	43	22	Total Rtn % Rank Cat
0.28	0.24	0.32	0.35	0.36	0.36	0.40	0.36	0.39	0.52	0.74	1.03	Income $
0.30	0.40	1.33	0.42	0.00	1.38	1.54	1.59	0.74	0.20	1.03	1.45	Capital Gains $
0.30	0.48	0.39	0.38	0.38	0.47	0.41	0.39	0.40	0.38	0.31	0.28	Expense Ratio %
1.66	1.55	1.36	1.36	1.36	1.63	1.52	1.57	1.56	1.79	1.67	1.57	Income Ratio %
13	21	15	19	19	18	24	28	23	26	1	17	Turnover Rate %
506	848	1,181	820	1,018	1,351	1,282	1,305	2,219	4,706	5,650	6,628	Net Assets $mil

Rating and Risk

Time Period	Load-Adj Return %	Morningstar Rtn vs Cat	Morningstar Risk vs Cat	Morningstar Risk-Adj Rating
1 Yr	19.68			
3 Yr	33.23	+Avg	-Avg	★★★★★
5 Yr	25.75	+Avg	-Avg	★★★★
10 Yr	16.53	High	Avg	★★★★★
Incept	14.78			

Other Measures	Standard Index S&P 500	Best Fit Index GS NATR RES
Alpha	20.6	6.4
Beta	0.99	0.98
R-Squared	13	98
Standard Deviation	18.72	
Mean	33.23	
Sharpe Ratio	1.46	

Portfolio Analysis 09-30-06

Share change since 06-06 Total Stocks:91	Sector	PE	Tot Ret%	% Assets
⊖ ExxonMobil Corporation	Energy	11.1	39.07	7.18
⊖ Chevron Corporation	Energy	9.0	33.76	5.81
⊖ ConocoPhillips	Energy	6.5	26.53	4.36
⊕ Total SA ADR	Energy	10.6	19.24	4.31
⊖ Schlumberger, Ltd.	Energy	22.3	31.07	3.55
⊕ Valero Energy Corporatio	Energy	6.3	-0.33	3.29
BHP Billiton, Ltd. ADR	Ind Mtrls	10.8	21.15	3.12
BP PLC ADR	Energy	10.4	7.94	2.89
⊖ BG Grp	Energy	—	—	2.82
⊕ ENI SpA ADR	Energy	4.4	27.38	2.75
⊖ Marathon Oil Corporation	Energy	6.1	54.68	2.46
⊖ Transocean, Inc.	Energy	27.1	16.07	2.39
⊕ Baker Hughes Inc.	Energy	9.9	23.68	2.11
⊕ Weatherford Internationa	Energy	15.2	16.56	2.09
⊕ Occidental Petroleum Cor	Energy	8.0	24.32	1.98
⊕ Petroleo Brasileiro S.A.	Energy	10.4	51.12	1.92
Royal Dutch Shell PLC AD	Energy	—	—	1.86
⊕ Halliburton Company	Energy	11.2	1.11	1.77
⊖ GlobalSantaFe Corporatio	Energy	16.3	24.06	1.76
⊕ Statoil ASA ADR	Energy	11.2	19.17	1.68

Current Investment Style

Value Blnd Growth — Large Mid Small

Market Cap	%
Giant	54.3
Large	33.9
Mid	11.7
Small	0.0
Micro	0.0

Avg $mil: 46,691

Value Measures		Rel Category
Price/Earnings	10.12	0.80
Price/Book	2.37	0.92
Price/Sales	0.87	0.69
Price/Cash Flow	5.98	0.85
Dividend Yield %	1.43	1.38

Growth Measures	%	Rel Category
Long-Term Erngs	11.79	0.74
Book Value	18.70	1.29
Sales	22.57	1.21
Cash Flow	32.01	1.14
Historical Erngs	46.86	1.02

Profitability	%	Rel Category
Return on Equity	27.33	1.28
Return on Assets	12.44	1.27
Net Margin	14.91	0.97

Industry Weightings	% of Stocks	Rel Cat
Oil & Gas	51.3	1.6
Oil/Gas Products	13.8	1.3
Oil & Gas Srv	25.3	0.8
Pipelines	0.7	0.7
Utilities	0.0	0.0
Hard Commd	5.0	0.6
Soft Commd	0.0	0.0
Misc. Indstrl	0.0	0.0
Other	4.0	0.5

Composition

● Cash	6.0	
● Stocks	92.6	
● Bonds	0.0	
● Other	1.3	
Foreign (% of Stock)	42.1	

Investment Style
Equity
Stock %

▼ Manager Change
▽ Partial Manager Change

Growth of $10,000
— Investment Values of Fund
— Investment Values of S&P 500

Vanguard Equity-Inc

	Ticker	Load	NAV	Yield	Total Assets	Mstar Category
	VEIPX	None	$25.30	2.7%	$5,293 mil	Large Value

Governance and Management

Stewardship Grade: B

Portfolio Manager(s)

John Levin & Co., which had previously managed 20% of the fund's assets, was removed as an advisor to the fund in September 2005. Now Wellington Management runs 60% of the fund's assets, and Vanguard's Quantitative Equity Group manages the remaining 40%. Wellington's John Ryan--who has been with this fund since January 2000--boasts more than 20 years of investment experience. QEG's James Stetler use a quantitative-based approach in managing his portion of the portfolio.

Strategy

The fund's two advisors seek stocks that are cheap and offer high dividend yields relative to the market. This tack often leads the team to pick up stocks that are temporarily under a cloud and hold them until they turn around. The upshot is that the fund tends to lag when growth stocks rule the roost, but it has been a steady performer over time. The fund's emphasis on cheap, high-yielding stocks, along with its broadly diversified portfolio, has kept volatility in check.

Performance 12-31-06

	1st Qtr	2nd Qtr	3rd Qtr	4th Qtr	Total
2002	3.61	-8.58	-17.94	8.52	-15.65
2003	-5.73	15.74	0.40	14.24	25.14
2004	1.33	1.69	1.15	8.96	13.57
2005	-1.19	1.52	2.71	1.30	4.37
2006	4.95	1.24	6.29	6.81	20.62

Trailing	Total Return%	+/- S&P 500	+/- Russ 1000 VI	%Rank Cat	Growth of $10,000
3 Mo	6.81	0.11	-1.19	66	10,681
6 Mo	13.53	0.79	-1.19	36	11,353
1 Yr	20.62	4.83	-1.63	19	12,062
3 Yr Avg	12.66	2.22	-2.43	41	14,299
5 Yr Avg	8.58	2.39	-2.28	45	15,092
10 Yr Avg	9.91	1.49	-1.09	27	25,726
15 Yr Avg	11.48	0.84	-1.55	33	51,045

Tax Analysis	Tax-Adj Rtn%	%Rank Cat	Tax-Cost Rat	%Rank Cat
3 Yr (estimated)	11.16	42	1.33	53
5 Yr (estimated)	7.36	45	1.12	60
10 Yr (estimated)	8.25	25	1.51	48

Potential Capital Gain Exposure: 22% of assets

Morningstar's Take by Dan Culloton 11-20-06

Exchange-traded funds don't phase Vanguard Equity-Income.

A host of exchange-traded funds (essentially mutual funds that can be bought and sold throughout the day on an exchange) tracking indexes that rank stocks by yield rather than by the value of all their outstanding shares have emerged in recent years. They purport to offer lower costs and higher yields than conventional mutual funds at a time when more companies are raising or initiating their dividends and an aging population is demanding more income-generating investments. Even Vanguard has jumped into the fray with two dividend focused index funds, including the recently launched Vanguard High Dividend Yield ETF. This fund stands up well to the new competition.

First, it has something the dividend-focused ETFs, none of which are older than three years, do not have: A decent long-term track record. Although it tends to look pokey in highly speculative periods (it dropped to the category's bottom quartile in 1999

and 2003) the fund's pre- and post-tax 10-year annualized returns through Oct. 31, 2006, beat more than 70% of its large-value peers.

Second, the fund has a proven management team and strategy. Vanguard has tinkered with the subadvisory assignments at this fund over the years, but the current managers have solid credentials. Wellington Management's John Ryan, who runs about 60% of the assets, has picked dividend-paying stocks for Vanguard Wellesley Income for more than 20 years, and Vanguard's quantitative equity group is accomplished.

Ryan's contrarian instincts have been a good fit for this fund's mandate--investing in cheap, above-average-yielding stocks. He increased his sleeve's helping of energy stocks early in the decade when they were unpopular and has been trimming them in the last couple of years as the oil patch got popular. Finally, the fund's yield and expense ratio are competitive with those of the new dividend ETFs. This fund still holds its own.

Address:	P.O. Box 2600 Valley Forge PA 19482 800-662-2739	Minimum Purchase:	$3000	Add: $100	IRA: $3000
		Min Auto Inv Plan:	$3000	Add: $50	
		Sales Fees:	No-load		
Web Address:	www.vanguard.com	Management Fee:	0.30%		
Inception:	03-21-88	Actual Fees:	Mgt:0.30%	Dist: —	
Advisor:	Vanguard Advisers, Inc.	Expense Projections:	3Yr:$103	5Yr:$180	10Yr:$406
Subadvisor:	None	Income Distrib:	Quarterly		
NTF Plans:	Vanguard NTF				

Historical Profile
Return	Above Avg
Risk	Below Avg
Rating	★★★★ Above Avg

89% 92% 91% 95% 90% 95% 97% 99% 95%

Growth of $10,000
— Investment Values of Fund
— Investment Values of S&P 500

Investment Style
Equity
Stock %

▼ Manager Change
▽ Partial Manager Change

Performance Quartile (within Category)

1995	1996	1997	1998	1999	2000	2001	2002	2003	2004	2005	2006	History
16.69	18.32	22.39	24.73	23.17	24.44	22.71	18.70	22.31	23.50	22.79	25.30	NAV
37.34	17.39	31.17	17.34	-0.19	13.57	-2.34	-15.65	25.14	13.57	4.37	20.62	Total Return %
-0.24	-5.57	-2.19	-11.24	-21.23	22.67	9.55	6.45	-3.54	2.69	-0.54	4.83	+/-S&P 500
-1.02	-4.25	-4.01	1.71	-7.54	6.56	3.25	-0.13	-4.89	-2.92	-2.68	-1.63	+/-Russ 1000 VI
4.77	3.89	3.70	2.89	2.65	2.66	2.10	2.13	3.10	2.69	2.93	3.15	Income Return %
32.57	13.50	27.47	14.45	-2.84	10.91	-4.44	-17.78	22.04	10.88	1.44	17.47	Capital Return %
11	73	17	16	77	29	43	32	78	43	67	19	Total Rtn % Rank Cat
0.60	0.64	0.67	0.64	0.65	0.61	0.51	0.48	0.57	0.60	0.68	0.71	Income $
0.17	0.58	0.89	0.83	0.87	1.14	0.60	0.00	0.42	1.17	1.05	1.42	Capital Gains $
0.45	0.42	0.45	0.39	0.41	0.43	0.47	0.46	0.45	0.32	0.31	0.31	Expense Ratio %
4.27	3.69	3.25	2.80	2.59	2.59	2.26	2.21	2.61	2.61	2.80	2.94	Income Ratio %
31	21	22	23	18	36	31	21	55	36	42	26	Turnover Rate %
1,103	1,425	2,100	2,939	2,874	2,561	2,250	1,931	2,590	3,162	2,818	3,306	Net Assets $mil

Rating and Risk

Time Period	Load-Adj Return %	Morningstar Rtn vs Cat	Morningstar Risk vs Cat	Morningstar Risk-Adj Rating
1 Yr	20.62			
3 Yr	12.66	Avg	Low	★★★
5 Yr	8.58	Avg	-Avg	★★★
10 Yr	9.91	+Avg	-Avg	★★★★
Incept	11.66			

Other Measures	Standard Index S&P 500	Best Fit Index Russ 1000 VI
Alpha	3.3	-0.6
Beta	0.81	0.86
R-Squared	85	92
Standard Deviation	6.08	
Mean	12.66	
Sharpe Ratio	1.49	

Portfolio Analysis 09-30-06

Share change since 06-06 Total Stocks:153	Sector	PE	Tot Ret%	% Assets
Bank of America Corporat	Financial	12.4	20.68	3.55
AT&T, Inc.	Telecom	18.2	51.59	3.13
ExxonMobil Corporation	Energy	11.1	39.07	2.50
Citigroup, Inc.	Financial	13.1	19.55	2.39
⊕ General Electric Company	Ind Mtrls	20.0	9.35	1.94
Wyeth	Health	17.2	12.88	1.79
⊕ Altria Group, Inc.	Goods	16.3	19.87	1.62
⊕ Wells Fargo Company	Financial	14.7	16.82	1.54
⊕ UBS AG	Financial	—	29.62	1.49
Pfizer Inc.	Health	15.2	15.22	1.43
Abbott Laboratories	Health	24.3	26.88	1.43
Kimberly-Clark Corporati	Goods	22.7	17.55	1.28
Vanguard Value ETF	—	—	—	1.27
Dow Chemical Company	Ind Mtrls	10.0	-5.44	1.22
Verizon Communications	Telecom	15.9	34.88	1.21
FPL Group	Utilities	17.7	35.49	1.18
⊕ Bristol-Myers Squibb Com	Health	23.1	19.93	1.14
Dominion Resources, Inc.	Utilities	17.8	12.56	1.10
⊕ Chevron Corporation	Energy	9.0	33.76	1.09
⊖ J.P. Morgan Chase & Co.	Financial	13.6	25.60	1.08

Current Investment Style

Value Blnd Growth — Large Mid Small

	Market Cap	%
	Giant	42.5
	Large	38.4
	Mid	18.1
	Small	0.9
	Micro	0.0
	Avg $mil:	36,417

Value Measures		Rel Category
Price/Earnings	14.23	1.04
Price/Book	2.41	1.09
Price/Sales	1.35	1.04
Price/Cash Flow	5.71	0.85
Dividend Yield %	3.13	1.34

Growth Measures	%	Rel Category
Long-Term Erngs	9.42	0.91
Book Value	6.56	0.83
Sales	7.31	0.81
Cash Flow	0.79	0.13
Historical Erngs	9.91	0.61

Profitability	%	Rel Category
Return on Equity	19.16	1.07
Return on Assets	9.50	0.97
Net Margin	13.38	1.03

Sector Weightings	% of Stocks	Rel S&P 500	3 Year High Low
☌ Info	9.31	0.47	
Software	0.00	0.00	0 0
Hardware	0.40	0.04	3 0
Media	2.70	0.71	3 1
Telecom	6.21	1.77	6 4
☎ Service	46.80	1.01	
Health	10.09	0.84	10 6
Consumer	3.30	0.43	3 2
Business	3.04	0.72	3 1
Financial	30.37	1.36	33 30
Mfg	43.90	1.30	
Goods	16.24	1.90	16 10
Ind Mtrls	15.25	1.28	20 15
Energy	6.00	0.61	13 6
Utilities	6.41	1.83	10 6

Composition

● Cash	4.9
● Stocks	95.1
● Bonds	0.0
● Other	0.0
Foreign (% of Stock)	4.4

MORNINGSTAR® Funds 500

Vanguard Eur Stk Idx

	Analyst Pick	Ticker VEURX	Load None	NAV $35.95	Yield 2.6%	Total Assets $25,865 mil	Mstar Category Europe Stock

Governance and Management

Stewardship Grade: B

Portfolio Manager(s)

Vanguard indexing guru Gus Sauter, who managed this fund since its 1990 inception, became the shop's CIO and stepped down as official manager in early 2006. Though Sauter still oversees Vanguard's indexing effort, the fund's day-to-day manager is Duane Kelly, who has been at Vanguard for more than 15 years.

Strategy

This fund tracks the MSCI Europe Index, a capitalization-weighted benchmark of the region's largest markets and stocks. The index is dominated by the U.K. market and financial services stocks and has only minimal exposure to smaller-cap shares. The large number of stocks in its portfolio dilutes its exposure to individual names. It does not own any stocks in the former Communist countries of Central and Eastern Europe. The fund does not hedge its currency exposure.

Performance 12-31-06

	1st Qtr	2nd Qtr	3rd Qtr	4th Qtr	Total
2002	0.05	-4.05	-22.84	10.77	-17.95
2003	-9.25	22.30	3.89	20.30	38.70
2004	0.82	2.25	1.19	15.86	20.86
2005	0.38	-1.11	8.14	1.78	9.26
2006	10.58	2.68	5.69	10.94	33.12

Trailing	Total Return%	+/- MSCI EAFE	+/- MSCI Eur	%Rank Cat	Growth of $10,000
3 Mo	10.94	0.59	-0.52	61	11,094
6 Mo	17.25	2.56	-0.48	54	11,725
1 Yr	33.12	6.78	-0.60	47	13,312
3 Yr Avg	20.69	0.76	-0.24	54	17,580
5 Yr Avg	14.88	-0.10	0.01	59	20,009
10 Yr Avg	10.58	2.87	0.11	68	27,338
15 Yr Avg	11.55	3.69	0.19	75	51,528

Tax Analysis	Tax-Adj Rtn%	%Rank Cat	Tax-Cost Rat	%Rank Cat
3 Yr (estimated)	20.11	46	0.48	24
5 Yr (estimated)	14.23	57	0.57	41
10 Yr (estimated)	9.80	50	0.71	13

Potential Capital Gain Exposure: 30% of assets

Historical Profile

Return	Average
Risk	Average
Rating	★★★ Neutral

95% 93% 98% 99% 96% 92% 97% 97% 98%

▼ Manager Change
▽ Partial Manager Change

Growth of $10,000
— Investment Values of Fund
— Investment Values of MSCI EAFE

31.0 / 24.0 / 17.0 / 10.0

Performance Quartile (within Category)

Investment Style
Equity
Stock %

History	1995	1996	1997	1998	1999	2000	2001	2002	2003	2004	2005	2006
NAV	14.02	16.57	20.13	25.28	28.83	25.99	20.25	16.21	22.00	25.99	27.70	35.95
Total Return %	22.28	21.26	24.23	28.86	16.66	-8.21	-20.30	-17.95	38.70	20.86	9.26	33.12
+/-MSCI EAFE	11.07	15.21	22.45	8.93	-10.37	5.98	1.12	-2.01	0.11	0.61	-4.28	6.78
+/-MSCI Eur	0.66	0.17	0.43	0.36	0.73	0.19	-0.40	0.43	0.16	-0.02	-0.16	-0.60
Income Return %	2.72	2.57	2.24	2.59	1.98	1.47	1.73	1.98	2.84	2.64	2.69	3.34
Capital Return %	19.56	18.69	21.99	26.27	14.68	-9.68	-22.03	-19.93	35.86	18.22	6.57	29.78
Total Rtn % Rank Cat	15	94	19	17	81	69	57	66	45	40	72	47
Income $	0.32	0.36	0.37	0.52	0.50	0.42	0.45	0.40	0.46	0.58	0.70	0.92
Capital Gains $	0.04	0.06	0.08	0.14	0.15	0.05	0.00	0.00	0.00	0.00	0.00	0.00
Expense Ratio %	0.35	0.35	0.31	0.29	0.29	0.29	0.30	0.33	0.32	0.27	0.27	0.27
Income Ratio %	2.66	2.45	2.19	1.97	1.99	1.64	2.08	2.24	2.76	2.67	2.84	3.35
Turnover Rate %	2	4	3	7	7	8	3	15	6	5	5	6
Net Assets $mil	1,017	1,595	2,432	4,479	6,106	5,611	4,405	3,998	6,252	9,220	11,580	18,461

Rating and Risk

Time Period	Load-Adj Return %	Morningstar Rtn vs Cat	Morningstar Risk vs Cat	Morningstar Risk-Adj Rating
1 Yr	33.12			
3 Yr	20.69	Avg	-Avg	★★★
5 Yr	14.88	Avg	Avg	★★★
10 Yr	10.58	Avg	Avg	★★★
Incept	10.70			

Other Measures	Standard Index MSCI EAFE	Best Fit Index MSCI Eur
Alpha	1.5	-0.1
Beta	0.94	0.99
R-Squared	87	99
Standard Deviation	9.61	
Mean	20.69	
Sharpe Ratio	1.70	

Portfolio Analysis 09-30-06

Share change since 06-06 Total Stocks:598	Sector	Country	% Assets
⊕ HSBC Hldgs	Financial	U.K.	2.61
⊕ BP	Energy	U.K.	2.54
⊕ GlaxoSmithKline	Health	U.K.	1.93
⊕ Total SA	Energy	France	1.81
⊕ Nestle	Goods	Switzerland	1.75
⊕ Novartis	Health	Switzerland	1.69
⊕ Royal Dutch Shell	Energy	U.K.	1.58
⊕ UBS AG	Financial	Switzerland	1.54
⊕ Roche Holding	Health	Switzerland	1.51
⊖ Vodafone Grp	Telecom	U.K.	1.39
⊕ Royal Bank Of Scotland G	Financial	U.K.	1.37
⊕ AstraZeneca	Health	U.K.	1.22
⊕ Banco Santander Central	Financial	Spain	1.17
⊕ Royal Dutch Shell	Energy	U.K.	1.17
⊕ Sanofi-Synthelabo	Health	France	1.13
⊕ BNP Paribas	Financial	France	1.12
⊕ ING Groep	Financial	Netherlands	1.03
⊕ Barclays	Financial	U.K.	1.02
⊕ Nokia	Hardware	Finland	1.01
⊕ BBVA	Financial	Spain	0.98

Current Investment Style

Value Blnd Growth — Large Mid Small

Market Cap	%
Giant	56.5
Large	29.8
Mid	13.2
Small	0.5
Micro	0.0

Avg $mil: 37,478

Value Measures		Rel Category
Price/Earnings	12.93	1.01
Price/Book	2.21	1.03
Price/Sales	1.03	0.94
Price/Cash Flow	7.94	1.04
Dividend Yield %	3.60	1.13

Growth Measures	%	Rel Category
Long-Term Erngs	11.34	0.82
Book Value	6.68	0.76
Sales	6.46	1.09
Cash Flow	5.28	0.70
Historical Erngs	20.76	0.95

Composition

Cash	0.6	Bonds	0.0
Stocks	97.6	Other	1.7
Foreign (% of Stock)	100.0		

Sector Weightings	% of Stocks	Rel MSCI EAFE	3 Year High	3 Year Low
◔ Info	12.73	1.08		
Software	0.67	1.20	1	0
Hardware	3.48	0.90	4	3
Media	2.33	1.27	3	2
Telecom	6.25	1.12	10	6
☞ Service	49.10	1.04		
Health	9.20	1.29	11	9
Consumer	5.00	1.01	5	4
Business	3.98	0.79	4	4
Financial	30.92	1.03	31	25
Mfg	38.17	0.93		
Goods	10.64	0.81	12	11
Ind Mtrls	11.96	0.78	12	9
Energy	10.44	1.46	13	10
Utilities	5.13	0.98	5	4

Regional Exposure	% Stock		% Stock
UK/W. Europe	100	N. America	0
Japan	0	Latn America	0
Asia X Japan	0	Other	0

Country Exposure	% Stock		% Stock
U.K.	36	Germany	10
France	14	Italy	6
Switzerland	11		

Morningstar's Take by Dan Lefkovitz 11-15-06

Over the next several years, we expect Vanguard European Stock Index's performance to weaken on an absolute basis but strengthen relative to its peers.

Europe continues to soar. While countries like China and India capture all the headlines, European markets have quietly posted years of stellar gains. The MSCI Europe Index, which this fund tracks, has climbed on the back of low interest rates, corporate restructuring, merger and acquisition activity, and, perhaps most importantly, strong companies benefiting from global growth. European currencies have also been appreciating. That has translated into gains for U.S. investors who bought this fund with dollars. In dollar terms, the fund has gained 28% for the year to date through Nov. 14, 2006, bringing its average annual gain over the trailing three-year period to 22.75%.

Investors shouldn't get too accustomed to these sorts of numbers. Europe is bound to cool off eventually, whether because of rising interest rates, valuations, or currency effects.

On a relative basis, though, we expect this fund's profile to improve. Over the past five years, the fund has gotten its clock cleaned by narrow offerings that focus on Eastern Europe or small-cap stocks, which have skewed the small Europe-stock category. For the same reasons mentioned above (with the possible addition of political risk in Eastern Europe), these areas could very well pass the baton to the Western European large caps that dominate this portfolio. The baton may already be passing. The fund is beating nearly two thirds of its peers so far in 2006. It hasn't looked this good since 1998.

We consider this fund the best option for investors looking for a mainstream Europe fund. (Be aware that most broad foreign funds are Europe-heavy.) Vanguard's indexing team is topnotch and fees are rock-bottom. Most Europe funds have high fees, putting them at a substantial disadvantage.

Address:	PO Box 2600 Valley Forge PA 19482 800-662-7447	Minimum Purchase:	$3000 Add: $100 IRA: $3000
		Min Auto Inv Plan:	$3000 Add: $50
Web Address:	www.vanguard.com	Sales Fees:	No-load, 2.00%R
Inception:	06-18-90	Management Fee:	0.22%
Advisor:	The Vanguard Group, Inc.	Actual Fees:	Mgt:0.22% Dist: —
Subadvisor:	None	Expense Projections:	3Yr:$87 5Yr:$152 10Yr:$343
NTF Plans:	Vanguard NTF	Income Distrib:	Annually

Vanguard Explorer

| | Analyst Pick | Ticker VEXPX | Load Closed | NAV $74.71 | Yield 0.4% | Total Assets $11,935 mil | Mstar Category Small Growth |

Governance and Management

Stewardship Grade: B

Portfolio Manager(s)

The fund's assets are divided among six advisors, one of which experienced a manager change at the end of 2005. Rob Soucy of Grantham, Mayo, Van Otterloo & Co. (GMO) retired in December 2005, handing the reins to Sam Wilderman, a nine-year GMO veteran, with Chris Darnell staying on in an oversight role. The five other managers on the fund are Vanguard's quantitative equity group, Ed Antoian of Chartwell Investment Partners, Jack Granahan from Granahan Investment Management, Ken Abrams of Wellington Management, and Ford Draper Jr. of Kalmar Investments.

Strategy

Vanguard farms out this fund's assets to six subadvisors, each of which operates independently. Two management teams--Vanguard's quantitative equity group, and Sam Wilderman from Grantham, Mayo, Van Otterloo & Co.--use quantitative models to pick stocks. The other four seek to add value through detailed fundamental analysis. Although each of the managers has a distinct approach to growth investing, they all are valuation-sensitive. As a result, the overall portfolio has typically had less exposure to highly speculative issues than its typical peer.

Performance 12-31-06

	1st Qtr	2nd Qtr	3rd Qtr	4th Qtr	Total
2002	1.33	-14.05	-18.47	6.22	-24.58
2003	-4.35	22.39	9.00	13.06	44.25
2004	5.01	-0.01	-5.18	14.26	13.75
2005	-3.16	3.79	5.42	3.14	9.28
2006	11.45	-6.64	-1.64	7.18	9.70

Trailing	Total Return%	+/- S&P 500	+/- Russ 2000 Gr	%Rank Cat	Growth of $10,000
3 Mo	7.18	0.48	-1.59	63	10,718
6 Mo	5.43	-7.31	-1.43	46	10,543
1 Yr	9.70	-6.09	-3.65	54	10,970
3 Yr Avg	10.89	0.45	0.38	32	13,636
5 Yr Avg	8.21	2.02	1.28	34	14,837
10 Yr Avg	10.25	1.83	5.37	32	26,533
15 Yr Avg	11.36	0.72	4.26	14	50,227

Tax Analysis	Tax-Adj Rtn%	%Rank Cat	Tax-Cost Rat	%Rank Cat
3 Yr (estimated)	9.71	33	1.06	40
5 Yr (estimated)	7.52	32	0.64	36
10 Yr (estimated)	8.53	32	1.56	64

Potential Capital Gain Exposure: 14% of assets

Morningstar's Take by Dan Culloton 11-30-06

Vanguard Explorer still has what it takes.

This closed fund relies on the wisdom of its crowd of managers. The offering divides its assets among six subadvisors. Five of them are privately held money managers with large rosters of experienced managers and analysts; one is Vanguard's quantitative equity group, which also is staffed by seasoned pros. Each manager has its own method. Sam Wilderman of Grantham, Mayo, Van Otterloo, and James Troyer of Vanguard, who together manage half of the portfolio's assets, use computer models. The rest rely on variations of fundamental research. John Granahan of Granahan Investment Management groups his picks into core growth, more aggressive pioneers, and undervalued special situations. Ken Abrams of Wellington Management taps a large pool of analysts to find stocks with solid balance sheets and financing. Ed Antoian of Chartwell Investment Partners stresses companies benefiting from secular trends, new products, or other catalysts. And Kalmar

Investments' Ford Draper Jr. likes double-digit growers at reasonable prices.

Perhaps equally as important as veteran management is this fund's low expense ratio. Its 0.51% levy is deep in the bottom quartile of all no-load small-cap funds and has fallen over time.

Those are big advantages, and the fund is going to need them. Its large asset base could make it harder to outperform. At more than $11 billion in assets, it's one of the largest offerings in its peer group. Splitting the fund among different advisors helps, but the portfolio already owns more than 1,000 stocks and has a high R-squared, which measures how much a fund's returns are explained by its benchmark. It's an open question how much bigger the fund can get without becoming more index-like.

So far, however, the fund has competed well as it has grown. Vanguard also has capped existing owners' annual investments to $25,000 to further control assets. So, there's no reason to leave now.

Address:	PO Box 2600 Valley Forge PA 19482 800-997-2798	Minimum Purchase: Min Auto Inv Plan: Sales Fees:	Closed Closed No-load
Web Address:	www.vanguard.com	Management Fee:	0.53%
Inception:	12-11-67	Actual Fees:	Mgt:0.53% Dist: —
Advisor:	American Century Investment Management	Expense Projections:	3Yr:$179 5Yr:$313 10Yr:$701
Subadvisor:	None	Income Distrib:	Annually
NTF Plans:	Vanguard NTF		

Add: —	IRA: —	
Add: —		

Historical Profile

Return	Average
Risk	Below Avg
Rating	★★★ Neutral

| 90% | 89% | 88% | 87% | 90% | 92% | 94% | 94% | 96% |

▼ Manager Change
▽ Partial Manager Change

Growth of $10,000
■ Investment Values of Fund
— Investment Values of S&P 500

33.0
26.0
20.0
15.0
10.0

Performance Quartile (within Category)

1995	1996	1997	1998	1999	2000	2001	2002	2003	2004	2005	2006	History
49.95	53.83	55.30	56.71	68.62	60.09	60.32	45.49	65.62	74.57	75.10	74.71	NAV
26.60	14.04	14.57	3.52	37.26	9.22	0.56	-24.58	44.25	13.75	9.28	9.70	Total Return %
-10.98	-8.92	-18.79	-25.06	16.22	18.32	12.45	-2.48	15.57	2.87	4.37	-6.09	+/-S&P 500
-4.44	2.78	1.62	2.29	-5.83	31.65	9.79	5.68	-4.29	-0.56	5.13	-3.65	+/-Russ 2000 Gr
0.56	0.54	0.46	0.36	0.41	0.36	0.17	0.01	0.00	0.00	0.31	0.43	Income Return %
26.04	13.50	14.11	3.16	36.85	8.86	0.39	-24.59	44.25	13.75	8.97	9.27	Capital Return %
67	63	63	50	65	20	26	33	50	40	23	54	Total Rtn % Rank Cat
0.24	0.27	0.25	0.20	0.23	0.25	0.11	0.01	0.00	0.00	0.23	0.32	Income $
4.00	2.83	5.85	0.30	8.03	13.91	0.00	0.00	0.00	0.07	6.21	7.42	Capital Gains $
0.68	0.63	0.62	0.62	0.74	0.71	0.72	0.70	0.72	0.57	0.51	0.46	Expense Ratio %
0.52	0.51	0.45	0.37	0.36	0.36	0.24	-0.01	-0.08	-0.11	0.16	0.36	Income Ratio %
66	51	84	1	79	123	77	69	77	82	80	96	Turnover Rate %
1,648	2,264	2,541	2,464	3,136	4,488	4,648	3,508	6,126	8,230	8,295	8,627	Net Assets $mil

Rating and Risk

Time Period	Load-Adj Return %	Morningstar Rtn vs Cat	Morningstar Risk vs Cat	Morningstar Risk-Adj Rating
1 Yr	9.70			
3 Yr	10.89	Avg	-Avg	★★★
5 Yr	8.21	Avg	Avg	★★★
10 Yr	10.25	Avg	-Avg	★★★★
Incept	9.60			

Other Measures	Standard Index S&P 500	Best Fit Index Russ 2000 Gr
Alpha	-4.0	1.3
Beta	1.73	0.84
R-Squared	77	97
Standard Deviation	13.48	
Mean	10.89	
Sharpe Ratio	0.60	

Portfolio Analysis 09-30-06

Share change since 06-06 Total Stocks:1109	Sector	PE	Tot Ret%	% Assets
⊖ Vanguard Small Cap ETF	—	—	—	1.03
⊖ Akamai Technologies, Inc	Software	26.0	166.53	0.81
⊖ O'Reilly Automotive, Inc	Consumer	20.4	0.16	0.67
⊕ Swift Transportation Co.	Business	13.0	29.41	0.63
⊕ Cephalon, Inc.	Health	28.6	8.76	0.61
⊕ Dun & Bradstreet Corpora	Business	23.1	23.64	0.59
⊖ MSC Industrial Direct Co	Business	21.6	-1.47	0.57
⊖ Red Hat, Inc.	Software	58.8	-15.63	0.56
⊕ Foundry Networks, Inc.	Hardware	39.8	8.47	0.51
⊕ Idexx Laboratories	Health	30.4	10.17	0.49
⊕ Alliance Data Systems Co	Business	29.1	75.48	0.47
⊕ Helix Energy Solutions G	Energy	10.6	-12.59	0.45
⊕ American Eagle Outfitter	Consumer	21.6	105.48	0.44
⊕ Terex Corporation	Ind Mtrls	18.2	117.44	0.44
⊕ Affiliated Managers Grou	Financial	32.5	31.00	0.43
⊖ Donaldson Company, Inc.	Business	21.3	10.22	0.42
⊖ Citrix Systems, Inc.	Software	27.4	-5.85	0.41
⊕ Henry Schein, Inc.	Health	24.0	12.24	0.41
⊕ MPS Group, Inc.	Business	21.1	3.73	0.39
⊕ CapitalSource, Inc.	Financial	15.7	32.16	0.38

Current Investment Style

Value Blnd Growth — Large Mid Small

Market Cap	%
Giant	0.0
Large	0.7
Mid	57.0
Small	36.8
Micro	5.5

Avg $mil: 2,019

Value Measures		Rel Category
Price/Earnings	17.08	0.81
Price/Book	2.66	0.97
Price/Sales	1.13	0.72
Price/Cash Flow	7.29	0.76
Dividend Yield %	0.57	1.24

Growth Measures	%	Rel Category
Long-Term Erngs	15.70	0.88
Book Value	7.95	0.76
Sales	10.74	0.90
Cash Flow	14.56	0.69
Historical Erngs	21.07	0.87

Profitability	%	Rel Category
Return on Equity	15.28	1.23
Return on Assets	7.87	1.18
Net Margin	9.44	1.09

Sector Weightings	% of Stocks	Rel S&P 500	3 Year High Low	
◐ Info	20.15	1.01		
Software	6.73	1.95	8	6
Hardware	11.04	1.19	15	10
Media	1.19	0.31	3	1
Telecom	1.19	0.34	3	1
☞ Service	55.27	1.20		
Health	16.57	1.37	20	17
Consumer	11.97	1.56	15	12
Business	16.74	3.96	17	14
Financial	9.99	0.45	10	7
◫ Mfg	24.58	0.73		
Goods	5.92	0.69	6	5
Ind Mtrls	12.42	1.04	12	8
Energy	5.59	0.57	9	4
Utilities	0.65	0.19	1	0

Composition

● Cash		3.5
● Stocks		96.5
● Bonds		0.0
● Other		0.0
Foreign (% of Stock)		2.1

Investment Style
Equity
Stock %

 MORNINGSTAR® Funds 500

Vanguard ExtMktIdx

	Ticker	Load	NAV	Yield	Total Assets	Mstar Category
	VEXMX	None	$38.68	1.2%	$12,747 mil	Mid-Cap Blend

Governance and Management

Stewardship Grade: B

Portfolio Manager(s)

Vanguard's indexing guru, Gus Sauter, has taken on a supportive role at this offering. In April 2005, he handed off the day-to-day managerial responsibilities to Donald Butler, who has been with Vanguard since 1992 and has worked with Sauter on this offering since 1997.

Strategy

In September 2005, this fund made the jump from its old benchmark, the Dow Jones Wilshire 4500 Index, to the newly created S&P Completion Index. The change didn't bring about dramatic changes. But unlike the Wilshire index, the new bogy screens out profit-challenged firms and companies with limited operating histories.

Performance 12-31-06

	1st Qtr	2nd Qtr	3rd Qtr	4th Qtr	Total
2002	1.86	-10.03	-15.50	5.81	-18.06
2003	-3.30	21.30	7.51	13.73	43.43
2004	5.93	0.11	-1.84	14.04	18.71
2005	-3.32	5.47	5.44	2.57	10.29
2006	9.80	-3.94	-0.30	8.67	14.27

Trailing	Total Return%	+/- S&P 500	+/- S&P Mid 400	%Rank Cat	Growth of $10,000
3 Mo	8.67	1.97	1.68	26	10,867
6 Mo	8.34	-4.40	2.51	56	10,834
1 Yr	14.27	-1.52	3.95	40	11,427
3 Yr Avg	14.37	3.93	1.28	26	14,960
5 Yr Avg	11.95	5.76	1.06	23	17,584
10 Yr Avg	9.70	1.28	-3.77	80	25,239
15 Yr Avg	11.36	0.72	-2.27	76	50,227

Tax Analysis	Tax-Adj Rtn%	%Rank Cat	Tax-Cost Rat	%Rank Cat
3 Yr (estimated)	14.15	18	0.19	8
5 Yr (estimated)	11.70	19	0.22	13
10 Yr (estimated)	8.18	73	1.39	37

Potential Capital Gain Exposure: 28% of assets

Morningstar's Take by Marta Norton 11-27-06

Vanguard Extended Market Index has lost its expense advantage to a close rival, but we still consider it a good option.

It's rare that a Vanguard index fund is solidly beaten on expenses, but that's exactly what has happened here. This fund charges a low 0.25% expense ratio, but in 2004, rival Fidelity Spartan Extended Market Index tipped the scales in its favor by slashing its expenses to 0.10%. The kind of differential might seem negligible, but even the slightest expense advantage can have an impact in the indexing world, where returns can vary by hundredths of a percentage point. In fact, since the Fidelity fund cut its expenses, it has edged out this fund by a handful of basis points.

Even given this fund's blunted edge in expenses, we wouldn't recommend that current investors throw it over for its Fidelity competitor. Such a move could result in serious tax consequences. Any benefit realized from a lower expense ratio could easily be offset by capital gains taxes triggered by the swap.

Also, this fund's 2005 benchmark switch from the Dow Jones Wilshire 4500 Index, which the Fidelity fund tracks, to the S&P Completion Index has its advantages. Both indexes own domestic stocks not included in the S&P 500 Index, and thus have similar profiles. But investors wanting a cheaply constructed, broad-based portfolio may have an easier time keeping things under the same roof by pairing this fund with Vanguard 500 Index. All Standard & Poor's indexes rely on the same committee-governed approach. Further, S&P screens out unprofitable companies, which should give the fund a higher-quality bent than it historically has had, and may make it less volatile than its Fidelity competitor.

There are still plenty of good reasons to own this fund, even though it isn't the cheapest out there. Investors interested in well-diversified mid- and small-cap exposure should consider it a viable option.

Address:	PO Box 2600	Minimum Purchase:	$3000	Add: $100	IRA: $3000
	Valley Forge PA 19482	Min Auto Inv Plan:	$3000	Add: $50	
	800-997-2798	Sales Fees:	No-load		
Web Address:	www.vanguard.com	Management Fee:	0.23%		
Inception:	12-21-87	Actual Fees:	Mgt:0.23%	Dist: —	
Advisor:	Vanguard Advisers, Inc.	Expense Projections:	3Yr:$80	5Yr:$141	10Yr:$318
Subadvisor:	None	Income Distrib:	Annually		
NTF Plans:	Vanguard NTF				

Historical Profile

Return Average
Risk Above Avg
Rating ★★★ Neutral

| 98% | 98% | 97% | 99% | 98% | 99% | 100% | 99% | 100% | | |

Investment Style
Equity
Stock %

▼ Manager Change
▽ Partial Manager Change

37.0
32.0
25.0 **Growth of $10,000**
20.0 ■ Investment Values of Fund
15.0 — Investment Values of S&P 500
10.0

Performance Quartile (within Category)

1995	1996	1997	1998	1999	2000	2001	2002	2003	2004	2005	2006	History
24.07	26.20	30.75	30.63	37.07	26.62	23.09	18.74	26.66	31.36	34.26	38.68	NAV
33.80	17.65	26.69	8.35	36.22	-15.51	-9.17	-18.06	43.43	18.71	10.29	14.27	Total Return %
-3.78	-5.31	-6.67	-20.23	15.18	-6.41	2.72	4.04	14.75	7.83	5.38	-1.52	+/-S&P 500
2.87	-1.60	-5.56	-10.77	21.50	-33.02	-8.56	-3.53	7.81	2.23	-2.27	3.95	+/-S&P Mid 400
1.62	1.43	1.39	1.23	1.10	0.73	0.82	0.78	1.14	1.07	1.05	1.36	Income Return %
32.18	16.22	25.30	7.12	35.12	-16.24	-9.99	-18.84	42.29	17.64	9.24	12.91	Capital Return %
24	67	55	51	19	94	85	65	19	26	44	40	Total Rtn % Rank Cat
0.30	0.34	0.36	0.37	0.32	0.26	0.21	0.18	0.21	0.28	0.33	0.47	Income $
0.40	1.72	1.91	2.17	3.64	4.43	0.81	0.00	0.00	0.00	0.00	0.00	Capital Gains $
0.25	0.25	0.23	0.23	0.25	0.25	0.25	0.26	0.26	0.25	0.25	—	Expense Ratio %
1.51	1.42	1.30	1.21	1.04	0.81	0.83	0.88	1.01	1.05	1.12	—	Income Ratio %
15	22	15	27	26	33	20	17	8	17	27	—	Turnover Rate %
1,523	2,099	2,723	2,939	4,221	3,881	3,115	2,629	4,259	5,484	5,441	6,172	Net Assets $mil

Rating and Risk

Time Period	Load-Adj Return %	Morningstar Rtn vs Cat	Morningstar Risk vs Cat	Morningstar Risk-Adj Rating
1 Yr	14.27			
3 Yr	14.37	+Avg	+Avg	★★★★
5 Yr	11.95	+Avg	Avg	★★★★
10 Yr	9.70	-Avg	+Avg	★★
Incept	12.30			

Other Measures	Standard Index S&P 500	Best Fit Index DJ Wilshire 4500
Alpha	0.6	-0.7
Beta	1.48	1.02
R-Squared	79	100
Standard Deviation	11.41	
Mean	14.37	
Sharpe Ratio	0.96	

Portfolio Analysis 09-30-06

Share change since 06-06 Total Stocks:3383

	Sector	PE	Tot Ret%	% Assets
⊕ Genentech, Inc.	Health	48.7	-12.29	1.26
⊕ American Tower Corporati	Telecom	—	37.57	0.51
⊕ Celgene Corporation	Health	—	77.56	0.50
⊕ DirecTV, Inc.	Media	26.5	76.63	0.50
⊕ Host Hotels & Resorts, I	Financial	51.9	33.95	0.39
⊕ GlobalSantaFe Corporatio	Energy	16.3	24.06	0.39
⊕ NYSE Group	Financial	—	94.40	0.38
⊖ General Growth Propertie	Financial	—	15.09	0.38
⊖ Cognizant Technology Sol	Business	52.9	53.49	0.34
⊖ Peabody Energy Corporati	Energy	17.3	-1.48	0.32
⊕ NII Holdings, Inc.	Telecom	45.9	47.53	0.32
⊕ Expeditors International	Business	34.4	20.54	0.31
⊖ Las Vegas Sands, Inc.	Consumer	75.7	126.70	0.31
⊖ AvalonBay Communities, I	Financial	68.7	49.69	0.30
⊖ Precision Castparts Corp	Ind Mtrls	25.4	51.40	0.28
⊖ Noble Energy, Inc.	Energy	11.7	22.48	0.26
⊖ Akamai Technologies, Inc	Software	26.0	166.53	0.26
⊖ CH Robinson Worldwide, I	Business	30.1	11.88	0.25
⊖ Kraft Foods, Inc.	Goods	18.0	30.52	0.25
⊖ Ultra Petroleum Corporat	Energy	30.4	-14.44	0.24

Current Investment Style

Value Blnd Growth — Large Mid Small

Market Cap	%
Giant	1.5
Large	4.1
Mid	52.3
Small	31.0
Micro	11.0

Avg $mil: 2,127

Value Measures		Rel Category
Price/Earnings	16.94	1.05
Price/Book	2.21	0.98
Price/Sales	1.12	1.00
Price/Cash Flow	7.40	0.88
Dividend Yield %	1.23	0.95

Growth Measures	%	Rel Category
Long-Term Erngs	13.62	1.07
Book Value	6.06	0.73
Sales	7.23	0.81
Cash Flow	12.14	1.43
Historical Erngs	16.00	0.89

Profitability	%	Rel Category
Return on Equity	12.65	0.79
Return on Assets	6.74	0.84
Net Margin	10.58	0.97

Sector Weightings	% of Stocks	Rel S&P 500	3 Year High Low
↻ Info	15.51	0.78	
Software	3.76	1.09	4 3
Hardware	6.50	0.70	8 6
Media	2.76	0.73	6 3
Telecom	2.49	0.71	2 1
⊂ Service	56.15	1.22	
Health	12.15	1.01	12 11
Consumer	9.65	1.26	12 9
Business	11.17	2.64	12 8
Financial	23.18	1.04	27 23
Mfg	28.33	0.84	
Goods	5.25	0.61	7 5
Ind Mtrls	11.18	0.94	12 8
Energy	7.81	0.80	9 5
Utilities	4.09	1.17	4 3

Composition

● Cash	0.2	
● Stocks	99.8	
● Bonds	0.0	
○ Other	0.0	
Foreign (% of Stock)	0.0	

Vanguard Global Equity

	Ticker	Load	NAV	Yield	Total Assets	Mstar Category
	VHGEX	None	$22.92	1.3%	$4,964 mil	World Stock

Governance and Management

Stewardship Grade: B

Portfolio Manager(s)

Until October 2004, when Acadian Asset Management was added as a subadvisor, Jeremy Hosking had been the sole manager of the fund since its August 1995 inception. He's been with Marathon, the fund's original subadvisor, since 1986. Before that, he was a portfolio manager with GT Capital Management. Acadian put John Chisholm, Ronald Frashure, and Brian Wolahan in charge. AllianceBernstein's international value team, which joined as a subadvisor in April 2006, is led by Kevin Simms and includes Sharon Fay and Henry D'Auria. They've established an excellent record at AllianceBernstein International Value.

Strategy

Longtime subadvisor Marathon Asset Management was joined by Acadian Asset Management on Oct. 22, 2004. Marathon uses a fairly strict value discipline but will buy tech and telecom firms if their valuations and prospects are appealing. It's also willing to buy small- and mid-cap stocks. Acadian uses a quantitative strategy that looks at more than 20,000 securities and screens for value, growth, and quality. AllianceBernstein's value team joined as third subadvisor in April 2006. Vanguard does not hedge foreign-currency exposure.

Performance 12-31-06

	1st Qtr	2nd Qtr	3rd Qtr	4th Qtr	Total
2002	8.29	-1.75	-18.83	9.30	-5.61
2003	-4.34	18.92	9.58	15.93	44.51
2004	4.27	-0.50	0.31	15.38	20.09
2005	-0.28	-0.11	9.62	2.37	11.77
2006	8.56	0.42	3.24	9.80	23.59

Trailing	Total Return%	+/- MSCI EAFE	+/- MSCI World	%Rank Cat	Growth of $10,000
3 Mo	9.80	-0.55	1.43	30	10,980
6 Mo	13.37	-1.32	0.16	40	11,337
1 Yr	23.59	-2.75	3.52	15	12,359
3 Yr Avg	18.38	-1.55	3.70	21	16,590
5 Yr Avg	17.74	2.76	7.77	4	22,627
10 Yr Avg	12.35	4.64	4.71	15	32,043
15 Yr Avg	—	—	—		

Tax Analysis	Tax-Adj Rtn%	%Rank Cat	Tax-Cost Rat	%Rank Cat
3 Yr (estimated)	17.47	16	0.77	43
5 Yr (estimated)	17.06	2	0.58	46
10 Yr (estimated)	10.90	13	1.29	65

Potential Capital Gain Exposure: 20% of assets

Morningstar's Take by Kai Wiecking 12-26-06

Vanguard Global Equity has undergone dramatic changes, but it retains much of its appeal.

This fund built an exceptionally strong track record under the stewardship of subadvisor Marathon Asset Management. From the fund's inception on August 15, 1995, through October 22, 2004, the fund's average annual return of 10.4% represents the sixth-best result among the 47 funds in the world-stock category with that much history. Lead manager Jeremy Hosking achieved those numbers by applying a strict value discipline, which helped the fund hold up particularly well in the bear market of 2000-02. His flexibility to delve into mid- and small-cap names also significantly contributed to this success.

However, as assets grew, Vanguard added Boston-based quant shop Acadian Asset Management as an additional subadvisor in late 2004. The addition changed the profile of the fund: Acadian's models incorporate various short-term factors and thus lead to much higher portfolio turnover. Its approach is also more benchmark-oriented than Marathon's more contrarian philosophy. Acadian's addition thus arguably led to a dilution of Marathon's very active, yet long-term-oriented, management style, but at the same time increased diversification and reduced volatility for the fund.

Vanguard added a third subadvisor in April 2006, when AllianceBernstein's international value team, which has assembled a remarkable record at AllianceBernstein International Value, joined the fray. The team's approach resembles that of Marathon in its value discipline and low turnover, but is more dedicated to large-cap stocks.

Those investors who chose the fund precisely for Marathon's distinctive style may be disappointed by the changes here. But we think the fund remains a fine core holding, thanks to a combination of three strong and experienced subadvisors, and a low expense ratio typical of Vanguard.

Address:	P O Box 2600 Valley Forge PA 19482 800-662-6273
Web Address:	www.vanguard.com
Inception:	08-14-95*
Advisor:	Acadian Asset Management Inc, Marathon-L
Subadvisor:	None
NTF Plans:	Vanguard NTF

Minimum Purchase:	$3000	Add: $100	IRA: $3000
Min Auto Inv Plan:	$3000	Add: $50	
Sales Fees:	No-load		
Management Fee:	0.76%		
Actual Fees:	Mgt:0.69%	Dist: —	
Expense Projections:	3Yr:$255	5Yr:$444	10Yr:$990
Income Distrib:	Annually		

Historical Profile

Return	Above Avg
Risk	Average
Rating	★★★★ Highest

| 94% | 92% | 95% | 92% | 93% | 93% | 93% | 96% |

▼ Manager Change
▽ Partial Manager Change

Growth of $10,000
— Investment Values of Fund
— Investment Values of MSCI EAFE

Performance Quartile (within Category)

1995	1996	1997	1998	1999	2000	2001	2002	2003	2004	2005	2006	History
10.53	11.84	11.98	12.06	14.14	12.62	11.58	10.83	15.45	18.06	19.51	22.92	NAV
5.69*	15.59	6.91	9.39	25.95	-0.17	-3.73	-5.61	44.51	20.09	11.77	23.59	Total Return %
—	9.54	5.13	-10.54	-1.08	14.02	17.69	10.33	5.92	-0.16	-1.77	-2.75	+/-MSCI EAFE
—	2.11	-8.85	-14.93	1.00	13.02	13.07	14.28	11.40	5.37	2.28	3.52	+/-MSCI World
—	1.33	1.94	2.17	1.49	1.84	0.95	0.69	1.20	1.36	1.33	1.59	Income Return %
—	14.26	4.97	7.22	24.46	-2.01	-4.68	-6.30	43.31	18.73	10.44	22.00	Capital Return %
—	52	84	71	64	11	4	17	13	50	15		Total Rtn % Rank Cat
0.07	0.14	0.23	0.26	0.18	0.26	0.12	0.08	0.13	0.21	0.24	0.31	Income $
0.00	0.19	0.44	0.75	0.84	1.17	0.44	0.02	0.07	0.27	0.44	0.88	Capital Gains $
0.57	0.85	0.71	0.68	0.71	0.70	1.08	1.11	1.05	0.90	0.80	0.72	Expense Ratio %
2.04	1.53	1.67	1.47	1.39	1.88	1.10	0.86	1.14	1.47	1.60	1.76	Income Ratio %
—	29	24	34	36	31	27	14	13	19	83	88	Turnover Rate %
42	107	126	128	145	143	158	251	826	1,270	2,676	4,964	Net Assets $mil

Rating and Risk

Time Period	Load-Adj Return %	Morningstar Rtn vs Cat	Morningstar Risk vs Cat	Morningstar Risk-Adj Rating
1 Yr	23.59			
3 Yr	18.38	+Avg	Avg	★★★★
5 Yr	17.74	High	Avg	★★★★★
10 Yr	12.35	+Avg	-Avg	★★★★★
Incept	12.74			

Other Measures	Standard Index MSCI EAFE	Best Fit Index MSCI World
Alpha	-1.2	2.7
Beta	1.00	1.16
R-Squared	90	94
Standard Deviation	9.92	
Mean	18.38	
Sharpe Ratio	1.44	

Portfolio Analysis 09-30-06

Share change since 06-06 Total Stocks:625	Sector	Country	% Assets
⊕ ING Groep	Financial	Netherlands	1.96
⊕ BNP Paribas	Financial	France	1.87
China Mobile	Telecom	Hong Kong	1.87
☼ Caterpillar Inc.	Ind Mtrls	United States	1.67
⊕ Nucor Corp.	Ind Mtrls	United States	1.52
⊕ ConocoPhillips	Energy	United States	1.52
⊕ Banco Santander Central	Financial	Spain	1.51
⊕ Canon	Goods	Japan	1.18
⊕ AstraZeneca	Health	U.K.	1.17
⊕ AmerisourceBergen Corpor	Health	United States	1.09
⊕ Royal Dutch Shell	Energy	U.K.	0.86
⊕ King Pharmaceuticals, In	Health	United States	0.83
⊕ ExxonMobil Corporation	Energy	United States	0.81
⊕ Chubb Corporation	Financial	United States	0.80
☼ Allianz	Financial	Germany	0.77
Cummins, Inc.	Ind Mtrls	United States	0.76
Metropolitan Life Insura	Financial	United States	0.73
⊕ Costco Wholesale Corpora	Consumer	United States	0.69
⊕ Carolina Group	Financial	United States	0.68
Bear Stearns Companies,	Financial	United States	0.66

Current Investment Style

Value Blnd Growth — Large Mid Small

Market Cap	%
Giant	35.8
Large	39.1
Mid	21.3
Small	3.4
Micro	0.5
Avg $mil:	18,873

Value Measures		Rel Category
Price/Earnings	12.37	0.80
Price/Book	1.96	0.82
Price/Sales	0.90	0.69
Price/Cash Flow	5.20	0.60
Dividend Yield %	2.39	1.10

Growth Measures	%	Rel Category
Long-Term Erngs	11.09	0.87
Book Value	9.30	1.04
Sales	8.84	1.06
Cash Flow	16.39	1.67
Historical Erngs	21.36	1.14

Composition

Cash	3.5	Bonds	0.0
Stocks	95.7	Other	0.8
Foreign (% of Stock)			58.2

Sector Weightings	% of Stocks	Rel MSCI EAFE	3 Year High	Low
☎ Info	17.36	1.47		
🖥 Software	0.26	0.46	1	0
💻 Hardware	4.99	1.29	7	5
🎤 Media	4.10	2.24	9	3
📶 Telecom	8.01	1.44	9	7
⚙ Service	46.32	0.98		
🏥 Health	6.80	0.96	7	5
🛒 Consumer	5.11	1.03	10	5
💼 Business	6.76	1.33	11	7
💲 Financial	27.65	0.92	28	15
🏭 Mfg	36.31	0.89		
🔧 Goods	7.58	0.58	11	7
🔩 Ind Mtrls	18.76	1.22	21	13
🔥 Energy	8.43	1.18	11	3
💡 Utilities	1.54	0.29	2	1

Regional Exposure	% Stock		
UK/W. Europe	30	N. America	45
Japan	9	Latn America	1
Asia X Japan	13	Other	2

Country Exposure	% Stock		
United States	42	France	5
Japan	9	Hong Kong	5
U.K.	9		

Morningstar® Funds 500

Vanguard GNMA

Ticker VFIIX	**Load** None	**NAV** $10.21	**Yield** 5.1%	**SEC Yield** 5.07%	**Total Assets** $23,069 mil	**Mstar Category** Intermediate Government

Governance and Management

Stewardship Grade: B

Portfolio Manager(s)

Thomas Pappas took over from longtime manager Paul Kaplan in June 2006. Pappas has worked in the background with Kaplan on this fund since 1986, and even longer at the fund's advisor Wellington Asset Management.

Strategy

This offering focuses exclusively on plain-vanilla GNMA pass-throughs, avoiding exotic mortgage-backed securities. Manager Thomas Pappas doesn't make big interest-rate bets, either. He keeps the portfolio's duration (a measure of interest-rate sensitivity) close to those of similar funds and holds expenses down by keeping trading to a minimum.

Historical Profile

Return	High
Risk	Average
Rating	★★★★ Highest

Investment Style: Fixed Income
Income Rtn %Rank Cat

▼ Manager Change
▽ Partial Manager Change

Growth of $10,000
— Investment Values of Fund
— Investment Values of LB Aggr

Performance Quartile (within Category)

1995	1996	1997	1998	1999	2000	2001	2002	2003	2004	2005	2006	History
10.43	10.22	10.43	10.45	9.86	10.24	10.38	10.75	10.50	10.44	10.30	10.21	NAV
17.04	5.24	9.47	7.14	0.78	11.22	7.94	9.68	2.49	4.13	3.33	4.33	Total Return %
-1.43	1.61	-0.18	-1.55	1.60	-0.41	-0.50	-0.57	-1.61	-0.21	0.90	0.00	+/-LB Aggr
-1.30	2.47	-0.12	-2.71	3.01	-2.02	0.71	-1.82	0.13	0.65	0.68	0.85	+/-LB Govt
7.93	7.21	7.27	6.83	6.59	7.16	6.59	5.82	4.86	4.69	4.70	5.17	Income Return %
9.11	-1.97	2.20	0.31	-5.81	4.06	1.35	3.86	-2.37	-0.56	-1.37	-0.84	Capital Return %
40	5	18	63	12	44	14	35	20	10	2	14	Total Rtn % Rank Cat
0.73	0.73	0.72	0.69	0.67	0.68	0.66	0.59	0.51	0.48	0.48	0.52	Income $
0.00	0.00	0.00	0.01	0.00	0.00	0.00	0.00	0.00	0.00	0.00	0.00	Capital Gains $
0.30	0.29	0.27	0.31	0.30	0.27	0.27	0.25	0.22	0.20	0.20	0.21	Expense Ratio %
7.04	7.22	7.16	6.97	6.56	6.63	6.85	6.24	5.51	4.73	4.61	4.67	Income Ratio %
35	7	12	3	7	5	8	8	17	26	53	38	Turnover Rate %
6,908	7,399	8,725	10,993	12,548	13,911	15,531	21,792	19,408	18,858	13,890	12,869	Net Assets $mil

Performance 12-31-06

	1st Qtr	2nd Qtr	3rd Qtr	4th Qtr	Total
2002	1.01	3.64	3.32	1.40	9.68
2003	1.04	1.00	-0.19	0.62	2.49
2004	1.59	-1.24	2.53	1.23	4.13
2005	0.09	2.13	-0.02	1.10	3.33
2006	-0.12	-0.70	3.63	1.49	4.33

Trailing	Total Return%	+/- LB Aggr	+/- LB Govt	%Rank Cat	Growth of $10,000
3 Mo	1.49	0.25	0.65	6	10,149
6 Mo	5.18	0.09	0.77	6	10,518
1 Yr	4.33	0.00	0.85	14	10,433
3 Yr Avg	3.93	0.23	0.73	3	11,226
5 Yr Avg	4.76	-0.30	0.12	10	12,618
10 Yr Avg	6.00	-0.24	-0.01	6	17,908
15 Yr Avg	6.22	-0.28	-0.08	6	24,723

Tax Analysis	Tax-Adj Rtn%	%Rank Cat	Tax-Cost Rat	%Rank Cat
3 Yr (estimated)	2.20	4	1.66	83
5 Yr (estimated)	2.91	13	1.77	86
10 Yr (estimated)	3.68	9	2.19	95

Potential Capital Gain Exposure: -1% of assets

Rating and Risk

Time Period	Load-Adj Return %	Morningstar Rtn vs Cat	Morningstar Risk vs Cat	Morningstar Risk-Adj Rating
1 Yr	4.33			
3 Yr	3.93	High	Avg	★★★★
5 Yr	4.76	+Avg	Avg	★★★★
10 Yr	6.00	High	-Avg	★★★★★
Incept	8.56			

Other Measures	Standard Index LB Aggr	Best Fit Index LB Mort
Alpha	0.3	-0.2
Beta	0.74	0.98
R-Squared	92	96
Standard Deviation	2.51	
Mean	3.93	
Sharpe Ratio	0.27	

Morningstar's Take by Michael Herbst 12-18-06

Vanguard GNMA is a great option for risk-sensitive investors.

This fund comes out swinging thanks in part to its very low fees. Its expense ratio clocks in at 0.21%, which is less than third the typical no-load intermediate-term government-bond fund's 0.66% levy. It's especially important for investors to choose funds with very low fees when it comes to government-bond funds because their managers have fewer ways to beat competitors given the similarity of the bonds they buy. The low fees also help the fund provide a higher payout to shareholders--the fund's yield measures 5.0% as of Nov. 30, 2006, which is 49 basis points higher than the intermediate-term government-bond category average.

There is another distinction. The fund only buys AAA rated GNMA bonds. Most in the intermediate-government category lace their portfolios with U.S. Treasuries and agency paper as well as a stash of corporate bonds. Because this fund focuses on GNMA bonds, manager Thomas Pappas (who took over from longtime manager Paul Kaplan in June 2006) cannot meaningfully mix up the portfolio when other areas of the bond market look more appealing. On the other hand, there's virtually zero credit risk here.

While the narrow focus of the fund suggests that it could lag other more-diversified funds at times, the fund's plain-vanilla mortgage-bond portfolio has not really hampered returns thus far. In fact, the funds 4.41% gain for the year-to-date period through Dec. 18, 2006, easily beats its typical rival's. Pappas thinks the risk/reward profile of mortgage bonds is superior to other bond types over long stretches of time. And the data supports his claim thus far: The fund consistently lands in the top decile of its peer group.

There is a lot to like here. The fund's cheap fees, tried-and-true strategy, and historically high payout ratio all argue in its favor.

Dieter Bardy contributed to this report.

Address:	PO Box 2600 Valley Forge PA 19482 800-997-2798
Web Address:	www.vanguard.com
Inception:	06-27-80
Advisor:	Wellington Management Company LLP
Subadvisor:	None
NTF Plans:	Vanguard NTF

Minimum Purchase:	$3000	Add: $100	IRA: $3000
Min Auto Inv Plan:	$3000	Add: $50	
Sales Fees:	No-load		
Management Fee:	0.17%		
Actual Fees:	Mgt:0.17%	Dist: —	
Expense Projections:	3Yr:$68	5Yr:$118	10Yr:$268
Income Distrib:	Monthly		

Portfolio Analysis 09-30-06

Total Fixed-Income:28654

	Date of Maturity	Amount $000	Value $000	% Net Assets
GNMA 5%	09-15-33	273,519	266,288	1.15
GNMA 6%	08-15-32	239,149	242,372	1.04
GNMA 5.5%	09-15-33	190,836	189,727	0.82
GNMA 6%	08-15-32	159,309	161,490	0.70
GNMA 5%	10-15-35	144,845	140,653	0.61
GNMA 5.5%	04-15-33	138,114	137,311	0.59
GNMA 5.5%	09-15-33	125,830	125,099	0.54
GNMA 5%	09-20-35	110,815	107,331	0.46
GNMA 5.5%	01-20-34	107,902	107,005	0.46
GNMA 5.5%	03-15-33	99,710	99,193	0.43
GNMA 5.5%	11-15-33	96,288	95,729	0.41
GNMA 7%	11-15-31	78,381	81,176	0.35
GNMA	08-15-36	72,732	74,591	0.32
GNMA 5.5%	09-15-34	70,857	70,401	0.30
GNMA 7%	11-15-33	65,241	67,523	0.29
GNMA 5%	04-15-33	67,040	65,310	0.28
GNMA 5.5%	01-15-35	64,592	64,176	0.28
GNMA 6%	10-15-32	62,836	63,670	0.27
GNMA 7%	07-15-33	60,738	62,883	0.27
GNMA 5.5%	08-15-33	62,075	61,714	0.27

Current Investment Style

Duration: Short Int Long
Quality: High Med Low

1 figure provided by fund

Avg Eff Duration[1]	4.5 Yrs
Avg Eff Maturity	7.2 Yrs
Avg Credit Quality	AAA
Avg Wtd Coupon	5.65%
Avg Wtd Price	99.85% of par

Coupon Range	% of Bonds	Rel Cat
0% PIK	0.0	0.0
0% to 6%	91.3	1.1
6% to 8%	8.5	0.6
8% to 10%	0.2	0.1
More than 10%	0.0	0.0

1.00=Category Average

Credit Analysis	% bonds 09-30-06		
AAA	100	BB	0
AA	0	B	0
A	0	Below B	0
BBB	0	NR/NA	0

Sector Breakdown	% of assets
US Treasuries	0
TIPS	0
US Agency	0
Mortgage Pass-Throughs	96
Mortgage CMO	0
Mortgage ARM	0
US Corporate	0
Asset-Backed	0
Convertible	0
Municipal	0
Corporate Inflation-Protected	0
Foreign Corporate	0
Foreign Govt	0

Composition			
Cash	3.8	Bonds	96.2
Stocks	0.0	Other	0.0

Special Securities	
Restricted/Illiquid Secs	0
Exotic Mortgage-Backed	0
Emerging-Markets Secs	0
Options/Futures/Warrants	No

Vanguard Gr Idx

	Ticker	Load	NAV	Yield	Total Assets	Mstar Category
	VIGRX	None	$29.77	0.8%	$12,680 mil	Large Growth

Governance and Management

Stewardship Grade: B

Portfolio Manager(s)

In April 2005, Gerard O'Reilly assumed control of this offering, replacing longtime manager Gus Sauter. O'Reilly, who has been with Vanguard since 1992, also manages Vanguard REIT Index and Vanguard Total Stock Market Index.

Strategy

Since 2003, this fund has tracked the MSCI U.S. Prime Market Growth Index. This index represents growth stocks contained in the MSCI U.S. Prime Market 750 Index (which contains the 750 largest companies--in terms of free-float market capitalization--in the U.S.). MSCI defines style (growth versus value) using an eight-factor model that includes measures ranging from dividend yield to long-term historical sales per share. MSCI also employs buffer zones to limit the migration of stocks between the growth and value camps. The buffer zones should help keep the fund's portfolio turnover low.

Performance 12-31-06

	1st Qtr	2nd Qtr	3rd Qtr	4th Qtr	Total
2002	-0.87	-16.30	-14.07	7.04	-23.68
2003	-0.91	11.57	3.24	10.33	25.92
2004	1.49	1.51	-4.88	9.40	7.20
2005	-3.56	2.12	3.59	3.00	5.09
2006	3.30	-3.94	3.79	5.85	9.01

Trailing	Total Return%	+/- S&P 500	+/- Russ 1000Gr	%Rank Cat	Growth of $10,000
3 Mo	5.85	-0.85	-0.08	41	10,585
6 Mo	9.86	-2.88	-0.24	28	10,986
1 Yr	9.01	-6.78	-0.06	30	10,901
3 Yr Avg	7.09	-3.35	0.22	48	12,281
5 Yr Avg	3.37	-2.82	0.68	39	11,802
10 Yr Avg	7.15	-1.27	1.71	31	19,949
15 Yr Avg	—	—	—	—	—

Tax Analysis	Tax-Adj Rtn%	%Rank Cat	Tax-Cost Rat	%Rank Cat
3 Yr (estimated)	6.89	41	0.19	13
5 Yr (estimated)	3.15	36	0.21	22
10 Yr (estimated)	6.77	18	0.35	13

Potential Capital Gain Exposure: 2% of assets

Morningstar's Take by Reginald Laing 11-15-06

Vanguard Growth Index makes a fine long-term holding, and now may be a good time to buy it.

This fund tracks the MSCI U.S. Prime Market Growth Index--a good representation of the large-growth universe. Thus, it gives you exposure to all the mid- to mega-cap stocks that fit MSCI's criteria for growth, and it does so for the very reasonable expense ratio of 0.22%.

Now may be an opportune time to buy this index offering, too, as this fund, and the large-growth universe it approximates, has been down-and-out for so long relative to the broader market. For the trailing five years through Nov. 14, 2006, this fund's 3.32% annualized gain might have outpaced the 2.9% return of the typical large-growth fund, but it's well shy of the 15.4% return of the average small-value fund, its stylistic opposite. Another measure of this fund's potential attractiveness, Morningstar's equity analysts estimate that seven out of this index's top 10 holdings are presently trading at discounts to their fair value--with retailer

Wal-Mart and beverage company PepsiCo trading at steep discounts. That means these stocks could have some upside potential (though they could stay undervalued, too).

If market leadership rotates back to large-growth stocks--and it's bound to happen eventually--it will be a boon to this fund. That's because style-specific index funds generally look best (not only relative to the market, but to their category) when the portion of the Morningstar Style Box they represent leads all others. When that happens, this fund--which is almost fully invested in large-growth and charges far less than its typical peer--will have a chance to stand out.

There are other reasons beyond a potentially bright immediate future to own this fund, though. It's a good long-term holding. Low costs, attentive management, broad diversification, tax efficiency, and a strong track record give it enduring appeal for those looking for growth exposure.

Address:	PO Box 2600 Valley Forge PA 19482 800-997-2798
Web Address:	www.vanguard.com
Inception:	11-02-92
Advisor:	Vanguard Advisers, Inc.
Subadvisor:	None
NTF Plans:	Vanguard NTF

Minimum Purchase:	$3000	Add: $100	IRA: $3000
Min Auto Inv Plan:	$3000	Add: $50	
Sales Fees:	No-load		
Management Fee:	0.19%		
Actual Fees:	Mgt:0.19%	Dist: —	
Expense Projections:	3Yr:$71	5Yr:$124	10Yr:$280
Income Distrib:	Quarterly		

Historical Profile

Return	Average
Risk	Below Avg
Rating	★★★★ Above Avg

Investment Style: Equity Stock %

97% 100% 100% 98% 98% 100% 100% 99% 100%

▼ Manager Change
▽ Partial Manager Change

Growth of $10,000
— Investment Values of Fund
— Investment Values of S&P 500

38.0
31.0
24.0
17.0
10.0

Performance Quartile (within Category)

1995	1996	1997	1998	1999	2000	2001	2002	2003	2004	2005	2006	History
13.97	16.90	22.53	31.67	39.43	30.57	26.42	19.95	24.92	26.41	27.54	29.77	NAV
38.06	23.74	36.34	42.21	28.76	-22.21	-12.93	-23.68	25.92	7.20	5.09	9.01	Total Return %
0.48	0.78	2.98	13.63	7.72	-13.11	-1.04	-1.58	-2.76	-3.68	0.18	-6.78	+/-S&P 500
0.88	0.62	5.85	3.50	-4.40	0.21	7.49	4.20	-3.83	0.90	-0.17	-0.06	+/-Russ 1000Gr
1.96	1.59	1.37	0.98	0.72	0.32	0.61	0.86	0.88	1.19	0.78	0.87	Income Return %
36.10	22.15	34.97	41.23	28.04	-22.53	-13.54	-24.54	25.04	6.01	4.31	8.14	Capital Return %
19	17	6	14	61	84	17	28	64	57	61	30	Total Rtn % Rank Cat
0.20	0.22	0.23	0.22	0.23	0.13	0.19	0.23	0.18	0.30	0.21	0.24	Income $
0.00	0.14	0.25	0.12	1.04	0.00	0.00	0.00	0.00	0.00	0.00	0.00	Capital Gains $
0.20	0.20	0.20	0.22	0.22	0.22	0.22	0.23	0.23	0.22	0.22	—	Expense Ratio %
1.71	1.57	1.19	0.92	0.64	0.33	0.67	0.97	0.77	1.14	0.75	—	Income Ratio %
24	29	26	29	33	33	31	23	44	24	23	—	Turnover Rate %
271	787	2,365	6,644	15,232	11,162	8,445	6,094	7,586	7,711	6,761	6,707	Net Assets $mil

Rating and Risk

Time Period	Load-Adj Return %	Morningstar Rtn vs Cat	Morningstar Risk vs Cat	Morningstar Risk-Adj Rating
1 Yr	9.01			
3 Yr	7.09	Avg	-Avg	★★★
5 Yr	3.37	Avg	-Avg	★★★
10 Yr	7.15	Avg	-Avg	★★★★
Incept	9.63			

Other Measures	Standard Index S&P 500	Best Fit Index Russ 1000Gr
Alpha	-4.2	0.2
Beta	1.17	1.00
R-Squared	90	99
Standard Deviation	8.50	
Mean	7.09	
Sharpe Ratio	0.47	

Portfolio Analysis 09-30-06

Share change since 06-06 Total Stocks:421	Sector	PE	Tot Ret%	% Assets
⊖ Microsoft Corporation	Software	23.8	15.83	3.84
⊕ Procter & Gamble Company	Goods	23.9	13.36	3.22
⊕ Johnson & Johnson	Health	17.5	12.45	3.05
⊕ Cisco Systems, Inc.	Hardware	30.1	59.64	2.22
⊕ Wal-Mart Stores, Inc.	Consumer	16.9	0.13	1.95
⊕ Intel Corporation	Hardware	21.0	-17.18	1.90
⊕ PepsiCo, Inc.	Goods	21.5	7.86	1.71
⊕ American International G	Financial	17.0	6.05	1.51
⊕ Google, Inc.	Business	61.5	11.00	1.37
⊕ Amgen, Inc.	Health	29.1	-13.38	1.34
⊖ Oracle Corporation	Software	26.7	40.38	1.20
⊖ Home Depot, Inc.	Consumer	13.5	1.01	1.19
⊕ Schlumberger, Ltd.	Energy	22.3	31.07	1.16
⊕ UnitedHealth Group, Inc.	Health	20.8	-13.49	1.05
⊕ Goldman Sachs Group, Inc	Financial	12.4	57.41	1.04
⊕ Apple Computer, Inc.	Hardware	37.6	18.01	1.04
⊕ Walt Disney Company	Media	21.0	44.26	1.02
⊕ IBM	Hardware	17.1	19.77	1.01
⊕ American Express Company	Financial	20.9	19.09	0.99
⊕ Motorola, Inc.	Hardware	11.8	-8.17	0.98

Current Investment Style

Value Blnd Growth — Large Mid Small

Market Cap	%
Giant	42.6
Large	40.0
Mid	17.4
Small	0.0
Micro	0.0

Avg $mil: 35,871

Value Measures		Rel Category
Price/Earnings	18.91	0.98
Price/Book	3.22	0.97
Price/Sales	1.71	0.88
Price/Cash Flow	11.62	1.02
Dividend Yield %	0.97	0.94

Growth Measures	%	Rel Category
Long-Term Erngs	14.45	1.01
Book Value	11.70	1.01
Sales	11.78	1.02
Cash Flow	15.00	0.89
Historical Erngs	22.94	1.00

Profitability	%	Rel Category
Return on Equity	21.82	1.07
Return on Assets	11.25	1.02
Net Margin	13.41	0.94

Sector Weightings	% of Stocks	Rel S&P 500	3 Year High	Low
↻ Info	30.75	1.54		
🖳 Software	7.00	2.03	8	6
💻 Hardware	16.55	1.79	21	16
🎙 Media	5.63	1.49	6	4
📶 Telecom	1.57	0.45	2	1
⊏ Service	46.20	1.00		
🩺 Health	17.19	1.43	22	17
🛒 Consumer	12.43	1.62	14	12
🏢 Business	7.89	1.87	9	6
💲 Financial	8.69	0.39	10	6
🏭 Mfg	23.05	0.68		
🛢 Goods	8.33	0.97	11	8
⚙ Ind Mtrls	8.67	0.73	10	3
🔋 Energy	5.73	0.58	7	2
💡 Utilities	0.32	0.09	1	0

Composition

● Cash		0.0
● Stocks		100.0
● Bonds		0.0
● Other		0.0
Foreign		0.0
(% of Stock)		

 **MORNINGSTAR® Funds 500**

Vanguard Gr & Inc

	Ticker	Load	NAV	Yield	Total Assets	Mstar Category
	VQNPX	None	$35.76	1.6%	$7,802 mil	Large Blend

Governance and Management

Stewardship Grade: B

Portfolio Manager(s)

John Cone took over as sole manager of this fund in July 1999, but he has been involved with its quantitative models since the early 1980s. Cone is one of six portfolio managers at the fund's advisor, Franklin Portfolio Associates. They are supported by one research analyst who focuses on valuation modeling and five IT analysts devoted to the firm's computerized model.

Strategy

Using a quantitative approach, management attempts to build a stock portfolio with risk comparable to that of the S&P 500 Index but that can outperform the index on an annual basis. Computer models rank a universe of 4,000 stocks on broad classifications of value, discounted cash flows, and earnings momentum. The models then build a portfolio with industry weights that are close to the index's, but the fund sports small overweightings (versus the index) in attractive stocks and underweights those with poor risk/reward profiles.

Performance 12-31-06

	1st Qtr	2nd Qtr	3rd Qtr	4th Qtr	Total
2002	-0.07	-12.14	-16.04	5.91	-21.92
2003	-2.99	14.96	3.36	12.90	30.15
2004	2.18	1.34	-1.53	8.97	11.11
2005	-1.21	1.16	3.03	2.77	5.82
2006	3.73	-2.01	5.07	6.75	14.01

Trailing	Total Return%	+/- S&P 500	+/- Russ 1000	%Rank Cat	Growth of $10,000
3 Mo	6.75	0.05	-0.20	42	10,675
6 Mo	12.16	-0.58	-0.20	35	11,216
1 Yr	14.01	-1.78	-1.45	55	11,401
3 Yr Avg	10.26	-0.18	-0.72	41	13,405
5 Yr Avg	6.38	0.19	-0.44	33	13,624
10 Yr Avg	8.85	0.43	0.21	20	23,350
15 Yr Avg	10.91	0.27	0.11	25	47,267

Tax Analysis	Tax-Adj Rtn%	%Rank Cat	Tax-Cost Rat	%Rank Cat
3 Yr (estimated)	10.01	29	0.23	11
5 Yr (estimated)	6.09	28	0.27	18
10 Yr (estimated)	7.54	26	1.20	55

Potential Capital Gain Exposure: 17% of assets

Morningstar's Take by Dan Culloton 11-20-06

Vanguard Growth & Income won't disappoint.

This fund doesn't do anything that will get it on the cover of glossy personal finance magazines or mentioned in lists of hot funds to own now. It just plods along using a quantitative model to build a portfolio that sticks close to the sector allocations and risk and size features of the S&P 500, and tries to beat it by choosing more promising stocks. To do that, the fund's models rank thousands of stocks by a variety of valuation, momentum, and manager behavior factors.

There are a lot of funds that rely on computers to sift stocks through similar sieves. It's hard to argue with this fund's execution, though. Plodding along has meant beating the S&P 500 in nine of the last 10 calendar years. It has been just as successful against the average large-blend fund as well.

Some key pieces are in place to help the fund be just as consistent in the future. The fund has an experienced manager, John Cone of Franklin Portfolio Associates, who is supported by a

decent-sized staff of portfolio managers and analysts. Furthermore, the fund's expense ratio is almost one third of the median no-load large-cap fund's, which gives its benchmark-conscious approach a smaller hurdle to clear than rivals'. The fund's fees are higher than many large-blend index funds that cover the same territory, though.

Don't expect too much from this fund. It won't blow its benchmark or peers out of the water. Through Oct. 31, 2006, its 15-year return was just 30 hundredths of a percent better than the index's. The fund also has high turnover for a large-blend fund and has made some big capital gains distributions in the past (the years from 1996 to 2000 saw some large payouts), so it may not be as tax-efficient as an index or tax-managed fund.

Nevertheless, this fund is a fine core holding for a tax-deferred account.

Address:	PO Box 2600 Valley Forge, PA 19482 800-997-2798	Minimum Purchase:	$3000	Add: $100	IRA: $3000
		Min Auto Inv Plan:	$3000	Add: $50	
		Sales Fees:	No-load		
Web Address:	www.vanguard.com	Management Fee:	0.38%		
Inception:	12-10-86	Actual Fees:	Mgt:0.38%	Dist: —	
Advisor:	Franklin Portfolio Associates, LLC	Expense Projections:	3Yr:$128	5Yr:$224	10Yr:$505
Subadvisor:	None	Income Distrib:	Semi-Annually		
NTF Plans:	Vanguard NTF				

Historical Profile

Return	Average
Risk	Average
Rating	★★★ Neutral

Investment Style: Equity / Stock %

97% 97% 98% 98% 97% 99% 99% 99% 99%

▼ Manager Change
▽ Partial Manager Change

Growth of $10,000
— Investment Values of Fund
— Investment Values of S&P 500

Performance Quartile (within Category)

	1995	1996	1997	1998	1999	2000	2001	2002	2003	2004	2005	2006	History
NAV	19.95	22.23	26.19	30.76	37.08	32.06	28.20	21.75	27.94	30.61	31.89	35.76	
Total Return %	35.93	23.06	35.59	23.94	26.04	-8.97	-11.13	-21.92	30.15	11.11	5.82	14.01	
+/-S&P 500	-1.65	0.10	2.23	-4.64	5.00	0.13	0.76	0.18	1.47	0.23	0.91	-1.78	
+/-Russ 1000	-1.84	0.61	2.74	-3.08	5.13	-1.18	1.32	-0.27	0.26	-0.29	-0.45	-1.45	
Income Return %	2.71	2.05	1.97	1.29	1.08	0.97	0.94	1.01	1.57	1.51	1.61	1.76	
Capital Return %	33.22	21.01	33.62	22.65	24.96	-9.94	-12.07	-22.93	28.58	9.60	4.21	12.25	
Total Rtn % Rank Cat	38	29	7	46	19	65	42	47	22	38	49	55	
Income $	0.42	0.40	0.42	0.33	0.33	0.35	0.30	0.29	0.34	0.42	0.49	0.56	
Capital Gains $	0.74	1.82	3.18	1.28	1.28	1.47	0.00	0.00	0.00	0.00	0.00	0.00	
Expense Ratio %	0.47	0.38	0.36	0.36	0.37	0.38	0.45	0.45	0.46	0.42	0.37	0.34	
Income Ratio %	2.25	1.97	1.74	1.27	1.04	1.02	1.02	1.02	1.39	1.35	1.53	1.65	
Turnover Rate %	59	75	66	47	54	65	41	70	88	79	84	93	
Net Assets $mil	909	1,285	2,142	5,161	8,816	8,968	6,925	4,495	5,483	6,224	5,217	5,314	

Rating and Risk

Time Period	Load-Adj Return %	Morningstar Rtn vs Cat	Morningstar Risk vs Cat	Morningstar Risk-Adj Rating
1 Yr	14.01			
3 Yr	10.26	Avg	Avg	★★★
5 Yr	6.38	Avg	Avg	★★★
10 Yr	8.85	+Avg	Avg	★★★★
Incept	11.78			

Other Measures	Standard Index S&P 500	Best Fit Index S&P 500
Alpha	-0.4	-0.4
Beta	1.04	1.04
R-Squared	95	95
Standard Deviation	7.38	
Mean	10.26	
Sharpe Ratio	0.93	

Portfolio Analysis 09-30-06

Share change since 06-06 Total Stocks:118	Sector	PE	Tot Ret%	% Assets
⊖ ExxonMobil Corporation	Energy	11.1	39.07	4.29
⊕ Bank of America Corporat	Financial	12.4	20.68	3.83
⊕ General Electric Company	Ind Mtrls	20.0	9.35	3.63
⊕ IBM	Hardware	17.1	19.77	2.92
⊕ Cisco Systems, Inc.	Hardware	30.1	59.64	2.73
⊕ Goldman Sachs Group, Inc	Financial	12.4	57.41	2.48
⊕ Johnson & Johnson	Health	17.5	12.45	2.33
⊕ News Corporation, Ltd. A	Media	—		2.22
⊖ Hewlett-Packard Company	Hardware	19.3	45.21	2.12
⊕ TXU Corporation	Utilities	12.8	11.19	2.03
⊖ ConocoPhillips	Energy	6.5	26.53	1.97
Lehman Brothers Holdings	Financial	12.2	22.75	1.95
⊖ AT&T, Inc.	Telecom	18.2	51.59	1.94
✵ Aflac, Inc.	Financial	15.2	0.30	1.91
⊕ Lowe's Companies Inc.	Consumer	15.6	-6.05	1.83
⊖ Merck & Co., Inc.	Health	19.1	42.66	1.73
⊕ Lockheed Martin Corporat	Ind Mtrls	17.3	46.98	1.71
⊖ Caremark RX, Inc.	Health	23.6	10.90	1.63
⊖ Target Corporation	Consumer	19.3	4.65	1.52
Norfolk Southern Corpora	Business	14.0	13.73	1.47

Current Investment Style

Value Blnd Growth — Large Mid Small

Market Cap	%
Giant	47.2
Large	39.1
Mid	13.7
Small	0.0
Micro	0.0

Avg $mil: 48,205

Value Measures		Rel Category
Price/Earnings	13.43	0.87
Price/Book	2.65	1.04
Price/Sales	1.35	0.96
Price/Cash Flow	8.24	0.98
Dividend Yield %	1.84	1.05

Growth Measures	%	Rel Category
Long-Term Erngs	11.71	0.99
Book Value	10.58	1.17
Sales	13.94	1.44
Cash Flow	18.17	1.76
Historical Erngs	21.54	1.16

Profitability	%	Rel Category
Return on Equity	22.29	1.15
Return on Assets	12.01	1.16
Net Margin	15.27	1.14

Sector Weightings	% of Stocks	Rel S&P 500	3 Year High	Low
↻ Info	19.35	0.97		
▤ Software	1.06	0.31	5	1
▦ Hardware	12.89	1.40	14	10
▥ Media	2.55	0.67	4	2
▣ Telecom	2.85	0.81	4	2
⊄ Service	45.90	0.99		
▥ Health	11.95	0.99	15	12
▤ Consumer	8.53	1.12	10	7
▣ Business	4.82	1.14	6	3
$ Financial	20.60	0.93	23	19
◪ Mfg	34.75	1.03		
▨ Goods	7.01	0.82	11	7
✿ Ind Mtrls	14.49	1.21	15	9
▣ Energy	9.98	1.02	11	7
▣ Utilities	3.27	0.93	4	2

Composition

	%
● Cash	0.9
● Stocks	99.1
● Bonds	0.0
● Other	0.0
Foreign	0.0
(% of Stock)	

Vanguard Growth Equity

✓ Analyst Pick	**Ticker** VGEQX	**Load** None	**NAV** $11.06	**Yield** 0.0%	**Total Assets** $754 mil	**Mstar Category** Large Growth

Governance and Management

Stewardship Grade: B

Portfolio Manager(s)

A team from subadvisor Turner Investment Partners calls the shots here. Lead manager Robert Turner has run the fund since its 1992 inception and draws on the expertise of the firm's 10 sector analysts. Comanagers Chris McHugh, who also leads Turner Midcap Growth, and Mark Turner assist him.

Strategy

This fund's managers combine quantitative screens with fundamental and technical analysis to pick stocks. They think earnings expectations drive stock prices, and they pay close attention to earnings revisions and surprises. If one of the fund's holdings fails to meet its earnings or revenue targets, they are quick to sell it. They keep the fund sector-neutral relative to the Russell 1000 Growth Index, which gives it an above-average weighting in tech stocks.

Performance 12-31-06

	1st Qtr	2nd Qtr	3rd Qtr	4th Qtr	Total
2002	-3.11	-18.84	-16.49	5.18	-30.94
2003	0.30	17.42	6.39	10.58	38.56
2004	1.85	-0.21	-6.97	11.42	5.35
2005	-5.07	3.27	6.12	3.69	7.88
2006	6.05	-5.97	1.25	5.14	6.15

Trailing	Total Return%	+/- S&P 500	+/- Russ 1000Gr	%Rank Cat	Growth of $10,000
3 Mo	5.14	-1.56	-0.79	57	10,514
6 Mo	6.46	-6.28	-3.64	77	10,646
1 Yr	6.15	-9.64	-2.92	59	10,615
3 Yr Avg	6.45	-3.99	-0.42	58	12,062
5 Yr Avg	2.91	-3.28	0.22	45	11,542
10 Yr Avg	6.03	-2.39	0.59	49	17,959
15 Yr Avg	—	—	—		—

Tax Analysis	Tax-Adj Rtn%	%Rank Cat	Tax-Cost Rat	%Rank Cat
3 Yr (estimated)	6.45	48	0.00	1
5 Yr (estimated)	2.88	40	0.03	4
10 Yr (estimated)	3.85	62	2.06	91

Potential Capital Gain Exposure: -60% of assets

Morningstar's Take by Paul Herbert 11-14-06

Will Vanguard Growth Equity shine during a recovery in large-growth stocks?

The obvious response to that question is "yes." Back when big, growing companies led the market during the late 1990s, this aggressive-growth fund delivered very strong total returns. Its managers focus on stocks featuring high growth rates and earnings momentum characteristics, making the fund almost as growth-oriented as funds in its category come. Just like they were during the previous decade, the fund's average growth measures are higher than its typical peer's.

But after examining the fund's makeup a bit more closely, we're going with "maybe" as our answer. Management's search for companies on the upswing necessarily leads them to favor smaller stocks within the large-cap space. Its average market cap is nearly always below the large-growth norm, and its stake in mid-caps is nearly always higher. But favoring such stocks could perhaps put the fund at a disadvantage if the ignored, and

hence cheap, mega-cap growth heroes of yesteryear, such as Microsoft and Wal-Mart, that some rivals favor carry the banner in a recovery. In fact, the fund has lagged a bit recently, due at times in part to the relative success of blue chips.

That alone isn't reason to disqualify the fund, though. We can't predict the precise nature of a resurgence in large-growth stocks. A rebound could well rest upon the success of the fastest-growing stocks, and if so, this fund would have a great chance of going to the head of the class.

Besides, as we've written many times in the past, investors should think about large-growth stocks right now because maintaining exposure to the category makes sense from a long-term portfolio planning perspective. Although we must repeat that this fund remains a racy offering that works best as a supporting player, we continue to recommend it for large-growth exposure because of its low costs, long-tenured managers, and their unwavering commitment to their approach.

Address:	P.O. Box 2600 Valley Forge PA 19482 800-662-2739
Web Address:	www.vanguard.com
Inception:	03-11-92
Advisor:	Turner Investment Partners, Inc.
Subadvisor:	None
NTF Plans:	Vanguard NTF

Minimum Purchase:	$10000	Add: $100	IRA: $3000
Min Auto Inv Plan:	$10000	Add: $50	
Sales Fees:	No-load		
Management Fee:	0.85%		
Actual Fees:	Mgt:0.85%	Dist: —	
Expense Projections:	3Yr:$281	5Yr:$488	10Yr:$1084
Income Distrib:	Annually		

Historical Profile

Return Average
Risk Above Avg
Rating ★★★ Neutral

	97%	98%	98%	99%	99%	100%	99%	100%

Investment Style Equity Stock %

▼ Manager Change
▽ Partial Manager Change

43.6
32.4
24.0
17.0
10.0

Growth of $10,000
— Investment Values of Fund
— Investment Values of S&P 500

Performance Quartile (within Category)

1995	1996	1997	1998	1999	2000	2001	2002	2003	2004	2005	2006	History
14.53	12.76	11.71	14.44	17.27	13.28	9.64	6.64	9.18	9.66	10.42	11.06	NAV
29.96	19.23	31.35	38.07	53.60	-23.10	-27.41	-30.94	38.56	5.35	7.88	6.15	Total Return %
-7.62	-3.73	-2.01	9.49	32.56	-14.00	-15.52	-8.84	9.88	-5.53	2.97	-9.64	+/-S&P 500
-7.22	-3.89	0.86	-0.64	20.44	-0.68	-6.99	-3.06	8.81	-0.95	2.62	-2.92	+/-Russ 1000Gr
0.79	0.04	0.00	0.00	0.00	0.00	0.00	0.19	0.30	0.12	0.01	0.01	Income Return %
29.17	19.19	31.35	38.07	53.60	-23.10	-27.41	-31.13	38.26	5.23	7.87	6.14	Capital Return %
62	52	22	23	16	86	81	79	9	77	35	59	Total Rtn % Rank Cat
0.09	0.01	0.00	0.00	0.00	0.00	0.00	0.02	0.02	0.01	0.00	0.00	Income $
0.85	4.59	4.82	1.60	4.52	0.00	0.00	0.00	0.00	0.00	0.00	0.00	Capital Gains $
0.94	1.06	1.02	1.00	0.92	0.72	0.59	0.43	0.42	0.61	0.82	0.88	Expense Ratio %
0.78	0.85	-0.25	-0.42	-0.42	-0.19	-0.10	0.12	0.25	0.14	0.01	-0.04	Income Ratio %
178	178	178	250	328	303	357	273	220	162	147	147	Turnover Rate %
106	90	90	124	203	916	728	541	846	787	749	754	Net Assets $mil

Rating and Risk

Time Period	Load-Adj Return %	Morningstar Rtn vs Cat	Morningstar Risk vs Cat	Morningstar Risk-Adj Rating
1 Yr	6.15			
3 Yr	6.45	Avg	+Avg	★★★
5 Yr	2.91	Avg	+Avg	★★★
10 Yr	6.03	Avg	+Avg	★★
Incept	8.59			

Other Measures	Standard Index S&P 500	Best Fit Index Russ MG
Alpha	-6.3	-5.2
Beta	1.43	0.94
R-Squared	80	94
Standard Deviation	11.02	
Mean	6.45	
Sharpe Ratio	0.33	

Portfolio Analysis 09-30-06

Share change since 06-06 Total Stocks:81

	Sector	PE	Tot Ret%	% Assets
⊖ General Electric Company	Ind Mtrls	20.0	9.35	3.97
⊕ Cisco Systems, Inc.	Hardware	30.1	59.64	3.74
⊕ Google, Inc.	Business	61.5	11.00	3.28
⊖ PepsiCo, Inc.	Goods	21.5	7.86	2.85
⊖ Gilead Sciences, Inc.	Health	40.6	23.51	2.33
☼ Procter & Gamble Company	Goods	23.9	13.36	2.23
⊕ Apple Computer, Inc.	Hardware	37.6	18.01	2.03
⊕ International Game Tech.	Consumer	34.3	52.07	2.00
☼ Texas Instruments, Inc.	Hardware	16.9	-9.82	1.84
☼ Baxter International Inc	Health	24.3	24.81	1.83
☼ Abbott Laboratories	Health	24.3	26.88	1.73
☼ News Corporation, Ltd. A	Media			1.66
⊖ Micron Technology, Inc.	Hardware	24.1	4.88	1.60
⊖ Goldman Sachs Group, Inc	Financial	12.4	57.41	1.59
⊖ Applied Materials	Hardware	19.5	3.89	1.56
⊖ NII Holdings, Inc.	Telecom	45.9	47.53	1.53
☼ Motorola, Inc.	Hardware	11.8	-8.17	1.53
⊖ Roche Holding AG ADR	Health	34.2	20.41	1.49
⊖ Comcast Corporation A	Media	45.2	63.31	1.48
⊕ UBS AG	Financial	—	29.62	1.47

Current Investment Style

Value Blnd Growth — Large Mid Small

Market Cap	%
Giant	35.5
Large	38.9
Mid	25.6
Small	0.0
Micro	0.0

Avg $mil: 28,448

Value Measures		Rel Category
Price/Earnings	21.87	1.14
Price/Book	3.85	1.16
Price/Sales	2.27	1.17
Price/Cash Flow	12.93	1.14
Dividend Yield %	0.79	0.77

Growth Measures	%	Rel Category
Long-Term Erngs	15.61	1.09
Book Value	10.02	0.86
Sales	11.33	0.98
Cash Flow	20.42	1.22
Historical Erngs	26.12	1.14

Profitability	%	Rel Category
Return on Equity	19.52	0.96
Return on Assets	10.72	0.97
Net Margin	14.58	1.02

Sector Weightings	% of Stocks	Rel S&P 500	3 Year High Low	
ⓘ Info	28.53	1.43		
▣ Software	3.89	1.13	8	2
▣ Hardware	18.76	2.03	25	18
▣ Media	3.15	0.83	5	0
▣ Telecom	2.73	0.78	3	0
⊛ Service	45.99	1.00		
▣ Health	18.52	1.54	25	18
▣ Consumer	8.47	1.11	14	8
▣ Business	8.92	2.11	9	2
▣ Financial	10.08	0.45	10	7
⊟ Mfg	25.48	0.75		
▣ Goods	9.31	1.09	12	6
▣ Ind Mtrls	12.80	1.07	17	6
▣ Energy	3.37	0.34	4	1
▣ Utilities	0.00	0.00	1	0

Composition

● Cash		0.0
● Stocks		100.0
● Bonds		0.0
○ Other		0.0
	Foreign (% of Stock)	9.9

M∩RNINGSTAR® Funds 500

Vanguard Health Care

Analyst Pick ✓

Ticker VGHCX	**Load** Closed	**NAV** $145.52	**Yield** 1.4%	**Total Assets** $26,884 mil	**Mstar Category** Specialty-Health

Governance and Management

Stewardship Grade: B

Portfolio Manager(s)

Ed Owens, who has been running the show since the fund's 1984 inception, may not be as daring as some of his rivals, but he's one of the best in the business. Three health-care analysts assist him.

Strategy

Manager Ed Owens employs a measured, low-turnover approach. He maintains exposure to five areas of the health-care industry: international stocks, pharmaceuticals, services, devices, and biotechnology. He then makes modest adjustments where he finds the best valuations. He likes to buy his stocks cheap and hold them for the long run.

Historical Profile

Return	High
Risk	Low
Rating	★★★★ Highest

82% 91% 85% 89% 88% 93% 92% 90% 92%

Investment Style
Equity
Stock %

▼ Manager Change
▽ Partial Manager Change

Growth of $10,000
■ Investment Values of Fund
— Investment Values of S&P 500

74.4 / 67.4 / 47.8 / 33.8 / 24.0 / 17.0 / 10.0

Performance Quartile (within Category)

1995	1996	1997	1998	1999	2000	2001	2002	2003	2004	2005	2006	History
49.82	58.35	71.88	96.85	95.21	132.74	116.84	96.16	120.57	126.79	139.45	145.52	NAV
45.17	21.36	28.57	40.80	7.04	60.56	-6.87	-11.36	26.58	9.51	15.41	10.81	Total Return %
7.59	-1.60	-4.79	12.22	-14.00	69.66	5.02	10.74	-2.10	-1.37	10.50	-4.98	+/-S&P 500
-9.57	2.70	-8.31	1.71	11.07	22.72	5.97	9.45	7.15	4.96	7.09	3.93	+/-DJ Hlthcare
1.61	1.50	1.35	1.19	1.02	1.19	0.79	0.82	1.04	0.93	1.23	1.54	Income Return %
43.56	19.86	27.22	39.61	6.02	59.37	-7.66	-12.18	25.54	8.58	14.18	9.27	Capital Return %
69	16	46	3	56	34	31	3	71	45	16	12	Total Rtn % Rank Cat
0.57	0.74	0.78	0.84	0.97	1.07	1.03	0.96	1.00	1.11	1.54	2.10	Income $
1.02	1.29	2.14	3.08	7.14	15.93	5.46	6.53	0.10	4.00	5.08	6.66	Capital Gains $
0.40	0.45	0.38	0.40	0.36	0.39	0.34	0.31	0.29	0.28	0.21	0.25	Expense Ratio %
1.58	1.57	1.41	1.28	1.13	0.92	1.03	0.84	0.86	0.91	1.02	1.29	Income Ratio %
25	13	7	10	11	27	21	13	25	13	13	14	Turnover Rate %
1,473	2,662	4,466	9,268	10,421	18,467	16,241	13,752	17,645	19,606	16,787	16,329	Net Assets $mil

Performance 12-31-06

	1st Qtr	2nd Qtr	3rd Qtr	4th Qtr	Total
2002	3.12	-9.32	-10.01	5.32	-11.36
2003	-2.62	15.98	0.29	11.76	26.58
2004	1.90	2.76	-2.73	7.52	9.51
2005	-0.12	5.55	6.26	3.02	15.41
2006	2.85	-0.43	7.35	0.79	10.81

Trailing	Total Return%	+/- S&P 500	+/- DJ Hlthcare	%Rank Cat	Growth of $10,000
3 Mo	0.79	-5.91	-0.92	77	10,079
6 Mo	8.20	-4.54	-2.47	40	10,820
1 Yr	10.81	-4.98	3.93	12	11,081
3 Yr Avg	11.88	1.44	5.30	14	14,004
5 Yr Avg	9.46	3.27	6.72	10	15,714
10 Yr Avg	16.36	7.94	6.71	1	45,503
15 Yr Avg	16.33	5.69	6.31	1	96,689

Tax Analysis	Tax-Adj Rtn%	%Rank Cat	Tax-Cost Rat	%Rank Cat
3 Yr (estimated)	10.92	10	0.86	44
5 Yr (estimated)	8.51	9	0.87	69
10 Yr (estimated)	14.81	1	1.33	68

Potential Capital Gain Exposure: 4% of assets

Rating and Risk

Time Period	Load-Adj Return %	Morningstar Rtn vs Cat	Morningstar Risk vs Cat	Morningstar Risk-Adj Rating
1 Yr	10.81			
3 Yr	11.88	+Avg	Low	★★★★
5 Yr	9.46	+Avg	Low	★★★★★
10 Yr	16.36	High	Low	★★★★★
Incept	19.19			

Other Measures	Standard Index S&P 500	Best Fit Index DJ Hlthcare
Alpha	4.3	5.5
Beta	0.58	0.79
R-Squared	32	87
Standard Deviation	7.10	
Mean	11.88	
Sharpe Ratio	1.17	

Portfolio Analysis 09-30-06

Share change since 06-06 Total Stocks:82	Sector	PE	Tot Ret%	% Assets
⊖ Eli Lilly & Company	Health	17.3	-5.16	4.81
⊕ Schering-Plough Corporat	Health	36.6	14.63	4.65
Roche Holding	Health	—	—	3.89
Forest Laboratories, Inc	Health	22.5	24.39	3.73
Sanofi-Synthelabo	Health	—	—	3.46
AstraZeneca	Health	—	—	3.39
Novartis	Health	—	—	2.94
Cardinal Health, Inc.	Health	20.8	-5.82	2.91
McKesson, Inc.	Health	18.1	-1.26	2.87
Amgen, Inc.	Health	29.1	-13.38	2.63
⊖ Abbott Laboratories	Health	24.3	26.88	2.59
⊖ CVS Corporation	Consumer	19.7	17.60	2.48
Takeda Chemical Industri	Health	—	—	2.39
⊖ Humana	Health	21.8	1.80	2.19
Astellas Pharma	Health	—	—	2.16
⊖ Gilead Sciences, Inc.	Health	40.6	23.51	1.96
⊖ Medtronic, Inc.	Health	23.8	-6.29	1.93
⊖ Becton, Dickinson and Co	Health	23.9	18.34	1.93
⊖ Pfizer Inc.	Health	15.2	15.22	1.84
⊖ Genzyme Corporation	Health	50.8	-13.00	1.72

Current Investment Style

Value Blnd Growth — Large Mid Small

Market Cap	%
Giant	42.6
Large	44.5
Mid	11.5
Small	1.3
Micro	0.0

Avg $mil: 30,246

Value Measures		Rel Category
Price/Earnings	20.48	0.90
Price/Book	3.50	0.97
Price/Sales	1.37	0.52
Price/Cash Flow	13.45	0.83
Dividend Yield %	1.21	1.44

Growth Measures	%	Rel Category
Long-Term Erngs	12.89	0.88
Book Value	9.79	1.16
Sales	10.71	0.90
Cash Flow	13.36	1.20
Historical Erngs	9.73	0.54

Profitability	%	Rel Category
Return on Equity	18.25	1.51
Return on Assets	9.20	2.37
Net Margin	13.31	1.22

Industry Weightings	% of Stocks	Rel Cat
Biotech	16.7	0.5
Drugs	42.6	1.4
Mgd Care	9.3	0.8
Hospitals	2.2	1.8
Other HC Srv	0.8	0.5
Diagnostics	2.7	2.0
Equipment	11.8	0.9
Good/Srv	5.3	1.5
Other	8.7	2.9

Composition

● Cash	8.2
● Stocks	91.8
● Bonds	0.0
○ Other	0.0
Foreign	30.4
(% of Stock)	

Morningstar's Take by Christopher Davis 12-27-06

Fortunately, Vanguard Health Care continues to go its own way.

This closed offering is distinctive without being flashy. Rather than trading at a rapid clip and piling into the sector's fastest-growing names, as is the case with most health-care investors, manager Ed Owens moves slowly, spreads his bets across health-care industries, and runs his portfolio with a contrarian bent. And while many of his rivals have only recently begun to invest meaningfully overseas, Owens has done so all along. Indeed, foreign stocks account for 27% of assets, nearly twice the health-care category norm.

The fund's foreign stake has actually grown in recent years. In 2003, Owens began ratcheting up the fund's exposure to European and Japanese drugmakers like AstraZeneca and Takeda Chemical. Although U.S.-based pharmaceutical stocks were also out of favor, Owens looked abroad where he thought both valuations and drug pipelines were more attractive. Since then, foreign drug stocks

have generally outpaced their U.S. counterparts, helping propel the fund to the top of the category heap last year and in 2006.

With domestic pharma continuing to lag, Owens has been modestly hiking the fund's weighting in the area. Meanwhile, he's been trimming long-term winners like AstraZeneca and Genentech. The move is vintage Owens: Indicative of his valuation-conscious ethos, he gravitates to out-of-favor areas in health care. But in reflecting his attention to diversification, Owens hasn't moved whole-hog into U.S. drug stocks, nor has he completely abandoned European pharma or biotech.

The long-term results of that approach are superb: Not only is the fund's 10-year record the category's best, but its volatility, as measured by standard deviation, is the group's lowest. Its giant asset base will make that feat tough to replicate, but given Owens' skill and the fund's ultra-low price tag, it's still a superior investment.

Address:	PO Box 2600 Valley Forge, PA 19482 800-997-2798	Minimum Purchase:	Closed	Add: — IRA: —
		Min Auto Inv Plan:	Closed	Add: —
		Sales Fees:	No-load, 1.00%R	
Web Address:	www.vanguard.com	Management Fee:	0.15% mx./0.05% mn.	
Inception:	05-23-84	Actual Fees:	Mgt:0.22%	Dist: —
Advisor:	Wellington Management Company, LLP	Expense Projections:	3Yr:$80	5Yr:$141 10Yr:$318
Subadvisor:	None	Income Distrib:	Annually	
NTF Plans:	Vanguard NTF			

Vanguard Hi-Yld Corp

		Ticker	Load	NAV	Yield	SEC Yield	Total Assets	Mstar Category
✓	Analyst Pick	VWEHX	None	$6.22	7.0%	7.06%	$9,371 mil	High Yield Bond

Governance and Management

Stewardship Grade: B

Portfolio Manager(s)

This fund is subadvised by Wellington Management Company. Earl McEvoy has run this offering since 1984. He also runs Vanguard Long-Term Investment-Grade and the bond portion of Vanguard Wellesley Income's balanced portfolio, both of which have been strong performers.

Strategy

This fund invests mainly in higher-quality junk bonds, with the bulk of assets parked in BB and B rated credits, along with a smattering of investment-grade bonds. Manager Earl McEvoy's approach is predicated on error avoidance. He generally seeks companies with steady-to-improving revenues and a relatively stable customer base. Although he is willing to bet on particular sectors, positions in individual issuers are kept relatively small to ward off blowups.

Historical Profile

Return Average
Risk Below Avg
Rating ★★★ Neutral

| 63 | 75 | 69 | 72 | 63 | 59 | 38 | 40 |

Investment Style
Fixed Income
Income Rtn %Rank Cat

▼ Manager Change
▽ Partial Manager Change

Growth of $10,000
— Investment Values of Fund
— Investment Values of LB Aggr

Performance Quartile (within Category)

1995	1996	1997	1998	1999	2000	2001	2002	2003	2004	2005	2006	History
7.85	7.87	8.08	7.83	7.39	6.69	6.29	5.88	6.38	6.44	6.17	6.22	NAV
19.15	9.55	11.91	5.62	2.49	-0.88	2.90	1.73	17.20	8.52	2.77	8.24	Total Return %
0.68	5.92	2.26	-3.07	3.31	-12.51	-5.54	-8.52	13.10	4.18	0.34	3.91	+/-LB Aggr
1.76	-2.87	-0.72	5.04	-0.79	4.33	-2.88	-1.38	-10.73	-3.44	0.51	-3.69	+/-CSFB Glb HY
9.83	9.12	9.08	8.54	8.32	9.01	9.28	8.39	8.39	7.45	7.04	7.32	Income Return %
9.32	0.43	2.83	-2.92	-5.83	-9.89	-6.38	-6.66	8.81	1.07	-4.27	0.92	Capital Return %
17	95	80	7	73	15	57	22	92	77	42	87	Total Rtn % Rank Cat
0.68	0.69	0.69	0.66	0.63	0.64	0.60	0.51	0.48	0.46	0.44	0.44	Income $
0.00	0.00	0.00	0.03	0.00	0.00	0.00	0.00	0.00	0.00	0.00	0.00	Capital Gains $
0.34	0.34	0.29	0.28	0.29	0.28	0.27	0.27	0.26	0.23	0.22	0.25	Expense Ratio %
9.13	8.85	8.92	8.63	8.26	8.34	9.07	9.02	8.42	7.65	7.26	7.01	Income Ratio %
33	38	23	45	31	20	16	29	29	52	51	44	Turnover Rate %
2,900	3,563	4,571	5,380	5,699	5,270	5,160	5,433	7,095	7,317	5,212	5,112	Net Assets $mil

Performance 12-31-06

	1st Qtr	2nd Qtr	3rd Qtr	4th Qtr	Total
2002	1.30	-1.84	-3.22	5.72	1.73
2003	4.27	5.98	1.31	4.69	17.20
2004	1.97	-1.01	4.30	3.07	8.52
2005	-1.71	2.59	0.61	1.30	2.77
2006	1.59	-0.52	3.51	3.47	8.24

Trailing	Total Return%	+/- LB Aggr	+/- CSFB Glb HY	%Rank Cat	Growth of $10,000
3 Mo	3.47	2.23	-0.98	78	10,347
6 Mo	7.10	2.01	-1.05	64	10,710
1 Yr	8.24	3.91	-3.69	87	10,824
3 Yr Avg	6.47	2.77	-2.15	77	12,069
5 Yr Avg	7.55	2.49	-3.52	76	14,390
10 Yr Avg	5.92	-0.32	-1.17	32	17,774
15 Yr Avg	7.79	1.29	-1.11	46	30,809

Tax Analysis	Tax-Adj Rtn%	%Rank Cat	Tax-Cost Rat	%Rank Cat
3 Yr (estimated)	3.86	66	2.45	51
5 Yr (estimated)	4.71	77	2.64	53
10 Yr (estimated)	2.74	30	3.00	26

Potential Capital Gain Exposure: -15% of assets

Morningstar's Take by Bridget Hughes 12-08-06

Look beyond Vanguard High-Yield Corporate's recent performance.

This high-yield Analyst Pick hasn't performed well of late. Through Dec. 7, 2006, its 7.43% five-year return lands just in the category's worst quartile, showing weakness relative to peers in 2003, 2004, and 2006. (To be fair, returns so far this year through November have been more compressed in this category, so this fund's near-8% gain isn't as far away from top-performing funds' as its 17.2% result was in 2003.)

Although we'd like to see our picks perform better, the fund's results are in line with its character. Lead manager Earl McEvoy continues to emphasize upper-tier credits (within the high-yield, or "junk" arena), particularly now that spreads--that is, yield differences between lower- and higher-rated bonds--are marginally tighter (smaller) than they were last year. (In other words, McEvoy doesn't feel he's getting paid enough in yield to take on too much credit risk.) That's hurt, as

lower-rated bonds, particularly CCCs, have performed exceptionally well. Further, while high-yield bonds aren't generally as sensitive to rate changes as, say, Treasuries certainly, this fund's higher credit breakdown means that it responds more to rate changes than its peers with junkier portfolios. If rates fall, the fund should do well. If spreads widen, the fund should do well. When the opposite happens, as has been the case, however, the fund lags.

While the credit profile has these certain implications for performance, there are other points always in this fund's favor. Specifically, McEvoy has much experience, and subadvisor Wellington has hired another high-yield analyst, bringing the total to 10. As can be expected from any Vanguard fund, expenses are much lower than its peers', giving the fund a sustainable advantage. One other plus has been this fund's below-average level of volatility, which should help investors stick with the fund during tough shorter-term periods.

Address:	PO Box 2600 Valley Forge PA 19482 800-997-2798
Web Address:	www.vanguard.com
Inception:	12-27-78
Advisor:	Wellington Management Company, LLP
Subadvisor:	None
NTF Plans:	Vanguard NTF

Minimum Purchase:	$3000	Add: $100	IRA: $3000
Min Auto Inv Plan:	$3000	Add: $50	
Sales Fees:	No-load, 1.00%R		
Management Fee:	0.21%		
Actual Fees:	Mgt:0.22%	Dist: —	
Expense Projections:	3Yr:$80	5Yr:$141	10Yr:$318
Income Distrib:	Monthly		

Rating and Risk

Time Period	Load-Adj Return %	Morningstar Rtn vs Cat	Morningstar Risk vs Cat	Morningstar Risk-Adj Rating
1 Yr	8.24			
3 Yr	6.47	-Avg	-Avg	★★
5 Yr	7.55	-Avg	-Avg	★★
10 Yr	5.92	Avg	-Avg	★★★
Incept	9.27			

Other Measures	Standard Index LB Aggr	Best Fit Index CSFB Glb HY
Alpha	2.9	-1.4
Beta	0.55	0.88
R-Squared	28	86

Standard Deviation	3.41
Mean	6.47
Sharpe Ratio	0.92

Portfolio Analysis 09-30-06

Total Fixed-Income:341	Date of Maturity	Amount $000	Value $000	% Net Assets
Gmac 8%	11-01-31	106,730	112,333	1.26
US Treasury Note 5.5%	05-15-09	109,750	112,100	1.26
Sungard Data Sys 9.125%	08-15-13	99,835	103,454	1.16
Qwest 8.875%	03-15-12	93,455	101,515	1.14
Charter Comms Oper 144A	04-30-12	97,100	97,828	1.10
Ford Motor Cr 7%	10-01-13	104,530	97,182	1.09
US Treasury Note 4.875%	07-31-11	90,000	91,040	1.02
US Treasury Note 5.625%	05-15-08	83,420	84,541	0.95
Mgm Mirage 8.5%	09-15-10	78,475	83,772	0.94
Reliant Engy 6.75%	12-15-14	86,930	82,584	0.93
Charter Comms Oper 144A	04-30-14	78,890	80,271	0.90
Insight Midwest L P / In	11-01-10	77,295	80,194	0.90
R H Donnelley 8.875%	01-15-16	76,260	76,737	0.86
Midwest Generation 8.75%	05-01-34	71,220	76,472	0.86
Aes 144A 9%	05-15-15	70,215	75,306	0.84
Nrg Engy 7.375%	02-01-16	75,045	74,670	0.84
El Paso Prodtn Hldg 7.75	06-01-13	72,250	74,056	0.83
Tenet Healthcare 9.875%	07-01-14	74,005	73,820	0.83
Hertz 144A 8.875%	01-01-14	68,500	71,583	0.80
Xerox 9.75%	01-15-09	65,875	71,310	0.80

Current Investment Style

Duration
Short Int Long
Quality High Med Low

Avg Eff Duration¹ 4.3 Yrs
Avg Eff Maturity 6.3 Yrs
Avg Credit Quality BB
Avg Wtd Coupon 7.71%
Avg Wtd Price 100.97% of par

¹figure provided by fund

Coupon Range	% of Bonds	Rel Cat
0% PIK	1.6	0.3
0% to 8%	62.7	1.2
8% to 11%	36.7	0.8
11% to 14%	0.5	0.1
More than 14%	0.1	0.5

1.00=Category Average

Credit Analysis	% bonds 09-30-06		
AAA	3	BB	50
AA	0	B	43
A	0	Below B	2
BBB	2	NR/NA	0

Sector Breakdown	% of assets
US Treasuries	4
TIPS	0
US Agency	0
Mortgage Pass-Throughs	0
Mortgage CMO	0
Mortgage ARM	0
US Corporate	86
Asset-Backed	1
Convertible	0
Municipal	0
Corporate Inflation-Protected	0
Foreign Corporate	6
Foreign Govt	1

Composition			
Cash	1.3	Bonds	98.7
Stocks	0.0	Other	0.0

Special Securities	
Restricted/Illiquid Secs	13
Exotic Mortgage-Backed	0
Emerging-Markets Secs	Trace
Options/Futures/Warrants	No

MORNINGSTAR® Funds 500

Vanguard Hi-Yld T/E

	Ticker	Load	NAV	Yield	SEC Yield	Total Assets	Mstar Category
	VWAHX	None	$10.89	4.5%	4.00%	$5,714 mil	Muni National Interm

Governance and Management

Stewardship Grade: B

Portfolio Manager(s)

Reid Smith took over day-to-day management of this fund in 1996. Bob Auwaerter sets the fund's duration range.

Historical Profile
Return High
Risk Above Avg
Rating ★★★★ Highest

	1	1	1	1	1	2	2	2

Investment Style
Fixed Income
Income Rtn %Rank Cat

▼ Manager Change
▽ Partial Manager Change

20.8
18.8
16.4 Growth of $10,000
14.0 — Investment Values of
12.0   Fund
10.0 — Investment Values of
          LB Muni

Performance Quartile
(within Category)

1995	1996	1997	1998	1999	2000	2001	2002	2003	2004	2005	2006	History
10.76	10.63	10.93	10.97	10.04	10.50	10.48	10.67	10.81	10.83	10.80	10.89	NAV
18.13	4.46	9.24	6.45	-3.38	10.73	5.34	7.30	6.35	4.98	4.34	5.53	Total Return %
0.67	0.03	0.05	-0.03	-1.32	-0.95	0.21	-2.30	1.04	0.50	0.83	0.69	+/-LB Muni
0.96	-0.08	0.01	-0.31	-2.13	-0.03	0.72	-2.87	0.65	0.83	1.60	0.82	+/-LB Muni 10YR
6.50	5.61	5.78	5.40	5.36	5.95	5.62	5.46	4.98	4.76	4.63	4.66	Income Return %
11.63	-1.15	3.46	1.05	-8.74	4.78	-0.28	1.84	1.37	0.22	-0.29	0.87	Capital Return %
6	19	5	8	79	25	12	84	2	2	2	2	Total Rtn % Rank Cat
0.61	0.59	0.60	0.58	0.57	0.58	0.58	0.56	0.52	0.50	0.49	0.49	Income $
0.00	0.00	0.05	0.07	0.00	0.00	0.00	0.00	0.00	0.00	0.00	0.00	Capital Gains $
0.21	0.20	0.19	0.20	0.18	0.19	0.19	0.17	0.17	0.15	0.15	0.16	Expense Ratio %
6.15	5.66	5.56	5.28	5.33	5.74	5.43	5.30	4.94	4.71	4.55	4.56	Income Ratio %
33	19	27	24	22	32	18	18	17	24	15	15	Turnover Rate %
1,988	2,039	2,320	2,767	2,753	3,143	2,650	2,669	2,668	2,764	1,745	1,845	Net Assets $mil

Strategy

The fund differs from many high-yield offerings in that its credit quality is fairly high. Management invests at least 80% of the fund's assets in municipal securities rated BBB and above. Management adjusts the fund's duration (a measure of interest-rate sensitivity) within a specified range depending on its interest-rate outlook. Typically, the fund is less sensitive to rate changes than its average muni-national long-term peer.

Performance 12-31-06

	1st Qtr	2nd Qtr	3rd Qtr	4th Qtr	Total
2002	1.04	3.27	3.22	-0.37	7.30
2003	0.68	3.39	0.48	1.67	6.35
2004	1.44	-1.51	3.67	1.35	4.98
2005	-0.08	3.22	0.11	1.05	4.34
2006	0.47	0.12	3.62	1.24	5.53

Trailing	Total Return%	+/- LB Muni	+/- LB Muni 10YR	%Rank Cat	Growth of $10,000
3 Mo	1.24	0.13	0.32	2	10,124
6 Mo	4.91	0.36	0.14	3	10,491
1 Yr	5.53	0.69	0.82	2	10,553
3 Yr Avg	4.95	0.67	1.09	2	11,560
5 Yr Avg	5.70	0.17	0.24	2	13,194
10 Yr Avg	5.63	-0.13	-0.07	3	17,293
15 Yr Avg	6.32	0.06	0.04	1	25,074

Tax Analysis	Tax-Adj Rtn%	%Rank Cat	Tax-Cost Rat	%Rank Cat
3 Yr (estimated)	4.95	1	0.00	1
5 Yr (estimated)	5.70	2	0.00	1
10 Yr (estimated)	5.60	1	0.03	13

Potential Capital Gain Exposure: 3% of assets

Rating and Risk

Time Period	Load-Adj Return %	Morningstar Rtn vs Cat	Morningstar Risk vs Cat	Morningstar Risk-Adj Rating
1 Yr	5.53			
3 Yr	4.95	High	+Avg	★★★★★
5 Yr	5.70	High	Avg	★★★★★
10 Yr	5.63	High	+Avg	★★★★★
Incept	7.33			

Other Measures	Standard Index LB Muni	Best Fit Index LB Muni 10YR
Alpha	0.7	1.1
Beta	0.97	0.83
R-Squared	97	97
Standard Deviation	3.02	
Mean	4.95	
Sharpe Ratio	0.55	

Portfolio Analysis 09-30-06

Total Fixed-Income:461	Date of Maturity	Amount $000	Value $000	% Net Assets
New Jersey St Transn Tr	12-15-21	79,000	92,105	1.67
California Statewide Cmn	03-01-45	75,000	78,984	1.43
New Jersey St Tran 5.5%	02-01-09	61,405	61,496	1.12
Michigan St Hosp Fin Aut	11-15-46	55,000	57,852	1.05
New Jersey Econ Dev Auth	09-01-26	45,000	53,179	0.97
Massachusetts St Wtr Res	07-15-19	43,700	52,176	0.95
Memphis Tenn Elec Sys 5%	12-01-16	40,000	42,810	0.78
Minneapolis Minn Health	11-15-32	39,000	41,957	0.76
California Statewide Cmn	05-15-25	37,785	38,859	0.71
Greenville Cnty S C Sch	12-01-27	35,000	36,881	0.67
Connecticut St Dev Auth	09-01-28	35,250	36,864	0.67
PUERTO RICO PUB FIN	08-01-27	34,000	36,782	0.67
NORTH CAROLINA CAP FACS	10-01-39	35,000	36,611	0.66
BRAZOS RIV TEX HBR NAV D	05-15-33	35,200	35,897	0.65
New Jersey Econ Dev Auth	04-01-31	30,500	35,877	0.65

Current Investment Style

Duration Short Int Long / Quality High Med Low

¹Avg Eff Duration	5.4 Yrs
Avg Eff Maturity	7.3 Yrs
Avg Credit Quality	AA
Avg Wtd Coupon	5.18%
Avg Wtd Price	106.69% of par

¹figure provided by fund

Credit Analysis % bonds 09-30-06

AAA	38	BB	2
AA	20	B	1
A	12	Below B	0
BBB	16	NR/NA	11

Special Securities

Restricted/Illiquid Secs	Trace
Options/Futures/Warrants	No

Top 5 States % bonds

CA	14.5	TX	5.3
NJ	11.1	FL	4.2
NY	9.1		

Composition

Cash	3.8	Bonds	96.2
Stocks	0.0	Other	0.0

Sector Weightings

	% of Bonds	Rel Cat
General Obligation	20.8	0.56
Utilities	9.2	0.98
Health	11.7	1.30
Water/Waste	10.4	1.14
Housing	3.8	0.72
Education	8.1	0.63
Transportation	8.1	1.54
COP/Lease	0.9	0.36
Industrial	26.9	2.92
Misc Revenue	0.0	—
Demand	0.0	0.00

Morningstar's Take by Dan Culloton 12-20-06

The secret of Vanguard High-Yield Tax-Exempt's success is not much of a secret.

This fund's low expense ratio explains most of its advantage over its peers. Its 0.15% expense ratio is just about the lowest in both the high-yield muni and muni-national long categories. (The fund falls in the latter category because of the high quality of its portfolio). Indeed, the levy is less than a fourth of the median for similar no-load funds. That allows the fund to deliver a competitive yield while taking on less risk than its peers.

That is not to say the fund lets its expenses do all of the work. Longtime manager Reid Smith tries to add value with measured moves. For example, with the Federal Reserve nearing the end of its rate-raising cycle, Smith extended the fund's option-adjusted duration (a measure of interest-rate sensitivity) out to a point slightly ahead of its custom benchmark, which has a duration of about six years. That makes the fund a little more interest-rate sensitive than it has been in the past, but no more so than its typical rival.

The fund is an incrementalist when it comes to security selection, too. It keeps close to three quarters of its money in bonds rated A or higher (nearly three times the stake of the average high-yield muni funds). It also tries to add as much value by avoiding trouble. For instance, recently Smith has been shunning securities used to fund real estate-related projects such as long-term care facilities. Typically, tenants have to sell their homes to finance their moves and they may be less likely to put their houses on the block if the residential real estate market continues to cool, Smith said.

It's a plain-vanilla approach but one that has been hard for competitors to match. The fund has finished at least in the top quartile in eight of the previous 10 years. Through November 2006, the fund has outpaced 97% of its peers. It has served investors well over the long term and should continue to do so in the future.

Address:	PO Box 2600 Valley Forge PA 19482 800-997-2798	Minimum Purchase:	$3000 Add: $100 IRA: $0
Web Address:	www.vanguard.com	Min Auto Inv Plan:	$3000 Add: $50
Inception:	12-27-78	Sales Fees:	No-load
Advisor:	Vanguard Advisers, Inc.	Management Fee:	0.14%
Subadvisor:	None	Actual Fees:	Mgt:0.14% Dist: —
NTF Plans:	Vanguard NTF	Expense Projections:	3Yr:$52 5Yr:$90 10Yr:$205
		Income Distrib:	Monthly

Vanguard Infl-Prot Secs

✓ Analyst Pick

Ticker	Load	NAV	Yield	SEC Yield	Total Assets	Mstar Category
VIPSX	None	$11.78	3.6%	2.26%	$9,593 mil	Inflation-Protected Bond

Governance and Management

Stewardship Grade: A

Portfolio Manager(s)

Experienced. John Hollyer and Ken Volpert have worked in the investment industry since 1987 and 1982, respectively. Hollyer runs two other Vanguard funds, and Volpert is the firm's bond index fund guru.

Strategy

The goal here is to provide inexpensive exposure to the inflation-protected bond market. Most of management's actions involve trying to identify undervalued issues along the inflation-protected bond-maturity spectrum. Historically, the fund has stuck exclusively with Treasury issues.

Historical Profile
Return	Average
Risk	Below Avg
Rating	★★★ Neutral

Investment Style
Fixed Income
Income Rtn %Rank Cat

91 50 19 5 17

▼ Manager Change
▽ Partial Manager Change

16.0
14.0 **Growth of $10,000**
12.0 ▬ Investment Values of Fund
10.0 ▬ Investment Values of LB Aggr

Performance Quartile (within Category)

	1995	1996	1997	1998	1999	2000	2001	2002	2003	2004	2005	2006	History
NAV	—	—	—	—	—	10.35	10.62	11.84	12.21	12.57	12.16	11.78	
Total Return %	—	—	—	—	—	5.92*	16.61	8.00	8.27	2.59	0.43		
+/-LB Aggr	—	—	—	—	—		-0.83	6.36	3.90	3.93	0.16	-3.90	
+/-LB US Treas TIPS	—	—	—	—	—		-0.28	0.04	-0.40	-0.19	-0.25	0.02	
Income Return %	—	—	—	—	—		4.37	4.39	3.85	4.70	5.53	3.54	
Capital Return %	—	—	—	—	—		3.24	12.22	4.15	3.57	-2.94	-3.11	
Total Rtn % Rank Cat	—	—	—	—	—		64	15	31	23	24	20	
Income $	—	—	—	—	—	0.27	0.45	0.46	0.45	0.57	0.68	0.43	
Capital Gains $	—	—	—	—	—	0.01	0.07	0.06	0.12	0.07	0.05	0.00	
Expense Ratio %	—	—	—	—	—		0.25	0.25	0.22	0.18	0.20		
Income Ratio %	—	—	—	—	—		6.38	3.92	4.55	3.46	4.83		
Turnover Rate %	—	—	—	—	—		122	75	108	63	47		
Net Assets $mil	—	—	—	—	—	148	772	2,988	4,557	7,182	5,440		

Performance 12-31-06

	1st Qtr	2nd Qtr	3rd Qtr	4th Qtr	Total
2002	1.51	5.77	7.96	0.60	16.61
2003	2.62	3.46	0.24	1.47	8.00
2004	5.00	-3.04	3.87	2.40	8.27
2005	-0.34	2.90	0.06	-0.02	2.59
2006	-2.14	0.48	3.52	-1.34	0.43

Trailing	Total Return%	+/- LB Aggr	+/- LB US Treas TIPS	%Rank Cat	Growth of $10,000
3 Mo	-1.34	-2.58	0.03	36	9,866
6 Mo	2.14	-2.95	-0.08	20	10,214
1 Yr	0.43	-3.90	0.02	20	10,043
3 Yr Avg	3.71	0.01	-0.14	13	11,155
5 Yr Avg	7.04	1.98	-0.15	29	14,052
10 Yr Avg	—	—	—		
15 Yr Avg	—	—	—		

Tax Analysis	Tax-Adj Rtn%	%Rank Cat	Tax-Cost Rat	%Rank Cat
3 Yr (estimated)	2.03	11	1.62	70
5 Yr (estimated)	5.31	1	1.62	16
10 Yr (estimated)	—	—		

Potential Capital Gain Exposure: -2% of assets

Rating and Risk

Time Period	Load-Adj Return %	Morningstar Rtn vs Cat	Morningstar Risk vs Cat	Morningstar Risk-Adj Rating
1 Yr	0.43			
3 Yr	3.71	+Avg	Avg	★★★★
5 Yr	7.04	Avg	-Avg	★★★
10 Yr	—	—	—	
Incept	7.52			

Other Measures	Standard Index LB Aggr	Best Fit Index LB Govt
Alpha	-0.1	0.6
Beta	1.37	1.28
R-Squared	75	77
Standard Deviation	5.07	
Mean	3.71	
Sharpe Ratio	0.11	

Morningstar's Take by Paul Herbert 12-28-06

Though it may not be for everyone, this fund remains a formidable option.

When we last wrote about Vanguard Inflation-Protected Securities, we talked about the intuitive appeal of the securities in which it invests. Specifically, Treasury Inflation-Protected Securities' (TIPS) values are adjusted upward with inflation. We did not address a drawback of owning mutual funds devoted to these bonds, though: Namely, TIPS' values are adjusted downward in the event of deflation, i.e., when the value of the Consumer Price Index (CPI) falls. That shortcoming can make their income streams variable. Shareholders here have witnessed the results of this process first hand. The CPI's value fell earlier this autumn, wiping out the fund's income. The fund did not pay a dividend in December.

We see this episode as part and parcel of owning TIPS, and as a result, we aren't worked up about it. In fact, other inflation-protected funds, such as iShares Lehman TIPS Bond, have had to forgo dividends, too. The lesson is that investors shouldn't rely on TIPS funds if they're looking for continuous dividend payments.

That limitation doesn't overwhelm the case for TIPS or for this fund. Inflation remains an ongoing concern for investors, and TIPS funds are a straightforward way to combat its effects. And this fund is one of the cheapest of the bunch. It charges less than half as much as the average no-load fund in the category does. In addition to assisting on the return front, low fees further allow the managers to take a less-risky approach. For one, they stick almost exclusively with TIPS. Plus, they use tactics such as highlighting cheaper bonds along the maturity spectrum, trading opportunistically among newly offered and seasoned TIPS bonds, and swapping TIPS for nominal Treasury bonds when those traditional issues offer higher yields.

Thanks to the success of their maneuvers and low fees, the fund hasn't had any trouble beating its peers over the short or long run.

Address:	PO Box 2600	Minimum Purchase:	$3000	Add: $100	IRA: $3000
	Valley Forge PA 19482	Min Auto Inv Plan:	$50	Add: —	
	800-662-6273	Sales Fees:	No-load		
Web Address:	www.vanguard.com	Management Fee:	0.18%		
Inception:	06-29-00*	Actual Fees:	Mgt:0.17%	Dist: —	
Advisor:	Vanguard Advisers, Inc.	Expense Projections:	3Yr:$64	5Yr:$113	10Yr:$255
Subadvisor:	None	Income Distrib:	Quarterly		
NTF Plans:	Vanguard NTF				

Portfolio Analysis 09-30-06

Total Fixed-Income:16

	Date of Maturity	Amount $000	Value $000	% Net Assets
US Treasury Bond 2.375%	01-15-25	1,006,995	1,104,808	11.45
US Treasury Note 2%	01-15-14	878,200	948,607	9.83
US Treasury Note 1.875%	07-15-13	843,500	910,355	9.44
US Treasury Note 1.625%	01-15-15	805,590	816,703	8.47
US Treasury Note 0.875%	04-15-10	682,400	694,543	7.20
US Treasury Bond 3.625%	04-15-28	429,575	669,869	6.95
US Treasury Note 2%	07-15-14	608,670	644,077	6.68
US Treasury Note 3%	07-15-12	537,500	631,258	6.54
US Treasury Note	01-15-16	581,525	582,643	6.04
US Treasury Note 3.875%	01-15-09	456,120	582,248	6.04
US Treasury Note 4.25%	01-15-10	431,350	551,897	5.72
US Treasury Bond 3.875%	04-15-29	284,400	455,029	4.72
US Treasury Bond 2%	01-15-26	343,875	338,144	3.51
US Treasury Note 3.5%	01-15-11	247,325	302,918	3.14
US Treasury Note 2.375%	04-15-11	100,000	102,638	1.06
US Treasury Bond 3.375%	04-15-32	71,100	101,282	1.05

Current Investment Style

Duration: Short Int Long
Quality: High Med Low

¹ figure provided by fund

Avg Eff Duration¹	6.0 Yrs
Avg Eff Maturity	9.7 Yrs
Avg Credit Quality	AAA
Avg Wtd Coupon	2.50%
Avg Wtd Price	115.88% of par

Coupon Range	% of Bonds	Rel Cat
0% PIK	0.0	0.0
0% to 6%	100.0	1.0
6% to 8%	0.0	0.0
8% to 10%	0.0	0.0
More than 10%	0.0	0.0

1.00=Category Average

Credit Analysis	% bonds 09-30-06		
AAA	100	BB	0
AA	0	B	0
A	0	Below B	0
BBB	0	NR/NA	0

Sector Breakdown	% of assets
US Treasuries	0
TIPS	98
US Agency	0
Mortgage Pass-Throughs	0
Mortgage CMO	0
Mortgage ARM	0
US Corporate	0
Asset-Backed	0
Convertible	0
Municipal	0
Corporate Inflation-Protected	0
Foreign Corporate	0
Foreign Govt	0

Composition			
Cash	2.2	Bonds	97.8
Stocks	0.0	Other	0.0

Special Securities	
Restricted/Illiquid Secs	0
Exotic Mortgage-Backed	0
Emerging-Markets Secs	0
Options/Futures/Warrants	No

MORNINGSTAR® Funds 500

Vanguard Ins L/T TE Inv

	Ticker	Load	NAV	Yield	SEC Yield	Total Assets	Mstar Category
	VILPX	None	$12.64	4.5%	3.80%	$3,213 mil	Muni National Long

Governance and Management

Stewardship Grade: B

Portfolio Manager(s)

Reid Smith has managed the fund since 1992 and is responsible for the day-to-day operations. Bob Auwaerter sets the fund's duration range.

Strategy

This fund invests at least 80% of its assets in municipal bonds that have principal and interest payments guaranteed by a third-party insurer. The fund's overall credit quality is very high. Management adjusts the fund's duration within a specified range, but it is generally less sensitive to interest-rate fluctuations than its average category peer. Management rotates between states and sectors based on assessments of relative value.

Historical Profile

Return	High
Risk	Above Avg
Rating	★★★★ Highest

	10	11	11	23	29	23	15	12

Growth of $10,000
- ■ Investment Values of Fund
- — Investment Values of LB Muni

20.8 / 18.8 / 16.4 / 14.0 / 12.0 / 10.0

▼ Manager Change
▽ Partial Manager Change

Investment Style
Fixed Income
Income Rtn %Rank Cat

Performance Quartile (within Category)

1995	1996	1997	1998	1999	2000	2001	2002	2003	2004	2005	2006	History
12.60	12.34	12.62	12.65	11.65	12.54	12.37	12.91	12.93	12.82	12.63	12.64	NAV
18.60	4.02	8.64	6.14	-2.91	13.61	4.30	10.03	5.77	3.93	3.37	4.92	Total Return %
1.14	-0.41	-0.55	-0.34	-0.85	1.93	-0.83	0.43	0.46	-0.55	-0.14	0.08	+/-LB Muni
-2.37	-0.44	-2.20	-0.68	1.77	-1.63	-0.57	0.00	-0.56	-2.63	-1.71	-0.94	+/-LB Muni 20YR
6.14	5.46	5.58	5.32	5.22	5.70	5.08	4.89	4.61	4.61	4.59	4.66	Income Return %
12.46	-1.44	3.06	0.82	-8.13	7.91	-0.78	5.14	1.16	-0.68	-1.22	0.26	Capital Return %
24	28	67	14	12	7	33	12	18	45	35	29	Total Rtn % Rank Cat
0.67	0.67	0.67	0.66	0.64	0.65	0.62	0.59	0.58	0.58	0.58	0.58	Income $
0.00	0.07	0.08	0.07	0.00	0.00	0.08	0.08	0.12	0.02	0.04	0.02	Capital Gains $
0.21	0.20	0.19	0.20	0.19	0.19	0.19	0.17	0.17	0.15	0.15	0.16	Expense Ratio %
5.82	5.46	5.47	5.22	5.20	5.48	5.00	4.80	4.57	4.50	4.52	4.60	Income Ratio %
7	18	18	16	17	34	21	20	17	18	15	19	Turnover Rate %
2,017	1,949	2,091	2,268	2,153	2,439	1,847	1,962	1,944	1,875	1,027	947	Net Assets $mil

Performance 12-31-06

	1st Qtr	2nd Qtr	3rd Qtr	4th Qtr	Total
2002	0.86	3.89	5.24	-0.22	10.03
2003	1.04	2.97	0.16	1.50	5.77
2004	1.23	-2.37	4.06	1.06	3.93
2005	-0.62	3.54	-0.35	0.82	3.37
2006	0.17	-0.13	3.70	1.14	4.92

Trailing	Total Return%	+/- LB Muni	+/- LB Muni 20YR	%Rank Cat	Growth of $10,000
3 Mo	1.14	0.03	-0.29	29	10,114
6 Mo	4.88	0.33	-0.63	14	10,488
1 Yr	4.92	0.08	-0.94	29	10,492
3 Yr Avg	4.07	-0.21	-1.76	36	11,271
5 Yr Avg	5.58	0.05	-1.18	13	13,119
10 Yr Avg	5.70	-0.06	-0.88	11	17,408
15 Yr Avg	6.31	0.05	-0.77	8	25,039

Tax Analysis	Tax-Adj Rtn%	%Rank Cat	Tax-Cost Rat	%Rank Cat
3 Yr (estimated)	4.03	25	0.04	15
5 Yr (estimated)	5.48	14	0.09	26
10 Yr (estimated)	5.60	7	0.09	39

Potential Capital Gain Exposure: 6% of assets

Rating and Risk

Time Period	Load-Adj Return %	Morningstar Rtn vs Cat	Morningstar Risk vs Cat	Morningstar Risk-Adj Rating
1 Yr	4.92			
3 Yr	4.07	+Avg	High	★★★★
5 Yr	5.58	+Avg	+Avg	★★★★
10 Yr	5.70	High	+Avg	★★★★★
Incept	7.91			

Other Measures	Standard Index LB Muni	Best Fit Index LB Muni 10YR
Alpha	-0.4	0.2
Beta	1.18	1.02
R-Squared	97	98
Standard Deviation	3.71	
Mean	4.07	
Sharpe Ratio	0.23	

Morningstar's Take by Brian Smith 12-20-06

Vanguard Insured Long-Term Tax Exempt's success is directly traceable to its low fees.

This fund earns our praise because it wallops long-term municipal competitors' expense ratios. At only 0.15% of assets, its levy is very far below a typical no-load peer's 0.65% charge. That built-in advantage allows the fund to pay out more yield than most peers without taking on added risk. In fact, more than 90% of its bonds are rated AAA, which is about 30 percentage points higher than its typical category rival's stake. That high-quality tilt should soothe the nerves of credit-risk-averse investors.

By mandate, this insured fund takes little credit risk, but it's not as defensive on interest rates. Manager Reid Smith's colleague, Bob Auwaerter, sets Vanguard's overall interest-rate outlook. Auwaerter still believes that the U.S. Federal Reserve has removed most inflation threats from the economy, which leads him to think that rates may stay relatively stable in the near future. The fund's 5.5-year duration (a measure of interest-rate sensitivity) is a reflection of that. Given the lack of overwhelming evidence in any one direction, this stance makes sense to us, too.

The fund's upper-quality focus combined with active interest-rate management and the all-important low expense ratio benefits shareholders. The fund's trailing five- and 10-year returns through Nov. 30, 2006 rank in the category's best quintile. The fund's year-to-date return is more in line with that of its peers, many of which have benefited recently from their added exposure to mid- and lower-rated bonds.

But this fund is ideally suited to tax-free investors who want to take no credit risk. Its consistently executed strategy, low fees, and able manager argue strongly in its favor.

Dieter Bardy contributed to this report.

Portfolio Analysis 09-30-06

Total Fixed-Income:288	Date of Maturity	Amount $000	Value $000	% Net Assets
Maryland St Health & Hig	08-15-38	62,055	72,349	2.30
Louisville & Jefferson C	05-15-31	51,960	55,840	1.78
New Jersey St Tran 5.5%	02-01-10	47,340	47,411	1.51
PUERTO RICO PUB FIN	08-01-30	40,000	42,977	1.37
MIAMI-DADE CNTY FLA EXPW	07-01-39	39,015	41,195	1.31
St Cloud Minn Health Car	05-01-26	37,665	40,357	1.29
California St 5%	08-01-24	37,225	39,658	1.26
New Jersey St Transn Tr	12-15-21	34,000	39,640	1.26
Michigan St Trunk Line R	11-01-26	35,765	36,832	1.17
New Jersey St Tpk Auth 6	01-01-13	30,000	34,705	1.11
Monroe Cnty Mich Econ De	09-01-22	25,000	32,930	1.05
Golden St Tob Securitiza	06-01-35	30,000	31,373	1.00
Massachusetts St 5.5%	12-01-22	25,580	30,048	0.96
Regl Transn Auth 7.2%	11-01-20	24,000	29,900	0.95
New Jersey Econ Dev Auth	12-15-20	25,000	28,390	0.90

Current Investment Style

	1Avg Eff Duration	6.0 Yrs
	Avg Eff Maturity	8.0 Yrs
	Avg Credit Quality	AAA
	Avg Wtd Coupon	5.11%
	Avg Wtd Price	106.81% of par

1figure provided by fund

Credit Analysis % bonds 09-30-06

AAA	95	BB	0
AA	5	B	0
A	0	Below B	0
BBB	0	NR/NA	0

Top 5 States % bonds

CA	11.4	IL	7.0
NJ	9.4	MA	5.5
TX	8.1		

Composition

Cash	0.4	Bonds	99.6
Stocks	0.0	Other	0.0

Special Securities

Restricted/Illiquid Secs	0
Options/Futures/Warrants	No

Sector Weightings

	% of Bonds	Rel Cat
General Obligation	30.4	1.08
Utilities	10.5	1.01
Health	12.7	1.22
Water/Waste	19.8	2.01
Housing	0.3	0.05
Education	7.6	0.77
Transportation	11.6	1.35
COP/Lease	1.1	0.46
Industrial	5.9	0.49
Misc Revenue	0.0	—
Demand	0.0	0.00

Address:	PO Box 2600 Valley Forge PA 19482 800-997-2798	Minimum Purchase:	$3000	Add: $100	IRA: $0
		Min Auto Inv Plan:	$3000	Add: $50	
		Sales Fees:	No-load		
Web Address:	www.vanguard.com	Management Fee:	0.14%		
Inception:	10-01-84	Actual Fees:	Mgt:0.14%	Dist: —	
Advisor:	Vanguard Advisers, Inc.	Expense Projections:	3Yr:$52	5Yr:$90	10Yr:$205
Subadvisor:	None	Income Distrib:	Monthly		
NTF Plans:	Vanguard NTF				

Vanguard Intm Bd Idx

	Ticker	Load	NAV	Yield	SEC Yield	Total Assets	Mstar Category
	VBIIX	None	$10.25	4.9%	4.96%	$6,228 mil	Intermediate-Term Bond

Governance and Management

Stewardship Grade: B

Portfolio Manager(s)

Ken Volpert has been the manager of this fund since its 1994 inception. Volpert's team, which includes six credit analysts, runs all of Vanguard's fixed-income index offerings, including the Short-Term Bond Index and Long-Term Bond Index, as well as Total Bond Market Index.

Strategy

This fund's goal is to approximate the performance of the Lehman Brothers 5-10 Year Government/Credit Index, which is composed of U.S. Treasuries, agency debentures, and corporate bonds. Although the duration (a measure of interest-rate sensitivity) and other key characteristics of the index are carefully replicated, the fund does not hold every security in the index, and management selects specific corporate bonds based on fundamental credit research.

Historical Profile

Return	Above Avg
Risk	High
Rating	★★★★ Above Avg

Return boxes: 17 | 24 | 19 | 13 | 12 | 16 | 12 | 16

Performance 12-31-06

	1st Qtr	2nd Qtr	3rd Qtr	4th Qtr	Total
2002	-0.67	3.36	5.77	2.08	10.85
2003	1.82	4.57	-0.74	-0.03	5.65
2004	3.77	-3.88	4.41	1.04	5.22
2005	-1.28	4.08	-1.29	0.33	1.75
2006	-1.35	-0.56	4.62	1.24	3.91

Trailing	Total Return%	+/- LB Aggr	+/- LB 5-10YR	%Rank Cat	Growth of $10,000
3 Mo	1.24	0.00	0.16	43	10,124
6 Mo	5.92	0.83	0.24	9	10,592
1 Yr	3.91	-0.42	0.10	52	10,391
3 Yr Avg	3.62	-0.08	-0.02	34	11,126
5 Yr Avg	5.43	0.37	-0.49	15	13,026
10 Yr Avg	6.49	0.25	-0.19	6	18,754
15 Yr Avg	—	—	—	—	—

Tax Analysis	Tax-Adj Rtn%	%Rank Cat	Tax-Cost Rat	%Rank Cat
3 Yr (estimated)	1.87	36	1.69	66
5 Yr (estimated)	3.51	15	1.82	66
10 Yr (estimated)	4.16	6	2.19	68

Potential Capital Gain Exposure: -2% of assets

History

	1995	1996	1997	1998	1999	2000	2001	2002	2003	2004	2005	2006	
NAV	10.37	9.96	10.20	10.48	9.51	10.02	10.28	10.75	10.69	10.68	10.36	10.25	
Total Return %	21.03	2.55	9.41	10.09	-3.00	12.78	9.28	10.85	5.65	5.22	1.75	3.91	
+/-LB Aggr	2.56	-1.08	-0.24	1.40	-2.18	1.15	0.84	0.60	1.55	0.88	-0.68	-0.42	
+/-LB 5-10YR	-0.40	-0.14	-0.02	-0.05	-0.12	0.34	0.46	-2.18	-0.32	-0.08	-0.08	0.10	
Income Return %	7.40	6.44	6.85	6.53	6.18	7.10	6.69	5.97	5.06	4.85	4.71	4.92	
Capital Return %	13.63	-3.89	2.56	3.56	-9.18	5.68	2.59	4.88	0.59	0.37	-2.96	-1.01	
Total Rtn % Rank Cat	13	73	38	2	86	5	12	5	31	13	54	52	
Income $	0.66	0.65	0.66	0.65	0.63	0.65	0.65	0.60	0.53	0.51	0.49	0.50	
Capital Gains $	0.03	0.00	0.00	0.07	0.03	0.00	0.00	0.01	0.12	0.05	0.01	0.00	
Expense Ratio %	0.20	0.20	0.20	0.20	0.20	0.21	0.21	0.21	0.20	0.18	0.18	—	
Income Ratio %	6.55	6.54	6.64	6.23	6.33	6.83	6.33	5.75	4.91	4.75	4.68	—	
Turnover Rate %	71	80	56	77	120	81	135	141	98	84	76	—	
Net Assets $mil	346	457	687	1,102	1,449	1,642	2,096	2,415	2,749	3,501	3,009	2,929	

Investment Style
Fixed Income
Income Rtn %Rank Cat

▼ Manager Change
▽ Partial Manager Change

Growth of $10,000
— Investment Values of Fund
— Investment Values of LB Aggr

Performance Quartile (within Category)

Rating and Risk

Time Period	Load-Adj Return %	Morningstar Rtn vs Cat	Morningstar Risk vs Cat	Morningstar Risk-Adj Rating
1 Yr	3.91			
3 Yr	3.62	Avg	High	★★★
5 Yr	5.43	+Avg	High	★★★★
10 Yr	6.49	High	High	★★★★
Incept	6.56			

Other Measures	Standard Index	Best Fit Index
	LB Aggr	LB 5-10YR
Alpha	-0.2	0.0
Beta	1.37	1.00
R-Squared	99	100
Standard Deviation	4.50	
Mean	3.62	
Sharpe Ratio	0.10	

Portfolio Analysis 09-30-06

Total Fixed-Income:855	Date of Maturity	Amount $000	Value $000	% Net Assets
US Treasury Bond 11.25%	02-15-15	208,735	303,580	4.90
US Treasury Note 4%	02-15-14	273,885	263,316	4.25
US Treasury Bond 8.75%	05-15-17	154,775	206,649	3.34
US Treasury Bond 9.875%	11-15-15	142,075	196,751	3.18
US Treasury Bond 9.25%	02-15-16	132,375	178,148	2.88
US Treasury Bond 7.25%	05-15-16	123,150	147,626	2.38
US Treasury Note 4%	02-15-15	110,975	106,206	1.71
US Treasury Note 4.25%	11-15-13	102,000	99,753	1.61
US Treasury Bond 10.625%	08-15-15	63,280	90,540	1.46
US Treasury Note 4.75%	05-15-14	87,150	87,872	1.42
FHLMC 4.875%	11-15-13	72,550	72,172	1.16
FNMA 4.625%	10-15-13	66,500	65,221	1.05
FHLMC 5.125%	07-15-12	64,000	64,611	1.04
US Treasury Note 4.375%	12-31-07	63,500	63,123	1.02
FHLMC 4.5%	07-15-13	64,500	62,869	1.01
FNMA 6.125%	03-15-12	55,410	58,536	0.94
US Treasury Note 4.75%	11-15-08	54,000	54,059	0.87
FNMA 5%	03-15-16	53,125	53,174	0.86
FHLMC 5%	07-15-14	51,100	51,268	0.83
FHLMC 5.75%	01-15-12	49,375	51,254	0.83

Current Investment Style

Duration: Short Int Long
Quality: High Med Low

¹figure provided by fund

Avg Eff Duration¹	5.9 Yrs
Avg Eff Maturity	7.6 Yrs
Avg Credit Quality	AA
Avg Wtd Coupon	6.14%
Avg Wtd Price	106.75% of par

Coupon Range	% of Bonds	Rel Cat
0% PIK	0.3	0.0
0% to 6%	64.6	0.9
6% to 8%	17.7	0.8
8% to 10%	10.6	2.2
More than 10%	7.1	10.1

1.00=Category Average

Credit Analysis	% bonds 09-30-06		
AAA	52	BB	0
AA	11	B	0
A	18	Below B	0
BBB	19	NR/NA	0

Sector Breakdown
	% of assets
US Treasuries	33
TIPS	0
US Agency	15
Mortgage Pass-Throughs	0
Mortgage CMO	0
Mortgage ARM	0
US Corporate	46
Asset-Backed	0
Convertible	0
Municipal	0
Corporate Inflation-Protected	0
Foreign Corporate	3
Foreign Govt	2

Composition
Cash	1.1	Bonds	98.9
Stocks	0.0	Other	0.0

Special Securities
Restricted/Illiquid Secs	Trace
Exotic Mortgage-Backed	0
Emerging-Markets Secs	2
Options/Futures/Warrants	No

Morningstar's Take by Sonya Morris 11-27-06

Despite its quirks, Vanguard Intermediate-Term Bond Index makes a strong case for itself.

Most intermediate-term bond funds keep a close eye on the Lehman Brothers Aggregate Bond Index, which is the benchmark for the domestic investment-grade bond universe. This fund, however, charts a slightly different course by tracking the Lehman Brothers 5-10 Year Government/Credit Index. Consequently, its portfolio looks different from its peers. For example, its benchmark is entirely devoid of mortgages, while its typical rival dedicates a third of assets to that sector. And it holds more bonds with slightly longer maturities.

This positioning has implications for the fund's performance. For example, when mortgages outperform, it is likely to lag. And because it holds more longer-term bonds, it tends to suffer more than its peers when interest rates rise, as its 1999 showing illustrates. Not surprisingly, this fund has experienced more volatility than its typical rival.

However, despite its slightly different profile, this fund's long-term results have been quite consistent with the Lehman Brothers Aggregate Index. According to its R-squared statistic (a measure of correlation), 99% of the variations in its returns can be explained by movements in that flagship index. And its 10-year trailing returns differ from that index by just 0.25%. That's been enough to lift this fund past the majority of its rivals over time. Its five- and 10-year annualized returns rank among the best in the category.

Those results can partly be attributed to this fund's tiny 0.18% expense ratio, which gives it a head start right out of the gate. Also, by keeping fees low, it passes more of its income stream on to shareholders. Its yield consistently ranks in the category's top 25%.

This fund's idiosyncrasies may put off investors seeking broad sector diversification and a smooth ride. But for everyone else, we think this is a fine choice for a core holding.

Address:	PO Box 2600 Valley Forge PA 19482 800-997-2798	Minimum Purchase: Min Auto Inv Plan: Sales Fees:	$3000 $3000 No-load	Add: $100 IRA: $3000 Add: $50
Web Address:	www.vanguard.com	Management Fee:	0.15%	
Inception:	03-01-94	Actual Fees:	Mgt:0.15%	Dist: —
Advisor:	Vanguard Advisers, Inc.	Expense Projections:	3Yr:$58	5Yr:$101 10Yr:$230
Subadvisor:	None	Income Distrib:	Monthly	
NTF Plans:	Vanguard NTF			

Morningstar® Funds 500

Vanguard Int-Tm US Trs

Ticker	Load	NAV	Yield	SEC Yield	Total Assets	Mstar Category
VFITX	None	$10.76	4.7%	4.48%	$3,974 mil	Intermediate Government

Governance and Management

Stewardship Grade: B

Portfolio Manager(s)

David Glocke assumed day-to-day management of this fund in May 2001. He was assisted by the head of Vanguard's fixed-income team, Ian MacKinnon. The duo also ran Vanguard Short-Term Treasury and Vanguard Long-Term U.S. Treasury. However, Bob Auwaerter replaced MacKinnon, who retired in June 2003. We expect Auwaerter, who is a veteran of the firm's fixed-income group, to ably succeed MacKinnon.

Strategy

This offering typically keeps 85% of its assets in Treasuries and the balance in government-agency bonds. Management avoids mortgages, which are the predominant securities in the average intermediate-government fund, and the fund tends to court more interest-rate sensitivity than its typical peer.

Historical Profile

Return	High
Risk	High
Rating	★★★★★ Highest

	45	39	24	26	18	26	15	13

Investment Style
Fixed Income
Income Rtn %Rank Cat

▼ Manager Change
▽ Partial Manager Change

Growth of $10,000
- Investment Values of Fund
- Investment Values of LB Aggr

Performance Quartile (within Category)

1995	1996	1997	1998	1999	2000	2001	2002	2003	2004	2005	2006	History
10.88	10.42	10.67	11.14	10.13	10.85	11.03	11.79	11.40	11.26	10.93	10.76	NAV
20.44	1.92	8.96	10.61	-3.52	14.03	7.55	14.15	2.37	3.40	2.32	3.14	Total Return %
1.97	-1.71	-0.69	1.92	-2.70	2.40	-0.89	3.90	-1.73	-0.94	-0.11	-1.19	+/-LB Aggr
2.10	-0.85	-0.63	0.76	-1.29	0.79	0.32	2.65	0.01	-0.08	-0.33	-0.34	+/-LB Govt
7.11	6.13	6.41	6.07	5.75	6.59	5.90	5.38	4.19	4.51	4.62	4.68	Income Return %
13.33	-4.21	2.55	4.54	-9.27	7.44	1.65	8.77	-1.82	-1.11	-2.30	-1.54	Capital Return %
4	73	40	3	86	1	23	2	22	35	27	63	Total Rtn % Rank Cat
0.66	0.65	0.65	0.63	0.62	0.65	0.62	0.58	0.48	0.50	0.51	0.50	Income $
0.00	0.00	0.00	0.00	0.00	0.00	0.00	0.18	0.18	0.02	0.08	0.00	Capital Gains $
0.28	0.28	0.25	0.27	0.27	0.27	0.28	0.29	0.28	0.26	0.24	0.26	Expense Ratio %
6.05	6.34	6.26	6.19	5.76	5.96	6.25	5.60	4.93	4.14	4.45	4.59	Income Ratio %
128	56	42	30	63	66	56	33	110	34	61	66	Turnover Rate %
1,195	1,270	1,506	1,864	1,705	1,761	1,971	2,685	2,296	2,160	1,761	1,696	Net Assets $mil

Performance 12-31-06

	1st Qtr	2nd Qtr	3rd Qtr	4th Qtr	Total
2002	-0.59	5.47	8.32	0.51	14.15
2003	1.08	2.54	-0.72	-0.52	2.37
2004	3.14	-3.22	3.20	0.39	3.40
2005	-0.93	3.53	-0.93	0.69	2.32
2006	-1.23	-0.25	3.96	0.70	3.14

Trailing	Total Return%	+/- LB Aggr	+/- LB Govt	%Rank Cat	Growth of $10,000
3 Mo	0.70	-0.54	-0.14	84	10,070
6 Mo	4.69	-0.40	0.28	28	10,469
1 Yr	3.14	-1.19	-0.34	63	10,314
3 Yr Avg	2.95	-0.75	-0.25	41	10,911
5 Yr Avg	4.98	-0.08	0.34	5	12,751
10 Yr Avg	6.16	-0.08	0.15	3	18,181
15 Yr Avg	6.48	-0.02	0.18	5	25,646

Tax Analysis	Tax-Adj Rtn%	%Rank Cat	Tax-Cost Rat	%Rank Cat
3 Yr (estimated)	1.28	45	1.62	79
5 Yr (estimated)	3.11	8	1.78	87
10 Yr (estimated)	3.98	4	2.05	82

Potential Capital Gain Exposure: -1% of assets

Morningstar's Take by Michael Herbst 12-18-06

Low fees drive Vanguard Intermediate-Term U.S. Treasury's appeal, but there's more to it.

This fund's low, low expense ratio is one of its most appealing aspects. At 0.26%, its expense ratio is much lower than the average no-load intermediate-term government bond fund's 0.66% charge. When aiming for an income payout superior to peers', a fund's expense ratio matters more in bond categories than probably anywhere else. Low fees are working here: The fund s 4.57% yield stands over 60% of its rivals .

That fat yield is impressive, considering the fund takes virtually zero credit risk. That's because this fund is one of the few in its category that focuses on U.S. Treasuries. Meanwhile, most of the fund's peers split their portfolios among U.S. Treasury, agency, and mortgage bonds and TIPs. While this fund will certainly be held back when those areas of the market are running strong, it also all but eliminates credit risk.

Despite its lack of diversity, the fund has delivered the goods for shareholders. The fund's five- and 10-year returns through Nov. 30, 2006, sit comfortably in the category's top decile. Those strong results come partly from the fund's typically more aggressive interest-rate positioning.

Manager David Glocke doesn't think further interest rate hikes are likely soon, because he thinks Federal Reserve chairman Ben Bernanke is willing to allow prior monetary policy to wind its way through the economy. Therefore, the fund remains neutral on interest rates, relative to the fund's custom benchmark, and the fund's duration is 5 years. Duration is a way to measure how sensitive a fund is to changes in interest rates; if rates move up 1%, this fund will lose 5%, and vice versa (all other things being equal). This fund's duration is a bit longer than its typical rival's, making it more reactive to any rate changes.

For investors partial to U.S. Treasuries, this fund is a good fit.

Dieter Bardy contributed to this report.

Rating and Risk

Time Period	Load-Adj Return %	Morningstar Rtn vs Cat	Morningstar Risk vs Cat	Morningstar Risk-Adj Rating
1 Yr	3.14			
3 Yr	2.95	Avg	High	★★★
5 Yr	4.98	High	High	★★★★★
10 Yr	6.16	High	High	★★★★★
Incept	6.80			

Other Measures	Standard Index	Best Fit Index
	LB Aggr	LB Govt
Alpha	-0.8	-0.2
Beta	1.19	1.11
R-Squared	98	99
Standard Deviation	3.91	
Mean	2.95	
Sharpe Ratio	-0.06	

Portfolio Analysis 09-30-06

Total Fixed-Income:47	Date of Maturity	Amount $000	Value $000	% Net Assets
US Treasury Bond 8.75%	05-15-17	459,700	613,773	15.78
US Treasury Note 3.625%	05-15-13	411,000	388,329	9.98
US Treasury Note 4.25%	08-15-13	354,000	346,478	8.91
US Treasury Note 6.5%	02-15-10	303,500	321,045	8.25
US Treasury Note 4%	11-15-12	251,000	243,078	6.25
US Treasury Note 4%	02-15-14	207,500	199,493	5.13
US Treasury Note 4.375%	08-15-12	194,000	191,969	4.94
US Treasury Note 4.875%	05-15-12	156,000	158,170	4.07
US Treasury Note 4%	04-15-10	157,000	153,959	3.96
US Treasury Note 3.875%	02-15-13	154,000	147,888	3.80
Private Expt Fdg 7.25%	06-15-10	135,920	146,368	3.76
Private Expt Fdg 5.87%	07-31-08	123,100	124,788	3.21
US Treasury Bond 9.125%	05-15-18	84,000	116,629	3.00
US Treasury Bond 9%	11-15-18	68,000	94,393	2.43
US Treasury Note 4.25%	11-15-13	86,000	84,105	2.16
Private Expt Fdg 4.95%	11-15-15	65,000	64,492	1.66
Private Expt Fdg 5.75%	01-15-08	60,000	60,487	1.56
Private Expt Fdg 6.07%	04-30-11	51,000	53,171	1.37
US Treasury Note 3.875%	09-15-10	53,000	51,642	1.33
Arab Rep Egypt 4.45%	09-15-15	40,000	38,518	0.99

Current Investment Style

Duration: Short / Int / Long

Quality: High / Med / Low

1 figure provided by fund

Avg Eff Duration[1]	5.2 Yrs
Avg Eff Maturity	6.4 Yrs
Avg Credit Quality	AAA
Avg Wtd Coupon	5.68%
Avg Wtd Price	107.08% of par

Coupon Range	% of Bonds	Rel Cat
0% PIK	0.0	0.0
0% to 6%	61.9	0.8
6% to 8%	16.6	1.1
8% to 10%	21.6	10.0
More than 10%	0.0	0.0

1.00=Category Average

Credit Analysis		% bonds 09-30-06	
AAA	100	BB	0
AA	0	B	0
A	0	Below B	0
BBB	0	NR/NA	0

Sector Breakdown

	% of assets
US Treasuries	81
TIPS	0
US Agency	13
Mortgage Pass-Throughs	0
Mortgage CMO	1
Mortgage ARM	0
US Corporate	2
Asset-Backed	1
Convertible	0
Municipal	0
Corporate Inflation-Protected	0
Foreign Corporate	0
Foreign Govt	0

Composition

Cash	1.6	Bonds	98.4
Stocks	0.0	Other	0.0

Special Securities

Restricted/Illiquid Secs	Trace
Exotic Mortgage-Backed	0
Emerging-Markets Secs	0
Options/Futures/Warrants	No

Address:	PO Box 2600 Valley Forge PA 19482 800-997-2798
Web Address:	www.vanguard.com
Inception:	10-28-91
Advisor:	Vanguard Advisers, Inc.
Subadvisor:	None
NTF Plans:	Vanguard NTF

Minimum Purchase:	$3000	Add: $100	IRA: $3000
Min Auto Inv Plan:	$3000	Add: $50	
Sales Fees:	No-load		
Management Fee:	0.22%		
Actual Fees:	Mgt:0.23%		
Expense Projections:	3Yr:$84	5Yr:$146	10Yr:$331
Income Distrib:	Monthly		

Vanguard Intl Explorer

		Ticker	Load	NAV	Yield	Total Assets	Mstar Category
✔ Analyst Pick		VINEX	Closed	$21.06	2.5%	$2,858 mil	Foreign Small/Mid Growth

Governance and Management

Stewardship Grade: B

Portfolio Manager(s)

A team from Schroder Investment Management runs this fund, which used to be called Schroder International Small Companies until Vanguard adopted it. Four regional portfolio managers (two on Europe, one on Japan, and one on Pacific/Asia ex-Japan) choose stocks, while team leader Matthew Dobbs determines the fund's regional allocation and portfolio structure. Besides this team of five, there are 13 analysts, making this bench one of the category's deepest. They also interact with Schroders' team of 70 analysts around the world.

Strategy

Like most at subadvisor Schroders, this fund's team takes a growth-at-a-reasonable-price approach, although it leans a bit more toward growth than value. At least two thirds of the portfolio's buys must have capitalizations of $1.5 billion or less, but the team isn't afraid to let its winners ride into the $4 billion to $5 billion range. That said, it does a better job than many of its peers at sticking with small companies. The fund invests largely in developed markets and has had particular success in peripheral European countries. Vanguard uses fair-value pricing and does not hedge foreign-currency exposure.

Performance 12-31-06

	1st Qtr	2nd Qtr	3rd Qtr	4th Qtr	Total
2002	4.07	-0.50	-19.96	3.91	-13.88
2003	-5.98	27.66	14.95	14.06	57.37
2004	10.37	0.00	0.42	18.88	31.77
2005	2.94	1.01	10.42	4.95	20.49
2006	13.73	-1.86	3.70	12.41	30.10

Trailing	Total Return%	+/- MSCI EAFE	+/- MSCI Wd xUS	%Rank Cat	Growth of $10,000
3 Mo	12.41	2.06	2.29	73	11,241
6 Mo	16.57	1.88	2.35	48	11,657
1 Yr	30.10	3.76	4.39	32	13,010
3 Yr Avg	27.36	7.43	7.26	28	20,659
5 Yr Avg	22.86	7.88	7.61	29	27,993
10 Yr Avg	15.83	8.12	7.87	30	43,472
15 Yr Avg	—	—	—	—	—

Tax Analysis	Tax-Adj Rtn%	%Rank Cat	Tax-Cost Rat	%Rank Cat
3 Yr (estimated)	25.53	27	1.44	57
5 Yr (estimated)	21.72	30	0.93	80
10 Yr (estimated)	13.47	58	2.04	90

Potential Capital Gain Exposure: 32% of assets

Historical Profile

Return	Average
Risk	Below Avg
Rating	★★★★ Above Avg

Investment Style: Equity, Stock %

Percentages (by year): 94% 93% 92% 99% 92% 82% 97% 98% 93%

▼ Manager Change
▽ Partial Manager Change

Growth of $10,000
— Investment Values of Fund
— Investment Values of MSCI EAFE

Scale marks: 39.4 / 32.4 / 24.0 / 17.0 / 10.0

Performance Quartile (within Category)

1995	1996	1997	1998	1999	2000	2001	2002	2003	2004	2005	2006	History
—	9.91	8.00	9.32	15.72	12.55	9.58	8.19	12.82	16.34	17.92	21.06	NAV
—	-0.82*	-14.13	25.98	90.29	-2.68	-22.52	-13.88	57.37	31.77	20.49	30.10	Total Return %
—	—	-15.91	6.05	63.26	11.51	-1.10	2.06	18.78	11.52	6.95	3.76	+/-MSCI EAFE
—	—	-16.40	7.29	62.31	10.68	-1.13	1.92	17.95	11.39	6.02	4.39	+/-MSCI Wd xUS
—	—	0.14	0.46	0.09	0.59	1.12	0.63	0.82	1.87	2.45	3.24	Income Return %
—	—	-14.27	25.52	90.20	-3.27	-23.64	-14.51	56.55	29.90	18.04	26.86	Capital Return %
—	—	100	19	26	16	53	45	25	6	68	32	Total Rtn % Rank Cat
—	0.01	0.01	0.04	0.01	0.09	0.14	0.06	0.07	0.24	0.40	0.58	Income $
—	0.00	0.50	0.70	1.96	2.61	0.00	0.00	0.29	1.35	1.65	Capital Gains $
—	—	—	1.50	1.50	1.50	1.50	1.50	1.04	0.73	0.57	—	Expense Ratio %
—	—	—	0.21	0.33	0.53	-0.26	0.15	1.13	1.52	1.96	—	Income Ratio %
—	—	—	32	82	81	86	48	11	60	21	—	Turnover Rate %
—	—	6	4	12	17	26	111	644	1,865	2,858	Net Assets $mil

Rating and Risk

Time Period	Load-Adj Return %	Morningstar Rtn vs Cat	Morningstar Risk vs Cat	Morningstar Risk-Adj Rating
1 Yr	30.10			
3 Yr	27.36	+Avg	-Avg	★★★★
5 Yr	22.86	Avg	-Avg	★★★
10 Yr	15.83	Avg	-Avg	★★★★
Incept	15.47			

Other Measures	Standard Index MSCI EAFE	Best Fit Index MSCI EAFE
Alpha	4.7	4.7
Beta	1.10	1.10
R-Squared	86	86
Standard Deviation	11.21	
Mean	27.36	
Sharpe Ratio	1.95	

Portfolio Analysis 09-30-06

Share change since 06-06 Total Stocks:214

	Sector	Country	% Assets
Sika	Business	Switzerland	1.54
⊕ HOCHTIEF	Business	Germany	1.46
⊕ Bilfinger Berger	Business	Germany	1.38
⊕ Red Electrica de Espana	Utilities	Spain	1.36
⊕ Geberit	Consumer	Switzerland	1.28
⊕ Nexity	Financial	France	1.23
⊕ Enagas	Energy	Spain	1.23
⊕ MTU Aero Engines Hldgs	Ind Mtrls	Germany	1.16
ACEA	Utilities	Italy	1.14
Saft Groupe, Bagnolet	—	France	1.08
⊕ YIT	Business	Finland	0.99
Pt Bk Agroniaga Tbk	—	Indonesia	0.97
⊖ BKW FMB Energie	Utilities	Switzerland	0.95
⊕ Techem	Business	Germany	0.94
⊕ Groupe Bourbon Sa	Consumer	France	0.94
Azimut Hldg	Financial	Italy	0.93
SIG	Ind Mtrls	U.K.	0.93
⊕ CIR Grp	Ind Mtrls	Italy	0.92
OKO Bank Grp	Financial	Finland	0.90
⊖ Jelmoli Hldg Ag	Consumer	Switzerland	0.87

Current Investment Style

Value Blnd Growth — Large/Mid/Small

Market Cap	%
Giant	0.0
Large	6.2
Mid	65.2
Small	24.0
Micro	4.6
Avg $mil:	1,642

Value Measures		Rel Category
Price/Earnings	16.44	1.05
Price/Book	1.82	0.75
Price/Sales	0.85	0.77
Price/Cash Flow	5.49	0.70
Dividend Yield %	2.48	1.21

Growth Measures	%	Rel Category
Long-Term Erngs	13.75	0.67
Book Value	10.18	1.08
Sales	5.92	0.47
Cash Flow	11.28	0.75
Historical Erngs	17.87	0.79

Composition

Cash	2.7	Bonds	0.0
Stocks	93.3	Other	4.0
Foreign (% of Stock)			100.0

Sector Weightings	% of Stocks	Rel MSCI EAFE	3 Year High	Low
ⓘ Info	4.88	0.41		
Software	0.21	0.37	2	0
Hardware	3.36	0.87	3	2
Media	1.17	0.64	3	1
Telecom	0.14	0.03	2	0
⊜ Service	62.27	1.32		
Health	3.40	0.48	4	3
Consumer	14.79	2.99	18	13
Business	26.15	5.16	27	19
Financial	17.93	0.60	21	17
ⓜ Mfg	32.85	0.80		
Goods	6.49	0.49	16	6
Ind Mtrls	18.70	1.21	21	12
Energy	2.44	0.34	2	2
Utilities	5.22	1.00	5	2

Regional Exposure	% Stock		
UK/W. Europe	68	N. America	1
Japan	19	Latn America	1
Asia X Japan	12	Other	0

Country Exposure	% Stock		
U.K.	19	Switzerland	9
Japan	19	France	6
Germany	10		

Morningstar's Take by Kai Wiecking 12-21-06

Vanguard International Explorer continues to be one of the best options of its kind.

International small-cap managers often justify their high expense ratios with the extensive research effort required to effectively manage that asset class. As in so many other cases, Vanguard proves here that it can be done rather well on the cheap. The firm is better than most in passing on economies of scale to investors, and with this fund's assets now at more than $2.5 billion, its price tag has dropped to only 0.48%, making it the cheapest offering in the foreign small/mid-growth category by a country mile. Many investors don't pay much attention to cost when times are good, as they certainly have been for this asset class since late 2002. But the extended bull run of small international stocks has gotten long in the tooth, and leaner times are arguably ahead. That's when moderate expenses show their true worth, as potentially slim returns aren't further reduced by juicy management fees.

But low costs by themselves don't guarantee a fund's long-term success. This vast and underresearched market offers many inefficiencies that can be exploited by skilled managers. Schroders' Matthew Dobbs certainly fits that bill. And he is supported by one of the deepest and most experienced teams of analysts around. Dobbs applies a moderate-growth style here, making this offering more appealing to investors who can't stomach the volatility associated with more-aggressive growth approaches.

But even Dobbs' team can't always avoid trouble. They were surprised when German premium television provider Premiere lost the rights to that country's soccer league, causing the stock price to implode. Still, Dobbs' preference for sustainable growth stocks with good earnings visibility helped the fund weather the correction in May and June of 2006. Predictably, the fund is lagging in the low-quality-driven year-end rally. But for the long term, this fund is a keeper.

Address:	PO Box 2600 Valley Forge PA 19482 800-997-2798	Minimum Purchase:	Closed	Add: —	IRA: —
		Min Auto Inv Plan:	Closed	Add: —	
		Sales Fees:	No-load, 2.00%R		
Web Address:	www.vanguard.com	Management Fee:	0.44%		
Inception:	11-04-96*	Actual Fees:	Mgt:0.44%	Dist: —	
Advisor:	Schroder Investment Mgt N. America Inc.	Expense Projections:	3Yr:$160	5Yr:$280	10Yr:$628
Subadvisor:	None	Income Distrib:	Annually		
NTF Plans:	Vanguard NTF				

Ⓜ Morningstar® Funds 500

Vanguard Intl Gr

	Ticker	Load	NAV	Yield	Total Assets	Mstar Category
	VWIGX	None	$23.81	2.0%	$15,840 mil	Foreign Large Blend

Governance and Management

Stewardship Grade: B

Portfolio Manager(s)

Roughly two thirds of assets are run by Schroder Investment Management. Richard Foulkes, who had overseen that money since 1981, retired on Oct. 31, 2005, passing the mantle to Virginie Maisonneuve and Matthew Dobbs. The former joined Schroders in November 2004 fter holding positions at Martin Currie and Clay Finlay. Dobbs has been number two on the fund since 1999 and also runs Vanguard International Explorer. A separate team from Baillie Gifford Overseas, led by James Anderson, manages one third of the portfolio.

Strategy

Like her predecessor, Richard Foulkes, current lead manager Virginie Maisonneuve devotes roughly two thirds of assets to core growth stocks that are well-positioned, run by shareholder-friendly management teams, and trading fairly cheaply. A portion of the portfolio will be reserved for "noncore" holdings that are shorter-term plays, driven in part by top-down analysis. The fund's second subadvisor, Baillie Gifford, uses more of a classic-growth approach and is long-term focused. Both managers venture opportunistically into emerging markets. The fund is not currently hedging its foreign currency exposure.

Performance 12-31-06

	1st Qtr	2nd Qtr	3rd Qtr	4th Qtr	Total
2002	0.40	-4.31	-20.80	8.06	-17.79
2003	-7.57	17.88	7.70	14.57	34.45
2004	6.20	-2.22	0.18	14.35	18.95
2005	-0.53	-1.07	11.58	4.73	15.00
2006	9.90	-0.13	3.82	10.28	25.66

Trailing	Total Return%	+/- MSCI EAFE	+/- MSCI Wd xUS	%Rank Cat	Growth of $10,000
3 Mo	10.28	-0.07	0.16	47	11,028
6 Mo	14.49	-0.20	0.27	48	11,449
1 Yr	25.66	-0.68	-0.05	39	12,566
3 Yr Avg	19.79	-0.14	-0.31	29	17,189
5 Yr Avg	13.70	-1.28	-1.55	40	19,002
10 Yr Avg	8.03	0.32	0.07	30	21,649
15 Yr Avg	9.53	1.67	1.49	22	39,174

Tax Analysis	Tax-Adj Rtn%	%Rank Cat	Tax-Cost Rat	%Rank Cat
3 Yr (estimated)	18.51	31	1.07	56
5 Yr (estimated)	12.78	40	0.81	64
10 Yr (estimated)	6.95	30	1.00	47

Potential Capital Gain Exposure: 26% of assets

Morningstar's Take by Kai Wiecking 01-05-07

Vanguard International Growth remains a very solid choice.

We think that Vanguard has found a winning combination here with the fund's two subadvisors complementing each other rather well. London-based Schroders manager Virginie Maisonneuve has thus far been able to fill the shoes of her retired predecessor, Richard Foulkes. Like Foulkes, Maisonneuve invests in a valuation-conscious, low-turnover growth style complemented by some bolder, more tactical holdings. Prior to joining Schroders, she had started her investment career at Edinburgh-based Martin Currie. Scotland's capital is not only the home of the world's oldest mutual fund launched in 1868, it also houses the fund's other subadvisor, Baillie Gifford. The team at Baillie Gifford, led by manager James Anderson, employs more of a classic-growth approach. Anderson assembled a strong track record at the U.K.-based fund Baillie Gifford International. His sleeve of the portfolio now accounts for about one third of assets and receives most of the inflows.

The fund is well on track to deliver its fourth straight year of above-average returns within the foreign large-blend category. Solid stock selection within financials, with picks such as Deutsche Bank enjoying strong gains, as well as contributions from less obvious areas such as the consolidating European utilities industry, led by French holding Suez, are among the reasons why the fund is well ahead of its benchmark. Exposure to telecoms from emerging markets also helped, while an underweight in U.K. banks detracted from relative performance.

But investors should bear in mind that global stock markets won't rally indefinitely. If and when the next bear market comes around, the importance of low expenses will come back to the fore. In that regard, there are few better options than this fund, with its rock-bottom price tag of 0.55%. All told, this fund is a winner.

Address:	PO Box 2600 Valley Forge PA 19482 800-997-2798
Web Address:	www.vanguard.com
Inception:	09-30-81
Advisor:	Baillie Gifford Overseas Ltd
Subadvisor:	None
NTF Plans:	Vanguard NTF

Minimum Purchase:	$3000	Add: $100	IRA: $3000
Min Auto Inv Plan:	$3000	Add: $50	
Sales Fees:	No-load, 2.00%R		
Management Fee:	0.60%		
Actual Fees:	Mgt:0.55%	Dist: —	
Expense Projections:	3Yr:$202	5Yr:$351	10Yr:$786
Income Distrib:	Annually		

Historical Profile

Return	Average
Risk	Average
Rating	★★★ Neutral

Growth of $10,000 — Investment Values of Fund / Investment Values of MSCI EAFE

Investment Style: Equity, Stock %

▼ Manager Change
▽ Partial Manager Change

Performance Quartile (within Category)

1995	1996	1997	1998	1999	2000	2001	2002	2003	2004	2005	2006	History
15.02	16.46	16.39	18.77	22.49	18.87	15.01	12.16	16.13	18.86	21.01	23.81	NAV
14.89	14.65	4.12	16.93	26.34	-8.60	-18.92	-17.79	34.45	18.95	15.00	25.66	Total Return %
3.68	8.60	2.34	-3.00	-0.69	5.59	2.50	-1.85	-4.14	-1.30	1.46	-0.68	+/-MSCI EAFE
3.48	7.78	1.85	-1.76	-1.64	4.76	2.47	-1.99	-4.97	-1.43	0.53	-0.05	+/-MSCI Wd xUS
1.49	1.26	1.28	1.34	1.39	0.98	1.27	1.20	1.73	1.95	1.96	2.52	Income Return %
13.40	13.39	2.84	15.59	24.95	-9.58	-20.19	-18.99	32.72	17.00	13.04	23.14	Capital Return %
12	36	68	30	85	13	27	62	38	29	39	39	Total Rtn % Rank Cat
0.20	0.19	0.21	0.22	0.26	0.22	0.24	0.18	0.21	0.31	0.37	0.53	Income $
0.21	0.55	0.52	0.16	0.90	1.42	0.04	0.00	0.00	0.00	0.32	2.04	Capital Gains $
0.58	0.56	0.57	0.59	0.58	0.53	0.61	0.67	0.69	0.63	0.58	0.55	Expense Ratio %
1.53	1.35	1.26	1.39	1.42	1.26	1.19	1.28	1.57	1.69	1.89	2.52	Income Ratio %
31	22	22	37	37	48	48	40	59	45	48	45	Turnover Rate %
3,676	5,569	6,809	7,723	9,681	8,900	6,088	4,768	6,424	8,097	8,871	11,800	Net Assets $mil

Rating and Risk

Time Period	Load-Adj Return %	Morningstar Rtn vs Cat	Morningstar Risk vs Cat	Morningstar Risk-Adj Rating
1 Yr	25.66			
3 Yr	19.79	+Avg	Avg	★★★★
5 Yr	13.70	Avg	+Avg	★★★
10 Yr	8.03	Avg	Avg	★★★
Incept	13.15			

Other Measures	Standard Index MSCI EAFE	Best Fit Index MSCI EAFE
Alpha	-1.0	-1.0
Beta	1.06	1.06
R-Squared	97	97
Standard Deviation	10.16	
Mean	19.79	
Sharpe Ratio	1.53	

Portfolio Analysis 09-30-06

Share change since 06-06 Total Stocks:135	Sector	Country	% Assets
Royal Bank Of Scotland G	Financial	U.K.	2.39
⊕ SAP	Software	Germany	1.92
⊖ Tesco	Consumer	U.K.	1.90
Deutsche Bank AG	Financial	Germany	1.74
⊖ BG Grp	Energy	U.K.	1.71
Rio Tinto	Ind Mtrls	U.K.	1.69
Roche Holding	Health	Switzerland	1.68
Suez	Utilities	France	1.54
Mitsubishi UFJ Financial	Financial	Japan	1.49
⊕ Novartis	Health	Switzerland	1.47
⊖ Vodafone Grp	Telecom	U.K.	1.43
⊕ ORIX	Financial	Japan	1.41
⊖ Allied Irish Banks	Financial	Ireland	1.33
⊖ Societe Generale Grp	Financial	France	1.31
⊖ Petroleo Brasileiro S.A.	Energy	Brazil	1.30
Daewoo Shipbuilding & Ma	Ind Mtrls	Korea	1.28
⊕ Sanpaolo IMI	Financial	Italy	1.26
Nestle	Goods	Switzerland	1.23
⊖ L'Oreal	Goods	France	1.18
Barclays	Financial	U.K.	1.15

Current Investment Style

Value Blnd Growth — Large Mid Small

Market Cap	%
Giant	57.0
Large	34.6
Mid	8.5
Small	0.0
Micro	0.0
Avg $mil:	29,401

Value Measures		Rel Category
Price/Earnings	15.05	1.15
Price/Book	2.39	1.10
Price/Sales	1.31	1.13
Price/Cash Flow	8.36	1.00
Dividend Yield %	3.52	1.21

Growth Measures	%	Rel Category
Long-Term Erngs	11.78	1.00
Book Value	9.55	1.05
Sales	8.44	1.29
Cash Flow	10.41	1.26
Historical Erngs	22.87	1.12

Composition

Cash	3.6	Bonds	0.0
Stocks	92.6	Other	3.8
Foreign (% of Stock)			100.0

Sector Weightings	% of Stocks	Rel MSCI EAFE	3 Year High	Low
☉ Info	8.31	0.70		
▣ Software	2.60	4.64	3	0
▣ Hardware	1.92	0.50	5	2
◓ Media	0.68	0.37	4	1
☎ Telecom	3.11	0.56	8	3
☞ Service	47.24	1.00		
▨ Health	8.49	1.19	8	4
▤ Consumer	7.59	1.53	10	5
▣ Business	4.05	0.80	8	4
$ Financial	27.11	0.90	27	17
⊔ Mfg	44.44	1.09		
▨ Goods	17.15	1.31	21	16
⚙ Ind Mtrls	16.49	1.07	20	15
◔ Energy	8.62	1.21	11	6
▼ Utilities	2.18	0.42	7	2

Regional Exposure	% Stock		
UK/W. Europe	62	N. America	2
Japan	20	Latn America	5
Asia X Japan	11	Other	0

Country Exposure	% Stock		
U.K.	27	Switzerland	7
Japan	20	Germany	6
France	10		

Vanguard Intl Value

	Ticker	Load	NAV	Yield	Total Assets	Mstar Category
	VTRIX	None	$40.27	2.0%	$7,681 mil	Foreign Large Blend

Governance and Management

Stewardship Grade: B

Portfolio Manager(s)

The fund is managed by three separate subadvisors. Hansberger Global Investors has been overseeing the portfolio since August 2000 and has experienced some attrition on its team--most notably the diminished role of firm founder Thomas Hansberger. Ron Holt and Aureole Foong now jointly oversee the fund. In April 2004, Vanguard assigned AllianceBernstein's value team to about one fourth of the portfolio. That team also oversees AllianceBernstein International Value. In 2006, Gabrielle Boyle and Michael Powers of Lazard International Equity Select were added as a third subadvisor.

Strategy

The team from Hansberger applies a "normalized earnings" approach that focuses on companies whose shares are cyclically depressed. The picks sometimes don't look cheap by traditional measures because they stray into nontraditional value sectors. Meanwhile, the team from AllianceBernstein applies more of a classic-value approach that uses both quantitative modeling and fundamental analysis. The fund is not currently hedging its foreign currency exposure. Lazard is looking for sustainable financial productivity at attractive valuations.

Performance 12-31-06

	1st Qtr	2nd Qtr	3rd Qtr	4th Qtr	Total
2002	4.53	-1.60	-20.75	6.30	-13.35
2003	-9.51	20.77	10.40	17.60	41.90
2004	4.19	0.04	1.50	13.21	19.77
2005	0.87	-0.83	11.93	5.36	17.96
2006	11.09	0.03	4.21	9.80	27.15

Trailing	Total Return%	+/- MSCI EAFE	+/- MSCI Wd xUS	%Rank Cat	Growth of $10,000
3 Mo	9.80	-0.55	-0.32	67	10,980
6 Mo	14.43	-0.26	0.21	50	11,443
1 Yr	27.15	0.81	1.44	21	12,715
3 Yr Avg	21.56	1.63	1.46	10	17,963
5 Yr Avg	17.17	2.19	1.92	7	22,084
10 Yr Avg	9.33	1.62	1.37	14	24,400
15 Yr Avg	9.11	1.25	1.07	28	36,980

Tax Analysis	Tax-Adj Rtn%	%Rank Cat	Tax-Cost Rat	%Rank Cat
3 Yr (estimated)	20.24	11	1.09	57
5 Yr (estimated)	16.19	6	0.84	67
10 Yr (estimated)	7.65	17	1.54	81

Potential Capital Gain Exposure: 20% of assets

Morningstar's Take by Kai Wiecking 12-27-06

Vanguard International Value is different animal these days, but it is still an appealing option.

With the addition of two new subadvisors in the past two years, this fund has lost its focus, but gained diversification and maneuverability. For more than four years, between August 2000 and December 2004, Hansberger Global Investors was the sole subadvisor here, running the portfolio in an opportunistic style that made it a better fit in the foreign large blend category than the foreign large value category. Then, on the last day of 2004, Bernstein's value team led by Kevin Simms was assigned a slice of the portfolio. Simms' team came with the recommendation of a strong track record at its own funds, pursuing a more-traditional value style. In March 2006, Lazard's Gabrielle Boyle and Michael Powers were added as a third subadvisor; their track record at Lazard International Equity Select is less than inspiring

Performance here has remained strong, however, as this fund continues to outpace most of its foreign large-blend competitors. In fact, the fund is well on track to deliver its seventh consecutive calendar year of top-quartile returns. In 2006, strong stock selection rather than any particular regional or industry biases gave this offering its edge. Picks such as Franco-Luxembourgish steel produce Arcelor delivered strong returns, as the company was taken over by it Indian competitor Mittal Steel. During the second half of the year, European airline stocks Lufthansa and Air France-KLM were added, as part of an ongoing theme of cost cutting and restructuring, and both picks have paid off handsomely thus far.

All told, we still think highly of this fund. It remains to be seen whether the addition of Lazard was a good decision by Vanguard, but at least two great management teams and very modest cost argue in the fund's favor.

Address:	PO Box 2600 Valley Forge PA 19482 800-997-2798	Minimum Purchase:	$3000 Add: $100 IRA: $3000
		Min Auto Inv Plan:	$3000 Add: $50
		Sales Fees:	No-load, 2.00%R
Web Address:	www.vanguard.com	Management Fee:	0.46%
Inception:	05-16-83	Actual Fees:	Mgt:0.40%
Advisor:	Hansberger Global Investors, Inc.	Expense Projections:	3Yr:$141 5Yr:$246 10Yr:$555
Subadvisor:	None	Income Distrib:	Annually
NTF Plans:	Vanguard NTF		

Historical Profile

Return	Above Avg
Risk	Above Avg
Rating	★★★★ Above Avg

Investment Style: Equity Stock %

98% 94% 92% 94% 92% 96% 90% 92% 92%

▼ Manager Change
▽ Partial Manager Change

Growth of $10,000
■ Investment Values of Fund
— Investment Values of MSCI EAFE

26.0 / 22.0 / 18.0 / 14.0 / 10.0

Performance Quartile (within Category)

	1995	1996	1997	1998	1999	2000	2001	2002	2003	2004	2005	2006	History
	31.11	27.54	22.64	25.09	29.12	26.03	22.07	18.83	26.24	30.93	34.82	40.27	NAV
	9.65	10.22	-4.58	19.46	21.77	-7.42	-14.05	-13.35	41.90	19.77	17.96	27.15	Total Return %
	-1.56	4.17	-6.36	-0.47	-5.26	6.77	7.37	2.59	3.31	-0.48	4.42	0.81	+/-MSCI EAFE
	-1.76	3.35	-6.85	0.77	-6.21	5.94	7.34	2.45	2.48	-0.61	3.49	1.44	+/-MSCI Wd xUS
	2.54	2.67	2.57	4.76	2.63	2.53	1.15	1.31	2.44	1.83	1.81	2.53	Income Return %
	7.11	7.55	-7.15	14.70	19.14	-9.95	-15.20	-14.66	39.46	17.94	16.15	24.62	Capital Return %
	65	67	98	15	92	9	7	19	6	19	15	21	Total Rtn % Rank Cat
	0.79	0.82	0.69	1.06	0.66	0.73	0.30	0.29	0.46	0.48	0.56	0.88	Income $
	2.52	5.77	2.95	0.90	0.73	0.19	0.00	0.00	0.00	0.00	1.10	3.09	Capital Gains $
	0.47	0.50	0.49	0.52	0.59	0.53	0.64	0.65	0.62	0.56	0.50	0.45	Expense Ratio %
	2.29	2.50	2.36	2.77	2.54	1.94	1.93	1.80	2.46	1.99	2.26	2.61	Income Ratio %
	47	82	37	39	41	78	37	26	27	74	32	36	Turnover Rate %
	988	917	777	806	1,045	835	895	1,104	1,704	2,663	4,127	7,681	Net Assets $mil

Rating and Risk

Time Period	Load-Adj Return %	Morningstar Rtn vs Cat	Morningstar Risk vs Cat	Morningstar Risk-Adj Rating
1 Yr	27.15			
3 Yr	21.56	+Avg	+Avg	★★★★
5 Yr	17.17	High	+Avg	★★★★★
10 Yr	9.33	+Avg	Avg	★★★★
Incept	12.04			

Other Measures	Standard Index MSCI EAFE	Best Fit Index MSCI Wd xUS
Alpha	0.5	0.5
Beta	1.06	1.05
R-Squared	95	95
Standard Deviation	10.37	
Mean	21.56	
Sharpe Ratio	1.65	

Portfolio Analysis 09-30-06

Share change since 06-06 Total Stocks:215	Sector	Country	% Assets
⊕ Total SA	Energy	France	1.89
ING Groep	Financial	Netherlands	1.84
⊕ Vodafone Grp	Telecom	U.K.	1.70
⊕ ENI	Energy	Italy	1.53
⊕ Credit Suisse Grp	Financial	Switzerland	1.37
⊖ Canon	Goods	Japan	1.37
⊖ AstraZeneca	Health	U.K.	1.28
Credit Agricole	Financial	France	1.26
Royal Bank Of Scotland G	Financial	U.K.	1.24
⊕ BNP Paribas	Financial	France	1.22
HBOS	Financial	U.K.	1.20
⊖ E.On	Utilities	Germany	1.14
⊕ Novartis	Health	Switzerland	1.01
⊕ Sanofi-Synthelabo	Health	France	0.97
⊕ Sumitomo Mitsui Financia	Financial	Japan	0.96
Carrefour	Consumer	France	0.94
Renault	Goods	France	0.90
⊕ HSBC Hldgs	Financial	U.K.	0.90
⊕ Nissan Motor	Goods	Japan	0.89
⊕ Societe Generale Grp	Financial	France	0.88

Current Investment Style

Value Blnd Growth — Large Mid Small

Market Cap	%
Giant	58.1
Large	31.9
Mid	9.2
Small	0.8
Micro	0.0

Avg $mil: 28,327

Value Measures		Rel Category
Price/Earnings	7.45	0.57
Price/Book	1.86	0.86
Price/Sales	1.07	0.92
Price/Cash Flow	7.14	0.86
Dividend Yield %	3.42	1.17

Growth Measures	%	Rel Category
Long-Term Erngs	10.69	0.91
Book Value	9.80	1.07
Sales	7.05	1.08
Cash Flow	6.63	0.80
Historical Erngs	8.68	0.43

Composition

Cash	5.5	Bonds	0.0
Stocks	92.3	Other	2.2
Foreign	(% of Stock)		99.6

Sector Weightings	% of Stocks	Rel MSCI EAFE	3 Year High	Low
☎ Info	12.82	1.08		
Software	0.76	1.36	1	0
Hardware	3.84	0.99	6	3
Media	2.64	1.44	3	0
Telecom	5.58	1.00	7	5
☞ Service	46.15	0.98		
Health	6.88	0.97	9	7
Consumer	3.35	0.68	6	3
Business	3.42	0.67	7	2
Financial	32.50	1.08	33	24
Mfg	41.01	1.00		
Goods	14.99	1.14	17	13
Ind Mtrls	12.94	0.84	19	13
Energy	9.37	1.31	12	6
Utilities	3.71	0.71	4	2

Regional Exposure	% Stock		
UK/W. Europe	57	N. America	4
Japan	21	Latn America	4
Asia X Japan	12	Other	2

Country Exposure	% Stock		
Japan	21	Switzerland	5
U.K.	20	Germany	5
France	14		

Morningstar® Funds 500

Vanguard IntTm Inv-Gr Fd

	Ticker	Load	NAV	Yield	SEC Yield	Total Assets	Mstar Category
	VFICX	None	$9.71	5.0%	5.19%	$5,197 mil	Intermediate-Term Bond

Governance and Management

Stewardship Grade: B

Portfolio Manager(s)

Manager Bob Auwaerter is responsible for the fund's day-to-day management and has been with the fund since its 1993 inception. Ian MacKinnon (former head of Vanguard's fixed-income group) previously set the fund's duration range. Auwaerter, his successor, has assumed that role. The team also includes an assistant portfolio manager, six credit analysts, and traders.

Strategy

Traditionally, this fund has invested mainly in midquality (A and BBB rated) investment-grade corporate bonds. Since a July 2004 modification to its mandate, though, the managers can invest a bit more broadly. The fund's duration is limited to a range of 4.75 to 6.25 years, which typically makes it a bit more sensitive to rate shifts than most of its intermediate-term bond peers. Manager Bob Auwaerter also invests modestly in highly rated asset-backed securities when the outlook for corporates dims.

Performance 12-31-06

	1st Qtr	2nd Qtr	3rd Qtr	4th Qtr	Total
2002	0.01	2.90	5.50	1.57	10.28
2003	1.97	4.01	-0.20	0.42	6.29
2004	3.12	-3.21	3.85	1.07	4.75
2005	-0.87	3.31	-0.83	0.41	1.97
2006	-0.95	-0.30	4.20	1.49	4.43

Trailing	Total Return%	+/- LB Aggr	+/- LB 5-10YR	%Rank Cat	Growth of $10,000
3 Mo	1.49	0.25	0.41	23	10,149
6 Mo	5.75	0.66	0.07	11	10,575
1 Yr	4.43	0.10	0.62	26	10,443
3 Yr Avg	3.71	0.01	0.07	29	11,155
5 Yr Avg	5.51	0.45	-0.41	13	13,076
10 Yr Avg	6.29	0.05	-0.39	12	18,405
15 Yr Avg	—				

Tax Analysis	Tax-Adj Rtn%	%Rank Cat	Tax-Cost Rat	%Rank Cat
3 Yr (estimated)	1.93	33	1.72	68
5 Yr (estimated)	3.54	14	1.87	70
10 Yr (estimated)	3.89	13	2.26	75

Potential Capital Gain Exposure: -1% of assets

Morningstar's Take by Dan Culloton 11-20-06

There are only a couple of reasons to own Vanguard Intermediate-Term Investment-Grade, but they're pretty good ones.

The most obvious and effective arrow in this fund's quiver is its low expense ratio. Its 0.21% levy is less than one third of the median expense ratio of no-load intermediate-term bond funds. That gives the offering a built-in advantage over its rivals over the long term.

This fund's second attractive feature flows from the first. Its low expenses allow the fund to avoid taking outlandish risks to provide a competitive yield and potential total return. However, with a portfolio mostly full of corporate bonds and a longer-than-average duration (a measure of interest-rate sensitivity), the fund is no wallflower. Indeed, its volatility, as measured by standard deviation, is above the category average, and it has looked a little haggard for short periods in the past when rates rise or non-corporate-bond sectors lead the market.

Over longer periods, though, the fund, which is broadly diversified over more than 500 bonds, has delivered above-average risk-adjusted returns. Because the fund's expense hurdle is lower than the vast majority of its peers, there's no pressure to load up on riskier but higher-yielding--and possibly higher-returning--bonds below investment grade. The fund usually owns some bonds rated BB or lower, but it can afford to keep that stake small (it was less than 2% of the fund on Oct. 31, 2006) without ceding much ground to rivals.

This is a simple approach that has served the fund well over time. It has completed seven of the last 10 calendar years in the top half of the category and never ended an annual campaign in the bottom fourth of its peer group. Many of the pieces are in place for continued success: veteran management, a repeatable strategy, a high-quality portfolio, and rock-bottom expenses. All this makes the fund a good choice to use for dedicated corporate-bond exposure.

Address:	PO Box 2600	Minimum Purchase:	$3000	Add: $100	IRA: $3000
	Valley Forge PA 19482	Min Auto Inv Plan:	$3000	Add: $50	
	800-997-2798	Sales Fees:	No-load		
Web Address:	www.vanguard.com	Management Fee:	0.18%		
Inception:	11-01-93	Actual Fees:	Mgt:0.18%	Dist: —	
Advisor:	Vanguard Advisers, Inc.	Expense Projections:	3Yr:$68	5Yr:$118	10Yr:$268
Subadvisor:	None	Income Distrib:	Monthly		
NTF Plans:	Vanguard NTF				

Historical Profile

Return	Above Avg
Risk	Above Avg
Rating	★★★★ Above Avg

| 18 | 15 | 9 | 10 | 9 | 13 | 14 | 15 | | | |

▼ Manager Change
▽ Partial Manager Change

Growth of $10,000

■ Investment Values of Fund
— Investment Values of LB Aggr

20.5 / 17.5 / 15.0 / 12.5 / 10.0

Performance Quartile (within Category)

1995	1996	1997	1998	1999	2000	2001	2002	2003	2004	2005	2006	History
10.15	9.75	9.94	10.03	9.21	9.49	9.73	10.11	10.13	10.07	9.78	9.71	NAV
21.39	2.78	8.94	8.30	-1.53	10.70	9.42	10.28	6.29	4.75	1.97	4.43	Total Return %
2.92	-0.85	-0.71	-0.39	-0.71	-0.93	0.98	0.03	2.19	0.41	-0.46	0.10	+/-LB Aggr
-0.04	0.09	-0.49	-1.84	1.35	-1.74	0.60	-2.75	0.32	-0.55	0.14	0.62	+/-LB 5-10YR
7.60	6.49	6.75	6.53	6.40	7.42	6.88	6.19	5.31	4.79	4.73	5.10	Income Return %
13.79	-3.71	2.19	1.77	-7.93	3.28	2.54	4.09	0.98	-0.04	-2.76	-0.67	Capital Return %
11	65	55	28	57	36	10	10	26	24	41	26	Total Rtn % Rank Cat
0.66	0.64	0.64	0.63	0.62	0.66	0.63	0.59	0.52	0.47	0.47	0.49	Income $
0.00	0.02	0.01	0.08	0.05	0.00	0.00	0.00	0.08	0.06	0.02	0.00	Capital Gains $
0.28	0.28	0.25	0.26	0.27	0.25	0.22	0.21	0.20	0.20	0.20	0.21	Expense Ratio %
6.46	6.70	6.61	6.51	6.25	6.60	7.17	6.99	5.87	4.90	4.70	4.71	Income Ratio %
97	78	85	69	71	67	85	118	84	55	40	51	Turnover Rate %
361	617	868	1,181	1,457	1,920	2,015	2,498	2,747	3,145	2,451	2,432	Net Assets $mil

Rating and Risk

Time Period	Load-Adj Return %	Morningstar Rtn vs Cat	Morningstar Risk vs Cat	Morningstar Risk-Adj Rating
1 Yr	4.43			
3 Yr	3.71	+Avg	High	★★★★
5 Yr	5.51	+Avg	+Avg	★★★★
10 Yr	6.29	+Avg	+Avg	★★★★
Incept	6.19			

Other Measures	Standard Index LB Aggr	Best Fit Index LB 5-10YR
Alpha	0.0	0.1
Beta	1.14	0.83
R-Squared	98	99
Standard Deviation	3.75	
Mean	3.71	
Sharpe Ratio	0.13	

Portfolio Analysis 09-30-06

Total Fixed-Income:510	Date of Maturity	Amount $000	Value $000	% Net Assets
US Treasury Note 4.875%	02-15-12	166,800	169,120	3.37
US Treasury Note 4.25%	08-15-13	83,900	82,117	1.64
US Treasury Note 4%	02-15-14	80,200	77,105	1.54
US Treasury Note 4.25%	11-15-13	78,630	76,898	1.53
General Elec Cap 5.875%	02-15-12	49,600	51,149	1.02
Wal Mart Stores 4.125%	02-15-11	34,000	32,730	0.65
US Treasury Note 4.25%	08-15-14	33,400	32,586	0.65
United Tech 6.35%	03-01-11	30,600	31,970	0.64
Wachovia Cap Tr Iii FRN	03-15-42	31,500	31,565	0.63
Mbna Cc Master Tr 2006-2	06-15-15	31,000	31,095	0.62
Daimler-Benz North Amerc	09-08-11	30,000	29,860	0.59
LEHMAN BROS HLDGS	05-17-13	28,000	28,492	0.57
Nabisco 7.55%	06-15-15	25,000	28,470	0.57
Hsbc Fin Cap Tr Ix FRN	11-30-35	27,500	27,504	0.55
France Telecom Sa 7.75%	03-01-11	25,000	27,390	0.55
General Elec Cap 6%	06-15-12	25,000	25,987	0.52
Citigroup FRN	06-09-09	25,700	25,771	0.51
Usaa Cap 144A 4.64%	12-15-09	26,000	25,566	0.51
Amer Gen Fin Medtm Srnt	06-01-13	25,000	25,554	0.51
Citibank Ccit 2005-A8 FR	10-20-14	25,000	25,085	0.50

Current Investment Style

Duration: Short Int Long

Quality: High Med Low

¹ figure provided by fund

Avg Eff Duration¹	5.0 Yrs
Avg Eff Maturity	6.5 Yrs
Avg Credit Quality	A
Avg Wtd Coupon	5.28%
Avg Wtd Price	100.31% of par

Coupon Range	% of Bonds	Rel Cat
0% PIK	3.0	0.4
0% to 6%	74.1	1.0
6% to 8%	24.1	1.1
8% to 10%	1.7	0.4
More than 10%	0.1	0.1

1.00=Category Average

Credit Analysis		% bonds 09-30-06	
AAA	29	BB	1
AA	14	B	0
A	35	Below B	0
BBB	21	NR/NA	0

Sector Breakdown	% of assets
US Treasuries	11
TIPS	0
US Agency	0
Mortgage Pass-Throughs	0
Mortgage CMO	1
Mortgage ARM	0
US Corporate	75
Asset-Backed	9
Convertible	0
Municipal	0
Corporate Inflation-Protected	0
Foreign Corporate	2
Foreign Govt	1

Composition			
Cash	2.3	Bonds	97.2
Stocks	0.0	Other	0.4

Special Securities	
Restricted/Illiquid Secs	11
Exotic Mortgage-Backed	0
Emerging-Markets Secs	Trace
Options/Futures/Warrants	No

Vanguard IntTm T/E

Analyst Pick ✓

	Ticker	Load	NAV	Yield	SEC Yield	Total Assets	Mstar Category
	VWITX	None	$13.35	4.2%	3.70%	$14,605 mil	Muni National Interm

Governance and Management

Stewardship Grade: B

Portfolio Manager(s)

Christopher Ryon has had day-to-day responsibilities for this fund since 1991. Bob Auwaerter, Vanguard's fixed-income director, sets the fund's duration range.

Strategy

This fund invests in municipal securities from many states. It invests at least 75% of assets in bonds rated AAA, AA, or A. No more than 20% of assets can be invested in bonds rated BBB. Up to 5% can be invested in below-investment-grade bonds. Management makes modest duration bets within a specified range, depending on its interest-rate outlook. However, the fund's rate sensitivity tends to be below average.

Performance 12-31-06

	1st Qtr	2nd Qtr	3rd Qtr	4th Qtr	Total
2002	0.91	3.57	3.25	-0.00	7.91
2003	0.60	2.57	0.29	0.94	4.46
2004	1.22	-1.92	3.30	0.66	3.23
2005	-0.70	2.61	-0.32	0.67	2.24
2006	0.13	-0.01	3.22	1.05	4.43

Trailing	Total Return%	+/- LB Muni	+/- LB Muni 10YR	%Rank Cat	Growth of $10,000
3 Mo	1.05	-0.06	0.13	7	10,105
6 Mo	4.30	-0.25	-0.47	15	10,430
1 Yr	4.43	-0.41	-0.28	15	10,443
3 Yr Avg	3.29	-0.99	-0.57	26	11,020
5 Yr Avg	4.44	-1.09	-1.02	39	12,426
10 Yr Avg	4.85	-0.91	-0.85	27	16,058
15 Yr Avg	5.59	-0.67	-0.69	28	22,612

Tax Analysis	Tax-Adj Rtn%	%Rank Cat	Tax-Cost Rat	%Rank Cat
3 Yr (estimated)	3.30	18	0.00	1
5 Yr (estimated)	4.42	29	0.02	8
10 Yr (estimated)	4.82	21	0.03	13

Potential Capital Gain Exposure: 2% of assets

Historical Profile

Return	Above Avg
Risk	Average
Rating	★★★★ Above Avg

	12	9	16	14	16	20	15	14

Investment Style
Fixed Income
Income Rtn %Rank Cat

▼ Manager Change
▽ Partial Manager Change

20.8 / 18.8

16.4 **Growth of $10,000**
14.0 ─ Investment Values of Fund
12.0
10.0 ─ Investment Values of LB Muni

Performance Quartile (within Category)

1995	1996	1997	1998	1999	2000	2001	2002	2003	2004	2005	2006	History
13.36	13.23	13.42	13.48	12.77	13.27	13.27	13.66	13.70	13.58	13.33	13.35	NAV
13.64	4.20	7.06	5.76	-0.50	9.24	5.05	7.91	4.46	3.23	2.24	4.43	Total Return %
-3.82	-0.23	-2.13	-0.72	1.56	-2.44	-0.08	-1.69	-0.85	-1.25	-1.27	-0.41	+/-LB Muni
-3.53	-0.34	-2.17	-1.00	0.75	-1.52	0.43	-2.26	-1.24	-0.92	-0.50	-0.28	+/-LB Muni 10YR
5.60	5.12	5.18	5.02	4.89	5.18	4.87	4.62	4.15	4.10	4.11	4.25	Income Return %
8.04	-0.92	1.88	0.74	-5.39	4.06	0.18	3.29	0.31	-0.87	-1.87	0.18	Capital Return %
51	30	72	38	10	54	18	68	33	30	34	15	Total Rtn % Rank Cat
0.68	0.67	0.67	0.66	0.65	0.65	0.63	0.60	0.56	0.55	0.55	0.56	Income $
0.01	0.00	0.05	0.04	0.00	0.00	0.03	0.04	0.00	0.00	0.00	0.00	Capital Gains $
0.21	0.20	0.19	0.21	0.18	0.18	0.19	0.17	0.17	0.14	0.16	0.16	Expense Ratio %
5.35	5.09	5.07	4.93	4.83	5.03	4.77	4.48	4.13	4.05	4.06	4.19	Income Ratio %
12	14	15	14	17	17	13	13	19	10	12	8	Turnover Rate %
5,770	6,123	6,891	7,896	7,920	8,925	6,653	7,338	6,970	6,897	4,682	4,901	Net Assets $mil

Rating and Risk

Time Period	Load-Adj Return %	Morningstar Rtn vs Cat	Morningstar Risk vs Cat	Morningstar Risk-Adj Rating
1 Yr	4.43			
3 Yr	3.29	+Avg	+Avg	★★★★
5 Yr	4.44	+Avg	Avg	★★★★
10 Yr	4.85	+Avg	-Avg	★★★★
Incept	5.94			

Other Measures	Standard Index LB Muni	Best Fit Index LB Muni 10YR
Alpha	-0.9	-0.5
Beta	0.94	0.81
R-Squared	97	98
Standard Deviation	2.96	
Mean	3.29	
Sharpe Ratio	0.02	

Portfolio Analysis 09-30-06

Total Fixed-Income:1120

	Date of Maturity	Amount $000	Value $000	% Net Assets
Garden St N J Preservati	11-01-28	140,220	171,761	1.23
California St Econ Recov	07-01-15	93,700	102,106	0.73
New Jersey St Transn Tr	12-15-20	83,500	97,070	0.69
New Jersey Econ Dev Auth	09-01-23	81,630	95,694	0.69
Missouri St Hwys & Trans	05-01-24	88,030	94,473	0.68
CALIFORNIA ST DEPT WTR R	05-01-16	77,880	86,435	0.62
Massachusetts St 5.5%	11-01-16	75,000	85,148	0.61
North Carolina Mun Pwr A	01-01-18	69,720	75,056	0.54
California Statewide Cmn	05-15-25	73,000	73,968	0.53
New Jersey Econ Dev Auth	09-01-24	60,000	70,502	0.50
CALIFORNIA ST DEPT WTR R	05-01-15	61,875	68,449	0.49
Memphis Tenn Elec Sys 5%	12-01-09	60,140	62,750	0.45
Triborough Brdg & Tunl A	01-01-10	55,325	59,542	0.43
BRAZOS RIV TEX HBR NAV D	05-15-33	58,000	59,148	0.42
Massachusetts St 5.5%	11-01-16	50,000	56,766	0.41

Current Investment Style

Avg Eff Duration[1]	4.9 Yrs
Avg Eff Maturity	6.2 Yrs
Avg Credit Quality	AA
Avg Wtd Coupon	5.19%
Avg Wtd Price	106.88% of par

[1]figure provided by fund

Credit Analysis % bonds 09-30-06

AAA	66	BB	0
AA	20	B	0
A	5	Below B	0
BBB	3	NR/NA	5

Top 5 States % bonds

CA	12.1	NY	8.8
TX	9.3	NJ	8.6
MA	9.1		

Composition

Cash	6.6	Bonds	93.4
Stocks	0.0	Other	0.0

Special Securities

Restricted/Illiquid Secs	0
Options/Futures/Warrants	No

Sector Weightings

	% of Bonds	Rel Cat
General Obligation	40.8	1.10
Utilities	21.2	2.24
Health	4.1	0.45
Water/Waste	9.2	1.00
Housing	1.0	0.19
Education	4.5	0.35
Transportation	8.9	1.69
COP/Lease	2.4	0.99
Industrial	7.5	0.82
Misc Revenue	0.0	—
Demand	0.3	0.90

Morningstar's Take by Dan Culloton 12-20-06

Vanguard Intermediate-Term Tax-Exempt's low expenses are reason enough to like it, but it has other desirable attributes.

This fund is cheap. Its 0.16% expense ratio is just about the lowest available to retail investors in the muni national intermediate category. That gives the fund a big head start because expenses consume less of its yield, and ultimately its total return, than its peers. More importantly, the small levy lets the fund's manager build yield without taking on as much risk at its rivals do.

In essence the fund is able to be as cautious as a tortoise and still keep up with the hares. It keeps more than 95% of its portfolio in securities rated A or better, while its typical category peer has less than 90% its assets in bonds of similar quality. Yet, thanks to a low expense ratio, the fund's roughly 4% yield is more than competitive with other more venturesome funds.

The fund manages duration, a measure of interest-rate sensitivity, carefully as well. Veteran manager Christopher Ryon keeps the portfolio's duration within bands set by Vanguard's fixed-income director. With the Federal Reserve apparently at the end of its cycle of interest-rate hikes, the fund has moved its duration out a tad longer than its internal benchmark. That exposes the fund to more interest-rate risk, but no more than its typical peer.

Such a sober approach has a lot of appeal to risk-conscious investors and has served this fund's shareholders well over the long term. The current market environment, however, also may play to this fund's strength. The difference between the yields of bonds with risk profiles closer to that of U.S. Treasury bonds and those of lower-rated securities remains pretty small. So, this fund and its higher-quality portfolio is getting paid almost as much as its competitors that assume more risk with lower-quality portfolios.

This Analyst Pick doesn't give any ground while playing it safe.

Address:	PO Box 2600	Minimum Purchase:	$3000	Add: $100 IRA: $0
	Valley Forge PA 19482	Min Auto Inv Plan:	$3000	Add: $50
	800-997-2798	Sales Fees:	No-load	
Web Address:	www.vanguard.com	Management Fee:	0.14%	
Inception:	09-01-77	Actual Fees:	Mgt:0.14%	Dist: —
Advisor:	Vanguard Advisers, Inc.	Expense Projections:	3Yr:$52	5Yr:$90 10Yr:$205
Subadvisor:	None	Income Distrib:	Monthly	
NTF Plans:	Vanguard NTF			

MORNINGSTAR® Funds 500

Vanguard LifeSt Cons Gr

	Ticker	Load	NAV	Yield	Total Assets	Mstar Category
	VSCGX	None	$16.59	3.1%	$5,567 mil	Conservative Allocation

Governance and Management

Stewardship Grade: B

Portfolio Manager(s)

The fund's trustees oversee the percentage of assets allocated to each of the underlying funds, and they rarely make changes. All of the underlying funds are overseen by experienced and talented managers. Asset Allocation is run by savvy veteran Tom Loeb, for example.

Strategy

This fund of funds invests at least 50% of assets in bonds, but that stake can go as high as 75%. That's because it invests about 25% of its assets in Vanguard Asset Allocation, which actively shifts between the S&P 500 Index and U.S. Treasury bonds based on projected long-term trends. The fund also invests approximately 30% in Total Bond Market Index, 20% in Total Stock Market Index, 20% in Short-Term Investment-Grade, and 5% in Total International Stock Index.

Historical Profile

Return	Above Avg
Risk	Average
Rating	★★★★ Above Avg

Investment Style: Equity, Stock %

32% 36% 31% 39% 39% 42% 46% 45% 45%

▼ Manager Change
▽ Partial Manager Change

Growth of $10,000
■ Investment Values of Fund
— Investment Values of DJ Mod

26.8
22.0
18.0
14.0
10.0

Performance Quartile (within Category)

	1995	1996	1997	1998	1999	2000	2001	2002	2003	2004	2005	2006	History
	11.68	12.14	13.40	14.71	15.10	14.71	14.06	12.82	14.54	15.26	15.49	16.59	NAV
	24.35	10.36	16.81	15.88	7.86	3.12	-0.08	-5.36	16.57	8.02	4.45	10.62	Total Return %
	4.55	-0.30	4.91	3.56	-9.47	4.79	2.72	1.41	-10.81	-4.95	-2.54	-1.68	+/-DJ Mod
	6.19	1.47	2.71	4.15	0.00	-3.67	-3.30	-1.34	-1.09	-0.99	-0.24	3.16	+/-DJ 40%
	4.82	4.61	4.69	4.47	4.35	4.74	4.01	3.53	3.00	2.99	2.91	3.40	Income Return %
	19.53	5.75	12.12	11.41	3.51	-1.62	-4.09	-8.89	13.57	5.03	1.54	7.22	Capital Return %
	26	50	17	9	25	61	56	76	21	15	19	13	Total Rtn % Rank Cat
	0.47	0.53	0.56	0.59	0.63	0.70	0.58	0.49	0.38	0.43	0.44	0.52	Income $
	0.12	0.20	0.19	0.20	0.11	0.16	0.04	0.04	0.00	0.00	0.00	0.25	Capital Gains $
	—	—	—	—	—	—	—	—	—	—	—	0.25	Expense Ratio %
	5.14	4.86	4.61	4.32	4.34	4.73	3.78	3.79	2.92	2.74	2.95	—	Income Ratio %
	1	2	1	3	5	9	14	12	5	5	7	—	Turnover Rate %
	219	462	803	1,416	1,748	1,897	2,026	2,193	2,924	3,650	4,324	5,567	Net Assets $mil

Performance 12-31-06

	1st Qtr	2nd Qtr	3rd Qtr	4th Qtr	Total
2002	0.43	-3.78	-6.74	5.02	-5.36
2003	-1.02	9.02	1.98	5.93	16.57
2004	2.48	-0.74	0.89	5.25	8.02
2005	-1.11	1.93	2.04	1.55	4.45
2006	2.45	-0.49	4.12	4.22	10.62

Trailing	Total Return%	+/- DJ Mod	+/- DJ 40%	%Rank Cat	Growth of $10,000
3 Mo	4.22	-1.37	1.18	20	10,422
6 Mo	8.51	-0.28	1.95	13	10,851
1 Yr	10.62	-1.68	3.16	13	11,062
3 Yr Avg	7.67	-3.05	0.63	14	12,482
5 Yr Avg	6.61	-3.41	-0.12	16	13,772
10 Yr Avg	7.55	-1.00	-0.15	10	20,706
15 Yr Avg	—	—	—		

Tax Analysis	Tax-Adj Rtn%	%Rank Cat	Tax-Cost Rat	%Rank Cat
3 Yr (estimated)	6.66	9	0.94	45
5 Yr (estimated)	5.53	13	1.01	41
10 Yr (estimated)	5.97	11	1.47	34

Potential Capital Gain Exposure: 14% of assets

Rating and Risk

Time Period	Load-Adj Return %	Morningstar Rtn vs Cat	Morningstar Risk vs Cat	Morningstar Risk-Adj Rating
1 Yr	10.62			
3 Yr	7.67	+Avg	Avg	★★★★
5 Yr	6.61	+Avg	+Avg	★★★★
10 Yr	7.55	+Avg	Avg	★★★★
Incept	8.91			

Other Measures	Standard Index DJ Mod	Best Fit Index DJ Mod
Alpha	-0.2	-0.2
Beta	0.62	0.62
R-Squared	90	90
Standard Deviation	3.86	
Mean	7.67	
Sharpe Ratio	1.12	

Portfolio Analysis 09-30-06

Total Stocks:0 Share change since 06-30-06	Sectors	P/E Ratio	YTD Return %	% Net Assets
⊕ Vanguard Total Stock Mkt	—	—	—	19.95
⊕ Vanguard Total Intl Stock	—	—	—	5.02

Total Fixed-Income:0	Date of Maturity	Amount $000	Value $000	% Net Assets
Vanguard Total Bond Marke		154,211	1,539,021	29.95
Vanguard Short-Term Inves		96,905	1,022,347	19.89

Morningstar's Take by William Samuel Rocco 11-03-06

Vanguard LifeStrategy Conservative Growth is distinctive in several respects.

This fund's asset mix isn't as staid as most of its peers' are. In addition to a 20% stake in a large-blend offering and a 5% stake in a foreign large-blend offering, this fund has a 25% position in a hybrid offering, Vanguard Asset Allocation, with the leeway to go all stocks, bonds, or cash based on its manager's quantitative model. This means that this fund's asset mix varies and includes much more than the conservative-allocation norm of 35% in equities whenever Vanguard Asset Allocation invests heavily or completely in stocks.

The benefits of this fund's relatively adventurous asset stance have been quite clear in recent years. Vanguard Asset Allocation has tilted heavily toward equities since mid-2002, and while that was burdensome initially, it has been a boon over the past several years, as stocks have walloped bonds. And thanks to that big edge, as well as the quality of its underlying pure-stock and pure-bond funds,

this fund boasts top-quintile three- and five-year returns.

This fund's strengths don't end there. It also has earned superior 10-year returns, as Vanguard Asset Allocation's composition calls have generally been on the mark in the past. (That fund's long-term gains are very competitive with broad market indexes, such as the S&P 500 Index.) The other underlying offerings also have been pretty successful over time.

Despite its generally oversized equity stake, this fund has not been significantly more volatile than the typical conservative-allocation vehicle. That's because its two pure-equity funds are pretty diversified, its two pure-bond funds are fairly conservative, and Vanguard Asset Allocation has generally been patient as well as accurate with its moves.

This fund, which also enjoys the benefits of low costs, is a superior option for reserved one-stop shoppers.

Address:	PO Box 2600 Valley Forge PA 19482 800-997-2798
Web Address:	www.vanguard.com
Inception:	09-30-94
Advisor:	Vanguard Advisers, Inc.
Subadvisor:	None
NTF Plans:	Vanguard NTF

Minimum Purchase:	$3000	Add: $100	IRA: $3000
Min Auto Inv Plan:	$3000	Add: $50	
Sales Fees:	No-load		
Management Fee:	0.00%		
Actual Fees:	Mgt:0.00%	Dist: —	
Expense Projections:	3Yr:$80	5Yr:$141	10Yr:$318
Income Distrib:	Quarterly		

Equity Style

Style: Blend
Size: Large-Cap

Value Measures		Rel Category
Price/Earnings	14.59	0.97
Price/Book	2.46	1.01
Price/Sales	1.36	0.98
Price/Cash Flow	7.19	0.90
Dividend Yield %	2.00	0.93

Growth Measures	%	Rel Category
Long-Term Erngs	11.35	1.00
Book Value	8.38	1.05
Sales	9.19	1.03
Cash Flow	8.91	0.99
Historical Erngs	14.77	0.86

Market Cap %			
Giant	47.0	Small	2.8
Large	34.4	Micro	0.9
Mid	14.9	Avg $mil:	35,488

Fixed-Income Style

Duration: Interm-Term
Quality: High

Avg Eff Duration [1]	3.6 Yrs
Avg Eff Maturity	5.5 Yrs
Avg Credit Quality	AA
Avg Wtd Coupon	4.87%

[1]figure provided by fund as of 09-30-06

Sector Weightings	% of Stocks	Rel DJ Mod	3 Year High Low	
☁ Info	19.06	—		
▣ Software	3.25	—	4	3
▣ Hardware	8.83	—	10	9
▣ Media	3.29	—	4	3
▣ Telecom	3.69	—	4	3
☐ Service	47.41			
▣ Health	12.07	—	13	12
▣ Consumer	7.58	—	9	8
▣ Business	4.73	—	5	4
▣ Financial	23.03	—	23	21
▣ Mfg	33.54			
▣ Goods	8.78	—	10	9
▣ Ind Mtrls	12.14	—	13	11
▣ Energy	9.07	—	10	6
▣ Utilities	3.55	—	4	3

Composition

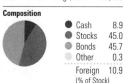

● Cash	8.9	
● Stocks	45.0	
● Bonds	45.7	
○ Other	0.3	
Foreign	10.9	(% of Stock)

Mɔrningstar® Funds 500

Vanguard LifeSt Growth

	Ticker	Load	NAV	Yield	Total Assets	Mstar Category
	VASGX	None	$23.87	2.0%	$8,783 mil	Large Blend

Strategy

This fund of funds invests about 25% of assets in Vanguard Asset Allocation , which actively shifts between the S&P 500 Index and U.S. Treasury bonds based on projected long-term trends. As a result, this fund's equity allocation fluctuates within a fairly wide range of 65% to 90% of assets. The fund also invests approximately 50% in Vanguard Total Stock Market Index, 15% in Vanguard Total International Stock Index, and 10% in Vanguard Total Bond Market Index.

Performance 12-31-06

	1st Qtr	2nd Qtr	3rd Qtr	4th Qtr	Total
2002	0.75	-8.65	-14.91	7.47	-15.84
2003	-3.41	15.20	3.84	11.23	28.52
2004	2.86	0.38	-0.54	9.62	12.58
2005	-1.65	1.57	4.58	2.30	6.88
2006	5.05	-1.20	4.58	6.99	16.13

Trailing	Total Return%	+/- S&P 500	+/- Russ 1000	%Rank Cat	Growth of $10,000
3 Mo	6.99	0.29	0.04	33	10,699
6 Mo	11.89	-0.85	-0.47	42	11,189
1 Yr	16.13	0.34	0.67	18	11,613
3 Yr Avg	11.80	1.36	0.82	19	13,974
5 Yr Avg	8.61	2.42	1.79	12	15,113
10 Yr Avg	8.54	0.12	-0.10	26	22,693
15 Yr Avg	—	—	—	—	—

Tax Analysis	Tax-Adj Rtn%	%Rank Cat	Tax-Cost Rat	%Rank Cat
3 Yr (estimated)	11.19	16	0.55	25
5 Yr (estimated)	8.01	12	0.55	36
10 Yr (estimated)	7.60	24	0.87	38

Potential Capital Gain Exposure: 24% of assets

Historical Profile

Return	Above Avg
Risk	Below Avg
Rating	★★★★ Above Avg

Investment Style: Equity, Stock %

▼ Manager Change
▽ Partial Manager Change

Growth of $10,000
■ Investment Values of Fund
— Investment Values of S&P 500

Return percentages across years: 60% 74% 59% 79% 78% 81% 85% 84% 85%

Performance Quartile (within Category)

1995	1996	1997	1998	1999	2000	2001	2002	2003	2004	2005	2006	History
12.36	13.68	16.04	18.79	21.41	19.59	17.43	14.36	18.16	20.04	21.00	23.87	NAV
29.24	15.41	22.26	21.40	17.32	-5.44	-8.86	-15.84	28.52	12.58	6.88	16.13	Total Return %
-8.34	-7.55	-11.10	-7.18	-3.72	3.66	3.03	6.26	-0.16	1.70	1.97	0.34	+/-S&P 500
-8.53	-7.04	-10.59	-5.62	-3.59	2.35	3.59	5.81	-1.37	1.18	0.61	0.67	+/-Russ 1000
3.14	2.85	2.79	2.57	2.41	2.41	1.90	1.85	1.96	2.16	2.06	2.35	Income Return %
26.10	12.56	19.47	18.83	14.91	-7.85	-10.76	-17.69	26.56	10.42	4.82	13.78	Capital Return %
78	92	81	54	64	47	26	10	34	22	34	18	Total Rtn % Rank Cat
0.31	0.35	0.38	0.41	0.45	0.51	0.37	0.32	0.28	0.39	0.41	0.49	Income $
0.15	0.23	0.29	0.27	0.16	0.17	0.06	0.00	0.00	0.00	0.00	0.00	Capital Gains $
											0.26	Expense Ratio %
3.67	3.18	2.84	2.53	2.50	4.73	1.53	2.12	1.79	1.79	2.09	—	Income Ratio %
1	—	1	2	1	9	7	7	2	5	4	—	Turnover Rate %
217	629	1,184	1,924	3,177	3,738	3,726	3,281	4,754	6,040	7,001	8,783	Net Assets $mil

Rating and Risk

Time Period	Load-Adj Return %	Morningstar Rtn vs Cat	Morningstar Risk vs Cat	Morningstar Risk-Adj Rating
1 Yr	16.13			
3 Yr	11.80	+Avg	-Avg	★★★★
5 Yr	8.61	+Avg	-Avg	★★★★
10 Yr	8.54	+Avg	Low	★★★★
Incept	10.45			

Other Measures	Standard Index S&P 500	Best Fit Index Russ 1000
Alpha	1.6	1.3
Beta	0.95	0.92
R-Squared	95	96
Standard Deviation	6.72	
Mean	11.80	
Sharpe Ratio	1.23	

Portfolio Analysis 09-30-06

Share change since 06-06 Total Stocks:0	Sector	PE	Tot Ret%	% Assets
⊕ Vanguard Total Stock Mkt	—	—	—	49.89
⊕ Vanguard Asset Allocatio	—	—	—	24.98
⊕ Vanguard Total Intl Stoc	—	—	—	15.02
⊕ Vanguard Total Bond Mark	—	—	—	10.00

Morningstar's Take by William Samuel Rocco 11-03-06

Vanguard LifeStrategy Growth provides exceptional broad exposure at a very low price.

This fund of funds delivers ample diversification in one package. It devotes 50% of its assets to Vanguard Total Stock Market Index and 15% of its assets to Vanguard Total International Stock Index, so it always has a sizable and broad overseas stake as well as a big and wide-ranging domestic position. It also always has an expansive slug of investment-grade bonds, due to its 10% investment in Vanguard Total Bond Market Index. And its fourth underlying offering, Vanguard Asset Allocation, adds to its diversification value because that offering tracks the Lehman Brothers Long-Term Treasury Index and the S&P 500 Index after making marked composition calls.

This fund's exceptionally diversified portfolio is available at an extremely low price. It does not add on its own layer of fees--as many funds of funds do--and all four of its underlying offerings are cheap. Thus, it sports a very fetching 0.26%

average weighted expense ratio.

This fund has much more than portfolio and price appeal. Its three-, five-, and 10-year returns all rank in the large-blend group's top third, as its stock breadth has been a boon in recent years, Vanguard Asset Allocation's composition calls have generally been on the mark, and its low costs and Vanguard indexing skill have consistently paid off. The fund has also been less volatile than its average peer, thanks to its bond stake and overall breadth.

All this means that this fund is a terrific option for one-stop shoppers who are seeking long-term capital appreciation without taking on too much risk. One-stop shoppers with more conservative goals should note that there are three other Vanguard LifeStrategy funds with more reserved makeups.

Current Investment Style

Value Blnd Growth — Large Mid Small

Market Cap	%
Giant	45.5
Large	33.1
Mid	16.4
Small	3.7
Micro	1.2

Avg $mil: 31,017

Value Measures		Rel Category
Price/Earnings	15.08	0.98
Price/Book	2.39	0.93
Price/Sales	1.30	0.93
Price/Cash Flow	7.20	0.85
Dividend Yield %	2.08	1.19

Growth Measures	%	Rel Category
Long-Term Erngs	11.52	0.97
Book Value	8.24	0.91
Sales	8.80	0.91
Cash Flow	8.71	0.84
Historical Erngs	17.62	0.95

Profitability	%	Rel Category
Return on Equity	18.88	0.97
Return on Assets	9.58	0.92
Net Margin	13.31	0.99

Sector Weightings	% of Stocks	Rel S&P 500	3 Year High Low	
↻ Info	18.58	0.93		
Software	3.10	0.90	4	3
Hardware	8.46	0.92	10	8
Media	3.18	0.84	4	3
Telecom	3.84	1.09	4	4
⊂ Service	47.42	1.03		
Health	11.70	0.97	12	12
Consumer	7.38	0.96	9	7
Business	4.98	1.18	5	5
Financial	23.36	1.05	23	21
Mfg	34.01	1.01		
Goods	8.97	1.05	10	9
Ind Mtrls	12.43	1.04	13	11
Energy	9.03	0.92	10	6
Utilities	3.58	1.02	4	3

Composition

	%
● Cash	5.1
● Stocks	84.5
● Bonds	9.9
● Other	0.5
Foreign	17.2
(% of Stock)	

MORNINGSTAR® Funds 500

Vanguard LifeSt Income

Ticker	Load	NAV	Yield	Total Assets	Mstar Category
VASIX	None	$13.93	3.9%	$1,690 mil	Conservative Allocation

Governance and Management

Stewardship Grade: B

Portfolio Manager(s)

The fund's trustees oversee the percentage of assets allocated to each of the underlying funds, and they rarely make changes. All of the underlying funds are run by experienced and talented managers.

Strategy

This fund of funds invests predominantly in bond funds, but its equity exposure can fluctuate between 5% and 30%. That's because it invests about 25% of assets in Vanguard Asset Allocation, which actively shifts between the S&P 500 Index and U.S. Treasury bonds based on projected long-term trends. The fund also invests approximately 50% in Vanguard Total Bond Market Index, 20% in Vanguard Short-Term Investment-Grade, and 5% in Vanguard Total Stock Market Index. The fund does not have any dedicated foreign-stock exposure.

Performance 12-31-06

	1st Qtr	2nd Qtr	3rd Qtr	4th Qtr	Total
2002	0.16	-1.18	-2.49	3.74	0.12
2003	0.08	6.20	1.01	3.18	10.77
2004	2.43	-1.41	1.75	3.17	6.01
2005	-0.88	2.25	0.74	1.11	3.23
2006	1.11	-0.28	3.97	2.96	7.93

Trailing	Total Return%	+/- DJ Mod	+/- DJ 40%	%Rank Cat	Growth of $10,000
3 Mo	2.96	-2.63	-0.08	67	10,296
6 Mo	7.05	-1.74	0.49	38	10,705
1 Yr	7.93	-4.37	0.47	50	10,793
3 Yr Avg	5.71	-5.01	-1.33	53	11,813
5 Yr Avg	5.55	-4.47	-1.18	46	13,101
10 Yr Avg	6.95	-1.60	-0.75	19	19,580
15 Yr Avg	—	—	—	—	—

Tax Analysis	Tax-Adj Rtn%	%Rank Cat	Tax-Cost Rat	%Rank Cat
3 Yr (estimated)	4.42	47	1.22	65
5 Yr (estimated)	4.20	47	1.28	65
10 Yr (estimated)	5.08	18	1.75	63

Potential Capital Gain Exposure: 8% of assets

Historical Profile

Return Above Avg
Risk Below Avg
Rating ★★★★ Above Avg

	17%	15%	16%	19%	20%	22%	26%	25%	25%	

Investment Style
Equity
Stock %

▼ Manager Change
▽ Partial Manager Change

26.8
22.0 Growth of $10,000
18.0 ─ Investment Values of Fund
14.0 ─ Investment Values of DJ Mod
10.0

Performance Quartile (within Category)

1995	1996	1997	1998	1999	2000	2001	2002	2003	2004	2005	2006	History
11.54	11.55	12.43	13.22	12.82	13.01	12.86	12.32	13.20	13.53	13.49	13.93	NAV
22.99	7.65	14.23	13.17	2.82	8.06	4.06	0.12	10.77	6.01	3.23	7.93	Total Return %
3.19	-3.01	2.33	0.85	-14.51	9.73	6.86	6.89	-16.61	-6.96	-3.76	-4.37	+/-DJ Mod
4.83	-1.24	0.13	1.44	-5.04	1.27	0.84	4.14	-6.89	-3.00	-1.46	0.47	+/-DJ 40%
5.04	5.66	5.56	5.16	5.32	5.92	5.06	4.35	3.53	3.45	3.52	4.06	Income Return %
17.95	1.99	8.67	8.01	-2.50	2.14	-1.00	-4.23	7.24	2.56	-0.29	3.87	Capital Return %
32	75	34	18	76	12	9	18	71	52	55	50	Total Rtn % Rank Cat
0.49	0.64	0.63	0.63	0.69	0.74	0.65	0.55	0.43	0.45	0.47	0.54	Income $
0.09	0.21	0.10	0.19	0.07	0.08	0.02	0.00	0.00	0.00	0.00	0.07	Capital Gains $
											0.25	Expense Ratio %
5.76	5.66	5.54	5.24	5.37	5.84	4.87	4.64	3.53	3.31	3.47	—	Income Ratio %
4	22	6	3	11	17	4	10	4	4	4	—	Turnover Rate %
121	151	244	449	555	632	809	1,028	1,404	1,654	1,708	1,690	Net Assets $mil

Rating and Risk

Time Period	Load-Adj Return %	Morningstar Rtn vs Cat	Morningstar Risk vs Cat	Morningstar Risk-Adj Rating
1 Yr	7.93			
3 Yr	5.71	Avg	-Avg	★★★
5 Yr	5.55	Avg	-Avg	★★★
10 Yr	6.95	+Avg	-Avg	★★★★
Incept	8.10			

Other Measures	Standard Index DJ Mod	Best Fit Index DJ Mod
Alpha	-0.4	-0.4
Beta	0.38	0.38
R-Squared	61	61
Standard Deviation	2.91	
Mean	5.71	
Sharpe Ratio	0.83	

Portfolio Analysis 09-30-06

Total Stocks:0 Share change since 06-30-06	Sectors	P/E Ratio	YTD Return %	% Net Assets
⊖ Vanguard Total Stock Mkt	—	—	—	5.02

Total Fixed-Income:0	Date of Maturity	Amount $000	Value $000	% Net Assets
Vanguard Total Bond Marke		82,353	821,888	49.94
Vanguard Short-Term Inves		30,989	326,932	19.86

Morningstar's Take by William Samuel Rocco 11-03-06

Conservative income-oriented investors should be very comfortable at Vanguard LifeStrategy Income.

This fund has two major advantages over its peers when it comes to yield. The first is its asset mix. This fund of funds never devotes less than 70% of its assets to bonds--and it invests even more in that asset class whenever Vanguard Asset Allocation shifts toward fixed-income securities--while most conservative-allocation offerings keep 50% to 60% of their assets in bonds. (Please note that Vanguard Short-Term Investment Grade, which is 20% of this fund's assets, invests some of its portfolio in bonds with maturities of less than one year, and such securities show up as cash in our composition breakdown.)

This fund's cost structure also serves to enhance its yield. Unlike many funds of funds, this one does not tack on its own layer of fees, and its four underlying funds are cheap, so it sports an average weighted expense ratio of just 0.25%. And due to its expense edge, as well as its asset-allocation

advantage, this fund's yield is normally much higher than the conservative-allocation norm and rather attractive in its own right.

This fund's strengths don't end there. Thanks to the moderating influence of its yield, as well as its cautious asset mix and the conservative nature of most of its underlying offerings, this fund has been significantly less volatile than most of its peers and pretty tame in absolute terms.

Conservative income-oriented investors should like these traits, but they should also recognize that this fund's approach has drawbacks. This fund's oversized bond position puts it at a real disadvantage during rising-rate environments and during sustained equity rallies, as its so-so returns in recent years attest. Therefore, interested investors should be prepared for periods of sluggish performance and should expect solid rather than superior long-term returns.

Address:	PO Box 2600 Valley Forge PA 19482 800-997-2798	Minimum Purchase:	$3000	Add: $100	IRA: $3000
		Min Auto Inv Plan:	$3000	Add: $50	
		Sales Fees:	No-load		
Web Address:	www.vanguard.com	Management Fee:	0.00%		
Inception:	09-30-94	Actual Fees:	Mgt:0.00%	Dist: —	
Advisor:	Vanguard Advisers, Inc.	Expense Projections:	3Yr:$80	5Yr:$141	10Yr:$318
Subadvisor:	None	Income Distrib:	Quarterly		
NTF Plans:	Vanguard NTF				

Equity Style

Style: Blend
Size: Large-Cap

Value Measures		Rel Category
Price/Earnings	15.24	1.01
Price/Book	2.55	1.05
Price/Sales	1.43	1.03
Price/Cash Flow	7.15	0.90
Dividend Yield %	1.90	0.89

Growth Measures	%	Rel Category
Long-Term Erngs	11.23	0.99
Book Value	8.56	1.08
Sales	9.69	1.09
Cash Flow	9.22	1.02
Historical Erngs	17.18	1.00

Market Cap %			
Giant	49.2	Small	1.3
Large	36.6	Micro	0.4
Mid	12.5	Avg $mil:	44,657

Fixed-Income Style

Duration: Interm-Term
Quality: High

Avg Eff Duration [1]	3.9 Yrs
Avg Eff Maturity	6.0 Yrs
Avg Credit Quality	AA
Avg Wtd Coupon	5.04%

[1]figure provided by fund as of 09-30-06

Sector Weightings	% of Stocks	Rel DJ Mod	3 Year High Low	
↻ Info	19.94	—		
Software	3.53	—	4	3
Hardware	9.47	—	11	9
Media	3.49	—	4	3
Telecom	3.45	—	4	3
☞ Service	47.07			
Health	12.71	—	13	12
Consumer	7.80	—	9	8
Business	4.31	—	5	4
Financial	22.25	—	22	20
Mfg	32.99	—		
Goods	8.49	—	9	8
Ind Mtrls	11.83	—	13	11
Energy	9.28	—	10	6
Utilities	3.39	—	4	3

Composition

	%
● Cash	8.9
● Stocks	25.5
● Bonds	65.5
○ Other	0.2
Foreign (% of Stock)	0.0

Vanguard LifeSt Mod Grth

	Ticker	Load	NAV	Yield	Total Assets	Mstar Category
	VSMGX	None	$20.36	2.6%	$9,802 mil	Moderate Allocation

Governance and Management

Stewardship Grade: B

Portfolio Manager(s)

The fund's trustees oversee the percentage of assets allocated to each of the underlying funds, and they rarely make changes. All of the underlying funds are run by very experienced and talented managers.

Strategy

This fund of funds devotes about 25% of assets to Vanguard Asset Allocation, which actively shifts between the S&P 500 Index, U.S. Treasury bonds, and cash based on projected long-term trends. The fund also invests approximately 35% in Vanguard Total Stock Market Index, 30% in Vanguard Total Bond Market Index, and 10% in Vanguard Total International Stock Index. Its equity allocation can range from 45% to 70% of assets.

Historical Profile

Return	Above Avg
Risk	Average
Rating	★★★★ Above Avg

Investment Style: Equity, Stock %

46% 55% 45% 59% 59% 62% 65% 64% 65%

Growth of $10,000
— Investment Values of Fund
— Investment Values of DJ Mod

Performance Quartile (within Category)

1995	1996	1997	1998	1999	2000	2001	2002	2003	2004	2005	2006	History
12.11	12.97	14.81	16.86	18.18	17.25	15.93	13.87	16.61	17.91	18.47	20.36	NAV
27.94	12.71	19.77	19.03	12.01	-0.88	-4.48	-10.32	22.40	10.57	5.69	13.31	Total Return %
8.14	2.05	7.87	6.71	-5.32	0.79	-1.68	-3.55	-4.98	-2.40	-1.30	1.01	+/-DJ Mod
3.17	1.37	0.57	6.64	-0.84	-5.32	-4.64	0.22	-1.66	-0.60	-0.31	3.04	+/-DJ US Mod
3.68	3.66	3.81	3.47	3.29	3.57	2.87	2.69	2.54	2.67	2.53	2.94	Income Return %
24.26	9.05	15.96	15.56	8.72	-4.45	-7.35	-13.01	19.86	7.90	3.16	10.37	Capital Return %
34	69	51	19	41	62	46	36	30	24	35	17	Total Rtn % Rank Cat
0.36	0.44	0.49	0.51	0.55	0.64	0.49	0.43	0.35	0.44	0.45	0.54	Income $
0.13	0.23	0.21	0.25	0.13	0.14	0.06	0.00	0.00	0.00	0.00	0.00	Capital Gains $
—	—	—	—	—	—	—	—	—	—	—	0.25	Expense Ratio %
4.42	3.98	3.72	3.43	3.47	3.59	2.69	2.98	2.39	2.36	2.61	—	Income Ratio %
1	3	2	5	3	12	16	15	5	6	8	—	Turnover Rate %
235	826	1,358	2,202	3,441	3,911	4,243	3,985	5,649	7,002	8,023	9,802	Net Assets $mil

Performance 12-31-06

	1st Qtr	2nd Qtr	3rd Qtr	4th Qtr	Total
2002	0.63	-6.11	-10.77	6.39	-10.32
2003	-2.23	12.23	2.85	8.46	22.40
2004	2.83	-0.29	0.36	7.45	10.57
2005	-1.40	1.93	3.20	1.90	5.69
2006	3.63	-0.92	4.48	5.62	13.31

Trailing	Total Return%	+/- DJ Mod	+/- DJ US Mod	%Rank Cat	Growth of $10,000
3 Mo	5.62	0.03	0.95	26	10,562
6 Mo	10.35	1.56	2.45	18	11,035
1 Yr	13.31	1.01	3.04	17	11,331
3 Yr Avg	9.81	-0.91	0.69	20	13,241
5 Yr Avg	7.76	-2.26	0.16	15	14,531
10 Yr Avg	8.19	-0.36	-0.40	24	21,972
15 Yr Avg	—	—	—	—	—

Tax Analysis	Tax-Adj Rtn%	%Rank Cat	Tax-Cost Rat	%Rank Cat
3 Yr (estimated)	9.02	14	0.72	34
5 Yr (estimated)	6.93	12	0.77	45
10 Yr (estimated)	6.95	16	1.15	25

Potential Capital Gain Exposure: 20% of assets

Rating and Risk

Time Period	Load-Adj Return %	Morningstar Rtn vs Cat	Morningstar Risk vs Cat	Morningstar Risk-Adj Rating
1 Yr	13.31			
3 Yr	9.81	+Avg	Avg	★★★★
5 Yr	7.76	+Avg	Avg	★★★★
10 Yr	8.19	+Avg	Avg	★★★★
Incept	9.81			

Other Measures	Standard Index DJ Mod	Best Fit Index DJ Mod
Alpha	0.1	0.1
Beta	0.86	0.86
R-Squared	94	94
Standard Deviation	5.24	
Mean	9.81	
Sharpe Ratio	1.22	

Portfolio Analysis 09-30-06

Total Stocks:0 Share change since 06-30-06	Sectors	P/E Ratio	YTD Return %	% Net Assets
⊕ Vanguard Total Stock Mkt	—	—	—	34.99
⊖ Vanguard Total Intl Stock	—	—	—	9.98

Total Fixed-Income:0	Date of Maturity	Amount $000	Value $000	% Net Assets
Vanguard Total Bond Marke	273,732	2,731,843		29.94

Morningstar's Take by William Samuel Rocco 11-03-06

Vanguard LifeStrategy Moderate Growth has much more than cost appeal.

This fund starts off with a big edge over other moderate-allocation offerings. While many funds of funds tack on their own layer of fees, this one does not, and all four of its underlying offerings are quite cheap. Consequently, it has an average weighted expense ratio of 0.25%, which makes it one of the very cheapest options in its category and 74 basis points, or hundredths of a percent, less expensive than the median for no-load moderate-allocation offerings.

This fund provides real composition calls as well as lots of diversification for its low price. It devotes one fourth of its portfolio to Vanguard Asset Allocation--which can go all stocks, bonds, or cash based on its manager's models--so its equity stake can range from 45% to 75%. It divides the rest of its portfolio among three expansive index funds. Vanguard Total Stock Market Index delivers exposure to thousands of U.S. stocks across the

market-cap and industry ranges, for example, whereas Vanguard Total International Stock Index is actually a combination of three regional index offerings and provides exposure to the shares of almost 2,000 overseas companies.

This fund's attractions don't end there. Due to the overall accuracy of Vanguard Asset Allocation's composition calls (that fund's long-term gains are very competitive with broad market indexes, such as the S&P 500 Index), as well as the quality of the other three underlying offerings, this fund has earned strong returns. It has been no more volatile than its average peer and sports a relatively attractive yield, though it often has a bigger stock stake than the group norm, thanks to its breadth and low costs, respectively.

For all these reasons, this fund is a superior option for investors seeking an all-in-one fund with a moderate risk/reward profile.

Address:	PO Box 2600 Valley Forge PA 19482 800-997-2798
Web Address:	www.vanguard.com
Inception:	09-30-94
Advisor:	Vanguard Advisers, Inc.
Subadvisor:	None
NTF Plans:	Vanguard NTF

Minimum Purchase:	$3000	Add: $100	IRA: $3000
Min Auto Inv Plan:	$3000	Add: $50	
Sales Fees:	No-load		
Management Fee:	0.00%		
Actual Fees:	Mgt:0.00%	Dist: —	
Expense Projections:	3Yr:$80	5Yr:$141	10Yr:$318
Income Distrib:	Semi-Annually		

Equity Style

Style: Blend
Size: Large-Cap

Value Measures		Rel Category
Price/Earnings	14.35	0.94
Price/Book	2.42	0.98
Price/Sales	1.33	0.97
Price/Cash Flow	7.20	0.89
Dividend Yield %	2.04	1.06

Growth Measures	%	Rel Category
Long-Term Erngs	11.40	0.97
Book Value	8.32	0.97
Sales	9.01	1.01
Cash Flow	8.80	0.89
Historical Erngs	14.05	0.79

Market Cap %			
Giant	46.1	Small	3.4
Large	33.5	Micro	1.1
Mid	15.8	Avg $mil:	32,450

Fixed-Income Style

Duration: Interm-Term
Quality: High

Avg Eff Duration [1]	4.6 Yrs
Avg Eff Maturity	7.1 Yrs
Avg Credit Quality	AAA
Avg Wtd Coupon	5.43%

[1] figure provided by fund as of 09-30-06

Sector Weightings	% of Stocks	Rel DJ Mod	3 Year High Low	
↻ Info	18.71	—		
Software	3.14	—	4	3
Hardware	8.58	—	10	8
Media	3.21	—	4	3
Telecom	3.78	—	4	4
☜ Service	47.54			
Health	11.82	—	12	11
Consumer	7.49	—	9	7
Business	4.90	—	5	5
Financial	23.33	—	23	21
☐ Mfg	33.75	—		
Goods	8.89	—	10	9
Ind Mtrls	12.26	—	13	11
Energy	8.99	—	10	6
Utilities	3.61	—	4	3

Composition

		%
● Cash		5.2
● Stocks		64.9
● Bonds		29.6
○ Other		0.2
Foreign		15.0
(% of Stock)		

MORNINGSTAR® Funds 500

Vanguard Lg-Tm T/E

Analyst Pick ✓

Ticker VWLTX	**Load** None	**NAV** $11.32	**Yield** 4.6%	**SEC Yield** 3.85%	**Total Assets** $2,384 mil	**Mstar Category** Muni National Long

Governance and Management

Stewardship Grade: B

Portfolio Manager(s)

Christopher Ryon assumed day-to-day responsibilities for this fund in 1996. Ian MacKinnon, who as Vanguard's fixed-income director set the fund's duration range, retired in June 2003. He has since been replaced by Bob Auwaerter.

Strategy

This fund's strategy is fairly straightforward. Its duration (a measure of interest-rate sensitivity) is typically shorter than the category norm, and at least 75% of its assets are required to be invested in bonds rated A or better. Management attempts to add value by making modest duration shifts and rotating among states and sectors.

Historical Profile

Return Above Avg
Risk High
Rating ★★★★ Above Avg

	14	13	12	19	21	20	16	14

Investment Style
Fixed Income
Income Rtn %Rank Cat

▼ Manager Change
▽ Partial Manager Change

20.8
18.8
16.4 **Growth of $10,000**
14.0 ■ Investment Values of Fund
12.0
10.0 ■ Investment Values of LB Muni

Performance Quartile (within Category)

1995	1996	1997	1998	1999	2000	2001	2002	2003	2004	2005	2006	History
11.09	10.95	11.29	11.26	10.31	11.07	10.98	11.48	11.54	11.48	11.27	11.32	NAV
18.72	4.42	9.29	6.02	-3.53	13.32	4.54	10.12	5.21	4.12	3.07	5.16	Total Return %
1.26	-0.01	0.10	-0.46	-1.47	1.64	-0.59	0.52	-0.10	-0.36	-0.44	0.32	+/-LB Muni
-2.25	-0.04	-1.55	-0.80	1.15	-1.92	-0.33	0.09	-1.12	-2.44	-2.01	-0.70	+/-LB Muni 20YR
6.21	5.41	5.51	5.24	5.14	5.68	5.16	4.99	4.65	4.61	4.56	4.68	Income Return %
12.51	-0.99	3.78	0.78	-8.67	7.64	-0.62	5.13	0.56	-0.49	-1.49	0.48	Capital Return %
24	17	42	19	25	7	25	9	33	37	49	18	Total Rtn % Rank Cat
0.60	0.59	0.59	0.58	0.57	0.57	0.56	0.54	0.52	0.52	0.51	0.52	Income $
0.00	0.02	0.06	0.12	0.00	0.00	0.03	0.05	0.00	0.00	0.04	0.00	Capital Gains $
0.21	0.20	0.19	0.21	0.18	0.19	0.19	0.17	0.17	0.15	0.15	0.15	Expense Ratio %
5.87	5.45	5.37	5.13	5.13	5.46	5.07	4.80	4.59	4.57	4.49	4.61	Income Ratio %
35	26	9	18	15	25	16	15	11	11	17	8	Turnover Rate %
1,114	1,142	1,291	1,537	1,487	1,746	1,187	1,248	1,146	1,127	641	638	Net Assets $mil

Performance 12-31-06

	1st Qtr	2nd Qtr	3rd Qtr	4th Qtr	Total
2002	1.13	3.79	5.38	-0.45	10.12
2003	0.72	2.97	0.12	1.33	5.21
2004	1.38	-2.50	4.33	0.97	4.12
2005	-0.66	3.28	-0.36	0.83	3.07
2006	0.16	-0.19	3.91	1.24	5.16

Trailing	Total Return%	+/- LB Muni	+/- LB Muni 20YR	%Rank Cat	Growth of $10,000
3 Mo	1.24	0.13	-0.19	14	10,124
6 Mo	5.20	0.65	-0.31	6	10,520
1 Yr	5.16	0.32	-0.70	18	10,516
3 Yr Avg	4.11	-0.17	-1.72	33	11,284
5 Yr Avg	5.51	-0.02	-1.25	19	13,076
10 Yr Avg	5.64	-0.12	-0.94	12	17,309
15 Yr Avg	6.32	0.06	-0.76	7	25,074

Tax Analysis	Tax-Adj Rtn%	%Rank Cat	Tax-Cost Rat	%Rank Cat
3 Yr (estimated)	4.09	22	0.02	8
5 Yr (estimated)	5.48	14	0.03	12
10 Yr (estimated)	5.58	8	0.06	26

Potential Capital Gain Exposure: 5% of assets

Rating and Risk

Time Period	Load-Adj Return %	Morningstar Rtn vs Cat	Morningstar Risk vs Cat	Morningstar Risk-Adj Rating
1 Yr	5.16			
3 Yr	4.11	+Avg	High	★★★★
5 Yr	5.51	+Avg	High	★★★★
10 Yr	5.64	+Avg	+Avg	★★★★
Incept	6.53			

Other Measures	Standard Index LB Muni	Best Fit Index LB Muni NY
Alpha	-0.3	-0.2
Beta	1.20	1.23
R-Squared	98	98
Standard Deviation	3.72	
Mean	4.11	
Sharpe Ratio	0.24	

Portfolio Analysis 09-30-06

Total Fixed-Income:241	Date of Maturity	Amount $000	Value $000	% Net Assets
New York St Environmenta	06-15-20	37,090	40,063	1.76
Massachusetts St Wtr Res	07-15-19	32,000	38,207	1.67
Texas Mun Pwr Agy	09-01-13	38,730	29,704	1.30
Lower Colo Riv Auth 5.87	05-15-16	27,490	29,244	1.28
Texas Mun Pwr Agy	09-01-17	39,170	24,957	1.09
Garden St N J Preservati	11-01-28	20,000	24,499	1.07
Manchester N H Arpt 5.62	01-01-30	23,000	24,461	1.07
San Diego Calif Uni Sch	07-01-27	20,000	23,731	1.04
San Bernardino Cnty Cali	08-01-24	18,000	23,562	1.03
Highlands Cnty Fla Healt	11-15-36	22,200	23,504	1.03
WISCONSIN ST CLEAN WTR R	06-01-11	20,500	22,813	1.00
Philadelphia Pa Wtr & Wa	06-15-10	20,000	22,326	0.98
Massachusetts St Wtr Res	08-01-31	21,000	22,289	0.98
Texas City Tex Indl Dev	10-01-20	17,000	22,089	0.97
Chicago Ill Met Wtr Recl	01-01-11	20,000	21,927	0.96

Current Investment Style

Duration: Short Int Long
Quality: High Med Low

¹Avg Eff Duration	6.2 Yrs
Avg Eff Maturity	8.4 Yrs
Avg Credit Quality	AA
Avg Wtd Coupon	5.09%
Avg Wtd Price	106.18% of par

¹figure provided by fund

Credit Analysis		% bonds 09-30-06	
AAA	65	BB	0
AA	18	B	0
A	4	Below B	0
BBB	3	NR/NA	10

Top 5 States	% bonds		
TX	12.5	MA	7.3
CA	12.1	IL	5.4
NY	10.3		

Composition			
Cash	8.6	Bonds	91.4
Stocks	0.0	Other	0.0

Special Securities	
Restricted/Illiquid Secs	0
Options/Futures/Warrants	No

Sector Weightings	% of Bonds	Rel Cat
General Obligation	28.4	1.01
Utilities	17.5	1.68
Health	6.9	0.66
Water/Waste	17.8	1.81
Housing	0.9	0.14
Education	8.1	0.71
Transportation	6.2	0.72
COP/Lease	3.1	1.33
Industrial	11.0	0.91
Misc Revenue	0.0	—
Demand	0.0	0.00

Morningstar's Take by Brian Smith 12-21-06

Vanguard Long-Term Tax Exempt Fund puts its cost edge to good use.

As the low-cost leader this fund beats the competition through its economic advantage. Its 0.15% expense ratio easily beats its typical municipal long-term rival's 0.65%. Low fees give it a big head start over rivals and are especially helpful during periods of tight returns. For example, for the year-to-date period through Nov. 30, 2006, only 47 basis points separate a fund that ranks in the category's top quartile from the median fund in the group. The fund's much-smaller levy has thus been a big contributor this year, pushing its return for the period into the category's top quartile.

The fund's low fees help drive its bond-picking, too. Instead of venturing into lower-rated bonds to offer a competitive yield, manager Christopher Ryon stashes most of the portfolio's assets in bonds rated AAA or AA. Only 8% of the fund's Oct. 31, 2006, portfolio resides in bonds rated below AA, whereas its typical peer owns 17 percentage points

more in riskier issues. One potential negative side effect of a lower-credit-risk portfolio might be a slimmer payout, but, again thanks to the fund's low fees, it delivers a 4.5% yield, which ranks in the peer group's top quintile.

While credit risk isn't a problem here, the fund doesn't shy away from accepting some interest-rate risk. Currently, Ryon feels comfortable embracing more responsiveness to changes in interest rates because he thinks that the U.S. Federal Reserve is nearing the end of its rate-hiking campaign. The fund's 6.4-year duration weighs in at half a year longer than its typical peer. Investors should remember: If Ryon's wrong and rates shoot up unexpectedly, the fund may give up more ground than less-rate-sensitive rivals.

We think that the fund continues to represent a reliable option for long-term tax-avoiding investors. Its low fees continue to separate it from competitors, and its consistent and enviable long-term record shows that its strategy works.

Address:	PO Box 2600, Valley Forge PA 19482, 800-997-2798
Web Address:	www.vanguard.com
Inception:	09-01-77
Advisor:	Vanguard Advisers, Inc.
Subadvisor:	None
NTF Plans:	Vanguard NTF

Minimum Purchase:	$3000	Add: $100	IRA: $0
Min Auto Inv Plan:	$3000	Add: $50	
Sales Fees:	No-load		
Management Fee:	0.14%		
Actual Fees:	Mgt:0.14%	Dist: —	
Expense Projections:	3Yr:$52	5Yr:$90	10Yr:$205
Income Distrib:	Monthly		

Vanguard Long-Tm InvGrde

✓ **Analyst Pick**

	Ticker	Load	NAV	Yield	SEC Yield	Total Assets	Mstar Category
	VWESX	None	$9.25	5.6%	5.65%	$5,711 mil	Long-Term Bond

Governance and Management

Stewardship Grade: B

Portfolio Manager(s)

Earl McEvoy of esteemed subadvisor Wellington Management Company has managed this fund since March 1994. McEvoy also runs Vanguard High-Yield Corporate and the bond portion of Vanguard Wellesley Income's balanced portfolio, where he has posted impressive results.

Strategy

The fund invests mainly in high-quality corporate bonds, but it may also invest up to 20% of assets in Treasuries and other government securities. Starting in mid-2001, the fund could invest up to 5% of assets in high-yield debt, but it has barely endeavored to do so yet. The fund's duration is kept within 20% of the Lehman Brothers Long Credit A or Better Index's, meaning that it tends to be more sensitive to interest-rate shifts than are many of its long-term bond peers. Over the past year or so, the fund's duration has ranged from 9.1 to 11.5 years.

Historical Profile

Return	Above Avg
Risk	Above Avg
Rating	★★★★ Above Avg

Investment Style: Fixed Income
Income Rtn %Rank Cat

▼ Manager Change
▽ Partial Manager Change

Growth of $10,000
— Investment Values of Fund
— Investment Values of LB Aggr

Performance Quartile (within Category)

	1995	1996	1997	1998	1999	2000	2001	2002	2003	2004	2005	2006	History
	9.48	8.79	9.26	9.29	8.11	8.45	8.68	9.23	9.27	9.55	9.52	9.25	NAV
	26.40	1.20	13.78	9.21	-6.23	11.76	9.57	13.22	6.26	8.94	5.13	2.86	Total Return %
	7.93	-2.43	4.13	0.52	-5.41	0.13	1.13	2.97	2.16	4.60	2.70	-1.47	+/-LB Aggr
	-3.55	1.06	-0.74	-2.56	1.42	-4.40	2.29	-1.59	0.39	0.38	-0.20	0.15	+/-LB LongTerm
	8.05	6.79	7.21	6.56	6.25	7.30	6.86	6.60	5.85	5.77	5.53	5.61	Income Return %
	18.35	-5.59	6.57	2.65	-12.48	4.46	2.71	6.62	0.41	3.17	-0.40	-2.75	Capital Return %
	56	55	42	9	58	5	34	16	68	20	17	90	Total Rtn % Rank Cat
	0.63	0.62	0.61	0.59	0.56	0.57	0.56	0.56	0.53	0.52	0.52	0.52	Income $
	0.00	0.15	0.07	0.21	0.06	0.00	0.00	0.00	0.00	0.00	0.00	0.00	Capital Gains $
	0.32	0.31	0.28	0.32	0.30	0.30	0.30	0.32	0.31	0.28	0.25	0.25	Expense Ratio %
	7.37	7.03	7.06	6.87	6.26	6.59	7.02	6.48	6.24	5.64	5.58	5.35	Income Ratio %
	43	49	30	33	43	7	17	39	33	11	16	9	Turnover Rate %
	3,356	3,412	3,637	4,153	3,724	3,704	3,550	3,753	3,851	4,213	4,224	4,187	Net Assets $mil

Performance 12-31-06

	1st Qtr	2nd Qtr	3rd Qtr	4th Qtr	Total
2002	-0.59	4.29	7.96	1.16	13.22
2003	1.96	6.48	-2.18	0.04	6.26
2004	4.90	-5.01	6.48	2.67	8.94
2005	0.70	6.97	-3.22	0.86	5.13
2006	-3.63	-1.88	7.25	1.42	2.86

Trailing	Total Return%	+/- LB Aggr	+/- LB LongTerm	%Rank Cat	Growth of $10,000
3 Mo	1.42	0.18	0.37	52	10,142
6 Mo	8.77	3.68	0.83	19	10,877
1 Yr	2.86	-1.47	0.15	90	10,286
3 Yr Avg	5.61	1.91	0.10	24	11,779
5 Yr Avg	7.22	2.16	-0.16	35	14,170
10 Yr Avg	7.30	1.06	-0.42	17	20,230
15 Yr Avg	7.79	1.29	-0.28	1	30,809

Tax Analysis	Tax-Adj Rtn%	%Rank Cat	Tax-Cost Rat	%Rank Cat
3 Yr (estimated)	3.59	16	1.91	64
5 Yr (estimated)	5.06	35	2.01	61
10 Yr (estimated)	4.74	16	2.39	90

Potential Capital Gain Exposure: 4% of assets

Rating and Risk

Time Period	Load-Adj Return %	Morningstar Rtn vs Cat	Morningstar Risk vs Cat	Morningstar Risk-Adj Rating
1 Yr	2.86			
3 Yr	5.61	+Avg	High	★★★★
5 Yr	7.22	+Avg	+Avg	★★★
10 Yr	7.30	+Avg	+Avg	★★★★
Incept	8.83			

Other Measures	Standard Index LB Aggr	Best Fit Index LB LongTerm
Alpha	1.5	0.1
Beta	2.25	1.01
R-Squared	93	99
Standard Deviation	7.59	
Mean	5.61	
Sharpe Ratio	0.33	

Portfolio Analysis 09-30-06

Total Fixed-Income:249	Date of Maturity	Amount $000	Value $000	% Net Assets
Illinois St Go Bds 5.1%	06-01-33	129,625	124,196	2.23
FHLMC 6.25%	07-15-32	95,400	110,757	1.99
General Elec Cap 6.75%	03-15-32	95,975	110,157	1.98
FNMA 6.625%	11-15-30	83,925	101,062	1.81
Deutsche Telekom Intl Fi	06-15-30	79,000	96,047	1.72
France Telecom Sa 8.5%	03-01-31	63,175	82,505	1.48
At&T Wireless Svcs 8.75%	03-01-31	52,725	67,543	1.21
Natl Rural Utils Coop Fi	03-01-32	50,000	64,380	1.15
FHLBA 5.5%	07-15-36	60,000	63,194	1.13
New York Life Ins 144A 5	05-15-33	57,775	59,082	1.06
President&Fellow Harvard	10-01-37	55,000	59,034	1.06
Hartford Life 7.375%	03-01-31	47,500	57,072	1.02
Intl Busn Machs 7%	10-30-25	50,000	57,003	1.02
Hydro-Quebec 9.4%	02-01-21	40,000	56,321	1.01
Wal Mart Stores 7.55%	02-15-30	45,000	55,416	0.99
Intl Bk For Recon&Dev 7.	01-19-23	43,320	54,389	0.98
Aluminum 6.75%	01-15-28	45,000	50,490	0.91
Hbos Plc Medium Tm Sb Nt	11-01-33	46,500	47,452	0.85
Dow Chem 7.375%	11-01-29	40,000	46,776	0.84
Bellsouth 6%	11-15-34	49,000	46,102	0.83

Current Investment Style

Duration: Short / Int / Long
Quality: High / Med / Low

1 figure provided by fund

Avg Eff Duration[1]	11.5 Yrs
Avg Eff Maturity	21.9 Yrs
Avg Credit Quality	A
Avg Wtd Coupon	6.84%
Avg Wtd Price	111.47% of par

Coupon Range	% of Bonds	Rel Cat
0% PIK	0.0	0.0
0% to 6%	25.2	0.6
6% to 8%	61.8	1.4
8% to 10%	13.0	1.2
More than 10%	0.1	0.1

1.00=Category Average

Credit Analysis	% bonds 09-30-06		
AAA	13	BB	0
AA	24	B	0
A	48	Below B	1
BBB	13	NR/NA	1

Sector Breakdown — % of assets

US Treasuries	0
TIPS	0
US Agency	6
Mortgage Pass-Throughs	0
Mortgage CMO	0
Mortgage ARM	0
US Corporate	83
Asset-Backed	0
Convertible	0
Municipal	4
Corporate Inflation-Protected	0
Foreign Corporate	6
Foreign Govt	1

Composition

Cash	0.3	Bonds	99.7
Stocks	0.0	Other	0.0

Special Securities

Restricted/Illiquid Secs	6
Exotic Mortgage-Backed	0
Emerging-Markets Secs	0
Options/Futures/Warrants	No

Morningstar's Take by Lawrence Jones 12-20-06

Vanguard Long-Term Investment-Grade faces challenges, but low costs ensure it a fighting chance.

This fund gains part of its edge from its low expense ratio. At just 0.25%, the fund's expense ratio is much lower than its typical no-load long-term bond-category peer's 0.93%. One significant benefit of owning a lower-fee fund is that costs don't eat away at much of the fund's yield. As a result the fund is able to provide more income and return than its typical peer.

The lower expense ratio also means that the fund has less reason to take on much credit risk. Because manager Earl McEvoy gains a sizable edge from the fund's low fees, he can buy mostly high-quality bonds without sacrificing return; currently, the fund dedicates just 15% of its assets to bonds rated BBB (just a notch above junk-bond level) and lower, compared with 35% for its average competitor. We like this distinction, as it gives the fund a uncommon profile--a high-quality portfolio with low fees.

One risk here, however, is the fund's sometimes extreme interest-rate sensitivity. The fund's benchmark is the Lehman Brothers Long Credit A or Better Index, which tends to be more sensitive to rate changes than the category norm. That's why the fund's duration is often much different than its typical peer's. In fact, the fund's recent 11-year duration, for example, was more than three years longer than its average rival's. And since the fund has been quite a bit more sensitive to rising rates, its modest 3.57% year-to-date return, through Dec. 19, 2006, is understandable. Long-term bonds have been beaten up this year as short-term bond yields have risen, shrinking demand for long-dated issues.

Even though this year has been disappointing, we still like the fund. Its low fees, stable management, and high-quality portfolio should help it in days to come.

Dieter Bardy contributed to this report.

Address:	PO Box 2600, Valley Forge PA 19482, 800-997-2798
Web Address:	www.vanguard.com
Inception:	07-09-73
Advisor:	Wellington Management Company, LLP
Subadvisor:	None
NTF Plans:	Vanguard NTF

Minimum Purchase:	$3000	Add: $100	IRA: $3000
Min Auto Inv Plan:	$3000	Add: $50	
Sales Fees:	No-load		
Management Fee:	0.26%		
Actual Fees:	Mgt:0.22%	Dist: —	
Expense Projections:	3Yr:$80	5Yr:$141	10Yr:$318
Income Distrib:	Monthly		

M⊙RNINGSTAR® Funds 500

Vanguard Long-Tm US Try

Analyst Pick ✓

	Ticker	Load	NAV	Yield	SEC Yield	Total Assets	Mstar Category
	VUSTX	None	$11.13	4.9%	4.62%	$2,174 mil	Long Government

Governance and Management

Stewardship Grade: B

Portfolio Manager(s)

David Glocke assumed management responsibilities in May 2001. He joined the firm in 1997. Ian MacKinnon, the head of Vanguard's fixed-income group, had worked on the fund since its 1986 inception. However, Bob Auwaerter recently replaced MacKinnon, who retired on June 30.

Strategy

Management invests primarily in long-term U.S. Treasury bonds. Most holdings won't mature for at least 10 years, and the fund strives to maintain an overall average maturity between 15 and 25 years. As a result, it tends to be more sensitive to interest-rate movements than is its average peer. Management does not make big duration bets, however, and keeps that figure within a half year of the Lehman Brothers Long-Term U.S. Treasury Index's. The fund can also invest in government-agency bonds, but that allocation hasn't exceeded 15% of assets in recent years.

Performance 12-31-06

	1st Qtr	2nd Qtr	3rd Qtr	4th Qtr	Total
2002	-1.49	5.97	11.64	0.12	16.67
2003	1.40	5.05	-2.57	-1.07	2.68
2004	5.24	-5.23	5.94	1.38	7.12
2005	0.56	7.59	-2.56	1.13	6.61
2006	-3.49	-1.29	6.28	0.50	1.74

Trailing	Total Return%	+/- LB Aggr	+/- LB LTGvtBd	%Rank Cat	Growth of $10,000
3 Mo	0.50	-0.74	-0.07	23	10,050
6 Mo	6.81	1.72	-0.28	52	10,681
1 Yr	1.74	-2.59	-0.32	30	10,174
3 Yr Avg	5.13	1.43	-0.38	28	11,619
5 Yr Avg	6.84	1.78	-0.27	46	13,921
10 Yr Avg	7.41	1.17	-0.34	46	20,438
15 Yr Avg	7.75	1.25	-0.33	38	30,638

Tax Analysis	Tax-Adj Rtn%	%Rank Cat	Tax-Cost Rat	%Rank Cat
3 Yr (estimated)	3.19	34	1.85	84
5 Yr (estimated)	4.75	46	1.96	81
10 Yr (estimated)	5.10	42	2.15	73

Potential Capital Gain Exposure: 6% of assets

Morningstar's Take by Michael Herbst 12-18-06

Vanguard Long-Term U.S. Treasury's cost advantage makes it hard to beat.

This fund makes its mark by offering more competitive fees than everyone else. Its 0.26% expense ratio is 22 basis points lower than the next-cheapest option, and less than one half the category's average expense ratio of 0.65%. Expenses always matter, but do so even more in a category where returns tend to be bunched so tightly. The fund's 2.53% gain for the year to date through Dec. 14, 2006, beats its typical peer's by 0.92%.

To be sure, there are other differences. Notably, this portfolio owns nothing but U.S. Treasuries, while most of the fund's typical peers devote a portion of their assets to mortgage and agency bonds and Treasury Inflation-Protected Securities. This fund avoids those issues because Vanguard offers other funds that dedicate their portfolios to non-Treasury bonds. This specialization might lead it to lag when other areas of the market thrive,

meaning that investors who want greater diversification should choose another option.

There's another risk, though it's currently muted. Because of its concentrated and long-term bond focus, the fund is very sensitive to changes in interest rates. Manager David Glocke and Vanguard's fixed-income chief Bob Auwaerter, who guides duration (a measure of interest-rate sensitivity) for all Vanguard fixed-income funds, think that since the U.S. Federal Reserve has increased interest rates 17 times, a neutral-to-guarded duration tone is warranted. The fund's 10.0-year duration is slightly shorter than that of its benchmark--the Lehman Long Treasury Index--and 1.1 years shorter than its typical peer's.

Given volatile interest rates in recent years, it's no surprise that returns aren't more impressive. However, given this fund's absolute low fee advantage and long-experienced manager, we think long-term investors will be rewarded.

Dieter Bardy contributed to this report.

Address:	PO Box 2600 Valley Forge PA 19482 800-997-2798
Web Address:	www.vanguard.com
Inception:	05-19-86
Advisor:	Vanguard Advisers, Inc.
Subadvisor:	None
NTF Plans:	Vanguard NTF

Minimum Purchase:	$3000	Add: $100	IRA: $3000
Min Auto Inv Plan:	$3000	Add: $50	
Sales Fees:	No-load		
Management Fee:	0.24%		
Actual Fees:	Mgt:0.23%	Dist: —	
Expense Projections:	3Yr:$84	5Yr:$146	10Yr:$331
Income Distrib:	Monthly		

Historical Profile

Return	Average
Risk	Average
Rating	★★★ Neutral

20	17	21	37	14	25	8	8

▼ Manager Change
▽ Partial Manager Change

Growth of $10,000
■ Investment Values of Fund
— Investment Values of LB Aggr

22.6
19.0
16.0
13.0
10.0

Performance Quartile (within Category)

1995	1996	1997	1998	1999	2000	2001	2002	2003	2004	2005	2006	History
10.79	9.96	10.64	11.36	9.67	10.90	10.76	11.76	11.37	11.51	11.55	11.13	NAV
30.09	-1.26	13.90	13.05	-8.66	19.72	4.31	16.67	2.68	7.12	6.61	1.74	Total Return %
11.62	-4.89	4.25	4.36	-7.84	8.09	-4.13	6.42	-1.42	2.78	4.18	-2.59	+/-LB Aggr
-0.81	-0.42	-1.22	-0.36	0.07	-0.57	-0.03	-0.32	0.07	-0.82	0.00	-0.32	+/-LB LTGvtBd
7.66	6.25	6.67	6.10	5.57	6.61	5.67	5.59	4.90	5.17	5.04	4.87	Income Return %
22.43	-7.51	7.23	6.95	-14.23	13.11	-1.36	11.08	-2.22	1.95	1.57	-3.13	Capital Return %
40	50	64	53	45	58	27	73	42	60	46	30	Total Rtn % Rank Cat
0.67	0.65	0.64	0.63	0.61	0.62	0.60	0.59	0.56	0.57	0.57	0.55	Income $
0.23	0.01	0.00	0.00	0.12	0.00	0.00	0.15	0.14	0.07	0.14	0.05	Capital Gains $
0.28	0.27	0.25	0.27	0.27	0.28	0.29	0.29	0.28	0.26	0.24	0.26	Expense Ratio %
7.02	6.57	6.66	6.38	5.69	5.98	6.00	5.52	5.19	4.81	5.02	4.82	Income Ratio %
85	105	31	18	22	43	49	64	100	64	38	25	Turnover Rate %
917	918	1,035	1,416	1,224	1,358	1,373	1,682	1,489	1,444	1,422	1,293	Net Assets $mil

Rating and Risk

Time Period	Load-Adj Return %	Morningstar Rtn vs Cat	Morningstar Risk vs Cat	Morningstar Risk-Adj Rating
1 Yr	1.74			
3 Yr	5.13	+Avg	Avg	★★★★
5 Yr	6.84	Avg	Avg	★★★
10 Yr	7.41	Avg	Avg	★★★
Incept	8.22			

Other Measures	Standard Index LB Aggr	Best Fit Index LB LTGvtBd
Alpha	1.0	-0.3
Beta	2.20	0.98
R-Squared	94	100
Standard Deviation	7.40	
Mean	5.13	
Sharpe Ratio	0.28	

Portfolio Analysis 09-30-06

Total Fixed-Income:25	Date of Maturity	Amount $000	Value $000	% Net Assets
US Treasury Bond 7.875%	02-15-21	196,581	258,258	11.83
US Treasury Bond 6.125%	08-15-29	177,300	208,964	9.57
US Treasury Bond 8.125%	08-15-19	133,173	175,622	8.04
US Treasury Bond 6%	02-15-26	153,000	175,018	8.01
US Treasury Bond 6.375%	08-15-27	110,650	132,814	6.08
US Treasury Bond 6.125%	11-15-27	111,000	129,801	5.94
US Treasury Bond 8.125%	05-15-21	92,875	124,786	5.71
US Treasury Bond 6.25%	08-15-23	101,500	117,819	5.39
US Treasury Bond 7.125%	02-15-23	83,000	104,230	4.77
US Treasury Bond 8.75%	08-15-20	70,000	97,672	4.47
US Treasury Bond 8.5%	02-15-20	71,500	97,419	4.46
US Treasury Bond 8.875%	02-15-19	56,000	77,306	3.54
US Treasury Bond 6.75%	08-15-26	59,000	73,234	3.35
US Treasury Bond 6.875%	08-15-25	52,000	64,951	2.97
Private Expt Fdg 4.95%	11-15-15	65,000	64,492	2.95
US Treasury Bond 6.625%	02-15-27	50,000	61,469	2.81
US Treasury Bond 8.75%	05-15-20	41,860	58,244	2.67
US Treasury Bond 8.125%	08-15-21	32,000	43,105	1.97
US Treasury Bond 6.5%	11-15-26	31,050	37,609	1.72
US Treasury Bond 8%	11-15-21	23,000	30,763	1.41

Current Investment Style

Duration: Short / Int / Long — Long
Quality: High / Med / Low — High

1 figure provided by fund

Avg Eff Duration[1]	10.0 Yrs
Avg Eff Maturity	16.6 Yrs
Avg Credit Quality	AAA
Avg Wtd Coupon	7.16%
Avg Wtd Price	125.31% of par

Coupon Range	% of Bonds	Rel Cat
0% PIK	0.0	0.0
0% to 6%	12.2	0.2
6% to 8%	56.9	3.8
8% to 10%	30.9	5.7
More than 10%	0.0	0.0

1.00=Category Average

Credit Analysis	% bonds 09-30-06		
AAA	100	BB	0
AA	0	B	0
A	0	Below B	0
BBB	0	NR/NA	0

Sector Breakdown	% of assets
US Treasuries	97
TIPS	0
US Agency	3
Mortgage Pass-Throughs	0
Mortgage CMO	0
Mortgage ARM	0
US Corporate	0
Asset-Backed	0
Convertible	0
Municipal	0
Corporate Inflation-Protected	0
Foreign Corporate	0
Foreign Govt	0

Composition			
Cash	0.3	Bonds	99.7
Stocks	0.0	Other	0.0

Special Securities	
Restricted/Illiquid Secs	0
Exotic Mortgage-Backed	—
Emerging-Markets Secs	0
Options/Futures/Warrants	No

Investment Style
Fixed Income
Income Rtn %Rank Cat

Vanguard LtdTm T/E

| | Analyst Pick | Ticker VMLTX | Load None | NAV $10.71 | Yield 3.3% | SEC Yield 3.52% | Total Assets $6,586 mil | Mstar Category Muni National Short |

Governance and Management

Stewardship Grade: B

Portfolio Manager(s)

Pam Wisehaupt-Tynan has managed the fund since the start of 1997. She has been with Vanguard since 1981 as an accountant and assistant portfolio manager. Bob Auwaerter, who leads the firm's fixed-income group, sets broad interest-rate policy.

Strategy

The fund invests in high-quality municipal issues with a combined average maturity of three to four years. At least three fourths of its bonds must be invested in the top three credit-rating categories. Management adjusts the fund's duration within a specified range, depending on its interest-rate outlook.

Historical Profile

Return: Above Avg
Risk: Average
Rating: ★★★★ Above Avg

Investment Style
Fixed Income
Income Rtn %Rank Cat

▼ Manager Change
▽ Partial Manager Change

Growth of $10,000
— Investment Values of Fund
— Investment Values of LB Muni

20.8
18.8
16.4
14.0
12.0
10.0

Performance Quartile (within Category)

	1995	1996	1997	1998	1999	2000	2001	2002	2003	2004	2005	2006	History
	10.76	10.71	10.77	10.85	10.55	10.73	10.85	11.11	11.07	10.92	10.71	10.71	NAV
	8.57	4.08	5.10	5.12	1.47	6.35	5.58	6.31	2.79	1.53	1.11	3.33	Total Return %
	-8.89	-0.35	-4.09	-1.36	3.53	-5.33	0.45	-3.29	-2.52	-2.95	-2.40	-1.51	+/-LB Muni
	-0.30	-0.36	-0.38	-0.09	-0.49	0.12	-1.01	-0.41	0.11	-0.25	0.24	0.28	+/-LB Muni 3YR
	4.76	4.53	4.51	4.35	4.29	4.58	4.48	3.87	3.15	2.90	3.05	3.32	Income Return %
	3.81	-0.45	0.59	0.77	-2.82	1.77	1.10	2.44	-0.36	-1.37	-1.94	0.01	Capital Return %
	22	29	49	8	29	26	7	29	27	29	48	28	Total Rtn % Rank Cat
	0.48	0.48	0.47	0.46	0.46	0.47	0.47	0.41	0.35	0.32	0.33	0.35	Income $
	0.00	0.00	0.00	0.00	0.00	0.00	0.00	0.00	0.00	0.00	0.00	0.00	Capital Gains $
	0.21	0.21	0.19	0.21	0.18	0.18	0.19	0.17	0.17	0.14	0.16	0.16	Expense Ratio %
	4.51	4.51	4.46	4.27	4.25	4.45	4.40	4.80	3.19	2.89	3.01	3.23	Income Ratio %
	35	27	28	35	14	32	19	17	13	8	17	27	Turnover Rate %
	1,683	1,789	2,023	2,391	2,569	2,932	2,104	2,773	3,256	3,494	2,169	1,930	Net Assets $mil

Performance 12-31-06

	1st Qtr	2nd Qtr	3rd Qtr	4th Qtr	Total
2002	0.36	2.93	2.20	0.70	6.31
2003	0.64	1.34	0.58	0.20	2.79
2004	0.81	-1.27	1.64	0.36	1.53
2005	-0.65	1.24	0.13	0.39	1.11
2006	0.22	0.54	1.79	0.76	3.33

Trailing	Total Return%	+/- LB Muni	+/- LB Muni 3YR	%Rank Cat	Growth of $10,000
3 Mo	0.76	-0.35	0.13	27	10,076
6 Mo	2.56	-1.99	-0.02	20	10,256
1 Yr	3.33	-1.51	0.28	28	10,333
3 Yr Avg	1.98	-2.30	0.08	37	10,606
5 Yr Avg	3.00	-2.53	0.00	26	11,593
10 Yr Avg	3.85	-1.91	-0.19	20	14,590
15 Yr Avg	4.25	-2.01	-0.20	40	18,670

Tax Analysis	Tax-Adj Rtn%	%Rank Cat	Tax-Cost Rat	%Rank Cat
3 Yr (estimated)	1.98	30	0.00	1
5 Yr (estimated)	3.00	22	0.00	1
10 Yr (estimated)	3.85	15	0.00	1

Potential Capital Gain Exposure: -1% of assets

Rating and Risk

Time Period	Load-Adj Return %	Morningstar Rtn vs Cat	Morningstar Risk vs Cat	Morningstar Risk-Adj Rating
1 Yr	3.33			
3 Yr	1.98	+Avg	Avg	★★★★
5 Yr	3.00	+Avg	Avg	★★★★
10 Yr	3.85	+Avg	Avg	★★★★
Incept	5.03			

Other Measures	Standard Index LB Muni	Best Fit Index LB Muni 3YR
Alpha	-1.7	0.0
Beta	0.43	0.94
R-Squared	88	96
Standard Deviation	1.42	
Mean	1.98	
Sharpe Ratio	-0.89	

Morningstar's Take by Lawrence Jones 12-21-06

Vanguard Limited-Term Tax-Exempt continues to display virtues that make it one of our favorites.

This fund's low costs continue to give it a strong and sustainable competitive advantage over its muni-national short-term category rivals. The fund's expense ratio, currently 0.16%, makes it the lowest-priced offering in the category. A cost advantage of 0.46% against the typical no-load peer may not appear to be much, but it gives the fund a huge lead over the competition in a category where just a few percentage points separate the winners from the losers.

The cost advantage achieved here allows veteran manager Pam Wisehaupt-Tynan to concentrate on purchasing high-quality bonds. The fund, for instance, currently holds more than 85% of assets in bonds rated AA or better, a higher percentage than is typical in the category. Added to this, the fund often holds a significant portion of its assets (currently about 43%) in insured municipal bonds, further strengthening its credit quality.

However, though the fund is able to avoid significant credit risk, it does take on some interest-rate risk, which adds to volatility. The fund's benchmark, composed of a custom peer group, carries slightly more interest-rate risk than the typical peer fund will. But even so, this fund keeps its risk profile constrained enough so that conservative investors can feel comfortable here.

The fund's long-term performance is testament to both the advantage low costs provide and management's careful guidance. Its trailing 10-year total return of 3.86% through Nov. 30, 2006, bests 81% of category rivals. The fund has also delivered yields that typically rank in the category's top quartile. And though low costs contributed to these results, we're also impressed with Wisehaupt-Tynan's near decade-long tenure here, where she's provided capable management.

In sum, the fund's low expenses, high credit quality, and solid management continue to make this Analyst Pick a favorite.

Address:	PO Box 2600 Valley Forge PA 19482 800-997-2798	Minimum Purchase:	$3000 Add: $100 IRA: $0
		Min Auto Inv Plan:	$3000 Add: $50
		Sales Fees:	No-load
Web Address:	www.vanguard.com	Management Fee:	0.14%
Inception:	08-31-87	Actual Fees:	Mgt:0.13% Dist: —
Advisor:	Vanguard Advisers, Inc.	Expense Projections:	3Yr:$52 5Yr:$90 10Yr:$205
Subadvisor:	None	Income Distrib:	Monthly
NTF Plans:	Vanguard NTF		

Portfolio Analysis 09-30-06

Total Fixed-Income:612

	Date of Maturity	Amount $000	Value $000	% Net Assets
New Jersey St Transn Tr	12-15-36	66,455	66,455	1.01
Engy Northwest Wash Elec	07-01-11	45,365	48,075	0.73
SUFFOLK CNTY N Y WTR AUT	06-01-31	40,000	39,969	0.60
MATAGORDA CNTY TEX NAV D	11-01-29	38,970	38,989	0.59
Texas St Tpk Auth 5%	06-01-08	36,300	37,145	0.56
New York N Y 5.25%	08-01-09	35,110	36,665	0.55
Kansas St Dept Transn Hw	09-01-13	32,590	35,307	0.53
Tarrant Cnty Tex Health	02-15-33	35,000	35,000	0.53
MICHIGAN ST CTFS PARTN C	09-01-31	33,000	34,797	0.53
CALIFORNIA ST	09-01-13	32,125	34,660	0.52
Clark Cnty Nev Sch Dist	06-15-08	33,555	34,642	0.52
New Jersey St Transn Tr	12-15-11	30,000	32,305	0.49
METROPOLITAN GOVT NASHVI	10-01-44	30,890	32,199	0.49
Jea Fla St Johns Riv Pwr	10-01-08	31,000	31,857	0.48
Clark Cnty Nev Sch Dist	06-01-08	30,735	31,461	0.48

Current Investment Style

Duration: Short Int Long
Quality: High Med Low

¹Avg Eff Duration	2.2 Yrs	
Avg Eff Maturity	2.5 Yrs	
Avg Credit Quality	AA	
Avg Wtd Coupon	4.85%	
Avg Wtd Price	103.49% of par	

¹figure provided by fund

Credit Analysis	% bonds 09-30-06		
AAA	52	BB	0
AA	33	B	0
A	7	Below B	0
BBB	5	NR/NA	3

Top 5 States	% bonds		
NY	12.6	FL	6.3
TX	10.0	NJ	4.7
CA	7.3		

Composition			
Cash	16.7	Bonds	83.3
Stocks	0.0	Other	0.0

Special Securities	
Restricted/Illiquid Secs	0
Options/Futures/Warrants	No

Sector Weightings	% of Bonds	Rel Cat
General Obligation	51.2	1.56
Utilities	9.5	1.18
Health	8.1	0.81
Water/Waste	6.8	0.91
Housing	0.9	0.10
Education	5.6	0.65
Transportation	6.2	1.20
COP/Lease	1.8	1.01
Industrial	7.9	0.49
Misc Revenue	0.0	—
Demand	2.0	2.96

MORNINGSTAR® Funds 500

Vanguard Mid Cap Growth

	Ticker	Load	NAV	Yield	Total Assets	Mstar Category
	VMGRX	None	$17.07	0.2%	$811 mil	Mid-Cap Growth

Governance and Management

Stewardship Grade: B

Portfolio Manager(s)

In February 2006, Chartwell Investment Partners was added as a second advisor to this fund. Then in June 2006, Vanguard gave the remaining half of the portfolio to William Blair & Co, taking the fund's original advisor, Provident Investment Counsel, entirely out of the picture. Ed Antoian and Mark Cunneen manage Chartwell's portfolio. Both have several years of managerial experience, and Antoian also runs a sleeve of Vanguard Explorer. The William Blair sleeve is run by the firm's mid-growth team, Harvey Bundy, Robert Lanphier, and David Ricci, who have delivered solid results at similar separate accounts.

Strategy

The management teams from both this fund's advisors share many traits. Both employ a research-intensive approach that focuses on rapidly growing midsized firms. They also both favor names with high-quality management teams that are committed to enhancing shareholder value. However the managers from Chartwell Investment Partners tend to trade frequently, whereas the team from William Blair takes a longer-term view and prefers firms that can deliver steady, sustainable growth over a period of years.

Performance 12-31-06

	1st Qtr	2nd Qtr	3rd Qtr	4th Qtr	Total
2002	0.07	-15.71	-15.45	0.20	-28.54
2003	1.39	19.45	6.38	10.85	42.81
2004	2.15	-1.09	-6.04	17.32	11.38
2005	-3.36	1.68	8.43	2.43	9.13
2006	11.65	-5.52	0.43	6.40	12.72

Trailing	Total Return%	+/- S&P 500	+/- Russ MG	%Rank Cat	Growth of $10,000
3 Mo	6.40	-0.30	-0.55	56	10,640
6 Mo	6.86	-5.88	-1.04	36	10,686
1 Yr	12.72	-3.07	2.06	23	11,272
3 Yr Avg	11.07	0.63	-1.66	48	13,702
5 Yr Avg	6.93	0.74	-1.29	42	13,980
10 Yr Avg	—	—	—	—	—
15 Yr Avg	—	—	—	—	—

Tax Analysis	Tax-Adj Rtn%	%Rank Cat	Tax-Cost Rat	%Rank Cat
3 Yr (estimated)	10.24	43	0.75	38
5 Yr (estimated)	6.46	40	0.44	31
10 Yr (estimated)	—	—	—	—

Potential Capital Gain Exposure: 8% of assets

Morningstar's Take by Dan Culloton 11-29-06

A lot has happened to Vanguard Mid Cap Growth in a short time; the long-term effects aren't clear.

Some near-term ramifications are apparent, though. The fund has new management, portfolio turnover will be higher this year, expenses will tick up, and a big capital gains distribution is headed shareholders' way.

Manager changes usually raise yellow flags. In this case it's not surprising Vanguard would make a change here, because the fund's former subadvisor, Provident Investment Counsel, turned in boom or bust results and didn't really compensate fund owners for the gyrations. Still the arrival of two new subadvisors will take some time to digest.

The teams that now divide this portfolio, Chartwell Investment Partners and William Blair & Co., both boast experienced managers and analysts who use fundamental analysis to pick profitable companies with strong growth prospects. The biggest differences between them is that Mark Cunneen and Ed Antoian of Chartwell trade more and emphasize companies that have secular trends, new products, or other catalysts filling their sails. Meanwhile, Harvey Bundy, Robert Lanphier, and David Ricci of William Blair stress companies with enduring competitive advantages and hold them longer. Separate accounts managed by each team have decent records, though it's hard to say how the strategies will interact.

It's clear, however, that the fund has had to trade more this year as the new managers remade the portfolio. Vanguard estimates the fund's expense ratio also could increase by as much as 20 hundredths of a percent to 0.57% due to the changes. The fund's levy still will be less than half that of the median no-load mid-cap fund's, though. Of more immediate concern is the estimated $2.69 per share capital gains distribution (more than 13% of the fund's net asset value) this offering will pay in December. That should cause taxable investors to balk at this fund now. Others should hold out, too, until the managers prove themselves.

Address:	PO Box 2600 Valley Forge PA 19482 800-997-2798	Minimum Purchase:	$10000	Add: $100	IRA: $3000
		Min Auto Inv Plan:	$10000	Add: $50	
		Sales Fees:	No-load		
Web Address:	www.vanguard.com	Management Fee:	0.54%		
Inception:	12-31-97*	Actual Fees:	Mgt:0.54%	Dist: —	
Advisor:	Chartwell Investment Partners, LP	Expense Projections:	3Yr:$183	5Yr:$318	10Yr:$714
Subadvisor:	None	Income Distrib:	Annually		
NTF Plans:	Vanguard NTF				

Historical Profile

Return	Average
Risk	Above Avg
Rating	★★★ Neutral

Investment Style: Equity, Stock %

99% 97% 93% 95% 94% 95% 97% 96% 94%

▼ Manager Change
▽ Partial Manager Change

Growth of $10,000
— Investment Values of Fund
— Investment Values of S&P 500

31.0 / 26.0 / 20.0 / 15.0 / 10.0

Performance Quartile (within Category)

1995	1996	1997	1998	1999	2000	2001	2002	2003	2004	2005	2006	History
—	—	10.00	12.63	22.09	18.92	14.12	10.09	14.41	16.05	17.51	17.07	NAV
—	—	0.00*	26.30	83.33	12.96	-25.37	-28.54	42.81	11.38	9.13	12.72	Total Return %
—	—	—	-2.28	62.29	22.06	-13.48	-6.44	14.13	0.50	4.22	-3.07	+/-S&P 500
—	—	—	8.44	32.04	24.71	-5.22	-1.13	0.10	-4.10	-2.97	2.06	+/-Russ MG
—	—	—	0.00	0.00	0.00	0.00	0.00	0.00	0.00	0.03	0.25	Income Return %
—	—	—	26.30	83.33	12.96	-25.37	-28.54	42.81	11.38	9.10	12.47	Capital Return %
—	—	—	24	24	20	73	65	21	69	61	23	Total Rtn % Rank Cat
—	—	0.00	0.00	0.00	0.00	0.00	0.00	0.00	0.00	0.01	0.04	Income $
—	—	0.00	0.00	0.94	6.71	0.00	0.00	0.00	0.00	0.00	2.68	Capital Gains $
—	—	—	1.04	1.39	2.14	1.39	1.24	0.48	0.34	0.39	0.47	Expense Ratio %
—	—	—	-0.43	-1.03	-1.76	-1.02	-1.02	-0.18	-0.05	0.01	0.26	Income Ratio %
—	—	—	167	174	206	149	44	106	102	80	159	Turnover Rate %
—	—	—	7	19	29	33	35	304	512	619	811	Net Assets $mil

Rating and Risk

Time Period	Load-Adj Return %	Morningstar Rtn vs Cat	Morningstar Risk vs Cat	Morningstar Risk-Adj Rating
1 Yr	12.72			
3 Yr	11.07	Avg	+Avg	★★★
5 Yr	6.93	Avg	+Avg	★★★
10 Yr	—	—	—	
Incept	11.80			

Other Measures	Standard Index S&P 500	Best Fit Index Mstar Mid Growth TR
Alpha	-3.2	-2.5
Beta	1.63	1.02
R-Squared	71	93
Standard Deviation	13.32	
Mean	11.07	
Sharpe Ratio	0.62	

Portfolio Analysis 09-30-06

Share change since 06-06 Total Stocks:117	Sector	PE	Tot Ret%	% Assets
⊕ Paychex, Inc.	Business	30.4	5.62	2.61
⊕ Fastenal Company	Business	27.8	-7.37	2.04
⊕ Corporate Executive Boar	Business	46.2	-0.97	1.90
⊕ MedImmune, Inc.	Health	—	-7.57	1.63
⊕ E*Trade Financial Corpor	Financial	17.6	7.48	1.62
⊕ IntercontinentalExchange	Financial	—	—	1.61
⊕ Jabil Circuit, Inc.	Hardware	18.8	-33.33	1.53
⊕ Tractor Supply	Consumer	20.7	-15.55	1.53
⊕ Laureate Education, Inc.	Consumer	27.1	-7.39	1.38
⊕ MSC Industrial Direct Co	Business	21.6	-1.47	1.36
⊖ Bed Bath & Beyond, Inc.	Consumer	20.1	5.39	1.33
⊖ Lamar Advertising Compan	Business	—	41.75	1.28
⊖ Pharmaceutical Product D	Health	24.3	4.26	1.27
⊕ Rockwell Collins, Inc.	Ind Mtrls	23.7	37.70	1.23
⊖ Cognizant Technology Sol	Business	52.9	53.49	1.21
⊕ J2 Global Communications	Telecom	26.6	27.52	1.21
⊖ Smith International, Inc	Energy	17.0	11.59	1.20
⊕ Investors Financial Serv	Financial	17.9	16.09	1.17
⊕ Grant Prideco, Inc.	Energy	15.2	-9.86	1.16
⊕ Activision	Software	—	25.47	1.15

Current Investment Style

Value Blnd Growth — Large Mid Small

Market Cap	%
Giant	0.0
Large	12.5
Mid	75.7
Small	11.7
Micro	0.0

Avg $mil: 4,525

Value Measures		Rel Category
Price/Earnings	22.68	1.11
Price/Book	3.52	1.10
Price/Sales	2.30	1.31
Price/Cash Flow	13.49	1.18
Dividend Yield %	0.57	0.90

Growth Measures	%	Rel Category
Long-Term Erngs	18.15	1.12
Book Value	13.32	1.05
Sales	16.82	1.68
Cash Flow	20.89	1.13
Historical Erngs	26.96	1.08

Profitability	%	Rel Category
Return on Equity	17.41	0.97
Return on Assets	9.80	1.05
Net Margin	12.25	1.05

Sector Weightings	% of Stocks	Rel S&P 500	3 Year High Low	
☁ Info	19.05	0.95		
Software	6.14	1.78	14	6
Hardware	9.86	1.07	20	9
Media	0.02	0.01	5	0
Telecom	3.03	0.86	7	2
⚙ Service	61.48	1.33		
Health	16.44	1.36	24	14
Consumer	13.87	1.81	15	6
Business	20.32	4.80	20	10
Financial	10.85	0.49	12	2
Mfg	19.47	0.58		
Goods	3.16	0.37	11	1
Ind Mtrls	8.03	0.67	12	3
Energy	8.23	0.84	14	4
Utilities	0.05	0.01	0	0

Composition

	%
● Cash	6.4
● Stocks	93.6
● Bonds	0.0
○ Other	0.0
Foreign	1.6
(% of Stock)	

Vanguard Mid Cap Idx

	Ticker	Load	NAV	Yield	Total Assets	Mstar Category
	VIMSX	None	$19.78	1.3%	$17,967 mil	Mid-Cap Blend

Governance and Management

Stewardship Grade: B

Portfolio Manager(s)

In 2005, Vanguard's index maven Gus Sauter handed off the daily managerial chores here to Donald Butler, who has been with the firm since 1992 and has worked with Sauter on this fund since its inception. Butler also handles the day-to-day management of Vanguard Extended Market Index and Vanguard Institutional Index. As Vanguard's chief investment officer, Sauter still serves in a supervisory role here.

Strategy

The fund adopted the MSCI U.S. Mid-Cap 450 Index as its benchmark in 2003. Unlike its former benchmark, the S&P Mid-Cap 400 Index, this fund doesn't screen for firms with limited operation histories. However, it employs a more sophisticated methodology that should more closely approximate the group norm. It also uses buffer zones to limit the migration of stocks between market-cap bands, which should help limit turnover.

Performance 12-31-06

	1st Qtr	2nd Qtr	3rd Qtr	4th Qtr	Total
2002	6.71	-9.35	-16.56	5.79	-14.61
2003	-4.45	16.31	6.28	13.57	34.14
2004	4.65	1.09	-0.94	14.84	20.35
2005	-0.45	4.43	6.33	3.06	13.93
2006	7.54	-2.90	1.30	7.38	13.60

Trailing	Total Return%	+/- S&P 500	+/- S&P Mid 400	%Rank Cat	Growth of $10,000
3 Mo	7.38	0.68	0.39	53	10,738
6 Mo	8.78	-3.96	2.95	52	10,878
1 Yr	13.60	-2.19	3.28	45	11,360
3 Yr Avg	15.92	5.48	2.83	16	15,577
5 Yr Avg	12.28	6.09	1.39	18	17,845
10 Yr Avg	—	—	—	—	—
15 Yr Avg	—	—	—	—	—

Tax Analysis	Tax-Adj Rtn%	%Rank Cat	Tax-Cost Rat	%Rank Cat
3 Yr (estimated)	15.70	10	0.19	8
5 Yr (estimated)	11.98	16	0.27	17
10 Yr (estimated)	—	—	—	—

Potential Capital Gain Exposure: 28% of assets

Morningstar's Take by Sonya Morris 11-29-06

The fine Vanguard Mid Capitalization Index has a long list of pleasing attributes.

An inventory of this fund's many strengths should begin at the expense line. With a price tag of just 0.22%, this is one of the cheapest mid-blend funds available. Low costs are crucial to the success of index funds because they use their expense advantage to edge past rivals over time.

Furthermore, this fund's low fee structure helps make management's job of tracking the index easier. But Vanguard's indexing team is a skillful lot, and they've demonstrated their capabilities here by making up some of the ground lost to expenses. Since mid-2003, when the fund switched its benchmark to the MSCI US Mid-Cap 400 Index, it has generated average annual returns that fall just 0.15% shy of the index's. It has also tracked its benchmark closely on a calendar-year basis. In 2004 it lagged its index by just 0.17%, and in 2005 it fell short of its bogy by a tiny margin of 0.01%.

That's been enough to lift this fund to the top of the category. Its average annual returns since its 1998 inception surpass 84% of its peers. And since it adopted the MSCI benchmark, its trailing returns rank in the category's top 20%.

That fine pretax record has paved the way to an impressive posttax showing as well. The fund's three-year tax-cost ratio (which expresses tax costs in the form of an expense ratio) of 0.17% ranks among the lowest 10% in the category. Indexing is an inherently tax-efficient strategy because trading is kept to a minimum. And this fund's turnover has trended significantly lower since it adopted the MSCI benchmark, which employs a methodology that takes steps to keep turnover in check. Management also attempts to enhance the fund's tax friendliness by employing tactics such as tax-loss harvesting (when it can do so without venturing too far from its benchmark).

All told, this fund's low costs, skillful management, and fine, tax-efficient record make it easy to recommend.

Address:	PO Box 2600	Minimum Purchase:	$3000	Add: $100	IRA: $3000
	Valley Forge PA 19482	Min Auto Inv Plan:	$3000	Add: $50	
	800-997-2798	Sales Fees:	No-load		
Web Address:	www.vanguard.com	Management Fee:	0.19%		
Inception:	05-21-98*	Actual Fees:	Mgt:0.19%	Dist: —	
Advisor:	Vanguard Advisers, Inc.	Expense Projections:	3Yr:$71	5Yr:$124	10Yr:$280
Subadvisor:	None	Income Distrib:	Annually		
NTF Plans:	Vanguard NTF				

Historical Profile

Return	Above Avg
Risk	Average
Rating	★★★★ Above Avg

	1995	1996	1997	1998	1999	2000	2001	2002	2003	2004	2005	2006	History
	—	—	—	10.79	11.30	12.21	11.81	9.88	13.13	15.64	17.63	19.78	NAV
	—	—	—	8.35*	15.32	18.10	-0.50	-14.61	34.14	20.35	13.93	13.60	Total Return %
	—	—	—	—	-5.72	27.20	11.39	7.49	5.46	9.47	9.02	-2.19	+/-S&P 500
	—	—	—	—	0.60	0.59	0.11	-0.08	-1.48	3.87	1.37	3.28	+/-S&P Mid 400
	—	—	—	—	0.74	0.70	0.58	0.79	1.23	1.23	1.22	1.40	Income Return %
	—	—	—	—	14.58	17.40	-1.08	-15.40	32.91	19.12	12.71	12.20	Capital Return %
	—	—	—	—	56	26	50	43	56	19	11	45	Total Rtn % Rank Cat
	—	—	—	0.05	0.08	0.08	0.07	0.09	0.12	0.16	0.19	0.25	Income $
	—	—	—	0.05	0.94	0.98	0.25	0.13	0.00	0.00	0.00	0.00	Capital Gains $
	—	—	—	0.25	0.25	0.25	0.25	0.26	0.26	0.22	0.22	—	Expense Ratio %
	—	—	—	1.19	0.99	0.90	0.83	0.85	1.20	1.26	1.36	—	Income Ratio %
	—	—	—	44	38	51	24	20	73	16	18	—	Turnover Rate %
	—	—	—	206	605	1,614	2,049	2,267	3,610	5,234	6,399	7,677	Net Assets $mil

Rating and Risk

Time Period	Load-Adj Return %	Morningstar Rtn vs Cat	Morningstar Risk vs Cat	Morningstar Risk-Adj Rating
1 Yr	13.60			
3 Yr	15.92	+Avg	Avg	★★★★
5 Yr	12.28	+Avg	Avg	★★★★
10 Yr	—	—	—	—
Incept	11.85			

Other Measures	Standard Index S&P 500	Best Fit Index Mstar Mid Core
Alpha	2.4	1.8
Beta	1.40	0.94
R-Squared	82	97
Standard Deviation	10.60	
Mean	15.92	
Sharpe Ratio	1.15	

Portfolio Analysis 09-30-06

Share change since 06-06 Total Stocks:450	Sector	PE	Tot Ret%	% Assets
⊕ American Tower Corporati	Telecom	—	37.57	0.66
⊕ CSX Corporation	Business	15.4	37.05	0.63
⊕ Qwest Communications Int	Telecom	—	48.14	0.61
⊕ ProLogis Trust	Financial	33.5	34.02	0.61
⊕ AES Corporation	Utilities	33.4	39.23	0.58
⊕ Micron Technology, Inc.	Hardware	24.1	4.88	0.55
⊕ Seagate Technology	Hardware	23.7	34.47	0.53
⊕ GlobalSantaFe Corporatio	Energy	16.3	24.06	0.53
⊕ T Rowe Price Group	Financial	26.1	23.27	0.52
⊕ Sempra Energy	Utilities	10.7	28.10	0.51
⊕ Archstone-Smith Trust	Financial	59.0	43.93	0.51
⊕ Chesapeake Energy Corp.	Energy	6.1	-7.74	0.50
⊕ Office Depot, Inc.	Consumer	22.9	21.56	0.50
⊕ Host Hotels & Resorts, I	Financial	51.9	33.95	0.49
⊕ Kinder Morgan, Inc.	Energy	20.8	19.22	0.49
⊕ Liberty Capital A	Media	—	—	0.49
⊕ Boston Properties, Inc.	Financial	14.9	62.75	0.49
⊕ Humana	Health	21.8	1.80	0.47
⊕ Public Storage, Inc.	Financial	46.2	47.46	0.47
⊕ Constellation Energy Gro	Utilities	17.6	22.70	0.46

Current Investment Style

Market Cap	%
Giant	0.0
Large	13.2
Mid	86.8
Small	0.0
Micro	0.0

Avg $mil: 6,334

Value Measures		Rel Category
Price/Earnings	15.90	0.99
Price/Book	2.41	1.07
Price/Sales	1.17	1.04
Price/Cash Flow	9.07	1.07
Dividend Yield %	1.37	1.05

Growth Measures	%	Rel Category
Long-Term Erngs	12.57	0.99
Book Value	8.50	1.02
Sales	9.91	1.11
Cash Flow	10.66	1.26
Historical Erngs	19.13	1.07

Profitability	%	Rel Category
Return on Equity	16.66	1.04
Return on Assets	8.45	1.05
Net Margin	12.05	1.11

Sector Weightings	% of Stocks	Rel S&P 500	3 Year High Low
⟳ Info	17.32	0.87	
Ⓝ Software	2.73	0.79	3 3
Ⓗ Hardware	9.19	0.99	13 9
Ⓜ Media	1.94	0.51	3 2
Ⓣ Telecom	3.46	0.99	3 1
⟲ Service	50.66	1.10	
Ⓗ Health	10.33	0.86	11 10
Ⓒ Consumer	10.31	1.35	12 10
Ⓑ Business	8.97	2.12	10 7
Ⓢ Financial	21.05	0.95	21 18
⟶ Mfg	32.03	0.95	
Ⓖ Goods	7.25	0.85	8 7
Ⓘ Ind Mtrls	9.07	0.76	12 9
Ⓔ Energy	9.80	1.00	12 7
Ⓤ Utilities	5.91	1.69	6 6

Composition

● Cash	0.1	
● Stocks	99.9	
● Bonds	0.0	
● Other	0.0	
Foreign	0.3	
(% of Stock)		

M⟨RNINGSTAR® Funds 500

Vanguard Morgan Gr

	Ticker	Load	NAV	Yield	Total Assets	Mstar Category
	VMRGX	None	$18.98	1.1%	$7,526 mil	Large Growth

Governance and Management

Stewardship Grade: B

Portfolio Manager(s)

In January 2006, Jim Stetler replaced Gus Sauter as manager of the 30% sleeve managed by Vanguard. Sauter had been gradually reducing his managerial duties at this and other funds since becoming Vanguard's chief investment officer in 2003. Stetler is assisted by Joel Dickson, who heads up Vanguard's Quantitative Equity Group. Wellington Management's Robert Rands, who recently announced his retirement, has been replaced by Paul Marrkand, formerly the manager of Putnam Vista. John Cone (who was added to the team in April 2000) has guided Vanguard Growth & Income to strong returns.

Strategy

Two of the fund's three managers, John Cone and Jim Stetler, use quantitative approaches to beat their respective benchmarks. Cone attempts to beat the Russell Midcap Growth Index, while Stetler tries to top the MSCI U.S. Prime Market Growth Index. Paul Marrkand, who manages 40% of the portfolio, looks for moderately priced growth stocks that have the potential to surge. Although it has a growth bias, the portfolio is still fairly well diversified across sectors and individual issues, typically courting less price risk than most funds in the category.

Performance 12-31-06

	1st Qtr	2nd Qtr	3rd Qtr	4th Qtr	Total
2002	-1.85	-14.28	-14.78	6.67	-23.52
2003	-1.35	16.64	3.98	11.78	33.73
2004	2.69	1.38	-4.59	11.22	10.47
2005	-3.86	3.76	4.67	4.48	9.09
2006	5.25	-3.86	2.34	7.28	11.09

Trailing	Total Return%	+/- S&P 500	+/- Russ 1000Gr	%Rank Cat	Growth of $10,000
3 Mo	7.28	0.58	1.35	13	10,728
6 Mo	9.95	-2.95	-0.31	30	10,979
1 Yr	11.09	-4.70	2.02	16	11,109
3 Yr Avg	10.22	-0.22	3.35	13	13,390
5 Yr Avg	6.49	0.30	3.80	11	13,694
10 Yr Avg	8.30	-0.12	2.86	15	22,197
15 Yr Avg	10.22	-0.42	2.20	22	43,043

Tax Analysis	Tax-Adj Rtn%	%Rank Cat	Tax-Cost Rat	%Rank Cat
3 Yr (estimated)	9.91	11	0.28	19
5 Yr (estimated)	6.27	10	0.21	22
10 Yr (estimated)	6.50	21	1.66	82

Potential Capital Gain Exposure: 14% of assets

Morningstar's Take by Reginald Laing 11-07-06

As a manager transition nears completion, the case for Vanguard Morgan Growth remains strong.

At year's end, manager Robert Rands will retire from the Wellington Management team that runs 40% of this fund. Rands, who has helmed this sleeve since 1994, will be replaced by Paul Marrkand, formerly of Putnam Investments.

Though Rands is this fund's longest-tenured manager, we're not overconcerned about the impact of his departure. First, by their nature, multimanager funds like this one are designed to better withstand manager departures. Moreover, we regarded Marrkand highly when he was at Putnam Vista, and Wellington chose him as Rands' successor after an exhaustive interview process. More important, under Rands' tutelage, Marrkand has comanaged the Wellington sleeve for most of the past year, in which time the fund has prospered. Last, it's worth noting that the talented research team dedicated to this particular strategy, as well as the firm's vast central analyst pool, remains intact.

The other portfolio managers--Jim Stetler of Vanguard's Quantitative Equity Group and John Cone of Franklin Portfolio Associates, who each run 30% of the fund--continue to ply their quantitative strategies. QEG's Stetler tries to beat a large-growth index by making modest bets against it. Franklin's Cone makes slightly bigger bets on sectors and on the individual companies in his mid-growth benchmark. These benchmark-conscious quant strategies aren't very bold, but they don't need to be. They're designed to edge past their respective benchmarks, and are assisted in that effort by this fund's very low expenses.

Indeed, a 0.39% expense ratio is this offering's biggest advantage. The fund won't top the category in any single year. But those low fees, combined with talented managers following sound strategies, will make the fund difficult to beat over long stretches of time.

Address:	PO Box 2600
	Valley Forge PA 19482
	800-997-2798
Web Address:	www.vanguard.com
Inception:	12-31-68
Advisor:	Franklin Portfolio Associates, LLC
Subadvisor:	None
NTF Plans:	Vanguard NTF

Minimum Purchase:	$3000	Add: $100	IRA: $3000
Min Auto Inv Plan:	$3000	Add: $50	
Sales Fees:	No-load		
Management Fee:	0.42%		
Actual Fees:	Mgt:0.39%	Dist: —	
Expense Projections:	3Yr:$132	5Yr:$230	10Yr:$518
Income Distrib:	Annually		

Historical Profile

Return	Above Avg
Risk	Average
Rating	★★★★ Above Avg

94% 91% 86% 96% 92% 95% 94% 93% 94%

▼ Manager Change
▽ Partial Manager Change

Growth of $10,000
■ Investment Values of Fund
— Investment Values of S&P 500

Performance Quartile (within Category)

1995	1996	1997	1998	1999	2000	2001	2002	2003	2004	2005	2006	History
14.09	15.63	17.54	19.72	22.92	17.08	14.63	11.15	14.87	16.32	17.71	18.98	NAV
35.98	23.30	30.81	22.26	34.10	-12.51	-13.60	-23.52	33.73	10.47	9.09	11.09	Total Return %
-1.60	0.34	-2.55	-6.32	13.06	-3.41	-1.71	-1.42	5.05	-0.41	4.18	-4.70	+/-S&P 500
-1.20	0.18	0.32	-16.45	0.94	9.91	6.82	4.36	3.98	4.17	3.83	2.02	+/-Russ 1000Gr
1.33	1.02	1.05	1.05	0.78	0.67	0.44	0.27	0.36	0.71	0.58	1.15	Income Return %
34.65	22.28	29.76	21.21	33.32	-13.18	-14.04	-23.79	33.37	9.76	8.51	9.94	Capital Return %
27	21	26	78	52	51	20	27	18	27	26	16	Total Rtn % Rank Cat
0.15	0.14	0.16	0.18	0.15	0.15	0.08	0.04	0.04	0.11	0.10	0.20	Income $
1.16	1.53	2.52	1.43	3.08	2.95	0.05	0.00	0.00	0.00	0.00	0.50	Capital Gains $
0.48	0.51	0.48	0.44	0.42	0.40	0.41	0.48	0.50	0.44	0.39	0.41	Expense Ratio %
1.10	0.97	0.93	0.96	0.71	0.73	0.49	0.37	0.31	0.32	0.82	0.95	Income Ratio %
76	73	76	81	65	94	53	104	91	88	88	90	Turnover Rate %
1,471	2,054	2,795	3,555	5,066	4,661	3,493	2,576	3,789	4,563	4,781	5,592	Net Assets $mil

Rating and Risk

Time Period	Load-Adj Return %	Morningstar Rtn vs Cat	Morningstar Risk vs Cat	Morningstar Risk-Adj Rating
1 Yr	11.09			
3 Yr	10.22	+Avg	Avg	★★★★
5 Yr	6.49	+Avg	Avg	★★★★
10 Yr	8.30	+Avg	Avg	★★★★
Incept	10.96			

Other Measures	Standard Index S&P 500	Best Fit Index Russ MG
Alpha	-2.1	-0.8
Beta	1.30	0.83
R-Squared	85	95
Standard Deviation	9.69	
Mean	10.22	
Sharpe Ratio	0.72	

Portfolio Analysis 09-30-06

Share change since 06-06 Total Stocks:344

	Sector	PE	Tot Ret%	% Assets
⊖ Microsoft Corporation	Software	23.8	15.83	2.98
⊖ Oracle Corporation	Software	26.7	40.38	2.25
⊕ Cisco Systems, Inc.	Hardware	30.1	59.64	1.75
⊕ Walt Disney Company	Media	21.0	44.26	1.62
⊕ ConocoPhillips	Energy	6.5	26.53	1.15
⊕ Manpower, Inc.	Business	20.7	62.53	1.13
⊕ GlobalSantaFe Corporatio	Energy	16.3	24.06	1.06
⊕ Accenture, Ltd.	Business	22.0	29.32	1.06
⊕ Network Appliance, Inc.	Hardware	56.7	45.48	1.04
⊖ Freeport-McMoRan Copper	Ind Mtrls	7.7	13.08	1.02
⊕ Abbott Laboratories	Health	24.3	26.88	1.01
⊖ AstraZeneca PLC ADR	Health	18.7	13.28	1.00
⊕ Boeing Company	Ind Mtrls	41.2	28.38	0.97
⊕ Parker Hannifin Corporat	Ind Mtrls	13.2	18.00	0.97
⊕ News Corporation, Ltd. A	Media	—	—	0.95
⊖ Procter & Gamble Company	Goods	23.9	13.36	0.93
⊕ Johnson & Johnson	Health	17.5	12.45	0.90
⊕ Merck & Co., Inc.	Health	19.1	42.66	0.90
⊕ PepsiCo, Inc.	Goods	21.5	7.86	0.89
⊕ Joy Global, Inc.	Ind Mtrls	15.1	22.11	0.88

Current Investment Style

Value Blnd Growth — Large Mid Small

Market Cap	%
Giant	32.6
Large	27.5
Mid	39.2
Small	0.7
Micro	0.0

Avg $mil: 20,412

Value Measures		Rel Category
Price/Earnings	16.13	0.84
Price/Book	3.18	0.96
Price/Sales	1.32	0.68
Price/Cash Flow	9.48	0.83
Dividend Yield %	1.15	1.12

Growth Measures	%	Rel Category
Long-Term Erngs	14.22	0.99
Book Value	10.28	0.89
Sales	11.25	0.97
Cash Flow	21.26	1.27
Historical Erngs	20.63	0.90

Profitability	%	Rel Category
Return on Equity	22.96	1.13
Return on Assets	11.29	1.03
Net Margin	13.48	0.95

Sector Weightings	% of Stocks	Rel S&P 500	3 Year High Low
↻ Info	28.16	1.41	
Software	7.43	2.15	9 6
Hardware	14.70	1.59	20 14
Media	4.67	1.23	8 4
Telecom	1.36	0.39	3 1
⊑ Service	44.18	0.96	
Health	16.17	1.34	22 16
Consumer	8.48	1.11	16 8
Business	10.54	2.49	11 5
Financial	8.99	0.40	10 6
⊡ Mfg	27.65	0.82	
Goods	5.66	0.66	7 5
Ind Mtrls	13.56	1.14	14 4
Energy	7.52	0.77	8 2
Utilities	0.91	0.26	1 0

Composition

● Cash	6.3
● Stocks	93.7
● Bonds	0.0
● Other	0.0
Foreign	5.6
(% of Stock)	

Vanguard Prec Mtls Mining

✔ **Analyst Pick**

Ticker	Load	NAV	Yield	Total Assets	Mstar Category
VGPMX	Closed	$28.00	1.6%	$3,394 mil	Specialty-Precious Metals

Governance and Management

Stewardship Grade: B

Portfolio Manager(s)

Graham French, a portfolio manager with M&G Investment Management, has been at the helm since June 1996 and is backed by a team of analysts. M&G, a U.K. firm, has approximately $175 billion under management.

Strategy

Manager Graham French focuses on large, low-cost global mining companies with solid balance sheets and good management at reasonable valuations. The fund's mandate was changed in 2004 to allow investments in a wide range of mining companies, which has meant a doubling of names in the portfolio and exposure to a much broader range of commodities, including coal, uranium, copper, and nickel. The fund also now holds more larger-cap names than its precious-metals rivals, which dampens its diversification potential compared with more gold-focused offerings.

Performance 12-31-06

	1st Qtr	2nd Qtr	3rd Qtr	4th Qtr	Total
2002	25.93	4.30	-9.06	11.64	33.35
2003	-8.17	14.30	23.18	23.32	59.45
2004	-2.56	-12.16	13.94	10.80	8.09
2005	4.37	1.15	27.53	6.80	43.79
2006	21.52	4.44	-6.69	13.20	34.06

Trailing	Total Return%	+/- MSCI EAFE	+/- MSCI W Me&M	%Rank Cat	Growth of $10,000
3 Mo	13.20	2.85	-3.75	88	11,320
6 Mo	5.63	-9.06	-6.06	80	10,563
1 Yr	34.06	7.72	-0.50	42	13,406
3 Yr Avg	27.73	7.80	0.74	1	20,839
5 Yr Avg	34.68	19.70	8.32	33	44,311
10 Yr Avg	13.90	6.19	—	5	36,748
15 Yr Avg	11.52	3.66	—	14	51,321

Tax Analysis	Tax-Adj Rtn%	%Rank Cat	Tax-Cost Rat	%Rank Cat
3 Yr (estimated)	26.13	1	1.25	57
5 Yr (estimated)	32.74	34	1.44	56
10 Yr (estimated)	12.54	4	1.19	68

Potential Capital Gain Exposure: 39% of assets

Morningstar's Take by Karen Wallace 12-20-06

Investors should stick with Vanguard Precious Metals and Mining.

This fund's standout performance of the last few years hasn't gone unnoticed. Assets increased from around $670 million at the end of 2003 to $3.3 billion recently; it's now the largest fund in the category by far. Commendably, Vanguard closed the fund to new investors in February 2006 in order to preserve longtime manager Graham French's investing flexibility.

One of the secrets to the fund's success in recent years has been its broader mandate. Unlike most category rivals, a significant percentage of this fund's assets is not devoted to precious metals. French can invest in copper and platinum as well as base metals (such as lead, aluminum, and nickel) and coal producers. This diversification has been a boon in recent years, as most of these industries have risen along with gold and, in some cases, have outpaced gold's rise. For example, strong demand from both developed and industrializing nations

such as China and India have buoyed the price of copper and nickel.

But investors should be aware that this fund may not always fire on all cylinders. Commodities markets don't always move in sync, which could lead this fund to underperform its gold-focused peers when the gold price is soaring and other commodities are in the dumps.

However, the fund's broader mandate, in addition to French's focus on low cost-producers with strong cash flows, has meant the fund is less volatile (as measured by standard deviation) than its category peers.

In short, although this fund is still highly volatile given its focus on a volatile sector, French has delivered impressive risk-adjusted returns over all long-term time periods. In addition, at 40 basis points, the fund's fees are among the cheapest in the category--they're even in line with the fees of exchange-traded fund options.

Address:	PO Box 2600 Valley Forge, PA 19482 800-997-2798	Minimum Purchase: Min Auto Inv Plan: Sales Fees:	Closed Closed No-load, 1.00%R	Add: — Add: —	IRA: —
Web Address: Inception: Advisor: Subadvisor:	www.vanguard.com 05-23-84 M&G Investment Management Ltd. None	Management Fee: Actual Fees: Expense Projections: Income Distrib:	0.30% mx./0.10% mn. Mgt:0.37% 3Yr:$128 Annually	Dist: — 5Yr:$224	10Yr:$505
NTF Plans:	Vanguard NTF				

Historical Profile

Return Above Avg
Risk Low
Rating ★★★★ Highest

	90%	95%	96%	96%	94%	98%	97%	97%	95%

▼ Manager Change
▽ Partial Manager Change

Growth of $10,000
— Investment Values of Fund
— Investment Values of MSCI EAFE

Performance Quartile (within Category)

1995	1996	1997	1998	1999	2000	2001	2002	2003	2004	2005	2006	History
11.98	11.63	6.97	6.61	8.41	7.58	8.55	10.89	16.38	16.69	23.20	28.00	NAV
-4.48	-0.75	-38.92	-3.91	28.82	-7.34	18.33	33.35	59.45	8.09	43.79	34.06	Total Return %
-15.69	-6.80	-40.70	-23.84	1.79	6.85	39.75	49.29	20.86	-12.16	30.25	7.72	+/-MSCI EAFE
—	—	—	—	-21.22	16.22	17.23	37.63	-4.88	-5.79	10.13	-0.50	+/-MSCI W Me&M
1.34	1.76	1.12	1.29	1.51	2.38	5.20	5.77	8.58	0.88	1.44	2.13	Income Return %
-5.82	-2.51	-40.04	-5.20	27.31	-9.72	13.13	27.58	50.87	7.21	42.35	31.93	Capital Return %
83	82	44	21	1	56	100	32	1	1	42		Total Rtn % Rank Cat
0.17	0.21	0.13	0.09	0.10	0.20	0.39	0.49	0.93	0.14	0.24	0.49	Income $
0.00	0.07	0.00	0.00	0.00	0.00	0.00	0.00	0.86	0.56	2.54		Capital Gains $
0.25	0.60	0.50	0.62	0.77	0.77	0.65	0.63	0.60	0.55	0.48	0.40	Expense Ratio %
2.04	1.38	1.07	1.41	1.33	1.42	2.94	3.45	2.14	1.61	1.32	1.68	Income Ratio %
4	5	19	26	23	28	17	52	43	15	36	20	Turnover Rate %
549	497	293	311	382	315	371	527	669	894	2,485	3,394	Net Assets $mil

Rating and Risk

Time Period	Load-Adj Return %	Morningstar Rtn vs Cat	Morningstar Risk vs Cat	Morningstar Risk-Adj Rating
1 Yr	34.06			
3 Yr	27.73	High	Low	★★★★★
5 Yr	34.68	Avg	Low	★★★★★
10 Yr	13.90	+Avg	Low	★★★★★
Incept	8.55			

Other Measures	Standard Index MSCI EAFE	Best Fit Index MSCI W Me&M
Alpha	-4.5	0.5
Beta	1.85	1.02
R-Squared	55	91
Standard Deviation	23.70	
Mean	27.73	
Sharpe Ratio	1.03	

Portfolio Analysis 09-30-06

Share change since 06-06 Total Stocks:41	Sector	Country	% Assets
Lonmin	Ind Mtrls	U.K.	9.37
⊖ Anglo Platinum ADR	Ind Mtrls	South Africa	6.67
IMPALA PLATINUM	Ind Mtrls	South Africa	6.22
⊕ Aber Diamond Corporation	Ind Mtrls	Canada	5.40
⊖ Meridian Gold, Inc.	Ind Mtrls	Canada	4.62
⊕ Rio Tinto Ltd	Ind Mtrls	Australia	4.60
⊕ Centerra Gold Inc	Ind Mtrls	Canada	4.19
⊖ Barrick Gold Corporation	Ind Mtrls	Canada	4.06
Eramet	Ind Mtrls	France	3.93
Consol Energy, Inc.	Energy	United States	3.55
⊕ K+S Grp	Ind Mtrls	Germany	3.40
Johnson Matthey	Ind Mtrls	U.K.	3.31
⊕ Imerys	Ind Mtrls	France	3.02
⊕ Peabody Energy Corporati	Energy	United States	3.00
Iluka Resources Ltd	Ind Mtrls	Australia	2.82
⊖ First Quantum Minera	Ind Mtrls	Canada	2.78
⊕ Rio Tinto	Ind Mtrls	U.K.	2.58
⊕ FMC Corporation	Ind Mtrls	United States	2.35
⊕ Sims Grp Ltd	Business	Australia	2.31
Agrium, Inc.	Ind Mtrls	Canada	2.16

Current Investment Style

Value Blnd Growth — Large Mid Small

Market Cap	%
Giant	14.1
Large	3.7
Mid	78.3
Small	3.5
Micro	0.3
Avg $mil:	4,477

Value Measures		Rel Category
Price/Earnings	13.84	0.67
Price/Book	2.96	0.85
Price/Sales	1.56	0.29
Price/Cash Flow	9.60	0.78
Dividend Yield %	3.33	2.69

Growth Measures	%	Rel Category
Long-Term Erngs	16.61	0.88
Book Value	9.56	0.88
Sales	11.43	0.53
Cash Flow	14.20	0.35
Historical Erngs	18.35	0.68

Composition

Cash	5.4	Bonds	0.0
Stocks	94.6	Other	0.0
Foreign (% of Stock)		87.7	

Sector Weightings	% of Stocks	Rel MSCI EAFE	3 Year High	Low
☁ Info	0.00	0.00		
Software	0.00	0.00	0	0
Hardware	0.00	0.00	0	0
Media	0.00	0.00	0	0
Telecom	0.00	0.00	0	0
Service	4.40	0.09		
Health	0.00	0.00	0	0
Consumer	0.00	0.00	0	0
Business	4.40	0.87	4	0
Financial	0.00	0.00	0	0
Mfg	95.61	2.34		
Goods	0.00	0.00	0	0
Ind Mtrls	87.49	5.67	100	85
Energy	8.12	1.14	12	0
Utilities	0.00	0.00	0	0

Regional Exposure	% Stock		
UK/W. Europe	29	N. America	37
Japan	0	Latn America	2
Asia X Japan	16	Other	16

Country Exposure	% Stock		
Canada	25	Australia	16
U.K.	18	United States	12
South Africa	17		

MORNINGSTAR® Funds 500

Vanguard PRIMECAP

	Ticker	Load	NAV	Yield	Total Assets	Mstar Category
	VPMCX	Closed	$68.94	0.6%	$31,504 mil	Large Blend

Governance and Management

Stewardship Grade: B

Portfolio Manager(s)

The fund's five managers employ an unusual management structure. They share ideas but make autonomous buy and sell decisions, with each managing a percentage of assets independently. Howard Schow, Theo Kolokotrones, and Joel Fried manage the lion's share of the fund's assets and have considerable experience, while Mitchell Milias and Alfred Mordecai oversee smaller portions. The team is supported by nine analysts, eight of whom have joined the firm since 2000.

Strategy

The fund's managers follow a contrarian-growth approach. They look for swiftly growing firms, but they like to buy them on the cheap--usually when they're out of favor. They're particularly fond of companies with high unit growth. The fund often has outsized sector weightings because many of the managers' favorites are clustered in particular industries, such as hardware.

Historical Profile

Return	High
Risk	High
Rating	★★★★ Highest

	92%	86%	88%	92%	91%	93%	93%	95%	97%

Investment Style
Equity
Stock %

▼ Manager Change
▽ Partial Manager Change

Growth of $10,000
— Investment Values of Fund
— Investment Values of S&P 500

49.2
42.2
32.4
24.0
17.0
10.0

Performance Quartile (within Category)

1995	1996	1997	1998	1999	2000	2001	2002	2003	2004	2005	2006	History
26.23	30.08	39.57	47.66	62.07	60.38	51.52	38.66	53.04	62.30	65.31	68.94	NAV
35.48	18.31	36.83	25.41	41.34	4.47	-13.35	-24.56	37.75	18.31	8.49	12.30	Total Return %
-2.10	-4.65	3.47	-3.17	20.30	13.57	-1.46	-2.46	9.07	7.43	3.58	-3.49	+/-S&P 500
-2.29	-4.14	3.98	-1.61	20.43	12.26	-0.90	-2.91	7.86	6.91	2.22	-3.16	+/-Russ 1000
1.10	0.77	0.67	0.89	0.57	0.80	0.47	0.41	0.54	0.84	0.62	0.67	Income Return %
34.38	17.54	36.16	24.52	40.77	3.67	-13.82	-24.97	37.21	17.47	7.87	11.63	Capital Return %
42	76	5	40	4	17	75	82	6	2	21	78	Total Rtn % Rank Cat
0.22	0.20	0.20	0.35	0.27	0.49	0.28	0.21	0.21	0.45	0.39	0.44	Income $
0.59	0.73	1.30	1.52	4.65	4.05	0.53	0.00	0.00	0.00	1.91	4.00	Capital Gains $
0.58	0.59	0.51	0.51	0.51	0.48	0.50	0.49	0.51	0.46	0.45	0.46	Expense Ratio %
0.99	0.69	0.69	0.78	0.50	0.80	0.58	0.42	0.56	0.48	0.85	0.64	Income Ratio %
7	10	13	13	19	11	7	11	12	9	12	10	Turnover Rate %
3,237	4,204	8,186	11,210	17,912	21,762	18,096	12,999	18,356	22,998	21,067	22,372	Net Assets $mil

Performance 12-31-06

	1st Qtr	2nd Qtr	3rd Qtr	4th Qtr	Total
2002	1.34	-17.37	-17.39	9.05	-24.56
2003	-0.85	16.88	6.23	11.91	37.75
2004	5.17	3.42	-0.88	9.75	18.31
2005	-3.93	1.04	7.14	4.32	8.49
2006	6.84	-2.85	3.70	4.33	12.30

Trailing	Total Return%	+/- S&P 500	+/- Russ 1000	%Rank Cat	Growth of $10,000
3 Mo	4.33	-2.37	-2.62	97	10,433
6 Mo	8.20	-4.54	-4.16	93	10,820
1 Yr	12.30	-3.49	-3.16	78	11,230
3 Yr Avg	12.97	2.53	1.99	9	14,417
5 Yr Avg	8.42	2.23	1.60	13	14,981
10 Yr Avg	12.64	4.22	4.00	3	32,880
15 Yr Avg	14.43	3.79	3.63	3	75,526

Tax Analysis	Tax-Adj Rtn%	%Rank Cat	Tax-Cost Rat	%Rank Cat
3 Yr (estimated)	12.39	8	0.51	24
5 Yr (estimated)	8.03	11	0.36	24
10 Yr (estimated)	11.71	2	0.83	36

Potential Capital Gain Exposure: 36% of assets

Rating and Risk

Time Period	Load-Adj Return %	Morningstar Rtn vs Cat	Morningstar Risk vs Cat	Morningstar Risk-Adj Rating
1 Yr	12.30			
3 Yr	12.97	High	High	★★★★★
5 Yr	8.42	+Avg	High	★★★★
10 Yr	12.64	High	High	★★★★★
Incept	15.26			

Other Measures	Standard Index S&P 500	Best Fit Index Russ MG
Alpha	0.6	2.0
Beta	1.28	0.79
R-Squared	83	87
Standard Deviation	9.60	
Mean	12.97	
Sharpe Ratio	0.99	

Morningstar's Take by David Kathman 12-13-06

Vanguard Primecap remains an excellent core holding for those lucky enough to own it.

This fund's enormous $30 billion asset base has not prevented it from shining recently. After a couple of off years during the bear market, it has rebounded strongly to post one of the large-blend category's best records since then, trouncing the category and the S&P 500 in each of the past three years. It has slowed down a little in the choppy market of 2006; as of mid-December, it was behind its category peers and the S&P 500 for the year to date.

We don't think that modest slowdown is necessarily a result of the fund's swelling asset base, because the fund's structure allows it to handle a lot of assets without too much trouble. Not only does it traffic mainly in liquid large-cap stocks, but the portfolio is divided into five sleeves, each run more or less independently by a different comanager on the Primecap team. The comanagers don't move in lockstep, but they all follow the same long-term, low-turnover approach, such that the portfolio's annual turnover has averaged just 10%.

We also remain confident because the Primecap management team is one of the best in the business, having put together an outstanding track record over the past 20 years. The team uses a contrarian growth approach to stock-picking, and is not afraid to make bold bets on sectors it likes, such as technology and health care. Its willingness to hold on to stocks through thick and thin means that sometimes the fund goes through a dry spell, but those have been more than outweighed by the good times. The fund's 10- and 15-year records are both among the best in the large-blend category.

The fund's closing in March 2004 has slowed its asset growth, nearly all of which now comes from the low-cost Admiral shares. Potential new investors who are shut out here might consider Vanguard Primecap Core, a similar fund from the same team at a higher (but still reasonable) price.

Address:	PO Box 2600 Valley Forge PA 19482 800-997-2798
Web Address:	www.vanguard.com
Inception:	11-01-84
Advisor:	PRIMECAP Management Co.
Subadvisor:	None
NTF Plans:	Vanguard NTF

Minimum Purchase:	Closed	Add: —	IRA: —
Min Auto Inv Plan:	Closed	Add: —	
Sales Fees:	No-load, 1.00%R		
Management Fee:	0.50% mx./0.15% mn.		
Actual Fees:	Mgt:0.44%		
Expense Projections:	3Yr:$148	5Yr:$258	10Yr:$579
Income Distrib:	Annually		

Portfolio Analysis 09-30-06

Share change since 06-06 Total Stocks:125	Sector	PE	Tot Ret%	% Assets
FedEx Corporation	Business	17.2	5.40	4.85
Adobe Systems Inc.	Software	48.1	11.26	4.16
⊕ Texas Instruments, Inc.	Hardware	16.9	-9.82	3.18
⊕ Novartis AG ADR	Health	22.2	11.29	3.15
⊕ Eli Lilly & Company	Health	17.3	-5.16	2.84
Biogen Idec, Inc.	Health	NMF	8.64	2.66
⊕ Pfizer Inc.	Health	15.2	15.22	2.52
Microsoft Corporation	Software	23.8	15.83	2.44
Oracle Corporation	Software	26.7	40.38	2.40
⊕ Medtronic, Inc.	Health	23.8	-6.29	2.38
Potash Corporation of Sa	Ind Mtrls	26.0	80.04	2.35
⊖ ConocoPhillips	Energy	6.5	26.53	2.21
Micron Technology, Inc.	Hardware	24.1	4.88	2.09
DirecTV, Inc.	Media	26.5	76.63	1.93
⊖ Union Pacific Corporatio	Business	17.4	15.87	1.90
⊖ Roche Holding	Health			1.67
⊕ Sony Corporation ADR	Goods	43.2	5.50	1.51
⊕ Intuit	Software	20.9	14.48	1.50
⊖ Corning Inc.	Hardware	25.5	-4.83	1.47
⊖ Hewlett-Packard Company	Hardware	19.3	45.21	1.42

Current Investment Style

Value Blend Growth — Large Mid Small

Market Cap	%
Giant	35.0
Large	52.3
Mid	11.4
Small	1.3
Micro	0.0

Avg $mil: 30,727

Value Measures		Rel Category
Price/Earnings	17.08	1.11
Price/Book	2.72	1.06
Price/Sales	1.49	1.06
Price/Cash Flow	9.23	1.09
Dividend Yield %	0.92	0.53

Growth Measures	%	Rel Category
Long-Term Ergs	12.65	1.07
Book Value	8.19	0.91
Sales	10.43	1.08
Cash Flow	13.39	1.30
Historical Ergs	19.70	1.06

Profitability	%	Rel Category
Return on Equity	16.79	0.86
Return on Assets	9.06	0.87
Net Margin	12.75	0.95

Sector Weightings	% of Stocks	Rel S&P 500	3 Year High Low	
☞ Info	34.34	1.72		
Software	12.77	3.70	13	7
Hardware	16.86	1.82	18	16
Media	4.02	1.06	5	4
Telecom	0.69	0.20	1	1
☞ Service	45.05	0.97		
Health	21.63	1.79	24	19
Consumer	5.55	0.73	8	5
Business	12.18	2.88	14	12
Financial	5.69	0.26	7	5
☞ Mfg	20.60	0.61		
Goods	3.83	0.45	4	3
Ind Mtrls	10.33	0.87	12	10
Energy	6.44	0.66	10	6
Utilities	0.00	0.00	0	0

Composition

● Cash	2.9	
● Stocks	97.1	
● Bonds	0.0	
○ Other	0.0	
Foreign	12.7	(% of Stock)

Vanguard PRIMECAP Core

Analyst Pick ✓

	Ticker	Load	NAV	Yield	Total Assets	Mstar Category
	VPCCX	None	$12.61	0.8%	$2,556 mil	Large Growth

Governance and Management

Stewardship Grade:

Portfolio Manager(s)

Howard Schow, Mitch Milias, Theo Kolokotrones, Joel Fried, and Alfred Mordecai, who also run Vanguard Primecap and Vanguard Capital Opportunity, split the management duties here, with each manager running a sleeve of assets independent of the others. They're supported by a team of nine analysts, each of whom typically follows two disparate industries. More-experienced analysts also chip in to manage a slice of the fund's assets.

Strategy

This fund's strategy is reminiscent of Vanguard Primecap's, with firms propelled by secular growth drivers taking center stage. As such, names are typically drawn from industries boasting improving unit growth, with the health-care, consumer-discretionary, and semiconductor areas playing prominent roles. This fund shares many stocks with Vanguard Primecap, but each fund has some top holdings that are absent in the other fund. It also shares Primecap's low-turnover style and valuation-conscious, contrarian investing ethos.

Performance 12-31-06

	1st Qtr	2nd Qtr	3rd Qtr	4th Qtr	Total
2002	—	—	—	—	—
2003	—	—	—	—	—*
2004	—	—	—	—	—*
2005	-0.88	2.76	5.17	4.63	12.08
2006	5.61	-2.16	4.16	4.35	12.31

Trailing	Total Return%	+/- S&P 500	+/- Russ 1000Gr	%Rank Cat	Growth of $10,000
3 Mo	4.35	-2.35	-1.58	77	10,435
6 Mo	8.69	-4.05	-1.41	45	10,869
1 Yr	12.31	-3.48	3.24	12	11,231
3 Yr Avg	—	—	—	—	—
5 Yr Avg	—	—	—	—	—
10 Yr Avg	—	—	—	—	—
15 Yr Avg	—	—	—	—	—

Tax Analysis	Tax-Adj Rtn%	%Rank Cat	Tax-Cost Rat	%Rank Cat
3 Yr (estimated)	—	—	—	—
5 Yr (estimated)	—	—	—	—
10 Yr (estimated)	—	—	—	—

Potential Capital Gain Exposure: 9% of assets

Morningstar's Take by David Kathman 12-13-06

Investors shut out of closed Vanguard Primecap have a fine option in Vanguard Primecap Core.

This fund was created in late 2004 as an alternative to the very popular Vanguard Primecap, which has been closed to new investors since March 2004. It has already attracted more than $2 billion in assets, but that still makes it much smaller and nimbler than the $30 billion Primecap fund. One consequence of that smaller asset base is a higher expense ratio, 0.72% versus Primecap's 0.45%, but that's still a very reasonable price tag for an actively managed large-cap fund.

The best thing this fund has going for it is the Primecap management team, who have put together an outstanding record over the past 20 years and were Morningstar's 2003 Domestic Stock Managers of the Year. They use the same basic strategy across all their funds, looking for stocks with a lot of growth potential but reasonable valuations--often because of temporary problems--and holding them for a long time.

This fund looks very similar to Vanguard Primecap in many ways. Both focus on large-cap stocks, with about 15% in mid-caps, and both have a modest growth tilt and very similar sector weightings. However, the two portfolios are not identical. Some top holdings in Primecap, such as FedEx and Adobe, have been in that fund for years but are much less prominent here because their valuations weren't attractive enough when the managers were building this portfolio. On the other hand, this fund's smaller asset base has let the managers more quickly build up prominent positions in such promising stocks as Sepracor and ASML Holding.

This fund has outperformed Primecap in its short life, but such short time periods don't mean much. The key point is that both are great funds from a topnotch team of managers, well worth considering as core funds. The fact that this fund remains open to new investors overshadows its slightly higher price tag.

Address:	P.O. Box 2600 Valley Forge, PA 19482 800-662-2739
Web Address:	www.vanguard.com
Inception:	12-09-04
Advisor:	PRIMECAP Management Co.
Subadvisor:	None
NTF Plans:	Vanguard NTF

Minimum Purchase:	$10000 Add: $100 IRA: $10000
Min Auto Inv Plan:	$10000 Add: $50
Sales Fees:	No-load, 1.00%R
Management Fee:	0.50% mx./0.20% mn.
Actual Fees:	— Dist: —
Expense Projections:	3Yr:$230 5Yr:$401 10Yr:$894
Income Distrib:	Annually

Historical Profile
Return
Risk
Rating   Not Rated

Investment Style
Equity
Stock %

81%   88%   92%

▼ Manager Change
▽ Partial Manager Change

Growth of $10,000
— Investment Values of Fund
— Investment Values of S&P 500

12.1
11.4
10.7
10.0
9.0

Performance Quartile (within Category)

1995	1996	1997	1998	1999	2000	2001	2002	2003	2004	2005	2006	History
—	—	—	—	—	—	—	—	—	10.25	11.41	12.61	NAV
—	—	—	—	—	—	—	—	—	—	12.08	12.31	Total Return %
—	—	—	—	—	—	—	—	—	—	7.17	-3.48	+/-S&P 500
—	—	—	—	—	—	—	—	—	—	6.82	3.24	+/-Russ 1000Gr
—	—	—	—	—	—	—	—	—	—	0.49	0.83	Income Return %
—	—	—	—	—	—	—	—	—	—	11.59	11.48	Capital Return %
—	—	—	—	—	—	—	—	—	—	13	12	Total Rtn % Rank Cat
—	—	—	—	—	—	—	—	—	0.00	0.05	0.10	Income $
—	—	—	—	—	—	—	—	—	0.00	0.03	0.11	Capital Gains $
—	—	—	—	—	—	—	—	—	—	—	0.60	Expense Ratio %
—	—	—	—	—	—	—	—	—	—	—	0.90	Income Ratio %
—	—	—	—	—	—	—	—	—	—	—	5	Turnover Rate %
—	—	—	—	—	—	—	—	—	—	238	2,556	Net Assets $mil

Rating and Risk

Time Period	Load-Adj Return %	Morningstar Rtn vs Cat	Morningstar Risk vs Cat	Morningstar Risk-Adj Rating
1 Yr	12.31			
3 Yr	—	—	—	—
5 Yr	—	—	—	—
10 Yr	—	—	—	—
Incept	13.18			

Other Measures	Standard Index S&P 500	Best Fit Index
Alpha	—	—
Beta	—	—
R-Squared	—	—
Standard Deviation	—	
Mean	—	
Sharpe Ratio	—	

Portfolio Analysis 09-30-06

Share change since 06-06 Total Stocks:103	Sector	PE	Tot Ret%	% Assets
⊕ Eli Lilly & Company	Health	17.3	-5.16	3.21
⊕ Novartis AG ADR	Health	22.2	11.29	3.11
⊕ Medtronic, Inc.	Health	23.8	-6.29	2.76
⊕ Intuit	Software	20.9	14.48	2.45
⊕ ASML Holding NV	Hardware	31.3	22.66	2.40
⊕ Pfizer Inc.	Health	15.2	15.22	2.27
⊕ Corning Inc.	Hardware	25.5	-4.83	2.03
⊕ Schlumberger, Ltd.	Energy	22.3	31.07	2.03
⊕ GlaxoSmithKline PLC ADR	Health	17.6	7.95	2.02
Oracle Corporation	Software	26.7	40.38	2.00
⊕ Bed Bath & Beyond, Inc.	Consumer	20.1	5.39	1.93
⊕ Southwest Airlines, Co.	Business	23.2	-6.65	1.92
⊕ Sony Corporation ADR	Goods	43.2	5.50	1.91
Roche Holding	Health			1.91
Texas Instruments, Inc.	Hardware	16.9	-9.82	1.89
⊕ Boston Scientific Corpor	Health		-29.85	1.75
Sepracor, Inc.	Health	NMF	19.34	1.71
⊕ Amgen, Inc.	Health	29.1	-13.38	1.65
⊕ Intel Corporation	Hardware	21.0	-17.18	1.58
Microsoft Corporation	Software	23.8	15.83	1.57

Current Investment Style

Value Blnd Growth — Large Mid Small

Market Cap	%
Giant	38.8
Large	48.5
Mid	12.7
Small	0.0
Micro	0.0

Avg $mil: 31,705

Value Measures		Rel Category
Price/Earnings	18.14	0.94
Price/Book	2.81	0.85
Price/Sales	1.98	1.02
Price/Cash Flow	11.11	0.98
Dividend Yield %	0.99	0.96

Growth Measures	%	Rel Category
Long-Term Erngs	13.92	0.97
Book Value	9.11	0.79
Sales	10.82	0.93
Cash Flow	10.52	0.63
Historical Erngs	16.21	0.70

Profitability	%	Rel Category
Return on Equity	19.76	0.97
Return on Assets	9.71	0.88
Net Margin	12.91	0.91

Sector Weightings	% of Stocks	Rel S&P 500	3 Year High	Low
↻ Info	32.27	1.61		
🖥 Software	8.20	2.38	8	5
💻 Hardware	17.48	1.89	18	16
📶 Media	5.75	1.52	7	5
☎ Telecom	0.84	0.24	1	1
☞ Service	47.32	1.02		
⚕ Health	24.08	2.00	25	21
🛒 Consumer	8.91	1.16	9	5
💼 Business	6.73	1.59	9	7
$ Financial	7.60	0.34	9	7
🏭 Mfg	20.43	0.60		
⚙ Goods	4.34	0.51	5	3
⚗ Ind Mtrls	10.32	0.86	13	10
🔋 Energy	5.77	0.59	9	5
💡 Utilities	0.00	0.00	0	0

Composition

● Cash	8.4
● Stocks	91.6
● Bonds	0.0
○ Other	0.0
Foreign	17.8
(% of Stock)	

M RNINGSTAR® Funds 500

Vanguard REIT Index

	Ticker	Load	NAV	Yield	Total Assets	Mstar Category
	VGSIX	None	$25.58	3.7%	$11,447 mil	Specialty-Real Estate

Governance and Management

Stewardship Grade: B

Portfolio Manager(s)

Gerard O'Reilly was named the day-to-day manager of this fund in 2005. O'Reilly has been with Vanguard since 1992 and has been involved with the fund since 1996. Gus Sauter still oversees Vanguard's quantitative equity group in his role as the firm's chief investment officer, but he is no longer the named portfolio manager.

Strategy

This fund is designed to track the performance of the MSCI U.S. REIT Index, although the Wilshire REIT Index is a more common benchmark for real estate funds. Thus, the fund is beholden to the decisions that MSCI (Morgan Stanley Capital International) makes in adding or subtracting REITs from its index.

Performance 12-31-06

	1st Qtr	2nd Qtr	3rd Qtr	4th Qtr	Total
2002	8.08	4.79	-8.48	0.10	3.75
2003	1.01	12.27	9.47	9.27	35.65
2004	11.75	-5.95	8.13	15.06	30.76
2005	-7.34	14.65	3.56	1.70	11.89
2006	14.79	-1.37	9.39	9.07	35.07

Trailing	Total Return%	+/- S&P 500	+/- DJ Wilshire REIT	%Rank Cat	Growth of $10,000
3 Mo	9.07	2.37	0.10	71	10,907
6 Mo	19.31	6.57	0.31	35	11,931
1 Yr	35.07	19.28	-1.06	46	13,507
3 Yr Avg	25.49	15.05	-1.88	59	19,762
5 Yr Avg	22.70	16.51	-1.14	66	27,811
10 Yr Avg	14.18	5.76	-1.11	62	37,662
15 Yr Avg	—	—	—	—	—

Tax Analysis	Tax-Adj Rtn%	%Rank Cat	Tax-Cost Rat	%Rank Cat
3 Yr (estimated)	23.36	45	1.70	36
5 Yr (estimated)	20.40	62	1.87	51
10 Yr (estimated)	11.80	64	2.08	63

Potential Capital Gain Exposure: 42% of assets

Morningstar's Take by John Coumarianos 12-28-06

Vanguard REIT Index's pros outweigh its cons.

This fund benefits from many of the same features that assist other index funds. Its expense ratio, which has come down over the years, is the lowest among retail funds in the real estate category. Moreover, the fund's turnover has typically been less than 20% annually since 2002. This minimizes trading costs and capital gains distributions, which can cut into returns. Because REITs (real estate investment trusts) are typically high-yielding stocks, with a large percentage of their total return coming from dividends, a low expense ratio, leaving much of the fund's yield intact, is a particular boon in this category as it can be in bond categories.

Unfortunately, this fund's structural advantages have been negated in the recent climate, while some of its disadvantages have been as salient as ever. This has allowed some of the better actively managed funds to outpace the benchmark. First, yield hasn't mattered that much, with REITs appreciating dramatically in recent years. In other words, yield has been a much smaller part of total return over the last five years than previously, minimizing this fund's structural advantage in the form of its low expense ratio.

Second and more importantly, because this fund is limited to a REIT index, it cannot invest in real estate operating companies (REOCs), such as Starwood Hotels, Marriott International, Brookfield Properties, and St. Joe. Not being organized as REITs allows these businesses to keep their earnings in order to finance future growth, and many of them have posted strong returns over the past few years. This fund, which tracks the MSCI REIT Index, has not been able to own them.

While the fee advantage should reassert itself in a more normal return environment, the limited opportunity set is permanent. Still, this fund remains a decent choice, as long as investors limit their expectations given the category's recent multiyear surge.

Address:	PO Box 2600
	Valley Forge, PA 19482
	800-997-2798
Web Address:	www.vanguard.com
Inception:	05-13-96*
Advisor:	Vanguard Advisers, Inc.
Subadvisor:	None
NTF Plans:	Vanguard NTF

Minimum Purchase:	$3000	Add: $100	IRA: $3000
Min Auto Inv Plan:	$3000	Add: $50	
Sales Fees:	No-load, 1.00%R		
Management Fee:	0.22%		
Actual Fees:	Mgt:0.18%	Dist: —	
Expense Projections:	3Yr:$68	5Yr:$118	10Yr:$268
Income Distrib:	Quarterly		

Historical Profile

Return	Average
Risk	Above Avg
Rating	★★★ Neutral

Growth of $10,000
— Investment Values of Fund
— Investment Values of S&P 500

▼ Manager Change
▽ Partial Manager Change

| 95% | 95% | 94% | 95% | 94% | 98% | 98% | 97% | 98% |

Performance Quartile (within Category)

1995	1996	1997	1998	1999	2000	2001	2002	2003	2004	2005	2006	History
—	12.62	14.16	11.08	9.85	11.56	12.13	11.84	15.18	18.79	19.80	25.58	NAV
—	30.41*	18.76	-16.32	-4.04	26.35	12.35	3.75	35.65	30.76	11.89	35.07	Total Return %
—	—	-14.60	-44.90	-25.08	35.45	24.24	25.85	6.97	19.88	6.98	19.28	+/-S&P 500
—	—	-0.91	0.68	-1.47	-4.69	-0.01	0.15	-0.41	-2.38	-2.11	-1.06	+/-DJ Wilshire REIT
—	—	4.77	4.81	6.21	6.72	7.19	6.40	6.74	5.92	5.11	4.82	Income Return %
—	—	13.99	-21.13	-10.25	19.63	5.16	-2.65	28.91	24.84	6.78	30.25	Capital Return %
—	—	89	56	62	69	19	53	59	69	58	46	Total Rtn % Rank Cat
—	0.34	0.59	0.67	0.67	0.64	0.81	0.76	0.78	0.88	0.94	0.94	Income $
—	0.04	0.18	0.14	0.11	0.18	0.00	0.00	0.00	0.07	0.22	0.12	Capital Gains $
—	—	—	0.36	0.24	0.26	0.33	0.33	0.28	0.27	0.24	0.21	Expense Ratio %
—	—	—	5.50	4.66	5.19	5.98	5.73	4.35	4.90	4.10	2.91	Income Ratio %
—	—	—	2	29	12	21	10	12	7	17	Turnover Rate %
—	—	469	1,278	924	875	1,094	1,230	1,784	3,051	4,663	6,066	Net Assets $mil

Rating and Risk

Time Period	Load-Adj Return %	Morningstar Rtn vs Cat	Morningstar Risk vs Cat	Morningstar Risk-Adj Rating
1 Yr	35.07			
3 Yr	25.49	Avg	+Avg	★★★
5 Yr	22.70	Avg	+Avg	★★★
10 Yr	14.18	-Avg	Avg	★★★
Incept	16.14			

Other Measures	Standard Index S&P 500	Best Fit Index DJ Wilshire REIT
Alpha	12.3	-0.8
Beta	1.24	0.97
R-Squared	28	100
Standard Deviation	16.21	
Mean	25.49	
Sharpe Ratio	1.30	

Portfolio Analysis 09-30-06

Share change since 06-06 Total Stocks:106

	Sector	PE	Tot Ret%	% Assets
⊕ Simon Property Group, In	Financial	58.3	36.98	5.93
⊕ Equity Residential	Financial	NMF	34.64	4.36
⊖ Equity Office Properties	Financial	—	64.28	4.31
⊕ ProLogis Trust	Financial	33.5	34.02	4.14
⊕ Vornado Realty Trust	Financial	37.1	51.14	4.11
⊕ Archstone-Smith Trust	Financial	59.0	43.93	3.45
⊕ Host Hotels & Resorts, I	Financial	51.9	33.95	3.34
⊕ Boston Properties, Inc.	Financial	14.9	62.75	3.32
⊕ Public Storage, Inc.	Financial	46.2	47.46	3.21
⊕ General Growth Propertie	Financial	—	15.09	3.06
⊕ Kimco Realty Corporation	Financial	30.1	44.91	2.75
⊕ AvalonBay Communities, I	Financial	68.7	49.69	2.65
⊕ Developers Diversified R	Financial	40.5	39.65	1.81
⊕ Macerich Company	Financial	—	33.91	1.62
⊕ Apartment Investment & M	Financial	—	55.18	1.57
⊕ Duke Realty Corporation	Financial	74.7	28.98	1.49
⊕ AMB Property Corporation	Financial	29.8	23.30	1.44
⊕ SL Green Realty Corporat	Financial	57.8	77.73	1.43
⊕ Regency Centers Corporat	Financial	55.7	37.58	1.40
⊕ Liberty Property Trust	Financial	18.9	20.85	1.26

Current Investment Style

Value Blnd Growth — Large Mid Small

Market Cap	%
Giant	0.0
Large	40.1
Mid	43.9
Small	15.2
Micro	0.9
Avg $mil:	5,395

Value Measures		Rel Category
Price/Earnings	17.19	0.91
Price/Book	2.90	1.02
Price/Sales	4.17	1.00
Price/Cash Flow	14.95	0.97
Dividend Yield %	4.37	1.08

Growth Measures	%	Rel Category
Long-Term Erngs	6.51	0.84
Book Value	-2.84	NMF
Sales	9.95	0.91
Cash Flow	—	—
Historical Erngs	2.67	0.19

Profitability	%	Rel Category
Return on Equity	10.82	0.94
Return on Assets	9.77	1.05
Net Margin	26.47	0.99

Sector Weightings	% of Stocks	Rel S&P 500	3 Year High Low
⌖ Info	0.00	0.00	
📠 Software	0.00	0.00	0 0
💻 Hardware	0.00	0.00	0 0
📶 Media	0.00	0.00	0 0
📞 Telecom	0.00	0.00	0 0
☎ Service	100.00	2.16	
🏥 Health	0.00	0.00	0 0
🛒 Consumer	0.00	0.00	0 0
🏢 Business	0.00	0.00	0 0
💲 Financial	100.00	4.49	100 100
🏭 Mfg	0.00	0.00	
Goods	0.00	0.00	0 0
Ind Mtrls	0.00	0.00	0 0
Energy	0.00	0.00	0 0
Utilities	0.00	0.00	0 0

Composition

		%
●	Cash	2.1
●	Stocks	97.9
●	Bonds	0.0
○	Other	0.0
	Foreign	0.0
	(% of Stock)	

Vanguard Selected Value

Analyst Pick ✓

	Ticker	Load	NAV	Yield	Total Assets	Mstar Category
	VASVX	None	$21.09	1.5%	$4,584 mil	Mid-Cap Value

Governance and Management

Stewardship Grade: B

Portfolio Manager(s)

Manager Jim Barrow, whose firm runs approximately 80% of this portfolio, took the fund's reins in March 1999. He has more than 30 years of investment experience and has built a fine long-term record as lead manager of Vanguard Windsor II. Comanager Mark Giambrone joined Barrow at this fund's helm in late 2002. Vanguard added a second subadvisor, Donald Smith & Co., to the fund in May 2005. The team from Donald Smith handles the remaining 20% of the portfolio.

Strategy

Managers Jim Barrow and Mark Giambrone, who run the bulk of the portfolio, invest in stocks with very low valuations and high dividend yields. This often leads them to companies that are out of favor with most investors. A second subadvisor, Donald Smith & Co., also uses a deep-value approach, seeking companies that are trading cheaply relative to their tangible book values. Both managers concentrate heavily in individual stocks, meaning the fund's performance swings will be more pronounced than some of its rivals.

Performance 12-31-06

	1st Qtr	2nd Qtr	3rd Qtr	4th Qtr	Total
2002	11.95	-6.27	-18.22	5.13	-9.79
2003	-6.54	19.05	5.49	15.21	35.21
2004	4.79	2.69	0.00	11.86	20.38
2005	3.49	3.96	1.34	1.52	10.67
2006	2.65	0.31	7.16	7.95	19.11

Trailing	Total Return%	+/- S&P 500	+/- Russ MV	%Rank Cat	Growth of $10,000
3 Mo	7.95	1.25	-0.55	50	10,795
6 Mo	15.68	2.94	3.35	2	11,568
1 Yr	19.11	3.32	-1.11	19	11,911
3 Yr Avg	16.64	6.20	-2.13	19	15,869
5 Yr Avg	14.12	7.93	-1.76	15	19,356
10 Yr Avg	10.17	1.75	-3.48	64	26,341
15 Yr Avg	—				

Tax Analysis	Tax-Adj Rtn%	%Rank Cat	Tax-Cost Rat	%Rank Cat
3 Yr (estimated)	15.73	11	0.78	20
5 Yr (estimated)	13.35	12	0.67	23
10 Yr (estimated)	9.33	47	0.76	15

Potential Capital Gain Exposure: 20% of assets

Morningstar's Take by Sonya Morris 11-20-06

Vanguard Selected Value is the complete package.

This mid-value fund boasts many of the traits we look for in a mutual fund. First of all, a seasoned and successful manager calls the majority of the shots. Jim Barrow, of subadvisor Barrow, Hanley, Mewhinney & Strauss, runs more than 80% of this portfolio. He has more than 30 years of investment experience and has been on the job here since March 1999. He has also managed the bulk of Vanguard Windsor II to fine effect since 1985. Barrow is supported by a team of experienced equity analysts, and in 2002, team member Mark Giambrone stepped up to assume comanager duties.

Barrow and Giambrone ply a consistent and disciplined strategy, another characteristic that argues in this fund's favor. The pair scours the mid-cap universe for stocks with ample dividend payouts that are trading at relatively cheap prices. That frequently leads them to beaten-down areas of the market, and it also results in rather lumpy

sector allocations. For example, because of management's fondness for dividends, the fund typically has a light technology allocation and a heavy presence in financials and utilities. That leaves the fund vulnerable to downturns in its favored areas, but thus far, it hasn't been more volatile than its typical rival. And over the long haul, management's straightforward and consistent strategy has yielded impressive results. Since Barrow look over the fund, its average annual returns outrank 70% of its peers.

All due credit goes to management for these fine results, but its job here has been made easier by this fund's tiny price tag. With its 0.51% expense ratio (per its most recent prospectus), this fund is the cheapest actively managed mid-value fund on the market. Furthermore, because of management's long-term orientation, turnover here is appealingly low, which should help keep a lid on trading costs. With these many fine attributes, this fund ranks among our favorites.

Address:	PO Box 2600 Valley Forge PA 19482 800-997-2798
Web Address:	www.vanguard.com
Inception:	02-15-96*
Advisor:	Barrow, Hanley, Mewhinney & Strauss Inc.
Subadvisor:	None
NTF Plans:	Vanguard NTF

Minimum Purchase:	$25000	Add: $100	IRA: $25000
Min Auto Inv Plan:	$25000	Add: $50	
Sales Fees:	No-load, 1.00%R		
Management Fee:	0.49%		
Actual Fees:	Mgt:0.49%	Dist: —	
Expense Projections:	3Yr:$164	5Yr:$285	10Yr:$640
Income Distrib:	Annually		

Historical Profile
Return	Above Avg
Risk	Average
Rating	★★★ Neutral

Investment Style: Equity, Stock %

	100%	96%	89%	97%	97%	96%	97%	91%	92%

▼ Manager Change
▽ Partial Manager Change

Growth of $10,000
— Investment Values of Fund
— Investment Values of S&P 500

26.0 / 22.0 / 18.0 / 14.0 / 10.0

Performance Quartile (within Category)

1995	1996	1997	1998	1999	2000	2001	2002	2003	2004	2005	2006	History
—	10.91	12.28	10.39	9.94	11.43	12.97	11.46	15.23	18.07	18.86	21.09	NAV
—	10.81*	17.40	-11.77	-2.72	17.45	14.99	-9.79	35.21	20.38	10.67	19.11	Total Return %
—	—	-15.96	-40.35	-23.76	26.55	26.88	12.31	6.53	9.50	5.76	3.32	+/-S&P 500
—	—	-16.97	-16.85	-2.61	-1.73	12.66	-0.15	-2.86	-3.33	-1.98	-1.11	+/-Russ MV
—	—	0.46	0.65	1.54	2.41	1.49	1.85	2.27	1.71	1.60	1.70	Income Return %
—	—	16.94	-12.42	-4.26	15.04	13.50	-11.64	32.94	18.67	9.07	17.41	Capital Return %
—	—	85	93	83	62	24	34	47	41	31	19	Total Rtn % Rank Cat
—	0.06	0.05	0.08	0.16	0.24	0.17	0.24	0.26	0.26	0.29	0.32	Income $
—	0.11	0.46	0.33	0.00	0.00	0.00	0.00	0.00	0.00	0.85	1.05	Capital Gains $
—	—	0.75	0.74	0.65	0.73	0.63	0.70	0.74	0.78	0.60	—	Expense Ratio %
—	—	0.75	0.60	0.58	1.31	2.40	1.67	1.63	2.05	1.78	—	Income Ratio %
—	—	—	32	47	102	40	67	50	40	35	—	Turnover Rate %
—	—	106	191	149	187	196	995	1,094	1,422	2,300	4,584	Net Assets $mil

Rating and Risk

Time Period	Load-Adj Return %	Morningstar Rtn vs Cat	Morningstar Risk vs Cat	Morningstar Risk-Adj Rating
1 Yr	19.11			
3 Yr	16.64	+Avg	-Avg	★★★★
5 Yr	14.12	+Avg	Avg	★★★★
10 Yr	10.17	Avg	+Avg	★★
Incept	10.35			

Other Measures	Standard Index S&P 500	Best Fit Index Mstar Mid Value
Alpha	5.7	1.0
Beta	0.99	0.83
R-Squared	73	77
Standard Deviation	7.98	
Mean	16.64	
Sharpe Ratio	1.58	

Portfolio Analysis 09-30-06

Share change since 06-06 Total Stocks:57	Sector	PE	Tot Ret%	% Assets
⊕ Tech Data Corporation	Business	—	-4.39	3.23
⊖ Pinnacle West Capital	Utilities	21.9	27.04	3.07
⊖ Carolina Group	Financial	—	52.24	2.88
⊕ Reynolds American, Inc.	Goods	15.9	43.87	2.57
⊕ Whirlpool Corporation	Goods	13.0	1.11	2.55
⊕ Advance Auto Parts, Inc.	Consumer	16.5	-17.64	2.54
⊖ Sherwin-Williams Company	Goods	15.4	42.73	2.53
⊕ Coventry Health Care, In	Health	15.4	-12.13	2.46
⊕ Willis Group Holdings, L	Financial	17.0	10.34	2.43
⊕ Xcel Energy, Inc.	Utilities	16.9	30.53	2.38
Hillenbrand Industries	Health	15.4	17.62	2.33
⊕ Axis Capital Holdings, L	Financial	5.9	8.78	2.25
⊖ Radian Group, Inc.	Financial	8.6	-7.86	2.24
⊕ Stanley Works	Ind Mtrls	15.9	7.22	2.23
⊕ American Power Conversio	Ind Mtrls	58.9	41.75	2.19
⊖ People's Bank	Financial	45.5	47.71	2.16
⊖ Royal Caribbean Cruises	Consumer	16.0	-6.78	2.15
⊕ Family Dollar Stores, In	Consumer	24.1	20.22	2.15
⊕ New York Community Banco	Financial	19.1	3.54	2.12
⊖ Ryder System, Inc.	Business	13.4	26.29	2.06

Current Investment Style

Value Blnd Growth — Large Mid Small

Market Cap	%
Giant	0.0
Large	5.9
Mid	89.2
Small	4.8
Micro	0.1
Avg $mil:	4,675

Value Measures		Rel Category
Price/Earnings	14.91	1.01
Price/Book	1.86	0.93
Price/Sales	0.70	0.72
Price/Cash Flow	7.55	1.00
Dividend Yield %	2.15	1.19

Growth Measures	%	Rel Category
Long-Term Erngs	11.69	1.06
Book Value	3.00	0.43
Sales	5.45	0.71
Cash Flow	-4.66	NMF
Historical Erngs	8.04	0.55

Profitability	%	Rel Category
Return on Equity	10.19	0.71
Return on Assets	6.22	0.85
Net Margin	7.79	0.74

Sector Weightings	% of Stocks	Rel S&P 500	3 Year High	Low
↻ Info	2.21	0.11		
Software	0.00	0.00	0	0
Hardware	2.21	0.24	3	0
Media	0.00	0.00	0	0
Telecom	0.00	0.00	0	0
Service	61.11	1.32		
Health	12.59	1.04	13	7
Consumer	10.78	1.41	20	10
Business	9.74	2.30	11	3
Financial	28.00	1.26	28	25
Mfg	36.69	1.09		
Goods	10.63	1.24	16	10
Ind Mtrls	12.13	1.02	20	10
Energy	3.47	0.35	7	3
Utilities	10.46	2.99	14	10

Composition

	%
● Cash	7.9
● Stocks	92.1
● Bonds	0.0
● Other	0.0
Foreign	6.5
(% of Stock)	

 MORNINGSTAR® Funds 500

Vanguard Sh-Tm Bd Idx

Analyst Pick ✓

	Ticker	Load	NAV	Yield	SEC Yield	Total Assets	Mstar Category
	VBISX	None	$9.89	4.3%	4.76%	$5,260 mil	Short-Term Bond

Governance and Management

Stewardship Grade: B

Portfolio Manager(s)

Greg Davis assumed management duties in January 2005, but Ken Volpert, who runs Vanguard Total Bond Market Index, sets a good deal of the fund's strategy. Davis is no stranger to index funds, having successfully managed offshore funds for Vanguard including Vanguard's European Government Bond Index, which tracked its index well.

Strategy

The fund strives to approximate the returns of the Lehman Brothers 1-5 Year Government/Credit Index, which includes U.S. Treasury, government agency, and investment-grade corporate bonds. Mortgage-backed securities are not included in the index. Although the duration and other key characteristics of the index are carefully replicated, the fund does not hold every security in the index.

Historical Profile
Return **Above Avg**
Risk **Above Avg**
Rating ★★★★ **Above Avg**

Investment Style: Fixed Income
Income Rtn %Rank Cat

▼ Manager Change
▽ Partial Manager Change

Growth of $10,000
— Investment Values of Fund
— Investment Values of LB Aggr

Performance Quartile (within Category)

	1995	1996	1997	1998	1999	2000	2001	2002	2003	2004	2005	2006	History
	10.07	9.92	10.00	10.10	9.73	9.96	10.19	10.32	10.28	10.14	9.92	9.89	NAV
	12.89	4.55	7.04	7.63	2.08	8.84	8.88	6.10	3.37	1.70	1.31	4.09	Total Return %
	-5.58	0.92	-2.61	-1.06	2.90	-2.79	0.44	-4.15	-0.73	-2.64	-1.12	-0.24	+/-LB Aggr
	0.01	-0.12	-0.09	-0.00	-0.01	-0.07	-0.15	-2.02	0.02	-0.15	-0.13	-0.13	+/-LB 1-5 YR
	6.76	6.00	6.19	5.90	5.49	6.35	5.85	4.53	3.23	2.99	3.51	4.38	Income Return %
	6.13	-1.45	0.85	1.73	-3.41	2.49	3.03	1.57	0.14	-1.29	-2.20	-0.29	Capital Return %
	26	39	28	5	56	22	4	40	27	43	59	43	Total Rtn % Rank Cat
	0.62	0.59	0.60	0.57	0.54	0.60	0.57	0.45	0.33	0.30	0.35	0.43	Income $
	0.00	0.00	0.00	0.07	0.03	0.00	0.07	0.02	0.06	0.01	0.00	0.00	Capital Gains $
	0.20	0.20	0.20	0.20	0.20	0.21	0.21	0.22	0.20	0.18	0.18	—	Expense Ratio %
	6.28	5.93	6.03	5.68	5.48	6.16	5.45	5.63	3.17	2.97	3.50	—	Income Ratio %
	65	65	88	112	108	74	156	139	111	92	106	—	Turnover Rate %
	208	327	446	709	1,156	1,287	1,680	2,553	3,041	3,795	2,951	2,731	Net Assets $mil

Performance 12-31-06

	1st Qtr	2nd Qtr	3rd Qtr	4th Qtr	Total
2002	-0.05	1.92	2.79	1.33	6.10
2003	1.15	1.77	0.30	0.12	3.37
2004	1.66	-1.80	1.76	0.11	1.70
2005	-0.69	1.65	-0.20	0.56	1.31
2006	0.08	0.46	2.47	1.04	4.09

Trailing	Total Return%	+/- LB Aggr	+/- LB 1-5 YR	%Rank Cat	Growth of $10,000
3 Mo	1.04	-0.20	0.03	50	10,104
6 Mo	3.53	-1.56	-0.01	24	10,353
1 Yr	4.09	-0.24	-0.13	43	10,409
3 Yr Avg	2.36	-1.34	-0.13	48	10,725
5 Yr Avg	3.30	-1.76	-0.47	41	11,763
10 Yr Avg	5.07	-1.17	-0.27	19	16,398
15 Yr Avg	—	—	—		—

Tax Analysis	Tax-Adj Rtn%	%Rank Cat	Tax-Cost Rat	%Rank Cat
3 Yr (estimated)	1.08	45	1.25	58
5 Yr (estimated)	1.91	37	1.35	56
10 Yr (estimated)	3.12	17	1.86	62

Potential Capital Gain Exposure: -3% of assets

Rating and Risk

Time Period	Load-Adj Return %	Morningstar Rtn vs Cat	Morningstar Risk vs Cat	Morningstar Risk-Adj Rating
1 Yr	4.09			
3 Yr	2.36	Avg	+Avg	★★★
5 Yr	3.30	Avg	+Avg	★★★
10 Yr	5.07	+Avg	Avg	★★★★
Incept	5.25			

Other Measures	Standard Index LB Aggr	Best Fit Index LB 1-5 YR
Alpha	-1.1	-0.1
Beta	0.56	1.01
R-Squared	91	99
Standard Deviation	1.94	
Mean	2.36	
Sharpe Ratio	-0.46	

Portfolio Analysis 09-30-06

Total Fixed-Income:682	Date of Maturity	Amount $000	Value $000	% Net Assets
US Treasury Note 4.375%	12-31-07	161,225	160,267	3.08
US Treasury Note 4.25%	10-15-10	154,600	152,668	2.93
US Treasury Note 4.875%	04-30-11	140,875	142,437	2.73
US Treasury Note 4.5%	02-15-09	139,725	139,201	2.67
US Treasury Note 5.125%	06-30-11	106,075	108,396	2.08
US Treasury Note 4.125%	08-15-10	101,875	100,188	1.92
US Treasury Note 4.875%	05-31-08	97,925	98,093	1.88
US Treasury Note 3.375%	02-15-08	99,825	97,937	1.88
FNMA 5.75%	02-15-08	93,500	94,350	1.81
US Treasury Note 4.375%	01-31-08	90,100	89,565	1.72
US Treasury Note 2.625%	05-15-08	87,075	84,204	1.62
FNMA 7.25%	01-15-10	77,000	82,384	1.58
US Treasury Note 3.5%	02-15-10	81,850	79,024	1.52
US Treasury Note 3%	02-15-08	80,325	78,417	1.51
FHLMC 5.25%	05-21-09	74,500	75,140	1.44
US Treasury Note 5.625%	05-15-08	65,700	66,583	1.28
US Treasury Note 4.75%	03-31-11	61,425	61,799	1.19
FHLMC 5.75%	04-15-08	60,500	61,144	1.17
FNMA 6%	05-15-08	58,075	58,964	1.13
US Treasury Note 4.5%	02-28-11	56,975	56,752	1.09

Current Investment Style

Duration: Short Int Long
Quality: High Med Low

¹ figure provided by fund

Avg Eff Duration¹	2.5 Yrs
Avg Eff Maturity	2.8 Yrs
Avg Credit Quality	AAA
Avg Wtd Coupon	4.76%
Avg Wtd Price	100.34% of par

Coupon Range	% of Bonds	Rel Cat
0% PIK	3.7	0.4
0% to 6%	84.0	1.0
6% to 8%	13.5	0.8
8% to 10%	1.7	0.7
More than 10%	0.9	1.9

1.00=Category Average

Credit Analysis	% bonds 09-30-06		
AAA	74	BB	0
AA	8	B	0
A	10	Below B	0
BBB	7	NR/NA	0

Sector Breakdown	% of assets
US Treasuries	41
TIPS	0
US Agency	25
Mortgage Pass-Throughs	0
Mortgage CMO	0
Mortgage ARM	0
US Corporate	27
Asset-Backed	1
Convertible	0
Municipal	0
Corporate Inflation-Protected	0
Foreign Corporate	1
Foreign Govt	2

Composition			
Cash	4.1	Bonds	95.9
Stocks	0.0	Other	0.0

Special Securities	
Restricted/Illiquid Secs	Trace
Exotic Mortgage-Backed	0
Emerging-Markets Secs	Trace
Options/Futures/Warrants	No

Morningstar's Take by Annie Sorich 12-21-06

Vanguard Short-Term Bond Index remains one of our favorites.

Even though this fund hasn't outperformed the short-term bond category during the past two years, we're sticking by our Analyst Pick. In fact, this fund is not designed to beat its peers. Instead, it imitates the Lehman Brothers 1-5 Year Government/Credit Index, which is a compilation of U.S. Treasury, agency, and corporate bonds.

On that front, the fund does an excellent job. It's impossible to own all 1700 names in the benchmark, but instead the fund's management uses a sampling technique that mirrors the main qualities of the index, such as duration, sector allocation, and credit quality. The fund's R-squared relative to the Lehman index (a figure showing how closely two investment returns are related) over the trailing three-years through November 2006, is 99. Such a reading suggests that virtually all of fund's performance is attributed to that of the index, speaking to the high quality of its management.

Still, investors may wonder why the index has trailed its peers. The index omits mortgage-backed and most asset-backed securities, which on average comprise 28% of its peers portfolios. In addition, the credit quality of the fund is higher than most other funds in the category. Both mortgage-backed and lower-quality bonds tend to be less sensitive to interest rates, which harmed the fund's relative performance when interest rates were rising during most of 2005 and 2006.

More importantly, the fund's main advantage lies with its low costs. With an expense ratio 0.18%, it's one of the least expensive ways for investors to buy short-term bond exposure. Consider that its typical no-load competitor charges 0.74%. These low fees allow the fund to offer an above-average yield although it owns higher credit quality bonds, and to post competitive long-term returns.

We think investors should stay with this high-quality offering.

Address:	PO Box 2600 Valley Forge PA 19482 800-997-2798	Minimum Purchase:	$3000	Add: $100	IRA: $3000
		Min Auto Inv Plan:	$3000	Add: $50	
Web Address:	www.vanguard.com	Sales Fees:	No-load		
Inception:	03-01-94	Management Fee:	0.15%		
Advisor:	Vanguard Advisers, Inc.	Actual Fees:	Mgt:0.15%	Dist: —	
Subadvisor:	None	Expense Projections:	3Yr:$58	5Yr:$101	10Yr:$230
NTF Plans:	Vanguard NTF	Income Distrib:	Monthly		

Vanguard ShtTm Fed

	Analyst Pick	Ticker	Load	NAV	Yield	SEC Yield	Total Assets	Mstar Category
	✓ Analyst Pick	VSGBX	None	$10.28	4.0%	4.74%	$2,580 mil	Short Government

Governance and Management

Stewardship Grade: B

Portfolio Manager(s)

Ron Reardon took over from John Hollyer in January 2005. Reardon, who joined Vanguard in 2001, had been on the firm's mortgage and derivatives team. As with Vanguard's other bond funds, this offering's broad interest rate policy is set by Bob Auwaerter, who has led the firm's fixed-income group since Vanguard veteran Ian MacKinnon retired at the end of June 2003.

Strategy

Its sister fund, Vanguard Short-Term Treasury, must keep 80% of its assets in Treasuries, but this offering has no such restriction. In fact, management usually holds a very modest Treasury stake, preferring to hold agency bonds and mortgages. Those securities typically pay a bit more in yield than Treasuries, without taking on much additional credit risk. Duration is typically kept between two and 2.5 years.

Performance 12-31-06

	1st Qtr	2nd Qtr	3rd Qtr	4th Qtr	Total
2002	0.45	2.94	3.26	0.78	7.61
2003	0.83	0.95	0.12	0.08	1.99
2004	1.37	-1.50	1.38	0.12	1.36
2005	-0.33	1.37	0.06	0.70	1.80
2006	0.34	0.60	2.36	0.97	4.32

Trailing	Total Return%	+/- LB Aggr	+/- LB 1-5 YR GOVT	%Rank Cat	Growth of $10,000
3 Mo	0.97	-0.27	0.03	40	10,097
6 Mo	3.35	-1.74	0.01	34	10,335
1 Yr	4.32	-0.01	0.31	13	10,432
3 Yr Avg	2.48	-1.22	0.14	20	10,763
5 Yr Avg	3.39	-1.67	0.04	19	11,814
10 Yr Avg	5.02	-1.22	-0.07	13	16,320
15 Yr Avg	5.27	-1.23	-0.10	8	21,606

Tax Analysis	Tax-Adj Rtn%	%Rank Cat	Tax-Cost Rat	%Rank Cat
3 Yr (estimated)	1.28	13	1.17	47
5 Yr (estimated)	2.02	17	1.33	59
10 Yr (estimated)	3.15	9	1.78	58

Potential Capital Gain Exposure: -3% of assets

Historical Profile

Return Above Avg
Risk Average
Rating ★★★★ Above Avg

32	27	26	31	43	41	45	46	

Investment Style
Fixed Income
Income Rtn %Rank Cat

▼ Manager Change
▽ Partial Manager Change

Growth of $10,000
— Investment Values of Fund
— Investment Values of LB Aggr

Performance Quartile (within Category)

1995	1996	1997	1998	1999	2000	2001	2002	2003	2004	2005	2006	History
10.25	10.11	10.13	10.26	9.90	10.17	10.48	10.70	10.58	10.41	10.26	10.28	NAV
12.26	4.75	6.46	7.22	2.07	9.18	8.61	7.61	1.99	1.36	1.80	4.32	Total Return %
-6.21	1.12	-3.19	-1.47	2.89	-2.45	0.17	-2.64	-2.11	-2.98	-0.63	-0.01	+/-LB Aggr
-0.40	0.15	-0.65	-0.43	0.11	0.09	-0.03	-0.08	-0.17	-0.18	0.32	0.31	+/-LB 1-5 YR GOVT
6.36	6.11	6.24	5.91	5.66	6.31	5.52	4.19	2.97	2.78	3.26	4.11	Income Return %
5.90	-1.36	0.22	1.31	-3.59	2.87	3.09	3.42	-0.98	-1.42	-1.46	0.21	Capital Return %
49	16	61	25	32	32	6	37	20	40	14	13	Total Rtn % Rank Cat
0.60	0.61	0.61	0.58	0.57	0.61	0.55	0.43	0.31	0.29	0.33	0.41	Income $
0.00	0.00	0.00	0.00	0.00	0.00	0.00	0.13	0.02	0.02	0.00	0.00	Capital Gains $
0.28	0.27	0.25	0.27	0.27	0.27	0.28	0.31	0.26	0.22	0.20	0.20	Expense Ratio %
5.53	5.93	6.09	6.04	5.68	5.64	6.10	5.07	3.90	2.86	2.77	3.29	Income Ratio %
57	74	57	94	107	93	169	80	136	81	49	51	Turnover Rate %
1,404	1,339	1,429	1,635	1,521	1,502	1,783	2,851	2,673	2,432	1,698	1,513	Net Assets $mil

Rating and Risk

Time Period	Load-Adj Return %	Morningstar Rtn vs Cat	Morningstar Risk vs Cat	Morningstar Risk-Adj Rating
1 Yr	4.32			
3 Yr	2.48	+Avg	Avg	★★★★
5 Yr	3.39	+Avg	Avg	★★★★
10 Yr	5.02	+Avg	Avg	★★★★
Incept	6.17			

Other Measures	Standard Index LB Aggr	Best Fit Index LB 1-5 YR GOVT
Alpha	-1.0	0.0
Beta	0.44	0.83
R-Squared	90	98
Standard Deviation	1.58	
Mean	2.48	
Sharpe Ratio	-0.49	

Morningstar's Take by Annie Sorich 11-10-06

Vanguard Short-Term Federal is one of our favorites.

It's no accident that this fund is the only Analyst Pick in the short-term government category. We believe low expenses are essential in aiding consistent outperformance, especially in the short-term government category, where often, 100 basis points can separate the bottom and top quartile. The fund's expense ratio is 0.20% of assets, making it one of the cheapest options in the category.

In part due to its low expenses, this fund can afford to take a mild tact (in terms of credit quality) in its approach to bond selection without worrying about ways to generate its chart-topping returns. Manager Ron Reardon can invest in a variety of agencies, Treasuries, or government mortgage-backed securities. A majority of the fund's assets are usually dedicated to agency bonds, which are bonds issued by federal agencies such as Fannie Mae. They tend to have higher yields than Treasuries because they are only implicitly backed by the government. Reardon finds agency bonds particularly attractive right now because he believes these federal agencies are recovering from their fiscal woes of years past. Still, he is valuation conscious, and hasn't been adding much to the portfolio because an increase in foreign demand and a lack of new issuance has priced these bonds too richly for his liking.

The fund has performed well in 2006. For the first six months of the year, it had a short duration (a measure of interest rate risk) relative to its peers when interest rates were rising. Reardon has since lengthened the duration from around 1.8 years earlier in the year to 2.1 years, taking a more neutral stance with the Fed's pause in rate increase. He did this by adding some longer-term Treasuries to the fund, as opposed to the more expensive agency-backed bonds.

Overall, the combination of smart management and low fees makes this a winning choice.

Portfolio Analysis 09-30-06

Total Fixed-Income:81	Date of Maturity	Amount $000	Value $000	% Net Assets
FNMA 7.125%	06-15-10	157,975	169,697	6.29
FNMA 7.25%	01-15-10	100,000	106,992	3.97
FHLMC 5.25%	07-18-11	100,000	101,379	3.76
FNMA	06-15-08	100,000	100,461	3.72
FHLMC 4.875%	02-17-09	100,000	99,896	3.70
FHLBA 4.875%	03-05-08	100,000	99,718	3.70
FNMA	06-01-10	100,000	98,878	3.67
FNMA 3.8%	01-18-08	100,000	98,411	3.65
FNMA 5.75%	02-15-08	96,000	96,873	3.59
FHLMC 4.625%	08-22-08	75,000	74,461	2.76
FNMA 5.5%	10-01-21	60,000	59,970	2.22
FNMA 4.75%	02-01-08	59,920	59,618	2.21
FHLMC 7%	03-15-10	50,000	53,287	1.98
FNMA 5.125%	04-15-11	50,000	50,428	1.87
FNMA 4.875%	04-15-09	50,000	49,974	1.85
FHLMC 5%	10-18-10	50,000	49,624	1.84
FHLBA 4.625%	02-18-11	50,000	49,536	1.84
FNMA 4%	01-26-09	50,000	48,957	1.82
FHLBA 3.375%	02-15-08	50,000	48,878	1.81
FNMA 3.25%	08-15-08	50,000	48,490	1.80

Current Investment Style

Duration: Short Int Long
Quality: High Med Low

1 figure provided by fund

Avg Eff Duration[1]	2.1 Yrs
Avg Eff Maturity	2.3 Yrs
Avg Credit Quality	AAA
Avg Wtd Coupon	4.84%
Avg Wtd Price	100.69% of par

Coupon Range	% of Bonds	Rel Cat
0% PIK	7.5	0.7
0% to 6%	82.1	1.0
6% to 8%	17.9	1.3
8% to 10%	0.0	0.0
More than 10%	0.0	0.0

1.00=Category Average

Credit Analysis	% bonds 09-30-06		
AAA	100	BB	0
AA	0	B	0
A	0	Below B	0
BBB	0	NR/NA	0

Sector Breakdown	% of assets
US Treasuries	2
TIPS	0
US Agency	62
Mortgage Pass-Throughs	14
Mortgage CMO	0
Mortgage ARM	0
US Corporate	0
Asset-Backed	0
Convertible	0
Municipal	0
Corporate Inflation-Protected	0
Foreign Corporate	0
Foreign Govt	0

Composition			
Cash	22.1	Bonds	77.9
Stocks	0.0	Other	0.0

Special Securities	
Restricted/Illiquid Secs	0
Exotic Mortgage-Backed	—
Emerging-Markets Secs	0
Options/Futures/Warrants	No

Address:	PO Box 2600 Valley Forge PA 19482 800-997-2798	Minimum Purchase:	$3000	Add: $100	IRA: $3000
		Min Auto Inv Plan:	$3000	Add: $50	
		Sales Fees:	No-load	
Web Address:	www.vanguard.com	Management Fee:	0.20%	
Inception:	12-31-87	Actual Fees:	Mgt:0.17%	Dist: —
Advisor:	Vanguard Advisers, Inc.	Expense Projections:	3Yr:$64	5Yr:$113	10Yr:$255
Subadvisor:	None	Income Distrib:	Monthly	
NTF Plans:	Vanguard NTF			

MORNINGSTAR Funds 500

Vanguard Short-Tm Trs

	Ticker	Load	NAV	Yield	SEC Yield	Total Assets	Mstar Category
	VFISX	None	$10.28	4.2%	4.53%	$3,501 mil	Short Government

Governance and Management

Stewardship Grade: B

Portfolio Manager(s)

David Glocke assumed day-to-day management duties of this fund in May 2000. He is assisted by the head of Vanguard's fixed-income team, Bob Auwaerter, who has been setting the firm's interest-rate policy since Vanguard veteran Ian MacKinnon retired at the end of June 2003.

Strategy

Management is required to keep at least 80% of assets in Treasuries, and although it does hold agency bonds, it leaves the mortgage-backed market to its sibling, Vanguard Short-Term Federal. Manager David Glocke typically keeps the portfolio's duration between 2.0 and 2.5 years and avoids big interest-rate bets.

Historical Profile

Return	Above Avg
Risk	Average
Rating	★★★★ Above Avg

Investment Style: Fixed Income / Income Rtn %Rank Cat

▼ Manager Change
▽ Partial Manager Change

Growth of $10,000
— Investment Values of Fund
— Investment Values of LB Aggr

Performance Quartile (within Category)

1995	1996	1997	1998	1999	2000	2001	2002	2003	2004	2005	2006	History
10.32	10.17	10.21	10.37	10.01	10.27	10.53	10.83	10.64	10.47	10.33	10.28	NAV
12.11	4.39	6.51	7.36	1.85	8.83	7.80	8.02	2.38	1.03	1.77	3.77	Total Return %
-6.36	0.76	-3.14	-1.33	2.67	-2.80	-0.64	-2.23	-1.72	-3.31	-0.66	-0.56	+/-LB Aggr
-0.55	-0.21	-0.60	-0.29	-0.11	-0.26	-0.84	0.33	0.22	-0.51	0.29	-0.24	+/-LB 1-5 YR GOVT
6.58	5.84	6.08	5.53	5.23	6.10	5.19	4.02	2.57	2.65	3.12	4.25	Income Return %
5.53	-1.45	0.43	1.83	-3.38	2.73	2.61	4.00	-0.19	-1.62	-1.35	-0.48	Capital Return %
52	31	60	21	40	38	23	29	7	60	17	42	Total Rtn % Rank Cat
0.63	0.59	0.60	0.55	0.53	0.59	0.52	0.42	0.27	0.28	0.32	0.43	Income $
0.00	0.00	0.00	0.02	0.02	0.00	0.01	0.11	0.17	0.00	0.00	0.00	Capital Gains $
0.28	0.27	0.25	0.27	0.27	0.27	0.27	0.29	0.28	0.26	0.24	0.26	Expense Ratio %
5.33	6.14	5.77	5.80	5.27	5.27	5.91	4.82	3.70	2.52	2.65	3.19	Income Ratio %
126	93	86	83	132	124	296	102	165	125	108	93	Turnover Rate %
869	966	998	1,184	1,235	1,200	1,394	2,211	2,086	1,886	1,383	1,331	Net Assets $mil

Performance 12-31-06

	1st Qtr	2nd Qtr	3rd Qtr	4th Qtr	Total
2002	0.28	3.08	3.66	0.81	8.02
2003	0.78	1.17	0.25	0.17	2.38
2004	1.20	-1.34	1.16	0.02	1.03
2005	-0.36	1.41	0.03	0.69	1.77
2006	0.20	0.64	2.08	0.81	3.77

Trailing	Total Return%	+/- LB Aggr	+/- LB 1-5 YR GOVT	%Rank Cat	Growth of $10,000
3 Mo	0.81	-0.43	-0.13	72	10,081
6 Mo	2.90	-2.19	-0.44	63	10,290
1 Yr	3.77	-0.56	-0.24	42	10,377
3 Yr Avg	2.18	-1.52	-0.16	37	10,668
5 Yr Avg	3.36	-1.70	0.01	21	11,797
10 Yr Avg	4.89	-1.35	-0.20	21	16,119
15 Yr Avg	5.17	-1.33	-0.20	20	21,300

Tax Analysis	Tax-Adj Rtn%	%Rank Cat	Tax-Cost Rat	%Rank Cat
3 Yr (estimated)	1.01	26	1.15	45
5 Yr (estimated)	1.99	18	1.33	59
10 Yr (estimated)	3.07	15	1.74	53

Potential Capital Gain Exposure: -2% of assets

Rating and Risk

Time Period	Load-Adj Return %	Morningstar Rtn vs Cat	Morningstar Risk vs Cat	Morningstar Risk-Adj Rating
1 Yr	3.77			
3 Yr	2.18	Avg	Avg	★★★
5 Yr	3.36	+Avg	Avg	★★★★
10 Yr	4.89	+Avg	Avg	★★★★
Incept	5.32			

Other Measures	Standard Index LB Aggr	Best Fit Index LB 1-5 YR GOVT
Alpha	-1.2	-0.3
Beta	0.42	0.78
R-Squared	89	98
Standard Deviation	1.49	
Mean	2.18	
Sharpe Ratio	-0.73	

Morningstar's Take by Annie Sorich 11-13-06

Vanguard Short-Term Treasury has a lot to offer more conservative investors.

This fund stands out from its peers on several fronts. First, this is a fund for style purists. It invests only in those securities backed by the full faith and credit of the U.S. government, which is particularly attractive to more risk-adverse investors. Most of its assets are dedicated to Treasuries or cash, with a small slice in agency bonds, whereas most rival short-term government funds dedicate more of their portfolios to mortgage-backed securities, which carry slightly more credit risk. This fund also distinguishes itself with rock-bottom expenses. At 0.26% of assets, its expense ratio is one of the slimmest in the category, which is especially important when the top- and bottom-performing funds in its category are often separated by as few as 100 basis points.

This low expense ratio gives the fund an automatic head start, but management has also made some savvy moves. For example, the fund greatly benefited this year from its duration (a measure of interest rate risk) strategy. Throughout the first half of the year, manager David Glocke reduced duration to 1.8 years (it normally sits between 2.0 and 2.5). This emphasis on shorter-term securities offered some protection from declining prices as the Fed continued to raise interest rates through mid-year. Now duration at the fund is in a more neutral position, which means it should do well if rates start to drop.

Despite its narrow focus, the fund's trailing three-, five-, and 10-year returns all land in the category's top half. Still, this fund's conservative approach can cause it to lag during shorter time periods. For example, when agencies and mortgaged-backed securities rally, this fund's performance might not stack up to the rest of the short-term government category.

This fund's low expenses and conservative risk-reward profile coupled with above-average returns make it a fine choice.

Portfolio Analysis 09-30-06

Total Fixed-Income:37	Date of Maturity	Amount $000	Value $000	% Net Assets
US Treasury Note 4.25%	11-30-07	604,000	599,657	17.50
US Treasury Note 4.875%	05-31-08	510,000	510,877	14.91
US Treasury Note 4%	06-15-09	412,875	406,360	11.86
US Treasury Note 2.625%	05-15-08	260,000	251,428	7.34
US Treasury Note 4%	04-15-10	220,535	216,263	6.31
US Treasury Note 4.625%	02-29-08	210,000	209,475	6.11
US Treasury Note 4.875%	04-30-08	200,000	200,282	5.85
US Treasury Note 4.375%	12-15-10	198,000	196,329	5.73
US Treasury Note 4.5%	02-15-09	150,000	149,438	4.36
US Treasury Note 3.875%	05-15-09	75,000	73,606	2.15
Private Expt Fdg 7.25%	06-15-10	64,080	69,006	2.01
US Treasury Note 4.875%	07-31-11	50,000	50,578	1.48
Private Expt Fdg 3.4%	02-15-08	45,000	44,014	1.28
US Treasury Note 5.125%	06-30-11	35,000	35,766	1.04
US Treasury Note 4.875%	04-30-11	30,500	30,838	0.90
Private Expt Fdg 6.07%	04-30-11	29,000	30,235	0.88
US Treasury Note 3.5%	02-15-10	25,000	24,137	0.70
FNMA 7.25%	01-15-10	20,000	21,398	0.62
FHLMC 6%	06-15-11	20,000	20,894	0.61
Private Expt Fdg 6.67%	09-15-09	17,000	17,794	0.52

Current Investment Style

Duration: Short / Int / Long
Quality: High / Med / Low

1 figure provided by fund

Avg Eff Duration[1]	1.9 Yrs
Avg Eff Maturity	2.0 Yrs
Avg Credit Quality	AAA
Avg Wtd Coupon	4.27%
Avg Wtd Price	99.53% of par

Coupon Range	% of Bonds	Rel Cat
0% PIK	2.7	0.2
0% to 6%	94.9	1.1
6% to 8%	5.1	0.4
8% to 10%	0.0	0.0
More than 10%	0.0	0.0

1.00=Category Average

Credit Analysis		% bonds 09-30-06	
AAA	100	BB	0
AA	0	B	0
A	0	Below B	0
BBB	0	NR/NA	0

Sector Breakdown % of assets

US Treasuries	87
TIPS	0
US Agency	6
Mortgage Pass-Throughs	0
Mortgage CMO	0
Mortgage ARM	0
US Corporate	0
Asset-Backed	0
Convertible	0
Municipal	0
Corporate Inflation-Protected	0
Foreign Corporate	0
Foreign Govt	0

Composition

Cash	6.8	Bonds	93.2
Stocks	0.0	Other	0.0

Special Securities

Restricted/Illiquid Secs	0
Exotic Mortgage-Backed	—
Emerging-Markets Secs	0
Options/Futures/Warrants	No

Address:	PO Box 2600, Valley Forge PA 19482 / 800-997-2798
Web Address:	www.vanguard.com
Inception:	10-28-91
Advisor:	Vanguard Advisers, Inc.
Subadvisor:	None
NTF Plans:	Vanguard NTF

Minimum Purchase:	$3000	Add: $100	IRA: $3000
Min Auto Inv Plan:	$3000	Add: $50	
Sales Fees:	No-load		
Management Fee:	0.22%		
Actual Fees:	Mgt:0.23%	Dist: —	
Expense Projections:	3Yr:$84	5Yr:$146	10Yr:$331
Income Distrib:	Monthly		

Vanguard Sht-Tm Inv-Grade

	Ticker	Load	NAV	Yield	SEC Yield	Total Assets	Mstar Category
	VFSTX	None	$10.56	4.4%	4.99%	$17,726 mil	Short-Term Bond

Governance and Management

Stewardship Grade: B

Portfolio Manager(s)

Seasoned and proven. Bob Auwaerter is responsible for the fund's day-to-day management and has been with the fund since 1984. He also sets the fund's duration, a duty assumed from outgoing fixed-income chief Ian MacKinnon (whom Auwaerter succeeds). The team also includes an assistant portfolio manager, six credit analysts, and traders.

Strategy

Traditionally this fund has invested mainly in midquality (A and BBB rated) investment-grade corporate bonds. A July 2004 modification allowed its managers to invest a bit more broadly, though. The fund's duration is limited to a range of 1.75 to 2.75 years, which typically makes it a bit less sensitive to rate shifts than most of its short-term bond peers. Manager Bob Auwaerter can also invest in highly rated asset-backed securities because the short-term corporate-bond supply can become scarce at times, he said.

Performance 12-31-06

	1st Qtr	2nd Qtr	3rd Qtr	4th Qtr	Total
2002	0.26	1.25	2.27	1.34	5.22
2003	1.39	1.89	0.40	0.46	4.20
2004	1.53	-1.30	1.50	0.39	2.11
2005	-0.38	1.55	0.24	0.77	2.20
2006	0.52	0.79	2.31	1.28	4.99

Trailing	Total Return%	+/- LB Aggr	+/- LB 1-5 YR	%Rank Cat	Growth of $10,000
3 Mo	1.28	0.04	0.27	16	10,128
6 Mo	3.62	-1.47	0.08	21	10,362
1 Yr	4.99	0.66	0.77	10	10,499
3 Yr Avg	3.09	-0.61	0.60	10	10,956
5 Yr Avg	3.74	-1.32	-0.03	21	12,015
10 Yr Avg	5.16	-1.08	-0.18	14	16,539
15 Yr Avg	5.53	-0.97	-0.05	14	22,420

Tax Analysis	Tax-Adj Rtn%	%Rank Cat	Tax-Cost Rat	%Rank Cat
3 Yr (estimated)	1.73	10	1.32	65
5 Yr (estimated)	2.20	20	1.48	68
10 Yr (estimated)	3.10	18	1.96	75

Potential Capital Gain Exposure: -2% of assets

Morningstar's Take by Paul Herbert 12-28-06

Vanguard Short-Term Investment Grade's moving parts have helped out lately, but we also like it for its enduring traits.

This fund cruised past its average short-term bond category peer in 2006. In the first half of the year, manager Robert Auwaerter and his team positioned the fund to thrive when interest rates climb. They kept the fund's duration, which measures rate sensitivity, relatively short. They also bought bonds with yields that reset at higher levels as rates rise, including mortgage- and other asset-backed fare, as well as floating-rate corporate issues when they looked cheap relative to fixed-rate bonds. For the most part, these moves paid off, as the Federal Reserve continued to ratchet interest rates higher.

But as we mentioned in July, the particular tilts mentioned above weren't permanent. And Auwaerter and crew had begun shifting gears, as they have became more convinced that the Fed's rate-hiking process was nearing an end. Therefore,

they accepted a bit more rate risk, distributed the fund's assets more evenly among bonds maturing in one to five years, and allowed the fund's weightings in some variable-rate bonds to drift lower. This positioning set the fund up perfectly for the rally that would take hold in August after the Fed paused to assess the impact of its 17 rate hikes.

But the less-temporary elements of the fund's profile will probably be more meaningful in the long run. Most importantly, it owns a huge fee edge, which allows it to deliver a bigger yield without stretching into lower-rated bonds. Thus, though the fund has a meaty weighting in corporate bonds--currently about 70% of assets--meaning that its value will fluctuate with that segment of the market to a degree, it has been able to avoid harrowing losses associated with owning those bonds.

In all, the fund's various elements combine into a very attractive package.

Address:	PO Box 2600
	Valley Forge PA 19482
	800-997-2798
Web Address:	www.vanguard.com
Inception:	10-29-82
Advisor:	Vanguard Advisers, Inc.
Subadvisor:	None
NTF Plans:	Vanguard NTF

Minimum Purchase:	$3000	Add: $100	IRA: $3000
Min Auto Inv Plan:	$3000	Add: $50	
Sales Fees:	No-load		
Management Fee:	0.16%		
Actual Fees:	Mgt:0.18%	Dist: —	
Expense Projections:	3Yr:$68	5Yr:$118	10Yr:$268
Income Distrib:	Monthly		

Historical Profile

Return	Above Avg
Risk	Average
Rating	★★★★ Above Avg

| | 17 | 12 | 9 | 5 | 6 | 17 | 26 | 30 | |

Growth of $10,000

— Investment Values of Fund
— Investment Values of LB Aggr

▼ Manager Change
▽ Partial Manager Change

20.5
17.5
15.0
12.5
10.0

Performance Quartile (within Category)

1995	1996	1997	1998	1999	2000	2001	2002	2003	2004	2005	2006	History
10.91	10.75	10.81	10.84	10.53	10.65	10.82	10.79	10.80	10.66	10.51	10.56	NAV
12.74	4.79	6.95	6.57	3.31	8.17	8.14	5.22	4.20	2.11	2.20	4.99	Total Return %
-5.73	1.16	-2.70	-2.12	4.13	-3.46	-0.30	-5.03	0.10	-2.23	-0.23	0.66	+/-LB Aggr
-0.14	0.12	-0.18	-1.06	1.22	-0.74	-0.89	-2.90	0.85	0.26	0.76	0.77	+/-LB 1-5 YR
6.68	6.25	6.36	6.30	6.24	6.94	6.55	5.47	4.12	3.43	3.62	4.49	Income Return %
6.06	-1.46	0.59	0.27	-2.93	1.23	1.59	-0.25	0.08	-1.32	-1.42	0.50	Capital Return %
28	32	32	43	17	34	23	59	12	27	13	10	Total Rtn % Rank Cat
0.67	0.66	0.66	0.66	0.66	0.71	0.68	0.58	0.44	0.36	0.38	0.46	Income $
0.00	0.00	0.00	0.00	0.00	0.00	0.00	0.00	0.00	0.00	0.00	0.00	Capital Gains $
0.28	0.27	0.25	0.28	0.27	0.25	0.24	0.24	0.23	0.21	0.18	0.21	Expense Ratio %
5.66	6.23	6.18	6.17	6.08	6.21	6.76	6.18	5.27	3.80	3.31	3.68	Income Ratio %
69	62	45	45	46	52	54	69	59	33	37	31	Turnover Rate %
3,743	4,587	4,601	5,428	6,799	7,341	7,383	8,668	11,120	13,122	10,409	10,377	Net Assets $mil

Rating and Risk

Time Period	Load-Adj Return %	Morningstar Rtn vs Cat	Morningstar Risk vs Cat	Morningstar Risk-Adj Rating
1 Yr	4.99			
3 Yr	3.09	+Avg	Avg	★★★★
5 Yr	3.74	+Avg	Avg	★★★★
10 Yr	5.16	+Avg	Avg	★★★★
Incept	7.39			

Other Measures	Standard Index LB Aggr	Best Fit Index LB 1-5 YR
Alpha	-0.3	0.4
Beta	0.40	0.72
R-Squared	91	98

Standard Deviation	1.43
Mean	3.09
Sharpe Ratio	-0.12

Portfolio Analysis 09-30-06

Total Fixed-Income:666	Date of Maturity	Amount $000	Value $000	% Net Assets
US Treasury Note 3.5%	02-15-10	190,000	183,439	1.04
Santander Us Debt S A 14	09-19-08	119,400	119,425	0.68
Bbva U S Sr S A Uniperso	04-17-09	117,500	117,504	0.67
Banc Amer Fdg 2006-H CMO	10-25-36	101,422	101,863	0.58
Morgan Stanley FRN	01-15-10	100,900	101,422	0.58
Sequoia Mtg Tr 2006-1 CM	09-20-46	99,738	99,870	0.57
CHUBB	08-16-08	97,900	98,316	0.56
Bear Stearns Arm Tr 2006	09-25-36	98,000	98,164	0.56
Wells Fargo Mbs 2006-Ar1	09-25-36	97,800	97,800	0.56
Royal Bk Scotland Plc Mt	07-21-08	97,700	97,705	0.56
Bmw Floorplan Mstr Tr 20	10-17-08	97,500	97,501	0.56
US Treasury Note 4%	04-15-10	95,000	93,160	0.53
Slm FRN	07-27-09	89,220	89,259	0.51
Hbos Plc Medium Term Sr	11-30-07	89,900	88,169	0.50
Citigroup FRN	06-09-09	81,000	81,224	0.46
US Treasury Note 3.125%	10-15-08	80,000	77,587	0.44
Caterpillar Finl Svcs Mt	08-11-09	74,100	74,099	0.42
Rfmsi Series Tr 2006-Sa2	08-25-36	74,106	73,901	0.42
LEHMAN BROS HLDGS	07-18-11	69,400	70,644	0.40
US Treasury Note 3.375%	10-15-09	70,000	67,550	0.38

Current Investment Style

Duration: Short Int Long
Quality: High Med Low

¹ figure provided by fund

Avg Eff Duration¹	1.7 Yrs
Avg Eff Maturity	2.5 Yrs
Avg Credit Quality	AA
Avg Wtd Coupon	3.81%
Avg Wtd Price	99.74% of par

Coupon Range	% of Bonds	Rel Cat
0% PIK	18.8	2.1
0% to 6%	87.0	1.1
6% to 8%	10.4	0.7
8% to 10%	2.5	1.1
More than 10%	0.0	0.1

1.00=Category Average

Credit Analysis		% bonds 09-30-06	
AAA	36	BB	2
AA	23	B	0
A	24	Below B	0
BBB	15	NR/NA	0

Sector Breakdown	% of assets
US Treasuries	4
TIPS	0
US Agency	0
Mortgage Pass-Throughs	5
Mortgage CMO	5
Mortgage ARM	0
US Corporate	49
Asset-Backed	17
Convertible	0
Municipal	0
Corporate Inflation-Protected	0
Foreign Corporate	1
Foreign Govt	0

Composition			
Cash	19.0	Bonds	79.9
Stocks	0.0	Other	1.1

Special Securities	
Restricted/Illiquid Secs	11
Exotic Mortgage-Backed	0
Emerging-Markets Secs	Trace
Options/Futures/Warrants	No

Investment Style
Fixed Income
Income Rtn %Rank Cat

Vanguard Sht-Tm TE

			Ticker	Load	NAV	Yield	SEC Yield	Total Assets	Mstar Category
Analyst Pick			VWSTX	None	$15.57	3.0%	3.45%	$4,058 mil	Muni National Short

Governance and Management

Stewardship Grade: B

Portfolio Manager(s)

Pam Wisehaupt-Tynan has managed the fund since the start of 1997 as well as its sibling, Vanguard Limited-Term Tax Exempt, which has an excellent record. She has been with Vanguard since 1981 as an accountant and assistant portfolio manager.

Strategy

The fund invests in high-quality municipal issues with a combined average maturity of one to two years. Management adjusts the fund's duration within a specified range, depending on its interest-rate outlook. The fund's short maturity and use of variable-rate notes make it look a lot like a tax-free money market fund, but with greater return potential and price volatility.

Historical Profile
Return: Below Avg
Risk: Low
Rating: ★★ Below Avg

Investment Style: Fixed Income
Income Rtn %Rank Cat

	1995	1996	1997	1998	1999	2000	2001	2002	2003	2004	2005	2006	History
	57	62	58	46	70	71	63	70					
	15.62	15.58	15.58	15.63	15.45	15.56	15.68	15.80	15.75	15.63	15.53	15.57	NAV
	5.99	3.69	4.07	4.32	2.58	4.91	4.75	3.49	1.64	1.12	1.65	3.26	Total Return %
	-11.47	-0.74	-5.12	-2.16	4.64	-6.77	-0.38	-6.11	-3.67	-3.36	-1.86	-1.58	+/-LB Muni
	-2.88	-0.75	-1.41	-0.89	0.62	-1.32	-1.84	-3.23	-1.04	-0.66	0.78	0.21	+/-LB Muni 3YR
	4.08	3.92	4.02	3.95	3.76	4.17	3.98	2.71	1.96	1.89	2.29	3.00	Income Return %
	1.91	-0.23	0.05	0.37	-1.18	0.74	0.77	0.78	-0.32	-0.77	-0.64	0.26	Capital Return %
	91	57	86	74	6	79	58	81	80	51	25	30	Total Rtn % Rank Cat
	0.61	0.60	0.62	0.60	0.58	0.63	0.61	0.42	0.31	0.29	0.35	0.46	Income $
	0.00	0.00	0.01	0.01	0.00	0.00	0.00	0.00	0.00	0.00	0.00	0.00	Capital Gains $
	0.21	0.20	0.19	0.20	0.18	0.18	0.19	0.17	0.17	0.14	0.16	0.16	Expense Ratio %
	3.88	3.90	3.91	3.90	3.71	4.03	4.04	2.80	2.01	1.86	2.16	2.85	Income Ratio %
	32	33	34	36	56	45	47	53	25	10	30	49	Turnover Rate %
	1,410	1,452	1,492	1,657	1,917	2,117	1,359	2,022	2,153	2,164	1,305	1,110	Net Assets $mil

Growth of $10,000
— Investment Values of Fund
— Investment Values of LB Muni

Performance Quartile (within Category)

Performance 12-31-06

	1st Qtr	2nd Qtr	3rd Qtr	4th Qtr	Total
2002	0.32	1.48	1.00	0.64	3.49
2003	0.46	0.56	0.46	0.15	1.64
2004	0.46	-0.30	0.79	0.18	1.12
2005	-0.01	0.75	0.46	0.44	1.65
2006	0.54	0.66	1.22	0.80	3.26

Trailing	Total Return%	+/- LB Muni	+/- LB Muni 3YR	%Rank Cat	Growth of $10,000
3 Mo	0.80	-0.31	0.17	22	10,080
6 Mo	2.04	-2.51	-0.54	60	10,204
1 Yr	3.26	-1.58	0.21	30	10,326
3 Yr Avg	2.01	-2.27	0.11	33	10,615
5 Yr Avg	2.23	-3.30	-0.77	70	11,166
10 Yr Avg	3.17	-2.59	-0.87	67	13,663
15 Yr Avg	3.43	-2.83	-1.02	93	16,584

Tax Analysis	Tax-Adj Rtn%	%Rank Cat	Tax-Cost Rat	%Rank Cat
3 Yr (estimated)	2.01	26	0.00	1
5 Yr (estimated)	2.23	62	0.00	1
10 Yr (estimated)	3.17	65	0.00	1

Potential Capital Gain Exposure: -1% of assets

Rating and Risk

Time Period	Load-Adj Return %	Morningstar Rtn vs Cat	Morningstar Risk vs Cat	Morningstar Risk-Adj Rating
1 Yr	3.26			
3 Yr	2.01	Avg	Low	★★★
5 Yr	2.23	-Avg	-Avg	★★
10 Yr	3.17	-Avg	Low	★★
Incept	4.75			

Other Measures	Standard Index LB Muni	Best Fit Index LB Muni 3YR
Alpha	-1.4	-0.7
Beta	0.16	0.38
R-Squared	72	91
Standard Deviation	0.63	
Mean	2.01	
Sharpe Ratio	-2.08	

Morningstar's Take by Lawrence Jones 12-21-06

Vanguard Short-Term Tax-Exempt's star rating doesn't capture the virtues that make it one of our favorites.

Low fees continue to give this fund a strong and sustainable competitive advantage over its muni-national short-term category peers. The fund's expense ratio, currently 0.16%, makes it, along with its sibling Vanguard Limited-Term Tax-Exempt, the lowest-priced offering in the category. A cost advantage of 0.46% against the typical no-load peer may not appear like much, but it gives the fund a huge lead over category rivals, given the narrow range of returns within the group.

This cost advantage allows veteran manager Pam Wisehaupt-Tynan to concentrate on maintaining the fund's high quality, enabling her to avoid having to take on much credit risk to generate reasonable yield. For example, the portfolio currently holds more than 90% of assets in bonds rated AA or better, a considerably higher percentage than is typical in the category. Added to

this, the fund often holds a significant segment of its assets (currently around 37%) in insured municipal bonds, further strengthening credit quality here. Moreover, Wisehaupt-Tynan also keeps interest-rate risk at bay by maintaining a defensive duration (a measure of interest-rate sensitivity) positioning relative to category rivals. This approach helps make this fund one of the least volatile in the category. True, the fund's conservative nature can cause it to lag peers during bond-market rallies, but the protection it offers during periods of rising rates, such as 2005, helps make a strong case for its judicious strategy.

Finally, we're also impressed with Wisehaupt-Tynan's experience. With close to a decade-long tenure here, she's provided solid management and has guided this fund well through the years. Though its relative performance appears middling, this fund's safety and stability make it an excellent short-term muni option.

Portfolio Analysis 09-30-06

Total Fixed-Income:281	Date of Maturity	Amount $000	Value $000	% Net Assets
FLORIDA HURRICANE CATAST	07-01-08	45,000	46,098	1.15
Engy Northwest Wash Elec	07-01-10	42,450	44,533	1.11
LOUISIANA ST MUN NAT GAS	03-15-14	40,000	40,000	1.00
New York N Y City Indl D	05-01-29	37,675	37,675	0.94
METROPOLITAN GOVT NASHVI	10-01-44	35,675	37,187	0.93
Texas St Tpk Auth 5%	06-01-08	36,115	36,956	0.92
San Antonio Tex Elec & G	02-01-08	34,320	35,075	0.87
CALIFORNIA ST DEPT WTR R	05-01-08	33,000	33,794	0.84
Kenton Cnty Ky Arpt Brd	07-01-32	32,635	32,635	0.81
HUNTSVILLE ALA HEALTH CA	06-01-34	30,000	30,482	0.76
SUFFOLK CNTY N Y WTR AUT	06-01-31	30,000	29,977	0.75
Chicago Ill Wtr Rev Seco	11-01-30	29,200	29,200	0.73
CYPRESS-FAIRBANKS TEX IN	02-15-20	27,810	28,732	0.71
North Carolina St 5%	02-01-08	27,585	28,139	0.70
HARRIS CNTY TEX TOLL RD	08-15-21	25,000	25,850	0.64

Current Investment Style

¹Avg Eff Duration	1.1 Yrs
Avg Eff Maturity	1.2 Yrs
Avg Credit Quality	AA
Avg Wtd Coupon	4.60%
Avg Wtd Price	102.01% of par

¹figure provided by fund

Credit Analysis % bonds 09-30-06

AAA	49	BB	0
AA	41	B	0
A	7	Below B	0
BBB	1	NR/NA	2

Special Securities

Restricted/Illiquid Secs	Trace
Options/Futures/Warrants	No

Sector Weightings

	% of Bonds	Rel Cat
General Obligation	38.2	1.16
Utilities	12.2	1.52
Health	9.6	0.96
Water/Waste	8.9	1.20
Housing	2.0	0.22
Education	8.3	0.96
Transportation	8.5	1.63
COP/Lease	1.0	0.56
Industrial	9.7	0.60
Misc Revenue	0.0	—
Demand	1.6	2.35

Top 5 States % bonds

TX	15.6	IL	5.9
NY	10.5	PA	5.5
CA	7.3		

Composition

Cash	35.0	Bonds	65.0
Stocks	0.0	Other	0.0

Address:	PO Box 2600	Minimum Purchase:	$3000	Add: $100	IRA: $0
	Valley Forge PA 19482	Min Auto Inv Plan:	$3000	Add: $50	
	800-997-2798	Sales Fees:	No-load		
Web Address:	www.vanguard.com	Management Fee:	0.13%		
Inception:	09-01-77	Actual Fees:	Mgt:0.13%	Dist: —	
Advisor:	Vanguard Advisers, Inc.	Expense Projections:	3Yr:$52	5Yr:$90	10Yr:$205
Subadvisor:	None	Income Distrib:	Monthly		
NTF Plans:	Vanguard NTF				

Vanguard SmCp Gr Idx

	Ticker	Load	NAV	Yield	Total Assets	Mstar Category
	VISGX	None	$18.34	0.3%	$2,982 mil	Small Growth

Governance and Management

Stewardship Grade: B

Portfolio Manager(s)

Gerard O'Reilly was named lead manager in May 2005, when previous manager Gus Sauter stepped down to concentrate on his duties as Vanguard's chief investment officer. O'Reilly has been with Vanguard since 1992 and also skippers Vanguard Total Stock Market Index, Vanguard Value Index, and Vanguard Growth Index.

Strategy

This fund tracks the MSCI U.S. Small Cap Growth Index, which uses an eight-pronged classification system to identify small-growth stocks. The index also employs buffer zones, which limit the migration of stocks into and out of the index. The buffers should help keep portfolio turnover and trading costs low and tax efficiency high.

Historical Profile

Return	Above Avg
Risk	Below Avg
Rating	★★★★★ Highest

Investment Style: Equity, Stock %

97% 100% 98% 100% 99% 99% 100% 99% 99%

▼ Manager Change
▽ Partial Manager Change

18.0
15.0 **Growth of $10,000**
12.5 — Investment Values of Fund
10.0 — Investment Values of S&P 500
7.0

Performance Quartile (within Category)

	1995	1996	1997	1998	1999	2000	2001	2002	2003	2004	2005	2006	History
	—	—	—	9.53	11.38	10.97	10.87	9.17	13.08	15.16	16.43	18.34	NAV
	—	—	—	-4.77*	19.80	1.59	-0.78	-15.41	42.88	16.06	8.64	11.95	Total Return %
	—	—	—	—	-1.24	10.69	11.11	6.69	14.20	5.18	3.73	-3.84	+/-S&P 500
	—	—	—	—	-23.29	24.02	8.45	14.85	-5.66	1.75	4.49	-1.40	+/-Russ 2000 Gr
	—	—	—	—	0.37	0.03	0.14	0.23	0.24	0.15	0.26	0.33	Income Return %
	—	—	—	—	19.43	1.56	-0.92	-15.64	42.64	15.91	8.38	11.62	Capital Return %
	—	—	—	—	81	33	29	6	59	24	28	38	Total Rtn % Rank Cat
	—	—	—	0.03	0.04	0.00	0.02	0.03	0.02	0.02	0.04	0.05	Income $
	—	—	—	0.00	0.00	0.57	0.00	0.00	0.00	0.00	0.00	0.00	Capital Gains $
	—	—	—	0.25	0.25	0.27	0.27	0.27	0.27	0.23	0.23	—	Expense Ratio %
	—	—	—	0.63	0.33	0.03	0.11	0.24	0.21	0.13	0.27	—	Income Ratio %
	—	—	—	—	82	136	74	61	108	41	39	—	Turnover Rate %
	—	—	—	90	167	356	357	388	907	1,435	1,726	2,208	Net Assets $mil

Performance 12-31-06

	1st Qtr	2nd Qtr	3rd Qtr	4th Qtr	Total
2002	3.59	-8.97	-14.63	5.09	-15.41
2003	-3.60	18.78	9.90	13.54	42.88
2004	6.04	1.08	-5.71	14.83	16.06
2005	-4.22	4.41	6.40	2.10	8.64
2006	13.29	-6.72	-2.36	8.50	11.95

Trailing	Total Return%	+/- S&P 500	+/- Russ 2000 Gr	%Rank Cat	Growth of $10,000
3 Mo	8.50	1.80	-0.27	39	10,850
6 Mo	5.93	-6.81	-0.93	41	10,593
1 Yr	11.95	-3.84	-1.40	38	11,195
3 Yr Avg	12.18	1.74	1.67	24	14,117
5 Yr Avg	11.28	5.09	4.35	9	17,064
10 Yr Avg	—	—	—	—	—
15 Yr Avg	—	—	—	—	—

Tax Analysis	Tax-Adj Rtn%	%Rank Cat	Tax-Cost Rat	%Rank Cat
3 Yr (estimated)	12.14	13	0.04	1
5 Yr (estimated)	11.22	6	0.05	1
10 Yr (estimated)	—	—	—	—

Potential Capital Gain Exposure: 24% of assets

Morningstar's Take by Reginald Laing 12-14-06

Vanguard Small Cap Growth Index is a relatively tame way to own a volatile corner of the style box.

Small-growth is an inherently volatile corner of Morningstar's style box. Small companies are less diversified across different lines of business, and have less heft with which to weather lean economic times, than their larger counterparts. And growth companies tend to have high valuation multiples, which can compress quickly if revenue or earnings growth fails to keep up with market expectations. That translates to volatility: For the trailing 10 years through Nov. 30, 2006, the standard deviation (a common measure of volatility) of the typical small-growth fund was 25.9, versus 16.6 for the average small-value offering.

This Vanguard index offering is a sensible way to gain exposure to small-growth stocks, though. First, its broad diversification ensures the fund isn't overallocated to a particular company or sector. That should help limit volatility here a bit. Another virtue is the fund's use of buffer zones, which keep

stocks from migrating out of the index when they leave the index's market-cap and style range. That keeps portfolio turnover and trading fees low--and tax efficiency high: The fund's trailing three-year annualized gain through Dec. 12, 2006, ranks in the category's top 25%, but its aftertax gains rank in the top 20%.

A side effect of the buffer zones is this fund's large mid-cap stake, which stands at 38.6% of assets. But what the fund loses in style purity it gains in stability, as midsized firms should provide ballast if the economy and financial markets hit turbulence--further tempering the volatility associated with small-growth funds. The buffer zones also allow the fund to more fully capture the upside of former small caps after they've rallied their way into mid-cap territory.

The fund's biggest draw, however, is its very cheap 0.23% expense ratio, which gives it an advantage on its small-growth competition. This is a pretty decent option.

Rating and Risk

Time Period	Load-Adj Return %	Morningstar Rtn vs Cat	Morningstar Risk vs Cat	Morningstar Risk-Adj Rating
1 Yr	11.95			
3 Yr	12.18	+Avg	Avg	★★★★
5 Yr	11.28	+Avg	-Avg	★★★★★
10 Yr	—			
Incept	8.14			

Other Measures	Standard Index S&P 500	Best Fit Index Russ 2000 Gr
Alpha	-3.3	2.0
Beta	1.81	0.91
R-Squared	74	99
Standard Deviation	14.42	
Mean	12.18	
Sharpe Ratio	0.65	

Portfolio Analysis 09-30-06

Share change since 06-06 Total Stocks:936

	Sector	PE	Tot Ret%	% Assets
⊕ Level 3 Communications,	Telecom	—	95.12	0.64
⊕ Covance, Inc.	Health	28.4	21.34	0.51
⊕ Roper Industries, Inc.	Ind Mtrls	24.8	27.83	0.47
⊕ FMC Technologies, Inc.	Energy	19.7	43.59	0.44
⊕ Denbury Resources, Inc.	Energy	16.0	21.99	0.41
⊕ Range Resources Corporat	Energy	16.8	4.62	0.40
⊕ O'Reilly Automotive, Inc	Consumer	20.4	0.16	0.38
⊖ Dade Behring Holdings, I	Health	26.3	-2.13	0.38
⊖ Affiliated Managers Grou	Financial	32.5	31.00	0.38
⊕ Crown Holdings, Inc.	Goods	—	7.12	0.38
⊕ Ametek, Inc.	Ind Mtrls	18.9	12.94	0.37
⊕ Jones Lang LaSalle, Inc.	Financial	18.6	84.32	0.37
⊕ ResMed, Inc.	Health	40.1	28.48	0.36
⊕ VCA Antech, Inc.	Health	26.5	14.15	0.36
⊕ Thomas & Betts Corporati	Hardware	19.1	12.68	0.36
⊕ Global Payments, Inc.	Business	24.7	-0.49	0.36
⊕ Stericycle, Inc.	Business	44.1	28.23	0.35
⊖ ITT Educational Services	Consumer	26.8	12.59	0.35
⊕ Helix Energy Solutions G	Energy	10.6	-12.59	0.35
⊕ Idexx Laboratories	Health	30.4	10.17	0.34

Current Investment Style

Value Blnd Growth — Large Mid Small

Market Cap	%
Giant	0.0
Large	0.0
Mid	38.6
Small	54.5
Micro	6.9

Avg $mil: 1,463

Value Measures		Rel Category
Price/Earnings	19.67	0.94
Price/Book	2.83	1.04
Price/Sales	1.30	0.83
Price/Cash Flow	7.15	0.74
Dividend Yield %	0.28	0.61

Growth Measures	%	Rel Category
Long-Term Erngs	17.41	0.98
Book Value	9.65	0.92
Sales	2.04	0.17
Cash Flow	17.65	0.83
Historical Erngs	22.18	0.91

Profitability	%	Rel Category
Return on Equity	14.24	1.15
Return on Assets	6.87	1.03
Net Margin	8.47	0.98

Sector Weightings

	% of Stocks	Rel S&P 500	3 Year High	Low
↻ Info	20.61	1.03		
Software	6.37	1.85	8	6
Hardware	9.96	1.08	15	9
Media	1.29	0.34	3	1
Telecom	2.99	0.85	3	2
☞ Service	50.89	1.10		
Health	18.36	1.52	21	18
Consumer	11.21	1.47	14	11
Business	14.52	3.43	15	13
Financial	6.80	0.31	8	6
↺ Mfg	28.51	0.84		
Goods	6.23	0.73	6	4
Ind Mtrls	13.17	1.10	14	8
Energy	8.85	0.90	11	5
Utilities	0.26	0.07	1	0

Composition

● Cash	0.5
● Stocks	99.5
● Bonds	0.0
● Other	0.0
Foreign (% of Stock)	0.4

Address:	PO Box 2600 Valley Forge PA 19482 800-997-2798	Minimum Purchase:	$3000	Add: $100	IRA: $3000
		Min Auto Inv Plan:	$3000	Add: $50	
		Sales Fees:	No-load		
Web Address:	www.vanguard.com	Management Fee:	0.19%		
Inception:	05-21-98*	Actual Fees:	Mgt:0.19%	Dist: —	
Advisor:	Vanguard Advisers, Inc.	Expense Projections:	3Yr:$74	5Yr:$130	10Yr:$293
Subadvisor:	None	Income Distrib:	Annually		
NTF Plans:	Vanguard NTF				

MORNINGSTAR® Funds 500

Vanguard SmCp Idx

	Ticker	Load	NAV	Yield	Total Assets	Mstar Category
	NAESX	None	$32.62	1.1%	$13,663 mil	Small Blend

Governance and Management

Stewardship Grade: B

Portfolio Manager(s)

In 2005, Michael Buek became this fund's listed manager, taking over from Gus Sauter, Vanguard's chief investment officer. Buek has been with Vanguard since 1987 and has helped manage this fund since 1991. Buek also manages the venerable Vanguard 500.

Strategy

This fund tracks the MSCI U.S. Small Cap 1750 Index, which contains the smallest 1,750 of the top 2,500 publicly traded companies in the United States (ranked by market capitalization). Because it pulls in a passel of mid-cap names, its median market cap is a tad higher than that of the Russell Index, which was this fund's benchmark until May 2003.

Historical Profile

Return: Average
Risk: Above Avg
Rating: ★★★ Neutral

96% 98% 98% 99% 99% 99% 100% 99% 100%

Investment Style
Equity
Stock %

▼ Manager Change
▽ Partial Manager Change

Growth of $10,000
- Investment Values of Fund
- Investment Values of S&P 500

Performance Quartile (within Category)

History	1995	1996	1997	1998	1999	2000	2001	2002	2003	2004	2005	2006
NAV	18.61	20.23	23.75	21.20	23.60	19.44	19.82	15.66	22.60	26.83	28.52	32.62
Total Return %	28.74	18.12	24.59	-2.61	23.13	-2.67	3.10	-20.02	45.63	19.90	7.36	15.66
+/-S&P 500	-8.84	-4.84	-8.77	-31.19	2.09	6.43	14.99	2.08	16.95	9.02	2.45	-0.13
+/-Russ 2000	0.29	1.63	2.23	-0.06	1.87	0.35	0.61	0.46	-1.62	1.57	2.81	-2.71
Income Return %	1.53	1.46	1.36	1.29	1.27	1.11	1.16	0.97	1.30	1.17	1.08	1.27
Capital Return %	27.21	16.66	23.23	-3.90	21.86	-3.78	1.94	-20.99	44.33	18.73	6.28	14.39
Total Rtn % Rank Cat	39	77	59	36	26	91	69	72	39	43	42	42
Income $	0.23	0.27	0.27	0.30	0.27	0.26	0.23	0.19	0.20	0.26	0.29	0.36
Capital Gains $	0.45	1.44	1.11	1.55	2.08	3.02	0.00	0.00	0.00	0.00	0.00	0.00
Expense Ratio %	0.25	0.25	0.23	0.24	0.25	0.27	0.27	0.27	0.27	0.23	0.23	—
Income Ratio %	1.58	1.51	1.38	1.39	1.25	1.17	1.16	1.11	1.17	1.13	1.08	—
Turnover Rate %	28	28	29	35	42	49	39	32	39	19	18	—
Net Assets $mil	971	1,713	2,652	2,768	3,553	3,577	3,545	2,943	4,871	6,247	5,902	6,808

Performance 12-31-06

	1st Qtr	2nd Qtr	3rd Qtr	4th Qtr	Total
2002	3.99	-7.81	-21.37	6.10	-20.02
2003	-4.53	22.21	8.65	14.89	45.63
2004	6.59	1.00	-2.26	13.95	19.90
2005	-3.79	4.84	5.21	1.17	7.36
2006	12.20	-4.72	-0.26	8.47	15.66

Trailing	Total Return%	+/- S&P 500	+/- Russ 2000	%Rank Cat	Growth of $10,000
3 Mo	8.47	1.77	-0.43	40	10,847
6 Mo	8.18	-4.56	-1.20	38	10,818
1 Yr	15.66	-0.13	-2.71	42	11,566
3 Yr Avg	14.19	3.75	0.63	36	14,890
5 Yr Avg	11.64	5.45	0.25	53	17,342
10 Yr Avg	10.03	1.61	0.59	75	26,008
15 Yr Avg	12.06	1.42	0.59	75	55,177

Tax Analysis	Tax-Adj Rtn%	%Rank Cat	Tax-Cost Rat	%Rank Cat
3 Yr (estimated)	13.94	20	0.22	5
5 Yr (estimated)	11.35	35	0.26	8
10 Yr (estimated)	8.77	61	1.15	34

Potential Capital Gain Exposure: 32% of assets

Rating and Risk

Time Period	Load-Adj Return %	Morningstar Rtn vs Cat	Morningstar Risk vs Cat	Morningstar Risk-Adj Rating
1 Yr	15.66			
3 Yr	14.19	Avg	Avg	★★★
5 Yr	11.64	Avg	Avg	★★★
10 Yr	10.03	-Avg	+Avg	★★
Incept	—			

Other Measures	Standard Index S&P 500	Best Fit Index Russ 2000
Alpha	-0.4	1.4
Beta	1.61	0.90
R-Squared	77	99
Standard Deviation	12.63	
Mean	14.19	
Sharpe Ratio	0.86	

Morningstar's Take by Reginald Laing 12-13-06

Vanguard Small Cap Index doesn't rank in the category elite, but it's better than most of its peers.

This fund, which charges only 0.23%, is among the cheapest in the small-blend category. Expenses are especially important here, as this offering passively owns roughly 1,500 of the stocks in its MSCI index and relies on low fees to edge past a majority of small-blend competitors.

Since adopting the MSCI bogy in May 2003, this fund has outgained its typical peer by a comfortable margin. For the trailing three years through Dec. 12, 2006, its 15.1% annualized return outpaced those of two thirds of its competitors. While investors can't expect such strong absolute gains every year, this fund's low fees should ensure a competitive category ranking over time. Moreover, its broad exposure limits stock- and sector-specific risk, which should keep volatility below the average for this somewhat volatile category.

The fund's high tax efficiency gives it a further leg up versus its peer group. Because the index employs buffer zones--which limit stocks' migration into and out of the fund--its turnover should be even lower than that of comparable index funds. That means taxable investors here will be able to keep a greater percentage of their profits than will owners of higher-turnover funds. Low turnover also controls trading costs, which aren't reflected in a fund's expense ratio but come out of assets.

Last, although active managers historically have taken advantage of small caps' relative inefficiency to outpace their indexing peers, finding a good small-cap manager (whose fund is still open and not already swamped with assets) is a tall order, now that small caps have been on a multiyear run and investors have flooded into the hottest performing of these funds.

By its passive nature, this fund won't likely top the small-blend category in any given calendar year--or even over long stretches of time. But it's still a good option for investors seeking no-frills exposure to small caps.

Address:	PO Box 2600 Valley Forge PA 19482 800-997-2798	Minimum Purchase:	$3000	Add: $100	IRA: $3000
		Min Auto Inv Plan:	$3000	Add: $50	
		Sales Fees:	No-load		
Web Address:	www.vanguard.com	Management Fee:	0.20%		
Inception:	10-03-60	Actual Fees:	Mgt:0.20%	Dist: —	
Advisor:	Vanguard Advisers, Inc.	Expense Projections:	3Yr:$74	5Yr:$130	10Yr:$293
Subadvisor:	None	Income Distrib:	Annually		
NTF Plans:	Vanguard NTF				

Portfolio Analysis 09-30-06

Share change since 06-06 Total Stocks:1728

	Sector	PE	Tot Ret%	% Assets
⊕ Level 3 Communications,	Telecom	—	95.12	0.31
⊕ Camden Property Trust	Financial	32.0	32.17	0.25
⊕ Covance, Inc.	Health	28.4	21.34	0.24
⊕ Federal Realty Investmen	Financial	53.5	44.88	0.24
⊕ Roper Industries, Inc.	Ind Mtrls	24.8	27.83	0.22
⊕ FMC Technologies, Inc.	Energy	19.7	43.59	0.21
⊕ HCC Insurance Holdings I	Financial	16.5	9.39	0.21
⊕ Ventas, Inc.	Financial	32.4	38.19	0.21
⊕ Northeast Utilities	Utilities	33.5	47.76	0.21
⊕ Reckson Associates Realt	Financial	46.0	31.78	0.21
⊕ Denbury Resources, Inc.	Energy	16.0	21.99	0.20
⊕ Plains Exploration & Pro	Energy		19.63	0.19
⊕ Range Resources Corporat	Energy	16.8	4.62	0.19
⊕ OGE Energy Corp	Utilities	15.8	55.73	0.19
⊕ Harsco Corporation	Ind Mtrls	16.3	14.65	0.19
⊕ Mack-Cali Realty Corpora	Financial	34.0	24.56	0.19
⊕ Integrated Device Techno	Hardware		17.45	0.19
⊕ O'Reilly Automotive, Inc	Consumer	20.4	0.16	0.18
⊕ CMS Energy Corporation	Utilities		15.09	0.18
⊕ Conseco, Inc.	Financial	23.9	-13.77	0.18

Current Investment Style

Value Blnd Growth — Large Mid Small

Market Cap	%
Giant	0.0
Large	0.0
Mid	40.3
Small	52.7
Micro	6.9

Avg $mil: 1,467

Value Measures		Rel Category
Price/Earnings	16.62	1.00
Price/Book	2.06	0.98
Price/Sales	0.99	1.01
Price/Cash Flow	6.72	0.96
Dividend Yield %	1.45	1.36

Growth Measures	%	Rel Category
Long-Term Erngs	13.03	0.93
Book Value	5.81	0.77
Sales	5.50	0.62
Cash Flow	8.29	0.65
Historical Erngs	13.75	0.82

Profitability	%	Rel Category
Return on Equity	11.94	0.93
Return on Assets	6.48	0.91
Net Margin	9.84	1.02

Sector Weightings	% of Stocks	Rel S&P 500	3 Year High Low
↻ Info	14.62	0.73	
▣ Software	3.88	1.12	5 4
▣ Hardware	7.35	0.80	9 7
▣ Media	1.52	0.40	2 1
▣ Telecom	1.87	0.53	2 1
⊊ Service	53.78	1.16	
▤ Health	10.11	0.84	12 10
▤ Consumer	10.13	1.32	12 10
▤ Business	11.14	2.63	11 10
▤ Financial	22.40	1.01	23 22
⊔ Mfg	31.60	0.94	
▤ Goods	5.91	0.69	6 4
▤ Ind Mtrls	15.02	1.26	16 13
▤ Energy	6.33	0.65	8 5
▤ Utilities	4.34	1.24	5 4

Composition

● Cash	0.2	
● Stocks	99.8	
● Bonds	0.0	
○ Other	0.0	
Foreign	0.4	(% of Stock)

Vanguard SmCp VI Idx

	Ticker	Load	NAV	Yield	Total Assets	Mstar Category
	VISVX	None	$17.05	1.8%	$5,134 mil	Small Value

Governance and Management

Stewardship Grade: B

Portfolio Manager(s)

In 2005, Michael Buek became this fund's listed manager, taking over from Gus Sauter, Vanguard's chief investment officer. Buek has been with Vanguard since 1987 and has helped manage this fund since 1991. Buek also manages Vanguard Small Cap Index and the venerable Vanguard 500.

Strategy

In May 2003, Vanguard replaced this fund's former bogy, the S&P SmallCap 600/Barra Value Index, with the newly minted MSCI U.S. Small Cap Value Index, which consists of the cheapest stocks (as determined by its eight-pronged classification scheme) in the small-cap universe. The index uses bands to limit the migration of stocks between market-cap and style boundaries, thus limiting turnover.

Historical Profile
Return Average
Risk Average
Rating ★★★ Neutral

| | 97% | 97% | 100% | 99% | 100% | 100% | 100% | 99% | 99% |

Investment Style
Equity
Stock %

▼ Manager Change
▽ Partial Manager Change

19.6
16.0 **Growth of $10,000**
13.0 — Investment Values of Fund
10.0 — Investment Values of S&P 500
7.0

Performance Quartile (within Category)

1995	1996	1997	1998	1999	2000	2001	2002	2003	2004	2005	2006	History
—	—	—	8.74	8.45	9.65	10.29	8.52	11.49	13.97	14.56	17.05	NAV
—	—	—	-12.47*	3.35	21.88	13.70	-14.20	37.19	23.55	6.07	19.24	Total Return %
—	—	—	—	-17.69	30.98	25.59	7.90	8.51	12.67	1.16	3.45	+/-S&P 500
—	—	—	—	4.84	-0.95	-0.32	-2.77	-8.84	1.30	1.36	-4.24	+/-Russ 2000 VL
—	—	—	—	0.80	1.00	0.71	0.90	2.32	1.96	1.88	2.12	Income Return %
—	—	—	—	2.55	20.88	12.99	-15.10	34.87	21.59	4.19	17.12	Capital Return %
—	—	—	—	51	40	61	78	71	21	55	25	Total Rtn % Rank Cat
—	—	—	0.06	0.07	0.08	0.07	0.09	0.20	0.23	0.26	0.31	Income $
—	—	—	0.00	0.50	0.50	0.55	0.28	0.00	0.00	0.00	0.00	Capital Gains $
—	—	—	0.25	0.25	0.27	0.27	0.27	0.27	0.23	0.23	—	Expense Ratio %
—	—	—	1.13	0.96	1.16	0.97	0.93	2.07	2.15	1.96	—	Income Ratio %
—	—	—	—	80	82	59	57	109	30	28	—	Turnover Rate %
—	—	—	113	204	317	802	1,176	1,730	2,947	3,446	4,314	Net Assets $mil

Performance 12-31-06

	1st Qtr	2nd Qtr	3rd Qtr	4th Qtr	Total
2002	10.41	-4.15	-22.50	4.62	-14.20
2003	-7.98	19.39	7.48	16.19	37.19
2004	7.14	0.89	1.13	13.03	23.55
2005	-3.35	5.26	4.01	0.24	6.07
2006	11.05	-2.72	1.72	8.52	19.24

Trailing	Total Return%	+/- S&P 500	+/- Russ 2000 VL	%Rank Cat	Growth of $10,000
3 Mo	8.52	1.82	-0.51	48	10,852
6 Mo	10.38	-2.36	-1.43	27	11,038
1 Yr	19.24	3.45	-4.24	25	11,924
3 Yr Avg	16.05	5.61	-0.43	20	15,629
5 Yr Avg	12.96	6.77	-2.41	63	18,392
10 Yr Avg	—	—	—		—
15 Yr Avg	—	—	—		—

Tax Analysis	Tax-Adj Rtn%	%Rank Cat	Tax-Cost Rat	%Rank Cat
3 Yr (estimated)	15.62	6	0.37	5
5 Yr (estimated)	12.35	48	0.54	15
10 Yr (estimated)	—		—	

Potential Capital Gain Exposure: 25% of assets

Rating and Risk

Time Period	Load-Adj Return %	Morningstar Rtn vs Cat	Morningstar Risk vs Cat	Morningstar Risk-Adj Rating
1 Yr	19.24			
3 Yr	16.05	+Avg	Avg	★★★★
5 Yr	12.96	Avg	Avg	★★★
10 Yr	—	—	—	
Incept	10.19			

Other Measures	Standard Index S&P 500	Best Fit Index Mstar Small Value
Alpha	2.4	0.6
Beta	1.43	0.95
R-Squared	74	98
Standard Deviation	11.40	
Mean	16.05	
Sharpe Ratio	1.09	

Morningstar's Take by Reginald Laing 12-26-06

Vanguard Small Cap Value Index is decent, though it will have trouble keeping up its recent pace.

This fund has benefited recently from a favorable market. For the past several years, small-value equities have posted double-digit yearly gains and led all other style categories. So, this offering--which invests in more than 900 micro- to mid-cap value stocks and charges an extremely cheap expense ratio--has posted strong absolute and relative returns: For the trailing three years through Dec. 22, 2006, it delivered a 16.1% annualized gain--a better record than 77% of its peers.

However, market conditions won't always be so favorable, and it's unlikely this fund will maintain its recent pace indefinitely. If, in the coming years, its small-value universe falters relative to the rest of the market, its absolute returns could be far less impressive. Its relative returns might suffer, too, as actively managed peers could outmaneuver the index by investing in bigger and more growth-oriented stocks, which this fund forsakes.

That doesn't mean you should avoid this offering. It remains one of the lowest-cost options in the category, and its broad exposure limits stock- and sector-specific risk. Moreover, this fund's use of buffer zones, which limit the migration of stocks into and out of the index, should limit portfolio turnover, making it tax-efficient and keeping trading costs (which come out of assets but aren't included in a fund's published expense ratio) low. And as money has flowed into hot-performing small-value funds in recent years, finding a good active manager with capacity can now be a challenge. Last, because this fund tracks a less commonly followed index, management can add and delete holdings without worrying about front-runners, who buy stocks in anticipation of their being added to the bogy (and bid up by indexers) and can hurt investors' returns.

Overall, we think this is a decent small-value option.

Portfolio Analysis 09-30-06

Share change since 06-06 Total Stocks:973

	Sector	PE	Tot Ret%	% Assets
⊕ Camden Property Trust	Financial	32.0	32.17	0.47
⊕ Federal Realty Investmen	Financial	53.5	44.88	0.45
⊕ Ventas, Inc.	Financial	32.4	38.19	0.40
⊕ Northeast Utilities	Utilities	33.5	47.76	0.39
⊕ Reckson Associates Realt	Financial	46.0	31.78	0.39
⊕ Plains Exploration & Pro	Energy	—	19.63	0.37
⊕ OGE Energy Corp	Utilities	15.8	55.73	0.36
⊕ Harsco Corporation	Ind Mtrls	16.3	14.65	0.36
⊕ Mack-Cali Realty Corpora	Financial	34.0	24.56	0.36
⊕ Integrated Device Techno	Hardware	—	17.45	0.36
⊕ CMS Energy Corporation	Utilities	—	15.09	0.35
⊕ Conseco, Inc.	Financial	23.9	-13.77	0.35
⊕ Sierra Pacific Resources	Utilities	12.2	29.06	0.35
⊕ Ryder System, Inc.	Business	13.4	26.29	0.35
⊕ Lubrizol Corporation	Ind Mtrls	16.6	18.17	0.34
⊕ BRE Properties, Inc.	Financial	71.6	48.20	0.34
⊕ Ann Taylor Stores Corpor	Consumer	16.6	-4.87	0.34
⊕ Brandywine Realty Trust	Financial	—	24.09	0.33
⊕ Energen Corporation	Energy	13.9	30.75	0.32
⊕ OfficeMax, Inc.	Consumer	—	98.81	0.32

Current Investment Style

Value Blnd Growth — Large Mid Small

Market Cap	%
Giant	0.0
Large	0.0
Mid	41.9
Small	51.1
Micro	7.0

Avg $mil: 1,470

Value Measures		Rel Category
Price/Earnings	14.66	0.95
Price/Book	1.67	0.94
Price/Sales	0.81	1.01
Price/Cash Flow	6.38	1.04
Dividend Yield %	2.54	1.61

Growth Measures	%	Rel Category
Long-Term Erngs	10.25	0.82
Book Value	4.19	0.77
Sales	7.70	1.04
Cash Flow	2.10	0.26
Historical Erngs	9.95	0.87

Profitability	%	Rel Category
Return on Equity	9.88	0.92
Return on Assets	6.12	1.00
Net Margin	11.09	1.23

Sector Weightings	% of Stocks	Rel S&P 500	3 Year High	Low
↻ Info	9.14	0.46		
▣ Software	1.60	0.46	2	1
▣ Hardware	4.95	0.54	6	3
▣ Media	1.74	0.46	2	1
▣ Telecom	0.85	0.24	1	0
⊂ Service	56.43	1.22		
▣ Health	2.50	0.21	4	2
▣ Consumer	9.12	1.19	9	8
▣ Business	8.03	1.90	8	6
▣ Financial	36.78	1.65	39	36
⊔ Mfg	34.44	1.02		
▣ Goods	5.61	0.66	6	5
▣ Ind Mtrls	16.72	1.40	20	17
▣ Energy	4.01	0.41	6	3
▣ Utilities	8.10	2.31	9	8

Composition

		%
● Cash		0.6
● Stocks		99.4
● Bonds		0.0
● Other		0.0
Foreign		0.5
(% of Stock)		

Address:	PO Box 2600 Valley Forge PA 19482 800-997-2798	Minimum Purchase:	$3000	Add: $100	IRA: $3000
		Min Auto Inv Plan:	$3000	Add: $50	
		Sales Fees:	No-load		
Web Address:	www.vanguard.com	Management Fee:	0.20%		
Inception:	05-21-98 *	Actual Fees:	Mgt:0.20%	Dist: —	
Advisor:	Vanguard Advisers, Inc.	Expense Projections:	3Yr:$74	5Yr:$130	10Yr:$293
Subadvisor:	None	Income Distrib:	Annually		
NTF Plans:	Vanguard NTF				

Morningstar® Funds 500

Vanguard STAR

	Ticker	Load	NAV	Yield	Total Assets	Mstar Category
	VGSTX	None	$20.95	2.7%	$13,858 mil	Moderate Allocation

Governance and Management

Stewardship Grade: B

Portfolio Manager(s)

This fund of funds owns 11 actively managed offerings and boasts several well-known and talented managers. Its trustees oversee its asset allocation but rarely alter the lineup.

Strategy

This fund of funds invests in 11 Vanguard funds to build a diversified portfolio. The goal is a stable asset allocation of 62% stocks, 25% intermediate- and long-term bonds, and 12% short-term bonds. The equity portion tilts toward two large-value funds (Windsor and Windsor II), but it also includes large-growth and small-growth offerings (Morgan Growth and Explorer) and two foreign-stock funds (International Growth and International Value).

Historical Profile

Return	Above Avg
Risk	Average
Rating	★★★★ Above Avg

| | 60% | 59% | 58% | 60% | 58% | 60% | 59% | 59% | 60% |

Investment Style
Equity
Stock %

▽ Manager Change
▽ Partial Manager Change

31.0
25.0 **Growth of $10,000**
20.0 ■ Investment Values of Fund
15.0 — Investment Values of DJ Mod
10.0

Performance Quartile (within Category)

1995	1996	1997	1998	1999	2000	2001	2002	2003	2004	2005	2006	History
15.03	15.86	17.38	17.96	18.21	17.81	16.44	14.35	17.20	18.74	19.60	20.95	NAV
28.64	16.11	21.15	12.38	7.13	10.96	0.50	-9.87	22.70	11.60	7.44	11.64	Total Return %
8.84	5.45	9.25	0.06	-10.20	12.63	3.30	-3.10	-4.68	-1.37	0.45	-0.66	+/-DJ Mod
3.87	4.77	1.95	-0.01	-5.72	6.52	0.34	0.67	-1.36	0.43	1.44	1.37	+/-DJ US Mod
4.73	3.96	3.75	3.36	3.42	3.74	3.27	2.94	2.73	2.57	2.52	2.98	Income Return %
23.91	12.15	17.40	9.02	3.71	7.22	-2.77	-12.81	19.97	9.03	4.92	8.66	Capital Return %
25	36	35	57	71	10	14	30	29	13	13	39	Total Rtn % Rank Cat
0.59	0.59	0.59	0.58	0.61	0.64	0.55	0.48	0.39	0.44	0.47	0.58	Income $
0.57	0.98	1.20	0.98	0.40	1.65	0.87	—	—	—	0.06	0.33	Capital Gains $
—	—	—	—	—	—	—	—	—	—	—	0.36	Expense Ratio %
4.12	3.71	3.46	3.18	3.21	3.57	2.91	3.07	2.60	2.39	2.44	—	Income Ratio %
13	18	15	16	10	17	6	12	15	6	6	—	Turnover Rate %
4,842	5,863	7,355	8,083	8,087	8,119	8,242	7,217	9,134	10,763	12,168	13,858	Net Assets $mil

Performance 12-31-06

	1st Qtr	2nd Qtr	3rd Qtr	4th Qtr	Total
2002	1.09	-6.20	-9.43	4.94	-9.87
2003	-1.81	12.12	2.75	8.48	22.70
2004	3.55	-0.22	0.40	7.59	11.60
2005	-1.07	2.64	3.34	2.38	7.44
2006	3.32	-1.36	4.15	5.18	11.64

Trailing	Total Return%	+/- DJ Mod	+/- DJ US Mod	%Rank Cat	Growth of $10,000
3 Mo	5.18	-0.41	0.51	45	10,518
6 Mo	9.55	0.76	1.65	30	10,955
1 Yr	11.64	-0.66	1.37	39	11,164
3 Yr Avg	10.21	-0.51	1.09	15	13,386
5 Yr Avg	8.16	-1.86	0.56	11	14,802
10 Yr Avg	9.19	0.64	0.60	12	24,090
15 Yr Avg	10.38	1.17	0.99	17	43,990

Tax Analysis	Tax-Adj Rtn%	%Rank Cat	Tax-Cost Rat	%Rank Cat
3 Yr (estimated)	9.23	13	0.89	43
5 Yr (estimated)	7.17	9	0.92	55
10 Yr (estimated)	7.25	12	1.78	67

Potential Capital Gain Exposure: 27% of assets

Rating and Risk

Time Period	Load-Adj Return %	Morningstar Rtn vs Cat	Morningstar Risk vs Cat	Morningstar Risk-Adj Rating
1 Yr	11.64			
3 Yr	10.21	+Avg	Avg	★★★★
5 Yr	8.16	+Avg	Avg	★★★★
10 Yr	9.19	+Avg	Avg	★★★★
Incept	11.12			

Other Measures	Standard Index DJ Mod	Best Fit Index DJ Mod
Alpha	0.3	0.3
Beta	0.89	0.89
R-Squared	95	95
Standard Deviation	5.36	
Mean	10.21	
Sharpe Ratio	1.25	

Portfolio Analysis 09-30-06

Total Stocks:0 Share change since 06-30-06	Sectors	P/E Ratio	YTD Return %	% Net Assets
⊖ MF Vanguard/Windsor II	—	—	—	16.30
⊕ Vanguard Windsor	—	—	—	8.88
⊖ Vanguard PRIMECAP	—	—	—	6.99
⊕ Vanguard U.S. Growth	—	—	—	6.95
⊖ Vanguard Morgan Growth	—	—	—	6.90
⊖ Vanguard International Va	—	—	—	6.29
⊖ Vanguard International Gr	—	—	—	6.25
⊕ MF Vanguard Explorer Fund	—	—	—	4.17

Total Fixed-Income:0	Date of Maturity	Amount $000	Value $000	% Net Assets
Vanguard GNMA		160,085	1,631,270	12.33
Vanguard Short-Term Inves		153,085	1,615,048	12.21

Morningstar's Take by William Samuel Rocco 11-03-06

Vanguard STAR still has real appeal despite the manager changes at a few of its underlying offerings.

Three of this fund of fund's underlying funds have had manager changes during the past year. Vanguard International Value added a third subadvisor, Lazard, in July 2006. Thomas Pappas replaced Paul Kaplan as the lead manager of Vanguard GNMA in June 2006. And at Vanguard Morgan Growth, Jim Stetler replaced Gus Sauter as lead manager on the Vanguard sleeve in January 2006, and Paul Markand replaced Bob Rand as the lead manager on the Wellington sleeve in December 2005.

Nonetheless, we still believe in these three underlying offerings. While the Lazard team hasn't shone at its other charge--and it's not yet clear that it will add a lot of value--the team is part of a respected firm and the other two subadvisors are good, so Vanguard International Value remains fairly attractive. Pappas worked with Kaplan for 20 years before taking over Vanguard GNMA. He has considerable analyst support and has kept that winning fund's strategy intact, so there's significant reason for optimism there. And there are ample grounds to believe Vanguard Morgan Growth will continue to be successful going forward: Stetler was very involved with running his sleeve before taking it over; Markand did a nice job at his prior charge and is supported by the same impressive team of analysts as his predecessor; and the third manager remains in place.

Meanwhile, this fund's other underlying funds are an excellent lot and combine with Vanguard International Value, GNMA, and Morgan Growth to provide exceptional diversification in one package. This fund boasts strong three-, five-, and 10-year returns as well as a moderate risk profile. And it is quite attractively priced.

This fund remains a great option for one-stop shoppers.

Address:	PO Box 2600 Valley Forge PA 19482 800-997-2798	Minimum Purchase: Min Auto Inv Plan: Sales Fees:	$1000 Add: $100 IRA: $1000 $1000 Add: $50 No-load
Web Address:	www.vanguard.com	Management Fee:	0.00%
Inception:	03-29-85	Actual Fees:	Mgt:0.00% Dist: —
Advisor:	Vanguard Advisers, Inc.	Expense Projections:	3Yr:$116 5Yr:$202 10Yr:$456
Subadvisor:	None	Income Distrib:	Semi-Annually
NTF Plans:	Vanguard NTF		

Equity Style
Style: Blend
Size: Large-Cap

Value Measures		Rel Category
Price/Earnings	13.94	0.91
Price/Book	2.38	0.96
Price/Sales	1.29	0.94
Price/Cash Flow	6.92	0.85
Dividend Yield %	1.98	1.03

Growth Measures	%	Rel Category
Long-Term Erngs	11.75	1.00
Book Value	8.84	1.03
Sales	9.36	1.05
Cash Flow	10.23	1.04
Historical Erngs	13.27	0.74

Market Cap %		
Giant	44.3	Small 2.9
Large	35.7	Micro 0.4
Mid	16.8	Avg $mil: 29,706

Fixed-Income Style
Duration: Long-Term
Quality: High

Avg Eff Duration [1]	6.3 Yrs
Avg Eff Maturity	11.2 Yrs
Avg Credit Quality	AA
Avg Wtd Coupon	5.56%

[1]figure provided by fund as of 09-30-06

Sector Weightings	% of Stocks	Rel DJ Mod	3 Year High Low
⌖ Info	20.68	—	
▩ Software	4.33	—	4 3
▩ Hardware	9.90	—	11 9
▩ Media	3.24	—	4 3
▩ Telecom	3.21	—	3 3
⌨ Service	46.83	—	
▩ Health	14.69	—	15 14
▩ Consumer	5.45	—	9 5
▩ Business	6.29	—	7 6
▩ Financial	20.40	—	21 19
▩ Mfg	32.49	—	
▩ Goods	9.53	—	10 8
▩ Ind Mtrls	12.81	—	14 11
▩ Energy	7.22	—	9 7
▩ Utilities	2.93	—	4 2

Composition

●	Cash	5.7
●	Stocks	59.6
●	Bonds	34.2
○	Other	0.5
	Foreign	26.3 (% of Stock)

Vanguard Strategic Eq

	Ticker	Load	NAV	Yield	Total Assets	Mstar Category
	VSEQX	None	$23.64	1.1%	$7,133 mil	Mid-Cap Blend

Governance and Management

Stewardship Grade: B

Portfolio Manager(s)

Early in 2006, James Troyer, a veteran member of Vanguard's Quantitative Equity Group, took over the day-to-day management of this fund. However, former managers Gus Sauter and Joel Dickson will retain supervisory roles. Troyer, who has been with Vanguard since 1989, has long been responsible for the firm's quantitative research.

Strategy

Quantitative models, designed by Vanguard's Quantitative Equity Group, call the shots at this offering. Management consults the models to construct a portfolio with moderate valuations, strong earnings growth, and sector weightings similar to those of the MSCI U.S. Small and Mid-Cap 2200 Index. The models consider myriad factors, including revisions to analysts' earnings estimates and changes in insider ownership.

Performance 12-31-06

	1st Qtr	2nd Qtr	3rd Qtr	4th Qtr	Total
2002	4.46	-6.98	-15.07	5.24	-13.14
2003	-0.92	18.95	8.10	12.89	43.83
2004	5.93	0.76	-1.35	14.44	20.49
2005	-1.87	5.04	5.39	1.23	9.97
2006	9.12	-2.93	-0.69	7.83	13.43

Trailing	Total Return%	+/- S&P 500	+/- S&P Mid 400	%Rank Cat	Growth of $10,000
3 Mo	7.83	1.13	0.84	41	10,783
6 Mo	7.08	-5.66	1.25	66	10,708
1 Yr	13.43	-2.36	3.11	46	11,343
3 Yr Avg	14.55	4.11	1.46	23	15,031
5 Yr Avg	13.43	7.24	2.54	11	18,778
10 Yr Avg	12.41	3.99	-1.06	35	32,214
15 Yr Avg	—	—	—	—	—

Tax Analysis	Tax-Adj Rtn%	%Rank Cat	Tax-Cost Rat	%Rank Cat
3 Yr (estimated)	13.35	22	1.05	46
5 Yr (estimated)	12.60	11	0.73	46
10 Yr (estimated)	10.85	30	1.39	37

Potential Capital Gain Exposure: 16% of assets

Morningstar's Take by Dan Culloton 11-20-06

The recently reopened Vanguard Strategic Equity may have won a battle against asset bloat, but the war continues.

This fund recently reopened to new investors after closing its doors in late April. At the time, the fund's decent record, as well as its focus on hot smaller-cap stocks, attracted lots of new shareholders. At more than $7 billion the fund was, and still is, one of the largest in the mid-blend category. Net cash flows into the fund, however, have dropped off considerably since Vanguard shut this fund, and the family concluded in early November it was safe to take new investments again, albeit at a higher $10,000 minimum.

There's evidence to support that the closing helped cool inflows at this fund, though two consecutive quarters of losses in the middle of 2006 also played a role. There's also not much sign that the fund's size is impeding its ability to execute its strategy, which consists of using quantitative models to find mid- and small-cap stocks with moderate valuations and strong growth prospects. The fund's turnover hasn't changed dramatically, so it appears that the managers are not having problems trading, and it still doesn't look like the fund would have much trouble unwinding its top positions. For example, it owns less than a half a day's trading volume in engine maker Cummins.

Still, it would have been more comforting if the fund stayed shut. It's particularly important for mid- and small-cap funds to keep their asset bases under control because their trading can have a larger impact on the prices of the stocks they are buying and selling. This fund still keeps more than a fourth of its assets in small caps, and its management team also runs the new Vanguard Strategic Small-Cap Equity, which ploughs some of the same fields as this one.

It remains a decent choice. The management team is experienced, and it has a clearly defined strategy, competitive long-term record, and low fees. Keep it, but also keep an eye on its waistline.

Address:	P O Box 2600
	Valley Forge PA 19482
	800-997-2798
Web Address:	www.vanguard.com
Inception:	08-14-95 *
Advisor:	Vanguard Advisers, Inc.
Subadvisor:	None
NTF Plans:	Vanguard NTF

Minimum Purchase:	$10000	Add: $100	IRA: $3000
Min Auto Inv Plan:	$3000	Add: $50	
Sales Fees:	No-load		
Management Fee:	0.38%		
Actual Fees:	Mgt:0.38%	Dist: —	
Expense Projections:	3Yr:$128	5Yr:$224	10Yr:$505
Income Distrib:	Annually		

Historical Profile

Return	Above Avg
Risk	Average
Rating	★★★★ Above Avg

Investment Style: Equity / Stock %

| 97% | 93% | 97% | 94% | 97% | 99% | 100% | 99% | 100% |

▽ Manager Change
▽ Partial Manager Change

Growth of $10,000
— Investment Values of Fund
— Investment Values of S&P 500

38.0 / 31.0 / 24.0 / 17.0 / 10.0

Performance Quartile (within Category)

	1995	1996	1997	1998	1999	2000	2001	2002	2003	2004	2005	2006	History
NAV	10.76	12.56	14.60	14.53	16.76	14.58	15.23	13.10	18.71	21.43	21.93	23.64	NAV
	7.76*	25.03	26.22	0.61	19.25	7.46	5.42	-13.14	43.83	20.49	9.97	13.43	Total Return %
	—	2.07	-7.14	-27.97	-1.79	16.56	17.31	8.96	15.15	9.61	5.06	-2.36	+/-S&P 500
	—	5.78	-6.03	-18.51	4.53	-10.05	6.03	1.39	8.21	4.01	-2.59	3.11	+/-S&P Mid 400
	—	1.67	1.11	1.03	1.10	1.25	0.96	0.85	0.99	0.75	0.98	1.19	Income Return %
	—	23.36	25.11	-0.42	18.15	6.21	4.46	-13.99	42.84	19.74	8.99	12.24	Capital Return %
	—	23	57	84	44	63	35	30	17	18	47	46	Total Rtn % Rank Cat
	0.08	0.18	0.14	0.15	0.16	0.21	0.14	0.13	0.13	0.14	0.21	0.26	Income $
	0.00	0.71	1.08	0.00	0.37	3.03	0.00	0.00	0.00	0.96	1.44	0.98	Capital Gains $
	0.06	0.38	0.40	0.43	0.46	0.49	0.54	0.50	0.50	0.45	0.40	0.35	Expense Ratio %
	2.22	1.78	1.28	0.93	1.00	1.31	1.06	0.94	1.04	0.83	0.99	1.18	Income Ratio %
	—	106	85	71	51	83	82	73	100	66	75	80	Turnover Rate %
	75	153	474	535	626	745	879	914	1,980	3,746	5,614	7,133	Net Assets $mil

Rating and Risk

Time Period	Load-Adj Return %	Morningstar Rtn vs Cat	Morningstar Risk vs Cat	Morningstar Risk-Adj Rating
1 Yr	13.43			
3 Yr	14.55	+Avg	+Avg	★★★★
5 Yr	13.43	+Avg	Avg	★★★★
10 Yr	12.41	Avg	Avg	★★★
Incept	13.77			

Other Measures	Standard Index S&P 500	Best Fit Index DJ Wilshire 4500
Alpha	0.3	-0.9
Beta	1.56	1.06
R-Squared	78	96
Standard Deviation	12.07	
Mean	14.55	
Sharpe Ratio	0.92	

Portfolio Analysis 09-30-06

Share change since 06-06 Total Stocks:777	Sector	PE	Tot Ret%	% Assets
⊖ AmerisourceBergen Corpor	Health	26.5	8.90	1.03
Parker Hannifin Corporat	Ind Mtrls	13.2	18.00	1.02
⊖ Fiserv, Inc.	Business	19.6	21.15	1.01
⊖ Safeco Corporation	Financial	8.8	12.89	0.97
⊖ Nordstrom, Inc.	Consumer	21.9	33.35	0.96
⊕ Whirlpool Corporation	Goods	13.0	1.11	0.96
⊕ Freeport-McMoRan Copper	Ind Mtrls	7.7	13.08	0.95
⊕ Cummins, Inc.	Ind Mtrls	8.4	33.23	0.92
⊖ Darden Restaurants, Inc.	Consumer	17.4	4.37	0.89
⊖ Radian Group, Inc.	Financial	8.6	-7.86	0.86
⊖ Barr Pharmaceuticals, In	Health	18.7	-19.54	0.85
⊕ Ameriprise Financial, In	Financial	—	—	0.84
⊕ Qwest Communications Int	Telecom	—	48.14	0.83
⊕ Manpower, Inc.	Business	20.7	62.53	0.82
VF Corporation	Goods	16.7	52.02	0.81
⊕ Computer Sciences Corpor	Business	23.7	5.39	0.80
⊕ Indymac Bancorp, Inc.	Financial	8.8	20.80	0.78
⊕ CSX Corporation	Business	15.4	37.05	0.77
⊕ Patterson-UTI Energy, In	Energy	5.7	-28.72	0.74
⊕ Helmerich & Payne, Inc.	Energy	10.7	-20.48	0.73

Current Investment Style

Value Blend Growth / Large Mid Small

Market Cap	%
Giant	0.0
Large	9.3
Mid	63.0
Small	25.9
Micro	1.8
Avg $mil:	3,332

Value Measures		Rel Category
Price/Earnings	13.11	0.81
Price/Book	2.22	0.98
Price/Sales	0.90	0.80
Price/Cash Flow	4.15	0.49
Dividend Yield %	1.39	1.07

Growth Measures	%	Rel Category
Long-Term Erngs	13.50	1.06
Book Value	6.97	0.84
Sales	7.00	0.79
Cash Flow	15.00	1.77
Historical Erngs	23.66	1.32

Profitability	%	Rel Category
Return on Equity	18.44	1.16
Return on Assets	9.64	1.20
Net Margin	12.51	1.15

Sector Weightings	% of Stocks	Rel S&P 500	3 Year High	Low
⟳ Info	14.06	0.70		
Software	1.95	0.57	3	2
Hardware	7.47	0.81	10	7
Media	1.80	0.47	3	1
Telecom	2.84	0.81	3	2
⟲ Service	52.13	1.13		
Health	10.33	0.86	11	10
Consumer	9.91	1.30	13	10
Business	9.66	2.28	10	7
Financial	22.23	1.00	22	19
⟳ Mfg	33.81	1.00		
Goods	7.00	0.82	7	5
Ind Mtrls	13.47	1.13	16	13
Energy	8.13	0.83	9	5
Utilities	5.21	1.49	6	5

Composition

		%
●	Cash	0.0
●	Stocks	100.0
●	Bonds	0.0
●	Other	0.0
	Foreign	0.2
	(% of Stock)	

MORNINGSTAR® Funds 500

Vanguard Target Rtmt 2025

Analyst Pick ✓

	Ticker	Load	NAV	Yield	Total Assets	Mstar Category
	VTTVX	None	$13.04	2.2%	$4,605 mil	Target-Date 2015-2029

Governance and Management

Stewardship Grade: B

Portfolio Manager(s)

A team led by experienced index-fund manager Duane Kelly oversees this and other Target Retirement Funds. Because this fund is composed of various Vanguard index offerings, shareholders tap into the company's skill at running index funds.

Strategy

This fund emphasizes capital growth and income. Initially, it invests 17.5% of assets in Vanguard Total Bond Market Index, 66% in Vanguard Total Stock Market Index, 9.7% in Vanguard European Stock Index, 4.6% in Vanguard Pacific Stock Index, and 2.2 % in Vanguard Emerging Markets Index. Allocation to fixed-income securities will increase gradually as the fund nears its target date.

Historical Profile

Return	Average
Risk	Below Avg
Rating	★★★★ Above Avg

Investment Style: Equity / Stock %
59% 58% 57% 80%

▼ Manager Change
▽ Partial Manager Change

Growth of $10,000
■ Investment Values of Fund
— Investment Values of DJ Mod

Performance Quartile (within Category)

	1995	1996	1997	1998	1999	2000	2001	2002	2003	2004	2005	2006	History
	—	—	—	—	—	—	—	—	10.51	11.39	11.77	13.04	NAV
	—	—	—	—	—	—	—	—	—	10.11	5.45	13.24	Total Return %
	—	—	—	—	—	—	—	—	—	-2.86	-1.54	0.94	+/-DJ Mod
	—	—	—	—	—	—	—	—	—	-4.60	-3.26	-1.04	+/-DJ Tgt 2025
	—	—	—	—	—	—	—	—	—	1.71	2.11	2.46	Income Return %
	—	—	—	—	—	—	—	—	—	8.40	3.34	10.78	Capital Return %
	—	—	—	—	—	—	—	—	—	23	66	31	Total Rtn % Rank Cat
	—	—	—	—	—	—	—	—	0.06	0.18	0.24	0.29	Income $
	—	—	—	—	—	—	—	—	0.00	0.00	0.00	0.00	Capital Gains $
	—	—	—	—	—	—	—	—	—	—	—	0.20	Expense Ratio %
	—	—	—	—	—	—	—	—	—	—	2.33	—	Income Ratio %
	—	—	—	—	—	—	—	—	—	—	3	—	Turnover Rate %
	—	—	—	—	—	—	—	—	—	30	708	4,605	Net Assets $mil

Performance 12-31-06

	1st Qtr	2nd Qtr	3rd Qtr	4th Qtr	Total
2002	—	—	—	—	—
2003	—	—	—	—	—*
2004	2.85	-0.28	0.37	6.95	10.11
2005	-1.32	2.14	2.79	1.78	5.45
2006	3.23	-1.32	4.34	6.55	13.24

Trailing	Total Return%	+/- DJ Mod	+/- DJ Tgt 2025	%Rank Cat	Growth of $10,000
3 Mo	6.55	0.96	-0.07	32	10,655
6 Mo	11.17	2.38	1.28	30	11,117
1 Yr	13.24	0.94	-1.04	31	11,324
3 Yr Avg	9.55	-1.17	-2.98	28	13,147
5 Yr Avg	—	—	—	—	—
10 Yr Avg	—	—	—	—	—
15 Yr Avg	—	—	—	—	—

Tax Analysis	Tax-Adj Rtn%	%Rank Cat	Tax-Cost Rat	%Rank Cat
3 Yr (estimated)	8.96	20	0.54	14
5 Yr (estimated)	—	—	—	—
10 Yr (estimated)	—	—	—	—

Potential Capital Gain Exposure: 9% of assets

Rating and Risk

Time Period	Load-Adj Return %	Morningstar Rtn vs Cat	Morningstar Risk vs Cat	Morningstar Risk-Adj Rating
1 Yr	13.24			
3 Yr	9.55	Avg	-Avg	★★★★
5 Yr	—	—	—	—
10 Yr	—	—	—	—
Incept	10.91			

Other Measures	Standard Index S&P 500	Best Fit Index DJ Mod
Alpha	0.3	0.3
Beta	0.81	0.81
R-Squared	93	93
Standard Deviation	4.96	
Mean	9.55	
Sharpe Ratio	1.23	

Portfolio Analysis 09-30-06

Total Stocks:0 Share change since 06-30-06	Sectors	P/E Ratio	YTD Return %	% Net Assets
⊕ Vanguard Total Stock Mkt	—	—	—	62.46
⊕ Vanguard European Stock I	—	—	—	9.63
⊕ Vanguard Pacific Stock In	—	—	—	4.56
Vanguard Total Stock Mark	—	—	—	2.31
⊖ Vanguard Emerging Mkts St	—	—	—	1.98

Total Fixed-Income:0	Date of Maturity	Amount $000	Value $000	% Net Assets
Vanguard Total Bond Marke		75,542	753,910	19.07

Morningstar's Take by Marta Norton 12-19-06

Vanguard Target Retirement 2025's changes make us like it even more.

This fund has several strong points. It offers investors planning to retire in or around 2025 a broadly diversified portfolio of Vanguard index funds. We like that much of the fund's equity exposure comes from Vanguard Total Stock Market Index, which covers the entire domestic universe, including the often-underweighted small-cap market. We also like Vanguard Total Bond Market Index, whose management does an exemplary job of tracking Lehman Brothers Aggregate Bond Index. The fund's gradual transition to a more conservative profile (approximately five years after its target year it should offer the same 30/70 stock/bond exposure as Vanguard Target Retirement Income) should make the fund attractive to investors who want to take a hands-off approach to asset allocation. And because the fund limits its investments to Vanguard index funds, it offers a hard-to-beat 0.20% expense ratio.

Our one complaint has been the fund's heavy fixed-income stake. Because it held roughly 40% in bonds, the fund frequently lagged its target retirement 2015-2029 peers, many of whom had fewer bond investments in order to stash more in higher-returning stocks. Vanguard's new allocation scheme addresses this weakness. It has upped its equity stake to about 80%, with around 16.5% of its assets devoted to international stocks alone. This change means the fund will likely keep better pace with its peers, albeit while increasing its return volatility. (Previously the fund's volatility, as measured by its standard deviation of returns, was below those of many of its peers.) Still, we think the new allocation is an improvement. The new structure may very well provide investors with more money during retirement.

Because these changes only improve an already good option, we think investors fitting the fund's profile and wanting a single retirement fund have little reason to invest elsewhere.

Address:	P.O. Box 2600 Valley Forge, PA 19482 800-997-2798	Minimum Purchase:	$3000	Add: $100 IRA: $3000
		Min Auto Inv Plan:	$3000	Add: $50
		Sales Fees:	No-load	
Web Address:	www.vanguard.com	Management Fee:	0.00%	
Inception:	10-27-03	Actual Fees:	—	Dist: —
Advisor:	Vanguard Advisers, Inc.	Expense Projections:	3Yr:$64	5Yr:$113 10Yr:$255
Subadvisor:	None	Income Distrib:	Quarterly	
NTF Plans:	Vanguard NTF			

Equity Style

Style: Blend
Size: Large-Cap

Value Measures		Rel Category
Price/Earnings	14.09	0.95
Price/Book	2.37	1.00
Price/Sales	1.29	1.00
Price/Cash Flow	7.24	1.00
Dividend Yield %	2.07	1.03

Growth Measures	%	Rel Category
Long-Term Erngs	11.49	0.97
Book Value	8.19	0.96
Sales	8.69	1.01
Cash Flow	8.70	0.90
Historical Erngs	13.14	0.75

Market Cap %			
Giant	43.5	Small	5.0
Large	31.5	Micro	1.7
Mid	18.3	Avg $mil:	26,636

Fixed-Income Style

Duration: Interm-Term
Quality: High

Avg Eff Duration [1]	4.6 Yrs
Avg Eff Maturity	7.1 Yrs
Avg Credit Quality	AAA
Avg Wtd Coupon	5.43%

[1]figure provided by fund as of 09-30-06

Sector Weightings	% of Stocks	Rel DJ Mod	3 Year High Low
↻ Info	18.17		
🖥 Software	3.03	—	4 3
💾 Hardware	8.21	—	9 8
🎤 Media	3.11	—	4 3
☎ Telecom	3.82	—	4 4
☕ Service	48.04		
🏥 Health	11.54	—	12 11
🛒 Consumer	7.46	—	9 7
📋 Business	5.29	—	6 5
💲 Financial	23.75	—	24 22
🏭 Mfg	33.78		
🏗 Goods	8.90	—	10 9
⚙ Ind Mtrls	12.35	—	13 11
🛢 Energy	8.82	—	10 6
💡 Utilities	3.71	—	4 3

Composition

● Cash	0.6	
● Stocks	80.2	
● Bonds	18.9	
○ Other	0.3	
Foreign	19.7	(% of Stock)

Vanguard Tx-Mgd App

	Ticker	Load	NAV	Yield	Total Assets	Mstar Category
	VMCAX	None	$33.62	1.4%	$3,992 mil	Large Blend

Governance and Management

Stewardship Grade: B

Portfolio Manager(s)

Michael Buek, who has been with Vanguard since 1987 and has worked on index funds since 1991, has worked on this fund since its 1994 inception. He took over as lead manager in 2005. The fund's former manager, Gus Sauter, who also is Vanguard's CIO and index specialist, still supervises this offering and others run by Vanguard's quantitative equity group. Buek has also taken over for Sauter on Vanguard 500 Index, Vanguard Small Cap Index, Vanguard Small Cap Value Index, and Vanguard Tax-Managed Small Cap.

Strategy

Although this isn't an index fund, manager Michael Buek uses a sampling technique to match the key characteristics of the Russell 1000 Index. Its returns have tended to correlate very highly with those of its bogy. However, Buek adds a twist by favoring the lowest-yielding stocks in the index to limit taxes. To further minimize capital gains distributions, Buek may sell stocks at a loss to offset gains, liquidating the highest-cost shares first.

Performance 12-31-06

	1st Qtr	2nd Qtr	3rd Qtr	4th Qtr	Total
2002	0.12	-14.64	-17.74	8.88	-23.45
2003	-2.31	16.02	3.49	12.30	31.72
2004	2.32	1.50	-2.61	10.49	11.75
2005	-1.71	2.25	4.43	2.42	7.49
2006	4.53	-2.15	4.79	6.75	14.42

Trailing	Total Return%	+/- S&P 500	+/- Russ 1000	%Rank Cat	Growth of $10,000
3 Mo	6.75	0.05	-0.20	42	10,675
6 Mo	11.86	-0.88	-0.50	43	11,186
1 Yr	14.42	-1.37	-1.04	48	11,442
3 Yr Avg	11.18	0.74	0.20	25	13,743
5 Yr Avg	6.74	0.55	-0.08	29	13,856
10 Yr Avg	8.65	0.23	0.01	24	22,924
15 Yr Avg	—	—	—	—	—

Tax Analysis	Tax-Adj Rtn%	%Rank Cat	Tax-Cost Rat	%Rank Cat
3 Yr (estimated)	10.60	21	0.19	9
5 Yr (estimated)	6.50	23	0.22	15
10 Yr (estimated)	8.42	14	0.21	4

Potential Capital Gain Exposure: 36% of assets

Historical Profile

Return Above Avg
Risk Above Avg
Rating ★★★ Neutral

Investment Style
Equity
Stock %

▼ Manager Change
▽ Partial Manager Change

Growth of $10,000
■ Investment Values of Fund
■ Investment Values of S&P 500

99% 99% 99% 99% 98% 100% 100% 99% 100%

36.0 / 31.0 / 25.0 / 20.0 / 15.0 / 10.0

Performance Quartile (within Category)

1995	1996	1997	1998	1999	2000	2001	2002	2003	2004	2005	2006	History
13.28	15.95	20.18	25.68	34.17	30.59	25.73	19.49	25.43	28.05	29.80	33.62	NAV
34.38	20.93	27.29	27.90	33.55	-10.13	-15.34	-23.45	31.72	11.75	7.49	14.42	Total Return %
-3.20	-2.03	-6.07	-0.68	12.51	-1.03	-3.45	-1.35	3.04	0.87	2.58	-1.37	+/-S&P 500
-3.39	-1.52	-5.56	0.88	12.64	-2.34	-2.89	-1.80	1.83	0.35	1.22	-1.04	+/-Russ 1000
0.90	0.83	0.75	0.64	0.48	0.35	0.56	0.80	1.22	1.44	1.26	1.60	Income Return %
33.48	20.10	26.54	27.26	33.07	-10.48	-15.90	-24.25	30.50	10.31	6.23	12.82	Capital Return %
52	58	60	28	8	82	85	73	16	30	28	48	Total Rtn % Rank Cat
0.09	0.11	0.12	0.13	0.12	0.12	0.17	0.21	0.24	0.37	0.35	0.48	Income $
0.00	0.00	0.00	0.00	0.00	0.00	0.00	0.00	0.00	0.00	0.00	0.00	Capital Gains $
0.20	0.20	0.17	0.19	0.19	0.19	0.18	0.17	0.17	0.14	0.14	—	Expense Ratio %
0.97	0.91	0.70	0.62	0.47	0.36	0.60	0.87	1.09	1.40	1.25	—	Income Ratio %
7	12	4	5	12	17	13	10	11	5	8	—	Turnover Rate %
254	517	893	1,479	2,378	2,643	1,678	1,154	1,466	1,596	857	832	Net Assets $mil

Rating and Risk

Time Period	Load-Adj Return %	Morningstar Rtn vs Cat	Morningstar Risk vs Cat	Morningstar Risk-Adj Rating
1 Yr	13.27			
3 Yr	10.81	+Avg	Avg	★★★★
5 Yr	6.74	+Avg	+Avg	★★★
10 Yr	8.65	+Avg	+Avg	★★★
Incept	11.22			

Other Measures	Standard Index S&P 500	Best Fit Index Russ 1000
Alpha	0.0	-0.3
Beta	1.10	1.07
R-Squared	98	99
Standard Deviation	7.68	
Mean	11.18	
Sharpe Ratio	1.01	

Portfolio Analysis 09-30-06

Share change since 06-06 Total Stocks:626

	Sector	PE	Tot Ret%	% Assets
ExxonMobil Corporation	Energy	11.1	39.07	3.04
General Electric Company	Ind Mtrls	20.0	9.35	2.65
Citigroup, Inc.	Financial	13.1	19.55	1.78
Microsoft Corporation	Software	23.8	15.83	1.72
Bank of America Corporat	Financial	12.4	20.68	1.71
Procter & Gamble Company	Goods	23.9	13.36	1.53
Johnson & Johnson	Health	17.5	12.45	1.46
Pfizer Inc.	Health	15.2	15.22	1.40
American International G	Financial	17.0	6.05	1.14
Cisco Systems, Inc.	Hardware	30.1	59.64	1.09
J.P. Morgan Chase & Co.	Financial	13.6	25.60	1.08
⊕ Altria Group, Inc.	Goods	16.3	19.87	1.05
Chevron Corporation	Energy	9.0	33.76	0.94
Wal-Mart Stores, Inc.	Consumer	16.9	0.13	0.92
IBM	Hardware	17.1	19.77	0.86
Intel Corporation	Hardware	21.0	-17.18	0.85
PepsiCo, Inc.	Goods	21.5	7.86	0.84
⊕ AT&T, Inc.	Telecom	18.2	51.59	0.79
⊕ Wells Fargo Company	Financial	14.7	16.82	0.76
Amgen, Inc.	Health	29.1	-13.38	0.67

Current Investment Style

Value Blnd Growth — Large Mid Small

Market Cap	%
Giant	42.2
Large	31.0
Mid	26.6
Small	0.2
Micro	0.0

Avg $mil: 32,985

Value Measures		Rel Category
Price/Earnings	15.46	1.01
Price/Book	2.57	1.00
Price/Sales	1.42	1.01
Price/Cash Flow	7.11	0.84
Dividend Yield %	1.56	0.89

Growth Measures	%	Rel Category
Long-Term Erngs	11.77	1.00
Book Value	9.83	1.09
Sales	10.63	1.10
Cash Flow	11.42	1.11
Historical Erngs	18.16	0.98

Profitability	%	Rel Category
Return on Equity	19.63	1.01
Return on Assets	10.73	1.03
Net Margin	13.71	1.02

Sector Weightings	% of Stocks	Rel S&P 500	3 Year High Low	
☎ Info	20.28	1.01		
Software	3.57	1.03	4	3
Hardware	9.60	1.04	13	9
Media	3.79	1.00	5	4
Telecom	3.32	0.95	3	3
Service	49.10	1.06		
Health	13.65	1.13	15	13
Consumer	8.97	1.17	12	9
Business	5.50	1.30	6	5
Financial	20.98	0.94	21	18
Mfg	30.62	0.91		
Goods	7.83	0.92	8	8
Ind Mtrls	11.01	0.92	12	9
Energy	8.85	0.90	10	7
Utilities	2.93	0.84	3	1

Composition

	%
● Cash	0.0
● Stocks	100.0
● Bonds	0.0
● Other	0.0
Foreign (% of Stock)	0.0

Morningstar's Take by Dan Culloton 11-20-06

Vanguard Tax-Managed Capital Appreciation's success is an open secret.

This fund proves it doesn't take a different structure or complicated strategy to be a good choice for taxable accounts. There are some who believe there's no way any conventional mutual fund can compete with exchange-traded funds or separate accounts when it comes to tax efficiency. This fund, however, has done--and should continue to do--quite well with the traditional mutual fund format by adhering to a simple formula: low costs, low turnover, broad diversification, and savvy tax-loss selling.

This fund may look and smell like an index fund, but it's really not. Manager Michael Buek uses computers and statistical models to construct a portfolio that resembles the sector allocations and risk characteristics of the Russell 1000 Index, but doesn't include all the stocks in that benchmark. The fund avoids high-yielding stocks to reduce its income distributions. Buek further manages taxable distributions by harvesting tax losses that can be used to offset gains and, when he has to make other changes, by selling the highest-cost-basis shares first.

This strategy has been quietly effective. The fund has never issued a capital gains distribution. Its long-term tax-cost ratio (a measure of how much taxes affect a fund's performance) as well as its aftertax results are better than the vast majority of its large-blend peers, including competing ETFs, such as iShares Russell 1000 Index, that are supposed to be more tax-friendly.

Of course, there are costs. The fund has tended to be a bit more volatile than its peers because of its aversion to high-yielding stocks. Dividends can smooth out a fund's total returns by offering a cushion in times of trouble, and downplaying them gives this offering a rough edge.

It's a worthy core holding for taxable accounts, though, because of its low fees, experienced management, and simple, well-executed strategy.

Address:	PO Box 2600 Valley Forge PA 19482 800-997-2798	Minimum Purchase:	$10000 Add: $100 IRA: $0
		Min Auto Inv Plan:	$10000 Add: $50
		Sales Fees:	No-load, 1.00%R
Web Address:	www.vanguard.com	Management Fee:	0.12%
Inception:	09-06-94	Actual Fees:	Mgt:0.12% Dist: —
Advisor:	Vanguard Advisers, Inc.	Expense Projections:	3Yr:$160 5Yr: — 10Yr: —
Subadvisor:	None	Income Distrib:	Annually
NTF Plans:	Vanguard NTF		

Morningstar® Funds 500

Vanguard Tax-Mgd Bal

Analyst Pick ✓

	Ticker	Load	NAV	Yield	Total Assets	Mstar Category
	VTMFX	None	$20.02	2.8%	$662 mil	Conservative Allocation

Governance and Management

Stewardship Grade: B

Portfolio Manager(s)

Michael Perre, who has been with Vanguard since 1990 and has worked on the equity portion of this fund since 1999, runs the show here now. Vanguard's indexing guru and chief investment officer Gus Sauter provides oversight. The fixed-income portfolio is run by Chris Ryon, who joined the team here in 1996.

Strategy

The fund invests half of its assets in stocks selected to match the key characteristics of the Russell 1000 Index, emphasizing those issues with low dividend yields. The bond portion consists of intermediate-term, high-quality municipal issues. The fund uses trading techniques, such as selling losers to offset gains, to minimize capital gains.

Historical Profile

Return	Above Avg
Risk	High
Rating	★★★★ Above Avg

Investment Style: Equity / Stock %

Investment Style percentages: 48% 47% 46% 47% 47% 49% 49% 47% 48%

▼ Manager Change
▽ Partial Manager Change

Growth of $10,000
— Investment Values of Fund
— Investment Values of DJ Mod

26.8 / 22.0 / 18.0 / 14.0 / 10.0

Performance Quartile (within Category)

	1995	1996	1997	1998	1999	2000	2001	2002	2003	2004	2005	2006	History
NAV	11.85	12.92	14.67	16.74	18.87	18.30	17.18	15.54	17.72	18.49	18.88	20.02	
Total Return %	24.52	12.21	16.55	16.93	15.49	-0.50	-3.54	-7.08	17.05	7.16	4.80	9.09	
+/-DJ Mod	4.72	1.55	4.65	4.61	-1.84	1.17	-0.74	-0.31	-10.33	-5.81	-2.19	-3.21	
+/-DJ 40%	6.36	3.32	2.45	5.20	7.63	-7.29	-6.76	-3.06	-0.61	-1.85	0.11	1.63	
Income Return %	3.30	3.07	2.89	2.68	2.59	2.62	2.54	2.53	2.86	2.74	2.65	2.94	
Capital Return %	21.22	9.14	13.66	14.25	12.90	-3.12	-6.08	-9.61	14.19	4.42	2.15	6.15	
Total Rtn % Rank Cat	23	19	19	7	3	86	81	84	17	28	12	27	
Income $	0.32	0.36	0.37	0.39	0.43	0.49	0.46	0.43	0.44	0.48	0.49	0.55	
Capital Gains $	0.00	0.00	0.00	0.00	0.00	0.00	0.00	0.00	0.00	0.00	0.00	0.00	
Expense Ratio %	0.20	0.20	0.17	0.19	0.20	0.20	0.19	0.18	0.17	0.12	0.12	—	
Income Ratio %	3.06	3.04	2.77	2.63	2.52	2.61	2.64	2.69	2.58	2.70	2.64	—	
Turnover Rate %	5	5	7	7	13	15	21	24	16	15	10	—	
Net Assets $mil	39	63	120	207	330	400	419	416	498	561	606	662	

Performance 12-31-06

	1st Qtr	2nd Qtr	3rd Qtr	4th Qtr	Total
2002	0.52	-5.41	-6.01	3.98	-7.08
2003	-0.58	9.04	1.80	6.06	17.05
2004	1.70	-0.39	0.51	5.25	7.16
2005	-1.13	2.42	1.95	1.52	4.80
2006	2.17	-1.04	4.04	3.70	9.09

Trailing	Total Return%	+/- DJ Mod	+/- DJ 40%	%Rank Cat	Growth of $10,000
3 Mo	3.70	-1.89	0.66	38	10,370
6 Mo	7.89	-0.90	1.33	20	10,789
1 Yr	9.09	-3.21	1.63	27	10,909
3 Yr Avg	7.00	-1.30	-0.04	24	12,250
5 Yr Avg	5.91	-4.11	-0.82	34	13,326
10 Yr Avg	7.25	-1.30	-0.45	14	20,136
15 Yr Avg	—	—	—		

Tax Analysis	Tax-Adj Rtn%	%Rank Cat	Tax-Cost Rat	%Rank Cat
3 Yr (estimated)	6.26	14	0.69	27
5 Yr (estimated)	5.35	16	0.53	10
10 Yr (estimated)	6.90	2	0.33	1

Potential Capital Gain Exposure: 19% of assets

Rating and Risk

Time Period	Load-Adj Return %	Morningstar Rtn vs Cat	Morningstar Risk vs Cat	Morningstar Risk-Adj Rating
1 Yr	9.09			
3 Yr	7.00	+Avg	+Avg	★★★★
5 Yr	5.91	Avg	+Avg	★★★
10 Yr	7.25	+Avg	High	★★★★
Incept	8.63			

Other Measures	Standard Index DJ Mod	Best Fit Index Russ 1000
Alpha	-0.7	-0.2
Beta	0.61	0.52
R-Squared	83	86
Standard Deviation	3.98	
Mean	7.00	
Sharpe Ratio	0.92	

Portfolio Analysis 09-30-06

Total Stocks:613

Share change since 06-30-06	Sectors	P/E Ratio	YTD Return %	% Net Assets
ExxonMobil Corporation	Energy	11.1	-5.19	1.49
General Electric Company	Ind Mtrls	20.0	0.91	1.30
Citigroup, Inc.	Financial	13.1	-1.17	0.91
Microsoft Corporation	Software	23.8	0.23	0.90
Bank of America Corporati	Financial	12.4	0.11	0.83
Procter & Gamble Company	Goods	23.9	-0.98	0.75
Pfizer Inc.	Health	15.2	1.00	0.69
Johnson & Johnson	Health	17.5	0.74	0.68
American International Gr	Financial	17.0	-0.18	0.53

Total Fixed-Income:139

	Date of Maturity	Amount $000	Value $000	% Net Assets
TENNESSEE ENERGY ACQUISIT	09-01-16	7,500	8,088	1.27
South Carolina Transn Inf	10-01-13	5,700	6,252	0.98
Phoenix Ariz Civic Impt 5	07-01-15	5,525	6,051	0.95
New Jersey St Tpk Auth 5.	01-01-25	5,000	5,893	0.92
Massachusetts Bay Transn	07-01-22	5,000	5,555	0.87
Univ Tex Univ Revs 5.25%	08-15-18	4,900	5,504	0.86
Cleveland Ohio Pub Pwr Sy	11-15-20	5,000	5,400	0.85
Ohio St Wtr Dev Auth 5%	06-01-17	5,000	5,386	0.84
Univ Colo Entpr Sys 5%	06-01-23	5,025	5,367	0.84

Equity Style

Style: Blend
Size: Large-Cap

Value Measures		Rel Category
Price/Earnings	15.36	1.02
Price/Book	2.58	1.06
Price/Sales	1.40	1.01
Price/Cash Flow	7.95	1.00
Dividend Yield %	1.54	0.72

Growth Measures	%	Rel Category
Long-Term Erngs	11.85	1.05
Book Value	9.58	1.20
Sales	10.95	1.23
Cash Flow	12.39	1.37
Historical Erngs	18.84	1.09

Market Cap %			
Giant	43.7	Small	0.3
Large	30.6	Micro	0.0
Mid	25.4	Avg $mil:	34,419

Fixed-Income Style

Duration: Interm-Term
Quality: High

Avg Eff Duration [1]	4.7 Yrs
Avg Eff Maturity	6.0 Yrs
Avg Credit Quality	AAA
Avg Wtd Coupon	5.12%

[1]figure provided by fund as of 09-30-06

Sector Weightings	% of Stocks	Rel DJ Mod	3 Year High Low
☗ Info	20.66	—	
Software	3.84	—	4 3
Hardware	10.13	—	13 10
Media	3.49	—	4 3
Telecom	3.20	—	3 2
☗ Service	49.69		
Health	13.68	—	15 13
Consumer	9.59	—	12 10
Business	5.78	—	7 5
Financial	20.64	—	21 18
☗ Mfg	29.65		
Goods	7.37	—	9 7
Ind Mtrls	10.84	—	11 9
Energy	9.24	—	11 7
Utilities	2.20	—	2 1

Composition

	%
● Cash	0.5
● Stocks	48.4
● Bonds	51.2
○ Other	0.0
Foreign (% of Stock)	0.0

Morningstar's Take by Dan Culloton 11-20-06

It doesn't get any simpler or cheaper than this for tax-conscious investors.

Vanguard Tax-Managed Balanced offers most of what you need for the core of a taxable portfolio. It relies on a no-fuss, no-muss strategy that pairs an index-fund-like portfolio of low-yielding Russell 1000 stocks with a sleeve of high-quality federally tax-exempt municipal bonds. That structure alone keeps the fund's taxable income to a minimum, but equity manager Michael Perre further enhances the fund's tax efficiency by realizing losses to offset gains and keeping turnover low. And when he has to trade, he first sells the shares that cost the fund the most to buy, thereby keeping recognized gains to a minimum.

The result is a broadly diversified package of mostly large-cap stocks and AAA rated bonds. The fund usually keeps more of its assets in equities than its typical peer does, which can make it a bit more volatile, as measured by standard deviation. The bigger stock helping also leaves the fund vulnerable when the stock market swoons (it lost money from 2000 and 2003, for example). In the last three years, however, the offering's equity bias has been a boon as the stock market has generally trended up. The strategy has held up well over time, as well. Returns on a pre- and post-tax basis rank in the conservative-allocation category's top quartile over most trailing periods.

Low expenses are a big factor behind the fund's success. Its expense ratio is the lowest in its peer group and allows it to offer marketlike returns, yet still pull ahead of the pack in the long run.

The fund doesn't have everything. There is no international or small-cap exposure, so this is not for one-stop shoppers. But you don't have to look far for funds to complete a portfolio. Vanguard's Tax-Managed International and Tax-Managed Small Cap share many of the same traits and would complement this fund well.

Taxable investors could do far worse.

Address:	PO Box 2600, Valley Forge PA 19482, 800-997-2798
Web Address:	www.vanguard.com
Inception:	09-06-94
Advisor:	Vanguard Advisers, Inc.
Subadvisor:	None
NTF Plans:	Vanguard NTF

Minimum Purchase:	$10,000	Add: $100	IRA: $0
Min Auto Inv Plan:	$10,000	Add: $50	
Sales Fees:	No-load, 1.00%R		
Management Fee:	0.10%		
Actual Fees:	Mgt:0.10%	Dist: —	
Expense Projections:	3Yr:$154	5Yr: —	10Yr: —
Income Distrib:	Quarterly		

Vanguard Tax-Mgd Intl

	Ticker	Load	NAV	Yield	Total Assets	Mstar Category
	VTMGX	None	$14.13	2.4%	$1,879 mil	Foreign Large Blend

Governance and Management

Stewardship Grade: B

Portfolio Manager(s)

Duane Kelly, one of the senior members of Vanguard's capable indexing team, handles the day-to-day managerial chores here. He has been actively involved with this fund since its inception. Kelly also manages Vanguard Emerging Markets Stock Index and Vanguard European Stock Index.

Strategy

The fund uses a sampling technique to match the key characteristics of the MSCI EAFE Index, which tends to favor large-cap stocks. To minimize capital gains distributions, manager Duane Kelly may sell stocks at a loss to offset gains, liquidating highest-cost shares first.

Historical Profile

Return	Above Avg
Risk	Average
Rating	★★★★ Above Avg

| | 96% | 98% | 99% | 98% | 92% | 97% | 98% | 99% |

▼ Manager Change
▽ Partial Manager Change

Growth of $10,000
— Investment Values of Fund
— Investment Values of MSCI EAFE

Performance Quartile (within Category)

	1995	1996	1997	1998	1999	2000	2001	2002	2003	2004	2005	2006	History
NAV	—	—	—	—	11.96	10.14	7.79	6.43	8.76	10.33	11.48	14.13	
Total Return %	—	—	—	—	20.01*	-14.29	-21.94	-15.62	38.67	20.25	13.60	26.00	
+/-MSCI EAFE	—	—	—	—	-0.10	-0.52	0.32	0.08	0.00	0.00	0.06	-0.34	
+/-MSCI Wd xUS	—	—	—	—	-0.93	-0.55	0.18	-0.75	-0.13	-0.87	0.29		
Income Return %	—	—	—	—	0.92	1.23	1.80	2.38	2.31	2.49	2.93		
Capital Return %	—	—	—	—	-15.21	-23.17	-17.42	36.29	17.94	11.11	23.07		
Total Rtn % Rank Cat	—	—	—	—		35	53	35	16	14	58	36	
Income $	—	—	—	—	0.04	0.11	0.13	0.14	0.15	0.20	0.26	0.34	
Capital Gains $	—	—	—	—	0.00	0.00	0.00	0.00	0.00	0.00	0.00	0.00	
Expense Ratio %	—	—	—	—		0.35	0.35	0.35	0.31	0.28	0.23	—	
Income Ratio %	—	—	—	—		0.96	1.24	1.49	2.04	2.33	2.34	—	
Turnover Rate %	—	—	—	—		7	5	20	7	9	5	—	
Net Assets $mil	—	—	—	—		135	241	327	334	514	825	1,621	

Performance 12-31-06

	1st Qtr	2nd Qtr	3rd Qtr	4th Qtr	Total
2002	1.03	-2.16	-20.00	6.71	-15.62
2003	-8.24	19.32	8.10	17.16	38.67
2004	4.36	0.55	-0.54	15.23	20.25
2005	-0.27	-1.26	11.01	3.92	13.60
2006	9.27	0.96	3.95	9.88	26.00

Trailing	Total Return%	+/- MSCI EAFE	+/- MSCI Wd xUS	%Rank Cat	Growth of $10,000
3 Mo	9.88	-0.47	-0.24	63	10,988
6 Mo	14.22	-0.47	0.00	56	11,422
1 Yr	26.00	-0.34	0.29	36	12,600
3 Yr Avg	19.84	-0.09	-0.26	27	17,211
5 Yr Avg	15.03	0.05	-0.22	19	20,140
10 Yr Avg	—	—	—		
15 Yr Avg	—	—	—		

Tax Analysis	Tax-Adj Rtn%	%Rank Cat	Tax-Cost Rat	%Rank Cat
3 Yr (estimated)	19.30	19	0.45	24
5 Yr (estimated)	14.47	15	0.49	39
10 Yr (estimated)	—			

Potential Capital Gain Exposure: 29% of assets

Rating and Risk

Time Period	Load-Adj Return %	Morningstar Rtn vs Cat	Morningstar Risk vs Cat	Morningstar Risk-Adj Rating
1 Yr	26.00			
3 Yr	19.84	+Avg	Avg	★★★★
5 Yr	15.03	+Avg	Avg	★★★★
10 Yr	—	—	—	—
Incept	6.74			

Other Measures	Standard Index MSCI EAFE	Best Fit Index MSCI EAFE
Alpha	-0.1	-0.1
Beta	1.00	1.00
R-Squared	99	99
Standard Deviation	9.58	
Mean	19.84	
Sharpe Ratio	1.62	

Morningstar's Take by Dan Culloton 01-03-07

Vanguard Tax-Managed International is a great choice for tax-sensitive investors.

This fund, like Vanguard's other tax-managed funds, shows that it's not impossible for conventional mutual funds to be both tax conscious and successful. All this fund does is follow a few simple rules: It keeps turnover low, harvests losses when possible, and, of course, keeps expenses modest.

This fund uses a quasi-indexing approach that allows it to keep its turnover rate in the single digits. The fund, however, can diverge slightly from its benchmark, the MSCI EAFE Index, from time to time to sell stocks at a loss to offset gains. When veteran manager Duane Kelly has to sell for other reasons, such as to match changes in the index, he will unload the highest-cost shares (those with the lowest potential capital gains) first.

The result is a fund that offers investors broad exposure to large-cap foreign developed-market stocks and strong returns on an absolute and tax-adjusted basis. The fund has never distributed a capital gain (though it has paid out some income) and its pre- and posttax results over the trailing three and five years were in the top fourth of the foreign large-blend category through the end of November 2006.

The fund's rock-bottom expense ratio is its biggest and most enduring advantage. The levy is about one fifth of that of the typical no-load foreign large-cap fund's. In fact, it is one of the cheapest foreign large-blend funds retail investors can buy, cheaper even than a lot of index funds and exchange-traded funds, such as iShares MSCI EAFE Index and Vanguard Total International Stock Index. (This fund, though, requires a $10,000 minimum investment and charges a 1% redemption fee.) That allows the fund to patiently track its benchmark and grind ahead of rivals on costs over the long term.

This is a solid option for taxable accounts.

Portfolio Analysis 09-30-06

Share change since 06-06 Total Stocks:1113

		Sector	Country	% Assets
⊕	BP	Energy	U.K.	1.84
⊕	HSBC Hldgs	Financial	U.K.	1.80
⊕	Toyota Motor	Goods	Japan	1.35
⊕	GlaxoSmithKline	Health	U.K.	1.32
⊕	Total SA	Energy	France	1.25
⊕	Nestle	Goods	Switzerland	1.20
⊕	Novartis	Health	Switzerland	1.16
⊕	Royal Dutch Shell	Energy	U.K.	1.11
⊕	UBS AG	Financial	Switzerland	1.06
⊕	Roche Holding	Health	Switzerland	1.04
⊖	Vodafone Grp	Telecom	U.K.	0.98
⊕	Mitsubishi UFJ Financial	Financial	Japan	0.96
⊕	Royal Bank Of Scotland G	Financial	U.K.	0.95
⊕	AstraZeneca	Health	U.K.	0.84
⊕	Royal Dutch Shell	Energy	U.K.	0.81
⊕	Banco Santander Central	Financial	Spain	0.80
⊕	Sanofi-Synthelabo	Health	France	0.78
⊕	BNP Paribas	Financial	France	0.77
⊕	ING Groep	Financial	Netherlands	0.71
⊕	Barclays	Financial	U.K.	0.69

Current Investment Style

Value Blnd Growth — Large Mid Small

Market Cap	%
Giant	54.9
Large	31.9
Mid	12.7
Small	0.4
Micro	0.1

Avg $mil: 28,304

Value Measures		Rel Category
Price/Earnings	10.00	0.76
Price/Book	2.03	0.94
Price/Sales	1.03	0.89
Price/Cash Flow	8.04	0.96
Dividend Yield %	3.15	1.08

Growth Measures	%	Rel Category
Long-Term Erngs	11.11	0.94
Book Value	8.45	0.93
Sales	5.94	0.91
Cash Flow	4.27	0.52
Historical Erngs	9.61	0.47

Composition

Cash	0.0	Bonds	0.0
Stocks	98.5	Other	1.5
Foreign (% of Stock)			100.0

Sector Weightings

	% of Stocks	Rel MSCI EAFE	3 Year High	Low
↻ Info	11.46	0.97		
🖳 Software	0.56	1.00	1	0
💻 Hardware	3.81	0.99	5	4
🎙 Media	1.91	1.04	2	2
☎ Telecom	5.18	0.93	8	5
☞ Service	47.96	1.02		
🛡 Health	7.87	1.11	9	7
🛒 Consumer	5.17	1.04	5	4
🏢 Business	4.98	0.98	5	5
💲 Financial	29.94	1.00	30	25
🏭 Mfg	40.56	0.99		
🏷 Goods	12.83	0.98	15	13
⚙ Ind Mtrls	15.14	0.98	16	13
🔋 Energy	7.62	1.07	9	8
💡 Utilities	4.97	0.95	5	4

Regional Exposure

	% Stock		% Stock
UK/W. Europe	68	N. America	0
Japan	24	Latn America	0
Asia X Japan	8	Other	0

Country Exposure

	% Stock		% Stock
U.K.	24	Switzerland	7
Japan	24	Germany	7
France	10		

Address:	PO Box 2600 Valley Forge PA 19482 800-997-2798
Web Address:	www.vanguard.com
Inception:	08-17-99*
Advisor:	Vanguard Advisers, Inc.
Subadvisor:	None
NTF Plans:	Vanguard NTF

Minimum Purchase:	$10000	Add: $100	IRA: $0
Min Auto Inv Plan:	$10000	Add: $50	
Sales Fees:	No-load, 1.00%R		
Management Fee:	0.15%		
Actual Fees:	Mgt:0.15%	Dist: —	
Expense Projections:	3Yr:$180	5Yr: —	10Yr: —
Income Distrib:	Annually		

Vanguard Tax-Mgd SmCap R ✔ Analyst Pick

	Ticker	Load	NAV	Yield	Total Assets	Mstar Category
	VTMSX	None	$25.72	0.8%	$1,883 mil	Small Blend

Governance and Management

Stewardship Grade: B

Portfolio Manager(s)

In 2005, Vanguard named Michael Buek manager of this offering. Previously, the firm's index guru, Gus Sauter, was listed as manager, but since his promotion to chief investment officer in March 2003, he has gradually stepped back from the day-to-day management of this fund. That task now falls to Buek, an 18-year Vanguard veteran who has assisted Sauter on this fund since its inception.

Strategy

Manager Michael Buek uses a sampling technique to match the key characteristics of the S&P SmallCap 600 Index, which has lower turnover than the other popular small-cap benchmark, the Russell 2000. To ensure tax efficiency, the fund emphasizes those stocks with low dividends. In addition, to minimize capital gains distributions, the fund may sell stocks at a loss to offset gains, and Buek liquidates highest-cost shares first.

Performance 12-31-06

	1st Qtr	2nd Qtr	3rd Qtr	4th Qtr	Total
2002	6.84	-6.27	-18.41	4.72	-14.44
2003	-5.76	19.68	6.93	14.85	38.51
2004	6.19	3.67	-1.30	13.05	22.84
2005	-2.02	3.99	5.40	0.33	7.74
2006	12.80	-4.84	-1.40	7.87	14.16

Trailing	Total Return%	+/- S&P 500	+/- Russ 2000	%Rank Cat	Growth of $10,000
3 Mo	7.87	1.17	-1.03	56	10,787
6 Mo	6.36	-6.38	-3.02	68	10,636
1 Yr	14.16	-1.63	-4.21	59	11,416
3 Yr Avg	14.75	4.31	1.19	26	15,110
5 Yr Avg	12.36	6.17	0.97	37	17,908
10 Yr Avg	—	—	—	—	—
15 Yr Avg	—	—	—	—	—

Tax Analysis	Tax-Adj Rtn%	%Rank Cat	Tax-Cost Rat	%Rank Cat
3 Yr (estimated)	14.61	16	0.12	2
5 Yr (estimated)	12.19	26	0.15	5
10 Yr (estimated)	—	—	—	—

Potential Capital Gain Exposure: 41% of assets

Morningstar's Take by Dan Culloton 01-03-07

Vanguard Tax-Managed Small Cap has more pros than cons.

The fund's expense ratio is hard for retail investors to beat. At 0.14%, its levy is a fraction of the median expense ratio for no-load small-cap funds. It's even lower than all rival exchange-traded funds, which are known for their low fees, except its cousin Vanguard Small Cap ETF. Investors trade some flexibility for low costs because this fund requires a $10,000 minimum investment and charges a 1% redemption fee on shares sold within five years of purchase. But they also get a huge head start on higher-cost funds in the bargain.

That's not all that's low. The fund's tax-smart strategy--which involves opportunistically realizing capital losses that can be used to offset future gains--has given this fund a lower tax-cost ratio than most of its rivals', including ETFs such as iShares Russell 2000 Index, that have a more tax-friendly structure. This means taxes have taken a smaller bite of this fund's returns than they have

of most rivals'.

Even without the tax benefits, the fund's sensible portfolio would merit attention. Manager Michael Buek tries to match the sector allocations and risk characteristics of the S&P SmallCap 600 Index and keeps turnover low. The fund is well diversified across industries and individual stocks, and since its benchmark requires constituents to be profitable, it's less susceptible to speculative performance swings. So volatility, as measured by standard deviation, has been below the category average, and performance has been competitive.

Nevertheless, this fund, like all small-cap offerings, has enjoyed considerable tail winds in recent years as little stocks have generally outperformed bigger ones. That advantage will dissipate eventually, so investors have to be willing to acknowledge that this fund's near future may not be as good as its recent past.

It's still a strong candidate for taxable portfolios, though.

Address:	PO Box 2600 Valley Forge PA 19482 800-997-2798
Web Address:	www.vanguard.com
Inception:	03-25-99*
Advisor:	Vanguard Advisers, Inc.
Subadvisor:	None
NTF Plans:	Vanguard NTF

Minimum Purchase:	$10000	Add: $100	IRA: $0
Min Auto Inv Plan:	$10000	Add: $50	
Sales Fees:	No-load, 1.00%R		
Management Fee:	0.12%		
Actual Fees:	Mgt:0.12%	Dist: —	
Expense Projections:	3Yr:$160	5Yr: —	10Yr: —
Income Distrib:	Annually		

Historical Profile
Return	Average
Risk	Average
Rating	★★★ Neutral

	1995	1996	1997	1998	1999	2000	2001	2002	2003	2004	2005	2006	History
					99%	99%	99%	100%	100%	100%	99%	100%	
	—	—	—	—	12.61	14.23	14.92	12.67	17.44	21.25	22.70	25.72	NAV
	—	—	—	—	26.28*	14.16	5.44	-14.44	38.51	22.84	7.74	14.16	Total Return %
	—	—	—	—	—	22.54	17.33	7.66	9.83	11.96	2.83	-1.63	+/-S&P 500
	—	—	—	—	—	16.46	2.95	6.04	-8.74	4.51	3.19	-4.21	+/-Russ 2000
	—	—	—	—	—	0.59	0.60	0.64	0.86	0.99	0.93	0.87	Income Return %
	—	—	—	—	—	12.85	4.84	-15.08	37.65	21.85	6.81	13.29	Capital Return %
	—	—	—	—	—	49	58	37	70	18	39	59	Total Rtn % Rank Cat
	—	—	—	—	0.05	0.07	0.09	0.10	0.11	0.17	0.20	0.20	Income $
	—	—	—	—	0.00	0.00	0.00	0.00	0.00	0.00	0.00	0.00	Capital Gains $
	—	—	—	—	0.19	0.20	0.20	0.17	0.17	0.14	0.14	—	Expense Ratio %
	—	—	—	—	0.70	0.64	0.63	0.68	0.77	0.96	0.92	—	Income Ratio %
	—	—	—	—	—	27	64	25	21	21	19	20	Turnover Rate %
	—	—	—	—	194	368	568	601	929	1,282	1,458	1,756	Net Assets $mil

Manager Change ▼
Partial Manager Change ▽

Growth of $10,000
— Investment Values of Fund
— Investment Values of S&P 500

Performance Quartile (within Category)

Investment Style
Equity
Stock %

Rating and Risk

Time Period	Load-Adj Return %	Morningstar Rtn vs Cat	Morningstar Risk vs Cat	Morningstar Risk-Adj Rating
1 Yr	14.16			
3 Yr	14.75	+Avg	Avg	★★★★
5 Yr	12.36	Avg	Avg	★★★
10 Yr	—	—	—	
Incept	13.66			

Other Measures	Standard Index S&P 500	Best Fit Index Mstar Small Core
Alpha	0.4	-1.4
Beta	1.57	0.96
R-Squared	70	98
Standard Deviation	12.86	
Mean	14.75	
Sharpe Ratio	0.88	

Portfolio Analysis 09-30-06

Share change since 06-06 Total Stocks:595	Sector	PE	Tot Ret%	% Assets
⊖ Roper Industries, Inc.	Ind Mtrls	24.8	27.83	0.68
Oshkosh Truck Corporatio	Ind Mtrls	17.1	9.47	0.65
✿ Public Storage, Inc.	Financial	46.2	47.46	0.62
⊕ Energen Corporation	Energy	13.9	30.75	0.58
⊕ Helix Energy Solutions G	Energy	10.6	-12.59	0.55
⊕ Cerner Corporation	Software	37.1	0.10	0.54
⊖ Idexx Laboratories	Health	30.4	10.17	0.54
⊕ Frontier Oil Corporation	Energy	8.1	53.75	0.54
⊕ Respironics Inc.	Health	26.8	1.83	0.53
⊕ Essex Property Trust	Financial	NMF	44.29	0.52
Maverick Tube	Ind Mtrls	—		0.52
⊖ ResMed, Inc.	Health	40.1	28.48	0.51
⊕ NVR, Inc.	Consumer	6.2	-8.12	0.50
⊖ Manitowoc Company, Inc.	Business	27.2	137.42	0.49
⊕ Southern Union Company	Energy	—	20.09	0.49
⊕ Trimble Navigation Ltd.	Hardware	29.7	42.94	0.48
⊕ Carpenter Technology Cor	Ind Mtrls	11.7	46.55	0.48
⊖ Global Payments, Inc.	Business	24.7	-0.49	0.48
⊕ UGI Corporation	Utilities	16.3	36.31	0.47
⊖ Landstar System, Inc.	Business	18.1	-8.30	0.47

Current Investment Style

Value Blnd Growth — Large Mid Small

Market Cap	%
Giant	0.0
Large	0.7
Mid	27.6
Small	63.9
Micro	7.8

Avg $mil: 1,271

Value Measures		Rel Category
Price/Earnings	16.11	0.97
Price/Book	2.20	1.04
Price/Sales	0.98	1.00
Price/Cash Flow	6.82	0.98
Dividend Yield %	0.87	0.81

Growth Measures	%	Rel Category
Long-Term Erngs	13.67	0.98
Book Value	9.24	1.22
Sales	11.14	1.26
Cash Flow	18.25	1.44
Historical Erngs	18.90	1.13

Profitability	%	Rel Category
Return on Equity	14.63	1.13
Return on Assets	8.48	1.19
Net Margin	10.22	1.05

Sector Weightings	% of Stocks	Rel S&P 500	3 Year High	Low
↻ Info	13.11	0.66		
Software	5.21	1.51	5	4
Hardware	6.64	0.72	8	6
Media	0.00	0.00	0	0
Telecom	1.26	0.36	1	1
☞ Service	47.85	1.04		
Health	10.51	0.87	13	10
Consumer	9.81	1.28	13	10
Business	10.48	2.48	11	9
Financial	17.05	0.77	17	15
⊔ Mfg	39.06	1.16		
Goods	7.23	0.85	7	6
Ind Mtrls	20.37	1.71	21	19
Energy	7.72	0.79	10	6
Utilities	3.74	1.07	4	3

Composition

● Cash	0.0
● Stocks	100.0
● Bonds	0.0
● Other	0.0
Foreign (% of Stock)	0.2

Vanguard Tot Stk

		Ticker	Load	NAV	Yield	Total Assets	Mstar Category
Analyst Pick		VTSMX	None	$34.09	1.5%	$85,096 mil	Large Blend

Governance and Management

Stewardship Grade: B

Portfolio Manager(s)

In 2005, Gus Sauter, Vanguard's vaunted index pro, passed the baton to Gerard O'Reilly, a longtime member of Vanguard's indexing team who has assisted Sauter on this fund since 1994. As Vanguard's chief investment officer, Sauter will retain a supervisory role here.

Strategy

In 2005, this fund dumped its old benchmark, the Wilshire 5000, in favor of a new bogy, the MSCI U.S. Broad Market Index. Both indexes include nearly all publicly traded domestic stocks. It would be impractical to own each smaller company in the index, so, among the tiniest firms, management selects a representative sample. In an effort to boost returns by a few basis points, the manager uses various techniques, including securities lending.

Performance 12-31-06

	1st Qtr	2nd Qtr	3rd Qtr	4th Qtr	Total
2002	0.97	-12.69	-16.84	7.82	-20.96
2003	-3.14	16.46	3.60	12.40	31.35
2004	2.58	1.28	-1.82	10.31	12.52
2005	-2.40	2.18	4.01	2.17	5.98
2006	5.37	-1.99	4.50	7.04	15.51

Trailing	Total Return%	+/- S&P 500	+/- Russ 1000	%Rank Cat	Growth of $10,000
3 Mo	7.04	0.34	0.09	32	10,704
6 Mo	11.86	-0.88	-0.50	43	11,186
1 Yr	15.51	-0.28	0.05	28	11,551
3 Yr Avg	11.26	0.82	0.28	24	13,773
5 Yr Avg	7.42	1.23	0.60	21	14,303
10 Yr Avg	8.57	0.15	-0.07	26	22,756
15 Yr Avg	—	—	—		—

Tax Analysis	Tax-Adj Rtn%	%Rank Cat	Tax-Cost Rat	%Rank Cat
3 Yr (estimated)	10.94	18	0.29	14
5 Yr (estimated)	7.07	18	0.33	22
10 Yr (estimated)	8.03	17	0.50	18

Potential Capital Gain Exposure: 6% of assets

Historical Profile

Return	Above Avg
Risk	Above Avg
Rating	★★★★ Above Avg

| | 99% | 97% | | 97% | 99% | 100% | 98% | 99% |

Investment Style
Equity
Stock %

▼ Manager Change
▽ Partial Manager Change

Growth of $10,000
— Investment Values of Fund
— Investment Values of S&P 500

31.0 / 25.0 / 20.0 / 15.0 / 10.0

Performance Quartile (within Category)

1995	1996	1997	1998	1999	2000	2001	2002	2003	2004	2005	2006	History
15.04	17.77	22.64	27.42	33.22	29.26	25.74	20.07	25.99	28.77	30.00	34.09	NAV
35.79	20.96	30.99	23.26	23.81	-10.57	-10.97	-20.96	31.35	12.52	5.98	15.51	Total Return %
-1.79	-2.00	-2.37	-5.32	2.77	-1.47	0.92	1.14	2.67	1.64	1.07	-0.28	+/-S&P 500
-1.98	-1.49	-1.86	-3.76	2.90	-2.78	1.48	0.69	1.46	1.12	-0.29	0.05	+/-Russ 1000
2.48	1.94	1.83	1.46	1.21	1.02	1.02	1.14	1.64	1.72	1.65	1.76	Income Return %
33.31	19.02	29.16	21.80	22.60	-11.59	-11.99	-22.10	29.71	10.80	4.33	13.75	Capital Return %
38	58	41	48	26	85	41	39	17	23	47	28	Total Rtn % Rank Cat
0.28	0.29	0.32	0.33	0.33	0.34	0.30	0.29	0.33	0.45	0.47	0.52	Income $
0.09	0.11	0.27	0.13	0.32	0.14	0.00	0.00	0.00	0.00	0.00	0.00	Capital Gains $
0.25	0.22	0.20	0.20	0.20	0.20	0.20	0.20	0.20	0.19	0.19	—	Expense Ratio %
2.14	1.86	1.65	1.44	1.15	1.04	1.11	1.32	1.49	1.70	1.62	—	Income Ratio %
3	3	2	3	3	7	4	4	11	4	12	—	Turnover Rate %
1,571	3,531	5,093	9,308	18,133	16,856	15,781	14,254	24,059	31,718	29,785	39,095	Net Assets $mil

Rating and Risk

Time Period	Load-Adj Return %	Morningstar Rtn vs Cat	Morningstar Risk vs Cat	Morningstar Risk-Adj Rating
1 Yr	15.51			
3 Yr	11.26	+Avg	Avg	★★★★
5 Yr	7.42	+Avg	Avg	★★★★
10 Yr	8.57	+Avg	+Avg	★★★★
Incept	10.89			

Other Measures	Standard Index S&P 500	Best Fit Index Russ 1000
Alpha	0.1	-0.3
Beta	1.10	1.07
R-Squared	98	99
Standard Deviation	7.70	
Mean	11.26	
Sharpe Ratio	1.02	

Portfolio Analysis 09-30-06

Share change since 06-06 Total Stocks:3727	Sector	PE	Tot Ret%	% Assets
⊕ ExxonMobil Corporation	Energy	11.1	39.07	2.68
⊕ General Electric Company	Ind Mtrls	20.0	9.35	2.43
⊕ Citigroup, Inc.	Financial	13.1	19.55	1.63
⊕ Bank of America Corporat	Financial	12.4	20.68	1.62
⊖ Microsoft Corporation	Software	23.8	15.83	1.60
⊕ Pfizer Inc.	Health	15.2	15.22	1.37
⊕ Procter & Gamble Company	Goods	23.9	13.36	1.34
⊕ Johnson & Johnson	Health	17.5	12.45	1.27
⊕ J.P. Morgan Chase & Co.	Financial	13.6	25.60	1.08
⊕ Altria Group, Inc.	Goods	16.3	19.87	1.06
⊕ American International G	Financial	17.0	6.05	0.97
⊕ Chevron Corporation	Energy	9.0	33.76	0.95
⊕ Cisco Systems, Inc.	Hardware	30.1	59.64	0.93
⊕ IBM	Hardware	17.1	19.77	0.84
⊕ AT&T, Inc.	Telecom	18.2	51.59	0.84
⊕ Wal-Mart Stores, Inc.	Consumer	16.9	0.13	0.82
⊕ Intel Corporation	Hardware	21.0	-17.18	0.79
⊕ Wells Fargo Company	Financial	14.7	16.82	0.76
⊕ Verizon Communications	Telecom	15.9	34.88	0.72
⊕ PepsiCo, Inc.	Goods	21.5	7.86	0.71

Current Investment Style

Value Blnd Growth — Large Mid Small

Market Cap	%
Giant	41.1
Large	31.2
Mid	19.5
Small	6.1
Micro	2.1

Avg $mil: 26,900

Value Measures		Rel Category
Price/Earnings	15.48	1.01
Price/Book	2.49	0.97
Price/Sales	1.37	0.98
Price/Cash Flow	7.18	0.85
Dividend Yield %	1.81	1.03

Growth Measures	%	Rel Category
Long-Term Erngs	11.50	0.97
Book Value	8.26	0.91
Sales	9.28	0.96
Cash Flow	9.64	0.93
Historical Erngs	16.90	0.91

Profitability	%	Rel Category
Return on Equity	18.25	0.94
Return on Assets	9.97	0.96
Net Margin	13.43	1.00

Sector Weightings	% of Stocks	Rel S&P 500	3 Year High Low	
⟳ Info	19.47	0.97		
Software	3.59	1.04	4	3
Hardware	9.14	0.99	10	9
Media	3.42	0.90	5	3
Telecom	3.32	0.95	3	3
⟳ Service	48.45	1.05		
Health	12.61	1.05	13	12
Consumer	8.08	1.06	10	8
Business	5.36	1.27	6	5
Financial	22.40	1.01	23	20
⟳ Mfg	32.09	0.95		
Goods	7.93	0.93	9	8
Ind Mtrls	11.61	0.97	12	10
Energy	9.05	0.92	10	6
Utilities	3.50	1.00	4	3

Composition

● Cash	0.5
● Stocks	99.5
● Bonds	0.0
● Other	0.0
Foreign (% of Stock)	0.1

Morningstar's Take by Dan Culloton 11-20-06

Vanguard Total Stock Market Index doesn't have to hang its head.

This fund has seen a lot of rivals emerge. There's been an explosion of exchange-traded funds offering different ways to track the market in recent years. The new ETFs range from funds tracking indexes that weight their constituents by fundamental factors, such as dividends, to offerings that use quantitative stock-picking models in an effort to beat traditional benchmarks. At the same time, some conventional index funds tracking similar benchmarks have slashed their expense ratios and now undercut this fund.

Nevertheless, this fund still stands up to the tougher competition. Its index, the MSCI U.S. Broad Market Index, encompasses virtually every domestic stock, so it's suitable as a core (or sole) U.S. equity holding. And while the fund is no longer the cheapest total market fund on the lot, it remains among the cheapest large-blend funds one can own. Its 0.19% expense ratio is less than a fifth of

that of the median no-load large-cap fund.

Furthermore, the fund is run by an experienced indexer, Gerard O'Reilly, who knows how to control tax and transaction costs. Indeed the fund's tracking error, or the amount by which it trails its benchmark, is usually no more than the size of its expense ratio, which indicates the fund's manager does a good job aping the index.

Finally, the fund's long-term track record also remains strong and looks even better on an aftertax basis. Low turnover helps keep this fund tax-efficient, but O'Reilly also puts a premium on managing taxes. Indeed, the fund's tax-cost ratio and aftertax returns for the five-year period ending Oct. 31, 2006, are even better than those of competing total market ETFs, which are supposed to be more tax-efficient due to their structure.

Because this fund owns more small caps than other core funds, it may look a bit sluggish in the future if small stocks surrender market leadership, but it's still an excellent long-term holding.

Address:	PO Box 2600 Valley Forge PA 19482 800-997-2798	Minimum Purchase:	$3000	Add: $100	IRA: $3000
		Min Auto Inv Plan:	$3000	Add: $50	
		Sales Fees:	No-load		
Web Address:	www.vanguard.com	Management Fee:	0.17%		
Inception:	04-27-92	Actual Fees:	Mgt:0.17%	Dist: —	
Advisor:	Vanguard Advisers, Inc.	Expense Projections:	3Yr:$61	5Yr:$107	10Yr:$243
Subadvisor:	None	Income Distrib:	Quarterly		
NTF Plans:	Vanguard NTF				

MORNINGSTAR® Funds 500

Vanguard Total Bd Idx

Analyst Pick ✓

	Ticker	Load	NAV	Yield	SEC Yield	Total Assets	Mstar Category
	VBMFX	None	$9.99	4.8%	4.96%	$39,926 mil	Intermediate-Term Bond

Governance and Management

Stewardship Grade: B

Portfolio Manager(s)

Ken Volpert has been the manager of this fund since 1992. Volpert's team, which includes eight credit analysts, runs all of Vanguard's fixed-income index funds, including Short-Term Bond Index, Intermediate-Term Bond Index, and Long-Term Bond Index.

Strategy

The fund strives to approximate the performance of the Lehman Brothers Aggregate Bond Index, which is a commonly used proxy for the broad, investment-grade U.S. bond market. The duration (a measure of interest-rate sensitivity) and other key characteristics of the index are carefully replicated, but the fund does not hold every security in the index. Instead, in an effort to pick up additional yield and return, it tends to hold a higher percentage of short-term corporate bonds or asset-backed securities and fewer short Treasuries than does its index.

Performance 12-31-06

	1st Qtr	2nd Qtr	3rd Qtr	4th Qtr	Total
2002	0.06	2.80	3.71	1.47	8.26
2003	1.30	2.57	-0.12	0.18	3.97
2004	2.71	-2.49	3.09	0.95	4.24
2005	-0.47	2.99	-0.75	0.65	2.40
2006	-0.73	-0.20	3.85	1.35	4.27

Trailing	Total Return%	+/- LB Aggr	+/- LB 5-10YR	%Rank Cat	Growth of $10,000
3 Mo	1.35	0.11	0.27	33	10,135
6 Mo	5.25	0.16	-0.43	22	10,525
1 Yr	4.27	-0.06	0.46	34	10,427
3 Yr Avg	3.63	-0.07	-0.01	33	11,129
5 Yr Avg	4.61	-0.45	-1.31	47	12,528
10 Yr Avg	5.96	-0.28	-0.72	26	17,841
15 Yr Avg	6.30	-0.20	-0.69	38	25,003

Tax Analysis	Tax-Adj Rtn%	%Rank Cat	Tax-Cost Rat	%Rank Cat
3 Yr (estimated)	1.99	31	1.58	58
5 Yr (estimated)	2.83	48	1.70	57
10 Yr (estimated)	3.74	19	2.10	58

Potential Capital Gain Exposure: -1% of assets

Morningstar's Take by Sonya Morris 11-27-06

Vanguard Total Bond Market is the quintessential core bond holding.

This fund tracks the Lehman Brothers Aggregate Index, the flagship benchmark for bond investors. Indeed, the "Lehman Agg," as it is familiarly known, is as ubiquitous in the bond world as the S&P 500 Index is in the equity arena.

Indexing is hugely popular among stock investors, but the strategy isn't as prevalent in the fixed-income realm. Nevertheless, indexing has the potential to be an even more potent strategy for bond investing. That's because bond returns typically fall within a narrow range, making it even more challenging for active bond managers to add incremental value. Furthermore, fixed-income managers tend to be more benchmark-conscious than their equity counterparts, which makes the task of outperforming even more difficult.

In addition, bond-index funds have rock-bottom expense ratios that give them an advantage over more-expensive active funds. Witness this fund's tiny 0.20% expense ratio, which is among the lowest in the intermediate-term bond category. That low expense hurdle has helped this fund edge out the competition over time and contributed to its competitive long-term track record. What's more, by keeping fees low, the fund can pass more of its income stream on to shareholders. Without doing anything fancy, it has managed to consistently deliver above-average yields, and for the past four years, its income payout has ranked in the category's top third.

This fund's charms go beyond its low price tag. It provides investors exposure to a broad swath of domestic investment-grade bonds. And after a slight misstep in 2002, when the fund's returns strayed too far from its benchmark's, Vanguard's fixed-income team tightened risk controls, and the fund has since tracked its bogy quite closely.

All told, this is a great choice to anchor a fixed-income portfolio.

Address:	PO Box 2600
	Valley Forge PA 19482
	800-997-2798
Web Address:	www.vanguard.com
Inception:	12-11-86
Advisor:	Vanguard Advisers, Inc.
Subadvisor:	None
NTF Plans:	Vanguard NTF

Minimum Purchase:	$3000	Add: $100	IRA: $3000
Min Auto Inv Plan:	$3000	Add: $50	
Sales Fees:	No-load		
Management Fee:	0.17%		
Actual Fees:	Mgt:0.17%	Dist: —	
Expense Projections:	3Yr:$64	5Yr:$113	10Yr:$255
Income Distrib:	Monthly		

Historical Profile

Return	Above Avg
Risk	Average
Rating	★★★★ Above Avg

22	23	22	19	17	27	25	23	

Investment Style
Fixed Income
Income Rtn %Rank Cat

▼ Manager Change
▽ Partial Manager Change

Growth of $10,000
■ Investment Values of Fund
— Investment Values of LB Aggr

- 20.5
- 17.5
- 15.0
- 12.5
- 10.0

Performance Quartile (within Category)

1995	1996	1997	1998	1999	2000	2001	2002	2003	2004	2005	2006	History
10.14	9.84	10.09	10.27	9.56	9.96	10.15	10.38	10.31	10.27	10.06	9.99	NAV
18.18	3.58	9.44	8.58	-0.76	11.39	8.43	8.26	3.97	4.24	2.40	4.27	Total Return %
-0.29	-0.05	-0.21	-0.11	0.06	-0.24	-0.01	-1.99	-0.13	-0.10	-0.03	-0.06	+/-LB Aggr
-3.25	0.89	0.01	-1.56	2.12	-1.05	-0.39	-4.77	-2.00	-1.06	0.57	0.46	+/-LB 5-10YR
7.31	6.51	6.76	6.36	6.19	6.99	6.53	5.77	4.67	4.42	4.47	4.93	Income Return %
10.87	-2.93	2.68	2.22	-6.95	4.40	1.90	2.49	-0.70	-0.18	-2.07	-0.66	Capital Return %
45	39	36	19	34	20	23	57	63	42	19	34	Total Rtn % Rank Cat
0.65	0.64	0.65	0.62	0.62	0.65	0.63	0.57	0.47	0.45	0.45	0.48	Income $
0.00	0.00	0.00	0.04	0.02	0.00	0.00	0.01	0.00	0.02	0.00	0.00	Capital Gains $
0.20	0.20	0.20	0.20	0.20	0.22	0.22	0.22	0.22	0.20	0.20	—	Expense Ratio %
6.66	6.54	6.54	6.10	6.26	6.72	6.21	5.63	4.46	4.29	4.40	—	Income Ratio %
36	39	39	57	55	53	67	75	66	44	59	—	Turnover Rate %
2,405	2,953	5,129	7,765	9,477	11,180	14,116	16,676	17,032	19,479	21,643	23,769	Net Assets $mil

Rating and Risk

Time Period	Load-Adj Return %	Morningstar Rtn vs Cat	Morningstar Risk vs Cat	Morningstar Risk-Adj Rating
1 Yr	4.27			
3 Yr	3.63	+Avg	+Avg	★★★★
5 Yr	4.61	Avg	Avg	★★★
10 Yr	5.96	+Avg	Avg	★★★★
Incept	6.96			

Other Measures	Standard Index	Best Fit Index
	LB Aggr	LB Aggr
Alpha	-0.1	-0.1
Beta	1.02	1.02
R-Squared	100	100
Standard Deviation	3.31	
Mean	3.63	
Sharpe Ratio	0.12	

Portfolio Analysis 09-30-06

Total Fixed-Income:10244	Date of Maturity	Amount $000	Value $000	% Net Assets
US Treasury Note 4.375%	01-31-08	555,950	552,648	1.48
US Treasury Note 4.375%	12-31-07	502,300	499,316	1.34
US Treasury Bond 8.75%	05-15-17	274,485	366,481	0.98
US Treasury Note 4%	02-15-14	351,745	338,171	0.91
US Treasury Note 4.25%	01-15-11	311,750	307,463	0.83
US Treasury Bond 8.5%	02-15-20	222,140	302,666	0.81
US Treasury Note 4.625%	02-29-08	296,150	295,410	0.79
US Treasury Bond 7.25%	05-15-16	244,125	292,645	0.79
FHLMC 5.75%	04-15-08	250,680	253,350	0.68
US Treasury Bond 10.625%	08-15-15	153,700	219,911	0.59
US Treasury Note 3.375%	10-15-09	223,470	215,649	0.58
US Treasury Bond 6.125%	08-15-29	182,015	214,521	0.58
US Treasury Note 4.125%	08-15-10	213,671	210,133	0.56
US Treasury Note 6.5%	02-15-10	196,130	207,468	0.56
US Treasury Bond 8.125%	08-15-19	156,245	206,048	0.55
Chase Issuance Tr 2005-1	12-15-10	203,326	203,497	0.55
Bk One Oneseries 2003-6a	02-15-11	200,000	200,520	0.54
US Treasury Note 4.5%	02-15-09	194,460	193,731	0.52
US Treasury Bond 8.875%	02-15-19	137,025	189,159	0.51
US Treasury Note 3%	02-15-08	191,100	186,561	0.50

Current Investment Style

Duration: Short Int Long
Quality: High Med Low

¹ figure provided by fund

Avg Eff Duration¹	4.6 Yrs
Avg Eff Maturity	7.1 Yrs
Avg Credit Quality	AAA
Avg Wtd Coupon	5.43%
Avg Wtd Price	103.23% of par

Coupon Range	% of Bonds	Rel Cat
0% PIK	0.9	0.1
0% to 6%	73.7	1.0
6% to 8%	19.0	0.9
8% to 10%	5.7	1.2
More than 10%	1.5	2.2

1.00=Category Average

Credit Analysis	% bonds 09-30-06		
AAA	79	BB	0
AA	5	B	0
A	8	Below B	0
BBB	8	NR/NA	0

Sector Breakdown	% of assets
US Treasuries	26
TIPS	0
US Agency	10
Mortgage Pass-Throughs	34
Mortgage CMO	2
Mortgage ARM	0
US Corporate	19
Asset-Backed	6
Convertible	0
Municipal	0
Corporate Inflation-Protected	0
Foreign Corporate	1
Foreign Govt	1

Composition			
Cash	0.9	Bonds	99.0
Stocks	0.0	Other	0.0

Special Securities	
Restricted/Illiquid Secs	Trace
Exotic Mortgage-Backed	0
Emerging-Markets Secs	Trace
Options/Futures/Warrants	No

MORNINGSTAR® Funds 500

Vanguard Total Intl Stk

Governance and Management

Stewardship Grade: B

Portfolio Manager(s)

The fund is made up of three component Vanguard funds. Vanguard indexing expert Gus Sauter managed all three until 2005, when other Vanguard individuals stepped forward and took day-to-day responsibility for them. However, Sauter, now chief investment officer at Vanguard, still has oversight of the funds.

Strategy

This fund of funds is made up of Vanguard's three regional index funds: Vanguard European Stock Index, Vanguard Pacific Stock Index, and Vanguard Emerging Markets Stock Index. It aims to track a customized index. It does not hedge its currency exposure. Vanguard uses fair-value pricing on some days.

Historical Profile

Return: Above Avg
Risk: Average
Rating: ★★★★ Above Avg

	94%	91%	0%	99%	95%	92%	97%	97%	97%

Investment Style
Equity
Stock %

Growth of $10,000
— Investment Values of Fund
— Investment Values of MSCI EAFE

Performance Quartile (within Category)

1995	1996	1997	1998	1999	2000	2001	2002	2003	2004	2005	2006	History
—	10.14	9.87	11.19	14.31	11.83	9.28	7.72	10.64	12.60	14.27	17.67	NAV
—	0.55*	-0.77	15.60	29.92	-15.61	-20.15	-15.08	40.34	20.84	15.57	26.64	Total Return %
—	—	-2.55	-4.33	2.89	-1.42	1.27	0.86	1.75	0.59	2.03	0.30	+/-MSCI EAFE
—	—	-3.04	-3.09	1.94	-2.25	1.24	0.72	0.92	0.46	1.10	0.93	+/-MSCI Wd xUS
—	1.68	2.13	1.88	1.40	1.39	1.69	2.46	2.40	2.33	2.82	Income Return %
—	-2.45	13.47	28.04	-17.01	-21.54	-16.77	37.88	18.44	13.24	23.82	Capital Return %
—	92	39	72	44	38	31	10	11	34	27	Total Rtn % Rank Cat
—	0.16	0.17	0.21	0.21	0.20	0.17	0.16	0.19	0.26	0.29	0.40	Income $
—	0.02	0.02	0.01	0.01	0.05	0.00	0.00	0.00	0.00	0.00	0.00	Capital Gains $
—											0.31	Expense Ratio %
—	1.51	2.19	2.18	2.04	1.68	0.05	2.24	1.75	1.54		Income Ratio %
—	—	6	2	1	3	2	5	2	3		Turnover Rate %
—	280	903	1,375	2,570	2,920	2,900	2,994	5,279	8,516	20,070	Net Assets $mil

Performance 12-31-06

	1st Qtr	2nd Qtr	3rd Qtr	4th Qtr	Total
2002	1.72	-2.75	-19.72	6.92	-15.08
2003	-7.90	19.55	8.71	17.25	40.34
2004	4.61	-0.36	0.27	15.62	20.84
2005	-0.08	-0.71	11.68	4.31	15.57
2006	9.46	0.06	3.97	11.21	26.64

Trailing	Total Return%	+/- MSCI EAFE	+/- MSCI Wd xUS	%Rank Cat	Growth of $10,000
3 Mo	11.21	0.86	1.09	22	11,121
6 Mo	15.62	0.93	1.40	21	11,562
1 Yr	26.64	0.30	0.93	27	12,664
3 Yr Avg	20.93	1.00	0.83	13	17,685
5 Yr Avg	16.08	1.10	0.83	10	21,076
10 Yr Avg	7.78	0.07	-0.18	37	21,153
15 Yr Avg	—				

Tax Analysis	Tax-Adj Rtn%	%Rank Cat	Tax-Cost Rat	%Rank Cat
3 Yr (estimated)	20.28	11	0.54	29
5 Yr (estimated)	15.44	9	0.55	43
10 Yr (estimated)	7.10	27	0.63	19

Potential Capital Gain Exposure: 31% of assets

Rating and Risk

Time Period	Load-Adj Return %	Morningstar Rtn vs Cat	Morningstar Risk vs Cat	Morningstar Risk-Adj Rating
1 Yr	26.64			
3 Yr	20.93	+Avg	+Avg	★★★★
5 Yr	16.08	+Avg	Avg	★★★★
10 Yr	7.78	Avg	Avg	★★★
Incept	7.33			

Other Measures	Standard Index MSCI EAFE	Best Fit Index MSCI EAFE
Alpha	-0.4	-0.4
Beta	1.08	1.08
R-Squared	99	99
Standard Deviation	10.32	
Mean	20.93	
Sharpe Ratio	1.60	

Portfolio Analysis 09-30-06

Share change since 06-06 Total Stocks:0	Sector	Country	% Assets
⊕ Vanguard European Stock	—	United States	58.29
⊕ Vanguard Pacific Stock I	—	United States	26.84
⊕ Vanguard Emerging Mkts S	—	United States	14.75

Morningstar's Take by Gregg Wolper 12-27-06

Besides this fund's appealing attributes, two other factors must be considered for anyone currently thinking of buying it.

Like all Vanguard index-trackers, Vanguard Total International Stock Index has very low costs--its expense ratio of just 0.32% for 2006 is far below the average for actively managed foreign large-blend funds. And its portfolio provides some exposure to emerging-markets stocks, unlike nearly all index-tracking rivals that include only the developed markets of the MSCI EAFE Index. Though emerging markets carry more risk of volatility, given the number of solid companies located there, it's getting harder and harder to justify excluding them entirely, so this fund's structure makes it especially suitable for investors who want to own just one international fund. And Vanguard's experienced investment team is able to track the returns of the underlying indexes about as closely as anyone.

However, note that most foreign markets and foreign currencies have been on rallies for the past several years, providing juicy returns for this fund. For the trailing three-year period through Dec. 26, 2006, it has posted an annualized 21.5% gain. The fact that emerging markets have been especially strong has allowed this fund to top indexing rivals that only track EAFE. This fund has also beaten plenty of actively managed rivals, resulting in an 11th-percentile ranking for the period. But it would be unrealistic to expect such large gains as a matter of course, or that emerging markets will outperform every year.

What's more, as the latter markets have powered ahead, that component has become a bigger and bigger part of this passive portfolio. Once just 8% of assets, emerging markets were up to 15.4% at the end of November 2006. That's not necessarily a dangerous level, but it does add risk. If you last checked this fund a few years ago, keep in mind that it has changed and has much more in emerging markets now.

Address:	PO Box 2600 Valley Forge PA 19482 800-997-2798
Web Address:	www.vanguard.com
Inception:	04-29-96*
Advisor:	Vanguard Advisers, Inc.
Subadvisor:	None
NTF Plans:	Vanguard NTF

Minimum Purchase:	$3000	Add: $100	IRA: $3000
Min Auto Inv Plan:	$3000	Add: $50	
Sales Fees:	No-load, 2.00%R		
Management Fee:	0.00%		
Actual Fees:	Mgt:0.00%	Dist: —	
Expense Projections:	3Yr:$100	5Yr:$174	10Yr:$393
Income Distrib:	Annually		

Current Investment Style

Value Blend Growth — Large Mid Small

Market Cap	%
Giant	53.2
Large	32.5
Mid	13.4
Small	0.8
Micro	0.1
Avg $mil:	25,061

Value Measures		Rel Category
Price/Earnings	10.29	0.78
Price/Book	1.99	0.92
Price/Sales	1.03	0.89
Price/Cash Flow	7.51	0.90
Dividend Yield %	3.21	1.10

Growth Measures	%	Rel Category
Long-Term Erngs	11.54	0.98
Book Value	8.25	0.90
Sales	6.97	1.06
Cash Flow	5.51	0.67
Historical Erngs	9.85	0.48

Composition

Cash	0.7	Bonds	0.0
Stocks	97.1	Other	2.3
Foreign (% of Stock)			99.9

Sector Weightings	% of Stocks	Rel MSCI EAFE	3 Year High	Low
☎ Info	13.16	1.11		
🖥 Software	0.76	1.36	1	1
🖥 Hardware	4.52	1.17	5	4
🎙 Media	1.83	1.00	2	2
📞 Telecom	6.05	1.09	9	6
⚙ Service	45.99	0.97		
⚕ Health	7.06	0.99	9	7
🛒 Consumer	4.89	0.99	5	4
🏢 Business	4.99	0.98	5	5
💲 Financial	29.05	0.97	29	24
🏭 Mfg	40.85	1.00		
Goods	12.89	0.98	16	13
Ind Mtrls	15.41	1.00	16	13
Energy	8.03	1.12	9	8
Utilities	4.52	0.86	5	4

Regional Exposure	% Stock		
UK/W. Europe	59	N. America	0
Japan	20	Latn America	3
Asia X Japan	15	Other	3

Country Exposure	% Stock		
U.K.	21	Switzerland	6
Japan	20	Germany	6
France	8		

MORNINGSTAR® Funds 500

Vanguard Tx-Mgd Gr

	Ticker	Load	NAV	Yield	Total Assets	Mstar Category
	VTGIX	None	$30.87	1.7%	$3,107 mil	Large Blend

Governance and Management

Stewardship Grade: B

Portfolio Manager(s)

Michael Perre took over this fund early in 2006. He's been with Vanguard since 1990 and has managed the equity portion of Vanguard Tax Managed Balanced since 1999. This fund's former manager, Gus Sauter, who also is Vanguard's chief investment officer and index expert, still supervises Perre and other members of Vanguard's quantitative equity group.

Strategy

The fund attempts to mimic the S&P 500. To minimize capital gains distributions, its manager may sell stocks at a loss to offset gains, liquidating the highest-cost shares first. The fund also takes steps to deter market-timers, whose activity can lead to more selling, by imposing redemption fees on short-term investors and by requiring a $10,000 minimum investment.

Historical Profile

Return: Above Avg
Risk: Average
Rating: ★★★★ Above Avg

	98%	99%	99%	99%	98%	100%	100%	99%	100%

Investment Style
Equity
Stock %

▼ Manager Change
▽ Partial Manager Change

Growth of $10,000
— Investment Values of Fund
— Investment Values of S&P 500

Performance Quartile (within Category)

1995	1996	1997	1998	1999	2000	2001	2002	2003	2004	2005	2006	History
13.16	15.89	20.88	26.55	31.81	28.66	24.93	19.15	24.23	26.36	27.15	30.87	NAV
37.53	23.03	33.31	28.67	21.12	-9.03	-11.93	-21.95	28.53	10.83	4.87	15.73	Total Return %
-0.05	0.07	-0.05	0.09	0.08	0.07	-0.04	0.15	-0.15	-0.05	-0.04	-0.06	+/-S&P 500
-0.24	0.58	0.46	1.65	0.21	-1.24	0.52	-0.30	-1.36	-0.57	-1.40	0.27	+/-Russ 1000
2.58	2.14	1.77	1.40	1.19	0.94	1.05	1.31	1.79	1.95	1.83	1.90	Income Return %
34.95	20.89	31.54	27.27	19.93	-9.97	-12.98	-23.26	26.74	8.88	3.04	13.84	Capital Return %
15	30	15	16	34	65	51	47	34	41	58	22	Total Rtn % Rank Cat
0.25	0.28	0.28	0.29	0.31	0.30	0.30	0.33	0.34	0.47	0.48	0.51	Income $
0.00	0.00	0.00	0.00	0.00	0.00	0.00	0.00	0.00	0.00	0.00	0.00	Capital Gains $
0.20	0.20	0.17	0.19	0.19	0.19	0.17	0.17	0.17	0.14	0.14	—	Expense Ratio %
2.37	2.04	1.62	1.32	1.11	0.96	1.44	1.44	1.63	1.89	1.78	—	Income Ratio %
6	7	2	4	4	5	5	9	5	8	10	—	Turnover Rate %
98	235	579	1,352	2,240	2,427	1,606	1,077	1,321	1,395	806	784	Net Assets $mil

Performance 12-31-06

	1st Qtr	2nd Qtr	3rd Qtr	4th Qtr	Total
2002	0.24	-13.32	-17.10	8.36	-21.95
2003	-3.19	15.37	2.64	12.12	28.53
2004	1.70	1.71	-1.89	9.21	10.83
2005	-2.12	1.36	3.59	2.04	4.87
2006	4.20	-1.45	5.65	6.67	15.73

Trailing	Total Return%	+/- S&P 500	+/- Russ 1000	%Rank Cat	Growth of $10,000
3 Mo	6.67	-0.03	-0.28	46	10,667
6 Mo	12.70	-0.04	0.34	20	11,270
1 Yr	15.73	-0.06	0.27	22	11,573
3 Yr Avg	10.39	-0.05	-0.59	38	13,452
5 Yr Avg	6.18	-0.01	-0.64	38	13,496
10 Yr Avg	8.43	0.01	-0.21	29	22,464
15 Yr Avg	—				

Tax Analysis	Tax-Adj Rtn%	%Rank Cat	Tax-Cost Rat	%Rank Cat
3 Yr (estimated)	10.04	29	0.32	15
5 Yr (estimated)	5.79	32	0.37	24
10 Yr (estimated)	7.98	18	0.42	14

Potential Capital Gain Exposure: 27% of assets

Rating and Risk

Time Period	Load-Adj Return %	Morningstar Rtn vs Cat	Morningstar Risk vs Cat	Morningstar Risk-Adj Rating
1 Yr	15.73			
3 Yr	10.39	Avg	-Avg	★★★
5 Yr	6.18	Avg	Avg	★★★
10 Yr	8.43	+Avg	Avg	★★★★
Incept	11.29			

Other Measures	Standard Index S&P 500	Best Fit Index S&P 500
Alpha	0.0	0.0
Beta	1.00	1.00
R-Squared	100	100
Standard Deviation	6.91	
Mean	10.39	
Sharpe Ratio	1.01	

Portfolio Analysis 09-30-06

Share change since 06-06 Total Stocks:508

	Sector	PE	Tot Ret%	% Assets
⊖ ExxonMobil Corporation	Energy	11.1	39.07	3.32
⊖ General Electric Company	Ind Mtrls	20.0	9.35	3.03
⊖ Citigroup, Inc.	Financial	13.1	19.55	2.04
⊖ Bank of America Corporat	Financial	12.4	20.68	2.02
⊖ Microsoft Corporation	Software	23.8	15.83	1.96
⊕ Pfizer Inc.	Health	15.2	15.22	1.72
⊕ Procter & Gamble Company	Goods	23.9	13.36	1.64
⊖ Johnson & Johnson	Health	17.5	12.45	1.58
⊕ American International G	Financial	17.0	6.05	1.43
⊖ J.P. Morgan Chase & Co.	Financial	13.6	25.60	1.36
⊕ Altria Group, Inc.	Goods	16.3	19.87	1.33
⊕ Chevron Corporation	Energy	9.0	33.76	1.19
⊕ Cisco Systems, Inc.	Hardware	30.1	59.64	1.17
⊕ AT&T, Inc.	Telecom	18.2	51.59	1.05
⊖ IBM	Hardware	17.1	19.77	1.04
⊕ Wells Fargo Company	Financial	14.7	16.82	1.01
⊕ Wal-Mart Stores, Inc.	Consumer	16.9	0.13	1.01
⊖ Intel Corporation	Hardware	21.0	-17.18	0.99
⊕ Verizon Communications	Telecom	15.9	34.88	0.90
⊕ PepsiCo, Inc.	Goods	21.5	7.86	0.89

Current Investment Style

Value Blnd Growth — Large Mid Small

Market Cap	%
Giant	51.2
Large	38.0
Mid	10.7
Small	0.1
Micro	0.0

Avg $mil: 50,531

Value Measures		Rel Category
Price/Earnings	15.18	0.99
Price/Book	2.56	1.00
Price/Sales	1.44	1.03
Price/Cash Flow	7.11	0.84
Dividend Yield %	1.92	1.10

Growth Measures	%	Rel Category
Long-Term Erngs	11.17	0.95
Book Value	8.61	0.95
Sales	9.76	1.01
Cash Flow	9.11	0.88
Historical Erngs	17.21	0.93

Profitability	%	Rel Category
Return on Equity	19.63	1.01
Return on Assets	10.79	1.04
Net Margin	14.04	1.05

Sector Weightings	% of Stocks	Rel S&P 500	3 Year High	Low
↻ Info	19.98	1.00		
Software	3.49	1.01	5	3
Hardware	9.53	1.03	11	9
Media	3.46	0.91	4	3
Telecom	3.50	1.00	4	3
☞ Service	46.77	1.01		
Health	12.71	1.05	13	12
Consumer	7.72	1.01	9	8
Business	4.06	0.96	5	4
Financial	22.28	1.00	22	20
Mfg	33.26	0.98		
Goods	8.64	1.01	10	8
Ind Mtrls	11.89	1.00	13	12
Energy	9.32	0.95	10	6
Utilities	3.41	0.97	4	3

Composition

● Cash		0.0
● Stocks		100.0
● Bonds		0.0
● Other		0.0
Foreign		0.0
(% of Stock)		

Morningstar's Take by Dan Culloton 11-20-06

Recent management changes won't trip up Vanguard Tax-Managed Growth & Income.

This fund has changed managers again. Michael Perre replaced Corey Holeman as lead manager in April 2006. Holeman had only been in control since 2005, when Vanguard CIO Gus Sauter and former manager of this fund dialed back his role here. The fund didn't lose a step during the previous change, though, and shouldn't now. Perre has been with Vanguard for 16 years and has worked on the equity portion of Vanguard Tax-Managed Balanced since 1999. Members of Vanguard's quantitative equity group, which runs this and the family's other tax-managed and index funds, also work closely together and still report to Sauter.

This fund also still has many other attributes that make it a good core holding. Its most-obvious selling point is its low expense ratio, which is a fraction of the median fee for no-load large-cap funds and even lower than a lot of exchange-traded funds in its peer group. Second, but no less important, is its simple and sensible strategy: It stays diversified and keeps turnover low by sticking close to the S&P 500 (it's virtually an index fund), and it minimizes taxable distributions via savvy trading. Indeed, historically the fund has been able to avoid capital gains distributions altogether, giving it 10-year aftertax returns through Oct. 31, 2006, that ranked ahead of 85% of its peers. The fund's five-year tax-adjusted results even beat shorter-lived rival ETFs, such as iShares S&P 500 Index, which have the advantage of a more tax-efficient structure.

There are reasons to be optimistic about this fund apart from tax sensitivity, though. Many of its holdings still look attractive from a fundamental perspective. The S&P 500 has jumped recently, but several of its top holdings, including Microsoft, Johnson & Johnson, and Wal-Mart, still look cheap relative to their estimated fair values, according to Morningstar stock analysts.

This is still a solid fund for a taxable portfolio.

Address:	PO Box 2600 Valley Forge PA 19482 800-997-2798	
Web Address:	www.vanguard.com	
Inception:	09-06-94	
Advisor:	Vanguard Advisers, Inc.	
Subadvisor:	None	
NTF Plans:	Vanguard NTF	

Minimum Purchase:	$10000	Add: $100 IRA: $0
Min Auto Inv Plan:	$10000	Add: $50
Sales Fees:	No-load, 1.00%R	
Management Fee:	0.12%	
Actual Fees:	Mgt:0.12%	Dist: —
Expense Projections:	3Yr:$160	5Yr: — 10Yr: —
Income Distrib:	Quarterly	

Vanguard U.S. Gr

	Ticker	Load	NAV	Yield	Total Assets	Mstar Category
	VWUSX	None	$18.18	0.5%	$5,847 mil	Large Growth

Governance and Management

Stewardship Grade: B

Portfolio Manager(s)

Alliance Capital ran the fund solo from June 2001 through mid-April 2004. Alan Levi is the lead manager at Alliance. He's backed by 25 analysts, and roughly 80% of each analyst's compensation is tied to his or her ability to identify strong stocks for the portfolio. In April 2004, Vanguard hired William Blair to run about a third of the fund. John Jostrand is the lead manager from William Blair.

Strategy

On the Alliance side, analysts assign stocks "buy," "sell," or "hold" ratings based on growth and valuation traits. To ensure that the cream rises to the top, they must assign roughly equal numbers of sells and buys. The two managers then further winnow down the universe based on analysts' ratings, growth forecasts, and valuation multiples, ultimately selecting 40 to 45 names for the portfolio. The Blair team seeks 30 to 40 high-quality growth companies it thinks have the potential for strong long-term earnings growth, placing a premium on predictable earnings and accounting integrity.

Performance 12-31-06

	1st Qtr	2nd Qtr	3rd Qtr	4th Qtr	Total
2002	-7.80	-20.71	-16.55	5.23	-35.80
2003	-0.25	10.64	4.06	9.81	26.10
2004	1.91	1.42	-5.87	10.00	7.03
2005	-5.50	5.10	5.79	5.79	11.15
2006	1.78	-7.72	4.09	4.09	1.77

Trailing	Total Return%	+/- S&P 500	+/- Russ 1000Gr	%Rank Cat	Growth of $10,000
3 Mo	4.09	-2.61	-1.84	82	10,409
6 Mo	8.35	-4.39	-1.75	51	10,835
1 Yr	1.77	-14.02	-7.30	88	10,177
3 Yr Avg	6.58	-3.86	-0.29	56	12,107
5 Yr Avg	-0.40	-6.59	-3.09	91	9,802
10 Yr Avg	1.42	-7.00	-4.02	96	11,514
15 Yr Avg	5.12	-5.52	-2.90	93	21,149

Tax Analysis	Tax-Adj Rtn%	%Rank Cat	Tax-Cost Rat	%Rank Cat
3 Yr (estimated)	6.53	47	0.05	4
5 Yr (estimated)	-0.47	88	0.07	8
10 Yr (estimated)	0.57	94	0.84	39

Potential Capital Gain Exposure: -100% of assets

Morningstar's Take by Dan Culloton 11-13-06

Vanguard U.S. Growth's forecast calls for improvement.

This decade has not been good to this fund. It has battled hurricane force headwinds since its longest-tenured manager arrived five years ago. If large-cap stocks have been out of favor, the giant-cap growth stocks this fund prefers have been sent to the doghouse. And this fund, whose average market capitalization is higher than more than 80% of its peers, has spent time there, too.

The fund could be ready for a reprieve, though. It's hard to remember the last time growth outperformed value for an extended period. But managers here (and even at some value funds) have been saying for some time that big growth stock valuations are as attractive as they have been in decades. When large growth takes its turn in the sun, this fund will look better. Indeed, though this fund owns some richly valued stocks such as Google and Goldman Sachs Group, it also devotes a lot of money to growth stocks that Morningstar stock analysts think are trading below their fair value estimates, such as health insurer WellPoint.

Other factors bode well for this fund's future. Manager Alan Levi, who runs nearly 70% of the portfolio's assets, is a seasoned investor whose other funds, particularly AllianceBernstein Growth, have done well when growth has been in favor. Levi taps the fundamental research of a large staff of AllianceBernstein analysts to find stocks with sustainable competitive advantages and the ability to consistently exceed consensus earnings estimates. His approach gives the fund an edgy profile, with big helpings of aggressive stocks such as Qualcomm, Genentech, and Legg Mason. John Jostrand of William Blair, who manages the rest of the fund, tempers the offering a bit with consistent growers.

The fund's growth-oriented mega-cap style, veteran management, research-driven process, and low expenses give it a good shot at looking much better when blue-chip growth stocks rally.

Address:	PO Box 2600
	Valley Forge PA 19482
	800-997-2798
Web Address:	www.vanguard.com
Inception:	01-06-59
Advisor:	Alliance Capital Management L.P.
Subadvisor:	None
NTF Plans:	Vanguard NTF

Minimum Purchase:	$3000	Add: $100	IRA: $3000
Min Auto Inv Plan:	$3000	Add: $50	
Sales Fees:	No-load		
Management Fee:	0.51%		
Actual Fees:	Mgt:0.51%	Dist: —	
Expense Projections:	3Yr:$170	5Yr:$296	10Yr:$665
Income Distrib:	Annually		

Historical Profile

Return Low
Risk Above Avg
Rating ★ Lowest

| | 92% | 98% | 98% | 98% | 99% | 100% | 97% | 95% | 96% |

Investment Style
Equity
Stock %

▼ Manager Change
▽ Partial Manager Change

Growth of $10,000
— Investment Values of Fund
— Investment Values of S&P 500

Values: 38.0 / 31.0 / 24.0 / 17.0 / 10.0

Performance Quartile (within Category)

1995	1996	1997	1998	1999	2000	2001	2002	2003	2004	2005	2006	History
20.35	23.74	28.70	37.49	43.53	27.65	18.85	12.06	15.16	16.18	17.95	18.18	NAV
38.44	26.05	25.93	39.98	22.28	-20.17	-31.70	-35.80	26.10	7.03	11.15	1.77	Total Return %
0.86	3.09	-7.43	11.40	1.24	-11.07	-19.81	-13.70	-2.58	-3.85	6.24	-14.02	+/-S&P 500
1.26	2.93	-4.56	1.27	-10.88	2.25	-11.28	-7.92	-3.65	0.73	5.89	-7.30	+/-Russ 1000Gr
1.89	1.28	1.14	0.66	0.56	0.11	0.13	0.22	0.39	0.30	0.22	0.48	Income Return %
36.55	24.77	24.79	39.32	21.72	-20.28	-31.83	-36.02	25.71	6.73	10.93	1.29	Capital Return %
17	10	52	18	78	80	90	91	62	59	17	88	Total Rtn % Rank Cat
0.29	0.26	0.27	0.19	0.21	0.05	0.04	0.04	0.05	0.05	0.04	0.09	Income $
0.57	1.62	0.89	2.31	2.02	7.45	0.00	0.00	0.00	0.00	0.00	0.00	Capital Gains $
0.44	0.43	0.42	0.41	0.39	0.36	0.44	0.50	0.55	0.53	0.52	0.58	Expense Ratio %
1.59	1.32	1.13	0.69	0.59	0.24	0.13	0.20	0.32	0.19	0.30	0.34	Income Ratio %
32	44	35	48	49	76	135	53	47	71	38	48	Turnover Rate %
3,624	5,532	8,055	13,624	19,068	16,232	9,180	5,030	6,086	5,411	5,015	4,573	Net Assets $mil

Rating and Risk

Time Period	Load-Adj Return %	Morningstar Rtn vs Cat	Morningstar Risk vs Cat	Morningstar Risk-Adj Rating
1 Yr	1.77			
3 Yr	6.58	Avg	+Avg	★★★
5 Yr	-0.40	Low	+Avg	★
10 Yr	1.42	Low	+Avg	★
Incept	—			

Other Measures	Standard Index S&P 500	Best Fit Index Russ 1000Gr
Alpha	-6.0	-0.8
Beta	1.39	1.21
R-Squared	80	90
Standard Deviation	10.65	
Mean	6.58	
Sharpe Ratio	0.35	

Portfolio Analysis 09-30-06

Share change since 06-06 Total Stocks:72	Sector	PE	Tot Ret%	% Assets
⊕ Goldman Sachs Group, Inc	Financial	12.4	57.41	3.92
⊕ Genentech, Inc.	Health	48.7	-12.29	3.71
⊕ Schlumberger, Ltd.	Energy	22.3	31.07	3.58
⊕ Google, Inc.	Business	61.5	11.00	3.24
⊖ Apple Computer, Inc.	Hardware	37.6	18.01	3.22
⊖ WellPoint, Inc.	Health	17.2	-1.38	3.11
⊕ Qualcomm, Inc.	Hardware	26.6	-11.32	3.04
Legg Mason	Financial	25.1	-19.99	3.02
⊕ Caremark RX, Inc.	Health	23.6	10.90	2.86
⊖ Danaher Corporation	Ind Mtrls	22.0	30.02	2.83
⊕ Teva Pharmaceutical Indu	Health	20.7	-27.22	2.55
⊕ Gilead Sciences, Inc.	Health	40.6	23.51	2.37
⊕ American International G	Financial	17.0	6.05	2.28
⊕ Advanced Micro Devices	Hardware	18.5	-33.50	2.06
⊕ Procter & Gamble Company	Goods	23.9	13.36	2.02
⊖ Citigroup, Inc.	Financial	13.1	19.55	1.77
⊖ UnitedHealth Group, Inc.	Health	20.8	-13.49	1.77
⊕ J.P. Morgan Chase & Co.	Financial	13.6	25.60	1.70
⊖ Kohl's Corporation	Consumer	22.6	40.80	1.69
⊕ Boeing Company	Ind Mtrls	41.2	28.38	1.68

Current Investment Style

Value Blnd Growth — Large/Mid/Small

Market Cap	%
Giant	50.3
Large	44.8
Mid	4.9
Small	0.0
Micro	0.0

Avg $mil: 42,367

Value Measures		Rel Category
Price/Earnings	20.57	1.07
Price/Book	3.21	0.97
Price/Sales	2.26	1.16
Price/Cash Flow	13.27	1.17
Dividend Yield %	0.82	0.80

Growth Measures	%	Rel Category
Long-Term Erngs	15.80	1.10
Book Value	13.35	1.15
Sales	15.17	1.31
Cash Flow	21.85	1.30
Historical Erngs	26.45	1.15

Profitability	%	Rel Category
Return on Equity	19.41	0.95
Return on Assets	12.19	1.11
Net Margin	16.93	1.19

Sector Weightings	% of Stocks	Rel S&P 500	3 Year High	Low
↻ Info	26.87	1.34		
Software	3.44	1.00	12	3
Hardware	20.23	2.19	23	19
Media	3.20	0.84	4	2
Telecom	0.00	0.00	0	0
☞ Service	51.70	1.12		
Health	23.89	1.98	28	21
Consumer	5.49	0.72	12	5
Business	4.61	1.09	6	0
Financial	17.71	0.80	19	13
Mfg	21.43	0.63		
Goods	4.61	0.54	7	2
Ind Mtrls	11.69	0.98	12	3
Energy	5.13	0.52	6	0
Utilities	0.00	0.00	0	0

Composition

	%
Cash	4.1
Stocks	95.9
Bonds	0.0
Other	0.0
Foreign (% of Stock)	6.7

MORNINGSTAR® Funds 500

Vanguard U.S. Value

	Analyst Pick	Ticker	Load	NAV	Yield	Total Assets	Mstar Category
		VUVLX	None	$14.74	1.5%	$1,512 mil	Large Value

Governance and Management

Stewardship Grade: B

Portfolio Manager(s)

Rob Soucy, who had managed day-to-day operations on this fund since its June 2000 inception, retired at the end of 2005. But Chris Darnell, who manages GMO's entire quant effort, will continue to oversee the process. Darnell comanages a number of GMO funds with superior long-term records. Sam Wilderman, a nine-year veteran of GMO's emerging-markets operation, has taken over the day-to-day operations from Soucy. Moreover, the quantitative equity team, which also manages a number of other large-cap value funds under the GMO banner, remains in place.

Strategy

Three quantitative models pick stocks here. One model screens for "classic value" stocks, which are simply cheap relative to the market. Another looks for companies with improving fundamentals and share price momentum. And a third screens for companies selling at a discount to GMO's estimates of their "intrinsic value," as measured by returns on equity and other factors. Because GMO picks stocks from the broad-based Russell 3000 Index, it holds mid- and small caps in this portfolio. It also keeps sector weightings reasonably close to those of the index and limits individual position sizes.

Performance 12-31-06

	1st Qtr	2nd Qtr	3rd Qtr	4th Qtr	Total
2002	5.14	-9.20	-17.72	7.86	-15.27
2003	-6.59	18.70	2.08	15.09	30.26
2004	3.91	0.00	0.55	8.83	13.70
2005	-1.16	3.53	2.06	1.85	6.37
2006	4.23	-2.78	6.52	5.71	14.10

Trailing	Total Return%	+/- S&P 500	+/- Russ 1000 VI	%Rank Cat	Growth of $10,000
3 Mo	5.71	-0.99	-2.29	90	10,571
6 Mo	12.60	-0.14	-2.12	56	11,260
1 Yr	14.10	-1.69	-8.15	91	11,410
3 Yr Avg	11.33	0.89	-3.76	68	13,799
5 Yr Avg	8.78	2.59	-2.08	41	15,232
10 Yr Avg	—	—	—	—	—
15 Yr Avg	—	—	—	—	—

Tax Analysis	Tax-Adj Rtn%	%Rank Cat	Tax-Cost Rat	%Rank Cat
3 Yr (estimated)	10.47	54	0.77	30
5 Yr (estimated)	8.09	32	0.63	34
10 Yr (estimated)	—	—	—	—

Potential Capital Gain Exposure: 12% of assets

Morningstar's Take by Dan Culloton 11-20-06

It's worth waiting around for Vanguard U.S. Value's revival.

This fund has struggled to keep up with the large-value category for much of the last year because it owned less than its peers did of what was hot, such as REITs and industrial and utilities stocks. We think this fund will be on the comeback trail before long, though. It already has shown signs of life. In the three months ending Oct. 31, 2006, it left 79% of its competitors behind, as falling commodity prices and a cooling economy sent investors scurrying for the perceived safety of the large classic growth stocks--such as drugmakers Pfizer and Merck--that have become common in this fund.

Three months of strong performance is too short a time to declare a turnaround (the only way anyone will know for sure is in hindsight), but it's still a good sign. You would expect a fund that has been snapping up stocks like Wal-Mart to do well when large core stocks do well, as they did in the three

months ending Oct. 31. And this fund behaved as expected, which vindicates its stock-selection process.

Not that we were too worried. The fund's management team follows a rigorous three-tiered quantitative strategy that looks first for Russell 3000 stocks trading below their intrinsic value, second for shares that look cheap relative to the broad equity market, and last for Russell 3000 Value stocks showing positive price momentum. This has proved to be a disciplined and dispassionate way to build a diversified portfolio of stocks with prices that lowball their prospects. The fallen growth stocks this fund likes, such as Home Depot, don't have to recapture their glory days, but the fund's models indicate they still deserve higher valuations, even with slower growth, the managers said.

The fund's consistent process, low costs, and deep, seasoned management team mean it should have plenty of good years ahead of it.

Address:	P.O. Box 2600
	Valley Forge PA 19482
	800-997-2798
Web Address:	www.vanguard.com
Inception:	06-29-00 *
Advisor:	American Century Investment Management
Subadvisor:	None
NTF Plans:	Vanguard NTF

Minimum Purchase:	$3000	Add: $100	IRA: $3000
Min Auto Inv Plan:	$3000	Add: $50	
Sales Fees:	No-load		
Management Fee:	0.37%		
Actual Fees:	Mgt:0.37%	Dist: —	
Expense Projections:	3Yr:$125	5Yr:$219	10Yr:$493
Income Distrib:	Annually		

Historical Profile
Return	Average
Risk	Average
Rating	★★★ Neutral

Investment Style: Equity, Stock %

92% 92% 94% 95% 99% 97% 95%

▼ Manager Change
▽ Partial Manager Change

15.5
12.5 — Growth of $10,000
10.0 — Investment Values of Fund
— Investment Values of S&P 500
5.0

Performance Quartile (within Category)

	1995	1996	1997	1998	1999	2000	2001	2002	2003	2004	2005	2006	History
	—	—	—	—	—	11.24	11.47	9.56	12.27	13.75	13.48	14.74	NAV
	—	—	—	—	—	12.97*	2.94	-15.27	30.26	13.70	6.37	14.10	Total Return %
	—	—	—	—	—	—	14.83	6.83	1.58	2.82	1.46	-1.69	+/-S&P 500
	—	—	—	—	—	—	8.53	0.25	0.23	-2.79	-0.68	-8.15	+/-Russ 1000 VI
	—	—	—	—	—	—	0.89	1.39	1.88	1.63	2.04	1.71	Income Return %
	—	—	—	—	—	—	2.05	-16.66	28.38	12.07	4.33	12.39	Capital Return %
	—	—	—	—	—	—	19	29	31	42	39	91	Total Rtn % Rank Cat
	—	—	—	—	—	0.08	0.10	0.16	0.18	0.20	0.28	0.23	Income $
	—	—	—	—	—	0.00	0.00	0.00	0.00	0.00	0.88	0.41	Capital Gains $
	—	—	—	—	—	0.58	0.51	0.54	0.63	0.49	0.39	0.39	Expense Ratio %
	—	—	—	—	—	2.08	1.67	1.36	1.72	1.61	2.08	2.09	Income Ratio %
	—	—	—	—	—	18	54	46	50	56	52	57	Turnover Rate %
	—	—	—	—	—	107	436	451	534	881	1,013	1,512	Net Assets $mil

Rating and Risk

Time Period	Load-Adj Return %	Morningstar Rtn vs Cat	Morningstar Risk vs Cat	Morningstar Risk-Adj Rating
1 Yr	14.10			
3 Yr	11.33	Avg	+Avg	★★★
5 Yr	8.78	Avg	Avg	★★★
10 Yr	—	—	—	—
Incept	9.19			

Other Measures	Standard Index S&P 500	Best Fit Index Russ 1000 VI
Alpha	0.7	-3.9
Beta	1.03	1.05
R-Squared	85	85
Standard Deviation	7.67	
Mean	11.33	
Sharpe Ratio	1.03	

Portfolio Analysis 09-30-06

Share change since 06-06 Total Stocks:351	Sector	PE	Tot Ret%	% Assets
⊕ Pfizer Inc.	Health	15.2	15.22	5.47
⊕ Citigroup, Inc.	Financial	13.1	19.55	4.64
⊕ Verizon Communications	Telecom	15.9	34.88	4.21
⊕ Merck & Co., Inc.	Health	19.1	42.66	3.58
⊕ AT&T, Inc.	Telecom	18.2	51.59	3.46
⊖ American International G	Financial	17.0	6.05	2.32
⊖ ExxonMobil Corporation	Energy	11.1	39.07	2.25
⊖ Fannie Mae	Financial	—	24.34	2.15
⊕ Home Depot, Inc.	Consumer	13.5	1.01	2.03
⊖ Wal-Mart Stores, Inc.	Consumer	16.9	0.13	1.90
⊕ Morgan Stanley	Financial	12.3	45.93	1.80
⊖ Bank of America Corporat	Financial	12.4	20.68	1.74
Altria Group, Inc.	Goods	16.3	19.87	1.70
⊕ J.P. Morgan Chase & Co.	Financial	13.6	25.60	1.62
⊕ Freddie Mac	Financial	23.3	7.06	1.44
⊖ Hewlett-Packard Company	Hardware	19.3	45.21	1.24
⊕ National City Corporatio	Financial	12.0	13.67	1.16
⊕ Washington Mutual, Inc.	Financial	13.4	9.62	1.15
⊖ UnitedHealth Group, Inc.	Health	20.8	-13.49	1.14
⊕ Lowe's Companies Inc.	Consumer	15.6	-6.05	1.12

Current Investment Style

Value Blnd Growth — Large / Mid / Small

Market Cap	%
Giant	50.0
Large	27.5
Mid	19.0
Small	3.5
Micro	0.0
Avg $mil:	37,419

Value Measures		Rel Category
Price/Earnings	13.23	0.96
Price/Book	2.15	0.97
Price/Sales	0.87	0.67
Price/Cash Flow	3.32	0.50
Dividend Yield %	2.25	0.97

Growth Measures	%	Rel Category
Long-Term Erngs	10.21	0.98
Book Value	8.29	1.05
Sales	7.50	0.83
Cash Flow	3.89	0.64
Historical Erngs	10.22	0.63

Profitability	%	Rel Category
Return on Equity	17.04	0.95
Return on Assets	10.22	1.04
Net Margin	13.04	1.01

Sector Weightings

	% of Stocks	Rel S&P 500	3 Year High	Low
↻ Info	15.62	0.78		
▯ Software	0.50	0.14	2	0
▯ Hardware	3.71	0.40	5	3
▯ Media	1.80	0.47	2	0
▮ Telecom	9.61	2.74	10	7
⊆ Service	67.18	1.45		
▮ Health	15.57	1.29	16	8
▯ Consumer	12.89	1.68	16	12
▮ Business	3.81	0.90	4	3
▮ Financial	34.91	1.57	35	22
◻ Mfg	17.20	0.51		
▮ Goods	7.42	0.87	12	7
▮ Ind Mtrls	5.13	0.43	10	5
▮ Energy	4.29	0.44	12	4
▮ Utilities	0.36	0.10	6	0

Composition

● Cash	4.7
● Stocks	95.3
◐ Bonds	0.0
○ Other	0.0
Foreign	0.0
(% of Stock)	

Vanguard Val Idx

	Ticker	Load	NAV	Yield	Total Assets	Mstar Category
	VIVAX	None	$26.58	2.2%	$10,896 mil	Large Value

Governance and Management

Stewardship Grade: B

Portfolio Manager(s)

In 2005, Vanguard began listing Gerard O'Reilly as this fund's day-to-day manager. Former manager, Gus Sauter, has scaled back his managerial responsibilities since becoming the firm's CIO in 2003. O'Reilly has been with Vanguard since 1992, and he's worked closely with Sauter on this offering since 1994. He also runs Vanguard Total Stock Market Index, Vanguard Growth Index, and Vanguard Small Cap Growth Index.

Strategy

This fund tracks the MSCI U.S. Prime Market Value Index, which consists of the value stocks within a universe of the 750 largest U.S. companies (in terms of free-float market cap). MSCI classifies stocks as growth or value using an eight-factor model and also employs "buffer zones" to limit the migration of stocks between the growth and value camps and, thus, turnover.

Performance 12-31-06

	1st Qtr	2nd Qtr	3rd Qtr	4th Qtr	Total
2002	1.32	-10.69	-20.45	9.88	-20.91
2003	-5.61	20.27	2.24	13.93	32.25
2004	2.12	1.56	1.24	9.80	15.29
2005	-0.42	1.70	4.08	1.60	7.09
2006	5.29	0.91	6.63	7.82	22.15

Trailing	Total Return%	+/- S&P 500	+/- Russ 1000 VI	%Rank Cat	Growth of $10,000
3 Mo	7.82	1.12	-0.18	26	10,782
6 Mo	14.96	2.22	0.24	12	11,496
1 Yr	22.15	6.36	-0.10	7	12,215
3 Yr Avg	14.68	4.24	-0.41	12	15,082
5 Yr Avg	9.54	3.35	-1.32	25	15,771
10 Yr Avg	9.46	1.04	-1.54	36	24,692
15 Yr Avg	—	—	—	—	—

Tax Analysis	Tax-Adj Rtn%	%Rank Cat	Tax-Cost Rat	%Rank Cat
3 Yr (estimated)	14.26	7	0.37	14
5 Yr (estimated)	9.06	16	0.44	24
10 Yr (estimated)	8.13	29	1.22	31

Potential Capital Gain Exposure: 20% of assets

Morningstar's Take by Reginald Laing 12-22-06

Vanguard Value Index has benefited from a strong market in large-value stocks, but remains attractive.

Style-specific index offerings tend to have their best relative performance when the segment of the market they track is in favor. Such has been the case recently with this fund. As large-value has comfortably outpaced the other squares of the Morningstar Style Box in the past year, this fund's nearly pure large-value exposure and low expense ratio have lifted it relative to its category: For the trailing 12 months through Dec. 21, 2006, its 20.9% gain topped those of 93% of its large-value peers.

Of course, recent performance isn't a strong predictor of future returns, and one can't expect this fund to trounce its peer group indefinitely. In particular, when market leadership rotates elsewhere, this fund may have difficulty keeping up: Its actively managed peers will be able to drift into more growth-oriented stocks or down the market-cap ladder when those segments of the

market pull ahead, while this passive fund will mostly have to stick to its corner of the style box.

But the case for this fund is as compelling as ever. First, it's one of retail investors' cheapest options in the category. So, while active managers might outpace this fund over short periods by chasing this or that hot area of the market, this fund's sizable expense advantage should make it tough to beat over long stretches of time. Also, even though this fund has posted strong gains recently, there's reason to think it still has room to appreciate. Of this fund's top 10 holdings, nine are trading at discounts to what Morningstar's stock analysts consider their fair value--financial-services company J.P. Morgan Chase at a sizable discount--which should at least give investors here a decent margin of safety.

Looking longer term, we think this fund has enduring merit for value-leaning investors in search of a core fund.

Address:	PO Box 2600	Minimum Purchase:	$3000	Add: $100	IRA: $3000
	Valley Forge PA 19482	Min Auto Inv Plan:	$3000	Add: $50	
	800-997-2798	Sales Fees:	No-load		
Web Address:	www.vanguard.com	Management Fee:	0.18%		
Inception:	11-02-92	Actual Fees:	Mgt:0.18%	Dist: —	
Advisor:	Vanguard Advisers, Inc.	Expense Projections:	3Yr:$68	5Yr:$118	10Yr:$268
Subadvisor:	None	Income Distrib:	Quarterly		
NTF Plans:	Vanguard NTF				

Historical Profile
Return Above Avg
Risk Above Avg
Rating ★★★ Neutral

99%	98%	98%	100%	100%	100%	100%	99%	100%		

Investment Style
Equity
Stock %

▼ Manager Change
▽ Partial Manager Change

Growth of $10,000
— Investment Values of Fund
— Investment Values of S&P 500

38.0
31.0
24.0
17.0
10.0

Performance Quartile (within Category)

1995	1996	1997	1998	1999	2000	2001	2002	2003	2004	2005	2006	History
14.80	17.02	20.85	22.51	22.89	22.87	18.90	14.65	18.95	21.35	22.29	26.58	NAV
37.03	21.78	29.77	14.64	12.57	6.08	-11.88	-20.91	32.25	15.29	7.09	22.15	Total Return %
-0.55	-1.18	-3.59	-13.94	-8.47	15.18	0.01	1.19	3.57	4.41	2.18	6.36	+/-S&P 500
-1.33	0.14	-5.41	-0.99	5.22	-0.93	-6.29	-5.39	2.22	-1.20	0.04	-0.10	+/-Russ 1000 VI
3.64	2.62	2.22	1.77	1.66	1.60	1.44	1.68	2.56	2.44	2.62	2.68	Income Return %
33.39	19.16	27.55	12.87	10.91	4.48	-13.32	-22.59	29.69	12.85	4.47	19.47	Capital Return %
12	26	26	32	20	67	91	72	18	24	32	7	Total Rtn % Rank Cat
0.40	0.38	0.37	0.36	0.36	0.36	0.32	0.32	0.37	0.46	0.55	0.59	Income $
0.00	0.57	0.75	0.99	1.96	0.98	0.98	0.00	0.00	0.00	0.00	0.00	Capital Gains $
0.20	0.20	0.20	0.22	0.22	0.22	0.22	0.23	0.23	0.21	0.21	—	Expense Ratio %
3.06	2.54	2.05	1.72	1.59	1.60	1.51	1.80	2.38	2.40	2.63	—	Income Ratio %
27	29	25	33	41	37	38	26	48	18	21	—	Turnover Rate %
496	1,016	1,796	2,421	3,378	3,450	3,018	2,197	2,921	3,592	3,376	4,417	Net Assets $mil

Rating and Risk

Time Period	Load-Adj Return %	Morningstar Rtn vs Cat	Morningstar Risk vs Cat	Morningstar Risk-Adj Rating
1 Yr	22.15			
3 Yr	14.68	+Avg	-Avg	★★★★
5 Yr	9.54	+Avg	+Avg	★★★
10 Yr	9.46	Avg	+Avg	★★★
Incept	12.07			

Other Measures	Standard Index S&P 500	Best Fit Index Russ 1000 VI
Alpha	4.6	0.0
Beta	0.89	0.96
R-Squared	87	98
Standard Deviation	6.60	
Mean	14.68	
Sharpe Ratio	1.65	

Portfolio Analysis 09-30-06

Share change since 06-06 Total Stocks:413	Sector	PE	Tot Ret%	% Assets
⊕ ExxonMobil Corporation	Energy	11.1	39.07	5.97
⊕ General Electric Company	Ind Mtrls	20.0	9.35	5.39
⊕ Citigroup, Inc.	Financial	13.1	19.55	3.63
⊕ Bank of America Corporat	Financial	12.4	20.68	3.59
⊕ Pfizer Inc.	Health	15.2	15.22	3.05
⊕ J.P. Morgan Chase & Co.	Financial	13.6	25.60	2.40
⊕ Altria Group, Inc.	Goods	16.3	19.87	2.35
⊕ Chevron Corporation	Energy	9.0	33.76	2.11
⊕ AT&T, Inc.	Telecom	18.2	51.59	1.86
⊕ Wells Fargo Company	Financial	14.7	16.82	1.70
⊕ Verizon Communications	Telecom	15.9	34.88	1.59
⊕ Wachovia Corporation	Financial	12.9	12.02	1.57
⊕ Coca-Cola Company	Goods	21.7	23.10	1.39
⊕ ConocoPhillips	Energy	6.5	26.53	1.37
⊕ Merck & Co., Inc.	Health	19.1	42.66	1.34
⊕ BellSouth Corporation	Telecom	—	—	1.14
⊕ Time Warner, Inc.	Media	19.6	26.37	1.12
⊕ Abbott Laboratories	Health	24.3	26.88	1.09
⊕ Morgan Stanley	Financial	12.3	45.93	1.03
⊕ Merrill Lynch & Company,	Financial	14.2	39.28	1.01

Current Investment Style

Value Blnd Growth — Large Mid Small

Market Cap	%
Giant	51.5
Large	32.0
Mid	16.5
Small	0.0
Micro	0.0

Avg $mil: 49,881

Value Measures		Rel Category
Price/Earnings	13.02	0.95
Price/Book	2.17	0.98
Price/Sales	1.28	0.98
Price/Cash Flow	5.17	0.77
Dividend Yield %	2.70	1.16

Growth Measures	%	Rel Category
Long-Term Erngs	9.39	0.90
Book Value	7.53	0.95
Sales	9.24	1.03
Cash Flow	5.98	0.99
Historical Erngs	14.56	0.90

Profitability	%	Rel Category
Return on Equity	17.07	0.95
Return on Assets	10.02	1.02
Net Margin	14.62	1.13

Sector Weightings	% of Stocks	Rel S&P 500	3 Year High	Low
↻ Info	10.27	0.51		
Software	0.31	0.09	2	0
Hardware	2.69	0.29	4	2
Media	1.94	0.51	4	2
Telecom	5.33	1.52	5	4
⊖ Service	48.78	1.06		
Health	8.85	0.73	9	5
Consumer	3.56	0.47	4	3
Business	1.39	0.33	2	1
Financial	34.98	1.57	36	33
Mfg	40.96	1.21		
Goods	8.19	0.96	8	7
Ind Mtrls	13.46	1.13	20	12
Energy	13.00	1.33	16	11
Utilities	6.31	1.80	6	5

Composition

● Cash	0.2	
● Stocks	99.8	
● Bonds	0.0	
● Other	0.0	
	Foreign	0.1
	(% of Stock)	

MORNINGSTAR® Funds 500

Vanguard Wellesley Inc

Analyst Pick ✓

	Ticker	Load	NAV	Yield	Total Assets	Mstar Category
	VWINX	None	$21.81	4.1%	$12,612 mil	Conservative Allocation

Governance and Management

Stewardship Grade: A

Portfolio Manager(s)

This fund boasts one of the most experienced management teams around. Earl McEvoy has been running the fixed-income portfolio for more than two decades. Jack Ryan, who also runs part of Vanguard Equity-Income, has been managing the equity portion of this fund since 1986. Both are senior vice presidents at Wellington Management.

Strategy

Comanager Jack Ryan, who runs the equity portion of the fund, is a yield-oriented contrarian. The fund typically has little exposure to growth-oriented sectors such as technology. The fund's bond stake (about 60% of assets) is run by veteran manager Earl McEvoy, who keeps the portfolio concentrated in higher-quality issues. The fund often has a longer duration (a measure of interest-rate sensitivity) than many of its peers, leaving it vulnerable to rising rates.

Historical Profile

Return	High
Risk	Average
Rating	★★★★ Highest

Investment Style: Equity / Stock %

Percentages: 36% 40% 37% 36% 36% 39% 39% 37% 38%

▼ Manager Change
▽ Partial Manager Change

Growth of $10,000
■ Investment Values of Fund
— Investment Values of DJ Mod

Scale: 30.8 / 26.8 / 22.0 / 18.0 / 14.0 / 10.0

Performance Quartile (within Category)

	1995	1996	1997	1998	1999	2000	2001	2002	2003	2004	2005	2006	History
NAV	20.44	20.51	21.86	22.12	18.85	20.34	19.91	19.90	20.91	21.58	21.07	21.81	NAV
Total Return %	28.91	9.42	20.19	11.84	-4.14	16.17	7.39	4.64	9.66	7.57	3.48	11.28	Total Return %
+/-DJ Mod	9.11	-1.24	8.29	-0.48	-21.47	17.84	10.19	11.41	-17.72	-5.40	-3.51	-1.02	+/-DJ Mod
+/-DJ 40%	10.75	0.53	6.09	0.11	-12.00	9.38	4.17	8.66	-8.00	-1.44	-1.21	3.82	+/-DJ 40%
Income Return %	6.84	5.82	6.01	5.31	5.20	5.74	5.06	4.65	4.44	4.08	4.08	4.42	Income Return %
Capital Return %	22.07	3.60	14.18	6.53	-9.34	10.43	2.33	-0.01	5.22	3.49	-0.60	6.86	Capital Return %
Total Rtn % Rank Cat	1	61	9	27	97	7	5	4	76	22	47	10	Total Rtn % Rank Cat
Income $	1.14	1.16	1.20	1.13	1.12	1.06	1.00	0.91	0.87	0.84	0.87	0.92	Income $
Capital Gains $	0.28	0.60	1.44	1.14	1.25	0.40	0.86	0.40	0.00	0.38	0.67	0.67	Capital Gains $
Expense Ratio %	0.34	0.31	0.31	0.31	0.30	0.31	0.33	0.30	0.31	0.26	0.24	0.25	Expense Ratio %
Income Ratio %	5.96	5.74	5.47	5.05	5.22	5.39	4.88	4.72	4.33	4.06	3.98	4.21	Income Ratio %
Turnover Rate %	30	26	36	32	20	28	24	43	28	23	18	19	Turnover Rate %
Net Assets $mil	7,181	7,013	7,646	8,498	6,976	6,558	6,495	7,484	8,439	9,268	7,614	7,743	Net Assets $mil

Performance 12-31-06

	1st Qtr	2nd Qtr	3rd Qtr	4th Qtr	Total
2002	2.01	1.09	-3.88	5.57	4.64
2003	-1.56	7.98	-1.32	4.54	9.66
2004	2.21	-1.41	3.10	3.55	7.57
2005	-0.27	2.91	0.62	0.21	3.48
2006	0.99	1.01	5.27	3.63	11.28

Trailing	Total Return%	+/- DJ Mod	+/- DJ 40%	%Rank Cat	Growth of $10,000
3 Mo	3.63	-1.96	0.59	42	10,363
6 Mo	9.09	0.30	2.53	9	10,909
1 Yr	11.28	-1.02	3.82	10	11,128
3 Yr Avg	7.40	-3.32	0.36	18	12,388
5 Yr Avg	7.29	-2.73	0.56	10	14,217
10 Yr Avg	8.62	0.07	0.92	5	22,861
15 Yr Avg	9.38	0.17	1.26	13	38,377

Tax Analysis	Tax-Adj Rtn%	%Rank Cat	Tax-Cost Rat	%Rank Cat
3 Yr (estimated)	5.87	20	1.42	78
5 Yr (estimated)	5.73	11	1.45	77
10 Yr (estimated)	6.08	7	2.34	94

Potential Capital Gain Exposure: 10% of assets

Morningstar's Take by Dan Culloton 11-20-06

Vanguard Wellesley Income's contrarian instincts serve it well.

You might ask, "How can you call a fund with a nearly 14% stake in what has been, until recently, one of the hottest sectors of recent years--energy--a contrarian?" History shows this fund has negotiated the recent years' energy rally with its cross-grain investor credentials intact, though. Equity manager John Ryan increased the stock sleeve's energy stake early in the decade, peaking at 19% of stocks in March 2004, while the Russell 1000 Value's energy helping was around 10%. As energy has rallied and claimed a bigger portion of the index and rivals' portfolios, Ryan has reined in the fund's exposure to such stocks. What's more, virtually all of the fund's energy-stock exposure is in major integrated oil firms, such as Royal Dutch Shell and ExxonMobil, that aren't as richly valued as other areas in the sector.

If that doesn't convince you that the fund hasn't lost its penchant for the out of favor, consider its purchase in the first half of 2006 of drugmaker Bristol-Myers Squibb. Ryan thought the market missed the company's strong cash flow and drug pipeline as it fretted over generic competition for its Plavix blood thinner and tactical mistakes by the firm's management.

The fund also has maintained its discipline on the fixed-income side. Earlier this year, manager Earl McEvoy extended duration (a measure of interest-rate sensitivity) out a bit because he thinks the economy, though slowing, won't sink into a recession.

The fund's longer-than-average duration and the equity portfolio's focus on high-yielding stocks, including many utilities stocks, make the fund more sensitive to interest rates. Out-of-favor stocks such as Bristol-Myers can take a while to work out, too. Still, the fund's veteran managers, low expenses, and consistent approach make it a worthwhile long-term holding.

Rating and Risk

Time Period	Load-Adj Return %	Morningstar Rtn vs Cat	Morningstar Risk vs Cat	Morningstar Risk-Adj Rating
1 Yr	11.28			
3 Yr	7.40	+Avg	Avg	★★★★
5 Yr	7.29	+Avg	Avg	★★★★
10 Yr	8.62	High	Avg	★★★★★
Incept	10.70			

Other Measures	Standard Index DJ Mod	Best Fit Index Mstar Large Value
Alpha	1.4	0.1
Beta	0.36	0.34
R-Squared	41	48

Standard Deviation	3.38
Mean	7.40
Sharpe Ratio	1.20

Portfolio Analysis 09-30-06

Total Stocks:57 Share change since 06-30-06	Sectors	P/E Ratio	YTD Return %	% Net Assets
AT&T, Inc.	Telecom	18.2	-5.43	2.27
Bank of America Corporati	Financial	12.4	0.11	2.23
⊖ ExxonMobil Corporation	Energy	11.1	-5.19	1.86
Citigroup, Inc.	Financial	13.1	-1.17	1.73
FPL Group	Utilities	17.7	-0.29	1.70
⊕ Altria Group, Inc.	Goods	16.3	2.52	1.27
BellSouth Corporation	Telecom	—	—	1.26
⊕ General Electric Company	Ind Mtrls	20.0	0.91	1.15
PNC Financial Services Gr	Financial	8.7	1.22	1.15

Total Fixed-Income:372	Date of Maturity	Amount $000	Value $000	% Net Assets
Illinois St Go Bds 5.1%	06-01-33	91,400	87,572	0.72
General Elec Cap 6.75%	03-15-32	74,050	84,992	0.70
FHLBA 4.375%	03-17-10	80,000	78,712	0.64
President&Fellow Harvard	10-01-37	68,000	72,988	0.60
FHLMC 7%	03-15-10	64,000	68,207	0.56
Landwirtschaftliche Rente	07-15-08	67,000	65,980	0.54
KREDITANSTALT FUR WIEDERA	01-23-08	60,000	58,764	0.48
European Investment Bank	05-15-14	54,000	52,837	0.43
Wal Mart Stores 6.875%	08-10-09	50,000	52,355	0.43

Equity Style

Style: Value
Size: Large-Cap

Value Measures		Rel Category
Price/Earnings	13.43	0.89
Price/Book	2.47	1.02
Price/Sales	1.41	1.01
Price/Cash Flow	9.46	1.19
Dividend Yield %	3.47	1.62

Growth Measures	%	Rel Category
Long-Term Erngs	8.73	0.77
Book Value	7.31	0.92
Sales	10.80	1.22
Cash Flow	0.01	0.00
Historical Erngs	11.66	0.68

Market Cap %			
Giant	53.8	Small	0.0
Large	40.9	Micro	0.0
Mid	5.4	Avg $mil:	59,106

Fixed-Income Style

Duration: Interm-Term
Quality: High

Avg Eff Duration [1]	5.2 Yrs
Avg Eff Maturity	7.8 Yrs
Avg Credit Quality	AA
Avg Wtd Coupon	5.57%

[1]figure provided by fund as of 09-30-06

Sector Weightings	% of Stocks	Rel DJ Mod	3 Year High Low
☎ Info	12.35	—	
Software	0.40	—	0 0
Hardware	0.40	—	0 0
Media	0.00	—	0 0
Telecom	11.95	—	12 7
Service	38.50		
Health	6.88	—	7 4
Consumer	0.00	—	0 0
Business	1.55	—	2 0
Financial	30.07	—	33 30
Mfg	49.15		
Goods	11.18	—	11 8
Ind Mtrls	13.60	—	19 13
Energy	11.15	—	19 11
Utilities	13.22	—	17 10

Composition

● Cash	3.0
● Stocks	37.9
● Bonds	59.0
● Other	0.1
Foreign	5.4
(% of Stock)	

Address:	PO Box 2600 Valley Forge PA 19482 800-997-2798	Minimum Purchase:	$3000	Add: $100 IRA: $3000
		Min Auto Inv Plan:	$3000	Add: $50
Web Address:	www.vanguard.com	Sales Fees:	No-load	
Inception:	07-01-70	Management Fee:	0.22%	
Advisor:	Wellington Management Company, LLP	Actual Fees:	Mgt:0.22%	Dist: —
Subadvisor:	None	Expense Projections:	3Yr:$77	5Yr:$135 10Yr:$306
NTF Plans:	Vanguard NTF	Income Distrib:	Quarterly	

Morningstar® Funds 500

Vanguard Wellington

Analyst Pick	Ticker	Load	NAV	Yield	Total Assets	Mstar Category
✔	VWELX	None	$32.43	2.9%	$45,718 mil	Moderate Allocation

Governance and Management

Stewardship Grade: A

Portfolio Manager(s)

Paul Kaplan, the manager of this fund's bond portfolio, retired on June 30, 2006. His replacement, John Keogh, has been with Wellington Management, this fund's subadvisor, since 1983 and has worked with Kaplan on this fund for the last two years. Ed Bousa, who took over the equity portfolio at the end of 2002, did a solid job managing Putnam Equity Income from late 1992 through early 2000. Kaplan, Keogh, and Bousa each have more than $1 million invested in the fund.

Strategy

This fund's fixed-income sleeve got a new manager in mid-2006, but we don't expect drastic changes to the strategy. The bond portfolio typically emphasizes high-quality issues, but it has often taken on a modest amount of interest-rate risk. On the stock side, Ed Bousa looks for dividend-paying companies with modest valuations and decent fundamentals. The fund is typically light on technology stocks and has plenty of exposure to value-oriented fare.

Performance 12-31-06

	1st Qtr	2nd Qtr	3rd Qtr	4th Qtr	Total
2002	3.30	-4.58	-11.04	6.17	-6.90
2003	-3.35	12.55	1.37	9.50	20.75
2004	2.19	0.41	1.65	6.58	11.17
2005	-0.53	1.71	4.22	1.31	6.82
2006	2.99	0.69	5.07	5.48	14.93

Trailing	Total Return%	+/- DJ Mod	+/- DJ US Mod	%Rank Cat	Growth of $10,000
3 Mo	5.48	-0.11	0.81	32	10,548
6 Mo	10.83	2.04	2.93	13	11,083
1 Yr	14.93	2.63	4.66	8	11,493
3 Yr Avg	10.93	0.21	1.81	11	13,650
5 Yr Avg	8.94	-1.08	1.34	7	15,344
10 Yr Avg	9.79	1.24	1.20	8	25,446
15 Yr Avg	11.01	1.80	1.62	8	47,911

Tax Analysis	Tax-Adj Rtn%	%Rank Cat	Tax-Cost Rat	%Rank Cat
3 Yr (estimated)	9.46	10	1.33	67
5 Yr (estimated)	7.64	7	1.19	73
10 Yr (estimated)	7.69	9	1.91	77

Potential Capital Gain Exposure: 21% of assets

Historical Profile

Return	High
Risk	Average
Rating	★★★★ Highest

	60%	65%	63%	67%	65%	66%	65%	65%	65%

▼ Manager Change
▽ Partial Manager Change

37.0
32.0
25.0 **Growth of $10,000**
20.0 ▬ Investment Values of Fund
15.0 ── Investment Values of DJ Mod
10.0

Performance Quartile (within Category)

1995	1996	1997	1998	1999	2000	2001	2002	2003	2004	2005	2006	History
24.43	26.15	29.45	29.35	27.96	28.21	27.26	24.56	28.81	30.19	30.35	32.43	NAV
32.92	16.19	23.23	12.06	4.41	10.40	4.19	-6.90	20.75	11.17	6.82	14.93	Total Return %
13.12	5.53	11.33	-0.26	-12.92	12.07	6.99	-0.13	-6.63	-1.80	-0.17	2.63	+/-DJ Mod
8.15	4.85	4.03	-0.33	-8.44	5.96	4.03	3.64	-3.31	0.00	0.82	4.66	+/-DJ US Mod
5.08	4.40	4.34	3.89	3.94	3.88	3.41	3.12	3.15	3.07	3.01	3.27	Income Return %
27.84	11.79	18.89	8.17	0.47	6.52	0.78	-10.02	17.60	8.10	3.81	11.66	Capital Return %
7	34	21	59	82	10	6	10	45	17	18	8	Total Rtn % Rank Cat
0.97	1.06	1.12	1.13	1.14	1.07	0.95	0.84	0.77	0.88	0.90	0.98	Income $
0.28	1.11	1.57	2.44	1.50	1.48	1.12	0.00	0.00	0.91	0.97	1.40	Capital Gains $
0.33	0.31	0.29	0.31	0.30	0.31	0.36	0.36	0.36	0.31	0.29	—	Expense Ratio %
4.37	4.08	3.97	3.68	3.74	3.77	3.42	3.18	3.00	2.99	2.93	—	Income Ratio %
24	30	27	29	22	33	33	25	28	24	24	—	Turnover Rate %
12,656	16,190	21,812	25,761	25,529	22,799	21,724	19,495	24,326	28,328	26,251	29,675	Net Assets $mil

Investment Style

Equity
Stock %

Rating and Risk

Time Period	Load-Adj Return %	Morningstar Rtn vs Cat	Morningstar Risk vs Cat	Morningstar Risk-Adj Rating
1 Yr	14.93			
3 Yr	10.93	High	-Avg	★★★★★
5 Yr	8.94	High	Avg	★★★★★
10 Yr	9.79	+Avg	Avg	★★★★★
Incept	8.38			

Other Measures	Standard Index DJ Mod	Best Fit Index Russ 1000 VI
Alpha	1.9	-0.2
Beta	0.75	0.67
R-Squared	85	90
Standard Deviation	4.81	
Mean	10.93	
Sharpe Ratio	1.54	

Portfolio Analysis 09-30-06

Total Stocks:111

Share change since 06-30-06	Sectors	P/E Ratio	YTD Return %	% Net Assets
Bank of America Corporati	Financial	12.4	0.11	2.21
General Electric Company	Ind Mtrls	20.0	0.91	1.95
Citigroup, Inc.	Financial	13.1	-1.17	1.65
AT&T, Inc.	Telecom	18.2	-5.43	1.54
⊕ Chevron Corporation	Energy	9.0	-2.83	1.47
⊕ Total SA ADR	Energy	10.6	-4.37	1.46
ExxonMobil Corporation	Energy	11.1	-5.19	1.42
Exelon Corporation	Utilities	—	-2.67	1.29
⊖ Abbott Laboratories	Health	24.3	2.81	1.28

Total Fixed-Income:2330

	Date of Maturity	Amount $000	Value $000	% Net Assets
US Treasury Bond 5.25%	02-15-29	364,975	385,848	0.90
US Treasury Note 5%	08-15-11	230,000	234,421	0.54
FNMA 3.25%	11-15-07	100,000	97,987	0.23
Household Fin 6.375%	10-15-11	75,000	78,589	0.18
Proc & Gambl Pft Shr Tr &	01-01-21	60,008	75,408	0.18
Japan Fin 4.625%	04-21-15	75,000	72,563	0.17
Illinois St Go Bds 5.1%	06-01-33	75,000	71,859	0.17
SIEMENS FIN NV	10-17-16	69,650	70,976	0.16
BARCLAYS BK PLC	12-15-49	70,000	70,662	0.16

Equity Style

Style: Value
Size: Large-Cap

Value Measures		Rel Category
Price/Earnings	14.60	0.96
Price/Book	2.42	0.98
Price/Sales	1.50	1.09
Price/Cash Flow	4.81	0.59
Dividend Yield %	2.42	1.25

Growth Measures	%	Rel Category
Long-Term Erngs	10.40	0.89
Book Value	7.27	0.84
Sales	9.67	1.09
Cash Flow	4.40	0.45
Historical Erngs	12.53	0.70

Market Cap %			
Giant	59.5	Small	0.0
Large	35.6	Micro	0.0
Mid	4.8	Avg $mil:	61,637

Fixed-Income Style

Duration: Interm-Term
Quality: High

Avg Eff Duration [1]	4.6 Yrs
Avg Eff Maturity	7.0 Yrs
Avg Credit Quality	AA
Avg Wtd Coupon	5.65%

[1]figure provided by fund as of 09-30-06

Sector Weightings	% of Stocks	Rel DJ Mod	3 Year High Low	
⟳ Info	16.64	—		
Software	1.68	—	2	1
Hardware	5.24	—	7	5
Media	4.54	—	5	3
Telecom	5.18	—	6	4
⟲ Service	40.30	—		
Health	11.05	—	11	9
Consumer	4.95	—	5	2
Business	5.49	—	8	5
Financial	18.81	—	20	18
Mfg	43.06	—		
Goods	7.96	—	9	7
Ind Mtrls	16.08	—	19	16
Energy	13.46	—	17	12
Utilities	5.56	—	6	5

Composition

	%
Cash	4.6
Stocks	65.1
Bonds	30.2
Other	0.1
Foreign (% of Stock)	17.3

Morningstar's Take by Dan Culloton 11-20-06

Vanguard Wellington has gotten more accessible.

Vanguard in November 2006 lifted restrictions meant to quell inflows into this fund. There is no longer any annual limit to the amount of money investors can put into this offering, though new owners would still need $10,000 to open an account. Due to this fund's status as one of the biggest funds in the moderate-allocation category, we wouldn't have minded if Vanguard left the limitations in place. It's important to control asset flows because when a fund grows too large, it can be hard for the manager to buy and sell stocks without affecting the securities' prices and hurting the portfolio's performance. For that reason, we'll be watching this fund closely for signs of bloat.

But for now, the fund's girth shouldn't keep anyone from considering it. Vanguard's decision earlier this year to increase the fund's minimum initial investment and to restrict additional investments from existing fund owners helped stem inflows, and the fund family has been proactive in

this area in the past. Furthermore this offering's value-oriented, cross-grain style also lends itself well to managing large sums. Equity manager Ed Bousa often buys when most others are selling, as recent health-care purchases such as Medtronic show.

There are other reasons to have confidence in the fund. Few funds can compete with its 0.29% expense ratio, and it has two solid managers at the helm. John Keogh took over the bond side of the portfolio from Paul Kaplan earlier this year, but he's worked on this portfolio before and has been with subadvisor Wellington Management for more than two decades. Bousa has managed portfolios since 1992 and has skippered the fund's equity side for nearly four years. Together, they patiently craft a broadly diversified portfolio of high-quality bonds and dividend-paying stocks with generally low valuations. That combination has produced consistently strong long-term returns. So it's all right to stay the course with this fund.

Address:	PO Box 2600 Valley Forge PA 19482 800-997-2798	Minimum Purchase:	$10000	Add: $100	IRA: $10000
Web Address:	www.vanguard.com	Min Auto Inv Plan:	$10000	Add: $50
Inception:	07-01-29	Sales Fees:	No-load
Advisor:	Wellington Management Company, LLP	Management Fee:	0.28%
Subadvisor:	None	Actual Fees:	Mgt:0.28%	Dist: —
NTF Plans:	Vanguard NTF	Expense Projections:	3Yr:$97	5Yr:$169	10Yr:$381
		Income Distrib:	Quarterly

Vanguard Windsor

	Ticker	Load	NAV	Yield	Total Assets	Mstar Category
	VWNDX	None	$18.64	1.4%	$24,176 mil	Large Value

Governance and Management

Stewardship Grade: B

Portfolio Manager(s)

Wellington Management runs roughly two thirds of the fund's assets. On June 30, 2004, David Fassnacht of Wellington took over lead-management responsibilities from Charles Freeman, who had been in charge since late 1995. Fassnacht, in turn, is backed by a deep and experienced team. Since mid-1999, Sanford C. Bernstein has managed 30% of the fund's assets. Bernstein is a value shop, but it takes a more diversified approach.

Strategy

Vanguard Windsor likes them cheap: Its managers buys stocks when they've fallen hard. They readily add to holdings on weakness--including cyclical issues and fallen growth names--and are not shy about grabbing mid-cap names when they look attractive.

Historical Profile
Return Average
Risk High
Rating ★★★ Neutral

96%	96%	96%	98%	95%	94%	96%	95%	95%

▼ Manager Change
▽ Partial Manager Change

Growth of $10,000
— Investment Values of Fund
— Investment Values of S&P 500

38.0
31.0
24.0
17.0
10.0

Investment Style
Equity
Stock %

Performance Quartile (within Category)

1995	1996	1997	1998	1999	2000	2001	2002	2003	2004	2005	2006	History
14.53	16.59	16.98	15.57	15.17	15.29	15.64	12.00	16.26	18.07	17.15	18.64	NAV
30.15	26.36	21.97	0.81	11.57	15.89	5.72	-22.25	37.01	13.38	4.99	19.35	Total Return %
-7.43	3.40	-11.39	-27.77	-9.47	24.99	17.61	-0.15	8.33	2.50	0.08	3.56	+/-S&P 500
-8.21	4.72	-13.21	-14.82	4.22	8.88	11.31	-6.73	6.98	-3.11	-2.06	-2.90	+/-Russ 1000 VI
3.68	2.84	1.94	1.48	1.74	1.79	1.31	1.09	1.38	1.61	1.47	1.65	Income Return %
26.47	23.52	20.03	-0.67	9.83	14.10	4.41	-23.34	35.63	11.77	3.52	17.70	Capital Return %
70	9	91	88	23	22	13	78	7	46	58	35	Total Rtn % Rank Cat
0.46	0.41	0.32	0.25	0.27	0.27	0.20	0.17	0.17	0.26	0.27	0.28	Income $
1.38	1.33	2.88	1.23	1.90	1.85	0.31	0.00	0.00	0.09	1.56	1.53	Capital Gains $
0.43	0.29	0.27	0.27	0.28	0.31	0.41	0.45	0.48	0.43	0.36	0.35	Expense Ratio %
3.01	2.75	1.89	1.31	1.56	1.75	1.37	1.16	1.27	1.32	1.47	1.50	Income Ratio %
32	34	61	48	56	41	33	30	23	28	32	38	Turnover Rate %
13,646	16,738	20,915	18,188	16,700	16,615	16,027	10,999	14,681	16,385	13,362	14,699	Net Assets $mil

Performance 12-31-06

	1st Qtr	2nd Qtr	3rd Qtr	4th Qtr	Total
2002	0.96	-13.36	-20.22	11.41	-22.25
2003	-3.75	18.77	4.77	14.39	37.01
2004	2.52	0.90	-1.68	11.46	13.38
2005	-1.99	1.81	2.07	3.09	4.99
2006	4.78	-0.88	4.19	10.29	19.35

Trailing	Total Return%	+/- S&P 500	+/- Russ 1000 VI	%Rank Cat	Growth of $10,000
3 Mo	10.29	3.59	2.29	2	11,029
6 Mo	14.91	2.17	0.19	13	11,491
1 Yr	19.35	3.56	-2.90	35	11,935
3 Yr Avg	12.42	1.98	-2.67	47	14,208
5 Yr Avg	8.64	2.45	-2.22	43	15,134
10 Yr Avg	9.79	1.37	-1.21	30	25,446
15 Yr Avg	12.44	1.80	-0.59	14	58,051

Tax Analysis	Tax-Adj Rtn%	%Rank Cat	Tax-Cost Rat	%Rank Cat
3 Yr (estimated)	11.12	42	1.16	46
5 Yr (estimated)	7.74	39	0.83	45
10 Yr (estimated)	7.76	36	1.85	69

Potential Capital Gain Exposure: 23% of assets

Rating and Risk

Time Period	Load-Adj Return %	Morningstar Rtn vs Cat	Morningstar Risk vs Cat	Morningstar Risk-Adj Rating
1 Yr	19.35			
3 Yr	12.42	Avg	+Avg	★★★
5 Yr	8.64	Avg	+Avg	★★★
10 Yr	9.79	Avg	High	★★★
Incept	12.58			

Other Measures	Standard Index S&P 500	Best Fit Index Russ 1000
Alpha	0.9	0.6
Beta	1.14	1.11
R-Squared	92	93
Standard Deviation	8.21	
Mean	12.42	
Sharpe Ratio	1.09	

Morningstar's Take by Dan Culloton 11-20-06

Vanguard Windsor can test your patience, as well as reward it.

This fund specializes in ostracized stocks. Accordingly, it occasionally looks out of favor itself, as it leaves popular market neighborhoods for shunned ones. This is why the fund has lagged most of its large-value peers in 2005 and for much of 2006 (though it improved in recent months). The fund shaved its energy exposure as those stocks ran up and moved into one-time growth darlings whose share prices have languished even as they have remained profitable.

Over time, however, manager David Fassnacht's contrarian predilections should serve this fund well. Indeed, while Fassnacht thinks the growth rates of many energy firms are peaking and not enough to justify their valuations, he believes some traditional growth stocks, such as Cisco Systems, still look cheap. Cisco rebounded smartly in 2006, but Fassnacht thinks it still could post steady double-digit earnings and cash-flow growth due to

its position as a leading supplier of broadband network gear. The fund's other subadvisor, a team from Sanford C. Bernstein, also has been finding more opportunities among larger and more growthier fare.

This migration has pushed the fund more toward the large-blend section of the Morningstar Style Box, which should help the portfolio hold up well relative to its peers if large-growth stocks rally. Indeed, this fund vaulted to the top decile of the large-value category in the three months ending Oct. 31, 2006, as software and hardware stocks led other sectors. However, even with its affinity for classic growth stocks, the portfolio's average valuation measures, such as price/cash, are below the category average, and several of the fund's holdings are priced under Morningstar equity analysts' fair value estimates.

All told, this fund's low costs, experienced management, and consistent contrarian strategy make it a valuable holding.

Portfolio Analysis 09-30-06

Share change since 06-06 Total Stocks:134

	Sector	PE	Tot Ret%	% Assets
Cisco Systems, Inc.	Hardware	30.1	59.64	4.55
⊖ Bank of America Corporat	Financial	12.4	20.68	4.35
⊖ Citigroup, Inc.	Financial	13.1	19.55	3.91
⊕ Comcast Corporation	Media	—		3.43
⊕ Wyeth	Health	17.2	12.88	3.30
Microsoft Corporation	Software	23.8	15.83	3.25
Tyco International, Ltd.	Ind Mtrls	15.7	6.83	2.85
Sprint Nextel Corporatio	Telecom	30.2	-10.44	2.48
Sanofi-Aventis ADR	Health	42.9	7.33	2.20
⊖ Alcoa, Inc.	Ind Mtrls	12.0	3.49	2.09
⊕ Applied Materials	Hardware	19.5	3.89	1.76
⊕ American International G	Financial	17.0	6.05	1.63
⊖ ExxonMobil Corporation	Energy	11.1	39.07	1.61
⊖ Goodrich Corporation	Ind Mtrls	12.9	12.95	1.48
⊕ Arrow Electronics, Inc.	Business	12.4	-1.50	1.46
E.I. du Pont de Nemours	Ind Mtrls	18.4	18.64	1.45
⊕ R. H. Donnelley Corporat	Business	—	1.82	1.37
Flextronics Internationa	Hardware	45.1	9.96	1.20
⊕ Time Warner, Inc.	Media	19.6	26.37	1.20
ACE, Ltd.	Financial	10.6	15.41	1.18

Current Investment Style

Value Blnd Growth — Large Mid Small

Market Cap	%
Giant	54.5
Large	27.9
Mid	16.8
Small	0.7
Micro	0.0

Avg $mil: 44,994

Value Measures		Rel Category
Price/Earnings	13.94	1.02
Price/Book	1.85	0.83
Price/Sales	1.05	0.81
Price/Cash Flow	4.81	0.72
Dividend Yield %	2.05	0.88

Growth Measures	%	Rel Category
Long-Term Erngs	10.72	1.03
Book Value	8.44	1.07
Sales	5.40	0.60
Cash Flow	6.46	1.07
Historical Erngs	15.17	0.94

Profitability	%	Rel Category
Return on Equity	15.77	0.88
Return on Assets	8.00	0.82
Net Margin	11.00	0.85

Sector Weightings	% of Stocks	Rel S&P 500	3 Year High	Low
↻ Info	29.45	1.47		
Software	4.16	1.21	4	1
Hardware	11.70	1.27	13	8
Media	7.85	2.07	8	6
Telecom	5.74	1.64	6	2
Service	43.93	0.95		
Health	13.16	1.09	13	12
Consumer	2.67	0.35	10	2
Business	5.69	1.35	7	4
Financial	22.41	1.01	29	22
Mfg	26.63	0.79		
Goods	4.97	0.58	5	2
Ind Mtrls	15.11	1.27	17	13
Energy	5.68	0.58	10	6
Utilities	0.87	0.25	2	1

Composition

		%
● Cash		5.0
● Stocks		94.9
● Bonds		0.0
● Other		0.0
Foreign		11.9
(% of Stock)		

Address:	PO Box 2600 Valley Forge PA 19482 800-997-2798	Minimum Purchase:	$3000	Add: $100	IRA: $3000
		Min Auto Inv Plan:	$3000	Add: $50	
		Sales Fees:	No-load		
Web Address:	www.vanguard.com	Management Fee:	0.35%		
Inception:	10-23-58	Actual Fees:	Mgt:0.35%	Dist: —	
Advisor:	Sanford Bernstein & Company, Inc.	Expense Projections:	3Yr:$119	5Yr:$208	10Yr:$468
Subadvisor:	None	Income Distrib:	Semi-Annually		
NTF Plans:	Vanguard NTF				

MORNINGSTAR® Funds 500

Vanguard Windsor II

	Ticker	Load	NAV	Yield	Total Assets	Mstar Category
	VWNFX	None	$34.75	2.1%	$48,585 mil	Large Value

Governance and Management

Stewardship Grade: B

Portfolio Manager(s)

Jim Barrow of subadvisor Barrow, Hanley, Mewhinney & Strauss handles slightly more than half the assets here. He has been on the fund since its inception in 1985 and also manages the mid-cap-oriented Vanguard Selected Value, where he has a strong record. Windsor II's other advisors are Hotchkis and Wiley, Equinox Capital Management, Tukman Capital Management, and Vanguard's quantitative equity group.

Strategy

This is a true-blue value fund. Manager Jim Barrow searches for low-P/E, high-dividend-paying stocks. He isn't afraid to snap up a number of stocks in beaten-down sectors. Consequently, the fund sometimes has sector weightings that are very different from its average rival's.

Historical Profile

Return: Above Avg
Risk: Average
Rating: ★★★★ Above Avg

	92%	93%	89%	92%	92%	98%	98%	96%	96%

▼ Manager Change
▽ Partial Manager Change

Growth of $10,000
■ Investment Values of Fund
— Investment Values of S&P 500

39.4
31.0
24.0
17.0
10.0

Performance Quartile (within Category)

1995	1996	1997	1998	1999	2000	2001	2002	2003	2004	2005	2006	History
20.66	23.83	28.62	29.85	24.97	27.20	25.59	20.80	26.49	30.73	31.33	34.75	NAV
38.83	24.18	32.37	16.36	-5.81	16.86	-3.40	-16.86	30.08	18.31	7.01	18.25	Total Return %
1.25	1.22	-0.99	-12.22	-26.85	25.96	8.49	5.24	1.40	7.43	2.10	2.46	+/-S&P 500
0.47	2.54	-2.81	0.73	-13.16	9.85	2.19	-1.34	0.05	1.82	-0.04	-4.00	+/-Russ 1000 VI
3.69	3.07	2.78	2.25	2.29	2.46	2.01	2.00	2.56	2.20	2.19	2.50	Income Return %
35.14	21.11	29.59	14.11	-8.10	14.40	-5.41	-18.86	27.52	16.11	4.82	15.75	Capital Return %
5	15	9	22	95	20	48	42	32	7	32	50	Total Rtn % Rank Cat
0.58	0.63	0.66	0.64	0.68	0.61	0.55	0.51	0.53	0.58	0.67	0.78	Income $
0.69	1.16	2.19	2.67	2.50	1.24	0.15	0.00	0.00	0.88	1.46	Capital Gains $
0.39	0.39	0.37	0.41	0.37	0.37	0.40	0.42	0.43	0.37	0.35	0.33	Expense Ratio %
3.27	2.92	2.49	2.16	2.08	2.36	2.10	2.12	2.31	2.07	2.14	2.28	Income Ratio %
30	32	30	31	26	26	10	41	29	22	28	34	Turnover Rate %
11,013	15,700	24,376	31,538	26,902	25,083	22,429	17,739	22,766	29,016	29,064	31,569	Net Assets $mil

Investment Style
Equity
Stock %

Performance 12-31-06

	1st Qtr	2nd Qtr	3rd Qtr	4th Qtr	Total
2002	4.03	-8.68	-17.16	5.65	-16.86
2003	-4.23	18.80	0.43	13.84	30.08
2004	4.76	2.02	0.54	10.11	18.31
2005	0.33	2.47	4.03	0.06	7.01
2006	3.57	0.70	6.35	6.60	18.25

Trailing	Total Return%	+/- S&P 500	+/- Russ 1000 VI	%Rank Cat	Growth of $10,000
3 Mo	6.60	-0.10	-1.40	73	10,660
6 Mo	13.37	0.63	-1.35	39	11,337
1 Yr	18.25	2.46	-4.00	50	11,825
3 Yr Avg	14.40	3.96	-0.69	15	14,972
5 Yr Avg	10.12	3.93	-0.74	16	16,193
10 Yr Avg	10.24	1.82	-0.76	21	26,509
15 Yr Avg	12.37	1.73	-0.66	17	57,512

Tax Analysis	Tax-Adj Rtn%	%Rank Cat	Tax-Cost Rat	%Rank Cat
3 Yr (estimated)	13.63	9	0.67	26
5 Yr (estimated)	9.42	12	0.64	35
10 Yr (estimated)	8.65	17	1.44	44

Potential Capital Gain Exposure: 29% of assets

Rating and Risk

Time Period	Load-Adj Return %	Morningstar Rtn vs Cat	Morningstar Risk vs Cat	Morningstar Risk-Adj Rating
1 Yr	18.25			
3 Yr	14.40	+Avg	-Avg	★★★★
5 Yr	10.12	+Avg	Avg	★★★★
10 Yr	10.24	+Avg	Avg	★★★★
Incept	13.05			

Other Measures	Standard Index S&P 500	Best Fit Index Russ 1000 VI
Alpha	4.9	0.8
Beta	0.80	0.87
R-Squared	80	91
Standard Deviation	6.17	
Mean	14.40	
Sharpe Ratio	1.70	

Portfolio Analysis 09-30-06

Share change since 06-06 Total Stocks:292	Sector	PE	Tot Ret%	% Assets
⊕ General Electric Company	Ind Mtrls	20.0	9.35	3.34
⊕ Pfizer Inc.	Health	15.2	15.22	2.96
⊕ Wells Fargo Company	Financial	14.7	16.82	2.61
⊖ Bank of America Corporat	Financial	12.4	20.68	2.59
⊖ Altria Group, Inc.	Goods	16.3	19.87	2.59
⊕ Citigroup, Inc.	Financial	13.1	19.55	2.53
⊕ Occidental Petroleum Cor	Energy	8.0	24.32	2.28
ConocoPhillips	Energy	6.5	26.53	2.16
⊖ Verizon Communications	Telecom	15.9	34.88	2.10
⊕ Bristol-Myers Squibb Com	Health	23.1	19.93	2.07
⊕ J.P. Morgan Chase & Co.	Financial	13.6	25.60	2.04
Imperial Tobacco Group P	Goods	27.5	35.28	2.03
⊕ Allstate Corporation	Financial	8.7	23.38	1.95
⊕ Exelon Corporation	Utilities	—	19.79	1.95
⊕ Duke Energy Corporation	Utilities	8.2	30.15	1.85
WellPoint, Inc.	Health	17.2	-1.38	1.80
⊕ SLM Corporation	Financial	14.1	-9.76	1.78
⊕ Wyeth	Health	17.2	12.88	1.77
Nokia Corporation ADR	Hardware	18.9	13.44	1.71
BellSouth Corporation	Telecom	—	—	1.55

Current Investment Style

Value Blnd Growth — Large Mid Small

Market Cap	%
Giant	46.5
Large	43.0
Mid	10.5
Small	0.1
Micro	0.0

Avg $mil: 47,938

Value Measures		Rel Category
Price/Earnings	13.50	0.98
Price/Book	2.26	1.02
Price/Sales	1.28	0.98
Price/Cash Flow	5.21	0.78
Dividend Yield %	2.56	1.10

Growth Measures	%	Rel Category
Long-Term Erngs	9.73	0.94
Book Value	7.56	0.95
Sales	10.83	1.20
Cash Flow	4.96	0.82
Historical Erngs	15.91	0.99

Profitability	%	Rel Category
Return on Equity	17.15	0.96
Return on Assets	9.32	0.95
Net Margin	13.03	1.01

Sector Weightings	% of Stocks	Rel S&P 500	3 Year High Low
↻ Info	11.89	0.59	
▤ Software	1.19	0.34	1 0
▤ Hardware	4.42	0.48	5 2
◉ Media	1.53	0.40	3 2
▤ Telecom	4.75	1.35	5 2
⊆ Service	46.10	1.00	
▤ Health	12.67	1.05	13 9
▤ Consumer	3.94	0.52	4 3
▤ Business	2.21	0.52	5 2
⑀ Financial	27.28	1.22	30 25
▤ Mfg	42.01	1.24	
▤ Goods	14.25	1.67	14 11
✿ Ind Mtrls	11.52	0.96	17 11
▲ Energy	8.28	0.84	15 8
▤ Utilities	7.96	2.27	9 6

Composition

● Cash	4.1
● Stocks	95.9
● Bonds	0.0
● Other	0.0
Foreign	8.4
(% of Stock)	

Morningstar's Take by Sonya Morris 12-07-06

This fund recently loosened up its purchase constraints, but there's still reason to be vigilant about its size.

Back in April, Vanguard restricted individual investments into this fund to $25,000 per year to help quell flows into this popular offering. That apparently did the trick, as flows did indeed level off, and in November, Vanguard removed the annual contribution limit. (The $10,000 initial investment requirement remains in place.)

The pace of assets entering this fund has slowed, but the portfolio's size is still worth watching. At more than $47 billion in assets, this is the fourth largest fund in the large-value category. Vanguard has skirted the size issue by farming out portions of the portfolio to five different advisors. Barrow, Hanley, Mewhinney & Strauss, the firm that runs approximately 60% of the portfolio, manages a total of $50 billion in large-value assets. Consequently, the firm has closed all of its large-value strategies and no longer takes new

asset flows from this fund.

It's important to monitor the size of a manager's asset base because he can become hamstrung if his portfolio grows too large. But at this point, we think the team from Barrow Hanley (lead by seasoned investor Jim Barrow) can handle its load because they trade infrequently, and when they do trade, their contrarian style means they are often buying when others are selling, and vice versa.

We like Barrow's independent ways, and he's produced solid results here and at his other charge, Vanguard Selected Value, but as this fund grows, Barrow's influence has waned, and some of the other advisors have taken on a larger role, particularly Equinox Capital Management and Vanguard's quantitative equity group. But we're heartened that each of those managers has produced competitive results elsewhere.

Given its size, this fund may not be as agile as it once was, but we think its talented lineup of managers and low costs will keep it in the game.

Address:	PO Box 2600 Valley Forge PA 19482 800-997-2798	Minimum Purchase:	$10000	Add: $100 IRA: $10000
		Min Auto Inv Plan:	$10000	Add: $50
Web Address:	www.vanguard.com	Sales Fees:	No-load	
Inception:	06-24-85	Management Fee:	0.34%	
Advisor:	Armstrong Shaw Associates Inc.	Actual Fees:	Mgt:0.34%	Dist: —
Subadvisor:	None	Expense Projections:	3Yr:$116	5Yr:$202 10Yr:$456
		Income Distrib:	Semi-Annually	
NTF Plans:	Vanguard NTF			

M☉RNINGSTAR® Funds 500

Wasatch Core Growth

	Ticker	Load	NAV	Yield	Total Assets	Mstar Category
	WGROX	Closed	$39.81	0.3%	$1,340 mil	Mid-Cap Growth

Governance and Management

Stewardship Grade: A

Portfolio Manager(s)

J.B. Taylor joined Wasatch as an analyst in 1996 and took over this fund's day-to-day operations at the start of 1999. Longtime Wasatch manager Sam Stewart stepped down in 2005 to oversee the firm's research efforts. Taylor is now joined by Paul Lambert, an analyst at Wasatch since 2000.

Strategy

Management seeks firms that will deliver consistent earnings-growth rates of between 15% and 25% during a three- to five-year time horizon. It also demands that a potential holding's trailing P/E be less than or equal to management's projection of the firm's sustainable earnings-growth rate. That tack has resulted in only minimal exposure to the tech sector and less volatility than the fund's typical peer.

Historical Profile

Return	Above Avg
Risk	Average
Rating	★★★★ Above Avg

Investment Style: Equity, Stock %

90% 92% 87% 78% 95% 95% 99% 98% 100%

▼ Manager Change
▽ Partial Manager Change

Growth of $10,000
— Investment Values of Fund
— Investment Values of S&P 500

59.0 / 43.6 / 32.4 / 24.0 / 17.0 / 10.0

Performance Quartile (within Category)

1995	1996	1997	1998	1999	2000	2001	2002	2003	2004	2005	2006	History
15.96	17.19	20.22	19.57	22.80	28.71	34.60	26.68	36.92	43.23	40.76	39.81	NAV
40.42	16.54	27.55	1.56	19.35	37.39	28.82	-22.89	38.46	21.65	3.26	6.68	Total Return %
2.84	-6.42	-5.81	-27.02	-1.69	46.49	40.71	-0.79	9.78	10.77	-1.65	-9.11	+/-S&P 500
6.44	-0.94	5.01	-16.30	-31.94	49.14	48.97	4.52	-4.25	6.17	-8.84	-3.98	+/-Russ MG
0.43	0.44	0.17	0.00	0.00	0.00	0.00	0.00	0.08	0.60	1.45	0.33	Income Return %
39.99	16.10	27.38	1.56	19.35	37.39	28.82	-22.89	38.38	21.05	1.81	6.35	Capital Return %
22	53	21	88	84	1	1	37	33	4	91	66	Total Rtn % Rank Cat
0.05	0.07	0.03	0.00	0.00	0.00	0.00	0.00	0.02	0.22	0.63	0.14	Income $
0.29	1.31	1.62	0.00	0.48	2.32	2.14	0.00	0.00	1.32	3.28	3.56	Capital Gains $
1.50	1.50	1.50	1.44	1.44	1.38	1.32	1.29	1.25	1.21	1.20	1.17	Expense Ratio %
0.29	0.40	0.44	-0.50	-1.07	-0.86	-0.66	-0.02	-0.02	0.34	1.30	0.38	Income Ratio %
88	62	81	63	79	75	51	76	47	47	42	42	Turnover Rate %
62	90	69	39	57	30	32	32	1,455	1,723	1,669	1,340	Net Assets $mil

Performance 12-31-06

	1st Qtr	2nd Qtr	3rd Qtr	4th Qtr	Total
2002	10.14	-9.24	-26.37	4.75	-22.89
2003	-7.53	27.16	6.92	10.14	38.46
2004	9.07	-1.32	-3.17	16.72	21.65
2005	-4.12	6.56	-0.59	1.66	3.26
2006	8.83	-8.03	0.69	5.85	6.68

Trailing	Total Return%	+/- S&P 500	+/- Russ MG	%Rank Cat	Growth of $10,000
3 Mo	5.85	-0.85	-1.10	67	10,585
6 Mo	6.57	-6.17	-1.33	40	10,657
1 Yr	6.68	-9.11	-3.98	66	10,668
3 Yr Avg	10.25	-0.19	-2.48	57	13,401
5 Yr Avg	7.43	1.24	-0.79	36	14,310
10 Yr Avg	14.62	6.20	6.00	6	39,138
15 Yr Avg	14.53	3.89	4.40	4	76,522

Tax Analysis	Tax-Adj Rtn%	%Rank Cat	Tax-Cost Rat	%Rank Cat
3 Yr (estimated)	8.91	59	1.22	59
5 Yr (estimated)	6.63	37	0.74	51
10 Yr (estimated)	13.36	4	1.10	38

Potential Capital Gain Exposure: 24% of assets

Rating and Risk

Time Period	Load-Adj Return %	Morningstar Rtn vs Cat	Morningstar Risk vs Cat	Morningstar Risk-Adj Rating
1 Yr	6.68			
3 Yr	10.25	Avg	Avg	★★★
5 Yr	7.43	Avg	+Avg	★★★
10 Yr	14.62	High	-Avg	★★★★★
Incept	14.30			

Other Measures	Standard Index S&P 500	Best Fit Index Mstar Mid Core
Alpha	-4.0	-4.7
Beta	1.63	1.10
R-Squared	75	88
Standard Deviation	12.87	
Mean	10.25	
Sharpe Ratio	0.57	

Portfolio Analysis 09-30-06

Share change since 06-06 Total Stocks:74	Sector	PE	Tot Ret%	% Assets
⊖ Copart, Inc.	Business	25.4	30.10	5.32
⊕ SCP Pool, Inc.	Goods	21.4	6.25	5.24
⊕ O'Reilly Automotive, Inc	Consumer	20.4	0.16	4.73
⊕ AmeriCredit Corporation	Financial	11.2	-1.80	3.38
⊕ Pediatrix Medical Group,	Health	25.0	10.42	3.34
⊕ NVR, Inc.	Consumer	6.2	-8.12	3.15
⊕ SRA International, Inc.	Business	25.3	-12.44	2.83
⊕ MSC Industrial Direct Co	Business	21.6	-1.47	2.63
⊕ SEI Investments Company	Business	26.8	61.73	2.53
⊕ Global Imaging Systems,	Ind Mtrls	16.4	26.77	2.48
⊕ United Surgical Partners	Health	35.6	-11.82	2.34
⊕ Commerce Bancorp, Inc.	Financial	23.6	3.89	2.33
⊖ UTI Bank Ltd	Financial	—		2.23
⊖ Knight Transportation, I	Business	21.4	-17.31	2.20
⊖ First American Corporati	Financial	8.6	-8.61	2.15
⊖ PSS World Medical, Inc.	Health	27.7	31.60	2.04
⊕ Guitar Center, Inc.	Consumer	16.6	-9.10	2.02
⊕ Sunrise Senior Living, I	Health	18.5	-8.87	2.01
⊕ Strayer Education, Inc.	Consumer	30.1	14.34	2.00
⊖ Redwood Trust, Inc.	Financial	11.0	56.92	2.00

Current Investment Style

Value Blnd Growth — Large / Mid / Small

	Market Cap	%
	Giant	0.0
	Large	5.7
	Mid	53.8
	Small	37.1
	Micro	3.4
	Avg $mil: 2,035	

Value Measures		Rel Category
Price/Earnings	16.66	0.81
Price/Book	2.60	0.81
Price/Sales	1.34	0.76
Price/Cash Flow	9.43	0.83
Dividend Yield %	1.06	1.68

Growth Measures	%	Rel Category
Long-Term Erngs	15.59	0.96
Book Value	13.86	1.09
Sales	14.82	1.48
Cash Flow	10.09	0.55
Historical Erngs	20.94	0.84

Profitability	%	Rel Category
Return on Equity	19.21	1.07
Return on Assets	12.18	1.30
Net Margin	13.80	1.19

Sector Weightings	% of Stocks	Rel S&P 500	3 Year High Low	
☎ Info	6.65	0.33		
Software	0.69	0.20	1	0
Hardware	5.96	0.65	9	4
Media	0.00	0.00	0	0
Telecom	0.00	0.00	1	0
☞ Service	78.57	1.70		
Health	14.21	1.18	21	11
Consumer	20.49	2.68	26	19
Business	19.42	4.59	20	9
Financial	24.45	1.10	39	24
Mfg	14.78	0.44		
Goods	7.91	0.93	8	2
Ind Mtrls	2.86	0.24	3	1
Energy	4.01	0.41	4	0
Utilities	0.00	0.00	0	0

Composition

● Cash	0.0	
● Stocks	99.8	
● Bonds	0.0	
● Other	0.2	
Foreign	12.7	(% of Stock)

Morningstar's Take by John Coumarianos 12-19-06

We think Wasatch Core Growth is poised for another great run.

Wasatch has an illustrious history in small-cap growth investing. The firm's founding philosophy values sustainable high returns on invested capital on par with earnings growth, recognizing that it's important to account for the amount of capital required to achieve growth. Except for a light stake in technology, this fund is representative of the shop's style, owning small-caps and smaller mid-caps displaying 15% annual growth rates, outsized returns on assets, and wide margins.

While investing in businesses with sustainable profitability is an eminently reasonable approach, it's worked poorly the past few years. Since the end of the bear market in 2002, investors have seemed spooked by stocks that appear expensive on a price/earnings basis, even when their underlying businesses sport solid prospects for future profitability and earnings growth. Meanwhile, apparently cheaper cyclical stocks have been the darlings.

Still, managers J.B. Taylor and Paul Lambert are sticking to their guns, as they continue to own growing businesses such as ambulatory surgical center operator United Surgical Partners. Despite a recent earnings stumble, the managers think this business is poised to benefit from the trend toward outpatient surgery and its ability to forge joint venture operations with for-profit hospitals. Taylor and Lambert also own smaller outfit Laureate, which they think should benefit from the same demand for education as a means toward higher wages. Laureate has displayed powerful international growth that the managers think they snagged at a reasonable price.

The emphasis on highly profitable growing companies will serve this fund well in the long run, despite its recent stumble. We've seen the assets in this fund decline by nearly 18% over the past year, and we predict that those who have fled this closed fund will regret their decision.

Address:	PO Box 2172 Milwaukee, WI 53201-2172 800-551-1700	Minimum Purchase:	Closed	Add: —	IRA: —
		Min Auto Inv Plan:	Closed	Add: —	
		Sales Fees:	No-load, 2.00%R		
Web Address:	www.wasatchfunds.com	Management Fee:	1.00%		
Inception:	11-28-86	Actual Fees:	Mgt:1.00%	Dist: —	
Advisor:	Wasatch Advisors Inc.	Expense Projections:	3Yr:$381	5Yr:$660	10Yr:$1455
Subadvisor:	None	Income Distrib:	Annually		
NTF Plans:	CommonWealth NTF, Fidelity Instl-NTF				

Wasatch Glob Sci & Tech

	Ticker	Load	NAV	Yield	Total Assets	Mstar Category
	WAGTX	None	$14.79	0.0%	$137 mil	Specialty-Technology

Governance and Management

Stewardship Grade: B

Portfolio Manager(s)

Ajay Krishnan has managed this fund since its 2000 inception. In January 2006, he took more of an advisory role and passed day-to-day management responsibility to Noor Kamruddin and James Gulbrandsen. Krishnan still serves as a comanager here, but he is taking a bigger roll on Wasatch Ultra Growth. Management draws on Wasatch's general research pool.

Strategy

This fund seeks out general growth themes, such as the development of the global wireless infrastructure, and looks for second-tier beneficiaries of that growth. It likes to see companies with three-year growth rates above 25% that trade at a discount to that rate. The fund's focus lands on small-cap tech firms, which are a core strength for Wasatch. The fund's small-cap focus will hurt when the market favors safer, large-cap behemoths.

Performance 12-31-06

	1st Qtr	2nd Qtr	3rd Qtr	4th Qtr	Total
2002	-4.68	-24.91	-21.33	28.21	-27.80
2003	-10.88	28.94	14.26	12.76	48.04
2004	-0.74	-1.33	-14.42	14.48	-4.05
2005	-3.18	4.98	9.91	4.23	16.43
2006	13.20	-7.93	1.09	10.05	15.95

Trailing	Total Return%	+/- S&P 500	+/- ArcaEx Tech 100	%Rank Cat	Growth of $10,000
3 Mo	10.05	3.35	4.42	8	11,005
6 Mo	11.25	-1.49	-0.40	34	11,125
1 Yr	15.95	0.16	11.27	13	11,595
3 Yr Avg	9.01	-1.43	1.13	25	12,954
5 Yr Avg	6.72	0.53	1.76	6	13,843
10 Yr Avg	—	—	—	—	—
15 Yr Avg	—	—	—	—	—

Tax Analysis	Tax-Adj Rtn%	%Rank Cat	Tax-Cost Rat	%Rank Cat
3 Yr (estimated)	8.69	22	0.29	41
5 Yr (estimated)	6.54	6	0.17	36
10 Yr (estimated)	—	—	—	—

Potential Capital Gain Exposure: 18% of assets

Morningstar's Take by Kai Wiecking 11-13-06

Investors in Wasatch Global Science & Technology should proceed with caution.

There's no denying the fact that this fund has achieved an enviable track record since it was launched at the end of 2000. Its trailing average five-year return of 9.3% as of Nov. 10, 2006, leaves 97% of its competitors in the technology category in the dust. But several factors make us skeptical as to whether this successful run can be repeated.

Topping the list of long-term concerns is the fund's unjustifiably high cost. There's simply no reason why investors should be charged 1.95% here, when the fund's typical no-load specialty peer charges 1.25%. This expense hurdle will likely come to haunt the fund when times are tougher. In fact, 2004 serves as a good example, as the fund lost 4.1% that year and trailed 89% of its peers.

We're also a bit concerned about management. Lead manager Ajay Krishnan relinquished the day-to-day responsibilities of running the portfolio at the beginning of 2006. Taking over are two

colleagues with no prior experience managing mutual funds. It's still early for an assessment, but thus far Noor Kamruddin and James Gulbrandsen have been up to the task. In a rather difficult year, their stock selection has mostly panned out. New holdings such as Singaporean storage-company MMI Holdings are performing strongly. It probably helps that Kamruddin has some first-hand experience in the industry: She used to be a software-development engineer. But it remains to be seen how the pair will handle truly challenging markets.

This fund's steep price tag and unproven management detract from its appeal, as does the fact that valuations in small-cap tech names have in many cases reached dizzying heights once again. Given Wasatch's expertise in small-cap stocks, we wouldn't bet against this fund, but we wouldn't recommend it either.

Address:	PO Box 2172 Milwaukee, WI 53201-2172 800-551-1700
Web Address:	www.wasatchfunds.com
Inception:	12-19-00*
Advisor:	Wasatch Advisors Inc.
Subadvisor:	None
NTF Plans:	Fidelity Retail-NTF, Schwab OneSource

Minimum Purchase:	$2000	Add: $100	IRA: $1000
Min Auto Inv Plan:	$1000	Add: $50	
Sales Fees:	No-load, 2.00%R		
Management Fee:	1.50%		
Actual Fees:	Mgt:1.50%	Dist: —	
Expense Projections:	3Yr:$616	5Yr:$1060	10Yr:$2293
Income Distrib:	Annually		

Historical Profile

Return	High
Risk	Average
Rating	★★★★ Above Avg

Investment Style: Equity, Stock %

76% 84% 83% 94% 91% 94%

▼ Manager Change
▽ Partial Manager Change

Growth of $10,000
— Investment Values of Fund
— Investment Values of S&P 500

14.0
12.0
10.0
6.0

Performance Quartile (within Category)

	1995	1996	1997	1998	1999	2000	2001	2002	2003	2004	2005	2006	History
NAV	—	—	—	—	—	10.29	11.33	8.18	12.11	11.62	13.26	14.79	
Total Return %	—	—	—	—	—	2.90*	12.35	-27.80	48.04	-4.05	16.43	15.95	
+/-S&P 500	—	—	—	—	—		24.24	-5.70	19.36	-14.93	11.52	0.16	
+/-ArcaEx Tech 100	—	—	—	—	—		27.94	5.53	-4.10	-15.78	9.07	11.27	
Income Return %	—	—	—	—	—		0.00	0.00	0.00	0.00	0.00	0.00	
Capital Return %	—	—	—	—	—		12.35	-27.80	48.04	-4.05	16.43	15.95	
Total Rtn % Rank Cat	—	—	—	—	—		1	6	65	89	3	13	
Income $	—	—	—	—	—		0.00	0.00	0.00	0.00	0.00	0.00	
Capital Gains $	—	—	—	—	—	0.00	0.18	0.00	0.00	0.00	0.27	0.59	
Expense Ratio %	—	—	—	—	—		1.95	1.95	1.95	1.95	1.95	1.94	
Income Ratio %	—	—	—	—	—		-1.50	-1.90	-1.87	-1.66	-1.15		
Turnover Rate %	—	—	—	—	—		94	95	88	55	58		
Net Assets $mil	—	—	—	—	—		31	29	74	77	137		

Rating and Risk

Time Period	Load-Adj Return %	Morningstar Rtn vs Cat	Morningstar Risk vs Cat	Morningstar Risk-Adj Rating
1 Yr	15.95			
3 Yr	9.01	+Avg	Avg	★★★★
5 Yr	6.72	High	Avg	★★★★
10 Yr	—	—	—	—
Incept	8.11			

Other Measures	Standard Index S&P 500	Best Fit Index Mstar Mid Growth TR
Alpha	-7.9	-6.8
Beta	2.14	1.32
R-Squared	67	87
Standard Deviation	18.00	
Mean	9.01	
Sharpe Ratio	0.39	

Portfolio Analysis 09-30-06

Share change since 06-06 Total Stocks:112	Sector	PE	Tot Ret%	% Assets
⊕ Infosys Technologies Ltd	Software	—	—	2.34
⊖ Cognizant Technology Sol	Business	52.9	53.49	2.34
⊕ Maxim Integrated Product	Hardware	23.1	-14.06	2.21
MMI Hldgs Ltd	Hardware	—	—	2.08
Micrel, Inc.	Hardware	24.5	-6.99	1.99
O2Micro International, L	Hardware	40.0	-16.01	1.92
Lma Intl N.V.	—	—	—	1.92
PLX Technology, Inc.	Hardware	NMF	51.63	1.88
⊖ SRA International, Inc.	Business	25.3	-12.44	1.86
⊕ Microchip Technology, In	Hardware	27.2	4.37	1.86
⊕ National Semiconductor	Hardware	16.1	-12.17	1.66
Power Integrations, Inc.	Hardware	—	-1.51	1.61
IntraLase Corporation	Health	48.1	25.52	1.59
Unisteel Technology Ltd	Ind Mtrls	—	—	1.56
TGS Nopec	Energy	—	—	1.52
⊕ Texas Instruments, Inc.	Hardware	16.9	-9.82	1.52
⊕ United Surgical Partners	Health	35.6	-11.82	1.47
Taiwan Semiconductor Man	Hardware	18.9	18.75	1.47
RaySearch Laboratories	Energy	—	—	1.45
⊕ Qualcomm, Inc.	Hardware	26.6	-11.32	1.40

Current Investment Style

Value Blnd Growth — Large Mid Small

Market Cap	%
Giant	9.7
Large	10.9
Mid	29.1
Small	30.4
Micro	19.9
Avg $mil:	1,814

Value Measures		Rel Category
Price/Earnings	20.82	0.86
Price/Book	3.50	1.08
Price/Sales	2.59	0.93
Price/Cash Flow	11.79	0.91
Dividend Yield %	0.61	1.39

Growth Measures	%	Rel Category
Long-Term Erngs	22.43	1.31
Book Value	3.00	0.31
Sales	17.68	1.42
Cash Flow	22.91	1.15
Historical Erngs	2.19	0.08

Profitability	%	Rel Category
Return on Equity	17.70	1.13
Return on Assets	10.67	1.15
Net Margin	15.26	1.10

Industry Weightings	% of Stocks	Rel Cat
Software	7.0	0.3
Hardware	2.6	0.2
Networking Eq	3.3	0.4
Semis	39.8	2.2
Semi Equip	8.5	1.7
Comp/Data Sv	1.3	0.1
Telecom	0.0	0.0
Health Care	19.5	4.0
Other	18.1	1.0

Composition

		%
●	Cash	2.2
●	Stocks	94.3
●	Bonds	0.0
●	Other	3.5
	Foreign	40.1
	(% of Stock)	

Mᴏʀɴɪɴɢsᴛᴀʀ® Funds 500

Wasatch Heritage Growth

 Analyst Pick

Ticker	**Load**	**NAV**	**Yield**	**Total Assets**	**Mstar Category**	
WAHGX	None	$11.67	0.0%	$246 mil	Mid-Cap Growth	

Governance and Management

Stewardship Grade:

Portfolio Manager(s)

This is the first time that Chris Bowen and Ryan Snow have managed a public mutual fund portfolio. The former joined Wasatch in 2001, while the latter has an additional year at the firm under his belt. Most recently, Bowen has been a member of the analyst team supporting Wasatch Core Growth, while Snow has been part of the crew supporting Wasatch Small Cap Growth.

Strategy

This fund invests in companies that are between $3 billion and $20 billion in size. Managers Chris Bowen and Ryan Snow use the same fundamentally driven growth process that's popular at Wasatch. Although the managers occasionally buy high-priced stocks, investors can expect a more moderate growth approach here. Also, investors should expect the fund to own stocks that have grown too large for Wasatch's small-cap portfolios.

Performance 12-31-06

	1st Qtr	2nd Qtr	3rd Qtr	4th Qtr	Total
2002	—	—	—	—	—
2003	—	—	—	—	—
2004	—	—	-1.69	13.01	— *
2005	-3.23	3.80	2.14	1.92	4.58
2006	3.17	-5.21	2.80	5.46	6.01

Trailing	Total Return%	+/- S&P 500	+/- Russ MG	%Rank Cat	Growth of $10,000
3 Mo	5.46	-1.24	-1.49	71	10,546
6 Mo	8.40	-4.34	0.50	22	10,840
1 Yr	6.01	-9.78	-4.65	72	10,601
3 Yr Avg	—	—	—	—	—
5 Yr Avg	—	—	—	—	—
10 Yr Avg	—	—	—	—	—
15 Yr Avg	—	—	—	—	—

Tax Analysis	Tax-Adj Rtn%	%Rank Cat	Tax-Cost Rat	%Rank Cat
3 Yr (estimated)	—	—	—	—
5 Yr (estimated)	—	—	—	—
10 Yr (estimated)	—	—	—	—

Potential Capital Gain Exposure: 12% of assets

Historical Profile

Return
Risk
Rating

Not Rated

Investment Style
Equity
Stock %

89%   93%   98%

▼ Manager Change
▽ Partial Manager Change

Growth of $10,000
━ Investment Values of Fund
━ Investment Values of S&P 500

13.0
12.0
11.0
10.0

Performance Quartile
(within Category)

1995	1996	1997	1998	1999	2000	2001	2002	2003	2004	2005	2006	History
—	—	—	—	—	—	—	—	—	11.14	11.34	11.67	NAV
—	—	—	—	—	—	—	—	—	—	4.58	6.01	Total Return %
—	—	—	—	—	—	—	—	—	—	-0.33	-9.78	+/-S&P 500
—	—	—	—	—	—	—	—	—	—	-7.52	-4.65	+/-Russ MG
—	—	—	—	—	—	—	—	—	—	0.13	0.01	Income Return %
—	—	—	—	—	—	—	—	—	—	4.45	6.00	Capital Return %
—	—	—	—	—	—	—	—	—	—	86	72	Total Rtn % Rank Cat
—	—	—	—	—	—	—	—	—	0.00	0.01	0.00	Income $
—	—	—	—	—	—	—	—	—	0.00	0.30	0.35	Capital Gains $
—	—	—	—	—	—	—	—	—	—	0.95	0.95	Expense Ratio %
—	—	—	—	—	—	—	—	—	—	-0.01	0.01	Income Ratio %
—	—	—	—	—	—	—	—	—	—	5	54	Turnover Rate %
—	—	—	—	—	—	—	—	—	—	202	246	Net Assets $mil

Rating and Risk

Time Period	Load-Adj Return %	Morningstar Rtn vs Cat	Morningstar Risk vs Cat	Morningstar Risk-Adj Rating
1 Yr	6.01	—	—	—
3 Yr	—	—	—	—
5 Yr	—	—	—	—
10 Yr	—	—	—	—
Incept	8.69			

Other Measures	Standard Index S&P 500	Best Fit Index
Alpha	—	—
Beta	—	—
R-Squared	—	—
Standard Deviation	—	
Mean	—	
Sharpe Ratio	—	

Portfolio Analysis 09-30-06

Share change since 06-06 Total Stocks:68	Sector	PE	Tot Ret%	% Assets
⊖ Apollo Group, Inc. A	Consumer	15.9	-35.54	3.83
⊖ WellPoint, Inc.	Health	17.2	-1.38	3.56
⊕ Infosys Technologies Ltd	Software			3.20
⊖ NVR, Inc.	Consumer	6.2	-8.12	3.18
⊖ Zimmer Holdings, Inc.	Health	24.5	16.22	3.00
⊖ Caremark RX, Inc.	Health	23.6	10.90	2.92
⊖ Amphenol Corporation	Hardware	24.9	40.57	2.66
⊕ Maxim Integrated Product	Hardware	23.1	-14.06	2.58
⊖ Bed Bath & Beyond, Inc.	Consumer	20.1	5.39	2.38
Commerce Bancorp, Inc.	Financial	23.6	3.89	2.00
⊖ Harley-Davidson, Inc.	Goods	18.5	38.81	1.95
⊖ Covance, Inc.	Health	28.4	21.34	1.94
⊖ CDW Corporation	Business	20.4	23.33	1.93
⊖ Linear Technology	Hardware	21.6	-14.44	1.92
⊖ Lincare Holdings Inc.	Health	19.3	-4.94	1.89
⊕ L-3 Communications Holdi	Hardware	20	11.04	1.88
⊕ Lowe's Companies Inc.	Consumer	15.6	-6.05	1.87
⊕ Coach, Inc.	Goods	32.1	28.85	1.86
⊖ National Semiconductor	Hardware	16.1	-12.17	1.80
⊖ Esprit Hldgs Ltd	Consumer	—	—	1.79

Current Investment Style

Value Blnd Growth — Large Mid Small

Market Cap	%
Giant	10.4
Large	35.3
Mid	52.5
Small	1.8
Micro	0.0

Avg $mil: 10,208

Value Measures		Rel Category
Price/Earnings	15.78	0.77
Price/Book	2.94	0.92
Price/Sales	1.56	0.89
Price/Cash Flow	10.68	0.94
Dividend Yield %	0.98	1.56

Growth Measures	%	Rel Category
Long-Term Erngs	14.68	0.90
Book Value	14.73	1.16
Sales	18.61	1.86
Cash Flow	15.19	0.82
Historical Erngs	23.94	0.96

Profitability	%	Rel Category
Return on Equity	25.99	1.45
Return on Assets	16.86	1.80
Net Margin	16.87	1.45

Sector Weightings	% of Stocks	Rel S&P 500	3 Year High Low	
↻ Info	23.14	1.16		
🖥 Software	3.79	1.10	4	1
💻 Hardware	19.35	2.09	19	9
🎙 Media	0.00	0.00	0	0
📶 Telecom	0.00	0.00	4	0
⊂ Service	67.72	1.47		
🩺 Health	19.98	1.66	21	17
🛒 Consumer	25.18	3.29	32	25
💼 Business	8.53	2.02	11	7
💲 Financial	14.03	0.63	23	14
⊔ Mfg	9.14	0.27		
🏭 Goods	4.40	0.51	5	4
⚙ Ind Mtrls	0.00	0.00	0	0
🔋 Energy	4.74	0.48	6	0
💡 Utilities	0.00	0.00	1	0

Composition

		%
● Cash		2.0
● Stocks		97.9
● Bonds		0.0
● Other		0.0
	Foreign	10.1
	(% of Stock)	

Morningstar's Take by John Coumarianos 12-17-06

We think Wasatch Heritage Growth is poised for greatness.

Wasatch has an illustrious history in small-cap growth investing. The firm's founding philosophy emphasizes sustainable high returns on invested capital as much as it does earnings growth, recognizing that it's important to account for the amount of capital required to achieve growth. Wasatch launched this fund in mid-2004 in an effort to maintain exposure to businesses that had outgrown the small-cap category but still displayed the high profitability that Wasatch investors require.

Unfortunately, the past few years have been a miserable time to invest in businesses with sustainable profitability. Since the end of the bear market in 2002, investors have been spooked by stocks that appear expensive on a price/earnings basis, even when their underlying businesses sport solid prospects for future profitability and earnings growth. As a result, the cyclical, lower P/E

businesses have been the darlings.

We think this situation can't last. Managers Chris Bowen and Ryan Snow concede that some holdings such as education provider Apollo are having problems, including management turnover and options accounting difficulties. However, the profitability and growth prospects remain strong for this business as the U.S. moves more toward a knowledge-based economy.

This penchant for stocks transitioning to a slower growth phase in their life cycle can lead to volatility. Investors often penalize a sock too harshly for slowing growth and then slowly bid the price back up when they regain confidence. (Home improvement retailer Lowe's comes to mind.) Bowen and Snow are willing to wait for this readjustment.

Because Wasatch closes funds early, we think it would be smart to buy this fund now. Should the fund rebound and asset pour in, it may be too late to get on board.

Address:	PO Box 2172
	Milwaukee, WI 53201-2172
	800-551-1700
Web Address:	www.wasatchfunds.com
Inception:	06-18-04
Advisor:	Wasatch Advisors Inc.
Subadvisor:	None
NTF Plans:	Fidelity Retail-NTF, Schwab OneSource

Minimum Purchase:	$2000	Add: $100	IRA: $1000
Min Auto Inv Plan:	$1000	Add: $50	
Sales Fees:	No-load, 2.00%R		
Management Fee:	0.70%		
Actual Fees:	Mgt:0.70%	Dist: —	
Expense Projections:	3Yr:$311	5Yr:$543	10Yr:$1209
Income Distrib:	Annually		

Wasatch Micro Cap

	Ticker	Load	NAV	Yield	Total Assets	Mstar Category
	WMICX	Closed	$6.64	0.0%	$623 mil	Small Growth

Governance and Management

Stewardship Grade: B

Portfolio Manager(s)

Robert Gardiner has managed this offering since its inception in mid-1995. He was an analyst at Wasatch before the fund was launched and has been employed at the firm for more than 20 years. Dan Chace supports him as comanager. Although a few dedicated analysts form this fund's "team," all Wasatch funds pull from the same larger pool of analysts.

Strategy

Managers Robert Gardiner and Dan Chace consider only firms with market caps of less than $1 billion--up from $750 million before September 2003--for inclusion in this portfolio. They blend some of the market's fastest-growing firms with more-steadily growing names. These slower-growth names, which are usually growing earnings by at least 15%, have made this offering less volatile than its typical peer.

Performance 12-31-06

	1st Qtr	2nd Qtr	3rd Qtr	4th Qtr	Total
2002	1.82	-7.73	-19.32	13.25	-14.17
2003	-4.37	27.44	8.89	12.92	49.84
2004	5.25	1.44	-8.80	15.73	12.70
2005	-2.45	7.69	3.98	1.64	11.02
2006	12.42	-5.31	0.30	9.63	17.05

Trailing	Total Return%	+/- S&P 500	+/- Russ 2000 Gr	%Rank Cat	Growth of $10,000
3 Mo	9.63	2.93	0.86	18	10,963
6 Mo	9.96	-2.78	3.10	10	10,996
1 Yr	17.05	1.26	3.70	11	11,705
3 Yr Avg	13.56	3.12	3.05	15	14,645
5 Yr Avg	13.50	7.31	6.57	3	18,836
10 Yr Avg	23.59	15.17	18.71	1	83,144
15 Yr Avg	—	—	—		—

Tax Analysis	Tax-Adj Rtn%	%Rank Cat	Tax-Cost Rat	%Rank Cat
3 Yr (estimated)	10.90	21	2.34	78
5 Yr (estimated)	11.27	6	1.96	86
10 Yr (estimated)	20.31	1	2.65	92

Potential Capital Gain Exposure: 25% of assets

Morningstar's Take by Andrew Gogerty 12-21-06

Investors with a stake in Wasatch Micro Cap can't do much with it, and there's no reason to.

Like its siblings, this fund taps Wasatch's strength of uncovering financially healthy companies with strong competitive advantages. At this offering, comanagers Rob Gardiner and Dan Chace limit their potential universe to stocks with a market cap of less than $1 billion exhibiting 15% or greater year-over-year earnings growth. We're fond of this level-headed approach given that the micro-cap arena is loaded with many unproven, speculative firms.

But don't mistake this prudence for conventional thinking. Gardiner and Chace pay little attention to the fund's asset mix, instead relying on the quality of their picks to drive returns and the portfolio's profile. In fact, that the fund's stake in foreign stocks--currently 27%--dwarfs the 8% category norm has keyed its recent success. Overseas consumer stocks such as athletic shoe maker China Hongxing Sports have not been impacted by

interest-rate and oil-price concerns seen in the U.S. in 2006. That performance, combined with strong picks in the domestic technology sector has kept the fund ahead of its peers despite its relatively light exposure to energy and industrial stocks, which Chace says often fall short of their earnings growth hurdles.

This willingness to go their own way is a major factor of the fund's consistent, long-term success, and the key to its ability to continue to outperform. In addition, Wasatch has a laudable history of preserving the fund's ability to own micro-cap gems in a meaningful way by slamming the door on asset flows. Not only is the fund closed to new investors, but current shareholders are currently prohibited from adding to their investment. Not only does this nip the urge to chase returns in the bud, but may serve as an indirect signal for investors to re-examine their asset mix. That's probably a good idea given the strong performance of small- and micro-cap stocks in recent years.

Address:	PO Box 2172 Milwaukee, WI 53201-2172 800-551-1700	Minimum Purchase:	Closed	Add: —	IRA: —
		Min Auto Inv Plan:	Closed	Add: —	
		Sales Fees:	No-load, 2.00%R		
Web Address:	www.wasatchfunds.com	Management Fee:	2.00%		
Inception:	06-19-95*	Actual Fees:	Mgt:2.00%	Dist: —	
Advisor:	Wasatch Advisors Inc.	Expense Projections:	3Yr:$682	5Yr:$1169	10Yr:$2513
Subadvisor:	None	Income Distrib:	Annually		
NTF Plans:	CommonWealth NTF, Fidelity Instl-NTF				

Historical Profile

Return	High
Risk	Average
Rating	★★★★ Highest

	89%	89%	87%	80%	96%	92%	92%	94%	94%

Investment Style
Equity
Stock %

▼ Manager Change
▽ Partial Manager Change

Growth of $10,000
— Investment Values of Fund
— Investment Values of S&P 500

18.0 / 78.0
50.0
30.0
10.0

Performance Quartile (within Category)

1995	1996	1997	1998	1999	2000	2001	2002	2003	2004	2005	2006	History
2.83	3.03	3.76	3.99	4.79	4.90	6.61	5.26	7.24	6.93	6.36	6.64	NAV
41.50*	13.66	35.32	18.98	32.86	37.53	49.99	-14.17	49.84	12.70	11.02	17.05	Total Return %
—	-9.30	1.96	-9.60	11.82	46.63	61.88	7.93	21.16	1.82	6.11	1.26	+/-S&P 500
—	2.40	22.37	17.75	-10.23	59.96	59.22	16.09	1.30	-1.61	6.87	3.70	+/-Russ 2000 Gr
—	0.00	0.00	0.00	0.00	0.00	0.00	0.00	0.00	0.00	0.00	0.00	Income Return %
—	13.66	35.32	18.98	32.86	37.53	49.99	-14.17	49.84	12.70	11.02	17.05	Capital Return %
—	69	6	14	70	2	1	3	27	47	16	11	Total Rtn % Rank Cat
0.00	0.00	0.00	0.00	0.00	0.00	0.00	0.00	0.00	0.00	0.00	0.00	Income $
0.00	0.18	0.33	0.36	0.42	1.55	0.60	0.34	0.59	1.06	1.34	0.80	Capital Gains $
2.50	2.50	2.50	2.50	2.46	2.38	2.32	2.28	2.24	2.19	2.18	2.14	Expense Ratio %
-0.76	-1.53	-1.64	-2.28	-2.22	-1.76	-1.76	-2.21	-2.13	-1.95	-1.58	-1.39	Income Ratio %
	84	99	81	57	69	58	62	50	56	50	46	Turnover Rate %
46	82	121	154	168	243	473	368	562	574	575	623	Net Assets $mil

Rating and Risk

Time Period	Load-Adj Return %	Morningstar Rtn vs Cat	Morningstar Risk vs Cat	Morningstar Risk-Adj Rating
1 Yr	17.05			
3 Yr	13.56	+Avg	Avg	★★★★
5 Yr	13.50	High	Avg	★★★★★
10 Yr	23.59	High	-Avg	★★★★★
Incept	25.21			

Other Measures	Standard Index S&P 500	Best Fit Index Mstar Small Growth
Alpha	-0.9	4.7
Beta	1.64	0.80
R-Squared	63	83
Standard Deviation	14.19	
Mean	13.56	
Sharpe Ratio	0.74	

Portfolio Analysis 09-30-06

Share change since 06-06 Total Stocks:130	Sector	PE	Tot Ret%	% Assets
Big 5 Sporting Goods Cor	Consumer	19.5	13.33	2.68
O2Micro International, L	Hardware	40.0	-16.01	2.01
⊕ Amsurg Corporation	Health	18.6	0.61	1.98
⊖ Raffles LaSalle Ltd	Consumer	—	—	1.93
⊕ Keystone Automotive Indu	Ind Mtrls	22.8	7.81	1.80
PLX Technology, Inc.	Hardware	NMF	51.63	1.80
⊕ Power Integrations, Inc.	Hardware	—	-1.51	1.77
Lma Intl N.V.	—	—	—	1.74
⊕ Providence Service Corpo	Health	24.4	-12.71	1.73
⊕ Guitar Center, Inc.	Consumer	16.6	-9.10	1.57
Micrel, Inc.	Hardware	24.5	-6.99	1.53
LECG Corporation	Business	19.3	6.33	1.53
⊖ ICON PLC ADR	Health	—	83.28	1.48
Pericom Semiconductor Co	Hardware	50.2	43.92	1.48
⊖ CorVel Corporation	Financial	53.6	275.75	1.48
⁂ Clarica Life Ins Pfd	—	—	—	1.46
⊕ SM&A	Business	22.7	-29.53	1.40
IntraLase Corporation	Health	48.1	25.52	1.32
⊖ MMI Hldgs Ltd	Hardware	—	—	1.32
⊖ Ports Design	Consumer	—	—	1.30

Current Investment Style

Value Blend Growth — Large Mid Small

Market Cap	%
Giant	0.0
Large	0.0
Mid	13.0
Small	37.8
Micro	49.2

Avg $mil: 434

Value Measures		Rel Category
Price/Earnings	18.22	0.87
Price/Book	2.40	0.88
Price/Sales	1.38	0.88
Price/Cash Flow	10.07	1.04
Dividend Yield %	1.02	2.22

Growth Measures	%	Rel Category
Long-Term Erngs	19.02	1.07
Book Value	14.06	1.34
Sales	13.78	1.16
Cash Flow	7.99	0.38
Historical Erngs	16.77	0.69

Profitability	%	Rel Category
Return on Equity	15.57	1.26
Return on Assets	10.12	1.52
Net Margin	9.13	1.05

Sector Weightings	% of Stocks	Rel S&P 500	3 Year High Low
⚙ Info	27.48	1.37	
🖳 Software	5.38	1.56	5 3
💻 Hardware	21.19	2.29	21 18
🎬 Media	0.53	0.14	1 0
📶 Telecom	0.38	0.11	0 0
☐ Service	57.23	1.24	
⚕ Health	18.56	1.54	32 19
🛒 Consumer	16.84	2.20	17 13
💼 Business	9.37	2.22	13 7
💲 Financial	12.46	0.56	16 11
⚒ Mfg	15.28	0.45	
🔧 Goods	4.32	0.51	5 3
⚙ Ind Mtrls	6.73	0.56	7 5
🔥 Energy	4.23	0.43	4 1
💡 Utilities	0.00	0.00	0 0

Composition

● Cash	1.8
● Stocks	93.6
● Bonds	0.0
● Other	4.6
Foreign (% of Stock)	26.0

 M⚙RNINGSTAR® Funds 500

Wasatch Small Cap Growth

	Ticker	Load	NAV	Yield	Total Assets	Mstar Category
	WAAEX	Closed	$36.88	0.0%	$1,255 mil	Small Growth

Governance and Management

Stewardship Grade: A

Portfolio Manager(s)

Jeff Cardon joined Wasatch as an analyst in 1980 and has been managing this offering since late 1986. All Wasatch funds share the same pool of analysts, and the firm's 10 portfolio managers often hold the same names across several funds. Wasatch is known for its close-knit management team and superb research, and it has never suffered a portfolio manager departure.

Strategy

Manager Jeff Cardon looks to buy firms with market caps of less than $1.5 billion that are growing their earnings by at least 20%. He does buy companies with growth rates that are significantly higher than 20%, but he blends them with steadier growers to keep a lid on volatility. He occasionally lets his winners run, which means the portfolio is sometimes home to mid- and large-cap names.

Performance 12-31-06

	1st Qtr	2nd Qtr	3rd Qtr	4th Qtr	Total
2002	-4.03	-12.63	-16.42	9.32	-23.39
2003	-5.88	25.79	5.19	10.35	37.43
2004	1.40	2.27	-5.39	15.53	13.36
2005	-2.69	6.74	0.60	0.60	5.14
2006	8.80	-8.01	0.71	7.55	8.40

Trailing	Total Return%	+/- S&P 500	+/- Russ 2000 Gr	%Rank Cat	Growth of $10,000
3 Mo	7.55	0.85	-1.22	57	10,755
6 Mo	8.31	-4.43	1.45	22	10,831
1 Yr	8.40	-7.39	-4.95	65	10,840
3 Yr Avg	8.91	-1.53	-1.60	58	12,918
5 Yr Avg	6.35	0.16	-0.58	51	13,605
10 Yr Avg	13.93	5.51	9.05	8	36,845
15 Yr Avg	13.54	2.90	6.44	1	67,179

Tax Analysis	Tax-Adj Rtn%	%Rank Cat	Tax-Cost Rat	%Rank Cat
3 Yr (estimated)	7.74	55	1.07	41
5 Yr (estimated)	5.64	49	0.67	38
10 Yr (estimated)	12.00	6	1.69	71

Potential Capital Gain Exposure: 25% of assets

Morningstar's Take by John Coumarianos 01-05-07

We're not used to seeing Wasatch Small Cap Growth in the middle of the pack, but that's not a reason to sell it now.

This fund has looked like a bear-market darling that hasn't played much offense in recent years. After traversing the bear market (2000-02) with aplomb by posting three straight annual top-third small-growth category finishes, the fund has had a string of subpar performances. Its 6.4% annualized five-year return through 2006 puts it in the middle of the small-growth category, and its cumulative return for the period trails both the Russell 2000 and Russell 2000 Growth Indexes'.

We think this recent performance is an anomaly, and the fund's sound investment process should guide it to better days. Although the fund rose 8% for a middling category finish in 2006, its holdings sported a 20% earnings-growth rate. The fund's holdings also boast higher margins and returns on capital than those of its peers. It's true that veteran manager Jeff Cardon is willing to pay a little extra

for excess profits and robust earnings growth, but his process isn't oblivious to price, either. For example, he recently exited a long-held position in fashion retailer Chico's FAS for valuation reasons before the market knocked it down.

Cardon also has made efforts to find businesses in the volatile and cyclical energy sector, which has traditionally not been a Wasatch hunting ground. He recently purchased Emeco Holdings, an Australian company that leases equipment to energy businesses working in the Canadian tar sands. True to the Wasatch style, Cardon figures that Emeco's fortunes are less subject to commodity prices than the energy companies'.

Still, this fund's bread-and-butter will continue to be companies such as health-care-consulting firm Healthways. Cardon thinks this fast-grower's ability to lower health-care costs for businesses will be in huge demand, and he's impressed with its cash-flow generation. Over a long period, Cardon has proved the virtues of this approach.

Address:	PO Box 2172 Milwaukee, WI 53201-2172 800-551-1700
Web Address:	www.wasatchfunds.com
Inception:	12-08-86
Advisor:	Wasatch Advisors Inc.
Subadvisor:	None
NTF Plans:	CommonWealth NTF, Fidelity Instl-NTF

Minimum Purchase:	Closed	Add: —	IRA: —
Min Auto Inv Plan:	Closed	Add: —	
Sales Fees:	No-load, 2.00%R		
Management Fee:	1.00%, 0.28%A		
Actual Fees:	Mgt:1.00%	Dist: —	
Expense Projections:	3Yr:$375	5Yr:$650	10Yr:$1433
Income Distrib:	Annually		

Historical Profile

Return	Above Avg
Risk	Below Avg
Rating	★★★★ Above Avg

94%	95%	91%	80%	87%	94%	92%	94%	96%

Investment Style
Equity
Stock %

▼ Manager Change
▽ Partial Manager Change

Growth of $10,000
■ Investment Values of Fund
— Investment Values of S&P 500

Performance Quartile (within Category)

1995	1996	1997	1998	1999	2000	2001	2002	2003	2004	2005	2006	History
23.87	23.86	24.60	22.97	29.00	27.82	33.99	26.04	35.61	39.46	36.70	36.88	NAV
28.12	5.20	19.23	11.17	40.87	16.80	24.17	-23.39	37.43	13.36	5.14	8.40	Total Return %
-9.46	-17.76	-14.13	-17.41	19.83	25.90	36.06	-1.29	8.75	2.48	0.23	-7.39	+/-S&P 500
-2.92	-6.06	6.28	9.94	-2.22	39.23	33.40	6.87	-11.11	-0.95	0.99	-4.95	+/-Russ 2000 Gr
0.00	0.00	0.00	0.00	0.00	0.00	0.00	0.00	0.00	0.00	0.00	0.00	Income Return %
28.12	5.20	19.23	11.17	40.87	16.80	24.17	-23.39	37.43	13.36	5.14	8.40	Capital Return %
66	92	44	27	62	9	3	29	79	43	58	65	Total Rtn % Rank Cat
0.00	0.00	0.00	0.00	0.00	0.00	0.00	0.00	0.00	0.00	0.00	0.00	Income $
0.54	1.22	3.69	3.07	2.71	5.85	0.45	0.00	0.17	0.77	4.82	2.92	Capital Gains $
1.47	1.50	1.50	1.48	1.44	1.38	1.36	1.31	1.25	1.20	1.18	1.18	Expense Ratio %
-0.37	-0.65	-0.39	-0.60	-0.79	-0.84	-0.83	-1.25	-1.08	-0.91	-0.62	-0.64	Income Ratio %
29	73	48	56	46	72	40	51	63	41	36	41	Turnover Rate %
294	219	172	157	182	240	934	786	1,258	1,357	1,361	1,255	Net Assets $mil

Rating and Risk

Time Period	Load-Adj Return %	Morningstar Rtn vs Cat	Morningstar Risk vs Cat	Morningstar Risk-Adj Rating
1 Yr	8.40			
3 Yr	8.91	Avg	-Avg	★★★
5 Yr	6.35	Avg	Avg	★★★
10 Yr	13.93	High	-Avg	★★★★
Incept	13.84			

Other Measures	Standard Index S&P 500	Best Fit Index DJ Wilshire 4500
Alpha	-5.7	-6.6
Beta	1.71	1.13
R-Squared	78	90
Standard Deviation	13.25	
Mean	8.91	
Sharpe Ratio	0.47	

Portfolio Analysis 09-30-06

Share change since 06-06 Total Stocks:97	Sector	PE	Tot Ret%	% Assets
⊕ O'Reilly Automotive, Inc	Consumer	20.4	0.16	5.41
⊕ Copart, Inc.	Business	25.4	30.10	3.80
⊕ Knight Transportation, I	Business	21.4	-17.31	3.65
⊕ Guitar Center, Inc.	Consumer	16.6	-9.10	3.38
⊖ FactSet Research Systems	Business	33.8	37.91	3.21
⊕ Techne Corporation	Health	29.5	-1.12	2.84
HDFC Bank, Ltd. ADR	Financial	36.8	49.14	2.50
United Surgical Partners	Health	35.6	-11.82	2.33
⊕ Power Integrations, Inc.	Hardware		-1.51	2.31
⊕ Amsurg Corporation	Health	18.6	0.61	2.18
⊕ Hibbett Sporting Goods,	Consumer	29.8	7.20	2.15
Strayer Education, Inc.	Consumer	30.1	14.34	2.03
⊖ ICON PLC ADR	Health		83.28	1.89
⊕ Bank of the Ozarks, Inc.	Financial	16.4	-9.32	1.86
Tessera Technologies, In	Hardware	35.4	56.05	1.74
⊕ Micrel, Inc.	Hardware	24.5	-6.99	1.73
⊕ Stantec, Inc.	Business			1.47
⊖ Resources Global Profess	Business	29.2	21.95	1.41
Qiagen NV	Health	38.1	28.77	1.37
⊕ Silicon Laboratories, In	Hardware	45.5	-5.48	1.36

Current Investment Style

Value Blnd Growth — Large Mid Small

Market Cap	%
Giant	0.0
Large	2.6
Mid	31.9
Small	56.4
Micro	9.0

Avg $mil: 1,298

Value Measures		Rel Category
Price/Earnings	20.36	0.97
Price/Book	2.91	1.07
Price/Sales	1.89	1.20
Price/Cash Flow	13.08	1.36
Dividend Yield %	0.35	0.76

Growth Measures	%	Rel Category
Long-Term Erngs	16.99	0.96
Book Value	17.57	1.68
Sales	16.75	1.41
Cash Flow	12.61	0.60
Historical Erngs	23.11	0.95

Profitability	%	Rel Category
Return on Equity	14.69	1.18
Return on Assets	8.48	1.27
Net Margin	12.04	1.39

Sector Weightings	% of Stocks	Rel S&P 500	3 Year High Low
↻ Info	16.58	0.83	
Software	2.38	0.69	5 2
Hardware	12.80	1.39	14 11
Media	0.00	0.00	1 0
Telecom	1.40	0.40	3 1
⊆ Service	76.52	1.66	
Health	23.94	1.99	31 19
Consumer	20.67	2.70	23 18
Business	20.51	4.85	21 16
Financial	11.40	0.51	15 9
Mfg	6.89	0.20	
Goods	3.38	0.40	5 1
Ind Mtrls	1.65	0.14	4 1
Energy	1.86	0.19	2 0
Utilities	0.00	0.00	0 0

Composition

● Cash	0.1	
● Stocks	96.5	
● Bonds	0.0	
○ Other	3.4	

Foreign 17.3 (% of Stock)

Wasatch Small Cap Value

	Ticker	Load	NAV	Yield	Total Assets	Mstar Category
	WMCVX	Closed	$5.01	0.7%	$681 mil	Small Blend

Governance and Management

Stewardship Grade: B

Portfolio Manager(s)

Jim Larkins and John Mazanec are responsible for the fund's day-to-day management. Larkins and Mazanec had worked as analysts before assuming their current positions. All Wasatch funds pull from the same pool of analysts, and the shop--which has never suffered a portfolio manager departure--is known for its close-knit, team-based management approach.

Strategy

Management won't buy firms with market caps greater than $2.5 billion (recently increased from $1.5 billion), but it has historically kept the portfolio's median market cap much smaller, typically less than $500 million. The managers look for either growth stocks that have stumbled or relatively undiscovered names that are selling at a discount to management's estimate of their growth rates.

Historical Profile

Return	Above Avg
Risk	Average
Rating	★★★★ Above Avg

Investment Style: Equity, Stock %

99% 89% 89% 82% 86% 97% 98% 98% 98%

▼ Manager Change
▽ Partial Manager Change

Growth of $10,000
— Investment Values of Fund
— Investment Values of S&P 500

39.4 / 32.4 / 24.0 / 17.0 / 10.0

Performance Quartile (within Category)

	1995	1996	1997	1998	1999	2000	2001	2002	2003	2004	2005	2006	History
	—	—	2.01	2.18	2.69	3.15	4.10	3.43	5.30	5.53	5.01	5.01	NAV
	—	—	0.50*	8.46	28.09	29.04	33.63	-16.34	54.57	21.58	4.75	14.84	Total Return %
	—	—	—	-20.12	7.05	38.14	45.52	5.76	25.89	10.70	-0.16	-0.95	+/-S&P 500
	—	—	—	11.01	6.83	32.06	31.14	4.14	7.32	3.25	0.20	-3.53	+/-Russ 2000
	—	—	—	0.00	0.00	0.00	0.00	0.00	0.00	0.00	1.24	0.76	Income Return %
	—	—	—	8.46	28.09	29.04	33.63	-16.34	54.57	21.58	3.51	14.08	Capital Return %
	—	—	—	6	21	9	1	54	8	29	68	50	Total Rtn % Rank Cat
	—	—	0.00	0.00	0.00	0.00	0.00	0.00	0.00	0.00	0.07	0.04	Income $
	—	—	0.00	0.00	0.09	0.31	0.10	0.00	0.00	0.78	0.72	0.71	Capital Gains $
	—	—	—	1.95	1.95	1.95	1.92	1.81	1.78	1.73	1.72	1.68	Expense Ratio %
	—	—	—	-1.02	-1.54	-1.02	-0.31	-0.44	-0.43	-0.26	0.94	0.81	Income Ratio %
	—	—	—	114	106	67	41	69	69	56	43	40	Turnover Rate %
	—	—	2	17	21	63	558	475	741	820	713	681	Net Assets $mil

Performance 12-31-06

	1st Qtr	2nd Qtr	3rd Qtr	4th Qtr	Total
2002	14.39	-4.90	-28.03	6.85	-16.34
2003	-4.37	25.91	11.86	14.75	54.57
2004	10.75	-2.90	-2.98	16.52	21.58
2005	-5.61	6.32	2.16	2.17	4.75
2006	11.38	-2.69	-2.58	8.76	14.84

Trailing	Total Return%	+/- S&P 500	+/- Russ 2000	%Rank Cat	Growth of $10,000
3 Mo	8.76	2.06	-0.14	30	10,876
6 Mo	5.96	-6.78	-3.42	72	10,596
1 Yr	14.84	-0.95	-3.53	50	11,484
3 Yr Avg	13.51	3.07	-0.05	48	14,625
5 Yr Avg	13.59	7.40	2.20	24	18,910
10 Yr Avg	—	—	—	—	—
15 Yr Avg	—	—	—	—	—

Tax Analysis	Tax-Adj Rtn%	%Rank Cat	Tax-Cost Rat	%Rank Cat
3 Yr (estimated)	10.61	61	2.55	78
5 Yr (estimated)	11.84	29	1.54	68
10 Yr (estimated)	—	—	—	—

Potential Capital Gain Exposure: 23% of assets

Morningstar's Take by Andrew Gogerty 12-21-06

We remain fans of Wasatch Small Cap Value.

Investors fortunate to get a spot in this closed small-blend fund have had a lot to smile about. The fund's long-term trailing returns outpace the category norm, and its calendar-year results have also been consistent. And, by keeping a close eye on assets through multiple closings, Wasatch has ensured that comanagers Jim Larkins and John Mazanec will continue to have the flexibility to own hidden small- and micro-cap gems in the future.

That said, management's willingness to chart their own course--and not the fund's long-term record--is why this fund continues to be a solid investment. Larkins and Mazanec pay little attention to the fund's sector biases and rather rely solely on the quality of their picks to drive returns. The fund has had little exposure to commodity-linked industrial stocks because the team isn't comfortable with the capital-intensive profile of the sector. This stance combined with more than one-third of its assets in financial stocks

has held back returns in recent years. But the firm is standing firm on picks such as lender United Pan Am Corp., saying that the market is undervaluing the firm's potential for higher loan volumes as its branch mix matures.

Though the fund has underperformed in 2005 and 2006, there's a case for staying put here. Like its siblings, this offering focuses on uncovering financially strong companies with entrenched competitive advantages for the long-term. Here management focuses on firms with market caps of less than $2.5 billion that have dominant positions in their respective industries. But, unlike some other Wasatch offerings this fund doesn't focus on sequential earnings growth, but rather battered stocks with the potential to generate high returns on equity. We think this focus is prudent, especially given the outperformance of small-cap stocks in recent years. In fact, shareholders should moderate their expectations, but overall this fund remains a solid holding.

Address:	PO Box 2172
	Milwaukee, WI 53201-2172
	800-551-1700
Web Address:	www.wasatchfunds.com
Inception:	12-17-97*
Advisor:	Wasatch Advisors Inc.
Subadvisor:	None
NTF Plans:	CommonWealth NTF, Fidelity Instl-NTF

Minimum Purchase:	Closed	Add: —	IRA: —
Min Auto Inv Plan:	Closed	Add: —	
Sales Fees:	No-load, 2.00%R		
Management Fee:	1.50%		
Actual Fees:	Mgt:1.50%	Dist: —	
Expense Projections:	3Yr:$542	5Yr:$934	10Yr:$2030
Income Distrib:	Annually		

Rating and Risk

Time Period	Load-Adj Return %	Morningstar Rtn vs Cat	Morningstar Risk vs Cat	Morningstar Risk-Adj Rating
1 Yr	14.84			
3 Yr	13.51	Avg	-Avg	★★★
5 Yr	13.59	+Avg	+Avg	★★★★
10 Yr	—	—	—	—
Incept	18.26			

Other Measures	Standard Index S&P 500	Best Fit Index DJ Wilshire 4500
Alpha	0.3	-1.5
Beta	1.42	1.04
R-Squared	62	87
Standard Deviation	12.36	
Mean	13.51	
Sharpe Ratio	0.83	

Portfolio Analysis 09-30-06

Share change since 06-06 Total Stocks:102

	Sector	PE	Tot Ret%	% Assets
⊕ Keystone Automotive Indu	Ind Mtrls	22.8	7.81	3.00
⊖ Hub International, Ltd.	Financial	24.8	22.88	2.60
⊖ Redwood Trust, Inc.	Financial	11.0	56.92	2.48
⊕ Beacon Roofing Supply, I	Consumer	17.8	-1.74	2.41
⊖ Northstar Realty Finance	Financial	13.4	79.48	2.10
⊕ Monro Muffler/Brake, Inc	Consumer	25.3	16.59	2.07
Dollar Financial Corpora	Financial	NMF	132.36	2.00
⊕ Global Imaging Systems,	Ind Mtrls	16.4	26.77	1.92
⊕ Vitran Corporation, Inc.	Business	11.5	-11.83	1.90
Fidelity Natl Finl	Financial	—	—	1.86
AmeriCredit Corporation	Financial	11.2	-1.80	1.80
Housing Development Fina	Financial	—	—	1.77
⊕ Ultra Petroleum Corporat	Energy	30.4	-14.44	1.73
Pericom Semiconductor Co	Hardware	50.2	43.92	1.64
Big 5 Sporting Goods Cor	Consumer	19.5	13.33	1.59
MCG Capital Corporation	Financial	11.3	54.30	1.57
UTI Bank Ltd	Financial	—	—	1.55
⊕ Saxon Engy Svcs	Energy	—	—	1.51
⊕ Placer Sierra Bancshares	Financial	18.8	-12.31	1.51
McGrath RentCorp	Consumer	18.0	12.67	1.48

Current Investment Style

Value Blnd Growth — Large/Mid/Small

Market Cap	%
Giant	0.0
Large	3.6
Mid	15.8
Small	39.9
Micro	40.7

Avg $mil: 707

Value Measures		Rel Category
Price/Earnings	14.63	0.88
Price/Book	1.63	0.77
Price/Sales	0.77	0.79
Price/Cash Flow	6.15	0.88
Dividend Yield %	3.32	3.10

Growth Measures	%	Rel Category
Long-Term Erngs	13.42	0.96
Book Value	10.97	1.45
Sales	11.08	1.25
Cash Flow	7.56	0.60
Historical Erngs	16.27	0.97

Profitability	%	Rel Category
Return on Equity	12.78	0.99
Return on Assets	7.41	1.04
Net Margin	14.13	1.46

Sector Weightings	% of Stocks	Rel S&P 500	3 Year High	Low
☍ Info	10.06	0.50		
▣ Software	1.77	0.51	2	0
▣ Hardware	8.29	0.90	9	2
▣ Media	0.00	0.00	0	0
▣ Telecom	0.00	0.00	1	0
▣ Service	67.17	1.45		
▣ Health	5.12	0.42	12	5
▣ Consumer	15.59	2.04	22	15
▣ Business	9.19	2.17	10	5
▣ Financial	37.27	1.67	44	37
▣ Mfg	22.78	0.67		
▣ Goods	3.85	0.45	4	1
▣ Ind Mtrls	11.08	0.93	14	11
▣ Energy	7.85	0.80	8	1
▣ Utilities	0.00	0.00	1	0

Composition

	%
Cash	1.0
Stocks	98.3
Bonds	0.0
Other	0.7
Foreign (% of Stock)	12.3

Morningstar® Funds 500

Wasatch Ultra Growth

	Ticker	Load	NAV	Yield	Total Assets	Mstar Category
	WAMCX	Closed	$24.04	0.0%	$305 mil	Small Growth

Governance and Management

Stewardship Grade: A

Portfolio Manager(s)

Lead manager Karey Barker has led this offering since its 1992 inception. Comanager Ajay Krishnan was an analyst on this fund before being elevated to his current position in early 2000.

Strategy

Management looks to buy firms with market capitalizations of no more than $5 billion that it thinks are capable of growing earnings by 25% or more annually. This approach has produced a portfolio that is almost entirely composed of names in the technology and health-care sectors. Management lets winners run and typically keeps about half of the fund's assets in its top 10 picks.

Historical Profile
Return	Average
Risk	Above Avg
Rating	★★★ Neutral

85% 89% 90% 78% 84% 95% 95% 95% 96%

▼ Manager Change
▽ Partial Manager Change

40.8
31.0
24.0
17.0

Growth of $10,000
— Investment Values of Fund
— Investment Values of S&P 500

10.0

Investment Style
Equity
Stock %

Performance Quartile (within Category)

1995	1996	1997	1998	1999	2000	2001	2002	2003	2004	2005	2006	History
18.29	18.94	16.71	19.77	21.48	21.41	24.20	19.68	28.17	26.84	24.05	24.04	NAV
58.77	3.57	-0.51	24.81	17.46	25.97	18.26	-18.68	44.52	-0.82	3.58	7.31	Total Return %
21.19	-19.39	-33.87	-3.77	-3.58	35.07	30.15	3.42	15.84	-11.70	-1.33	-8.48	+/-S&P 500
27.73	-7.69	-13.46	23.58	-25.63	48.40	27.49	11.58	-4.02	-15.13	-0.57	-6.04	+/-Russ 2000 Gr
0.00	0.00	0.00	0.00	0.00	0.00	0.00	0.00	0.00	0.00	0.00	0.00	Income Return %
58.77	3.57	-0.51	24.81	17.46	25.97	18.26	-18.68	44.52	-0.82	3.58	7.31	Capital Return %
5	95	94	5	83	4	5	14	47	96	75	73	Total Rtn % Rank Cat
0.00	0.00	0.00	0.00	0.00	0.00	0.00	0.00	0.00	0.00	0.00	0.00	Income $
0.19	0.00	2.00	0.74	1.47	5.39	0.92	0.00	0.26	0.97	3.78	1.78	Capital Gains $
1.75	1.75	1.75	1.75	1.75	1.75	1.75	1.71	1.57	1.50	1.50	1.48	Expense Ratio %
-0.71	-1.27	-1.48	-1.54	-1.49	-1.19	-1.39	-1.67	-1.50	-1.39	-1.30	-1.19	Income Ratio %
46	121	103	91	77	135	123	78	76	67	65	76	Turnover Rate %
130	100	61	63	43	55	177	389	595	449	374	305	Net Assets $mil

Performance 12-31-06

	1st Qtr	2nd Qtr	3rd Qtr	4th Qtr	Total
2002	-1.32	-16.58	-17.07	19.13	-18.68
2003	-8.74	29.29	9.52	11.84	44.52
2004	0.39	-1.41	-13.67	16.07	-0.82
2005	-5.37	5.55	4.36	-0.64	3.58
2006	10.85	-9.64	0.00	7.13	7.31

Trailing	Total Return%	+/- S&P 500	+/- Russ 2000 Gr	%Rank Cat	Growth of $10,000
3 Mo	7.13	0.43	-1.64	64	10,713
6 Mo	7.13	-5.61	0.27	30	10,713
1 Yr	7.31	-8.48	-6.04	73	10,731
3 Yr Avg	3.30	-7.14	-7.21	94	11,023
5 Yr Avg	5.32	-0.87	-1.61	60	12,958
10 Yr Avg	10.90	2.48	6.02	25	28,139
15 Yr Avg	—				

Tax Analysis	Tax-Adj Rtn%	%Rank Cat	Tax-Cost Rat	%Rank Cat
3 Yr (estimated)	1.76	93	1.49	59
5 Yr (estimated)	4.34	62	0.93	54
10 Yr (estimated)	9.03	29	1.69	71

Potential Capital Gain Exposure: 15% of assets

Rating and Risk

Time Period	Load-Adj Return %	Morningstar Rtn vs Cat	Morningstar Risk vs Cat	Morningstar Risk-Adj Rating
1 Yr	7.31			
3 Yr	3.30	Low	+Avg	★
5 Yr	5.32	Avg	+Avg	★★★
10 Yr	10.90	+Avg	Avg	★★★
Incept	12.45			

Other Measures	Standard Index S&P 500	Best Fit Index Mstar Small Growth
Alpha	-12.3	-5.5
Beta	1.95	0.92
R-Squared	71	88
Standard Deviation	15.98	
Mean	3.30	
Sharpe Ratio	0.08	

Portfolio Analysis 09-30-06

Share change since 06-06 Total Stocks:78	Sector	PE	Tot Ret%	% Assets
United Surgical Partners	Health	35.6	-11.82	4.00
Silicon Laboratories, In	Hardware	45.5	-5.48	3.31
ArthroCare Corporation	Health	34.1	-5.27	3.08
⊕ Knight Transportation, I	Business	21.4	-17.31	2.95
⊖ Healthways, Inc.	Health	50.4	5.44	2.90
⊖ O'Reilly Automotive, Inc	Consumer	20.4	0.16	2.89
⊖ Pediatrix Medical Group,	Health	25.0	10.42	2.70
⊖ SRA International, Inc.	Business	25.3	-12.44	2.64
⊖ Cognizant Technology Sol	Business	52.9	53.49	2.53
LECG Corporation	Business	19.3	6.33	2.49
Microchip Technology, In	Hardware	27.2	4.37	2.48
⊖ Psychiatric Solutions, I	Health	43.7	27.75	2.39
⊖ Tessera Technologies, In	Hardware	35.4	56.05	2.30
⊕ Providence Service Corpo	Health	24.4	-12.71	2.26
Guitar Center, Inc.	Consumer	16.6	-9.10	2.19
⊖ HDFC Bank, Ltd. ADR	Financial	36.8	49.14	2.17
⊖ IntraLase Corporation	Health	48.1	25.52	2.07
⊕ Kyphon, Inc.	Health	56.5	-1.05	2.05
Power Integrations, Inc.	Hardware	—	-1.51	1.81
Micrel, Inc.	Hardware	24.5	-6.99	1.70

Current Investment Style

Value Blnd Growth (Large Mid Small)

	Market Cap	%
	Giant	0.0
	Large	4.0
	Mid	25.2
	Small	57.0
	Micro	13.8
	Avg $mil:	1,319

Value Measures		Rel Category
Price/Earnings	25.07	1.19
Price/Book	3.18	1.16
Price/Sales	2.45	1.56
Price/Cash Flow	14.63	1.52
Dividend Yield %	0.25	0.54

Growth Measures	%	Rel Category
Long-Term Erngs	22.23	1.25
Book Value	16.04	1.53
Sales	21.63	1.82
Cash Flow	24.82	1.17
Historical Erngs	24.60	1.01

Profitability	%	Rel Category
Return on Equity	13.09	1.06
Return on Assets	8.80	1.32
Net Margin	11.18	1.29

Sector Weightings	% of Stocks	Rel S&P 500	3 Year High Low
↻ Info	30.90	1.55	
▣ Software	3.35	0.97	10 3
▣ Hardware	24.85	2.69	25 17
▣ Media	1.20	0.32	2 0
▣ Telecom	1.50	0.43	6 1
⊄ Service	63.58	1.38	
▣ Health	30.75	2.55	38 25
▣ Consumer	11.32	1.48	15 6
▣ Business	15.00	3.55	24 13
▣ Financial	6.51	0.29	13 5
⊔ Mfg	5.52	0.16	
▣ Goods	1.70	0.20	2 1
▣ Ind Mtrls	2.11	0.18	3 1
▣ Energy	1.71	0.17	3 0
▣ Utilities	0.00	0.00	0 0

Composition

● Cash	0.7
● Stocks	96.4
● Bonds	0.0
● Other	2.9
Foreign	12.2 (% of Stock)

Morningstar's Take by John Coumarianos 11-05-06

Investors who bail out of Wasatch Ultra Growth are making a mistake.

Funds as aggressive as this one invariably go through hot and cold streaks, and during the last three years, this fund has been in an arctic deep frost. This fund's strategy is to buy stocks under $5 billion in market capitalization (the amount of shares outstanding multiplied by the share price) that are growing their earnings by 20% or more annually. Companies growing this quickly usually exhibit great price volatility because so much anticipated growth is priced into their stocks. Any decline in earnings (or perceived decline) can send prices down dramatically. Therefore, it's not unusual for the fund to lag its category. Over the past decade, the fund has finished in the top or bottom quartile of the small-growth category every calendar year except one, including back-to-back bottom-decile finishes in 1996 and 1997.

Fortunately, the fund has been near the top of its peer group more often than it's been near the bottom. In 2002's difficult year for growth stocks, the fund dropped 18%, but this compares favorably with a 28% loss for the average small-growth fund and a 30% loss for the Russell 2000 Growth Index. Additionally, its long-term performance is stellar: It's returned 191% cumulatively for 10 years through October 2006, versus 143% for its typical peer and 65% for the Russell 2000 Growth Index.

We think the fund's recent poor performance isn't likely to last. Top two holdings United Surgical Partners and Silicon Laboratories have struggled this year, but both businesses garner narrow-moat ratings from Morningstar analysts for their competitive advantages. United Surgical receives no payments from Medicare or Medicaid, and Silicon Labs makes unique mixed-signal chips, which are expensive and time-consuming for competitors to duplicate.

We've noticed assets leaving the fund lately, as some investors have become impatient, but we think those sticking around will be rewarded.

Address:	PO Box 2172 Milwaukee, WI 53201-2172 800-551-1700	Minimum Purchase:	Closed	Add: —	IRA: —
		Min Auto Inv Plan:	Closed	Add: —	
		Sales Fees:	No-load, 2.00%R		
Web Address:	www.wasatchfunds.com	Management Fee:	1.25%		
Inception:	08-17-92	Actual Fees:	Mgt:1.25%	Dist:—	
Advisor:	Wasatch Advisors Inc.	Expense Projections:	3Yr:$475	5Yr:$819	10Yr:$1791
Subadvisor:	None	Income Distrib:	Annually		
NTF Plans:	Fidelity Retail-NTF, Schwab OneSource				

Weitz Hickory

	Analyst Pick	Ticker WEHIX	Load None	NAV $39.96	Yield 0.5%	Total Assets $387 mil	Mstar Category Mid-Cap Blend

Governance and Management

Stewardship Grade: A

Portfolio Manager(s)

Rick Lawson ran the fund from its 1993 inception through 2002. Firm founder Wally Weitz took his place at the end of 2002. Weitz has built great long-term records at Weitz Value and Weitz Partners Value. The firm has seven investment professionals, including a recently added small-cap analyst. The firm's analysts and managers are generalists and do not specialize in any one industry.

Strategy

Historically, the fund has emphasized out-of-favor stocks that its management thinks are cheap relative to the present value of their future cash flows, and it has frequently made large individual stock and sector bets. Together, these tendencies have led the fund's performance to deviate sharply from its peers'. Although the fund is valuation-conscious, it can provide an exceedingly bumpy ride. It changed managers at the end of 2002 and will likely be a bit less concentrated.

Historical Profile

Return	Average
Risk	Above Avg
Rating	★★★ Neutral

Investment Style: Equity, Stock %

85% 97% 98% 96% 95% 92% 80% 92% 97%

▼ Manager Change
▽ Partial Manager Change

Growth of $10,000
— Investment Values of Fund
— Investment Values of S&P 500

Performance Quartile (within Category)

1995	1996	1997	1998	1999	2000	2001	2002	2003	2004	2005	2006	History
14.66	18.80	23.70	30.98	39.65	27.55	26.26	18.42	26.99	32.86	32.71	39.96	NAV
40.49	35.36	39.17	33.01	36.67	-17.24	-4.65	-29.31	47.95	22.61	-0.22	22.80	Total Return %
2.91	12.40	5.81	4.43	15.63	-8.14	7.24	-7.21	19.27	11.73	-5.13	7.01	+/-S&P 500
9.56	16.11	6.92	13.89	21.95	-34.75	-4.04	-14.78	12.33	6.13	-12.78	12.48	+/-S&P Mid 400
1.28	0.00	0.40	0.41	0.04	0.00	0.00	0.54	1.39	0.85	0.23	0.63	Income Return %
39.21	35.36	38.77	32.60	36.63	-17.24	-4.65	-29.85	46.56	21.76	-0.45	22.17	Capital Return %
11	3	6	1	17	95	75	95	14	9	96	7	Total Rtn % Rank Cat
0.14	0.00	0.07	0.10	0.01	0.00	0.00	0.14	0.25	0.23	0.08	0.21	Income $
0.07	1.04	1.91	0.45	2.56	5.29	0.01	0.00	0.00	0.00	0.00	0.00	Capital Gains $
1.50	1.50	1.50	1.46	1.30	1.23	1.22	1.25	1.32	1.30	1.21	1.20	Expense Ratio %
-0.20	0.33	0.33	-0.13	0.48	-0.44	-0.27	-0.08	0.78	0.96	0.65	0.28	Income Ratio %
20	28	28	29	40	46	22	18	64	50	58	65	Turnover Rate %
5	10	22	539	913	466	339	195	235	344	335	387	Net Assets $mil

Performance 12-31-06

	1st Qtr	2nd Qtr	3rd Qtr	4th Qtr	Total
2002	2.86	-14.51	-28.89	13.05	-29.31
2003	-2.44	25.28	3.43	17.04	47.95
2004	6.93	0.91	3.06	10.25	22.61
2005	-4.56	5.10	-3.61	3.20	-0.22
2006	4.59	0.84	4.61	11.31	22.80

Trailing	Total Return%	+/- S&P 500	+/- S&P Mid 400	%Rank Cat	Growth of $10,000
3 Mo	11.31	4.61	4.32	7	11,131
6 Mo	16.44	3.70	10.61	3	11,644
1 Yr	22.80	7.01	12.48	7	12,280
3 Yr Avg	14.53	4.09	1.44	24	15,023
5 Yr Avg	9.46	3.27	-1.43	63	15,714
10 Yr Avg	12.11	3.69	-1.36	42	31,365
15 Yr Avg	—				

Tax Analysis	Tax-Adj Rtn%	%Rank Cat	Tax-Cost Rat	%Rank Cat
3 Yr (estimated)	14.34	16	0.17	8
5 Yr (estimated)	9.21	50	0.23	14
10 Yr (estimated)	11.10	25	0.90	13

Potential Capital Gain Exposure: 2% of assets

Rating and Risk

Time Period	Load-Adj Return %	Morningstar Rtn vs Cat	Morningstar Risk vs Cat	Morningstar Risk-Adj Rating
1 Yr	22.80			
3 Yr	14.53	+Avg	-Avg	★★★★
5 Yr	9.46	Avg	+Avg	★★
10 Yr	12.11	Avg	+Avg	★★★
Incept	13.91			

Other Measures	Standard Index S&P 500	Best Fit Index DJ Wilshire 4500
Alpha	4.1	3.5
Beta	0.97	0.64
R-Squared	54	63
Standard Deviation	9.02	
Mean	14.53	
Sharpe Ratio	1.20	

Portfolio Analysis 09-30-06

Share change since 06-06 Total Stocks:32	Sector	PE	Tot Ret%	% Assets
⊖ Redwood Trust, Inc.	Financial	11.0	56.92	8.17
⊕ Countrywide Financial Co	Financial	9.8	26.22	7.29
⊖ Berkshire Hathaway Inc.	Financial	—		6.45
⊖ Cabela's, Inc.	Consumer	20.0	45.36	5.32
Tyco International, Ltd.	Ind Mtrls	15.7	6.83	4.71
Liberty Interactive A	Media	—		4.52
⊖ UnitedHealth Group, Inc.	Health	20.8	-13.49	4.52
Cumulus Media, Inc. A	Media	—	-16.28	4.10
⊖ Coinstar, Inc.	Business	38.9	33.90	3.96
Liberty Capital A	Media	—		3.71
⊖ Fannie Mae	Financial	—	24.34	3.59
⊖ Liberty Global, Inc.	Media	—		3.54
⊖ Dell, Inc.	Hardware	18.4	-16.23	3.53
⊕ IAC/InterActiveCorp	Consumer	40.6	31.26	3.26
AutoZone, Inc.	Consumer	15.3	25.95	2.53
⊕ Wells Fargo Govn't Fund	—			2.52
Wal-Mart Stores, Inc.	Consumer	16.9	0.13	2.26
Comcast Corporation	Media	—		2.25
⊖ Telephone and Data Syste	Telecom	—		2.25
Six Flags, Inc.	Goods	—	-32.04	2.16

Current Investment Style

Value Blnd Growth — Large Mid Small

Market Cap	%
Giant	30.3
Large	17.7
Mid	14.9
Small	25.4
Micro	11.8
Avg $mil: 7,547	

Value Measures		Rel Category
Price/Earnings	14.41	0.90
Price/Book	1.72	0.76
Price/Sales	1.22	1.09
Price/Cash Flow	7.01	0.83
Dividend Yield %	1.83	1.41

Growth Measures	%	Rel Category
Long-Term Erngs	10.91	0.86
Book Value	-2.66	NMF
Sales	14.32	1.61
Cash Flow	18.45	2.18
Historical Erngs	41.24	2.31

Profitability	%	Rel Category
Return on Equity	9.76	0.61
Return on Assets	5.98	0.74
Net Margin	5.08	0.47

Sector Weightings	% of Stocks	Rel S&P 500	3 Year High Low
⟳ Info	27.99	1.40	
Software	0.61	0.18	1 0
Hardware	3.62	0.39	4 0
Media	20.54	5.42	24 18
Telecom	3.22	0.92	10 3
⟲ Service	63.09	1.37	
Health	7.53	0.62	17 0
Consumer	19.12	2.50	29 17
Business	4.07	0.96	5 0
Financial	32.37	1.45	40 30
⟱ Mfg	8.92	0.26	
Goods	4.09	0.48	4 0
Ind Mtrls	4.83	0.40	8 0
Energy	0.00	0.00	0 0
Utilities	0.00	0.00	0 0

Composition

● Cash	0.0
● Stocks	97.5
● Bonds	0.0
● Other	2.5
Foreign (% of Stock)	0.0

Morningstar's Take by Todd Trubey 11-07-06

Weitz Hickory is as tough and flexible as the wood that shares its name.

We're confident enough to make this fund an Analyst Pick, but maybe investors shouldn't watch its volatile returns. It resides in the grab-bag mid-blend category, where its finish during the last four years has twice been in the bottom decile and twice in the top 15% of the group. The fund's nifty 16% gain for the year to date through Nov. 3, 2006, is in the group's top 5% but clashes sharply with last year's 0.22% loss.

The areas driving the relative and absolute return shifts are financials and media. Manager Wally Weitz's preference for out-of-favor firms with strong future cash-flow expectations tends to push him toward areas that are cash-rich but not capital-intensive. While the media sector, where this fund has 7 times the weighting of its typical peer, was out of favor in 2005, it's back to the fore in 2006. The three Liberty entities, CBS, and Comcast have all helped this fund quite a bit. And

in financials, top holdings Redwood Trust and Berkshire Hathaway, have boosted returns this year.

The fact is that the source of our zeal--the fund's investment style--can't be separated from the fund's erratic short-term nature. Like famed investor Warren Buffett, Weitz believes in focused portfolios (this fund holds but 32 stocks). Weitz and Buffett also agree that smart investing stems from a focus on the best opportunities, despite the lumpy returns they may drive. Buffett's influence is also evident in the fund's unusual mix of fundamentals, which lands it in the mid-blend category. All picks depend on a clear-cut, discounted cash-flow model; but some lean more on low valuations, and others on growth forecasts.

Because Weitz Value, also an Analyst Pick, mainly targets larger firms and holds a few more stocks, we see this as both the most pure and challenging Weitz fund to own. For those who understand it, we highly recommend this fund.

Address:	1125 South 103 Street Omaha NE 68124-6008 800-304-9745
Web Address:	www.weitzfunds.com
Inception:	04-01-93
Advisor:	Weitz Wallace R & Co.
Subadvisor:	None
NTF Plans:	Schwab OneSource

Minimum Purchase:	$5000	Add: $0	IRA: $4000
Min Auto Inv Plan:	$100	Add: $100	
Sales Fees:	No-load		
Management Fee:	1.00% mx./0.80% mn., 0.22%A		
Actual Fees:	Mgt:1.00%	Dist:—	
Expense Projections:	3Yr:$381	5Yr:$660	10Yr:$1455
Income Distrib:	Semi-Annually		

Weitz Partners Value

	Ticker	Load	NAV	Yield	Total Assets	Mstar Category
	WPVLX	None	$24.43	0.5%	$2,035 mil	Large Value

Governance and Management

Stewardship Grade: A

Portfolio Manager(s)

Wally Weitz has been at the helm of this offering since its inception, and he also manages Weitz Hickory and Weitz Value. He owns Wallace Weitz & Co. and is a major shareholder in the firm's funds.

Strategy

Manager Wally Weitz looks for companies trading well below the price he thinks a rational private buyer would pay. To determine the latter, he relies mostly on discounted cash-flow analysis, often trying to look out 10 years or more. His price discipline and analysis of a business's long-term cash flows typically keep him out of expensive, unpredictable firms' stocks. Weitz will buy controversial names, load up on individual sectors where he finds bargains, and will hold cash when he can't find names that meet his criteria. This fund is designed for taxable accounts.

Performance 12-31-06

	1st Qtr	2nd Qtr	3rd Qtr	4th Qtr	Total
2002	-0.38	-13.30	-13.30	10.86	-16.99
2003	-4.31	18.16	0.21	10.66	25.38
2004	4.84	-1.28	2.35	8.55	14.99
2005	-3.85	1.98	-3.39	3.00	-2.42
2006	3.29	2.36	5.28	10.07	22.53

Trailing	Total Return%	+/- S&P 500	+/- Russ 1000 VI	%Rank Cat	Growth of $10,000
3 Mo	10.07	3.37	2.07	2	11,007
6 Mo	15.88	3.14	1.16	4	11,588
1 Yr	22.53	6.74	0.28	5	12,253
3 Yr Avg	11.20	0.76	-3.89	70	13,750
5 Yr Avg	7.43	1.24	-3.43	66	14,310
10 Yr Avg	14.30	5.88	3.30	1	38,059
15 Yr Avg	14.97	4.33	1.94	1	81,053

Tax Analysis	Tax-Adj Rtn%	%Rank Cat	Tax-Cost Rat	%Rank Cat
3 Yr (estimated)	9.95	62	1.12	44
5 Yr (estimated)	6.64	60	0.74	40
10 Yr (estimated)	12.83	1	1.29	35

Potential Capital Gain Exposure: 27% of assets

Morningstar's Take by Todd Trubey 12-05-06

It's clear to us that Wally Weitz hasn't lost his touch.

Toward the end of 2005, Weitz Partners Value's calendar-year return looked bad: Its 2.4% loss trailed 98% of its large-value category rivals. But now it seems 2005 was a rare short-term period when this fund was out-of-sync with the market. It rebounded in 2006, gaining 20% through December 4 and beating more than three quarters of its peers. This year should be the eighth time in 10 calendar years that the fund tops its typical rival.

It's crucial to grasp that the same traits that hurt the fund last year helped it this year. Manager Wally Weitz focuses his attention on a limited number of firms with steady businesses--those he can buy at a discount. For much of 2003 through 2005, such drab fare was out of favor while commodity firms were hot. That meant this fund's cheap holdings got cheaper--and we'll note that Weitz is one of the few investors we know of who truly sounds excited when that happens. In his

Sept. 30, 2005, shareowner letter, he pointed to six of the largest and cheapest stocks in the fund. Their average gain during the subsequent 12 months was 16%--with Comcast and Redwood Trust each surging more than 50% in 2006 after falling more than 20% in 2005.

The ability to look beyond short-term troubles and market skepticism is rare and a key part of this fund's strategy. For example, Weitz bought computer maker Dell in the late spring of 2006, when the market was fixated on Hewlett-Packard taking its market-share crown. Dell was also dogged by apparent problems in foreign markets and in the laptop market in the U.S. But Weitz admired the firm's agility and relatively strong margins; plus, he thought it had corrected some recent problems. The fund bought nearly 2 million shares in the second quarter and again in the third quarter, and the stock has since soared 26%.

It's this straightforward discipline that should keep this fund a long-term winner.

Address:	1125 S 103rd St Omaha NE 68124-1071 800-304-9745
Web Address:	www.weitzfunds.com
Inception:	05-31-83
Advisor:	Weitz Wallace R & Co.
Subadvisor:	None
NTF Plans:	Fidelity Retail-NTF, Schwab OneSource

Minimum Purchase:	$5000	Add: $0	IRA: $4000
Min Auto Inv Plan:	$100	Add: $100	
Sales Fees:	No-load		
Management Fee:	1.00%		
Actual Fees:	Mgt:1.00%	Dist: —	
Expense Projections:	3Yr:$362	5Yr:$628	10Yr:$1386
Income Distrib:	Semi-Annually		

Historical Profile

Return	Above Avg
Risk	Average
Rating	★★★★ Above Avg

| | 73% | 75% | 72% | 77% | 86% | 77% | 69% | 91% | 91% |

Investment Style
Equity
Stock %

▼ Manager Change
▽ Partial Manager Change

Growth of $10,000
▬ Investment Values of Fund
▬ Investment Values of S&P 500

- 59.0
- 43.6
- 32.4
- 24.0
- 17.0
- 10.0

Performance Quartile (within Category)

1995	1996	1997	1998	1999	2000	2001	2002	2003	2004	2005	2006	History
10.39	11.52	15.45	17.68	20.02	21.51	20.87	17.15	21.48	23.90	22.77	24.43	NAV
38.66	19.04	40.64	29.13	22.02	21.07	-0.86	-16.99	25.38	14.99	-2.42	22.53	Total Return %
1.08	-3.92	7.28	0.55	0.98	30.17	11.03	5.11	-3.30	4.11	-7.33	6.74	+/-S&P 500
0.30	-2.60	5.46	13.50	14.67	14.06	4.73	-1.47	-4.65	-1.50	-9.47	0.28	+/-Russ 1000 VI
2.86	0.55	0.00	1.08	0.28	2.63	0.98	0.24	0.11	0.39	0.63	0.62	Income Return %
35.80	18.49	40.64	28.05	21.74	18.44	-1.84	-17.23	25.27	14.60	-3.05	21.91	Capital Return %
7	58	1	1	3	11	33	43	76	26	98	5	Total Rtn % Rank Cat
0.24	0.06	0.00	0.17	0.05	0.50	0.21	0.05	0.02	0.08	0.15	0.14	Income $
0.85	0.79	0.53	1.67	1.23	1.88	0.26	0.13	0.00	0.70	0.40	3.19	Capital Gains $
1.27	1.23	1.24	1.25	1.24	1.19	1.13	1.08	1.08	1.13	1.13	1.14	Expense Ratio %
0.82	0.51	1.11	0.34	1.57	1.77	1.77	0.69	0.76	0.16	0.61	0.49	Income Ratio %
51	37	30	36	29	5	29	10	20	11	22	36	Turnover Rate %
74	95	134	292	1,143	1,948	2,978	2,327	2,811	2,893	2,074	2,035	Net Assets $mil

Rating and Risk

Time Period	Load-Adj Return %	Morningstar Rtn vs Cat	Morningstar Risk vs Cat	Morningstar Risk-Adj Rating
1 Yr	22.53			
3 Yr	11.20	Avg	Avg	★★★
5 Yr	7.43	Avg	-Avg	★★★
10 Yr	14.30	High	Avg	★★★★★
Incept	15.09			

Other Measures	Standard Index S&P 500	Best Fit Index Mstar Large Core TR
Alpha	2.6	1.9
Beta	0.72	0.77
R-Squared	52	54
Standard Deviation	6.90	
Mean	11.20	
Sharpe Ratio	1.12	

Portfolio Analysis 09-30-06

Share change since 06-06 Total Stocks:37	Sector	PE	Tot Ret%	% Assets
⊕ Countrywide Financial Co	Financial	9.8	26.22	6.58
Tyco International, Ltd.	Ind Mtrls	15.7	6.83	5.81
⊖ Berkshire Hathaway Inc.	Financial	13.2	24.89	5.53
UnitedHealth Group, Inc.	Health	20.8	-13.49	5.37
⊖ Wal-Mart Stores, Inc.	Consumer	16.9	0.13	4.42
⊖ Liberty Interactive A	Media	—	—	4.38
American International G	Financial	17.0	6.05	4.34
⊕ Washington Post Company	Media	21.8	-1.53	4.25
⊖ Fannie Mae	Financial	—	24.34	4.15
Liberty Capital A	Media	—	—	3.72
Telephone and Data Syste	Telecom	—	—	3.56
⊖ Liberty Global, Inc.	Media	—	—	3.30
⊖ Dell, Inc.	Hardware	18.4	-16.23	3.21
⊕ IAC/InterActiveCorp	Consumer	40.6	31.26	3.19
Redwood Trust, Inc.	Financial	11.0	56.92	3.03
WellPoint, Inc.	Health	17.2	-1.38	2.55
News Corporation, Ltd. A	Media	—	—	2.47
⊖ Expedia, Inc.	Consumer	—	-12.44	2.23
Comcast Corporation A	Media	45.2	63.31	2.21
Berkshire Hathaway Inc.	Financial	—	—	2.09

Current Investment Style

Value Blnd Growth		Market Cap	%
	Large	Giant	51.6
	Mid	Large	24.4
	Small	Mid	16.8
		Small	6.7
		Micro	0.5
		Avg $mil: 29,000	

Value Measures		Rel Category
Price/Earnings	14.35	1.05
Price/Book	1.87	0.84
Price/Sales	1.42	1.09
Price/Cash Flow	4.85	0.72
Dividend Yield %	1.71	0.73

Growth Measures	%	Rel Category
Long-Term Erngs	11.72	1.13
Book Value	2.92	0.37
Sales	14.03	1.56
Cash Flow	13.48	2.22
Historical Erngs	17.33	1.07

Profitability	%	Rel Category
Return on Equity	13.29	0.74
Return on Assets	7.85	0.80
Net Margin	8.12	0.63

Sector Weightings	% of Stocks	Rel S&P 500	3 Year High Low
↻ Info	34.96	1.75	
Software	0.00	0.00	0 0
Hardware	3.52	0.38	4 0
Media	27.53	7.26	31 24
Telecom	3.91	1.11	15 4
⊑ Service	57.38	1.24	
Health	8.69	0.72	9 1
Consumer	14.42	1.88	16 13
Business	0.75	0.18	1 0
Financial	33.52	1.51	44 34
⊟ Mfg	7.66	0.23	
Goods	1.29	0.15	3 1
Ind Mtrls	6.37	0.53	7 0
Energy	0.00	0.00	0 0
Utilities	0.00	0.00	0 0

Composition

● Cash	8.9	
● Stocks	91.1	
● Bonds	0.0	
○ Other	0.0	
Foreign	0.0	(% of Stock)

Weitz Value

Analyst Pick

	Ticker	Load	NAV	Yield	Total Assets	Mstar Category
	WVALX	None	$40.26	0.7%	$3,147 mil	Large Value

Governance and Management

Stewardship Grade: A

Portfolio Manager(s)

Wally Weitz has been at the helm of this offering since its inception, and he also manages Weitz Hickory and Weitz Partners Value. He owns Wallace Weitz & Co. and is a major shareholder in the firm's funds. We believe he is one of the best fund managers in the business. The firm's research staff includes six investment professionals.

Strategy

Manager Wally Weitz looks for companies trading well below the price he thinks a rational private buyer would pay. To determine the latter, he relies mostly on discounted cash-flow analysis, often trying to look out 10 years or more. This practice typically keeps him out of expensive, unpredictable firms' stocks. Weitz will buy controversial names, load up on individual sectors where he finds bargains, and hold cash when he can't find stocks that meet his criteria. This fund is designed for tax-advantaged accounts.

Performance 12-31-06

	1st Qtr	2nd Qtr	3rd Qtr	4th Qtr	Total
2002	-0.12	-12.46	-14.89	11.39	-17.10
2003	-3.83	19.47	0.62	11.35	28.73
2004	5.59	-1.20	2.31	8.44	15.74
2005	-4.14	1.90	-3.23	2.85	-2.77
2006	2.57	2.56	4.81	10.52	21.85

Trailing	Total Return%	+/- S&P 500	+/- Russ 1000 VI	%Rank Cat	Growth of $10,000
3 Mo	10.52	3.82	2.52	1	11,052
6 Mo	15.84	3.10	1.12	5	11,584
1 Yr	21.85	6.06	-0.40	9	12,185
3 Yr Avg	11.10	0.66	-3.99	71	13,713
5 Yr Avg	7.91	1.72	-2.95	56	14,632
10 Yr Avg	14.29	5.87	3.29	1	38,026
15 Yr Avg	14.56	3.92	1.53	2	76,824

Tax Analysis	Tax-Adj Rtn%	%Rank Cat	Tax-Cost Rat	%Rank Cat
3 Yr (estimated)	9.71	66	1.24	49
5 Yr (estimated)	6.94	52	0.90	48
10 Yr (estimated)	12.52	1	1.55	51

Potential Capital Gain Exposure: 28% of assets

Morningstar's Take by Todd Trubey 12-05-06

We think Wally Weitz hasn't lost his touch.

Toward the end of 2005, returns looked bad here, but that episode now looks like a rare yet predictable short-term period when this fund was out of sync with the market. Last year the fund's 2.77% loss trailed 98% of large-value category rivals. In 2006, the fund's 19% gain through Dec. 4 puts it in the top quintile of that group--which should make for the ninth time in the past 10 calendar years that the fund tops its average rival. It's crucial to grasp that the same traits that hurt last year helped this year.

Manager Wally Weitz focuses his attention on a limited number of firms with steady businesses--those he can buy at a discount. For much of 2003 through 2005, such drab fare was out of favor while commodity firms were hot. That meant this fund's cheap holdings got cheaper--and we'll note that Weitz is one of the few investors we know of who truly sounds excited when that happens. In his Sept. 30, 2005, shareowner letter,

he pointed to six of the largest and cheapest stocks in the fund. Their average gain in the next 12 months was 16%--with Comcast and Redwood Trust surging over 50% each so far in 2006 after falling over 20% each in 2005.

The ability to look clearly beyond short-term troubles and market skepticism is rare and crucial to a fund like this one. In late spring 2006, Weitz bought computer-maker Dell when the market was fixated on Hewlett-Packard taking its market share crown and other problems. Weitz, meanwhile, admired the firm's agility and relatively strong margins--plus, he thought it had corrected some recent problems. The fund bought nearly 2 million shares in the second quarter and again in the third quarter. After reporting some margin improvements, Dell shares have surged 26% so far in the fourth quarter of 2006.

We continue to appreciate Weitz's straightforward discipline. His stock-picking skill should keep this fund a long-term winner.

Address:	1125 South 103 Street Omaha NE 68124-6008 800-304-9745
Web Address:	www.weitzfunds.com
Inception:	05-09-86
Advisor:	Weitz Wallace R & Co.
Subadvisor:	None
NTF Plans:	Fidelity Retail-NTF, Schwab OneSource

Minimum Purchase:	$5000	Add: $0	IRA: $4000
Min Auto Inv Plan:	$100	Add: $100	
Sales Fees:	No-load		
Management Fee:	1.00% mx./0.80% mn., 0.22%A		
Actual Fees:	Mgt:0.97%	Dist: --	
Expense Projections:	3Yr:$356	5Yr:$617	10Yr:$1363
Income Distrib:	Semi-Annually		

Historical Profile

Return	Above Avg
Risk	Average
Rating	★★★★ Above Avg

Growth of $10,000
- ▬ Investment Values of Fund
- ─ Investment Values of S&P 500

▼ Manager Change
▽ Partial Manager Change

Investment Style
Equity
Stock %

	63%	82%	76%	81%	87%	76%	67%	87%	91%	

Performance Quartile (within Category)

1995	1996	1997	1998	1999	2000	2001	2002	2003	2004	2005	2006	History
18.38	20.59	25.15	29.07	33.08	35.22	34.29	27.92	35.78	37.70	35.42	40.26	NAV
38.37	18.70	38.93	28.95	20.97	19.62	0.24	-17.10	28.73	15.74	-2.77	21.85	Total Return %
0.79	-4.26	5.57	0.37	-0.07	28.72	12.13	5.00	0.05	4.86	-7.68	6.06	+/-S&P 500
0.01	-2.94	3.75	13.32	13.62	12.61	5.83	-1.58	-1.30	-0.75	-9.82	-0.40	+/-Russ 1000 VI
2.93	0.68	1.59	0.73	1.30	1.56	1.06	0.58	0.55	0.59	0.99	0.81	Income Return %
35.44	18.02	37.34	28.22	19.67	18.06	-0.82	-17.68	28.18	15.15	-3.76	21.04	Capital Return %
9	62	1	1	3	13	30	44	42	21	98	9	Total Rtn % Rank Cat
0.42	0.13	0.31	0.17	0.37	0.49	0.37	0.20	0.15	0.21	0.37	0.28	Income $
1.08	1.10	2.61	3.01	1.67	3.42	0.67	0.32	0.00	3.30	0.86	2.55	Capital Gains $
1.42	1.35	1.29	1.27	1.26	1.19	1.11	1.06	1.08	1.11	1.10	1.12	Expense Ratio %
1.06	0.91	0.93	0.87	1.35	1.39	36.00	0.87	0.76	0.57	0.95	0.64	Income Ratio %
28	40	39	39	36	31	36	13	18	12	26	40	Turnover Rate %
149	261	366	1,197	2,680	3,317	4,150	3,236	4,063	4,502	3,244	3,147	Net Assets $mil

Rating and Risk

Time Period	Load-Adj Return %	Morningstar Rtn vs Cat	Morningstar Risk vs Cat	Morningstar Risk-Adj Rating
1 Yr	21.85			
3 Yr	11.09	Avg	Avg	★★★
5 Yr	7.91	Avg	Avg	★★★
10 Yr	14.29	High	Avg	★★★★★
Incept	13.47			

Other Measures	Standard Index S&P 500	Best Fit Index DJ Wilshire 4500
Alpha	2.7	2.6
Beta	0.70	0.44
R-Squared	48	50
Standard Deviation	6.94	
Mean	11.10	
Sharpe Ratio	1.10	

Portfolio Analysis 09-30-06

Share change since 06-06 Total Stocks:36	Sector	PE	Tot Ret%	% Assets
⊖ Berkshire Hathaway Inc.	Financial	13.2	24.89	7.64
⊕ Countrywide Financial Co	Financial	9.8	26.22	6.61
Tyco International, Ltd.	Ind Mtrls	15.7	6.83	5.95
UnitedHealth Group, Inc.	Health	20.8	-13.49	4.70
⊖ Liberty Interactive A	Media	—	—	4.48
⊖ Fannie Mae	Financial	—	24.34	4.34
⊖ Washington Post Company	Media	21.8	-1.53	4.28
⊖ Wal-Mart Stores, Inc.	Consumer	16.9	0.13	4.23
American International G	Financial	17.0	6.05	4.22
Redwood Trust, Inc.	Financial	11.0	56.92	4.16
Liberty Capital A	Media	—	—	3.80
⊕ Dell, Inc.	Hardware	18.4	-16.23	3.23
⊕ IAC/InterActiveCorp	Consumer	40.6	31.26	3.20
⊖ Liberty Global, Inc.	Media	—	—	3.05
⊖ Comcast Corporation A	Media	45.2	63.31	3.03
Telephone and Data Syste	Telecom	—	—	2.65
WellPoint, Inc.	Health	17.2	-1.38	2.61
⊖ News Corporation, Ltd. A	Media	—	—	2.44
⊖ Expedia, Inc.	Consumer	—	-12.44	2.28
⊖ Washington Mutual, Inc.	Financial	13.4	9.62	1.75

Current Investment Style

Value Blnd Growth
Large Mid Small

Market Cap	%
Giant	51.5
Large	24.4
Mid	15.8
Small	6.3
Micro	2.0

Avg $mil: 28,466

Value Measures		Rel Category
Price/Earnings	14.38	1.05
Price/Book	1.81	0.82
Price/Sales	1.49	1.15
Price/Cash Flow	3.21	0.48
Dividend Yield %	2.03	0.87

Growth Measures	%	Rel Category
Long-Term Erngs	11.35	1.09
Book Value	1.75	0.22
Sales	13.86	1.54
Cash Flow	16.51	2.72
Historical Erngs	20.27	1.26

Profitability	%	Rel Category
Return on Equity	12.36	0.69
Return on Assets	7.77	0.79
Net Margin	8.42	0.65

Sector Weightings	% of Stocks	Rel S&P 500	3 Year High	Low
⌖ Info	35.42	1.77		
🅝 Software	0.00	0.00	0	0
🅗 Hardware	3.55	0.38	4	0
🅜 Media	27.82	7.34	31	23
🅣 Telecom	4.05	1.15	15	4
⌦ Service	57.75	1.25		
🅗 Health	8.01	0.66	8	1
🅒 Consumer	12.49	1.63	16	10
🅑 Business	0.00	0.00	1	0
🅢 Financial	37.25	1.67	45	37
⌐ Mfg	6.84	0.20		
🅖 Goods	0.32	0.04	4	0
🅘 Ind Mtrls	6.52	0.55	8	0
🅔 Energy	0.00	0.00	0	0
🅤 Utilities	0.00	0.00	0	0

Composition

	%
● Cash	8.6
● Stocks	91.4
● Bonds	0.0
○ Other	0.0
Foreign	0.0
(% of Stock)	

MORNINGSTAR® Funds 500

Westcore Midco Growth

	Ticker	Load	NAV	Yield	Total Assets	Mstar Category
	WTMGX	None	$7.45	0.0%	$184 mil	Mid-Cap Growth

Governance and Management

Stewardship Grade: B

Portfolio Manager(s)

Will Chester, this fund's longtime analyst and comanager, took the helm in June 2005, succeeding Todger Anderson. (Anderson, the fund's skipper since its 1986 inception, will continue to play a limited role here.) Chester has been a part of the research process for more than 19 years. Nine industry analysts and comanagers work on the fund and corresponding institutional accounts, and make buy and sell decisions.

Strategy

This fund reflects the advisor's institutional background. It delivers straightforward exposure to mid-cap growth stocks. Management looks for companies with at least 15% earnings--growth rates that also boast good sales growth and returns on equity. It buys leaders in emerging industries and uses discounted cash-flow analysis to identify the ones with significant upside ahead of them.

Performance 12-31-06

	1st Qtr	2nd Qtr	3rd Qtr	4th Qtr	Total
2002	2.96	-10.66	-14.77	4.67	-17.94
2003	1.70	20.67	4.50	10.10	41.19
2004	4.81	-0.72	-6.36	15.43	12.48
2005	-6.95	3.02	4.32	4.64	4.64
2006	9.09	-6.22	1.88	7.61	12.15

Trailing	Total Return%	+/- S&P 500	+/- Russ MG	%Rank Cat	Growth of $10,000
3 Mo	7.61	0.91	0.66	33	10,761
6 Mo	9.63	-3.11	1.73	15	10,963
1 Yr	12.15	-3.64	1.49	26	11,215
3 Yr Avg	9.70	-0.74	-3.03	63	13,201
5 Yr Avg	8.87	2.68	0.65	23	15,295
10 Yr Avg	8.60	0.18	-0.02	51	22,819
15 Yr Avg	10.06	-0.58	-0.07	40	42,116

Tax Analysis	Tax-Adj Rtn%	%Rank Cat	Tax-Cost Rat	%Rank Cat
3 Yr (estimated)	8.69	62	0.92	46
5 Yr (estimated)	8.27	21	0.55	39
10 Yr (estimated)	5.02	72	3.30	97

Potential Capital Gain Exposure: 23% of assets

Morningstar's Take by Karen Dolan 12-10-06

Westcore Midco Growth Fund's minuses are starting to overshadow its pluses, in our eyes.

We've become increasingly skeptical of some of management's actions here. For example, the fund lagged its peers in 2005 because it didn't have much in rallying energy stocks. We were happy with the reason: The team said its approach didn't work well with the cyclical, commodity-dependent sector. Thus, we had a harder time buying the team's decision to jump in later. Through the end of November, the fund had parked 8.5% of assets in energy stocks, which is nearly 20% more than the mid-growth category average.

To be sure, the fund primarily is exposed to oil-services companies possessing many of the characteristics the team seeks. But we're still not convinced that management can consistently add value in the inherently cyclical sector. After all, this isn't the first time the fund jumped into an industry well into a rally; it loaded up on telecom service providers in early 2000 and later got stung by them.

All told, we've become wary of management's response to weak times here, which has sometimes been to chase areas the team missed and should have missed, given its approach. Such moves have led to shifting results over the years. The fund has not been able to maintain above-average returns for the three- and five-year periods consistently.

Despite those lackluster returns, the fund still has plenty of saving graces. It boasts reasonable expenses, a seasoned lead manager, and a straight shot at mid-cap growth stocks. Its attention to valuation has kept it out of some of the more speculative stocks and tempered its downside. We've also liked the small boutique-like investment culture backing it. However, we're keeping a close eye on execution and would like to see stronger performance come from an unswerving application of its approach.

Address:	1625 Broadway Denver CO 80202 800-392-2673
Web Address:	www.westcore.com
Inception:	08-01-86
Advisor:	Denver Investment Advisors LLC
Subadvisor:	None
NTF Plans:	Fidelity Retail-NTF, Schwab OneSource

Minimum Purchase:	$2500	Add: $100	IRA: $1000
Min Auto Inv Plan:	$1000	Add: $100	
Sales Fees:	No-load, 2.00%R		
Management Fee:	0.65%, 0.30%A		
Actual Fees:	Mgt:0.65%	Dist: —	
Expense Projections:	3Yr:$347	5Yr:$601	10Yr:$1327
Income Distrib:	Annually		

Historical Profile
Return Average
Risk Average
Rating ★★★ Neutral

85%	84%	91%	86%	91%	95%	94%	95%	98%

▼ Manager Change
▽ Partial Manager Change

Growth of $10,000
— Investment Values of Fund
— Investment Values of S&P 500

33.0
26.0
20.0
15.0
10.0

Performance Quartile (within Category)

1995	1996	1997	1998	1999	2000	2001	2002	2003	2004	2005	2006	History
19.76	20.06	19.66	18.92	20.06	6.41	5.74	4.71	6.65	7.48	7.81	7.45	NAV
27.42	16.99	14.89	10.40	59.31	-17.51	-10.45	-17.94	41.19	12.48	4.64	12.15	Total Return %
-10.16	-5.97	-18.47	-18.18	38.27	-8.41	1.44	4.16	12.51	1.60	-0.27	-3.64	+/-S&P 500
-6.56	-0.49	-7.65	-7.46	8.02	-5.76	9.70	9.47	-1.52	-3.00	-7.46	1.49	+/-Russ MG
0.00	0.00	0.00	0.00	0.00	0.00	0.00	0.00	0.00	0.00	0.00	0.00	Income Return %
27.42	16.99	14.89	10.40	59.31	-17.51	-10.45	-17.94	41.19	12.48	4.64	12.15	Capital Return %
77	48	72	69	42	83	30	16	25	61	85	26	Total Rtn % Rank Cat
0.00	0.00	0.00	0.00	0.00	0.00	0.00	0.00	0.00	0.00	0.00	0.00	Income $
0.72	3.02	3.24	2.50	8.85	9.96	0.00	0.00	0.00	0.00	0.02	1.32	Capital Gains $
0.94	1.08	1.14	1.13	1.15	1.15	1.15	1.15	1.15	1.14	1.11	1.09	Expense Ratio %
-0.03	-0.42	-0.70	-0.71	-0.63	-0.81	-0.72	-0.75	-0.57	-0.62	-0.62	-0.34	Income Ratio %
50	63	61	76	116	118	191	67	49	53	84	127	Turnover Rate %
547	570	603	491	300	176	119	89	168	194	195	184	Net Assets $mil

Rating and Risk

Time Period	Load-Adj Return %	Morningstar Rtn vs Cat	Morningstar Risk vs Cat	Morningstar Risk-Adj Rating
1 Yr	12.15			
3 Yr	9.70	Avg	Avg	★★★
5 Yr	8.87	+Avg	Avg	★★★★
10 Yr	8.60	Avg	Avg	★★★
Incept	12.22			

Other Measures	Standard Index S&P 500	Best Fit Index Russ MG
Alpha	-4.5	-3.1
Beta	1.63	1.05
R-Squared	82	93
Standard Deviation	12.38	
Mean	9.70	
Sharpe Ratio	0.55	

Portfolio Analysis 11-30-06

Share change since 10-06 Total Stocks:71	Sector	PE	Tot Ret%	% Assets
⊖ Coach, Inc.	Goods	32.1	28.85	2.69
⊖ T Rowe Price Group	Financial	26.1	23.27	2.42
⊖ NII Holdings, Inc.	Telecom	45.9	47.53	2.21
⊖ Activision	Software	—	25.47	2.16
⊕ Davita, Inc.	Health	21.1	12.32	2.14
⊖ International Game Tech.	Consumer	34.3	52.07	2.10
⊖ NVIDIA Corporation	Hardware	33.4	102.46	2.08
⊖ Gamestop Corporation A	Goods	33.9	73.19	1.94
⊖ Eaton Vance Corporation	Financial	25.8	22.47	1.92
⊖ AMR Corporation	Business	—	35.99	1.88
⊕ Take-Two Interactive Sof	Software	—	0.34	1.86
⊖ Ambac Financial Group, I	Financial	10.9	16.52	1.85
⊖ Digital River, Inc.	Business	38.3	87.59	1.83
⊖ Polo Ralph Lauren Corpor	Goods	25.5	38.77	1.82
⊖ Noble Corporation	Energy	15.5	8.19	1.82
⊕ Electronic Arts, Inc.	Software	91.2	-3.73	1.78
⊖ Dover Corporation	Ind Mtrls	16.7	22.85	1.78
⊖ State Street Corporation	Financial	22.4	23.22	1.77
⊕ Range Resources Corporat	Energy	16.8	4.62	1.76
⊖ Digene Corporation	Health	90.4	64.28	1.75

Current Investment Style

Value Blnd Growth — Large / Mid / Small

Market Cap	%
Giant	1.6
Large	18.4
Mid	63.9
Small	16.1
Micro	0.0

Avg $mil: 5,324

Value Measures		Rel Category
Price/Earnings	21.95	1.07
Price/Book	3.53	1.10
Price/Sales	1.74	0.99
Price/Cash Flow	11.55	1.01
Dividend Yield %	0.33	0.52

Growth Measures	%	Rel Category
Long-Term Erngs	17.22	1.06
Book Value	14.02	1.10
Sales	12.06	1.21
Cash Flow	19.48	1.05
Historical Erngs	14.72	0.59

Profitability	%	Rel Category
Return on Equity	17.30	0.96
Return on Assets	9.32	0.99
Net Margin	12.53	1.08

Sector Weightings	% of Stocks	Rel S&P 500	3 Year High Low	
Info	25.50	1.28		
Software	10.10	2.93	13	8
Hardware	10.12	1.10	13	8
Media	0.78	0.21	5	0
Telecom	4.50	1.28	5	0
Service	52.76	1.14		
Health	17.93	1.49	25	17
Consumer	12.16	1.59	15	9
Business	9.70	2.29	15	7
Financial	12.97	0.58	15	8
Mfg	21.76	0.64		
Goods	8.74	1.02	11	6
Ind Mtrls	4.31	0.36	7	2
Energy	8.71	0.89	10	4
Utilities	0.00	0.00	0	0

Composition

	%
● Cash	2.4
● Stocks	97.5
● Bonds	0.0
● Other	0.0
Foreign (% of Stock)	1.6

Western Asset Cr Bd Inst

Analyst Pick ✓

	Ticker	Load	NAV	Yield	SEC Yield	Total Assets	Mstar Category
	WATFX	None	$11.34	4.5%	4.30%	$5,650 mil	Intermediate-Term Bond

Governance and Management

Stewardship Grade: B

Portfolio Manager(s)

Ken Leech, Western Asset's chief investment officer, and Steve Walsh, the firm's deputy investment chief, oversee the management team, which has a fine record. Each member of the team manages the fund's holdings in a different market sector. Compared with rivals in the fixed-income world, Western Asset has very large groups of credit analysts and risk analysts.

Strategy

In general, the fund is more aggressive than most of its peers. For example, management makes bolder duration adjustments (plus or minus 20% of its benchmark's duration) than many of the category's more conservative offerings. It also takes on added credit risk on occasion. Overall, though, it is a true core bond holding, with a focus on investment-grade bonds and a broadly diversified portfolio.

Performance 12-31-06

	1st Qtr	2nd Qtr	3rd Qtr	4th Qtr	Total
2002	0.51	2.44	2.68	2.82	8.70
2003	2.78	4.17	-0.50	1.17	7.77
2004	2.60	-2.21	3.58	1.33	5.30
2005	-0.92	3.24	-0.34	-0.04	1.91
2006	-0.39	-0.13	4.59	1.71	6.24

Trailing	Total Return%	+/- LB Aggr	+/- LB 5-10YR	%Rank Cat	Growth of $10,000
3 Mo	1.71	0.47	0.63	13	10,171
6 Mo	6.38	1.29	0.70	6	10,638
1 Yr	5.84	1.51	2.03	8	10,584
3 Yr Avg	4.33	0.63	0.69	9	11,356
5 Yr Avg	5.88	0.82	-0.04	7	13,307
10 Yr Avg	6.83	0.59	0.15	3	19,361
15 Yr Avg	7.24	0.74	0.25	6	28,533

Tax Analysis	Tax-Adj Rtn%	%Rank Cat	Tax-Cost Rat	%Rank Cat
3 Yr (estimated)	2.64	8	1.62	60
5 Yr (estimated)	3.99	6	1.79	64
10 Yr (estimated)	4.37	4	2.30	79

Potential Capital Gain Exposure: 1% of assets

Morningstar's Take by Paul Herbert 11-29-06

Western Asset Core Bond looks like it's hitting its stride.

Though such an outcome seemed less certain in June, this fund is having another great year in 2006. Its managers had been expecting the U.S. Federal Reserve to pause in its interest-rate-hiking campaign much sooner than it had--the bank last inched up the Fed funds rate to 5.25% in June. The fund suffered a bit during the year's first six months by taking on added interest-rate risk and holding exposure to inflation-protected bonds. But since the Fed stopped, the fund has been sitting pretty, as it stuck with its bullishness on rates, and other decisions such as favoring lower-quality corporate bonds and an overweighting in mortgage-backed securities have paid off. Its 6.37% year-to-date gain (as of Nov. 28, 2006) beats 97% of similar funds'.

The downside of this success is that fewer areas represent compelling values now, but the managers still spy opportunities in spots. High valuations and some looming risks have led them to take a neutral stance on the corporate sector. They have also kept the fund's duration (a measure of interest-rate sensitivity) fairly close to the Lehman Brothers Aggregate Index's. They still think there's value in some areas of the corporate market, though, among the bonds of utilities and the financing arms of automakers. And, since rates may not move up or down much in the short term, they think mortgage bonds, particularly Fannie Mae mortgages, have a lot of appeal.

Plus, this fund's many built-in advantages should help to keep it in the game over the long term. Many readers may not know much about Western Asset, but the firm is one of the largest bond managers going, with more than $500 billion in assets under management. That size allows the firm to hire and retain scores of top managers and analysts, invest in analytics and risk-control measures, and keep costs low.

The fund remains one of our top intermediate-term picks.

Address:	100 Light Street Baltimore MD 21202 888-425-6432	Minimum Purchase:	$1000000 Add: $0 IRA: $0
		Min Auto Inv Plan:	$0 Add: —
		Sales Fees:	No-load
Web Address:	www.westernasset.com	Management Fee:	0.45% mx./0.40% mn.
Inception:	09-04-90	Actual Fees:	Mgt:0.41% Dist: —
Advisor:	Western Asset Management Company	Expense Projections:	3Yr:$144 5Yr:$252 10Yr:$567
Subadvisor:	None	Income Distrib:	Monthly
NTF Plans:	N/A		

Historical Profile

Return High
Risk High
Rating ★★★★ Highest

Investment Style: Fixed Income
Income Rtn %Rank Cat

▼ Manager Change
▽ Partial Manager Change

Growth of $10,000
— Investment Values of Fund
— Investment Values of LB Aggr

Performance Quartile (within Category)

	1995	1996	1997	1998	1999	2000	2001	2002	2003	2004	2005	2006	History
	11.40	11.14	11.41	11.12	10.28	10.87	11.10	11.37	11.59	11.48	11.21	11.34	NAV
	20.92	3.73	10.13	8.36	-1.69	13.34	9.48	8.70	7.77	5.30	1.91	5.84	Total Return %
	2.45	0.10	0.48	-0.33	-0.87	1.71	1.04	-1.55	3.67	0.96	-0.52	1.51	+/-LB Aggr
	-0.51	1.04	0.70	-1.78	1.19	0.90	0.66	-4.33	1.80	0.00	0.08	2.03	+/-LB 5-10YR
	6.69	5.97	6.53	5.95	5.75	7.31	6.15	5.36	4.20	3.42	4.28	4.60	Income Return %
	14.23	-2.24	3.60	2.41	-7.44	6.03	3.33	3.34	3.57	1.88	-2.37	1.24	Capital Return %
	14	34	15	26	61	2	10	44	17	12	44	8	Total Rtn % Rank Cat
	0.66	0.66	0.71	0.65	0.62	0.73	0.65	0.58	0.46	0.38	0.48	0.55	Income $
	0.04	0.01	0.12	0.56	0.03	0.00	0.13	0.09	0.18	0.31	0.00	0.00	Capital Gains $
	0.50	0.50	0.50	0.50	0.50	0.50	0.50	0.50	0.49	0.49	0.46	0.45	Expense Ratio %
	6.98	6.30	6.40	6.00	5.70	6.30	6.80	5.60	4.90	3.50	3.40	4.30	Income Ratio %
	258	266	385	227	484	260	387	595	439	465	407	540	Turnover Rate %
	398	539	624	682	683	740	883	1,271	1,990	2,912	3,879	4,549	Net Assets $mil

Rating and Risk

Time Period	Load-Adj Return %	Morningstar Rtn vs Cat	Morningstar Risk vs Cat	Morningstar Risk-Adj Rating
1 Yr	5.84			
3 Yr	4.33	High	+Avg	★★★★
5 Yr	5.88	High	High	★★★★
10 Yr	6.83	High	High	★★★★
Incept	8.09			

Other Measures	Standard Index LB Aggr	Best Fit Index LB. U.S. Univ. Bd
Alpha	0.7	0.2
Beta	1.02	1.04
R-Squared	95	96
Standard Deviation	3.42	
Mean	4.33	
Sharpe Ratio	0.36	

Portfolio Analysis 09-30-06

Total Fixed-Income:953	Date of Maturity	Amount $000	Value $000	% Net Assets
FNMA 5%		804,550	773,076	8.39
FNMA 5.5%		544,800	536,628	5.82
FNMA 6%		533,920	536,274	5.82
Dbirs Deutsche 0wr021254	10-11-10	206,790	204,149	2.21
EuroDollar (Fut)	12-18-06	183,000	173,237	1.88
US Treasury Note (Fut)	12-29-06	150,500	158,801	1.72
US Treasury Bond 4.5%	02-15-36	148,943	142,718	1.55
US Treasury Note 5.125%	05-15-16	131,530	136,442	1.48
Dbirs Db 0wr021098	10-05-08	115,540	114,533	1.24
FNMA 6.5%		90,850	92,497	1.00
Irs Rec 5.628 Db 0wr0324	07-13-11	83,870	85,817	0.93
EuroDollar (Fut)	03-17-08	85,250	81,188	0.88
Irs Rec 5.693 Fixed Db 0	07-21-16	77,910	81,042	0.88
Thornburg Mtg Tr 2006-1	01-25-36	65,984	65,870	0.71
Russian Federation FRN	03-31-30	49,315	55,040	0.60
Residential Asset Sec 20	02-25-19	56,170	54,274	0.59
Wamu Mtg Cert 2005-Ar11	08-25-45	53,984	54,110	0.59
US Treasury Bond 2.375%	01-15-25	53,132	53,988	0.59
Greenpoint Mtg Fdg 2006-	09-25-46	53,368	53,368	0.58
Greenpoint Mtg Fdg 2006-	10-25-46	52,900	52,905	0.57

Current Investment Style

Duration: Short / Int / Long
Quality: High / Med / Low

¹ figure provided by fund

Avg Eff Duration¹	4.0 Yrs
Avg Eff Maturity	—
Avg Credit Quality	AA
Avg Wtd Coupon	4.89%
Avg Wtd Price	99.51% of par

Coupon Range	% of Bonds	Rel Cat
0% PIK	2.7	0.4
0% to 6%	85.0	1.2
6% to 8%	13.8	0.6
8% to 10%	1.2	0.2
More than 10%	0.0	0.2

1.00=Category Average

Credit Analysis	% bonds 09-30-06		
AAA	79	BB	3
AA	6	B	1
A	4	Below B	0
BBB	7	NR/NA	4

Sector Breakdown	% of assets
US Treasuries	8
TIPS	0
US Agency	2
Mortgage Pass-Throughs	33
Mortgage CMO	12
Mortgage ARM	0
US Corporate	15
Asset-Backed	3
Convertible	0
Municipal	0
Corporate Inflation-Protected	0
Foreign Corporate	1
Foreign Govt	0

Composition			
Cash	22.1	Bonds	70.6
Stocks	0.0	Other	7.4

Special Securities	
Restricted/Illiquid Secs	2
Exotic Mortgage-Backed	—
Emerging-Markets Secs	Trace
Options/Futures/Warrants	No

MORNINGSTAR® Funds 500

Westport R

	Ticker	Load	NAV	Yield	Total Assets	Mstar Category
	WPFRX	None	$19.21	0.0%	$48 mil	Mid-Cap Blend

Governance and Management

Stewardship Grade:

Portfolio Manager(s)

Seasoned. Ed Nicklin has been running money at Westport since 1997. He comanages Westport Select Cap with Andy Knuth. Nicklin built a great record at Evergreen Growth & Income before joining Westport.

Strategy

Manager Ed Nicklin uses an approach that's similar to one he used quite effectively at his former charge, Evergreen Growth & Income. He looks for stocks of all sizes that are trading at low multiples relative to their long-term growth prospects. Nicklin is willing to make big sector bets and isn't afraid to buy stocks in nontraditional value sectors such as technology. Thus, the portfolio typically has a mix of value and growth stocks. Nicklin also has a long time horizon and keeps turnover to a minimum.

Historical Profile
Return Average
Risk Below Avg
Rating ★★★ Neutral

91%	93%	81%	83%	94%	90%	99%	97%	97%

Investment Style
Equity
Stock %

▼ Manager Change
▽ Partial Manager Change

Growth of $10,000
— Investment Values of Fund
— Investment Values of S&P 500

26.8
22.8
18.0
14.0
10.0

Performance Quartile
(within Category)

1995	1996	1997	1998	1999	2000	2001	2002	2003	2004	2005	2006	History
—	—	10.00	11.22	14.75	14.37	14.55	12.09	15.64	18.05	18.87	19.21	NAV
—	—	0.00*	12.20	46.13	8.68	3.99	-16.91	29.36	16.86	11.61	13.27	Total Return %
—	—	—	-16.38	25.09	17.78	15.88	5.19	0.68	5.98	6.70	-2.52	+/-S&P 500
—	—	—	-6.92	31.41	-8.83	4.60	-2.38	-6.26	0.38	-0.95	2.95	+/-S&P Mid 400
—	—	—	0.00	0.00	0.00	0.00	0.00	0.00	0.00	0.00	0.00	Income Return %
—	—	—	12.20	46.13	8.68	3.99	-16.91	29.36	16.86	11.61	13.27	Capital Return %
—	—	—	40	8	59	39	61	82	42	32	49	Total Rtn % Rank Cat
—	—	0.00	0.00	0.00	0.00	0.00	0.00	0.00	0.00	0.00	0.00	Income $
—	—	0.00	0.00	1.60	1.69	0.39	0.00	0.00	0.23	1.28	2.17	Capital Gains $
—	—	—	1.49	1.49	1.50	1.50	1.50	1.50	1.50	1.50	—	Expense Ratio %
—	—	—	-0.53	-0.53	-0.81	-0.54	-0.83	-0.83	-0.82	—		Income Ratio %
—	—	—	63	68	48	15	40	9	30			Turnover Rate %
—	—	—	6	10	15	12	16	25	27	35		Net Assets $mil

Performance 12-31-06

	1st Qtr	2nd Qtr	3rd Qtr	4th Qtr	Total
2002	1.17	-4.96	-17.51	4.77	-16.91
2003	-7.20	18.63	6.56	10.27	29.36
2004	4.20	0.24	-1.22	13.26	16.86
2005	3.19	3.61	3.63	0.74	11.61
2006	6.94	-3.07	2.91	6.18	13.27

Trailing	Total Return%	+/- S&P 500	+/- S&P Mid 400	%Rank Cat	Growth of $10,000
3 Mo	6.18	-0.52	-0.81	80	10,618
6 Mo	9.28	-3.46	3.45	46	10,928
1 Yr	13.27	-2.52	2.95	49	11,327
3 Yr Avg	13.89	3.45	0.80	33	14,773
5 Yr Avg	9.69	3.50	-1.20	59	15,879
10 Yr Avg	—	—	—		—
15 Yr Avg	—	—	—		—

Tax Analysis	Tax-Adj Rtn%	%Rank Cat	Tax-Cost Rat	%Rank Cat
3 Yr (estimated)	12.87	26	0.90	39
5 Yr (estimated)	9.10	52	0.54	32
10 Yr (estimated)	—		—	

Potential Capital Gain Exposure: 37% of assets

Morningstar's Take by Karen Wallace 12-01-06

Westport Fund can compete in most markets.

Manager Ed Nicklin invests with conviction. This fund holds just over 30 stocks, and position sizes tend to be pretty large. The fund's largest holding, Precision Castparts, takes up around 6.8% of assets. In addition, the fund tends to have large concentrations in particular sectors--the fund's software weighting, for instance, is more than 3 times the mid-cap blend category median, and its energy weighting is more than double.

One might assume that would lead to volatile, if not streaky, performance. But it hasn't. In fact, the fund's standard deviation is well below the category median, and the fund has been a pretty consistent performer, in both absolute and relative terms, in most market environments. One way Nicklin controls volatility is that he's very valuation-sensitive. He likes companies with improving cash flow, and he prefers to pick up stocks when they're selling at low price-to-earnings multiples.

Nicklin has had a good record of finding undervalued stocks that are poised for rebound. For instance, top-holding Precision Castparts, which the fund has owned for more than six years, has soared nearly 40% per year over the past five years, on an annualized basis. Though Nicklin has trimmed a little this year on valuation and to control the size of the position, he is still optimistic about the firm's prospects as he expects that demand for the firm's products (components for aerospace and energy markets) will continue to be strong in the next few years.

In addition, even though Nicklin is valuation-sensitive, he isn't afraid to venture into growthy areas of the market--hence the fund's big software and energy weightings. The result is a portfolio that tends to hold on to its gains in down markets and has enough juice to keep pace in market rallies.

Address:	253 Riverside Avenue Westport CT 06880 888-593-7878	Minimum Purchase:	$2500	Add: $0	IRA: $2000
		Min Auto Inv Plan:	$1000	Add: $100	
		Sales Fees:	No-load		
Web Address:	www.westportfunds.com	Management Fee:	0.90%		
Inception:	12-31-97*	Actual Fees:	Mgt:0.90%	Dist: —	
Advisor:	Westport Advisers LLC	Expense Projections:	3Yr:$493	5Yr:$857	10Yr:$1882
Subadvisor:	None	Income Distrib:	Annually		
NTF Plans:	Fidelity Retail-NTF, Schwab OneSource				

Rating and Risk

Time Period	Load-Adj Return %	Morningstar Rtn vs Cat	Morningstar Risk vs Cat	Morningstar Risk-Adj Rating
1 Yr	13.27			
3 Yr	13.89	Avg	-Avg	★★★★
5 Yr	9.69	Avg	-Avg	★★★
10 Yr	—	—	—	
Incept	12.74			

Other Measures	Standard Index S&P 500	Best Fit Index Russ MG
Alpha	2.7	3.6
Beta	1.08	0.71
R-Squared	67	79
Standard Deviation	9.04	
Mean	13.89	
Sharpe Ratio	1.13	

Portfolio Analysis 09-30-06

Share change since 06-06 Total Stocks:32	Sector	PE	Tot Ret%	% Assets
⊖ Precision Castparts Corp	Ind Mtrls	25.4	51.40	6.87
Caremark RX, Inc.	Health	23.6	10.90	6.16
Praxair, Inc.	Ind Mtrls	20.8	14.01	5.85
EOG Resources	Energy	10.1	-14.62	5.34
Laboratory Corporation o	Health	24.3	36.44	5.32
Anadarko Petroleum Corp.	Energy	5.2	-7.44	4.33
Synopsys	Software	—	33.25	3.90
Amphenol Corporation	Hardware	24.9	40.57	3.67
Abbott Laboratories	Health	24.3	26.88	3.60
CACI International, Inc.	Business	20.9	-1.53	3.53
SunTrust Banks, Inc.	Financial	14.1	19.81	3.44
CA, Inc.	Software	NMF	-19.10	3.28
Cox Radio, Inc.	Media	21.7	15.77	3.22
Pall Corporation	Health	29.1	30.60	3.05
Claire's Stores, Inc.	Consumer	19.2	14.94	3.03
Cullen/Frost Bankers, In	Financial	16.5	6.45	2.97
FedEx Corporation	Business	17.2	5.40	2.79
International Rectifier	Hardware	24.0	20.78	2.76
Pogo Producing Company	Energy	4.7	-2.16	2.63
MRO Software, Inc.	Business	—	—	2.54

Current Investment Style

Value Blnd Growth — Large Mid Small

Market Cap	%
Giant	3.7
Large	33.4
Mid	47.3
Small	15.6
Micro	0.0

Avg $mil: 6,666

Value Measures		Rel Category
Price/Earnings	16.83	1.05
Price/Book	2.42	1.07
Price/Sales	1.71	1.53
Price/Cash Flow	9.39	1.11
Dividend Yield %	0.70	0.54

Growth Measures	%	Rel Category
Long-Term Erngs	11.92	0.94
Book Value	11.23	1.35
Sales	13.57	1.52
Cash Flow	14.02	1.66
Historical Erngs	20.23	1.13

Profitability	%	Rel Category
Return on Equity	15.77	0.99
Return on Assets	8.77	1.09
Net Margin	14.09	1.30

Sector Weightings

	% of Stocks	Rel S&P 500	3 Year High Low
⟳ Info	22.66	1.13	
Software	9.09	2.63	13 8
Hardware	10.26	1.11	10 5
Media	3.31	0.87	7 2
Telecom	0.00	0.00	0 0
⟲ Service	45.30	0.98	
Health	18.64	1.55	25 17
Consumer	3.11	0.41	9 3
Business	13.16	3.11	17 13
Financial	10.39	0.47	13 7
⟰ Mfg	32.04	0.95	
Goods	1.91	0.22	2 1
Ind Mtrls	14.76	1.24	15 9
Energy	15.37	1.57	17 4
Utilities	0.00	0.00	1 0

Composition

● Cash	2.8	
● Stocks	97.2	
● Bonds	0.0	
○ Other	0.0	
Foreign (% of Stock)	0.0	

Westport Select Cap R

	Ticker	Load	NAV	Yield	Total Assets	Mstar Category
	WPSRX	Closed	$24.56	0.0%	$1,020 mil	Mid-Cap Blend

Governance and Management

Stewardship Grade:

Portfolio Manager(s)

Andy Knuth has been with Westport since the 1980s, serving as comanager at Managers Special Equity since 1985. Ed Nicklin had a good record managing Evergreen Growth & Income for 10 years before joining Westport in 1997. He also manages Westport.

Strategy

Comanagers Andy Knuth and Ed Nicklin look for stocks trading at modest price multiples relative to their long-term growth prospects. They aren't afraid to invest in companies that are out of favor as long as their long-term business models look strong. Another facet of their strategy that we find appealing involves seeking firms that have a catalyst for improved earnings or those that are likely to benefit from merger and acquisition activity. They typically have a long time horizon and keep turnover to a minimum.

Historical Profile
Return   Below Avg
Risk   Below Avg
Rating   ★★ Below Avg

	91%	87%	84%	77%	86%	93%	99%	97%	98%

Investment Style
Equity
Stock %

▼ Manager Change
▽ Partial Manager Change

28.4
22.8
18.0
14.0
10.0

Growth of $10,000
■ Investment Values of Fund
— Investment Values of S&P 500

Performance Quartile (within Category)

1995	1996	1997	1998	1999	2000	2001	2002	2003	2004	2005	2006	History
—	—	10.00	11.54	16.47	18.23	19.45	16.49	21.79	24.06	24.16	24.56	NAV
—	—	0.00*	15.40	42.72	13.60	8.22	-15.22	32.14	10.43	8.63	12.41	Total Return %
—	—	—	-13.18	21.68	22.70	20.11	6.88	3.46	-0.45	3.72	-3.38	+/-S&P 500
—	—	—	-3.72	28.00	-3.91	8.83	-0.69	-3.48	-6.05	-3.93	2.09	+/-S&P Mid 400
—	—	—	0.00	0.00	0.20	0.00	0.00	0.00	0.00	0.00	0.05	Income Return %
—	—	—	15.40	42.72	13.40	8.22	-15.22	32.14	10.43	8.63	12.36	Capital Return %
—	—	—	36	10	43	27	52	67	93	57	57	Total Rtn % Rank Cat
—	—	0.00	0.00	0.00	0.03	0.00	0.00	0.00	0.00	0.00	0.01	Income $
—	—	0.00	0.00	0.00	0.45	0.28	0.00	0.00	0.00	1.99	2.59	Capital Gains $
—	—	—	1.50	1.43	1.27	1.24	1.29	1.34	1.35	1.31	—	Expense Ratio %
—	—	—	-0.39	-0.33	0.13	-0.33	-0.74	-0.74	-0.70	-0.74	—	Income Ratio %
—	—	—	19	10	15	11	4	12	9	2	—	Turnover Rate %
—	—	21	80	110	210	314	456	467	440	440		Net Assets $mil

Performance 12-31-06

	1st Qtr	2nd Qtr	3rd Qtr	4th Qtr	Total
2002	3.03	-7.83	-15.27	5.37	-15.22
2003	-5.52	17.78	5.71	12.33	32.14
2004	3.52	-0.99	-2.10	10.05	10.43
2005	1.07	5.06	0.51	1.78	8.63
2006	5.96	-3.71	2.84	7.13	12.41

Trailing	Total Return%	+/- S&P 500	+/- S&P Mid 400	%Rank Cat	Growth of $10,000
3 Mo	7.13	0.43	0.14	56	10,713
6 Mo	10.18	-2.56	4.35	38	11,018
1 Yr	12.41	-3.38	2.09	57	11,241
3 Yr Avg	10.48	0.04	-2.61	81	13,485
5 Yr Avg	8.60	2.41	-2.29	76	15,106
10 Yr Avg	—	—	—	—	—
15 Yr Avg	—	—	—	—	—

Tax Analysis	Tax-Adj Rtn%	%Rank Cat	Tax-Cost Rat	%Rank Cat
3 Yr (estimated)	9.53	69	0.86	37
5 Yr (estimated)	8.04	64	0.52	31
10 Yr (estimated)	—	—	—	—

Potential Capital Gain Exposure: 42% of assets

Rating and Risk

Time Period	Load-Adj Return %	Morningstar Rtn vs Cat	Morningstar Risk vs Cat	Morningstar Risk-Adj Rating
1 Yr	12.41			
3 Yr	10.48	-Avg	-Avg	★★
5 Yr	8.60	-Avg	-Avg	★★
10 Yr	—	—	—	—
Incept	13.23			

Other Measures	Standard Index S&P 500	Best Fit Index DJ Wilshire 4500
Alpha	-0.2	-1.1
Beta	1.05	0.73
R-Squared	66	84
Standard Deviation	8.90	
Mean	10.48	
Sharpe Ratio	0.81	

Morningstar's Take by Karen Wallace 12-01-06

Westport Select Cap's consistent style delivers.

This is a fairly concentrated fund--currently, it holds about 50 stocks, and position sizes tend to be pretty large. In addition, the fund tends to have large concentrations in particular sectors--the fund's consumer-services and health-care weightings, for instance, are more than 2 times the mid-cap blend category median.

One might assume that would lead to volatile, if not streaky, performance. But it hasn't. In fact, the fund's standard deviation is well below the category median, and the fund has been a pretty good performer in absolute terms in most market environments. One way managers Ed Nicklin and Andy Knuth control volatility is that they're very valuation-sensitive. They particularly like companies with a catalyst for improving earnings, and they prefer to pick up stocks when they're selling at low price-to-earnings multiples. They've had pretty good success with that consistently applied strategy: For instance, one of the fund's

longtime holdings, discount retailer Big Lots, has risen more than 80% this year as the company's restructuring efforts have borne fruit.

In addition, the managers construct the portfolio using so-called "internal hedges," or positions in sectors or industries that tend to counterbalance one another. For instance, when the fund's energy picks are sagging, as they are this year, the fund's consumer stocks tend to pick up the slack.

Though the fund's relative returns will rarely top the category, the fund holds on to investors' capital admirably, with low volatility. We are optimistic that the fund's conservative style will continue to perform well for investors in a variety of market environments.

Investors should note that though the fund's retail share class remains closed, the advisor reopened the fund's institutional shares, in part to fund additional stock purchases and also to dilute future capital gains to current shareholders.

Portfolio Analysis 09-30-06

Share change since 06-06 Total Stocks:49

	Sector	PE	Tot Ret%	% Assets
⊖ Caremark RX, Inc.	Health	23.6	10.90	6.04
Universal Health Service	Health	23.6	19.31	5.25
⊖ ITT Educational Services	Consumer	26.8	12.59	4.24
Precision Castparts Corp	Ind Mtrls	25.4	51.40	3.80
Houston Exploration Comp	Energy	13.6	-1.93	3.56
Hilb Rogal & Hobbs Compa	Financial	17.5	10.67	3.41
⊖ Darden Restaurants, Inc.	Consumer	17.4	4.37	3.26
Orient-Express Hotels, L	Consumer	50.0	50.53	3.25
CACI International, Inc.	Business	20.9	-1.53	2.86
Fisher Scientific Intern	Health	—		2.78
Charles River Laboratori	Health	—	2.08	2.71
BankUnited Financial Cor	Financial	13.1	5.31	2.52
DeVry, Inc.	Consumer	34.4	40.26	2.41
Big Lots, Inc.	Consumer	46.2	90.84	2.40
Pogo Producing Company	Energy	4.7	-2.16	2.39
Ruby Tuesday, Inc.	Consumer	16.4	7.30	2.23
⊖ People's Bank	Financial	45.5	47.71	2.19
Brown & Brown, Inc.	Financial	22.9	-6.98	2.08
Applebee's International	Consumer	21.9	10.16	1.85
Triad Hospitals, Inc.	Health	15.5	6.63	1.76

Current Investment Style

Value Blnd Growth   Large Mid Small

Market Cap	%
Giant	0.0
Large	6.4
Mid	53.0
Small	37.5
Micro	3.1
Avg $mil:	2,655

Value Measures		Rel Category
Price/Earnings	19.28	1.20
Price/Book	2.14	0.95
Price/Sales	1.28	1.14
Price/Cash Flow	8.27	0.98
Dividend Yield %	0.50	0.38

Growth Measures	%	Rel Category
Long-Term Erngs	12.95	1.02
Book Value	10.03	1.21
Sales	11.33	1.27
Cash Flow	8.05	0.95
Historical Erngs	7.82	0.44

Profitability	%	Rel Category
Return on Equity	16.59	1.04
Return on Assets	7.90	0.98
Net Margin	11.10	1.02

Sector Weightings	% of Stocks	Rel S&P 500	3 Year High Low
↻ Info	9.78	0.49	
▣ Software	4.56	1.32	9 5
▣ Hardware	2.35	0.25	4 2
▣ Media	1.89	0.50	9 2
▣ Telecom	0.98	0.28	3 1
⊂ Service	71.06	1.54	
▣ Health	21.34	1.77	21 15
▣ Consumer	22.21	2.90	22 14
▣ Business	9.69	2.29	14 10
▣ Financial	17.82	0.80	20 18
▣ Mfg	19.17	0.57	
▣ Goods	3.30	0.39	4 3
▣ Ind Mtrls	8.08	0.68	8 4
▣ Energy	7.79	0.79	11 7
▣ Utilities	0.00	0.00	0 0

Composition

		%
● Cash		2.5
● Stocks		97.5
● Bonds		0.0
○ Other		0.0
Foreign (% of Stock)		3.3

Address:	253 Riverside Avenue Westport CT 06880 888-593-7878
Web Address:	www.westportfunds.com
Inception:	12-31-97 *
Advisor:	Westport Advisers LLC
Subadvisor:	None
NTF Plans:	Fidelity Retail-NTF, Schwab OneSource

Minimum Purchase:	Closed	Add: —	IRA: —
Min Auto Inv Plan:	Closed	Add: —	
Sales Fees:	No-load		
Management Fee:	1.00%		
Actual Fees:	Mgt:1.00%	Dist: —	
Expense Projections:	3Yr:$452	5Yr:$782	10Yr:$1713
Income Distrib:	Annually		

MORNINGSTAR® Funds 500

Westwood Balanced AAA

Ticker	**Load**	**NAV**	**Yield**	**Total Assets**	**Mstar Category**
WEBAX	None	$11.65	1.7%	$155 mil	Moderate Allocation

Governance and Management

Stewardship Grade:

Portfolio Manager(s)

Equity manager Susan Byrne is the founder and chief investment officer of Westwood Holding Group and has a terrific long-term record as a stock-picker here and at Westwood Equity. Mark Freeman has managed the bond portfolio since December 2000. He has been an analyst on the fund since 1998. Eight industry analysts assist the managers.

Strategy

Equity manager Susan Byrne scours the domestic-equity universe for companies that have posted positive earnings surprises but have yet to see upward estimate revisions from analysts. If the fundamentals check out, she's interested. The fund generally stakes about 60% of assets in stocks. Its bond sleeve is a conservative, intermediate-term portfolio.

Historical Profile

Return	Above Avg
Risk	Below Avg
Rating	★★★★ Above Avg

Investment Style: Equity, Stock %

| 63% | 61% | 61% | 60% | 61% | 58% | 59% | 67% | 56% |

▼ Manager Change
▽ Partial Manager Change

Growth of $10,000
■ Investment Values of Fund
— Investment Values of DJ Mod

Performance Quartile (within Category)

1995	1996	1997	1998	1999	2000	2001	2002	2003	2004	2005	2006	History
8.89	9.68	11.00	11.88	11.71	11.62	10.99	9.99	11.19	11.95	12.01	11.65	NAV
31.16	18.11	22.45	11.51	7.75	11.49	-3.26	-6.99	14.38	8.84	9.29	12.41	Total Return %
11.36	7.45	10.55	-0.81	-9.58	13.16	-0.46	-0.22	-13.00	-4.13	2.30	0.11	+/-DJ Mod
6.39	6.77	3.25	-0.88	-5.10	7.05	-3.42	3.55	-9.68	-2.33	3.29	2.14	+/-DJ US Mod
2.88	2.57	2.77	2.27	2.13	2.45	2.13	2.19	2.22	1.96	1.66	1.92	Income Return %
28.28	15.54	19.68	9.24	5.62	9.04	-5.39	-9.18	12.16	6.88	7.63	10.49	Capital Return %
14	16	25	63	68	9	33	10	94	51	3	25	Total Rtn % Rank Cat
0.20	0.23	0.27	0.25	0.25	0.28	0.25	0.24	0.22	0.22	0.20	0.23	Income $
0.13	0.58	0.56	0.12	0.81	1.10	0.00	0.00	0.00	0.00	0.85	1.61	Capital Gains $
1.25	1.32	1.25	1.17	1.20	1.19	1.17	1.22	1.23	1.22	1.25	1.27	Expense Ratio %
2.47	2.62	2.60	2.37	2.06	2.21	2.23	2.25	2.10	1.92	1.67	1.78	Income Ratio %
133	111	110	77	86	65	37	78	56	41	56	2	Turnover Rate %
9	31	81	142	160	148	163	150	160	140	147	148	Net Assets $mil

Performance 12-31-06

	1st Qtr	2nd Qtr	3rd Qtr	4th Qtr	Total
2002	1.13	-2.75	-9.19	4.13	-6.99
2003	-3.27	9.64	0.72	7.07	14.38
2004	1.45	-0.01	2.45	4.73	8.84
2005	1.65	1.97	3.95	1.44	9.29
2006	3.98	0.81	3.24	3.88	12.41

Trailing	Total Return%	+/- DJ Mod	+/- DJ US Mod	%Rank Cat	Growth of $10,000
3 Mo	3.88	-1.71	-0.79	89	10,388
6 Mo	7.24	-1.55	-0.66	87	10,724
1 Yr	12.41	0.11	2.14	25	11,241
3 Yr Avg	10.17	-0.55	1.05	16	13,372
5 Yr Avg	7.30	-2.72	-0.30	21	14,223
10 Yr Avg	8.48	-0.07	-0.11	19	22,568
15 Yr Avg	10.37	1.16	0.98	19	43,930

Tax Analysis	Tax-Adj Rtn%	%Rank Cat	Tax-Cost Rat	%Rank Cat
3 Yr (estimated)	8.28	22	1.72	86
5 Yr (estimated)	5.85	27	1.35	83
10 Yr (estimated)	6.73	19	1.61	57

Potential Capital Gain Exposure: 9% of assets

Rating and Risk

Time Period	Load-Adj Return %	Morningstar Rtn vs Cat	Morningstar Risk vs Cat	Morningstar Risk-Adj Rating
1 Yr	12.41			
3 Yr	10.17	+Avg	-Avg	★★★★
5 Yr	7.30	+Avg	-Avg	★★★★
10 Yr	8.48	+Avg	Low	★★★★
Incept	10.70			

Other Measures	Standard Index DJ Mod	Best Fit Index Russ 1000 VI
Alpha	1.7	-0.3
Beta	0.68	0.62
R-Squared	76	83
Standard Deviation	4.62	
Mean	10.17	
Sharpe Ratio	1.44	

Morningstar's Take by Kerry O'Boyle 12-11-06

Investors now have access to Westwood Balanced's excellent management team and strategy elsewhere at a cheaper price.

Westwood Management, subadvisor to this and a number of other funds, is in the awkward position of no longer owning the funds that bear its name. Having entered into a joint venture with Gabelli Funds in 1994 to handle marketing, distribution, and administrative operations, Westwood now can't get its funds back. The situation has reached a head for Westwood as fund stewardship and fees have become a big issue for investors in the wake of the industry trading scandal in 2003.

As a result, the firm has rolled out its own lineup of funds bearing the WHG brand, the latest being WHG Balanced on Sept. 10, 2006. That fund, also led by veteran manager Susan Byrne, is run in the exact same manner as this fund and the firm's institutional accounts. The fees for WHG Balanced are capped at 1%, well below this fund's 1.25% annual charge. Plus, in late September, Westwood

lowered the minimum initial investment for the WHG funds, including this one, from $100,000 to $5,000.

Byrne has built a top-quartile record in the moderate-allocation category over nearly 15 years here, despite the added weight of its hefty expense ratio. At the beginning of 2006, she reduced the fund's stake in equities to 55% of assets in the belief that the 5% risk-free return on cash is too good to pass up in today's uncertain market. That move helped the fund weather the early-summer stock market correction better than most rivals, though it has been a bit of an anchor the past three months.

We're big fans of Byrne's moderate approach to this balanced offering and her long-term-focused style of investing. But we can no longer recommend this fund knowing that she's available elsewhere at a cheaper price in another fund run by her own firm, an organization that ee think will be better stewards of investor interests.

Portfolio Analysis 09-30-06

Total Stocks:49 Share change since 06-30-06	Sectors	P/E Ratio	YTD Return %	% Net Assets
ExxonMobil Corporation	Energy	11.1	-5.19	1.63
⊕ Burlington Northern Santa	Business	15.2	-0.89	1.58
Allstate Corporation	Financial	8.7	0.25	1.53
Bank of America Corporati	Financial	12.4	0.11	1.52
⊖ Verizon Communications	Telecom	15.9	-0.07	1.49
⊕ Colgate-Palmolive Company	Goods	27.6	0.72	1.49
⊖ Phelps Dodge Corp.	Ind Mtrls	12.7	-1.81	1.49
⊖ Motorola, Inc.	Hardware	11.8	-9.53	1.47
⊖ General Mills, Inc.	Goods	19.1	0.00	1.47

Total Fixed-Income:31	Date of Maturity	Amount $000	Value $000	% Net Assets
FNMA 4.375%	03-15-13	2,500	2,424	1.61
US Treasury Note 4.75%	05-15-14	2,250	2,270	1.51
FHLMC 5%	07-15-14	2,000	2,007	1.33
US Treasury Note 3.375%	02-15-08	2,000	1,963	1.30
FNMA 3.25%	11-15-07	2,000	1,961	1.30
US Treasury Note 4.25%	08-15-15	2,000	1,946	1.29
Sec Cap Pac Tr 7.2%	03-01-13	1,600	1,721	1.14
US Treasury Note 5.125%	05-15-16	1,500	1,556	1.03
FHLBA 5.375%	05-18-16	1,500	1,546	1.03

Equity Style
Style: Blend
Size: Large-Cap

Value Measures		Rel Category
Price/Earnings	12.76	0.84
Price/Book	2.35	0.95
Price/Sales	1.24	0.91
Price/Cash Flow	8.07	1.00
Dividend Yield %	1.78	0.92

Growth Measures	%	Rel Category
Long-Term Erngs	12.09	1.03
Book Value	13.33	1.55
Sales	15.22	1.71
Cash Flow	13.95	1.41
Historical Erngs	21.66	1.21

Market Cap %			
Giant	37.4	Small	0.0
Large	56.1	Micro	0.0
Mid	6.5	Avg $mil:	42,803

Fixed-Income Style
Duration: —
Quality: —

Avg Eff Duration [1]	—
Avg Eff Maturity	—
Avg Credit Quality	—
Avg Wtd Coupon	4.81%

[1]figure provided by fund

Sector Weightings	% of Stocks	Rel DJ Mod	3 Year High Low
⌖ Info	13.66	—	
Software	3.27	—	4 0
Hardware	5.20	—	8 4
Media	0.00	—	4 0
Telecom	5.19	—	5 2
⌖ Service	44.95		
Health	2.58	—	5 0
Consumer	9.38	—	9 1
Business	7.80	—	8 1
Financial	25.19	—	26 21
⌖ Mfg	41.39		
Goods	7.15	—	10 6
Ind Mtrls	15.17	—	28 15
Energy	14.17	—	23 12
Utilities	4.90	—	5 0

Composition
● Cash	13.7
● Stocks	56.3
● Bonds	30.0
● Other	0.0
Foreign (% of Stock)	1.2

Address:	One Corporate Center Rye NY 10580 800-422-3554	Minimum Purchase:	$1000	Add: $0	IRA: $250
		Min Auto Inv Plan:	$0	Add: $100	
Web Address:	www.gabelli.com	Sales Fees:	No-load, 0.25%S		
Inception:	10-01-91	Management Fee:	0.75%		
Advisor:	Gabelli Advisers, Inc.	Actual Fees:	Mgt:0.75%	Dist:0.25%	
Subadvisor:	Westwood Management Corp	Expense Projections:	3Yr:$397	5Yr:$686	10Yr:$1511
NTF Plans:	Fidelity Retail-NTF, Schwab OneSource	Income Distrib:	Quarterly		

WF Adv Common Stk Z

	Ticker	Load	NAV	Yield	Total Assets	Mstar Category
	STCSX	Closed	$20.00	0.0%	$1,116 mil	Mid-Cap Blend

Governance and Management

Stewardship Grade: C

Portfolio Manager(s)

Dick Weiss has been on board since 1991. Ann Miletti was named comanager of the fund in October 2001 after serving as an associate manager for several years. A team of six analysts assists them.

Strategy

Dick Weiss and Ann Miletti search for stocks that are trading at discounts to their estimates of their private market values. They use the same strategy on the sell side, shedding stocks when they reach their price targets. The managers' price targets are generous enough, however, that the fund's price multiples can be substantially higher than its average peer's. They also keep the fund diversified by sector, giving it larger weightings than its typical peer in growth areas such as technology.

Performance 12-31-06

	1st Qtr	2nd Qtr	3rd Qtr	4th Qtr	Total
2002	2.68	-14.77	-17.97	12.46	-19.26
2003	-1.06	18.04	4.66	13.47	38.70
2004	2.89	-0.61	-3.66	11.62	9.96
2005	0.16	2.06	4.70	4.65	12.01
2006	8.13	-2.25	2.04	6.91	15.31

Trailing	Total Return%	+/- S&P 500	+/- S&P Mid 400	%Rank Cat	Growth of $10,000
3 Mo	6.91	0.21	-0.08	64	10,691
6 Mo	9.10	-3.64	3.27	49	10,910
1 Yr	15.31	-0.48	4.99	32	11,531
3 Yr Avg	12.40	1.96	-0.69	54	14,200
5 Yr Avg	9.72	3.53	-1.17	59	15,901
10 Yr Avg	11.10	2.68	-2.37	58	28,651
15 Yr Avg	13.73	3.09	0.10	24	68,885

Tax Analysis	Tax-Adj Rtn%	%Rank Cat	Tax-Cost Rat	%Rank Cat
3 Yr (estimated)	9.77	66	2.34	84
5 Yr (estimated)	8.17	64	1.41	81
10 Yr (estimated)	8.59	65	2.26	89

Potential Capital Gain Exposure: 18% of assets

Morningstar's Take by Andrew Gogerty 11-30-06

We can't pound the table for Wells Fargo Advantage Common Stock.

To be sure, this mid-blend fund does have a few things in its favor. Manager Dick Weiss has more than two decades of experience evaluating whole companies--not just stocks--something we don't see changing. His focus on private market value (the price a potential buyer would pay for the entire firm) goes beyond the typical discounted cash-flow analysis and includes a qualitative assessment of everything from management to suppliers to a company's foothold in the marketplace. Weiss has also signaled his confidence in his approach by investing more than $1 million alongside fund shareholders.

The fund's history is dotted with pockets of success, but ultimately its record has been unspectacular. Weiss' style portends relative sector biases such as energy and media names, which has helped push the fund past its peers thus far in 2006 and in 1999. But the fund isn't a one-trick pony, as his team's somewhat unique approach to valuation has allowed the fund to participate in both value- and growth-led markets. In addition, the team keeps the potential volatility from its higher-flying names in check by limiting individual position sizes (single holdings rarely top 3% of assets). Overall, though, the fund's long-term profile hasn't offered much more than a competitive risk/reward profile--middling category returns have been coupled with modest volatility. That's not exactly a compelling argument.

What's more, this lackluster history is tagged with high fees. Fund expenses here and at sibling Opportunity are above the mid-cap median. In total, the team's research process is leveraged across nearly $6 billion, and we feel investors deserve lower fees from Wells Fargo. So, while there are certain things to like here, we'd ultimately suggest investors go elsewhere first.

Address:	525 Market Street San Francisco CA 94163 800-368-3863
Web Address:	www.wellsfargofunds.com
Inception:	12-29-89
Advisor:	Wells Fargo Funds Management, LLC
Subadvisor:	Wells Capital Management
NTF Plans:	Schwab OneSource

Minimum Purchase:	Closed	Add: —	IRA: —
Min Auto Inv Plan:	Closed	Add: —	
Sales Fees:	No-load		
Management Fee:	0.75% mx./0.60% mn.		
Actual Fees:	Mgt:0.75%	Dist: —	
Expense Projections:	3Yr:$458	5Yr:$807	10Yr:$1793
Income Distrib:	Annually		

Historical Profile

Return	Average
Risk	Average
Rating	★★★ Neutral

| | 88% | 91% | 86% | 85% | 86% | 94% | 94% | 90% | 83% |

Investment Style
Equity
Stock %

▼ Manager Change
▽ Partial Manager Change

40.8
31.0
24.0
17.0
10.0

Growth of $10,000
— Investment Values of Fund
— Investment Values of S&P 500

Performance Quartile (within Category)

1995	1996	1997	1998	1999	2000	2001	2002	2003	2004	2005	2006	History
19.77	20.24	21.02	21.06	25.21	20.16	19.78	15.97	22.15	22.65	21.77	20.00	NAV
32.41	20.47	24.04	6.60	40.35	-1.20	-1.70	-19.26	38.70	9.96	12.01	15.31	Total Return %
-5.17	-2.49	-9.32	-21.98	19.31	7.90	10.19	2.84	10.02	-0.92	7.10	-0.48	+/-S&P 500
1.48	1.22	-8.21	-12.52	25.63	-18.71	-1.09	-4.73	3.08	-6.52	-0.55	4.99	+/-S&P Mid 400
0.71	0.59	0.20	0.00	0.00	0.21	0.00	0.00	0.00	0.00	0.00	0.00	Income Return %
31.70	19.88	23.84	6.60	40.35	-1.41	-1.70	-19.26	38.70	9.96	12.01	15.31	Capital Return %
30	43	64	62	12	80	60	71	32	94	24	32	Total Rtn % Rank Cat
0.12	0.11	0.04	0.00	0.00	0.04	0.00	0.00	0.00	0.00	0.00	0.00	Income $
2.21	3.35	3.86	1.32	4.03	4.46	0.04	0.00	1.65	3.56	5.11	Capital Gains $
1.20	1.20	1.20	1.20	1.20	1.20	1.30	1.30	1.40	1.30	1.31	—	Expense Ratio %
0.50	0.30	0.00	0.00	-0.10	-0.10	-0.10	-0.30	-0.40	-0.40	-0.38	—	Income Ratio %
92	91	117	103	80	95	89	65	42	42	33	—	Turnover Rate %
1,061	1,244	1,565	1,440	1,733	1,719	1,703	1,476	1,437	1,187	1,061	999	Net Assets $mil

Rating and Risk

Time Period	Load-Adj Return %	Morningstar Rtn vs Cat	Morningstar Risk vs Cat	Morningstar Risk-Adj Rating
1 Yr	15.31			
3 Yr	12.40	Avg	Avg	★★★
5 Yr	9.72	Avg	+Avg	★★★
10 Yr	11.10	Avg	Avg	★★★
Incept	15.46			

Other Measures	Standard Index S&P 500	Best Fit Index Russ MG
Alpha	-0.5	0.6
Beta	1.38	0.90
R-Squared	79	92
Standard Deviation	10.65	
Mean	12.40	
Sharpe Ratio	0.86	

Portfolio Analysis 10-31-06

Share change since 07-06 Total Stocks:67	Sector	PE	Tot Ret%	% Assets
EOG Resources	Energy	10.1	-14.62	2.10
⊖ Noble Corporation	Energy	15.5	8.19	2.09
Apache Corporation	Energy	7.8	-2.30	2.03
⊖ Cablevision Systems A	Media	—	84.55	1.98
⊖ Smith International, Inc	Energy	17.0	11.59	1.57
⊖ Activision	Software	—	25.47	1.56
MedImmune, Inc.	Health	—	-7.57	1.56
Cooper Cameron Corporati	Energy	21.8	28.14	1.56
⊖ Foundry Networks, Inc.	Hardware	39.8	8.47	1.50
Altera Corp.	Hardware	24.8	6.21	1.45
⊖ Kohl's Corporation	Consumer	22.6	40.80	1.43
HCC Insurance Holdings I	Financial	16.5	9.39	1.43
✷ Eclipsys Corporation	Software	—	8.61	1.40
Marshall & Ilsley Corp.	Financial	15.2	14.38	1.39
⊖ Trimble Navigation Ltd.	Hardware	29.7	42.94	1.39
⊖ Liberty Global, Inc. A	Media	14.6	29.56	1.37
⊖ Sysco Corporation	Consumer	25.2	20.96	1.36
Republic Services, Inc.	Business	20.7	9.91	1.34
Advance Auto Parts, Inc.	Consumer	16.5	-17.64	1.34
⊕ SkyWest, Inc.	Business	10.9	-4.58	1.33

Current Investment Style

Value Blnd Growth (Large Mid Small)

Market Cap	%
Giant	4.4
Large	18.2
Mid	62.0
Small	15.5
Micro	0.0

Avg $mil: 5,460

Value Measures		Rel Category
Price/Earnings	16.71	1.04
Price/Book	2.63	1.16
Price/Sales	1.17	1.04
Price/Cash Flow	8.87	1.05
Dividend Yield %	0.81	0.62

Growth Measures	%	Rel Category
Long-Term Erngs	14.09	1.11
Book Value	8.75	1.05
Sales	10.19	1.14
Cash Flow	9.01	1.06
Historical Erngs	12.11	0.68

Profitability	%	Rel Category
Return on Equity	12.98	0.81
Return on Assets	6.85	0.85
Net Margin	10.69	0.98

Sector Weightings	% of Stocks	Rel S&P 500	3 Year High Low	
↻ Info	32.76	1.64		
Software	8.79	2.55	9	2
Hardware	15.09	1.63	15	5
Media	8.83	2.33	11	8
Telecom	0.05	0.01	3	0
⊂ Service	39.51	0.86		
Health	7.73	0.64	14	6
Consumer	11.67	1.53	15	11
Business	7.73	1.83	12	5
Financial	12.38	0.56	14	9
⬑ Mfg	27.76	0.82		
Goods	3.72	0.44	10	2
Ind Mtrls	12.61	1.06	14	6
Energy	11.38	1.16	16	11
Utilities	0.05	0.01	2	0

Composition

	%
● Cash	15.1
● Stocks	83.2
● Bonds	0.0
○ Other	1.6
Foreign (% of Stock)	2.9

MORNINGSTAR® Funds 500

WF Adv Opportunity Inv

	Ticker	Load	NAV	Yield	Total Assets	Mstar Category
	SOPFX	None	$41.64	0.2%	$2,052 mil	Mid-Cap Blend

Governance and Management

Stewardship Grade: C

Portfolio Manager(s)

Dick Weiss has been on board since 1991. Ann Miletti was named comanager of the fund in October 2001 after serving as an associate manager for several years. A team of six analysts assists them.

Strategy

Dick Weiss and Ann Miletti search for stocks that are trading at discounts to their estimates of their private market values. They use the same strategy on the sell side, shedding stocks when they reach their price targets. Management's price targets are generous enough, however, that the fund's price multiples can be substantially higher than its average peer's. They also keep the fund diversified by sector, giving it larger weightings than its typical peer in growth areas such as technology.

Historical Profile
Return Average
Risk Average
Rating ★★★ Neutral

Investment Style
Equity
Stock %

83% 88% 85% 82% 86% 96% 87% 89% 86%

▼ Manager Change
▽ Partial Manager Change

Growth of $10,000
— Investment Values of Fund
— Investment Values of S&P 500

Performance Quartile (within Category)

	1995	1996	1997	1998	1999	2000	2001	2002	2003	2004	2005	2006	History
	33.35	35.26	37.41	38.62	44.69	42.35	39.29	28.70	39.45	46.40	44.87	41.64	NAV
	27.27	18.14	23.45	15.49	33.39	8.57	-4.80	-26.95	37.46	17.62	7.22	11.75	Total Return %
	-10.31	-4.82	-9.91	-13.09	12.35	17.67	7.09	-4.85	8.78	6.74	2.31	-4.04	+/-S&P 500
	-3.66	-1.11	-8.80	-3.63	18.67	-8.94	-4.19	-12.42	1.84	1.14	-5.34	1.43	+/-S&P Mid 400
	0.78	0.77	0.30	0.14	0.22	0.43	0.17	0.00	0.00	0.00	0.00	0.23	Income Return %
	26.49	17.37	23.15	15.35	33.17	8.14	-4.97	-26.95	37.46	17.62	7.22	11.52	Capital Return %
	52	61	68	35	24	60	76	90	36	34	69	62	Total Rtn % Rank Cat
	0.21	0.25	0.10	0.05	0.08	0.17	0.07	0.00	0.00	0.00	0.00	0.09	Income $
	1.63	3.82	5.75	4.47	6.35	5.64	0.95	0.00	0.00	0.00	4.93	8.44	Capital Gains $
	1.30	1.30	1.20	1.20	1.20	1.20	1.40	1.40	1.40	1.40	1.36	—	Expense Ratio %
	0.70	0.60	0.30	0.20	0.20	0.50	0.02	-0.20	-0.40	-0.60	-0.46	—	Income Ratio %
	92	103	94	86	81	87	88	71	60	42	35	—	Turnover Rate %
	1,328	1,770	1,925	2,038	2,537	3,337	3,664	2,507	2,709	2,406	1,965	1,825	Net Assets $mil

Performance 12-31-06

	1st Qtr	2nd Qtr	3rd Qtr	4th Qtr	Total
2002	0.94	-16.59	-20.53	9.17	-26.95
2003	-4.32	21.41	5.85	11.79	37.46
2004	4.97	3.02	-1.48	10.40	17.62
2005	-3.00	3.71	4.48	2.01	7.22
2006	4.97	-2.80	3.34	5.98	11.75

Trailing	Total Return%	+/- S&P 500	+/- S&P Mid 400	%Rank Cat	Growth of $10,000
3 Mo	5.98	-0.72	-1.01	86	10,598
6 Mo	9.53	-3.21	3.70	44	10,953
1 Yr	11.75	-4.04	1.43	62	11,175
3 Yr Avg	12.12	1.68	-0.97	61	14,094
5 Yr Avg	7.19	1.00	-3.70	89	14,150
10 Yr Avg	10.77	2.35	-2.70	65	27,811
15 Yr Avg	12.86	2.22	-0.77	59	61,390

Tax Analysis	Tax-Adj Rtn%	%Rank Cat	Tax-Cost Rat	%Rank Cat
3 Yr (estimated)	10.33	61	1.60	64
5 Yr (estimated)	6.16	87	0.96	60
10 Yr (estimated)	8.73	63	1.84	63

Potential Capital Gain Exposure: 18% of assets

Rating and Risk

Time Period	Load-Adj Return %	Morningstar Rtn vs Cat	Morningstar Risk vs Cat	Morningstar Risk-Adj Rating
1 Yr	11.75			
3 Yr	12.12	Avg	-Avg	★★★
5 Yr	7.19	-Avg	+Avg	★★
10 Yr	10.77	Avg	Avg	★★★
Incept	14.66			

Other Measures	Standard Index S&P 500	Best Fit Index Russ MG
Alpha	-0.1	1.1
Beta	1.26	0.81
R-Squared	80	89
Standard Deviation	9.66	
Mean	12.12	
Sharpe Ratio	0.90	

Portfolio Analysis 10-31-06

Share change since 07-06 Total Stocks:68

	Sector	PE	Tot Ret%	% Assets
Praxair, Inc.	Ind Mtrls	20.8	14.01	2.21
⊖ Weatherford Internationa	Energy	15.2	16.56	2.12
Apache Corporation	Energy	7.8	-2.30	1.92
⊖ Cablevision Systems A	Media	—	84.55	1.90
Waters Corporation	Health	24.9	29.55	1.72
⊕ Transocean, Inc.	Energy	27.1	16.07	1.69
Accenture, Ltd.	Business	22.0	29.32	1.65
⊖ GlobalSantaFe Corporatio	Energy	16.3	24.06	1.54
Cadence Design Systems	Software	47.5	5.85	1.53
⊖ Comcast Corporation	Media	—		1.52
⊖ Interpublic Group of Com	Business	—	26.84	1.52
⊖ IMS Health, Inc.	Health	17.4	10.77	1.51
⊖ Ensco International, Inc	Energy	11.0	13.12	1.50
⊕ Red Hat, Inc.	Software	58.8	-15.63	1.49
⊖ Target Corporation	Consumer	19.3	4.65	1.48
⊖ J.B. Hunt Transport Serv	Business	15.6	-6.93	1.48
⊖ Staples, Inc.	Consumer	19.6	18.58	1.47
⊖ NiSource, Inc.	Utilities	21.8	20.51	1.42
AutoNation, Inc.	Consumer	15.0	-1.89	1.41
⊖ E.W. Scripps Company	Media	33.1	5.05	1.39

Current Investment Style

Value Blnd Growth — Large Mid Small

Market Cap	%
Giant	1.6
Large	43.0
Mid	49.8
Small	5.4
Micro	0.1

Avg $mil: 8,067

Value Measures		Rel Category
Price/Earnings	16.02	1.00
Price/Book	2.32	1.03
Price/Sales	1.19	1.06
Price/Cash Flow	9.04	1.07
Dividend Yield %	1.02	0.78

Growth Measures	%	Rel Category
Long-Term Erngs	13.86	1.09
Book Value	6.88	0.83
Sales	9.23	1.04
Cash Flow	14.26	1.68
Historical Erngs	16.27	0.91

Profitability	%	Rel Category
Return on Equity	17.74	1.11
Return on Assets	7.39	0.92
Net Margin	10.59	0.97

Sector Weightings

	% of Stocks	Rel S&P 500	3 Year High	Low
↻ Info	29.53	1.48		
Software	6.88	1.99	7	3
Hardware	14.11	1.53	14	7
Media	8.51	2.25	13	8
Telecom	0.03	0.01	4	0
☞ Service	44.26	0.96		
Health	10.20	0.85	10	7
Consumer	15.46	2.02	17	12
Business	7.78	1.84	14	8
Financial	10.82	0.49	11	9
☐ Mfg	26.22	0.78		
Goods	4.00	0.47	6	3
Ind Mtrls	9.93	0.83	12	7
Energy	10.46	1.07	16	10
Utilities	1.83	0.52	5	1

Composition

	%
● Cash	12.0
● Stocks	86.4
● Bonds	0.0
○ Other	1.6
Foreign (% of Stock)	5.5

Morningstar's Take by Andrew Gogerty 12-01-06

We can't pound the table for Wells Fargo Advantage Opportunity.

To be sure, this mid-blend fund does have a few things in its favor. Manager Dick Weiss has more than two decades of experience evaluating whole companies--not just stocks--something we don't see changing. His focus on private market value (the price a potential buyer would pay for the entire firm) goes beyond the typical discounted cash-flow analysis and includes a qualitative assessment of everything from management to suppliers to a company's foothold in the marketplace. Weiss has also signaled his confidence in his approach by investing more than $1 million alongside fund shareholders (comanager Ann Miletti has between $500,000 and $1 million invested as well).

The fund's history is dotted with pockets of success, but ultimately its record has been unspectacular. Weiss' style portends relative sector biases such as energy and media names, which has helped push the fund past its peers at times, such as in 1999 and 2003-2004. But the fund isn't a one-trick pony, as his team's somewhat unusual approach to valuation has allowed the fund to participate in both value- and growth-led markets. In addition, the team keeps the potential volatility from its higher-flying names in check by limiting individual position sizes (single holdings rarely top 3% of assets). Overall, though, the long-term profile hasn't offered much more than a competitive risk/reward profile--middling category returns have been coupled with modest volatility. That's not exactly a compelling argument.

What's more, this lackluster history is tagged with high fees. Fund expenses here and at sibling Common Stock are above the mid-cap median. In total, the team's research process is leveraged across nearly $6 billion, and we feel investors deserve lower fees from Wells Fargo. So, while there are certain things to like here, we'd ultimately suggest investors go elsewhere first.

Address:	525 Market Street San Francisco CA 94163 800-368-1030	Minimum Purchase:	$2500 Add: $100 IRA: $1000
		Min Auto Inv Plan:	$2500 Add: $100
Web Address:	www.wellsfargofunds.com	Sales Fees:	No-load
Inception:	12-31-85	Management Fee:	0.75% mx./0.60% mn.
Advisor:	Wells Fargo Funds Management, LLC	Actual Fees:	Mgt:0.75% Dist:—
Subadvisor:	Wells Capital Management	Expense Projections:	3Yr:$457 5Yr:$800 10Yr:$1768
		Income Distrib:	Annually
NTF Plans:	Fidelity Retail-NTF, Schwab OneSource		

WF Adv S/T Muni Bd Inv

	Ticker	Load	NAV	Yield	SEC Yield	Total Assets	Mstar Category
	STSMX	None	$9.79	3.6%	—	$650 mil	Muni National Short

Governance and Management

Stewardship Grade: D

Portfolio Manager(s)

Lead manager Lyle Fitterer took over this portfolio in March 2000. He also manages Wells Fargo Advantage Municipal Bond and Wells Fargo Advantage Ultra Short-Term Municipal Income.

Strategy

Manager Lyle Fitterer sticks primarily with short-term municipal bonds. He favors midquality bonds and isn't afraid to throw the occasional high-yield security into the mix. Fitterer doesn't make big interest-rate bets, and the fund's duration is typically shorter than the category average. He limits new BBB purchases to 1% of assets or less and BB purchases to 0.5% of assets or less.

Historical Profile
Return High
Risk Average
Rating ★★★★★ Highest

	8	8	12	11	6	2	3	6

Investment Style
Fixed Income
Income Rtn %Rank Cat

▼ Manager Change
▽ Partial Manager Change

20.8
18.8
Growth of $10,000
16.4 ■ Investment Values of Fund
14.0
12.0 ─ Investment Values of LB Muni
10.0

Performance Quartile (within Category)

1995	1996	1997	1998	1999	2000	2001	2002	2003	2004	2005	2006	History
9.77	9.74	9.92	9.97	9.63	9.64	9.70	9.79	9.84	9.84	9.79	9.79	NAV
5.37	4.87	6.93	5.55	1.17	5.05	5.17	5.08	4.02	3.21	2.67	3.65	Total Return %
-12.09	0.44	-2.26	-0.93	3.23	-6.63	0.04	-4.52	-1.29	-1.27	-0.84	-1.19	+/-LB Muni
-3.50	0.43	1.45	0.34	-0.79	-1.18	-1.42	-1.64	1.34	1.43	1.80	0.60	+/-LB Muni 3YR
4.96	5.16	5.03	5.03	4.67	4.93	4.55	4.14	3.50	3.16	3.18	3.64	Income Return %
0.41	-0.29	1.90	0.52	-3.50	0.12	0.62	0.94	0.52	0.05	-0.51	0.01	Capital Return %
100	8	5	1	38	67	29	54	3	1	3	12	Total Rtn % Rank Cat
0.47	0.49	0.48	0.49	0.46	0.46	0.43	0.39	0.34	0.31	0.31	0.35	Income $
0.00	0.00	0.00	0.00	0.00	0.00	0.00	0.00	0.00	0.00	0.00	0.00	Capital Gains $
0.80	0.70	0.70	0.60	0.60	0.60	0.60	0.60	0.60	0.70	0.66	0.66	Expense Ratio %
4.80	5.10	5.00	4.80	4.70	4.80	4.50	4.10	4.10	3.10	3.07	3.40	Income Ratio %
227	—	26	16	23	49	74	68	84	69	75	129	Turnover Rate %
133	145	181	264	282	312	511	126	528	499	655	647	Net Assets $mil

Performance 12-31-06

	1st Qtr	2nd Qtr	3rd Qtr	4th Qtr	Total
2002	0.92	1.99	1.61	0.47	5.08
2003	0.94	1.81	0.53	0.69	4.02
2004	0.76	-0.22	1.72	0.92	3.21
2005	0.41	1.00	0.59	0.64	2.67
2006	0.55	0.69	1.54	0.82	3.65

Trailing	Total Return%	+/- LB Muni	+/- LB Muni 3YR	%Rank Cat	Growth of $10,000
3 Mo	0.82	-0.29	0.19	17	10,082
6 Mo	2.38	-2.17	-0.20	33	10,238
1 Yr	3.65	-1.19	0.60	12	10,365
3 Yr Avg	3.17	-1.11	1.27	2	10,981
5 Yr Avg	3.72	-1.81	0.72	2	12,004
10 Yr Avg	4.24	-1.52	0.20	1	15,148
15 Yr Avg	4.31	-1.95	-0.14	27	18,832

Tax Analysis	Tax-Adj Rtn%	%Rank Cat	Tax-Cost Rat	%Rank Cat
3 Yr (estimated)	3.17	1	0.00	1
5 Yr (estimated)	3.72	2	0.00	1
10 Yr (estimated)	4.24	1	0.00	1

Potential Capital Gain Exposure: -2% of assets

Rating and Risk

Time Period	Load-Adj Return %	Morningstar Rtn vs Cat	Morningstar Risk vs Cat	Morningstar Risk-Adj Rating
1 Yr	3.65			
3 Yr	3.17	High	-Avg	★★★★★
5 Yr	3.72	High	-Avg	★★★★★
10 Yr	4.24	High	Avg	★★★★★
Incept	4.31			

Other Measures	Standard Index LB Muni	Best Fit Index LB Muni 3YR
Alpha	-0.3	0.6
Beta	0.24	0.54
R-Squared	68	80
Standard Deviation	0.82	
Mean	3.17	
Sharpe Ratio	-0.10	

Morningstar's Take by Andrew Gogerty 11-17-06

High fees tarnish Wells Fargo Advantage Short-Term Municipal Bond's otherwise appealing profile.

Low costs are a strong selling point for any mutual fund, but expenses matter even more so among bond offerings. Given their narrower range of potential returns compared with equities, bond-fund winners and losers are typically separated by a smaller margin. Unfortunately, Wells Fargo has done little to help this fund out. The fund's 0.66%-of-assets expense ratio still remains higher than that of the median no-load short-term municipal offering, even though we find it hard to believe there were no economies of scale to be gained after the merger of the former Strong funds into the Wells Fargo complex.

Though the fund's returns would look even better if its fees were lower, manager Lyle Fitterer has been able to keep the fund competitive. The fund's three- and five-year trailing returns through Nov. 13, 2006, top nearly every category peer.

Fitterer makes full use of the fund's flexibility. He looks across the credit spectrum for mispriced bonds relative to comparable issues, and as a result, the fund has had upwards of 40% of assets invested in bonds rated BBB and below during his tenure.

But over the past year, Fitterer has been playing more defense than offense. He's been upgrading the credit quality of the portfolio, taking gains from the fund's strong-performing high-yield issues and investing in higher-quality bonds, saying that lower-quality issues are not offering a significant premium for the added risk of their current prices. In fact, the fund's stake in bonds rated BBB and below has fallen from 36% to 25% of assets since June 2005.

Overall, this fund does have appeal, as Fitterer has done a good job utilizing the fund's credit flexibility. But even those willing to accept this credit profile should consider other options until Wells Fargo lowers fees.

Address:	525 Market Street San Francisco CA 94163 800-222-8222
Web Address:	www.wellsfargofunds.com
Inception:	12-31-91
Advisor:	Wells Fargo Funds Management, LLC
Subadvisor:	Wells Capital Management
NTF Plans:	Fidelity Retail-NTF, Schwab OneSource

Minimum Purchase:	$2500	Add: $100	IRA: $1000
Min Auto Inv Plan:	$50	Add: $50	
Sales Fees:	No-load		
Management Fee:	0.40% mx./0.25% mn., 0.45%A		
Actual Fees:	Mgt:0.39%	Dist: —	
Expense Projections:	3Yr:$317	5Yr:$586	10Yr:$1354
Income Distrib:	Monthly		

Portfolio Analysis 09-30-06

Total Fixed-Income:278

	Date of Maturity	Amount $000	Value $000	% Net Assets
Tobacco Settlement Auth	06-01-25	15,725	16,829	2.68
AURORA COLO MULTIFAMILY	12-20-40	12,750	12,753	2.03
Tobacco Settlement Auth	06-01-35	10,670	11,636	1.85
BEXAR CNTY TEX REV REV B	08-15-22	9,655	10,267	1.64
MONROE CNTY N Y INDL DEV	11-15-32	8,500	10,195	1.62
District Columbia 5.5%	06-01-12	8,000	8,444	1.34
DISTRICT COLUMBIA REV BD	06-01-19	7,400	7,400	1.18
Wyandotte Cnty Kans City	12-01-12	7,250	7,232	1.15
Rhode Island St Partn Ct	10-01-16	7,000	7,176	1.14
Texas Water Dev Brd Sr L	07-15-13	7,075	7,087	1.13
Delaware Valley Pa Regl	07-01-27	7,000	7,060	1.12
North Little Rock Ark El	07-01-10	6,500	6,870	1.09
Badger Tob Asset Securit	06-01-17	6,375	6,803	1.08
Ashland Ky Pollutn Ctl R	11-01-09	6,330	6,711	1.07
Illinois Dev Fin Auth	05-01-31	6,675	6,675	1.06

Current Investment Style

¹Avg Eff Duration		1.6 Yrs
Avg Eff Maturity		—
Avg Credit Quality		AA
Avg Wtd Coupon		5.06%
Avg Wtd Price		102.37% of par

¹figure provided by fund

Credit Analysis	% bonds 09-30-06		
AAA	52	BB	4
AA	10	B	1
A	14	Below B	0
BBB	19	NR/NA	0

Top 5 States	% bonds		
TX	10.0	WI	4.5
PA	7.3	NY	4.3
IA	6.7		

Composition			
Cash	12.0	Bonds	88.0
Stocks	0.0	Other	0.0

Special Securities	
Restricted/Illiquid Secs	0
Options/Futures/Warrants	No

Sector Weightings	% of Bonds	Rel Cat
General Obligation	13.4	0.41
Utilities	7.1	0.88
Health	21.0	2.10
Water/Waste	8.0	1.08
Housing	16.4	1.77
Education	6.0	0.69
Transportation	1.5	0.29
COP/Lease	4.1	2.25
Industrial	21.3	1.32
Misc Revenue	0.0	—
Demand	1.3	1.94

MORNINGSTAR® Funds 500

William Blair Intl Gr N

	Ticker	Load	NAV	Yield	Total Assets	Mstar Category
	WBIGX	Closed	$27.70	1.2%	$6,266 mil	Foreign Large Growth

Governance and Management

Stewardship Grade: B

Portfolio Manager(s)

George Greig is in his second stint with this offering. He helped launch the fund in 1992 and has done well since returning in 1996. Before joining William Blair, he was a founding partner of PBHG.

Strategy

Manager George Greig looks for companies with good growth prospects, high returns on equity, and low debt. He also considers qualitative elements such as corporate culture and strength of management. Greig isn't solely a top-down investor, but he often uses themes such as Asian economic growth to help drive his stock picks. An emerging-markets stake of 10% to 15% is not uncommon here. Greig looks across the market-cap range for his picks, and multinationals often rub shoulders with tiny, unknown names in this portfolio. William Blair instituted a fair-value-pricing policy on this fund in 2003.

Performance 12-31-06

	1st Qtr	2nd Qtr	3rd Qtr	4th Qtr	Total
2002	1.81	-0.82	-19.13	3.88	-15.18
2003	-5.71	17.85	11.79	14.48	42.21
2004	5.36	-2.29	-0.47	15.63	18.48
2005	-0.27	1.77	12.13	6.89	21.65
2006	9.83	-3.54	4.27	11.40	23.06

Trailing	Total Return%	+/- MSCI EAFE	+/- MSCI Wd xUS	%Rank Cat	Growth of $10,000
3 Mo	11.40	1.05	1.28	39	11,140
6 Mo	16.15	1.46	1.93	22	11,615
1 Yr	23.06	-3.28	-2.65	55	12,306
3 Yr Avg	21.05	1.12	0.95	15	17,738
5 Yr Avg	16.43	1.45	1.18	11	21,396
10 Yr Avg	14.94	7.23	6.98	1	40,245
15 Yr Avg	—	—	—	—	—

Tax Analysis	Tax-Adj Rtn%	%Rank Cat	Tax-Cost Rat	%Rank Cat
3 Yr (estimated)	19.87	12	0.97	58
5 Yr (estimated)	15.74	6	0.59	53
10 Yr (estimated)	13.19	3	1.52	92

Potential Capital Gain Exposure: 28% of assets

Morningstar's Take by Arijit Dutta 12-20-06

William Blair International Growth is still a keeper.

This closed fund has encountered some hardship this year, but things aren't as bad as they might have been. Its 16% loss during the May-June market correction, though painful, was only a point more than the foreign large-growth average. Considering that small-cap and emerging-markets stocks were among the hardest-hit assets in the correction, the fund actually held up well. (This all-cap portfolio's average market cap of $13 billion is only one third of the foreign large-growth average, and its 19% emerging-markets stake is twice the group norm.) Moreover, rather than panic, manager George Greig held his ground, so the fund has benefited from the recovery in small caps and emerging markets since June.

Greig's calm reaction to this adversity is based on sound analysis. Greig didn't see business slowing among the companies on his team's coverage list, so he didn't anticipate a prolonged slump in world markets. Thus, he even bought some aggressive emerging-markets names on weakness, such as wind-power generator Suzlon Energy of India. Based on Greig's calculation, Suzlon got unduly punished in the correction considering the company's robust profit outlook. Using similar logic, he's held on to some of the relatively sluggish developed-market stocks in the portfolio, such as top holdings Rolls-Royce and AstraZeneca. Those stocks have slowed the fund down this year, but Greig has faith in his analysis of their merit.

Overall, his aggressive management style has its pitfalls, but Greig has consistently managed to avoid any potholes. Greig runs a vast, go-anywhere portfolio, which gives him a lot of room to find growth stocks in overlooked areas, should any parts of the market become overheated. Through the years, he has wielded that flexibility to great effect by identifying opportunities most rivals overlooked. We think the fund will continue to benefit from great stock selection.

Address:	222 W Adams St	Minimum Purchase:	Closed	Add: —	IRA: —
	Chicago IL 60606	Min Auto Inv Plan:	Closed	Add: —	
	800-635-2886	Sales Fees:	No-load, 0.25%S, 2.00%R		
Web Address:	www.wmblair.com	Management Fee:	1.00%		
Inception:	10-01-92	Actual Fees:	Mgt:1.00%	Dist:0.25%	
Advisor:	William Blair & Co.	Expense Projections:	3Yr:$452	5Yr:$779	10Yr:$1702
Subadvisor:	None	Income Distrib:	Annually		
NTF Plans:	Fidelity Retail-NTF, Schwab OneSource				

Historical Profile

Return	High
Risk	Average
Rating	★★★★★ Highest

| 93% | 97% | 92% | 85% | 85% | 89% | 95% | 97% | 96% |

Investment Style
Equity
Stock %

▼ Manager Change
▽ Partial Manager Change

Growth of $10,000
■ Investment Values of Fund
— Investment Values of MSCI EAFE

42.2
32.4
24.0
17.0
10.0

Performance Quartile (within Category)

1995	1996	1997	1998	1999	2000	2001	2002	2003	2004	2005	2006	History
13.12	13.95	13.14	14.62	24.03	17.93	15.48	13.13	18.65	22.09	25.22	27.70	NAV
7.21	10.20	8.39	11.46	96.25	-8.10	-13.66	-15.18	42.21	18.48	21.65	23.06	Total Return %
-4.00	4.15	6.61	-8.47	69.22	6.09	7.76	0.76	3.62	-1.77	8.11	-3.28	+/-MSCI EAFE
-4.20	3.33	6.12	-7.23	68.27	5.26	7.73	0.62	2.79	-1.90	7.18	-2.65	+/-MSCI Wd xUS
1.05	0.52	0.56	0.18	0.00	0.32	0.00	0.00	0.16	0.03	0.51	1.49	Income Return %
6.16	9.68	7.83	11.28	96.25	-8.42	-13.66	-15.18	42.05	18.45	21.14	21.57	Capital Return %
63	67	30	71	4	2	9	28	16	26	11	55	Total Rtn % Rank Cat
0.13	0.07	0.08	0.02	0.00	0.08	0.00	0.00	0.02	0.01	0.11	0.37	Income $
0.00	0.43	1.86	0.00	4.49	3.97	0.00	0.00	0.00	0.00	1.51	2.91	Capital Gains $
1.48	1.44	1.43	1.36	1.35	1.59	1.60	1.51	1.50	1.47	1.42	—	Expense Ratio %
0.87	0.19	0.01	0.09	-0.43	-0.44	-0.11	-0.36	0.05	-0.16	0.16	—	Income Ratio %
77	89	102	98	122	116	112	73	57	79	70	—	Turnover Rate %
90	105	129	140	40	116	189	527	1,355	2,062	3,128	4,191	Net Assets $mil

Rating and Risk

Time Period	Load-Adj Return %	Morningstar Rtn vs Cat	Morningstar Risk vs Cat	Morningstar Risk-Adj Rating
1 Yr	23.06			
3 Yr	21.05	+Avg	+Avg	★★★★
5 Yr	16.43	+Avg	Avg	★★★★
10 Yr	14.94	High	Avg	★★★★★
Incept	13.97			

Other Measures	Standard Index MSCI EAFE	Best Fit Index MSCI Wd xUS
Alpha	-1.3	-1.3
Beta	1.16	1.14
R-Squared	94	94
Standard Deviation	11.27	
Mean	21.05	
Sharpe Ratio	1.48	

Portfolio Analysis 11-30-06

Share change since 10-06 Total Stocks:173	Sector	Country	% Assets
⊕ ABB Ltd	Ind Mtrls	Switzerland	2.01
⊕ L'Oreal	Goods	France	2.01
⊕ Roche Holding	Health	Switzerland	1.99
⊕ Tesco	Consumer	U.K.	1.98
⊕ HBOS	Financial	U.K.	1.94
⊕ Rolls-Royce Grp	Ind Mtrls	U.K.	1.86
⊕ Denso	Ind Mtrls	Japan	1.85
⊕ ORIX	Financial	Japan	1.79
⊕ CapitaLand Ltd	Financial	Singapore	1.76
⊕ Reckitt Benckiser	Goods	U.K.	1.72
⊕ AstraZeneca	Health	U.K.	1.68
Hon Hai Precision Indust	Hardware	Taiwan	1.52
⊕ LVMH Moet Hennessy L.V.	Goods	France	1.51
⊕ DANONE Grp	Goods	France	1.49
⊕ BNP Paribas	Financial	France	1.37
⊕ BG Grp	Energy	U.K.	1.34
Saipem	Business	Italy	1.32
⊕ Macquarie Bank Ltd	Financial	Australia	1.32
☼ Veolia Environnement	Business	France	1.26
⊕ Northern Rock	Financial	U.K.	1.23

Current Investment Style

Value Blnd Growth — Large Mid Small

Market Cap	%
Giant	32.8
Large	36.8
Mid	27.1
Small	3.2
Micro	0.0

Avg $mil: 13,401

Value Measures		Rel Category
Price/Earnings	19.85	1.29
Price/Book	3.44	1.31
Price/Sales	1.78	1.26
Price/Cash Flow	13.26	1.37
Dividend Yield %	2.23	0.92

Growth Measures	%	Rel Category
Long-Term Erngs	16.81	1.24
Book Value	10.41	0.95
Sales	14.14	1.62
Cash Flow	17.81	1.46
Historical Erngs	13.78	0.60

Composition			
Cash	3.2	Bonds	0.0
Stocks	96.3	Other	0.4
Foreign (% of Stock)			99.8

Sector Weightings	% of Stocks	Rel MSCI EAFE	3 Year High	3 Year Low
⟳ Info	8.25	0.70		
🗔 Software	2.58	4.61	5	2
🖳 Hardware	3.19	0.83	7	2
🎤 Media	1.22	0.67	2	0
📞 Telecom	1.26	0.23	3	1
⟳ Service	56.87	1.20		
➕ Health	9.45	1.33	13	7
🛒 Consumer	10.95	2.21	15	9
🏢 Business	12.93	2.55	13	7
💲 Financial	23.54	0.78	28	21
⟳ Mfg	34.87	0.85		
🛠 Goods	16.89	1.29	22	14
🔧 Ind Mtrls	12.07	0.78	13	7
🔋 Energy	4.82	0.67	7	1
💡 Utilities	1.09	0.21	5	1

Regional Exposure		% Stock
UK/W. Europe	56	N. America 3
Japan	11	Latn America 7
Asia X Japan	21	Other 2

Country Exposure		% Stock
U.K.	19	Switzerland 7
France	12	Hong Kong 5
Japan	11	

William Blair Sm-Cp Gr N

	Ticker	Load	NAV	Yield	Total Assets	Mstar Category
	WBSNX	Closed	$25.41	0.0%	$1,256 mil	Small Growth

Governance and Management

Stewardship Grade: B

Portfolio Manager(s)

Michael Balkin and Karl Brewer managed this offering from its December 1999 inception until March 2005, when Balkin departed to run a hedge fund. Brewer has remained as a manager since that time, and Colin Williams was promoted from an analyst on the team to comanager in June 2006.

Strategy

Management uses a combination of bottom-up and top-down analysis to pick stocks. It looks for industry and sector trends that can spur growth and prefers companies that have strong catalysts for sustainable sales and earnings growth. The thing that sets it apart is its valuation consciousness and a contrarian streak that leads the team to jump in when a stock is promising but beaten down.

Historical Profile
Return High
Risk Average
Rating ★★★★★ Highest

Investment Style
Equity
Stock %

100% 93% 92% 91% 93% 96% 95%

▼ Manager Change
▽ Partial Manager Change

Growth of $10,000
— Investment Values of Fund
— Investment Values of S&P 500

29.0
21.0
15.0
10.0
5.0

Performance Quartile (within Category)

	1995	1996	1997	1998	1999	2000	2001	2002	2003	2004	2005	2006	History
NAV	—	—	—	—	10.19	13.16	16.58	13.72	21.83	25.72	23.76	25.41	
Total Return %	—	—	—	—	1.90*	33.68	25.99	-17.25	61.87	27.24	1.18	14.12	
+/-S&P 500	—	—	—	—	—	42.78	37.88	4.85	33.19	16.36	-3.73	-1.67	
+/-Russ 2000 Gr	—	—	—	—	—	56.11	35.22	13.01	13.33	12.93	-2.97	0.77	
Income Return %	—	—	—	—	—	0.00	0.00	0.00	0.00	0.00	0.00	0.00	
Capital Return %	—	—	—	—	—	33.68	25.99	-17.25	61.87	27.24	1.18	14.12	
Total Rtn % Rank Cat	—	—	—	—	—	3	2	9	10	3	86	24	
Income $	—	—	—	—	0.00	0.00	0.00	0.00	0.00	0.00	0.00	0.00	
Capital Gains $	—	—	—	—	0.00	0.43	0.00	0.00	0.36	2.01	2.30	1.71	
Expense Ratio %	—	—	—	—	1.60	1.60	1.59	1.62	1.52	1.49	1.49	—	
Income Ratio %	—	—	—	—	-1.60	-0.75	-1.15	-1.37	-1.19	-1.27	-1.23	—	
Turnover Rate %	—	—	—	—	—	433	147	133	103	109	80	—	
Net Assets $mil	—	—	—	—	3	12	24	328	476	489	703		

Performance 12-31-06

	1st Qtr	2nd Qtr	3rd Qtr	4th Qtr	Total
2002	-0.42	-3.94	-21.37	10.02	-17.25
2003	-3.94	30.20	12.35	15.19	61.87
2004	8.75	2.57	-1.81	16.17	27.24
2005	-5.05	0.94	7.38	-1.69	1.18
2006	11.99	-5.49	0.80	6.96	14.12

Trailing	Total Return%	+/- S&P 500	+/- Russ 2000 Gr	%Rank Cat	Growth of $10,000
3 Mo	6.96	0.26	-1.81	67	10,696
6 Mo	7.81	-4.93	0.95	25	10,781
1 Yr	14.12	-1.67	0.77	24	11,412
3 Yr Avg	13.68	3.24	3.17	13	14,691
5 Yr Avg	14.50	8.31	7.57	3	19,680
10 Yr Avg	—	—	—	—	—
15 Yr Avg	—	—	—	—	—

Tax Analysis	Tax-Adj Rtn%	%Rank Cat	Tax-Cost Rat	%Rank Cat
3 Yr (estimated)	12.15	13	1.35	52
5 Yr (estimated)	13.50	1	0.87	51
10 Yr (estimated)	—	—	—	—

Potential Capital Gain Exposure: 14% of assets

Rating and Risk

Time Period	Load-Adj Return %	Morningstar Rtn vs Cat	Morningstar Risk vs Cat	Morningstar Risk-Adj Rating
1 Yr	14.12			
3 Yr	13.68	+Avg	Avg	★★★★
5 Yr	14.50	High	Avg	★★★★★
10 Yr	—			
Incept	18.96			

Other Measures	Standard Index S&P 500	Best Fit Index Russ 2000 Gr
Alpha	-1.2	3.8
Beta	1.70	0.85
R-Squared	66	88
Standard Deviation	14.33	
Mean	13.68	
Sharpe Ratio	0.74	

Morningstar's Take by Kerry O'Boyle 12-11-06

The addition of a new comanager at the fine William Blair Small Cap Growth doesn't change much.

In June 2006, Colin Williams was promoted from analyst to comanager at this fund. The move fills the hole left by the departure of Michael Balkin roughly a year ago, but overall it doesn't change things a whole lot. Karl Brewer, a manager since the fund's inception, remains, and Williams has been working on the fund as a technology analyst since 2002.

That's good news for shareholders because this closed fund has returned to fine form after a relatively disappointing year--its first--in 2005. Williams noted that their bottom-up stock research had caused them to trim back their stakes in aggressive areas such as tech and industrials earlier this year. Thus, the fund endured the summer market correction better than most of its small-growth rivals, which were battered severely. It has maintained that advantage during the subsequent rally as seen in the fund's top quartile ranking for the year to date through Dec. 8, 2006.

Although a number of managers viewed the mid-year market correction as a buying opportunity, the fund mostly held back. Williams did say that they did add to their stake in top-holding Laureate Education, which they thought had been unfairly punished along with the rest of the online education industry, despite its greater exposure to the less competitive international market. And the fund initiated new positions in two firms, Silicon Laboratories and F5 Networks, that they thought had competitive technological advantages over their competitors.

All told, last year's weak showing is looking more like an aberration than a trend. We applaud the firm for once again closing the doors to new investors at a manageable asset size, even though we think fees here could be lower. This remains an excellent vehicle for shareholders wishing to maintain exposure to small-cap growth stocks.

Address:	222 W Adams St
	Chicago IL 60606
	800-635-2886
Web Address:	www.wmblair.com
Inception:	12-27-99*
Advisor:	William Blair & Co.
Subadvisor:	None
NTF Plans:	Fidelity Retail-NTF, Schwab OneSource

Minimum Purchase:	Closed	Add: —	IRA: —
Min Auto Inv Plan:	Closed	Add: —	
Sales Fees:	No-load, 0.25%S, 1.00%R		
Management Fee:	1.10%		
Actual Fees:	Mgt:1.10%	Dist:0.25%	
Expense Projections:	3Yr:$472	5Yr:$814	10Yr:$1780
Income Distrib:	Annually		

Portfolio Analysis 11-30-06

Share change since 10-06 Total Stocks:80	Sector	PE	Tot Ret%	% Assets
⊕ Laureate Education, Inc.	Consumer	27.1	-7.39	4.03
Volterra Semiconductor C	Hardware	94.9	0.00	2.47
⊖ ValueClick, Inc.	Business	46.8	30.48	2.44
⊕ Integra LifeSciences Hol	Health	43.2	20.11	2.23
⊕ DJO, Inc.	Health	50.0	55.26	2.20
Santarus, Inc.	Health	—	47.74	2.13
⊕ Healthways, Inc.	Health	50.4	5.44	2.12
J2 Global Communications	Telecom	26.6	27.52	2.09
⊕ Coinstar, Inc.	Business	38.9	33.90	2.02
⊖ Jarden Corporation	Goods	32.0	15.39	2.02
⊕ ValueVision Media, Inc.	Consumer	—	4.29	1.96
⊖ F5 Networks, Inc.	Hardware	49.5	29.76	1.96
⊕ Rackable Systems, Inc.	Hardware			1.91
⊕ Silicon Laboratories, In	Hardware	45.5	-5.48	1.83
⊕ Nuance Communications, I	Software		50.20	1.79
⊕ WebEx Communications, In	Software	36.5	61.30	1.76
⊕ PSS World Medical, Inc.	Health	27.7	31.60	1.71
⊕ Hornbeck Offshore Servic	Business	12.5	9.17	1.67
⊕ American Medical Systems	Health	69.9	3.87	1.57
⊕ WNS (Holdings) Limited A	Business			1.53

Current Investment Style

Value Blnd Growth — Large Mid Small

Market Cap	%
Giant	0.0
Large	0.0
Mid	13.8
Small	50.4
Micro	35.8
Avg $mil: 798	

Value Measures		Rel Category
Price/Earnings	25.07	1.19
Price/Book	2.29	0.84
Price/Sales	1.74	1.11
Price/Cash Flow	11.43	1.18
Dividend Yield %	0.08	0.17

Growth Measures	%	Rel Category
Long-Term Erngs	19.97	1.12
Book Value	14.81	1.41
Sales	16.65	1.40
Cash Flow	26.46	1.25
Historical Erngs	8.38	0.35

Profitability	%	Rel Category
Return on Equity	8.46	0.68
Return on Assets	1.59	0.24
Net Margin	9.29	1.07

Sector Weightings	% of Stocks	Rel S&P 500	3 Year High Low	
⊙ Info	22.64	1.13		
Software	7.81	2.26	14	8
Hardware	10.18	1.10	11	3
Media	2.45	0.65	4	1
Telecom	2.20	0.63	4	0
⊜ Service	64.57	1.40		
Health	25.80	2.14	26	12
Consumer	14.33	1.87	15	11
Business	20.66	4.88	29	16
Financial	3.78	0.17	10	4
⊔ Mfg	12.79	0.38		
Goods	4.74	0.55	8	2
Ind Mtrls	2.71	0.23	7	3
Energy	5.34	0.54	7	4
Utilities	0.00	0.00	0	0

Composition

	%
● Cash	2.3
● Stocks	94.8
● Bonds	0.0
● Other	2.9
Foreign (% of Stock)	7.3

Morningstar® Funds 500

Tables and Charts

This section breaks down the performance of the Morningstar Categories and lists the best-and worst-performing funds.

Please see Page 550 for Category Index

Performance Summary–Equity Funds

Morningstar's Open-End Fund Universe

Category	2006 Total Return % 1st Quarter	2nd Quarter	3rd Quarter	4th Quarter	2006	Annualized Total Return % 3 Year	5 Year	10 Year
Domestic Equity	**7.39**	**-2.99**	**1.26**	**6.93**	**12.70**	**10.93**	**8.21**	**9.17**
Large Value	4.87	-0.09	5.22	7.19	18.18	12.27	8.38	8.80
Large Blend	4.65	-2.07	4.33	6.74	14.15	10.05	5.92	7.79
Large Growth	3.72	-4.81	2.60	5.56	6.93	7.15	2.88	5.88
Mid-Cap Value	6.41	-1.36	2.16	8.04	15.89	14.01	11.55	10.86
Mid-Cap Blend	7.65	-2.82	1.02	7.75	13.92	12.87	10.51	10.99
Mid-Cap Growth	9.06	-5.60	-0.89	6.86	9.01	10.85	6.48	8.31
Small Value	10.74	-3.29	0.16	8.44	16.26	14.04	13.85	12.39
Small Blend	12.01	-4.43	-0.71	8.39	15.06	13.49	11.72	11.24
Small Growth	12.83	-7.06	-2.41	7.89	10.49	9.22	6.12	8.02
Long-Short	1.95	1.59	1.11	2.46	7.06	5.35	4.68	7.41
International Equity	**11.13**	**-2.40**	**3.24**	**12.92**	**26.69**	**23.14**	**18.52**	**9.77**
Europe Stock	13.01	0.37	4.54	12.62	33.55	23.31	19.16	12.85
Latin America Stock	17.27	-3.40	5.16	22.40	44.35	45.47	31.90	16.51
Diversified Emerging Mkts	12.50	-4.99	5.33	17.85	32.38	28.97	25.99	10.10
Diversified Pacific/Asia	9.32	-3.31	1.77	10.64	18.73	20.91	16.63	6.89
Pacific/Asia ex-Japan Stk	15.06	-1.02	5.65	21.16	45.81	24.28	21.93	6.98
Japan Stock	4.51	-7.59	-2.10	3.74	-1.76	13.89	11.69	2.96
Foreign Large Value	9.52	0.20	4.15	10.09	25.94	20.26	16.41	10.68
Foreign Large Blend	9.71	-0.63	3.75	10.42	24.82	18.83	13.19	7.37
Foreign Large Growth	9.89	-1.67	3.26	10.89	23.78	17.96	12.54	6.85
Foreign Sm/Mid Val	11.74	-1.87	2.31	12.66	26.45	22.88	20.90	13.51
Foreign Sm/Mid Grth	13.13	-3.11	1.57	13.64	26.73	25.44	21.07	13.86
World Stock	7.95	-1.75	3.44	8.95	19.51	15.50	10.78	8.68
Specialty Stock	**9.09**	**-2.15**	**2.31**	**8.79**	**18.69**	**16.24**	**13.70**	**10.30**
Specialty-Communications	10.34	-6.75	4.97	11.08	19.95	15.71	5.58	8.01
Specialty-Financial	5.39	-1.58	5.45	6.88	16.84	12.55	11.30	11.57
Specialty-Health	3.61	-6.83	4.95	2.84	4.15	7.70	3.46	9.79
Specialty-Natural Res	8.02	3.50	-8.99	8.00	10.14	25.22	20.74	13.00
Specialty-Precious Metals	20.81	1.32	-6.37	14.82	31.71	16.63	33.00	8.35
Specialty-Real Estate	13.76	-1.12	8.33	10.07	33.61	25.02	22.98	14.60
Specialty-Technology	7.62	-9.64	3.88	6.05	7.14	5.74	1.08	6.54
Specialty-Utilities	3.18	3.92	6.27	10.57	26.01	21.34	11.42	10.53
Balanced	**4.08**	**-1.08**	**3.33**	**5.26**	**11.76**	**8.70**	**7.41**	**7.50**
Conservative Alloc	2.00	-0.49	3.19	3.43	8.18	5.70	5.60	5.91
Moderate Allocation	3.48	-1.28	3.65	5.06	11.26	8.36	6.09	7.12
World Allocation	5.60	0.52	3.22	6.37	16.67	13.44	12.40	10.00
Target-Date 2000-2014	2.30	-0.89	3.57	3.93	8.60	6.11	5.39	6.08
Target-Date 2015-2029	4.40	-1.82	3.94	6.11	12.45	8.77	6.88	7.38
Target-Date 2030+	5.60	-2.26	3.71	7.31	14.40	10.69	7.60	7.73
Convertibles	5.15	-1.35	2.03	4.63	10.74	7.82	7.93	8.30
Total Equity Fund Average	**8.34**	**-2.26**	**2.52**	**8.96**	**18.35**	**15.62**	**12.59**	**9.29**
Total Fund Average	**5.20**	**-1.41**	**2.78**	**6.04**	**13.12**	**11.22**	**9.90**	**7.77**

Index Benchmarks

Domestic Equity

S&P 500	4.21	-1.44	5.67	6.70	15.79	10.44	6.19	8.42
Wilshire 5000	5.61	-1.91	4.31	7.32	15.97	11.54	7.65	8.67
Wilshire 4500	9.26	-3.43	0.48	9.48	16.07	14.92	12.38	9.74
Russell 2000	13.94	-5.02	0.44	8.90	18.37	13.56	11.39	9.44
S&P 400	7.63	-3.14	-1.08	6.99	10.32	13.09	10.89	13.47

International Equity

MSCI EAFE	9.40	0.70	3.93	10.35	26.34	19.93	14.98	7.71
MSCI World	6.60	-0.51	4.47	8.37	20.07	14.68	9.97	7.64
MSCI Europe	10.76	2.54	5.63	11.46	33.72	20.93	14.87	10.47
MSCI Pacific	6.70	-2.97	0.41	7.93	12.20	17.86	15.51	3.20
MSCI Latin America	14.86	-4.10	4.43	21.13	39.34	39.61	27.87	12.69
MSCI Emerging Markets	11.51	-5.11	4.10	17.28	29.18	27.26	23.52	6.73

Performance Summary–Fixed-Income Funds

Morningstar's Open-End Fund Universe

| Category | 2006 Total Return % | | | | | Annualized Total Return % | | |
	1st Quarter	2nd Quarter	3rd Quarter	4th Quarter	2006	3 Year	5 Year	10 Year
Specialty Bond	**1.56**	**-0.06**	**3.23**	**3.12**	**8.00**	**6.87**	**9.20**	**6.44**
Bank Loan	1.85	0.98	1.62	1.97	6.55	5.58	5.60	4.97
Emerg Mkts Bd	2.36	-2.51	6.14	4.88	10.96	11.56	15.40	10.53
High Yield Bond	2.60	-0.11	3.25	4.04	10.14	7.52	8.93	5.32
Multisector Bond	0.89	-0.28	3.53	2.68	6.95	6.01	8.54	6.06
World Bond	0.10	1.61	1.59	2.02	5.38	3.68	7.54	5.30
General Bond	**-0.21**	**0.11**	**3.07**	**1.32**	**4.32**	**3.24**	**4.27**	**5.17**
Ultrashort Bond	0.89	0.96	1.47	1.29	4.70	2.74	2.55	4.09
Short-Term Bond	0.34	0.51	2.03	1.10	4.01	2.34	3.15	4.59
Intermediate-Term Bond	-0.51	-0.21	3.53	1.29	4.12	3.34	4.62	5.51
Long-Term Bond	-1.57	-0.84	5.24	1.58	4.43	4.52	6.77	6.49
Government Bond	**-1.74**	**-0.41**	**3.91**	**0.21**	**1.82**	**3.13**	**4.87**	**5.51**
Short Government	0.12	0.31	2.23	0.95	3.66	2.08	2.93	4.46
Intermediate Government	-0.59	-0.28	3.29	1.03	3.43	2.80	3.89	5.16
Long Government	-4.37	-2.00	6.84	0.12	0.11	4.57	6.37	7.02
Inflation-Protected Bond	-2.10	0.32	3.26	-1.28	0.09	3.07	6.30	5.38
Municipal Bond	**0.33**	**0.05**	**2.98**	**0.94**	**4.33**	**3.53**	**4.59**	**4.73**
High Yield Muni	1.29	0.77	3.27	1.68	7.14	6.64	6.67	5.40
Muni National Long	0.30	-0.08	3.29	1.01	4.59	3.88	4.99	4.96
Muni National Interm	0.01	-0.02	2.96	0.72	3.67	2.81	4.27	4.64
Muni Single ST Long	0.38	-0.09	3.21	1.04	4.53	3.74	4.84	4.94
Muni Single ST Inter	0.02	-0.11	3.03	0.81	3.77	2.92	4.28	4.62
Muni Short	0.32	0.42	1.55	0.61	2.92	1.77	2.57	3.45
Muni NY Int/Sh	0.05	-0.08	2.94	0.71	3.64	2.76	4.37	4.72
Muni NY Long	0.41	-0.15	3.42	1.05	4.76	3.92	5.11	5.09
Muni CA Int/Sh	0.15	0.01	2.83	0.70	3.71	2.60	3.79	4.28
Muni CA Long	0.32	-0.15	3.32	1.06	4.56	4.30	5.01	5.17
Total Fixed-Income Average	**0.14**	**-0.04**	**3.21**	**1.35**	**4.69**	**4.14**	**5.59**	**5.31**
Total Fund Average	**5.20**	**-1.41**	**2.78**	**6.04**	**13.12**	**11.22**	**9.90**	**7.77**

Index Benchmarks

Government and Corporate

Lehman Brothers Aggregate	-0.65	-0.08	3.81	1.24	4.33	3.70	5.06	6.24
Lehman Brothers Government	-0.91	0.02	3.54	0.84	3.48	3.20	4.64	6.01
Lehman Brothers Mortgage	-0.07	0.01	3.63	1.60	5.22	4.17	4.85	6.16
Consumer Price Index	1.06	1.25	0.20	-0.49	2.02	2.90	2.60	2.40
US 90-Day Treasury Bill	1.15	1.24	1.30	1.29	5.06	3.27	2.50	3.76

Specialty Bond

First Boston High Yield	3.09	0.39	3.54	4.45	11.93	8.62	11.07	7.09
Salomon Brothers World Government	-0.41	3.17	1.44	1.80	6.12	2.93	8.41	5.24

Municipal Bond

Lehman Brothers Muni	0.25	0.03	3.41	1.11	4.84	4.28	5.53	5.76
Lehman Brothers CA Muni	0.36	0.00	3.49	1.22	5.13	4.92	5.61	5.88
Lehman Brothers NY Muni	0.30	0.01	3.30	1.07	4.73	4.10	5.43	5.81

Performance Summary 1992–2006: Equity Funds

Morningstar's Open-End Fund Universe

Category	1992 TR%	# of Funds	1993 TR%	# of Funds	1994 TR%	# of Funds	1995 TR%	# of Funds	1996 TR%	# of Funds	1997 TR%	# of Funds
Domestic Equity	**12.44**	**745**	**14.85**	**916**	**-0.94**	**1162**	**28.64**	**1461**	**19.76**	**1729**	**24.51**	**2207**
Large Value	10.36	142	14.19	173	-1.10	213	32.13	275	19.76	325	27.25	397
Large Blend	8.99	189	11.90	229	-0.44	285	33.35	336	21.61	390	28.05	518
Large Growth	7.81	163	11.85	201	-1.32	251	32.35	302	19.32	358	25.79	447
Mid-Cap Value	15.63	26	17.20	29	1.39	35	27.12	40	20.92	45	25.98	54
Mid-Cap Blend	15.75	39	16.05	47	-1.76	63	28.91	83	19.33	100	25.36	117
Mid-Cap Growth	9.72	78	15.08	96	-1.93	122	34.11	169	18.12	196	20.60	264
Small Value	19.42	21	16.67	28	-0.92	35	23.87	44	23.05	58	29.52	71
Small Blend	16.17	31	16.45	41	-1.58	60	27.16	79	23.77	91	27.12	119
Small Growth	10.48	51	16.28	67	-1.07	93	33.27	128	18.86	161	19.13	215
Long-Short	10.02	5	12.85	5	-0.62	5	14.12	5	12.82	5	16.27	5
International Equity	**-3.66**	**141**	**45.90**	**187**	**-2.23**	**272**	**5.18**	**418**	**13.97**	**544**	**2.96**	**692**
Europe Stock	-6.00	10	30.19	10	5.64	11	16.67	17	25.72	21	23.04	29
Latin America Stock	1.88	3	66.48	4	-15.81	6	-20.77	8	26.13	8	27.44	8
Diversified Emerging Mkts	-3.13	4	77.10	5	-7.02	12	-0.44	46	14.82	58	-0.60	84
Diversified Pacific/Asia	-5.29	4	58.46	5	-5.89	6	5.67	6	4.40	9	-16.78	9
Pacific/Asia ex-Japan Stk	7.02	2	62.39	5	-20.63	13	-0.65	28	11.92	33	-30.09	37
Japan Stock	-20.66	5	23.27	6	18.06	6	-3.06	6	-12.48	12	-14.77	13
Foreign Large Value	-2.24	15	36.72	19	2.55	24	13.39	31	15.51	51	9.18	64
Foreign Large Blend	-4.66	43	33.80	63	-1.39	81	10.87	110	12.97	140	6.92	183
Foreign Large Growth	-2.74	13	40.29	18	-2.03	24	9.58	45	13.46	61	6.70	71
Foreign Sm/Mid Val	-1.86	3	41.92	4	1.64	9	7.63	15	17.17	21	0.84	27
Foreign Sm/Mid Grth	-9.08	1	49.48	2	-0.94	3	5.67	5	21.53	5	9.02	13
World Stock	2.86	38	30.74	46	-0.91	77	17.56	98	16.51	125	14.56	154
Specialty Stock	**8.95**	**113**	**26.73**	**126**	**-0.60**	**155**	**29.83**	**200**	**20.55**	**238**	**14.90**	**297**
Specialty-Communications	15.77	5	28.38	7	-1.35	9	29.11	9	10.48	11	28.53	11
Specialty-Financial	34.71	13	16.92	15	-2.68	15	46.02	16	31.88	16	47.09	25
Specialty-Health	-2.96	14	4.30	19	4.75	21	48.57	25	13.50	27	21.96	35
Specialty-Natural Res	2.64	20	22.58	21	-1.57	24	20.78	30	32.48	37	2.31	41
Specialty-Precious Metals	-16.16	21	81.54	21	-11.12	24	4.20	25	10.59	30	-40.98	30
Specialty-Real Estate	16.22	8	20.81	8	-1.73	12	14.42	27	34.35	42	22.16	59
Specialty-Technology	12.37	16	23.73	16	18.33	19	48.07	27	19.83	31	11.21	44
Specialty-Utilities	9.02	16	15.57	19	-9.43	31	27.47	41	11.32	44	26.92	52
Hybrid	**8.67**	**149**	**14.86**	**186**	**-4.21**	**245**	**24.56**	**335**	**13.35**	**401**	**17.80**	**537**
Conservative Alloc	9.77	11	12.91	18	-4.17	24	20.71	38	10.00	52	13.66	88
Moderate Allocation	8.12	105	11.87	129	-2.06	175	26.41	228	14.70	266	19.94	349
World Allocation	8.37	9	19.74	10	-2.65	12	19.73	18	12.84	24	11.92	30
Target-Date 2000-2014	2.48	2	12.49	3	-7.19	5	22.98	11	9.65	11	14.35	14
Target-Date 2015-2029	—	—	—	—	—	—	27.25	3	13.33	3	21.04	4
Target-Date 2030+	—	—	—	—	—	—	31.60	6	16.96	6	24.86	7
Convertibles	14.61	22	17.28	26	-4.98	29	23.22	31	15.96	39	18.84	45
Total Equity Fund Average	**5.58**	**1148**	**28.21**	**1415**	**-1.77**	**1834**	**20.51**	**2414**	**16.84**	**2912**	**14.17**	**3733**
Total Fund Average	**6.46**	**2118**	**21.81**	**2637**	**-2.73**	**3422**	**18.95**	**4372**	**12.89**	**5119**	**12.15**	**6169**

Index Benchmarks

Domestic Equity

	1992	1993	1994	1995	1996	1997
S&P 500	7.62	10.08	1.32	37.58	22.96	33.36
Wilshire 5000	8.97	11.28	-0.06	36.45	21.21	31.29
Wilshire 4500	11.76	14.54	-2.65	33.39	17.25	25.69
Russell 2000	18.41	18.88	-1.82	28.45	16.49	22.36
S&P 400	11.91	13.95	-3.56	30.93	19.25	32.25

International Equity

	1992	1993	1994	1995	1996	1997
MSCI EAFE	-12.17	32.56	7.78	11.21	6.05	1.78
MSCI World	-5.23	22.50	5.08	20.72	13.48	15.76
MSCI Europe	-4.71	29.28	2.28	21.62	21.09	23.80
MSCI Pacific	-18.40	35.69	12.83	2.78	-8.58	-25.49
MSCI Latin America	11.69	50.66	-0.99	-15.03	18.87	28.34
MSCI Emerging Markets	9.03	71.66	-8.72	-6.91	3.93	-13.45

Performance Summary 1992–2006: Equity Funds
Morningstar's Open-End Fund Universe

1998 TR%	1998 # of Funds	1999 TR%	1999 # of Funds	2000 TR%	2000 # of Funds	2001 TR%	2001 # of Funds	2002 TR%	2002 # of Funds	2003 TR%	2003 # of Funds	2004 TR%	2004 # of Funds	2005 TR%	2005 # of Funds	2006 TR%	2006 # of Funds
9.93	**2766**	**24.95**	**3331**	**6.36**	**3953**	**-2.61**	**4727**	**-17.58**	**5520**	**33.78**	**6358**	**13.73**	**7052**	**6.92**	**7856**	**12.70**	**8747**
11.00	456	5.89	524	10.00	595	-3.25	682	-18.00	835	28.73	977	13.25	1111	5.87	1239	18.18	1359
21.27	642	19.64	781	-3.15	941	10.52	1078	-21.45	1238	27.90	1401	10.40	1574	6.00	1754	14.15	1989
31.08	573	38.13	659	-11.86	803	20.48	990	-26.82	1109	29.18	1284	8.16	1405	6.61	1547	6.93	1691
2.08	72	10.19	92	20.20	105	6.38	121	-12.99	186	36.14	243	18.76	268	8.25	304	15.89	377
9.45	142	24.82	176	9.21	201	0.74	249	-16.44	310	37.86	338	16.34	378	9.19	428	13.92	459
17.68	320	60.76	388	-2.00	450	17.17	586	-25.86	665	36.19	764	13.87	823	10.03	902	9.01	995
-6.31	98	6.00	137	19.06	171	15.44	187	-9.42	220	42.73	269	20.93	304	5.81	347	16.26	387
-5.03	174	15.76	229	13.51	271	8.05	326	-16.44	386	43.59	434	18.83	489	6.97	554	15.06	599
5.50	281	61.77	327	-4.16	395	-9.00	477	-28.33	532	46.15	603	11.87	648	5.91	726	10.49	793
12.54	8	6.57	18	12.79	21	3.75	31	-0.03	39	9.33	45	4.92	52	4.56	55	7.06	98
2.41	**892**	**62.17**	**1074**	**-17.65**	**1206**	**-15.64**	**1368**	**-12.91**	**1614**	**45.04**	**1817**	**20.71**	**1964**	**23.47**	**2088**	**26.69**	**2330**
12.62	39	39.50	48	-5.59	57	14.14	73	-9.64	89	40.60	96	22.38	107	15.57	111	33.55	118
-37.28	8	60.66	14	-15.52	14	-6.47	14	-20.01	18	62.24	18	38.58	18	53.89	18	44.35	18
-25.90	103	70.20	114	-29.62	124	-3.10	143	-5.75	168	55.41	188	23.83	194	31.78	207	32.38	234
-1.34	15	87.35	15	-30.85	15	17.77	15	-10.78	15	41.32	20	17.39	22	27.13	22	18.73	22
-5.21	52	73.30	60	-24.58	67	-1.48	72	-8.95	78	54.22	80	13.07	86	21.28	94	45.81	108
4.93	19	10.12	33	-33.67	33	30.41	38	-12.96	42	38.14	44	13.96	47	32.69	49	-1.76	49
10.59	82	28.62	96	-3.55	110	14.36	117	-11.85	147	39.17	162	21.95	177	13.32	182	25.94	210
13.17	236	38.38	275	-15.45	321	21.64	363	-16.86	435	33.56	485	17.39	537	14.82	583	24.82	648
14.07	89	55.90	112	-20.18	122	23.03	143	-18.43	174	34.98	194	15.97	206	15.13	222	23.78	246
12.03	34	56.63	36	-11.91	45	16.19	50	-6.35	58	51.44	66	23.83	73	18.83	76	26.45	79
16.87	29	84.02	40	-13.64	46	23.22	61	-14.51	64	53.78	73	24.72	82	25.35	83	26.73	103
14.39	186	41.37	231	-7.25	252	15.90	279	-18.88	326	35.64	391	15.47	415	11.80	441	19.51	495
11.63	**401**	**30.75**	**488**	**9.38**	**598**	**-9.85**	**822**	**-9.41**	**935**	**39.78**	**1043**	**15.64**	**1129**	**15.56**	**1246**	**18.69**	**1335**
43.13	12	56.82	16	-30.00	17	29.23	40	-39.61	41	45.56	41	20.84	41	7.56	44	19.95	44
5.98	47	-2.31	58	27.59	76	-1.74	96	-9.23	115	32.88	118	14.05	122	7.05	135	16.84	137
20.73	50	18.79	58	56.96	84	-10.88	131	-27.05	158	31.78	183	9.87	188	9.46	202	4.15	212
-24.98	59	31.23	66	30.31	69	10.44	72	-3.04	83	32.72	93	27.45	104	38.58	130	10.14	151
-10.16	31	6.78	37	-16.51	37	19.22	40	63.74	46	57.34	55	-8.21	59	30.84	62	31.71	62
-15.77	80	-2.80	110	26.99	127	9.93	144	4.51	159	36.87	193	32.13	241	11.57	272	33.61	300
54.75	64	19.90	83	-31.23	126	34.58	232	-41.89	259	56.95	277	4.77	288	5.79	302	7.14	317
19.32	58	17.55	60	10.93	62	21.05	67	-22.70	74	24.15	83	24.19	86	13.62	99	26.01	112
13.09	**632**	**14.77**	**735**	**0.94**	**806**	**-4.76**	**884**	**-7.98**	**1004**	**20.55**	**1213**	**9.43**	**1561**	**5.30**	**1876**	**11.76**	**2356**
9.16	108	5.40	124	4.04	134	-0.24	158	-3.66	177	13.10	249	5.79	339	3.07	418	8.18	540
13.87	411	10.78	487	2.21	532	-4.36	575	-12.05	626	20.67	725	8.97	840	4.95	934	11.26	1039
8.20	33	17.31	34	6.40	37	-3.79	43	-1.80	47	24.21	66	14.63	78	8.71	78	16.67	106
13.50	16	9.09	19	2.70	23	-0.54	23	-4.11	37	13.67	43	6.82	88	3.68	124	8.60	186
19.99	5	15.53	6	-3.95	8	-6.96	8	-11.14	15	20.73	18	9.17	52	5.79	100	12.45	172
23.54	9	19.47	11	-7.86	15	12.14	16	-15.68	36	25.33	42	11.31	87	7.27	143	14.40	231
3.40	50	25.82	54	3.02	57	-5.32	61	-7.41	66	26.11	70	9.29	77	3.61	79	10.74	82
8.46	**4691**	**36.35**	**5628**	**-1.80**	**6563**	**-8.81**	**7801**	**-12.48**	**9073**	**36.23**	**10431**	**15.59**	**11706**	**13.85**	**13066**	**18.35**	**14768**
7.06	**7467**	**22.40**	**8685**	**2.23**	**9894**	**-3.42**	**11434**	**-4.60**	**13035**	**25.24**	**14855**	**11.50**	**16487**	**9.64**	**18158**	**13.12**	**20145**
28.58		21.04		-9.10		11.89		-22.10		28.68		10.88		4.91		15.79	
23.43		23.56		-10.89		10.97		-20.86		31.64		12.62		6.24		15.97	
8.63		35.49		-15.77		-9.30		-17.81		43.72		18.57		10.27		16.07	
-2.55		21.26		-3.02		2.49		-20.48		47.25		18.33		4.55		18.37	
19.12		14.72		17.51		-0.61		-14.53		35.62		16.48		12.56		10.32	
19.93		27.03		-14.19		21.42		-15.94		38.59		20.25		13.54		26.34	
24.32		24.95		-13.19		16.80		-19.89		33.11		14.72		9.49		20.07	
28.50		15.93		-8.40		-19.90		-18.38		38.54		20.88		9.42		33.72	
2.41		57.63		-25.78		-25.39		-9.29		38.48		18.98		22.64		12.20	
-38.06		55.48		-18.38		-4.24		-24.79		67.06		34.77		44.92		39.34	
-27.67		64.09		-31.90		-4.68		-7.97		51.59		22.45		30.31		29.18	

Category	1992 TR%	1992 # of Funds	1993 TR%	1993 # of Funds	1994 TR%	1994 # of Funds	1995 TR%	1995 # of Funds	1996 TR%	1996 # of Funds	1997 TR%	1997 # of Funds
Specialty Bond	**9.53**	**128**	**14.00**	**149**	**-3.78**	**182**	**16.79**	**235**	**17.28**	**294**	**9.35**	**355**
Bank Loan	6.21	4	5.70	4	6.60	4	7.84	4	6.75	5	7.21	5
Emerg Mkts Bd	—	—	—	—	12.30	2	21.69	11	44.44	15	13.01	23
High Yield Bond	17.26	70	18.75	76	-3.14	89	17.35	107	13.46	131	13.31	152
Multisector Bond	10.21	25	16.13	31	-5.06	39	17.76	58	11.35	73	9.20	82
World Bond	4.43	29	15.41	38	-5.00	48	19.31	55	10.41	70	4.03	93
General Bond	**6.72**	**201**	**9.68**	**285**	**-2.59**	**368**	**16.28**	**454**	**4.12**	**500**	**8.88**	**569**
Ultrashort Bond	4.54	13	3.82	20	1.97	25	7.75	32	6.11	34	6.20	38
Short-Term Bond	5.75	46	6.76	79	-1.04	98	11.63	120	4.52	131	6.57	153
Intermediate-Term Bond	7.42	139	10.89	181	-4.22	238	18.09	291	3.44	322	9.06	364
Long-Term Bond	9.18	3	17.24	5	-7.08	7	27.66	11	2.42	13	13.67	14
Government Bond	**5.80**	**139**	**11.95**	**174**	**-3.90**	**225**	**19.10**	**268**	**2.42**	**298**	**10.00**	**322**
Short Government	5.89	34	6.29	51	-1.06	70	12.00	84	3.80	99	6.81	106
Intermediate Government	6.44	93	8.42	110	-4.04	140	17.02	168	2.84	183	8.81	199
Long Government	7.36	9	18.01	9	-6.37	11	30.63	12	-1.84	12	16.53	13
Inflation-Protected Bond	3.51	3	15.09	4	-4.14	4	16.76	4	4.86	4	7.83	4
Municipal Bond	**8.47**	**502**	**11.30**	**614**	**-5.14**	**813**	**15.27**	**1001**	**3.76**	**1115**	**8.23**	**1190**
High Yield Muni	8.36	26	11.96	29	-4.70	42	16.25	47	4.34	54	9.75	60
Muni National Long	9.01	102	12.53	107	-6.55	137	17.34	164	3.47	183	9.21	196
Muni National Interm	8.25	38	10.83	54	-3.46	83	14.13	99	3.71	113	7.65	124
Muni Single ST Long	8.66	112	12.46	134	-6.78	186	17.04	237	3.54	258	9.07	259
Muni Single ST Inter	8.52	80	11.76	115	-5.43	156	15.80	186	3.57	211	8.13	233
Muni Short	6.64	19	6.64	28	-0.38	35	7.94	47	3.82	53	5.15	56
Muni NY Int/Sh	9.26	14	11.00	19	-4.81	23	14.59	28	3.56	32	8.27	37
Muni NY Long	9.60	44	12.70	47	-7.33	53	16.92	71	3.39	78	9.08	80
Muni CA Int/Sh	7.68	10	10.55	19	-4.59	23	14.03	29	4.24	30	6.76	35
Muni CA Long	8.74	57	12.60	62	-7.36	75	18.65	93	3.94	103	9.21	110
Total Fixed-Income Average	**7.86**	**970**	**11.62**	**1222**	**-4.19**	**1588**	**16.44**	**1958**	**6.53**	**2207**	**8.89**	**2436**
Total Fund Average	**6.46**	**2118**	**21.81**	**2637**	**-2.73**	**3422**	**18.95**	**4372**	**12.89**	**5119**	**12.15**	**6169**

Index Benchmarks

Government and Corporate

	1992	1993	1994	1995	1996	1997
Lehman Brothers Aggregate	7.40	9.75	-2.92	18.47	3.63	9.65
Lehman Brothers Government	7.23	10.66	-3.38	18.34	2.77	9.59
Lehman Brothers Mortgage	6.96	6.84	-1.61	16.80	5.35	9.49
Consumer Price Index	2.97	2.81	2.60	2.53	3.38	1.70
US 90-Day Treasury Bill	3.59	3.12	4.45	5.79	5.26	5.31

Specialty Bond

	1992	1993	1994	1995	1996	1997
First Boston High Yield	16.66	18.91	-0.97	17.39	12.42	12.63
Salomon Brothers World Government	5.53	13.27	2.34	19.04	3.62	0.23

Municipal Bond

	1992	1993	1994	1995	1996	1997
Lehman Brothers Muni	8.82	12.28	-5.17	17.46	4.43	9.19
Lehman Brothers CA Muni	—	—	-6.38	19.30	4.43	9.43
Lehman Brothers NY Muni	—	—	-5.02	17.24	4.74	9.84

Performance Summary 1992–2006: Fixed-Income Funds

Morningstar's Open-End Fund Universe

1998 TR%	# of Funds	1999 TR%	# of Funds	2000 TR%	# of Funds	2001 TR%	# of Funds	2002 TR%	# of Funds	2003 TR%	# of Funds	2004 TR%	# of Funds	2005 TR%	# of Funds	2006 TR%	# of Funds
-0.85	**446**	**7.94**	**551**	**2.90**	**610**	**4.64**	**675**	**6.59**	**743**	**19.58**	**810**	**9.03**	**878**	**3.52**	**952**	**8.00**	**1049**
6.49	5	5.96	8	5.58	19	1.82	35	0.77	49	10.56	50	5.08	55	4.56	70	6.55	84
-20.69	31	27.58	43	11.47	43	13.17	44	12.59	48	30.26	51	12.15	54	11.44	56	10.96	63
0.04	208	4.86	284	-6.83	316	2.48	357	-1.24	386	24.63	430	10.05	472	2.55	508	10.14	543
0.70	94	3.50	103	0.92	112	3.92	112	7.02	119	18.35	125	8.93	137	2.14	149	6.95	167
9.22	108	-2.20	113	3.37	120	1.83	127	13.81	141	14.10	154	8.96	160	-3.07	169	5.38	192
6.43	**653**	**-0.02**	**742**	**8.40**	**853**	**7.68**	**979**	**6.75**	**1121**	**4.83**	**1306**	**3.46**	**1469**	**2.05**	**1615**	**4.32**	**1694**
5.02	48	4.44	49	6.75	54	5.82	71	2.82	82	1.58	96	1.34	113	2.51	133	4.70	137
6.18	165	2.07	177	7.88	204	7.33	229	5.68	250	2.78	313	1.67	371	1.44	416	4.01	438
7.26	426	-1.32	493	9.64	570	7.76	654	8.20	759	5.37	865	4.09	951	1.80	1025	4.12	1074
7.26	14	-5.25	23	9.34	25	9.80	25	10.29	30	9.59	32	6.72	34	2.43	41	4.43	45
8.52	**370**	**-2.25**	**398**	**13.55**	**425**	**5.88**	**458**	**11.92**	**487**	**3.09**	**566**	**4.93**	**615**	**2.91**	**665**	**1.82**	**722**
6.64	119	1.17	127	8.42	132	7.27	140	6.95	145	1.45	158	1.36	167	1.23	169	3.66	175
7.59	223	-1.46	238	11.09	259	6.98	282	9.26	300	1.84	338	3.09	353	1.89	358	3.43	376
14.15	18	-10.92	21	22.12	22	1.89	22	16.29	25	1.79	27	7.72	28	6.41	30	0.11	34
5.69	10	2.20	12	12.57	12	7.37	14	15.19	17	7.29	43	7.53	67	2.12	108	0.09	137
5.52	**1307**	**-3.17**	**1366**	**9.79**	**1443**	**4.30**	**1521**	**7.81**	**1611**	**4.43**	**1742**	**3.46**	**1819**	**2.86**	**1860**	**4.33**	**1912**
5.43	62	-4.50	70	5.75	80	5.06	92	6.12	94	7.03	99	6.55	102	6.37	107	7.14	108
5.44	217	-4.64	231	11.12	244	4.01	255	8.46	266	4.97	275	3.87	284	3.16	289	4.59	297
5.61	130	-2.33	139	9.47	152	4.38	162	8.67	193	4.21	220	2.87	241	1.86	244	3.67	260
5.47	286	-4.71	296	11.34	308	4.31	320	8.27	325	4.77	325	3.80	325	2.91	326	4.53	330
5.49	257	-2.95	261	9.80	270	4.40	281	8.37	294	4.20	316	2.92	325	2.06	329	3.77	338
4.54	63	0.65	69	5.81	72	4.81	79	5.08	85	2.39	100	1.17	120	1.20	132	2.92	133
5.75	42	-2.78	45	10.30	48	4.13	49	8.83	56	4.15	67	2.68	72	1.95	72	3.64	76
5.81	88	-4.68	88	12.08	92	3.70	95	8.84	101	5.01	113	3.71	114	3.29	114	4.76	114
5.58	41	-0.92	43	9.19	49	4.47	53	7.52	58	3.27	75	2.55	79	1.91	85	3.71	92
6.04	121	-4.85	124	13.05	128	3.76	135	7.92	139	4.31	152	4.43	157	3.93	162	4.56	164
4.81	**2776**	**-0.05**	**3057**	**8.71**	**3331**	**5.24**	**3633**	**8.07**	**3962**	**7.56**	**4424**	**4.92**	**4781**	**2.87**	**5092**	**4.69**	**5377**
7.06	**7467**	**22.40**	**8685**	**2.23**	**9894**	**-3.42**	**11434**	**-4.60**	**13035**	**25.24**	**14855**	**11.50**	**16487**	**9.64**	**18158**	**13.12**	**20145**

1998	1999	2000	2001	2002	2003	2004	2005	2006
8.69	-0.82	11.63	8.44	10.25	4.10	4.34	2.43	4.33
9.85	-2.23	13.24	7.23	11.50	2.36	3.48	2.65	3.48
6.96	1.86	11.16	8.22	8.75	3.07	4.70	2.61	5.22
1.61	2.68	3.44	1.60	2.42	1.87	3.30	3.40	2.02
5.01	4.87	6.32	3.67	1.68	1.05	1.43	3.34	5.06
0.58	3.28	-5.21	5.78	3.11	27.93	11.96	2.26	11.93
15.30	-4.27	1.59	-0.99	19.49	14.91	10.35	-6.88	6.12
6.48	-2.06	11.68	5.13	9.60	5.31	4.48	3.51	4.84
6.93	-2.79	12.68	5.20	8.45	4.86	5.50	4.14	5.13
6.88	-2.03	12.01	4.84	9.67	5.30	4.28	3.31	4.73

Domestic-Equity Funds
Morningstar Funds 500 Universe

Leaders

Page	Cat	Fund Name	Total Return%*	Morningstar Rating	Style	Sales Charge%
		One Year (12/29/2006)				
299	SR	Morgan Stan Ins US R/E A	38.85	★★★★★		None
395	SR	T. Rowe Price Real Est	36.75	★★★★		None
259	SR	JPMorgan U.S. Real Est A	36.21	★★★		5.25
487	SR	Vanguard REIT Index	35.07	★★★		None
192	SR	Fidelity Real Estate Inv	32.84	★★★		None
418	SR	Third Avenue RealEst Val	30.16	★★★		None
386	SC	T. Rowe Price Med & Tele	28.55	★★★★★		None
139	SU	Eaton Vance Utilities A	28.51	★★★★★		5.75
144	MG	FBR Small Cap	28.49	★★★★★		None
86	SB	Aston/TAMRO Small Cap N	27.84	★★★★		None
		Three Year (12/29/2006)				
451	SN	Vanguard Energy	33.23	★★★★★		None
194	SN	Fidelity Sel Energy Serv	31.22	★★		None
299	SR	Morgan Stan Ins US R/E A	30.90	★★★★★		None
259	SR	JPMorgan U.S. Real Est A	29.22	★★★		5.25
395	SR	T. Rowe Price Real Est	28.93	★★★★		None
192	SR	Fidelity Real Estate Inv	26.97	★★★		None
91	MG	Baron Partners	25.54	★★★★		None
391	SN	T. Rowe Price New Era	25.50	★★★★		None
487	SR	Vanguard REIT Index	25.49	★★★		None
139	SU	Eaton Vance Utilities A	24.57	★★★★★		5.75
		Five Year (12/29/2006)				
180	MB	Fidelity Leverage Co Stk	27.08	★★★★★		None
451	SN	Vanguard Energy	25.75	★★★★★		None
299	SR	Morgan Stan Ins US R/E A	25.33	★★★★★		None
395	SR	T. Rowe Price Real Est	24.95	★★★★		None
358	SV	Schneider Small Cap Val	24.31	★★★★★		Clsd
259	SR	JPMorgan U.S. Real Est A	23.74	★★★		5.25
192	SR	Fidelity Real Estate Inv	23.70	★★★		None
357	MB	RS Value A	23.11	★★★		4.75
487	SR	Vanguard REIT Index	22.70	★★★		None
418	SR	Third Avenue RealEst Val	22.26	★★★		None
		Ten Year (12/29/2006)				
518	SG	Wasatch Micro Cap	23.59	★★★★★		Clsd
144	MG	FBR Small Cap	17.87	★★★★★		None
109	MG	Calamos Growth A	17.77	★★★★		4.75
295	MB	Meridian Value	17.50	★★★★		None
386	SC	T. Rowe Price Med & Tele	17.44	★★★★★		None
349	SV	Royce Opportunity Inv	17.34	★★★★		None
299	SR	Morgan Stan Ins US R/E A	17.06	★★★★★		None
321	LB	Oakmark Select I	17.05	★★★★		None
451	SN	Vanguard Energy	16.53	★★★★★		None
461	SH	Vanguard Health Care	16.36	★★★★★		Clsd

Laggards

Page	Cat	Fund Name	Total Return%*	Morningstar Rating	Style	Sales Charge%
		One Year (12/29/2006)				
426	LG	Touchstn Snds Cp Sel Gr Z	−6.50	★★★		None
409	LG	TCW Select Equities I	−5.12	★★		None
331	SN	PIMCO CommRealRetStrD	−3.46	★		None
51	LG	AmCent Ultra Inv	−3.28	★★★		None
246	SH	Janus Global Life Sci	−1.95	★★★		None
48	LG	AmCent Select Inv	−1.79	★★		None
140	SH	Eaton Vance Wld Health A	−0.01	★★★		5.75
193	ST	Fidelity Sel Electronics	0.30	★★		None
115	LG	Chase Growth	1.41	★★★★★		None
109	MG	Calamos Growth A	1.45	★★★★		4.75
		Three Year (12/29/2006)				
193	ST	Fidelity Sel Electronics	1.54	★★		None
48	LG	AmCent Select Inv	2.07	★★		None
314	ST	Northern Technology	2.27	★★★		None
354	SG	RS Diversified Growth A	2.57	★★		4.75
51	LG	AmCent Ultra Inv	3.02	★★★		None
521	SG	Wasatch Ultra Growth	3.30	★★★		Clsd
409	LG	TCW Select Equities I	3.58	★★		None
397	ST	T. Rowe Price SciTech	3.69	★★★		None
196	ST	Fidelity Sel Technology	4.24	★★★		None
140	SH	Eaton Vance Wld Health A	4.78	★★★		5.75
		Five Year (12/29/2006)				
193	ST	Fidelity Sel Electronics	−2.30	★★		None
508	LG	Vanguard U.S. Gr	−0.40	★		None
314	ST	Northern Technology	−0.33	★★★		None
397	ST	T. Rowe Price SciTech	0.04	★★★		None
48	LG	AmCent Select Inv	0.48	★★		None
103	SG	Brown Cap Small Co Instl	0.54	★★		Clsd
354	SG	RS Diversified Growth A	0.74	★★		4.75
51	LG	AmCent Ultra Inv	1.12	★★★		None
230	LG	GAMCO Growth AAA	1.32	★★★		None
85	LG	Aston/Montag Growth N	1.39	★★★★		None
		Ten Year (12/29/2006)				
397	ST	T. Rowe Price SciTech	1.22	★★★		None
508	LG	Vanguard U.S. Gr	1.42	★		None
222	MB	FPA Paramount	3.28	★★		2.00
389	LG	T. Rowe Price New Amer	4.31	★★★		None
433	LG	USAA Aggressive Growth	4.50	★★★		None
48	LG	AmCent Select Inv	5.31	★★		None
51	LG	AmCent Ultra Inv	5.42	★★★		None
151	LG	Fidelity Blue Chip Grth	5.61	★★★		None
311	LB	Nicholas	6.02	★★★		None
460	LG	Vanguard Growth Equity	6.03	★★★		None

*Three-, five-, and 10-year returns are annualized.

International-Equity Funds

Morningstar Funds 500 Universe

Leaders

One Year (12/29/2006)

Page	Cat	Fund Name	Total Return%*	Morningstar Rating	Style	Sales Charge%
385	LS	T. Rowe Price Latin Amer	51.24	★★★★		None
252	FG	Janus Overseas	47.21	★★★★★		None
390	PJ	T. Rowe Price New Asia	36.12	★★★★		None
320	FA	Oakmark Intl Small Cap I	34.90	★★★★		Clsd
79	FA	Artisan Intl Val	34.46	★★★★		None
119	FR	Columbia Acorn Intl A	34.16	★★		5.75
484	SP	Vanguard Prec Mtls Mining	34.06	★★★★★		Clsd
366	EM	SSgA Emerging Markets	33.46	★★★★		None
69	EM	Amer Funds New World A	33.42	★★		5.75
80	FR	Artisan Intl Sm Cap	33.18	★★★★		Clsd

Three Year (12/29/2006)

Page	Cat	Fund Name	Total Return%*	Morningstar Rating	Style	Sales Charge%
385	LS	T. Rowe Price Latin Amer	49.61	★★★★		None
322	EM	Oppenheimer Develop MktA	32.98	★★★★		5.75
372	EM	T. Rowe Price Emg Mkt St	32.50	★★★★		None
252	FG	Janus Overseas	32.21	★★★★★		None
366	EM	SSgA Emerging Markets	31.70	★★★★		None
450	EM	Vanguard Em Mkt Idx	29.06	★★★		None
320	FA	Oakmark Intl Small Cap I	28.25	★★★★		Clsd
80	FR	Artisan Intl Sm Cap	28.15	★★★★		Clsd
119	FR	Columbia Acorn Intl A	28.06	★★		5.75
484	SP	Vanguard Prec Mtls Mining	27.73	★★★★★		Clsd

Five Year (12/29/2006)

Page	Cat	Fund Name	Total Return%*	Morningstar Rating	Style	Sales Charge%
484	SP	Vanguard Prec Mtls Mining	34.68	★★★★★		Clsd
385	LS	T. Rowe Price Latin Amer	34.07	★★★★		None
41	SP	AmCent Global Gold Inv	30.77	★★		None
322	EM	Oppenheimer Develop MktA	30.76	★★★★		5.75
80	FR	Artisan Intl Sm Cap	27.61	★★★★		Clsd
372	EM	T. Rowe Price Emg Mkt St	27.49	★★★★		None
366	EM	SSgA Emerging Markets	27.28	★★★★		None
413	EM	Templeton Devel Mkts A	26.29	★★★		5.75
450	EM	Vanguard Em Mkt Idx	25.69	★★★		None
320	FA	Oakmark Intl Small Cap I	24.99	★★★★		Clsd

Ten Year (12/29/2006)

Page	Cat	Fund Name	Total Return%*	Morningstar Rating	Style	Sales Charge%
322	EM	Oppenheimer Develop MktA	19.07	★★★★		5.75
385	LS	T. Rowe Price Latin Amer	17.94	★★★★		None
261	FB	Julius Baer Intl Eqty A	16.99	★★★★★		Clsd
45	FR	AmCent Intl Disc Inv	16.61	★★★		Clsd
383	FR	T. Rowe Price Intl Disc	16.33	★★★		None
303	ES	Mutual European A	16.09	★★★★		5.75
468	FR	Vanguard Intl Explorer	15.83	★★★★		Clsd
216	FA	First Eagle Overseas A	15.82	★★★★		Clsd
320	FA	Oakmark Intl Small Cap I	15.50	★★★★		Clsd
324	WS	Oppenheimer Glob Oppor A	15.45	★★★		5.75

Laggards

One Year (12/29/2006)

Page	Cat	Fund Name	Total Return%*	Morningstar Rating	Style	Sales Charge%
324	WS	Oppenheimer Glob Oppor A	11.00	★★★		5.75
247	WS	Janus Global Opps	11.19	★★★		None
177	FR	Fidelity Intl Sm Cp	14.22	★★★		Clsd
94	IH	BlackRock Global Alloc A	15.94	★★★★		5.25
87	WS	Atlas Global Growth A	16.02	★★★★		None
190	DP	Fidelity Pacific Basin	16.16	★★★★		None
269	FV	Longleaf Partners Intl	17.07	★		None
417	FA	Third Avenue Intl Value	17.13	★★★		Clsd
323	WS	Oppenheimer Glob A	17.38	★★★★		5.75
213	WS	Fidelity Worldwide	17.42	★★★		None

Three Year (12/29/2006)

Page	Cat	Fund Name	Total Return%*	Morningstar Rating	Style	Sales Charge%
257	WS	Janus Worldwide	9.61	★★		None
247	WS	Janus Global Opps	10.10	★★★		None
269	FV	Longleaf Partners Intl	13.35	★		None
94	IH	BlackRock Global Alloc A	13.49	★★★★		5.25
213	WS	Fidelity Worldwide	14.39	★★★		None
59	IH	Amer Funds CplncBldr A	14.56	★★★		5.75
41	SP	AmCent Global Gold Inv	14.64	★★		None
68	WS	Amer Funds New Persp A	15.08	★★★		5.75
415	WS	Templeton Growth A	15.51	★★★★		5.75
87	WS	Atlas Global Growth A	15.59	★★★★		None

Five Year (12/29/2006)

Page	Cat	Fund Name	Total Return%*	Morningstar Rating	Style	Sales Charge%
257	WS	Janus Worldwide	3.89	★★		None
247	WS	Janus Global Opps	9.21	★★★		None
46	FG	AmCent Intl Growth Inv	10.59	★★★		None
87	WS	Atlas Global Growth A	10.83	★★★★		None
213	WS	Fidelity Worldwide	10.96	★★★		None
384	FG	T. Rowe Price Intl Stk	11.15	★★		None
269	FV	Longleaf Partners Intl	11.47	★		None
42	WS	AmCent Global Gr Inv	11.50	★★★		None
68	WS	Amer Funds New Persp A	11.84	★★★		5.75
323	WS	Oppenheimer Glob A	11.96	★★★★		5.75

Ten Year (12/29/2006)

Page	Cat	Fund Name	Total Return%*	Morningstar Rating	Style	Sales Charge%
384	FG	T. Rowe Price Intl Stk	5.82	★★		None
257	WS	Janus Worldwide	6.82	★★		None
41	SP	AmCent Global Gold Inv	6.85	★★		None
390	PJ	T. Rowe Price New Asia	7.05	★★★★		None
506	FB	Vanguard Total Intl Stk	7.78	★★★★		None
469	FB	Vanguard Intl Gr	8.03	★★★		None
189	FB	Fidelity Overseas	8.25	★★★		None
213	WS	Fidelity Worldwide	8.59	★★★		None
413	EM	Templeton Devel Mkts A	8.70	★★★		5.75
414	FV	Templeton Foreign A	8.88	★		5.75

*Three-, five-, and 10-year returns are annualized.

Fixed-Income Funds
Morningstar Funds 500 Universe

Leaders

Page	Cat	Fund Name	Total Return%*	Morningstar Rating	Style	Sales Charge%
One Year (12/29/2006)						
152	HY	Fidelity Capital & Inc	13.04	★★★★★	—	None
58	HY	Amer Funds Amer H/I A	12.19	★★★★	▦	3.75
313	HY	Northeast Investors	12.10	★★★	—	None
187	EB	Fidelity New Markets Inc	11.89	★★★	—	None
138	HY	Eaton Vance Inc Boston A	11.29	★★★★	▦	4.75
249	HY	Janus High-Yield	11.10	★★★★	▦	None
271	MU	Loomis Sayles Bond Ret	10.99	★★★★★	▦	None
171	HY	Fidelity High Income	10.74	★★★★	—	None
340	HY	Pioneer High Yield A	10.60	★★	▦	4.50
381	HY	T. Rowe Price Hi-Yld	9.75	★★★★	▦	Clsd
Three Year (12/29/2006)						
187	EB	Fidelity New Markets Inc	11.83	★★★	—	None
332	EB	PIMCO Emerg Mkts Bd D	10.80	★★★	▦	None
152	HY	Fidelity Capital & Inc	10.16	★★★★★	—	None
313	HY	Northeast Investors	9.44	★★★	—	None
271	MU	Loomis Sayles Bond Ret	8.62	★★★★★	▦	None
138	HY	Eaton Vance Inc Boston A	8.48	★★★★	▦	4.75
58	HY	Amer Funds Amer H/I A	8.47	★★★★	▦	3.75
171	HY	Fidelity High Income	7.91	★★★★	—	None
381	HY	T. Rowe Price Hi-Yld	7.79	★★★★	▦	Clsd
249	HY	Janus High-Yield	7.70	★★★★	▦	None
Five Year (12/29/2006)						
187	EB	Fidelity New Markets Inc	15.61	★★★	—	None
332	EB	PIMCO Emerg Mkts Bd D	15.09	★★★	▦	None
271	MU	Loomis Sayles Bond Ret	13.32	★★★★★	▦	None
152	HY	Fidelity Capital & Inc	13.12	★★★★★	—	None
138	HY	Eaton Vance Inc Boston A	10.47	★★★★	▦	4.75
272	IB	Loomis Sayles GlbBd Ret	10.40	★★★★	▦	None
171	HY	Fidelity High Income	10.21	★★★★	—	None
60	IB	Amer Funds CapWrldBd A	10.01	★★★	▦	3.75
382	IB	T. Rowe Price Intl Bd	9.74	★★★	▦	None
58	HY	Amer Funds Amer H/I A	9.66	★★★★	▦	3.75
Ten Year (12/29/2006)						
271	MU	Loomis Sayles Bond Ret	9.31	★★★★★	▦	None
479	GL	Vanguard Long-Tm US Try	7.41	★★★	▦	None
138	HY	Eaton Vance Inc Boston A	7.37	★★★★	▦	4.75
381	HY	T. Rowe Price Hi-Yld	7.30	★★★★	▦	Clsd
478	CL	Vanguard Long-Tm InvGrde	7.30	★★★★	▦	None
58	HY	Amer Funds Amer H/I A	7.28	★★★★	▦	3.75
401	MU	T. Rowe Price Spect Inc	7.06	★★★	▦	None
249	HY	Janus High-Yield	6.97	★★★★	▦	None
410	CI	TCW Total Return Bond I	6.88	★★★★★	▦	None
526	CI	Western Asset Cr Bd Inst	6.83	★★★★★	▦	None

Laggards

Page	Cat	Fund Name	Total Return%*	Morningstar Rating	Style	Sales Charge%
One Year (12/29/2006)						
405	GL	T. Rowe Price US Try L/T	1.07	★★★	▦	None
479	GL	Vanguard Long-Tm US Try	1.74	★★★	▦	None
329	CI	Payden Core Bond	2.21	★★★	▦	None
333	IB	PIMCO For Bd USD-Hdgd D	2.48	★★★	▦	None
478	CL	Vanguard Long-Tm InvGrde	2.86	★★★★	▦	None
197	MS	Fidelity Sh-Int Muni Inc	2.96	★★★	▦	None
348	CI	Robeco WPG Core Bond	3.12	★★★★	▦	None
467	GI	Vanguard Int-Tm US Trs	3.14	★★★★★	▦	None
403	MS	T. Rowe Price T/F Sh-Int	3.26	★★★★	▦	None
493	MS	Vanguard Sht-Tm TE	3.26	★★	▦	None
Three Year (12/29/2006)						
197	MS	Fidelity Sh-Int Muni Inc	1.94	★★★	▦	None
403	MS	T. Rowe Price T/F Sh-Int	1.94	★★★★	▦	None
480	MS	Vanguard LtdTm T/E	1.98	★★★★	▦	None
493	MS	Vanguard Sht-Tm TE	2.01	★★	▦	None
491	GS	Vanguard Short-Tm Trs	2.18	★★★★	▦	None
336	CS	PIMCO Low Duration D	2.23	★★★	▦	None
437	MS	USAA Tax Ex Short-Term	2.27	★★★★	▦	None
489	CS	Vanguard Sh-Tm Bd Idx	2.36	★★★★	▦	None
490	GS	Vanguard ShtTm Fed	2.48	★★★★	▦	None
176	GI	Fidelity Interm Govt	2.49	★★★	▦	None
Five Year (12/29/2006)						
493	MS	Vanguard Sht-Tm TE	2.23	★★	▦	None
330	UB	Payden Limited Maturity	2.34	★★★	▦	None
367	UB	SSgA Yield Plus	2.42	★★	▦	None
403	MS	T. Rowe Price T/F Sh-Int	2.94	★★★★	▦	None
437	MS	USAA Tax Ex Short-Term	2.95	★★★★	▦	None
480	MS	Vanguard LtdTm T/E	3.00	★★★★	▦	None
197	MS	Fidelity Sh-Int Muni Inc	3.05	★★★	▦	None
489	CS	Vanguard Sh-Tm Bd Idx	3.30	★★★★	▦	None
336	CS	PIMCO Low Duration D	3.30	★★★	▦	None
360	UB	Schwab YieldPlus Inv	3.30	★★★★★	▦	None
Ten Year (12/29/2006)						
493	MS	Vanguard Sht-Tm TE	3.17	★★	▦	None
403	MS	T. Rowe Price T/F Sh-Int	3.84	★★★★	▦	None
437	MS	USAA Tax Ex Short-Term	3.84	★★★★	▦	None
480	MS	Vanguard LtdTm T/E	3.85	★★★★	▦	None
197	MS	Fidelity Sh-Int Muni Inc	3.88	★★★	▦	None
367	UB	SSgA Yield Plus	3.91	★★	▦	None
330	UB	Payden Limited Maturity	4.08	★★★	▦	None
532	MS	WF Adv S/T Muni Bd Inv	4.24	★★★★★	▦	None
382	IB	T. Rowe Price Intl Bd	4.33	★★★	▦	None
472	MI	Vanguard IntTm T/E	4.85	★★★★	▦	None

*Three-, five-, and 10-year returns are annualized.

Category Averages

Category	P/E Ratio	P/B Ratio	P/CF Ratio	Average Mkt Cap $Mil	Top Three Sectors % of Stock			Cash %	Turnover %	Yield %	Expense %	Potential Cap Gains Exp%	Alpha	Beta	R²
Domestic Equity	**18.8**	**2.9**	**18.8**	**23463**	19	14	12	3.7	85	0.4	1.43	3	3.1	0.95	77
Large Value	15.2	2.4	15.2	43514	29	13	11	3.6	62	1.0	1.34	16	2.2	0.93	81
Large Blend	16.9	2.8	16.9	38200	22	13	13	3.9	69	0.9	1.30	10	−0.5	1.03	87
Large Growth	21.3	3.8	21.3	32382	17	14	13	3.1	98	0.2	1.45	−22	−4.6	1.26	78
Mid-Cap Value	15.9	2.1	15.9	6935	24	16	10	4.9	73	0.7	1.41	11	2.1	1.19	74
Mid-Cap Blend	17.6	2.5	17.6	5553	19	15	11	4.7	104	0.4	1.43	13	0.4	1.30	73
Mid-Cap Growth	22.9	3.7	22.9	5584	16	13	12	3.2	109	0.1	1.56	−20	−2.8	1.53	71
Small Value	16.5	1.9	16.5	1108	24	20	10	4.4	65	0.3	1.55	17	0.8	1.41	66
Small Blend	18.1	2.3	18.1	1262	19	18	12	4.0	81	0.2	1.46	14	−0.7	1.57	69
Small Growth	23.3	3.2	23.3	1184	17	15	12	3.4	114	0.0	1.67	−11	−6.0	1.81	68
International Equity	**16.7**	**3.1**	**16.7**	**21147**	22	20	13	3.8	75	0.9	1.67	5	3.1	0.90	70
Europe Stock	15.4	3.3	15.4	26981	28	17	13	5.3	106	1.3	1.75	17	1.7	1.08	77
Latin Amer Stock	15.4	4.0	15.4	19333	27	17	15	5.9	54	0.7	1.84	38	8.1	1.88	62
Div Emerging Mkts	14.8	2.8	14.8	9901	19	17	14	3.6	76	0.7	1.90	25	−0.4	1.57	75
Div Pac/Asia	18.7	2.5	18.7	8468	26	23	17	2.1	70	0.3	1.72	−27	−1.7	1.19	72
Pac/Asia ex-Japan	15.7	2.9	15.7	8866	25	12	12	3.2	87	0.7	2.01	26	0.5	1.25	56
Japan Stock	18.1	2.3	18.1	7832	28	20	19	10.3	136	0.7	1.66	−12	−5.3	1.06	36
Foreign Large Value	14.4	2.4	14.4	27060	28	16	14	4.4	42	1.3	1.42	20	1.0	0.95	90
Foreign Large Blend	16.0	3.0	16.0	27701	29	15	15	3.5	71	1.2	1.57	13	−1.3	1.03	93
Foreign Large Growth	18.6	3.8	18.6	23231	24	18	16	2.1	86	0.7	1.71	3	−3.0	1.10	90
Foreign Sm/Mid Val	16.3	2.7	16.3	2929	27	17	14	4.1	124	1.8	1.68	7	1.2	1.09	81
Foreign Sm/Mid Grth	19.6	3.7	19.6	2962	27	18	13	2.3	78	0.4	1.77	17	1.0	1.26	80
World Stock	17.6	3.1	17.6	25640	20	14	14	4.1	66	0.7	1.66	2	−2.5	0.92	79
Specialty Stock	**23.9**	**3.2**	**23.9**	**14054**	24	16	13	11.2	158	1.4	1.71	−40	4.2	0.68	59
Communications	21.4	2.8	21.4	14698	61	23	7	4.3	238	0.5	1.62	−88	0.3	1.78	61
Financial	15.3	2.1	15.3	23571	96	1	1	4.4	178	0.8	1.67	13	2.1	1.00	56
Health	24.4	4.2	24.4	19482	97	1	1	4.1	130	0.1	1.77	−22	−1.4	0.87	33
Natural Resources	13.4	2.9	13.4	14529	72	23	2	11.4	196	0.9	1.50	12	14.2	1.02	16
Precious Metals	25.9	4.7	25.9	4120	98	2	—	5.9	86	2.0	1.56	26	−16.8	2.18	44
Real Estate	32.4	2.8	32.4	5869	95	3	1	3.4	85	2.5	1.54	27	12.0	1.21	29
Technology	27.4	3.8	27.4	13246	48	21	12	3.6	188	0.0	1.85	−193	−10.8	2.10	67
Utilities	17.9	2.4	17.9	15631	66	22	10	3.7	88	2.3	1.41	13	12.4	0.59	26
Balanced Fund	**17.9**	**2.8**	**17.9**	**28401**	25	12	11	10.0	66	—	1.50	—	2.8	0.46	71
Conservative Alloc	16.9	2.8	16.9	31287	26	13	11	15.5	57	2.7	1.47	5	−1.2	0.50	74
Convertible	19.2	3.0	19.2	23719	26	13	12	5.7	61	2.3	1.42	5	−2.9	1.06	80
Moderate Allocation	17.0	2.8	17.0	31125	23	13	12	8.5	69	2.0	1.42	5	−1.0	0.83	83
World Allocation	16.0	2.7	16.0	26492	26	12	11	18.1	60	2.0	1.35	12	2.5	1.00	78

Category	Duration	Maturity	Average Credit Quality	Avg Wtd Coupon	Avg Wtd Price	Cash %	Turnover %	Yield %	Expense %	Potential Cap Gains Exp%	Alpha	Beta	R²
Specialty Bond	**4.1**	**6.8**	**BB**	**7.52**	**108.71**	**8.3**	**87**	**5.8**	**1.24**	**−33**	**6.0**	**0.48**	**21**
Bank Loan	0.3	5.1	BB	4.10	102.24	6.6	60	6.3	1.35	−6	2.2	−0.02	1
High Yield Bond	4.0	6.5	B	7.85	108.56	6.6	80	6.8	1.24	−49	3.9	0.40	13
Multisector Bond	4.6	7.7	A	6.35	109.29	14.4	112	4.9	1.26	−17	2.3	0.78	51
World Bond	5.1	7.5	AA	4.78	155.23	26.7	180	2.9	1.25	−5	0.2	0.79	34
Emerg Mkts Bd	6.2	11.8	BB	7.63	106.26	10.2	129	5.4	1.46	−3	7.3	1.53	50
General Bond	**3.6**	**6.7**	**AA**	**4.90**	**153.61**	**14.2**	**157**	**4.7**	**1.01**	**−6**	**0.9**	**0.47**	**47**
Long-Term Bond	7.8	16.2	A	6.14	104.05	9.0	144	4.8	0.94	−4	0.6	1.50	89
Interm-Term Bond	4.6	7.9	AA	5.22	103.27	11.3	200	4.3	1.03	−3	−0.3	0.91	94
Short-Term Bond	2.1	3.3	AA	4.55	313.31	19.8	99	3.9	0.98	−7	−1.1	0.41	82
Ultrashort Bond	0.7	2.3	AA	3.42	98.90	26.4	65	4.3	0.77	−8	−0.6	0.10	44
Government Bond	**4.5**	**7.4**	**AAA**	**4.44**	**101.66**	**11.9**	**210**	**3.8**	**1.04**	**−6**	**−1.2**	**1.27**	**85**
Long Govt	11.1	15.8	AAA	4.27	94.79	5.0	467	3.9	1.06	−4	0.5	2.50	89
Interm Govt	4.2	7.1	AAA	5.01	100.08	10.3	222	4.2	1.09	−6	−0.8	0.83	95
Short Govt	2.4	3.1	AAA	4.63	99.70	18.3	155	3.9	0.96	−8	−1.4	0.48	86
Municipal Bond	**5.3**	**11.2**	**AA**	**5.23**	**105.64**	**2.3**	**29**	**3.6**	**1.02**	**3**	**−0.8**	**0.91**	**92**
High Yield Muni	6.3	15.1	BBB	5.81	104.49	1.6	35	4.5	1.08	0	2.5	0.72	81
Muni National Long	6.0	12.8	AA	5.33	106.63	1.3	36	3.8	1.06	3	−0.4	0.98	93
Muni National Interm	5.0	7.4	AA	5.25	106.66	2.4	45	3.5	0.92	2	−1.3	0.90	95
Muni NY Long	6.4	13.8	AA	5.32	106.53	0.6	29	3.9	1.04	4	−1.4	1.01	92
Muni NY Int/Sh	5.0	8.3	AA	5.16	106.78	2.8	26	3.3	1.03	3	−1.4	0.91	94
Muni CA Long	6.1	14.7	AA	5.07	103.70	1.2	23	3.9	1.05	5	−0.0	1.05	94
Muni CA Int/Sh	4.5	6.3	AA	4.94	105.36	5.2	31	3.3	0.88	3	−1.5	0.83	93
Muni Single ST Long	5.5	13.8	AA	5.20	105.37	0.8	18	3.8	1.08	4	−0.5	0.94	93
Muni Single ST In/Sh	5.2	9.4	AA	5.15	105.75	1.7	27	3.6	1.00	3	−1.2	0.91	94
Muni Short	1.9	3.4	AA	4.70	102.71	12.9	50	3.0	0.84	−3	−1.8	0.34	70
Inflation-Protected Bond	6.6	9.9	AAA	2.67	110.01	10.0	187	3.3	0.98	−8	−0.7	1.34	75

Lowest Expense Ratio

Morningstar Funds 500 Universe

Domestic Equity

Page	Cat		Expense Ratio %
		Actively Managed Funds	
461	SH	Vanguard Health Care	0.25
511	CA	Vanguard Wellesley Inc	0.25
451	SN	Vanguard Energy	0.28
512	MA	Vanguard Wellington	0.29
452	LV	Vanguard Equity-Inc	0.31
459	LB	Vanguard Gr & Inc	0.34
498	MB	Vanguard Strategic Eq	0.35
514	LV	Vanguard Windsor II	0.35
513	LV	Vanguard Windsor	0.36
449	LV	Vanguard Dividend Growth	0.37
481	MG	Vanguard Mid Cap Growth	0.39
509	LV	Vanguard U.S. Value	0.39
483	LG	Vanguard Morgan Gr	0.41
442	MA	Vanguard Asset Alloc	0.41
454	SG	Vanguard Explorer	0.46
485	LB	Vanguard PRIMECAP	0.46
445	MG	Vanguard Cap Opp	0.49
488	MV	Vanguard Selected Value	0.49
131	LV	Dodge & Cox Stock	0.52
128	MA	Dodge & Cox Balanced	0.53
		Index Funds	
203	LB	Fidelity Spar 500 Inv	0.10
205	LB	Fidelity Spar Tot Mkt Inv	0.10
501	CA	Vanguard Tax-Mgd Bal	0.12
507	LB	Vanguard Tx-Mgd Gr	0.14
500	LB	Vanguard Tx-Mgd App	0.14
503	SB	Vanguard Tax-Mgd SmCap R	0.14
99	LB	Bridgeway Blue-Chip 35	0.15
441	LB	Vanguard 500 Index	0.18
504	LB	Vanguard Tot Stk	0.19
443	MA	Vanguard Bal Idx	0.20
510	LV	Vanguard Val Idx	0.21
487	SR	Vanguard REIT Index	0.21
458	LG	Vanguard Gr Idx	0.22
482	MB	Vanguard Mid Cap Idx	0.22
495	SB	Vanguard SmCp Idx	0.23
496	SV	Vanguard SmCp Vl Idx	0.23
494	SG	Vanguard SmCp Gr Idx	0.23
455	MB	Vanguard ExtMktIdx	0.25
444	LG	Vanguard FTSE Soc Idx Inv	0.25
126	SB	DFA U.S. Micro Cap	0.55
		Average Expense Ratio	**0.95**

International Equity

Page	Cat		Expense Ratio %
		Actively Managed Funds	
484	SP	Vanguard Prec Mtls Mining	0.40
468	FR	Vanguard Intl Explorer	0.48
470	FB	Vanguard Intl Value	0.50
469	FB	Vanguard Intl Gr	0.55
59	IH	Amer Funds CpIncBldr A	0.57
41	SP	AmCent Global Gold Inv	0.67
73	FV	American Beacon IntEq Ins	0.70
130	FV	Dodge & Cox Intl Stock	0.70
68	WS	Amer Funds New Persp A	0.71
456	WS	Vanguard Global Equity	0.72
61	WS	Amer Funds CapWrldGI A	0.73
62	FB	Amer Funds EuroPac A	0.76
275	FV	MainStay ICAP Intl I	0.80
257	WS	Janus Worldwide	0.85
189	FB	Fidelity Overseas	0.86
236	FV	Harbor Intl Instl	0.87
384	FG	T. Rowe Price Intl Stk	0.89
252	FG	Janus Overseas	0.89
178	FB	Fidelity Intl Disc	1.01
213	WS	Fidelity Worldwide	1.01
		Index Funds	
204	FB	Fidelity Spar Intl Inv	0.10
502	FB	Vanguard Tax-Mgd Intl	0.20
453	ES	Vanguard Eur Stk Idx	0.27
450	EM	Vanguard Em Mkt Idx	0.42
		Average Expense Ratio	**1.08**

Lowest Expense Ratio

Morningstar Funds 500 Universe

Taxable Bond

Page	Cat		Expense Ratio %
		Actively Managed Funds	
490	GS	Vanguard ShtTm Fed	0.20
471	CI	Vanguard IntTm Inv-Gr Fd	0.21
457	GI	Vanguard GNMA	0.21
492	CS	Vanguard Sht-Tm Inv-Grade	0.21
478	CL	Vanguard Long-Tm InvGrde	0.25
462	HY	Vanguard Hi-Yld Corp	0.25
467	GI	Vanguard Int-Tm US Trs	0.26
491	GS	Vanguard Short-Tm Trs	0.26
479	GL	Vanguard Long-Tm US Try	0.26
330	UB	Payden Limited Maturity	0.40
348	CI	Robeco WPG Core Bond	0.43
129	CI	Dodge & Cox Income	0.44
168	GI	Fidelity Government Inc	0.44
198	CS	Fidelity Sh-Term Bond	0.44
174	CI	Fidelity Interm Bond	0.44
410	CI	TCW Total Return Bond I	0.44
179	CI	Fidelity Invt Grade Bond	0.45
167	GI	Fidelity Ginnie Mae	0.45
185	CI	Fidelity Mtg Sec	0.45
176	GI	Fidelity Interm Govt	0.45
		Index Funds	
466	CI	Vanguard Intm Bd Idx	0.18
489	CS	Vanguard Sh-Tm Bd Idx	0.18
505	CI	Vanguard Total Bd Idx	0.20
210	CI	Fidelity U.S. Bond Index	0.32
		Average Expense Ratio	**0.60**

Municipal Bond*

Page	Cat		Expense Ratio %
		Actively Managed Funds	
465	ML	Vanguard Ins L/T TE Inv	0.15
463	MI	Vanguard Hi-Yld T/E	0.15
477	ML	Vanguard Lg-Tm T/E	0.15
480	MS	Vanguard LtdTm T/E	0.16
472	MI	Vanguard IntTm T/E	0.16
493	MS	Vanguard Sht-Tm TE	0.16
208	ML	Fidelity Tax-Free Bond	0.17
175	MI	Fidelity Interm Muni Inc	0.36
197	MS	Fidelity Sh-Int Muni Inc	0.42
186	ML	Fidelity Municipal Income	0.45
50	MI	AmCent Tax-Free Bond Inv	0.49
403	MS	T. Rowe Price T/F Sh-Int	0.51
402	ML	T. Rowe Price T/F Inc	0.53
436	ML	USAA Tax Ex Long-Term	0.55
435	MI	USAA Tax Ex Interm-Term	0.55
71	MI	Amer Funds T/E Bd A	0.56
437	MS	USAA Tax Ex Short-Term	0.56
224	ML	Franklin Fed T/F Inc A	0.61
532	MS	WF Adv S/T Muni Bd Inv	0.66
		Index Funds	
		None	
		Average Expense Ratio	**0.39**

* There are only 19 municipal-bond funds in the Morningstar Funds 500 universe, none of which are index funds.

Lowest Turnover Rate
Morningstar Funds 500 Universe

Domestic Equity

Page	Cat		Turnover Rate %
		Actively Managed Funds	
225	LB	Franklin Growth A	2
529	MA	Westwood Balanced AAA	2
528	MB	Westport Select Cap R	2
279	LB	Mairs & Power Growth	3
144	MG	FBR Small Cap	3
474	LB	Vanguard LifeSt Growth	4
361	LB	Selected American S	4
264	LG	Legg Mason P Aggr Grow A	4
123	SF	Davis Financial A	5
486	LG	Vanguard PRIMECAP Core	5
475	CA	Vanguard LifeSt Income	6
228	MB	Gabelli Asset AAA	6
229	SV	Gabelli Sm Cp Growth AAA	6
300	LV	Muhlenkamp	6
124	LB	Davis NY Venture A	6
497	MA	Vanguard STAR	6
133	LB	Dreyfus Appreciation	7
223	MV	Franklin Bal Sh Invmt A	7
473	CA	Vanguard LifeSt Cons Gr	7
268	LB	Longleaf Partners	7
		Index Funds	
205	LB	Fidelity Spar Tot Mkt Inv	6
126	SB	DFA U.S. Micro Cap	7
203	LB	Fidelity Spar 500 Inv	7
441	LB	Vanguard 500 Index	7
500	LB	Vanguard Tx-Mgd App	8
507	LB	Vanguard Tx-Mgd Gr	10
504	LB	Vanguard Tot Stk	12
487	SR	Vanguard REIT Index	17
495	SB	Vanguard SmCp Idx	18
482	MB	Vanguard Mid Cap Idx	18
503	SB	Vanguard Tax-Mgd SmCap R	20
510	LV	Vanguard Val Idx	21
458	LG	Vanguard Gr Idx	23
102	SB	Bridgeway UI-Sm Co Mkt	26
455	MB	Vanguard ExtMktIdx	27
496	SV	Vanguard SmCp VI Idx	28
443	MA	Vanguard Bal Idx	31
494	SG	Vanguard SmCp Gr Idx	39
99	LB	Bridgeway Blue-Chip 35	41
444	LG	Vanguard FTSE Soc Idx Inv	51
		Average Turnover Rate %	**55.81**

International Equity

Page	Cat		Turnover Rate %
		Actively Managed Funds	
292	PJ	Matthews Pacific Tiger	3
41	SP	AmCent Global Gold Inv	5
430	FA	Tweedy, Browne Glob Val	6
130	FV	Dodge & Cox Intl Stock	7
341	WS	Polaris Global Value	10
236	FV	Harbor Intl Instl	12
319	FV	Oakmark International I	14
269	FV	Longleaf Partners Intl	17
484	SP	Vanguard Prec Mtls Mining	20
431	FB	UMB Scout International	23
323	WS	Oppenheimer Glob A	23
61	WS	Amer Funds CapWrldGI A	26
59	IH	Amer Funds CpIncBldr A	26
414	FV	Templeton Foreign A	26
302	WS	Mutual Discovery A	26
325	FG	Oppenheimer Intl Grth A	26
119	FR	Columbia Acorn Intl A	27
216	FA	First Eagle Overseas A	28
87	WS	Atlas Global Growth A	28
215	IH	First Eagle Glbl A	29
		Index Funds	
204	FB	Fidelity Spar Intl Inv	2
506	FB	Vanguard Total Intl Stk	3
502	FB	Vanguard Tax-Mgd Intl	5
453	ES	Vanguard Eur Stk Idx	6
448	FB	Vanguard Dev Mkts Idx	10
450	EM	Vanguard Em Mkt Idx	26
		Average Turnover Rate %	**50.43**

Best Five-Year Tax-Adjusted Returns

Morningstar Funds 500 Universe

Domestic Equity

Page	Cat		5-Year Tax-Adjusted Return %
		Highest	
180	MB	Fidelity Leverage Co Stk	26.2
451	SN	Vanguard Energy	24.6
395	SR	T. Rowe Price Real Est	23.1
299	SR	Morgan Stan Ins US R/E A	22.8
357	MB	RS Value A	21.7
192	SR	Fidelity Real Estate Inv	21.6
102	SB	Bridgeway Ul-Sm Co Mkt	21.0
418	SR	Third Avenue RealEst Val	21.0
144	MG	FBR Small Cap	20.6
487	SR	Vanguard REIT Index	20.4
358	SV	Schneider Small Cap Val	20.3
259	SR	JPMorgan U.S. Real Est A	19.7
194	SN	Fidelity Sel Energy Serv	19.1
391	SN	T. Rowe Price New Era	18.9
386	SC	T. Rowe Price Med & Tele	16.5
91	MG	Baron Partners	16.1
82	MV	Artisan Mid Cap Value	16.1
283	LG	Marsico 21st Century	15.8
113	LB	CGM Focus	15.7
399	SB	T. Rowe Price Sm Val	15.6
		Average 5-Year Tax Adjusted Return	**8.6**

Taxable Bond

Page	Cat		5-Year Tax-Adjusted Return %
		Highest	
187	EB	Fidelity New Markets Inc	12.4
332	EB	PIMCO Emerg Mkts Bd D	11.3
271	MU	Loomis Sayles Bond Ret	10.8
152	HY	Fidelity Capital & Inc	10.4
272	IB	Loomis Sayles GlbBd Ret	9.0
382	IB	T. Rowe Price Intl Bd	7.8
60	IB	Amer Funds CapWrldBd A	7.7
206	MU	Fidelity Strategic Inc	7.3
171	HY	Fidelity High Income	7.3
381	HY	T. Rowe Price Hi-Yld	6.5
401	MU	T. Rowe Price Spect Inc	6.2
313	HY	Northeast Investors	6.1
138	HY	Eaton Vance Inc Boston A	6.1
335	HY	PIMCO High-Yield D	5.9
58	HY	Amer Funds Amer H/I A	5.8
340	HY	Pioneer High Yield A	5.6
249	HY	Janus High-Yield	5.6
478	CL	Vanguard Long-Tm InvGrde	5.1
462	HY	Vanguard Hi-Yld Corp	4.7
129	CI	Dodge & Cox Income	4.2
		Average 5-Year Tax Adjusted Return	**4.9**

International Equity

Page	Cat		5-Year Tax-Adjusted Return %
		Highest	
385	LS	T. Rowe Price Latin Amer	33.6
484	SP	Vanguard Prec Mtls Mining	32.7
41	SP	AmCent Global Gold Inv	30.5
322	EM	Oppenheimer Develop MktA	27.8
372	EM	T. Rowe Price Emg Mkt St	26.8
366	EM	SSgA Emerging Markets	25.9
80	FR	Artisan Intl Sm Cap	25.0
450	EM	Vanguard Em Mkt Idx	25.0
413	EM	Templeton Devel Mkts A	24.0
292	PJ	Matthews Pacific Tiger	23.2
320	FA	Oakmark Intl Small Cap I	22.9
383	FR	T. Rowe Price Intl Disc	22.2
390	PJ	T. Rowe Price New Asia	22.1
468	FR	Vanguard Intl Explorer	21.7
341	WS	Polaris Global Value	20.7
130	FV	Dodge & Cox Intl Stock	20.4
417	FA	Third Avenue Intl Value	20.3
216	FA	First Eagle Overseas A	19.8
69	EM	Amer Funds New World A	19.5
308	FR	Neuberger Ber Intl Inv	19.4
		Average 5-Year Tax Adjusted Return	**16.5**

Municipal Bond

Page	Cat		5-Year Tax-Adjusted Return %
		Highest	
436	ML	USAA Tax Ex Long-Term	6.1
208	ML	Fidelity Tax-Free Bond	6.0
463	MI	Vanguard Hi-Yld T/E	5.7
186	ML	Fidelity Municipal Income	5.7
477	ML	Vanguard Lg-Tm T/E	5.5
465	ML	Vanguard Ins L/T TE Inv	5.5
402	ML	T. Rowe Price T/F Inc	5.5
435	MI	USAA Tax Ex Interm-Term	4.9
175	MI	Fidelity Interm Muni Inc	4.8
224	ML	Franklin Fed T/F Inc A	4.6
472	MI	Vanguard IntTm T/E	4.4
50	MI	AmCent Tax-Free Bond Inv	4.4
71	MI	Amer Funds T/E Bd A	4.4
532	MS	WF Adv S/T Muni Bd Inv	3.7
480	MS	Vanguard LtdTm T/E	3.0
197	MS	Fidelity Sh-Int Muni Inc	3.0
437	MS	USAA Tax Ex Short-Term	3.0
403	MS	T. Rowe Price T/F Sh-Int	2.9
493	MS	Vanguard Sht-Tm TE	2.2
		Average 5-Year Tax Adjusted Return	**4.5**

Fund Name Changes

Morningstar Funds 500 Universe

Previous Name	Current Name	Date of Change
Allianz RCM Global Technology Instl	Allianz RCM Technology Instl	03/2006
ABN AMRO/Montag & Caldwell Growth N	Aston/Montag & Caldwell Growth N	12/2006
ABN AMRO/TAMRO Small Cap N	Aston/TAMRO Small Cap N	12/2006
Merrill Lynch Global Allocation A	BlackRock Global Allocation A	09/2006
Scudder Fixed Income Instl	DWS Core Fixed Income Inst	02/2006
Delphi Value Retail	E*TRADE Delphi Value Retail	11/2006
Fidelity Asset Manager	Fidelity Asset Manager 50%	09/2006
Fidelity Asset Manager: Growth	Fidelity Asset Manager 70%	09/2006
Fidelity Asset Manager: Aggressive	Fidelity Asset Manager 85%	09/2006
Gabelli Growth AAA	GAMCO Growth AAA	01/2006
Janus Core Equity	Janus Fundamental Equity	06/2006
Janus Mercury	Janus Research	12/2006
Smith Barney Aggressive Growth A	Legg Mason Partners Aggressive Growth A	04/2006
ICAP Equity	MainStay ICAP Equity I	08/2006
ICAP International	MainStay ICAP International I	08/2006
ICAP Select Equity	MainStay ICAP Select Equity I	08/2006
RS Diversified Growth	RS Diversified Growth A	10/2006
RS Emerging Growth	RS Emerging Growth A	10/2006
RS MidCap Opportunities	RS MidCap Opportunities A	10/2006
RS Value	RS Value A	10/2006
Royce Value Inv	Royce Value Service	05/2006
TCW Galileo Dividend Focused I	TCW Dividend Focused I	02/2006
TCW Galileo Opportunity I	TCW Opportunity I	02/2006
TCW Galileo Select Equities I	TCW Select Equities I	02/2006
TCW Galileo Total Return Bond I	TCW Total Return Bond I	02/2006
TCW Galileo Value Added I	TCW Value Added I	02/2006
TCW Galileo Value Opportunities I	TCW Value Opportunities I	02/2006
Constellation Clover Small Cap Value	Touchstone Diversified Small Cap Value Z	11/2006
Constellation Sands Cap Select Growth I	Touchstone Sands Capital Select Growth Z	11/2006
UMB Scout WorldWide	UMB Scout International	10/2006

Category Index

Fund Categories

BL	Bank Loan Bond	**IB**	World Bond	**MY**	Muni New York Long
CA	Conservative Allocation	**IH**	World Allocation	**PJ**	Pacific ex-Japan Stock
CI	Intermediate-Term Bond	**IP**	Inflation Protected Bond	**SB**	Small-Cap Blend
CL	Long-Term Bond	**JS**	Japan Stock	**SC**	Speciality-Communications
CS	Short-Term Bond	**LB**	Large-Cap Blend	**SF**	Speciality-Financials
CV	Convertible Bond	**LG**	Large-Cap Growth	**SG**	Small-Cap Growth
DP	Diversified Pacific Stock	**IO**	Long-Short	**SH**	Specialty-Health
EB	Emerging Markets Bond	**LS**	Latin America Stock	**SI**	Muni Single-State Interm
EM	Diversified Emerging Markets	**LV**	Large-Cap Value	**SL**	Muni Single-State Long
ES	Europe Stock	**MA**	Moderate Allocation	**SP**	Specialty-Precious Metals
FA	Foreign Small/Mid Value	**MB**	Mid-Cap Blend	**SN**	Specialty-Natural Resources
FB	Foreign Large Blend	**MC**	Muni California Long	**SR**	Specialty-Real Estate
FG	Foreign Large Growth	**MF**	Muni California Int/Sh	**ST**	Specialty-Technology
FR	Foreign Small/Mid Growth	**MG**	Mid-Cap Growth	**SU**	Specialty-Utilities
FV	Foreign Large Value	**MI**	Muni National, Intermediate-Term	**SV**	Small-Cap Value
GI	Intermediate-Term Government Bond	**ML**	Muni National, Long-Term	**TA**	Target-Date 2000-2014
GL	Long-Term Government Bond	**MN**	Muni New York Int/Sh	**TB**	Target-Date 2015-2029
GS	Short-Term Government Bond	**MS**	Muni National, Short-Term	**TC**	Target-Date 2030+
HM	High-Yield Muni	**MU**	Multisector Bond	**UB**	Ultrashort Bond
HY	High-Yield Bond	**MV**	Mid-Cap Value	**WS**	World Stock

Summary Pages

This section offers the essential risk and return data for all 500 funds in a table format, allowing you to make quick comparisons across funds.

Domestic-Equity Funds

Page		Cat	Style Box	NAV	1Yr	Annualized 3Yr	5Yr	10Yr	Yield %	Performance	Risk	Morningstar Rating	Expense Ratio %	Sales Charge %
	Total Return % through 12-29-06									**Morningstar Rating Statistics** through 12-29-06				
	S&P 500				**4.91**	**14.38**	**0.54**	**9.07**						
35	Aegis Value	SV		14.41	17.79	11.55	13.82	—	0.7	Avg	Low	★★★	1.42	None
36	Allianz RCM Tech Ins	ST		41.51	4.98	10.47	6.33	15.13	0.0	High	Avg	★★★★	1.24	None
37	AmCent Capital Val Inv	LV		8.35	19.71	12.35	9.43	—	1.5	+Avg	Avg	★★★★	1.10	None
38	AmCent Equity Growth Inv	LB		25.64	14.14	11.76	7.70	8.79	0.9	+Avg	+Avg	★★★★	0.67	None
39	AmCent Equity Income Inv	LV		8.58	19.45	11.26	10.21	12.30	2.1	+Avg	Low	★★★★	0.98	None
43	AmCent Growth Inv	LG		22.20	7.94	7.54	2.71	6.56	0.1	Avg	Avg	★★★	1.00	None
44	AmCent Inc & Growth Inv	LV		33.30	17.17	11.53	7.71	9.18	1.7	Avg	+Avg	★★★	0.67	None
47	AmCent Large Co Val Inv	LV		7.58	19.81	12.56	9.74	—	1.7	+Avg	Avg	★★★★	0.84	None
48	AmCent Select Inv	LG		36.73	−1.79	2.07	0.48	5.31	0.4	-Avg	-Avg	★★	1.00	None
49	AmCent Small Cap Val Inv	SV		9.74	15.52	15.11	12.97	—	0.5	Avg	-Avg	★★★	1.25	Clsd
51	AmCent Ultra Inv	LG		27.11	−3.28	3.02	1.12	5.42	0.0	-Avg	Avg	★★★	0.99	None
52	AmCent Value Inv	LV		7.59	18.51	12.49	9.91	10.88	1.5	+Avg	-Avg	★★★★	0.99	None
53	AmCent Veedot Inv	MG		6.43	10.10	7.54	6.65	—	0.0	Avg	Avg	★★★	1.50	None
54	AmCent Vista Inv	MG		17.11	9.05	11.20	9.21	6.69	0.0	Avg	Avg	★★★	1.00	None
55	Amer Funds Amcap A	LG		20.02	8.63	8.47	6.12	11.00	0.8	+Avg	Low	★★★★	0.65	5.75
56	Amer Funds Amer Bal A	MA		19.02	11.81	7.89	7.65	9.69	2.4	Avg	-Avg	★★★	0.59	5.75
57	Amer Funds Amer Mut A	LV		29.21	16.24	10.54	7.91	9.45	1.9	-Avg	Low	★★★	0.56	5.75
63	Amer Funds Fundamen A	LB		40.05	19.24	14.90	10.60	11.14	1.4	+Avg	Avg	★★★★★	0.60	5.75
64	Amer Funds Grth Fund A	LG		32.87	10.94	12.37	8.01	12.94	0.8	High	Avg	★★★★★	0.63	5.75
65	Amer Funds Inc Fund A	MA		20.36	**20.29**	11.99	10.97	10.12	4.3	+Avg	-Avg	★★★★	0.53	5.75
66	Amer Funds Inv Co Am A	LV		33.51	15.94	10.80	8.00	10.47	2.1	Avg	Low	★★★	0.55	5.75
67	Amer Funds New Econ A	LG		26.70	14.73	13.11	8.23	9.56	0.7	High	+Avg	★★★★	0.79	5.75
72	Amer Funds WashingtonA	LV		34.86	18.04	10.34	7.56	9.88	1.8	-Avg	-Avg	★★	0.57	5.75
74	American Beacon SmCVl Pln	SV		21.38	15.36	14.46	16.12	—	0.6	+Avg	+Avg	★★★★	1.10	Clsd
75	Ameristock	LV		43.79	17.95	6.52	4.25	10.48	3.7	-Avg	-Avg	★★	0.79	None
76	Ariel	MB		51.81	10.35	10.75	10.52	13.11	0.0	Avg	-Avg	★★★★	1.07	None
77	Ariel Appreciation	MB		48.33	10.94	8.90	8.68	12.76	0.0	-Avg	Avg	★★★	1.16	None
81	Artisan Mid Cap Inv	MG		30.46	9.65	11.11	6.52	—	0.0	Avg	Avg	★★★	1.18	Clsd
82	Artisan Mid Cap Value	MV		20.18	14.20	**18.50**	**16.96**	—	0.3	High	Avg	★★★★★	1.20	Clsd
83	Artisan Small Cap	SG		18.20	6.92	11.77	7.41	7.18	0.0	Avg	Avg	★★★	1.15	Clsd
84	Artisan Small Cap Value	SV		18.08	19.11	17.02	16.57	—	0.0	+Avg	-Avg	★★★★	1.17	Clsd
85	Aston/Montag Growth N	LG		25.49	8.07	5.83	1.39	6.24	0.2	Avg	Low	★★★★	1.03	None
86	Aston/TAMRO Small Cap N	SB		19.55	**27.84**	13.57	15.36	—	0.0	+Avg	+Avg	★★★★	1.30	None
88	Baron Asset	MG		59.80	14.64	17.90	10.80	9.35	0.0	+Avg	-Avg	★★★★	1.33	None
89	Baron FifthAveGr	LG		13.11	10.17	—	—	—	0.0	—	—		1.39	None
90	Baron Growth	SG		49.88	15.50	**15.62**	12.30	13.81	0.0	High	Low	★★★★★	1.31	None
91	Baron Partners	MG		22.34	21.55	**25.54**	16.82	15.33	0.0	High	High	★★★★	1.35	None
92	Baron Small Cap	SG		22.83	11.83	13.96	13.17	—	0.0	High	Low	★★★★★	1.33	None
93	Bjurman, Barry MicroCp Gr	SG		20.87	4.52	6.19	10.51	—	0.0	Avg	+Avg	★★★	1.52	Clsd
95	Bogle Small Cap Gr Inv	SB		24.48	15.29	14.41	14.39	—	0.0	+Avg	+Avg	★★★★	1.35	Clsd
96	Brandywine	MG		34.29	11.09	12.85	8.14	7.96	0.0	+Avg	-Avg	★★★★	1.08	None
97	Brandywine Blue	LG		31.70	10.89	12.76	9.92	8.84	0.0	High	Avg	★★★★★	1.12	None
98	Bridgeway Balanced	CA		12.54	6.65	7.08	6.89	—	2.2	+Avg	+Avg	★★★★	0.94	None
99	Bridgeway Blue-Chip 35	LB		8.06	15.42	6.56	5.04	—	1.4	-Avg	+Avg	★★	0.15	None
100	Bridgeway Small-Cap Gr	SG		14.27	5.31	11.59	—	—	0.0	+Avg	+Avg	★★★	0.81	None
101	Bridgeway Sm-Cap Val N	SV		16.16	12.77	16.31	—	—	0.0	+Avg	High	★★★	0.77	None
102	Bridgeway Ul-Sm Co Mkt	SB		19.54	11.48	11.70	**21.27**	—	0.4	+Avg	+Avg	★★★★	0.65	None
103	Brown Cap Small Co Instl	SG		32.60	15.67	6.72	0.54	10.24	0.0	-Avg	Avg	★★	1.19	Clsd
104	Buffalo MicroCp	SG		13.03	12.54	—	—	—	0.0	—	—		1.51	None
105	Buffalo Mid Cap	MG		15.01	5.68	11.94	9.43	—	0.0	+Avg	+Avg	★★★★	1.02	None
106	Buffalo Small Cap	SG		26.94	13.95	14.86	11.22	—	0.0	+Avg	+Avg	★★★★	1.01	None
107	Calamos Convertible A	CV		19.03	9.13	6.46	7.56	10.42	4.0	Avg	Avg	★★★	1.12	Clsd
108	Calamos Gr & Inc A	CV		31.46	9.84	9.19	9.75	**13.93**	1.9	+Avg	+Avg	★★★★	1.05	4.75
109	Calamos Growth A	MG		53.90	1.45	9.29	9.35	17.77	0.0	+Avg	Avg	★★★★	1.19	4.75
112	Century Sm-Cp Sel Inv	SG		23.94	9.27	8.26	13.28	—	1.2	+Avg	Low	★★★★	1.35	Clsd
113	CGM Focus	LB		34.69	14.95	17.42	**17.25**	—	2.2	High	High	★★★★★	1.07	None
114	Champlain Small Co Adv	SG		12.33	14.03	—	—	—	0.0	—	—		1.41	None
115	Chase Growth	LG		18.99	1.41	9.71	6.12	—	0.3	+Avg	-Avg	★★★★★	1.18	None
116	Chesapeake Core Growth	LG		18.07	7.22	6.34	5.43	—	0.0	+Avg	+Avg	★★★★	1.35	None
117	Clipper	LB		91.98	15.28	6.78	6.55	12.22	1.1	+Avg	-Avg	★★★★	1.11	None

Domestic-Equity Funds

| | | | | | Total Return % through 12-29-06 | | | | | Morningstar Rating Statistics through 12-29-06 | | | | |
| | | | | | | Annualized | | | | | | | | |
Page		Cat	Style Box	NAV	1Yr	3Yr	5Yr	10Yr	Yield %	Performance	Risk	Morningstar Rating	Expense Ratio %	Sales Charge %
	S&P 500				**4.91**	**14.38**	**0.54**	**9.07**						
118	Columbia Acorn A	MG		29.02	14.13	15.93	14.23	—	0.1	High	-Avg	★★★★★	1.03	5.75
120	Columbia Acorn Select A	MG		26.18	19.32	16.03	13.26	—	0.1	High	Low	★★★★★	1.26	5.75
121	Columbia Acorn USA A	SG		28.02	7.95	13.47	11.61	—	0.0	+Avg	-Avg	★★★★	1.31	5.75
122	Davis Appr & Income A	CV		29.71	**15.19**	**11.45**	**11.67**	8.54	2.0	+Avg	Avg	★★★★	1.07	4.75
123	Davis Financial A	SF		47.48	**18.74**	12.88	9.78	12.10	0.0	Avg	Avg	★★★	0.98	4.75
124	Davis NY Venture A	LB		38.52	15.12	12.71	9.44	10.67	0.7	+Avg	-Avg	★★★★	0.87	4.75
125	Delafield	MV		25.64	**20.38**	15.53	14.86	13.21	0.7	+Avg	+Avg	★★★★	1.33	None
126	DFA U.S. Micro Cap	SB		15.70	16.16	13.27	15.16	13.48	1.8	+Avg	+Avg	★★★	0.55	None
127	Diamond Hill Small Cap A	SV		25.03	7.03	16.03	16.57	—	0.3	+Avg	Avg	★★★★	1.45	Clsd
128	Dodge & Cox Balanced	MA		87.08	13.86	11.20	10.68	11.79	2.4	High	Avg	★★★★★	0.53	Clsd
131	Dodge & Cox Stock	LV		153.46	18.53	15.60	**12.84**	14.23	1.3	High	Avg	★★★★★	0.52	Clsd
132	Domini Social Equity	LB		33.42	12.58	7.87	4.82	7.60	0.8	Avg	+Avg	★★★	0.95	None
133	Dreyfus Appreciation	LB		43.79	16.26	8.53	4.98	7.86	1.4	Avg	-Avg	★★★	0.92	None
134	Dreyfus Prem Bal Opp J	MA		20.28	9.63	5.00	5.05	9.34	1.9	Avg	+Avg	★★★	1.01	Clsd
136	E*TRAD Delphi Value Ret	MV		18.46	17.65	12.19	11.08	—	0.2	Avg	-Avg	★★★	1.57	None
139	Eaton Vance Utilities A	SU		13.25	**28.51**	**24.57**	**16.33**	**14.05**	2.5	High	Avg	★★★★★	1.08	5.75
140	Eaton Vance Wld Health A	SH		11.31	−0.01	4.78	2.13	12.29	0.0	Avg	Avg	★★★	1.49	5.75
141	Excelsior Val & Restruct	LV		52.54	14.88	14.67	11.31	13.80	0.9	High	High	★★★★	1.05	None
142	Fairholme	MB		28.99	16.72	18.37	15.14	—	0.8	High	Low	★★★★★	1.00	None
143	FAM Value	MB		49.65	8.73	10.28	9.68	11.83	0.6	Avg	Low	★★★	1.18	None
144	FBR Small Cap	MG		53.85	**28.49**	19.76	**20.78**	**17.87**	0.0	High	Avg	★★★★★	1.50	None
145	Fidelity	LB		35.84	13.67	9.64	5.45	8.28	0.9	Avg	Avg	★★★	0.56	None
146	Fidelity Adv Small Cap T	SG		22.14	9.67	13.26	9.98	—	0.0	+Avg	-Avg	★★★★	1.51	3.50
147	Fidelity Asset Mgr 50%	MA		16.11	9.19	6.18	5.22	7.42	2.9	Avg	Avg	★★★	0.71	None
148	Fidelity Asset Mgr 70%	MA		16.25	10.33	6.68	4.94	6.84	2.4	-Avg	+Avg	★★	0.79	None
149	Fidelity Asset Mgr 85%	LG		13.35	12.40	10.24	5.31	—	1.6	+Avg	+Avg	★★★★	0.87	None
150	Fidelity Balanced	MA		19.43	11.65	11.09	9.98	10.84	2.0	High	+Avg	★★★★★	0.63	None
151	Fidelity Blue Chip Grth	LG		44.31	5.54	5.27	1.69	5.61	0.5	Avg	-Avg	★★★	0.61	None
153	Fidelity Capital Apprec	LG		27.11	13.80	10.24	9.85	10.08	0.4	High	+Avg	★★★★	0.90	None
154	Fidelity Contrafund	LG		65.20	11.52	14.26	11.52	11.01	0.5	High	Low	★★★★★	0.88	Clsd
155	Fidelity Convertible Sec	CV		25.33	15.13	10.37	8.24	11.87	1.9	+Avg	High	★★★★	0.69	None
156	Fidelity Disciplined Eq	LB		29.02	14.58	12.28	7.95	9.21	0.6	+Avg	-Avg	★★★★	0.87	None
157	Fidelity Discovery	LB		12.85	13.94	8.78	5.34	—	0.9	Avg	Avg	★★★	0.61	None
159	Fidelity Dividend Growth	LB		31.68	14.67	7.90	4.27	9.68	1.4	Avg	Avg	★★★	0.59	None
160	Fidelity Equity-Inc	LV		58.55	19.81	12.13	8.70	9.38	1.5	Avg	Avg	★★★	0.67	None
161	Fidelity Equity-Inc II	LV		24.24	13.73	9.35	7.95	9.09	1.4	Avg	Avg	★★★	0.62	None
163	Fidelity Exp & Multinatl	LG		22.98	8.43	12.40	8.90	12.89	0.2	High	Avg	★★★★★	0.81	None
169	Fidelity Growth & Income	LB		31.15	10.71	7.69	4.02	7.15	0.7	Avg	Low	★★★	0.65	None
170	Fidelity Growth Company	LG		69.71	9.56	11.72	5.58	9.56	0.0	High	High	★★★★	0.94	Clsd
172	Fidelity Independence	LG		21.96	12.26	11.49	7.60	9.72	0.5	High	+Avg	★★★★★	0.72	None
180	Fidelity Leverage Co Stk	MB		28.97	17.57	**19.79**	**27.08**	—	0.4	High	High	★★★★★	0.85	None
181	Fidelity Low-Priced Stk	MB		43.54	17.76	16.08	15.63	15.34	0.7	High	-Avg	★★★★★	0.87	Clsd
182	Fidelity Magellan	LG		89.52	7.22	7.04	3.17	6.99	0.4	Avg	-Avg	★★★	0.56	Clsd
183	Fidelity Mid Cap Value	MV		16.67	14.50	16.63	12.86	—	0.5	Avg	Avg	★★★★	0.81	None
184	Fidelity Mid-Cap Stock	MG		29.14	14.78	13.26	6.99	12.70	0.0	+Avg	Avg	★★★★	0.69	Clsd
188	Fidelity New Millennium	MG		29.40	13.53	9.23	7.48	13.87	0.0	+Avg	+Avg	★★★	0.80	Clsd
191	Fidelity Puritan	MA		19.97	14.78	9.50	8.12	8.74	2.8	+Avg	Avg	★★★★	0.62	None
192	Fidelity Real Estate Inv	SR		36.37	32.84	26.97	23.70	15.09	1.0	Avg	Avg	★★★	0.82	None
193	Fidelity Sel Electronics	ST		43.83	0.30	1.54	−2.30	8.32	0.1	Avg	+Avg	★★	0.88	None
194	Fidelity Sel Energy Serv	SN		67.50	8.64	31.22	19.28	14.19	0.0	+Avg	High	★★	0.91	None
195	Fidelity Sel Health Care	SH		125.06	4.98	10.06	4.84	10.22	0.1	Avg	Low	★★★★	0.87	None
196	Fidelity Sel Technology	ST		67.89	7.51	4.24	2.35	8.75	0.0	+Avg	+Avg	★★★	0.93	None
199	Fidelity Small Cap Indep	SG		21.05	14.59	13.51	9.32	8.97	0.2	+Avg	Low	★★★★	0.75	None
200	Fidelity Small Cap Stock	SB		19.01	12.37	11.64	11.21	—	0.0	Avg	Avg	★★★	0.93	Clsd
201	Fidelity Small Cap Value	SB		14.00	15.65	—	—	—	0.0	—	—	—	1.06	None
202	Fidelity Small Cap Retire	SB		16.03	9.45	11.17	7.84	—	0.0	-Avg	Low	★★	1.05	None
203	Fidelity Spar 500 Inv	LB		97.97	15.71	10.34	6.08	8.27	1.5	Avg	Avg	★★★	0.10	None
205	Fidelity Spar Tot Mkt Inv	LB		39.58	15.73	11.35	7.44	—	1.3	+Avg	Avg	★★★★	0.10	None
207	Fidelity Strategic RRet	CA	—	10.15	4.89	—	—	—	3.3	—	—	—	0.79	None
212	Fidelity Value	MV		80.60	15.09	16.81	14.23	12.00	0.7	+Avg	Avg	★★★★	0.72	None

Bold numbers indicate *highest* return for the listed time period in each category.

Domestic-Equity Funds

		Cat	Style Box	NAV	Total Return % through 12-29-06				Yield %	Morningstar Rating Statistics through 12-29-06				
Page					1Yr	Annualized 3Yr	5Yr	10Yr		Performance	Risk	Morningstar Rating	Expense Ratio %	Sales Charge %

	S&P 500				4.91	14.38	0.54	9.07						
214	First Eagle Fund of Am Y	MB		25.97	15.79	12.67	10.15	11.95	0.0	Avg	Low	★★★	1.43	Clsd
217	Forward Hoover Sm-Cp Eq	SG		20.47	9.43	13.77	10.38	—	0.1	+Avg	-Avg	★★★★	1.73	None
219	FPA Capital	SV		41.44	5.42	11.43	13.00	12.69	1.4	-Avg	Avg	★★	0.83	Clsd
220	FPA Crescent	MA		26.40	12.43	11.15	**12.43**	11.52	1.9	High	+Avg	★★★★★	1.39	Clsd
222	FPA Paramount	MB		16.18	4.76	10.85	11.04	3.28	0.9	-Avg	Avg	★★	0.85	2.00
223	Franklin Bal Sh Invmt A	MV		66.71	16.35	17.37	14.53	13.16	1.2	+Avg	-Avg	★★★★	0.91	Clsd
225	Franklin Growth A	LB		41.63	14.16	11.25	5.92	7.43	0.3	-Avg	Avg	★★★	0.91	5.75
227	Franklin Income A	CA		2.66	**19.12**	**10.82**	**12.01**	**9.62**	5.4	High	High	★★★★★	0.64	4.25
228	Gabelli Asset AAA	MB		47.38	21.84	14.01	10.66	12.81	0.6	Avg	Low	★★★★	1.37	None
229	Gabelli Sm Cp Growth AAA	SV		31.20	19.17	15.38	14.87	13.76	0.0	+Avg	-Avg	★★★★	1.44	None
230	GAMCO Growth AAA	LG		30.62	6.28	7.06	1.32	6.97	0.0	Avg	+Avg	★★★	1.49	None
232	Greenspring	MA		23.43	12.29	9.16	9.94	8.15	2.5	+Avg	+Avg	★★★★	1.16	None
234	Harbor Capital App Instl	LG		33.35	2.33	8.46	2.89	7.52	0.2	+Avg	+Avg	★★★	0.68	None
237	Harbor Large Cap Val Inv	LV		19.23	15.63	11.54	—	—	0.7	Avg	-Avg	★★★	1.10	None
239	Homestead Value	LV		35.94	17.82	14.46	10.84	9.94	1.5	+Avg	-Avg	★★★★	0.76	None
241	Janus	LG		28.14	10.59	6.38	2.81	6.12	0.3	Avg	Avg	★★★	0.87	None
242	Janus Balanced	MA		24.41	10.56	9.00	6.60	9.70	1.8	+Avg	-Avg	★★★★	0.79	None
243	Janus Contrarian	LB		16.83	**24.58**	**21.01**	15.69	—	1.9	High	High	★★★★★	0.93	None
244	Janus Enterprise	MG		47.45	13.22	15.04	8.20	7.37	0.0	+Avg	Avg	★★★	0.95	None
245	Janus Fundamental Equity	LB		25.91	10.28	13.44	8.09	11.84	0.4	High	Avg	★★★★★	0.89	None
246	Janus Global Life Sci	SH		19.66	−1.95	7.90	2.27	—	0.0	Avg	Avg	★★★	0.96	None
248	Janus Growth & Income	LG		38.26	7.82	10.71	5.83	10.71	1.4	High	-Avg	★★★★★	0.87	None
250	Janus Mid Cap Val Inv	MV		23.81	15.25	14.01	14.61	12.76	3.0	Avg	Avg	★★★	0.92	None
251	Janus Orion	MG		9.86	18.64	18.13	10.74	—	0.2	+Avg	Avg	★★★★	1.01	None
253	Janus Research	LG		24.95	8.65	8.74	3.82	8.57	0.1	+Avg	Avg	★★★	0.92	None
254	Janus Sm Cap Val Instl	SV		26.16	12.57	11.82	10.18	14.47	4.9	Avg	-Avg	★★★	0.79	Clsd
255	Janus Twenty	LG		54.62	12.30	15.04	7.71	9.91	0.6	High	+Avg	★★★★★	0.86	Clsd
256	Janus Venture	SG		62.45	**23.58**	13.84	10.83	10.31	0.0	+Avg	+Avg	★★★★	0.87	Clsd
258	Jensen J	LG		26.93	14.01	6.02	4.25	9.49	0.8	+Avg	Low	★★★★	0.85	None
259	JPMorgan U.S. Real Est A	SR		22.62	36.21	29.22	23.74	—	1.2	Avg	Avg	★★★	1.21	5.25
262	Kalmar Gr Val Sm Cp	SG		16.81	6.17	8.02	8.60	—	0.0	Avg	-Avg	★★★	1.29	None
263	Legg Mason Opp Prim	MG		18.94	13.41	11.25	14.33	—	0.0	+Avg	High	★★★★	2.08	1.00
264	Legg Mason P Aggr Grow A	LG		115.66	7.98	10.36	4.31	**14.78**	0.0	+Avg	+Avg	★★★★	1.13	5.75
265	Legg Mason Spec Invt Pr	MB		38.92	7.80	9.71	13.21	13.07	0.0	+Avg	High	★★★	1.76	None
266	Legg Mason Value Prim	LB		72.72	5.85	7.67	7.75	12.14	0.0	+Avg	High	★★★	1.68	None
267	LKCM Small Cap Equity Ins	SB		21.98	14.98	17.11	13.80	11.91	0.0	+Avg	-Avg	★★★★	0.99	None
268	Longleaf Partners	LB		34.86	21.63	10.53	10.78	12.77	0.4	+Avg	Avg	★★★★	0.91	Clsd
270	Longleaf Partners Sm-Cap	SV		30.12	**22.33**	15.85	16.58	14.51	1.7	+Avg	Low	★★★★★	0.93	Clsd
273	Lord Abbett Affiliated A	LV		15.28	17.61	11.02	7.78	9.95	1.2	Avg	Avg	★★★	0.83	5.75
274	MainStay ICAP Equity I	LV		45.03	20.17	14.06	7.57	9.95	1.3	+Avg	Avg	★★★	0.80	None
276	MainStay ICAP Sel Eq I	LV		41.62	20.60	15.83	10.53	—	1.2	+Avg	Avg	★★★★	0.80	None
277	MainStay MAP I	LB		37.54	16.44	13.83	10.41	13.38	0.5	High	Avg	★★★★★	0.95	None
278	Mairs & Power Balanced	MA		63.06	12.10	9.47	8.35	10.14	2.9	+Avg	Avg	★★★★	0.84	None
279	Mairs & Power Growth	LB		77.10	10.24	10.73	9.52	12.33	1.2	High	-Avg	★★★★★	0.70	None
281	Managers Fremont Mic-Cap	SG		35.63	12.26	6.22	4.72	11.59	0.0	Avg	+Avg	★★★	1.56	Clsd
282	Managers Special Equity M	SB		83.59	12.12	10.33	8.35	9.90	0.0	-Avg	Avg	★★	1.40	None
283	Marsico 21st Century	LG		15.23	**18.65**	**16.10**	15.83	—	0.9	High	+Avg	★★★★★	1.39	None
284	Marsico Focus	LG		19.29	8.60	9.99	7.79	—	0.1	High	-Avg	★★★★★	1.25	None
285	Marsico Growth	LG		20.09	6.58	9.17	7.40	—	0.0	High	-Avg	★★★★★	1.26	None
287	Masters' Select Equity	LB		15.69	9.34	9.22	6.82	10.12	0.0	+Avg	High	★★★	1.19	None
288	Masters' Select Small Co	SG		14.86	9.68	11.80	—	—	0.0	+Avg	-Avg	★★★★	1.30	None
289	Masters' Select Value	LB		16.34	16.77	11.73	9.65	—	0.3	High	+Avg	★★★★★	1.21	None
291	Matrix Advisors Value	LB		57.50	16.31	6.83	6.92	10.57	0.8	+Avg	High	★★★	0.99	None
294	Meridian Growth	MG		39.24	15.81	9.97	10.08	12.73	0.0	+Avg	-Avg	★★★★	0.85	None
295	Meridian Value	MB		35.60	18.67	12.02	10.41	**17.50**	1.0	+Avg	-Avg	★★★★	1.09	None
298	MFS Total Return A	MA		16.18	11.56	8.67	7.21	8.75	2.4	Avg	Low	★★★	0.90	5.75
299	Morgan Stan Ins US R/E A	SR		28.23	**38.85**	**30.90**	**25.33**	**17.06**	1.5	High	-Avg	★★★★★	0.89	None
300	Muhlenkamp	LV		87.15	4.08	11.82	10.64	13.29	0.9	+Avg	High	★★★	1.06	None
301	Mutual Beacon A	LV		16.61	20.65	14.46	11.37	11.62	1.3	+Avg	Low	★★★★	1.17	5.75
304	Mutual Qualified A	LV		21.76	18.94	15.30	11.63	11.63	1.5	+Avg	Low	★★★★	1.16	5.75

Bold numbers indicate *highest* return for the listed time period in each category.

Domestic-Equity Funds

Total Return % through 12-29-06 · Morningstar Rating Statistics through 12-29-06

Page		Cat	Style Box	NAV	1Yr	3Yr (Annualized)	5Yr	10Yr	Yield %	Performance	Risk	Morningstar Rating	Expense Ratio %	Sales Charge %
	S&P 500				**4.91**	**14.38**	**0.54**	**9.07**						
305	Mutual Shares A	LV		25.91	17.98	13.77	10.54	11.10	1.6	+Avg	Low	★★★★	1.11	5.75
306	N/I Numeric Inv Sm CapVl	SV		17.36	19.82	17.16	19.52	—	0.9	High	Avg	★★★★★	0.54	Clsd
307	Neuberger Ber Genesis Inv	SB		33.36	7.31	14.04	13.64	**13.91**	1.3	+Avg	Low	★★★★	1.02	Clsd
309	Neuberger Ber Fasciano In	SG		42.14	4.86	6.59	7.48	7.74	0.0	Avg	Low	★★★	1.20	None
310	Neuberger Ber Part Inv	LB		31.05	13.19	16.77	10.21	8.91	0.6	High	High	★★★★★	0.82	None
311	Nicholas	LB		58.38	9.34	8.88	5.36	6.02	1.3	-Avg	-Avg	★★★	0.77	None
312	Nicholas II I	MG		22.93	8.25	8.71	6.42	6.96	0.3	-Avg	Low	★★★	0.67	None
314	Northern Technology	ST		12.26	5.51	2.27	−0.33	7.11	0.0	Avg	Avg	★★★	1.25	None
315	Oak Value	LB		28.16	14.18	6.74	3.98	8.53	0.3	Avg	+Avg	★★	1.29	None
316	Oakmark Equity & Inc I	MA		25.88	10.82	9.92	9.88	**13.27**	1.8	High	Avg	★★★★★	0.86	None
318	Oakmark I	LB		45.92	18.26	9.25	6.94	8.58	0.9	+Avg	-Avg	★★★★	1.05	None
321	Oakmark Select I	LB		33.48	13.60	9.33	8.09	**17.05**	1.1	+Avg	+Avg	★★★★	0.99	None
326	Oppenheimer Main Street A	LB		40.66	14.91	9.95	6.34	7.60	0.9	-Avg	-Avg	★★★	0.92	5.75
327	Osterweis	MB		26.48	11.36	12.65	10.95	15.28	0.7	+Avg	Low	★★★★	1.26	None
328	Pax World Balanced	MA		24.53	10.71	9.78	7.17	9.52	1.5	+Avg	Low	★★★★	0.96	None
331	PIMCO CommRealRetStrD	SN	—	13.88	−3.46	10.25	—	—	2.8	Low	Low	★	1.24	None
339	Pioneer A	LB		48.10	16.39	11.40	6.55	9.70	0.9	Avg	Avg	★★★	1.08	5.75
342	Presidio	SB		13.64	15.59	—	—	—	0.0	—	—	—	1.50	None
343	PRIMECAP Odyssey Agg Gr	MG		14.34	21.57	—	—	—	0.0	—	—	—	1.25	None
344	PRIMECAP Odyssey Growth	LG		13.90	14.85	—	—	—	0.1	—	—	—	1.25	None
345	Putnam Fund for Gr&Inc A	LV		20.00	15.82	10.56	6.81	7.36	1.0	Low	Avg	★★	0.89	5.25
346	Rainier Sm/Mid Cap	MG		36.67	14.67	16.51	13.09	11.79	0.0	High	Avg	★★★★★	1.21	Clsd
347	Robeco BostPtn SmCpll Inv	SV		21.40	15.66	13.15	13.24	—	0.1	Avg	+Avg	★★★	1.77	Clsd
349	Royce Opportunity Inv	SV		13.04	18.76	13.50	15.97	**17.34**	0.0	+Avg	High	★★★★	1.14	None
350	Royce Premier Inv	SB		17.66	8.81	16.09	14.90	13.73	0.4	+Avg	Low	★★★★	1.13	Clsd
351	Royce Special Equity Inv	SV		19.72	14.00	8.74	13.61	—	0.5	-Avg	Low	★★	1.14	None
352	Royce Total Return Inv	SV		13.75	14.54	13.36	13.25	12.89	1.1	Avg	Low	★★★★	1.12	None
353	Royce Value Service	SB		11.06	16.76	**21.47**	16.17	—	0.1	+Avg	High	★★★★	1.28	None
354	RS Diversified Growth A	SG		24.13	8.06	2.57	0.74	11.27	0.0	-Avg	+Avg	★★	1.63	4.75
355	RS Emerging Growth A	SG		35.66	9.45	8.27	2.19	10.04	0.0	-Avg	+Avg	★★	1.54	4.75
356	RS MidCap Opport A	MG		14.17	9.43	10.43	8.03	9.73	0.0	Avg	Avg	★★★	1.34	4.75
357	RS Value A	MB		27.43	16.37	18.89	23.11	6.50	1.1	Avg	Avg	★★★	1.39	4.75
358	Schneider Small Cap Val	SV		21.66	21.08	**19.16**	**24.31**	—	0.8	High	High	★★★★★	1.10	Clsd
359	Schneider Value	LV		22.78	**23.34**	**17.12**	—	—	0.4	High	High	★★★★★	0.85	None
361	Selected American S	LB		46.06	15.19	12.33	9.00	11.12	0.6	High	-Avg	★★★★★	0.90	None
362	Selected Special Shares S	MB		13.98	17.74	12.44	10.61	9.97	0.8	Avg	Avg	★★★	1.12	None
363	Sequoia	LB		152.75	8.34	6.91	6.86	11.57	0.0	+Avg	-Avg	★★★★	1.00	Clsd
364	Skyline Spec Equities	SV		25.99	18.71	15.35	14.90	11.94	0.0	+Avg	Avg	★★★	1.47	None
365	Sound Shore	LV		39.19	16.56	12.82	9.85	10.51	0.5	+Avg	+Avg	★★★★	0.98	None
368	T. Rowe Price Balanced	MA		21.29	13.73	9.81	8.06	8.19	2.4	Avg	Avg	★★★	0.69	None
369	T. Rowe Price BlChpGr	LG		35.73	9.73	8.29	4.54	7.46	0.4	+Avg	-Avg	★★★★	0.85	None
370	T. Rowe Price Cap Apprec	MA		20.62	14.54	**12.16**	12.22	12.18	2.2	High	Avg	★★★★★	0.76	None
371	T. Rowe Price Div Growth	LB		25.36	16.45	10.43	6.57	7.86	1.3	Avg	-Avg	★★★★	0.75	None
373	T. Rowe Price Eq Inc	LV		29.55	19.14	12.64	9.35	10.13	1.6	+Avg	Avg	★★★★	0.71	None
374	T. Rowe Price Fincl Svcs	SF		21.38	15.98	11.40	**10.92**	**13.57**	1.8	+Avg	Avg	★★★★	0.93	None
376	T. Rowe Price Glob Tech	ST		6.71	10.00	10.38	**7.15**	—	0.0	High	-Avg	★★★★★	1.50	None
378	T. Rowe Price Grth & Inc	LB		22.14	14.44	9.17	4.91	6.68	1.3	-Avg	Avg	★★★	0.76	None
379	T. Rowe Price Gr Stk	LG		31.63	14.05	10.24	6.25	9.20	0.6	+Avg	-Avg	★★★★★	0.72	None
380	T. Rowe Price Health Sci	SH		26.13	9.58	**12.95**	7.44	12.45	0.0	+Avg	+Avg	★★★★	0.91	None
386	T. Rowe Price Med & Tele	SC		43.18	**28.55**	**24.25**	**16.47**	**17.44**	0.0	High	Avg	★★★★★	0.92	None
387	T. Rowe Price Mid Gr	MG		53.69	6.79	13.23	9.59	11.63	0.1	+Avg	-Avg	★★★★	0.80	Clsd
388	T. Rowe Price Mid Val	MV		25.42	20.24	16.02	14.99	**14.18**	0.9	High	-Avg	★★★★★	0.82	Clsd
389	T. Rowe Price New Amer	LG		31.38	7.24	7.52	3.74	4.31	0.0	Avg	Avg	★★★	0.91	None
391	T. Rowe Price New Era	SN		46.00	17.00	25.50	19.79	13.16	1.2	Avg	Low	★★★★	0.68	None
392	T. Rowe Price New Horiz	SG		32.29	7.39	12.32	9.20	8.63	0.0	+Avg	Avg	★★★★	0.84	None
394	T. Rowe Price Pers Inc	CA		15.84	9.64	8.24	7.76	7.74	2.9	+Avg	+Avg	★★★★	0.78	None
395	T. Rowe Price Real Est	SR		25.33	36.75	28.93	24.95	—	2.4	+Avg	Avg	★★★★	0.85	None
397	T. Rowe Price SciTech	ST		20.96	7.10	3.69	0.04	1.22	0.0	-Avg	Avg	★★★	1.00	None
398	T. Rowe Price Sm Stk	SB		34.23	12.78	13.25	10.52	11.34	0.1	Avg	-Avg	★★★	0.92	Clsd
399	T. Rowe Price Sm Val	SB		41.21	16.24	16.68	16.32	13.42	0.6	+Avg	Low	★★★★	0.84	Clsd

Bold numbers indicate *highest* return for the listed time period in each category.

Domestic-Equity Funds

Page		Cat	Style Box	NAV	Total Return % through 12-29-06				Yield %	Morningstar Rating Statistics through 12-29-06				
					1Yr	Annualized 3Yr	5Yr	10Yr		Performance	Risk	Morningstar Rating	Expense Ratio %	Sales Charge %
	S&P 500				**4.91**	**14.38**	**0.54**	**9.07**						
400	T. Rowe Price Spect Grth	LB		20.40	16.37	13.63	9.59	8.93	0.8	High	+Avg	★★★★★	0.86	None
406	T. Rowe Price Value	LV		27.05	19.75	13.66	9.75	10.94	1.0	+Avg	+Avg	★★★★	0.90	None
407	TCW Dividend Focused I	LV		13.30	18.45	—	—	—	1.7	—	—	—	0.87	None
408	TCW Opportunity I	SB		14.72	11.44	10.23	10.93	10.58	0.0	Avg	+Avg	★★	1.16	None
409	TCW Select Equities I	LG		19.10	−5.12	3.58	3.07	7.86	0.0	Avg	High	★★	0.89	None
411	TCW Value Added I	SB		12.99	18.21	6.67	6.66	—	0.0	Low	High	★	1.62	None
412	TCW Value Opportunities I	MB		22.62	12.90	9.94	7.57	—	0.3	-Avg	+Avg	★	0.92	None
418	Third Avenue RealEst Val	SR		34.64	30.16	24.03	22.26	—	2.4	-Avg	Low	★★★	1.14	None
419	Third Avenue Sm-Cap Val	SB		25.83	11.43	14.50	13.22	—	1.6	+Avg	Low	★★★★	1.13	Clsd
420	Third Avenue Value	MB		59.46	14.69	19.15	14.49	13.50	5.4	High	-Avg	★★★★★	1.10	None
421	Thompson Plumb Growth	LB		48.95	14.96	5.32	4.16	11.84	0.7	Avg	High	★★★	1.08	None
423	Thornburg Value A	LB		39.29	21.95	12.72	7.76	12.04	0.8	+Avg	+Avg	★★★★	1.34	4.50
424	Torray	LB		41.57	13.74	7.46	6.20	9.10	0.2	Avg	Avg	★★★	1.07	None
425	Touchstn Dvrsf S/C Val Z	SV		19.24	15.83	12.77	10.56	13.51	0.0	Avg	+Avg	★★	1.23	None
426	Touchstn Snds Cp Sel Gr Z	LG		7.77	−6.50	6.85	3.73	—	0.0	Avg	+Avg	★★★	1.36	None
427	Turner Midcap Growth	MG		29.21	6.72	9.91	5.92	13.42	0.0	+Avg	+Avg	★★★	1.20	None
428	Turner Small Cap Growth	SG		28.76	13.36	10.32	7.46	8.68	0.0	Avg	+Avg	★★★	1.25	Clsd
429	Tweedy, Browne American	MV		24.33	11.62	7.71	5.55	8.81	1.0	-Avg	Low	★★	1.36	Clsd
432	Undiscovered Mg BehGrlns	MG		24.06	4.02	6.69	9.56	—	0.0	Avg	High	★★★	1.30	None
433	USAA Aggressive Growth	LG		33.01	5.37	8.49	3.00	4.50	0.0	Avg	Avg	★★★	0.99	None
438	Van Kampen Comstock A	LV		19.25	16.06	12.45	8.41	11.98	1.9	Avg	+Avg	★★★	0.80	5.75
439	Van Kampen Eq and Inc A	MA		9.12	12.53	10.69	8.72	11.04	2.1	+Avg	Avg	★★★★	0.78	5.75
440	Van Kampen Growth & IncA	LV		22.08	16.01	13.25	9.58	11.37	1.4	Avg	-Avg	★★★	0.80	5.75
441	Vanguard 500 Index	LB		130.59	15.64	10.30	6.07	8.34	1.6	Avg	Avg	★★★	0.18	None
442	Vanguard Asset Alloc	MA		28.78	16.02	10.61	7.68	9.22	2.0	+Avg	+Avg	★★★★	0.41	None
443	Vanguard Bal Idx	MA		21.36	11.02	8.30	6.62	7.92	2.8	Avg	Avg	★★★★	0.20	None
444	Vanguard FTSE Soc Idx Inv	LG		9.21	13.09	8.42	4.73	—	1.3	+Avg	Avg	★★★★	0.25	None
445	Vanguard Cap Opp	MG		36.68	16.78	15.43	10.63	15.56	0.2	High	Avg	★★★★★	0.49	Clsd
446	Vanguard Capital Value	LV		12.68	18.90	12.65	7.82	—	1.0	Avg	High	★★	0.60	None
447	Vanguard Convertible Sec	CV		13.64	12.94	8.88	9.01	9.02	3.1	Avg	+Avg	★★★★	0.86	None
449	Vanguard Dividend Growth	LV		14.57	19.58	11.43	6.56	6.87	1.8	-Avg	-Avg	★★	0.37	None
451	Vanguard Energy	SN		64.63	**19.68**	**33.23**	**25.75**	**16.53**	1.6	High	Avg	★★★★★	0.28	None
452	Vanguard Equity-Inc	LV		25.30	20.62	12.66	8.58	9.91	2.7	+Avg	-Avg	★★★★	0.31	None
454	Vanguard Explorer	SG		74.71	9.70	10.89	8.21	10.25	0.4	Avg	-Avg	★★★	0.46	Clsd
455	Vanguard ExtMktIdx	MB		38.68	14.27	14.37	11.95	9.70	1.2	Avg	+Avg	★★★	0.25	None
458	Vanguard Gr Idx	LG		29.77	9.01	7.09	3.37	7.15	0.8	Avg	-Avg	★★★★	0.22	None
459	Vanguard Gr & Inc	LB		35.76	14.01	10.26	6.38	8.85	1.6	Avg	Avg	★★★	0.34	None
460	Vanguard Growth Equity	LG		11.06	6.15	6.45	2.91	6.03	0.0	Avg	+Avg	★★★	0.88	None
461	Vanguard Health Care	SH		145.52	**10.81**	11.88	**9.46**	**16.36**	1.4	High	Low	★★★★★	0.25	Clsd
473	Vanguard LifeSt Cons Gr	CA		16.59	10.62	7.67	6.61	7.55	3.1	+Avg	Avg	★★★★	0.25	None
474	Vanguard LifeSt Growth	LB		23.87	16.13	11.80	8.61	8.54	2.1	+Avg	-Avg	★★★★	0.26	None
475	Vanguard LifeSt Income	CA		13.93	7.93	5.71	5.55	6.95	3.9	+Avg	-Avg	★★★★	0.25	None
476	Vanguard LifeSt Mod Grth	MA		20.36	13.31	9.81	7.76	8.19	2.7	+Avg	Avg	★★★★	0.25	None
481	Vanguard Mid Cap Growth	MG		17.07	12.72	11.07	6.93	—	0.2	Avg	+Avg	★★★	0.39	None
482	Vanguard Mid Cap Idx	MB		19.78	13.60	15.92	12.28	—	1.3	+Avg	Avg	★★★★	0.22	None
483	Vanguard Morgan Gr	LG		18.98	11.09	10.22	6.49	8.30	1.1	+Avg	Avg	★★★★	0.41	None
485	Vanguard PRIMECAP	LB		68.94	12.30	12.97	8.42	12.64	0.6	High	High	★★★★★	0.46	Clsd
486	Vanguard PRIMECAP Core	LG		12.61	12.31	—	—	—	0.8	—	—	—	0.60	None
487	Vanguard REIT Index	SR		25.58	35.07	25.49	22.70	14.18	3.7	Avg	+Avg	★★★	0.21	None
488	Vanguard Selected Value	MV		21.09	19.11	16.64	14.12	10.17	1.5	+Avg	Avg	★★★	0.49	None
494	Vanguard SmCp Gr Idx	SG		18.34	11.95	12.18	11.28	—	0.3	+Avg	-Avg	★★★★★	0.23	None
495	Vanguard SmCp Idx	SB		32.62	15.66	14.19	11.64	10.03	1.1	Avg	+Avg	★★★	0.23	None
496	Vanguard SmCp VI Idx	SV		17.05	19.24	16.05	12.96	—	1.8	Avg	Avg	★★★	0.23	None
497	Vanguard STAR	MA		20.95	11.64	10.21	8.16	9.19	2.7	+Avg	Avg	★★★★	0.36	None
498	Vanguard Strategic Eq	MB		23.64	13.43	14.55	13.43	12.41	1.1	+Avg	Avg	★★★★	0.35	None
500	Vanguard Tx-Mgd App	LB		33.62	14.42	11.18	6.74	8.65	1.4	+Avg	+Avg	★★★	0.14	None
501	Vanguard Tax-Mgd Bal	CA		20.02	9.09	7.00	5.91	7.25	2.8	+Avg	High	★★★★	0.12	None
503	Vanguard Tax-Mgd SmCap R	SB		25.72	14.16	14.75	12.36	—	0.8	Avg	Avg	★★★	0.14	None
504	Vanguard Tot Stk	LB		34.09	15.51	11.26	7.42	8.57	1.5	+Avg	+Avg	★★★★	0.19	None
507	Vanguard Tx-Mgd Gr	LB		30.87	15.73	10.39	6.18	8.43	1.7	+Avg	Avg	★★★★	0.14	None

Bold numbers indicate *highest* return for the listed time period in each category.

Domestic-Equity Funds

Page		Cat	Style Box	NAV	Total Return % through 12-29-06 1Yr	Annualized 3Yr	5Yr	10Yr	Yield %	Performance	Risk	Morningstar Rating	Expense Ratio %	Sales Charge %
	S&P 500				**4.91**	**14.38**	**0.54**	**9.07**						
508	Vanguard U.S. Gr	LG		18.18	1.77	6.58	−0.40	1.42	0.5	Low	+Avg	★	0.58	None
509	Vanguard U.S. Value	LV		14.74	14.10	11.33	8.78	—	1.5	Avg	Avg	★★★	0.39	None
510	Vanguard Val Idx	LV		26.58	22.15	14.68	9.54	9.46	2.2	+Avg	+Avg	★★★	0.21	None
511	Vanguard Wellesley Inc	CA		21.81	11.28	7.40	7.29	8.62	4.1	High	Avg	★★★★★	0.25	None
512	Vanguard Wellington	MA		32.43	14.93	10.93	8.94	9.79	2.9	High	Avg	★★★★★	0.29	None
513	Vanguard Windsor	LV		18.64	19.35	12.42	8.64	9.79	1.4	Avg	High	★★★	0.36	None
514	Vanguard Windsor II	LV		34.75	18.25	14.40	10.12	10.24	2.2	+Avg	Avg	★★★★	0.35	None
515	Wasatch Core Growth	MG		39.81	6.68	10.25	7.43	14.62	0.3	+Avg	Avg	★★★★	1.17	Clsd
516	Wasatch Glob Sci & Tech	ST		14.79	**15.95**	9.01	6.72	—	0.0	High	Avg	★★★★	1.94	None
517	Wasatch Heritage Growth	MG		11.67	6.01	—	—	—	0.0	—	—	—	0.95	None
518	Wasatch Micro Cap	SG		6.64	17.05	13.56	13.50	**23.59**	0.0	High	Avg	★★★★★	2.14	Clsd
519	Wasatch Small Cap Growth	SG		36.88	8.40	8.91	6.35	13.93	0.0	+Avg	-Avg	★★★★	1.18	Clsd
520	Wasatch Small Cap Value	SB		5.01	14.84	13.51	13.59	—	0.7	+Avg	Avg	★★★★	1.68	Clsd
521	Wasatch Ultra Growth	SG		24.04	7.31	3.30	5.32	10.90	0.0	Avg	+Avg	★★★	1.48	Clsd
522	Weitz Hickory	MB		39.96	**22.80**	14.53	9.46	12.11	0.5	Avg	+Avg	★★★	1.20	None
523	Weitz Partners Value	LV		24.43	22.53	11.20	7.43	**14.30**	0.5	+Avg	Avg	★★★★	1.14	None
524	Weitz Value	LV		40.26	21.85	11.10	7.91	14.29	0.7	+Avg	Avg	★★★★	1.12	None
525	Westcore Midco Growth	MG		7.45	12.15	9.70	8.87	8.60	0.0	Avg	Avg	★★★	1.09	None
527	Westport R	MB		19.21	13.27	13.89	9.69	—	0.0	Avg	-Avg	★★★	1.45	None
528	Westport Select Cap R	MB		24.56	12.41	10.48	8.60	—	0.0	-Avg	-Avg	★★	1.31	Clsd
529	Westwood Balanced AAA	MA		11.65	12.41	10.17	7.30	8.48	1.7	+Avg	-Avg	★★★★	1.27	None
530	WF Adv Common Stk Z	MB		20.00	15.31	12.40	9.72	11.10	0.0	Avg	Avg	★★★	1.31	Clsd
531	WF Adv Opportunity Inv	MB		41.64	11.75	12.12	7.19	10.77	0.2	Avg	Avg	★★★	1.36	None
534	William Blair Sm-Cp Gr N	SG		25.41	14.12	13.68	**14.50**	—	0.0	High	Avg	★★★★★	1.49	Clsd

International-Equity Funds

Page		Cat	Style Box	NAV	Total Return % through 12-29-06 1Yr	Annualized 3Yr	5Yr	10Yr	Yield %	Performance	Risk	Morningstar Rating	Expense Ratio %	Sales Charge %
	S&P 500				**4.91**	**14.38**	**0.54**	**9.07**						
41	AmCent Global Gold Inv	SP		19.63	27.03	14.64	30.77	6.85	0.2	Avg	+Avg	★★	0.67	None
42	AmCent Global Gr Inv	WS		10.74	18.16	17.12	11.50	—	0.5	Avg	Avg	★★★	1.30	None
45	AmCent Intl Disc Inv	FR		15.20	31.52	26.21	21.55	**16.61**	0.0	+Avg	+Avg	★★★	1.47	Clsd
46	AmCent Intl Growth Inv	FG		12.52	25.00	17.77	10.59	9.20	0.7	Avg	Avg	★★★	1.23	None
59	Amer Funds CpIncBldr A	IH		61.11	**22.04**	14.56	12.97	11.26	3.6	Avg	-Avg	★★★★	0.57	5.75
61	Amer Funds CapWrldGI A	WS		41.93	22.36	18.79	16.70	13.79	2.1	High	-Avg	★★★★★	0.73	5.75
62	Amer Funds EuroPac A	FB		46.56	21.87	20.89	15.20	11.23	1.6	+Avg	-Avg	★★★★	0.76	5.75
68	Amer Funds New Persp A	WS		31.74	19.87	15.08	11.84	11.91	1.5	Avg	Avg	★★★	0.71	5.75
69	Amer Funds New World A	EM		48.44	33.42	25.35	21.91	—	1.8	Low	Low	★★	1.12	5.75
70	Amer Funds Sm World A	WS		39.07	22.96	19.05	14.56	9.59	1.6	+Avg	+Avg	★★★	1.01	5.75
73	American Beacon IntEq Ins	FV		23.91	26.45	20.30	**16.24**	**10.33**	2.2	Avg	Avg	★★★	0.70	None
78	Artisan International Inv	FG		28.99	25.56	19.80	12.48	12.88	1.4	+Avg	+Avg	★★★★	1.20	None
79	Artisan Intl Val	FA		27.93	34.46	25.10	—	—	1.5	Avg	-Avg	★★★★	1.25	None
80	Artisan Intl Sm Cap	FR		21.83	33.18	**28.15**	**27.61**	—	2.7	+Avg	Avg	★★★★	1.53	Clsd
87	Atlas Global Growth A	WS		26.61	16.02	15.59	10.83	13.14	0.6	+Avg	+Avg	★★★★	1.31	None
94	BlackRock Global Alloc A	IH		18.16	15.94	13.49	12.84	11.17	1.9	Avg	Avg	★★★★	1.09	5.25
111	Causeway Intl Value Inv	FV		19.70	25.74	19.66	17.24	—	0.9	Avg	Avg	★★★	1.21	Clsd
119	Columbia Acorn Intl A	FR		40.07	**34.16**	28.06	20.85	—	0.7	-Avg	-Avg	★★	1.30	5.75
130	Dodge & Cox Intl Stock	FV		43.66	28.01	**25.56**	20.78	—	1.3	+Avg	High	★★★★	0.70	None
158	Fidelity Diversified Int	FG		36.95	22.52	19.78	17.27	13.16	0.9	+Avg	-Avg	★★★★★	1.07	Clsd
162	Fidelity Europe	ES		39.36	25.18	**24.02**	15.87	10.87	1.0	Avg	+Avg	★★★	1.07	None
177	Fidelity Intl Sm Cp	FR		24.93	14.22	24.16	—	—	0.2	Avg	+Avg	★★★	1.25	Clsd

Bold numbers indicate *highest* return for the listed time period in each category.

International-Equity Funds

Page		Cat	Style Box	NAV	Total Return % through 12-29-06				Yield %	Morningstar Rating Statistics through 12-29-06				
					1Yr	Annualized 3Yr	5Yr	10Yr		Performance	Risk	Morningstar Rating	Expense Ratio %	Sales Charge %
	S&P 500				**4.91**	**14.38**	**0.54**	**9.07**						
178	Fidelity Intl Disc	FB		37.92	24.22	20.58	17.77	11.28	1.0	High	+Avg	★★★★★	1.01	None
189	Fidelity Overseas	FB		44.80	20.49	17.73	13.66	8.25	1.1	+Avg	High	★★★	0.86	None
190	Fidelity Pacific Basin	DP		27.35	**16.16**	**20.65**	**17.54**	**8.90**	0.5	+Avg	-Avg	★★★★	1.05	None
204	Fidelity Spar Intl Inv	FB		44.14	26.15	19.81	14.85	—	1.9	+Avg	Avg	★★★★	0.10	None
213	Fidelity Worldwide	WS		20.11	17.42	14.39	10.96	8.59	0.8	Avg	Avg	★★★	1.01	None
215	First Eagle Glbl A	IH		45.80	20.50	**17.90**	**19.99**	**14.56**	2.5	High	Avg	★★★★★	1.20	Clsd
216	First Eagle Overseas A	FA		25.08	22.29	20.32	22.62	**15.82**	3.2	Avg	Low	★★★★	1.18	Clsd
218	Forward Intl Small Co Inv	FR		18.96	29.51	27.20	—	—	0.2	Avg	Avg	★★★	1.45	None
235	Harbor Intl Growth Inv	FG		13.57	23.59	17.69	—	—	0.0	Avg	+Avg	★★★	1.39	None
236	Harbor Intl Instl	FV		62.04	**32.69**	23.67	20.07	**12.64**	2.3	+Avg	High	★★★★	0.87	None
247	Janus Global Opps	WS		14.07	11.19	10.10	9.21	—	0.6	Avg	+Avg	★★★	1.02	None
252	Janus Overseas	FG		46.30	**47.21**	**32.21**	**19.19**	14.42	1.2	High	High	★★★★★	0.89	None
257	Janus Worldwide	WS		50.46	17.90	9.61	3.89	6.82	1.3	-Avg	Avg	★★	0.85	None
260	Julius Baer Intl Eq II A	FB		15.09	28.62	—	—	—	0.2	—	—	—	1.36	None
261	Julius Baer Intl Eqty A	FB		42.23	**31.75**	**23.86**	**20.02**	**16.99**	0.6	High	+Avg	★★★★★	1.31	Clsd
269	Longleaf Partners Intl	FV		18.91	17.07	13.35	11.47	—	0.1	Low	Avg	★	1.64	None
275	MainStay ICAP Intl I	FV		39.10	24.30	23.40	16.82	—	2.6	+Avg	+Avg	★★★★	0.80	None
286	Marsico Intl Opp	FG		16.91	23.95	20.01	17.68	—	0.2	High	Avg	★★★★★	1.60	None
290	Masters' Select Intl	FB		18.74	23.61	20.48	15.78	—	1.9	+Avg	+Avg	★★★★	1.08	Clsd
292	Matthews Pacific Tiger	PJ		23.71	27.22	24.34	**23.55**	**9.51**	1.0	+Avg	Avg	★★★★	1.31	Clsd
302	Mutual Discovery A	WS		30.15	23.02	19.05	14.93	13.12	1.8	+Avg	Low	★★★★	1.39	5.75
303	Mutual European A	ES		24.19	26.96	21.85	**17.10**	**16.09**	2.3	+Avg	Low	★★★★	1.37	5.75
308	Neuberger Ber Intl Inv	FR		24.48	25.18	26.46	20.29	11.42	1.1	Avg	-Avg	★★★	1.25	Clsd
317	Oakmark Global I	WS		25.28	24.18	17.59	18.85	—	1.1	High	+Avg	★★★★★	1.18	None
319	Oakmark International I	FV		25.45	30.60	21.08	17.53	12.36	1.5	+Avg	+Avg	★★★	1.10	None
320	Oakmark Intl Small Cap I	FA		22.89	**34.90**	**28.25**	**24.99**	15.50	2.2	+Avg	Avg	★★★★	1.41	Clsd
322	Oppenheimer Develop MktA	EM		41.21	25.19	**32.98**	**30.76**	**19.07**	1.1	+Avg	Avg	★★★★	1.37	5.75
323	Oppenheimer Glob A	WS		73.51	17.38	16.61	11.96	13.39	0.7	+Avg	Avg	★★★★	1.08	5.75
324	Oppenheimer Glob Oppor A	WS		35.93	11.00	19.19	14.22	**15.45**	0.3	+Avg	High	★★★	1.13	5.75
325	Oppenheimer Intl Grth A	FG		27.86	29.61	19.86	14.10	10.87	0.8	+Avg	High	★★★	1.41	5.75
341	Polaris Global Value	WS		19.98	**24.57**	19.40	**21.05**	—	0.8	High	Avg	★★★★★	1.29	None
366	SSgA Emerging Markets	EM		23.43	**33.46**	31.70	27.28	11.49	1.4	+Avg	Avg	★★★★	1.25	None
372	T. Rowe Price Emg Mkt St	EM		32.41	32.01	32.50	27.49	12.20	0.7	+Avg	+Avg	★★★★	1.27	None
375	T. Rowe Price Glob Stock	WS		22.64	22.50	**19.82**	12.13	9.44	0.4	Avg	Avg	★★★★	1.18	None
383	T. Rowe Price Intl Disc	FR		47.48	27.65	26.42	22.83	16.33	0.6	Avg	Avg	★★★	1.28	None
384	T. Rowe Price Intl Stk	FG		16.83	19.26	16.45	11.15	5.82	1.2	-Avg	Avg	★★	0.89	None
385	T. Rowe Price Latin Amer	LS		37.74	**51.24**	**49.61**	**34.07**	**17.94**	0.8	+Avg	-Avg	★★★★	1.29	None
390	T. Rowe Price New Asia	PJ		14.21	**36.12**	**26.85**	23.22	7.05	1.3	+Avg	Avg	★★★★	1.05	None
413	Templeton Devel Mkts A	EM		28.28	28.29	27.31	26.29	8.70	1.8	-Avg	-Avg	★★★	1.97	5.75
414	Templeton Foreign A	FV		13.64	19.93	16.16	13.32	8.88	2.1	Low	-Avg	★	1.16	5.75
415	Templeton Growth A	WS		25.66	21.81	15.51	13.14	10.85	1.8	Avg	-Avg	★★★★	1.05	5.75
416	Templeton World A	WS		19.42	20.89	16.00	12.84	10.08	1.6	Avg	Avg	★★★★	1.06	5.75
417	Third Avenue Intl Value	FA		21.94	17.13	20.85	21.54	—	4.6	Avg	Low	★★★	1.53	Clsd
422	Thornburg Intl Value A	FB		28.48	25.62	20.29	16.89	—	1.0	+Avg	-Avg	★★★★	1.44	4.50
430	Tweedy, Browne Glob Val	FA		30.93	20.14	18.50	12.80	12.84	1.4	-Avg	Low	★★★	1.38	Clsd
431	UMB Scout International	FB		32.66	21.51	19.70	13.94	11.16	1.0	+Avg	-Avg	★★★★	1.03	None
448	Vanguard Dev Mkts Idx	FB		12.58	26.18	19.81	14.98	—	2.4	+Avg	Avg	★★★★	0.29	None
450	Vanguard Em Mkt Idx	EM		24.21	29.07	29.06	25.69	9.28	1.6	Avg	Avg	★★★	0.42	None
453	Vanguard Eur Stk Idx	ES		35.95	**33.12**	20.69	14.88	10.58	2.6	Avg	Avg	★★★	0.27	None
456	Vanguard Global Equity	WS		22.92	23.59	18.38	17.74	12.35	1.3	+Avg	Avg	★★★★★	0.72	None
468	Vanguard Intl Explorer	FR		21.06	30.10	27.36	22.86	15.83	2.6	Avg	-Avg	★★★★	0.48	Clsd
469	Vanguard Intl Gr	FB		23.81	25.66	19.79	13.70	8.03	2.1	Avg	Avg	★★★	0.55	None
470	Vanguard Intl Value	FB		40.27	27.15	21.56	17.17	9.33	2.0	+Avg	+Avg	★★★★	0.50	None
484	Vanguard Prec Mtls Mining	SP		28.00	**34.06**	**27.73**	**34.68**	**13.90**	1.6	+Avg	Low	★★★★★	0.40	Clsd
502	Vanguard Tax-Mgd Intl	FB		14.13	26.00	19.84	15.03	—	2.4	+Avg	Avg	★★★★	0.20	None
506	Vanguard Total Intl Stk	FB		17.67	26.64	20.93	16.08	7.78	2.3	+Avg	Avg	★★★★	0.31	None
533	William Blair Intl Gr N	FG		27.70	23.06	21.05	16.43	**14.94**	1.2	High	Avg	★★★★★	1.42	Clsd

Bold numbers indicate *highest* return for the listed time period in each category.

Fixed-Income Funds

Page		Cat	Style Box	NAV	Total Return % through 12-29-06				Yield %	Morningstar Rating Statistics through 12-29-06			Expense Ratio %	Sales Charge %
					1Yr	Annualized 3Yr	5Yr	10Yr		Performance	Risk	Morningstar Rating		
	LB Agg				**2.43**	**3.62**	**5.87**	**6.16**						
40	AmCent Ginnie Mae Inv	GI		10.16	3.99	3.31	4.03	5.37	4.9	Avg	-Avg	★★★	0.57	None
50	AmCent Tax-Free Bond Inv	MI		10.79	4.10	3.06	4.44	5.01	3.8	+Avg	Avg	★★★★	0.49	None
58	Amer Funds Amer H/I A	HY		12.61	12.19	8.47	9.66	7.28	7.3	+Avg	+Avg	★★★★	0.65	3.75
60	Amer Funds CapWrldBd A	IB		19.22	7.60	**5.20**	10.01	**5.84**	3.3	Avg	Avg	★★★	0.91	3.75
71	Amer Funds T/E Bd A	MI		12.53	4.76	4.16	5.21	5.36	4.0	+Avg	Avg	★★★★	0.56	3.75
129	Dodge & Cox Income	CI		12.57	5.30	3.63	5.49	6.52	4.9	High	-Avg	★★★★★	0.44	None
135	DWS Core Fixed Income Ins	CI		10.69	4.26	4.00	5.09	6.33	4.7	+Avg	Avg	★★★★	0.55	None
137	Eaton Vance Fltg Rt A	BL		10.19	6.22	4.70	—	—	6.3	Low	Low	★	1.03	2.25
138	Eaton Vance Inc Boston A	HY		6.53	11.29	8.48	10.47	7.37	7.3	+Avg	Avg	★★★★	1.06	4.75
152	Fidelity Capital & Inc	HY	—	8.89	**13.04**	**10.16**	**13.12**	8.09	6.0	High	High	★★★★★	0.77	None
164	Fidelity Float Rt Hi Inc	BL	—	9.95	**6.37**	**5.02**	—	—	6.2	-Avg	-Avg	★★	0.82	None
167	Fidelity Ginnie Mae	GI		10.77	4.13	3.66	4.35	5.57	4.8	+Avg	Low	★★★★	0.45	None
168	Fidelity Government Inc	GI		10.04	3.53	3.18	4.49	5.64	4.2	+Avg	+Avg	★★★★	0.44	None
171	Fidelity High Income	HY	—	9.06	10.74	7.91	10.21	5.64	6.9	+Avg	Avg	★★★★	0.76	None
174	Fidelity Interm Bond	CI		10.26	4.26	3.07	4.64	5.73	4.3	Avg	-Avg	★★★	0.44	None
175	Fidelity Interm Muni Inc	MI		9.97	3.97	3.42	4.89	5.20	3.9	+Avg	Avg	★★★★	0.36	None
176	Fidelity Interm Govt	GI		9.97	3.64	2.49	3.88	5.31	4.2	Avg	Avg	★★★	0.45	None
179	Fidelity Invt Grade Bond	CI		7.37	4.82	4.03	5.20	6.08	4.6	+Avg	Avg	★★★★	0.45	None
185	Fidelity Mtg Sec	CI		11.05	4.84	3.92	4.86	5.97	4.8	+Avg	Low	★★★★	0.45	None
186	Fidelity Municipal Income	ML		12.77	4.78	4.39	5.86	**5.88**	4.1	+Avg	Avg	★★★★	0.45	None
187	Fidelity New Markets Inc	EB		14.80	**11.89**	**11.83**	**15.61**	**12.13**	5.7	Avg	-Avg	★★★	0.94	None
197	Fidelity Sh-Int Muni Inc	MS		10.19	2.96	1.94	3.05	3.88	3.0	Avg	Avg	★★★	0.42	None
198	Fidelity Sh-Term Bond	CS		8.87	4.58	2.86	**3.76**	4.98	4.4	+Avg	Avg	★★★★	0.44	None
206	Fidelity Strategic Inc	MU	—	10.64	8.15	6.87	9.63	—	5.2	+Avg	Avg	★★★★	0.75	None
208	Fidelity Tax-Free Bond	ML		10.79	4.83	4.48	6.04	—	3.9	High	High	★★★★	0.17	None
209	Fidelity Total Bond	CI		10.45	5.12	4.34	—	—	4.5	High	Avg	★★★★★	0.45	None
210	Fidelity U.S. Bond Index	CI		10.86	4.33	3.65	5.18	6.24	4.6	+Avg	Avg	★★★★	0.32	None
211	Fidelity Ultra-Short Bd	UB		10.01	4.90	3.05	—	—	4.9	+Avg	-Avg	★★★★	0.45	None
221	FPA New Income	CI		10.85	4.79	2.98	4.33	5.85	4.6	Avg	Low	★★★	0.62	3.50
224	Franklin Fed T/F Inc A	ML	—	12.17	5.08	**4.91**	5.55	5.41	4.4	+Avg	Low	★★★★	0.61	4.25
226	Franklin Hi Yld T/F A	HM	—	11.02	**7.45**	6.58	6.57	**5.63**	4.8	Avg	Avg	★★★	0.63	4.25
233	Harbor Bond Instl	CI		11.56	3.91	3.98	5.54	6.63	4.4	High	Avg	★★★★★	0.58	None
249	Janus High-Yield	HY		9.83	11.10	7.70	8.26	6.97	7.3	+Avg	Low	★★★★	0.87	None
271	Loomis Sayles Bond Ret	MU		14.25	**10.99**	**8.62**	**13.32**	**9.31**	5.2	High	+Avg	★★★★★	1.00	None
272	Loomis Sayles GlbBd Ret	IB		15.28	**7.98**	4.09	**10.40**	—	2.7	+Avg	Avg	★★★★	1.00	None
280	Managers Fremont Bond	CI		10.23	3.47	3.91	5.34	6.71	4.7	High	+Avg	★★★★★	0.60	None
296	Metro West Low Dur M	CS		9.45	**6.19**	**4.05**	3.52	—	4.6	+Avg	+Avg	★★★★	0.58	None
297	Metro West Total Ret	CI		9.73	**7.03**	**5.08**	5.53	—	5.0	+Avg	+Avg	★★★★	0.65	None
313	Northeast Investors	HY	—	7.76	12.10	9.44	9.12	5.65	6.8	Avg	-Avg	★★★	1.23	None
329	Payden Core Bond	CI		10.13	2.21	2.88	4.78	5.80	4.7	Avg	+Avg	★★★	0.45	None
330	Payden Limited Maturity	UB		9.87	4.51	2.71	2.34	**4.08**	4.3	Avg	-Avg	★★★	0.40	None
332	PIMCO Emerg Mkts Bd D	EB		11.05	9.35	10.80	15.09	—	5.0	Avg	+Avg	★★★	1.25	None
333	PIMCO For Bd USD-Hdgd D	IB		10.18	2.48	4.62	4.83	—	2.8	Avg	Low	★★★	0.95	None
334	PIMCO For Bd (Unhdgd) D	IB		10.18	6.17	—	—	—	2.9	—	—	—	0.95	None
335	PIMCO High-Yield D	HY		9.89	9.00	7.38	8.55	—	6.7	Avg	+Avg	★★★	0.90	None
336	PIMCO Low Duration D	CS		9.91	3.43	2.23	3.30	—	4.2	Avg	Avg	★★★	0.75	None
338	PIMCO Total Ret D	CI		10.38	3.66	3.67	5.19	—	4.4	+Avg	+Avg	★★★★	0.75	None
340	Pioneer High Yield A	HY		10.82	10.60	6.51	9.21	—	4.8	-Avg	+Avg	★★	1.06	4.50
348	Robeco WPG Core Bond	CI		10.53	3.12	3.20	5.06	6.21	4.1	+Avg	+Avg	★★★★	0.43	None
360	Schwab YieldPlus Inv	UB		9.69	**5.41**	**3.65**	**3.30**	—	5.0	High	Avg	★★★★★	0.58	None
367	SSgA Yield Plus	UB		9.94	5.02	3.21	2.42	3.91	5.0	-Avg	Low	★★	0.59	None
377	T. Rowe Price GNMA	GI		9.37	3.86	3.47	4.33	5.61	5.0	+Avg	-Avg	★★★★	0.66	None
381	T. Rowe Price Hi-Yld	HY		7.04	9.75	7.79	9.60	7.30	7.3	+Avg	-Avg	★★★★	0.77	Clsd
382	T. Rowe Price Intl Bd	IB		9.69	7.55	3.23	9.74	4.33	3.2	Avg	+Avg	★★★	0.86	None
393	T. Rowe Price New Inc	CI		8.92	4.13	3.86	4.92	5.62	4.6	Avg	Avg	★★★★	0.67	None
401	T. Rowe Price Spect Inc	MU		12.19	8.38	6.14	8.01	7.06	4.5	Avg	-Avg	★★★	0.73	None
402	T. Rowe Price T/F Inc	ML		10.05	5.14	4.38	5.48	5.47	4.4	+Avg	-Avg	★★★★	0.53	None

Bold numbers indicate *highest* return for the listed time period in each category.

Fixed-Income Funds

Page		Cat	Style Box	NAV	Total Return % through 12-29-06				Yield %	Morningstar Rating Statistics through 12-29-06			Expense Ratio %	Sales Charge %
					1Yr	Annualized 3Yr	5Yr	10Yr		Performance	Risk	Morningstar Rating		
	LB Agg				**2.43**	**3.62**	**5.87**	**6.16**						
403	T. Rowe Price T/F Sh-Int	MS		5.34	3.26	1.94	2.94	3.84	3.2	+Avg	+Avg	★★★★	0.51	None
404	T. Rowe Price T/F Hi-Yld	HM		12.14	6.88	**6.59**	**6.65**	5.59	4.8	Avg	Avg	★★★	0.70	None
405	T. Rowe Price US Try L/T	GL		11.37	1.07	4.07	5.79	6.78	4.5	Avg	-Avg	★★★	0.63	None
410	TCW Total Return Bond I	CI		9.47	5.27	4.60	5.55	**6.88**	4.8	High	-Avg	★★★★★	0.44	None
434	USAA Income	CI		12.11	4.16	3.88	5.02	6.11	4.8	+Avg	+Avg	★★★★	0.59	None
435	USAA Tax Ex Interm-Term	MI		13.20	4.59	3.98	4.95	5.28	4.2	High	-Avg	★★★★★	0.55	None
436	USAA Tax Ex Long-Term	ML		13.96	4.76	4.72	**6.16**	5.77	4.4	High	Avg	★★★★★	0.55	None
437	USAA Tax Ex Short-Term	MS		10.61	3.54	2.27	2.95	3.84	3.6	+Avg	Avg	★★★★	0.56	None
457	Vanguard GNMA	GI		10.21	**4.33**	3.93	4.76	6.00	5.1	High	Avg	★★★★★	0.21	None
462	Vanguard Hi-Yld Corp	HY		6.22	8.24	6.47	7.55	5.92	7.0	Avg	-Avg	★★★	0.25	None
463	Vanguard Hi-Yld T/E	MI		10.89	**5.53**	**4.95**	**5.70**	**5.63**	4.5	High	+Avg	★★★★★	0.15	None
465	Vanguard Ins L/T TE Inv	ML		12.64	4.92	4.07	5.58	5.70	4.6	High	+Avg	★★★★★	0.15	None
466	Vanguard Intm Bd Idx	CI		10.25	3.91	3.62	5.43	6.49	4.9	+Avg	High	★★★★	0.18	None
467	Vanguard Int-Tm US Trs	GI		10.76	3.14	2.95	**4.98**	**6.16**	4.7	High	High	★★★★★	0.26	None
471	Vanguard IntTm Inv-Gr Fd	CI		9.71	4.43	3.71	5.51	6.29	5.0	+Avg	+Avg	★★★★	0.21	None
472	Vanguard IntTm T/E	MI		13.35	4.43	3.29	4.44	4.85	4.2	+Avg	Avg	★★★★	0.16	None
477	Vanguard Lg-Tm T/E	ML		11.32	**5.16**	4.11	5.51	5.64	4.6	+Avg	High	★★★★	0.15	None
478	Vanguard Long-Tm InvGrde	CL		9.25	2.86	5.61	7.22	7.30	5.6	+Avg	+Avg	★★★★	0.25	None
479	Vanguard Long-Tm US Try	GL		11.13	**1.74**	5.13	6.84	7.41	4.9	Avg	+Avg	★★★	0.26	None
480	Vanguard LtdTm T/E	MS		10.71	3.33	1.98	3.00	3.85	3.3	+Avg	Avg	★★★★	0.16	None
489	Vanguard Sh-Tm Bd Idx	CS		9.89	4.09	2.36	3.30	5.07	4.3	+Avg	+Avg	★★★★	0.18	None
490	Vanguard ShtTm Fed	GS		10.28	**4.32**	2.48	3.39	**5.02**	4.0	+Avg	Avg	★★★★	0.20	None
491	Vanguard Short-Tm Trs	GS		10.28	3.77	2.18	3.36	4.89	4.2	+Avg	Avg	★★★★	0.26	None
492	Vanguard Sht-Tm Inv-Grade	CS		10.56	4.99	3.09	3.74	**5.16**	4.4	+Avg	Avg	★★★★	0.21	None
493	Vanguard Sht-Tm TE	MS		15.57	3.26	2.01	2.23	3.17	3.0	-Avg	Low	★★	0.16	None
505	Vanguard Total Bd Idx	CI		9.99	4.27	3.63	4.61	5.96	4.9	+Avg	Avg	★★★★	0.20	None
526	Western Asset Cr Bd Inst	CI		11.34	5.84	4.33	**5.88**	6.83	4.5	High	High	★★★★★	0.45	None
532	WF Adv S/T Muni Bd Inv	MS		9.79	**3.65**	**3.17**	**3.72**	**4.24**	3.6	High	Avg	★★★★★	0.66	None

Bold numbers indicate *highest* return for the listed time period in each category.

Supplementary Information

This section contains a glossary of investment terms. It explains how to use the data found in this publication to make better investment decisions.

Glossary

The following is a complete alphabetical listing of the terms and features found in the pages of Morningstar Funds 500.

A

Actual Fees
see Expenses and Fees

Address
Usually the location of the fund's distributor, this is where to write to receive a prospectus.

Advisor
This is the company that takes primary responsibility for managing the fund.

Alpha
see Modern Portfolio Theory Statistics

Analysis
see Morningstar's Take

Analyst Picks
We highlight a few of our favorites in each investment category. Funds that make the cut as Fund Analyst Picks have terrific long-term records, experienced managers, and moderate to low costs. However, we sometimes relax one of these criteria when a fund is truly superior in the other areas. For example, if a fund is supported by a number of talented, experienced analysts, we won't necessarily drop it from our picks list when there is a manager change. Also, a fund that is closed to new investors can still be a pick as long as it is still available to existing investors, and we think it's still a good investment. (For instance, we would give kudos to a fund that closes in a timely manner, before its asset base swells to the point that it's difficult to execute the fund's strategy.) There is no upper limit on the number of funds that can be named Analyst Picks in a category, but in major groups such as large blend, there are normally five to seven. Smaller categories often have fewer picks. A fund may be dropped from the list due to a shift in investment style, poor performance, a management change, organizational turmoil at the fund company level, and/or an increase in costs.

Average Credit Quality
see also Credit Analysis
Average credit quality gives a snapshot of the portfolio's overall credit quality. It is an average of each bond's credit rating, adjusted for its relative weighting in the portfolio. For the purposes of Morningstar's calculations, U.S. government securities are considered AAA bonds, nonrated municipal bonds generally are classified as BB, and other nonrated bonds generally are considered B.

Average Effective Duration
Average effective duration provides a measure of a fund's interest-rate sensitivity. The longer a fund's duration, the more sensitive the fund is to shifts in interest rates. The relationship among funds with different durations is straightforward: A fund with a duration of 10 years is expected to be twice as volatile as a fund with a five-year duration. Duration also gives an indication of how a fund's net asset value (NAV) will change as interest rates change. A fund with a five-year duration would be expected to lose 5% of its NAV if interest rates rose by 1 percentage point, or gain 5% if interest rates fell by 1 percentage point. Morningstar surveys fund companies for this information.

Average Effective Maturity
see also Average Nominal Maturity
Average effective maturity is a weighted average of all the maturities of the bonds in a portfolio, computed by weighting each bond's effective maturity by the market value of the security. Average effective maturity takes into consideration all mortgage prepayments, puts, and adjustable coupons. (Because Morningstar uses fund company calculations for this figure and because different companies use varying interest-rate assumptions in determining call likelihood and timing, we ask that companies not adjust for call provisions.) Longer-maturity funds are generally considered more interest-rate sensitive than their shorter counterparts.

Average Historical Rating
see Historical Profile, Rating and Risk

Average Nominal Maturity
see also Average Effective Maturity
Listed only for municipal-bond funds, this figure is computed by weighting the nominal maturity of each security in the portfolio by the market value of the

security, then averaging these weighted figures. Unlike a fund's effective maturity figure, it does not take into account prepayments, puts, or adjustable coupons.

Average Stock Percentage

see also Composition

For stock-oriented funds, we provide a yearly average stock position calculated by averaging all reported composition numbers for the year. These averages provide a valuable complement to the current composition numbers; investors can compare a fund's current level of market participation with its historical averages.

Average Weighted Coupon

see also Coupon Range

Average weighted coupon is computed by averaging each bond's coupon rate adjusted for its relative weighting in the portfolio. This figure indicates whether the fund is opting for a high- or low-coupon strategy and may serve as an indicator of interest-rate sensitivity, particularly for mortgage-backed funds or other funds with callable bonds. A high coupon frequently indicates less sensitivity to interest rates; a low coupon, the opposite.

Average Weighted Price

Average weighted price is computed for most bond funds by weighting the price of each bond by its relative size in the portfolio. This number reveals whether the fund favors bonds selling at prices above or below face value (premium or discount securities, respectively) and can also serve as an indicator of interest-rate sensitivity. This statistic is expressed as a percentage of par (face) value. It is not calculated for international-bond funds, because their holdings are often expressed in terms of foreign currencies.

B

+/- Benchmark Index

see Indexes

Best Fit Index

see also Indexes and Modern Portfolio Theory Statistics

The Best Fit Index is the market index whose monthly returns have correlated the most closely with a given fund's in the most recent 36 consecutive months.

Morningstar regresses the fund's monthly excess returns against those of several well-known market indexes. Best Fit signifies the index that provides the highest R-squared, or correlation with a given fund.

Beta

see also Modern Portfolio Theory Statistics

Beta, a component of Modern Portfolio Theory statistics, is a measure of a fund's sensitivity to market movements. It measures the relationship between a fund's excess return over T-bills and the excess return of the benchmark index. Equity funds are compared with the S&P 500 Index; bond funds are compared with the Lehman Brothers Aggregate Bond Index.

C

Capital Gains $

Capital gains are the profits received and distributed from the sale of securities within a fund's portfolio. This line shows a summary of the fund's annual capital gains distributions expressed in per-share dollar amounts. Both short- and long-term gains are included, as are options premiums and distributions from paid-in capital.

Capital Return %

see also Income Return % and Total Return

Morningstar provides the portion of a fund's total returns that was generated by realized and unrealized increases in the value of securities in the portfolio. Frequently, a stock fund's returns will be derived entirely from capital return. By looking at capital return and income return, an investor can see whether the fund's returns come from capital, from income, or from a combination of the two. Adding capital and income return will produce the fund's total return.

Category

see Morningstar Category

Composition

see also Average Stock Percentage

The composition percentages provide a simple breakdown of the fund's portfolio holdings, as of the date listed, into general investment classes at the bottom of the Portfolio Analysis section. Cash encompasses both actual cash and cash equivalents (fixed-income securities with maturities of one year or less). Negative percentages of cash indicate that the portfolio is leveraged, meaning it has borrowed against its own assets to buy more securities or that it has used other techniques to gain additional exposure to the market. The percentage listed as Stocks incorporates only the portfolio's straight common stocks. Bonds include every fixed-income security with a maturity of more than one year, from government notes to high-yield corporate bonds. Other includes preferred stocks (equity securities that pay dividends at a specified rate), as well as convertible bonds and convertible preferreds, which are corporate securities that are exchangeable for a set amount of another form of security (usually shares of common stock) at a prestated price. Other also includes all those not-so-neatly categorized securities, such as warrants and options.

Country Exposure

For each international portfolio, the country exposure information displays the top five countries in which the fund is invested. This information is gathered directly from the portfolios given by the fund companies.

Coupon Range

see also Average Weighted Coupon
Taxable-bond funds feature a table listing the breakdown of each portfolio's bond coupons, or rates of interest payments. The coupon range is designed to help an investor complete the picture suggested by the average weighted coupon statistic.

These ranges differ according to Morningstar Category and, due to changing interest rates, are subject to alteration over time. Whatever the breakdown may be, the first number is always exclusive and the second number is always inclusive. A range of 8% to 10%, for example, would exclude bonds that have a weighted coupon rate of exactly 8% but would include bonds with a weighted coupon rate of 10%. High-yield bond funds include "PIKs" in their coupon breakdown, which are payment-in-kind issues that make interest payments in the form of additional securities rather than cash.

The overall percentage of bond assets that fall within each coupon range is noted in the % of Bonds column. The Rel Cat column compares a fund with others in its Morningstar Category. The category average is set at 1.0.

Credit Analysis

see also Average Credit Quality
This section depicts the quality of bonds in a bond fund's portfolio. The credit analysis shows the percentage of fixed-income securities that fall within each credit-quality rating as assigned by Standard & Poor's or Moody's. Bonds issued and backed by the government, as well as those backed by government-linked organizations such as Fannie Mae and Freddie Mac, are of extremely high quality and thus are considered equivalent to bonds rated AAA, which is the highest possible rating a corporate issue can receive. Bonds with a BBB rating are the lowest grade that are still considered to be investment grade. Bonds that are rated BB or lower (often called junk bonds or high-yield bonds) are considered to be speculative. Any bonds that appear in the NR/NA category are either not rated by Standard & Poor's or Moody's, or did not have a rating available at the time of publication.

Current Investment Style

see also Investment Style Box
For equity funds, this section lists a fund portfolio's current averages for various portfolio statistics, including price/earnings, price/cash flow, and historical earnings growth. To provide perspective, we compare these measures with the funds' category average.

For bond funds, this section lists a portfolio's current duration, as well as averages for effective maturity, credit quality, weighted coupon, and price. These numbers are helpful in determining how much interest-rate and credit risk the portfolio currently has. For example, funds with high durations typically are very sensitive to changes in interest rates, whereas those with durations of just a year or two tend to be relatively insensitive to interest-rate changes. Funds with AAA or AA average credit-quality rankings take on less credit risk than those with, for example, B ratings, which indicate the portfolio holds a lot of high-yield (or junk) debt.

Morningstar currently uses price/cash flow, price/book, and median market cap to categorize foreign funds. This section also compares international-stock funds' current valuations with those of the MSCI EAFE Index, which is the most widely used benchmark for international offerings. Funds with low valuations typically hold stocks that aren't expected to grow rapidly, and therefore land in one of the value style boxes.

By contrast, portfolios with high valuations typically hold fast-growing issues.

D

Distributor

The distributor, also known as the fund underwriter, is the company that distributes the shares of the fund. This task usually includes promoting the fund and preparing and sending out fund literature.

Dollar-Cost Averaging

see Minimum Automatic Investment Plan

Duration

see Average Effective Duration

E

Emerging-Markets Securities

see Special Securities

Equity Style

see Investment Style Box

Exotic Mortgage-Backed Securities

see Special Securities

Expense Projections

see Expenses and Fees

Expense Ratio %

see also Expenses and Fees

The annual expense ratio, taken from the fund's annual report, expresses the percentage of assets deducted each fiscal year for fund expenses, including 12b-1 fees, management fees, administrative fees, operating costs, and all other asset-based costs incurred by the fund. Portfolio transaction fees, or brokerage costs, as well as initial or deferred sales charges, are not included in the expense ratio.

The expense ratio, which is deducted from the fund's average net assets, is accrued on a daily basis. If the fund's assets, listed in the lower part of the History

section, are small, the expense ratio can be quite high because the fund must meet its expenses from a restricted asset base. Conversely, as the net assets of the fund grow, the expense percentage should ideally diminish as expenses are spread across the wider base.

Expenses and Fees

see also Expense Ratio % and Load

Morningstar distinguishes among the myriad fees and expenses encountered with mutual funds. The different expenses and their characteristics are listed below.

Sales Fees

Also known as loads, sales fees list the maximum level of initial (front-end) and deferred (back-end) sales charges imposed by a fund. The scales of minimum and maximum charges are taken from a fund's prospectus. Because fees change frequently and are sometimes waived, it is wise to examine the fund's prospectus carefully for specific information before investing.

B (12b-1)

The 12b-1 fee represents the maximum annual charge deducted from fund assets to pay for distribution and marketing costs. This fee is expressed as a percentage. Some funds may be permitted to impose 12b-1 fees but are currently waiving all or a portion of the fees. Total allowable 12b-1 fees, excluding loads, are capped at 1% of average net assets annually. Of this, the distribution and marketing portion of the fee may account for up to 0.75%. The other portion of the overall 12b-1 fee, the service fee(s), is listed separately and may account for up to 0.25%. Often, funds charging a relatively low 12b-1 fee will allow shareholders to convert into a share class without the fee after a certain number of years. (These are normally deferred-load funds.) When this is the case, we note the conversion feature and the number of years after which it applies. Investors should check the fund's prospectus for full details.

D (Deferred Load)

Also called a contingent deferred sales charge or back-end load, a deferred load is an alternative to the traditional front-end sales charge, as it is deducted only at the time of sale of fund shares. The deferred-load structure commonly decreases to zero over a period of time. A typical deferred load's structure might have a 5% charge if shares are redeemed within the first year of ownership, and decline by a percentage point each year thereafter. These loads are normally applied to the lesser of original share price or current market value. It is important to note that although the deferred load declines each year, the accumulated annual distribution and services charges (the total 12b-1 fee) usually offsets this decline.

L (Front-End Load)

The initial sales charge or front-end load is a deduction made from each investment in the fund. The amount is generally based on the amount of the investment. Larger investments, both initial and cumulative, generally receive percentage discounts based on the dollar value invested. A typical front-end load might have a 4.75% charge for purchases of less than $50,000, which decreases as the amount of the investment increases. For those with $1 million to invest, the entire front-end load is waived. Investors who have significant assets and work with a financial advisor are therefore better off buying front-load shares than deferred-load shares.

No-Load

This label denotes the fund as a true no-load fund, charging no sales or 12b-1 fees.

R (Redemption Fee)

The redemption fee is an amount charged when money is withdrawn from the fund before a predetermined period elapses. This fee does not go back into the pockets of the fund company, but rather into the fund itself and thus does not represent a net cost to shareholders. Also, unlike contingent deferred sales charges, redemption fees typically operate only in short, specific time clauses, commonly 30, 180, or 365 days. However, some redemption fees exist for up to five years. Charges are not imposed after the stated time has passed. These fees are typically imposed to discourage market-timers, whose quick movements into and out of funds can be disruptive. The charge is normally imposed on the ending share value, appreciated or depreciated from the original value.

S (Service Fee)

The service fee is part of the total 12b-1 fee, but is listed separately on the page. Capped at a maximum 0.25%, the service fee is designed to compensate financial planners or brokers for ongoing shareholder-liaison services, which may include responding to customer inquiries and providing information on investments. An integral component of level-load and deferred-load funds, the fees were previously known as a trail commission. Only service fees adopted pursuant to Rule 12b-1 are tracked. Despite the implication of its name, service fees do not act as compensation for transfer agency or custodial services.

W (Waived)

This indicates that the fund is waiving sales fees at the time of publication. A fund may do this to attract new shareholders. Call the fund's distributor to ensure that the waiver is still active at the time of investment.

Management Fee

The management fee is the maximum percentage deducted from a fund's average net assets to pay an advisor or subadvisor. Often, as the fund's net assets grow, the percentage deducted for management fees decreases. Alternatively, the fund may compute the fee as a flat percentage of average net assets. A portion of the management fee may also be charged in the form of a group fee (G). To determine the group fee, the fund family creates a sliding scale for the family's total net assets and determines a percentage applied to each fund's asset base. The management fee might also be amended by or be primarily composed of a performance fee (P), which raises or lowers the management fee based on the fund's returns relative to an established index (we list the maximum by which the fee can increase or decrease).

It might also be composed of a gross income fee (I), a percentage based on the total amount of income generated by the investment portfolio.

The letter A denotes an administrative fee, which is the fund's maximum allowable charge for its management-fee structure, excluding advisor fees. Costs associated with Securities and Exchange Commission compliance may also be included under this label. Administrative fees often operate on a sliding scale and include the costs of basic fund operations, such as leasing office space. Investors should note that there is not necessarily a total expense differential between funds with disclosed administrative fees and funds without. Most funds roll administrative costs into their management fees; other funds, especially those with out-of-house administration, prefer to break them out. For this reason, we include administrative fees in the Management Fee area.

Actual Fees

Taken from the fund's prospectus, this area qualifies the management and 12b-1 distribution and service fees. Actual Fees most commonly represent the costs shareholders paid for management and distribution services over the fund's prior fiscal year. If fee levels have changed since the end of the most recent fiscal year, the actual fees will most commonly be presented as a recalculation based on the prior year's average monthly net assets using the new, current expenses. Although contract-type management and distribution costs are listed in a fund's prospectus, these are maximum amounts, and funds may waive a portion, or possibly all, of those fees. Actual Fees thus represent a close approximation of the true costs to shareholders.

Expense Projections (Three-, Five-, and 10-Year)

The SEC mandates that each fund list its expense projections. Found in the fund's prospectus, these figures show how much an investor would expect to pay in expenses, sales charges (loads), and fees over the next three, five, and 10 years, assuming a $10,000 investment that grows by 5% per year with redemption at the end of each time period. Expense projections are commonly based on the past year's incurred fees or an estimate of the current fiscal year's fees, should a portion of the overall fee structure change as of the printing of the fund's most current prospectus. Newer funds are required to print expense projections for only one- and three-year time periods because longer-term projections may not be possible to estimate.

F

Fixed-Income Style

see Investment Style Box

G

Growth

see also Investment Style Box and Value

Often contrasted with a value approach to investing, the term growth is used to describe an investment style in which a manager looks for equity securities with high rates of revenue or earnings growth. A company's valuations are generally not emphasized as much as they are in value-style investing.

Growth of $10,000

see also Performance

The Growth of $10,000 graph shows a fund's performance based on how $10,000 invested in the fund would have grown over time. The returns used in the graph are not load-adjusted. The growth of $10,000 begins at the fund's inception, or the first year listed on the graph, whichever is appropriate. Located alongside the fund's graph line is a line that represents the growth of $10,000 in either the S&P 500 Index (for stock funds and hybrid funds) or the LB Aggregate Index (for bond funds). Both lines are plotted on a logarithmic scale, so that identical percentage changes in the value of an investment have the same vertical distance on the graph. This provides a more accurate representation of performance than would a simple arithmetic graph. The graphs are scaled so that the full length of the vertical axis represents a tenfold increase in investment value. For securities with returns that have exhibited greater than a tenfold increase over the period shown in the graph, the vertical axis has been compressed accordingly.

Growth Measures

Long-Term Earnings Growth

Earnings are what are left of a firm's revenues after it pays all of its expenses, costs, and taxes. Companies whose earnings grow faster than those of their industry peers usually see better price performance for their stocks. Projected earnings growth is an estimate of a company's expected long-term growth in earnings, derived from all polled analysts' estimates. When reported for a mutual fund, it shows the weighted average of the projected growth in earnings for each stock in the fund's portfolio. This measure helps determine Morningstar's growth score for each stock and the overall growth orientation of the fund.

Historical Earnings Growth

Historical earnings growth shows the rate of increase in a company's earnings per share, based on up to four periodic time periods. When reported for a mutual fund, it shows the weighted average of the growth in earnings for each stock in the fund's portfolio. This measure helps determine Morningstar's growth score for each stock and the overall growth orientation of the fund.

Sales Growth

Sales growth shows the rate of increase in a company's sales per share, based on up to four periodic time periods, and it is considered the best gauge of how rapidly a company's core business is growing. When reported for a mutual fund, it shows the weighted average of the sales-growth rates for each stock in the fund's portfolio. This measure helps determine Morningstar's growth score for each stock and the overall growth orientation of the fund.

Cash Flow Growth

Cash flow tells you how much cash a business is actually generating—its earnings before depreciation, amortization, and noncash charges. Sometimes called cash earnings, it's considered a gauge of liquidity and solvency. Cash-flow growth shows the rate of increase in a company's cash flow per share, based on up to four time periods. When reported for a mutual fund, it shows the weighted average of the growth in cash flow for each stock in the fund's portfolio. This measure helps determine Morningstar's growth score for each stock and the overall growth orientation of the fund.

Book Value Growth

Book value is, in theory, what would be left over for shareholders if a company shut down its operations, paid off all its creditors, collected from all its debtors, and liquidated itself. In practice, however, the value of assets and liabilities can change substantially from when they are first recorded. Book value growth shows the rate of increase in a company's book value per share, based on up to four periodic time periods. When reported for a mutual fund, it shows the weighted average of the growth rates in book value for each stock in the fund's portfolio. This measure helps determine Morningstar's growth score for each stock and the overall growth orientation of the fund.

H

Historical Profile, Star Rating, and Overall Assessment

see also Morningstar Category

The star rating displayed in the Historical Profile section is a fund's overall risk-adjusted star rating. The star ratings for the three time periods in the Rating and Risk section are combined here. In ascending order, these categories are Lowest (1 star), Below Average (2 stars), Neutral (3 stars), Above Average (4 stars), and Highest (5 stars). Funds less than three years old are listed as Not Rated.

History

see also individual listings of terms in History section

The History section is a table of annual information providing performance and expense statistics along with relative comparisons on a yearly basis. The Overview pages found at the beginning of each category list some of the same statistics, but these are calculated as averages for each fund category (with the exception of net assets, which is an aggregate figure).

I

Inception

The date of inception is the date on which the fund commenced operation. If an asterisk appears next to the date that indicates the fund's inception was not on the first business day of the year. Returns for that partial year appear in the History section of the page. (Those returns are also marked with an asterisk.)

Income $

Income reflects the dividends and interest generated by a fund's holdings. This area shows a fund's yearly income distribution expressed in per-share dollar amounts.

Income Distribution

Income distribution represents the number of times per year that a fund intends to make income payments (from either dividends or interest). A fund generally makes distributions monthly, quarterly, semiannually, or annually.

Income Ratio %

The fund's income ratio reveals the percentage of current income earned per share. It is calculated by dividing the fund's net investment income by its average net assets. (Net investment income is the total income of the fund, less expenses.) An income ratio can be negative if a fund's expenses exceed its income, which can occur with funds that have high costs or tend to emphasize capital gains rather than income. Because the income ratio is based on a fund's fiscal year and is taken directly from the fund's annual shareholder report, it may not exactly correspond with other calendar-year information on the page.

Income Return %

see also Capital Return % and Total Return
Income return is that portion of a fund's total returns that was derived from income distributions. Income return will often be higher than capital return for bond funds, and typically lower for stock funds. Adding the income return and the capital return together will produce the fund's total return.

Income Return Percentile Rank

This ranking shows how a fund's income distributions have stacked up against other funds in its category. Each calendar year features a ranking, with 1 being the highest percentile and 100 the lowest. We use the income-return figures printed in the History section to determine the rankings. This ranking is calculated over a trailing 12-month figure.

Indexes

see also Best Fit Index

Benchmark Index
A benchmark index gives investors a point of reference for evaluating a fund's performance. In all cases where such comparisons are made, Morningstar uses the S&P 500 Index as the basic benchmark for stock-oriented funds. The Lehman Brothers Aggregate Bond Index is used as the benchmark index for all bond funds. We also provide a comparison with a secondary, specialized benchmark. Because the S&P 500 Index is composed almost entirely of large-cap domestic stocks, it is a good performance measure for large-cap domestic-stock funds and the overall market, but other comparisons are less useful. Comparing a foreign

large-value fund with the S&P 500 Index, for example, does not show how the fund has done relative to foreign stock markets, so a fund's total return in the History and Performance sections is compared with a more specialized index.

Industry Weightings

see also Relative Comparisons and Sector Weightings
For specialty funds (also called sector funds), we replace the standard sector weightings, which include broad industry classifications such as hardware, with a breakdown of the fund's weightings in the sector's subindustries, or subsectors. Each sector has its own breakdown of subsectors, which can help investors determine which specific areas of an industry the fund invests in and how pure its focus is. The industry weightings show at a glance whether a fund is conservatively diversified across a sector, betting on just a couple of risky subsectors to charge up returns, or crouching defensively in the mildest corner of the specialty. The fund's weightings relative to its category average are also shown.

Each specialty's breakdown also includes an Other classification, but a large weighting there doesn't mean the fund is investing outside of its specialty. This is merely a catchall designation to classify the stocks that don't meet the exact criteria for any specific subsector. It's impossible to capture every nook and cranny of the sprawling technology category, for example, in the eight subsectors included on the page. Thus, a fair number of tech stocks fall into Other.

Investment Style Box

see also Current Investment Style, Growth, Investment Style History, Market Capitalization, Morningstar Category, and Value
To eliminate confusion about the many fund types, Morningstar designed the style box, a visual tool for better understanding a fund's true investment strategy. Based on an analysis of a fund's portfolio, the Morningstar style box is a snapshot of the types of securities held by the fund. The style box is calculated with methodology similar to that used to assign the Morningstar Categories. By providing an easy-to-understand visual representation of stock and fund characteristics, the Morningstar style box allows for informed comparisons and portfolio construction based on actual holdings, as opposed to assumptions based on a

fund's name or how it is marketed. The style box also forms the basis for Morningstar's style-based fund categories and market indexes.

Domestic-Stock Style Box
The Morningstar domestic-stock style box is a nine-square grid that provides a graphical representation of the "investment style" of stocks and mutual funds. It classifies securities according to market capitalization (the vertical axis) and growth and value factors (the horizontal axis). Note: Fixed-income funds are classified according to credit quality (the vertical axis) and sensitivity to changes in interest rates (the horizontal axis).

Stock Style Box

Risk	Investment Style			Average Weighted Market Capitalization
	Value	Blend	Growth	
Low ◯	Large-cap Value	Large-cap Blend	Large-cap Growth	Large
Moderate ◯	Mid-cap Value	Mid-cap Blend	Mid-cap Growth	Mid
High ◯	Small-cap Value	Small-cap Blend	Small-cap Growth	Small

Within the stock style box grid, nine possible combinations exist, ranging from large-cap value for the safest funds to small-cap growth for the riskiest.

How It Works
Style box assignments begin at the individual stock level. Morningstar determines the investment style of each individual stock in its database. The style attributes of individual stocks are then used to determine the style classification of stock mutual funds.

The Horizontal Axis
The scores for a stock's value and growth characteristics determine its placement on the horizontal axis of the stock style box:

Value Score Components and Weights

Forward-looking measures

Price/projected earnings	50.0%

Historical-based measures

Price/book	12.5%
Price/sales	12.5%
Price/cash flow	12.5%
Dividend yield	12.5%

Growth Score Components and Weights

Forward-looking measures

Long-term projected earnings growth	50.0%

Historical-based measures

Historical earnings growth	12.5%
Sales growth	12.5%
Cash flow growth	12.5%
Book value growth	12.5%

Growth and value characteristics for each individual stock are compared with those of other stocks within the same capitalization band and are scored from zero to 100 for both value and growth. To determine the overall style score, the value score is subtracted from the growth score.

The resulting number can range from 100 (for low-yield, extremely growth-oriented stocks) to -100 (for high-yield, low-growth stocks). A stock is classified as growth if the net score equals or exceeds the "growth threshold" (normally about 25 for large-cap stocks). It is deemed value if its score equals or falls below the "value threshold" (normally about -15 for large-cap stocks).

If the score lies between the two thresholds, the stock is classified as "core."

The thresholds between value, core, and growth stocks vary to some degree over time, as the distribution of stock styles changes in the market. However, on average, the three stock styles each account for approximately one third of the total free float in each size category.

The Vertical Axis

Rather than a fixed number of large-cap or small-cap stocks, Morningstar uses a flexible system that isn't adversely affected by overall movements in the market to classify stocks as small, medium, or large. Large-cap stocks account for the top 70% of the capitalization of the Morningstar domestic-stock universe; mid-cap stocks represent the next 20%; and small-cap stocks represent the balance. The Morningstar stock universe represents approximately 99% of the U.S. market for actively traded stocks.

Moving from Individual Stocks to Funds

A stock fund is an aggregation of individual stocks and its style is determined by the style assignments of the stocks it owns. By plotting all of a fund's stocks on the stock style grid, the range of stock styles included in the fund immediately becomes apparent. An asset-weighted average of the stocks' net value/growth scores determines a fund's horizontal placement: value, growth, or blend.

A fund's vertical placement is determined by its "market cap," which is defined as the geometric mean of the market capitalization (or average weighted market cap) for the stocks it owns, where:

Cap1 = the capitalization of stock 1 and W1 = the % weight in the portfolio and the geometric mean of market capitalization

$$=(Cap1^{W1})(Cap2^{W2})(Cap3^{W3})(Cap4^{W4})...(CapN^{WN})$$

For a simple example, consider a fund that owns just three stocks:

25% stake in Stock A, market cap = $1.85 Billion
35% stake in Stock B, market cap = $3.56 Billion
40% stake in Stock C, market cap = $8.58 Billion

Its geometric mean of market capitalization would equal:

($1.85 bil $^{.25}$)($3.56 bil $^{.35}$)($8.58 bil $^{.40}$) = $4.30 Billion

Note that this number is larger than the fund's median market cap—the capitalization of the median stock in its portfolio. That's because stock C, with a relatively higher market cap, occupies the biggest slice of the portfolio. The geometric mean better identifies the portfolio's "center of gravity." In other words, it provides more accurate insight into how market trends (as defined by capitalization) might affect the portfolio.

Style box assignments for stocks are updated each month. Assignments for funds are recalculated whenever Morningstar receives updated portfolio holdings for the fund.

Using the Style Box

In general, a growth-oriented fund will hold the stocks of companies that the portfolio manager believes will increase earnings faster than the rest of the market. A value-oriented fund contains mostly stocks the manager thinks are currently undervalued in price and will eventually see their worth recognized by the market. A blend fund might be a mix of growth stocks and value stocks, or it may contain stocks that exhibit both characteristics.

Understanding how different types of stocks behave is crucial for building a diversified, style-controlled portfolio of stocks or mutual funds. The Morningstar style box helps investors construct portfolios based on the characteristics, or style factors, of all the stocks and funds that portfolio includes.

Methodology Changes

We made significant changes to the style box methodology for domestic stocks and stock funds, effective June 30, 2002. Previously, a stock or fund's horizontal placement within the style box was determined by two factors: its combined relative price/book and price/earnings ratios. Our new system uses an enhanced 10-factor model, with separate scores for value and growth characteristics. The new methodology better measures the characteristics of individual stocks and is also more in line with the way portfolio managers look at stocks.

We also made changes to the way we determine capitalization bands and calculate a fund's market capitalization. Instead of basing the size breakpoints using a specific number of stocks, Morningstar now defines large-cap stocks as those that account for the top 70% of the domestic-stock market, mid-cap stocks as those that account for the next 20%, and small caps for the remaining 10%.

For mutual funds, we switched from using median market capitalization to the geometric mean of market capitalization (or average weighted market-cap). The latter method results in a number that better represents how market trends (as defined by capitalization) might affect the portfolio.

International-Stock Style Box

These style boxes are similar to the domestic-stock style box described above.

On the vertical axis, international-stock funds are grouped as small-, mid-, and large-cap funds. Rather than using a fixed number of large-cap or small-cap stocks, Morningstar uses a flexible system that isn't adversely affected by overall movements in the market. World equity markets are first divided into seven style zones: United States, Latin America, Canada, Europe, Japan, Asia ex-Japan, and Australia/New Zealand. The stocks in each style zone are further subdivided into size groups. Giant-cap stocks account for the top 40% of the capitalization of each style zone; large-cap stocks represent the next 30%; mid-cap stocks represent the next 20%; small-cap stocks represent the next 7% and micro-cap stocks represent the smallest 3%. For value-growth scoring, giant-cap stocks are included with the large-cap group for that style zone, and micro-caps are scored against the small-cap group for that style zone.

On the horizontal axis, international-stock funds, like their domestic counterparts, are separated into value, blend, and growth funds. Morningstar uses 10 different stock characteristics to measure value and growth, and this produces more accurate and stable stock and portfolio style assignments. Morningstar uses both forward- looking and historical-based components to ensure that information available to active portfolio managers is incorporated in the model. This robust approach to style analysis is a powerful lens for under-standing stocks, funds, and portfolios.

Bond Style Box

Domestic- and international-bond funds feature their own Morningstar style box, which focuses on two pillars of bond performance: interest-rate sensitivity and credit quality. Morningstar splits bond funds into three groups of rate sensitivity as determined by duration (short, intermediate, and long) and three credit-quality groups (high, medium, and low). These groupings graphically display a portfolio's average effective duration and credit quality. As with stock funds, nine possible combinations exist, ranging from short duration/high quality for the safest funds to long duration/low quality for the more volatile.

Along the horizontal axis of the style box lies the interest-rate sensitivity of a fund's bond portfolio based

Bond Style Box

Risk	Duration			Quality
	Value	Blend	Growth	
Low ○	Short-term High Quality	Interm-term High Quality	Long-term High Quality	High
Moderate ○	Short-term Medium Quality	Interm-term Medium Quality	Long-term Medium Quality	Medium
High ◉	Short-term Low Quality	Interm-term Low Quality	Long-Term Low Quality	Low

Within the bond style box grid, nine possible combinations exist, ranging from short duration or maturity/high quality for the safest funds to long duration or maturity/low quality for the riskiest.

on average effective duration. This figure, which is calculated by the fund companies, weights each bond's duration by its relative size within the portfolio. Duration provides a more accurate description of a bond's true interest-rate sensitivity than does maturity because it takes into consideration all mortgage prepayments, puts and call options, and adjustable coupons. Funds with an average effective duration of less than 3.5 years qualify as short term. Funds with an average effective duration of greater than or equal to 3.5 years and less than or equal to six years are classified as intermediate. Funds with an average effective duration of greater than six years are considered long term. (The duration ranges are slightly different for municipal-bond funds: Less than 4.5 years is short term; 4.5 to seven years is intermediate; greater than seven years is long term.)

Along the vertical axis of a bond style box lies the average credit-quality rating of a bond portfolio. Funds that have an average credit rating of AAA or AA are categorized as high quality. Bond portfolios with average ratings of A or BBB are medium quality, and those rated BB and below are categorized as low quality. For the purposes of Morningstar's calculations, U.S. government securities are considered AAA bonds, non-rated municipal bonds generally are classified as BB, and all other nonrated bonds generally are considered B.

For hybrid categories, both stock and bond style boxes appear on the page.

Investment Style History

see also Investment Style Box

A fund's Morningstar style box position can change over time, perhaps because of a manager or strategy change or because market forces affect a portfolio's price ratios. To give investors an idea of how a fund's investment style has varied, a row of style boxes is included above the Performance Graph section. Each style box shows where a fund placed at the end of the calendar year. This feature chronicles such aspects as consistency in investment style, or it may help explain why a stock fund did especially well or poorly during growth- or value-driven periods. It could also shed light on why a bond fund performed well or poorly in periods when lower-quality issues were in favor.

Investment Value

see Performance

IRA Purchase

see Minimum Purchase

L

Load

see also Expenses and Fees

Load denotes either a fund's maximum initial or deferred sales charge. For initial, or front-end loads, this figure is expressed as a percentage of the initial investment and is incurred upon purchase of fund shares. For deferred sales charges (also known as back-end loads or contingent deferred sales charges), the amount charged is based on the lesser of the initial or final value of the shares sold. If the fund does not have a load and remains open to investors, "None" appears. We list "12b-1 only" in this space if the fund has no sales fees, but does have a 12b-1 fee. If the fund no longer offers shares to new investors, "Closed" is listed here. A percentage followed by a W indicates that, at the time of publication, the fund is waiving its load for the general public.

Load-Adjusted Return %

For this statistic, total returns are adjusted downward to account for sales charges and are listed for the trailing one-, three-, five-, and 10-year periods. For funds with front-end loads, the full amount of the load is deducted.

For deferred, or back-end loads, the percentage charged often declines the longer shares are held. This charge, often coupled with a 12b-1 fee, usually disappears entirely after several years. Morningstar adjusts the deferred load accordingly when making this calculation. For funds that lack a 10-year history, we provide an annualized load-adjusted return figure for the period since the fund's inception.

M

Management Fee

see Expenses and Fees

Manager

see Portfolio Manager

Manager Change

see also Portfolio Manager

It is important for investors to know how much of a fund's performance can be attributed to current management. We track manager changes by using two symbols, which indicate when a full or partial manager change has occurred. The symbol (▼) marks a total manager change, when an entirely new manager or team of comanagers assumed fund leadership. The symbol (▽) indicates a partial change, when at least one manager remains with the fund while another joins or leaves.

Market Cap

see also Market Capitalization

Shown for domestic-stock funds, this section gives investors a view of the different sizes of companies in a fund's portfolio. Every month, we break down a stock portfolio into five different sizes of companies by their market capitalization and show what percentage of a fund's stock assets is devoted to each. Instead of using stationary market-cap cutoffs, we base our boundaries on percentiles: We call the largest 1% of U.S. companies Giant, the next 4% Large, the next 15% Medium, the next 30% Small, and the bottom 50% Micro. The Market Cap section is designed to help investors complete the picture suggested by the median market cap statistic. While average weighted market cap pinpoints the size of the average holding, this section allows investors to see the whole range of companies held by the fund.

Market Capitalization (Average Weighted)

see also Market Cap and Relative Comparisons

For domestic-stock offerings, this measures the portfolio's "center of gravity," in terms of its market-cap exposure. A market capitalization is calculated for each stock. Its weight in the average weighted market cap calculation is then determined by the percentage of stocks it consumes in the overall portfolio. For example, a stock that is a 10% position in a fund will have twice as much influence on the calculation than a stock that is a 5% stake. See Investment Style Box for a more-detailed explanation.

Maturity

see Average Effective Maturity and Average Nominal Maturity

Mean

see Standard Deviation

Minimum Automatic Investment Plan

(Min Auto Inv Plan)

This indicates the smallest amount with which an investor may enter a fund's automatic-investment plan—an arrangement where the fund takes money on a monthly, quarterly, semiannual, or annual basis from the shareholder's checking account. Often, the normal minimum initial purchase requirements are waived in lieu of this systematic investment plan. Studies indicate that regular automatic investment (also known as dollar-cost averaging) can be a very successful investment plan for long-term investors.

Minimum Purchase

Minimum purchase indicates the smallest investment amount a fund will accept to establish a new account. Also noted is the smallest additional purchase a fund will accept in an existing account. (This figure follows the designation ADD). "None" indicates initial or additional investments can be of any amount. In addition, we include the smallest permissible initial investment a fund will accept in an individual retirement account (IRA). If the fund does not offer an IRA program, N/A will appear.

Modern Portfolio Theory Statistics

Alpha, beta, and R-squared are components of Modern Portfolio Theory (MPT), which is a standard financial and academic method for assessing the performance of a fund, relative to a benchmark. To understand how to use MPT stats, readers may want to begin with the following explanation of R-squared, then move to beta, and finally to alpha. The three statistics should be used in conjunction with one another.

Morningstar bases alpha, beta, and R-squared on a least-squares regression of the fund's excess return over Treasury bills compared with the excess returns of the fund's benchmark index (the S&P 500 for stock-oriented funds and the Lehman Brothers Aggregate Bond Index for bond funds). These calculations are computed for the trailing 36-month period.

Morningstar also shows additional alpha, beta, and R-squared statistics based on a regression against the Best Fit Index. The Best Fit Index for each fund is selected based on the highest R-squared result from separate regressions on a number of indexes. (See also Best Fit Index. If the standard index already has the highest R-squared, it will be shown again as the Best Fit Index.) For example, many high-yield funds show low R-squared results and thus a low degree of correlation when regressed against the standard bond index, the Lehman Brothers Aggregate. These low R-squared results indicate that the index does not explain well the behavior of most high-yield funds. Most high-yield funds, however, show significantly higher R-squared results when regressed against the CSFB High-Yield Bond Index.

Both the standard and best-fit results can be useful to investors. The standard index R-squared statistics can help investors plan the diversification of their portfolio of funds. For example, an investor who wishes to diversify and already owns a fund with a very high correlation (and thus a high R-squared) with the S&P 500 might choose not to buy another fund that correlates closely to that index. In addition, the Best Fit Index can be used to compare the betas and alphas of similar funds that show the same Best Fit Index.

Alpha

Alpha measures the difference between a fund's actual returns and its expected performance, given its level of risk (as measured by beta). A positive alpha figure indicates the fund has performed better than its beta would predict. In contrast, a negative alpha indicates a fund has underperformed, given the expectations established by the fund's beta. Many investors see alpha as a measurement of the value added or subtracted by a fund's manager.

There are limitations to alpha's ability to accurately depict a fund's added or subtracted value. In some cases, a negative alpha can result from the expenses that are present in the fund figures but are not present in the figures of the comparison index. Alpha is completely dependent on the accuracy of beta: If the investor accepts beta as a conclusive definition of risk, a positive alpha would be a conclusive indicator of good fund performance.

Beta

Beta is a measure of a fund's sensitivity to market movements. It measures the relationship between a fund's excess return over T-bills and the excess return of the benchmark index. Morningstar calculates beta using the same regression equation as the one used for alpha, which regresses excess return for the fund against excess return for the index. This approach differs slightly from other methodologies that rely on a regression of raw returns.

By definition, the beta of the benchmark (in this case, an index) is 1.00. Accordingly, a fund with a 1.10 beta has performed 10% better than its benchmark index after deducting the T-bill rate in up markets and 10% worse in down markets, assuming all other factors remain constant. Conversely, a beta of 0.85 indicates that the fund has performed 15% worse than the index in up markets and 15% better in down markets. A low beta does not imply that the fund has a low level of volatility, though; rather, a low beta means only that the fund's market-related risk is low. A specialty fund that invests primarily in gold, for example, will usually have a low beta (and a low R-squared), as its performance is tied more closely to the price of gold and gold-mining stocks than to the overall stock market. Thus, although the specialty fund might fluctuate wildly because of rapid changes in gold prices, its beta will remain low.

R-squared

R-squared ranges from 0 to 100 and reflects the percentage of a fund's movements that are explained by movements in its benchmark index. An R-squared of 100 means that all movements of a fund are completely correlated with movements in the index. Thus, index funds that invest only in S&P 500 stocks will have an R-squared very close to 100. Conversely, a low R-squared indicates that very few of the fund's movements are explained by movements in its benchmark index. An R-squared measure of 35, for example, means that only 35% of the fund's movements can be explained by movements in its benchmark index. Therefore, R-squared can be used to ascertain the significance of a particular beta or alpha. Generally, a high R-squared will indicate a more reliable beta figure. If the R-squared is low, then the beta explains less of the fund's performance.

Morningstar Category

see also Historical Profile and Investment Style Box
While the investment objective stated in a fund's prospectus may or may not reflect how the fund actually invests, the Morningstar Category is assigned based on the underlying securities in each portfolio.

The Morningstar Category helps investors make meaningful comparisons among funds. The categories make it easier to build well-diversified portfolios, assess potential risk, and identify the top-performing funds.

The following is a list and explanation of the categories. We place funds in a given category based on their portfolio statistics and compositions over the past three years. If the fund is new and has no portfolio history, we estimate where it will fall before giving it a more permanent category assignment. When necessary, we may change a category assignment based on recent changes to the portfolio.

Stock Funds

Domestic-Stock Funds

Funds with at least 70% of assets in domestic stocks are categorized based on the style and size of the stocks they typically own. The style and size divisions reflect those used in the investment style box: value, blend, or growth style and small, medium, or large. Based on their investment style over the past three years, diversified domestic-stock funds are placed in one of the nine categories shown below:

Large Growth	Mid-cap Growth	Small Growth
Large Blend	Mid-cap Blend	Small Blend
Large Value	Mid-cap Value	Small Value

Morningstar also includes several other domestic-stock categories: Communications, Financial, Health Care, Natural Resources, Precious Metals, Real Estate, Technology, Utilities, Convertible Bond (convertible-bond funds have at least 50% of their assets invested in convertible securities), Conservative Allocation (conservative-allocation funds invest in both stocks and bonds, with just 20% to 50% of assets in stocks), and Moderate Allocation (moderate-allocation funds invest in both stocks and bonds, with more than 50% in stocks), Long Short (long short funds take long positions in securities that appear attractive and short positions in securities that appear to be unattractive), Target Date 2000-2014 (target-date portfolios provide diversified exposure to stocks, bonds, and cash for those investors who have a specific date in mind—in this case, the years 2000-2014), Target Date 2015-2029, and Target Date 2030+.

International-Stock Funds

Stock funds that have invested 40% or more of their equity holdings in foreign stocks (on average over the past three years) are placed in an international-stock category, based on the parameters listed below.

Europe: at least 75% of stocks invested in Europe.

Latin America: at least 75% of stocks invested in Latin America.

Diversified Emerging Markets: at least 50% of stocks invested in emerging markets.

Diversified Asia/Pacific: at least 65% of stocks invested in Pacific countries, with at least an additional 10% of stocks invested in Japan.

Asia/Pacific ex-Japan: at least 75% of stocks in Pacific countries, with less than 10% of stocks invested in Japan.

Japan: at least 75% of stocks invested in Japan.

Foreign Large Value: a majority of assets invested in large-cap foreign stocks that are value-oriented (based on low price/book and price/cash flow ratios, relative to the MSCI EAFE Index).

Foreign Large Blend: a majority of assets invested in large-cap foreign stocks, where neither growth nor value characteristics predominate.

Foreign Large Growth: a majority of assets invested in large-cap foreign stocks that are growth-oriented (based on high price/book

and price/cash flow ratios, relative to the MSCI EAFE Index).

Foreign Small/Mid-Cap Value: a majority of assets invested in small- and mid-cap foreign stocks that are value-oriented (based on low price/book and price/cash flow ratios, relative to the MSCI EAFE Index).

Foreign Small/Mid-Cap Growth: a majority of assets invested in small- and mid-cap foreign stocks that are growth-oriented (based on high price/book and price/cash flow ratios, relative to the MSCI EAFE Index).

World: an international fund having more than 20% of stocks invested in the United States.

World Allocation: a fund with stock holdings of greater than 20% but less than 70% of the portfolio where 40% of the stocks and bonds are foreign. Also, must have at least 10% of assets invested in bonds.

Bond Funds

Funds with 80% or more of their assets invested in bonds are classified as bond funds. Bond funds are divided into two main groups for classification purposes: taxable bond and municipal bond.

Note: For all bond funds, maturity figures are used only when duration figures are unavailable.

Taxable-Bond Funds

Long-Term Government: at least 90% of bond portfolio invested in government issues with a duration of greater than six years, or an average effective maturity of greater than 10 years.

Intermediate-Term Government: at least 90% of bond portfolio invested in government issues with a duration of greater than or equal to 3.5 years and less than or equal to six years, or an average effective maturity of greater than or equal to four years and less than or equal to 10 years.

Short-Term Government: at least 90% of bond portfolio invested in government issues with a duration of greater than or equal to one year and less than 3.5 years, or an average effective maturity of greater than or equal to one year and less than four years.

Inflation Protected: inflation-protected bond portfolios primarily invest in fixed-income securities that increase coupon and/or principal payments at the rate of inflation. These bonds can be issued by any organization, but the U.S. Treasury is currently the largest issuer of these types of securities.

Long-Term Bond: focuses on corporate and other investment-grade issues with an average duration of more than six years, or an average effective maturity of more than 10 years.

Intermediate-Term Bond: focuses on corporate and other investment-grade issues with an average duration of greater than or equal to 3.5 years but less than or equal to six years, or an average effective maturity of greater than or equal to four but less than or equal to 10 years.

Short-Term Bond: focuses on corporate and other investment-grade issues with an average duration of greater than or equal to one but less than 3.5 years, or an average effective maturity of greater than or equal to one but less than four years.

Ultrashort Bond: used for funds with an average duration or an average effective maturity of less than one year. This category includes general corporate and government bond funds, and excludes any international, convertible, multisector, and high-yield bond funds.

High-Yield Bond: at least 65% of assets in bonds rated below BBB.

Multisector Bond: seeks income by diversifying assets among several fixed-income sectors, usually U.S. government obligations, foreign bonds, and high-yield domestic debt securities.

Bank Loan: invests primarily in floating-rate bank loans instead of bonds. In exchange for their credit risk, they offer high interest payments that typically float above a common short-term benchmark.

World Bond: at least 40% of bonds invested in foreign markets.

Emerging-Markets Bond: at least 65% of assets in emerging-markets bonds.

Municipal-Bond Funds

High-Yield Municipal: Municipal fund that over the past three years has kept an average of 50% or more of assets in issues rated BBB or below. For the purposes of this calculation, nonrated issues are considered to be high-yield debt.

Muni National Long-Term: a national fund with an average duration of more than seven years or an average maturity of more than 12 years.

Muni National Intermediate-Term: a national fund with an average duration of greater than or equal to 4.5 years but less than or equal to seven years, or an average maturity of greater than or equal to five years but less than or equal to 12 years.

Muni New York Long-Term: a fund with at least 80% of assets in New York municipal debt, with an average duration of more than seven years or an average maturity of more than 12 years.

Muni New York Intermediate/Short: a fund with at least 80% of assets in New York municipal debt, with an average duration of up to seven years.

Muni California Long-Term: a fund with at least 80% of assets in California municipal debt, with an average duration of more than seven years or an average maturity of more than 12 years.

Muni California Intermediate/Short: a fund with at least 80% of assets in California municipal debt, with an average duration of up to seven years.

Muni Single-State Long-Term: a single-state fund with an average duration of more than seven years or an average maturity of more than 12 years.

Muni Single-State Intermediate: a single state fund with an average duration of greater than or equal to 4.5 years but less than or equal to seven years, or an average maturity of greater than or equal to five years but less than or equal to 12 years.

Muni National Short-Term: focuses on municipal debt/bonds with an average duration of less than 4.5 years or an average maturity of less than five years.

Morningstar Risk-Adjusted Rating
see Rating and Risk

Morningstar Style Box
see Investment Style Box

Morningstar's Take
The analysis interprets and enhances the numerical data that appear on the page in an effort to provide an assessment of a fund's worth. To accomplish this, a Morningstar analyst scrutinizes past shareholder reports, puts historical performance into the perspective of market trends, and whenever possible, interviews the

fund manager or another fund official. Although many people are involved in producing the Morningstar page, the analyst is ultimately responsible for its content.

N

NAV
see Net Asset Value

Net Assets
see also Total Assets
This figure gives the fund's asset base, net of fees and expenses, at year end of past calendar years and at month end for the current year.

Net Asset Value
A fund's net asset value (NAV) represents its per-share price. A fund's NAV is derived by dividing the total net assets of the fund by the number of shares outstanding.

No-Load
see also Expenses and Fees
This label denotes the fund as a true no-load fund, charging no sales or 12b-1 fees.

NTF Plans
This indicates which No Transaction Fee programs offer the fund. Wrap programs are not included in this section.

O

Options / Futures / Warrants
see Special Securities

Other Measures
see Modern Portfolio Theory Statistics, Sharpe Ratio, and Standard Deviation

P

Partial Manager Change
see Manager Change

P/E
see Price/Earnings Ratio

Percent of Assets (% Assets)
see % Assets entry in Portfolio Analysis

Percentile Rank (% Rank)
see also Performance
Located in the Performance and History sections, these rankings allow investors to compare a fund's total returns with those of other funds.

In the Performance section, we compare the fund's total return for various time periods against the same Morningstar Category (% Rank Cat). In the History section, we compare a fund's calendar-year total returns with its category's (Total Rtn % Rank Cat). In both sections, a fund's total returns are ranked on a scale from 1 to 100 where 1 represents the highest-returning 1% of funds and 100 represents the lowest-returning funds. Thus, in the Performance section, a percentile rank of 15 under the % Rank Cat column for the trailing three-month period indicates that the fund's three-month return placed in the top 15% of all funds in its category for that time period.

Performance
see also Percentile Rank, Tax Analysis, and Total Return
The tables in this section display the fund's total return figures for various time periods. The trailing total returns are as of the date listed in the section heading above. The trailing total returns are accompanied by relative statistics that allow readers to compare the returns with appropriate indexes and category averages.

Investment Value Graph
The Investment Value graph line shows a fund's performance trend, derived from the fund's historical growth of $10,000. It provides a visual depiction of how a fund has amassed its returns, including the performance swings its shareholders have endured along the way. The growth of $10,000 begins at the date of the fund's inception, or if the fund has been in existence for more than 12 years, then growth of $10,000 begins

at the first year listed on the graph. Also, featured in the graph is the performance of an index (S&P 500 or MSCI EAFE), which allows investors to compare the performance of the fund with the performance of the benchmark index.

Quarterly Returns

The first section provides the fund's quarterly and year-end total returns for the past five years. The quarterly returns are compounded to obtain the year-end total return shown on the right. (Calculating the sum of the four quarterly returns will not produce the year-end total return because simple addition does not take into account the effects of compounding.)

Total Return %
see also Total Return

This figure is calculated by taking the change in net asset value, reinvesting all income and capital gains distributions during the period, and dividing by the starting net asset value.

+/- S&P 500
see also Indexes

This statistic measures the difference between a stock fund's total return and the total return of the S&P 500 Index. A negative number indicates that the fund underperformed the index by the given amount, while a positive number indicates that the fund outperformed the index by the given amount. For example, a listing of -2.0 indicates that the fund underperformed the index by 2 percentage points. The difference between each stock fund's performance and the S&P 500 Index is listed. Bond funds are compared with the Lehman Brothers Aggregate Bond Index. The next column shows the same performance figure relative to another more specialized benchmark index.

% Rank Cat
See also Percentile Rank

Morningstar lists each fund's total return for various time periods against the funds in the same Morningstar Category (% Rank Cat). One is the highest or best percentile ranking and 100 is the lowest, or worst.

Growth of $10,000

This column shows the current value of a $10,000 investment made at the beginning of each of the

time periods listed. These calculations are not load- or tax-adjusted.

Performance Quartile Graph

The Performance Quartile graph is a representation of the fund's calendar-year total-return percentile rank among funds in the same category. A more specific version of this information is presented numerically in the History section (Total Rtn % Rank Cat). The black bar on the graph represents the quartile in which the fund's performance ranking falls. If the top quarter of the graph is shaded, for example, the fund performed among the top 25% of its category that year.

Portfolio Analysis

Occupying much of the right side of the page is the Portfolio Analysis section. Prominent in this section are the fund's most recently reported top securities (excluding cash and cash equivalents for all but short-term bond funds), ranked in descending order by the percentage of the portfolio's net assets they occupy. With this information, investors can more clearly identify what drives the fund's performance.

Morningstar makes every effort to gather the most up-to-date portfolio information from a fund. By law, however, funds are required to report this information only four times during a calendar year, and they have two months after the report date to release the shareholder report and portfolio. Therefore, it is possible that a fund's portfolio could be five months old or more at the time of publication. We print the date the portfolio was reported. Older portfolios should not be disregarded, however; although the list may not represent the exact current holdings of the fund, it may still provide a good picture of the overall nature of the fund's management style.

Items that pertain to the fund's portfolio are detailed below:

Total Stocks/Total Fixed-Income

Total Stocks indicates the total number of stock securities in a fund's portfolio, and Total Fixed-Income denotes the number of bond securities a fund holds. These do not simply refer to the stocks or bonds listed on the page; rather, they represent all stocks and bonds in the portfolio. These listings can be quite useful for gaining greater insight into the portfolio's diversification.

Share Change

Applied only to common stocks, the share change entry indicates the change in the number of shares of each stock from the previously reported portfolio. The share change column is dated and represents the change from the portfolio received just prior to the current one on the page. For stock funds, we indicate whether a fund has enlarged, reduced, or initiated new positions with the following symbols: (⊕) for purchases, (⊖) for sales, and (✻) for new holdings.

Security

This column lists the names of the stock or bond securities held as of the portfolio date. For stock holdings, this line typically displays just the name of the issuing company. Other stock labels are included where appropriate, such as ADR, which distinguishes an American Depositary Receipt. Bond holdings, however, will usually include more information to differentiate among the many types of bonds available. For most bonds, the coupon rate is listed as a percentage figure after the name of the bond. Adjustable-rate mortgages and floating-rate notes will have ARM or FRN (or IFRN for inverse-floating rate notes) listed after the name of the bond to indicate that the coupon rate is variable. Some adjustable-rate bond listings will include the formula by which the coupon rate is calculated, which is usually a fixed percentage plus some benchmark value. Securities followed by the abbreviation IO are interest-only securities, or those that consist only of the interest portion of a security, not the principal portion. PO indicates a principal-only security that sells at a discount to par and carries a coupon rate of zero.

Sector

see also Sector Weightings

The industry sector of each stock holding is reported in this column. This gives investors greater insight into where a fund's top holdings are concentrated and where its vulnerabilities lie. For specialty funds, we list each stock's subsector.

P/E

see also Price/Earnings Ratio

To add depth to the average P/E number for the entire portfolio (listed under Current Investment Style), the P/E ratio for each stock is reported here. NMF means the stock's P/E is 100 or more. A dash means the company has no earnings or the figure is not available.

YTD Return %

The year-to-date stock returns show whether one or two big winners (or losers) are driving fund performance, or a lot of little successes. In some cases, losses in top holdings can suggest a bargain-hunting strategy if a position in a losing stock is new or expanded.

% Assets

The % Assets column indicates what percentage of the portfolio's net assets a given security constitutes. Morningstar calculates the percentage of net assets figure by dividing the market value of the security by the fund's total net assets. If a given security makes up a large percentage of the fund's net assets, the fund uses a concentrated portfolio strategy, at least with respect to the security in question. If, however, the percentage figures are low, then the manager is simply not willing to bet heavily on a particular security.

Date of Maturity

see also Average Effective Duration

Maturity, located in the portfolio section for bond funds only, indicates the date on which a bond or note comes due. This information can be used in determining the portfolio's basic fixed-income strategy. For example, if most of these dates are a year or two away, the fund is taking a conservative, short-term approach. The maturity dates listed here, however, are not adjusted for calls (rights an issuer may have to redeem outstanding bonds before their scheduled maturity) or for the likelihood of mortgage prepayments. Thus, they might not accurately state the actual time to repayment of a bond, and might overstate a portfolio's sensitivity to interest-rate changes.

Amount

Found on bond-fund pages, the amount column refers to the size of the fund's investment in a given security as of the portfolio date listed above. The size is enumerated in thousands. For bonds, this figure reflects the principal value of the security in thousands of dollars.

Value

Value simply gives the market value of a particular security in thousands of dollars as of the portfolio date. The value column allows investors to gauge whether a fixed-income security is selling at a premium or a discount to its face value, as reflected in the amount column.

Portfolio Manager(s)

see also Manager Change

The portfolio manager is the individual or individuals responsible for the overall fund strategy; as well as the buying and selling decisions for the securities in a fund's portfolio. To help investors know who is running a fund, we detail management with a brief biography. We note the manager's background, experience, analytical support, other funds managed, and whether the manager invests in his or her own fund.

Potential Capital Gain Exposure

see Tax Analysis

Price/Book Ratio

see also Relative Comparisons

The price/book ratio of a fund is the weighted average of the price/book ratios of all the stocks in a fund's portfolio. Book value is the total assets of a company, less total liabilities. A company's P/B ratio is calculated by dividing the market price of its outstanding stock by the company's book value, and then adjusting for the number of shares outstanding. (Stocks with negative book values are excluded from this calculation.) In computing a fund's average P/B ratio, Morningstar weights each portfolio holding by the percentage of equity assets it represents; larger positions thus have proportionately greater influence on the final P/B. A low P/B may indicate that the stocks are bargains, priced below what the companies assets could be worth if liquidated.

Price/Cash Flow

see also Relative Comparisons

Price/cash flow is a weighted average of the price/cash flow ratios of the stocks in a fund's portfolio. Price/cash flow represents the amount of money an investor is willing to pay for a dollar of cash generated from a particular company's operations. Price/cash flow shows the ability of a business to generate cash and can be an effective gauge of liquidity and solvency. Because accounting conventions differ among nations, reported earnings (and thus P/B ratios) may not be comparable across national boundaries. Price/cash flow attempts to provide an internationally standardized measure of a

firm's stock price relative to its financial performance. In computing the average, Morningstar weights each portfolio holding by the percentage of stock assets it represents; larger positions thus have proportionately greater influence on the fund's final price/cash flow ratio.

Price/Earnings Ratio

see also Relative Comparisons

The price/earnings ratio of a fund is the weighted average of the price/earnings ratios of the stocks in a fund's portfolio. The P/E ratio of a company, which is a comparison of the price of the company's stock and its estimated earnings per share, is calculated by dividing these two figures. In computing the average, Morningstar weights each portfolio holding by the percentage of stock assets it represents; larger positions thus have proportionately greater influence on the fund's final P/E. A high P/E usually indicates that the market will pay more to obtain the company's earnings because it believes in the firm's ability to increase its earnings. (P/E can also be artificially inflated if a company has very weak earnings, which may be temporary. For example, during recessions, cyclical firms' earnings fall and their P/Es rise.) A low P/E indicates the market has less confidence that the company's earnings will increase; however, a fund manager with a value investing approach may believe such stocks have been overlooked or undervalued and have potential for appreciation.

Profitability Measures

Return on Assets (ROA)

This measures how effectively companies use their assets to generate profits. The formula for an individual firm is net income divided by assets. Companies with high returns on assets include software firms and beverage companies. Both types of companies frequently generate high profits but have relatively small investments in plant, equipment, and other assets. Firms with low returns on assets are typically in manufacturing or other capital-intensive industries. Companies with low returns on assets tend to have low valuations and are mostly held by value funds; by contrast, growth managers favor firms with high returns on assets. A fund's ROA is equal to the weighted average ROA of its individual holdings.

Return on Equity (ROE)

This calculation reveals how effectively management has invested shareholders' equity, which is the amount of money initially invested in the business plus retained earnings. ROE is simply net income divided by average shareholder equity. A high ROE is often a sign that a company's management uses its resources wisely, and the company is often located in a growing industry with high barriers to entry. For example, thanks to its dominance of the software operating-systems market, Microsoft usually sports high ROEs. By contrast, companies with low ROEs frequently operate in stagnant industries in which there is overcapacity. For example, automakers frequently earn low returns on equity. Companies with high ROEs generally have better business models, but as a reflection of that, their share prices are often expensive. Growth managers typically prefer companies with high and rising ROEs, while valuation concerns may lead value managers to buy firms with low ROEs. A fund's ROE is the weighted average of its individual holdings' ROEs.

Net Margin

We arrive at net margin by dividing a firm's net income (after all expenses, including taxes) by its sales. This measures how effective a company is at wringing profits out of each dollar of revenues. Companies with high net margins tend to have strong competitive positions, while those with low net margins often operate in highly price-competitive industries such as retailing. Companies that consistently earn high net margins include pharmaceuticals and successful software companies. Low-margin businesses include supermarkets and other retailers. High-margin firms earn superior returns but also garner premium valuations, so the stocks are often too expensive for value managers. At the fund level, net margin represents the weighted average of the individual stocks' net margins.

R

Rank
see Percentile Rank

Rating and Risk
see also Historical Profile
In this section, Morningstar includes load-adjusted returns and several risk measures and proprietary statistics.

Morningstar Return vs. Category
This represents an assessment of a fund's excess return over a risk-free rate (the return of the 90-day Treasury bill) in comparison to similar funds, after adjusting for all applicable loads and sales charges. In each Morningstar Category, the top 10% of funds earn a High Morningstar Return, the next 22.5% Above Average, the middle 35% Average, the next 22.5% Below Average, and the bottom 10% Low. Morningstar Return is measured for up to three time periods (three, five, and 10 years). These separate measures are then weighted and averaged to produce an overall measure for the fund. Funds with less than three years of performance history are not rated.

Morningstar Risk vs. Category
Here we show an assessment of the variations in a fund's monthly returns in comparison to similar funds, with an emphasis on downward variation. The greater the variation, the larger the risk score. If two funds have precisely the same return, the one with greater variations in its return is given the larger risk score. In each Morningstar Category, the 10% of funds with the lowest measured risk are described as Low Risk, the next 22.5% Below Average, the middle 35% Average, the next 22.5% Above Average, and the top 10% High. Morningstar Risk is measured for up to three time periods (three, five, and 10 years). These separate measures are then weighted and averaged to produce an overall measure for the fund. Funds with less than three years of performance history are not rated.

Regional Exposure
All international-stock funds, as well as precious-metals funds, feature a regional exposure listing. This table displays the percentage of the fund's total net assets invested in the U.K./Western Europe, Japan, Asia ex-Japan, North America, and Latin America. Below the regional information on each page, we list the five largest country exposures. The information in this section is gathered from portfolios and is the most recently available.

Relative Comparisons

see also Market Capitalization, Price/Book Ratio, Price/Cash Flow, and Price/Earnings Ratio

At various places in the Portfolio Analysis section, Morningstar shows how an individual fund compares with the average of all funds within its category (Rel Cat) or a benchmark index (Rel S&P 500). The category average (or index) is always set equal to 1.00. For example, a municipal-bond fund with a utilities weighting of 1.50 relative to its category has 50% more in utilities issues than its average peer. Stock statistics are displayed in comparison with the S&P 500 Index. In this case, 1.00 represents the index. A relative P/B ratio of 0.43, for example, indicates that the fund's P/B is 57% lower than that of the index.

Restricted/Illiquid Securities

see Special Securities

Return

see Historical Profile and Total Return

Risk

see Rating and Risk, Modern Portfolio Theory Statistics, and Standard Deviation

R-squared

see Modern Portfolio Theory Statistics

S

Sales Fees

see Expenses and Fees

Sector Breakdown for Fixed-Income Funds

The fixed-income sector illustrates the type of bonds a fund owns. These sectors help investors compare and understand the sector exposure of each mutual fund. These data are especially useful for comparing two funds that may be in the same Morningstar Category. The fixed-income sectors are calculated for all domestic taxable-bond portfolios. It is based on the securities in the most recent portfolio. This information shows the percentage of bond and cash assets invested in each of the 14 fixed-income sectors.

Morningstar groups all fixed-income assets into the following sectors:

U.S. Government

U.S. Treasuries

This sector includes all conventional fixed-rate debt issued by the Treasury department of the United States government. (For example, this sector excludes TIPS.) Some examples of this type of debt are Treasury bonds and Treasury notes. Treasury bills are included under % Cash, because they mature in less than 12 months.

TIPS

TIPS are inflation-indexed debt issued by the U.S. Treasury. (The term TIPS derives from their former name, Treasury Inflation-Protected Securities.) These bonds have principal and coupon payments that are linked to movements in the Consumer Price Index. They are a defensive measure against expectations of inflation, which typically erodes the real yield of conventional bonds. Even if inflation fears are in check, these bonds can benefit when the yields fall on traditional Treasuries. These unique securities act very differently than any other fixed-rate bond, and their volatility can change over time, depending on the level of interest rates.

U.S. Agency

This sector includes debt securities issued by government agencies—such as the Federal National Mortgage Association (FNMA), also known as Fannie Mae, or the Federal Home Loan Mortgage Corporation (FHLMC), also known as Freddie Mac—to raise capital and finance their operations. These "debentures" are not secured by physical assets, so they differ from most of the mortgage bonds that are issued by these agencies.

Mortgage

Mortgage Pass-Throughs

These are fixed-income securities that represent a claim to the cash flows associated with a pool of mortgages. The bondholders are entitled to a share of the principal and interest payments paid by the homeowners. The majority of these bonds are issued by a government agency such as FNMA, GNMA, or FHLMC. A few private corporations and banks also securitize and package mortgages in this way, and those are also included in this sector.

Mortgage CMO

Collateralized mortgage obligations (CMO) are similar to pass-through mortgage securities, but investors have more control over whether they will be paid sooner or later. CMOs are structured by time, so that some investors can line up for the first series of cash flow payments, while others may choose to put themselves at the end of the line. A fund manager would buy a late-paying CMO if he or she believed that there would be a lot of mortgage refinancing in the near term. This would protect the fund from getting its money back too early, which would require it to be reinvested at a lower interest rate. Most CMOs are based on mortgages from government agencies, such as FNMA and GNMA.

Mortgage ARM

Adjustable-rate mortgage (ARM) securities are backed by residential home mortgages where the interest rate is reset periodically in relation to a benchmark. Most ARMs are from government agencies, such as FNMA and GNMA.

Credit

U.S. Corporate

This sector includes all fixed-income securities that are issued by corporations domiciled in the United States. Corporate bonds are issued with a wide range of coupon rates and maturity dates.

Asset-Backed

Asset-backed securities are based on the expected cash flow from such things as auto loans, credit-card receivables, and computer leases. The cash flows for asset-backed securities can be fixed (auto loans have a defined payment schedule and a fixed maturity, for example) or variable (credit-card debt is paid at random intervals). These securities typically range in maturity from two to seven years.

Convertible

Convertible bonds give the owner an opportunity to convert the bond to a certain number of shares of common stock at a certain price. As the stock approaches that price, the option to convert becomes more valuable and the price of the convertible bond also rises. These securities usually provide lower interest payments, because the option to convert to stock could potentially be quite valuable at some point in the future.

Municipal

Local and state governments issue municipal bonds in order to raise money for operations and development. This financing is sometimes used to build or upgrade hospitals, sewer systems, schools, housing, stadiums, or industrial complexes. Some municipal bonds are backed by the issuing entity while others are linked to a revenue stream, such as from a tollway or a utility. Municipal bonds are exempt from federal tax and often from state and local taxes, too. The tax break allows municipal governments to sell the bonds at a lower interest rate, because the investor gets an additional tax benefit.

Corporate Inflation-Protected

Inflation-protected securities are similar to TIPS, but they are issued by a private entity rather than by the U.S. government. These bonds are linked to an index of inflation, and the principal and coupon payments increase when inflation increases. As with TIPS, these securities behave quite differently than conventional bonds.

Foreign

Foreign Corporate

These fixed-income securities are issued by corporations that are based outside of the United States.

Foreign Government

These fixed-income securities are issued by governments outside the United States.

Cash

Cash can be cash in the bank, certificates of deposit, currency, or money market holdings. Cash can also be any fixed-income securities that mature in less than 12 months. Cash also includes commercial paper and any repurchase agreements held by the fund. Because this data point is based on only the cash and bond assets in the fund, it can be different from the % Cash in the composition breakdown, which is expressed as a percent of total assets.

Sector Weightings/Economic Spheres

Morningstar divides the stock market into three broad "economic spheres," each of which contains four specific industry sectors. Sectors are based on what companies actually do. That is, unlike some other sector classification systems, sectors aren't based on expected behavior of the stocks of these companies.

Economic spheres with their major inclusive sectors:

👁 *Information Sphere*
Made up of the Software, Hardware, Media, and Telecommunications sectors.

⌨ *Service Sphere*
Made up of the Health Care, Consumer Services, Business Services, and Financial Services sectors.

🏭 *Manufacturing Sphere*
Made up of the Consumer Goods, Industrial Materials, Energy, and Utilities sectors.

Sectors with their major inclusive industries:

⬉ *Software*
Companies engaged in the design and marketing of computer operating systems and applications. Examples include Microsoft and Oracle.

💻 *Hardware*
Manufacturers of computer equipment, communication equipment, semiconductors, and components. Examples include IBM, Cisco Systems, and Intel.

🎙 *Media*
Companies that own and operate broadcast networks and those that create content or provide it for other media companies. Examples include Time Warner, Walt Disney, and Washington Post.

📱 *Telecommunications*
Companies that provide communication services using fixed-line networks or those that provide wireless access and services. Examples include Verizon and Alltel.

🩺 *Health Care*
Includes biotechnology, pharmaceuticals, research services, HMOs, home health, hospitals, assisted living, and medical equipment and supplies. Examples include Abbott Laboratories, Merck, and Cardinal Health.

🛒 *Consumer Services*
Includes retail stores, personal services, home builders, home supply, travel and entertainment companies, and educational providers. Examples include Wal-Mart, Home Depot, and Expedia.

📄 *Business Services*
Includes advertising, printing, publishing, business support, consultants, employment, engineering and construction, security services, waste management, distributors, and transportation. Examples include Manpower, R.R. Donnelley, and Southwest Airlines.

💲 *Financial Services*
Includes banks, finance companies, money-management firms, savings and loans, securities brokers, and insurance companies. Examples include Citigroup, Washington Mutual, and Fannie Mae.

🚗 *Consumer Goods*
Companies that manufacture or provide food, beverages, household and personal products, apparel, shoes, textiles, autos and auto parts, consumer electronics, luxury goods, packaging, and tobacco. Examples include PepsiCo, Ford Motor, and Kraft Foods.

⚙ *Industrial Materials*
Includes aerospace and defense firms, companies that provide or manufacture chemicals, machinery, building materials, and commodities. Examples include Boeing, DuPont, and Alcoa.

🔥 *Energy*
Companies that produce or refine oil and gas, oilfield services and equipment companies, and pipeline operators. Examples include ExxonMobil, Schlumberger, and BP.

💡 *Utilities*
Electric, gas, and water utilities. Examples include Duke Energy, Exelon, and El Paso.

Sector weightings are also calculated in-house for municipal-bond funds. Although they are generally listed in order of descending credit risk, the categories are not as neatly divided as the stock sector weightings. General obligation bonds, which garner income from the municipality's tax revenues, are listed first (though some perceive these as risky if the issuing municipality is shaky). Revenue-based municipal-bond sectors follow. Near the bottom of the list are lease-backed and industrial-activity bonds, which are generally considered more risky for investors to hold. Demand notes, however, are unrelated to the other types of municipal bonds and hold little credit risk due to their short durations.

Municipal-bond classifications:

General Obligation
General obligation bonds, which are repaid from general revenue and borrowings rather than from the revenue of a specific project or facility.

Utilities
Electricity, gas, nuclear power, dams, telephones.

Health
Hospitals, nursing homes, retirement facilities.

Water/Waste
Water, sewers, sanitation, irrigation, drainage

Housing
Single and multifamily housing.

Education
Colleges and universities, independent and unified school districts, student loans, tuition.

Transportation
Transportation by air, water, road, or railroad.

COP/Lease
Certificates of participation and lease bonds, used to finance a variety of public endeavors.

Industrial
Economic and industrial development, pollution control, resource recovery, conventions, expositions, stadiums, hotels (typically backed by a business or corporation rather than by a municipality).

Misc Revenue
Miscellaneous revenue bonds.

Demand
Short-term municipal securities.

SEC Yield
see also Yield
SEC yield is a standardized figure that the Securities and Exchange Commission requires funds to use to calculate rates of income return on a fund's capital investment. SEC yield is an annualized calculation that is based on a trailing 30-day period. This figure will often differ significantly from Morningstar's other yield figure, which reflects trailing 12-month distributed yield, because of differing time periods as well as differing accounting policies. For example, SEC yield is based on a bond's yield to maturity, which takes into account amortization of premiums and discounts, while Morningstar's distributed yield is based on what funds actually pay out.

Share Change
see Portfolio Analysis

Sharpe Ratio
The Sharpe ratio is a risk-adjusted measure developed by Nobel Laureate William Sharpe. It is calculated using standard deviation and excess return to determine reward per unit of risk. First, the average monthly return of the 90-day Treasury bill (over a 36-month period) is subtracted from the fund's average monthly return. The difference in total return represents the fund's excess return beyond that of the 90-day Treasury bill, a risk-free investment. An arithmetic annualized excess return is then calculated by multiplying this monthly return by 12. To show a relationship between excess return and risk, this number is then divided by the standard deviation of the fund's annualized excess returns. The higher the Sharpe ratio, the better the fund's historical risk-adjusted performance.

Short Sales
Short sales are bets that a stock will fall. To sell short, a mutual fund borrows shares from one party and then sells them to another on the open market. The fund's managers hope the stock drops, because they would be able to buy the shares back at a lower price and then return them to the lender. The difference between the original price and the price management pays to buy the shares back is the profit or loss. Short sales can slow returns in a rising market, but reduce losses or even produce gains in a falling market. One of the risks of short sales is that the maximum gain is 100%, but potential losses are unlimited.

Special Securities

This section shows a fund's exposure to a variety of complex or illiquid securities, including derivatives. The percentage of total net assets represented by each type of security is listed to the right of each group. Some securities may fall under more than one type.

Restricted/Illiquid Securities

Restricted and illiquid securities are issues that may be hard to accurately price and difficult to sell because an investor may be unable to find a buyer quickly. Private placement issues and 144(a) securities are both included here. Both types have varying degrees of liquidity and are exempt from some of the cumbersome registration and disclosure requirements that public offerings usually face.

Emerging-Markets Securities

Debt or equity securities from emerging markets are listed here. These figures are calculated from the most recently available portfolio. Morningstar classifies as emerging markets anything aside from the following developed markets: Australia, Austria, Belgium, Canada, Denmark, Finland, France, Germany, Greece, Hong Kong, Ireland, Italy, Japan, the Netherlands, New Zealand, Norway, Portugal, Singapore, South Korea, Spain, Sweden, Switzerland, Taiwan, the United Kingdom, and the United States. This list is subject to change as markets become more developed or vice versa.

Exotic Mortgage-Backed Securities

This section indicates how much of a fund's net assets are held in unusual mortgage-backed derivatives. Specifically, we delineate those securities that see their price changes magnified when interest rates or mortgage-prepayment speeds change. Because not all mortgage-backed derivatives have these traits, we include the following: interest-only (IOs) and principal-only paper (POs), inverse floating-rate securities (IFRNs), and Z-tranche collateralized mortgage obligation issues, all of which are fairly clearly labeled in a fund's shareholder reports. Kitchen-sink bonds—a complex mix of interest-only bonds, principal-only bonds, and cast-off CMO tranches—are also tallied here. For stock funds, which rarely hold mortgage-backed issues of any kind, we combine exotic mortgage-backed securities with structured notes. Municipal-bond funds do not have an exotic mortgage-backed section in the Special Securities box.

Options/Futures/Warrants

Options and futures may be used speculatively, to leverage a portfolio, or cautiously, as a hedge against risk. We don't show the percentage of assets devoted to options or futures because it is difficult to determine from shareholder reports how much of a portfolio is affected by an options or futures contract. We also include forward contracts and warrants in this area.

Standard Deviation

Standard deviation is a statistical measure of the range of a fund's performance. When a fund has a high standard deviation, its range of performance has been very wide, indicating that there is a greater potential for volatility. The standard deviation figure provided here is an annualized statistic based on 36 monthly returns. By definition, approximately 68% of the time, the total returns of a given fund are expected to differ from its mean total return by no more than plus or minus the standard deviation figure. Ninety-five percent of the time, a fund's total returns should be within a range of plus or minus 2 times the standard deviation from its mean. These ranges assume that a fund's returns fall in a typical bell-shaped distribution. In any case, the greater the standard deviation, the greater the fund's volatility has been.

For example, an investor can compare two funds with the same average monthly return of 5%, but with different standard deviations. The first fund has a standard deviation of 2, which means that its range of returns for the past 36 months has typically remained between 1% and 9%. On the other hand, assume that the second fund has a standard deviation of 4 for the same period. This higher deviation indicates that this fund has experienced returns fluctuating between -3% and 13%. With the second fund, an investor can expect greater volatility.

Mean

The mean represents the annualized average monthly return from which the standard deviation is calculated. The mean will be the same as the annualized trailing, three-year return figure for the same time period.

Star Rating

see Historical Profile and Rating and Risk

Stewardship Grade

Morningstar's Stewardship Grade for funds goes beyond the usual analysis of strategy, risk, and return. The Stewardship Grade allows investors and advisors to assess funds based on factors that we believe influence the manner in which funds are run; the degree to which the management company's and fund board's interests are aligned with fund shareholders; and the degree to which shareholders can expect their interests to be protected from potentially conflicting interests of the management company.

We assign each fund a letter grade from A (best) to F (worst). Funds are graded on an absolute basis. There is no "curve." Each fund receives a grade based on Morningstar analysts' evaluation of five factors: Regulatory Issues, Board Quality, Manager Incentives, Fees, and Corporate Culture.

Each factor is worth a maximum of 2 points, for a total of 10 possible points. Points for each component are awarded in increments as small as 0.5 point. With the exception of Regulatory Issues, the worst possible score a fund can receive in each component is zero. For Regulatory Issues, the minimum score possible is -2. We assign each fund's overall letter grade as follows:

A: 9 - 10 points

B: 7 - 8.5 points

C: 5 - 6.5 points

D: 3 - 4.5 points

F: 2.5 points or fewer

For ease of use, we translate funds' scores for each of the five individual factors into the following qualitative terms:

Excellent = 2 points

Good = 1.5 points

Fair = 1 point

Poor = 0.5 point

Very Poor = 0 points and below

Morningstar's Fiduciary Grade for funds is entirely different from the Morningstar Rating for funds, commonly known as the star rating. There is no relationship between the two.

Strategy

While the Morningstar Category gives investors an idea of what sorts of investments a manager makes, it does not fully capture the nuances of a manager's approach to picking stocks or bonds. In this section, Morningstar analysts explain what criteria a manager uses in selecting securities and how risky a given approach may be. On the equity side, the strategy description often focuses on what size and type of company a manager prefers, along with a discussion regarding how he or she balances growth and value factors. With bond funds, the strategy section explains whether the manager makes interest-rate and credit-quality bets, or whether management attempts to add value with individual security selection.

Style Box

see Investment Style Box

Subadvisor

In some cases, a fund's advisor employs another company, called a subadvisor, to handle the fund's day-to-day management. If the fund employs a subadvisor, the portfolio manager probably works for the fund's sub-advisor, not the fund's advisor.

Systematic Investment $

see Minimum Automatic Investment Plan

T

Tax-Adjusted Return %

see Tax Analysis

Tax Analysis

The information provided in the Tax Analysis section can be used to evaluate a fund's aftertax returns and its efficiency in achieving them. Additionally, the potential capital gain exposure figure can provide a glimpse at a shareholder's vulnerability to taxation. All these figures can help an investor judge which funds have used tax-friendly strategies. They can also aid in deciding which funds are best suited to tax-deferred accounts and which serve better as taxable investments.

Tax-Adjusted Return

The Tax-Adj Rtn % column shows an estimate of a fund's annualized aftertax total return for the three-, five-, and 10-year periods, excluding any capital gains effects that would result from selling the fund at the end of the period. Consistent with SEC guidance regarding tax-adjusted returns, these figures reflect the maximum load paid by fund shareholders. To determine this figure, all income and short-term (less than one year) capital gain distributions are taxed at the maximum federal rate at the time of distribution. Long-term (more than one year) capital gains are taxed at a 20% rate. The aftertax portion is then reinvested in the fund. State and local taxes are ignored, and only the capital gains are counted for tax-exempt funds, because the income from these funds is nontaxable.

The category percentile rank (% Rank Cat) for each fund's tax-adjusted return is also listed. This ranking helps investors compare a fund's estimated aftertax performance with that of other funds in the category.

Tax-Cost Ratio

This represents the estimated percentage-point reduction in an annualized return that has resulted from income taxes over the past three-, five-, and 10-year periods. The calculation assumes investors pay the maximum federal rate on capital gains and ordinary income.

Potential Capital Gain Exposure

Morningstar calculates potential capital gain exposure to give investors some idea of the potential tax consequences of their investment in a fund. We cannot predict what a fund's taxable distributions might be, but we can offer some clues based on a fund's liquidation liability. The figure shows whether a fund has consistently distributed taxable gains or has been relatively tax-efficient.

A mutual fund's assets are composed of paid-in (investment) capital, appreciation or depreciation of this capital, and any undistributed net income. Paid-in capital is simply the monies investors have put into the fund (which can decrease should shareholders decide to redeem their shares). Any appreciation of this capital may eventually be taxed. Our potential capital gain exposure figure shows what percentage of a fund's total assets represent unrealized (or at least undistributed) capital appreciation.

Capital appreciation can be either unrealized or realized. In the first case, the fund's holdings have increased in value, but the fund has not yet sold these holdings; taxes are not due until the fund does so. Realized net appreciation (commonly called realized gains) represents actual gains achieved by the sale of holdings; taxes must be paid on these realized capital gains, which the fund must distribute each year if it can't offset them with realized losses. Unrealized appreciation may turn into realized gains at any time, should the fund's management decide to sell the profitable holdings. Thus, our formula includes unrealized appreciation as part of the potential capital gains exposure.

A negative potential capital gains exposure figure means that the fund has greater net losses than it has gains. This likely indicates that the fund has or will have a tax-loss carryforward, which would mean that some amount of future gains could be offset by past losses.

To keep our calculation current, we update the information between shareholder reports by accounting for a fund's market losses or gains, the sale or redemption of shares, and the payment of capital gains. This updated figure is not quite as precise as the one stated in the shareholder report, but it is more current and therefore more relevant to the investor.

Telephone Numbers

These are the local and toll-free (if available) numbers that an investor may use to contact the fund, call for a prospectus, or get marketing information.

Ticker

A ticker is the symbol assigned to the fund by the NASDAQ system. The ticker is commonly used to locate a fund on electronic price-quoting systems.

Top Five States

We display the five states or U.S. territories in which a municipal-bond fund invests most heavily and the percentage of the portfolio each state or territory represents. This information reflects the holdings of the portfolio on the page.

Total Assets

see also Net Assets

This figure reflects the total assets of all the fund's share classes at the end of the most recently reported month.

Total Cost

see Expenses and Fees

Total Return % Rank Cat

see Percentile Rank and Performance

Total Return

see also Capital Return % and Income Return %

All references to total return represent a fund's gains over a specified period of time. Total return includes both income (in the form of dividends or interest payments) and capital gains or losses (the increase or decrease in the value of a security). Morningstar calculates total return by taking the change in a fund's NAV, assuming the reinvestment of all income and capital gains distributions (on the actual reinvestment date used by the fund) during the period, and then dividing by the initial NAV.

Unless marked as load-adjusted total returns, Morningstar does not adjust total return for sales charges or for redemption fees. (Morningstar Return and Morningstar Risk-Adjusted Ratings do incorporate those fees.) Total returns do account for management, administrative, and 12b-1 fees and other costs automatically deducted from fund assets. The quarterly returns, listed in the Performance section, express the fund's return for each individual quarter; the total shown on the right is the compounded return for the four quarters of that year. An asterisk next to the total return number indicates that the return is calculated for a partial quarter or partial year because the fund began operations during that time period.

Total Stocks/Total Fixed-Income

see Portfolio Analysis

Turnover Rate %

The turnover rate provides a rough measure of the fund's level of trading activity. This publicly reported figure is calculated by the funds in accordance with SEC regulations, and Morningstar gathers the information from fund shareholder reports. A fund divides the lesser of purchases or sales (expressed in dollars and excluding all securities with maturities of less than one year) by the fund's average monthly assets. The resulting percentage can be loosely interpreted to represent the percentage of the portfolio's holdings that have changed over the past year. The turnover ratio is most accurate,

however, when a fund's asset base remains stable. A low turnover figure (typically less than 30%) might indicate that the manager is following a buy-and-hold strategy. High turnover (more than 100%) could be an indication of an investment strategy involving considerable buying and selling of securities.

V

Value $000

see Portfolio Analysis

Value

see also Growth and Investment Style Box

The investment style commonly referred to as a value approach focuses on stocks that an investor or fund manager thinks are currently undervalued in price and will eventually have their worth recognized by the market. It is often contrasted with a growth-style approach to investing.

Value Measures

Price/Projected Earnings

Projected earnings are the consensus analyst opinion of how much a company will earn during its next fiscal year. Price/projected earnings represents the amount investors are paying for each dollar of expected earnings per share. When reported for a mutual fund, it shows the weighted average of the price/projected earnings ratio for each stock in the fund's portfolio. This measure helps determine Morningstar's value score for each stock and the overall value orientation of the fund.

Price/Book Value

Book value is, in theory, what would be left over for shareholders if a company shut down its operations, paid off all of its creditors, collected from all of its debtors, and liquidated itself. In practice, however, the value of assets and liabilities can change substantially from when they are first recorded. Many investors use the price/book ratio—the ratio of a company share price to its total book value per share—as a way to value a stock. If the share price is less than total equity per share, the company is selling for less than its break-up value. When reported for a mutual fund, it shows the weighted average of the price/book ratio for each stock in the fund's portfolio. This measure helps determine Morningstar's value score for each stock and the overall value orientation of the fund.

Price/Sales

Price/sales represents the amount investors are paying for each dollar of sales generated by the company. Price/sales is usually a less volatile measure than either price/earnings or price/book and can be especially useful when evaluating companies with volatile earnings. When reported for a mutual fund, it shows the weighted average of the price/sales ratio for each stock in the fund's portfolio. This measure helps determine Morningstar's value score for each stock and the overall value orientation of the fund.

Price/Cash Flow

Cash flow tells you how much cash a business is actually generating—its earnings before depreciation, amortization, and noncash charges. Sometimes called cash earnings, it's considered a gauge of liquidity and solvency. Price/cash flow represents the amount investors are paying for each dollar generated from a company's operations. When reported for a mutual fund, it shows the weighted average of the price/cash flow ratio for each stock in the fund's portfolio. This measure helps determine Morningstar's value score for each stock and the overall value orientation of the fund.

Dividend Yield

Dividends are the per-share amount taken from a company's profits and paid to shareholders. Dividend yield is equal to a company's annual dividend divided by its share price. It works as a kind of valuation measure—the lower the yield, the more investors have to pay for each dollar of dividends. Investors often consider stocks with high dividend yields potentially undervalued investments. When reported for a mutual fund, it shows the weighted average of the dividend yield for each stock in the fund's portfolio. This measure helps determine Morningstar's value score for each stock and the overall value orientation of the fund.

Y

Yield

see also SEC Yield

Yield, expressed as a percentage, represents a fund's income return on capital investment for the past 12 months. This figure refers only to interest distributions from fixed-income securities and dividends from stocks. Monies generated from the sale of securities, from options and futures transactions, and from currency transactions are considered capital gains, not income. Return of capital is also not considered income. NMF (No Meaningful Figure) appears in this space for those funds that do not properly label their distributions. We list N/A if a fund is less than one year old, in which case we cannot calculate yield. Morningstar computes yield by dividing the sum of the fund's income distributions for the past 12 months by the previous month's NAV (adjusted upward for any capital gains distributed over the same period).

*Manager Index includes only the three longest-tenured managers on each fund.

Bradford, Patrick T.
93 Bjurman, Barry Micro-Cap Growth

Bradley, Harold S.
48 American Century Select Inv

Brady, Brian
45 American Century Intl Discovery Inv

Brayman, Scott T.
114 Champlain Small Company Adv

Brennan, Brian J.
405 T. Rowe Price U.S. Treasury Long-Te

Brewer, Karl W.
534 William Blair Small Cap Growth N

Brooks, Joshua H.
345 Putnam Fund for Growth & Income A

Brown, Christopher D.
328 Pax World Balanced

Brown, Christopher H
328 Pax World Balanced

Brown, Christopher H.
328 Pax World Balanced

Brown, Eddie C.
103 Brown Capital Mgmt Small Co Instl

Browne, Christopher H.
429 Tweedy, Browne American Value
430 Tweedy, Browne Global Value

Browne, Connor
423 Thornburg Value A

Browne, William H.
429 Tweedy, Browne American Value
430 Tweedy, Browne Global Value

Brugere-Trelat, Philippe
303 Mutual European A

Brynjolfsson, John B.
238 Harbor Real Return Instl
331 PIMCO CommodityRealRet Strat D
337 PIMCO Real Return D

Buek, Michael H.
441 Vanguard 500 Index
495 Vanguard Small Cap Index
496 Vanguard Small Cap Value Index
500 Vanguard Tax-Managed Capital App
507 Vanguard Tax-Managed Grth & Inc
503 Vanguard Tax-Managed Small Cap Ret

Buller, Steven J.
192 Fidelity Real Estate Investment

Bundy, Harvey H
481 Vanguard Mid Cap Growth

Buntrock, Kenneth
272 Loomis Sayles Global Bond Ret

Burlingame, Steve A.
409 TCW Select Equities I

Burn III, Harry
365 Sound Shore

Butler, Daniel B.
114 Champlain Small Company Adv

Butler, Donald M.
455 Vanguard Extended Market Idx
482 Vanguard Mid Capitalization Index

Byrne, Susan M.
529 Westwood Balanced AAA

Calamos, Jr, John P.
109 Calamos Growth A
110 Calamos Market Neutral Income A

Calamos, Nick P.
107 Calamos Convertible A
108 Calamos Growth & Income A
109 Calamos Growth A

Calamos, Sr., John P.
107 Calamos Convertible A
108 Calamos Growth & Income A
109 Calamos Growth A
110 Calamos Market Neutral Income A

Callahan, Kevin W
112 Century Small Cap Select Inv

Callinan, James L.
355 RS Emerging Growth A

Cameron, Bryan C.
130 Dodge & Cox International Stock

Canakaris, Ronald E.
85 Aston/Montag & Caldwell Growth N

Cancelmo Jr., Richard P.
98 Bridgeway Balanced

Cardon, Jeff
519 Wasatch Small Cap Growth

Carey, John A.
339 Pioneer A

Carlson, Charles vK.
232 Greenspring

Carlson, John H.
187 Fidelity New Markets Income

Carlson, Marina T.
83 Artisan Small Cap

Carr Jr., David R.
315 Oak Value

Castegren, Hakan
236 Harbor International Instl

Cates, G. Staley
268 Longleaf Partners
269 Longleaf Partners International
270 Longleaf Partners Small-Cap

Cepukenas, Craigh A.
83 Artisan Small Cap

Chace, Daniel
518 Wasatch Micro Cap

Chamby, Dan
94 BlackRock Global Allocation A

Chase, Jr., Derwood S.
115 Chase Growth

Chen, Huachen
36 Allianz RCM Technology Instl

Cheng, Ren Y.
165 Fidelity Freedom 2010
166 Fidelity Freedom 2020

Chester, William S.
525 Westcore Midco Growth

Chin, David
132 Domini Social Equity

Chizmarova, Ellie
74 American Beacon Small Cp Val Plan

Chow, C. Robert
161 Fidelity Equity-Income II

Clark, Chad M.
320 Oakmark International Small Cap I

Clark, Jerome A.
396 T. Rowe Price Retirement 2015

Coats Jr., Larry D.
315 Oak Value

Cohen, David L.
214 First Eagle Fund of America Y

Cohen, Timothy J.
169 Fidelity Growth & Income

Coleman, Jonathan
244 Janus Enterprise

Cone, John S.
459 Vanguard Growth & Income
483 Vanguard Morgan Growth

Conelius, Mike
382 T. Rowe Price International Bond

Cordisco, Larry
295 Meridian Value

Corkins, David J.
241 Janus

Linehan, John D.
406 T. Rowe Price Value

Lippman, William J.
223 Franklin Balance Sheet Investment A

Liss, Michael
52 American Century Value Inv

Lob, Roger M.
277 MainStay MAP I

Loeb, Thomas F.
442 Vanguard Asset Allocation

Lovelace, James B.
59 American Funds Capital Inc Bldr A

Lovelace, Robert W.
62 American Funds EuroPacific Gr A

Lynn, Brent A.
252 Janus Overseas

Lyon, Robert H.
274 MainStay ICAP Equity I
275 MainStay ICAP International I
276 MainStay ICAP Select Equity I

MacMillan, James A.
94 BlackRock Global Allocation A

Madden, Mark H.
322 Oppenheimer Developing Markets A

Maissoneuve, Virginie
469 Vanguard International Growth

Male, Bob
104 Buffalo Micro Cap
105 Buffalo Mid Cap
106 Buffalo Small Cap

Malley, Thomas R.
246 Janus Global Life Sciences

Mallon, Mark L.
37 American Century Capital Val Inv
47 American Century Large Co Val Inv

Maloney, Michael
364 Skyline Special Equities

Mangum, Charles
159 Fidelity Dividend Growth

Manno Jr., Anthony R.
259 JPMorgan U.S. Real Estate A

Maran, Edward
423 Thornburg Value A

Margard, James R.
346 Rainier Small/Mid Cap Equity

Mariappa, Sudi
333 PIMCO Foreign Bond (USD-Hedged) D
334 PIMCO Foreign Bond (Unhedged) D

Marsico, Thomas F.
284 Marsico Focus
285 Marsico Growth
433 USAA Aggressive Growth

Martin, William
38 American Century Equity Growth Inv
41 American Century Global Gold Inv

Matthews, Brian W.
329 Payden Core Bond
330 Payden Limited Maturity

Maurer, Gary S.
274 MainStay ICAP Equity I

May, Jim
132 Domini Social Equity

Mazanec, John
520 Wasatch Small Cap Value

McCarthy, Steven J.
366 SSgA Emerging Markets

McConnell, Christine
164 Fidelity Floating Rate High Income

McCrickard, Gregory A.
398 T. Rowe Price Small-Cap Stock

McDermott, Eugene Andrew
269 Longleaf Partners International

McDermott, John
141 Excelsior Value & Restructuring

McEvoy, Earl E.
462 Vanguard High-Yield Corporate
478 Vanguard Long-Term Investment-Grade
511 Vanguard Wellesley Income

McGee, Margaret
223 Franklin Balance Sheet Investment A

McGinley, Douglas
175 Fidelity Intermediate Municipal Inc

McGregor, Clyde S.
316 Oakmark Equity & Income I
317 Oakmark Global I

McHugh, Christopher K.
427 Turner Midcap Growth
428 Turner Small Cap Growth
460 Vanguard Growth Equity

McLaughlin, Michael
218 Forward International Small Co Inv

McQuaid, Charles P.
118 Columbia Acorn A

McVail, William C.
428 Turner Small Cap Growth

Mendes, Louis
119 Columbia Acorn International A

Mewbourne, Curtis
332 PIMCO Emerging Markets Bond D

Milano, Joseph M.
389 T. Rowe Price New America Growth

Miletti, Ann M.
530 Wells Fargo Advantage Common Stock
531 Wells Fargo Advantage Opportunity I

Milias, Mitchell J.
486 Vanguard PRIMECAP Core

Millen, Robert G.
258 Jensen J

Miller III, William H.
289 Masters' Select Value

Miller, Bill
263 Legg Mason Opportunity Prim
266 Legg Mason Value Prim

Miller, Mary J.
402 T. Rowe Price Tax-Free Income

Miller, Robert J.
50 American Century Tax-Free Bond Inv

Mobius, Dr. J.
413 Templeton Developing Markets A

Moffett, James L.
431 UMB Scout International

Mohn, Robert A.
118 Columbia Acorn A
121 Columbia Acorn USA A

Mollenhauer, Eric
209 Fidelity Total Bond

Monoyios, Nikolaos D.
326 Oppenheimer Main Street A

Monrad, Bruce H.
313 Northeast Investors

Monrad, Ernest E.
313 Northeast Investors

Montgomery, John
99 Bridgeway Blue-Chip 35 Index
100 Bridgeway Small-Cap Growth N
101 Bridgeway Small-Cap Value N
102 Bridgeway Ultra-Small Company Marke

Moore, Jeffrey
179 Fidelity Investment Grade Bond

Moore, Scott A.
39 American Century Equity Income Inv
52 American Century Value Inv

Mordecai, Alfred W.
343 PRIMECAP Odyssey Aggressive Growth

Morris, Peter R.
239 Homestead Value

Morrow, James
193 Fidelity Select Electronics
196 Fidelity Select Technology

Muhlenkamp, Ronald H.
300 Muhlenkamp

Mulally, James R.
60 American Funds Capital World Bd A
61 American Funds Capital World G/I A

Mullarkey, Christopher
277 MainStay MAP I

Mullarkey, Michael J.
277 MainStay MAP I

Mullick, S. Basu
310 Neuberger Berman Partners Inv

Murchison, Murdo
414 Templeton Foreign A
415 Templeton Growth A
416 Templeton World A

Murphy, James M.
404 T. Rowe Price Tax-Free High-Yield

Musser, Peter M.
346 Rainier Small/Mid Cap Equity

Myers, Charles L.
202 Fidelity Small Cap Retirement

Myers, Lisa F.
414 Templeton Foreign A
415 Templeton Growth A
416 Templeton World A

Ngim, Andrew
75 Ameristock

Nicholas, Albert O.
311 Nicholas

Nicholas, David O.
311 Nicholas
312 Nicholas II I

Nicholls, Dale O.
190 Fidelity Pacific Basin

Nicklin Jr., Edmund H.
527 Westport R
528 Westport Select Cap R

Notkin, Mark
152 Fidelity Capital & Income

Notzon III, Edmund M.
368 T. Rowe Price Balanced
394 T. Rowe Price Personal Strat Income
400 T. Rowe Price Spectrum Growth
401 T. Rowe Price Spectrum Income

Nygren, William C.
318 Oakmark I
321 Oakmark Select I

O'Boyle, Kevin C.
342 Presidio

O'Brien, Timothy
134 Dreyfus Premier Balanced Opportunit

O'Donnell, Helen
42 American Century Global Growth Inv

O'Donnell, Robert G.
56 American Funds American Balanced A

O'Neil, Ford G.
174 Fidelity Intermediate Bond
209 Fidelity Total Bond
210 Fidelity U.S. Bond Index

O'Reilly, Gerard C.
458 Vanguard Growth Index
487 Vanguard REIT Index
487 Vanguard REIT Index
494 Vanguard Small Cap Growth Index
504 Vanguard Total Stock Mkt Idx
510 Vanguard Value Index

Ober, Charles M.
390 T. Rowe Price New Asia
391 T. Rowe Price New Era

Odegard, Mark N.
364 Skyline Special Equities

Olivier, Kenneth E.
128 Dodge & Cox Balanced
129 Dodge & Cox Income
131 Dodge & Cox Stock

Orndorff, Christopher
329 Payden Core Bond
330 Payden Limited Maturity

Osterweis, John S.
327 Osterweis

Ostrer, Neil
456 Vanguard Global Equity

Owens, Edward P.
461 Vanguard Health Care

Page, Scott H.
137 Eaton Vance Floating Rate A

Palmieri, V. Jerry
225 Franklin Growth A

Pangaro, Gonzalo
385 T. Rowe Price Latin America

Pappas, Thomas L.
457 Vanguard GNMA

Pariseau, Robert R.
436 USAA Tax Exempt Long-Term

Patel, Margaret D.
340 Pioneer High Yield A

Paton, Ben
177 Fidelity International Small Cap

Payden, Joan
329 Payden Core Bond

Payne, Jeffrey S.
525 Westcore Midco Growth

Peck, Andrew
88 Baron Asset

Pell, Richard C.
261 Julius Baer International Equity A
260 Julius Baer International Equity II

Perkins, Robert Hun
254 Janus Small Cap Value Instl

Perkins, Shep
184 Fidelity Mid-Cap Stock

Perkins, Thomas H.
250 Janus Mid Cap Value Investor
254 Janus Small Cap Value Instl

Perkins, Thomas M.
250 Janus Mid Cap Value Investor
254 Janus Small Cap Value Instl

Perks, Edward D.
227 Franklin Income A

Permut, Steven
50 American Century Tax-Free Bond Inv

Peron, Matthew
314 Northern Technology

Perre, Michael
443 Vanguard Balanced Index
444 Vanguard FTSE Social Index Inv
501 Vanguard Tax-Managed Balanced
507 Vanguard Tax-Managed Grth & Inc

Perry, Dina N.
63 American Funds Fundamental Invs A
65 American Funds Inc Fund of Amer A
68 American Funds New Perspective A
307 Neuberger Berman Genesis Inv

Peters, Samuel M.
265 Legg Mason Special Investment Prim

Petersen, Stephen R.
160 Fidelity Equity-Income
191 Fidelity Puritan

Phillips Jr., John D.
513 Vanguard Windsor

Pickett, Robert
367 SSgA Yield Plus

Segal, F. Dav
302 Mutual Discovery A
305 Mutual Shares A

Segalas, Spiros
234 Harbor Capital Appreciation Instl

Sellecchia, Vincent
125 Delafield

Senser, Jerrold K.
274 MainStay ICAP Equity I
275 MainStay ICAP International I
276 MainStay ICAP Select Equity I

Sertl, Jr., George O
82 Artisan Mid Cap Value
84 Artisan Small Cap Value

Shackelford, Daniel O.
393 T. Rowe Price New Income

Shafer, Regina
435 USAA Tax Exempt Intermediate-Term
437 USAA Tax Exempt Short-Term

Shanahan, R. Michael
55 American Funds Amcap A
57 American Funds American Mutual A
64 American Funds Grth Fund of Amer A
66 American Funds Invmt Co of Amer A

Sharpe, Chris
206 Fidelity Strategic Income
207 Fidelity Strategic Real Return

Shaw, Jeff
237 Harbor Large Cap Value Inv

Shelon, Jonathan
165 Fidelity Freedom 2010
166 Fidelity Freedom 2020

Shiel, J. Fergus
153 Fidelity Capital Appreciation

Shiffman, Dan
40 American Century Ginnie Mae Inv

Simon, Bobe
203 Fidelity Spartan 500 Index Investor
204 Fidelity Spartan International Inde
205 Fidelity Spartan Total Market Index

Slome, Wade W.
51 American Century Ultra Inv

Small Jr., John
53 American Century Veedot Inv

Smet, John H.
56 American Funds American Balanced A

Smith, Bonnie L.
293 Merger

Smith, Donald G.
488 Vanguard Selected Value

Smith, Gibson
242 Janus Balanced
249 Janus High-Yield

Smith, Reid
463 Vanguard High-Yield Tax-Exempt
465 Vanguard Insured Long-Trm T/E

Smith, Robert W.
379 T. Rowe Price Growth Stock

Snow, Ryan
517 Wasatch Heritage Growth

Sohn, Minyoung
245 Janus Fundamental Equity
248 Janus Growth & Income

Sola, Michael F.
397 T. Rowe Price Science & Tech

Sommer, Mark
197 Fidelity Short-Intermediate Muni In

Soviero, Thomas T.
155 Fidelity Convertible Securities
180 Fidelity Leveraged Company Stock

Spears, John D.
429 Tweedy, Browne American Value
430 Tweedy, Browne Global Value

Sprauer, Scott
133 Dreyfus Appreciation

Stanske, Frederick W.
432 Undiscovered Mgrs Behavioral Growth

Stattman, Dennis W.
94 BlackRock Global Allocation A

Stephens, Andrew C.
81 Artisan Mid Cap Inv

Sterling, Joseph B.
41 American Century Global Gold Inv

Stetler, James P.
452 Vanguard Equity-Income
483 Vanguard Morgan Growth

Studzinski, Edward
316 Oakmark Equity & Income I

Sullivan, Gerard P.
51 American Century Ultra Inv

Sullivan, Jerry
51 American Century Ultra Inv

Sustersic, Frank L.
428 Turner Small Cap Growth

Suvall, Susan I.
411 TCW Value Added I
412 TCW Value Opportunities I

Swaffield, Payson F.
137 Eaton Vance Floating Rate A

Tasho, Philip D.
86 Aston/TAMRO Small Cap N

Taylor, Daniel M.
306 N/I Numeric Investors Small Cap Val

Taylor, J.B.
515 Wasatch Core Growth

Taylor, Robert A.
317 Oakmark Global I

Teach, Stuart E.
239 Homestead Value

Tedder, Alexander
46 American Century Intl Growth Inv

Thay, Victor Y.
163 Fidelity Export & Multinational

Thompson, Christine Jones
186 Fidelity Municipal Income
208 Fidelity Tax-Free Bond
352 Royce Total Return Inv

Thompson, John C.
421 Thompson Plumb Growth

Thompson, John W.
421 Thompson Plumb Growth

Thompson, Richard
199 Fidelity Small Cap Independence

Thomson, Justin
383 T. Rowe Price International Discove

Thorndike, Alexander L.
112 Century Small Cap Select Inv

Tillinghast, Joel C.
181 Fidelity Low-Priced Stock

Tolson, Susan M.
58 American Funds American Hi Inc Tr A

Toney, Kevin
39 American Century Equity Income Inv

Toraasen, Trygve
162 Fidelity Europe

Torray, Robert E.
424 Torray

Trauner, Keith D.
142 Fairholme

Trevisani, Wendy
422 Thornburg International Value A